THE ENCYCLOPEDIA OF

Country Living

AN OLD FASHIONED RECIPE BOOK

UPDATED NINTH EDITION

THE ENCYCLOPEDIA OF

Country Living

AN OLD FASHIONED RECIPE BOOK

UPDATED NINTH EDITION

by Carla Emery

ILLUSTRATED BY CINDY DAVIS AND DAVID BERGER

SASQUATCH BOOKS
SEATTLE

First printing of updated ninth edition, 2003

Printed in the United States of America
Distributed by Publishers Group West
10 09 08 07   6 5

The following authors and publishers have generously given permission to use extended quotations from copyrighted works: From *Gardening Under Cover* by William Head. Copyright 1984, 1989 by Amity Foundation. Published by Sasquatch Books. Reprinted by permission of the publisher. From *Winter Harvest Cookbook* by Lane Morgan. Copyright 1990 by Lane Morgan. Published by Sasquatch Books. Reprinted by permission of the publisher. From *Growing Vegetables West of the Cascades* by Steve Solomon. Copyright 1989 by Steve Solomon. Published by Sasquatch Books. Reprinted by permission of the publisher. From *The Complete Guide to Landscape Design, Renovation and Maintenance: A Practical Handbook for the Home Landscape Gardener.* Copyright by Cass Turnbull. Reprinted by permission of the author. From "Remove the Toxic Waste Dump from Your Home . . . " by Rodney L. Merrill as published in *Backwoods Home Magazine* (January/February 1991). Copyright by Rodney L. Merrill. Reprinted by permission of the author. From "Bury Your Own Dead" by Carl Watner as published in *Backwoods Home Magazine* (May/June 1992). Copyright by Carl Watner. Reprinted by permission of the author.

Cover design: Karen Schober
Interior design: Lynne Faulk Design
Composition: Valerie Brewster, Lynne Faulk, Magrit Baurecht, pdbd.

Library of Congress Cataloging in Publication Data
        The encyclopedia of country living : an old fashioned recipe book / by Carla Emery : illustrated by Cindy Davis and David Berger.—
updated 9th ed.
             p. cm.
        Includes index.
        ISBN 1-57061-377-X
        1. Home economics—Handbooks, manuals, etc. I. Title.
        TX158.E45 2003
        640—dc21   2002191140

Published by
Sasquatch Books
119 South Main Street, Suite 400
Seattle, Washington 98104
(206) 467-4300
www.sasquatchbooks.com

To contact the author:
Carla Emery
P.O. Box 133
San Simon, AZ 85632
520-678-2271
doncarla@vtc.net
www.carlaemery.com

Contents

ACKNOWLEDGMENTS

So many people have helped me during the years I've been working on this book, I can't begin to list everyone here. Please forgive me if you should be named and you aren't.

Thank you, God.

Thank you, all of my original subscribers. You bought into a dream, not knowing it was then just a dream and not yet a book. Thank you, everyone who worked so hard in those early days to help me make that dream a reality. All of you—and everyone who ever bought a book from me—made it possible for me to keep writing new, improved editions.

And thank you, all of my contributors. The larger and more complete this book has become, the more I have depended on those more knowledgeable and experienced than I in particular areas. You'll find their names in this book—people who contributed a recipe, a piece of advice, or an anecdote, as well as those who provided whole sections of information on specific topics. Those people are sharing firsthand knowledge gleaned from years of experience; without them, this book never could have happened.

I'm also grateful to the people in the publishing and book trade world who helped make this ninth edition a reality. I'm grateful to Patty Merrill, from Powell's Books for Cooks in Portland, for bringing my book to the attention of Sasquatch. My thanks to Chad Haight, Sasquatch Books publisher, for making the offer; to editor Anne Depue for wise advice gently given and for always being there; to food and garden writer Lane Morgan for her expert review and suggestions; and to Pam Milberg for updating and verifying the accuracy of my mail-order entries and for advising me on the section headings in each chapter. I'm grateful to Cindy Davis for letting me reuse her classic set of illustrations; to David Berger and Dave Albers for creating additional ones; to the design and composition team of Lynne Faulk, Magrit Baurecht, and Valerie Brewster for giving the book a whole new look; to Joan Gregory and Nancy Deahl for helping pull the design, illustration, and production stages together. And I'm grateful to the copy editors and proofreaders—Sherri Schultz, Kim Carlson, Marianne Moon, Julie Hoffman, and others—for their expert attention and for making sure that I won't keep my world record for typos and goofs!

Finally, my apologies to all the people who sent me information and recipes that I couldn't individually give them credit for, or that I wasn't able to include (we had to drop 60,000 words to make everything fit). Maybe we can put them in the next edition!

—Carla Emery

Here are some poems readers have shared with me. A dear lady named Maude Dougharty sent the first one to me back when I was first publishing this book, and it's appeared in every edition since. The second poem was sent to me in January 1994 by Julie Ryan of Connecticut. I love it!

MAMA'S MAMA

Mama's Mama, on a winter's day,
Milked the cows and fed them hay,
Slopped the hogs, saddled the mule,
And got the children off to school.
Did a washing, mopped the floors,
Washed the windows and did some chores.
Cooked a dish of home-dried fruit,
Pressed her husband's Sunday suit,
Swept the parlor, made the bed,
Baked a dozen loaves of bread.
Split some wood and lugged it in,
Enough to fill the kitchen bin,
Cleaned the lamps and put in oil,
Stewed some apples she thought might spoil,
Churned the butter, baked a cake,
Then exclaimed: "For Mercy's sake,
The calves have got out of the pen!"
Went out and chased them in again,
Gathered the eggs and locked the stable,
Returned to the house and set the table,
Cooked a supper that was delicious,
And afterwards washed all the dishes,
Fed the cat, sprinkled the clothes,
Mended a basket full of hose,
Then opened the organ and began to play,
"When You Come to the End of a Perfect Day."
　　　　　—Anna Rees Henton
　　　　　　Age 85, 1953

OUT IN THE FIELDS WITH GOD

The little cares that fretted me,
　　I lost them yesterday,
Among the fields, above the sea,
　　Among the winds at play;
Among the lowing of the herds,
　　The rustling of the trees,
Among the singing of the birds,
　　The humming of the bees.
The foolish fears of what may happen,
　　I cast them all away
Among the clover-scented grass,
　　Among the new-mown hay.
Among the rustling of the corn,
　　Where drowsy poppies nod,
Where ill thoughts die and good are born—
　　Out in the fields with God.
　　　　　—Author Unknown
　　　　　　Attributed to Elizabeth Barrett Browning
　　　　　　and Imogen Guiney

WHAT THIS BOOK IS

This book has been written—and rewritten—over a span of 32 years. Like a geological deposit, it has layers. The first layer was the ambitious 12-page table of contents I started compiling back in 1969. That's when I first got to thinking about this book. I wanted to put into one work everything someone would want or need to know about family food production. I wanted it to be a complete reference, an encyclopedia of information and skills, a practical resource anyone could use.

The "back to the land" movement had started happening then—a tremendous out-migration from cities to country. I was living in a tiny town in northern Idaho, and the newcomers were everywhere, full of urgent questions about growing plants and raising animals. So the next layer of the book got written as I tried to answer their questions, encourage them in the hard moments, and help them adapt to the harsh realities of country living. I was struggling to create for them an affordable, single-volume reference work on raising and preparing food—every kind of food, every step of the way—from planting a seed in the garden or mating animals to preparing a meal.

I was also trying to preserve the precious knowledge of an older generation of homesteaders—knowledge that was rapidly disappearing as that generation passed on. It seemed that traditional, "old-time" technologies were being cast aside as people flocked to petroleum-based technologies and centralized supply systems. I wanted to help record and preserve the traditional methods. They offer a workable alternative to petroleum-dependent technologies, and as we continue to deplete the earth's oil deposits, the old, self-sufficient methods will become more and more important to know.

Mrs. Harless and Imogene Kepford were among the first old-timers I talked to. I visited their homes—where they always made me feel welcome—and listened to them, enjoying their blunt, charming, pioneer language. Their amazing knowledge about every aspect of home food production humbled me. I began trying out what they told me—and writing it down. Then I'd return to their homes to ask more questions, and I'd write those answers down too. When Mrs. Harless died unexpectedly about a year after I met her, I felt as though I'd lost a mother. And I realized how much harder and faster I needed to work on my project.

Today, a general ignorance about food production—as well as the lack of land on which to grow plants or raise animals—makes most people captive consumers. Unlike their great-grandparents, the urbanized members of today's society are almost totally dependent on other people to produce their food, clothing, and shelter—and they're subject to the market prices for those essential commodities. Many people spend their lives a paycheck away from hunger or homelessness—because they must pay other people to supply their most basic needs.

I love education and books because they empower people. That's what this book is all about: providing you with the information you need to do things on your own, instead of paying someone else to do them for you.

Another layer of this book comes from the many people who have contributed to it. I've been helped by an army of persons who have shared recipes, advice, and information gained from years of experience. And every time I finished another edition of this book, people wrote to me with corrections, or with more information, or with important questions I hadn't answered. The book grew and improved edition after edition, prodded by those interactions with readers. So this isn't *only* "Carla's Book." Often I just had the humble task of stitching together information from other people, guided by the knowledge and experience I do have.

It took me four years to complete the first edition of this book. During that time, I was a lonely rural housewife, grateful for my pen pals from all over the country—wonderful people who read early parts of the book and shared with me recipes, advice, and encouragement. As I continued writing the book, I kept thinking about those faraway but precious friends, and I began including personal thoughts and memories in my book, sharing with my readers stories about myself, my past, my life. Thus, another layer emerged.

For this updated ninth edition, I added several more layers. I described mushroom cultivation and aquaculture, and updated the book to give advice on problems such as killer bees, global warming, and pesticide contamination in food. Because the international swapping of seeds has made a multitude of non-native, exotic plants available, I added extensive instructions for growing and cooking those plants. This information is useful to city folks as well, now that so many "new" fruits, vegetables, and herbs are appearing in supermarkets. I also added websites and e-mail addresses for over 1,500 mail-order sources.

In fact, as this book has evolved, I've thought of more and more ways it could be useful to city- as well as country-dwelling people. I've begun to think of it as—and have strived to build it into—a basic kitchen reference work, so packed with reliable, practical information that any family, urban or rural, would want to own it.

Is that the final layer? If the last 32 years are any indication, probably not!

WHO THIS BOOK IS FOR

This book is written for everyone. I kid you not. It's interesting reading, a valuable reference, and a useful source of recipes and how-to-do-it information. If you're in the suburbs with space enough for a little garden, you'll find it even more useful. If you dream of someday living on enough land for a garden and maybe a few animals, it's a great wish book and guide to that transition. If you live out of town where you can have a big garden and livestock, you'll get even more use out of this book. Even if you already know a lot about growing food, I've tried to make the book a resource that will help you learn even more, or point you to other places where you can network and get more information. But I want city-dwelling readers to know they're just as important to me as the country folks, and I've tried hard with this ninth edition to address urban needs too.

I think there can be a satisfaction in doing your own thing, in learning new skills, in producing from scratch. I also think the ability to act independently is personally empowering and can be a survival factor in crisis. I'd like to make clear, however, that I don't expect you to do everything in this book. It would take 200 hours a day—or more—to do it all! I did most of it at one time or another and wrote about whatever I was doing while it was fresh in my mind. It may sound as if I was doing it all at the same time, but that's not true.

I also don't want you to think I'm preaching about "from-scratch" procedures as though they're the only righteous way. You can cut down a tree using a cross-cut saw or a chain saw. Some people get great satisfaction from working with a cross-cut saw, sharing the task with a neighbor on the other end of the saw. Other people, with family to keep warm and little time for other things, need the expediency of a chain saw. Modern methods can save you time. I've learned to use a computer. It sure beats having to retype a whole page just to change a few sentences. Every person has to strike a balance between doing for themselves and letting themselves be done for. It's not weak to compromise; it's absolutely necessary.

A spunky lady, Barb Lasley of Ramah, NM, wrote me, "Having been reared on a farm in southwest Wisconsin, I now exist as a parody to your book, because my microwave heats the lard to proper soap temperature and my Kenmore dishwasher cleans up after. My Oster Kitchen Center grinds my meat and turns out great pasta and bread dough while my washer and dryer are busy doing the laundry. I can't imagine living better than we do, with fresh food, homemade soap, clean air, non-chlorinated water, and all the TLC that's necessary to make a house a home. If modern conveniences infringe upon those qualities, I fail to see where."

Although I've written this collection of food-growing information and along the way lived, loved, and extolled—and also probably idealized—the rural life, I don't want you to feel pushed in that direction unless it is truly right for you. Going back to the land is not, for me, a religion. It's not the only right or happy way to live. And there are lots of country-type skills and food self-sufficiency ideas in this book that you can make use of even in town!

There have always been lots of Canadians, Australians, and New Zealanders in my family of readers and back-to-the-landers. I used to get happy letters from Americans who had moved to Mexico to make new homes there. I also hear from missionaries all over the world who have moved from "modern" living to the bush and are having to learn from-scratch cooking. I've tried hard to make this book something that could be of use to ever more people in ever more places. I've added new grains, vegetables, and fruits—many of which are grown more frequently in other countries than in the United States.

So there are as many styles of "country living" as there are people and places. Whatever and wherever yours is, thank you for being my reader. You give meaning and joy to my life by being out there on the receiving end of this book, which has been, more or less, my life's work.

This is sometimes a very personal book, a letter to a friend.

ABOUT THE TIME TRAVELING IN THIS BOOK

The contents have gradually accumulated over 32 years (to date), expanding from all points like an accordion—or a universe. I added new things as I learned them, rewrote sections I wasn't satisfied with, and confided new personal events. So it enlarged—less regularly than the growth rings on a tree, but more systematically than a scrapbook just gradually gaining pages and mementos.

That's why you may encounter perhaps jarringly different styles, tones, and contexts. I can't change that; you'll just have to bear with me. This book is different from most because of its time-jumping. You may encounter me as a recently married young mother living on 3 acres, or on a larger farm, or even in the city. I may be running a School of Country Living, doing media appearances to get out the news about my book for sale—or living very quietly. On some pages I'm having babies, surrounded by toddlers; elsewhere I'm middle-aged, divorced, a grandmother.

I started writing this book around 1969. I'm writing this section in 1994. A few entries are dated, but mostly you'll have to guess when I wrote each passage. So buckle your time-traveler's quick-switch seat belt, and away we go!

Oddments

ODDMENTS CONTENTS

INTRODUCTION

If you've considered moving to the country—yes! But don't move to the country in search of a notion of freedom that pictures you lying on the grass all of a fine summer's day, chewing on a succession of hay straws. True freedom doesn't mean a vacuum. In the kind of freedom I'm talking about, you work 12-hour days in the summer. Finding freedom is a strange kind of paradox, anyway—like the spiritual truths that you can actually get by giving, and that you can conquer by simply loving and having faith.

But first, a definition. What really is "country"? To me, "urban" means a place where you can't grow any of your own food. "Suburban" means you can have a garden but not food animals like chickens, pigs, or goats. Real "country living" means really having the right and opportunity to grow both food plants and animals. A block of apartments plopped into the middle of a cow pasture 10 miles from the supermarket isn't real "country." It's guaranteed commuter clog and developer's profit (buying cheap agricultural land and turning it into urban-density, perpetual-rent housing). If you can't have even a garden, you're in phony country. This book is about real country living—growing your family's food, both plant and animal.

So moving to a more rural area means being able to grow more—or most—of your own food. Home-grown food will taste better and be healthier and more affordable. And to grow your own food is to be in a very special and personal relationship with those species that feed you. When you plant seeds, you make a promise that you will be there to care for the plants as they grow. You will spread manure and till the ground before you plant those seeds. When they start to grow, you'll pull the weeds that threaten to stifle the plants and give them precious water to drink. For the animals, you promise to love them, feed them, doctor them, and forgive them the aggravations they cause you. In return,

by their flesh they will help sustain you and your family. The animals and plants you are possessed by give you freedom from food shortage and freedom from unwanted chemicals in your food.

There are people who can freeze or dry all the family's meat, grow their own grain, bake their own bread, and make all their own soap products. All they buy at the grocery store are spices, salt, and toilet paper. I admire such people, but please don't think I'm one of them. At one time or another I've tried to do a lot of those things, but never all at the same time. Such a person doesn't have time for much else, and I've got this book to write!

I love this life and I recommend it, but now let me do a little debunking. The rewards are largely the spiritual cultivation that work and austerity bestow. The easy way to do things is to do one thing and do it well. But if you commit yourself to this kind of life, you're committing yourself to trying to do a hundred incompatible and competitive things, and like as not, in your first year 75 of them will fizzle. It happens to me constantly. I've never yet grown a three-pound tomato. I

have a friend who grows big ones, but I'm happy to get them store size. Furthermore, the goats never give as much milk as the references say they will, nor do the hens lay as faithfully. My garden doesn't produce like anybody's magazine article, and it doesn't look like any of the photographs. I will add, however, that it does feed us.

At least some of the orchard crop usually gets attacked by some combination of animals and disease. This year [1971] the robins took most of the cherries, the fungus got into the pears, and an early frost prevented the apricots and peaches from bearing fruit. The bees don't make as much honey as they are supposed to. Everything that eats requires more feed than you expect, and by fall you can toboggan from the house to the barn across all that manure. Nobody dares step onto the front porch barefoot, and I wouldn't even suggest having a picnic in the yard.

But if I don't let the chickens roam around the side of my organic garden, armies of insects come. Thousands of grasshoppers and potato bugs and tomato worms—long green monsters with horns and big mouths. All kinds of hungry, creeping, crawling, leaping things. And nothing that is supposed to stay confined does. We are constantly having to put some animal back in its appointed place. They go over, under, through, or—failing that—the children leave gates and cage doors wide open. In the mechanical realm, any machine that we want urgently and can manage to get started will break down later, usually after half a day. Cars and trucks are regularly subject to gas shortages, flat tires, ruined spark plugs, expired batteries, burnt-out generators, or worse.

We often have sick animals that require first aid. In the spring especially, the kitchen doubles as a veterinary hospital. Nevertheless, we invariably lose some of our crop of baby animals. The milk goats get horrible gashes on their teats from trying to jump barbed-wire fences. Cows occasionally eat nails or wire and would die of lingering indigestion if we didn't feed them a magnet. Some baby chicks always smother or drown or get trampled by a galloping old hen, run over by the car, or squeezed by the baby. Baby pigs catch cold, and goslings are the most vulnerable of all to fatal chills. Baby calves and goats are sometimes taken by diarrhea or more serious diseases. I will add that this does not apply to kittens and puppies. They all live to grow up and reproduce themselves in

cheerful abundance—providing they have no market value.

And last but not least, this ideal of rural living turns out to be pathetically dependent on city money. My husband, Mike, has to drive 28 miles each way and be away in town all day to make it. The land was so expensive. Even with a town job, it's hard to earn enough to pay for it. And everything else costs money too: the constant mechanical repairs, the gas to commute to work, a spring supply of garden seed. And all the animals and plants require store props —buckets, medicine, machinery, housing . . . Fencing is very expensive too.

We'd like to pay ourselves back by selling farm products, but it's hard

to make a profit. Seems like farmers are the only people who buy retail and sell wholesale. And the job that pays for the farm also means that Mike is away every day and works long days because of commuting and overtime.

With all these things that require so much time and effort (and where you save money is by doing it yourself), the woman is the Johnny-on-the-spot when the bull goes through the fence, the pigs suddenly appear in the garden, the pickup gets a flat tire, or the house catches on fire. The homestead can be hard on a woman and a marriage. So be reminded of all these realities, and then relax. Admit you can't do everything. The most important thing is to survive! That means keeping your spiritual, mental, and physical health—and keeping your family happy and together.

MAKING THE MOVE
Letters to Carla

People who make the brave move from urban to rural are very dear to my heart, the ones I talk to in my mind when I'm writing. And they talk back. Over the years I've gotten letter after letter from readers who have done country living all their lives or for many years—or who are just beginning or just thinking about it. My readers have taught me a lot. I get a lot of "Hooray, Carla, we're on the land at last" letters, and the letter writers' routes back to the land were as individual as the people taking them.

Edith Brown, Vaughn, WA, wrote me, "Chauncey and I moved from Seattle last Valentine's Day to retire on our 40 acres that we bought for taxes 40 years ago. I had always vowed I would never live on a farm as I felt four years of homestead living in my early years were more than enough. When we came to look at our property a year and a half ago, the apple trees in the old, old orchard were in full bloom and a sight to behold. We observed that folks were preparing to move to the property across the road from our place so our dead-end road would begin to have some life. I changed my mind. Last summer, Chauncey raised a tremendous garden and we can hardly believe all the improvements made in the past year. We bought a used mobile home, an old truck, new tractor, rototiller and other equipment from sale of stock in our machine shop so we have enjoyed a very busy, but happy year."

Barbara Ingram and her husband made the move to the northern Idaho forestland in midlife: "If you are moving to an undeveloped piece of ground, there are three things you must have: 1) Groceries, six months' to a year's supply to keep you until you can get started. 2) Hand tools, all you can accumulate. 3) And all the junk you can haul. Too many people give all their stuff away, get out here, and find

they could have used it—or traded it for something they could use. We came to our five undeveloped acres 2½ years ago. We brought with us an 8-foot by 35-foot trailer ready to fall apart and loaded to capacity with stuff and groceries. And $20 and high hopes. The first year, bang! I got pregnant, which was impossible. We had been married for 9 years. [Several other women besides Barbara have told me that, after despairing of being able to conceive, their first year in the country or even wilderness also brought their first baby.]

"Two months ago we bought a generator. So now we have electricity for such things as a washing machine. But for two years we lived with no plumbing, no electricity, and no gas. We have a spring 300 feet from the house. We hauled water in buckets until Bob started hauling it in barrels with the jeep. With a band saw we built a large room on the trailer, a chicken house, a goat shed, rabbit hutches, and fences. Our added room on the trailer cost only $120 and it's 12 × 35 feet. (We tore down an old barn for materials.) Bob has a job now at a shake mill but the first year there was no job to be had. Thank goodness for the groceries. Now we have a pair of peacocks, 25 hens laying 60 dozen eggs a month, a nanny and billy goat, rabbits everywhere (what we don't eat, we sell), and a Jersey cow named Julie. It takes guts, hard work, and a big faith that the Lord will help you over the humps. But it can be done by middle-aged people with no money. We are stronger, healthier, and feel younger, even if we do go to bed after a 16-hour day, year-round, dead tired. It's a good tired!"

Marion Earnhart and her husband left the details of their move in God's hands: "God led us to sell or give away everything we had and take only what would fit in our VW Bug. After traveling through Oregon, Idaho, Wyoming, Colorado, back through Wyoming and Montana, we were on our way to Canada when we ran out of food, money and things to sell. We spent the night in a little city park praying every minute. The next day my husband got a job that kept us going until we found a ranch job that included a place to live. I am now in the middle of nowhere, on a ranch, trying to figure out how they get those great big cows into those little tiny packages I'm used to buying. Amazing!!! Actually I spend most of my time chasing down the flies in my kitchen and trying to keep my husband's stomach halfway full."

Working on somebody else's farm is a good education, but Linda Lanigan and her husband wanted their own place. They told me about the long, serious road of apprenticeship they took to get there: "We are both from large cities. We left seven years ago and first went to Oklahoma, where a buddy of my husband's from Vietnam had a job for us on a large dry-land wheat farm, where they also fed out a couple hundred steers a year. We learned a lot, mainly that we didn't want to stay there, but that we definitely wanted to farm and live in the country! Next was Colorado, more experience—but Colorado is more of a resort state (and was too expensive). So we came to Idaho where we worked for a large rancher. My husband learned a lot about flood irrigation and all about cows and calves, caring for 3,000 head.

"After five years of hard-earned experience and below-poverty wages we felt we were ready to work our own place. We spent a year looking for just the right one. It had to be perfect, including an owner who would help us find financing. Working all those years for farmers and ranchers, averaging about 50 cents an hour, there wasn't any chance to save a down payment, though we did manage to collect most of the things necessary to a small homestead: a couple of milk cows and goats, chickens, rabbits, horses, a good tiller for my garden (I paid for it by custom tilling), a large pressure canner, butter churn, etc.

"Well, we found our place, got a really good deal. We went to FHA and they were willing to finance us because of our experience. But still, we will be doing everything we can in order to make payments. My husband has a full-time job working for the county. He operates the grader, plowing snow in winter and fixing roads during the summer. I drive the school bus. So we have two salaries, plus the sale of steers, plus my husband's shoeing and breaking and training a few horses each summer."

Patricia Twait, Cylinder, IA, wrote me, "I remember my mother rendering lard and making soap. She was so glad to quit doing those things and here you are telling how to do them. I loaned her the book to read and she laughed. Everything does go in cycles, doesn't it? My husband and our two sons and I moved to the country 8 years ago. It has been a very hard way to make a living. We farm 314 acres of corn and soybeans and farrow to finish about 1,000 hogs

a year. I work as a school media specialist so we do have a monthly paycheck coming in."

Margie Becker of Cottonwood, CA: "Two years ago my family and I lived in a duplex in San Diego. My husband and I worked around the clock, 7 days a week, running a doughnut shop. This is no exaggeration—24- and 36-hour shifts were common. Then in February 1990, my husband's father died of cancer. My daughter, who is emotionally disabled, was really getting out of control and headed back into the hospital. Visiting my mother-in-law, I saw your book on her bookshelf and, for lack of anything better to do, I started to read it. I ended up having to share it with my husband who became as absorbed by your book as I was.

"We traded our little Toyota for a Ford van, sold all our stuff, and loaded up ourselves, 3 kids, and 2 dogs to look for our little piece of ground. We lived and traveled like that for almost 6 months until we finally found our home: 47.9 acres in Northern California's Shasta County. We view Mt. Shasta and Mt. Lassen from our front yard and not a neighbor for two miles in any direction, but the neighbors we do have are the greatest. We never would have made it without their help.

"We now have a herd of 26 goats (and it's growing), 5 hogs, and almost 100 chickens. We have been hauling our water for the last two years but this summer we finally have enough money to put in our own well. I cannot believe the change in my daughter since her diet was changed to natural foods without all of the sugars, dyes, and preservatives. That, combined with all of the fresh air and exercise she gets shepherding the goats, is really having an effect on her attitude and weight. We still work long, hard days and we still work 7 days a week, but it's different when I am not doing it to make some fat cat that I don't even know a little bit richer. This is for me!"

I also get letters from old-timers on the land like Cathy Peterson, Catawba, WI: "Many years ago I bought a copy of your 'cookbook' at a rummage sale—a young couple of the 'back to the land' era had decided to return to a more 'civilized' area! We are dairy farmers. We have 8 children, 4 of them still at home. Both my husband and I have to work off the farm to pay the bills! There is a lot of work to do—but we also are active in church, 4-H, and a community food program."

Some of my readers are the children of parents like the Petersons, struggling to bring their precious memories to life again: "My name is Missy Kolb. I am 24 years old. I live in Mt. Airy, MD. I am originally from a small valley burg in the mountains of West Virginia called Burlington. We always had a big garden, canned our own peaches, tomatoes, pickles, applesauce, peas, beans, etc. We put up our own hogs, steers, deer, and turkey. I met my husband, married him, and we moved here in 1988. Then I realized that there was so much that I had been used to but never thoroughly learned how to do. I'd stirred apple butter kettles since I could hold a paddle, but never bothered to find out how much sugar, which apples are best, etc. I could clean and pack produce in jars from dawn to dusk. I could check seals and mix syrups and brines, but had no idea how to operate the pressure cooker!"

Some ex-urbanites adapt easily and happily, but for some the transition period brings real hardships of body and soul. Mike (from Idaho) and I (from Montana) both went to graduate school in New York (that's where we met) and felt very out of place there. I'm sure it can be the same agony in reverse when a city native emigrates to a rural area.

The problem I hear about most often from isolated wives newly moved from city to country is desperate loneliness. Ricky Witz, Armstrong, IL, wrote me, . . . "4½ months and I still didn't know even a single neighbor—the closest one lives over 1 mile away. But finally, through a series of coincidences, and as a result of prayer, I met a neighbor down the road about 1½ miles!" So I urge you, plead with you: Join something! Join two or three somethings! Whatever there is around. Because they won't join you. You've got to make that first step of accepting and integrating with them. Trust me, it will turn out far better than your worst fears, though maybe not as good as your highest hopes.

The problem husbands most dread—and most often encounter—is joblessness and a shortage of money. If you give up, it will probably be because of one of those two problems—or both. A reader named Darlene wrote me, "Two and a half years ago, my husband and I decided to give up a comfortable suburban life (home and job) and move to an island in the Strait of Juan de Fuca, Washington. Island living had a lot of pros and cons. Our four children (aged 12, 13, 14, 15) loved and feared the place. We were terribly lonely. Meaningful work escaped us. We decided to leave after only 6 months."

That's how it is. Some never move to the country at all. Some go but leave after a time. Some go and like it; they put down roots and stay.

BOOKS AND PERIODICALS FOR EDEN SEEKERS:
The best recent entry in this field is *How to Find Your Ideal Country Home: A Comprehensive Guide,* by Gene GeRue (**www.ruralize.com**). My favorite feature in this monumental and well-researched book for prospective buyers of rural property is its many maps: weather maps, sociology maps, pollution maps, etc. *How to Buy Land Cheap* by Edward Preston is about buying land from county, federal, state, and city governments. Interesting but results not guaranteed (as Heinlein says, "TANSTAAFL"). *How to Quit the Rat Race Successfully* by John F. Edwards is a basic master guide to the decision making and process involved in relocating to rural land. *Moving to the Country* by Robert McGill is a collection of what-happened-then stories of those who made the big move. It follows them from the 1960s to the 1980s and was written by an extension service agent in Missouri. Good insights. *The Eden Seekers Guide* by William L. Seavey surveys "best" states, Western counties, small towns, Costa Rica, islands, etc. Interesting. *Finding and Buying Your Place in the Country* by Les Scher is a top-notch, thorough, and up-to-date book for real-world buyers. *Surveying Your Land* by Charles E. Lawson covers surveys, deeds, and title searches

and includes a buyer's checklist.

Don Mitchell has written a series of country-living books: *Moving UpCountry* about making the move, *Living UpCountry* about being there, and *Growing UpCountry* about raising children there.

There are also periodicals for prospective land buyers, but be cautious of the sales pitch. *Rural Property Bulletin* is a monthly catalog "packed with bargains of farms, ranches, acreages, rural homes, survival retreats, hunting/fishing land, waterfront, small town, nationwide listings by owners and agents." It's $16/yr for bulk mail; $18, first-class (12 issues); $3/sample; 888-FARM-BUY; 402-376-2985; PO Box 369, Bassett, NE 68714; **info@ruralproperty.net; www.cnweb.com/rural.** *Montana Land Magazine* lists Montana real estate; $10/yr (4 issues); PO Box 30516, Billings, MT 59107-0516. William and Cynthia Reid specialize in finding you the perfect homestead, large or small—for you and your poultry and livestock; 2313 SW 120th, Seattle, WA 98146, **Reidpnw@hotmail.com; www.homeseattle. com.**

The Homesteaders

"Homesteading" has more than one meaning. It used to mean qualifying for free government land because you lived on it, built a house on it, and so on. Now it means living on the land and trying for at least some degree of home production of your needs, especially food. When people who were raised in cities try to accomplish that, I believe it can be every bit as much of a challenge for them as crossing the plains was for our pioneer ancestors. People go to all kinds of places to do their homesteading: the suburbs of their city, the mountains of Appalachia or the western United States, the northeastern United States, the Midwest, northern California, Alaska, Canada, Mexico. No matter where you are— or go—if you can grow a garden and raise some animals, you're a homesteader. And a fortunate human being!

THE HOMESTEADER TYPE: Who are these people? I've been getting to know them for nearly 25 years now by reading their wonderful letters. They are young, just graduated, just married, just beginning. They are in the middle years, making the massive change, starting all over. They are elderly, just retiring, free for the first time and determined to finish their years living their country dream. Are they "hippies"? "Squares"? Hippies, yes, living in communes, in all sorts of extended families. Or living alone. Or in traditional families. And conservatives, yes, folks prepared to survive a collapse of the economy or society— Latter-Day Saints preparing for a time of trials, Christians getting ready for the Last Days. Or environmentalists trying to preserve some chunk of Mother Earth, eager to practice what they preach and discover an agriculture and technology that can maintain human society on a flourishing blue-green planet for a million years rather than degrade and destroy it in a hundred.

Alternative Families and Economics. Helpful readers have made me understand that there are other ways to live on the land besides the husband-works-wife-keeps-house style of my own experience. Some are weekend farmers who can get away to their piece of earth only two days a week but still find satisfaction and a family food supply there. Some people "buy" a share in a farm and visit and work there during weekends and vacations, although the real responsibility resides with a full-time manager. I've talked to "house-

husbands" such as John Herrington of Greely, CO, who manages the farm and cares for his 17-month-old baby while his wife works. "Sometimes it gets pretty hectic," he told me. "Sometimes I wish she'd come home and let me go out." Often both spouses work; often it's the only way they can hang on to their beloved land. I've also met people who buy and hold their land in common but own their homes, plants, and animals individually.

One brave lady, Martha Wells of Normangee, TX, told me about her version of country living: "Howdy, from Texas! In 1984, I finally moved to the family farm. My husband did not know anything about farm life before moving here. And, with his working off the farm, a lot of 'man-things' are left to me. I want to let your readers know, a woman *can do* a lot more than she suspects! I knew how to string the hay baler and run the tractor, so guess who gets to do the hay baling each year! (After getting tired of having to fix the baler after the men used it, I took over that job.) I run commercial Brahma × Hereford-type cows. When they get penned and wormed, branded, or whatever, I do the penning and separating. Actually crawling in to castrate or give shots, yes, I occasionally lose my nerve and require help! I always assist in the delivery of my brood sows and castrate my own boar pigs also."

Commercial Farmers. Farmers who earn their living producing agricultural products typically have college degrees in agriculture and highly mechanized and incorporated farms. That's not a sin. Most farms are incorporated, not so much to be tax write-offs as to try to keep the farm in the family at inheritance-tax time. The dream is equally meaningful for these people, who have long-established roots in their land and a proud family tradition of farming. They are always living on the brink, always struggling to do more work than there is time for, to pay more bills than there is money for, to find ways to improve their production and their land, and they are ever conscious that a year or even just an incident of poor management could cause them to lose the farm forever.

I am concerned that chemical fertilizer, herbicides, and pesticides upset the local ecology and poison groundwater supplies that all area residents, rural or urban, depend on. I'd like to see farms progress as rapidly as possible toward nonpolluting technologies, but I understand the risk and agony of economically hard-pressed farmers wrestling with the monetary side of those choices.

CHOOSING AND BUYING YOUR LAND

This book is mainly about how to grow food. To do that, you need access to land—your own or yours to work with. You need at least enough for a garden and maybe also some animals—space for a hen house and rabbit pens, pasture, and a barn for goats or a cow. You have to think way ahead to get your piece of land. You have to make sacrifices and maybe work two jobs to boot. But you can do it if you really want to.

I've seen too many people sink all their money into a piece of land, only to discover they can't find jobs in the area, the land isn't fertile, they don't like the area after all, etc. I strongly recommend that you first rent and try to find work in the area you're interested in. Once you have commenced earning a living there, you can gradually, and more knowledgeably, shop for land while you rent.

But Where?

Here are some factors to consider when choosing where to look for land.

CAN YOU GET A JOB NEAR THERE? Would some kind of special training make it more possible for you to earn a living there? Jobs in really rural areas are scarce, and openings go first to local people (and they should). Rural jobs are often highly specialized, such as logging or operating farm equipment (you have to be a skilled mechanic too). If you are city-raised, you don't know anything about these things, and potential employers understand that even better than you. You'll have to learn your way around—learn where to ask and whom to ask for. You may want to pick a spot near a university or medium-sized town—if that is a place where you'd have a marketable skill. Unless you have a large and dependable private income, stay near a place where you are sure you can find work, probably a city of some size.

CAN YOU AFFORD LAND THERE? On the other hand, land prices near the cities are high because of the heavy competition for properties, and property taxes are high too. You have to go hundreds of miles from any major metropolitan area to find land at its true agricultural value. An area receiving a flood of immigrants can change its nature very quickly. Certain very scenic and well-publicized areas are attracting so many new residents that the influx is creating problems with sewage disposal and pressure on the school system, not to mention that whole valley bottoms of fertile land are getting covered with homes. (Better to put the house on your untillable hillside and reserve the flat for garden, cropland, or pasture.) Land in that sort of too-quickly growing area is already expensive and getting more so. So if there are frequent "land for sale" signs and you see new

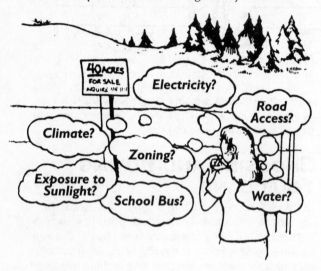

homes left and right, consider looking elsewhere. And if you take a creek, timber, and a view of a snow-capped mountain range off your list of necessities, you'll get a better price and fewer neighbors.

CAN YOU DO WHAT YOU CARE ABOUT THERE? Do you just want a cottage for vacation getaways? Or a full-time place where you'll live year-round, grow food in a good garden, and have a pasture for animals and a woodlot for firewood? Or do you plan to vacation there now but live there full-time after it's paid for? Do you love fishing and want access to clean trout water? Or to a good deer hunting area? Do you want an existing home on the place or the adventure of building your own? Do you want neighbors close or scarce and far away? Do you want store, school, and church close for convenience and economy? Or far away for privacy?

HOW MUCH LAND? A reader named Tom wrote and asked me, "How much land do you need for a few cows, hogs, chickens, ducks, etc." Good question. First of all, figure out the space you need for buildings, driveways, and lawns. Then add the space you want for a garden—and animals.

A Half Acre. This would allow you to keep a couple hives of bees, plant a fruit orchard, and keep a few grazing animals, such as 2 milk goats, 2 weaner pigs, 3–12 hens, and some rabbits. If you have water, you could add a few ducks or geese. Put your orchard around the perimeter of your land, so you can have a permanent grass pasture in the center of it. If you divide up the pasture with electric fence and rotate at intervals of 3 weeks or less, you can get more out

of it. You'll need housing and yarding for all your animals, so they can be confined when the grass shows signs of failing under the onslaught. On just a half acre, you'll have to compromise with livestock between a confined lifestyle and some opportunities to get out on pasture. But a half acre is really *very* small.

An Acre. Remember, we're not counting the house, lawn, etc. An acre is twice as good, of course, as a half. You could consider keeping a breed sow in place of the two weaner pigs and profiting by her piglets. If you hate goat milk, you might keep a small breed of cow instead, although this is still rather small for a cow. You could raise a half-dozen goslings as well as chickens and rabbits. Your animals will be able to get a greater part of their diet from grazing.

Two Acres. This would be enough to comfortably pasture a cow and grow a sizable garden and orchard, if all the soil is good and there's plenty of water to irrigate it. Three, four, or five acres would be better.

Ten Acres. This is a mini-farm. You can install one or more ponds for raising fish and have numerous waterfowl too. You have enough land to have a nice grain patch or other field crop in rotation, in addition to your pasture and pond.

Twenty Acres. With twenty acres of good garden land, you could probably make your family's living by growing something.

Here we are talking about acres of fertile, irrigable ground. But they're hard to find, and costly. You're more likely to be offered wooded areas, steep hillsides, swamps, or shallow soils. But much depends on the skill of the gardener: the one before you, and the one you are. There are people who have made lush garden spots in the arctic and in the tropics, on salt soil and on bare rock, and in abandoned gravel pits.

HOW DO YOU KNOW IF THE LAND IS FERTILE? My friend Frank Ryset is a real estate agent. He's an honest and sincere man. I asked him that and he asked me, "How high is the sagebrush? If the sagebrush was only up to his boot tops, my dad didn't think it was worth plowing, but if it reached up to the horse's belly he judged we could make that land produce. So how deep is the grass? How tall and lush are the trees? Have the berry bushes borne fruit? Consider also that you may be able to increase the production by building up the soil. A soil testing service can be located through your Yellow Pages or county agent, or you can do it yourself using a purchased kit. Soil chemistry tests tell you in precise, technical terminology that land's potential productivity." (More on this in Chapter 2.)

Buying Your Land

Land is expensive if it's good for gardening or pasture. Turnover is slow, so you may have to wait for a piece that's in your desired location. If the demand is high, you may have to be ready to leap when your chance does come along. Prices may be high already and higher as time passes. Required down payments may be large. Or sometimes prices and down payments get into a lowering trend for a while; that's a good time to buy. Cash really talks in land deals; so does property you already own and can trade. But sometimes you can swing a deal with less money down than you might think, if you keep trying. Interest will be a heavy additional financial load on any contract you are paying off over time.

Stay within commuting distance, or bring all the city money with you that you can. Jobs are easier to find in the city, and wages are much higher. Of course, the problem with city money is that land on the edge of a town costs more than it does in a very remote or agriculturally poor area. Try to spend that money so that you get the best value for it. In general, the sooner you buy the better—now rather than twenty years from now, because land prices tend to rise over the long haul. Investing in land is a pretty safe place to put your money, because land seems to be in-flation-proof (its value increases proportionate to inflation). Land does not depreciate (decrease in value with time) as do cars, mobile homes, and boats. Instead, land becomes worth more with time, because while things can be manu-factured in greater numbers all the time, there is only one earth (and ever more people wanting a piece). Land is generally cheaper per acre in big hunks (by the hundred acres) than in little ones (1–5 acres), but most people can't afford a hundred acres. If you want a place to grow food, I'd suggest you get started with your house/lawn plus 3–5 acres of good, tillable, rainy-climate or irrigable land.

DEALING FOR LAND: Don't wait for a land promoter to shove a deal under your nose. Be prepared to personally work at finding and dealing for your piece of land. Watch the local newspaper's legal notices section for announce-ments of places being sold because of unpaid taxes, estate auctions, and mortgage foreclosures. Studying the paper will also inform you about local prices. If you want to work with a real estate agent, start by calling several of them and compare what happens. You could then choose one agent and work exclusively through that person, or you could look at properties with several of them. *There is never a charge for you to be shown property by an agent.*

Sale "by Owner." You could also deal directly with an owner. Some owners prefer to deal directly with you, so that they get all of your down payment, rather than work through a real estate agent. They'll advertise "by owner." Without a real estate agent in the picture, you might be able to make the purchase for somewhat less cash down. To find an owner who wants to sell, drive around and look for "sale by owner" signs, and watch the advertisements. Or put in your own ad describing how many acres you want, whether with or without buildings, what type of land, and how much money you can put down. Here's an example:

> **WANTED TO BUY:** 15+ acres suitable for gar-den or pasture in Scrumptious School District. Buildings not necessary . . . [your telephone number]

Give the ad lots of time. Let it run all year if need be. It worked for us!

When You Visit Property That's for Sale. You'll probably be with an owner or agent, ask a lot of questions, take your time, and look at as nearly everything as you can. It's im-portant, sooner or later, to walk every step of the property line with the owner so you'll know exactly where it is. (Then double-check that information with another source.) The more information you have, the better you can judge the property; also, if you buy the land, you'll need to know all that info.

Don't Talk Final Prices in a Hurry. If possible, get 3 good prospects before you make a deal. This will give you per-spective on what's available and how much it costs. On the

other hand, if you've studied the market and know what you want and what a good price is, and a bargain comes along—be prepared to move fast!

Preparing Your Offer. Don't make it for everything you have in cash, or the most you think you could pay, unless the owner is taking sealed bids. Make it for the smallest amount down and the smallest total price you think has a chance. You'll need the rest of your cash to get started on the place and to use as a cushion.

The Counteroffer. The owner may say no. He may revise his terms downward a little, though, and give them to you as his counteroffer. You may accept them or come back with your own counteroffer—somewhat better terms than you first offered, maybe a higher monthly payment. Avoid offer-ing a higher rate of interest. Keep those interest costs as low as possible, because they will really cost you.

Interest. Calculate how much each interest point will cost you in cash. If possible, choose the deal with the lowest rate of interest. There's an old saying that you pay for a place twice: once in principal (the original price) and once in interest. But that was in the old days, when interest rates were lower. Now you might pay for it more than once over in interest.

Payments. Your contract will most likely call for a regular monthly payment for a stated number of years, such as $500 a month for 25 years. Or your payment plus all the interest due might be payable on a certain date annually or semiannually, such as $5,000 a year plus interest, payable November 1. (That's called "amortization.") Large farm-type parcels are often handled on a payment-plus-interest, or amortized, basis. A November payment date assumes you have just sold your crop and have your year's cash in the bank.

Real Estate Agents. These folks get sizable fees, usually the day after the contract is signed, because their fee is paid out of the down payment. On a $30,000 deal, for example, the real estate company typically may get $3,000 cash. The agent who has been personally helping you may get $1,000 of that. So the down payment has to be $5,000 if the owner requires at least $2,000 down for himself. In most of the real estate deals I've been involved in, if an agent was also involved, the majority of the down payment asked went to pay the real estate company's fee.

HOUSE BUYING AND FIXING INFO: You'll find what you need to know about asbestos, formaldehyde, healthy lighting, lead, noise, radon, security, and water in *The Healthy Home* by Linda Mason Hunter. (Radon is a naturally occurring but carcinogenic gas that seeps out of certain soils into basements. You can find a radon testing kit or a radon testing service on the Internet. Or look in your Yellow Pages under "Radon" for somebody local.) Buyer brokering and agents' obligations are covered in Sloan Bashinsky's 115-page book, *Home Buyers: Lambs to the Slaughter. The Com-plete Book of Home Inspection* by Norman Becker covers in-specting and estimating. For real estate language and law, read *All America's Real Estate Book* by Carolyn Janik and Ruth Rejnis; it covers building and remodeling as well as buying. *Housewise* by Suzanne Brangham guides those planning on buying and improving an old "fixer" of a house. Another guide to fixers is *The Old House Journal Compendium,* edited by Clem Labine and Carolyn Flaherty. *Your Low-Tax Dream House* by Steve Carlson, a tax assessor, focuses on property tax issues.

AN AGENT'S REBUTTAL: *Ninth edition, August 1992.* Mary Ashby Purington, Clinton, MT, wrote me, "Having been a real estate agent, then an independent broker, for 20 years, I'd like to offer some insights."

Agent Services for the Seller. "The agent earns his or her money from the seller by screening potential buyers for credit-worthiness and ability to pay. (How many owner-sellers know how to obtain credit reports on would-be buyers?) Sellers also pay agents for explaining zoning, water rights, and covenants, etc. Informing the buyer of these things is the responsibility of the agent, legally and morally. Agents also handle important details like setting up an escrow properly. I've seen escrows set up without an agent in which a quitclaim deed from a previous buyer who had defaulted was not included, thus clouding the title. This sort of problem comes to light when a title search is made, an automatic step for a good agent."

Agent Services for the Buyer. Legally an agent works for the seller, but he or she helps the buyer by providing information on the availability of suitable property, taking the buyer to visit that property, explaining details about it, and then helping to negotiate a deal. Agents usually have access to listings of all local properties for sale by all brokerages, through what is called a multiple-listing service. Mary added, "A real estate agent or broker knows the market value of property in his/her area, thus saving you lots of

time. But try to find out *before* you talk to agents in person what local prices are, by making lots of phone calls on ads and trying to determine for yourself the range of prices."

Split Commissions. "If a property that sounds especially attractive to you is represented by your ultimate nightmare agent, don't despair: an agent you like may be able to get it for you. Acreages are less likely to be sold by brokers belonging to a multiple-listing service, but it's common practice for them to cooperate with one another and split commissions."

Agent as Matchmaker. "An otherwise improbable deal is more likely to occur when there's a go-between to take the heat. Emotions can safely be vented on the agent without damaging the chances for an eventual deal. Think of agents as marriage brokers who'll match-make you and the land you want."

Choosing Your Agent. "You'll find many different person-

alities among real estate agents. Visit with as many as it takes, preferably face-to-face, until you find a person with whom you feel comfortable. But be aware that some of them will 'grab on' like bulldogs if they decide you're a serious buyer, and it may take very firm rejection before you convince that person you *are not* going to be his/her prospect! If you're inclined to trust the 'soft-sell,' easygoing type of agent, be aware that seduction can feel good—until you wake up and realize you've been had! Because in the end, you must look out for yourself." Let me add that an agent who has lived and worked in one place for a long time will be well known in a small community. Ask around and learn his or her reputation. Does the agent have a record of cheating people, of selling bad land at inflated prices to dreamy-eyed would-be city escapees?

CONTINGENCIES: "It's a good idea for a buyer to make a list of requirements and specify them—things such as a water right—as contingencies in a sales contract, especially if they are not easily researched. A contingency is saying, 'I agree to buy *if* I have first water rights to such-and-such a creek,' only the legalese 'contingent on having' is used in place of 'if I have.' Contingencies are useful if you fear a property may sell to someone else before you have a chance to check it out." Here are some specific aspects you should check into before buying—or make part of your deal as the "contingencies" Mary referred to.

Access Rights and Road Matters. Are there road access rights to the property, or could you be one day surrounded by people who padlock their gates and can legally prevent you from going home? Real estate agent Frank Ryset advised, "Land can be cheap and easy to buy, but if there is no road to get to it, or if the road is good only for four months out of the year, your land value is worth only one-third the value of land that you can drive to year-round." Will you have to put in a road? Find out what legal restrictions apply and how much that would cost. Even a short driveway can be expensive. Figure on 10-feet wide in all its straight places and 14 feet wide anywhere it curves.

You'll want to either pave, concrete, or gravel the surface. A gravel road needs a slight slope from the center to the edge of about ¼ inch per foot to make it shed water. A gravel road also needs more gravel added every few years to fill in ruts and maintain traction. If your road goes over a creek, or a place where there is a creek after rain, you'll want to install a culvert there.

Water. Be especially careful to double-check whatever is said about water and septic rights. A secure—and unpolluted!—water supply is necessary unless you're going to truck it in weekly (which some homesteaders, especially desert dwellers, do!) Not all land has water underneath it, even if there is water running over or under the adjacent property. The only way to know for sure is to try drilling a well before you buy. Before you buy undeveloped land, find out how much it will cost to drill a well, pipe water in, or put in an aqueduct to bring water to you. Availability of water to irrigate land and produce the crops you want to raise to live is important! The best time to check on water supply is when the weather is hot and dry; springs that run in April are often dry by August. And find out if there is a land use requirement—a condition imposed by county health boards stating that only one sewage system can be put on a 5-acre parcel, for example, depending on the percolation or absorption rate of the land. Growth management laws are causing a real tightening up on water requirements. Note: Water rights can be bought as well as sold. You could deal to buy the right to an unused spring, for example, on an adjacent piece of land.

For lots more info on doing your own setup of a country water system, read *Cottage Water Systems: An Out-of-the-City Guide to Pumps, Plumbing, Water Purification, and Privies,* by Max Burns (1999). It's available from Cottage Life Books; 54 St. Patrick St., Toronto, ONT M5T 1V1 CANADA. Or read *The Home Water Supply: How to Find, Filter, Store and Conserve It* by Stu J. Campbell (1983). Order from Storey Books, Pownal, VT 05261.

Septic Rights. Unless your property is on a city sewer line that you could hook up to, you'll have to provide your own. That usually involves installing a septic tank and leach field. But government officials won't let you do that unless they judge the land permeable enough to absorb that water as it gradually drains out of the septic tank through the "leach lines" (long pipes with holes in them). So before you buy, get a county inspector to perform a percolation test to see if there's a spot on your land that will be okayed for percolation. *If the land won't percolate, don't buy!*—unless there's some truly possible and legal option. (More on water in Chapter 2.)

Assignable Lease. If you are told there is an "assignable lease," check that too. It sounds good, but it might not be true.

Electricity/Phone Costs. It could easily cost you thousands of dollars to bring in electricity and/or a phone if the property isn't already connected. The phone and electric companies will probably cooperate in getting their services to you, but you'll have to pay for it. Ask them what procedure you should follow to get their services, and how much it will cost. For either overhead or underground lines, they will charge by the foot. Compare that with how much an independent power system, such as a solar-power system ($5,000–10,000), would cost for power. You might well be ahead with private power! And consider buying some form of wireless telephone service.

Schooling. The school bus may not be willing or able to pick up your children at your prospective home. State or local school district policies or regulations might strictly forbid home schooling and militantly enforce that proscription. Frank warned, "Maybe today you don't have any desire or need to have a school bus coming by your door. But in 10 years you may have acquired some young ones. If you have to board your children out for schooling—what's life? That's 9 months of separation." On the other hand, home schooling is legal in some states, such as Montana and Washington.

Zoning and Building Codes. Frank said, "In the West, some of our counties are zoned and some are not. Or sometimes part of a county is restricted, while another portion is still clear of this type of ordinance. You can't ignore codes." I don't like zoning laws that require you to waste land in cosmetic lawns or that say you can't keep rabbits or chickens. People shouldn't have to be slaves to a standard of appearance that says everybody has to look rich and that makes it illegal to use your land to help grow your food. That's so far away from reality; it denies that we live by God's gifts of food, created by plants that grow in dirt

strengthened by manure—and by dairy products stroked from animals that have given birth so they will make milk to feed their babies and ours, and that give their extra males to be our meat, nurturing us as we have nurtured them.

Furthermore, the modern concept of zoning canonizes our petroleum dependence, our society's constant and excessive driving. It has widely separated business from factory from home from farm from school and church and shopping mall. A century ago, before the automobile, cities were much smaller, and the rural countryside was dotted with hamlets every 6–12 miles. Each little town consisted of a cluster of homes, a church or two, a school, and essential stores and industrial enterprises. Outside that tiny urban center were the gardens, orchards, cultivated fields, and farms with livestock yards where much of the town's food was raised. Beyond that were often "woods," where wild animals survived.

For efficient transportation, this arrangement was ideal. People could walk to most of the places that we now drive to: children to and from school, adults to work and the store. The setup also fostered a strong social fabric: neighbors who truly looked after each other, a school that was managed by the local parents in a very positive way. The economy was sustainable and nonpolluting. Well, both cars and zoning laws are going to continue to be with us for a while.

Acreage Limitations. Frank explained, "You find this land you like and it looks like it will produce. Now go to the county zoning board to find out if in that area there are any acreage limitations, meaning how many acres per living unit is the requirement of the county? Maybe they won't let you buy less than 5 acres, for example, 5 acres per family."

Timber. "Timber utilization is another fast-approaching zoning restriction. Under these regulations you aren't able to fell trees on your property without permission of the zoning officer of the county." If you're buying in a forested area, another consideration is the possibility of a forest fire that could burn your buildings. Fire insurance is always costly, and a house in a place considered at risk for forest fire may not be insurable at all.

Owner-Built Home. You may have been dreaming of a log cabin made from the trees on your property, or a budget shelter constructed from scavenged materials. But the county zoning board might consider it illegal for you to build your own home unless you are capable of meeting every detail of a conventional building code. So find out for sure if you can do it yourself and under what limitations. Incidentally, many homesteaders bring in a cheap used trailer house, or do build their own. Use your land wisely. Don't cover up a fifth of your land with a big expensive sprawling house and another big hunk with lawn that's mostly there to look at. Keep your house small and use that land like a real farmer with a big garden and animals in a pasture.

For home building info, see the Chelsea Green and Storey book lists ("Homestead Book or Video Dealers," this chapter). *Storey's Basic Country Skills* is a good starting place. The Builders Booksource offers mail-order and retail books on architecture, design, and construction, plus a free newsletter. For titles on seismic retrofit of buildings, building codes, landscaping, etc., contact 800-843-2028; fax 510-845-7051; 1817-4th St., Berkeley, CA 94710; **service@ buildersbooksite.com; www.buildersbooksite.com.** Home Planners offers mail-order books and residential blueprints; books, 800-322-6797; blueprints, 800-521-6797; fax 800-224-6699; 3275 W. Ina Rd., Ste. 110, Tucson, AZ 85741; **www.eplans.com.** For inside finishing info (doors, windows, plumbing, wiring, etc.), see *Housebuilding—A Do-It-Yourself Guide* (encyclopedic coverage) and *The Owner-Builder and the Code* by Kern, Kogon, and Thallon; these cover things you need to know about. *How to Build in the Country* by D. J. Berg tells you how to choose a site, plan, design, build, decorate, and landscape.

Home-Based Business. You may have an idea for starting a business at home, but the zoning for your area may not permit that, or there may be some highly inconvenient restrictions or taxes on such businesses. Find out before you sink money into it.

Covenants. Frank advised, "When buying in a 'subdivision' or in an already laid-out area, be sure you check for covenants upon future owners to restrict what they will build. There have been covenants where only one family could occupy a building, or only one house be built per 10 acres, or even that you can't have a pig on the property."

Balloon Payment. "Read the fine print of any contract," Frank warned, "and have your own lawyer do that also. And never sign a contract that contains a balloon payment clause unless you understand it. For example, I knew a fellow who bought an apartment house for $62,000 with payments of just $500 a month. He knew it was a good deal, but it never worried him until after 8 years, when he went to his lawyer to ask what the 'balloon payment' was that the contract said was coming due in 2 years. His lawyer explained that the 'balloon payment' meant the entire rest of the principal and interest became due and payable on that date, 2 years from then. So he lost the apartment house and everything he had invested in it. Most of his payments had been going for interest, so he hadn't yet paid off enough principal to have acquired enough 'equity' for the bank to be willing to loan him any money to make the balloon payment."

Title Search and Title Insurance. A title search determines whether there are any liens, water rights, back taxes, judgments, etc., against the property. A title company will do this search for you for a reasonable fee. Another worthwhile expenditure is for title insurance. Frank, teller of cautionary real estate tales, said: "Another friend of mine didn't worry about getting title insurance for the property he had just bought. It was a piece of land in the center of a block. He had his own private driveway; no one else came in and out of there. He lived on it for three years. Then one morning his neighbor had built a fence across his driveway. He went to the sheriff and to the county. What he discovered was that his driveway was entirely under the control of the other owner. It took a long court battle and almost as much in legal fees as he had paid for the house to secure a permanent, open easement to his property."

ASK! Asking questions, many questions of many sources, is the essence of wise buying. Be very conservative and careful in your dealing. You're going to have to live with this real estate contract a long time. Double-check everything the owner or real estate agent tells you with other sources.

1. Ask the Agriculture Stabilization and Conservation Service (ASCS); it's a government agency that gives free advice. Or ask your county extension agent if you have a choice. The agent may even be willing to walk over the land with you and point out features to keep in mind. The Soil Conservation Service agent for the county might also be available to walk the land with you and explain erosion and water aspects. He or she is the right person to ask whether a pond is practical, what the soil depth is over bedrock, etc. Or you can get that information on your own, because the Soil Conservation Service has available maps for the entire country that identify flood plains, soil type (color, texture), seasonal high water table, degree of slope, depth of bedrock, possible use of land for farming or forestry, and suitability of soil for septic system.

2. Ask the agent or clerk where you can see the U.S. Geological Service topographic map of the area. It will show elevations by means of contour lines, as well as roads, water, towns, etc. The place where you find the topographical map will probably also have aerial photographs of the entire region, so you can look at the property that way too.

3. Ask the town or county clerk what the tax rate is and how it's collected. Find out what the assessed value of the property has been, and what the tax bill actually was the past three years. Ask if the property tax rate is rising and when the assessor last reevaluated it. Bear in mind that if it hasn't been reassessed for many years, the past tax bills won't be typical of what you'll have to pay, because the sale to you will probably trigger a new assessment.

4. Ask the local planning board for maps that show the growth plan.

5. Ask the zoning commission to see a map of zones and their restrictions. This office will probably also be able to tell you what zoning and other regulations affect your prospective property. Also ask if there is a growth plan; is there a housing development or a mall, for instance, planned near your possible property? Ask what services will be available to that property: water? sewage disposal? garbage collection? road maintenance? Ask what their road-building specifications are.

6. Ask the neighbors next door what seasonal changes the property has and what its history and important points are. Does the gushing spring that's there in May dry up in August? They may give you a very different story than does the owner or agent.

7. Hire a local attorney as your lawyer. He'll know his way around with the people and information sources involved. Ask him what rights have been sold to or away from the land—water? mineral? Ask the lawyer or your real estate agent if any previous surveys or soil tests (for septic rights) have been done and how they turned out. (Ask to see the survey map.)

8. If it hasn't been surveyed, a rather expensive but valuable source of further information would be to hire your own surveyor to tell you exactly how many acres the property comprises and exactly where the property lines are. This is especially critical if the old land description takes as reference points things that no longer exist.

9. Ask a knowledgeable person to advise you on the condition of the buildings, their foundation, wiring, etc.

10. If you are participating in a property auction, either oral or by sealed bid, ask the auctioneer and/or the selling party ahead of time what the exact procedures are.

11. An assessor makes a living determining the market value of property. If you want an expert opinion, you can buy it.

CLOSING THE DEAL

IMPORTANT: Even if you negotiate your own deal, have a lawyer read over your contract and advise you before you sign it!

Down Payment. Sooner or later, your deal will be set, and all you'll need to close it will be enough money for the down payment. It's best if you have this saved up. The bank probably won't loan you any money unless you're already prosperous, in which case you don't need my advice. It's against the law to borrow money to put down on an FHA deal. If you must borrow, it's best to borrow from your parents or close friends rather than from interest-charging banks or loan companies. And consider this: If you borrow money to make the down payment, for the first couple years you'll be paying every month:

- On the land/home contract.
- To return the money borrowed to make the down payment.
- For housing if the land is "unimproved."
- For fire insurance if there are existing buildings (your contract will require you to have it).
- For stocking the land—seeds, animals, fences. (Tool cost depends completely on how many you buy and what kind they are—i.e., a spade or a tractor. When you set out to grow your own food, there's no end to the things you probably would like to buy. But you just have to do what you can with what you can afford.)
- For transportation.
- For property taxes (high in or near urbanized areas).

This combination is a heavy burden. It has to be an amount you can afford.

Escrow. A willing owner would probably have his own lawyer draw up a contract, since he will have dealt in land before and will know a lawyer. He'll split the fee with you and will choose a bank or escrow company to hold the contract in escrow (keep it safe until you have paid the last dime on it—30 years later or whenever). Only then will you get your deed from the escrow holder, enact a fulfillment deed, and become the legally recorded owner of the property. In the meantime, you send your regular payments to the bank or escrow service. It records receipt of them, takes out its small handling fee, and then passes the remaining money on to the owner.

Paying Off. It is typical of these contracts that if you are over 10 days late with a payment, the owner can send you a certified letter of warning and can soon take back his farm, complete with your down payment, everything you've paid up till then, and the property improvements you've made. That is a very hot seat to have to sit in for umpteen years, but there really isn't any other way to get land if you can't pay all cash up front. (And many owners don't want cash because they want the price plus interest, and because they want their income spread out for tax purposes.)

Be sure, however, that your contract stipulates that you can pay off sooner if you can and want to. That way, if you should strike it rich, you can get out from under the debt more quickly. The long payoff period is a good bet for owners, some of whom make a habit of selling their land to people they figure can't make it. When the suckers eventually get behind on their payments, the original owners can repossess it, together with improvements, and keep it—or sell it to another hopeful sucker.

YOUR LAND IS A SPIRITUAL RESPONSIBILITY: Whoever you are, whatever your faith, the land you live on is a spiritual responsibility. With privilege comes responsibility!

We all have to become political activists, fighting the sources of pollution everywhere we find them! If we don't fight, it will keep on happening. And don't be reluctant to study science. On the contrary, we who are trying to cure these planetary ills desperately need knowledge. We need expert chemists to tell us which poisons are in our food and water and how they're getting there. We need technicians to test our air, drinking water, and garden soil for toxic pollutants that could get into our bodies. We need scientists to tell us what's happening with the greenhouse effect, the hole in the ozone layer, vanishing or unhealthy forests, and vanishing plants and animals. We need to be told just how unhealthy it now is to eat the various ocean and lake fish species, where the radioactivity has leaked to now, and how likely the storage sites or power plants are to blow up. These are good-guy scientists, and a veritable army of them is absolutely necessary if this fight is to be won.

The moral person takes responsibility for his or her entire life, and afterlife, and the lives of those given to us as a

---

A LITTLE BIT OF LAND

A little bit of land is all I ask.
Just a small place to call my own,
where I can put down roots, so deep
  so deep,
that great-grandchildren still will
  call it home.
Is it so much to ask?
a lane of trees,
bringing birdsong and colored leaves,
a grape arbor, the roses beyond,
sweet lilacs holding in their arms,
the lawn.
Tulips, and yellow daffodil,
spattered up and down the cellar hill,
sweet gurgling brook, fresh and cool,
the brush beyond
sheltering grouse and sage,

and shy sweet deer.
Oh aching heart, hungry hungry soul.
What little bit to make a grateful
  whole.
Is there no spot in all this universe?
a little valley, with a cabin home,
a bit of garden I can call my own,
I would not bruise the land, or tear
  it apart,
but keep it beating with a happy
  blooming heart.
Each bit of soil, which God had
  surely blessed,
would be a cozy home for seeds to
  rest,
and grow and nourish, comforting
  all men,

with fruit and shade, and food for
  every soul.
A little bit of land, to call my own,
within its small confines, a loving
  home,
and fertile soil
no matter the toil,
I would so grateful be
if God would take a little chance on
  me
and give me a small plot of lonely
  sod
that needs a gentle hand, and God.

— *Jennie Senrud Hutton*

responsibility—and the tomorrow of this great gift of a planet! This is one of those times in history when everybody truly has to stand up and be counted. You're either for planetary death by poison or you're for a responsible, protective stewardship that will recover and maintain healthy soil, air, and water. There's no in-between. At the rate we're going, the next 10, 20, or, at the most, 50 years, will decisively tip the balance one way or the other. Now that modern times have arrived, from this time forward there can never be a letting up of this vigilance, this policing and regulation of government and industry's tendency and capacity to pollute.

There is change, good change, coming. New, more efficient technologies are now the leading edge in world business. More and more people are calling for ambitious long-term plans to save the environment. When we're awakened and aroused to the point at which people do what's needed even without legislation to force them, that's the best of all possible systems. Environmental issues are now global, and no single country's laws can solve them— although every country that enacts enlightened legislation is helping! Fixing what's wrong is going to require the creation of some totally new technologies, the transformation of some familiar ones, and the return to some very old ones. It can happen. It has to. Industry and government have to be willing, or forced, to include the ecological impact in their calculation of the true value of any product or result. They, and we, can't make decisions or set goals without taking into consideration the damage inflicted on the environment. We have to be willing to pay the many prices to avoid irreparable environmental damage.

INFORMATION PLEASE
Government Resources

YOUR COUNTY EXTENSION AGENT: There is a county agent in every county in the country, even very urban ones! These wonderful people are there to, among other things, answer your questions. Your agent is an expert on local rural matters and can advise you about local laws, pests, how much land in that particular area is required to carry a specified number of livestock, and so on. The agent may also give you helpful information about local politics. For example, is there conflict between ranchers accustomed to open-ranging their herds and homesteaders who don't like having range cattle wandering onto their private land and devouring their gardens? Who, if anybody, does the law require to build the fence? The agent can probably identify your bug problem and suggest a remedy—which may or may not be organic in nature.

You can find your county's extension service office in the phone book or by asking the state office. Or inquire of your local county government, probably under "Extension." The offices operate under the Cooperative Extension Service System, which is administered by a state university. Every state has a land grant institution whose mission is to do research appropriate to the local area and extension service. The extension service is paid for by taxes, and anyone is entitled to its assistance. The agents are information specialists, trained to consult a vast network of sources and researchers about any problem they don't have immediate answers to.

I asked Jan Grant (a Very Responsible Person in the King County [Washington] Extension Service, founder of the Master Food Preserver Program, and a professor at Washington State University) to go over this book and make sure there wasn't anything life-threatening in it. She did that, and much more. With painstaking care, she read each chapter in manuscript form; then she sat with me

and carefully explained things I didn't understand but needed to. She eagerly supplied me with heaps of additional and up-to-the-minute research materials, especially for Chapter 7, "Food Preservation." I am awed by the breadth of her knowledge and the care with which she evaluated my every statement. I'm humbly grateful for her willingness to help and for the considerable time and effort that demanded of her, but she says it's just part of her job.

AGRICULTURE CLASSES AND CLUBS: In a rural area, your children will be able to take agriculture classes at school, join Future Farmers of America (FFA) or Future Homemakers of America (FHA), and, best of all, participate in 4-H, a terrific learning opportunity. The local ag teacher is also a good person to ask questions.

STATE AGRICULTURAL COLLEGES: Every state has a land-grant agricultural university. That school has specialists who could help you identify local problem weeds, plant and animal parasites, and diseases—and suggest control methods to help you with every problem associated with regionally suited crops. Most of these folks are entwined in the agribusiness/big government comradeship and boost pesticides and chemical fertilizers. They may offer unwelcome solutions after they identify the problem. But it's a help to know exactly what you're up against, even if you disagree with the expert on how to deal with it. Most ag departments have at least token representation from the organic side. Some state ag colleges have terrific programs for homesteaders, especially the University of Michigan at Kalamazoo, whose Tillers International has contributed greatly to the comeback of oxen, and renewal of many other old-time agricultural skills.

ALABAMA: 114 Duncan Hall, Auburn University, AL 36849-5612; **apowell@aces.edu.**

ALASKA: 907-474-7188; U. of Alaska, PO Box 757200, Fairbanks, AK 99775.

ARIZONA: 520-621-7621, fax 520-621-7196, U. of Arizona, College of Agriculture and Life Sciences, Forbes Bldg., Tucson, AZ 85721; **egsander@ag.arizona.edu.**

ARKANSAS: 479-575-2000; U of Arkansas, Fayetteville, AR 72701; **www.uark.edu/.**

CALIFORNIA: U. of California, 300 Lakeside Dr., 6th Floor, Oakland, CA 94612.

COLORADO: Colorado State U., Fort Collins, CO 80523-1101.

CONNECTICUT: 860-486-1987; U. of Connecticut, 1376 Storrs Rd., W. B. Young Bldg., Box 4036, Storrs, CT 06269-4036. **www.canr.uconn.edu.**

DELAWARE: U. of Delaware, Townsend Hall, Newark, DE 19717; **ag.udel.edu.**

DISTRICT OF COLUMBIA: U. of the District of Columbia, 901 Newton St. NE, Washington, DC 20017. Or contact USDA Extension Service, Room 5509 South Building, Washington, DC 20250.

FLORIDA: 352-392-1961; fax 352-392-8988; U. of Florida, Institute of Food and Agricultural Sciences, College of Agricultural and Life Sciences, Office of the Dean; 2001 McCarty Hall/PO Box 110270, Gainesville, FL 32611-0270; **www.cals.ufl.edu.**

GEORGIA: U. of Georgia, College of Agriculture, Athens, GA 30602.

HAWAII: U. of Hawaii at Manoa, Honolulu, HI 96822.

IDAHO: U. of Idaho, Agriculture Science Bldg., Moscow, ID 83843.

ILLINOIS: U. of Illinois, 1301 W. Gregory, Mumford Hall, Urbana, IL 61801.

INDIANA: 317-494-8488, Purdue U., West Lafayette, IN 47906.

IOWA: Iowa State U., 110 Curtis Hall, Ames, IA 50011.

KANSAS: Kansas State U., Extension, 123 Umberger Hall, Manhattan, KS 66506-3401; **www.oznet.ksu.edu.**

KENTUCKY: U. of Kentucky, College of Agriculture, Lexington, KY 40506.

LOUISIANA: Louisiana State U., Knapp Hall, University Station, Baton Rouge, LA 70803.

MAINE: U. of Maine, Winslow Hall, Orono, ME 04469.

MARYLAND: 301-405-2072; U. of Maryland, College of Agriculture & Natural Resources, College Park, MD 20742; **www.agnr.umd.edu.**

MASSACHUSETTS: U. of Massachusetts, College of Food and Natural Resources, Amherst, MA 01002.

MICHIGAN: Bulletin Office, 517-355-0240, fax 517-353-7168, Michigan State U., 10-B Agriculture Hall, East Lansing, MI 48824-1039.

MINNESOTA: Extension Service, U. of Minnesota, 240 Coffey Hall, 1420 Eckles Ave., St. Paul, MN 55108-6068.

MISSISSIPPI: Mississippi State U., Box 9601, Mississippi State, MS 39762.

MISSOURI: U of Missouri, University Hall, Columbia, MO 65211.

MONTANA: Montana State U., College of Agriculture, Bozeman, MT 59717.

NEBRASKA: U. of Nebraska, Agriculture Hall, Lincoln, NE 68583.

NEW HAMPSHIRE: U. of New Hampshire, College of Life Sciences and Agriculture, Durham, NH 03824.

NEW JERSEY: Rutgers U., Cook College, 88 Lipman Dr., Room 104, New Brunswick, NJ 08901-8525; **ocpa@aesop.rutgers.edu; cook.rutgers.edu.**

NEW MEXICO: New Mexico State U., Box 3 AE, Las Cruces, NM 88003.

NEW YORK: Cornell U., Roberts Hall, Ithaca, NY 14853.

NORTH CAROLINA: 919-515-2011; North Carolina State U., Raleigh, NC 27695; **www.ncsu.edu/.**

NORTH DAKOTA: North Dakota State U., Box 5437, Fargo, ND 58105.

OHIO: Ohio State U., 2120 Fyffe Rd., Columbus, OH 43210.

OKLAHOMA: Oklahoma State U., Agriculture Hall, Stillwater, OK 74078.

OREGON: Oregon State U., Ballard Hall, Corvallis, OR 97331.

PENNSYLVANIA: Penn. State U., 323 Agriculture Adm. Bldg., University Park, PA 16802.

PUERTO RICO: U. of Puerto Rico, Rio Piedras, Puerto Rico 00928.

RHODE ISLAND: U. of Rhode Island, Woodward Hall, Kingston, RI 02881.

SOUTH CAROLINA: Ag & Forestry Research; 864-656-3141; Clemson U., 104 Barre Hall, Clemson, SC 29634-0151; **www.clemson.edu/agforestryresearch/.**

SOUTH DAKOTA: South Dakota State U., Box 2207, Brookings, SD 57007.

TENNESSEE: 865-974-7114; U. of Tennessee; 121 Morgan Hall, Knoxville, TN 37996-4530; **clnorman@utk.edu; www.utextension.utk.edu.**

TEXAS: Texas A & M, College Station, TX 77843.

UTAH: Utah State U., State Extension Service, Logan, UT 84322.

VERMONT: 802-656-2980; fax 802-656-0290, U. of Vermont, College of Agriculture and Life Sciences, 108 Morrill Hall, 146 University Place, Burlington, VT 05405.

VIRGINIA: Virginia Polytechnic Inst. and State U., Burruss Hall, Blacksburg, VA 24061.

WASHINGTON: Washington State U., College of Agriculture and Home Economics, PO Box 646242, Pullman, WA 99164-6242.

WEST VIRGINIA: West Virginia U., State Extension Service, Morgantown, WV 26506.

WISCONSIN: 608-263-5110; U. of Wisconsin, Agriculture Extension, 432 N Lake St., Madison, WI 53706.

WYOMING: U. of Wyoming, Box 3354, Univ. Station, Laramie, WY 82071.

USDA CONTACTS

Ag-in-the-Classroom "is a grassroots program coordinated by the USDA whose goal is to give students more awareness of the role of agriculture in the economy and society"; Kathleen Cullinan, Program Leader; 202-720-6825; fax 202-690-0062; Ag in the Classroom, USDA, 1400 Independence Ave. SW, Stop 2251, Washington, DC 20250-2251; **kcullinan@intranet.reeusda.gov.**

Agricultural Marketing Service can help you research potential markets. Write AMS, USDA, Room 2503-S, Washington, DC 20250.

Foreign Agricultural Service (FAS), Information Division, Room 4644-S, Washington, DC 20250-1000, provides info on U.S. trade and the world situation for most ag products.

Meat and Poultry Hotline: 800-535-4555.

National Agricultural Statistics offers federal ag stats on their home page: **www.usda.gov/nass.** Then choose Publications, then Reports by Commodity. Then choose your commodity.

National Agriculture Library takes requests for a search for any agricultural book or for general information on any ag topic: Document Delivery Services Branch, 6th Floor, 10301 Baltimore Blvd., Beltsville, MD 20705-2351; 301-504-5755; **www.nal.usda.gov.** NAL offers "Sustainable Agriculture in Print: Current Books, Videocassettes in the NAL Collection Pertaining to Alternative Farming Systems," and "IPM and Biological Control of Weeds." Their "Calendar of Events Related to Sustainable Agriculture" is an 8-page listing of national and regional seminars and conferences.

Office for Small-Scale Agriculture, USDA, Washington, DC 20250-2200; 202-401-4640, is a good place to ask questions about any aspect of farming, especially marketing.

ATTRA: A U.S. agency, funded by the Fish and Wildlife Service since 1987, called Appropriate Technology Transfer for Rural Areas, offers free info booklets and question-answering service (takes 2 to 4 weeks) for farmers wanting to grow food using organic/sustainable methods. "Within the agricultural industry there is a growing interest in changing away from farming practices that lead to water pollution, soil erosion, and chemical residues in our food." Contact: ATTRA, 800-346-9140; PO Box 3657, Fayetteville, AR 72702. (If you have an urgent question, such as how to deal organically with a weed or pest problem, contact your extension agent for a quick answer.)

ONLINE INFO: There are different ways of accessing information online after you have used your computer's modem to connect to the Internet. You can get online just to exchange e-mail with friends who are interested in the same subjects as you, and that can be a good source of information. The next step up is to go surfing, looking at websites and digging online for the info you need. And there are online homestead discussion groups you can subscribe to. Martha in Texas writes: "The problem is that you may not only get topics of interest, but also many e-mails of no interest. Still, they are an excellent mode of transmitting information to a like-minded group of people. Usually, the discussion group has a list moderator or owner and a parent Web page where digests of e-mail topics are archived, and log-on and unsubscribe information can be found. Another huge group is the Organic Garden Discussion List. Quite often, the BioDynamic groups, SANET and OGL, have people who 'cross post' topic information, so when something of interest comes up (such as Monsanto's horrifying terminator gene), it shows up again and again on all related list groups." Here are some worthwhile discussion groups and websites:

Homesteading and Frugal Living News is a list managed by Harry and Josie Meekins, Wyoming homesteaders: **wrp@trib.com; w3.trib.com/~wrp/HFLN.htm.**

National Gardening offers a free e-mail newsletter, online articles/library, message boards, seed swap, and events calendar: PO Box 51106, Boulder, CO 80322-1106; **www.garden.org.**

Nebraska Sustainable Agriculture Society can put you in touch with other state organizations: 402-254-2289; PO Box 736, Hartington, NE 68739; **www.netins.net/showcase/nsas.**

Northeast Organic Farming Association (NOFA-VT) is an alliance of consumers, gardeners, and farmers who support local, organic agriculture: 802-434-4122; **www.nofavt.org.**

Sustainable Agriculture Society is a great place to find info on organic and renewable farming methods. To help you network with helpful people and groups, ATTRA created the Sustainable Agriculture Network Directory of Expertise: 301-504-6425; **san@sare.org; www.sare.org.** One visitor said, "These are some of the most positive, innovative, and energetic people that I've met. . . . They are really enthused about the future of agriculture!"

Back-to-the-Landers' Books and Magazines

You will want lots of help besides this book. If you get interested in any particular subject, the material in this book can be a starting point, but by all means look in your bookstore or public library, or at the list of specialty country-skills book dealers later in this chapter, for more detailed information. You really can't know too much.

INTER-LIBRARY LOAN: Not all the books recommended throughout this book are available through your bookstore. But they probably are available through your library. If they aren't in your local library, ask about getting them from another library via "inter-library loan," one of the true blessings of modern times. Your local librarian can do a computer search to see if the book you want is available in *any* library in the country. If it is, the librarian will request it for you from that distant library! You'll be able to check it out as soon as it arrives in the mail. So throughout this book, I list book references whether or not the books are still "in print" (offered for sale by the publisher). I get most of my books from my library, which can usually find out-of-print books as efficiently as in-print ones—and I'm assuming yours is just as good.

GENERAL BOOKS ABOUT FOOD SELF-SUFFICIENCY AND COUNTRY LIVING: Here follows my annotated, opinionated bibliography. Most of these books are out of print, but your local librarian can help you obtain them.

The Almanac of Rural Living by Harvey C. Neese (Troy, ID: N & N Resources, 1976). Reprints of a mass of government ag pamphlets.

Back to Basics by *Reader's Digest* staff (New York, 1981). Wide coverage, shallow depth.

Backyard Farming by Ann Williams (London: Bowering Press, 1978). A broad but not deep survey of the subject from an Englishwoman's point of view.

The Basic Essentials of Survival by James E. Churchill (ICS Books).

The Complete Book of Self Sufficiency by John Seymour (Faber, 1976). John Seymour is one of the foremost British authors writing in this field. Together with his wife, Sally, he also wrote the classic *Farming for Self-Sufficiency: Independence on a 5-Acre Farm* (New York: Schocken Books, 1973) and *The Self-Sufficient Gardener,* found below on this list.

Country Women: A Handbook for the New Farmer by Sherry Thomas and Jeanne Tetrault (Cloudburst Press). Good source of info about animals and building; published in Canada.

The Encyclopedia of Country Living: An Old Fashioned Recipe Book by Carla Emery (Seattle: Sasquatch Books, 2003). The best there is, and it keeps coming out in new editions that are better yet!

Farming for Self-Sufficiency: Independence on a 5-Acre Farm by John and Sally Seymour. A beloved classic of the English "smallholders" movement.

Five Acres and Independence: A Practical Guide to the Selection and Management of the Small Farm by M.G. Kains. First published in 1935 by Greenberg, revised and enlarged by Kains. Fifty-one chapters with a little of everything (like this one). Good!

The Foxfire Series (I, II, III, etc.), edited by Eliot Wigginton. This longtime English teacher at a private boarding school in the Appalachians annually sent his students out to interview elderly hill people about old-time ways. Back-to-the-landing from those who never left. Not always the most practical source, but always worth reading.

Future Is Abundant: A Guide to Sustainable Agriculture (1982). An annotated bibliography published by the Tilth organization. Full of valuable ideas for everyone, but aimed at the Pacific Northwest.

The Golden Age of Homespun by Jared van Wagenen, Jr. (Cornell University Press, 1953). Beautifully written by one of the last of the true "old-timers." He says U.S. rural population reached its maximum between about 1860 and 1880. At that time there were more country people and a greater number of individual farms than ever before or since.

Grow It! by Richard W. Langer (New York: Saturday Review Press, 1972). Good in both breadth and depth of coverage. Reliable info.

The Guide to Self-Sufficiency by John Seymour.

The Harrowsmith Reader by the editors of *Harrowsmith* magazine (Camden House, 1978). There's a series of these collections of articles from *Harrowsmith*. Any and all are worth reading but are not systematic in topic.

The Home & Farm Manual: A Pictorial Encyclopedia of Farm, Garden, Household, Architectural, Legal, Medical and Social Information, Classic 1884 Edition by Jonathan Periam (New York: Crown Publishers, reprinted 1984). An extraordinary book—humbling when you consider they knew that much over 100 years ago. Illustrated by over 1,200 exquisite engravings.

Home Food Systems by editors at Rodale (Emmaus, PA: Rodale Press, 1981). An annotated gadget catalog, but the notes are copious, entertaining, and useful.

The Homesteader's Handbook by James E. Churchill (Harrisburg, PA: Stackpole Books, 1974). (There are a number of books with this title; titles can't be copyrighted, only the text inside a book.)

The Homesteader's Handbook by Rich Israel and Reny Slay (1973). Fun and folksy.

The Homesteader's Handbook by Martin Lawrence (New York: Mayflower Books).

How to Live on Almost Nothing and Have Plenty by Janet Chadwick.

Husbandry: The Sure, Cheap Way to Plenty and Prosperity in the Country (1998) by Nathan Griffith is an encyclopedic collection of Mr. Griffith's lifetime of homestead experience: HCR 68, Box 185-CL, Trout, WV 24991, **www.cobblemead.com.**

Living off the Country for Fun and Profit by John L. Parker (Ontario, CA: Bookworm Publishing, 1978).

Living on a Few Acres by the U.S. Dept. of Agriculture. A useful book-length collection of articles written by extension agents in 1978.

Managing Your Personal Food Supply: How to Eat Better for Less by Taking an Active Role in Producing, Processing, and Preparing Your Food, edited by Ray Wolf, an editor at Rodale Press.

The Manual of Practical Homesteading by John Vivian (Emmaus, PA: Rodale Press, 1975). Good information but choppy presentation.

The Owner-Built Homestead: A How-to-Do-It Book by Barbara Kern and Ken Kern. Site selection, water development, soil management, farming, farm machinery, bulk processing and marketing, etc. Excellent.

Practical Skills: A Revival of Forgotten Crafts, Techniques, and Traditions by Gene Logsdon (1985), who also has written classics on small-scale grain growing, aquaculture, berry raising, and gardening and *The Contrary Farmer's Invitation to Gardening* (1997). His books are now offered by Chelsea Green Publishing Co. All are superbly researched, carefully illustrated, and a pleasure to read because he is a fine human being as well as an honest, articulate, independent thinker and careful researcher.

Self-Sufficient Country Living by D.S. Savage (St. Martin's Press, 1978).

The Self-Sufficient Gardener: A Complete Guide to Growing and Preserving All Your Own Food by John Seymour (Garden City, NY: Doubleday & Co., 1979).

Storey's Basic Country Skills: A Practical Guide to Self-Reliance, edited by Deborah Burns (1999). This collage of info and pix from the stable of Storey authors is especially helpful in plumbing, carpentry, and home improvement, but offers a bit of everything in the homestead line.

Successful Small-Scale Farming: An Organic Approach by Karl Schwenke (Storey Books, 800-441-5700; **www.storey. com**). This old classic is pitched to both professional and entry-level small-scale farmers, heavy on the organic info.

The University of California Small Farm Center has compiled loose-leaf sheets on 37 organic, ethnic, and unusual agricultural options for a small farmer, including arugula, bok choy, endive, kiwano, and tomatillo, as well as seed sources, cultivation and production methods, marketing alternatives and bibliography. Send $30, payable to UC Regents, to ANR Publications, U. of California, 6701 San Pablo Ave., Oakland, CA 94608-1239, (510) 642-2431.

Village Technology Handbook. Big book of tips with a focus on appropriate, elementary technology for developing nations. Send $19.95 to VITA; 703-276-1800; fax 703-243-1865; Ste. 710, 1600 Wilson Blvd., #500, Arlington, VA 22209; **vita@vita.org; www.vita.org**.

When Technology Fails: A Manual of Self-Reliance & Planetary Survival by Mathew Stein is a practical guidebook for developing a sustainable lifestyle and being prepared for any emergency or disruption due to natural or manmade causes. Mat offers great technical info for hands-on inclined folks in this book; 505-989-9590; fax 505-989-9519; Clear Light Publishers, 823 Don Diego, Santa Fe, NM 87501; **clpublish@aol.com; www.clearlightbooks.com**.

HOMESTEAD BOOK OR VIDEO DEALERS: These offer more useful and enjoyable books than you have money to buy, alas! But pick and choose, and you'll benefit from what you can order. Many back-to-the-land magazines also sell books geared to their audience's interests.

American Nurseryman Publishing specializes in mail-order horticultural books, software, and videos. Free catalog; 800-621-5727; fax 312-782-3232; 77 W. Washington St., Ste. 2100, Chicago, IL 60602-2904; **books@amerinursery.com; www.amerinursery.com**.

Aspen Cabin Wilderness Bookstore sells books on wilderness living, survival, gardening, homesteading, hunting, fishing, construction, etc. Catalog $1; 800-397-6584; Aspen Cabin, 5038-J Sixth Ave., Kenosha, WI 53140-3402.

Astragal Press offers unusual craft books for instruction, antique tools, blacksmithing, carriage building, tinsmithing, coppersmithing, woodworking. Free catalog; 5 Cold Hill Rd., Ste. #12, PO Box 239, Mendham, NJ 07945-0239; **astragalpress@attglobal.net**.

Atlan Formularies is where Kurt Saxon compiles and reprints technical articles and books from years past (1700s? through early 1900s) that deal with "survival and self-sufficiency"; 870-437-2999; PO Box 95, Alpena, AR 72611; **cary@survivalplus.com; www.survivalplus.com**.

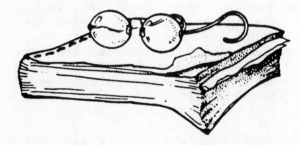

Back Forty Books offers retail or mail-order books on agriculture, native ways, and health. Free catalog; 764-596-4379; fax 740-596-3079; 26328 Locust Grove Rd., Creola, OH 45622.

CEV Multimedia markets FFA and ag-science curriculum videos and audios. Pricey ($50 to $100), slick, and high-tech. Interesting, sizable videocassette catalog $1.50. Topics such as *Budding and Grafting*, 25 min.,

$95, *Introduction to Greenhouse Management*, $95, *Sheep Management Practices—I* (lambing, docking, castration procedures, etc.), 55 min., $79, etc. Contact: 800-922-9965; fax 800-243-6398; PO Box 65265, Lubbock, TX 97464; **cev@cev-inc.com; www.cev-inc.com**.

Chelsea Green Publishing offers Gene Logsdon's books and a couple hundred (!!!) more on every aspect of sustainable living, alternative building methods, renewable energy, gardening, small farming, etc. Large free catalog; 802-295-6300; 800-639-4099; fax 802-295-6444; PO Box 428, White River Junction, VT 05001; **publicity@chelseagreen.com; www.chelseagreen.com**. They also publish a free e-mail newsletter called "The Hub" and periodic paper newsletters called *The Junction*.

Cobblemead Publications, HCR 68, Box 185-M5, Trout, WV 24991; **www.cobblemead.com**. Nathan Griffith publishes and markets his own books (*Husbandry, How to Cheaply Get Land . . .*), an 1859 reprint (*Our Farm of Four Acres . . .*), and used books of the homestead genre.

Eureka Resources sells books on homesteading, gardening, energy; backpacking, wildlife, survival; health, nutrition, medicine; crafts, tools, alternative building methods; legal self-help. Catalog $2. PO Box 2356, Martinez, CA 94553.

Food Products Press, a division of Haworth Press, offers numerous ag books, such as its seven titles under Aquaculture (*Recent Developments in Catfish Aquaculture*, etc.). It also publishes dozens of agribusiness journals and ag college textbooks. Haworth is a print reflection of the power structure, profit orientation, and organizational trends of modern agriculture; 607-722-5857, ext. 375; fax 607-722-6362 (for textbooks); 10 Alice St., Binghamton, NY 13904-1580; **www.haworthpress.com**. (See *Journal of Sustainable Agriculture* under "Magazines and Newsletters.")

Good Farming Books sells new and out-of-print books on responsible agriculture, livestock, poultry, gardening, rural life. Catalog $1; Robert Gear, 413-337-4844; Box 1137, Greenfield, MA 01302.

Horizon Publishers offers a line of books on camping, wilderness survival skills, and Indian crafts; three Dutch oven cookbooks; three great books on food drying; and more on food storage and sprouting. *Leather Makin': A Manual of Primitive and Modern Leather Skills* covers tanning. Contact: 801-295-9451; fax 801-295-0196; PO Box 490, 50 South 500 West, Bountiful, UT 84011.

Lindsay Publications has reprinted many old-time manuals on making things from scratch: 815-935-5353; fax 815-935-5477; PO Box 538, Bradley, IL 60915; **www.lindsaybks.com**.

Rodale Press: They've been a major contributor in this area and still are, with many good books in print. Write or call for their list: 215-967-5171; 33 East Minor St., Emmaus, PA 18098.

Storey Publishing: How-To Books for Country Living is one of the largest publishers/distributors in this field. The mission is "to serve our customers by publishing practical information that encourages personal independence in harmony with the environment." Free catalog: 800-441-5700; fax 800-865-3429; 210 MASS

MoCA Way, North Adams, MA 02147; **storey@storey. com; www.storey.com.**

USDA. You can find out about USDA print and diskette publications by calling 212-512-1800 or 202-512-1530. Or mail to Superintendent of Documents, PO Box 371954, Pittsburgh, PA 15250-7954. You can search the online Publications Reference file at **www. access.gpo.gov/su_docs/.**

Volunteers in Technical Assistance (VITA) is a private, nonprofit international development organization operated by 4,000+ volunteers. It offers self-sufficiency info to individuals and groups in developing countries: agriculture, food processing, renewable energy, water supply, sanitation, house construction, and small business development. It also runs a matchmaking service connecting Western experts with needs in developing nations. If you're expert on anything agricultural or relevant to basic how-to, write VITA and offer to help. It might be the beginning of a beautiful adventure! You can help from your armchair via letter. Free publications catalog: 703-276-1800; Suite 710, 1600 Wilson Blvd., #710, Arlington, VA 22209; **vita@vita.org; www.vita.org.**

Williamson Publishing puts out good animal care books. Free catalog: 800-234-8791; fax 802-425-2102; PO Box 185, Charlotte, VA 05445; **jane@williamson books.com.**

MAGAZINES AND NEWSLETTERS: You'll enjoy and find useful both articles and ads in the periodicals listed below. This list is of general ones that are pitched to back-to-the-landers, do-it-yourselfers, and animal/plant/earth lovers. Specialized magazines, newspapers, and newsletters are listed in this book under their specific topics. Your author's choices for "best magazines for back-to-the-landers," based on my measures of their page quantity, quality, and relevance of articles, are, as of 2002, *Countryside, Mother Earth News,* and *Backwoods Home.* My other two favorites on a homestead-related subject are *Home Power* (independent systems for rural or urban homes using wind, water, solar, or hydrogen energy) and *Green Prints,* the "Weeder's Digest."

Acres U.S.A. is a monthly magazine presenting refreshingly radical info on agriculture, medicine, soil building, and organic/sustainable farming, livestock, herb production, etc., that can pay: "A Voice for Eco-Agriculture." They announce eco-farming meetings and events across North America, list eco-suppliers, and sell good land-lover's books. Subscription rates are $27/yr in U.S.; $32/yr outside U.S.: 800-355-5313; 512-892-4400; fax 512-892-4448; PO Box 91299, Austin, TX 78709-1299; **info@acres.com; www. acresusa.com.**

AgVentures, 11950 W. Highland Ave., Blackwell, OK 74631; **agventures@aol.com;** 888-474-6397; 580-628-4551; fax 580-628-2011; **www.agventures.com.** Detailed articles describing small farm projects with profit potential: raising livestock, herbs, animals, mushrooms, etc. Six issues/yr for $21. Recommended.

American Agriculturist, Farm Progress Co., 191 S. Gary Ave., Carol Stream, IL 60188; 708-690-5600.

(The) Avant Gardener is a horticultural news service in a monthly 8-page newsletter for educated gardeners: $24/yr; Box 489, New York, NY 10028.

BackHome provides good, unpretentious articles on self-reliant living, homeschooling, healthy and nutritious food preparation, alternative building methods, solar/renewable energy technologies, organic gardening, and cottage industries: $21.97 (6 issues/yr). There are 66 total pages, about 45 of them articles, the rest ads. Publisher Richard Freudenberger and associates (many of whom staffed the original *Mother Earth News*) are carefully nonreligious and nonpolitical in presentation: 800-992-2546; PO Box 70, Hendersonville, NC 28793; **www.backhomemagazine.com.**

Backwoods Home Magazine is a great resource for folks who value personal independence and a self-reliant lifestyle, with good-quality articles on owner-built housing, alternative energy, gardening, health, self-employment, country living, etc. Publisher/editor Dave Duffy promotes high morals, work ethic, and a largely Libertarian view of things: $19.95/yr (6 issues); $35.95 for 2 yrs; 800-835-2418, fax 541-247-8600, PO Box 712, Gold Beach, OR 97444; **editor@backwoodshome.**

com; www.backwoodshome.com.

The Backwoodsman has a muzzle-loading and knife focus. Also, Indian lore, gardening, old-time skills and technologies such as trapping, tanning, Dutch oven cooking, hunting, historical articles, and announcements of reenactments (gatherings where folks dress and behave like persons from a designated historical period). It's $18/yr (6 issues); sample $3; 719-783-9028; PO Box 627, Westcliffe, CO 81252; **bwmmag@iris.net; www.backwoodsmanmag.com.**

Biodynamics is published by the Biodynamic Farming and Gardening Association. They provide a free list of farmers practicing Community Supported Agriculture. Very intense about the biodynamic science, art, and religion of gardening. They grow *great* gardens; $45/yr (6 issues); 800-516-7797; 888-516-7797; PO Box 29135, San Francisco, CA 94129-0135; **www.biodynamics. com.**

Caelum et Terra is a thoughtful Catholic quarterly, with a land and self-sufficiency orientation; $20/yr; PO Box 1494, Wooster, OH 44891.

Common Sense at Home Newsletter & Books, a 12-pg newsletter of how-tos for homeschooling, homekeeping, thrift, gardening, issues of the day, book reviews, etc. Selling the basic how-to books, $6 for 4 issues/yr. Free issue: CSAHNB, PO Box 784, Warsaw, MO 65355; **csah@ lakeozarknet.**

Country is a color photo magazine featuring lovely rural scenes; no ads. Reiman Publications offers a free sample issue "for those who live in or long for the country." A 2-yr (6 issues/yr) sub costs $19.96/yr; 414-423-0100; 5925 Country Lane, PO Box 994, Greendale, WI 53129-0994; **www.reimanpub.com.**

Country Folks is a weekly agricultural newspaper with your choice of New England, Pennsylvania, and two New

York editions. *Country Folks Farm Chronicles* covers North Carolina, Virginia, Maryland, and Delaware. *Dairy Farm* covers NC, SC, GA, FL, LA, KY, TX, MO, MS monthly. Write for subscription rates to Lee Publications, PO Box 121, 8113 Slate Hwy. 5, Palatine Bridge, NY 13428.

Countryside Magazine, W11564 Highway 64, Withee, WI 54498; 715-785-7979; fax 715-785-7414; **csymag@midway.tds.net; countrysidemag.com.** A classic in this field, mostly reader-written. You'll soon feel like "family." This magazine is one of the oldest in the field but stays abreast, too. "Countryside reflects and supports the simple life, and calls its practitioners homesteaders . . . reverence for nature and a preference for country life; a desire for maximum personal self-reliance and creative leisure; a concern for family nurture and community cohesion; a certain hostility towards luxury; a belief that the primary reward of work should be well-being rather than money; a certain nostalgia for the supposed simplicities of the past and an anxiety about the technological and bureaucratic complexities of the present and the future; and a taste for the plain and functional." Recommended! Black-and-white, 148+ pages; $18/yr (6 issues); sample $3.

Country Woman has color, slick pages, and lots of appeal for farm/ranch and suburbanite wives who live in or long for the country; recipes, gardening, crafts, etc. No advertising. Six issues/yr for $16.98; 5400 S. 60th St., Greendale, WI 53129-1404; **www.countrywoman magazine.com.**

The Draft Horse Journal, PO Box 670, Waverly, IA 50677; 319-352-4046. Published by Cedar Creek Publishing, Inc., Lynn Telleen, editor. Quarterly publication dedicated to the draft horse industry. $25/yr.

Ecology Action Newsletter is a quarterly newsletter focused on sustainable mini-farming and useful for gardeners, homesteaders, and fans of nonpolluting energy systems. Cost: $15 for newsletter only; $30 Ecology Action membership; 5798 Ridgewood Rd., Willits, CA 95490.

Farm and Dairy is a weekly newspaper focused on OH, PA, WV areas: $28/yr, $48/2 yrs, 44-pg news/ads section; 60-pg auction guide (205 auctions listed the week I'm looking at); 38-pg classifieds section (785 ads). Lots and lots of news, weekly Bible study, recipes: 330-337-3419; fax 330-337-9550; 800-837-3419; Box 38, Salem, OH 44460; **www.farmanddairy.com.**

Farm and Ranch Living serves an audience of commercial farm and ranch families with human-interest stories, a 4-month farm/ranch diary in each issue, humor, rural nostalgia, old-time tractor talk, 4-H, retired farmer column, and events. Color pictures; no ads; $17.98/yr, sample issue $2. Contact: 414-423-0100; fax 414-423-8463; 5925 Country Lane, Greendale, WI 53129; **farmandranchliving.com; reimanpub.com.**

Farming Magazine is "the only magazine helping small-scale farmers make a good living, and a good life, from the land . . . wants to help you make farming profitable, enjoyable, and something your children will want to do." Cost is $18/yr; PO Box 85, Mt. Hope, OH 44660.

The Fence Post is a 200-pg farm paper, published weekly for 23,500 paid subscribers. It has 32 full-color pages, 60% ads (farm real estate, machinery, fences) and farm calendar announcements; auctions, 4-H/FFA and horse events, etc. Plus human interest stories, syndicated columnists, photo contests, recipe pages, kid's page, cartoons, and poetry. Cost is $37/yr; 970-686-5691; fax 970-686-5694; 423 Main St., Windsor, CO 80550; **sweeney@thefencepost.com.**

The Furrow is a big tractor company's (John Deere) sales aid, and, of course, slick and well written; 913-310-8302; 11145 Thompson Ave., Lenexa, KS 66219, **jdmail@banta.com.**

Gentle Spirit focuses on liberal Christian and nonviolence topics, plus garden, homeschooling, and homesteading items. Published monthly except August; $22/yr; 425-747-7703; PO Box 246, Wauna, WA 98395, **www.gentlespiritcom.**

(The) Gentle Survivalist Newsletter, published in southern Utah since 1991, is read by deep thinking, sustainably oriented, survivors of modern materialism: "Walk softly, yet self-sufficiently on Mother Earth." Great poetry; Native American items. This 14-pg monthly costs $22 for 4 issues/yr; sample $2; Box 4004, St. George, UT 84770; **gentle_survivalist@yahoo.com; www.infowest.com/gentle.**

Good Life Journal is the meeting place for Christians living more with less. Reader-written quarterly newsletter focused on simple, sustainable, good stewardship. Sample $4; $16/yr; $30/2 yrs; PO Box 9522, Ft. Wayne, IN 46899-9522.

Green Prints, a.k.a. "Weeders Digest," is an 80-pg illustrated b/w quarterly that shares the joy, humor, frustration, and heart of gardening. It's the human (not how-to) side; $19.97/yr; 828-628-1902; PO Box 1355, Fairview, NC 28730; **www.greenprints.com.** Recommended!

(The) Homesteader is a bimonthly paper published by the Catholic homestead movement "to better the world by helping people to homestead with Christian principles." Articles on medicinal herbs, hand tools, gardening, log cabins, workhorses, nonelectric living, and thoughts on homesteading. For info, send 3 stamps to 19 Delaware Square, Norwich, NY 13815.

Homesteader's Connection is a 24-pg, newspaper-format, bimonthly that covers homesteading and simple living, featuring dairy and meat goats, small livestock, gardening, alternative energy, etc. Cost is $18/yr; sample $2. Contact Publisher Andy Oliver; 915-653-5438; PO Box 5373, San Angelo, TX 76902; **www.homesteaders connection.com.**

Horticulture is a big money media production of garden advice plus ads; 1 yr for $19.95: 800-234-2415; PO Box 51455, Boulder, CO 80323-1455; **hcul@neodata.com.**

Hortideas is a small but significant magazine in which Greg and Pat summarize magazines, reports, and books about plant research in plain English; paper, $25/yr, e-mail version $15; 750 Black Lick Rd., Gravel Switch, KY 40328, **gwill@mis.net; www.users.mis-net/~gwill.**

Journal of Sustainable Agriculture provides articles such as "The Effect of Dry Matter Level on Effluent Loss and Quality Parameters of Potato Based Silage," "Neighborhood Effects of Growth, Seed Yield, and Weed Biomass for Three Perennial Crops in Polyculture," "An Upbeat Look at Government Policies and Proposals Involving Cattle and Sustainable Agriculture," etc. Agribusiness discovering the profit potential in organic ag. Cost is $38/yr for 4 issues. This one is published by the mega-mono of agribusiness publishing (dozens of journals and books catering to the college ag/big ag clientele): Food Products Press, a division of Haworth Press; 607-722-5857, ext. 375; fax 607-722-6362 for textbooks; 10 Alice St., Binghamton, NY 13904-1580; **www.haworthpress.com.**

Lancaster Farming: This $19/yr newspaper (published every Saturday) has a circulation of 50,000+ in the mid-Atlantic and Northeast. Contact: Andy Andrews, Editor, 717-626-1164; 1 East Main St., Ephrata, PA 17522; **farming@lancnews.infi.net; www.lancasterfarming.com.**

Luddite Journal contains intelligent articles on simple living and related subjects by an association of Quaker and Mennonite/Amish authors. The 32 pages on life, land, and spirit are printed by nonelectric technology (wood cuts, manual press!); $11/yr for 3 issues, published irregularly, payable to Scott Savage. No telephone; 60805 Pigeon Point, Barnesville, OH 43713.

Maine Organic Farmer & Gardener is published by the Maine Organic Farmers and Gardeners Association (MOFGA) on 56 newspaper-style pages (6 issues/yr). It covers northeastern U.S. organics, farms, crafts, draft animal news, activities, and ads. Membership costs $25 individual, $35 family, $15 elder or student, and also buys admission to the Association's huge Sept. "Common Ground Country Fair" and Nov. "Farmer-to-Farmer Conference" on sustainable ag systems. Membership also gets you discounts on supplies and notice of training conferences, programs, and activities, 207-568-4142; PO Box 170, Unity, ME 04988-0170.

Mother Earth News offers lots of solid info for suburban and rural folks from good writers who are living the life. It's a super bargain at $12.95/yr (6 issues) or $22.95/2 yrs for this 146-pg magazine, 80 pgs articles, remainder ads; 785-274-4300; 1503 SW 42nd St., Topeka, KS 66609; **motherearthnews.com.** Recommended!

National Gardening used to be chemical/mainstream, but is now organic in attitude. Cost is $12.95/yr (6 issues), 40 pages. But their big deal is web services: free e-mail newsletter, online articles/library, message boards, seed swap, and events calendar; PO Box 51106, Boulder, CO 80322-1106; **www.garden.org.**

The Natural Farmer, published by the Northeast Organic Farming Association (NOFA), provides great how-to articles on organic techniques, interviews with organic farmers, updates on certification standards, organic news, research, and legislation. Also job, land, equipment, and product listings, letters, and editorials; $10 for 4 issues/yr. Contact: 802-434-4122; 411 Sheldon Rd., Barre, MA 01005; **JACKKITT@aol.com; www.nofavt.org.**

New England Farm Bulletin is a monthly that features an annual almanac and summer directory of all fairs and farmers markets in New England, plus farm classified ads: PO Box 67, Taunton, MA 02780, costs $17/yr.

Organic Gardening is the magazine that introduced me to organic growing. They defined and popularized the term "organic." They've fought intelligently, endlessly, and creatively for a better, healthier, toxic-free life for people and the soil. But they've also gone urban/suburban

in recent years and are not relating to and serving the rural homestead contingent as well as they used to. Cost is $24.96/yr for 6 issues. The issue I looked at had 28 pages of articles and related pix and a total of 50 pages (remainder being ads); 800-666-2206; PO Box 7320, Red Oak, IA 51591; **orggard@aol.com; www.organicgardening.com.**

(The) Permaculture Activist is a quarterly of ecological design. Articles and books on gardening, trees, agroforestry, natural building, community, energy and technology, and local economics. Cost $20/yr; $37 for 2 yrs; 828-669-6336; PO Box 1209, Black Mountain, NC 28711; **info@permacultureactivist.net; www.permacultureactivist.net.**

Permaculture Connections: Southeast Permaculture Network News focuses on practical permaculture in the southeastern U.S.; PO Box 1303, Waynesville, NC 28786; 704-452-5716; $5/yr, quarterly.

(The) Potter's Daughter is "a magazine for Rural Christian Women" focused on at-home moms, nonchemical gardening, handcrafts, family, evangelism ("KJV only"), recipes, and money-saving tips; 36 pgs; free classified ads for subscribers; U.S. $20/yr for 6 issues; $38/2 yrs; sample $4; 270-352-0059; 420 E. Spring St, Radcliff, KY 40160; **thepottersdaughter@yahoo.com; www.pottersdaughter.com.**

Progressive Farmer, 2100 Lakeshore Dr., PO Box 2581, Birmingham, AL 35212. Also has a *Southwest Edition.* Respected monthly alternative ag news source; $13/yr; **www.progressivefarmer.com.**

Rural Heritage, "20 years in support of farming and logging with horses, mules and oxen," provides solid articles, apprenticeship postings, a draft animal events calendar, and annual updates to their *Work Horse, Mule & Oxen Directory and Guide.* Cost is $26/yr for 6 issues, 108 pgs; $47 for 2 yrs. Great, free book/video catalog; 281 Dean Ridge Lane, Gainesboro, TN 38562-5039; 931-268-0655; **www.ruralheritage.com.**

Ruralife is a 40-pg monthly cooperative publication free to member public electric utility consumers in parts of Oregon, Washington, Alaska, Idaho, Nevada, northern California, Montana, Wyoming, Utah, and elsewhere. Lonely-hearts, classified, and recipe-swapping sections plus some articles: PO Box 558, Forest Grove, OR 97116; 503-357-2105.

Small Acreage Farming supports Community Supported Agriculture; $16/yr, 6 issues; fax 208-764-2332; PO Box 219, Fairfield, ID 83327.

Small Farmer's Journal: The Quarterly Magazine about Craftsmanship in Farming, Culture in Agriculture, and Farming with Work Horses & Mules, Lynn Miller, PO Box 1627, 325 Barclay Way, Sisters, OR 97759; 541-549-2064; fax 541-549-4403; **farmer@smallfarmersjournal.com.** Classified ads for country apprenticeships or workers. No ads for pesticides, tobacco, alcohol, or petro-powered items. This international magazine is "an ongoing encyclopedic book-like publication covering everything and anything of interest to the independent family farmer, and those who dream of having their own place." SFJ advocates the lifestyle and values of small-scale independent family farming. Recommended! B/w, 11 x 14 in., 127 pgs; $30/yr ($40/yr Canada and Mexico); single copy $6.

Small Farm Today. Intelligent, informed, practical focus on moneymaking for the small farm: 64 pgs; $23.95/yr (6 issues). Dedicated to preservation and promotion of small farming, rural living, and agripreneurship; plants and animals. Focus on alternative and traditional crops, livestock, and direct marketing. Spunky, practical small farmer's bimonthly that takes on the big guys in plain language. Organic emphasis. Great classifieds and calendar of events. The **Small Farm Today Seminar and Trade Show** near Columbia, MO, is a great annual event for the small farm community. The *Breeders Directory,* part of the magazine, is a good way to find exotic or homestead breeds. Contact Ronald E. Macher, Editor, 800-633-2535; 573-687-3525; 3903 W. Ridge Trail Rd., Clark, MO 65243-9525; **smallfarm@socket.net; www.smallfarmtoday.com.**

FOREIGN MAGAZINES AND BOOK DEALERS

Farming Press Ltd. offers lots of books and videos on British/Irish agriculture: Wharfedale Rd., Ipswich, Suffolk, ENGLAND; **www.farmgate.co.uk** is also the website for *Farming News, Dairy Farmer, Pig Farmer,* and *Arable Farming* magazines.

Granny Smith's Bookshop is an Aussie seller of books on useful plants, fruits, nuts, tree crops, permaculture, organic growing, farm trees, etc. "Best selection in Australasia, drawn from worldwide sources"; free lists; 08-9388 1965; fax 08-9388 1852; PO Box 27, Subiaco, WA 6008 AUSTRALIA; **granny@AOI.com.au; www.AOI.com.au/granny.**

Grass Roots is "Australia's Most Popular Self-Sufficiency Magazine." Articles; event listings; reader letters; new agey; land ads; Au $36.30/yr in Australia; Au $50/yr; overseas (bank draft/credit card only). Contact Grass Roots, PO Box 117, Seymour 3661, AUSTRALIA; 03-5792-4000; fax 03-5792-4222.

Hartley & Marks, Box 79, Brackendale, BC VON 250 CANADA. Or PO Box 147, Pt Roberts, WA 98281; 604-739-1771; fax 604-738-1913. Some homesteading-type books in their list.

Natural Life is a Canadian-based magazine that reports organic, eco-conscious, humanist news, ads, and event announcements. It's $24/yr; U.S. address: Box 112, Niagara Falls, NY 14304. Phone/fax 519-442-1404. Or PO Box 340, St. George, ONT N0E 1N0 CANADA.

(The) Soil Association Organic Book Catalogue offers organic gardening and agriculture books, including *The Concise Book of Organic Growing and Small Livestock* by Meike and David Watkins. They carry all the European books on rural living and self-sufficiency that are in English—more than 250 titles. 0272-290139 (24-hr order line); 1992, 86 Colston St., Bristol, BS1 5BB ENGLAND.

Smallholder is "The practical monthly" for English (or English-speaking) small farmers. What we call "homesteaders," the English call "smallholders." Emphasis on livestock, but there are also plant articles; £35/yr: High St., Stoke Ferry, King's Lynn, Norfolk PE33 9SF ENGLAND.

Smallholder Bookshop, proprietor Valerie Charlesworth, stocks nearly 600 titles of books and videos, which are sent worldwide. These cover livestock, poultry, organics, horticulture, crops, fencing and hedging, building, country crafts, rural interests, and much more; (44) 1366-500466; fax 501122 for a booklist; **www.smallholderbooks.co.uk.**

Town and Country Farmer is pitched to Aussie food-growers, straddling all farm sizes and growing persuasions (organic, non-). Articles on livestock, herbs, sustainability, soil fertility, etc. I counted 59 pages of articles in the 68-pg total, but more than a few were infomercials by advertisers: PO Box 798, Benalla, Vic. 3672 AUSTRALIA.

Warm Earth: Focused on organic gardening and healthy living, this is "Australia's down-to-earth organic gardening magazine." Articles on growing fruit, vegetables, and herbs organically in gardens or small acreage and on managing poultry and other animals. Books, too; Au $26/ yr sub; Warm Earth Publishing, 'Kiah' Cottage, Kenilworth Qld. 4574, AUSTRALIA; **warmearth@powerup.com.au; www.powerup.com.au/~warmearth.**

Looking for Love?

Have you, a person who longs to live in the country, been looking for love in all the wrong places? Instead, run a personal ad in one of the homestead magazines. An ad in your favorite is likely to be answered by someone who suits you. In 2000, Don DeLong saw my picture and answered my online ad at **www.oneandonly.com.** Three days later, I drove from Nevada to Arizona to meet him. We married and are living happily ever after.

You might subscribe to *Sweetheart Magazine.* These folks give great weekend parties, drawing singles mostly from ID, MT, ND, and WY. Contact: PO Box 514, St. Ignatius, MT 59865; **www.sweetheartmag.com. www.Christiancafe.com** is another online romantic site with many rural-dwelling members. Midwesterners will enjoy *Singles in Agriculture (SIA).* This national organization, which provides introductions to unmarried rural people, has 1,200+ members of all ages. It began in 1984 with a letter to the editor in *Farm Journal.* There have been 300+ marriages of people who met through SIA. It offers national conventions, campouts, regional activities, and chapters in IL, OH, IN, TX, MO, IA, KS, NE, OK, and WI, a Rocky Mountain chapter (Western USA), and a Northern Great Plains chapter (ND, SD, and MN). Membership $28, with directory $35. Contact: 815-947-3559; 118 E. Front Ave., Stockton, IL 61085.

Mail-Order Suppliers

Chef's Catalog sells every imaginable kitchen gadget, poultry shears, etc. Free catalog from 800-884-CHEF; fax 972-401-6400; PO Box 620048, Dallas, TX 75262-0048; **www.chefscatalog.com.**

Christian Family Resources. Their 50-pg "Healthy Living Catalog" lists water distillers and filters, grain mills, juicers, books, etc. (catalog $3, refundable with order); 719-962-3228; fax 719-962-3232; PO Box 405, Kit Carson, CO 80825; **www.cfamilyresources.com.**

Cumberland General Store sells churns, windmills, copper kettles, nest eggs, root beer extract, wood stoves, buggies, hand pumps, and many other old-fashioned items that are otherwise hard to purchase. Lid lifters, replacement parts for oil/kerosene lanterns, parts for food grinders, and a host of other items for living a simpler life. It costs $4 for a 289-pg catalog;

800-334-4640; fax 931-456-1211; #1 Highway 68, Crossville, TN 38555; **info@Cumberlandgeneral. com; www.Cumberlandgeneral.com.**

Lehman's Hardware offers 3,500+ items, including non-electric and old-fashioned kitchen and farm tools, cheese- and sausage-making equipment, grinders, slaw cutters, gasoline- or hand-operated clothes washers, kerosene refrigerators, iron cookware, crocks, kegs, and churns. Catalog $3; 888-438-5346; 330-857-5757; fax 330-857-5785; PO Box 41, Kidron, OH 44646; **info@Lehmans.com; www.Lehmans.com.**

Modern Farm's free color catalog lists items for home security, gardening, housewares, tools, work clothes, and picking accessories; 307-587-5946; 1825 Big Horn Ave., Cody, WY 82414.

The Urban Homemaker is dedicated to teaching and pro-moting "old-fashioned skills for contemporary people"; bread and yogurt making, canning, etc. Their catalog of kitchen appliances, tools, etc., promotes thrift, self-sufficiency, and healthy homemade foods; 800-55-BREAD; **UrbanHome@aol.com; www.urbanhome maker.com.**

Wisemen Trading and Supply offers Gem Dandy electric butter churns, wind-up solar radios and flashlights, de-hydrators, canners, canning tools and books, hand washers (Yukon plunger), etc. 8971 Lentzville Rd., Athens, AL 35614; 888-891-8411; 256-729-8868; fax 256-729-6788; **contact@wisementrading.com; www.wisementrading.com.**

SOURCES OF ORGANICALLY GROWN FOOD AND BULK FOODS FOR STORAGE

When you buy organic, you're preserving your and your family's health, and every dollar you spend is also working to save the planet from agricultural toxics! The catalogs usually tell you which items are organically grown.

For much more detailed lists of mail-order suppliers of organic food, get *Safe Food: Eating Wisely in a Risky World* by Debra Lynn Dadd (Los Angeles: Jeremy P. Tarcher, Inc., 1990) or *Nontoxic, Natural, and Earthwise* by Michael F. Ja-cobsen, Ph.D., Lisa Y. Lefferts, and Anne Witte Garland (Center for Science in the Public Interest, 1991). Below are some of my favorites, including food co-ops—groups of families who have joined together to buy more healthy food at lower (wholesale) prices. They usually order once a month, provide their own containers, and enjoy working together! Because food is heavy and shipping costs money, first look to see who's closest to you. Then consider other factors, too.

At **www.coopdirectory.org** you'll find co-ops all over the U.S.

Canned meats and seafood last 18 months, or longer. TVP, canned salmon, and sardines last 2 or 3 years.

Azure Standard is an organic and natural food distributor serving OR, WA, ID, MT, ND, CA, HI, AK, and northwest VT; David Stelzer, 541-467-2230, ext. 12, 79709 Dufur Valley Rd., Dufur, OR 97021; **david@ azurefarm.com; www.azurestandard.com.**

Blooming Prairie Warehouse, "Member Services Dept.," 2340 Heinz Rd., Iowa City, IA 52240, 319-337-6448. Food co-op serving IA, IL, IN, KS, MI, MN, MO, NE, SD, WI, and WY residents.

Cordonnier Meats sells drug-free canned beef, chicken, turkey, or pork (also organic veggies/fruits); 3333 Russia-Houston Rd., Russia, OH 45363; 937-295-2297; **BertCordonnier@yahoo.com.**

Emergency Essentials sells 1-year food supplies, etc.; 800-999-1863; 362 Commerce Loop #6, Orem, UT 84058-5157; **www.BePrepared.com.**

Essentials 2000 sells emergency foods and supplies; 800-775-1991; PO Box 158, Nevada City, CA 95959; **sales@essentials2000.com; www.essentials2000.com.**

Farm Country General Store specializes in service to homeschooling Christian families. Some organic food. 168-pg catalog, $2, refundable with order; 309-367-2844; 731 North Fork Rd., Metamora, IL 61548; **fcgs@homeschoolfcgs.com; www.homeschoolfcgs. com.**

Food Storage Solutions is an outlet for Perma Pak's one-year food storage packages, water filters, grain mills, etc.; 888-452-3663; 1868 N. 170 W., Tooele, UT 84074-9312.

Great River Organic Milling offers great prices and prod-ucts, but 1,000-lb. minimum order! 507-457-0334; fax 507-452-7507; PO Box 73, Winona, MN 55987; **gromnrb@hbci.com; www.greatrivermilling.com.**

Happy Hovel Storable Foods sells organic and natural foods, egg and water preservers, grain mills, books, and services for those who want to be self-sufficient. The *Food Storage & Self Sufficiency Handbook & Catalog* is $7 postpaid; 360-894-5984; 800-637-7772; PO Box 781, Yelm, WA 98597; **haphov@seanet.com; www. happyhovel.com.**

Harvest Pantry sells bulk food products, herbs, and sup-plements. Their website contains much info and won-derful recipes; 605 E Kansas Plaza, Garden City, KS 67846; 620-275-7572; 888-332-6644; **harvest@pld.com; www.harvestpantry.com.**

Health Food Mart offers organic and bulk storage foods, grain mills, water filters, and other self-sufficiency items; 785-235-9710; fax 785-235-9716; 1507 SW 21st St., Topeka, KS 66604-3172; **healthfoodmart@ mcleodusa.net.**

Jaffe Bros. has shipped gourmet organic foods (including organic coffee) worldwide for 54 years; 760-749-1133; PO Box 636, Valley Center, CA 92082-0636.

Major Surplus & Survival sells foods for long-term stor-age; 435 W Alandra Blvd., Gardena, CA 90248; 800-441-8855.

Mountain People's Warehouse sells bulk grains and foods wholesale from their warehouses in Auburn, CA, and Auburn, WA, to health food stores, small co-ops, and any group that can collect their minimum order of $200 for warehouse pickup, $250 UPS, or $50 if delivered. CA: 800-679-6733; 530-889-9531; 12745 Earhart Ave., Auburn, CA 95602. WA: 253-333-6769; 22 30th St. NE, Ste. #102, Auburn, WA 98002; PO Box 1856, Auburn, WA 98071-1856.

Natural Lifestyle offers bulk natural foods, herbs, and more; 800-752-2775; 16 Lookout Dr., Asheville, NC 28804-3330; **www.natural-lifestyle.com.**

Natural Way Mills offers storage foods packed with nitrogen in pails; 218-222-3677; fax 218-222-3408; 24509-390th St. NE, Middle River, MN 56737. Nice folks; don't do the computer thing.

Northbend Trading Post ships storage foods, water storage containers, emergency kits, books, self-sufficiency products, etc.; 435-427-9390; fax 435-427-5016; PO Box 193, 40 S. State, Fairview, VT 84629.

Northeast Cooperatives is a distributor to consumer buying clubs in 22 states in the Northeast, Southeast, and Midwest. They offer a wide selection of natural foods, organic produce, herbs, etc., at savings over retail prices. Visit their website for more info on buying clubs and to find a buying club near you: PO Box 8188, Brattleboro, VT 05304; **www.northeastcoop. com.** For info on starting a buying club, call 800-344-9939, ext. 132; or 888-936-9648, ext. 3330; or e-mail **bcservices@northeastcoop.com.**

Ozark Cooperative Warehouse is a great resource, founded in 1976, for persons who sell, or buy, organic products. They distribute 6,000+ natural food products (organic grains, flowers, beans, carrots, organic milk and eggs, natural meats, etc.). They serve buying clubs and stores in 13 states in the South and Midwest (AR, TX, OK, MO, KS, AL, GA, MS, FL, TN, LA, etc.) with scheduled refrigerated and frozen delivery on their own trucks. They also offer a terrific free newsletter with valuable food info; 479-521-4920; PO Box 1528, Fayetteville, AR 72702; **new@ozark.coop; www.ozark.coop.**

Preparedness Center operates two websites that offer thousands of products (updated weekly), including food storage; water filters and purifiers; self-reliance, and outdoor survival items; 800-547-4223; **sales@ preparedness.com; www.preparedness.com** and **www.safetycentral.com.**

Tucson Cooperative Warehouse is a food co-op for AZ, NM, west TX, CO, UT, NV, and southern CA; 800-350-2667; 350 S. Toole Ave., Tucson, AZ 85701.

Walton Feed supplied storage foods for the White House and Congress as Y2K loomed; **www.waltonfeed.com;** 135 N. 10th St., PO Box 307, Montpelier, ID 83254; 800-847-0465; fax 208-847-0467.

Yellowstone River Trading; 800-585-5077; PO Box 3235, Bozeman, MT 59772; **www.yellowstonetrading.com.**

Schools of Country Living

For two summers, I operated one. It turned out I'm better at writing than at running a school, so now I'm leaving that to the experts. The following list of schools doesn't even scratch the surface. Through your local extension agent or college, you can probably find out about master gardener, master food preserver, and other such training programs offered in your county. These programs offer free training ending in your certification. In return for your 50-some hours of training, you are then expected to spend 75–100 hours of community service in your area.

The 4-H programs for young people are wonderful, and adults can learn a lot by helping them, or by taking classes at an agricultural college, each of which has animal and plant specialties suited to its geographical situation. (Just hold firm for the nontoxic, organic approaches despite the chemical agribusiness presence.) You could major in botany (classifying and observing plants), horticulture (gardening), or agriculture (growing food for big buyers using big machines).

Denise LaPole wrote me about being a volunteer at Living History Farms, Des Moines, IA, at the 1900 site! You can visit "the living museum of 17th-century Plymouth,"

Plymouth Plantation; PO Box 1620, Plymouth, MA 02362; 508-746-1622; fax 508-746-4978.

ALHFAM is the Association for Living History, Farm and Agricultural Museums; its members bring history to life in the U.S., Canada, and other countries. It helps both paid and volunteer museum staff at these many member museums; 440-685-4410; 8774 Rt. 45 NW, N. Bloomfield, OH 44450; **sheridan@orwell.net; www.ALHFAM.org.**

Aprovecho Research Center, located on 40 acres of timbered land in rainy Oregon, offers residential internships in organic gardening, sustainable forestry, solar cookers, hay boxes, solar design, alternative building, etc. The lifestyle is authentic; the gardens are fabulous; $1,800–$2,500 for the 10-week course; 541-942-8198 (8 to 5, M-F), 80574 Hazelton Rd., Cottage Grove, OR 97424; **apro@efn.org; www.efn.org/~apro.**

Back to Basics offers audiotaped classes: "Organic Gardening," "Long-Term Food Storage and Preserving the Harvest," and "Setting up the Self-Sufficient Homestead." A 6-tape set (9 hours) is $40; 828-452-2866; PO Box 1138, Waynesville, NC 28786; **garden_girrl@ yahoo.com.**

Bullock Brothers' Homestead, Orcas Island, WA, is where Sam Bullock, "Cosmic Bob," teaches "a path to right livelihood" at his 17-year-old permaculture homestead. He offers courses in useful edible and medicinal plants for landscaping; permaculture design and consulting; workshops, internships, field-trip opportunities, a month-long ecological design and sustainable living apprenticeship; and a course on "Water Harvesting." Contact: 360-567-5447; PO Box 107, Deer Harbor, WA 98243; **www.sustainablelivingnews.com;** or **www.permacultureportal.com.** His website lists permaculture design courses, both his and around the world.

Catholic Homesteading Movement has taught homestead skills on a working homestead since 1961. Classes include an intensive week, 7 to 10 hours per day, of general homesteading skills: medicinal herbs, intensive gardening, home dairying with goats and cows, draft horses, log cabin building, etc. Or choose among Herbalism Week, Survival Workshop, Horse Working Workshop, Homebirth and Midwifery Week, Log Cabin Workshop, Fruit and Nut Tree Workshop, and/or Organic Gardening Course! Cost is $395 for a one-week workshop. For info, send 3 stamps to 19 Delaware Square, Norwich, NY 13815.

Central Rocky Mountain Permaculture Institute has a permaculture demonstration farm and market garden on the forest garden concept. It integrates trees, shrubs, plants, and animals. Their intensive permaculture design course is held twice a year: a 10-day course in the spring, a 14-day course in the fall. They offer a 5-week self-reliance internship that includes the design course plus apprenticeship in permaculture principles, composting, marketing, greenhouse building, companion planting, succession planting, pest management, seed collecting, and designing integrated systems of food production, housing, technology, and community development. Contact: call/fax 970-927-4158; PO Box 631, Basalt, CO 81621; **jerome@ crmpi.org; www.crmpi.org.**

Country Living Field Day is a huge educational field day (yearly, last Saturday in September), geared to small and part-time farmers and their families: continuous exhibits on apple cider pressing; aquaculture; poultry, rabbit, and turkey production; sheep, hog, and goat production; beekeeping; taxidermy; and maple syrup production. There are also exhibits, workshops, farm tours, and seminars on hundreds of different sustainable ag topics related to livestock, crops, natural resources, and marketing. Sponsored by the USDA, Ohio State U. Extension; 330-627-4310; 32 W. Main St., Carrollton, OH 44615-1336; **carroll.osu.edu/country living.htm.**

Deutsch Country Days is held at Luxenhaus Farm, a typical German hill farm as it would have been in the 1850s, plus 20 restored Missouri log and period structures and a covered bridge located 3 miles NE of Marthasville, MO. The long-standing annual weekend teaches and demonstrates 75+ skills of the early Germans in Missouri: candle dipping, soap making, weaving, crocheting, quilting, chair caning, bladesmithing/blacksmithing, woodworking, carving, lace making, hearth cooking, sorghum pressing/cooking, log hewing/splitting/sawing, period musicians, farm animals, and costumed artisans using ancestral tools; 636-433-5669; fax 636-433-5275; 5437 Highway "O," Marthasville, MO 63357-2357; **luxenhaus@yhti.net; www. deutschcountrydays.org.**

Ecology Action offers 6-month internships or a 3-year professional program. The focus is intensive, sustainable food production. 5798 Ridgewood Rd., Willits, CA 95490.

Ecovillage Training Center offers an immersion experience in sustainable living: courses and workshops, internships, and special demonstrations in green lifestyles. Set among the Farm's 1,700 acres of woods and meadows, ETC is a living laboratory: organic garden, forests, and wetlands. Their courses include Solar Installation (**sei@solarenergy.org**), Permaculture Fundamentals and Practicum, Natural Buildings (2 to 10 days of wattle and daub, mud and stone, turf and timber, straw, cob, and wood construction), Ecovillage Design, etc. Or do an apprenticeship in organic food production, natural buildings, and wetlands construction for $450/month (includes board and lodging, courses, and training in organic gardening). For info or to register: 931-964-4474 or 4324; fax 931-964-2200; 560 Farm Rd., PO Box 90, Summertown, TN 38483-0090; **ecovillage@thefarm.org.**

Gardener's Supply Company offers a professional correspondence course in plant science and ecology, leading to certification as a Master Horticulturist. 800-863-1700; fax 800-551-6712; 128 Intervale Rd., Burlington, VT 05401; **info@gardeners.com; www. gardeners.com.**

Good Earth Farm School, 1702 Mountain View Rd., Buena Vista, VA 24416, 540-261-8874, offers high-quality speakers on all aspects of growing and marketing profitably, in 3- to 4-day intensive workshops with experts such as Joel Salatin (author), Preston Sullivan (ATTRA), Andy Lee (author), and Steve Muntz (Heifer Project International).

Good Farming Apprenticeship Network includes internships involving working with draft animals. You'll find more info in *Rural Heritage* magazine; 931-268-0655; 281 Dean Ridge Lane, Gainesboro, TN 38562; **rural heritage.com/apprenticeship/.**

Maine Organic Farmer's and Gardener's Association (MOFGA) runs the Common Ground Fair, a wonderful annual educational event. They also sponsor a great apprenticeship program matching farm workers to such situations as a small-scale dairy, a nonelectric backwoods homestead, a spinning/weaving sheep farm, a maple-sugaring/cider-pressing outfit, or an organic market garden. Learn skills in organic farming and market gardening, livestock care, CSAs, homesteading, draft animals, etc. Room, board, small stipend for labor, $20 application fee. Contact Farm Apprenticeship Program; 207-568-4142; PO Box 170, Unity, ME 04988; **mofga@mofga.org; www.mofga.org.**

Mount Pleasant, John and Jenny White, Peny Bont, Carmarthen, Dyfed SA33 6PP ENGLAND; 0994-484315. Self-sufficiency courses. Send SASE or international reply coupon.

National Agricultural Center and Hall of Fame, 630 Hall of Fame Dr. (N. 126th St.), Bonner Springs, KS 66012; 913-721-1075; fax 913-721-1202. This center was chartered by Congress to honor America's farmers. It's both an educational tour of the importance of agriculture and a celebration of outstanding achievements by farmers. See thousands of historical relics and an extensive collection of rural art: the first farm truck, steam engines, threshing machines, a covered wagon, Harry Truman's plow, ice harvesting tools, etc., all displayed in a 172-acre setting. The nearby National Poultry Museum is now open as well.

Occidental Arts and Ecology Center, near Santa Rosa, CA, offers one-day, weekend, and two-week residential permaculture training courses such as "Starting and Sustaining Intentional Communities," "Surface Water Management for Home Owners," "Introduction to Gourd Craft," "Organic Gardening," "Seed Saving," "Sustainable Forestry," and "Carpentry for Women." Magnificent gardens, high-quality art, permaculture with an activist left-wing/San Francisco ambience; 707-874-1557; 15290 Coleman Valley Rd., Occidental, CA 95465; **oaec@oaec.org; www.oaec.org.**

Ogden Publications sells a Farm Museum Directory. These educational places demonstrate old-time farming. Ogden also publishes a directory of antique farm equipment shows (more than 1,200 are held nationwide each year); 800-678-4883; 1503 SW 42nd St., Topeka, KS 66609.

(The) Permaculture Activist: A Quarterly Voice for Permanent Culture in North America offers training in organic, sustainable land use and management through one-week intensive courses and residencies. Also training in natural building, community skills, and more. 828-669-6336; PO Box 1209, Black Mountain, NC 28711; $19/yr, $45/3 yrs.

Jeff Poppen writes about organic and biodynamic farming (his book is *The Barefoot Farmer*), runs a 300-acre CSA, is a TV garden commentator, and holds workshops

("Herbs," "Organic Gardening," etc.) at his place; Box 163, Red Boiling Springs, TN 37150; **barefoot farmer@hotmail.com; www.barefootfarmer.com.**

Rodale Institute Experimental Farm, 611 Siegfriedale Rd., Kurtztown, PA 19530; 610-683-1400; fax 610-683-8548. Offers several internships, both paid and unpaid, April through December. Areas: tour guides, office, soil health, produce marketing.

Solar Energy International offers a weekend course on building and using a solar cooker and courses and internships on many other renewable energy topics; PO Box 715, Carbondale, CO 81623; 970-963-8855; fax 970-963-8866; **sei@solarenergy.org; www.solar energy.org.**

Solar Living Institute "promotes sustainable living through inspirational environmental education" . . . workshops in solar power design and installation; retrofitting a house for energy efficiency and healthy interiors; electric vehicles; solar cooking; how to build a solar business; hydrogen energy, wind energy; alternative construction (straw bale, adobe, bamboo, stone, etc.); wastewater design; fish ponds; gardening; herbs; etc. The Institute is based in the Real Goods Solar Living Center and also sponsors "the nation's premier energy fair, SolFest," and 20+ internships per year for college students; 707-744-2017; fax 707-744-1682; PO Box 836, Hopland, CA 95449; **www.solarliving.org.**

Sustainable Farming Internships & Apprenticeships: For more than a decade, this ATTRA service has helped hundreds of family farms find interns/apprentices. Listing is free and includes contact info and detailed descriptions of the farm, room and board arrangements, time frames, etc. The list is updated at the beginning of each year; **www.attra.org/attra-rl/intern.html.** To list your farm in the next update, contact Katherine Adam, NCAT/ATTRA, PO Box 3657, Fayetteville, AR 72702; 800-346-9140; **kadam@ncat.org.** The great folks at ATTRA also provide a free booklet, *Sustainable Agriculture Curricula: K-12,* which covers curricula, publications, and electronic resources for teaching about sustainable ag in schools. Or order their *Educational & Training Opportunities in Sustainable Agriculture,* which lists (organic, alternative, or sustainable ag) internships in both U.S. and international institutions and organizations, as well as at farms outside the U.S.!

S.W.E.A.T. (Society of Workers in Early Arts and Trades) publishes a newsletter, "The Rag," and takes part in fairs and exhibits put on by local chapters all over the U.S.; **cinbair@hotmail.com; www.sweatrag.org.**

Tillers International, 5239 S. 24th St., Kalamazoo, MI 49002; 616-344-3233; 800-498-2700; **Tillersint@ aol.com; www.wmich.edu/tillers/.** More than 40 workshops and classes on a wide range of traditional skills.

Trumkinland is Fran and Carl Ogren's homestead, which they've turned into a school to teach self-sufficiency skills: putting up hay (some loose, some cut by scythe); farming with draft horses; raising rabbits, pigs, sheep, goats, dairy cows, horses, llamas, ducks, turkeys; using guardian dogs; spinning; tanning hides; etc. Contact: PO Box 502, Northport, WA 99157; **mypage.goplay.com/trumkinland/.**

Union Agricultural Institution provides training in the biodynamic gardening method: "BD agriculture attends to both soil and heavens, earth and cosmos." Conferences. Fringe science, but great gardens and great food! Contact: 8475 Dockery Rd., Blairsville, GA 30512; **uai@alltel.net; www.unionag.org.**

Willing Workers on Organic Farms. WWOOF is a wonderful worldwide program. To purchase your very affordable membership and address directory, write WWOOF in Australia at Mt. Murrindal Co-op, W. Tree 3885, Victoria, AUSTRALIA. Or call 03-5155-0218 or 03-5155-0342.

About Nonpolluting Energy Resources

MAGAZINES AND ORGANIZATIONS: These are the technologies of the future!

Alternative Energy Institute. For technical details on the "many potential breakthrough technologies being pursued by freethinking inventors, engineers, and physicists," read *Turning the Corner: Energy Solutions for the 21st Century,* by Mark McLaughlin, the lead writer/researcher of the Alternative Energy Institute. You'll learn about advanced electromagnetic theory; Mach's principle and impulse engines; anomalous gravitational/inertial mass effects, etc. He says these will be future mainstream science, that we have begun a transition from fossil fuels to a world economy based on hydrogen and electricity as primary energy carriers. AEI works to educate the public about the developing energy crisis, those who are searching for solutions, and to encourage development of these new technologies; PO Box 7074, Tahoe City, CA 96145; 530-583-1720; fax 530-583-5153; **www.altenergy.org.** At **www.eren.doe.gov** you'll find the Department of Energy's "Energy Efficiency and Renewable Energy Network," with much info, 80,000 articles, and 600+ links!

Chelsea Green Publishing offers *The Independent Home: Living Well with Power from the Sun, Wind, and Water* by Michael Potts; *The Solar Electric House* by Steven Strong; *Wind Power for Home and Business* by Paul Gipe; *American Intensive Gardening: Growing Food Year-Round with Solar Appliances* by Gretchen and Lea Poisson; and many more focused on sustainable living; PO Box 428, White River Junction, VT 05001-0131; 802-295-6444; orders 800-639-4099; **www.chelseagreen.com.** Free catalog.

Home Power Magazine brings you realistic, cost-effective info about private, renewable energy sources for home or business: photovoltaics, wind, micro-hydro, batteries, efficient appliances. It connects you with a worldwide network of solar-active people (43 percent of readers own PV modules). Issues are 144 to 164 pgs, 94 pgs of articles last I looked; the remaining pages are ads for renewable energy companies. Cost is $22.50 for 6 issues/yr. *Recommended.* Home Power Publishing also puts out great books; 800-707-6585 or 541-512-0201; fax 541-512-0343; PO Box 520, Ashland, OR 97520; **richard.perez@homepower.com; www.homepower. com.**

Solar Energy International is a nonprofit organization that works to promote renewable energy. They teach hands-on workshops on solar installation, micro-hydropower, wind power, solar home design, and alternative home building technologies; 970-963-8855; PO Box 715, Carbondale, CO 81623; **sei@solarenergy.org**; **www.solarenergy.org**. They sponsor a community solar cookout every July and take interns on a work/study/trade basis.

Solar Nova Scotia is a not-for-profit organization that promotes energy conservation and renewable forms of energy; RR 1, McGrath's Cove, West Dover, NS B0J 3L0 CANADA; 902-852-4758.

SUPPLIERS: For local companies, check your Yellow Pages under "Power" or "Solar."

Abraham's Solar: Mick Abraham gives solar advice, etc. at 800-222-7242; PO Box 957, Pagosa Springs, CO 81147; **abrahamsolar@hotmail.com**.

Alternative Power offers mail-order and retail alternative power systems. Free flyer; 608-637-2722; fax 608-637-8507; 2857 N. Summit Ave., Milwaukee, WI 53211-3439; **altpower@frontiernet.net**; **www.nopowernoproblem.com**.

Backwoods Solar Electric Systems will help you set up an independent solar, wind, or hydro energy system. Catalog $3; 208-263-4290; fax 208-265-4788; 1395 Rolling Thunder Ridge, Sandpoint, ID 83864; **info@backwoodssolar.com**; **www.backwoodssolar.com**.

China Diesel Generators sells their excellent product a lot cheaper than the competition. A 10-kilowatt Kodiak is priced at $2,895; 870-427-9621; PMB 160, 605B 62/65 North, Harrison, AR 72601; **chinadiesels.com**; **chinagenerators.net**.

Cumberland General Store sells windmills, etc. A page in their catalog that compares all the windmill brands is a good one-stop shopping aid; $4 for a 289-pg. catalog; 800-234-4640; fax 931-456-1211; #1 Highway 68, Crossville, TN 38555; **info@Cumberlandgeneral.com**; **www.Cumberlandgeneral.com**.

Gaiam Real Goods (Real Goods and Jade Mountain were bought by a corporate giant, Gaiam) sells energy-efficient and energy-independent products: photovoltaic-, wind-, and hydro-powered systems; super-efficient refrigerators; composting toilets; instantaneous and solar hot water heaters; compact fluorescent lighting; water conservation aids; and books. Free catalog; 800-919-2400; 360 Interlocken Blvd., Ste. 300, Broomfield, CO 80021; **www.gaiam.com**. The classic *Real Good Solar Living Sourcebook*, regularly updated, covers renewable energy sources, sustainable living practices, alternative construction, homesteading, and off-the-grid living, plus alternative vehicles. Thousands of products and technical details; 608-pg paperback, $30. Their retail store (707-744-2100), and Institute for Solar Living (707-744-2017) are at 13771 S. Highway 101, Hopland, CA 95449; **techs@realgoods.com**; **www.realgoods.com**. Or 800-919-2400 (orders).

Independent Power and Light: What you need to get power from the sun, wind, or water: photovoltaic modules, hydroelectric power, composting toilets, wind generators, special refrigerators, solar ovens, inverters, motors, pumps, lights, fans, etc. Free consultation. Fair, honest, expert service from William Davis, 406-333-4944; PO Box 186, 103 Capricorn Dr., Emigrant, MT 59027.

Kansas Wind Power sells wind and solar electric systems,

energy-efficient products, LED flashlights, water pumps, fans, solar cookers, wood-fired water heaters, grain mills, water purifiers, composting toilets, hydraulic ram pumps, fence chargers, tankless water heaters, shortwave radios, books, propane refrigerators, heaters, lights, etc. Catalog $4; 785-364-4407; 13569-214th Rd., Holton, KS 66436-8138.

Kyocera Solar manufactures photovoltaic modules (solar collectors) and will sell direct to you with a 25-year warranty; 780-951-6330; fax 800-544-6466; 7812 E. Acoma Dr., Scottsdale, AZ 85260; **www.kyocerasolar.com**.

Lehman's Non-Electric Catalog offers windmills, hydraulic rams, etc.; catalog $3; 888-438-5346; 333-857-5757; **www.Lehmans.com**.

Mountain Pass Wind Co. has designed and sold wind and solar systems since 1981. Many used parts in stock for 12- and 32-volt windchargers. They also sell wind speed instruments, Whisper 1000-watt wind machine (any voltage); 406-547-2266; PO Box 394, White Sulphur Springs, MT 59645; **Steveahicks@yahoo.com**.

New England Solar Electric sells wind, water, solar, gas private systems. Contact 413-238-5974; fax 413-238-0203; 64-pg catalog/design guide $3; 401 Huntington Rd., PO Box 435, Worthington, MA 01098; **nesolar@newenglandsolar.com**.

Old Mill Mercantile, 14580 Wallin Mountain Rd., West Fork, AR 72774; 501-839-8269; **www.oldmillmercantile.com**. Offers tools, wood-burning stoves and water heaters, steam engines, and many alternative energy items.

The Ram Co. offers Fleming Hydro-rams and solar pumps, in cooperation with Energy Outfitters of Oregon; 247 Llama Lane, Lowesville, VA 22951; 800-227-8511; 804-277-8511; fax 804-277-8333; **rhfleming@earthlink.net**; **www.ibt.et/ramco**.

Solar Components Corporation, 121 Valley St., Manchester, NH 03103; 603-668-8186. The Energy Saver's Catalog: **www.solar-components.com**. Solariums, solar aquatic wastewater treatment tanks, solar storage tubes, solar glazing, climate control for your greenhouse or sun space.

Solar Electricity designs RV, cabin, water pumping, and total home power systems, solar modules, controllers, batteries, inverters, water pumps, energy-efficient lights, and propane appliances. Their 124-pg catalog costs $4.95. Contact: PO Box 1499, Hamilton, MT 59840.

Solar Survival is a sun power specialist! Plans for solar pods, cones, reprints of useful books; Box 250, Harrisville, NH 03450.

Solar Survivor has been in business for 22 years selling mostly UL-approved solar electric panel systems and micro-wind generators; 316-554-0911; 5119 S. Mt. Carmel, Wichita, KS 67217.

Southwest Wind Power: 800-245-0311.

Sunelco (now a division of Golden Genesis) offers solar chargers for portable computers and solar, wind, and hydro private energy systems. There's a good catalog that helps you plan your system; 406-363-6924; order 800-338-6844; store at 100 Skeels St., PO Box 787, Hamilton, MT 59840-0787; **sunelco@montana.com**; **www.sunelco.com**.

Triple A Solar Supply: 800-245-0311; **www.aaasolar.com**.

THOUGHTS ON CLEAN, RENEWABLE ENERGIES: As you can see from the above lists, a brave new generation of scientists continues to struggle to save the planet by finding ways to harness renewable, non-petroleum, non-nuclear, nonpolluting energy sources to replace the coal, oil, and nuclear technologies that put our collective future desperately at risk.

Concerned about the ever-rising price of petroleum products as well as the greenhouse effect and the long-range risk of nuclear accidents, many people are developing a private energy supply of an earth-friendly nature. If you also buy, install, and use one of these hopeful technologies, your dollars work to support research in the field. You set a positive example that there can be practical alternatives. And because of you, one more household joins the transition to safe energy systems that *must* happen on a large scale. The research and development of wonderful alternative energy technologies that have already taken place will be in vain unless it is widely adopted by individuals, communities, and corporations. On the community level, please be a voice urging commercial sources of energy to also make this transition.

For a fun immersion in the technology, products, and people of the renewable energy scene, visit a renewable energy fair! The Mid-West Renewable Energy Association's annual expo is held at the fairgrounds at Custer, WI, in late June; 715-592-6595; **info@the-mrea.org; www.the-mrea.org.** About 95 miles north of San Francisco, SolFest is held every August, offering workshops, speakers, and a host of vendors showcasing the latest in renewable energy and sustainable living technologies; 707-744-2017; **isl@rgisl.org; www.solarliving.org.**

When making alcohol for use as a fuel, you can easily get a free permit from the Bureau of Alcohol, Tobacco and Firearms (ATF), which will make what you're doing legal. Further information is available from Lindsay Publications, PO Box 538, Bradley, IL 60915: *Distillation of Alcohol & De-Naturing* by F. B. Wright (reprint of a 1918 book) and *Practical Distiller* by Leonard Monzert (reprint of a classic 1889 text). *The Secrets of Building an Alcohol Producing Still* by Vincent R. Gingery (1994) is available from PO Box 318, Rogersville, MO 65742; 417-890-1965; **gingery@cland.net.**

There are five varieties of alternative energy sources that are suitable for individual families: wind, water, solar, methane, and wood (also, paper or grass) burning. For communities, thermal energy (from heat sources deep in the earth) and wave energy (for communities that are near waters with strong tides) are also good possibilities. Of the options for families, the cleanest and most environmentally kind are wind, water, and solar. There are numerous small companies eager to help you apply these better energy technologies. They advertise in the homesteader periodicals. There is a good chance that conversion will be tax-deductible, and it will definitely reduce your electric bill!

A sixth exciting new technology is not yet at the homestead level, but it's worth mentioning: hydrogen fuel. Mazda, for example, is currently working hard on a car fueled by hydrogen. Proponents tout hydrogen as a clean and renewable fuel that emits no carbon-dioxide gases and does not contribute to smog.

Many companies offer electric bikes, cars, or conversion kits, or print plans for you to turn your gas guzzler into an electric-powered vehicle. Electro Automotive sells electric car components and a Basic or Deluxe universal conversion kit to transform your gas-burner, providing experienced tech support and design help. Catalog is $6; PO Box 1113, Felton, CA 95018; **www.electroauto.com.**

Energy Conservation. If you have the opportunity to build a house from scratch, make one so well insulated in roof and walls and so well designed that solar heat can do most or all of the job. Or consider an underground house: they reduce heating and cooling problems to a minimum. They use your land efficiently too, because you can put a garden or grass on top! They are naturally the best insulated, most heat-holding in winter, and most cool-keeping in summer. There are wonderful books on how to build underground homes! It's a neglected technology that really deserves widespread application.

If you install your own energy system in your home, I bet you will become more conservation-minded than you were in the past. Walk around your home with pencil and paper, writing down everything you own that plugs into an electrical socket or that is fueled by natural gas or some form of gasoline or fuel oil. Now go back over that list of energy-eating things and decide which ones you absolutely must have. Cross out and discard the rest. The things you are left with determine how much energy you have to be able to generate. The next step is to choose your source.

Choosing a System. Which energy-generating system is most suitable for your environment? Can it independently come up with the conservation-reduced sum of your energy needs? Environment is everything in this decision. If you live in the treeless desert, a wood cookstove isn't practical. Water power wouldn't be practical there either. But prairies and deserts do tend to be windy and cloudless, so a windmill generator for electricity and solar panels for hot water and home heating would work. In rainy climates, solar heat isn't practical except as a supplement, but that's where the mighty forests grow, so wood for cooking and heating becomes practical—if air pollution isn't an issue. (It is in many half-developed areas.)

Water Power. The important questions are how far your water falls and how fast it flows. Does it drop inches or feet? Measure the velocity of your stream in feet per second by throwing in a floater and timing its travel. The hydraulic ram is a wonderful, simple mechanical technology for bringing water into your home without electricity. You can install one if you have a creek with some drop to it. The ram uses the energy of falling water to pump water uphill to where you need it. The pamphlet *Manual of Information: Rift Rams* costs $2 from Lehman's; 888-438-5346; **info@lehmans.com.** Ram pumps are available from The Ram Co., 804-277-8511; fax 804-277-8333; 247 Llama Lane, Lowesville, VA 22951; **rhfleming@earthlink.net; www.ibt.et/ramco.**

The old-fashioned waterwheel, like all the other renewable, clean power technologies, is undergoing wonderful technological progress and is now well worth considering. Your wheel diameter should be 3–6 times the drop amount. All-welded steel undershot wheels, etc., for people with potential waterpower are available from Fitz Waterwheel Co., 118 Sycamore Ct., Collegeville, PA 19426; 215-489-6256. Ready-made water power units are now available that can generate power from a surprisingly small flow of water. But then you have to worry about drought. The amount of electricity you can get depends on the volume of the water flowing, the amount of altitude it loses crossing your property, and the nature of the stream bed. The best private

---

KEEPING A HOUSE COOL WITHOUT AIR CONDITIONING

1. If you cook, bake, and can in the house rather than in an outdoor summer kitchen or campfire, do it in the evening so the house will have all night to cool off. But minimize cooking by serving salads, raw fruit, cool herb teas, and grilled or quickly heated foods.

2. Get cool air indoors. After the sun goes down and the outside air becomes cool, open all your windows and get as much of that good cool air inside as possible. Using fans, especially an attic fan, will help accomplish that quickly. (A fan doesn't need as much energy as does air conditioning, and it doesn't use chemical refrigerants!) In the morning, close all your windows to keep in that wonderful cool night air you collected.

3. Ceiling fans are inexpensive to operate and can help keep rooms cooler.

4. Hang heavy insulating blankets in all south- and west-facing windows, at least while the sun is shining on them. The more you can prevent summer sun from directly shining into your house's rooms, the cooler they will be.

5. A cool shower before the afternoon nap or bedtime helps keep both grown-ups and children cool.

6. Drink lots of pure water or water with a little fruit juice added.

7. Arrange your work schedule as they do in hot desert countries: Take a siesta or stay inside quietly in your coolest room during the hottest afternoon hours. Make up for it by working in the evening, when the temperatures are comfortable, doing what in winter you would have done in the afternoon. Plan to do hard mental jobs in the morning and expect to have brain meltdown during the hot hours, compensated for by that nap or undemanding time. It's a simple physiological fact that we don't think and function as well under extreme heat.

---

water generators now are generally turbine units working in small creek situations.

Methane. Anybody with manure has a potential methane generating system. Methane gas production is now possible with as few as 2 cows, although for most efficient production it takes a lot of animals in a confined situation. Once you are set up and getting methane, it's easy to use; you burn it as you would natural gas. It won't work with cows grazing in a pasture unless they have diapers on. The manure has to be quite fresh to give good results, which means frequent collection—and that is work.

Also keep in mind that your methane generator won't work well in cold, or even chilly, weather, because this is a fermenting process. And if it does work well, you have the risk of some idiot lighting a match in the wrong place and blowing your farm off the map. You have to do some minor converting to make natural gas appliances work with your private methane system. You'll want to add an odorant like that supplied in commercial natural gas—which gives you an olfactory warning if you have a leak, before you pass out forever. In India now, the government has a program to distribute operational one-family methane-generating plants. They work so efficiently that the owner of a few cows can make enough methane to meet the energy needs for his family. (See *Methane: Planning a Digester* by Peter-John Meynell, 1978.)

Wind Power. Windmill power generation was getting quite common and well developed in the midwestern United States before government subsidizing of rural electrification put private windmill manufacturers out of business. Now windmill-generator manufacturers are going again with a vastly improved new generation of windmills and battery storage setups. There are several brands available in varying prices, but they all need wind to make them work. A wind generator can indeed power an entire house, and such generators are available in a wide range of sizes, large enough to power any electric home—if you live where you can get at least an 8-mph average wind velocity. If your area is windy, and your electric company's rates are high, wind power would be a good choice. But the bigger the wind charger you buy, of course, the more it will cost. So think of ways you could save on electricity before you go shopping. Incidentally, dollar for dollar, in a windy place, a wind generator will produce more electricity than equal dollars spent on solar panels. The problem with wind machines is that, like all machines, they need occasional maintenance, whereas solar panels just lie there and do it practically forever. Most libraries have or can get you books on wind generators. The classic is *Wind and Windspinners* by Michael Hackleman and David House.

The National Renewable Energy Laboratory conducts technical research and licensing of wind technologies for the U.S. Department of Energy; 1617 Cole Blvd., Golden, CO 80401-3393; 303-275-3000; **www.nrel.gov.** *Common Sense Wind Energy,* by the California Office of Appropriate Technology, covers everything about wind machines except building your own. *Windmills and Wind Motors,* by F. E. Powell, is a reprint of an old book with diagrams and details on making your own. Both are available from Eureka Resource, PO Box 2356, Martinez, CA 94553; catalog #2.

The National Climatic Data Center stores weather records, which includes wind speed records for many places. This info can help you choose the best size and type of wind turbine. If you pay them a little, they'll provide you with complete weather data for your area: NCDC, Federal Building, 151 Patton Ave., Asheville, NC 28801-5001; 828-271-4800; fax 828-271-4876; **orders@ncdc.noaa.gov; www.ncdc.noaa.gov.**

The world's best-selling wind generator, the Air 403, is made in Flagstaff, AZ. It generates 400 watts in a 28-mph wind. Price is $590. You can buy it through any dealer in alternative energy systems for private homes.

If wind is a risk, build a shelter. Or buy one. You can buy a prefab, watertight, galvanized steel shelter, size options of 4 to 20 people, including a ventilation system, from Storm Chaser Shelters, Inc., 1200 Lawson Rd., Ft. Worth, TX 76131; 817-847-9000; **treyt@flash.net.**

Sun Power. Solar hot water heaters are generally roof-mounted solar panels combined with hookups to the hot water system. Unfortunately, they work better in the summer than in the winter, for obvious reasons. But the technology is simple, and almost any halfway mechanically minded backyard tinkerer could come up with a working version. There aren't any worse dangers involved than a broken water pipe and hot water momentarily failing. Heating a home with solar power can be as simple as having windows on the south side and lots of insulation, or as complex as installing a battery of solar panels to conduct heat indoors. Also consider the new systems for generating electricity by solar power—exciting cutting-edge technology! To learn more, read *The Solar Electric Independent Home Book* by Jeffrey Fowler ($18.95), *The New Solar Electric Home* by Joel Davidson ($20.95), and *The New Solar Home Book* by Bruce Anderson. And talk to an alternative energy dealer-specialist.

To me, the scientists who research in this field and the struggling young companies that do manufacturing and retailing are all heroes. It doesn't matter how hard it is or how long it takes or how much adaptation it requires: we have to overcome the obstacles and discover, master, and widely distribute clean, renewable energy technologies until they are finally at work in every home and business.

Wood Power. Did you know that back during World War II there were thousands of wood-burning vehicles on the roads of Europe? Yes! The technology of wood-powered transportation and wood-powered generators to make electricity exists! For books, videos, and info call 417-336-2869; or visit **www.sensiblesteam.com**.

Muscle Power. You can turn exercise into useful power using a bicycle-powered generator. You provide the bicycle. You have to build the stationary support for it so that when you pedal, the bike doesn't go anywhere and your energy goes to charge a 12-volt battery. For rechargeable batteries, call Gaiam Real Goods at 800-919-2400.

STORAGE IN CASE OF EMERGENCY

Nobody schedules hurricanes, tornadoes, destructive winter storms that take down the power lines, earthquakes, riots, and so on, but they do occasionally happen. How can you cope with primitive conditions—expected or unexpected? Find out the risks in your region and what you should do to prepare; I can't tell you everything here. But I'll tell you what to keep in storage in case of disaster, and how to cope with the more usual run of problems.

Do develop a well-stocked storage area, just in case. Keep on hand food to eat, water to drink, a way to cook and keep warm and see in the dark, a toilet method, bedding to keep you warm, and medical supplies. Store a few battery-operated radios and some extra batteries for them. In addition, have a plan for how you can get along with no electricity, no running water, no operational toilet, and no road access in or out of your immediate environs for a while.

SUPPLIES: The following companies specialize in emergency supplies.

Andreas Industries, Inc., offers a *Practical Preparedness* catalog ($3) with discount disaster shelters, alternative energy supplies, etc.: PO Box 70131, Eugene, OR 97401-0107; 541-746-6828; **www.practical preparedness.com**.

Christian Family Resources, PO Box 405, Kit Carson, CO 80825; 719-962-3228.

Emergency Essentials: 800-999-1863; 362 S. Commerce Loop #6, Orem, UT 84058-5157; **www.BePrepared. com**.

Essentials 2000 sells emergency foods and supplies for backpacking and camping; 800-775-1991; PO Box 158, Nevada City, CA 95959; **sales@essentials2000. com; www.essentials2000.com**.

Major Surplus & Survival, 435 W. Alondra Blvd., Gardena, CA 90248; 800-441-8855; 310-324-8855; fax 310-324-6909; **www.majorsurplusnsurvival.com**. Offers preparedness and survival goods, plus military surplus.

NITRO-PAK Preparedness Center has sold preparedness gear and foods for 18 years: freeze-dried and dehydrated foods; emergency heat, light, and cooking gear; 72-hr. kits; water storage containers and filters; first-aid kits and supplies; potassium iodide tablets; solar water distillers; solar flashlights and radios; grain mills; preparedness books; etc. Contact: 800-866-4876; 435-654-0099; fax 435-654-3860; 151 N. Main St., Heber City, UT 84032; **www.nitro-pak.com**.

Out N Back: Outdoor Food and Equipment, 1797 S. State St., Orem, UT 84097; 800-533-7415; fax 801-224-0982; **sales@outnback.com; www.outnback.com**.

Preparedness Center operates two websites: **www. preparedness.com** and **www.safetycentral.com**. They offer thousands of products, updated weekly, including food storage, water filters and purifiers, self-reliance, and outdoor survival items: 800-547-4223; **sales@ preparedness.com**.

Ready Made Resources offers solar, hydro, wind, and preparedness equipment; catalog $3; 239 Cagel Rd., Tellico Plains, TN 37385; 800-627-3809; **www.ready maderesources.com**.

Sam Andy offers long-term storage foods and emergency preparedness supplies, publications, and videos; 972-887-9336; fax 972-717-1332; PO Box 141741, Irving, TX 75014. Or Sam Andy; 719-269-3030; 596 McDaniel Blvd. #111, Canon City, CO 81212. Website: **SAMANDY.COM**.

Survival Center, PO Box 234, McKenna, WA 98558; 800-321-2900; fax 360-458-6778; **sales@survivalcenter. com; survivalcenter.com**.

Wisemen Trading and Supply, 8971 Lentzville Rd., Athens, AL 35614; 256-729-8868; fax 256-729-6788; **wisemen@iol-12.net; www.integrityonline12.com/ wisemen.**

Yellowstone River Trading, 2010 W. Koch St., Bozeman, MT 59718; 800-585-5077; fax 406-586-6955; **YRTR@ aol.com; www.yellowstonetrading.com.**

VEHICLES: In the trunk of your car, keep a few blankets, a warm coat, walking shoes in summer, and warm boots suitable for hiking in the worst weather in winter.

MEDICAL: In general, store aspirin, bandages, antibiotic ointment, and a supply of your regular prescription items, plus personal sanitation supplies. Incidentally, unscented sanitary napkins are excellent compresses for a bleeding wound.

FOOD: Eat up all the stuff in your refrigerator first. After that, eat canned goods. Don't open the freezer unless power will be out more than three days. (It may stay frozen that long if unopened.) If power is going to be out longer and you have a way to cook, you can cook everything practically instantly and preserve it by canning. But you'll need an operational stove and enough lids and jars. For a long-term food storage plan, one reader recommended the *Food Storage Handbook* by Cathy and Dan Brimhall (Helena and Billings, MT: Falcon Press Publishing).

Canned goods are the backbone of an emergency food supply because they're precooked, store without refrigeration, and can be eaten without being heated. Store the sizes that would make easy meals for your family, feeding them without leaving excess leftovers to spoil. You'll need an average of 3 cans per family member per day of your emergency. So figure the worst that could happen, and store twice that much. It'll be a lot of cans. Store foods your family likes to eat, so that once a year or so you can use them up in your regular diet and replace them with fresh ones. Full-meal cans of food such as beef stew, chicken and noodles, or canned spaghetti dinner are handy for emergency food. Kids will weather this sort of emergency easiest if their emergency food supply is basically familiar foods. Assume clean water will be precious unless you have a private supply, so store a week or two's supply of disposable plates and silverware.

WATER: The basic rule of quantity for long-term drinking water storage is ½ gallon per family member per day, usually stored in gallon plastic jugs. Rinse them and change the water once every 6 weeks or so if you're using plastic. If you store water in glass gallon jars, it needs to be changed for freshness only about once every three years. Save more water for washing and flushing. If you know a disaster may be coming, fill all the sinks, the bathtub, and any other sizable containers—such as clean plastic garbage cans—with water. Then you'll have that plus your regular stored water. *NOTE: Don't drink the water from a waterbed, even in an emergency. An algaecide in that water is poisonous. Don't drink swimming-pool or pond water unless you boil it for 5 minutes before drinking it or add iodine tablets (purchase from a pharmacy or campers' supplier) or regular liquid laundry bleach. Don't use (drink) a bleach, such as fabric softener, that has anything in it besides sodium hypochlorite. Add 2 or 3 drops of bleach for each quart of water. If you're desperate enough to use some water that doesn't look clean and clear, add 5 drops of bleach per quart.*

Water Storage Summary. So you'll have a long-term store of drinking water in gallon containers plus garbage cans filled at the last minute. Plus you store pure bleach to purify water in case you have to use questionable outside sources. If you have to haul water to your site, get as much per trip as you can by using the biggest containers you can find. (See "Water" in Chapter 2.)

Diapers. If you have children in diapers and usually use cloth diapers—which require a lot of water for washing— you might want to keep a supply of disposables in your emergency box, too.

Toilet. Where do you live? If you live out in the woods, you can go out behind a tree if need be. If you live in an apartment, that isn't an option; you could purchase a chemical toilet ahead of time against such an emergency, plus a supply of heavy-duty plastic trash bags to empty it into. Either way, store 1 roll of toilet paper per family member per week you are preparing for.

EMERGENCY LIGHT: When I was a little girl, rural electrification was just reaching rural Montana, and we were all very excited about it. We kept plenty of matches in a watertight metal box though, in case the electricity failed and we had to fall back on older technologies. Always keep on hand a way of making light if the electricity goes off. All the adults in the house should have a few candles, a candle holder, and a box or book of matches right with them in their rooms, situated so that the candle could be lit and mounted in a firm position even when struggling to see in the dark. In addition to the candles, a few kerosene lamps, Coleman lanterns, "barn lights," or other such devices would be helpful.

How Many Candles? You almost can't have too many. When you are depending on them, they burn down all too fast. The general rule is to store at least three candles per day you are storing for, or 21 per week; but it's good to have more. Fat ones burn down more slowly than thin ones. If you happen onto a candle sale, buy a bunch. They keep just about forever. Liquid wax candles or 100-hour candles are sold by **www.candleservices.com.**

Instant Candles. Mike and I were in New York City during the famous 12-hour blackout of Manhattan, which happened shortly before we met. We were both graduate students at Columbia University. I simply went to sleep early. Mike went to a classmate's house with friends, where they conducted jolly conversation by the light of strings burning in cooking oil. This Montana farmer's daughter met her Idaho cowboy in an Irish pub on Amsterdam Avenue there in N.Y.C. He was wearing his cowboy boots when I first laid eyes on him, and by the next morning I knew I was in love. I was 27 years old. We've been married 9 years now and have 5 children. It was the real thing.

That's how I learned that, in an emergency, you can make an instant candle out of a string, with one end lying in some cooking oil (or any fat, even bacon grease) in a dish and the other end hanging over the edge and burning. You get more light if you use 7 or 8 strings. They're very smoky, but if you're desperate for light, anything will do. Bacon grease smokes, as does oil, but you wouldn't use this unless you needed it, in which case smoke would be secondary. (Much more on how to make candles can be found later on in this chapter.)

Outdoor Lights. A powerful, portable battery-operated light and extra batteries for it is the cleanest, safest, easiest emergency lighting system. Carry one in your car, and keep one or two in your emergency kit at home. We used Coleman lanterns for night trips to the barn before we got electric barn lights. They're still good for making outdoor light for farming, camping, or hunting, although "barn lights" and electric lamps are also good options now. They're all very portable in the lighted state. Many camping/hunting stores carry them. You have to buy a special fuel for Coleman lanterns, but a little of it goes a long way. You also have to buy a "mantle," which functions as a wick and lasts pretty long unless a curious little finger pokes it. In that case, it immediately shatters into ashes, and you have to install a new one to have light again. Don't throw away your instruction booklet, because they can seem complicated until you get used to them.

NOTE: Be careful! Coleman fuel is explosive like gas, whereas kerosene (see below) has no flashpoint. Both kerosene and Coleman fuel are poisonous, but kerosene is safer to burn.

LED (light-emitting diode) flashlights are a new superefficient light source. You can see the whole array of LEDs at **www.ccrane.com.** Free catalog: 800-522-8863; 1001 Main St., Fortuna, CA 95540.

Aladdin Industries, Lamp Division, PO Box 100255, Nashville, TN 37224; 800-456-1233, specializes in nonelectric lighting.

Kerosene Lamps. I remember kerosene lamps in our house. Electric lights were such an improvement—more light, no odor, no lamps to fill or wicks to turn up or lamp glasses to clean or break. Kerosene lamps are good indoors but not outdoors because they blow out easily. For kerosene lamps, call Major Surplus and Survival, 800-441-5588. After years of absence, kerosene lamps and lamp fuel are back in hardware stores now. Practice using yours when you have plenty of light, so it will be easy when you need to light it in the dark. A mail-order source of kerosene (or gasoline) table lamps, whole or parts (wicks, etc., sold separately), is Lehman's Non-Electric Catalog (888-438-5346; **www.Lehmans.com**).

Smoke Detector. Since you might be burning all those flames to help you cook and see, better also make sure you have a battery-powered smoke detector.

Emergency Heat. Plan a way of heating and cooking without electricity, and store a fuel supply for that system. For most people, that backup is a wood burner, even a fireplace. But fireplaces are not heat-efficient and are tough to cook on, so a wood stove, properly installed with a stovepipe, is better. Keep a supply of newpapers and kindling for starting fires and wood for burning, or you'll be burning your furniture if it's that or freeze. To keep the fire going for heat and bottle warming, you have to train yourself to wake up and put more fuel in the stove when needed.

NOTE: You absolutely cannot use charcoal grills or hibachis to heat a house. They give off carbon monoxide, a colorless, odorless, poisonous gas that has killed a lot of people who tried that. A propane or gasoline camp stove can be used in the house, and propane stores well.

LIVING SIMPLY ("PRIMITIVELY")

Actually, coping with natural disasters and living a deliberately simple life have some similarities, if you're prepared for them. Natural disasters tend to cause a sudden loss of electricity, gas, and running water—resulting in primitive living that you didn't want to happen, aren't used to, and probably aren't fully prepared for. For those who endure it, especially women, the distinction between camping, wilderness living, and making it through a natural disaster when the power is off may be very blurred. *Living with Nature* by Art Ludwig includes both principles of primitive/simple living and a powerful argument for living thus.

Years ago I received a memorable letter from a young couple who were squatting on national forestland in Alaska. They lived there year-round in a tipi, and there in the tipi their first baby was born during winter. That's a hard way to

live, and though I'm all for getting out on the land, I don't know that I'd recommend that particular style. It's best to own your own piece of earth if you can. That way you can feel like you're building something permanent that nobody can chase you from and that your children can inherit—and their children from them. Then you can plant things like sugar maples, which take a long time to mature, and feel that you and your descendants will reap the fruits of your labor. Nevertheless, there's an education for us in what Che Che Gammon wrote me:

"First, we built an ozan type roof for the 'inner roof' of the tipi out of scrap canvas. By connecting it to the liner inside the tipi, we were able to keep more heat in. The next problem was the floor. We had to make the floor stay warm, even though it was freezing all the time. We used a chain saw and made sawdust by cutting up biscuits of wood. After laying down about 6 inches of sawdust, we decided that would be enough. Then more scraps of canvas were used to cover the floor. Then we laid down deer hides I stretched and scraped all over the tipi for more warmth.

"The next problem was the biggest one by far: what to use for heat. We used an open fire for a while, but I knew that the diapers I'd be washing by hand would be really sooty if I dried them in that manner. So this was not the answer. Next we tried a small airtight stove. After cooking on it for a while and trying to bake one loaf of bread at a time in my Dutch oven, we decided again this really wouldn't be ideal. So we found an old wood stove and patched her up, and we were happy to find this solved our problem of heat and cooking and also the drying of clothes.

"When we had picked this site for our tipi, the creek was of great concern. We were lucky enough to pick one that didn't freeze up in winter, or didn't run dry in summer. It is fed by an underground stream. It isn't too far from our tipi, so we pack the water in with big buckets and I have a huge water boiler on the stove for hot water anytime we need it. Also if it rains a lot, like it does here, a rain barrel is the answer. We take our baths in two galvanized buckets (the same ones I wash in).

"During the winter, the tipi was real dark inside. The 'ozan' we put up was working, but we never thought about the light problem. A couple of kerosene lamps were acquired and some candles were made. It was not the best light, but you could see a lot better.

"Though our problems seemed to be getting smaller, there were still many things to consider, one of which was food. One thing that really helped us out was that during the summer we went fishing for salmon and I canned it up. I also picked a lot of goose tongue and canned that. With all the different kinds of berries growing wild, I soon discovered the trick of making jams and canning berries. We also grew a garden of considerable size of root crops and other vegetables. (Seaweed makes a good fertilizer!) During the winter there was deer we hunted to eat and soon different kinds of fowl. We are also very lucky where we live to have crab. Everything seems to be plentiful here. Especially love."

BOOKS AND CLASSES: During 1998 and 1999, a number of survival books appeared, of widely varying quality, including *The Emergency Disaster Survival Guidebook* by Doug King (1994), available from amazon.com or from ABC Preparedness, PO Box 795, Sandy, UT 84091 ($7.95, free shipping). It contains compact, practical, basic survival instructions with checklists to prepare for various possible emergencies. *Primitive Wilderness Living & Survival Skills,* by John and Geri McPherson (1993), has great info on primitive survival skills: bow and arrow making, container and cordage and fire making, hide tanning, pottery, sinew extraction and sewing, shelters, and tools. Order from Prairie Wolf, PO Box 6, Randolph, KS 66554. Since a picture is worth a thousand words, it's better to take a class and watch the teacher doing it.

Earth Knack: Bart and Robin Blankenship teach students and interns Stone Age living skills such as basketry, pottery, using simple tools, and soap making. They wrote *Earth Knack: Stone Age Skills for the 21st Century* (1996), a well-illustrated text in this field. (Order it from Gibbs Smith, PO Box 667, Layton, UT 84041.) To ask about classes, contact PO Box 508, Crestone, CO 81131; 719-256-4909; **www.earthknack.com.**

Hollowtop Outdoor Primitive School: Tom Elpel teaches brain tanning of hides, identification of edible wild plants, and survival on actual wilderness treks at his school; 406-685-3222; 12 Quartz St., Pony, MT 59747; **www.hollowtop.com.** His website offers links to articles on primitive living and many other primitive living schools. Tom's book, *Participating in Nature:*

Thomas J. Elpel's Guide to Primitive Living Skills (1999), covers hide tanning, fire building, cooking, shelter building, and edible plants.

The Society of Primitive Technology is a nonprofit focused on the practice, teaching, and researching of primitive technology. If you join, you get *The Bulletin of Primitive Technology* twice a year and can network with other persons developing this type of skill, find out when classes/workshops are scheduled, and read reviews of new books in this field and notices about where to get supplies and tools. Members, plus editor David Wescott, published their articles on fire making, building permanent shelters, making cordage, glue, hunting, and other tools in *Primitive Technology: A Book of Earth Skills* (1999). This comprehensive and fascinating book is published by Gibbs Smith, PO Box 667, Layton, UT 84041. Contact the Society at PO Box 905, Rexburg, ID 83440; phone/fax 208-359-2400; **www.hollowtop.com/spt-html/spt.html.**

Tom Brown Jr's Tracking, Nature, and Wilderness Survival School offers training in traditional Native American fishing, hunting, trapping, and tracking, all with low-tech, homemade tools. There's also a book: *Tom Brown's . . . .* Contact: 908-479-4681; fax 908-479-6867; PO Box 173, Ashbury, NJ 08802; **www.tracker school.com.**

GREEN DESIGN AND CONSTRUCTION IDEAS: Robert Bolman, Chairman of the Eugene, OR, chapter of the Northwest Ecobuilding Guild, is campaigning for new building codes that will let folks build "environmentally appropriate housing." He gives slide shows and talks on sustainable housing; 541-344-7196; 888 Almaden St., Eugene, OR 97402. Patrick Newberry, who is building an earthbag and hybrid home, is a guide and inspiration to others; Rt. 1, Box 245B, Mauk, GA 31058; **goshawk@gnat.net.** Ole Ersson experiments in low-impact urban living: rainwater harvesting, straw bale construction, waterless toilets, compost heating, rooftop gardening. Ole and his wife created an amazing sustainable home in the middle of Portland, OR; **krishna@rdrop.com; www.rdrop.com/users/krishna.**

The Healthy House Institute provides info to identify and avoid indoor toxic air pollution and other house-caused health problems; 430 N. Sewell Rd., Bloomington, IN 47408; phone/fax 812-332-5073; **www.hhinst.com.**

Home Energy Magazine editors wrote *No Regrets Remodeling: Creating a Comfortable, Healthy Home That Saves Energy* (1997). At their website you can order the book, or print articles from the magazine's searchable archive of great energy conservation and home performance info; 510-524-5405; fax 510-486-4673; 2124 Kittredge St., PMB 95, Berkeley, CA 94704; **contact@homeenergy.org; www. homeenergy.org.**

Environmental Building News is a monthly technical newsletter on green design and construction, focused on energy efficiency and construction styles that minimize ecological impacts; 802-257-7300, ext. 101; fax 802-257-7304; 122 Birge St., Ste. 30, Brattleboro, VT 05301. Their website, **www.buildinggreen.com,** has articles and links. They also publish the *GreenSpec Product Directory* (info on green building products, etc.). Center for Maximum Potential Building Systems is a nonprofit org that develops and promotes green building technologies. At their website, **www.cmpbs.org,** you'll find *Green Builders Sourcebook:* info on green building technologies, sustainable sources, and links to other green sites.

Natural Home ($24/6 issues) promotes earth-friendly and healthy mainstream homes; 800-340-5846; 201 E. Fourth St., Loveland, CO 80537; **www.naturalhome mag.com.**

BUILDING MATERIALS: This section is about "alternative home building," a fascinating array of uncommon options in housing. Charmaine Taylor ("Taylor Publishing") produces *The Dirt Cheap Builder's Catalog* and is author of "The Dirt Cheap Houses Guidebook on Disk," *All About Lime—A Guide for Natural Building; Low-Cost Construction: Building with Paper and More; Ancient Earth Dwellings; Safe Rainwater Collection; Build a Rocket Stove Cooker;* etc. She does a mail-order business in books and videos on natural building (rammed earth, adobe, straw bale, papercrete, travel-trailer homesteading, underground . . .), and simple, sustainable living; PO Box 6985, Eureka, CA 95502; phone/fax 888-441-1632; **www.dirtcheapbuilder.com.** The Fox Maple School of Traditional Building teaches workshops on all sorts of building methods, including straw/clay, cob, straw bales covered with earth plaster, wattle and daub, etc.; Corn Hill Rd., PO Box 249, Brownfield, ME 04010; 207-935-3720; fax 207-935-4575.

Wood: *Shelters, Shacks, and Shanties* by D. C. Beard (one of two founders of the Boy Scouts) is a reprint of a 1914 classic. It covers primitive shelters that you can build with just an axe and a knife: hogans, longhouses, lean-tos, wigwams, simple log cabins, etc. *How to Build a Hodgepodge Lodge* by Dave Hodges is a guide to low-cost log cabin construction, including sewage, well, water heater, etc. *Build Your Own Low-cost Log Home* and *Log Building Standards: The Building Code for Handcrafted Log Homes*, were both written by Roger Hard. *Log Building Construction Manual* (1999) is by Robert Chambers, a teacher of log home building; **www.log building.org.** Or get *How To Build This Log Cabin for $3,000* by John McPherson, from Prairie Wolf, PO Box 96, Randolph, KS 66554. *The Complete Book of Cordwood Masonry Housebuilding* by Rob Roy covers the cordwood and mortar building method.

Yurt: Want to live in a yurt? These tent-type structures are derived from the Mongolian nomads' traditional round dwelling. They can travel in the back of a pickup, are easily set up, and can be used as a cheap home, bunkhouse, or camp dwelling. Contact Pacific Yurts, 77456 Highway 99 S., Cottage Grove, OR 97424; 800-944-0240; fax 541-942-0508; **yurts@pacinfo.com; www.yurts.com.** They make year-round ones certified to endure 100 lb./sq. ft. of snow load or 100-mph winds.

Tipi: For building and living in a tipi (and other Indian crafts), read *The Indian Tipi: Its History, Construction, and Use* by Reginald Laubin and Gladis Laubin (1989), available from U. of Oklahoma Press, 1005 Asp Ave., Norman, OK 73019-0445. The Laubins described portable hunting tipis as about 12 ft. in diameter. A regular family lodge was 18 to 20 ft. across. Such a tipi was supported by poles 22 to 28 ft. long. To buy a tipi or tipi accessory, contact Nomadics Tipi Makers, 17671 Snow Creek Rd., Bend, OR 97701; phone/fax 541-389-3980; **www.tipi.com.**

Adobe, Cob, or Cast Earth: Joe Tibbets teaches the latest construction methods at his Southwest Solar Adobe School; PO Box 153, Bosque, NM 87006; 505-861-1255; fax 505-

861-1304; **www.adobebuilder.com.** For the latest methods, materials, and designs for cast earth, rammed earth, and adobe building, subscribe to his magazine, *Adobe Builder;* $19.95/4 issues per yr. Cast Earth, 4022 E. Larkspur, Phoenix, AZ 85032; 602-404-1044; **www.castearth. com,** teaches that building process, guided by Harris Lowenhaupt.

Paul Graham McHenry Jr.'s guides to do-it-yourself mud building, *Adobe: Build It Yourself* (1998) and *Adobe and Rammed Earth Buildings: Design and Construction*, are available from 800-426-3797 or 520-621-1141; U. of Arizona Press, 355 S. Euclid, Ste. #103, Tucson, AZ 85719; **orders@uapress.arizona.edu.** Professional builders should read *Buildings of Earth and Straw: Structural Design for Rammed Earth and Straw-Bale Architecture* (1996) by Bruce King. Jim Graham, Sun & Earth Enterprises, is a general contractor who specializes in energy-efficient construction and classic adobe homes: 1108 Gardner, Las Cruces, NM 88001; 505-521-3537. For an Aussie view, read *The Mud Brick Adventure* by Andrew Bianco.

Straw Bale: For the brighter side of this choice, read Chelsea Green's *The Straw Bale House* by Athena Swentzell Steen et al. (1994); and *Build It with Bales: A Step-by-Step Guide to Straw-Bale Construction, Version Two* by Matts Myhrman and S. O. MacDonald (1998). To network with straw bale builders and natural builders, subscribe to *The Last Straw Journal;* $28/4 issues per yr; HC 66, Box 119, Hillsboro, NM 88042; 505-895-5400; **thelaststraw@ strawhomes.com; www.strawhomes.com.** Taylor Publishing offers *How to Build Your Elegant Home with Straw Bales* by Carol Escott and Steve Kemble. It's both video and manual: 90 minutes of video, 690-pg. manual; $59.

Papercrete: Books and videos on building with papercrete are available from Charmaine, including her own book, *All About Papercrete and Other Alternative Building Materials.* Mike McCain "has mixer, will travel," and gives papercrete workshops; 505-531-2201. The amazing Talmath Mesenbrink both builds with papercrete for hire and teaches "solar stuff and alternative building workshops"; 709-256-4197; c/o General Delivery, Crestone, CO 81131. Laura and Gordon Solbert created *Building with Papercrete*, a book and video; 505-526-1853; PO Box 23E, Radium Springs, NM 88054; **earth@zianet.com.**

Sod or Thatched Roof: Colin McGhee, Master Thatcher, is a delightful Irishman who dwells in the U.S. and offers a complete thatched roofing service: total thatching, repairs, advice, and assistance, and occasional workshops on his ancient craft! Contact: 540-923-4707; **thatchit@aol.com; www.thatching.com.**

Mothering When It Gets Very Cold

Summer is manageable just about anywhere. It's the other three seasons, especially winter, that you want to really prepare for. You have to prepare to keep warm and also keep fed. (There's not much wild food forage outdoors in February.) Yet you, me, and everybody else could get along with a lot less heat if we had to.

CLOTHING CHILDREN AND CHANGING BABIES: Keep children dressed in plenty of dry clothes. Long underwear is a good idea, or long, heavy "pantyhose" for girls if they are wearing dresses. Learn how to change clothes quickly or under the covers in bed. To keep from having to change (and chill) the babies so often, use two or three cloth diapers at once rather than just one. (Be sure and wash them only in a very mild soap, and rinse well so they don't irritate tender skin.) These extra diapers are also good insurance against the babies having wet outer clothes and are especially needed at night. If your baby is still soaking through into clothes and bedding at night, you'll just have to train yourself to wake up and change the child as often as necessary to keep him or her dry, and thus warm. (Wet, by definition, is cold.) Stake out a warm spot near the stove and set it up for your diaper-changing area. Have everything close at hand and ready so you can work very fast during the time the baby's body has to be exposed to the cold. A big thick rug near the heat stove will do. You can lay the baby there, kneel beside, and accomplish the job.

For more info on cloth diapers, read *Diaper Changes: The Complete Diapering Book and Resource Guide* by Theresa Rodriguez Farrisi; 877-285-4337; Homekeepers, Box 439, Richland, PA 17087; **diaperchanges@homekeepers.com; www.diaperchanges.com.**

BABY BOTTLES: Keep a kettle on the stove. You can warm baby milk bottles whenever you need them by just setting them in the hot water. They'll be ready very quickly. Infants can stand a lot of cold if they're kept warmly wrapped, are accustomed to it, and regularly get warm milk in their tummies. Don't feed them cold milk, and keep them out of drafts. If you are cooking over an open fire, you'll have to use your own body as a bottle warmer when you are without a fire. Put the bottle inside your clothes, between your breasts if they are ample enough for the job or inside your belt, tight against your body. That will at least take the chill off the milk if you are warm-blooded. Fix a bottle and take it to bed with you to keep it warm if you expect a night feeding when the fire will be out. Use the tight cap; put the nipple on only when you're ready to feed to prevent leakage. Canned baby formula keeps sweet a lot better than "regular" milk under these conditions. If you can't nurse, what you really need is a lactating animal— such as a goat, cow, or sheep—to share her milk with you and your baby!

BATHING UNDER PRIMITIVE CONDITIONS: Use your clothes boiler or a big galvanized tin tub for baths. That's what my mother used. In winter, when you're heating with one wood stove in a chilly, drafty tent or cabin, the children run a risk of colds every time you give them a bath. So once a week in winter is enough. Don't bathe children at all under those conditions if they have any sign of a cold, even if the cold goes on and on. The dirt won't really harm them, but a chill almost certainly will worsen the cold. Instead, just spot-wash them when and where needed—face, hands and privates. When you're ready to bathe them, heat the kitchen, heat the water, and then run them through the tub one at a time (using the same water if need be), with a good scrubbing but no lingering. Rinse them with a tea kettle or pitcher just as they are ready to step out of the tub. Quickly wrap the wet children in thick, dry towels for a brisk drying off, and then it's back into warm clothes pronto.

ADJUSTING HOT WATER TEMPERATURE: For any purpose (baths, dishes, clothes washing, shampoos), first boil water in your usual container. Then pour hot water until your working pan is partly full. Now pour in cold water, stirring with your hand once in a while to mix it up and check the temperature. Pour and mix until you have the combined temperature just right for your purpose. This system makes the most of your pan space, doesn't use up all your hot water at once, and gets just the water temperature you want.

SLEEPING WARM: Be sure to keep small children's feet covered. Thick warm sleeping suits that have built-in foot coverings—I call them "zoot suits"—are the best thing I know for keeping toddlers warm at night. They cover a child from neck to toe. I buy the heaviest weight I can get. For extra cold weather, give them socks, pants and a T-shirt inside the zoot suit. If it's colder than that at night, or if you have a child who doesn't stay under the covers, put 2 or even 3 zoot suits on him or her at bedtime (or daytime), one right on top of another. If you have the hairless variety or a child that's very prone to head colds or earaches, rig up a nightcap. You can use a sweat shirt with a hood or a soft bonnet that ties under the chin—but not too tight. If you have a big thick rug on the floor by the heat stove, the children will naturally go there to dress in the morning and to fall asleep at night.

The adult version of the wonderful zoot suit is long underwear together with a pair or two of warm socks— good for sleeping clothes when it gets awfully cold, and in the daytime too under other clothing! And in cold weather, use sheet blankets for everybody. Sheet blankets are much warmer than sheets; they are light blankets meant to be used as sheets. Use lots of heavy, thick blankets and quilts on top of the sheet blankets to complete the bed. Being miserably cold much of the day is manageable if you can sleep snugly warm at night. So have plenty of bedding and let the little ones sleep two by two or more. They help keep each other warm as well as cheerful. In cold weather you can easily fit 6 children into a double bed because they instinctively make themselves small and cuddle up. (In summer they'll spread out and need more bed space.)

BED-WETTING: It can be a real problem to keep young (bed-wetting) children warm at night. Housebreak them in the spring; if you haven't won by fall, go back to diapers for the rest of the winter. If they're too big for diapers but still wet the bed, cover the mattress with plastic and dry the bedding every day (no use trying to wash it every day when you have no washer and dryer). When the child wakes up and cries because his sleeping clothes and bed are wet, just help him or her out of the wet clothes into something dry (be prepared), and bed the child back down in a dry place, such as with his or her head at the other end of the bed. Or pull off the wet sheets and put the kid a couple layers up, between some blankets.

The important thing is not to make yourself or the child miserable over it. This happens more to mothers (and to more mothers) than they'll admit—most of them, I think. Fighting it by anger, hitting, or shaming does more harm to the child than the wet bedding. I used to assure my offspring that by the time they got old enough to date, the problem would be gone, and sure enough it was.

SICKNESS: Winter is also sickness time for children. Have a copy of a good baby book that covers symptoms, their diagnosis, and treatment, and have a flashlight or something on hand to read it by. Crises always happen in the middle of the night, usually Saturday night (unless you have a Seventh-Day Adventist doctor, in which case it would be Friday night). And make sure the children have all their immunization shots and get them as young as possible. Whooping cough is very much around, masquerading as a cold that hangs on and on in children who have not been immunized against it. Even very small babies can get it, and they will be desperately ill if they do.

Keeping the House Warm

THE STOVE: When you heat with wood, the fire goes out in the stove or fireplace after you go to bed. (The fire builder in cold weather is every morning's hero!) I was raised that way, and I live that way. There are ways to keep warm, and in this section I'm passing them on. Check the damper on your wood-burner to make sure it's closed, so you won't lose heat up the chimney. If your heat stove is in the kitchen, a nice wide, high doorway—about twice or more the usual width, with no door of course—will help heat circulate into an adjoining room where you want it, such as your living room. (For lots more on stoves, wood, etc., see Chapter 6.)

NEWSPAPER USES: If getting firewood is a problem, have you considered burning newspapers? You can roll them up tightly and make your own sort of Presto log. You can make an emergency blanket for the bed out of them too.

THE BATHROOM: This is an important room. People using the bathroom immensely appreciate warmth. If pipes are not at risk of freezing, close off the bathroom and heat it only when needed. You can put a little quick-response electric space heater in there, if you have electricity, to be turned on only when someone is using the room. But if you have water pipes in the bathroom that might freeze and burst (and that can happen if it gets cold enough, even if you leave the water running), then keeping the pipes warm enough is even more important than keeping people warm! *If you leave water running, it is less likely to freeze;* running water can withstand a lot more cold before freezing up than can standing water in the pipes. The colder it is, the larger the volume of water you must keep running to keep it from freezing. Let it run in both your kitchen and bathroom.

HOUSE INSULATING

Windows. If you're cold and don't have heavy thermal drapes that can completely cover your windows, hang heavy-textured blankets over them. Wave your hand slowly around suspicious areas—such as around the sides of your windows and above and below your doors—to find out where cold drafts are coming in. Then plug those holes by tacking or taping newspaper or plastic over the windows and adding an insulating lining to the edges of the door. Storm windows on the outside of windows help insulate. If you don't have the regular glass kind of storm window, improvise by nailing a layer of heavy, clear plastic over the outside of all windows. Tack it down all the way around the outside edges of the window, nailing strips of cardboard or thin wood on top of the plastic to prevent it from ripping off in strong winds. We do this every fall and take it off every spring. With the plastic storm windows on the outside and heavy curtains on the inside, not much heat is lost.

Doors. If you don't have an enclosed porch to buffer the air flow between outside and inside the house every time that door opens, install storm doors to hold in your heat. (Even with a porch, they're a good idea.) Make sure the storm doors have good springs so they will stay tightly shut. You don't need but one door in wintertime. Seal off the oth-

ers and you'll save heat. Frances E. Render of Billings, Montana (where it really gets cold) wrote me a great "dire emergency" method for sealing doors and windows that let cold in around the edges: Tear cloth strips, wring them out in water, and poke them in those drafty cracks. As they freeze, they will expand and make a perfect seal. Frances has used this trick "on the north side during temperatures of −30 to −40°F with a strong wind and it worked great!" It helps to have a porch-type enclosure outside with one operating door.

Sealing Off Spaces. If you don't have doors on the pantry, closets, and similar non–lived-in spaces that don't need to be heated, hang blankets or plastic curtains over their openings. Seal off as many infrequently used rooms as you can for the duration of the cold weather. Keep the bedroom doors shut so you don't have to heat those rooms during the daytime. For more ideas, read *Superinsulated Houses and Air-to-Air Heat Exchangers* by William A. Shurcliff.

If you do all these things, and your fire is burning fine, by now you ought to be feeling warmer. Still cold? Try the Eskimo technique for keeping warm. Always wear lots of clothes, eat rich food, and take a dog to bed—a nice furry variety. If you're still cold, take two dogs to bed, or three. If you're still cold—get married! If that doesn't do it, I give up!

Giving Birth by Yourself

A comprehensive and fully illustrated training manual for midwives is *Hearts & Hands: A Midwife's Guide to Pregnancy and Birth* (1997), by Elizabeth Davis. It's available from Celestial Arts, PO Box 7123, Berkeley, CA 97407. The *Emergency Childbirth Handbook* by Barbara Anderson and Pamela Shapiro is good for an amateur to read in preparation for the possibility of an unexpected delivery. I first was inspired to do natural childbirth by reading *Birth Without Fear*, an inspiring and reassuring 1940s classic by an English doctor. *Spiritual Midwifery,* by Ina Mae Gaskin, puts natural birth into perspective with a moving collection of photos and birth stories from the '70s stage of her "hippie" community.

Most childbirth manuals don't say what to do if you're giving birth alone, although it's not uncommon for women to give birth while completely alone. So I wrote the following section, which is better than nothing.

TOILET BABIES: Whether it is your first birth or your tenth, it is possible to mistakenly interpret labor phenomena as frequent urges to urinate or move your bowels. No two labors are exactly alike, so just because you never made that mistake before doesn't mean it can't happen. If you are having a premature child, or if you tend to have easy deliveries, this misinterpretation of labor as urges to toilet is a special risk for you. I shared a ward room with a lady to whom this had happened. It was her third baby and she thought she was having the stomach flu with diarrhea. Maybe she did have it. But frequent bowel movements can have a close relationship with labor. That's why the old-timers used to think you could start a woman into labor by giving her a big dose of castor oil. Sometimes it worked.

So my friend made one trip to the potty after another. Finally she sat on it one more time and something very big slipped into the water of the toilet bowl. She immediately realized she had delivered her baby, scooped up the child, and had her husband, who was home, take them both to the hospital. Baby and mother were fine. But the next time my friend was expecting a baby, she made sure she was at the hospital for her delivery. I've since heard of several other cases of "bathroom babies."

WILDERNESS BABIES: Years ago I read in a magazine the true story of a young couple living in the Alaskan wilderness who were accidentally separated before the woman's delivery. They had been planning to fly down to the Lower 48 for the baby's birth. But a freak accident trapped the husband and his friend with the plane in one part of Alaska, incommunicado for several months, while the wife was left alone. She had a warm cabin and plenty of food and fuel. When she realized her husband wasn't coming back, she spent her waiting days making warm Eskimo-type clothing for her baby and gathering dried moss to use as diaper material. She delivered safely and fed her newborn by nursing. When her husband and his friend were finally able to escape from their own entrapment and return, three months later, mother and child were fine, though terribly lonely.

HOSPITAL BABIES: Most of the mothers I know about who've been forced to give birth alone have done so in U.S. hospitals. That may amaze you. It worries me and is a good reason why I want you to know what to do if you find yourself giving birth alone. One of the saddest stories I know is the true story of a black couple whose first child was born in a large big-city hospital. They had married late in life and were both clean-living, deeply religious people. She was given a narcotic early in labor. The staff was having a busy night and were all in the delivery room with another woman or on errands elsewhere in the hospital at the moment that she delivered. Her husband was out in the fathers' waiting room.

She delivered a baby who would otherwise have been full-term and completely healthy, except that the cord was wrapped twice around its neck. As it delivered, that cord pulled tight around the neck, cutting off oxygen to the brain. The mother had been anesthetized enough to be quite fuddled, but she knew she'd given birth, and she lay there and screamed for 10 solid minutes trying to attract help. When help finally came, it was almost too late. The tight cord around the baby's neck had caused not only a shortage of oxygen to its brain but also hemorrhaging in the brain due to prolonged pressure. The baby was successfully resuscitated, but because it had been without oxygen for 10 minutes and because of the hemorrhaging, it was severely and irreversibly brain-damaged.

If only the mother had refused the narcotic, she would have been more conscious and able to cope with her situation, and her baby would have had better resistance to the trauma it had to endure. If only she had known that after giving birth alone, she needed to immediately sit up, pick up her baby, see what it needed, and take care of those needs herself—in this case, quickly unwinding the cord from around the baby's neck.

My mother gave birth to me alone in a hospital too. The nurses didn't think she was making much progress and had all gone to lunch. Mother realized that she was delivering. She told me, "With my last ounce of strength, I reached up and managed to push the emergency buzzer above the bed." (Always find out where the emergency button is as soon as you get to your labor room, and *use it* if you need to!) But by the time a nurse showed up, I had already been born. I emerged "in the veil" (that's what my mother's generation called unbroken membranes), so I couldn't breathe until somebody broke them and exposed my face to the air. (Mother said an old woman working at

the hospital told her that any child born in the veil was destined to grow up to be somebody very special.) It could easily have been another tragedy if not for the staff's quick response to the call button.

So you see, there is a practical reason for allowing husbands to sit with their wives in labor rooms as well as delivery rooms; it beefs up the help-power and makes sure somebody is there all the time. But if nobody is there, for your baby's sake you will manage.

WHAT TO DO IF YOU MUST DELIVER A BABY ALL ALONE: If you have had no anesthetic (and please, for your baby's sake and yours, don't have any), the moment your baby completely delivers, you will get a terrific jolt of adrenaline into your system and be totally alert and able to cope with anything. Before this, during the stage where you've been pushing the baby out through your birth canal, you're in a naturally semi-conscious state, submerged in total concentration on the physical process of moving your baby to freedom. But the moment your baby is entirely out of your body, all that sluggishness is instantly swept away in a sudden, morning-clear reawakening of your ability to think, plus a jolt of pure energy to power you to accomplish whatever is needed. (I know the phenomena of this post-birth transition well. I had 6 babies with no anesthetic!)

So you'll have a terrific urge to sit up and look at the baby lying between your legs. That is exactly what you must do. It is urgent to discover if the cord is wrapped around the baby's neck. If it is, gently unwind the baby's head from it. Don't pull on the cord; don't do anything that tightens it. Just pick up the baby and wind it out of the cord. (Practice now with a doll and a cord until it feels simple to free the neck.) If your baby's face is covered by intact membranes the way mine was, you must tear them open with your fingers and free the baby's head so it can breathe. No need to panic. The baby still receives oxygen through the umbilical cord for about 5 minutes after the birth. But if the baby's face is blue, that means the oxygen isn't getting through and it *really* needs to take a breath.

Make sure your baby's mouth is clear of mucus. You can scoop it out with your finger while holding the baby upside down. If the baby is still not breathing, give it a gentle slap on the buttocks or on the bottoms of the feet while you have it upside down. The upside-down position is best for encouraging drainage of any glop that may still be in the baby's nose and mouth.

Once you are sure your baby is breathing, your next priority is to make sure it doesn't chill. Newborn babies don't make heat as well as we do. Your baby has been at 98.6°F for 9 months. And it's wet. Too much chilling can kill it. Wrapping it in a cool blanket won't help. Your infant doesn't yet have the ability to warm up its own blanket; it will just lose more body heat to the cool blanket. The best thing is to put the naked baby inside your clothing, right next to your warm skin, but with its head safely able to get air. And cover it warmly there.

Now try to get your baby to nurse by touching it on the side of the mouth with your closest nipple. If you can get the baby to nurse, that not only warms it but also helps it breathe, because the act of sucking helps clear its mouth of glop by means of the swallowing reflex. In the meantime, you've probably delivered the afterbirth.

There's no big rush about the cord. Make sure you have these other things taken care of first. Don't tie it until there is no more pulse in it. Then tie it at 2 points in the cord a couple inches apart, and cut between them. The flopping tag end left on the baby is natural. Just leave it be. It will dry up and drop off on its own after a week or two. Don't try to hurry it. That would do more harm than good.

The baby's delivered, and mother and child are fine! But somewhere I have to place the topic of home burial, and since death is the natural successor to life, though hopefully a long-distant event, I'll go on to that.

How to Care for Your Dead

In most states it is legal for family and friends to care for their own dead. There was a wonderful article on this subject in one of my favorite magazines ("Walking that last mile with a loved one . . . a guide to caring for your own dead" by Carl Watner, *Backwoods Home Magazine*, May/June 1992):

"Even today, in 41 states, a family or support group has the right to handle all death arrangements without the assistance of outside professionals. In the other nine states, if the family (and friends) can find a cooperative funeral director they may, if they wish, 'take on at least some of the duties usually assigned to a funeral home.' . . . In Lisa Carlson's book *Caring For Your Own Dead*, she writes that this can be one of 'the most meaningful' ways 'to say goodbye to someone you love.' Like home schooling, home birth, and home care (hospice) for the terminally ill, home funerals allow us to take control of critical areas of our lives . . . Participation of close friends and family in construction of a casket, transportation of the body, preparation of the grave, scattering of 'ashes,' or other related activities helps them accept the fact of death—both emotionally and intellectually. For most people who have done it, involvement in a home funeral is a special time, not frightening or aversive. In effect, it is 'going the last mile' with the deceased, and customizing their last rites. By not turning over the funeral responsibilities to people who never knew the deceased as an individual human being, we not only offer our last respects but engage in an emotional process which helps us cope with their death. To be around the body of one who has just died gives us the 'unparalleled opportunity,' as one death educator has put it, 'to let go gently into the light,' 'to act out one's grief by confronting the reality of death.'

"Certainly the decision to care for your own dead should be taken seriously, discussed beforehand, and accepted by all concerned relatives . . . Not everyone will want nor be able to cope with a funeral without an undertaker . . . If you live in an area where at-home funerals are not common, then you should be prepared to expect hesitancy and even resistance on the part of those normally involved in the process . . . but if you have studied the law and know what you are doing, their unwillingness and indecision should be easily overcome. Plenty of advance planning and forethought is necessary. Timing is important, as cemeteries and crematories have cut-off hours. Death is certainly part of life, much as we are conditioned to reject this idea. Active involvement following the death of a loved one or friend is actually a labor of love. It is often the best type of grief therapy . . . "

MORE INFORMATION: Carl Watner recommended most highly *Caring for Your Own Dead* by Lisa Carlson. He wrote, "Must reading. Presents a detailed study of all aspects of home funerals, plus analyses on a state-by-state basis." His second choice is Ernest Morgan's *Dealing Creatively with*

Death: A Manual of Death Education and Simple Burial, whose 168 pages ($12.95) cover how to get dignity, simplicity, and economy in funeral arrangements, how to cope with bereavement, how to provide hospice care at home and relate to dying persons, and how to safeguard your right to die (forms and legal information included). It contains directories of grief support groups; memorial societies in the United States and Canada; eye, organ, and tissue banks; and an annotated bibliography of books, pamphlets, periodicals, and audiovisuals having to do with death-related problems. Both books are available from Upper Access Book Publishers; 800-310-8320; fax 802-482-7730; Box 457, Hinesburg, VT 05461; **www.upperaccess.com**. Also see *Affairs in Order: A Complete Resource Guide to Death and Dying* by Patricia Anderson (1991).

Backwoods Housekeeping

KEEPING FOOD COOL IN HOT WEATHER

The Pantry. An old-time pantry was a room away from heat sources which was warm enough in winter that food in it didn't freeze but was about the coolest room in the house in summer because it was kept tightly shut off from heat sources. Some old-timers kept butter and such in the cellar or basement in the summer, where it would be cool enough not to melt. Nevertheless, old-time cooks made only enough food to be quickly eaten up, so storage of cooked leftovers just wasn't the issue then that it is today. And people in the old days weren't accustomed to drinking cold beverages and cold food. They didn't mind "lukewarm" stuff.

Cold-Water Milk Cooler. Just run cool water into a tub and then set your milk can in it.

Iceless Refrigerator. This is basically a box with a tray on top for water and a cloth drape down over the sides, into which water seeps from the tray on top. There are shelves inside the box. It keeps food cooler than it would be otherwise.

Spring House. Spring water and well water are generally on the cool side. You can take advantage of that by building a well-insulated room over a spring outlet. The spring water runs through it and out an opening at the downhill end. The cool water from underground is made to run through a flat traylike space. Set your cans and crocks and bowls of dairy products and leftovers right down into the cool water. The cooler your water, of course, the cooler it will keep your food. You can do something similar by making a coolerbox where water runs through from a cool well.

Kerosene Refrigerator. There was and is such a thing. Lehman's has them: 888-438-5346; **info@lehmans.com**.

ICE HARVEST: If you live where there's a real winter, you can dam up a spring, make a pond, and save ice. In the winter when the pond ice is frozen hard and thick, cut it into blocks and pull them up into the cave. The old-timers had a special "ice saw" for this

Margaret Kerrick, West Roxbury, MA, wrote me, "There was no refrigeration when I was a child, and so when the ponds froze over, all the men in the community would gather with their teams and sleighs and saws, and cut ice from the ponds. They would haul out huge cakes of ice after sawing it; they must have measured 2 feet square or more, and anywhere from 9 inches to a foot thick. Everyone had an icehouse where the ice was stored between layers of sawdust. It was pulled up a long chute, by means of ice tongs and a rope, from the sleigh to the icehouse, and there it kept perfectly all winter.

"Our men in Spring Hill, Pennsylvania, where I grew up, didn't have any power saws, so they chopped a hole in the ice and then got the crosscut saw in and sawed the cakes out. Then they tilted ice tongs onto the free cake and tied a rope to it, and it was then hauled out of the water with a team of horses and pulled up into a sleigh. When the sleigh was loaded, it was drawn by horses to the icehouse of the particular farm that was being served that day. On arrival at the icehouse, the tongs were attached to each cake of ice in turn, and this ice was pulled up into the icehouse and covered with sawdust, brought in usually from a local sawmill. It was hard, cold work, and the men came in for dinner with huge appetites. My mother cooked gargantuan meals, and delicious ones too—huge slabs of salt ham, mashed potatoes, squash, pickles, jelly, bread, and apple pie. Those men would consume about 3 loaves of bread at a meal. The ice lasted very well until the next year's harvest.

"We used 1 cake very day to put in the milk vat to cool the milk, and on Sunday, my father would get out an extra cake to make ice cream with. Also we used half a cake at a time in our old wooden house refrigerator. The ice cake was placed in the top compartment, which was lined with tin or zinc. As it melted, a small pipe carried the water to a container in the cellar. This kept the food cool, but nothing like today's refrigerators."

Making an Ice Cave. Up on the south bank, dig back in until you have a sizable cave. Store by putting in an insulating layer like straw or sawdust, then a layer of ice, then the straw or sawdust again, then ice, until the cave is full. With enough ice in there to start with, you'll have ice until the last part of summer. Good for making ice cream or using in an old-time icebox. You can also keep dairy products and leftover food cool by setting them in a tub of water that has a chunk of ice in it.

An Old-Time Icebox. The simplest pioneer system was to dig a hole in the ground, put sawdust in it for a liner, and then put in a block of ice. Put food in there, with a heavy, insulated lid on top. For an inhouse icebox, wrap a chunk of ice in insulating material such as cloth or paper. Put it in a wooden box, maybe lined with metal and thick enough to be well-insulated. Set the food in there with it. Have a way for the melting water to drain and be caught in a pan!

Now to the subject of how to cook without electricity.

SOLAR COOKERS: Solar cookers are a wonderful technology that works every sunny day using the sun's energy to cook food and pasteurize water and milk: no cost! no pollution!

Barbara Kerr wrote me, "Solar cookers can be used as the major stove for a family, as an occasional cooker, or for novelty. They come in three main types: solar boxes, parabolic cookers, and solar panel cookers. There are innumerable ways to home-make solar cookers and many different designs and models for sale. To understand the underlying principles for solar cookers, check out **solarcooking.org/sbcdes.htm#heat_principles** and **solarcooking.org/intuit1.htm. solarcooking.org** is the basic whole solar archives. Browsing it can be fascinating. Check out the Reflective Open Box (ROB) design; it is the quickest to make and will cook a single pot containing enough food to serve 4 to 6 people. It also presents the CooKit, a new solar-panel design of solar cooker. CooKit is the cheapest manufactured solar cooker, yet it can feed 4 to 6 people. Plans for both are available through the archives."

Capturing Heat: Five Earth-Friendly Cooking Technologies and How to Build Them, published by Aprovecho Research Center, is a small book costing $6; 541-941-8198; **apro@efn.org.** The most complete paperback book on this subject is *Heaven's Flame: A Guide to Solar Cookers,* by Joseph Radabaugh. Order it from Home Power Publishing, PO Box 275, Ashland, OR 97520; **www.homepower.com.** You can buy books on solar cooking, solar cookers, a black pot, a water pasteurization indicator, and video from Solar Cookers International; 916-455-4499; fax 916-455-4498; 1919 21st St., Ste. 101, Sacramento, CA 95814-6827; **info@solarcookers.org.**

The Expanding World of Solar Box Cookers contains detailed solar box cooking info plus plans for homemade solar cookers. You can order it for $15 from author Barbara Kerr, a longtime expert in this field who invented the solar wall oven, a solar cooker attached to the outside of the house which can be reached through a doorway in her kitchen wall. A video on her Sustainable Living Center costs $17. Her basic plans for a Sustainable Emergency Kitchen cost $3 (plus SASE); 928-536-2269; PO Box 576, Taylor, AZ 85939; **bkerr@cybertrails.com.** *Favorite Recipes from Solar Cooks/Solar Box Cooking* is out of print, but the entire text can be found on the web at **www.solarcooking.org/recipes.**

Vegas Trailer Supply hosts solar living seminars that are usually free; 702-457-4265; fax 702-457-1662; 3076 E. Fremont, Las Vegas, NV 89104; **mike-little@vegastrailer.com; www.vegastrailer.com;** or **www.greensun.org.**

PERIODICALS AND SOLAR COOKOUTS

Citizens for Solar holds a solar cookout and potluck every spring at Catalina State Park just north of Tucson, AZ, to educate the public on solar cooking, photovoltaics, solar water heating systems, and other solar-powered applications.

Solar Cooker Review is a newsletter published two or three times a year by Solar Cookers International (an organization that helps communities use the sun's power to cook food and pasteurize water). It lists their various items for sale, including teaching and development materials, CooKits, and the water pasteurization indicator known as the WAPI. The *Review* is sent to persons who contribute money ($10/yr) or news about solar cooking projects. It publishes info from solar cooking projects in the developing world. There are free plans to make a CooKit solar cooker from a 3 ft. x 4 ft. piece of cardboard, glue, and aluminum foil: **www.solarcooking.org/cookit.htm.** They also sell solar cookbooks. *Cooking with Sunshine,* by L. Anderson and R. Palkovic ($10; for vegetarians using fish and poultry); *Eleanor's Solar Cookbook,* by E. Shimeali ($10; includes red meat recipes and solar canning); *Solar Cooking Primer,* by H. Kofalk ($12; vegan recipes only). Contact: Solar Cookers International; 916-455-4499; fax 916-455-4498; 1919 21st St., Ste. 101, Sacramento, CA 95814-6827; **info@solarcookers.org; solarcooking.org.**

THE CAMPFIRE KITCHEN: You need a good place to build your fire and plenty of fuel for all its stages. You will be glad for a work table—maybe a plank between two stumps, so you don't have to set everything on the ground. Anything that can be cooked in frying pans, kettles, or reflector ovens can be managed with a campfire. Don't use pans with handles that will burn. Handles that aren't metal will promptly burn or melt. If they're all you have, let them do it, and then you can get on with it. Stick to simple ingredients and simple procedures when you're cooking, because you didn't bring your kitchen. If you are able to plan ahead to do all your cooking over an open fire, you especially need one or two cast-iron frying pans, a Dutch oven, a campfire coffeepot, and a big pan to heat dish and washing water in.

A folding grill to hold pans secure and level is very helpful. You can buy a folding grill and many other helpful items from the Campmore catalog; 800-226-7667.

Starting a Fire. Campfire cooking means starting a fire and controlling it until you don't need it any more. There's a real skill to it, which you'll acquire with practice. The easiest way to do camp cooking is to pack a proper wood cookstove, set it up in your camp, and use it. Gather wood on dry days and store it under shelter to use on wet ones. You can do this in a semi-permanent camp. If you're living on the trail, start a fire like this: Lay a little mound of really flammable dry stuff in an open place, on dirt or sand if you can, and away from dry brush or grass. (Please don't start a forest fire!) Place very loosely wadded toilet paper, dry grass, the wrappers from tin cans, or one of my book brochures crumpled up on top of that. You crumple it because paper doesn't burn well flat. You've got to get air in there. Now make a tipi of very slender dry sticks over that, then bigger and bigger ones over that. Set aside some yet bigger ones to add later. Use 3 matches bunched together to start the fire.

Frying. Try to allow enough time to let a good roaring blaze burn down to coals. When desperate, though, you can fry on a flame. Have a circle of big flat-topped rocks around the outside of your fire circle. They will help hold the heat.

Stewing. Just make a place for your kettle down in there among the rocks. Some tribes of native Americans cooked their meat by digging a hole, lining it with a hide, filling it with water, and then adding hot rocks and pieces of meat. This had to be the first crock pot!

Baking. Use a reflector oven, Dutch oven in a hole, or build a mud oven.

Building a Mud Oven. If you have clay soil, this is a natural. Start by building a strong, dome-shaped frame of willow branches and sticks about 2 feet wide by 3 feet long. Cover your branch canopy with a layer of mud 6–12 inches thick. Cut a square opening at one end to be your oven door. At the top opposite end, insert a large tin can that is open at both ends; that will be your chimney. After the mud is completely dry, build a fire inside and burn out all your wooden framework. Cool and scrape the insides clean. To bake in your mud oven, first build a fire inside it and heat the mud to red-hot. Then rake out the fire and put in your sourdough bread, bannocks, stew, or roast. Close the door with a slab of flat rock, and it should bake wonderfully.

If you like playing in the mud, you can build a wood-fired kiln and produce pots and dishes, too. You'll find instructions in *Low Fire: Other Ways to Work in Clay,* by Leon I. Nigrosh (Davis Publications; 800-533-2847; 50 Portland St., Worcester, MA 01608; **www.davis-art.com**), and in *Wood-Fired Stoneware and Porcelain* by Jack Troy (Krause Publications, 700 E. State St., Iola, WI 54945).

Bread in a Clay Pot. Randee Greenwald wrote me from West Africa, "We bake soybean bread using an oven made of a large, heavy pot that has been partially filled with sand. It works great over a wood fire. If you want circulation, you just cut off the tops and bottoms of small tomato paste cans and place them on top of the sand and under the bread pan."

Phyllis Vallette, a Wycliffe Bible translator living with the Fulani, a semi-nomadic cattle-herding people in Ouagadougou, Burkina Faso (also in West Africa), wrote me, "When we live in the bush I make my own bread, but in small batches—every 2 or 3 days, about a kilo of flour. I don't have an oven (a big factor for me to go easy on the butane, as it is expensive and a bother to pack in from the city). At one time I made an interesting oven from a super-size clay pot, on its side, with a floor of stones and a fire underneath. It worked okay after we built a mud-brick house around it to keep off the wind, but I had to watch and feed the fire every 5 minutes. I hate to consume so much firewood in this environment. But then I learned from a veteran missionary how to bake in a Dutch oven, on top of my stove; easier and, on the lowest flame, almost as cheap. Actually, I don't have a real Dutch oven—I use my pressure cooker, which is heavy aluminum."

Baking in a Pressure Cooker. "When I form my loaves I grease the pan liberally and set them down in (I divide the lot in 3 balls, to help prevent it falling in the center). When it's risen, I set on the biggest burner, lowest flame, and cover to keep the heat in (no pressure). When the bread is cooked through and firmish (like "bake and serve" rolls), I tip it out onto a rack or towel, take it up with the potholders, and slip it gently back in head-down. In another 5 or 10 minutes the top is golden too. With the years of experimenting, I've gotten more versatile. I make pizzas (with fully cooked toppings), custard-type pies and quiches, coffeecakes (yeast-risen—a regular cake is too soft), cookies or crackers, etc. I've gotten so used to making pie shells in the frying pan that I prefer it to the oven, even in the city—same for biscuits. And the pressure cooker with pressure is suitable for all recipes that say to put a pan of water in the oven with a dish. I do lots of souffles, bread puddings, egg custard, etc. that way. The pressure cooker is also great for the tough beef we get in market—zebu, the Brahma-type with a hump for surviving dry season."

And that's a good introduction to the subject of cast iron in general and Dutch ovens in particular.

CAST-IRON COOKWARE: When I was younger my favorite pans were cast iron. Now they're stainless steel. Both kinds are healthy and long-lasting, with no coating to chip or scratch. Cast-iron pans can even be set in the middle of a campfire or in an underground oven with no damage. Iron cookware is also good for campfire cooking because it evens out the heat and holds it. And they don't get lost because they are too heavy for the kids to lug away. They will, however, crack if you overheat them, and rust if you haven't coated them and let them sit wet after washing.

I have a smallish iron fry pan, a big iron fry pan, and a big Dutch oven for stewing, roasting, boiling spuds, and so on. You can buy cast-iron muffin pans called "gem pans." You can use any muffin recipe in a gem muffin pan, but here's one that is guaranteed to work.

☙ *GEM MUFFINS First grease your iron gem pan and put it in a hot oven (about 400°F). Now sift together 1 c. flour and 2 t. baking powder, or just mix them well if you don't have a sifter. In another bowl break an egg, beat it, and add 1 t.*

sugar, a pinch of salt, and 1 T. melted butter or cooking oil. Now add the flour alternately with ½ c. milk. You could double or triple this recipe if you need to. By now your gem pans should be smoking hot. Pour the batter into the individual cups. Bake. They will need only about 10 minutes to get done.

Waffle Iron

Gem Pan

Skillets

Dutch Oven

Griddle

Mail-Order Cast Iron. You can order a full line of cast-iron cookware from Lehmans (888-438-5346; **info@lehmans.com**) or perhaps through your local kitchen store. It's usually best to buy cast iron from the closest outlet you can, because freight costs on the bigger ones are so great. (A 45-gal. cast-iron kettle weighs 250 lb.) "Bails," which are overarching metal handles, are optional for all pots and are available at a small extra cost. Lehman's offers sugar kettles of 6-, 10½-, and 12½-qt. capacities; English pots in 5-qt., 3-gal., and 6½-gal. capacities; and kettles in 23-, 33-, and 45-gal. capacities. You'd be surprised how many different styles of cooking pans you can buy in cast iron: a French fryer with basket, a stew pan, griddles of various sizes and shapes, French bread and breadstick pans, and more.

Cast-Iron Tea Kettle. You can also get a cast-iron teapot, but I think that's the one use for which cast iron is not suitable. Witness: Evvalynda Hoover, Cheyenne, WY, wrote me about the "cast-iron tea kettle my husband gave me for a gift. I find either it rusts or the water tastes like residual of the seasoning, and I feel bad having such a lovely gift sit idle."

Seasoning Cast Iron. Baked beans, stews, roasts, etc. can be left in seasoned Dutch ovens treated in the following way without worrying about rust or metallic taste, since there is no exposed metal. Outdoor cooking doesn't hurt the seasoning.

1. New iron cookware has a factory-applied preseasoning coating. So first wash your pan thoroughly with a mild dishwashing liquid. Rinse and dry completely with a dishcloth. (Never let your cast-iron cookware drain dry. That's inviting rust.)
2. Now grease the inside with suet or vegetable shortening. Rub the grease in. Lightly grease the outside of the pan also. Wipe away any surplus. Do the same for the lid if it has one.
3. Place in 250–275°F oven and let season ("bake") for 8 to 10 hours, or leave overnight. Gaylen Lehman (an ironware dealer) wrote me, "Some people will protest

vociferously that you should use 400°F for 2–3 hours. At these temps the seasoning often glazes and burns, and can ruin the pot. Don't you believe them!"
4. Do not put on any lid while treating it, since it will stick on and you will need a crowbar to pry it open again.
5. Let cool naturally. Your pot is now ready for use.
6. Or you can apply a second coat—or more. Just repeat the procedure. If the first coat is spotty and has bare spots, don't worry. Just apply a second, even possibly a third, coat; that will coat the bare spots.

Recoating. If the coating gets scratched or is burned off by overheating, just recoat as per above instructions.

Cleaning Cast Iron. Treat your seasoned cast-iron ware as you would a Teflon-coated pan. Don't use a scraper inside it; that could gouge off the coating. Don't use a metal scratch pad to clean it; that could create deep scratches in the surface, which food will then stick in. Use a plastic cleaning pad if you must. Dry your Dutch oven after every washing. Grease it if you want. I don't follow the school of thought that says you shouldn't wash an iron pan. That's unreal. If you are having trouble with an iron pan rusting, recoat and/or grease it after every washing. My Dutch oven must be at least 40 years old though, and it hasn't rusted yet.

Cooking in Cast Iron. Don't cook with cast iron at a temperature higher than 300–350°F, or the pan may crack. Don't leave a pan on high heat with no liquid in it. First it will get red-hot, and then it will crack and be ruined. Your pan will get blacker with use, and that's what it's supposed to do. Mine are all coal-black. Never cook food high in acid content in a cast-iron (or aluminum!) pan. The acid will work on the pan, and your dish will pick up more iron content than will taste good. Your pan is for cooking only; don't store food in it unless it's well-seasoned (the pan, not the food).

DUTCH OVEN COOKERY: A Dutch oven is made of heavy iron and comes in basic sizes from 8 to 16 inches across and 4 to 6 inches deep. My iron Dutch oven is my very favorite kettle. If I had to give up all but one of my pans and pots, it is the one I'd keep. It has a tightfitting lid that holds in the steam when that's what I want. The heavy iron heats evenly, so I'm safer from scorching in that kettle than in any other. I can make it do for a frying pan in a pinch. I can cook a moist, good roast in it with ¼ cup of water because it holds the steam so well. It's ideal for cooking on a campfire. You can put it right in the coals of an open fire or use a bean hole. You can use it to bake a roast, boil a stew, bake bread and biscuits, boil potatoes, or fry fish.

Some Dutch ovens have three short legs, like a tripod. That's good for camping use, but I vastly prefer the flat-bottomed kind in the kitchen. They always have tight-fitting lids that are slightly domed in the center. The lid has a handle, and sometimes the outer rim is turned up (flanged) for the purpose of holding hot coals when you're having cookouts. But flanging isn't essential, because the pot itself has a bail (handle).

Dutch Oven in a Hole. Dig a hole at least twice as deep and wide as your kettle. Build a fire in it and let it burn until there are plenty of red coals. Scrape a depression or remove some coals. Set the oven down in the hole and cover it with the removed coals. Then cover oven, coals and all, with the dirt you dug out to make your pit. The dirt cover should end up being at least 4 inches thick. If you aren't very confident of your bed of coals, you could build another fire on top of the dirt. Wait 4 to 8 hours, and your beans or roasted meat or stew should be just fine. This is best for one of those huge Dutch ovens, I think, when you're planning on serving 20 or more people. For 40 people, use 2 or 3 Dutch ovens in the same hole (make it bigger).

Roasting in a Dutch Oven. I often put the frozen roast into the Dutch oven, especially if it's some wild meat that we got into the freezer in the nick of time. On the evening of the day I thaw it, such meat will be on the verge of spoiling, but if I thaw and cook it at once, it's safe. I mix in a little water, seasonings, and chopped onion or any other vegetables added just for flavor. (Vegetables meant for eating wait until the last hour to go in.) Add the lid and cook as long as it takes. Depends on the size of the roast. I start the oven at 400°F and then finish at 350°F or lower if I have the time. The slower I cook it, the better I like the results.

A good cook would preheat the Dutch oven, grease it, and sear the roast (that means fry it all over the outside) to brown it before adding the water and the lid and cooking it. I'm usually in too much of a rush. After the roast is done, while Daddy Mike is carving it, I toss a handful of flour into the good brown juices left in the pan and churn it like crazy with the eggbeater to get ahead of the lumps. Then I add salt and put it on the table for gravy. Baked potatoes are a natural with a Dutch oven dinner. We have them with a choice of gravy, butter, or homemade cream cheese whipped (just like dairy sour cream).

Deep-Fat Frying in a Dutch Oven. The Dutch oven is good for this—better than any other container. The only problem is that it ties up your Dutch oven, so maybe you'll want to invest in two if you love deep-fat fried food. My husband does. I fill the kettle half full of home-rendered lard, heat it to where it is just starting to smoke, and commence to fry. Homemade French fries are good. Don't add the fries until they promptly float. Stand by on the ready to fish out the ones that are done, or else they will just proceed to burn. Burned stuff will taint your whole kettle of grease. French fry just before the meal and take the food out onto a towel to soak up the extra grease. French-fried bland vegetables are good—like summer squash, peeled and sliced ½ inch thick, or green tomatoes. Dip the vegetables in beaten egg (add a little milk to stretch it), then in flour, then in egg again, then in flour.

To make hotcakes in a Dutch oven, fry on the oiled, heated bottom of the oven or on the upside-down lid if you have that shape of lid. Okay in a pinch, but I'd rather use a frying pan or griddle.

➢ *OTHER BATTERS From Moscow Writer's Bloc (my first writer's critique group—thanks for all the educating you did of me!): Combine ½ beer and ½ flour, or ½ flour and ½ pancake mix.*

➢ *ONION RINGS Peel and slice the biggest onions you have. Then break the rings into groups of about 3, dip into the batter, and fry. Green pepper rings are also good. If you didn't burn anything, you can just keep the grease in the Dutch oven in your refrigerator between uses. Clarify by cooking some potato in it and straining when it gets dark. You can serve leftover French-fried food by warming it up to sizzling again in the oven (not the Dutch oven).*

Baking in a Dutch Oven. To make bread, grease oven and preheat. Set raised and ready loaf into the oven. Or pour in

your corn bread or cake batter. Make sure the Dutch oven is level. Cover. Set oven into bean hole prepared as above. Cover with coals and dirt and leave 3 hours. Preheating is very important to all Dutch oven baking. Or you can bake with a few coals under and a lot over, right by the fire or on top of the ground. Or you can bake in your Dutch oven in the stove oven.

Biscuits, Pies, Corn Bread, Etc.: Preheat oven and lid. Grease oven. For biscuits, put them in the bottom as the pan is sitting in the coals. You don't need to cut them out—just break off chunks of fairly firm dough. Turn them over when browned and then set the lid on the oven. Put the coals on the lid. It will take about 10 minutes, and you'll learn by experience just how many coals are needed. Cook pies in a pie pan inside the oven. To make corn bread, just grease your oven and pour in the batter. You don't need to preheat.

➢ *CAMPFIRE COBBLER From Brian Pruiett, Basin, WY: "You need a seasoned Dutch oven, greased to be safe. A lid with raised rim is preferable. Preheat the Dutch oven just until it's warm. While the fire burns to coals (use a type of wood that makes good coals, e.g., red alder, maple, elm without bark, juniper, etc.), make about 2 c. piecrust dough and collect about 1 qt. cobbler 'makins.' (Amounts of dough and makins, of course, vary depending on number coming to supper.) Makins can be anything from canned fruit cocktail to huckleberries—including sliced apples, blackberries, juneberries, peaches, you name it; sweeten to taste, more for tart fruit like green apples or almost-ripe berries. Line the oven with the dough on the bottom and about halfway up the sides. Hold back ½ c. dough. Pour in makins. Now, if you have a rolling pin and cutting board, roll out the ½ cup of dough you held back, cut it into strips, and criss-cross them on top of the makins. Pinching the edges onto the shell is nice, but optional. In absence of a board, I usually pinch off pieces of dough, roll them into cylinders between my palms, and pat them flat before laying them across the makings.*

"Now comes the hardest part: cooking. Experience is the best teacher when different types of wood, altitude, and weather conditions are involved. The way I judge heat is (on calm days) by holding out my palm 18 or 20 inches from the hot coals. If I can hold it there for only 8 or 10 seconds, it's a good bed of coals for cooking. Nest the oven into a bed of coals, with coals up the sides to the level of the cobbler inside. Cover the lid on the oven with coals. This is where a raised rim is a blessing, particularly for keeping coals out of the cobbler when checking on it. Check your cobbler after 20 minutes. If the makins are bubbling and the top crust is baked through, it's ready to eat. If not, then keep checking at 5-minute intervals until done. Now if you sprinkle some cinnamon and sugar across the top, you've got a sure-fire crowd pleaser from Sitka to Salinas."

➢ *POET'S HEARTH BREAD Dallas A. Sall, a Northwestern poet, wrote me, "I, like yourself, know the many trials that come with the writing of a book and all that goes with it. Many times in these past years I have wondered if the effort was worth it. But the words keep coming, so I keep at it. I have chosen to winter this year in a small cabin in the High Desert of eastern Oregon, just out of Sisters. Here, in the peace and quiet, I am working on a new book of poetry as well as a book about the old Indian Medicine Society. Here's the recipe for my favorite bread. At the cabin, I have been making it in the outside fire pit as I have no cookstove. I find that I like it better in the Dutch oven, or maybe it seems better because of the extra effort.*

"Ingredients: 5 c. flour (3 c. to mix with ground wheat, 2 to knead in), 2 c. stone-ground whole wheat, 2 T. or 2 pkg. dry yeast, 1 T. salt, 2 c. milk, 3 T. butter, 3 T. honey. Mix dry ingredients. Heat milk, butter, and honey and add to them. Mix, turn out on board, and knead in flour. Let rise in buttered bowl until double. Divide into three balls. Knead and let rise again. Bake on sheet covered with cornmeal at 375°F for about 45 minutes, or until hollow-sounding. In the wilderness I make this into two balls and bake in two 10-inch Dutch ovens in a pit."

Country Clothing

A friend of mine wears homemade quilted britches for cold mornings out. She cuts them out of an old blanket of flannel, a little larger than for regular sewing. Then she puts the patches on the separated pieces until they are covered like a quilt, sews up her seams, and adds a drawstring for a belt.

I used to wear bib overalls. They're even less attractive but handier. I could bring back 3 dozen eggs from a foray into the hayloft or carry home a batch of baby chicks in those many deep pockets. Whatever the outfit, I need to be able to drop to my knees for a spurt of weeding in the garden without worrying about either my knees or my clothes. They are cool in summer and cover me in all the places I need to be covered for climbing over fences, into fruit trees, or under the house. I don't think it makes good sense to buy clothes that have to be sent to a cleaner.

Scott Miller wrote me of himself and his wife, Kathy, "We are conservative Mennonites. Our church teaches simplicity in all areas of life, and we tend to be basically a rural-oriented people . . . By the way, it is possible to wear dresses on the farm. Just keep lots of aprons on hand, and wear knee boots when you're in the mud." My friend and neighbor, Imogene, dresses like that—aprons and dresses. Looks pretty, too.

OF CLOTHING AND DIRT: The modern philosophy seems to be that you wear a garment part of one day and then put it in the wash. It wasn't so in the old hand-washing days. Clothes were washed when they were dirty, *really* dirty. Frequent machine washing and drying, especially in the automatic dryer, takes a toll on our clothes. All that "lint" means you have that much less clothes, towels, and bedding. My mother wanted day clothes to be carefully folded and laid out to wear again the next day. She wanted night clothes folded and put under the pillow for wearing again the next night—until wash day. Aprons covered dresses and were whisked away only as company knocked on the door. There were Sabbath clothes, which were not allowed to get dirty, and everyday ones, which were not expected to be clean.

NATURAL CLOTHING FIBERS: The big four that you can make clothes from without starting with an oil well are cotton, linen (from the flax plant), wool, and silk. Cotton has very good abrasion resistance, and there are now clothes made from organically grown cotton! The others have only fair resistance, which is why cotton is the fiber of choice for the likes of coveralls and jeans. Cotton and linen both have good sunlight resistance and so are good for outdoor work clothing. Wool has fair resistance to damage by sunlight. Silk has low resistance, and its exposure to sunshine should be minimized. Wool is the best of these fabrics

for wrinkle resistance, and it's good to pack and good to wear on long days when you want to keep looking fresh. Silk is the second best of the four for wrinkle resistance. Both cotton and linen are likely to wrinkle unless they're starched, which transforms that situation and is why the old-timers starched cottons and linens before ironing them if they were for dress-up.

Wool and silk both need special handling when cleaning, since the fibers are weaker when wet than when dry. When washing them, use neutral or slightly alkaline soap. Never use chlorine bleaches on them, as they literally damage the fibers. Wool is damaged by dry heat, so if you have to iron it, use a steam iron on a wool setting. *Never wash wool in hot water, because it will be ruined by shrinking.* Cotton and linen are both attacked by mildew (which is no problem to wool or silk), so they must be protected against dampness in storage. On the other hand, these two are able to endure frequent hard laundering and harsh soaps. They can also both be ironed at high, dry temperatures. *However, do not press sharp creases into linen.*

WASHING BY HAND: If you're washing diapers by hand, use diaper liners or some kind of water-absorbent paper or skin-gentle moss to keep the glob of glop from really getting into the cloth. Then do the washing every morning first thing after breakfast, so you'll have it done and out of the way. To wash dishes or clothes, heat the water first and have lots, if possible, so you can change water frequently. In the old days, "washing" clothes meant boiling them, which is also a natural technique for agitation—and sterilization!—when you think about it. Those cotton and linen garments were boiled in a pan on the stove or in a big kettle over a campfire outside. My mother used to boil dirty dishtowels on the wood-stove top with a little lye to get them clean and white. When the wash water gets dirty, switch the rinse water into its place for wash water, throw out the dirty old wash water, and get new rinse water.

Add soap and lots of water, as hot as your hands can stand it. Then comes the elbow grease. I push the clothes in and out of the water, counting as I go: maybe 100 squishes of the water through the material for this one, only 25 for something less dirty. The essence is to loosen the dirt from the surface of the fabric and to carry it away by squishing that water right through the weave of the cloth. Some people like to work with a washboard or use a plunger in the bathtub. A rubber toilet-type plunger is actually easier on the clothes and still gets them clean. The good thing about a plunger is your hands don't get raw from the detergent.

Rinse in at least 2 waters to get out as much of the soap as you can. Then wring out the water by twisting each piece all the way from end to end to squeeze it out. Hang up to dry; a clothesline made of rope or wire stretched high between two points is handiest. You can just throw the clothes over on a calm summer day. But if the wind is blowing or the sun not hot or if you are trying to dry indoors, you had better use clothespins so you can hang the clothes out with as few doublings as possible. If you're using clothespins to hang clothes out in the dead of winter, dipping them in salt water first will keep them from freezing to the clothes. Or dry indoors on a clothesline or on fold-up racks.

I don't want to romanticize hand washing. This is how to do it. But when I think back on the times I've hand-washed clothing for 9 people, including a couple in diapers and a bed-wetter—spending most of one day a week washing, hanging out, bringing in—for months at a time—it makes me think the washing machine is a wonderful modern convenience and everybody ought to be blessed with one!

Non-Electrical Washing Machines. Washers that don't use electricity are available by mail from Lehman's. There is a James Hand Washer with wringer. You push a rod back and forth to cause the agitation action in the 16-gallon tub and use a hand crank to run the wringer. You can get a washboard, a clothes stomper, or a gas-engine-powered washing machine there also. Another system: If you have a car and a bumpy road, put your laundry into a 5-gallon bucket with a tight lid and then into your car before you go to town. Driving over the rough road agitates and washes your clothes!

FLATIRONS: These old-fashioned irons were heated on top of the wood stove. A different model was kept heated by hot coals put into a hollow chamber inside the iron. To iron with flatirons, you need two or more so one can be heating while you are ironing with the other. But as far as I'm concerned, the best way to handle the ironing problem is to keep everybody in the kind of clothes that don't require ironing—Levis, sweat shirts, and long underwear!

Quilting

The classic quilt style and the only one I've made, being of a practical mind, is the "crazy" quilt. This means the quilt cover is made by fitting and sewing together pieces of every size, shape, and kind of material. The results are usually very interesting! The total should be blanket-sized to fit the bed you have in mind. A quilt is a total of three layers. The stuff in the middle is wool, feathers, commercial batting, or old blankets (perhaps ones that have sprung holes or gotten out of shape) that still have lots of good in them. I strongly advise against commercial batting, because after every washing there seems to be less of it, so your quilt is less fluffy and less warm.

The crazy-quilted top hides whatever is providing the real warmth in the middle layer. The bottom layer is made of any material you prefer. I like flannel because it's cozy in bed. (I'm an advocate of sheet blankets, which are practically extinct. They are so warm and nice if you're in a chilly house.) Some people use cotton—plain or a pretty print.

You can mail-order quilting stuff from Oklee Quilting Supply, PO Box 279, Oklee, MN 56742; 800-777-7403. They sell batting in four different weights, broadcloth in 30 colors, stuffing and pillow forms.

SHRUNKEN WOOL BLANKET QUILT: I know that hot water shrinks wool, but I keep forgetting and shrinking wool anyway. Then came Joanne Tack, Curlew, WA, who taught me how to make a wonderful, warm "shrunken sweater blanket." She doesn't shrink things herself, of course, but she makes use of ruined sweaters that come through a free used-clothing exchange she created. She said, "They must be at least 80 percent wool (if you can tell) and already shrunken. You can get them as trash from a laundromat or thrift shop. Save up until you have a couple pillowcases full so you can develop a color scheme, such as squares or stripes. You can get one good-sized block out of a sleeve and one or two out of the front and back. Assemble quilting-style. The finished blanket will have an up side and a down side, with the raw seams on the down side—or stitch a lining over that side. Bind around the edge with strips of some cloth."

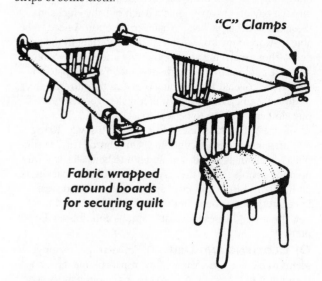

"C" Clamps

Fabric wrapped around boards for securing quilt

HOW TO MAKE A QUILTING FRAME: The three layers of the traditional quilt are put together on a quilting frame to be tied. The frame stretches the quilt and raises it off the floor. But I've tied quilts without a frame, just by spreading it all out on the floor and fighting with it until I won. To make a frame, you need four boards to make a rectangular shape somewhat bigger than you want your quilt to be. You fasten them together at the four corners with "C" clamps that you can buy at a hardware store. Or nail them or tie them. You double over a long strip of cloth, like one torn from an old sheet, and staple it the whole length of each board, so you have something to pin your quilt top to. Now you want to get the quilting frame up off the ground, so you set it on chair tops, boxes, or whatever else seems handy.

TYING: The layers are fastened together with wool yarn sewn through at intervals back and forth across the quilt and tied above each stitch, with the little ends left dangling on the top side for appearance's sake. About 8 people can tie a quilt in 1 to 1½ hours. If your quilt is such that you can't readily wash the center layer (wool or feathers), don't tie. Instead, make a fitted "bag" to serve as the cover, with just big loose stitches on one side, so you can get it off when you need to wash the cover and stitch it up again afterwards, with the unwashable filling in its own cover inside the bag. (More under "Sheep" in Chapter 11.)

STUFFING: Good stuffings come from a wide variety of animal and plant sources. You can stuff quilts, pillows, etc., with wool (see "Sheep" in Chapter 11), feathers (see the end of Chapter 9), cattail fur (see Chapter 5), Angora fur (see "Rabbits" in Chapter 11), or cotton. You need a warmish climate like Alabama or California to grow cotton. Grow it until the "bolls" break open and you can see the beautiful cotton in there. Card it with wool cards, and stuff with it.

Candle Making

For more information, read *Manufacture of Soaps and Candles* by W.T. Brannt (published in Philadelphia, 1888), *Making Homemade Soaps and Candles* by Phyllis Hobson (Vermont: Garden Way Publishing, 1975), and *A Technical Treatise on Soap & Candles* by R.S. Cristiani (Philadelphia: Henry Carey Baid & Co., 1881).

MAIL-ORDER CANDLE-MAKING SUPPLIES: Blossomland Supply specializes in candle-making equipment; 616-473-3917; 800-637-5262; PO Box 74, Berrien Center, MI 49102; **katherine@blossomland.com; www.blossomland. com.** Or look up **www.pourette.com**, which sells soap-making kits, candle molds, and candle-making supplies. Or the International Guild of Candle Artisans; **www.igca.net.**

DIMENSIONS AND BURNING RATES: A tallow candle ½ inch in diameter and 6 inches in length burns approximately 3 hours. If 1 inch wide and 6 inches long, it burns 8 hours. If 2 inches wide and 9 inches long, it burns 48 hours.

MELTING POINTS: Different kinds of candle waxes have different melting points. A melting point of 125–165°F is best. A "harder" wax or fat has a higher melting point. Candles with low melting points tend to lose their shape and droop in hot weather. Try to get the hardest wax you can, considering the materials you have to choose from. From that point of view, bacon grease is harder than cooking oil. Sheep fat is harder, cow harder yet, and deer, goat, and elk fats that shouldn't be used for making soap (they are too hard and cause curds) are best of all for candle making because they have the highest melting points. Beeswax melts at 145°F.

STEARIC ACID: The reason one kind of fat is harder than another is because it has more natural stearic acid in it. You can harden animal fat by adding beeswax in any proportion or by adding alum or stearic acid. Alum, stearic acid, or beeswax combined with tallow will raise its melting point and generally improve it.

☙ *PIONEER ALUM/TALLOW CANDLES Five pounds of alum was dissolved in 10 gallons of water and boiled until dissolved. Then they added 20 pounds of tallow and boiled an hour more. Then the mixture was stirred well and skimmed to take the wax off the top. When the wax was cool, it was strained through thick muslin into molds, or candles were made by the dipping method. You can buy stearic acid from suppliers of candle materials. A druggist can order alum for you.*

SUBSTANCES SUITABLE TO SUPPORT A WICK: Candles can be a by-product of butchering, made from deer, goat, or beef tallow. Or of beekeeping, made from beeswax. Where you can grow bayberry plants, they can be made from bayberry wax. From this book's point of view, those blocks of paraffin you buy at hobby shops for candle making are the least interesting—but most common—kind of candle wax.

Paraffin. This is a waxy fraction of petroleum. It's not the kind of thing you can do yourself unless you have an oil well and a refinery. This commercial wax for candle making is sold in blocks. You can save all your old candle ends, remelt them, and add to the material. *Heat paraffin wax only over low heat. The wax is volatile and explodes easily when overheated.* Use a coffee can or big vegetable can. A pot with handle and a spout for pouring is the nicest of all. Put the wax in the can and put the can into a bucket of water to create a double-boiler effect. *To prevent explosion, never put paraffin wax directly on a heating element.*

Tallow. Save your firm, clean hunks of fat from butchering, about 2 pounds of tallow for each dozen candles you plan to make. Render out the tallow as you do in lard making, by heating to melt it and then straining through a cloth. Then skim your candle tallow off the top. It helps in final appearance to go through the whole procedure again with your once-skimmed tallow: Melt, strain, and skim to get your final candle-making tallow.

Beeswax. Beeswax candle fans believe these are the absolute best quality as well as the easiest to make. You can make candles out of beeswax if you have beehives and they are doing well enough so that you have extra wax. But keeping your wax in comb for them to store honey in, so they don't have to take time and effort to build more comb, is probably a better use of it. Not robbing the beeswax increases your total honey production. But if you must harvest it, see Chapter 11 under "Bees" for how to prepare beeswax for candle making. Make sure your wax is clean before you start.

To shape beeswax, you cut or press. You can cut beeswax with a knife if you slightly warm the knife beforehand. You can press the beeswax around the wick in the shape you prefer. Warmed slightly, beeswax is very pliable. Or you can melt the beeswax like tallow, and hand-dip your candles. To make it harder, add ½ ounce stearic acid per 1 lb. wax. Melt beeswax by the directions for paraffin, never over direct heat. *If your beeswax starts to burn, put a tight lid or baking soda over it to smother.* Set a container of cold water close by to dip the candle into after its immersion in the melted wax. If you can, buy thin, flat sheets of beeswax from regular candle suppliers. You make candles out of the sheets by rolling a sheet up around the wick. Beeswax candles are better in hot weather than the tallow ones. They don't drip or smell, and they take a long time to burn.

☙ *SHEEP-BEE CANDLES Mix proportions of ½ melted, strained sheep fat with ½ melted, strained beeswax. This was a highly regarded old-time formula.*

Bayberry. You can make fine vegetarian candles out of the waxy grey berries of the bayberry bush if you live where the plants will grow. It grows naturally in the wet soil near the sea on the East Coast. The wild East Coast bayberry looks like a shrub or small tree and grows as much as 8 feet tall. The western bayberry, a relative, can be found growing on the West Coast. If you live in the Southeast or westward to Texas, look for a member of this family called the wax myrtle. All of them grow berries from which candle wax can be extracted. However, some of these plants are endangered, and it is illegal to pick their berries.

You can buy plants and grow your own. They do well in poor, acid soil, pH 4.5–5.5. (Lack of acidity is a problem for this plant.) Gather when ripe, late in the autumn. Throw into a copper kettle full of boiling water. When the fat melts out of them and floats at the top of the water, skim it off into another container. Remelt that fat and strain in order to achieve wax of a fine transparent green color. To make dipped bayberry candles, leave the melted wax on just enough low heat to keep it liquid. Then dip wicks into the wax, let harden, dip again, and so on, until the desired size of candle is achieved. You can extend bayberry wax by mixing it with beeswax or paraffin.

WICKING: You can buy wicking or make your own. If you are a spinner, you can loosely spin hemp, tow, cotton, or milkweed "silk" for wicks. Or just twist the material together tightly as best you can. You can make wicks out of common rushes by stripping part of the outer bark from them, leaving the pith bare. You can make a wick out of string or make long cotton wicks out of cloth strings made by tearing cotton rags. (Cotton cloth should have a good boiling before being made into wicking, to get out the dyes and various additives that you don't want to breathe.) It helps to braid it. For wicking you could also use old wicks from used candles, string, commercial wicking from candle suppliers, or pipe cleaners. A wire center makes it burn brighter. A wick too narrow for the diameter of your candle will not be strong enough and will let the flame get drowned in the melting wax. A wick that is too thick will smoke. To improve the final action, soak your wicking of cotton, hemp, tow, or milkweed silk in limewater and saltpeter; limewater alone; vinegar; or saltpeter alone. Then dry.

Rush Lights. These go way, way back. They are made by dipping a dry and fibrous long plant (a rush) into a can of melted fat (a firm one like mutton or deer would be best). Cool and dip again. Repeat. This will create a floppy candle that will give a useful candle-type light.

Mullein Leaf Wicking. People who live where the mullein leaf grows can make a primitive candle using this leaf for wicking. Put mud in the bottom of a small flat can. Roll a dry mullein leaf and bury partially in the center of the mud. Let the mud dry completely. Pour hot bacon grease or some other tallow around the leaf and let it harden. When needed, simply light the leaf, and it will burn. The leaf will also burn by simply being placed in a dish or shell of fat. Roll the leaf tightly and proceed as above.

SHAPING THE CANDLE: You create and shape your candle by a method specific to the kind of material you're working with, your personal preference, and the final results you want to get. Candles are easy to make and can be wonderful works of art, and lots of people make them simply for fun. Commercial wax is usually poured into a mold. You can buy all kinds and shapes of molds, metal or plastic, from candle craft suppliers. Large molded candles act as their own base and last longer. (Tapered candles require a candleholder to burn, as do dipped candles.) You can make homemade molds out of yogurt or cottage-cheese containers. They can then be peeled off when you're done. Milk cartons will work, too. If you use tin-can molds, you'll have to take off the bottom and jam the candle on through after it has set up hard. Old-time candle molds were made of metal, but they were shaped to make candles that were long and narrow, like dipped ones. A functional candle mold can also be made out of wood, like a bullet mold with

the two halves hinged together and a special opening for the wick. You grease or oil the inside of the mold, close the mold, pour wax into the top, cool, and then open to get the finished candle.

MOLDING A CANDLE: Get the wick into place by first dipping it into the wax and then pulling it out long and straight. Then attach it to a wire or nail across the open top of the mold so that it hangs down the center. Then pour the melted tallow or other material in carefully around the wick. With commercial wax you can pour the wax first, let it set a few minutes, and then stick the wick down in while the wax is still liquid in the middle. You can put 2 or 3 (or more) wicks into a big candle if you want to. After the candle material is poured into the mold, let it stay overnight to cool; then warm it a little to loosen.

Molded Beeswax Candles. Just proceed in the regular way. Have a mold with a wick in it. Melt the pure beeswax and pour it in around the wick. Pour your wax into the molds at 180–185°F. That gives a nice sheen on the outside, and you're less likely to get bubbles. But don't get burned.

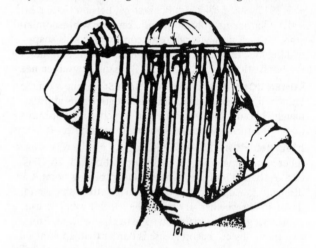

MAKING DIPPED CANDLES: Lay sheets of paper under the candle rods and all over where you expect to be working, in order to protect your floors. This is very time-consuming and tends to make a mess. To work with a small amount of tallow or wax, you need a tall container, since you can't make an 8-inch candle from a 6-inch container. A 2-inch diameter would be sufficient; use metal if possible.

Making Dipped Candles with Paraffin Wax. You have to have a double-boiler-type arrangement with your tube that holds the wax being in a pan of water (also tall). When working with commercial wax, you can also use a cooling tube of lukewarm water. Use this to dip your candle in after it comes out of the hot wax. Stroke, blow, or pat the water with a cloth if it clings to the wax after being in the cooling tube.

Making Dipped Tallow Candles. Tie a wick to a stick and dip into melted tallow. Let harden and then dip again. Continue in this way until your candle is big enough to suit you. You can make more than 1 candle at a time by tying several wicks to a stick and dipping them all at once.

To do it as they did in colonial days, lay two long poles between two chairs. Across these poles, at regular intervals, lay smaller sticks 15 to 18 inches long called "candle rods." To each candle rod, attach 6 to 8 carefully straightened candlewicks. The wicking is twisted strongly one way and then doubled. The loop is then slipped over the candle rod and the two ends twisted the other way around each other to make a really firm wick. The rod, with its row of wicks, is dipped into the melted tallow in the pot and then returned to its place across the poles. For the first dip, wet your wicks in the tallow. They will probably want to float, and you'll have to help them into it. When cool, straighten and smooth them. Then dip again. It is better if they go in obliquely rather than perpendicularly. Each candle rod is dipped in regular turn, thus giving the rod time to cool and harden between dips. If the bottoms get too large, hold them in the hot grease until part melts off. After they have hung all night to cool, you can cut off the bottom and trim around the base to get a nice bottom that will fit into your candleholder.

Making Dipped Beeswax Candles. Dipped candles use beeswax more economicaly than molded ones. Have ready 2 containers. One has your melted wax in it. The other contains ice water. You can dip 6 or 8 at a time if you have a holder that will suspend that many wicks at once. You dip in the wax and then in the ice water. Then dip in the wax again, then in the ice water again, and so on until you have your candle where you want it.

More Dipping Tips. Tying a small weight (such as a little steel bolt) to the bottom of the wick will help keep it straight. After 1 or 2 dips, pull wick straight. Another hint is to alternate dips into the hot wax with dips into cool water to speed cooling. But you can't dip into the wax again until the candle is dry (you can wipe it dry). About 30 dips makes an average candle.

If you were a colonial housewife making a whole winter's supply of dipped candles, you would use a large kettle, preferably about 2 feet across, containing half hot water and half rendered tallow. If you had them, you would have added beeswax and powdered alum to make the candles harden better. You would keep the tallow hot in your kettle and add more tallow and water as fast as each is used up. To phase out, you would just keep adding more hot water as the tallow got used up.

COLOR AND SCENT: You can color your candles and scent them the same way as you do soap, but with even more freedom since you aren't going to use the results on your skin. For coloring you can use crayons. You can't use food coloring because it is water-based and won't combine with the wax. Special candle-wax colorings, scentings, and all kinds of arty possibilities can be bought from said suppliers if you want to make your candles very, very nice to sell or give away. Or experiment with herbal colorings and scents from Chapter 5.

COOLING AND STORING CANDLES: Don't cool candles in the refrigerator or freezer. They crack and become brittle. Do store in a dry, cool, dark place. But return to room temperature well before you plan to burn them; that way they will burn slower and won't drip as much. Don't store tapered candles upright because they may bend; store them on their sides.

MONEY MANAGEMENT
The Three Steps to Profit

First you have to produce your raw material. Second you harvest, clean, refine or process, and package it. Third you sell it. Each of these steps is very different from the others.

Each is critical, can't be left out, and must be done well.

PRODUCING: The essential here is to figure out what the combination of your particular piece of earth, climate, etc., and you as a human being can produce most abundantly and economically, and what will be most saleable. It's likely that has already been figured out, and everybody in your county is growing it. But you might think of something new.

PROCESSING: Whatever you create has to be prepared for the marketplace. This process will be unique to your particular product but, in general, you want it to look clean and attractive, be portable, and be packaged in unit amounts convenient for your buyer. Complex processing may be involved, as in the making of fancy goat cheese. You may have to master—or even create—a new processing technology.

SELLING: You can sell all your product directly to one middleman or through one middleman. But the secret of profit is to process your own product and sell it to the retailer, or best of all the consumer, yourself. That's best because the profit is on the retail end. However you sell, you have to sell at a profit. You can't allow yourself to lose money on every item. Price your product to fairly reflect your expenses in producing it and include a reasonable profit for you. Then sell it.

Whatever your marketing system, make yourself an expert on that particular process. If it's mail-order, check out books on the mail-order business. Take small business courses, read books, and talk to experts. But don't believe everything you read or hear. Keep learning and gaining experience. Carefully inform yourself about what already exists in your product line and how it is produced, packaged, and marketed. Then you are ready to offer your item in an effectively competitive manner.

Don't be timid. The only way I know to make a living selling is to be a flagrant promoter. That's not vanity. That's tirelessly getting out the word that your product exists, what it's good for, and how people can buy it. So if you have eggs for sale, tell friends, put flyers on bulletin boards all around your area, run an ad in local newspapers, and check with your local food co-op and other stores that might carry farm-fresh eggs. If you are selling game birds, tell your friends, feed dealer, county agent, shooting preserves, local restaurants, and specialty markets. If you are selling art objects made from goose eggs or dried herbs, contact area craft stores and craft fairs. Create business cards with your name, address, phone number, and product description and pass them out generously. If you want to develop a clientele that comes directly to your home to buy, use roadside signs, cleverly designed to catch the eye of passing motorists. They should include your name, address, directions to your home, phone number, and what it is you're selling. For a larger operation, you can advertise in specialty magazines. Radio advertising is a possibility. The station will be glad to help you create an ad.

Or you can direct-sell. One common system for farms near urban areas is called Community Supported Agriculture (CSA). You sign up members who pay a yearly fee and so much a month for 5 or 6 months, during which you'll give them a box or bag of produce once a week. When their organic produce is ready, you might have them U-pick it, or you might pick it for them. One way or another, as time goes by, you'll acquire repeat business and a steady clientele, but you can never stop looking for new customers, because old ones get lost to natural causes like moving away.

Bio-Dynamic Farming and Gardening Ass'n: 610-469-8788; fax 610-469-8789; 800-516-7797; PO Box 550, Kimberton, PA 19442; **biodynamics@aol.com; www.biodynamics.com.**

CSANA (Community Supported Agriculture of North America); c/o WTIG, 818 Connecticut Ave. NW, Ste. 800, Washington, DC 20006.

Bob and Bonnie Gregson wrote an excellent handbook called *Rebirth of the Small Family Farm: A Handbook for Starting a Successful Organic Farm Based on the Community Supported Agriculture Concept* (1996). Cost is $9.95 (postpaid); PO Box 2542, Vashon Island, WA 98070; **bbgrgson@cs.com.**

Growing for Market Newsletter; PO Box 3747, Lawrence, KS 66046.

Robyn Van En and Elizabeth Henderson co-authored another guide to CSA, *Sharing the Harvest* (1999); $25; Fulton Center for Sustainable Living, Wilson College, 1015 Philadelphia Ave., Chambersburg, PA 17201; **info@csacenter.org; www.csacenter.org.**

Selling Processed Food. There's a lot of demand for organically grown food that is prepared ahead for harried urban housewives who want to feed their children chemical-free food but don't have time to make spaghetti sauce, etc. from scratch. There's also a good demand for ethnic foods and health (low-fat, low-cholesterol, low-sugar, high-fiber) foods. If you can get your product into the center of the urban market, you've got it made, because those people have to buy food. If you grow your own ingredients or buy them wholesale, you can prepare canned goods and market them through regular supermarket channels. Rent a "commercial kitchen" and spend the day peeling, stirring, and cooking or whatever it takes. One day in a commercial kitchen with all your family working hard from morning to night can yield as much as 60 cases of a canned product.

To send your product mainstream, you have to start with a carefully tested and precise recipe so you can list ingredients and amounts on the label the way the law requires. Your jars/packages will also need a nice label designed by a talented artist. If the label covers only part of the jar, then shoppers can also see the nice food in there. Or make the label bigger and add to it a recipe or a cute story. Or shrink-wrap a brochure, recipe, or recipe booklet to the lid, or do in-store demonstrations with free tastes and recipes. Also look for a specialty-foods market and work to enter it, and/or look for regular retail distributors in nearby large urban areas. Expect the process to take time.

There are FDA regulations on labeling and health department regulations on cooking equipment, but it's probably more possible than you think to start your own line of processed foods. You don't need to buy expensive equipment because you can lease a certified kitchen, perhaps most affordably in the evenings or on weekends. Churches, schools, restaurants, athletic clubs, and country clubs are all places that may have a certified kitchen you could rent. Your state has agencies that exist to help beginners like you to learn the regulations and make your way through the maze. There is probably also a state organization dealing with this field that has annual conferences where packaging and labeling companies and others display their wares, and seminars discuss the latest FDA laws. *From Kitchen to Market: Selling Your Gourmet Food Specialty* by Stephen F. Hall is a helpful book.

Successful homesteader/entrepreneur Deb from Hillsboro, OH, wrote me, "The real secret of success is starting small with minimum expense and reinvesting the profit back into the business . . . The main thing, I think, is to do something you love—not just be out to make money. It really shows in your product."

Elly Mocello, Rothschild, WI, did that: "This Chicago girl has learned (from you) how to garden, can, preserve, butcher, dehydrate, etc., way beyond her wildest dreams. I . . . moved to the town of Wausau, WI, in 1974 . . . I now own and operate a bakery and deli with catering in a suburb of Wausau known as Rothschild. My baked goods are made from scratch. So are the soups, sandwiches, pies, etc., I sell. I also have a variety of jams and jellies that I 'put up' (590 this year!) using all fresh fruits. Business has been excellent. I also take all of this to our home Farmer's Market twice a week June through Oct. People do want real food!"

14 PRINCIPLES FOR MAKING A PROFIT ON THE FARM

1. Save your money until you have enough to buy your start of land and seed or starter livestock. That money is your initial working capital.
2. Raise a crop of something uncommon but with a solid potential market. That way it will sell easily and bring a good price.
3. Or plan to hit the market with your product at a time when other producers don't, so you can take advantage of out-of-season scarcity. Be very aware of the overproduction or shortage status of your proposed product in the present marketplace, and figure out what that status will be when your crop is ready for market.
4. When you have your product ready to go, you've only just begun. Work just as hard, boldly, and creatively at marketing it as you did at raising it.
5. Sell retail rather than wholesale whenever possible, so you can collect the middleman's profit.
6. Don't spend the return on the sale of your crop on anything beyond dire operational necessities. Try to keep all, or as much as possible, of that income as your working capital. That way you'll be able to buy more seed, or better starter livestock, or more land for the next income-producing project.
7. When you have to spend money, make an effort to find bargains or to negotiate them. In general, buy cheap and sell dear.
8. Invest in stock, land, etc., when prices are in a slump, when you can get it cheap.
9. Buy quality foundation seed or livestock. Don't buy animals sight unseen. Do take advantage of any connections you have to get good ones at good prices. If you buy animals that are pregnant, you're off to a running start.
10. Take excellent care of your plants and animals, daily if appropriate, day and night if need be. Unless they survive and thrive, you have no profit.
11. Constantly learn about your product field. Subscribe to the periodicals in that area. Join your product association; attend meetings, conventions, showings, demonstrations. Take appropriate classes in or out of a regular classroom setting.
12. When in doubt, ask your county extension agent or some other knowledgeable source for assistance. Don't

just stumble in the dark.

13. Pay all your bills on time so that your creditworthiness is top notch. That way, when you need a line of credit at the feed store, you can get it.

14. Keep close track of all your expenses and your income so you can see exactly how you're doing and what you might change to do better.

How to Pinch a Penny

Don't buy anything new if you can help it. Write what you need on a list, and then watch and wait. You probably don't need it all anyway. Never buy on impulse. Buy only what's on your list. If you see something you like, go home and think about it. If it was really that good, you can put it on next month's list. Attend auctions and yard sales; go to secondhand stores. If you can't find a bargain, wait.

Buy out of season; for animals, that's fall, because everybody is trying to buy them in the spring, when the grass is bursting out all over, but people don't want the expense and bother of feeding and caring for them through winter. It's winter, too, for gardening and farming equipment. In the summer, hunt for stoves and heaters and your winter fuel supply. Buy your vehicles used enough to be a bargain but not old enough to be constantly breaking down. Shop auto junkyards for used parts when you have breakdowns. Then don't risk that precious heap with cross-country adventures. Stay home.

You don't need an automatic washer unless you have children; you can wash by hand. You don't need a dryer at all—a clothesline will do in summer, with a clothes rack standing near the stove or clotheslines in the basement for winter. Learn to patch. You don't need new sheets; learn to sleep between patched ones or between blankets. Stop washing so much and using bleach and machine drying, and all your clothes will last longer. You don't need a freezer. You could can it all. Advertise for used jars. You don't need an electric stove or oil heater if you have dead trees on the place (better yet, use wind, water, or solar energy). You don't have to have a telephone; use postcards.

Buy your rototiller used in the dead of winter, when prices are down. Or cheaper yet, spade your garden to break up the clods, and then rake. Then hoe to keep the weeds down. Don't buy a snowthrower. Stay home when it's that bad, or take the time to tunnel by hand. You don't

need a chain saw right now. There's bound to be somebody around who has one already and will make wood with you on halves for the help. You don't need a power mower. Get a hand mower, or picket a goat in the yard, or just let it grow.

You don't need to paint the inside of the house; wash the walls instead. Lots of women would accept even living in a tent to get started living in the country. I spent a summer in one once, and it's a very happy memory. With the money saved (that would have been rent) by the tent living, I was able to buy a very small trailer to live in by the time really cold weather came. Don't buy buildings—build them, and buy your material used. Scout around and you'll find out where to get used 2 × 4s, cement blocks, and tin sheets for roofing and siding and used bricks. You can mix and lay your own cement, or tear down somebody's unwanted old building in return for the materials.

You may have to do without dogs and cats so you won't have to feed them. Instead, get animals that can forage and reproduce themselves, such as Chinese white geese, goats, and banty chickens. Maybe somebody will give you a start in banty chickens or a kid goat to raise if you make friends and are sincere. Rabbits are easy to come by. You only need two; they are as prolific as the tradition says. Pigs are fairly cheap too. Feed the farm animals your leftovers, and get out and scrounge for them as well. Offer to take away neighbor families' garbage, and they may save it for you if they don't have animals of their own.

Neighbors will give you starts of horseradish, strawberries, raspberries, Egyptian onions, and lots of other perennials if you'll let them know ahead of time in early spring and late fall, when they are digging the excessive growth out of their gardens. If they don't give it away, they'll be throwing it away, and they'd just as soon give it away. Help people with their haying in return for some hay. They'll be happy to save on the cash outlay.

Learn to live off what you can raise and to raise what you want to live off. Plan ahead for several cash crops (in case one or two fail) because you can't make it without cash. A good job is the most reliable "cash crop." Buy cheap and sell dear. The theme song of all this: Take what somebody else doesn't want and, with a little extra effort, make it work. And do the job yourself. To become a homesteader is to become a curious combination of poor and rich. You'll be poor in loose cash but richer than you ever were before, because you'll have a piece of earth that is yours. You'll probably look destitute. This doesn't trouble many young couples, but for older couples trying to make the change, often it isn't easy to move from an urban middle class to a rural lower class along with all the rest of the culture shock involved. It hurts to look poor and know everybody else is thinking that.

I remember one trip to buy goats, when I was very pregnant, accompanied by three little ones, and had accidentally donned one of my boots and one of Mike's. The two boots, of course, didn't in the least match, and I was generally dressed for coping with animals rather than people. We stopped at a little restaurant along the highway to eat. A wonderfully neat and scrubbed and uptight-looking couple with two uptight-looking little children were seated at the table next to us; the husband kept looking at us.

When I went up to pay my bill, the restaurant man told me that man (who had already left with his family) had paid it for us. I was embarrassed and furious. I wanted to run after him and explain that, although I might look poor, I wasn't. That he had his big new car and the next month's rent on his apartment in town, but we had 115 acres and a growing flock of goats and money enough to buy an occasional meal along the road too. And happy, healthy children who knew how to clamber up a mountain just like the goats, yell like hooligans, and put a seed under the dirt just like you're saying a prayer, and on and on and on like that.

But he was already gone. The restaurant man wouldn't accept my money, and my boots indeed didn't match. There was nothing to do but go on down the road and get the new goats.

How to Buy at Auction: In rural areas, both livestock and movable objects are often sold at auction. These auctions are advertised in the newspaper and on flyers for miles around. They are fun, educational, and a great way to acquire things you need at reasonable prices. At the auction, householders offer their household goods and/or machinery for sale by auction right there on their property. You may have to drive many miles, but if you are interested in obtaining working "antiques" at a reasonable price, this is one of the best ways.

The price you pay at an auction is affected by the wealth of the town where the auction is held, the number of buyers present, and the popularity of the item being sold. In our area (a wheat farming community), September is the worst time to go to an auction. The wheat farmers are the most prosperous single economic class in the area. In September they have just gotten paid for their crop, and they live far enough from easy shopping to be willing to pay a "new" price for a used item.

The best time to be at an auction is either right at the beginning or near the end. The crowd is thinnest then and competitive bidding least lively. Your natural enemy will be the antique dealer. But you and he (or she) may not always see eye to eye on what is of value. A wheelbarrow in good condition for $1.50 might be a real buy to you and of no value to the dealer. To avoid making a bad buy, try to get to the auction early enough to carefully examine all the merchandise while it is spread out for people to look at. Note what you want to bid on and decide the top price you would pay for it. That way you can make sure you're present when something you want comes up, and you will know whether the antique chamber pot has holes in the bottom; you won't get swept away in the excitement of the contest and pay more than the object is really worth to you. The best auction attitude is that you would like to have your chosen items, but you could live without them if need be.

When bidding, you have to catch the eye of the auctioneer or the assistant on the platform. Once you get in your first bid or two, the auctioneer will be watching for your bid, will understand how you are signaling, and will even wait for you to think awhile if things are going slowly. But the first time you bid, you should nod your head or wave your arms or yell, if necessary, to get his or her eye to signal that you are "in." Make sure you're not bidding against your spouse. I've seen that happen several times. Make sure you're not bidding accidentally. My husband once bought a cake by scratching his head!

Hang back as long as possible before opening a bid. Then leave it as low as possible. I recommend bidding a quarter on anything for an opener. I've gotten many an interesting and useful item for a quarter that way. If there are several items of a kind, and the auctioneer announces that they will be sold to the highest bidder (who is to take as many as he or she wants), stop bidding. Almost certainly the winning bidder will not want all the items. After the winner of the bid has named the items he or she wants, the bidding will be reopened on the remaining items. If the item was overbid (and it was probably was), and no one wants the rest at that price, the auctioneer will then re-auction the remainder, arriving at a lower sale price—and still lower until all the items are finally sold.

Payment is made by check or cash. Anytime you want to leave the sale, go up to the auction clerk—the person who is recording each sale by price and the name or num-

ber of person buying—and ask for your total, telling him your name or number. The clerk will add it up, and you'll pay on the spot. Driving a pickup to the sale makes it easier for you to get your new stuff home. Just gather up the things you bought and take them. If you didn't drive a pickup, maybe you could buy one there! Sometimes an auction is a good place to get a bargain vehicle, if your bank account can handle the cash transaction.

Don't get into a contest with somebody who is bidding unreasonably high. It isn't worth it. Such a person is probably a novice at auctions and is determined to be brave and buy that particular item no matter what the cost. He or she is playing to win, not by common sense, and will get the item, of course. Keep in touch with used market prices on the kind of items you shop for, and then you'll know when it's a bargain and when it isn't.

A 10-Step Plan to Straighten Out Your Finances: Most people have too much debt and too little savings. It's a relief to get out of debt, and it's a wonderful feeling to save money. It all starts with your decision to do that! After that big decision, the next thing you do is find out where all the money is going right now. Before you can get ahead, you have to realize where you've been. That means learning just what your current spending habits are. That's Step 1.

Below is a 10-step plan to get your money under real control, have what you truly need, and get some enjoyment out of life too! But first there's the pain of looking into the possible black hole of your pocketbook. What you don't know really can hurt you terribly in the case of finances, hurt you even more than finding out. Tell yourself: no pain, no gain! Then work your way through this 10-point path to financial recovery!

1. It's easy to track your spending if you use checks. If you have a checking account, get out your old checkbooks and a sheet of paper. Write down the basic categories like food, clothing, utilities, home payment, etc. Go through your checkbooks from at least the past 3 months, and assign every single check to a category. (Add more categories as you need them.) When you've done that, divide each total by 3 (if you totaled 3 months), and that gives you an average picture of how much you've spent in each category each month.

2. Where does the rest of your money go? The checkbook doesn't cover it all. To find this out, buy or create a pocket diary to carry with you. In it keep a "dollar diary" to track your cash expenditures, even little ones. Anything you spend habitually can add up fast, maybe more than you realized: daily cups of coffee; a magazine, newspaper, or book; bus fares. Multiply anything little by 365 days a year, and you're suddenly looking at a substantial sum. Keep your dollar diary for at least 2 weeks, but preferably 1 month—long enough to have a clear picture of your cash spending pattern. Then you're done with Stage 1.

3. Find out what your credit status is. Ask at your bank or look in the Yellow Pages under "Credit" for a credit reporting service. For $10 or so, they'll give you a print-out of your public record. Anybody who wants to check your credit rating can get that record; you should know what they're seeing!

4. Analyze all your bills. List them. How much is your total indebtedness? Sort the bills into categories. What are most of them for? For future reference, could any of them have been avoided? Are any of them overdue? How many dollars' worth is overdue? How long has it been overdue? Are you in debt trouble? Credit can be a blessing if it enables you to feed your livestock through a hard winter or buy your piece of land, but it can also be your enemy. Is your debt load so great that your budget couldn't handle a crisis: a sudden new expenses, a sudden loss of income? A financial expert would consider you to have an excessive debt load if:
   - Your debt payments exceed 33–40 percent of your gross income.
   - You pay only the minimum due on accounts instead of being able to progress toward paying them off.
   - You use one credit card to make payments on other ones.
   - Your indebtedness is staying the same or getting worse.
   - You put off one bill to pay another.
   - You are past due with basic expenses like rent and utilities.
   - You apply for additional credit cards because you've reached the limit on your current ones.
   - You get advances on paychecks.
   - You tap your savings for everyday living expenses.

5. Change your life so you don't have to worry about money or hate/fear the mail. How drastically you act depends on how bad things are. If you are bouncing checks, close your checking account, open a savings account instead, and pay your bills with money orders or in cash. That way people can't pressure you to give them a check. Doing without a problem checking account will save you money and your reputation. If you are overusing credit cards, cut them all up and flush them down the toilet. (Consider the Eureka Resource catalog's stirring words: "Credit cards are an instrument of the Corporate Hologram, the New World Virtual Reality, which is conspiring to enslave you by controlling your economy with records, privilege of buying and selling, identification, surveillance, and market research.") Carry cash instead. Keep emergency cash hidden at home that a relative or friend can bring or wire you for an emergency away from home.

6. Plan to save money. You've taken steps to avoid spending more than you have. But you want to do better than that, to save money so you can have a cushion against emergencies and take advantage of the bargains cash buyers get! Look for the places in your budget where you can save money. What can you do without? Even little items add up. If you can avoid spending $3 a day, that's a savings of $100 a month.

7. Now lay out your monthly budget. Include money for yourself, for your necessities, and to pay on your debts. When you get paid, pay yourself first, but make sure the rest of it goes where you budgeted it and doesn't get diverted. It's hard to say no to people you love for things they really want—even really need—but keep in mind that you're setting an example for their own future economic survival. Nobody can buy everything he or she wants. Most of us can't even buy very much of what we want. So we need to get along with what we do have—and what we can afford. Nevertheless, it's nice to think things could be better, that life could be easier. It could—if you spend less and/or earn more.

8. Choose and apply these ways to spend less: Generic prescription drugs? Buying on sale? Packing a lunch? Writing instead of phoning? Buying in bulk? Car pooling or riding the bus instead of driving? Staying away from stores? Swapping skills with friends and neighbors instead of hiring people to do things? Getting books from the library instead of buying or renting entertainment? Eating at home instead of in restaurants? Eating meatless? Growing more of your food? Preserving more of what you grow to make it last? Making your own gifts or giving services instead of things? Repairing instead of replacing? Using self-service gas stations and paying cash for gas where a cash discount is given? Changing your car insurance to a maximum-deductible policy?

9. The other side of the budget coin is to earn more. Here are ideas to increase your income: Rent out a spare room? Have a garage sale? Take a course that could help you get a better-paying job? Second job at night or on weekends? Sign up with temporary-help agency? Do free-lance work in your field? Advertise what you're good at in your neighborhood? Start a small business at home? Ask for overtime work at your job? Look for a job with better employee benefits, especially health insurance?

10. The final achievement is to have a substantial and growing savings account. That's your cushion against emergencies, and your down payment for a home with garden space or with acreage for livestock, or your

capital for starting a business that's going to provide even more income or allow you to do the kind of work you really want to. It does take money to make money. So you have to hold some back to reinvest as capital and maintain enough to be able to live frugally. It's paradoxical but true that it's most expensive to always live poor: throwing money down the rent hole, paying interest on credit purchases, unable to get the bargains that require cash.

So budget an amount to be saved per month. Most banks will make an automatic deposit from your checking account to your savings account if you tell them to. Take it out on payday, and don't let yourself make withdrawals except for one of the above reasons. If you get a bonanza, like a raise or a bonus or your tax refund check, assign most or part of it to the savings account. (Spend at least a little of it; that helps keep down the stress level.) Interest will help make your savings grow once it becomes a long-standing habit.

LEE'S WISDOM: Lee Bannister, a Palouse farmer's son, advises, "Buy land when nobody wants it. Know your marketplace. The farmers who make money are good businessmen. If you're out on a limb to the bank, the bank is going to eventually own your farm because crop failure is periodic and inevitable. You stay out of debt by being frugal. You look at how much money you can afford to spend, and you don't spend more than that. And keep a cushion—enough put away to carry you through a couple bad years. A lot of farmers who make money do it by staying out of debt, using *older* (work wearing a dust mask when there's no cab), *little* equipment, and working for wages during the day and then going home and farming by night."

HEALTH MATTERS

Where There Is No Doctor: A Village Health Care Handbook, by David Werner, Carol Thurman, and Jane Maxwell (1992), is the classic. It's written for people with no medical training in a rural situation and offers info on first aid, symptoms, treatment, drug side effects, etc. Order from Hesperian Foundation: 510-845-1447; fax 510-845-9141; 1919 Addison St., Ste. 304, Berkeley, CA 97407; **hesperian@hesperian.org; www.hesperian.org.** The companion volume, *Where There Is No Dentist,* by Murray Dickson (1999), covers dental hygiene, temporary fillings, pulling teeth, etc. The top first aid and CPR manual is *The American Red Cross First Aid & Safety Handbook* (1992). For preventive medicine, get *Healthwise Handbook: A Self-Care Guide for You* by Donald W. Kemper (1999). A supplementary volume for Werner's book is *Medicine for Mountaineering & Other Wilderness Activities,* James A. Wilderson, M.D., Editor (5th edition, 2001; 800-553-4453; **www.mountaineers books.org**).

The most advanced text for surgical procedures under doctorless emergency conditions (care of wounds, amputations, burn care, etc.) is *Ditch Medicine: Advanced Field Procedures for Emergencies* by Hugh L. Coffee (1993; Paladin Press, PO Box 1307, Boulder, CO 80306). Planning wilderness or third world travel? Get *A Comprehensive Guide to Wilderness and Travel Medicine* by Eric A. Weiss, M.D. (1997; Adventure Medical Kits, PO Box 43309, Oakland, CA 94624).

Lyme Disease

When I started this book 25 years ago, I'd never heard of AIDS or Lyme disease. Now I know a brave young divorced woman in Spokane, WA, who is dying from AIDS. She used to live for her backpacking weekends into the woods. Her beloved 12-year-old only child, a daughter, is crippled from Lyme disease. Times change and not always for the better. Both of those are new diseases, arrived since the first edition of this book. Lyme disease was first identified in 1978.

In my childhood, ticks were just a darned nuisance, little bloodsucking buggers that crawled onto man and beast in the spring and stayed too long. Once in a while, rarely, somebody got Rocky Mountain spotted fever from them. But Lyme disease is now the most common tick-transmitted illness and a serious public health problem, and case numbers are increasing. For current info, call 800-886-LYME. Or send a SASE to Lyme Disease Foundation, 1 Financial Plaza, 18th Floor, Hartford, CT 06103-2601.

WHERE IS LYME? Europe, Asia, and Australia, and almost every state in the United States have cases: 497 U.S. cases reported to the CDC in 1982, 5,700 in 1988, 9,677 in 1992. Ninety percent of the reported cases are in 8 hot spots for the infection: the northern coast of California, Connecticut, Massachusetts, Minnesota, New Jersey, New York, Rhode Island, and Wisconsin. As of 1993, the Northeast and northern Midwest had most of the cases. In most other places Lyme is still rare or nonexistent, but where it's bad it can be awful. *The New York Times* (June 15, 1993) reported that "in some high-risk counties nearly 5 percent of residents came down with the disease last year." Even within those counties, the disease tends to be very localized. From the *Times* again, Dr. Alan Steer, discoverer of the disease, said: "There are roads where someone in almost every house has had Lyme, and 5 miles away there is almost none."

WHEN IS LYME? People get infected between April and October, most usually between May and July. The peak Lyme season is June 15 to August 15.

LYME CONDITIONS: Besides the time of year, you need four other things for Lyme to be a possibility where you live: deer; rodents, especially mice (or birds); the Lyme spirochete infesting the tick population; and the particular kind of tick that will carry Lyme. It's really unfortunate that just when we need to plant more trees, here comes this disease; suddenly, having woods—and deer—on your property becomes a definite risk factor.

Lyme Ticks. The tick that usually carries Lyme disease on the West Coast is the "black-legged tick"; the usual carrier elsewhere is the "deer tick." Deer ticks winter on white-tailed deer, but they get around on field mice. They pick up Lyme disease from dining on rodents or birds. The big ugly ticks that come home on dogs (or kids) and have to be pulled off aren't the carriers of Lyme. The ticks that carry Lyme disease are the size of a pinhead. They're hard to see unless you look carefully—or feel them bite.

Lyme Spirochetes. The Lyme beastie, *Borellia burgdorferi,* is a spirochete, like syphilis. Like syphilis, a Lyme infection has 3 stages of symptoms and the third stage can be very serious indeed.

DIAGNOSIS: The place to start is to find out if your area has the 4 necessary elements. If you have no deer, mice, or deer ticks, or your deer ticks don't (yet?) carry Lyme, there's nothing to worry about. Lyme's hard to correctly identify and is very commonly misdiagnosed. It's easier for doctors to diagnose when it's in the more advanced stages—but then it's harder to treat successfully. The 3 symptom stages are as follows:

Stage 1 Symptoms. A doughnut-shaped red rash and a "flu" occur within days or weeks of the bite. In *Backwoods Home Magazine* (Feb./March 1990), Rodney L. Merrill wrote: "The most commonly recognized warning sign is the 'bull's-eye rash'—a round, expanding red rash surrounding a lighter red area. There is sometimes a puffy area (bull's-eye) at the center where the tick bite occurred." Having the rash means you should for sure head to the doctor for treatment, but not having it doesn't necessarily mean you're free of the infection. As for the "flu," Merrill lists "fever, chills, sore throat, swollen glands or testicles, abnormal fatigue resembling mononucleosis, sleeping difficulties, stiffness in the neck, chronic joint and muscle pain."

Stage 2 Symptoms. Some weeks or months after the bite, the Lyme sufferer experiences a variety of heart or nervous abnormalities such as irregular heartbeat or paralysis of a nerve.

Stage 3 Symptoms. Merrill says untreated Lyme that has been there for years can result in "unexpected premature labor or symptoms of phlebitis, meningitis, rheumatoid or other types of arthritis, multiple sclerosis, Alzheimer's disease, Lou Gehrig's disease, or Bell's palsy (twitching and loss of muscle control in the cheeks, lips, and eyelids)." The *Times* lists "a severe intermittent arthritis of 1 or 2 joints, generally the knees, or an inflammation of the brain or nerves . . ."

Blood Test—You could go to the doctor and take the Lyme disease blood test. If it says you have Lyme, maybe you do and maybe you don't. This test, which looks for antibodies to Lyme, is notorious for giving false positives. In fact, if you keep taking the test, sooner or later you're sure to get a "positive." Recent research at a Lyme referral clinic found that the disease had been falsely diagnosed in 77 percent of the cases sent to them. On the other hand, if the test says you don't have it, there's a chance that it's wrong and you do. The bottom line for Lyme disease identification is a skilled medical diagnosis rather than the test, though we all wish it could be otherwise.

TREATMENT: Early treatment with big doses of powerful antibiotics is the best way to stop Lyme in its tracks forever. However, antibiotics generally are successful against it at any stage. Stage 3 patients may need a month of intravenous antibiotics.

PREVENTION: Here's what Merrill, public health people, and *The New York Times* advise:

1. When in woods, brush, or tall grass, wear socks and shoes, pants with bottoms tucked into shoes, and a tucked-in shirt with a snug collar, long sleeves, and cuffs. Merrill: "Wear light-colored clothes so that dark-colored ticks are easier to spot." Avoid brush and leaf litter.
2. Apply insect repellent containing DEET to exposed skin and socks, lower pant legs, sleeve cuffs, and collar. Reapply as needed. For children, apply repellent to clothing, not skin.
3. After an outing, shower to wash away unattached ticks. Merrill: "Ticks wander around the body for several hours looking for a choice spot to set up camp, so if you take a shower as soon as you return home, giving

special attention to warm and furry areas, chances are good for flushing them to tick heaven." Do a daily full-body exam on people and pets, keeping in mind that Lyme ticks are the size of a pinhead before feeding. Merrill: "*Shower-inspect children.* Although the immature ticks are hard to detect, it is still a good idea to thoroughly inspect children and pets with a jaundiced eye and a ruthless attitude toward moving freckles."
4. Remove all ticks promptly with fine-point tweezers placed on the mouth parts of the tick, not the head or body, as close to the skin as possible. Wash the body area where the tick was, and swab with alcohol.
5. Make your yard inhospitable to ticks, removing leaf litter and keeping soil relatively dry. Clean up borders; use an insecticide (Sevin, Dursban, or Tempo) once or twice per summer to treat the yard edge and a little way into adjacent wooded areas. Keep deer out of your yard.
6. Watch for the bull's-eye lesion, red with a clearing in the center, that may follow infection. If you suspect infection, get medical help promptly.

Now here's what Carla advises:

1. Give up woodsy outings in tick season.
2. Eat venison. Deer hunting needs to get extremely popular in Lyme areas, because that's the best way to break the spirochetes' life cycle—aside from using pesticides on your yard, land, children, and self. You won't have Lyme ticks where you don't have deer!

Non-Lyme (Big) Ticks

The best way to kill a tick, I think, is to drop him into the flame of your stove, or put him on an electric burner until you're sure he's dead. They don't crush easily. Or else pull the head part away from the body part, or tear open the body part. To remove a tick that isn't just walking around (one that is dug in and feeding), use tweezers or your fingers, but be sure to get a firm hold on the little head part. Otherwise, you may just pull him apart. Don't assume that just because you've got his head in the tweezers, he's dead—he isn't.

If you think this is brutal talk about a fellow life form, you've never worn a tick. The worst tick season here is May. We have to check dogs and kids every day and have gotten as many as 20 at a time off a dog. Ticks eat only twice in their lives, but when they feed, they feast. They usually go to the head end of their victim, and that helps you to find them.

Poisonous Bites

Children are most at risk for these bites because adults know enough to carefully avoid such critters, but kids may be fascinated by them. And children are more likely to die from their stings or bites than adults are because risk is a matter of how much body weight there is for the poison to distribute itself through. That's why children under 3 are likely to die from such a bite, but adults will probably recover—unless they're over 60, which again increases the risk. So for starters, you have to teach your children to avoid bugs with long tails, spiders, and snakes in general until they can seriously discriminate the OK ones from the bad guys.

SCORPIONS: They live in warm-climate zones. Most of the 20 U.S. varieties are based in the Southwest, but one kind is winter-hardy and is found even in Alberta, Canada. Scorpions have long movable tails with a stinger on the end that injects poison. Scorpion poison can paralyze muscles, including the heart muscle.

BLACK WIDOW SPIDERS: They are found throughout the United States. If you get a look at the belly, there is an hourglass shape—bright red or bright yellow—on it. If, however, all you're seeing is the spider's back, it's hard to tell. Black widow poison is similar to scorpion. Florence Merrifield from Mexico wrote me, "My neighbor had 3 dogs. Two got black widow spider bit and died in ½ hour."

First Aid for Scorpion/Black Widow Bites

1. Slowest possible absorption of venom results in milder symptoms and less possibility of death.
2. So, if possible, put ice on wound. If bite or sting is on a limb, ice the entire limb if possible.
3. If the bite is on a limb, use a limited-tightness tourniquet, and do so carefully. You want the arteries to continue to carry blood into the area, but the veins to be inhibited from carrying blood away from it. *Don't shut off blood flow completely.*
4. *Do not give stimulants.* They speed up absorption of venom.
5. *Avoid physical exertion by the victim.* This also speeds up absorption. So keep the victim still rather than walking.
6. *Don't apply heat, chemical cauterization, herbal stimulants, or anything containing alcohol to the wound.* All these speed up absorption and make the doctor's job more difficult.
7. *Get expert medical assistance.* If the identity of the stinging or biting culprit is known for sure, a doctor can give the victim an effective antivenin—unless the victim is allergic to horse serum, and many people are.
8. If the victim is allergic, a doctor can give only supportive treatment for symptoms, and the body must deal with the venom on its own.

BROWN RECLUSE SPIDER: This spider is at home all over North America. Its bite results in a sizable area of rotting flesh all around where the bite happened. Take the victim to the doctor right away. The doctor can't counteract the venom but can help the victim stay alive until it works its course, which can take months.

SNAKES: Most snakes are not poisonous, but some are: the copperhead, coral snake, water moccasin (or cottonmouth), and the many kinds of rattlesnake.

Rules for Snaky Places and Times of Year

1. Don't go out without the protection of a pair of heavy snake boots if you live where snakes are numerous, grumpy, and poisonous. The thicker the shoe leather, the better. Boots that cover not only the foot but also the calf (at a distance from the calf) are best.
2. Stay alert for the presence of snakes. Discover them before you're on top of them. Snakes don't ordinarily chase people. People practically step on them, and then they bite. So see the snake first, and then backtrack like greased lightning till you're well out of its way.
3. Never put your foot or hand down until you can first see what's there. In other words, stay on the trail, and keep your eyes on where you're about to step. If around water, keep in mind that snakes may be in trees.
4. Send a dog with the kids when they go out alone, because it will probably notice the snake before they do and bark to warn them, probably risking its life for them. A dog saved my children in just that way, more than once!

5. I always used to make the children go out in snake season at least in pairs, or else stay home, so that if one had a problem, the other could go for help.
6. *If a bite happens, also follow rules for scorpion/black widow bites. And get medical help as soon as possible.*
7. If you don't own a basic first-aid handbook, get one and read it.

MEASUREMENTS: METRIC EQUIVALENTS

Until everyone agrees on one system of measurement, we'll have to keep converting. On the following pages are some tables comparing metric amounts and measurements to those we use in the United States. For an easy introduction to metric cooking, read *Metric Cooking for Beginners,* by Ginevera Barta.

DISTANCE/LENGTH

Unit	Abbrev.	Meters	U.S. Equivalent
Kilometer	km.	1,000	0.62 mile
Hectometer	hm.	100	109.36 yards
Dekameter	dam.	10	32.81 feet
Meter	m.	1	39.37 inches
Decimeter	dm.	0.1	3.94 inches
Centimeter	cm.	0.01	0.39 inch
Millimeter	mm.	0.001	0.039 inch

AREA

Unit	Abbrev.	Square Meters	U.S. Equivalent
Square kilometer	sq. km.	1,000,000	0.3861 square mile
Hectare	ha.	10,000	2.47 acres
Are	a.	100	119.60 square yards
Square centimeter	sq. cm.	0.0001	0.155 square inch

VOLUME

Unit	Abbrev.	Cubic Meters	U.S. Equivalent
Cubic centimeter	cu. cm. or cc.	0.000001	0.061 cubic inch
Cubic decimeter	cu. dm.	0.001	61.023 cubic inch
Cubic meter	cu. m.	1	1.307 cubic yards

Speech bubble: HEAPING GRAM SPOON? SCANT LITER? KILO CAKE?

MASS/WEIGHT

Unit	Abbrev.	Grams	U.S. Equivalent
Metric ton	t.	1,000,000	1.102 short tons
Kilogram	kg.	1,000	2.2046 lb.
Hectogram	hg.	100	3.527 oz.
Dekagram	dag.	10	0.353 oz.
Gram	g.	1	0.035 oz.
Decigram	dg.	0.10	1.543 grains
Centigram	cg.	0.01	0.154 grains
Milligram	mg.	0.001	0.015 grain

1 liter liquid (water) weighs 1 kilogram.

MILLILITERS TO TEASPOONS/TABLESPOONS/CUPS
(Rounded Off)

Metric	U.S. Equivalent
1 ml.	¼ t.
2 ml.	½ t.
5 ml.	1 t.
7 ml.	1½ t.
10 ml.	2 t.
15 ml.	1 T.
30 ml.	1 fl. oz. or 2 T.
45 ml.	3 T.
50 ml.	3 T.
60 ml.	¼ c.
75 ml.	⅓ c.
125 ml.	½ c.
200 ml.	¾ c.
250 ml.	1 c.
375 ml.	1½ c.
500 ml.	2 c.
750 ml.	3 c.
875 ml.	3½ c.

.95 l. = 1 qt.

1 l. = 1 qt. + ¼ c.

3.8 l. = 1 gal.

These equivalents are rounded off. They're fine for cooking, but I wouldn't try to do industrial chemistry with them! One milliliter equals .004 cup. To compute other rounded milliliter equivalents, multiply .004 by the number of milliliters, and the answer is the number of cups you need.

CAPACITY

Unit	Abbrev.	Liters	Cubic	U.S. Equivalent Dry	U.S. Equivalent Liquid
Kiloliter	kl.	1,000	1.31 cubic yards		
Hectoliter	hl.	100	3.53 cubic feet	2.84 bushels	
Dekaliter	dal.	10	0.35 cubic feet	1.14 pecks	2.64 gallons
Liter	l.	1	61.02 cubic inches	0.908 quart	1.057 quarts
Deciliter	dl.	0.10	6.1 cubic inches	0.18 pint	0.21 pint
Centiliter	cl.	0.01	0.61 cubic inch		0.338 fluid ounce
Milliliter	ml.	0.001	0.061 cubic inch		0.27 fluid dram

CUPS/QUARTS/GALLONS TO MILLILITERS

U.S.	Metric Equivalent
½ c.	118 ml.
1 c.	236 ml.
1¾ c.	413 ml.
2 c. (1 pt.)	472 ml.
4 c. (1 qt.)	946 ml.
4 qt. (1 gal.)	3785 ml.

GRAMS TO POUNDS (Rounded Off)

Metric	U.S. Equivalent
250 g.	½ lb.
300 g.	¾ lb.
500 g.	1 lb.
600 g.	1¼ lb.
700 g.	1½ lb.
1 kg.	2.2 lb.

One pound equals 454 grams.

U.S. TO METRIC PAN SIZES

U.S.	Metric Equivalent
8 × 1½ inches	20 × 4 cm.
9 × 1½ inches	23 × 4 cm.
13 × 9 × 3 inches	33 × 23 × 5 cm.
9 × 5 × 3 inches	23 × 12.5 × 5 cm.

FORMULAS FOR METRIC/U.S. CONVERSIONS

Original Measurement	Multiply by	Result
Ounces	28.3	Grams
Grams	0.0353	Ounces
Pounds	453.59	Grams

Pounds	0.45	Kilograms
Ounces	30	Milliliters
Cups	0.24	Liters
Inches	2.54	Centimeters
Centimeters	0.39	Inches

To convert a Fahrenheit temperature, subtract 32; then multiply that number by 5 and divide by 9 to get the Celsius equivalent. To convert a Celsius temperature, multiply by 9, divide that by 5, and then add 32 to get the Fahrenheit equivalent.

METRIC WEIGHT EQUIVALENTS OF COMMON FOOD MEASURES (Rounded Off)

Food	Amount	Gram Equivalent
Baking powder	1 t.	3.65 grams
Biscuit mix	1 c.	115 grams
Butter	1 c.	224 grams
Cinnamon	1 t.	1.1 grams
Cooking oil	1 c.	210 grams
Cornmeal	1 c.	152 grams
Flour	1 c., sifted	115 grams
Milk	1 c.	244 grams
Milk	1 qt.	976 grams
Pancake mix	1 c.	130 grams
Pecans	1 c., chopped	120 grams
Salt	1 t.	6 grams
Sugar	1 T.	12.5 grams
Sugar	1 c.	200 grams
Vanilla	1 t.	5 grams
Walnuts	1 c., chopped	124 grams

MISCELLANEOUS RECIPES

NOTE: *Throughout this book, "t." stands for "teaspoon," "T." stands for "tablespoon," "c." stands for "cup."*

First, here's a recipe for a happy home: Combine 4 c. love, 2 c. loyalty, 3 c. forgiveness, 1 c. friendship, 5 t. hope, 2 t. tenderness, 4 qt. faith, and 1 barrel of laughter. Take the love and loyalty and mix it thoroughly with faith. Blend it with tenderness, kindness, and understanding. Add friendship and hope. Sprinkle abundantly with laughter. Bake it with sunshine. Serve daily with generous helpings.

I've never tried any of the following recipes; I'm not sure anybody should! But if you try one, let me know what happens.

❧ **TURKEY STUFFING** *Combine 3 eggs, 1 t. salt and pepper, 1 green pepper cut up, 1 c. celery cut up, 2½ c. washed, unpopped popcorn, and 3 c. washed, uncooked rice. Mix well. Stuff turkey loosely. Put in the oven at 350°F. Bake until popcorn pops and blows the hind end off the turkey.* On May 28, 1976, somebody let me know how this turned out! *"Dear Carla Emery, I have tried your turkey stuffing. But it was a flop; the rice was dry and still hard, and not even one corn popped. I had to throw out the whole stuffing. What went wrong? My husband was mad."*

❧ **STONE SOUP** *A poor man's specialty. Start with one large, smooth, clean, round stone. Add ½ teaspoon salt and ample water. Boil 2 hours. In the meantime, ask around at your neighbors for possible other ingredients. At the end of 2 hours, add any vegetables or meat (check the mousetrap) that you have been able to lay hands on. Cook 1 more hour. Remove the stone (save it for the next batch) and eat the soup. Speaking of mice . . .*

❧ **MOUSE PIE** *First catch 5 fat field mice. Then boil 1 c. macaroni 10 minutes. While it is cooking, skin and gut the field mice; then fry long enough to fry out some of the excess fat. Grease a casserole with some of this fat and put a layer of cooked macaroni in it. Add ½ onion, sliced, and 1 medium-sized can of tomatoes; add salt and pepper to taste. Add field mice and cover with remaining macaroni. Sprinkle top with 1 c. cracker crumbs seasoned with salt, pepper, and butter. Bake at 375°F about 20 minutes, or until mice are well-done. Note: If it is difficult to find or catch field mice, a good substitute is about 10 "little pig" sausages.* Ruth Thoreland, Yakima, WA, gave me this one!

❧ **ELEPHANT STEW** *You'll need 1 medium-sized elephant, 2 rabbits (optional), and salt and pepper. Cut the elephant into small bite-sized pieces. Add enough brown gravy to cover. Cook over kerosene fire about 4 weeks at 465°F. This will serve 3,800 people. If more are expected, the 2 rabbits may be added, but do this only in emergency. Most people do not like hare in their stew.*

❧ **MUSGOES** *One day a lady invited me in for dinner with her family. She said, "We're having Musgoes." I had to ask, "What are Musgoes?" She answered, "I just go to the refrigerator and point, saying, 'This musgo, that musgo!'"* Courtesy of John Ramem, Jamestown, ND.

❧ **RECIPE FROM A TEXAS NEWSPAPER!** *This recipe is great if you're tired of the same old turkey or ham for a holiday dinner. It's guaranteed to elicit excited oohs and aahs from your guests, and it's so delicious you won't have to worry about leftovers. You'll need 1 whole camel, medium-sized; 1 whole lamb, large-sized; 20 whole chickens, medium-sized; 110 gal. water; 5 T. black pepper; salt to taste; 12 kilos rice; 2 kilos pine nuts; 2 kilos almonds; 1 kilo pistachio nuts; and 60 eggs. Skin, trim, and clean the camel, lamb, and chickens*

and boil until tender (be sure your pot is big enough). Cook rice until fluffy. Fry nuts until brown and mix with the rice. Hard-boil the eggs and peel them. Then stuff the chickens with eggs and rice. Stuff the camel with the lamb and more rice. Place the camel on a large tray and broil briefly. To serve, place remaining stuffed chickens on the tray around the camel. Decorate surplus heaped rice with boiled eggs and nuts.

❧ **NORTHERN BEATEN BISCUITS (A YUKON RECIPE)** *Mix 1 c. lard with 4 qt. flour until you have got the lard consumed in the flour. Add 1 T. salt and enough cold water to make a stiff dough. Knead into round shapes. Place on a stump and beat 1,500 times with the flat of an axe. Bake in a mud oven.*

The following 3 recipes were written by first-graders from the Cloverdale Grade School in Hebo, OR.

❧ **COOKIES WITH CHOCOLATE CHIPS** *"Put eggs and powder in dough; then you stir it with a thing you use for stirring. Put the chocolate chips in. Turn oven onto 10. Cook for about an hour and a half."* By Troy.

❧ **POTATO CHIP RECIPE** *"Peel some (about 5) potatoes. Then slice them. Put them in a big kettle. Put boiling water in it. Put it on a big plate, with paper on it so it won't burn the plate. Then you eat them."* By Brittany.

❧ **MACARONI AND CHEESE** *"You set the table. Then you wait for your dad to come home. Then you start eating the macaroni and cheese."* By Latina.

KEY TO MYSTERY SCRIPTURE CAKE INGREDIENTS

1 c. water, 1 c. sugar, 1 c. raisins, 1 t. oil, 1½ t. spices. Stir. Boil. Cool. Then add 2 c. flour, 1 t. leavening, ¼ t. salt, ½ c. nuts. Beat. Bake. And eat.

⊃ PENNSYLVANIA DUTCH SCRIPTURE CAKE *Read the verses and bake the (spice) cake. "And behold there was a cake baken!"—1 Kings 9:16.*

Mix Judges 5:25 (½ c. butter); 1 Kings 4:22 (2 c. flour); Leviticus 2:13 (½ t. salt); 1 Samuel 30:12 (1 c. chopped dried figs); Jeremiah 6:20 (1½ c. sugar); Luke 13:21 (2 t. baking powder); Genesis 24:11 (½ c. water); 1 Samuel 30:12 (1 c. raisins); Isaiah 10:14 (3 eggs); 1 Kings 10:10 (cinnamon, mace, cloves); Proverbs 24:13 (1 T. honey); Genesis 43:11 (½ c. chopped almonds). Blend butter, sugar, spices, and salt. Beat egg yolks and add. Sift in baking powder and flour. Then add the water and honey. Put fruits and nuts through food chopper and flour well. Follow Solomon's advice for making good boys (first clause of Proverbs 23:14). Fold in stiffly beaten egg whites. Bake 1 hour in 375°F oven.

⊃ MYSTERY SCRIPTURE CAKE *You've had one to practice on. See if you can figure this one out from scratch! Matthew 10:42, 1 c. Jeremiah 6:20, 1 c. 1 Samuel 25:18, 1 c. Matthew 25:4, 1 t. II Chronicles 9:9, 1½ t. Psalms 35:23. Isaiah 38:21. Luke 16:24. Then add: 1 Kings 4:22, 2 c. 1 Corinthians, 1 t. Luke 14:34, ¼PP t. Genesis 43:11, ½ c. Isaiah 2:4. Leviticus 26:26. Luke 15:23. (See box for answers if you're stumped.)*

Christiane Henningsen of Walton, Nova Scotia, wrote: "My husband and I emigrated to Nova Scotia in 1983 with a suitcase each and a tent. We pitched the tent near the woods, then started building a 12- by 14-foot cabin, which we moved into in September. (A mathematician and a lawyer don't build very fast.) The cabin had a cast-iron wood stove but no water or electricity, yet we lived in that little structure for nearly 3 years (our son was born there), while my husband built the house, starting with a hammer and saw. Now, 11 years later, the house is nice, and we have running water. There always was a garden."

Introduction to Plants

INTRODUCTION TO PLANTS CONTENTS

INTRODUCTION

Very little of our world is now pristinely clean in the old-time, pre-petroleum sense. The sad fact is that in these modern times we live in a sea of pollutants. Tiny particles of these potentially health-damaging chemicals are in the air we must breathe, the water we must drink, and the food we must eat. But pollution is always a point somewhere on a spectrum: It can be worse, it can be better. If you learn what and where the worst pollution problems are, you can protect yourself and your family.

I used to believe the cities were the polluted places and that rural living guaranteed clean everything—air, water, soil. I've undergone a rude awakening from that assumption. I've discovered that the urban areas in which political power is centered and where pollution decisions are usually made routinely send polluting industries and toxic waste out to rural areas, where "nobody" lives.

So when you're looking for a place to live in the country, or if you already live there, you're quite likely to encounter a nearby nuclear power plant or nuclear waste dump; a weapons storage site, practice range, or testing site; a toxic waste incinerator (downwinders get the exposure); or a toxic or not-as-toxic waste/garbage dump site. More such facilities are being built all the time as industrial and urban areas desperately seek ways to unload their ever-growing mountains of nuclear, chemical, and just-plain-garbage waste. There have even been incidents in which forest dwellers, their children, or livestock were sickened by overhead or roadside chemical spraying.

NOTE: Know who is dumping or plans to dump, and what and where they plan to dump, in your region. So much money can be made in both legal and illegal dumping that it's realistic to be a little suspicious.

The only real solution is for a society not to produce this type of waste. But that's hard, if not impossible, in our type of economy and world. There are no easy or absolute answers. But if you have an existing or would-be polluter in your area, it's simple self-defense to fight to keep your region from being a dumping ground. You have to. And a lot of local battles can add up to a national trend. It is a sad truth, however, that any toxics you successfully fight will just be taken to some other less-organized, less-resistant area.

POLLUTION MATTERS

POLLUTION FIGHTERS: Margaret Mead once said, "Never doubt that a small group of thoughtful, committed citizens can change the world. Indeed, it's the only thing that ever has." Almost every state has one or more organizations fighting toxic pollution that can give you the real facts and assistance.

This problem is correctable. "Rachel Environmental Weekly" is an online listing of relevant announcements: **www.rachel.org**. The following organizations fight toxic pollution. Join one!

Appalachia—Science in the Public Interest: 606-256-0077; fax 606-256-2779; 50 Lair St., Mount Vernon, KY 40456-9806; aspi@kih.net; www.a-spi.org.

Beyond Pesticides/National Coalition Against the Misuse of Pesticides publishes a good quarterly magazine, *Pesticides and You*, which informs on the latest scientific info, industry moves, and counter-moves ($15 low income; $25 regular): 202-543-5450; fax 202-543-4791; Ste. 200, 701 E St. SE, Washington, DC 20003; **info@beyondpesticides.org; www. beyondpesticides.org.**

Citizens Environmental Coalition offers ($3) "A Citizens' Guide to Understanding Measurements of Toxic and Radioactive Concentrations"—fascinating and useful for anybody with a scientific bent: 518-462-5527; 33 Central Ave., Albany, NY 12210.

Concern, Inc., produces plain-English publications for activists, organizers, and public officials; "Pesticides in Our Communities: Choices for Change," "Global Warming and Energy Choices," "Household Waste: Issues and Opportunities," "Drinking Water: A Community Action Guide," etc. First copy is $4 each plus $1.50 postage; each additional copy is 50 cents.

Contact: 202-328-8160; 1794 Columbia Rd. NW, Washington, DC 20009.

Environmental Health Coalition: 619-235-0281; 1717 Kettner Blvd., San Diego, CA 92101.

Great Lakes United is an international coalition of more than 1,800 individuals and 150 groups working to protect the Great Lakes and St. Lawrence River Basin from pollution. Join and get their newsletter, *Bulletin of Pollution Prevention*: 716-886-0142; State University at Buffalo, Cassety Hall, 1300 Elmwood Ave., Buffalo, NY 14222. Their Canadian address is 4525 Rue de Rouen, Montreal, Quebec, H1V 1H1 CANADA.

Human Ecology Action League provides info on toxic exposures: nervous system poisons, indoor air pollution, and irritants, allergens, sensitizers. They offer printed materials such as "How Chemicals in Your Environment Can Affect Your Health" ($.30 ea.); "Pesticide Close-Up" ($7); and "Pesticide Avoidance and Clean-up" ($16): 404-248-1898; PO Box 49126, Atlanta, GA 30359; **HEALNatnl@aol.com.**

National Toxics Campaign, PO Box 206, Allston, MA 02134.

Northcoast Environmental Center focuses on sustaining the environmental quality of northwestern California. It publishes *ECONEWS*, sent to members. Contact: 707-822-6918; fax 707-822-0827; 575 H St., Arcata, CA 95521; **nec@igc.org; www.necandeconews.to.**

Northwest Coalition for Alternatives to Pesticides, 541-344-5044; fax 541-344-6923; PO Box 1393, Eugene, OR 97440; **info@pesticide.org; www.pesticide.org.**

Washington Toxics Coalition: 206-632-1545 ext. 17; fax 206-632-8661; 4649 Sunnyside Ave. N., Ste. #540, Seattle, WA 98103; **info@watoxics.org; www.wa toxics.org.**

Air Pollution

The air we breathe, the winds that blow—those used to seem like a simple matter. Now we know so much more, with so much yet to learn, and nothing is simple anymore. Air pollution is a problem for plants as well as people.

PLANT DAMAGE FROM AIR POLLUTION: Plant food can be unhealthy to eat because of airborne lead pollution. In fact, plants are typically even more sensitive to pollution than people. (If you're looking at a home in a neighborhood where the plants don't look healthy, I'd look elsewhere.) Urban plants are most often sickened by ozone, sulfur dioxide, and hydrogen fluoride in the air. Plants can get sick as soon as 24 hours after exposure. The healthiest plants may be the most affected by air pollution because they are more active in growth and thus are taking in more of the problem chemical.

Ozone. Ozone pollution interferes with photosynthesis. The damage to leaves is visible on the upper leaf surfaces rather than the lower ones. The leaves of cucumber, spinach, parsley, nasturtium, or zucchini plants get a bleached stippling. Green beans, lima beans, grapes, and white potato leaves get a dark pigmented stippling. Really severe air pollution can even cause leaves to turn yellow and drop. Woody plants aren't as vulnerable to air pollution as herbaceous ones.

Hydrogen Fluoride and Sulfur Dioxide. These gases are usually worst near the factory that spews them out. Sulfur dioxide comes from plants that burn high sulfur petroleum or coal. Plants get tan areas or spots between the veins of leaves. These lesions will go all the way through leaves and be visible on both top and bottom. Tomatoes, apples, and roses are especially susceptible. Hydrogen fluoride comes from industries that make aluminum, ceramics, phosphate fertilizers, or steel. Cherries, blueberries, corn, grapes, and peaches are all sensitive to it, and their leaf margins will get brown. (Conifers' needle tips die. Affected deciduous trees can grow a new crop of leaves and survive, but affected conifers usually die.)

GLOBAL WARMING: The earth's climate is always changing, getting either cooler or warmer by some extremely tiny amount. Normally the forecast for 10,000 years in the future would be another glacial epoch. But right now the weather is in a warming curve due to the "greenhouse effect." If our petroleum-based civilization keeps burning fuel at current or increased rates, some scientists project that the concentration of CO_2 (carbon dioxide) in the earth's air will be double the preindustrial levels by the year 2030—and will continue on up as long as the amount of greenhouse gases in the air increases.

Stopping the Warming Trend

1. People all over the world switch from burning wood and fossil fuels to using draft animal, wind, water, geothermal, tidal/wave, solar, and hydrogen energy. Those energy sources don't emit CO_2. Yes, I know cows emit a little methane, but nothing like a tractor.
2. In a desperate crash effort, a new generation of scientists comes up with the breakthrough technologies to make this necessary transition bearable by combining the best of pre-petroleum science with whole new postpetroleum technologies. Nuclear power isn't the answer. It's a terrible polluter of another sort.

3. A major global effort stops the current trend of deforestation. Sulfur- and coal-fueled power plants that create forest-killing acid rain are shut down everywhere. Citizens worldwide race to reforest, planting trees that remove carbon dioxide from the air faster than the windstorms caused by a warmer atmosphere can blow them down (and faster than lumberjacks can cut them down). And the tree planters win!

4. Worldwide CFC production ends.

If those 4 changes are accomplished within the next decade, scientists estimate that the progress of global warming will greatly slow and will have nearly stopped by 2099. Anything short of the above 4 accomplishments means both greater warming and warming for a longer period of time. Right now the earth's temperature is projected to very slowly but steadily increase for the foreseeable future . . . until human beings planetwide change in the above ways. That's a big order, but step 4 is well on the way to accomplishment already [1993], so obviously change is possible.

I can reassure you on one important point. Global warming will not continue until the earth is a cinder. The entire earth's climate might become tropical, but that's it. That's because the warming trend will stop when the earth's oil supply is exhausted (if not sooner), which will happen. Then there'll have to be a jarring readjustment, whether folks are ready or not—and all the nonpetroleum food-growing technologies could be useful indeed!

But for a bunch of reasons, there ain't a snowball's chance in hell that what's necessary to absolutely stop the warming will happen in the next decade. And even if it does, there will still have been some global warming. So . . .

Family Defense Strategies Against Global Warming. Strategies 1–6 were extracted and extrapolated from National Resource Defense Council data in *The Rising Tide* by Lynne T. Edgerton.

1. Both the frequency and wind velocity of storms coming off the ocean onto land will continue to increase as long as the atmosphere's average temperature increases. It is during the periodic extremes of these storms that the most damage and suffering is likely to occur to your property and family. No matter where you live, be prepared for high winds. Be prepared to do without normal services such as electricity or shopping for long periods of time.

2. Earth-sheltered, or underground, housing for people and livestock is far more energy-efficient: It stays warm in winter and cool in summer. It's also the housing type that's most protected from violent windstorms. So consider evolving toward underground or earth-sheltered housing in any new construction you do for yourself and your livestock.

3. These storms may be either "hot" or "cold" in nature. Or there may be episodes, without accompanying wind, of either unprecedentedly hot or cold, wet or dry, weather. So plan and prepare for your family, livestock, and plants to survive all those extremes.

4. A warming earth is causing polar ice to melt. The level of the oceans is gradually rising, slowly but steadily. Erosion of beaches and flooding of low islands and coastal areas during storms is going to happen at an ever-increasing rate until the earth's heating trend stops. Salt water will be invading and shifting to dominance in areas where salt water and fresh water meet and mix. The health of many fish and shellfish populations will be threatened as their environmental conditions change to favor salt-water species—and salt-water pests. So if you live on the ocean-front (most risky) or in a coastal area, especially a low-lying coastal lowland, consider moving to an inland, more water- and wind-sheltered site.

5. Because most plants (and some animals) are best adapted to a narrow climatic zone, be prepared to gradually shift to more "southern" food-producing species, both plant and animal, as the climate warms. Botanists predict that some native wild species will die off, since forests can't uproot and move 150 miles north to adapt to changing climate. They'll have to be replaced with species that can thrive under the new conditions. And then replaced again?

6. Because rainfall in rain-prone areas and storms of all sorts are going to increase in frequency and intensity, inland as well as near the ocean (worst there), expect increasingly remarkable storm runoffs. Don't build on or near any water channel or floodplain. Build only well above it.

7. Consider moving toward a colder climate. Then you stay ahead of destructive warm-climate insects (such as fire ants and "killer" bees) as well as problematic human and animal diseases associated with tropical and subtropical climate zones.

8. Buy land, get it paid for, live on it, and grow chemical-free food, thus ensuring an adequate, safe food supply for your family and your descendants. Keep a supply of food in storage against the unexpected. Buy your home; consider building or buying space to rent. It's a solid investment.

9. Cherish green and living things and an unpolluted environment. Buy land and protect it from toxic and nuclear waste dumping, nuclear construction, deforestation, water pollution, plant and animal species destruction, shotgun hunting (lead pollution), and soil-eroding or polluting farming practices.

10. Join an effective community support system—or several of them. Individuals and families survive hard times better when they are organized for cooperation and have a heartfelt and clearly understood commitment to care for each other.

11. Consider long-term consequences. Plan for the next 20 years rather than the next 2, for the next 50 rather than the next 5.

12. Learn extra skills and save money so you can quickly switch your location or lifestyle should that be necessary.

TESTING FOR RADIOACTIVITY: By 2030, the state of Idaho's Idaho Nuclear Engineering Laboratory (INEL) Oversight Program figures that the U.S. government will own more than 83,000 metric tons of high-level radioactive nuclear waste. The government has only until 1998—when it takes control of the waste from the nation's commercial nuclear power plants—to find a permanent waste repository for the huge amounts we already have. High-level nuclear waste is unspeakably dangerous. What could possibly be a "safe" depository for products that will remain deadly for the next 10,000 years?! But the stuff is already leaking: from power plants and weapons testing and storage sites.

Water Pollution

HARD WATER: Ground water may have dissolved minerals in it, making it "hard water." Just what is in it depends on where you live, so treatments differ. This is a kind of natural pollution and usually isn't a health threat, just a nuisance. One old-time midwestern system for treating wash water so it wouldn't make clothes gray was to dissolve lye in hot water and let it stand until a white scum or settling developed at the bottom. Then they skimmed or poured off the top, cleaner water to be the clothes-washing water and discarded the sediment. Borax helps too.

AGRICULTURAL CHEMICAL POLLUTION: "Chemical fertilizers" basically means nitrate fertilizers, which are all manmade. Where chemical fertilizer is laid on the ground, nitrates can be a major problem in the water supply. Pesticides and nitrates from the fertilizers quickly soak down into the soil through a zigzag pathway of ground crevices, root holes, and worm tunnels. Once contaminated, ground water stays that way year-round.

Excess nitrates from artificial fertilizer end up not only in the drinking water but also in the food plants. Plants raised using this type of fertilizer rather than green manure or natural animal manure contain unnaturally high levels of nitrates. Most of the commercial foods we eat, especially vegetables and most especially green leafy vegetables, are grown using nitrate fertilizers, and they accumulate nitrates in their edible parts. When we eat them, a significant fraction of the nitrate gets reduced in our bodies to nitrite. Nitrite can react with amine compounds (which are present in your body at all times) to form nitrosamines, which are known carcinogens. There's no doubt about the potential problems that nitrosamines can cause in a body. But there are certain things that inhibit the formation of nitrosamines. Among those are vitamin C and E. Many plants are rich in these. The nitrosamine problem is worse for infants and very young children because their bodies tend to transform a higher percentage of the nitrates into nitrites, making them likely to end up with more carcinogens in their bodies than adults. (The preceding facts were carefully explained to me by Martin Pall, an old friend who has a Ph.D. in biochemistry, is a professor at Washington State U., and is writing a book on the subject.)

A friend of mine in Idaho moved onto her dream place, a small rural acreage, only to discover 6 months later that her baby was sick. She learned that water with a high nitrate content causes "blue-baby" anemia by reducing the blood's ability to transport oxygen. *If you have a newborn baby, for sure get your water tested for nitrates!* Dairy cattle or goats that drink high-nitrate water will give milk that is also too high in nitrates and that cannot be legally sold. High nitrate levels in drinking water have also been linked to birth defects, high blood pressure, anemia, gastric cancer, and worsening of other illnesses.

In addition to nitrates, researchers have started finding atrazine, alachlor, cyanazine, and other manmade compounds in ground water. This is because millions of pounds of these artificial molecular chains are now being injected every year into our living biosphere—all of them deadly "biocides." There is an enormous supply of biocides and an eager, lucrative market. It's all so recent that we don't fully know yet how badly years of drinking chemically tainted water can affect a person. We do know that certain cancers, including breast cancer in women, are significantly more common among persons exposed to pesticides, and that there are higher rates of cancer among children in the most pesticide-polluted rural communities.

If your drinking water is contaminated, don't drink it until it's been through a distilling process. If you can also provide family dairy animals with distilled water to drink, so much the better.

WATER TESTING: Get your water tested. If it's bad, you'll probably want to get a water distiller and drink and cook only with that water. Every state has a certified laboratory that will test water samples. The tests, however, may be limited in extent and expensive. Make a preliminary phone call to get location and price, and plan to deliver the sample to the lab within 6 hours. Important tests include a coliform count, which reveals whether there is sewage in your water supply, and tests for heavy metals, which are not uncommon but are very unhealthy. And if you live in an agricultural area, test for nitrates.

Read *Don't Drink the Water (Without Reading This Book): The Essential Guide to Our Contaminated Drinking Water and What You Can Do About It* by Lono Kahuna Kupua O'o (1998). It's available from Kali Press, PO Box 2169, Pagosa Springs, CO 81147. It has up-to-date and accurate presentations of health problems posed by various drinking water contaminants and gives good counsel on how to test your own water and what to do about various problems. A slightly older book, but one with great evaluations of specific products, is *The Drinking Water Book: A Complete Guide to Safe Drinking Water,* by Colin Ingram (1991; Ten Speed Press, PO Box 7123, Berkeley, CA 94707).

You can buy one-item water tests from Lowe's Home Improvement Centers for $10 to $18 each. They test for sediment, chlorine, or fluoride. It's good to know that, but you need to know more. Every state has a certified laboratory that will test water samples. These tests, however, may be limited in extent and expensive.

National Testing Laboratories, Ltd., offers the Watercheck (testing for 75 contaminants, $125) or Watercheck with Pesticide Option (testing for 95 contaminants; $155). This latter one is a broad-spectrum drinking water analysis that I recommend. If you want to test for lead coming from plumbing in a home, order their First Draw and Flush Lead test ($40). They can also do a simple test for presence or absence of *E. coli* ($35). Their Quick-Screen test determines

your water softening needs. Included on this test are iron, alkalinity, hardness, pH, and TDS ($55). This test can be used as a "post-check" after a softener has been set up, to see how well the system is working. For rural areas, there's a quickie BNLC test: bacteria, nitrate, lead, and copper ($90). Contact them at 6555 Wilson Mills Rd., Ste. 102, Cleveland, OH 44143; 800-458-3330; fax 440-449-8585; **www.ntllabs.com**. Each water test report is accompanied by a Corrective Action Brochure that offers recommendations on how to deal with water concerns once they're identified. National Testing Laboratories must receive the sample within 30 hours for results of bacteria testing to be valid. The 94 most common pollutants are:

Metals: Aluminum, arsenic, barium, cadmium, chromium, copper, iron, lead, manganese, mercury, nickel, selenium, silver, sodium, zinc.

Inorganics: Total alkalinity, chloride, fluoride, nitrate, nitrite, sulfate, hardness, pH, total dissolved solids, turbidity.

Microbes: Coliform bacteria.

PCBs, pesticides, and herbicides: Alachlor; Aldrin; Atrazine; Chlordane; Dichloran; Dieldrin; Endrin; Heptachlor; Heptachlor Epoxide; Hexachlorobenzene; Hexachloropentadiene; Lindane; Methoxychlor; Pentachloronitrobenzene; polychlorinated biphenyls (PCBs); Silvex 2,4,5-TP; Simazine; Toxaphene; Trifluralin; 2,4-D.

Organic chemicals, trihalomethanes: Bromoform, bromodichloromethane, chloroform, dibromochloromethane, benzene, vinyl chloride, carbon tetrachloride, 1,2-dichloroethane, trichloroethylene (TCE); 1,4-dichlorobenzene, 1,1-dichloroethylene, 1,1,1-trichloroethane; bromobenzene, bromomethane; chlorobenzene; chloroethane; chloromethane; 2-chlorotoluene; 4-chlorotoluene; dibromochloropropane; dibromomethane; 1,2-dichlorobenzene; 1,3-dichlorobenzene; dichlorodifluoromethane; 1-1-dichloroethane; trans-1,2-dichloroethane; cis-1,2-dichloroethane; dichloromethane; 1,2-dichloropropane; trans-1,3-dichloropropane; cis-1,3-dichloropropane; 2,2-dichloropropane; 1,1-dichloropropane; 1,3-dichloropropane; ethylbenzene; ethylenedibromide; styrene; 1,1,1,2-tetrachloroethane; 1,1,2,2-tetrachloroethane; tetrachloroethane; 1,2,3-trichlorobenzene; 1,2,4-trichlorobenzene; 1,1,2-trichloroethane; trichlorofluoromethane; 1,2,3-trichloropropane; toluene; xylene; methyl-tert-butyl-ether.

If you're looking for a specific thing in your water and it's not on this list, go to a local water testing lab and arrange for testing for that specific item. For not only a test, but also advice and sales of remediation equipment, contact Naturally Pure Alternatives; 800-736-7877; 575 Live Oak Ave., Ukiah, CA 95482-3730. They use the above company for their testing, offering the big one (95 pollutants) for $146 (2002). After receiving your test results, you can call and ask any questions you have about the results. They'll advise you on the best management of any problems in your water supply.

Harmless Cleaning Agents and Other Eco-Safe Formulas

In the Jan./Feb. 1991 issue of *Backwoods Home Magazine*, Rodney Merrill, Ph.D. and M.P.H. (master's in public health), wrote, "Americans use more chemical cleaners and disinfectants per person than any other people on Earth. Some analysts say we have a neurotic obsession with odors, germs, and cleanliness. The advertising industry has helped push our obsession to the limits by bombarding us daily with hundreds of radio and TV commercials that sell us chemical solutions that will wash away our fears.

"But many of these advertised chemical solutions pose serious threats to the members of our households, the genetic integrity of unborn children, and the viability of the natural environment—in exchange for solving imaginary, invented, and inconsequential problems. But there are no-tox or low-tox natural alternatives that work as well or better than their commercial counterparts and are far cheaper to buy." The material in this section on eco-safe cleaning agents is quoted from his great article.

THE BASIC INGREDIENTS

Ammonia. "This is ammonium hydroxide dissolved in water. It is the active ingredient in a lot of cleaners. Ammonium hydroxide is a natural grease cutter and costs about $1.50 per gal., much cheaper than spray cleaner at $3.50 per qt. Ammonia evaporates and becomes nitrogen gas again. As long as you provide plenty of ventilation and never combine it with other chemical cleaners, ammonia is safe to use."
CAUTION: *"Without proper ventilation, nitrogen can suffocate you by displacing oxygen in the air. If you mix ammonia with other commercial cleaners, especially chlorine bleach, you risk turning your house into a gas chamber!"*

Distilled White Vinegar. "Vinegar is just about the most natural substance you can find. The active cleaning ingredient in vinegar is acetic acid, which can be used for a variety of acidifying and oxidizing tasks. Brown cider vinegar will do the job, but distilled white has less odor."

Baking Soda. "Sodium bicarbonate is a good deodorizer and a mild abrasive."

Bleach. "Laundry bleach is 5 percent sodium hypochlorite no matter whose name is on the label. It's an oxidizer and a natural germ killer. Chlorine bleach, as it is commonly called, is an excellent disinfectant and cleaner, and it's a powerful bacteriostatic for drinking water. Bleach plays an important role in halting the spread of contagious diseases.

"The trouble is, once chlorine enters lakes and streams, it combines with organic matter to create methane gas. The gas is then transformed into numerous cancer-causing agents called trihalomethanes. Therefore, the general rule for chlorine bleach should be: When a powerful disinfectant is crucial, use chlorine bleach—but only then."
CAUTION: *"Deadly chlorine gas results if you mix chlorine bleach with acids, such as commercial toilet cleaners, or with ammonia."*

Borax. "Borax is sodium borate. At about $3 per 5-lb. box, it's a good phosphate-free water softener and it makes an effective but mild abrasive when used dry or damp."

Cornstarch. "Starch extracted from corn is used as a thickening agent and as an extra-fine polish that imparts a sheen to glass and other surfaces."

Lemon. "The active cleaning ingredient in lemons is citric acid. Lemons acidify and oxidize, and they smell nice."

Mineral Oil. "Although a refined petroleum product, mineral oil is a low-tox, economical, and versatile lubricant that can be used in place of a great many highly toxic solvent-based products."

Salt. "Sodium chloride (common table salt) has mild antiseptic and disinfecting qualities. It also has abrasive qualities. And it's incredibly cheap."

Soap Flakes. "Natural soap is made with lye and some kind of fat or oil. Old-fashioned, natural soap is fully biodegradable into nonpoisonous substances. Detergents resemble soaps in their ability to emulsify oil and hold dirt in suspension, but they are very different chemically. Detergents are made with petroleum products and phosphate conditioners. Detergents are biodegradable, but their end products are pollutants."

Washing Soda. "'Washing soda' is hydrated sodium carbonate, an alkali similar to lye but much less powerful. It's available at most grocery stores."

ABOUT AIR FRESHENERS. "Most chemical 'air fresheners' are air contaminators and health hazards. Most contain petroleum distillates, toluene, chlorinated hydrocarbons, ketones, and a myriad of other dangerous organic solvents. A few actually deaden unwanted odors, but most are designed to deal with *you,* not the odor. Most mask natural odors by overpowering them with a stronger chemical one, or they coat your nasal passages with an oily film to impair your ability to smell, or they attack your nasal passages with nerve-deadening agents. With the last 2 methods, anyone who walks into the room can smell the odor—but you can't."

SINK, TUB, AND TOILET CLEANERS

Sink Stain Remover. "Bleach is an environmental hazard and should not be used frivolously. Chlorinated sink cleaners are frivolous. But there is a simple, natural alternative. Lemon juice is a natural oxidizer, which gives it a mild bleaching action. For stained sinks, cut open an over-the-hill lemon and wipe the sink down with lemon juice. Let it work for about 10 minutes. Then sprinkle borax or baking soda, and scour."

Shower/Tub Mildew Remover. "Avoid commercial mold and mildew preparations. Most are made with ingredients nobody needs filling the air of their home: formaldehyde, phenol, pentachlorophenol, or kerosene. For mildew, instead just dilute 2 t. white vinegar in 1 qt. warm water.

Apply with a soft cloth. Dry with squeegee, old towels, or discarded T-shirts."

Scouring Powder (Cleanser). "Bon Ami is a good and natural scouring powder, and it's available at your grocery store or supermarket. For most jobs, a special scouring powder is an unnecessary expense. Another way is to sprinkle borax or baking soda on a damp sponge, and scour. These are the main ingredients in expensive cleansers anyway. Without the petrochemical additives, natural cleansers may require slightly more elbow grease, but they do less damage to the environment and to the item being cleaned."

Toilet Bowl Cleaner. "Toilet bowl cleaners are among the most obscene inventions to date. For the sake of a shiny toilet, we flush a mixture of acids, phosphates, petrochemical fragrances, and dyes into the environment. The 'automatic' type treats the world to this poison cocktail every single time the toilet is flushed. Instead, pour a bucket of water into the toilet to lower the water level. Sprinkle a few tablespoons of baking soda around the inside of the bowl. Drizzle in enough vinegar to dampen the baking soda. Add sufficient 'elbow grease' to a toilet brush. Flush the toilet. This method will clean, shine, and deodorize your toilet bowl with minimal pollution."

DRAIN CLEANER: "Plungers and metal 'snakes' are the most environmentally friendly drain openers in the world. Use them first, second, and third." [Carla: I use the toilet stomper. Just keep doubling until it works. If 10 stomps in quick succession doesn't do it, I try 20. If not 20, 40 ought to work!] "If that doesn't work, then try mixing ½ c. vinegar and ½ c. bicarbonate (baking soda) into 2 c. boiling water and pouring it down the drain. Let it stand for 3–5 minutes and flush with hot water. Commercial drain openers are extremely caustic, which makes them corrosive to plumbing, dangerous to have around children, and toxic to the environment. They are expensive as well. If you just can't give up the monthly drain cleaner habit, this concoction will be a lot easier on the plumbing, friendlier to the environment, and less hazardous to kids because it doesn't even exist until you mix it up. And it's cheap."

OVEN CLEANER: "Everything just said about commercial drain openers is the same for commercial oven cleaners because they are only slightly different formulations using the same active ingredients. There are 2 alternative approaches to oven cleaning. The first is to keep a box of salt handy and sprinkle fresh spills generously while still hot. Salt will absorb most spills and become an ashlike powder that can be brushed away after the oven has cooled off. For periodic cleaning of build-up, preheat the oven to 200°F and turn off heat. Place 2 c. straight ammonia in a shallow (nonaluminum) pan on the middle rack. Close the oven door tight and leave overnight. The hot ammonia gas works its way into the grease film and turns it into a soaplike sludge that can be wiped off. *Remember, use plenty of ventilation when working with ammonia.* (If you put brown-stained Pyrex dishes in the oven during ammonia treatment, they will be cleaned at the same time.)"

FURNITURE POLISH: "There would be far fewer poisoned children and much less air, land, and water pollution if everyone would stop buying commercial furniture polish. Instead, melt 1 T. carnauba wax into 2 c. mineral oil and 1 t. lemon oil. Apply a light coating with a soft cloth. Wipe off excess and polish with another clean soft cloth. Discarded T-shirts are ideal for this job."

GOOD SOAPS AND LAUNDRY AIDS: "Don't be fooled by 'No Phosphates!' detergents. Most detergent manufacturers who plaster 'no phosphate' slogans on their boxes are substituting nitrioltriacetic acid (NTA), which chokes the life out of lakes and streams the same way as phosphates. Worse, nitrosamines like NTA are carcinogens even at extremely low doses. That's why few detergent companies list ingredients."

NOTE: "*Synthetic soaps (detergents) were made to wash synthetic clothes. So the first recipe for cutting down on detergent pollution is to buy only clothes made of natural fibers: cotton, wool, linen.*"

Good Laundry Soaps. "At the supermarket, you can have confidence in Simple Green, Ivory Soap, and Bon Ami products."

Multi-Purpose Soap Gel. "You can make an all-purpose soap gel. Grate a bar of pure natural soap (like Ivory) into a mixing bowl. Measure the shavings, and then pour an equal amount of boiling water over them. Let the mixture stand about 5 minutes until soap has melted. Smooth remainder with a wire whip. Soap gel can be used to refill existing bottles for dishes, hand washing, and laundry (natural fibers)."

Automatic Dishwasher Soap. "You can save a lot of money and a lot of environmental damage if you make your own dishwasher formulation. If you have 'soft' water, you might get by with straight borax. For 'hard' water, you may need to tinker with adding washing soda until you get just the right ratio. Use exactly as you would the commercial preparations."

A PARTING PERSPECTIVE. "In the name of sparkling toilets, whiter shirts, and odorless armpits, most Americans fill their homes and apartments with a veritable arsenal of biological and chemical weapons known to cause severe environmental damage and such medical problems as muscle weakness, chronic fatigue, lung and respiratory illness, liver and kidney damage, cancer, a variety of birth defects, and even mental depression, confusion, and psychosis. There's no getting around it: Sometimes a natural cleaner just does not pack the punch of its toxic counterpart. Sometimes we have to take a stand for a brighter future over a shinier Crapper; for a clean bill of health over spotless glasses; for a ring around the collar rather than a noose around our necks."

Thank you, Rodney, for the wake-up call. In Rodale's *Book of Practical Formulas: Easy-to-Make, Easy-to-Use Recipes for Hundreds of Everyday Activities and Tasks,* you'll find more than 500 nontoxic homemade alternatives to toxic products.

About Unhealthy Residues in Food

Farm workers who are exposed to toxics *both* in the workplace and in their diet are at greatest risk for pesticide-induced cancers and neurotoxin poisoning. Around the world, uneducated, unwarned agricultural workers are getting sick and dying of those exposures. But all who eat those foods are at long-term risk too. Mercury, radioactive particles, PCBs, carcinogens, and nerve poisons ("neurotoxins"—cumulative poisons that cause reduced mental ability) are all possible ingredients in your food.

Agricultural poisons include "pesticides" that kill insects, "herbicides" that kill weeds, fungicides that kill molds, and rodenticides that kill rats and mice. Agent Orange, for example, was a neurotoxic herbicide. These days, starting at our mother's breast, we begin to accumulate poisons and continue all our life.

Lane Morgan, who's from northeast Washington, says, "They grow a lot of cole crops in the Skagit Valley, and they use Diazinon for the rootfly maggot and Malathion for the caterpillars. Plus the seed would be treated with Captan (maybe that's been banned recently—I know strawberry growers are mad because they aren't supposed to use it any more). Hard to believe that stuff wouldn't turn up in the harvested rutabagas and cauliflowers. The general point is that we should assume our bought food has residues and protect ourselves accordingly."

As with Captan, the list of allowed chemicals in the United States constantly evolves. There also is typically a long time period between concern about a pesticide and its actual banning. And many chemicals that used to be widely used in the United States, such as DDT, are no longer legal here, but they can be and are still used overseas—and they can legally enter the United States on the huge amounts of imported food that our supermarkets carry, often without identifying the country of origin. Children are at greatest risk from residues. They eat more fruit than do adults, and fruit is the most heavily contaminated kind of food. Their neurological systems are still developing and thus are at special risk for damage by neurotoxins. So when you have to eat grocery-store rather than home-grown foods, look for organically grown food.

When you can't grow your own or buy organic, here's your next line of self-defense.

TIPS TO MINIMIZE EATING POISONOUS RESIDUES

1. When eating meat or fish, discard the fat.
2. Don't eat organ meats: liver, brains, sweetbreads, kidneys, heart, or gizzard. The poisons tend to concentrate in organs.
3. Avoid smoked foods and cured meats such as bacon and ham. They contain potentially carcinogenic nitrates and nitrites as well as the usual run of contaminants.
4. Meat from young animals is less likely to be contaminated than meat from older ones. Contamination is a lifelong accumulation.
5. About food from water: Choose fish over shellfish, ocean fish over river or lake fish, deep-ocean fish over shore- or bottom-feeding fish. In the case of meat-eating predator fish, choose small fish over large fish (the more they eat, the more they grow and the more food-chain poisons have accumulated in their bodies). Fish-farm fish are normally raised in water that doesn't contain PCBs, mercury, or other chemicals, so they're the best of all from that point of view; however, they are typically fed small doses of antibiotics every day.
6. When eating dairy products, eat products that are skim or as nearly skim as possible. The best dairy foods are skim milk, nonfat yogurt, and nonfat cottage cheese.
7. But use butter rather than margarine! You *need* some fat in your diet to be healthy—for your brain to do its best. Margarine is much worse for you than butter!
8. Choose fruits and vegetables that can be peeled. Wash them with unscented dish soap and rinse well. Then peel before eating. Forget everything you've heard about vitamins from eating peelings. A baked potato with peel has an average 30 percent more pesticide residue than a peeled, boiled one. It's even worse with waxed fruits and vegetables. The wax that is applied to them typically contains fungicides (another poison). In addition, the wax layer seals in the previous layers of pesticides; if waxed, you can't wash anything off. But you can still peel some residues away.
9. Peeling doesn't guarantee that there are no residues. Cooked foods are always safer from the residue point of view, although cooking destroys vitamins. The "systemic" kinds of poisons get into the flesh of the fruit or vegetable rather than just lodging on the peel. Cooking detoxifies some—but not all—of them.
10. Concentrated fruit products have concentrated residues. Raisins, prunes, jams, jellies, fruit juices, and wine are all more likely to have residues than single fruits, because they're made of concentrations of fruit.
11. Sweeteners are low-residue foods. This really turns the long-standing wisdom on its ear. For some reason or other, honey, corn syrup, maple syrup, and molasses—and yes, white sugar too—are all exceptionally low-residue foods and therefore are good from this point of view! Chocolate, however, is sometimes contaminated.

A beautiful final word to the heartbreaking subject of pollution comes from Maggie: "Dear Carla, What you wrote on how the land is your spiritual responsibility is the truest statement I've ever read. I have friends who are Christians, and when I talk about farming and caring for the earth—recycling, composting, using no insecticide—they think I'm nuts. They always say, 'The Lord is coming back, so it does not matter. We can never save the earth.' But at least I take care of my bit of the earth as God leads, and it's wonderful."

ORGANIC FARMERS: It's harder to risk the survival of a commercial farm by switching to organic practices. But it's coming! By 1987, about 100,000 of the nation's 2.1 million farmers had made the switch, and more were considering it. There's a growing market for organic food, and you can save money by not buying chemicals.

WATER

Water falls out of the sky as rain and collects and runs across the top of the ground in streams and rivers, soaks deep into the earth and lies there, or gently flows in the form of "ground water." Ground water can be lying there in sheets all over underground, or it can be located only in "veins," underground streams. A spring is a natural appearance of that ground water, sheet or vein, flowing out of a hole in the ground. When you drill down to the water-saturated level and pump water up for your use, you have a well. A large-scale drainage basin or series of linked basins is a "watershed." Water constantly evaporates from oceans —but also from rivers, soil, and plants. When enough water gets up into the air, it comes down again as rain.

WELL-READ: *Waterhole* by Bob Mellin tells how to dig your own well with hand tools, step by step from planning to well casing and installing a pump. Good bibliography of sources. *Wells and Septic Systems* by Max and Charlotte Alth (latest edition revised by Duncan) deals with wells and septic systems too. Very thorough. *The Drinking Water Book* by Colin Ingram covers pollutants, testing, water types, water purifiers, and distillers, including sources. *The Water Heater Workbook* by Larry and Suzanne Weingarten tells all about water heaters. All these books are available from Eureka Resource, PO Box 2356, Martinez, CA 94553.

Being Frugal with Water

Water is everything to an agricultural project, be it plant or animal. A field situated in a subirrigated stream bottom can carry 4 times as many animals—or more—as desert land. You have to have some water: to drink, to wash your face, to water your animals and your plants. But most of us don't need nearly as much as we've gotten used to thinking we do, although pasture and hay sure will do more with water on it: An unirrigated hayfield around here will produce 2 cuttings a year; with irrigation, lots of dry, hot weather, and diligence you could get 5 cuttings . . . and that's in northern Idaho. But household water use is something else.

Last year it got so cold here it actually froze 3 feet down and froze our water line, which runs 800 feet uphill from a spring in the canyon bottom. The water stayed frozen from then (December 1) until spring, and I did everything water-related using buckets of water hauled by my precious husband from the stock tanks, or from 50-gal. drums that I hauled from town after the stock-tank water was used up. That really gives a person some new angles on water.

We are all accustomed to wasting water. If you're skeptical, uncouple the trap under your bathroom sink and replace it with a bucket. That way you have to empty all the water that flows through your sink by hand into your tub or toilet. You'll quickly see what I mean. If that doesn't convince you, do the same thing under your kitchen sink! Somebody researched the question and discovered that when water has to be carried from a well, people use an average of 8 gal. a day. If you give them a pump attached to their kitchen sink, they'll use more—up to 10 gal. per person per day. If you give them running hot water in the kitchen, they'll use 20 gal. a day. And if you put in a complete pressurized plumbing system, they'll use 30 gal. a day.

Did you know that you use 8–20 gallons of water every time you take a bath in a bathtub, 3 to 5 more every time you flush a toilet, and 1 or 2 every time you use the bathroom

sink? In my travels, I've been amazed that it seems as if the dryer the area, the more water the local citizens use. In dry southern California, where they bring their water in from far away, water seems abundant in a way that amazes me.

At our home, all our water is pumped up a hill from a tiny spring, and then it flows into the house by an unpressurized gravity system from a cistern up the hill. So when I encounter pressurized plumbing, all that pressure startles me and seems wasteful. I'm not prepared for all the water that comes shooting out of the faucet. Running hot water is such a luxury. I used to live without it, and when I had it again, I counted it as one of the grandest things in life. One thing about our water system—if we use too much, we'll run out of that precious resource too. So we've learned to be careful, especially in summer when the flow is lowest and we need it most for irrigating the garden.

COMPOST TOILETS: In addition to the outhouse, now there is a "biological toilet." It's a self-contained system that requires no water, chemicals, or septic tank. It's easy to install and is available from various manufacturers.

BioLet USA sells a waterless, composting toilet: 800-524-6538; fax 740-498-4073; PO Box 548, Newcomerstown, OH 43832; **info@biolet.com; www.biolet.com.**

Envirolet waterless and low-water toilet system is manufactured and sold by Sancor: U.S. 800-387-5126, Canada 800-387-5245; fax 416-299-3124; 140-30 Milner Ave., Toronto, ON M1S 3R3, CANADA; **info@envirolet.com; www.envirolet.com.**

Porta-Loo, a bucket toilet, is available from Christian Family Resources: PO Box 195, Kit Carson, CO 80825; 719-962-3228.

Sun-Mar offers a $1,000 composting toilet; 905-332-1314; fax 905-332-1315; 5035 N. Service Rd., Burlington, ON L7L 5V2, CANADA; **compost@sun-mar.com; www.sun-mar.com.**

GRAYWATER RECYCLING: A reader who lives on a desert island in the South Caribbean wrote me, "My dad has set up an underground hose network running from our septic tanks to various parts of the garden, both front and back." That's an idea whose time is coming for many folks.

Create an Oasis with Greywater: Your Complete Guide to Managing Greywater in the Landscape, by Art Ludwig, is the best book on this subject. It tells how to design and build a graywater system to recycle the house's wastewater for landscape and garden uses. *The Builder's Greywater Guide* tells how to deal with codes and inspectors when installing such a system. Order from Oasis Design, 5 San Marcos Trout Club, Santa Barbara, CA 93105-9726; **www.oasis design.net.**

Your Water Source

PURITY: It used to be that any mountain stream in the Northwest was guaranteed pure water. Now it's likely contaminated with *Giardia*, a nasty little parasite. Nowadays the purest water around is what comes from your home distiller, if you have one. Water from underground should be good, unless it's contaminated with agricultural chemicals.

Short of distilling, rainwater is the purest water you can get, but even that's not as dependably pure as it used to be. These days it may have acid in it. Or it (as well as the air you breathe) may be contaminated if you live downwind from a toxic-waste incineration plant or any other source of air pollution, such as a city or an industry. Your rainwater may contain radioactivity if somebody's nuclear power plant or weapon test blew up upwind, since rain brings radioactive particles, like all airborne particles, down to earth at a greatly increased rate. Otherwise, rainwater's great stuff.

You can order a distiller from Ralph at Health Mart, 1507 SW 21st St., Topeka, KS 66604. For a solar still, go to **www.purwater.com**. The best, most affordable ready-made filter unit is the Basic Necessity filter: 4 filters, using 5-gal. buckets for intake and collection of purified water. If you like stainless steel, the British Berkfeld Water Filter is $259 for a 3-candle filter; $279 for a 5-candle filter, the "Big Berkie." This is a good system in price, effectiveness, and the fact that you can clean a clogged filter and reuse it. Look for dealers on the Internet. Katadyn sells another good line of filters. A wide selection is available from Wisemen: **www.wisementrading.com**.

RAINWATER: It used to be that almost every home where ground water was scarce had eave troughs to catch rainwater and direct it into cisterns. Few people collect rainwater now, although it's still a worthwhile water source. To systematically collect it, equip all your buildings with good metal gutters set up to drain into prepared containers. If the rainwater is dirty, strain it through several thicknesses of cloth. Keep a separate cistern for this rainwater, which you can collect whenever feasible and use for washing—even for drinking and cooking if you're careful about cleanliness and the types of metal you use. I once met a family on a tight budget who bought a spent gravel pit for their "homestead." It had no soil or water source at all. Undeterred, the husband brought in enough soil to eventually create a wonderful garden and pasture! He also installed a sophisticated rainwater collection system on the rooftops of all his buildings, and he built an absolutely *huge* underground storage container for that water. They could make it through dry seasons on their stored rainwater and irrigate the land as well!

DOWSING TO FIND WATER: If you try the old-fashioned method called "dowsing," the results may surprise you. It really does work, if you've got the talent. I've tried it with a bunch of people, and about half of them had the gift. It seems to run in families, though. If both parents have it, all their kids usually will too. Over on the School of Country Living property, we dowsed all over the place and located an iron pipe, which somebody else had placed in there, that actually runs a continual stream of good water. It was a literal godsend since it was just where we needed irrigation water for our garden. We traced it underground by dowsing way up the hill and finally came to a point where the pipe stuck out of the ground in midair, dry as a bone. It's a mystery I'm not going to take a chance of messing up by trying to understand further—there is the pipe, dry at one end and water coming out the other. Maybe there's a crack in the middle and underground water enters.

If you start asking around, you will probably hear of somebody who can come and dowse your place. Or write the American Society of Dowsers, PO Box 24, Danville, VT 05828-0024. Ask them for "contact" people in your area. They have a national membership book listing both individuals and dowser organizations around the country. Or check out the literature on dowsing.

Your dowser will find you a good place to dig for a well. Or you can try it yourself. Some people can and some

can't, and nobody knows why or why not. Mike can, and I've never tried. He's better at climbing up and down mountains and around in the brush than me, anyway. He uses an unwound coat hanger. He's a one-man water department, clambering down the mountain to see what has gone wrong every time I turn the faucet and no water comes out. The trouble with selfsufficiency is that you also have to be able to be self-sufficient for upkeep and repair, and there tends to be a lot of it with any system.

If you want to try dowsing for yourself, unwind 2 metal coat hangers to make straight wires out of them. Take the end of one in each hand and hold them somewhat loosely pointed straight out in front of you, parallel to each other. Walk around. If they want to cross and make an X, you have dowsed yourself some water flowing underground. Of course, I know people whose rods swing out instead of in. Anyway, they'll do something.

Metal rods seem to work better than the traditional forked twig. Some people hold it from shoulder level, others at waist level. To start, walk very slowly over a known vein of water or buried water pipe. Talk to yourself and to the rod while you're doing it—not because the rod understands but because it will help you concentrate. If you are experimenting with pipes bringing water to your house, it helps to have water running in the pipe. A forked twig, unlike wires (which turn either in or out), will pull down. Mark the spot on the ground where you got the reaction. You may think you'll remember the spot, but sometimes it's hard to find again. Now walk back toward the spot from another direction and mark where you get the reaction again. Working like this at the School property, we discovered a round-shaped wet area that would be the perfect spot to dig a well . . . or maybe there was once a well there that has been covered on top. Right now we don't need a well, so it doesn't matter, because we found 13 springs on the School grounds.

A SPRING: This is a place where water literally comes out of the ground. It is a real blessing. If you've got a spring, you can improve it by digging it out so the water doesn't just seep up in a mudhole. You can get it tiled around where the water comes out, and/or sink a pipe in there to catch the water and bring it to a stock watering tank or down to your house (put the buildings downhill from the spring and you'll have a perfect water system set up).

Bury your pipe over 3 feet deep, or whatever the neighbors tell you the frost line is in that area, so it won't freeze in winter. For summer usage only, bring it down in a cheap plastic pipe. Springs can be very deceiving. For one thing, they tend to be seasonal. They may run wonderfully in the rainy season and dry up completely in the dry times, when you need them most. They may be good in a cycle of good years and dry up in a cycle of dry years. They have a tendency to move and come out someplace else, where you may or may not be able to rediscover them. Generally, the bigger the water flow, the safer you are. You can measure the flow by taking a bucket of known quantity and a watch to the spring and counting how many gallons you get in a minute. You're safest with a flow that will equal 100–150 gal. per day.

A WELL: If you don't have a spring on your place, you can consider drilling a well. Nowadays it's pretty near a given that you'll hook up electricity before you even start drilling the well, and that the hookup has to have a permit and be state-inspected. But in the old days they just dug a hole and then brought water up using either a bucket or a cranked pump. It had a lever you moved up and down to bring up the water. But an electrically powered system is by far the most convenient.

First you must find a competent drilling contractor—unless you want to try digging the well by hand. Chances are that hand digging won't work. To find a drilling contractor, use the Yellow Pages and newspaper ads. Inquire into the money side of it in advance. Try to find somebody a neighbor will recommend. In general, though, I must say that in all too many places, ground-water pumping is in trouble—because of ever-worsening pollution and because water tables almost everywhere are steadily falling. As a result, people have to dig ever deeper to get well water. And there's always the risk of a well going dry, forcing you to dig a deeper one.

The deeper a well is drilled, the more expensive the drilling. And the deeper a well is, the higher the daily cost of pumping water out of it. Where water is abundant, wells can be used to supply both house water and irrigation water, but where water tables are falling, irrigation from wells tends to become too expensive or too big a drain on the water supply. Usually the higher the elevation, the deeper you have to go for water. Last I heard [1992], in northern Idaho a drilled and cased well cost $21 per foot, and the average drilling depth needed to hit water was 75 feet. If you use a hydraulic ram pump, you can pump water for free.

Lane Morgan says, "One problem with an electric well is that when the power goes out, the water is gone too. That's a bummer in itself, and it also means you can't keep a trickle going to keep the pipes from freezing and breaking. (Same problem with a nonelectric furnace that has an electric motor.) So if you live in a winter storm zone and you have plumbing, *be sure* you have a system to drain your pipes. We didn't used to, but we sure do now. And if the storm is likely to leave you housebound, *be sure* you have emergency water stored somewhere."

You can get water out of a well without using electricity by taking the top off and letting down a long, narrow, round container on the end of a rope. Mark Barnett makes the Living Water well bucket at his home at 608 Lockhart Rd., Hartselle, AL 35640, 256-751-4318. It costs $47, is made of PVC plastic with stainless steel hardware, holds 1½ gal., and fits down a 4- or 6-in. diameter well casing (specify which when you order). Or get a 5-qt. PVC well bucket for $35, custom-built for any size casing, from my friend, Claire Grimes: 205-669-7466; 255 Powers Rd., Wilsonville, AL 35186.

EMERGENCY HAND PUMPS: The Stalwart emergency hand pump is brass with stainless steel on top. It is the most slender hand pump on the market (widest part is 1³/₈ in., yet it pumps up to 5 gal./min.) and it will slip down through the pump seal inside the casing beside your existing submersible. Any time the power goes off, use the hand pump to draw water. Works down to 170 ft. deep. Cost is $425 plus pipe ($18/5 ft). Contact inventor/builder Paul Miller: 620-623-4081; Rt. 1, Box 88, Hanston, KS 67849.

Another hand pump designed to be a built-in option to your electric water pump can be custom made for you by John Medicraft, 21255-370th Ave., Roseau, MN 56751. Simple Pump Co. also makes a back-up hand pump that goes down your well casing, plus a 12-volt gear motor attachment (battery or solar); 1603 Esmerelda Ave., Minden, NV 89423; 877-782-0109; **keith@simplepump.com; www.simplepump.com.** Baker Mfg. makes an old-fashioned, long-handled, cast-iron well pump: 800-356-5130; 133 Enterprise St., Evansville, WI 53556; **Monitor@baker-mfg.com; www.bakermfg.com.** Rintoul's Hand Pumps sells a variety of hand-operated water pumps. Some are designed for drinking water; others can be used as back-up sump pumps. Harvey Rintoul wrote, "Make sure that hand pump installations meet local health requirements for keeping contaminants out of well water. Or use a licensed pump installer. Test all water before drinking it." 519-596-2612, RR #2, Tobermory, ON N0H 2R0, CANADA; **hrintoul@handpumps.com; www.handpumps.com.** Lehman's Hardware also offers hand pumps: 888-438-5346; 330-857-5757; **www.Lehmans.com.**

Moving Water

HAULING WATER: I remember living in a house that didn't have "running water"; it didn't have water at all except that carried there in a bucket. We used an outhouse for our toilet. I hauled water up a hill from the creek in a bucket and poured that water into a tank on the back porch. For hot water, we heated water on the stove until we got a stove that had a tank built right onto one side of it where the water heated more or less automatically, as long as you had a fire in the stove. We took baths in a round tub in the middle of the kitchen floor. Depending on how scarce water was, we might all use the same water or each have our own. The Fuller Brush salesman offered a bucket that had an attached hose with a body brush on the end of it. That allowed us to take showers in the washtub!

Years later, as a young woman, I lived for a while in Wyoming in a tiny community where every person trucked in their water in big tanks from 30 miles away or so—every drop of it. Then I moved to a tent on the bank of the Wind River outside Thermopolis, Wyoming. There I had a whole river full of running water right outside my front door, but none in a faucet. (If it had stayed summer forever, I might never have left.)

Nowadays, people who have to haul their water usually do so in 15gal. food-quality plastic barrels.

PLUMBING: If you have "plumbing," you have an automatic system for bringing water to your house in a pipe and making it come out a faucet. Plumbing is a recent invention. The introduction of plumbing—along with electricity, all the electric appliances, and the telephone—easily convinced old-time homemakers that modern times were an absolute blessing.

DRAINAGE: You can have too much water as easily as too little. Waterlogged soil suffocates plant roots, increases the chance of disease, and drains heat from the soil. If your land has poor drainage, you can dig a ditch, lay drain tiles just below the surface, or use "leaky" pipe made from recycled tires. That will channel water away from your garden. Another way to cope is to build raised beds, which make your garden soil drain better and help keep plant roots above the water table.

IRRIGATION SYSTEMS: Old-time watering means a watering can for small jobs as well as some irrigation system: water running downhill, directed into ditches that either temporarily flood or run near your plants. I remember helping my dad irrigate that way—hard work in the hot sun. But most watering systems nowadays are more easily managed.

Here we have heavy spring rains from February to June. Then it suddenly turns hot, and there may not be another significant rainfall until the fall rains come. All the early crops like carrots, green onions, and peas do fine, but any crop that matures later than June has to be watered.

Irrigation Supplies. Any good gardening-supply store or catalog has a whole section of equipment to help you water your garden. You can get a system that will water house plants while you're away, traditional watering cans like the one Peter Rabbit encountered, all sorts of watering hoses (including soaker types), and a variety of sprinkler systems. (Mellinger's has an excellent offering.) You can use seasonal above-ground watering systems or permanent, automatic, below-ground systems. For vegetable gardening, above-ground watering is most suitable. A canvas soaker hose works well. You can buy inexpensive, nonelectric timers that shut the water off automatically, or electric timers that turn water on or off at preset times. Modern technology makes possible automatic watering, with the time of day, where, and how much to water all managed by computer. For a long-term orchard, below-ground watering may be preferable. Drip is more water frugal than sprinkler. Dripworks is a specialist: 180 Sanhedrin Circle, Willits, CA 95490-8753; 800-522-3747; fax 707-459-9645; **dripworks@pacific.net; www.dripworksusa.com.** They offer mail-order systems and design service. Free catalog.

Bucket. Another way to water is to carry the water in buckets and dump it on the plant. Don't laugh. I know a lady who has a magnificent orchard and garden, and that's how she has always done it. A watering can is more sightly but operates on the same principle.

Inverted Bottle. To water a tree or some such while you're gone for several days, get a jar, bottle, or jug that has a small neck opening, and fill it with water. Stick it into the ground upside down next to the plant. The water will gradually soak into the ground.

Drip Hose. This irrigation system is the best if you live in a water-shortage area. It uses a special hose that has small holes that let water drip out. It's good for desert areas. Small plastic tube "emitters" about ⅛ inch in diameter are in-

serted into a larger tube and spaced so the bed of plants is watered evenly. Water is applied slowly to the plants to completely saturate the root zone. Watering by this sort of trickle is most effective for the plants, and you lose less by evaporation than with spray systems. A porous hose or pipe with holes in it that lets out a slow steady flow of water is a "trickle" system.

Soaker Hose. We've never been blessed with enough water pressure to make a trickle system work, however, so we use a soaker hose. It's a long hose with tiny holes along one side and the end capped so water is forced to spray up and out through the holes. It sprays up 3 to 5 feet through the holes (depending on your water pressure) and has a gentle soaking action that is good for young, tender plants and older ones too. We hook up two of them, one behind the other, to cover more territory. The whole thing is on the end of about 200 feet of hose, so I can take the water wherever I want it in our big garden. If you try to make the water run uphill, you lose water pressure correspondingly.

Rainbird Sprinkler. If you have good water pressure, you can use a rainbird sprinkler—that's a contraption that fits on the end of the hose and jerks back and forth, spraying water over quite a large circle as it goes. It is adjustable to water in a full circle, half circle or quarter circle. You can set it up wherever you want it. Just pound the sharp pointed metal stake side into the ground wherever you want it to sprinkle.

Ditch Irrigation. You can bring a heavy flow of water into your garden through ditches. You then flood the garden with it, if you have lots, or else run it down little ditches alongside each row of plants. Old-time ditch irrigation for field crops waters a portion at a time using a system of ditches and dams. The ditches are just plain old "V"s gouged in the dirt by a ditcher machine, and they carry the water where you want it to go. At the place where you want the water to stop and pour out of the ditch, you plug the ditch with a dam of mud scooped up in your shovel from the ground beside. You have to spend all day out there either leaning on the shovel or digging with it to keep the water moving and achieve the fine distinction between leaving the ground too dry and washing out the crop.

My father used to irrigate this way. I recommend an irrigating costume of shorts, hip waders, and straw hat. The exact placement of the ditches is a fine art. The water has to flow downhill, of course, but you want it to flow slowly, so it won't wash out your dams, which means contouring the ditches appropriately to the slope of your land. Then they should be a reasonable distance from each other, say 15 to 20 feet for a hayfield. Every field is different, and the first summer's experience will correct all your original estimates.

You need a top ditch to feed from your water source down to the field. This ditch has to divert the water from somewhere higher than the field so that gravity makes it flow down to the field. That ditch feeds into one along the top side of your field from which all the contour ditches branch off. You dam the top ditch wherever you want the water to flow into a contour ditch, and cut out the side of the top ditch to let the water flow out of it. Start with the lower end and work your way back because you are weakening your ditch sides doing this. The top ditch is several feet deep. The contour ditches are less deep—6–12 inches —to facilitate overflow.

But where will your irrigation water come from? Your well? Spring? The community irrigation ditch? You have to apply and pay annually for your water use. You are allowed only as many cubic feet of water as you pay for, calculated by the inches of water and the time it flows. You want to pump water from your nearby river or lake? That is also not necessarily okay. River and lake water is often polluted. And you have to get permission from your state government before using it.

I've never known farmers to fight more bitterly about anything than they do about water. I've personally known cases of near murder happen along ditch lines, when a man down the line wasn't getting the water he was paying for and walked up the line to discover somebody else was diverting it onto his own ground.

Pipes. Another way to carry water on a large scale—for hay or truck gardening—is with a system of irrigation pipes. But these are expensive. They can be either permanently installed or movable. You can buy movable irrigation pipe that isn't unreasonably heavy or pipe that comes with built-in wheels. You buy heavy-duty sprinklers to go with it and a big pump to draw your water. This assumes you have a river, big pond, or artesian well in your field to draw from.

SECRETS OF PLANT WATERING

1. Plants can absorb food from the soil only if it is in solution. So in effect, plants must have damp feet in order to eat.
2. A desert is usually rich farmland that happens to be lacking water. If you add water by irrigation, those arid lands will bloom. Only land whose topsoil has eroded or that has poisonous minerals in the topsoil is true desert. Water supply and temperature are the 2 great determinants of what plants can be grown where.
3. The best time to water is in the morning. Plants do most of their growing during the day and need the water for photosynthesis. Watering in the morning also allows plants to dry out by evening, which reduces the chance of mildew and rot.
4. Mulching helps to keep soil moist as well as to suppress weeds. (But wait until the ground gets thoroughly warm before putting on mulch.)
5. Plant species differ a lot in water requirements. Vegetables need a lot of water. Most vegetables are about 85 to 90 percent water. Flowers, trees, and bushes can all survive longer without water than vegetables.
6. Erosion happens when wind or water moves soil. If you garden or farm on sloping land, you risk erosion. Grass planted in strips across slopes, summer mulches, and winter cover crops help prevent erosion. Strategically placed diversion ditches also help.
7. Watering must be faithful. If stunted by water shortage, many vegetables never grow normally again.
8. Watering needs to be generous. Almost all vegetables produce much more with abundant water than with a skimpy supply. For a minimum, your garden needs about an inch of water a week, from either the sky or your irrigation system.
9. Surface runoff, puddling, and evaporation are all wastes of water.
10. For newly planted seeds, water often enough to keep the soil continually moist—morning and evening, sprinkling every day until they are up. You want them to come up as fast as possible. The moist ground also helps discourage wild birds and the family poultry from digging up the seeds and eating them.
11. Once your plants are well started, give them a good soaking rather than morning and evening sprinkles. Light sprinkles encourage shallow root systems because unless the soil gets wet to the level of the deeper roots, the shallow roots develop at the expense of the deeper ones. But those shallow roots can't do as good a job of finding soil nutrients. Because the surface of the soil dries out faster than the deeper soil, shallow watering also creates a vicious cycle in which more frequent watering is needed to keep the plants from wilting. Deep soakings, on the other hand, encourage deep root systems, and deep roots don't have to be watered as often.
12. For that "deep" watering, you want to water until the soil is wet to a depth of 4 to 6 inches. How long that takes depends on how fast your irrigation system delivers water and how fast your soil type absorbs it. When the soil gets dry, water again, to a depth of about 4 inches.

SOIL
Soil Texture, Layers, Depth

The rest of this book is about how to grow your own food, every kind of it, every step of the way, and in such a way that it won't contain residues! Growing naturally disease- and pest-resistant plants starts with helping your soil be as alive and healthy as possible.

"Soil" is a mixture of mineral particles of various sizes, an amount of organic material (at some stage of decay), water, and air.

NONLIVING PARTS OF SOIL: It's helpful to be able to answer 5 basic questions about your garden soil:

1. Is it sand, silt, clay, or loam?
2. What are its layers?
3. How deep is it?
4. What's its pH?
5. What are the nutrient levels?

If you don't know the answers, you can still have a great garden by adding lots and lots of organic fertilizer. But you can garden more knowledgeably and confidently if you know those answers.

PARTICLE SIZE: Soils are defined according to how large or small their particles are. Particles can range from big rock chunks, such as in a gravel pit, down to clay soils at the other extreme. You can do an easy test to find out your soil type by just picking up and rubbing some of your garden dirt between your fingers. Notice whether it feels gritty, silky, sticky, or otherwise. A gritty-feeling soil is sandy. You can see the individual sand particles in sandy soil. A silky-feeling soil is "silt." You can see the individual particles under a microscope. A sticky feeling soil is a clay type. Those particles are so small it takes an electron microscope to see them. Dirt that isn't gritty or sticky is "loam," the "otherwise." There are other soil types too, such as peat and chalk soils. Most soils are actually a mixture of the types, though, rather than a pure one.

Sandy vs. Clay. Soils that are toward the sandy end of the spectrum have many spaces containing air and are easy to cultivate, drain well, and warm up quickly in the spring. They can be quickly cultivated in preparation for planting and soon reach good germination temperatures. The problems with sandy soils are that they drain too quickly and don't hold moisture, so they have to be watered more often, and that easy drainage causes nutrients to leach out. Soils toward the clay extreme contain few air spaces and tend to pack together tightly. Clay soils are hard to till, especially when damp. They hold moisture fairly well and drain slowly, but they can hold too much water, become soggy, and make plants so waterlogged that they die. On the other hand, clay soils hold their fertility; it doesn't wash away from them as it does from sandy soils.

Loam. The basic way to improve whatever kind of soil you have is always the same—add organic matter. If you add enough organic matter over a few years, you'll have a nice loam, the best soil. "Loam" means a soil that is neither very clayey nor very sandy. It's sort of inbetween and has lots of organic material in it. A good rule of thumb is that if you are looking at a deep soil (2 or 3 feet) that has a real good crop of something—even grass or weeds—and if it's dry on top within a couple days after a rain, that's what you want. The dryness means the soil drains enough to dry out, so it isn't a swamp (which you couldn't till), and yet it holds nutrients. The luxuriant weed patch or grass growing there proves that it has abundant nutrients.

SOIL LAYERS: Here's where you consider the answer to the second question, what the soil layers in your garden are.

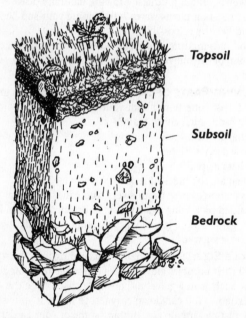

Topsoil

Subsoil

Bedrock

Topsoil. The top 6 inches are the most important part of your garden soil. That's where about 75 percent of the microscopic organisms live. That's where earthworms crawl about and do their beneficial thing. That's the layer that you usually add fertilizers to and mulch over.

Subsoil. However, the lower layers are important too. Tomato roots can go as far as 6 feet down. Many plants grow roots down 4 or 5 feet. Most go down beyond the 6-inch line. To help keep those lower layers loose, cut off plants to be harvested and leave their roots in the ground. As they grow, the roots will open small passageways for air and water, which future crops will benefit from. If you let them decompose in the ground, those openings will better remain. Abundant earthworms also help break up and fertilize this layer; they can even gradually penetrate hardpan.

Hardpan. This is the compacted, often clayey bottom layer of soil, sometimes called bedrock. Essentially, it isn't broken up much and there isn't much life in it. Nevertheless, some

powerful roots do penetrate down here, some earthworms come, and water trickles through where it can.

SOIL DEPTH: Logically, the next thing to think about is how deep each layer of your soil is. To find out, take your spade and dig a hole about a foot square at several different places on your land or in your potential garden—or at each end of your garden if you already have one. You'll see a distinct color change as the layer of topsoil gives way to the subsoil. The subsoil is lighter. You'll know when you've come to the hardpan because it's so hard. Your "soil depth" is the distance between ground surface and the hardpan.

Soil Composition

To produce soil that yields the best garden, pasture, or field crop, start with a soil test and add what you're lacking. Dirt in any particular area is probably low in some elements and high in others. In some places it is so low in a particular substance that animals that eat feed grown on that ground are malnourished. If your animals have a mysterious health problem, this is one possible cause. Your vet or county extension agent probably already knows about the local soil deficiency and can advise you.

GROUND UNDER TIMBER: This soil presents special problems. Falling pine needles make the ground under pine trees very acidic, and you can't garden there unless that is corrected. The presence of the trees means not enough sunlight is going to come through to grow anything very well. And your plants will have heavy competition for water and nutrients, because the trees are plants too—big, strong ones. So you'll have to clear a place for the garden, and clearing timber isn't easy. Then you'll have to haul in a bunch of stuff to neutralize the soil—or wait a long time.

SOIL TESTING: You can buy a soil testing kit from any mail-order gardening supplier or possibly from your local garden store. A "soil tester" tells you when to fertilize. It gives an accurate 10-second test measuring the combined amount of nitrogen, phosphorus, and potash in your soil. Or you can send out your soil to be tested (ask your extension agent where).

Preparing a Soil Sample for Testing

1. Fall is the best time of year to test. If you're having a professional analysis done, you avoid the spring rush. If you're doing it on your own, you can plan your garden accordingly for fall and spring fertilizing.
2. Dig a 6-inch-deep hole with a trowel at 4 different spots in your garden, each at some distance from the other. But don't take soil from any place that legumes, such as beans or peas, were growing in the past year's garden.
3. Take a scoop of soil from the 6-inch level of each hole.
4. Mix those scoops well in a container.
5. Take out about 1½ c. of your mixed soil, spread it out, and dry at room temperature. (Drying at high heat will make the test give a false result, saying you need lime.)

Testing for pH. "pH" means the acidity or alkalinity of your soil. It's a matter of life or death in canning. When gardening, it's useful to know your soil's pH because some plants are picky about the pH they'll do best in. The pH scale runs from 1 to 14; a pH of 7 is right in the middle and means a neutral soil, neither alkaline nor acid. Numbers bigger than 7 mean alkalinity. Numbers smaller than 7 mean acidity. Most veggies do well in about the 6 to 6.5

range. For about $20 you can buy an "acid/alkaline soil tester" or "pH computer" that can accurately determine your soil's pH in 1 minute.

SOIL NUTRIENTS: A reader asked me, "Is there a certain type of soil necessary for growing produce as opposed to field crops?" The answer is that you need good soil for both field crops or produce. Some types of produce do best in clay, some in sand. Nevertheless, you can grow almost any plant in almost any soil if you have enriched it with enough manure and other organic material and pour on enough water in the growing season. And the richer your soil is, the more plants you can grow in it and the bigger harvest they'll give—up to a point, anyway. Manure adds humus to sandy soils, which otherwise have the problem of draining too fast. Manure changes them so they can hold water (and nutrients) longer. Manure loosens up a clayey soil, whose big problem is that it won't drain well enough, and thus makes it possible for crops, especially root crops, to do better in clay. Good soil can come from manure, sawdust, straw, or household table scraps—anything that was once alive.

Plants can make food from sunshine in their green leaves and stems. They can also make it from nutrients in the soil. In fact, in order to thrive and give good harvests, most plants need plenty of both sunshine and fertile soil. Wherever plants grow, they are taking these materials from the ground. But some plants by their nature take more from the ground than others. Those kinds of plants are called "heavy feeders." For a heavy-feeder crop that needs rich, fertile soil, prepare by spreading manure or some other organic material onto the field and then tilling it in, or grow a legume or green manure crop and till that in, or spread manure or compost—or all of the above.

Legumes. Legumes actually give back more nutrients to the soil than they take. For more info, see the introduction to legumes in Chapter 4.

Fertilizers. You have to keep adding fertilizers to your garden, orchard, pastures, and fields if you want the very best production from them. (Animals pasturing in a field take care of that naturally.) You replenish every year to take the place of what you took away in the form of harvest. Under natural circumstances, the fruits spill onto the ground and rot, and the upper part or the entire plant collapses and dies on the ground when the cold weather comes, with rotting fruit and plants gradually turning into fertilizing material that will feed future plant generations.

But when you garden, and thus carry away a harvest, every year your soil gets poorer and poorer—unless you fertilize every year to replace what you have carried away. If you don't fertilize, every year your garden plants get weaker and spindlier and your harvest gets smaller. In earlier times, people who didn't know any better used to cut down trees, farm the land until the stored-up organic material was used up and they couldn't get a decent crop any more, and then cut more trees to start a new farm. That kind of growing is always a tragedy because the exhausted land, without a forest to build it back up again and protect the soil with a perpetual leaf mulch, is very likely to lose its topsoil to erosion. Then a forest will have a hard time growing there in the future.

So don't think of soil as something constant, unchanging, and unchangeable. That just isn't so. Any soil, especially garden soil, is in a process of constant change, with organic material being taken out by the plants and being put back by the plants—or by the humans. You should

really work at your fertilizing. It's quite possible that if you make an effort to get more energy into your soil, your garden could produce 5 times as much food for your family as it does right now.

What's "Organic"? In this context, "organic" material means material left over from something that was once alive —plant, animal, tree, seaweed, leaf, sawdust. Any organic material is a natural fertilizer. Manure is also organic and natural and is a good fertilizer. A "chemical fertilizer" is the opposite of organic in that it is basically a petroleum product. In garden stores you can buy a range of both organic and chemical fertilizers.

You can also make your own organic fertilizer. Compost, green manure, and manure, together with bedding from where your animals live, are your 3 big options for home-grown fertilizer. These home-grown fertilizers are also "organic" in the sense of the word that means "free of toxic chemicals." "Natural fertilizing" basically means returning to the soil all the plant and animal residues that came from it originally. You can collect the best animal fertilizer from where your animals sleep: their manure. You can make the best "vegetable" fertilizer-compost.

Compost. This is simply decayed organic material. Anything that was once alive makes good compost: leaves, coffee grounds, grass clippings, kitchen food scraps. But avoid meat, fat, cooking oils, and grease; they're slow to decompose and their odors could attract rodents. In general, you make a pile of the stuff; a bottomless wooden box at least 3 × 3 × 3 feet works well. Turn your pile with a pitchfork once a week to sort of stir it, and keep it damp with a hose. Manure works the same way: Pile it up outside the barn and let it winter there. You really don't need to do anything else. In spring it will be ready to put on. Fresh organic material isn't ready for your plants to absorb. It can do more harm than good if you try to hurry it along. Manure that isn't well rotted will kill your plants. Composting is, in a nutshell, a set of techniques for hurrying up natural decomposition so you can get that organic material on your garden more quickly.

You can compost right in the garden. In the fall, spread a layer of decayable stuff on the ground: grass clippings, leaves, weeds, vegetable scraps. Spread a 2-inch layer of manure on top of that. Now scatter lime or wood ashes saved from your wood cookstove on top of that, and cover with straw. Red worms are better than earthworms at helping this process along, but once composting starts, garden worms will come. Water occasionally if the weather isn't doing the job. When you are ready to cultivate in the spring, dig this all into the upper 4 or 5 inches of your ground.

Try Stu Campbell's 1990 revision of the classic *Let It Rot! The Gardener's Guide to Composting* or *Don't Waste Your Wastes—Compost 'Em: The Homeowner's Guide to Recycling Yard Wastes* by Bert Whitehead (1991). Or order *Urban Home Composting: Rodent-Resistant Bins and Environmental Health Standards* for $10 from City Farmer, 604-685-5832; fax 604-685-0431; 801-318 Homer St., Vancouver, BC V6B 2V3, CANADA.

Incidentally, "City Farmer" is Canada's Office of Urban Agriculture, which helps urban folks start organic food gardens in their back and front yards, on balconies and rooftops, in community open spaces, in schoolyards and classrooms, and in hospitals and seniors' homes! It's presently also working to teach the public how to compost yard trimmings and food scraps. City Farmer runs a Demonstration Garden, including a Compost Demonstration Garden, at 2150 Maple St. in Vancouver, BC. Staff members give tours there and answer questions about composting on their Compost Hotline, (604) 736-2250. City Farmer also helps people and organizations develop urban agricultural programs. They have a large, unique library on the subject, and it's available to researchers by appointment. City Farmer also organizes courses and workshops on urban agricultural subjects and publishes handbooks.

Meanwhile, in the United States, the old meaning of the word "compost" is being perverted to include ground-up municipal solid waste. There's growing pressure to dispose of city garbage, once it's ground into tiny soil-like particles, by spreading it over farmers' fields as "fertilizer." It really would be just a cheap way for cities to camouflage plastic, metal, etc., as dirt and get rid of their waste. There would be compostable organic material in that stuff, but that wouldn't excuse the slow but steady pollution of the soil with lead and other heavy metals and bad stuff that would come with it—to say nothing of the burden of non-biodegradable ground plastic and metal. The food grown in such soil would be polluted. But desperate urban waste-disposal bureaucracies are pushing this plan hard because it would open up all of agricultural America as a new landfill area for them!

A friend of mine who works for the EPA attended a National Extension Compost Utilization Conference in Minneapolis in June 1993, where the agenda actually was to push this plan. She said the meeting was attended mostly by representatives from municipal waste agencies advocating the plan and by university researchers who don't like the idea but can't afford to reject the money they're being paid to study it. She said there's lots of big money pushing it because the need to hide garbage is so great.

She told me that near the end of the conference, one brave researcher stood up and asked, "Does anybody here really think this is a good idea? Raise your hand if you think spreading this stuff over the cropfields of America is a good idea." The silence was deafening. Not one person there raised a hand! But she said it's going to happen anyway unless there's effective citizen resistance, which at the moment is nowhere in sight. Contact one of the toxic-pollution fighting organizations listed at the beginning of this chapter for help in organizing to stop this.

Preparing to Plant: Fertilizing. The most foolproof fertilizing system is to annually test your soil to see what it needs, and then add the organic material that will supply that need —in addition to your regular annual layer of compost, green manure, and/or animal manure and bedding. Some growers add lots of compost; some add lots of manure; some add both. We manure the ground in spring and fall and scatter leaves from town in the fall to build up the soil. The manure truly makes a significant difference in the size of crop and the workability of the soil.

Earthchild Marie Stanley, Davenport, WA, wrote me to supplement the above meager info: "To begin your garden, you fertilize. It's best to add everything in the spring. Each 100 square feet needs a cup of ground-up alfalfa (smashed rabbit pellets will do), 2 lb. bonemeal, 10 lb. rock phosphate, 25 lb. greensand, 2 lb. granite dust, and 10 lb. wood ashes. If none of these are available, just add a commercial fertilizer and/or compost. The garden needs 3 inches or more of compost each year. That's why serious gardeners also have rabbits or goats. Compost has been called 'black gold': well worth digging for!"

GREEN MANURE: This is another way of fertilizing your ground. The crops most suitable for green manure are those that grow very fast, make a lot of organic material, and can handle growing in cool fall weather, after the regular harvest is done, or in early spring. Green manuring is more practical for a field or big garden than for a little one, although some great gardeners manage it on small plots too. You grow the crop and then plow it back under, where it enriches the ground as it decomposes. It's that simple. The green manure system may delay the rest of your garden, though, and of course you can't do it where you have perennials.

Rye grass, buckwheat, and alfalfa are probably the most popular green manure crops. Barley, oats, clover, and other legume crops are also good green manures. But check with your gardening neighbors, because the green manure that's best for you depends partly on where you live. For example, crimson clover is very good in the Puget Sound/maritime Northwest area. You can grow alfalfa or red clover together with tall, grassy grains. The hay crop won't really take off until after you harvest the grain. You can either plow the hay crop under in the fall for green manure, or you can harvest it for livestock feed the following summer.

Buckwheat. Buckwheat is a popular green manure crop. If you plant it into newly plowed-up pasture ground, it will not only smother out weeds and grasses but also add huge amounts of natural, healthy fertilizer to your soil. And the process of plowing it in further chops and buries perennial grasses and weeds. For even more weed-choking ability, plant a second buckwheat crop the day after you plow under (or harvest the grain from) the previous one. Or you can follow any spring crop of grain or vegetables with a second crop of green manure. Plow that one under the same way. If your green manure crop was a quick grower like buckwheat, you might be able to plant yet a third green manure crop! Yes, as many as 3 in one summer! For this third weed-choking, green-manuring crop, plant something that won't seed, such as annual ryegrass, unless you plan to raise a buckwheat grain crop in that place next spring! Plant the third crop thickly. It will die off over winter. In the spring, plow under what's left, and plant your garden or grain or whatever in the fertile, loose soil you created in one miraculous summer. There'll be scarcely a remnant of those original pasture plants left to bother with.

Tilling Under Green Manure. An extremely dense green manure crop may need to be cut with a scythe or mowed one or more times before you till it in, depending on what system you're using for tilling. And even so, you might have to till several times to get it well turned under and broken up. Hand digging in such a crop is hard work, and it's hard, though possible, to do it well. Don't plow your fertilizer in too deep. You want it in the topsoil. When you till under your green manure, that's a good time to add any other fertilizers planned for the land. If your green manure is reasonably well chopped up and mixed in with the dirt, it will compost nicely.

Planting in Green Manure. You have to wait until the tilled-in green manure has had time to compost before you plant seeds there. If you have warm soil temperatures plus rain, you have ideal composting conditions. In that case you can plant in only about 3 weeks. Don't try to shorten that composting time. An active underground composting process causes a temporary nitrogen shortage. You'll know the green manure is ready to have seeds or transplants put in when it has decomposed to the point of looking just like the rest of your dirt.

ANIMAL MANURE: Manure is home-grown fertilizer, a valuable by-product of keeping animals. If you have a lot of animals and a nearby stream or wetland, check with your extension agent about laws. Manure piles usually have to be covered if they are located within 200 feet of a stream or wetland. There are charts that say how much nitrogen, phosphorus, and potassium is in each animal's manure. And it's true they're all different. But it also depends on the animal's age, size, and feed—and on the manure's length of time in storage. (More on this in Chapter 8.)

Manure Management. Modern times have brought with them the science of manure management along with laser technology and atomic physics. Even with a few animals and reasonable bedding for them, you may have several tons of manure to compost each year. (When fresh, it is "hot" and might kill plants. After it has composted, it is wonderful for the garden.) You either spread it on the land on which you'll grow food and feed, or sell it to somebody who wants that good natural fertilizer. If you have lots of animals that are confined, you'll have lots of manure to deal with. If you have a few animals that are living in pasture you'll scarcely notice the animals' manure, yet it will be helping to keep their pasture green.

No-Bedding System. Big operations with lots of confined animals and strict environmental laws are rightly concerned about managing manure. One design system eliminates bedding, using slatted floors instead. The manure falls between the floor slats and lands in a space beneath the building. But as an organic grower, you are endeavoring to live as a part of nature's natural cycles, so your animals' manure and the organic bedding too are a blessing rather than a problem.

Need for Bedding. There's urine and there's feces. Pigs make more urine than other animals; up to 40 percent of their manure is urine. The urine from any animal is good stuff, worth keeping. An animal's urine contains half of the nitrogen the animal gives off, 6 percent of the phosphorus, and 60 percent of the potassium. So half of the animal's potential nutritional value to your field or garden is in its urine. But that's the part you lose without bedding to trap and hold it. The smaller the pieces your bedding is made of, the better it holds urine; good materials include chopped straw, ground corn cobs, wood shavings, and, better yet, sawdust. Chopped straw, for example, holds twice as much urine as unchopped.

Care of Manure Until Spreading. Most small farms clean out the manure from the chicken house, goat barn, etc. twice a year (spring and fall), so that's something to consider when you design those buildings: Make the roofs high enough to allow bedding to build up for that long. That's called the "deep litter" system. Adding new layers of bedding gives you more rich compost, keeps the bedding dry (on top), and keeps the odor down. Animals stay cleaner and warmer. (Roaming chickens are a good way to keep summer flies under control.) When barn-cleaning time does come, with maybe 3 feet of manure-laden bedding to haul

out, you've still got a big job ahead of you, but your manure will be in good condition, already largely composted in the deeper layers, so you can directly spread and till it in.

Spreading. Your timing must be right. You can't spread manure onto snowy ground. You can't spread it onto a growing garden or crop. And sometimes you can't wait all that long to get it out of the barn. In that case, the manure needs time enough to compost in a pile before it is spread, because it needs to heat-process so the nutrients will be ready for release. Make your barnyard or field compost piles at least 5 or 6 feet deep (to avoid water leaching) and not more than 6 feet wide; they can be as long as you want. Cover them with plastic or dirt. Make sure the pile doesn't get too dry, because if it does, it will lose a bunch of its nitrogen and other fertilizer elements. Spread it and till it in when that becomes possible.

So it's best if the manure is in your barn, in a compost pile in your field, or spread onto your garden or field and then immediately plowed or disked into the soil. That's the best way to handle it, because manure is perishable. It shouldn't ever dry out completely or be repeatedly rained on so that water runs clear through it and carries the good stuff away into a creek or down into the water table. Weathering makes it lose nitrogen. *Don't let manure dry out, and don't let it leach out.*

So you should time the deep-litter spring barn cleaning for several weeks before your spring plowing. Take the manure and stack it into compost piles. Make them high enough so rain won't leach out the good stuff. Turn the piles enough so the composting process will be done before plowing. Then you spread the manure and plow it in—except for one pile or so, which you'll hold back for "sidedressing."

In the fall, do the same thing again: Clean your barns and make compost piles of the manure in the garden. Only this time you can combine any garden residues with the manure for joint composting. You can disk in that manure after it is done composting. Minimize the time between when you take the compost out of the compost pile and when you get it under your ground, because the fermentation gases being produced are good stuff and you need to capture them in the soil for your plants, not let them escape into the air.

MANURE DANGERS

1. Don't gather bat guano from caves. It contains a fungus that can cause respiratory disease in humans, and disturbing the caves can threaten endangered species.
2. Dog and cat manure should not be used in your garden because they may carry diseases.
3. Don't use sewage sludge from a treatment plant unless it has been tested and guaranteed free of contamination by heavy metals.
4. Don't put fresh manure on plants because the ammonia in it can damage them.
5. Horse manure tends to contain hay and weed seeds. Make sure it is composted well enough to kill the seeds before applying it.

Cultivating the Soil

NO-TILL REASONING: Not all agree that cultivation is necessary or desirable. The worry is erosion. Topsoil is so precious; nature needs millennia to make it. When land is plowed up and then left bare much of the year, all the topsoil can be washed away in a few generations. For example, before the plow touched the Great Plains of our Midwest, all the topsoil was tightly held by native grasses that had root systems so extensive that some statistician calculated that the root hairs of one single stalk, laid end to end, would stretch 300 miles. Those roots were bound together in clumps, and they held the precious soil tightly in their tenacious, protective grasp.

The plow tore up and destroyed those grasses. Corn, a shortrooted plant, was planted in rows, and bare dirt lay between the corn plants. Between plants and between crops, the soil was exposed to rain and wind. It took only a few decades for those once-great grasslands to turn into the awful "dust bowl" in which dust often lay 6 inches deep and terrible dust storms were stirred up whenever the wind blew. In *Plowman's Folly* (1943), Edward H. Faulkner argued very effectively that plowing was the basic cause of the tragic erosion of soil nutrients and the soil itself.

Not only are soil erosion statistics horrifying, but topsoil continues to be lost wherever there is cultivation (or clearcutting of timber). One scientist calculated the average loss of topsoil from cultivated land at 12 tons per acre per year. Yes, soil is constantly being made by the action of earthworms, roots, etc., as they break minerals off the bedrock layer and by organic matter on the top of the soil as it decays, but the rate of topsoil formation is, at best, about 1 inch per 100 years—1.5 tons per acre per year.

The severity of erosion depends on how fine the soil texture is, how strong the winds blow, how much rain falls, how steep the land's slope is, and whether the land is bare only every few years (as with hay crops) or mostly bare more of the time (as with row crops). The story of erosion is one of inexorable, creeping, perpetual loss, though, whether fast or slow, as long as there is cultivation (unless the soil is constantly rebuilt by organic techniques—and many organic gardeners do that!). For this reason, some soil specialists recommend "no-till" methods of agriculture. More moderate but sympathetic voices accept cultivation but urge management to keep the vulnerable, loose soil under a protective cover as much of the time as possible—under mulch in summer and green manure in the winter.

No-till advocates also point out that both the microbiotic soil life and structure of the soil also suffer from extensive, repeated cultivation. Rototillers kill earthworms, mess up bugs, and demolish the soil's natural crumb structure. One variety of no-till gardening does work. In this method, the land is double-dug once to make a raised bed and is heavily fertilized. (See "Double-Digging," later in this section. After that, it is never dug up again. In order to do this, you need 2 things. First, you must have so much organic material in the soil that even if it was initially heavy clay, it has now become loose humus. Secondly, you have to use a bed system in which you *never* walk on the soil. That keeps it from compacting. You also must keep the soil fertile enough to have lots of earthworms. Every earthworm is a tiny tilling machine, constantly burrowing tunnels into the dirt through which water, air, and nutrients can go down to plant roots.

TILLING: But virtually all gardeners do till before planting. There are 3 good reasons to cultivate.

1. Cultivating breaks up the ground. For good plant growth, it's important to have the soil well prepared. That means having it broken up into fine particles. You want to loosen the soil enough so you can plant seeds into the ground and easily pull weeds out, and so the plant roots can quickly and easily grow down and out to find the growing materials they need in the soil—food and water. It's technically possible to just make a seed trench with a pickax, plant the seed, and cover it by kicking the clods back over with your boot—but you won't get much of a crop if that's all the cultivating you do. With deeply dug, well-loosened soil, vegetables grow bigger. With both loose and fertile soil, you can plant them closely ("intensive," or "wide row," style).

2. Cultivating works in your fertilizer. When you till under the leftover pea and bean vines, etc., from the summer's garden, you are green-manuring. When your compost or manure piles are ready to be spread on the garden, you want to till in the fertilizer enough to get it mixed up and stirred around with the dirt.

3. Cultivating fights weeds.

First Cultivation. If you are turning over virgin soil that hasn't been cultivated before, the fall is the best time. That will allow all winter for the weed seeds, roots, and grass to decompose. Heavy matted grass, though, probably won't decompose over just one winter. Cultivate again in the spring and a few more times as you let it lie fallow that summer to finish rotting. But if you really need that land to produce food right away, do the spring plowing and then plant. You'll get a crop, but it may be more weedy.

Routine Cultivation. Many growers routinely plow in the fall; this turns under organic material from the previous crop so it can decompose over the winter season and enrich the ground. Then they plow again in the spring, when the planting season is coming up again. That spring plowing is the most necessary one.

When to Cultivate in the Spring. Don't start tilling your ground in the spring until it has pretty much dried. Sandy soils will be ready before clay ones. A good test of whether the soil is ready for the plow is to pick up a ball of soil, press it together, and then drop it onto the ground from 3 feet up. If your ball doesn't break apart when dropped, the soil is definitely still too wet. If you try to cultivate ground that's too wet, especially clayey wet ground, you'll get dreadful lumps that resist breaking up afterwards and hinder root growth. On the other hand, don't linger. Be out there as soon as you can. Early cultivation gives you time to add more organic matter to the soil and still have enough time for it to naturally compost for a few weeks before planting time. And, of course, you can't start your effective "growing season" until your soil is prepared for planting!

Rototillers are expensive to buy new. Advertise in a wanted-to-buy column in your newspaper for a used one. There are lots of models of rototillers. Some have outer tines you can take off to allow a narrower space between rows. Buying a small one also saves. The Mantis tiller weighs just 20 pounds, tills down to 10 in., and has a 2-cycle engine (Mantis, 1028 Street Rd., Southampton, PA 18966-9941). The Troy-Bilt is a well-known larger tiller: 1 Garden Way, Troy, NY 12179; 800-260-1133; **www.troybilt.com.**

CULTIVATING WITH HAND TOOLS: *How to Select, Use and Maintain Garden Equipment* (Ortho Books, 1982) is a good book on choosing, using, and caring for these hand tools. For all sorts of traditional tools (including those for milling and hulling grains), contact the Olden Days Store, 5939 Guide Meridian, Bellingham, WA 98226; 360-647-0975; 800-738-4358. Adrian B. DeBee runs this store. Down to Earth Home and Garden is another West Coast supplier of hand tools: 532 Olive St., Eugene, OR 97401; 541-342-6820; **www.home2garden.com.** In the East, there's Walt Nicke, who specializes in garden tools and has a free catalog: 800-822-4114; fax 508-887-9853; 36 McLeod Lane, PO Box 433, Topsfield, MA 01983; **www.gardentalk.com.**

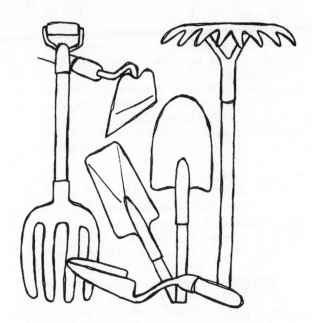

If you're "plowing" by hand, you do it with a spade, or a "spading fork," which looks like a pitchfork except that it has wide tines. Then you break up clods with a hoe. Then rake to smooth the seed bed, level the dirt, spread fertilizers, and pull any remaining clods or rocks out of the seedbed.

Lane Morgan says, "I think if you are going to do a lot of double-digging or raised bed work, it's worth it to buy or make a Ubar digger. I got mine from Territorial. The tines are 18 inches long, so you can dig a bed in one go, with much less strain on your back, and they are steel, so they don't cave in the first time they meet a rock. They are expensive, but I have been able to quit using the rototiller entirely in most of the garden, so it evens out over time in saving fuel and repairs."

You weed by hand or with a hoe. There are several styles of hoes, some with narrow blades (the "finger hoe" is the narrowest, "Reisch hoe" is less narrow), some with wide ones ("onion hoe"). Another weeding tool is the hand cultivator that you pull through the soil, or the "push cultivator," which is a hoe in a fixed mount behind a wheel; you push it through the soil while walking behind it. All your hoe-type tools need occasional sharpening, but on the *inside edge only*. That is the side facing up when pulled toward your body. A sharp blade does its job easier and better.

For close-in hand weeding or digging holes for transplants, a trowel beats fingernails. It's the pro gardener's upgrade of the big spoon. Even if you have a rototiller, you need all this stuff too because times will come when you'll

need the finesse that hand tools allow, like working around perennials.

First Digging. Hand digging is exceptionally hard work. But if you use the no-till system, you have to do it only the first year. Even if you plan to spade it up every year, the first year usually gets the biggest effort, since many gardeners double-dig the first time.

First, mark the sides of your new garden by string tied to stakes at each corner. If you can, it's a good idea to then cover the whole bed-to-be with 6 inches of good rotted compost or manure before you even start your deep digging. Then you will be spading in that compost as you go. You dig down something like a foot for a single-dug garden.

A good way to organize your digging is to start on one side, going the long way, and dig a trench to the depth you need, laying the dirt from the first trench in a garden cart. Then dig out another strip right beside it. Fill the one you just dug with the dirt you are now taking out of the new one—and so on. How you handle the returning dirt depends on whether this is virgin soil with tight clumps of grass in it, or ground that has been cultivated before and doesn't have a problem like that. If it has the grass problem, take each sod chunk after you dig it up, shake it over your garden plot to get the good topsoil out, and then toss the grass/roots part over onto a compost heap. Doing this will make your chopping stage easier, and you won't have all that upside-down grass trying to grow again.

If this is dirt that doesn't have so much growing stuff in it, however, just put the dirt back in. But lay it in upside down, plant roots to the top, grass or whatever to the bottom. That kills a lot of the grass/roots, and they'll begin to compost. After you've dug out the last trench, haul the garden cart around and lay that dirt from the first trench into your last one.

Now that you have it all dug up, let it sit a few days. Then lay on the rest of the fertilizing materials you want to add. Now go through your garden about 3 times, one after the other, hacking at clods with a hoe. You're now trying to get the soil broken down to a fine texture, and also well mixed. The deep digging (and fertilizing) helps plants sink deep, healthy roots and really get at the minerals they need.

Double-Digging. The most thorough way to prepare a seed bed is "double-digging." In this case, you loosen the soil down to 20 to 24 inches deep. As in regular digging, you first take a shovelful of topsoil out and move it over. But then you take your spading fork and use it to loosen the next foot of soil down (don't take the fork out; just wobble it around). Then refill your trenches as with single digging.

Preparing Later Gardens. After the first year most gardeners working only with hand tools take life easier. They either use a no-till system and don't dig at all, or they spade the garden in a simple one-two rather than do all that careful dirt shifting. To do this, just go through the garden, digging down about a foot and turning the dirt over in each hole. In a week, come back and spade again, but go down only about 4 inches this time. Come back several more times and spade or chop with a hoe that top 4 inches (or even as few as 2 inches) of soil. When your soil is broken up fine, nice and crumbly and fairly smooth on top, you're ready to plant.

Powered Cultivation. You need some kind of power source if you are farming over an acre. To spade even an acre by hand is asking a lot of yourself. For just an acre or so of ground, you can prepare the ground using a tractor or draft animal pulling a plow, your rototiller, or hand labor. If you're planting several acres or more, you could use a small farm tractor or draft animal. You can handle up to 2 or even 3 acres with a rototiller plus maybe asking a neighbor to come in and plow it once in the spring for you. If you're going to cultivate more than that, you need a draft animal or a tractor of your own. The basic farm machine for cultivating larger areas is something that can power other things: a team of horses or oxen or a tractor. Or a rototiller for in-between sizes.

Animal-Powered Cultivation

Like goat people, animal traction folks form strong bonds with each other, reflected in their many events and publications.

BUYING DRAFT ANIMALS

Eastern States Draft Horse Sale is held in Columbus, OH, once a year. For more info, contact Chrissy Steinbrick; call/fax 419-734-2013; 5910 E. Port Clinton Rd., Marblehead, OH 43440; **belgian@cros.net.**

Topeka Draft Horse Auction is your chance to buy young harness-trained horses, experienced draft teams, and horse-drawn farm implements. There are two draft horse and three carriage auctions each year: Robert Bale; 260-593-2522; fax 260-593-2258; PO Box 279, Topeka, IN 46571; **auction@topekanet.com; www. Auctions-USA.com.**

Waverly Midwest Horse Sale happens twice a year in Iowa. Contact Ron Dean, PO Box 355, Waverly, IA 50677; 319-352-2804 for more info.

DRAFT ANIMAL ORGANIZATIONS AND ACTIVITIES

Horse Progress Days is an annual July trade show at the Vernon J. Yoder Farm, Arcola, IL, where manufacturers and distributors demonstrate new horse-powered farming and logging equipment. Also, draft horses and mules of all breeds and demonstrations of field work in 1- to 12-horse hitch-ups; plowing, hay making, logging, etc. Info: Neil M. Hostetler, 217-543-2217; 130 E. County Rd. 200 N., Arthur, IL 61911. Or Vernon J. Yoder; 217-268-3444; 650 E. County Rd. 400 N., Arcola, IL 61910; **progress@ruralheritage.com; rural heritage.com/progress/.**

Iowa-Minnesota Horse Plowing Association offers fun and fellowship with horse and mule plowing. Contact Judson and Carol Schrick; 563-382-5086; 2378 Trout River Rd., Decorah, IA 52101.

Mid-South Drovers Ass'n, c/o Joyce Hetrick, 288 Heifer Creek Rd., Springfield, AR 72157; 501-354-5025 or 501-450-1448; **joyce@heifercreek.com; www.heifer creek.com.**

North American Horse & Mule Loggers Association, c/o Tim Carroll, President; 507-325-4197; Rt. 1 Box 114, Lyle, MN 55953; **tecarrol@smig.net.**

Tennessee's Great Celebration Mule Show: Mary Lynn Reed; 931-684-4915; PO Box 1010, Shelbyville, TN 37162; **www.twhnc.com.**

WXICOF specializes in donkey and mule books: 636-828-5100; fax 636-828-5431; 914 Riske Lane, Wentzville, MO 63385; **wxicof.com/ratite.htm.**

DRAFT ANIMAL PERIODICALS

The Brayer, published by the American Donkey and Mule Society, is the "world's largest single source of info and services for donkeys, mules, and zebra hybrids." Joining ($20/yr) gets you *The Brayer,* and more. Contact: PO Box 1210, Lewisville, TX 75067; 972-219-0781; fax 972-420-9980; **adms@juno.com; www.lovelong ears.com.**

The Carriage Journal is published 5 times/yr by the Carriage Association of America, a world organization of people interested in horse-drawn vehicles: Jill Ryder, Executive Director; 856-935-1616; fax 856-935-9362; 177 Pointers-Auburn Rd., Salem, NJ 08079; **carrassc@ mindspring.com; www.caaonline.com.**

Draft Horse Journal is a quarterly magazine (250+ pages!) produced by Lynn Telleen, Editor, for 30+ years. It reports on shows and sales, does features on horse farmers and breeders, provides horse management tips and bloodlines, and gives info on horse machinery. It's $25/yr ($30 foreign); 319-352-4046; PO Box 670, Waverly, IA 50677.

Driving Digest deals with harnessed equines (miniature donkeys to draft horses); $24 for about 64 pages, 6

issues/yr; 419-929-6781; PO Box 110, New London, OH 44851.

Feather and Fetlock is a quarterly magazine (80+ pages) covering the Canadian heavy horse scene, especially showing; U.S. $36/yr; 403-337-2342; PO Box 9, Cremona, ALB T0M 0R0, CANADA.

Heavy Horse World is the U.K.'s draft horse magazine. It's $37 U.S. airmail (4/yr); $30 surface mail. Call/fax +44 01730 812419; Lindford Cottage, Church Lane, Cocking, Midwest, West Sussex U29 0HW U.K.; **heavy horse@mistral.co.uk; www.heavyhorseworld.co.uk.**

Mules and More is a monthly magazine for mule, wagon, and harness enthusiasts; $24/yr. Editor Sue Cole; 573-646-3934; PO Box 460, Bland, MO 65014; **mules@socket.net; www.mulesandmore.com.**

Rural Heritage has been published since 1976 in support of farming and logging with horses, mules, and oxen. Articles on training and using draft animals for farming and logging; 108 pages in 6 issues/yr for $26/yr USA; $32/yr Canada. *The Evener Work Horse, Mule & Oxen Directory and Guide* ($6.25 by itself) is an annually updated supplement to the magazine. The *Directory* lists sources in 35 categories, including harness, horse farming implements, draft horses, mules, oxen, workshop schedules, and stock sales; 931-268-0655; 281 Dean Ridge Lane, Gainesboro, TN 38562; **www.rural heritage.com.**

Small Farmers Journal prints practical draft horse info in addition to general articles for small, independent family farmers. Cost is $30 for 128 large-size pages, 4 issues/yr; L. R. Miller, Editor; 541-549-2064; fax 541-549-4403; PO Box 1627, Sisters, OR 97759-5039.

ANIMAL TRACTION BOOKS: The Mischka Farm Draft Horse Bookstore offers a beautiful draft horse calendar and 100+ books and videos (free catalog) on draft horses: PO Box 224, Oregon, WI 53575; **www.mischka.com.** Many animal traction books and videotapes are offered by the Rural Bookstore (931-268-0655; **ruralheritage.com**). *Draft Horses: An Owner's Manual* by Beth Valentine (a vet) and Mike Wildenstein (a farmer) covers the health problems and disorders that affect draft horses. *Work Horse Handbook* by Lynn R. Miller (1981) is a classic text with hundreds of photos and drawings teaching you about the care and feeding, hitching and driving of draft horses. *Training Workhorses/Training Teamsters,* also by L. R. Miller, covers training horses to work in harness on the farm, in the woods, and on the road, how to correct behavior problems of work horses, and how to train people to drive and work horses. *Haying with Horses, Horsedrawn Plows and Plowing,* and *Horsedrawn Tillage Tools* are Miller's most recent books. *Draft Horses Today,* by Robert Mischka, is a basic review of the modern draft horse scene with hundreds of color photos by this gifted photographer.

HARNESS SUPPLIERS

Cumberland General Store Catalog, Rt. 3, Box 479, Crossville, TN 38555. Harness, implements, tools. Catalog.

Detweller's Harness Shop, Rt. 1, Box 228, Hazleton, IA 50641. Catalog.

McKee's Horse & Buggy, PO Box 27, 101 E. Main, Drakesville, IA 52552; 515-722-5222; fax 515-722-3771. "Your complete driving horse supply shop." Harness, shafts, wheels, and springs, bells, books, farm

equipment. Illustrated catalog, $2.

Meader Supply Corp., 23 Meaderboro Rd., Rochester, NH 03867; 800-4-HORSES. Harness, hardware, halters, bits and bridles, books and videos, carts, wagons, yokes, horse-drawn equipment, trailers, etc. Free catalogs.

Midwest Leather & Harness, Rt. #2, Box 153, Paris, MO 65275; 816-327-5278. Farm, single driving, and logging harness, collars, harness parts, etc. Call for catalog.

Miller Harness Company, 235 Murray Hill Parkway, East Rutherford, NJ 07073; 800-553-7655; fax 800-526-6389; **millerharness.com.** Free catalog.

Stitch 'n Hitch: Mari Lintin sells farm, pulling, and buggy collars and harnesses. Complete catalog online, or send $3; 931-484-2203; 3200 Hebbertsburg Rd., Crab Orchard, TN 37723; **stitchnhitch@multipro.com; rural heritage.com/harness/.**

John Thompson (died 1995) left wonderful plans to build horse-drawn vehicles of every sort (and books). His plans are now offered by Roger Morgan. Catalog is U.S. $8; 1 Lamb Lane, Ponthir, Newport, South Wales NP18 1HA UNITED KINGDOM.

DRAFT ANIMALS TO WATCH: This is just the tip of the iceberg. See the draft animal magazines for more current info.

Howell Living History Farm puts on the Howell Farm Plowing Match for horses, oxen, and mules on the Saturday of Labor Day weekend with both professional and novice competition levels: 609-737-3299; 101 Hunter Rd., Titusville, NJ 08560.

Living History Farms, 10 miles northwest of Des Moines, IA, recreates four time periods: a 1700 Iowa Indian site; an 1850 pioneer farm (with oxen); an 1875 frontier town; and a 1900 farm (with draft horses). Open May 1 to mid-October; 515-278-2400 (recorded messages).

Ross Farm demonstrates oxen and horse-powered farm operations and ox shoeing. Daily operation May to October: 902-689-2210; Rt. 12, New Ross, NS B0J 2M0, CANADA. For info and publications: Director, Nova Scotia Museum, 1747 Summer St., Halifax, NS, CANADA; **rossfarm@gov.ns.ca; rossfarm.museum. gov.ns.ca.**

TRAINING IN USE OF DRAFT ANIMALS

Amish Farmer, Eli J. C. Yoder, 445 S. Mill St., Sugar Creek, OH 44681; 216-852-4603, offers hands-on driving instruction at his horsemanship school for beginners.

Good Farming Apprenticeship Network: rural heritage.com/apprenticeship/.

Howell Living History Farm. For info on their 10-week internship on the care, training, and use of oxen, contact Rob Flory: fax 609-737-6524; **thefarm@bell atlantic.net; www.howellfarm.org.**

Ridgewind Farm offers horse logging workshops taught by Jason Rutledge, Regional Director of the North American Horse & Mule Loggers Association. Scholarships are available. The training program begins with an intensive course on basic forestry, restorative/sustainable timber management, and animal-powered skidding techniques, followed by a 10-week apprenticeship. You'll learn the essentials of a Healing Harvest: care and handling of draft horses, including harnessing, driving techniques, and log skidding; directional timber felling and chainsaw safety; skid trail placement and loading site selection; silviculture; sustained yield forestry principles used in choosing trees for harvest; and Green Certification marketing; 540-651-6355; fax 540-651-3914; 8014 Bear Ridge Rd., Copper Hill, VA 24079; *rutledge@swva.net; www.draftwoodforestproducts.com*. He also sells horse-logged Appalachian wood products for construction or remodeling.

Rural Heritage's "Calendar of Events" lists more workshops, draft horse/mule sales, etc.

Tillers International offers workshops in sustainable ag, international rural development, blacksmithing, hand tool woodworking, rope making, timber framing, and draft animal skills; 800-498-2700; 616-344-3233; 5239 S. 24th St., Kalamazoo, MI 49002; **Tillersint@aol.com; www.wmich.edu/tillers/.** Another Tillers International school is at 816-795-8200, ext. 1-260; 22807 Woods Chapel Rd., Blue Springs, MO 64015.

BLACKSMITHING AND FARRIER SKILLS: Blacksmithing is taught at Tillers International and also at the Turley Forge Blacksmithing School: 505-471-8608; 919-A Chicoma Vista, Santa Fe, NM 87507; **teeweld@msn.com.** The major U.S. supplier of barrier and blacksmithing supplies is Centaur Forge, Ltd.

DRAFT HORSES: A horse can outpull a little Ford tractor, especially in cold and deep snow when the tractor won't even move. A horse can pull 16-foot logs. A team can pull a ton for a short distance but won't be able to keep it up. They can easily pull 300 lb. all day long. But remember to stop and rest them often. There is an old saying that if you want to have a good pulling horse, always leave one pull in him. That means quit working him while he is still pulling.

To get yourself started with draft horses, you need one or a team. Consider subscribing to the *Small Farmer's Journal.* It's the homesteader's magazine that takes the greatest interest and gives the most exposure to draft horse topics. In fact, it used to have "draft horse" in its name.

When you go to buy one, take someone with you who knows them. They're expensive but don't cost nearly as much as a tractor. Then you need harness. Hopefully you can buy a set from the same person who sells you the horses because harness is hard to find. Make sure you know how to harness and hitch them up before you bring them home. Have the seller show you how. Otherwise, you will have a hard time figuring it out for yourself later on. If the wooden parts of the harness—called "hames"—seem dry, you can oil them with tung oil or neat's-foot oil. Put it on hot and rub it in well. Same for the leather.

Practice is important for any draft animal. Hitching up the animals and using them every day helps them stay at their best (and keeps you in practice too). When you are first training draft animals to pull, load them very lightly. Gradually, over time, increase the load. Pat the animal and let it know you appreciate it after a good hard pull. That moment of sincere thanks really makes a difference in the quality of future performance you'll get. Horses aren't nearly as dumb as many people think. And they've got feelings too. On a terribly hot 105°F day, bring your animal in at noon with you. Give it a 2-hour break in the shade. (The break will also help you.)

The state of your horses' feet is important. Don't buy an animal with badly split hooves. Bring in the horseshoer, or "farrier," regularly. Around here there are a couple that run continuous advertisements in the newspapers. Horseshoes are vital if your animal is going to be walking on pavement or gravel a lot because both are especially hard on hooves, which nature didn't design for such hard surfaces. But even if your horses work on dirt, their hooves can stand some trimming.

Draft horse breeding is a good cause and potentially profitable. But keeping a draft horse stud is not all fun and games. They are so big, and any male is a potentially mean animal. We have neighbors that keep a stud. They take beautiful care of their horses, but one day he simply up and bit a big chunk out of the lady's face. That was an Arabian stud. A draft horse stud could be twice the weight. If he is somewhere near where a mare is in heat, he could be very hard to handle no matter how nice his disposition. You can artificially inseminate horses just like cows or goats. Four to six weeks before a draft mare foals (has a baby), it's time to let her quit working. Until then it's okay to work her. A month after she foals, you can get her back into harness. Working again soon after foaling will help keep her in shape.

Machinery for Cultivation

ROTOTILLER: A rototiller is a little gas-powered tilling machine that you follow down its path. We use a spring-tooth harrow on the ground in the spring; then we till with the rototiller once before planting and several times at later intervals to take out weeds. Some people love rototillers. The typical, organic rototiller gardener tills both spring and fall and cultivates with the machine again during spring and summer as needed for weeds. Some tillers have shredder/grinder attachments that help make compost. When organic gardeners combine tilling with lots of mulching, manuring, and composting, they can produce wonderful soil that just keeps getting better and deeper.

Rototillers are expensive to buy new; used ones are cheaper. Advertise in a wanted-to-buy column in your newspaper. Most gardeners around here plow their garden in early spring and then come through and rototill—and they rototill several more times through the summer as needed to keep the weeds down. There are lots of models of rototillers. Some have outer tines you can take off to allow a narrower space between rows.

A rototiller can play the same role as a disk, spring-tooth, or spike-tooth harrow—except most rototillers can't plow. If you have a rear-tined, self-propelled rototiller, you can supposedly make it plow too—that's why the Troy-Built people say they're so special. But a rototiller really doesn't plow nearly so well as a tractor pulling a plow. And you haven't a chance trying to plow with a regular rototiller. The little front-tined ones won't cut unplowed earth at all.

TRACTOR: These come in all sizes (as do horses). If a draft animal is not for you, then you need a tractor: one small enough to be affordable and yet big enough to do your work. Small riding tractors are fine for orchards and little jobs. You don't want a farm-size tractor on 10 acres or less. There are now some companies with lines of machinery especially for truck farms, orchards, vineyards, or homesteads.

Before you buy your first tractor, consider what you'll use it for. You don't want it either underpowered or overpowered. If you underpower (buy too small a tractor), it won't get your job done and will wear out sooner. If you overpower, you are wasting money on gas and are inefficient. There's a distinction between diesel and gas engines. A diesel 50-horsepower engine is really powerful, but 50 horsepower in gas isn't as powerful. Educate yourself about the choices before you buy: Talk to a dealer of farm equipment like John Deere or Allis Chalmers, and talk to your neighbors. If you have mechanical skills, look around for some used equipment.

My beloved friend and neighbor, Janice Willard, a veterinary student and a farm manager, wrote me about this section, "I think you slighted tractors a bit. Tractors have an advantage over horses (and I am an avowed horse lover), because they need little care when you are not using them. When I went to buy my tractor, an old farmer gave me this advice: 'There are 3 important things to look for in a tractor—condition, condition, and condition.' It's true. A well-cared-for tractor is more important than year and model. Tractors are beautiful machines because they are built strictly for function. They put out huge amounts of work and reliability with only a little repair and maintenance. I trade tune-ups and maintenance work with a mechanical friend for occasional use of the machine. My tractor is a '64 Massey Fergeson. I paid $4,000 for it. It is the most dependable machine I have ever owned and one of the best investments I have ever made. If you live where it snows, be sure to get chains for your tractor."

Lee Bannister, Pullman, WA, advises: "It helps money-wise if you can do your own mechanicing. If you aren't willing to tinker with machinery and spend time with it, you won't make it farming. Used, affordable equipment is going to need a lot of work. You can get parts for the older machines for almost nothing by buying the basic one and then buying a junked one for parts."

FARM IMPLEMENTS: Your power source needs a few appropriate tools or "implements" to pull: machines for tilling, weeding, harvesting, manure-spreading, and so on. Exactly what implements you need depends on what you grow and how much of it. Implements, like tractors, come in all sizes. Each implement has a specific action on the soil or plant. You have to decide what combination you want. Most of the machinery is designed for large-scale farming, but there are some for small and labor-intensive farms such as orchards and truck gardens. It's hard to find horse- and oxen-drawn implements, but it can be done. You may have to do some renovating.

The most recent great book on how to correctly operate a disk and a spring-tooth harrow and properly plow a field is *Successful Small-Scale Farming* by Karl Schwenke (1979). It explains all about farm machinery and soil care (as well as cash crops, specialty crops, storing and marketing produce, measuring acreage, building fences and stone walls, etc.). *Tools for Homesteaders, Gardeners and Small-Scale Farmers* (Rodale Press, 1978) has info on draft animals as well as tractors. *Using Field Machinery* by W.F. Boshoff (London: Oxford U. Press, 1968) covers equipment run by animal power as well as tractors and implements. *Farm Implements for Arid and Tropical Regions* by H.J. Hopfen (1969) is available in French and English editions from UNIPUB, United Nations, New York, NY. It is part of the Food and Agriculture Organization (FAO) Better Farming Series and covers hand tools and animal-powered machinery. *Farm Implements in the Making of America* by Paul C. Johnson (1976) and *Farm Tools Through the Ages* by Michael Partridge

(1973) are other good resources for learning about animal-powered implements.

Plow. Land that hasn't been cultivated recently (or ever) needs a good plowing to start with. You can get that plowing done in either the spring or the fall. If you plow in the fall, you'll have more work to do next spring. The old-timers said you could judge a man's character and the probable success or failure of his entire future life by looking at the evidence of one day's work behind a plow: Was it careful? Did he get a lot accomplished? Plowing, like all the rural skills, is an art as well as a science. Plowing a straight furrow sets the tone for all the field cultivation and harvesting that will follow and is rightfully something to be proud of.

To plow is to break the soil, loosen it, and turn it over. If you are cultivating virgin ground, plowing is the first step, no matter what you do later. Plowing actually turns the soil over to a given depth, usually 4 to 6 inches. You set the plow to turn the soil to the exact depth you want.

A plow can have one blade or a whole row of them. Each blade is called a "bottom," so a 5-bottom plow has 5 cutting blades. But a plow is not always the best option. The plow is appropriate in soils where you have humus that extends below the plowing depth. If you have very shallow topsoil, a plow is not a good tool for you because you don't want to bury the topsoil. Your precious topsoil is a nice organic material with worms and compost and energy, and you want more rather than less of it.

All over northern Minnesota the topsoil is kind of thin. Lots of farmers there come through instead with a chisel plow in the spring. That's a tool that sends 7 or 14 fingers down in there to open up the soil. The chisel plow breaks up hardpan; it helps the water soak in and helps enable roots to grow down and get trace minerals, yet it does not disturb the surface. But in most areas the topsoil isn't that thin, so plowing is fine.

The most efficient way to plow a sizable field is to go around from the outside in, turning left at each corner. Then the only wasted land will be 4 little triangular-shaped pieces at the corners. If there's a small slough (a chronically wet place), a jutting rock, or a sudden hillock in the field, just plow around it. Don't plow through soggy ground. You run the risk of miring the tractor, and plowing will make it even more wet.

Disk. A disk is an implement that cuts up the big chunks turned up by the plow with rolling disk-shaped blades when it's pulled over the ground.

Spring-Tooth. This implement comes in all types and sizes, but basically it has iron teeth that are dragged over the ground like a multi-tined rake. To plant a seed and get it to grow well, your seed bed must be fine, well-broken-down particles of earth. If the clods are too large, air gets in there and your soil dries out. Then you've got little dry seeds

lying between big chunks of earth. This implement's teeth break the little chunks into even finer chunks and smooth the soil surface to get it ready for seeding. With enough power, some farmers plow and then pull a disk with a spring-tooth attached behind the disk. How many times you pull the spring-tooth over the same field depends on your soil and on how easy it is to break up.

Earthworms

PRE-TEST: True or false?

1. If you cut a worm in half, you'll end up with 2 worms.
2. Worms have lips.
3. A worm has no brain.
4. It takes 2 worms to create another.
5. Rabbits and worms have nothing in common.

Earthworms are good to fish with, good for your birds to eat, good for recycling kitchen wastes, and good for your garden soil. They can be wild or domesticated. Wild worms in your garden tunnel and loosen soil. Also, in their process of digestion, worms actually reduce soil acidity and complete the composting process of freeing up plant nutrients. Over time these busy worms build good topsoil by breaking up and enriching the subsoil under it—even hardpan under that. And earthworm tunneling makes homes for many smaller animals who also make for healthier plants.

Pam Milberg wrote most of this section (later I tinkered with it somewhat). She's my volunteer assistant. She checked all my topics to make suggestions for improved arrangement and also sent letters to every mail-order address listed in this book to verify the information listed.

WORM INFO AND PRODUCTS: *The Worm Book,* by Loren Nancarrow and Janet Hogan Taylor, is an amusing, informative, fascinating, and complete guide to gardening and composting with worms. *Worms Eat My Garbage* by Mary Appelhof is an easy-to-read guide to raising worms that's equally suited to urban and rural folks. Her company sells supplies to worm growers: Worm's Way, 7850 N. State Rd. 37, Bloomington, IN 47414-9477. *Harnessing the Earthworm* by Thomas J. Barrett (Bookworm Publishing Co.) gives in-depth, scientific facts on worms and how to grow them. *Raising Earthworms for Profit* by Earl B. Shields tells how to raise worms to sell. An older classic is *Earthworms for Ecology and Profit* by Ronald E. Gaddie, Sr. and Donald E. Douglas. For online worm info, visit **www.worm digest.org**.

BUYING WORMS: The number or amount of worms you use will depend on the size of your household and the amount of garbage you want consumed. The rule of thumb is 2 lb. worms per 1 lb. garbage. For instance, if you produce 1 lb. organic and compostable garbage a day (or an average 7 lb. per week), you would use 2 lb. worms in the worm bed container. You can buy either "pit-run" or "breeder" worms. Breeders do lay cocoons quicker than the average pit-run worms, but they still take some time getting used to their new home before beginning to breed. Pit-run are cheaper, are usually younger, and will reproduce well soon after you get them . Because red worms are so popular for growers and fishermen, it's easy to purchase them year-round. Try your hardware store, bait shop, or garden store—or maybe a gas station, if you're in a rural fishing area.

WORM WORDS

Bait worms: Worms that fishermen use to catch fish.

Bed: The place where domesticated worms live.

Bedding: The soil of worms' bed.

Bin: A container for worms.

Breeders: Worms that lay cocoons relatively quickly.

Castings: Dirt, etc. that has gone through a worm's digestive tract and out its hind end. Very good stuff for your soil.

Pit-run worms: This term refers to worms of all ages and sizes, averaging 2,000 to a pound.

Vermicomposting: The process of using worms to decompose kitchen waste (or other organic materials, such as manure/straw bedding from the barn) into rich castings that make wonderful fertilizer for plants and gardens.

WORM VARIETIES: The most common earthworms in the United States, western Asia, and Europe are in the *Lumbricidae* family, which has 220 species or types.

EARTHWORM PRE-TEST ANSWERS

1. False. One half may continue to live, depending on where the cut is made.
2. True. They actually have 3 lips.
3. False. Not only does a worm have a brain, it also has 5 hearts!
4. True. The red wriggler is bisexual but still needs to mate with another worm before laying its eggs. It will be blessed with hatched-out babies in 20 to 30 days.
5. False. These 2 animals have a good symbiotic relationship.

Garden Worms. These are the worms you find in your yard. Fishermen don't like them because they turn white in water. They are usually sold along with a red wriggler to provide the buyer with some big worms. These are not the best kind for your compost bin.

Nightcrawler, African. *Lumbricus terrestris,* also known as the "rain worm, "dew worm," or "orchard worm," averages 5 inches long but can grow to as much as 1 foot long in adulthood. African nightcrawlers are adapted to warm weather and die quickly in cold water or cold air. They are slow breeders, reproducing only every 2 years. Don't bother with them.

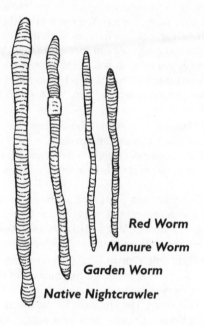

Red Worm
Manure Worm
Garden Worm
Native Nightcrawler

Nightcrawler, Native. Steelhead fishermen prefer these. You find them on lawns and golf courses after a heavy night rain. Native nightcrawlers are slow breeders too, but fishermen like the fact that they can handle cold temperatures and cold water. They require lots of soil for indoor growing and can't tolerate temperatures over 50°F. They don't like having their bedding disturbed, so although they are good in your garden, they aren't too useful in your kitchen-waste recycling bin.

Red Worms. These "red wrigglers" (also known as the "manure worm" or "red hybrid") are the best for doing the job in your household compost bin. Two of the most commonly used red worms are *Lumbricus rubellus* and *Eisenia foetida. Rubellus* is the most likely of the two to be found living in your dirt, but the soil must contain lots of organic material for it to live there. This is a popular worm for growing in a worm bed because it is capable of consuming large quantities of garbage, reproduces quickly, and thrives in a worm bin. The red worm has alternating red and buff stripes. Adults are 1½ to 3 inches long. The red worm produces young every 7 days. The worm reaches full maturity in 9 months, but it is capable of mating at 2 to 3 months. It lives up to 15 years. This worm is good for fishing because it stays active (doesn't drown) and remains red in the water.

Sewer Worms. They can be found in manure piles and identified by the bright rings around their bodies. They grow quite large but are not good bait.

USES FOR EARTHWORMS: You can raise worms for bait or for vermicomposting. Some additional benefits of using worm castings in your garden are reduced insect damage and better texture. One gardener said she felt she'd hit upon a miracle when she started this. She no longer needs to use a rototiller, only a trowel!

Worms for Bait and Moneymaking. The demand for bait is quite high. In the Seattle area, for example, millions of worms for bait are sold each week! Growing worms is easy; it's a potentially profitable hobby or part-time job for at-home mothers, retirees, or anybody who needs extra cash. And it's a great project for kids! The older the worms, the better they are for bait. Nightcrawlers and red worms are good varieties; garden worms are not a good choice for bait because they turn white in the water and die quickly. Sewer worms are sometimes sold to fishermen since they are large, but due to their sour taste, they aren't good bait either.

Selling Bait Worms. Place an ad in the paper; post a notice in your front yard, the local hardware store, or gas station; or advertise in *Field and Stream.* Be prepared to fill big orders. People may want 500 to 5,000 worms. Package in "bait bags." The worms can't crawl out of those.

Worms Produce Fertilizer. Worms can be used to make fertilizer for your garden out of your household garbage or other organic material. Aristotle referred to the earthworm as the "intestines of the world." These lowly creatures eat dirt and organic matter. They combine this food with their digestive juices and excrete a mixture of organic and inorganic material called "castings." The castings improve both soil structure and its ability to hold moisture. Worm castings are practically neutral in pH; they're a water-soluble humus, a perfect fertilizer for plants. Both country and city gardeners can improve their soil by raising worms and using their castings in the garden.

WORM BIN: This is about the container your worms will live in.

Materials. Your worm bin can be made of wood, metal, or plastic. All are equally good, but if you use wood it should be exterior-grade and not aromatic, because aromatic woods (redwood, cedar, etc.) are hard on the worms. Wooden worm boxes wear out. If you let the box dry out once in a while, it will keep longer; building 2 boxes and alternating them allows for that. Painting the wood with something like polyurethane varnish or epoxy also helps protect the wood. Otherwise a wood box will last only 2 or 3 years. *If using a ready-made container, be sure it was not used to hold pesticides. Thoroughly scrub any plastic container you use.* You can build or place your bin outdoors if you live in a mild climate.

Size. The container should be no deeper than 12 inches; 8–12 inches is a good size. The worms tend to stay on the surface, so a deep container is unnecessary and will only encourage the growth of smelly microorganisms, which live where there is little or no oxygen. The width of your bin depends on how much organic garbage your household produces, if you're using the worms to recycle garbage. Your bin should have 1 square foot of surface for each pound of garbage you'll be adding per week. (An average person produces about 2 lb. of garbage per week.) So for a family of 2, a $2 \times 2 \times 8$-foot bin is generally good.

Building Your Own Wooden Worm Bin. See *Raising Earthworms for Profit* by Earl B. Shields for more instructions for building outdoor bins. To build a box for worms that will be composting household garbage, see the instructions in *Worms Eat My Garbage* by Mary Appelhof.

WORM BEDDINGS: Worm beddings not only provide moisture to the bin but also give you a place to bury the garbage. If left a long time, the bedding would be entirely converted into castings by the worms. (You won't leave the worms in the bin that long, though.) The lighter the bedding, the easier it is for the worms to make their way around the box.

Worms in nature enjoy living in organic material such as decaying leaves and rotten logs. Soil is not a necessary bedding ingredient, although you might want to add a handful to the bedding to help the worms' gizzards break down the food. But soil is heavy, and too much makes your bin difficult to move around. Powdered limestone is also a good addition: It adds grit, reduces acidity, and provides calcium for worm reproduction. Or you can use pulverized egg shells for calcium.

NOTE: Do not use slake or hydrated lime. It will kill your worms.

Here are some other common beddings:

Shredded Cardboard. Corrugated cardboard works well. It's light and fluffy and moistens easily. Before wetting, however, this cardboard gives off a fine dust that may be harmful to breathe.

Shredded Paper. Paper is easy to come by. It dries out more quickly than cardboard, but it doesn't give off the problem dust. You can use printed paper; the ink in newsprint doesn't hurt worms. Newspapers, in fact, are the cheapest and easiest worm bedding to get. To prepare the newspaper, just tear it lengthwise into strips 1 to 3 inches wide. Narrow strips are better because the wider the strip, the more quickly it dries out.

Manure. Manure makes good bedding for worms. The odor decreases after the worms are introduced. Adding peat moss makes the manure lighter.

Leaves. Decaying leaves are also good bedding. Avoid using leaves that have been exposed to the lead-laden exhaust from cars. The only problem with leaves is that they can make it harder for the worms to move around.

Peat Moss. Commercial worm growers use peat moss as bedding because it stays damp longer than the others, but it has no food value and is highly acidic. Before adding peat moss to the bed, soak it in water a few hours; that removes some of the acidity. Peat moss is best when combined with other bedding materials: Make peat moss one-third to one-half of the mix. In that role, it improves water retention and makes material like manure less dense.

NOTE: Keep cats out of the worm bin. Cat manure can spread toxoplasmosis, an infection caused by a nasty parasite which, if breathed in by a pregnant woman, can cause brain damage to the unborn child. Also, the ammonia in urine can kill worms.

WORM FOOD

Amount. Too much food will "sour" your worm bed; the worms won't be able to keep up, and it'll smell bad. If you give them too little food, your worms will start getting smaller, and some will die. This happens if your worms have reproduced more worms than your garbage or other feeding schedule can handle. Their population will stabilize at the amount your food for them will support. Over time you'll get a feel for how much to feed.

Frequency. Growing bait worms and harvesting them regularly calls for regular feedings. Worms for vermi

composting can get fed as much kitchen garbage as you have. You can let it build for a few days and give it to them once or twice a week.

How to Feed. As you dump the food out on top of the bin, don't always put it in the same place. In fact, try to put it in a different place each time on about a nine-day feeding cycle. Dig a shallow hole, put the garbage in it, and cover with 1 inch of bedding. Covering the bin with a plastic sheet holds in moisture.

Feeding Kitchen Scraps. Worms can eat any vegetable or fruit leavings and waste. They eat uneaten pasta and potatoes. Unlike most garbage-eating animals, they can eat rotten leftovers! Send the coffee grounds, tea leaves, and coffee filters to your worm bin too. You can also send them meat, although rotting meat smells worse than most garbage. If the meat is chopped, they can process it faster. And if you mix the chopped meat with something organic like sawdust, it won't smell as bad. Meat is rich in nitrogen, and that's something your worms need. Worms can't eat plastic or metal.

Feeding Manure. One of the foods worms thrive on is manure, especially rabbit or horse manure.

NOTE: The manure from recently wormed animals kills worms. Before getting manure someplace, learn the seller's worming schedule.

Rabbits make lots of manure, so put a tray under your rabbit cages and collect this valuable stuff for your worm bin. *Rabbit manure should be soaked with limestone flour for 24 hours to neutralize the acid in the urine before giving it to worms.*

How to Feed Bait Worms. The idea is to fatten up these worms. Once you've figured out the number of beds you want, feed the worms 2 weeks for propagation and 2 more weeks for fattening. Then pick out the fat worms for fishing or for sale. Keep their beds moist by watering. You may not have to water every day, but water enough so that when you squeeze a handful of bedding, it drips. If the beds drip on their own, you've watered too much. After watering, sprinkle chicken mash on the top for worm feed. You'll soon get a feel for how much will be eaten before the next scheduled feeding. If you overfeed, the bed will sour. There's a supplement called SW60 that decreases breeding age by 3 weeks; if you're in a hurry, buy some from a feed store and add to the manure and mash you're feeding the worms.

☛ *WORM FOOD Mix 1 part screened topsoil and 1 part vegetable matter (grass clippings, kitchen waste, etc.). Peat moss is more water-absorbent than food scraps. If the manure is fresh, add more topsoil to prevent heating. Heating forces the worms to the bottom of the bin, where they won't eat or breed. The topsoil also absorbs odors and adds body to the mixture. Add chicken mash or cornmeal to provide the carbohydrates, protein, and fats the worms need for nutrition and to help in the formation of egg capsules. Mix very well.*

BASIC WORM CARE: The less you mess with the worms, the better. Feeding them once or twice a week is sufficient. While feeding, note whether their bedding is staying moist and any other changes. As the worms eat the food and bedding, you'll see more castings. This higher proportion of castings to bedding is not the best thing for worms. If your worms are for bait, get them out of there before they start shrinking instead of growing. On the other hand, if your goal is to grow rich humus for your garden and house plants rather than fishing worms, you can let the worms stay in the bin longer.

Harvest. You will be harvesting either big worms for bait or the old bedding and accumulated castings for your garden.

Method 1. Move the old bedding to one side of the bin and fill the empty side with new bedding. Put the worms' food on the side with the new bedding, and they'll move over there. Then you can just carry off the old vermicompost.

Method 2. Move all the bedding and its worms to a big piece of plastic. Divide the big pile into several smaller piles. Prepare fresh bedding for your worms in their bin. Now shine a bright (100-watt) light on the outside of the piles. The light causes the worms to dig deeper inside. Every 10 minutes, take away the outside layer of vermicompost. Keep doing that every 10 minutes until you get to the worms. Move them into their new bedding.

USING WORM CASTINGS: Put the castings on your house plants about ¼ inch deep. Repeat every 2 months. Use plenty of water periodically to rinse off some salt, which castings contain in abundance. Vermicompost contains some bedding material and is not as decomposed as castings, which contain less salt. High salt content can cause slowed plant growth. You might want to experiment with different kinds of potting mixes, using worm castings, peat moss, perlite for aeration, and/or sand or garden soil for body.

To feed potted plants or transplants, try making a tea from the castings by soaking them in water. Then use the tea to water your plants. Or place the castings in holes where you're going to transplant vegetables or fruit trees; this will give them an added boost.

One less conventional method of using worms is to dig holes for them throughout your garden. "Bury" the worms in the holes, covering them with manure, weeds, and soil. Be sure to keep these holes watered (and covered). The worms will turn the burial materials into castings and then move out to other parts of the garden. Periodically add weeds and other vegetation to the holes to keep the worms fed.

PLANNING YOUR GARDEN

Gardening is fun, educational, profitable—and popular for those very good reasons. For every $1 you spend on your garden (once you have the land), you'll get back about $5 in produce—or more. It's a good investment of time too.

Somebody figured out that for every hour you spend working in your garden you can harvest about $15 worth of produce. In climates with icy winters, gardens begin in the winter, when you're cold and housebound. Then you read, dream, and plan.

GARDENING INFO: *Sunset New Western Garden Book,* written by the editors of *Sunset* magazine, is a big book with small print, jam-packed with reliable information about gardening from the Pacific Coast over to the eastern slopes of the Rockies—especially good on the Pacific rain forest and desert ecosystems. For a good complement to this book, one that is strong where I'm weak (and weak where I'm strong), I recommend the Rodale classic *How to Grow Vegetables and Fruits by the Organic Method. Better Vegetable Gardens the Chinese Way* by P. Chan complements the Western point of view. *Knott's Handbook for Vegetable Growers* by O. A. Lorenz and D. N. Maynard (1980) is very professional, good techno stuff.

Because gardening practices can vary so much in different climate zones, it's especially helpful if you can find regional gardening books such as *Growing Vegetables West of the Cascades* by Steve Solomon (Seattle: Sasquatch Books, 1989), which is great if you're on the Pacific Northwest coast. In addition to books, you can get in-person training by joining your county extension agent's Master Gardener program!

GARDEN SUPPLIES: *Tools for Agriculture,* by John Boyd (1995), from VITA, is a new, enlarged edition of the well-known catalog listing 1,000+ manufacturers and suppliers of low-cost ag implements. Advice is given for choosing 3,000 products, from hand tools to animal-powered and small-engine equipment. *Tools for Agriculture: A Buyer's Guide to Appropriate Equipment for Smallholder Farmers* (4th ed., London), by Ian Carruthers and Marc Rodriguez, is an expert guide to small-scale farming equipment, matching available tools to good farming choices. *How to Select, Use and Maintain Garden Equipment* (Ortho Books, 1982) is a good book on choosing and caring for hand tools.

A. M. Leonard: Sensible Tools for the Serious Gardener offers a free 84-pg catalog of garden tools, etc.: 241 Fox Dr., PO Box 816, Piqua, OH 45356; 800-543-8955; fax 800-433-0633; **www.amleo.com**.

Down to Earth Home, Garden and Gift is a specialist in hand tools: 532 Olive St., Eugene, OR 97401; 541-

Small, First Garden
Bush beans
Bush peas
Leaf lettuce
Onions from sets
Summer squash
Swiss chard (no spinach)
Tomatoes (if you've the climate for them)

Small Garden, Experienced Gardener
Choose compact varieties.
Beans
Brussels sprouts
Cabbage
Carrots
Celery
Corn, sweet
Kale
Peas
Popcorn, dwarf
Tomato

Salad Garden
Carrots
Chives
Cucumbers
Green peppers
Green onions
Lettuce (various kinds)
Parsley
Radishes (red/white)
Tomatoes

Other greens

Basic Temperate Zone Family Garden
Asparagus (a perennial)
Beets
Bush beans
Cabbage
Carrots
Corn, early and late
Cucumbers
Dill
Eggplant
Green peppers
Kidney beans
Leaf and loose-head lettuces
Muskmelon
Onion sets and/or onion seed
Potatoes
Pumpkin
Radishes
Squash, summer
Squash, winter
Sunflowers
Swiss chard
Tomatoes
Turnips
Watermelon

Edible Flower Garden
Nichols Garden Nursery specializes in edible flowers (for address, see "Vegetable Seed Catalogs").
Anise hyssop

Bean
Bergamot
Borage
Calendula petals
Carnation petals
Chives
Chrysanthemum
Cresses
Cucumber
Dandelion
Dill
Fennel, bronze
Garlic
Lavender, English
Lemon mint petals
Marigold
Mints (not pennyroyal!)
Nasturtium
Oregano
Pansy
Pineapple sage
Rose petals
Rosemary
Safflower
Sage
Squash
Sweet cicely
Thyme
Viola odorata

342-6820; or their other location at 2498 Willamette St., Eugene, OR 97405; 541-349-0556; **www.home2garden.com.**

Gardener's Supply Company offers a wide variety of earth-friendly products for gardeners: greenhouses, compost bins, hand tools, trellises, etc. 128 Intervale Rd., Burlington, VT 05401; 800-863-1700; **info@gardeners.com; www.gardeners.com.**

Gardening with Kids: 877-538-7476; 1100 Dorset St., So. Burlington, VT 04503; **www.kidsgardening.com.**

Gardens Alive! 50-pg. catalog; organic tilt: 5100 Schenley Place, Lawrenceburg, IN 47025; 812-537-8650; fax 812-537-5108; 812-537-8651; **76375.2160@compuserve.com.** Their seeds are jobber—that is, they don't grow their own, but buy from others and resell.

Harmony Farm Supply offers drip and sprinkler irrigation systems, organic fertilizers, ecological pest controls, beneficial insects, tools and horticultural supplies, books, seeds, and lab services (soil, water, and plant testing). 128-pg. catalog. Recommended! Contact: PO Box 460, Graton, CA 95444; 707-823-9125; fax 707-823-1734; **info@harmonyfarm.com; www.harmonyfarm.com.**

Integrated Fertility Management offers fertilizers, soil amendments, etc.: fax 509-662-6594; 1422 N. Miller St. #8, Wenatchee, WA 98801; **philu@televar.com;** **www.agricology.com.**

Lee Valley Tools, Ltd., sells mail-order woodworking and gardening supplies: catalog $5; 1090 Morrison Dr., Ottawa, ON K2H 1C2, CANADA; U.S. 800-871-8150; Canadians call 800-267-8767; fax 800-513-7885; **www.leevalley.com.**

Let's Get Growing! "Bringing Nature, Ecology, Science, Habitats, Gardens, Art, and Music to Your Class"—garden supplies for school programs: 1800 Commercial Way, Santa Cruz, CA 95065; 800-408-1868; fax 408-476-1427; **www.letsgetgrowing.com.**

Mantis Garden Tools sells mail-order and retail garden supplies. Free catalog; 1028 Street Rd., Southampton, PA 18966; 800-366-6268; fax 215-357-1071; **mantisgardentools.com.**

Walt Nicke specializes in garden tools and offers a free catalog: 800-822-4114; fax 508-887-9853; 36 McLeod Lane, PO Box 433, Topsfield, MA 01983; **www.gardentalk.com.**

Peaceful Valley Farm Supply sells seeds, fertilizers, weed and pest controls, tools, season extenders (row covers, shade cloth, greenhouses, cold frames, etc.), irrigation, composting and propagation supplies, soil testing, earthworms, bat houses, deer repellents. Organic. Contact PO Box 2209, Grass Valley, CA 95945; 888-784-1722; **www.groworganic.com.**

EARTHCHILD MARIE'S EARLIEST GARDEN

Spacing (Inches)	Amount to Plan per Person	Expected Harvest Date	Crop and Variety Name	Remarks	Needs Full Sun	Transplants	Seeds
18	3	June	Broccoli		x	x	
4	8	June	Beets	Use thinnings as greens; plant with coffee	x		
18	2	June	Cabbage		x	x	
2	20	June	Carrots	Coffee in row repels wireworms	x		
12	4	June	Early sweet corn		x	x	
6	4	June	Kohlrabi		x		x
18	3	June	Head lettuce	Bigger if grown in plastic tunnel		x	x
18	3	May–June	Leaf lettuce			x	x
18	3	May–June	Tender greens				x
2	6	May–June	Onion sets and plants	Thinnings = green onions	x	x	
12	2	May–June	Parsley			x	
18	1	Aug–Sept	Cherry tomatoes	Cage them	x		x
4	12	June	Pole peas		x		x
4	12	June	Bush peas		x		x
12	3	May–June	Early spuds	Reds or cobblers	x		x
4	12	June	Snap peas		x		x
4	12	June	Chinese peas		x		x
1	12	May–June	Radishes	Coffee in row	x		x
12	3	May	Spinach	Cover with box 8pm–10am after June 1			x

Start transplants on March 1; plant out on April 15. Sow seeds April 1 and April 15.

Cover plot with plastic on March 1 to defrost the soil. After planting, replace the plastic until April 15 or until the soil is 40°F. Cover garden with plastic on hoops at night until May 15.

Worm's Way sells supplies for indoor and outdoor gardening: lighting, hydroponics, natural pest control, and worm composting info: 800-316-1261; 7850 N. State Rd. 37, Bloomington, IN 47404-9477; **www.wormsway.com.**

Laying Out the Garden

You have 5 big, complicated questions to answer before your garden is fully planned.

1. Where will it be?
2. How will you arrange the plants in the site?
3. What will you plant in it?
4. When will you plant?
5. Will you use indoor starting/transplanting, cloches, cold frames, and/or a greenhouse to extend your season?

WHERE WILL IT BE? If you really want to have a garden, you can. I've heard from people who live in sunless rooms and have them filled with fragrant green stuff growing under special lights. I've read letters from and visited garden lovers in Nevada and New Mexico, where the natural soil is actually poisonous to plant life or untillable in the most literal sense. They literally built their own soil by bringing in sand, clay, and organic material and mixing, matching, and mulching until they had a mixture that would grow a garden. I've heard from a family that lives on a bare rock cliff and raises a wonderful yearly garden in 4 × 8 foot redwood boxes, 12–14 inches deep. I know Alaskans who do most of their gardening in greenhouses and desert dwellers who do part of it under light wooden slat roofs to keep out the extreme sun.

Water Supply. Some gardens are limited by their water supply—either by how much water they have (you need 1 inch per week from sky or hose) or by how far they can deliver that water. Unless you live in an area with dependable, abundant spring-to-fall rains, don't plan a vegetable garden someplace you can't get water to. Actually drag the hose out and make sure you can get water to all the area you're planning to garden. On the other hand, some land is too wet. In that case, you need a garden site with adequate drainage. Unless you're growing cranberries or water chestnuts, too much water isn't a good thing. If you have a drainage problem, you may have to design a ditching system to take water off or a levee system to keep it out—or grow rice.

Available Sunlight. Pick the sunniest spot available for a start because that's another thing your plants have to have—a minimum of 6 hours a day of sunshine. Hook up your water system in the middle of the sunny spot and see how much gets wet. Then you'll know you have both water and sunshine!

EARTHCHILD MARIE'S SPRING GARDEN

Spacing (Inches)	Amount to Plan per Person	Expected Harvest Date	Crop and Variety Name	Remarks	Needs Full Sun	Transplants	Seeds
8	3	June–July	Bush beans			x	x
4	3	July	Pole beans	Trellis			x
2	8	July	Beets		x		x
2	20	June–July	Carrots		x		x
12	1	July	Cauliflower		x	x	
12	3	June–July	Swiss chard		x	x	
12	4	July	Corn				x
12	1	—	Foxglove	Plant is bug repellent			x
2	12	June–July	Onions				x
12	1	—	Mint	Plant is bug repellent		x	
3	8	July–Aug.	Parsnips		x		x
12	1	—	Petunias	Plant is bug repellent			x
12	3	June	Potatoes	Reds or cobblers	x		x
—	3	July–Aug.	Cherry tomatoes	Cage them	x		x
18	3	July	Leaf lettuce	Cover with boxes after June 15, 8pm–10am			x
18	3	July	Head lettuce	Cover with boxes after June 15, 8pm–10am			x

Start transplants April 1; plant out on May 15. Sow seeds May 1 and May 15.

Water in the morning. Cover with plastic on hoops at night until May 15.

Slope. One of the best protections against erosion is to locate your garden on flat ground. Extremely sloping ground should be kept under permanent plant cover to prevent erosion. Less sloping land can be cropped if need be, but try hard to keep that ground protected by a crop (garden plus green manure or succession planting) at least three-fourths of the time to minimize soil loss. Only quite level ground—"bottom land"—is fairly immune to erosion.

Lead in Soil. I used to complain bitterly about lawns that take up good ground. I'd say, "What is a lawn? It's grass that no animal is going to eat, occupying ground where no vegetable, berry, or fruit is going to grow." I noted that gardens were invariably in the backyard, as if using the ground to grow food instead of that cosmetic grass was a shameful thing. I've learned better. Gardens belong in the backyard—because of lead pollution. The more traffic that goes by your garden, the more lead content there is in the soil; the most dangerous soil is that within 100 feet of a street. If you want to grow food for yourself and your family, you need ground that's away from traffic.

Lead is a toxic heavy metal. Even a little of it can cause severe and permanent damage, especially if young children eat it. Lead is invisible, but if it is present in the soil, it will find its way into every plant that grows there, including parts you harvest for food. I've heard that near stop signs and stoplights the lead content is the worst, up to 5 times normal. That's why neighborhood gardens in urban areas with high traffic density are not as great as they sound—unless you truck in lead-free dirt. Jan Clark, a researcher at the U. of Washington, has found that organic matter in soil can help tie up lead. So one answer is lots of compost. Still, if you live in town, your *backyard* is the best place for the garden!

The other common source of lead contamination in garden soil is lead-based paint that has been scraped off onto the ground around your building. Any wooden house built before the 1950s, when lead was banned in exterior house paints, probably has lead-contaminated soil around the edges of it. Assume the contamination goes out to about 10 feet.

To test the lead level in your soil, inquire at a local Environmental Protection Agency office, county extension service, or toxics lab. To deal with this pollution, remove the top 3 inches of your soil and replace it with new, safe topsoil.

Plot Size. You're lucky if you can make your garden any size you want. In that case, plant according to how many people are being fed, how much they'll eat, and what they like to eat. Ideally, plant about 50 square feet of garden for each person you're feeding, not counting paths. An acre of garden is a minimum for me. But most people are limited by space available. Many are also limited in that they don't have time to keep up with a big garden. You need to know the size of your garden in square feet and in acres, because garden products are often packaged for certain sizes. For easy arithmetic, use multiples of 10. About 200 × 200 feet equals an acre. (See measurement conversion tables in Chapter 1.) Use graph paper for your plot plans.

Plot Shape. Both rectangular and square plots are typical, although you can actually work with any shape you please. You can have several small plots or one big one.

EARTHCHILD MARIE'S LATE SPRING GARDEN

Spacing (Inches)	Amount to Plan per Person	Expected Harvest Date	Crop and Variety Name	Remarks	Needs Full Sun	Transplants	Seeds
8	3	Aug.	Bush beans				x
4	3	Aug.	Pole beans	Trellis			x
8	3	Aug.	Bush limas				x
4	3	Aug.	Pole limas	Trellis			x
—	1	—	Foxglove	Plant is bug repellent		x	
2	20	Aug.	Carrots		x		x
—	2	—	Marigolds	Plant is bug repellent		x	
8	4	Aug.–Sept.	Celery		x	x	
12	4	Sept.	Corn		x		x
18	2	Aug.	Cucumbers		x	x	x
12	2	Aug.	Miniature eggplant		x	x	
—	1	—	Mint	Plant is bug repellent		x	
24	3	Aug.	Bush cantaloupe		x	x	x
18	4	Aug.	Head lettuce				x
18	4	Aug.	Leaf lettuce				x
—	1	—	Petunias	Plant is bug repellent		x	
12	3	Aug.	Peppers		x	x	
1	12	July	Radishes				x
18	6	Sept.	Spuds	Mulch well	x	x	
24	3	Sept.	Yams		x	x	
24	2	Aug.	Bush summer squash		x	x	
24	3	Sept.	Late & Longkeeper tomatoes	Cage them		x	x

Start transplants May 1; plant out June 15. Sow seeds June 1 and June 15.

Water in the morning. Seeds need 50°F soil; transplants, 60° soil.

HOW TO ARRANGE PLANTS? Now you plan how to arrange your plants within the garden site, dealing with matters of beds or rows and planned paths. There are 3 main questions to answer:

1. Will you plant in double-dug, raised beds or use regular tilling, which treats the entire garden area the same way until you plant? If you're going to make beds, what shape and how large? (See "Raised Beds and Wide Rows.")

2. If you are doing a plain garden rather than raised beds, are you going to plant single rows, double (or triple) rows, or "wide" rows?

3. How wide will your paths be? This depends partly on your preference but also on your cultivating method. If you hoe out weeds, you can make narrow (and also uneven) paths between the vegetable rows. But if you plan to rototill, the space between rows must be wide enough so your tiller can get between them without tearing out your vegetables. In a large garden, you may need to make some paths wide enough to bring in a wheelbarrow. In a garden on a slope, it's a good idea to garden in raised beds that have protective sides to hold the dirt in, and to have strips of grass between the garden patches to prevent soil from working its way downhill.

Your Garden on Paper. It helps to use graph paper. Advice from Earthchild Marie: "Show trees, yard, house, garage, fences, flower beds, etc. If you have a compass, add the cardinal points symbol. If not, sketch in the afternoon shadows; then also show the morning shadows. Most garden plants prefer morning sun if there has to be a choice. Greens and beans need the least sun." Do be sure to place the tallest plants where they won't cause morning shade for smaller ones. After making that preliminary sketch, the next step is to choose your varieties. Then you can finish laying out your garden plan.

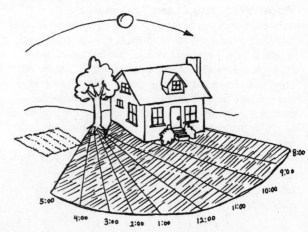

EARTHCHILD MARIE'S SUMMER GARDEN

Spacing (Inches)	Amount to Plan per Person	Expected Harvest Date	Crop and Variety Name	Remarks	Needs Full Sun	Transplants	Seeds
8	3	Sept.	Bush beans				x
4	3	Sept.	Pole beans	Trellis			x
8	3	Sept.	Bush limas		x		x
4	3	Sept.	Pole limas	Trellis			x
2	8	Sept.	Beets		x		x
18	3	Sept.	Broccoli	9-star is perennial	x	x	
18	2	Oct.	Brussels sprouts		x	x	
18	3	Sept.	Cabbage		x	x	
—	1	—	Foxglove	Plant is bug repellent		x	
2	20	Sept.	Carrots		x		x
—	2	—	Marigolds	Plant is bug repellent		x	
18	3	Oct.	Cauliflower		x	x	
12	1	Oct.	Chicory			x	
24	1	Sept.	Kale		x		x
—	1	—	Petunias	Plant is bug repellent		x	
18	4	Oct.	Corn		x		x
18	4	Sept.	Head lettuce				x
18	4	Sept.	Leaf lettuce				x
—	1	—	Mint	Plant is bug repellent		x	
4	8	Oct.	Parsnips		x		x
6	4	Sept.	Kohlrabi		x		x
6	6	Oct.	Winter radishes		x		x
6	6	Oct.	Rutabagas		x		x
6	6	Oct.	Turnips		x		x

Start transplants June 1; plant out July 15. Sow seeds July 1 and July 15.

Water in the evening. To conserve moisture, cover freshly planted seeds with wood or plastic until they emerge.

Perennials. It's wonderful to be able to go out and harvest without having planted! Perennials are plants that come back all by themselves year after year. Rhubarb, asparagus, Jerusalem artichokes, fruit and nut trees, berry bushes and strawberries, certain onions, garlic, and many herbs are perennials. When planting perennials, it's important to place them on the edge of your garden for safety, so that when you plow in spring you can get the job done without tearing out your precious perennials. Or give them a special area—your orchard and berry patch.

WHAT WILL YOU PLANT? Once you've decided exactly what you want to plant, you can complete your plans by deciding the exact arrangement in your garden of each vegetable type. In general, concentrate on the sources of food that will yield the biggest harvest for the least work. Then add a few more for exploration or fun. The varieties you can raise depend on your elevation, the part of the country you live in, your rainfall or water supply, and so on.

Your first garden is almost certain to have some failures. You'll grow to understand its peculiarities over time. But I'm sure you'll be able to raise something that first year.

Companion Planting. Some people use a companion planting system, based on which plants are supposed to be most supportive to each other. But not everybody is convinced that all those so-called good companions are truly that. Some scientifically inclined folks regard some of it as fact but the rest as hokum. For much more info read "Companion Planting: Basic Concepts & Resources" at **www.attra.org/attra-pub/complant.html.**

The "Garden Ideas" lists show you some possible choices for different kinds of gardens.

Secrets of Getting the Most from a Small Garden
Knox Cellars is dedicated to discovering how to do intensive gardening on city lots. They grow dozens of fruit trees by the espalier method and pollinate them with their own colonies of Orchard Mason bees. Their website, **www.knox cellars.com/,** features the most recent issue and several back issues of *Urban Farmer.* Most people pay their way onto the mailing list by buying something from them: bees, a book, or audiotape. They write an *Urban Farmer* from time to time, when the mood strikes, sharing interesting things they have learned about bees, bugs, or gardening.

1. Make use of semishaded areas unsuitable for tomatoes or root vegetables by growing leafy vegetables like lettuce, chard, mustard, or endive there.
2. Don't overplant herbs. Two parsley or chive plants can quite likely produce all you need unless your family is large.

Earthchild Marie's Late Summer Garden

Spacing (Inches)	Amount to Plan per Person	Expected Harvest Date	Crop and Variety Name	Remarks	Needs Full Sun	Transplants	Seeds
12	3	Oct.	Bush beans				x
18	4	Oct.	Chinese cabbage (Taisai or Pakchoi)				x
4	20	Oct.	Carrots	In open cold frame	x		x
18	4	Oct.	Swiss chard	In open cold frame			x
18	1	Oct.	Kale	In open cold frame			x
18	4	Oct.	Sweet corn		x		x
18	4	Oct.	Head lettuce				x
18	4	Oct.	Leaf lettuce				x
18	4	Oct.	Mustard greens	In open cold frame			x
6	12	Oct.	Bush peas		x		x
6	12	Oct.	Snap peas		x		x
6	12	Oct.	Chinese peas (white-flowered)			x	x
3	12	Sept.	Radishes		x		x
18	4	Oct.	Spinach		x		x
18	1	Winter	Cherry tomatoes	In open cold frame		x	
6	6	Oct.	Turnips		x		x

Start transplants July 1; plant out July 15. Sow seeds Aug. 1 and Aug. 15.

Water in the evening. To conserve moisture, cover freshly planted seeds until they emerge. After Sept. 15, cover garden at night with plastic.

3. Avoid sprawling varieties. You can plant 6 rows of carrots, beets, or onions in the same square footage that one row of squash would take because squash simply will spread out all over the place, but root vegetables don't. So limit or refuse summer squash, winter squash, cucumbers, watermelons, muskmelons, cantaloupes, and corn, because they take more space than they're worth. Or use the recently developed compact "bush" kinds of melons, squash, cucumbers, and pumpkins.

4. Consider interplanting so that fast-maturing vegetables use the space between slower-maturing ones that will later spread; for instance, plant radishes or lettuce between vine plants like squash or pumpkin. They mature so fast that you get a crop before the vines need that space.

5. Give preference to continuously bearing vegetables; for instance, choose chard over spinach, because spinach has a brief period of productivity but then is done for the whole summer. Chard will keep making harvest for you until frost kills it. Other continuous bearers are tomatoes, broccoli, kale, lima beans, squash of all sorts, eggplant, peppers, cucumbers, chard, and Brussels sprouts.

6. Use wide-row and succession planting methods to give you the most vegetable productivity per square foot. For instance, peas have a relatively brief production season, but they produce heavily while they are at it, and then you can till up the ground they were in and plant something else. Succession planting works best with a long growing season, but in most places peas, lettuce, radishes, beets, and carrots mature quickly enough that you have time for a second crop if you plant as soon as the first is harvested.

7. Harvest daily in season. Broccoli, cucumbers, summer squash, beans, and chard, for example, will stop producing if they aren't harvested. But if you keep them faithfully and regularly harvested, then they keep producing and you maximize their production.

8. Encourage your garden to grow up rather than across: Try climbing beans (pole or runners) or cucumbers trained to grow up something. Use a big vine such as runner beans, kiwi, or grapes to screen out an ugly area, make shade, or hang from a basket.

9. Plant tall crops such as corn or sunflowers on the north end of the garden so they don't shade other plants.

10. Practice deep watering; it allows you to plant closer together because the roots will go down instead of spreading sideways.

Check out *Success with Small Food Gardens* by Louise Riotte; *How to Grow More Vegetables than You Ever Thought Possible on Less Land than You Can Imagine* by J. Jeavons (1979), a classic on the intensive method; *Growing Vegetables the Big Yield/Small Space Way* by D. Newcomb (1981); *The Integral Urban House* by the Farallones Institute (Sierra Club Books, 1979); and *The Complete Urban Gardener* by Joan Puma (1985). The National Gardening Association offers info at **www.nationalgardening.com** and **www.kids gardening.com**.

Spring Planting Dates

Crop	March 20	March 30	April 10	April 20	April 30	May 10
Asparagus*	Feb. 1–March 10	Feb. 15–March 20	March 10–April 10	March 15–April 15	March 20–April 15	March 10–April 30
Beans, lima	April 1–June 15	April 15–June 20	April 1–June 30	May 1–June 20	May 15–June 15	May 25–June 15
Beans, snap	March 15–May 25	April 1–June 1	April 10–June 30	April 25–June 30	May 10–June 30	May 10–June 30
Beet	Feb. 15–May 15	March 1–June 1	March 10–June 1	Mar 20–June 1	April 1–June 15	April 15–June 15
Broccoli, sprouting*	Feb. 15–March 15	Feb. 15–March 15	March 15–April 15	March 25–April 20	March 20–April 20	April 15–June 1
Brussels sprouts*	Feb. 15–March 15	Feb. 1–March 20	March 15–April 15	March 25–April 20	March 25–April 20	April 15–June 1
Cabbage*	Feb. 1–March 1	Feb. 15–March 10	March 1–April 1	March 10–April 1	March 15–April 10	April 1–May 15
Cabbage, Chinese	+	+	+	+	+	April 1–May 15
Carrot	Feb. 15–March 20	March 1–April 10	March 10–April 20	April 1–May 15	April 10–June 1	April 20–June 15
Cauliflower*	Feb. 10–March 10	Feb. 20–March 20	March 1–March 20	March 15–April 20	April 10–May 10	April 15–May 15
Celery and celeriac	March 1–April 1	March 15–April 15	April 1–April 20	April 15–May 1	April 15–May 1	April 20–June 15
Chard	Feb. 20–May 25	Feb. 20–May 25	March 15–June 15	March 20–May 1	April 1–June 15	April 20–June 15
Chervil and chives	Feb. 15–March 10	Feb. 15–March 15	March 1–April 1	March 10–April 10	March 20–April 20	April 1–May 1
Chicory, witloof	June 1–July 1	June 1–July 1	June 10–July 1	June 15–July 1	June 15–July 1	June 1–June 20
Collards*	Feb. 15–May 1	March 1–June 1	March 1–June 1	March 10–June 1	April 1–June 1	April 15–June 1
Corn salad	Jan. 1–March 15	Jan. 15–March 15	Feb. 1–April 1	Feb. 15–April 1	March 1–April 1	April 1–June 1
Corn, sweet	March 15–May 1	March 25–May 15	April 10–June 1	April 25–June 15	May 10–June 1	May 10–June 1
Cress, upland	Feb. 20–March 15	March 1–April 1	March 10–April 15	March 20–May 1	April 10–May 10	April 20–June 1
Cucumber	March 1–May 1	April 15–May 15	April 10–May 15	April 20–June 1	May 1–June 15	May 15–June 15
Eggplant*	April 1–May 1	March 10–April 10	April 20–June 1	May 1–June 1	May 10–June 1	May 15–June 1
Endive	March 1–April 1	March 10–April 10	April 20–June 1	April 25–June 1	April 25–June 1	June 1–June 15
Fennel, Florence	March 1–April 1	March 10–April 10	March 20–May 1	April 10–May 15	May 15–June 1	April 15–June 1
Garlic	Feb. 1–March 1	March 1–April 1	March 15–April 15	March 20–May 1	April 1–May 1	April 15–May 15
Horseradish*	—	—	Feb. 20–March 20	March 10–April 10	March 15–April 15	April 1–May 1
Kale	Feb. 20–March 10	Feb. 20–March 20	March 1–March 20	March 20–April 20	April 1–April 20	April 10–May 15
Kohlrabi	Feb. 20–March 15	Feb. 20–April 1	March 1–April 1	March 20–May 1	April 1–May 10	April 10–May 15
Leek	Feb. 15–March 10	Feb. 15–March 15	Feb. 15–April 1	March 20–April 1	April 1–April 20	April 15–May 15
Lettuce, head*	Feb. 1–April 1	Feb. 15–April 15	March 1–April 1	March 20–April 15	April 1–May 1	April 15–May 15
Lettuce, leaf	Feb. 1–May 1	March 1–April 1	March 15–May 15	March 20–May 15	April 1–June 1	June 1–June 15
Muskmelon	April 20–June 1	April 10–May 15	April 20–June 1	May 1–June 15	May 15–June 15	May 20–June 10
Mustard	Feb. 20–April 1	March 1–April 1	April 20–June 1	April 20–May 1	May 1–June 1	April 1–May 1
Okra	April 20–June 1	April 10–June 15	May 1–July 1	May 10–June 10	May 10–June 10	May 20–June 10
Onion*	Feb. 10–March 10	Feb. 20–March 20	March 1–April 1	March 15–April 10	April 1–May 1	April 10–May 1
Onion, seed	Feb. 10–March 10	Feb. 1–March 20	March 1–April 1	March 15–April 1	April 1–May 1	April 1–May 1
Onion, sets	Feb. 1–March 20	Feb. 1–March 20	March 10–April 1	March 20–April 20	April 15–May 10	April 15–May 15
Parsley	Feb. 15–March 15	March 1–April 1	March 10–April 10	March 20–May 1	April 1–May 1	April 15–May 15
Parsnip	Feb. 15–March 15	March 1–April 1	March 10–April 10	March 20–May 1	April 1–May 1	April 15–May 15
Peas, black-eyed	April 1–July 1	April 15–July 1	May 1–July 1	May 10–June 15	May 15–June 15	—
Peas, garden	Jan. 15–March 1	Feb. 10–March 15	Feb. 20–March 20	March 10–April 10	April 1–May 10	April 15–June 10
Pepper*	Feb. 15–March 1	April 10–June 1	May 1–June 1	May 10–June 1	May 15–June 10	May 20–June 10
Potato	Feb. 10–March 15	Feb. 20–March 20	March 10–April 1	March 15–April 10	March 20–May 10	April 1–June 1
Radish	Jan. 20–May 1	Feb. 15–May 1	March 1–May 1	March 10–May 10	March 20–May 10	April 1–June 1
Rhubarb*	—	Feb. 15–May 1	March 1–April 1	March 10–April 10	March 20–May 10	May 1–June 1
Rutabaga	Jan. 15–March 1	Feb. 1–March 1	Feb. 1–March 1	—	—	May 1–June 1
Salsify	Feb. 15–March 1	March 15–March 15	March 10–April 15	March 20–May 1	April 1–May 15	April 15–June 1
Shallot	Feb. 1–March 10	Feb. 15–March 15	March 1–April 1	March 15–May 1	April 1–May 1	April 10–May 1
Sorrel	Feb. 1–March 10	Feb. 1–March 10	Feb. 20–April 1	March 1–April 15	April 15–May 15	April 15–June 15
Soybean	April 10–June 30	April 20–June 30	May 1–June 30	May 10–June 20	May 15–June 15	May 25–June 10
Spinach	Jan. 15–March 15	Feb. 1–March 20	Feb. 15–March 15	March 1–April 15	March 20–April 20	April 1–June 15
Spinach, New Zealand	April 1–May 15	April 10–June 1	April 20–June 1	May 1–June 15	May 1–June 15	May 10–June 15
Squash, summer	April 10–May 15	April 20–June 1	April 20–June 15	May 1–May 30	May 1–May 30	May 10–June 15
Sweet potato	April 20–June 1	April 20–June 1	May 1–June 10	May 10–June 10	May 20–June 10	May 10–June 10
Tomato	April 10–June 1	April 10–June 1	April 20–June 1	May 5–June 10	May 10–June 10	May 15–June 10
Turnip	Feb. 20–March 20	Feb. 20–March 20	Feb. 20–March 20	March 10–April 1	March 20–May 1	April 1–June 1
Watermelon	April 1–May 1	April 10–May 15	April 20–June 1	May 1–June 15	May 15–June 15	June 1–June 15

This table gives the range of dates for safe spring planting of vegetables in the open. The date at the top of each column represents the average date of the last freeze in the area; choose the date that fits your area, and read down that column.
*Plants +Generally fall-planted

EARTHCHILD MARIE'S FALL GARDEN

Spacing (Inches)	Amount to Plan per Person	Expected Harvest Date	Crop and Variety Name	Remarks	Needs Full Sun	Transplants	Seeds
4	20	Winter	Carrots				x
12	4	Nov.	Leaf lettuce				x
3	12	Oct.	Radishes				x
12	4	Nov.	Mustard greens				x
12	8	Nov.	Turnip greens				x
12	4	Nov.	Spinach				x
12	8	Nov.	Swiss chard				x
4	12	Nov.	Onion sets/seeds			x	x
4	12	Nov.	Leeks			x	x
4	12	Nov.	Garlic			x	
—	4	Oct.	Tomatoes	Pull up garden plants; ripen in greenhouse			
—	4	Oct.	Peppers	Dig up garden plants			
—	—	—	Rhubarb	In cold frame or pot			
—	—	—	Nettles or dandelions	In pot			

Start transplants Aug. 1; plant out Sept. 15. Sow seeds Sept. 1 and Sept. 15.

Water in the morning. Close cold frames at night. Cover garden at night with plastic on wire frames. Bring plants into the greenhouse on Oct. 1. As each planting bed is harvested, add 3 inches of finished compost, dig it all up for spring, and plant a cover crop such as clover to add nitrogen for next year's garden.

EARTHCHILD MARIE'S WINTER GARDEN

- Oct. 1: Plant peas outside for spring and mulch well. Bring in herbs and cold-frame plants to greenhouse; use large pots. Plant radishes and Asian brassicas in large pots in greenhouse. Cover rest of outdoor crops with a plastic tunnel at night.
- Oct. 30: Pile straw or dry leaves on the fall garden. Cover with 6-mil (.006 inch) plastic. Harvest from the ends of the rows or beds until December if you pick veggies only at noon and cover everything back up immediately.
- Nov.: Third coldest month of the year. Eat the veggies you brought into the greenhouse. Plan next year's garden and make a "Seeds Needed" list.
- Dec.: Make salads with the greenhouse veggies you planted in October. Enjoy your ripened tomatoes. Order seeds.
- Jan.: Coldest month of the year. Begin sprouting grains for salads in the greenhouse or kitchen. Try planting a few Chinese brassicas in pots.
- Feb.: Second coldest month of the year. Make a hotbed in the greenhouse and start planting salad greens and Chinese brassicas in flats. Set a cold frame on your rhubarb, asparagus, or strawberry plants. Cover some daffodils and crocus plants with a cold frame. Think spring!

Winter Garden. Winter gardening right out in the garden can be done, of course, anywhere in the South, but some plants can also make it in the maritime climate of the northwestern United States (between the mountains and the ocean) and in Appalachia, northern California, and the south Atlantic coast. In such areas, and sometimes farther north, you can harvest these plants direct from the garden from Nov. through April.

Brussels sprouts (Nov.–Dec.)
Carrots (Nov.–Dec.)
Chinese cabbage (Nov.–Dec.)
Leeks (Nov.–Dec.)
Parsnips (Nov.–Dec.)
Salsify (Nov.–Dec.)
Kale (Nov.–March)
Leaf lettuce, grown in house/greenhouse (Nov.–April)
Witloof chicory (Jan.–March)
Jerusalem artichokes (whenever ground isn't frozen)
Asparagus (April)
Dandelion greens (April)
Parsley (April)
Swiss chard, if you have plants from previous year (April)

USDA PLANT HARDINESS ZONES

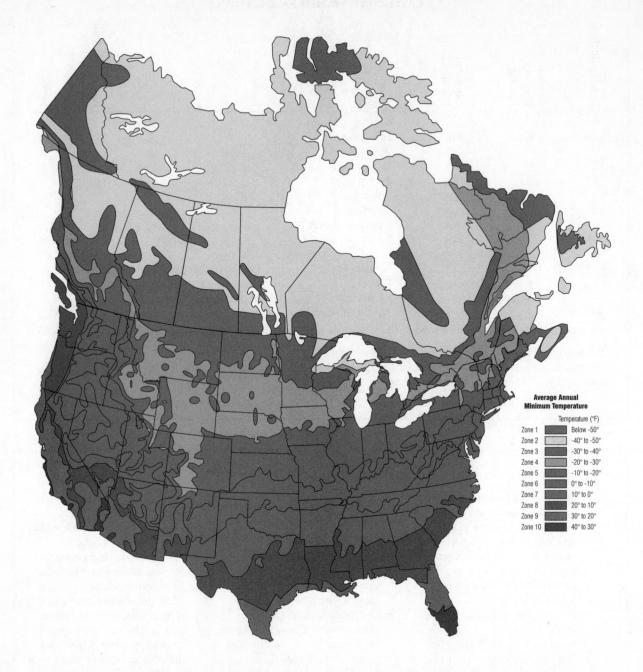

	Average Annual Minimum Temperature
	Temperature (°F)
Zone 1	Below -50°
Zone 2	-40° to -50°
Zone 3	-30° to -40°
Zone 4	-20° to -30°
Zone 5	-10° to -20°
Zone 6	0° to -10°
Zone 7	10° to 0°
Zone 8	20° to 10°
Zone 9	30° to 20°
Zone 10	40° to 30°

For more on off-season gardening, see the "Undercover Gardening" section, and read Winter Gardening in the Maritime Northwest by Binda Colebrook (Seattle: Sasquatch Books, 1989) and The New Organic Grower's Four-Season Harvest by Eliot Coleman, which covers cold-season vegetables in the garden and in cold frames, portable greenhouses, and root cellars (Chelsea Green). If you live in the northeastern United States, also read Intensive Gardening Round the Year by Doscher, Fisher, and Kolb (1981). Go to www.attra.org/attra-pub/nursery.html to read "Sustainable Small-Scale Nursery Production." And order the Ball Red Book, which is a good reference book for greenhouse production: 888-888-0013; PO Box 9, Batavia, IL 60510; www.growertalks.com.

Crop Rotation. Commercial farmers plant the same crop year after year; they hold down the pests with poisons and supply the "fertility" with other chemicals. Organic farmers realize that the insects simply get more resistant and the soil more depleted, and that a better answer is crop rotation. It's smart to move each kind of plant around in the garden every year. For example, you could avoid root maggot by not putting cabbage in the same place twice. If you don't plant the same crop in the same place 2 years in a row, that way at least the bugs will have to hunt every year to find it.

Rotation helps fertility too. Because some crops add fertility and some take it away, always follow the ones that add (such as legumes) with the ones that take (such as corn). Here are some tried-and-true rotation systems for larger, single-crop fields. (See Chapter 3 for others.)

- 3-year rotation: Potatoes; wheat; clover
- 4-year rotation: Wheat; clover; corn; peas or beans
- 5-year rotation: Clover; corn; peas or beans; tomatoes; wheat

Fallow. If a field is let "rest" for a year and no crop planted in it, but it's still tilled several times to keep out weeds, that's called letting it "lie fallow." You can grow a crop 2 years and then let the field lie fallow the third. The advantages of fallowing are that the land settles, organic material that has been tilled under has time to compost, bug and weed species die out, and the ground accumulates moisture. The problem with fallowing is that it risks erosion and wastes good crop land that could be producing a harvest or growing a green-manure crop.

WHEN WILL YOU PLANT?
Planting dates can vary drastically. They depend on which hemisphere you live in and your altitude, basic climate, cropping system (single or double), plant variety, and intended use of the crop—for example, as grain or as green manure. To make planting decisions, you need some basic facts about your climate and the plants you want to grow.

Climate Zone. A valuable thing to know is what climate zone you live in. Your county extension agent can tell you, or you can refer to the map on page 90. When reading garden books and shopping in garden catalogs or nurseries, knowing your zone helps you tell what information is applicable to you and what plant species are suited for your land.

Growing Season. Your "growing season" is the number of days your plants will take to become mature, plus some more time for you to harvest them. If you live in a cold place such as Minnesota or Vermont, you have a shorter growing season than if you live in North Carolina or Texas. So find out the usual frost-free span for where you live: the number of days from the last killing frost in spring to the first killing frost in fall.

Spring and Fall Frost Dates. Your average local spring and fall frost dates, given in 2-week estimates, are available from your county extension agent and are a key planning tool. Some plants go in before the expected date of the last spring frost. Most go in after, and some go in long after.

Pushing the Limits of the Growing Season. The usual growing season extends from the spring frost date (and maybe an extra 2–3 weeks if you're lucky and it's earlier than usual, which is a risk you can take) to the fall frost date. Actually, the fall date is not a simple, single one. This is because a light frost will ruin tomatoes, but certain other plants can keep on growing and producing for a while—until you have a hard freeze. That may not happen for even 2 or 3 months later, depending on what zone you live in. (For late fall and winter gardening, see the "Cold Frames" section under "Undercover Gardening.")

For maximum production, many gardeners push their growing season to the limits and beyond. They plant early enough to risk losing some of that first planting (seeds are cheap). If they have to replant, no big deal; they just do it. They also plant late enough in the fall to risk missing out on harvesting something, but frequently they luck out—because, you see, those frost "dates" are just average, nothing absolute. In any particular year you've got 50 percent odds of being able to stretch the growing season—and 50 percent odds that it'll be somewhat shorter than predicted.

Soil Temperature. This is the other key indicator for proper planting time. Every seed has a soil temperature below which it will not grow and above which it grows, but slowly. (Soil temperatures of various seeds are listed in

Knott's Handbook for Vegetable Growers by Lorenz and Maynard.) You can literally take the soil's temperature, and some people do in order to plant seed when the soil is in the best temperature range for a particular plant. However, most people don't bother with that. There may be another temperature above which it grows rapidly. On the other end, of course, there's such a thing as soil that's too warm.

There are so many different vegetables and each one is a little different, but here are some basic categories:

Frost-Tender Plants. Frost-tender vegetables can't survive a light frost. Don't plant frost-tender vegetables, either seeds or transplants of started plants, until after the last even light frost. ("Frost" means when the temperature gets down around 32°F or lower, because that is freezing.)

Corn is frost-tender. Basically, frost-tender plants are semitropical or tropical natives that we manage to grow in the warmest part of a temperate-zone growing season. You plant corn after most of your other garden vegetables—after the lettuce, peas, beans, beets, chard, turnips, cabbage, and so on—but shortly before the most tender plants of all: cucumbers, muskmelons, watermelons, and squash.

Semihardy Plants. These vegetables can live through a light frost but not a hard one. You'll have to find out the average frost dates for your area. Generally these are planted right on the last frost date. If you wait a couple extra weeks, you'll be safer but your harvest will be later. If you plant earlier than the average frost date, you may be lucky that particular year and be able to start harvesting sooner. Or you may be unlucky and lose all your plants and have to replant.

Hardy Plants. Semihardy and hardy vegetables can live through some degree or other of frost; just how much depends on the particular vegetable. Peas, beets, and kale are in this class. They can be planted as soon as you can get the ground ready in the spring, or you can plant them in midsummer for a late fall crop. These seeds germinate at relatively low temperatures and can be planted 2 to 3 weeks before the expected last frost date.

If you buy the variety your neighbor is using, you're safe planting when he or she does. If you're buying seed from outside your region, ask the seed company for advice —and start with a small, experimental plot.

The "Spring Planting Dates" table, created by the USDA, is a good basic planting schedule for vegetables.

EXTENDED SEASON GARDENING: Here are some methods gardeners use to allow them to eat fresh foods from their garden even longer than nature would ordinarily allow.

Succession Planting. "Succession planting" means planting another crop as soon as you've harvested the previous one. That keeps all your garden ground constantly producing.

Warm-Season vs. Cool-Season Plants. Tomatoes, eggplant, green peppers, watermelon, cantaloupe, and cucumbers are warm-season crops. They are injured or killed by frost, and their seeds won't come to life in cold soil. They won't grow well until your days are hot. Cool-season crops, on the other hand, grow wonderfully in wet, chilly spring weather. Lettuce, spinach, carrots, and broccoli are cool-season crops. From cool-season plants, you typically harvest leaves, roots, or stems (rather than the seeded fruit you harvest from the warm-season vegetables). If the weather turns hot, a cool-season plant tends to "bolt"—it produces flowers and seeds instead of the leaves, roots, and stems that you want to harvest. Succession gardeners plant cool-season vegetables to catch the cool part of their season. They put in the warm-season vegetables timed to catch the right part for them: the heat.

Double-Cropping. This is a basic 2-plant succession. Any garden crop that is harvested and out of there by midsummer, such as peas or beans, leaves a space where another crop can then be planted and still have time to mature before fall frost. That's "double-cropping." Green manure crops, quick-maturing corn, and buckwheat are good possibilities. Another double-cropping pattern starts with a fall-planted crop of winter grain. After it is harvested in mid-summer the next year, a batch of quick-maturing vegetables can be planted where the grain used to be.

Multi-Crop Succession System. From Earthchild Marie: "Divide your garden space into thirds. One third of the available space will be planted in April, one third in May, and one third in June. In July, April's garden will be finished and that space replanted. August's and September's gardens will go in where May's and June's were."

NOTE: *"The secret is to plant something every 2 weeks and to pick something every single day of the year!"*

"The worksheets [Earthchild Marie's planting worksheets have been reproduced on these pages] describe exactly what, when, and how you plant everything. Be sure to record the variety names you plant on the worksheets. Use a pencil so you can use the worksheets over and over. On a separate copy of the plot, plan where each kind of plant is to grow in the garden. When finished, photocopy. One copy goes into your gardening notebook. One copy (encased in plastic) is stapled to the door of your toolshed for easy reference all year long. If you are lucky enough to have a greenhouse, keep the third copy there."

Earthchild Marie lives near Spokane, Washington. In adapting her planting worksheets for your own use, adjust the planting dates and varieties according to where you live.

YOUR GARDEN RECORD: Your first garden is the hardest one to plan because everything is theoretical. To plan subsequent gardens, you can just adapt the plan you used in the previous year, making changes based on what you have learned. Don't wait until winter to think about lessons learned from your summer garden; you might forget too much. It helps to keep weekly notes, even during the busy growing and harvesting months. A big calendar with plenty of space to write those notes in will do. Keep your record going all summer. You'll be so glad you did when you sit down to order again. Write down:

1. The varieties you planted.
2. How much seed you used and how many feet of row you were able to plant with it.
3. Any problems that developed—for example, poor germination, an attack by some insect or disease, or poor performance in dry weather.
4. When you were able to begin harvesting.
5. Whether the yield was good.
6. What you want to do differently next year, and what to do the same way.

Next Year's Garden Plan. Although seed catalogs don't usually arrive until January, do a preliminary plan of your new garden in the fall, as soon as you get some relief from harvest work. Do it while you still remember the successes and difficulties of the just-past gardening season. Use the winter months to consider all the results of last summer's

garden, figure out what changes you want to make, and plan next year's garden as exactly as possible. Based on the summer's experience, consider changing some varieties or quantities.

Words of warning: No 2 gardening years are exactly alike. Weather changes. Pests and pestilences appear and disappear. So 2 or 3 seasons give you a better picture than just one. And things can still change.

BUYING SEEDS, SAVING SEEDS, AND PLANT PROPAGATION

You don't have to buy seeds; you can grow your own. There are some seeds that you don't even have to plant in the garden; you can just plant them in a jar and eat sprouts!

Buying Seeds

If you're doing out-of-season planting you'll need seed catalogs, since grocery stores carry seeds only in the peak planting seasons of spring and summer. If you live way out of town you'll need catalogs for your propagated plant stock too, because nurseries are in the city. At a store, avoid buying seeds that have been situated either where direct sun touches them or near a heat source; a lot of them are probably dead. If the seed packet is dated, get one for the current year.

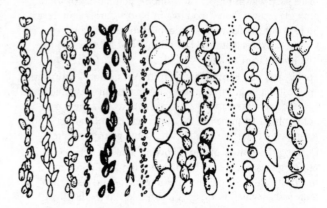

COMMON SEED PACKET/CATALOG PHRASES

Certified seed: Seed that, like a registered animal, has a predictable heredity. You can save your own seed from a certified parent or any nonhybrid variety.

Days-to-maturity: A figure that represents the average number of days from planting to first harvest. It's usually given as a number in parentheses, usually between 28 and 140. Order plants that have a days-to-maturity number that is at least a few less than your usual frost-free period.

Grows in shade: Grows in filtered sunlight, like what comes through tree branches—not absolute shade.

Likes full sun: Won't grow well in an area where there's shade even part of the day.

Perennial: A plant that will live for years (for example, asparagus, artichokes, and rhubarb).

Resistant: Able to naturally withstand insect or disease attack better than a non-resistant plant.

Self-seeder: A plant that may become a weedy pest.

Tolerant: Able to put up with a certain amount of disease or pest damage. A "tolerant" plant isn't as hardy as a "resistant" one. The catalog will indicate what diseases the plant is tolerant of or resistant to by initial. For example, the Beefmaster tomato resists "VFN": verticillium wilt, fusarium wilt, and nematodes.

Treated seed: Seed that contains a deadly chemical to prevent soil fungi diseases. *Do not eat treated seed or feed it to animals.* Treated seed might be yellow, pink, or white. Treating the seed prevents diseases called "damping off" and "soil rot." These are most likely to strike in cool, wet soil early in the spring, but organic seed houses and growers get along without them.

Zone: Find out which USDA zone (1–10) you live in. The catalog often tells you what zone a variety is best suited for, and that's important information.

PRINCIPLES OF CHOOSING SEEDS

1. Look for early and late varieties to extend your growing season. Remember that varieties which do well in the spring may not be as successful in the fall.
2. Be picky about the firms you give your business to. Don't be seduced by color pictures and imaginative promises. Most seed-selling houses are brokers. They place orders for seeds all over the place and then resell them to you. Many of those seeds come from foreign countries, but some houses grow their own. If they do, they'll probably say so. I favor small, regional companies that follow organic principles.
3. Every area has different growing conditions. Ask gardeners who live near you what varieties they have best success with. Your local extension agent is another info source. Order from catalogs directed to your particular climate zone.
4. Note info on new varieties, characteristics of plants, and instructions for growing them.
5. Look for varieties that are resistant to whatever problems are prevalent in your area.
6. The same variety is sometimes sold by different companies under different names. Latin names are the best guide to what species you're getting. Patented names give you precise variety identities, but it's illegal to save seed from a patented plant.
7. You have to evaluate all the characteristics of various varieties: earliness, tolerance/resistance, flavor, compactness, yield, etc., and then choose one or several. Each one has advantages and disadvantages.
8. Store seeds in a dry, cool room. (They are living but dormant.)
9. If you plan to save your own seed—once you have your first mature plants—buy "open-pollinated" rather than "hybrid" varieties. Don't buy patented.
10. When buying seeds by mail, order early to get the best selection and avoid the delays associated with peak sales periods.
11. You can both get and give bargain seeds through seed-swap organizations. (See "Saving.Seeds ")

Besides all that's here, there are three wonderful source books:

Cornucopia II: A Source Book of Edible Plants, by Stephen Facciola, can be purchased for $45 from Kampong Publications, 1870 Sunrise Dr., Vista, CA 92084. This big reference work, years in the making (a kindred soul! When a compulsive gets inspired. . .) lists descriptions and seed/plant sources for 3,000 species of food plants and 7,000 varieties, plus names and addresses of more than 1,300 firms and institutions that offer gourmet, heirloom, ethnic, wild, and standard edibles from around the world. More useful for gourmet cooks, however, than for gardeners.

Garden Seed Inventory, by Kent Whealy of the Seed Savers Exchange, is an inventory of mail-order seed catalogs that lists all the nonhybrid vegetable seeds still offered in the U.S. and Canada: more than 5,700 seed varieties, 223 mail-order sources. Helps you find varieties adapted to your growing conditions. (More than 4,000 varieties of tomatoes, etc.) Paperback, 502 pgs; $22 from Seed Saver Publications, 3076 N. Winn Rd., Decorah, IA 52101; **tara@seedsavers.org.**

Source List of Plants and Seeds, by R. T. Isaacson, is now in its fifth edition. Order either a softcover copy or the web version for $39.95: Andersen Horticultural Library; 952-443-1405; PO Box 39, Chanhassen, MN 55317; **plantinfo.umn.edu.**

Vegetable Seed Catalogs

Listed below are firms offering general garden seed catalogs, including some specialized firms that offer vegetable seeds as well as their specialties. (In subsequent chapters' entries about various vegetables and other plants, these firms are simply mentioned by name; you can get the address from this section.) Sometimes I mention if the catalog is black and white ("b/w") or color. Personally I prefer the b/w folks because they're doing the environmentally wiser, less-leaded option. I wish I had enough space to tell you everything about the special, interesting offerings and bargains of each particular source; instead I've listed highlights for most of them.

In addition to the following list, there are 2 other sizable plant catalog lists in this book: the fruit and berry nursery list in Chapter 6 and the herb specialty businesses listed in Chapter 5. Some other specialty nurseries are listed with the entry for the relevant food—for instance, rosariums are listed in the rose section in Chapter 5.

ARCTIC, CANADIAN, NORTHLAND SPECIALISTS

Try these Down South to beat the bugs! Check out **www.ptialaska.net/~pbabcock/patch/** for garden info from Fairbanks, Alaska!

Alberta Nurseries & Seeds Ltd. specializes in garden seed for areas with a short growing season. Exports only garden seed; bulbs and plants are available only in Canada. Catalog free in Canada; $2 to U.S. and other countries: retail 403-224-3545; wholesale 403-224-3546; Bowden, ALB T0M 0K0, CANADA; **dectool@telusplanet.net; www.gardenersweb.com.**

Allen, Sterling & Lothrop specializes in seeds adapted to the climate of northern New England. Catalog $1 (refunded with order): 207-781-4142; 191 U.S. Rt. 1, Falmouth, ME 04105.

Comstock, Ferre & Co. sells dependable New England varieties (since 1820) of vegetables and herbs. Big b/w catalog, $3 (refunded with order). Inquire for bulk/wholesale prices; 860-571-6590, 263 Main St, Wethersfield, CT 09109, **www.comstockferre.com.**

William Dam Seeds specializes in short-season vegetable varieties from foreign countries. Conscientiously organic, all seeds untreated. Catalog $1; 905-628-6641; fax 416-627-1729, Box 8400, Dundas, ON L9H 6M1, CANADA; **willdam@damseeds.com; www.damseeds.com.**

Gardenimport offers a 2-yr subscription (4 issues/yr) to their full-color 60-pg catalog for $4; 905-731-1950; fax 905-881-3499, PO Box 760, Thornhill, ON L3T 4A5, CANADA.

Good Seed Co. is dedicated to encouraging genetic diversity in home gardens by selling open-pollinated, heirloom, and homestead seeds adapted for the northern garden. Complete catalog online, or send for a seed list: 195 Bolster Rd., Oroville, WA 98844; 509-486-1047; **moonmt@televar.com**; **www.goodseed.net**.

High Altitude Gardens specializes in high-altitude hardy veggies, including Spartan sweet corn; 180 varieties of open-pollinated, untreated seeds. Catalog $2. 208-788-4363; fax 208-788-3452, 4150-B Black Oak Dr, Hailey, ID 83333-8447; **www.seedstrust.com**.

Johnny's Selected Seeds carries a wide selection (700+) of vegetable seeds, culinary, medicinal, and aromatic herb seeds, plus gardening tools, garden supplies, etc. They specialize in cool-season vegetables that do well in Albion. They also sell seeds in bulk: 207-437-4301; fax 800-437-4290; Foss Hill Rd, RR 1, Box 2580, Albion, ME 04910-9731; **info@johnnyseeds.com, www. johnnyseeds.com**.

Rawlinson Garden Seed, 1979 Rte. 2 Hwy., Sheffield NB E3A 8H9, CANADA; 506-446-3882; fax 506-357-2256; **rawlinson@fundy.net**. Specializes in untreated, short-season vegetables and herbs. Modest catalog free in Canada, $1 to U.S. (refunded with order).

Salt Spring Seeds offers amaranth, tampala, quinoa, various wheats, runner beans, hull-less barley, hull-less oats, etc., all grown organically: 250-537-5269; Box 444, Salt Spring Island, BC, V8K 2W1, CANADA; **www.saltspringseeds.com**.

Stokes Seeds gives a 96-pg, 8½ x 11 in. color catalog—half veggies, half flowers; 800-263-7233, fax 888-834-3334. The Canadian company serves U.S. customers from PO Box 548, Buffalo, NY 14240-0548, Canadians write 39 James St., Box 10, St. Catharines, ON L2R 6R6, CANADA, **stokes@stokeseeds.com, www. stokeseeds.com**.

T & T Seeds Ltd. specializes in vegetables and fruits for northerners; 204-895-9964; fax 204-895-9967; Box 1710, Winnipeg, Manitoba R3C 3P6, CANADA; **orders@ttseeds.mb.ca; www.ttseeds.mb.ca**.

Vesey's Seeds, Ltd.: Free catalog. 902-368-7333; fax 902-566-1620; York, Prince Edward Island C0A 1P0, CANADA; **www.veseys.com**.

TROPICAL/SUBTROPICAL

(The) Banana Tree is a worldwide subtropical and tropical seed and bulb specialist. They grow everything that they offer on their tropical farms, including a big selection of bananas, and ship worldwide. Everything comes with brief growing instructions. Catalog on Internet: 610-253-9589; fax 610-253-4864; 715 Northampton St., Easton, PA 18042; **faban@enter.net; www.banana-tree.com**.

Digger's Mail Order specializes in Australian varieties, carries tree tomato: 03-5987-1877; fax 03-5981-4298105; Latrobe Parade, Dromana, 3936, AUSTRALIA.

Eden Organic Nursery Services offers open-pollinated and hybrid seeds for peppers, organic tobacco, medicinal/healing plants, vegetables, vines, tropical plants, and organic gardening supplies: 954-455-0229; fax 954-458-5976; PO Box 4604, Hallandale, FL 33008; **info@eonseed.com; www.eonseed.com/**.

Native Seeds/SEARCH offers heirloom vegetable seeds of the desert and mountain Southwest, great chile collection, multicolored popcorn, great sorghum assortment including cotton and desert foods for diabetes control. B/w catalog $1: Southern Arizona Gourd Ass'n c/o Kasin Hunter, 520-746-1563; PO Box 26037, Tucson, AZ 85726; **nss@azstarnetcom; www.nativeseeds.org**.

Park Seed Co. offers a color 8½ x 11 in. catalog of seeds/plants for folks in the Southeast U.S. or California: 800-845-3369; fax 864-941-4206; 1 Parkton Ave.; PO Box 46, Greenwood, SC 29647; **info@parkseed. com; www.parkseed.com**.

Phoenix Seeds offers common and unusual vegetables, culinary and medicinal herbs, plus trees; catalog: 03-6267-9663; PO Box 207, SNUG 7054, AUSTRALIA.

Southern Exposure Seed Exchange offers 550+ varieties of open-pollinated, heirloom seeds of vegetables, flowers, and herbs, plus seed-saving and growing supplies. The $2 catalog includes growing info; after you order, the catalog is free. They encourage you to save seed from endangered species: 540-894-9480; fax 540-894-9481; PO Box 460, Mineral, VA 23117; **gardens@southernexposure.com; www.southern exposure.com**. Online forum for discussing gardening, farming, organics, seeds, seed saving, etc.

BULK SEED PURCHASES: You may buy bulk seeds at discount from Abundant Life Seed Foundation, Evergreen Y.H. Enterprises, Johnny's Selected Seeds, R.H. Shumway's, Seeds of Change, etc. (listed above and below).

Twilley Seed Co. supplies bulk seeds (mostly hybrid vegetables) for roadside, u-pick, and truck gardeners. Free 90-pg color catalog. Ornamental corn seed (blue, pink, red, Indian): 800-622-7333; fax 864-227-5108; PO Box 4000, Hodges, SC 29653-4000; **www.twilley seed.com**.

OPEN-POLLINATED/HEIRLOOM & ORGANIC SEEDS

Abundant Life Seed Foundation is a nonprofit that specializes in untreated, open-pollinated, and rare/endangered species; offers seed screens, quinoa, amaranth, heirloom corn, flax, Egyptian onions, orach, etc. Order the catalog and join a community of brave idealists pursuing organic, biodynamic, sustainable agriculture. Projects include World Seed Fund (open-pollinated seeds for poor farmers), building a new dorm for apprentices, finding more gardeners for their Seed Growers Network, and training residential students who work with master gardeners in seed production. B/w catalog $2. A $20 membership gets you their newsletter, and your money is donated to the project of your choice. Will sell seeds in bulk: 360-385-5660; fax 360-385-7455; PO Box 772, Port Townsend, WA 98368; **abundant@olypen.com; www.abundantlifeseed.org**.

Bountiful Gardens specializes in organic gardening supplies, nonhybrid seeds, and garden grains (wheat, oats, barley). Good selection of books on organic gardening and food self-sufficiency with a small garden. Free catalog; garden workshops, internships: 707-459-6410; fax 707-459-1925; 18001 Shafer Ranch Rd., Willits, CA 95490-9626; **bountiful@sonic.net, www. bountifulgardens.org**.

Fedco is a grower co-op that offers a good variety of their own grown untreated hybrid and open-pollinated seeds and supplies for the organic grower: 207-873-7333; fax 207-872-8317; PO Box 520, Waterville, ME 04903; **www.fedcoseeds.com.**

Heirloom Seeds offers herb and vegetable seed (all non-hybrid, no chemical treatments or genetically engineered; certified organic), plus books, insect control products, and gardening supplies: catalog $1; Box 245, W. Elizabeth, PA 15088-0245; phone/fax 412-384-0852; **mail@heirloomseeds.com; www.heirloom seeds.com.**

Native Seeds/Search offers a catalog featuring Southwestern seeds: 520-622-5561; 526 N. 4th Ave., Tucson, AZ 85705; **info@nativeseeds.org; www.nativeseeds.org.**

Redwood City Seed sells no hybrids or genetically modified seeds, just 280 great heirloom vegetables and herbs. Earth-loving, organic-principled folks; emphasis on seeds for home food growers. Small-print, packed, free b/w catalog; PO Box 361, Redwood City, CA 94064; 650-325-7333; **www.ecoseeds.com.**

Seed Savers Exchange offers a 40-pg color catalog of heirloom vegetables, all open-pollinated. A truly unique selection of outstanding vegetables, flowers, and herbs: 297 varieties produced by networking home gardeners. Free catalog: 3076 N. Winn Rd., Decorah, IA 52101; **catalog@seedsavers.org; www.seedsavers.com.**

Seeds of Change: 51-pg color catalog of heirloom seeds, all certified organic and open-pollinated: good herb collection, amaranth, runner bean, echinacea. Dedicated to preserving biodiversity. Option to buy seeds in bulk; seed saver training: PO Box 15700, 3205 Richards Lane, Santa Fe, NM 87506-5700; 888-762-7333; fax 888-329-4762; **soc.customer.service@seedsof change.com; www.seedsofchange.com.**

Select Seeds specializes in antique flowers. Free catalog: 180 Stickney Hill Rd., Union, CT 06076; 860-684-9310; fax 800-653-3304; **info@selectseeds.com; www.selectseeds.com.**

Sow Organic Seeds offers organic herb, vegetable, and flower seeds. Their website has info on saving seeds and a free, printable online catalog: 888-709-7333; 1573 Wilson Ct., Eugene, OR 97402; **www.organic seed.com.**

Talavaya Seeds is a nonprofit that collects and preserves open-pollinated Indian food crops. Catalog $1. "Talavaya is a Hopi word for the time of day just before dawn, when the farmer goes to his fields and the Great Spirit receives his prayers": PO Box 50, Caballo, NM 87931-0050.

Victory Seed Company is working to preserve open-pollinated and heirloom seed varieties for home gardeners. No unstable modern hybrids or genetically modified seeds. All seed chemically untreated and many are organically grown or from certified organic growers. Catalog $2 (refunded with order). 503-829-3126; PO Box 192, Molalla, OR 97038; **info@VictorySeeds.com; www.VictorySeeds.com.**

SPECIALTY SEED CATALOGS

(The) Cook's Garden specializes in European vegetables and herbs for gourmet cuisine: arugula, celery root, chicories, plus glass canning jars with old-fashioned rubber rings from Germany. Organic emphasis; "largest selection of lettuce and salad greens in the world." You are invited to tour their gardens in Burlington, VT. Catalog $1: 800-457-9703; fax 800-457-9705; PO Box 535, Londonderry, VT 05148; or Box 5010, Hodges, SC 29653-5010; **info@cooksgarden.com; www.cooks garden.com.**

Dutch Gardens offers a catalog/website with flower bulbs and plants shipped direct from Holland: 144 Intervale Rd., Burlington, VT 05401; 800-944-2250; **www. dutchgardens.com.**

Evergreen Y.H. Enterprises sells hybrid or nonhybrid Oriental vegetable seeds; small packets or bulk. Books on Oriental cuisine: PO Box 17538, Anaheim, CA 92817; **eeseedsYH@aol.com; www.evergreenseeds.com.**

Howard Dill Enterprises sells seed for "world's largest" and "smallest" pumpkins and squash, and many other pumpkin, squash, and gourd varieties: 902-798-2728; fax 902-7980842; RR 1, 400 College Rd., Windsor, Nova Scotia B0N 2T0, CANADA; **www.howard dill.com.**

J. L. Hudson, Seedsman, specializes in heirloom vegetables and Zapotec Indian seeds, and sponsors a seed exchange. Catalog $1. No phone: Star Rte. 2, Box 337, La Honda, CA 94020; **www.JLHudsonseeds.net.**

Kitazawa Seed Co. specializes in Japanese and other Asian vegetable seeds. Interesting, free price list for wholesale, mail-order, or bulk buyers: 510-595-1188; fax 510-595-1860; PO Box 13220, Oakland, CA 94661-3220; **kitaseed@pacbell.net; kitazawaseed.com.**

Le Jardin du Gourmet specializes in French vegetables and herbs, beans, peas, seeds from France, leeks, garlic, and rocambole. Catalog and 4 sample packets of herb seeds and recipes cost $1: 802-748-1446; PO Box 751, St. Johnsbury Center, VT 05863; **www. ArtisticGardens.com.**

Nichols Garden Nursery specializes in rare seeds and varieties for short- and variable-season areas and the Pacific Northwest. Good herb section, plus a potpourri of gardening supplies, tea bags to make your own herb tea blends, potpourri kit, corks/corkers, etc. Free 70-pg b/w and color catalog: 1190 N. Pacific Hwy., Albany, OR 97321; 541-928-9280; fax 800-231-5306; **nichols@gardennursery.com.; www. gardennursery.com.**

Shepherd's Garden Seeds sells gourmet vegetables, culinary herbs, and garden supplies. Call 800-482-8915 for garden advice and info on *The Gardener's Magazine*. They also have a marvelous demonstration garden, White Flower Farm. It's on Rt. 63 south of the center of Litchfield, CT; 30 Irene St., Torrington, CT 06790; 800-503-9624; 860-496-9624; fax 860-482-0532; 6116 Hwy. 9, Felton, CA 95018; **www. whiteflowerfarm.com.**

Vermont Bean Seed Co. offers a free 90-pg color catalog. Specialty in antique and gourmet vegetables: 803-663-0217; fax 888-500-7333; Garden Lane, Fair Haven, VT 05763; **www.vermontbean.com.**

Willhite Seed Company specializes in melons. Free 60-pg color catalog: 817-599-8656; PO Box 23, Poolville, TX 76487; **www.willhiteseed.com.**

GENERAL SEED CATALOGS

Burgess Seed & Plant Co. has a basic selection of fruits and vegetables; 48-pg color catalog: 905 Four Seasons Rd., Bloomington, IL 61701; 309-663-9551.

W. Atlee Burpee Co. has some of everything in their free 123-pg color catalog: 800-888-1447; fax 800-487-5530; 300 Park Ave., Warminster, PA 18974; **www.burpee.com**.

D. V. Burrell Seed Growers Co. sells vegetable and herb seed, including gourds and lots of open-pollinated varieties; also, chemicals, books, and tools; free 98-pg catalog: PO Box 150, Rocky Ford, CO 81067; 719-254-3318; fax 719-254-3319.

Crosman Seed Co. has served the home gardener for more than 160 years with flower, vegetable, promotion seed packets, and grass seed. Free packet listing: 800-446-7333; fax 585-586-6093; PO Box 110, East Rochester, NY 14445; **www.crosmanseed.com**.

DeGiorgi Seed Co. offers basic vegetables, and their specialty of Italian veggies. Free catalog: 6011 N St., Omaha, NE 68117-1634; 402-731-3901; **www.degiorgi seed@aol.com**.

Gourmet Gardener, 8650 College Blvd., Overland Park, KS 66210; 913-345-0490. Herb, vegetable, and flower seeds from around the world. Catalog $2.

Gurney's Seed & Nursery Co. offers a basic selection of seeds, trees, plus gardener's supplies. Free color catalogs—spring and fall: 812-539-2499; fax 812-537-9059; 812-539-2502; **www.gurneys.com**. Same outfit ("Gardens Alive!") now owns Gurney's, Henry Field's, Spring Hill Nurseries, Michigan Bulb Co., and Breck's. They're basically "jobber"—meaning they don't grow their own, but buy from other growers and resell.

Harris Seeds offers a free 80-pg catalog of seeds and seed-starting supplies: 800-514-4441; fax 877-892-9197; 355 Paul Rd., PO Box 24966, Rochester, NY 14624-0966; **gardeners@harrisseeds.com**; **www.harris seeds.com**.

Henry Field's Seed & Nursery Co. sells vegetables and fruit in their free colorful 88-pg spring and fall catalogs: 415 N. Burnett, Shenandoah, IA 51602; fax 800-357-4149; orders 800-235-0845; service 800-798-7842; **www.henryfields.com**.

Ed Hume Seeds specializes in basic vegetable seeds suited to cool summers in the Pacific Northwest. Catalog $1: PO Box 1450, Kent, WA 98035; **HumeSeeds@ aol.com**.

J. W. Jung Seed has a complete selection of vegetables, fruit, and nursery stock, but summer/fall catalog is almost all flowers: 800-247-5864; 800-297-3123; fax 800-692-5864; 335 S. High St., Randolph, WI 53957; **info@jungseed.com**; **www.jungseed.com**.

Mellinger's offers garden supplies and a free 8½ x 11-in. seed and garden supply catalog with more than 4,000 items! Seeds, trees, shrubs, bulbs, perennials, *plus* all the supplies to make them grow including greenhouses: PO Box 157, N. Lima, OH 44452; 800-321-7444; fax 330-549-3716; **mellgarden@aol.com**; **www.mellingers.com**.

Peaceful Valley Farm Supply sells bulk vegetable seeds, cover crops, garden supplies, etc.: PO Box 2209, Grass Valley, CA 95945; 888-784-1722; fax 530-272-4792; **www.groworganic.com**.

Pinetree Garden Seeds offers a free large catalog of seeds (also kitchen gadgets, garden aids, books): 207-926-3400; fax 888-52-SEEDS; Box 300, 616A Lewiston Rd., New Gloucester, ME 04260; **pinetree@super seeds.com**; **www.superseeds.com**.

R. H. Shumway's has a large, charming old-fashioned b/w catalog entirely focused on vegetables. Wholesale prices for bulk seed purchases of selected varieties: 803-663-9771; fax 888-437-2733; PO Box 4, Graniteville, SC 29829; **www.rhshumway.com**.

Territorial Seed Co. sells mole traps, natural insecticide and fertilizer products, vegetable varieties suited to gardening "west of the Cascades" (maritime Northwest), and *winter* harvest veggies; 124-pg catalog: 541-942-9547; fax 541-942-9881; orders 888-657-3131; PO Box 158, Cottage Grove, OR 97424-0061; **tertrl@ territorial-seed.com**; **www.territorialseed.com**.

Thompson & Morgan is an English seed company whose U.S. branch offers many rare or unique seed varieties. Large, free color catalog: 800-274-7333; fax/info 888-466-4769; PO Box 1308, Jackson, NJ 08527-0308; **www.thompson-morgan.com**.

About Latin Plant Names

Plant catalogs and garden books usually give plants at least 2 names: a popular one and a Latin one. The Latin names have one important advantage: there's only one per plant. And that one Latin name is the same in every country and in every language. Or, more accurately speaking, there is *supposed* to be only one Latin name for each plant, but sometimes seed houses—or even botanists!—don't agree on the Latin name of a plant or even on its botanical family, such as whether or not it's a legume!

But the confusing array of English-language names for a particular vegetable or herb is typically much worse than the Latin naming. As it is, a person could go bonkers looking at seed catalogs and trying to figure out what plant some of those fancy, meant-to-sell, English-language variety names really mean. So I apologize in advance for all the scientific names of plants in Latin I'm going to throw at you in this book, but for me, starting with the Latin and avoiding trade names made it much simpler.

Incidentally, I honestly think there should be a law requiring all seed catalogs to give the Latin name for each plant whose varieties they offer as well as some agreed-upon common name. Then they wouldn't just think up their own or pick something "exotic," as now sometimes happens. It's so hard for seed shoppers when the same plant may appear in 5 different catalogs under 5 entirely different names. A regulation like that would be like that wonderful law that requires companies to list ingredients in order of amount on food containers: openness and truth in labeling!

Here's a summary of how Latin naming of plants works.

KINGDOMS: All living creatures are assigned to one of 5 categories called "kingdoms." The nonmeat foods we eat come from either kingdom Fungi (mushrooms, truffles) or kingdom Plantae (apples, turnips, wheat . . .). Each of the kingdoms is subdivided into "phyla." The singular of that is "phylum." The fungi we eat from kingdom Fungi, which has five phyla in all, come from either the phylum Basidiomyocota (mushrooms), or the phylum Ascomycota (baker's and brewer's yeasts; truffles). Nearly all of your nonmeat food-unless you're a major mushroom eater—comes from kingdom Plantae.

Kingdom Plantae. This is divided into 2 big subgroups: the gymnosperms and the angiosperms. There are nine gymnosperm phyla, but most of them don't contain plants with edible parts. Plants such as conifer trees, ferns, ginkgo trees, and mosses are gymnosperms. The angiosperms, or flowering plants division, has only one phylum, named Angiospermophyta. The plants of that one phylum of angiosperms are the ones that we human beings—as well as all the animals we depend on for food—live on! Angiospermophyta is itself subdivided into 2 great divisions called "classes": the Monocotyledoneae and the Dicotyledoneae. The class Monocotyledoneae is called the "monocots" for short. The class Dicotyledoneae is called the "dicots."

Monocots and Dicots. Monocots have seeds with 1 seed leaf (1 cotyledon), leaves that are narrow with parallel veins, flower parts that appear in multiples of 3, and no stem cambium (cells that produce wood). Dicots have seeds that start out with 2 cotyledons, broad leaves with a central midrib and veins that branch out from that, flower parts that grow in multiples of 4 or 5, large colorful flower petals, and sometimes woody stems.

Orders and Families

Each class, monocot or dicot, is subdivided into "orders." Each of those orders is again subdivided into "families." The order name is frequently ignored in describing a plant. Both order names and family names end with "eae," so it's easy to get them confused. If you want to see all the order names organized with all the family names that go under each order, look under "angiosperm" in the Macropedia of the *Encyclopedia Britannica*. The order Poaceae is important because it contains the family Gramineae, also known as the "grasses," the grain plants that feed humankind.

The more frequently encountered family names have English equivalents that are more commonly used in talking about them. Thus Rosaceae is also called the rose family, Solanaceae the nightshade family, Asteraceae the sunflower family, and so on. There are far more dicot than monocot families. But the monocots are still tremendously important as a food base for the larger animals on earth because of the monocot order Poaceae. The table "Important Monocot Families" lists the main monocot families (usually ignoring the orders).

IMPORTANT MONOCOT FAMILIES

Latin Name	Common Name	Some Members
Arecaceae	Palm family	Coconut palm, date palm
Bromeliaceae	Bromeliad family	Pineapple
Gramineae	Grass family	Wheat, bamboo, grasses (corn, rice)
Juncaceae	Rushes family	Rushes
Liliaceae	Lily family	Lily, tulip, all onions
Musaceae	Musa family	Banana

Members of the family Gramineae, also known as the "grasses," all have jointed stems and slender, sheathing leaves. (Go out and look at one; you'll see!) The bamboos, grass grains (wheat, rye, oats, barley), and the sorghums are all of family Gramineae. The members of that family are so important as a food source for us that their species take up most of one big chapter in this book (Chapter 3, "Grasses, Grains, and Canes"). Coconuts, dates, pineapples, and bananas are other important monocot foods in tropical climates. Almost all of our other important foods come from the dicot families.

IMPORTANT DICOT FAMILIES

Latin Name	Common Name	Some Members
Apiaceae	Carrot family	Carrot, parsley
Asteraceae	Sunflower family	Dandelion, sunflower
Brassicaceae	Crucifer ("cabbage") family	Cabbage, cauliflower, kale, turnip
Cucurbitaceae	Cucurbit ("gourd") family	Cucumber, melon, pumpkin, squash
Lamiaceae	Mint family	Lavender, mint
Leguminoseae	Legumes	Alfalfa, beans, peanuts, peas
Rosaceae	Rose family	Apple, rose
Solanaceae	Nightshade family	Pepper, potato, tomato

The dicot order Fabaceae is like the monocot order Poaceae in that it contains one overwhelmingly important food-producing family for both domestic animals and people. That family, Leguminoseae, commonly called the legumes, includes alfalfa, clover, beans, and peas. The legumes, together with the grass grains, are the 2 fundamental foods that feed humanity and its livestock.

GENERA: Each family is subdivided into genera, the singular of which is "genus." (The genera were created by a famous old-time European botanist named Linnaeus, who assigned to a genus every plant in the world that he had ever heard about.) When you look at Latin names in a seed catalog or plant encyclopedia, what you usually see is the genus name (capitalized) followed by the species name (not capitalized). Generally the name of the plant's botanical family is mentioned too. You can expect plants in the same genus to be quite similar in flower, fruit, and growing characteristics and to be subject to the same diseases and the same insect attackers.

For example, the genus of all the onion varieties is *Allium*. Its family is Liliaceae, the lily family, a monocot. "Allium" is the Latin word for "garlic" (one of the onions). Garlic (*Allium sayivum*) is a single species inside that larger *Allium* genus, all of which have Latin names that start with *Allium*. So chives' botanical name is *Allium schoenoprasum*. Garlic chives are *Allium tuberosum*. Shallots are *Allium ascalonicum*. Globe onions are *Allium cepa*. Leeks are *Allium ampeloprasum*. The Welsh onion is *Allium fistulosum*. Rocambole is *Allium scorodorprasum*.

Another botanical convention followed in this book is that when plants of the same genus are mentioned repeatedly, the genus is abbreviated after the first mention, using only the first letter and a period—for instance, in the above paragraph, *Allium cepa* would be abbreviated as *A. cepa*.

Variety. When there are different varieties within the species, as is frequently true, the species name is followed by "var."—which stands for "variety"—and then its variety name. Tree, or "topset," onions are classed as a variety of globe onions (*Allium cepa*). But anyway, a "variety" is supposed to be a subspecies (inside a species group) that has minor variations which are consistently passed on to the progeny of that plant. So the Latin name for tree onions is *Allium cepa* var. *viviparum* or, as varieties are more briefly written—omitting the "var."—*Allium cepa viviparum*. The same is true of potato onions, which are named *Allium cepa* var. *aggregatum. So here's the taxonomic structure for potato onions:*

Kingdom: *Plantae*

Phylum: *Angiospermophyta*

Class: *Monocotyledoneae*

Order: *Liliae*

Family: *Liliaceae (Lily)*

Genus: *Allium*

Species: *Cepa*

Variety: *Aggregatum*

There are two long-time systems for remembering the basic names and sequential order of these groupings of kingdom, phylum, class, order, family, genus, and species. One is "King Philip Came Over For Good Soup." The other is "Kindly Place Cover On Fresh Green Spicy Vegetables." That last one takes it all the way down to the "V" for "variety."

Group. Sometimes there is only one plant type in a species; that's really nice. But often there are several. And sometimes there are so many distinct varieties of a species that it just gets crazy. That's true of the Crucifer genus *Brassica*. For a situation like genus *Brassica*, botanical taxonomists break it down one step further and give similar varieties a special "group" name.

For example, the species of *Brassica oleracea* includes as varieties broccoli, Brussels sprouts, cabbage, cauliflower, collards, kale, and kohlrabi! So those are subdivided by "group." Cauliflower and broccoli are both *Brassica oleracea*, Botrytis group. Kale and collards are *Brassica oleracea*, Acephala group. Cabbage is *Brassica oleracea*, Capitata group. Brussels sprouts are *Brassica oleracea*, Gemmifera group. Kohlrabi is *Brassica oleracea*, Gongylodes group. The related species of *Brassica rapa* contains both turnips and Chinese cabbage as varieties, which is equally hard for the non-expert to understand: How can Chinese cabbage be more like a turnip than a cabbage? However, it is some comfort that turnips are *Brassica rapa*, Rasifera group, and Chinese cabbage is *Brassica rapa*, Pekinensis group.

Cultivar. The word "cultivar" means the same thing as "variety," except it's an English word instead of a Latin one and suggests that somebody somewhere owns the rights to sell the seed. A cultivar is a subspecies of a plant species that has predictable features which will be passed on from generation to generation. The cultivar's name is capitalized. For example, in the cauliflower section of a seed catalog, you might see "Snow King F1," "Late Queen," or "Purple Cape." Those are cultivar names.

Botanical experts who classify plants sometimes don't agree with each other and sometimes don't agree with the previous generation of experts on a plant's particular classification and therefore its botanical family and proper Latin name. That's why you may see the same plant listed with one Latin name in one place and another somewhere else. Usually names are standard, but one source may be much older than another—or an author may be just plain nervy and may fake a Latin name for the heck of it. Who knows? Even exact science can be woefully inexact.

MORE INFO: If you liked this, you'll love the *International Code of Botanical Nomenclature* (1988) or *Hortus Third* (Macmillan, 1976). Those books are the court of last resort for folks who want official Latin names; the ones listed in them are supposed to be *correct*.

Saving Seeds

Bananas, potatoes, and many herbs are reproduced by propagation rather than by planting seeds. Propagation means burying a piece of the progenitor plant. But most of the common garden vegetables are always planted from seed: seed that you buy, save from your own plants, or swap with other seed savers.

BOOKS FOR SEED SAVERS: *Seed to Seed: Seed Saving Techniques for the Vegetable Gardener* by Suzanne Ashworth is a complete guide for saving the seeds of 160 vegetables. For each vegetable it gives the botanical classification, method of pollination, isolation distance, caging technique, seed harvest, and methods of drying, cleaning, and storage, plus a source list for seed-saving supplies and instructions in how to sell surplus seeds. Another good book on seed saving is *Seeds of Change: The Living Treasure* (Harper San Francisco, 1993).

Still another is *Saving Seeds: The Gardener's Guide to Growing and Storing Vegetable and Flower Seeds* by Marc Rogers (1990). Peter Donelan's book *Growing to Seed* is a good one on home seed production (available from Bountiful Gardens). Also check out "Vegetable and Herb Seed Growing," a pamphlet by Douglas C. Miller (1977). Nancy Bubel's solid 1978 work, *Seed Starter's Handbook*, includes 84 pages on collecting and storing seed. And then there's *Growing and Saving Vegetable Seeds* by Marc Rogers.

For the history of plant extinctions and politics of genetic diversity, read *Plant Extinction: A Global Crisis* by Dr. Harold Koopowitz and Hilary Kaye (1983) and *Seeds of the Earth: A Public or Private Resource?* by Pat Roy Mooney (London: Canadian Council for International Co-operation, 1979).

SUPPLIES: Bountiful Gardens, Abundant Life, and Southern Exposure Seed Exchange are companies that specialize in supplying open-pollinated seeds and also offer seed-saving supplies. Bountiful Gardens has a "Seed Saver's Kit" that includes silica gel to absorb moisture, data-keeping forms, and instructions. Abundant Life offers books on the subject and testing screens. For a hand thresher for seeds or grains, contact Alan Dong, I-Tech, P.O. Box 413, Veneta, OR 97487, (503) 935-6419.

SEED SNAPS

Seed Savers Exchange (SSE). Send a long SASE to Seed Savers Exchange for free info about this nonprofit organization of more than 8,000 gardeners who search for endangered vegetable seeds (old-time varieties that are not being propagated by seed companies) and grow them; 563-382-5990; 3076 N. Winn Rd., Decorah, IA 52101; **sse@ rconnect.com; www.seedsavers.org.** Kent Whealy founded the SSE in 1975 after an elderly, terminally ill relative gave him seeds of 3 garden plants that the family had brought from Bavaria 4 generations earlier. Whealy started trying to locate other gardeners who were also keeping seeds their families had passed on from generation to generation. These "heirloom" garden seeds are still being kept by elderly gardeners in rural areas and ethnic enclaves; often they've been grown on the same farm by different generations of the same family for 100 years or more, but these days the new generation often quits gardening and leaves the land. SSE members find these precious seeds, save them, plant them, save them again, and share them.

You don't have to keep heirloom seeds to join SSE, though; the only requirement is that you want to try growing some of them. You obtain seeds by writing directly to the members, who list their varieties in *Seed Savers Yearbook*. Membership costs $30; $35 for Canada or Mexico; $45 for other countries. SSE also maintains a Preservation Garden, holds a Campout Convention each year for members, and teaches how to save all your own seeds and keep genetic lines pure. It also maintains a plant finder service to help people find specific varieties for which they are searching.

PLANT REPRODUCTION

Flowering. Seeds follow the flowering. A late frost is a risk with any flowering plant, such as nut and fruit trees; it kills the vulnerable flowers and ends all hope for a crop that year—either for fruit or the seeds within them. If the blossoms survive without freezing, the next critical step is pollination.

Pollination. The pollen is carried to the plant's ovaries either by wind or by some variety of insects, depending on the variety of plant. Without the carrier, you will have no harvest. If the carrier is bees rather than wind, as with almonds, the trees can be planted farther apart. But if all the area's bees get killed by pesticides, there'll be no tree harvest that year for bee-pollinated plants.

Annuals. Annuals flower and then, in every place where there was a flower, they make seed. They do this the same summer you plant them. Radishes and spinach are annuals. When an annual is ready to flower, it stops putting energy into the food part you would ordinarily grow it for; instead, it uses the food in the seed-making process and stores it in the seeds themselves. When saving seed from an annual, try to get seed from the last one to go to seed, because you want to select offspring that will make food as long as possible before making seeds—especially with leafy plants like lettuce and spinach.

Biennials. Root vegetables are generally biennials. A biennial takes 2 years instead of one to make seed. The first year a carrot grows, for example, it never makes a flower. Instead it makes a root and stores food in it. It's the next spring that things get exciting seedwise: That carrot sends up a long stalk, much longer and taller than most annuals could, because the carrot has all that stored food from the first summer's growth in its root to draw on. (The carrot becomes woody and inedible as the food is pulled back out of it.) The tall stalk flowers, and then seeds develop in each place where there was a flower.

SEED SAVING: I'm just skimming it here. See each plant's individual entry for more on how to save its seeds, and see the books mentioned for the best and most complete info of all. *It matters which plant you save seed from!* Choose the best possible heredity for the offspring. (Same as when you choose a spouse!)

Volunteers. Some plants are "self-seeders," and from them you will get lots of "volunteers." A garden that has been gardened for years tends to contain lots of volunteers, or plants that grew because of their progenitors' efforts, not yours. Potatoes, squash, dill, Jerusalem artichokes, and sunflowers often make up volunteers. Volunteer potatoes grow when you miss digging up some. The squash grows from the fruit you forgot to harvest. The dill and sunflower drop some seeds before you get there to harvest the seed heads. Volunteer spinach and radishes are common too. Whenever hardy plants get a chance, they'll go to seed in your garden. But for better management, you can practice seed selection

and seed saving.

Patented Varieties. A new situation in the seed world is the development of patented varieties from which even amateurs are legally prohibited from saving seed. Packets of patented seed should be so marked.

Hybrid vs. Open-Pollinated. If you're even considering saving your own seed, read the fine print on the seeds you buy to start with. Don't buy "hybrid" varieties. If they don't say "nonhybrid," they are probably a hybrid. Hybrids are famous for their vigor and productivity, but they don't usually breed true; rather, they will revert to one hereditary side or the other, thus losing some of their desirable qualities. Your "open-pollinated" variety (that means one not pollinated under artificially controlled conditions) probably won't be as big, colorful, or heavily producing as a hybrid. But learning how to save your own seeds is interesting for you and your children, it preserves old-fashioned varieties, and it can save you money. Serious seed savers are concerned that so many useful old plant (and animal) varieties are being lost while most of the varieties grown are hybrids. That genetic sameness in crops makes them more vulnerable to disease and insect afflictions.

Saving Seed from Fruits. Fruited plants such as melons, tomatoes, green peppers, and eggplant make their seed inside the fruit. First comes the flower and then the fruit! In this case, you let the seed-bearing fruit get fully ripe. Then scoop out the seeds and let them dry. Spreading them out on a newspaper works well.

Flower Seed. You can save the seeds from almost any flower that has a flower head—a zinnia is one example. Go out in the fall, when the flowers are dry. Remember the colors. Snip off flower heads with scissors and dry the heads. Store in a dry place for winter. In the spring, break apart the head. The zinnia has about 100 seeds to a pod.

COPING WITH WEEDS IN SEED: It's absolutely essential that your seed be clean of weed seeds. You don't want to plant weeds with your new crop! This is most often a problem with seeds harvested in bulk, such as grain seeds. If you can see weed seeds in seed grain, there's a problem waiting to happen. Get rid of them before planting. In fact, you need to get the weeds out whether you're going to use the grain for seed or table.

Seed Cleaning. If you are saving seeds in bulk or have weedy seeds, you need a seed cleaner. It's a machine cleaner that literally shakes the grain over a sequence of wire mesh screens, which sift out all the objects too big or too small to match the specific grain size you're working with: weed seed, dirt, chaff, and undersized, weak grain or grass seeds.

You could buy an old-time one; they used to be common on farms. Or you could buy a new one. Models come in various sizes, according to how much seed grain you want to clean. But that costs money, a tight item for most of us. So for cleaning small quantities of seed, the cheapest way is to make your own.

Homemade Seed-Cleaning Sieves. Buy ⅛-inch, 3/16-inch, and ¼-inch wire mesh squares—18 inches square. Staple or nail the wire tightly onto a wooden side frame—in effect, onto the bottom of a wooden box. You can make the wooden box sides using wood strips that are 18 inches long, as high as you need (maybe 2 inches), and 1 inch wide.

You end up with 3 cleaners, each with a mesh of a different size. If the weed seeds are smaller than your grain

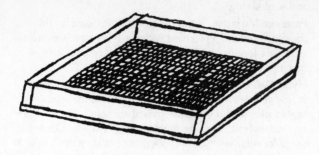

seed, what falls through the mesh when you shake the grain-weed mixture in the box will be the weeds. If the weed seeds are bigger than the type of grain seed you're saving, then you do the operation exactly in reverse. Screen onto a cloth and save what falls through for your seed crop and kitchen use. But save the weed seeds too. Cook them long enough to ensure they can't ever germinate. Then they're good pig and chicken feed! (Unless you've got poisonous plants to contend with.)

Bountiful Gardens, Abundant Life, and Southern Exposure Seed Exchange are companies that specialize in supplying open-pollinated seeds and also offer seed-saving supplies. Bountiful Gardens has a "Seed Saver's Kit" that includes silica gel to absorb moisture, date-keeping forms, and instructions. Abundant Life offers books on the subject and testing screens. For thresher designs for seeds or grains, contact Alan Dong, I-Tech, PO Box 413, Veneta, OR 97487; **agronomy.ucdavis.edu/LTRAS/itech/**. He also offers tool designs for a rice huller, seed storage, and weed burner.

SEED STORAGE: See Chapter 3 for much more on seed storage. In general, keep dry. Label each container with the plant name and the year the seeds were grown. Glass canning jars store seeds well. Don't dry your seeds with artificial heat; you'll kill the tiny life stored within them, and besides, too much dryness can kill them. But protect them from dampness in storage, because too much moisture is bad for them too. Get your seeds well dried, and then store them in glass or plastic sealed with freezer tape (freezer tape won't let moisture through in either direction, and that's just what you want). Store them under cool conditions, and then they will last as long as their individual ability allows. What I mean is that some seeds last better than others anyway: squash, radish, turnip, and lettuce seeds are very hardy, for instance, whereas onion, spinach, and corn seeds are less so.

Stratifying Home-Grown Seeds. Seeds from herbs grown in places other than your hometown often fail. The safest seeds for you are those grown in your own or your neighbors' gardens, since they are acclimated. You'll have better success with cold-climate seeds if you "stratify" them before planting. In fact, some seeds will not grow at all without this treatment. That means freezing and thawing them. Put them in your freezer in a paper or plastic package and leave them there at least overnight. Now take them out and let them thaw completely. Do this to the package at least 3 times.

Germination Rates. Remember that no seed, wherever it's from—your garden or the professional seedsman—is going to germinate 100 percent. Fifty percent is more realistic, so save more than just the bare minimum. Seeds are living things and can have all kinds of troubles. They get old and die, and that affects germination rates too.

Testing Seed for Germination. If for some reason you're using old grain for seed, or grain that you lack confidence in, or if you just want to know what to expect, test the seed's germination rate. Put a sample of your grain seed on a cotton flannel cloth between 2 dinner plates, or between moist blotting papers. Keep the cloth or papers constantly moist and at a moderate temperature. The smaller your germination percentage, the thicker you'll have to plant that seed to get the stand you want in your garden or field.

Vegetative Propagation

Well, back to the subject of plant reproduction. "Vegetative propagation" is reproducing plants any way other than by seeds. It works for some plants and not for others. Dividing a clump and layering are nonseed propagation methods. Check out *Plant Propagation by P.M. Browse* (1979), *Secrets of Plant Propagation* by Lewis Hill, and *Plant Propagation in Pictures* by M. Free (1979).

DIVIDING ROOT CLUMPS: This works nicely with certain multistemmed plants. Dig up a plant that is at least 2 years old, and divide the roots and their connected stems. Be gentle and let the plant find its own natural separations. Try not to tear the roots as you pull them apart. Don't use a knife. If you're having a real hard time, leave the roots in a bucket of water overnight. That will help relax them and make it easier.

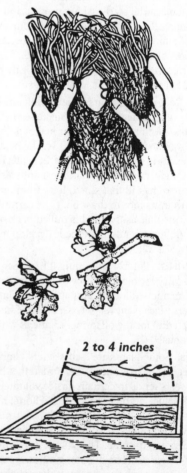

2 to 4 inches

ROOT CUTTING: Lemon balm, comfrey, mint, and horseradish are some of the herbs you can propagate by root cuttings. For a root cutting, you literally cut off a piece of root from an established plant (at least 2 years old) and then plant it in a new place to make a new plant. The piece of root you cut off for replanting should be at least 2 inches long. If the root is small, thin, and just not husky-looking, take a longer piece—up to 4 inches.

LAYERING: With certain shrubs, you can bend a branch over and cover it in the middle with a layer of dirt. The covered middle will eventually grow roots. Then you can cut that new plant away from the old one and transplant where you want it.

TUBERS: Tubers are something else again. Here the plant sends up a stalk, flowers prettily above ground, and then finishes the job underground by making potatoes with eyes or some such. It's sort of a combo of flowering and vegetative reproduction. You cut the potato apart, being careful not to harm the eyes and with each piece having at least one eye. Plant, and from every eye a new plant grows.

PLANTING AND GROWING YOUR GARDEN
Planting

DIRECTION: If water flows lengthwise across your field, plant in rows crosswise. That protects your land from erosion. If the water flows crosswise, plant lengthwise. If the land is level, make rows any direction you want; lengthwise is usually easiest.

ROW PLANTING: This is the style most of us were raised with. In the old days, rows were 30 inches between because the horse pulling the cultivator needed that much space to get through. But in a kitchen garden that people can hoe, rows might be only a foot apart. In this book, ideal spacing for rows, if you're doing single rather than wide rows, is given with the planting directions for each vegetable.

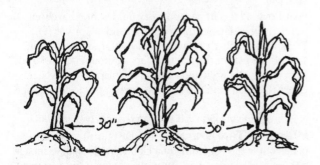

RAISED BEDS AND WIDE ROWS: Basically, you plant in rows, hills, or wide rows. The "wide" row is a strip of spaced but dense planting, unlike a single-row planting. This type of gardening makes the most of limited space for good growing efficiency. With either raised beds or wide-row gardening, you have a long, narrow bed. The "raised bed" is raised; the "wide row" is simply a long, narrow bed in your regular garden area that is planted with a wide row of something rather than a single row. You can do your whole garden or only part of it in wide rows; you can do your whole garden or only part of it in raised beds.

How to Make a Raised Bed. Your seed bed is literally raised because of double-digging that loosens the soil, adds air, and raises the ground level 3 or 4 inches. It's raised even more by the fertilizer you add and mix in. Some gardeners make the beds 2 × 10, others 3 × 10. The wider size gives

you more production. Your width is limited by your ability to reach the center of the bed with your hands from the outside all around to weed, thin, or harvest as needed.

1. Dig deep to make your planting "bed." Dig the ground up by hand (see "Double-digging" in the "Cultivating the Soil" section) or with a powered tool. Each bed will be about 4 feet wide and as long as convenient before you need a walkway between (maybe 8 feet).
2. Fertilize. If you can, cover the whole bed-to-be with 6 inches of good rotted compost or manure before digging. After digging, let the bed set a few days. Then lay your fertilizer on top, and proceed to break up clods and mix it in at the same time. For example, sprinkle a dusting of bone meal, an inch or more of well-rotted manure, and some wood ashes over the top. Then rake or cultivate this fertilizer into the top 3 to 6 inches.
3. Soak the resulting soil with a gentle spray. If you did it all right so far, your "raised bed" is indeed higher than the ground around it.

Planting Your Wide Row (or Raised Bed). Maybe you're used to gardens planted in rows that are a rototiller's width apart. That's fine if you have enough room to do it. But in the raised-bed or wide-row method, your plants grow close together, so close that the outer leaves of plants will touch as they approach mature size, or sooner. Whether you are setting out transplants or planting from seed, you are going to space way closer than you ever have before. The result is a spaced but dense mass of plants. If you dig it deep enough, fertilize it richly enough, water it generously enough, and weed it carefully enough, that little piece of earth will be able to support all those plants.

A "HILL": This is a cluster of a few plants with the soil between them kept as clear of weeds as possible, just like with rows. Sometimes the soil is actually hoed up from every side to make a literal "hill" about 6 inches higher than the surrounding dirt. On the other hand, in very dry areas, the hill should actually be a depression in the dirt, a hole that will better collect and hold rainwater. Hill planting is especially valuable in desert areas and where hot, drying winds blow. It will help the plants get started to place a windbreak on the side the wind usually blows from—anything sizable, even a rock or shingle, will shield them. In such a climate, the middle plants of the cluster—the most protected ones—may yield best.

Hill planting is common for corn, pole beans, melons, cucumbers, winter squash, some kinds of summer squash, and watermelons are possible hill crops. Thus, except for corn and beans, the hill crops are all vine-type plants that need to spread out over the ground. They all love heat and can't be planted until the soil has really warmed up, around June 1 here. Hill crops are not very practical in a small garden because they are space hogs—the small cucumber the least so, the huge winter squashes (which grow in rows 12 feet apart with 6 feet between hills) the most so. Hilling is not as important in light soil, but it does help you see where you planted until the plants get going. Don't hill in extremely sandy soil, because a hill of sand dries out too fast and your plants will probably die. In clay-type soil, hilling really helps your plants to grow.

My husband Mike makes a hill by standing about where he wants the hill with a hoe. He hoes the topsoil toward himself in a semicircle to make a "hill" about 6 inches high and about 1 to 1½ feet in diameter.

PLANTS PER ACRE: The size of your garden or field has to be a factor. If you calculate your plants per acre, there's an ideal number. For corn it's 16,000. If corn plants are more crowded than that, you'll likely just have less yield per plant, so the total per acre yield will be about the same. So you don't gain anything by crowding plants past the land's capacity to nourish them. Any plants can be grown closer than these directions say if you get plenty of manure or compost into the soil and are desperate.
NOTE: *Replant as soon as you're sure a crop isn't making it. You can plant potatoes, beans, and onion sets clear up to July 15. Those are basic keep-you-alive foods. Just keep them well watered.*

Save your seed packets. But don't tack them on posts at the end of each row, because you'll end up losing them to rain, kids, animals, or wind. Then you'll be sorry, because the back of the seed packet often contains good information about growing that plant, from preparing the ground right through to harvesting.

COPING WITH BIRDS: Birds love to eat corn and other large seeds right after they sprout. A well-made scarecrow that moves in a breeze really will help keep them away, especially if you supply it with real people-clothes, shiny foil hanging strips for "hands," and a foil face. It also helps if you go out to the garden several times a day during the large-seed germination period.

Starting Transplants

To do serious self-sufficient gardening, including starting early and growing late, you'll need to grow your own transplants. Commercial seedlings are usually not available except during the times of peak consumer demand. I set out cabbages, tomatoes, green peppers, and eggplant every year. It's cheaper to start your own sets from seed than to buy them from a local nursery. Try not to mail-order them.

Eggplants, green peppers, tomatoes, and cabbage have to be started in the house and then transplanted to the garden. I think head lettuce is better off raised from seed in the garden, although I've seen recommendations to start it indoors. But this depends on your climate. Start your plants for transplanting about 2 to 2½ months before you plan to set them out. They will germinate easily indoors, where the moderate temperatures that are comfortable for humans are generally perfect for seed germination too. Make your soil mixture in the fall, before the ground gets too wet: 1 part well-rotted compost and 2 parts dirt. Fill your containers to the top with dirt.

SUNSHINE: Start your seeds in the house or greenhouse rather than in a cloche or cold frame, because most seeds require much warmer soil to germinate than they need to grow. Inside you can give them ideal conditions in their tender early stages. They don't need much space. You can grow your transplants on a windowsill that's sunny at least part of the day. For more plants, make shelves across your window. Remove anything underneath that could be harmed by dripping water.

WATER: You'll want to water the plants every other day or whenever they look dry. Several light waterings beat one big flood, which has a tendency to go right through, leaving the plant still dry.

CONTAINERS

Milk Cartons? Mary Ann Shepherd, Del Mar, CA, wrote me, "I use milk cartons as collars to blanch celery, around

my new lettuce seedlings to discourage cutworms, and to start all sorts of cuttings (both flowers and vegetables) and seeds. For collars, cut off tops and bottoms. For all else, cut off tops (or open up) and use a tri-cornered beverage opener ('church key') to cut a drain hole on all four sides at the bottom (not in the bottom itself). When I go to transplant I slit the sides and bottom and plant the whole thing —the carton eventually disintegrates and you don't disturb the roots that way. My pine seedlings take about a year to germinate and grow to about 4 inches tall, and they have lived happily in milk cartons for up to 2 years before I've transplanted them."

Cardboard Boxes. I sometimes start the plants in "seed flats" (for me, that means a cardboard box with dirt in the bottom) and then transplant to tin cans. If I don't get them out of there pretty fast, the bottoms get too soggy.

Cans. Cans of any size are good. I like those big tins that canned hams come in, and gallon tins are great. You have to punch small holes in the bottom. Big containers of dirt are better than small ones. I use 1 plant to 1 soup can or peat pot once they are started in the seed flats, or about 6 to a ham can.

Peat Pots. Plants in peat pots dry out fast and have to be watered every day. Set them out, pot and all, or you'll be breaking off roots that have grown right into the pot side. Tear off the part of the rim that's above ground to prevent it from acting as a wick and causing the plant to lose water. Other than that, and the fact you have to pay for them, peat pots are great.
NOTE: *Be sure to label each flat with the variety of plant in it.*

WHEN TO TRANSPLANT? The best time to set transplants out is the beginning of a cloudy, rainy spell. Cabbage sets are hardy and can go out in the garden when you plant your green onions. But in my garden, if I plant too early I risk losing my plants to cutworms. A little later is perfect. Tomato sets can go to the garden when you're positive the frosts and near-frosts are over. Green pepper and eggplant sets should wait till the nights are not cold at all. Because plants I set out too early may be wiped out by cutworms or cold, I first set out a sampling and then wait a few days to see what happens before setting out the rest. Or you can harden off . . .

HARDENING OFF: You can do this by setting your containers outside during the warmer hours of the day, longer each day, before actually transplanting them into the garden. Or you can do it by transplanting your tender young plants from the house or greenhouse into a cold frame, where they will stay 2 or 3 weeks, gradually getting used to cold air and chilly nights before they go out into the regular garden in yet another transplant. For hardening plants, leave the lid of the cold frame up a bit more each day—unless you need to protect the plants from a spell of cold weather.

HOW TO TRANSPLANT? To set out plants with dirtless roots, make a mud bath to plant them in. It's cold, dirty work. If they have their own dirt—for instance, plants in a peat pot that you'll plant pot and all—give them a wet hole to sit in and plenty of good water for the next few weeks. A hot, dry spell, even in May, can wipe out new, unwatered sets because their root systems haven't yet had a chance to get normally established. To set them out from a can, dig a hole and shake the plants out of the can (it's easier if the soil is soaked ahead of time). Separate them, keeping as much dirt on the roots as you can, and try not to damage the roots. Set a plant in your hole, pack dirt in around it, and give it a good soaking. Give tomato plants plenty of room to spread. They get big.

For Easy Spacing. From Earthchild Marie: "Your garden tools—shovel, rake, hoe—can be marked with a 3-corner file at 6-inch intervals for ease in setting transplants at the proper spacing. Trowel handles, marked every 3 inches, are convenient for smaller seeds and for setting transplants into the soil."

Undercover Gardening

The following section is often indebted to one of the basic books in this field, William Head's *Gardening Under Cover: A Northwest Guide to Solar Greenhouses, Cold Frames, and Cloches* (Seattle: Sasquatch Books, 1989).

For fall and winter gardening in chilly or cold climates, and very early spring growing, cover is essential. A garden under cover is protected from rain, frost, wind, and cold. There are 4 styles of light-transparent, cold-protective covering for plants: floating plastic row covers, cloches, cold frames, and greenhouses.

UNDERCOVER GARDEN SUPPLIERS: Check the Yellow Pages in your area. Or contact:

Charley's Greenhouse & Garden specializes in supplies for hobby greenhouses: gardening supplies, climate controls, greenhouse equipment, and more than 100 greenhouse kits (from 2 x 6 ft. to 16 x 37 ft.). Free catalog: 800-322-4707; fax 800-233-3078; 17979 State Rt. 536, Mt. Vernon, WA 98273; **tamara@charleys greenhouse.com; www.charleysgreenhouse.com.**

Mellinger's offers a good selection of light row and plant covers, soil heating cables, greenhouses, cold frames, etc.: PO Box 157, N. Lima, OH 44452; 800-321-7444; fax 330-549-3716; **mellgarden@aol.com; www. mellingers.com.**

Teufel Nursery sells both wholesale and retail. Their catalog lists many unusual items, including greenhouse aids: 503-646-1111; 12345 NW Barnes Rd., Portland, OR 97229. Or in Washington: 425-482-1112; 6303-233rd Place SE, Woodinville, WA 98072; **www.teufel.com.**

INFO ON INDOOR GARDENING: These books detail methods of gardening under cover that are more advanced than plants on a shelf or windowsill that gets lots of sunshine. *Greenhouse Gardener's Companion* is by Shane Smith, director of Cheyenne Botanical Gardens; **shane@botanic. org.** William Head's *Gardening Under Cover: A Northwest*

Guide to Solar Greenhouses, Cold Frames, and Cloches (1989); *Intensive Gardening Round the Year,* by P. Doscher, T. Fischer, and K. Kolb (1981); *Successful Cold-Climate Gardening* by L. Hill (1981); and *Building and Using Coldframes,* by C. Siegchrist (1980) are also useful.

ADVANTAGES OF GARDENING UNDER COVER

Heat Is Trapped. When a cat lies in a pool of sunlight that is streaming through a glass window on a cold but sunny day, the sun's rays are transformed. The visible sunlight has radiant energy that becomes heat energy when it strikes the cat's fur and other surfaces inside the room. Some of this heat is reflected and radiated into the air inside. As heat, it

cannot easily pass back through the glass, so inside the window the air warms up. A covering over a garden bed acts in the same manner. When light strikes the soil and plants, it is converted into heat, and it warms the environment within the covered space. This warmth speeds up all life processes, including the growth and development of the garden plants.

Protection from Damaging Rain. In the maritime climate of much of the Pacific Northwest, rain is a major cause of crop failure. Wet conditions encourage diseases that rot stems and leaves of plants and may rot germinating seeds. Heavy rains compact the surface of the soil and can wash seeds out of their shallow soil cover. In very cold weather, wet ground freezes to a depth of several inches.

Frost and Wind Protection. Coverings particularly protect plants from late-spring and early-fall frosts. Frosts usually occur after a sunny day during which the soil has been warmed. At night, warm air rises and is replaced by freezing air. A covering slows down this air exchange and helps prevent freezing. Winds can knock over plants and lower air temperatures dramatically, even on otherwise sunny days. The cover protects against that, too.

Flexibility in Plant/Harvest Dates. How many times have you set out plants only to see them killed by a frost or to watch them sit without growing until warm weather finally arrived? How many times have you nursed your tomato plants through summer only to see the fruit destroyed by an early fall frost or rainstorm? By gardening under cover, you can plant seeds at 2-week intervals over a span of 4 to 8 weeks and discover how much earlier and later you can start your garden beyond the dates recommended on the seed packet. And food, herbs, and flowers grown out of season sell for higher prices.

More Crop Variety. Many less hardy vegetable and ornamental plant varieties that normally would not do well in your area can be grown successfully under cover.

Faster Plant Growth. Vegetables and flowers should be grown to maturity as soon as possible because the faster a vegetable grows, the better its chances of resisting disease and surviving bad weather. Plants grown quickly will also be less likely to become stunted and will even taste better. You can also grow more food in less time from that one bit of earth.

Example: In one test in the Pacific Northwest, lettuce planted March 2 and grown inside a cloche was ready for first harvest by midApril. Lettuce planted on the same date in open beds was not ready for harvest until mid-May. In addition, the total harvest of lettuce per square foot was 3 to 4 times greater in the cloche as in the open beds!

Another example: In the same way, tomatoes started and reared in a greenhouse matured earliest. Those planted inside, transplanted to cloches after 4 weeks, and reared there were ready for first picking only 12 days later than the greenhouse ones. But those transplanted to an open garden were not ready for harvest until 5 weeks later than those growing under cloche.

Less Insect Damage. Early-spring and late-fall plantings avoid most garden pests. Crops left in the ground during the winter rarely have insect damage because most of the bad bugs are not eating during that season. The later you plant in the spring, the more likely your plants will have bug bites. Midsummer undercover plantings also escape attack by many pests by maturing in late fall or winter.

CLOCHE: A cloche (pronounced "klosh") is a lightweight covering for a plant or plants that can easily be moved. A cloche is the simplest cover to build and use. It can easily be moved to different parts of the garden to cover different plants. When the cloche is put on over tender young plants in early spring, it's called a "hot cap." Unlike cold frames, cloches allow light to reach a plant from every direction. You can reuse cloches to cover as many as 3, 4, or more crops in the same year. Cloches are especially well suited for use in the maritime Northwest, where plants need protection from excessive rain and cold winds more than from very low temperatures. The weaknesses of cloches are their vulnerability to heavy wind and their inability to keep plants as warm as cold frames or greenhouses.

Cloche Materials. A cloche can be made of anything that transmits light, so the possibilities for design are nearly limitless. They can be made of cheap materials—cheaper than those needed to make a cold frame or greenhouse. To cover a row of plants or a section of garden, you can build one large cloche or a series of modular cloches that link together. The word "cloche" is French for bell. In Europe, gardeners have covered plots for centuries, and in the 1600s, French market gardeners used a glass jar in the shape of a bell to cover a plant. Now cloches for individual plants may be made of waxed paper, plastic, fiberglass, or glass. Or your cloche may be a big, plastic-covered tunnel or tent that covers entire rows of plants. A wide variety of cloches are available commercially, with an equally wide range in prices.

When open-air gardening begins in the summer, wash your cover material, dry, and store in a *shady* place until needed in the fall.

Homemade Cloche Design. You can scrape together a cloche by making halfcircle hoop rows out of old coat hangers and then covering them with plastic. Or cut out the top, bottom, or side of any 1-gal. plastic or glass jug. To cover a wide raised bed, use sections of hog-wire fencing curved to fit the beds and covered with plastic. But people who speak carpenterese will find much better cloche plans for both tunnel and tent styles in *Gardening Under Cover.*

Tunnel: In general, the tunnel style is made by stretching 4-mil polyethylene plastic sheeting over a line of half-circle hoops. The hoops are bent and fastened to strips at the top and bottom sides so they will stay put. For example, you could put the plastic over 6 × 6-inch mesh concrete-reinforcing wire. The reinforcing-wire cloche looks like the tunnel style except the wire is arched from where it is nailed to a 10-foot lumber plank over to the other side, where it is nailed to a parallel plank. Then the plastic is put over that. The 2 end openings are covered with more plastic.

To ventilate a tunnel cloche, on cloudy days you open the end away from the wind. On sunny days you can open both ends. A breeze is created by the warm air leaving the cloche. As the weather gets warmer, you'll be able to leave one end open continuously. When the weather gets hot, of course, you take off the plastic and put it away until fall, when the weather gets cold again.

Tent: This cloche is lighter, portable, and easier to build than the tunnel. It has 4- or 6-mil polyethylene plastic sheeting stretched over an umbrella-tent–style support.

Using a Cloche. Cloches can be placed over any area of your garden, large or small, that you want to protect. To water, weed, and harvest, you lift the cloche off the bed, tilt up one end, or take off the plastic. If your cloche has no natural opening, you must remember to ventilate by propping up one side.

COLD FRAME: Cold frames are temporary structures that cover and protect plants in the garden. They extend the growing season into the fall or through the winter, or help plants get an early start in spring. These temporary structures can be set down over plants in the garden, opened by day, shut at night, and removed when not needed. A cold frame is more rigid and heavy than most cloches, harder to move. It is usually more expensive and time-consuming to build than a cloche—but, once built, is far more durable. A cold frame provides more protection from weather than a cloche but less than a greenhouse. In a mild maritime climate like the Willamette Valley of Oregon, a cloche can get many plants safely through the winter. But since cold frames stay warmer inside than cloches, if you live where there is severe winter cold, you'll need to use one of these for weather that's too much for a mere cloche to handle. You can start frost-tender plants from seed in a cold frame the same way you would start them in a tin can in your house. Or use a cold frame to harden off transplants from the house before sending them on to the garden.

A cold frame is basically a glass or clear plastic window, the lid of a bottomless box. Wherever the box is set down, the ground under it becomes the bottom of the box. Inside the cold frame, you are creating a special area of milder climate. A cold frame is usually a permanent structure.

Choose suitable kinds of plants for the cold-frame style of gardening. Oriental greens such as Green Wave, Mizuna mustard, Florida broad-leaf mustard, Chinese broad-leaf mustard, and edible chrysanthemum (all available from Abundant Life Seed Foundation) are good. Siberian kale and corn salad are good too. The mustards have a remarkable rate of growth and are somewhat slug-resistant. *Winter Gardening in the Maritime Northwest: Cool Season Crops for the Year-Round Gardener* by Binda Colebrook will help.

Soil. The place where you construct a cold frame should have good garden soil—soil that contains enough organic material to drain adequately and that is also very fertile. Consider adding manure too. In a cold climate, self-heating soil can be very helpful! Goat, horse, chicken, rabbit, or pigeon manures give off a lot of heat as they age. If you put a 6- to 8-inch layer in the cold frame, it will turn it into a "hotbed." But wait until it's cooled down some—a week at least—before you plant in there.

Glazing Material. This is the glass or glass substitute in the top of your cold frame or greenhouse windows. Most glazings allow the same amount of light penetration. Where they vary widely is in cost and breakability or durability. Polyethylene is cheapest by far but lasts only 1 or 2 years. Fiberglass is commonly used because it's a good compromise between low cost and long lifespan. Untempered glass is midprice but vulnerable to breakage; it's best used only on vertical installations or small cold frames. Tempered glass is an excellent glazing material and can frequently be purchased inexpensively as blemished or used patio doors. It seems as if every year new glazing products, such as double-wall acrylics, are invented.

Cold Frame Design. A "cold frame" has low opaque walls that support the transparent overhead material, usually a glass or clear plastic lid in a frame. The frame is hinged so it can be raised to let you in to work with your plants and to let in air, but it can also stay down to keep out cold. A cold frame with insulation around all its sides (such as 1½ inches thick) will be warmer inside than one that isn't. In very cold climates, you can also insulate the lid of the cold frame. (In that case, you have to be faithful about lifting it off when the sun's up!) All of the books I have recommended in this section contain more ideas and instructions for building cold frames. In general, the designs are for either portable or permanent cold frames.

Portable: An old-time style of cold frame, called a "light," is as portable as a cloche, though it is heavier. A "light" is basically glass in a frame that fits over some sort of wooden-sided box, which sits on the ground over the plants. Or it can be made of straw, as Earthchild Marie wrote me: "The classic cold frame is straw bales with old windows laid on them at an angle."

From Bill Rogers in Wyoming: "I make them light and portable so that I can put them over vegetables not yet ripened in the fall. In the spring, I locate the frames near a rock or other shelter, exposed to maximum sunlight. Thus I obtain a month or 6 weeks additional on each end of the season, and I have ripe tomatoes or cantaloupes or other vegetables that otherwise I could not have in our short growing season. The earth is over a heavy bed of manure for starting. And for both starting and finishing, I make sure there is plenty of water. I use window sashes from houses that are being wrecked; otherwise the cost of glass would run hot frames out of sight. I use scrap lumber for the frames but extend its life by painting—likewise the window frames and putty."

Permanent: These are at least semipermanent. You pick the best place in your garden for the cold frame, build it there, and there it stays. The best site for a cold frame is well drained, receives the most sunshine possible, and has steady, gentle air movement yet is protected from cold north winds. A gentle slope is good because it will drain easily.

Sunshine. Your site should receive full sun from 9am to 3pm because during the colder months, 90 percent of the sun's energy is received between these hours. Beware of shading, and remember that the sun is at a lower angle during fall, winter, and early spring, so trees and buildings to the east, south, and west are more likely to cast shade on your site. For a cold frame to receive maximum winter light, the long axis of the structure should be oriented east-west. The difference in light intensity due to orientation is not great during the summer, when the sun is high in the sky, but it's an important difference in the winter, when the sun is low.

You can combine a raised-bed garden and a cold-frame or cloche design and get good results. The drier soil of a raised bed retains heat better than does wet soil. Rodale Press of Emmaus, PA, offers plans for a "grow frame." *Gardening Under Cover* has 2 top-notch designs with full construction details: one for a 4 × 4-foot grow space; the other for a 4 × 8-foot Hermeyer cold frame, 30 inches high at the

BASIC ORGANIC GARDENER'S PLANT DEFENSE

1. The best defenses against bacterial and fungus problems are well-nourished soil, plenty of sunshine, and plenty of water.
2. Consider companion planting with these plants, which have pest-repellent talents and/or attract pest-eating bugs: marigolds, alliums, evening primrose, wild buckwheat, baby blue eyes, candytuft, bishops flower, black-eyed Susan, strawflowers, nasturtiums, angelica, and yarrow. All are offered by Clyde Robin Seed Co., PO Box 2366, Castro Valley, CA 94546; 510-785-0425; fax 510-785-6463; **stevenra@clyderobin.com; www.clyderobin.com.** More than 250 pages of gardening info and photos. Free catalog.
3. To combat greenhouse insect pests, careful screening is the simple, basic answer.
4. In urban areas, the "plant doctor" is the equivalent of the rural vet. You can get a beloved plant diagnosed and treated by the doc's house call, although it costs. It's more likely to need more or less water or more or less light than to suffer from a disease.
5. Move each vegetable's planting place around in your garden every year. This helps avoid a build-up of one kind of pest or pestilence in a part of your garden. Don't let them just lie in wait to eat the same stuff next year. Move the target!
6. Buy resistant seed varieties.
7. Use diatomaceous earth to combat slugs and snails. (It must be dry to work.)
8. Use beneficial insects: ladybugs, predatory mites, praying mantis, beneficial nematodes, parasitic wasps, mealy bug destroyers, etc.
9. Set traps for larger pests.
10. Use sprays of environmentally safe (biodegradable), natural (plant-originated) material such as garlic, hot pepper, pyrethrum, nicotine, or rotenone as a last resort. Or mulch with coffee grounds, etc.
11. Don't leave disease-infected plants in the garden, and don't put them on the compost pile. This goes for clubroot, late blight in tomatoes and potatoes, and any other soilborne contagion. Put them on a separate trash pile or burn them.

---

back and 18 inches high at the front with transparent material for its front panel to allow in more light.

CLOCHE AND COLD-FRAME MANAGEMENT: Think temperature and humidity. Ventilate! And water as needed.

Ventilation. Except during long freezing periods, open your cold frame or cloche during the day and close it at night. Venting is needed to control temperature and humidity and to provide a change of air for the plants. Venting helps prevent outbreaks of mold and other diseases. (For more venting ideas, see the section on tunnel cloche design earlier.)

Water. Watering "as needed" is not simple! The more you vent, the more you'll have to water, because venting lets moist air escape, and the movement of air through a cold frame or cloche can quickly dry out soil. On the other hand, when a cold frame or cloche is closed, moisture that would otherwise escape to the air condenses on the glazing and returns back to the soil; it's kind of a mini-planet. During damp and cloudy periods, you may not have to water for weeks at a time. To determine if your plants need water, dig down 4 to 6 inches into your bed. If the soil is dry to that depth, water. Or if your plants begin to wilt, water.

Hotbed. A hotbed is used to start tender crop seedlings. You make one by adding to your bed a source of heat, such as an electric heat cable equipped with a thermostat. Or make a nonelectric hotbed by filling the bed with a 2½-foot layer of rich, fairly fresh manure, a manure/bedding mix, or raw compost and keeping it wet at night. Put a few inches of straw and then 4 to 6 inches of nice topsoil over that, so your seeds are about 8 inches over the manure. It will keep heating for up to 3 months.

GREENHOUSE DESIGN AND CONSTRUCTION: A "greenhouse" is a glass or plastic-walled building large enough for people to stand and move around in. Greenhouses can extend the living space of a home while at the same time expanding the garden. "Solar" greenhouses are the only kind of interest to ecology- and budget-conscious people.

Good books on the topic include *The Food- and Heat-Producing Solar Greenhouse* by B. Yanda and R. Fisher (1981); *The Complete Greenhouse Book* by P. Clegg and D. Watkins (1978); *A Solar Greenhouse Guide for the Pacific Northwest* by T. Magee (1979); *The Passive Solar Energy Book* by E. Mazria (1979); and *The Solar Greenhouse Book*, edited by J. C. McCullagh (1978).

The truly dedicated may also wish to check out *Growing Under Glass* by K. A. Beckett (1981); *The City Greenhouse Book* by P. Chapel (1980); *Rodale's Encyclopedia of Indoor Gardening,* edited by A. M. Halpin (1980); *Horticultural Management of Solar Greenhouses in the Northeast* by M. Klein (1980); *Greenhouse Operation and Management* by P. V. Nelson (1985); *Gardening for All Seasons* by New Alchemy Institute (1983); *The Bountiful Solar Greenhouse* by S. Smith (1982); and *Growing Food in Solar Greenhouses* by D. Wolfe (1981). The wonderful Helen and Scott Nearing wrote *Building and Using Our Sun-Heated Greenhouse: Grow Vegetables All Year Round* (1977).

Secrets to a Successful Greenhouse Business by T. M. Taylor (1991) comes from a professional greenhouse designer and one of the nation's largest growers. This book will save you money if you want to set up a professional greenhouse operation. It covers organic greenhouse growing, and provides a Nationwide Plant Buyers List and directory for best grower supplies. It tells how to sell to big chains or local markets, how to choose varieties, how to build or buy a greenhouse, including a simple solar greenhouse with poly roof. Send $19.95 (+ $3 s/h) to GreenEarth Publishing: 407-242-2241; 800-927-3084; 5205 Lake Washington Rd., Melbourne, FL 32934; **www.greenhousebusiness.com.**

HYDROPONICS: Hydroponics is a method of growing crops without soil in a tank of nutrient-rich water. The nutrients are supplied in a liquid form, circulated in the trough. Plants are supported by a mesh or some such so that their roots are in the solution but their stem and leaves are out of it. Most hydroponic systems rely heavily on synthetic fertilizers and relatively high energy and equipment costs; thus, they're the opposite of what advocates of organic farming and sustainable agriculture are striving toward. An even more exciting concept combines fish farming with hydroponic vegetable growing.

The D. W. Aqua Farm in Barnstable, MA, has a thriving aqua farm that combines hydroponically growing vegetables, herbs, and flowers with producing striped bass. State-of-the-art technology makes possible a closed-circuit, balanced, controlled environment that produces as much as 20,000 lb. of bass per year as well as organic (no pesticides are used) vegetables, herbs, and flowers year-round. The hydroponic tanks are situated in connected greenhouses. All the nutrients for the plants come from the fish, and the farm's contract to provide food and flowers for an inn and restaurant chain pays for the hydroponic setup.

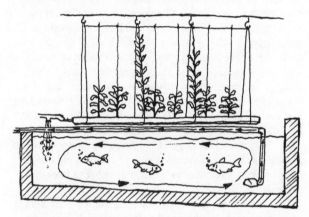

Hydro-Gardens offers wholesale supplies for serious hydroponic growers. Catalog, of course: PO Box 25845, Colorado Springs, CO 80936; phone/fax 800-634-6362; **HGI@Hydro-Gardens.com; www.hydro-gardens.com.**

For much more info on this, subscribe to *Aquaponics Journal*, a bimonthly magazine for hydroponic gardeners who are also raising fish. Cost is $49/yr; 209-742-6869; fax 209-742-4402; PO Box 1848, Mariposa, CA 95338; **info@ aquaponics.com; www.aquaponics.com/.**

The *Growing Edge Magazine* is a bimonthly on high-tech garden systems like hydroponics, bioponics, aquaponics, etc. Cost is $27/yr; 800-888-6785; fax 541-757-0028; PO Box 1027, Corvallis, OR 97339; **tom_alexander@ growingedge.com; www.growingedge.com.**

There's more info on aquaponics at **www.attra.org/ attra-pub/aquaponic.html,** and at **www.hydroponics. com.au,** a marvelous Australian magazine's website.

COPING WITH THE COMPETITION: WEEDS, PESTS, AND PESTILENCE
About Weeds

The number one thing to keep in mind here is that self-defending plants are the easiest ones to grow but in order to grow, they need carbon dioxide, water, and 13 elements that come from the soil. By keeping their soil well fertilized, providing air to their roots with loose, earthwormy soil, and watering as needed, you'll maximize the plant's chance of looking after itself. Nevertheless . . .

There is only so much plant food in your garden, and you've worked really hard to get it there. If your garden has one weed for every vegetable plant, then half your soil-type plant food is going to the weeds and half to your vegetable plants. That means your vegetable plants will be half as big and healthy and productive as they could be if there were no weeds. It isn't quite that simple, but that's the general idea. You want to kill existing weeds and turn them into green manure. You certainly want to get rid of annual-type weeds before they have a chance to go to seed. If you let that happen, you could have 3 generations of pigweed happily growing side by side in a single summer, even in a shortish growing season.

WEEDING BY HAND OR CULTIVATION: You can control weeds in pasture by hand, or you can put sheep in there. (See the section on sheep in Chapter 11.) For cultivated crops, you have to weed before you plant as well as while your crops are up. It's very important to get the ground tilled up really well in the spring, before you plant your rows, to get rid of the weeds that have already started; then weed at intervals as the weeds seem to be gaining again—every couple weeks or so during the growing season. Come through between your rows with a rototiller or a hoe. Weed by hand inside the row close between and beside the plants. There's a secret to easy weeding: never let the weeds get a head start on you! And it's always better to take a weed out root and all, of course, than to cut through it.

My objection to the rototiller is that, like all machines, it is not sufficiently discriminating. It can't go around a lovely volunteer that is in the middle of the row. It helps to have everything in long, straight rows that have been preplanned to be wide enough so you can go back and forth between with the rototiller. Our rototiller can be made shorter or longer in its bite, and that's a help.

Once the crops are planted, I do the close-in weeding—stooping over, kneeling, or sitting with my bottom on some newspaper or piece of cardboard when the ground is damp. The best time to handweed is right after a rain, when the ground is really damp. Then those long-rooted weeds come right up. They seem to relax their roots when the ground is wet and the soil gets soft. When it gets hot, the roots really grab again. To machine-weed, wait for drier ground so the tiller forks won't gum up in mud. If you rototill clay soil while it's damp, you really make a mess.

Some people don't believe in weeding. I do, but sometimes I don't have the time or strength to do a really good job. A crop will definitely do better if it doesn't have to compete with a lot of weeds for the available minerals, water, and sunshine. Some crops can resist weeds better than others. Peas, corn, squash, and beans are pretty good that way.

MULCHING: I wasn't sure where in this book I should put "Mulching." Should I put it with watering? Mulching is an important technique of conserving your soil moisture. Should I put it with weeding? Mulching is a useful method of smothering weeds. Or should I put it with fertilizing? The lower layers of an organic mulch tend to compost and enrich the soil underneath. But a lot of "mulches" now are just a plastic sheet. Whatever its category, mulching is a useful method in your garden. Check out *The Mulch Book: A Guide for the Family Food Gardener* by Stu Campbell (1973) to learn everything about mulch known by the 1970s. Look in a garden supply catalog for the most recent techno-mulches.

Mulching for Weed Control. Mulching has limitations as a weed control method. It doesn't discourage morning glory weed, of which I have lots. You don't know about morning glory? Happy innocence! I used to have nightmares about the stuff—seriously!

A single, week-old morning glory plant already has a root 5 inches long. (I'm speaking of the wild weed type, not the kind you buy to climb your fence and display pretty flowers.) You can kill a morning glory plant if you dig it up root and all and are careful not to leave it lying on dirt in the rain (in which case it will reroot itself). Otherwise, when that same plant is 6 weeks old, the root is 12 inches long, and if you try to dig it out and fail to get all the root, it will regrow from what's left of the root. After 10 weeks, the root is 34 inches long and has buds on the lateral roots, and you've lost the battle. By the end of the summer, the roots will be 4 feet deep, with side branches reaching 5 feet in every direction. After 2 summers, the original plant will be a patch 17 feet wide with roots 19 feet deep.

We finally found a different answer to morning glory. You build a pigpen right on top of it and leave the pigs rooting happily there for a few years. Then move the pigpen, and Lo! No morning glory and lots of good manure!

And never mulch with hay. I once did that. Yes, I was that dumb. And soon a lush stand of grass from the seeds contained in it grew everywhere I had laid it. I'll never do that again! The grass was worse to get rid of than any of the other stuff I was trying to cover.

Plastic. Black plastic has its fans. Here's what my friend Barb Ingrams from Stites, Idaho, wrote to me: "We don't have too big of a garden spot, but it was big enough for my family. Glenn rototilled up the spot and then we laid black plastic over the whole thing. We both have backs that bother us, so this is done to eliminate a lot of weed pulling. Black has to be used so no sunlight can make weeds grow. For plants, cut holes about the size of the top of a 3-lb. coffee can. For the rows of vegetables, take a board about the size of 1 × 4 or 1 × 6 feet—depending on what the veg-

etable is. Cut around the board on both sides and lift the strip out. Plant as usual. Instead of black plastic this year, we are going to try newspapers, planted in the same manner as for the plastic. In between the rows, lay boards in the middle; that makes walking much easier and you don't pack the dirt down as bad. With the plastic, the ground seems to hold in the heat better, and also the water. For tomato plants, the holes have to be quite a bit larger than for pepper or some other plants. We had a tomato plant grow over 4 feet, and it was just a volunteer. With newspapers, instead of picking up the papers at the end of the season, just turn them under when you till. Saves a lot of time."

Coping with Pests and Pestilence

If you plant and then find that something else ate most of a crop before you got there, you won't be the first person it ever happened to. The number of possible plant diseases and plant-devouring insect species, to say nothing of fungi and garden-munching mammals, is legion.

PEST CONTROL INFO: There's fun-to-read, reliable info in *Bugs, Slugs and Other Thugs: Controlling Garden Pests Organically* by Rhonda Massingham Hart (1991). Another good entry in this field is *Common-Sense Pest Control* by William Olkowski, Sheila Daar, and Helga Olkowski, a huge encyclopedia of "least-toxic" methods of dealing with pests that afflict home, garden, pets, or human bodies. The Olkowskis founded a nonprofit organization called the Bio-Integral Resource Center that answers members' questions about least-toxic pest controls and publishes *Common-Sense Pest Control Quarterly* and *The IPM Practitioner* (a monthly for professionals); PO Box 7414, Berkeley, CA 94707; 510-524-2567; **www.birc.org**. "IPM" stands for "integrated pest management," a commercial farmer/gardener's philosophy of trying least-toxic methods first, but going to toxics if organic doesn't work.

Older classics in this area include *Garden Pests and Diseases* by Audrey Brooks and Andrew Halstead (1980), the *Rodale Garden Insect, Disease & Weed Identification Guide* by Miranda Smith and Anna Carr (1988), *Rodale's Color Handbook of Garden Insects* by Anna Carr (1979), *The Bug Book* by Helen and John Philbrick (1974), *Pests of the Garden and Small Farm: A Grower's Guide to Using Less Pesticide* by Mary Louise Flint; and *Rodale's Chemical-Free Yard and Garden*.

SOURCES OF BENEFICIAL INSECTS: The history of this is that in the 1970s, 2 greenhouse pests, whitefly and spider mite, developed a resistance to pesticides and threatened to wipe out greenhouse tomato and cucumber crops. Growers turned to natural biological control agents such as parasites and predators for control, and it worked! Since then, the firms in the following list have learned how to mass-produce these "biological control agents" and how to release them at the best timing and rate.

The basic "beneficial insects" are the predatory mite that attacks spider mites, green lacewing, praying mantis, whitefly parasite, mealybug destroyer, fly parasite, lady beetle, aphid parasite, red scale parasite, cabbage–root-maggot predator, and predators of other soil-dwelling pests (*Neoplectana* sp.). The following people are specialists in this wonderful new business area. They know their stuff. Ask here first!

Arbico is a large supplier of organic products such as beneficial insects and organisms, organic fertilizers, weed and disease control remedies, botanicals and traps, and biological fly and mosquito control. Very interesting free catalog: PO Box 8910, Tucson, AZ 85738-0910; **www. arbico.com.** You'll find a big list of insectaries and insect distributors at **www.cdpr.ca.gov/docs/ipminov/bensuppl. htm.** Biocontrol Network helps home gardeners with their bug/disease problems: **www.biconet.com.** Rincon-Vitova Insectaries is a large marketer in this area, which avoids small orders: 800-248-2847 (BUGS); **bugnet@rincon vitova.com; www.rinconvitova.com.**

MUSHROOMS

Mushrooms are really neither "vegetable" nor "animal." Although technically classified as "plants," fungi curiously straddle the plant and animal kingdoms. They don't make food from sunshine and air as plants do. Instead they extract it from decaying matter and make it into fresh and concentrated protein food for us, the way a cow turns grass into the fine protein foods of milk and meat. Molds (for making antibiotics), yeasts (for making bread, brew, and vinegar), and truffles are related fungi.

MYCOLOGICAL SOCIETIES: A mycological society is a fungus lovers' club. There are more than 100 mycological societies in North America. The societies at Boston and San Francisco, in particular, are large and venerable institutions. Here follow a few. For others, ask the North American Mycological Association.

Canadian Mushroom Grower's Association: 416-421-3179; fax 416-423-8453; 8 Trimontium Cr., Toronto, ON M2C 5N7, CANADA.

Los Angeles Mycological Society: 213-897-1844; Natural History Museum, Botany, 900 Exposition Blvd., Los Angeles, CA 90007.

North American Mycological Association publishes a yearly directory of most amateur mycological societies in North America; 304-744-1654; 10 Lynn Brooke Place, Charleston, WV 25312-9521; **brightcloud@ mciworld.net.**

Puget Sound Mycological Society: 206-522-6031; Center for Urban Horticulture, GF-15, U. of Washington, Seattle, WA 98195.

Vancouver Mycological Society: 604-878-9878; Box 181, 101-1001 W. Broadway, Vancouver, BC V6H 4E4, CANADA; **vancouver_myco@yahoo.com; www. geocities.com/vancouver_myco/.** Membership costs $15/yr and gets you their newsletter, *Mycofile.*

MUSHROOM WORKSHOPS: Fungi Perfecti give workshops on how to generate spawn, prepare substrate, inoculate, and maximize yield (plus five mushroom strains to

take home). Western Biologicals gives similar workshops: one for beginners, one for professionals. Or attend a "Mushroompeople Workshop" at The Farm. (Details under "Mushroom-Growing Supplies.") Videos and correspondence or personal classes on identifying wild mushrooms are offered by Outdoor Eduquip: 909-796-8501; 24414 University Ave. #34, Loma Linda, CA 92354.

PATENTS: Mike Hess, my mushroom-growing friend, says, "Patents have been filed for various processes to grow one of the more sought-after mushrooms—morels (*Morchella esculenta*). "Morel-growing on a commercial scale hasn't happened yet, but the general belief is that it's just a matter of time. Soon morels will be available in grocery stores the way button mushrooms, *Agaricus bisporus,* are today."

MUSHROOM PERIODICALS

McIlvanea & Mycophile: Journal of American Amateur Mycology. North American Mycological Association membership gets you a subscription to their newsletter, $15/yr (6 issues). Contact NAMA: 304-744-1654; 10 Lynn Brooke Place, Charleston, WV 25312-9521.

Spore Prints: Bulletin of the Puget Sound Mycological Society. 206-522-6031; PSMS, Center for Urban Horticulture, Box 354115, U. of Washington, Seattle, WA 98195-4115; **www.psms.org.**

BOOKS: Check out *The Biology and Cultivation of Edible Mushrooms,* edited by Chang and Hayes (1978). It has 33 chapters by scientists worldwide, which describe cultivation of a jillion mushroom varieties using many different methods. The sequel, edited by Chang and Quimio, is *Tropical Mushrooms: Biological Nature and Cultivation Methods.* It emphasizes Southeast Asian varieties; the info is good. *Mushrooms in the Garden* by Helmut Steineck (1984, tr. from German) is a *great* book for beginners who want a mushroom patch in their garden. *The Mushroom Cultivator* by Paul Stamets and J. S. Chilton (1983) is highly regarded. And Paul (member of PSMS) has a new 615-pg. update and companion guide to the old classic called *Growing Gourmet and Medicinal Mushrooms* with 16 pages of color pix; cost $49.95. Get both of Stamets' books from Agarikon Press, Box 2233, Olympia, WA 98507. Also see *Growing Wild Mushrooms* by Bob Harris (1989); and *Mushrooms and Truffles: Botany, Cultivation, and Utilization,* a hard-to-find classic by Rolf Singer (1961).

If you want to grow and market shiitake mushrooms, read *Growing Shiitake Mushrooms in a Continental Climate* by Maryellen Kozak and Joe Krawczyk, for growing shiitake mushrooms on natural logs. It's available from several of the listed suppliers. Also check out *Shiitake Growers Handbook: The Art and Science of Mushroom Cultivation* by Paul Przbylowicz and John Donoghue. *Is Shiitake Farming for You?* by R. Kerrigan (1982) discusses techniques and potential profits. Also read "Cultivation of shiitake, the Japanese forest mushroom: a potential industry for the United States" by G. F. Leatham in *Forest Products Journal* 32 (8): 29-35, 1982; and "Shiitake mushrooms: consumption, production, and cultivation" by D. J. Royse, L. C. Schisler, and D. A. Diehle in *Interdisciplinary Science Reviews* 10 (4): 329-335, 1985, for growing shiitake on sawdust.

START-UP KITS: These kits are a nice way to experiment and are fine for beginners. Many garden catalogs offer a basic mushroomgrowing kit together with directions, such as

Bountiful Garden's "Mushroom Farm In-A-Box," a 3-month supply. Similar start-ups are offered by Mushroom Supply Co. (see list of suppliers), Henry Field, Mellinger's, and Gurney. Edmund Scientific offers a button mushroom kit. Their astonishing, delightful catalog offers 4,000+ science products, including bunches of project kits and tools. Great resource here for homeschoolers and parents of scientifically inclined children: 609-573-6250; 7782 Edscorp Bldg., Barrington, NJ 08007. For higher-tech mushroom cultivation . . .

MUSHROOM-GROWING SUPPLIES

Field & Forest Products is very good and probably the biggest supplier in the country, offering spawn, books, and supplies. The owners of FFP wrote *Growing Shiitake Mushrooms in a Continental Climate:* 800-792-6220; N3296 Kozuzek Rd., Peshtigo, WI 54157; **FFP@mari.net.**

Fungi Perfecti is where mushroom guru Paul Stamets offers classes, supplies, starter kits, equipment, and expertise. Free brochure; sizable catalog, $4.50; 360-426-9292; PO Box 7634, Olympia, WA 98507; **myco media@aol.com; www.fungi.com.**

Hardscrabble Enterprises sells spawn for shiitake; books (*Shiitake Growers Handbook; Growing Shiitake Mushrooms in a Continental Climate*) and supplies. Conscientious, generous service. Info packet, $4; 304-358-2921; PO Box 1124, Franklin, WV 26807; **hardscrabble@mountain.net.**

Mushroompeople, since 1976, has offered premium spawn for shiitake, oysters, lion's mane, maitake, and reishi—

and cultures, tools, handbooks, cookbooks, field guides, videos, and gifts for the commercial and home cultivator. Free catalog from The Farm; 931-964-2200; PO Box 220, Summertown, TN 38483-0220.

Northwest Mycological Consultants offers books and supplies for mushroom culture. Besides numerous shiitake strains, they offer spawn of these other edible fungi: button, meadow, shaggy mane, velvet-stem enoki, (Ling Zhi) reishi, hen of the woods, morel, Nameko, yellow oyster, *Pleurotus eryngii,* oyster, angel wings, grey oyster, *Pleurotus sapidus, Polyporous umbellatus,* and wine-red Stropharia. Catalog $2 from 541-753-8198; 702 NW 4th St., Corvallis, OR 97330.

Rainforest Mushroom Spawn: Jeff Chilton, 604-886-7799; Box 1793, Gibsons, BC V0N 1V0, CANADA.

Western Biologicals is where Bill Chalmers offers books, supplies, and spawn for shiitake strains, many oyster mushroom strains (white, brown, pink, blue, golden, king, abalone, shimeji), lion's mane, golden giant, almond mushroom, shaggy mane, nameko, white button, portobello, enoki, reishi, and meitake. Hands-on workshops; call/fax 604-856-3339; PO Box 283, Aldergrove, BC V4W 2T8, CANADA; **western@ prismnet.bc.ca.**

Hunting Wild Mushrooms

I don't have anything in this book about identifying and collecting wild mushrooms—except this: *Don't do it from a book. Join a mushroom club.* To gather wild edible mushrooms, start by going out with experienced people. You'll learn more safely and surely about wild mushroom identification that way than you ever could from a book. *NOTE: Please think twice before gathering scarce mushrooms. Many varieties in many places are now near extinction because of overharvesting, although the problem is not so much hobbyists' harvesting but rather people's gathering them to sell here and overseas.*

The most beautiful and edible-looking wild mushrooms are often the most poisonous. The deadliest of all, the *Aminita phalloides,* or "death cap," is very similar to the *Agaricus campestris,* an edible relative of the commercial button mushroom. And the poisonous *Galerina marginata,* which grows on wood, looks very like the edible *Armillaria mellea.* Even experienced mushroom hunters have confused these two.

CARLA'S SIMPLE BUTTON-GROWING SYSTEM: It's easier than most people think if you do the basics right. The easy-goingest mushroom grower I know is a remarkable Florida lady named Rachel Jackson. She lives on the Linger Longer Ranch at Barberville, FL, and is always looking for sharecroppers who will come, trailer and all, and help garden her land in return for three-quarters of the produce. She throws old mushrooms on the compost pile and around the barn, often blending them first and sprinkling the blended mixture so it will grow like seed.

The problem with Rachel's system is that edible mushrooms can so much resemble deadly poisonous varieties—and an unexpected wild variety could easily grow up in the middle of your outdoor crop. For example, the jack o'lantern mushroom much resembles the chanterelle; the only real differences are that the jack o'lantern has a near-golden-yellow flesh and is poisonous, while the chanterelle has almost whitish flesh and is good to eat. That's one reason why my friend Mike Hess emphasizes sterile conditions so much. If you grow mushrooms under controlled (sterile) conditions, you know exactly what you've got.

So it's better to start out by buying spawn from a seed company. "Spawn" means started mushroom growth (the mycelium) rather than spores (the true mushroom seeds). The easiest way to start is with a "kit," which will include everything, already put together and sterilized for you. But here's a step-by-step procedure for growing a mushroom crop if you're doing it from scratch rather than from a kit.

1. Where? Decide where you're going to grow mushrooms —in a cave or fallout shelter, under the kitchen sink, or whatever. Mushrooms are the only "plant" crop that doesn't need light to grow, since they make food from manure and other decaying organic material rather than from sunshine. In fact, until the mushroom is actually ready to fruit, its growth is held back by the presence of light. So mushrooms are best grown in a basement, cellar, cave, or mine; in the dark, damp space between the floor of any building you have and the ground under it; or in a windowless building like a garage or barn, as long as it doesn't get too cold inside.

Commercial growers build special mushroom houses where they keep the temp at 55–65°F. Your growing place will work best if the temp hovers around 45–60°F, but the mushrooms won't die unless they either freeze or get way too hot.

2. In What Containers? The growing boxes can be heavy, waxed cardboard, but wooden boxes hold up better in the long run. Make your boxes at least 6 to 8 inches deep. You can just spread them out. Or to use space more efficiently, build a shelf arrangement for them. Make the bottom shelf at least 6 inches above the floor. Make the next shelves 2 feet above each other. You can go as high as the ceiling height allows.

3. In What Soil? Mushroom-growing soil is called "compost," and that's basically what it is. Different mushrooms grow best in different soils. Shaggy mane mushrooms like horse manure. Shiitake and Enoke like a sawdust/bran mix. Buttons and oysters will grow on this mixture:

Start with 4 parts grass or straw. The compost process goes best if you plan to work a 500-lb. lot at a time. Shred the grass or straw (lawn-mowing clippings work too). Wet it with nonchlorinated water, cover, and let soak several days. Now you're going to make a compost heap. Spread out your straw/grass a few inches high. Spread a layer of *fresh* cow, horse, or other manure over it. (Mike Hess says, "Horse manure's the best. Cow and pig are inferior and to be avoided.") Spray with water and keep adding more layers the same way until you're out of shreddings and manure. Cover with plastic and let 'er heat! After 5 days, start checking every day to see how the center temp is doing. When the temp starts dropping, turn and circulate the heap, water as needed, cover, and continue composting. You're done when turning no longer results in an increased temp. You have to let the manure age enough so that it won't heat up to more than 85°F, which would harm your mushrooms.

4. Bake the Growing Soil. This sterilization step is really important; please don't skip it. (You'll hear much more about sterilization from Mike later.) Mushrooms have quite a few natural enemies: bugs, worms, molds. This step protects them; it also ensures that you won't grow any kind of mushroom-toadstool–looking thing except exactly what you intend to. Bake each box, dirt and all, in your oven at 200°F for at least 1 hour. Let the oven get hot before you start timing the hour. Other ways to accomplish this are to compost the manure mixture beforehand and make sure it gets up to at least 170°F. After your soil has cooled down to no more than 70°F, make sure it's loose and not hard-packed. If the compost is so dry that it doesn't feel moist to the touch, spray before planting.

5. Load Growing Boxes. Put your growing mix into the boxes 6 to 10 inches deep. Don't pack it tightly. Smooth the top with a fork.

6. Plant the Spawn. Dried spawn keeps a long time in a cool and dry place, but spawn that is moist must be refrigerated or planted right away. Sprinkle spawn over the surface. Then sprinkle more pasteurized manure-compost mixture a couple inches deep over that; work the spawn flakes with your hands gently into the soil mixture; or lift some soil, spread the spawn with a teaspoon, and then replace the soil over it. Make these plantings about 8 inches apart.

7. Maintain Humidity and Dampness. Now sprinkle with lukewarm water and plan on keeping the mixture wet. It works best if you water with as fine a spray as you can manage. Check often enough to make sure the mushroom bed doesn't dry out, because if you let it completely dry out, that could be the end of your hoped-for mushroom crop. For a single, small box, it helps at first to put a damp cloth over the tray. Or rig up some constantly dripping water to keep humidity high in your mushroom-growing area. On the other hand, you can drown your mushrooms with too much water. If you can squeeze some of the growing mixture in your hand and no water comes out, it's still on the okay side. A plastic tent over your growing boxes helps hold in humidity without keeping the dirt itself oversoaked.

8. Do Casing. About 4 weeks after you plant your spawn in the boxes, your mushroom crop is ready to . . . "flower"? . . . "fruit"? . . . grow mushrooms. For, believe it or not, the mushroom you eat is a sort of flower. Or maybe it's more of a fruit.

The mushroom, in the form of that mycelium, does most of its early growing below ground, where the food is. It doesn't create the part of the plant that you think of as a proper mushroom until conditions trigger its reproductive phase. There has to be enough of a mycelium, which then builds and feeds the mushroom.

When mycelia—silky white threads that look like cotton—have grown out from each of your planting sites until they almost meet, it's casing time. You may even already see the first sign of life from your mushrooms above ground—a small knob growing above ground from that mycelium underneath. Mike Hess: "If the mushroom forms a 'knob' above ground before casing, then casing is probably unnecessary. But no knob will form, generally, until *after* you case. That's what casing is for."

Casing works because it's a layer of soil that's not sterilized and, for some unknown reason, the introduction of vigorous microscopic critters atop your mycelium growth at this stage triggers fruiting! So casing encourages the mycelium to make an aboveground mushroom flower/fruit. Here's how to do it: Sprinkle on anywhere from ½ to 1 inch of screened clay loam (or plain loam, but not sand and not soil with any partly rotted composting material in it).

9. Ventilate. During the fruiting stage, the plants need some fresh air. Don't overdo it to the point of drafts, but have enough air circulation so that the natural metabolic gases can't accumulate. At the same time, the mushroom-growing place needs to have a temp as nearly steady as possible in the 50–60°F range.

10. Pick. About a week or 10 days after the casing, you'll see mushrooms starting to form. Ten days after that, you'll be able to start picking. Harvest every day. Pick them just before they open out. (Also see "Harvest and Preparation.") When you pick, twist to prevent pulling up lots of "root," which would cause damage to the mycelium. Water as needed, just enough so the growing soil stays damp. But if you see spotted mushrooms, that means you need more ventilation and much less water. Your beds will now continue to grow mushrooms for about 3 to 6 more months, as long as the good temperature conditions hold and bugs and other competition stay out.

11. Raise Your Own Spawn. A box where mushrooms have been grown for several months has what is called "running spawn" all through it, at the level where you first planted spawn. You can use that dirt (unpasteurized, of course) to plant other boxes. If you dry the dirt in an airy but shaded place, you can store it under dry, dark, cool (but above freezing) conditions for maybe up to 10 years. Or the used box of soil will be a good addition to your garden or potted plants.

Harvest and Preparation

Button mushrooms don't all grow at the same speed, and those that are the same age aren't necessarily the same size. You may be harvesting as long as 2 or 4 months. Twist them out of the soil carefully. Don't leave any little pieces behind if you can help it, because those little pieces can rot and cause trouble for the rest of the crop. Pick them when closed and still white. Otherwise you'll have an overgrown mushroom. If you want to use them fresh, don't wash them and try not to bruise them, and they'll keep fairly well for about a week in an uncovered dish in the refrigerator.

ON "MATURE" BUTTONS: Lane Morgan says, "Not all mushrooms are best tiny. People should experiment. The big, mature button mushrooms often have a lot more flavor than the babies, and I like them better in many recipes. We have a mushroom farm nearby, and when they have extras they sell 'matures' for 10 lb. for $6. They're great for soup. I pickle some, and saute and freeze a bunch to add to tomato sauce later."

PREPARING: Clean the mushrooms by washing them thoroughly. Trim stems. Leave whole or slice. The small ones can be left whole and the large ones sliced. But Lane Morgan says, "Never wash a mushroom. They soak up the water just like a sponge, lose their flavor, and make whatever you cook with them watery too. If you grow them yourself in sterilized soil and harvest them carefully, how dirty are they going to be? My mother uses a special little soft brush to clean mushrooms. I use a dry dishrag or paper towel." If you're going to can them, though, you want that dirt out of there.

PRESERVING: Because of the nature of mushrooms, unless you live in a drafty tent you have a chance of growing them fresh year-round. Nevertheless, they can be preserved by drying, freezing, or canning.

Drying. Mike Hess: "Some mushrooms are excellent dried and rehydrated later. Morels, shiitake, and some oysters dry well. In fact, I've heard it argued that shiitake mushrooms are considerably better dried and rehydrated! Once you've dried them to a crisp, store them in airtight bags or jars. As added precaution against bugs eating your stores, freeze the containers for a couple of days before storage. If there are any eggs in there, that ought to kill them."

So here's how to dry them. Clean the mushrooms, slice thin (about ¼ inch), and dry until brittle. That will take a couple of days in the sun—less if you dry them at 110–140°F in an oven or dehydrator. You can add dried mushrooms directly to soup or revive them by soaking in water.

Freezing. Clean and cut into pieces no larger than an inch across. Then use one of these 2 methods.

Method 1: Prevent darkening by soaking the mushrooms 5 minutes in a mixture of 1 pt. water and 1 t. lemon juice (or ½ t. citric acid powder). Drain. Steam or blanch 2 to 4 minutes (longer for larger ones). Dip in cold water. Drain, pack, and freeze.

Method 2: Saute in butter or some such until tender. Chill, pack, and freeze.

Canning

USDA caution: Do not can wild mushrooms.

Trim stems and remove discolored spots. Soak in cold water 10 minutes to remove clinging soil; then wash in clear water. Leave small mushrooms whole. Cut large ones into halves or quarters. Cover with water in pan and boil 5 minutes. Pack hot. Add salt if desired. For better color, add ⅛ t. crystalline ascorbic acid per pint. Cover mushrooms with fresh boiling water. Pack in pint or half-pint jars only. Pressure-can only. Processing time for half-pints is the same as for pints: 45 minutes. If using a weighted-gauge canner, set at 10 lb. pressure at 0–1,000 feet above sea level; at higher altitudes, set at 15 lb. If using a dial-gauge canner, set at 11 lb. pressure at 0–2,000 feet above sea level; 12 lb. at 2,001–4,000 feet; 13 lb. at 4,001–6,000 feet; 14 lb. at 6,001–8,000 feet; or 15 lb. above 8,000 feet.

🐚 *MARINATED WHOLE MUSHROOMS You'll need 7 lb. small whole mushrooms, ½ c. bottled lemon juice, 2 c. olive or salad oil, 2½ c. white vinegar (5 percent), 1 T. oregano leaves, 1 T. dried basil leaves, 1 T. canning or pickling salt, ½ c. finely chopped onion, ¼ c. diced pimento (optional), 2 cloves garlic cut in quarters, and black peppercorns. Select very fresh, unopened mushrooms with caps less than 1¼ inches in diameter. Wash. Cut stems, leaving ¼ inch attached to cap. Add lemon juice and water to cover. Bring to boil. Simmer 5 minutes. Drain mushrooms.*

Mix olive oil, vinegar, oregano, basil, and salt in a saucepan. Stir in onions and pimento and heat to boiling. Place ¼ garlic clove and 2 to 3 peppercorns in each half-pint jar. Fill half-pint jars with mushrooms and hot, well-mixed oil-vinegar solution. Leave ½-inch headspace. Adjust lids and process in a boiling water bath. Process in half-pints only. At 0–1,000 feet above sea level, process 20 minutes; from 1,001–3,000 feet, 25 minutes; from 3,001–6,000 feet, 30 minutes; and above 6,000 feet, 35 minutes. Or use lower-temperature pasteurization (see the pickling section of "Cucumbers" in Chapter 4).

RAW OR COOKED? Home-grown mushrooms are more tasty and tender than store ones. But Mike warns: "Besides the obvious rule *'Know what kind of mushroom it is,'* there is a lesser-known one, *'Cook all mushrooms.'* Not even a cute little store-bought white button mushroom should be eaten raw. The reason is we don't digest raw mushrooms very well, and raw mushrooms will screw up your innards. The problem is chitin, the material that makes up a mushroom's cell walls. Chitin is what an insect's shell is made of."

Lane Morgan contends, "The little buttons are nice for eating raw (and for delicate dishes). Angelo Pellegrini [gourmet cook and cookbook author] ate raw mushrooms by the bushel and was hale well into his 80s, so it's not cut and dried."

Mushroom Toxins. Mike: "Toxins are another reason to cook mushrooms. Probably not something a cultivator need worry about, but many wild mushrooms—*Gyromitras*, for example—contain toxins that are broken down or driven off by heat. *Cook wild mushrooms with the lid off, so the fumes can escape.*" (See the book *Mushrooms Demystified*.)

Mushroom Allergies. Mike: "Also, there are some mushroom-allergic folks out there. So it's possible that the mushroom I can eat a plate of will make you mildly ill. That's why, among mushroom hunters, there's a rule: *Always try just a few bites of a new mushroom first. Wait 24 hours to be sure.* If

you have no reaction the first time, try more the next time. Thus you work up slowly to that heaping plate of morels.

"Funny thing about morels. In some parts of the world, morels are left alone as poisonous. I was at a foray once and a gal was talking about how one member of their group had gotten sick on the same dinner that 3 others had enjoyed completely. When he heard that, one fellow asked if the guy was Russian. It turns out not only that he was, but that, of several people this fellow had heard of with morel intolerance, all were Russian."

Lane Morgan adds: "One other weird thing. Shaggy manes are a favorite of mine, but some people can't digest them (or the other *Coprinis* species) in the presence of alcohol. So wine-with-dinner folks should plan their menus accordingly."

Mushroom Recipe Ideas. To cook, add only a little water and cook at a simmering temperature; don't cook any longer than necessary, or they will get tough. Add seasonings after cooking rather than before; that helps keep them tender. Ten or 15 minutes of cooking with a tight cover should do it. You can store cooked mushrooms in the refrigerator and use in other recipes for the next few days.

Or you can fry mushrooms in a little butter for 3 to 8 minutes, add salt and pepper, and serve on toast or mix with other foods. Or you can broil them by brushing with melted butter; broiling; seasoning with salt, pepper, and nutmeg; and serving. If you add a cup of cooked mushrooms to any white sauce, you can serve them as creamed mushrooms or as a sauce on cauliflower, peas, fish, ham, tongue, or toast.

For more recipes see *Joe's Book of Mushroom Cookery* by Jack Czarnecki; *A Mushroom Feast* by Jane Grigson, a cookbook for wild mushrooms; *Wild Mushroom Recipes* by the Puget Sound Mycological Society, which contains 200 more wild mushroom recipes that can also be used for home-grown ones; *Shiitake Sampler* by Janet Bratkovich, which includes 49 recipes for shiitake mushrooms; and *Wild About Mushrooms: The Mycological Society of San Francisco Cookbook* by Louise Freedman. Lane Morgan recommends Margaret McKenny's *The Savory Wild Mushroom* (U. of Washington Press) as a good source of recipes as well as hunting tips.

🐚 *HOMEMADE MUSHROOM SOUP Clean ½ lb. fresh mushrooms and chop them up. Pour boiling water over them and then pour it off. Melt 4 T. lard or drippings, add 4 T. flour, mix together, and brown the flour lightly. Add 1 minced clove garlic, 1 T. chopped onion, and 1 T. chopped parsley and continue browning. Add mushrooms; cover and let simmer for 10 minutes. Add 2 medium-sized potatoes that have been cubed and cooked, 1½ qt. water, a very small bay leaf, 1 T. vinegar, and a dash of marjoram, salt, and pepper to taste. Cook 10 minutes more. If you have sour cream around, add a couple of tablespoons before serving for extra goodness. Or serve grated Cheddar cheese on top.*

🐚 *SIMPLY MUSHROOM SOUP Chop up 1 c. onion, 1 c. celery, and 4 c. fresh mushrooms, and saute the mixture in butter. Add 2 T. flour and brown. Then add 7 c. milk, season with salt and pepper or whatever you like, simmer a half hour, and serve.*

🐚 *ENGLISH MUSHROOM/BASIL SOUP From Vickey of Westmeston, West Sussex, England: In a covered pan, cook in olive oil or butter until soft 1 large finely chopped onion* and ½ lb. finely chopped mushrooms. Heat 2 c. stock. Add it to the onion-mushroom mix and continue to cook until the vegetables are cooked through. Add 1 t. fresh or dried basil and 1 c. cool milk that has been premixed with 2 T. cornstarch. Combine, cook, and stir until thick and creamy. Add salt and pepper to taste. Serve piping hot with homemade bread.

✒ *MUSHROOM BURGERS* Stir together in a bowl ¼ lb. cleaned, finely chopped mushrooms, 1 large finely chopped onion, ¼ c. bread crumbs (the homemade kind), 2 beaten eggs, ¾ c. grated Cheddar cheese, and salt, pepper, and oregano to taste. Form into hamburger-type patties and fry in a pan on very low heat. Tastes even better if you put some garlic slices in the pan to float around and cook with it. Done when crisp on the outside and moist inside.

ABOUT SPROUTS AND VEGETARIAN DIETS

Sprouts

Legume and grain seeds are most frequently eaten as sprouts: any beans—soy, fava, lima, pinto, garbanzos—and peas, lentils, fenugreek, and alfalfa seeds. I've also heard of sprouting corn and barley—and buckwheat, sunflower seeds, dill, flax, pumpkin, beet, and lettuce seeds. The same general procedure works for them all.

SPROUTING INFO, BOOKS, SUPPLIES: ATTRA's pamphlet on "Sprouts and Wheatgrass Production and Marketing" is at **www.attra.org/attra-pub/sprouts.html.**

Good books on sprouting are *The Sprout Garden* (800-695-2241); and *Sprout for the Love of Everybody: Nutritional Values of Sprouts and Wheatgrass* (800-593-2665). *Sprouts: The Miracle Food* and *Sproutman's Kitchen Garden Cookbook,* by Steve Meyerowitz, are also useful. Steve also sells sprouting products: 413-528-5200; PO Box 1100, Great Barrington, MA 01230; **Sproutman@Sproutman.com; www. Sproutman.com.** *Sprouting for All Seasons: How and What to Sprout, Including Delicious, Easy-to-Prepare Recipes,* by Bertha B. Larimore, is a plain-speaking (no colored pages, no cute illustrations) complete guide to sprouting anything, any way, plus recipes to use sprouts (801-295-9451).

International Sprout Growers Association is a professional organization of professional sprout growers and their suppliers. Join and you get a subscription to their newsletter, *Sprouter's Journal,* an invitation to their annual convention, etc. They offer recipes, sprout nutrition, and growing info: 413-253-6965; PO Box 2214, Amherst, MA 01004-2214; **sprout1221@aol.com; www.isga-sprouts.org.**

Life Sprouts offers organic sprouting seeds and sprouting supplies: 800-241-1516; PO Box 150, Hyrum, UT 84319. Sprout House sells 30 kinds of sprouting seeds, 4 types of sprouters, books, and juicers: 800-SPROUTS; fax 607-278-5337; PO Box 754131, Parkside Station, Forest Hills, NY 11375; **www.sprouthouse.com.** Johnny's Selected Seeds also sells sprouting seeds; **www.johnny seeds.com.**

SPROUTING CONTAINERS: You can sprout seeds in all kinds of containers. You can buy 3-decker Lucite sprouting trays, use a cheesecloth or nylon-lidded jar, or grow them in an earthenware sprouter with a bottom saucer or in a suspended cotton or nylon bag. Ellen Hanshaw, Port Angeles, WA, shared her way of sprouting: "I use an $8 \times 8 \times 2$-inch glass baking dish lined with 5 layers of white terry cloth soaked with warm water. Sprinkle over 1½ t. alfalfa seeds. I lightly lay a plastic bag over the top, put the dish where it won't get direct sunlight, and 4 days later have a full dish of sprouts, with no rinsing or watering in between time."

Tribest Corp. sells an electric sprouter ($100) that sprinkles water and wafts air over the seeds: 888-254-7336; fax 562-623-7160; 14109 Pontlavoy Ave., Santa Fe Springs, CA 90670; **service@tribest.com; www.freshlifesprouter. com.** Back to Basics sells a wheatgrass growing kit, sprouter, and wheatgrass juicer: 801-571-7349; **www.back tobasicsproducts.com.** Commercial suppliers market a wheatgrass sprouter for $895 that would grow enough sprouts to supply your whole neighborhood.

SPROUTING TIPS

1. *Don't ever eat potato or tomato sprouts. They are poisonous.*
2. *Don't sprout seeds that have been sold for planting in the garden, because they've probably been treated with poisonous fungicides.* Always buy untreated seeds to sprout. They're available at food co-ops and natural food stores or from seedhouses that specialize in untreated seeds.
3. Use clean water for rinsing sprouts. If you must use city tap water, allow it to sit in a window for a day before using. Use cool rinse water, never warm.
4. You can hurry bigger seeds by first soaking them in some warm water overnight. Some people lay them on several layers of wet paper towels. Allow about 5 days to get them sprouted. It may happen faster.
5. Don't put your sprouts in direct sunlight.
6. Little whiskers that grow on your sprouts are rootlets starting. Just trim them off.
7. Beans, lentils, and so on have hulls that you can eat. If you don't like them, put the sprouts in a bowl of cold water, rub them gently, and the hulls will come off and float so you can discard them.
8. The bigger seeds like bean, pea, and lentil are done when the sprout is an inch long. Smaller seeds make smaller sprouts, of course. But actually, the general length of your sprouts doesn't matter—it's just a matter of your personal preference. Sample the sprouts each day to find when they best suit your taste, and harvest them then.
9. Sprouts can be stored for a week in the refrigerator or for a long time in the freezer.
10. Sprouts can be used in any kind of cooking, but for full nutritional value they should be eaten raw.

COMPLETE SPROUTING CHART

Seed	Method	Amount/ Qt. Jar	Seed Soak Time (Hours)	Best Temp (°F)	Rinses/Day	Days to Sprout	Length at Harvest (Inches)
Adzuki bean	Jar	½ c.	5–10	65–85	3–5	2–4	½–1½
Alfalfa	Jar or tray	2 T.	3–6	60–85	2–3	4–6	½–2
Almond	Jar or towel	2 c.	10–12	70–85	2–3	0–2	0–⅛
Barley	Jar	1½ c.	6–10	68–80	2–3	1–2	0–¼
Buckwheat (unhulled)	Soil	—	8–14	65–80	—	8–15	4½–6
Cabbage	Jar	3 T.	4–8	60–85	2–3	3–5	1–1½
Chia	Clay	—	—	65–85	—	3–5	1–1½
Chinese cabbage	Jar	3 T.	3–6	65–85	2–3	4–5	1–1½
Clover	Jar or tray	2 T.	3–6	60–85	2–3	4–6	1½–2
Corn	Jar	1½ c.	10–14	68–85	2–3	2–3	¼–½
Cress	Clay	—	—	50–72	—	4–5	1–1½
Fenugreek	Jar or soil	¼ c.	4–8	65–85	2	3–6	1–2
Flax	Clay	—	—	65–80	—	0–5	1–1½
Garbanzo bean	Jar	1 c.	8–12	68–85	3–4	2–4	½
Kidney bean	Jar	¾ c.	8–12	68–85	3–4	2–4	½–1
Lentil	Jar	¾ c.	5–8	60–85	2–3	2–4	¼–1
Lettuce	Jar or soil	3 T.	3–6	65–85	2–3	4–5	1–1½
Millet	Jar	1½ c.	5–7	70–80	2–3	1–2	0–⅛
Mung bean	Jar	⅓ c.	5–10	68–85	3–5	3–5	1–3
Mustard	Jar or soil	3 T.	4–6	65–85	2–3	4–5	1–1½
Oats	Jar or towel	1½ c.	3–5	68–80	1–2	1–2	0–¼
Pea	Jar or soil	2 c.	7–10	50–72	2–3	2–3	¼–½
Peanut	Jar	1 c.	8–12	68–85	2–3	3–5	¼–¾
Pinto bean	Jar	¾ c.	8–12	68–85	3–4	3–4	½–1¼
Popcorn	Jar	1½ c.	10–14	68–85	2–3	2–3	¼–½
Psyllium	Clay	—	—	65–80	—	4–5	¾–1½
Pumpkin	Jar	1½ c.	4–6	65–85	2	0–2	0–⅛
Quinoa	Jar	⅓ c.	2–4	55–80	2–3	1–4	¼–1¼
Radish	Jar or soil	3 T.	4–8	60–85	2–3	4–5	1–2
Rice	Jar	1½ c.	12–15	55–80	2–3	1–3	0–⅛
Rye	Jar or soil	1 c.	6–10	50–72	2	2–3	¼–½
Sesame	Jar	2 c.	6–8	68–80	3–4	2–3	⅛
Soybean	Jar	¾ c.	4–8	65–85	3–4	3–4	½–2
Spinach	Jar or soil	3 T.	4–6	65–85	2–3	3–6	1–2
Sunflower (hulled)	Jar	1 c.	2–4	60–80	2	0–4	0–1
Sunflower (unhulled)	Soil	—	10–14	60–80	—	8–15	3½–6
Triticale	Jar or soil	1 c.	6–10	60–80	2	2–3	¼–1/2
Turnip	Jar or soil	3 T.	4–8	65–85	2–3	3–5	1–1½
Wheat	Jar or soil	1 c.	6–10	55–80	2	2–3	¼–1/2

LENTILS SPROUTED IN A JAR: Rinse seeds in lukewarm water and drain ½ c. lentils. Put into a 1-qt widemouthed jar. Add 2 c. lukewarm water. Fasten a square of cheesecloth or nylon stocking over the jar top with a rubber band or some such. Let stand overnight. The next morning, drain off the water. When you sprout your seeds, you can't leave them under water. They'll spoil. Turn your jar upside down until all the water has drained out. Now hold the jar on its side and gently shake it enough so the lentils get scattered all along one side of it. If you want white or light-colored sprouts, put the jar, still on that side, in a dark cupboard or closet. If you want green sprouts, put the jar in a place where there is light.

Each morning, run lukewarm water into the jar, leaving the cloth covering the top of it, and then drain until all the water is drained out. That's "rinsing" the sprouts. Again gently shake the jar until the lentils are all on the side.

Lentil sprouts are ready to use when ¼ inch in length. It takes about 4 to 5 days. Once they're the length you want (about an inch), store in the fridge. Use within a week. If roots develop, cut them off before use.

ALFALFA SPROUTED IN A JAR: Pat Crim of Fort Collins, CO, who has been helping me write this cookbook practically from the beginning, wrote me: "I sprout only alfalfa seeds, and the advantage to me is that it gives my family a source of fresh greens all winter and they are amazingly cheap. I just use a widemouthed mason jar with several layers of nylon net over the mouth and a canning ring to hold them on. I put the seeds in the jar and leave them in a warm, dark closet, taking them out 2 or 3 times a day to rinse them, until they are sprouted. It takes less time than going to the store for a head of lettuce."

BASIC JAR SPROUTING: Jar sprouting is so easy. To jar-sprout any variety of seeds, soak them in a jar for the length of time indicated in the "Complete Sprouting Chart." Use cheesecloth to cover the mouth of the jar, and hold it on there with a canning jar rim or rubber band. Rinse seeds and drain off water 2–4 times a day. Keep the jar at an angle facing down to allow for complete drainage.

EATING SPROUTS: Don't cook the sprouts more than 5 or 6 minutes. Too much cooking takes away their prime—except for soybean sprouts, which are tougher. You can mix them raw in salads. Rye and wheat sprouts can be eaten plain as a snack. You can add them to soups, casseroles, scrambled eggs, bread batters, or stewed tomatoes, but remember to do it just at the end, 5 minutes before serving, if it's a cooked dish. They make a good substitute in recipes calling for celery, which is something a lot of people (me included) can't grow. They have that nice crunchiness of celery. You can cook and serve them plain as a "vegetable" dish. Just steam, fry quickly in a little oil, or bake.

➢ *SPROUTED PEAS These are good served with salt, pepper, and a pinch of basil leaves. Cook them a half hour or so to get them tender. Add butter and serve.*

➢ *SPROUT SANDWICH Start with 2 slices of good whole wheat bread. Spread each half with cream cheese. Put on a layer of sliced cucumbers, one of sliced tomatoes, and one of sprouts. Put the top on the sandwich, slice in half, and enjoy.*

Vegetarianism

VEGETARIAN DIETS: When I first started writing this book I didn't know anything about the vegetarian way of eating. But readers, and life, have educated me. I've been exchanging letters for about a year now [1989] with a remarkable young lady named Ruth Miller. Age 13, she lives with her sister and parents on a small island, Bonaire, Netherlands Antilles, in the Southern Caribbean, where her parents manage a religious radio station called Trans World Radio. Ruth and her parents are long-time vegetarians—vegans, actually.

So I asked her to write a comparison of various vegetarian styles of eating. After a silence of several months, I received her reply: 70 hand-printed pages, solidly covered with small lettering on both sides! Her research was excellent. She made many suggestions for not only this particular section but also many other chapters. So when you see "vegan" in a recipe title, or "Ruth's," that's who it came from!

VEGETARIAN READING AND INGREDIENTS: Start with *The Mail Order Catalog for Healthy Eating* because it's such a huge listing of vegetarian/vegan books and products: Box 180, Summertown, TN 38483; 800-695-2241; **catalog@ usit.net; www.healthy-eating.com.** For from-scratch, out-of-the-garden cooking, check out *The Home-Grown Vegetarian* by Labine, Burrill, and Nolfi. I also recommend the *Around the World Vegetarian Cookbook, The Moosewood Cookbook,* and *The New Laurel's Kitchen* by Laurel Robertson (more than 500 vegetarian recipes and special sections on dietary needs of pregnant, elderly, infant, and sick persons). But then again, I never met a vegetarian cookbook (or a vegetable or a vegetarian) that I didn't like. *Vegetarian Times* is a popular magazine in this field: 800-829-3340; Canada and foreign call 904-446-6914; PO Box 5189, Pittsfield, MA 01203-5189. Powell's Books for Cooks & Gardeners stocks more than 10,000 recipe books: 800-354-5957; 3747 SE Hawthorne Blvd., Portland, OR 97214;

www.powells.com. They carried mine even when everybody else was calling it "out of print" (they are very persistent people). Especially their Patty Merrill, who is really the one responsible for this fine new commercial-edition book being in your hands. Patty wrote Sasquatch Books a couple of years ago and asked, "Why don't you put out Carla's book?" So Chad Haight, Sasquatch's publisher, wrote me a letter asking, "Will you?" I answered, "Yes," and here's the book!

THE KINDS OF VEGETARIANISM: Now here's Ruth! "I'm going to try hard and give you an overview and summary of some distinct schools of thought. I am speaking from firsthand experience on all these diets; these classifications are representative of my own experimentation with vegetarian diets. For me, vegetarianism started as a health diet. Now it involves a lifestyle and way of viewing the world. In general, if you crave stuff like coffee, chocolate, salt, fat, sugar . . . it's a sign of addiction, not health. But please, don't make vegetarianism into an excuse for eating a lot of chemicalized junk, especially commercial meat substitutes. My whole way of thinking about vegetarianism centers around doing what is absolutely best for my body. That includes not only staying away from animal products (for me) but also avoiding all sorts of processed foodstuffs. My motto is to eat it as close to its original state as possible."

Lacto-Ovo (or Lacto- or Ovo-) Vegetarian. Ruth: "This means one avoids meat, poultry, fish, etc., but eats milk and dairy products (lacto) and eggs (ovo). Or some eat just milk products or just eggs—in conjunction with fruit, vegetables, grains, etc., of course! Often such people try to make sure their diet equals a meat-inclusive diet in protein content, using a method called protein complementarity. Frances Moore Lappe has an informative book, *Diet for a Small Planet,* which takes this approach. Be careful on this diet, for many commercial dairy products are loaded with chemicals and saturated fat. For some people, a lacto-ovo vegetarian diet is the first step toward a total vegetarian diet."

Lacto-Ovo Vegetarian Recipes. Okay. Here I let Ruth turn it over to Melanie for a bit. Melanie Kohler, Haleiwa, HI, was my very first teacher (about '77) on vegetarian eating. She cooks a lot of lacto-ovo-vegetarian meals, the kind Ruth was just describing. Here's Melanie:

"Both my husband and I were born and raised as Seventh-Day Adventists (my father-in-law is an SDA minister). Danny grew up in California, but I'm a native Hawaiian (although I don't have any Hawaiian blood—I'm Portuguese, Chinese, Spanish, and Filipino). Danny's dad was transferred here to Hawaii to pastor our church while we were both in high school, and we've been sweethearts since then. We're now 26 and 27 years old, have a 2½-year-old miniature Danny, and live on 2⅓ acres of hilltop land about 40 miles from Honolulu.

"Not all Seventh-Day Adventists are vegetarians—I never have been one, but Danny was raised as one and got his eating habits changed while he was in the army. We are allowed to eat beef, lamb, chicken, turkey, and fish, but not unclean food such as pork and shellfish. But although we aren't vegetarians, we do have vegetarian meals about 2 or 3 times a week—both because we feel that it is healthful and to keep the cost of our food down (since we don't raise any livestock). You really can't beat vegetarian dishes (if prepared the right way) for tasty and, most of all, economical food!

"The Cottage Cheese Patties recipe that I sent you

earlier is one of our favorites. It's also my old standby to take to church potlucks, and I never have to take home any leftovers!"

☞ **COTTAGE CHEESE PATTIES** *Melanie: "Combine 1 c. cottage cheese, 1 c. bread crumbs, 1 c. rolled oats, 1 onion chopped fine, 2 T. chopped parsley, 2 to 3 eggs, and salt and sage to taste. Form into patties and fry. Place browned patties in baking dish. Cover with tomato sauce. Bake at 350°F for about 30 minutes or until gravy bubbles. This recipe should serve about 4 to 5 people.*

"I usually make several recipes of patties, cool them after frying, and then place them in plastic bags and put in the freezer. Then, whenever we have unexpected guests, get home late from work, or whatever, I can just take out however many patties I need, put them in a baking pan, pour tomato sauce over, and bake until bubbly. You can also pour cream of mushroom soup over to make the gravy, or use homemade brown gravy, or just eat the patties plain with a little ketchup. The mixture can also be formed into balls, fried, added to spaghetti sauce, and served over cooked spaghetti. Actually, you can fix up these patties just about any way you want—just use your imagination and whatever you have in your pantry!"

Melanie: "A couple of good recipes that I got while majoring in home economics at Walla Walla College in Washington state are for Walnut Cheese Patties and Imperial Roast."

☞ **WALNUT CHEESE PATTIES** *Melanie: "Mix together 6 chopped hard-cooked eggs, 1 c. cottage cheese, 1 ground onion, ¼ c. soft bread crumbs, 1 t. salt, ½ c. ground nuts, and 2 T. chopped parsley. Shape into patties; dip into beaten eggs and dry bread crumbs to coat. Brown lightly in hot oil and place in baking dish. Pour desired gravy (tomato sauce, mushroom soup, or brown gravy) over and bake at 350°F for 1 hour."*

☞ **IMPERIAL ROAST** *Melanie: "Mix together ¼ c. cooked brown rice (or white, if you don't have brown), 1 chopped hard-cooked egg, 2 c. dry cubed bread, 1½ c. chopped walnuts, 3 T. evaporated milk, 1½ t. salt, and ½ t. sage. Place in oiled pan to a depth of about 2 inches. Bake at 400°F for about 1 hour. Serve with gravy."*

☞ **EGGPLANT MAIN DISH** *Melanie: "If you like eggplant like I do, a very easy and tasty dish that can be used as either an entree or a side vegetable can be made as follows: Slice eggplants (as many as needed to feed your family) into approximately ½-inch-thick slices. Dip slices into beaten egg, and then dredge in mixture of flour, salt, and pepper. Fry slices in oil until golden brown and set aside. Chop 1 or 2 onions and fry in same pan until golden. Place a layer of eggplant slices in a greased baking dish, sprinkle with some of the sauteed onion, and pour some tomato sauce over. Repeat layers until all of the onions and eggplant slices are used up; end with a layer of tomato sauce over all. Bake at 350°F until bubbly (30–45 minutes)."*

Melanie: "A meatlike substitute can be made from the gluten of hard-wheat flour." (See the "Unleavened Breads" section of Chapter 3.)

"These next few recipes are some I've gotten at various times from different ladies in my church."

☞ **CARROT AND NUT LOAF** *Melanie: "Combine 2 c. ground raw carrots, 1½ c. dried bread crumbs, ⅓ c. milk (or more), 3 T. oil, 1 chopped onion, ½ c. chopped nuts, and salt to taste. Add 1 or 2 eggs if needed to moisten. Put into a greased baking dish, cover, and bake at 350°F for 1 hour. Uncover for the last few minutes to brown top."*

☞ **RUTH'S VEGAN CARROT LOAF** Here's Ruth's version: *"Mix 3 c. finely shredded carrots, 1 c. toasted bread crumbs, ½ c. (more or less) rice milk, 1 grated onion, 2 cloves garlic, 1½ t. curry powder, ½ c. sliced water chestnuts (or peeled, chopped broccoli stalks), and 2 T. tomato paste. Bake covered for an hour at 350°F."*

☞ **PRINCESS LOAF** *Melanie: "Saute ½ c. chopped onion and combine with ½ c. cooked brown rice, 2 beaten eggs, ½ c. evaporated milk, 1 c. bread crumbs, ½ c. sour cream, 2 T. margarine, 1 c. chopped walnuts, ½ t. sage, and 1 t. salt. Bake at 350°F for about 45 minutes."*

☞ **PECAN LOAF** *Melanie: "Mix together 4 eggs, 1 c. chopped pecans, ¼ c. chopped parsley, ¼ c. melted butter, ½ onion, chopped, 1 c. finely chopped celery, 2 c. oats, 3 c. milk, and salt to taste. Bake at 350°F for 45 to 60 minutes, or until loaf is set."*

☞ **EGG FOO YUNG** *Melanie: "This is another one of our old family favorites, prepared very simply with whatever we happen to have in the refrigerator or in the garden. I don't have any particular quantities for anything in this recipe—just vary it according to whatever you have and how many you plan to serve. I use home-sprouted mung bean sprouts, carrots (cut in slivers), green beans (sliced thin, diagonally), celery (cut same as beans), onions (sliced thin), bell peppers (sliced thin), etc. Canned bamboo shoots and water chestnuts may also be added for a more exotic touch, but they're really not necessary. Mix all ingredients (all vegetables are still raw) and add enough beaten eggs to hold together. Fry in large patties and serve hot with steamed rice and soy sauce. The vegetables should still be crunchy and the eggs a golden brown. A sweet-sour sauce to serve with the patties may also be made from soy sauce, brown sugar, vinegar or lemon juice, a pinch of salt, and cornstarch to thicken.*

"This is a good dish to prepare ahead—have all of the vegetables sliced and mixed ahead of time, and then add eggs right before dinner. Bring your electric skillet to the table and fry the egg patties right there at the dining table so your family can have them piping hot as they are ready for them.

"Well, Carla, I've been typing this straight through, and I'm pooped! After doing these few pages, it's even more of an amazement to me how you managed to ever do all of those 600-plus pages! And especially with 5 children around the place—I know what kind of trouble my little one can get into the minute I turn my back, and to multiply that by 5 just boggles my imagination! Love and aloha!"

See the soybean section in Chapter 4 for more recipes from

Ruth and Melanie. From here on, the diets and recipes have no animal products, milk, or eggs. My friend Mary at the Cooperative Extension office urged me to point out that *people who eliminate from their diet all animal products, including milk and eggs, risk iron, B-12, and calcium deficiency, and pregnant women are at particular risk on such a diet.* So there it is: On any of the following diets, please make sure you're getting enough iron, B-12, and calcium—*especially if you're pregnant!*

MACROBIOTICS: Melanie: "Macrobiotics is a complete lifestyle-diet (as most vegetarian diets become if you live that way long enough). In my experience, it is popular among people who are involved with meditation, yoga, and Eastern teachings. The main tenet seems to be a balance of yin and yang, with all foods being in one or the other category. This diet involves a lot of food-preparation and cooking techniques. There are books on Zen cookery in many bookstores."

RAW-FOOD VEGETARIAN: Back to Ruth: "You could classify this as the other extreme from lacto-ovo. The strict form confines the eater to a mainstay of fruits and above-ground, succulent vegetables. The "modified" raw-food eater adds sprouted grains and seeds. In the raw-food school of eating, there are very definite subdivisions, with various people promoting their differing opinions and research. Some say a diet of mostly raw fruit is best; others preach the glories of sprouting everything in sight and eating at least 4–8 oz. of nuts every day. It's a highly individual matter. Some people use an extreme form of the diet for a while, and then settle down to a modified form of the diet; others strictly stick to raw foods. When I was eating all raw foods, 60 percent of that was fruit. [See the section on sunflowers in Chapter 4 for protein dishes based on raw sunflower seeds.]

"But a word of warning. A few rather scary phenomena may temporarily accompany a change to a strict raw-food diet, especially if your previous diet has been very different from that. Often diarrhea or a flu-like reaction can result from the change in diet. This passes in a few days to a few weeks, depending on the individual.

"I don't follow a 100 percent raw diet any more, partly because of the unavailability of suitable vegetables and nuts here on Bonaire. But since I live in the tropics, I still do eat 50 percent of my food as fruit, and about 70–80 percent is uncooked, both fruits and veggies."

Raw-Food Vegetarian Recipes. All these recipes are from Ruth.

❧ *ALMOND MAIN DISH* "Try these for a different (raw-food) main dish! Get out your food grinder and start grinding almonds until you have a cup of almond butter. Now run through the grinder 2 c. chopped broccoli (flowers and stalks), 2 quartered red bell peppers, and ½ c. raisins that have been soaked overnight. Mix these vegetables with 2 c. 3-day lentil sprouts, 1 c. finely minced celery, and 6 minced tomatillos. Then add the almond butter and knead till well mixed. Use an ice cream scoop to make round balls. Serve balls in individual bowls with lettuce linings. Garnish with slivered almonds."

❧ *VEGETABLE NUT LOAVES* "One recipe is enough for 4 or 5 people. Natural Hygienists use this like tofu or seitan because it is endlessly versatile and can be molded into loaves, balls, or any other desired shapes. Combine 6 to 7 c. assorted shredded raw vegetables (anything from cabbage or celery to pumpkin, kohlrabi, zucchini, or sprouts), ½ c. nut meal (coarsely ground nuts that are not a butter), and ¾ c. nut butter (raw, freshly made)."

❧ *TROPICAL RAW PIE CRUSTS* "For 2 crusts: Mix 2 c. fresh shredded coconut, 1 c. almond butter, ½ c. grated apples, and 1 lb. chopped moist dates. For one 10-inch pie-plate crust: Use 1 lb. chopped dates, ½ c. finely grated apple, ½ lb. walnut butter, and 1½ c. finely grated fresh coconut. For a fig crust: Grind equal amounts of shelled raw almonds and unsoaked, dried figs together and press into pie plate."

❧ *NUT/DATE PIE FILLING* "Try ½ c. nut butter mixed with juice of 1 lemon, ½ c. pureed dates, 1 c. soaked pureed currants, and 3 c. grated tart apples. (Fruits can be varied to taste and need.)"

❧ *BANANA COCONUT PIE FILLING* "Mash 4 ripe bananas and mix with 1 c. grated fresh coconut. (If you put coconut with half a vanilla bean in an airtight container for a while, it adds an extra twist.) Put mix into piecrust. Set in freezer for an hour before serving."

❧ *PECAN PIE FILLING* "Crush 1 c. shelled unroasted pecans and then mix with 1 c. mashed banana, 1 c. ground dried figs, and some cinnamon and nutmeg. Pour into piecrust. Top with whole pecans. Chill before serving."

Soup the Natural Hygiene Way. Ruth: "When you make soup this way, heat the kettle and the serving bowls and have the ingredients at room temperature before preparing, but don't cook the soup. (You heat the kettle with boiling water.) The soup ends up being as warm as you can eat it without burning your tongue, but the enzymes are still intact! (You can prepare the soup in a kettle that has been heated and is still standing in hot water.) Here are some of examples:

❧ *TOMATO SOUP* "Blend 3 c. tomato juice (fresh!) with ½ cup favorite nut butter. Pour into heated kettle (a bowl of hot water, not a pan heating on the stove). Stir in 2 finely chopped tomatoes and half of a finely chopped red bell pepper. When soup is thoroughly warm, serve in heated bowls."

❧ *MINESTRONE* "Blend 4 c. tomato puree and ½ c. fresh nut butter. Place in water-heated kettle. Add 1 c. corn sliced off the cob (uncooked, fresh), 1 c. freshly shelled peas, 1 diced tomato, 1 minced bell pepper, some diced celery, and ½ c. shredded carrot."

❧ *PEA SOUP* "Blend 3 big tomatoes with 2 c. fresh green peas and the flesh of 1 avocado. Place in water-heated kettle. Stir in 1 finely chopped celery stalk, 1 finely chopped bell pepper, and 1 more c. fresh peas. Serve in heated bowls."

❧ *BORSCHT* "For each person, use 2 c. diced raw beets, 1 c. warm liquid (water or beet juice), juice of half a lemon, and ¼ c. nut butter. Liquefy in blender and then warm it. Some people like it thicker, with more nut butter."

ORGANIC VEGAN: Ruth: "This is the diet my whole family and I presently follow. We call it 'vegan' for short. The formal definition of an organic vegan diet is no salt, processed fat, or refined sugar; no meat, fish, or poultry; and no milk or eggs. It takes a little thinking, planning, and doing to get going with this diet, but gradually you'll discover a wide variety of things to do with grains, beans, vegetables, and fruits that can more than adequately meet your nutritional requirements. Things you'd never thought of before! And you are much healthier on this type of diet. *The McDougall Plan* by John McDougall, M.D. (Piscataway, NJ: New Century Publishers, Inc., 1983), which is available at most natural food stores, covers this type of diet. Here's how you adapt recipes to a vegan diet . . . "

Sugar- and Salt-Free. "If you really miss the sugar or salt, be patient. Taste buds can be trained to enjoy the flavors of unsalted, unsugared foods. If you're eating food the way it comes from nature, the flavor is unbeatable, and you can supplement it with herbs and spices. The body does need sodium but not sodium chloride. You can get all the sodium you need, properly balanced with potassium, from fruits and vegetables. Tamari, which is a natural soy sauce from Japan with no chemicals added, can be used as a nice salt substitute for flavoring. Natural sugar in fruits, plain sugar cane, and other unprocessed sweets such as sorghum, molasses, maple syrup, and honey are all right to use."

Oil-Free. "Natural fats are found in avocadoes, bananas, nuts, and seeds. In bread making, fat and oil are totally unnecessary. We make great bread using flour, water or vegetable juice, and yeast only! No sugar, salt, or fat. Here are some tips we use for eliminating fat while keeping flavor:

"Saute or fry without oil. Use ¼–½ c. water or vegetable stock with herbs to saute onions, etc. If need be, you can just shine a griddle with oil. Shortenings and oils can be totally and completely left out of recipes for baked goods like muffins and most breads (shortbread and pound cake you shouldn't be eating anyway!). When moisture and extra sweetness is needed, substitute applesauce or mashed banana for oil and sugar. Eggs can also be eliminated with a bit of experimentation. Try a few spoonfuls of wheat flour to hold something together; in the pancake/pudding-type recipes, some steamed/mashed potato or cauliflower holds things together nicely. For mayonnaise or sour cream, we substitute sesame-seed butter (oil poured off the top) whipped with water and lemon juice to proper consistency. Or soft tofu."

Vegan Flavor. "It's amazing how you can develop a new, healthy cooking style so that you don't even miss the old foods. (It takes about 3 months.) Your taste buds really start to respond to the flavors of the natural foods, herbs, and spices; salty, fatty, sugary food just tastes gross! A hint for flavor: Steamed vegetables have more taste than boiled ones. It's easy to get in the habit of steaming instead of boiling using a little collapsible steam basket. (We have 2!) The flavors of 2 different vegetables stay separate if you steam instead of boil them. Nutrients are also well-preserved because the water doesn't touch the food. Herbs in the water add a different twist; the leftover water is great for soup stock. Tamari and miso also help make vegan soup but are not necessary (or always available on Bonaire). Mashed beans are wonderfully versatile for dressings and dips." (See Chapter 3 and Chapter 4, especially the dried bean and soybean sections, for more by Ruth.)

➤ *RUTH'S STEAMED VEGAN MEDLEY* "I like this simple, flavorful dish! Steam a beet, a potato, a turnip, a carrot, a stalk of broccoli, a zucchini, and ⅛ head cabbage for each person (add or delete any vegetables). Keep all warm until time to serve. Serve drizzled with lemon juice. Or slice the vegetables and tubers into matchsticks and bake them in a covered casserole. Serve that also with lemon juice."

Vegan Meal Planning. Ruth: "Breakfast can be skipped, or many people like to eat fruit for it—or some hot cereal if it's a cold winter. Lunch can be soup and sandwiches or your main meal. For supper, instead of featuring a main dish plus side dishes, you might like to try serving 3 lesser dishes together. Always serve a huge raw salad first, then maybe a starchy grain or vegetable and some steamed ones, or an elaborate dish. Or just add some cooked beans or grain to the salad and call it a meal. We like to concentrate on the main dishes and forgo dessert, but you could sometimes serve fruit or a honey-fruit-bread for a dessert."

VEGAN PREPARATION PRINCIPLES AND SUBSTITUTIONS: This is what I extracted from those many pages and scores of recipes from Ruth, trying to boil it down to what she actually does.

Do Steam, Bake, or Saute. Avoid boiling. Steaming, baking, or the quick-fry method called sauteing are the healthiest ways to cook vegetables if you want to protect and preserve their vitamin content. To saute, use water or tomato juice or tomato sauce instead of oil. Or "shine" your pan by rubbing with a cut potato instead of using oil. Or just use enough cooking oil for that "shine." Never fry in deep fat.

Don't Use Animal or Processed Fat. Substitute banana, avocado, nuts, tahini (blended sesame seeds), or other oily seeds daily in order to get a natural source of unprocessed, vegetarian fat in your diet (which your brain and body need to function normally).

Boullion Cube Substitute. Substitute a slug of tamari or a spoonful of miso.

Meat, Milk, or Egg Substitute. Substitute bread crumbs soaked in rice milk (or soy milk) to hold a dish together. For the taste, add a mashed block of tofu that has been marinated in a mixture of tamari, water, sage, basil, and oregano. Or substitute gluten (see the section on unleavened breads in Chapter 3), seed protein dishes (see the sunflower section in Chapter 4), or soybean products (see soybean section in Chapter 4).

Marinade. When appropriate, marinate foods in lemon juice or tamari; add herbs as desired.

Salad Dressing Substitute. Use lemon juice as the base, varied with a little water, or half and half with tamari, or a drop of Tabasco sauce. No oil. Ruth eats salad every day, usually as the main dish at dinnertime, before the cooked food. Her salads are about ½ to ⅓ lettuce, the rest being any or all of these: cabbage, tomato, sweet pepper, all sorts of sprouts (especially lentil sprouts), onion, cauliflower, mushrooms, green beans, peas. They're all chopped up and tossed with dried herbs, garlic powder, and her choice of spices.

Milk Substitute. Use soy milk diluted with 2 parts water. But cereals and such cooked in apple juice are wonderful plain or with applesauce. Or use rice milk: In blender, process 4 c. water with 1 c. cooked brown rice until smooth. Refrigerate; shake before using. Makes 1 qt. Or use nut milk: Blend 4 c. water with ¾ c. blanched almonds. May be strained before refrigeration. Use just as you would dairy milk. Shake before using. Makes 1 qt. (Other nuts can also be used.)

Mayonnaise Substitute. Ruth uses plain lemon juice, a nut butter whipped with water, or soft creamy tofu with lemon juice.

GREASELESS WHITE SAUCE OR GRAVY *Ruth: "Use as much water as you need sauce, and about one-fourth as much whole wheat flour. Toast the flour over dry heat in a skillet for about 5 minutes, stirring constantly. Take from heat. Gradually whisk in water, blending well; then return to low heat and stir occasionally until thickened. Season as desired (nice seasoning blends include basil, dill, cumin; basil, tarragon, marjoram; thyme, sage, oregano; or your own). Use when white sauce is needed."*

Sugar Substitute. For each 1½ c. sugar in a recipe, use 1 c. frozen apple juice concentrate. When suitable, thicken apple juice to a runny paste by boiling with arrowroot or cornstarch, as for making a pie.

Cheese Substitute. In a casserole recipe, use bread crumbs, herbs, and a dash of tamari in place of cheese.

Salt, Pepper, and Butter Substitute. Use herbs. And I note that Ruth and her family frequently use "a dash of tamari" or a bit of miso for flavoring—both high-salt items. So they *are* getting this necessity for life somehow. But obviously, unlike most of us, they're not getting too much of it, and that's the good news.

Some years back, I wanted to do a really thorough rewrite of the chapter on vegetables [Chapter 4] because I'd learned so much more since I first wrote it. I also knew so much more about what people wanted and needed to know from the letters they had written me asking questions. So on one of my trips around the country talking about country living, I wrote about vegetables in all my spare time. I came back home with pages and pages of manuscript, scribbly looking but full of information ready to be typed up. After I got my scribbling done, I threw out the many wonderful letters and other source material that I used in writing it.

Well, it happened that those scribbles all got lost. That really hurt. They never did turn up.

Did you ever hear of that fellow in England, a long time ago, who wrote a huge wonderful history of England? He had just finished it. It took him something like 7 years to write the thing. And a new housecleaner, while he was away from home for the day, threw the entire manuscript in his fireplace and burned it up. (She didn't mean to do anything bad. She thought it was trash.)

You remember what he did then? He sat down and wrote it all over again. It became a very famous book, and students studied it for generations. He was a great man.

I had that happen to me once before. Back in my college days, I decided to write a novel—a great novel, nothing halfway for me. I was about 24. Managed to spend a whole summer in Canada writing, and more time other places too (mostly at home), until there was a pile of manuscript pages about 2 inches high, mostly typed on only 1 side of the pages. Raggedy emotional poetical stuff—but still, it was my life's work to date. I had outlined it to be an allegory on 5 levels. I was going to be right up there with Goethe and Dante.

My mother died when I was 20. She was an English teacher all her life, longed to be a writer, and would have been proud to think her daughter was one. She did write part of a novel, back in the days when the Southern historical novel was a big thing—everybody wanted to do a *Gone with the Wind*—and sent it to a publisher. He wrote back and said he liked it. Then she wrapped it up carefully in brown paper and string and never touched it again—I think maybe because she was writing about her own very unhappy childhood as an alcoholic's daughter in Mobile, Alabama.

When she died, my father gave me the manuscript. I couldn't read it right then. The pain was too new and too great. I decided I would read it later, after I wasn't hurting so much. In the meantime, I set out to write my own novel and hoped she would be proud of me. I threw out everything I'd ever written before—poems, short stories. I didn't want to lean on past accomplishments. I wanted to put it all into this new manuscript. I worked a lot and for a long time, until it seemed right to let it rest a while, come back and look at it later, and then figure out what to do with it next.

About then, I got an opportunity to go overseas to Taiwan (I was a college student then, studying Chinese). I jumped at the chance to go and learn from people who were born speaking the language. I left all my books, most of them with my name written in them by my mother (she always gave me books for Christmas and birthdays), and my manuscript and hers in a house in Casper, Wyoming (why I left them there would be a whole other story). I was overseas for a year and a half.

When I came back I felt ready to read Mother's novel and go back to work on mine. I learned my stuff had been moved from that house into a man's garage. But when I got there, the man who owned the garage told me that just a week before he had cleaned the garage, and the stuff he couldn't give away he had sent to the Casper city landfill. At the landfill they kept a constant fire going with the flammable trash. I went there and looked—in vain. I cried and walked around the edge of the dump, seeing the smoke curl up everywhere. I was too late. Mother's manuscript and mine had been burned. I really thought I'd never write again.

I did, though. But I never wrote the same as before. I didn't ever again hide away my stuff to meditate on it, perfect it, wait on it, and dream of publishing a perfect masterpiece some far-off day, as I'd done before. Instead, I wrote small pieces and tried to share them any way I could before something happened to them—before they got burned or some such. I took poems to a street corner in Greenwich Village. There I wore a sandwich board that announced "Poems for Sale." When it came time to first share this recipe book, I mimeographed copies and peddled them.

Sounds nuts, doesn't it? But it worked. Every reader on that street corner taught me something by the expression on their face, by where they lingered and where they flipped pages. Every interaction with a reader defined me to myself more earnestly as a writer and fired me up to go home and try again, harder. And every reader fulfilled a rite of passage from my heart and mind to theirs that somehow was the intended destiny of those words I wrote—and without which passage I was wretched.

So that's how I learned way back then that it's better to put an unfinished, imperfect book into a reader's hands than to risk having a someday-to-be-absolutely-perfect manuscript burning in a dump. I learned that if I get material published somehow, it's safely "out there." That way, if I lose my copy, I can always borrow one from a reader and carry on the task of trying to get it right—or righter—in the next edition!

CHAPTER THREE

Grasses, Grains & Canes

OLD-TIME HARVESTING TECHNOLOGY

SHOCKING, THRESHING, AND WINNOWING

EATING FRESH, RAW SUGAR CANE

SOURDOUGH BREADS AND STARTERS

HARVESTING SWEET CORN

UNLEAVENED, EGG, AND ACID-BASE LEAVENED BREADS

RAISING BREAD IN A CHILLY KITCHEN

MILLET, OATS, RYE, AND SORGHUMS

WHEATY READING

COOKING PERFECT RICE

STORAGE TECHNOLOGY

Grasses, Grains & Canes Contents

INTRODUCTION

Of Book Writing, My Childhood, and Grain Growing

For you, this is near the beginning of my book. For me, as I write, it is near the end. [Written in first edition, 1974.] I started with the back of the book. I didn't know how to write when I started and wanted to do my learning in some dark corner where it would be as unnoticeable as possible, so I wrote "Definitions and Measures" first. Then "Home Industries" and "Herbs." Then I wrote "Sours" and the first part of "Meats" except the introduction. Then I wrote the first and last sections of "Dairy" and all the "Oddments." [In later editions of the book, some of these chapters were eliminated and some of the material moved into other chapters.] Then I did the rest. It's been a long journey, 4 years in time. Three babies have been born since I started, making a total of 5 children, 4 of them preschoolers. I've been through some hard and deep periods of adjustment with my children, my husband, my friends and neighbors, and God. And all along I struggled to bring this book to life as if it were a kind of baby, too—a child part brain, part spirit, part paper and ink.

I wrote it always under pressure. Not just the pressure of other responsibilities and the never-completely-resolved question of whether I even had the right to take so much of myself from my housework and my husband and the children to do something like this. Not just money pressure as I took every spare cent of ours over all those years for my electric typewriter, mimeograph machine, advertising, paper, and so on. Not just pressure of knowing I was a little fish in a big ocean where big fish eat little fish—big companies with research staffs that discover what books the public wants, then order them written, printed, advertised, and sold, and then go on to the next book—and thus knowing that the idea that was such a good idea 4 years ago has already been done and redone in the 4 years since, while I mopped floors and comforted children and listened to my husband's troubles and wondered if I was ever going to finish it at all.

The real pressure was simply that I couldn't stop. Maybe it's like having a compulsion. I swore off time and time again. Promised my husband, myself, God, that I was through. And kept going back. In the end I felt that God wanted me to finish and helped me find a way to write that didn't really harm my family. But it made me slow, and I'm finishing this book now in the knowledge that when I advertise "Candles, Sausage Making, Cheese," I'm not offering something completely new any more. But I have faith that this book is a better one, maybe because it did all come about so slowly and because I was living it even when I couldn't be writing it. And because it isn't just a textbook written by a staff in a library. There's a lot of my soul in this book. When I sit down at the typewriter now, I feel as if I'm starting to write another letter to an old friend who will really understand—kind of like the way I feel when I pray.

I also kept going back because a certain group of people wouldn't hear of me stopping. They were the people who answered my first little ad when I figured I could get my book written in a couple of months. That was in 1971. I sent them those first 3 chapters I wrote, and (bad as they now seem to me) those people, who paid $3.50 each for the book I proposed to write, from then till now just wouldn't let me quit. They besieged me with the most loving and beautiful letters insisting that my book was needed and that I could write and declaring that they were willing

to wait, however long it took, but I must not give up. So when I write, I'm writing to them: people whose letters I often had no time to answer or took 2 years to answer. But I figured if I put the time instead into writing the book, they would prefer that anyway. In this book, when I say, "A friend gave the recipe to me," sometimes I mean a neighbor down the road, but sometimes I mean a correspondent across the nation or even in Turkey, France, or Haiti. Those first chapters traveled so far.

Here I am at the typewriter with a little girl in a red polka-dot maxidress sitting in my lap. She's 3 and her name is Rebecca. We all call her Becca. She's been fighting with Luke, who, though just 2, has the approach of a professional football player, and she needs comfort. Danny, 5, is sitting in the big overstuffed chair pretending something. Sara, 7 months, is crawling around on the floor looking for something she hasn't tasted or touched before. Dolly is at school, Mike is at work, and I'm going to tell you all I knew, know, and could find out about grains.

In a way, it's an easy subject for me. Before my father went into the sheep and cattle business, he was a wheat rancher in the hard wheat area around Clyde Park, Montana. That's the same wheat that is now sold as "organic" because the farmers raise it without fertilizer or pesticides (or irrigation). We would get 15 bushels to the acre on a terrible stand and 80 to 100 on a fabulously good one. Usually it was around 40. We suffered losses from grasshoppers, hail, and drought, and from cloudbursts that beat down the stalks so flat to the ground that the combine couldn't pick up the heads to cut and thresh them. But in good years, like right after World War II, when the price was up and yields were good, my father made as much as $10,000 a year.

It was all done on a big-scale commercial basis. During the busy seasons of tilling and planting, the tractors went night and day, with big headlights on them at night. We had our own underground gas tanks and gas pumps above ground to keep the equipment running. In combining season, the big combines went round and round the fields catching up the golden waves of grain in their great revolving paddles. I sat high up in the combine's hopper and played with the wheat flowing into it in a steady orange stream. The wheat came out of a spout from the complex threshing machinery below. The driver drove the combine, and I sat up there in that hopper watching myself get covered with wheat: first my feet, then my knees, and finally my arms.

Or I would crawl up on top of the grain and amuse myself with all the fascinating bugs that came along with the grain: grasshoppers in all sizes and colors—yellow legs, orange legs, blue legs, green legs, and all sorts of combinations; dear little ladybugs, red with black spots; and ugly old green bugs that we called stinkbugs because they had such an awful odor. When the hopper was heaping full of grain, it would be unloaded into the back of a waiting truck. About 3 hopperfuls would fill our truck. Then it would be off, driving to unload at the granary in Clyde Park. Another truck would wait in its place at the field to get filled with the hopperfuls of grain from the combine.

Daddy Harshbarger wasn't always so highly organized and mechanically oriented. When he met my mother, he was farming near Ellensburg, Washington, with a team of horses, very much the way his father, a Quaker dairy farmer, had lived outside Xenia, Ohio. Daddy's mother was a Dunkard. When she had crossed the denominational line to marry that Quaker, a lot of tongues clucked and said it would never work, but they stayed married 'til death did them part, 5 children and some 50 years later. Daddy's people on both sides were honest, hardworking, conservative Pennsylvania Dutch and Germans. Change wasn't necessarily welcome to them.

But the first year Daddy was married to Mama (who had been working as a schoolteacher when he met her), change came regardless of whether he was willing. Potato bugs got his potato crop. A drought got his alfalfa. Something else took his third crop. Daddy had figured no way could he lose all 3 crops, being as they were different, in the same year—but he did. By summer's end the young man, married only a few months and his wife now pregnant, had gone broke and been forced off his rented land.

They auctioned off both teams of horses and everything else they owned and bought a little Model-something-or-other car, and went to California *Grapes of Wrath*-style, having heard there was lots of work down there. But there wasn't. They ended up broke in Los Angeles. I was born January 19, 1939, while my father spent day after day going from door to door in search of a job—any job. He and my mother finally took a training course to be domestic servants, and then the school got them a job. My father was butler and chauffeur to the movie star Dorothy Lamour. Really! My mother became her cook and housekeeper. I was boarded out with an aunt so they could get the job.

When I think about it now, I bet Dorothy was proud of her butler. He wasn't awfully tall, but he stood up so straight, he seemed taller than he was. He had coal black hair, very white skin where he wasn't exposed to the sun a lot, a big nose like butlers are supposed to have, and stern blue eyes when he wanted to look at you like that. He also loved to speed. When Dorothy would tap him on the shoulder from her stylish seat in the rear and say, "Faster, Carl, faster!" those eyes would twinkle and he'd happily go faster. When Daddy got older, he had 2 laugh wrinkles for every worry wrinkle. That's how he was.

Well, it took Carl 5 years of buttering in California, logging in Oregon, and doing defense work at Washington shipyards to finally work his way back to another farm. This time he mechanized all the way. Then he had 5 postwar years of big crops and good prices. The annual fall wheat check would come in, and Daddy would go to town and buy the latest model of Mercury, and my mother would mutter darkly as he drove it faster and faster. He always passed everything on the road. Although he was a brilliant driver, Mother and I were both scared to death to drive with him. We weren't made of the same stuff as Dorothy, I guess. But speeding and all, Daddy was still a solid Quaker gentleman in his heart and in the way he treated his family.

So I understand well the commercial, mechanized kind of wheat ranching, but as for the technology of raising just enough for your own family's needs—sowing and threshing by hand—I'm a beginner, trying to learn as much as I can. Here's everything I've been able to find out . . .

ABOUT GRASSES, GRAINS, AND CANES

The grass family comes close to basically supporting all the animal life on earth. Green grass is pasture. Dried grass is hay. The edible seeds are our grain, rich food for both people and their livestock. Corn, wheat, rye, barley, rice, oats, flax, sorghums, sugar cane, bamboos, and many other species are all grasses. Many of them are also valuable as green manure crops, raised to be plowed into the soil to fertilize it. All grasses have jointed stems and narrow leaves that grow from joints in the stems. At its base each leaf is wrapped like a sheath around the stem. There are also some non-grass plants that grow seeds and are considered "grains"; millet, amaranth, quinoa, and buckwheat, for instance, are non-grass grains whose seeds make cereal and bread.

BOOKS ON GRAIN RAISING: The best books on grain raising by organic or non-petroleum methods, for basically family use, are "antiques." Don't let that stop you. They are superb sources of practical, time-tested information. *The International Library of Technology: Wheat, Oats, Barley, Rye, and Buckwheat, Corn, Hay and Pasture Crops . . .* (Scranton, PA: International Textbook Co., 1911) was originally offered as the basic text for a correspondence course on farming. An even better old book is *The Home & Farm Manual: A Pictorial Encyclopedia of Farm, Garden, Household, Architectural, Legal, Medical and Social Information, Classic 1884 Edition* by Jonathan Periam (New York: Crown Publishers, 1984), reprinted in the 1980s. And then there is

INTRODUCTORY GRAIN QUIZ

Here's a pre-test for you, just for fun. (Find the answers later in this chapter!)

1. Deer are eating your wheat. Which basic grain can you plant instead that deer won't eat, but you, your livestock, and family can?

2. If you live at a 7,000-foot elevation in the Colorado Rockies, which grain can you grow?

3. If your land is just a swamp next to a river, which grain can you grow?

4. If your land is leached-out sand, which grain can you grow?

5. If you get behind on your work and only get the field plowed and no more, which grains can you throw onto those clods, till in afterwards, and count on good results from?

6. If your ground is loaded with barnyard manure, which grain should you grow?

7. If you are in a hot, dry place—hot enough for corn, but too dry for it—which grain can you grow?

8. If you live where winters get down to –40°F, the summers are short and cloudy, and the soil is of poor quality, which grain can you grow?

9. If you needed to raise tons of quality hay within 2 months, which grain can you plant?

10. If you want to grow a heavy-producing, top bread-making grain, which one should you plant?

11. If you just plowed up a pasture and want a plant that can wipe out any grass trying to come back, which grain should you plant?

12. If you want to raise your own pancake syrup, but maple trees aren't an option, which member of the grass family should you plant?

13. If you want to be able to winter horses, sheep, pigs, and rabbits entirely on home-grown feed, from a crop that can be grown, cut, dried, and stored just like hay but that provides nutritious grain as well as grass protein, which grain should you grow?

14. If you want a grain that will produce over a pound of seed per plant, which one should you grow?

15. If you want to start your family every morning on pancakes made from the most nutritious grain of all, which one should you plant?

16. Which grain can you plant in your garden in July, on ground freed up by harvesting vegetables, that will give you a good crop before frost?

17. If you have a plowed-under alfalfa field, which grain can you plant there next year that will feed a person for a day for every kernel you plant?

18. If there's no irrigation water this year and only 90 days left in the growing season, which grain might yet produce 50 bushels per acre?

19. Which grain can be stored untreated in an airtight 5 gal. can, left in an unheated mountain cabin for 25 years, and still have 98 percent sprouting ability?

20. Which grain will grow up to 12 stalks, each with a fully developing seed head, out of every single seed you plant?

Hint: Some of these questions have the same grain for an answer.

---

the unique treasure of Gene Logsdon's 1977 book, *Small-Scale Grain Raising* (Emmaus, PA: Rodale Press).

ATTRA's "Organic Small Grain Production" is at **www.attra.org/attra-pub/smallgrain.html**. "Grain Processing: Adding Value to Farm Products" is at **www.attra.org/attra-pub/grainpro.html**. Or order free print versions of both: 800-346-9140.

OF PLANTING, GROWING, AND HARVESTING GRAIN

Planning Ahead

Which grain will you grow? Well, what do you like to eat? One family I know uses 4 bushels of wheat, 1 bushel of oats, and 2 bushels of shelled corn a year. Raising your own grain may require less space than you thought. A family rice paddy can produce copiously in a very small area. Organic, handraised wheat will produce at least 40 bushels per acre, and quite possibly more, up to 80 or so. That means a patch of wheat 20 × 55 feet or 10 × 100 feet could produce a bushel or two—probably a year's supply of wheat for a family of 4. An acre could provide you with a ton or more. You can plant any size patch of grain—30 square feet, 1,000 square feet, or acres of it—if you have the land. Plant whatever's right for you.

Grain	Square Feet to Grow 1 Bushel
Barley	10 × 90
Buckwheat	10 × 130
Corn, field	10 × 50
Oats	10 × 60
Rye	10 × 150
Sorghum, grain	10 × 60
Wheat	10 × 100

An acre of corn can produce over 150 bushels of grain, plus stalks and cobs that are good livestock feed. That corn can maintain one pig, a milk cow, a beef steer, and 30 laying hens for a year, plus cornmeal for your family. To break that down, figure 12 bushels of corn to get a weaner pig to butchering weight, a bushel of grain per year to provide a good grain supplement for one sheep plus a lamb, 6 bushels to supplement for a milk cow, 6 for a calf you're raising for beef. You might choose to grow wheat, buckwheat, and rye for baking, sweet corn for a vegetable, and oats, corn, and a hay mix for your collection of livestock. You could easily do all that on 5 acres. And you would have healthy milk, eggs, and meat because all the food that went to make them would be free of residues if you farm without using poisons.

But also choose your grains to be suitable to your soil and climate. Your county agent can tell you what common grains and varieties are being most successfully grown in your area. Find out the length of the growing season in your area and compare that with the shortest period of time required to mature a crop of the grain you're investigating. If you're trying something unusual, start with a small area and see how it grows. Next year, if results are good, you can plant more.

If you intend to raise a year's supply of some basic grain like wheat, plan your area to plant according to how much grain you need to harvest. If you have in storage 40 lb. for each child in your family and 300 lb. for each adult, that should be plenty for your year's supply until the next harvest. On the other hand, the concept of having an extra few years' supply probably goes farther back than Moses and is still sound: enough to eat and enough to plant too. The starving people are the ones whose storage ran out and who ate their seed or who have no land to plant.

Steve Solomon, a gardening expert whose books include *Growing Vegetables West of the Cascades* (Seattle: Sasquatch Books, 1989), wrote of planting hand-grown grains: "Yields may be expected to range from 20 to 60 bushels per acre (25 to 75 lb. per 1,000 square feet), so the serious grower must consider plots of several thousand square feet."

The one thing you can't plan ahead for is the specific weather of your upcoming growing season. The wrong kind of weather can transform the best-laid plans into disaster. A very dry summer can ruin some grains. An exceptionally cloudy and wet late summer can drastically reduce harvest. The Palouse area wheat farmers still talk of the fall of 1893, when there was such unending rain they couldn't harvest any of their grain. A plague of locusts or rabbits or hail can be equally destructive. A severe hailstorm with big heavy stones or a torrential downpour that beats everything into the ground can ruin your grain crop. Most full-time grass-grain farmers carry hail insurance, because they're almost certain to lose some or most of the crop during a certain percentage of the years, when hailstones happen to fall on their fields.

It helps if you have more than one kind growing, but nothing is ever for sure when you're farming. That's why it's so important to put away both cash savings and food surpluses in a good year, in case you have to go a year or more without a harvest. It happens. It's not a matter of if, but when.

"SPRING" AND "WINTER" VARIETIES: Specific grains are covered in the alphabetical guide to grains that follows this introductory material. The varieties are discussed under each grain, but there is one general pattern that occurs repeatedly: rye, wheat, barley, and oats don't have to be planted in the spring. You can plant "winter" varieties in the fall. "Spring" varieties are planted in the spring and harvested in the summer. "Winter" varieties are planted in September or later, and harvested the next summer.

Snow Insulation. Grains will start to grow and then will die back in winter, but they won't kill off completely unless you have terribly cold weather with no snow cover. It's good to have snow covering the ground during all your really cold weather because it insulates the crop underneath and prevents it from freezing. Last December there was a prolonged spell of below-freezing weather—10° or more below zero—and no snow cover. A lot of farmers around here lost their winter wheat crop, and a lot of water mains (including ours) froze up that ordinarily would have been buried deeply enough to be all right.

Stooling. The other thing that can go wrong with winter grain is "stooling," in which the grain develops a real stalk. That's trouble because grain in the stalk or "stool" stage is more easily winterkilled. That's another good reason for not planting winter grain too early. You can also hold back stooling by sending animals in to graze; that holds it off until it's too cold to grow any more.

Winter/Spring Varieties Compared. In most years the winter wheat will make it through all right and do better than the spring wheat. For example, the average yield for hard red spring wheat is 3.7 lb. per 100 square feet, compared to 4.3 lb. per 100 square feet for hard red winter wheat. The winter wheat does better because the next spring it has a head start and takes off with the first warmth, just like my February peas. More seed is usually planted for winter grain than spring in order to make sure that plenty makes it through. So a winter variety is generally a bigger producer than a spring one, but there is a slightly higher risk factor involved for a winter variety; a torrential downpour shortly after seeding could wash out your seed, or an extra-freezing-cold winter with no snow cover to keep the plants snugly warm underneath could kill your whole crop. But if you do lose the winter grain crop, you'll have time to plant another one of a spring variety.

Winter grain that is planted in September and then gets rained on comes up within a week and looks like a newly planted lawn, green and lovely. You can let the cows graze on it, but don't overdo it. The grain needs to gather some energy to winter on. When cold weather comes, the grain will turn brown and look dead. But it isn't. It's a grass, and next spring it will magically reappear and recommence growing up and up, from 2 to 4 feet high depending on how much moisture it gets, how fertile the soil is, and what kind of plant it is.

ANSWERS TO INTRODUCTORY GRAIN QUIZ

1. Bearded barley	8. Rye	15. Buckwheat
2. Quinoa	9. Oats	16. Buckwheat
3. Wild rice	10. Wheat	17. Corn
4. Rye	11. Buckwheat	18. Millet
5. Rye or oats	12. Sorghum	19. Wheat
6. Corn	13. Oats	20. Rice
7. Amaranth	14. Amaranth	

So the kind of grain, spring or winter, that you plant depends on what time of year you are planting it. It also depends on what part of the country you are planting in. Different types are better suited to special season lengths and amounts of rainfall and soil types.

It's all somewhat complicated, and you really would do best to ask your local granary (which buys grain from farmers), feed store, seed store, or any grain-growing farmer in your area to find out what types are generally raised in your area.

AMOUNT TO PLANT: Figure it in pounds, pecks, or bushels per acre. But pecks and bushels are uncertain amounts. There are 4 pecks to a bushel, and you can convert from bushels to pounds if you know the official per-bushel weight for a particular grain. But in the past, those official bushel weights have been different in different parts of the country and at different times. They are basically just an agreed-on average.

Exact amounts to plant are generally announced by companies that sell seed, so they're usually on the generous side. But if you are broadcast seeding rather than drilling, order extra seed, because you will lose a lot of your seed to birds or failure to cover all your soil with seed. (For information on these planting methods, see "Broadcasting" and "The Drill.") Also plant in proportion to the amount of moisture your crop will get: use more seed for an area with higher rainfall, because extra rain allows plants to grow more densely in an area. On the other hand, if you're short of money or seed, you probably can grow more grain with less seed than you think because of tillering (see "Tillers"). A basic rule of thumb is that 1 lb. of seed grain will increase to about 50 lb. of eating grain, and you want to plant 12 seeds per foot.

Crop	Pounds/Bushel
Alfalfa	60
Barley	48
Buckwheat	50
Clover, red	50
Clover (others)	60
Corn, field	56
Flax	56
Oats	32
Rye	56
Sorghum, cane (sweet)	50
Spelt	40
Wheat	60

Tillers. A stalk that holds a grain head is called a tiller, but usually anything more than the first stalk is referred to as a "tiller." Grass grains can have tillers. When they grow on corn, they are called "suckers" and are considered a minor matter because they don't bear serious ears but do add a little forage. But in other grasses, the more tillering, the better yield, because their tillers are identical twins to the first stalk and bear just as much grain. So your total yield from a single plant would be its number of "ears" or "heads" (usually one per tiller), multiplied by the number of kernels or grains per head, multiplied by the average weight of each grain. So you can get more than one head per grain you plant.

A further beauty of tillers is that often a lower rate of seeding will result in the grain plants growing more tillers per plant, resulting in a yield about as good as if you'd planted heavier. Even corn, though it won't produce good ears on the suckers, will produce more and larger ears if not planted thickly—for example, at the rate of 2,000 plants on a tenth of an acre (rather than 3,000). You might even get a better grain crop planting at a lower rate! On the other hand, you can't make 1 seed cover a whole field, no matter how good your soil is. Experiment to discover what works best for you.

Of Seed and Soil

WHERE TO BUY FIELD GRAIN SEED: If you're needing much seed, it's going to be expensive to ship those heavy grains from far away. The cheapest seed source would probably be your local grain elevator. They might not know exactly what variety they're selling you, but you can be sure it will grow in your area. Or, if you live in a farming area, ask around and find a "seedsman" who wholesales grain, hay, and other field crop seeds to farmers. He or she will know the varieties and will happily sell you some, even though you don't need a whole truckload. Or plant feed grain from a feed store. Seed Savers Exchange is another good source for homestead varieties. NC+ Organics is a supplier of organic row crop seeds, including grains. They offer helpful info on growing and marketing organic grains in their newsletter and online forum: 800-279-7999; 3820 N. 56th St., Lincoln, NE 68504; ncorganics.com/index. htm. Almost any mail-order seed catalog offers one or more grains. This chapter often lists seed sources in the special grain sections.

About Treated Seed. The seed that you buy from a seed company will be either "treated" or "untreated."
NOTE: If you have "treated" seed grain, don't eat it. It's lethal! Don't let little kids get into it. Don't use the sacks it came in to hold any food product!

If you live in an area where grain varmints are well established, things can go wrong if you use untreated seed. Lee Bannister, Pullman, WA, told me, "I saved my own grain for seed wheat, but I found out if you don't treat the wheat, you'll get only half the yield because the worms will eat it. The first year you'll be OK. Next year better plant extra so the worms can have some. The next year it will be worse. Finally they'll get it all. In former days it was quite common to treat your own."

HOME-GROWN SEED: After your first crop, you can hold back part of your crop from year to year for seed, unless you have a hybrid (which doesn't breed or doesn't breed true). For most seed grains, if you just keep them dry they will store very easily, just like dried peas or beans. But some seed grains have special procedures. Be sure that your seed is well matured, according to the specific directions for your type of grain, and free of broken grains (or just plant extra to compensate for the broken ones—which won't sprout). In general, your seed needs to be healthy and young enough to germinate readily and make strong sprouts.

Drying Grain for Seed. For seed, the grain should dry in the shock for a month or more before threshing. When stored in a pile, threshed grain that is not totally dry will heat up enough to destroy its capacity for germination (but not its food value). If you're in a hurry to thresh, you can accomplish drying with small quantities by spreading and frequently stirring the grain. Don't dry on a surface that could get hot enough to kill the seeds. Also see "Seeds" in Chapter 2.

MANURE: Corn and wheat need some manure, but some grass grains, such as oats, rice, and rye, are actually harmed by too-rich soil. Too much nitrogen in their soil fuels excess stalk growth, and they grow so tall they're then likely to fall over. That's called "lodging" or the grain going "down." It usually ruins the crop. Hard winds, hail, or feet can all cause it. Grass grains go down particularly easily, especially when heads are heavy with a good yield of grain. Plant geneticists have worked to develop varieties with short, stiff stalks that stay up better. Plant chemists have discovered that too much nitrogen in the soil contributes to the problem because it fosters long, moist stems. They've also learned that potassium is the element by which the plant stiffens its stalks; lack of potassium can cause lodging.

TILLING: For most of the grain crops, the ground needs to be well tilled and loose for the seeding operation. Grain generally gives a better yield if it's planted in a more finely broken-up soil. The Good Book says, "He who tills his land will have plenty of bread, but he who follows frivolity will have poverty enough" (Proverbs 28:19).

PLANTING THE SEED: Seed can be planted by drilling or broadcasting. Commercial grain farmers seed their huge fields using a "drill" pulled by a tractor. Any grain does a little better drilled than broadcasted. On the other hand, a big drill is an expensive, unwieldy machine, totally unsuitable for small grain plots—or very wet ground. On ground that is too wet for drilling, and for a small patch of grain, you broadcast. Or use a row seeder, which is a miniature, manual version of the drill.

Broadcasting. The simplest broadcast system is walking out to the field with a bag of seed in one hand, scooping up seed, and flinging it out on the ground. It helps to have the bag arranged like a sling, hanging over one shoulder, so you don't have to literally "carry" it. Then your hands are free to dip in and scatter the seed as you walk through the field, though many people have one smart hand and one dumb one and get along best letting just the smart one dip in and scatter the seed.

Your goal is to lay down about 1 seed per square inch. You could get more even coverage by walking the patch lengthwise to plant and then doing it all again walking widthwise. The old-time system for broadcasting a large field was to lay down sacks of seed grain at both ends of the field. The sower also brought along two large stakes with a handkerchief tied to the top for extra visibility. The sower set one stake on each side, planning to cast the grain out in a strip 12 feet wide on each walk-across. Each time you get to a stake, you move it the right distance to be your target the next time you're headed that way. The guide stakes help keep your lines straight and keep you where you need to be in the field.

Broadcasting Machines. Despite its simplicity, reaching into a bag and flinging the seed out around you is the most inefficient way of broadcasting. It's hard to get the seed scattered evenly, and it's hard to get all the ground covered when you have more than 10 square feet to work on. So consider buying a broadcasting machine. There are several kinds.

One is the "horn" sower, which works by swinging the horn back and forth, spraying seed out in a steady flow in front of you. Once you learn to use it, it makes possible a steadier lay-down of seed than you can manage using hand flinging alone.

A broadcast seeder scatters seed on the ground anywhere you walk. There are several types of hand seeders available. The HandiSpread is a simple machine that you wear strapped to your body. It has a bag that can hold up to 35 lb. of grain seed. You fill the holder with seed, set the machine for the speed of release you want, and go. At the bottom, there's a fan fastened to a crank. As you walk through the field, you turn the crank, which turns the fan

and blows the seed out in front of you. It has 8 settings so you can select the planting density you want. It spreads from 8 to 30 feet. With practice you'll learn how fast to walk and crank to get the approximate amount of seed scattered that you want. (Of course, you can handily sow grain by the acre with this tool.) This seeder type is found in garden centers and hardware stores as a "lawn seeder." Or get it from Lehman's (888-438-5346; **www.Lehmans.com**).

Another, older type of broadcasting machine was essentially a hopper on wheels with the fan on the bottom; you pushed it in front of you, and the seed sprayed out ahead and to the sides. Other kinds of broadcasters operate from the power take-off of a tractor. The most high-tech broadcast seeder of all, of course, is the airplane, which is routinely used to plant commercial rice crops and often also wild rice and other grains and forage grasses.

Row Planters. These planting machines are for crops that are to be planted in rows—most any regular garden crops and, among the grains, usually corn or certain of the sorghums. They are seed boxes on wheels with machinery that lets the seeds fall down through a planting tube into a pre-specified depth in the soil at your choice of regular intervals—every ½ inch or 2 inches or whatever. They can be handwheeled or horse-drawn. If you are planting more than 5 acres, you could use a horse-pulled 2-row planter; for larger acreage yet, use a 4-row planter. But the old-time horse-drawn implements are hard to find now, and the new models are very expensive. For homestead-size human-powered single-row planters, "Plant-Rite" and "Dial-A-Seed" are some welcome brand names.

The Steve Solomon Grain-in-Rows System: Steve plants grain about 1 inch deep, in rows 12 inches apart. "To facilitate weed control and harvesting, it is well worth the trouble to make the row spacing precise. To uniformly plant that much area, I use an Earthway one-row-at-a-time seeder, an inexpensive but durable plastic and aluminum machine that has served me well since 1973."

The Drill. For planting solid stands on large fields, the drill is the most sophisticated row planter. It's a horse- or tractor-drawn machine that can plant many rows at the same time, at precise depths, in straight rows, with designated distances between the rows. It also covers the seed—all in one operation. It's a set of pipes with no back at the bottom, which are dragged through the prepared soil at the same time that seeds are gradually dropping down each pipe. The metal front of the pipe opens a furrow (a little trench) in the ground. The seed falls down into the furrow and gets covered by the natural falling of the dirt back into the furrow. You set the drill to plant just the right amount in parallel rows, usually about 3 inches apart. Older drills plant a total 7-foot width on a pass, newer models a 10-foot swath.

COVERING THE SEED: In general, any seed planted on sandy or similarly loose soil can go relatively deep and be okay. Seed planted on clay or other dense soil should go in more shallowly. After broadcasting, you need to go back and try to cover the seed with an inch or so of dirt. That isn't easy, but if seed is lying on top of the ground, birds and other creatures will come and fill their tummies, so cover your seed as fast as you can. After broadcasting, go over the ground with a hand tool like a rake and cover it up. Rake it under or roll it down as you would grass seed. Or come through lightly again with your tiller. For a larger field, if you can, after broadcasting have somebody on a tractor go over the ground pulling a spiketooth harrow or a disc. Those tools won't get it all covered at the same depth. The easiest system of all for covering broadcast seed is to plant on well-tilled soil just before a long, hard rain. Then the rain beats the seed further into the ground and splashes a nice wet mud cover over it. Or if you plant in the very early spring, the combination of rains, freezing, and thawing will do the job of covering it for you.

But unless you have the luck of a wet spring, the germination rate won't be very good with uncovered seed. That's why, if you plan to broadcast, you should automatically go to the high end of the amount-to-plant poundage. That allows for the expected losses. Even so, you probably won't get as good a stand from broadcasting as you would with a drill, but it will be good enough.

Then there is nothing left to do but struggle all spring to keep people and animals from walking in your grain field. They are certain to step on the tiny young plants, an abuse that most of the plants couldn't recover from.

The Growing Grain

OF FEET AND GRAIN: Most grains require much less care than does a vegetable patch. In fact, you shouldn't walk around in your grain field to weed or do anything else: feet are deadly to the tender grass grains once they get tall, past

the "lawn" stage—unless they're planted in rows that you can walk between (and they usually aren't). Every step of man or beast in your closely planted, nearly ripe grain field wipes out part of the crop because the stalks are tall and very fragile and once bent over, they don't stand up again.

COPING WITH WEEDS: You have 4 options.

1. Plant buckwheat and amaranth. They are such fast growers that they are weedlike themselves and can race to maturity safely ahead of the competition.

2. Plant into a very thoroughly prepared field. Most grain fields are planted in a solid mass across the field, so they can't be cultivated or weeded once planted. So till as much as you can before and after your grain crop to keep weeds from getting a hold in the field. Do a good fall cultivation and another in the spring, as early as you can. Try to kill every weed seed that has germinated. Wait 2 weeks, or however long it takes, for the field to look greenish again. That color is evidence of another bunch of weed seeds that has now germinated. Cultivate again to kill all those new weed plants. If you got started early enough, you could give it yet another treatment; otherwise, go ahead and plant your grain. After that, your grain crop is on its own as far as competing with the weeds goes.

3. Pour on herbicides—chemicals that poison broadleaf plants but not grasses. Commercial grain, unless it's "organic," is raised using various chemical fertilizers, herbicides, or pesticides. Of course, that just selects for herbicide-resistant offspring of those weeds. I'd reject this option.

4. Weed grain that has been planted in rows. Corn and sometimes sorghum are usually planted in rows rather than in a mass. And you can plant any other grain that way using the Steve Solomon system. Steve advises: "Keep weeds thoroughly hoed between rows while plants are less than knee-high. Weedy fields are low-yielding and very difficult to harvest, and make it very difficult to obtain clean, pure grain. A couple of spring weedings will probably be sufficient. Twelve-inch row spacing just permits one to carefully walk in the patch. For weeding I've found possessing a diverse and well-sharpened hoe collection very helpful. Do not irrigate."

GRAZING THE YOUNG GRAIN: The grass grains can be used as pasture early in the year if you let it grow at least a month first, so that the plants have a strong root system to come back from like a lawn does after it's mowed. After that first month of growing, you could let chickens, a few sheep, or a cow in there for the next month, if the ground isn't too muddy. Use good judgment to be careful not to let it be damaged. You have to decide how desperate for pasture, or for grain, you are. After a month of grazing, I wouldn't let any livestock in there but chickens. They'll eat some grain, but they have to be fed anyway so it comes out even.

OF WATERING NON-ROW GRAIN CROPS: You won't be able to water if you have densely planted stands, unless it rains, or you have flood irrigation as with the rices, or you put a huge sprinkler in place before the grain comes up so you don't trample it moving the sprinkler in and out. Or else you plant such a small patch of grain that you can water by sprinkling from outside the patch. Most grain is grown by depending on rain and learning to do a rain dance when needed. Or praying for something to fall from the sky. But not hail!

Harvesting Grain

GRASS GRAIN MATURITY STAGES: The grass grains differ somewhat, but in general they go through a series of ripening stages, each less moist than the one before.

Heading Out. Your grass grain is said to "head out" when the seed head forms at the top. That will usually happen within two months after it starts growing in the spring. Now harvest time is coming up.

Milk Stage. If you press the grain between your thumb and finger, a milky juice can be pressed out.

Dough Stage. In the early dough stage, when you press the grain there's no milk, but the kernel is still soft enough to mash. After a little more ripening, you can shell dough-stage kernels out in your hand, but when you bite one or press your thumbnail into the center of it, you can still make a dent.

Dead Ripe. When the kernels are totally dry, they are dead ripe. How many times I went with my father to the field and watched as he snapped the head of a stalk of wheat and rubbed it apart between his fingers to get a look at the kernels and see how hard they were. He wanted grain so hard that it shattered out of the husk relatively easily and couldn't be dented at all with his fingernail. That's dead ripe.

WHEN? When a combine is used, harvesting is timed to coincide with dead-ripe grain. When grain is hand-harvested, however, there is so much more handling to do that you risk losing your grain off the heads onto the ground by shattering if you wait until it's dead ripe to harvest. Instead, reap after the grain has stopped being milky but before it shatters too easily. Hand-harvested grain is cut and then cured in the sunshine, and during that curing time its kernels finish hardening from the dough stage to dead ripe.

Grain harvest time moves from south to north. For example, winter wheat is ripening down South around June 1, but wheat harvesting in Canada doesn't begin until early August. That's why professional combiners have an annual pattern of moving from south to north following the harvest. That much is general and always true. But for you, one harvest experience may be very different from another because weather may differ so much year to year. Harvest needs to take place during a prolonged spell of hot, dry weather. Some areas, some years, provide that. Sometimes it rains all harvest season, and salvaging the crop is impossible. Combine crews wait until the grain is dead ripe, the weather is hot and dry, and morning is far enough along that all the dew has completely evaporated from the grain, leaving it dry and brittle. Then they accomplish all the operations in one swoop. Still, the grain is further dried in the granary before it can be safely stored. With quality weather prediction, harvesting is a surer thing now.

Don Winter, a Nova Scotia homesteader, wrote me, "My wheat crop grew beautifully this year due to my liming last fall and in spite of fog. However, after cutting by hand with a sickle, and bundling and stooking [English term for shocking], I let it stand about 2 weeks in the field. When I went to bring it in to the barn, it had turned black (some of it) with, I presume, fungus. This is a very damp area, near the salt water. Next year I will cut the wheat and bundle and immediately move it into the barn to dry. Will it dry properly inside?" Yes, it will—if the crop is small and "inside" is warm, dry, and large so that the drying can be accomplished fast enough.

MODERN HARVESTING: Nowadays most cutting and threshing of grain is done on big stands by a combine, a machine that combines those 2 operations. Present-day combines are huge space-age machines that cost huge sums (in 1987 the cheapest combine cost $150,000). They are quite a sight rolling down the highways around here, usually four or so in a line, with flag vehicles in front and behind as they travel from one farmer's fields to another. The combines are generally owned by a combining company that harvests a farmer's grain in return for a percentage of the crop, about one-third. Those combines are not so different from the kind I rode in as a little girl—just much, much bigger. And the cabs are very sophisticated: a little house atop all that fine machinery, complete with air conditioning.

The combines cut the stalks, thresh the grain from the stalks, and then separate the threshed grain from the stalks, now called "straw." The machine pours the threshed grain into its hopper and broadcasts the straw back onto the field to be plowed under and composted. It accomplishes all this on something like a 16- or 18-foot swath in a flash, and it moves fast too. (These machines did only an 8-foot swath when I was a little girl.)

OLD-TIME HAND (NON-PETROLEUM-USING) HARVESTING TECHNOLOGY

If you don't have a combine or a reaper, you can harvest your grass-type grain by hand.

Mowing

Start by "mowing" or cutting the stalks. You could use an old-time horse-drawn mower, or you could mow with hand tools. When you mow, avoid getting grass and other weedy growth cut and bound with the grain. That stuff causes fermentation and heat in the stack because it generally stays moist longer than the grain stems. The old-timers had lots of uses for the straw and cut the grain off close to the ground. You might want to leave a taller stubble in the field, maybe 8 inches tall. Tall stubble will return nutrients to the soil, inhibit erosion, and give cover to wildlife.

Sickle. You can cut grains and grasses with a sickle. (The sickle-bar tractor mowers used to cut hay aren't suitable for grain because they run over it, shelling out some of your grain.) Lightweight hand sickles are available at most hardware stores. The sickle is best for short, rough, or patchy growth. It has a short handle and a long blade, which may have a straight or a serrated edge; serrated is better for grain cutting. The sickle was humankind's first harvesting implement, but even a very strong and hard-working person couldn't cut more than half an acre a day with one. It a misery to the back to use it for very long because for each cut, you have to bend over in order to cut near ground level: grab a clutch of grain heads with one hand; put in the sickle blade with the other, starting on the opposite side of the grain stalks from you and pulling it toward you with a sawing motion. The goal is to cut the stalks with such a gentle motion that you minimize the loss of grain to spillage. If you can cut the heads higher up on the stalk, it's not so hard on your back, and that's the way it's done with a "harvest knife."

The Harvest Knife. An Asian version of the sickle is the harvesting knife. It's small. You hold it in your hand, bend your finger around the plant stem, and sever it. You continue holding the grain head in your knife hand and cut new ones to add to it until you get a handful, which is then transferred to the other hand until it's holding a bunch large enough to bundle or put in a container. The blessing of this method is that it works very well with grain that has fallen over or that has unevenly ripe areas in the field or on various parts of the plant itself.

Scythe. A scythe is far better than a sickle for harvesting grain. There are different styles of scythe for grain, weed, or bush mowing. A scythe has a handle about 6 feet long, called a "snath," and a long, gently curved blade, which is the "scythe" proper. The snath has a handhold on it that enables an easy, comfortable, swinging motion, each arc swinging into the grain in front of you and cutting a swath about 2 feet across. (Trying to go wider can do more harm than good to your motion.) The scythe's blade should come against the grain at about a 45° angle rather than squarely, at a 90° angle. Cut the stalks about 3–4 inches above ground. If there is no cradle, just let them fall in that long swath.

With practice you'll soon get a natural, rhythmic, unhurried but steady motion with it that you can keep up for a long time and actually enjoy. You'll discover that scything in different varieties of grain differs as stalk stiffness differs. In general, barley and rye are easier to cut than wheat. In old-time harvests, mowing (what scything is called) was done by a group of men moving through the field of golden grain side by side. Their carefully measured movements were subtly synchronized so as to cut all the grain in front of them and yet not collide with each other, like the motions of a well-trained rowing crew. An experienced scyther can cut 1 or 2 acres a day, laying the grain evenly in a swath. For a beautiful description of how to use a scythe, read "Grow Wheat in Your Garden," *Organic Gardening,* January 1972. For more on how to mow hay, chop weeds, and bring in small grains using hand tools, get *The Scythe Book* by David Tresemer (1980).

Scythe with a Cradle. This works best of all. The "cradle" is 4 fingerlike wooden rods, which look like oversized fork tines, attached above the blade of the scythe. The scyther is now called a "cradler." The cradle catches the wheat in its fall as the scythe cuts it. The motion of the scythe and

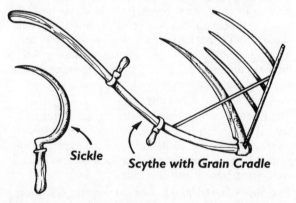

Sickle   *Scythe with Grain Cradle*

cradle's swing causes the wheat to form a pile. After several strokes of the blade, the cradle gets full of cut grain and is emptied into the bundler's arms or tossed out in one heap for you to come back later and make into a sheaf. To dump the cradle, bring it back and up in order to let the grain

slide gently into a neat pile on the ground. You can buy a scythe from Cumberland General Store or Lehman's (they also offer replacement snaths and hardware to put them on: 888-438-5346; **www.Lehmans.com**). It's important that either sickle or scythe be kept sharp. Lehman's also sells sickle grinders for this purpose. The old-timers say that for grain, you should whet the blade with a rough stone; for grass, use a very fine-grained one.

WINDROWS: The horse-drawn mower leaves the grain in "windrows." The cradler can dump the cradle into the arms of a binder or into a pile ready to be made into a sheaf by a bundler. Or the cradler can windrow it. If the grain isn't ripe when cut or isn't dry, it's definitely windrowed. The windrows look like long, narrow rows. They lie about 8 to 10 feet apart. The space allows the wind to get in there and dry out the grain. To make a windrow, the cradler dumps at the end of each cutting swing. You start the swing of the scythe on your right side, pull it through in front of you, and then empty the cradle directly to the left of your feet. All the grain heads will be at the same side of the windrow. Let the windrows lie in the sun from 2 to 6 days, depending on the weather and how wet the grain was to start with. When they're dry, you proceed. This all assumes you have sunshine during the entire time the grain is in the windrows. Extended rain while the grain is lying in the windrows will greatly lower any value of the straw as livestock feed; it can also lower the quality of the grain.

Raking the Windrows. Hand-rake into a pile for binding, enough to make a bundle that, when brought together, will be at least 6 inches in diameter. (The old-timers had a special type of rake called a "grain rake" for this purpose. It was all wood with widely spaced, smooth, round rake tines.) Then bind.

Binding

When wheat and rye are hand-reaped, they are usually directly bound by hand into sheaves, without windrowing, and then left sitting up in shocks in the field to finish ripening and to further dry before the threshing. Binding the grain is a big job that is harder and requires more skill than cutting it. The old-time binders, who walked behind the cradlers all day to bind, moved close behind the harvesters' heels. The best of them could work one per scyther, but we lesser modern folks generally must plan for 2 binders to work behind each mower. The grain end of the bundle is called "the head"; the cut ends, the "butt."

MAKING A SHEAF: A sheaf is a bundle of straw tied together, the grain heads all at the same end. Sizes vary a lot. The old-timers routinely made very large sheaves, their measure being the largest amount a person could hug in front of themselves by putting both arms around the stalks. Those big ones were made from windrowed grain. Smaller sheaves are made when following the scyther's grain cradle. The cradle is considered full enough to make a proper-sized sheaf when it is 8 to 12 inches in diameter. Then the grain is unloaded into the binder's waiting arms. That style of binder does his or her job without allowing the grain to touch the ground until it is bound. If the grain will be bound later, it is gently dumped out of the cradle into a pile to await the binder's touch.

TYING THE SHEAF: Expert binders tie by feel in front of their stomach, working at the side of the bundle farthest from them. They tie using either twine or a handful of the grain straw itself and a binder's knot.

Single-Band "Binder's Knot." Take a handful of stalks of the grain, wrap them around the outside of all the rest, twist the ends together below the grain heads, and tuck them under the band. Grain with nice long straw can be bound with a single band. To do that, grab in one hand a solid fistful of stems from the bundle right under the heads. Hold in your other hand the other end of it. Holding the

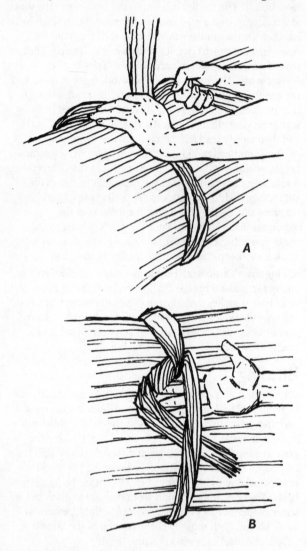

A

B

band, get the whole bundle in front of you and wrap the band around the middle of the bundle. You can do this with the bundle lying on the ground, or you can work by feel on the other side of the bundle in front of you with the two loose ends of the band you're holding. When the band is tightly drawn around the bundle, give the two separated ends a half twist to unite them, and the resulting single "rope" is tucked under the band to keep it from coming loose.

Double Band. If the grain stalks are too short to go around the bundle, make a "double band" by dividing your fistful of banding grain just below the heads into 2 halves, twisting one around the other and tucking the end back to hold it in place, and then using the 2 ends to bind the bundle as with a "single" band, ending with the twist and tuck of the

binder's knot. A double band has 2 binder's knots, one on each side: one made with 2 heads, the other with 2 butts.

If you can't master the binder's knot, no matter. In our modern times there's always baling twine and a more usual knot!

Machine Binders. The "selfbinding harvester" or "binder" was a transitional machine between the human binder and the combine (which dispensed with the binding step). It cut a swath 6 feet wide, bundled the resulting grain into sheaves, and then deposited them in piles. It took about 3 horses to pull it, and it could cut and bind about 10 acres a day. Scott Thompson, Tremont, IL, wrote me, "It's possible to cut, bind, and shock by hand, but believe me, a grain binder saves a heckuva lot of work!"

Curing the Grain

Grain that is cut by hand is generally cut before it's dead ripe so it will be less likely to shatter during handling. The "curing" is time for the ripening and drying to finish so that threshing can be done. So whether the grain is lying in a windrow or is bound into sheaves, the sheaves are not taken directly to thresh. Instead they are set up in shocks in the field for further curing there, taken under shelter to stack, or made into a rick. If you have only a little grain and a lot of threat of rain, put the heads into paper bags and leave the bags with tops wide open on a high shelf in a warm room. If you have enough roofed space to hold lots of grain, then it's best to get the sheaves in there before they get seriously rained on because, despite the most expertly constructed shocks, rain will reduce the straw's nutritional value, if not the grain's. But if you have more grain than sheltering space and need to dry outdoors, shocking is a traditional method for outdoor drying of grain and straw.

SHOCKING: The bundles of bound grain should be stood up into "shocks" as soon as possible. The principle of the shock is that with the grain heads elevated up off the ground in the air, they stay dry better. And if they do get rained on, they dry more quickly and thoroughly in a shock than on the ground. If a hard wind blows them over, put them back up again. How long you leave the grain shocked depends on the weather. It might be a few days or longer, all depending on how ready the grain is to be threshed (hard enough yet?), and how ready you are to thresh it (got friends coming to help?). In dry weather, it can stay shocked 3 weeks to a month and benefit from the curing time.

The shocks can be constructed either round or long in shape: about 6 to 8 bundles for a little shock, or 10 to 14 for a big one. Bigger ones provide more weather protection for the grain inside but don't dry out quite as fast. Round shocks also give more protection from weather. Long shocks hasten the drying process.

The Round Shock. Round shocks are roughly teepee-shaped arrangements of individual sheaves brought to-gether and leaned on each other toward the center. To make a "round" shock, you basically just stack bundles around the outside, leaning into the center.

Two-Shock Start-Up. To make the very simplest round shock, start with 2 sheaves (the bound bundles of grain). Push the cut ends of the grain firmly into the ground to po-sition the bundles, and rub their head ends together to make them stay up. Lean two more in the opposite sides of the first two, and so on until you have the number you want.

Four-Shock Start-Up. A more sophisticated shock design starts with 4 sheaves stood up all in a row on the ground, with the 2 endmost ones slanting inward at the top toward the others. As with the previous system, the butts are pressed firmly into the ground to make them stand up. Then 3 sheaves are placed on each side of those.

Long Shock. These are standing shocks in 2 parallel rows leaning on each other at the center. Long shocks are usually 5, or even 6, bundles long. They are made in a north-south direction to maximize sun exposure to both sides.

Capping the Shock. If it isn't going to rain on the shocks, you don't need to cap them. If it is, capping needs to be done, and carefully. Then the central grain heads will be protected by a rain cap created by a sheaf or two laid over the top of the heads. The capping sheaf or sheaves are bent in half before being spread over the shock's top. You can cap with either 1 or 2 sheaves. To cap with 1 sheaf, pick it up, hold the butt end against your stomach with one arm, and fold the stems over that arm using your other hand to make a "V" shape. That bending of the straw is called "breaking" the bundle. Now set the bent cap over the shock like an upside-down V. It's capped.

But to cap with 2 sheaves provides extra protection. To accomplish that, take up the first capping sheaf and divide its head end into 2 separate bundles. Now break them away from each other, each toward the center tying band on its side. Lay that on top of the shock, butt to the east. Now take up the second capping sheaf and break it right at the

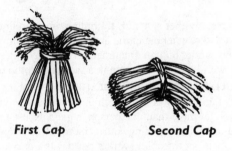

First Cap   **Second Cap**

Finished Shock

center, where it is bound, to make an upside-down "V" shape. Lay that one on top of the shock with its butt to the west and slightly spread out to protect the heads beneath. If the shocks end up getting rained on, you may want to keep the cap sheaves separated after you remove them, thresh them separately, and feed that grain to livestock. You could "cap" instead by throwing a plastic over when the weatherman predicts rain and pulling it off after the sun comes back.

Keep and treasure this knowledge of how to harvest grain every step of the way without use of petroleum products. It's a valuable alternative technology—the original one—now on the brink of extinction.

Building an Old-Time Rick to Store Unthreshed Grain

If the weather is dry while your grain is in the shocks, it will dry out well enough to go directly to threshing, and well enough that it will keep in the bin without excessive heating. But wet weather while the grain is shocked may cause sprouting or molding. So in a wetter climate, sheaves of grain may be better off stored in a stack or in a barn mow —or, nowadays, baled. It can be stored like that to use for livestock feed or to await threshing. In the old days it was also sometimes stored unthreshed until the previous year's grain supply for family and livestock ran out, and threshed only then. If you want to leave your grain unthreshed and make it into a haystack—"a rick"—to withstand the rain and stay safely stored a while, here's how.

NOTE: Don't stack the sheaves until the grain is entirely hard and the stalks completely dried. Wetness in the rick generates heat, which causes spoilage.

BUILDING THE RICK BASE: Decide where you'll put the rick. If you have a raised, hard floor with open sides and a roof on top, that's ideal. If you need to build the rick completely outside, choose a well-drained place. There build a foundation of brush or boards in a circular shape on the ground to keep the grain sheaves at least 7 to 12 inches above the damp ground. Lay the base in such a way that air is able to circulate under there. (Or place the rick on plastic or tarp.) Plan for a base diameter of no more than 10–15 feet. It's better to have several small ricks with 10 feet or so separating them than one big one. You don't want somebody falling off and getting killed, and the topmost peak of a well-built rick will be almost exactly as high as the foundation is wide. Another reason to limit the rick's size is that curing grain creates heat. If the heat becomes too intense, the quality of your grain could be harmed—or the stack could catch on fire. Build the rick's base of sheaves on top of the foundation by following these 3 rules:

1. Cut ends (the butts) always point to the outside. You start at the center of the foundation with a few sheaves, heads toward the center. Then lay a row of bundles around the center pile, extending out from the center like rays from a sun, butts toward the outside, of course. The next row outward is laid in by placing the head ends at the band level of the previous circle and creating a new layer outward like that. You keep adding in the same fashion until you get to the edge of the foundation, each circular band being wider and farther out than the previous one.

2. The bundle always slopes downward toward the butts in order to shed any rain that the wind drives in there. So as you build, you keep the center high (by adding a few extra sheaves there) and the outside of each bundle lower. After the first layer is built, you go back to the center and start a second one. Add a few extra bundles at the center in order to get your tilt right for the rest of the layer. And so on like that, layer above layer of sheaves. Build your rick layers full and solid all the way across. The sheaves should be as tightly placed against each other as possible, with no hollows. The old-timers used to say they were making it so tight that a rat couldn't get in!

3. The rick walls are shaped like a corn crib's, sloping farther out the higher it goes. So the first few layers of

sheaves extend out to just the edge of your foundation, but the next few are just a little larger in diameter, and the next few larger yet, and so on. Thus the upper edges form a roof over over the lower ones—until you get to where the topmost "roof" of your rick starts.

THE RICK'S ROOF: You start building the roof when you're up to one-third of the expected completed height of the rick. That allows you to make a roof that's as steeply pitched as possible, so it will shed rain well. Then you start building the sheaf layers back from the edge, laying in the sheaves like shingles. Make the roof as steeply pitched as possible, which is accomplished by making the layers smaller very, very gradually. If you make them smaller too fast, your roof will be too flat. Continue to keep the middle part of each layer higher to shed water.

To finish the center point, shove a pole into the absolute center of your stack. About 4–6 feet long will work as long as there's plenty sticking out at the top. When you arrive at the center point—the end, the peak—tie straw tightly to the pole to keep rain from getting in at the middle of the rick. The old-timers skillfully thatched the rick roof with more threshed straw. But nowadays the making of a rick roof isn't necessary. You can just throw a tarp or plastic over the whole thing and anchor that with tires tied to the sides. Or make it under a shed.

STORING SHEAVES IN THE MOW OF A BARN: The "mow" is the upstairs of a traditional barn, which had places for the livestock to live downstairs and a big open place to store winter feed for them upstairs. You could store sheaves in the mow instead of in a rick—or do both. Before storing in a mow, clean and sweep it. Place the sheaves starting against the wall and working toward the center, with the butts toward the walls. Build the center of the stack higher, with the sheaves tilted down toward the butt end as in a rick. Cover the pile with loose straw or with sheaves turned butt up to discourage thieving birds.

Rodent control is important. Get several cats, and keep them a little hungry!

Threshing

Threshing is the process of separating the grain from the straw, which is the dry stalk of the tall grass, and the chaff, which is the outer seed hulls. A combine both cuts and threshes. If you have money to spend and more than a few acres, renting a custom combiner to do your threshing is the quickest, easiest way. But they are likely to refuse to come for less than 10 acres. Lacking the use of a combine, carry your cut and cured sheaves of grain to the threshing floor. This can be a wood, hard dirt, or even cement floor, but choose one that won't be harmed by the pounding and that won't lose grain into cracks.

FLAIL: A flail is used to beat the grain off the "ear." The basic structure of a flail is a stick connected by a thong to another stick—the first stick for holding and swinging, the other for thumping the grain pile. So it's a wooden handle at the end of which a stouter and shorter stick is hung (usually with a leather thong) so as to swing freely. You can make a flail out of a broom handle or similar-length stick. (A wide, flat flail works better than one made from a round broomstick end though.) Cut off a section about a foot long from one end of the broom handle or stick. Drill a hole through each end where you cut them apart. Attach the cut

piece back to the broom handle with a thong or wire. Now you have a homemade flail. To use it, hold the long end and beat the grain with the loose end.

You can use other items as flails. Here in modern times, a plastic baseball bat does a good job. A rubber hose section can work even better. Other threshers favor the system of banging sheaves over the back of a chair, barrel, or

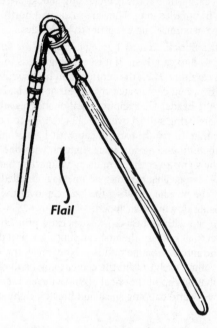

Flail

sawhorse. Another system is trampling the grain underfoot —in a basket in a hole in the ground in Native American cultures, under human or animal feet in many other parts of the world. Or put the grain in a sack and stomp on that.

A FULL-SCALE HAND THRESHING: Threshing is hard work, traditionally done on a chilly fall or early winter day. It's a job for more than one person, a good excuse to invite friends over. For planning your person-power, figure that 10 bushels per threshing worker per day is a busy day's work. So the more bushels you have to thresh out, the more help you can use. Here's the old-time American procedure:

1. Bring and unbind the sheaves. Lay the grain on the floor in two long rows, each with heads to the center, or arranged in a circle with heads to the center.
2. The flailers beat a steady tattoo with the flail on the grain heads. As often as necessary, another person shifts the straw with a pitchfork to keep the heads concentrated where the flailers' blows are striking. Then turn the sheaves over and beat again. Do this until all the grain is beaten out of the heads.
3. When the flailing is done, lift the straw up off the grain with a pitchfork, shaking it just enough to make the grain and chaff fall out. Remove the straw to where you're going to store it for livestock bedding, feed, or mulch.
4. The heavier grain and chaff will be lying on the floor. Shovel it up for the winnowing. Sweep up what remains after the shoveling.

If you have a large enough threshing floor and enough helpers . . . Divide the floor and the helpers into thirds (plus extras for the flailing section) and keep rotating, with one team laying out sheaves on a third of the floor. Flailers and their straw-shifting assistants work on the second third.

The third group gathers up grain that has already been flailed out on the last third of the floor. After all the grain is gathered up, a new batch of sheaves is laid out, and so on, keeping the production line moving.

THRESHING USING ANIMALS: Unbind the sheaves and spread them all over the threshing floor. Unshod draft animals are best. (Old-timers might have chosen a smooth, hard clay surface on a hilltop where a good winnowing breeze would come through for the threshing place. Or they'd drive the animals over a wooden floor that had special cracks built into it to let the grain fall through.) Drive the animals over the grain in a circle. Unless your animals are accustomed to that heavy a diet of grain, muzzle them so your beloved beasts won't founder themselves on the unaccustomedly rich diet. Keep turning over the straw, shaking out the grain and chaff.

This method is slow, so somebody invented a hand-cranked thresher machine called the "groundhog." Then came a horse-powered thresher, and then steam and gas ones.

MACHINE THRESHING: Allen Dong and Roger J. Edberg invent low-tech food processing machines and give the technology away. I kid you not. They have a set of instructions to convert a leaf shredder/wood chipper into a grain thresher. They have declared all their inventions mentioned in this book public domain. They have thresher designs for seeds or grains, and also designs for a rice huller, seed storage, and flame weeder. To get free info, write I-Tech: PO Box 413, Veneta, OR 97487; or visit **agronomy.ucdavis. edu/LTRAS/itech/**. You can use a "seed cleaner" or a "fanning mill" as a final stage to thresh grain. You pour a mixture of grain and debris into a hopper at the top of the machine. It passes over a series of shaking screens. These get rid of anything either larger or smaller than the grain kernels. NASCO sells the Vac-A-Way Seed Cleaner and Grader, both hand-driven and motor-driven units (and also moisture testers!): 800-558-9595; 901 Janesville Ave., PO Box 901, Fort Atkinson, WI 53538-0901; **info@ncacofa. com; www.nascofa.com.**

Scott Thompson wrote me, "Hi Carla! Threshing ended in the 1940s as a general farm practice, but a few thresher-men decided a few years later to get some of the old engines out and thresh again just for old times' sake. I attended my first threshing show in 1978 at Pontiac, IL, and have been involved with a threshing club and shows ever since. These shows highlight many aspects of farm life and Americana besides old-time threshing. They offer antique tractors and engine displays and old-time crafts and professions. But the heart of any good show is always the threshing! They range in size from small shows like ours that go for one day and host a few hundred people to mammoth events that last a week and draw a quarter of a million folks. Shows can be excellent sources for machine parts, as well as new friends and fun!

"The scythe and the flail are tools Christ knew, but threshing the grain out by hand with a flail . . . Well, a more labor-intensive chore you have never known! If you don't knock your block off learning the rhythmic swing of the flail, you'll be panting like a steam engine before you knock the grain out of 2 bundles! The threshing machine is, in my opinion, man's greatest accomplishment. Before this machine, farmers could produce only enough grain to feed their own family and livestock, with darn little left to sell. And the best part is, unlike old tractors, which have gone

through the roof in price (collectors, you know!), an old binder or thresher can still be found resting in a barn or shed exactly where it was parked the last day of threshing, and be had for a reasonable price. A working binder should bring around $100 [1992] or so, a thresher, oh . . . $200 to $300. It really depends. The fellow might just be happy to see them used again! The cheap ones are the gas threshers. Old steam-powered threshers will bring many, many thousands of dollars.

"Steam engines burned renewable resources: wood, straw, and coal. While it involved more labor to feed the fire, many steam threshers were equipped to be straw burners and burned what was often the waste product of the day! What the farmer didn't save as bedding (and off a 40-acre field, that's a whale of a lot of bedding!) ran the machine. A true tragedy of our modern times is that some entrepreneur doesn't produce a simple, inexpensive steam engine for export into Third World countries. Outside of oil and general repairs, this power source would be virtually free. And with applications of modern technology, I'd bet my boots there'd be a domestic market too! How about it, inventors!

"These were relatively very simple machines, and many parts can be fabricated, or, as the old-timers did, trussed up with baling wire! Every thresher ran on about the same principle, though they had running speeds and settings all their own. Your best bet is to find some old-timer who actually ran a machine to help get you started. The network of hobbyists includes many people who would gladly help a new thresherman and woman get off on the right foot. Or if you don't have anybody close to help, a letter requesting a copy of a field manual will often get results.

"To that end, there are 2 publications that are very helpful to anyone wishing to get into threshing." One is *The Iron Men Album Magazine;* 785-274-4377; 1503 SW 42nd St., Topeka, KS 66609-1265; **lmcdaniel@ogdenpubs.com**. "While readers are mostly hobbyists and collectors, there are also many fellows who actually lived this life, and a letter to the editor can elicit tons of responses!"

Gas Engine Magazine is a monthly publication for collectors of antique gas engines: 800-678-4883; 1503 SW 42nd St., Topeka, KS 66609-9925; **www.gasengine magazine.com.** And they provide a great service to all who love to attend these old-time threshing celebrations by putting out an annual *Steam and Gas Engine Show Directory,* available for $5 in March of every year.

Now back to Scott: "Old-time threshing takes man-power. Even later threshers designed for small farms, which could be operated by only two men (or even one!), required another two people to load wagons with bundles to bring to the machine and pitch them into the feeder. These days, when horses are scarce, another small farm tractor or even a pickup truck can be used to pull the hayracks of bundles from the field to the thresher. Straw, blown through the windstacker at the rear of the machine, can be baled right at the spot, and the stack grows. You'll also need a wagon or truck bed to catch the grain as it comes out the grain auger of the machine, and someone to haul it away and replace it with another wagon.

"The threshing crew could, at a minimum, still require 5 or 6 men. Big threshing rigs needed 15 to 20. You can see why combines were so quickly accepted. But for sheer old-time fellowship and camaraderie, threshing was hard to beat. The neighbor-needing-neighbor element is sadly lacking in today's farm life. Sure, it's more work, and not too cost-effective. But if you have a couple neighbors with some big kids just crazy enough to try it, it can be a lot of fun!

"Well, Carla, that's about it. Please feel free to use my name, address, and phone as a contact on any of these things. I may not know near all the answers, but I can sure recommend where they may go for help!" Contact Scott Lee Thompson, 12109 Mennonite Church Rd., Tremont, IL 61568, (309) 925-3932.

Of Dehusking and Winnowing

DEHUSKING: The husks of some grains like wheat or rye are loosely attached and pop off in the threshing process. For grains like them, you thresh, winnow, and use. Oats, barley, wild rice, and other grains with adhering husks that won't snap off easily require an additional step to get those husks off the grain after the threshing and before the milling (grinding). In general, you first heat the grain to loosen the husk; then grind it in a burr mill set about a $\frac{1}{16}$-inch width, in a roller mill, or in a blender; and then sift out as much of the husks from the flour as you can. For dehusking details, see this chapter's entries on specific grains.

WINNOWING: You're "winnowing" when you separate the grain from the remnants of straw and the chaff of husks. The easiest way to winnow is to pour the grain from a high place in a light breeze to a container below—as much as 20 feet high. The breeze will carry the lighter straw and chaff away. For example, while standing on a stepladder on a windy day, you can shake the grain from a bucket down onto a tarp below. Or stand on a good floor with doors open at either end of the room to cause a draft to blow through. Or use a fan, which will provide any desired speed of wind at your convenience.

Winnowing Basket. This is a large, flat, shallow platterlike light basket. Fill the winnowing basket with the grain mixed with chaff, lift it up, and pour the mixture over the basket's side in a thin stream. With a good wind, winnowing is quickly finished!

CHAFF: Save that chaff! It's wonderful organic material that can be used for livestock bedding or for mulch in your garden. Before storing, be sure your wheat is free of weed seeds as well as chaff.

STRAW: Those long, lovely yellow stalks left after the grain is threshed out are called straw. The straw can be left in the field to decay and nourish the soil (it's called "stubble" there), or gathered up from the field after combining and taken to shelter in your barn, or built into an outside strawstack.

The Strawstack. The traditional barnyard strawstack was a big heap of straw, easily built. Make your stack several times the height of a cow. Then turn the cows in. They'll eat and rub the lower part of the stack away so that it ends up looking like a big mushroom, and that's its rain-shedding roof! In cold weather the stack provides shelter for animals. They'll eat and burrow their way in. Your horses, cows, pigs, and poultry will all enjoy hanging around a strawstack, and after it's gone you'll have terrifically rich ground there for a garden patch!

Building a Strawstack Pig Shelter. Because of their worm problems, pigs can be best off if they are regularly moved. You can build an excellent temporary shelter for a sow and her family by making a simple wooden outer frame for their shelter and piling up straw over that. Inside it will be warm enough even for baby pigs.

Other Uses of Straw. Straw makes wonderful bedding for livestock (your goats or rabbits, for instance), nesting-box material, and poultry-house floor covering. Straw keeps tender plants warmer in cold weather and is useful in the garden in general as mulch. The chickens will pick out any grain you missed. Straw can also be baled and sold or can be woven into things.

OF DRYING, STORING, GRINDING, AND CEREAL

Civilization began in large part because of grain and grain storage. A storehouse of grain is true insurance against the lean years and enables some of us to study, write, and teach while others grow the food. To store best, grain needs to be very dry. Even if your grain was harvested by a combine or by hand in very dry weather, you should dry it further before storing.

Storage Technology

NOTE: The dryer, the better! And don't wash your grain before storage!

MOISTURE METER: At every stage of the way, from deciding when to harvest to planning your storage, it is useful to know the exact water content of your grain. For example, insects can't reproduce in grain when its moisture content is below 10 percent. Any grain elevator can do moisture testing for you. Just hand-thresh about a gallon sample and take it in for testing. You can buy and use a moisture meter yourself, but they might be pricey. For sources, inquire from your seedsman.

SUN DRYING: First, you need a day of full sun. Then spread your grain out thinly on some clean surface. A little grain can be dried on a tray, a lot on sheets of plastic or cloth. Stir it occasionally. Take the grain inside at night so it doesn't pick up moisture again from the dew. It will take at least 1 or 2 days to get it fully dried. Grain that is already contained in sacks can be further dried by leaving them outside in the sun and breeze even as long as a few weeks. Just leave the whole sacks in the sun, but not sitting right on the ground, and be sure to turn them once a day! Or dry in a dehydrator, oven, or homemade dryer. *Damp grain tends to mold if sealed!*

DEHYDRATOR: For small amounts of grain, spread your grain (already partially dried in the field) up to a half-inch deep on the dehydrator trays. Dry at 115°F 12–18 hours (longer if needed), stirring occasionally.

GRAIN DRYER: For large amounts you can buy a mechanical grain dryer or purchase the help of somebody who has one. The dryer is used after combining by forcing warm air through the pile of stored grain. It dries first where the air enters the pile and last where it leaves it. If you have grain in a big pile in a bin, check on it once in a while. If it's getting too hot in the middle, spread it out for more equal drying and cooling.

STORAGE CONTAINERS

Sacks. You can buy new gunnysacks at a feed-and-seed store or make your own. Don't use any sack that has held commercial seed grain; *the grain may have been treated with mercury.* Store sacks on end on a slatted floor in a dry room with plenty of air circulation. If dampness in the grain is any concern, turn the bags upside down after 2 days of storage, and again each week for the first month. Grain in cloth mesh bags will store more safely if the moisture content is a little higher than it should be for storage in a big bin. But it will naturally be like that from absorbing humidity from the air.

Cans. The most pest-proof way to store grain is to shift it out of any paper or cloth containers into plastic or metal cans with tightfitting lids. For small quantities you can both move and store in 5-gal. cans with airtight lids. They are available in both metal and plastic. For large amounts you can use big garbage cans. Metal cans, over the years, will eventually get rust holes through which insects and moisture can enter. They will last longer if you avoid setting them directly on cement or dirt floors. So lay down wooden planks to put them on, or set them on wooden shelves.

"Bin." For larger amounts yet, metal granaries are available. A "bin" means any storage room for grains, shelled corn, or dried beans or peas. A bin is tightly built of wood, concrete, or steel so the tiny kernels don't leak out and no moisture or rodents can get in. You can buy them in various sizes and styles, or make your own. But don't store grain in a bin until the moisture is 14 percent or less—down to 10 percent if possible. A "postripening process" occurs in freshly harvested, stored grain, during which both its moisture and temperature increase. With too much moisture and heat, mold starts to grow. At higher temperatures yet, the grain may be damaged and blackened from heat. The ultimate storage bin of modern times is the "grain elevator." These high towers have high-tech ventilating systems so they can hold a lot of grain, dry it as needed, and disperse surplus heat generated by the grain so there's no fire. (Once in a while, one burns anyway!)

NOTE: Don't store grains in a damp root cellar. Freezing doesn't hurt grains, so you can store in an unheated room or outbuilding, or on a porch (not in a garage).

Fighting Pests in Grain

Trouble with bugs in stored grain can be really bad. It's hard to store a sizable quantity of grain for very long without bugs and mice getting into it. It's best not to let bugs get into stored grain, because once you have them, it can be a terrible struggle. The insect eggs can be invisible to the naked eye, carried right into your storage from the field. If you have an insect problem in storage, there will be kernels with insect holes and insect chew marks—along with the adult insects, alive or dead. If the bugs are coming in from the field, the only totally effective treatments are freezing, heating, or carbon dioxide. After you freeze or heat grain, sift to get rid of bug bodies and debris, repackage, and seal.

SECRETS OF MINIMIZING INSECT DAMAGE TO STORED GRAIN

1. Don't store near an "old shed." It's liable to be full of critters looking for food.
2. The grain should be very dry—down to 10 percent if possible.
3. Clean your grain to make sure there are no green leaves or twigs in it. They drastically raise the moisture count.
4. Store the varieties of grains that don't have bug problems in your area. Barley, buckwheat, corn, oats,

sorghum, and soybeans are less likely to have insect problems than wheat and dried beans. Use up first the ones that do have insect problems.
5. Don't keep any grain with which you have insect problems stored over a year. Use it up by the winter's end, feed it to the livestock, or plant it. That way bugs can't get a full annual life cycle going.
6. Store in insect-proof, rodent-proof containers in a cool, dry place.
7. Inspect stored food of any sort, including grain, regularly to check for insect or rodent problems or too much heating going on.

TREATMENTS FOR INSECT INFESTATIONS IN PACKAGED GRAINS: If you are storing dried grain or legumes in cans and believe you have insects or insect eggs in your grain, you can defend your harvest in any of the following ways:

Carbon Dioxide. Dry ice changes into carbon dioxide, which displaces oxygen out of your storage container. Carbon dioxide doesn't harm your grain in the least, but it does discourage insect and mold growth, which require oxygen. In general, use ½ lb. dry ice per 100 lb. grain. For containers that are made to seal airtight (usually these are 5-gal. cans), put 1 T. crushed dry ice on the bottom of the can, pour in the grain, wait 1 hour, put on the lid, and seal airtight. For food stored in a metal ("garbage") can, line it with 2 tough-grade plastic sacks, the second right inside the first. Pour in a 1-inch layer of grain, add a chunk of dry ice, and finish filling the can with grain (not so full that you can't tie the bags shut). Tie the bags, leaving enough space for the oxygen to get out as the dry ice melts into carbon dioxide. Let alone for 12 hours; then tie the bags as tightly shut as you can and put a lid on the can. Tape the lid to the can to make an airtight seal if you can.

Pit Preservation. A very primitive version of carbon dioxide preservation was used by Stone Age farmers. They first dug a pit in soil that would be staying dry, then lined the pit with woven straw, then put in the grain, and finally sealed the pit totally airtight with clay. Grain sealed like that gave off enough carbon dioxide over time to preserve it.

Heat Treatment. Spread the grain ¼ inch or less deep in a tray and heat at 140°F for 30 minutes—or at 125°F for 1–2 hours. Then pour in and put on the lid. (But your germination rate will be harmed.)

"Dry Canning." Kathryn Dodds, Independence, MO, does this: "Lentils, rice, oats, beans, split peas, barley, powdered milk—any grain except oily types can be canned in this way. The storage time is from 30 years to indefinitely. I can a dry soup mixture—lentils, rice, dried onions, and salt—this way. Sterilize clean jars in a 200°F oven for 30 minutes. Then fill the sterilized jars. The filled jars—without lids—are then returned to the 200°F oven for 2 hours. Jars are removed one at a time and a bay leaf is added (to grains only). Wipe rim of jar with a damp paper towel; then place a sterilized lid on jar, followed by a screw lid. For this type of canning, you leave the screw top ring on until used. Make sure the jar is definitely sealed."

Freezer Treatment. Store (sealed to keep out moisture!) in the freezer 4 days before shifting to dry storage. That will kill most insects and their eggs.

Bay Leaves. This is the least reliable, but bay leaves scattered through your grain may deter wimpy varmints; the more bay leaves, the stronger the deterrent.

Diatomaceous Earth. Any worm that crawls across D.E. or ingests some gets sliced open and bleeds to death. Any bug that breathes it tends to die. **These microscopic bits of glass aren't good for your lungs, either, so wear a mask while working with it.**

Use "natural grade" or "food-grade" D.E. only. The quality of these deposits greatly varies. You can order food-grade D.E. from Mack Byard, Box 99, Elk Falls, KS 67345; 316-329-4327. Perma-Guard D.E. carries a food-grade designation from the FDA and can be ground directly into flour with the grain. Order from 115 Rio Bravo S.E., Albuquerque, NM 87105; 505-873-3061; **www.permaguard. com.** A 50-lb. bag costs about $25.

For each 5-gal. container of grain or beans to be stored, add 1¼ c. (about 3 oz.) diatomaceous earth. Or about 1 full cup per 40 lb. grain. Just dump the D.E. on top of the grain, or pour the food and D.E. into the container in alternate layers: a layer of food, a dusting of D.E., and so on.

MICE: If you don't keep your grain in lidded containers, the mice will find it. If you have mice, you'll know it because they invariably leave their little dark calling cards mixed in with whatever they are eating. Despite the fact that I have a large, expert mouse catcher on patrol (a gray cat named Smokey), my cellar is afflicted with mice. Those critters can climb straight up a wooden or concrete wall to get on a shelf. They'll gnaw a hole in the corner of anything gnawable—such as thin plastic—until the contents spill out. The grain stored in the barn needs to be in mouseproof containers too. We keep it in a special small room for livestock feedstuffs, which helps keep out the bigger animals too.

Once I had a cat that I refused to feed; I kept her on an exclusive diet of mouse. She did succeed in absolutely exterminating a mouse population in both house and barn and thrived on it. But after the mice were all gone, she wasn't interested in my handouts and moved on to the birds and baby chicks. She wiped out $30 worth of young chickens the following spring, so I finally took her to the pound and traded her in for Smokey. Smokey catches mice for fun rather than hunger, and she isn't nearly as efficient.

ERGOT

NOTE: Warning about ergot—read text below!

Wheat, rye, wild rice, and other cereal grains can have ergot fungus. It's rare but possible—especially when harvest has to take place in cool, damp weather, and stored grain has some dampness in it. *Don't ever eat moldy grain, or feed it to livestock.* Don't eat it even if you know for sure it is not ergot, because there are other kinds of grain molds that can make you sick, too, and some are highly carcinogenic!

Ergot is a fungus disease. It can strike both wild grasses and cereal grains, especially rye, rice, and wild rice. Its scientific name is *Claviceps purpurea*. It's spread by the wind and insects. The fungus attacks the developing grain inside its husk and produces a hard black or dark purple body that replaces the normal kernel in its position in the husk. The sclerotia (those dark ergot masses) are larger than regular kernels and have slightly curved, crescent-moon–type shapes.

Ergot grows on damp grain—in the field or in storage. If you encounter something that might be ergot in grain of any variety, don't eat it. Don't feed it to your animals either, because ergot is likely to cause miscarriage. Call your county extension agent and ask him or her where you can get your grain examined for ergot. Then you can know for

sure and either quit worrying or get rid of the fungus.

Coping with Ergot-Contaminated Seed Grain. If you do have ergot, don't plant any of that grain, because the seed will carry the fungus with it. Best to plant a non-grass grain crop on that land for at least 3 years. That will starve out the ergot, although it is said that all the fungus will die if you use seed at least 2 years old. If in desperation for seed grain, it is possible to remove ergot sclerotia from grain by soaking and stirring the seed grain in extremely salty water. The sclerotia will float up to the top and can be skimmed away. Wash off the salt.

Ergot Poisoning. In the 1300–1400s, ergot was a tremendous problem in the rye bread in Europe. Ergot is a poison; a dose of it can cause violent contractions of involuntary muscles, miscarriage, hallucinations, coma, and even death. Mild ergotism can cause extremities to tingle or have a burning sensation. That's why in the Middle Ages the disease was called "St. Anthony's fire." Ergotism can also cause disorderly speech, odd gestures, strange postures, and convulsive fits of various degrees of severity. In modern medicine an extract of ergot is used to induce labor because it causes involuntary uterine contractions. LSD can also be extracted from ergot. The root cause of the bizarre "mass hysteria" in the Middle Ages and the "bewitched" symptoms of those testifying against the Salem "witches" are now considered by some medical historians to have been unidentified ergot poisoning.

The Salem trial records describe numerous incidents when young girls were stricken with violent fits. At that time the fits, miscarriages, etc., were believed to be caused by torture from invisible, evil entities. In *Science* magazine, writer Linda R. Caporeal explained that "Accusations of choking, pinching, pricking with pins, and biting by the specter of the accused formed the standard testimony of the afflicted in almost all the examinations and trials. The choking suggests the involvement of the involuntary muscular fibers that is typical of ergot poisoning; the biting, pinching, and pricking may allude to the crawling and tingling sensations under the skin experienced by ergotism victims . . ." Luckily, after a series of deplorably damp summers, the next harvest season in Salem was finally dry. And the witch trials ended.

Other Reading. Read *Ergot and Ergotism* by George Barger (London: Gurney & Jackson, 1931). An issue of *Science* some years ago contained the great above-mentioned article speculating on ergot poisoning as a probable cause for the Salem witch trials; succeeding issues printed supporting letters from experts. More recently, *The Economist,* May 16, 1992 (vol. 323, no. 7759, p. A31) carried the article "Misogyny, Ergot, or Envy? The Salem Witch Trials." The March/April 1990 issue of *In Health* (vol. 4, no. 2, p. 11) offers the article "Let Them Eat Wheat," which speculates that ergot poisoning was a factor in the French Revolution.

Grinding Your Grain

If you've never eaten food made from freshly ground grain, you've never realized how flat and insipid the flour you're used to really tastes. You can home-grind all the grains, including rye, wheat, corn, rice, barley, and oats, as well as soybeans, chestnuts, peanuts, lentils, and dried peas to make a variety of flours. In the old days you took your grain to a mill and had the miller grind it. For payment, old-time law stipulated that the miller was entitled to one-tenth part of what he ground—except for corn, in which case the cut was one-seventh. That's because *corn is the hardest of all grains to grind.* When you're shopping, keep in mind that some mills can handle anything but corn. The basic tip is to make sure your food is dry before you put it through.

BARGAIN GRAINS FOR GRINDING: If you just want to experiment a little with grinding, popcorn is available at any grocery store. Make it into cornmeal. If you are survival-minded or if you like the taste and nutritional value of home-ground flour, but won't be growing it yourself, you can still have your own grain in storage. You can buy grain from health food stores, food co-ops, and by mail—whole as "berries," rolled as "flakes," ground coarse for cereal, or ground fine for bread flour.

The cheapest way to get whole grains for home grinding is by going to a grain elevator and buying grain there, just as the farmers do to feed their stock. It's fine for human consumption too. It will have some dust and weed seeds and a few husks in it. As you need it, winnow or wash it, pick out the remaining husks by hand, grind, cook, and eat. If there's no grain elevator around but you have a Latter-Day Saint (Mormon) friend, they can also help you buy wheat in quantity for long-term storage, because Mormons are advised to have a year's supply of food in storage. (If you don't know a Mormon, call their nearest church, listed in your phone directory.) Or see the list of mail-order sources under "Bulk Foods for Storage" in Chapter 1.

GROUND GRAIN FOR LIVESTOCK FEED: Grain can be fed whole or ground. Some grains, like corn, will go straight on through an animal if they aren't at least partly ground beforehand. It matters which grain you have, how dry/hard and large the kernel is, and what your animal is. Experiment with different grains and coarsenesses of grind. Many farms are equipped with large burr, hammer, or roller mills mainly to grind grain for chickens and livestock.

FINE AND COARSE: Almost all the grinders are adjustable for "fine" or "coarse" grinding. "Grits" are made by cracking grain on one of the coarser settings and then removing the "fines" by sifting. The coarser grits are cooked in water or milk, being then a type of hot cereal. Mills with the finest settings produce a "cake" flour. One cup of grain will usually (but not always—depends on the grain) grind into about 1½ c. flour.

STORING HOME-GROUND FLOUR: Don't make all your grain into flour at once. Whole-grain cornmeal or wheat flour or any other flour ground at home loses quality—flavor and vitamins—almost literally every hour it waits between the grinding and the baking. Home-ground flour and cornmeal has a higher lipid (oil) content and is not degerminated or bleached. It's therefore better food for you and any other form of life, so it won't keep like store-bought flour—unless you freeze it. As soon as your grain is ground, the oxidation processes begin; ultimately they will turn the fat in it rancid. Rancid fat is not deadly poisonous; it's merely slightly harmful to eat and unpleasant to taste.

Weevils and other insects are also more inclined to get into and be a noxious presence in flour than whole grain. Home-ground flour can also absorb odor and dampness, so it's best to store it in an airtight container—for a small quantity, a glass jar; for large quantities, one of the 5-gal. metal or plastic cans that you can buy with fitted lids. Best of all is to grind the flour just before using it. If you plan to keep it more than a week, freeze it!

NONELECTRIC GRINDERS: Back when I first wrote this book and the back-to-the-land movement was beginning, none of us usually came right out and said it, but we were all reacting to having grown up with the imminent horror of all-out nuclear war, and each of us was preparing to survive the nuclear destruction of the underpinnings of urban civilization. Nonelectric grinding was a requirement of that projected scenario.

Mortar and Pestle. You can use a mortar made of a hollowed block of wood, with a heavy chunk of wood for a pestle, but stone works better. Find a flat, smooth rock with a center depression large enough to grind on and a smooth rock to grind with.

Hand-Cranked Models. A typical home grain grinder sets on a tabletop. There is usually a large screw clamp to provide firm attachment to a bench or table while you are grinding. The hand models work as long as you have the strength and will to turn the crank. Hand grinders come in various sizes. The Family Grain Mill, made in Germany, provides the best-quality flour of any of the grinders—bread quality with only one grinding! It is not too hard to turn and is reasonably priced (about $130). But its plastic parts have been known to break. These mills are available from Linda Yoder, PO Box 100, Mark Center, OH 43536; 419-542-6275. When it comes to grinders, you definitely get what you pay for. A cheaper hand mill would not be able to produce consistently fine flour. Also, cheap mills are much harder to turn and cannot be motorized—which most people want to do sooner or later.

With the small, bargain hand grinders, it is hard work to get grain fine enough so as to not have chunks in it. The worst of the manual grinders produces a "fine meal" rather than a "flour" on the first grind. In order to get a flour grind, you have to crank very hard and put it through more than once. Then sift out the "grits" and put through again, and so on until you are satisfied with your flour. Feed the grits to your livestock, or cook for cereal.

POWERED GRINDING: Electric grinding is easy and quick, and blenders are easy to buy. They will work to grind a small amount of grain at any one time, such as the grain for your day's cooking needs. But grinding is hard on blender blades, and they can't handle bulk jobs. In most commercial mills today, flour is made by crushing the grain between a series of rollers, much like a wringer washing machine. The expensive electric models for home use can put out around 10 to 16 lb. of flour per hour, depending on size, and cost several hundred dollars. They are kitchen appliances. You plug one in and pour your grain in the hopper, and it grinds your baking flour. One or two quarts of grain at a time is about right for a small family.

Stone Mill. "Stone grinding" means that the grain is reduced to flour texture by rubbing against a stone surface in a manner similar to the old-style water-powered gristmills. Stone wheel mills, whether electric- or hand-powered, cannot be used for soybeans because of the oil from the beans, but they will produce a fine flour. Incidentally, the more a grinder grinds, the better job it does, because the stones grind themselves into a better and better fit.

Burr Mill. This type of mill crushes the grain between a stationary heavy wheel and a revolving one. These are good for people who want to grind feed for livestock as well as their own meal and flour. A burr mill grinds finer than a hand-cranked household mill, although you may need to run it through more than once—maybe 3 times for baking flour. A burr mill is also the answer for folks who want to grind flour in larger quantities than household mills can handle. The drawback of a burr mill is that it grinds any grain fine but will not grind unthreshed grain-straw combinations. Incidentally, don't run the burrs on empty. It wears them out faster.

Roller Mill. You can buy an attachment for some household mills that will make rolled oats, wheat, or rye flakes ($99 attachment for the Family Grain Mill). Or get the Marga Grain Roller/Flaker, which has three hardened steel rollers and can be adjusted to make different grades of either flour or flakes, $70 from the Urban Homemaker (see "Buying Your Grinder" below). A roller-type mill is the best for rolling and flaking grains, but it's not good for making flours. They are less expensive than hammer mills and require less power. They work by mashing the grain between two clothes-wringer-type rollers. You can set a roller mill to hull, crack, and grind grain. The grain will be quite fine, but not fine enough for baking. A good roller mill with crusher rollers can chop corn or grain on the stalk, wet or dry, into silage. A roller mill is what you need if you want to grow one of the grains that doesn't thresh clean and must be dehulled after threshing and before grinding (such as oats or barley).

Hammer Mill. Hammer mills do big grinding jobs. They also use a lot of electricity and cost a lot. The hammer mill basically grinds anything. You can put whole grain right on the stalk into a hammer mill, and it will turn out a fine livestock feed that includes roughage and avoids threshing. You can mix the feed beforehand and then mill it, and grind corn on the cob. In some cases you can adjust these grinders to make cornmeal, too, but usually a hammer mill always lets some coarser material through and won't make a baking-quality flour.

BUYING YOUR GRINDER: Shop around, comparing prices and available models. Because there is such a confusing array of choices, tell the grinder salesperson your size of household; what grains or seeds you plan to grind, shell, or crush for oil; and, if you'll be also be grinding feed for livestock, how many and what kind. Health food stores or co-ops sometimes have grinders for sale, but they're not as likely to be able to give you expert advice. Grinders are now available that can operate either by hand or by electricity at the flip of a switch. The Country Living Grain Mill can even grind moist, oily items like oil seeds ($380 from Urban Homemaker). The Quaker City Grinding Mill will mill grains, beans, corn, coffee, and even nuts ($190 from Urban Homemaker). For family milling of wheat, I recommend the Family Grain Mill (available from many outlets). Health food stores and co-ops often have grinders for sale. The Braun Coffee/Grain Mill can't mill corn or beans, but it has 24 fineness settings and is only $70 (Urban Homemaker). Magic Mill is another popular home grinder.

Back to Basics Products designs and produces specialty kitchen tools and appliances: grain mills (also peelers, slicers, strainers, food dryers, juicers, meat grinders, sprouters, smoothie machines, etc.). Their hand mill retails for $80. Free catalog: 801-571-7349; 11660 S. State St., Draper, UT 84020-9455; fax 801-571-6061; **www.backtobasicsproducts.com.**

C. S. Bell makes hammer mills and burr or grist mills. The hammer mills are good for livestock and poultry feed preparation, grinding yard waste for compost, or fruit, vegetable, and grain processing for kitchen use. The mill weighs 54 lb. Its auger shaft is supported by two bronze bearings with oilers; the grinding disks self-align. Hand crank optional. Their mills can grind bones, hull sunflower seeds, or make bread flour in two grinds: 419-448-0791; Box 291, Tiffin, OH 44883; **sales@csbellco.com; www.csbellco.com.**

Christian Family Resources sells many different grinders. Their free catalog compares the mills based on speed, effort, burrs, hopper capacity, motor, country of origin, size, warranty, etc.: 719-962-3228 (1–5pm M–F, Mountain Time); PO Box 405, Kit Carson, CO 80825; **www.cfamilyresources.com.**

Cumberland General Store sells stone burr mills, etc., ranging in capacity from 150 to 1,250 lb./hr. Catalog, $4; 615-484-8481; 800-334-4640; Number 1, Hwy. 68, Crossville, TN 38555.

Electro-Mechano makes a good, high-speed electric mill that works by shattering grain into flour. Suited for a big family or small bakery. No hand crank option: 414-272-4050; 242 E. Erie St., Milwaukee, WI 53202.

K-TEC makes a very good high-speed electric (no manual option) micronetic chamber grain mill for $199–240; 800-748-5400; 1206 S. 1680 W., Orem, UT 84058; **www.blendtec.com.**

Kuest Enterprises manufactures a good-quality, high-volume electric mill with stainless steel burrs able to deal with dry or oily grains, including a commercial-size grinder. Detachable handle for hand cranking: Box 110, Filer, ID 83328; 208-326-4084.

Lehman's Hardware carries 12 grinder models, both hand and power, in full price and performance range (high-quality hand mill for $950). Check out their comparative performance chart: 330-857-5757; 888-438-5346; **info@lehmans.com; www.lehmans.com.**

R & R Mill Co. sells hand-cranked and motorized mills for home use: 801-563-3333; 45 W. First N., Smithfield, UT 84335.

Retsel Corp. manufactures the Little Ark (hand) and the Mil-Rite (electric with optional hand crank)—interchangeable stone and metal burrs, a lifetime warranty, and no answering machines! The Mil-Rite has a removable hand crank for optional hand operation: 208-254-3737; fax 208-478-5779; PO Box 37, McCammon, ID 83250; **www.RETSEL.com.**

Rocky Top General Store sells a heavy-duty power mill with 1,400-lb. capacity as well as smaller mills. Free catalog; 865-882-8867; fax 865-882-9056; PO Box 1006, Harriman, TN 37748; **rockytopgen@msn.com.**

Survival Center offers the Country Living Mill, and more; $2 catalog; 800-321-2900; PO Box 234, McKenna, WA 98558.

Urban Homemaker has a wonderful selection of kitchen grain grinders (and much else!!!): 800-55-BREAD; **UrbanHome@aol.com; www.urbanhomemaker.com.**

Vita-Mix sells a blender that can grind grain or make juice: 800-848-2649; **www.vitamix.com.**

Cereal

Throw away your notions about cereal and start over. I'm talking about the cereal you make yourself. You can get 2 kinds of cereal from your home grinder, one on the coarse grind and one on the fine. If you have more settings, you can get more kinds. Or you can cook the whole grain for still another variety. The amount of time you cook a cereal depends on the size of the pieces it is ground into and whether it has been presoaked. With store cereals, it depends on how much it has been precooked. I think cereals are nicest cooked in a double boiler or steamer, or baked in the oven.

BASIC COOKING PROCEDURE: The general rule is the larger your particles, the longer they will take to soften and the more water they will absorb. For cereals ground as fine as cornmeal (or finer), you add the cereal slowly to rapidly boiling water, stirring at the same time. In the case of fine-particled cereal, stir continuously until it has set and not at all afterward if possible. Cook until done. Watch carefully so it doesn't scorch, or cook in a double boiler. Particularly fine-grained, flour-type cereals should be first mixed with cold liquid to keep them from lumping, or made gravy-style.

COOKING WHOLE GRAINS: Cooking in a double boiler is the safest method. Cooking in a pressure cooker is the shortest. Cooking whole brown rice, barley, or other medium-hard grains takes 40–45 minutes in a regular pan or 20 minutes in a pressure cooker. Cooking cracked wheat or precooked or soft grains takes only 20–30 minutes regular, 5–10 pressure. Whole wheat berries, whole rye, whole oats, and other very hard grains take 1 hour or more regular, 35 minutes in the pressure cooker. When pressure cooking grains, be sure to use enough water, especially for the hard grains. They soak up a lot!

Homemade Quick-Cooking Cereal. Coarse grains like whole or cracked grains take a while to cook. You can speed that up by precooking them for 2 or 3 minutes in boiling water and then letting them soak in that liquid for several hours, or better yet overnight. Then they will cook up faster then they would have otherwise.

COOKING GROUND GRAINS: You can thicken the cereal in any recipe by adding more grain, or thin it by using less. You can cook it in milk instead of water, in part milk and part water, in all water, or in a fruit sauce. You can add raisins, dried, fresh, or canned fruit, nuts, any sweetening, or yogurt at any stage. Salt isn't necessary. In general, about 4 parts liquid to 1 part cereal is appropriate for coarsely ground cereals from the whole grain. Rolled cereals take 2 parts liquid to 1 part cereal. A "gruel" means a very thin cereal. A "mush" is a medium one, and a "porridge" means a very thick one.

Precooked Cereal. This is how you can have homemade cereal for breakfast without getting up earlier than you want to. Cook it the day before and refrigerate overnight. If you cooked it in a double boiler, it can be warmed up in the same container. Or start it very late in the evening and let cook all night at a low temperature. If you plan to warm up cracked wheat, oatmeal, or another coarse grain preparation, use an extra ½ c. water when you make it the night before. It also helps if you heat the milk or cream to be used on warmed-up cereal. I like cereal for lunch with the children, too. And, ah, yes, it is modern times, and cereal reheats nicely in a microwave.

Letters from Cereal Lovers. Wendy Neidhardt of Fox, AR, wrote me, "I put stone-ground cornmeal or ground wheat berries in boiling water (adding slowly so as not to disturb boiling) and cook for no longer than 15 minutes. I sometimes add instant powdered milk at the end of the cooking process, stir, and let sit for a minute to increase the protein content." Maureen Darby of Leslie, AR, wrote me too: "I recommend pressure cooking for grains. I think it cooks them better and conserves more food value . . . because they don't need such long cooking. We eat cracked grain or oats or cornmeal every morning for breakfast. I believe it would lose much of its food value if overcooked. I cook our cornmeal and rolled oats about 10 minutes, just in a pot on the stove. The cracked grain gets about 15 minutes' cooking time." I've been told that grains that are ground really fine like a flour can be boiled as little as 5 minutes. Some people recommend that this fine cereal be poured into a pan with cold water and then constantly stirred until the gruel comes to a boil. Then continue stirring until it is finished cooking, thick, and smooth.

BASIC GRAIN RECIPES

GRAIN AND VEGETABLES *If you have leftover whole or cracked grain, any kind that isn't mushy but still can be separated into the individual grains, you can make this dish. Peel and chop 1 onion, 1 celery stalk, and 1 green pepper or carrot for every cup of grain you're going to use. Brown the onion in a little oil until soft. Then stir in your grain and continue cooking until it is warmed through. Add a pinch of salt, 2 c. boiling water, and the chopped vegetables. Cover and simmer until the vegetables are finished cooking. Season with a pinch of thyme and basil and a slice of garlic.*

EGG FOO YUNG WITH LEFTOVER COOKED GRAIN *Cut up onions and either celery, carrots, peppers, or some other vegetable or combination you prefer. Fry the vegetables in some oil until they look done enough. Add precooked grain and stir it into a mixture with the vegetables. Season with salt and soy sauce. Add 2 beaten eggs and stir together until cooked.*

GRAIN SOUP *Use 1 c. grain to 4 c. water. Simmer an hour or so with a little salt and whatever else you want to add—vegetable, meat, etc. This is a good place to hide leftovers for a nourishing and tasty recycling.*

LEFTOVER GRAINS SALAD *Toss 2 or 3 c. cooked grains (all the same or a mixture of them) together with your favorite salad fixings, such as green pepper, red pepper, radishes, cucumber, sunflower seeds, parsley and other fresh herbs, onion, any selection of lettuces, and dressing (vinegar and oil works well with this). To serve, line a bowl with lettuce leaves and pour the salad mixture in. If you'd rather have a specific recipe, see below.*

☙ *MINTY LEFTOVER GRAIN SALAD Combine 2–3 c. cooked grain, 4 cubed tomatoes, 1 c. fresh mint, 1 c. chopped parsley, 1 c. chopped green onions, and a chopped green pepper. Premix ½ c. lemon juice, 4 T. oil, a pinch salt, and a dash pepper, and mix with salad.*

☙ *LEFTOVER GRAINS PUDDING Preheat your oven to 325°F. Butter a baking dish large enough to hold your pudding. Combine 3 eggs, 1½ c. milk, and ¼ c. honey, and beat well. Add 1 t. vanilla, ½ t. nutmeg, ½ c. raisins, and 2 c. leftover cooked grain. Pour into your baking dish and bake until set. Good hot or cold. Best with fresh berries on top.*

There just aren't quick and easy answers to the big questions of life. There is no way to seal yourself off from trouble, pain, and difficulty. No philosophy of life is going to work for you that doesn't accept those things and find a productive function for them. Yes, I mean it—find a way to turn worry and suffering into something worthwhile. You can accomplish that by directing yourself with all your heart to struggle for truly worthwhile goals. Then the beatings you take will have been for a noble cause, and you can be sustained by the hope of prevailing over your obstacles in the end. But when you do win, you can't just sit there and live on past glory. There's no such thing as standing still in this life. You're either trudging forward or slipping backward. For the sake of your own fullest aliveness, you have to look around the day after that victory and find some new challenges, even bigger and better ones to be having troubles for.

Now on to amaranth, and all the other good and useful individual grains—and canes—that have sustained human life since the Old Stone Age became the New Stone Age. They are the foundation of your diet, the staff of your life, the contents of your food storage system that guards you from disaster.

The entry for each grain lists mail-order sources of that grain; if you'd like to order, see the list of nurseries and seed suppliers in Chapter 2 for addresses.

GRAIN AMARANTH

The naming of amaranths in seed catalogs is very confusing because there are ancient names, modern but local names, names under which the plant is sold as an ornamental, and Latin names. Amaranths are annuals and are a domesticated, lovely, useful relative of pigweed. They are broadleafed plants, not grasses, but grain amaranths produce large amounts of seeds that resemble a cereal-type grain.

All the amaranths grow vigorously, as tall as 4–6 feet or more, depending on the variety and conditions. They are hardy and bug-resistant, and at least one variety can be persuaded to grow in just about any given place. (Domesticated amaranths aren't nearly as aggressive as the weed varieties, however, and lack the strong taproot of the weeds.) On an equal-sized piece of ground in a hot, dry climate, amaranth will outproduce corn and at the same time use less water. It can do that because of its special chemistry, which makes it able to use water more efficiently.

The Jefferson Institute offers info on "new crops,"

including amaranth, available in print or online: 573-449-3518; 601 Nifong Blvd., Ste. 1D, Columbia, MO 65203; **info@jeffersoninstitute.org; www.jeffersoninstitute.org.** Nu-World Foods offers amaranth recipes, seed, FAQs, and an Amaranth Grower Resource Center: 630-369-6819; fax 630-369-6851; PO Box 2202, Naperville, IL 60567; **sales@nuworldamaranth.com; www.nuworld amaranth.com.**

Growing Grain Amaranth

VARIETIES: Basically, the amaranths come in 3 main divisions: the "grain amaranths," grown for seeds; the "vegetable amaranths," grown for their stems and green leaves (which are harvested and cooked like the related plants Swiss chard and spinach); and the weedy amaranths such as pigweed. (For information on vegetable amaranths, see also "Leafy Greens" in Chapter 4.) The amaranth seedhead colors are wonderful: red, orange, golden, or "burgundy" purple. Depending on the variety, seeds are cream-colored, golden, pink, or white. (Wild weedy amaranths all have black seeds.)

The preferred grain amaranths are *Amanthus hypochondriacus* and *A. cruentus* (both from Mexico and Guatemala) and *A. caudatus* (native to the Peruvian Andes). *A. caudatus* is the best variety to grow at altitudes above 7,000 feet and is the most resistant to chilling. *A. hypochondriacus* and *A. cruentus* are not frost-hardy. On the other hand, *A. cruentus* is the one dual-purpose species of grain amaranth, supplying both greens and grain. You may get as much as 1 lb. seed per amaranth plant. The seeds are tiny, barely bigger than the proverbial mustard seed, 1,000–3,000 seeds per gram. But each plant produces them in huge numbers, as many or more than 50,000 to a plant. Harvests vary widely depending on variety and conditions—and how well that particular variety is suited to those growing conditions. In Pennsylvania experiments, Rodale got 1,600 lb./acre. California growers have doubled that.

CLIMATE: There are distinct varieties adapted to almost any latitude, but you definitely need the correct one, because many of the amaranths are responsive to length of day—and length of day depends on your latitude and your season. The tropics have days of even length, uniformly short. Temperate latitudes alternate short days in winter with long days in summer. Thus certain Mexican amaranths will mature and set seed only in a Pennsylvania greenhouse in winter because only then are the days short enough! If you buy from a local seed company, they will already have figured out what variety is right for your region.

Both the grain and vegetable amaranths love heat, but grain amaranth is also extraordinarily drought-resistant. Native to the Americas, grain amaranth was nearly as important as corn and beans to pre-Columbian agriculture. It has been grown without irrigation in regions with as little as 7–8 inches of annual rainfall. Grain amaranth once grew wild in Arizona and southern Utah, and is still grown widely in rural Mexico. Amaranth is now a staple crop for hill tribes of India, Pakistan, Nepal, Tibet, Mongolia, and China as well. You can plant grain amaranth if you live in a somewhat dry area or on tropical highlands, or plant it as a dry-season crop if you live in a monsoon area.

PLANTING: The amaranth grain available in health food stores will generally grow fine when planted. Or you can order seed from Abundant Life (five varieties), Gurney, Johnny's, Salt Spring Seeds, Seeds of Change, Southern Exposure Seed Exchange, Bountiful Gardens, and Nu-World Foods (above).

Grain amaranths can thrive in any well-drained, neutral or basic (pH above 6) soil. (Some varieties will tolerate alkaline, acidic, or even slightly saline soils, but they're hard to find.) The patch or field should be fairly level and well cultivated—no clods to smother these tiny seeds! And make it fairly level, because these seeds are so very small. Plant after all danger of frost is over, in full sun, no more than 1/3–1/2 inch deep. Amaranth is planted densely: 130,000 plants per acre for grain amaranth.

WATER AND WEEDING: Since it is slow-maturing, get it in early. To get started, both grain and vegetable amaranths need their soil kept damp. After that, grain amaranths do well in a dry, warm climate, but vegetable amaranths need frequent watering right to the end of their growing season. Amaranth planted in rows can be weeded by hand or machine during the early stages. You want to avoid weeds that might get their seeds mixed with the amaranth grain harvest, because the tiny amaranth seeds are extremely difficult to separate out. Once they get well established, the plants are sufficiently luxuriant in foliage that they tend to shade out the competition and don't need to be weeded any more.

Harvest and Use

Most grain amaranths are mature after 4–5 months—quicker in monsoon climates, slower in highland regions (even as long as 10 months there). Some varieties of grain amaranth in experimental settings have been harvested by machine, but more commonly amaranth is handharvested. Hand harvesting persists because the central flower head usually matures and dries before the seeds on lower branches do. This varying maturity of seed-bearing branches is not a problem to a hand harvester, who can choose and pick. After being plucked from the plant, the grain is dried in the sun and then threshed and winnowed—the seed is heavier than its chaff.

SAVING YOUR OWN SEED: The seeds of weedy amaranths have been known to live as long as 40 years. Domesticated varieties are not so hardy, as is the way of things, but if kept in a dry container at room temperature, they have been found to still be able to sprout and grow after several years. High humidity, however, causes the seeds to more quickly lose viability.

USING AMARANTH GRAIN: The grainlike seeds of amaranth are rich in the amino acids that are missing in other grains such as sorghum, millet, barley, and wheat. So adding amaranth to any protein-limited diet improves its nutrition. For this reason, amaranth grain products are especially good for babies, children, and pregnant and nursing women. If you have surplus grain amaranth, chickens like it. Or you can sprout it.

You can boil the seeds to make a thin or thick cereal. Or grind them into flour, add to wheat flour, and make breadstuffs. (Substitute amaranth flour for 1/4 of the wheat flour.) Amaranth flour contains no gluten, so it can't make raised bread, but it makes a sweet light-colored flour that cooks well into unleavened flatbreads like chapatis or tortillas.

☙ *POPPED AMARANTH In a wok or fry pan, pop the seeds. Then mix them with honey or molasses and shape into a popcorn-type ball. Or eat the popped amaranth seeds as a cold cereal with milk and a sweetening, or use them as a breading for meats or vegetables. Or bake them whole in bread. But if seeds are too old or dry, they lose their ability to pop.*

BAMBOO

Bamboo is a primitive kind of grass, a common tropical Asian plant that likes warm, humid places and lower elevations. But there are varieties that can grow in northern places. I know of people who have had success with bamboo in California, Louisiana, Florida, Arkansas, and Washington; and I'm sure there are others, elsewhere in the United States. Bamboo can be a valuable food plant as well as provide a useful crafting material. The bamboo leaves can be fed to livestock. In Japan, most country-living families have a private or communal bamboo patch. Bamboo is a perennial, but it needs a constant supply of water. Once you get a stand going, you can harvest shoots to eat and also have the ornamental, treelike mature stalks with all their possibilities as a craft material.

You might read *The Book of Bamboo,* by David Farrelly; and *Bamboo on the Farm,* by Daphne Lewis. *Hardy Bamboos for Shoots & Poles: Thirty Varieties of Bamboo for Farms in USDA Zones 7, 8, 9,* by Daphne Lewis, helps you choose the right bamboo for your specific microclimate. To find books, visit the American Bamboo Society Bookstore: 512-345-3852; 6501 E Hill Dr. #110, Austin, TX 78731; **Support@ AmericanBamboo.org; www.bamboo.org/abs/BooksOn Bamboo.html.** The ABS has chapters all over the U.S. (and the world), an annual conference, and a bimonthly magazine, *Bamboo Science and Culture;* 518-458-7618; fax 518-458-7625; 750 Krumkill Rd., Albany, NY 12203-5976; **abs@bamboo.org; www.bamboo.org.** Their Tradewinds Bamboo Nursery also carries a good assortment of bamboo books, proceedings, journals, and tech reports, plus tools and plants: 541-247-0835. The website has FAQs and general bamboo info: **gib@bamboodirect.com; www.bamboo direct.com.**

Adam and Sue Turtle are the editors of *Temperate Bamboo Quarterly,* an indispensable popular journal on bamboo ($28/4 issues/yr). They co-founded the American Bamboo Society's Southeastern Highland Chapter. They've established a bamboo park that is the largest collection of bamboo (200 species, 22 genera) east of the Mississippi River. They also operate a bamboo nursery called "Our Nursery": 931-964-4151; 30 Myers Rd., Summertown, TN 38483; **www.thefarm.org/businesses/bamboo/bam98a. html.** They teach classes such as bamboo basket making, and bamboo design and construction (5 days for $350). Check out **www.growit.com/bamboo** for their Bamboo Institute of TN.

James Clever, the "Bamboo Gardener," distributes Daphne Lewis's books and carries an extensive listing of books, catalogs, newsletters, proceedings, reprints, and back issues of old newsletters and journals on bamboo and Japanese gardening, plus young bamboo plants and tools for digging and dividing. His website also is rich in links to other bamboo sites: 206-782-3490; PO Box 17949, Seattle, WA 98107; **bambuguru@earthlink.net; www.bamboo gardener.com/.**

The European Bamboo Society is a loose federation of national European bamboo societies, meeting at a yearly conference, in a different country each year. Their website's INDEX has links to bamboo info and pages from around the world: **www.bodley.ox.ac.uk/users/djh/ebs/**.

Bamboos at EarthCare Nursery in Australia has a website with good-quality photos of bamboo species, plus descriptions and online slide shows, cooking info, recipes, and, of course, things to buy: **http:/www.earthcare. au/bamboo.htm**. The Bamboo Society of Australia offers links, gallery of bamboo pix, list of their club chapters, and one of Aussie bamboo nurseries at **www.bamboo.org/abs/**. *The Bamboo Handbook*, by Durnford Dart, is 120 pages about growing eight bamboo species on an Aussie farm for five years.

Growing Bamboo

VARIETIES: There are hundreds—some grown for ornamentals, some for crafts material, some for the edible shoots, and some for all three. (All species of bamboo actually have edible shoots, but some taste better than others.) Some varieties can grow as much as 30 feet a year, up to 120 feet tall and 8 inches in diameter. The Mimosa bamboo can grow 13 inches in 24 hours when abundantly watered. Moso (*Phyllostachys moso*) is the kind most often grown to harvest the edible shoots. But if uncut, it can get 80 feet tall. Moso is usually about 3 inches in diameter. It can grow as much as 2 inches per hour. (Ancient Oriental execution method: stake the victim onto the ground with a bamboo shoot under his heart. I kid you not.) Sweet-shoot (*Phyllostachys dulcis*) is another edible variety. These shoots have a sweet flavor that reminds you of sugar cane. Green sulphur (*Phyllostachys sulphurea viridis*) is yet another edible variety of bamboo. Mankino and Taiwan giant are commercially important varieties raised in subtropical climates such as Taiwan. Makino is a naturally slender variety with poles 1–1½ inches in diameter. A complete listing of bamboo species and their suppliers in the U.S. is available in print from the American Bamboo Society (see above), and at **www.bamboo.org/abs/SpeciesSourceList.html**.

PLANTING: You can buy and plant bamboo sections only in the spring. With 25 years of full-time growing experience, Adam and Sue Turtle's business, "Our Nursery," is a great resource. Their website (see above) has a "Bamboo under Cultivation" list that summarizes bamboos adapted to temperate growing conditions by species, height, diameter, and hardiness temperature categories, all available to mail order! Tradewinds Bamboo Nursery and the Bamboo Gardener (also see above) are other good sources. For the best yield, you want to start with thoroughly plowed, well-drained, weedfree, acid soil. Bamboo planted in a temperate zone should have full sun. In hottest areas, however, it can do well in partial shade. Plant in late spring after all frost danger is past and the soil is warm. Bamboo needs to start in well-fertilized soil and must be kept moist the entire first year. (After that, bamboo can endure drought.) Plant bamboo before its sprouting season begins; in a semi-tropical climate, that would mean from early September to early December. In a slightly less tropical climate, the bamboo is planted in early April. You can transplant normal young bamboo or plant rhizome (stem) sections. Usually bamboo is raised from those sections of a mature plant, cut apart and laid under dirt, rather than from seed. Plant like sugar cane in 2-foot-long chunks 6 feet apart. For Moso, the giant variety, plant 10–15 feet apart. Cover with 1 inch of dirt.

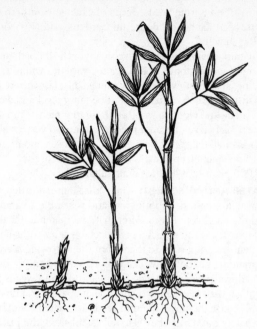

Bamboo grows amazingly fast when given its 2 basic requirements of fertile soil and warmth. It can handle some weedy competition once it gets going. It takes about 10 years to get a bamboo plantation well developed, either by planting rhizomes or transplanting young bamboo plants. It can stay outside all year if the temperature doesn't get below 0°F. Young plants are less hardy and need winter mulching. For more tropical varieties or colder winters, bring the bamboo in during the cold weather. You can lop off their tops and limit height to 12 feet or so. You can also prune out older ones.

Containing Bamboo. Install a root-impenetrable barrier around your bamboo patch. It has to go down at least 2 feet deep to work. So plant inside a 2-foot-deep metal or concrete root barrier, or in a sunken old tub, or grow it entirely in a large container. There are two kinds of bamboo, one of which (*Phyllostachys*) is invasive and the other (*Bambusa*, the clumping species) not so. Unfortunately, the best-tasting kinds are all varieties of *Phyllostachys*, the "runner." Bamboo containment is necessary because, under natural conditions, the runner varieties reproduce by sending a root outward and then sending up a sprout from that root. The root runs underground for an indeterminate distance, but far enough to surprise you, and then the sprout comes up (even through asphalt!). Lane Morgan (a Northwest gardening expert) says, "You need an underground barrier or your bamboo will spread and become a real pest. Watch out for drainfield invasions in particular."

Harvesting and Cooking Bamboo

The new shoot of the bamboo plant is eaten asparagus-style. Harvest enough every spring so your grove doesn't get too crowded, but don't take them all. The bamboo grove needs some new plants to stay healthy. The season for cutting sprouts in subtropical Taiwan is May to September. A dense area of bamboo stems is called a "cane brake." When harvesting, be careful not to damage nearby shoots. The taller the bamboo shoots get, the less tender and edible they are. How you harvest depends on the species.

THICK-SHOOT SPECIES: Just as, or soon after, the shoot emerges from ground level in the early spring, dig down and cut it off several inches below ground with a knife. If you heap up soil around the shoot of these bamboo species as they grow, you get extra-wide and -long tender shoots, because being underground keeps them tender. A better system is to add 6 extra inches of dirt if you know where the shoot will come up.

THIN-SHOOT SPECIES: The varieties of bamboo that have shoots only 1–2 inches wide don't need the dirt-heaping treatment. But don't let them get taller than a foot before harvesting. Cut off at ground level with pruning shears. Peel them one section at a time.

COOKING: Bamboo shoots deteriorate in quality as fast as they grow. They are best eaten or preserved the same day they are cut. If you've eaten only canned sprouts, you haven't experienced real bamboo. To prepare shoots, first remove the tough, tight-fitting outside husks until you have peeled down to the white inside. Cut off the base of the sprout and discard with the husks. Cut the hollow bamboo tube into thin slices. What you do next depends on whether your shoots are of the bitter or non-bitter variety.

Bitter. Moso and other bitter-while-raw varieties (which is most of the bamboos) can't be eaten raw. Boil 10 minutes. Throw out that water. Add fresh water. Boil 10 more minutes.

Non-Bitter. These can be eaten raw in salads or with a vegetable dip.

USING AND PRESERVING BAMBOO: Serve your boiled bamboo slices hot in stir-fry recipes or soups, or fry them in miso. Or serve cooked and then chilled, mixed into a potato or green salad. To freeze bamboo, bag slices (boiled if bitter) in plastic and freeze. To dry bamboo, boil the shoots 15 minutes, slice, salt, and dry.

BAMBOO CRAFTS: The best "wood" comes from un-crowded stands. The possible uses are almost infinite: giant bamboos make water pipes, fences, sheds, handles for fruit pickers, kitchen utensils, primitive masts for sailboats, weapons for hunting, fishing rafts, and furniture. The small-in-diameter kinds of bamboo can be used to create screens and window and wall coverings. Slender bamboo is used to make garden stakes, baskets, mats, screens, bird-cages, and chopsticks.

BARLEY

Barley was grown in ancient Egypt, and until the 16th century it was the chief bread plant of Europe. It looks at first glance like a short variety of wheat. Today most home grain growers prefer wheat to barley because the outer husks of U.S.-grown barley varieties are tough and stick tightly to the kernel, so they don't thresh easily like wheat and rye. So don't raise barley for household consumption unless you have access to a pearling machine or a roller mill—or are going to put the barley, husk and all, through a grinder, as does one lady I know. There's plenty of bran in her diet! Barley is a hardy grain that will grow in alkaline soils and survive summer frost. And it yields well, possibly better than wheat. Barley matures so quickly that it's useful to plant a hay crop with it. When the barley is harvested, the legume goes on to be green manure or a perennial hay field.

If you have deer eating your grain crops, a bearded, "roughawned" barley variety is one they'll leave strictly alone, because the awns are mean stickers about 3 inches

long with fishhook barbs that, like porcupine quills, go into skin and won't come out! For the same reason, don't cure awned barley for hay, though you can pasture it until in early stages.

Growing Barley

VARIETIES: There are 3 categories to consider: the row number, whether it's winter or spring barley, and whether it has beards and husks.

Rows. There is "6-row" and "2-row" barley. Six-row barley literally has 6 up-and-down rows of kernels on each head. Two-row barley has only 2 rows, because it has a mutation that causes the other 4 rows to not develop. (The old-timers also had a 4-row barley.) Don't mix 2-rowed and 6-rowed seed if you're planning to malt, because they take different times to sprout. The advantage of 2-rowed barleys is that they pearl easiest because their kernels are more uniform in size.

Winter/Spring. You can also choose between winter (2 or 6-rowed) and spring (2-row) types. In general, use the same kind of barley (winter or spring) as you would wheat. So in the southern United States, plant winter types; in the north, spring types. Don't plant winter barley unless your average winter temperature is higher than 20°F.

Beards and Husks. You can get "bearded" and do without deer (they don't like to eat it), or "beardless" and do without prickly awns. Beardless is easier to handle and can be used to make hay, but has weak stems and a tendency to lodge. You can also choose between the tough-to-dehull regular varieties and the "hull-less" kinds that are naturally "naked" or "huskless." But these are mostly available in low-tech societies and are harder to obtain in the United States. And hull-less doesn't yield as well as hulled and isn't used for malting. Abundant Life and Bountiful Gardens offer bearded barley (*Hordeum vulgare*). Bountiful Gardens also offers hull-less barley.

CLIMATE: The big argument for barley is that it is adapted to the north temperate zone—and requires less moisture for growth than any of the other cereal grasses. It's heavily grown in the United States, Canada, northern Europe, Russia, China, India, Argentina, and Ethiopia—and also across northern Africa, on the high plateaus of Tibet, in the Andes Mountains of South America, and north of the Arctic Circle. But it does best where the ripening season is long and cool, rainfall moderate rather than heavy, and soil well drained (no wet feet for this grain!). Barley yields better in the northern United States and Canada than in the southern United States. Barley likes clay soils but not sandy ones. Barley grows in an alkaline soil better than any other grain; it reacts the worst to an acid soil (pH of at least 6.0 needed). Barley is grown in the oases of the Sahara because it can stand high temperatures if the humidity is low. But if both temperatures and humidity are high, it doesn't do so well. Winter barley is more hardy than oats but less so than wheat or rye.

GOOD BARLEY ROTATIONS: Barley doesn't do well planted in the same soil year after year. It needs to be part of a rotation. You manage that by double-cropping, or in a 2-, 3-, 4-, or 5-year rotation. Don't plant barley after corn; it can pick up scab (*Gibberella zeae*) from the corn, and scab-infected barley can be poisonous to pigs.

Double-Cropping. Here's how double-cropping works in California's Central Valley. Since barley is ready to harvest there in about 60 days, it is combined about June 10; a second crop is planted within 2 weeks and is harvested in late September or early October. You could plant barley followed by soybeans in the milder north, barley-sorghum in the south.

Rotations. For a 2-year rotation, you can simply alternate barley and wheat, barley and potatoes, or barley and oats (oats help a root-rot problem barley can get). A good 3-year rotation for dry land is to alternate fallow, wheat, and barley. Here's a good 5-year rotation for irrigated land.
1. The first year, plant a barley/alfalfa mixture. Then harvest barley when it's ready and alfalfa at the end of the summer.
2. The second and third years, take 3 cuttings of alfalfa off the field each summer.
3. The fourth year, plant corn, which benefits from the preceding alfalfa.
4. The fifth year, plant vegetables.
5. The next year, you're back to the beginning, planting your barley/alfalfa mixture, which will do well even in depleted soil.

PLANTING: Seed winter barley in the early autumn (10 days to 2 weeks earlier than winter wheat) at 1¼–3½ lb. per 1,000 square feet—or about 100 lb. per acre. Here's another formula: for every bushel of barley you want to harvest, plant a 10 × 85-foot area. A bushel of barley weighs about 48 lb. Barley yields from 35 to 90 bushels an acre, depending on fertility, etc. Plant 1–2 inches deep. Or figure 100 lb./acre if grown alone and for grain; 120 lb. for crop to be pastured or if seeding on the late side. For spring barley, plant 50 lb./acre in dry areas, 120 on irrigated land or for a forage crop or for a delayed planting. Barley seed that isn't fully cleaned of awns will plug a drill and must be broadcast. *NOTE: Be careful that no barbed barley awns work their way into tender places on child, man, or beast!*

Harvesting and Using Barley

HARVESTING: Barley ripens before wheat, 60–70 days after spring planting, or 60 days after spring growth begins in fall-planted barley. It is mature when the straw is yellow and the heads droop. Because of the sharp, hard beards, it's best to handle barley as little as possible during harvest. Combining works best. If you use a threshing machine, you may need to run the barley through twice to get off all the beards and outer husks. Combine only when fully ripe and when kernels are at less than 14 percent moisture. (Straw will feel dry, and kernel will snap when bitten.) To cut by hand, harvest a few days earlier than for combining, while

there's still considerable moisture in the grain and straw, to avoid shattering. Make medium-sized shocks that are loose enough to allow air circulation. Threshing barley can be a little tricky because if it's too moist (above 20 percent), any setting able to remove the beards tends to crack or skin the grain. That doesn't matter for table use, but it kills the germ and so messes up the grain for sprouting or seeding. The barley will machine-thresh best if it's fully mature and very dry.

MALT: "Malt" means a grain, generally barley, that has been softened by soaking in water and then allowed to sprout. The sprouting develops the enzyme "diastase," which converts to sugar the starch of the malt and any raw grain mixed with it. Because of this, malt is important in the beer brewing process. If you want to delve into the chemistry of it, see *Barley and Malt: Biology, Biochemistry, Technology*, edited by A.H. Cook (1962).

Sprouting Barley. You have to wait 6 weeks after harvesting. Only then will the seeds have finished maturing enough to be able to sprout. Then soak the seeds (on or off the heads is OK). At about 60°F, they'll sprout in about 5 days. At this sprouting stage, the grain is called "green malt." Green malt is usually dried in a kiln and is sometimes roasted like coffee.

You can make a simple homemade malt by drying the sprouted grain. Then you literally "crack" the green malt by going over it with a rolling pin till it has an almost flourlike fineness. Now toast or roast it until you have your chosen flavor of malt: pale, medium, dark, or very dark. "Malt extract" is a malt-flavored syrup. "Malted milk" is powdered milk combined with powdered malted barley and/or wheat.

THE HUSK PROBLEM: Any barley variety that has a husk needs to be dehulled or "pearled." First you toast the grain. (See "Wild Rice.") Then grind. A pearling machine is equipped with wire brushes or a stone-mill process that grinds the grain between the stones to take off the barley kernel's hull and outer layers. A hammer mill will work if you remove the screen and run it at half the usual speed. Both electric and hand-cranked barley hullers have been manufactured and marketed, especially by seed equipment outlets. You can do a halfway job with a blender, too.

Pearling. Whatever style of machine you have, it's important to keep the barley moving inside it. After the first few minutes of pearling, stop and sift out the hulls and flour. Then briefly pearl again; then sift again. After 3 pearlings, the hull and kernel coating should be all removed. Now you have "pot barley." After 5–6 pearlings, the little bit of the barley kernel that remains (most of the vitamins are gone) is commercially called "pearled barley." Starting with 100 lb. barley, figure on getting 65 lb. pot barley or 35 lb. pearled barley. You'll get a bunch of barley flour along the way in the pearling process. Pot barley makes good soup, and is, of course, considerably more nutritious than the ground-on-down "pearled" barley.

BARLEY FOR LIVESTOCK FEED: Rabbits, pigs, and other livestock can eat barley whole. Chickens can eat it after it's cracked or hulled so they can easily digest it. Make sure rough-awned varieties are clean of beards. Otherwise, the animals can get sore mouths. Larger animals can eat it in the husk but, like poultry, they'll get more food value out of it and like it better if it's chopped, sprouted, or hulled first. (If you put the barley through a chopper, do a coarse chop.) In fact, barley is frequently hulled for livestock as well as people. You can add the sifted hulls to animal feed. For chickens or other livestock, you can soak the unthreshed barley head. When the seeds sprout, feed the whole thing to them. It's a good winter source of vitamins.

COOKING POT OR PEARLED BARLEY

➤ **BARLEY CEREAL** *Whole barley takes longer to cook than most grains. A cup of dry barley makes about 4 c. cooked barley. For every ½ c. barley, provide 1 c. boiling water. Sprinkle barley into the boiling water. Reduce heat and simmer until tender (1½ hours, maybe). Drain. Add butter and honey, or cream and honey.*

➤ **SCOTCH BROTH** *Soak 1 c. barley in 1 qt. water overnight. In the morning add a sizable hunk of mutton or lamb on the bone and water enough to cover all. Simmer until the meat and barley are tender. Add vegetables in season, or what you have stored. Season to taste. Thicken soup with some flour and serve.*

➤ **BAKED BARLEY** *Soak 6 T. pearled barley in cold water overnight. In the morning pour off the water and put the barley in a baking dish. Pour 7 c. boiling water over it. Add salt, if desired, and bake in a moderate oven (325°F) about 2½ hours, or until the barley is completely soft and all the water is absorbed. When it is half done, add about 4 T. sugar or a pour of honey mixed with grated lemon peel. You can eat it warm with cream or serve cold molded in cups with cream on the side. Or make with raisins. For sweetening, serve with applesauce on the side. You can also make it nice by stirring in raisins before you serve it. Get the raisins ready by pouring boiling water over them and letting them stand until they soften before stirring them in.*

➤ **BARLEY PUDDING** *Wash ½ c. pearled barley. Presoak for an hour to partially soften. Combine barley, 4 c. milk, ⅓ c. honey, ½ t. salt, ½ t. cinnamon, and 1 T. shortening. Pour into a buttered baking dish. Bake at about 300°F for 3 hours. Stir it 3 times during the first hour to keep the barley from settling in the pudding.*

➤ **BARLEY WATER** *This is a traditional beverage for invalids. Soak 1 T. pearl barley overnight in 3 c. water. In the morning simmer slowly, stirring frequently, until the barley is very soft and your liquid is reduced to 1 cup. Strain. Add salt to taste.*

➤ **BARLEY STEW** *Cook 2 lb. stewing meat until tender. About a half hour before you expect the meat to get done, set 1½ c. pot or pearled barley to soak in cold water. When the meat is done, add the barley and your choice of vegetables such as sliced carrots, snapped beans, potato chunks, and chopped onion. Cook until the vegetables and barley are tender. Add your favorite seasonings (salt? pepper? chopped parsley? paprika?), and serve.*

➤ **BARLEY BURGERS OR MEATLOAF** *Mix together 1 lb. ground meat, 2 beaten eggs, 1½ c. cooked barley, some finely chopped onion, and your favorite burger seasonings to taste. Shape into patties and fry or shape into a meatloaf (bread-loaf-shape) and bake at 350°F until cooked through.*

COOKING WITH BARLEY FLOUR: You get some barley flour as a by-product of pearling. Or you can grind pot or pearled barley into flour. Roller milling works well. Or you can make it straight from the threshed barley still in the husk, ground husk and all. If the barley flour is unparched,

breads made with it will have a slightly bitter taste. Barley breads are a sweet-tasting, low-starch product. They can be made to leaven by adding some wheat flour or baking powder. A plain loaf of all-barley bread can be made by simply substituting barley flour for white flour in a bread recipe. The loaf will be small, heavy, and very moist, like an unleavened or sourdough bread. Barley breads are crumbly when warm. Let them cool before slicing and you'll have better luck.

Parching. Toast the barley flour in your oven in a flat pan until it is darkened. In the Middle Ages, "black barley bread" was a staff of peasant life. "Black" referred to the fact that it was parched. It tastes better that way, although I've tried it both ways and parching isn't absolutely necessary.

➤ **BARLEY WHOLE WHEAT BREAD** *This does rise, stays wonderfully moist, and is delicious! Dissolve 1 heaping T. dry yeast in 1 c. warm water. Combine 2 T. corn oil, 1 T. salt, and 2½ c. warm water. Add the yeast mixture. Add 2 c. barley flour and enough whole wheat flour to make a dough. Knead until done. Divide into 2 loaves and put into greased loaf pans. Let rise until doubled in bulk. Bake at 425°F for 20 minutes, then at 275°F for 40 minutes.*

➤ **BARLEY MUFFINS** *I recommend these! Sift together 2½ c. barley flour, 2 t. baking powder, and a dash salt. Beat 2 eggs slightly. Combine eggs, ¼ c. rich cream, and ¼ c. honey with dry ingredients and mix well. Pour batter into muffin tins (makes a big dozen) and bake at 400°F for 25 minutes.*

➤ **STEAMED BARLEY BROWN BREAD** *Sift 2 c. cornmeal, 1 c. barley flour, 2 t. baking powder, ½ t. soda, and 1 t. salt. Combine 1 c. molasses and 2 c. cold water and then stir into flour mixture. Put into 3 pint cans and steam for 4 hours.*

➤ **POTATO AND BARLEY DROP COOKIES** *Put ingredients together in the order given: 1 egg lightly beaten, 1 c. mashed potatoes, ¼ c. melted butter or other fat, ¾ c. corn syrup or molasses, 1⅓ level c. barley flour, 2 level t. baking powder, ½ t. salt, and ½ t. vanilla. Beat egg, potato, and fat to a cream. Mix in corn syrup or molasses. Then add sifted dry ingredients. A half cup of nutmeats or dried fruit may be added. Drop by spoonfuls on well-greased cookie sheet and bake in moderate oven.*

➤ **BARLEY PASTRY** *Sift 2 level c. barley flour, ¼ level t. baking powder, and ½ t. salt; cut in 6 T. shortening. Add very cold water to make a soft dough. Mix well and press into pie plate with your hands, ¼ inch thick. Patting it into shape gives more satisfactory results than rolling. This is enough for 2 crusts.*

BUCKWHEAT

Buckwheat is one of the cereal grains that is not a grass. Originally from China, it's a member of the knotweed family, related to weeds dock and sorrel. The bushlike plants grow about 3 feet high and have heart-shaped leaves. But in the kitchen, it's a standard "grain"—in fact, an exceptionally nutritious one. The pioneer women who routinely sent their families out for a day of school or work on a start of buckwheat pancakes were indeed giving them the best possible start for a hard day's work.

But buckwheat has many other uses. It's valuable for beekeepers because it bears abundant white flowers (with hints of pink or red) starting about 4 weeks after planting.

The plants will continue to bloom until killed by frost, still flowering when most other pollen sources are failing. Buckwheat-blossom honey—dark-colored and richly flavored—is considered a delicacy and can be bottled and sold as a specialty. Buckwheat is rich in rutin, a substance that controls certain types of hemorrhaging.

And buckwheat is the best crop to use to smother out perennial grasses. If it is planted thickly, it soon forms a dense canopy of leaves that blocks off the sun from the unwanted plants below. So if you've plowed up old pasture for a garden, immediately plant buckwheat. It's also a valuable green manure crop. Plow it under just as it starts to blossom (about 6 weeks after planting). You can till under even a very thick stand of buckwheat with a rototiller because the stems are hollow and tender. In fact, you can turn it under even with a spade; it keeps the soil under it very moist and loose.

Growing Buckwheat

Buckwheat grows especially well in moist, cool climates and cold areas, from Pennsylvania north into Canada. But it grows acceptably well in many other regions. Buckwheat is also a good grain choice if you have poor soil, especially if it's sticky, dense clay, because buckwheat roots break that up and make it loose. Buckwheat is not a good choice if you have nitrogen-rich soil. It will grow too tall and be likely to fall over. There's lots more info at **www.jefferson institute.org** and at **www.ext.nodak.edu/extpubs/ plantsci/crops/a687w.htm**.

PLANTING BUCKWHEAT: Order seed from Bountiful Gardens, Farmer Seed, Johnny's, or Territorial. There is one type of buckwheat recommended for a green forage crop and another for the grain, so be sure to get the right one for your purposes.

When to Plant for Grain. Buckwheat grain should generally be harvested after 90–110 days. Dry, hot weather during seed formation cuts your yield, so if your summers are like that, consider planting in July for a better-yielding crop by frost. In general, plant 12 weeks before your first expected fall killing frost. Buckwheat grows fine in hot weather; the heat inhibits only the seed-making part of its life cycle.

When to Plant for Green Manure. For a green manure crop, plant buckwheat as early as 1–2 weeks before your expected last killing frost of spring—or as late as 4–6 weeks before the first fall frost. Buckwheat seed is cheap. If you lose it to a frost, replant, but odds are it will grow fine. In warm weather, buckwheat sprouts and grows quickly. Spring-planted green-manure buckwheat can be ripe and ready for harvest in June. Or buckwheat can be seeded with rye in July. (After harvest, the rye continues to grow, producing grain or a crop for plowing under the next spring.)

How Much to Plant. For every bushel of buckwheat grain you want to grow, plant an area of 10 × 130 feet. Plant 1¼ lb. buckwheat seed per 1,000 square feet, about 3 to 4 pecks (50 lb.) per drilled acre, or 4–5 pecks per broadcast acre. (A bushel of buckwheat weighs 48 lb.) If planting buckwheat for a smother or green manure crop, also plant it thickly: 3–4 lb. per 1,000 square feet. Plant 1½ inches deep.

Harvesting and Storing

Unlike a stand of grass grain, which usually ripens pretty much all at once, any one buckwheat plant at mid-season will have flowering buds, green grains, *and* ripe seed on it. The grain starts maturing in 70–86 days—maybe even 60 if planted at midsummer. If you thresh too early, you lose the late-coming kernels. If you wait too long, the early-maturing seeds fall out onto the ground. Because the stems of mature buckwheat become brittle and lodge (fall over and break) easily, harvest before a hard wind or rain storm hits, if possible, to prevent crop losses. Also, plan to do it in the middle of a prolonged dry spell. In general, when most of the grain is completely developed and you have had a light frost, get busy and combine or cut it, because buckwheat is killed by the slightest frost and, after dying, quickly becomes very brittle. To maximize your yield, harvest late enough to get as many mature seeds as possible, but before serious shattering begins.

For a preview of the coming grain, just go out and strip off a few cupfuls of the grain into a container you've brought with you. Take that into the house, grind, and bake. But that doesn't give you a winter's supply. For that, you combine or mow by hand. Use the general routines described in the opening of this chapter to cut, bundle, shock, and thresh. Field-dry the buckwheat grain or dry it under cover, but it must be absolutely bone dry when you thresh. If moisture is in the forecast, cover with plastic or take it under shelter. After buckwheat plants die, they become so brittle that the seed easily threshes out (in field) on the threshing floor. A typical yield is 25 to 50 bu./acre.

VOLUNTEER BUCKWHEAT: What falls to the ground will grow next year. You don't need to plow to have another crop. If you don't want volunteer buckwheat in that place the next year, harvest soon after the *first* seed matures, *before* the plant scatters seeds! If you cut in cloudy weather or while it's still damp with dew, that helps avoid shattering, too.

STORING: Buckwheat stores best at 12–13 percent moisture. Chickens, goats, and rabbits love it! You can store unthreshed buckwheat and feed it to them, straw and all.

BUCKWHEAT HULLS: The buckwheat seed has a sizable hull, about 40 percent of its weight. You can grind up the whole thing or dehull it. The hulls actually add good nutritional value; ground unhulled buckwheat makes a darker flour as well as a much better food. However, if you must dehull . . .

Dehulling. Toast the seeds (see "Wild Rice") and grind them; then stop and sift out hulls with your flour sifter (see "Barley"). Big outfits use a commercial-sized dehuller.

Buckwheat Recipes

BUCKWHEAT GREENS: Lane Morgan says, "Tibetans and Nepalis use buckwheat greens as a salad. It's about the only green vegetable they can grow at high altitudes." She has a recipe for them in her *Winter Harvest Cookbook* (Seattle: Sasquatch Books, 1990).

KASHA RECIPES: Use your buckwheat whole as "kasha" or ground into buckwheat flour. Kasha is made from whole, "green" buckwheat. "Green" means not toasted yet; after toasting, it's called kasha. Dry-roast your buckwheat kernels under a low flame for about 15 minutes until they turn a nice brown color. You can substitute kasha in any recipe where you'd use rice. It makes a good cooked breakfast grain.

❧ *KASHA, EGG, AND ONION To 1 c. kasha add 1 T. butter or oil, stir over heat, and let melt and coat the grains. Add 1 beaten egg and stir constantly over high heat until the egg is dry. Add 2 c. boiling water (otherwise it spits like crazy). Add some chopped onions that have been sauteed in butter. Put the lid on and lower the heat. Let simmer on low, low heat for 20 minutes. When done, dish into bowls and eat.*

❧ *KASHA PIROGEN Make a basic piecrust dough, but add 3 or 4 eggs so that the dough is more elastic than regular piecrust dough. Roll it out to piecrust thickness. Cut into 2-inch (or larger) squares. Take a square in the palm of one hand; take a spoonful of cooked kasha in the other and place it in the center of the square. Moisten the edges of the square and fold it over, using a slight pressure on the edges to seal. When you have a batch of squares filled, drop them into boiling water. Leave them in the water 2 or 3 minutes and they're done. Eat immediately or fry in butter until crisp and brown. Jeanie Karp gave me this recipe. She used to live in the Bronx. Now she's my neighbor down the road.*

❧ *RUTH'S VEGAN KASHA Serve cooked kasha with chopped vegetables that have been sauteed in some vegetable stock with a dash of tamari and favorite herbs and spices.*

RECIPES FOR BUCKWHEAT FLOUR: Molasses is sometimes used in buckwheat recipes to improve the color of the product, since without it the breads are a blah gray color, but I don't mind the color and love the taste. Always shine your griddle with a bit of fat before starting, and drop batter by tablespoonfuls to make dollar-sized pancakes. They're good with butter and honey, sour cream—or what have you. Any kind of buckwheat griddle cake makes a fine quick lunch as well as a breakfast. All buckwheat pancakes tend to be doughy; adding even just a trace of wheat flour helps counteract that.

❧ *BUCKWHEAT OVERNIGHT YEAST PANCAKES Dissolve 1 t. dry yeast in a little warm water. Add 1 t. sugar, enough lukewarm water to measure 4 cups, ½ t. salt, and enough buckwheat flour to make a thin batter (about 3¼ cups). Let it work overnight. In the morning add 2 T. molasses. Stir it down, pour onto griddle in dollar-sized pancake dollops, and cook.*

❧ *BUCKWHEAT OVERNIGHT YEAST PANCAKES WITH CORNMEAL Pour 2 c. boiling water over ½ c. cornmeal. When it has cooled to lukewarm, add 2 t. dry yeast and then*

1 T. molasses, ½ t. salt, and 2 c. buckwheat flour. Let it rest overnight. In the morning dissolve ½ t. soda in ⅓ c. hot milk and mix well with batter. This also can be made into a sourdough recipe by simply holding back some of the batter to use in place of the yeast in future recipes.

❧ *SOURDOUGH BUCKWHEAT CAKES Save a cup of the batter from either of the above yeast recipes. If you keep your starter in a cool place, such as a refrigerator, and use it (holding out a cup of the new mix for the next starter) every couple of days, you'll have the traditional sourdough buckwheat cakes every morning for breakfast. Make the new batch using the cup of the starter to replace the yeast, and 1 cup water.*

❧ *SOURDOUGH BUCKWHEAT PANCAKES WITH SODA Make the original batter using sour milk or buttermilk for the liquid. Let the batter rest overnight. Mix in ½ t. soda in the morning before cooking the pancakes.*

❧ *ALMOST-INSTANT BUCKWHEAT CAKES Take as much or little of your buckwheat flour as you think you'll need, and add enough sour cream to make a pancake batter that's on the thick side. About 1 c. liquid to 1½ c. flour is right. Stir in 2 T. molasses and ½ t. soda.*

❧ *BUCKWHEAT MUSH METHOD #1 Place 2 c. water and a pinch of salt in a saucepan and bring to a brisk boil. Keep at the boiling point and add 1 c. buckwheat flour. Believe it or not, do not mix the buckwheat flour into the water. Just leave it there and let boil for 5 minutes. Now make a hole in the center of the flour with a wooden spoon and boil again for 10 minutes. Pour off half the water and set aside. Now mix well the buckwheat flour and remaining water. Add 2 T. hot melted butter. Cover and cook over low heat 5 more minutes. If it seems too dry to you, pour in some more of the extra water you poured off before and mix it in. For an extra-tasty touch, fry 3 slices of cut-up bacon until brown and crisp and pour over the buckwheat mush before serving.*

❧ *BUCKWHEAT MUSH METHOD #2 Mix your buckwheat flour with cold water first, 1 c. flour to 1 c. cold water. Then gradually stir it into 4 c. boiling water in the top of a double boiler. Cover and simmer for 15 minutes.*

❧ *FRIED BUCKWHEAT MUSH Cut it up after it has gotten cold and set, fry in a little oil, and serve with butter and syrup, same as cornmeal mush. Or bake and serve with honey or applesauce.*

> **BUCKWHEAT ROLL** *Sift together 3 c. buckwheat flour and 1 t. salt. Combine with 1½ c. boiling water or enough boiling water to make a manageable, workable dough. You've got to make this recipe quickly while the dough is still hot; otherwise, it won't handle well. Lay the dough on a floured table or breadboard and roll out about ¼ inch thick. Sprinkle on something sweet—honey, jelly, or ¼ c. sugar and ¼ c. rendered fatback cracklings, if you want the genuine Slovenian touch. Or sprinkle with chopped fruit and a dribble of honey, vegan-style. Roll it up like a jelly roll and lay in a greased baking pan. Bake at 350°F for 1 hour.*

> **SOBA (BUCKWHEAT NOODLES)** *Combine 2 eggs, ⅓ c. powdered milk, 1 t. salt, and enough buckwheat flour for a stiff dough (it will take about a cup). Roll out on a surface covered with wheat flour. Cut in ¼-inch strips. Dry for 30 minutes. Drop into boiling water gradually so boiling doesn't stop. Add 1 T. powdered sage to water for seasoning. Cook until done, drain, and serve with butter. Soba is a Japanese favorite, served in miso broth and Asian pasta salads.*

> **BUCKWHEAT-RYE YEAST BREAD** *Angie McLure, Kirkland, WA, highly recommends this one! "Stir ¼ c. molasses into a cup of just-lukewarm water. Add 2 t. dry yeast. While it's soaking, combine 2 c. buckwheat flour, 2 c. rye flour, 2 c. whole wheat flour, 1 c. sesame seeds, ¼ c. oil, and 1 c. water and blend well. Now add the yeast solution and work the dough until it's in a ball. Oil the outside of your bread ball and set to rise in a greased bowl in a warm place until it doubles in bulk. This will take a long time, maybe 3 hours. Then shape into loaves, put into your pans, let rise again, and bake."*

CORN

Corn was first created by the genius of native Americans thousands of years ago from an annual grass that had an extraordinarily high natural mutation rate. There's nothing comparable to it among all the wild grasses; corn was created by farmers' careful seed selections over the millennia (and is still being thus "created").

Corn is a space and soil/nitrogen hog, but it gives abundantly in return for what it gets. Corn is good for homesteaders because it can easily be grown on a small plot without draft animals or farm machinery. Your family can do it all: plant, weed, water, harvest, husk, and shell by hand. Corn is a sensible crop to be ambitious about. It yields generously. You plant one kernel and get about 750 back: 25 bushels per acre if you do everything absolutely wrong, 90 or much more if you do it right. It can provide high-quality food for every man and beast on the place. A single corn plant can produce enough grain to feed a person for a day. It's a bread, it's a vegetable, it's a decoration. The husks can be made into paper, rope, or stuffing. The cobs provide fuel to burn. The stalks and leaves are as good as hay for winter feeding.

ATTRA's "Organic Sweet Corn Production" manual is online at **www.attra.org/attra-pub/sweetcorn.html**. More info is at **www.agrypurdue.edu/ext/corn/**, a.k.a. King-Corn.org, and "The Corn Growers' Guidebook."

Names and Kinds of Corn

The Latin name for corn is *Zea mays*. The word "Zea" is ancient Greek for "cereal" and comes from the verb "to live." Similarly, the native American word for corn was "maize,"

which meant "that which sustains." To Europeans, the word "corn" meant and still means the hard kernels of any common grain: wheat, oats, barley . . . or maize. That's why the pioneers called maize "corn"—and why Europeans are still confused when we say "corn." If you are speaking to a European, call the plant "maize," and then there will be no misunderstanding.

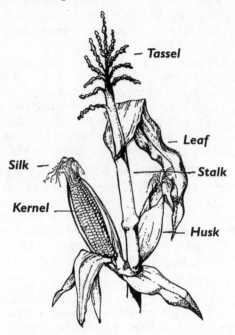

Corn's high mutation rate has made possible many varieties to choose from, one for almost any climate or use. To help you sort out the hundreds of possible choices—there's a different array in each seed catalog—here follows a basic pathway through the possibilities. First you choose one or more of the eight basic corn varieties and then make secondary choices within those categories: color, hybrid or open-pollinated, standard size or dwarf (if available). Really, I've never met a bad corn variety. But with experiment and experience, you'll find one or more varieties and/or timed plantings (early, mid-season, or late) that survives insects or disease better, yields better, or suits you or your needs better than the others. Then you'll favor that one.

The 8 basic corns, in roughly chronological order of development, are Indian (hominy and flour) corn, popcorn, pod corn, flint corn, dent corn, sweet (and supersweet) corn, high-lysine corn, and waxy maize. Some of these corns, including Indian corn, popcorn, flint, and dent, are sometimes referred to as "field corn" because they are left in the field to dry on the cob and are stored on the cob. Sweet corn, on the other hand, is picked fresh from the stalk and hurried into the house to be frozen, canned, or dried.

INDIAN CORN: All the original corns, of course, were native American, or "Indian." It was they who originally developed the flour, hominy, pod, popcorn, flint, and dent varieties, and all the colors and color combinations of corn. Current books on Indian corn/beans/squash, etc., growing methods include *Native American Gardening Stories, Projects and Recipes,* by Michael J. Caduto and Joseph Burchac; *Buffalo Bird Woman's Garden: Agriculture of the Hidatsa Indians;* and *Brother Crow, Sister Corn: Traditional American Indian Gardening,* by Carol Buchanan. For a fascinating in-depth study of traditional corn growing throughout the Americas, read the classic *Indian Corn in Old America* by Paul Weatherwax (New York: Macmillan, 1954).

Another great corn book is *Corn Among the Indians of the Upper Missouri* by George F. Will (1917). In that book he described 104 significant, different varieties of corn traditionally raised by the native Americans of that region alone. Now all but a few of the varieties he spoke of are gone forever, allowed to die out in the blind rush toward oneness, the worship of uniformity: all corn is yellow, all corn is hybrid, all corn is of the sweet, field, or popping variety. Only that's not true, or shouldn't be.

By "Indian corn" we now usually mean old-time genetic lines of corn. There are many of these ancient varieties, and they come in many unusual and pretty colors of kernels—yellow, white, blue, black, pink, red, or colors in combination—and in many sizes and climate adaptations. Indian corn can be dried to make flower arrangements or heaped in a decorative basket in the middle of the Thanksgiving table. Indian blue corn has now achieved supermarket popularity as blue corn chips.

Some varieties of Indian corn are called "flour corn" because the special kind of soft starch they have grinds to a fine flour rather than the flint/dent type that makes the familiar cornmeal. Mandan Bride is one such "flour" corn—98 days to maturity and multicolored. Taos Blue Flour is another. Mandan Clay is a red flour corn. Whatever color you start with, you'll get that color of flour (or cornmeal if you grind it only as far as coarse).

The varieties of Indian corn that are left are a treasure. Corn seed is viable only a few years. You have to keep planting a corn variety to keep it from becoming extinct. Here and there, despite all the vicissitudes of history in the Americas over the last several hundred years, brave souls have faithfully planted these few remaining antique breeds year after year and kept them going. Other devoted preservers have struggled to discover these remnants of old-time strains in order to help distribute and protect them.

You can buy Indian corn from Abundant Life (Mandan Bride, Mandan Black, Taos Blue Flour, Hopi Blue Flint, Hopi Pink, and Hopi White), Johnny's (Mandan Bride), Good Seed (Mandan Clay red flour corn), Talavaya (Hopi Turquoise, "pale blue kernels make delicious flour"), and Redwood City, which offers about 20 varieties.

POPCORN: Popcorn (*Zea mays* var. *praecox* or *everta*) is the only kind of corn that pops and turns inside out. It is considered by archaeologists to be the most ancient of the corns, popped and served for thousands of years. All popcorns are late maturing, 95–120 days. The nonhybrid popcorns are shorter than other corns (3–5 feet) and have smaller ears; the kernel is smaller too and is unique in having a point. They can handle more drought, less fertility, and more crowding (space rows 2–3 feet apart). Some hybrid popcorns have kernels twice the original size.

Popcorn's on the tough side unless you pop or grind it (makes great cornmeal). That toughness is what makes it able to pop. Compared to other corns, popcorn has an extra-hard outer covering (endosperm). When it has some moisture content (about 12 percent) and is heated, pressure builds up inside the tough endosperm that is preventing that water vapor from escaping until the whole thing explodes with a pop!

There are white, black, yellow, strawberry, blue, and multicolored popcorn varieties, but they all turn white when popped. Strawberry (hybrid) and Japanese hull-less (open-pollinated) are good varieties. You can get popcorn seed from Abundant Life, Johnny's, Farmer Seed, Redwood City, Harris, Shumway, and Southern Exposure, etc.

POD CORN: This old-time Indian corn is described as growing each individual kernel enclosed in a separate "pod" or husk. The result is a very leafy plant that is most useful as a forage corn. Native Seeds/Search catalog carries it: 520-622-5561; 526 N. 4th Ave., Tucson, AZ 85705; **info@nativeseeds.org; www.nativeseeds.org,**. Or buy pod corn seeds from DeeDee Wick, 4055 W. Myers Rd., Covington, OH 45318. Or from Stokes Seeds: 800-263-7233; **www.stokeseeds.com.**

DENT: Kernels of "dent" corn (*Zea mays* var. *indentata*) literally get a dent in the top of the kernel when they mature and dry on the cob. Dent and flint are both ancient native American types of corn, and there are many varieties of either one, some very old. Dents are the most commonly grown corn for livestock feed. Dent is also a good kind to "parch." You can use immature dent, a field corn, like sweet corn for roasting ears and table corn, though it won't be quite as tasty. But field corn is mainly grown for livestock feed (both fresh feed and silage) and for cornmeal and hominy making. Field corn has bigger, taller stalks, larger ears, and greater resistance to almost anything than sweet corn. It has the heaviest yields of both ears and silage of all the corns: an amazing 150–300 bushels per acre for commercial farmers, who usually raise a yellow or white dent hybrid.

Field corn basically comes in 2 colors: yellow or white. The white is a late-maturing Southern field corn variety with white kernels that makes white cornmeal. The white isn't quite as nourishing as yellow cornmeal though. White corn seed (also popcorn seed and a full line of sweet corn, including open-pollinated sweet corns) is available from the Schlessman Seed Co., Milan, OH 44846; **seedco@acc norwalk.com; www.schlessman-seed.com.**

And you can get four different kinds of dent (Reid's yellow, Boone Co. white, Krug's yellow, and Henry Moore yellow) from Leonard and Gerald Borries, 217-857-3377; 16293 E. 1400th Ave., Teutopolis, IL 62467. Time out for a word about this remarkable family. Although surrounded by a sea of hybrids, the Borries' dad, Joseph, never quit growing the dents of his childhood. He was one of only 5 stubborn corn growers who kept open-pollinated old-time field corns alive during the era when hybrids theatened to take over. But after the terrible 1970 corn blight epidemic in the hybrid fields, his blight-free varieties made a sudden comeback! "Open-pollinated corn will also produce more silage because the stalks grow larger. Quite a few dairymen are buying it for that," Joseph said. And it will dry down fast. The Borries family does a clover, corn, corn, soybeans, wheat rotation. Dad Joseph is retired now. Like him, the Borries sons always have to be looking for new customers because, since the corn they sell is open-pollinated, once you make a purchase, you have all the seed corn you'll need from then on! They'll mail any amount anywhere for a very reasonable price. Send SASE for more info.

FLINT: Kernels of flint (*Zea mays* var. *indurata*) don't get a dent because flint has less soft starch than dent corn. So, true to the name, flint kernels are harder than dent kernels and don't shrink when drying. The flints are all late-maturing, 100–120 days, but you have a better chance of getting a flint mature than a late sweet corn because they handle cool, wet weather better. They are also better nutritionally than most other varieties, make good cornmeal, and have outstanding capacity for crib storage. Kernels of dried flint corn aren't wrinkled like sweet, or indented as with dent, or small and pointed as with popcorn; they are smooth and hard.

There are open-pollinated, old-time Indian flints with interesting colors: black, blue, purple, or red. Rainbow flint has multicolored ears (available from Olds). Garland flint has kernels that range from yellow to red (Johnny's). Flint corns are frequently sold for decoration purposes. You can also buy flint varieties from Gurney, Nichols, and Abundant Life.

SWEET CORN: Sweet corn (*Zea mays* var. *rugosa*) was the first corn variety developed by European immigrants to the New World. First appearing in the 1880s, it is a mutation in which the kernels contain sugar in a water solution as well as some starch, though the sugar quickly changes to starch after picking. Open-pollinated sweet corns have an additional advantage in that they tend to ripen over a period of time rather than all at once as do the hybrids, giving you a longer sweet corn season and more time to get the crop preserved. Sweet corns are sweeter. That's the only thing going for them. Indian, popcorn, flint, or dent all tend to be more disease-resistant, less dependent on highly fertile soil, and more vigorous in germination and growth than the sweet corns. Dent corn has a larger ear with many more kernels than sweet corn. Field corn plants are larger and thus provide more livestock forage when stalk and leaves as well as ears are used as feed.

But corn on (or off) the cob, your table vegetable, is normally grown from one of the sweet corn varieties. It is a variety that you would ordinarily can, freeze, or use fresh as a part of your dinner menu. You can pick field corn and use it like sweet corn, but it won't be as sweet and delicious. You can make cornmeal or hominy out of sweet corn if you dry it like field corn. Most sweet corn is yellow, but there are also white kinds and a green one. The sweet corns are subdivided by maturity date. You can get an "early," a "mid-season," or a "late" sweet corn.

Early. "Early" corn generally means about 53 to 68 days to maturity, but cold weather could make that longer. Any of the three could be planted in early summer, but early corn can be planted when soil temperature is around 55–70°F. You plant early corn where your warm season is short; if you live up high or way up north, you want a quick-maturing corn. Or you plant early corn to double-crop a limited garden area because, given a reasonably long summer, you could follow it with a quick-growing vegetable crop or a cover crop. In general, early corn will cooperate and grow more readily in cool weather than will mid-season or late corn. Even in warmer climates, some people choose to make plantings of early corn every 10 days or so from first planting time on to midsummer. And, since corn growing slows down in late summer when days are getting shorter, an "early" variety is also the best choice for your very latest planting. Early corn gets only 4 to 6 feet high and has smallish ears. It can be planted closer together than later corns. Figure on thinning it to 6 inches.

Golden Midget (65 days) is a very specialized early sweet corn—the one that has ears with edible centers, "baby corn." At maturity the ears are 3 to 4 inches long and can be pickled, steamed, or stir-fried, all on the cob. (Don't let them get overmature!)

Mid-Season. "Mid-season" corn takes 69 to 86 days to maturity. Mid-season and late corn need a warmer soil, 60–80°F. Usually the longer the corn takes to mature, the bigger the ear and the more ears you get. So mid-season and late corns yield better than early. Thin to 8 inches for mid-season corn. Early Golden Bantam is a good yellow, 5-foot-tall, very sweet, midseason, open-pollinated variety with 6½-inch ears. Most mid-season types grow 6–8 feet tall. Gardening and food writer Lane Morgan's favorite sweet corn is Burgundy Delight, "a hybrid midseason bicolor from Johnny's Selected Seeds. We shuck it and steam it about 5 minutes. It's heaven. It will hold its prime sweetness for several days in the field. We have harvested excellent corn from mid-August until early October from 2 plantings."

Late. "Late" corn takes 87 to 92 days to mature and usually is larger yet. Thin to 12 or 18 inches for late corn. Country Gentleman is a classic white, late, 7-foot tall, open-pollinated sweet corn (kernel rows not regular). It bears 1–2 ears/stalk and the ears are 7–8 inches long. Stowell's Evergreen is another white, late, many-kerneled, open-pollinated classic dating back to at least the 1800s. Golden Bantam is an open-pollinated, yellow late classic (introduced 1902) with slender ears 5½ to 6½ inches long. The usual late corn grows 7–10 feet tall and has the largest ears of any of the three.

Every seed house carries a good selection of sweet corns—early, mid-season, and late.

Supersweets Selection continues to develop the sweets. Now we also have the "supersweets," which are even sweeter and also hold their sugar for a longer time before changing it to starch. Many of them, however, will lose some of their value if cross-pollinated by another variety. But Shumway's Everlasting Heritage series of sweet corns have the ability to hold their sugar content up to 14 days and despite cross-pollination. But Lane Morgan complains, "A lot of people these days are into the supersweets, but I don't like them personally. I like my corn to taste like corn, and the supersweets taste like a candy bar."

HIGH-LYSINE CORN: This recently developed variety has more lysine, which makes it a nearly complete protein food. Regular corn is short on the amino acid lysine, which is why you eat it together with beans, which are rich in lysine, in order to have a complete protein. High-lysine corn is raised like dent corn and is used mainly for livestock feed, although it could also be a fine field corn for human use. Order from Crow's Hybrid Corn Co., PO Box 157, Kentland, IN 47951.

WAXY MAIZE: This is another new corn, an extra-digestible cornstarch specialist.

OTHER CONSIDERATIONS IN CHOOSING YOUR CORN VARIETY: After you've made your choices from the basic 8 varieties, you'll have the further choice of hybrid or open-pollinated, dwarf or standard size, and disease-resistant or susceptible.

Hybrid vs. Open-Pollinated. Hybrid corn varieties were first developed in the 1930s and are famous for their husky, early productivity, but you can't save the seed and get that marvel to happen again. And because they all have exactly the same genetic makeup, they will ripen basically all at the same time. Lane Morgan defends hybrids: "If you are growing field corn, the money you save can compensate for the lower yield. But when it comes to sweet corn, the flavor is the thing, and the hybrid varieties do deliver. People will need to realize that they won't get the same flavor from the old-time varieties, especially in cooler climates." Well, flavor is a matter of opinion. A more painful pro-hybrid argument is the one that hybrid sweet corns produce twice the yield of open-pollinated ones. That's why so few open-pollinated varieties now survive.

Standard or Dwarf. Almost the only problem with corn as a garden plant is its size. It takes a lot of room for what you get. Some Indian corns and all nonhybrid popcorns are on the small side as corns go, but typical sweet corn stalks grow 5–7 feet tall (some up to 15 feet). Stalks that size should be planted 6–18 inches apart (depending on your variety). You'll harvest only 2 or 3 ears per stalk from all that space. So rather than plant 50 percent of a small-sized garden in corn, consider succession planting or interplanting—or dwarf corn.

Dwarf corn is also ideal if you are gardening in containers. Dwarf sweet corn grows 3 to 4 feet tall, and can be crowded up more than any of the other varieties (4–6 inches apart). But the ears are also significantly dwarfed, half the size of standards. Native American dwarf corns have further value, because they are the species that are best adapted for drought and high-altitude regions. Golden Midget is a good dwarf yellow sweet corn, early and hybrid. It grows 2½ to 3 feet high and bears 4-inch ears, 2 ears per plant, with 8 rows of kernels. The white midget takes longer to mature. Use dwarf corn as you would any sweet corn.

Disease Resistance. Corn is subject to a legion of pests, but there are varieties resistant to many of them. For example, if there is corn bacterial wilt disease in your area, you will want to get a variety that is resistant to it. Early yellow corns are most susceptible. You can get wilt-resistant corn from Burpee, Harris, Stokes, and the Vermont Bean Seed Co.

Planning for Corn

SUNLIGHT: Corn likes a hot summer. Plant where it will get at least 6 hours of good full sunlight a day and preferably more. The hotter your weather, the better your corn will thrive. Corn has a heat-loving tendency because originally it was a tropical plant that thrived only in subtropical or temperate zones during the part of the year when the weather is truly warm. In your planning, also consider what the corn plants will shade. They're usually placed at the north end of the garden to minimize that.

SOIL: Corn will grow on almost any kind of soil. However, in more northern climes it tends to start better in sandy soil because that kind warms up most quickly in the spring. Light, sandy-type soil will germinate corn days or even weeks sooner than would a clay soil. But it will grow fine in heavy, clayey soil too, once it gets warm enough to grow. In light soil, you can plant early varieties of corn; in

heavy soil, it's best to plant late varieties. And in heavy soil, don't plant until the weather is true germinating temperature; otherwise you risk seed that rots before it grows. Corn likes wood ashes or lime too; the best pH for it is 6.0 to 6.8.

FERTILITY: All the corns but popcorn need to have soil containing plenty of green manure, barnyard manure, or dead fish (actually, any decaying substance)! A 1-inch spread of livestock manure is about right. It's best if you get it in there in time to compost and get diffused into the soil. Try to put it in the previous fall before planting, because early-planted seed in contact with manure has a tendency to rot rather than germinate. On the other hand, if you're not antsy to have the earliest corn around, you can fertilize almost any time: green manure planted in the fall and plowed under in the spring, side dressings of manure and mulching during the growing season. Corn is a grain high in nourishment. It pulls that nourishment not only out of the sunshine but also out of the soil. The better nourished the soil, the better your harvest of corn.

Corn Crop Rotations. Avoid planting corn in the same part of the garden or field year after year. That's called "continuous corn." The only way you can get away with that is to really pour the fertilizer—and eventually the insecticides—onto the land, because corn insects will move in there and gradually build strength year after year. The best plant to come before corn in a rotation is some kind of alfalfa or clover. So if you are ready to plow under a hay field, corn is the best grain to plant in that place the next year. A perfect crop rotation is vegetable, wheat, clover, corn, and around again. If this is a big field that you don't want to grow vegetables in, then a good rotation is alfalfa or clover for a couple years, a year of corn, and then a year of wheat or another non-corn grain. In general, figure 2 years of something else, then a year of corn.

SUCCESSION PLANTINGS? MATURING DATES? For sweet corn, we usually plant an early one and then a mid-season or late one (or both). And we also plant some early corn in succession, every 10 days, 2 weeks, or 3 weeks until midsummer. Succession planting especially helps if you are planting hybrid sweet corn, which tends to ripen all at once and needs to be processed while at its peak. Then a growing system that staggers the canning, freezing, or drying really helps. If you plan to sell sweet corn at a truck garden stand, succession planting is also a good idea. On the other hand, if you're planting any other corn but sweet, then it can be left in the field until you get around to it, and it's fine to have 5 acres all ripen at once. Another good type of succession is planting a corn crop after another crop is harvested, like an early corn after peas.

Of Succession Plantings and Weather. Corn needs lots of heat to grow. Sometimes the first part of our summer is chronically wet, cloudy, and cool. The corn will sprout reluctantly, grow a few inches, and then just seem to stand still, as if it's never going to do anything. If cool, rainy, cloudy weather continues day after day, week after week, your corn will scarcely grow no matter what kind you planted—until the long, hot days of sunshine in midsummer come, that is. Then it takes off as if on signal and grows so fast you can practically see the difference from day to day, up and up so fast and high you'll be amazed, and then straight on into making ears. Then suddenly you have loads of sweet corn to be harvested, because corn happens all at once when it does. This behavior can wipe out your best-laid plans of succession planting and planting seeds with varying maturity dates, because with a cool June none of them will grow very fast, but once the sunshine gets going, the late ones will all seem to be hurrying to catch up.

WHEN TO PLANT? Corn is a grass like wheat, rye, and oats, but it's by far the tenderest one. If corn earworm is a problem to you, check with your local extension agent to find out when it comes out in your county. Each summer there is a first and then a second earworm hatch. If you can arrange your corn harvest to take place right in between the 2 hatches, you can save yourself a lot of trouble. And don't plant until danger of frost is over. Plant early varieties from a week before the frost-free date and on, mid-season and late ones 1 to 2 weeks after that date—or later. You need to be concerned about frost not only because a late frost could kill your whole crop, forcing you to replant, but also because germination requires warm soil.

Soil Temperature for Corn Germination. Corn seed won't come up until the temperature down in the soil, where the seed is lying, is at least 55°F in loamy or sandy soil, 60°F in clayey soil. It takes even more warmth than that for a good germination rate: 60–70°F three inches down. You can get a "soil thermometer" and stick it in the ground to find out what the temperature is down there.

Planting and Growing Corn

CORN PLANTING PATTERNS: Unlike the other cereals, all of which can be sown by broadcast, corn seeds should be planted in a designated pattern, at specific intervals or distances, and in separated rows. Corn is planted in those spaced ways no matter how big the field. It's usually put in rows, though some folks hill it.

In Rows. Space your corn rows according to the method of weeding you're going to use. If you plan to rototill out the weeds, make the rows rototiller-width plus a little. Tractor cultivators designed specially for corn can be adjusted to fit row widths of 36–42 inches. Make them that wide. If you're going to cultivate using a horse, the rows have to be 40 inches apart to squeeze the horse between them. If you are going to hoe out the weeds by hand, you could plant as close as 20 inches row to row.

In Hills. To plant old-time style in hills, put 5 or 6 seeds about 1½ inches deep in concentrations 2½ to 3 feet apart each way. Thin out to 3 to 5 stalks per hill. The situation where "hill" planting really pays off is in a very dry area. The native Americans made a water-collecting depression in the ground for each little group of corn plants. It also helps if the soil is unfertile and the hills far apart; the little "hill" family will pollinate each other.

In Wide Rows. Space plants 10 inches apart in each direction in a bed 3 × 6 feet or 3 × 10 feet.

In Containers. If you are growing your corn in tubs or boxes, plant in groups to ensure pollination. Plant directly into your container. Thin to 4-inch spacing.

Interplanted. Or plant as the native Americans traditionally did. Grow the beans with the corn year by year—several pole bean plants or limas next to each stalk of corn. The beans will climb the corn stalks so you won't have to put up poles. In that case, space the corn plants a foot apart. Plant the bean seeds about 6 inches from the corn after the corn has gotten half a foot high. Native Americans sometimes planted squash or melons in the spaces between

corn plants. Plant squash at the same time as the corn. (In that case, cut the corn stalks as soon as the ears are harvested in order to let more sunshine in on the melons.) They sometimes planted quinoa in there too.

THE PLANTING TOOL: You can poke a hole in the ground with your finger or a deer's antler to drop a seed in and then cover it up. There used to be a tool with a hollow point called a "corn planter" or a "jab planter." You poked it into the ground where you wanted to plant, moved a handle, and it dropped your chosen number of kernels from a seed container on the side into the hole. You pulled it out,

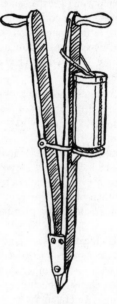

dirt fell around the seed, and it was done. The jab planter was also great for planting corn in hills, replanting, and planting any large seeds such as beans and peas, but it's no longer available new. You can buy a more modern wheel-type row planter that has six seed dispensers for planting more than 20 different vegetables from Lehman's (888-438-5346; **www.Lehmans.com**). You just push it down the rows, and it plants every seed at the correct depth and spacing. For commercial-sized cornfields, there are big horse- or tractor-pulled corn planters. I never have owned any of those; I just keep doing it by hand and am content so doing. But then I don't plant acres.

TRANSPLANTING: In very short season areas, you can start corn indoors in a container as much as 4 weeks ahead, then move to the garden a week or two after your last frost date. Be careful to keep corn roots intact and undisturbed. Transplanting can be hard on corn. But as Lane Morgan, who lives in cold, wet northwestern Washington state, says, "With our often soggy Mays and Junes, sometimes it's transplanted corn or no corn. It actually does pretty well if transplanted to good soil. It sulks a week or two and then takes off."

CORN PLANTING GUIDELINES
1. For every bushel you want to grow, plant a 10 × 50-foot area.
2. You can handle up to 5 acres of corn without fancy machinery if you need it and you're not afraid of work.
3. Make corn rows 24–30 inches apart for short varieties and/or weeding by hoe. Make them 36–40 inches apart for taller varieties and/or rototiller or other mechanical cultivation.

4. You'll need ½ lb. seed to plant every 75 hills, 6 to 8 lb. seed to plant an entire acre; or ¼ lb. to plant each 100-foot row.

5. Plant the seeds 1 inch deep if planting early, 1½ to 2 inches deep for later plantings.

6. Unless you're very short of seed, folks usually plant a seed every 3–4 inches for early or mid-season sweet, dent, or flint corn and every 4–10 inches for late corn. For organically grown field corn, 6–12 inches apart is usual. The pioneers planted 8–15 inches apart because seed was so precious, and they replanted where seeds didn't germinate.

7. On the average, 1 out of 4 seeds won't germinate.

8. Corn seed will keep its germination ability only about 3 years.

9. The plants should break ground in 7–10 days. Thin to 8–10 inches apart for standard plants.

10. You'll harvest an average of 2 ears per corn plant. You can count on an average of 50 ears per 100-foot row, if the plants are 15 inches apart and rows 2½ feet apart.

BIRDS: From planting time until the corn is up a few inches, you may have to deal with hungry birds. Put up a scarecrow. Or lay out strings, cat's cradle style, over your planting; that disturbs them. And find lots of reasons to be in the garden.

THINNING: I hate to thin and throw away a precious corn plant! I'm always so grateful for every stalk that grows. I just try to give them extra-good care, and we do get a fine crop. But many expert gardeners do thin their corn crop.

REPLANTING CORN: Not every kernel will grow. Where plants are missing, you may want to come back through and replant rather than waste the space. Or transplant the plants you've thinned to fill in.

WEEDING: Here also, corn is different from most other grasses and grains. Cultivate right before you plant, and plant late enough so the corn won't just sit there and wait while the weeds grow. Then weed, trying hard to keep out plants that compete with corn (the heavy feeder) for nourishment and water. At first you can cultivate fairly deep and close to the plant—even before it comes up!. But get all your deep cultivating (like rototilling) done while the corn is still young and doesn't yet have a highly developed root system, because if the tiller tears up tender corn roots, it can do more harm than good. Even just knee-high corn has a root system that stretches out about 15 inches, and corn roots grow close under to the ground surface. So when weeding larger corn plants, don't dig down more than 1 to 1½ inches.

A Weeding Schedule. One good plan is to first come through with the tiller 10 days after the corn is up. (Then you can see where the rows are.) Till again two weeks later. After that, don't rototill in there any more, but do the third weeding by hand with a hoe. Hoe shallowly to protect corn's highly developed root system. Another approach is to till only until the corn gets knee-high, or maybe even hip-high. Then stop—unless you're pulling weeds by hand, which is what I do.

"Suckers." These little mini-corn stalks will sprout from the bases of your corn plants. Some books tell you to tear them off, but that's compulsive neatness and can actually harm your yield. In fact, the sucker leaves make more food for the main plant and more cornstalk forage or compost—or whatever you're using the stalks for.

WATERING: Corn needs moisture to germinate, and it needs periodic irrigation or rainfall to grow. When the hot days come and your corn is growing fast, remember that, although corn rejoices in heat, you've got to give it plenty to drink while the heat is on. If not enough rain falls, sprinkle or irrigate regularly; each time, water until the ground is wet at least 4 inches down. If you have the ground mulched, feel underneath for moisture. If the ground feels dry, irrigate. "Silking" means you can see pollen on the tassels atop the corn stalks and silks on the coming ears of corn. This means your corn has entered the pollinating stage. Before and after silking, corn especially needs lots to drink.

SECRETS OF CORN POLLINATION

1. Pollen is made by the "tassel" at the top of the corn plant, the male part. For each kernel, there is one silk, the female "flower" of the plant, which extends from the outside of the husk inside to that particular kernel.

2. Each silk has to be pollinated with a grain of pollen, or it won't complete the process and make its corn kernel. If you've seen an ear of corn in which some kernels weren't there, those are kernels whose silks didn't get pollinated.

3. Corn pollen is carried by wind from where it's made by the tassels down to the silks of nearby plants. If corn is planted only in a single row, you risk the pollen all blowing away without touching a silk. But if there are several short rows of corn next to each other, your chances of thorough pollination are good.

4. For that reason, *block planting is necessary for good pollination*. Whether you plant in rows or hills, plant so you have at least 4 adjacent rows of corn that form a square-shaped corn area rather than 1 super-long row of corn.

5. All corn varieties will cross with all other corn varieties. Broom corn is a sorghum, not a true corn, so it won't cross with corn.

6. Commercial seed growers separate their corn plantings for seed by at least 1,000 feet to prevent cross-fertilizing because a stiff breeze can carry pollen a long way. For home corn-seed production, plant separate varieties at least 250 feet apart, preferably with a building, hedge, or row of trees—or at least a couple rows of sunflowers!—between them. Or choose corn varieties that are far enough apart in maturity dates (at least 2 weeks) that their flowering won't happen at the same time. Or plant different varieties at sufficiently different times that they won't flower together.

7. Corn is different from other garden plants in that cross-pollination can also be a problem for the quality of your harvest this year! The pollen that fertilizes any particular corn silk will influence the nature of the harvested kernel as well as its heredity. This is because corn does a curious thing called "double fertilization" in which the pollen grain becomes the heredity of that kernel—and an identical-twin bit merges to become half the nature of the corn kernel that will develop from that silk. For example, if sweet corn is fertilized by field corn, the kernels will be only half as sweet as they would have been, becoming half like field corn.

8. Unbroken heavy rains during pollination can interfere with or prevent normal fertilization. (Not that we can do anything about the weather . . . but I include this in case it explains what went wrong with your corn.)

DISEASES AND INSECTS: If you plant corn and then discover something else ate part of it before you got your turn, you won't be the first person it ever happened to. Corn has troubles with plant diseases and insects, but 90 percent of the damage is generally in fields of hybrid corn. So plant nonhybrid seed. The next defense is to rotate your corn year after year into different parts of your land. That way, when the corn-eating beasties hatch out and look around for corn, you can at least make them work to find it. Another line of defense is succession planting, because generally one crop will get it the worst and somehow the others will get through much better. It's a matter of the fine timing of beastie life cycles. Against bacterial and fungus problems, the best defense is well-nourished plants, plenty of sunshine, and plenty of water. Against corn borers, it helps to faithfully harvest your corn a little on the early side; then remove each stalk from the garden as fast as you have picked the last ear, and shred or bury all the stalks. If you leave them out in the garden as is, the borers will shelter through the winter in them and emerge even more destructively next year.

But the most common and serious insect problem with corn is the corn earworm, especially in the South. You can endure earworm depredations, which are generally only around the tip of the cob and can be cut away, or you can hand-pick borers and earworms on a reasonable-sized patch of corn. But that's impossible if you have more than an acre or so, and it's a nasty job too. One defense against corn earworm larvae is to cut the silks off close to the ear tip and then compost them safely away from the corn, because it's in the silks that the earworm larvae will be first located. Keep doing that about every 4 days until harvest. Start cutting as soon as pollination is over. You can tell that because the silks dry and turn brown. But when the silks dry is also when the earworms move from eating on the silks to eating on the kernels, so cut the silks off quick enough to catch the critters before they move in.

The most popular way to fend off earworms is to put mineral oil on the corn silks. Mrs. Grimshaw wrote me from Cedar City, UT, that she has used the mineral oil system for years. She wrote, "We have a long-snouted oil can that gets it right into the tip of the ear. One drop to each ear right down to the tip through the silk kills the larvae of the corn worm. It really works!" Some gardeners spray the mineral oil on with a squirt bottle. *Don't squirt mineral oil onto all-green silks because their pollination hasn't been completed, and the oil can interfere with it and cause deformed ears.*

SAVING YOUR OWN SEED: Select the kind of corn you want to grow year after year (not hybrid). Plant and grow it. Choose the best plants and mark them in the field with a strip of cloth. If it's early corn you need, choose the earliest ears. If it's big corn you want, choose from the tallest, thickest stalks with the longest ears. Don't save from just one ear or one plant. That's inbreeding, and it can result in stunting and other bad qualities.

For perfect control of pollination when there are several varieties growing, cover each ear destined to be seed corn with a paper (*not plastic*) bag before it starts showing any silk. Tie the bag closed (replace if it gets rain-or wind-frayed). When you can observe pollen on the tassels, cut off a tassel, take off a bag from an ear *on a different plant,* and rub the silk of that ear with it. Then replace the bag. Keep the bags on until the silks turn brown, which means that

pollination is complete. If you take off the bags, mark the ears some other way to distinguish them from the food ears.

To harvest and store seed corn, choose at least a dozen of the best ears from the best plants. (That prevents inbreeding.) Leave them on the plants at least a month longer than you would for sweet corn harvest. Light frost won't damage dried corn in the field, but hard freezes can kill corn seed, so harvest before they come. Strip back their husks, tie them together with string, and hang the bundle from a ceiling nail. Or hang the ears on strings from a wire. Seed corn is best stored with the ears not touching and with air circulating between them. *Don't shell out the corn from the ears until the cob and kernels are completely hard and dry.* Then you can select even between individual kernels of corn on the ear. For example, you may want to collect only the largest kernels. Store the kernels in a dry, cool, well-ventilated place where they will be safe from rodents.

Viability of Seed Corn. Corn is one of the least hardy grains for survivability in the seed. Alternate freezing and thawing will hurt it. Weather that's too warm and moist can cause grains to sprout prematurely, which uses up the nutrients in the seed. Even with good care, you really can't depend on corn keeping good germination power for more than 5 years. Planting it within 1 year would be best; if that's not possible, try to plant it at least within 2 or 3 years. Whenever you plant it, keep extra seed in reserve. But if disaster does happen, you could still start with only 1 viable seed and have bushels again after only a few years.

Harvesting Sweet Corn

Harvesting traditional sweet corn has the feeling of a rush job from start to finish. It may be as few as 7 to 10 days from the time the first ears are ready to eat until the last ears are in the last stage of maturity and have to be harvested or else. If you're using an open-pollinated or supersweet variety, it may not be such a rush job. It helps that not all the ears get ripe at once. The ones nearest the top of the plant generally ripen first, the lower ones later. So you watch your corn patch for the first ripe ears, then go back through it every day or two while the harvest is on, getting the next ones that are ready.

IS THE SWEET CORN READY? There is one day of absolute perfection in corn ripeness, but you can actually start harvesting and eating several days before it, and continue several days after. How do you know when it is? Well, not by the seed catalog "number of days to maturity," because your local temperatures, soil, rainfall, etc. can change that. You tell by looking. Really underripe corn kernels are small and not very tasty. Really overripe corn kernels are tough and tasteless, and you'll be mad at yourself for having let the golden moment pass you by. In general, your corn will be ready 3 weeks after the tassels begin to shed pollen.

Watch the Silk. A mature corn ear has dark-green husks and dried brown silk. Corn is starting to get dangerously near the overmature stage when the silk gets really dark brown or black. It may feel nice and plump, but it won't stay prime for more than a few more days. If you think the silk looks dried enough, double-check by observing the milk.

Observe the Milk. Pull back a husk a couple inches to see if the kernels have filled out. Puncture a kernel with your thumbnail. The juice that comes out is the corn "milk." Clear juice means the corn is not yet ready. As every day goes on, the milk changes. Some people prefer to gather ears when the milk is still thin and sweet. Some wait until the milk is white and thicker and the kernels are fuller and more mature. The milk is thickening because the sugar in it is gradually changing to starch. The chosen stage is up to you. I think perfect corn should practically squirt out milk when you dent it. Corn that's getting a little overripe will be moist but won't squirt. Really thick, "doughy," and yellow juice means prime harvest time has come and gone.

Uses for Overripe Sweet Corn. You can still get some good out of it. Make cream-style corn (use one of the recipes in this section that contains added ingredients). If your corn is so dry it looks more like popcorn, then follow the instructions for making hominy or cornmeal in the sections on harvesting and eating field corns (dent, flint, popcorn, and Indian corn). Or feed it, stalks and all, to animals.

PLUCKING AN EAR OFF ITS STALK: Twist and snap away the ear with one hand while holding the stalk firmly with the other hand. Be careful not to damage the stalk itself because that will make it hard for the plant to finish up the other ears still in the making.

Preserving or Eating Sweet Corn

Once you have the ears separated from the stalk, don't leave them sitting very long. All fruits and vegetables taste better when garden fresh, but few are in the same class with corn in the rate of deterioration from parent plant to table. Sweet corn on the stalk is literally sweet. But half its sugar becomes starch during a day's storage at 86°F. At a lower storage temperature, the sugar still turns into starch, but not quite so quickly. If you've never tasted anything but store-bought corn on the cob, this has never been an issue with you: all store corn has long since turned to starch, and in the absence of a choice it's good eating. But having gone to the trouble of growing your own sweet corn, it's exciting to taste the real thing.

To best preserve that sweetness, don't remove the corn-husk after picking until your corn is actually being prepared for cooking or preserving. The unhusking hastens that change from sugar to starch. And keep the corn as cool as you can while it is waiting to be worked on. And keep the time span from field to table as short as possible. Don't go out in the morning and pick bushels of corn unless you're sure you're going to be able to spend all day processing it, because if it hangs around on your counter until the next day, it will suffer a real taste loss. Ideally, getting corn from field to canning jar, deep freeze, or drying tray takes less than 3 hours. If you must store it, keep the corn in its husk in the coldest part of your refrigerator short of freezing.

DRYING: You can dry sweet corn, like field corn, on the stalk and on the cob for making cornmeal, hominy, or parched corn. (See "Harvesting Dent, Flint, Popcorn, and Indian Corn.") However, to dry sweet corn in its prime, harvest as near the perfect stage as possible—but on the immature side. Then husk it and blanch it. Blanching sets the "milk" so it isn't runny any more. That way you don't lose it when you cut open the kernels.

Setting the Milk by Boiling or Steaming. Put ears in boiling hot water and leave there just long enough for the water to return to a boil. Or steam by putting the ears in a large kettle that has about 1½ inches of boiling water in the bottom. Stack the corn in there criss-crossed so the steam

can get to it all. Cover and let steam 7 to 10 minutes. Now cool the blanched corn enough so you can start cutting off the kernels.

Cutting Off Kernels. Next you cut the corn off the cob, somewhere between half and three-fourths of the way to the cob. If you don't cut very close to the cob, scrape the remaining corn onto the tops of the corn kernels laid out on your drying trays. When experienced, you'll be able to cut off kernels and roll the cob slightly so that rows of kernels fall onto your drying trays (enamel broiler trays or large cookie sheets or some such) with the cut side up. The rows of corn should be as close together as possible, but don't have the corn more than one row thick up and down, or it won't dry as quickly or be as nice. A corn holder helps. Just hammer a stainless-steel nail through your bread board (or any wooden board). To use, push the stem end of the corn ear down onto the nail where it sticks out of the board. The nail holds the ear in place while you're cutting off kernels. Or use a saw-tooth corn cutter. This tool fits around the ear of corn and removes kernels as you twist and turn it about the cob.

Drying. Dry in a dehydrator at 120°F. In an oven, dry the first 15 minutes at 250°F; then finish drying at 100–140°F. Leave the oven door propped open. After the first 8 to 10 hours, stir once in a while, pushing the outside kernels to the center and the center ones to the outside, since the outside kernels have a tendency to dry first. Be careful to keep the heat down as you get nearer the end. Or you can sun-dry. But it helps if you can dry in the oven 10 or 15 minutes and then finish drying in the sun. You'll need dry, hot weather. Figure about 2 days to finish sun drying, much less if using an oven or dehydrator. Dry till it's brittle and hard. Store in covered glass containers or bags in a cool, dry place.

Cooking Dried Corn. Pour boiling water over your dried corn to start (2 c. water/1 c. dried corn). Then cook on low heat until corn feels tender (about an hour). When the corn is tender, drain off the water, cover the corn with milk, add seasoning, and serve. (To cook corn kernels that have been dried on the ear is different—a much harder, longer project. See "Harvesting Dent, Flint, Popcorn, and Indian Corn.") Then use your reconstituted corn in any corn recipe.

FREEZING WHOLE EARS IN THE HUSK: Whole ears of corn will fill your freezer quickly, but it is possible to freeze them. In fact, freezing the ears in the husk is the quickest, easiest system, and it preserves vitamins the best. Gather the ears. Remove the silks. Then smooth the inner husks back over. Pack the whole, unhusked ears into plastic bags, about 6 per package, and put them in the freezer. No blanching is needed. They'll keep well at least 6 months.

To cook them, thaw just enough to remove the husks. You can hasten that by holding them under cold running water. Then lay in a pan of cold water. Heat to boiling. Boil about a minute. Take off heat. Leave the ears in the hot water 5 minutes more. Then eat. Or you can turn these into kernel corn by letting them thaw enough so you can cut the kernels off the cob.

FREEZING HUSKED EARS: Blanch and then chill them. It helps to have more than one person working at this freezing game, especially with corn. Since corncobs don't fit nicely into colanders, one system is to tie a batch of ears in a dishtowel, suspend it on the end of a stick for blanching, and then dunk it into Ice Waters 1 and 2. Then you can untie and let them out for cutting off the cob. Or sometimes I just dump ears into a big kettle of boiling water. Then when it boils up again, I fish the ears of corn out using two potato mashers, one in each hand. I've seen books that say blanch 6–8 minutes, but that's too long for me. Then I put ears into Ice Water 1, then into Ice Water 2. To freeze ears out of the husk, bag them at this point and put into the freezer.

Whole-Kernel and Cream-Style Corn. "Cream-style" corn means loose kernels cut off the cob. No real cream is involved unless you make the "gourmet" recipe. Each 35 pounds of sweet corn on the husk will yield about 14 to 17 frozen pints of whole-kernel corn. After each ear is blanched and then comes out of Ice Water 2, hold the cob upright on a wooden cutting board, and with a sharp knife cut the kernels away close to the cob. When you have a good-sized pile, bag them up and put the bags of cream-style corn in the freezer. "Whole-kernel corn is cut from the cob at about two-thirds the depth of the kernel, and cream-style corn is cut from the cob at about the center of the kernel and the cob is then scraped." That's from a book, and it's unreal. When I am processing 200 ears of corn, I just grab the ear and whack down wherever the blade may land. Don't scrape it afterwards, but move on to the next. Give the cobs to the pigs. Call it "cream-style" anyway. I freeze all my corn cut from the cob that way.

☙ *GOURMET FROZEN CORN Combine 15 c. freshly cut corn kernels with ½ lb. butter (or margarine), 1 qt. milk (Gertrude Johnson substitutes evaporated milk or light cream), and salt and pepper to taste. Pour into baking pan. Heat thoroughly in 325°F oven, stirring every 15 minutes until the butter is all melted and mixed through. Then cool, divide into your packages, and freeze.*

☙ *VEGAN CREAM-STYLE CORN Measure your freshly cut corn kernels into a pan. For every quart of kernels, add 1 c. boiling water into which 1 T. cornstarch has been stirred. (Salt, pepper, herbs, and pimiento for seasoning are optional.) Heat the mixture to a boil; continue on low heat for 5 minutes (stir enough to prevent scorching!). Now move your pan into a sink of ice water and chill. Package and freeze. To cook, warm in the top of a double boiler.*

PREPARING CUT/FROZEN CORN: I just warm it, drain the water (for the pigs or the gravy), add butter, and serve. If there is leftover corn (which there seldom is), I can make fritters or soup with it or warm it up to serve again. If you freeze all your sweet corn homestyle, you'll sometimes want to serve it in a way besides buttered corn. See "Corn Recipes" below.

CANNING KERNEL CORN: Figure each 8 to 16 ears of corn will yield 2 pt. cut corn. Husk corn ears and remove silks. Wash ears. Then cut the corn off the cob at two-thirds kernel depth without blanching or scraping.

Hot Pack. Add 1 c. hot water for each 1 qt. corn. Heat to boiling. Pack corn loosely into clean, hot jars. Pour enough cooking water over the corn in the jar to cover it, leaving 1 inch headspace. The water you pour on may be plain or salted, up to ½ t. per pint or 1 t. per quart. Put lids on. Pressure-can only—pints 55 minutes, quarts 85 minutes. See the "Altitude Adjustments for Pressure Canning" table for the correct pressure; it's different depending on your altitude and the type of canner you're using.

ALTITUDE ADJUSTMENTS FOR PRESSURE CANNING

	Processing Pressure	
Altitude	Dial Gauge	Weighted Gauge
Under 1,000 feet	11 lb.	10 lb.
1,001–2,000	11 lb.	15 lb.
2,001–4,000	12 lb.	15 lb.
4,001–6,000	13 lb.	15 lb.
6,001–8,000	14 lb.	15 lb.
8,001 or more	15 lb.	15 lb.

Raw Pack. Not much difference. Proceed as above to prepare corn and cut off kernels. Pack kernels into jars without shaking or pressing them down. Add salt if wanted. Pour over enough boiling water to cover. Leave 1 inch headspace. Processing times are the same as for hot pack above.

CANNING CREAM-STYLE CORN: Shuck, remove silk, and wash ears. Cut kernels from cob at half kernel depth. Then scrape remaining corn from cob with table knife.

Hot Pack. Add 1 pt. boiling water for each quart of corn. Heat to boiling. Pack into clean, hot *pint jars only*. (It's not safe to can this in quart jars.) Leave 1 inch headspace. Optionally, add ½ t. salt. Put on lids. Pressure-can only for 85 minutes. See the "Altitude Adjustments for Pressure Canning" table for the correct pressure; it's different depending on your altitude and the type of canner you're using.

Raw Pack. Loosely pack in pint jars only. Add salt and boiling water. Leave 1 inch headspace. Process as for hot pack, except the processing time is 95 minutes instead of 85.

PRESERVING BY SALTING DOWN: Remove the husk and silk, and cook the corn as if you were having it for supper. Cool and cut the kernels off the cobs as if you were going to freeze them. Layer the cut corn into a clean crock, sprinkling salt between the layers. (See "Kraut Making" under "Cabbage" in Chapter 4.) Pour over a salt brine made by using ½ c. pickling salt per 1 gal. water. Add enough liquid to be sure the corn is covered. Cover the crock with a plate, and weight the plate down with something clean (such as a quart jar full of water with a tight lid on it) so that it holds absolutely *all* the corn under the brine. Throw a cloth over the crock's top. If there's a chance the plate won't keep all the corn down, first cover the corn with a cloth that's large enough to extend over the sides of the crock. Then, on top of the cloth, put a board cut to fit or a plate that will fit inside the sides of the crock as closely as possible, right down on top of the corn. Weight the flat thing with a jar filled with water or a boiled rock or some such. Be sure that there is always enough brine to cover the corn. *If the brine is evaporating, add more.* If scum forms, remove it and wash the cloth.

To eat the salted corn, first thoroughly rinse to remove as much of the salt as possible. (The old-timers would leave it in a sieve under running water for a while.) Then eat it straight, or fry in bacon grease, or serve hot and buttered.

SILK/HUSK TEA: Incidentally, you can make a nice "herbal" tea from the broth of corn silk and/or husks. It has a corny flavor. Or you can actually throw them into the soup pot and get some good out of them that way. (Or give to the animals. Or compost.)

CORN RECIPES: Ruth, from Bonaire, wrote me, "We eat our corn on the cob uncooked! In fact, I know many folks who agree with me that it tastes much more satisfying this way. Try it. No salt, butter, or pepper—just tasting the sweetness of the corn." Other folks like to roast corn in its husk: Keep your sweet corn in the husk, soak it in water, and then roast in a pit.

No matter how you cook your ears—boiled or roasted, oven or grill—serve by rolling them in melted butter and eat joyously with your hands, one on each end of the cob. Make sure there is something like a napkin for people to wipe their hands and faces on afterwards.

➷ *BEST CORN ON THE COB For the very best-tasting corn of all, put your water on the boil, go out to pick the corn, run all the way from the field to the kitchen, and husk and cook it! Or for the super-absolute best, don't boil the corn at all—roast it in a 375°F oven for about 15 minutes. (Remove all but the inner layers of husks, take out the silk, and tie the ends of the remaining husk together with string.) Never salt corn until after you are all done cooking, because the salt tends to toughen it. You can roast corn on a grill over coals as well as in the oven. If using a grill, shuck the corn first, lay the ears on the grill, and turn them every so often until roasted on all sides. It will take about 10 minutes.*

➷ *CORN CAKES FROM LEFTOVER ROASTED OR BOILED CORN When you have leftover boiled or roasted ears, split the kernels lengthwise with a sharp knife and scrape the corn from the cobs, leaving the hulls on the cobs. For every 6 ears of corn done this way, combine corn with 3 eggs, add salt and pepper to taste, form into small cakes, and fry to a nice brown.*

➷ *VEGAN CACHAPAS These are Venezuelan corn cakes made from fresh, raw corn. Scrape the corn off the cob and put it through a food mill. Add some pressed-out cane juice (or honey). Add enough flour to give it a thick pancake-batter consistency. Pour out enough for a good-sized pancake onto a lightly shined griddle. (Rub griddle with a cut, raw potato for that; don't use grease.) Don't overcook—they should be very tender and moist when served. From Ruth in Bonaire, who adds, "Cachapas are traditionally served stacked 2-on-a-plate, either plain or with sliced white cheese in between."*

➷ *SUCCOTASH An old-time native American dish, this combination provides a nearly complete protein. Cook together beans (traditionally lima beans) and corn; if you like, add tomatoes, squash, etc.*

➷ *VEGAN CORN Mix corn with curry powder to taste and a squirt of lemon juice. Cook for 5 minutes; don't overcook.*

➷ *VEGAN CORN-STUFFED PEPPERS Mix together uncooked corn kernels, any sort of cooked beans, tomato sauce,* and cumin to taste. Stuff into green peppers or cabbage leaves. Place into a baking dish. Bake for 20 minutes or so with just enough water or tomato juice to keep it moist.

➷ *CORN PUDDING Combine 1 qt. corn off the cob, 2 c. milk, 2 beaten eggs, 1 T. butter, and salt and pepper to taste. Pour into a greased casserole. Sprinkle dried bread crumbs moistened with melted butter (or margarine) over top. Set casserole in low-sided pan of water. Bake at 350°F 45–50 minutes.*

➷ *GERTRUDE JOHNSON'S CORN FRITTERS Combine 1 c. cooked corn, 1 t. baking powder, ⅓ c. flour, 1 egg, a pinch salt, and a dash pepper, plus enough milk to get a thin batter. The thinner the batter, the better the fritters. Fry like a pancake in hot fat.*

➷ *CORN SOUP Boil a beef soup bone in 1 gal. water with salt. Skim. Season. When meat is well done, remove bone. Add corn from 12 ears. Just as corn is tender, add 1 T. butter. Add tomatoes, too, if you like.*

➷ *CREAM OF CORN SOUP Cut corn kernels from 3 ears of corn. Put the cobs into enough water to cover, and cook 30 minutes. Strain and add the corn pulp to the boiling corn water; cook about 15 minutes. If you want to make this from frozen cream-style corn or leftover cooked corn, use 2 c. corn cut from the cob. Now add 2 c. milk and a dash of salt and pepper, thicken with a little white sauce made from butter and flour, and serve.*

➷ *CORN CROQUETTES Melt 4 T. butter. Add 1 c. milk. Separate 2 eggs. Beat whites and yolks lightly. Add yolks to milk mixture, then whites. Add 1 qt. cream-style corn, 1 c. flour, and salt or pepper to taste. Fry one side and then the other in hot oil or lard. Drain and serve right away.*

Harvesting Dent, Flint, Popcorn, and Indian Corn

TIMING: With the varieties of corn that are harvested for popcorn or for making cornmeal or hominy, you have more time than with sweet corn. But timing still matters. The timing of field corn cutting is a delicate balancing of needs; don't cut the stalks (with ears still on them) until the dent kernels are fully dented. Flint kernels should look glazed and be so hard they cannot possibly be indented by pressure of your fingernail. The stalks should look brown and dry. If you cut stalks sooner than that, the ears won't be able to properly mature; they're likely to mold while stored and will act sticky in the grinder. When the ears are ready to be gathered, you'll feel how they crisply break off from the stalks. Wait until this stage to gather ears, whether from standing stalks or shocked ones. A more modern measure is to gather the ears when they are down to 20 percent moisture or less, because with greater moisture they won't store safely. In these modern times, corn is artificially dried at the grain elevator to make sure it's dry enough for good keeping. However, when dried too fast and at too high a temperature, both the germination ability and the nutritional value of the corn can be harmed.

On the other hand, if your weather is cool and rainy, and the weather prediction is for endless more downpours, you really have no choice but to cut the stalks and bring them into some covered place that has good air circulation in order to finish their drying. And freezing and snow don't improve corn still on the stalk. You could just go out all winter, bringing in ears as needed—it's been done that way—but deer and other critters are likely to harvest too, and the longer the stalks stand uncut in the field, the more nutritional value they lose. So people generally prefer to do a systematic harvest once the ears have pulled in all the nutrition they will, and then have those ears stored close to the house or barn when the worst weather rolls in.

Some harvest when the bottom leaves have lost all their color and the top ones some. In the temperate zone, definitely wait until after it has frosted. Some folks wait 4 or 5 weeks after the first fall frost to cut stalks. But climates and needs differ a lot. (Some corn-growing places don't have frost.) With experience, you'll learn what you prefer. Harvesting corn is essentially a two-step process because you're dealing with both the ears and the stalks with their leaves, and each requires a separate process. Which to do first?

Pick Ears First? Or Cut Stalks? You can pluck the ears off the standing stalks first and come along and get the stalks later; or you can cut the stalks, make them into shocks to finish drying, and then harvest from the shock. If you're making silage, you pick ears first. (A friend grows his winter pig feed by planting 3 acres of field corn. He broadcasts seeds by hand, then covers the seed with a tractor pulling a spiketooth harrow, and then makes all that corn into silage.)

Husk Ears First? Or Later? It saves an extra handling if you just husk the ear the moment after you pull it off the stalk and before you throw it into the truck. On the other hand, corn stored in the husk tends to keep better and suffer less insect damage, so wise old-timers usually wait.

Shell Sooner? Or Later? Old-timers shelled off the kernels only when absolutely necessary. They keep better on the cob.

HARVESTING THE STALKS: To make silage, cut as soon as possible, bundle, and carry off for silage cutting. To dry corn for fodder, you can usually leave corn in the field for weeks or even months without heavy loss. If you are planning to just leave the stalks in the field, they still need to be shredded or somehow hastened to a composting end. (A combine with appropriate header and screens would do the job in a short time: pick, husk, and even shell the corn, and shred the stalk and cob and blow the pieces back onto the ground for green manure. Combine when corn moisture is below 30 percent.)

Cutting Stalks. Then come along with a corn knife (also called a "corn hook") and cut stalks at the base, around 4 inches above ground, or else yank them out of the ground. A corn knife has a straight blade, about 1½ feet long. It should be kept very sharp. If you want to cut but don't have a corn knife, use a sickle or whatever you can muster. Or you may prefer the old-time foot cutter for corn, which is a steel blade that straps to your leg at just the right height to cut off the cornstalk with a kick and no bending over! (Available from Lehman's, 888-438-5346; **www.Lehmans.com**.)

Bundling. Different bundlers have different techniques. The most efficient is to cut with one hand and gather in the cut stalk with your other hand until you're holding as many stalks as is comfortable. Then set them carefully down for later tying and shocking and go on cutting. What you do next depends on the style of shock you'll make. Some folks tie every bundle. When they have a bundle of 10 to 20

stalks, they tie them with string or something.

Shocking the Stalks. If your cut corn needs more drying, or if you have no indoor storage space, or if you prefer the corn quality from outdoor drying, shock it—unless your weather will be absolutely too wet for field drying. First make small shocks (use all the corn from about 40 square feet) because your corn will dry better in a smaller shock.

A Simple Shock. Lean 2 bundles head to head and 2 more on each side of them, tipi-style, to start the shock. Then lean 4 more around the outside of those to make the shock stand up and stay put. Some tie only those first few bundles of the shock and then lean armfuls of unbound stalks against the others till they have 15 to 20 bundles in there. Then tie twine or a flexible cornstalk (binder's knot) tightly around the whole thing to hold it together. The trouble with this style of shocking, however, is that it's hard to get it started because it has such a tendency to fall over. That's why the old-timers used a different system.

Old-Time Shock. Start with uncut corn. Stand in the center of where your shock is to be placed. Tie together the tops of *uncut* stalks from 4 different directions in a reasonable approximation of a shock shape. Cut other stalks in the area and lean them into the support already created. As the last step, tie your shock around the middle by twisting one stalk around the others and fixing with a binder's knot.

Tightening a Shock. To tighten a big corn shock, it helps to use a "shock tightener." This is a long enough rope or strap to go around, with a stopper on one end so you can hook it tight for a moment. You throw the rope around the shock, pull it as tight as you possibly can, and hook it. While the shock tightener is holding it, tie with twine. Then undo the tightener and go on to the next.

Sorting and Making the Fodder Shock. Later, maybe in November (wait at least until after the first heavy frost), take the shocks apart and pull the ears off the stalks. The ear corn goes to the crib. Reshock the stalks, which you're probably saving for winter livestock fodder, into a single big "fodder shock." You can leave the fodder shock there for weeks or for the winter. Its outer leaves will shed water and keep the insides as dry as hay in a haystack.

CORN FOR LIVESTOCK FEED

Grazing the Corn. Green cornstalk leaves are good food, but be cautious because animals can bloat on fresh green corn or get diarrhea. Dried corn doesn't carry that risk. So consider grazing it, but introduce it to the animals gradually if it's still green. Sheep can graze in grown corn without harming it much; they'll eat the lower leaves and leave the stalks up. Pigs will push down the stalks and fatten themselves on the corn. Cows will eat the stalks.

Feeding Dried Whole Corn/Stalk Mixes. After the corn dries, you can begin feeding to livestock husked ears, unhusked ears, stalks, or bundles from your fodder shock in the field. Or from storage in the barn, where you can lean cornstalk bundles upright around the walls of the haymow or lay them flat, like logs. To feed barn-stored cornstalks, you toss a dried, stored bundle down to the animals just like hay. Feed sheep, goats, cows, and horses leaves, stalks, ears—on or off the stalk. They'll eat the cob and all. Rabbits will relish ear corn and leaves. For pigs and chickens, you don't have to shell ear corn; they'll eat the kernels off the cob themselves. But pigs, to some extent, and chickens definitely will digest it better with at least a coarse grind.

Corn as Nutrition. Corn is not a complete food for either animals or people. It lacks protein, so both for people and animals it needs to be combined with a legume to complete the protein, and with another grain (or hominy) for the missing niacin. That's why you should mix corn feed with some oats, soybeans, or wheat—especially soybeans (your protein). The usual proportions are two-thirds corn and one-third a mix of oats (or some other grain) and soybeans. Chickens will thrive on a similar mix, choosing it over the commercial stuff.

Shredded, Ground Corn/Stalks. If you have a shredder, after drying in the field and bringing in the crop, you have the option to shred stalks, ears, and all; and bag, store, and feed like that. But if you separate out the ears, shell off the kernels, and grind those separately to a cornmeal consistency, your pigs and chickens will be able to get more nutritional value.

Non-Feed Uses for Stalks. If you feed your animals stalks and all, they'll leave what they don't want to eat. That material makes good bedding for them. If you don't have stock to feed, or need the green manure, shred and compost the cornstalks or just spread them like manure. If you have a big plow or disc, use it to work the stalks and roots back into the soil with them. There are giant varieties of corn whose stalks have traditionally been used by the native peoples in Central America (particularly Guatemala) to make fences and house walls. Bundles of stalks make good insulation for animal quarters. Just lean bundles around the inside or outside walls. The denser you pack them, the warmer your beasts will be. Florence Merrifield wrote me about seeing, on the bus to Guadalajara, three horses being led, each laden with a load of cornstalks stacked as high as the horse was tall. She said, "From the side all you could see were legs and a moving stack."

HARVESTING CORN EARS: Another way to proceed is to let the ears dry on standing corn and then pick them and deal with the cornstalks afterward and separately. Just come out with your wheelbarrow or pickup, tear the ears off the stalks (either standing or shocked), and throw them in one at a time. It takes a good picker 8 hours or so to gather the ears from an acre of corn.

Corn Gleaning. If you live in commercial corn-growing areas, you can help harvest fields you never planted by getting permission to glean the left-behind ears after the corn-picking machine is finished. If a farmer has used a corn sheller to harvest his fields, there won't be enough left to bother, but a cornpicker is kinder to the gleaner; it leaves more behind. The best places to hunt are at the ends of rows, on the ground, and in the places where the corn-picker first entered the field. You can also glean cornstalks by asking neighbors if they want theirs. Some will be glad to have the stalks go away without any effort on their part or willing to help you gather winter feed for your animals.

Corn Ears Under Cover. Put ears into an airy place to finish drying. Though it's best if the field corns dry completely on the stalk before you harvest them, ears that aren't dry enough to store safely can be carried on through to the necessary dryness inside your oven, or stacked over a pilot light, or piled near your wood cookstove or heater. Then store them husked in gunnysacks in a dry shed or room. Or, if you are having trouble drying your corn, peel back the husk to the butt of the corn and tie together bunches of

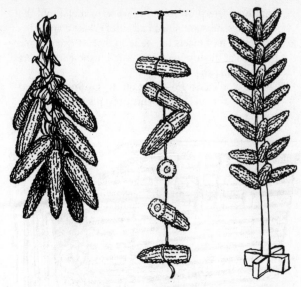

husks. Then hang up the corn bunches for about a month. (Hanging is rodent-proof.) If all that husk gets in the way, pull off all but a few of the inner husks, leaving those attached. Then tie together or French braid the ears by those remaining husks, with a new ear added on for each twist. Hang them on wires or poles or walls. You can braid a bushel of corn into one string. Or put them in net onion bags or nylon panty hose and hang up to dry. It's traditional to hang popcorn, corn for parching, and seed corn. You could hang corn for cornmeal, hominy, and livestock food too, but it's far more efficient to use a corn crib for larger quantities.

The Corn Crib. But if you have a large amount of corn to store, or just want more convenience, put it in a corn crib. A corn crib is an outdoor storage space for ears of corn. The crib's design allows the corn to finish drying inside it and keeps any objectionable amount of rain or snow from getting at it. (A long spell of rainy weather puts it to the greatest test.)

BUILDING A CORN CRIB: Ear corn is safe to crib when moisture's down to 20 percent or less. In cold weather, corn will store safely at higher moistures. Corn will keep as long as a year in a crib. Each cubic foot of crib space will store ⅖ bushel of corn. If your crib is rectangular, you can compute bushels of corn by multiplying length × width × height and then dividing the answer by 2½ (or multiplying by 0.4).

1. Build a rectangular box standing by itself rather than next to another building. It must not be more than 4 feet wide at the base. A wider crib wouldn't have air circulation good enough to keep the corn inside from molding. Typical crib dimensions would be 4 feet wide, 6 feet long, and 6 feet high. That size of crib would hold 75 bushels.

2. Make the walls of wire mesh or boards. If boards, they must have cracks 1 to 2 inches wide between them. The spaces are to let enough air in and out of the crib to dry the ears, but note that cracks wider than 1 inch admit English sparrows and other birds. (To totally prevent bird robbing, staple a wire mesh over all the openings.) Boards can be almost any width in the 2- to 6-inch range.

3. Build walls that steadily slant slightly outward from the bottom up to where they meet the roof. This makes rain less likely to get into the crib.

4. Supply a waterproof, slanting wood or metal roof that overhangs substantially on all sides. Make a space where the roof meets the walls so that air can get into the corn at the top to compensate for the width there being greater than 4 feet.
5. Set the whole crib 1½–3 feet off the ground on wood, concrete, or metal "legs." This prevents critters from coming in.

6. Make the legs vermin-proof by giving them circular overhangs (toadstool-shape), which vermin can't crawl up over. A leg with an upside-down plate on top of it, or any comparable arrangement, accomplishes the same thing. An alternative way to keep out rodents is to place a sheet of tin over the supports and under the crib. The sheet should be wider than the crib and support stones so vermin cannot crawl up over it.
7. The crib has a door or opening in one end through which you can load and unload. There is a traditional tool for unloading called a "corn drag," a rake with 4 tines, all of them almost pitchfork-length. It's useful because cribbed corn gets settled in the crib and needs to be literally dragged out.

THE HUSKING: The ear of corn is sheathed in leaflike tight wraparounds called "husks." Another term for the husk is the "shuck," so "shucking corn" is the same as husking it. Different varieties have different kinds of husks, some of them worse than others to peel off. Husking can be done in the field before you cut and shock. Or later—whenever—you can take apart a shock, get the ears out, put the shock back together until needed for livestock feed, and take the ears to husk. Or you can eventually store the shocks in the barn and husk at leisure. Or the ears can be stored unhusked in the crib until you need them or are ready to husk. There isn't any single right way. Husking is work, but it can also be fun, a good time to have friends over, tell stories, eat good food, and give thanks for the harvest—a "husking bee."

Husking Tools. John H., Moscow, ID, told me: "I remember sitting around with mounds of corn beside us and throwing the husked ear out in the middle of the floor, and each person had their own cornhusking tool." A cornhusking tool helps when you have hundreds of ears to peel. Native Americans first invented the "husking peg." It's a round, smooth, pointed object 3–4 inches long and ½ inch wide

with an attached leather thong to hold it on the fingers. The purpose is to tear the husk loose using just one quick jerk down. Originally of antler, bone, or wood, husking pegs are now made of steel, leather bands, and leather straps to fit over gloves that protect your fingers. (Three different styles are available from Lehman's, P.O. Box 41, Kidron, OH 44636, (216) 857-5441, catalog $2.) Otherwise too much husking can cause blisters and misery.

Uses for Husks. The inner husks are different from the outer ones—more thin, tough, and paperlike. Cornhusks don't split like regular leaves. Even after drying, you can moisten the inner husks, and they will be flexible and strong again. You can pull off, bundle, and store husks till needed. Use to wrap tamales, or shred husks to make a stuffing material for mattresses and cushions. You can moisten husks; tear them into strips; and braid, weave, or twist those strips into ropes, mats, baskets, or dolls. Husks were used by ancient native Americans to wrap articles (just as we do with paper). You can also soak them in hot water and make a pleasant tea.

Making an Old-Time Cornhusk Bed. The husks need to be slit. Drive a few large nails through a board, file the nails sharp at the point, and then pull the husks across the nails to slit them into shreds an inch or less wide. Or use an old carving fork for this. Then put the shreds out to dry in an attic or the loft of an outbuilding. If you have enough husks to be picky, reject the weatherworn outer ones and take only the thin, papery inner ones. When a sufficient amount has been prepared, buy your ticking. That should be a heavy, very tough twill ticking weave made especially for making pillows and mattresses. Fill the tick as desired. The fuller it is of shredded cornhusks, the stiffer it will be. The husk mattress is not washable, but the outer tick can be taken off and washed, and the husks sunned and then sewn back into the tick.

SHELLING: There are some South American corn varieties with loosely attached kernels. You can shell those by just holding them up and shaking over a container. But our kinds are more work. When the corn is really dry, you can shell all the ears at once or you can shell them a few at a time on winter evenings. (If the corn isn't dry enough, it won't shell easily.) Push on the dry kernels with your thumb or thumbs, and the kernels will just pop right off the cob. Too much of that, though, and you'll end up with blistered fingers! Or scrape the ears on a stick, bone, or any firm metal edge.

Beating Bag. In old Yucatan, corn was shelled using a long, loosely woven mesh bag. The bag was hung hammock-style between two trees. One end of the bag was arranged lower than the other. The workers put the ears of dried corn into the higher end of the bag. Three workers hit the bag with sticks in rapid sequence, over and over. The shelled corn fell out the mesh holes into containers waiting underneath. The cobs worked their way down and out the lower end of the bag, where 3 other workers checked the cobs. Ones that still had grains of corn attached were put back into the high end of the beating bag. Periodically, the two teams switched jobs.

Corn Shellers. You can buy a "hand corn sheller" from Lehman's, Box 41, Kidron, OH 44635. It's a round metal ring that slips over the cob to shell it. The C. S. Bell Co. sells a mechanical corn sheller to process big amounts (**www.csbell.com**). Or you can get a small electric one, or a big tractor-powered one.

Uses for Corncobs. They make nice children's play-things—building logs and such. When added to a fireplace fire, they make a bright light. They can be used for smoking hams and bacon instead of apple and other hard woods. They can be used like firewood. They have a traditional use as toilet "paper" for the outhouse. Native Americans made them into bottles by hollowing the center and making a stopper for each end.

☙ *CORNCOB JELLY* *Break 12 corncobs into small pieces. Boil in 3 pt. water for 30 minutes. Then strain. To 3 cups corn juice, add the juice of 1 lemon and a box of commercial pectin. Bring to a boil. Add 3 c. sugar and boil 3 minutes longer. Pour into jars and seal.*

WINNOWING: If you have chaff, pour the corn from one pan to another to get rid of it.

STORING THE DRIED KERNELS: Put kernels into tightly lidded containers and store in a cool, dry place. The drier your shelled corn, the better it stores: 13 percent or less moisture is safe. But you can't use corn dried above 110°F for seed—it won't germinate well. It's okay for animal feed and grinding, though, even when dried at 180–200°F.

GRINDING CORN: After the corn kernels are really hard and dry, you can put them through your grinder. For cereal, grind to medium coarseness and stop. One cup dried corn makes about ¾ c. cornmeal. Home-ground cornmeal is a little coarser than commercial cornmeal. Keep it in the refrigerator, if you have one, and use it within a reasonable period of time. Warmth is what's hard on your cornmeal—and the fact that it will absorb odors.

Eating Dent, Flint, Popcorn, and Indian Corn

You could be in terrible shape for money and still make it if you had some dried corn. Your shoes might get holes; you could stuff cornhusks in the bottoms. You could shell off the corn and burn the cobs for warmth. And you could eat the corn with water if you don't have anything else. The exact recipe you make depends on how much water you add. If you add just a little water to your cornmeal, you make a kind of corn bread. If you add somewhat more, you've got cornmeal gruel. For variety you could make hominy from wood ashes, water, and corn; but if you've truly got a food shortage, don't do that because you lose some nutritional value. If you have some fat of any sort, you have shortening to add to your bread. Some dried fruit, honey, or maple syrup gives you an Indian pudding. Add beans and you've got succotash. Add meat and you have a stew. You can tell I'm a corn lover!

☙ *COOKING WHOLE, DRIED, SHELLED CORN KERNELS* *Pour boiling water over the kernels. Let soak overnight. Then cook on low heat 4 to 5 hours.*

PARCHED CORN: Parched corn looks like the inside part popped or expanded inside the tough hide of the kernel. Each kernel will about double in size when parched. Sue Windover, Holland, MI, wrote me, "During World War II, my great-aunt and uncle ran a small gas station in Fryan, Ohio. They were unable to buy peanuts for their nut dispenser. So my aunt made parched corn to use instead. It was so popular, they continued even after peanuts were again available." Ruth Kellogg, Elk City, ID, wrote me that parched corn was a trail food to native

Americans and trail blazers of the old West. The following recipes combine their pieces of advice. For each of them, start with field-dried ears of corn. Husk and then pry off the kernels. Don't cut, because you want the kernels intact.

☙ *OVEN-PARCHING* *Put kernels in a hot oven in one layer on a cookie sheet, stirring until they are brown and crunchy. After they are baked, add just enough oil so some salt will stick. (Without the oil, the parched corn will keep forever, if you could keep people from eating it!)*

☙ *FRY-PARCHING* *Heat about 2 t. lard in a covered heavy pot. Pour in a handful of corn kernels. Cook over medium-high heat, covered. When the popping is completed, drain on a towel. Sprinkle with salt and serve.*

☙ *CRISPY CORN* *Moisten ½ c. cornmeal in ½ c. cool water. Add 1 t. salt to 2½ c. of boiling water. Now gradually stir the cornmeal mix into the hot water. Cook over medium heat, constantly stirring, until thick. Now shift to very low heat, cover the mush, and cook another half hour, stirring once in a while. In the meantime, prepare drying trays by covering them with plastic. After the cornmeal is cooked, drop it onto the covered tray, a dollop (scant teaspoonful) at a time. Spread each crisp dollop out quite thin (press with back of a spoon that has been dipped in water). Don't let one crisp touch another. Place in hot sunshine to dry. After about 6 hours, you can peel away the plastic. Turn each crisp upside down and set directly on the tray. Continue drying until fully dry and brittle. To dry these in an oven or mechanical dryer, heat at 150°F.*

CORNMEAL AND WATER BREADS

☙ *HOECAKES* *These are also called pone, flatbread, or Johnnycakes. Moisten 2 c. cornmeal with ½ c. cool water. Heat 2 c. salted-to-taste water to boiling. Add about 3 T. shortening to the water (if you have it and want to use it). Combine the cornmeal and boiling water, stirring constantly. Let stand, covered, until it cools down enough to work with. Now form into your shapes for cooking. Lay your dozen or so hoecakes on a greased pan to bake. There's a specially shaped iron baking pan that you can buy to bake these in, or you can bake them in a greased iron frying pan. Takes a little over half an hour in a 350°F oven. It takes some work to eat because it isn't flabby soft. (It helps to serve with melted butter or hot gravy poured over.)*

☙ *CORN DODGERS* *Make salted cornmeal and water dough as above. Wrap a sizable chunk in wet cornhusks. Press into a flat form. The pioneers baked these in the hot coals and ashes, but you can do it in an oven.*

CORNMEAL BREADS

These have more ingredients than just cornmeal and water, and they are even better tasting and more nourishing for you.

☙ *CORNMEAL WAFFLES* *Pour 1½ c. boiling water over 1 c. cornmeal. Add ¼ c. melted butter. Stir in 1½ c. buttermilk. Separate 2 eggs and stir in the yolks. Sift 1 c. flour with 1½ t. baking soda and ½ t. salt. Blend dry ingredients with cornmeal mixture. Beat the 2 egg whites you have waiting and fold them into batter. Bake in your waffle iron until crisp and brown. Very light.*

☙ *CORN/WHEAT BREAD* *Combine 1 c. cornmeal, 1 c. home-ground (or whole) wheat flour, ½ t. salt, and 1 T. bak-*

ing powder in a bowl. In another bowl stir together 1 egg, ½ c. honey, and 1 c. milk. Pour the liquid ingredients into the dry ones and stir together. Add 2 T. melted butter (or lard). (Betty Gehrke, Montesano, WA, wrote me, "I didn't add the melted butter and they were real good anyway. Makes me wonder what the fat in a recipe does but add calories.") Stir a moment more, but don't overstir, because you don't want to stir your bubbles out. Pour into a greased 8-inch square baking pan. Bake at 425°F about 25 minutes.

❧ VEGAN CORN/WHEAT BREAD Another recipe from Ruth in Bonaire: Combine 1 c. cornmeal, 1 c. whole wheat flour, 3 t. baking powder, and 1 t. of cinnamon or ½ t. chili powder along with a pinch of oregano. Mix. Stir 1 T. honey into 1½ c. warm water. Now stir the honey/water mix into the dry ingredients until just mixed. Bake in a nonstick pan about 20 minutes at 375°F or so.

❧ CORN GEMS Maybe you've seen old-time cast-iron gem pans in your favorite hardware store, and maybe you've wondered what you're supposed to bake in those peculiarly shaped spaces. Well, here is an old-time corn gem recipe. (If you don't have gem pans, just use a regular muffin pan!) Follow the Corn/Wheat Bread recipe above except use 2 eggs instead of one, and 2 t. baking powder instead of 1 T. Preheat your gem pans, grease them, and pour in the batter. The muffins will take about 15 minutes to bake in a 400°F oven. You can make oatmeal and whole wheat gems, too.

❧ SOUTHERN SPOON BREAD Mrs. Donald E. Woodliff, Petersburg, TN, who likes to grind her own cornmeal, wrote me, "One of our favorite recipes is this one for Southern Spoon Bread. Scald 2 c. milk. Add ½ c. cornmeal. Cook together until thick. Add 1 t. salt, ½ t. baking powder, 2 T. sugar, and 2 T. melted butter. Beat the yolks of 3 separated eggs and add to cornmeal mixture. Let it cool a few minutes while you are beating the 3 egg whites to soft peaks, and then fold the beaten egg whites into your batter. Pour into a well-buttered 1½ qt. casserole. Bake at 375°F 30–45 minutes, or until golden brown and puffed like a souffle. A refreshing substitute for either a bread or vegetable."

❧ REAL SOUTHERN HUSH PUPPIES WITH WHITE CORN-MEAL Mrs. Phil R. Cahoon, Citrus Heights, CA, wrote me, "Hush puppies are a bread all true Southerners eat with fish. First you fry a big mess of fish. (A 'mess' means enough to feed everyone that's there and any more that may show up.) Fry fish dipped in cornmeal in deep fat, then drain. Hush puppies are always, I must repeat, always, fried in the fish grease, after the fish; otherwise you would just have fried corn bread. Make as many as you have people, but the recipe should serve 5 or 6 people.

Combine 2 c. white cornmeal, ½ c. flour, ½ t. salt, ½ t. soda, ½ t. baking powder, 1 c. chopped onion. and 1 egg in a bowl. Add enough buttermilk to make a batter, not too thin!

Drop by tablespoonfuls in the hot fish grease. The hush puppies will be a golden brown when done. Turn as needed to brown evenly."

Another friend wrote me, "Those things are best thrown to the dogs to get them to shut up . . . 'Hush Puppies!'"

❧ NO-FISH HUSH PUPPIES Mrs. Edna Chavez, Cypress, CA, wrote me about a goof in one of my cracker recipes and sent me this one while she was at it. "Some people think you must have fish with hush puppies, but I make them for after-school snacks: 1 c. cornmeal, 1 c. flour, a dash of salt, ½ t. soda, and 1 egg. Add as much chopped onion as you like. We like lots. Mix all together with enough milk to make a very stiff dough. Drop by teaspoonfuls into hot oil. Fry on one side. Turn to brown the other side, then drain. They taste a lot like onion rings. We love them."

Using Leftover Corn Bread

❧ SOUR MILK CORN BREAD PUDDING Crumble 1 c. (more or less) of dried corn bread crumbs. Soak them in 2 c. sour milk for about a half hour. Add 1 beaten egg, ½ c. raisins, ½ t. soda, and ¼ t. cinnamon, and bake at 325°F until it begins to set. Then spread 4 T. molasses over the top and bake until a firm crust has formed.

❧ PUDDING FROM LEFTOVER CORN BREAD Crumble enough leftover corn bread to measure 1 cup. Add 2 c. milk and 2 egg yolks. Gently fold in 2 beaten egg whites. Bake slowly in a dish set in a pan of hot water for about 1 hour. Optionally, sweeten with molasses or sugar. Or add currants or raisins.

❧ CORN BREAD STUFFING Combine 4 c. crumbled corn bread with 4 c. crumbled white bread (or brown), 1 medium onion, chopped, 1 t. sage or poultry dressing, salt and pepper to taste, and the broth from your cooked giblets. Moisten with more broth or milk as needed. This is enough stuffing for a 10-lb. turkey. If you are stuffing a chicken, cut the recipe in half.

CORNMEAL MUSH: The easiest way to make cornmeal mush is to mix your cornmeal with enough cold water to thoroughly moisten it, and then add it to boiling water a bit at a time, stirring constantly. Or if you have a very quick arm, you could just sprinkle the cornmeal, stirring constantly, into rapidly boiling water. If you don't get it mixed very fast, it has a tendency to lump. Salt to taste. It will cook in half the time over direct heat, but you'll have to be careful to prevent scorching or sticking, so if you have time, make it in a double boiler. Figure 30 minutes over direct heat or 1 hour in the double boiler. (The exact amount of time will be unique for your particular variety of corn and grind of cornmeal.) You can hurry it some by soaking it overnight. The same applies to grits and hominy. Cook them in the same water in which they were soaked. About 3 c. water should be right for each ½ c. cornmeal; that includes the cold water you use to moisten it. Mush is done when the spoon can stand up straight by itself. Don't be afraid to make a lot of cornmeal mush because there are good uses for the leftovers.

❧ ITALIAN POLENTA Cook your cornmeal in chicken broth. Serve with butter and grated cheese on top and meat on the side.

❧ WHAT TO DO WITH LEFTOVER CORNMEAL MUSH If you are going to make fried mush, just be sure to get your leftover cornmeal mush poured into another pan before it gets cold. It has to be still hot to pour right into the loaf pan. Smooth the surface after pouring. Use a pan of such size that the mush will be about 2 inches deep. Optionally, break up your leftover bacon and add it to the leftover corn mush before pouring it into a pan to set. Let cool until firm. When you are ready to fry your mush (for breakfast the next morning, maybe, or for lunch the next day), turn the cornmeal out of the mold or cut ¾-inch slices and lift them out. Then follow one of these recipes!

🍃 **CLASSIC FRIED LEFTOVER CORNMEAL MUSH** Fry your slices in a little oil as is — first one side, then the other. Or first roll them in flour until dry, and then fry. Or roll in flour and then beaten egg, or in egg and then crumbs, or in flour and then egg and then crumbs! And then fry. Fry in some oil or butter over a medium-to-hot heat, turning once, just long enough to heat through and put a nice brown crust on the outside. Serve with syrup and butter.

🍃 **SPOON-FRIED MUSH** Owa Malone, Portland, OR, wrote me about a recipe failure. (I am so glad when someone writes to tell me a recipe is bad. That way I can fix it in the next edition!) She also said, "I wanted to share with you my Missouri mother's way of making fried mush. She cooked it the same as any mush, but instead of chilling, molding, and slicing for frying, she just dropped large spoonfuls of the fresh mush into hot fat and fried it until brown and crisp."

🍃 **FRIED MUSH AND BACON** Fry your bacon until done. Remove it from pan, but put it someplace where it will keep warm. Dip your cold cornmeal mush slices into flour, egg, and crumbs. Fry in the hot bacon fat until brown and crisp on both sides. Drain on absorbent paper or cloth and serve with the bacon.

🍃 **CREAMY LEFTOVER MUSH** Slice the set mush into slices 1 inch thick, then make cubes about 1 inch square. Put the cubes into cereal bowls. Pour hot rich milk or cream over the cubes. Let the dishes stand in a warm place (like your warming oven—or the microwave) until the cornmeal is heated through; then serve. Or slice the cold cornmeal mush thin, brush each slice with thick sweet cream, and brown in a medium oven until heated through.

🍃 **VEGAN LEFTOVER MUSH** Use above recipe, but substitute applesauce for the milk or cream. My editor says I've got too many cornmeal mush recipes. Is she right? Maybe other people just don't relate to cornmeal mush as positively as I do . . . I stubbornly left them all in. Well, here's something more highly developed of the cornmeal sort . . .

🍃 **POLENTA PIZZA** From Ruth of Bonaire. "Combine 1 c. cornmeal, 1 c. cold water, and 1 t. salt. Stir that mix vigorously into 2 c. boiling water and keep stirring as it cooks (about 5 minutes) till thick. Remove from heat. Add ⅓ c. grated parmesan cheese. Then take a spoonful of it out, beat that with 1 egg, and then beat it back into the cornmeal for 1 minute. Let stand to cool. Then use wet hands and spatula to press into a thick crust in a buttered 9-inch pie plate. Now let it stand several hours to get fairly dry. Then bake for 45 minutes at 350°F. (Brush with oil after 30 minutes of baking.) For topping, saute ½ c. each minced green pepper and onion and season it with oregano and black pepper. Sprinkle 1 c. grated cheese onto your hot baked cornmeal crust. Spread pepper and onion over this. Arrange a sliced tomato over

that. Top with another ½ c. grated cheese. Broil until bubbly. Serve immediately."

CORN PUDDINGS

🍃 **OLD-TIME MOLASSES OR "INDIAN" PUDDING** Heat 2 c. milk in the top of a double boiler. Pour ¼ c. cornmeal into ½ c. cold milk and stir until mixed. Then add the mixture of cornmeal and cold milk gradually to the hot milk, stirring constantly. Cook 15 minutes more, stirring occasionally. Add 2 T. butter, ½ c. molasses, cinnamon, and ginger to taste. Add another 1½ c. milk. Pour into baking dish and bake in a slow (250°F) oven about 3 hours.

🍃 **VEGAN RAISIN/RICE CORN PUDDING** Combine 1 c. cornmeal and ½ c. (cold) cooked rice. Soak ⅓ c. raisins in boiling water; then drain and chop. Add to cornmeal with 2 c. boiling water (or less) and 1½ rounded t. baking powder. Bake in ungreased dish at 350°F until center is firm.

COOKING WITH CORN FLOUR: Corn grain ground to a flour consistency is "cornstarch." It's useful for thickening gravies and sauces same as you would with wheat flour. However, cornstarch, if overcooked, can thin out again.

HOMINY: Flint corn, other field corns, Indian corn, and any hard corn will make hominy. You are ready to use a hominy recipe once you have dried and shelled your corn. Hominy-making time of year here is about October. Choose a soda, lye, or lime method. Lye cuts the outside husk best, but you have to do a lot more rinsing. *If using lye, see the warnings and first aid treatments for lye burns under "Soap Making" in Chapter 8.* Incidentally, you can make a sort of hominy from shelled wheat using these same recipes. No matter which recipe you decide to use, read the first one for general orientation, since it has a lot of hints I don't repeat afterwards.

Why bother making hominy? Well, if you have lots of good food, there's no need. But after corn traveled from the Americas to Europe and Africa and became standard fare for poor people, epidemics of pellagra, a disease caused by niacin deficiency, followed. The native Americans never got pellegra because they made part of their corn into hominy through an alkaline process that just happened to release the corn's niacin content in a way that regular cooking could not. (They also regularly combined corn with beans, not only growing but also eating them together. Beans supply the 2 nutritional elements missing in regular corn—tryptophan and niacin. In China, rice and soybeans are traditionally combined for the same result; in India, wheat and lentils, or wheat and split peas.)

By the way, if you like hominy and grits, you'd love the *Good Old Grits Cookbook* by Bill Neal and David Perry. It is a huge collection of lore and recipes—even how to get mail-order grits! Available from Eureka Resource, P.O. Box 53565, San Jose, CA 95153.

Boiled Soda Method Hominy. For each 2 gal. shelled corn, use ⅓ c. baking soda and 1 gal. water. Make sure you have enough liquid to cover your corn kernels with at least 2 inches over. Remember each grain will puff up to 3 or 4 times the dried size, so allow for expansion. Use a big pan like a 5-gal. granite (enamel ware) canner or an iron kettle. *Don't use aluminum, copper, tin, or zinc.* Optional: Let soak overnight before commencing to boil. Now boil corn heavily about 2 hours—until you can feel the hulls slip off when you pick up the corn in your fingers. While boiling, keep covered. Add more water if needed.

This is the ticklish thing: The hulls are too coarse to eat and have to come off, but when the hulls slip, there is nothing to protect the corn from the soda water. So drain the soda water off before the hulls come off so the soda won't leach out all the good stuff in the corn. Replace the soda water with fresh water. Now it increases in volume. Change the water at least one more time, more if you like. When the corn has doubled in bulk, wash it very hard in a continuous flow of water in a dishpan or colander, rubbing it with your hands to let out the hulls. (Beware of clogging the sink!) Don't worry about the black spot at the bottom of the kernel. It's just the end of the germ showing.

Pour fresh water over the corn and cook again. You could add salt and sweetening at this time, or wait to do that until serving time. Add salt to taste, and maybe 2 heaping tablespoons of sugar or honey for sweetening. Cook until you can comfortably chew the kernels. It will be done after about 4 hours of boiling. Cool. Drain.

Freezing, Drying, or Canning Hominy. To freeze, now's the time. Just package and freeze. (To use frozen hominy, just thaw it in water; then drain off the water and continue by your favorite hominy recipe.) To dry hominy, drain thoroughly and follow directions for beans. To can, boil freshly made hominy until it is almost tender. To hot pack, pack into clean, hot *pint jars only*. (Not safe to can this in quart jars.) Add enough liquid from cooking to cover hominy, but leave 1 inch headspace. Optionally, add ½ t. salt. Put on lids. Pressure-can only, for 95 minutes. See the "Altitude Adjustments for Pressure Canning" table for the correct pressure; it's different depending on your altitude and the type of canner you're using.

ALTITUDE ADJUSTMENTS FOR PRESSURE CANNING

	Processing Pressure	
Altitude	Dial Gauge	Weighted Gauge
Under 1,000 feet	11 lb.	10 lb.
1,001–2,000	11 lb.	15 lb.
2,001–4,000	12 lb.	15 lb.
4,001–6,000	13 lb.	15 lb.
6,001–8,000	14 lb.	15 lb.
8,001 or more	15 lb.	15 lb.

Other Ways to Make Hominy

➤ **UNBOILED SODA-METHOD HOMINY** In a crock or a large good-quality plastic can, put corn to soak in soda water. Use 4 level T. baking soda per 1 gal. water. Keep covered in a cool place. Test every day to see if the hulls are ready to come off. They usually take more than a week. When the hulls are loosened, wash them away under plenty of running water. This hominy can be stored in a solution of 1 c. pickling salt per 1 gal. water until wanted. Then rinse and soak in fresh water, changing water several times.

➤ **LIME HOMINY** Dissolve 2 heaping T. powdered lime in 4 qt. water. Add 2 qt. corn. Stir. Set on low heat. Cook until hulls loosen. Drain and rinse several times with cold water while rubbing hulls off. Rinse until water comes out clear and all lime is gone.

➤ **BOUGHTEN LYE HOMINY** Dissolve 4 T. lye in 2 gal. cold water. (One level tablespoon lye equals ½ oz.) Keep your spoon dry! Add 2 qt. corn and boil a half hour. Take off

the heat and let the corn soak in the solution about another 20 minutes. Skim out the corn and commence rinsing and working to get the hulls off. When the hulls are all off (and the dark kernel tips removed if you want), cover the hominy with fresh water and bring to a boil. Then change water and bring to a boil again, and so on at least 4 times. Then cook in a final water until the hominy is tender.

Recipes for Using Hominy

➤ **PLAIN BUTTERED HOMINY** Rinse and soak overnight in fresh water 1 c. or more of your hominy. Next day cover it with water, put a loose lid on the pan, and and boil it until all the water has evaporated. Stop before the hominy burns! Now stir in a little butter and serve. This is a traditional dish in South America, where corn and hominy came from.

➤ **HOMINY, BACON, AND EGGS** Mrs. H.J. Clough of Long Beach, CA, is a hominy lover and sent me this recipe: Boil several cups of hominy until tender. Fry 4 slices of bacon per person. Drain off bacon fat. Add the drained hominy. Cook in the pan where the bacon was fried until the hominy is well warmed. Then add an egg and milk mixture, just as if you were going to scramble eggs by themselves. Stir constantly until the egg part of the mixture is cooked. Serve with buttered toast for a breakfast or with a salad for a quick dinner.

➤ **HOG AND HOMINY** Mix together in an unlidded casserole or oven pan 2½ c. hominy, 1 lb. browned hamburger or sausage, 1 sliced onion, and 2 or 3 c. tomatoes. Cook in oven almost an hour, then serve.

Hominy Grits Recipes

➤ **HOMINY GRITS** First thoroughly dry your hominy. Then put it through a grinder set for coarse. Dry some more and then store for use. To cook, add boiling water and salt to taste and cook until done. Homemade grits may take as long as 4 hours to cook properly. Use about 3½–4 parts water to 1 part grits. You can hasten the cooking time by soaking grits overnight beforehand. (Cook them in the water in which you soaked them.) Grits are good plain with just a dab of butter.

➤ **FRIED LEFTOVER GRITS** Pour warm cooked grits into a rectangular dish—like a buttered bread pan. Let grits cool and get firm. The next meal, or whenever you're ready, cut the firm grits into slices and brown them slowly in hot fat or butter just as you would fried cornmeal mush.

➤ **LEFTOVER GRITS CROQUETTES** Combine 3 c. cooked grits with 2 eggs and seasoning. Form into flat round cakes. Dip into beaten egg, then bread crumbs, then again into egg. Fry in hot lard or butter until brown. (If short of eggs, use 1 egg extended with a little milk.)

Hominy Flour (Masa Harina) Recipes

➤ **MASA FLOUR** Make hominy by any directions and dry it. Grind to flour fineness.

➤ **MASA TORTILLAS** Moisten masa flour to make a soft dough. Pat a chunk out thin or shape in a tortilla press to make cakes about 5 inches in diameter. Fry on a lightly greased griddle, turning frequently, until thoroughly cooked.

➤ **AREPAS** From Ruth of Bonaire, Netherlands Antilles: "Arepas are called 'Venezuelan hamburgers' and are traditionally made from white cornmeal prepared like Mexican masa harina. They are eaten for breakfast, lunch, or supper;

you slit them halfway open, hollow them out, and fill them with white cheese or beans (black), tuna fish or chicken salad, scrambled eggs, or a meat-vegetable mixture. To make them, you shape them like large English muffins about 12 cm. in diameter and 3 cm. high [5 inches wide and 1 inch high]. Then bake on a grill or griddle. Stir 1⅓ c. boiling water into 2 c. fresh cornmeal. Let stand a few minutes to absorb liquid. Should be very thick. Stir in 2 T. oil. Shape into round cakes and bake on a grill, griddle, or in a preheated oven (400°F) until edges are brown—15 minutes or so. Serve warm."

TAMALES: A traditional tamale has three layers. Outside is the cornhusk. Just inside that comes an "envelope" of cornmeal. A meat mixture is inside the cornmeal layer—or mixed with the cornmeal. Or you can make a veggie tamale.

Cornhusks. These hold the tamale together on the outside and are the first layer you put down. The soft inner husks of green corn are best to use, but you can also use tougher husks. Trim away the top and bottom ends of the husk. Leave them about 6 inches long and rinse in boiling water. If you have to use very tough husks, soaking them in cold water for a few hours beforehand will help. Wipe them dry before using.

Cornmeal "Envelope." Mix 4 c. yellow cornmeal, 1 t. salt, 2½ c. stock (left over from cooking the meat part of the filling), and ¼ lb. fat (lard works well). Beat this thoroughly to make it light.

Meat Filling. Boil 1 lb. meat (any kind: chicken, beef, goat) with 1 onion, 2 garlic cloves, and a couple bay leaves. When the meat is tender, save the stock to use in making the envelope for cooking it. Dice the meat and saute the cubes in a bit of oil. (If you are rushed, you can just shred or chop or grind the meat instead of sauteing it.) For "hot" tamales, add chili powder. For regular tamales, add some mashed garlic or just salt and paprika. You could add a few olives or raisins to each portion of meat as you put it into the tamale. Or green pepper, chopped onion and celery, tomatoes, cream-style corn, or whatever else you have . . .

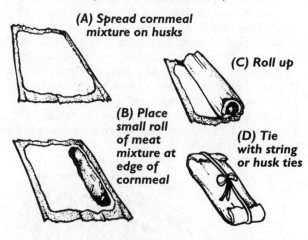

(A) Spread cornmeal mixture on husks

(C) Roll up

(B) Place small roll of meat mixture at edge of cornmeal

(D) Tie with string or husk ties

Meat-Cornmeal Combination. Boil a chicken until tender. Cool and remove all the bones. Save the broth. Add any or all of the following ingredients or anything else you have that sounds good: ½ lb. seeded raisins, minced; ½ c. pitted olives; a fresh red pepper, chopped fine; 6 hard-boiled eggs, chopped (if you decide on the eggs, mix them in after the cornmeal). Make a paste with 2 c. yellow cornmeal moistened with the reserved hot chicken stock. Season

to taste with salt and onion juice. Add enough water so you can cook it in a double boiler, stirring, about 15 minutes. Then combine with the meat mixture.

Shaping the Tamales. Spread your cornmeal envelope on each layer of husks you want to fill. If you are using a meat, cornmeal combination; just lay on the husks as much filling as they will reasonably contain, and then wrap. Using the cornmeal outer envelope, put the filling in the middle of your cornmeal layer. It helps to shape the meat into rolls the size of your little finger before you put them on the cornmeal paste. Now roll it up. Fold both ends of the husking down like you would the wrapping paper around a gift. Now tie it closed.

Tying up Your Tamales. Use husk ties or string, or just stack them in your steamer for cooking and hope they stay together. It's safer to tie. To make husk ties, tear some husks into strips and use like string.

Cooking the Tamales. You either steam or boil them. To steam them, use a steamer or rig up a makeshift one by making a rack in the top part of your canning kettle. Stack the tamales in it or on it, and cook until well done. To boil tamales, put a kitchen lid in the bottom of a deep kettle. Cover that with extra husks. Stack the tamales on top of that. Add the boiling stock that you cooked the meat in. You may add a few dried red peppers if you want the tamales extra hot. Cover tightly and cook until well done.

☙ *AFRICAN FERMENTED TAMALES Stir 4 c. boiling water into 4 c. cornmeal (stir fast so it doesn't lump). Cool to lukewarm. Stir in 2 T. unflavored yogurt. Cover the mixture with a damp cloth and let ferment 8–24 hours. Then add 2 t. salt and stir dough into 2 c. boiling water. Spoon this mixture onto husks, fold shut, and steam until done.*

POPCORN: Popcorn takes longer to mature than most sweet corns. Harvest it as you would other field corns, first drying it in the field. Then hang it in the house like seed corn and dry another 3–4 weeks. The kernels of popcorn need to be hard on the outside in order to get the proper explosion of the remaining moisture at the center of the kernel when it's heated. Popcorn is the hardest of all corns to shell. To keep from hurting your hand, shell by rubbing one ear of corn against another or cover your hand with an old sock before you rub kernels away from the cob. Store popcorn in tightly lidded glass jars (so kernels don't become too dry to pop). If you have bulk popcorn and need to store it in the open, choose a cool place (so further drying is less likely).

Reasons for Failure to Pop Well. A 12–14 percent moisture content is the key to good popping; it must be not too moist and not too dry inside the kernel. Popcorn will keep poppin', even after 3 years or more in storage, if the moisture level is right. The most common reason that popcorn fails to pop well is that it got too dry. If it sits in the pan and the kernels get a dark-colored, scorched look, some of them partly split, the problem is definitely dryness. To cure that, add 1 T. water per quart jar of corn, put the lid on as tightly as you can, and shake thoroughly 3 times a day for the next 3 days. Then try popping a little of it. If it still doesn't pop, give it another water treatment the same as before. (Watch for mold!)

Occasionally the problem is just the opposite, that your popcorn is too moist: it pops, but with a louder-than-usual noise, and the puffed kernels may look small and ragged and be tough to eat. In that case, spread in pans and slowly dry under low heat.

Popping. Dutch ovens are good popcorn poppers. So is an iron frying pan with a lid. So are commercial poppers. Allow ½ c. dry corn for every 1 gal. popped corn that you want. Melt about 1 T. cooking oil in your Dutch oven or some other heavy pan with a tight-fitting lid. When the oil is hot enough to get broken lines across it and is just starting to smoke, it's ready for the popcorn. Add the popcorn, cover, and cook over medium heat. Shake the pan on top of the heat constantly until you don't hear much more popping; then hurriedly take it off the heat to prevent burning. (It may seem frugal to try to get the last kernels to pop, but it's really wasteful because you risk burning the already-popped ones, and they start to get tough.) To butter the popcorn, just melt some butter in another pan, pour it over the popcorn, and stir to mix. Sprinkle with salt if you like.

✍ **WARMED-UP POPCORN** *You can make a big bag of popped popcorn and keep it to use later. Warm it up in your dehydrator or oven. Serve plain or with seasoning. Re-heated, you'll be surprised how good it can taste!*

✍ **POPCORN CEREAL** *Eat leftover popcorn for breakfast with milk, sweetening, and fruit.*

✍ **MAKE-IT-YOURSELF POPCORN FLAVORING** *A powdered, favorite herb? Such as a chili-powder/cumin mix, or some grated or melted cheese stirred into the melted butter? Nuts or seeds? Dried fruit? Caramel or maple syrup? A mixture of peanut butter and melted butter? Whatever the flavoring, just mix together with your freshly popped popcorn and serve!*

✍ **CINNAMON-RAISIN POPCORN MIX** *Mix together 2 T. melted butter, 3 T. brown sugar, ½ t. ground cinnamon, ¼ c. raisins, and about ¼ c. apple chunks. Toss together with 8–10 c. freshly popped popcorn.*

✍ **CURRIED POPCORN** *Combine 1 t. curry powder with a pinch of garlic powder. Toss with 8–10 c. popcorn.*

✍ **CHEESE-COATED POPCORN** *Grate cheese to make ½ cup. Sprinkle cheese onto still-warm popped corn. Mix well. If you bake this for 15 minutes, it will dry out and be crisper.*

✍ **HONEY-NUT GOURMET POPCORN** *Mix together 2 qt. freshly popped corn, 1 c. chopped peanuts, 1 c. raisins, and 1 c. sunflower seeds. Heat ½ c. honey and ½ c. water together in a pan, stirring, until you get to hard-ball stage. Add ½ c. butter and stir to melt. Pour the sweet mix over the dry mixture, stirring until the kernels are all coated. Spread it out on 2 greased cookie sheets. Bake 15 minutes at 350°F.*

✍ **PICKLED CORN EARS** *From Etta Jaderborg, Chapman, KS: Use immature popcorn ears, not more than 2–3 inches long. Don't work with too many at a time. Drop them in boiling, salted water. Add 1 T. salt to each qt. water. Drop in the corn; let stand for 3 minutes. Drain and pack tightly in small sterile jars to stand upright. Make a hot syrup of 1 qt. vinegar, 1 T. sugar, and 2 T. mixed pickling spices tied in a cloth sack. Pour that over the hot packed corn. Then add ¼ pod of hot dried red pepper to each jar and seal. They should be ready in 2 weeks.*

✍ **POPCORN CAKE** *This is something different and fun for a child's birthday party. In a double boiler (or kettle over hot water), melt together ½ lb. butter and 4½ oz. apple caramel.*

When that is melted and blended, add a package of marshmallows and a cup of peanuts and stir well. Now pour the coating slowly over the popcorn, mixing as you pour until it's all coated. Press the coated popcorn into a greased angel food cake pan. When cooled (put in refrigerator if in a hurry), remove from pan onto a plate. (If it sticks, run a little hot water over the outside of the pan.) Slice with a serrated knife when ready to serve. It's not really health food, but I believe in serving something besides homemade bread and carrot sticks on birthdays. It's only once a year!

✍ **POPCORN BALLS** *Boil together 1 c. white Karo syrup, 1½ c. sugar (white or brown), ½ c. butter, and 4 t. vinegar until a thread of the syrup snaps when tested in cold water. Have ready 8 qt. freshly popped corn. Pour syrup, while hot, over the corn, stirring with a spoon until well mixed. Set out a pan of cold water next to where you'll be working. Wet your hands in the cold water and begin to press the corn into balls, working as quickly as you can. Then cool the balls on a greased cookie sheet. Optional: Before pouring over the syrup, premix a cup of shelled peanuts into the popcorn.*

✍ **CRACKER JACKS** *Violet Stewart sent me this one: "Start with 8 or 9 cups of popped corn. Put into a dishpan with enough room to move it around easily. In a separate pan, combine 2 c. packed brown sugar, 1 stick margarine or butter, 1 t. salt, ¾ c. white syrup or light sorghum, and 1 t. vanilla. Cook together at a full rolling boil for 5 minutes. If it spins a thread, it is ready. Add ½ t. soda. (Hold pan over dishpan of corn before adding soda so that if it runs over, it will fall on the corn.) Stir a moment. Pour over popped corn. Stir until all is coated well. Put in a roaster in 200°F oven for 1 hour. Look now and then—some ovens are hotter. Stir occasionally so it will not get in one mass. Store in a covered container. It keeps well."*

MILLET

Millet has been human food for thousands of years. Millet grains are tiny, round kernels to start with, but they swell hugely when cooked. In the United States, millet is used mostly in birdseed mixtures. But that's our ignorance. Millet is a basic starch food in many countries of the world. Once you could see it growing in the Red River Valley of North Dakota . . . or all over northern China, where it was *the* staple food before the introduction of rice. Phyllis Vallette, a missionary in Burkina Faso, Africa, wrote me, "Millet is the staple cereal here, the only grain that grows fast enough for the short rainy season." She's right.

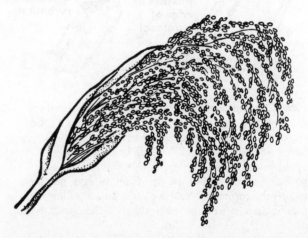

Millet is grown in the United States as a pasture and hay crop as well as for birdseed grain. Millet here has the reputation of a forage crop that can be fed as little as 30 days after it's planted. No legume hay can grow that fast. If you give millet 3 months, it can yield more than 5 tons per acre. Harvested for grain, you can get 50 bushels or more per acre.

It's good in drought areas because it can go dormant when the rains stop and then start growing again when it rains, showing no harmful effects for the delay. It's good for places with poor soil because soil quality doesn't matter with millet. It's good for weedy ground because, like buckwheat, millet grows fast and thick and can out-compete the weeds. It's good for a short-season grain crop because it grows so fast. It provides good nutritional value if you also grow buckwheat, another easy crop, because millet and buckwheat are true amino acid complements; if eaten together, they provide a complete protein.

Like buckwheat, you can plant millet late, after a patch of vegetables has been harvested. Chickens love it. They'll peck out the grain from the straw. For other livestock, millet can be stored without threshing and fed in winter as is. Millet is also unusual in that it is the only alkaline grain, so people with acidosis or bad breath have reason to eat it!

Varieties

The millets are a collection of rather loosely related grains, each main category being of a different genus. Millet has five very distinct types and many subspecies of those. The basic ones are "African," proso, fox or foxtail, pearl, and teff. Each variety's seed heads look quite different from the others.

"AFRICAN MILLET": This differs from proso, foxtail, pearl, and teff in that it is not a real millet but rather a variety of sorghum grown for pasture and hay. (See "Grain Sorghums.")

PROSO MILLET: Proso (*Panicum miliaceum*) is also called "broomcorn" millet because it has a head that spreads out like a broom. Proso is the millet traditionally used for grain and flour in Asia but mainly for birdseed and cattle feed in the United States. Proso millet does comparatively well in poorish and dryish soils. To feed proso to livestock, first grind it. But chickens can eat it plain. Proso varieties can be gotten with grain that is red, white, or yellow. Bountiful Gardens offers seed for a proso millet that grows 1–4 feet high and has hairy stems (a good hay maker).

FOXTAIL MILLET: Foxtail (*Setaria italica*) makes good hay and pasture. It is chosen over proso as a forage crop because it has less hair on the stems. Foxtail is a later-maturing millet. The variety of foxtail called Japanese makes twice as much silage as an equal acreage of oats and just about as much corn. Japanese millet grows 5 feet tall and, unlike corn, will regrow even after it is cut. It is said to be the best millet for forage.

PEARL MILLET: The varieties of pearl millet (*Pennisetum glaucum*) look like a cattail and are actually called "cattail millet" in some places. Pearl millet is a southern variety. It will thresh out of its hulls, which makes it a good choice if you are raising millet for your family's food. You can order pearl millet seed from Mellinger's. It can also be used as a green manure and to choke out weeds. If growing it for green manure, plow under at 5 weeks. Ready to harvest for grain about 9 weeks after planting. Plant 1–1¼ lb. per 1,000 square feet.

TEFF: Teff (*Eragrostis abyssinica*) is the world's smallest grain, a grass grain from Ethiopia that most resembles millet and is usually considered to be a millet variety. It is also grown as a forage and hay crop. It is an important cereal crop in Africa. Like buckwheat, it makes great, nourishing breakfast pancakes when ground into flour. Substitute teff in any non-wheat flour, millet, or millet flour recipe. You can order teff seed from Abundant Life or Seeds of Change. They offer white-seeded teff, a standard variety for grain production. Redwood City carries a brown-seeded variety and sends a leaflet of 11 recipes using teff with seeds. Plant in spring by broadcasting, and rake seeds in lightly. They'll germinate in a week and be ready to harvest in about 100 days. For more info and recipes, see Rebecca Wood's article, "Teff," in *East West,* August 1988.

Planting, Harvesting, and Using Millet

PLANTING: You can plant birdseed and then pick out the best millet heads to save for your own seed. I've read elsewhere that millet must not be planted until corn is started up and the nights are warm, since it is not cold-hardy, but gardening writer Steve Solomon says it should be "sown just before the last anticipated frost and harvested late in July to mid-August." Plant about 30 lb./acre of Japanese millet, more if broadcast—1 inch deep. Plant other millets at 45 lb. per acre. Plant small varieties solid. Tall, large varieties do best in rows. To plant millet in your garden, plant in rows, but thickly.

HARVESTING: Harvest like buckwheat, but before the grain is totally ripe. Then let it dry and finish ripening in a place where birds can't get it. Birds are crazy about millet, which is why most American millet production is sold to be part of birdseed mixes, but this can be a real problem at harvest time. That's why homestead millet growers usually cut off the heads a day or two before they are ripe and the birds move in. In *Growing Vegetables West of the Cascades*, Steve Solomon wrote, "When the birds have taken about 10 percent of the seed, I harvest with a sickle, making large bundles to dry under cover. Millet, being weak-strawed, is best dried in bundles hung upside down under cover where the birds can't get to it." During that indoor drying, the millet finishes ripening. Then it's time to thresh, which is easy.

HULLING: Steve Solomon wrote, "Compare the flavor of freshly hulled millet to that stale stuff obtained from the health-food store and you'll never want to buy hulled millet again. The seed coats are easily removed by running the seeds through a hand mill with the grinding plates about ¹⁄₁₆ inch apart and then sifting out most of the cracked hulls from the gritty and denser seed pieces and washing out the remainder of the hulls before cooking the millet like porridge."

COOKING WITH MILLET: A pound of millet will make a greater volume of cereal than any other grain. Millet has a bland flavor compared to other grains. That makes it good for thickening soups and stews. Millet is a little weird because when it is cooked in water, an okra-like gooey stuff rises to the surface. When cooking millet, it's best to stir with a bamboo or wet wooden spoon, which is less likely to stick to the grain. Millet doesn't have enough gluten to make raised breads, but it can be used in unleavened breads such as chapatis. Add ½ c. millet per loaf of other bread for a nicer texture and added nutrition. Buckwheat and millet are a good nutritional combo. *The Book of Whole Grains* by Marlene Anne Bumgarner (New York: St. Martin's Press, 1976) has a whole chapter of millet recipes, and the same on grain sorghum, etc. It's a treasure!

☙ *NUTTY FLAVORED MILLET Before using millet in a recipe where it will be combined with other ingredients, first brown it in a frying pan with a very little oil; then go ahead and use it in your recipe. This toasting makes it more flavorful.*

☙ *BASIC COOKED MILLET Heat 1 qt. water to boiling. Add 1 c. millet and ½ t. salt, and stir a moment. Then cover the pan, turn down the heat to lowest setting, and cook for a half hour—or until the water is all taken up by the grain and it is soft. It's important to keep the lid on and the steam in. Millets and stoves vary. You may even need to add a little more water. Put through a food mill or grinder for a "mashed potato" effect. On the other hand, if you steam instead of boil and simmer, you'll end up with fluffy kernels.*

☙ *BREAKFAST TUO ZAAFI This is a replay of the above, North African style. Mix 1 c. cold water with 1 c. coarsely ground millet meal. Put 3 c. water on to boil. When it boils, stir the meal and water combination into the boiling water. Like cornmeal, this must be stirred constantly, or there may be lumps. Now turn the heat down to low and cook, with frequent stirring, until your porridge is thickened to stiff. For everyday use, serve with your favorite sweetener and milk. For special times, add chopped nuts, raisins, dried fruit, butter, or chopped apples. To make Supper Tuo Zaafi, cook millet the same way, but serve with gravy or a mushroom or vegetable sauce instead of with milk and sweetener.*

☙ *MILLET SOUP Cook millet with onions, celery, carrots, and potatoes until everything is tender and the broth is tasty. Season and serve.*

☙ *MILLET CASSEROLE Bake millet with cheese, broccoli, sesame seeds, and enough liquid to keep it moist.*

☙ *MILLET BREAKFAST PUDDING Combine 3 c. cooked millet, 2 eggs, ½ c. milk, honey or sorghum to taste, and 1 c. dried prune pieces (or other fruits). Sprinkle nutmeg (or other spices) on top. From Gen MacManiman, Fall City, WA.*

OATS

Oats—both grain and straw—are good winter food for pigs, horses, sheep, or rabbits. Oat straw is the most nutritious of the grass grain straws for feeding animals. Rabbits can eat oats in the hull very well, but chickens can't, preferring wheat or any ground grain—or hulled oats. Oats used to be important because they were the main grain fed to workhorses. Now the usual farmload puller eats gasoline instead of oats, and everybody's worrying about Middle Eastern politics instead of the weather.

Planting and Growing Oats

CLIMATE: Although oats originally come from Central Asia, they do best in cool, moist climates. They actually yield heavier in more northern areas. They are easy to grow and can do well in a wide range of climates and soils as long as they get ample moisture. Oats yield better on acid land than do barley or wheat. They don't tolerate arid conditions or high altitudes well. Oats need more moisture than the other grains. In fact, up to a point, the more mois-

ture they get, the better they'll yield. That makes sense when you consider they're a relative of wild rice. But unlike that close relative, there is a limit. Oats do not thrive in a chronically soggy soil. So oats do well in the northern United States, Canada, northern Europe, and Scotland.

Scotland's production of oats prompted the famous Englishman Dr. Johnson to scoff at his Scottish friend, the equally famous Mr. Boswell, "They feed men in Scotland what in England they only feed to horses." Boswell retorted, "Yes. Better men. Better horses."

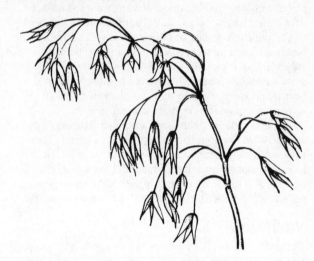

VARIETIES: All oats are genus *Avena*. Regular northern, spring-planted, white oats are *Avena sativa*. (Spring varieties are sown unless your winters are very mild.) You can order *A. sativa* seed from Bountiful Gardens. Red oats, *A. byzantina*, is now a less common type, a winter variety planted in the fall in more southern areas. There is a wild oat called *A. fatua* that can be used in pasture or hay mixes, but it is avoided because it tends to become a noxious weed in grain fields. The old-time seed catalogs commonly listed many additional kinds of oats. My 1885 one lists spring and winter varieties; white, black, gray, yellow, and red oats; and a choice of plump-grained or slender-grained varieties. The catalog states that the black and brown varieties are hardier and better yielding than the white, with "Black Tartarian" recommended as the best of all. But I don't know where you could find a seed for Black Tartarian now. It's probably extinct. So it goes: White shirts. White bread. White toilets. White oats . . .

Hull-less Oats (A. nuda). This variety has been cultivated in England for over 300 years. Its drawbacks are that it shatters more easily in the field, yields lower, takes more losses from birds, and is more likely to be lost to a spring freeze than is wheat or rye. The advantage of hull-less oats is that they're as convenient to thresh and grind as are wheat or rye; they're much easier for the do-it-yourselfer to process into oatmeal than are hulled oats. Steve Solomon, in *Growing Vegetables West of the Cascades*, wrote, "Ordinary oat hulls are sharp, bitter and incredibly tough. Without a full-scale mill it is nearly impossible to efficiently groat the oats (separate seed from hull) . . . Once you try making oatmeal porridge from recently cracked oat groats instead of from stale, rancid, rolled oats, you'll be more interested in growing your own." Seed for a variety of hull-less oats called "Freedom" is available from Southern Exposure Seed Exchange. Bountiful Gardens also sells it.

WHEN TO PLANT: The ground should be well prepared the fall before seeding. Plant spring varieties in spring as soon as the ground is ready to cultivate and get ready for seeding. That's sometime between mid-March and June 1, depending on how far north you live. For oats, hurry: the sooner they're planted, the better, because they grow best before warm, dry weather sets in. They grow fine under clouds. They'll probably be the first field crop you plant. Plant winter oats between October 1 and December 1. Or between January 1 and April 1. The later you plant, the poorer your crop will be. Steve Solomon wrote, "Hull-less oats aren't nearly as winter-hardy as wheats or ryes; if they freeze out, these may be resown in very early spring since oat seed germinates in chilly soil."

HOW MUCH TO PLANT: Seed at the rate of 2 to 4 bushels per acre. If you broadcast, use the higher number. A bushel of oats weighs an average 32–38 lb. Heavier oats have more seed inside the hull and will usually grow better. Cover with 1 to 1½ inches of soil, or 2–3 inches where there is a problem of dryness.

Harvesting and Using Oats

HARVESTING OAT HAY: Another choice with oats is to raise oats for hay, pasture, or winter stock food. We let the larger animals feed on oats in the field while the crop is still green. Then we mow and bale what's left for winter food for the livestock. Oats can be cut at any stage for livestock feed, but animals consume them most easily when they are harvested in the milk stage. So all we need to do is bale in the summer and unbale in the winter, and the animals get bulk and grain without our having to sheave, dry, mill, or roll.

HARVESTING OAT GRAIN: Mature oats are 2–5 feet high depending on the variety and soil fertility. Oats are harvested when half the leaves are green and the grain has just finished the milk stage and gone into the dough stage. A well-filled oat head has 30–150 grains per stalk. Cut and let cure 1–2 days. Then sheave, and set up the sheaves in long, narrow shocks running north and south to cure. Oats need more drying than barley or wheat. If rain's a threat, move them to a shed, or mow and dry there as long as it takes—2 days to 2 weeks.

Then your oats will be cured. Haul the sheaves carefully to your threshing area and thresh. A yield of 30–40 bushels per acre is fine, although a 90–100-bushel yield has been reported on good ground. Now you've got a bunch of fine horse feed—or people food, once it's hulled, unless you grew *A. nuda*. You'll have oat straw left over from the threshing, about 2 lb. per pound of grain harvested.

HULLING: To prepare oats for human food, you must thoroughly remove the hull. Oats in the hull are about 30 percent hull, and that hull is all pure indigestible fiber. The grain inside is higher in protein than any other, but how do you get at it?

Roasting. Hulling is easier if you first heat the oats. Commercial processors toast the grain for an hour and a half. That loosens the hulls as well as reduces the moisture content. To accomplish this at home, follow the directions for parching under "Wild Rice."

Milling. Then you mill. It works well to now grind oats between two millstones that are set very precisely apart so that the space between them is narrow enough for the millstones to scrape off the oat hulls without crumbling the precious

groats inside. This is called a burr mill. Set the grinder to ¹⁄₁₆-inch clearance between grinding burrs. Or you can hull the oats in a roller mill; Sears sells a family-sized one. Then winnow out the hulls in the wind or before a fan.

Blender "Milling." Or you can do a barely satisfactory job in a heavy-duty blender. The blender actually cuts up the oats, but in the process it chops the hulls too, and some of them will fall off. So you put the oats into the blender, run it a moment, and then sift, and the little stuff is oat flour. The blender system is inefficient and wasteful but better than nothing. Some people grind the oats in the blender and cook them, hulls and all. It's good for their cholesterol count!

COOKING WITH OATS: We now know that eating oats can reduce cholesterol and lower blood pressure. Good stuff. You can buy hulled oat groats from health food stores or mail-order outlets specializing in whole grains (see the list in Chapter 1). Or you can buy the ones sold for animal feed. Whole groats can be used in soups the same as barley or can be made into porridge. Or you can grind oat groats in a regular grinder—the same kind you'd use for wheat. Oats, like barley, don't leaven, so you can't make a good bread out of oat flour alone, unless it's a very thin tortilla-like bread—an oatcake. But you can add oat flour to any other bread (or cookie!) recipe. Many oat recipes originated in Scotland, where oats have long been the staff of life in the form of oatcakes and porridge.

❧ *OAT PORRIDGE If you are making porridge out of home-ground groats, you first grind and then cook. The coarser you grind, the longer it will need to cook. Don Winters, Nova Scotia, Canada, wrote me, "I grind ⅔ c. of oat groats (hulled oat berries), giving 1 c. of cracked oats and flour. Bring 2 c. water to boil. Add the oats and flour. Simmer for 20 minutes until water is taken up by oats. I add 2 t. cinnamon and ½ c. raisins after 10 minutes or so. This will serve 2 or 3 people. I like it with real maple syrup over it." I usually serve it with milk or cream and a sweetening. But for a special touch, add some brown sugar, raisins, or cream just before serving. It's also nice if you stir in fruit: peaches or apricots or . . .*

❧ *GROAT CEREAL Put oat groats, salt, and water in a casserole. Use 2 parts water to 1 part groats. Plan on cooking it a long, long time. (Put it on the night before you want it for breakfast.)*

❧ *ROLLED OAT CEREAL Use 1 part rolled oats to 2½ parts water. Pour the oats into the boiling water. Reduce heat to medium. Wait about 10 minutes for the oats to cook. Remove the pan from the heat, cover, wait 5 more minutes, and serve. Cook in a double boiler with a tight lid. Good with raisins or chopped apples added shortly before you take it off the heat.*

Oat Flour. Put groats or rolled oats through a grain mill or twice through a regular food grinder.

❧ *OATCAKES This was often made in old Scotland. Mix your oat flour with enough water to make a dough. Knead as you would bread. Then roll out as thin as you can. Cut into squares. Fry on an iron plate or griddle or in a pan that is shiny with oil. Serve warm with butter and honey or . . . Ruth, who lives in Bonaire (Netherlands Antilles), wrote me, "We make oatcakes by shaping batter into rounds about 1 cm (⅓ inch) thick and then cutting into pie-shaped wedges before baking in a very slow oven. Good cold with honey too."*

OAT FLOUR APRICOT FRITTERS *Sift together ½ c. oat flour, ½ c. rice flour (health food stores carry it), and 1 t. baking powder. Add 1 t. honey, a pinch salt, 1 egg, ¼ c. milk, and 1 c. stewed apricots. Drop mixture by tablespoonfuls into hot deep fat. Fry until a golden brown. Drain. You can roll in powdered sugar for a fancy touch. Doesn't make but a dozen.*

GRANOLAS: When I was a little girl, I liked a bowl of raw rolled oats with milk and honey for breakfast in the summertime. Then somebody came along and invented granola, which is even better. You'll have to visit your health food store (or grocery store) for some of these ingredients. It's pretty hard to grow almonds, coconuts, and carob in your yard unless you live in southern California. Granola recipes are fun to make, so good to eat, and so healthy! Store any granola in an airtight container. It will keep several weeks. It's best stored in the freezer or in plastic bags or jars in the refrigerator.

BASIC UNCOOKED GRANOLA *Here are proportions for any amount. Make your recipe one-half cereal, and have at least half of that half be rolled oats and the rest be some kind of other rolled cereal like wheat flakes or rye flakes. Then add one-fourth dried fruit or some kind of fruit (even fresh, if you're going to eat the granola right away), one-fourth nuts or seeds and sweetening, and extras like maybe powdered milk or wheat germ. I can guarantee you it will be good to eat. You can eat this make-your-own granola anytime after you've given it a good shaking to mix all ingredients together. Shaking it in a big grocery bag works well. It helps if you use brown sugar rather than molasses or honey for the sweetening; that way you don't have anything wet and sticky in there! You can make a cold breakfast cereal by pouring over cold milk over granola and eating as is. You can make a hot cereal for a winter's morning by cooking granola a short time in a little water.*

PRUNEOLA *I got this recipe from Sunray Orchards (Myrtle Creek, OR 97457), which offers wonderful organic prunes by mail-order. Pit and snip into small pieces 1 lb. prunes. Set aside. Combine with ½ c. vegetable oil: 1 lb. rolled oats (not the quick-cook kind), 1 c. shredded coconut, 1 c. chopped unblanched almonds, 1 c. hulled sunflower seeds, 1 c. wheat germ, and ½ c. honey. Heat to just under a boil and mix well. Spread about ⅓ to ½ of the mixture in a thin layer in a large shallow pan. Bake in a 325°F oven for 25 minutes, stirring occasionally. Repeat with remaining mixture, or use 2 or 3 pans. When all the mixture has been baked, stir in the small pieces of prunes. Break mixture into small pieces, if necessary. Let cool completely. Store in a tightly covered container or in plastic bags. Makes about 3 lb.*

BASIC BAKED GRANOLA *Mix together 1 c. rolled oats, 1 c. rolled whole wheat, ½ c. grated dried coconut, ⅓ c. wheat germ, ½ c. chopped nuts (almonds, cashews or peanuts), ½ c. hulled sunflower seeds, and 7 t. sesame seeds, if you can get them. Now heat to just under a boil 5 T. honey, 5 t. vegetable oil, and 1 t. vanilla. Mix with dry ingredients. Spread about ⅓ to ½ of the mixture in a thin layer in a large shallow pan. Bake in a 325°F oven for 25 minutes, stirring occasionally. Repeat with remaining mixture, or use 2 or 3 pans. Then add ¼ c. seedless raisins or chopped dried fruit like prunes, dates, currants, or apricots. Be sure to stir in the fruit while the granola is still warm. Store.*

NUTTY GRANOLA *Start by getting out 6 c. rolled oats, 2 c. grated or preshredded coconut, 2 c. nuts (any kind—almonds, cashews, walnuts—only chop them up somewhat), ⅔ c. sesame seeds or sunflower seeds, ⅔ c. bran flakes, and ⅔ c. wheat germ. Take each of the preceding ingredients by itself and roast in a 300°F oven until lightly toasted. Now combine. Pour over and stir in ½ c. oil and ½ c. honey (or molasses, sorghum, or maple syrup). When you have it stirred together really thoroughly, roast in the oven again at 250°F until golden brown. Now stir in 2 c. chopped dried fruit —any kind or a mixture. Serve with milk.*

SUN-DRIED GRANOLA *In your big bread bowl, first put 5 c. oatmeal. Mix ½ c. honey, ½ c. hot water, ½ c. oil, and 2 t. vanilla. Pour liquid over oatmeal. Now add 1 c. sunflower seeds, 1 c. sesame seeds, 1 c. flaxseed, 1 c. grated coconut, ¾ c. chopped nuts, and ¾ c. chopped dried fruit. Mix well. Spread thinly to dry for at least 2 days.*

HIGH-PROTEIN GRANOLA *Combine 5 c. old-fashioned oatmeal, 1 c. powdered milk, 1 c. wheat germ, 1 c. sesame seed, 1 c. soy flour, 1 c. sunflower seeds, 1 c. chopped nuts, and 1 c. coconut. Mix all that thoroughly. In a blender, combine 1 c. honey, ¾ c. cooking oil, and ¾ c. water. Then mix the liquid mixture with the dry one. Spread out your granola on 2 cookie sheets. Bake 1 hour at 250°F, stirring about every 15 minutes. Optional: While granola is still warm and fresh from the oven, you can mix in dates or raisins.*

FAT-FREE/DAIRY-FREE GRANOLA *Toast equal amounts of rolled oats and rolled wheat and/or barley flakes in an oven on cookie tins until brown. (Optional: Before baking, stir in mixture of equal parts honey and hot water.) If you didn't use liquid, watch carefully to prevent burning. When grain is toasted (or dry), combine with about ⅓ as much chopped dried fruit as you have cereal. You can also add nuts or sunflower seeds. From Ruth of Bonaire, Netherlands Antilles.*

Other Ways to Use Granola. Add a cup or two to your bread or cake (you'll have to add more liquid, too), or to poultry stuffing, cabbage roll stuffing, or apple stuffing. Eat it plain as a snack or use it as an ice cream topping. Serve stirred into yogurt instead of with milk. Or use it as a topping on cooked fruit. Or make candy out of it by mixing it with peanut butter, honey, and powdered milk and rolling into little individual balls. Or start with an egg and 2 T. milk, add enough granola to make a batter, and fry in a greased skillet for pancakes (top with yogurt).

QUINOA

October 1992. For the last 5 weeks, I've been going to barter fairs every weekend selling books, off in the most rural areas of eastern Washington and northern Idaho. At one fair in the Okanogan Highlands, where the stars at night look so big and bright you feel that you could just reach up and grab one, I happened on a quinoa (pronounced "keenwa") booth. "Oh," I said to the lady with delight. "Could I buy some seed from you?"

"No," she stated firmly. "You can buy quinoa porridge, or flour, or quinoa grain for soups, but we don't sell seed. We've spent 5 years developing our supply source direct from the high Andes and have too much invested to risk that."

Well, phooey all over you, I thought in unspoken retort, as I silently walked away. Sorry about that, Lady, but

I'll lay odds you're growing it yourself right in this lovely mountain valley. It's a perfect place for quinoa. And you may not like it, but in the new edition of my book I'm going to tell anybody who reads it how to grow quinoa. Yes, and where they can get seed right here in the United States. Some types of information I think should be public by God-given right, including where to get seeds and how to grow and process food. So here it is . . .

Quinoa, like amaranth, is another non-grass grain, a domesticated lamb's-quarters. It's a native of the Andes Mountains of South America and is a staple grain in parts of Peru, Bolivia, and southern Chile. Called the "mother grain" by the Incas, quinoa is a tiny seed whose color depends on the variety. Its advantages are its ability to handle droughts, cold weather, high elevations, and infertile soil. It resembles millet and amaranth.

Planting and Growing Quinoa

ORDERING QUINOA SEED: Abundant Life offers 12 varieties of quinoa, including the low-saponin Dulce Saj. Bountiful Gardens has three; Ecology Action, Hudson, Irish Eyes/Garden City, Seeds of Change, Territorial, and Bountiful Gardens also offer it. I learned a lot of what I know about quinoa from Steve Solomon's books. He wrote, "Quinoa from the health-food store won't sprout, because it's scarified to remove most of the saponins and eliminate the need for long soaking." Variety matters. Get the best for your particular climate. Quinoa seed stays viable 4 years or more.

CLIMATE: Colorado and New Mexico are good places to grow quinoa. It thrives in the 6,000–7,000-foot zone in the central Rocky Mountain area, in northern California and northward near the Pacific Ocean, and in the interior Northwest as well. Extremely hot weather actually holds back the seed setting process of this crop. According to Steve Solomon, "Its seeds sprout in chilly soil, and its frost-hardy seedlings may tolerate night temperatures in the low 20s."

PLANTING: Sow in spring in fertile soil as soon as the soil is warm (April or May). Steve Solomon again: "Quinoa must be sown early while there remains adequate soil moisture . . . early sowing—leading to the earliest possible harvest when weather is most likely to be dry—is essential . . . One organic farmer in the dry highlands of eastern Washington's Cascade foothills grows quinoa like wheat, because when crowded and under competition, the plants don't branch, but instead concentrate the harvest into a single seed head that can be harvested with a combine like wheat. I think the gardener will do better planting in rows about four feet apart, the seed sprinkled thinly in the row and gradually thinned to about eight inches in the row . . . Far less than an ounce of seed will sow 100 row feet, yielding 25 to 50 pounds of seed."

Keep the seedbed damp until it has germinated. You can eat the young greens you get from thinning the plants; they're nutritious and tasty. Quinoa will grow about 4 feet high. Steve Solomon wrote, "Keep quinoa well-weeded to allocate all soil moisture to the crop. With only a little fertilizer, quinoa grows fast to a magnificent six or seven feet tall, with numerous bushy side shoots."

Harvesting and Using Quinoa

HARVESTING: About mid-summer, it grows a sizable seed head heavy with tiny seeds. Harvest when dead ripe. You can thresh out the grain directly from the field, but threshing will be easier if you harvest and then dry the plants indoors a while more before the flailing. Steve Solomon: "The main hazard is rain. Should the drying seed be moistened, it will sprout right in the head; so if rain threatens once the seed is drying, the plants should be cut, bundled, and hung to finish under cover . . . When the heads are dry, thresh the seed by walking on the stalks, spread on a tarp. Clean by pouring the seed back and forth between two buckets in a mild breeze."

OF QUINOA AND SAPONIN: Steve Solomon: "The seed coat contains a bitter, somewhat poisonous soap or saponin that prevents insect damage and bird predation, but also must be removed before we can eat the grain. Fortunately, the saponin can, with patience, be soaked out at home; commercially grown quinoa, which is beginning to appear in health-food stores, conveniently has the saponins and seed coat mechanically removed." Wash only as much quinoa as you're going to cook and eat very soon. The saponin coating needs to be on if the grain is to be stored.

Steve Solomon's Saponin Soak-Out. "Soak a pint of dry seed overnight in a half-gallon mason jar with a screen lid such as is used to sprout alfalfa, then drain and refill. Continue soaking the seed and rinsing with cold water two to four times a day. Some varieties have harder seed coats containing more saponin than others, and the hardness of your water will regulate the effectiveness of soaking. The foaming saponins may be removed in 36 hours at best; when the water stops foaming when rinsed, the seed is ready for cooking. If 72 hours of rinsing and soaking pass with no end to the foaming, bring the seed to a boil for only a moment, pour off the hot soapy water, cover again, boil rapidly again for only a moment, and pour off the water a second time. Now the seed is ready to cook."

Other Saponin Wash-Out Systems. Blend about ½ cup of quinoa with cold water at lowest speed. Keep pouring off the foaming water and adding fresh water. Repeat until the blending doesn't release any more foam. Another system is to make yourself a quinoa-washing bag out of a loose-weave cloth like muslin. Then put in the grain, tie the bag shut, and wash in a series of cold-water baths until there's no more foam released.

COOKING QUINOA: Steve Solomon: "Add enough water to just about cover the soaked grain; simmer for 20 minutes or so. The cereal is good any time of day. Nutritionally it is oil-rich, and leaves you feeling satisfyingly full for a long time, much like oats." Quinoa grain has a delicate flavor and twice the protein of rice.

Substitute in any rice recipes. Quinoa will expand to four times the original bulk in the cooking, so 1 cup of the uncooked grain will give you 4 cups to serve.

TOASTED QUINOA Some cooks prefer to make their recipes with toasted quinoa because of the peanutty flavor it develops during toasting. To toast, first rinse quinoa. Then cook in a frying pan over medium heat. Shake the pan once in a while. In about 15 minutes, it will be dried and have a golden brown color. That's your toasted quinoa. If you put it in a container with an airtight cover, it will keep as long as a month. Use toasted quinoa to substitute for chopped nuts, seeds, or rice in any recipe.

☞ *HOT BREAKFAST QUINOA* Stir 1 c. rinsed (and toasted, if you like) quinoa into 2 c. boiling water. Add ½ t. cinnamon and ½ c. raisins or any other small or chopped dried fruit. Cover and cook on low heat until the quinoa has absorbed all liquid, 15–20 minutes.

☞ *SUPPER QUINOA* Cook the quinoa in a chicken or beef stock (don't add salt). For a curry quinoa, mix in 1 t. curry powder. Quinoa is wonderful in a stew of any sort. Add it to your cooked meat and vegetables as the last thing, because quinoa will absorb so much of your liquid.

☞ *QUINOA IN AND ON BREADSTUFFS* Toss some quinoa into any recipe to add nutritional value. Sprinkle toasted quinoa on the top of a batter-bread or very soft dough for a sesame-seed effect.

RICE

A culture's staple food is usually a starchy food. You can define countries by the grain their diet is built around, and in a lot of the world that grain is rice. Like wheat, oats, rye, and barley, rice is a member of the grass family, an annual whose seeds are planted in spring and ripen in fall. Rice especially resembles oats, particularly the water oat called "wild rice." Each rice seed sends up as many as 12 stalks ("tillers"), each of which may grow a seed head, so it can produce 2 to 3 times as much grain as wheat from an equal-size field. The two essentials for growing most rice varieties are plenty of clean water and a growing season with a minimum of 40 days of temperatures above 70°F.

U.S. agribusiness grows rice in large fields whose levees and contour, laid out by surveyors, are marvels of engineering. Seed and chemicals are sprayed onto the field from an airplane that covers several hundred acres a day. Huge machines till and level, combine and ditch. But in most other countries, rice is grown with hand labor in household "garden" plots or small family fields called "paddies," raising enough to feed the family and a little extra to sell. And it has been and can be grown that way in the United States, too.

MORE INFO: For a wonderful, detailed, homey description of rice growing by a private family in their garden, read David Spiekerman's article in *Organic Gardening*, Dec. 1975. The most thorough and enjoyable book is *Rice*, a plump little hardcover (1955) by English scientist D.H. Grist, who compulsively but passionately surveys in painstaking detail the rural, manual rice-growing methods of every area of the world. Most of the other resources on growing rice either are published by agricultural schools of the rice-growing states or else are short articles in scholarly journals, and all these are addressed to large, commercial growers. But *Rice in the United States: Varieties and Production* (Ag Handbook No. 289, USDA, 1973) is a book-length monograph of potential value to smaller growers as well. The best source of all may be *Rice* by Sylvia A. Johnson (Minneapolis, MN: Lerner Publications Co., 1985). Although supposedly a "juvenile" book, it contains valuable information about small-scale, family rice growing, translated from a Japanese original. And it's loaded with beautiful color photos of rice in various stages of growth.

SUPPLIES FOR RICE GROWERS: Seed for upland/paddy rice (*Oryza sativa*), 120 days, is available from Southern Exposure. Quality will be the same as commercial brown rice. Plants yield 5 lbs./100 sq. ft., 2,500–7,200 lbs./acre. This seed grows from Albany, New York, south to Florida. Plant in April/May and harvest in September. *NOTE: Requires dehusking before cooking. Dehusking procedures for small-scale gardeners and growers are included with your order!*

Rice Varieties, Climates, and Rotations

The rice genus, called *Oryza*, has about 25 main species and thousands of varieties of those species, each indigenous to some part of the world where it has usually been cultivated for hundreds—even thousands!—of years.

LOWLAND AND UPLAND, WETLAND AND DRYLAND RICES: The rices are divided into two general types: "lowland" and "upland." Lowland will not tolerate dry ground; upland can't stand to get its feet wet. So lowland rice is the semi-aquatic, wet-paddy kind that is irrigated for most of its growth period, the basic *Oryza sativa*. But among the multitude of rices, there are also numerous upland varieties.

Upland Rice. This one can be grown without irrigation, like any other dryland cereal grain. An upland rice variety is used in the Thai mountains (4,500 feet above sea level) and in the Himalayas (9,000 feet). Even upland rice benefits from fairly abundant rainfall over 3 to 4 months. But the hardiest upland varieties can go maybe 20–30 days without water. Upland rice can produce a harvest on stored soil moisture and infrequent rains, but yields are only 30–70 percent of what flooded rice can do given similar soil and climate. So lowland kinds are preferred in places that have enough water for it. In 1850, upland rice was being grown in Missouri, Illinois, and Iowa, but now U.S. commercial rice crops are all lowland. However, upland rice is not extinct.

COMMON/AROMATIC/GLUTINOUS: Another way of classifying rice species is into the 3 great families of "common," "glutinous," and "aromatic" rices. U.S. rice is almost all "common."

Common Rices. These have no distinctive flavor or odor and none of the "glutinous" or "waxy" nature. They are further subdivided according to kernel type: long-grained rice, medium-grained rice, and short-grained rice. In the United States, long- and medium-grained rice are basic cooking rices. Short-grained rice is the kind that puffed rice is made from—and that's all it's used for.

Glutinous/Non-Glutinous. Japanese rice is the *Oryza sativa Japonica* variety, highly glutinous when boiled. Most other countries, however, grow non-glutinous rices.

Aromatic or Scented. The rice varieties that have a discernable odor or flavor are a distinct group known as "aromatic" or "scented" varieties. They are common in India and Southeast Asia. Basmati is an aromatic variety. Though low-yielding, aromatic rices are valued enough to sell at twice the price and so have been saved from extinction.

Maturation Period: Early, Medium, Long:

There are rice varieties also categorized by maturation period. Some early varieties can be as quick as 100–120 days. Some late ones may need as long as 170 days. The mediums fall in between. In general, rice with a long maturation period grows more tillers than short-season rice. Each tiller will carry a fully developed seed head, so a rice of long maturation period generally gives a bigger yield.

Climate: In its origins, rice is a tropical plant, but in cultivation it is grown in temperate zones as well as subtropical and tropical ones. There are rice fields on all continents except Antarctica—in Africa, Australia, North and South America, Italy and Spain in southern Europe—but most of all in Asia. Not only is rice grown in at least the southern belt of temperate zones, but yields are often significantly higher in temperate compared to tropical zones! Rice in the United States is a significant commercial crop in Arkansas, Louisiana, Mississippi, Texas, and California. Some rice has also been grown in Missouri, Oklahoma, South Carolina, and Tennessee. The United States, in fact, is a significant rice-exporting country. At some time or other rice has been tried in most southern states.

Rice can be grown farther north in the United States, especially in a family-sized plot. The Japanese cultivate it quite successfully on their northern island of Hokkaido, which has a climate resembling that of New England. Korean farmers cope with severe winters and a short summer by early planting in nursery areas that are flooded every night, enough to completely submerge the plants and protect them from frost, and then drained in the morning.

To get the best yielding rice crop, you need a long growing season with a high average temperature during that season; the heat can be either humid or dry. In a humid area such as the southern United States, less irrigation water is needed for rice than in a dry, hot area such as California, where the water evaporates at a greater rate; that's the main difference.

Double-Cropping and Rotations

Double-Cropping Rice. In many areas, 2 or 3 crops of rice are grown every year. In monsoon climates, a crop is grown during each monsoon (Sri Lanka has 2 per year). By double-cropping you could theoretically double your yield. However, since slow-maturing varieties yield more heavily than the fast-maturing ones used in double-cropping, it's not a simple doubling. In Taiwan, 2 crops are generally grown, each 100–160 day varieties.

In southern Taiwan they sow in early December; in northern Taiwan, during the second or third week of February. The "nursery" stage is 14–40 days. Transplanting to the field is done from mid-January to late March for the first crop. Seeds for the second crop are sown in southern Taiwan in mid-June, in the north in early July. In southern Taiwan, the first crop is harvested from late May to early July, the second from October to December. The yield of the second crop is about 10–20 percent less than that of the first.

Crop Rotations Including Rice. Rice is subject to lots of insect and weed problems. Although it is remarkable for having been continuously produced for years—sometimes centuries—on the same land, even in Asia, rotations are sometimes done—and with good results. It starves out the pests between rice seasons and adds nutrients, so crop rotation typically increases the yield of the rice crop. In the United States, rice has sometimes been followed by fall-planted oats and then potatoes the next year. Or rice followed by soybeans (for beans or hay) or lespedeza (hay). Or soybeans followed by a winter green manure crop, plowed in and followed by 2 years of rice. Or soybeans, oats, rice.

Given a long enough growing season, 2 crops can be grown during the warm months—for example, rice followed by vegetables that handle cool weather better. In even warmer zones, three crops a year are possible: two of rice and one of vegetables grown during the winter season.

Fish-Rice Rotations. To do vegetable or dryland grain or bean rotation, you have to have land that can be dried out. Some rice land is naturally marshy and never dries out; in that case, you can rotate with a fish crop! The fish most commonly raised in rice paddies are buffalo and bass, or catfish. This takes advantage of the waterholding capacity of the paddy. And not only are fish a marketable crop in their own right, they also leave behind a rich organic fertilizer. The rotation is uaually 2 years fish, then 2 years rice; or 1 year fish, then 1 or 2 years rice. The fish years should be limited because growing fish too long creates excess fertility, giving the rice weak stalks that tend to fall over. If you want fish for more than 1 year, follow the fish crop with soybeans, grain sorghum, or corn, and then grow rice. In that case, the rice stalks will be all right.

The Paddy and the Planting

Soil types don't matter much to rice, but water availability does. Lowland rice thrives and produces best when its soil is flooded during part or all of its growing period. So it's grown in a special floodable, drainable field called a "paddy." The paddy needs to be located near a dependable supply of fresh water that is available for irrigation. The field must be level enough so that when it is flooded, the water will be almost equally deep in all parts. Yet it must be slightly sloped throughout, just enough so the water can be drained off when necessary. The Persian water wheel and the shadouf are two ancient, practical methods of lifting water out of a well or lower source into a paddy.

Levees: The raised earthen sides of the paddy that hold the water inside it like a bowl are called "levees." The levees can be permanent or plowed out every year and then put back in. The levee has to be located in just the right place so the depth of water inside its paddy is even. That means building the levee on the contour, on the line of equal elevation. If you're rich, you can hire a surveyor. If you're regular, you can struggle with a carpenter's level and some trial and error. Make the levees solid enough to hold water and high enough to hold 3 to 6 inches of water.

Making a Small Paddy. Till the ground you have chosen until it is loose and able to become a fine mud. Around the edge of your paddy-to-be, dig a small ditch. The ditch should be deep enough that it will provide enough dirt to make a levee (dike) on the outside of the ditch that is at least a foot high. (A foot deep and a foot wide, or 1½ feet deep and 6 inches wide, would also work.) After you get your levee built, if you are concerned that it may leak (and it will), you can vastly reinforce it by laying plastic from the far side of the levee ridge down to the bottom of the ditch. Level the paddy bottom. Do a test flooding, and it's ready for planting.

Terracing. In a temperate zone and on ground that is not naturally level, paddies can be created by terracing. That means creating a series of steplike level fields, one above another, cut into the slope of the hillside. In the Northern Hemisphere, the best side of a hill for rice is the south side, because it gets the most sunshine.

Paddy Irrigation in Delta Land. Most of the great rice areas in Asia are in river deltas. In a natural delta region, there's a time of year when the river begins to swell and overflow its low-level channel. On the old-time Mississippi, that time was the end of February until about June 1. To raise rice in a natural delta area, you dig a ditch from the river downhill to a field that can be thus flooded, making a water gate where it meets the river. Make your delta paddies narrow and almost parallel to the river, inclining off from the river bank. Bank them all around with levees to hold in the water.

THE WATER: Flooding increases the yield of the rice, so an adequate water supply is important. Rice can be irrigated from a nearby river, from a reservoir where spring rainwater or winter snow melt is captured, or from springs or wells. The irrigation setup for rice can be as simple as a hose leading from your well to your garden paddy, on up to complexes of reservoirs, aqueducts, ditches, and water gates into the field and drainage gates out of it. The pumping system can be as simple as gravity or a waterwheel or can be electrically powered and monitored. If the irrigation and drainage systems work, that's the essence of it. You can't raise rice with salt water; that will kill it. You can't raise rice with discolored, scum-coated, or toxic water either. Fresh river water is better for rice than well water because fresh water carries silt and fertilizer. The plants grow best if their water is never stagnant, ever gently flowing.

Water Temperature. Unlike wild rice, regular rice does not do well with cold water. Flooding rice with water that's too cool will drastically delay the seeds' germination and the plants' maturation. Water coming out of a well or river is typically too cool for rice, which needs its irrigation water to be no less than 70°F. So it's good practice to have a shallow holding area for such cool water where the sunshine can have time to warm it up before it goes onto the rice plants. If you do send cool water onto the paddy, the rice growing nearest the water inlet will be most affected and may ripen as much as 7 to 10 days later than the rest. If the whole field is irrigated with water below 65°F in temperature, harvest can be delayed about 30 days past the normal time. Yields will be highest if the water averages around

80°F, but above 85°F is too much of a good thing, and the yield goes down again.

Water Amount. The rice will grow well if you flood it as little as 1 inch deep. Flooding is also used by commercial growers to control weeds, though, and at least 4 inches depth is needed for that. On the other hand, more than 6.4 inches is bad for the rice because it inhibits tillering (and costs more in water purchase or pumping). So growers try to hold the water between 4 and 6 inches. They keep track of that by "depth stakes" in the field that are painted with color codes to show depth. In the South, 2.8 to 3.8 acre-feet of water are used to produce a rice crop, but about ⅓ of that will be from rainfall. In California, where there is less rainfall and more evaporation, growers figure use from 4.3 to 14.8 acre-feet in a season. For a one-time flooding on average soil, it takes 1 acre-foot of water to flood a paddy 6 inches deep. Some farmers flood the field and then let out the water several times through the season. But in California, fields remain continuously flooded until just before harvest, when they are drained.

Water Drainage. Floodings and drainings are a science learned by long experience and exercised like an art depending on soil wetness, air temperature (flood to protect from freezing), weeds (drain to kill water weeds and to weed; flood to kill dryland weeds), disease, insects, harvest schedule, etc. Drain slowly by stopping the flow of water into the paddy. The water already on the field will diminish over the following days. This makes lodging (falling over) of the plants less likely.

Mosquitoes. Rice land tends to produce mosquitoes as well as rice. Pesticides just create pesticide-immune mosquitoes. A variety of fish called "mosquito fish," if stocked in the paddy at the rate of at least 100 fish per acre, can wipe them out in 3 days. An easier way to deal with mosquito larvae is to drain the paddy at night. Mosquitoes can't breed there unless the standing water stays put.

THE SOIL: The paddy soil must be of a sort that will hold rather than lose the water. Clay of any sort, loams, and silt loams are all good because they prevent water loss from seepage. Porous soils can work if they are over a clay or other hardpan layer that will hold the water. If the rice is to be dry-planted, the soil should be worked to a fine texture, but if the rice is to be broadcast on top of water, the seedbed should be cloddy, with lumps up to 4 inches across. The rough seedbed will prevent the seed from drifting with water currents and keep it more evenly distributed in the field.

Soil Fertility. Rice stubble and weeds plowed under to decompose add fertility. More nitrogen fertilizer means more yield—but only up to the point at which excess nitrogen causes the rice stalks to get weak and easily fall over. The traditional fertilizer has been manure, which rice makes use of very well. Planting legume green manure crops immediately preceding the rice crop increases rice yield 30–50 percent.

Cultivation. For dry ground, cultivate as usual for grain. In very deep mud and naturally swampy land that can never be dried out, you can cultivate by driving large animals through the field repeatedly until they've trampled down all the weeds and worked the mud soft. Rough surfaces can be leveled by dragging a board through the paddy behind an animal.

HOW TO PLANT: There are a myriad procedures for planting rice—and they all work. Rice can be planted on dry ground or onto ground covered with water. It can be broadcast by hand or machine, or drilled on dry ground that is then flooded, or the seed can be sprayed from an airplane. Water seeding is preferred if you're fighting grass weed, because the water drowns it out. If planted dry, or drilled, the seed is covered 1½ to 2 inches. Rice usually won't germinate until it gets wet enough from daily rain or flooding. On the other hand, rice that has been planted under soil cannot emerge through both 1–3 inches of soil and a thick layer of water on top of that. For that reason, the water that is sent in to soak the seed after planting is drained for a while very soon afterward. Rice seed finds it easier to get started in sandy soils than in clay soils, so for clay soils, plant seeds more shallowly. Furthermore, seed can be planted directly into the paddy or first planted in a nursery and later transplanted. Direct seeding saves about two-thirds of the labor needed to raise a crop.

TRANSPLANTING RICE: Where land is scarce and labor is plentiful, transplanting has been an efficient way of maximizing land productivity because another crop can be growing in the paddy while the seedlings are in the nursery bed. Transplanting also helps overcome the limitations of a short growing season and the weed-management problems. Some Japanese writers insist that transplanting increases the rice crop; some American researchers insist it makes no difference. In the United States almost all rice growing is done by agribusiness: seed sown by airplanes, harvested by combine. Most Japanese rice is grown at the family level with lots of hand labor and tender, loving care—and transplanted. U.S. government rice experimental stations reported, "None of the varieties at any of the stations produced significantly higher average yields when transplanted than when directly sown." Do whichever feels right.

The Nursery. A family-sized nursery bed is just a miniature paddy, about 2 × 4 feet. Locate it in a warm place that gets lots of sunshine. Make sure the soil has lots of rich compost. Pre-flood and drain to make mud. Broadcast sprouted seeds or press unsprouted seeds into the mud carefully, so that they aren't completely covered. Scatter over them a light sand layer followed by a light mulch layer. As soon as they germinate, flood the soil. When the seedlings are big enough that the primary leaves have emerged, begin to very gradually drain so the seedlings have time to adapt to direct exposure to air and sunshine. The nursery doesn't have to be kept flooded all the time.

Readiness to Transplant. Rice seedlings from a nursery must be transplanted at about 4–5 inches high, 30–40 days of maturity (seedlings that aren't flooded don't develop as fast). The best way of all to measure transplant readiness is when 5 or, at the most, 6 long, thin leaves have been grown. Then the seedling is ready to be moved from the nursery to the paddy. Don't delay beyond the 5–6-leaf stage. Otherwise, they'll be too developed for the transition.

How to Transplant. You can do this either without or with dirt on the roots. Without soil is the more common practice. Pull seedlings, being careful not to damage roots, rinse any remaining dirt off roots, and tie into handy-sized bundles. Out in the paddy, the transplanter holds a clump of seedlings in one hand, selects 2–6, and pulls them off with the other hand. These are then pushed into the mud to root. Thus there are "hills" or clumps of 2 to 6 rice plants

every 4 to 17 inches (usually 6 inches) depending on rice variety and grower preference.

To transplant with soil, pull up the nursery seedlings in small bunches. Don't worry about perfect capture of every root. They'll be all right. In Asia there is a special hoe for this purpose. The hoe blade is used to lift an area of seedlings complete with the soil in their vicinity. They are planted in the field like that, with their adhering soil still attached, either by setting them carefully down or by throwing them down into the mud as the planter steps backwards.

Plant close enough together for a good yield, far enough apart to allow a person to walk between the clumps to pull weeds. If a seedling loses its grip and floats to the top, just gently push its root end back into the mud again. Two weeks after transplanting, the rice plants will have re-established their root systems in the dirt.

WEEDING: Water on the paddy will of itself kill the land weeds. But then water weeds may grow. If you broadcast-seeded, you can't weed. If you planted or transplanted in rows, you can. Hand weeding is easy in a paddy because the weeds can't get firmly rooted in the mud. Just wade out, pull up the bad guys, and stick them back into the mud upside-down (for green manure). Or stuff them into a bag hooked on your belt. The weeding is traditionally done in bare feet because that way your toes can feel and avoid damaging the rice plants. Weed 2 weeks after transplanting. In another method, the paddy is temporarily dried out 1–3 times during the growing season, weeded, and then re-flooded. In that case you can see what you're doing and wear shoes! Rather than hand weeding, you could come between the rows pulling a hoe or another weeding instrument.

Harvesting and Processing Rice

From the moment the rice plant's stem begins to swell (the "heading") until harvest, don't let anybody go into the rice paddy—not to weed or anything! All the while the plants are heading, it's important to keep the paddy flooded with at least an inch of water. A few plants may not head at all, and some may head only partly. Some may get insect damage. But 95 percent of your crop should be fine.

THE HARVEST DATE: The mature rice stalk is 3–5 feet tall, turning yellow, with heavy heads drooping downward. The heads don't all emerge at once; some can be as much as a month earlier than others. As a general rule of thumb, when one-tenth of the rice has headed out, harvest is about 35 to 45 days off. Very heavy crops take longer to maturity, as much as 55 days from that first heading. Rice needs to be harvested at just the right stage, then dried to a safely low moisture content. The right stage at which to drain rice from the point of view of grain quality is when the rice is fully headed and the heads are turned down and ripening in the upper parts. This stage is usually reached about 2 to 3 weeks before you'll want to cut. Harvest when the last few grains at the bottom are in a doughy state and the higher ones are all ripe. If you harvest your rice too soon (when immature), your yield will be less and there will be a lot more breakage of the doughy kernels in the subsequent steps. On the other hand, rice that is left in the field too long, until overripe, shatters severely during harvest. So the ideal time for harvest is right between the underripe and overripe stages. That stage will also make the best seed grain. When the grain is just right, you proceed as rapidly as possible to get the job done.

DRAINING THE WATER FOR HARVEST: If rice is being harvested by heavy machinery, the water has to be drained far enough ahead so the soil can get dry enough to hold the equipment. On the other hand, the water needs to be on the rice long enough so it will reach maturity. Your drainage date will be individual depending on your experience of your type of soil, drainage method, and weather conditions. Every soil dries at a slightly different rate. On commercial farms, soil is drained an average 3 to 5 days before cutting the grain. But garden farmers can let the rice dry in the paddy as long as a month after the yellow straw, head-drooping stage.

CUTTING: Cut 6–18 inches above ground. Spread evenly and thinly to let dry. Dry at least 24 hours in dry weather before binding, and wait to bind until the dew has dried off. A good system is to cut from sunrise to noon. Then bind the previous day's cutting from noon to sunset. Shock up the bound rice for a week. If you have a great deal of rice, it can go from the shock to a rick 30 feet long × 8 feet wide × 10 feet high. Or into a circular heap about 9 feet in diameter × 9 feet high. Or better yet, into a shed that's roofed and has a back side but is open on the front for good air circulation. It can dry in the stack for up to 3 months. Throw a tarp over an unprotected rick to shed rain. Rice threshes most easily after it's fully mature.

THRESHING: Proceed by the general directions given near the beginning of this chapter. Rice can be threshed almost as soon as cut, or dried first for a short or longer time and then threshed. In many parts of the world you can obtain motor-operated rice threshers.

Uses for Rice Straw. About 1100–1500 lb. of rice straw are produced per acre. You can use it as livestock feed (mix with chaff from the winnowing and bran from the milling), organic fertilizer, mulch, or cooking-fire fuel. You can also use rice straw for mattress stuffing and woven matting.

Yields. Yields vary extremely. In 1966 the highest average yield in the world was in Australia: 6,690 lb. per acre. The lowest were in Brazil and India: 1,370. Japan's average was 4,610. The U.S. average was 4,440. U.S. organic rice growers get about 2,500 lb./acre; chemical growers get 5,000. With double-cropping you can almost double a single-crop yield.

PROCESSING: If you dry rice by spreading it out in the sun and occasionally stirring it, you probably won't have much problem. But commercial growers use artificial dryers and great care, because rice kernels in the dryer are more likely than any other grains to "check" (shatter) when dried. Overripeness or too much hot sun can also cause checking. If drying artificially, dry at no higher than 100°F for seed grain, and no more than 110°F if you're going to dry the grain in just one in-and-out operation. If your oven or dryer is warmer than that, you're safest drying in 2-minute shifts with 12–24-hour cooling periods between. Checking happens if the outer kernel dries faster than the inner, so the cooling periods allow the kernel's moisture to shift around enough to even out again between outer and inner parts. Then they won't crack. But don't let the rice "rest" long enough to be at risk of mold or fungus. Keep sending it back to the dryer until it is fully dried.

Hulling. Rice kernels, after threshing, are still covered with a green-brownish husk or "hull." Leave them that way for storage because once they are hulled out; they don't keep nearly as well. Hull out only a few days' worth at a time for cooking. You can remove hulls by hand, but it's tedious;

pounding, rolling, or grinding is more efficient. But even professionals break about 20 percent of the kernels in the process.

To pound the hulls off, put the rice in a sturdy container that resembles a very large mortar. Then pound with a wooden pestle. Two or three people can pound at the same time, or the pestle can be lifted and dropped onto the grain by hand, foot, or water power. It helps to have a really big, heavy pestle to let fall on the rice in the mortar again and again. It takes a good bit of pounding before all the hulls are off and can be winnowed away. (For a small-scale hulling system, see "The Grain Sorghums.")

Rice hulling machines may operate on the same principle as oat hullers, grinding between 2 stones. (See "Hulling" under "Oats.") Or they may work like sorghum grain hullers with a pounding action. After hulling, rice is separated into hulls and what is called "unpolished" rice or "brown rice." After hulling, rice must be winnowed to separate out the chaff.

Allen Dong and Roger J. Edberg invented a way to make a homemade rice huller and then declared this invention public domain. This huller also hulls millet, sesame, spelt, and wheat, and it will remove saponins from quinoa. For more info, write I-Tech, PO Box 413, Veneta, OR 97487. Or visit **agronomy.ucdavis.edu/LTRAS/itech/**.

"Polishing." The more your rice is pounded in the mortar or ground between surfaces, the more of the good stuff is removed. If the rice is further polished, enough to take off all the bran, germ, vitamins, and fat (contained in its darker outer layers), the result is that perfectly white, polished rice that is the usual table fare. What gets thrown away is the "rice bran." White rice is "polished rice"; it looks clean, but you could get vitamin deficiencies from eating it if you had no other foods. A young man of macrobiotic fame is said to have gone into the wilderness for 6 months with nothing more than a sack of brown rice, a bag of lentils, and a gallon of soy sauce, and emerged just as healthy as when he left! He wouldn't have been in such good shape if his rice had been white.

Storing. Unlike wheat, brown rice will eventually go rancid. Store it in an airtight container. Under reasonably cool conditions, it will keep 6 to 18 months. It goes bad more quickly in hot, humid climates

Rice Cooking

COOKING PERFECT RICE: Years ago, a lady walked up to me and complained, "There's no recipe for cooking brown rice in your book." Well, there is now! Use a heavy pan with a tight-fitting lid. If you briefly saute the uncooked kernels in a little oil before adding the water, your rice will turn out non-gummy with nicely separated grains.

How Much Water to Add? After you put rice (brown or white) in the pot but before you saute it, push your finger down through the rice to touch the pan's bottom. See how far up your finger the rice extends. Saute the rice. Now just barely touch the top of the rice with the top of that finger and add water until it comes up as high on your finger as the rice did. That works unless your rice is deeper than 1 inch. In that case, add water until the water is an inch (no more!) above the level of the rice.

Finish Cooking the Rice. If you like, add a pinch of salt. Now cover pot and heat. When steam begins to seep out from under the lid, take the pan off the heat for 5 minutes.

Then cook on your lowest heat setting for 25 more minutes. *Once the steaming starts, don't lift the lid until the rice is done!* Lifting the lid will spoil the steaming process. Let the rice cool 10 minutes, stir well, and serve.

Ruth of Bonaire told me that one of her favorite meals is rijsttafel: "This meal is Indonesian in origin but has now become more Dutch than East Indian. 'Rijsttafel' means 'rice table' and consists of a huge assortment of various warm toppings to put on rice—which is served in a huge basin in the middle of all the topping-dishes (like 25 at a time)."

➢ *NASI GORENG* Ruth again! *"Each cook makes this differently, but here is the basic format so you can be sure you end up with a similar dish. You'll need to cook 1 lb. of rice for every ½ lb. of meat, and have as many onions, etc., as meat in volume. Get out your biggest frying pan. While your rice is cooking, fry up the meat (chicken, pork, beef, goat, etc.) in small pieces in it, along with onions, green peppers, etc. Add ketjap manis (see "Seasoning Mixes" in Chapter 5). And add curry powder, cumin, more gingerroot, garlic, coriander, and red pepper until you think it's a bit over-spicy (the rice dilutes the spices). Now add the cooked rice to the spiced meat mixture in the frying pan along with another good glug of ketjap manis. Mix it all together thoroughly. When the rice is brownish-colored from the sauce, serve immediately. (For an extra-authentic touch, make an omelet of 2 or 3 eggs, or scramble them. Cut omelet into strips when cooked and lay that on top of the rice mixture.)"*

➢ *BROCCOLI AND BROWN RICE* Saute 1 large chopped onion in a little fat or oil. Add 3 c. chopped broccoli and saute a couple more minutes. Add 1 minced or crushed clove garlic, 2 c. cooked brown rice, and ½ c. grated cheese. In a separate bowl beat 4 eggs. Add ½ c. milk and a bit each of freshly ground black pepper and nutmeg. Stir into the broccoli-onion-rice mixture. Cover with another ½ c. of shredded cheese or cheese slices. Now pour into a 2-qt. casserole dish, cover, and bake at 350°F till cheese topping has melted.

SECRETS OF RICE COOKING

1. Don't overcook the rice. That will tend to make it sticky instead of fluffy.
2. Don't stir the rice while it's cooking. That disturbs the starch on the surface of the grains and causes them to clump.
3. Be aware of the kind of rice you're using. Italian arborio and Japanese glutinous rices are supposed to stick together.
4. Don't use too much water.
5. If your rice is tough, it wasn't cooked long enough. Brown rice and short-grained rices take longer to cook than white and long-grained rices.

WILD RICE

Wild rice is actually a member of the oat rather than the rice family, a water-oat. It grows wild in shallow lakes and along riverbanks in the northern United States and Canada. The Sioux called it "pshu" and the Chippewas "man-om-in," and it was the basic food for the northern residents of the lakes and rivers between the Mississippi and Lake Superior. Other names for this plant: "Indian rice," "water oats," "water rice," and the Latin scientific name of the Northern wild rice variety, *Zizania palustris*. When this *Zizania* is called "wild rice" in discussions with Asians, they get confused. You have to explain that it's not the same thing as the wild rices related to true rice (*O. sativa*), of which there are many—all more appropriately called "wild rice" by Asians.

There are other varieties of *Zizania*: Interior wild rice, Southern wild rice, and Estuarine wild rice. But the Northern variety, *Z. palustris,* is the one North Americans commonly gather, plant, harvest, and eat; and that's the one they mean when they speak of "wild rice." Plant geneticists have recently created new varieties of *Zizania* wild rice; like corn, it has the convenient and unusual characteristic of having separate male and female flowers.

MORE READING: I know of only one book about growing and processing wild rice, but there are many, many useful magazine articles going back to the 1920s. The book is small but very good: *Wild Rice in Canada* by S.G. Aiken, P.F. Lee, D. Punter, and J.M. Stewart, who based their work on the original monograph by William G. Dore. It lists the magazine articles.

Growing Wild Rice

GROWING CONDITIONS: Under natural conditions, Northern wild rice is found growing along river shores in the shallow water and in lakes. The plant thrives best in rivers that have rushing floodwaters in the spring and water depths of about a foot, although it can grow in water as deep as 3 feet. In deeper water, the plants get spindly, late-flowering, and poor-producing because too much of their energy has to go into stalk. It produces best per acre in water 6–12 inches deep in midsummer. Incidentally, what keeps the grass standing up in all that water is many small air spaces, like tiny balloons, located all through its tissue.

In lakes, wild rice is generally concentrated near the water inlets and outlets because of its need for aerated, clean, moving water. It can grow on bottoms that are mud, sand, or gravel—and even on bare and rocky ones—as long as it can find some small crevices for seedling roots to hold on, but wild rice does best in soft-textured sediments. It won't grow in murky water; water loaded with sewage, industrial wastes, detergents, or floating oil; or water covered with floating algae, scum, or other debris that prevents light from shining down into the water. It likes sunlight under or above the water. A large population of carp can be a problem because the fish's habit of thrashing about in shallow water can uproot wild rice. Powerboats also destroy wild rice stands because of the waves they create.

Wild rice won't grow in brackish water or sea water, nor does it produce well when crowded by other aquatic plants. For that reason, some growers tear out or till up competition like reeds and cattails before introducing wild rice. But it will grow well, even becoming self-seeding, almost anywhere there is fairly fresh, shallow, flowing water that's both temperate and tropical. And it will gradually, naturally spread downstream from where it's introduced—but not upstream.

Thus wild rice is sometimes deliberately introduced to waters it hasn't grown in before, or artificially helped to expand into adjacent areas and there harvested for home use or sale. In recent years, it has been also grown paddy-style, like Asian rice. (This development makes the name "wild rice" less true than ever.)

WILD RICE SEED

Buying. Packaged wild rice from the store won't sprout because of processing. You can buy live seed from Wildlife

Nurseries, PO Box 2724, Oshkosh, WI 54903-2724; 920-231-3780; fax 920-231-3554. (They also sell wild rice for table use, and a book of 101 wild rice recipes for $9.50.) Or buy your wild rice seed from Richter's, Box 26, Goodwood, ON L0C 1A0, CANADA.

Harvesting. If you're trying to establish wild rice in a new area, the seed will be a problem. It's best to harvest the seed from one place, move it to the new place you want to plant, and promptly throw it in the water there. If you do that, the germination of your seed will be almost 100 percent. If you must wait a few days before planting the seed, first soak it in water because while it waited in dry storage, the hulls absorbed air. If unsoaked, it is likely to float away from where you want it to sink and grow next spring.

When wild rice is allowed to fully ripen on the stalk and then collected, sprouting rates are best. Poor sprouting results if the seeds are taken from the stalk when not fully mature. Ability to sprout is also harmed if the seed is spread out to dry in the sun, maybe because it gets too hot. But if gathered when fully ripe and dry, not subjected to any further drying, and not handled roughly, wild rice seed will retain its sprouting ability for a couple weeks out of water. Storing clean seed that is free of smashed grains and caterpillar bodies also helps avoid decay. But long-term dry storage simply doesn't work. Less than half your seed would germinate after a month of dry storage, about a tenth after 6 weeks, almost none after 7 weeks. You can't plant packaged wild rice from the store. That won't sprout at all because of its processing.

Storing. For temporary, brief storage longer than 2 weeks, scatter wild rice seed in sphagnum moss, sawdust, sand, or mud and refrigerate. To store all winter, place in mud and submerge in water outdoors; it may germinate as well as 100 percent when planted the next spring. It's important that the seeds be scattered in the storage substance and not concentrated. Whatever you have them in, place that in wooden boxes, and sink the boxes into water. If it's water with animals in it, cover the box with a fine-mesh wire to protect your seed from hungry critters. Another way to store wild rice seed all winter is in a porous cloth bag in cold water (about 35°F) that is regularly changed. Changing the water discourages decay. If you can store seed in a natural, strong flow of clean water, that's best of all.

Wild rice seed won't grow too soon. Seeds will not germinate for at least 3 months after harvest, no matter what. They must also experience freezing or near-freezing temperatures to break their dormancy. Freezing solid doesn't hurt them as long as the temperature lowers very gradually. Once spring does approach, you need to get that seed planted because the grains will germinate, and if they aren't safely out of the storage medium and under water when they do, they won't survive.

PLANTING CONDITIONS: You have to have lots of running water! You also need a field that can be flooded with it. If you have those, wild rice is a possible crop for you, a good new use for marginal bottomland, one that can benefit both you and the nearby wildlife. Turning marshland into wild rice land is one use for wetlands that tends to please both the Soil Conservation Service and the farmer. Wherever you grow wild rice, the bird hunting will be good. Wild rice is also pursued by insect pests, particularly a variety of caterpillar, and is occasionally afflicted with ergot. Most commercial wild rice is not organically grown.

If you can acquire the water and have a way to construct a water channeling system and paddy levees, it can be done. One way is to use a low-lying field adjacent to a river. Cultivate to get rid of other plants. In mid-September, let the water in until it reaches a depth of 1 foot (or at least 6 inches), and immediately seed. The water can be left in place, but it needs to have circulation in and out for a good harvest. After harvest the land can be drained, dried, cultivated, and reflooded for seeding.

PLANTING: Let enough wild rice escape your harvesting to fall into the water and seed next year's crop. Wild rice is an annual grass, of course, and has to be reseeded every year. The seeds drop into the water in late summer, sink quickly to the bottom, and lie there dormant until spring, when they germinate, take root, and grow. Wild rice seeds can't grow unless covered by at least 1 or 2 inches of water. The stalks appear above water about mid-June, eventually growing several feet above its surface.

For artificial planting, you'll want about 20 lb. of wet seed for each acre to plant. Plant in the fall to have wild rice growing the next spring. Take your seed bag out in a very steady boat or raft because you can broadcast it most effectively from a standing position. Or if the water is shallow and the bottom firm enough, you can wade through the areas you want to seed. Or just throw seed from the shore. Large-scale seeding can be done by airplane. Don't harvest at all the first year after you plant. That allows the crop to become seed for an even better crop the following year. In addition, plant more seed in that second year in the places you missed during the first one.

Harvesting Wild Rice

WATER LEVEL FOR HARVEST: Wild rice can handle torrential flooding in the spring, but it needs a stable—or gradually lowering—water level as harvest approaches. Flooding can destroy the harvest. A sudden drop in water level can cause the plants to collapse onto the water.

RIPENING: In early August, the oat-type, loosely branched seed head is produced at the top of the stem. The kernel is first light green, then olive brown, and finally brown or black. When ripening, the formerly pale-green stalks turn yellow. Once the seed is ripe and hard, the slightest wind will shake off the ripe grains into the water, and the birds and other wildlife will eagerly feed on it. This is harvest time! On public wild rice stands, there may be complex and strictly enforced harvesting rules, usually a variation of the traditional Indian harvest system.

INDIAN HARVEST: The hard, ripe seed is harvested by boat, two people to a canoe, one to pole and one to harvest. The harvester holds a stick in each hand. With one stick, the grain heads are gently bent over the edge of the boat. With the other stick, they're tapped to make their ripe grain fall down into the bottom of the boat. Then those stalks are released, the poler moves the boat forward, and the harvester does it again with another clump of wild rice.

Repeated Harvesting, Indian Style. Not all the seeds of a head of wild rice get ripe at once, so harvest gently, bending the long grass over the gunwale of your boat carefully so as not to break the stems, hitting the heads hard enough to make the ripe grains fall onto the collector pad in your boat but not so hard that you damage the unripe grains. Since the grain ripens over a week or two, you'll be back a few

more times before the harvest period is over, doing exactly the same thing: collecting the portion of the seeds that are ripe enough to easily fall from your experienced blow with the flail stick.

Sheaved Wild Rice. Here's another Indian harvest method. When the heads are green and won't lose grains from the handling, a lone boater ties a mass of heads together to form a sheaf. Then the sheaf is allowed to ripen naturally while being somewhat protected by its density from the birds and from shattering into the water. (A modern version of this is to tie a plastic bag over the sheaf head.)

COMMERCIAL: Commercial wild rice growers may harvest with more sophisticated equipment. The ideal machine gently shakes off the ripe grains and catches them without damaging any stems, so the grain can continue ripening. Al Bruner, co-owner of the St. Maries Wild Rice Co., harvests from airboats powered by an airplane propeller and equipped with a front-end header that knocks the ripe kernels off their stalks into a scoop. Dense stands of wild rice can be profitably harvested by canoe, but where it grows sparsely over a wide area, mechanized harvesting is a great advantage. Or the best of the crop can be gathered by hand and then the machine sent through to make a last sweep of it. If a harvesting machine crushes the stalks after harvest by passing over them, it's going to be the last harvest visit for that year anyway.

By mid-September all the seeds will have been harvested, been eaten by wildlife, or fallen into the water. afterward, the plant stalks die and fall into the water as well.

Processing and Using Wild Rice

Three more steps remain before the wild rice you harvested is ready for market or your kitchen. It has to be cured, parched, and threshed.

CURING: Freshly harvested "green" wild rice is invariably on the damp side. It must commence drying, or "curing," almost immediately, or souring and mold will develop, especially in broken or crushed grains. Another purpose of the curing period is to give the immature grains a chance to ripen. Given this opportunity, a good number of the soft grains will get hard and gain the dark brown or black color of a ripe grain. The grain can be moved from the boat to a drying place in burlap or cotton sacks or in any other handy container.

Native American Method. On a day of full sun, the native Americans spread the freshly harvested grain in a thin layer on skins, bark sheets, or an exposed large stretch of flat rock. They stirred it once in a while and put it in a shelter if there was a risk of rain or dew reversing the drying. Wild rice so dried would store without rotting until the next step, parching, could be accomplished.

Commercial Cure Process. It's basically the same. The green rice is spread out as thinly as possible on a large pavement in the hot sun, and is turned over or stirred once or more per day. It takes several days of this to get it dry enough that the immature grains have finished ripening and decay isn't a risk.

PARCHING: The purpose of parching is to complete the drying of the grain and loosen the hull. The wild rice hull is easily removed after being heated. The heat applied should be just enough (and no more) to swell the grains enough to force apart what up until then have been tightly closed hulls. Too much heat could cook the grains, make them pop, or even burn them, so the amount of heating must be very closely controlled.

Native American Method. In 1885 this description of a native American parching process was recorded by the USDA: "It [the grain] is laid on scaffolds about four feet high, eight wide, and twenty to fifty long, covered with reeds and grass, and a slow fire is maintained beneath for thirty-six hours, so as to parch slightly the hull, that it may be removed easily." Another native American method of parching was to pour about a half bushel of the grain into a bark basket or bowl, which was then hung over an outdoor fire. The grain was stirred continually, so it wouldn't burn, while it was heated to the necessary temperature to break open the hulls.

Commercial Parching Oven. This is a metal cylinder large enough to hold about a bushel of wild rice at a time. It rotates over a fire and is either hand-cranked or electric-powered. To keep the temperature for the process even and not too high, the rotation is continuous and the size of the grain load limited. The parching continues until there is no more visible water vapor escaping from the barrel holding the grain. After the steaming has completely stopped, the grain is dumped into a thin spread on a drying surface. The final vestiges of water vapor will escape there as it cools. The final result should be grain with firm, hard kernels that are perfectly dry. The leaf fragments and caterpillars that accidentally got harvested together with the grain will be bone-dry too. Next comes the hulling, or threshing.

THRESHING: The 1885 report continued: "To separate [kernels] from the chaff or husk, a hole is made in the ground a foot wide and one deep, and lined with skins. About a peck of rice is put in at a time; an Indian steps in, with a half jump, on one foot, then on the other, until the husk is removed . . . The hull adheres tightly, and is left on the grain." To do it this way, the hole is best located in hard ground.

The commercial hulling method is an electric machine in which the grain is rotated in a large cylinder, similar to the parching oven, and is simultaneously flailed with pieces of rubber garden hose attached to a central axle. At the optimum beating speed, the kernels shell out easily. The ideal huller flails hard enough to accomplish the threshing but not so roughly that kernels are broken. In real life, some kernels always get broken.

WINNOWING: The traditional method was to toss up into the wind the grain mixed with chaff and dirt. The modern hulling machine uses an air stream that carries the light material away from the grain.

SCREENING: The modern process adds a step of passing the hulled grain over vibrating screens to get rid of small or broken grains. But for home use, don't screen; it's all good food. For the gourmet marketplace, though, only the large, unbroken kernels can be sold.

WILD RICE RECIPES

➤ *WILD RICE/MUSHROOMS CASSEROLE Wash 1 c. wild rice and cook it 15 minutes in boiling water. Brown a cup of sliced mushrooms in butter. Make a white sauce of 1 c. (or more if needed) milk, 2 T. flour, and ¼ c. butter. Drain rice and pour into a greased casserole dish. Pour mushrooms on top and white sauce over all. Sprinkle with salt and pepper. Cover with a thin layer of bread crumbs. Bake at 350°F for 15–20 minutes, or until crumbs are brown.*

➤ *THREE-WAY ELEGANCE Cook wild rice. Toss with sliced mushrooms and snow peas that have been sauteed in butter.*

RYE

Rye looks and grows a lot like wheat and barley, except that it grows much taller than either of those, 6–7 feet high. Its seed head is "bearded" like barley. Originally from central Asia, rye thrives in cool climates and poor soils, including sand. Lyme grass is a wild relative of rye. Rye kernels are larger than wheat ones and will thresh out just as easily as wheat. Unlike oats, they have no problem hull. Rye is the cereal grain least injured by disease and insects; it's even hardier than wheat, the best survivor of all the grass family of grains. Sandy ground is okay. Acid soil is okay. Soil of very low fertility is okay. (Just the opposite of corn, rye actually does better in low-fertility soil because surplus nitrogen causes excess stalk growth and then lodging.) It will grow after a single plowing, in a seedbed so rough that

wheat would do badly. Rye threshes more easily than any other grass grain. However, if you have land that is suitable for growing wheat, you may want to plant that instead, since rye doesn't yield as much per acre as does wheat. But some gardeners plant rye between their garden rows in late summer to control the mud, and then till it in with their spring plowing for green manure, hay, or straw.

Planting and Growing Rye

VARIETIES: Rye, like wheat, comes in both "spring" and "winter" varieties. Different varieties are suited to different climatic regions. It also comes in steps of strongness in flavor called "light," "medium," or "dark" rye. If you plan to save some rye for seed, grow just one kind, for rye is wind-pollinated, and varieties readily cross.

Winter and Spring Rye. This variety can be grown either for grain, green manure, or green fodder. Plant in the fall 2 to 3 weeks before frost. For a green manure crop, till it in next spring after it has gotten to be almost a foot high. But if you live in the northern United States or Canada, winter rye kills off too much to make the best grain crop. Plant spring rye instead, in early spring, and harvest it in late summer. You can order winter rye seed from Ronniger's, cereal rye from Abundant Life or Bountiful Gardens.

Annual Ryegrass. This can be used as a green manure crop. It grows only a couple feet tall and doesn't produce a table grain. Plant 2 to 3 lb. per 1,000 square feet or 25 per acre (24 lb. per accepted bushel of ryegrass). Best time to plant is midsummer right on to a few weeks before first frost time. Annual ryegrass can be planted in all soils, all climates. It grows fast. Winter cold will kill it. As it dies, it forms a protective mat over the soil that prevents erosion and deep freezing.

Perennial Ryegrass: This is a lawn seed. Don't grow this variety for either a grain or a green manure crop because it's not a grain crop and it's very persistent in coming back, as is proper for a lawn grass but not for a green manure crop.

CLIMATE: It will grow where it's too cold for wheat. Rye can also grow in warmer areas—although it won't germinate if the temperature is over 85°F. But its most valuable trait is its unusual tolerance for cold. Rye will germinate at 33°F and grow any day the temperature is above 40°F. Even a –40°F period won't kill it! If you have poor soil and a cold climate, consider rye for your bread flour. It can manage to grow and make a crop with less moisture than wheat or oats, though you get a larger yield with more moisture. The high plains of eastern Colorado, North and South Dakota, and Nebraska are rye-growing areas of the United States. In Russia and Germany it's an important bread grain.

WHEN TO PLANT: Plant the same as wheat, except on poor soils plant 1 to 3 weeks before wheat-planting time. Plant winter rye earlier for a green fodder than for a grain crop. In the central United States, plant by September 15 for fodder, by September 30 for grain.

HOW MUCH: Plant an area about 10 × 150 feet for every bushel of rye you want to grow. There are 56 lb. per bushel of rye. Plant 1½ to 2½ inches deep: 1½ bushels per acre for a grain crop, 2 to 2½ bushels for a grazing or hay crop, 1 lb. per 1,000 square feet for a green manure crop. But in a dry climate, plant only half the usual rate. In old-time England, the rye and wheat seeds were often planted premixed, and then the two grains were reaped, threshed, ground, and baked together. The result was called "maslin" bread. I always add at least a handful of rye flour to my wheat bread. Tastes good.

GREEN FODDER: Rye is husky enough that you can let animals graze on winter rye in the late fall and again in early spring—but not when the ground is muddy, because they would damage the grain by trampling it. After a spring grazing, keep them away from it long enough for it to grow tall enough to be cut down in another good grazing or mowed for hay—or allow it time enough to mature a grain crop.

Harvesting and Processing

RYE HAY: Cut just as the heads start to bloom. Gather up immediately into small curing bundles. Let cure in the sun a few days. Turn over, spread out, and cure some more. Then stack or store in your barn.

RYE GRAIN: Your rye will ripen about a week before your wheat. Harvest when the kernels are in the dough stage, as you would wheat. Cut, bind, shock, and thresh. You can thresh directly out of the field, or store and thresh later. If you cut and shock, make sure to let the kernels dry thoroughly (to avoid ergot). In 1850, yields averaged 14 bushels per acre, with many folks getting 35. If you have a roller mill, you can "flake" kernels into a rolled rye. With a grinder you can make grits for cereal or flour for bread.

RYE STRAW: This is the longest of any of the grass grains, so it has excellent possible craft uses. In the old days they made hats, matting, thatched houses, "corn dolls," baskets, fans, packing material, and horse bedding from it.

EATING: Rye flour is darker in color and stronger in flavor than wheat. But the real drawback of rye, as compared to wheat, is its lower gluten content. Rye breads are usually made with at least half wheat flour. Even so, they are heavy, and it's harder to get them baked clear through than it is for wheat-flour breads. Rye doesn't have quite as much nutritional value as wheat, but it's by no means poor. It makes good sprouts. Rye doesn't absorb moisture like wheat flour, so cut down on liquids when you are substituting in recipes, or else use correspondingly more rye flour. Anything with rye flour in it that you knead will tend to be sticky. Sourdough rye bread is an excellent moist bread that keeps well (recipe in "Sourdough Recipes" under "Yeast Breads"). Caraway, anise, and orange peel are good flavors in rye baking. So are spices, brown sugar, and molasses.

❧ *RYE FRUIT BREAD Cut up dried prunes, discarding the seeds, or any other kind of home-dried fruit until you have ½ cup. Sprinkle a little flour over them so they won't stick together. Sift together 2½ c. rye flour, ½ t. salt, 2 t. baking powder, and ½ t. soda. Combine ¼ c. molasses, 1½ c. water, and 2 T. cooking oil or melted lard. (If you use melted lard, have your water warm.) Combine with dry ingredients, add the fruit, and mix well. Pour into a greased loaf pan. Bake about an hour in a 350°F oven.*

Here follow some excellent recipes from the Mary Mill Service, Fisher Flour Mills Co. These recipes will work with your home-ground rye flour too.

❧ *ALL-RYE SNACK BREAD Makes 1 loaf 4 × 8 × 2½ inches. Preheat oven to 350°F. Besides 2½ c. Fisher's rye flour, you'll need 1 t. salt, 2 t. baking powder, ½ c. sliced pressed figs, ½ t. soda, 1½ c. lukewarm water, ¼ c. molasses, and 2 T. oil or melted shortening. Sift Fisher's rye flour with salt and baking powder. Add figs and stir enough to coat the fruit with flour. Put soda in a 2-cup measure or larger, add lukewarm water and molasses, stir until it foams a little, and then dump all at once into the center of flour mixture. Pour oil on top and stir until smooth. Grease the loaf pan well (bottom only), and smooth in the dough well up on sides of pan. Bake at 350°F for 55 minutes. Cut sides of loaf away*

from pan immediately on taking from the oven. Cool on rack before storing. Optionally, add ¼ to ½ t. each of caraway and anise seeds to the above recipe and omit the figs. Or use ½ c. moist seeded or seedless raisins instead of the figs.

❧ *BUTTERMILK RYE BREAD Substitute buttermilk for the 1½ c. water in the recipe and increase soda to 1 teaspoon. Omit baking powder.*

❧ *RYE SCONES (WHEATLESS, EGGLESS, MILKLESS) Makes 8 wedges. Use a pancake griddle, if possible, or a heavy frying pan. Do not grease. Sprinkle with ½ c. sifted Fisher's rye flour and heat until flour begins to color slightly (medium heat is best). Besides flour you'll need ¼ to ½ t. salt and 1 c. mashed Irish potatoes. The wetness of the potatoes may make more or less flour necessary. To preserve the potatoes' flavor, it is best to steam them in their jackets, but leftover mashed potatoes (without milk, if for a milkless diet) are satisfactory. Sift the salt with the flour, add to the potato, and work well with fingers. Sprinkle Fisher's rye flour on a board or paper towel. Pat out the mixture into a 9-inch round. Crimp the edges like a pie. Cut in 8 or 9 pie-shaped wedges, lift to hot griddle, and cook 5 minutes on each side. Eat hot with butter and syrup, or what you prefer.*

❧ *RYE PASTRY Makes a 2-crust, 9-inch pie. Preheat oven to 450°F. Besides 2 c. Fisher's rye flour, you'll need 1 t. salt, ⅔ c. shortening, and 3 to 4 T. water. Sift and measure rye flour. Sift again with salt. Cut half of shortening into dry ingredients until they are the consistency of cornmeal. Cut in remaining shortening to lumps the size of a pea. Sprinkle water over dry ingredients, tossing aside dampened particles. Use only enough water to hold particles together. Knead until smooth. Roll out about ⅛ inch thick. For baked pie shell, fit in pan and bake at 450°F for 10 to 12 minutes.*

❧ *RYE QUICK BREAD (WHEATLESS) Makes one 1½-pound loaf. Preheat oven to 325°F. Besides 2½ c. unsifted Fisher's rye flour, you'll need ¾ T. salt, 1 T. baking powder, 1 T. sugar, 1 well-beaten egg, 1½ c. milk, and 2 T. melted butter or salad oil. Optional: 1 T. caraway seeds or grated orange peel. Combine dry ingredients. Beat egg with milk; add melted butter or salad oil and combine with dry ingredients. Stir in caraway seeds or orange peel. Bake in well-greased loaf pan at 325°F for 1 hour. Let stand in pan for 15 minutes before turning out onto a rack.*

❧ *RYE GRIDDLE CAKES You'll need 2½ c. Fisher's rye flour, ½ t. salt, 1 t. soda, 1 beaten egg, 1¾ c. sour milk or buttermilk, 1 T. melted butter, and ¼ c. honey. Spoon flour from sack lightly. Measure and mix with salt and soda. Beat egg; add milk, butter and honey; and beat gradually into dry ingredients until smooth. Bake on lightly greased griddle, turning but once. (Sweet milk may be used in place of sour milk or buttermilk, but the griddle cakes will not be as tender. If using sweet milk, omit the soda and add 4 t. baking powder.)*

❧ *RYE FLOUR CAKE You'll need 7 T. butter or margarine, 1 c. granulated sugar, 2½ c. Fisher's rye flour, ½ t. salt, ½ t. cinnamon, ½ t. ginger, ¾ t. nutmeg, 2½ t. baking powder, 1 c. milk or orange juice, and 1 t. vanilla. Cream the shortening and add sugar gradually, beating well. Sift together dry ingredients 3 times. Add to the first mixture, alternating with the liquid. Add vanilla and beat well. (If you use orange juice, omit vanilla.) Pour into 2 well-greased, wax-paper-lined, 8-inch layer pans. Bake at 375°F for 35 to 50 minutes.*

> **RYE FLOUR PORRIDGE** *Mix 1 c. Fisher's rye flour, 1 t. salt, and 1 c. cold water into a smooth paste. Stir the mixture into 4 c. boiling water in the top of a double boiler. Cook about 20 minutes, stirring once in a while. Serve with molasses and butter.*

Here are some other good rye recipes.

> **RYE-WHEAT CEREAL** *Esther R. McMenamin, Kennewick, WA, makes a cereal from coarse ground rye and wheat mixed together, 1 part rye to 2 parts wheat. Cook (add a pinch salt) in 2 parts water to each 1 part cereal for about an hour. Serve with milk or cream and sweetening.*

> **STEAMED RYE** *You can serve rye as your starchy item the same way you would rice. (You can substitute whole wheat in this recipe if you want.) Wash 2 c. raw (unroasted) whole rye and then soak in 4 c. water or soup stock for 3 hours. Now add 1 t. salt and simmer until the grain is tender and all water is absorbed. (You may have to add more water, stock, tomato juice, or soy sauce to get it tender because it may take so long that your original water steams off.)*

> **FLAKED RYE** *Looks like rolled oats. You can buy it at a health-food store. To use it as a breakfast cereal, boil 2 c. water and a pinch of salt. Slowly stir in 1 c. flaked rye. Reduce heat to simmer and cover pan tightly. Cook until all water is absorbed. Eat with honey and cream. Good!*

> **RYE AND LENTIL** *This dish is awesomely healthy for you. Chop up an onion and a carrot. Fry them in a very little oil briefly until tender. Then mix them with 1½ c. cooked rye and 1½ c. cooked lentils. Stir in ¼ t. each of thyme, sage, and pepper. Moisten with a pour of tomato juice. Pack into a casserole dish and steam, bake, or microwave until hot.*

THE SORGHUM FAMILY

The sorghums (also called "milo") are bonafide members of the grass family, though a rather distinct branch, *Sorghum vulgare*. Originally from Africa, sorghum grain is still a major cereal on that continent. The plant looks somewhat like corn but, instead of growing ears, it develops its seeds in a cluster on top of the stalk called the "head." The sorghum family has 4 basic subgroups: broomcorns, grain sorghums, sweet/forage sorghums, and pasture grass sorghums such as Johnson grass and Sudan grass. Sorghum likes sandy, well-drained soil. Like corn, it needs nitrogen-rich, fertile ground—though it isn't quite as needy as corn in that regard, so green or animal manuring is helpful for sorghum.

CLIMATE: The sorghums will grow anywhere you can grow corn, but you need at least 100 frost-free days after you plant. Sorghum seed won't germinate in cold soil; it needs a soil temperature of at least 70°F for germination. (Broomcorn is an exception; it can handle colder climates than the others.) Sorghum will thrive even in places that are too hot and dry to grow corn, because sorghum has the ability to actually go into a kind of hibernation during a dry period and then come out of it and continue growing when it gets water again. It needs lots of water at some time or other though, but it is better than corn at waiting for it or finding water hidden in the soil. So sorghum will outproduce corn in a dry climate; in an even dryer climate, it will grow when corn won't.

SORGHUMS FOR LIVESTOCK: Feed as green chop or

silage, or make into hay. To harvest for silage, cut in the late doughy stage. If you want to strip leaves for feeding, do so before frost or you'll lose them. *Be cautious about feeding fresh green sorghum leaves and stalks to animals, especially rabbits. It may disagree with them.* But sorghum that is ensiled or dried will never be a problem and is very nourishing.

SECRETS OF SORGHUM SEED

1. For numerous sorghum varieties, contact Seeds of Change or Southern Exposure Seed Exchange (grain and sweet sorghums, broomcorn).
2. Plant sorghum in a rotation schedule to avoid a buildup of cane bugs, diseases, and soil depletion.
3. Unlike the other two domesticated "canes" (bamboo and sugar cane), the sorghums are raised from seed, and anyone growing any kind of sorghum—except a hybrid!—can easily save seed at harvesting time.
4. Your only risk of not breeding true is from other wind-transported pollen. Sorghum will cross-pollinate with other sorghums and with Sudan grass. So plant the sorghum that you plan to save seed from in isolation from any other variety of sorghum, tame or wild. Recommended isolation distance is at least 1,300 feet.
5. At harvest time, as the heads are cut, select your choice of the fullest, best-developed ripened seed heads.
6. Air-dry them as soon as they are removed from the plant. Then thresh. About 75 percent of the weight of your dry, whole heads will turn out to be seeds.
7. Store the dry seed in an airtight container to protect from insect damage.
8. Professional growers usually treat seed with a fungicide before planting, ½ T. Thiram per lb. of seed.
9. Sorghum requires a fine-tilled, weed-free soil because the young plants germinate slowly and are not husky at first. (Once they get going, sorghum plants will usually do well.)
10. Plant about 10 days to 2 weeks after corn time.

Broomcorn

Broomcorn first came to the United States when Ben Franklin went traveling and saw it in Hungary. He brought back seeds and began making new-style brooms from this other variety of sorghum. Broom making used to be a much bigger industry in Illinois before synthetics, but there is still enough broomcorn grown there to keep about a dozen broom companies going. It's a nice cottage industry because broomcorn is easy to grow and making brooms doesn't require complex, expensive machinery. Real broomcorn straw makes a better broom than petroleum, too. You could grow enough broomcorn on a mere acre to make a thousand brooms, but making the brooms would be a lot of work.

PLANTING AND GROWING BROOMCORN

Varieties: You grow broomcorn for its stiffbranched, elongated top, which is used to make brooms and brushes. Different varieties of broomcorn range from 2 to 5 feet high. You can buy broomcorn seed from Bountiful Gardens.

Climate: Broomcorn will grow anywhere corn will, and you raise it basically the same way as corn. Commercial broomcorn is grown in the Midwest, the South, and Mexico.

Planting: Plant your seeds 4 inches apart in rows about 30 inches apart, 1½ inches deep. The small seeds are likely to plant thicker than that, so thin after the plants come up. Thin again to 8 inches or even 12 inches distant. Planted like that, a 10-foot row will provide enough tassels to make one, or maybe two, brooms. Weed and water as you would sweet corn.

HARVESTING AND MAKING BROOMS

Harvesting for Broom Making: By late summer, your broomcorn plants will have reached the late bloom stage. Before the seeds have fully developed (while they are still green), bend down the stalks from a point 2 or 3 feet below the top tassel. Let them dry like that, still rooted in your garden, for several days. Then cut off the top brush plus 6 inches of stalk below. Or you can wait for the tassels to turn yellow or even reddish for a more attractive color—but late harvesting like that results in broomcorn that is less sturdy for real work. Pull off the leaves. Spread out the strawlike brush on a clean surface in the sun to dry-cure for 3 weeks before you try to make a broom. Bring in at night or if precipitation is expected. They're dry enough for broom making when tassels spring back after you gently bend them.

Harvesting for Seeds: Wait until after the seeds are ripe. Left in the field, the plant will finish maturing, the brush will turn yellow, and seeds will form in clusters that grow like corn tassels at the tip of the stem. Then cut. Thresh out the seeds by scraping them out. Use them like any sorghum grain. The seeds are also good for birdfeed. And save some for next year's crop.

Broom Making: Copy your favorite model of broom in the stores. The easiest to make are round "fireplace" brooms. Those are also the traditional Halloween witch-riding kind. You can make them without any machinery. Just comb the seeds out of the tassels. Allow 4–8 inches of stem plus the tassel length. Whatever length you choose, trim all the stems to that length. Trim away part of the stalk on one side; this makes a thinner "neck" to bind. "Insides" are the short straws. "Hurl" is the long straws. A broom of all hurl is the best kind, but you can make good brooms with the insides slipped inside the hurl and not have to waste any straw. Prepare your broom handle from straight young wood, and cut it 4 or 5 feet long.

Soak your tassels in boiling water to soften them. Take them out; while they're still hot and wet, bind them very tightly with twine or wire around the end of the broom handle. Bent-over nails can also help anchor them. One way to do it is to put in two nails, bend them over, tie your twine to the lowest nail, wrap it around stalks, and then fasten at upper nail. Better yet is to use the nails to help get you started, but then discard them as you create your

finished product. You can make 1 or 2 tiers of bound-on tassels. If 2 tiers, one will go on lower than the other. Then trim off evenly the sweeping base straws. As they dry, they'll shrink tight around your handle.

The two kinds of sorghums left to talk about, grain sorghum and sweet sorghum, are so important and complex that they have their own sections, coming up next.

THE GRAIN SORGHUMS

Sorghum grain is marketed under the variety names of "kafir" or "milo" as well as "grain sorghum." It's commonly grown in the United States (Great Plains and Southwest) for a livestock grain feed, but in Africa and Asia it's an important food grain for people. In fact, human use of this cereal grain dates back to the Assyrians, Mesopotamians, and Egyptians.

Of Varieties, Planting, and Growing

VARIETIES: You can use the seed of a sweet sorghum or a broomcorn like a grain sorghum if it happens to be a light-colored "yellow endosperm sorghum." But real grain sorghum is the best tasting, most healthy, most digestible sorghum grain. Grain sorghum varieties vary in height, from 2 feet, to a common 4½ feet, up to even 15 feet or more. Most varieties have multicolored brown, yellow, and red seeds mixed in various degrees. The brown part contains tannin, so the more brown in the seed, the less pleasant the grain tastes to most animals or humans. (But chickens love the grain no matter what.) For the best grain sorghum, you want one that has a comparatively thin seed coat and none of that bitter taste. There are excellent new grain sorghums along those lines. Available from Redwood City, Bountiful Gardens, and DeGiorgi. Or get Black African, a drought-resistant and easily hand-threshed grain sorghum, from Seeds of Change.

ROTATIONS AND DOUBLE-CROPPING: You can substitute sorghum for corn in any rotation and do fine. Southern farmers take advantage of sorghum's need for late planting to double-crop—for instance, with wheat as the first harvest followed by a grain sorghum crop.

AMOUNT TO PLANT: You can expect to harvest 100–180 bushels per irrigated acre, 50–100 bushels per dryland acre, 25–50 from a half acre. For fractions of dryland acres, here are some optimistic estimates: 25 bushels per ¼ acre, 12 per ⅛ acre, 6 per 1/16 acre. For every 4 rows, each 50 feet long, expect to harvest 1 bushel of grain. Plant in rows as you would corn—12 to 30 inches apart—about 10 days later than corn. But sorghum planted too thick may have weak stalks that tend to fall over. The specific amount to plant per unit area depends on variety, water availability, and how far apart you're making your rows. Typically, you'll need 2–4 lb. seed per ordinary dryland acre, or 8–10 lb. seed per well fertilized, irrigated acre.

GROWING: Tend as you would corn, cultivating while the plants are young to keep out weeds. The biggest problem with growing yellow endosperm sorghum is usually that birds love it so much. If you have a small crop, you can protect the maturing clusters from birds by covering sorghum with paper bags.

Harvesting, Processing, and Using

HARVESTING: Wait until the seed heads are dry. They're ripe and ready when the grain threshes out easily. The perfect timing is when the grain is hard but not yet falling off. Combine or, by hand, cut off about 12 inches of stalk together with the seed head.

Finishing Drying. Hang tied bundles, or spread heads on a clean floor. In northern climates, grain sorghum usually has to be harvested and dried indoors or artificially, because if you let near-ripe sorghum grain stand in a wet field too long, it may mold. But grain sorghum can be hard to dry inside as well. For one thing, the heads don't dry evenly in the field, so they're likely to come indoors with damp spots still in them. Drying unthreshed sorghum is also hard because the heads are so compact that air doesn't circulate freely through them. So you may have to give the grain extra attention and extra airing or heating to get it dry and prevent spoiling.

Threshing. Sorghum is one of the easiest grains to thresh. Once dry, the seed heads can be threshed by hand or with any other type of thresher. You can thresh as needed, or all at once. To thresh out a dried sorghum seed head by hand, hold it over a clean cloth or some such, and rub it vigorously between your two gloved hands. Rub as if the seed head was a lump of clay that you're shaping into a ball. The seed will fall right out, along with bits of hull and stem that you next must winnow out. About 75 percent of the weight of your dry, whole heads will turn out to be seeds.

Sorghum Grain for Livestock. You can feed sorghum grain to any animal; they'll eat unthreshed seed heads. But they need other feeds too. Moreover, your animals may get more good out of the grain if it's ground, rolled, or parched first to break open the outer layer.

HUSKING: You can grind your sorghum grain whole to make a flour, and the flour will have more food value for you if it's made from the unhusked grain. But if you want to use grain sorghum like rice, then it has to be husked ("decorticated"). Sorghum is tougher than barley to dehusk, but it can be done. Sorghum can be dehusked in any rice mill (it can also be parboiled same as rice). Or you can husk sorghum grain (or any of the other grains) by hand, using the following procedure:

1. Dry grain well in the sun.
2. Remove dirt by winnowing.
3. Wash and remove sand and stones.
4. Pound the moist kernels in a wooden mortar to remove the chaff.
5. Winnow again after pounding.
6. Pound once more.
7. Winnow again until chaff is completely removed.
8. Optional: Now use a seed-cleaning sieve to sort the kernels into 2 sizes: the largest two-thirds of the kernels to be saved to cook whole, the smallest third to be ground for flour.
9. To create "pearled" sorghum, follow directions for pearling barley (see "Pearling" under "Barley"). Sorghum "bran" is the "flour" that results from the pearling; it has a good part of the vitamins in it. So cook the pearled sorghum like rice, but add the bran to your bread recipes so you don't lose the vitamins. Or make a coarse grind of the whole kernel and use in recipes that call for "cracked wheat" or "meal."

10. Or grind fine to make a flour. Light-colored varieties of sorghum grain make white flour. Darker or multicolored grains make a greyish flour, sometimes with very dark specks in it—equally edible, but not as marketable.

STORING: In the north, sorghum grain stores easily. In the south, raiding insects may come in from the field with the grain. In that case you'll need to treat the grain (see "Fighting Pests in Grain" earlier in this chapter) and then store in airtight containers. To store sorghum flour, lightly roast it first to get rid of excess moisture. Then store in an airtight container, but the sooner you use it, the better.

COOKING SORGHUM GRAIN: Grain for grain, sorghum has as many calories as and more protein than rice (it has almost as much protein as wheat). It has more calcium, iron, and vitamin A, and more of all the B vitamins, than rice does! Serve whole sorghum grain using any recipe for unground wheat. You can boil unground sorghum grain and eat it like any cooked cereal. Or prepare whole like rice and substitute in any rice recipe, since sorghum closely resembles rice in its cooking qualities. Or use for part of the rice in a rice recipe. Or grind partially for a cracked cereal. Or grind fine to make flour from sorghum grain. Use sorghum flour in any recipe the same as you would rice flour. Use it mixed with at least ⅓ wheat flour unless you're making a flatbread or cookies! *The Book of Whole Grains* by Marlene Anne Bumgarner (St. Martin's Press, 1976) has a whole chapter of recipes for sorghum grain!

It takes time for sorghum flour to absorb water. For baked recipes, it's always a good idea to combine your sorghum flour and liquid and let it rest at least 30 minutes and up to 3 hours before proceeding to let the sorghum absorb the liquid as thoroughly as possible.

I am indebted to Farm Women's Agricultural Extension of Peradeniya, Sri Lanka, for most of the following recipes. Sometimes those Sri Lankan ladies steam the sorghum flour in their steamer for a while before they add water to it. Otherwise they let it soak or use it in a boiled form.

➤ *COOKED PLAIN SORGHUM* In a pan add 4 c. water (or soup stock) to 1 c. sorghum. Stir in ½ t. salt, cover, and cook on low heat for about an hour.

➤ *SPANISH SORGHUM* In a frying pan brown a chopped large onion. Add 2 c. cooked sorghum and 1 c. cooked tomatoes. Stir in salt, pepper, basil, or other seasonings to taste and heat through.

➤ *RICE-SORGHUM* Combine 1 c. rice, 1 c. sorghum grain, 6 c. water, and salt to taste. Cook like rice until done.

➤ *ROTI* Mix 1 c. sorghum flour, ½ c. wheat flour, ½ c. fresh coconut scrapings, salt to taste, and a little water—enough to enable it to stick together so you can knead it well. Divide into several portions. Flatten each portion into ¼-inch-thick rounds. Cook them on a "roti" (or griddle) until both sides are done.

➤ *PITTU* Combine 2 c. sorghum flour, 1 c. freshly scraped coconut meat, and salt to taste. Mix together to form little granules, adding as much as ¼ c. water if necessary. Now place mixture in the pittu mold, which will hold about a handful. In Sri Lanka this is made of bamboo and consists of 3 woven cup-shapes in a framework meant to stand over boiling water in your pot and be steamed. You can substitute a cup, packing it lightly, to shape the pittu. Then turn out the packed raw pittus and steam them by comparable arrangement. It helps to steam at quite a high temperature until done—about 10 to 15 minutes.

☙ **STRING-HOPPERS** These are Sri Lankan sorghum noodles. Start by steaming 2 c. sorghum flour to pre-moisten it. Then sieve the steamed flour into a bowl. Add salt to taste. Mix enough boiling water into the sorghum flour to make a soft mixture. Now squeeze this dough through your noodle press onto a greased bamboo string-hopper mat, on which you will then steam them until done. Western readers will have to contrive some comparable system for steaming your string-hoppers.

☙ **PEARLED SORGHUM** Combine 1 part sorghum to 2 parts water and cook like brown rice.

☙ **SORGHUM PUDDING** Combine 1 c. cooked pearled sorghum (see above), 2/3 c. sugar, 1/4 t. vanilla, 1/2 t. cinnamon, 1 c. milk, 1/2 c. raisins, 1 T. butter, and 2 eggs. Bake at 400°F for 45 minutes to 1 hour.

☙ **SORGHUM MASA TORTILLAS** First you make the sorghum hominy. (See "Hominy" under "Corn" for background information.) Combine 5 c. grain sorghum, 15 c. water, and 1 heaping T. powdered lime in a pan (not aluminum, copper, tin, or zinc). Cook on low heat until hulls loosen (20 to 40 minutes). Soak mixture for 4 hours. Now drain and rinse until most all of the lime is removed. Dry your sorghum hominy in the sun or dehydrator until thoroughly dry. Grind into flour. You now have a sorghum masa. Add enough liquid to shape masa into dough balls. (Or use a corn masa tortilla recipe.) Then press the dough ball between wax papers with a tortilla press. Cook tortilla on a hot griddle (500–600°F) one minute on each side.

☙ **SORGHUM BISCUITS** Sift together 1/4 lb. sorghum flour, 1/4 lb. wheat flour, and 1 t. baking powder. Cream together 1/2 c. butter or margarine and 1/4 lb. sugar. Work butter/sugar mix in with the flour. Add 2 well-beaten egg yolks. Knead well. Add milk as needed until a smooth dough forms. (You'll need between 1/4 and 1/2 c. milk.) Flatten the dough onto your floured wooden bread board. Roll to a thickness of 1/8 inch. Use your biscuit cutter to cut into rounds (or fancy shapes). Arrange them on a greased and flour-dusted cookie sheet, leaving a little space between each biscuit. Bake at 350°F for about 15 minutes.

☙ **SORGHUM GRAIN PANCAKES** Combine 1 1/2 c. sorghum flour (made from either grain or sweet sorghum seeds), 1/2 t. salt, 2 T. brown sugar, and 3 t. baking powder and mix well. Separate 3 eggs into yolks and whites. Beat the egg yolks, combine with 1 c. milk, and then add that to your dry ingredients. Beat the egg whites to soft peaks, and fold into your batter. Bake in a greased, hot pan. Turn when they get bubbly on top.

☙ **SORGHUM COOKIES** Combine 1 1/4 c. flour, 1/4 c. sorghum flour, 3/4 t. baking soda, 1/2 t. salt, 3/4 c. sugar, 1/2 c. shortening, 1/4 c. molasses, and 1 egg. Blend very thoroughly. Now stir in 1/2 c. chopped nuts and mix them in well too. Drop by rounded teaspoonfuls onto a greased cookie sheet. Bake at 375°F for 8 to 10 minutes. Cool 1 minute and serve.

☙ **SORGHUM BRAN MUFFINS** Heat oven to 400°F. Grease bottoms of 12 medium muffin cups. Beat 1 egg. Stir in 1 c. milk and 1/4 c. salad oil. Mix in 2 c. flour, 1 t. cinna-

mon, 1/2 c. sorghum bran, 1/2 c. brown sugar, 3 t. baking powder, 1/2 t. salt, and 1/2 t. nutmeg until flour is moistened. Fill muffin cups two-thirds full. Bake 20 to 25 minutes or until golden brown. Immediately remove from pan.

☙ **SORGHUM BROWNIES** Sift together 1 1/4 c. wheat flour, 1/4 c. sorghum flour, 1 t. baking powder, 1/2 t. salt, and 1/2 c. cocoa. Beat 3 eggs. Mix in with eggs 1 1/2 c. sugar, 1 t. vanilla, and 1/2 c. butter or margarine. Add the flour mixture to the egg mixture and stir together well. Optional: add chopped nuts. (You may need to add a little water to this batter.) Pour into a greased cake pan. Bake at 375°F for 25 to 30 minutes. Cool slightly and cut into squares.

☙ **SORGHUM MEAL BREAD** In a large mixing bowl, combine 3/4 c. flour, 1 c. sorghum meal, 3 T. sugar, 2 t. baking powder, and 1 t. salt. In a separate bowl combine 1 egg, 1 c. milk, and 1/4 c. cooking oil. Add moist ingredients to dry ones. Stir until all dry particles are moistened. Pour into well-greased 8-inch-square pan. Bake at 400°F for 25 to 30 minutes until golden brown.

☙ **TOMATOEY SORGHUM** Saute 1 c. uncooked pearled sorghum in 2 T. shortening with 2 large sliced onions and 1 chopped green pepper. Add 1 c. canned tomatoes, 1/2 t. salt, 3 c. boiling water, and 1/4 t. chili powder, and cook on low heat until sorghum grain is tender. (Add more water as needed.)

☙ **SORGHUM MUFFINS** Sift together 1 2/3 c. flour, 1/3 c. sorghum flour, 2 t. baking powder, and 1/2 t. salt. In another bowl, combine 1 beaten egg, 1 1/3 c. milk, and 1/4 c. melted (and then somewhat cooled) butter or margarine. Add that all at once to the flour mixture. (Make a depression in the center of the flour mixture before adding egg mixture.) Stir lightly, just until liquid is absorbed. Batter will be lumpy. Spoon into 12 greased medium-sized muffin pan cups, filling each cup two-thirds full. Bake in hot oven for 25 minutes or until golden brown.

THE SWEET/FORAGE SORGHUMS

A piece of sweet sorghum is as delicious to chew on as a stick of candy. Forage and sweet sorghums grow way taller than corn. The sweet and forage varieties are linked, because forage sorghums are more leafy and have stalks that contain more sugar than grain sorghums. There's also a sub-category of varieties that are specialized for molasses making. But if you plant sorghum for syrup, you can still have a sorghum grain harvest, and the leaves, seeds, and pressed-out stalks can be fed to animals. The seed yield, in addition to your syrup and forage harvests, can also be heavy: 500 lb. of seed per acre and up. One ounce of seeds will plant a 50-foot row.

Planting and Growing

CLIMATE FOR SWEET SORGHUM: In general, the forage/sweet sorghums thrive in areas that are more humid than those for which grain sorghums are specialized. Tennessee and Kentucky are leading sorghum syrup states. It is said that the most southern-grown sorghum, i.e., the longest-to-maturity varieties, are the best; but good sorghum can actually be grown over a wide area of the South and Midwest. Even here in our lowland Idaho valley, a neighbor raised a crop of sweet sorghum and made syrup! But do experiment with the longest-to-maturity varieties that you can grow in your particular area, because those should produce the best sorghum syrup. Raymond Weaver, a professional sorghum maker from Sale Creek, TN, wrote me, "Dear Carla: I specialize in sorghum, so quite naturally I checked out your article and seems like the most helpful thing I could do is give you some meat to go on those bones and some yardsticks to go by." On varieties, he said, "We planted Dale, one from the U. of Miss., and Honey Drip. We found Dale far superior to the other two."

GETTING SWEET SORGHUM SEED: Seed is available from Park, Redwood City, and Shumway. Four varieties—Dale, M-81-E, Topper 76-6, and Thei's—can be ordered from the Agriculture Experiment Station, Mississippi State U., Box 9811, Mississippi State, MS 39762; 662-325-2390; **msucares.com/crops/sorghum/descriptions.html.** The next year, plant your own seed. All the varieties of sweet sorghum are naturally self-pollinated and easy to save seed from.

HOW MUCH TO PLANT: A few ounces will plant a 50 × 50-foot plot. The recommended seeding rate per acre is about 3 lb. Raymond says, "The standard is 100 gal. per acre. Yields of over 400 gal. have been recorded, though. If you can estimate the bushels of corn a piece of ground will produce, a good rule of thumb is 2 gal. syrup for each bushel of corn. Another rule of thumb is 1 gal. for each 100 feet of row (at 130 gal./acre). For the beginner, I recommend a plot 50 × 50 feet. This will give you enough to cut your teeth on, and you'll be glad you didn't get in any deeper (750 feet of row or 7½ gal.)."

HOW TO PLANT: Sorghum does not come up well in cold ground. Plant 2 weeks after the last frost. Plant in hills or rows. The conventional wisdom is to plant 4 seeds to a hill with hills 18 inches distant, or plant in rows your best cultivating width apart, with plants 6 inch distant. Raymond adds, "Shake the seed into the row, letting it dribble out the side of your hand between thumb and index finger. You want a seed about every 2 inches. This will give you a good sure stand. When 1 inch high, thin to 6–8 inches apart and weed. It's really important not to have it too thick. A thinned stand gives you good big stalks. I remove my suckers (tillers) when cane is 24 inches high."

Harvesting, Stripping, and Pressing

NOTE: Once you begin harvesting sweet sorghum cane, you must keep at it until the job is done. This is one crop that can't wait anywhere along the process.

WHEN TO HARVEST: The seeds are first milky, then increasingly tough and doughy, then hard. For syrup making, you cut sooner than you would for grain. You cut after the milky stage and before the hard stage, meaning in the tough, doughy ("hard dough") stage, while your thumbnail can cut the seed. Raymond says, "It is better to get it a little early than a little late. If you wait longer, the syrup will get darker and stronger." But also take into consideration the weather. The old-timers warn against making molasses on a rainy day. A clear but chilly day is considered ideal for the boiling down. Harvest before frost to prevent loss of the leaves if you plan to use them for fodder.

STRIPPING THE CANE: "Stripping time" means cutting, stripping, and topping. To harvest the cane for syrup, strip

off the leaves and leave to dry for fodder. Then, using a corn knife, cut off the stalks near the ground and bundle them with the heads all at the same end. Have available a wooden tabletop or some other suitable setup for cutting off the heads so you don't get dirt into the cane. There cut the seed clusters off the cane tops. (You'll hang or spread them someplace for drying.) The remainder of the stalk goes to your syrup press.

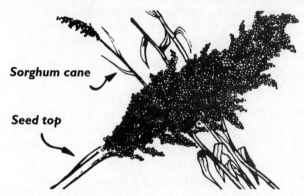

Sorghum cane

Seed top

Raymond adds: "We make strippers out of old saws by removing the handle and putting on our own homemade one. It should be light (but strong) and shaped like a hoe handle. The toothed edge is good to knock off the leaves. The first 6 inches of the back edge can be sharpened like a sickle blade to cut off stalks and head. One hour's work to strip 100 feet of row is a good rule of thumb. Haul to the mill and protect it from [moisture in general] rain, cattle, and frost. [Don't pile near heat either.] Estimates of stripping time will improve with experience."

THE PRESSING PROBLEM: Press the green syrup out of the canes as soon as possible after cutting them. It's best of all if the canes go directly from the field to the mill. The basics of milling cane are to somehow crack open the tough outside shell of the stalk and then press out the juice from the soft inside of the stalk; your syrup is then made from that juice. In the old days, cut sorghum was hauled to a horse- or mule-powered mill. When the animal got tired, farmers would feed him tidbits of the cane and lead him around his circle some more. The animal-powered rollers pressed out the juice by walking round and round, pulling or pushing the end of a long pole attached to reduction gears. The cane juice being squeezed out from between the rollers was directed through several strainers and then into a holding tank. In an ideal setup, there was a gravity-fed connection right from the holding tank to the evaporator pan.

If you don't have your own mill, it's easiest to locate a neighbor with a press and trade labor for service. Or maybe you could find and buy an old mill. They're easiest to find in the South. Otherwise, you'll have to improvise some way to cut, chop, or grind up the stalks and then squeeze them. A cider press? It may not have pressure enough to get all the juice. But the wringers of an old-fashioned wringer washer will work.

Well, that's an ignorant northerner talking. Raymond retorts, "If you have more than a few feet of row you better have a sorghum mill. The cider press is going to get old pretty fast. Your 50 × 50 foot patch is likely to produce 60 to 80 gal. of juice. That will be a very good day's work with a cider press—maybe more. If you have a three-roller horse-drawn mill, you should get about 15 gal. an hour (green juice). It takes one man sticking cane and one man carrying cane in, removing pomace (crushed stalk) and staying after the horse. Juice should not be ground more than 24 hours in advance. In my case we start grinding Saturday morning and grind all day. Counting late starts, breakdowns, tired horses, and low yield we usually end up with about 80 gal. They finish grinding about noon Sunday, just as we are pulling off the first molasses [from the evaporator]. That way we know just how much juice we are going to have and, most important, we are not likely to run out of juice."

Pressed-Out Cane. The cane that has been pressed dry of juice is good winter feed for cattle or good mulch for the garden.

Boiling Down

When Raymond referred to "green juice," he was being literal. The juice that is pressed from the sorghum stalks is a green color. It will turn the familiar brown during the boiling down. The basics of the boiling-down stage are to evaporate the pressed-out juice until it is thick enough to be called a syrup and to purify it, very similar to making maple syrup. Raymond: "I wish I could tell you that sorghum is a breeze, but it's not. It's a lot of hard work and long hours, especially until you find out what you're doing. Cooking syrup is the most challenging thing I have ever done in my life. I guess every syrup maker has had some scorches." As with the pressing, the easiest way to start is to find a neighbor who's set up and making syrup and trade labor for getting your syrup boiled. If not . . . For more on sorghum making, read *Foxfire III*, edited by Elliot Wigginton (1975).

BOILING TIMES AND YIELDS: Raymond: "You should get 1 gal. of syrup for each 10 gal. of juice you put in the pan. We got 35 gal. of syrup from 275 gal. of juice, or about 7.5 to 1. The beginner should make about 2 gal. of syrup an hour. Figure about 3 hours to boil it down. It's done whenever you decide you're done."

THE EVAPORATOR: You boil down the syrup in a big evaporator tray over a fire. The tray is about 5 feet wide and 16 feet long. It is set up to have a very slight tilt from the beginning (higher) end to the ending (lower) end. Evaporator trays have been made with anywhere from 3 to 10 compartments between the beginning and finish. Each compartment is made by a ridge of metal that creates a pan inside the larger pan. Each is connected with the next one by one narrow opening that can, if wanted, be plugged by sticking a rag or some such into it. But normally the syrup will simply flow naturally and gradually through the opening from one compartment to the next lower one. The opening of the very last evaporator section is equipped with a spigot so you can easily pour the finished syrup into a strainer or containers.

Of buying sorghum evaporators ready-made, Raymond advises, "Avoid the galvanized pans with soldered seams. This puts hot syrup in direct contact with zinc and lead. The galvanization eventually wears off, and you know where it goes [into the syrup]! I use black iron with beaded seams. It would be better with welded seams. I'm not that skilled a welder, though. Stainless and copper are too expensive." Other sorghum makers have been troubled by metal getting into the syrup and at best, spoiling the taste—at worst, making it totally unhealthy to consume. The syrup is a high-acid product, so stainless steel is really preferable for working with it.

THE FIRE: This very large, flat metal evaporator has to have a heat source. It's traditionally suspended somehow over a long, low fireplace. Old-timers built 3 connecting walls of a mixture of mud and Johnson grass: one to support each of the long sides of the evaporator pan and one to support the spigot end—with a high smokepipe emerging through the otherwise closed-off lower end. They built the fire under the upper end. The draft was arranged so that heated air would move under the length of the evaporator and finally emerge through the smokepipe. That way the fire was hottest where the syrup was most liquid and least likely to burn. The fire needed to be kept burning in as steady and moderate a manner as possible.

THE EVAPORATOR CREW: "I recommend that the beginner start out with 5 people on the pan: the syrup maker, 2 skimmers, a backup syrup maker, and a relief skimmer. When you're learning, it's better to have too much help and cut down than to have too little and be run ragged. Estimates of pan crew should improve with experience. Watch your hot syrup. It could cook you to the bone." *NOTE: Never! Never! Never pick up a pan full of hot syrup. One slip could be fatal.*

THE SYRUP MAKER'S RESPONSIBILITIES: The "syrup maker" oversees the whole operation and bears heavy responsibilities.

1. There must be plenty of juice on hand so the process doesn't have to shut down unexpectedly to wait for more juice. This is when the syrup is most likely to scorch.
2. The proper amount of juice must be in the pan. Too much can cause it to boil over and make it finish slowly. Too little will make it scorch.
3. The skimmers must be doing a good job skimming off the green scum of surface foam.
4. The proper amount of fire must be under the pan. Too much fire will make it boil over; if there's not enough, it takes forever to finish.
5. The syrup should move from compartment to compartment in the evaporator pan so that it is ready just as it reaches the final one.

Rate of Flow. "The syrup in each successive section [of your evaporator] must be a little thicker than that in the preceding section. If one section gets ahead of the section in front of it, it will scorch before it gets to the spout. Don't pull your syrup too fast. If you do, you'll leave a bare spot behind your pusher that will scorch before the syrup can run in and cover it."

Skimming. "The boiling down coagulates the foreign materials in the syrup, which rise to the top. They're then called 'skimmings' and must be skimmed off with a ladle. The skimmer has to stay on the job because if the materials aren't skimmed off, they'll make the syrup taste bitter."

Chalking. "The syrup tends to chalk near the end. This is a white coating of starch that looks like white paint. As it builds up, the bottom side will brown and then char. Later, pieces of this charred chalk will break loose, giving the syrup a scorched taste. The syrup maker must keep the chalk scraped off the bottom of the pan with something like a spatula. Or else cut off the syrup flow, empty the last few sections, and scrub them out clean before continuing. This past year I had a scorch, so I cut off the syrup flow with a rag, and we scrubbed the last 4 sections clean. They were badly chalked. Even though the chalk was not charred, we noticed a definite improvement in the quality of the syrup when we resumed."

Judging Finish Temperature. "The most important job of all for the syrup maker is judging when to pull the syrup [when it's finished cooking]. One old saying is that it's ready when the bubbles get as big as a bull's-eye. A better way is to pull it when it begins to thread. Dip your pusher into the finishing syrup and hold it up in the air, letting the syrup drip back into the pan. If it immediately breaks into a stream and then breaks into little drops, you have a light syrup (226°F) just right for pancakes. City folks tend to prefer a thin mild syrup like this, which is easy to pour. If the stream falls about a foot before it breaks into drops, it's getting pretty thick. This is the way old-time country people usually like it. The thicker it gets, the richer (stronger) the flavor."

Twenty years later, Raymond wrote me again: "After I wrote that letter I had a bad experience with some syrup that I didn't cook down enough. Dark caught us, and I simply misjudged it. It got a mold on it and began to ferment. We lost it all. In view of this experience, I cannot recommend a finishing temperature of less than 230°F."

Using a Candy Thermometer. The best way of all to know when to pull your syrup is to use a candy thermometer. From Raymond's original letter: "I prefer the kind in a glass tube with a pencil clip on it. This can give the beginner a big edge on the experienced syrup maker. You want 226–230°F, depending on how thick and strong-flavored you want it. Don't take your thermometer out of hot syrup and wash it off. It will crack. Let it cool a minute first. Don't let it get water inside the tube. It will fog up so bad you can't read it." A syrup hydrometer gives a 35–36 degree Baume reading for syrup with proper density. A hydrometer gives a reading of specific gravity (.990 to 1.170), sugar by weight (1 to 22 percent), and potential alcohol by volume (1 to 22 percent). You can mail-order a hydrometer from Lehman's, 888-438-5346; **www.Lehmans.com.** They also stock a syrup test kit that includes a candy thermometer and hydrometer.

Straining. "Be sure and strain your syrup through cheesecloth because the syrup will have a few yellow jackets and honeybees in it. You don't want to bottle them. I use aluminum screen under the cheesecloth for support."

Cooling. For the best-quality sorghum, quick cooling is essential. Cool the syrup at least to 190°F to fill small bottles, 180°F before filling large ones. Raymond: "You'll need about 100 gal. of water. We carried ours until we got the shed built over the pan. Now we just set two drums under the low end [of the roof] a month or so before we make." Or situate your evaporator near a cold spring.

Storing. Store in containers with tight lids.

Names—"Sorghum Syrup" vs. "Molasses": Some writers say that "molasses" is only the dark dregs from the bottom of the barrel; others say that "molasses" is the product resulting from boiling down the sorghum syrup. Raymond says, "I'm not sure feed molasses is sorghum. Sorghum is not a true molasses. It is a syrup. A true molasses is a syrup from which at least some of the sugar has been removed." My dictionary suggests that both extremes are true: that specifically, molasses is the syrup left when sugar has been extracted, but in general, "a molasses" can be the result of the boiling down of any sweet syrup.

Syrup for Livestock: Sorghum syrup can be made both for table use and for food for animals—horses, cows, etc! Don't mix syrup with feed too far ahead or it will dry out. A reader of mine named Hazel gets 2 tons mixed at a time for her household's 1 milk cow and 5 goats. Their formula for feed mix is as follows: 3 sacks (100 lb. each) cottonseed hulls; 2 sacks (100 lb. each) cottonseed meal; salt; calcium; 100 lb. of sorghum syrup; and the rest of the weight in dry corn (shuck, cob, and all). The skimmings from your boiling off are also good cattle feed.

Making Brown Sugar: These instructions come from a farm handbook written in the mid-19th century, *The Home and Farm Manual.* I haven't tried them, nor do I know of anybody else who has. But that book as a whole is dependable, so here goes:

1. Start out by stripping, cutting, and milling the cane.
2. After the green syrup comes from the mill, filter it through thick, clean cloth fixed into a basket. The filtering is to get out as much fiber, cellulose, and starch as can be thus captured.
3. Add enough milk of lime (meaning lime "slaked and mixed with water") to the green syrup to get a slightly alkaline result (changes red litmus paper to blue). A little too much lime won't hurt the results.
4. Boil the juice and milk of lime mixture a quarter hour. Skim off the scum that rises. It should be a "pale straw color."
5. Filter it again.
6. Evaporate by boiling until the syrup is around half of its starting amount.
7. Turn the heat down low to continue the evaporation and constantly stir because from here on, it is at considerable risk of scorching at the pan bottom.
8. Test the syrup once in a while by removing a little and allowing it to cool to see if it has gotten dense enough for crystallization to occur. It must become "as dense as sugar-house molasses, or tar."
9. When you do have it that dense, take off the heat and put in "tubs or casks" to await the natural granulation. (Lehman's sells wood barrels and kegs of 10, 22, and 30 gal.) In 3–4 days, sugar crystals should start forming. After the mass solidified, the old-time sugar makers scooped it into canvas or cloth bags that were made in the shape of a cone. These were hung over a container for the molasses—because the only portion of the once-liquid syrup that remains liquid after the crystallization takes place is now true molasses, and it can be obtained by letting the cones hang to drip. Molasses being as it is, it will drip off much better in a warm room, 80–90°F. Let the bags hang and drip at least several days. The residue in the bag should be "good brown sugar."
10. Your brown sugar can be refined, bleached, and recrystallized to make it the familiar white sugar of commerce, but I prefer brown anyway and am going to stop the instructions here.

🥄 **SORGHUM ROAST** *Rub the top and sides of a ham or a plain pork roast with sorghum syrup before baking it. That's all I do, and it comes out just delicious.*

🥄 **THICK MOLASSES SAUCE** *Boil 1 c. molasses with 2 T. butter for 5 minutes. Cool. Add 2 T. lemon juice.*

☞ *MOSTLY MOLASSES SAUCE Boil together for 15 or 20 minutes 1 c. molasses, ½ c. water, 1 T. butter, a pinch each of salt and cinnamon, and 1 T. vinegar.*

SPELT

See "Wheat Varieties" under "Wheat."

SUGAR CANE

Sugar cane (*Saccharum officinarum*) is a subtropical grass. This is an entirely different plant than the sweet sorghum varieties from which sorghum syrup is made. You can't get sorghum syrup from sugar cane or vice versa. In the United States sugar cane is, or has been, grown commercially in Hawaii, Louisiana, and Florida. According to my 1885 book on farming, places farther south get better sugar cane yields. It said that Louisiana could grow from 1,200 to 1,800 lb. of sugar per acre, but Mauritius could produce 3,000–5,000 lb. per acre and Cuba could get up to 7,000. Modern yields are usually way bigger than those listed in that old-time reference.

GROWING SUGAR CANE: Cane is a giant grass that can grow as high as 15 feet. It likes lots of sun and water. It is not raised from seed; instead, stalks are cut into pieces that are planted in rows. A new plant comes up—and sends down roots—at each node (joint) of the buried cane. To harvest, you strip the leaves from the stems and cut the stalks. They can be cut into foot-long sections for people to enjoy fresh.

EATING FRESH, RAW SUGAR CANE: Some of your sugar cane is sure to be gnawed on plain by the children. They cut off a stick about a foot long and peel it enough so they can get their teeth into the softer inside. They take a bite, chew and suck it until all the sweetness is out, then spit out the tough fibers that will noways chew up, and take another bite.

SUGAR CANE JUICE: This is the liquid that comes out when sugar cane is put through a cider-press-type machine. The juice is thin but very tasty. It can be used as a table syrup and as a substitute for sugar or another sweetening in any recipe, keeping in mind that it adds to your volume of liquid as well as sweetens it. Making sugar from sugar cane juice is essentially an expensive industrial process that simply can't be duplicated at home.

TEFF

See "Varieties" under "Millet."

WHEAT

Wheat eating started 10,000–15,000 years ago in the Tigris, Euphrates, and Nile valleys. It's a good basic grain to plant. You can grow a crop of wheat even in your backyard if you can keep people and dogs from trampling the tender stalks. You can harvest, store, and grind it—all without expensive or inconvenient machinery. On a fraction of an acre, you can grow a year's supply of wheat for your family and your animals. Wheat makes the lightest breads because it has the most gluten of any grain, and gluten is the substance that holds air bubbles.

WHEATY READING: *This Was Wheat Farming: A Pictorial History of the Farms and Farmers of the Northwest Who Grow the Nation's Bread* by Kirby Brumfield (Seattle: Superior Publishing Co., 1968), is a treasure chest of old photos of wheat-growing procedures. *The Wheat Album: A Picture and Story Scrapbook of Wheat Harvests in Years Gone By* by Kirby Brumfield (Seattle: Superior Publishing, 1974) is a similar and equally valuable book.

Planting and Growing Wheat

WHEAT VARIETIES: Choosing and finding the right wheat variety may be harder than you think. Redwood City offers 9 wheat varieties for small growers—mostly unusual varieties. But in *Growing Vegetables West of the Cascades,* Steve Solomon warns: "Except in the rain shadow of the Olympics where rainfall amounts to less than 20 inches, I don't think it would be possible for maritime Northwest wheat to form enough gluten/protein for decent yeast bread. Besides becoming relatively soft on my ground, the hard varieties I've tested also develop very thin straw, yield very poorly, and, despite their small seed heads, lodge (fall over) easily. Unfortunately, those very high-yielding, strong-strawed, soft white varieties grown commercially in the Willamette are too low in gluten to even make chapatis that don't crumble like cake. However, I'm very successfully growing a soft red winter wheat from Ohio called Logan that yields very big and has just the right gluten content to make chapatis that don't get too tough to chew (which is what happens when they're made with high-protein bread wheats) and yet don't fall apart. I get an amazingly fine satisfaction from eating home-grown chapatis dipped in home-grown beans, all sustainably producible without irrigation."

Wheat in general is genus *Triticum.* Most of the wheats are varieties of common wheat (*Triticum vulgare*), including the "hard" and "soft" wheats, both winter and spring types. The soft wheats are suited to a climate with more rainfall than the hards. There's also the variety *T. compactum,* or "club wheat," which grows well in the Pacific Northwest. *T. durum* is the durum wheat that has larger kernels than the others and makes good macaroni.

Turkey red (dark hard) winter wheat, dark hard spring wheat, and Marquis wheats store best. Hard red winter wheat, because of its high gluten content, makes the best bread (rises higher and easier). Soft red winter wheat contains slightly less gluten and is used commercially as a pastry flour—makes good piecrusts. But actually you can make acceptable bread out of it too. Soft wheat has a trifle less protein; durum wheat is the highest in protein content and can stretch the farthest when cooked. So that's the best kind for making spaghetti, macaroni, and noodles. Soft white wheat is considered the most inferior type, but it makes manageable noodles and buns. Those are the wheat varieties grown in the United States. Worldwide there are about 15,000 other distinct varieties, some of which will grow in almost any climate, hot or cold, wet or dry. A hard red spring wheat, *T. aestivum,* is available from Bountiful Gardens. It's a high protein (over 12 percent) grain.

Spelt. Spelt (*T. spelta*) is an old-time variety of hard wheat. My dictionary says it has "lax spikes and spikelets containing two light red kernels." Author Gene Logsdon says it's taller than regular wheat and has a long head, resembling rye. But it's very different from the easy-threshing other wheats, Gene reports, because the seed coat hangs on and has to be dehulled like those of oats or rice, making it less desirable for people food than other wheats because of the difficulty in hulling it. But then again, it's no worse in that regard than oats or rice. It contains gluten and can be baked just like wheat.

Spelt is hardy and reliable as a green manure, a pasture crop, or a livestock feed (in an unthreshed state). The hulls make it hard to separate out weed seed from the harvested grain, so spelt seed tends to carry along weed seeds. And it tends to suffer from smut. Spelt-flour products are hot in the food co-op right now. But I wonder if that's really "spelt" or if they're using Early Stone Age wheat (see below). Plant spelt like wheat, 2½ bushels per acre. Harvest like oats. Spelt flour, whole hulled kernels, toasted flakes, bread mixes, pastas, *The Spelt Cookbook,* and *Easy Bread Making for Special Diets* are available from Purity Foods; 517-351-9231; 2871 W. Jolly Rd., Okemos, MI 48864; **www.purity foods.com.** You can buy spelt seed there too: **bill@purity foods.com.**

Triticale. This is a recently developed, manmade grain, a cross of wheat (*Triticum*) and rye (*Secale*). An item for specialty stores. It is not as winter-hardy as wheat, nor does it produce as well. It is also somewhat more susceptible than wheat to developing ergot. It makes better bread than rye. Its protein content is better than older varieties of wheat but not as good as more modern ones. Plant and harvest it just like wheat. Some organic farmers have harvested 55 bushels of triticale per acre, but others get less. Gurney and Bountiful Gardens carry triticale seed. To cook with it, substitute it for rye in rye recipes.

Kamut, a.k.a. Polish wheat or Astraakan wheat, is the most drought-tolerant of wheats. Seed is available from Bountiful Gardens.

Early Stone-Age Wheat. This one is so distantly related that it isn't even a *Triticum;* its scientific name is *Einkhorn hornemanii.* It's pretty wonderful stuff, an ancient wheat that may have been first cultivated by humans as much as 10,000 years ago in Europe. It's a high-protein grain (18 percent). There are 2 seed rows on each head, and it's bearded. Most exciting, like rice, it grows numerous seed heads on each plant—as many as 90 if uncrowded. Seed available from Bountiful Gardens and Redwood City.

CLIMATE: All the North American wheats are very hardy; the hard reds are the hardiest of all. Wheat can stand a cold winter, a short summer, and a relatively dry climate, but it needs a growing season of 150 days and a high probability of a dry harvest season. It thrives on a low-temperature, high-light environment. Excessively high summer temperatures make it mature so fast that its yield is reduced. A moisture shortage also causes a smaller harvest. An area with a short growing season and a cool, damp harvest season is not good for wheat; your crop is likely to spoil in the field. About 15–35 inches of rain per year is just right—if the rainfall pattern is typically a cool, damp growing season followed by dry, warm days for ripening and harvest. Wheat's requirement of a dry harvest season can't be argued with. There isn't much time between when wheat is ripe enough to harvest and when you're too late because the crop has gotten so ripe that the heads have shattered and scattered the kernels or molded in the shocks.

SOIL: Wheat doesn't like acid, sandy, or soggy soil. Almost as much as corn, wheat needs soil with plenty of manure-type nutrients to do well. Supply enough nitrogen, but not too much, because if there's too much nitrogen in the soil, the wheat may fall over unless you have a strong-strawed kind.

SOME WHEAT NUMBERS

- One peck of wheat will feed 1 grown person for 2 weeks.
- Four ounces of wheat seed will plant 10 square feet and yield about 1 lb. wheat.
- There are about 16,000 wheat berries in a pound.
- A bushel of good wheat weighs at least 60 lb.
- For every 10 × 110-foot area you plant, you'll harvest about 1 bushel of wheat.

WHEN TO PLANT: Plant winter wheat right around the usual time of your first frost. Plant spring wheat around the usual time of your last killing frost in the spring. Try not to be late. The later you plant wheat after the ideal time, the less your yield may be, because summer heat depresses grain production. Wheat germinates at as low as 39°F, but it does better in the 60s. Because the Hessian fly damages early-planted wheat, don't plant until your extension agent announces the "fly-free date." (The date varies in different areas.)

HOW MUCH AND HOW: The best amount to plant varies widely according to your particular circumstances and variety, so experiment, and good luck! Try to have the ground free of weeds, especially vetch. Try 3 lb. for 1,000 square feet, 90–120 lb. per acre. Expect a return of 15–90 bushels per acre. (Even 15 is still a lot of wheat!) Durum kernels are larger than spring wheat kernels, so if planting that kind, plant an extra peck per acre. Plant 3–5 pecks per acre of hard red winter wheat, 6 pecks per acre for soft red winter wheat. For sure, plant 1–2 inches deep. To plant in rows with a hand planter, make the rows 4 inches apart. Otherwise, broadcast.

Harvesting, Storing, and Using Wheat

WHEN TO HARVEST: Wheat is one of the slower grains to mature; it takes winter wheat 40–50 days from heading to harvest. The wheat is close to harvest time when it has grown tall, has headed out with a big "bushy" top full of those wonderful grain seeds, and has started looking dry and turning yellow all over (some varieties turn a brownish red).

HOW TO HARVEST: To harvest by hand, do it at this time, when the straw is just turning yellow and the grain can be dented but not mashed (seed at 20–35 percent moisture). If combining, wait 7–10 days more, until the whole grain head is brittle and the grain of wheat is so hard you can't dent it with your thumbnail (14 percent moisture), for the grain must be completely dry when combined. Wait even for the dew to go off and for a sunny day. If it rains, you have to wait until the grain gets completely dry again. But if you leave the wheat too long, the heads will shatter and spill the grain onto the ground. To harvest by hand, cut, bundle, and shock to cure. Then thresh, winnow, and store. Grind as needed. Wheat straw is useful as nesting, bedding, and litter material for animals; mulch for the garden; and green manure for the field.

STORING: Wheat will keep indefinitely as long as the moisture content is under 10 percent and the storage location relatively cool. A reader named Hazel wrote me, "Dear Carla: A little experiment finished last year was interesting. We opened a 50-lb. can of hard winter wheat that had been stored for 25 years in a cabin which had no heat during subfreezing periods of the year. The summer heat probably seldom went above 76°F. The can was airtight and was produced to store food for human consumption. After being stored with no preservatives for so long and under less than optimal conditions, 98 percent of the wheat sprouted!" Nevertheless, it's wise to use your oldest storage wheat first, and then replace it with fresher stuff.

EATING WHEAT
For a cookbook written for freshly ground whole grain flour (it's different from store flour), get *The Amazing Wheat Book* by LeArta Moulton: 801-374-1858; LM Publications; 509 E. 2100 N., Provo, UT 84604.

Tudy Kile wrote me in 1983, "Greetings from Rwanda . . . a little republic in the center of Africa. We live in a beautiful spot on the shores of Lake Kivu on an old coffee plantation (abandoned by the previous owner in 1960 . . .), which became a haven for us and many other missionary families from the Congo (now Zaire) during the Independence evacuations and the wars there of 1964 and 1967, when we lost all of our earthly possessions but praised the Lord for 10 minutes allowed in which to flee. We've done that so many times during our 35 years of missionary service. Now it is 'I'; my husband was killed by accidental electrocution in March. After having worked so many years to get the hydro-electric plant operational for our large village of Bible School students and vocational school for 150 boys, I must confess I did sneak in a little 'Why, Lord?' but not for long because I know the Lord *does not make mistakes.*"

Tudy asked me about wheat: "I can find nothing in your book about roasting. Is wheat to be roasted or is it not? I roast the kernels (after washing, debugging, and destoning—the local stores add rocks, etc., to make the wheat weigh more—and drying) in my electric fry pan (which can be used only in 'off-hours' when there's not too heavy a load on the system). I find 400°F the best for wheat. I rewind the kitchen timer to remind me every 5 minutes to take a look at it. Right now, the wheat is finished and we are roasting coffee—something that you don't have to do."

My answer to that question would be . . . It depends. Here in the United States, wheat doesn't usually need to be washed, debugged, or destoned—or roasted either—before

grinding. But if you have your reasons (or if it feels right), do it!

Eating Unground Wheat

WHEAT GRASS *Start out by sprouting the regular way until the sprouts are as long as the seed. Then uncover and water once in a while. If you have them on something like a sponge that will hold the dampness well, the sprouts should keep growing until they look like grass; it takes about 7 days. The best time to eat them is when they're 1–2 inches long. You eat the entire seed and grass blade. Full of vitamins! If you put wheat grass in your juicer, you'll have a nourishing drink. Or use wheat grass in salads or sandwiches. Wheat grass will enrich unleavened or leavened breads and taste good baked into them. Ground wheat sprouts are good added to butter for a special spread.*

COOKED UNGROUND WHEAT *I just love it. And so does Greta Forbish, Portland, OR, who lives in what is "now termed a 'depressed area' though in my youth it was a respectable lower middle-class district and quite safe for a lone teenager to walk 8 blocks to the library after dark, or for a group of giggling girls to attend the local movie theater and thrill to Hoot Gibson or Clara Bow and come back without being molested. (Local movie theater is now showing X-rated films—'Girls on Parade,' 'Maisie's Bedroom,' 'The Men in Her Life,' etc. And here I am still dreaming of John Gilbert and Norma Shearer.)*

"During my early years, mother cooked whole wheat. Papa bought this in 5-lb. sacks from a local hay, grain, and feed store. Mother sorted it over each night and removed the spears and other residue and soaked it to skim off the chaff. After we got our gas range, she cooked it overnight in a double boiler with plenty of salted water, and by morning it had swelled to double its bulk and could be eaten with enthusiasm and sugar and cream, although I always preferred a dollop of butter and a sprinkle of brown sugar. I used this with my older children (now 42 and 40) and they loved it."

FRUMENTY *"Frumenty" is whole wheat cooked for cereal. Seems like everybody has their own favorite way of cooking it. Process 30 minutes in a pressure cooker. Or on top of the stove in a double boiler (simmer 4–6 hours). Or soak 24 hours in water enough to cover; then put the wet wheat in a covered oven dish, cover with water, and let cook in a slow oven for 12 hours. Or presoak the whole wheat in water (2⅔ c. water per 1½ c. wheat berries) for 8 to 10 hours; then bring wheat and soaking water to a boil with 1 t. salt. Boil gently until tender and the kernels break open. Serve like Greta's mother did, with cream or butter or sweetening added at the table. For fruity frumenty, mix your cooked wheat with milk and dried fruit before serving it. Stir up, cook together a few moments, and then set out to eat.*

To make vegan frumenty, reader Ruth from Bonaire suggests, "Serve with chopped dried fruit stirred in the last 20 minutes of cooking. Enjoy without the milk. Or use soy milk diluted with 2 parts water. Grain cooked in apple juice is wonderful with applesauce, or plain."

WHOLE WHEAT CASSEROLE *Bring 3 c. tomato juice, canned tomatoes, or 1½ c. tomato sauce (plus 1½ c. water) to a boil. Add 1 c. wheat. Simmer on the stove top or bake in a 250°F oven until the wheat is tender. Add more liquid as needed while it's cooking. Once the wheat is cooked, add 1 chopped onion, 1 lb. browned, ground meat, 2 minced garlic* cloves (or 1 t. garlic salt), ½ c. chopped green peppers, 1 c. corn, ½ t. salt, and a bay leaf. Basil or oregano is good too! Let simmer more until the flavors are soaked in. Now cover with 1 c. grated cheese and bake in the oven, uncovered, 15 minutes more, until the cheese is bubbly. Optional: leave out the meat. Another option: make it with water rather than tomato juice.

OF CRACKED WHEAT, BULGUR, AND COUSCOUS:

Bulgur, cracked wheat, and couscous are all more or less interchangeable in recipes.

Couscous. I didn't know about couscous until Cindy Roundy from Ludlow, VT, wrote me, "When visiting Algeria in October 1974 I picked up one of the ultimate treats of the world. 'Couscous' is coarsely ground wheat, usually accompanied by a bowl of lamb or chicken stew." Here's Cindy's recipe.

➢ *COUSCOUS Spread 2 c. couscous on a baking sheet. Sprinkle with water and lightly mix to moisten all grains. Place couscous in a colander lined with something, or use a special couscous cooker. Cover and steam 20 minutes. Stir couscous. Steam 20 minutes more. Stir in a little butter and place on platter. Meanwhile, place 1 c. chopped carrots and 1 c. chopped turnip in pan under colander. Cook until almost tender. Drain. Add salt and pour 3 c. homemade vegetable broth all over. Add 1 c. peas, 2 c. cooked garbanzo beans, and 1 c. cooked chicken. Heat until boiling. Pour stew over couscous on platter.*

➢ *COUSCOUS FROM A BOX Food writer Lane Morgan says, "Our couscous from a box cooks a lot faster and easier. Boil 2 minutes, stirring, in stock or water. Let sit off heat for 10–15 minutes. That's it. It's great—light and fluffy and soaks up pan juices." (It's quick 'cause it's precooked.)*

Bulgur. Bulgur is wheat that has been boiled, then dried, then cracked. You can use bulgur in any recipe that calls for cracked wheat, and vice versa; note that bulgur cooks faster because it has been precooked and dried. You can substitute bulgur for rice or mashed potatoes in any recipe.

➢ *COOKING COMMERCIAL BULGUR One cup dry bulgur makes 2½ cups cooked. Measure out equal parts of bulgur and boiling water and combine. Add a pinch of salt. Cover and wait 20 minutes to an hour. Stir and taste. Not all bulgurs are the same. If it's still tough, add ¼ cup more of boiling water, cover, and steam some more.*

➢ *MAKING BULGUR Start with a kettle large enough that you can fit a small pan into it. The kettle must have a tight-fitting lid and a steamer rack on the bottom of it. Pour water into the large kettle up to the rack level. Put 1 c. water, 1 c. cracked wheat, and ½ t. salt into the pan. Set it on the rack inside the large one. Don't cover the pan, but cover the kettle tightly. Heat on high for 15 minutes, and then steam at a lower temperature until the wheat has absorbed all the water in the pan. Store in fridge, covered. It won't keep more than a couple weeks.*

➢ *BULGUR BREAKFAST Heat bulgur. Serve with milk and sweetening. If you like, add raisins.*

➢ *BELL PEPPERS STUFFED WITH BULGUR Combine 2½ c. bulgur, ½ lb. ground meat, 1 c. water, and your favorite herbs and seasonings. Let that mixture wait while you cut 3 peppers (green or red) into lengthwise halves (cut out and discard all inside parts). Now fill your pepper "bowls" with*

the bulgur mix. Lay in a baking dish. Pour tomato puree over them. Bake at 375°F for about an hour.

➢ *TABOULI For recipes for this popular bulgur salad, see "Mint" and "Parsley" in Chapter 5.*

➢ *HOMEMADE BULGUR "POSTUM" Parch bulgur under broiler or in oven until dark brown. (Don't burn it!) Grind to a fine consistency. To make your drink, put ¼ c. powder into 2–4 c. hot water (depending on how strong you prefer it!). Add honey (or brown sugar), 1 T. vanilla, a dash of nutmeg, and a pour (or much more!) of milk. Served with whipped cream on top, this is a gourmet drink!*

➢ *RUTH'S BULGUR "SAUSAGE" From Ruth of Bonaire: "Soak 1½ c. bulgur (cracked wheat) in 1½ c. boiling hot water till fluffy (30 minutes) and drain. To bulgur, add 3 T. finely minced sweet pepper, 3 T. minced onion, 5 crushed garlic cloves, 4 T. whole wheat flour, 2 T. paprika, ¼ c. tamari, 1½ T. sage, and 3 T. nutritional yeast. Mix well with hands. Form into patties or rolls. Fry (without oil) until browned (3 minutes per side)."*

Cracked Wheat. If you grind wheat very coarsely, you have "cracked wheat."

➢ *CRACKED WHEAT CEREAL Simmer ½ c. cracked wheat in 2½ c. water until tender. (Instead of cracked wheat, you can use wheat grits that you have sifted out of your wheat flour after grinding it.) It will be done in 1–3 hours, depending on the size of your chunks. Add salt to taste while cooking. Serve hot with a slosh of rich, thick cream and some fresh blackberries or whatever you like with your cereal.*

➢ *FRIED WHEAT MUSH Pour leftover cracked wheat breakfast cereal or graham porridge into a bread pan to get cold and set; then slice and fry it to make a hot mush. Serve with butter and syrup.*

➢ *CRACKED WHEAT BREAD From Pat Brunton, Maple Valley, WA: Bring to a boil and simmer until tender: 1 c. cracked wheat, 1 T. salt, 4 T. shortening, and 2 c. water. Dissolve 3 T. yeast in 1 c. warm water. Put all that in a large bowl, add 8 T. molasses, 1 can (13 oz.) evaporated milk, and 5 c. flour, and mix. Add another 5 c. (more or less) flour. Flour your hands. Knead dough (sort of push it together!) till dough sticks in a ball. Grease ball and let rise till doubled in bulk. Knead again; put in 6 loaf pans and let rise. Bake at 350°F about 40 minutes. Pat advises, "While it is baking, have a nap—the smell of home-baked bread eliminates the need for dusting, scrubbing, and all those stupid things."*

➢ *"POPPED" WHEAT In your heavy iron frying pan or Dutch oven (no lid needed), heat 1 T. oil to very hot (or pop it in a dry pan). Now add about ½ c. whole wheat. As soon as it starts to get hot, begin to agitate the pan over the heat. The wheat will pop just a little, like parched corn, but the kernels will be easy to chew. Serve plain, or buttered and salted like popcorn. Or serve with milk and a sweetening for a breakfast cereal. Or grind to make a raw or cooked breakfast cereal.*

GRAHAM WHEAT RECIPES:

"Graham" is an old-time word for home-ground flour or flour that is a trifle on the coarse side.

➢ *RAW GROUND WHEAT CEREAL Grind your wheat fine enough to chew without cooking. Pour milk and sweetener over a small bowl of it and eat it like a dry cereal.*

🐝 *GRAHAM MUSH* *This is the quickest wheat cereal you can make. Grind your wheat as fine as baking flour. For every 1 c. flour, add 1 c. cold water and ½ t. salt. Mix into a smooth paste. Then stir the mixture into 4 c. boiling water in the top of a double boiler. Cook until it tastes done and is of a nice cereal consistency. It will take maybe 20 minutes. Good with any dried fruit cooked in with it and served with milk or butter and sweetening. Or cook in all or part milk. Or cook in applesauce or any other fruit sauce, or a few cups of blackberries that have been stewed and put through a sieve to get out the seeds.*

🐝 *TRAVELER'S BREAD* *Geraldine Strusek of Carmel Valley, CA, wrote me a beautiful letter about her Minnesota childhood. "There in that big old kitchen was love, food, and a secure kind of feeling that comes over you as you enter its warm kingdom." My mother's kitchen was like that too! Geraldine said to grind 2 cups of northern wheat. Then add dried fruit (figs, dates, raisins, prunes) and nuts crushed fine. Stir with cold water as briskly as you can (to get air bubbles in it) until quite stiff. If you got it too sticky, add more wheat flour until you can cut it in cakes from a roll ½ inch thick. Bake.*

BRAN: If you are grinding hard wheat into flour, you can sift out bran; what's left is a relatively light flour for piecrusts or light muffins.

Before I get on to the wonderful world of wheat breads, here's . . .

UNLEAVENED, EGG, AND ACID-BASE LEAVENED BREADS

To "leaven" bread means to lighten it and make it rise with air bubbles. Unleavened bread won't cook through unless it is rolled as flat and thin as a tortilla. If you want to cook a loaf of bread, it has to be leavened by either yeast or baking powder. They both manufacture carbon dioxide inside the the dough, which causes it to "rise." So breads can be unleavened, leavened with air beaten into eggs (or just air beaten into the batter), or leavened with agents that make bubbles: baking powder, soda and sour milk or some other acidic food, commercial yeast cultures, or wild yeast (sourdough and salt-rising breads).

Leavening breads goes way back, at least to the Egyptians, Greeks, and Romans and probably farther, given that wheat has been raised for 10,000–15,000 years and any ground, moistened, sweetened wheat gets discovered by wild yeast in no time. "Yeast" is a microscopic-sized plant of the fungus category. It is common in dirt and floats unseen in air. There are many varieties of yeast, some better suited to baking, some to brewing. When yeast plants consume sugar, they create carbon dioxide bubbles and alcohol.

The transition from accidental "proofing" to deliberate leavening from yeast in the air, and then to the purposeful addition of a yeast (sourdough) culture to bread dough, was quick. The old-time bread ingredient variously called "start," "railroad," "everlasting," or "potato" yeast is a captured wild yeast turned into a home-maintained variety. Some persons got lucky and captured a yeast strain that had better flavor and better produced the desired bubbles. These folks loaned "starters" of their prized culture to friends. They learned how to dry or freeze portions of it and share them that way. Then an enterprising person with such a superior strain started charging for starts, and thus the commercial yeast business began.

You can leaven bread containing wheat flour because of its phenomenon of "gluten," which stretches to make a bubble when carbon dioxide gas is released inside the bread (either by yeast or baking powder chemistry).

The Klondike gold rush brought to prominence another way of doing it. You can't catch wild yeast in the Klondike in February. So they kept a culture going in the famous sourdough pot, and it got really sour. But from that came the first "baking powder." Refined soda was coming on the market, and the bread makers discovered that a pinch of soda added to a cup of sourdough (acid) made bubbles practically instantly in the batter. So instead of messing around with real sourdough breads, they started living on pancakes that they leavened by combining their soda with their homemade acid.

Well, soda can combine with any acid and do the same thing, so recipe books soon included recipes for breads and cakes leavened with soda and vinegar, soda and lemon juice, and soda and molasses (yes, it contains acid too) as well as soda and sourdough. Then cream of tartar came on the market, and with it recipes combining soda and cream of tartar to get the same reaction. Some people premixed it themselves in the right proportions and combined it with cornstarch to help keep their powder dry until they wanted the acid and base to react. That's the homemade baking powder you've heard about. Finally some started selling these mixes, and those were the first commercial baking powders. Since then, they've found different and stronger dry acids to use in place of cream of tartar; those are your "double-acting" and "triple-acting" baking powders.

Unleavened Breads

The Jewish Passover bread (matzoh) that looks like a cracker is one kind of unleavened bread. But any flat cracker could be an unleavened bread, if it's made without soda or baking powder. Tortillas, chapatis, and any other very thin, flat breads are usually unleavened. Bread with no bubbles in it at all has to be thin and flat so it can cook through. To make unleavened breads, you basically just mix water and flour, roll out flat and thin, and cook a few minutes on each side in a dry frying pan.

TORTILLAS: This unleavened bread can be made out of all kinds of flours: ground hominy (masa), cornmeal, wheat flour, etc. (For a masa tortilla recipe, see "Hominy Flour (Masa) Recipes" under "Corn.") It's the shape of the end product rather than the ingredients that makes a tortilla a tortilla. If you want to read the best book in the world about making tortillas, see *The Tortilla Book* by Diana Kennedy. My vegan reader Ruth from Bonaire says that if you use masa to make tortillas, you don't need shortening.

☙ *CORNMEAL TORTILLAS Stir 1 c. boiling water into 1 c. cornmeal. Add salt and a couple teaspoons bacon grease and mix. Pat into thin cakes and bake on a griddle the same as for masa tortillas (see "Hominy Flour (Masa) Recipes" under "Corn"). If you make tortillas out of flour and mashed potatoes, you have lefse (a Scandinavian dish). If you make the tortilla out of flour, you get another kind.*

☙ *LUPE'S TORTILLA DE HARINA Merry Collins of Kennewick, WA, told me this easy way to make tortillas, easy because "all the ingredients are warm and liquid. Mix together 3 c. flour, 1 T. baking powder, 1 t. salt, 3 T. vegetable oil, and 1 c. very hot water. Form a large dough ball. Let rest for a few minutes. Form small dough balls. Grab as much as you can pull off in your left palm. That's just the right amount. Make the glob of dough round by pulling the edges in but keeping it against the left palm. It makes the top nice and smooth. Then the balls are rolled out with a rolling pin until round and flat, put them on an ungreased preheated griddle (cast iron) at a medium heat. After bubbles begin forming, turn and cook on the other side. We store them in a crockery pot with a lid or in a plastic bowl. They should be stacked inside a clean dishtowel. It took me quite a while to be able to get these tortillas rolled out round. I used to get teased about my tortillas. They were so misshapen."*

Hazel's Rollout System. "When ready, make small balls and set aside about 8 or 10. With hands slightly moist, dip them in flour. Now work the balls into flat round disks. Either roll out or, as I do, turn the dough and stretch it until you have a tortilla with no holes, about the size of a bread-and-butter plate and about ⅛ inch thick. I cook mine on a lightly greased griddle—that flat kind (do not fry). Cook on both sides. A little scorch won't hurt. Just don't burn holes. As they come off the griddle, place between 2 towels or a folded towel. This will soften the tortillas so you can roll them when you get to the filling."

Tortilla Press. At a little fair where I sold my books last weekend, the lady who was selling wonderful from-scratch pancakes bartered breakfast for a big family for their tortilla press and considered it well worth it. You can buy a similar little press that turns out one nice tortilla at a time in the blink of an eye. No rolling with a pin, no struggle, no mess, no time wasted. I recommend it!

Taco Fillings. For the filling part, make tortillas into a sandwich sort of thing and fold over or roll up. For a quick filling, try peanut butter and jam. Or tomato chunks with melted cheese. Or you could get serious about it and fill them with some grated cheese or homemade cottage cheese, garden leaf lettuce, chunks of garden-ripened tomato, homemade taco sauce, and homemade refried beans. Then you have a wonderful meal that is not only food for the body but entertainment for the whole family.

Taco night at the Emery house is Daddy Mike's night to cook. It happens when he wants to give me an evening off

and has become both a rite of love and great fun for all. I love standing back and letting Daddy slave over the hot stove. The children slice tomatoes, grate cheese, and shred lettuce. Grated turnip is wonderful with tacos too, and so is radish, especially the long white kind. We try to find something new to put in the tacos every time we eat them just for the fun of it.

☙ *CHAPATIS This is a traditional bread from India. Combine 2 c. ground wheat flour (or corn, bean, or rice flour), 2 T. oil (or melted fat of some sort), ¾ c. water, and ½ t. salt. Knead as you would tortillas; make little balls the size of a golf ball. Let rest about 1½ hours. Roll out flat and thin. Cook on griddle. Don't oil the griddle—oil each side of the chapati! Best eaten warm, right from pan to plate. If you have leftovers, reheat when ready to eat them; that will make them soft and tasty again. Ruth says, "Omit oil and salt. Make 'golf balls' and then flatten them, brush them lightly with oil, and roll into a ball again. Repeat. Then roll out thinly and bake, without oiling the pan. That's how the East Indians from Trinidad do it."*

☙ *ROTI From Ruth: "Another from India. Make chapati dough. Meanwhile, have some green split peas or lentils cooking. Then make balls of dough and roll out. Put a spoonful of mashed (drained if necessary) peas on each round of dough, roll up again, and knead each ball separately to mix in peas. Then roll out thinly and bake on griddle. Rotis are usually about 18 inches in diameter! They are served with a filling of curried vegetables heaped in the middle and the edges of the roti folded over it. You eat it with your right hand, by tearing off pieces of roti and scooping up some curried vegetables with the bread. (Left hands are used for purposes other than eating! Bad breach of etiquette to eat with your left hand.)"*

☙ *RUTH'S EGGLESS CREPES "Combine 2 c. cornmeal, 1 c. whole wheat flour, and 3 c. water. Leave it in a warm place to ferment about 8 hours, or overnight. (Cover bowl with a cloth.) Ladle ¼ c. batter onto nonstick frying pan, spread thinly. (Batter tends to separate. Stir often!) Do not flip until top has dried out. Then loosen and cook other side. These are hard to make at first; practice makes perfect! Serve with anything rolled up inside, like a bean-tomato mixture."*

☙ *RUTH'S EVEN EASIER EGGLESS CREPES! Combine ¾ c. whole wheat flour of pastry-flour quality, 1 c. soy or rice milk, 4 T. cornstarch, and 1 small mashed banana. Cook about 7 T. batter at a time in a skillet shined with a cut raw potato. Flip when top is dry. Fill with a mixture of applesauce, raisins, and cinnamon for a dessert crepe. Or fill with a mix of several mashed potatoes and a mashed carrot for a main-course dinner crepe.*

Breads Leavened with Eggs and Beating

"Quick" breads are breads leavened with air beaten into eggs or the batter, with baking soda, or with baking powder. That's quick compared to yeast breads, which make you wait a couple of hours for the yeast to work. Sponge cakes and popovers are leavened simply with air beaten in. The problem in these batters is to get and keep in as much air as possible. The egg whites and egg yolks are usually beaten separately and all the ingredients mixed well. Then the egg white is folded in—gently, to keep from driving out the air that has been whipped into the eggs. The more air you have in the batter, the larger the volume of batter and the finer the texture. Air-leavened batters should be baked or cooked at a relatively low temperature for as long as it takes.

When the egg whites are beaten, air is trapped in them and the eggs become fluffy and white. Then the eggs containing the air are mixed with the flour and other ingredients and put into the oven to bake. Air expands when heated, and this makes the cake "rise." When you cut the cake, you can see the holes made in it by the expanding air bubbles.

POPOVER BATTERS: Thoroughly beat these at least several minutes with your eggbeater or blender. Then pour immediately into your baking container, preferably preheated to reduce the baking time and help keep the air bubbles. Use a hot oven to start with until your batter has risen all it can from the expansion of the air bubbles as they heat; then reduce the temperature to prevent burning.

➣ *POPOVERS Preheat and grease a muffin pan, 8 custard cups, or a regular popover pan. Preheat the oven to 450°F, because you want to get those right into a hot oven. Mix 1¼ c. flour, ¼ t. salt, 1 t. sugar, 1 c. milk, and 2 well-beaten egg yolks. Beat the batter thoroughly and then fill the popover spaces about half full of batter. Bake at a hot temp. 20 minutes, then turn the oven down and continue baking until the popovers suit you. Some people like them dry inside and prick the popovers and then leave them in 20 minutes more. Good for breakfast.*

➣ *CREPES (For years I called this recipe "crepes suzette" until Sylvia Nelson, Hillsdale, WY, corrected me: "Crepes suzette is a fancy dessert, liberally loaded down with orange liqueur. What is in your book is simply crepes. Don't mind me —I used to work as a proofreader." Sylvia, I am so grateful when somebody catches an error and tells me!)*

When I recently was 9 months pregnant, avoiding salt, and also trying life without baking powder and soda, these crepes were a mainstay. They are bland alone but delicious spread fresh and hot with sour cream, apple butter, or what you like; roll them up and eat, or eat them with a fork like a pancake. I'm sure you'll like them. Ingredients: 4 or more eggs, separated, 1½ c. milk, 1 c. flour. Mix flour, milk and egg yolks. Beat whites stiff and fold in. Grease a round frying pan enough to make it shine, and heat it medium-hot. Pour in a ladleful of the batter; if the pan is not level, keep turning it until the batter makes a round pancake covering the bottom. When the bottom is done, turn and cook on the other side. Serve immediately. Cook as slowly and gently as possible for maximum tenderness and tastiness. The more eggs you use in them, the nicer they are.

Acid-Base Leavenings

SODA COMBINED WITH AN ACIDIC FOOD: The "acidic food" could be sour milk, buttermilk, vinegar, cream of tartar, molasses, lemon juice, or any combination thereof. When sour milk is used, the acid that reacts with the soda is lactic acid. Soda always means baking soda, or "bicarbonate of soda," $NaHCO_3$ ("sodium hydrogen carbonate"). Soda is a base, and when the base and the acid are both in solution and able to contact each other, the resulting chemical reaction releases a harmless gas (carbon dioxide), which makes bubbles in your batter and "leavens" the bread. Always sift the soda with the flour.

The Proper Soda/Acid Proportion. Use ½ t. baking soda per 1 c. sour milk or buttermilk. Molasses varies in acidity, so if you have molasses as your acid in a recipe, you have to approximate: ½ t. soda will be right for ½–1 c. molasses. You could use 1 c. molasses to be safe. A half teaspoon of soda is the right amount to combine with 1 T. vinegar or 1 T. lemon juice. A half teaspoon of baking soda plus acidic liquid equals 2 t. baking powder in leavening power. I wouldn't use soda in a food unless there's an equivalent amount of acid in your recipe. Excess soda means you'll have a soda taste and no nutritional value from it unless it's a treatment for excess stomach acid.

A Soda Substitute. If you can't buy soda—if you're in the wilderness, or the jungle—what can you substitute? Marie Oesting, Ocean Park, WA, sent me that answer: "In the real old days, they used to leaven with wood ash. Ashes are alkaline. If you add a teaspoon of ash to a mixture that contains an acid, such as real sour cream, buttermilk from slightly soured milk, or yogurt, then the two make bubbles. You have to work *fast* because the bubbles don't last very long. It won't produce as 'light' a biscuit, so make them thin."

Soda/Food-Acid Leavened Breads. I like breads that use soda and natural food acids for leavening. Here are some of my favorites.

➣ *HOBO BREAD Boil 2½ c. water. Pour it over 2 c. raisins and 4 t. soda. Let that mixture rest overnight. Next morning, add 1 c. sweetening (brown or white sugar, honey, molasses —less if supplies are short). Also add 4 T. shortening (oil, melted lard or butter, bacon grease, etc.), 4 c. of some kind of flour, and a pinch of salt. Pour the resulting batter into 3 loaf pans. Each should be about half full. (The Depression-era hobos baked this in 1-lb. coffee cans.) Bake at 350°F for about 1 hour. Cool before removing from pan.*

➣ *PIONEER SOFT GINGERBREAD Combine 3 c. molasses, 1 c. rich cream, 1 c. melted butter, and 2 beaten eggs. Sift together 6 c. flour, 2 t. soda, and 2½ t. ginger (you might want more ginger). Mix wet ingredients with dry ones. Bake at 350–375°F for 45 minutes. This makes a lot of gingerbread!*

➣ *MODERN SOFT GINGERBREAD Sift together 1 t. soda, 1 t. ginger, 1 T. cinnamon, 1 t. cloves, a pinch salt, and 3 c. whole wheat flour. In a separate bowl combine 1 c. brown sugar, 1 c. oil (or melted butter), 3 beaten eggs, 1 c. sour milk, and 1 c. molasses. Now beat dry ingredients into the liquid. Pour into a greased and floured 8 × 12-inch pan. Bake at 375°F for 30–45 minutes.*

➣ *JEANIE JOHNS' CAKE Mix in a pan 1½ c. flour, 1 c. sugar, 3 T. cocoa, 1 t. baking soda, and ½ t. salt. Melt 6 T. shortening and stir in. Add 1 T. vinegar, 1 c. cold water, and 1 t. vanilla. Make holes in the batter and stir. Bake immediately in a preheated 350°F oven for 25 to 30 minutes.*

➣ *BOSTON BROWN BREAD This traditional recipe works well with home-ground grains. Combine 1 c. whole wheat flour, 1 c. rye flour, 1 c. corn flour, 1½ t. soda, and ½ t. salt. Add ¾ c. molasses and 2 c. buttermilk. Pour the batter into a greased 2-qt. container. Cover loosely. Set container on a rack in a large kettle. Pour boiling water into the outer kettle. Fill it halfway to the top of a brown bread mold. Cover kettle with a tight-fitting lid. Cook over medium heat 3½ hours. The water around the outside of the mold shold be boiling all that*

1. Add the soda, or the dry mixture containing the soda, last.
2. Avoid stirring the batter very much once the soda has been added. Overmixing will knock out the gas that you need to raise your dough.
3. Get your batter into the pan and from there into the oven as quickly as possible to preserve the leavening effect.
4. For each teaspoon of double-acting baking powder called for in a recipe (or each 2 t. single-acting baking powder), substitute ¼ t. baking soda plus ½ c. sour milk or buttermilk. Let the ½ cup sour milk or buttermilk replace ½ c. sweet milk or other fluid called for in your recipe.

time (you'll need to add more). Then remove brown bread container from water, use a knife to cut it loose from the sides of its container, turn upside down, and dump out the bread. It's best served hot.

☙ *RHUBARB NUT BREAD* Combine 1½ c. brown sugar, ½ c. vegetable oil, ⅔ c. water, 1 c. buttermilk, 1 egg, and 1 t. vanilla extract in a big bowl. Beat those ingredients until well mixed. Add 2½ c. whole wheat flour, ½ t. salt, and 1 t. soda and again mix well. Now stir in 1½ c. finely chopped rhubarb and ½ c. nuts. Divide the batter between 2 greased 8 × 4 × 2-inch loaf pans. Bake at 325°F for about 1 hour. This is delicious!

☙ *HOMEMADE GRAPE NUTS* Ingredients: 3½ c. sifted whole wheat flour, 1 t. soda, ½ c. brown sugar, 2 c. sweet milk, 2 T. vinegar, and ½ t. salt. Mix flour, soda, sugar, and salt. Add sour milk and beat until smooth. Spread dough ¼ inch thick on a greased cookie sheet. Bake in a 375°F oven about 15 minutes. When cool, grind in a food chopper. Don't dry it completely or you'll get flour. Let it finish drying after grinding. Before serving, mix in anything else you would like, such as nuts or fruit. You can bag and tie with wire in family-sized portions. Handy for an instant breakfast.

BAKING POWDERS

Soda/Cream of Tartar Baking Powders. These are basically a mixture of soda, cream of tartar, and cornstarch (or flour). The purpose of the cornstarch is to keep the base (soda) and acid (cream of tartar) separated until the liquid hits them. It also prevents water vapor in the air from causing the powder to form a solid cake.

Cream of Tartar. This one is potassium hydrogen tartrate, $KHC_4H_4O_6$. Cream of tartar is naturally found in grape juice. If you make your own grape juice, you may notice floating crystals of crude tartar, also called "argol." In home-canned grape juice that has been sitting quietly in storage for several months, you get big chips of argol on the bottom of the jar. This crude tartar is less soluble in alcoholic fluid than in water and so is deposited at an even greater rate if wine is made from grape juice. The argols that form when wine is made are about 90 percent cream of tartar. You can pulverize them to make cream of tartar. Soda reacts with cream of tartar much more slowly than it does with molasses, sour milk, and lemon juice—hence its usefulness as an ingredient in baking powder.

Homemade Baking Powder. You can make your own; a woman named Mrs. Essemen sent me the recipe [1975]. "Using a scale, measure out 350 grams (12½ oz.) of cream of tartar, 150 grams (5½ oz.) bicarbonate of soda, and 100 grams (3½ oz.) cornstarch. You could use flour instead of cornstarch if you want, and the exact amount isn't awfully

important. Or, if you want to make a huge quantity in pounds, use 1 lb. cream of tartar and ½ lb. soda. As you see, the general proportion of cream of tartar to soda in homemade baking powder is 2 to 1. Usually a little extra cream of tartar is included to make sure all the soda is acted on. You don't have to be absolutely precise, especially with the cornstarch. If you can manage a rounded-off ounce, that's close enough. To mix, sift them together 10 times. Spread out to dry if there is any dampness in your batch."

A gentleman from Metairie, LA, made a batch of Mrs. Essemen's baking powder. It worked fine for him, but he calculated that the cost was more than 5 times that of the same amount of store-bought baking powder. He wrote [1977] and asked me, "What is the use of that expensive formula?" I didn't have a good answer. Quite often, making things yourself will be more expensive than buying them. And invariably it is more work and trouble than grabbing a box or bottle off the supermarket shelf. Maybe the recipe is here to give you an option, or to help you better understand what is in the store's box of baking powder. Anyway, I'm proud of Mrs. Essemen for knowing how to make her own baking powder and grateful to be able to share her know-how.

Saleratus. I learned that when baking powder first appeared in the United States about 1790, many cooks made their own, and it was no big deal. They called it "saleratus." Any old-time recipe that calls for "saleratus" means a soda/cream of tartar single-acting baking powder. Wilma Litchfield, a wonderful Utah grandmother, sent me her saleratus recipe.

☙ *SALERATUS (OLD-TIME BAKING POWDER)* For every cup of flour in your recipe, combine 2 t. cream of tartar, 1 t.

ONE TEASPOON DOUBLE-ACTING BAKING POWDER EQUALS

- 1½ t. phosphate baking powder
- 2 t. homemade (or single-acting) baking powder
- ½ t. soda plus 1 c. sour butter-milk

- ½ t. soda plus 1 c. sour milk
- ½ t. soda plus 1 T. vinegar plus 1 c. sweet milk
- ½ t. soda plus 1 T. lemon juice plus 1 c. sweet milk

- ½ t. soda plus ½–1 c. molasses (use 1 c. when in doubt)
- ½ t. soda plus 1 t. cream of tartar

BAKING POWDER RATIO TO FLOUR

- 1 t. baking powder per 1 c. flour for cakes in which eggs are used

- 2 t. baking powder per 1 c. flour for biscuits, muffins, and waffles

- ¾ T. baking powder per cup flour for buckwheat and whole-grain flours and flours when eggs are not used

---

bicarbonate of soda, ½ t. salt, and ½ t. cornstarch. Sift these ingredients together twice. Then add to flour. (This is Mrs. Essemen's recipe on a teaspoon scale.) But Lea, whom I met at a barter fair (see her recipe for Gourmet Healthy Pancakes a little later on), uses 1 t. soda, etc. for 3-plus cups of dry ingredients rather than for every 1 cup flour.

1983. A letter arrived from Yvonne Parker, Baptist Theological Seminary, Lusaka, Zambia: "Dear Carla, My husband and I are Southern Baptist missionaries to Zambia, having served here since late 1978. Many times we go for long periods of time without seeing 'necessary' commodities for sale, and we do all 'from-scratch' cooking, even making marshmallows. We have just returned to Zambia after a time of furlough in the States, and there is no baking powder to be found. So . . . I turned to your book and found Mrs. Essemen's Baking Powder Recipe. If the gentleman from Metairie, LA, were living here, he would surely appreciate that recipe—no matter what the cost. We——and many others!—have taken your book around the world to help with the adjustments of learning to live in more 'basic' places than the affluent USA."

About the same time that Yvonne wrote me, I learned of research that suggested a posible link between excessive aluminum intake and development of Alzheimer's disease. For that reason, cautious people now try to reduce the aluminum in their diet. There are 5 ways to do that:

1. Don't cook or eat with aluminum utensils or aluminum foil, *especially in the presence of acids.*
2. Don't eat store pickles because they're made with an aluminum compound.
3. Don't use aluminum-based commercial baking powder or eat bakery and restaurant products because they're usually made with aluminum powders.
4. Avoid deodorants; most are aluminum-based.
5. Avoid beverages and other foods in aluminum cans (also because even the recycling of aluminum is a significantly polluting industry).

1993. I just heard of a research study that found *no* link between aluminum consumption and Alzheimer's. So maybe aluminum doesn't harm your health. Well, I know *for sure* the process of recycling aluminum, because an aluminum company wanted to truck in aluminum-can recycling wastes that nobody else wanted to the community dump at Moscow, Idaho, which happens (alas) to be a privately owned and for-profit dump. (There should not be *any* privately owned, for-profit dumps—too much temptation to hide toxics in them for big payoffs.) Returnable glass containers are environmentally much preferable to aluminum cans because recycling bottles doesn't result in tons of heavy-metal-laced salt that has to be piled somewhere forever.

Single or Double-Acting. "Single-acting" baking powder is the kind that contains soda and cream of tartar and just leavens once. "Double-acting" baking powder is a more sophisticated mixture that produces gas bubbles during mixing and again during baking. Double-acting baking powder has been considered to be the best. Its secret is that its acid is only moderately soluble. If the acid dissolves too easily, or if you wait too long or stir too much, the carbon dioxide gas will be released before, rather than during, the baking. Under the best of circumstances, the heat of the baking causes the completion of the chemical reaction and the final raising.

When using a single-acting baking powder recipe, remember: *Put what you're baking into the oven as soon as it is mixed.* When substituting a single-acting baking powder in a modern recipe that calls for double-acting baking powder, use between 1½ and 2 teaspoons of yours for every 1 t. specified.

Commercial Soda/Tartar Baking Powder. Katya Morrison, Mount Airy, MD, wrote me, "Royal is a baking powder that contains cream of tartar, tartaric acid (the acid of grapes), bicarbonate of soda, and starch. From what I understand, it is the best there is, but I have a hard time finding it. It works well with no bitterness."

LEA'S GOURMET HEALTHY PANCAKES Lea from Oregon says she buys her cream of tartar right at the grocery store. In barter-fair season, Lea travels with her two young daughters from gig to gig in a big school bus, and that's how I met her. She's tries hard to live right for Mother Earth, even on the fair circuit: no paper products, no plastic, no detergents. Lea serves her pancakes on regular dishes with stainless steel silverware. She makes the best pancakes I ever tasted. Combine ¼ c. millet, 1 c. white flour, 1 c. whole wheat flour, 1 t. baking soda, 2 t. cream of tartar, ½ t. salt, 2 T. sugar, ⅓ c. rice bran (or any other bran), ¼ c. cornmeal, ¾ c. rolled oats, and ¼ cup oil. Add 2 beaten eggs and enough milk to make a thin batter. Let it stand 5 minutes to thicken; then pour pancake-sized dollops and fry.

Phosphate Baking Powder. There is another baking powder available on the commercial market besides the soda-cream of tartar one (Royal) and the double-acting (Calumet, Clabber Girl, Davis). Double-acting baking powder uses sodium aluminum sulfate, $NaAl(SO_4)_2$, as the acidic component. The base in every powder is soda. Phosphate powders are about one-fourth less strong in leavening effect than the double-acting powders. Rumford and Dr. Price are brand names for phosphate powders. The phosphate baking powders are made with calcium phosphate, $CaH_4P_2O_8$, or sodium dihydrogen phosphate, NaH_2PO_4, as the acid part.

Baking Powder Bread Recipes

❧ **BANANA NUT BREAD** Ingredients: ⅔ c. peanut oil, 2½ c. unbleached flour, 1¼ c. honey, 6 large ripe bananas, mashed, 1¼ t. baking powder, 1 t. soda, and ¼ t. sea salt. Mix 2 minutes. Add ⅔ c. (goat's) milk, 2 eggs, and beat. Lastly, add ⅔ c. sunflower seeds (roasted). Bake at 350°F oven until done—can check with a toothpick, but usually 35 to 45 minutes will do. Makes 2 loaves.

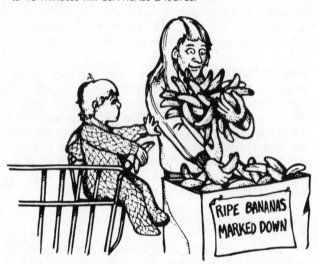

RIPE BANANAS MARKED DOWN

❧ **BAKING POWDER PANCAKES** Sift together into a bowl: 1 c. whole wheat flour, 1½ t. baking powder, and ½ t. salt. Separate 2 eggs. Beat the egg whites. In a separate bowl combine 1 c. milk, 2 egg yolks, and 2 T. oil or melted fat. Now add wet ingredients to dry ones and mix. Lastly, fold in the beaten egg whites. And fry 'em.

❧ **BAKING POWDER WAFFLES** Combine 1 c. whole wheat flour, 3 t. baking powder, a pinch of salt, and 2 t. sugar, and sift all together several times. Separate 2 eggs and beat the egg whites. Combine egg yolks and 1¼ c. milk. Add ¼ c. oil. Waffle batter is best if the batter is on the thin side and beaten hard. Now fold in the egg whites, and bake in waffle iron.

Indian Woman Bread

7th edition, 1976. A friend wrote to ask if I could help her find an "Indian woman" bread recipe. I didn't know one but published her request, and did I ever get native American bread recipes!

❧ **KIOWA BREAD** George Lawrence, Denver, CO, wrote me that for the past few years he has belonged to a YMCA group studying the life of the American Indian. George says to use biscuit dough with very little shortening. Flavoring is optional. Roll out, cut into squares, and make a few indentations with a knife in the squares. Drop into boiling fat and remove when golden brown.

❧ **YAVAPAI BREAD** Marion Stick, Phoenix, AZ, is of Pima Indian descent. They make wonderful fried bread. But her Pima Indians ate lunch together with the Yavapai Indians in the Superstition Mountains, and she was so enthused about their bread that she sent that recipe to me. Combine 2 c. flour, 1 t. salt, 2 t. baking powder, ½ c. powdered milk, and 1 T. sugar in a bowl. Gradually add enough warm water (about a cup) to make a soft dough. Divide dough in half and flour lightly. Pat a small amount into about an 8-inch circle (very thin). Fry quickly in hot oil (275°F and about 2½ or 3 inches deep). Drain on absorbent paper. While warm, dust with powdered sugar. Dough that is overhandled will tend to make a tough bread.

❧ **DOUGH BOD BREAD** Russell Shorten, Colfax, WA, wrote me, "One day I was making what I call 'dough bods,' and an old Indian friend came by and said his mother used to make them and called it 'Squaw Bread.' She cooked hers over an outdoor fire. You simply take bread dough at the stage you usually make it into a loaf (about enough to make a good-sized bun), flatten it with your hands, and fry it in a skillet of good hot grease. We eat it hot with butter and jelly."

Homemade Ready Mixes. The store mixes are cheap and easy but not very healthy. But the basic notion of combining enough dry ingredients ahead of time for maybe 7 to 10 bakings is a good one if you like baking-powder breads. If you do make your own mixes, they may be either more or less expensive than the ones you buy, depending on what ingredients you choose and how you supply them. You'll know for sure there are no preservatives. The only drawback to mixes, besides the fact they depend on baking powder, is that you aren't using freshly ground flour.

❧ **BASIC HOMEMADE BAKING MIX** Regular baking recipes have an average of about 9 ingredients. You can make your own 4-time mix recipe by combining the dry ingredients of your favorite recipe, quadrupling, and using as needed. Your mix won't perform well unless the premixed ingredients are thoroughly blended. Sift your dry ingredients together several times; then add the shortening and cut it in well. Store in the refrigerator any mixes that contain shortening. Mixes that contain only dry ingredients can be stored like your flour. Then all you need to do is combine your mix, the eggs, and milk (or other liquids). To use the mix, leave out the ingredients you've already got in, add the rest, stir, and cook.

❧ **HEALTHY BAKING MIX** Thoroughly combine 2½ qt. whole wheat flour, 1 qt. powdered milk, 1 c. soy flour, ½ qt. wheat germ, and ½ c. baking powder by sifting together several times. Cut in 1 qt. (4 c.) butter. To make pancakes of this, combine 1½ c. mix, 1 c. liquid, and 1 egg. To make fruit muffins, combine 1 egg, 1 c. milk, a little sweetening, and ½ c. apples or raisins. Dump that liquid into 3 c. mix and stir. Quickly pour batter into greased muffin tin. Bake at 400°F.

❧ **MISSOURI MIX** Combine ⅓ c. baking powder, 1 c. plus 2 T. powdered milk, 4 t. salt, and 9 c. flour. (You can make that half whole wheat flour and it will still perform fine.) Blend thoroughly by sifting together. Cut 1½ c. lard into flour mixture. Store in refrigerator and use within a month. Make biscuits by adding ½ c. water to 2 c. mix.

🍞 *HOMEMADE BISCUIT, DUMPLING, SHORTCAKE, WAF-FLE, MUFFIN, COFFEE CAKE, ETC. MIX If you have to do a lot of baking and you're really desperate for time, make this dry mix. To use, add enough milk to make a soft dough and proceed. You should store it in the refrigerator, where it will keep at least a month. Your basic proportions: for every cup flour, cut in 1 t. baking powder, ½ t. salt, and 3 T. shortening. Thus for 10 c. flour, sifted and measured, add 10 t. baking powder and 5 t. salt. Then mix and sift again. Cut in 1⅞ c. shortening (⅞ c. would be 1 c. minus 2 T.) until the mixture has a fine even crumb. Keep in a closed container.*

YEAST BREADS

I feel inadequate to tell you how to make yeast bread, which is paradoxical because it's probably the thing I do best. The problem is I never use a recipe. I've included in this book the recipes I learned to make bread from.

I make bread once every 10 days or so—whenever we get near to running out. I mix my liquid in a 5-gal. bucket. I bring up flour from the basement in another bucket and combine in my liquid bucket until I have it dry enough to turn out in the middle of my big round kitchen table, which is covered (over the tablecloth) with a heavy sheet of clear plastic. I finish adding flour there and knead the dough, and then let it rise right there in the middle of the table. I punch it down and commence putting it in pans. My children love bread-making day. They all get into the act. We make lots of rolls because it's something they can and like to do. So we make big rolls and little rolls, odd-looking rolls and worse-looking rolls. My only absolute demand is that their hands be washed before they help me. For them it's like modeling-clay day. For me it's a race to get as much of the dough into proper loaf shapes and loaf pans before they have the whole 5 gallons made into a mountain of rolls. I like loaf bread better because there's a smaller percentage of crust and it keeps better and serves better.

When we bake, we keep about 5 loaves at a time in the oven (but that's really too many to do it right). The first get rushed in before they are really done rising. The last ones may have had to be punched down in the pan to let rise again before they finally get a turn in the oven. The children go in the living room and wait for the cry of "hot bread." They they all come running and the first couple of pans of bread go down the hatch on the spot. My children can eat a loaf of bread just for a snack be-tween them all, and I like it too, so I have to figure on at least one loaf of bread consumed per day and more likely three. I use the bread in

other things, too, and that helps make it go. I make puddings and desserts, and stuff the roast chicken with seasoned bread.

So bread making here is on such a massive scale, and usually so chaotic with all my helpers, that we aren't too picky about the results. With all those pans in the oven at once, I have a problem with poor circulation of heat, and they tend to burn on the bottom. If that happens, I just slice off the whole bottom of the loaf and put it in the pig bucket. And my helpers haven't really reached a stage of high artistic perfection with their roll and loaf mixtures. But it seems to all get eaten up at an appallingly fast rate, and so soon it's time to make bread again. I bag up the bread and keep the extra loaves in the freezer, pulling out just one or two ahead of time to thaw. The frozen bread isn't as nice as fresh bread. And fresh bread isn't as nice as hot bread just out of the oven, but it's still our staff of life.

In this household you can eat bread anytime. The children usually have it with their breakfast and at intervals all day long. Some people don't believe in letting their children eat between meals, but my bread is so healthy I don't worry about it. They eat it at meals, too, and even if they didn't, I wouldn't mind, since what they were full of was my bread. When we go visiting, I usually take a loaf of bread as a hostess gift, and when someone comes to visit, I usually send a loaf home with them. If I'm tired or sick or didn't get home from shopping until 6 at night, I don't have to worry—there's always bread. Even the rabbits like my bread, and so does the cat.

I started out baking bread from recipes. I wish you could have seen my first 3 loaves. They were just awful, small and hard as a rock. I hadn't managed to make the bread rise, and then I overbaked it. There was no way to eat them. I threw them out. But gradually, over the years, I learned so much about bread making that now I know intuitively what will go with what and how much of it I can get away with adding. If you've never made much bread before, you too can start with recipes—plus all the general principles of bread making that I'm going to give you—and then eventually work your way off the rigid recipe and experiment. It's both fun and a practical way to recycle leftovers. Or maybe you'd be happiest finding one good recipe that always works for you and using that one forever. That's okay too.

How to Use Recipes from an Antique Cookbook

I wrote this section in February 1971. It was the first writing I did on this book.

I read about 50 antique recipe books before I started writing this section. That's how I figured these things out. It was sleuthing, and I really enjoyed it. Antique recipe books can work for you, if you know how to use them. They can be a functional part of your kitchen library, not merely sentimental curiosities on the shelf.

LEAVENING: This is invariably a problem in using old-time recipes. See "Acid-Base Leavenings" for lots more on old-time leavenings. If the recipe calls for yeast by the "teacup" or some such strong amount, it means liquid yeast; use any sourdough starter or homemade yeast recipe. Or, easier yet, substitute dry yeast. How much? For less than 6 c. flour, use 1 T. dry yeast. From 6 to 11 c. flour, use 2 T. From 11 to 26 c., use 3 T. Then fill the "teacup," or whatever, with water to match the desired liquid quantity. If the recipe calls for a yeast "cake," that means compressed yeast. Those pressed cakes of combined moist yeast and filler material rapidly disappeared from the marketplace after the introduction of dry yeast. For each "cake of yeast," substitute 1 T. dry yeast.

TEMPERATURES: In the old days it was assumed that everyone knew how to cook, so instructions for baking and cooking were vague. Anyway, there were no temperature controls on campfires, fireplaces, or early day ranges.

MEASURES: "Teaspoon" may not mean what you think. "Teaspoon" has changed from the old-time ratio of 4 t. per tablespoon to our present 3 t. per tablespoon. Worse yet, in some old books "teaspoon" and "tablespoon," when applied to dry materials, were understood to be a "rounded" quantity—meaning as much heaped above the rim of the spoon as below. "Heaping" meant as much of a dry ingredient as could be piled on the spoon without falling off. A "dessert-spoon" was half a tablespoon. That means it was the equivalent of 2 t. when 4 t. equaled 1 tablespoon. A "saltspoon" contained ⅛ teaspoon. A "dash" meant one shake of the shaker. A "pinch" then and now was as much as can be taken between the top of your finger and thumb. If you're not comfortable with "salt to taste," add ¼ t. salt per 2 c. flour.

"Cup" in old recipe books meant about one-fifth less than our present 8-oz. cup. "Teacup" meant what we would call a half-cup. "Wineglass" was the equivalent of our ¼ cup. When a recipe calls for "bowls," as some old mincemeat recipes do, use the same bowl consistently and guess from the quantity of ingredients how large a bowl is needed. (A 3-cup capacity is a good average guess.) There were 12 fluid oz. but 16 dry oz. per pound. Thus, a "pound" of molasses was 12 fluid oz., about 1½ cups. Recipe amounts were often given by weight rather than volume. You can buy an adequate kitchen scale in most hardware stores. A "hen's egg of butter" is 3 to 4 tablespoons. A "walnut-sized lump of butter" is 2 tablespoons. For "tumbler," "large coffee cup," and "glassful," you can substitute 1 cup.

FLOUR: Flour consistencies have varied over the years and with the brand. (For amounts to add, see "Yeast Bread Ingredients" a bit later on). Whole wheat flour was formerly sold in 2 grades. "Graham" flour was the heavier, containing more bran and coarse particles, and was considered the lowest class of brown flour. "Entire wheat flour" was the other grade. The entire wheat flour was usually intended when whole wheat flour was mentioned in a recipe, unless graham flour was specifically named. In old recipe books, "1 cup flour" means unsifted flour unless the recipe directs you to sift it. You can freely substitute one kind of wheat flour for another. It changes the color and the taste a little, but that's all.

SUGAR: "Loaf sugar" was sugar purchased in hard loaves or cones that averaged about 9 to 10 lb. apiece in weight. That's way back when. One cone would last thrifty people a year. The sugar cone was cut into lumps of equal size and regular shape with special "sugar shears." For "1 lump loaf sugar," substitute a modern sugar cube. For loaf sugar "crushed," substitute granulated sugar. Loaf sugar "ground in a mortar" meant loaf sugar crushed only to a particle size, similar to sand or fine gravel. "Powdered sugar" in the old recipe books meant a grade of fineness between granulated and confectioners' sugar. Granulated sugar had a weight of 2 c. per pound, powdered sugar a weight of 2⅔ c. per pound.

FLAVORING: You are safest if you learn to use judgment in flavoring. Lemons and eggs are not always of the same size anyway; nor are fruits always of the same degree of sweetness or acidity. When your old-time cookbook was written, flavorings were commonly adulterated, so you may need to reduce the suggested quantity of spices. If the recipe calls for ginger and the amount seems large, it meant ginger root, which was purchased whole and ground at home as needed. Home-ground ginger is not as strong as the powdered commercial product. To substitute store-ground ginger for ground root, reduce the amount to one-fourth of the quantity given. For "1 grated nutmeg," substitute 2¾ T. store-ground.

Get in the habit of tasting a pinch of mixture now and then, and you'll learn what to expect and be forewarned when all is not well. Be prepared to try an old recipe several times before getting all the kinks out of it. If the recipe is for a large amount, scale it down until your experimenting is done. After each trial, think about which measures may have been wrong and write down your guesses of what they should be. To be a real old-time cook, get to know what a teaspoon and tablespoon of a dry ingredient look like in the palm of your hand. Know how stiff or runny and how sweet, sour, or spicy you want your dish to be, and then trust your taste buds!

FRUITS AND VEGETABLES: Our great-grandmothers used some vegetables that are now usually sold in grocery stores. You can look for the names in your garden seed catalog and plant your own salsify, sorrel, leeks, and the like. In some cases, the plant is the same but over the years the name has changed. "Pieplant" means rhubarb; "vegetable marrow" means summer squash; "oyster plant" is salsify.

Bread-Making Equipment

Mixing Container. You need something large enough to mix in. For me that's a stainless steel bucket or a big stainless steel bowl. For you it could be any sort of bowl or pan. If you are working in an old-fashioned kitchen, substitute potato masher when you see "blender" in a recipe. And substitute an eggbeater or a big mixing spoon and some elbow grease for "electric mixer." A clock helps, but it isn't necessary.

Baking Pans. If things are grim, large-size (46-oz.) juice cans with one end neatly removed can be used to make do for baking bread, and so can large coffee cans. If you have pie tins or Pyrex oven-type plates, you can make dough into large rolls and bake it that way. Or you can make rolls and bake in a loaf pan. It's nicest if you can bake in a regular bread loaf pan. Any size or shape is fine—big or small. If you don't have a choice, any material is fine; if you do, I recommend glass loaf pans such as Pyrex, because you can see how the bottom crust is doing and take the bread out before it burns. I'm not enthused about those coated metals like Teflon because sooner or later they scratch, and then you're eating aluminum. And I avoid anything enameled (except canning kettles) because I turn around twice and they're chipped and rusting.

While I'm on the subject, I'll add that cast iron is my favorite for roasting and frying on top of the stove, and stainless pots with copper bottoms are the absolute best for cooking, especially dealing with fruits, if you can afford them. They are practically eternal, so they're a good investment. I always shun aluminum. It tends to dent, the handles scorch, it gets odd-looking with age, especially coffeepots—and it's accused of contributing to Alzheimer's. Pottery cookware is great; although it shares with glass the possibility of breakage, it's pretty tough.

OVEN: Any oven that can get up to 350°F will bake bread. If you can't get your oven hot, you can make biscuit-shaped things and cook them in a frying pan on top of the stove, turning once. Really very tasty! Or bake in a Dutch oven in a bed of coals.

Yeast Bread Ingredients

BASIC PROCEDURE FOR BREAD MAKING: Start with a yeast solution and add that to a liquid. A sweetening for the yeasties to feed on is helpful, plus some shortening, salt if you want, other things in the fruit and vegetable kingdoms, and finally your flours, the kneading process, and the rising, punching down, second rising, and baking.

YEAST: Use sourdough (homemade) or store-bought. There are different kinds of commercial yeast. "Brewer's yeast" won't raise bread. Neither will the dry yeast sold as a vitamin and protein supplement in health food stores.

Commercial Yeast Containers. You can buy yeast in a bulk 2-lb. package, a 4-oz. jar, or 2½ t. at a time in little foil packages. Don't buy the 2-lb. container unless you know you're going to use it all up reasonably soon. Yeast is alive, but it can live only so long confined to a jar. The 4-oz. jar is large enough to be more economical and small enough that the yeast will probably stay alive until you've used up the last of it. If you seldom make bread, buy those individual foil packets of yeast. One package is the equivalent of 1 T. yeast in any recipe. When I was younger, yeast was also sold in moist foil-wrapped cakes. Those are uncommon now, replaced by dry yeast. Substitute 1 pkg. dry for 1 cake of compressed. When we used the yeast cakes, we had to crumble them into the warm liquid. With the dry yeast, you just pour it in and stir it up.

Yeast Storage. Store any yeast in the refrigerator for the short term, or in the freezer for the long term. Unopened yeast in a jar or foil packet survives best in cool, dry storage. So don't keep it near your stove. In your fridge is best. There is an expiration date stamped on it, which is 1 year after packaging. But using it sooner is better. Don't open the foil packets until you're ready to use them. Once you've opened the jar, refrigerate. Best results if used up within 4–6 months. The moist compressed yeast keeps only 4–6 weeks, and that's only if it's kept refrigerated. If wet yeast

breaks easily, it's okay to use. If it feels mushy and soft, throw it out.

"Proofing" the Yeast. "Proofing" means testing yeast for life and liveliness. Mix yeast with your warm water and a little sweetener. Let it set about 20 minutes. If it is starting to get bubbly, it's okay; proceed. If it's just sitting there doing nothing, throw it out and restart with some different yeast.

Yeast Temperature. Yeast is a living organism, so don't pour really hot water in on top of it or you'll kill it. If it is too cold, it won't do any work for you either. A temperature on the warmish side of lukewarm is best—110–115°F. It is important to have your bread liquid the right temperature when you combine it with yeast—not just the liquid you dissolve the yeast in, but all of it, because if you throw in a lot of cold milk or water, you chill down the whole dough. You can warm a liquid very quickly and easily, but it takes a long time for a dough to warm up once you've got the flour in.

Yeast Food. A working yeast consumes some variety of sugar in order to manufacture its by-product—carbon dioxide bubbles. Its main product, of course, is more yeast, and that's why the action may start slowly and then get faster. The more yeast you start out with, the faster the bread will rise. Given time enough, even a little yeast can do the job. However, if you take too long, wild yeast will start working in there, and you may have a sourdough taste when you didn't plan on it. By "too long," I mean hours and hours. As yeast grows, it eats sugar and produces alcohol plus carbon dioxide gas. The alcohol will bake away, but the bubbles of gas get baked into position, and that makes your bread light and porous—which is the whole reason for bothering with yeast, although it does add some food value to your bread as well.

SECRETS OF MAKING YEAST BREADS

1. Warm up all your ingredients before combining, including the yeast—but not so hot as to kill it. It helps to use a thermometer until you get familiar with what works.
2. Dissolve dry yeast by sprinkling it over water—not any other liquid—to start it! Just substitute ¼ c. warm water per 2½ t. dry yeast for ¼ c. other liquid in the recipe. Stir the yeast into the water. Add ½ t. honey or sugar. After 5 minutes, stir that yeast-water mix into your other recipe liquid.
3. The commercial dry yeast dissolves best into 110–115°F water, but hotter water kills it. The best room temperature for raising your yeast dough is 80–90°F. Too low a temperature can result in a souring of the dough, which is okay if you like sourdough. Don't put your rising bowl right onto a radiator or wood-stove top, because that can get hot enough to kill the yeast.
4. The tiny plant cells that are "yeast" feed on the sugars in your dough. More sweetness feeds them better.
5. Blending or beating doesn't harm yeast.
6. A lot of dried fruits, eggs, nuts, salt, shortening, and/or sugar will hold back the rising. If you want light bread, dry ingredients (aside from wheat flour) should be no more than 25 percent by volume.
7. Breads made from all whole wheat flour take longer to rise and make heavier, denser loaves because the white part is the part that contains the gluten, and whole flour has a smaller percentage of the inner (white) kernel. Also, breads made from home-ground whole

wheat flour will be as much harder to leaven as the grind is coarser than your familiar commercially milled bread flour.

8. A good kneading helps get good gluten development. When you've finished kneading, the dough feels smooth and elastic and pops back out when poked. But too much kneading can interfere with gluten's bubble-holding ability. Fifteen minutes max.

9. When your dough has doubled in size, it's full of bubbles. You can't measure rising by time. Time to double depends on temperature and humidity. But you can test for doubling by pressing the tips of 2 fingers quickly, lightly into your dough. If the dent they make disappears right away, the dough should rise more. If it stays put, the doubling is accomplished. Now do something with it: bake it, or punch it down and shape and then let rise for baking. If you don't do one of those 2 things reasonably soon, the dough may fall.

10. Punching down breaks up oversized bubbles and gives you a finished bread with a finer texture.

LIQUID: The more liquid you start out with, the more bread you'll end up with. Your basic choice is milk, water,

or fruit juice. Water bread has a wheaty flavor and a lovely crust. It keeps better than milk bread. Potato water makes wonderful bread. (You can make potato water especially for your bread base. Just peel, dice, and boil the spuds. Then mash or blend the potatoes and their water together.) If you make the bread with milk, it has more food value and delicious flavor when fresh. Milk also gives it a fine texture. Using syrup, molasses, or honey for your sweeteners will help make a moist bread that stays soft and edible longer than it would otherwise.

Lukewarm Liquid. Make sure your liquids are warm. Many people scald unpasteurized milk to destroy an enzyme that supposedly makes bread gummy. I gave up doing that years ago when I got rushed for time and couldn't seem to see the difference anyway. To "scald" means to heat until bubbles form around the rim of the pan, not to actually boil. Then you have the problem of getting it cooled down so you can proceed with the bread making. I used to solve that by plopping my butter, which was right out of the refrigerator, into the middle of the scalded milk. That way the butter melted and milk cooled, and it pretty much came out the right temperature for adding the yeast solution.

Enough Liquid? At this point, I take a second look to see if I have enough liquid. If not, I add more. The volume of the final dough batch will be the same as my liquid plus almost half. With good rising, that amount doubled will be the final amount of baked bread, but usually it doesn't all rise that high.

SWEETENING: Sweetness feeds your yeast. Add any sort of sugar—white, brown, powdered, confectioners', candy dissolved in water, fruit juice, honey, maple syrup, or molasses. Keith Berringer, Midway, BC, Canada, told me that if he uses honey to start the yeast, he first boils the honey together with some water. Otherwise, he says, the enzymes are hard on the yeast. Molasses, honey, or sorghum syrup in a brown bread recipe makes the crust softer and helps keep it moist as well as sweet. Adding raisins or any fruit to the bread brings in quite a bit of sweetening too. Or you can make the yeast tough it out and find some natural sugars in the flour, which they can do.

SHORTENING: Any fat is "shortening": lard, butter, bacon grease, margarine, olive oil, and other vegetable oils. Any solid shortening should be melted before adding. Or you can use mashed banana or avocado, which are high-fat fruits. I know people who won't use any shortening and make beautiful breads, but if I try to do completely without it, the bread is too crumbly. The exact amount is really very flexible.

SALT: When the bread is spread with butter or other toppings, there's enough salt that way. You can leave all the salt out of any bread recipe and make perfectly delicious breads. On the other hand, if you like the taste of it but wonder how much to use, ¼ t. salt per 2 c. flour is about standard if you're not comfortable with "to taste."

OTHER THINGS: If you want your bread to rise well, limit other things in the recipe to no more than 25 percent of the volume of your wheat flour. I've reached the point in my bread making where I don't make a bread without some "other things." A whole wheat bread is improved so much by the addition of a quite large part of fruit, vegetable, or both. When I get ready to make bread, I start out by thoroughly searching the refrigerator and cupboards to see what I have: cereals, rice, corn bread or crusts, extra eggs (as we have in spring), leftover mashed potatoes, cooked squash or pumpkin, or canned fruit like apricots or peaches.

In egg season I can make a rich, delicious bread resembling the famous Jewish Challah by putting in a dozen eggs. For special occasions I use a lot of fruit. I pit canned cherries and use them with apricots or whatever fruit I have lots of. Raisins and nuts, if you have them, will be a welcome addition to the bread too. Leftover vegetables are fine. Mash any fruit or vegetable well before you put it in. My bread is never quite the same. I've turned out some batches that were so heavenly that I've been wishing ever since that I could do it again. I served one bread that was just loaded with applesauce, and I think it had some apple plum butter in it too, to Mike's boss and his family for dinner. Boss told his wife to "get that recipe." I couldn't tell her how. I wished I knew myself.

Sometimes we play guessing games on guests. What do you suppose is in the bread? They're unlikely to come up with such ingredients as the scrapings of a jar of peanut butter and half a box of tapioca. But I go very easy with ingredients like peanut butter and tomatoes. And I've never added meat, although I suppose a person could if it were precooked and ground. But come to think of it, "meat loaf"

is usually a meat/grain mixture; it can be a lot more grain than meat! And it's good.

FLOUR: The last ingredient you add to your yeast bread dough will be the flour. Part of that *must* be wheat flour. That's so you'll have gluten in the mix.

Gluten. When your liquid meets your wheat flour, the proteins in that flour begin bonding together in a special way that forms the wonderful substance called "gluten." (See "Special Breads.") Gluten is elastic and will hold bubbles and expand with them like bubble gum. It's contained in the white, starchy part of the wheat kernel. No matter how able a strain of yeast you have, the only dough it can make rise is one with wheat flour in it. You couldn't make barley flour or pea flour rise if you used a whole quart of yeast. White flour rises more readily than brown flour. A mixture of whole wheat flour and rolled oats and rye won't rise nearly as well as straight whole wheat flour. And the only part of the wheat flour the yeast can make rise is the starchy, white center of the kernel, so you can't make bread that rises out of wheat bran only. Whole wheat flour doesn't rise as high as all-white because its percentage of the white endosperm is lower, since it also contains all the outer non-gluten part of the kernel ground up in there—the part with the vitamins!

Have at least three-fourths of your flour be wheat flour for a light bread, one-half for a heavy one. But for the other one-fourth or one-half, you can use all kinds of grains. I've used leftover cooked cereals of all sorts, leftover puddings, dry cereals of all sorts that I figured weren't going to get eaten before they got stale, tapioca base, cornmeal, oatmeal, farina, and any sort of flour you can think of. It usually turns out fine. My favorite flavoring is a dollop of rye flour in the bread. Just a little adds a really nice taste. Breads that include flours that won't leaven don't rise so high or easily but, on the other hand, they have a close-grained moist quality and keep much longer than regular bread.

Phyllis Vallette wrote me from Burkina Faso, "Non-gluten grains can be substituted freely. If you're looking for recipes to use an unusual grain—trying to find uses for oat flour, which I hear is a new trend, or if you're given a bushel of barley or live by a sorghum field—you should definitely read through the recipes for corn, rye, etc., and try out anything interesting with the grain you have. With our local millet, I make a delicious spoon bread (i.e., souffle) that's sometimes pure millet, sometimes half corn meal. I use a corn chip recipe to make millet crackers. I sometimes use millet flour in my bread, using as much millet as you'd use of rye in rye bread—and so on."

Flour Consistencies. Consistencies have varied over the years and with the brand. If you're using a recipe that says "flour" but doesn't say how much, it's always safe to add flour like this:

- Add 1 measure flour per 1 measure liquid for pour batters.
- Add 2 measures flour per 1 measure liquid for drop batters.
- Add 3 measures flour per 1 measure liquid for a dough.
  Or like this:
- A crepe batter should be watery, a pancake batter thin, a waffle batter thin enough to pour—but thick enough to clump voluntarily on the waffle iron and not run over.

- Quick bread batters should be thick with just enough thinness to pour into the pan.
- Kneaded bread doughs should be thick and dry enough to handle without stickiness.

Adding Flour. I mix the bread with one hand, scooping up flour and pouring it in as needed with the other hand. Anybody else would use a spoon, but I'm the sort to just plunge right in there with my fist. I end up that way, anyway. The odd variety flours and other dry ingredients go in first. Then the basic whole wheat flour, since I want at least 50 percent of that. You learn when the dough has just the right amount of flour by experience. Add enough flour so the dough stops being sticky on your hands, and quit adding before it gets so tough and hard you can't knead it. The feel of the dough—and the look of it—will tell you.

Kneading and Rising

Kneading is a stretching motion applied to dough when more flour is to be added than can be either stirred or beaten into the mixture. Kneading is also used to make a dough smooth and even in texture. You place the dough on a flat surface and work it, pressing down with knuckles and then folding over, and repeating several times. After that, you give the yeast time to work and raise the bread. Both kneading and rising help make nice bread with a smooth texture that holds together and is properly porous.

I love to knead bread. It makes me calm and peaceful, just the way milking a cow does: I feel that I'm accomplishing something worth doing and there's no sense rushing about it. And it's not just me. I received this letter from a beautiful lady, Mary W. Lutzke of Sylvania, OH: "Dear Carla, Two children of my four are retarded, and to me the hardest prayer to say is 'Thy will be done' and mean it; but, once said, it is the happiest." And she sent a poem:

> *Bread*
> When times get tough
> And pressures seem intolerably high,
> I get a yen to give the yeast a try
> And taste and smell the ancient real bread stuff.
> Is it the punch and knead that mends my soul?
> The elemental peasant hidden deep?
> Or fragrant smells of childhood long asleep?
> The shiny growing life within my bowl?
> Oh, blessed time of trial, turn on your heat
> For I am yeast—swell, bubble, double, rise!
> As I pass on to younger nose and eyes
> The magic, healing nuances of wheat.

THE SPONGE METHOD: There are various patterns to the rising (yeast leavening). If you use a "starter," "sourdough," or "homemade yeast," it's better to use the sponge method. To do this, combine your homemade yeast, the liquids, and just enough flour to make a batter that will drop from a spoon. More precisely: add half of the flour to the liquid and yeast mixture and beat thoroughly. Set in a warm place and let that work and rise overnight—or for at least several hours, until the batter is light and yeasty. In the morning, or whenever, you finish by stirring in the remaining flour—or enough to make a dough of your desired stiffness. Then proceed with your kneading and so on. Some recipe books give you a sponge method for regular breads.

It's a way of doing it, but I don't really see the point with regular breads. I usually just mix the ingredients, knead the dough, and then let it do a first rising.

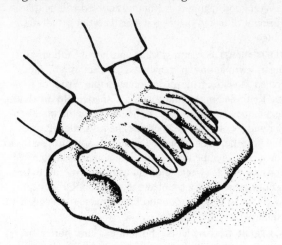

KNEADING THE DOUGH: First work the dough in your bowl, bucket, or whatever until it loses part of its stickiness. You are working it all into one big ball, sort of as if you were working with clay. If you rub your hands together, you can make little snakes of the dough between your fingers, and they will drop off. Then flour the place where you're going to knead. Any smooth, sturdy surface will do. Turn the dough out of your container into the middle of your floured kneading surface.

You "knead" by pulling up the dough side farthest from you and then pushing it into the top center of your ball. When you pull up the dough, your hands should be fingers down, as if you were playing the piano or typing. You punch the pulled-up dough into the center of your dough ball with the heels of your 2 palms. Give the whole ball of dough a quarter turn more or less, depending on how big it is. Then pull and punch again in the new place. Continue doing this as quickly and continuously as you can. You'll really develop a rhythm for it after a while, and it gets to be fun.

When you first begin, the dough will be soft and sticky and without a smooth surface. The longer you knead, the smoother the surface will be. It gradually loses much of its stickiness. If it doesn't, add more flour, but beware of adding too much. With white bread, when you can knead it on an unfloured dry board without immediately getting gummed up, you can consider the kneading done. If the surface of your dough ball breaks, that means you haven't really gotten all the flour worked in yet and should beware of adding more. With white flour, you'll really notice when the magic moment arrives. The dough changes from a tough, undisciplined glob of something somewhat firmer than goop to a smooth, cooperative, roundish mass. That's the time to quit and get it ready for a rising.

Sticky Dough When your hands feel sticky during your kneading, don't wash with water; dip them in flour to unstick and continue kneading. Limit the flour you add in working with a sticky dough. The most common problem beginners have is adding too much flour. They don't know from experience when to stop, and they knead in flour until the dough gets so hard they just can't knead any more, and that's too much! Too much and your bread will turn out too hard and dry — or crumbly; you just have to learn to knead a sticky dough. Whole wheat is stickier than white.

Other flours are progressively stickier. Rye is bad that way. It's helpful to dip your hands into the flour bucket regularly.

Dry Dough. If you are worried that you may have put too much flour in the dough, there is nothing to be done about it now. *You cannot add moisture after adding the flour and creating your dough ball.* Trying would make an awful, unmanageable mess. That's experience talking. So be careful to start with less flour and gradually work up, as you knead, to the perfect combination.

How Long to Knead? Kneading softens and develops the gluten. I've seen some really long kneading times recommended: as much as an hour in some old-time recipe books. But modern experts advise that gluten holds bubbles best if not overkneaded. So limit that pleasure to 15 minutes. The bread itself tells you by its feel when it's done. You'll learn that silky finished feel by experience. White bread cooperates best with this kneading process because it has the highest percentage of gluten, and kneading is a gluten game.

THE FIRST RISING: I've seen as many as 4 risings suggested in some recipes. Like everything else I do, for better or for worse I've discovered the easiest and briefest method: one rising after the kneading. After rising, you punch down, knead a couple more minutes, and shape into loaves. It rises a second time in the pan, and you bake it when it finishes rising.

The Bowl. Use a bowl that will hold twice the amount of your dough, because you expect it to at least double. Lightly grease or oil your bowl and put the dough ball in it.

Of Top Greasing. Some people advise greasing the top of the dough because otherwise it may develop a sort of crust before the bread ever sees the oven, just from a drying-out action, and that "crust" is hard to knead back in. But I don't have to do it. There's so much dough there that it just doesn't dry out, and I make such a moist dough anyway with all that stuff like squash and eggs and cherries in it. If you want to, though, now's the time. After you put the dough in the bowl, slide it over upside down, and the top that was on the bottom will now be greased.

Covering. Judge with your eye where in the bowl the top of the dough will be when the dough has doubled in amount. Cover with a clean cloth at that level to keep out specks and drafts.

Where? I leave my dough in the middle of the table, next to the warm wood stove. For a good rising of bread, you need a really warm kitchen—too hot to be comfortable. In summer, that's no problem. In winter, when I'm going to make bread, I get the wood stove going especially strong. It helps if your dough has its own warmth because you used nice warm liquid, but it will lose too much heat if your rising area is too cold.

WAYS TO RAISE BREAD IN A CHILLY KITCHEN

1. Set it in a gas oven whose pilot light keeps it warm inside.
2. Put it in a covered crock that has a light bulb hanging inside.
3. Set the rising bowl in an "off" oven but with a large pan of hot water beneath it that you change as needed.
4. Heat oven at low long enough to warm it up inside. Turn off. Set rising bowl inside.
5. Fill a steamer pan two-thirds full of hot water. Place a wire rack on top and set the bowl on that.

6. Set the bowl near (not on) a heat source like a stove or radiator.
7. Place a heating pad set for low inside a styrofoam insulated chest together with your bowl.

Check the Clock. On the average, it will take an hour for the first rising. Of course, if you used a lot of non-wheat flour in the bread, it may never get up to double. In that case, have a notion in your head when to give up and go on to the next step of punching down.

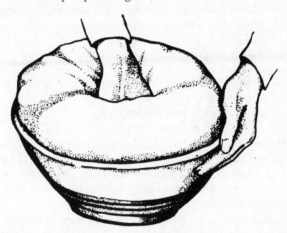

Punching Down. It's time to punch when you observe that your dough is up as far as you are going to let it get— preferably not so far that it is sagging by itself. To test its readiness, poke it gently with 2 fingers. If the indentation springs back a little or fills back in within a few minutes, it can rise some more. But if the hole stays put, it is finished rising and ready to punch down. If the dough collapses easily and stays down, it's more than ready for punching. Shove your working fist into the middle of the puffed ball of dough and push down as far as you can go. Then, with the same fist, punch the rest of the dough over and into the middle. Turn the ball over, put your cloth back over it, and let it rise again.

How Many Times to Rise. If I'm in a tremendous rush for the first couple loaves (for instance, if we are out of bread), I even let a couple loaves have the first rising in a bread pan and then bake them; this gives them a total of only one rising. Using the system I'm going to describe, you get 2 risings. Some people do 3 risings: let it rise, punch down, let it rise again, punch down, put it in your bread pans, let rise the third, and bake.

Shaping and Baking

I let the dough sit 15 minutes while I'm getting the bread pans oiled and ready. Then I shape my loaves, put them in the bread pans, and set the pans in that same warm place to rise enough to be baked. (The second rising is usually faster than the first one.) So after the bread's first rising, I call the children to make rolls and loaves.

SHAPING A LOAF: There's more than one way to do either one. I use a bread knife to cut off what I figure is enough for a loaf from one side of the dough ball. The conventional loaf pan size is 9 × 5 × 3 inches, but any vaguely approximate size will do. I aim to get the bread pan just a little over half full for a light (white) bread, or three-fourths full for a heavy one. When the bread doubles in amount, it will just nicely rise over the top of the pan. I fold the cut edges of each loaf piece to the underside and pinch them together to make a seal, gently molding it at the same time into a vaguely rectangular shape. I lay the dough loaf in the pan and press it down where it needs any more molding. If I goofed and haven't got enough dough, I cut off another piece, stick it in at one end, and patch them together, but it will not come out quite like a proper loaf.

A high school friend of mine, Virginia Boegli, has a much more sophisticated way of making loaves:

1. Flatten your piece of dough into a rectangle.
2. Stretch into a long strip by slapping dough on the table.
3. Fold into thirds, pressing out bubbles and sealing seams.
4. Fold up, starting on the long side. (The roll should be almost as long as your loaf pan.)
5. Pinch together ends and long seam.
6. Place in pan and grease the top.

Shaping Rolls. I pull a handful of dough out of the dough ball and pinch the torn edges together at the bottom to seal. I pat it into shape and set in the oiled pan. Once in the pan, either loaves or rolls should sit in a warm place until almost doubled in bulk.

Butter Top. I don't grease the top, never seem to think of it, but it is a good idea. Sometimes I butter the tops of white bread loaves when they come out of the oven. Just rub a hunk of butter over it. Makes a nice effect.

When to Bake? Don't let the bread rise too long before baking it. Bread can "fall" just the way cakes can. When the bubbles become big and visible and the whole affair looks spongy, falling is a serious risk. Punch down and let rise again. It doesn't have to be absolutely doubled before baking. Better safe than sorry. After all, your dough will rise further during the first quarter hour or so of baking. But when the loaf temperature gets up to around 140°F, the yeast cells die and there's no more rising except for some normal expansion from heat.

BAKING: The oven should be at least 350°F. An oven that won't get hot won't bake right. Baking causes the starch in the bread to get hard on the inside, and it develops a crust on the outside. The bread also gets somewhat drier as it bakes. A white loaf cooks quicker than any other kind; rolls are also pretty quick. Unleavened and sourdough breads take the longest. In general it takes 30–60 minutes to bake bread. If using a wood stove, you may need to put a pie plate or some kind of lid above the bread so the crust won't burn.

Done? Your bread should be done when the crust is sort of golden brown and the loaf sounds hollow when you rap it with your knuckles (be quick, so you don't burn them!) or tap it with your fingertips. If the loaf sounds hollow when tapped, it's done. When done, loosen the sides gently, if necessary, and turn out onto an oven grill to cool. Butter the top crust immediately for a softer crust. Wrapping a loaf of bread that is fresh out of the oven in a dishtowel while it's cooling also gives you a much nicer (softer) crust.

Serving. You are now in a class (upper) with the little red hen, who planted, harvested, and baked her own grain into bread! Cut your homemade bread with a serrated (sort of sawtooth) knife. Slice ½ inch thick if it is white bread that rose well; otherwise, slice thinner. Spread it with room-temperature (softened) butter or your favorite spread. Never cut more than will be eaten right away, since white bread

dries out very quickly and all breads dry out sooner or later. Some bread types are hard to slice—crumbly and easily mashed—when they are fresh out of the oven. They will firm up after sitting overnight.

Storage. Put bread in a plastic bag to retain moisture and soften the crust. Bread will freeze and keep indefinitely, so put the extra loaves in your freezer. For maximum freshness, freeze immediately after baking and cooling.

YEAST BREAD RECIPES

The easiest bread to make is a basic white bread. I never use white flour now. But if you are just learning to make bread, you might want to start with a recipe that uses 100 percent white or unbleached flour. It rises better and generally cooperates better. You can learn what you're doing with a white bread recipe and then move on to one that uses a heavier flour. Or you can just plunge in with any old recipe that takes your fancy, and enthusiasm will carry you over the difficulties. Here's the recipe I learned bread making with.

➢ *CARLA'S WHITE BREAD Scald 1 c. milk until there is a little rim of bubbles around the edge of the pan. Add 6 T. sugar, 2 t. salt, and 6 T. margarine or butter to the hot milk. When the milk mixture has cooled to lukewarm, proceed. Into your big bread bowl, measure 3 c. lukewarm water. Dissolve 2 pkg. yeast in the water. Add the milk mixture and about 5 c. white flour. Mix until smooth. Keep adding flour until you have a kneadable dough. Flour your breadboard, turn the dough out onto it, and commence kneading.*

Allow the dough to continue to absorb flour, and knead until smooth and elastic. When it is ready, let it rest while you wash out the mixing bowl, dry it, and then grease it inside very lightly. Put your dough into the greased bowl, turning it once to grease the top. Cover with a dishtowel and leave in a warm place until it doubles in bulk.

Punch down. Prepare 4 bread pans. Cut the dough carefully into 4 sections. Take 1 section at a time and fold under to turn in the severed edges, seal, and shape into a loaf. Put each loaf into a bread pan. Cover and let rise again until doubled in bulk. Bake in a preheated 400°F oven about 30 minutes.

➢ *VIRGINIA'S WHITE BREAD Mix 2½ c. liquid, 3 T. sugar, 1 T. salt, and 2 T. shortening. Dissolve 2 envelopes (or 2 T.) yeast in ¼ c. lukewarm water and add to other ingredients. Mix in with spoon, then by hand, 7 to 7¼ c. flour. Turn dough out on floured board and let rest about 10 minutes. Knead until smooth and elastic (8 to 10 minutes). Grease bread dough and put in a large bowl or pan. Cover with a cloth and let rise in a warm place out of drafts until doubled in bulk.*

You can test this by jabbing 2 fingers into the dough. If this causes the dough to slowly collapse, it is ready to punch down. Punch and fold it into a firm ball and let rise again untilalmost doubled in bulk. Divide into 2 pieces. Let dough rest on floured table 10 minutes. Shape into loaves. Put in pans. Grease. Let rise to just above top of loaf pans. Bake at 425°F for 25 to 30 minutes. Turn out on racks to cool. This dough may be used for sweet rolls, buns, cinnamon loaves, and cheese or onion loaves by adding the appropriate extra ingredients when shaping the bread.

➢ *GROSSMAMMA BAUM'S BASIC YEAST BREAD Grossmamma, who lives in Seattle, WA, has used this recipe for more years than most of us have lived. "Each time I make bread it is a little bit different. Use the basics, toss in raw* peanuts, sesame seed, sunflower seed, dried fruit. Use honey or molasses instead of sugar. Each time you have a new taste and texture. I won a blue ribbon at the Western Washington Fair last year. But when people asked me for the recipe, I could only give them the basic recipe and say I put in a little of this and that." For Grossmamma's basic 3 loaves: Use 3 c. warm water, 2 cakes (or packages) yeast, ½ c. sugar, 3 t. salt, 5 level T. shortening, and unsifted flour. Dissolve yeast in warm water, add sugar, salt and shortening. Add flour until no more can be added. Dough should be elastic. Knead and place in warm spot. Let rise until double in size. Punch down and knead again—pinch into loaves. Let rise approximately 1 hour. Bake at 350°F for 40 minutes. Wipe lightly over top of loaves with butter, oil, or shortening after removing from pans.

❧ WHOLE WHEAT BREAD #1
Scald 2 c. milk and ¼ c. water. Add 2 t. salt and ¼ c. honey (or molasses). Dissolve 2 T. dry yeast in ½ c. warm water. When the milk mixture is lukewarm, add it to the yeast mixture. Add 1 c. rye flour and enough whole wheat flour to make a workable dough. Knead. Wash and grease bowl. Return dough to bowl and grease top. Let rise until doubled in bulk. Punch down and let rise again. Cut dough into two parts. Shape each into a loaf. Put loaves in greased pans and let rise until doubled in bulk. Bake at 375°F for 35 to 40 minutes. Remove from pan. Butter the top crust. Leave out the rye flour if you want.

❧ WHOLE WHEAT BREAD #2
Scald ¾ c. milk until it just gets bubbles around the rim. Add ⅓ c. butter, cut up to help it dissolve in the hot milk. When the butter is dissolved, add ¼ c. sugar, 1 T. salt, and ⅓ c. molasses. In your large bread mixing bowl, dissolve 2 T. dry yeast in 1½ c. lukewarm water. Add milk mixture, then 5 c. whole wheat flour (no need to sift). When that is well mixed, add white flour enough to make a soft but kneadable dough. Knead on floured board until it feels done (300 times maybe). Wash and grease your bowl. Return dough to it and let it rise until doubled in bulk. Punch down the dough. Grease 2 regular-size bread pans. Divide the dough in half and shape each half into a loaf. Put the loaves into the bread pans and let them rise again until doubled in bulk. Bake at 400°F about 30 minutes. Remove from pan to cool. You may need to slip a knife in at the side to loosen the loaf.

❧ DORIS GRONEWOLD'S GOAT-MILK BROWN BREAD
Scald 3½ c. goat's milk. Add ¼ c. shortening, 6½ T. sugar, and 1½ T. salt to milk, and cool to lukewarm. Set aside 4 t. dry yeast dissolved in 1 c. warm water. Then add 1 c. finely ground wheat bran. Add yeast. Then finish off with whole wheat flour—9 cups or so. Let rest 10 minutes, then knead 10 minutes. Let this rise 2 hours. Punch down, let rise 1 hour again. Shape into 4 loaves. Let rise 1 hour. Bake in hot oven, 425°F. This bread is very moist and is a good moist keeper. Doris's children love it as toast, too, with jam and butter.

❧ RUTH'S EUROPEAN-STYLE BREAD
"One thing I noticed, when I was visiting in the States a couple years ago, is that the texture of North American bread is so cakelike—even whole grain bread. I think it's because of the additions like eggs, sugar, etc. In Europe, bread is generally denser, chewier, and altogether (in my opinion) more satisfying. Personally, I am shocked by the amount of sugar and fat in most American breads—you can't use cake as the staff of life! Here is my basic bread recipe:

Put 2½ c. warm water in a bowl and sprinkle in 2 T. dry yeast. After a few minutes (when bubbles start to form), add 3–4 c. whole wheat flour and beat well—until dough is smooth. Cover; let rise an hour or so. Now add 3–4 more cups whole wheat flour, one at a time (mix after each addition) and knead well on floured board until dough does not stick to hands or board (add more flour as you knead). Return to bowl, and let rise until doubled. Sprinkle flat baking tins with cornmeal. Divide dough in half. Shape each half into a roll and place on tin (optional: with sharp knife, slit each loaf lengthwise down the top about 1½ cm (½ inch). Cover and let rise. Bake in preheated oven at 300–350°F for 45 minutes to 1 hour (until golden brown and hollow-sounding when tapped). Remove from pan immediately. Makes 2 loaves."

❧ WHOLE WHEAT VEGAN SWEET ROLLS
"This can be varied in almost any imaginable way—with various flours, cooked mashed pumpkin and raisins, various herbs, fresh or dried fruit, applesauce, etc. You can make rolls of all shapes or braided loaves; you can let it rise once, twice, or three times for various textures; you can make sweet rolls by using applesauce in the dough, then rolling out thinly and sprinkling with a mixture of 3 parts cinnamon, 1 part ginger, and ½ part each nutmeg and cloves; then sprinkle on raisins and/or chopped dried apples, roll up, and slice buns off the roll. Bake in a pie tin and dip in a half honey-half water syrup when they come out of the oven. Cool and enjoy."

❧ RYE BREAD
The procedure is similar to the white and brown bread. Scald 1 c. milk. Add 1 T. butter and then 3 T. honey, 2 t. salt, and 1 T. sugar. In your bread bowl, dissolve 1 T. yeast in ¾ c. warm water. Add the milk mixture. Then add 2½ c. rye flour. (If you want to add caraway seeds, now's the time.) Mix well. Add enough white flour to make a soft but kneadable dough. Knead until done. Let rise, covered, in greased bowl until doubled in bulk. (It takes longer than others to rise.) Punch down.

Cut the dough in half. Mold each half into a ball. Grease a cookie sheet and sprinkle it with cornmeal. Flatten the top of your ball a little and put the round loaves on the baking sheets (if you prefer an oval shape, make that). Brush the loaves with 1 egg white beaten with 2 T. water. Let the loaves rise; then bake at 400°F for 25 minutes.

❧ MRS. ARTHUR JOHNS'S OATMEAL BREAD
Soften 2 T. yeast in ½ c. warm water and set aside. Combine 1½ c. boiling water, 1 c. oatmeal, ½ c. molasses, ⅓ c. shortening, and 2 t. salt. Cool to lukewarm. Add yeast. Stir in 2 c. white flour and 2 beaten eggs. Beat well. Add 4 c. more white flour (more or less) to make a soft dough. Grease top; cover tightly and refrigerate overnight. Shape into 2 loaves. Let rise until doubled in bulk. Bake at 375°F for 45 minutes.

❧ FRENCH BREAD
Combine 2½ c. warm water and 2 T. dry yeast. Add 2 t. salt and 1 T. melted butter. Add flour to make a dough (about 7 cups—no need to sift). The dough will be on the sticky side. Turn dough out of your bowl long enough to wash and then grease it. Put the dough back into the bowl, grease the top of it, and let it rise, covered, until it has doubled in bulk. Flour your breadboard.

Divide the dough in half and roll out each half with your rolling pin into a rectangle about ¼ inch thick. Now roll up the dough as if you were making a jelly roll, beginning at a wide side. Make the roll as tight as possible; when all done, seal the edges by pinching as tight as possible. Grease your cookie sheet and then sprinkle it with cornmeal. Put the loaves on it, spread a dishtowel across them, and let rise until doubled in bulk. Bake at 450°F for 30 minutes.

➤ **BAGELS** Sift together 8 c. flour, 1 T. salt, and 1 T. sugar. Soften 2 pkg. yeast in 2 c. lukewarm potato water. Combine yeast liquid with dry ingredients. Knead 10 minutes. Let rise to double. After punching down, pinch off sections to make a rope about 6 inches long, ¾ inch wide. Dampen ends and press them tightly together to make your "doughnut" shape. Set ½ gal. water on to boil. Add 2 T. sugar when it's at a hard boil. Then drop your bagels in, one at a time. After they rise, turn over 1 minute. Then lay the bagels on a greased baking sheet. Bake at 450°F about 10–15 minutes (until golden brown).

➤ **NO-FRY DOUGHNUTS** Just as if you were making bread, combine 2 pkg. yeast, ¼ c. warm water, ½ c. scalded lukewarm milk, ½ c. sugar, 2 eggs, 1 t. salt, ⅓ c. shortening, 1 t. nutmeg, 4½ c. flour, and ½ t. cinnamon. Knead, cover, and let rise for 50–60 minutes. Turn onto a floured board and roll with a rolling pin until dough is about ½ inch thick. Cut with a doughnut cutter and carefully lift with a spatula onto a greased cookie sheet. Brush with melted butter. Let rise until doubled in bulk. Bake at 425°F for 8 to 10 minutes. Brush with more butter. Dust with cinnamon and sugar. From the kitchen of Cathy Frame.

➤ **YEAST ROLLS** In preparation, measure 6½ c. flour. Combine 2 c. warm water (110–115°F) with 2 pkg. yeast and dissolve well. Now add ⅓ c. sugar, 1 T. salt, 2 c. flour, 2 eggs, and ⅓ c. shortening. Beat for 1 minute. Mix together well and let rest 20 minutes. Work in remaining flour (approximately 4½ c.). Shape dough into a long roll on a floured board. Cut half of recipe into 16 equal-sized pieces. Shape each into a ball. Lay the balls on a greased pan. Let rise, covered, for 45 minutes or longer. Bake at 375°F for 30 minutes. Brush tops with melted butter and serve hot.

➤ **ENGLISH MUFFINS** Dissolve 1 pkg. dry yeast in 1½ c. warm water. Add 3 T. sugar, ½ c. powdered milk, 1 t. salt, 1 beaten egg, and 3 T. butter. When that is well mixed, add about 4 c. flour. Let rise until doubled in bulk. Punch down. Shape into muffin shapes—flatten them enough. Oil a griddle and then scatter a little cornmeal on it. Fry them on the griddle like a pancake. Turn them over when one side is done to get the other side done. Serve warm. If you have trouble getting them done in the middle, you can slice in half and fry those insides too to finish the job.

➤ **PIZZA DOUGH** Dissolve 1 pkg. yeast in 2 T. warm water. Pour 1 c. boiling water over 2 T. shortening, and then let cool. When shortening mixture is lukewarm, add the yeast solution and then 1½ c. flour. Stir until smooth. Add 1½ c. more flour. Prepare 2 greased pizza pans. Grease hands.

Divide dough into halves and pat each into one of the pans. Let rise 2 or 3 hours. Bake until almost done. Then add your favorite toppings and finish baking.

Of Sourdough Breads and Starters

In the old days, people didn't use the current array of life-killing "cleaning agents," so a suitable baking yeast was quite likely to be around for the invitation, unless you were camping in the Klondike in February. Incidentally, the Klondike miners sometimes drank, straight, that floating layer of grain alcohol that sourdough produces—they called it "hooch." (I don't recommend the stuff.) Even now, if you put out something tempting to eat, like a bowl of lukewarm potato water, you may capture a fine supply of wild yeast.

But if you have a problem capturing a good wild yeast, then start from store yeast, or borrow a sourdough starter, or buy one. Even a sourdough starter begun from commercial yeast, over a period of time, will probably acquire wild yeasts, too. I have a friend in Georgia who gets not only wild yeast but wild mold in hers with no trouble at all. The more southerly, humid, and summerish your climate, the quicker the starter will start—or get into trouble. Trying to work with invisible livestock can be tricky.

Sourdough Sourness: Sourdough's flavor can be

sharp and biting, but not as sharp as you may fear. The painstaking pioneers, trying to reduce the bread's sourness, made fresh starter for every bread making. Starters vary in sourness depending on how long they've been working and also on what kind of yeast you have. You can control the sourness of your product by the length of time you let it work. There will always be some sourness, because typically sourdough yeasts must be given more time to work than commercial yeasts. The batter thickness will make a difference in the time involved, however. Too thin a sponge will tend to work very fast and burn itself out, while too thick a sponge works too slow. You'll have to learn to kind of keep an eye on it and adjust as you go.

Secrets of Sourdough

1. Wild yeasts are likely to be in the air, in soil, and on containers.
2. Wild yeasts cause a fermenting action that raises bread like that of tame yeast.
3. *Any container sourdough lives in should be non-metal!*
4. Don't use metal utensils in sourdough.
5. *Never put sourdough in a tightly covered container such as*

a sealed glass jar. It needs air to live, and it produces a gas that could explode the container.

6. To make bread with sourdough, make sure the bowl, the ingredients, and the place it rises are all warm; 80–95°F is best.

SOURDOUGH STARTERS FROM SCRATCH: When you try to catch a wild yeast, one of four things will happen:

- Nothing, in which case you try something different.
- Your mixture has a moldy, awful smell, in which case you throw it out and try something else.
- Your mixture has a light color and looks foamy or effervescent. It will leaven bread, but it tastes terrible. In that case, you've caught an effective yeast but not one that tastes good.
- The ultimate: it leavens and it also makes tasty bread.

❧ *GLEN HOWERTON'S STARTER Mix 1 c. flour with 1 c. water. Leave it covered with a light cloth 2 or 3 days.*

❧ *MILK AND WATER STARTER Mix 1 c. unpasteurized milk with a cup of flour. If your milk is pasteurized, let it stand 24 hours first. Leave covered with a light cloth in a warm place.*

❧ *STARTER WITH COMMERCIAL YEAST Mix 1 c. flour, 1 c. water, and 1 pkg. dry yeast.*

❧ *HAZEL'S STARTER Mix 1 pkg. dry yeast, 2½ c. warm water, 1 T. sugar, 1 T. salt, and 2 c. sifted flour. Dissolve yeast in ½ c. lukewarm water. Let stand 10 minutes. Stir and add remaining water, sugar, salt, and flour. Mix well. Let stand in a covered bowl for 3 days at room temperature (78–80°F). The container should be big enough to let the starter rise to about 4 times its starting size. Stir down every day.*

PRESERVING SOURDOUGH STARTER: You don't have to struggle to keep it going unless you like eating sourdough every day. It will slow down some if you keep it in the refrigerator until you want it again.

Drying. Before freezers, the old-timers, who may have had a problem with their yeast being overactive in warm weather, preserved it by drying. Dried yeast cakes should keep 5 months or so.

Homemade Yeast Cakes from Hops. You can buy hops at a health food store, put up for "tea." Boil a handful of the hops in 4 c. water for 30 minutes. Then mix in ½ c. whole wheat flour and let cool to lukewarm. Now add 3 pkg. dry yeast (or 1½ c. homemade liquid yeast). Let rise until very light. Thicken with cornmeal until stiff. Roll thin. Cut into 3-inch squares. Dry in the shade in clear, windy weather or in a warm (but not hot!) oven. Turn often to prevent souring. When dry, tie in a mesh bag and hang in a cool, dry place. To use, soak in warm water, about 2 c. per 3-inch square of homemade yeast cake. When cake is dissolved, go ahead with your recipe.

Reviving an Old Starter. Just stir it up and feed it. Add 1 c. lukewarm water, ½ c. flour, and 1 t. sugar. Cover and let stand in a warm place until it foams; then it's ready to use again.

Testing Liquid Yeast for Liveliness. Take a small quantity, add a little flour and sweetening to it, and set in a warm place. If fermentation begins within 15 or 20 minutes, you have good yeast. Don't let it overflow your container.

Replacing a Pour-Off. Whenever you use a starter, you pour off part of it. After you're done, or the next morning,

replace what you took out. You can do that by putting a surplus cup of your sponge back into your starter jar, or by just stirring in some more flour and water.

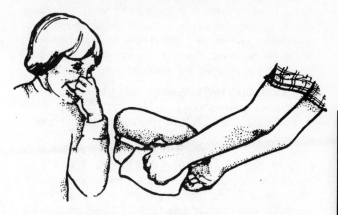

SOURDOUGH RECIPES: Sourdough bread is not as light as regular yeast bread, but some people, including me, enjoy its slightly sour flavor and fine compact texture. You can make all kinds of breads with a sourdough starter, and I love them all even though they are sour, moist, and heavy. My children hate my sourdough breads except when they're spread with butter and toasted, especially under a broiler. Then they love them. These recipes are appropriate for my starter, which is the 1 cup flour-1 cup water kind. (See Rita Davenport's *Sourdough Cookery* for more.)

The Sponge. Cooking with a sourdough starter for leavening usually begins with a sponge made the night before. A typical sponge is made by putting 1 c. of your starter in a bowl and then mixing in 2 c. warm water and 2½ c. flour. Mix well and let rest in a warm place a few hours or overnight (caution: the longer it works, the sourer your bread will taste). If you let it sit too long, the yeast uses up all the sugars and stops making bubbles. Starting it up again is as simple as adding more food. Figure on every rising stage taking longer, and the baking too. And sourdough won't rise much once it gets in the oven.

❧ *SOURDOUGH PANCAKES Mix 2 c. lively starter, 2 c. flour, 2 beaten eggs, 1 T. sugar, ½ t. salt, and 2 T. melted butter or oil, plus enough milk to make a good pourable batter (about 1½ cups, depending on how thick your starter is). Lastly, add 2 t. baking soda. Mix well; then let it rest a few minutes. Heat your griddle or frying pan. Shine it with oil before each panful of pancakes. Fry on medium heat. It helps to make dollar-sized pancakes. Be sure they are cooked through. You can't make good pancakes in a big pan on a little burner; you need even heat and heat over the entire bottom of your pan. Sourdough pancakes taste even sourer if underdone.*

❧ *SOURDOUGH WHOLE WHEAT PANCAKES The night before you plan to bake, combine 2½ c. whole wheat flour, 2 c. water, and ½ c. starter. This makes a lot of pancakes. If you have a small family, cut the recipe in half. In the morning, add 2 beaten eggs, 2 T. oil or melted butter, ½ t. salt, 2 T. honey, and enough milk to make an easily pourable pancake batter (probably about 1 cup). Then add 1 t. soda and mix well. Let it set a few minutes. Heat a griddle or frying pan moderately, shine it before each panful of cakes, make dollar-sized cakes, and cook them through.*

❧ **SOURDOUGH SODA BREAD** *The night before, mix together 1½ c. starter and 1½ c. warm water. Let work until morning. In the morning, add 2 t. soda and mix well. Then add ¼ c. melted butter, ½ c. sugar, and 1 t. salt. Add enough flour for a kneadable dough. Knead into shape, let rise, punch down, and let rise a second time. Again punch down and shape into loaves. Put the loaves into your greased loaf pan; let rise again. Bake in a moderate oven.*

❧ **SOURDOUGH WHOLE WHEAT BREAD** *This is a variety bread. It has quite a strong taste when first made, but it mellows a little with time. Makes a good appetizer or sampler, unless you really love strong dark breads. The night before, combine 4½ c. whole wheat flour, 1 c. starter, and 3¾ c. lukewarm water. In the morning, add 1 t. soda, ½ c. oil, 2 t. salt, and enough whole wheat flour to make a kneadable dough (about 5 cups). The dough tends to be sticky. Makes 2 loaves. Cut your kneaded dough into 2 parts. Make each into a loaf and put into greased loaf pans. Let rise in pan until almost doubled in bulk or till it is a little above the top of the pan. Keep it in a very warm place for the rising (maybe 2 hours). Bake 20 minutes at 425°F, then at least an hour longer at 375°F.*

❧ **HAZEL'S SOURDOUGH BREAD** *Ingredients: ½ c. milk or water (I use skim milk), 2 T. sugar, 2 T. shortening, 1 c. starter (use Hazel's), and 2–3 c. sifted flour. Scald milk, add sugar and shortening, and stir. Cool mixture to lukewarm and add starter. Stir in flour, adding enough to make a medium dough. Put onto a floured board or flat surface; knead about 10 minutes (it's hard work). Put into greased bowl and brush top lightly with melted shortening or cooking oil. Cover with a cloth and let stand in a warm place (80–85°F), with no draft on it, for about 1½–2 hours or until doubled in bulk. Punch down with spread fingers and let rise again to double size (about half an hour). Punch down as before, let it rest about 10 minutes, and then shape into loaves. Put loaves in small greased loaf pans. Let stand until doubled in bulk. It takes about 1 hour. Bake about 30–40 minutes in a 400°F oven. Just before putting bread in oven, put a pot of already boiling water in oven for 5 minutes. For a rich brown crust, brush with egg whites or milk—I use milk.*

❧ **SOURDOUGH RYE BREAD** *The night before, combine 1 c. starter, 3¾ c. warm water, 2 c. rye flour, and 2½ c. white flour. Let it set in a warm place. In the morning, add to the sponge ½ c. oil, 2 t. salt, and ½ t. soda. Stir it up. Add 5½ c. rye flour and 1 c. white flour. Knead 5 minutes. The dough will be softer and stickier than regular bread. Divide into loaves (depends on the size of your pan—I made 3) and place in oiled bread pans. Slit tops lengthwise down the middle. Leave it in a very warm room for as much as 5 hours; try to get it to rise at least 50 percent. (It rises soon after it goes into the oven.) Brush tops with water. Bake in preheated 425°F oven 20 minutes. Brush tops with water. Continue baking at 375°F oven for 1¼ hours.*

❧ **SOURDOUGH FRENCH BREAD** *Soften 1 pkg. yeast in 1½ c. warm water. Blend in 1 c. sourdough starter, 2 t. salt, and 2 t. sugar. Add 2½ c. flour. Beat a few minutes with a strong arm or mixer. Cover and let rise until it's bubbly. Combine ½ t. soda and 2½ c. flour, and stir that into your dough. Continue adding flour until you have a stiff dough. Knead on a floured surface almost 10 minutes. Divide your dough into 2 halves, cover with a cloth, and let rise in a warm place for*

10 minutes. Now shape into 2 French bread loaves. Place them, not touching, on a greased baking sheet. Let rise until it doubles and then bake at 400°F for 35–40 minutes. Just before your loaves are done, take them out of the oven long enough to generously spread butter on their tops. Then return to oven for a few minutes. Serve in about 1-inch slices, cut somewhat on the diagonal.

❧ **PLAIN BROWN SOURDOUGH BREAD** *The night before, mix 4½ c. whole wheat flour, 1 c. starter, and 3¾ c. lukewarm water. In the morning, your sponge will be light and bubbly. Add to it ½ t. soda, ½ c. oil, 2 t. salt, and enough flour to make a kneadable bread dough (about 5 cups, but the exact amount will vary with how thick your starter was). But be forewarned—the dough will stick to your hands more than usual kneaded bread. Knead about 5 minutes. Form into loaves. This recipe will make two 1 lb. loaves. Oil your bread pans.*

Let the bread rise in the pans until it is about a third larger. The exact amount of time needed will vary. Keep it in as pleasantly warm a place as you can. It will need at least 2 hours. Brush the tops with water when you are ready to bake. Bake 20 minutes in a preheated 425°F oven and then at least an hour at 375°F. I like this bread best hot from the oven and buttered, or wrapped in foil, plastic, or paper tightly for 2 days until the crust and center equalize their moisture. The same dough can be used for whole wheat muffins.

❧ **SOURDOUGH APPLESAUCE CAKE** *Mix 1 c. sourdough starter, 1 c. applesauce, 1½ c. white flour, and ¼ c. milk. In a separate bowl cream ¼ c. lard, ½ c. white sugar, and ½ c. brown sugar. Add 1 beaten egg, ½ t. cinnamon, ¼ t. cloves, ¼ t. nutmeg, ¼ t. allspice, a pinch of salt, and 2 t. soda. Combine this bowl with the contents of the other. Add a handful of dates, raisins, nuts, or whatever you like. Bake 1 hour in a moderate oven. Let the cake cook in the pan; then turn it out, upside down—carefully, because it is very fragile. It will be a moist, delicate treat. If you are a spice lover, you can double all the spice amounts.*

❧ **SOURDOUGH SPICED OATMEAL COOKIES** *Cream 1 c. lard with 1½ c. brown sugar. Add 1½ c. sourdough starter and 3 c. rolled oats. Sift together 1½ c. flour, ½ t. salt, 1 t. soda, 1 t. cinnamon, and ½ t. each cloves and allspice. Add dry ingredients to first bowl, mix well, and chill in the refrigerator a couple of hours. Tear off pieces of dough and pat into cookie shapes, or roll out on floured board and use your cookie cutter. Bake on greased cookie sheets 18 minutes at 400°F. The exact time will be affected by how big and thick you make them.*

❧ **SOURDOUGH CORNMEAL CAKES** *Beat well together 4 c. flour, 2 c. cornmeal, ½ c. milk, ½ c. starter, 3 eggs, and 2 t. salt. Let rise overnight in a warm place. Bake on a griddle in the morning.*

SERVING SOURDOUGH BREAD: I trim off the crust if it's hard. Then I spread the slice with butter and leave it under the broiler long enough to melt the butter, warm the bread through, and just start to toast the top. It's a great winter breakfast.

Last time I was at the paper wholesalers, they had a new stock boy—a young man, really. He loaded up my order, which the manager had pointed out to him. As I was about to leave, he called after me, "Hey, what are you going to do with all that paper?" I mumbled something about "Underground press . . ." and escaped.

People often come up to me in our small town here and, beaming or otherwise, commence, "I hear you're writing a book."

I want to be kind, and appropriate, but that opening leaves me speechless. This is the book that got turned down by the only publisher I had the courage to send it to, the book I feel so compelled to produce somehow, any way, that I'm mimeographing it on the cheapest paper (colored) and advertising it by passing out flyers from a little portable table at fairs.

If I were to answer (really honestly answer) that person, it would be like trying to explain to someone why you're in love with somebody who doesn't love you back. I suppose they just expect me to glow with pride and modestly murmur, "Yes." But I'm more likely to associate "writing a book" with "depression . . . guilt . . . stubbornness . . . dream . . . heart . . . cry . . . weary" and so on. At least that's what I associate with the kind of book a person tries to print and sell themselves, which this is.

Well, on to finding ways to avoid wasting leftover bread.

Using Leftover Breads

TOAST: Accidentally undercooked bread can happen to anybody (it has to me plenty of times), and the answer is to turn it into zwieback or melba toast: zwieback if it is coarse-grained, melba if fine. You can toast rye, French, or almost any other nonsweet bread. Toast it buttered or plain, under your broiler or on a grill, on a cookie sheet, or in a cake pan. The firmer the grain or the staler the bread, the more butter you need for good results. Put the slices about 9 inches away from the broiler. Watch carefully to prevent burning. The butter softens bread that is getting a little stale and revives its flavor.

➤ *CROUTONS (OR "CROUSTADES") Cut stale bread in ½-inch slices and remove crusts. Spread lightly with butter on one side if you like; then cut across to make cubes. Bake at 325°F for 15 to 20 minutes, until a golden brown, stirring occasionally. Serve with soup or sprinkle in salads.*

➤ *RUTH'S VEGAN CROUTONS "Leave out the butter. A sprinkle of garlic powder is nice, or better yet, a thin layer of pureed garlic cloves spread before toasting."*

➤ *HERBED CROUTONS Sprinkle with dried marjoram and onion or garlic salt. If no fat is in the recipe, and croutons are dried to crispness and tightly sealed, they can keep for months. Sun-dry 6–8 hours (stir occasionally). To dry in an oven or dryer, maintain at 145°F 4–6 hours.*

➤ *MILK TOAST This recipe fell out of favor during the period of domination of white bread, which was too salty and generally poor for this fine old-time dish. Make it instead with homemade bread. Most simply, toast some thinly sliced bread, butter it on each side, lay in a bowl, and pour hot (but not boiled) milk over it. For extra richness, use cream or part cream. It's traditional for invalids. I loved this for breakfast in early pregnancy, when my stomach was queasy. Very nourishing but light on the tummy.*

➤ *FRENCH TOAST Combine 1 c. milk, 2 slightly beaten eggs, a pinch of allspice or nutmeg, and a pinch of cinnamon. Dip each slice of bread long enough to coat each side but not to soak to the falling-apart state. Heat and shine your griddle, and brown the toast on each side in it. Serve immediately with syrup or jam and a little butter.*

MAKING AND USING BREAD CRUMBS: Some breads are easier to crumb while still moist. Others are best dried in your oven a while first. Close-grained and unleavened breads should, if possible, be crushed with a rolling pin or in a blender before they get rock-hard. Otherwise, if too hard, you'll have to grate to make crumbs, unless you manage to saw off small enough hunks to fit into your grinder or blender. Otherwise, keep crusts and leftover bread odds and ends like heels in a paper bag in a dry, warm place. Don't store stale bread wrapped in plastic or in a plastic container, because it will mold far more quickly in there.

To crush dried bread, put it in a paper bag and roll it into crumbs with a rolling pin. Or rub through a sieve or colander, or grate on a grater. Or put in a clean bag, tie it at the top, and rub the bag with your hands a few minutes. Or briefly "blend." Or put leftover rolls and torn-off chunks of stale bread into a pillowcase. Tie it firmly shut and put it through a dryer cycle! If there is any dampness remaining in the bread after making the crumbs, finish thoroughly drying them in your oven, food dryer, or sun in order to prevent mold. Then put the crumbs in a jar, put the lid on tightly, and keep dry until needed. Store rye, whole wheat, and cornmeal bread crumbs separately.

Thickening Gravies Bread crumbs toasted and rolled, ground, or grated to fineness can be used to thicken meat gravies.

Crumb Toppings. Put a thin layer of crumbs over your casseroles, or coat meats to be fried by dipping in beaten egg and then in crumbs.

➤ *BREWIS This is an old-time breakfast dish made with a cup of very fine dried rye or brown bread crumbs. Heat 2 c. rich milk to boiling. Then beat crumbs into it quickly. Serve at once with cream.*

➤ *CRUMB PANCAKES Grate until you have as many crumbs as you want. (This recipe was obviously created by me, because it's one-half guess and the other half golly.) Add 2 eggs if the bread was a relatively eggless one. Add milk until you have a pancake-type batter. Add a dribble of honey or some other sweetener such as molasses or brown sugar. Let rest a bit to give the larger crumb hunks and brown sugar time to soften. Mix. Pour out a pancake-type dollop and cook on a griddle. Serve with your butter and syrup, or in the way you usually serve pancakes.*

➤ *RECYCLED BREAD PUDDING Combine 2 c. crushed dry bread crumbs, 2 c. whole wheat flour, 3 t. baking powder, and 1 t. salt (if using salt-free homemade bread crumbs; otherwise, omit salt). To 2 c. milk, add 1 T. molasses and 1 beaten egg. Stir liquid into dry ingredients and bake in a greased bread pan at 350°F about 50 minutes.*

STUFFING RECIPES: Stuffings are generally, but not necessarily, bread-based. I like them made with homemade bread. And they're another good way to use leftover bread. You can make stuffing for a roast bird and bake it inside the bird, or you can bake it in a bread pan and serve it as a separate dish. You can stuff any piece of meat, like a roast or a rack of ribs, by cutting a large pocket in the meat, stuffing it, and sewing or fastening it shut with skewers. Stuffing ingredients are mixed in a bowl or pan with your hands until the seasonings are equally distributed through-out the mixture.

❧ *CARLA'S TURKEY STUFFING—Start by shredding several loaves of the most nourishing, tasty whole wheat bread you have. If it has good and interesting stuff in it like sunflower seeds, etc., that's great. It doesn't have to be stale, just delicious. Cut about 3 onions into reasonably small pieces and add. Add about 8 eggs. Maybe add some chopped celery. Add a bunch of powdered sage, oregano, and/or poultry seasoning. Mix thoroughly. It will proabably need more moisture to mix easily, so add just enough milk to turn it into a mass that's soft enough to work easily with your hands. Stuff the bird both fore and aft, and skewer shut. Pat any surplus stuffing down into a pan and bake.*

❧ *PRECISE-AMOUNT STUFFING RECIPE # 1 Combine 2 c. dried bread crumbs with ½ c. finely chopped onion and 2 T. melted butter. Season to taste with salt, pepper, sage, poultry seasoning, etc.*

❧ *PRECISE-AMOUNT STUFFING RECIPE # 2 Combine 2 c. dried bread crumbs with ½ c. chopped celery, ¼ c. chopped onion, 2 T. melted butter, and seasonings.*

❧ *PRECISE-AMOUNT STUFFING RECIPE # 3 For this turkey-sized batch of dressing, cook 3 c. chopped onion and 2 c. diced celery in 1 c. melted butter until tender. Toss together 1 gal. bread chunks with 1 t. salt, 1 t. sage, 1 t. marjoram, 1 t. thyme, 1 T. parsley, and ½ t. pepper. Combine butter mixture with bread mixture and moisten with 2 c. milk or water.*

❧ *ORANGE-PRUNE CRUMB STUFFING Saute 2 c. bread crumbs in ¼ c. melted margarine or butter. Add ¼ c. chopped, peeled orange, ¼ t. grated orange rind, ½ c. chopped celery, 1 c. chopped cooked (pitted) prunes, and ½ t. salt.*

❧ *BROWN RICE STUFFING Stuffings with strong and unusual tastes go well with wild or unusual-tasting meats. This rice stuffing will make a dull bird interesting or complement an exotic one. Cook 1½ c. brown (or wild) rice until tender. Saute 1 c. chopped onion and ½ c. fresh, sliced mushrooms in 2 T. melted butter. Add sauteed mixture to rice. Also add to rice ¼ t. each of sage, thyme, and savory. Mix stuffing thoroughly. Stuff bird with it and roast, or bake it separately and serve.*

Puddings Made with Leftover Bread. Times have changed. When I first wrote this chapter 20 years ago, the only breads available in stores were white, French, and a faintly brown-tinted bread otherwise indistinguishable from the white. That white was just like the absolutely cheapest white now available. I told a man back then that my book was going to have recipes for homemade bread in it, and he looked shocked. "You shouldn't tell people how to do that," he sputtered. "They . . . they . . . might try it!"

Back then, making things homemade had gotten somehow classed with using outhouses as the behavior of really backward people. As a society, we were being urged to be modern, and that was defined as being specialized. You were only supposed to do one thing and let somebody else do all the rest for you. The old-timers were at the other extreme. The farther back you go, the more different skills they had mastered and practiced that contributed to their survival.

Then came a generation that had grown up knowing that nuclear bombs were targeted on their cities, grown up with the threat of an imminent end to civilization hanging over them ever since they could remember. They were understandably disillusioned with modern times. As soon as they got old enough, bunches of them left the targeted cities and started practicing how to live without civilization so they'd be good at it when the time came. Along the way, they rescued the art of home bread making from Wonder bread, Miracle bread, or whatever.

That particular crisis seems to be past, and I'm so glad. But now we need to remember how to live with fewer petroleum products, no CFCs, and so on. The greenhouse effect . . . The ozone hole . . . Pollution damage everywhere . . . Poverty . . .

Well, here's how to make delicious, nutritious, old-time crumb puddings out of leftover bread.

❧ *BREAD PUDDING Soak 1½ c. chunked, dried bread in 2 c. milk (if your bread is fresh, toast it in the oven before making this). Add 1 T. sugar, 1 T. melted butter, 2 lightly beaten eggs, and 1 t. vanilla. Put into a buttered ovenproof dish. Set dish in a pan of hot water. Bake at 325°F about 30 minutes. Test by inserting knife. If the knife comes out clean, your pudding is done. Serve hot or cold with rich cream, berries, or a pudding sauce.*

❧ *WHOLE WHEAT CRUMB PUDDING Moisten 2 c. fine whole wheat crumbs with ½ c. thin cream. Add a cup or more of finely chopped fresh figs, 3 T. sugar, and 1 c. milk. Pour the mixture into a mold and steam about 2½ hours. Serve hot with rich cream or orange or lemon sauce.*

❧ *RYE (OR WHOLE WHEAT) CRUMB PUDDING Prepare 2 c. crumbs. They should be very dry; if necessary, give them a special oven heating. Cool and mix with ½ c. currant, wild plum, or other tart jam. Pour into a mold and chill until set. Serve with whipped cream.*

❧ *CRUMBS AND APPLESAUCE Line a buttered baking dish with dried crumbs ½ inch thick. Add a layer of applesauce, dot with butter, add a layer of crumbs, and so on. Use 1 c. thick applesauce for each 1 c. crumbs and about 1 T. of butter for each. When the dish is full, crumbs should be the top layer. Pat down until firm. Bake at 325°F for 45 minutes. Serve with whipped cream.*

❧ *CRUMBS AND SLICED APPLES Follow above recipe, but use 1 c. sliced apples per 1 c. bread crumbs. Sprinkle each layer of apples with 1 t. cinnamon, dot with 1 T. butter, and sprinkle with ⅓ c. brown sugar. When finished, add ½ c. water per 2 c. bread crumbs. Bake at 350°F for 45 minutes. Serve hot with whipped cream. You can use any kind of fruit in this recipe to make Crumbs and Fruit!*

SPECIAL BREADS: GLUTEN, CRACKERS, PASTAS, STEAMED OR BOILED BREADS, AND FRUITCAKES

Gluten

Gluten is a high-protein wheat flour product. It's sometimes used as a meat substitute by vegetarians and is healthy and enjoyable for any eater! The flour that's highest in protein makes the best gluten, of course, and that would be hard-wheat flour.

⋙ *MELANIE'S GLUTEN RECIPE From Melanie Kohler of Hawaii! "Mix 8 c. gluten flour with 4 to 5 c. water (amount of water needed will vary according to flour—dough should be about the same consistency as drop-biscuit dough). Knead mixture with hands for about 5 minutes, cover with water, and let stand for a few hours or overnight. Wash dough carefully under running water (this washes out all the starch and leaves behind the gluten, the protein part of wheat). What you will have left is the raw gluten, which can now be formed into "steaks" or ground up to use in roasts, etc. What I usually do is form the raw gluten into a roll and then slice off steaks from this roll. Boil these steaks in a broth that you make from onion, garlic, water, soy sauce, salt, brown sugar, and some oil. Simmer for about 1 hour in the broth; then let cool and store (still in the broth) in your refrigerator until you're ready to use it. We like these steaks dipped in beaten egg and then in cornflake crumbs, fried until golden brown and served with ketchup.*

"After being cooked in the broth, the steaks may also be soaked in teriyaki sauce made of shoyu (soy sauce), sugar, fresh garlic, ginger and water; and broiled right before serving. Or the teriyaki gluten steaks may be sliced, combined with your choice of fresh garden vegetables (onions, celery, green beans, broccoli, cauliflower, tomatoes, or whatever) and stir-fried over high heat until vegetables are just barely cooked and still crunchy. Serve immediately with hot steamed rice. A little bit of meat or gluten and whatever vegetables we happen to have on hand, stir-fried together like that and served with rice, are an old faithful standby around our house. Of course, we eat rice instead of potatoes with almost every meal. There is a strong Oriental influence here in Hawaii, along with the Western way of living that we have. The result is something uniquely Hawaiian."

⋙ *RUTH'S GLUTEN RECIPE Ruth Miller in Bonaire (Netherlands Antilles) eats lots of gluten, too. She wrote me, "Gluten is also called 'seitan.' Here's another method: Put 5 lb. whole wheat flour in a large bowl. Add water in small amounts, kneading until you have a soft ball. Cover and let stand 45 minutes. Then, under running water, wash and knead dough till bran is washed out and water is clear (takes 10 or 15 minutes). Drain off all the water.*

"Now you can do things with it like make mock ribs, roasts, turkeys, etc. Here's one such recipe: Knead gluten dough (from 5 lb. flour) with ½ c. chopped onions that have been sauteed in ½ c. peanut butter (optional), 2 T. brewer's yeast (adds extra flavor but also optional), 1 T. garlic powder, 1 T. paprika, ½ t. sage, ¼ c. tamari, and any other seasonings you feel like. There's endless variation. Then pull off pieces and form into whatever shapes (ribs, drumsticks, balls, etc.) you need, and bake at 350°F for 45 minutes or till crisp. Baste with a sauce of tomato sauce, tamari, and garlic (maybe some molasses for a barbecue flavor) during last 10 minutes. Or boil pieces in vegetable broth (sugar and oil not necessary) as Melanie does, and use as meatballs in spaghetti sauce, stir-fry with vegetables, slice in sandwiches, etc. It's about as versatile as ground hamburger."

⋙ *RUTH'S KISHKE "This is a vegan version of a Jewish sausage. Combine 2 stalks of finely chopped celery, 1 grated carrot, 1 finely chopped large onion, ¼ c. tamari, 1 c. whole*

wheat flour, ¼ c. wheat germ or nutritional yeast, and pepper, sage, oregano, and paprika to taste. If extra moisture is needed, use soy or rice milk. Mix together well. Divide in half. Form each half into a cylinder on aluminum foil. Then roll the foil around the cylinder to cover. Bake each roll at 350°F, 45 minutes. Then turn upside down and bake 45 minutes more. Unwrap foil to cool.

Crackers

"Cracker" means a flat dry bread. Home cracker making is a lost art I'd like to see revived. It's a lot healthier than feeding the children half-food/half-cookies, or the adults heavily salted treats. Instead you can make their crackers out of all healthy things!

ROLLING OUT: Be sure to roll out any cracker dough to uniform thickness so it will brown evenly in the oven. Janice Smith, Castle Rock, CO, wrote me, "I got a noodle-making machine with Green Stamps and have enjoyed it immensely. I also use it to roll out crackers or small amounts of pie dough to make our own Pop-Tart-type pastries. It rolls those things much thinner than I could with a rolling pin. It is one of those luxury-type tools, like the apple peeler, but it sure does make the job more enjoyable!"

STORING: If your crackers are good and dry, and in an airtight container, they might keep as long as a month, but homemade crackers don't have preservatives in them and aren't meant for long-term storage. If you are making crackers to store for a very long time, use vegetable oil instead of butter in the recipe, because butter crackers get stale faster. You can freeze crackers, but in the freezer they may soak up a little dampness, and that affects their crispness. Some kinds of crackers are best not stored at all—those that have a little dampness in them and taste better that way.

At first I had trouble finding cracker recipes. But finally I got together this really nice selection.

TOASTED BREAD CRACKERS: My favorite crackers are the ones where you make bread first and then slice and toast it to make your "cracker." There are two types—zwieback, which is delicious, healthy, and perfect for teething babies, and melba crackers, which are made from leftover bread. Zwieback is so good of itself that you don't need anything on it or with it. You can make a toasted-bread sort of cracker out of any homemade bread.

⋙ *BASIC BREAD CRACKER RECIPE Chill the bread for easier cutting. Then trim the crust off closely. Cut into ½-inch slices for a zwieback, ⅛–¼ inch thick for a melba. Make slices about 1½ inch wide and as long as you want. Spread* out on a cookie sheet. Bake in a preheated 350°F oven for about 20 minutes, or until dry and crisp clear through. Then store in a dry place, such as a tightly covered glass jar, or in a plastic bag in your freezer. Serve as needed. Good to keep on hand for the children.

➤ **ZWIEBACK** If you're not familiar with zwieback, buy a package at the store just to give you a notion of where you're trying to get to. Your homemade zwieback will taste and look very much like the store product. It's a great cracker for toddlers. Scald ½ c. milk; then cool. When lukewarm, add 2 T. yeast and dissolve. Add ¼ c. sugar or ¼ c. honey, ½ t. salt, 3 eggs, and enough flour to make a workable dough. Make the dough more tender than for regular bread (use less flour). Let rise in bowl until light. Shape into oblong rolls about 2 inches in diameter and 4 inches long. Space about 2 inches apart in a buttered pan in parallel rows. Let rise again. Rolls will more than double. Bake 20 minutes at 400°F. Remove from oven when agreeably browned. Let cool. Then chill in refrigerator. When cold, cut carefully into crosswise slices ½ inch thick —like store-bought bread slices. Brown evenly in the oven at 400°F about 10 minutes. They need to be dry all the way through.

➤ **MELBA TOAST** Slice day-old bread very thin and toast until it is very crisp. The bread should be fine-grained to start with so it will cut into thin, even slices. Unleavened bread works well. Any older bread that is thoroughly chilled will cut thinner than fresh, warm bread. Ideally, melba toast is a delicate brown all over and is totally dry. Cut the slices ⅛–¼ inch thick. Lay them in a pan side by side and bake in the oven at 250–325°F for 15 to 18 minutes.

➤ **RYE MELBA CRACKERS** This recipe gives you results closest to the little cellophane packets of rye melba crackers that you may have seen in restaurants. Start by making sourdough rye bread (for a recipe, see "Sourdough Recipes"). After your sourdough rye bread is made, chill it in the refrigerator. Cut off the crust and recycle. Cut the inside of the loaf into very thin slices, as near ⅛ inch as you can manage. Spread on a cookie sheet in a single layer, and bake at 250°F until completely crisp and dry.

➤ **HERBY BUTTERED RYE MELBA CRACKERS** Mix 1 t. dried marjoram (or 2 T. chopped fresh), 2 t. lemon juice, and ½ c. melted butter. Brush that mix over the toast and return to the oven for 10 minutes.

FROM-SCRATCH CRACKERS

➤ **QUICK RYE CRACKERS** Don't sift your rye flour. Combine 2 c. rye flour, ¾ c. unsifted white or unbleached flour, ½ c. wheat germ, ½ t. salt, 1 t. baking powder, and 6 T. butter or margarine. Cut in the butter with a pastry cutter or 2 knives until you have a mixture with particles about the size of cornmeal. Add ¾ c. milk and 1 slightly beaten egg. Mix, roll out, and cut into diamond shapes by making parallel lines one way diagonally and then the other. Lay the crackers onto a cookie sheet, prick with a fork, and bake at 325°F until lightly browned. Takes about 30 minutes.

➤ **UNLEAVENED RYE CRACKERS** You'll need 1 c. rye flour, 1 c. white flour, 1 t. sugar, ½ t. salt, ½ c. melted butter (cooled), and ½ c. milk. Stir the flours together. Add sugar and salt and stir. Combine butter and milk and pour that over dry ingredients, stirring with a fork until all is moistened. Gather your dough into a ball and knead until smooth. Pinch

off pieces the size of marbles and roll very thin to 3–4 inches in diameter. Prick with fork and put on lightly greased baking sheet. Bake at 400°F for 10 minutes, or until lightly browned. Makes 48 three-inch crackers. (Optional: Add 1 t. caraway seed to dough and sprinkle tops with coarse salt.)

➤ **BONNIE'S HEALTHY OATMEAL-WHEAT CRACKERS** Combine 3 c. quick rolled oats (or 2 c. quick, 1 c. plain), 2 c. whole wheat flour, ½ c. wheat germ, ½ c. white flour, and 2 t. sea salt. Put in blender to emulsify: 3 T. honey, ¾ c. oil, and 1 c. water (optional: 1½ c. grated cheese). Now add liquid to dry ingredients. Roll out and cut into shapes or press into baking sheet and score with a knife. Bake at 350°F for 15 to 20 minutes.

➤ **CRISPBREAD** To make this Swedish yeast cracker: In a big bowl, dissolve 2 T. yeast in ½ c. warm water. In a separate saucepan, melt 1 c. butter or margarine. Then add 1½ c. milk to the butter and heat just until lukewarm. Combine with your yeast mixture. Now add about 2 t. honey (doesn't have to be exact), 1 t. salt, and 2 c. whole wheat flour. (It's also good if made with rye flour, all or any percentage). Stir it up. Then add about 4 c. more unbleached or white flour. Knead your dough. Then let rise for 30 minutes. Knead again. Divide your dough into sections. Roll out very thin. If you want them to look authentic, use a knobbed rolling pin. Cut into rectangles about 2½ × 4 inches. You can roll it out right on your baking sheet, cut it there, and let it do its last rising there too, which makes it all easier. Let rise 30 minutes again. Bake at 350°F until light brown (15 to 20 minutes). Your pieces will have sort of grown back together where you cut them. Break the pieces away from each other on those seams.

➤ **SWEETLESS YEAST CRACKERS** This is a fine-tasting white cracker for people who don't like sweets. Not flaky, it is a very hard cracker. The night before, make a sponge using 3 c. flour, 3 T. margarine (cut into flour until very fine, or melt it and add with water), and 1 t. dry yeast. Mix well, cover, and let sit overnight or several hours. (Or make it in the morning and set in a warm place 3 to 4 hours, until risen.) When risen, add to the sponge 1 t. salt and ¼ c. milk mixed with 1 T. vinegar. Stir in as best you can. Then add about 2 c. flour, working in with a spoon and then your hands. More flour may be needed, enough to make a manageable dough. Divide into halves or fourths to make rolling out easier. Roll and stretch dough until it's thin. I prefer to use a Tupperware pastry sheet (a heavy plastic) and to not put much flour on it near the edges. That way I can roll the dough and kind of stick it to the edges of the plastic to hold it taut and thin. The dough is very elastic (if using white flour) and is hard to keep stretched any other way. Prick thoroughly and, if desired, sprinkle with salt. Cut with a pastry wheel or pizza cutter or knife. Bake on cookie sheets at 325°F for 20 to 30 minutes until lightly browned. Remove done crackers from sheet, and return the ones that aren't quite dry enough to the oven for another few minutes.

➤ **CREAM WAFERS** These are delicious, good hot or cold, and easy to make. Sift 1½ c. flour with ½ t. salt. Gradually add heavy cream (best with "real" cream) to make a dough. You'll need about ½ c. cream. Knead on a floured board until smooth and then roll as thin as possible. Prick with a fork and cut out with a cutter in whatever shapes you want; I prefer rounds. Arrange on a greased cookie sheet and bake at

400°F about 10 minutes, or until just delicately browned.

⏩ **GREAT CRACKERS** *From Esther Adams, Poulsbo, WA:* Combine 1½ c. white flour, ½ c. whole wheat flour, ½ c. sugar, and ½ t. salt. Using an electric mixer, food processor, or pastry cutter, mix in 3 T. butter (at room temperature) until mix is as grainy as cornmeal. Slowly add ½ c. milk (you may need a little more). Knead 5 minutes. Roll out a fistful at a time to ⅛ inch or thinner on lightly floured surface. Cut into 2-inch squares. Place squares on baking sheet (not touching). Sprinkle with salt. Prick each cracker with fork 2 to 3 times, and bake until golden brown.

⏩ **SOUR CREAM WHOLE WHEAT CRACKERS** Combine 1 c. sour cream, 1 T. melted butter, a pinch salt, ½ c. sugar, and 1 t. soda and mix all together well. Add enough whole wheat flour to make a stiff dough that can be rolled. Roll out to about a ⅛-inch thickness. Cut into the shapes you prefer and bake at 325°F for 30 minutes (or 400°F for 10 minutes). I like these.

⏩ **UNCOOKED SEED WAFERS** You dry these like a fruit leather. Get the ingredients from a health food store or food co-op. Get a little each of alfalfa seed, barley, buckwheat, corn, flaxseed, lentils, millet, mung beans, oats, rice, rye, sesame, wheat, and almonds. If you can't find them all, don't worry. Just leave out what you can't find. Combine in equal amounts, such as ¼ cup of each. Soak just as if you were going to sprout them. If some of them go ahead and sprout, don't worry—your crackers will still be fine. Put a cupful of the mixture at a time into your blender with just enough water so it will blend. Now add ¼ c. chia seeds (pre-ground) if you have them. If not, you can do without. Spread ¼ inch thick evenly over parchment or plastic. Dry in the sun, in a dryer, or in a very low oven. When dry enough, take away the paper or plastic and continue drying on a screen, turning as needed. Cut into pieces and serve or store.

⏩ **APPLE WAFERS** Combine ½ c. of the above mix with ½ c. chopped apples. Blend and dry like a fruit leather.

⏩ **CHEESE CRACKERS** This is a flaky (like piecrust), tasty cracker. Use any yellow cheese. You can grate a soft cheese on the big holes of the grater and then use your fingers to work it into the flour and margarine as you would make a piecrust. Grate a hard cheese as fine as possible. Rub 3 T. margarine into ¾ c. flour. Work in ½ c. grated cheese (measured after grating) and a dash of salt. Blend 1 egg yolk with 1 T. cold water and add. Work it into a soft dough. Roll out very thin and cut into rounds or whatever shapes you prefer. Bake at 350°F for 8 to 10 minutes (exactly how long depends on how thick your dough is). This and all the following wonderful cracker recipes were sent to me by Mrs. George Baker, who lives in Arizona.

⏩ **PRETZELS** Make a dough of 4 c. flour, 1 T. butter, ½ t. salt, 1 rounded t. dry yeast, and enough water to make a rollable dough. Let dough rest 20 minutes. Then roll out, cut into strips, and let dry a couple minutes. Shape into pretzels, pinching ends together. Let stand until they begin to rise. Make a solution of 1 level T. lye in ½ gal. boiling water, or 2 T. in a gallon. (Don't use an aluminum pan!). Put the pretzels in the boiling water. As soon as they come up to the top, take them out. Drain, brush with beaten egg yolk, and sprinkle with coarse salt or caraway seeds. Bake on an oiled baking sheet. Set oven as high as you can: 700°F if possible. (We did

it at 500°F.) And bake 10 minutes (2½ minutes if you have 700°F). Take out of the oven. Turn oven down to 400°F, set them back in and leave in until they are bone-dry. Drying time varies a lot according to how they are cut out and how thick they are. Break into desired lengths. Put into jar with tight lid and they'll keep. They aren't exactly like store pretzels, but it surprised me that they were something like them. Not something I'd bother with every day, though.

⏩ **GRUEL CRACKERS** Start with 2 c. gruel (your choice of rice, grain, soups, or vegetables all mixed up). Add ¼ c. oil and 1 t. salt or soy sauce to gruel. Now add 2 c. whole wheat flour. If you need more flour, use rye, buckwheat or barley flour, or corn or millet meal—up to 2 cups per loaf. Work until pliable but still slightly moist. Let set in a warm place or finish up at once. Brush a cookie sheet with oil or garlic butter, and sprinkle it with salt. Roll dough out to ⅛ inch thick. Cut into any shape. Place on greased cookie sheet. Bake at 425°F for 10 minutes. May also be deep-fried.

⏩ **RUTH'S VEGAN GRUEL CRACKERS** Omit salt and oil. (Don't deep-fry!) A good combination is 2 c. cooked split pea puree with 2 c. wheat flour and a bit of millet meal. Add any favorite herbs or spices.

⏩ **SWEDISH HARDTACK** You'll need 2 c. yogurt, ½ c. honey, ½ c. oil, 6 c. rye flour (3 c. rye and 3 c. whole wheat), 3 T. nutritional yeast, and 1 t. salt. Blend yogurt, honey, and oil. Stir in remaining ingredients. Dough should be stiff. Knead. Roll out very thin on floured board. Cut into any shape. Bake at 425°F about 15 minutes (watch them carefully to avoid scorching!) until brown. Wafers should be crisp and tender.

⏩ **SWEDISH CRISP BISCUITS** You'll need 1½ c. white flour, 2 c. coarse rye meal or flour, 1 T. sugar, 1 t. salt, ½ c. butter, and 1 c. milk. Sift flours into bowl and add sugar and salt. Divide butter into parts and dot over the flour. Rub in well with fingertips and add milk until you have a fairly stiff dough. Work well until smooth and glossy. When it comes away from the sides of the bowl, roll very thin, prick with fork, and cut into oblongs about 4 × 2½ inches. Bake on buttered tins at about 385°F to a nice golden brown. This is a delicious toast substitute.

Pastas

Pastas were originally made in China, then became an Italian specialty, and now are loved in the United States too. The Chinese still make pasta, which they call "mien," as I learned when I spent a year and a half living in Taipei, Taiwan, in a noodle-making district. If I were there now, I would run downstairs (I lived in a small apartment on the top floor of my building) and out the front door and beg to watch them make it. But my interest then wasn't noodles; it was learning to speak Chinese. I do remember, though, the miles of noodles hung out to dry in the hot tropical sun between poles, like low-slung telephone lines. When I looked out from my balcony, the view was noodles and more noodles—in sunshiny weather. When it rained, the noodles were all taken in, and the streets were just narrow, dirty, and sadly naked.

Spaghetti, macaroni, and all such ilk are the same basic dough recipe squeezed out into different shapes. "Macaroni" is a narrow, hollow tube. "Spaghetti" is smaller in diameter and has no hole in the middle. Even thinner spaghetti is called "vermicelli." Old-time "noodles" (as opposed to modern Asian ones) are broad and flat. Noodles are the easiest to make at home; you don't need any special equipment, although a rolling machine can be fun and very helpful too.

THE 7 SECRETS OF PASTA COOKING

1. Don't put the pasta in until the water is boiling hard.
2. The more water the better. The more water you start with relative to the amount of pasta, the faster you can cook it and the better your pasta will turn out.
3. Add a dollop of olive oil to your cooking water just before you take out the pasta, or toss your pasta with some oil after you drain it and before you add the sauce.
4. If your pasta is frozen, don't thaw first. Just drop it into the water frozen, stir gently to separate, and keep the water boiling.
5. Cook pasta until tender but not soft.
6. Don't rinse.
7. If you have a sauce, toss the cooked pasta with the warm sauce in a pre-warmed pan or bowl.

HOMEMADE NOODLES: Any homemade pasta is so good that once you've tried it, you'll never want to buy the store stuff again. Most store pasta is made of just flour and water, but your homemade noodles, to be really tasty, are made of flour and eggs! Making pasta other than noodles at home would require special equipment that isn't commonly available. But a little machine that will roll out various widths and thicknesses of noodles (or ravioli or cookies) is available from most kitchen supply stores.

My children love it when Mama decides to make noodles. It's almost as good as bread-making day. It's an act they can all get in on. Noodle dough is basically a couple of eggs, a pinch of salt, and all the flour the eggs can absorb to make a stiff dough. You can make noodles out of water rather than eggs, but then they will taste like store noodles—bland. Gertrude Johnson, Lamont, WA, advises adding about ¼ c. melted butter to the eggs, salt, and flour. She says it makes the dough easier to handle and "such tender noodles." Gertrude's always right!

You roll out the dough, cut it into narrow strips, separate them, and spread them out to dry. If you have sunshine, that will do the job. In winter you can dry them just on a tray. Or in your dehydrator. Nowhere is it written that you have to dry noodles before cooking them. You can make them and drop them directly into the pot damp and limp. They cook up fine. The thing about undried noodles is that they won't keep. If your noodles are really crisp and bone-dry, you can put them in a jar and they'll keep a month.

Some people knead their noodle dough, but I don't. I make it so stiff it would be miserable to try to knead it. Then I roll it as thinly as possible, cut into sections, pile about 4 sections atop one another, and slice off noodles. The thinner you can roll the dough, the quicker and easier the noodles will dry and the quicker they will cook. I cut

with a butcher knife. I dry either on the table, on trays in the sun, or in my fruit dryer in the sun.

My noodles aren't very thin or very narrow. They take anywhere from 20 minutes to a half hour to cook. Noodle meals here are famous for everybody standing around hungrily saying, "Mama, aren't the noodles done yet?" And then I fish out enough for everybody to try and we argue over how raw is edible. When they finally get done, they are really good, a meal to remember. And cheap. And it's easy to warm up your leftovers the next day for another meal—which will be delicious too.

If your dough is too moist, you'll have trouble with the noodles sticking together. In that case, dust the dough with cornstarch or cornmeal to keep them from gumming up. But if your noodles have too much loose flour on them, you'll have trouble with the stew thickening and burning on the bottom of the pan before you can get the noodles cooked. Practice makes perfect. If scorching is too great a risk, cook the noodles separately in boiling salted water.

Noodles are great with any stew, chicken or beef dish, or even in a vegetable soup. Or you can cook egg noodles plain and serve them just buttered, or with cheese cut into bits and stirred in with them. You can make noodles out of white flour, unbleached flour, or whole wheat flour. I don't know why you couldn't make them out of rye or barley or rice flour, too, though I've never tried that. To make lasagna noodles, just cut them wide—an inch is good.

Freezing Noodles. Make and cut out the noodles. Then lay the pasta on top of a sheet of wax paper. Cover with another sheet. Fold over and over into thirds. Place your noodle/paper bundle into a freezer bag and tie tightly shut. They'll keep like this in the freezer for as long as 1½ years.

Noodle Recipes

✎ *BASIC NOODLES This makes more than enough to thoroughly noodle up a stew: 2 eggs, a pinch of salt, and all the flour the eggs can absorb.*

✎ *DELICIOUS EGGY NOODLES Combine 6 eggs, 6 T. light cream or canned milk, 1 t. salt, and about 4½ c. flour. This dough can be kneaded. Divide into fourths. Roll out on lightly floured board till paper-thin. Dry 30 minutes. Cut into strips. Drop into boiling salted water and cook.*

LEFTOVER-YOLKS NOODLES This dangerously rich noodle is as delicious as most things that are bad for you. To ¼ c. egg yolks, add 1 T. rich cream plus enough flour to make your stiff noodle dough.

EGGLESS NOODLES Just an eggshell of water with a pinch of salt; then add flour. A teaspoon of butter and some special seasoning helps: a pinch of pepper, ginger, or nutmeg.

GREEN NOODLES Cook a small batch of your garden spinach or other greens. Drain and put through a sieve. Drain again. Combine 3 eggs, ½ c. of the spinach, 2 t. butter, and enough flour to make the dough.

POTATO NOODLES Use the equivalent of about 4 large potatoes, cooked and mashed. Leftover mashed spuds are also fine to start with. Now mix in 1 egg and a pinch of salt, and maybe a little nutmeg. Add enough flour to get a good noodle-type dough. Roll out, etc.

FETTUCCINE Use one of these noodle recipes. Cut in strips ½ inch wide. They should be flat, long, and ribbonlike.

RUTH'S VEGAN NOODLES "I never have used eggs in pasta-making! Just water or rice milk and flour. Sometimes tamari or spinach or mashed potato, sweet potato or squash. Or even beet puree—for red noodles! Rye flour noodles in a cabbage-tomato stew are great!"

LAPSHEVNIK This baked noodle main dish is a specialty of the Canadian Doukhobors, a vegetarian religious community. Boil 3 c. homemade noodles in plenty of salted water for about 8 minutes. Remove from heat and drain off water. When noodles have cooled to lukewarm, add 8 slightly beaten eggs, ½ c. cream, and 1 t. salt. After those ingredients are well mixed with the noodles, add 2 t. baking powder and mix well again. Now pour into greased baking pan and bake at 400°F for about half an hour. When done, cut into squares to serve. Offer melted butter as a sauce. (Optional: add ½ c. raisins!)

BAMI GORENG From Ruth of Bonaire. (This is the noodle version of the Nasi Goreng recipe under "Rice.") "The noodles are nests of 1 cm. (⅓ inch) wide noodles. If you've made nasi, you know about how many noodles, volume-wise, to use since the proportion (noodles to meat mixture) should be the same, only Bami will ultimately have more vegetables in the meat mixture. For Bami meat, use either pork or chicken (not beef or goat). Cut it into small strips. (The key to this dish is long and thin, whereas Nasi is small and chunky.) Cook meat with an equal amount of shredded cabbage, and add these spices: grated gingerroot (or lots of ground ginger), strips of onion (if you use lots and lots of leeks instead of onion, it will be more authentic!), celery sliced thinly, ketjap manis (see "Food Seasonings" in Chapter 5), and red pepper. (Add vegetables and spices only after the meat loses its redness.) When the meat is cooked thoroughly, add the cooked noodles and more ginger and ketjap manis. Serve on a platter or huge frying pan with egg strips, like for Nasi."

NON-NOODLE HOMEMADE PASTAS: Here are some other ways to use noodle dough.

PFARVEL AND SPAETZLE To make pfarvel, make a ball of stiff noodle dough and then grate it coarsely. Spread out the grated dough and let it dry. Then add the bits to boiling soup and cook 10 minutes.

Spaetzle is very like pfarvel. A kitchen specialty store could get you a "spaetzle machine." Spaetzle are tiny dumplinglike noodles. You mix a noodle dough; then the spaetzle are extruded through the holes in the machine directly into boiling water. Use spaetzle in soups and stews, or fry like hash browns.

NOODLE PUFFS Make your favorite noodle dough. Roll out and let lay until moderately dry. Fold over the dough into halves. With a floured thimble, cut out puffs. Press the thimble firmly enough so the edges stick together. (There'll naturally be a little pocket in the middle.) Fry the puffs in deep fat until golden brown and serve as soup crackers. Put them in the bowl and pour the soup over them.

RAVIOLI Make your favorite noodle dough, only use less flour so that your dough is just stiff enough to roll and hold its shape. Roll it very thin and let it dry on a cloth for about an hour. You can make the ravioli with either a cheese filling or a meat filling.

Cheese Filling: Blend together 1 lb. ricotta, ⅓ c. grated Romano, ½ t. fresh chopped parsley, 2 eggs, and a dash of salt. This is the real Italian thing.

Meat Filling: Combine ground cooked beef (or a mixture of ground cooked leftover meat and sausage, with half as much bread crumbs as ground meat), egg, some grated onion, chopped fresh parsley, and salt. Optional: pepper, nutmeg to taste, and the grated rind of a lemon.

Fill and Cook the Ravioli: Cut the dough into 3-inch squares. Place 1 t. filling into the middle of each square. Fold the square over to make a triangle. Press the edges well together to seal. Set down on a floured board and let dry an hour or more. Then have ready boiling salted water. Drop the ravioli in, a few at a time, until they're all in. Cook for 20 minutes. Serve with a gravy or a topping of grated cheese.

Steamed and Boiled Breads

DUMPLINGS: A biscuit-sized chunk of bread cooked as it floats on top of boiling soup or stew is a "dumpling." A dumpling bread shouldn't have very much shortening in it, or it will come apart in the water. You want to make a dough that's firm enough to hold together on the water but not floury, which could cause your stew to burn on the bottom. Wait to drop in dumplings until your stew is boiling hard. The pot should be about two-thirds full. If you sprinkle a little flour on the dumplings before dropping them in, that will be enough to make you a nice thick gravy if you stir them a moment in there. Figure on cooking them about 20 minutes. The dumplings are done when they don't taste doughy or floury any more.

FRANCIS WARD'S OLD-TIME BOILED DUMPLINGS Sent to me by Brian Pruiett, Basin, WY: "Mix some flour, a little grease, salt, and pot liquid to make a soft dough, just stiff enough not to stick to hands while rolling. Roll into marble-sized balls between palms and drop into boiling soup or stew."

BAKED EGG DUMPLINGS Combine 1 c. whole wheat flour, a pinch salt, and 3 t. baking powder. Then add ½ c. milk and 2 beaten eggs. Mix well. Drop the dumpling dough by teaspoonfuls on top of the meat and gravy. Bake at 450°F until the dumplings are done.

BOILED DUMPLINGS Cut 3 T. shortening into 4 c. flour that has been sifted with 4 t. baking powder. Add water and milk alternately to moisten, about a cup of each, until your *dough is moist but firm. Knead, roll out in flour, cut into 1 × 1½-inch sections, and cook.*

STEAMED BREADS (PUDDINGS): To the pioneers, "pudding" meant a hot, moist, spiced, and sweetened bread that was steamed or boiled in a bag. These were usually soda-leavened breads, so before starting to mix the pudding, you should have your ingredients ready, your pans greased (or your bag floured), and the water boiling in the pan, because you want to get the bread on the heat as soon as possible after mixing. In Great-Grandmother's day, she had a regular "steamer" to make it in, and they are again becoming available at hardware and kitchen stores.

The typical steel steamed pudding mold comes in many shapes, but basically they are bucket-shaped, plain or fluted on the sides, and often have a central tube like an angel food cake pan to help get the pudding cooked through. With glazed earthenware steamer pans, you put a cloth over the top, secured with a string tied around the outside edge. To use such a mold, grease and fill one-half to two-thirds full. If your recipe says to "steam" it but you don't have a steamer, don't despair. They're nice but not necessary. There are ways to make an adequate homemade substitute.

The "Inside" Pan of a Homemade Steamer. Pour your pudding into a well-greased (use butter) 2-qt. mold, bowl, basin, or casserole; or two 1lb. coffee cans; or as many greased 1-pint cans (16-oz. size), or cans a little bigger, as you need. *Be sure to use cans that are smooth, not ridged, on the inside. Fill the cans only about half full to allow for expansion during steaming.* Pour your pudding in. Cover with lids, cloth tied on with string, or aluminum foil; or leave uncovered. I leave them uncovered and haven't had soggy bread yet!

The "Outside" Steamer Pan. For your steamer pan, choose one that has a lid and is big enough to hold the pudding pans with room to spare. On the bottom of that pan, set a smaller pan, such as a baking pan, upside down. Or use crumpled foil, a rack, canning-jar lids, or whatever you can devise to keep the bread cans from sitting directly on the bottom of the steamer pan. Set your container(s) of bread batter in on top of that. Pour water to almost halfway around the cans; you want steam, not water, on top of the pudding. Put on the steamer cover and boil the water slowly until the time is up. Add to the water as it runs dry. Don't open the steamer and let cold air in on the pudding, except when necessary to replenish the water or near the end to see if it's done.

Steaming in a Pressure Cooker. Place a filled 1-qt mold on a rack in the bottom of a 4-qt. pressure cooker (for a larger mold, you need a larger pressure cooker). Add 3 c. water. Steam 20 minutes without pressure. Close vent. Steam 30 minutes at 10 lb. of pressure. This is equivalent to about 4 hours of steaming.

Steamed in a "Pudding Bag." In this old-time system, the bread was cooked in a bag over boiling water in a colander or perforated steamer with the lid on.

COOKING THE PUDDING: Steam until the pudding springs back when touched lightly in the center. When your pudding is done cooking, lift the can or mold out of the kettle and remove its cover, if any. Cool. Loosen the pudding around the edges with a knife and remove. To serve, offer the pudding hot, cut into slices, and with a sauce. To reheat in the mold, cover and steam 30 minutes or, if there is no mold, wrap in aluminum foil to reheat.

🍠 *HELEN'S CARROT PUDDING* Sift together 1 c. flour, 1 t. soda, ½ t. cinnamon, ½ t. allspice, ¼ t. cloves, and ¼ t. salt. Grate until you have 1 c. grated raw potato (no peel!) and 1 c. grated raw carrot (no peel). Combine grated vegetables and dry ingredients. Now add ½ c. melted shortening, 1 c. sugar, 1 c. raisins, and (optional) ½ c. chopped nuts. Mix well. Put in a greased pan and steam 3½ hours. Serve with a sauce from the "Pudding Sauces" section!

BOSTON BROWN BREADS: Traditionally, these all originated as steamed puddings (or even boiled-in-a-bag puddings).

🍠 *WHOLE WHEAT PUDDING* This is either a very tender, nice Boston Brown Bread or a firm pudding to be served with a sauce, as you choose. Take 2 c. whole wheat flour, ½ t. soda, and ½ t. salt, and mix together well. Stir in 1 c. milk and ½ c. molasses. Then add 1 c. chopped dates. Mix and pour into 3 buttered pint cans. Steam 2½ hours. Optional: Substitute for those chopped dates 1 c. ripe strawberries or blackberries (or any berries you like), raisins, chopped dried figs, or chopped apple. Nice served with whipped cream.

🍠 *PLAIN BOSTON BROWN BREAD* Beat 1 egg slightly. Combine it with ½ c. sugar and ½ c. molasses. Add 1 t. salt and ½ t. soda to 1 c. sour milk (or 1 c. sweet milk with 1 T. vinegar added; let it set a bit before using). Combine with egg mixture. Mix in 2¾ c. whole wheat flour. Butter 3 pint cans and divide the batter among them. Steam 1 hour. Then bake in a preheated 400°F oven for 25 minutes. The neighbor children love this hot from the oven, sliced and buttered.

🍠 *MRS. ESSEMEN'S BOSTON BROWN BREAD* Sift together 1 c. cornmeal, 1 c. rye meal, 1 c. whole wheat flour, and ½ t. salt. Add ¾ c. molasses, 1 c. sour milk, and ½ t. soda. Optional: ½ c. raisins. Mix and pour into washed and scalded vegetable cans. For me, this recipe makes four 13-oz. cans. Be sure to grease the cans well before putting your bread dough in. Steam for 3 hours.

🍠 *VEGAN BOSTON BROWN BREAD* Use above recipe, but omit sour milk and soda. Instead use ¾ c. to 1 c. water and 2 t. baking powder.

PUDDING SAUCES: The puddings above really need a sauce over them when served.

🍠 *HELEN'S HARD SAUCE* In a pan combine ½ c. sugar, 1 T. cornstarch, pinch salt, pinch nutmeg, and 1 c. boiling water. Cook until thickened. Then add 2 T. butter and 1½ T. lemon juice (juice of half a lemon). The pudding and sauce are good hot or cold. You can keep the sauce in a jar in the refrigerator and use as needed. Good on any of these boiled or steamed puddings.

BRANDY SAUCE *Combine 1 well-beaten egg, ½ c. butter, and 1 c. sugar. Add 2 T. boiling water. Put your mixture into the top of a double boiler and stir until the sauce boils. To prevent it from sugaring, keep it covered when you can't stir it, and when stirring, keep the sides stirred down into the mixture to prevent crystals from forming there. Then add 1½ t. brandy (or more). This is just right for fancy fruitcake-type puddings and whole wheat pudding. To warm up, add rich cream and mix well.*

HARD SAUCE *Cream 3 T. butter with ¼ c. powdered sugar and a dash of salt. Stir in 1 t. grated lemon peel and 1 t. lemon juice. Add ¾ c. more powdered sugar alternately with 1 T. cream. Beat sauce until fluffy. Good on fruit puddings.*

LEMON SAUCE *Good on molasses puddings. Combine ½ c. sugar, 1 T. cornstarch, a dash salt, and 1 c. water over heat, stirring constantly until thickening takes place and sauce boils for 1 minute. Stir in 1 t. grated lemon peel, the juice of ½ lemon, and 1 T. butter.*

ORANGE SAUCE *Good on carrot pudding. Mix ⅓ c. sugar, 1½ T. cornstarch, ¼ t. salt, 1 c. orange juice, ½ c. water, ½ t. grated lemon peel, and 1 t. lemon juice in a pan. Heat, stirring constantly, until thickening takes place and sauce boils 1 minute. Serve hot.*

FLAMING PUDDING *To add a festive touch to any pudding, soak sugar cubes in brandy or rum for about 5 minutes. Place the soaked sugar cubes around the plate in which the pudding has been placed. Light the sugar cubes and serve them flaming to your Christmas guests, or just to your family to brighten up a regular dinner. This will really make the children's eyes light up! The flame doesn't last very long, and it is easily blown out if you wish to do so.*

BOILED-IN-A-BAG PUDDING: When it says in your old-time recipe book, "Boil the pudding 3 hours and a half" or "boil the bread 3 hours and then bake it 10 minutes," it probably means to boil in a pudding bag. Boiling in a bag was standard in colonial times, when one big kettle per household was about it for pans. That big iron pot hung or set in the fireplace. The menu most days was stew. To make a side dish of pudding or bread (depending on how firm it turned out), the batter was tied up in a special boiling cloth and hung over the edge of the pot to boil inside it, in with the stew. They even made custards this way: "batter puddings." Such a custard comes out too broken up for modern tastes. But the breads are good. So set a big pot of water on to boil and make a bit of history for dinner! (If you want to follow this recipe but not bother with the bag, substitute a steamer mold. Or set an ovenproof bowl in a kettle of water with the top of the water not over the bowl.)

Preparing the Pudding Bag. The pudding bag was and is a cloth bag in which to pour a pudding or bread batter. *Use only undyed white cotton, such as a diaper.* Dip your pudding bag into very hot water. Shake off the excess water or wring it out. Rub with flour all over what will be the inside of the bag to get flour in all the spaces in the weave. Take some boiling water and slop it around on the flour until you have a kind of paste all over.

Filling and Tying the Bag. Now pour your pudding into the middle of the cloth that will become a bag. Don't fill it over half full. Pull up the cloth all around the sides. Tie it tightly shut with string or wire, *leaving room for the pudding to swell!*

Pudding in the Pot. Have your water boiling in a deep pot. All boiled puddings must be put quickly into hard boiling water. Put a small plate or saucer under the pudding bag if there is a possibility of it sticking to the bottom of the pan. *The water mustn't stop boiling all the time the bread is in there, and the pudding must always be covered with water.* You might need to weight it down with a plate on top. Boil 40 minutes or whatever it takes.

Serving a Boiled Pudding. If you want to serve the pudding hot, then as soon as it comes out of the boiling water, dip the bag into a pan of cold water before peeling off the cloth. A boiled pudding is best when sent directly from the pot to the table and served hot. To serve, slice off a portion and serve in a cereal bowl with rich cream or a pudding sauce poured over it.

Boiled-in-a-Bag Pudding Recipes

GENUINE PIONEER PUDDING *Combine 1 c. molasses, 1 c. water, 1 t. soda, and 1 t. salt. Thicken with flour enough to make a batter about the consistency of cupcake batter. Pour into pudding bag and boil until done. Serve with meat gravy or sauce poured over it.*

A MODERN VERSION OF AN ANCIENT MEAT-PIE PUDDING *Grate some suet (beef fat). Rub it into flour and add enough water to make a dough. Line the inside of a heatproof bowl with this. (Or substitute a modern piecrust dough!) Put a mixture of cooked meat and chopped onions into the middle. Place a layer of dough over the top of the meat mix and seal tightly all around the edges where it meets the side layer of dough. Wrap bowl and all in a pudding cloth. Lower into a big pan of boiling water and cook until done.*

Fruitcakes

Fruitcakes can be almost an everyday affair, or they can be a really high culinary art. I make a special bread at Christmas time that has pitted canned cherries and apricots and raisins and applesauce in it. Very popular with the children. I can't give you a recipe for it because, like all my other breads, I just put it together and it's never quite the same. If I had nuts I'd put some of those in too, but I have no nut trees on this place. Here is a recipe I do have, though, for an everyday sort of fruitcake.

EVERYDAY FRUITCAKE *Let the children have all they want of this. Mix 4½ c. whole wheat flour, 2½ c. rye flour, 2 t. salt, and ½ c. oil. Add "fruits"—1 c. raisins, ½ c. roasted sunflower seeds, ½ c. roasted pecans, almonds, or a mixture of nuts (but not peanuts), and ½ c. dried fruit, cooked enough to chop (prunes or apricots are good). Add enough water to make a dough (about 2⅔ cups). Knead and then make a loaf. One big loaf is better than 2 small ones.*

Put into a loaf pan and let rest overnight. Brush the top with water; then bake at 275°F for 1½ hours. When cooled to lukewarm, wrap tightly in foil or plastic wrap and let season before eating for at least a couple days, so the crust will soften and the flavor will improve.

RUTH'S HONEY FRUITCAKE *Mix 2 c. honey and ½ c. water. Then beat in 4 c. rye flour, 4 t. baking powder, 3 t. cinnamon, 1 t. allspice, and 1½ c. chopped dried fruit. Bake at 350°F in 2 round pans with a pan of boiling water in the oven bottom (about 40 minutes). Age about a week, wrapped in plastic.*

🐚 *UNCOOKED FRUITCAKE* *Soak 1 c. hulled raw almonds overnight in 2 c. water. Do the same with 1 c. hulled raw sunflower seeds. In the morning, discard water and grind nuts with 2 c. dried fruit (any combination) and ½ c. sliced banana (use a food processor). Press into a loaf pan. Serve thinly sliced. Will keep in the refrigerator up to 24 hours after making. From Ruth of Bonaire.*

GENERAL HINTS ON MAKING HOLIDAY FRUITCAKES:
These are the kind you serve at Christmas, Thanksgiving, and Easter. They can be fun because, since you make them so infrequently, you can really put yourself out.

1. To chop suet, sprinkle it liberally with flour while you are chopping it. That way it won't stick to the knife.
2. To separate seeded raisins and sticky candied fruit, immerse them in a bowl of flour, rubbing until you have them all separate and each coated with flour before adding to your batter.
3. When first baked, the cake may have a hard dry crust. During the aging period, the fruits and crust become moist, the flavors blend, and it "seasons." There's a real art to this aging of fruitcakes, and there are a number of different ways to accomplish the same end.

Aging a Cake. A well-made old-fashioned fruitcake should easily keep for 2 or 3 months. You need an airtight fruit-cake-type pan to store it in. You can buy them at hardware stores or in cooking specialty stores, if you don't have any around the house. Keep the can with the cake in it in a cool place to prevent mold. A cool basement, cellar, or refrigerator is fine. To help your cake keep or to send it through the mail, soak the outside of the cake with a brandy bath. There are several different ways to accomplish that. You can paint the brandy on with a pastry brush. Give it 2 or 3 brushings. If you get mold anyway, don't worry. Mold doesn't hurt a fruitcake. Just trim it off. If you're intending to eat it up soon, just wrap it tightly in foil or plastic. To make fruitcake last a very long time, though, you need to do more. They can be aged as long as 3 years, but a year is a more sensible amount. That way you can plan on baking your fruitcakes after the Christmas rush is over for the next Christmas. To make them last that long, you have to soak them with plenty of rum or brandy or some kind of strong alcoholic beverage. This prevents molding. Then wrap the cake in cheesecloth or some such cloth that has been soaked in the alcoholic beverage. Overwrap in either plastic or foil and put in an airtight tin in a cool place. Or bury in powdered sugar in an airtight tin and keep in a cool place. For very long storage, it helps to poke the cakes with a skewer sort of thing and pour a little brandy or rum into the holes. The airtight packing is to keep the alcohol preservative from evaporating.

If you're not confident and you'd like to keep an eye on what's happening, start out by soaking cheesecloth in brandy, and wrap each cake with about 4 lengths of cheesecloth. Then overwrap tightly with foil or plastic. Put it in a tin can and store in a cool place. Every 2 weeks, unwrap to see what's happening (and probably nibble). Resoak the cheesecloth, wrap it up, and pack again. This system is good for 6 weeks easily.

To decorate cakes for serving, wait until after the storage time is up and you are ready to serve them. It doesn't matter if it has been 2 weeks or 3 years. Make a glaze by combining ½ c. light corn syrup with 2 T. water in a pan. Bring to a full boil; then let cool off a little. Brush the sur-

face crumbs off your unwrapped fruitcake. Brush the cake with glaze. Then lay candied cherry halves, citron, and/or walnut halves on the cake for garnish, and brush again with the glaze.

To make a gift of fruitcake, wrap each one in plastic. Tie with a ribbon and decorate to suit yourself. Put it in a box and gift-wrap it if you're going to deliver it in person. To mail it, you'd better send it in something really strong, like a can. I've received enough mashed fruitcakes to have resolved that metal is the only way.

Freezing Fruitcake. Some say the fruitcakes you make ahead and freeze till needed taste the best of all, and they're definitely less work. Just bake, wrap, and freeze.

🐚 *CHRISTMAS PLUM PUDDING* *Before there was a fruit-cake, there was plum pudding at Christmas time. The ingredients are very similar, but you don't need to age it. It can be boiled in a bag, steamed in a bag, or steamed in a mold. Soak overnight in 1 c. of good brandy: 1½ lb. seedless raisins, ½ c. chopped almonds, 2 oz. finely chopped candied citron, and 2 c. finely chopped sour apples. Then add 1½ c. dry bread crumbs (toast them if necessary), 1 c. finely chopped beef suet, ½ c. sugar, 1 c. molasses, 3 eggs, ¼ c. flour, 1 t. each cinnamon and salt, and ½ t. each allspice and cloves. Grate the rind of a lemon and add. Mix well and pour into your buttered mold or floured pudding bag. Steam 4 to 8 hours—the longer the better. Serve with a brandy sauce. (Hard sauces that firm up when cool and become like frosting are traditional with plum pudding.)*

🐚 *MRS. F.W. FERRELL'S JAM CAKE* *This is a special holiday cake. Mrs. Ferrell always makes two of these in early November; the first is cut on Thanksgiving and the second is saved for Christmas. Cream together gradually ½ lb. butter and 3 c. sugar. Beat for 5 minutes. Separate 7 eggs. Beat egg yolks until light and lemon-colored. Beat egg whites separately until stiff and dry. Add yolks to butter-sugar mixture; then fold in egg whites. Dissolve 1 t. soda in 1 c. buttermilk. Boil 1 c. chopped pecans (or other nuts) and 3 c. chopped seedless raisins in 1 c. flour. Add buttermilk mixture, 1 c. wild plum jam (preferably homemade), 1 c. dewberry jam (or substitute strawberry or blackberry), 1 t. vanilla, and nut/raisin mix to the batter. Sift together 3 c. flour, 1 t. baking powder, and ½ t. each cinnamon, nutmeg, and cloves; add to batter. Beat* thoroughly. Note: Dough should not be too thick. Place in lined cake pans. Bake in slow oven (300°F). Cover with wax paper during last part of the baking. Makes 5 layers. Cover each layer, top, and sides generously with caramel icing (see following recipe). Decorate tops and sides of cake with whole pecan halves. This cake ripens like a fruitcake. To serve, slice thinly, since it is sweet as any confection, and very filling. It keeps for months. If the icing dries out, cover the cake with a slightly moist cheesecloth for a day or so.

🐚 **CARAMEL ICING FOR THE JAM CAKE** Ingredients: 6½ c. sugar, 2 c. milk, ½ c. butter, 1 t. vanilla, and 1 c. chopped pecans. Put 5 c. sugar, milk, and butter into a pan and bring to a boil. When boiling, add remaining 1½ c. sugar, which you have slowly melted in another iron skillet. Cook until a soft ball forms when mixture is dropped into cold water. Add vanilla and pecans. Beat well.

🐚 **MRS. NEELEY'S WHITE FRUITCAKE** Combine 2 oz. white raisins, ½ lb. light-colored citron, ½ lb. candied cherries, ½ lb. candied pineapple, 1 small fresh coconut, grated (save the coconut milk!), and 1 lb. chopped, blanched almonds. Sprinkle the fruit-nut mix with 1 c. flour and set aside. Cream 2 c. sugar with 1 c. shortening (your choice). Add alternately to creamed mixture 1 c. coconut milk (add water if nut was short on milk) and 3 c. flour (presifted with 2 t. baking powder). Add 1 t. vanilla, 1 t. lemon extract, and then floured fruits and nuts. Mix well. Beat 8 egg whites to stiff peaks. Fold them in carefully and lightly. Bake ½ hour at 250°F in a round tube pan 10 inches across and 4½ inches deep. Decorate with cherry halves and citron slices. It keeps well.

🐚 **OLD-FASHIONED FRUITCAKE** Put 6½ lb. of fruit and 1 lb. of nuts into a bowl and pour 1 c. dark rum over it all. Stir, cover, and let rest overnight. For fruit, use your favorite combination of typical fruitcake stuff—candied cherries, candied pineapple, citron, candied orange and lemon peel, and raisins. The golden and muscat raisins end up tasting better than the regular ones, I think. Currants are okay too. So are dates, figs, dried chopped apricots, chopped pitted prunes, and all sorts of home-dried fruits. For nuts you can use walnuts, pecans, Brazil nuts, almonds, filberts—any nuts except peanuts.

Cream together 1 lb. butter and 1 lb. brown sugar. Add 12 egg yolks (save the whites). Now add 4 c. flour; 1 t. each salt, ground allspice, and nutmeg; and 2 t. each cinnamon, mace, and cloves. Stir in the fruits and nuts too. Whip the 12 egg whites stiff and fold in. Bake in four 9 ½ × 4¾-inch or 12 × 5 × 3-inch loaf pans that have been oiled and, if possible, lined with parchment paper and then lightly oiled again.

It helps if you brush the tops of the cakes with milk. It takes a long time to bake these, and you should use about a 250°F oven. Figure 3½ hours for the large loaf pans, 2½ to 3 hours for the smaller ones. The toothpick test works. Let cool about 15 minutes before you try to peel off the paper.

🐚 **MOLASSES FRUITCAKE** Combine 3 c. dark raisins, chopped dates, or pitted prunes; 3 c. golden raisins or chopped dried apricots; and two 16-oz. pkg. mixed candied fruit or some equivalent. Stir in some brandy or rum (or apple juice if you want to avoid the alcohol). Let soak overnight. Now cream together 3 c. butter and 2½ c. sugar. Beat in a total of 12 eggs; then add 1 T. real vanilla extract and then a 12 oz. bottle of molasses or the equivalent in the homemade stuff. Now add 1 T. each grated orange and lemon peel. Sift together 7 c. flour, 2 t. soda, 2 t. salt, 2 T. each of ground cinnamon and nutmeg, and 1 T. ground cloves. Add 4½ c. chopped walnuts. Combine with egg-molasses mixture. Bake about 2 hours at 300°F in floured 9 × 5 × 3-inch loaf pans that are lined with foil or else greased and lined with parchment paper that has been oiled on top too. Use a toothpick to test for doneness. If you use foil, cool cakes completely before removing it.

In the Bible we often read of gleaners like Ruth and Naomi, who went into the fields following the harvesters to gather kernels that had been left behind. Shelley Dalen, Pasco, WA, wrote me about a modern version of that old principle of sharing food that would otherwise go unharvested.

"Have you heard of the gleaning programs that Community Action Agencies have going (at least in Washington and Oregon that I know of)? Living in the heart of farming country, there is a *great* deal of produce going to waste. We go out and glean what would otherwise rot on the trees or be plowed under. Everyone who gleans donates 25 percent of what they glean to Community Action. They in turn give it to local low-income programs like Head Start, the food banks, Salvation Army, senior citizen centers, and churches —sometimes even the jails! In addition, each gleaner has an "adoptee"—someone who, for some reason, can't go out and glean on their own. (I have a handicapped friend who watches my kids while I glean. In exchange, I split whatever I get with her.)

"The remainder goes to the gleaner. I hardly bought any fruit last year. We gleaned asparagus, pie and sweet cherries, raspberries, peaches, apricots, nectarines, carrots, corn, apples, potatoes, garlic, and grapes! Even got 100 lbs. of onions! If there isn't one in your area, it might be something to look into!"

Shelley's right. If there isn't a gleaning program in your area, are you the right person to start one? Every worthwhile thing started with one person who took it upon him- or herself to make it happen.

CHAPTER FOUR

Garden Vegetables

ALL THE ONIONS

NON-BRASSICA GREENS AND THE MOTLEY BRASSICA HORDE

LEAVES, STEMS, AND ROOTS WE EAT

EATING AN ARTICHOKE

LEGUME LORE

BUSH, POLE, SHELL, AND SNAP BEANS

FROM FAVA TO PEANUT, GARBANZO TO SOY

SEED RECIPE IDEAS

TO PEEL OR NOT TO PEEL

THE GOURD FAMILY

HARVESTING CANTALOUPES AND MUSKMELONS

SECRETS OF MAKING PICKLES

BIG CHANGES IN TOMATO CANNING

GARDEN VEGETABLES CONTENTS

4 | GARDEN VEGETABLES

INTRODUCTION

The vegetables are a motley and hard-to-organize horde, and there are more of them all the time as old-time vegetables are reintroduced and vegetables from around the world join the old stand-bys. I'd guess there are maybe 5 times as many different vegetables listed here as in the first edition of this book. But many of them are closely related and are similarly grown, harvested, preserved, and prepared.

So in this new edition I've changed to a dual organizational system, grouping vegetables either by botanical family or by the part of the plant that we eat. This allows me to present them in somewhat related groups rather than in a strictly alphabetized list. An alphabetized list would have amaranth greens near the beginning, lettuce in the middle, and spinach near the end, but here all three are grouped together in the section on greens.

The plant family sections are alliums (onion, garlic, etc.), brassicas

(cabbage, kale, cauliflower, etc.), cucurbits (gourd, squash, pumpkin, etc.), legumes (pea, bean, etc.), and nightshades (pepper, eggplant, tomato, etc.). The plant-part sections are "The Leaves We Eat" (all kinds of greens), "The Stems We Eat" (asparagus, cardoon, celeriac, celery, celtuce, Florence fennel, globe artichoke, and rhubarb), "Flower Seeds," and "The Roots We Eat."

If in doubt about where to find a particular plant, look in the index or table of contents. Sometimes I had a hard time figuring out where to place a vegetable. Okra ended up in the nightshade section because, although it isn't a nightshade, I think it is very much like one. Rutabagas and turnips are in the root rather than the brassica section (although they are brassicas) because they're grown, harvested, and stored like the usual root vegetable, and that seemed more important in their case.

Mail-order sources for various vegetables are listed in most entries. Look for the addresses of those firms in the source list in Chapter 2. If they're not listed, look in the source lists in Chapter 5 (for firms that primarily carry herbs) and Chapter 6 (for firms that specialize in trees and fruits).

I'm starting with "alliums" (the onions) because it starts with A and I like onions.

ALLIUM: ALL THE ONIONS

This section is dedicated to the great *Allium* genus—all the onions and their near (and also strongly flavored) relatives, totalling some 250 edible varieties worldwide! The alliums are from the lily family of the monocots, which means the onions are more closely related to grass than to carrots! They all are rich in sulphur, which gives them their vivid flavor—and their stink when rotting. The alliums include leeks, rocambole, Welsh onions, globe onions (sweet, red, yellows, etc.), pearl onions, potato onions, and top-set onions—and chives, garlic, elephant garlic, shallots, etc., as well.

Each of those has around 15 other common names, many of which are the same for different kinds of onions. Then there are the variety names in the seed catalogs, which are likely to be different from the common names. And varieties are frequently written about under the wrong name, sometimes even in garden manuals. In at least one case, experts recently changed the Latin designation for an allium variety; now some experts call it by one Latin name and others by another.

Allium Varieties

So if you're sometimes confused about which onion is which and what their differences are, you're in very good company. How to sort them out? I do it by reproductive similarities. This system isn't perfect, but it's better than nothing.

1. Cloves: Shallots, garlic, and elephant garlic all reproduce by division underground, making a "nest" or "head" of cloves that you divide and plant to get new ones.
2. Clones: Welsh onions and potato onions reproduce by dividing at the base—not into topless cloves like the garlics and shallots but into twins, quadruplets, octuplets, etc., very like the amoeba.
3. Top-sets: Tree ("top-set," "Egyptian," or "walking") onions reproduce by interesting little bulbs that grow from the tip-tops of their leaves and then are gradually bent down and planted by the parent plant. Like the tree onion, rocambole grows top-set bulbs, but it also reproduces by twinning underground like a Welsh or potato onion.
4. Seeds: Bunching onions, chives, garlic chives, pearl onions, leeks, and globe onions reproduce in the more familiar manner of flowering and then making seed.

For more onion info, read "All the Onions and How to Grow Them" from Garden Way and *Onions: A Handbook for Gardeners* by Marian Coonse. Southern Exposure (540-894-9480; **www.southernexposure.com**) carries a large variety of garlic and perennial onions. Irish Eyes–Garden City Seeds carries 40 garlic varieties, five of shallots, walking onions, netted onion bags, and burlap sacks! 509-925-6025; fax 509-925-9238; PO Box 307, Thorp, WA 98946; **www. irisheyes.com**. ATTRA's info roundup, "Organic Allium Production," is at **www.attra.org/attra-pub/allium.html**.

Scallions

Before I get seriously into those alliums, I'll explain about scallions. "Scallions" aren't a variety of onion. They're "green onions," the kind you can buy tied in bunches at the store. Lately seed catalogs are labeling as "scallions" all kinds of onion varieties, not just immature globes. A lot of onion varieties look like "scallions" at an immature stage, and some do at a mature stage. For scallions, you can use thinnings from your globe (winter) onions or young Welsh onions, which look enough like them to pass, or young top-sets with the root end trimmed off, or potato types. The White Lisbon variety is a good scallion variety. The following directions are best, however, for scallions grown from globe types.

GROWING: For scallions, plant in early spring or in the fall. If you live in the south, fall is best. In a temperate zone, if you plant in late fall and winter them over, you'll have scallions about the next March. It takes an average of 60 days to get scallions from seed. You can plant the seed fairly thickly and thin by harvesting. You can also plant onion sets instead of seeds for scallions. You'll get them a lot faster that way, in only a few weeks. If you plant sets in wide row, plant 2–3 inches apart each way. Rows can be planted wide-style, or single as close as a foot apart. To grow scallions in a pot, scatter seeds in a 12-inch pot and then gradually thin to about 18 plants. The soil in the container should be at least 8 inches deep, spacing ultimately 1 to 4 inches apart.

HARVESTING: They're "scallions" when thick as a pencil and at least 6 inches tall. You can keep on using them as they grow, harvesting as needed. But to be able to harvest at ideal size, the best system is to plant in succession. Pulling scallions actually improves conditions for the remaining onions by loosening their soil as well as removing competition.

SCALLION SALAD DRESSING *Chop up 6 scallions. Combine with 2 T. chopped parsley, 3 T. strongly flavored vinegar, and ½ c. oil. Add salt, pepper, or herbs. Shake well in a lidded container.*

DRYING: Trim away the white bottoms from the green tops. Chop tops and slice bottoms. Dry greens and whites separately, since greens will dry faster. Dry tops at 110°F, whites at 120°F. Or dry outdoors in an airy, shady place.

Allium Group I

The vegetables in this group (elephant garlic, garlic, and shallots) reproduce by making an underground head of cloves. Garlic and elephant garlic are 2 different species, but they are much alike in their cultivation and use.

The Garlic Press is a quarterly newsletter ($15/yr) published by the Garlic Seed Foundation. It covers tours, festivals, and research. David Stern, foundation director, maintains their garlic library and bibliography and networks with growers and researchers worldwide. He also answers specific questions: 315-587-9787; Rose Valley Farm, PO Box 149, Rose, NY 14542-0149.

ELEPHANT GARLIC: Elephant garlic (*Allium scorodoprasum* or *Allium ampeloprasum*) is a different species from regular garlic. Elephant garlic is significantly hardier than regular and can be grown as a perennial in most places. The plants are larger and require more garden space. The heads and cloves are much larger and are so mild that they can be used raw in salads or substituted in any onion recipe; they taste like a garlic-flavored onion. Other than that, grow and use like regular garlic.

GARLIC: *Allium sativum* has flat, grasslike leaves that grow 1–2 feet tall. Garlic is a hardy perennial (though usually grown like an annual), the strongest member of the onion family in its sulfide of allyl content—that good stuff that acts as wormer, disinfectant, etc. Shallots, its closest relative, are basically a mild-flavored garlic variety. Like shallots, garlic blooms (pink flowers), but it may or may not make seed depending on the variety and circumstances.

Instead garlic is usually propagated by garlic bulbs or "heads" that grow underground (roots go as deep as 2 feet). Each head is made up of a cluster of smaller ones, each called a "clove." Garlic is a type of onion, a semihardy perennial that, since it's not damaged by frost or light freezing, can be left in the garden over winter in the Pacific climate—or can be dug up and stored like onions. It's grown both for the kitchen garden and for commercial sale (it yields a good profit from a very small acreage). Store-bought garlic is usually too dry to plant. Buy a cluster of garlic cloves from a plant nursery or mail-order source.

There's more info in *Growing Great Garlic: The Definitive Guide for Organic Gardeners and Small Farmers,* by Ron L. Engeland (1991); 509-422-6940; **filaree@northcascades. net; www.filareefarm.com.** Ron also sells organic seed garlic. Irish Eyes–Garden City Seeds offers 40 kinds of garlic, including Red German garlic, favored for fine flavor, ease of peeling, and specialization where winters are cold; or Spanish Roja garlic, whose bulb wrappers have a light purple streaking; or Sicilian garlic, which is basically nonbolting. Other sources of seed garlic are The Montana Garlic Farm (406-932-4828; PO Box 1283, Big Timber, MT 59011) and Jim Baiar (406-892-4409; 490 Halfmoon Rd., Columbia Falls, MT 59912; **ginger@hotmail.com**).

Planting and Growing. For either garlic or elephant garlic: Plant in well-drained soil, pH 5.5 to 6.8. Garlic plants need full sun; fertile, moist soil; and a loose, even sandy or high-humus soil so the bulbs can easily spread out and grow. The best time of year to plant is late August to mid-October because garlic grows best during cool weather; during the fall and spring it will store energy with which it will ultimately make the cloves. If you want to plant in spring, do it as soon as the ground is no longer frozen (probably early

March). Plant where you want it to grow; garlic doesn't transplant. Garlic can thrive in a window box; a pot is too small for it.

In general, use 2 lb. of cloves (about 150 cloves to the pound) for each 50-foot row you want to plant. Plant individual cloves, or plant 2–3 cloves per site to compensate for nongrowers. *Plant with their points up!* And have those points sticking out of the ground just a bit, or else very, very shallowly covered with soil. Roots will grow from the bottom end of the clove. Plant each 2–3 inches deep and 3 inches apart in a row, bed, or wide row. Plant very shallow if you're planting on the late side of spring, but garlic needs cool temperatures while it's getting started (and heat while it's making bulbs). Or you can plant in the fall for a very northern garden (Canada) or for an earlier-maturing, larger-bulbed crop. Two pounds averages 300 cloves, which would plant about a 100-foot row. One planted clove will yield an average head of 15 cloves. Garlic is a good thing in your garden: It repels many insects and is compatible with most vegetables. For this reason and also because the garlic plant doesn't take up much space, it's often interplanted with vegetables (any kind but legumes, which it inhibits) or flowers (especially roses). Weed and loosen the soil around them with your hoe to help the heads grow and expand. Don't let them get dry. Garlic should be kept free of weeds.

Harvesting and Drying. You can cut and use the thin shoots like chives (another onion relative); a leaf or two now and then will do no harm. Once your garlic leaves get a foot high, stop watering. Harvest bulbs as soon as the leaves die and fall over (about August). Like onions, garlic doesn't make cloves until the last minute, the last 45 days of its growing season. To hurry them, knock over the aboveground shoots 90–110 days after planting. Don't cut off the leaves if you want to braid. In a few days you'll be able to loosen the dirt and pull up the whole plant. After digging, wash them well and let them dry in the sun until they are white (about a week).

Saving Bulbs/Seeds. Garlic will sometimes send up a tough stalk that flowers and makes seed. Sometimes the flowers contain little bulbs that look like tree onion top-sets. A better way is to divide and plant the cloves. Bulbs to save for seed should be dried at a day temp of less than 100°F, or in the shade. Garlic bulbs need a period of chill of at least 8 weeks, not below freezing but between 32°F and 50°F, before you plant them. The little skinny center cloves aren't so good for planting.

Storing for Kitchen Use. Dust off, trim off roots, and store in mesh or paper bags. They'll stay good that way at least several months, longer if your humidity is low. Bulbs for winter kitchen use are nice braided together by their dried stems and hung. Commercial garlic is stored at 35–40°F, 60–70 percent humidity, and can last 6–8 months.

Cooking with Garlic. Peel off a clove's papery outer layer and use the clove whole, chopped, minced, or crushed in a garlic press. In the kitchen, rub it on meat or add to salad dressing or tomato sauce. If your garlic gets a bitter taste when cooked, you cooked it over too high a heat. Garlic needs less time to cook than onions. Add the garlic after the onions. Garlic's good for you, and you can use more than you may think. A gourmet recipe calls for 2 lb. garlic plus 1 chicken. You can use 10 cloves per 1 qt. soup, 4 cloves per 1 meal-sized batch of spaghetti sauce, 3 in a salad dressing.

Or add to pickle mixtures. For more garlic recipes, read *The Great Garlic Cookbook* by Barbara Friedlander (Macmillan, 1975). Incidentally, the old-time cure for garlic breath is to chew raw parsley or celery leaves!

☙ *GARLIC POWDER* *Peel cloves; slice or chop, dry (120°F), and then grind or mortar or pound them into a powder. Homemade is usually stronger than store-bought. But dried garlic just isn't as good as fresh. Instead make . . .*

☙ *GARLIC BUTTER/BREAD* *Mince 3 cloves garlic. Mix with ½ c. melted butter. Add other herbs as desired. Let steep an hour. Spread on sliced French bread, heat under the broiler, and serve hot!*

☙ *VETERINARIANS' WEDDING ROAST* *I attended the marriage of 2 vet students. The main course was 2 stuffed, roasted turkeys, each basted and injected numerous times with garlic butter while roasting. One lb. garlic cloves had been whipped small and smooth in a blender. Then they were crushed, strained, and mixed with 2 lb. melted butter. The garlic butter was then injected into the barbecuing meat at various points and times with a regular vet syringe, which had a suitably large hypodermic needle! (The students told me they often do the same with other roasts besides turkey and with other liquids, such as red or white wine.)*

☙ *GARLIC PRESERVED IN OIL* *Peel and mince 1 head of garlic. Mix with vegetable oil. Store in a covered glass jar in fridge. It will stay good for months. A quarter teaspoon of this equals 1 garlic clove in a recipe.*

☙ *QUICK GARLIC SOUP* *Heat 12 cloves crushed garlic for about 8 minutes in 3 c. rich milk.*

☙ *ROAST GARLIC SPREAD* *Cut the tips off a whole head of garlic (don't peel or separate cloves). Wrap the head in foil; bake at 350°F until cloves get soft and pulpy. Squeeze the mush onto crackers, toast, or good fresh bread. From* The Good Food Guide, *edited by Lane Morgan (Sasquatch Books, 1992).*

Garlic as Medicine. Garlic has genuine antibiotic properties. Garlic juice, lemon juice, and some sweetening mixed in a cup of warm water are good for a sore throat. Garlic juice applied to ant bites helps make the pain go away. For a patient with a chest cold, mix garlic juice and a vapor rub ointment. Smooth that on a square of cloth, cover with another cloth, and place on chest. Garlic is also a diuretic that thins blood and lowers blood pressure. To prevent travelers' dysentery, eat a clove per day. It has been used to treat patients (humans and animals) who need worming and has no toxic side effects. To worm a large cat, give one crushed clove each month. So whether you use it for medical or culinary reasons, have at it!

☙ *GARLIC GARDEN SPRAY* *To fight insects and plant blights, blend several garlic cloves with some water and 1 T. cooking oil or soap emulsion. Strain. Dilute to 1 qt. and spray on. It works very well but must be done very often if you're in a serious battle situation.*

SHALLOTS: Shallots are a perennial member of the onion family. Their Latin name is *Allium ascalonicum* or *Allium cepa*, Ageratum group, depending on whom you ask. Shallots are a very close relative of garlic, easy to grow and generously productive. They are a hardy, temperate-zone plant. Like garlic, they reproduce by bulb division underground.

The "nest" of 3–10 or more shallot bulbs resembles a head of garlic cloves except that there are fewer cloves and no outer covering, unlike garlic. Shallots are basically a very mild-flavored garlic variety (see "Garlic"). The shoots grow about 8 inches tall and can be harvested and used like a green onion. Shallots do very well in a container.

Varieties. All shallots have hollow leaves, grow about a foot and a half tall, and make cloves. But some have purple flowers, some white; the best types don't flower or make seed at all.

Planting. Shallots would be a hardy perennial if you left them in the garden. But they are so easy to harvest and store indoors over winter that people usually grow them like an annual. Planting early—like February—is fine because they will germinate even despite low temperatures and are not harmed by freezing. An early start is advisable because they grow only from planting time until just past midsummer anyway, and they need about 100 days to get to maturity. So plant shallot cloves early in the spring, or else in the fall. Fall planting is best if your area has hot summers; in southern zones, plant them in the fall for a winter crop. Plant them 4 to 6 inches apart, pointed end up, and deep enough to get them at least a little covered. In a container, plant 1–2 bulbs per 6-inch pot, 4 per 12-inch pot. The dirt should be at least 8 inches deep. Place in full sun or a sunny window. The soil should be fertile, well-drained, and of average pH.

Harvesting. What you harvest is the bulbs; 8 to 15 will grow per each shallot you have planted. Wait until leaves die back and turn yellow-brown; then pull up, lifting the nest of bulbs out of the soil, and sun-dry it for 2–3 days. Cut off tops. Store as you would globe onions (in hanging stockings or net bags), braid like garlic, or put in an open-topped basket in a root cellar, where it is dry and cool. They actually keep better than the big onions. You can either leave some in the ground to keep them coming or save some of your harvest to plant next spring.

Using. Peel the clove as you would garlic. Use the same way you would an onion bulb to flavor foods, salads, or egg dishes.

NOTE: Unlike regular onions, shallots shouldn't be fried to the point of browning; that makes them develop a bitter taste.

Allium Group 2

Vegetables in this group (potato onions and Welsh onions) reproduce by dividing at the base to make "clones" or twins/quadruplets, etc.

POTATO ONION: This onion is classified as a variety of the basic globe onion, so it's *Allium cepa* var. *aggregatum*. Other common names are the "underground onion," the "multiplier," and the "Egyptian onion." The potato onion produces a large bulb 3 inches or wider at the base, which looks like that of your basic yellow globe onion. You'd never, ever mistake one for a globe onion; at the end of its growing season, instead of a single big round bulb on the bottom, there is a linked aggregation of maybe 8 to 16 bulbs down there. They are distinctly not "cloves," like those of garlic or shallots, but rather true "bulbs." Starts of potato onions are available from Irish Eyes–Garden City Seeds.

Planting. The earlier their start and the better your soil, the earlier in the spring you'll have scallions, and the larger the

individual potato bulbs may ultimately grow. So if you have a mild winter, plant even in January or February—"as early as the ground can be worked and is warming in the spring," Mr. Ronniger says. Or fall-plant fairly large bulbs for very early spring scallions. Ronniger's guidelines for fall planting: "In the far North, plant mid-October until November 1. In the deep South, plant mid-December until January 1. Somewhere in between, plant in November or right around Thanksgiving. Fall plantings are usually mulched with straw to protect them from freezing. Even so, these onions are extremely hardy, reportedly down to −20 to−25°F." If you have a harsher climate, plant as soon as the soil has thawed and dried enough to cultivate a little.

The bulbs should be planted just deeply enough so that there is about ⅛ inch of soil over them, about 8 inches apart. Don't transplant them or hoe close to them; it's too easy to damage the root. Mulching this onion variety can result in rotting. They do their dividing (and multiplying) in the spring.

Harvesting. Like the tree onion, the potato onion is a hardy perennial, but unlike the tree onion, many growers harvest every fall, hold out the bulbs they want for "seed," and plant again each spring. Potato onions tend to be done with their growing by midsummer (about mid-July). When their tops become a brownish-yellow shade, bend over the tops but leave the roots in place longer than you could for globes. Then harvest and cure as you would globe onions.

Sorting and Storing. Your potato onion clusters of bulbs will be of various sizes. Sort them. Store the largest ones for the cook's use. Plant some medium-sized bulbs in the fall for spring green onions. Save and store the smallest ones to plant like "sets" next spring for the main part of next year's crop. Potato onions are one of the best onion varieties for winter keeping, even better than yellow globes.

Use like any other onion; they taste the same, though on the mild side.

WELSH ONION: *Allium fistulosum* is the Asian equivalent of our globe onions; it's the traditional garden onion of the Orient, not of Wales! It's also known as the "Japanese onion," "cong bai," "Japanese bunching onion," and "ciboules." Welsh onions are considered "nonbulbing," but they really do get a significant swelling on the root if they get mature enough, as if they were half a leek and half a globe onion. They are very hardy. They reproduce by multiplying at the base, developing ever more dense clumps. In their young stage, they make great scallions. Fall-planted, they will overwinter in the garden and can be harvested until about May, when they'll either bolt or bulb. If planted early enough in the year, they'll divide (and multiply) at the base during winter, each plant becoming 4, 5, or even more. If planted in midsummer, they'll be ready for harvesting from February through May, but they are usually put in too late to divide. Welsh onions are one of the cold-hardiest alliums, being able to handle even temperatures below 0°F.

Planting. You can get White Lisbon, a good Welsh kind, from Territorial Seed Co. Other sources are Nichols, Le Jardin du Gourmet, Kitazawa, Johnny's, Park, Vermont Bean, Redwood City, etc. They are easy to grow. Average weeding and watering will be fine.

Using. They are fairly mild in flavor. You can harvest green tops from late winter (very early spring), through the summer, on to early winter. You can dig them up any time of year the ground isn't frozen. Serve slivered, chopped, or as scallions. They can be used same as any other onion. In the Orient they're enjoyed chopped into pancake batter; sauteed with tofu chunks flavored with sesame oil and soy sauce; fried with beef strips and flavored with soy sauce; made into a soup with lemon grass, mushrooms, and chicken stock; or served raw as salad, combined with sliced cukes and a vinegar dressing. You can use Welsh onion flowers in salads.

Storing. Welsh onions store best in the ground in your garden and taste best fresh.

Allium Group 3

Vegetables in this group (rocambole and tree onions) reproduce by growing small bulbs at the top of the plant.

ROCAMBOLE: *Allium scorodorprasum,* a form of *Allium sativum* (a.k.a. sand leek, Spanish garlic, Spanish shallot, and top-set garlic) is similar to the tree onion in being a hardy perennial that produces small bulblets at the top of each plant. You can propagate either by planting the top-set bulblets like those of a tree onion or by dividing at the base for replanting. If you're going to divide at the base, it's best to get it over with as soon in the springtime as you can. Plant bulbs or divisions spaced a half foot apart and about an inch underground. Otherwise, rocambole grows and is used like the other onions. Available from Richters and Nichols.

TREE ONION: Though lots of people call *Allium cepa* var. *viviparum* "Egyptian onions" or "top-sets," and I used to call them "multipliers," the majority now seems to be going with "tree onions," so I'll go along. They are a true native of the Americas, having been here before the white man arrived! They are a perennial onion—if you plant a row, you'll have it forevermore. Tree onions are the first edible thing in my spring garden. They'll take off long before the last frost; frosts don't bother them in the least. They are as persistent as chard. As well as they grow outside, though, they don't do well indoors or even in pots.

Harvesting Green Onions. After I go out and cut bunches of them to use as green onions, they immediately recommence growing. When you harvest a tree onion, *do not pull it up by the roots* as you would a green onion of the commoner sort that's been raised from seed (or from a set). You cut off a tree onion just above the ground, leaving the root, which promptly grows you another green onion. And so on. They get bigger and bigger. Eventually, as spring rolls along, their stalks become tough and inedible. Then it's farewell to green onions of the tree type, but by then other green things will be growing in your garden. Furthermore, once the tree top isn't good any more, its root has grown big enough so you can pull the whole thing, cut off the top, peel, and use the root like any large onion, although it will never get as large as a globe type. Tree onions never make big onion bulbs for winter onions as the globe onions do. Yet you can dig them up as needed through the winter, since they will be out there all winter, waiting for spring to take off again.

About Top-Sets. When the summer heat comes on, if you don't keep the green leaves cut off, the tree onion flowers and then grows a cluster of sets (bulblets) at the very tip-top of each long hollow green lead—they easily get 5 feet high if they've been generously watered. These onions are

similar to the regular sets of other types of onions except they grow in thin air instead of underground. If left alone, the stalk will next dry up, bend over, and deposit the sets somewhere on the ground. You will have more tree onions there next spring. But it's best to pick them and then plant them in a row exactly where you want them. Plant in the fall for earliest growth next spring, give to a friend, or dry to use in the kitchen.

Allium Group 4

Vegetables in this group (bunching onions, chives, garlic chives, globe and sweet onions, leeks, and pearl onions) reproduce by making seeds.

BUNCHING ONION: I don't know a Latin name for these, but they're distinct from the others. Seed companies sell them, and people grow and love them. They make great scallions. Park sells an Evergreen White Bunching Onion that grows in clusters of 4 to 9 and takes 120 days. True bunching onions are perennials. They never form a bulb; the white bottoms always stay thin and straight. Plant thickly in a block, in a place where they can stay and make it their own. It's possible to keep patches of bunching onions going for 10 or 20 years. Plant in early spring. The first year, don't harvest many. Let them go to seed and self-sow. Next spring they'll be the first edible thing in your garden, and from then on you can harvest as needed, although in early spring they're at their best.

CHIVES: Chives (*Allium schoenoprasum*) is a hardy perennial with deep green and hollow leaves. It grows 8–12 inches high. Chives and garlic chives are both nonbulbing, grasslike onions, but chives are smaller, the smallest culti-vated onion. Chives has tiny, lovely purple-to-rose–shaded flowers in midsummer and makes a nice border for a peren-nial bed.

Planting. You can order seeds from Thompson & Morgan, Le Jardin du Gourmet, Richters, Redwood City, etc. You can get starts of plants from Richters. Plant seeds ¼ inch deep in fertile soil in the early spring, in full sun in a place where they can stay for several years. Or start indoors and then transplant outside after the ground is warm. In the fall dig up part of a clump to transplant to an indoor pot. Then you'll also have fresh chives all winter. Do similar root divi-sion every 2–3 years in spring or fall to put more space be-tween clumps (figure 10 bulbs per clump, clumps set 10 inches apart). About 3 container plants provides enough for a family.

Harvesting. Chives are at their best in late spring. Cut off the thin grasslike top. Don't be afraid to cut your chives. They always seem able to recover and grow more, and cut-ting a plant keeps the leaves tender. You can also harvest the green-onionlike base and use it, but then it couldn't grow you more green tops. If you don't prevent flowering, fewer green leaves will grow. But the pomponlike flowers are pretty, so you could put 1 patch of chives in your flower garden. Withered leaves in spring means you should add fertilizer.

Saving Seed. Chives are a bee-pollinated perennial. If you were a professional gardener with several chive varieties, you'd have to raise each in isolation to give pure seed, but at home, crossing is almost never a problem with chives. The seed is black and very small. As soon as you can see it, harvest. Otherwise, you risk loss from shattering. Seeds re-main viable only about 2 years.

Preserving and Serving. To preserve, dry ¼-inch pieces at 110°F or in an airy place out of sunshine. Or freeze in little individual packages; they turn out nicer than dried. But fresh is nicest of all. To serve fresh, dried, or frozen chives, chop finely and add to green or potato salads, soups, fish, or sour cream, or mix with cottage cheese. Good with Jerusalem artichokes. Or add to white sauces or to eggs for scrambling.

GARLIC CHIVES: Garlic chives (*Allium tuberosum*), also known as Chinese chives or Oriental chives, are a different species from regular chives but are used in the same way. They are a hardy flowering (white) perennial. Because of their garlic flavor, you can also use them as a garlic substitute in any recipe.

Growing. Garlic chives differ from chives in that they are quicker to mature; have flat grasslike leaves rather than round, hollow ones; are less hardy (long harsh winters can kill unmulched plants); bear white flowers instead of purple; and have a delicate garlic flavor rather than an onion one. Unlike regular chives, garlic chives won't grow potted on your sunny windowsill in the winter; they turn dormant.

You can obtain garlic chive seed from Le Jardin du Gourmet, Redwood City, or Richters. The seed of garlic chives needs a warm start (70–80°F) and is usually started inside in flats. At transplanting time, work with them in a clump of about a dozen at once. Trim roots down to ½ inch, and plant them together out in the garden.

Propagating. Once they get to be several years old, divide them in spring as needed. Or in a southern climate, divide in the fall. To divide garlic chives, dig out the entire chives clump, wash the dirt away from its roots, trim them to a reasonable length, gently separate individual plants, and re-plant where you want them.

GLOBE ONION: Globe onions (*Allium cepa*) start out as green onions and then, if allowed to grow, end up with big roots and withered-away tops. They are as respectable and important as okra or peas. The onion-as-vegetable is important not only because it's good food but also because it's one of the garden's easiest vegetables to grow and one of the easiest to preserve over winter, even if all you have is an attic and a sack.

Varieties. Globes come in yellow, white, purple, red, Bermuda, and many other varieties. There are easily 50 different varieties. Ask the great gardeners in your neighborhood which globe onions they grow, or just start buying seed or sets and experimenting. In the South the Yellow

Bermuda, Granex, and Grano-type onions do well. Those kinds are planted in the fall and harvested in the spring, but they don't store well. In the middle between North and South, Sweet Spanish does well and stores well. The Bermuda won't winter-keep as well as the Sweet Spanish. In general, white varieties are milder and make better green onions; whites are also the kind you raise to get the little "pickling onions." Red varieties are sweetest of all but winter-keep the worst. Yellow varieties winter-keep the best. There are lots of good hybrids for the more northern zones; their problem is that they're hybrids. In the Northeast and Mideast, Southport White Globe, Southport Yellow Globe, Ebenezer, Early Yellow Globe, and Yellow Globe Danvers all do well and are very good long-storing onions. In very northern regions Early Harvest does well, but it's a hybrid.

Planting Seed. Seed catalogs may offer seed, sets, and/or plants. Seed is by far the cheapest way to start, sets are a little more expensive, and plants are the most expensive. But any of the three is cheaper than buying grown onions at the store. We plant onion seed to make green onions and sets and then harvest the sets and plant them the next year to grow the big onions. Onions really like wood ashes as well as the usual manure-compost stuff, so in the off-season you can get rid of some of your ash-pan ashes by dumping them where your onions will grow.

You can plant onion seed indoors as early as 6 weeks before the ground can be worked and transplant them later, but that's too much work for me. I just wait until the garden soil is more or less ready for some planting—as early as possible—and then plant them directly in the garden. Seed germinates best at 50–90°F. Allow 10 to 14 days. The more early top growth your onion makes, the bigger its bulb will be when the weather gets warm and the onion starts transferring food from leaves to root.

Planting Sets. Just make a shallow trench; put the sets in there, neck up, 2–3 inches apart; and cover to the neck with dirt. If you want to harvest green onions all summer long, plant onion seed or sets at intervals all spring. Summer is something else; it's much harder to get onion seeds going once dry hot weather sets in. Planting from seed you'll have green onions in 60–75 days; from sets, earlier yet; and from plants, in 25 or more days—quickest of all. But onion varieties and even individual onions differ widely in how quickly they grow—or whether they even grow at all. A certain part of the sets never do. Allow the seeds 2–4 months to grow to good-sized green onions, although you might be able to harvest them earlier. An easy way to raise winter onions is to plant seed the first summer to make sets, and then save the sets and plant again the next spring to make bulbs.

You can also plant sets in the late fall; with that head start, they will give you green onions about 2 weeks after they get going in the spring. With the right climate and the right onion, fall seeding makes growing globes for winter keeping even easier too. Walla Walla sweet onions are planted around August 25 to September 1. It's going through a cold winter that makes them sweet. Bermuda and Sweet Spanish onions are started in early September; the following spring, they'll take off to make those big lovely onions. Remember that they need long days to really put the growth on their bulbs.

Growing. Thin onions gradually as they grow by taking out the overcrowded ones and eating them. Either sets or

seed grow well in cool, wet spring weather. If your weather isn't wet, keep the onions well watered. You'll get the best results if you prevent the topsoil from drying clear out around them. When weeding, be careful not to disturb the shallow onion roots, because that may slow down their growth quite a bit.

Saving Sets. If you have seed-making onions, you can save either sets or seed. You get your first chance to save at the set stage, which generally comes way before the seed stage. Plant your seed and let the onion plants grow until the root bulb is about marble-sized. Then cure them by removing the tops and sun-drying the bottoms so they'll be able to overwinter. Store in a place that's cool, dry, and well ventilated, such as in a pair of worn-out panty hose. You need about a quart of sets to plant 100 feet of row. Figure the sets will shrink some over the winter and some won't grow. Plant next spring.

Mrs. Otto Kliewer of Frazer, MT, wrote me about another way to make "sets": "My mother-in-law tells me that if you have onions left over in the spring, you can cut them into sections and plant them, and each section will produce an onion. I have done that and it works!"

Saving Seeds. Onions produce seed by putting up one slender stalk that flowers and then makes seed. If you want your onions to keep putting their energy into making bulbs rather than divert it to making seed, just snap the flower stems off when they start to make flowers. Onion pollen is carried by insects; you can't have purebred seed unless you grow only one kind, have only one kind flowering at a time, or keep your different kinds quite separate. On the other hand, if they do cross, the results will be edible and may have hybrid vigor! Onions are biennial if you're going from seed to set and then from set to bulb. You save good bulbs from the plants you choose to be parents (your sets) and set them out the next spring. To keep seed-making plants from losing your onion seed by scattering before it is ripe on the plant, fasten a paper bag over the seed head with a rubber band. Then you can harvest seed, bag and all, when you're ready. But first give the insects a chance to do their job completely. Or you can gather your onion seed a little earlier and finish drying on a newspaper.

Onion seeds will last for years if well dried and sealed in glass where humidity can't get at them, but they will die in just a few months if you have them in a warm, humid place. Getting them too dry by artificial heating will kill them too. They are one of the shortest-lived seeds unless conditions are just right.

Harvesting Big Bulbs. In order to grow large, globe onions need long, sunny days. If they're planted from sets in the spring, a good part of them will be of storing size by fall. The ones that don't will simply be bigger sets to plant next spring. Most of my bulb onions never get as big as the store-bought ones, but that doesn't bother me a bit, because they're practically free and I have as many as I want, so there's just a little extra peeling. When the weather is hot enough to discourage growth, or you are satisfied with the onion size, or if they have started to dry up on top anyway, walk along your row and twist the green tops over. Ideally, onions are left in the ground until they are so mature that the tops dry up by themselves, but you can hurry them by twisting and breaking them over. Come back in a few days when you expect a spell of hot, sunny weather, and pull or dig them out of the ground.

Curing Bulbs. Let them sun-cure for 3 days: Spread them out on top of the ground until tops are thoroughly dry. Then sort. Bulbs that accidentally got cut with the spade go into the house to be used soon. Sets that for some reason didn't take off are cured some more (maybe 2 weeks in a shady, airy place) and then saved to be given another chance next year. They often make it the second time they are planted. The winter storage onions are cured some more and then bagged for keeping.

Storing. If properly cured and stored in a dry, airy place, many of your winter-keeper onions will last 4 or even 6 months. Every summer we bring in onions from sets by the gunnysackful for our winter supply. The trick is to cure them very well in the sun for 3 days or so before bringing in. Rip off the "set" portion before drying if you can. The onion grown from a set has 2 parts. One is small and extends up into a stiff hollow stem. That is the part you should rip off—or else the onions won't keep long.

After you bring your onions in from the field, continue drying them. We have tried all sorts of systems for this. You can braid them by the dry stems and hang them up in bunches with wire or twine around the bunch. Or put them in an "onion"-type bag or into old panty hose and hang them up. My current system, the easiest one yet, is to dump them into cardboard boxes and bring them into the kitchen. I check them occasionally by running my hands through the boxes, removing any damp ones. Any onion that feels the least bit damp is on the verge of spoiling. When the rest are absolutely bone-dry from the kitchen's heat (once that old wood cookstove starts going, it really gives them the treatment), they can go under the bed or into the attic—anywhere they won't freeze and will stay dry.

Slight freezing doesn't hurt them, provided you don't handle them while frozen. Good ventilation is very important to their storage place, and that's why they should be in some sort of loosely woven bag or hanging basket, or braided and hung up or some such, although I get away with a box. They do better stored dry and cool than dry and hot because with too much heat, they have a tendency to gradually dry away to layer upon layer of papery nothingness as winter goes by.

When we use our big winter onions, we take the largest first and gradually work our way down in size. That way if there are any left over come spring, they will be small ones suitable to use as sets in the spring planting.

Preserving. I think there's no point in trying to can or freeze onions when they are the easiest thing in the whole garden to keep year-round in a virtually "fresh" state by drying whole (I don't mean sliced and dried . . . I mean just like the big onions you buy in the store). They get stronger dried whole, but you expect strongness in an onion anyway. Here's how to dry them. It's a good start for making homemade onion powder!

Drying. For little pieces, slice onions up and down, from their stem to root ends, into fairly same-sized, ¼-inch-thick pieces and dry at 120°F. You can make an onion holder by putting 2 nails in your slicing board to hold the onion firmly. No blanching needed. Dry until light-colored and brittle. In an oven, dry below 135°F; onions can't stand more heat. Or sun-dry; it takes several days (take trays in at night). You can add dried onion to any soup, stew, etc.

Freezing. Be forewarned! A lady from Springfield, NJ, wrote me, "I have a small freezer chest, and when onions were on sale I froze some chopped onions. I put them in freezer bags and then in aluminum foil wrapping, and still they filled my freezer with such an odor that I finally ended up throwing them all out. What did I do wrong? My little 'bargain' in onions didn't prove to be a bargain at all for me."

Start by removing the outside skin, roots, and top. Chop. Bag *as airtight as you can,* and freeze. No blanching needed. It's handy to have some ready-chopped this way. They'll stay prime about 2 months in the freezer.

Weep No More. In an earlier edition of this book I mentioned crying over onions. Well, some thoughtful readers cured me of that. Frances Hanken wrote me from Lucerne Valley, CA: "Please, Carla, weep no more—all you need do is keep a supply of onions in the refrigerator. Then when you cut them up, you will find no tears at all. I've used onions in cooking for so many years, and since I've 'cooled it,' no tears for me!" Terry Bedard, Warner Robins, GA, told me her simple preventive: "Five to 10 minutes before using onions, put them in the freezer. It has no effect on the onion's texture or flavor, but it completely kills the strong fumes and just that easy, no more crying." Another reader told me: "I was told to hold a bread crust between my teeth. I figured out that meant to breathe through my mouth. It works!" Sarah Johnson, Kirkland, WA: "Onions make you cry because of the enzyme allinase. It bonds with sulphur and activates when exposed to air. Cutting under running water helps." Two other readers agreed with that system.

Cooking. Peel the paper skin off big ones, boil until done, and serve with a white or cheese sauce poured over them. Or bake big onions in their skins like potatoes, 30 to 40 minutes at 350°F. Or slice a bunch of onions, saute until golden in some cooking oil, and add sliced apples, raisins, and a dash of vinegar or lemon juice; cover and steam until the apples are softened. Salt and pepper to taste.

➢ *MOCK CHICKEN Finely chop 1 onion and cook in a little butter, but don't brown. Add a small skinned and chopped tomato, 1 t. mixed herbs, salt and pepper, and 1 beaten egg. Cook slowly until mixture thickens. Put on biscuits and garnish with parsley. From a Utah mother of 13 who knows how to stretch an onion!*

➢ *CREAMED ONIONS Make a white sauce by browning flour in melted butter. Thin it with cream or milk and cook it until it's gravylike. Boil whole onions in water; add a little salt to season. When they're tender, remove to a dish. Pour sauce over onions.*

➢ *ONION JUICE Cut a slice from the root end of the onion and scrape out the juice with the edge of a teaspoon. Or squeeze out juice using a lemon squeezer that you keep especially for this purpose.*

➢ *ONION POWDER Peel away the skin of large onions (1 onion gives 3 T. powder). Cut into thin slices. Dry them thoroughly. Then grind or pound to a fine powder. Keep in a shaker jar.*

➢ *ONION SALT Mix table salt and onion powder in whatever proportion you prefer.*

➢ *OLD-TIME ONION COUGH SYRUP From Clara Magers, Modesto, CA: "My mother took big red home-grown onions, sliced them, stacked them in alternate layers with sugar in a quart fruit jar, and let it set overnight. Then the next day she turned the jar upside down on a saucer, and the juice was cough medicine."*

LEEK: The leek (*Allium porrum*, a.k.a. *Allium ampeloprasum*, Porrum group) is grown for its fleshy stem, which is kind of like a bulb onion's root that goes up and up, 7½ to 9 inches long, 1 to 2 inches thick, depending on variety, etc. Leeks are harder to grow than globe onions. They don't make a bulb and aren't suitable for winter keeping by drying. On the other hand, you can harvest them at any time. And where winters are reasonably mild, leeks can winter through in the garden, pulled as needed.

Planting. A typical leek variety needs 105 to 130 days to get from germination to maturity for harvest. If you're going to start them in the house, plant them as early as 50 days before the frostfree date. Otherwise, plant in the garden 30 days before. If you plant them 6 inches apart, you could harvest 100 from a 50-foot row. Make rows about 2 feet. Plant ½ inch apart and ¼ inch deep. Then transplant to 3 or 4 inches apart. They'll be 7 to 10 days to germination. To grow leeks in a container, supply ¼ gal. soil for each plant. The container should be at least 1 foot deep. Leave 6 inches between plants, or distribute about 4 in a 12-inch pot. Both real hot and real cold weather hinder their growth.

Lane's Leek-Growing System. Leek-loving Lane says: "I have trouble growing storage onions, so I grow lots of leeks. They spend a full year in the garden, from planting until bolting, and I can't always spare the space that long. So I plant my year's supply crammed together in a seed bed. It will be a couple of months before they need transplanting, so you can grow a whole crop of greens in the space where they will go. And it's easier to space transplants than seeds. Cut off the top few inches when you transplant, and put the plants about 2 inches apart. That's so you can enjoy the scallion stage—delicious!—while thinning to 6 inches apart. Every few weeks, pull some soil up around the leek shaft, keeping it below the first leaf opening so you don't get dirt inside. That gives you more white shaft, which has the best flavor and texture. Garden books will tell you to plant in a trench and fill it in gradually, but my way is easier. Leeks and kale are my winter stalwarts. Only once in 14 years of northeasters, ice storms and blizzards have I lost them all." In a colder climate, mulching well with straw or some such or transplanting to a storage cold frame helps preserve leeks for winter eating.

Saving Seed. Leeks are biennial. Leeks for seed can stay in the garden all winter, even in the north. The next year they'll raise a seed stalk that bees will pollinate. Leeks do need isolation from closely related alliums to breed true. Seed is viable about 3 years. Follow directions for globe onions.

Root Cellar Storage. Dig them up from the garden, and root in sand or soil in a box in your cellar. If you water them once in a while, they'll keep a few months and maybe more.

Drying. Trim off roots and top. Slice ⅛ inch thick. Separate rings. Dry as you would globe onions.

Preparing. Leek is a very mellow onion. Fully mature leeks have a thick stem up to 2 inches wide and 4 to 6 inches high. Cut off roots and tops, leaving the white stem and the lower part of the leaves. The leeks' topmost leaves will probably be tough. Either discard them or put them in something that will be boiling a long time, like your stockpot. Wash them carefully, being sure to get rid of any dirt that got into the tops. A good system is to cut the leek in half from root to top and then hold it under running water or swish it in a pan of water, pulling off layers and rinsing each. Then shake dry. They're good substituted in almost any onion or asparagus recipe.

❧ *SAUTEED LEEKS* *Thinly slice leeks and cook over low heat with thinly sliced mushrooms.*

❧ *BOILED LEEKS* *Wash and trim, leaving about 1½ inches of the green top. Boil until tender. Drain. Serve with melted butter. Or cover the cooked stalks with salt, pepper, and grated cheese. Then set under the broiler until the cheese has melted. Or serve on toast, covered with a white sauce. Or drain, chill, and serve as a salad covered with French dressing.*

❧ *BAKED LEEKS* *Parboil 5 minutes in boiling water. Drain. Cut into 2-inch pieces and put into an ovenproof dish with salt, pepper, and enough meat stock or consomme to cover. Bake at 325°F for 30 minutes.*

❧ *LEEK SOUP* *This can be made in as many ways as onion soup. Boil leeks with pork and potatoes, or with beef and potatoes. Or cut the white part of the leek into thin slices and precook by frying before adding to the soup. Or make a cream soup and grate the leek before adding it. Serve with crackers or croutons.*

PEARL ONION: These are basically pickling onions, the tiny whites. They can be a European variety of onion, or another type of onion—usually a globe type grown as if for a set. When planting globes destined to be pickling onions, space closely (about 1 inch apart and rows as little as 8 inches apart) and keep an eye on them, because they'll be maturing early. Harvest as soon as they get nice and round but are still small. Territorial Seed Co. offers a variety of pickling onion.

True pearl onions resemble garlic in that they have just a single layer of vegetable flesh. They're attractive in the garden. Even at maturity, pearl onion bulbs are as small as a cherry. (Small white onions are frequently substituted in recipes for pearl onions, and they work just as well.) To cook with pearl onions, first dip them into boiling water. Then the skins slip off. They're so small that you don't have to cut them up. And they're really "tearless."

❧ *PICKLED ONIONS* *Small "pearl" onions are best. Use onions that are small and nearly the same size. Peel until the white is reached. When peeled, put them into a strong brine of salt and water for 24 hours, and then boil. Strain and dry the onions. Put them into jars or bottles and cover with boiled and cooled vinegar. Flavor with peppercorns, white mustard, sliced horseradish, and/or a little mace. Cover.*

❧ *FERN'S PICKLED PEARLS* *Start out with very small bulbs that you have saved set-style from "pearl" or any other sort of white-rooted onion. Fern Archibald, Morgantown, IN, sent this recipe; it has been in her family for 200 years! "Select small white onions. Peel (if held under water, will not affect eyes). After peeling, cover with a rather strong brine, keeping onions under by laying a plate on top. Let stand for 2 days. Drain and place in a new brine for same length of time. Then boil in still another brine for 3–4 minutes. After boiling, put them in clear, cold water to freshen. Leave them in the cold water 4–5 hours. Drain and pack in jars. Scatter whole cloves, pepper, and mace among them. Fill up the jars with scalding vinegar to each gallon of which has been added a cup of sugar. Seal while hot. Good in 4–5 weeks, but better in 3–4 months."*

❧ *ALMOST PLAIN CANNED TINY ONIONS* *Pour boiling water over them. Let them soak in it a few minutes. Drain and they'll easily peel. Now add onions to a boiling mix of vinegar and water (1 c. vinegar per 1 gal. water), bring to a boil, and boil 5 minutes. Separate onions and their liquid (save it!). Pack the onions into clean, hot jars (pints only), leaving 1 inch headspace. Add 3 T. salt to the gallon of vinegar-water and pour it over the onions in the jars. Put on lids. Pressure-can only for 25 minutes. If using a weighted-gauge canner, set at 10 lb. pressure at 0–1,000 feet above sea level; at higher altitudes, set at 15 lb. If using a dial-gauge canner, set at 11 lb. pressure at 0–2,000 feet above sea level; 12 lb. at 2,001–4,000 feet; 13 lb. at 4,001–6,000 feet; 14 lb. at 6,001–8,000 feet; or 15 lb. above 8,000 feet.*

THE LEAVES WE EAT
Introduction to Greens

Leaves. We eat them raw in salads and cooked in all kinds of dishes, getting strength from their vitamins as Popeye did. Basically, greens are edible-leaved plants. They're all annuals—or biennials and perennials planted each year from seed as if they were annuals—because the tender new leaves are the best.

CLIMATE/TIME OF YEAR: Climate and the time of year you want to harvest are factors in choosing what greens to plant. Some—endive, kale, lettuce, mustard, and spinach—do best if planted in early spring or in late fall but don't do well in hot weather, unless they get a lot of shade. If you live where summers are very hot, then chard, collards, and New Zealand spinach are best, although even they may need some shade if it's too hot.

Winter Greens. Most salad greens grow best in spring and fall, but it is possible to have salad year-round if you grow the right greens in the right way. Harold Okubo wrote me from West Jordan, UT, about his experience with winter greens: "We have always tried to produce most of our food at home. I have an advantage over most people as I'm a commercial truck farmer (Japanese origin). There are ways to have some green leaf crops most of the winter. Like spinach—if you drill a patch about August 15 in this area, by September 30 it will be large enough, and it will be good all winter. You can plant leaf and head lettuce in the fall of the year and let the young seedlings winter over. The

The most important thing is to know if you're saving seed from an annual (spinach, lettuce) or a biennial (beets, turnips, chard, kale, collards, Chinese cabbage). In the case of spinach, the plant stops putting energy into making leaves and instead puts up a long stalk. We say it is "bolting." It will flower on top of the stalk, and where each flower was, seed will come. Maybe they call it "bolting" because with spinach and lettuce it seems to happen fast. It isn't any use trying to harvest greens if they have started to bolt.

When saving seed from plants like spinach and lettuce, be choosy about which plants you save it from. You want one of the last to go to seed rather than one of the first, which is difficult to manage if you are basically raising it for a food crop rather than a seed crop.

Most of the greens seeds have good longevity. Lettuce, endive, kale, collard, and Chinese cabbage seeds keep well for 5 years; chard and mustard green seeds keep well for 4 years.

---

lettuce will be ready to eat by April or May. If you put a plastic tent over some, it will be earlier yet." F.E. Pennington, Kelso, WA, wrote me: "Let turnips or rutabagas live through the winter. When they start sprouting in February or March, getting ready to go to seed, pick those little sprouts of 2 or 3 inches. They make the finest greens in the world and are the first green thing you can get from the garden. They must be picked twice a week and are good for a month or 6 weeks—unless your area is so cold that they freeze out." (For more on this, see entries for individual greens in this chapter and the "Undercover Gardening" section in Chapter 2.)

CLASSIFICATION OF GREENS: Seems like, at the end of each of the 25 years since I started this book, there've been even more greens than before: old-fashioned leafy greens, leafy parts of other vegetables that can be cooked as greens, wild greens made tame, imports from every continent on earth (America, Africa, Asia, Europe), and tropical greens like Malabar spinach and chaya, a spinach that grows on trees. How to sort them out? I looked at the same problem 25 years ago and simplified by dividing the greens into 2 basic groups: lettuces, usually eaten raw, and spinach types, usually eaten cooked.

Now that system is too narrow and simple. There are so many leafy greens, so many odd ones; some are just slight variations on old themes, true, but others are wildly different. Back then I took my country roots and country-girl identity so seriously that I would have been insulted by the suggestion that I lean on Latin botanical classifications. I was inclined to hide the fact that I had had 8 years of college and an A in botany before I married Mike and we went back to our rural roots in the West. Then I liked hanging out with country old-timers who had another kind of literacy. I wanted so much to learn everything they knew that wasn't written down anywhere and get it recorded before they were all gone. I soaked up not only their verbal style but also some of their prejudices.

Now I'm not only older but, I hope, wiser, with more perspective on the sources and varieties of knowledge. Wise enough that I'm grateful for the labor of generations of humble, anonymous plant classifiers who have painstakingly sorted all these green leaves out into their respective families. It's also helpful to group the plant relatives because they tend to have similar cultivation needs and kitchen uses. That saves repeating tedious instructions. For example, the brassicas and goosefoots are more often cooked. The chicories are as likely to be eaten cooked as raw. The

dandelion/lettuce family members are usually presented raw as salad. If I couldn't think about and present these grouped into those botanical families, I don't know how I would make sense of it all—either to myself, or for you.

The Green Groups
I. Non-Brassicas
A. The carpetweed: New Zealand spinach
B. The chicories: endive, escarole, radicchio, and witloof
C. The dandelion/lettuce group: dandelion and 4 lettuces—butterhead, crisphead, looseleaf, and romaine
D. The goosefoot greens: amaranth, beet greens, Good King Henry, lamb's-quarters, Malabar spinach, orach, purslane, sea purslane, spinach, Swiss chard, and water spinach
E. The sagebrush tribe's entry: edible chrysanthemum
F. The only edible valerian: corn salad

II. Brassicas
A. The cabbagy brassicas: Brussels sprouts, cabbage, and Chinese cabbage
B. The edible flower-bud and stem brassicas: broccoli, cauliflower, kohlrabi, raab, and sea kale
C. The leafy brassicas: collards, cress, kale, mizuna, mustard, rape, rocket, turnip greens, tyfon, and watercress

There are some additional greens that are essentially used as flavoring agents rather than a main dish. If they seemed to me to be flavoring herbs rather than basic salad greens (coriander, parsley, etc.), or wild species rather than domesticated (nettle, poke salet, etc.), I discussed them in Chapter 5. But I put dandelion here with its lettuce relatives.

HARVESTING, COOKING, AND PRESERVING GREENS
Harvesting. There are 2 different ways: by cutting off the whole plant about 2 or 3 inches above the ground, and by picking only the outside leaves and leaving the center ones to develop. If you cut off chard, endive, lettuce, mustard, and spinach the first way, they'll grow back just like grass. But for collards, kale, and New Zealand spinach, you must do it the second way. Take those outer leaves by cutting with a scissors or snapping them off by hand. If you keep up with them, you'll keep the outer leaves tender. If they get ahead of you, the outer leaves are likely to get tough. In that case, give them to chickens, cows, etc., and go in another layer to get the now-tender ones.

Or you can harvest whole plants of either type by thinning. All greens need enough space for some air to circulate between them. That allows them to dry off after a wetting. Plants that are thickly pressed together and can't dry off are much more likely to have disease or insect problems.

Cooking. Which greens to eat cooked is really a matter of opinion. Some people eat anything and everything raw. Some greens you can eat raw at one stage or in small amounts, but at maturity (or over-maturity!) or in quantity you'll definitely want to cook them. An advantage of cooked greens is that you can preserve them by canning, freezing, or drying. You grow your big crop in the summer and preserve it, and then you're done for the year.

To cook greens, first wash your leaves. Boil with or without salt (I don't use it). To add flavor, use water in which meat or vegetables have been cooked. Or serve buttered and peppered. Or with vinegar. Or season with bacon drippings, salt, and hot sauce. Mustard, kale, and turnip greens are specially good cooked in the water in which the meat has cooked and then served with the meat. Here are some great recipes for cooked greens.

🌱 *SIMPLE HOMESTEAD SPRING DINNER MENU Gather 2 lb. of some early greens. Steam or boil to tenderness. In a frying pan heat 2 T. butter. Stir in 3 T. flour and brown the flour. Add the water from cooking your greens and mix well to make a sauce. Serve greens, "gravy," boiled potatoes, and boiled (or fried) eggs.*

🌱 *MASHED POTATO/GREENS CASSEROLE Steam 3 c. chopped greens plus a handful of chopped onions (green or globe) until tender. Layer in a casserole dish with leftover mashed potatoes. Bake at 375°F until heated through. Slice cheese on top and continue heating until it melts. Serve.*

🌱 *RICE/GREENS Simmer 3 c. chopped cooking greens in 2 c. stock or soup broth until tender. Add 1 or 2 c. leftover cooked rice (brown or white), and continue heating until warmed through. Add 1 t. butter or oil, salt, and pepper, stir, and serve.*

🌱 *GREENS ROLL-UPS Steam ½ lb. cooking greens. Then chop coarsely. Add ¼ c. chopped onion, ¼ c. chopped bell pepper, 1 T. oregano, 6 oz. tomato paste, and ½ t. each of paprika and garlic powder. This is the filling. For the wrappers, make a dough of 3 c. whole wheat flour and 1 c. water (like noodle dough). Knead and divide in 10 pieces. Roll each piece into a square ½ inch thick. Spoon filling onto wrappers. Fold over the 2 diagonally opposite corners (the filling should be in a diagonal down the center, with the other 2 corners folded over, so it sort of spills out at the open sides). Bake at 350°F for 15 minutes until crust is golden. From Ruth of Bonaire.*

Step-by-Step Greens Freezing
1. Wash off bugs and dust from leaves. Put a big pan of water on to boil. (I bring greens into the house by the 5-gal. bucket.)
2. Cut in lengths of about 2½ inches.

3. Drop a load of greens into the boiling water. Let boil 3 minutes. (You can also blanch by steaming or even stir-frying!)
4. Scoop greens into a colander to drain. (I fish the greens out of the water using 2 potato mashers, the same way I do corn on the cob, one masher on each side.)
5. Hold under running cold water just long enough so that you can handle them. Or cool (immediately!) in ice water.
6. Pack in baggies, squeeze out most of the air, and fasten the neck with one of those little wires or tie it in a knot. Pack enough chard in the baggie for 1 meal for your family.
7. Immediately put in the freezer.
8. When you want to eat frozen greens, just turn out the frozen lump into a little water. Thaw and heat. Either butter them or serve them with vinegar.

Drying. If you have a choice, I think freezing is the best way to keep greens, but more can be done with dried greens than you might think. To dry spinach, beet tops, Swiss chard, or any other greens, start by making sure they are well washed and the roots are cut away and discarded. You'll have better results with young leaves than with old ones. If the stems seem thick, separate them out and discard, or dry them separately, because stems take longer to dry than leaves do. Slice both the leaf stalks and stems into sections about ¼ inch long, spread out on your drying screens or trays, and dry. They're done when they crumble easily into your hand.

To use dried greens, pour boiling water over and then simmer, covered, until tender. Or crumble into soup or sauce; finely grind dried greens and add to anything from soup to salad; or use it mixed with other dried vegetable powders to make instant vegetable soup. You can use it like a seasoning powder too.

Canning Loose-Leafed Greens. It is safer and tastier to freeze greens than to can them. If you do can, you must use a pressure canner. Choose fresh, tender greens. Wash and cull out bad leaves. Remove tough stems and midribs. Make sure you have rinsed away all the dirt. Blanch by steaming, briefly boiling, or stir-frying until wilted. Loosely pack hot greens into hot jars. Optional: Add ¼ t. salt per pint, ½ t. per quart. Pour over enough boiling water to cover, but leave 1 inch headspace. Process in pressure canner: pints 70 minutes, quarts 90 minutes. If using a weighted-gauge canner, set at 10 lb. pressure at 0–1,000 feet above sea level; at higher altitudes, set at 15 lb. If using a dial-gauge canner, set at 11 lb. pressure at 0–2,000 feet above sea level; 12 lb. at 2,001–4,000 feet; 13 lb. at 4,001–6,000 feet; 14 lb. at 6,001–8,000 feet; or 15 lb. above 8,000 feet.

SALAD MAKING: In season we have salad every day. I send the children out to the garden to cut lettuce and pull a few green onions. My mother taught me to tear the lettuce with my fingers for the salad rather than cut it. So I tear it into pieces after washing and patting it dry inside a fuzzy towel. (Not all the way dry, of course, but near enough.) Then I add the young green onions, chopped fine; radishes, sliced thin; and dressing. Or grated peeled turnip. Some grated cabbage or carrot, too, or beets if I feel like it and have the vegetables. I use the part of the grater that makes long thin slivers.

A combination of different kinds of leaf lettuce, fresh from the garden, is delicious and full of vitamins. And you can add so many different things: chunks of garden tomato or grated green peppers, chopped green onion, or grated carrot. For salad dressing I usually make a mixture of two-thirds salad oil and one-third vinegar, and then add salt and garlic salt. For fancier dressings I add a little lemon juice, pepper, or a pinch of dry mustard. If you add any kind of seafood, pour on some lemon juice and use a mayonnaise dressing.

When people come up to me and say, "I hear you're writing a cookbook," I scarcely know what to say because what I really feel like is a noncook. My own personal cooking style is to cook foods as simply and quickly as possible. My great aim is just to somehow keep the 6 other mouths in this family so busy chewing that they can't complain. It's plain old-fashioned cooking. Lots of everything but nothing fancy. I've never made a pie in my life. Someday I'm going to. I'd really like to if I could just get around to it. I have made maybe a thousand loaves of bread—I've no idea how many. That's the staff of life here. That, and plain meat and gravy, potatoes, cooked vegetables, and the salad in season.

Homemade Salad Dressings. Next is a section on salad dressings. After that you'll find a section on how to make mayonnaise. This may seem like a strange place to put it, because you don't put mayonnaise on a tossed salad unless it also contains seafood, chicken, meat, eggs, or some such. But where else in this book would you put mayonnaise?

I make all my own salad dressings. Mine don't taste nearly as exotic as the store ones to me, but Mike claims they are much better. I don't offer much variety in the salad dressing department either. It's usually a vinegar and oil dressing, a wilted lettuce dressing, or homemade mayonnaise. Herbwise, though, I'm liable to throw in anything, and that really flavors them up.

For dressings for potato salad, see "Potatoes" under "Starchy Roots." For coleslaw dressing, see "Cabbage" under "The Wonderful, Motley Brassica Horde."

☙ *TWO-QUARTS SALAD DRESSING Mix together 1 qt. buttermilk and 1 qt. mayonnaise. Use wire whip or spoon,*

not a blender. Add 1 T. salt, ½ t. garlic powder, 1 T. dry onion (or fresh), ½ t. pepper, 1 T. dried parsley, ½ t. dry mustard, dash of red pepper, 1 T. chopped capers, and ½ t. celery salt. Stir to mix well. Keep in refrigerator.

☙ *BLUE CHEESE DRESSING Add 3 or 4 oz. blue cheese and 1 T. lemon juice to 1 cup of Two-Quarts Salad Dressing (see preceding recipe).*

If you want to eat raw greens other than lettuce, I recommend a wilted lettuce dressing because they are mostly on the strong side. I use lettuce for green salads and cook other greens.

☙ *WILTED LETTUCE DRESSING My mother's regular salad dressing was wilted lettuce dressing. That's because she had lard but not oil, and this is one kind of salad dressing that uses lard. It's a delicious salad dressing, one that you can vary in many ways. You can fry bacon or side meat to get your lard and then crumble the bacon or cooked meat bits into the salad. That's the best tasting. But you can also start out with straight lard. I usually thicken my wilted lettuce dressing with egg yolks. If you make a small amount of dressing, it doesn't actually wilt the lettuce; it just dresses it. If you make a lot and pour it over hot, it does wilt the lettuce, but it tastes good that way too.*

Use about 1 lb. greens. This is great for any greens, including the stronger, tougher ones like New Zealand spinach. Wash and pat dry. Fry about 5 slices bacon that have been cut into little pieces. (You can use lard or any other oil, if you don't have bacon or do like lard.) Take out the bacon and all the grease but about 2 T. Add 3 T. vinegar and 2 T. sour cream. Blend 1 t. flour with an egg (not in a blender) and stir into pan mixture. Add ½ t. salt and 1 T. sugar or the equivalent in honey. When the salad dressing is thickened and is boiling hot, pour it over your greens. Add crumbled bacon, toss a moment to mix, and serve immediately. This dressing has to be poured hot on the lettuce or it doesn't taste right. Serve immediately. You can enrich with mustard and onion salt. It's also good on leaf lettuce (as opposed to head lettuce).

☙ *FRENCH DRESSING This is our quick and easy, favorite dressing on fresh garden lettuce. Wash about 1 qt. lettuce and pat dry inside a towel. Tear into pieces. Mix ¼ c. oil, 1 T. vinegar, about 1 T. lemon juice, ⅓ t. salt, and ½ t. garlic salt. Toss with lettuce and serve.*

☙ *LOW-CAL GARDEN FRENCH DRESSING Puree together ½ c. tomato juice, 2 T. lemon juice, 1 T. onion, 1 T. green pepper, 1 T. honey, ¼ t. salt, a pinch pepper, and 1 clove garlic. Chill at least an hour.*

☙ *CLASSY ITALIAN DRY MIX FOR SALAD DRESSING You can make this ahead of time and then mix for your salad as needed. Combine ⅓ c. any grated dry cheese and 1 T. each of garlic powder, onion powder, paprika, celery seeds, and sesame seeds. Optional: Add other herbs or dry mustard. Mix well and store airtight.*

To make a salad, combine 1 T. of your Classy Mix with ¼ c. vinegar and ½ c. oil. For a low-calorie dressing, leave out the oil. Or combine 1 T. mix with ¼ c. mayonnaise, ¼ c. unflavored yogurt, or ¼ c. sour cream. For more of a salad-dressing consistency, add 2 T. water and shake energetically in a covered container.

☙ *SOUR CREAM DRESSING You can still make a nice dressing without the above herbs by mixing 1 c. sour cream,*

2 T. lemon juice, 2 T. vinegar, ½ t. dry mustard, a grind of pepper, and ½ t. salt.

Homemade Mayonnaise. I've never really understood just what makes a person decide to send me a particular recipe, but I can sure tell you for a fact that they come in bunches. I've gotten more letters with ideas for preventing gas from dried beans, remedies for wasp stings, and recipes for zucchini breads and zucchini pickles than anything else. But running a close second to these are recipes for homemade mayonnaise! Which from now on I'm calling "mayo" 'cause I can spell that.

Traditionally mayo is made with eggs. But raw eggs can be the source of salmonella poisoning, so I'm including only eggless recipes.

❧ **EGGLESS MAYO** *"In a blender, combine 3 T. lemon juice, 1 T. dry mustard, and 2 chopped garlic cloves until blended. Then, while the blender whirls, dribble from a cup of vegetable oil, drop by drop, until the mayonnaise has thickened. (You might not need a whole cupful of oil.) This makes only a bit more than a cup. The garlic and mustard do the work of the egg yolks. Don't try to reduce the recipe or it won't work." From Ruth of Bonaire.*

❧ **NATURAL HYGIENE MAYO** *Blend 2 c. seed cheese (for recipe, see beginning of "Flower Seeds" section) with a chopped scallion, a chopped cucumber, 1 t. kelp powder, and/or 1 T. tamari. Blend about 2 minutes till smooth and creamy. From Ruth.*

❧ **TOFU MAYO (SOYNAISE)** *Using a blender, blend 1 c. soft tofu with 2 T. lemon juice, 1 t. tamari, 1 T. frozen apple juice concentrate or honey, and a pinch of garlic powder. Blend until smooth, scraping down sides of blender jar. You may need to add water, depending on how firm or soft the tofu was to begin with. From Ruth.*

Mayo-Based Salad Dressings. Making your own mayonnaise is just the beginning of good things. Then comes homemade Tartar Sauce for your fishwiches and homemade Thousand Island Dressing for salads.

❧ **THOUSAND ISLAND DRESSING** *Combine 1 c. mayonnaise, ¼ c. ketchup or chili sauce or some tomato stuff, 2 t. parsley, 1 T. finely chopped onion, a cut-up hard-boiled egg, 2 T. cut-up fine green pepper (if you have it), and ½ t. sweet basil or dill. If you don't have all that, don't worry; make it with what you have. Taste to see if it needs more salt, pepper, or anything else.*

❧ **TAHINI ISLAND DRESSING** *This is Ruth of Bonaire's veggie version of Thousand Island Dressing: "Chop about 2 c. tomatoes and whirl in blender with some minced onion, minced dill pickles, and maybe some garlic. Then add the juice of ½ lemon and 2–3 T. tahini (or as much as you want) to thicken it to salad-dressing consistency."*

❧ **TARTAR SAUCE** *The simplest way is to add ¼ c. chopped pickles and 1 T. capers to 1 c. mayonnaise. Or use only 1 T. chopped pickle and add, in addition to the capers and mayo, 1 t. onion juice and a dash of dry mustard. Or to your cup of homemade mayo, add 1 t. each chopped green onion, green olives, parsley, and pickles and 1 T. tarragon vinegar.*

February 7, 1977. Back when I was reading books instead of writing one, I used to wonder so much about the people who wrote them—what they were like, what things were like when they were writing. I'm sitting here in a not-very-clean orange bathrobe. It's one of 3 things left in the house that I can still get into because I'm 9-plus months pregnant, running overdue as usual. I'm sitting on the side of my bed in moccasins typing at a little desk my mother bought me to study at when I was in high school—*wow*, does that ever seem a long time ago. The big front drawer of it is missing. Probably some kid or other dragged it away to play with and lost it years ago, but the top still works fine to hold the typewriter. Dolly, Danny, and Becca are all in school now. Luke and Sara are tumbling all around me playing their games—now on top of the bed, now under the covers, now under the bed! Their noises are happy noises, and that's what matters. Mike is out working. This is the year of our tenth anniversary and it's the best yet.

That sounds like a glib phrase. It's more than that. The fact is that our first years together were awful, just awful, in any category you want to name. It took us years to learn how to live the love that got us married in the first place and then seemed to simply get buried forever under the debris of everyday living and its problems. We toughed out all those years mainly because both of us really wanted to stay married on the principle of it if nothing else, because children have a right to both their parents, because we never gave up at the same time, and because deep down inside we loved each other even when all we could find or feel was hate. Over years and years there were so many times I stood in the doorway and pleaded to him, "Please don't go." And there were times when I cried and stormed and said, "I can't take it anymore and you can just go!" But I never, never told him to leave at the same moment he was saying he wanted to leave. It was like we got to take turns giving up, but at least one person hanging on was enough to keep it going.

I'm telling you that in case you think I'm a saint who never did anything wrong or crazy, who never had a problem that lasted more than 5 minutes. But aging has its blessings, like every crisis and every suffering: Slowly we learned about each other, learned to accept each other for what we were, and learned not to keep a head full of bad stuff about what he or she isn't or what happened last week, last month, or last year. Forgiveness is one of the basics that nourish love. If one of you has to forgive the other for the more spectacular sins, the other may have to forgive you for being dull and self-righteous. A lifetime is a long time to try to live together, and if you think your boat is never going to rock, that's unreal. You're going to go through all kinds of horrible real-life nightmares, and you're going to survive them, come out better, and be able to look back and see that, in a way, the hard times were blessings.

Next come all the non-brassica greens, in their family groups. The leafy brassicas lead the all-brassica section after that.

THE NON-BRASSICA GREENS

In "The Leaves We Eat," I divided the greens by their botanical families into 8 basic groups. Here are all the non-brassica greens: carpetweed (New Zealand spinach), chicories, dandelion/lettuces, goosefoot greens, sagebrush (edible chrysanthemum), and valerian (corn salad). Look in the next section for the brassica greens.

The Carpetweed

NEW ZEALAND SPINACH: *Tetragonia expansa* is the only vegetable in the family Tetragoniaceae, the "carpetweeds." New Zealand spinach actually loves hot weather and can handle even hot, dry soils—although it actually grows well almost anywhere. It's a trailing, ground-cover–type plant with succulent, small, triangular-shaped leaves. It originally came from New Zealand and Australia and also thrives by oceans. No bug or disease bothers it. This is a good, nutritious choice for your hot summer season. Slugs and snails don't bother this green! The only thing New Zealand spinach can't take is frost.

Planting. Seeds are available from Hudson, Redwood City, and Bountiful Gardens. It germinates slowly, but you can speed it up by soaking the seeds 24 hours before planting. New Zealand spinach grows much larger than regular spinach. Plant in rows maybe 3 feet apart. Thin to 8 to 10 inches apart. If you're growing it for hot-weather greens, plant it where it will have some shade in summer; it will taste better that way. It grows well in containers and is especially attractive in hanging baskets or flowing over the side of a planter box. In a container, put 1 in a 12-inch pot or 3 in a 2-foot tub. It can handle some drought, but its taste will not be as good unless you keep it well watered.

Saving Seed. New Zealand spinach is a wind-pollinated annual in temperate zones, but it's a self-reseeding perennial in the south. What is good about it for growing greens, though, is a problem for growing seed—it takes a *long* time to make seed. So plants for seed usually must be started indoors and transplanted out after all danger of frost is over. Plant 18 inches apart, rows 3 feet apart. Even the flowering and seed making happens very slowly. First there are flowers at the bottom of a plant, and then gradually the blooming works its way up. Each seed pod has only a few seeds in it. Those pods will shatter if they mature on the plant and lose the seed, so you need to bring the plants inside onto a newspaper or cloth surface to finish drying. Then you can shake the seed loose, discard the plants, and gather the seed. Seeds live about 5 years.

Harvesting. New Zealand spinach requires 40 to 55 days to maturity. Cutting off those growing tips every week keeps it growing tender new shoots. New Zealand spinach produces way better than its namesake. You can cut leaves off your New Zealand spinach for 3 or even 4 months. What you don't want to harvest is leaves that you let get old. They taste bitter and tough. You can eat stems but not flowers or pods. Jeannie Williams, Yoncalla, OR, who buys hers from Burpee, wrote me: "It can be picked over and over all summer, right up to a really hard freeze. The leaves slightly resemble ivy. My sister just whacks off the new growth, stems and all, but my sister-in-law picks each leaf separately." You can preserve by freezing.

Recipe Ideas. Serve raw in a salad with a strong-flavored dressing. Or cook together with barley and parsnip chunks—or with carrots, onions, potatoes, and meat (or just a meat bone)—for a soup. When cooked, it tastes like spinach. Or add to a vegetable/chicken mix in your wok and saute for an Asian dish. Or boil with herbs to tenderness; then chop, season, and mix with rich cream just before serving.

The Chicories

Chicory started out as a wild plant in the Mediterranean area. It's been cultivated and improved in Europe since the Middle Ages. (Old-time recipe books may call it "succory.") All the chicories (endive, escarole, radicchio, and witloof) have a sharp, somewhat bittersweet taste that's quite unlike the more familiar iceberg lettuce. Chicory is to lettuce as radish is to apple. But there are many varieties of chicory, some with quite different appearances and flavors. The chicories can be a hot-weather substitute for head lettuce, which gets buggy and rotten and stops growing when the real hot weather comes. You can eat chicories raw in a salad or cook the greens like spinach.

NOTE: Do not cook any of the chicories in an iron pan; that turns the leaves black!

NAMES: The naming of chicories is a zoo, a joke, a mishmash, a terror—or perhaps merely an extreme confusion. The botanical family is Compositae. The genus is *Cichorium* (chicory). Inside that genus, there are numerous wild and domesticated species of chicory and many varieties of each of those species.

Wild Chicory. Wild chicory grows in both Europe and the United States. Ours is a sturdy weed with little blue flowers and a root system that can penetrate any soil. When the greens are young, you can gather and use them in any chicory recipe. In the fall you can dig up wild chicory roots and force them like witloofs, or store and set them out in your garden—but I'd rather use the space for a domesticated chicory. There are so many highly developed, interesting varieties.

Domesticated Chicory. The 4 main domesticated chicory species are:

1. Asparagus chicory, grown for its fleshy stalks (not described in this book).
2. Root, "coffee," or "Magdeburgh" chicory, a perennial, whose 14–16-inch roots are dried, ground, and brewed to make a popular European beverage (seeds from Redwood City; for preparation see Chapter 5).
3. The loose-headed, leafy chicories. *Cichorium endivia* var. *crispa* is curly-leaved and is called "endive" or "curly endive." The other type, *Cichorium endivia* var. *latifolia,* has broad, flat leaves and is called "escarole." "Radicchio" (pronounced "rahd-EEK-ee-o"), a group of subspecies of the escaroles, is currently very popular. In Italian, "radicchio" means chicory, *any* chicory. In the United States, it means either loose-headed, red-leaved (when mature) varieties or radicchios that make little round iceberg-type heads.
4. Witloof chicory (*Cichorium intybus*) is grown for its big roots, which are then "forced" (coaxed to grow new green tops) in winter in the dark of your basement—tops that look like white romaine and are called "chicons" or "Belgian endive" or are misnamed "endive."

This being the section on greens, it's categories 3 and 4 that are covered below. In the following information, where one type of chicory differs from the others, its particular guidelines are given under its specific plant name. Recipe ideas given below for any one chicory variety are likely to work for any other, as long as you're in the same basic chicory category of loose-headed or witloof.

PLANTING: A further difficulty in classifying chicory is that a few of your plants are likely to look unlike the rest, since many of these species are not a single infallible type but grow from seed with a genetic scatter. Make sure they have enough nitrogen to grow fast, as they taste best if they go as quickly as possible from seed to maturity. Once started, chicory basically does the rest on its own, although it grows slowly compared to lettuce.

HARVESTING AND BLANCHING: Pick outer leaves, leaving the inner ones to grow. Or gradually thin, using the plants you've pulled as your table greens. All the chicories are less bitter if blanched, but the bitterness is caused by their abundant vitamins. The milder they taste, the less vitamins they have. So blanching is an option, but it's not necessarily the best one. On the other hand, some gardeners are eating so many vitamins that a few less is really no great loss! And they like to set a gourmet table.

ABOUT LOOSE-HEADED CHICORIES (ENDIVE/ESCAROLE)

Blanching. Do this when the weather is dry, the plant is dry, and you're expecting a couple weeks of dry weather. (If it rains, set the leaves free until they're dry again, and then start over; otherwise they're likely to rot.) Using both your hands, gather the outer leaves together and pull them up to cover the center. Fasten them thus with string, a large rubber band, or some such. Let blanch about 2 weeks. Best to harvest or at least check on them after that 2 weeks is up, because sometimes the covering causes plant crowns to start to rot.

Harvesting. Cut off the whole plant, within 1 or 2 inches of the root top. Hot weather tends to make endive and escarole get bitter and bolt. They store well, either in a root cellar or just in your fridge in a bag, if dried off on the outside before storing. Storage time makes their taste milder. Or leave in the garden and mulch, and they'll last like that.

ENDIVE: Called "chicorée frisée" in French, it is indeed curly and frizzy; it's also low-growing. Endive is very hardy and easy to grow, although if you live in a very rainy zone, some protection from endless rain will improve your harvest.

Planting. Endive can be harvested young, although it needs about 95 days to full growth. To prevent bolting, plant your spring crop as soon as your soil can be worked—around May 1—because endive is frost resistant. (See planting directions and container-growing advice under "The Lettuces." It all applies.) Most endive varieties don't do well in hot weather. If you have a relatively cool summer, you can direct-seed a crop into the garden in midsummer. Otherwise, plant your fall crop about August 1. Or get one of the varieties that cope well with hot weather and rarely bolt, such as Salad King Green Curled. Plant ¼ to ½ inch deep, rows 18 inches apart. Thin to a foot apart.

Using. Home-grown endive usually tastes much better than the store-bought product. After the first few frosts, the taste is best of all. After harvest, store inside a plastic bag in your fridge. Endive keeps for a surprisingly long time like that, and it gets milder when stored that way. The center leaves will always be paler and milder than the outside ones. Use those center leaves in a raw salad mixed with other greens and a somewhat sweet dressing. You can use the outer ones in a recipe for cooked chicory if they're too strong for you in the salad.

➢ *ENDIVE SALAD Slice endive lengthwise or crosswise into a salad. Some people pick off the green outer leaves and use only the light-colored, feathery leaves. I think they're all fine. Wash thoroughly and cut off discolored parts. Chill until crisp before making your salad. For a plain endive salad, serve with a French dressing and garnish with paprika and parsley (and rings of green pepper if you have it).*

➢ *ENDIVE POTATO SALAD Cut 2 c. boiled potatoes into slices and marinate 1 hour with salt and pepper, oil, and vinegar (a vinegar and oil "dressing"). Get ready 4 hard-boiled eggs. Prepare the endive. Mix sliced, marinated potatoes and endive. Arrange the boiled eggs in quarters over the top and pour French dressing over all.*

ESCAROLE: Countries around the Mediterranean enjoy escarole as a cooking green. This plant has green outer leaves; the leaves grow paler (and less bitter) as you move to its center. Unlike the leaves of curly endive, these are broad and wavy. Sometimes this plant is called "broadleaf endive." There is a headed green variety called "Pain du Sucre," "Italian lettuce," or "sugar hat." About 90 days to maturity. Plant like endive.

Recipe Ideas. You can fill the center of an escarole head with a rice/meat mix and bake. Or serve Italian-style, sauteed with sliced tomatoes, mushrooms, and chopped onion with spaghetti sauce poured over. Or serve German-style, sauteed with chopped cabbage and sausage. Or combine with milder greens and chopped salad vegetables, cheese bits, and a vinegar/oil dressing. Or combine with crushed garlic, sliced hard-boiled eggs, and chopped tomato with a vinegar/oil dressing. Or add to a tomato-rice-chicken soup. Or wrap leaves around meat or fish and bake. Or serve with a hot bacon-onion "wilted lettuce" dressing. You can use a radicchio in any of these recipes, too, since radicchio is an endive variety.

RADICCHIO: Some types of radicchio are hybrid, some open-pollinated. Radicchio will grow throughout the United States. It doesn't start out red. Your little plants will look as green as lettuce all the way up until when the cold fall weather

Radicchio

Endive

begins. Then, finally, their leaves will change to a range of reds, from pink to dark burgundy. They don't start out with the interesting shapes you see in stores either, like the Verona radicchio that resembles a small red cabbage or the Treviso variety that looks like a head of red romaine lettuce.

Recipe Ideas. Cook in chicken stock; add thick cream or cream sauce. Combine pureed chicory with cheese, egg, and broccoli, and bake. Cook together with meat, onions, and potatoes by placing a layer of chicory leaves over the rest. (For a chayote/radicchio salad recipe, see "Chayote" under "Exotic Squashes" in the "Squashes" section. See "Escarole" earlier in this section for other suitable recipes.)

☙ *BROILED RADICCHIO This is a good use for slightly raggedy plants. Preheat broiler to 450°F. Heat ½ c. olive oil in a small skillet. Add 2 sliced cloves garlic. Cook over low heat until garlic begins to turn color. Remove from heat and strain it. Add 2 T. fresh lemon juice and a dash each of salt and pepper. Cut 2 medium heads of radicchio in half lengthwise and brush surface with olive oil mixture. Place cut side down on a hot broiling pan. Cook 3 to 5 minutes, turning once, until radicchio is dull brown and edges are slightly crisped. Transfer to plates and pour remaining oil over the top. From Lane Morgan's Winter Harvest Cookbook (Sasquatch Books, 1990).*

WITLOOF: This variety of chicory is grown for its large root. The leaves are edible, but harvesting many—or any—harms the root's growth. You want as much energy stored in that root as possible. Don't start witloof plants too early in the spring because if the plants have gone to seed before you move them to the cellar, they can't be used for "forcing"—it doesn't work. So plant in late spring or early summer. Thin to 6 inches apart. Make rows at least 2 feet apart. The plants will grow as tall as 2 to 4 feet.
NOTE: Do not put raw manure in witloof's soil. It causes crooked roots.

Harvesting Roots. Dig up the roots in the fall after you've had a severe frost. They need to have been frozen to break their dormancy before being brought in. Then cut off the tops, leaving just an inch of so of stem. Pack them upright, with considerable soil still on the roots and soil between each root, in a container 17 to 21 inches deep that has holes in the bottom so surplus water can drain out. You can crowd them, and it doesn't matter how poor the soil is that they're packed in as long as it's about 10 inches deep (enough to cover them) and damp. Now spread 6 to 8 inches of sand or sawdust over the top of the root. (Sawdust is easier to clean off the chicons.) Witloof will last easily in a root cellar for a couple of months.

Growing Chicons. You "force" the witloof roots by moving them someplace 50°F or somewhat warmer (but over 60°F they have looser leaves and more bitter flavor) and beginning to water them weekly. Keep them in near-dark, as with newspapers over the box. The sprouts come at intervals, the first ones after about 20 days of moisture. When you see the tip top of the blanched, mild-flavored, crunchy, romaine-shaped top called a "chicon" or "Belgian endive" poke up you can harvest. Cut it off where it meets the root being careful not to cut off the bottom 1 inch of greens, the "root crown." Then leave the root in place and it will grow a second, smaller, chicon (maybe even a third). Chicons are good winter greens for either raw or cooked use, but they need to be used soon. Usually forcing is done anytime from

November to April. Spent witloof roots can be used to make chicory coffee (see Chapter 5) or fed to livestock.

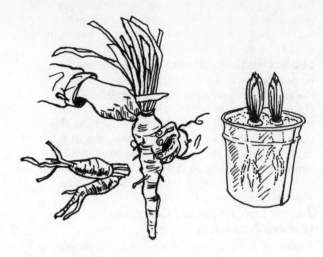

Keeping and Forcing Witloof in the Garden. In a mild winter climate, you can get your chicons this way. When the first frost comes, cut off the chicory tops without injuring the crowns. Now cover with dirt so that you end up scraping a ridge about 18 inches high. Leave it like that until around late December. Then take the dirt off one end of the row and cut off the white shoots. You cover the plants back up with dirt after this harvesting and mark with a stick to show how far down the row you harvested. You can keep coming back and working your way farther down the row. Be sure and harvest fairly often because if the chicory gets ahead of you and makes it through the ground, it will get bitter. And be sure to cover it back up after you harvest; that way, when you've come to the end of the row, you can just go back and start harvesting at the first end again all winter long, because many of those roots will make a second or even a third chicon!

Belgian Endive Recipe Ideas. Dunk into veggie dip and eat raw. Or steam and serve in halves or whole with Hollandaise sauce. Or boil until tender (takes only about 8 minutes and a little water) and serve with garlic butter. Or place in a baking dish, drizzle with lemon juice, dot with an herb butter mix, and bake. Or add to any soup.

☙ *COOKED CHICORY 1 Remove any discolored outside leaves. Cover the remaining head with boiling water and let stand for 5 minutes; then drain. Lay the head in a greased, shallow, ovenproof dish. Sprinkle with salt and pepper and squeeze a little lemon juice in each one. Add ¾ c. stock and dot each head with butter. Cover and cook with moderate heat. For the last 20 minutes, remove the cover, turn the chicory over, and let it brown.*

☙ *COOKED CHICORY 2 Leave stalks whole unless very large, in which case split them. Place in a frying pan and add beef or chicken stock until ½ inch deep. Salt to taste, cover, and cook gently until done. For variety you can serve it buttered or covered with white sauce.*

The Dandelion/Lettuce Group

DANDELION: I love those shining little flower suns. A cultivated dandelion (*Taraxacum officinale*) now is said to make better greens than wild dandelions, but I sure haven't grown them on purpose. But dandelions have uses: You can make a root "coffee" (see Chapter 5) from them, use them for dyeing (the blossoms make pale yellow dye; roots, yellow-brown), and more (keep reading) . . .

Peter Gail, Ph.D., is a wild food specialist who organizes The Annual Dandelion Cook-off, sponsors contest rules and prizes, and offers a book catalog including *The Dandelion Celebration: A Guide to Unexpected Cuisine*; Goosefoot Acres Press, 216-932-2145; fax 216-932-2187; PO Box 18016, Cleveland, OH 44118; **petergail@aol.com**.

Growing. Like most of us, I grow dandelions whether or not I intend to. Plant them as early as you like. Or cover with cloches or mulch existing plants in the fall for earliest spring growth. Dandelions are good container plants for apartment dwellers! Plant 2 seeds/inch. Thin (by using them) to 1 plant per 6 inches. Greens will be less bitter if they are grown from forced roots (chicons) or blanched by bunching up the leaves and tying them together so they get less sun, but I don't think it's worth the bother.

Harvesting. The greens will be ready 6 weeks after planting, the blossoms shortly after. Greens will be less bitter and coarse for use in salads if you pinch off the flower stalks. If you let them go to seed, you'll have volunteer dandelions there forever. A dandelion is not only a vigorous self-seeder (as we all know!), it also has a long tap root from which it can regenerate if you don't get it all out.

Using. Choose young, tender leaves. Wash. Add salad dressing. Leaves are good fixed wilted-lettuce–style with a hard-boiled egg. Or steam and season with 1 t. cider vinegar or lemon juice and generous butter. Reader Bobby Slover recommends: "As with many overly strong wild greens, prepare by boiling, pouring out water, and reboiling in new water. Simmer till done. You get enough vitamins." Start with quite a pile, as they boil down in amount.

Dandelion Buds. Some people gather only the buds instead of the flowers and preboil them a few minutes to remove some of the bitterness. But if you harvest them in early spring, they aren't particularly bitter. Cook as a vegetable mixed with onions. Serve with a seasoned (salt/pepper) butter sauce.

Dandelion Roots. Use like parsnips or salsify. Peel, slice, and simmer with a pinch of soda until almost fork-tender. Drain and then simmer until completely tender. Drain again. Season with salt, pepper, and butter.

Dandelion Chicons. Dig up large dandelion roots and proceed exactly as for witloof chicory. They'll grow the same.

⋙ *FRENCH-FRIED DANDELION BLOSSOMS* *From B. Rubinski, Quecreek, PA: "Did you ever French-fry dandelion blossoms? Sift ¾ c. flour and ½ t. salt into a bowl. Add ½ c. milk, 2 T. oil, and 1 beaten egg. Wash large fresh dandelion blossoms lightly, drain, and dip immediately into batter. (Make sure you leave a little stem to hold while dipping.) Dip each blossom into batter (drain excess batter over bowl) and drop a few at a time into hot oil heated to 375°F. Fry 2–3 minutes, turning occasionally, until golden brown. Drain."*

⋙ *DANDELION BLOSSOM FRITTERS* *Mildred Beitzel, Palouse, WA, wrote me: "These recipes are tasty and delicious, although that may sound strange if someone thinks of dandelions only as a bad weed to be pulled up and thrown away." Combine 1½ c. whole wheat flour, 2 t. baking powder, 1 T. sugar, and 1 t. salt. Add ½ c. milk, 1 beaten egg, and 1*

T. melted butter or oil. Mix well. Then stir in 2 c. rinsed dandelion blossoms. Drop by spoonfuls onto greased griddle and fry until golden brown.

⋙ *EASY FRIED DANDELION BLOSSOMS* *Gather blossoms in early morning. Rinse. Roll in beaten egg and then flour. Fry until golden brown.*

⋙ *DANDELION JELLY* *Pick 1 qt. of blossoms in the morning. Hold each flower by its calyx (the green base) and snip off the golden blossoms with scissors into your saucepans. Discard calyx. Boil blossoms in 1 qt. water for 3 minutes. Drain off 3 c. liquid. Add 1 package (1¾ oz.) powdered pectin and 2 T. lemon juice to the liquid. When it comes to a rolling boil, add 4½ c. sugar and a few drops of yellow food coloring. Boil about 3 minutes or until it reaches the jelly stage.*

LETTUCES: Lettuce growing goes back at least to the Greeks and Persians in 500 B.C. Columbus first brought lettuce seed to the Americas. There are many different kinds of lettuce, all *Lactuca sativa*. But they can be sorted into 5 basic types: butterhead, celtuce, crisphead, looseleaf, and romaine.

Butterhead. These are between head lettuce and pure leaf lettuce. They make a head but not a tight, blanched sort like crisphead lettuce. They are loose, leafy, and head-shaped. That gives them some of the best of both worlds. I don't even try to grow a crisphead lettuce in my garden, but every year I do grow some butterhead-type lettuce as well as leaf lettuce. Those are my 2 favorites in salads and, in my experience, the easiest to grow. Boston and Bibb lettuce are butterhead types, as is any lettuce described in a seed catalog as making a "loose head." The butterhead lettuces are green-leafed and healthy, have a wonderful garden-fresh flavor, and are ready to harvest only a little later than leaf lettuce. But butterheads, like crispheads, can't stand hot weather. You will have more wonderful lettuce than you can eat for a brief period. Then, when the weather turns hot, that's the end of it.

Celtuce. Celtuce has stems like celery and not much leaf. See "Celtuce" in "The Stems We Eat."

Crisphead. The most familiar crisphead is iceberg lettuce, the kind with the big, firm head that you buy in stores and eat in restaurants. Years ago it dominated the commercial lettuce market to the exclusion of all other salad greens, despite the fact that it has less color and taste and fewer vitamins and minerals than any other kind of lettuce. (It does store and transport well, though.) But crisphead lettuce is the hardest to grow in your home garden and is really the least desirable. And it takes twice as long to mature as leaf lettuce. The inside leaves of a head lettuce are blanched because the sun couldn't get at them. That's the reason for the milder taste and lower nutritional value. Hot weather, especially hot nights, is the worst thing for head lettuce; instead of making a head, it tends to go to seed and acquire a bitter taste in the process. Fulton, Great Lakes, and Imperial are varieties of crisphead lettuce. Space them 8 to 18 inches apart, wider for bigger heads.

Looseleaf. Looseleaf lettuces are the easiest to grow, the hardiest in hot weather, and the most nourishing. Slobolt is a famous hot-weather variety; Oak Leaf and Salad Bowl are 2 others. Once you're used to leaf lettuce, iceberg lettuce is almost too bland to bear. Leaf lettuce has at first experience a stronger taste, but you can soon get used to it and learn to love it. Leaf lettuce is ready long before the others, in 40 to 45 days, whereas head lettuce takes 80 to 95 days and needs all of it cool. There are many different varieties of looseleaf lettuce, including Simpson, Grand Rapids, and Salad Bowl.

Romaine. Also called "cos," this lettuce comes in several varieties such as Paris White, Valmaine, and Parris Island. Romaine leaves grow out of a tight central bunch and straight up instead of curling into a ball or waving loosely. Romaine tolerates more heat than head or butterhead lettuce but not as much as leaf lettuce. It's not as easy to grow as leaf lettuce, and it takes much longer. Germination is more spotty, so plant it thicker. Leaf lettuce matures in 40 to 45 days, while romaine needs 70 to 85 days; if you start romaine indoors and then transplant it, though, you'll enjoy its nutritious and flavorful leaves. It's often planted in late summer or fall in warm-climate places to avoid the heat. Plant ½ inch deep, ½ inch apart if you're going to transplant. Thin or transplant to 8 inches apart. Romaine varieties do best in the Pacific coast climate, but there's a limit to how much rain even romaine can appreciate, so consider a tunnel cloche.

When to Plant. In spring, plant hardy lettuce varieties at the same time as peas—as soon as you can get seed into the ground in the spring. They can endure some early freezes. If not, since seed's cheap, plant again. But leaf lettuce or any of the other noncrisphead lettuces are very perishable once harvested from the garden, and they don't last in the garden very long—an average of only 3 weeks. The answer to that is succession planting about every 2 or 3 weeks. With succession planting plus a cold frame, you can have lettuce every month of the year if you live in the South, and fresh lettuce for about 8 months of the year in a climate like the Midwest.

Winter Lettuce. To grow winter lettuce where it freezes, plant it in the garden in late summer (or in your cold frame in early fall), and then transplant to the cold frame right before first frost. There it will keep producing for some time. You can plant a fall crop in late July, another in early August, another in late August, and maybe even another in September. To save your latest crop during a frost, dig up plants, transplant them to pots or flats, and install in a sunny window inside your house, where they'll produce some more.

Avoiding Bolting. Lettuce is one of the seed makers that is triggered to mature by the long daylight periods of early summer. That means if you live in a warm part of the country where they grow lettuce all winter, and you plant your seed in October, your lettuce won't make seed until the following summer. The seed may lie dormant all winter, but it then comes up first thing in the spring. But if you plant it in late spring in the North, it soon makes seed. So for a longer harvest season and a delay of the seed making ("bolting"), plant as early in the spring as you can, indoors or out. In the very far south, you can grow lettuce in the winter months.

How to Plant. Lettuce likes deeply worked, crumbly soil that you have manured or composted the fall before,

because it has a puny root system that doesn't hunt for food effectively. The Cook's Garden offers many lettuce varieties, but every catalog has some. You can plant lettuce in the garden or start it indoors and transplant when in the 4-leaf stage. But I'm just too lazy to start it indoors and transplant when, with just a little more time, it will grow outdoors. Plant ¼ to ½ inch deep. For containers, put 1 plant in a 8-inch pot, 4 in a 12-inch pot. Their shallow roots can manage in a pot or flat only 6–8 inches deep. But plant several seeds and then thin.

Sun. For very hot weather choose looseleaf lettuce. But any lettuce seed is harder to sprout in hot weather. It helps to cover the newly planted seed with burlap or wet sawdust and keep it wet until after sprouting. Later you can shelter the lettuce from the sun by stretching burlap on upright sticks over the row like a light roof. In fact, professional growers grow lettuce under cheesecloth or fish netting laid over slats to cut back the sun's heat as much as 45 percent. They use a photographic light meter as a guide to getting the right amount.

Water. Lettuce needs water when the leaves begin to droop. If it doesn't rain, you'll have to irrigate. Base-type watering is a better irrigation for your lettuce than water sprinkled on because it's less inviting to bugs than moisture between the leaves. But sprinkling works if that's what you've got.

Air. Any lettuce will stand up better under heat if it is well thinned and air can get in there and circulate. When any kind of lettuce is crowded, the leaves may start to rot in heat. Then bugs move in by the millions. (Uncrowded lettuce has bugs too, but only some walking around that you can easily rinse off.) Speaking of pests, if slugs are a problem, install toads and leopard frogs. They like to rest under small piles of old hay or mulch during the day and hunt (slugs!) at night.

Thinning. Lettuce thinnings are good to eat—just cut off the root—so it helps your salad supply to thin in stages, as the plants need more room and as you need more lettuce! When thinning, be sure and pull the plant up root and all, because if you leave the root in there, it will try to grow again and pull nourishment from the other plants.

Saving Seed. Lettuce has a self-fertilizing (insect-pollinated) blossom, so even if you are growing several varieties in your own garden, they generally don't cross-pollinate. You can even save seed from varieties that have been grown separated by only one row of something else. The seed stalk develops by the fall of the first year. Stake the tall lettuce seed stalks (2 to 5 feet high) if they threaten to fall over and lose your seed. Seeds develop a couple of weeks after flowering, which goes on for about a month. So shaking the head into a paper bag every week or so gives you the most and cleanest seeds. Or, when all the seeds are fully developed, cut the seed stalks, dry on cloth or paper, and then shake off the rest of the seed. To save seed from fall plantings, mulch to get them through the winter to a bolting time. Lettuce seed survives about 5 years.

Harvesting. The nicest time to harvest in hot summer is early in the morning, before either you or the plants get hot. Then you wash your lettuce and put it in the refrigerator until you use it. If you cut lettuce leaves away fairly early in a plant's lifespan and it doesn't need thinning, keep watering; it'll keep growing more leaves for a while. That's especially true of leaf lettuces. Some of the special hot-weather varieties will let you keep harvesting for a surprising length of time. To use your lettuce like that, pick off outside leaves or cut so you leave about the bottom third of the plant. Then it will take off and grow again, for a while anyway.

Drying. There's no point in freezing or canning lettuce. Some people dry it, though. To do that, use tender inner leaves. Shred the leaves. Blanch until wilted. It takes about 1½ minutes in boiling water. Drain. Spread thinly over dehydrator trays or sun-drying trays. Dry at 120°F in a dehydrator or oven. Stir and rotate trays once in a while. When dry enough, a cool shred will crumble when rubbed between your fingers. Takes about 8–12 hours in a dehydrator, 2 or 3 days in the sun. Use dried lettuce in soups and in the recipes in "The Leaves We Eat."

The Goosefoot Greens

Amaranth is a more distant relative of this bunch, as are purslane and sea purslane. The rest (beet greens, Good King Henry, lamb's-quarters, Malabar spinach, orach, spinach, Swiss chard, and water spinach) are all closely related members of the family Chenopodiaceae—the beet, chard, spinach, and quinoa family.

Some food experts recommend that you boil the goosefoot greens before eating them. This is because they all contain more than the usual amount of oxalic acid (too much oxalate can cause kidney stones) and other chemicals that are harmful in excess. None of the goosefoot greens will send you to the hospital if you eat them raw in a salad. On the other hand, if you're going to eat a pound a day of them, I'd boil them before eating and discard the cooking water. Boiling flushes the bad guys (and unfortunately also some of the vitamins) into a solution that you can throw out.

AMARANTH, THE VEGETABLE: The various vegetable amaranths are also known as "Chinese spinach," "een choy," "hiyu," "tampala," "yin choy," "hin choy," "edible amaranth," and "amaranth spinach." Vegetable amaranths differ from the grain ones in requiring moisture throughout their growing cycle and in being able to tolerate as much as 15 inches of annual rainfall. This crop can be grown and harvested even during the downpours of West Africa's rainy season. Vegetable amaranths need well-manured ground. Amaranth greens are hardy in hot weather; they don't bolt, get bitter, or wilt. They are useful where summers are too hot for lettuce, spinach, or cabbage and in the soaking tropics. In the tropics amaranths will produce year-round and can reseed themselves naturally; they can also get places you don't want and become a nuisance. Ruth from Bonaire, an island in the Southern Caribbean with a forbiddingly desert climate, writes me that amaranth "grows wild on Bonaire. It grows in back of our house by the sewer. (Only place where anything grows.) We eat it steamed, drizzled with lemon juice." See "Grain Amaranth" in Chapter 3 for more information.

Planting. You can order from Burgess, Burpee, or Redwood City. Amaranth can be planted densely, up to 90 plants per square yard.

Harvesting. The leaves and stems can be eaten as soon as they get big enough to make it worth your effort, starting in 3–6 weeks. You can continue to cut greens off the plant weekly until the flowers develop. Then the leaves and stalks get fibrous and undesirable. Some varieties can put off that development for up 13 weeks after planting, some as long as 6 months. But sooner or later it happens.

Cooking. Cook amaranth leaves like turnip greens, collards, or spinach. Amaranth greens are rich in iron, calcium, vitamin A, and the same complementary amino acids, lysine and methionine, that make a complete protein in combination with other grains. Amaranth greens contain some oxalic acid and nitrate, almost exactly the same amount as in spinach, beet greens, and chard. If you want to detox, boil before eating.

➢ *BOILED VEGETABLE AMARANTH* Rinse the leaves and completely immerse in plentiful water. Boil 10 minutes. Discard water. Drain amaranth. Toss with vinegar and butter.

➢ *AMARANTH GREENS CASSEROLE* Butter a casserole dish. Mix 1 lb. cooked amaranth greens, 1 lb. cottage or ricotta cheese, and 1 beaten egg. Put mixture in the dish and bake at 350°F for a half hour.

BASELLA: See "Malabar Spinach."

BEET GREENS: This green tastes even better than chard. I'm putting about two-thirds chard and one-third beet greens into my freezer. I like the beety taste and the pretty red stems of the beet greens. So does Mike (whose idea this originally was). When harvested early and given plenty of water, the beets recover and grow more tops—or we can get greens from them when the roots are harvested. Use mixed with a bland lettuce, chopped onion, and hard-boiled egg to make a green salad. Or in a soup with carrots, potatoes, onion, and meat. Or boiled, drained, and served with butter.

GOOD KING HENRY: *Chenopodium bonus-henricus,* also known as "poor man's asparagus," or "wild spinach," is a wild perennial that can be cultivated. It used to be popular in European cottage gardens and is now enjoying somewhat of a comeback with the herb lovers. You can grow this plant to feed people or animals (chickens like it) or to use as green manure. Good King Henry prefers rich, well-drained soil plus half shade, although it can survive in full sun. Seeds are available from Bountiful Gardens, plants from Nichols.

Growing. Plant ⅛ inch deep, rows 18 inches apart, and thin to 12 inches apart. The plant will self-sow freely and keep itself going for years, so plant it in a wide bed in a place where it is welcome to stay. Because it's not picky about where it is, it's a perfect plant to put in a neglected place that undesirable weeds are currently occupying. It gets started early in the spring and grows 1 to 2 feet high, bearing arrow-shaped leaves. You can get even earlier spring growth by mulching with straw, and earlier growth yet by placing a bottomless box over some plants and covering it with a pane of glass, creating a greenhouse effect.

Eating. Good King Henry is an unusual green in that it shouldn't have its arrow-shaped leaves cut until after the first year. Substitute very young, tender leaves in any spinach or chard recipe. Then substitute shoots and flower buds in any asparagus recipe. Or break the leaves up, steam, and serve with a lemon sauce. Or add to a leaves to a vegetable soup. Or add whole leaves to other cooking-type greens, boil, and serve. Or stir-fry young shoots with sliced turnip and carrots and serve with a sweet-and-sour sauce. Or mix with avocado slices and other greens and serve with a strong-flavored salad dressing. You can also serve young shoots raw with a vegetable dip.

LAMB'S-QUARTERS: You can gather and use orach's wild relative, lamb's-quarters (*Chenopodium album*) the same way you use orach. Or buy the seed from Bountiful Gardens and plant it on purpose. The whole plant is edible. Grind seed as you would its relative, quinoa. Cook stems like a vegetable. Use leaves raw or cooked like spinach.

MALABAR SPINACH: This name applies to 2 *Basella* species, *Basella rubra* and *Basella alba*. It's also known as "Ceylon" or "Indian" spinach, "Malabar Nightshade," "Put" "Saan Choy," and "land kelp." This tropical goosefoot green comes from Southeast Asia and resembles the flowering white cabbage. It's a beautiful plant that does well in a hanging basket and is easily grown and quite productive. It's a good hot-weather substitute for spinach.

Seeds are available from Nichols, Redwood City, Bountiful Gardens, etc. Northerners start it indoors because it won't germinate until night temps are over 58°F, and it does best at higher temps than that. Outside, plant 1 inch deep, 1 inch apart, rows 2½ feet distant. Thin to 1 foot apart. Or transplant outdoors when frost is safely past. It needs plenty of water and something to climb. It will climb up a fence or trellis as high as 6 feet.

The leaves are large, thick, and dark green, and they taste milder than Swiss chard. Folks in the tropics wait and start cutting about 12 weeks after planting, but hurried northerners may start snipping in as little as 35 days. Can be eaten raw in salads or cooked. To cook, just steep a few minutes in very hot water. Malabar spinach leaves, when cooked, resemble kelp and have a thickening effect in soups just like okra. Pinch off flowers to keep the leaves growing. Leaves are good shredded and served in chicken stock with tofu chunks and ginger flavor. Incidentally, the red berries also thicken liquids. And they can be used to make a jelly.

ORACH: *Atriplex hortensis* used to be known as "mountain spinach" or "giant lamb's-quarters." Orach does best in regions where the spring is short and the soil is saline, alkaline, and dry—but it can do well in other places too. It produces longer and gives a larger total harvest than common spinach. It's a close relative of Good King Henry. Orach will go to seed in hot weather, so it's not the best green to plant for a midsummer harvest, unless you have Bountiful Garden's heat-resistant variety. It will self-seed.

Planting and Growing. Available from Abundant Life, Bountiful Gardens, etc., in a green and a beautiful red/purple (it changes to green when cooked) variety. Plant ¼ inch deep. Thin to 8 to 12 inches apart. Harvest young, when 4 to 6 inches, or else harvest the tender top growth, because lower leaves get tough. Left alone, it can grow as tall as 6 feet, but for salad keep pinching it back to a short, bushy plant. Or make succession plantings, figuring on maturity in 6 to 8 weeks after planting.

Using. Rabbits love it. People eat it raw or cooked. Pick and use fresh, since it gets limp fast. Substitute in any spinach recipe: Put a leaf in your sandwich, salad, quiche, casserole, cooked greens, etc. The flavor of cooked orach is sweet and mild, like spinach.

PURSLANE: *Portulaca oleracea* is a low-growing perennial that can thrive in any soil. Territorial's Garden Purslane is about 4 times as big, more succulent, and more upright than the wild one. Provide moisture until it gets started. After that it can also handle very dry conditions. Use leaves and stems in salad or cook like spinach. The flavor is sharp, but it's rich in vitamin C and omega-3 fatty acids that help prevent heart/circulatory problems. Bountiful Gardens and Territorial offer seed.

SEA PURSLANE: *Honkenya peploides,* also called sea chickweed, is a creeping, mat-forming seashore plant with fleshy leaves and tiny greenish white petals. The leaves and stems are edible. In Asia, sea purslane is used raw or made into pickles.

SPINACH: *Spinacia oleracea* responds to long days by going to seed. It reacts to hot weather, dry conditions, or bolting by getting bitter and tough. When it bolts, it also stops making new leaves. All the plant's energy then goes into stalk and flower. Spinach leaves don't get nearly as big as chard leaves.

That's the bad news. The good news is that spinach is a great-tasting early greens crop that is ready for harvest weeks before chard. It is the earliest next to dandelion greens. Lane Morgan says, "A lot of work has been done lately on bolt-resistant spinaches. Most of them are hybrids, but Territorial has at least one—Steadfast—that isn't. This means a nice June crop in this climate (north Pacific maritime), before the weather gets hot and the flavor suffers. (I think it's the daylight more than the heat that sets it off to bolt, but heat affects the taste.) But I love it most as a winter salad green—something to put with the mizuna and other strong-tasting stuff, and something to eat in early spring before the new lettuces get going. In this mild winter climate I harvest spinach from October to April, cutting leaves off as needed. That time of year bugs and disease don't bother it."

Planting. Plant spinach seed ¼ inch deep, 18 inches between rows, 12 inches between plants. Radish seeds germinate faster, so plant a few in there to mark the row. You can plant in a partial-shade site. Don't transplant thinnings; they don't do well. If container planting, put 4 plants in each 12-inch pot. You need at least ¼ gal. soil for each spinach plant, dirt at least 8 inches deep. Allow 3 to 6 inches between the plants.

Saving Seed. Spinach is a wind-pollinated, self-fertile annual. It won't cross with New Zealand spinach, but other spinach varieties will cross because spinach pollen is very fine and the wind carries it all over the place. So plant only one variety and hope you're far enough away from neighbors with closely related species while it is flowering. Save seed from late-bolting plants and good-sized, abundantly leafy ones. When plants get yellow, pull them out and hand-strip seeds from stalk. Seeds will remain viable about 5 years.

Harvesting and Preserving. Spinach will be grown in about 65 days. Cut off a little way above ground. Or pick it leaf by leaf like chard. It will keep growing unless it was about to bolt anyway. To preserve, follow the basic canning, freezing, and drying directions in "The Leaves We Eat." White crystals in canned spinach are just calcium oxalate; they can't be prevented and won't hurt.

Recipe Ideas. Put into a pie crust with a pimento-flavored white sauce and call it a mock meat pie. Or stir-fry with garlic in bacon grease. Or bake with layers of pasta/cheese mix alternating with layers of spinach. Or add to a mushroom soup or cream soup. Good in omelets. Great in quiche. Terrific baked with eggs and feta or another strong cheese. Good curried with potatoes. From gardening and food writer Lane Morgan: "Another good thing to do with spinach is steam it, add tamari, a little oil (sesame if you have it), and vinegar (rice vinegar if you have it), and let it marinate a while. Wonderful as a savory side dish with rice and tofu, tempura, or other Japanese-style dishes."

☙ *FRENCH SPINACH* From Karin Webber, Reseda, CA: *"You'll need 2 lb. fresh spinach, 1 large onion, 1 clove garlic, olive oil, butter, 2 beaten eggs, 1 c. freshly grated Parmesan cheese, salt, and freshly ground black pepper. Wash the leaves carefully, and the rest is easy as pie. Chop the onion and mince the garlic. Heat the olive oil in a very large kettle, and saute the onion and garlic in it for a few minutes. When the onion is transparent, add spinach and cover tightly. In about 3 minutes the spinach will be reduced to a fraction of its former bulk. Remove the lid and cook a few minutes longer. Remove from heat. Butter a medium-size baking dish. When spinach is somewhat cooled, stir in the 2 beaten eggs and ½ c. of the Parmesan cheese. Season with salt and pepper and pour mixture into baking dish. Sprinkle the remaining Parmesan over the top and dot with butter. Bake the spinach in a 275°F oven for about 10 to 15 minutes and serve steaming hot. It's delicious and it doubles easily."*

☙ *SPINACH LASAGNE* Make a batch of marinara (tomato sauce) and a batch of white sauce. Steam 1 lb. spinach until barely tender. Then chop it coarsely and combine with the white sauce. Also steam 3 large sliced zucchini. Now, into a 9 × 12-inch baking dish, spoon a thin layer of tomato sauce, a layer of uncooked wide noodles, one-third of the tomato sauce, a layer of half the zucchini slices, and half the spinach mixture. Then repeat noodle layer, tomato sauce layer, rest of zucchini, and rest of spinach. Finally, top with a last layer of noodles and the remaining one-third of tomato sauce. Bake at 350°F covered for a half hour and uncovered for another half hour. Let stand before serving. From Ruth of Bonaire.

SWISS CHARD: Botanically Swiss chard is a beet, *Beta vulgaris cicla*, with an undeveloped root and wonderful leaves. Gardeners in the hot interior United States favor it in the summer garden because it doesn't "bolt" the way spinach does. You can also plant it early because it's as hardy against spring frosts as it is against summer heat. Maritime gardeners often grow it for the winter garden too, planting in July, because it continues producing long after fall frosts. With some winter mulching, you can get early spring greens from this biennial from maybe February through May.

Planting. Fordhook Giant is a good kind. Ruby chard tends to be bitter. Plant as you would beets. To grow in a container, plant 1 to 2 seeds per inch, ½ inch deep. Later, thin some—eat the thinnings!

Saving Seed. Swiss chard is a wind-pollinated biennial. So for seed, don't cut it, and leave it in the ground all winter. In cold climates, cover with a thick mulch layer for protection. It will cross with similar species, so it needs to be isolated during the flowering next year. Chard seed lives about 4 years.

Harvesting. I like it stalk and all. (So do the chickens!) When it's up 6 inches or more, I go out with a bucket and

knife and whack off everything about 1 inch above the root level. It's quick and easy and it doesn't harm the plant at all. The chard will grow again. Depending on your soil and watering, in a few weeks or less, you have another crop, and another after that, and so on. When I get all the chard I want in the freezer, we till up their rows and plant them with potatoes or some other late crop.

There are 2 distinct stages at which you could harvest your chard. Harvest while young and small, like 6 inches tall, for a tender, spinachy green with very little "rib." That's my favorite way to eat it. But if you keep watering and don't cut it, you get tall, big leaves, each with a long, thick stem. That's the way some good friends of mine prefer to harvest it—getting 2 vegetables for one, the spinach-type leaf (but way tougher) plus the stem, which they use like celery.

Recipe Ideas. Combine chopped chard with nuts and raisins in a pie crust to make an interesting pie. Or wrap fish covered with tomato slices and an herb sauce inside chard leaves and bake. Or boil chard and serve with a cheese sauce. For very mature chard, cook stems and leaves separately because stems take longer.

Chard "Celery." Chard stems are a good substitute for celery. Chard is so much easier to grow than celery, and its texture and crunchiness, when raw, are similar, although the chard stems are a bit milder in flavor. Celia Sorenson, Spokane, WA, uses it that way. She chops them up in lettuce salads, egg salad sandwiches, and any dishes that call for "celery"—especially soup. Chard cooks more quickly than celery and has more nutrition too!

WATER SPINACH: *Ipomoea aquatica* is an Asian green, a.k.a. "ong choy" and "swamp cabbage." It's related to sweet potato and morning glory. This aquatic vegetable has long pointed leaves and hollow stalks. Harvest little young leaves and stems while they're still tender. If they get too large, they're too tough. This one's only eaten cooked except for the very smallest, most tender shoots. Once cooked, the leaves are tender, the stems firm but edible.

Recipe Ideas. Cut water spinach into pieces and stir-fry with assorted Asian veggies. Or boil small pieces, drain off cooking liquid, and serve with gravy or herb butter poured over. Or serve the tiniest shoots with a seasoned veggie dip. Or make a soup with water spinach, sliced carrots and turnips, and meat or fish pieces.

Sagebrush Tribe

EDIBLE CHRYSANTHEMUM: *Chrysanthemum coronarium* var. *spatiosum,* often called chop suey green, is also called "shungiku," "shingiku," "Garland Chrysanthemum," or "edible chrysanthemum." This chrysanthemum's leaves are fleshier and have a different shape than the ornamental chrysanthemum. Its has small yellow flowers and can grow up to 2 feet tall. It originated in China, spreading from there to Southeast Asia and Japan. It is still far better known among Asian gardeners than Westerners. The whole plant is edible: leaves, shoots, stems, and buds.

Growing. You can order seeds of the edible chrysanthemum from William Dam, DeGiorgi, Johnny's, Kitazawa, Nichols, and Park. Cover seeds ¼ inch deep. Plant any time between April and August. Thin to a 4-inch distance between plants. If you keep out weeds and provide reasonable water, chop suey green will produce generously. Leaves are ready 40 to 50 days after planting, when around 5 inches in length.

Harvesting. Requires 50 days to maturity. Then sever the side leaves (which are the most tender ones) just above the soil, or you pull or cut off the entire plant and use stem, leaves, and all. Chop suey green is likely to grow back from a cut stem. Harvest your winter crop from late August until early March. Harvest young plants up to a foot tall with still tightly closed flower buds. Once the flower buds fully develop, the leaves get stringy and too strong. Keeping them cut off can delay blooming. Succession sowing ensures a tender supply.

Using. *Do not eat this plant raw.* Cook briefly as you would spinach. You can substitute chop suey green in any spinach recipe, or stir-fry and serve with butter. It's good steamed and served with chopped lemon. Or make tempura with it by dipping each leaf in the batter, frying in hot oil, and serving in combination with other tempura vegetables. Chop suey green is a classic chop suey ingredient. It can also be used to make a Western vegetable soup by combining with potatoes, parsnips, onions, and carrots and cooking till done. Or saute Chinese-style with pork slivers and mushroom, water chestnut, bamboo, and broccoli slices; then serve with tamari sauce for a delicious main dish. Or use to make sukiyaki.

The Valerian

CORN SALAD: *Valerianella locusta* var. *olitoria* is Latin for corn salad, a.k.a. "lamb's lettuce," "fetticus," and "mache." The only name all gardeners agree on is the Latin one. The plant originated in mid-Europe, where it grows wild, and Europeans love it; the cultivated varieties are a standard market item there.

Opinions of its flavor differ also: some think it bland, but I think it has a fine, nutty taste. For some people the bland aspect is disagreeable. But most get used to it and can even get to like corn salad as one of their basic salad ingredients. In appearance, it's a small flat, ground-hugging plant with oval or round leaves. Corn salad is a special treasure if used as a winter green, because it is one of the few delicate-tasting greens you can harvest from your garden between late December and April, particularly in the South but also in more temperate zones.

It's an impractical green though, because it tends to germinate poorly, takes a very long time to grow (2–3 months) compared to other greens, and never gets very big; it remains just a little rosette of leaves. It does grow more quickly in warmer climates than in colder ones, and if planted in the fall, it gets going early in the spring. In fact, you can harvest corn salad any time it isn't frozen. But the most you can grow from a 100-foot row is a bushel.

Varieties. In Europe they grow *V. olitoria* or *V. eriocarpa* (Italian lamb's lettuce). *Eriocarpa* differs from *olitoria* mainly in having fuzzy rather than smooth leaves and in doing much better in a warm Mediterranean-type climate than in more chilly climates.

Climate. Corn salad is a very hardy annual, as long as your weather isn't hot. Plant in succession, starting as early in the spring as you can get to the garden, because once each planting of corn salad grows its tiny blue flowers and goes to seed, it won't make any more greens. If you live in a cool-summer area, you can succession-plant through the summer. In a hot summer area, you can manage a summer crop by planting corn salad where it will be shaded in the afternoon. Plant in August for your first fall crop. In September, plant again. One way to plant is simply to broadcast those tiny seeds over your bare garden. That's its natural growing cycle—to germinate from fall rains, winter in a small rosette, and then finish growing in spring. In fact, corn salad that is allowed to make its tiny blue flowers and go to seed will self-sow. But not right away. The seeds wait through the summer until fall, and only then do they sprout—about the time you're done harvesting other crops.

Planting. Le Jardin du Gourmet offers several varieties. Or order from Nichols, Abundant Life, Redwood City, DeGiorgi, Cook's Garden, Bountiful, or Vermont Bean. For a big crop cover with ½ inch of dirt and make rows as close as 1 foot apart. The seed is tiny and light (8,000 per oz.), hard to manage, and sometimes has many germination failures. Plant generously and then thin to a 3–4-inch distance between plants.

Growing. You can harvest the quicker growers for salad in the fall. When the ground is about to freeze, spread a light mulch on the remaining ones. Corn salad can be a surprisingly good green manure and can literally carpet your soil for winter ground cover despite its small size. The plants are often unharmed, even by freezing, and can be thawed and added to your salad. Many plants will make it through even a harsh winter, especially if mulched, to provide your winter and early spring greens. In the South, plant in late fall—no mulch needed.

Begin harvesting whenever you feel like picking a leaf. It will take 6 or 7 weeks after you planted for the corn salad to reach mature size. *Don't cut the leaves; pick them.* Or you can pull out the whole plant to harvest. Corn salad grows low to the ground, only about 3 inches tall, so wash carefully to make sure it hasn't brought any soil in with it. The best harvesting is from about September to May. If the leaves are handled gently so as not to bruise, they'll keep a week in your fridge.

Serving. Use individual leaves or whole heads. Always use absolutely fresh corn salad; it can't be preserved. Cut off the roots and wash it well by swishing in and out of water. Corn salad is the perfect balance, either raw or cooked, for bitter or strong-tasting greens such as rocket, sorrel, cress, and beet greens. It's even better as the only green in the salad. It can be eaten raw or cooked and can be substituted for virtually any green in any recipe. Serve corn salad leaves

Most brassicas are biennials (mustard and broccoli are annuals); you have to keep the plant alive through a winter to get seed. The potential crossings are usually a nightmare because broccoli, Brussels sprouts, cabbage, cauliflower, kale, kohlrabi, etc. (any or all), will cross if flowering within 100 yards of each other.

on a saucer with radish and carrot, a sliced hard-boiled egg, and a tangy salad dressing. Other ideas: Use to garnish protein dishes; include in stir-fry with other vegetables; break into smaller pieces and add to any strong-flavored soup; chop into pieces and saute with pork chops and caraway seeds; serve in a salad mixed with a chicory, tomato sections, and an olive oil-lemon juice dressing; or cook like spinach and serve with vinegar.

☙ *CORN SALAD AND ROCKET WITH BEETS* This gardener's salad is reprinted from the Nichols Garden Nursery catalog via Lane Morgan's Winter Harvest Cookbook. Ingredients: 4 c. mixed corn salad and rocket, 1 c. sliced cooked beets, 2 chopped green onions or very small leeks, ¼ c. olive oil, 3 T. red wine vinegar, 1 t. Dijon mustard, and salt and pepper. Wash greens, place in a bowl, and arrange beets and onions on top. Dress with oil, vinegar, mustard, and salt and pepper to taste.

THE WONDERFUL, MOTLEY BRASSICA HORDE

In this section are first cabbagy brassicas (Brussels sprouts, cabbage, and Chinese cabbage), then brassicas with edible flowers/stems (broccoli, cauliflower, kohlrabi, raab, and sea kale), and then leafy brassicas (collards, cress, kale, mizuna, mustard, rape, rocket, turnip greens, tyfon, and watercress). The brassica roots (radish, rutabaga, and turnip) are the only brassicas not here; they're in "Nonstarchy Roots." Most of these brassicas are very good for you, containing an anticancer substance and lots of vitamin A and C.

The Cabbagy Brassicas

This group includes Brussels sprouts, cabbage, and Chinese cabbage.

BRUSSELS SPROUTS: You are probably going to plant your seed indoors and then transplant outside. You're aiming to produce little cabbage-type heads. They can get as large as ping-pong balls, but don't let them, because bigger ones aren't as tasty. Brussels sprouts are a funny-looking, tall (2 to 4 feet) plant with a bunch of leaves at the top like a palm tree. The sprouts grow all around the sides of the stem.

Planting. You can buy red or green varieties. Plant seed indoors ¼ to ½ inch deep, 3 inches apart, figuring that the plants will grow indoors for 6 to 8 weeks before transplanting. Plan about 1 to 5 plants per family member. It germinates in 6 to 9 days. When you move them outside after hardening off, thin to 14 to 18 inches apart, rows about 30 inches apart. Set out almost as soon as soil can be worked in the spring; 65–90 average days to harvest after setting out plants. Seed planted in early April won't produce until September. For your fall crop, plant directly into garden around June 1 or later. First frosts won't kill your sprout plants in the fall. If space is tight, plant quick-maturing plants like lettuce, radishes, and green onions between the slow-growing broccoli plants.

Lane Morgan says, "Brussels sprouts are right up there with kale as superhardies, if you order the right English or Dutch seed from Territorial. If you plant a few different varieties, you can harvest them clear into April in a maritime climate [e.g., Northwest coast]. I've broken through the crusty snow to harvest them." Or move the plant to a cold frame or even your basement, and it will live and continue to produce a while.

Saving Seed. Saving seed probably isn't worth the trouble. The plant is a bee-pollinated biennial whose seeds are viable 5 years. It needs isolation to prevent problems with crossing. It's much like cabbage; see "Saving Seed" under "Cabbage" and "Broccoli."

Harvesting. Sprouts grow close-packed on the plant's main stem at the base of each leaf, starting from the bottom and working up. So you harvest the lowest sprouts first. Temperate-zone plants may produce to Thanksgiving. They're much better tasting after several frosts. You can pick once they're ½ inch wide on up to full-sized, 1 inch across, or even 1½ inch. Just grab the sprout with 2 fingers and give a little twist—or cut. In that case, don't cut too close to the stem because that can damage its ability to grow more sprouts. If harvested gently, 2 or 3 more sprouts may grow in where you picked that one. You should definitely harvest before they become tough or yellow. Once sprouts are growing, snap off all the leaves from the bottom half-foot of stem. After harvesting begins, snap off the leaves for the next few inches up. Doing that makes the plant grow taller and grow more sprouts (if the ground is fertile enough to support all that growth!). The plant will produce until it dies as long as you faithfully keep picking. You can get up to 100 sprouts per plant.

Root Cellar Storage. You can store sprouts in a porous bag for 3 to 5 weeks if they're in a very cold but also moist place. Or bring whole plants into your root cellar, and plant or merely hang them in there. But most folks leave them in the garden, because with luck you can keep picking sprouts there, even from under the snow, even as late as January.

Freezing. Sprouts taste better frozen than canned. Cut off stems and remove wilted or tough leaves. Sort by size and debug. Blanch large heads 5 minutes, medium ones 4 minutes, and small ones 3 minutes. Cool, drain, and pack in freezer bags.

Drying. Cut sprouts in half. Blanch in boiling water 3 to 5 minutes. Drain. Spread with cut side up on trays. Turn them over once a day. Dry when brittle, and dry clear to the center. Takes 18 to 24 hours in dehydrator or oven, several days in sun (bring in at night). To rehydrate, pour boiling water over and simmer until tender.

Canning. Canning Brussels sprouts is not recommended. But if you must: Boil sprouts in water at least 5 minutes. Save the water. Pack hot sprouts into clean, hot jars: *pints only.* Pour the cooking water over the sprouts. Leave 1 inch headspace. Optional: Add ½ t. salt to each jar. Process in a pressure canner for 95 minutes. If using a weighted-gauge canner, set at 10 lb. pressure at 0–1,000 feet above sea level; at higher altitudes, set at 15 lb. If using a dial-gauge canner, set at 11 lb. pressure at 0–2,000 feet above sea level; 12 lb. at 2,001–4,000 feet; 13 lb. at 4,001–6,000 feet; 14 lb. at 6,001–8,000 feet; or 15 lb. above 8,000 feet.

Cooking. Soak in salt water as you would to debug broccoli or prepare it for canning. Remove all blemished leaves. Small sprouts will cook tender in 7 or 8 minutes. Don't cook them until soft; that's too long, and they'll lose texture, shape, and vitamins. After steaming or boiling until tender, drain and serve buttered, with a sauce, or with a drizzle of lemon juice, vinegar, or tamari.

➣ *SPROUTS AND CHESTNUTS For a delicacy, if you live in chestnut country, prepare about 1 lb. Brussels sprouts. Skin ½ lb. chestnuts and boil separately until tender. Drain and mix the two together. Add a dash of tamari or lemon juice. Or add butter, salt, and pepper. Serve hot.*

CABBAGE: Cabbage is a standard crop around here, along with corn, peas, carrots, beets, turnips, and potatoes. It smells when either stored or cooked and may not be as interesting as some other veggies, but it's relatively easy to grow, a heavy producer in your garden, and nutritious; and late types store easily and well through winter in pit, cellar, or your garden. And the American Cancer Society advises us to eat cabbage to protect against cancer. What more do you need? Yea, cabbage!

Varieties. There are cabbage varieties with all kinds of maturing dates and sizes—from Little League, which makes a head about the size of a football in 60 days, to giant kinds that make 50-lb. heads but take a long time doing it. Plant a combination of early-, midseason-, and late-maturing cabbages. The earlies give your first harvest. The mid-seasons keep it up. The lates are the easiest, though slowest, to grow and are the best winter keepers. Cabbage takes up a lot of space, but you get a lot of food for it. The lates take more room in the garden than the earlies, and they yield more harvest. (Space earliest 18 inches apart, lates 24 inches.) And you have color choices: pink, red, lavender, blue, purple, white, cream, or green. And a choice of tight or loose heads: Savoy, a looseleafed cabbage with a wonderful taste, is hardy enough for a winter garden. In fact, Savoy is probably the best cabbage variety of all for the home garden.

When to Plant. For early spring cabbage in the South, plant seeds in an outdoor bed and then transplant to the garden before January 1. In the North plant the seeds in a hotbed or indoors during February and set the plants in the open ground as early as the soil can be worked. For a late crop in the North, plant the seeds in a protected bed in the open ground in May or June, and then transplant to the garden in July. We start cabbages from seed in the house and then set them out in spring, but maybe I'm working harder than I need to. Cathy Tate, Coulee City, WA, wrote me that she seeds cabbage, broccoli, kohlrabi, kale, cauliflower, etc., right into the ground as early as she can, along with the early peas. She says they can take the cold, even a snow, and that she's been doing this successfully for 4 years. If you are planning to store in a root cellar or a pit, plant a late cabbage crop, because early cabbage won't keep through the hot weather.

But when to plant also depends on whether you're planting an early, medium, or late cabbage variety. Plant earlies March to June. Plant middles from late May to early June. Plant lates from late May to late June for harvesting from August to April, depending on variety.

How to Plant. Soil needs to be fertile and nonacidic. A little cabbage seed will go a long way. Just 1 oz. produces 1,500 to 3,000 plants. Plant in full sunshine. Plant seed ¼–½ inch deep and 3 inches apart. Transplant in your garden to a few feet apart, rows 3 feet apart. They transplant best if you wait for a rain before setting them out, or soak your holes with water overnight before transplanting and give them a good soaking afterward too. If you are going through a period of dry, hot weather, keep them generously watered or even give the plants some shade with boards or leaves. For early cabbages, you want well-manured ground to hasten its growth. If container-planting, figure 1 cabbage per 8-inch pot.

Bugs. For really beautiful heads of county-fair quality, grow some plants inside a special house made of a wooden frame with fine wire mesh nailed over the top and sides. Or just scatter dill seed so it rests right between the cabbage leaves. Bugs don't like a house with dill in it. (I found that out accidentally when I had dill growing in my cabbage row.) Or plant thyme alongside cabbage in a row about 6 inches away. Bugs hate thyme too—and onions and garlic! Or frequently spray with a mix of boiled onion and garlic. An organic prevention for root maggots is to spread wood ashes around each plant, digging some ashes into the ground around the roots and replacing the ash after heavy rains, until maggot season is over at the end of June.

Saving Seed. Cabbage is an insect-pollinated biennial that will cross-pollinate with other cabbage varieties, unless you have them at least 100 yards distant. Choose the best plants, mark them, and carefully store them alive through winter in a container of soil or laid close together on a shelf in your root cellar. Some plants are self-sterile, so grow about 6 of them. Plants must be chilled enough to break dormancy before they'll grow the seed stalk. Set out the next spring. The branched, flowering seed stalk grows up through the middle of the head after it splits wide open. It speeds it up to cut a 1- to 2-inch–deep × on the top of the cabbage head to start the splitting. Support the seed stalks (they grow as tall as 5 feet). Cut stalk when pods are changing color. (They don't all get ripe at once, which makes it a tough call.) Dry on paper or cloth. Strip pods, put into bag, and beat. Winnow. Seed viable 5 years. See also "Broccoli."

Harvesting. You can pick the first or later cabbage heads at any size, as long as they haven't gotten big enough to split. Baby heads, boiled and buttered, are a real delicacy. When your early cabbage head is ready, cut it off, but leave the stem. The secret to getting a second crop of heads there is to cut close to the head, leaving most of the stem. And keep on watering. About 4 more heads will grow, each the size of a baseball. If a head is starting to crack open and you want to stall the harvest, giving the plant an 180° twist at ground level will break off some roots and slow its growth, because it's fertile soil and thriving health that causes growth. If the cracking continues, twist another 90°. Or give up and harvest it right away before it puts up its seed stalk through the crack. Cabbage heads can stand overnights down to 20°F, but if a serious freeze is approaching, it's time to finish the harvest. Late-planted, late varieties with firm, solid heads, picked just before the outside wrapping leaves lose their bright green color, store the best in pit or cellar. For that kind of storage, pull the plant out of the ground head, root, and all. Cut away the floppy outer leaves.

Cabbage Pit. The old-timers preserved cabbage by making sauerkraut and by pit or root-cellar storage. Don't put any diseased cabbages into pit or cellar storage. G.E. Marley, Hale, MO, wrote me: "You dig a pit about 2 or 2½ feet deep and line it with straw. Place cabbages, which have been pulled up roots and all, in the pit with the roots up, cover with straw, and shovel the dirt on top of the straw. Roll up a burlap sack or an old rug and leave it sticking out, so you can get into the pit after the snow covers it and the dirt is frozen. This keeps the cabbage nice and crisp all winter long." He keeps apples, turnips, and potatoes that way too.

An easier, though less dependable, version of Mr. Marley's system is to dig a trench in the garden, set the cabbage heads in it exactly upside down with the roots pointing straight up, and completely cover with dirt. It'll be harder to find the cabbages again, though. If you have more cabbage heads, you can enlarge the pit in diameter, making it circular. You can also stack the cabbages so that the root of each is covered by the head of another. Then cover them with straw and dirt. Your pit will be safer if you dig a drainage ditch leading downhill and away from the circular trench to avoid the possibility of water settling in there, and if you put the cabbages on a mound of dirt piled in the center of the pit to give them some extra drainage and protection. You can remove a few heads from time to time and cover the rest back up, and they'll be fine. Slight freezing does not injure cabbage, so you don't have to cover it as deeply as other pit-stored vegetables. A succession of heavy freezings and thawings, though, would certainly do them no good.

Root Cellar. You also can lay heads of cabbage in rows on shelves in a root cellar-type storage area, several inches apart, or hang the cabbages head down by a string tied around the root, or put them in layers on the floor with hay under and between. But if your root cellar has access to the house, you'll smell cabbage all winter! Heads keep best at 32 to 40°F and 90 percent humidity.

Freezing. Use young small heads. Shred them as for slaw or cut into small wedges. Blanch wedges in boiling water for 3 minutes, leaves for 2 minutes. If you are using whole leaves, blanch shreds for 1½ minutes. Cool, drain, and pack. That's what the experts say, but I take all the blanching times of vegetables with more than a few grains of salt. I know from considerable experience that it really doesn't matter that much. Don't worry about a half minute, or even a minute or two.

Drying. Use well-developed heads. Remove loose, bad outside leaves. Split the cabbage and get rid of the bitter core. Slice up the rest with a kraut cutter or some such, and spread on drying trays. Dry at about 120°F until brittle. The best way to use dried cabbage is to grind it up (in a seed mill, for instance) and use the powder as an addition to anything from soup to salad. The flavor will be good and it will be nutritious. You can powder lots of other dried vegetables that way, and a variety mixed together makes a great instant vegetable broth.

Canning. Canning cabbage is not recommended by the extension service. But if you must: Cut the cabbage as you would to cook it. Boil in water until you can pack it in jars easily—at least 5 minutes. Reserve cooking water. Pack hot cabbage into clean, hot jars: *pints only.* Pour cooking water over the packed cabbage. Leave 1 inch headspace. Optional: Add ½ t. salt to each jar. Process in a pressure canner for 95 minutes. If using a weighted-gauge canner, set at 10 lb. pressure at 0–1,000 feet above sea level; set at 15 lb. at higher altitudes. If using a dial-gauge canner, set at 11 lb. pressure at 0–2,000 feet above sea level; 12 lb. at 2,001–4,000 feet; 13 lb. at 4,001–6,000 feet; 14 lb. at 6,001–8,000 feet; or 15 lb. above 8,000 feet.

When you use the cabbage, pour off water and proceed with your recipe as you would if using fresh cabbage. Canning is a way to preserve early cabbage when it starts to burst. Use canned cabbage to make corned beef and cabbage, potatoes and cabbage, or fried cabbage.

Recipe Ideas. To prepare fresh cabbage, pull off the outer leaves. Cut out the stem, including the central core, which is bitter. Soak in salt water, if need be, to get out bugs. (Store-bought cabbage is so lovely and pure because it is heavily sprayed with insecticides. I'd rather have the bugs.) It cooks up faster if you shred it first. Caraway seed is good with boiled cabbage. Cabbage is also good raw, made into a salad (coleslaw). Red cabbage is a different color, but you can use it to make anything you can make with regular cabbage, including sauerkraut.

☙ *FRIED CORN AND CABBAGE From Alyce Townsend, Rock Port, MO: "Use any leftover boiled or roasted corn. Cut corn off cob. Put in skillet with some butter and/or bacon grease. Add whatever amount of fresh shredded cabbage. Put on lid and cook until cabbage is tender. Stir fairly often. Optional: Add 1 t. sugar."*

☙ *BUBBLE AND SQUEAK From Judith D. Smith, New Berlin, NY: "This is a leftover dish made on Monday or Tuesday after the big Sunday lunch. There's usually not much meat but lots of potatoes (mashed) and cooked cabbage. If there are other vegetables left, all the better. The potatoes, if not already mashed, should be mashed and all mixed up with the precooked, chopped cabbage. Chop any meat and onion really small and mix it in well. Now put it all in a frying pan and cook until brown. It will 'complain' about the heat by 'bubbling and squeaking'!"*

GRAMMA'S HOLIDAY FEAST CABBAGE
Judy Burley, Surrey, BC, Canada, sent a recipe her grandmother brought from Russia. Take 1 large or 2 small heads of cabbage (preferably the curly-leafed kind). Put in a pot with some boiling water to loosen leaves. Cover and set aside for 10 minutes. In a large bowl put 2 lb. minced beef and 1 lb. minced pork. Add salt, pepper, garlic, onions (1 or 2), a couple of eggs, and 2 or 3 handfuls of rice (not Minute Rice). Mix together well. Now carefully take the leaves off the cabbage. Put a small handful of meat mix in a large leaf and roll it up tightly. Put it in the bottom of a large roaster-sized container until you've used up all the meat mixture. You will have cabbage left over. Now put a layer of cabbage leaves over the rolls. Add 2 c. tomato juice and another layer of leaves. Cover this with spareribs, pork steak, or some such. Over this, add another 1½ c. sauerkraut, salt and pepper, and another 2 c. tomato juice. Now cover tightly and bake in a 350°F oven for 5 or 6 hours. By that time the smell will attract everybody for a long way around. We all love this. It is also great warmed up the next day."

RUTH'S VEGAN CABBAGE FEAST
Follow above recipe, except: "Steam cabbage to loosen leaves. For filling, use cracked wheat (bulgur) softened in boiling water, mixed with tomato sauce, onions, grated celery, chopped parsley, garlic, tamari, and sage. Then cover the rolls with tomato juice, sauerkraut, cabbage, and a dash of tamari. Bake it 30 minutes to an hour."

JEANIE'S CABBAGE ROLLS
Cook 1 c. brown rice. Steam 6 large cabbage leaves until tender. Saute a chopped onion and a green pepper together in butter. When the onion is transparent, add 1 lb. hamburger meat and ¼ c. water and fry. Combine cooked rice with hamburger. Stuff cabbage leaves with the mixture, fastening them together with toothpicks. Bake at 350°F for 30 minutes. Serve with ketchup.

RUTH'S VEGAN CABBAGE ROLLS
"For filling, mix 3 c. cooked rice, 1 c. tomato sauce, ½ lb. chopped mushrooms plus a chopped onion sauteed in ½ c. water plus a dash tamari, ¼ t. nutmeg, and some garlic. Stuff 14 leaves. Bake 30 minutes, covered with tomato sauce."

There are infinite variations on the theme of raw shredded cabbage served with a sweet-sour cream dressing. Vegan Ruth says: "For dressing, we use either a lemon juice mixture, soft tofu (like sour cream), or nut butter whipped with water." You can also use an oil-vinegar-mustard dressing.

VIOLA'S COLESLAW
Take about 2 c. chopped cabbage. Dress with 2 heaping T. sour cream, 1 scant t. vinegar, a pinch of salt and pepper, and a sprinkle of sugar (substitute a drip of honey if you can).

RUTH'S CARROT COLESLAW
"Use 3 parts shredded cabbage to 1 part shredded carrot. Dressing: 2 T. tahini whipped with ¼ c. lemon juice. Good stuffed in tomatoes, rolled in lettuce leaves, or plain!"

RUTH'S PRETTY COLESLAW
"For each person you're serving, use 2 c. shredded cabbage (red and green together is pretty), half a chopped bell pepper, and 1 chopped green onion. To make dressing, whip together (per person) ½ c. any fruit/vegetable juice (fresh!) and 1½ oz. nut butter. Serve on a platter atop a bed of fresh greens."

RUTH'S SAVOY CABBAGE ROLLS
"I love these! Carefully separate Savoy cabbage leaves (or use lettuce leaves if you don't have that soft cabbage) and pile on a serving platter. In another bowl, shred about 6 c. raw vegetables and mix with a vegetable juice/avocado or a juice/nut butter dressing. To eat, scoop vegetable mixture onto leaf, roll up, and enjoy."

Sauerkraut. "Kraut" is a process, not just a one-vegetable thing. It's shredding and salting and naturally fermenting a food. So you could put down green beans, sliced apples, green tomatoes, or cucumbers with your cabbage kraut. Or you can make kraut out of shredded turnips, with no cabbage in there at all, or out of green beans alone. But most often, sauerkraut means cabbage and salt. You can add extra flavor with a few grains of coriander or juniper berries, but I don't because we like our kraut plain.

Here's the USDA's kraut-making procedure. Use firm heads of fresh cabbage. Shred the cabbage and start the kraut between 24 and 48 hours after harvesting the cabbage heads. You'll use 1 c. canning or pickling salt per 25 lb. cabbage. Work with about 5 lb. cabbage at a time. Discard the outer leaves. Rinse heads under cold running water and drain. Cut heads in quarters and remove cores. Shred or slice to the thickness of a quarter. Put cabbage in a suitable fermentation container. (See "Fermented ('Brined') Cucumber Pickles.") Add 3 T. salt. Mix thoroughly, using clean hands. Pack firmly until salt draws juices from cabbage. Repeat shredding, salting, and packing until all cabbage is in the container. Keep the cabbage level at least 4 or 5 inches below the upper rim of the container.

If juice doesn't cover the cabbage, add boiled and cooled brine (1½ T. salt per 1 qt. water). Add plate and weights (see "Fermented Cucumber Pickles"). Cover container with a clean towel. Store at 70–75°F while fermenting. At temperatures between 70 and 75°F, kraut will be fully fermented in 3 to 4 weeks; at 60°F, fermentation may take 5 to 6 weeks. At temperatures lower than 60°F, kraut may not ferment; above 75°, it may become soft. Do not disturb the crock until fermentation is completed. You'll know it's done when the bubbling ceases. Check the kraut 2 to 3 times each week, and remove scum if it forms. Fully fermented kraut may be kept in the refrigerator for several months, or it may be canned. To can, either hot-pack or raw-pack as follows.

To hot-pack, bring kraut and liquid slowly to a boil in a large kettle, stirring frequently. Remove from heat and fill pint or quart jars rather firmly with kraut and juices, leaving ½ inch headspace. Process quarts in boiling-water bath for 15 minutes at 0–1,000 feet, 20 minutes at 1,001–6,000 feet, or 25 minutes above 6,000 feet. Process pints for 5 minutes less.

To raw-pack, fill pint or quart jars firmly with kraut and cover with juices, leaving ½ inch headspace. Adjust lids and use conventional boiling-water canner processing or lower-temperature pasteurization (detailed in "Pickles" section under "Cucumbers"). In a boiling-water bath, process quarts for 25 minutes at 0–1,000 feet, 30 at 1,001–3,000 feet, 35 at 3,001–6,000 feet, 40 above 6,000 feet. Process pints for 5 minutes less.

Here's another kraut procedure. This one's for old-time salted kraut. If you have a cold place like a dugout cellar to keep your kraut in, and if you make it in the fall after the worst heat is over, you can keep it all winter. But don't wait too long to make it, because your cabbage will dry out some and the juice will be hard to get. If you are making sauerkraut in hot weather, you should can the sauerkraut after it has finished fermenting.

Hack away the buggy leaves from your cabbage until you get down to the nice solid center. Then cut the cabbage into quarters and discard the hard core. If you were to use the core, it would make your kraut very bitter. Finely shred the cabbage. I shred it using a butcher knife on a wooden cutting board, but someday I'm going to splurge on an old-time slaw cutter. The cabbage shreds should be about the thickness of a dime, long and thin.

If you aren't brave enough to guess at the amounts as Great-Grandmother always did, weigh 5 lb. of the shredded cabbage on a food scale, measure 3 T. salt, and sprinkle over the cabbage. Mix with your hands a bit and then tamp. If you are brave enough, put cabbage into your 5-gal. crock to make about a 2-inch layer in the bottom. Tamp it down. Add 1 or 2 T. salt (to taste), and tamp down again. To "tamp" means to stomp the heck out of it with a heavy, blunt object. Wood seems to work the best. I use a whittled-down cedar fence post. You are done tamping when you've stomped so much that the juice comes out of the cabbage and just about covers it. Pack each layer in, salt, and then tamp until enough juice has come out to cover the shredded cabbage.

It's important to use the right amount of salt and mix it in well. Too little or uneven distribution of the salt can result in a soft kraut. Too much or uneven distribution of salt can result in a pinkish kraut, caused by the growth of certain types of yeast.

When you've shredded, salted, and tamped your way through all your heads of cabbage or to the top of your crock, cover the cabbage. Everybody has their own system. Mine is to use a cloth over the sauerkraut, then a plate just a little smaller than the diameter of the container, and a jar filled with water (with a lid on) on top of that. If you do it right, the brine comes just to the cover but not over it. As with crock pickles, the cabbage needs to be thoroughly under the juice. And it needs to be covered sufficiently to shut out air from the surface. Even so, your top layer may turn brown, in which case just throw away the off-color part when you get ready to use the crock. (Animals can eat it.) The rest of the kraut will be fine.

Now let your kraut ferment. It will start making gas bubbles; that tells you it's fermenting. Fermenting takes from 2 to 6 weeks, depending on how warm your weather

is. You know when the kraut is ready by taking a taste of it. Some people just leave it alone during this time. Others wash the cloth, the sides of the crock, and the lid every week. Home-fermented cabbage is fairly strong stuff. But I like it strong.

≫ *PICKLED RED CABBAGE* *Choose 1 hard red cabbage. Trim off the coarse outside leaves. Cut it in quarters. Core and remove the thickest stalks. Finely shred the cabbage. Put the shreds in layers on a dish, sprinkling each layer with salt, and leave until the following day. Boil 1 T. mixed pickling spice in 1 qt. vinegar for 5 minutes. Then leave until cold. Drain off all moisture from the cabbage and put into jars. Pour the cold, spiced vinegar over the cabbage. It should come to at least 1 inch above the cabbage. Weight the cabbage and cover the whole thing. It will be ready to use after 2 weeks. It won't keep well over 2 months, since it tends to soften. So use it in recipes like the ones that follow!*

Recipes Using Sauerkraut

≫ *GRANDPA SMITH'S MESS* *This is a complete meal-in-one sent to me by Eleanor Seberger of Cozad, NV. Boil potatoes with the skins on. Then make as many sausage cakes—with a few extras—as your family will need. Fry a batch of onions, chopped fine. Set aside the sausage and heat your sauerkraut in the sausage skillet. Let each person take a serving of each ingredient—sausage cakes, potatoes, onions, and sauerkraut. Cut with a knife, mix, and down with hot garlic bread or toast.*

≫ *SAUERKRAUT ONION BISCUITS* *Sauerkraut doesn't have to be served with sausage, though. Here's a vegetarian sauerkraut recipe. Everybody in my family loves these! When you bake bread, while you are letting your dough have its first rising, drain the juice from a pint of sauerkraut and then fry the sauerkraut and an equal (or smaller) amount of onion in a greased pan. When the dough has risen, roll it out with a rolling pin to less than ½ inch—as thin as you can get it. Cut the dough into 6- to 8-inch squares. Put a nice big heaping spoonful of the cooked mix in the middle of each one. Pinch together, let rise, and bake. If they come out just in time for supper—perfect! Imogene taught me how to make these. She and her family are vegetarians, but that doesn't mean they don't eat hearty meals!*

Imogene's one of my favorite people. She's a lady who doesn't go to town very often. She's never used a recipe book. She hasn't bought any detergents for at least 50 years because she makes all her own soap. Once I took her with me to a cafeteria. She had a glass of ice water and asked what the ashtray was for. She's my ideal. I wish I didn't know what they were for—not that I smoke, because I don't, but just to be that truly innocent of worldliness! Imogene and her family are Seventh-Day Adventists. They believe in staying away from the "world" and worldliness as much as possible. I'm in real sympathy with that point of view. As the poet Wordsworth wrote a long time ago, "The world is too much with us; late and soon/Getting and spending, we lay waste our powers . . . "

≫ *IMOGENE'S SAUERKRAUT DUMPLINGS* *Put water on in a kettle. Let it boil up. Get out a quart of sauerkraut, drain the juice off, and fry it in a little oil. Make a dough of flour, water, and salt that's the consistency of bread dough. With a sharp knife cut off pieces 1 inch long and about ⅓ inch thick. Put into the boiling water and let boil. When the dumplings* are boiled down so that there is no or very little water left, add the kraut. Mix and serve.

> **BAKED SAUERKRAUT, ONION, APPLE** *Combine sauerkraut, cored apple slices, and sauteed onion in a greased ovenproof dish. Dribble 1 T. molasses over the top and scatter a fat pinch of dry mustard over it. Bake at 350°F for 30 minutes.*

> **PORK BONES AND KRAUT** *Kraut goes well with any pork. Boil the pork bones (such as the backbone or ribs) until done. Cool enough to separate the meat from the bones and discard them. Add kraut and cook until done.*

> **FANCY RIBS AND KRAUT** *Brown your ribs. Cook them until about half done in your Dutch oven. Add 1 qt. kraut and potatoes; then add water to cover. Add drop dumplings. Cook until potatoes and dumplings are done.*

> **STEAK STUFFED WITH KRAUT** *Salt and pepper a big round steak. Add a layer of bacon and then lots of kraut. Roll it up and tie it with a string. Bake in your roaster in a moderate oven for an hour.*

CHINESE CABBAGE: "Chinese cabbage" is more closely related to mustard than to cabbage, although all are brassicas. They are more mild in taste, more delicate in texture, and more digestible than regular cabbages. Because Chinese cabbages do best planted for a late fall harvest, they are ideal for the winter garden, producing when most of your other greens are done. Chinese cabbages mature much faster than regular cabbage, as fast as 8 weeks. But they are grown, stored, and cooked much like cabbage. Chinese cabbages are especially well suited to stir-frying; most are mild in flavor and easy to cook.

Varieties. There are so many varieties of Asian cabbages, with so many different flavors, that if you don't know which you prefer, the best thing to do is to just start trying them out and seeing which grow best for you and which you like best. There are so many names for each plant—Japanese, Chinese, Korean, and American names—that distinguishing them can be tough. "Flat cabbage" is said to be the wild ancestor of all other cabbages. It is strong in flavor, comes from North China, and is very cold-hardy. Other than that, you have 2 main groups to choose from: the heading and the nonheading types. The heading ones are *Brassica rapa*, Pekinensis group: Chinese celery cabbage, michihli, nappa, and wong bok. Nappa is shaped like Romaine lettuce and is self-blanching; the others are rounded heads. The nonheading ones are *B. rapa*, Chinensis group: bok choy, Chinese mustard cabbage, and pak choi. These look like Swiss chard, with loosely bunching green leaves and a thick midrib.

Planting. Seed is available from any Asian-specialist seed house and from Burpee, Comstock, William Dam, DeGiorgi, Hudson, Johnny's, and Kitazawa. The seeds are very small; it doesn't take many to plant 100 feet. Plant 2 inches apart, 2½ feet between rows, ¼–½ inch deep. Thin out the extras when plants are 3 inches high, 4 weeks old, or have 5 true leaves. Thin nonheading types to 9 inches, heading types to 12–15 inches apart. The thinnings make good salad or can be cooked. In a container, plan for 1 per 8-inch pot.

Secrets of Growing Chinese Cabbage

1. It needs a very rich soil, one with lots of manure/compost. If your soil is not ultra-rich, add more manure/compost after thinning.

2. It needs a light, porous soil. If you have clay, add lots of compost.

3. Never let its roots get totally dry.

4. Mulch helps a spring crop stay moist in summer, but mulch shouldn't be put on a fall crop; it prevents the ground from getting the sun's warmth.

5. When you have a choice, water at ground level rather than from overhead. This discourages moisture-loving insects and diseases from living in the plants.

6. These photosensitive plants react to long days—if it's been a month or so since germination—by "bolting" (growing a flowering seed stalk), after which the crop will diminish. This is mainly a problem for spring-grown crops. Because of bug/worm problems, risk of bolting, and natural hardiness, many gardeners skip the spring crop and instead plant their Chinese cabbage in late July or early August (about 12 weeks before fall frost date) for a fall harvest. Or look for one of the new nonbolting varieties and use that for a spring crop.

7. It grows best when days are becoming shorter and temperatures are 60–65°F. It can grow right on into the winter, or at least stay alive, because it can endure frost down to 20°F without much damage.

8. To bear a spring/summer crop, it needs a cool-summer climate. To get that, in most areas, you start it indoors 8 to 10 weeks before the last frost date. Set out 4 to 6 weeks before that date. To discourage plants from bolting, cover them with something opaque in late afternoon to shorten their day and protect them from excess heat, because just 1 or 2 hot days can cause bolting, after which they become inedible.

9. If you start spring plants in seed flats, transplant before they get a month old, or you risk transplant shock (makes them bolt instead of heading). Since Chinese cabbage is set back (slowed) in growth by transplanting; for fall planting, seed directly if you can.

10. Transplanting is not a risk for fall planting. You can plant in a partly shaded site in late summer, and then transplant to full sun in September; you can even transplant again to a cold frame in November or so.

11. Thinning is important. Plants that don't have 6 inches between them won't get nearly as large and tender.

Saving Seed. Chinese cabbage is a bee-pollinated annual that bolts when the length of the day increases. The flowers of *Brassica rapa*, Pekinensis group, have both male and female parts and are self-sterile. The only other cabbages and brassicas they will cross with are other Chinese cabbages, turnips, radishes, rutabagas, and mustards (both wild and tame). But you can still manage to save seed if you grow the others for food but let only your Chinese cabbage flower. Seed viability is 5 years.

Harvesting. You can eat Chinese cabbage of any age. Some taste best after frost. To harvest heading types, pull out and cut off the head. To harvest nonheading ones, do the same, or just take off the outer leaves and come back to get new growth—as long as you leave at least 5 leaves at the center of the plant. Bugs and worms like to nibble on the spring crop, but the inside leaves should be fine. Just throw away messy outer leaves.

Root Cellar Storage. Heads for storage should be mature and solid. Get them into storage before your first severe frost. Store like regular cabbage but upright, because nappa cabbages get L-shaped if left lying on the side. If you keep

Chinese cabbages just above freezing in a very humid place, they will keep for 2 to 4 months.

Recipe Ideas. For *strong-tasting* cabbage: Use in kim chee; stir-fry with meat and strong spices (alcoholic beverage optional); use in cole slaw recipe; make miso and veggie soup; or boil and serve with garlic butter. For *mild-tasting* cabbage: Substitute it in any cabbage soup recipe. Or boil with tomatoes, onions, and a bone. Or finely chop and fry with tomatoes and thin-sliced, precooked meat. Or stir-fry Chinese-style, with small slices of tofu or pre-cooked meat, bamboo, onion, and lemon juice. Or serve raw, chopped like coleslaw, in a salad with shredded daikon radish, sliced cucumber, and strips of green pepper covered with a dressing of oil and vinegar or oil and soy sauce. Or combine sliced cabbage, radishes, and Jerusalem artichokes. Or roast meat on a bed of shredded nappa surrounded by onions and potatoes.

➢ *KIM CHEE From Lane Morgan's* Winter Harvest Cookbook: *"Kim chee is a generic name for a hot fermented pickle that is ubiquitous in Korea—where it accompanies every meal—and common in Japan. It can be made with vegetables ranging from spinach to cucumber, but it most commonly contains nappa cabbage and daikon radish and serves as a way to preserve these vegetables in quantity through the winter. The taste and smell are unforgettable. I love it, not only with Asian food but with grilled cheese sandwiches. There are a number of commercial brands with varying textures and firepower. It's also simple to make at home.*

"Put 1 medium head nappa cabbage (or regular cabbage, or spinach, or whatever—about 2 lb. of it) in a large bowl. Sprinkle with 2 T. salt and mix. Cover and let stand at room temperature until cabbage wilts to about half its original volume. This will take about 3 hours. Rinse well, drain, and return to bowl. Optional: add 1 c. julienned daikon radish or kohlrabi. Not optional: Add 2 green onions or small leeks, chopped; 3 minced cloves garlic; 1 to 2 t. chopped hot red pepper or cayenne; and 1 more t. salt. Mix well, pack into a quart jar, cover lightly, and let stand at room temperature until it is fermented to your taste. This will take from 1 to 4 days, depending on the temperature and your preference. Do not use a tight cover during fermentation. Strong forces are at work here, and you risk an eruption when the pressure is released. Some stores carry a bottled seasoning base for kim chee. Just prepare the vegetables as described above, omitting the garlic and red pepper, and pour on the bottled mixture before fermentation. Makes about 3½ cups."

The Edible Flower-Bud and Stem Brassicas

These include broccoli, cauliflower, kohlrabi, raab, and sea kale. As little plants, they all look about the same; they begin to look different only as they mature. They all require long, cool summers and need fertile, well-limed soil. Most have insect and disease problems, so don't plant brassicas in the same spot for 2 or 3 years. To hold off cutworms from new transplants, arrange a newspaper, cardboard, or metal collar around the stem.

I have trouble growing these because it's hot here in the summertime. You may think that surprising in north Idaho, but we live in a little pocket of low-altitude, warmer country here in the Potlatch River valley. As far north as this is, it's probably the warmest place anywhere short of the West Coast. Tomatoes, watermelon, cantaloupe, and grapes grow well here. People can grow good broccoli and cabbage in our steep-sided canyon, 1,500 feet up, but tomatoes are hard.

BROCCOLI: *Brassica oleracea botrytis cymosa* and *Brassica oleracea italica* are the Latin names for broccoli. The British call winter cauliflower "broccoli" and call broccoli "Calabrese" (because it comes from the Calabrian district of Italy). It's been grown in the Mediterranean and Middle East areas for at least the last 2,000 years. The part we eat is the "head," a mass of tiny unopened flower buds, plus its stem underneath. There are a myriad varieties: purple (turns green when cooked), white, or green; broccoli with odd and artistic head designs; and spring ("early"), fall, and overwintering specialists (Purple or White Sprouting or Nine Star Perennial). Plant those in late May, later in the south; the plant makes heads early the next spring.

Planting. A few plants can produce a lot of broccoli. Experiment with a half dozen to start with. Lane Morgan says, "Broccoli likes lots of light and not much heat, which is why gardeners in Alaska get heads a foot across (and cabbages the size of basketballs)." So gardeners plant it either very early for a spring crop or later for a fall crop—omitting the summer, as with kohlrabi.

From Seed. Plant in garden or seed flat. Spring broccoli planted directly in the garden does better but is a gamble. Timing is important when planting indoors for later transplanting. If you start too soon, the plants may outgrow their containers and get potbound or spindly. Plant ¼ to ½ inch deep and 3 to 4 inches apart. Allow 7 to 10 days for germination; 70–85°F is best. Then figure 5 to 7 weeks of growing before the time for transplanting, which should be in early spring. In a mild climate you can plant even in late January or early February. For a fall crop, start seed directly in the garden 10 to 12 weeks before the first fall frost date.

Fall Crops. Roberta Van Slyke, Cortland, NY, wrote me that she plants her broccoli so it will mature in cooler weather. She then keeps it mulched with grass clippings or straw. Lane Morgan (on the northwestern Washington coast) says, "What I like to do is plant hardy varieties (from Territorial) in late summer. They hunker down through the winter and then take off come spring. I am harvesting some this week (mid-June)." Fall crops have fewer worm problems.

Transplanting. You can buy plants and set them out, or set out your home-grown plants. Harden off before transplanting. You can get a jump-start for the spring crop by using a hot cap or cloche. It needs very fertile soil with some lime in it. Broccoli may have trouble with insects or disease, so don't plant it in the same place year after year. Gardeners argue about whether the best process for a spring planting is to transplant as soon as the ground can be worked, or 2 weeks before the frostfree date, or after it, or when day temps get around 50°F. The plants can stand some frost but not too much. Experiment. Set them 18 to 24 inches apart, rows 2 to 3 feet apart. Keep the crop well watered because a dry spell triggers premature heading.

Saving Seed. Cabbage, kale, Brussels sprouts, kohlrabi, broccoli, and cauliflower are all bee-pollinated. And they all belong to the same family and will cross, so you can save seed only if you are growing just one of them or have them very widely separated—which isn't much guarantee, given the way bees can cover ground. Except for spring-planted broccoli, all these plants are biennials, so you have to wait for the second year of growth for them to produce seed. Fall-planted broccoli makes seed the *next* spring. When the seed pods are mostly brown and dry, harvest, thresh out the seed, and winnow it clean. Viable 5 years.

Harvesting. Mature broccoli is a big plant, 2 to 4 feet high. Harvest before the central cluster that the plant first produces (which may be as much as 8 inches across) blossoms. You can feel the tightness of closed buds by rubbing your thumb over the broccoli head. As long as the buds feel tight, the cluster is still growing. When you can feel those buds begin to loosen up and spread out, harvest! Cut even if the head seems small to you. Drought or hot weather can bring on premature flowering. It's better to cut too early than too late. You can cut heads 1 or 2 weeks before they are actually mature. Not all your plants will mature at the same time, which also spreads out the harvest. Just be sure to cut the sprout while still tightly closed. Cut with stem attached. The stem as well as the head is good to eat. But cut high on the stalk; rot can result if you cut low enough to expose the hollow center of it.

A few days after the central sprout is cut, the plant begins to grow side sprouts, smaller versions of the central head, from where other leaves join the stem. Those side shoots are your second crop; they're as tasty and nutritious as the central sprout. Cut them also while the buds are still tightly clustered. None of those side shoots will get as big as the first one, but together they can give you some good meals. You must stay on the ball with your harvesting—check every 2 or 3 days. If you don't keep cutting regularly and a cluster gets away from you and manages to blossom, the plant will stop making clusters. You can get from 4 to 6 more cuttings from these side shoots. Their size will gradually decrease. But if you keep cutting, the plant keeps producing until frost finally kills it. If some do get past you to the yellowed or open-bud stage, they're still edible, although they won't taste as good and won't keep as well in storage. (Make them into soup!)

Preparing. Trim off outer leaves and anything woody. If the stalks are big, slice them lengthwise into pieces so that the flowerets are no more than 1½ inches across. If you have cabbage looper problems, soak the broccoli in a brine (4 t. salt per 1 gal. cold water) for 30 minutes to chase out the worms. Rinse and drain.

Freezing. Cut into pieces. Now pack and freeze without blanching. Or blanch stalks with 1½-inch heads for 3 minutes, smaller heads for 2 minutes. Chill, drain, and pack.

Drying. Start with fresh prime broccoli. Soak in brine as above. Rinse. Split stalks into thin strips. Blanch as above. Drain. Cut or chop strips into 2- to 3-inch, or finer, sections. Spread pieces on tray. Dry at 120°F until crisp and dry to center. To reconstitute, pour boiling water over and simmer until tender.

Canning. Canning broccoli is not USDA-recommended. If you must: Prepare and precook 3 minutes. Pack hot with cooking liquid and 1 t. salt per quart. Pack into *pints only.* Leave 1 inch headspace. Pressure-can only for 95 minutes. If using a weighted-gauge canner, set at 10 lb. pressure at 0–1,000 feet above sea level; at higher altitudes, set at 15 lb. If using a dial-gauge canner, set at 11 lb. pressure at 0–2,000 feet above sea level; 12 lb. at 2,001–4,000 feet; 13 lb. at 4,001–6,000 feet; 14 lb. at 6,001–8,000 feet; or 15 lb. above 8,000 feet.

Recipe Ideas. Broccoli is good raw in salads or with bean, tofu, and eggplant dips. Large broccoli stalks can be sliced at an angle and used like celery in salads, soups, and Chinese stir-fry dishes. For cooked broccoli, how long to cook depends on how big your sprouts are, so just keep testing for tenderness. Steamed or boiled broccoli is good with tamari or a cheese sauce or just buttered. Lane Morgan says, "Steam the broccoli about 10 minutes; then saute with a little oil and a lot of garlic. Mix with cooked penne or spiral noodles or some such. Sprinkle with Parmesan. Great quick dinner. If you want a little more protein, stir 1 or 2 beaten eggs into the hot noodles. Also good with cauliflower." Or stir-fry with sliced sweet peppers and garlic or with thin-sliced meat and other veggies. Or cook with mushrooms (or cabbage) and serve with butter or a sauce.

CAULIFLOWER: *Brassica oleracea botrytis* needs a cool, moist climate. And much more—for this is the most difficult brassica to grow. Get Territorial's seed catalog for the best growing instructions and choice of varieties.

Varieties. Cauliflower comes in white, green, and purple heads. It's ordinarily planted in the early spring to early summer in cold frames and then transplanted to the garden after 6 weeks—"summer cauliflower." Summer ones take little as 50 days from setting out in garden to harvest. Or plant "winter cauliflower" in spring for a fall/winter crop if you live where winters are cold but not severe, such as the Pacific Northwest coast. Winter types can mature 6 months after setting out to harvest. Overwintering varieties are meant to be planted in summer or fall in a mild climate to bear the next spring. In the southern United States, try the purple long-season type or a quick-growing type that's set out very early—or plant in late summer for a late fall crop. By using a combination of varieties, you can have an extended harvest season. For small gardens there are mini-cauliflower varieties.

Planting. Have the soil deeply worked even though cauliflower is shallow-rooted. Work in plenty of manure and compost, for cauliflower requires richer ground than any other brassica (but commercial fertilizers make it sick). Experimenters have grown cauliflower with as few as 2 hours of sunlight each day. Too much heat makes it head prematurely. So plant in a partially shady spot. Plant seed ¼ to ½ inch deep, 3 inches apart if you're doing it outdoors. If planting directly in garden, do so as soon as ground can be worked. Germination in 5 to 10 days. Grow for 5 to 7 weeks before setting out. Transplant a few plants to your garden 3 to 4 weeks before your last spring frost date (or as soon as your ground is workable); transplant more thereafter in succession. Set them 20 inches apart. It will be 60 to 100 days to maturity (depending on your variety) from the time of transplanting.

Growing. Cauliflower needs plenty of water, more if you have hot weather or a hot climate. Watch carefully to make sure you don't let the ground dry out. Water nightly on days when it doesn't rain. Heavy mulching helps combat weeds and hold moisture. If you don't mulch, be careful in your weeding, because cauliflower has a very shallow root system. It gets the same bunch of bugs and diseases as cabbage. If aphids get into the head, they're next to impossible to get out again.

Blanching. You can harvest your cauliflower either plain or "blanched." If you don't blanch it, your cauliflower won't be any less edible. You can just pare off the green or yellowed outside if you don't like the look of it. If you do blanch, it's the last step before you whack off the head and take it in the house. To blanch: once the heads are 3 to 5 inches in diameter, it's time. Pull those big outside leaves up across the cauliflower's head. Tie them together up there with a rubber band or string. Or just cover the head with a big leaf that's tucked in around its sides (more air circulation and less risk of rotting this way). Blanch for 4 to 12 days (longer in the fall). Now harvest.

Saving Seed. Cauliflower is a bee-pollinated biennial that will cross with a slew of other brassicas. You have to keep the plant alive during the winter; in a cold zone, this is best done by growing it in a pot until setting it out in your garden in the spring of its second year. In a warm zone, plant in midsummer and you can get seed next summer that will be ripe (first yellow, then brown) by fall. Cut and thresh like cabbage. Seed viable 5 years.

Harvesting. You can be really proud when you've gotten this far! Harvest any time you get a head 6 inches in diameter or larger. Once they get growing, the heads develop very fast. As with broccoli, be careful to harvest before the flower buds loosen and open. Cauliflower really loses its flavor and texture when the buds loosen. Cauliflower can't keep producing, unlike broccoli. You cut the head and it's done. Plant something else there. Cauliflower isn't as hardy against frost as cabbage, but once it starts to mature that head, light frost won't hurt it.

Root Cellar. Cauliflower freezes at 30°F. Cut off root. Leave on protective outer leaves. Wrap and pack with loose, moist sand in outdoor storage area (because it gives off strong odors) or in a root cellar, as near 32°F as possible, in moderately moist humidity. Keeps 2 to 8 weeks.

Freezing. Wash. Break into 1-inch chunks. To de-worm, soak 30 minutes in brine (4 t. salt/1 gal. water). Blanch 3 minutes. Rinse and drain; chill; package and freeze.

Drying. Prepare as for freezing through to blanching. Then spread pieces on drying trays. Dry at 120°F until chunks are crisp and dry clear to center. To use, pour boiling water over and simmer to tenderness.

Canning. Follow directions for broccoli.

Recipe Ideas. Soak in salted water. Cut off the green leaves. Eat them raw in a tossed salad or with a dip, or eat them cooked—steamed, boiled, or baked. Serve cooked cauliflower plain, buttered, with a cheese sauce or a vinegar-oil dressing, etc. Or stir-fry with broccoli and sweet red peppers.

🐟 *RUTH'S VEGAN BAKED CAULIFLOWER Bake a whole head in a covered dish; spread generously with stone-ground mustard before baking. Good cold or hot. Cooked, mashed cauliflower is a good substitute for eggs in a vegetable pudding-type dish.*

KOHLRABI: This is a fast-maturing, pest- and disease-free brassica whose edible part tastes like an apple, looks like an above-ground turnip (a close relative), and has the life cycle of a radish (another relative). You have a choice of white, purple, and king-size varieties. Plant breeders keep trying for ones with less tendency to get woody. If you like turnips but the cabbage root maggot is getting them, grow kohlrabi as a substitute. Kohlrabi behaves differently depending on the time of year it's planted. But the seeds are able to handle both cold and heat and can be planted directly into the garden.

Spring Crop. Small succession plantings are best because the harvest time for each planting is only about 2 weeks long. You want them to grow fast and do their growing while the weather is still cool, because slow growth and/or hot weather makes them hot and woody. Soil should be fertile. Plant 4 to 6 weeks before frostfree date. Or start inside 4 to 6 weeks before transplanting date, which will be between 5 weeks before and 2 weeks past the last frost time—as soon as the ground can be worked. Water supply should be faithful and generous. Weed carefully to keep out the competition.

Fall Crop. Plant in succession, starting in late July. Fall-planted kohlrabi will wait for harvest without the sort of hot/woody deterioration the spring ones get.

How to Plant. Plant ¼–½ inch deep, 6 to 9 days to germination. Thin to 3 to 6 inches between plants, 12 to 24 inches between rows. Thinnings can be transplanted elsewhere.

Saving Seed. This is a bee-pollinated, problem-crossing biennial. Seed viable 5 years. For seed, plant in fall. Mulch for the winter or keep in root cellar, cabbage-style, and replant in spring 2 feet apart. Grows seed stalk that second year. Harvest seed as you would cabbage.

Harvesting. Time to maturity depends on variety, maybe as little as 45 to 60 days or as much as 120 for the giant kind. You eat the enlarged stem, which has leaves growing out of it but looks like an above-ground root. *Harvest spring-planted kohlrabi when only 1 to 2 inches in diameter.* Fall kohlrabi should be okay until the size of a tennis ball or an orange. Don't let them get too large because they turn from tender and crunchy to woody. (Unless you planted the giant variety, which grows to 10 lb. or more and is said to stay tender.) The fall crop will be fine outdoors until temps get down to the low 20s. The early frosts will do no harm, and kohlrabi keeps better in the ground. In fact, fall kohlrabi can endure being frozen a time or two.

Root Cellar Storage. For cellar storage, dig up kohlrabi at a time when the soil is relatively dry. Cut off the outer leaves and root. They keep best in layers between moist sand, peat, or sphagnum moss. If you don't bed them as described, they will wither. Keep as cool as possible, short of freezing. If they get too warm, the roots will sprout new tops and become woody as all the stored food gets sent out to make new leaves.

Freezing. Scald 1 minute, cool, and package.

Drying. Cut leaves off bulbs. Peel bulbs. Cut into thin slices or small cubes. Blanch in boiling water about 3 minutes. Drain. Spread on drying trays. Dry at 120°F, stirring and rotating trays occasionally. Dry until crisp. Takes about 24 hours in dehydrator, 36 in oven, several days in sun. To rehydrate, pour boiling water over and simmer until tender.

Canning. Cut off tops and roots. Wash and peel. Leave whole or dice, as you prefer. Pack hot in *pints only.* Cover with boiling water. Leave 1 inch headspace. Pressure-can only for 40 minutes. If using a weighted-gauge canner, set at 10 lb. pressure at 0–1,000 feet above sea level; set at 15 lb. at higher altitudes. If using a dial-gauge canner, set at 11 lb. pressure at 0–2,000 feet above sea level; 12 lb. at 2,001–4,000 feet; 13 lb. at 4,001–6,000 feet; 14 lb. at 6,001–8,000 feet; or 15 lb. above 8,000 feet.

Recipe Ideas. When very young and tender, you can wash, trim, and eat raw kohlrabi like an apple, and it will taste sweet and fruity. Raw kohlrabi is best if crisped in ice water a quarter hour first. Shred like cabbage to make slaw salad. Or cook and serve with broiled mushrooms. Or bake unpeeled kohlrabi until done; then peel, slash in a few places, and season with salt, paprika, and butter. Or bake and season with a mixture of tamari and lemon juice. Or slice/dice and add to a tossed salad. Or saute with onion and then bake in a meat and onion casserole. Or serve raw strips with veggie dip. Or stir-fry with bamboo shoots. Or boil in a vegetable/meat soup. Or substitute in any celeriac or turnip recipe.

BUTTERED AND SAUTEED KOHLRABI Use only the bulb; remove the green (or purple or white) skin. Slice or cut into quarters. Boil until tender. Then either serve with butter, salt, and pepper to taste or brown in melted butter that has been seasoned with onion and curry powder.

CREAMED KOHLRABI Cut off the tops and roots of about 6 kohlrabi plants. Wash and peel; leave whole or dice. Cook in boiling water until tender. Make a white sauce of 2 T. butter, 2 T. flour, 2 c. milk, salt and paprika to taste, and an egg yolk, and pour over the drained kohlrabi before serving. Or serve with a cheese or tomato sauce.

BULB AND GREENS If you harvest them radish-sized, you can chop and stir-fry, greens and all. Some folks find the greens from bigger ones too strong. Others do this: Wash, peel, dice the bulb, and cook in salted water until tender. Cook the greens in another pan of boiling water until tender. Drain the greens and chop fine. Make a paste of butter and flour; add soup stock to make a sauce. Then add the chopped greens and, finally, the cooked kohlrabi.

RAAB: *Brassica rapa ruvo* is also called "rapa" and "rapini," but it's usually known as "broccoli raab." It's an Italian vegetable eaten leaves, buds, flowers, and all. It's kind of a loose-topped broccoli or, more precisely, the flowering stems of a turnip. Easier to grow than broccoli, it's a gardener's veggie you don't see in stores. Seed is available from Comstock (in spring "early" and fall "late" varieties), Territorial, Nichols, and Park; Johnny's has a purple version ("Han Tsai Tai"). Plant in February or March (will bolt in mid-May) and then again in the fall. Use planting directions under "Kohlrabi" for spring and fall crops. Harvest when flower stalks have developed buds, but the buds are not yet open.

Recipe Ideas. Stalks will need peeling. Stir-fry with garlic in olive oil and a bit of water. Or serve raw in strips with a sour cream dip. Or slice and make into a soup with beans and other veggies. Or boil in stock with potatoes, garlic, and greens. Or cook slices with meat and greens. Look in Italian (Tuscan) recipe books for more recipes.

SEA KALE: *Crambe maritama* is a European seashore perennial cultivated at least since the Romans. Like rhubarb, it starts early in spring. Grow the early shoots with a bucket over their head to blanch the tops. Sea kale does best in cool seashore regions.

Planting. If you start it from seed, you can't get a crop of shoots until the third year. If you start with a root cutting, you can harvest the next spring. Seed is available from Bountiful Gardens or Thompson & Morgan. Plant in fertile soil with your other perennials because it will keep yielding for many years. Allow each plant a space 3 or 4 feet wide. In late fall cut off the top leaves. In winter, mulch the plant with deep compost/manure for the best crop next year. Some folks keep a crown in their root cellar and force it for early greens.

Harvesting. When shoots are 4 to 12 inches tall, cut. Harvest can continue until the leaves start opening. Then you stop, take off the bucket, and let it store energy through the summer. Be sure and keep it in total darkness while growing shoots to eat, just like with witloof chicory. Light makes it turn bitter.

RECIPE IDEAS Boil and serve with a lemon or garlic butter mixture. Good cooked with pearl onions and served with a cheese sauce or a vinegar-oil dressing.

The Leafy Brassicas

There are lots to choose from in this group: collards, cress, kale, mizuna, mustard, rape, rocket, turnip greens, tyfon, and watercress.

COLLARDS: I've got at least a partial credential for talking about collards because my mother was born and raised in Alabama. She left around age 20, first for a job in a bank in New York City and then to take a teaching job as an English teacher in the practically brand-new, whistle-stop town of Clyde Park, Montana. They called her "Alabam" there, and from her I know about fried chicken, grits, okra, collards, and corn bread!

Collards (*Brassica oleracea* var. *acephala*) are a kind of kale that's easy to grow and disease-free. Collards are a traditional southern food because they tolerate heat; they're the only brassica that gets along in the South. But they can also handle cold. Each plant is a tall kale, a nonheading cabbage that grows on top of a stick stem about 1 to 4 feet high.

Planting. In the South they plant collards from July to November to eat during the fall and winter, or start them indoors early to be set out as soon as the ground can be worked in spring. If you live in the North and want to try collards, plant them early in the spring. Southern Seeds sells a Georgia variety with whitish stems and blue-green leaves that can stand hot summers as well as Vates, a quicker maturing, more cold-resistant kind. (Lane Morgan recommends Vates as the best northern variety.) Plant seed ½ inch deep and 1 inch apart if starting indoors, 5 to 7 weeks before setting out. Then set out 18 to 24 inches apart, rows maybe 30 inches apart. To raise them in a container, plan on growing 1 per 8-inch pot, ½ gal. soil per plant, at least 6 inches deep, plants as close as 12 to 14 inches apart. The seeds will germinate in 6 to 9 days.

Harvesting. Collards take 75–85 days to reach maturity, but even before that you can whittle leaves off them to eat. Pick lower leaves as needed, but don't cut the whole plant off if you want it to keep on producing. It's a good fall crop. Frost sweetens its flavor. Plants produce generously. It's easy to get more than you can use.

Cooking. Collards need to be cooked longer than most of the other greens, and you'll do better starting with young, tender leaves anyway. Roll up like a newspaper, chop them up, and then cook. They are generally cooked by boiling with some bacon or salt pork or frying with a little bacon fat. The juices left in the saucepan are called "pot likker" and should be sopped up with hot corn bread. Or cook in a pressure cooker: Steam with vent open for half a minute; cook at 15 lb. pressure for 4 more minutes. Add flavoring and serve. Or substitute for cabbage in a stuffed cabbage recipe.

CRESS: There are basically 3 brassica cresses. All have a flat or curly leaf and a small stem. Watercress belongs to a different genus and is listed separately later on.

Pepper Cress. Pepper cress (*Lepidium sativum*) is also called "cress," "common cress," "garden cress," "peppergrass," and "sai yeung choy." It is actually more of an herb: The leaves are so spicy they're a seasoning rather than a true green.

Upland Cress. Upland cress, or "winter cress" (*Barbarea verna*) gets confused with pepper cress. It's a hardy perennial grown like lettuce or spinach.

You can order pepper and upland cress from Abundant Life and Shumway. Serve using watercress recipes.

KALE: It's *B. oleracea acephala* in Latin, used to be called "borecole" in British seed catalogs, and is called "kale" in American catalogs. Kale handles cold and heat well. It can be raised from the deep South to Alaska. Southerners can plant even in September or October and grow kale through the winter. It's likely to be the hardiest vegetable you've ever raised. In fact, kale endures cold so well that in a climate like the Midwest, you can leave it out in the garden all winter and depend on it for greens. It can handle quite a lot of heat too, providing you supply adequate water. You see a lot of purple and curly ornamental varieties of kale planted for display in winter "flower" gardens.

Varieties. The kales are all nonheading species of the cabbage genus, of the mustard family (Cruciferae), of the order Brassica. Basically there are 3 big kale categories:
- Collards proper, *Brassica oleracea acephala*. (See "Collards," a few entries back.)
- Kales that are closely related to collards and are also called *Brassica oleracea acephala*. These resemble a frilly, headless cabbage that you harvest leaf by leaf. They are more cold-hardy than the others and transplant well. Members of this group are the very curly kinds like Scotch, Cottagers, or Thousand-Headed (the huge stuff you grow for stock feed). These *B. oleracea acephalas* are significantly different from the following kale category.
- *B. napus pabularia,* a family of "kale" that is actually a cousin to the rutabaga. Good varieties include Russian, Siberia, and Hanover. They have looser leaves, are more likely to be reddish-tinted, and don't transplant well. They are less hardy but are sweeter in summer! (For that data, thanks to Binda Colebrook, Kale Queen of the maritime Northwest!)

Planting. In the deep South, plant even in September or October. In the Pacific Northwest, west of the Cascades, Lane Morgan says she wouldn't bother with spring-planted kale. "It doesn't taste that good in the summer anyhow. We plant in July or August in the ground vacated by the early peas or lettuces." If you've got a transplanting kind, you can plant it indoors, ½ inch deep and 1 inch apart, and transplant to the garden 6 to 12 inches apart. Or start it in the garden and thin it there. You can plant kale in the garden as much as 40 days before your frostfree date. Or plant in midsummer. Plant rows 30 inches apart.

Germination should happen in 6 to 9 days. Thin to a foot apart. Or you can raise kale in a container. There'll be room for only 1 kale plant per 12-inch pot. There should be at least 3 gal. of soil in the pot, at least 12 inches deep. A good thick mulch will protect garden kale from freezing to death in the worst weather.

Be sure to keep it watered in summer, and don't plow it up in the fall—let it keep producing.

Harvesting. Kale is 55 to 70 days to maturity and can live through frosts. When cold weather comes along, you'll still have kale. It will grow right through all but the fiercest winters. If frost does succeed in cutting it back, as soon as things warm up a little it will sprout new leaves. You can harvest leaves as you need them; more will keep growing. Pick the large outside leaves and let the little center ones grow. Or harvest whole plants as you thin, to 4 to 6 inches apart at first, more later. Use the tough outer leaves for soup, the tender inner ones for salad. Gradually, as your plants get bigger, you'll want to do further thinning. Very cold weather slows the growth of greens, causing tougher outer leaves. But tough leaves are still great for soup. Kale is biennial and will start to grow again in the spring. Those tender new leaves can be yet another harvest for you.

Saving Seed. Kale is a bee-pollinated biennial. The Asian ones cross with rutabaga; English types cross with most other brassicas. Seeds are viable for about 5 years. See other brassica entries for more seed-saving info.

Cooking. This plant has lots of vitamins and minerals, more than any of the other garden greens. Kale leaves are too coarse for salad greens unless you use just the small, young, tender ones. Wash carefully and discard the hard pieces of stalk. Kale is good cooked with pork, like cabbage.

Or cook in salted water until tender, drain and chop fine, and return to the pan with butter, salt, and pepper to taste. Mix and melt the butter and serve hot on buttered toast pieces. You can figure that 3 c. raw kale from the garden will cook down to a cup of kale for the table. If you are using kale leaves in other recipes, you may need to give them a special parboiling beforehand. They are not only the most vitaminaceous and hardy green, they are also the hardest to soften up and make edible! On the other hand, try not to overcook it because that's bad too. You've got to catch that moment of perfection.

About classic kale soups, Lane Morgan says: "Caldo Verde is a staple dish of Portugal—it's a soup of kale, potatoes, and spicy sausage. I've seen lots of different versions, including a vegetarian one with more garlic and olive oil instead of sausage. Another one is Brose, an ancient Scottish soup that is kale and beef broth, thickened with a handful of toasted rolled oats. I'm not crazy about it, but it would definitely get you through a lean winter—true and original homestead food."

MIZUNA: Also known as "kyona," mizuna (*Brassica japonica*) is a mild-flavored mustardy green that's good in salads. It has attractive, feathery foliage and is not usually bothered by pests or pestilence. It's best suited for fall planting since it bolts quickly if planted in spring. Thin to 8 inches apart. Mizuna grows particularly well inside a winter cloche or frame. If you plant it in summer or fall, it will go to seed the following spring, around April. Seeds from Territorial. Mature mizuna has many thin, light-green stalks in a rosette shape with deeply cut leaves. To harvest, take individual leaves from the outside, and the plant will keep producing them.

MUSTARD: Mustard (*Brassica juncea*), also called "mustard greens" or "mustard spinach," is another traditional southern—and Asian—green, one of the first available in the spring. Mustard is stronger in taste and tougher in texture than spinach and chard. There are many varieties. The traditional southern ones are covered here. Pak choi is the only mustard that can be planted spring, summer, fall, or winter and won't bolt distressingly soon.

Planting. Start them as early as February or March in fertile soil; they grow fast and bolt when May comes. (Or plant in fall.) Make your first planting about 20 days before your frostfree date. Plant ¼ to ½ inch deep. Plant 3 or 4 seeds per inch. Make rows 18 to 24 inches apart. To grow mustard greens in a container, allow at least a 6-foot depth of soil and at least ¼ gal. soil per plant. You can grow 2 plants per 8-inch pot if you space them 4 inches apart. Your seeds will germinate in 5 to 8 days. This is a cool-weather crop, although some new varieties have better resistance to heat and drought than the old ones.

Growing. Let a lot of plants stay in the row for a while if you have flea beetle problems. Once they've grown past the stage at which flea beetles are a problem, gradually thin to 9 inches between plants. You can eat the thinnings, of course. Keep plants well watered since a water shortage makes them much "hotter" to eat. They're self-seeders.

Saving Seed. The mustard varieties are bee-pollinated; they cross with each other and with turnips and Chinese cabbages. They are very sensitive to length of day versus length of night ("photoperiodic") and will go to seed in May, when days lengthen and temperatures increase. There are new slow-to-bolt varieties. But old-style ones go to seed; that seed grows with the next watering and you can end up with several generations of mustard in a garden. To save seed, cut the stalk once half the seed pods have dried, dry on cloth, thresh, and winnow. Seed viable 7 years.

Harvesting. They are rapid growers, about 35 to 45 days to harvest. They're best cut when the leaves are 4 to 6 inches long, but definitely cut them before they get too big and tough. The younger they are, the less "hot" they are to eat. They will bolt as soon as the day length triggers them to do so. Fall-planted mustard greens will keep going through light frosts; in fact, early frosts improve their flavor. They generally do well under a cloche or some such.

Recipe Ideas. A few leaves are good in salad. Or stir-fry with other veggies. Or steam and serve with vinegar and beans. Or cook with meat and veggies as a soup or stew. Mustard is traditionally cooked with salt pork. Chinese mustard has thick stems and fuzzy leaves and is good only if very young and small.

RAPE: This brassica mustard green variety is milder flavored than either kale or collards, can be mature as fast as 3 weeks, and is easy to grow in any soil. It can be grown as a cover crop, for animal forage, as a cooking green, and for its oil-rich seeds (canola). See "Flower Seeds."

ROCKET: *Eruca vesicaria sativa*, or rocket, is also called "arugula," "garden rocket," and "Mediterranean salad." This sharp-flavored green, a mustard relative, is used in small quantities to add flavor to salads, much like sorrel. It's a fairly hardy brassica, Mediterranean in origin (still popular in southern Europe and Egypt as a salad green). It will grow almost anyplace.

Planting. You can order rocket seeds from Burpee, Comstock, Cook's Garden, William Dam, DeGiorgi, Gurney, Hudson, Le Jardin du Gourmet, Nichols, Park, Redwood City, Shepherd's, or Vermont Bean. You can plant in a cold frame in winter—or in the garden in spring, as early as you please, because rocket can and will germinate despite the very wettest, coldest spring soils—as long as the ground isn't frozen. Plant it in a "perennial" site because, Lane Morgan says, "rocket will self-seed like crazy. It remains good-tasting about 3 years. Then you need to start over because the self-seeded gets too funky to eat."

Rocket seems to pop out of the ground and up in a flash, just like its name. You can use rocket like radishes to mark or break ground for slow-germinating seeds. For a steady supply of the most tender leaves, it's best if you plant a few seeds every week and keep picking for a constant supply of new young plants, which are the most flavorful. Or plant late in the summer for a fall harvest. Rocket can survive light frosts. As it gets colder, add a cold frame, or pot and move inside. In the Deep South, rocket can be grown only during the winter months. Rows should be at least a foot apart, seed covered with ½ inch of dirt. Thin seedlings to 6 to 9 inches apart.

Growing. Once up, rocket requires the odd combination of full sun and 30 to 50 days of cool weather to properly mature. Rocket that grows during the hottest part of the summer is likely to go to seed prematurely and be too strong tasting. (It may help to provide afternoon shade and very regular, deep watering.) The best rocket grows in well-prepared, rich soil that is kept constantly moist. Pull out overmature and/or bolted plants unless you're saving them for seed.

Harvesting. If you're just getting acquainted with rocket, be advised that it is definitely a flavoring salad ingredient rather than a foundation green because of its rather odd, strong, spicy flavor. It's essential to harvest it very young, when it's at its mildest; the older it gets, the stronger the flavor, and the leaves getting tough and stringy too. For mildest flavor, pick when the leaves are only 3 to 6 weeks old and the plant is under 6 inches high. You can still harvest up to 10 inches high; then stop for sure. If you don't pick rocket early and keep it down, it can get 2 feet high, but leaves from a plant like that are so bitter and spicy-hot as to be totally undesirable for eating raw. Don't worry about damaging the plant by cutting it. Like chard, it will keep growing back. Rocket is best if it goes directly from garden to table. If you must store it, pull plants up, roots and all; wrap root end in wet paper towels or cloth; and keep in fridge. You can freeze rocket using the basic process for freezing greens.

Recipe Ideas. Serve with hummus in pocket bread. Its bright green leaves are attractive as well as flavorful when added to the blander lettuces in any salad, especially one with feta cheese. Add to quiche; to any soup, cream or clear; or to any tomato dish. The flowers are edible, too, and go nicely in a raw salad. Or substitute in any sorrel recipe. Cooking will tame the flavor somewhat. The Italians saute rocket and then mix it in with pasta, or combine it with other cooked greens such as mustard and turnip greens. You can even get some good from bitter, stringy old rocket leaves by boiling, pureeing, and adding to soup. Or combine boiled, pureed rocket (young or old) with sour cream and herbs.

TURNIP GREENS: I've seen baby turnips bundled and sold tops and all as "turnip greens." They'd be good that way too. But in my garden, turnip greens are prickly, bugs riddle the leaves, and the turnips can't recover if they lose their tops. There is a better variety for this purpose, called "raab"; its entry is a bit later on.

TYFON: Lane Morgan says, "Tyfon is a turnip/rape cross that is really versatile. It makes a good winter green manure here [north Pacific coast], plus you can eat it all year long if temps don't drop below 0°F. It tastes like a mild mustard green. Young leaves go in salads. Big ones need some cooking. Territorial sells it."

WATERCRESS: *Nasturtium officinale*, or watercress, used to be the last entry in this chapter, back when it was organized alphabetically. Now it's in the middle. It makes me think of the time I climbed the tallest mountain for miles around and discovered layers of fossilized seashells making up the broken, bare rocks at the very top of it. That really boggled my mind. The high point I'd toiled all day to reach was once the bottom of an ocean!

Well, speaking of water . . . Watercress grows in cold, deep springs. I've seen it growing only once—on the road to Jackson Hole, WY, coming in from the Southwest. Near the side of the road there is a small cold spring, and therein grows watercress. Just a spring along the highway, free and giving watercress to anyone who knew where to find it.

I believe God answers prayer, but I think He doesn't ordinarily just hand things out free. God gives us fruitful labors, and it is our job to do the laboring part. We show our faith in His will to bless us by working on, undismayed by the apparently uncrossable river or unclimbable mountain. If we work, really work—you can pray and work at the same time, and that's how I do a lot of mine—and constantly search in your mind for God's will in your work, what you should work for and how you should work at it—then the Fruit is certain. Not just earthly fruits but, even more important, spiritual fruits of knowing how to love and experiencing love, both God's and man's, and the deep and lovely satisfaction of seeing God make of your soul-self a beautiful and worthy one.

We get our water from a spring here. It's peculiar in that it moves around. About every 3 months there is no water, and Mike climbs down the canyon to find out where the spring went. He always finds it, digs it out enough to make the water flow easily, and resets the pipe that carries the spring water to the first tank, which is in the canyon, and from which it gets pumped up to the tank above our house. So it isn't really suitable for growing watercress.

Growing. Gene Logsdon has a nice section on growing watercress in his book *Getting Food from Water*. I now know that you can grow watercress under a drippy faucet or in a planter containing cool water—or even in dirt in a planter that gets watered generously each day. The main thing is to keep giving it lots of water. Commercial growers set out the plants and then flood the area as if they were growing rice. Watercress seed is available from Abundant Life or Shumway. The taste is best and mildest in early spring, before it flowers.

Recipe Ideas. Remove the roots. Pick over and wash the watercress thoroughly. Make sure there are no water bugs. Drain and chill. Use raw like chives. Or arrange on chilled plates and serve with French dressing. Or add chilled cucumbers, diced or cut in thin slices. Or add to a tossed green salad with sliced tomato. Or mix watercress, shredded lettuce, and nutmeats with lemon juice for a salad dressing. Or chop and toss into soup. Or chop into a quiche mixture. Or cook like spinach and serve with an herb butter.

☙ *WATERCRESS SANDWICHES Strip watercress from the stems and sprinkle it with salt, paprika, and lemon juice. Or mix seasoned cress with mayonnaise (about 1 ½ c. cress per ¼ c. mayonnaise). Good with homemade whole wheat bread. Or serve cress like lettuce in a sandwich, along with tomato slices and mayo.*

☙ *WATERCRESS SOUP Peel and slice a large onion or leek and about 1 ½ lb. potatoes, and put them in a pan with 6 c. soup stock (or 3 c. milk, 3 c. water). Keep back about a third of the leaves of a large bunch of watercress. Add the rest to the stock along with the stalks. Cook until the vegetables are soft and then sieve the whole thing. Add a little flour for thickening; then add the chopped watercress leaves that you held back. Simmer 5 minutes more before serving.*

THE STEMS WE EAT

These are plants whose food storage site—or whose part we prefer to harvest—is a fleshy stem. There are 3 types of fleshy-stemmed plants. One is the new-growth spears: asparagus, hops (see Chapter 5), and young globe artichoke spears. A second is the edible stems, called "chards" or "stalks": cardoon, celery, celtuce, and rhubarb. The third type is plants that develop a rootlike bulge in their stem and store food there in something that looks somewhat like an aboveground root: celeriac and Florence fennel.

If there is below-ground stem storage, as with water chestnut and lotus, that's called a "corm"; I've listed corms in the section on roots and tubers. The onions certainly store food in their stems, but they're in their own section ("Alliums").

Asparagus

This perennial does well almost anywhere in Canada and in the United States as far south as southern Georgia. It likes cool temperatures during the growing season and winters that are cold enough to provide a dormant season. Asparagus dislikes extremely hot summers. Once it starts producing, it may live and fruit for 20 or more years. It literally shoots up overnight in my garden in the early spring, the second edible thing (multiplier onions are even earlier, radishes a shade later). On the other hand, it takes up considerable space and may be both difficult and slow to get started producing.

There's great info on asparagus, planting to harvest, at **aggie-horticulture.tamu.edu/extension/easygardening/ asparagus/asparagus.html**. Also see **www.abs.sdstate.**

edu/hort/asparag.htm. And **www.attra.org/attra-pub/ asparagus.html**. And **www.ext.nodak.edu/extnews/ askext/vegetabl/1121.htm**. Asparagus terms and varieties are explained at **www.orst.edu/Dept/NWREC/asparagu. html**. There's an asparagus reference service at **www.msue. msu.edu/msue/iac/agnic/asparagus.html**.

The Ohio Asparagus School, Carl Cantaluppi chief teacher, is an annual school for market growers of asparagus at Piketon, Ohio. Or buy *The Proceedings of the Ohio Asparagus School;* 740-289-2071; **piketon.osu.edu**.

PLANTING ASPARAGUS

Choosing Seed or Roots

NOTE: Asparagus seeds are poisonous.

Will you grow asparagus from seed? Or from roots? From 1-year-old roots? Or from 2-year-old or 3-year-old roots? The younger the roots (called "crowns") are, the cheaper they are but the longer it takes them to produce, a difference measured in *years*. You will harvest lightly from seeds in 3 years, normally after 4. You will begin getting a heavy harvest from 1-year-old crowns in 3 years, from 2-year-old crowns in 2 years, from 3-year-old crowns after 1 year. (You can get a light harvest earlier than that.) If you do buy roots, plant 15 for each family member. Most northern growers plant roots in the early spring. Southern growers tend to plant them in the fall.

The "Purple Passion" asparagus variety is available from Pendleton's Country Market: 785-843-1409; 1446 E. 850th Rd., Lawrence, KS 66046. You can buy bulk asparagus seed from Nourse Farms (413-665-2658; **www.nourse farms.com**) or Jersey Asparagus Farms (856-358-2548; **jaf@jafinc.com**; **www.jerseyasparagus.com**).

Choosing the Site. You do this only once every 25 years, so it's worth investing some effort. Choose your site carefully, one where the asparagus plants will not be in danger of being plowed up. Putting them in a long row at one side of your garden works well. It should be sunny and well-drained—because asparagus dies in waterlogged ground! For either asparagus seed or roots, your seedbed soil should be light and rich. Cultivate *deeply*. If the soil is not loose and light—if it's heavy clay, for example—add a little sand and a lot of compost. Like artichokes, asparagus is a heavy feeder. Start it out with a compost- or manure-rich soil.

Planting Seed. Asparagus seed is usually planted in a special seedbed or in seed flats. You can also use seeds to occasionally replenish your permanent bed of asparagus plants. Or plant directly to your garden. Start by pouring lukewarm (not hot!) water over the seed, and let it soak until cool. Pour off that water and do the same thing 3 more times. Or else soak the seed 48 hours at 85 to 90°F if you have a way to control the temperature. Plant the seeds 2 inches deep and about ½ inch apart, in rows 18 inches apart, as early in the spring as possible. Plant some radish seed together with the asparagus to mark row location for cultivation because asparagus takes 3 weeks to germinate.

When the plants are 2 inches tall, thin to about 1 inch apart. Weed frequently enough to keep out weeds. Be careful not to cut or disturb the asparagus when cultivating. From a seedbed, transplant the following spring, using directions for asparagus roots. If you planted in seed flats, transplant to your permanent site when the plants are well rooted.

Planting Roots. Proceed with care. Dig trenches 18 inches deep in rows 4 feet apart. Why the deep trench? Because a thriving asparagus plant has a strong root system that spreads as much as 6 feet horizontally and goes 6 to 8 feet down. The deep digging of the soil before you plant helps with that spreading, and the deep trench ensures that you get the asparagus' root system established *below* cultivation level, so you can use a rototiller within much of that 6-foot horizontal root-spreading area. Cover the bottom of the trench with a 6-inch layer of well-rotted manure. Spread 6 inches of topsoil over that. Now set in the asparagus crowns, 12 to 18 inches apart. Cover them with 2 inches of soil. As they grow, gradually cover them with more soil. Keep them weedfree.

GENERAL UPKEEP FOR AN ASPARAGUS BED: Both new and established asparagus beds benefit from fertilizer. You'll get some harvest without it, but more with it. And the spears actually taste better if they've been raised in rich soil! Manure is best for asparagus, compost second-best. Every fall, cover it with a blanket of manure or compost. Early the next spring, fertilize heavily again with about 3 inches of manure. Mulch is fine too, 4–6 inches thick, except don't put it on very young plants that might have trouble growing up through it. Asparagus also likes wood ashes. Keep out the weeds until you can't get in there anymore because of the growing asparagus. Some gardeners like to renew their asparagus bed by adding new seed every 15 or 20 years.

HARVESTING

Saving Seed. Asparagus makes seed every summer. At the end of the season cut the plant, seeds and all, and hang in an airy place to dry. Then remove the berries, dry, and store. Some people remove the berries, soak, mash off the outer shells, wash under running water, dry again, and store them like that.

Harvest Males or Females? You would think by now (50 years of age and 7 children), I'd have this sex thing straight, but a very tactful gentleman named Frank A. Yurg of Troy, MT, informed me that I didn't. And alas, he was right. I had told my readers to harvest the females and leave the males. This I stated in print for a dozen years, frozen in embarrassing inaccuracy. Now I'm putting out this humbly corrected version: You harvest the males and leave the females. To further clarify, the males are the fat spears and the females are the skinny ferns that grow up and up, the thin stems that will bear seeds.

I frequently tell my children to be skeptical of what they read, to never take anything as absolute truth just because it's on the printed page. I explain, "Your mother writes books, and you know how very human and prone to error she is!" When researching, I see how often the Experts flat out don't agree with each other. Then I have to choose with whom to side—which is tough if I have no idea who is right. Or maybe they both are. Or maybe neither is.

But anyway, I think I finally understand about asparagus sexes. Shoots that are quite spindly, like a pencil, are female and should not be harvested. They are the ones that will grow into the leafy fronds that help nourish the roots. Those ferns also eventually make bright red berries that are the asparagus seeds (*poisonous!*).

When and How. Wait until the bed is established, according to root age. Harvest conservatively the third year (for 4 to 6 weeks), heavily the fourth year (5 to 10 weeks), and the same from then on. Begin cutting when spears are 4 to 6 inches high and a thumb's thickness, just before the scales at the tips begin to open. Cut them off at, or just below, ground level—be careful not to injure other spears. Or snap them off by hand. The texture of a spear that is on the verge of outgrowing you (getting too big) will be changing to tough and stringy. If the compact tip of the spear has started to open, you no longer have a young, tender stalk. Early morning is the best time to harvest, since a hot day actually makes the stalks tougher and dryer. Make it a habit to get out to the asparagus bed every single day (or at least every 2 days) during your harvesting season.

When you are harvesting asparagus, there's no doing it halfway. You've got to take every sizable spear, or you'll have none. A spear that isn't cut and that manages to flower will inhibit further shoot production from that root. So until you're done for the season, all thick shoots need to be snapped off. When you stop harvesting depends on when you started: the later you start, the later you stop. In general, you will stop heavy harvesting at mid-June or very early July (in New England), although you can harvest lightly from a well-established bed on into late fall. The way you "harvest lightly" is by taking only shoots that are more than ½ inch in diameter.

PREPARING AND PRESERVING: Wash and discard any tough bottoms. Get rid of the scales that cling tightly to the lower half of the spear. Just lift the tip of each with a paring knife and pull it off. Or use a potato peeler if you're in a hurry. Get your asparagus from ground to preservation system or table as fast as possible for best taste. If you aren't going to process or cook it right away, refrigerate it.

Freezing. Choose firm young spears. Remove scales and toss into piles by size. Steam-blanch similar-sized stalks 2 to 4 minutes. Pack and freeze.

Drying. Dry right after picking. Wash, drain, and split 3-inch tips into lengthwise pieces. Or split the entire stalk lengthwise into halves. Or cut into ½-inch slices. Blanch for 3 minutes in boiling water, or steam for 5 minutes. Drain thoroughly. Asparagus must be dehydrated relatively quickly—in strong sunlight or a dehydrator. Use dried asparagus in soups and sauces or, after simmering 30 minutes, as a vegetable dish.

Canning. First wash asparagus and cut off any tough ends. If canning whole spears, place them upright in a pan with the water level just below the tender tips. Boil 3 minutes. For canned asparagus sections, cut spears into pieces about 1 inch long, and boil them for 2 to 3 minutes. Then pack either spears or pieces into clean jars. Optional: Add salt. Cover with boiling water. Leave 1 inch headspace. Process in a pressure canner only: 30 minutes for pints, 40 minutes for quarts. If using a weighted-gauge canner, set at 10 lb. pressure at 0–1,000 feet above sea level; at higher altitudes, set at 15 lb. If using a dial-gauge canner, set at 11 lb. pressure at 0–2,000 feet above sea level; 12 lb. at 2,001–4,000 feet; 13 lb. at 4,001–6,000 feet; 14 lb. at 6,001–8,000 feet; or 15 lb. above 8,000 feet.

PICKLED ASPARAGUS *You'll need 8 pt. asparagus spears, 6 c. water, 6 c. white vinegar (5 percent), 6 T. salt, 2 t. pickling spice (remove cloves), and 1 clove of garlic per jar. Wash asparagus well in cool water. Cut into jar-length spears. Combine water, vinegar, salt, and mixed pickling spices (tied into a clean thin white cloth). Heat to boiling. Remove bag containing spices and pack asparagus into pint or quart jars* *(with tip ends down for easier removal). Put 1 clove garlic in each jar. Cover with boiling brine, leaving ½ inch headspace. Adjust jar lids. Process in boiling-water bath. For either pints or quarts, at up to 1,000 feet above sea level, process 10 minutes; at 1,001–6,000 feet, 15 minutes; and above 6,000 feet, 20 minutes. Or use lower-temperature pasteurization detailed in "Pickles" section under "Cucumbers."*

Recipe Ideas. The tender new tips are good raw. Just snap off and eat. Before boiling or steaming, first wash and remove any tough ends. Leave the spears long or cut into 2 lengths.

❧ *BOILED ASPARAGUS Add the tender tops after the stalks have boiled for 10 or 15 minutes, since they require less cooking. If you want to leave the stalks whole, stand them on end in the water so the tips are out; then lay them down as soon as the bottoms begin to get tender. Boiled asparagus is good served just with a little butter, vinegar, salt, and pepper. Or put a cream sauce on spears cooked whole, or cut into short pieces and serve on toast.*

❧ *ASPARAGUS SALAD Drain boiled asparagus, chill, cut into pieces, arrange on lettuce leaves, and serve with French dressing.*

❧ *FRIED ASPARAGUS Use only tender stalk tops. Precook until half-done. Tie stalks together, 5 or 6 to a bundle. Dip in beaten egg and then into flour. Fry in deep fat.*

❧ *ASPARAGUS SOUP This is a good way to make use of tough ends. Cut about 1 lb. asparagus into 1-inch pieces. Cook with a little salt until tender in 1 qt. water. Make a white sauce by stirring 4 T. flour into 4 T. melted butter. Add to soup along with 1 beaten egg yolk and a dash of rich cream.*

❧ *RUTH'S VEGAN ASPARAGUS "Steam instead of boiling; it's much more flavorful. Drizzle with lemon juice while hot."*

Cardoon

Cardoon (*Cynara cardunculus* or *Scolymus cardunculus*) is a tender perennial of the thistle family, an ancestor of the globe artichoke (similarly grown but a little hardier) and a cousin to Canadian thistle. It looks like a huge celery plant. Although it has been cultivated for its huge leaf stalks for over 30,000 years around the Mediterranean, especially northern Italy, it is little known and seldom grown in the United States. In the Seattle area, Angelo Pellegrini raised it, praised it, and described how to grow and cook it in *The Food Lover's Garden*. For more cardoon info, also see *Oxford Book of Food Plants* by Simons.

GROWING: Seed is available from DeGiorgi, Comstock, William Dam, Gurney, Nichols, Redwood City, etc. (Or propagate by root division, taking and replanting suckers.) In a temperate zone, start seed indoors in March. Transplant to garden after last frost, 3 feet apart because cardoons need space—they can get 6 feet tall and quite wide! You can plant them in trenches as you'd plant leeks, gradually filling the trenches in with dirt as the cardoons grow; this is a natural blanching system for the "cardoon heart." In a subtropical zone, cardoon plants can be planted directly into the garden and can also winter outside if temps don't drop below the high 20s; they'll make new growth in the spring.

BLANCHING: Unblanched, mature cardoon stalks are virtually inedible because of bitterness and toughness. When the leaves are almost full grown, tie them together near the

top. Then pile straw or some other covering around the head, and hoe up dirt against that. Leave that way for 2 to 4 weeks, and then harvest (it'll be ready around November). Some people bend the stems over into a trench and cover with a foot of dirt, leaving just a bit of leaf exposed at the top. Some cover with cardboard rather than dirt. Another blanching method is to harvest the entire plant before frost (leaving the roots on) and then keep it in a dark, root-cellar–type place for a month before using.

SAVING SEED: Lane Morgan writes from her home near the Canadian border in western Washington that her cardoons have flowered: "huge gorgeous flowers." Given enough time, seed follows the flowers, and the plant self-sows.

HARVESTING: You want very young stalks. Cut them off near the ground. Or choose the mild, tender, meaty, white-yellow leaf-ribs from the center. Avoid outer stalks, which are too tough. Trim off and discard the upper portion of the stalk. In a mild climate, if you harvest only part in the autumn and leave the plant in place, you'll get another harvest in the spring.

PREPARING AND PRESERVING: They'll store for as long as 7 days in your refrigerator. Before using, strip and trim each cardoon stalk to eliminate fuzziness. Discard every bit of leaf because of their bitterness. Cut into 2- to 4-inch sections. Unblanched cardoons must be boiled longer than blanched ones (as long as an hour) to make them tender.

Canning. Cardoon may be canned. In fact, this is probably the best preservation system for it. Use the times given for canning broccoli.

Recipe Ideas. Add to soups or stews. Dip in flour and egg, and then fry. Tea made by steeping cardoon leaf fuzz has been used in Europe as a substitute for rennet in the cheese-making process.

❧ *STEWED CARDOONS "This dish presents the unadorned flavor of cardoons. Once cooked, they can be sprinkled with a cup of grated cheese and run under the broiler, or covered with cream sauce and some bread crumbs and baked 20 minutes at 400°F." Remove any tough strings and slice 4 lb. cardoons (about 8 big stalks) into ½-inch pieces. Put 3 T. lemon juice in a bowl of cold water, add cardoons, and let stand for 15 minutes. Drain and cook about 20 minutes in 1 inch of lightly salted water. Drain again and put in medium skillet with 2 c. water, 3 T. olive oil, 2 sliced cloves of garlic, 2 T. chopped parsley, and salt and pepper to taste. Cook, covered, at low heat for 30 minutes. Remove cover and continue simmering until liquid has evaporated. From Lane Morgan's Winter Harvest Cookbook.*

❧ *CARDOONS PELLEGRINI Trim and slice 1 lb. cardoons into 2-inch pieces and blanch 3 or 4 minutes in boiling salted water. Remove and drain. (You can save the cooking water for soup.) Melt 2 oz. lean salt pork, minced and pounded to a paste; 2 T. olive oil; and 2 t. butter in a skillet. Add 3 shallots or 1 small onion, minced; 2 garlic cloves, and 1 T. chopped celery leaves. Saute gently, watching carefully so mixture does not brown. Add ⅓ c. tomato sauce, ⅓ c. beef or chicken stock, and 3 T. lemon juice. Simmer a few minutes until mixture is well blended. Add cardoons, cover, and cook until tender. Recipe from Angelo Pellegrini via Lane Morgan's Winter Harvest Cookbook.*

❧ *CARDOONS LYONNAISE "You can serve cardoons with a simple cream sauce, but the delicate artichoke flavor goes* especially well with the bit of lemon and Gruyere in this dish." Preheat oven to 425°F. Cut 1 lb. slender cardoons into bite-sized pieces and sprinkle with juice of half a lemon. Simmer about 30 minutes in a medium saucepan with just enough water to cover. Remove cardoons from heat, drain, and saute in 2 T. olive oil over medium heat until golden brown. Meanwhile, gently heat 1 c. vegetable stock and add 1 c. dry white wine. Melt 1 T. butter in small saucepan. Add 1 T. flour, stirring to mix thoroughly. Gradually add stock and wine mixture, stirring constantly. Cook gently until mixture thickens; simmer 5 more minutes and remove from heat. Stir in 1/2 c. grated cheese (Gruyere preferred) and the juice from the other half of the lemon. Put cardoons in shallow casserole. Pour sauce over and bake, uncovered, 10 to 15 minutes. From Lane Morgan's Winter Harvest Cookbook.

Celeriac

Apium graveolens var. *rapaceum*, a little-known relative of celery, is a valued winter veggie in Europe. Other names for it are "celery root," "knob celery," and "turnip-rooted celery." The edible part is its enlarged, knobby combination stem base/root crown/tap root. It does best if your weather is above 45°F and below 75°F. It's easier to grow and stores much better than celery but grows more slowly, is a chore to clean, and takes longer to cook. It can be eaten in soups and salads and as a vegetable.

PLANTING/GROWING: In warm zones, gardeners plant celeriac seed directly into the garden in late summer 1/8 inch deep. Temperate-zone gardeners must plant early in flats—February to April. Soil should be manure-rich and fairly moist. Spread seed generously; germination tends to be spotty and slow. Allow 15 to 20 days for germination and figure about 120 more to harvest. If the flat gets crowded before setting-out time in June, separate plants to 2–3 inches apart or individual pots. Harden off. Soak ground to muddiness before transplanting, and keep previous soil around the roots, since they may die if exposed to air. In the garden, thin to 4–6 inches between plants, 12–24 inches between rows. Keep well watered since dryness toughens the knob. Some people blanch celeriac and some don't. To blanch, hoe dirt up around the knobs for the final several weeks before harvest.

SAVING SEED: This is a biennial of the same species as celery. Setting out a house-planted start when night temps are still under 45°F can stimulate a seed stalk the first year instead of the "root." Follow directions for saving celery seed.

HARVESTING AND WINTER STORAGE: Start using celeriac roots when they are 2 inches thick. Harvest season starts about late September and lasts till spring. A late crop can be stored in the garden until needed if you have a mild climate. For temps below 18°F, bring dirt over and mulch over that to keep them from freezing. Or dig up the roots as ground-freezing weather gets closer, cut off all but an inch of the tops, and store in root cellar in dry or damp sand, as you would carrots. They will keep like that for months.

PREPARING: The part you eat is the enlarged root just above the ground, which usually grows to a diameter of 4 inches or so. Don't eat the leaves.

➣ *CELERIAC SALAD Ruth: "Slice celeriac thinly and then cut peel away. Slice into 'matchsticks.' Place in steamer basket; steam about 5–10 minutes until tender-crisp. Then toss with a dressing of mustard and diluted lemon juice. Serve*

chilled." Lane Morgan's dressing for celeriac salad: "Serve with a well-flavored mayonnaise. This is sensational with some shrimp or crab. Or just grate raw celeriac, sprinkle with lemon juice, and add to carrot slaw." Phyllis Valette: "Serve grated raw celeriac with vinaigrette. Wonderful!"

About Scrubbing/Peeling. Scrub the root thoroughly. If you peel it after cooking, it's easier to scrub. (Trim away those knoblike buds on the surface while you're at it.) But peeling it before cooking saves some scrubbing effort. Easiest of all is to cut first and then peel.

Precooking. For fastest cooking, peel first and then halve or quarter—or even slice or cube, in which case you may be able to cook this slow-cooking vegetable in 20 minutes. An uncut, freshly dug whole root, say 3 inches thick, might take an hour and a half of boiling or steaming with the lid on the pan to really get tender. Strangely enough, old celeriac will cook faster than the fresh kind. The cooking water from celeriac makes a good soup base or addition to any soup.

Recipe Ideas for Cooked Celeriac. Cooked celeriac tastes like celery flavored with English walnuts. Serve with tamari, lemon juice, melted butter, or a cheese or white sauce. Or dice and add to any stew or soup. Or add thin, shredded "chips" of lightly presteamed celeriac to a stir-fry mixture.

➣ *FRIED CELERIAC Cut the precooked "root" into slices 1/2 inch thick. Coat them with flour on both sides, dip into slightly beaten egg whites, and then dip into fine, dry bread crumbs. Fry in a little butter or oil over medium heat until lightly browned, first on one side and then the other. Sprinkle on a little salt and serve.*

Celery

Growing celery (*Apium graveolens dulce*) is slow and challenging. It's not a basic sustenance plant like carrots, potatoes, and tomatoes. But garden-fresh celery tastes better than any store-bought celery, so you might want to try for it.

VARIETIES: Don't plant the type of celery seed that's used for flavoring; that variety doesn't make an edible stalk, but it quickly produces abundant seed. Commercial-type celery is better adapted for intensive commercial growing in a suitable part of the country (celery probably originally grew in a swamp) than for your garden. Home gardeners may prefer one of the "nonblanching" varieties or "cutting celery," an ancestor to the commercial variety . . .

Cutting Celery. Lane Morgan: "We have good soil and coolish weather, so I've tried all kinds of celeries. Of all that temperamental clan, I think the easiest for the home gardener is 'leaf celery' ['cutting celery,' 'Chinese celery,' 'kin tsai,' or *Apium graveolens secalinum*]. Nichols sells it as French Celery Dinant. It has thin, leafy stalks that are too strong-tasting to eat raw but are fine for flavoring soup, tomato sauce, etc. [Use half as much to compensate for its stronger taste.] It is quicker, more disease resistant, and less prone to rot than the big blanching types." It's hardier too; if mulched, it can get through most winters to grow again in the spring.

WHEN TO PLANT: Celery takes 115 to 135 days to mature, and it likes cool weather. In northern areas with a cool summer, you have a chance of growing it in summer if you start it indoors or in a cold frame sometime in February through April. Then transplant to the garden. On average, celery plants spend 10 to 12 weeks indoors before transplanting to the garden. In a long-season, temperate climate, plant directly outside mid-April through May—that gets you a fall crop. It doesn't like hot weather, so in the South plant for maturing around late November or even late December.

HOW TO PLANT: Plant in very rich soil that has lots of manure and is loose and loamy, because celery is one of the heaviest-feeding plants. Commercial crops are usually grown on marsh or peat soils after they have been drained. Make a little ditch. Fill it with two-thirds fine-textured dirt and one-third rich compost. Plant on that, ¼ inch deep. Don't let the seedbed dry out even once until the plants are up, 10 to 15 days later. Then ease off on the water lest you drown them. You can start a multitude of plants in a small box. When the second leaves appear, transplant 1½ to 2 inches apart into larger boxes; then gradually harden them by exposure to open air and sunshine on warm days. When your weather is well past the last frost and dependably warm and the little celery plants are 5 or 6 inches high, set them out in the garden 12 inches apart, rows 18 inches apart.

If you live in an area where you can plant the seed directly into the garden, a light mulch over it will help it grow. After the plants come up, carefully remove the mulch. Fall celery is planted in the garden and then thinned in place or transplanted to better spacing when no more than 3 inches high. Celery takes a lot of water; it prefers flood irrigation to sprinkling because its roots are adapted to pulling water out of soaked bogs. Keep weeds out.

SAVING SEED: Celery is a self-fertile, insect-pollinated biennial. It will cross with celeriac or other celeries. In cold zones, choose your best plants in the fall. Dig them out, being careful not to harm roots. Replant them in dirt in something you can keep in a root cellar, the above-ground part mulched with straw. Replant in spring after last frost; trim rotted parts. In warm zones, plant for seed in July and transplant in January. Set out 2 feet apart because second-year growth gets high and wide. Later come tiny white blooms; still later, brown seeds. To avoid loss on the ground, shake the top heads (which mature seed first) into a bag once in a while. Cut and dry on cloth or paper. Seed viable 5 years.

BLANCHING: Blanching lightens color and makes the flavor milder. If you don't want to blanch, get a nonblanching variety. To blanch, raise the dirt level up 4 to 5 inches around the sides of the row, or plant the last 10 days or so.

HARVESTING: You can rob the plant of a stalk or leaf anytime through its growing period without ruining it. You can use harvesting as a way of thinning as soon as the plants get big enough to be worth the trouble. Half-grown celery is just as edible as the full-grown stuff. Cut plants at ground level and just leave the roots in the dirt to become compost. If your winters are mild, celery will survive in your garden to spring. Pick side stalks as needed. In this case, don't take off the entire head; that way the stalks can stay fresh and keep coming.

Root Cellar/Pit Storage. Dig before hard frosts and store in boxes, covered with slightly damp sand or dirt, in your root cellar. Or leave in the ground, cover entire row with at least 6 inches of dirt, and put a heavy mulch like straw over that. Or transplant to a cold frame in late fall, closely planted side by side, or transplant to a box of damp earth in your root cellar. *Don't wash before storage. Don't store with*

turnips or cabbage. Ideally, keep as cool as possible without actually freezing. Celery will keep 1 to 2 months.

Freezing. To freeze celery, you have to cook it first; some people don't like it that way. If you don't mind it, cut across the rib into about 1-inch sections. Steam-blanch 3 minutes, chill, drain, and package. You can freeze leaves to add to stews and soups—but freeze them separately.

Drying. Trim off leaves, etc., and rinse stalks. Cut stalks into really thin slices. Don't blanch. Spread slices on drying trays. Dry at 120°F in dehydrator or oven. Dry when crisp. To dry leaves: Rinse and shake dry. Chop or dry whole. Spread in a thin layer over your dryer tray. Dry outside in an airy, shaded area—or in oven or dehydrator at 110°F. Dry until crisp. Use to flavor stews, salads, soups, or any cooked dish. Use celery seed you've saved and dried in similar ways.

Canning. Add celery to your canned tomato sauce, substituting it for part of the pepper or onion in the recipe. Or add to canned meat or stock. To can it alone, use directions for canning broccoli.

CELERY VINEGAR *Combine ¼ lb. celery seed or 1 qt. fresh celery chopped fine, 1 qt. vinegar, 1 T. salt, and 1 T. sugar. Put celery in a jar; heat the vinegar, sugar, and salt; and pour in boiling hot over celery. Cool, cover tightly, and set away. After 2 weeks, strain and bottle.*

CELERY SOUP *Serve cooked celery with a white sauce made with cream to thicken the broth, a beaten egg yolk, and seasonings.*

Celtuce

This lettuce variety (*Lactuca sativa* var. *angustata*) is also called "asparagus lettuce" and "stem lettuce." It comes from China and combines celery and lettuce traits. The edible part is the enlarged seed stalk, not the leaves at the end of the stalk. Seed is available from Nichols and Kitazawa. Grow like a summer lettuce. Use the stalks like celery—either raw in salads, as sticks with dips, or cooked like asparagus and served with a sauce. Or stir-fry with meat and daikon chunks and serve with a Chinese sauce.

Florence Fennel

Florence fennel, or "finnochio" (*Foeniculum vulgare dulce*), is a relative of the herb called fennel. It's grown for the swollen stems at its base, which are cooked like a vegetable after the leaves are cut away. Florence fennel is an easy-to-grow perennial, but I don't care for its bitter, licorice, herb-type flavor.

GROWING: Seeds are available from William Dam and Redwood City. Plant between April and mid-July. Gradually thin to a foot apart. It matures quickly. Cover base of plant with dirt to blanch; this makes its flavor milder. Dig or pull to harvest when the bulb is 2½ to 3 inches wide. If allowed to grow larger, it gets stringy and tough. Later plantings can endure some frosts.

RECIPES: Eat raw or cooked. (It's milder-tasting when cooked.) Substitute in any celery recipe. The leaves go in salads, fish, soups, etc. The bulb can be used when it measures about 2 inches across. To cook, peel and slice the bulb and as much of the stalk as is tender. Cook in boiling salted water until tender-crisp. Drain. Sprinkle with salt, pepper, and butter—or grated Parmesan. Or slice and boil with green beans and serve with chopped parsley and butter. Or cook with meat and vegetables.

➤ *BENGALI EGGPLANT Preheat oven to 375°F. Split 3 eggplants lengthwise. Then cut each half lengthwise (cut side down) into ½-inch thicknesses to form fans. Leave stem ends attached. Cut 3 large tomatoes into thin slices, placing 1 slice between eggplant sections. In a large (nonstick) baking dish (9 × 13 inches or so), scatter 1 small, thinly sliced fennel bulb on bottom. Arrange eggplant in dish, gently forcing fan sections together to make it fit. Wedge any remaining tomato slices in between, as well as 2 cassia or bay leaves (broken in pieces). Scatter another thinly sliced fennel bulb on top along with 1 t. coriander seeds, ½ t. fennel seeds, ½ t. fresh-ground black pepper, 1 T. chopped fresh basil, and 1 T. chopped fresh cilantro. Cover dish and bake 1½ hours, until stem end of eggplant is soft to touch. Uncover and broil 3 inches from heat until fennel slices start to be brown-edged. Sprinkle with 2 more tablespoons each of chopped basil and cilantro. Serve hot or cold. From Ruth of Bonaire.*

Globe Artichoke

The globe artichoke was hard for me to classify. But the artichoke is unique among the food plants in that the part we eat is the base of the unopened flower bud—and the top of the bud's stem (aha!). Its closest (and only) edible relative is the cardoon, an edible stalk (second aha!). And you can also eat artichoke sprouts like asparagus (third aha!). So I listed it here.

The globe artichoke (*Cynara scolymus*) is a semihardy thistle variety that does nicely in California but not in Idaho. Globe artichokes have the reputation of being a difficult plant to grow. A perennial, thriving artichoke can be 5 feet high and 5 feet wide. Lane Morgan: "It's not a very defensible use of garden space—that huge plant for this exquisite little treat—but they are unbelievably good."

CLIMATE: The artichoke-growing center of the United States is Castroville, about 100 miles south of San Francisco, where fields of artichokes stretch literally mile after mile. Old-time varieties of globe artichoke hate cold and cannot normally be grown where there are ever zero-degree temperatures. They also don't grow to their full 5 × 5-foot size if winters are too cold or summers too hot for their systems. They do best in southern coastal areas with mild weather both in winter and in summer. If you live in a climate where artichokes are natural perennials, consider growing 5 plots of them, starting one in each of 5 consecutive years. After 5 years of production, you dig out those

particular plants, refertilize, and start over. But some gardeners in colder areas have to grow them as an annual, using recently developed, hardier, quicker-maturing varieties that will bear the first year. And that can work too.

SOIL: Artichokes don't thrive in heavy, clay soils. They need some sand and lots of humus. Like asparagus, globe artichokes are "heavy feeders" and will thrive according to how much manure or compost was mixed in with their soil to start with. They'll even take fresh chicken manure and love it. A lightly manured artichoke may live and bear pretty well for 3 or 4 years, although the buds it produces may be smaller each year. If you really load the manure on it, the plant might go to 6 years of production.

PLANTING SUCKERS: In California globe artichokes are perennials that are planted by cutting off and planting suckers. If you have a choice, don't save your own artichoke seed. Instead, use the system of transplanting sprouts (suckers). Six plants are enough for an average-sized family. You can buy dormant roots or young plants from California nurseries, or take starts off your own or a friend's artichoke. To do that, you plant the side shoots that come up from the base of the old plants. These are like sprouts, are called "suckers," and grow in the spring, from 2 to 20 per mature plant. (You can cut and eat them like asparagus if you don't want to use them to start new artichoke plants!) When the suckers are about a foot high, they're ready to take. Dig away the soil from the parent plant's crown. When you cut off each sucker, take a portion of the plant roots with it. Cut off the larger outer leaves. For best results, replant immediately. Transplant suckers, or plants grown from seeds or purchased from a nursery, as described below. If you plant suckers rather than seed, you may get a first-year crop, though buds are typically small.

PLANTING SEED: You can plant seed, but it won't bear much fruit the first year unless you have a new variety, the "annual artichoke," from Territorial. A further problem with artichoke seeds is that their offspring frequently revert to the thistle side of their heredity, so a certain percentage of them won't produce well for you. But they're the cheapest way to get started. Start seed indoors or in a greenhouse in February to mid-March in individual 3-inch pots. Six to 8 weeks later, when they have 3 or 4 leaves apiece, it's time to transplant them to your garden.

TRANSPLANTING: Place them 24 inches apart, hilled like squash, in rows 3 feet apart. Supply 1 c. concentrated fertilizer or 1 shovelful chicken manure, well worked into the hill of soil, before the transplanting. Keep them well watered. A frost will destroy young buds, though more will develop. If you have a blazing rather than a mild summer, on the other hand, you will need to use 8 to 12 inches of mulch and some shading system, in addition to the generous watering, at least until they are well started. Or you can plant suckers; they'll get going faster and bear the first year.

WINTERING: If you're in a subtropical zone, wintering will be no problem, but if your zone is marginal, it will require special attention. After the growing season is over, thin to your very best plants, about 1 every 4 feet. Cut plant off about 6 inches above the ground. Gardeners argue a lot about what to do next.

Mulch. Every northern artichoke grower has a favorite system—which may or may not work. In general, you cover the remaining stem with something, such as a mound of straw and then sheets of plastic over that. Or a mound of straw, covered by a layer of leaves, which is covered by a layer of dirt, which is covered by a basket. The nifty trick is that they need to be kept warm but they also need air. If you do this and your climate or your winter is only marginally cold, you might luck out and have a perennial artichoke. In the spring, remove the basket or plastic. The artichoke will come right up through the mulch on its own.

Dormant Root. Where the ground freezes solid, try creating dormant roots. Leave them in the ground until hard frost is forecast. Then dig the roots up carefully, cut the leaves back to an inch or two of the crown, and brush off loose dirt. Wrap the roots in something organic that allows air circulation—such as burlap. Store in a dry place at about 33–40°F. Plant in the spring using the directions for transplanting.

HARVESTING: You will be able to harvest annual artichokes during August and September. An individual plant will produce from 2 to 20 artichokes per season. Lane Morgan says: "When you grow your own, you have the wherewithal for dishes that shoppers never see. If you pick the chokes just bigger than egg-sized, you can slice them straight down the middle lengthwise and saute them like that. There's none of that thistly stuff in the middle."

The mature artichoke bud resembles a large scaly head, like the cone of a pine tree; it grows on the top of a long stalk (the flower stalk). Get the buds when they have finished growing but before they flower (open). What you are going to eat is the flower bud before it opens. If in doubt, cut too young. If you wait too long and the bud starts to open, the inside gets woody. Harvest faithfully, because if you keep taking the buds off so that no seed can form, the plants will continue to produce until the end of the season. It's handy to leave 1 or 2 inches of stem on the artichoke at this stage. Buds that mature in the hottest part of the summer are tougher than those that come before and after that heat.

PREPARING AND PRESERVING: Pull off the tough outer leaves. Cut off the prickly top with scissors. The edible portion is the thickened base of each scale and the bottom/center/core to which the leaflike scales are attached. That bottom center, or "heart," is the most tender and delicious part of the artichoke. *Basic rule on hearts: Soak them in lemon juice and water. Otherwise they turn dark.* You can store fruits in the refrigerator for up to 2 weeks if you must delay using them. Angelo Pellegrini's cookbook has good instructions on handling garden-grown artichokes and recipes for them.

Freezing. First pull away the outer leaves until you reach light yellow or white ones that are free of all green (same if you're going to freeze them). Then cut off the top of the bud and trim to a cone shape. Wash in cold water and keep under water with a plate on top to hold them under until all your hearts have been trimmed. Add ½ c. bottled lemon juice and water to cover. Boil 5 minutes and freeze (or pickle as in next paragraph).

Canned, Pickled Artichokes. Follow directions for freezing in preceding paragraph. For your pickling solution, mix in a pan 2 c. olive or salad oil, 2½ c. white vinegar (5 percent), 1 T. oregano leaves, 1 T. dried basil leaves, and 1 T. canning or pickling salt. Stir in ½ c. finely chopped onion and ¼ c. diced pimento (optional) and heat to boiling. (You can expand this recipe—double, triple, etc.—as needed.) Place ¼ garlic clove and 2 to 3 peppercorns in each *half-pint* jar.

Fill the half-pint jars with artichoke hearts. Pour over them your hot, well-mixed oil-vinegar solution. Leave ½ inch headspace. Adjust lids and use boiling-water bath processing: Process in half-pints only. At up to 1,000 feet above sea level, process 20 minutes; at 1,001–3,000 feet, 25 minutes; 3,001–6,000 feet, 30 minutes; and above 6,000 feet, 35 minutes.

EATING AN ARTICHOKE: Your first priority is to carefully distinguish between the edible parts and the nonedible parts. They're very close! Remember the thistle heritage! When the artichoke is very young and tender, the edible parts can be eaten raw as a salad. When it becomes hard, as it does very quickly, it must be cooked. Hearts can be cut up for a salad or stewed and served with a sauce.

➤ *BOILED WHOLE ARTICHOKE Boil with 2 T. lemon juice until you can easily remove a leaf. After boiling, drain upside down and then serve. One artichoke per person, served on a saucer or in a bowl, is about right. It's nicest to provide a little individual container of melted butter or mayonnaise at each plate for that dipping. The eater pulls scales with the fingers one by one from the cooked head. The thickened base of each scale is dipped in a sauce and then eaten by dragging it through your clenched teeth to scrape off the soft, good part from the tough upper part.*

➤ *OTHER ARTICHOKE SAUCES These are good on cold artichoke hearts: French salad dressing, Hollandaise sauce, or mayonnaise seasoned with lemon juice and mustard.*

➤ *FRIED ARTICHOKES AND MUSHROOMS Fried artichoke hearts go well with mushrooms. Use 1 part sliced mushrooms and 1 part sliced artichoke hearts. Season with salt and garlic powder and bake in a baking dish about 20 minutes.*

➤ *RUTH'S VEGAN ARTICHOKES For a tastier product with nutrients intact, steam instead of boiling. When done cooking but still hot, dribble lemon juice all over. Then you can eat plain or with a sauce of mustard, lemon juice, and rice milk. Or eat with a handful of ground nuts or seeds mixed with lemon juice and blended to dip consistency.*

Rhubarb

Rhubarb (*Rheum rhabarbarum*) is a hardy perennial from Siberia, a relative of buckwheat that grows on its own year after year once (20 years easily) it's started. A good plant for the northern third of the United States, it is one of the earliest spring producers. Rhubarb thrives on being frozen all winter.

PLANTING: Start with 2- or 3-year-old roots. Plant in spring or fall. For one family, 2 to 4 plants are plenty. Dig a hole in your perennial area, put a layer of compost/manure in it, and then put in the root. Cover with an inch of dirt. Separate plants by 2 to 4 feet, rows by 4 to 6 feet, because they'll end up big. Don't take any stalks the first year from spring-planted rhubarb. Fall-planted rhubarb may be lightly harvested next spring.

HARVESTING

NOTE: Rhubarb leaves eaten in large amounts, even when cooked, can cause convulsions and coma rapidly followed by death. The root is also poisonous.

The stalks are the edible part. Remove them by cutting or by twisting and pulling up and out. You can use them at almost any size, but it's kind of a waste to take them when less than 8 inches long. Generally people take the biggest ones first. Leave at least a third of them for the plant to make food from. Spring rhubarb is the nicest. Later the stalks get woody. Pulling off seed stalks will keep your rhubarb producing. Compost discarded leaves; don't give them to animals.

PROPAGATING: A 5-year-old (or older) plant is ready to be divided. Using a sharp-edged shovel, cut off parts of the root. They can be transplanted to make new plants. Rhubarb does send up a seed stalk after the first year, but the seeds don't always breed true to the parent, are more trouble, and reduce stalk production.

PRESERVING AND PREPARING

Drying. Thinly slice (or chop) unpeeled red stalks. If you are drying for a snack, sweeten them with a honey solution or sprinkle with sugar before drying. Then spread in a single layer over the drying surface. Dry in dehydrator or oven at 120°F. Stir and rotate trays as needed. To reconstitute dried rhubarb, just add boiling water in an equal amount and let set. If you add sugar and simmer, it makes a rhubarb sauce.

➤ *RHUBARB LEATHER In general, rhubarb is more of a trial than a blessing to me because it seems to require so much sweetening to make it edible. But you can make rhubarb leather by washing and cutting up your rhubarb pulp. Rhubarb and raspberries go very well together to make a mixed fruit leather. Rhubarb is so acidic that you can't dry it on any metal surface like a cookie sheet. You have to use plastic underneath and be careful not to let the pulp get under the plastic.*

Freezing. Wash stalks. Cut into ½-inch chunks. Blanch 1 minute—or don't blanch, as you prefer. Cool. Pack into containers or bags, close, and freeze. Optional: Pack it sprinkled with sugar or even covered with syrup (leave headspace).

Canning. Wash. Cut into ½-inch chunks. Mix in ½ to 1 c. sugar per 1 qt. rhubarb. Let set several hours to draw out juice. Now heat to a boil. Pour hot rhubarb and its syrup/juice into hot jars. Cover with hot liquid from cooking it, but leave ½ inch headspace. Process in a boiling-water bath. For either pints or quarts, at up to 1,000 feet above sea level, process 15 minutes; at 1,001–6,000 feet, 20 minutes; and above 6,000 feet, 25 minutes.

Cooking/Serving Rhubarb. This is some of the sourest stuff around. It used to be that the only way anybody ate it was with so much added sweetening that it ended up being dessert. But Ann Saling says, "You should eat it. Rhubarb is very low in calories, only 56 per pound. It contains valuable minerals. Its fiber is very healthful."

➤ *RHUBARB SAUCE Cut trimmed stalks into about 1½-inch sections. Most rhubarb, if cooked over very gentle heat, will make its own juice and needs no added water at all. Simmer until you have a nice-looking sauce. Sweeten to taste. Determined sugar-fighters manage by adding a sweet fruit juice or mixing rhubarb with a sweet fruit to make a combination sauce. Adding lemon juice helps; add 1 T. per 1 c. cooked rhubarb.*

LEGUMES
Introduction to Legumes

Legumes are part of the family Leguminosae, or the "pea" family. Legumes all have clusters of fruit that matures in pods. Beans are actually just a small subgroup of this huge category. There are about 200 edible species of legumes cultivated worldwide, with about 1,500 different varieties, 500 of them bean varieties!

LEGUME LORE: For more information on the less familiar legumes, see *Tropical Legumes: Resources for the Future* (National Academy of Sciences, 1979) and *Underexploited Tropical Plants with Promising Economic Value* (NAS, 1975). *Future Food* by Barbara Ford has chapters on beans and peanuts with lots of fascinating info. The Vermont Bean seedhouse specializes in legumes.

LEGUME SECTION ORGANIZATION: The peas (*Pisum sativum*) are listed first in this section. Then come the most numerous species of edible legumes, *Phaseolus vulgaris,* the "common" beans—from snap beans to shell beans. Next are the other *Phaseolus* beans, those not close enough to be *vulgaris*: adzuki, lima, mung, rice, runner, and tepary beans. More distantly related yet are the other legumes, which follow in alphabetical order by their common names: fava, garbanzo (a.k.a. chickpea), lentil, peanut, pigeon pea, the southern group (black-eye, crowder, field pea, pea bean, and yellow-eye), soybean, winged, and yardlong bean.

LEGUME BENEFITS: Legumes, particularly the *Phaseolus* genus of beans, are extremely important plants for 3 reasons:

- Since most of the common legumes are nitrogen fixers, they are great for renewing fertility in a crop rotation following heavy feeders, and they make perfect "green manure." *Till legume roots into your soil!*
- They dry easily and store well under the most simple care, even increasing their protein value in storage.
- Together with a grain, they make a complete protein. So, after grains, beans are the most important food on the planet.

Inoculant. You can buy inoculant from most places you buy seed. Make sure you get the right kind; there are different one for beans, peas, and vetch. The inoculant powder that you dust over your legume seed before planting can increase both your yield and your plants' storage of nitrogen in the soil because it adds nitrogen-fixing bacteria to your seeds. The bacteria create and live in those root nodules that "fix" nitrogen. Seed fungicides don't harm most inoculant bacteria. Inoculant can be stored up to a year in your refrigerator and still be viable if it is dry and in an airtight container. In the soil the bacteria can survive up to 3 years between plantings of their host type of plant. Gardeners report that it seems to help peas a lot more than beans.

Combining Beans and Grains. All over the world beans are regularly eaten in combination with a grain. Both grain and beans are good food, but no bean or grain by itself contains all the amino acids necessary for human health, unlike meat and dairy (and mushroom) products. For example, corn is low in lysine and tryptophan, 2 essential amino acids. Beans are rich in lysine and tryptophan but lack zein, which corn can provide. So grains and beans together are as good as drinking milk or eating steak. *But they must be eaten in the same meal for it to work.* You get the same result with

Another way to group legumes is by the 3 basic ways they're harvested and served:

1. "Snap beans" and "snap peas" are eaten pods and all while still young and tender—they "snap" in two when bent. Snow peas and sugar snap peas are part of this group.
2. "Green shell beans" are used while still green rather than when they're dried up, but the beans are shelled out of the pod and you eat only those green beans, not the pod too. Lima beans, regular peas, and flageolets (small, pale-green shell beans, revered in French cooking) are in this group.
3. "Shell" or "dry" beans are harvested only after they've dried on the vine, further dried until their moisture level is down to about 10 percent, and only then—after some length of time in storage—cooked and eaten. Kidney and pinto beans, garbanzos, the southerns, and split peas are in this group.

Fava, horticultural, mung, and scarlet runner beans can be used in any of these 3 ways.

---

corn and bean stew (succotash), baked beans and bread, beans with barley or rice, beans and pasta, or corn chips and bean dip.

Health Diet. Latest research [1994!]: Eat some legumes (soybeans are great) every day. They reduce your risk of both heart disease and cancer. Eating at least 5 servings of fruits and vegetables a day reduces by half your cancer risk. Carrots, sweet potatoes, kale, and other deep orange or dark green vegetables that are rich in beta carotene are especially effective cancer deterrents. And include an allium every day to protect against viruses, cancer, and heart disease. One garlic clove per day lowers cholesterol and thins the blood.

PISUM SATIVA: THE PEAS

People have been eating peas even longer than beans, at least as far back as the Bronze Age. Maybe that's because peas are the easiest vegetable to grow. The work is in all that picking and shelling afterwards.

Varieties

There are big peas and petit peas; big vines and dwarf ones (Little Marvel, Progress No. 9); spring peas and hardy "winter" ones; hot weather specialists such as Wando (good for the South); *Pisum sativum arvense,* the gray field pea popular for food in the Middle East and India but used more for animal feed or a green manure crop here; and bush peas and pole peas.

BUSH/POLE PEAS: Pole peas take longer to mature, and you have to rig up something 3 to 6 feet tall for them to climb (see "Pole Beans"), but they bear more pods and go longer. Lincoln comes on early; Alderman next for a nice succession. Bush pea height depends on your soil and climate. Mine get only between 1 and 2 feet high. Lane Morgan, in her pea-paradise maritime climate, says she has to add at least a foot (and some kind of support) to all the catalog estimates about pea vine height, "bush" or not.

SNAP PEAS: These combine traits of the snow pea (see next paragraph) and the regular green pea. Pick them when the peas are mature and can be either snapped like beans and used in the pod or shelled like old-time green peas. The Park variety can be eaten at any stage of development —like a snow pea, like a snap pea, or shelled. Lane Morgan says, "In my opinion, snow peas aren't worth the trouble because they are persnickety to grow and you don't get much. But sugar snaps are another matter. You get that wonderful, unbeatable garden pea flavor, with several times the bulk and without the trouble of shelling. What a great deal. You don't even have to cook 'em; they are so good raw. You do have to support the vines. I use chicken wire that has gotten too ragged to protect the chickens: Run some poles through it. Stick it up along the rows in the spring. Roll it up again in the fall. Every year I grow more sugar snaps and fewer English peas [English peas are regular peas, not sugar snaps or edible-pod peas]."

SNOW PEAS: If the seed directions tell you to pick the flat pod before the seeds inside have begun to form bumps, that's a "snow pea" or "edible-pod" pea (*Pisum sativum macrocarpon*). "Sugar" in the name also suggests the ability to be picked at the edible-pod stage. But "snow" guarantees it. These are the old-time Asian stir-fry specialists. They don't freeze or can as well as standard greens, but they're wonderful raw or briefly sauteed. There are both bush and climbing varieties, but even the "bush" types seem to long to climb. Plant as much as 6 (or even 8) weeks before your last spring frost date. In the Deep South, plant snow peas around October for a winter crop. Snow peas have only half the calories of English peas.

Planting and Growing

Peas are easy to raise in cool weather and hard in hot weather. They like cool nights and bright, cool days. In the South, plant in earliest spring or the fall. In a more moderate zone, plant in the later summer and get a fall crop. With

SAVING LEGUME SEED

This procedure is easy. It's the same for all legumes and the same as the process you use for making dried beans. Legumes can cross-pollinate, so if you are growing more than one kind, you'll get guaranteed pure seed only by having them flower at different times or by planting them at some distance from each other.

But legumes rarely cross—unlike squash and pumpkins, for instance—because legumes are self-pollinated. So although legumes are capable of crosses, the odds are against it if you have at least 1 row of some other crop between them (taller is better). If they do cross, the result, though unfamiliar, is sure to be edible.

Tag the best-looking plants to leave while you harvest from the rest. Then specially harvest them for seed. Leave seeds in the pod on the plant until completely dry, because those dried in the pod have a higher germination rate. Then shell and store in a dry, cool place. They keep for years. When shelling out, get rid of small, strangely shaped, sick, or otherwise weird ones.

---

cooler summers, you can do succession plantings (every 3 to 4 weeks) all summer, but I prefer planting a lot of them at the time when peas grow best here (early spring). Then I freeze and dry enough for the rest of the year.

Peas are a cheery thought to me all winter because they are the first thing I plant—about February 20. It doesn't matter if it's snowing or there is snow on the ground, as long as the ground isn't frozen. That date is long before my husband will even consider going into the garden. But not me. By then I'm just famished to play in the dirt. I grab my jar of home-grown pea seed and my pick and head for the garden.

Peas don't mind cold. You could plant them in the late fall if you wanted to. They have a wonderful instinct that tells them just when to wake up and start growing, and they won't grow until then. But the ones that I plant so early get going at the very first opportunity, so we have peas on our table 2 weeks before anybody else. There's another advantage to such early planting: Peas can be picked, shelled, and put to sleep in the deep freeze—all done—leaving me free to devote all my available time to the green beans, which will be coming up a week later. It's just awful trying to put up both peas and beans at the same time.

So I go out in my winter coat while everybody in the house is either laughing or sighing in sorrow at my strangeness. I muck through the cold, muddy ground to the chosen spot: somewhere on the side of the garden, where it will be safely out of the way when Mike tills later. I eye it, calculate vaguely where my row will go, walk to one end, and commence whacking with my pick. I used to spade the ground, but that's a terrible struggle in this clay soil when it is wet. The peas don't care anyway. All they need is a head start, and they'll beat the weeds anyway. So, using the pick, I manage to break open a row. (Last year I was 7 months pregnant when I did it—in fact, come to think of it, I've been pregnant a lot of years when I planted peas because I have had mostly spring babies—like the goats.)

Then I walk back and commence planting pea seeds. I don't drop them precisely at all; I just sort of dribble them through my fingers. It doesn't hurt peas to be a little crowded. Then I walk back, kick clods back over them as best I can, and go on to the next row. By 3 rows I'm either cold enough or tired enough to quit, but the first seeds are in. After that I try to get out and plant a few seeds every day. Planting seeds makes me happy. As long as I am putting seeds in the ground, I know spring will come, and by then I'm getting anxious for spring. I plant peas until the peas are all planted (we need 12 rows) and then put in some spinach.

By the time I have those in, it has warmed up enough for the onion sets, my husband has started taking walks to the garden on his own, and the multipliers are up. When the multipliers come up, spring has sprung for sure.

The rows of peas that I planted with the pick always turn out crooked—not merely curved but outright zigzag! —and too close together for the rototiller to squeeze between. My husband looks at them, sighs, and gets on with the chard, carrots, beans, and so on. Our garden is short on looks anyway. Nobody around here is decorator-minded. But it really does grow the food.

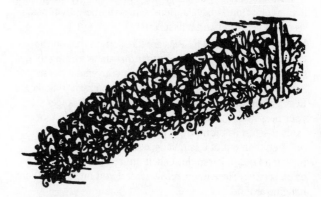

HOW TO PLANT: To do it right, till the ground first. Then make a long trench with the corner of your hoe. Space the seeds in it. Rake dirt over them; water and weed as needed. A pint or pound of seed plants about 100 feet in your garden. If you want to hurry them because you're trying to beat the heat or just want peas a week earlier, soak them in a flat dish. Spread them one pea deep in the dish, and add water until it comes halfway up the pea seed; when little sprouts show, plant right away before they rot. Plant 1 to 1½ inches deep, 2 to 3 inches apart, in rows 3 feet apart. The large pea seeds are easy to space when planting so that you won't need to thin later. They'll be 10 days to 2 weeks coming up (if they think the weather is warm enough to come up).

In a container, plant 12 seeds per 12-inch pot or 15 per square foot in a box. Or plant wide-row–style. That way, even overtall bush peas hold each other up, except for a few plants on the edges that fall over. Wide-row style is best for growing peas in the Deep South because the dense mass of plants helps keep them all cool, whereas in a single row they soon droop and fail from the heat. Mass peas choke out weeds too.

Peas hate dryness. But other than watering—and weeding if you have narrow rows—you don't have to do anything more until harvest.

Harvesting

First they flower; soon afterward they make pods. Start harvesting as soon as the pods are decently filled out. You need perfect timing: If you pick too soon, before the peas have gotten to their full size, you'll be wasting your and the pea vine's effort. But if you wait a few days too many, the peas will be yellow and hard and will have lost their good taste (although they'll still be fine to dry or make seed from). When picking pods, treat the vines gently, so you don't hurt them or pull out the roots. It helps to hold the vine with one hand as you pull off pods with the other one. They'll produce the most if you keep them well watered and well picked (pick every other day or so).

When farmers grow peas by the field, the crop is usually cut and windrowed; then it's left to sun-dry until a combine threshes out the peas from the pods.
NOTE: *If you're thinking about helping yourself to some peas, you'd best check with the farmer about his or her spraying schedule. If they've just been sprayed with parathion, you might not come out of that field alive.*

SAVING SEED: Peas are a self-fertile, insect-pollinated annual. Let peas for seed stay on the vine until the pods are well developed. Dry and then shell out of the pod. Pea seed lives a long time. I have a friend whose home-grown pea seed is 8 years old and still sprouts.

WHAT'S THE RUSH? Peas are like corn in that on the vine, they have lots of natural sugar that starts turning to starch as soon as they are picked. Peas' conversion doesn't happen as quickly as corn's, but it's quick enough to make fresh garden peas the best kind you'll ever taste. So get your peas from the plant to the pot—or frozen, dried, or canned—just as promptly as possible. Peas keep better in the shell than out of it (similarly, corn keeps better in the husk than out of it), so don't shell until just before cooking or preserving. Store in the refrigerator if you must keep them hanging around.
NOTE: *Don't wash peas before cooking or preserving. Just shell them out of clean pods; that's good enough.*

Preserving

For days on end we pick in the early morning or late evening, to avoid sunstroke, and shell the rest in our spare time. The emptied shells go to the pig. Peas are sorted as they are shelled. Those that have already started to get too hard or dry are not shelled; they are temporarily sorted into a special bucket for drying. (For details on the drying process, see "Harvesting" under "Shell (Dry) Beans.") It takes a lot of work and a lot of time to shell out a quart of peas. All the folks who come along get a batch of pea pods dumped in their laps, and we all sit on the porch and work. (Since I first published this, several people have written to me to say that they blanch peas in the pod, then shell, and then freeze and that the peas shell easier that way.)

DRYING: There are two ways to do it.
Old-time method: See "Harvesting" under "Shell (Dry) Beans"; basically the process is the same. Leave peas on the vine until the leaves have turned color and are clearly dying. Then pick the pods and shell out their peas. Finish drying them in an airy place in or out of sun.

Modern (dehydrator) method: Pick peas young and tender, as for freezing. Steam 8 to 10 minutes or dip in boiling water for 3 to 4 minutes. Spread on trays and dry. Either way, they are finished when shriveled and hard enough that they shatter if hit by a hammer. To dry sugar snap peas, wash, cut in ¼-inch pieces, and dry the same way you would string beans.

Splitting Peas. Buy commercially made split peas if you must have them; there's no point in trying to make them on your own. Pea farmers make them by first drying whole peas. Next the peas are soaked and steamed to loosen their fibrous outside seed coat, which is then removed. Then the peas are "shot" out so they hit hard against a kind of wall or "baffle" in a "splitter" machine. A natural break in the seed causes it to split in an exact half when that is done.

❧ *RUTH'S VEGAN CURRIED DRIED PEAS* "Cook soaked, dried peas for 40 minutes (be careful not to let them boil over or scorch) in water that's a thumbjoint above pea level, adding more if necessary. Then add a good jolt of curry powder and 1 t. of either cinnamon (for a sweet taste) or cumin (for an East Indian taste), and stir up the mixture. Add more water if needed, and cook, mashing occasionally, until it's a mush-puree consistency. Now serve as a cracker spread or over rice with chopped tomatoes and onions."

FREEZING: Once a day's batch is shelled, I lower a sieveful of peas into boiling water in a kettle. I leave it there until the water returns to a boil. A minute or two later, the peas have all changed color. That means they're done blanching. I lift them out, cool under running water, and pour into a bowl. I refill my sieve with peas and put them in the boiling water. While the water is in the process of coming to a boil again, I package the first batch for the freezer. (To freeze snow peas, remove stem and blossom ends, blanch as above, chill, and bag.) It's usually about 11 at night when I get the last sieveful done. To use frozen peas, just melt, warm, and serve.

CANNING: Tender, young peas are best. Gather, wash, and shell. Three to six pounds of peas will make 1 canned quart. Wash the shelled peas. (Canning snow, sugar, and edible pod peas is not recommended because they turn out badly.) Raw-pack or hot-pack; then process.

Raw Pack. Pack peas into jar without shaking or pressing down. Optional: Add salt. Pour boiling water over them, to within 1 inch of the jar top.

Hot Pack. Cover peas with boiling water. Boil 2 minutes. Pour loosely into hot jars. Allow 1 inch headspace. Optional: Add from a pinch to ½ t. salt per pint (up to 1 t. salt per quart). Pour boiling cooking liquid over, filling only up to within 1 inch of the jar top. Adjust lid.

Process. Pressure-can only. Process either pints or quarts for 40 minutes. If using a weighted-gauge canner, set at 10 lb. pressure at 0–1,000 feet above sea level; set at 15 lb. at higher altitudes. If using a dial-gauge canner, set at 11 lb. pressure at 0–2,000 feet above sea level; 12 lb. at 2,001–4,000 feet; 13 lb. at 4,001–6,000 feet; 14 lb. at 6,001–8,000 feet; or 15 lb. above 8,000 feet.

Recipe Ideas

ENGLISH PEAS: Add them to any salad or soup. Eat raw or cook only briefly to preserve best flavor and nutrition. Serve cooked peas plain, buttered, or in a stew, soup, or casserole.

SNOW PEAS: Open pods and stuff with herbed cream cheese for an appetizer. Or use in any Asian stir-fry dish—for instance, with beef or chicken strips and water-chestnut slices. Serve raw with a dip. Or serve sauteed in oil and hot with grilled mushrooms. Or use in salad.

SUGAR PEAS: Add to a meat-onion-potato stew. Or cook pods and all, and then drain and serve with Hollandaise or melted butter. Or chill and serve, covered with French dressing, as a salad. Or stir-fry in oil with sliced onion and celery until all are tender; then season with soy sauce and serve. Or serve with sweet-and-sour sauce over meatballs on a bed of brown rice.

THE PHASEOLUS BEANS

Bean eating is worldwide and goes way back—4,000 years in Europe, 5,000 in Asia. *Phaseolus vulgaris* are your "common" beans: the usual varieties of bush beans and pole beans and the common varieties that are dried, such as kidneys, pintos, and navy beans. These beans can be grown anywhere you have 3 frost-free months, but any touch of frost will kill them. In hot climates, they can be planted in fall, winter, or spring.

SOMETHING TO CLIMB. Pole beans are a vine rather than a bush plant. You can let them wander all over your ground, but they'll cover other plants; they also have a tendency to wind around and choke each other, which is even worse. They have no natural built-in support for their length; instead they need something to hang on to with their tendrils and to climb up. Climbing keeps them away from excessive moisture and destructive insects. Given the opportunity, they will grow only vertically. Your options include cornstalks, a trellis, poles, wire, and string.

Cornstalks. You can let them grow in your corn row and use the cornstalks for poles, but make sure you give the corn a head start. Or you can have them grow up a trellis or arbor structure or over your fence to save space.

Trellis. You can have ready 6–8-foot "poles." There are lots of different ways you can arrange them. You can stand a pole straight up beside each "hill" of seed (they aren't really dirt mounds — I just mean that you plant 4 to 6 seeds in the same general area and then thin to 3). Or you can arrange seeds and poles so that every 3 or 4 poles can be leaned together and tied at the top, tipi-style, with twine or some such.

Wire. Or you can try wire. Some big growers give their pole beans wire to climb. Others firmly believe that chicken and woven wire don't work as well as poles and vertical strings. Everybody agrees that pole beans given horizontal support on a grapevine-type structure don't do well because they tend to wind around them together and choke each other.

String. A compromise method is a top wire strung between a sturdy post at each end of your pole-bean row, with strings hanging down from it at intervals for the beans to climb up. Tie a wire or string near the base of the post or poles, and then you can tie the bottom of the string to that to keep it firmly placed. Or you can plant a pole at every other hill, or every third or fourth one, and run a string or wire along near the tops of those, with strings hanging down wherever you have a plant without a pole. One reader places poles about 2½ to 3 feet apart, crisscrosses twine between the poles, and plants 4 to 5 beans at the base of each pole.

Snap Beans

VARIETIES

Colors. They come in a number of colors. Most are green, but there are also purple- and yellow-podded varieties of both bush and pole beans. "Wax beans" are yellow-podded. The yellow beans have a smooth, almost translucent shell and a milder, more delicate flavor than green beans; some people enjoy the flavor, and some don't. Yellows are easier to pick than greens because the bright color is so obvious against the green, leafy background.

Bush Beans. Bush beans grow as a low, free-standing bush. Pole beans are vine varieties that have tendrils to cling with and need something to climb (see "Something to Climb"). Bush green beans are one of the easiest vegetables to grow. They will grow well even in poor soil. Their time from planting to picking can be around 60 days, which makes them good in a short-season climate. They cannot live through frost, but they can stand lots of heat if you keep them frequently watered.

Pole Beans. You don't have to stoop so much and hunt so hard to harvest pole beans, but putting up the poles is a nuisance. Because they will grow up rather than out, pole beans are a good choice when you have to garden in very little space. A commercial pole bean producer in the Oregon's Willamette Valley claims to grow 16 tons of pole beans per acre, "4 times what I could grow with bush beans." The beans he doesn't sell for snap beans, he leaves to dry in the field and then sells them as seed or shell beans. Even if you decide to grow pole beans, I'd advise you to put in a row or so of bush beans too, because bush beans will be producing 10 or so days before your pole beans. On the other hand, once they get started, pole beans have a longer harvest season than bush beans do, and with care the poles will keep making beans until frost finally kills the vines. Kentucky Wonder and Oregon Giants, which really produce, are many people's favorite pole bean.

The Romano is another important other pole bean variety. Also known as "Italian pole bean," Romanos are a traditional southern European variety that is wider, flat-podded, pest- and pestilence-resistant, and distinctive-tasting. The "Roma" is a bush variety of Romano. Available from Burgess, Burpee, Comstock, William Dam, DeGiorgi, Gurney, Harris, Nichols, Park, Redwood City, Shumway, Stokes, Thompson & Morgan, and Vermont Bean.

PLANTING

Planting Bush Beans. Put your first row in on the date of your supposed last frost. For a quicker start, presoak your seeds 1 to 4 hours in barely lukewarm water before you plant them. (Don't oversoak, or they'll split or rot.) Plant 1 inch deep and 3 to 5 inches apart. If you're short of garden space, you can make your rows as little as a foot apart, but only if you're planning on weeding by hand and with a hoe. Otherwise make your rows about 2–3 feet apart. You can figure that ½ lb. of seed will plant a 50-foot row. Bush beans do well in containers: dirt at least 12 inches deep, 6 inches between plants.

If you live in a very wet climate, cover your bean seed only shallowly, rather than with an inch or more of dirt, because bean seed is susceptible to rot and will survive better that way. If you are in control of the watering, don't overwater during this period for the same reason. If a killing frost takes your first planting, just replant and keep planting another row or so every week or 10 days through the spring. In 7 to 14 days your plants will be up. Seeds that germinate before a frost will be killed. But plants that are still not up at the time of a frost will come up, thrive, and mature ahead of seeds you plant after a frost (to replace plants killed by frost).

Planting Pole Beans. Plant in the early summer, when frost danger is over; pole beans are more sensitive to cold than bush beans or shell beans. Plant pole beans about 2 weeks later than you would the first row of bush beans. Pole beans also require a richer soil than any other bean except limas. Plant the beans in a straight row at the base of their support, or group a few seeds at every pole or other support. You'll need about ½ lb. seed to plant a 50-foot row. But that 50-foot row will yield about 50 lb. of beans—or more. Pole beans grow well in containers: Plant at least ½ inch deep, 1–2 gal. soil per plant, 4–6 inches between plants. Remember that they will grow 6 or 8 feet tall and have lots of leaves, so put them where they won't shade other vegetables and give them plenty of room. Expect 5 to 8 days before germination.

HARVESTING AND PRESERVING

Harvesting Bush Beans. Once your bush green beans start, they will bear for 4–5 weeks if you treat them right. Commercial bush bean varieties were developed for mechanized big-scale growers who needed a plant that would bear heavily and then mature all at the same time, enabling a harvesting machine to come along, cut off the whole plant, and harvest its beans. But gardeners' varieties of bush beans, if given regular watering and kept thoroughly picked, will keep producing for quite a while.

You can pick them at various stages; different people have different preferences. I like them best picked when they are still young enough that the beans inside the pods aren't completely filled out, especially if I'm freezing them. Older beans will give you more bean, but it won't be as tender. If you wait longer than that, they start to be dried out and tough. Plan on picking beans at least every 3 days while they are on. That way you should be able to stay ahead of them. Pick into a big paper shopping bag or basket or whatever you prefer. Early morning and after sunset are the times kindest to the picker, and the beans come off just as easily.

Bean vines aren't too husky and they pull up and bruise easily, so learn to handle them gently while picking. Bush green beans don't make the best dried beans, so there isn't any point in drying their seeds, unless you want to save your own seed. Can, freeze, or start your drying the same day if possible; at the latest, start the next morning.

Harvesting Pole Beans. All pole beans flower and grow beans from the bottom of the plant up. Some growers pinch away the very first, lowest flowers; that way the beans don't touch the ground, and the plant concentrates its energy a bit more on growing up. Otherwise, just use the directions for harvesting bush beans.

How to "Snap" Beans. Pick and snap into 1-inch lengths. Snap rather than cut; if you cut them, you will cut some of the beans inside the pods, and the pieces will fall out of the pod. Snap off both tips and throw the tips into your animal feed.

Freezing. Choose young, tender "baby" beans, 3 inches long, for best results. Wash and cut or snap off their stem and blossom ends. Wash, snap into the lengths you want, scald (boil 1 minute or steam 2–4 minutes). Drain and chill very, very well. Drain and pack in freezer bags. Frozen beans keep best if you steam rather than boil, drain well, freeze quickly, and don't thaw before cooking to serve.

Snap beans don't keep as well in the freezer as most other vegetables, so *don't thaw before you cook them.* You can put the frozen hunk right into the frying pan, being careful not to burn any, and cook there. If your beans have been in the freezer 6 months or so and are seriously losing their flavor, fry them with something flavorful like bacon grease or potatoes and onions.

Drying. Use immature beans (those that have not yet developed seeds in the pod). Wash. Snap off the ends and snap into about 1-inch pieces; cut lengthwise; or leave whole. Steam them 4 minutes or blanch in boiling water about 2 minutes. Drain well. Spread on trays in a single layer. Dry outside in full sun or in a dryer or dehydrator at 120°F. Stir beans and rotate trays as needed. Takes 7 to 14 hours if using artificial heat, a couple of days if sun drying. Done when hard and brittle.

COOKING DRIED SNAP BEANS *For each 1 c. dried beans, add 2 c. boiling hot water. Cook, covered, over low heat until beans are tender and plump again.*

Strung Beans. To use this pioneer method of making "leather-breeches beans," start with tender green beans. Wash and trim off the ends. Using a long needle and a long, strong thread, sew each bean onto the string by pushing the needle right through the center of the bean. As you work, you'll have to keep pushing the beans down to the knot end, until the thread is fully loaded with beans from knot end to needle. Then hang up the string of beans to dry by one end in a place that's warm but out of the sun. When beans are completely dry, you can store them in something else.

Canning. Wash, trim ends, and snap beans into 1- to 1½-inch lengths. Raw-pack tightly into jars. Optional: Add salt. Cover with boiling water. Or precook by boiling until pliable (about 5 minutes). Pack hot into hot jars, and cover with hot cooking liquid or fresh boiling water. Optional: Add ½ t. salt/pint, or 1 t. salt/quart. Leave 1 inch headspace. Pressure-can only: 20 minutes for pints, 25 minutes for quarts. If using a weighted-gauge canner, set at 10 lb. pressure at 0–1,000 feet above sea level; set at 15 lb. at higher altitudes. If using a dial-gauge canner, set at 11 lb. pressure at 0–2,000 feet above sea level; 12 lb. at 2,001–4,000 feet; 13 lb. at 4,001–6,000 feet; 14 lb. at 6,001–8,000 feet; or 15 lb. above 8,000 feet.

Canning Pickled, Dilled Beans. You'll need 4 lb. fresh tender green or yellow beans (5 to 6 inches long), 8 to 16 heads fresh dill, 8 cloves garlic (optional), ½ c. canning or

This is a French term for green beans that have been picked before the seeds inside have started to swell. The Park seedhouse suggests their "Mini-Green" and "Mini-Yellow" varieties be used for haricots verts. They are skinny and tender, and you serve them whole. Comstock, Johnny's, and Nichols also sell haricots verts.

For haricots verts, harvest while beans are very slim, lumpless, and no more than 7 inches long. Stir-fry with chopped green onion, fresh basil, and precooked bacon bits. Or bake with carrots, chicken, garlic, sage, and butter. Or mix with other chopped cooked veggies and serve with vinegar-oil dressing as a cold salad.

---

pickling salt, 4 c. white vinegar (5 percent), 4 c. water, and 1 t. hot red pepper flakes (optional). Wash and trim ends from the beans. Cut to 4-inch lengths. In each pint jar, place 1 to 2 dill heads and, if desired, 1 clove of garlic. Place beans upright in *pint* jars, leaving ½ inch headspace. Adjust lids. Process in water-bath canner. At up to 1,000 feet above sea level, process 5 minutes; at 1,001–6,000 feet, 10 minutes; and above 6,000 feet, 15 minutes. Or use lower-temperature pasteurization process (detailed in "Pickles" section under "Cucumbers").

Snap Bean Recipe Ideas. Add diced onion and bacon (or salt pork cut into small pieces) to your beans and cook, covered, until the beans are done, adding water as necessary. Or steam whole or in pieces, and serve with a sprinkle of tamari. Or steam with half as much onion; then marinate overnight in tamari and serve cold in a salad. Or serve long green beans raw in salads or with dips. For julienned ("French-style") beans, slice unsnapped beans lengthwise into slender strips (you can buy a "French-bean slicer"). Also see following recipe.

❧ *GREEN BEANS NICOISE Heat ¼ c. cooking oil in pan. Add 1 minced garlic clove, 1 c. chopped onion, and ¼ c. chopped green pepper, and saute a few minutes. Now pour in 2 c. canned tomatoes that have been mashed, blended, or forced through a strainer. Also add a bay leaf, 2 T. finely chopped parsley, and salt and pepper to taste. Simmer your sauce 15 minutes. Now add about 1½ lb. green beans. Cover the pan and simmer about ¾ hour.*

Romano Bean Recipe Ideas. Pick for snap beans while still quite immature. They taste different than other snap beans. Don't overcook; they cook more quickly than regular green beans. Harvest while still flat. String and snap them. Steam with mushrooms and serve with a sauce. Or stir-fry with other veggies, meat strips, and ginger. Or use in a soup with shell beans and meat.

Green Shell Beans

Green shell beans can be made from snap beans that have been let go a little longer and then shelled, from varieties grown specifically for this purpose (limas, flageolets, and horticultural beans), or from shell beans gathered on the early side and shelled. See "Lima Beans."

GROWING FLAGEOLET AND HORTICULTURAL BEANS:
These are bred for their large seeds, which are eaten at the green shell stage like limas (or as dry shell beans). Pick the pods after the seeds have fully formed but before they've started drying. You can use these as snap beans if you catch them early enough, although the pods tend to get tough and stringy quickly.

CANNING GREEN SHELL BEANS: Follow directions for canning fresh lima beans.

FREEZING GREEN SHELL BEANS: Blanch 1½ to 2 minutes. Thoroughly chill. Drain well. Pack into freezer bags or boxes, and freeze. *Don't thaw before cooking.*

GREEN SHELL BEAN RECIPE IDEAS: Steam or simmer in water till tender; serve with a little butter, a garlic-flavored white sauce, or a dollop of sour cream. Or stir-fry with a chopped garlic clove and several chopped onions, add a pour of soy sauce, and serve with rice. Or combine cooked green shell beans with leftover cooked sweet corn cut off the cob (or canned or frozen loose corn); then heat, stir in a dab of butter, and add salt and pepper and maybe a little cream to taste. Or boil, puree, season, and serve topped with chopped green onions and tomato sauce. Or cook with onions, beets, and carrots for soup. Or with meat, veggies, and herbs for soup. For commercial growing, see "Sustainable Dry Bean Production" at **www.attra.ncat. org/attra-pub/drybean.html.**

Shell (Dry) Beans

"Shell beans" are the many varieties of *Phaseolus vulgaris* that are dried on the vine, shelled, stored dry, and then served in chilis, soups, casseroles, etc. Basically you grow shell beans (beans for drying) just as you grow bush beans (almost all of them are bush rather than pole types), but you harvest them differently.

VARIETIES: All the beans described in the following paragraphs are *Phaseolus vulgaris* varieties. Soybeans, lentils, dried peas, garbanzos, and black-eyes are good shell "beans" too, and much of the following info also applies to them, but details about growing them are discussed elsewhere in this chapter. Snap bean varieties don't make the best shell beans, and shell beans don't make the best snap beans. There are a myriad special shell bean varieties, each slightly or substantially different from all the others in size, color, days to maturity, best climate for growing, etc. In general, large-seeded beans are easier to shell and will produce more per space than smaller-seeded beans will. Plant several types and then narrow it down for future gardens to the one(s) that produce best for you.

Black. The black bean is Latin America's favorite bean. Small, glossy black (a.k.a. turtle) beans grow on semi-vining bushy plants. They can be grown anywhere with 85 to 115 warm, frostfree days. If you have disease and insect problems, black beans are a good choice because they're especially resistant. Black beans are small, but they have more nutrients than pintos. Good in the South. Available from Park and Johnny's.

Horticultural. This popular homestead bean is also known as "wren's egg bean," "shell bean," and numerous other names. These beans are good as snap, green shell, or dried beans but are most commonly used as a green shell bean. There's a pole variety and a dwarf one, which takes about 60 days to produce green shell beans. Other varieties need 90 days for full, dried-bean maturity. Horticultural is a very popular kind of shell bean in all its varieties. It gets a high yield per square foot and is good canned and frozen. Available from Territorial.

Kidney. The kidney bean is Mexico's most popular bean and the one traditionally used in chili and kidney bean salads. It takes 95 days to maturity. Its pods are about 6 inches long. It's also available in other varieties, including a white bean called cannellini. It has been called the easiest shell bean to grow. Available from Territorial.

Pinto. The pinto can be grown anywhere with 85 to 105 warm, frostfree days. The fast variety is one of the fastest to mature and generally produces well. Grow pintos as you would pole beans.

Others. Other varieties include Boston, brown Dutch, California small white, Italian shell, and the following types.

- Coco: Can be used as snap beans, green shell beans, and dry beans; plump, black, relatively quick-cooking; from Territorial.
- Cranberry: Large, egg-shaped, reddish-brown seeds.
- Foul Madammas: a Middle Eastern bean.
- Great Northern: A big white bean with heavy yields; 90 days to maturity; bushy plant, good for short-season places, also can be harvested as green shell beans.
- Marrow: Popular kind.
- Navy: Traditional white soup bean; 95 days to maturity; prolific producer.
- Pink: California pink is a pole bean.

In general, shell beans are available from Burpee, Comstock, Gurney, Harris, Johnny's, Shumway, Stokes, Vermont Bean, etc.

PLANTING: Follow directions for planting bush or pole beans, whichever you have.

HARVESTING:

NOTE: These instructions for drying and threshing are appropriate for almost any legume, including peas.

Dried beans are so important to a subsistence diet . . .

Drying on the Vine. You can leave the bean pods hanging on the plants until they are fully mature and the beans inside have become so dry that they are very hard. If the rains will hold off long enough, it's ideal to wait until most of the leaves have yellowed or fallen off. But getting shell beans dry on the vine before they mold can be difficult in hot, humid climates—or in cool, perpetually rainy ones. If you're expecting rain, a way to deal with the matter in a hurry is to pull out the plants by the roots and move them into an airy but safely covered place to finish drying. Another problem with vine drying is that it reduces or stops further production.

Drying Off the Vine. So consider drying off the vine—in or out of the pod. Drying in the pod seems to work best for

most types of bean. Picking from the vines on a very dry day helps avoid mold. Our summers are very hot and dry, perfect for drying fruits and vegetables (except for the August hordes of wasps). The one place where you could goof is by not starting to dry them as soon as you pick them. If you leave them heaped up for very long, such as in a bucket or a pile—even in a very dry place—the lower layers will mold and get slimy. That means the whole bucketful is a loss, because those mold spores will be ahead of you. I use a sheet spread out on the ground in the full sun. I scatter the pods on it so there are none on top of each other. In the evening I gather up the corners of the sheet to make a sack and haul it all in so they won't get damp again in the night dew; I put them out again the next morning.

Drying right out in the sunshine really works better than drying indoors. But if you have lots of rain in summer or a rainy spell just when you are trying to dry pods, you can shell out the beans and finish drying them in your oven or dryer on trays. You are safest when the dried beans (or peas) are so hard and dry that they shatter when struck by a hammer.

Bean Threshing! Once your beans are dried, you can shell directly into your storage containers (which can be virtually anything), or you can thresh them out onto a clean floor and get the kids to pick them up for you. I generally leave the shelling for later in the season, after the rush is over. Folks who leave beans on the vine until the pods are dry, or who pull up the plants and let them dry in an airy place under cover, can thresh any time after the dried pods have become so dry they are brittle.

One easy threshing system is to put the pods (plants and all if that's how you harvested them) into a burlap bag. It works best if you resew it into a long, cylindrical shape. Have the bag open at the top, and hang it from something. You can stuff bean plants/pods in the top. Have it openable at the bottom but tied off with something for the time being. Put the brittle pods in there and then beat the bag with something like a stick. Periodically, open the bottom of the bag and let the loose beans that have collected at the bottom pour on down into a basket or some such. Or shell them out, pod by pod, by hand. Or hold several plants by the roots and whack them back and forth inside a large barrel-type container. Or flail a pile of them. Or stuff them into a sack with holes in the bottom and then stomp or beat on the sack. Or put the beans into a big tub and stomp on them to some lively tunes. Or buy a family-sized motorized pea sheller from Lehman's.

Winnowing and Final Drying. Pour from a container to a blanket outside on a windy day. Or sift across a seed-cleaning wire screen in the wind. If you doubt whether your seeds are dry enough, give them another week or two or three, spread out where they will finish drying. Don't waste those leftover bean plants and pods. Plow them back under or compost. If you've had trouble with disease, however, you should burn them.

STORING DRIED BEANS: Store both shelled and unshelled beans in a cool place. Conventional wisdom advises putting them in tightly lidded plastic, metal, or glass containers, but that may not work as well as keeping them in burlap sacks or other permeable material, out of rodents' reach. For some reason, storing peas and beans in airtight containers can result in growth of fungi, odd smells, spoilage, and lower viability of seed. The important thing is to keep the humidity down. But no matter how dry seed is to start with, it will end up as dry as the place where you store it. If you live in the South, you'll have a harder time keeping any dried food.

Insects. The basics of grain and bean storage are almost identical. But dried beans have a worse time of it with bugs than grains do. Storing beans in a bugproof container prevents mama bugs from getting in there to do their thing. If eggs or tiny insect larvae are already on or in beans that have been harvested, there are 3 basic responses: freezing, boiling, or baking. Unless you kill the bugs, they will destroy the beans, even if you put those beans into a tightly covered container.

Freezing: If you aren't planning to use the beans for seed, you can store them in the freezer temporarily or until needed. Two weeks at 0°F will take care of any bean weevils.

Boiling: Put the beans in a coarse sack or basket and dip into boiling water for just a minute or two. Then hang up to drip dry. That should get rid of the insects and won't harm the beans' ability to keep.

Baking: Heat in the oven at 250°F for 10 to 15 minutes with the door slightly open to prevent overheating. Just don't put in too many beans at once. Then put beans into that tightly covered container.

Bean Flour. If you have your own flour grinder, you can grind your own dried peas, lentils, soybeans, etc., to make a flour. The commercially produced pea and lentil flours are precooked, so your home-ground flours won't act exactly the same. These vegetable flours can be added to any bread-type recipe and are good that way. But don't substitute them for wheat flour. Bean flour will help you get more food mileage out of your beans if you have a lot of them some year.

COOKING DRIED BEANS AND PEAS: Some store-bought beans are partially precooked, so make sure, whatever recipe you use, that the home-dried beans are actually done before you commence with the rest of it. In general, they are soaked awhile and then cooked. If you cook them in the water in which they were soaked, you save nourishment. Then they are combined with something like pork, molasses, tomatoes, onions, or spices because they are awfully bland foods to eat alone.

Bean Cooking Times. Drier beans require longer cooking times. Assuming beans have been given a pre-treatment of 2 minutes of boiling followed by 1 hour of soaking, the average cooking times are 2 to 2½ hours for kidney, pink, cranberry, and pinto beans; 2½ hours for black beans; 2½ to 3 hours for great northern and marrow beans; and 3 to 3½ hours for navy, small white, and small red beans.

Pressure Cooking. Don't pressure-cook limas, butter beans, black-eyed peas, garbanzos, split peas, whole dried peas, or lentils because they foam too much and can clog the vent. Basic directions for pressure-cooking other beans: Presoak or merely wash them. Put beans into cooker, adding 3 to 4 cups of water per 1 c. beans. Never fill cooker more than one-third full. Bring beans to a boil. Add a little fat to water to reduce tendency to foam. Put lid on cooker. Set gauge for 15 lb. Keep heat so gauge jiggle is steady but not extremely fast. When cooking time is up, hold cooker under cold running water. Vent remaining steam and open. Assuming beans have been boiled and presoaked as above, pressure-cooking times for beans are 8 minutes for great northerns, marrows, and black beans (25 minutes

if unsoaked) and 10 minutes for navy, small white, and small red beans (30–35 minutes if unsoaked).

Oven-Cooked Beans. From Diane Stark, Corinne, UT: "Don't even soak them. Just wash and put in the oven for the night at about 300°F. Add double or triple usual amount of water so they don't cook dry in the night. Cook them in a good beanpot or casserole dish with a tight-fitting lid so the liquid doesn't evaporate. The next morning I salt and season them. Don't stir too much, as they are so tender they fall to pieces. It's fun to scoop out a few large spoonfuls, mash up, and cook refried beans for breakfast. And beans cooked this way never give you gas!"

BEAN PUREE: Any kind of dried beans can be boiled and then served as a wet mixture of mashed and whole beans plus some of the bean broth and seasonings. Call it "bean puree" or "fried beans." They're wonderfully adaptable. Season with cumin, cayenne, and coriander—or whatever. Put them in breads, cakes, and soups; on sandwiches; and so on. Here are some more fancy recipes for fried beans.

"REFRIED" BEANS Mash cooked beans fried in oil with onions and seasonings (like garlic, tomato puree, and red pepper) until the moisture has mostly evaporated, but don't let them burn! Good with little cubes of cheddar or jack-type cheese stirred in or sprinkled on top to melt. Ruth of Bonaire says, "Refried beans can be made without oil, either in a skillet or in the oven with water or juice for moisture. Use about ⅓ c. water for 3 c. cooked beans."

RUTH'S BEAN SPREAD Someday I betcha Ruth is going to write her own recipe book. It boggles my mind that she is only 13. "In a large pan, in ½ c. water, saute a finely chopped onion, a green pepper, 3 ribs celery, and about ½ c. coarsely shredded carrots for about 10 minutes. Then add about 3 c. cooked beans (garbanzos, navy beans, or any leftover beans), some crushed garlic, 1 T. curry powder (maybe a pinch of hot pepper), and a slug of tamari. Also add about 1–1½ c. water or vegetable-cooking water. Mix well. Then put the pan into the oven and bake the spread until the liquid is absorbed (about 1 hour at 350°F). Cool. Then mash with a potato masher. Chill before using. Good sandwich material."

Ruth's Many Uses for Plain Cooked, Mashed Beans. First cook them well. Mash and add some cooking water and/or lemon juice and spices. Use garbanzos for Middle Eastern dishes, pinto beans for Mexican, black beans for Caribbean, lentils for Egyptian.

1. Spread plain on bread or crackers.
2. Use as a dip for raw veggies.
3. Take mash with a thick consistency. Form into 1-inch balls. Roll in crumbs and deep-fry. (If done with garbanzos, this is falafel, which is eaten stuffed into pocket bread with tomatoes, onions, lettuce, and/or anything else you like.)
4. Heavily spice kidney-bean mash. Form into rolls and fry to make veggie hot dogs!
5. Thin with tomato juice and use as salad dressing.
6. Mix with chopped onion, tomato, pepper, zucchini, etc. Pile into a sandwich (rye bread) with mustard or something else for a mock chicken or egg salad. (Grated carrot with garbanzo mash is like mock salmon or deviled ham.)
7. Form into patties and fry as "hamburgers."
8. Mix with chopped veggies; stuff into hollowed-out zucchini, green peppers, eggplant, or tomato; and bake.

9. Roll up mashed beans (seasoned) with chopped veggies in large, steamed leaves of cabbage. Cover with tomato sauce. Bake until bubbly.

10. Make thick batter of 1 part cornmeal, 2 parts boiling water, and maybe a glug of cooking oil. Fry into large pancakes. Then spread with mashed beans, tomato sauce, and chopped onion. Roll up. Presto—a Mexican crepe!

11. Use your imagination. There are endless possibilities!

SAUCES FOR COOKED WHOLE BEANS: Because most dried beans are on the bland side, a tasty sauce can really improve them. See "Tomatoes" for good tomato sauce recipes. For a molasses sauce, combine 3 c. water from the bean cooking with 3 t. molasses, 1 t. vinegar, 1 t. salt, and ¾ t. dry mustard.

SHELL BEAN RECIPE IDEAS: Cook beans with pork; serve with rice. Saute precooked beans with green pepper strips and diced onion. Cook with onions, basil, and garlic, and serve with Parmesan cheese. Mix with a molasses sauce and serve with sliced tomatoes and guacamole. Make a soup with the beans and whatever veggies (meat optional) you have. Serve refried beans with fried potatoes and hamburgers. Bake beans with plenty of onion chunks and sorghum. Or bake with tomato sauce, onions, and mustard. Or make a stew from a combination of several kinds of beans plus veggie chunks. Serve cooked, chilled beans with vinegar/oil dressing in salad or on greens. Make a soup of beans, potatoes, greens, and spices.

➤ *RUTH'S VEGETARIAN FEIJOADA Bring to a boil and then simmer 2 hours: 2 c. black beans, 6 c. water, 2 large garlic cloves (crushed), 1 onion studded with 10 cloves, 2 chopped onions, and 1 chopped green pepper. Meanwhile, make sauce and refrigerate at least 2 hours: 6 chopped tomatoes, 1 bunch chopped scallions or leeks, ½ chopped onion, 1 crushed clove garlic, 3 T. lemon juice, and a dash Tabasco. Serve beans over cooked rice. Top with sauce.*

➤ *KIDNEY BEAN/HAMBURGER CHILI Saute a chopped onion in 2 T. butter until golden brown. Add 2 c. tomatoes, 1 lb. hamburger, 2 c. kidney beans that have been cooked up, 1 t. chili powder, and ½ t. salt. Simmer an hour, adding water as necessary.*

➤ *VEGAN KIDNEY BEAN CHILI Soak 2 c. dried kidney beans overnight. The next day, pour off water. Simmer beans with 2 onions and 2 peppers (both chopped), 6 crushed garlic cloves, 1 lb. skinned, chopped tomatoes, 2 c. tomato sauce, and 2–4 c. water, depending on how soupy you like it. Seasonings could be 1 T. each of chili powder and soy sauce (tamari). Optional ingredients are ½ lb. sliced mushrooms or 1 c. corn kernels (add those just a few minutes before serving). Simmer all for about 2 hours before serving.*

➤ *GARDEN BEAN SOUP From Melanie in Hawaii: "I just cook 1 or 2 c. red or pink beans, and then add whatever vegetables we happen to have growing in our garden—tomatoes, okra, peas, green beans, onions, celery, corn, etc. Season the soup with garden herbs—garlic, sweet basil, oregano, etc. Simmer a few hours. Add some macaroni about ½ hour before you're ready to eat. Serve with hot homemade bread and some fresh fruit salad!"*

➤ *FIRE STATION BEANS From George C. White, who just retired after 44 years with a fire department in the Fort*

Worth, TX, area: "This is a bean pot and not a chili. Some version is cooked in almost all the fire stations in Texas. The pinto beans are soaked overnight and then cooked slowly all day or until soft. Add bacon fat, salt pork, ham hock, backbone, knuckles, pig tails, or ears for seasoning—or ground beef. Brown meat with chopped onions, chopped or ground garlic, chopped celery, and chopped bell pepper. Other optional ingredients are brown sugar or molasses, mustard, oregano, mace, nutmeg, a few pods of whole chili, some cooked tomatoes, salt, and/or pepper. After adding meat and flavorings, simmer further until done. Serve with corn bread and fresh onions."

ABOUT FLATULENCE: Time to get earthy. As the old poem says, "Beans, beans, the musical fruit—the more you eat, the more you toot! Beans, beans, they're good for your heart, but the more you eat, the more you fart!" Yes indeed, the problem to be faced up to with eating dried beans is their gas-manufacturing tendency.

My mother-in-law really pushes beans and is always telling me how much protein they contain. Her son has firm control of his system and can deposit his total flatulence (gas) in the bathroom alone and behind the closed door in a maximum of 3 daily visits. I apparently come from a totally different—uncontrolled—genetic line. My mother had this problem and so do I. When it hits me, that's it. I've been standing in church singing a hymn and wanting to die with shame because everybody around me was wondering who had done the terrible thing, and I was afraid they'd figure it out just from the look on my face. At least the hymn covered the sound effects, but what about the many other times I make sounds which, to my embarrassed ears, resemble the backfire of our 1-ton truck going down the mountainside to town with the muffler off?

And beans have a cumulative effect. One unfortunate week I served chili for supper. The next day Mike happened to lunch where they served him chili again. That evening I was sick in bed and asked my 8-year-old daughter, Dolly, to feed everybody something. It turned out she decided the best answer was to open another jar of chili. In the middle of the night Mike announced there was a distinct possibility he was going to die. He didn't, but now we are careful about spacing our bean meals. (That was the week when Mike was in a conference room with a group of executive types, and even he was overcome by pressure to the point that the whole proceedings stopped while people wondered where it all was coming from.)

Since the first issue of this book came out, I've received in the mail a lot of helpful advice about how to keep beans from causing gas. J.O. Pettit, the salt-rising bread expert, told me to keep a cruet of vinegar on the table and add a pour of vinegar to each serving of beans. Janet Kieffer wrote me that her Mexican cooking teacher said 1 t. olive oil in a batch of beans helps take out the gas. Mrs. George Baker of Floresville, TX, wrote me to advise adding ¼ t. ginger to 1 lb. beans in cooking them.

Seventh edition. Now I have still more advice. Julia Reynolds from Galvin, WA, says if I blanch and freeze the dried beans as I would string beans, that will help the gas problems. Abbie Pyne from Twin Falls, ID, says the best way to cook beans to prevent gas is to add 1 T. castor oil for every 1 c. dry beans when you put them on to cook. "When the castor oil is cooked, it has no laxative effect and cuts the gas to almost none." My friend Lenna says for fewer explosions, don't soak them overnight. Angie says discarding the soaking water and cooking in fresh water helps. The scientists say if you eat beans regularly and increase your bean consumption gradually, your body will become accustomed to them and the tooting will be diminished. Lois Rumrill from Forks of Salmon, CA, says, "I always cook my dry beans upside down. That way they don't make you pass gas, they just make you hiccup!"

Why Flatulence? *Ninth edition.* It's because beans contain certain natural sugars called oligosaccharides in generous amounts, and when oligosaccharides encounter certain of the natural bacteria that make their home in everybody's digestive tract (normally unknown and unnoticed), gas gets manufactured. You can't change the bean. You can't change the microbe. You can't change the human be'in. That's just how it is. Best we should be kind to one another about it. But you *can* choose a low-flatulence legume!

Flatulence from Various Legumes. This must have been an interesting scientific project! Somebody actually measured, in a variety of subjects, the amount of flatulence emitted over a 3-hour period after a test meal of dried beans, starting from 4 hours after eating the beans. On a scale of 1 to 12, with 12 being the most gas-producing, the no-bean meal—peanuts and Fordhook limas—rated a 1. Green peas came in at 2.6, soybeans at 3.8, Ventura limas at 4.6, dried peas at 5.3, and mungs at 5.5. Then there was a sudden big jump to the big leagues of gas, with pinto beans at 10.6 and kidneys and California small whites at 11.4.

Other Phaseolus Beans (Alphabetical List)

The other *Phaseolus* beans besides the basic *Phaseolus vulgaris* bunch covered above are adzuki, lima, mung, rice, runner, and tepary beans.

ADZUKI BEAN: *Phaseolus angularis*, or adzuki, is a bush bean from Japan. It grows long, thin pods, each of which holds 7 to 10 small purplish seeds. Adzukis need 118 days to start bearing. They have a somewhat nutty flavor, are high in protein, and can be used all 3 ways: snap, green

shell, and dried shell. They can handle the climate in either long or short season areas. Use like shell beans.

LIMA BEAN: The lima bean (*Phaseolus limensis* or *P. lunatus*) is a lovely-tasting, tropical-origin green shell bean. But in my experience and in my climate (Idaho), you can't harvest from lima beans, bush or pole, as long as you can from green beans. They are a high-protein bean, wonderfully nutritious.

Varieties. Limas are not cold-weather–hardy. There are both bush and pole limas. Bush limas grow faster than pole limas, but pole limas keep pods off the ground so they don't acquire a yucky, earthy taste. Pole limas also yield more and longer.

Planting. Lima beans have a harder time sprouting than other beans. You need to have their soil very loose and crumbly to help them get up out of it. Sticky clay is hard for them to germinate through. Soaking the seed overnight before planting also helps, but don't more than half-cover the seed with water.

Don't plant until the ground is thoroughly warm. If the night temperature less than 65°F, you are certain to have germination problems. A minimum night temperature of 75°F is best. Or plant 7 to 15 days after final frost date. Allow 5 to 18 days for germination, 68 to 88 days to harvest.

Make your rows 30 inches apart and plant the seeds 4 to 8 inches apart in the row. Cover 1 to 1½ inches deep. Plant pole limas 3 to 4 plants per hill. Limas need lots of room for best production.

Harvesting and Processing. The shelling is a chore. To shell, cut a strip off one side. You'll find 2 to 5 beans per pod. Lima pods are never eaten. Eat green or dried.

Freezing. Green-shell limas are best preserved by freezing. First boil or steam-blanch them for 2–4 minutes. I once saw directions in a book that said to freeze lima beans, they should be sorted for size and the large ones blanched for 4 minutes, the medium-sized ones 3, and the small ones 2 minutes. Those directions must have been written in a public library . . . or else by a machine! Anyway, you blanch, cool, pack, and freeze.

Canning Fresh Lima Beans. Shell and wash young, tender beans. Then hot- or raw-pack. To hot-pack: Cover with boiling water. Return to boil. Loosely pack, leaving 1 inch headspace. Add salt if desired. Cover with boiling water. To raw-pack: Loosely pack to these headspaces: small beans 1 inch for pints, 1½ inch for quarts; large beans ¾ inch for pints, 1¼ inch for quarts. *Do not press down or shake jar.* Add salt if desired, along with enough boiling water to cover the beans.

Pressure-can only, 40 minutes for pints, 50 minutes for quarts. If using a weighted-gauge canner, set at 10 lb. pressure at 0–1,000 feet above sea level; set at 15 lb. at higher altitudes. If using a dial-gauge canner, set at 11 lb. pressure at 0–2,000 feet above sea level; 12 lb. at 2,001–4,000 feet; 13 lb. at 4,001–6,000 feet; 14 lb. at 6,001–8,000 feet; or 15 lb. above 8,000 feet.

Green Lima Recipe Ideas. Cook plain with a quick boil and serve with seasonings and butter. Or make a succotash with corn and cream. Or boil with lots of onions until tender, add cream, and serve. Or serve as a salad with other cooked, chilled veggies and a vinegar/oil dressing.

Drying. Use directions for drying shell beans. Or shell and steam 10 to 15 minutes, or boil 5 minutes; spread on tray ½ inch; stir often; and dry until beans are hard and brittle and break clean.

Cooking Dried Limas. Don't presoak. Boil until tender. Don't pressure-cook. They tend to get mushy and clog the valve. Use in any dried bean recipes.

MUNG BEAN: *Phaseolus aureus* is a bush-type annual that is most suited to a warm climate. Its seeds are green or yellow. The plants make excellent livestock forage. The classic Asian "bean sprout" is a sprouted mung bean. Mungs are the second most popular bean in Japan, after soybeans. Harvest and cook like a shelling bean. Seeds available from Comstock and Park.

RICE BEAN: *Phaseolus calcaratus* is its scientific name. It's edible, important in some places, and is harvested and cooked like a shell bean. That's all I know.

RUNNER BEAN: I first grew runner beans as flowers. The variety I grew was an eager climber with lots of orange blossoms that bore from midsummer on to frost. I planted them along my yard fence. They bloomed all summer, even through very hot weather, and were pretty. They had wonderful "Jack in the Beanstalk" seeds—big and colorful. The children loved to play with them. They made necklaces by sticking a hat pin through the beans while they were still soft and letting them dry several days like that. Then they strung them with whatever other items took their fancy. Then I discovered that the beans are edible. Now I know much more about them. They're available from Park, etc.

The runner bean (*Phaseolus coccineus* or *P. multifloris*) is also known as multiflora, painted lady, and Dutch caseknife bean. The runner is actually a perennial but is grown like an annual in the temperate zone. They come in orange-, scarlet-, white-, and red-and-white–flowered varieties. They thrive in hot, humid weather but need plenty of water.

Planting. Seeds are available from Comstock, William Dam, Field, Harris, Hudson, Redwood City, Shumway, Stokes, Thompson & Morgan, and Vermont Bean. Fifty beans will plant about 25 feet. If you start them inside, plant about 3 inches apart 3 to 4 weeks before last frost date. Set them out about a week after that date, or plant them directly outside, about 2 inches deep and 6 inches apart in double rows, one on each side of your climbing support for them. Keep them well watered until they get going. Runners must have something to climb—fence, wall, trellis, or poles (see "Something to Climb" and "Pole Beans"). They'll grow up to 10–12 feet high and are good for screening.

Saving Seed. Most beans don't cross-pollinate significantly, but runner varieties will, so grow just 1 kind at a time to save seeds.

Harvesting. Runners need 60 to 70 days to mature, depending on variety. The beans of some varieties may grow as long as 15 inches, but for snap beans, it's best to pick them quite young and much shorter. A 25-foot single row of runners will yield about 80 lb. of beans. To preserve them, you can freeze or can using snap bean recipes . . . or salt.

Salted Runner Beans. This old-time way of preserving runner beans works surprisingly well. Pick them while at their best, young and green. Slice by hand or with a julienne/French slicer. Lay the sliced beans down in a large

crock, in layers with salt between them. Use 1 lb. non-iodized salt for each 3 lb. beans. Press them down tight enough that there are no air pockets, but don't mash! After the crock is full, cover it. You must have enough salt to keep them from spoiling, because the salt is your only preserving agent. Later on, after the growing season is over and winter has stopped your garden bean production, you can have salted runner beans for dinner. To do that, take out a handful. Put them in a strainer and let sit under running water for an hour. Or rinse with *many* changes of water. Or boil in 3 changes of water. Then finish cooking them. (You can preserve other kinds of green beans this way too.)

Using. Runners can be eaten all 3 ways—snap, green bean, or dried bean. Their flavor is stronger than regular beans; it's good cooked but not raw. To eat green, choose very small ones that are only three-fourths grown, and leave whole; otherwise, slice. Boil or steam and serve with butter. Older pods can be saved and dried for eventual shelling. Use in any bean recipes.

TEPARY BEAN: *Phaseolus acutifolius* var. *latifolius,* commonly called the tepary bean, is an annual, vine-type, twining bean that originated in the southwestern United States and northern Mexico. It does best in those warm climate zones. The pods contain round, edible seeds in a range of colors: white, brown, bluish black, and yellow. Grow and use like southerns.

THE NON-PHASEOLUS BEANS

The non-*Phaseolus* beans are fava, garbanzo (a.k.a. chickpea), lentil, peanut, pigeon pea, the southern group (blackeye, crowder, field pea, pea bean, and yellow-eye), soybean, winged, and yardlong bean.

Fava Bean

Vicia faba is called fava bean (Italy), faba (southern Europe), and broad bean (England); in various other places it's called shell, English dwarf, or horse bean. They grew favas in ancient Egypt and China, in Europe in the Bronze Age, and in the Greek and Roman empires. The *Vicia* means that they're a vetch rather than a *Phaseolus* and that they're related to the southerns and the yardlong bean. The name "horse bean" refers to the fact that this vetch can be harvested for a good hay or can be grown as a summer green manure, winter cover, or spring green manure to be plowed under before the regular garden is planted. All the vetches build nitrogen in your soil, and their empty shells make good compost. *NOTE: There is a very rare inherited sensitivity to fava beans and their pollen. It's found mostly in males of Mediterranean ancestry. This allergy, if triggered, can result in a mild to severely toxic reaction.*

CLIMATE AND WHEN TO PLANT: Fava beans are popular now in England and Canada, and they should be in the United States west of the Cascades because they're perfect for the wet cool climate. They're also a good choice for a high altitude in a tropical zone. Favas can handle cold down to 20°F, but they can't take a hot summer. Plant favas in the spring, as soon as you can get into the garden (whenever you plant peas—February to mid-April). In the Deep South and mild coastal regions, favas do well planted in the fall, October to early November. Or start inside in late winter and then set them out in the garden in March.

PLANTING: Thompson & Morgan, Burpee, and Territorial offer them. Favas have many varieties, pod sizes (4–18 inches long), and degrees of heat and cold tolerance. Johnny's has a variety bred to endure hot weather. Bountiful Gardens has one that's frost-resistant to 10°F. *If you order an inoculant, get one for vetches, not for beans.* Soak seeds overnight; plant 4 to 5 inches apart, 1½ to 2 inches deep, rows 12 to 36 inches apart. If you have bean aphids, you'll find them virtually 100 percent clustered on the tender tops. Just pinch those off, aphids and all, and burn them or drop them into something deadly to the aphids. Don't put them on the compost pile, or they'll return with offspring.

HARVESTING: Fava flowers are edible and can be added to a salad. Mature favas are bushes from 3 to 5 feet tall. Early-planted favas will yield before your regular snap beans and maybe even before your peas! And it's best to harvest in May and early June because hot weather harms pod setting and flavor. After that, cut back to 2 inches and fertilize, and you may get a late summer harvest. Young fava leaves are edible and taste like peas.

USING: If the pods are small enough that there is no white cottony padding inside them, you can follow green bean procedures. The smaller you pick them, the better, because the pod gets tough fast. Harvest when they're even smaller than the size at which you'd take regular snap beans.

To shell out the young beans and use like green limas or green soybeans, drop the green fava beans out of their shells into boiling water for 30 seconds. Then move them to ice water. Now remove beans from their outer skins by slitting them with your thumbnail and pushing them out. They'll need a long cooking even when "green." Compared to green beans, green favas have 10 times as much protein and a different taste.

You can also dry them for soup beans, the most common way of using them. Madhur Jaffrey's *World-of-the-East Vegetarian Cookbook* has fava bean recipes. Among legumes, dried favas are second only to soybeans for protein content.

Garbanzo Bean (Chickpea)

Cicer arietinum is known as "garbanzo" in Spain; "chickpea" (although it's not a true pea) in England; "ceci" in Mexico/Latin America; "gram" (in India, where they are a staple of "dal," the national dish); "homino" in Italy; and "hummus" in Arab countries. This bush bean originated in the Middle Eastern section of the Mediterranean. Garbanzos need 65 to 100 days to mature, depending on the variety. They usually don't do well in a cool climate, but in warm ones they're popular.

PLANTING: Garbanzo seed (90 days) is available from Gurney's. White is the most common variety, but it also comes in black and red. Plant like peas, early, 1 inch deep, 3 to 4 seeds each foot, rows 36 inches apart.

RECIPE IDEAS: Garbanzos can't be used like a snap bean, but they can be used in green shell bean recipes. Prewash dried garbanzos carefully to get rid of dirt that can get into their wrinkles. Don't presoak. Boil 4 hours or until tender. If you pressure-cook them they get awfully foamy, although it can be done. Pressure-cook garbanzos about 30 minutes. They're often used as a salad ingredient after cooking and chilling because they taste almost like a nut. Then use in a dal, falafel, couscous, or hummus recipe. Or serve mixed with chopped onions and carrots and a curry sauce. Or grind and saute. Or saute cooked garbanzos in olive oil with chopped tomatoes, flavored with basil and thyme. Or blend with some sesame oil and lemon juice to make hummus. Or mix cooked garbanzos with tomatoes, anchovies, basil, thyme, and finally cooked macaroni. Or make sandwiches by cooking, mashing, and adding lemon juice to a spreadable consistency (and maybe a crushed garlic clove or two). Or marinate in the refrigerator for a day in a sauce of tamari, lemon juice, water, and favorite herbs and spices—or of cider vinegar, oil, salt, pepper, and an onion or two sliced in thin rings.

✒ *GARBANZO CUTLETS From Melanie Kohler, Haleiwa, HI: "Run 3 c. cooked garbanzos through a grinder (or mash by hand). Combine with 1 c. mashed potatoes, ½ c. onion (chopped fine), ¼ c. chopped parsley, and salt to taste. Mix thoroughly and form into walnut-sized balls. Fry in deep hot oil and serve hot." Or bake as balls or patties.*

✒ *GARBANZO MOCK ROAST Melanie: "Combine in any combination you wish mashed beans, eggs, bread crumbs, oatmeal, chopped nuts, salt, sage, milk, or whatever. Shape into a 'roast.' This is very good cold, sliced like meatloaf for sandwiches." Ruth of Bonaire: "Use rice milk, oatmeal, bread crumbs, and even cooked mashed cauliflower to hold it together. Sage makes for a sausage-like flavor."*

✒ *HUMMUS Puree 2 c. precooked garbanzos together with 1 garlic clove. Add ¼ c. olive oil and ¼ c. lemon juice. If it seems too thick, thin by adding a little water. Chill before serving. Optional: Stir in or sprinkle on top chopped parsley. It's good spread on crackers or wheat bread, a perfect protein complement, and a tasty dip for raw vegetable slices.*

Lentil

Lentils (*Lens culinaris*) go way back. Esau sold his birthright for lentils and bread. They take up a lot of space for what you get, so now they're usually grown as a field crop rather than as a garden crop. Most of the U.S. commercial supply is grown in the Palouse area of eastern Washington. Lentils used to be red or brown, depending on variety. The reds are "Chilean lentils." The browns are "Persian lentils." But there's an amazine variety of new kinds and colors. Washington State U. keeps inventing more.

CLIMATE: Lentils are cool-season–hardy and can stand light frosts. They can be grown in the summer in the northern United States and in the winter in the south. The rolling dry hills of eastern Washington and northern Idaho are the lentil-growing center of the United States. Seeds are available from Park ("sprouting seeds"). You can plant them in early spring. If you have several acres, lentils are good grown as a rotation crop with grain, or as a preliminary crop followed by a crop of late corn.

PLANTING, HARVESTING, AND SAVING SEED: Plant according to the directions for peas: early March to early April, 1 inch deep, 3 inches apart, rows 36 inches apart. They get only 12 to 18 inches high. To harvest, first let plants dry thoroughly in pods in the field, weather permitting. Dry as is, or cut and windrow them to cure in the sun. Large-scale growers use a type of combine to thresh and winnow them. Lentils grow in pods like peas or beans, but each pod contains only one or two of those little seeds. With home-saved lentil seed, the germination rate is best if you leave the seeds in the pods all winter. Be sure they are absolutely dry before you store them.

COOKING: Cooking lentils is fast and easy. Don't presoak lentils, especially not the reds, which soften even more than the greenish and brown ones. Don't pressure-cook lentils because they'll get too mushy and clog the vent. The varieties can be used in recipes interchangeably. To prepare, simply wash 1 lb. lentils (6 servings), place in a heavy saucepan, and add 5 c. cold water and 1 t. salt (optional). Bring to a boil, reduce to a simmer, and cook about 30 minutes, tightly covered. Or make a soup by cooking them with onions, carrots, turnips, celery, beef stock (or vegetable stock and miso), salt, pepper, and a bay leaf.

➤ *LENTILS AND CHEESE Simmer 1 lb. lentils until soft. Strain or mash. Chop 1 onion and saute in ¼ c. butter. Mix sauteed onion, butter, and some grated American cheese with the lentils, and season with salt and pepper to taste. Put all into a greased baking dish; sprinkle more grated cheese and butter bits over the top. Bake until browned.*

➤ *HONEY BAKED LENTILS Cook 1 lb. lentils; drain and reserve fluid. Mix the cooked lentils with 1 t. dry mustard, ½ t. powdered ginger, and 1 T. soy sauce. Add ½ c. chopped onion and 1 c. lentil liquid. Pour mixture into a baking dish and pour ½ c. honey over the top. Cover and bake at 350°F for 1 hour. Uncover dish for the last few minutes of baking to brown the top.*

➤ *LENTIL, WALNUT, AND RICE LOAF Saute 1 onion (chopped) in 2 T. oil or butter. Add ½ t. salt and ⅛ t. each thyme, garlic salt, and celery salt. Add to onions 2 eggs, 2 c. lentil puree, 1 c. chopped walnuts, and 1 c. cooked rice (brown or white). Pack mixture into a buttered loaf pan and bake at 350°F for 45 minutes or until slightly browned on top. Ruth's vegan version: "Saute onion in tamari instead of oil, use garlic powder instead of salt, and substitute ½ c. mashed cooked cauliflower and a spoonful of water for eggs. Use a nonstick pan."*

➤ *RUTH'S LENTIL BURGERS "Bring 1 c. lentils to a boil in 3 c. water. Add a finely chopped onion, a carrot, a celery stalk, and a crushed garlic clove. Reduce heat and simmer about ½ hour. Add ½ c. bulgur (or rice), 2 T. tomato sauce, 1 t. chili powder, and 1 t. mustard (prepared mustard). Cook 15 to 20 minutes more; then cool. Shape into patties*

and bake on a griddle or in a medium oven till browned (both sides)."

➤ *SLOPPY LENTILS Ruth: "Cook 2 c. dried lentils with chopped onion, carrot, and green pepper. After ½ hour, add 4 c. tomato sauce and parsley, basil, bay leaf, garlic, and tamari to taste. Simmer another ½ hour. Eat in pocket bread or over toast."*

Peanut

This Brazilian native (*Arachis hypogaea*, a.k.a. "goober" and "groundnut") likes long, hot summers of at least 4 months (5 is better). If you have that climate, they're easy to grow. If you live in the part of the United States that's north of Arkansas, out of their natural range, you can grow them—but you'll have to try harder. It's worth it, though, because freshly dug and home-roasted peanuts are delicious and healthy. Peanuts are an odd and interesting plant to watch growing. They have 2 sets of flowers, one that's showy yellow and another that forms the peanuts by bending over and growing into the ground. The peanuts develop underground.

VARIETIES: Peanut varieties are distinguished by shape when shelled. The Virginia peanut is long and slender, the Runner is small and stubby, and the Spanish is round. Virginia peanut varieties grow well in warm-climate gardens. Spanish peanut varieties are better for northern growing. Tennessee Red is the sweetest peanut; it has long shells with 3 or 4 nuts per shell. Early Spanish are best for northern growers.

PLANTING: If you're trying to grow peanuts in an area that is really too cold for them, it will probably be worth your while to prepare a special planting area for them. You can make long, 4-foot-wide beds, each of which can hold 3 rows, with the peanuts planted 1 foot apart and your rows 1 foot apart. Make sure your soil is sandy or loamy. Sandy soil helps lengthen peanuts' growing season because it warms up quickly. If their growing place is a sheltered site that slopes to the south, you're better off yet.

Tennessee Red seeds are available from Park and Redwood City. You can plant your peanuts either whole or shelled. Start with seed that you have bought from a seedsman rather than with store peanuts. You can plant nuts either in hulls or shelled. Unshelled peanuts grow more quickly, but you have to shell very carefully so that you don't break the papery inner skin. Don't plant until the ground is warm. Spanish peanuts grow a foot high, but Tennessee Reds can grow 2 feet high. Plant 12 inches apart and 1 inch deep, rows 24 to 30 inches apart.

HARVESTING

Green Stage. After the peanuts are well-formed but not yet fully mature because their hulls are still thin and soft, dig them up. Take the peanuts off the vines. Boil nuts inside hulls in salt water. After 5 to 10 minutes, remove from water, drain, salt, and roast in oven 10 to 15 minutes. You eat these nuts shells and all!

Digging Mature. Each healthy peanut plant with a chance to get its growing done will yield about ½ c. (40–50 pods) of shelled nuts. You must dig up the whole plant to get at the pods. Dig before frost; or dig after frost, when the vines start to turn yellow. Don't rush, because even dying vines are able to continue storing some food in the nuts. They are fully ready to dig when the shells appear fully shaped and when the pod insides have visible dark-colored veins. Dig with a fork, slowly lifting up the whole plant. Where the growing season is on the short side, your main crop will be under the center of the plant, because the peanuts on the outside edge won't have time to finish ripening.

Curing. Shake off the loose soil. Cure them in the sunshine for a few weeks, but bring in at threat of rain. In cold climates or wet weather, hang them on the vine to cure in an airy but shaded place like a shed or attic. They need to cure for about 2 months. When the leaves get dry enough to be crumbly, take the nuts off the vines, roast, and store. Or, if short of time or space, after 2 or 3 weeks of vine drying, pull off the peanuts, pile them lightly into cardboard boxes or onto newspaper, and dry like that another 2 or 3 weeks. *NOTE: Moist peanuts can get moldy. A common peanut mold produces aflatoxin, a dangerous carcinogen that is unaffected by heat. Never eat moldy peanuts. Discard them!*

STORAGE AND PREPARATION: You can save some of them for the next year's seed. To store peanuts briefly, shell, pack raw into airtight containers, and then refrigerate. For longer storage, freeze them. Roast only as needed because they taste best when freshly roasted.

Blanching. Put peanuts into boiling water and leave for 3 minutes. Pour off the water, skin, and spread out to dry. But if you are planning to make peanut butter, roasting is preferable.

Roasting. Spread out the peanuts in a shallow pan or on a cookie sheet and roast at 350°F. Stir frequently. The safest way to know when they are done is to remove and shell a nut at intervals. When the skin slips off easily and the nut itself is a light brown and tastes "roasted," they are done—probably 15 to 20 minutes. A properly roasted peanut ends up with a brittle shell and an inner skin that comes off easily.

Peanut Butter. Peanut butter is simply ground, mashed, or blended peanuts. The homemade kind is actually the best for eating and cooking, but it needs refrigeration and must be used up reasonably soon. It's good to leave it outside the fridge if you'll need it again the next day, though; it's easier to handle at room temp.

To make peanut butter, first skin peanuts. Then you can use a grinder, a mortar and pestle, or a blender to butter them.

Storage of Peanut Butter. Your homemade peanut butter won't keep as well as store-bought, because the kind you buy in stores is protected against rancidity by the addition of an antioxidant. You can solve that problem by either making peanut butter in small batches and keeping them in the refrigerator while they are being used up, or by canning your peanut butter. Also be aware that, unlike most store peanut butters, your homemade butter is unhomogenized and has no sweeteners, preservatives, or stabilizers. If the oil on your peanut butter starts to separate and rise, just turn the jar upside down or stir it together again.

Canning Peanut Butter. Pack closely into clean jars, filling to within 1 inch of the top. Put your lid and screw band on and tighten. Process 1 hour at simmering (about 180°F) in a water-bath canner.

⏩ *BLENDER PEANUT BUTTER Put 1 c. peanuts in a blender. You can add a maximum of 1 c. more after it gets going. Add about 2 T. vegetable oil per 1 c. peanuts. Add salt, if you want (like ½ t. salt per 1 c. nuts).*

⏩ *GRINDER, OR MORTAR/PESTLE, PEANUT BUTTER Put the nuts in the same proportions as above through the grinder several times, or mash them with the mortar and pestle until the consistency satisfies you. Mix in oil and salt in the later stages.*

⏩ *CRUNCHY PEANUT BUTTER If you are using a grinder, put through a part of your peanuts on the coarse grind, and then hold them out to add at the very end. Otherwise, cut up a portion of the peanuts by hand, or use a vegetable chopper, and stir them in last.*

⏩ *ULTIMATE PEANUT BUTTER Spanish peanuts contain a large amount of oil, which in this recipe is offset by the texture of Virginia peanuts. Use 2 parts Virginia peanuts to 1 part Spanish peanuts. You can add to any peanut butter recipe salt, sugar, or oil to taste. Different people like widely differing amounts of salt. It shouldn't be necessary to add oil to this recipe because the peanuts should have just the right amount all by themselves.*

⏩ *GORP Mix 1 part shelled, toasted, ground peanuts (you can use an ordinary hand meat chopper with the small-hole plate) with 1 part raisins. Put it all through the chopper about 3 times for the best flavor. Use more or fewer raisins to suit yourself. Works with walnuts or almonds too (put the almonds through the grater first).*

⏩ *RUTH'S PEANUT SAUCE "Peanut sauce is as Bonairean as gravy is North American. Try a small amount (you'll either love-it-can't-live-without-it or utterly despise it). Try first on baked or grilled chicken, grilled meat on skewers (called satay here), other plain meats, or rice. Stir together in a saucepan over gentle heat only until mixed (don't boil): ¼ c. water, ½ c. peanut butter, 6 T. ketjap manis (see Chapter 5), ¼ t. (or less) hot pepper, and ½ t. each of garlic powder, ground cumin, and curry powder. For authentic satay, marinate cubes of any kind of meat or chicken for at least 24 hours in a marinade of 2 parts ketjap or soy sauce, 1 part water, and equal amounts of curry powder, cumin, garlic, and hot pepper. Then thread meat cubes onto (bamboo) skewers and grill or barbecue. Serve with peanut sauce (or tomato ketchup if you hate peanut sauce)."*

⏩ *GROUNDNUT SAUCE FOR RICE Also from Ruth: "This is a West African recipe; peanuts are called groundnuts there. Mix ½ t. nutmeg and 1 T. chili powder into ¼ c. water. Heat this in a skillet and then add 4 thinly sliced onions and saute.*

Add 1 c. sliced mushrooms and 2 chopped bell peppers. Now add 1 c. ground peanuts (or ¾ c. chunky peanut butter) and 3 c. boiling water. Stir well and test for seasonings (tamari, garlic, nutmeg, and curry are good). Simmer till desired consistency; serve over rice. For a variation, saute the onion in tomato paste instead of water."

Pigeon Pea

Pigeon peas (*Cajanus cajun*), a *perennial* legume, are one of the most popular beans of India, where they, together with chickpea and lentil, are called "grams." If you live in a quite southern zone where it doesn't frost, this is an excellent legume for you. It takes at least 5 months to start bearing but then will continue for up to 5 years. It gets up to 8 feet tall, supporting that on woody stems, and is dense enough that some people grow it for a hedge as well as a food producer. Plant in full sun. The yellow flowers are pretty, and *Cajanus* seeds, though small, are highly nutritious. Use like green peas when seeds are very young and green, or else let mature and dry and use like shell beans. Seeds are available from Southern Seeds.

Southerns

Vigna sinensis, the southerns, consist of many important and closely related varieties. They all do well in the southern United States, so they're grouped together as the "southerns." Though often called "peas," all the southerns are closer botanically to *Phaseolus* than to *Pisum*; technically they are neither peas nor beans but are closest to the lentils and the yardlong bean, the other *Vignas*. The southerns originated in the world's tropical regions, but they can also grow in mild but warm climates (full sun and a long growing season, about 4 months of warm days and nights), basically anywhere corn will grow). They're drought-resistant. They're all good protein sources, nitrogen-fixers, green manure crops to grow and then plow under, or field crops to cut and dry for hay to feed livestock.

VARIETIES: The southerns are Africa's favorite legume (along with the peanut). They arrived in North America from Africa via slave ships. They're one of the oldest domesticated legumes, dating back to cave days. Popular varieties of southerns include "pea beans," which are very small in size; "crowders," which have seeds that seem tightly crowded into their pods; "black-eyed" and "yellow-eyed" peas (or "black-eyes" and "yellow-eyes"), so named because of a dark spot; and "field peas." Black-eyes and brown crowders (cowpeas) have been southern staples for generations.

Black-Eye. The classic black-eye grows pods up to a foot long that contain large, white seeds with black spots or "eyes." The plant takes 60–75 days to maturity. Eat either green shelled or dried. Ideal in the Deep South. Black-eyes require warm days and nights to mature.

Crowder. Mississippi Silver is a crowder pea variety, 65 days to maturity, a heavy yielder with 7–8-inch pods containing beans end to end. Brown crowders are called that because they turn brown when cooked. Crowders are easy to harvest and shell, a long-time Southern favorite.

PLANTING: You can order one or more of the southern varieties from Burpee, Burrell, Comstock, DeGiorgi, Gurney, Jackson and Perkins, Mellinger's, Park, Shumway, Twilley, and Vermont Bean. Don't put these seeds in your richest soil, or they'll make much plant and little bean. This legume enriches the soil and should be planted in your poorest soil. If planting southerns in the North, plant on the late side, not until after the soil and the nights have gotten warm. For a food crop, plant southerns in rows 3 feet apart, seeds spaced 2 to 3 inches apart. Cover with 1 inch of soil. For a green manure or hay crop, broadcast your seeds; about ¼ lb. seed will broadcast 100 square feet of field. Rake to cover them. Keep the growing plants well weeded because weeds harbor insect problems for southerns.

SAVING SEED AND HARVESTING: To save seed from this or any other *Vigna* species, pick before the pods are well developed. That way they can be easily shelled before the pods begin to dry out. Shell them out of the green pods and then dry. Southerns, especially cowpeas, are very frost-tender. Harvest when immature if you want to use them like snap beans. For green shell beans, harvest when the color has begun to fade. By then the seeds are about grown but haven't dried. For dry shell beans, let dry on the vine and then pick.

PRESERVING AND USING: Preserve using the directions given for other beans. Use like a snap bean in their very young stage. Or mature and dry them for shell beans. Presoak black-eyes and then boil 30 to 50 minutes. Pressure-cooking black-eyes is not recommended; they tend to mush and clog the vent. You can use "yellow-eyed peas" in any black-eyes direction or recipe.

Recipe Ideas. Serve as a stew with potatoes. Or mix with chilled cooked corn, boiled diced potatoes, bits of raw carrot and onion, basil, and mayo to make a cooked salad. Or bake precooked beans with onions, ham chunks, and molasses. Or fry precooked southerns with onions and sausage and serve with ketchup. Or roast meat on top of a bed of precooked southerns with a ring of carrots and potatoes around the edge. Or cook southerns with lots of onion (or another allium), puree with a slosh of milk, and serve with melted cheese on top. Or use in any other dried bean recipe.

Soybean

The soybean (*Glycine max*) is a vegetarian favorite, the lowest-starch, highest-protein bean. It's from China, is popular in Japan, and is valuable in parts of the world where, because dairy cows fall victim to tropical insects and disease, babies are fed a soybean milk. The average Japanese person eats about 60 soybeans every day, an average of 20 a meal!

SOY INFO: Check out William Shurtleff and Akiko Aoyagi's *The Book of Tofu* and *The Book of Tempeh*; Louise Hogler's *Tofu Cookery*; and *The New Farm Vegetarian Cookbook* (terrific huge catalog for health-conscious eaters: PO Box 180, Summertown, TN 38483; www.healthy-eating.com; 800-695-2241). The best book on soy nutrition is *The Simple Soybean and Your Health,* by Mark and Virginia Messina. Soybean recipes regularly appear in *Vegetarian Times* magazine. "Soyfoods: Adding Value to Soybeans" is at www.attra.org/attrapub/soyfoods.html. Soyfoods Association of America is a nonprofit trade organization that connects growers, bean processors, soyfood manufacturers, retailers, and consumers. It promotes soyfood use and offers nutritional info, recipes, and a listing of soyfood companies: 202-986-5600; fax 202-387-5553; info@soyfoods.org; www.soyfoods.org.

The Soyfoods Center, founded by Shurtleff and Aoyagi, is the largest computerized database/research center on soyfoods in the world, now having 59,000 documents. They sell 55 books on soyfood and consult on producing commercial soyfoods: 925-283-2991; fax 925-283-9091; PO Box 234, Lafayette, CA 94549-0234; **email@ thesoydailyclub.com; www.thesoydailyclub.com/ soyfoodscenter.asp.**

CLIMATE: Soybeans need heat to produce well. Some chill-tolerant kinds will produce modestly in more temperate zones but not in really cold places. The problem is that once the soybean plant starts blooming and making seed pods, it stops growing. If the plants are small when blooming begins, the harvest will be small. If the plant grows a long time before the changing length of the day signals it to begin making seed, the harvest can be large. Problems you may encounter growing a family plot of soybeans: They take a long time to mature, the yields are poor, pods spill beans on the ground, or the variety is not suited to your growing season. Difficulty with shelling and bland or even bitter taste are other problems. Soybeans do well in the Corn Belt and in the lower Mississippi River valley.

VARIETIES: In Asia, over 100 varieties are grown; elsewhere, you have fewer choices. Commercial farmers plant small-seeded varieties intended for mechanical processing into oil or for dry seeds. Soybeans used to be grown for animal forage, hay, green manure, or for silage (with sorghum), but bean hay is riskier than clover because it takes longer to cure. There are both high-protein and high-oil types. For green manure, choose a late-maturing kind to give it a chance to make more foliage, since soybeans don't add as much nitrogen to the soil from roots as other beans do, but they do enrich the soil greatly when the whole plants are plowed under. For eating, choose between "field soybeans" for drying or the "sweet or edible" soybeans for eating green shell-style. For biggest harvest, find the latest-maturing variety that can ripen in your summer's length before a killing frost. Envy and Fiskeby are for more northern latitudes. Available from Johnny's (which has more varieties than most), Burgess, Burpee, Comstock, William Dam, DeGiorgi, Gurney's, Kitazawa, Le Jardin du Gourmet, Nichols, Stokes, and Vermont Bean.

PLANTING: Follow basic directions for planting lima beans. Soil needs to be warm, at least 65°F, for germination. So plant about a week after your green beans, 1 inch deep, 1 to 2 inches apart, rows at least 1 foot apart. Later, thin to 2 to 4 inches apart. (The longer-maturing the variety, the taller and sprawlier-on-the-ground the plants will get.) To broadcast field soybeans, plant 100 lb. per acre or 4–5 lb. per 1,000 square feet. If seeding a field in rows, plant 40 lb. per acre; if drilling, 60–80 lb. per acre. The accepted weight of a bushel of soybeans is 60 lb. For green manure, plow under when the seeds are half-formed.

SAVING SEED AND HARVESTING: For seed: Because of soybean's tendency to shatter its pod and spill its seed, gather pods before full maturity and then dry, shell, and store them like other legumes. The bushlike plants mature all at once when triggered by the length of the day. If the bushes are able to grow long enough beforehand, each gets loaded with greenish, fuzzy, lumpy pods (up to 50 per plant), each with 2 or 3 oval-shaped beans. For green shell beans, start picking when the soybeans are green in the pod, ideally when the pods are just a bit short of fully mature. A soybean harvest is short, only 7 to 10 days. They don't hang on and wait for you to come and get them; rather, they'll turn from green to yellow in only a few days. Yellow is too late for green soybeans. For soybeans to dry, however, you pick when the leaves are 90 percent yellow and the pods are dry but haven't yet begun to shatter. Harvest like other beans for drying.

PREPARING: Soybeans plus corn provide complete protein in a diet. As a green shell bean they're as tasty as limas, or they can be dried and used in all kinds of interesting ways. Dried ones can be sprouted. *Don't ever eat soybeans raw or feed them to animals!* That's because soybeans contain "trypsin inhibitor"—a substance that, if not destroyed by lots of cooking, will "inhibit" (destroy) the trypsin enzyme made by your pancreas. Trypsin makes it possible for you to digest protein. Since protein is the main benefit you get from eating soybeans, cook them well. Soybeans are high in protein but low in flavor.

Green Shell Soybeans. If you have the kind you can eat green, use them in lima bean recipes. They are difficult to shell but are easier after cooked in the pods. At least blanch them (to deactivate the trypsin inhibitor) before eating. But usually folks boil the beans in the pods 5 to 8 minutes. Then shell out, finish steaming, and serve. To shell, break pods crosswise and squeeze out the beans. Food writer Lane Morgan says, "I've grown the green ones here. They do pretty well, but they are so tedious to shell, even after blanching, that I wouldn't be tempted to use them as a main homestead vegetable. Ruth and Melanie's suggestions to serve them in the pod as snacks are the best bet, in my opinion."

Green Soybean Recipe Ideas. To freeze them, boil in the pods about 5 minutes, and cool enough to shell. Shell directly into the containers you're going to freeze them in. To can them, use the directions for canning lima beans. Green soybeans can be served buttered as part of a meal; cooled and added to a salad; or cooked with tomatoes, green onions, and green peppers and then served. Or cook with corn, tomatoes, and garlic, and serve buttered. Or puree the green soybeans, combine with rice, and serve with a spicy sauce. Or stir-fry with a chopped allium and sliced cooked meat. Or cook in a soup with greens, onions, and miso paste for flavoring. Melanie says, "If fresh, I just boil them in the pods, and then we pop them into our mouths." Ruth says, "Boil in pod and then whisk to table. Each person has a small dish of soy sauce (tamari), dunks the whole pod in it, puts the whole thing in his mouth, shells inside the mouth, and discards the pod. Finger-lickin' good—on a par with corn-on-the-cob!"

ABOUT DRIED SOYBEANS

Harvesting for Drying. Soybeans must be allowed to dry on their plants. *Watch carefully so that you pick the pods immediately after the beans inside are dry (the beans will rattle in the pod) but while the stems are still green.* If you wait longer, the hulls will shatter and the beans will be lost onto the ground. After gathering, dry them further in an airy situation until they are good and dry. Then they store nicely for seed or for use in any dried soybean recipe.

Cooking Dried Soybeans. The 2 rules for successfully cooking dried soybeans are to thoroughly soak in plenty of water beforehand (and then throw out the water and use new water for cooking) and to pressure-cook or cook a long time. The minimum for cooking whole soybeans: Soak overnight, using 3 times as much water as beans to start with; throw out the soak water and cook another hour. Without the presoak, cook 4 to 6 hours or pressure-cook at 15 lb. for 20 to 30 minutes. Readers tell me that to cope with bitter-tasting soybeans, they boil them and then pour off the water.

To have soybeans ready to cook on short notice, you can go through the whole soaking process, spread in a single layer on large cookie sheets, freeze, and then store in containers in the freezer. You spread them out so they'll freeze separately; that way they thaw and cook up more quickly for you. When you want to cook your frozen beans, you can then skip the soaking process and cook them right away. Presoaked and frozen beans won't take quite as long to cook. Soybeans are done cooking when very soft—you can easily mash a bean between your tongue and the roof of your mouth or between your fingers. When pressure cooking, adding 1½ t. cooking oil per 1 c. beans helps prevent soybean seed hulls from stopping up the steam escape valve.

Flavorings for Cooked Soybeans. After you get them cooked, stir in some flavoring and just a little more water, and keep heated 10 minutes or so. Add one of these per 1 c. dried soybeans: 2 T. miso; 1 T. (or more) soy sauce; 2 t. lemon juice; some butter; chopped fried onion with miso and grated cheese stirred in; a sweetener, like molasses or honey, along with a little miso or soy sauce; chopped vegetables (the kind you can eat raw); or cooked vegetables seasoned with a little salt or soy sauce and maybe garlic. Or make a soup by adding vegetables and extra water to almost-cooked soybeans and cooking on until the veggies are done. Or serve with yogurt. Ruth suggests: "Cook soybeans and lentils half-and-half in a chili soup or stew. Or marinate whole cooked soybeans in the refrigerator in a mixture of tamari, water, lemon juice, and your favorite herbs and spices."

➤ *SOYBEAN LOAF From Melanie: "Combine 2 c. soybeans (soaked, cooked, and ground), 1 c. tomato sauce, 1 ground onion, 1 c. cubed cheese, ½ c. cornmeal, ¼ c. chopped ripe olives, 3 eggs, and salt and sage to taste. Bake at 350°F for 1 to 1½ hours."*

➤ *BAKED SOYBEANS From Melanie: "Mix together 6 c. cooked soybeans (2 c. dried), 3 T. molasses, 1 can tomato soup, 1 c. liquid from beans, the juice of 1 lemon, 1 T. oil, and salt to taste. Place in bean pot or baking dish. Put a whole onion in the center of the beans, and place several bay leaves on top. Bake at 325°F for 1 hour or longer, adding more bean liquid or tomato juice as needed to keep moist."*

➤ *SAVORY SOYBEAN PATTIES Melanie: "Grind 6 c. cooked soybeans. Add 1½ c. oats, ½ t. garlic salt, 2 T. soy sauce, ¼ t. salt, 2 eggs, and any other seasonings you feel in the mood for. Let mixture stand 10 minutes for the oats to absorb moisture. Drop by tablespoonfuls into oiled skillet. Fry till brown. Serve with homemade tomato sauce."*

➤ *SOYNUTS Lou Reed, Gillette, WY, advises soaking your soybeans in water overnight. Drain on a paper towel or cloth until dry. Then put beans in a fine wire strainer that looks like a big tea strainer, and cook in deep bacon grease until light brown. Add salt and onion salt (to deaden the "soy" taste).*

➤ *MEXICAN SOYNUTS Dry out the extra moisture from your cooked beans on a baking sheet in the oven. Fry in oil, ½ c. at a time, for 10 minutes or so. Serve crisp, golden brown, and salted.*

➤ *FAT-FREE SOYNUTS Roast precooked beans on a tray, sprinkled with salt if you like, at 350°F for an hour or more, stirring frequently. They're done when they smell toasted and are crunchy clear through. Or spread on an unoiled cookie sheet a layer of beans one bean thick, and toast overnight at a fairly low oven temp. Serve still warm with a little oil and salt. Or roast at 250°F for 2½ hours, shaking pans every 15 to 30 minutes. If you soak the beans in salt water before roasting, don't salt them afterward.*

SOY MILK: To make soy milk, be sure you start with the "edible" people-type soybean. Otherwise your soy milk won't have the best flavor. Use a soy milk machine or make it from scratch. Soy milk machines make soy milk in 12–20 minutes using a controlled cooking and grinding process. (They can also be used to make rice milk, nut milks, smoothies, etc.) Get more info from C. F. Resources (719-962-3228; **www.cfamilyresources.com**); or Chin Enterprises ($148; 617-423-1725, Boston, MA); or the SoyaJoy Soy Milk machine from Miriam Kramer ($150; 909-796-8501; 800-500-7342).

Or make your soy milk the old-fashioned way. Carefully clean the beans and soak overnight. Soak in 7 c. water per 1 lb. soybeans (2½ c. dried soybeans equal 1 lb.). Now drain off soaking water and thoroughly wash 3 times in separate clean water, stirring briskly. That stirring and rinsing helps get out the beany taste; it also helps heat up your beans (if you use hot water). While rinsing, keep the beans in a bowl with very hot tap water running slowly over them, and fill your blender with boiling water to get it hot for the next step.

Now you're going to blend your beans with hot water. But first, ready a large strainer by placing it over a deep kettle, bowl, or pail. Inside the strainer, lay unbleached muslin or nylon curtain material for a straining cloth—about 1 square yard or less, depending on your container size and how much soybean milk you're going to make. When your strainer is ready to go, you can get back to the blending. The following directions assume you have a 1-qt. blender; if not, adjust the quantities for the smaller or larger size of your blender. Put about 1½ c. of your soaked, hot soybeans into the blender. Add boiling water (about 2 c.) to fill the blender about two-thirds full. Put on the blender lid. Cover that with a big folded towel and keep children away because the steam pressure that builds when you start to blend might cause the lid to blow off. Run blender at low speed for 3 or 4 minutes and then at highest speed for about 5 more minutes.

The next step is to drain off and separate your soy milk from the remains of the blended soybeans. As each portion of beans and hot water is finished in the blender, dump it into your straining setup. Gather up the edges of the strainer cloth after most of the milk has run through, and put pressure on the soybean residue to get out as much more soy milk as you can. When you have blended and strained all your soybeans, put the residue from the strainer cloth back into your blender, together with 2 c. cold water. Blend. Drain and squeeze again. Now you have soybean milk. The exact amount of fluid in it is surprisingly flexible. For baby formula, the pound of beans you started out with should make about 1 gal. milk. If you don't have that much, simply add more water.

Now you cook it to get rid of that anti-trypsin agent that makes all the difference between an indigestible and a superdigestible, nourishing soy milk. You can do this in a deep kettle, but you have to stir it continually while it is boiling and watch it like a hawk to keep it from either scorching or boiling over. By far the safest and easiest way is to rig up some sort of double-boiler arrangement for heating the soy milk. Make sure it spends at least 30 minutes at top heat. Now quickly chill and store under refrigeration if possible because it spoils easily, just like real dairy products.

Soy Milk Baby Formula. Per each gallon soy milk, weigh out 100 grams (3½ oz.) of an edible oil like corn, soy, peanut, or safflower and 300 grams (10½ oz.) of corn syrup. Place oil in blender with as much hot soy extract as will fit (fill the blender three-quarters full). Blend. Add blended oil-soy milk mixture and corn syrup to rest of soy milk and bring to active boil again, so the oil and corn syrup will be sterilized too. Now cool and store. It will keep easily for 3 to 5 days under refrigeration.

Other Flavorings and Fortifiers. For cooking and for foods like white sauce, a more concentrated soy milk works better. If you make it more concentrated, Lo! It's soy cream. Optional flavorings for your soy cream are brown sugar, vanilla, and coconut flavoring.

Soy Milk Yogurt. From Ruth of Bonaire! "Use soy milk and add commercial yogurt for starter (or your own soy yogurt) at a ratio of 2 to 3 T. per quart of soy milk. Here's the procedure: Sterilize your jars by boiling about 2 minutes. Also boil the soy milk for 30 seconds, *stirring constantly*. Pour into the still-hot jars and cover them. Wait until the jar still feels hot but doesn't burn the inside of your arm when you touch it and hold it there. Then stir your starter into the yogurt with a sterilized spatula. Cover jars and place in a pan of warm water until yogurt separates cleanly from jar sides when the jar is gently tilted (Takes 4 to 6 hours). Thicker yogurt comes from thicker soy milk.

➣ *SOY YOGURT CREAM CHEESE Ruth: "Make this from soy milk yogurt instead of dairy yogurt." See yogurt cream cheese recipe in "Cheese Making" in Chapter 10.*

➣ *SOY YOGURT SOUR CREAM Ruth: "Blend 1 c. moist Soy Yogurt Cream Cheese (to be moist, it shouldn't hang too long) with 4 t. lemon juice and 1 t. frozen apple juice concentrate until smooth."*

➣ *SOY YOGURT COTTAGE CHEESE Ruth: "Let your yogurt cheese hang for more than 1 or 2 days, and it will turn into a curded-type cheese. You can use it just like dairy cottage cheese."*

➣ *SOY MILK ICE CREAM Ruth: "Here are 2 basic versions of soy milk ice cream to make in your crank freezer. Mix 3 c.*

soy milk, 2 medium mashed bananas (very ripe ones), and ½ c. honey. Freeze in an ice cream freezer. Or use 1 c. frozen apple juice concentrate, 3 c. soy milk, 2 t. real vanilla, and ¾ t. liquid lecithin. Blend well before freezing. This can be made into 'chocolate' by omitting the vanilla and using ¾ c. carob powder."

➣ *SOYSAGE Also from Ruth: "There are lots of ways to duplicate the taste and look of sausage without using meat at all. For this recipe, use 4 c. soy pulp (leftovers from making soy milk, after it's strained) or cooked ground soybeans. Mix with 2 c. whole wheat flour, 1 c. wheat germ, 2 c. liquid (soy milk, water, juice, or vegetable-cooking liquid), 1 c. nutritional yeast flakes (Saccaromyces cererisiae, which is grown in molasses and is bright golden yellow, not torula or 'brewer's yeast'), ¼ c. tamari or shoyu, 2 T. prepared mustard, 1½ t. fennel seed, 1 t. black pepper, 3 t. oregano, 1 t. sage, and 1 t. allspice. (These spices are just guidelines. Adjust as you prefer.) Shape mixture into any shape: patties, 'hot dogs,' rings, whatever. Place on a rack in a steamer and steam, covered, for 1½ hours. (For hot dog shapes or patties, it helps if they are wrapped in foil.) When they are cool, freeze until needed. Then bake or fry (in an ungreased cast iron skillet)."*

It's hard to believe the author of above recipes was only 13 when she sent me that information. She and I corresponded after that for years, even after she was going to college in the States. But then she got busy with her own life (as is appropriate for a young woman), and I haven't heard from her since.

TOFU: Tofu, or bean curd, is a staple in Asian cooking, especially in Chinese and Japanese dishes. It's 95 percent digestible compared to 68 percent for whole, cooked soybeans. It consists of the "milk" solids that are separated out of soy milk—the soy-milk equivalent of cottage cheese.

For much more info than I can squeeze in here, see John Ward's 1998 book, *An American's Introduction to Tofu* (**www.tofu.com/whatis.html**) and *The Book of Tofu*, a 433-pg paperback classic with 250 recipes, 175 illustrations, instructions, etc.

Making Tofu. To make cottage cheese, you sour the milk to get your curds and whey to separate (precipitate). You sour either naturally, by adding rennet, or by adding lemon juice (in the case of a whey cheese like ricotta). To make tofu, you can sour the soy milk by adding lemon juice, lime juice, cider vinegar, or some unfamiliar-sounding stuff like Epsom salts, calcium lactate, or calcium carbonate. As in cheese making, the exact amount of acid you must add is really quite flexible. So in general, to make tofu, start out by making soy milk with the recipe I already gave you. Don't worry if you end up with somewhat more or less than a gallon, because you can make tofu anyway. In fact, I think it helps a bit if it's a little more than a gallon (and thus more concentrated).

When your soy milk is done cooking and still hot but not boiling, like about 180°F, add your precipitant. If it's a chemical, dissolve it in 1 c. soy milk separately and then stir it gently into the rest. How much precipitant? Use 2–3 T. calcium lactate or calcium carbonate or ¼ c. lemon or lime juice or cider vinegar. Always stir in the same direction and pour in the precipitant mixture very slowly. It curdles quickly.

Now pour the milk into something in which it can set up, get firm, and take its shape. The Japanese pour the curd into large wooden frames with wire bottoms into which they sort of press it, and that helps drain out the extra whey. You can do something like that too by building a square frame of wood, taking a husky wire mesh across the bottom, laying cheesecloth or some sort of straining cloth in the frame over the wire, and then pouring the curd into that, making it spread out to an even thickness. You can put some gentle pressure on it to help the whey get out. But you don't have to use this system, even though it's nice to be able to dump out the whole slab and cut it into squares that look just like what the Japanese make. The bean curd will be just as good to eat if you drain it in a cloth laid inside any old strainer, with cloth over the top and a plate weighted on top to help press out the whey. That takes only a few minutes, and either way it's ready.

Storing Tofu. Cut into squares and keep them in cool water in your refrigerator until you use them. Change the water daily. Aging actually firms up your bean curd, making it easier to handle. Or freeze it. You may want to freeze it just for its effect on the curd, for tofu enters a freezer soft but comes out firm and dry enough to skewer (squeeze out any remaining water). To freeze it, you can first slice or cube it, or keep it in the full cake. Squeeze all the air out of its bag. It changes texture within 48 hours.

Seasoning/Cooking with Tofu. Tofu is almost tasteless in its own right, so add flavor or let it absorb flavor from whatever dish it's included in. Melanie Kohler from Hawaii: "One of the simplest ways I fix tofu is just to cut it in cubes approximately 1 inch square and put it in a bowl. It can be served just plain like that, or with shoyu (soy sauce) poured over, or with a sauce made of 2 T. soy sauce, 1 t. sugar, and some powdered garlic or ginger. Heat the sauce a minute or two, and then pour over the tofu. Sprinkle some chopped green onions or Chinese parsley (coriander or cilantro) on top and serve." Ruth adds: "Tofu cubes may also be added to stir-fried vegetables for a quick entree. Add just before serving so the tofu doesn't get all mashed in the cooking. Or add tofu cubes to a plain soup broth to make it more nourishing."

✎ *TOFU BALLS* Melanie: *"Mash, squeeze, and drain 1 block of tofu. Combine with the mashed tofu 2 carrots (grated finely), 1/4 c. chopped green onions, 1 c. chopped peanuts, 1 T. sugar, 1 1/2 t. salt, and 2 eggs. Form mixture into balls, roll in bread or cracker crumbs, and deep-fry until golden brown."*

✎ *TOFU CASSEROLE* Melanie: *"Cut tofu into cubes and fry lightly in a little oil. Place in a casserole dish, cover with tomato soup, and sprinkle grated cheese on top. Bake at 350°F until hot and bubbly. Cream of mushroom soup or plain brown gravy may be used instead of tomato, if you wish."* Ruth comments, *"Omit oil. If you use homemade tomato sauce instead of canned soup, you won't get all the sugar and chemicals."*

✎ *TOFU LOAF* Melanie: *"Mash a block of tofu and squeeze out as much water as possible. Combine the mashed tofu with 1 carrot (grated finely), 1/2 c. soft whole wheat bread crumbs, 2 T. mayonnaise, 1 onion (grated finely), 1 egg, and 1/2 t. salt. Mix well, pour into a greased pan, and bake at 375°F for 45–60 minutes or until lightly browned. Serve with ketchup, with brown gravy, or as is."*

✎ *VEGAN SOYBEAN LOAF* Ruth: *"Combine 2 1/2 c. mashed, cooked soybeans, 1 grated onion, 1 c. tomato sauce, 2 T. tamari, 2 t. curry powder (or 1 t. sage and 1 T. basil), and 1*

T. molasses. Mix together and add either more tomato juice or some arrowroot, depending on consistency (it should be on the thick side, but not too dry). Bake till done (an hour at 350°F)."

✎ *RUTH'S TOFU "BIG MAC"* *"Saute 2 chopped onions, 1/2 lb. chopped mushrooms, and 3 crushed garlic cloves in water until soft and water is absorbed. Mash 2 lb. tofu and combine with 3 c. rolled oats, 1 1/2 c. cooked, chopped, drained spinach, 4 T. tamari, 1 T. lemon juice, and 1 t. each of black pepper and paprika. Mix well before adding mushrooms and onions. Shape into patties. Bake (on nonstick baking tray) for 20 minutes at 350°F. Then flip and bake 10 more minutes. Serve on homemade buns with your favorite condiments. Delicious!"*

✎ *RUTH'S TOFU SALAD* *"This is like egg salad, I think. It's good as a sandwich filling or mounded on lettuce leaves with homemade crackers. Crumble 1 lb. (drained) tofu and mix with 1/4 c. pickle relish, 1 t. garlic powder, a few stalks of chopped celery, and 1 chopped green pepper. Optional: Add 1 T. honey. Add 1/4 c. eggless mayonnaise, soynaise, or whatever you use instead of mayonnaise (we use nut butter whipped with water, or soft creamy tofu with lemon juice)."*

✎ *RUTH'S TOFU PIZZA* *"Make a pizza crust of flour, water, and yeast-bread dough, using any combination of flours (a mix of whole wheat, rye, and cornmeal is nice). Bake the crust before proceeding. Puree in a blender peeled tomatoes, a good spoonful of oregano, a few cloves of minced garlic, and a pinch each of basil, thyme, and marjoram. Spread this sauce on crust when it's cool. On top of sauce put sliced mushrooms, olives, onions, etc., and chunks of soysage mixture (see following recipe). Serve pizza immediately."*

✎ *RUTH'S SOYSAGE MIXTURE* *"Soak 1/4 c. cracked wheat (bulgur) in boiling water for 30 minutes. Drain. Also drain and crumble 1 lb. (or less) of tofu and mix well with bulgur, 1 t. cumin, 1 1/2 T. sage, garlic powder, and 1/4 c. tamari. Good on pizza (see preceding recipe); can also be used in tacos instead of hamburger."*

✎ *TOFU COTTAGE CHEESE* Mash tofu to a cottage-cheeselike consistency. Stir in salt to taste, some concentrated soy milk to moisten, and/or 1/2 c. chopped chives per 2 c. soy cottage cheese. Or add chopped nuts, or serve with fresh fruit.

TEMPEH: SOYBEANS WITH CULTURE: To make tempeh (pronounced "TEM-pay"), soybeans are inoculated with a specific variety of mold, a mushroomy member of the fungus genus *Rhizopus* whose specialty is natural decay processes. It can be made from soybeans, other beans, a grain, or a mixture of grain types. Tempeh is Indonesian in origin. To see what you're aiming for, buy a sample from a food co-op or health food store. It's weird stuff, but I like it. You can eat it plain, chunked into a salad like strong-flavored cheese, or thinly sliced in a sandwich. Here are Ruth's tempeh-making instructions: "First cook the soybeans, and then cool and combine with vinegar and starter as follows."

Starter. You can buy a starter of tempeh culture from The Mail Order Catalog; PO Box 180, Summertown, TN 38483; 800-695-2241. Or from GEM Cultures: 707-964-2922; 30301 Sherwood Rd., Fort Bragg, CA 95437; **www.gem cultures.com**. GEM also sells a culture thermometer ($7), Kombucha Tea Fungus, nigari, miso, and kefir starters. Ruth:

"Once you get your first batch of tempeh started, you can start your next batch from your previous one if you let a small piece 'incubate' long enough to turn black, and then put it in a very small jar of water and shake vigorously. Remove black piece of tempeh and let jar set overnight (in the refrigerator). The little black spores will settle to the bottom. In the morning, pour off the water and use those starter spores to make your next tempeh: 1 t. starter for 2½ c. dry beans."

The Basic Mix. Ruth: "Boil your dry soybeans for 20 minutes. Then, leaving pot covered, turn off heat and let stand for about 2 hours. Next, split the beans—grab a handful and knead until the beans split in half (you can also use a potato masher for this). When all beans are split, return to pot with fresh water and boil for an hour. Skim off the hulls. Now drain off any water, and then roll the beans around in a big fuzzy towel to dry them. (If they are wet, you can be sure the tempeh will rot.) When beans are pretty cool to the touch, mix them with 2 T. vinegar and 1 t. starter per 2½ c. dry soybeans (as they measured *before* you cooked them). Mix each ingredient well before adding the other. Now pack a layer of the soybeans 1 cm. (about ½ inch) deep into a plastic bag, which will be your tempeh mold."

Proper Curing. Ruth: "With the tines of a fork, poke lots of holes all over the plastic bag. Place on a wire cooling rack so the air can circulate. [For basic background on working with fungi, see "Mushrooms" in Chapter 2.] Tempeh must be in a very warm place, like 30–35°C (about 85°F to 95°F). If you live in a colder (than tropical) climate, periodically check the temperature of the curing location with a thermometer. The curing place should also be open to normal airflow. A sunny window might be a good place in colder climates.

"As the curing process progresses, after 12 to 15 hours you will see condensation on the outside of the plastic bag containing the soybeans and a faint white mold beginning to form. After about 20 hours, the tempeh should be completely white. Then it will start to get gray and black spots in places; that means it is almost done. (Soybean tempeh isn't ready until the black/gray spots appear.) Tempeh takes between 19 and 26 hours to cure properly. If it is sliced, finished tempeh should appear solid, with no gaps between bean pieces. A thin slice should hold together well. It should smell like mushrooms or yeast dough. If it is slimy or sticky or smells strongly of ammonia, either all over or just on the bottom (too much moisture), or if it has a color other than white or gray/black, you should *not* eat it—*throw it away!* Bad tempeh is usually mushy; good tempeh is solid. If the mold does not fill in all the open spaces between beans, let it cure a while longer. Sometimes half of the piece gets done before the other half. In this case, cut off the finished part and leave the rest until it gets gray/black spots and is solid all the way through."

Preserving Tempeh. Ruth: "Refrigerate separate packages for up to 2 days. Because the mold is still active, it produces heat and should not be placed next to another piece of live tempeh in the fridge. Or cut into pieces, steam about 5 minutes to kill the mold, and freeze. You can also slice tempeh very thinly and dry it in the sun, oven, or dehydrator; you can then store it almost indefinitely."

Other Tempehs. Ruth: "Tempeh can be made from various beans, nuts (peanuts), and grains, alone or in any combination. (If using a combination, cook each separately, split and mix together when cool, and then add vinegar and starter.)

"Navy beans: Boil 15 minutes, let set 5 minutes, split, and boil 6 to 10 minutes, skimming hulls off.

"Kidney and pinto beans: Crack dry beans in a food mill, and then boil 20 minutes.

"Peanuts: Shell; boil 1½ hours. Use only half the amount of vinegar.

"Rice: Boil 10 minutes, drain, and flood with cold water. Layer rice in the plastic bag only half as deep as you would layer soybeans. Harvest when still white, before gray spots appear.

"Barley (pearled): Boil 15 minutes, drain, and rinse in cold water. Layer in bag half as deep as you would layer soybeans. Harvest when still white.

"Cracked wheat: Steam 20 minutes, stirring occasionally. Layer in bag half as deep as you would layer soybeans. Harvest when still white."

MISO AND SOY SAUCES: Miso is fermented soybeans, aged in wooden barrels for 3 years. It's dark-colored, it tastes like bouillon, and vegetarians substitute it any time a recipe calls for beef stock or bouillon cubes. See William Shurtleff's *Book of Miso: Savoury High-Protein Seasoning* for directions on how to make it.

Tamari. "Tamari soy sauce" is a term the natural foods industry uses to distinguish its soy sauce from chemically processed ones (which contain sugar, chemical additives, food coloring, etc.). But in traditional usage, "tamari" meant the liquid that collected at the top of a miso-fermenting tub. That tamari was then bottled and sold as a condiment.

Commercial Soy Sauce. Somebody from Hawaii sent me a newspaper clipping that described a reporter's visit to a shoyu (soy sauce) factory. He said a lot of store soy sauce is chemically produced and takes only 24 hours to make. But Diamond Shoyu is made from a mixture of roasted, crushed wheat and soybean meal that is first sprayed with hot water, and then pressure-cooked for an hour. Then a special mold is added. It sets in a warm place for 4 days and then in a salt solution in fermenting tanks for 10 to 12 months. At last the shoyu is filtered out from the solids, monosodium glutamate and a preservative are added, and it's ready for market.

   KATHY'S SOY SAUCE From Kathy Colin, Kailua, HI: Mix 10 c. soybeans, ½ c. molasses, ½ c. pure salt, and 6 gal. water. Cook until boiling. Lower heat and simmer 5 hours (should be about 5 gal. left). Strain. Pour into a 5-gal. glass jug. Seal airtight. Keep in a frequently sunlit spot like a window ledge or roof (remember, she lives in Hawaii!) for 1 year or more if it seems to need it and your patience is up to it. And, Kathy promises, "the resulting liquid will be a delectable light soy sauce."

Winged Bean

Psophocarpus tetragonologus purpurea is also called the winged pea, asparagus bean, asparagus pea, dambala, goa bean, and Manila bean. Its name refers to the 4 lengthwise ribs—"wings"—that develop on its seed pods. It's a remarkable tropical legume, a food plant from southern Asia that's widely grown in Asia and Europe but is little known in the United States. This is a pretty climbing plant (10 to 12 feet) that endures heat well but can't endure frost. It flowers only when the days are short. So your seasonal window of opportunity for growing it is narrow unless you live in a subtropical zone. It grows best with support—against fences or walls or with corn. Winged beans are said to prefer clay to sandy soils. It can self-seed. Southern Seeds says it "requires ample moisture and likes cool weather . . . should be planted in the fall-winter-spring season in the Deep South . . . is daylight-sensitive and will set flower only when the days are short . . . enhances soil fertility." Seeds are available from Hudson, Park, and Thompson & Morgan.

GREEN PODS: This is a very nourishing plant. It's one of the few whose every part is edible, tasty, and very good for you. After about 50 days, the seed pods will be mature enough to be eaten like snap beans—that is, you eat both the pod and the peas inside it. Harvest by the time they reach 1 inch long, or else they'll start to get tough. If you let the pods get beyond that young stage, you've got shell beans rather than snap beans. They're good steamed with pineapple and banana and served with pork steak. Or stir-fried with peanuts and strips of coconut meat and served with taro. Or boiled with sliced mushrooms, bamboo, and pork.

➢ *STIR-FRIED WINGED BEANS From Southern Seeds: "Heat wok. Add 2 T. peanut oil. Add ½ lb. winged beans, rinsed and cut up, and 1 diced, small onion. Stir-fry 5 to 8 minutes until crunchy but cooked. (To keep beans from drying out, add a little water as needed.) Blend 1 T. soy sauce, 1 t. Asian sesame paste (or 2 t. tahini or creamy peanut butter), minced garlic, and hot pepper flakes to taste. Add to beans; toss to coat. Season and serve hot."*

MATURE PODS: Discard the pod and use the seeds like green shell beans—roasted, boiled, steamed, or fried. Dried, shelled winged beans are good cooked casserole-style, with fish and corn added toward the end. Or make a soup with them, using any basic dried bean recipe. Or use in a soup with lots of onions, carrots, rice, and a bone. Or serve cooked plain beans in a molasses sauce with roast fish or beef. Or steam mature pods (2–3 inches long) 15 to 20 minutes; then eat them like artichoke leaves by dipping singly into an individual container of melted butter, eating off the tender outside of the pod. Throw away the tough center.

ROOTS, STEM, LEAVES, FLOWERS: Winged bean roots also bear small, edible tubers, which are high in both protein and potato-type starch! You can eat the tubers either raw or cooked potato-style. The stem and leaves are nourishing too and can be cooked and eaten. They taste like spinach. Add them to stews, soups, and other vegetable recipes. The flowers are edible too; steam or fry them.

Yardlong Bean

"Sesquipeddis" in vigna sesquipeddis means "foot and a half" in Latin. That's closer to the truth than "yard." This is the other important *Vigna* bean, closely related to the black-eyed pea. The yardlong bean is an Asian vegetable (a.k.a. long bean, Chinese long bean, asparagus bean, bodi, boonchi, and bow gauk) that gives huge yields. The plants average 2 to 3 feet long; they're definitely the longest bean around. They're very thin, about the diameter of a lead pencil, and they snap easily *if picked young*. They are climbing vines with pretty, large, lavender-white flowers. They are good hot-weather vegetables; they *love* heat. They grow best in temps of 95–100°F. They're easy to grow and cook; they're prolific producers and aren't usually bothered by bugs.

PLANTING: Seed is available from Burgess, William Dam, Kitazawa, Mellinger's, Nichols, and Park (green or purple). They need very warm conditions (60 to 90 hot days) and something to climb up that's 8–10 feet tall. Unlike many other legumes, this plant will benefit from rich soil with plenty of compost/manure in it. (See "Pole Beans.") Plant in your warmest, sunniest garden site. Start seeds indoors 2 to 3 weeks ahead in peat pots and then set out. Or plant seeds directly into garden 2 to 3 weeks after the date of your last spring frost. Plant ½ to 1 inch deep, 6 inches apart in rows, or 2 to 3 seeds per pole. Don't let them stay dry more than a week. They don't require much other care.

HARVESTING: Yardlongs are 75 to 80 days to maturity. Pick when 12–18 inches long (when the swelling of seeds inside is barely becoming visible). Keep picking to encourage further production. Yardlong beans don't store well in a refrigerator. Eat fresh, freeze, or can (using directions for snap beans). You can also eat the leaves (use them in spinach recipes).

SERVING: Yardlongs don't taste like the familiar snap bean, although they're prepared the same way. They have a flavor all their own—not crisp, sort of nutty, somewhat like asparagus but stronger. Some people like them; some don't. Traditional Asian uses include cutting the beans into snap-bean lengths and stir-frying with chopped veggies and sliced meat. You can spice up a long bean dish with bits of hot pepper and/or sliced ginger—or cool it down with tofu chunks and bean sprouts. Either way, season with soy sauce. Or bake the snap lengths with sliced onions, mushrooms, and almonds, covered with a white sauce in a casserole dish. Or tie a bean in a knot, dip in tempura batter, and deep-fry. Or use in any green-bean recipe.

FLOWER SEEDS

These include flax, poppy, rape, safflower, sesame, and sunflower. For a complete protein, serve seeds (or nuts) with legumes.

Basic Seed Recipe Ideas

Soft seeds are important to raw food eaters—especially sunflower seeds, because they're easy to grow. The following recipes are all from Ruth of Bonaire:

➢ *SEED CHEESE "Use 1½ c. hulled raw sunflower seeds and ½ c. hulled raw sesame seeds (or 2 c. sunflower seeds). Soak for 8 hours, drain, and let sprout for another 8 hours. Then pour 1 c. water into a blender and blend in seeds, bit by bit, with blender on highest speed, until you have a smooth paste (takes about 3–5 minutes). Pour mixture into a glass jar, cover with cloth, and let set about 8 hours. Afterwards, drain off the whey. Store, tightly covered, in refrigerator for up to 5 days. You can use ¼ c. of this cheese in your next batch to shorten curdling time up to 4 hours."*

➢ *SEED YOGURT "Proceed as above, but let mixture set only 4 to 6 hours. Don't drain off whey, but stir it in and refrigerate up to 5 days."*

➢ *SEED LOAF "Grind 2 c. lentil sprouts and mix with 2 grated carrots, 1½ c. seed cheese, ¼ c. chopped onion, ½ t. cumin, and a pressed garlic clove. Shape into a loaf or into individual forms. (For instance, use muffin tins for molds.) Sprinkle with poppy seeds if you like, and serve on lettuce leaves."*

➢ *SEED MILK "Blend 5 c. water with 1 c. soaked raw almonds, sunflower seeds, or sesame seeds. Start with only 1 c. water, and then add the rest when you have a paste, blending for 2 more minutes at high speed. Drain out the pulp and*

HOME-PRESSED OIL FROM SEEDS

Is there a way to make pressed-seed oils at home? For info on how to do this in a low-tech way, see "Small-Scale Oilseed Processing" at **www.attra.org/attrapub/oilseed. html.** ECHO offers online publications on oilseed crops, including *The Manual Screw Press for Small-Scale Oil Extraction*, by Kathryn H. Potts and Keith Machell, which covers every aspect: 941-543-3246; fax 941-543-5317; **echo@echonet.org; www.echonet.org.** Unlike ECHO, the Oilseeds Processing Program at Texas A&M U. has an agribusiness orientation in its research, but they do offer much info, short courses, and custom training: 979-845-2741; College Station, TX 77843-2476; **kcrhee@tamu.edu; www.tamu. edu/food-protein.** You can order a book on *Small Scale Oil Extraction from Groundnuts and Copra* from VITA (703-276-1800; **www.vita. org**). It covers the steps in getting oil from peanuts (groundnuts) and dried coconut (copra) using small-scale machines. Also see Bob Lead-

er's Producers' Natural Processing: 765-563-3437; fax 765-563-6753; **leader@pnpi.com; www.pnpi.com.**

The Taby Press is a screw press manufactured in Sweden: +46-19-228005; **info@oilpress.com; www.oilpress.com.** Various models are available for cold-pressing oil from rapeseed, linseed, flaxseed, sunflower seed, sesame seed, peanuts, mustard seed, poppy seed, cotton seed, etc. Bengt Jonsson is the builder and seller of the oilpress and also a farmer. Seedburo Equipment Co., "serving the grain, feed, and seed industries since 1912," also offers a press (312-738-3700; **www.seedburo.com**). Here's how to get oil from sunflower seeds. You can use the same procedures for any of the other seeds.

First, sunflower seeds must be dehulled before pressing. You can use any grain mill whose stones can be opened as wide as the seeds. But small seeds won't dehull at a setting for the largest-hulled ones, so it helps to presort the seeds using a

series of seed screens that shake out all but the largest seeds.

Next you press the seed. The simplest home extraction system is to just make a "butter" in the blender. Let the butter settle. Then pour off the oil that rises to the top. For larger-scale extraction with a press, see directions for making olive oil under "Tropical Fruits" in Chapter 6. Basically the seeds are pressed whole or ground—usually ground. Peanut oil is pressed from peanuts. Linseed (made from flax seed) oil is made by first crushing the seeds and then pressing for the oil. Similar procedures apply for safflower and other seed oils. The residue from pressing can be used as fertilizer, food for animals, or seed-cheese–type food for people.

Then you filter the oil. Pour it through a coffee filter. Filtered oil doesn't burn as badly when used for frying as does unfiltered. You can use unfiltered oil to make salad dressings and mayonnaise.

HOT-PRESSED OILS AND MARGARINE

I'm no fan of hot-pressed oils or margarine. Reader Abby Moran wrote me, "To make margarine, first the seeds are mashed and then a solvent (such as benzene) is added to remove the oil. The law states the solvent must be almost completely removed; no more than 1 part per million may remain. I don't want to eat anything that might contain "benzene"—even 1 part per million!

"And in addition, to get rid of the benzene, the oil is heated enough to boil off the solvent, which probably doesn't do its food value any good either. The solvent is used because with it you can get up to 95 percent of the oil, whereas if you just press with no solvent, you get only about 10 percent of the oil. Then the pulp is sieved out and the remaining oil is deodorized,

bleached, mixed with chemicals to solidify it, and combined with yellow dyes."

Friends of mine, two M.D.s married to each other, told me that a recent study showed that women live longer if they regularly eat butter rather than margarine. These doctors want all their friends to switch to butter—or "cold-pressed oils" (no solvent, no heat).

---

store in fridge up to 4 days. Use on cereal, in 'milkshakes' with fresh or frozen fruit, etc."

SEED FLOUR: Ground seeds can be used as a kind of flour. Add to baking recipes as you would any nonwheat flour, or stir into soups and gravies as a thickener.

Flower Seeds (Alphabetical List)

FLAX: Flax (*Linum usitatissimum*) is a member of the flax family (Linaceae). It's an annual that grows about 2 feet tall. Once flax was a main source of fabric for clothing. It used to be planted on most farms, back in the days when a fabric called linsey-woolsey was popular, because the stalks can be made into linen, an exceptionally durable fabric. (Mummies in ancient Egypt are wrapped in a finer grade of linen than

anybody now knows how to make.) Flax seeds are wonderful in dried fruit leathers and on crackers and desserts. They're also good livestock or poultry feed. Linseed oil is derived from the oil pressed from flax seeds.

Climate and Varieties. Flax used to be a common crop right here in Idaho, but flax plants are now rarely seen in the United States, except in North and South Dakota. The plant does well in cool, dry climates like the Dakotas, Canada, and Russia (where most of the world's supply is now grown). Some flax varieties are best for flax seed, others for fiber production. Abundant Life, Bountiful Gardens, William Dam, and Richters carry various kinds.

Planting Flax. Don't fertilize flax. It does fine in poor soil; the fertilizer would just encourage weeds, which flax can't compete with, since it doesn't shade the ground much. Plant in well-tilled, weed-free ground. The earlier you can get it into the ground for a running start on the remaining weed seeds, the better. Don't plant flax in a rotation following millet, sorghum, or Sudan grass; it doesn't cope well with their decaying roots. A successful rotation often used in Canada is rape, flax, and wheat.

Flax, either for seed or linen, is an annual, planted in the spring and harvested in the fall, except in warm parts of California, Texas, and Arizona. Plant just before corn planting time using the procedures for planting wheat. For seed, plant 1½ to 3½ pecks per acre—1½ in a dry climate, 3½ in a wet one. But for linen, plant at the heavy rate because thick stands produce more stalks and discourage branching, causing longer, smoother stalks (and longer, better flax fibers).

Harvesting for Seed. Flax grows fast and blooms early, by June even in the Dakotas. The fields of waving blue flowers are lovely. Flax continues to bloom even after the first seed is set, but in the North the later flowers won't have time to mature, so the harvest process begins as soon as most of the seed is almost ripe. The flax is cut, swathed, and left in the sun to finish ripening. Then the harvest is completed with a combine and a pickup reel. Flax doesn't give a big yield of seeds, only about 10 bushels per acre from an average crop, 30 from the best. Because of its tendency to contain weed seed, an extra screening is helpful.

Eating Flax Seed. Flax seed stays fresher if unground, but you can use it whole or ground. You can mix it into a bread or sprouting mixture. The oil pressed from flax seed makes a fine cooking oil.

✎ *FLAX SEED LEMONADE This is an old-time home remedy that's soothing for colds. Be careful not to crush the seeds, as their oil will make the drink nauseating. Pour 1 qt. boiling water over 4 T. flax seed. Steep 3 hours. Strain, sweeten to taste, and add the juice of 2 lemons. If too thick, add more water. Another way to make lemonade is to boil 3 T. seed in 6 c. water until reduced to 3 c. Then add lemon and sugar, strain, and serve. Pioneers kept a coffeepot of this on the back of the stove so they could drink it as often as they took a notion to.*

Flax for Linen. You harvest by pulling, not cutting, the stalks in order to have longer fibers. Flax will produce at least a ton of stalks per acre, and sometimes 2 or more, so the harvest from a small part of an acre will give 1 spinner plenty of flax to experiment with.

Flax Fiber Info. No. 133, *Flax & Linen*, is a useful reference. For their free catalog, contact Shire Publications, Ltd.: +44-1844-344301; fax +44-1844-347080; Cromwell House, Church St., Princes, Risborough, Bucks, U.K.; **shire@shire books.co.uk; www.shirebooks.co.uk**. *The Retting of Flax & Hemp,* by Paul W. Allen, M.S., Ph.D., comes from Caber Press (call/fax 503-735-3942; **tcl@teleport.com; www. teleport.com/~tcl**).

Steps in Making Linen
1. Pull the flax plants, roots and all. That's to preserve the total length of the fiber and prevent discolored ends.
2. Dry them out in the sun.
3. Cut, comb, or pull off the seeds and/or seed heads from the stems. You treat flax differently from wheat in that you don't beat off the seeds.
4. Soak flax in water or leave out in rainy weather for several weeks while the woody stems surrounding the

fibers rot. This step is called "retting." The soaking rots the pith and "bark." How long it takes to ret depends on your climate. In a warm climate and warm weather, 3 weeks can be enough. In a cooler area it may take 1½ months or longer. Your flax-soaking vat should be of wood or clay construction because metal drums will color the fiber. That doesn't matter if the flax is to be used for rough sacking material or rope, but it does matter if you want to make something nice from it.

5. When the retting is finished, again dry the fibers.
6. Soften, or "break," the fibers on a tool called a "flaxbrake." In this step you break the rotted pith out of the stem and knock loose the "bark" with a wooden mallet or stone or with a stick across the edge of a wooden bench. Starting at one end of a handful or bundle, beat and turn the bundle, working toward the middle. Then change ends and finish pounding the bundle, working from the end to the middle again.
7. Scrap the fibers with a "swingling knife." This causes the woody stem pieces around the fibers to loosen and drop to the ground.
8. Handful by handful, straighten the fibers, simultaneously removing the remaining stem pieces by combing with a steel-toothed brush called the "hetchel." Or comb fibers with regular wool-carding combs or even hair-type combs.
9. You'll end up with short fibers called "tow" and long fibers called "streak." These fine, fluffy linen fibers are

now ready to be spun into yarn on the spinning wheel.

10. Weave the linen and make tablecloths! Or make rope and sacks.

Afterthoughts. Phyllis Friesen wrote: "The biggest problem in raising your own flax is getting the proper seed. I carry the flax fiber in 'strick' [a bundle], along with silk fibers and cocoons for spinning, in my small mail-order business. I really started spinning flax and silk the hard way by learning alone. I knew no one spinning such fibers so had no one to turn to for advice. I have learned it's much easier to separate your strick of flax into about 4 or 5 bundles and then lay one of these bundles in your lap and proceed to spin the thread by pulling fibers from the end, rather than to tie it to the distaff as all the books recommend. Then you dip your fingers in water and keep the thread wet as you spin. Just a few fibers at a time are all you need. Then when you ply it, you do not need to use water. I used a cute gourd to make a water container for my wheel and tied it on with a thong."

POPPY: The poppy varieties are species of *Papaver*. They are related to the thistle and handle infertile soils well. Poppies overwinter and grow large, deep taproots that break up subsoil. Poppies make a great green manure because their taproots are tender and rot easily and their aboveground vegetation is also tender and so can be easily cultivated into the ground.

Or you can raise this crop for the seeds. The yield will be about 1,500 lb. per acre of dry land. Poppy seed is easy to harvest by hand. If you want to make oil from it, hand-pressing can accomplish the extraction. Your yield will be about half oil. You can make a sort of poppy "tahini" by grinding the seed in a blender. The result will be a sprightly tasting, mayonnaise-ish salad dressing. Poppies can be grown in tough northern climates, planted in the fall, and overwintered. For much more detail, see Steve Solomon's *Growing Vegetables West of the Cascades*.

RAPE (CANOLA): Rape is a leafy brassica (*Brassica napus*), so similar to mustard greens you grow it the same way; in fact, it is sometimes incorrectly called mustard greens. Here in Idaho there are beautiful fields of golden yellow rape that will end up in birdseed mixtures. It holds up under hot weather better than regular mustard (*Brassica juncea*). It's also a wonderful forage crop for sheep or pigs.

My pig-raising friend Stephen wrote me: "Canola is grown extensively in Canada as an oilseed crop: hence canola oil. It has great ability to draw bees. It blossoms for a month, during which time the bees have a feast. It grows fast and chokes out weeds too. If you decide to plant canola seed in rows, it will take about ½ oz. per 100-foot row. Or you can broadcast it at the rate of 3 oz. per 1,000 square feet. Plant it about 3 weeks before you buy your pigs, and they can start grazing on it right away. You can also plant some in the garden and save seed from it to grow for sprouts." Or press the seed to make "canola" oil. Rape is available from Johnny's.

SAFFLOWER: *Carthamus tinctorius*, a.k.a. "Mexican saffron," is a Compositae (daisy) family member, a relative of the chicories and the edible chrysanthemum (see "The Non-Brassica Greens"). It's also known as "false saffron" because the bright dye you can make from its large red or orange flower heads can be used, like saffron, to color food—and to make rouge! But safflower has additional uses too. It

is widely grown in order to harvest the oil-rich seeds (about 25 percent by weight). Safflower oil is a low cholesterol source of fat, rich in linoleic acid and vitamin E. The meal left over after the oil is extracted is good livestock feed. The seeds are very small, like tiny sunflower seeds. There are several varieties, some more thistlelike and spiny than others. You can order it from Redwood City or DeGiorgi.

Climate and Growth. The flowers do well in a somewhat dry climate such as in the western Plains states. Plant in any soil but in full sun. Wait until ground is warm to plant (March to May), and keep moist. It takes 120 days for the seeds to mature. Plant 1 inch deep, rows about 18 to 24 inches apart. Safflower is ordinarily grown as a large-scale field crop. Wait for virtually all the heads to be dry before you cut. Then use the directions for grain harvesting in the beginning of Chapter 3 to cut and thresh.

SESAME: *Sesamum orientale* (a.k.a. *Sesamum indicum*) flowers and then makes the delicious seeds used in baked goods. Sesame is as tender as cotton and does best in southern states. It's an annual that grows up to 2 feet high. Its flowers are pale rose or white. It's grown for the seed crop, which is eaten either raw, roasted, or crushed to get the oil. Sesame oil is great for soap making as well as for cooking. Plant sometime during March to May in full sun. Sesame seed needs to go into well-tilled soil that has had both manure and lime added. It's available from Redwood City.

> **SESAME SEED CRUST FOR ANY BREAD** *Before you bake your bread, take some warm water and work it into the top of the dough-loaf until it's goopy. Then work in as many sesame seeds as you want, and bake.*

> **TAHINI** *Blend sesame seeds into a smooth paste of mixed seed and oil. The oil will rise to the top after it sets a while, it can be used like any cooking oil. Use the solid portion like peanut butter or to thicken a salad dressing.*

> **TAHINI-YOGURT SALAD DRESSING** *Combine 2 T. vinegar, 1 crushed garlic clove, 2 T. tahini, juice from half a lemon, and salt and/or pepper to taste. Now gradually mix in about ⅔ c. unflavored yogurt. Good with strong-tasting greens.*

SUNFLOWER: *Helianthus annus*, native to the Americas, is a wonderful crop for hot, dry climates, high altitudes, low-temperature regions, and/or poor soils (but the more fertile the soil, the bigger your yield). The sunflower is great winter food for man and beast because it is one of the few plant sources of vitamin D! Sunflower seeds can be used as a grain substitute in livestock food, can add protein to human diets, and can be pressed for cooking oil. Crushed petals will dye yellow, roasted seed makes a "coffee," and stems provide a silky fiber (process like flax) or livestock forage (but animals like them better if mixed with molasses). Consider growing them as your "grain" if you live where corn can't make it, for you can substitute sunflower seeds for grain in poultry or other livestock rations or grow them for compost making. They do well as a broadcasted field crop. Yield will be 10 to 80 bushels per acre (the per-bushel weight for sunflower seeds is 30 lb.) depending on soil fertility, weed control, and water.

Varieties. All kinds are easy to grow. Their sizes range from 5 inches to 12 feet tall, with flowers from 2 inches to 2 feet in diameter. Small sunflowers are ornamentals, mid-size ones are grown commercially for mechanical harvesting, and giant ones (Mammoth Russian is the classic) are grown for home gardens because of their big seed heads and spectacular appearance. Choose between short- and long-season specialists and between "eating" and oil (longer to mature) types. Cook's Garden offers the largest selection in any U.S. catalog. Abundant Life, Burpee, Comstock, William Dam, DeGiorgi, Nichols, Redwood City, etc., offer one or more varieties.

Planting. To grow enough sunflower seed to press out a year's supply of oil for a family (about 3 gal.), you'd need maybe 3,000 square feet planted to sunflowers. (You'd have 20 lb. of seed pulp left over.) Sun is vital to sunflowers, so put them in an open, sunny place where these tall plants won't cause a problem by shading other plants—the north end of your garden, for instance. They prefer light, well-drained soil, pH 6.0–7.5 (slightly acid to alkaline). Plant as early as possible (longer growing means bigger yield), 2 weeks before the last frost.

For an even earlier crop, plant earlier and then again 2 weeks later, hoping for the best; or plant inside and transplant once plants have 4 leaves and are frost-hardy. Plant 4–8 lb. per acre for a field crop. Plant seeds ½ inch deep, 6 inches apart and rows 24–48 inches apart depending on variety. Thin as needed for the size of your variety when 3 or 4 inches high (thin to 4 feet apart for the biggest ones). About 8 to 10 weeks after planting, the flowers will begin to open and follow the sun from morning to night. If you are growing a giant, it may need staking.

Harvesting. Leave the sunflower heads on the plant until they are really dry. If your sunny weather holds, leaving them on until after the first frost won't hurt them, and you can let them ripen on the stalks. If birds are a problem, protect the heads with plastic mesh or cheesecloth tied loosely over but closed at the bottom to catch dropping seed.

Signs that sunflowers are ready to cut:
- The back of the head looks brown; there's no sign of green there anymore.
- The head appears dry.
- Florets in the middle of the flower are shriveled.
- The stem turns yellow near the flower's base.
- The whole head starts to noticeably droop.
- About half of the yellow petals have fallen off.
- The seeds are dry but have not yet fallen off.

Make sure you have sunflowers out of the garden before the heavy fall rains. Sunflowers need from 1 to 3 weeks of drying (more is better), either on or off the plant. Heavy frosts do not harm ripening seeds, meaning that your "growing season" can last that much longer. Cut the heads with 1 to 3 feet of stalk attached.

More Drying. Hang them by their stems separately if you have room, in bundles for a big crop. Hang in a dry, warm, airy place. Or spread them out on a wall or roof—seeds up —in the sunshine for a week (avoid birds and rodents). If outside, cover with cheesecloth or netting to protect from birds; put cloth or paper underneath to catch dropped seeds. Let the seeds finish ripening and drying. Check occasionally to make sure they aren't molding! In damp weather, molding is unavoidable if you try to dry outdoors.

Getting Seed off the Head. You can tell when heads are completely dry: The seed easily rubs out of the flower head. You can rub by hand or brush out the seed by means of a wire brush, curry comb, or fish scaler. Or remove the seeds by rubbing over a coarse (1-inch-mesh) screen that is fastened over a container. Large-scale growers use a regular thresher or combine at the soybean setting.

Storage. Storing seeds in the shell protects the vitamin content. If the seeds are still a bit damp, dry them some more.

Sunflower seed must be very, very dry (below 11 percent moisture) to store successfully. Store sufficiently dried seeds in small bags made of porous material; store in dry areas safe from bugs and rodents. Turn them over twice a week. Seeds must be drier yet to be successfully kept in glass or metal because the seeds are so likely to mold in that type of container. Don't try storing large quantities of sunflower seeds in a heap; these will also likely spoil. Sunflower seeds make good sprouts!

Roasted/Unshelled/Salted Seeds. Put the seeds in the bottom of a 3-gal. crock or some such. Add water to fill and half a box of salt (or use 2 gal. water and a 26-oz. box of salt). Stir and then leave to soak for a week. Now spread the seeds on a tray and roast in your oven at 350°F, stirring at least every 10 minutes to get the damp ones evenly distributed. It will take about an hour to dry them all through. Test to make sure, observing and cracking samples. The development of a whitish color shows they are getting done, and inside the shell they should be dry instead of still soggy. Watch carefully to prevent burning. After the seeds come out of the oven, they are done and ready to eat. Store in a cool, dry place.

Roasted/Shelled/Salted Seeds. Preheat oven to 350°F. Spread seeds on tray and bake 10 minutes. After they are cool, remove shells. Spread shelled seeds on the tray, sprinkle with salt, and bake again for 10 minutes. Cool. Store in container with tight lid.

Shelling. Sunflower seeds are good food for livestock as well as people. Animals will happily eat them whole. For people, shell by hand one by one—or get a grinder that can handle shelling sunflower seeds in bulk (Lehman's carries one: 888-438-5346; **www.Lehmans.com**).

Recipe Ideas. To press the seeds for oil, see "Home-Pressed Oil from Seeds" earlier in the "Flower Seeds" section. Sunflower seeds are high in nutrition and protein and worthy of main-dish status. Here are 2 such recipes.

☙ *VEGETABLE SEED ROAST Combine 4 medium-sized grated carrots, 6 sliced medium-sized boiled potatoes, 4 minced small onions, 1 T. chopped parsley, ½ c. chopped celery, ½ c. chopped spinach or beet tops, 1 c. chopped cabbage, 1 c. chopped sunflower seeds (or leave whole), 1½ c. whole wheat bread crumbs, ½ c. milk, 4 eggs, and 1 minced clove garlic or a little garlic salt. Mix well. Place in oiled pan. Dot top with butter or oil. Bake 2 hours at 250°F.*

☙ *SUNFLOWER LOAF Combine 2 c. cooked brown rice, 1 c. chopped sunflower seeds, ½ c. whole wheat bread crumbs (toasted), soy milk to moisten, 2 T. soy sauce, 2 T. chopped onion, 2 T. diced celery, and salt to taste. Mix thoroughly. If too dry, add in more soy milk. Bake in 325–350°F oven for 45 minutes.*

THE ROOTS WE EAT

The "roots" we eat come from plants that store food underground—in a root, tuber, or corm (a rounded, thickened, underground stem base). I've divided the roots into 2 big subcategories: starchy and nonstarchy (savory). The starchy roots, which tend to be a dietary mainstay wherever they're grown, include the potato and sweet potato as well as the lesser-known arrowhead, cassava, kudzu, malanga, taro, and yam. The nonstarchy roots, which are good for soups, stir-fry dishes, and salads, include the beet, carrot, radish, turnip, and many more.

Introduction to Roots

The typical root vegetable is a biennial that fills its root with stored food the first year it grows; the next spring, it draws on that food to make a tall seed stalk, flower, and seed. Because of this long-term survival strategy, root crops can cope well with poor soils.

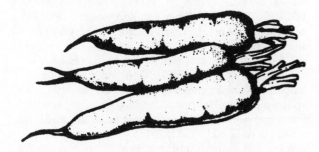

ABOUT THEIR SOIL: Because the root's the thing and it needs to be able to expand with stored food, all these plants produce best in soil that's well tilled—as deeply tilled as you expect the particular root to grow. It also helps if the soil is a light, sandy humus rather than a dense clay—or at least something in between. It also helps to have soil clean of rocks and clods, since roots can't go through those but must grow around them, producing weird shapes. Root crops thrive in a double-dug, raised bed because of the loose soil. They also do well in wide rows, so they're a good choice if you want to cram a lot of food production into a small space.

WATER FOR ROOT CROPS: A steady supply of moisture keeps the soil soft so the root can easily swell up. If the ground gets dry and rigid, the roots have trouble growing and, worse, can get tough-textured and bitter-tasting. The more claylike your soil, the greater the need for moisture.

STORING ROOTS

Garden Storage. In the South, you can leave root crops in the ground, right where they grew in your garden, until you need them. Where the ground freezes or gets covered by lots of snow, you have to mulch to keep roots in the garden. This works well up to about Zone 7 or more. To mulch, put a layer of mulch over the row that's deep enough so it won't freeze—maybe 1 or 2 feet high and covering at least 1 foot on each side of the row. Put black plastic over all to keep out rain. You can dig about a week's worth at a time. Use them up before spring comes and the root veggies start to sprout and get woody.

Secrets of Storing Roots in a Cellar

1. Plant your crop to be harvested as late as you can (the later it's harvested, the later it keeps).
2. Dig the roots following 2–3 days of dry garden conditions.
3. In the garden, cut off tops just above the crown, but don't cut off tail roots.
4. Before storing, let cure in the sun for an hour—but not more!
5. Don't wash, brush, or shake the garden dirt off them—it helps preserve them!
6. If any roots got cut in half, bruised, or broken, send them to the kitchen directly rather than to storage.
7. Store in food-quality plastic bags, closed at the top, with some holes cut in them; in a barrel; or in cardboard or wooden boxes, stacking the boxes on top of each other. Or put them in a pile in a corner with dirt thrown over them. Or use a permanent wooden bin. Potatoes stored this way in a root cellar will still be all right the following June, except they'll have lots of sprouts.
8. Wash the roots just before you're going to use them, never before storing them!
9. Light harms roots. A good root cellar is always dark except when you are actually in there getting stuff in or out.
10. Roots packed in sand tend to bring sand into the kitchen and even into the food, and the roots sometimes pick up an off-taste from the sand.

Trench/Pit Storage. If you don't have a root cellar, your safest alternative is a hole in the ground—or, better, a bunch of small pits, because once you open a pit it's best to take out all the vegetables at once. Putting a mixture of pit-storable root vegetables in each hole makes them easier to use up when that time comes. But don't store potatoes with apples, because apples give off a gas that encourages potatoes to sprout.

Dig down as far as you can fairly easily dig. Make a trench that's longer than it is wide, so it isn't such a struggle to get it covered with dirt. It doesn't matter if the ground is damp when you dig it. Line the hole's bottom and sides with cardboard from boxes, straw, leaves, or some such. Put your vegetables in loosely but in piles, not bags. Put your carrots in one area, potatoes in another, and so on. Mark on the outside with stakes so you'll know where to dig for what. Now cover the vegetables over with more cardboard.

A cloth, scrub brush, or especially one of those plastic, orange Tuffy pads will do the job of getting garden dirt off most young root vegetables. Just scrub . . .

A lot of the peel will come off with the dirt. It's exposure to the air that toughens the skin, making the skins a hindrance to good taste and making it necessary to peel the veggies to get rid of the bad-tasting skins.

Cover the cardboard with at least 1 foot of dirt. Or cover the vegetables all over with more straw, leaves, etc., and then put dirt over that. Cover with more for a colder winter.

It helps to have a ventilating pipe at the center. Cover it when it rains; when it turns bitterly cold, remove the pipe and fill in the hole with dirt. In the meantime, the pipe aids air circulation.

MORE ABOUT DIGGING: Don't dig the root vegetables that you plan to store until the last moment—that is, not until after the first light frosts, when you have signs that you are going to have a hard frost. (In Idaho that means sometime in October.) Then dig and transfer to storage in one operation. Don't wash the vegetables. When you get vegetables out of storage in the ground, take enough to hold you for a good while: 50 lb. of potatoes at a time and equivalent amounts of other vegetables. That way you don't have to dig out there any more than necessary.

See "Beet" and "Carrot" (under "Nonstarchy Roots") and "Cabbage" (under "The Cabbagy Brassicas") for more about winter storage systems.

STARCHY ROOTS
Potato

It isn't just because I live in Idaho, land of the famous baking spud, that I love potatoes. Nor is it just because my husband spent many a childhood hour walking down the rows in southern Idaho, picking up potatoes and dropping them into the potato sack hooked on a belt around his waist. Nor is it just because I'm the daughter of a 3-square-meals-a-day Pennsylvania Dutchman who included potatoes in all of those meals. No, potatoes are just naturally important. They are a starchy food that you can grow easily in large quantities in your own garden.

The potato's Latin name is *Solarium tuberosum*. It's a member of the nightshade family right along with tomatoes, peppers, and eggplant. It's one of the food plants that are native to the Americas, like corn, tomatoes, and pumpkins. Maybe you thought they came from Ireland, but they didn't originate there. The Incas in South America had the potato long before that. Then it came to Spain around 1700 and gradually spread all through Europe (including Ireland), from which it then came back to North America. Potatoes are an important part of being self-sufficient foodwise, because they are one of the wonderful root vegetables that winter so easily and simply. They are easy to save your own "seed" from because you plant potatoes, or pieces of potato, to grow potatoes. They do better in the northern United States than in the South.

There's more info at **www.potatonews.com.** For help with diseases, including late blight (new strains have seriously challenged commercial potato growers recently), see Oregon State U.'s **www.cropinfo.net/Potatoblight.htm** and **www.uidaho.edu/ag/plantdisease.**

NOTE: The leaves and stems of the potato plant are poisonous.

VARIETIES: There used to be just 2 kinds in the seed catalogs—reds and whites. The whites winter-stored and baked best; the reds tasted nicest as boiled new potatoes. Those facts are still true, but now there are zillions to choose from. Potatoes grow wild in the Andes mountain area, which contains thousands of both wild and tame varieties. Or contact Irish Eyes–Garden City Seeds for a large catalog and good selection of organically grown seed potatoes (50 varieties): 509-925-6025; PO Box 307, Thorp, WA 98946; **www.irish-eyes.com.** Or buy Maine Certified Organic seed potatoes farm-direct from Jim and Megan Gerritsen. They offer a free catalog and Rose Finn Apple, Yukon Gold, Russian Banana, All-Blue, Caribe, etc., for home or market gardener: 800-829-9765; 4931 Kinney Rd., Bridgewater, ME 04735; **woodpr@agate.net.** U.S. seed potatoes can't legally be shipped to Canada.

Your potato options include yellow, rose, blue skin/white flesh, blue skin/blue flesh, white, russet, red, black, purple, red skin/red flesh, red skin/gold flesh, color-splashed (multicolored), scab-resistant, best keeper, heirloom, and more. You can also choose between varieties that mature in early, mid-, and late season—and between quicker- and slower-maturing varieties (75 to 130 days). If you plant a quick-maturing variety early in the spring, you'll have new potatoes on your table more quickly.

SOIL: Like any root vegetable, in which the important action is underground, potatoes do best in a sandy or loamy soil that easily spreads apart. Cultivating the soil deep enough to give them stretching-out room helps too. They need lots of organic matter in the soil, but it's best if no manure is put on more recently than the previous fall. They definitely prefer an acid soil, so don't put wood ashes or lime on their ground.

CLIMATE: Potatoes grow best in fairly cool weather with long days. Light frosts don't kill potatoes, so they can be planted very early in the spring. The problem for them in the South is that warm soil temperatures, combined with a lot of moisture, tend to make them rot in the ground; they're much more subject to problems and don't keep as well. For a hot climate, look for the heat-resistant varieties, or plant in the winter and harvest in the spring.

POTATO "SEED": Potato plants will make seed, but it doesn't breed true to variety. The plant sends up a stalk and flowers prettily above ground, but for our use the seed-making job takes place underground, where the plant finishes making potatoes with eyes. The next spring, every eye has the capacity to sprout and grow a new potato plant. If you don't know what I mean by an eye, look at a potato. Each little round depression on the potato surface is an eye. The eyes are generally numerous on one end of the potato and are scattered more thinly over the rest of it. Each potato piece you plant must have at least one eye in it to grow a new plant. It also needs a chunk of potato behind that eye that's big enough to supply nourishment to the new plant so it can get up through the ground and reach the sunlight, where it can make its own energy.

Where to Get Seed Potatoes: Regular store potatoes don't make the best seed potatoes. The store kind are cheaper than specially bagged-up seed potatoes, but it may not be clear what variety they are, and they may have been treated with a chemical to inhibit sprouting. If they don't grow for you, a chemical is probably the cause. On the other hand, the "sets" that you buy in seed catalogs are often potatoes that have been cut into the smallest pieces the firm dares to, and they often have been treated with chemicals too. The ideal start is to buy seed potatoes of a known variety the first year—I recommend getting them from Ronniger's or from a neighbor who knows what kind they are—and to save your own after that.

Saving Seed: Potatoes are a self-pollinated annual, and old-time varieties actually do make seed. Gardeners just use the vegetative method to plant; only plant breeders bother with seed. The breeders use seed because you can't select genes by planting cut spuds, since every new plant is a clone; but if you're working with seed, you have a genetic spread just like with Mendel's peas. Potatoes flower, and their flowers are followed by a fruit that resembles a tiny tomato. It's called a "seed ball," and you can save the seed in it, tomato-style, and plant it next spring.

But usually people save some of their best spuds for "seed." You may be tempted to save the little bitty potatoes, but don't do that because you'll be selecting plants with the worst hereditary characteristic available—failure to mature in time. Instead, save for seed the potatoes that are best for eating or storing. For spring planting, choose from your storage the potatoes that look the most eager to sprout or that have sprouted, and let them go ahead and make potato plants in your garden.

Greening: Some people say it helps production if you "green" your seed potatoes before planting by laying them out for a couple of weeks in a place (indoors or out) that gets lots of light. They'll turn reddish or green and grow sprouts. Then you cut. *But remember, the green on potatoes is poisonous, as are the sprouts. I've heard of a child dying from eating potatoes that her dad had spread out in the yard to green up and sprout.* The green tastes so bad I don't see how anybody could be tempted, but children will eat strange-tasting things, as every parent knows.

How to Cut for Seed: Potatoes are the poor man's friend. Agricultural college researchers say that a large piece of potato with an eye grows better than a small piece with an eye, and that a whole potato grows best of all. But many a desperate gardener has planted potato peelings that have eyes in them and has gotten a fine crop of potatoes. The usual way to do it (and the way we do it) lies in between. When you cut the potato, make sure that each piece has at least one eye. Cutting through the middle of an eye may kill the sprout, so try to avoid that. You can get 3, 4, or 5 squarish pieces out of an average potato. We like to have several good eyes on each chunk; you get fewer chunks but often more sprouts from each potato.

Curing Seed: We don't do this because our area has no trouble with potato diseases. But if yours does, try these organic preservation methods: Dip the cut potatoes into wood ashes, or let them dry in the air for a few days before planting them. If you have enough moisture in the soil so the potatoes can take right off, though, these tactics aren't necessary.

PLANTING: How much seed? Well, I think any family would want to plant at least 50 lb. A peck of potatoes will plant 300 feet of row. Potatoes are such a staple that you may want to grow lots—maybe even a whole field of them.

When to Plant: Under natural conditions, the potato is a tropical perennial. But in the temperate zone, we grow it as an annual. Plant early potatoes as soon as you can get the ground worked—January in the extreme southern states, May in the cold states. The first crops are for kitchen use through the summer. In cold-weather climates, get in the first planting a month or 2 weeks before you've expected the last frost—anytime during March or April is great. We plant the first crop of potatoes as soon as we have the ground plowed and cultivated. For the earliest possible crop, plant 5 or 6 weeks before last spring frost date, use an early variety, and cover with mulch or hilled-up dirt if you hear a frost warning (they'll grow back up through it).

In the North, you can plant late potatoes in late May or all through June or even July, depending on your growing season, but planting too late will result in a smaller crop. We plant spuds every few weeks until midsummer. By then, every spare inch in the garden is in potatoes, including the areas where we grew early crops like spinach, peas, and greens. The latest-planted, latest-harvested potatoes will keep the best.

How to Plant: The easiest way to plant a big field of potatoes is to just make a furrow and drop pieces into the bottom of it. Make the rows 2½ feet apart. Plant 3 inches deep, or a few inches deeper if you're planting way before the last frost date, and 6 to 18 inches apart, depending on how good your soil is and how cramped you are for space. I plant 'em 6 inches apart (I'm always trying to squeeze in just a few more plants). Plant with the eye pointing upward! In 3 or 4 weeks you'll see the sprouts above the ground.

Straw Bed Planting: This simplifies the planting and harvesting, but the potatoes don't produce as well. Just place your seed potatoes on top of the soil. Then put a foot of straw mulch on top of them. (My husband Mike digs a trench, puts spuds in there, adds mulch or a little straw, and then covers it with some dirt.) Lastly, give them a good soaking to get them started if you don't expect rain. Make sure they don't get prematurely exposed to sun, or they'll get a greenish tint under their skins. At harvest time, rake back the straw and pick up your crop.

NOTE: If poisonous snakes live in your area, don't feel under the mulch for potatoes; rake it back instead, because a snake could be under there!

Instant Planting: This is another of Mike's methods. (He likes finding easy ways to do things!) But if your ground is sticky clay, the furrowing or straw bed methods will work better than this one. Go out into the garden with a box of seed potatoes, cut and ready to go, and a shovel. This is a good way to plant your very earliest potatoes. Force your garden spade straight down into the dirt, as far as you can get it if frost danger isn't past yet and you want them deep. Now lean forward on the spade handle until you've forced open a space in the dirt between the back of the spade blade and the dirt. Drop your seed potato in there, right into the open space you've made. Pull the spade out, leaving the seed potato planted in the hole. Gently step on the ground with your foot to settle the dirt back again. Walk to the spot in your row where you're going to plant the next set, and repeat the process.

Weeding and Watering: Potatoes need a good soaking at least once a week from either rainfall or your ingenuity and labor. As soon as your potatoes are up and you can see where the rows are, you can start fighting weeds. Keep weeding all the while the potatoes are growing, so they won't have competition for food and water.

HARVESTING: You can start harvesting potatoes even before the plants are finished making them. But the main crop won't be ready until the leaves on the potato plants start to yellow—or, better yet, until the whole vine starts to wither. That will be about 3 full months from when you planted them. I leave the first plantings in the ground rather than try to root-cellar them, and I just go out to dig every few days or so. That way I have new potatoes (which are the nicest) from the first harvest until the last, and those left in the ground can keep on growing until fall or as long as they are willing and able. When the vines die, that means the potatoes have stopped growing and are ready to dig. But in hot weather they keep better in the ground, so we dig only after it starts to stay cool all the time. We definitely dig them all before the ground freezes.

Digging: If you have nice loose or sandy soil or a straw bed, just poke around until you find some potatoes near the surface, gently wiggle them out, and firm up the soil around the plant again. The remaining tubers will keep growing. Or you can dig up a whole plant and take everything it has, digging from one end of the first row and proceeding systematically. For the big harvest, Mike spades and I feel around in the loosened dirt with my hands to find and bring up all the loosened potatoes.

Sorting: The children pop them into burlap bags. The very small potatoes and the ones that have been accidentally cut go into a special cardboard box to come directly into the kitchen and be used up first. The small ones are used after the nicked or cut ones. Use like "new potatoes." The potatoes that will be used right after the small ones go into the basement. The rest go into a root cellar or a pit in the garden.

Curing: Experts advise curing potatoes before storage by spreading them out where the temperature is around 60–75°F, but they're protected against sun, rain, and wind. Keep them there 1 to 2 weeks. During that time, they'll heal small surface cuts and thicken their skins.

NOTE: Don't leave potatoes lying out in the sunlight. That makes them taste awful and turn poisonous in and under the skin—everywhere they get that greenish tinge. Exposure to light, even if not direct sunlight, in storage will tend to have the same effect, though the greening will happen more gradually.

PIT AND CELLAR STORAGE: For a potato pit, dig a hole down to 2 feet below the frost line (that means the depth to which it freezes, and you just have to hope you figured it right). Put in the potatoes, cover with straw, and pile dirt over that. Lay a piece of tin or plastic over that to keep them dry. (Also see "Cabbage Pit" under the "Cabbage" entry.) Even store-bought potatoes should be stored in a cool, dark, ventilated place. In a root cellar, store in wooden boxes, baskets, or a bin, or right on the dirt floor. *Don't store near apples, because apples give off a gas that encourages potatoes to sprout!*

Storage Temperature: Most importantly, keep them cool and in darkness. Potatoes keep best between 40 and 50°F. Don't store in the fridge because temps below 40° can cause potato starch to turn to sugar in a disagreeable way. Temps warmer than 50° can trigger sprouting. But they keep a few months no matter what you do, as long as they're in a dark, dry place. After a few months, check them occasionally. When they start to sprout—warmth and light make it happen more quickly, but sooner or later they'll try anyway—snap the sprouts off unless the potatoes are for planting. In that case, plant them sprout and all. *They must not be allowed to freeze.* If they freeze, they're no good for human consumption anymore. They can still be fed to animals, but it's best to cook them first.

ABOUT SPROUTS AND PEELINGS

NOTE: I've said this before, but I'll say it again. Don't ever eat potato sprouts. Just snap off sprouts and throw away. Don't feed to any livestock. Don't eat skins or peels if they are tinted the least bit green. Cut away the green-tinted skins and any green under them before cooking. Potato leaves and stems are also poisonous. Peelings with a little green in them can go to big animals like pigs, but they make rabbits really sick. Regular non-green, nonsprouted potato peelings are fine food for chickens and animals.

PRESERVING POTATOES

Freezing: To preserve potatoes in your freezer, you have to cook them first. You can freeze boiled, mashed, or French-fried potatoes. The freezer life of French-fried potatoes isn't very long, though.

Drying: I don't think drying potatoes is very practical when they store so well in root cellars. But here's how to do it anyway.

Dried "raw": Wash, peel, and cut into ¼-inch shoestrings or ⅛-inch slices. Steam-blanch 6–8 minutes or boil 5–6 minutes. Drain and spread on tray in single layer. Dry in sun or in dehydrator or oven at 120°F. Turn potatoes and rotate tray now and then. Dry until brittle and semitransparent. It takes about 24 hours in dryer, 2 or 3 days in sun. But they will easily mold in storage if the least bit of moisture gets in there.

Dried cooked: Peel and cook, or cook and peel. (If you don't peel them, your dried potatoes will have a weird flavor.) Cook until nearly done but just a trifle firm. Put through a potato ricer to make shreds, or cut into thin slices. Spread on trays and dry until brittle. The ancient Incas made dried potatoes into a flour called "chuño" that was storable for years and was used in vegetable-meat mixes and sweet dishes.

To reconstitute dried potatoes, just pour boiling water over and simmer until done (about 50 minutes).

Canning: Canning potatoes carries above-average risk because of their density and the soil they may carry, so it's not recommended by the USDA. If you must: Wash, peel, and wash again thoroughly. Can them in ½-inch cubes rather than whole. To prevent darkening, dip in brine (1 t. salt per 1 qt. water). Drain. Cook 2 minutes in boiling water. Drain. Pack. Add salt if desired. Pour fresh hot water over, leaving 1 inch headspace. Process *in pressure canner only* for 35 minutes for pints, 40 minutes for quarts. If using a weighted-gauge canner, set at 10 lb. pressure at 0–1,000 feet above sea level; set at 15 lb. at higher altitudes. If using a dial-gauge canner, set at 11 lb. pressure at 0–2,000 feet above sea level; 12 lb. at 2,001–4,000 feet; 13 lb. at 4,001–6,000 feet; 14 lb. at 6,001–8,000 feet; or 15 lb. above 8,000 feet.

RECIPE IDEAS

New Potatoes: Potatoes that are fresh from the ground are a whole new eating experience if you haven't had them before. Delicious! Those tiny new potatoes are, I think, best and easiest served boiled in their jackets—which can then easily be slipped off by the cook, or you can eat them skins and all. New potatoes cook more quickly than those that have been stored.

Tiny Potatoes: I used to think that if small potatoes were left around for a while and their skins allowed to harden, they were scarcely worth the peeling and could just move on to the pig trough. But a reader wrote me: "A neighbor always gives me the ones less than 2 inches in diameter. I scrub them, raw-pack them in quart jars, add 1 t. salt per quart, cover with water, and pressure-can [see preceding section ("Canning") for times]. Very good for quick potato salad, fried, or in stew."

◆ *POTATO PANCAKES Margaret Larsen, Fields, OR, sent her mother's recipe: "She had chickens and grew plenty of potatoes. My mother considered this a one-dish meal. We always put warm applesauce or sour cream on top of the pancakes. Grate 4 medium-sized peeled potatoes and 1 large onion on your smallest-sized grater. (Do not blend in blender.) Add 4 egg yolks and a pinch salt. Whip whites of the 4 eggs and add them. In a skillet with a lid, fry till brown on each side, turning only once."*

◆ *RUTH'S VEGAN POTATO PANCAKES "Grate 1½ lb. potatoes and 2 small onions. Combine with 3 T. cornstarch, some parsley, and 2 T. tamari. Form mixture into patties and bake on a griddle or in medium oven until crisp."*

◆ *POTATO/ONION CASSEROLE Put alternate layers of*

sliced onions and potatoes into a casserole dish. Sprinkle a pinch of salt on each layer. Make the top layer potatoes. Sprinkle top with pepper and scatter butter lumps over it. Cover with boiling hot water. Bake an hour.

◆ *ALMOST NONFAT FRENCH FRIES Preheat oven to 450°F. Peel your potatoes and cut them into lengthwise strips about ½ inch thick. Keep strips in ice water until finished cutting. Drain, pat dry, put in bowl, and sprinkle with just a little oil. Mix using your hands to spread the oil evenly over the potatoes. Then bake in a bread pan until golden brown and tender, turning often (about ½ hour). Sprinkle with paprika, salt to taste, and serve.*

◆ *POTATO CHIPS These were called "Saratoga chips" in the old days. Peel potatoes and slice into thin shavings (use vegetable cutter), soaking in ice water an hour. Drain and dry in a towel. Put them in a wire frying basket and immerse it in preheated oil that's not too hot or too cold. Fry until they curl and are delicately brown. Shake them as free of fat as possible before lifting them away from the kettle. Drain on absorbent paper or cloth. Dust with salt. A big batch will last 20 days or so if you keep them in a cool, dry place and reheat in the oven until crisp before serving.*

◆ *STEAMED/BOILED SPUDS Steam or boil potatoes. Test for doneness with a fork. If it penetrates to the center easily with a little pressure, your potato is done, new or old. Drain right away or they'll keep soaking up water and get mushy. Potato water is good for making gravy and soups. Or steam/boil spuds with a few carrots and onions and serve, whole or mashed, with the vegetables.*

◆ *BAKED POTATOES Start with a baking-type (white) potato. Scrub the potato clean, and bake at 350°F until you can poke into the middle with a fork. Serve halved with all sorts of vegetables mashed in or on top, with cheese melted over, or with butter or sour cream.*

◆ *POTATO SALAD Basically, potato salad is diced cold boiled potatoes, cut-up hard-boiled eggs, chopped onions, and mayonnaise, thoroughly mixed together. Optional: Add chopped celery, diced pickle, olives or pimento, celery seed, dill, garlic powder, paprika, sugar, vinegar, horseradish, mustard, etc.*

◆ *HASH BROWNS Put just enough fat or oil into the frying pan to shine it. Grate the cold boiled potatoes into the pan and press down flat. Let fry until crisp on the bottom; then turn and let crisp on the other side. Or if the layer is very thin, fold over like an omelet. Hint from Julia Reynolds, Galvin, WA: "After you grate them, rinse in a colander under cold water, drain well, and after they are fried, they'll be just like what you get in a restaurant."*

◆ *MASHED POTATOES Cook peeled potatoes to tenderness; then drain (save water for gravy if you like). When I make these for supper, I usually cook extras and hold them back from the mashing to make hash browns for breakfast or potato salad for lunch the next day. Keep remaining spuds on very low heat if they are soggy. Mash thoroughly with a potato masher or electric mixer. Optional: Add a lump of butter, a slosh of milk, or salt and pepper. Mound in a serving bowl with maybe a dab of butter melting in a hollow in the middle and a sprinkle of paprika. They're nicest with gravy, a veggie, or a cream sauce.*

◆ *POTATO CAKES If your leftover potato is mashed rather*

than whole, you can make patties and fry them plain for breakfast the next morning. Or make potato cakes: Mix well 2 c. cold mashed potato, 2 beaten eggs, some chopped onion (green or otherwise), and a little chopped green pepper if you have it. Make into patties and fry them on each side.

Sweet Potato

What vegetable is another tropical starchy root from the ancient Americas; is grown like a potato but is not related to the potato; is a great poor-soil crop yet is one of the most nutritious foods from the garden (containing vitamin A, which helps prevent cancer and preserve night vision); is stored, cooked, and tastes like a winter squash; and is not a yam? Answer: the sweet potato, *Ipomoea batatas*!

Climate is a problem for sweet potatoes, though. They hate cold, love hot weather, and need about 100 days to grow baby bakers (150 to make big ones). If your July/August mean temperature is more than 80°F, you're in an ideal zone for sweet potatoes. Sweet potatoes will yield less elsewhere, but they can be grown as far north as southern New York, Michigan, and the Midwest. You'll find much good info in "Organic Sweet Potato Production," free from ATTRA (800-346-9140). Also see **www.orst.edu/Dept/ NWREC/swpotato.html**.

VARIETIES: The sweet potato comes in many colors: white, yellow, orange, red, and brown. The one with deep orange flesh does best south of mid-Virginia and is often called a "yam," although it's not a true yam. The one with creamy yellow flesh grows well north of there. The white kind is the boniato, also called "batato," "white sweet potato," or "Cuban sweet potato." Southern Seeds sells slips (sprouts) of the boniato and says it's "grown widely in Latin America and Asia and is sixth among the principal food crops of the world."

PROPAGATION: Buy plants from a local nursery or a mail-order house. You can get novel, red-fleshed, and heirloom varieties from Fred's Plant Farm (731-364-3754; PO Box 707, Dresden, TN 38225) or Steele Plant Co. (731-648-5476; PO Box 191, Gleason, TN 38229). You can buy organically grown slips from Sand Hill Preservation Center (563-246-2299; 1878 230th St., Calamus, IA 52729) or Mapple Farm (506-734-3361; **wingate@nbnet.nb.ca**). You need 80 plants for a 100-foot row. For each 25 plants that grow, you may be able to harvest about 30 lb. of sweet potatoes. They are perennials grown as annuals. Soil that's not too rich is best for them, since excess nitrogen will send growth to the vine instead of the root. They need well-cultivated, well-drained soil.

Growing Slips: The sweet potato, like the white potato, is not grown from seed but is propagated. The potato is a tuber with eyes that sprout, but the sweet potato is a true root with no eyes or buds. Nevertheless, if you keep a sweet potato around long enough, it will sprout (although some store sweet potatoes are treated to discourage that). Its sprouts are called "slips," and one sweet potato can grow 20 to 50 of them (smaller roots produce more slips). Start in about January. You can grow slips in quantity by bedding sweet potatoes about 3 inches apart, buried only about halfway, in a hotbed with soil at least a foot deep (or in a pan of water). Controlling temperature during this process is important—the plant has to stay *warm*!

Separating Slips: When a slip is about 6 to 10 inches long

and has a nice set of little roots, it's time to carefully pull it away from the original root. Or let them grow as is until it's time to transplant to the garden. To take off a bunch of them, start at one end and work toward the other. Hold the parent tightly with one hand and pull on the offspring with the other. Transplant to individual little pots or a hotbed for extra growing time, or move directly to the garden.

Planting Slips: Plant them 2 to 3 inches apart with the base 2 to 3 inches deep. A good time to plant in the hotbed is about 5 or 6 weeks before garden planting date. Keep them warm—at least 75°F—and moist. As you get nearer transplanting time, start giving the plants more cool air to get them hardened off before going outdoors. Plant 2 weeks after last frost time.

Planting Cuttings: Once the plants are up and making vines at least 3 to 4 feet long, you can remove 7- or 8-inch pieces (each containing at least 2 joints). Plant lying horizontally except for the last few inches, which should stick out of the ground. If you are gentle and pick a rainy spell for making and planting the cuttings, each cutting will grow roots and give you that many more sweet potato plants.

Planting/Growing Outdoors: Set plants about 1 to 3 feet apart, depending on variety, rows 2½ feet apart. If you're short of garden room, run the trailing morning-glory-type vines (4 to 16 feet long) up a garden fence. Or grow in a window box (at least a foot deep and well watered) with the vines trailing down. Once garden vines get going, they grow every which way and put down new roots wherever they take a notion to. You can't cultivate in there. Don't tear the vines loose from the ground if you can help it, because that hurts the plant and decreases your yield. This plant can handle a dry spell without harm; it may even be stimulated to make a better crop as a result.

HARVESTING: The sweet potatoes grow, and grow fast, during the last part of the plant's life—September and October. That's why planting too late or harvesting too early results in low yield and in skinny, low-starch roots. Another argument for leaving them to grow as long as possible is that the more mature sweets heal from nicks much better. The only way to know how big and numerous they're getting is to dig up a plant. You can't tell by looking at the vines—except that if they get limp and black after a hard frost, you need to harvest right away, because sweets not dug by the day after the vines die are said to keep and taste worse. But if the vines are merely frost-nipped on the tips, you can let them continue growing. If the weather doesn't freeze, you can leave them in the ground until needed.

Dig on a sunny, dry day when the soil is not wet. Dig with a potato fork very carefully from the side, not from the top. *Cut or bruised sweet potatoes won't winter-keep well, and they rot easily. Even after they are dug, you should still handle them gently. Gently separate each sweet potato from its top.* Sort out all bruised, cut, or tiny sweets for immediate use since they won't keep well.

Curing: Let them lie on the ground in the sunshine for 2 or 3 hours to dry thoroughly. In the South you can finish the job there: Let them lie in the sun another 10 to 14 days. They need temps of 80 to 85°F for that period. If you're in a cooler climate, do the 10 to 14 days at 80 to 90°F in the house, behind the wood stove, near your furnace, or in a car parked in the sun with windows lowered or raised as needed to manage temperature. Unlike any other curing vegetable I know of, sweets need it damp during their curing period. If the weather isn't humid, cover them with a slightly damp towel.

STORING OR PRESERVING: But, once cured, sweet potatoes need to stay dry (and well insulated)! So pack them individually in newspaper and then in boxes or baskets in a cool room. Or wrap individually in newspaper, package in paper bags, and hang the bags by twine from ceiling beams. Another system is to pack them in sawdust or feed grain. In that case, don't let them touch each other or the bottom or side of the container. Store at 45–55°F. They don't keep as dependably as white potatoes do, but they may last 3 to 5 months, and they'll get better-tasting each day of storage as starch is changed to sugar and their texture softens. When your stored sweet potatoes threaten to shrivel up, shift to another preservation system: freezing, canning, or drying.

Freezing: This is probably the next easiest way to preserve them. Wash, fill your oven with them, bake until tender, cool, bag in plastic, and freeze. Or steam instead of bake. Or peel and cut in halves before packaging. Or slice or mash, and then package and freeze.

Canning: Cook sweet potatoes in boiling water or steam for 20 to 30 minutes. Peel and cut into pieces. You can dry-pack them by just filling your jar with the hot pieces of sweet potato and putting the lid on, or you can wet-pack by covering the potato pieces with boiling water. Pack in pints only. Pressure-can only for 95 minutes. If using a weighted-gauge canner, set at 10 lb. pressure at 0–1,000 feet above sea level; set at 15 lb. at higher altitudes. If using a dial-gauge canner, set at 11 lb. pressure at 0–2,000 feet above sea level; 12 lb. at 2,001–4,000 feet; 13 lb. at 4,001–6,000 feet; 14 lb. at 6,001–8,000 feet; or 15 lb. above 8,000 feet.

Drying: Drying sweet potatoes is much like drying pumpkins. Peel, slice, and dry. Or boil the sweet potatoes until tender, slip off skins, slice ⅛ inch thick, and dry. Or cook, mash, and make dried leather (see leather-making in the "Drying" section of Chapter 7). Reconstitute dried sweet potato by pouring boiling water over and simmering to tenderness; use in puddings, pies, breads, etc.

COOKING: Cooking sweet potatoes in their skins preserves vitamins. Boiling or baking first and then skinning is easiest because they're hard to peel before cooking, and when peeled, they tend to turn black. To boil: Scrub, cover with water, cook until just tender, skin, and serve. To bake: Scrub, bake until tender (about an hour), wrap a few minutes in a towel after they come out of the oven, and serve. The wrap makes the skin tender and easy to get off.

Recipe Ideas: Sweet potatoes that have been cured taste best. You can boil, bake, broil, or glaze. Or serve them with cream, make them into croquettes, or fry slices in tempura batter. Or cut into small chunks and stir-fry with other vegetables. Or cut into slices, steam, and serve sprinkled with cinnamon—or mashed with cinnamon and orange juice. Or deep-fry long strips that have been dipped into tempura batter, and serve with fish. Or bake, cut in half, cover with cheese, melt the cheese, and serve. Or peel, chunk, and cook with meat and veggies for a soup. Or peel, quarter, steam, and serve with chopped green herbs and melted butter. Or precook, peel, chunk, and stir-fry with onions, green beans, garlic, and meat strips. Or make a pudding of 1½ c. cooked, mashed sweet potatoes, 2 T. honey, ⅓ c. orange juice, and 1 t. grated orange rind (eggs optional) baked at 350°F.

Substitute sweet potato in any pumpkin or squash recipe.

Sweet Potato Greens: The vine tips can be served as a green vegetable; they're good steamed. Or stir-fry with tofu cubes, garlic, and soy sauce.

Lesser-Known Starchy Roots

These include arrowhead, cassava, kudzu, malanga, taro, and yam.

ARROWHEAD: *Sagittaria latifolia* is also known as "bardang," "chee koo," "duck potato," and "kuwai." It's a hard, small (walnut-sized) tuber that's native to America but is now also grown in Asia. It's not an easy crop to grow because the tubers grow from underground runners that stray far from their origin. Raw arrowhead tastes unpleasant; the cooked stuff tastes like a sweet potato. Use like potatoes.

CASSAVA

NOTE: Cassava, like taro, contains prussic acid and must be boiled in water at least 1 hour to be sure all the acid is dispersed before you eat it or use it in a recipe.

Cassava is also known as "yuca," "manioc," and "mandiota." The edible part is its long root with brown skin, white flesh, and a hairy complex of veins. The importance of this tropical starchy root is that, like taro, it will grow where neither grains nor potatoes can. Use in recipes in the "Taro" section.

KUDZU: This aggressive, leguminous vine (*Puereria thunbergiana*) is Asian in origin but has now virtually taken over certain Appalachian areas. It looks, grows, and sprawls somewhat like a giant squash plant. Kudzu has one compensation: It produces very large, edible tubers. I wouldn't plant the stuff on purpose, although it is touted as an erosion control. It's true; once kudzu gets established, nothing much gets through to the soil. But *be cautious* and control it by clipping the runners back so it doesn't take over the state and so you don't get sued by all your neighbors for letting loose such a nuisance on them. In some places, people also harvest the greens for hay and forage. Here's how to cook the tubers.

Kudzu tubers have yellowish brown, fibrous outer peels and white flesh inside. Smaller roots have better flavor. All of them are somewhat on the bitter side. They aren't long on vitamins but are a starchy food like potatoes. *Peel them and discard the peels before cooking.* You can then boil them like potatoes and serve mashed with soy sauce; or make vegetable sticks of them and cook in any stir-fry; or slice thin and saute in a Chinese recipe; or grind, dry, and grind again to make a powder comparable in function to cornstarch; or steam.

MALANGA: This tropical plant (*Xanthosoma sagittifolium*) has a foot-long, brown-skinned corm and little 3-inch tubers connected to it; both corm and tubers are edible. Malanga is not the same thing as taro. It is basically a potato that can be grown in areas too hot for the familiar northern spud. It comes from tropical Latin America.

Malanga can be a basic starchy food since it contains minerals and even more starch than potatoes. You cook and use malanga very much like potato except that *you must always boil, drain, and peel it before using; that takes care of the bitter taste.* Peel, mash, and season like new potatoes; or cook, cube, and substitute for potatoes in a potato salad recipe. You can make a malanga soup using both malanga leaves and the cut-up roots. Mexicans like malanga boiled and then sauteed with hot sausage. They also make a stew of malanga, pork, and other vegetables, seasoned with cilantro.

TARO: Taro (*Manihot esculenta,* or *Colocasia esculenta*) is also known as "candala," "dasheen," "eddoe," "gabi," and "yautia." It's a Latin American staple whose leaves and roots are both edible if cooked. Taro is an important plant because it provides starch in tropical areas where neither potatoes nor grains can make it.

Leaf Recipe Ideas

NOTE: All taro leaves must be cooked 1 hour before eating. Don't let children chew on them. They contain prussic acid. Once thoroughly boiled or baked, they are fine and nourishing to eat. This is true even of the little leaves that may develop off your tuber.

Taro leaves can be boiled with a stew, added to a pot of dried beans, or wrapped around meat that will be thoroughly roasted. The bulbous "root," which is actually a corm, can be eaten too.

Root Recipe Ideas

NOTE: Taro roots also contain prussic acid and must be boiled at least 1 hour before you can be certain all the prussic acid is taken care of. After that, they are safe and nourishing food.

Boil the roots with onions, add seasonings, and serve. Or do like the father in *The Swiss Family Robinson*: First thoroughly press out the poisonous juice, grind it into a meal (the Brazilians call this "farinho"), and then cook it like a cereal. Or boil, mash, and serve with cooked meat chunks. Or use preboiled taro tubers in a stir-fry recipe, add to a stew with other vegetables, or bake in a casserole with meat, vegetables, and herbs.

YAM: If it has the Latin name *Dioscorea,* that means it's a true yam. The true yam resembles but is botanically quite different from the sweet potato, which is a dicot relative of the potato, another member of the nightshade family. Because "yam" is often mistakenly used as a name for sweet potatoes, a lot of people don't realize that the plants aren't related at all. The yam is not a dicot nightshade like the sweet potato and potato; it's a monocot like onion and asparagus. The harvested part is a fleshy, starchy tuber that may grow either deep underground or above ground in leaf axils like Brussels sprouts, depending on species. Most yams are tropical and prefer a 12-month growing season and lots of heat. The best places in the United States to grow them are Hawaii and Florida.

D. bulbifea is from Africa and is also known as "kush kush." It's the most familiar variety. It's orangy, with roughly the same dimensions as a sweet potato.

D. japonica is also known as "mountain yam," "tororo imo," "mountain potato," and "jinengo potato." This hardy perennial Chinese vine grows long underground tubers that are highly valued for food in Japan. It is most closely related to the yam, also a monocot. The Japanese grow it as they do burdock, in raised beds or boxes that can be dismantled. It takes 2 to 3 years to get a crop. Small aerial (and also edible) tubers that grow on the stems are the means of propagation. Available from Deep Diversity.

Yam Recipe Ideas. Boil, mash, and serve with butter like potatoes. Boil, puree, and mix with a sweetening like honey and maybe also a spice like cloves or cinnamon. Cook and then add a brown sugar-butter sauce. Slice and deep-fry to make a chip that is then served with a sour cream dip. Peel, grate, and sprinkle flakes on food that will be stir-fried. Stir-fry cubes together with tofu, veggies, and seasonings. Cook with meat and vegetables for a soup.

NONSTARCHY ROOTS

Lots of vegetables fit in this category: beet, burdock, carrot, chufa, Hamburg parsley, Jerusalem artichoke, jicama, lotus root, parsnip, radish, rutabaga, salsify, scorzonera, skirret, turnip, and water chestnut.

Beet

The common old garden beet (*Chenopodiacene beta vulgaris*) is a food that people either like or dislike. The beet isn't a very romantic food, but if you can grow it, it can be an eminently practical one—for you *and* your livestock! The beet is a goosefoot that's closely related to the chards. And you can cook and eat beet greens like chard. Most beets are good and easy winter keepers in garden, pit, or root cellar. Beets generally appreciate a cool climate and have little tolerance for hot weather. They don't like poor, clay soil either, but everything else is pretty much okay with them.

If you live in a place as far north as Peace River in Alberta, Canada, like Marie Jeanne Cartier, beets (and turnips)

are an ideal crop for you. She wrote me: " . . . back of our house you could walk through hill and dale practically up to the North Pole without passing a neighbor. I don't have any heat problems with beets—or turnips either. Hot weather never makes them tasteless and woody the way it does elsewhere. Here a beet can grow and grow and will always remain tender."

VARIETIES: Beets come in all kinds of shapes—short round-rooted or long varieties, small and large. The long varieties are best for pit storage, but you've got to loosen the ground deeper for them.

Mangels. Also called wurzel or "stock beets," these are usually grown for animal rather than people food, and are valuable in that role. They grow *very* large. You can winter your goats on mangel beets plus carrots and the big varieties of winter squash even if you can't grow hay. Every goat owner I know around here feeds mangel beets to their goats. Cows and pigs like them too. Folks usually cook them for the pigs. They vary in maturing time from about 45 to 150 days, but most are on the quick side.

Sugar Beets. Most commercial white sugar comes from sugar cane, but some comes from sugar beets, the sugar crop in temperate zones where cane won't grow. Sugar beets can't compete with cane in terms of sugar yield, though, and you can't make beet sugar without a factory. The raw beets don't even have a sweet taste. Sugar beets aren't good people food. They make fine animal feed, but don't feed the animals spoiled beets—that would make them sick.

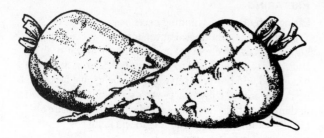

The sugar beet is a remarkable plant. Its taproot can be as much as 6 to 7 feet deep, and its smaller roots reach out in all directions. When you pull it out to harvest, the lower part of the taproot and the tiny rootlets remain in the ground. Sugar beets loosen the soil and draw food from lower levels than does your usual crop. They like sunshine and can handle a warmer climate than most table beets. You can get sugar beet seed from Gurney's. Seed in rows 18 inches apart when frost danger is past. Thin the seedlings to stand 9 inches apart in the row. Keep out the weeds. Harvest around October 1.

There are a lot of sugar beets grown around Colorado. I remember the smell of those processing plants: really rank. At the factory the top and small part of the neck of the beet are cut off. The beet is washed, thinly sliced, and exposed to running water, which dissolves the sugar. The beet juice containing sugar is black. Lime is added to make unwanted stuff clump together in the solution and then settle to the bottom (precipitate out). The remaining clear juice is then centrifuged to extract molasses and raw beet sugar, which is then put through several more procedures to make it white. The end product of all that grinding, crushing, heating, pressing, and adding of chemicals is granulated white sugar.

Making Sugar Beet Syrup. If you want to make sugar from sugar beets at home, the closest you can come is to make a syrup like this. Scrub beets well. Slice like cucumbers. Cover with boiling water and bring to a boil. Drain. The liquid you drained off is thin raw beet syrup. Evaporate to thicken, using low heat. You can use the surplus sliced beets and green leaves that you cut off for animal food (cows enjoy them), or compost them. Now back to growing regular table beets or mangel beets.

PLANTING: Beets dislike a heavy clay-type soil. Plant in soil that's deeply loosened. They like manure and compost, but unrotted manure will make them produce lots of leaves and little root. For fresh eating, canning, freezing, or drying, plant your beets as soon as the frost is out of the ground. You can plant at 2- or 3-week intervals after that, until within a few months of your first expected killing frost. For beets that you plan to store in pits or root cellars, later planting is better.

Two ounces of seed will generally plant about 100 feet of row. Plant ½ inch deep, seeds about 1 inch apart, and figure that they probably won't show above the ground for 2 or 3 weeks after that. If you carefully keep the soil moist while waiting for the seeds to germinate, they may appear in as little as 10 days.

THINNING: Beet seed, unless you get the kind called Monogram, is different from the usual case because every "seed" really is a clump of seeds, as many as 8. So it really doesn't matter how carefully you space the seed when planting—you will always have to thin beets. So using a thin-and-eat policy, gradually thin your beets as they grow so that they are ultimately 3 inches or further apart. The basic rule on thinning is simply that as soon as the plants begin to crowd each other, you should pull up every other one.

If you end up with a hole in your row, you can transplant some thinnings to fill it up. Young beets transplant easily if you are gentle. Set the beet plant in straight up and down in a hole deep enough to have room for all of it. Keep it well watered during the whole transplanting process. Give them a good soaking before you take them out and again when you have settled them in their new spot.

HARVESTING

Saving Seed. Beet pollen is wind-carried, and beet varieties will cross, so your safeguard is to plant only 1 variety. Beets will also cross with Swiss chard. Like carrots, beets are biennials; that means they store food in a root during the first summer and then grow stalk, flower, and seed from that root during the second summer. If you won't be cultivating the ground, you can pick out plants to save seed from and leave them in the row for 2 years until the process is finished, but odds are that they'll be in the middle of your garden and you'll need the rest of the row anyway. In that case leave them in the ground until late fall. Then dig up carefully, break off the leafy tops (leaving about ½ inch of stem), and store in a special place buried under dirt deep enough so they won't freeze. (How deep that is depends on where you live and your ability to predict how cold it's going to get.) In the spring, as early as you can, set the roots back out in a row with the tops just level with ground surface. That second summer they'll go ahead and make seed. When the seed is fully mature and dry, cut off the seed clusters, take them indoors, rub the seeds off the seed heads by hand, dry some more, and store.

Pit/Root-Cellar Storage. If you have a long growing season, use late-planted beets for root-cellar storage. Otherwise the beets will be oversized and woody—and table beets should be no more than 3 inches in diameter. Leave them in the ground as long as possible because they keep better there than anywhere else. When you are ready to move them, try to pick in dry weather. Whack off the green tops with a knife. Store where they'll keep moist and be as near freezing as possible without ever actually freezing. If they are too warm in storage, they'll sprout new tops and get woody inside. To bed in moist sand or sawdust, use a galvanized tub or wooden container. Make a layer of sawdust, a layer of beets, a layer of sawdust, and so on.

Container Deoxygenation. A friend told me about an old man in his 90s who stores his beets in a can with an airtight lid in a root cellar. In the center of the can he places a candle stub. Before closing the lid, he lights the candle. The candle burns until all the oxygen is used up. He says that is what keeps the vegetables from softening. Each time he goes back for more beets (or turnips), he lights the candle again. If you have a root cellar with a dirt floor, you can put your beets in small piles along the wall—not in large piles, because they're more likely to heat and decay. Or store them in your basement or root cellar in wooden boxes. Or do pit storage as described earlier in "Introduction to Roots."

Scrubbing. No matter what else you're going to do with your beets—unless it's root-cellar storage—start by giving them a good scrubbing with a brush and plenty of water to get off the dirt, and cut off all but an inch of the tops. See "Beet Greens" under "The Non-Brassica Greens" for how to manage the tops.

FREEZING: Cut off tops, wash, scald, and cook until tender. Peel, dice, chill, and package.

DRYING: By the time you boil them for about 15 minutes to get the skins off, you have blanched them. Slice ⅛ inch thick, and dry them. They are delicious if you start with young, tender beets. Real baby beets don't need any precooking. Just wash, peel, slice, and dry.

CANNING: First scrub roots very well. Then precook by either baking or boiling because raw-packing is not recommended for beets.

Precooking by Baking. Cut off tops and roots. You can put beets of any size together in the oven (conventional or microwave). They're all cooked when the biggest one is done. Then pour cold water over the hot, roasted beets, and you'll be able to slip off their skins. Dump the water.

Precooking by Boiling. Remove the entire beet top except for the closest 1–2 inches of stem. Leave the roots on; that keeps them from "bleeding" (losing nutrients). Sort beets according to size, and boil similar sizes together so they'll get done at about the same time. When fork-tender (in about 30 minutes), move them into cold water. Slip off skins, stems, and roots.

Cutting Up. You cut up beets to improve and even out heat penetration in your jar. If baby beets are smaller than 2 inches wide, they can be left whole. If they're larger, cut them into ½-inch cubes. Or slice ½ inch thick, and then quarter the slices.

Packing and Processing. Pack beets into hot jars. Cover with boiling water, leaving ½ inch headspace. Optional: Add ½ t. salt/pt., 1 t. salt/qt.; add 1 T. vinegar/pt., 2 T./qt. to preserve color. Process in a pressure canner only: pints for 30 minutes, quarts for 35 minutes. If using a weighted-gauge canner, set at 10 lb. pressure at 0–1,000 feet above sea level; set at 15 lb. at higher altitudes. If using a dial-gauge canner, set at 11 lb. pressure at 0–2,000 feet above sea level; 12 lb. at 2,001–4,000 feet; 13 lb. at 4,001–6,000 feet; 14 lb. at 6,001–8,000 feet; or 15 lb. above 8,000 feet.

PICKLED BEETS *Start by carefully scrubbing 7 lb. of beets (2 to 2½ inches in diameter) to remove all dirt. Now trim off beet tops, leaving on 1 inch of stem and roots to prevent nutrient loss. Wash well. Sort by size. Cover size-grouped beets with boiling water and cook until tender (25 to 30 minutes). Drain and discard liquid. Cool beets. Trim off roots and stems and slip off skins. Slice into ¼-inch slices. Peel and thinly slice.*

Combine 4 c. vinegar (5 percent), 1½ t. canning or pickling salt, 2 c. sugar, and 2 c. water. Put 2 cinnamon sticks and 12 whole cloves in a cheesecloth bag and add to vinegar mixture. Bring to a boil.

Add beets and 4 to 6 onions (2 to 2½ inches in diameter). Simmer 5 minutes. Remove spice bag. Fill pint or quart jars with hot beets and onions, leaving ½ inch headspace. Adjust lids. Process either pints or quarts in boiling-water canner. At up to 1,000 feet above sea level, process 30 minutes; at 1,001–3,000 feet, 35 minutes; 3,001–6,000 feet, 40 minutes; and above 6,000 feet, 45 minutes.

PICKLED WHOLE BABY BEETS *Follow above directions, but use beets that are 1 to 1½ inches in diameter. Pack whole; don't slice. You can leave out the onions.*

PREPARING

Eating Baby Beets. Thinning beets has a really good side. You can eat the thinnings. Eat the tops like greens. If they're big enough to have roots of any development, eat both tops and roots together. I boil top greens and bottom root with bacon and add butter at serving time. Delicious! I like beets best of all at the "baby" stage—that's around 1½ to 2 inches in diameter, about the size of a radish. Baby beets are also nice for eating, freezing, canning, or pickling.

Precooking Beets to Eat Fresh. Cut off tops. You may or may not leave a stub (leaving it prevents nutrient loss). Cover with boiling water, and boil until the beets are slightly soft to the touch. Another way to precook beets is to bake them in the oven. The bigger they are, the longer it takes. Drain and slip off the skins; no peeling is necessary. Cut off any remaining root tail and the stalk stub.

RECIPES

NOTE: Fresh garden beets have more color than most digestive systems can absorb, so your resulting bowel movement may appear to have "blood" in it. That's just beet color. Eating beets is absolutely not harmful—on the contrary, beets are very nourishing. And they're not harsh to digest, only startling to view in that manner.

BOILED BEETS *Try any precooked beet cut into slices and seasoned with salt, pepper, butter, and a little vinegar or lemon juice.*

SPECIAL BOILED BEETS *Cook, peel, and slice. Make a quick sauce by melting butter and stirring in chopped parsley, chives or other fine green onion, and garlic juice or finely chopped garlic. Now thicken sauce with a little flour and cook a few minutes. Add beets, a dash of vinegar, salt, and pepper, and let it simmer as long as you can—up to 30 minutes—to soak up the flavor before serving. Good with mashed potatoes.*

BEET SOUP *Here is a German recipe for the beet soup known in Europe as borscht. This is a famous, delicious way to eat beets. You can grow the ingredients in an American garden, of course! Cook 2 medium-sized diced potatoes, 1 c. shredded beets, 1 medium onion, and 1 t. salt until almost done. Keep soup on the thick side. Add 1 c. tomatoes or juice, ⅓ c. peas, and some dill weed (if you don't have it, you can do without it). Turn off heat. Carefully add 1 c. light cream so it won't curdle from the tomatoes. Heat, do not boil, and serve.*

QUICK BEET SOUP *Combine 2 c. milk, ½ c. beet juice, and seasonings.*

COLD BEET SALAD *Cook 1 lb. beets until tender. Cool, peel, and slice thinly. Combine 4 T. vinegar, 4 T. water, ½ t. sugar, 2½ t. caraway seeds, 1 chopped small onion, 1 t. ground cloves, 1 bay leaf, salt, pepper, and 4 T. oil. Pour over beets and let marinate several hours before serving.*

ORANGE/BEET JUICE *From Ruth of Bonaire: "Make fresh orange juice—enough to fill the blender two-thirds full. Then add ¼ c. peeled, cubed raw beet. Blend and then pour through a strainer, a bit at a time, mashing pulp with a spoon to extract the maximum amount of juice. You can eat the pulp—it's sweet! This juice looks and tastes like red Kool-Aid!"*

Burdock

The Japanese grow burdock, a very hardy monster weed—*Arctium lappa*, a member of the thistle family—for its sweet, edible, strange-tasting root and young shoots. Pretentious and curious people in this country have tried growing burdock root. It passes in elegant company as "beggars' buttons," "gobo," or "takinogawa," and some in Japan believe it helps virility.

Country dwellers know burdock best as "cocklebur," the weed with the Velcro seeds, those incredibly clinging burrs that can virtually ruin a sheep's fleece and that are so tough to pick out of any soft fabric you wore on a stroll through them. I'm inclined to think that growing the stuff should be a jailable offense—or at least a sue-able one. But people do grow it, and I have to perform my duty here; I won't censor information. (At least they're not poisonous.) So here goes. But if you do plant them, be warned: You've taken on a moral responsibility not to let them turn weedy, get away from you, and infest the county.

PLANTING: Seeds are available from Kitazawa, Nichols, and Seeds of Change. Plant for control and for easy harvesting. Japanese farmers plant burdock in a specially contrived growing box that sits on the ground, isolated from all other garden dirt, full of loose, rich, easy-digging soil. Plant in spring. Allow plenty of space because burdock is a big plant with huge leaves that will shade any nearby plants. Plant in any kind of soil. For the best roots, don't overwater, because you want the roots to probe downward in search of water. It grows slowly, so be patient; wait until fall to harvest.

HARVESTING: *Dig, don't pull.* Burdock is most easily harvested from soft, loose soil. Left overlong, burdock can get a root even 2 or 3 feet long. It's best harvested at about 18 inches and when still skinny, although the root can get very thick. But thinner roots will actually be more edible than the thicker ones, which tend to be tougher. Also, you need to get out all of the root, or the plant will come back from the remaining root whether or not you want it to.

PREPARING: Prepare burdock roots by scraping their outer surface using a dull knife until you can see the white flesh inside. Older, tougher roots will have to be peeled. As you work with burdock roots, your fingers will discolor as if you were husking walnuts. Put the scraped roots into acidic water (lemon juice or vinegar mixed with water) as soon as you've cleaned them. Burdock root is fibrous; pounding before you cook it softens and improves it. It is never eaten raw. Cut in strips or slices.

RECIPE IDEAS: Pound, slice, and add to a sukiyaki recipe. Or slice and cook in a little liquid with slivers of chicken, slices of mushroom, chopped onions, and herbs. Or stir-fry strips with crushed garlic and soy sauce. Or saute sliced burdock with thin strips of beef and soy sauce. Or make a soup of burdock slices, potatoes, carrots, onions, tomatoes, and a meat chunk. Or make as tempura. Or saute with Asian veggies and seaweed. Or substitute for carrot in any recipe that calls for cooked carrot.

Carrot

Daucus carota, I love you. There are so many hard things already in life—I'm not looking for more. Carrots are easy: quick to grow and mature, productive in a limited space, unscathed by diseases and insects (at least in my garden), cheerfully colored, delicious, and nourishing. And carrots are an easy, good winter keeper. Carrot is a vitamin A veggie, a preventer of eye problems. Carrots prefer cool, wet weather to grow in.

VARIETIES: Carrots come short-rooted or long-rooted. Most carrots take about 2 months to mature, a little longer for the long-rooted kinds. Short-rooted carrots are the thing to grow if you have very rocky ground, if the ground is shallowly cultivated, or if your growing season is extra-short. Long kinds may grow a foot long. If your soil has not been well loosened by cultivation or by organic matter or sand in it, a long carrot just can't make it down through and will end up having a weird stunted shape that is hard to deal with in the kitchen. In southern gardens the short, quick-growing varieties do better than the longer-rooted kinds.

PLANTING: Start planting carrots anytime in your deeply and finely tilled soil (no fresh manure), raked smooth on top, anytime after 25 days before your frostfree date. In the South, plant for spring or fall, not midsummer, growing. You can make succession plantings of carrots as often as you like, from the time the ground can be cultivated until it's too hot to plant carrots. In a longer-season zone, plant again in late summer for a fall crop, and those will be your best winter keepers. Rotate them into different parts of your garden in successive years.

Carrot seed is slow to germinate. Soaking it in a little water overnight before planting speeds it up a little. Ideally you plant the seed ¼ inch deep, ½ inch apart, at least 12 inches between rows. In a 12-inch pot (at least a foot deep), you could plant about 25, knowing you'll be thinning later. But carrot seed is so fine that your fingers won't be able to make that happen exactly. An ounce will plant 150 feet of row. So just space the seed as best you can, and take courage from the thought that, as with beets, the thinnings are good to eat. We plant carrots mixed with a little radish seed because the carrots are so slow to germinate (12 to 18 days) that the weeds will get started if we can't get out and cultivate. The radishes mark the row so we can get on with the hoeing and rototilling while the carrots are still waking up. Keep the place where you planted the seeds well watered and moist until they are up, and afterwards too.

THINNING: Start thinning your carrots when they are 2 or 3 inches high. Keep thinning enough to leave growing room for the ones that are left. Each time, before you thin, water the row well first. Then pull your chosen carrots carefully so they don't break off at the top or in the middle. Eat, freeze, can, or dry the carrots you have pulled out. Thinning also benefits the row by loosening the soil. Even after thinning, you still should be able to have a final harvest of about 200 carrots per 50-foot row.

SAVING SEED: Carrots are insect-pollinated biennials that will cross with other varieties and with wild carrots. So it is very hard to get pure seed where wild carrots (Queen Anne's Lace, etc.) grow or within a mile of other flowering carrots. Crossing with wild carrots will result in whitish, fibery, nonsweet roots. You have to overwinter your prospective parents. Choose your best plants and mark them. In the fall, break or twist off the tops, leaving only about an inch of green stem. Store those carrots buried under the ground deep enough so they won't freeze. Mark your spot. In the spring set them out in rows, with the crowns level with the ground, and off they'll go again. The second year they become inedible because they send all the food out of the root into the seed stalk, and the root gets woody. The seeds don't come or ripen all at once. First they come on the main stem and then on the branches. Wait until the greenish color disappears from the seeds and the branches they hang from. Then cut the stalks, air-dry further, rub out the seed by hand, and screen. Sift or winnow out the sticks, etc. A dozen carrot plants would probably give enough seed for your family. The seed stays healthy at least 3 years.

HARVESTING AND STORING: An average carrot needs 70 days from planting until full growth and readiness for final harvest. They are not ruined by slight freezing, being tougher that way than beets. In a mild winter, you can leave carrots in the garden, mulched for protection. But I don't do that. Once the whole crop froze on me. And come next spring, they start to get woody from the top down. (The woody place is right where the outer layer meets the inner core—where they change color. You can still use such woody carrots by starting your slicing from the tip and discarding what your knife can't pass through easily.)

Root Cellar/Pit. So we put the big, late carrots into the root cellar in October, *unwashed*, with the tops snapped off. It doesn't matter if carrots are accidentally cut by the spade when you're digging—they will still keep. They'll keep all winter in a barrel in a good root cellar; in a poor one, they'll keep in a galvanized or wooden tub or some such between layers of sawdust or moist sand arranged like this: layer of sawdust, layer of carrots, layer of sawdust, and so on. If you have a cool storage room with a dirt floor in the basement, store there in wooden boxes. Or store in a pit under straw and dirt.

Cleaning Carrots. The big job with any stage of carrot, including the baby stage, is washing off the dirt. Cut off the green tops. Carry them by the bucketful to the bathtub (at least that's where we do it), fill it with water, and scrub the carrots under running water with a copper mesh pad (not a soapy pad, of course), a Tuffy plastic scrub pad, or a scrub brush. Sometimes we do the job out in the yard with a big tin tub and a hose. It's a long, tedious job to get all those carrots completely free of dirt. Gail Prill, Mayville, MI, wrote me: "I throw my carrots (minus tops) in my washer machine. It does a terrific job, quick and easy. I do the same with my small baby potatoes." Once they're clean, the rest is

easy. If you have baby carrots, they're as tender as new potatoes and don't need to be peeled.

Freezing. Small carrots between ½ and 1 inch in diameter are the good ones for freezing. Bigger ones simply aren't good this way. Fifty pounds (about 1 bushel) of carrots will yield about 35 frozen pints. Wash and scrub baby carrots. Cut off tops and tips. Wash and peel bigger ones. Then cut those big ones into ½-inch chunks or slices. We freeze the babies whole, unpeeled. Just bring to a boil, bag up, and put in the freezer. Blanch the biggest, oldest ones as long as 5 minutes. Then chill, package, and freeze. Freezer carrots are not nearly as tasty as fresh ones, even when you use baby carrots, but they have the enormous advantage of being handy for the pot, clean and ready to go. They're fine with some seasoning or in a soup.

Drying. Use young, tender carrots. Wash, trim ends, and peel—or don't peel. Slice lengthwise into pieces about ⅛ inch thick. Or slice across ⅛ inch thick. Or dice. Optional: Steam-blanch 8–10 minutes. Spread in thin layer. Dry until tough and leathery. To reconstitute, pour boiling water over and simmer to tenderness.

Canning. Figure that you'll need 1 quart jar for every 2 to 3 lbs. carrots. Prepare as for freezing. Or instead of using chunks, you can make "sticks" but, of course, they can't be longer than 1 inch short of your jar top. Cover with boiling water in a pan. Bring to a boil. Pack into hot jars. Optional: Add ½ t. salt for pints, 1 t. for quarts. Add boiling cooking liquid. Leave 1 inch headspace. Adjust lids. Process in a pressure canner: 25 minutes for pints, 30 minutes for quarts. If using a weighted-gauge canner, set at 10 lb. pressure at 0–1,000 feet above sea level; set at 15 lb. at higher altitudes. If using a dial-gauge canner, set at 11 lb. pressure at 0–2,000 feet above sea level; 12 lb. at 2,001–4,000 feet; 13 lb. at 4,001–6,000 feet; 14 lb. at 6,001–8,000 feet; or 15 lb. above 8,000 feet.

Recipe Ideas. Garden-fresh carrots cook more quickly than store-bought ones, smaller ones more quickly than larger ones. They are tender when a sharp fork punches through with just a little pressure. Don't cook them long enough to get mushy. You can eat them raw or in soups. Or boil and serve creamed or with butter.

> *CARROT SALAD Here's a good winter dish. Grate 3 or 4 carrots. Add any kind of fruit or fruits in combination, such as home-dried fruit chopped into little bits; apples, oranges, bananas, dates, raisins, pears, pineapple, or coconut; or vegetables such as grated turnip, cabbage, or celeriac. Toss all together. Dress with mayonnaise mixed with a dribble of honey. Or dress with salt and lemon juice before you add the other ingredients. Optional: Add chopped nuts or green onion.*

> *FRESH CARROTS IN LEMON BUTTER Peel 8 to 10 fresh carrots. Leave whole if small; cut in lengthwise halves if large. Put the carrots in a cooking pan with about 1 inch of boiling water. Add ½ t. sugar or other sweetening, ¼ t. ground nutmeg, 2 T. butter or margarine, and shake over low heat for a few minutes. Sprinkle with 1 t. fresh lemon juice.*

> *VEGAN CARROTS Steam about a half dozen carrots. Don't salt them. Remove from heat and toss with 2 T. lemon juice, 2 t. water, ¼ t. nutmeg, and ½ t. cinnamon.*

> *CARROT RING Kay Arnold, who writes a wonderful cooking column for the Monte Vista Journal in Colorado, sent*

me this recipe: "Set oven at 350°F. Generously grease a 2-qt. ring mold. Prepare your carrot pudding: Beat 2 eggs into 2 c. milk. Add 1 T. flour or ¼ c. fine bread crumbs, 1 t. salt, and 1 t. sugar. Fold in 2 c. finely grated carrots. Pour mixture into mold and bake 30 to 40 minutes or until firm. Invert onto serving dish and fill center with creamed peas to which chopped celery or lettuce or tiny pearl onions have been added. Garnish with fresh parsley, and you have a vegetable dish to really serve with pride."

➤ *VEGAN CARROT RING* Ruth: "Set oven at 350°F. Spray a 2-qt. ring mold with lecithin (Pam cooking spray) or use a nonstick mold. Combine 2 c. finely grated carrots with 2 c. rice milk, ½ c. cooked, mashed cauliflower, 2 T. whole wheat flour, and ½ t. cinnamon. Pour mixture into mold and bake until firm. Serve with lightly steamed, plain peas in the center."

➤ *SWEET CARROT SOUP* Ruth: "Steam 2 lb. carrots, peel, and dice. Simmer with 3 c. vegetable stock until carrots are very tender. Puree in blender. Reheat, adding about 1½ c. orange juice and 2 T. honey. Serve when warmed through, garnishing with parsley and grated orange peel."

➤ *CARROTY BUNS/COOKIES* Start with a yeast bread or cake recipe. Substitute carrot puree, raisins, and apple juice for the liquid. Substitute molasses for the sweetener, and add some cinnamon. Bake in bun shapes, or roll out and cut with cookie cutters.

ABOUT VEGETABLE JUICES: Let me digress here a moment. Vegetable juice is a vegetarian delight and a healthy treat for anybody at any time, and I want to cover it somewhere in this book.

Juicing Equipment. But to get any vegetable juice except tomato, cucumber, or rhubarb—to make carrot juice, for instance—requires special equipment. And juicers can be expensive. A juicer produces 2 things—juice and pulp. A blender produces a pulpy juice; it liquefies the entire product by breaking down the tissue and suspending it in its own juice. You can get juices with a hand mill, too, but not very easily or efficiently—except cucumber juice. Ruth says, "Natural Hygienists like the Champion Juicer for its versatility as a juicer, grinder, and nut-butter maker.

Preparing Vegetables for Juicing. Wash or scrub them clean. Then put whole veggies into the juicer. To make juice from root vegetables, store them and make the juice as you need it. Freshly made juices taste best. A pound of any vegetable will yield about an 8 oz. glass of juice. *Don't store juice in a metal container; your juice may get a bad taste.*

Serving Juice. Spinach, broccoli, cabbage, celery, green pepper, beet, and watercress juices are most palatable in relatively small quantities and in combination with other juices—especially tomato and apple. Ruth from Bonaire (which is an island off the coast of Venezuela) wrote me: "In Venezuela, juices are very popular, and every home has a mechanical citrus press and a sturdy blender." The "best" vegetable juice combinations are very much a matter of individual preference. But try using juice for part of your liquid in any sort of bread or rolls! Use plain tomato juice, tomato combined with carrot or celery juice, or any sort of V-8ish mix. Everybody loves that—all those good vitamins jumping out and hitting your taste buds.

Carrot Juice. Carrot is the only "sweet" vegetable juice. Carrot pulp is relished by rabbits. Incidentally, don't drink more than 1 big glass of carrot juice per day, or you may

turn as orange as the carrot! (Some friends of mine did!) Here are some good recipes with carrot juice in them.

➤ *ORANGE-CARROT JUICE* From Ruth: "Squeeze fresh orange juice. Add carrot chunks, blend, and strain. This is like orange pop, I think."

➤ *CARROT-BEET-LETTUCE JUICE* Mix 1½ c. carrot juice, ¼ c. beet juice, and ¼ c. lettuce juice.

➤ *CARROT-CELERY-APPLE JUICE* Mix 1 part each carrot, celery, and apple juices.

➤ *CARROT-CELERY-SPINACH JUICE* Mix 1 part each celery, carrot, and spinach juices.

➤ *CARROT SHAKE* Mix ½ c. carrot juice and ½ c. milk.

➤ *CARROT AND EVERYTHING* Mix 1 c. carrot juice, ¼ c. parsley juice, ¼ c. spinach juice, ¼ c. what-have-you, and ½ c. of a different what-have-you! (This is an I-dare-you-to-experiment recipe!)

➤ *CABBAGE COMBO* Mix ¾ c. cabbage juice with ¼ c. celery, tomato, or carrot juice.

➤ *CELERY-CARROT JUICE* Mix ⅓ c. celery juice and ½ c. carrot juice.

➤ *PARSLEY-CARROT JUICE* Combine this with other juices; it isn't drunk by itself. It's especially good with carrot, celery, and lettuce juices. Try ½ c. carrot juice, ½ c. celery juice, and 1 T. parsley juice.

➤ *THE FAMOUS 8* If you have a juicer, experiment with blends of tomato, carrot, celery, beet, parsley, lettuce, watercress, and spinach juice.

Chufa

Chufa (*Cyperus esculentus*), also called "nutsedge," "nutgrass," and "ground almond," can be gathered wild or planted in your garden. It's good and tasty food for both people and animals. It looks like grass above ground. Harvest the tuberous roots in spring and early summer.

RECIPE IDEAS: Eat the sweet, nutty-tasting tubers raw like candy. Or cook with other vegetables in a soup. Or stir-fry with greens, peanuts, and other vegetables. Or boil with potatoes and onions and serve with a cream sauce. Or roast like peanuts and then add to a tossed salad. Or puree in a blender until of a nut-butter consistency. Or make into drinks served hot or cold (has an almond-coconut taste). Or grind and add to any baked goods (adds a nutty flavor).

Hamburg Parsley

Hamburg parsley (*Petroselinum crispum* var. *tuberosum*), also called "parsnip-rooted parsley" and "turnip-rooted parsley," is a variety of parsley grown for its crisp, white-fleshed, carrot-shaped root. It's very hardy and can be harvested, stored in a root cellar, and used in stews like any root vegetable.

PLANTING: Seeds are available from Burpee, William Dam, Farmer, Harris, Hudson, Johnny's, Jung, Nichols, Park, Stokes, etc. Hamburg grows fine in low-nitrogen soils, pH 6 to 7. In fact, excess nitrogen can cause it to make more top than root, so it shouldn't follow legumes. Don't add fresh manure during the growing season because that causes the root to fork in a bad way, although compost added the previous fall is a good thing. Hamburg can also handle an area of partial shade, such as under tall trees. Seed stays viable only about 3 years.

When to Plant. In a short-season area, plant outside as early as possible—on the frostfree date. Or plant indoors in peat pots no more than 6 weeks before the frostfree date and transplant on that date. It won't transplant well if the roots have developed for more than 6 weeks or are disturbed too much during the process. If you have a very mild winter, you can plant in late fall for a spring crop.

How to Plant. Plant presoaked seed about 2 per inch. Cover with ¼ inch dirt. You can make rows as close as a foot. Plant some radish seeds (about 1 every 3 inches) in the row to mark it for tilling since, like any parsley, it will take a month for the Hamburg to come up. Keep the seed row moist until the plants are up and well started. After that, expert gardeners put on a heavy mulch and don't water any more unless it gets radically dry. Thin first to an inch apart, later to 4 to 6 inches apart. Hamburg prefers cool weather, growing best in the 50–70°F temp range.

HARVESTING GREENS: The top of the plant is true parsley. You can harvest and use Hamburg parsley greens just like any other parsley (see "Parsley" in Chapter 5). The problem is that if you cut off more than 1 or 2 stems per plant, you'll harm its root development. So the best way to harvest Hamburg parsley greens is to refrain from clipping them until you dig up the roots. At that time, harvest the greens too, and freeze or dry for flavoring or garnish.

HARVESTING ROOTS: For greatest growth of the root (they'll get as long as 6 to 8 inches or more), Hamburg parsley needs a long season—seeds planted in March will have finished roots in October or November. But you can harvest the root whenever you like. Roots 5 to 7 inches long are the most tender and sweet. The longer you wait to harvest, the bigger they get, but roots larger than that are not as nice. If you wait to harvest until after several fall frosts, the sugar content of the roots will be greater. Hamburg is very frost-resistant and is not killed by it, although it won't grow at low temps. If your area is mild, put a heavy mulch over the plants and leave them in the ground all winter to harvest as needed. (Hamburg is a biennial and will bolt to seed the second year, when temps get up to 75°F.) Hamburg left in the ground will stay crisper than Hamburg in a root cellar, but if your ground freezes hard, dig up before that happens and store in a moist, cool (32–40°F) place, as you would carrots. They can last as long as 4 to 5 months that way.

USING HAMBURG ROOTS: Scrub well or precook. Peel to get rid of the hairy outer skin. But it's better to keep the peel on until after cooking; otherwise the roots discolor. Serve Hamburg roots raw in strips with any dip. Cooked Hamburg can be substituted in any parsnip or turnip recipe, although it has a milder flavor, more like celeriac, than those two. Add to stews and soups; it's good cooked together with roast beef.

Jerusalem Artichoke

The Jerusalem artichoke (*Helianthus tuberosus*) is from the sunflower family; it's not a relative of the globe artichoke at all. These perennial crunchy white tubers grow wild in the eastern part of the United States and Canada. Or they can be cultivated. In seed catalogs and stores, you might also see them called "crosne du Japon," girasole, Japanese artichoke, sunchoke, sunroot, and winter artichoke. Some

folks call them "chokes" for short, and I do too. Native Americans cultivated and used them for food. They do not suffer from any insect or disease—and can handily defeat any known weed in plant-to-plant combat. They can be an exceptionally useful food for diabetics since they are tasty and nutritious like potatoes.

Chokes are such prolific growers that they sometimes tend to take over the garden like a weed. But you can make use of that abundance. Dig your extras and feed them to the chickens, goats, or pigs. They are so easy to grow that you might want to plant extras on purpose to serve as part of your animal feed.

PLANTING: Choose an area of your garden where the choke's ambition to be the only vegetable in your entire garden can be curbed, where a 6–8-foot plant won't cause a problem by shading other plants, and where a perennial can live undisturbed. If you're starting a new patch, you'll need about 4 qt. of choke "seed" to plant a 50-foot row. You either plant them in rows, 1 seed every foot with 2 or 3 feet between your rows, or plant in "beds" about 4 × 4 feet, as some flowers grow. Plant 4 inches deep. You'll see the plants above dirt in 8–12 days.

Once the chokes get going, they'll choke the weeds. Give them a designated space and just let them grow as much as they want to in there. If you've planted some chokes last year, when spring comes they'll naturally start multiplying. You can either let them spread where they are or, if you must, dig them and replant in rows. To increase your artichoke crop quickly, cut them before planting, as you do with potatoes; that increases your "seed" amount. Just lay them one by one on a cutting board and cut an × on each one, which gives you 4 "seeds."

HARVESTING: It takes newly planted chokes about 130 days to be ready for harvest. The chokes look like small, light brown potatoes. Dig them anytime from after the first frost until spring, about October 1 to March 10, when the new growth starts. You could harvest about 1½ bushels per 50-foot row, but don't dig up too many at one time because they don't keep well.

STORING: Using a heavy mulch on chokes in the winter season will help prevent the ground from freezing and will make it easier for you when you want to dig some up. Freezing underground doesn't hurt the chokes, but it makes it kind of hard to dig them up. If you need to store them out of the garden, put them in plastic bags or in a container of damp sand. They keep best at 32–40°F, 90–95 percent humidity. But even so, chokes out of the garden will last only a few months. If you wash but don't peel and keep them in an airtight, refrigerator-type container or a plastic bag, they might last a month in your fridge.

TO PEEL OR NOT TO PEEL: That is the question. People can really get worked up over peelings. And so it is with Jerusalem artichokes: There are pro-peelers and anti-peelers. I don't think it makes a whole lot of difference, since if you have 'em, you have lots of 'em. But if you are an anti-peeler, just scrub well, remove any dark blemish, and slice off lumps. If you steam the chokes about 5 minutes, most of the skin will just slip off.

If you are a peeler, wash them thoroughly and then peel thinly with a vegetable peeler. If you're going to use them raw in salads, drop them into a bowl of cold water with some lemon juice or vinegar in it; otherwise they quickly turn black if exposed to the air. They can also be cooked in their skins and the skin removed after cooking. But if you boil them in the skins, you should remove the skins while they are quite hot, or you'll lose a lot of artichoke with them.

RECIPE IDEAS: Mix somewhat finely chopped cucumbers, 'chokes, apples, and nuts and moisten with mayonnaise for a kind of Waldorf salad. You can substitute them for water chestnuts or jicama in any recipe. Since they are free from starch, you can eat them uncooked. Raw Jerusalem artichokes are good grated or ground on a bed of lettuce with salad dressing and a bit of grated onion. Or served sliced and mixed in salads, where they taste like water chestnuts. Add to your salad dressing the leftover lemon juice that you marinated them in. Or cook them . . .

Boiling. Boil them quickly, since overcooking toughens them. Serve with a white sauce or a butter-lemon juice-parsley sauce. Chives and parsley really get along with artichokes.

Baking. First boil about 10 minutes. Then peel and arrange around the meat as you would potatoes, or put into a baking dish with dots of butter, salt, and pepper.

Pureeing. Cook until tender (in stock if you have it). Peel. Put through a sieve, or mash with a little butter and seasoning. (Garlic flavor is a good addition.)

Deep Frying. Cut into strips and fry in shallow oil until golden brown, or slice as thin as a penny and fry like potato chips in deep fat at 375°F.

⋙ *ARTICHOKE FRITTERS Dip chokes into a batter (mix egg, flour, milk, and salt) and fry in deep fat until golden brown.*

Jicama

Jicama, a Mexican vegetable, is also called "sincama," "sa gord," "yam bean," "Mexican potato," and "Mexican water chestnut." Its Latin name is *Pachyrhizus tuberosus*. The jicama sold in U.S. markets is a subtropical tuber (most suited for zones 9 and 10). It's the root of a climbing vine related to the legumes, so it also enriches your soil. Jicama resembles a flattish turnip both in its shape and in its white, crisp inside flesh. It tastes like a water chestnut crossed with an apple. (Good!) The best place to grow jicamas is in southern zones, where you can harvest as needed for months and an individual tuber may weigh up to 6 lb. However, gardeners everywhere except the most northern tier of states can grow tubers weighing at least ½ lb.

VARIETIES: The name jicama is used in South America and Mexico to mean the edible roots of several different plants. *Ipomoea bracteato* and *Exogonium jicama* are two of these from the morning glory family. *Dalia rosea* is a dahlia variety that Mexicans grow for its edible tuber as well as its lovely flowers. But the standard grocery-store jicama is *Pachyrhizus tuberosus* (also called *P. erosus*), a leguminous species. *P. tuberosus* itself has 2 varieties: jicama de agua, so called because its juice is clear, and jicama de leche, named for its milky juice.

PLANTING

NOTE: Jicama plant seeds are poisonous to humans and insects. The seeds contain rotenone, an organic insect poison that also kills fish, incidentally, so don't drop the seeds in your pond either. (You don't have to worry about bugs getting this crop!)

You can order jicama seeds from Exotica, Gurney, Hudson, Nichols, or Redwood City. Low-nitrogen soil is best for getting good roots rather than leafy growth. Plant outdoors on last frost date in coastal and southern areas. In northern climates, soak seed to speed germination; then start seed indoors in individual peat pots 4 to 8 weeks (or more) early —the colder your climate, the earlier you need to start them (120 days to harvest). Or plant in a large container.

GROWING: Keep moist until the plant is up. Transplant outside when the ground gets warm. In a short-season area, space plants about every ½ foot; the longer your season, the wider you should space the plants—up to a foot apart if you have a growing season as long as 7 months. In the south, the vines may grow 10 to 15 feet long. Consider providing a trellis or arbor for the glossy, heart-shaped leaves to climb. In the north, the plants will loaf until late summer and then take off, growing 10 to 15 feet in length, and make your harvest. This is a good plant to train up a trellis, arbor, or fence (plant 1 row on each side, staggered). It gets white or purple flowers (late in the season) and big, shiny, heart-shaped leaves. Pinch off every vine blossom to get the biggest, best-shaped jicama tubers. The plants need plenty of water to make crunchy roots. Mulching helps them. Water if they get dry under there.

HARVESTING

NOTE: Jicama flowers, leaves, seed pods, and seeds are all poisonous to humans—and also insects. The very young pods are not yet poisonous but develop poison as they mature. Keep the "beans" away from children. But there is absolutely no poison in the tubers.

Pinch off the first few flowers to save strength for later fruit. The longer your growing season, the bigger your jicamas will get. They can get up to grapefruit size and will still be juicy, slightly sweet, and good to eat. Start to harvest whenever you feel the roots are big enough to bother with, and continue harvesting as needed to season's end. In the tropics, you may still be harvesting as long as 2 years after you plant. In northern regions, the vines will die as the weather gets more chilly. Harvest before frost! If you do not wash them, jicamas will keep in a cool place (fridge or root cellar) up to a month.

USING: Jicama doesn't discolor after peeling and doesn't lose its crunchiness, so it's good for a vegetable tray. To prepare, peel thinly. Mexicans like them cubed and raw, sprinkled with red chili powder, lime juice, and salt. Or thinly slice and add to any variety of salad. Or cut into long sticks and dip into guacamole, or cook with a chicken or seafood stir-fry. Or boil, mash, and season with cilantro-flavored butter. Or cut in half, bake like a potato, and serve with chopped green onion and yogurt or sour cream. Or substitute in any recipe that calls for water chestnuts. When you have a big jicama, just cut off what you need and leave the rest for later. It keeps fine like that.

Lotus Root

The water lotus (*Nelumbo*) comes from Southeast Asia. A distant relative of the avocado, it is a perennial that can live in zones 5 to 10. (Don't let the roots freeze.) Seeds for *Nelumbo nucifera*, the Buddhist Sacred Lotus, are available from Deep Diversity. Lotus seeds remain fertile for hundreds of years. For quickest germination, you drill a tiny hole into the dense outside shell, wrap the seed in a lump of clay, and drop it into a body of shallow water such as a pool, a bog garden, or even a water container. Or propagate from rhizomes. It needs full sun.

RECIPE IDEAS: You harvest the edible, submerged, enlarged rhizomes that are strung together. Technically they aren't "roots," and they are not actually found underground. They grow along the top of the underwater soil. Their skin is reddish brown; the inside flesh is whitish-orange with holes. The texture is crunchy, the taste mild. The roots are best when young. To serve, peel raw lotus roots, slice across the width, and add to a salad. Or peel, cut into chunks, and add to any vetetable soup or stew. Or peel, cut into carrot-stick–type lengths, and add to any stir-fry. Or peel, boil, and mash. Or peel, slice, color with food coloring, and use to ornament other foods. Lotus leaves, flower petals, and seeds are edible too. Use leaves raw in salad or cooked as a green, but don't take too many off a plant.

Parsnip

The parsnip (*Pastinaca sativa*) is a member of the Apiaceae, or "carrot," family. It is just about the hardest-to-grow root vegetable. But parsnips are worth the trouble because of their winter-keeping ability. Parsnips come from northern Europe, and successfully growing them is just a matter of knowing what they need and giving it to them. A pale relative of the carrot, the parsnip resembles that vegetable in having a long tapered root (up to a foot long); smooth, light-colored skin; and a soft, sweet inside. More than any other vegetable in the garden (even the carrot), parsnips can handle and even thrive on being left in the garden all winter to be dug as needed. It's with soil, seed, and season that they have problems.

PLANTING

Soil. Parsnips need a deep, finely cultivated soil. If your soil is very sandy naturally, that makes it easy. They'll love it. If it's not, you have some work ahead of you. But the same manuring and composting treatment that benefits your other garden vegetables also helps parsnips. The parsnip patch in your garden needs more, though. You need to work the soil thoroughly, 1–1½ feet deep, getting out stones and such so the roots don't catch on them and get deformed and discouraged. A heavy clay soil is the hardest kind to get ready for parsnips. Working in extra cinders and compost will help make your soil loose and crumbly. You can work the soil without turning your good topsoil under and digging it to the bottom—it's good enough just to get the soil loose. Some people have grown parsnips 3 or 4 feet long for fun by digging the soil loose that deep and supplying plenty of manure-compost.

How to Plant. Parsnip seed doesn't keep well over a year or so. If it doesn't come up, the problem may be old seed. But don't despair too soon, because parsnip seed has the distinction of being slower to germinate, even under the best conditions, than any other kind of seed I know of. Figure on waiting 21 to 28 days after planting before you'll see something green above the ground! Parsnips must be planted very shallow and gently. They have trouble getting up if there is any sort of crust on your soil. Water well before you plant. Ideally plant ½ inch apart, although you can't possibly do that in real life because the seed is so fine. Cover very lightly, no more than ¼ inch deep. If you think the seeds need extra protection from birds or some such, add a ½-inch layer of peat moss or other light mulch, and remove it as soon as the parsnips begin to come up. In a short-summer climate, the right time to plant is immediately after your last frost date, since parsnips can't take the hot midsummer weather. Plant in the fall or early, early spring. The parsnip rows can be anywhere from 18 inches to 3 feet apart. If you choose 18 inches, be sure to get plenty of manure-compost into the soil.

Weeding and Thinning. Because parsnips are so slow to come up, you've got to do something extra to avoid losing them in weeds. So mix radish seed with your parsnip seed. The radish seed comes up fast and shows you where the parsnip row will be, and that makes it possible for you to cultivate and keep out the weeds without accidentally cultivating out your parsnips-to-be. After they get going, you can thin to 3 to 6 inches apart depending on how much space you can spare and how rich your soil is. Or let them go as long as you can and figure on eating the thinnings. Keep weeding faithfully all summer long.

HARVESTING

Saving Seed. Parsnip is an insect-pollinated biennial, so seed is made the second summer. Leave in the ground the ones you want to make seed, collect the seed when it's mature, and store for use. Collect parsnip seed generously, because you can't count on all the seed staying alive and germinating; having lots of extra seed is good insurance. Parsnip seeds stay viable only 1 to 2 years. (Also see "Saving Seed" under "Carrot.")

About Garden Frozen Parsnips. We rush sweet corn from garden to cooking pot because its abundant natural sugar starts changing to starch the minute it leaves the stalk. Parsnips reverse that process. They contain lots of starch which, when the plant freezes, changes to sugar! That's why you're ahead, tastewise, if you leave parsnips outside in the ground until after at least 3 weeks of frosty weather. Or you can leave them in the ground all winter, because more freezing only improves them. Tastewise they are best if left in the ground until spring. You can harvest them until they start to make new leaves. Then they'll get completely woody and inedible.

Digging. Basically, your harvest season for parsnips is from October to May. The technical problem is that you can't dig anything out of frozen ground but must do your harvesting during thaws; if you want parsnips and no thaw comes, you're out of luck. And you must *dig* parsnips. Pulling them is likely to result in a break at the halfway point of that long, skinny root. That's the advantage of some alternative preservation systems (see the next section). Or, after the first frosts, put a mulch over the parsnip row to keep it from freezing solid again.

PRESERVATION SYSTEMS

Root-Cellar Storage. Parsnips can be stored in a root pit: Lay right on the ground; cover with soil, then with straw or leaves, and then with a waterproof tarp or plastic. If you want to keep them in a root cellar, pack in moist soil. They will soon start to develop again in the spring. Then the roots all become too woody to eat. Or you can store dug-up parsnips between layers of damp sand in a tub in a cool outbuilding. Or preserve them by freezing or canning.

Freezing. About 50 lb. of parsnips will give you about 40 frozen pints. Trim off parsnip tops. Wash the roots well. Peel. Cut into ½-inch cubes or lengthwise into slices about ¾ inch thick. Scald 2 or 3 minutes. Cool in 2 successive ice-water baths. Package and freeze.

Drying. Avoid parsnips old enough to have a woody core. Slice or cut into chunks—or, easiest of all, shred with a salad maker. The shreds dry very quickly and evenly. Then you can reconstitute by overnight soaking and cook and eat. Or add to soups, stews, and casseroles. Or powder them and add to your instant vegetable soup mix.

COOKING: Generally speaking, you can catch parsnips at any of 3 stages. In the first, they are garden-fresh and young, starchy rather than sweet, but tender all through, without the woody center core that comes later. Stage 2 is when they are full grown and have their frost treatment but are still "young." Stage 3 is the "older parsnip."

Young Parsnips. Scrape rather than peel, wash, and French-fry or whatever. Some people like to eat parsnip tops, which taste a little like watercress and can be used in salads. Other people get an allergic reaction from wet parsnip leaves that blisters tender skin.

Older Parsnips. The large, older parsnips may taste better, but you've got a woody center core as well as a peel to get rid of. Really old parsnips get too woody to eat—you might as well let them go on and make seed. Boil unpeeled, washed parsnips until tender; it takes about 10 minutes for a 1-inch-wide parsnip. Now peel by skinning, as you would a potato, or run a razor blade the length of the parsnip, just cutting the skin, and roll out the vegetable. If the parsnip has a woody core, next slit it lengthwise down to the core and remove it. Or if you are going to cut the parsnip into sections, do that and then push the core out of each section.

Recipe Ideas. Serve boiled like carrots, with butter. Or bake 20 to 30 minutes at 350°F and serve with a brown-sugar glaze. Or add to a vegetable soup. Or cook slices in a frying pan with broccoli and other vegetables. Boiled parsnips are good served cold with mayonnaise. Or creamed. Cut in slices and brown in butter. Or add to any potato-turnip kind of stew or soup. Or mash and serve with salt, pepper, and butter. Or mash, season, and shape into cakes; lightly flour, fry till brown, and serve. Or glaze in a frying pan in a mixture of salt, pepper, butter, fruit juice, and brown sugar or honey. Or, instead of boiling, roast them in the jacket with meat as you would potatoes.

➤ *PARSNIP FRITTERS Boil 2 to 3 peeled and sliced parsnips in salted water. When tender, drain and dip parsnip chunks into a batter of ½ c. milk, 1 egg, ½ t. baking powder, a dash of salt, and enough flour to thicken batter to the consistency of griddle cakes. Fry in deep fat or cooking oil until golden brown. From Wilma Litchfield.*

Radish

Radishes are the vegetables that spring-starved fanatics get out and plant because they're early and quick—you might have the first ones to eat as soon as 3 weeks after planting. Children love to grow these brassica roots, because they grow so easily in a pot or outdoors. The quick red globe kinds are the most commonly grown, often to mark the rows of slower-germinating plants like carrots. Or you can plant them with parsnips or parsley; the robust radish sprouts help those frailer creatures break through the soil's crust. All parts of the radish are edible (but the leaves aren't usually eaten), and there's much you can do with them.

VARIETIES: *Raphanus sativus* is your basic radish, but there are many different varieties (red, white, yellow) with maturing dates ranging from 20 to 60 days. (Horseradish is not a radish.) The red radishes don't usually do as well once the days get short, but there are winter varieties that can be planted in the fall. Some radish varieties look and are used rather like turnips. One almost rootless variety is grown for its green top, which is used in salad, and one is grown for its seed pods! Every major Asian country developed its own favorite radish variety centuries ago, and Asians include radishes in their daily diet much more than we do. Available from Bountiful Gardens, Cook's Garden, Kitazawa (winters!), Nichols, Park, Shumway, and Territorial.

Red Radishes. The short "cherry" radish is the most familiar one in the United States: red skin, white flesh, green leaves, cherry-sized, quite hot. These are fast and easy, best for container growing. Use sliced (not peeled) in salads or as raw, edible garnishes. You can also boil them or add them to soup, as you would carrots. There are also long, red varieties. Use them raw like the small ones, or roast with meat, as you would turnips, or chop and saute them together with other vegetables.

White or "Winter" Radishes. These close relatives of the reds are generally larger, milder in flavor, harder to grow, and longer to mature. They also stay crisp longer—several weeks instead of several days. Icicle, a 4-inch white, is the quickest-to-mature long white; it straddles the categories of red and white. The other whites are the true "winter radishes," so called because they are often planted in mid- or late summer, harvested in fall, and stored during winter in damp sand. Winter radishes taste better cooked than the summer ones do. One of the best winter radishes is daikon.

Daikon. This is a very large (2–4 inches across, 6–20 inches long), white, Asian radish variety (*Raphanus sativus longi pinnatus.*) With its peppery taste (milder than the reds), it is the most popular Japanese vegetable, a fixture in Japanese cuisine. But writer Lane Morgan and some other folks say that daikon has a problem in the United States because it's so attractive to the cabbage-root-maggot butterfly. Plant in late summer (1 inch deep). They take a long time. Seeds are available from Cook's Garden, Johnny's, and Kitazawa. Harvest, store, and cook like any root vegetable.

Daikon contains diastase, a starch-digesting enzyme, so it goes well with a heavy-starch meal. Daikon leaves can be substituted in any cooked greens recipe. In Japanese edible art, daikon is carved into shapes such as a rectangular fish-net made of one continuous peeling of the daikon that is then laid over seafood dishes. The Japanese serve grated or slivered daikon with raw fish on rice (sushi) and with rice in general. Daikon can also be slivered and made into Instant Pickles (see recipe in "Cucumbers"). Or substitute in regular pickle recipes. Or use raw slices in green salad, stir-fry, or cook in soup.

Sakurajima. It takes 70 days to mature and needs as much room to grow as does a tomato plant. I've heard that a single specimen can get to 10, 20, or even 50 lb. in size. This variety is not eaten raw because it is extremely hot. Cook it turnip-style. Plant seeds 2 feet apart.

Lobak. This is a Korean radish, spicy rather than mild. It's white, with some pale green shading at base. It's as wide as a potato and is 6–8 inches long. You can cut into strips and serve with a dip, or use in the famous Korean relish called kim chee. It's good chopped into an omelet, sauteed as a side dish with carrots and onions, sliced in an avocado salad, or cooked in a soup.

Black Radishes. There is a Chinese black radish and a Black Spanish one. Some black radishes look like daikon (7–8 inches in length, 2–3 inches in diameter). Some are turnip-shaped. The black ones are also "winter radishes," so plant them like winter radishes and cook like turnips. Seed is available from William Dam.

Rat-Tail Radish. This "podding radish" is raised in order to harvest the long (9 inches or more!) seed pods, which develop late in the season. This is a very uncommon but fascinating-looking variety of radish. The seed pods are long and beanlike, but they are wide at one end and dwindle to a tip at the other. Rat-tail radishes are grown just like other radishes. Harvest after only a few weeks, while still tender. Use like edible-podded peas, or stir-fry or pickle them. The taste is moderately hot, like other radishes. Seed is available from Bountiful, Cook's Garden, and Seeds of Change.

PLANTING

When to Plant. Timing is critical to success with radishes. Reds can be planted as soon as the soil thaws and can be ready in 20 days. But wait to plant your salad crop until the lettuce that it will be served with is half-grown. Radish roots don't grow as well in summer's heat; compensate by planting late reds in a shady spot and mulching. Since reds don't last long, if you want a steady supply of radishes, you'll have to make successive plantings every 2 to 4 weeks —or else plant a combination of early-maturing and late-maturing varieties. The white winter radishes absolutely must be planted at such a time that they'll have cool weather when the root is maturing. Some varieties go entirely to leaf and seed and make hardly any root at all if they mature in summer instead of fall. But they can survive frosts. Plant about 8 weeks before the average date of your first fall frost.

How to Plant. Loose, humusy (but not nitrogen-rich) dirt is best for them. Fight root maggots by adding wood ashes to their soil and moving your radish plantings around. Plant ¼ to ½ inch deep. Red radishes don't need much room; plant 12 or more to an 8-inch container. Six-inch-deep soil is enough. They're soon grown and harvested, so just tuck them in anywhere. Let your density in planting be guided by expected radish size. Try to plant red radishes 2 inches apart; they'll end up closer, because the seed is so small and hard to control. Plant winter radishes 3–4 inches apart. They'll be up in 3 to 6 days. Thin enough so they have room to grow without deforming each other. The exact distance depends on how big a root you're expecting. If you're cramped for space, make your red-radish rows as close as 6 inches, your winter-radish rows 1½ foot apart.

Water. Poor soil or dryness slows up radishes' growth and can cause tough roots that are too hot. So for mildest radishes, keep their soil damp. With winter radishes, dryness results in woody as well as tough texture. If water is scarce, planting them in a comparatively shady spot helps keep their soil moist.

HARVESTING

Saving Seed. Radishes are bee-pollinated and self-incompatible; they may cross between varieties blooming within ¼ mile. The reds are annuals, the winters biennial. It can be hard to get seed unless there are plenty of bees, weather

under 90°F, and reasonable moisture. Radishes left in the ground past their prime soon send up a stalk, flower, and then form seed pods. Discard the early bolters. Let the seed pods develop, ripen, and dry on the stalk. If the stalk looks fragile, you can stake it to keep from losing the seed in case it falls over onto the ground. Then harvest the seed pods by breaking off the stalks. Don't open until you can rattle the seeds around in the pod. If they aren't dry enough to rattle, continue drying pods in a shady, airy place out of direct sunlight. Once dry enough to rattle, the pods will be easy to open. Spread out the seeds and continue drying. When completely dried, store in an envelope or jar marked with radish variety and year saved. Store in a dry place. They stay viable about 4 or 5 years. Radish sprouts have a nice pungent flavor. (Also see "Saving Seed" under "Carrot.")

Harvesting. Red radishes are one of the quickest-growing vegetables, about 50 days to harvest. But they have to be pulled, washed, and used promptly when they reach their prime—tender and young—which is soon gone, leaving them too pithy and soft to be very good. You can combine thinning with harvesting. Take the fattest ones early in the season, leaving the slower ones to catch up. Reds store best right in your fridge and will last up to a month.

Winter radishes can be pulled young and used like the reds (that's a good way to thin them). Once winter radishes mature, you have about 3 weeks before they lose their prime in the garden. After that, they gradually get tougher.

PRESERVING

Storing. So although winter radishes will survive if left in well-mulched ground to winter, they're normally dug up and stored in a root cellar. Digging them up stops the toughening process. Store winter radishes between layers of moist sand in a box or tub. (See "Introduction to Roots.") Or freeze them. You can also preserve red or winter radishes by drying or canning, but people usually don't bother.

Freezing. For winter radishes: Wash, peel, stir-fry briefly, package, and freeze. Good as a buttered vegetable and in stews, soups, and stir-fry dishes.

Drying. Wash, trim off top and root, and slice ⅛ inch thick. Spread over drying trays and dry until brittle. Good broken up into small pieces and scattered over a salad. Or use them like "chips" for dipping. Or add boiling water, simmer till tender, season, and serve.

Canning. Follow directions for canning carrots.

➢ *ROSY RADISH RELISH From Cathy Tate, a supergardener from Keller, WA: Makes 2½ pt. Use 3 c. stemmed radishes, 2 large ribs celery, 1 large mild red onion, 2 t. salt, 1 c. sugar, 1 T. mustard seed, 2 T. dill seed, ½ t. celery salt, and 1 c. cider vinegar. Put the radishes, celery, and onion through the coarse blade of a grinder, or chop them finely. Mix with the remaining ingredients and allow to stand for 3 hours. Bring to a boil in a large pan and cook 5 minutes. Pour hot into half-pint or pint jars, leaving ½ inch headspace. Process in boiling-water bath. At up to 1,000 feet above sea level, process 30 minutes; at 1,001–3,000 feet, 35 minutes; 3,001–6,000 feet, 40 minutes; and above 6,000 feet, 45 minutes.*

RAW RADISHES: My family enjoys occasional raw radishes, especially the first few batches from the garden. They're good plain or dipped in salt or mayonnaise. Radishes are also good grated or sliced thin in a tossed salad. You can add sliced raw radish to cucumber or tomato sandwiches on homemade or dark store bread. But with the first exciting appearance of radishes at the table, I go all out and make radish roses.

Radish Roses. Choose round radishes without blemishes. Wash. Trim off the roots and part of the stalk, leaving on a few of the best-looking short leaves. With a sharp knife, starting at the root end, peel down the red skin. Make about 5 of these "petals." Once you have the knack, the petals will open right out as you peel—the trick is to get them the right thickness and width. Experiment!

Radish Mouse. Cut off the widest end. Leave the other for the tail. Cut 2 ears (radish-rose–style). Stick in 1 large clove for the mouth and 2 very small ones for the eyes. Stick in a toothpick for the tail.

➤ *BRAISED RADISHES Also from Cathy Tate: Take 2 T. butter, 2 c. sliced radishes, 1 bouillon cube, ¼ c. hot water, ⅛ t. ground marjoram, and salt. Melt butter in saucepan, add radishes, and cook 5 minutes. Stir frequently. Dissolve bouillon in hot water (or substitute ¼ c. beef broth), add to radishes, and simmer 3–4 minutes. Add marjoram and serve as a hot vegetable.*

➤ *CREAMED RADISHES If you're still having trouble using up your radishes (I don't know any families who can eat all the radishes they can grow!), make this dish. It also makes use of your large, strongly flavored radishes. Wash, pare, and slice the radishes to about about 1½ cups. Boil until tender. Make a white sauce from 2 T. flour, 2 T. fat, 1 c. milk, salt, and pepper. Mix the sauce with the radishes and serve.*

➤ *RUTH'S VEGAN CREAMED RADISHES Steam radishes 5 minutes instead of boiling them. Make white sauce of 1 c. water or rice milk and ¼ c. whole wheat flour. (Toast flour over dry heat, remove, whisk in liquid, and then return to low heat, stirring occasionally till thickened.) Season with basil, tarragon, and/or marjoram.*

➤ *FRIED WINTER RADISH Cut into long strips. Dip each strip into beaten egg, then into crumbs, and then fry it.*

➤ *WINTER RADISH GREENS The greens of radishes are edible, especially those of winter radishes. Cut; throw out the stems and imperfect leaves. Wash and slice into salad-sized chunks or strips. Substitute in cooked leafy greens recipes.*

Rutabaga

The rutabaga (*Brassica napobrassica*), called "Swede" or "Swedish turnip" in England, is a cross between a turnip and a wild cabbage. It was created back in the Middle Ages. Rutabagas don't like hot weather and are a natural northern vegetable, good in the northern United States and cooler parts of Canada. Grow them as you would turnips, although they get bigger (4–5 inches wide) and take about a month longer to mature. They're fairly hardy but dislike heat.

PLANTING: Seed is available from William Dam, Territorial, etc. Like any root vegetable, rutabagas like a well-tilled, fertile soil. If you plant in early spring (good started in a cold frame), they'll probably do well for you unless you have a very hot summer. Hot weather during the later part of their growth causes big tops but small, tough roots. If you plant in June to mid-July, they'll mature in the cool, fall weather, and that will be better for them if you have a hot summer. Plant ¼–½ inch deep; thin to 8 inches apart

(crowded rutabagas don't get big), rows 2 feet apart. Expect 5 to 10 days to germination and about 90 days to harvest. They're pretty tough about frost; like parsnips, a light frost sweetens them. So wait to harvest them until after a few of those frosts. Or else mulch heavily so they don't freeze, and you'll be able to dig as needed.

HARVESTING AND PRESERVING: Harvest anytime you want to, once they're big enough to bother. The biggest roots are better livestock food than people food. Light frosting of the top growth improves the flavor, but freezing of the root gives it a bad flavor and shortens its keeping time.

Saving Seed. Rutabagas are biennial and bee-pollinated, and they will cross, just like beets and turnips, which are biennials too. Mulch to keep the plant alive over winter. Take off the cover early in spring. Seed lives about 5 years.

Storing. Store in a cellar the same way you would a turnip. Rutabagas store 2 to 6 months in any cool, moist darkness—a cellar, a pit, or a big box with sand, sawdust, moss, or dirt in it. If you have a crop and decide you don't like them, feed them to your cows, goats, etc. They will love them and the rutabagas can provide a substantial part of their winter nourishment.

Freezing. Harvest rutabagas while very young, small, and tender. Remove tops, wash, peel, and cut into ½-inch cubes. Scald 2 minutes, chill, and package. To cook them, just thaw, mash, and season.

Drying. Wash, peel, slice ⅛ inch thick, spread on trays, and dry until crisp. Eat dried slices plain, with dip, or chopped in salad or soup. Or pour boiling water over them and simmer until tender. Then mash and season.

COOKING. Store-bought rutabagas have usually been dipped in wax for preservation. Peel. They're good grated raw in salads. Or cook like turnips, but longer. Use in any winter soup or stew. Or cook and mash, or bake in pies, custards, and baked goods (substitute for pumpkin or squash in recipes). Or serve cooked with cream and nutmeg mashed in. Or boil, dice, and use in a veggie salad. Or roast with meat and other veggies.

Salsify

Salsify (*Tragopogon porrifolius*), also called "oyster plant" or "vegetable oyster" in old-time cookbooks, is a very hardy biennial of the family Compositae, grown for its long white root. The roots are hairy and off-white—not much to look at, not very sweet, but flavorful in a different way. Salsify is grown much like parsnips and has all the same problems. In addition, if salsify likes your climate, you have a problem of overabundance if you let it get away from you and do some self-seeding. Then it deserves the name of weed.

PLANTING: In the south, plant in summer for a winter crop. But if you plant before June or July in a warm climate, you may get seed instead of root, even though it is technically a biennial. In the north, plant in April, because it takes 120 to 150 days for the roots to get big enough that there's something left after the peeling. It's also good to plant early, because later plantings have a poorer germination rate. Seed is available from Thompson & Morgan, etc. Plant in very loose, well-tilled soil so that the long, slim roots can find their way down. Plant ½ inch deep, 2 inches apart (thickly due to poor germination); thin later to 6 inches apart. Salsify doesn't like soakings, so don't water unless it's truly bone-dry. Be careful when weeding so that you don't pull out your salsify plants, mistaking them for grass—which is just what salsify plants look like!

SAVING SEED: Salsify is a self-pollinated biennial with "perfect" flowers (meaning they have both male and female parts). You don't need to worry about it crossing with something. Choose the best of your roots to raise seed from in the spring. If your plants are crowded, replant at least a foot distant from each other and in rows 3 feet apart. In its second year, salsify shoots up to 4 feet or higher. In June it grows sizable purple blooms, which are followed by feathered seeds (like those of dandelions). *Don't let salsify seeds get away from you. That's how it can turn into a weed.* Choose your seed heads to save. Harvest in the morning. Dry a few days. Rub those dried heads between your hands to loosen and separate out their seeds. Winnow to clean. The seeds will keep for at least 2 years.

HARVESTING AND PRESERVING: The part you eat is the long, tapering white root; when boiled, mashed, and fried it supposedly has an oyster flavor. At maturity the roots are at least 8 inches long and an inch thick. They don't have their best flavor until they've been through frost, although the youngness, freshness, and tenderness of smaller ones right from the garden can make up for that.

Winter Storage. You can store salsify as you would beets, carrots, or parsnips, but out of the ground it has a tendency to shrivel. The best way of all to store salsify is to leave it right where it is growing. It can survive the winter right in the garden, even as far up as northern Vermont. But put over it a mulch, like a bunch of straw. That will keep the ground from freezing so hard that you can't dig up your salsify. Or you can dig it up in the spring. Or if you're leaving and want to take your salsify with you, dig up the roots, leave 1½ inches of stalk on them, and store between layers of damp sand in a root cellar. To store in the fridge, wash but don't peel. They'll keep several weeks.

Drying. Clean and scrub or peel salsify. Make ⅛-inch slices and then either dip them into mixture of 1 T. lemon juice per 1 qt. water, blanch about 3 minutes in boiling water, or steam about 4 minutes. Dry slices in a single layer in a dehydrator or oven at 120°F for about 18 hours. They're done when crisp. Or dry in full sun about 2 days (take inside overnight). Use plain as a snack, toss dried chips in salad, or grate for casserole topping. Or reconstitute with boiling water and simmer till tender.

COOKING: If the salsify is garden-fresh, just scrub the roots, scrape them, and boil or steam in a covered pan until they are fork-tender (10 to 20 minutes). With old or store-bought salsify, use 1 T. lemon juice in the boiling water to prevent darkening. After cooking till tender, serve with lemon juice. Or drain, season with butter, salt, pepper, and parsley if you have it. Or cover with a white sauce.

➤ *SALSIFY GREENS You can cook the fresh, slender leaves of spring using any cooked greens recipe. Or use raw in a salad.*

➤ *QUICK SALSIFY FRITTERS Mash cooked, seasoned salsify and shape into cakes. Roll the cakes in flour and brown in butter.*

➤ *RUTH'S SALSIFY FRITTERS Mash steamed salsify with tamari. Shape into cakes and fry on a skillet rubbed with a raw potato.*

➤ *MOCK FRIED OYSTERS Wash, trim, and cook a bunch*

of salsify in boiling salted water until tender. Drain and scrape off the skin. Mash. (If stringy, put mash through a colander.) For every 2 c. mashed salsify, add 1 t. flour, 1 T. butter, 1 beaten egg, salt, and pepper. Take a spoonful and shape it into an "oyster." Dip the oyster in flour or cracker crumbs. Brown in butter on each side in the frying pan.

➤ *CREAM OF SALSIFY SOUP Cook at least 3 salsify roots until tender. In another pan melt ¼ c. butter or margarine. Stir in ¼ c. flour. Gradually add 3 c. milk. Cook until thickened (stir constantly). Add salsify and seasonings (salt, pepper, and/or herbs) to taste.*

Scorzonera

Not only does *Scorzonera hispanica* come after "Salsify" in this alphabet of roots, but this long, slender root also tastes, looks, and is grown much like salsify. They are botanically related, although not as closely as scorzonera's other names of "black salsify" and "black oyster plant" would make you think. Like salsify, scorzonera is biennial, has leaves that look like a clump of grass, originated in the Mediterranean area, can grow throughout the United States, was used by the Romans and Greeks, and is important in Spanish and Russian cooking.

How is scorzonera different from salsify? *Scorzonera, like Jerusalem artichokes, contains inulin and can be a good carbohydrate food for diabetics.* It has yellow dandelion-like flowers rather than salsify's purple, and its roots are longer, straighter, and thinner. It's dark-colored rather than whitish on the outside, and it's brown inside. Scorzonera produces somewhat bigger harvests than salsify. You can order scorzonera seed from William Dam, DeGiorgi, Johnny's, or Redwood City.

HARVESTING: If you leave scorzonera roots in the ground for 2 growing seasons rather than just one, no harm is done and your roots will be bigger when you do harvest (as long as 18 inches). Be careful not to accidentally cut off the bottom section of that long, thin, straight root that just goes down and down. Also be careful not to break, scratch, or scrape the root because scorzonera "bleeds" through any such cut and literally loses flavor. The leaves are also edible and can be chopped and added to salads. It discolors when cut, so have ready some water or marinade with lemon juice or vinegar in it. Scrub the outside of the root well, but don't peel it; peeling seriously diminishes the flavor. If there is any bitterness, soaking in water before cooking will help. Cook and drain; *only then do you rub off the skin.*

RECIPE IDEAS: If your variety of scorzonera has a bitter taste, scrubbing the roots and soaking in water before cooking should help that. Scorzonera usually tastes much like salsify, with the same sweet flavor, and can be substituted in any salsify recipe. It takes about 45 minutes to cook to tenderness. Cook with carrots and potatoes/onions, or boil in any soup or stew. Or serve pureed with milk and butter, like mashed potatoes. Or serve plain, boiled scorzonera with melted butter or a white sauce. Or bake or fry it. Or thinly slice and serve in a vinegar marinade like instant pickles. Or cook first; then slice thin and marinate in that vinegar sauce.

➤ *GOURMET SCORZONERA Preheat oven to 400°F. Steam 2 lb. peeled scorzonera until tender (about 8 minutes). Remove from heat and dice when cool enough to han-*

dle. Mix together scorzonera and 1 medium minced onion, and spoon into greased casserole. Melt 2 T. butter in small pan. Stir in 1 T. flour and simmer 1 minute. Add 1 c. sour cream (heavy or light), plus salt and pepper to taste. Heat gently. Don't let it boil. Spoon cream sauce over vegetables and toss lightly to blend. Sprinkle with grated Swiss cheese and crumbs. Bake 15 to 20 minutes and serve. From Lane Morgan's Winter Harvest Cookbook (Sasquatch Books, 1990).

Skirret

Skirret (*Sium sisarum*) is part of the Apiaceae family (carrot, parsley, etc.). An Asian vegetable, it was discovered and adopted in Europe by the time of the Roman Empire, but it's little-known and seldom grown in the United States. Also called "zuckerwurzel," "crummock," and "suikerwortel" in Europe, skirret is a hardy perennial whose edible portion is a cluster of thick, knobby, grey roots that hang down under its crown, kind of like a handful of carrots, so you get about 8 roots from a plant instead of just one.

PLANTING: Skirret can be started from seed or from root divisions, but in the United States it's usually started from seed. Seed available from Nichols. Plant seed toward the end of March or early April for a fall crop. Plant in well-tilled, loose (sandy is best) soil. Plant in the autumn to get a spring harvest. Plant sparsely. Keep seedbed moist until germination. Once you can see what you've got, thin to about a foot apart. Weed and water like carrots. Because the leafy aboveground part of the skirret plant is so sparse, it doesn't shade its neighbors and does fine interplanted with something like lettuce, which will grow and get out of there.

To make root cuttings, follow the instructions for horseradish propagation (in Chapter 5) since, like that plant, skirret makes thin side roots which, once they develop an "eye" or "bud," can then be cut off and planted separately any time of year.

HARVESTING: Spring-planted skirret will be ready around October. Basically, you wait to harvest until the roots are big enough. Skirret is like salsify in that cool fall weather actually improves the crop and the roots get sweeter after frost. Also like salsify, you can leave skirret roots in the garden all winter, digging them up as needed. Or dig in the fall and store like carrots. The colder it is (short of freezing), the better skirret keeps.

COOKING: Clean the roots. Prepare like a carrot or parsnip, except also remove the woody core before cooking. Then boil and serve with butter. Or substitute in salsify or parsnip recipes. Or add to soup or stew. Or mash like potatoes. Or serve like broccoli, with a cheese sauce. Or grate and toss with a salad, like turnips or carrots.

Turnip

Seventh edition. After 2 months of hard work I'm nearing the end of the rewrite of this chapter. As of this moment I'm alternating typing with my new baby, Jacob, on my lap with not typing and holding him on my shoulder and patting him. He is just about the fussiest baby I've ever had. He has a bit of diarrhea, which is getting better, and a bit of a rash, and he sneezes several times a day. It's enough to keep me a nervous wreck. He sure is husky though. The more they yell, the more quickly the lungs and limbs get strong. That's true, if a small comfort, when you're trying to make a squally baby happy.

Turnips (*Brassica rapa*) are easy to grow and good for high altitudes and chilly climates (but switch to rutabaga in the coldest zones). In the South, turnips are a good winter vegetable. You can eat the top for greens. We really like the taste of turnip, both raw and cooked.

WHEN TO PLANT: Turnips have maturing times anywhere from 35 to 70 days. Turnips hate hot weather, especially hot nights, so plant either an early crop, about 35 days before the last spring frost date, or a late one (plant in July or August). If you try to grow turnips through a hot summer, you're likely to get a stringy, strong-tasting root. The late turnips won't be bothered as much with wireworms, and they are the only crop suitable for root-cellar storage. If you live in a really mild-wintered area, plant in late fall for a winter crop.

HOW TO PLANT: Prepare fertile, deeply cultivated soil. Turnips like wood ashes too. Plant seed ¼ inch deep and an inch or so apart, 5 to 10 days to germination. If you have really rich soil and are short of garden space, you can put rows of turnips as close as a foot apart or do intensive planting. In containers, plant about 3 in each 12-inch pot. To plant an acre of them (they're good winter animal feed), broadcast-sow and rake lightly to cover. Then give a good watering. When your turnips are 4 to 6 inches high, or when they start to crowd one another while trying to grow, start thinning—to about 6 inches apart. You can eat the thinnings . . . or freeze or can them.

HARVESTING

Saving Seed. Turnips are bee-pollinated, self-incompatible, biennial roots that easily cross with many other brassicas: turnip, radish, rape, mustard, rutabaga, Chinese cabbage, and the wild varieties of turnip and mustard. You're safe from crossing only if your seed bearers are not within ¼ mile of any of those related plants while both are flowering. But the problem the first year is to get the parent plant through the winter. In the coldest zones, dig and store the root, and then replant the next spring. In warmer areas, mulch and leave it in the garden. Allow 18 inches between seeding plants. After seed pods become yellow, cut the stalk and manage like cabbage. Turnip seed is very strong; with care it should keep its germinating power for 5 years or more.

Digging. Turnips can stand some frost. They'll keep on growing if you have some decent weather after the first frost. But the nicest ones for people food are no bigger than 3 inches in diameter. In very mild winter areas you can leave them in the ground and dig as needed until the weather gets so warm that they start to grow again, which ruins them for eating. Turnips can stand top frosting, but alternate freezing and thawing of the root will ruin them. After digging, cut off the tops. Definitely harvest before a hard freeze, or if the tops look yellow and withered.

STORING AND PRESERVING

Ground, Pit, or Cellar Storage. I have neighbors who raise huge, lovely turnips and store them in a root cellar. To do this, leave them in the ground until it's time for a heavy freeze. Then dig up—don't wash!—and store undamaged ones in a vegetable pit or root cellar. If your storage place is too warm, they may start to grow and get pithy. They'll keep 2 to 4 months. Turnips and rutabagas have an odor in storage that can affect celery.

Freezing. Because of my wireworm troubles, I harvest all my turnips early, peel, cut into chunks, blanch a few minutes, cool, bag, and freeze. When I want them, I just turn them out of the bag into a little water and thaw. I usually serve them mashed with a little butter and seasoning.

Canning. Use instructions under "Beet."

Drying. Use young, tender turnips. Peel, thinly slice, shred, or make into ¼-inch cubes. Spread on tray and dry at 120°F until hard and crisp. Use slices as a snack with with dip. Add dried bits to salad. If broken up in a blender, it can be added to any casserole or meat loaf. Or add to soup. Or reconstitute by pouring boiling water over and simmering till tender.

RECIPE IDEAS

Raw Turnips. These are good sliced thin and dipped into a seasoned sour-cream dressing (let each person do their own dipping) or served grated with such a dressing. Turnip slices are good with carrot sticks and celery; the sharper taste of the turnip slices complements the blander vegetables. I also love turnip grated, added to a tossed green salad, and served with a dressing.

➣ *TURNIP SLAW Prepare 4 c. pared and shredded turnips and 2 cored and diced red apples. Mix with 2 T. chopped parsley and 2 T. minced onion. Stir together ½ c. sour cream, 1 T. vinegar, 1 T. honey, and salt and pepper to taste. Combine dressing with vegetables.*

Cooked Turnips. Cook turnip greens like any cooked greens. Turnip roots can be eaten from 1 inch in diameter on up. Cook small ones whole. Slice larger ones about ½ inch thick. Small turnips can be cut into wedges and used in a stir-fry. Cook larger ones by steaming or boiling until tender enough to pierce with a fork. Serve plain or with lemon juice or tamari drizzled over cut surfaces while hot. Or add to any sort of potato, cabbage, or meat dish. Or make a pea-carrot-turnip soup. Or serve sliced cooked turnips with cream or a white sauce. Or cook in just enough stock or consomme to cover, and save liquid; take out and mash turnips, return them to the liquid, and simmer until all is absorbed. Or peel, slice, blanch, briefly precook, and then bake ½ hour in a sauce of dry mustard, brown sugar, maple syrup, salt, and pepper. Or roast with meat and other vegetables. Or wash and wipe turnips (but don't peel), bake until tender, peel, and serve either mashed or with a white sauce.

Water Chestnut

The water chestnut (*Eleocharis dulcis*) is a Chinese aquatic plant distantly related to chufa. You harvest the brown- or black-colored base of the stem, a corm. This tender perennial (suited for zones 7–10) will need protection from winter cold. Propagate by planting offsets (offshoots). Plant in a pool, a bog garden, or a large container of water. Harvest the corms in the fall. They're delicious fresh. If you blanch them, the skin easily comes off. To preserve the white color, store in water that has a little lemon juice or vinegar added. This vegetable stays crisp even when cooked. Serve raw sliced in a veggie salad, or plain with dip. Or add to an omelet, a soup, or a stir-fry dish (good with green beans).

Buy this and other wonderful aquatic plants from:

Lilypons Water Gardens: 800-999-5459; fax 800-879-5459; PO Box 10, 6800 Lilypons Rd., Buckeystown, MD 21717-0010; **info@lilypons.com; www.lilypons.com.**

Van Ness Water Garden: 800-205-2425; 909-982-2425; fax 909-949-7217; 2460 N. Euclid Ave., Upland, CA 91786-1199; **vnwg@vnwg.com; www.vnwg.com.**

Wicklein's Water Gardens: 800-382-6716; PO Box 9780, Baldwin, MD 21013; **sales@wickleinaquatics.com; www.wickleinaquatics.com/.**

THE GOURD FAMILY

These are squashes, melons, and cukes. Botanically, the gourds' closest relatives are the brassicas, that other great cluster of related food plants. Along with bean and cereal crops, edible gourds were humankind's first cultivated crops. Squashes, pumpkins, and chayote, developed by the civilizations of the ancient Americas, are now grown worldwide. Watermelon and muskmelon originated in Eurasia and Africa. They're all part of what's variously called the gourd family, "gourds" (but the gourds technically are an ornamental kind of squash), cucurbits (Latin for the squash portion of the family), or "melons" (another subdivision of the family). (Are you confused yet?) Most cucurbits are tropical perennials grown as annuals, so they generally won't germinate if your soil is cold and wet, although squashes are more tolerant of cold than the others.

Botanical Groups and Seed Saving

There are 3 main botanical groups of cucurbits (gourds):

- Squashes: Species of the *Cucurbita* genus, including all the squashes (summer, winter, and exotic) and pumpkins
- Melons: Netted and smooth-skinned muskmelons (*Cucumis melo*) and watermelon (*Citrullus lanatus*)
- Cucumbers: *Cucumis sativus,* including citron and all the cucumber varieties

SQUASHES: Seed saving is most complicated with the squash group because the group doesn't subdivide in a simple way. But you'll be able to save seed if you have just one kind each of *C. pepo* and *C. maxima* flowering at once. Or grow them at least 500 feet apart. Remove seed from *ripe* fruit, wash away the pulp, and spread out to dry. (See "Saving Seed" section in "Cucumbers.") If stored in a cool place, they will survive up to 7 years. To help you better understand what will and will not cross, here are the squashes' botanically based subdivisions.

Cucurbita maxima. All the big, hard-shelled winter squashes (Hubbards, Marblehead, Chestnut, and Sweetmeat), the giant types of pumpkins (Hungarian Mammoths, Big Macs, Buttercup, Boston Marrow, Delicious, Turban, etc.), and the Japanese varieties (Green Hokkaido, Orange Hokkaido, and Red Kuri).

These will not cross with *C. pepo* but will cross with each other and with *C. moschata.* The *C. maxima* members need a little more warmth to sprout and take several weeks more to mature (about 120 days) than do *C. pepo* members. They have the nicest seeds for eating, bigger vines, larger leaves, and a soft, round, hairy stem. If you don't get them completely mature, the seed won't germinate well and the flesh won't taste as good as it could. If thoroughly cured after harvest, they have very good storing qualities and maintain their quality and smooth texture all winter.

Cucurbita mixta. Less-familiar Asian varieties (cushaw squashes, certain tropical pumpkins). Will cross with each other and with *C. pepo.*

Most of the members of the gourd family have trailing ("running") vines with large, lobed leaves and pretty white or yellow edible flowers. Every year we set aside a big section of the garden for these vine-type crops that are planted in hills instead of rows—the cucumbers, watermelons, muskmelons, pumpkins, and summer and winter squashes. But space is a problem for lots of people, so some squashes now come in "bush" varieties, which have smaller fruits but don't spread out as far.

Or you can hold back the vines by picking off their fuzzy, growing tip. Not only do you save space, but you may increase fruit production and speed up fruit ripening if you continuously take off all the fuzzy ends starting in August. And they're edible. Use in any greens recipe.

Another method of compensating for the space the vines need stems from the fact that they start slowly, so it's a long time before they need all that space between the rows. You can grow early beans or peas between the squash rows and

then take them out after your harvest in June or July, when the cucurbits are starting to seriously run.

Or send the vines up instead of across by providing a trellis or pole. In that case, you tie the plant to the support at about 1-foot intervals, or just twist its stem gently around the support. Some will climb on their own. If you plant cukes next to chicken wire or staple the wire to poles next to the young plants, they will climb it as they grow.

4 | GARDEN VEGETABLES

Cucurbita moschata. Butternut, melon squash, and calabaza. These will cross with each other and with *C. maxima* and *C. pepo.* They are long-maturing (120 to 130 days) for seed or flesh and generally require even more heat than *maxima* or *pepo,* getting fully ripe only in the southern zones. They have a 5-sided corky but smooth stem, which flares out at the site where it meets the fruit.

Cucurbita pepo. All the summer squashes (crooknecks, zucchini, etc.), some winter squashes (acorn, Delicata, Benning's, Green Tint, Vegetable Gourd, Vegetable Spaghetti, White Bush Scallop, and Gem), common orange Halloween pumpkins, the lagenarias (including cocozelles and ornamental gourds), and 2 Japanese varieties (Hyuga Black and Kikuza White).

C. pepo members will not cross with *C. maxima* members, but they will cross with each other and with *C. moschata* and *C. mixta* members. *C. pepo* members have small seeds and are quickest to mature (about 90 days), thus best for northern gardeners. They come in bush or vine and have a 5-sided stem like *C. moschata,* 5-sided branches, and spines. For winter storage, the winter squash–type *C. pepo* members (such as acorns and pumpkins) don't require as much curing as *C. maxima* members, but they also don't keep their good flavor or texture longer than a couple of months.

CUCUMBERS: The cucumbers don't cross with any of the others, only with each other and with citron. Grow different cucumber varieties 1,000 feet apart, or hand-pollinate. Seeds are ripe only when fruit is dead-ripe and yellow. (See "Saving Seed" section in "Cucumbers.")

MELONS: The netted-skin cantaloupes don't cross with the smooth-skinned muskmelons, and neither cantaloupes nor muskmelons cross with watermelons, so you can raise all of these three in the same garden for seed. Seeds are ripe when the fruit is ripe enough to eat. (See "Saving Seed" section in "Cucumbers.")

Pollination and Flower Eating

Cucurbits usually have both male and female flowers on each plant, but sometimes plants have only one sex of flower, so always plant at least three to be sure they'll fruit. Another potential difficulty is that all cucurbits are bee-pol-

linated, and bees are sometimes scarce nowadays due to pesticide spraying. Lack of bees results in small or poorly shaped fruit or no fruit. If you have no bees, the only way to get a crop is to hand-pollinate.

HAND-POLLINATING CUCURBITS: There are 2 kinds of blossoms: males and females. You can tell a male by its thin stem. The female is bright yellow and generally has a tiny cucumber or pumpkin or such already formed at its base. When a male blossom is so full of ripe pollen that some will dust off on your fingertip, cut off the blossom and carefully touch the sticky stigmas in the center of each female blossom with this pollen. That solves your problem. There are typically more male than female flowers—although some recently developed plants have only female flowers (are "gynoecious"), and they bear more fruit.

CUCURBIT BLOSSOM RECIPE IDEAS: Fried squash blossoms are a traditional native American delicacy. But all the cucurbits have edible blossoms. If you pick only the male flowers (the ones with long, thin, upright stems), you won't be depriving yourself of any fruit.

➽ *SQUASH BLOSSOM FRITTERS From Jan Franco, Hamden, CT, who also wrote me these beautiful words: "I used to work in a library, and I love books and used to buy them when possible—being especially partial to anything with 'complete' in the title. Well, my husband says this is the first truly 'complete' book I have, because it's the only one that includes the most important topic: the Lord, in addition to all the self-sufficiency information. After all, no matter how self-sufficient we may be, we're all dependent on Him . . .*

"Pick a dozen or so male flowers. Pick at a time when the flowers are open to make sure there are no bees trapped inside. Make a batter from 1 egg, ¾ c. whole wheat (or white) flour, 1 t. baking powder, and a little milk. Coat the flower with batter and fry in a little oil until lightly browned. Yum. Also can be frozen; warm it in the oven. We use flowers from zucchini or pattypan squash. An Italian favorite!"

➽ *STUFFED BLOSSOMS Lane Morgan says, "You also can stuff blossoms with cheese and herbs before frying. Just sort of twist the flower tips into a spiral to hold the stuffing in."*

Eating Cucurbit Seeds

Originally, the flesh of the squashes was inedible. Students of ancient humankind think that the first parts of the squash plants that were eaten were the seeds. The seeds of almost any mature, large-seeded squash can be dried, roasted, and eaten. But over centuries, Incan, Mayan, and Toltec gardeners gradually selected the most promising seeds until they got the familiar edible-fleshed squashes.

The problem is shelling them. Some people chew and eat them shells and all, but they taste sort of woody that way. But modern seed savers have taken squash seed evolution one step farther, and now we have the Lady Godiva variety, whose seeds have no shells!

The following recipes will work with any *large* cucurbit (or gourd family) seeds.

PUMPKIN SEEDS My friend Jeanie gave me this recipe. She used to live in the Bronx, and now she lives down the road with her husband, mother, father, sister, and sister's husband. Open the pumpkin and remove the seeds. Let the seeds dry for 2 days. They can be spread on a tray or on newspaper. Just before roasting, rub the seeds between your fingers to remove that thin, papery outer skin. Then dry in the sun a few days, in the oven a few hours, or in the broiler under a low flame for about 15 minutes. (When they're brown and start popping out of the tray, they're done.) A moment before removing them from the oven, sprinkle them with tamari. Or just toast and then brush with melted butter and sprinkle with salt. In Latin America, roasted squash seeds are ground, transformed into a seasoning paste, and used to thicken and flavor sauces.

SALTED ROASTED PUMPKIN OR SQUASH SEEDS Wash seeds. Boil them in salted water (2–3 T. salt per 1 qt. water) for about 15 minutes. Drain. Spread on a cookie sheet with a little oil or melted butter. Roast in a moderate oven (350°F) until brown and crisp. Flavor as above.

Also see Watermelon Seeds recipe under "Watermelon."

The Gourd Family, Classified by Use

The following sections contain detailed information about growing and using each member of the gourd family. I've sorted the gourds into the following groups.

I. Squashes
    A. Summer squashes (zucchini, etc.)
    B. Winter squashes (including pumpkin)
    C. Exotic squashes (bitter melon, calabaza, chayote, fuzzy and winter melon, Lady Godiva, and spaghetti squash)
    D. Craft gourds (lagenarias, including cocozelle)
    E. Squash sponge (luffa)
II. Melons (cantaloupe, honeydew, and watermelon)
III. Cucumbers (including citron)

SQUASHES
Summer Squashes

When somebody tells you zucchini is Italian soul food, that's okay. But if they say zucchini came over on the boat with Columbus, inform them they've got the direction backwards. Both summer and winter squash are natives of the United States that migrated to Europe! A meal of squash, beans, corn, and venison was a basic native American supper. Summer squashes are grown, cooked, and preserved quite differently than are winter squashes (see next section). Zucchini, marrow, scalloped pattypan squash (or "white bush scallop" or "cymling"), cocozelle (see "Craft Gourds"), yellow crookneck, and yellow straightneck are some varieties of summer squash.

CLIMATE AND SOIL: I've never heard of a place you couldn't grow summer squash. The longer the growing season, the longer they bear. In 40 to 55 days your first young summer squash is ready to eat. There's no point in starting them indoors and transplanting because they can't take having their roots disturbed. Summer squashes need to be planted in warm soil, well past frost, and they need warm weather to grow in. They like well-manured, well-composted soil and wood ashes. Keep down the weeds.

PLANTING: How many plants? Summer squashes are prolific—especially zucchini! Even when small children plant and care for it, it grows. It blooms abundantly without fail and produces abundantly. Two plants are probably enough for a small family, 4 plants provide plenty for you plus some to give away to friends, and 8 plants give a large family a whole winter's supply. If you plant a whole package of zucchini seed, it will grow and grow and grow. There will be no way to eat, use, or give away all that summer squash—unless you have animals, that is. We grow it for pig feed. Plant summer squash 1 inch deep, 4 feet between hills and 4 feet between rows. For a container garden, plant 1 per 8-inch pot, 1 foot deep, 5 gallons of soil per plant, 2 feet between plants if they're in something like a window box.

HARVESTING: Pick your zucchini when they're small. You'll get the tastiest, tenderest ones if you harvest them very young, when they're less than 4 to 6 inches in diameter (if they're the kinds that grow long). Harvest when the skin is so tender that you can easily press your fingernail through it. You'll also be spared wondering how to use the extra pounds of veggies that will grow if you leave them on the vine a few days longer. As long as you keep picking, your plants keep producing. If you leave squashes unpicked, they get bigger, their skin gets tougher, and their seeds get bigger and tougher. But the squashes are still edible. If you're fully supplied and your summer squash plants are still producing—which they will do as long as you keep picking and frost hasn't arrived—you can quit watering them. Or let them grow the last squashes undisturbed for a seed crop. Or attack the plants with an ax while screaming!

PRESERVING: Cellar-store, freeze, can, or dry your summer squashes.

Cellar-Storing. Let the squashes grow as big as they will; pick and store in a cool place. They'll keep a couple of months or so. From Kat Atkins, Coquille, OR: "I save the huge zucchinis and put them in with the winter squash. They turn from green to yellow. Out of an average 20, I have to cut off a 6-inch section as one starts to soften. The rest I cook whole, cut in half and, depending on how we had it last, I clean it out and fill it with butter and syrup, honey, hot applesauce, or . . . Here I've already started my seedling plants for this year, and I have 2½ boxes of zucchini left. Maybe a cake?"

Freezing. Wash; peel if you like. Slice about ½ inch thick. Blanch about 3 minutes, chill, and package. This works fine with great huge summer squashes as well as with little ones. I don't freeze more than a few bucketfuls though, because my family just doesn't have that much desire for frozen zucchini.

Drying. Wash; peel if you like. Slice ⅛ inch thick. Recommended: Steam 6 minutes. Spread in thin layer. Turn as necessary while drying so they won't mildew. Dry until brittle. Dried summer squash is good with dips (eat like potato chips—it's better for you!). Try them with a yogurt-based dip or in soup.

☙ *ZUCCHINI CHIPS From Ruth of Bonaire: "Slice zucchini in ¼-inch slices and dunk in tamari. Sprinkle with paprika and then dry until crispy using a dehydrator (12 hours), a 100°F oven (16 hours), or the sun (time varies). Store in plastic bags at room temperature." Yellow straightneck squash is good fixed this way.*

☙ *DRIED OVERGROWN ZUCCHINI To manage overgrown zukes, cut into sections, peel, remove seeds, shred, and dry. Don't blanch. Use in soup and spaghetti sauce and in casseroles (mix with shredded cheese), where it will soak up broth and thicken.*

Canning. The USDA does not recommend canning summer squash. However, here are 2 recipes for summer squash combos that are recommended by the USDA.

☙ *CANNED TOMATOES WITH ZUCCHINI An average of 12 lb. of tomatoes and 4 lb. of zucchini is needed per 7-qt. canner load. An average of 7 lb. of tomatoes and 2½ lb. zucchini is needed per 9-pt. canner load. Wash tomatoes and zucchini. Scald and peel the tomatoes. Slice or cube the zucchini. Bring tomatoes to a boil and simmer 10 minutes. Add zucchini and boil gently 5 minutes. Fill jars with mixture, leaving 1 inch headspace. Add 1 t. salt per quart if desired. Adjust lids and process in a pressure canner: 30 minutes for pints, 35 minutes for quarts. If using a weighted-gauge canner, set at 10 lb. pressure at 0–1,000 feet above sea level; set at 15 lb. at higher altitudes. If using a dial-gauge canner, set at 11 lb. pressure at 0–2,000 feet above sea level; 12 lb. at 2,001–4,000 feet; 13 lb. at 4,001–6,000 feet; 14 lb. at 6,001–8,000 feet; or 15 lb. above 8,000 feet.*

☙ *SUMMER SQUASH BREAD-AND-BUTTER PICKLES, CANNED Substitute zucchini or any other slender (1 to 1½ inches in diameter) green or yellow summer squash for the cucumbers in the Bread-and-Butter Pickle recipe in the "Cucumbers" section.*

COOKING: Mary Ann Shepherd, Del Mar, CA, wrote me: "Last year we really overprogrammed on zucchini, and one of our house guests reported that when you visit the Shepherds, you have zucchini for breakfast (bread), lunch (raw in salads and pickled), dinner (as a vegetable—grated and stir-fried with mushrooms) and dessert (chocolate cake) as well as for canapes (raw sticks marinated in salad dressing or raw sticks to dunk with), and she expected the furniture to be made from it next year!"

Both these garden-to-table cookbooks have very good zucchini sections: *The Home Garden Cookbook, from Seed to Plate* by Ken and Pat Kraft and *The Kitchen Garden Book* by Stringfellow Barr and Stella Standard. Lane Morgan says: "I like *The Zucchini Cookbook* by Paula Simmons [Seattle: Pacific Search, 1975]. She has good recipes for stuffing the great big ones. The *Territorial Seed Co. Cookbook* has 33 mostly wholesome zucchini recipes, including my personal favorite."

RECIPE IDEAS: With zucchini that has been harvested young, frying, baking, or steaming give you better results than boiling because summer squash is mostly water anyway. You don't have to peel 'em unless they're old and tough-skinned. For more recipes suitable for summer squash, see "Using" under "Chayote" and "Recipe Ideas" under "Fuzzy Melon" (both are in the "Exotic Squashes" section).

Raw. Serve raw in sticks with a dip. Or serve grated or chunked in a tossed salad with a zesty dressing. Or make into a salad dressing: peel, de-seed, chop 2 or 3 large cucumbers, liquefy in blender, add a few squirts lemon juice and a dash of garlic powder (or 1 small minced clove), and thicken with tahini.

Sauteed. Slice and cook in butter 10 minutes. Or slice, dip in egg batter and then flour, and French-fry. Or fry in butter in a pan with chopped onions. Or mix chunks with chopped parsley and basil and add to an omelet. Or stir-fry with onions, carrots, meat strips, garlic, and a bay leaf. Or stir-fry with sliced mushrooms, sprouts, beef slices, tomato slices, and soy sauce. Or saute sliced zuke with precooked chopped onion and bacon, canned tomatoes, and a bit of seasoning (garlic, oregano, basil, salt, and pepper) until all is cooked and hot (from a precious saint, reader Tannis Prosser). Or stir-fry shredded summer squash and onions together in a little tamari with a pinch of curry, or use tomato sauce instead of tamari and add a pinch of basil and oregano (from Ruth of Bonaire).

Baked. Or bake in an oiled casserole dish (with tomatoes, garlic, and basil or fennel) with Parmesan cheese on top. Or bake in a casserole dish halved or quartered summer squash layered with pork chops and halved onions. Or slice into ½-inch slices, put into a baking dish, dot with butter, sprinkle with salt and finely chopped onion, add just enough water (or cream) to cover the bottom of the dish, cover, and bake until tender. Or slice into a baking dish, add enough tomato juice to barely cover, and bake—or cover with homemade tomato sauce mixed with a little soft tofu (this makes a good main dish). Or grate and add to any bread mix.

☙ *MASHED ZUCCHINI Mash 1 zucchini. Mix with 1 grated onion, 1 c. mashed cooked cauliflower, garlic, and a dash of tamari. Add ¼ c. whole wheat flour and ½ t. baking powder. Bake 1 hour at 350°F.*

Boiled. Boil in a little water until tender; then drain, season with butter, and serve. Or cook, mash, season, and serve.

Or boil briefly with cut-up green peppers and tomato, garlic, and oregano. Or simmer chunks with onions, tomatoes, and fennel until tender. Or slice zuke into frying pan; add 1 T. tamari, 1 T. water, a bunch of sliced green onions, and 1 T. chopped fresh herbs for each zuke; cover and steam until tender (about 5 minutes).

➤ *LANE'S MOM'S ZUCCHINI SOUP* *"My mom makes the best zucchini soup: Steam and puree a bunch of young zucchinis. Add a little milk and/or chicken stock, some sauteed onion, some parsley and dill or other herbs to taste, and a bit of salt and pepper. Serve hot or cold, with a little yogurt or sour cream on top. Use the nicest, youngest zucchinis for this —that's where the good flavor comes from."*

➤ *CHEESE SUMMER SQUASH* *Cut maybe 9 little squashes in half and steam in water 10 minutes. Then lay in a buttered ovenproof dish, sliced sides up. Sprinkle with salt and ½ t. sage. Dot with butter. Sprinkle about ½ c. grated Cheddar cheese over the top and put in 325°F oven until cheese is melted.*

➤ *SOUR CREAM SUMMER SQUASH* *Cut about 2 lb. squash into 1 inch slices. Sprinkle them with ½ t. salt. Let stand an hour and then drain. In a frying pan, saute squash in margarine or oil with ½ c. chopped onion. When squash is tender, add 1 c. sour cream mixed with 4 t. flour. Bring to a boil. Sprinkle with paprika and serve.*

➤ *BAKED SQUASH SOUFFLE* *From Arlene Jackson, Santee, CA: Boil 3 or 4 zucchini squashes until tender. Mash. Brown 1 diced medium-sized onion in margarine. Add to mashed zucchini some onion, grated cheese, 2 or 3 beaten eggs, a pinch of garlic, and salt and pepper to taste. Mix and pour into casserole. Dot with butter and, if desired, grated cheese (Parmesan) or cracker meal. Bake about 1 hour at 350°F. Slivered almonds browned in margarine can be added to topping.*

Winter Squashes

You never use winter squash when it's green and small, the way you do summer squash. You let winter squash thoroughly ripen on the vine. Winter squash tastes way different too. It's a very nourishing vegetable, different from summer squash that way too, resembling sweet potato in taste, texture, and uses.

VARIETIES: The winter squashes look very different on the outside, but all are grown, harvested, and prepared in a similar way, and they taste similar too. You can grow 5-lb. butternut or buttercup squashes, a 15-lb. Hubbard (a good pumpkin substitute in recipes), 25-lb. Marblehead squashes (seed available from Abundant Life), or 600-lb. giant pumpkins. The banana squashes get quite large too. Among the smallest winter squashes are the acorn, Delicata, and Sweet Dumpling squashes. All of those are just the right size for 2 servings. You can order Red Kuri and Pink Banana from Southern Seeds. Tahitian squash can be eaten like a summer squash when immature and treated like a winter squash when fully grown (up to 2 feet long). The "turban," or buttercup, squash can grow bigger than a foot in diameter and is a very good winter keeper. "Sweet dumpling" is a little one (4 inches across) from the Philippines. Use like an acorn. Delicata tastes best when its skin looks yellow and its stripes are nearly orange. The Asian "kabocha" squash, or "Japanese pumpkin," gets very big. The banana squash is a kabocha relative from Asia.

Pumpkin. Pumpkin is a kind of squash, a *C. pepo*. The pumpkins and the big winter squashes grow more pounds of flesh per plant than any other garden veggie I can think of. My problem has always been finding a way to use them other than letting the children make 6 jack-o'-lanterns apiece. When we harvest, the nicest ones are set aside to be jack-o'-lanterns. Lane Morgan says she likes to "go out in the field when they are getting big but are still green and thin-skinned, and incise the kids' names or designs or whatever into the skin with my thumbnail or a pocketknife. The cuts heal into a raised scar as the skin hardens (I've never had one rot from this treatment), and the result is a delight to the young ones when they search for their own monogrammed pumpkins at harvest time." After the jack-o'-lanterns have run their course, they go to the pigs.

Seeds from the world's biggest (500–700 lb.), smallest (2" x 3"), and many other varieties of pumpkin are available from pumpkin specialist Howard Dill Enterprises, RR#1, Windsor, Nova Scotia, B0N 2T0, CANADA; 902-798-2728; fax 902-798-0842.

PLANTING: Your winter squash will be ready to harvest in 80 to 120 days after planting, pumpkins in 100 to 120 days. Plant squash or pumpkins in early midsummer, after the weather is definitely past the last frost and has warmed up comfortably. Plant 1 inch deep, about 4 seeds to a hill, hills about 3 to 6 feet apart each way depending on your variety. Allow 7 to 10 days for germination. After the vines start to grow, be careful not to hurt them when weeding. And water—all winter squashes need lots of water, especially once they start making fruit.

HARVESTING AND CURING: Leave winter squash or pumpkins out there until after the first frost or longer, but don't let them freeze. Then go out and cut the stems about an inch from the fruit. Let cure in the field for a few days or up to 2 weeks, depending on your weather. Then bring them into the warmest room in your house for the next stage of curing. At temperatures of 80 to 85°F, the rind will harden and the fruit will heal its own surface cuts. But handle gently, because the fruit can't heal itself of bruises, and the bruised places will rot first. Squashes so blemished they won't keep go to the pigs. If the squashes freeze, as soon as they start to thaw they also start to spoil, and your only alternative is to cook them all right away; then mash and freeze them, or can them.

Storing. Commercial squash crops are stored here in special barns where a fire is kept burning all the time in cold weather, so they won't freeze before markets open up for them. Then they are cut into big chunks and sent to market in an insulated truck. *Stored squash and pumpkins must never* freeze. *That ruins them completely.* It's best if they don't touch each other in storage; they tend to go bad at the point where they touch one another. If your regular checks show that you have one with a bad spot, just cut out the spot and cook up the rest of it. We keep ours in the attic, spread out on newspapers. Fortunately, I have a very large, cool attic. Wooden shelves would work fine for them, too.

I read a university handout which says that at over 60°F they get too dry, and at under 50°F they get "chilling injury." Everybody around here simply does the best they can to keep them from getting frozen, and that's good enough. Everybody's system is different. You just have to think about all the nooks and crannies of your own set of buildings, and don't put the squash in the root cellar (don't put onions or pumpkins there either) because dampness really harms them and will soon result in rot. We eat acorn squashes during the first part of the winter and then switch to the Marbleheads. With luck, some of those big squashes harvested in October will still be fine in late March; at worst, they'll make it to February. The ones that go bad are passed on to the pig. After the Marbleheads are gone, frozen squash is the best thing. You can freeze squash in the late fall and all winter at your leisure.

Squashes for Fodder. The big winter squashes are useful as winter food for people and for animals too, especially goats. If you can't raise grain, you can winter your goats on stock beets, carrots, and squash, along with just a little purchased grain and hay. Cows or pigs will use winter squashes for winter feed too. Rotted squashes or bad spots you've cut out can go to the pig. Squashes have to be cut into pieces before you give them to the animals.

Cutting. Cutting big stored squash is really a job. The longer they have been in storage, the tougher the peel gets. You can open tough squashes by literally hammering a butcher knife through the shells. Or saw the shells. Always cut lengthwise.

PRESERVING SQUASH OR PUMPKIN

Freezing. Cut open your winter squash or pumpkin. Remove stringy fibers and seeds (save them for seed or snacks). Cut into pieces and cook until soft in as little boiling water as possible. Or steam in a pressure cooker or bake in the oven. You can bake a whole big squash; it takes about 2 hours. Then you cut open, remove seeds, and mash. Or bake or boil sections and, after the squash is cooked, scrape off the rind and mash the insides (use a masher or rotary colander or push through a sieve). (Using a masher is by far the easiest way.) Then package and freeze. There's no good way to cool it, so just don't put more in the freezer than it can handle each day.

I thaw a bag of frozen squash in a frying pan with a little water, butter, and honey. Mix well and serve hot. Substitute for sweet potatoes on Thanksgiving or at any other time. Around here, squash is much cheaper and easier to grow than sweet potatoes. You can use it in pies or add it to bread dough.

Drying. Pioneer Americans dried pumpkins a lot. Their method was generally to slice the pumpkin around in circles, scrape out the seeds and strings, peel it, and let the circles hang in the air, out of direct sunshine, until they were dried. Another method: Cut into small pieces, seed, peel, cut into 1-inch strips, and cut those ¼ inch thick. Or shred it. Dry until tough.

➣ *SQUASH/PUMPKIN LEATHER* Cook and puree. For each 2 c. puree, add ½ c. honey, ¼ t. cinnamon, and ⅛ t. each of nutmeg and cloves. (Other options: Combine with apple puree. For spices, substitute ginger and pumpkin pie spice. Sweeten with white or dark corn syrup rather than honey. For each 1 c. steamed squash, pumpkin, yam, or sweet potato, add 1 c. mashed banana, 1 t. pumpkin pie spice, ½ t. vanilla, and ½ c. chopped nuts; dry like a fruit leather.)

Canning. Wash; remove seeds. Cut into chunks and peel. Cut the peeled chunks into 1-inch cubes. Add just enough water to cover. Boil 2 minutes. Optional: Add salt. Put chunks into clean canning jar. Pour cooking liquid over, leaving 1 inch headspace. *Caution: Do not mash or puree before canning.* Process pints 55 minutes, quarts 90 minutes, in *pressure canner only.* If using a weighted-gauge canner, set at 10 lb. pressure at 0–1,000 feet above sea level; set at 15 lb. at higher altitudes. If using a dial-gauge canner, set at 11 lb. pressure at 0–2,000 feet above sea level; 12 lb. at 2,001–4,000 feet; 13 lb. at 4,001–6,000 feet; 14 lb. at 6,001–8,000 feet; or 15 lb. above 8,000 feet.

COOKING SQUASH AND PUMPKIN: Basically you start any recipe by boiling, baking, or pressure-cooking the flesh. If you then mash, you've got the equivalent of the canned pumpkin that is called for in most recipes. Just substitute from there.

Boiling. Halve the fruit and scoop out the seeds and stringy fibers that are mixed up with them. Peel and cut what's left into cookable-sized pieces. Boil until tender (a half hour or so). To pressure-cook, cook the peeled pieces 15 minutes at 15 lb. pressure.

Baking. Arrange your peeled pieces cut side down in some sort of baking pan. Bake about an hour at 400°F. Then scoop out the part that stayed soft and mashable. Another system is in Ruth's Vegan Squash Pie recipe a bit later on. Of that one, Lane Morgan says, "That's how I always prepare my pumpkins for pies, except I scrape out the seeds before I bake because I don't know how good they'd be for roasting after being cooked in all that moisture. You don't have to peel or chunk the pumpkin, and I hate peeling pumpkin. Don't use a rimless baking surface because the pumpkins will 'weep' as they cook. I save that liquid to get the puree going in the blender."

Instant Mashed Squash/Pumpkin. Blend 2 c. cut-up pumpkin with ½ c. water until smooth. If you aren't going to use your puree in a recipe where it will get cooked, you can cook it plain in a pan, but you have to stir constantly to prevent burning.

Recipe Ideas. For more recipes suitable for winter squash, see the recipe ideas under "Winter Melon" (in the "Exotic Squashes" section).

➣ *SQUASH HALF (OR CHUNK) BAKED IN THE SHELL*
This is my family's winter squash favorite. We use acorn squashes. I cut them in half (or into appropriate-sized baking sections) and remove seeds. In the cavity of each squash half, I sprinkle a little brown sugar and butter. Or some cooked bacon bits and butter. Or maple syrup. Or a honey/mustard mix. Or I mix ½ c. orange juice concentrate, ½ c. honey, salt, 2 T. butter, and ⅛ t. nutmeg and divide this among the squashes. Or combine prefried crumbled bacon (about 4 slices), half a small onion (cut up and sauteed), ½ c. brown sugar, a big pinch of ground cloves, and 1½ c. peeled apple

sections. In any case, put filled squashes in a loaf pan, sprinkle bacon bits on top, and bake in a loaf pan at about 350°F until fork-tender. Or stuff with a meat-loaf mix and bake. Or fill with a mixture of chopped apples, raisins, bread crumbs soaked in orange juice, a little honey, cinnamon, and cloves.

Then serve. Since it's hard for any child (or most adults) to eat an entire half of an acorn squash, we carve them up at the table and serve the pieces, trying hard not to lose much of the filling in the process. Then just spoon the squash off the rind into your mouth. Use mashed leftover squash in any baked goods (bread, cookies, cakes, and muffins).

❧ **SQUASH STUFFING** Mix together 2 c. mashed squash, 1 egg, 1 c. each finely chopped onion and celery, 1 T. chopped parsley, 1 chopped green pepper, 2 T. melted butter, ½ t. sage, and a dash of thyme.

❧ **VEGAN SQUASH PIE** From Ruth: Cut 1 large or 2 medium butternut squashes (you can substitute any other winter-keeper squash) in half lengthwise and bake, cut side down, for an hour (till very soft when forked). Discard seeds. Then scoop out flesh and puree in blender till smooth—add ½ c. maple syrup or honey, 1½ t. cinnamon, ½ t. nutmeg, ½ t. ginger, 2 T. tahini (sesame seed butter), and ½ c. rice (or soy milk). Bake in pie shell or glass baking dish at 375°F for 30 minutes, till slightly browned.

❧ **BANANA SQUASH SEEDS** The banana squash has very big seeds that taste great when roasted.

Pumpkin Recipe Ideas. Check out a copy of *The Pumpkin Eater Cook Book* by Phyllis E. Strohsahl, or substitute in a squash or sweet potato recipe. Or try one of these . . .

❧ **PUMPKREAM PIE** It was a red-letter day for me indeed when this one came in the mail from Esther Shuttleworth, mother of the famous editor of Mother Earth News (John): Mix together 1 c. granulated sugar, a pinch of salt, 1 t. cinnamon, ¼ t. cloves, and ¼ t. nutmeg. Beat in 2 eggs. Then add 1 c. well-cooked–down (cooked-dry) pumpkin. Add 1 c. thick cream or whipping cream. Bake in an 8-inch pie pan, which will be full, for 20 minutes at 425°F. Then reduce to 375°F and bake until it rises and then makes small cracks around the edge.

That reminds me of another exciting day. I answered the telephone, and it was a lady from California wanting to order a hardcover copy of the book for her grandchildren. The address she gave me was "Marian Anderson . . ." I asked, "Are you Marian Anderson, the great singer?" And she said, "Yes!" She had a strong, lovely voice, even just talking over the telephone, and she was a thoroughly enjoyable lady to talk to.

❧ **IVY'S PUMPKIN PIE FROM SCRATCH** Ivy Isaacson lives here in Kendrick and helped me a lot with mimeographing earlier editions of this book. I got a request in the mail for a pumpkin pie recipe from scratch, and Ivy offered hers. Here it is for everybody: Cut pumpkin in pieces; peel and cook in small amount of water. Drain well, mash, and put through strainer. Line a 9-inch pie pan with plain pastry. Set oven at 450°F. Mix 1½ c. of your cooked and strained pumpkin, ⅓ c. brown sugar, ⅓ c. white sugar, 1 t. cinnamon, ½ t. ginger, ¼ t. nutmeg, ½ t. salt, 2 slightly beaten eggs, 1½ c. milk, and ½ c. cream or evaporated milk. Pour into pie shell. Bake 10 minutes; then lower heat to 300°F and bake until firm (about 45 minutes). For spicier filling, add ¼ t. cloves.

❧ **VEGAN PUMPKIN PIE** From Ruth of Bonaire: "Take 2 c. cooked-down pumpkin, 1 c. rice cream cereal (cooked and cooled), 2 T. tahini, ½ c. apple juice (or ¼ c. juice and ¼ c. honey), 2 t. each of allspice and fresh grated ginger root, and ¼ t. cloves. Puree all that in a blender until very smooth, and then bake in an ungreased glass baking dish 30 minutes at 375°F or until set."

Exotic Squashes

These include the bitter melon, calabaza, chayote, fuzzy and winter melons, Lady Godiva, and spaghetti squash.

BITTER MELON: Bitter melon (*Momordica charantia*) is also known as "foo gwa," "balsam pear," "kareli," and "bitter cucumber." It's native to Asia and India. Perennial in the tropics, it can be grown annually in zones 5–10. The vine will climb up to 20 feet.

Using
NOTE: Don't eat the seeds of a ripe bitter melon. They'll make you sick.

The fruit is very bumpy and ridged on the outside; otherwise it resembles a light green cucumber. It does indeed taste somewhat bitter because of the quinine it naturally contains; the taste resembles quinine water. The fruits get more bitter as they get older, so harvest them when they're young. Soak in a brine for a half hour, or boil in a brine for 5 minutes, before using. For recipes, look in Indonesian, Sri Lankan, and Indian recipe books. Or boil, peel, take out seeds, mash like winter squash, and add spices. Or precook and then add to a stir-fry with either curry flavorings or garlic and soy sauce. Or add to any spicy soup. Or stuff and bake.

CALABAZA: *Cucurbita moschata* (or *Cucurbita foetidissima*) is like a large pumpkin, but it's not of the same cross-pollinating group as the regular pumpkins. Also called "Cuban squash," "calabazilla," and "green" or "Indian" pumpkin, it's grown a lot in Central and South America. It keeps like a winter squash and grows great in hot climates like Florida. The vines will cover a large area (they get up to 60 feet long) and produce prolifically.

Using. The shell is hard. Saw into it or use a big, sharp-edged knife. Substitute in any pumpkin or winter squash recipe, or use in stew, soup, casseroles, and breads. Or bake pieces with brown sugar and butter sprinkled on them. Or boil a chunk, mash like potatoes, and add seasoning. The taste resembles sweet potato. The blossoms are good eating, and so are the seeds if roasted.

CHAYOTE: Chayote fruit (*Sechium edule*) is shaped like an avocado and is green outside but white inside. Its many names include "brionne," "christophine," "chocho," "mango squash," "mirliton," and "vegetable pear." It comes from Central America, was grown by the Aztecs and Mayas, and is now popular in Latin America and India. Its vines are eager growers (30 to 100 feet a year, in a style resembling kudzu). It's a perennial in places where the ground doesn't freeze, such as Florida and California.

Planting. Chayote takes a long time to get going and needs a hot summer, which makes it a tricky crop to grow farther north, although in the hot interior it can produce if started indoors in March and transplanted later. It needs constantly moist, fertile soil and no frost. To start, plant sprouted fruits. You can start with grocery-store fruits, or mail-order them (Southern Seeds). As with other cucurbits, even though the vine gets so large, you need to plant several because some plants have flowers of only one sex. Plant them 10 feet apart in every direction and with something *strong* (fence, tree, outbuilding, high trellis) to climb on because the fruit shouldn't be on the ground. Plant the seed in compost or aged manure tilted at about 45 degrees, with the small end up and just barely sticking out of the ground. Or do vegetative propagation by planting the small shoots that grow off the crown (you'll have to keep a plant base alive all winter).

Harvesting. Chayote needs a minimum of 12 hours of sunlight per day to set off flower production. The first fruit will be ready about a month later. Once they get going, your vine will start fruiting in October and thereafter will produce fruit year-round unless stopped by cold. Night temps down to 40°F will terminate fruiting until next spring. But this cucurbit is quite different from the others in that it has many other edible parts besides the little squash: You can also eat its seed; harvest tender leaves from its growing tips anytime and use them raw or cooked; harvest young shoots in late spring and early summer and serve them asparagus-style; or dig up and eat the tubers, which resemble potatoes and can get big as 25 lb! In fact, in the tropics the tubers are an even more important chayote crop than its squash. Dig up the tubers as soon as your vine dies from cold, although the tubers will be small. To get good-sized ones, wait to harvest until after a vine is at least 2 years old. Discarded vines are good animal fodder.

Preserving. If you've got chayote, odds are you have too much fruit, because it's the Mexican equivalent of zucchini. If you wrap and store chayotes in the fridge, they keep for weeks. Or dice, blanch 2 minutes, chill, package, and freeze.

Using. Wash; take off stem and blossom ends. The male fruits will be smooth and the female ones prickly, but both are edible. You can eat very young chayotes unpeeled, raw, or cooked. For an older one, the peel gets tough and will need peeling. But older ones are sweeter because their starch changes to sugar. Peel, cut in half, and take out the seeds. You can eat the youngest chayote fruits raw, as in a salad, where it tastes a bit like cucumber. You can also make a pie of it using an apple pie recipe. The bland flavor needs help. Serve in strips with a spicy dip. Or boil, mash, and season. Or saute strips in any stir-fry dish. Or add to an onion/meat soup.

Fuzzy Melon: Fuzzy melon (*Benincasa hispida*) is a Chinese member of the gourd family; it's also known as "hairy melon" or "wax gourd." The many Asian varieties of this species come in various shapes. It's most comparable to our summer squash. The name "hairy melon" refers to its fuzzy, kiwi-like outside. In shape and color, it's like a fat green cuke. The melons can grow up to 2 lb. You'll be harvesting in late summer and fall.

Recipe Ideas. Wash your fuzzy melon, cut it in half, and scoop out the seeds and pulp. It has a spongy texture and a bland flavor. Substitute in any summer squash recipe. It's good when added to a stew or soup and cooked slowly. You can also prepare fuzzy melon by cleaning out the cavity and then stuffing it with a mixture of vegetables (shrimp is good too) and baking until all are cooked through. Or stuff with a mixture of poultry meat and mushrooms seasoned with crushed garlic cloves and ginger, and bake. Or saute strips of it with slivers of chicken and Asian greens, which is a favorite way the Chinese prepare it. The Japanese like it stir-fried in sesame oil with strips of carrot, broccoli, and tofu and served with soy sauce. Or make a plain fuzzy-melon stew by simmering chunks of the flesh slowly until fork-tender and then thickening with cornstarch.

Lady Godiva: This European *Cucurbita pepo* has naturally hull-less seeds! The seeds are about half protein and half polyunsaturated fat, with some other vitamins and minerals thrown in. Some Lady Godiva varieties have seeds that are good people food but flesh that isn't (it's good for animals, though). But Nichols sells a new hybrid whose seeds *and* flesh are good to eat. Grow it like a pumpkin (which it resembles). Harvest when cracks begin to appear where the fruit is attached to the vine. To prepare, halve the fruit, scrape out the seeds, and soak them in water (use the instructions in "Seed Saving" under "Cucumbers") until the seeds are nicely separated from the other stuff. Then spread them out to dry for up to a week. Add them to recipes, eat straight as a snack, roast, mix with sunflower (or other flower) seeds and grind for a spread, or press for oil. (For roasting and oil-pressing directions, see "Flower Seeds.")

Spaghetti Squash: This thin-skinned *Cucurbita pepo* is full of long strands of flesh instead of a solid mass like the others. It's also, and appropriately, called "vegetable spaghetti." Nichols carries an improved 85-day variety. Plant and grow like other cucurbits. When ripe and ready, it looks yellow. Some people claim it cures and stores as well as a *maxima*. Others prefer to preserve by cooking and then packaging and freezing the "spaghetti."

Preparing. It's usually first cooked whole, either boiled (about a half hour) or baked (poke with a fork and bake about 90 minutes at 350°F). Then cut in half lengthwise and take out the seeds and central pulp. Rake out the shreds of "spaghetti." There will be enough to cover a big plate. Stir cream and melted cheese in with the strands and serve. Or serve with plain salt, pepper, and butter. Or serve with pasta sauce, chili, garlic butter, or mushroom soup. Or preboil and then cook in a casserole mix with meat chunks. Or stir-fry the strands with onions, carrots, and garlic and serve stirred in with real spaghetti. Or substitute for the noodles in a lasagna recipe. Or cook, chill, and toss some squash strands with a green salad.

Winter Melon: Winter melon is another Chinese variety of *Benincasa hispida*. It's also called a "wax gourd" because the green skin gets coated with a waxy material when it matures. It needs a hot climate and takes 150 days to mature. (Seed is available from Southern Seeds.) Use when young, like a zucchini squash. Just cut into slices, steam, and serve with soy sauce. Or, if left on the vine, this variety can get as heavy as 35 lb. and then is treated like a winter squash.

The Chinese sometimes scoop out the cavity of such a very large winter melon and serve soup in it. For special occasions, they may create ornate carvings from the outer skin. Harvest very late in the year; cure and store like a pumpkin or winter squash (hence its name, "winter melon").

Recipe Ideas. Scoop out the winter melon's flesh and cook it with black mushrooms to make a soy-flavored soup. Or bake sections. Or simmer flesh slowly with bamboo shoots, thicken with cornstarch, and serve. Or steam with other vegetables and mushrooms and serve with soy sauce. Or use as an ingredient in a chicken and shiitake mushroom stew.

Craft Gourds

"Bottle gourd" or "hard-shell" squashes (*Lagenaria siceraria*) are easy to grow and are quite durable, as vegetable products go. Grow as you would other squashes or pumpkins. If you love doing crafts, these are the melons for you! Except for cocozelle (discussed a bit later on), craft gourds are inedible; they're simply gourds with interesting shapes and colored patterns that are dried whole to look at or make useful objects out of. People who live in the Southwest have the easiest time with gourds because they both grow and dry so well in that climate.

Archaeologists tell us that early human societies were making lagenaria gourd containers even before they had discovered how to turn clay into pottery or stems into baskets. They used the largest ones for storing grain and seeds, the smaller ones for dishes. The lagenaria "bottle gourd" is indeed of a suitable shape for a liquid container. The bowls and baskets aren't sturdy enough to be cooked in over a fire, but you can drop heated stones in them to cook. They make fine children's toys, little dishes, and doll bathtubs. A big burlap bag full of them makes marvelous winter entertainment for the children. You can hang them to display by punching a hole in the top and running string or leather through. And they can be flower vases.

You grow a lagenaria until the stem has dried, pick it, dry it, use a strong household disinfectant to wipe off all the dirt (including invisible fungi that otherwise could cause rotting), and then wax and polish it. A good wax car polish looks fine. These squashes can be made into bowls, skimmers, dippers, bottles, seed holders, and birdhouses.

MORE INFO: See *Traditional American Crafts* by Betsy B. Creekmore (New York: Hearthside Press, 1968), *Gourd Craft* by Carolyn Mordecai (New York: Crown, 1977), and *The Art of Drying Plants and Flowers* by Mabel Squires (New York: Bonanza Books, 1958).

VARIETIES: The lagenarias come in a delightful array of varieties, mainly named for their shapes or uses: ball, bottle (vase or liquid container), "canteen" or "bushel" (great bowls or "baskets," depending on size), club (good rattle), dipper (ladle, planter), dumbbell (small ones can be made into salt shakers with a wood plug in the center bottom), and penguin (bowls with interesting matching lids). They range widely not only in shape but also in size and color.

Garden catalogs generally list both small and large varieties. To start with, you could plant one of the "mixed" packets, which will give you an interesting assortment. Gourds come in an amazing array of sizes and styles. Stokes Seeds offers a good assortment of both large (Cave Man's Club, Giant Bottle, Dipper, and Birdhouse) and small (Miniature Bottle, Miniature Ball, etc.) gourds. Nichols also offers an outstanding collection: 10 small types and 9 large ones. Southern Seeds offers them as well.

Cocozelle. *Lagenaria longissima* is the exception among lagenarias: It's grown to eat rather than to carve. It's a variety of the Italian cocuzza squash. Seed is available from Southern Seeds. It produces like a zucchini, grows well in an area like southern Louisiana, and is great to eat when just 18 to 24 inches (that's immature for it!). Bake, steam, or add to a casserole.

PLANTING: The lagenarias, like the luffas, are tropical plants that thrive in hot, humid weather and need a long growing season, at least 100 to 110 days. You can direct-seed them into the garden and harvest before frost only if you live in the southern United States. Plant seeds a foot apart if in rows; 2 to the hill, hills 6 feet apart, if in hills. In more northern zones, start them in peat pots (2 seeds per pot, ½ inch deep) some weeks before your last frost date, and then transplant to the garden after the dirt has warmed up. In the coldest zones, they can only be grown in a greenhouse, where they will thrive and provide dense foliage as well as flowers and fruits.

Gourds are best grown as climbers—over a fence, for instance, to keep them out of the dirt—unless the growing instructions say otherwise. That's because the position in which they grow can affect the ultimate shape of the gourds. Lagenarias do best in soil that is light and only moderately provided with nitrogen, although humus is good for them. Excess nitrogen tends to make them produce more leaves and fewer gourds. Lagenarias need full sunlight and regular enough watering that their dirt never completely dries out.

CLIMBING: Inside or out, plant any lagenaria next to something the vines can climb: a fence, trellis, or sash. Strange but true: Experiments have shown that craft gourds produce much better—even 2 or 3 times as much—if their vines are tied up with string or in some fashion supported up off the ground. However, some of the lagenarias need to develop on the ground either to have the right shape or because of their weight. If having the melons sitting on the ground seems to be a problem, protect the fruits by slipping some clean dry mulch (such as straw) under them.

Large Bottle Gourd. This one grows 12 inches long, 8 to 10 inches in diameter, with a somewhat hourglass shape. In Mexico it's still used to make water bottles. It also makes a great birdhouse. To form a bottle with a flat, stable bottom, stand the gourd upright while young and still growing. Seeds are available from Southern Seeds. You can take off just the tip and discard it, clean out the seed cavity, and make a vase. If you do the same thing but keep the top for a lid, you have a nice bottle. If you cut about two-thirds of the way up and keep the top, you have a nice bowl with a lid.

Bushel Gourd. This one makes a large, round "bushel basket." It is basically pumpkin-shaped but with smoother sides, and it grows from 12 to 18 inches in diameter. Mature fruits can weigh as much as 30 to 100 lb. Seeds are available from Southern Seeds. Its large vine needs lots of room. Let the fruits fully mature on the vine. Then pick, dry, and cure.

Dipper Gourd. This variety is also called "siphons." Its fruit makes excellent ladles, planters, and vases as well as dippers. The gourd has a narrow neck, which becomes the dipper's handle, and a wide but flattish body, 6 to 8 inches in diameter on that larger end. The plant does best when provided with something like a trellis to grow on.

SECRETS OF LAGENARIA HARVESTING AND CUTTING

1. Pick the gourds when completely ripe. Don't let them frost. You can give them a little more time by protecting them with paper or cloth from the first light frosts. They'll be ready to be picked any time after the stems have become dry and shriveled. Leave several inches of stem when cutting. Be careful not to injure or bruise them while handling.

2. Let them dry several days to 2 weeks.

3. Dip into diluted bleach or alcohol, dry the gourd, and that's it. Or, if you want to decorate the gourd skin, remove the outer skin by rubbing it off with steel wool until all of that waxy outermost layer is off. Or wrap each gourd in a towel that has been soaked in liquid household cleanser, and let the gourd soak for at least 3 hours. That softens the outside skin layer. Take the gourd out of the towel. Scrape off the outer skin. Getting it off enables the rest of the gourd to quickly finish drying. (Or else skip this and wait until you've finished cleaning and scraping the gourd [see the next "Secrets" list]. Then take off the outer papery skin by giving it a quick scalding in boiling water. A light scraping then will take off the rest.)

4. Spread out the gourds to dry in a dry, well-ventilated place, making sure the gourds don't touch each other. Turn them regularly until the drying is completed—usually 3 or 4 weeks. (You can also hang them to dry, but don't let them touch each other.) As a gourd dries, the seeds get loose and rattle and the gourd gets light. A gourd rattle makes a fine toy or child's musical instrument.

5. Let the size and shape of the gourd suggest its use to you. Refer to one of the following cutting patterns. To cut a lagenaria, first draw a line on it with a pencil. Use something small and pointed to punch open a spot on the line. Finish the cut with a fine-toothed saw and steady pressure. Or, if you're like me, just brace the gourd and hammer the knife through it, or chop with a hatchet. They're hard to cut. For more precision, use a drill, saber saw, or keyhole saw. Make your first cut where you want it, because it's very difficult to trim, although some gourd varieties are softer than others.

6. Proceed to the next list of "Secrets" to finish your gourd.

For a Bowl. Choose a round gourd. Cut off one end, or cut the gourd across the middle, depending on whether you want a wide mouth or a tapered shape. To make yourself a "set," choose matching gourds.

Dipper. For a dipper, choose a gourd with a long, nicely shaped neck. The neck will be your handle. Lay the gourd on its side. Cut off the top half from the base of the neck to the other end of the gourd. If one side is flatter than the other, let that be the bottom of your dipper.

Skimmer. To make a skimmer, proceed as for a dipper. Then perforate the bottom and sides of the dipper with a nail in lots of places, creating a slotted-spoon effect. Finish drying. Then you can dip up scum from your stew pot with it, and the juice will flow back into the kettle through the holes. Or you can scoop vegetables out of a soup or use the gourd as a sieve.

Bottle or Vase. Choose a gourd with the appropriate shape. Test it to see if it can stand up on its bottom. Cut off the neck to make the shape you desire. Remove seeds, pulp, and fibers through the neck hole as it softens up. You can make another kind of vase by cutting a gourd in half lengthwise, hollowing it out, and putting flowers in it to use as a centerpiece. Some prople waterproof the inside with paraffin.

Toys. Gourds make good toys: dolly bathtubs, cups for dolls to drink out of, and so on. You can make a lantern from a really big gourd by cutting out one whole side, leaving the neck and base intact so it will stand up. Hollow it out and then put a candle inside. Start with a large gourd—if your gourd is too small, the sides will scorch and get kind of stinky.

Bird Feeder. To make a bird feeder, cut out an entry hole for the bird and let the gourd dry. Then hollow it out. Hang it up outside fairly securely and put some birdseed in it. Birds will climb in and eat.

Birdhouses. The big, round, pumpkin-sized gourds are good for these. Cut a hole that's big enough to let you hollow out the gourd. Hang it in a tree by punching a hole and putting leather through it. For a lot more detail and to learn which size the entrances should be to attract a certain type of bird, look up "Gourds Make Attractive Birdhouses" in *Organic Gardening* (Aug. 1971, p. 54).

SECRETS OF LAGENARIA DESEEDING AND FINISHING

1. Cutting has now enabled you to get at the inside seeds and pulp. If they're hard to scrape out, set the gourd in a warm place for another few days before removing the seeds. Don't scrape the inside of the gourd too hard at any particular point; otherwise the shell will become thin and may shrivel. After taking out the seeds, wash the inside of the gourd and stand it in a fairly warm place for a few days. If you're working down a long narrow neck to make a vase or bottle, it will help to fill the gourd with water for about 3 hours and then scrape with a suitable long instrument (such as a metal spoon). Then soak and repeat until it's all cleaned out.

2. Gourd makers recommend using steel wool to finish cleaning both the inside and the outside of the gourd.

3. To decorate a lagenaria, first pencil your pattern onto it. Then paint, stain, or carve with any engraving tool or just a sharp knife.

4. When gourds are finished and completely dry, polish them to ensure that they will keep well. Shellac, varnish, or spray with a clear cellulose lacquer.

5. How long will decorative gourds keep? Temperature and humidity are important factors, but gourds should keep at least several years, although as time passes they will lose some of their natural color. You can make them look nice if you wax them with floor wax and polish them with a soft cloth.

Squash Sponge: Luffa

The luffas are a totally different gourd species (*Luffa*) than the lagenarias. The luffa (sometimes spelled "loofa") originated in Asia and has as about as many names as there are seed catalogs. One of its most common names is "vegetable sponge" because the skeleton of this gourd is the "luffa sponge" you can buy from your health-food store. It's also known as "towel gourd" or "dishcloth gourd." Asian specialty catalogs may use its Chinese names.

Luffa sponges can be used as bathing sponges, boat or kitchen scrubbers, filters, insulation, and packing material. You can use them to make baskets, mats, and slippers. Luffa is also edible!—unlike the lagenarias. In fact, in much of the tropical world, luffas are grown not only for their summer squash-type fruits and the spongy skeletons of mature fruits left to dry on the vine but also for their edible flowers, leaves, and seeds!

LUFFA VARIETIES: There are 2 basic kinds of luffa: "ridged" and "smooth." You can tell their seeds apart by looking, because the seeds of ridged luffa are wrinkled and winged. The seeds of smooth luffa are smooth and wingless.

Ridged Luffa. Its Latin name is *Luffa acutangula*. Its Chinese name is "Sze Kwa." Some call ridged luffa "Chinese okra" because each fruit resembles a large, long, dark green, club-shaped (wider at one end) okra. It's also known as "angled luffa" because of its odd, S-curved shape. Ridged luffa grows wild in Indonesia and India. In most of Asia, luffa is grown for both food and sponges. At full maturity, they're about a foot long. Ridged or "angled" luffas grow long and slender, with leathery furrows down their length. To prepare them for eating, cut those long ridges off the sides, since they're too stiff to eat.

Smooth Luffa. Its Latin name is *Luffa aegyptiaca*. But its scientific name is unclear because it's also been called *L. cylindrica*, *L. macrocarpa*, and *L. marylandica*. The fruits are significantly bigger than the ridged kind. They're light green and smooth-skinned, and they're straight cylinders rather than S curves.

PLANTING AND GROWING: Luffas are grown much like lagenarias. Allowed a long growing season, they are easy to grow and produce as prolifically as zucchini. You can order luffa seed from Exotica, Gurney, Hudson, Johnny's, Nichols, Redwood City, Shumway, and Thompson & Morgan.

Luffa seeds have unusually hard outer coats and thus are slow to germinate. It helps to start by soaking them at least 12 hours. If you plant them indoors, keep the pot in a dark place in a warm room. Even so, figure on waiting several weeks before seeing a sprout. As soon as the sprout shows, transfer the pot to a situation with good light. At the 2-inch point, cull the weaker-looking plant in a pot. At 3 inches, it's ready to be transplanted outdoors (plant in the evening). It becomes an attractive plant with yellow flowers.

HARVESTING: Gather fruits when young and tender—*no more than 6 inches long*. Longer, older luffa rapidly develops a stringy quality. Luffa has a mild flavor and lots of vitamin B complex.

Recipe Ideas. You can substitute raw luffas in any recipe that calls for raw cucumbers. Or substitute cooked luffas in any recipe for cooked summer squash or okra. Or steam to cook and then add sugar, vinegar, sesame oil, and ginger to flavor. Or cut into strips and saute with other slivered or chopped Chinese vegetables in a little hot sesame oil. Or cut in half the long way; partly scoop out inside; stuff with a mixture of onions, cooked rice, marjoram, and thyme; and bake 40 minutes at 350°F. Or make into a soup by cooking chopped luffa together with sliced shiitake mushrooms, fresh peas, sliced bamboo, or other vegetables. Or cook cut-up chunks of luffa, tomato, onion, and basil in a casserole (sprinkle cheese on top). Or boil, puree, season with a bit of soy sauce, and serve. Or make a Chinese-style stew: Add luffa and other Asian veggies to a cooked pork soup, thicken the broth, and serve. The Japanese prepare chunks of luffa tempura-style.

Luffa Greens and Flowers. You can gather luffa leaves any time and use them raw in salads or cook them like spinach. Luffa bears large, yellow flowers. The plant will bear more fruit if you pick the first several flowers. Substitute them in any recipe for dandelion blossoms!

Luffa Sponges. To get the sponges, you really need to live in a southern zone or have the plants in a greenhouse. First you let the luffas grow past eating size, on to complete maturity on the vine. They will get from 1 to 2 feet long before they quit growing and will be several pounds in weight. To reap the very best sponges, let them stay undisturbed on the vines, where they will first grow to that fully mature size, then ripen, and then dry. If possible, let them dry there until the stem turns yellow and the skin gets dry, paper-thin, and faded in color. Then peel them like an orange. Don't wait until they are fully yellow to peel. Greener skin means a more tender sponge. Yellower skin means a wiry, harsh sponge. (You can soften sponges by boiling them in water 5 minutes.)

When the time comes to harvest the luffas, cut them away from their vine using a keen-edged blade. Dry at least 10 days more, or until their outsides have gotten hard and turned to a brown color. Now open the big end of the luffa. Shake out all its seeds. Get rid of any remaining outer skin, strings, or seeds and rinse out the center of it. Immerse the luffa sponge in water and leave it there 12 hours. Now peel off the outside layer. Dry in the shade. If you need white sponges for some reason, soak your dried sponges for 30 minutes in water that has a little bleach added.

MELONS

This section includes cantaloupe, honeydew, and watermelon. Nichols, Seeds of Change, and Shumway all offer outstanding melon collections. Small cantaloupes can be as quick as 65 days to maturity; watermelons may take as long as 95 days. Good varieties for the north are honeydew and Persian melons.

HEAT: Melons grow best where the summer is hot, dry, and almost constantly sunny—the hotter, the better the flavor. (Cloudy, rainy weather literally stops melons' growth.) Squash are the hardiest cucurbits; cucumbers, a little less hardy; cantaloupes, less hardy; and watermelons, still less. Melons have deep taproots, so they're good at finding water on their own. And direct watering cools off this heat-needing plant and slows down its growth. So if you live in a marginal climate for melons and want to help them along, don't water them—or water only around the edge of the hill, not on the plants. If you don't have plenty of subsoil water, you do need to water them somehow when the weather is hot, at least 1 to 2 inches per week.

PLANTING: If you live in a northern temperate zone, plant your cantaloupe and watermelon seeds as early as you dare. If the seeds rot, plant them again. If those seeds rot, plant again. The longer the season you can manage to give your plants, the better your harvest will be. Allow plenty of room between plants. Keep out the weeds, and you'll get fine melon crops.

You can get a head start on the summer heat by starting plants from seed indoors, several weeks before your last frost date. Transplant after a week of hardening off or set out under a plastic cover, which will keep your ground warm. If you plant in succession every week, you might get a jump on the season if there's a warm spring. You can plant 1 or 2 cantaloupes or bush watermelons in a container the size of half a whiskey barrel; use 5 gal. soil per plant, 12 inches deep and 2 feet between plants. Near harvest time, when frost is coming, pick and discard any little melons that aren't going to make it. Then the plants can concentrate their energy on ripening the hardier melons.

Now on to more species-specific info . . .

Cantaloupe

Cucumis melo is Latin for both the smooth-skinned muskmelons and the netted-skin cantaloupes, although those two are too distantly related to cross-pollinate. Cantaloupes are raised on a truck-garden scale all up and down the bottom of our valley. The bottom is the warmest place of all. Plant 1 inch deep, 6 feet between hills and 6 feet between rows. Allow a week or two to germination and about 90 days to harvest.

HARVESTING CANTALOUPES AND MUSKMELONS: You may find wasps eating your melons. Wasps will nibble at the shell until they get a hole; then they'll eat out a chamber inside the hole, causing the melon to rot inside. If this happens, harvest any melons that are under attack; that minimizes the damage. These melons are ready to pick when the skin starts to get yellowish; they soften up a little and detach readily from the vine. American melons also usually crack away from the stem a little when they are ripe and ready. *Don't pick them green. Cantaloupes and muskmelons (and also watermelons) do not ripen any more after picking.* If the only cantaloupes you've eaten before are those from supermarkets, you've never enjoyed a genuinely ripe melon, since store melons are all picked green and stay that way. A cantaloupe picked green will keep 4 to 6 weeks if stored at 40 to 50°F, but a fully ripe cantaloupe keeps only a week or two. A melon picked green can get softer and can ultimately rot, but it can't get any sweeter.

☙ *CANTALOUPE SWEET PICKLES Cut 12 unripe melons into quarters. Peel the tough outer rind and the mushy, stringy inner surface of each melon. Place fruit in a jar in vinegar to cover, and leave overnight. In the morning, to each pint of vinegar, add ¾ lb. sugar, 1 T. cloves, ½ T. mace, and 4 large sticks of cinnamon, broken into small pieces. Boil the vinegar and spices, and remove the melons to jars. Boil the syrup 30 minutes longer. Pour it hot over the fruit in jars and seal.*

Watermelon

Watermelon, *Citrullus lanatus,* is the best fruit in the world if you're thirsty. It comes from Africa, where early farmers in semi-desert areas developed it as a source of water during droughts. People have lived with no other source of water but watermelon juice for as long as 6 weeks.

Seems like some people can grow watermelon and some can't. I have neighbors who grow fields of watermelon to sell on a truck-garden basis, but I can't seem to grow even one big one. (I've just about decided to quit wasting my time and stick to cantaloupes, which are much easier for me to grow.) Shumway has a great watermelon collection. There are even small watermelon varieties, such as Sugar Bush, that can be grown in a container.

PLANTING: Plant outdoors a week after last frost date, 1 inch deep, 8 feet between hills and 8 feet between rows. Allow a week or two for germination and about 100 days to harvest.

TESTING WATERMELON FOR RIPENESS: Using the thump test, rap the melon with your knuckles; if it sounds hollow, it's ready. The plug test is surer: With a pocketknife, cut a round cork-shaped plug from the side of the watermelon, pull it out, and have a look at what's inside. If it's white, you've been way overeager. If it's pink, it's coming but is not ready yet. If it's bright pink, you can eat the plug and harvest the melon, or slip the plug back in the melon and leave it until you're ready to serve it fresh off the vine for dinner. Another test is to look and see whether the place where the melon skin is lying on the ground has turned kind of white—then it's ripe.

FREEZING MELON: I think the best way to eat a watermelon is to cut it in pieces, start eating, and continue until you're full. But Lane Morgan says mushed-up, frozen watermelon makes good kids' popsicles. And a new neighbor of mine who has lived entirely on raw food for many years freezes melon chunks. He cuts 1-inch chunks from the heart of melons like casabas and honeydews. He doesn't include any rind. If just dicing the melon hasn't given him enough juice for packaging, he mashes a little extra melon to give him juice to pour over the fruit. He packages it in plastic baggies. Here's the extension service's way: Cut the melon into slices, balls, or cubes. Pour cold, light syrup to cover. (Optional: Add 1 t. lemon juice per 1 c. syrup for flavor.) Cover and freeze.

☙ *WATERMELON SEEDS One thing they haven't put on the American market yet is watermelon seeds. But Alice Shattuck wrote me that when her grandmother (and Alice is a grandmother herself!) and her mother used to cook up a lot of watermelon for syrup, they would save all the seeds. They washed the seeds, boiled them a little, dried them off, and spread them on wooden trays to dry in the sun.*

CUCUMBERS

Cucumis sativus, the cucumber genus (of which citron is a member), is easy to grow if you have a warm summer and can avoid insect and disease problems. Before World War II, especially in the South, people had simply given up trying to grow cucumbers because they suffered so from diseases. Then seed companies came out with disease-resistant hybrids that solved most problems—except the cucumber beetle. As with tomatoes, there are a jillion varieties: the familiar green salad cuke, various thin-skinned pickling kinds, little yellow-colored "lemon" cucumbers, long crooked ones from Asia, the Japanese "kyuri" (which they use unpeeled), citron, and so on.

CITRON: Citron looks like a small, round watermelon but is solid clean through, with uniformly green flesh and green seed. (Don't confuse it with the citrus fruit that resembles a large lemon and is also called citron.) Citron is eaten only pickled, preserved in sugar syrup, or candied. You can substitute citron-melon preserves for store-bought citron in fruit cakes, plum puddings, and mincemeat.

LEMON CUCUMBERS: This round, tennis-ball–sized fruit may have a few spines on the skin; just rub them off. Otherwise it's just another cuke.

Planting and Growing

WHEN TO PLANT: Cucumbers are less hardy than winter squashes but are more hardy than melons. Wait to plant or transplant into the garden until the weather is truly warm, after the corn, at the same time that you would plant watermelon—about a week after your last frost date. (A frost would be the end for them.) In a very hot climate like that of the Mississippi Gulf Coast, an early spring planting (February or March) and a late summer one do best. Cucumbers like a warm summer and lots of sunshine.

HOW TO PLANT: Cucumbers need well-manured, well-tilled ground and plenty of water all through their growing season. We plant from seed directly in the garden around June 1, which is when we can start to trust the weather to be and stay warm here. Cucumbers are only 55 to 65 days to maturity, so a late start still gives you time for a good crop if you have a reasonably long growing season.

It's possible to transplant cucumbers, but it's a little risky because they don't do well if their root system is disturbed. So if you start them inside, do so using a system that lets you set them out in the garden in the same block of dirt in which they grew inside—little peat pots, for instance. Or plant in the garden under paper or plastic, which gives you a little extra safety as the weather is warming up.

Most people plant them in hills, 4 to 5 feet apart each way, 1 inch deep. Allow 7 to 10 days for germination, about 75 days to maturity. If you want to plant cucumbers in rows instead of hills, make the rows about 7 feet apart, and thin the plants to 12 to 18 inches apart in the row.

CONTAINER AND TRELLIS GROWING: Cucumbers do exceptionally well in containers, and they produce for city dwellers even in rooftop gardens. You can fit 3 bush cucumber plants into a container the size of half a whiskey barrel. Provide at least 3 gal. soil per plant, at least 1 foot deep, plants at least 6 inches apart. In the garden, you can crowd them more if you give the vines something to climb up. Lane Morgan says she usually uses trellises with hers "to save space and make life harder for the slugs."

THINNING AND WEEDING: In hills, thin to about 4 plants per hill if you have well-composted or manured soil, less if you don't. But don't thin until the plants are at least 3 weeks old, because they have a high fatality rate and you may end up with too few. Weeding in your cucumber patch can be done thoroughly and with a rototiller while the little plants are at home on cucumber hill. But when they start "running," as it's called, with long, leafy stems covering the ground every which way, that's the end of the cultivating. You can still weed by hand, though.

WATERING: Cucumbers need plenty to drink, especially after they start making cucumbers. A cucumber is 95 percent water, which has to come from somewhere. Figure on a deep watering at least once a week. You don't have to water every piece of ground the running vine is covering. If you're short of water, concentrate it near the hill where the primary roots are. Once the cucumber vines start bearing fruit, as long as you keep watering, they will keep bearing cucumbers until the frost kills them. A few vines can produce a lot of cucumbers before the summer is over. But if you let your vines dry out badly, the cucumbers will taste so bitter that you won't be able to eat them, and even the very little ones that have experienced such a drought will grow up with that bitter taste. So if they do dry out badly, it's a good idea to pick off all the cucumbers, water the plant well, and let it start from scratch again.

BEETLES AND DISEASES: Cucumber beetles do their damage while the plant is young, before it starts to run. They attack the lower part of the stem and the underside of the leaves. Commercial farmers generally have more trouble with them than do home gardeners. It doesn't take a whole lot of cucumber plants to give your family a good supply. If you live in cucumber-beetle country, you can protect the little plants by covering them with frames over which you have stretched fly screen or mosquito netting—wooden box-type frames set into the dirt, for instance, or wire frames with the edges of the netting held down by covering with dirt. When the plants have grown big enough to hold their own, you can store away the whole rigging for use next year. It helps control diseases if you destroy the old vines and cucumbers by burning at the end of each year and don't plant cucumbers in the same place in your garden 2 years in a row. If you've never grown cucumbers before, the best way to find out what problems you will face is to simply plant some and see what happens.

Saving Seed

The cucumber is a self-fertile, annual, fruited plant that makes its seed inside the fruit. In this it resembles the entire gourd family—pumpkin, squash, and so on—and also the

nightshade fruits—tomatoes, green peppers, and eggplant. The "fruit" in this case is the cucumber itself.

CROSSES: Cucumbers are cross-pollinated, with the pollen being carried from one flower to another by insects. That means any one cucumber variety will easily cross with another. But cucumbers will not cross with watermelon, muskmelon, pumpkin, or squash—only with other cucumber varieties. So to avoid crosses, pick one open-pollinated cucumber variety and plant just that. Or separate varieties by ¼ mile (preferable) or by at least 100 feet, with some natural barrier like a house in between. That works if you have no gardening neighbors.

SELECTING: Choose your best-looking cucumber fruits from your best-looking vines; really pay attention to health. The cucumbers intended for seed must be left to ripen on the vine. Mark them with a stake or some kind of tag so that somebody doesn't come along and accidentally pick them off.

HARVESTING AND STORING: After being green, your cucumbers for seed will turn yellow and then brown. The skin will become hard, almost like a gourd. Then it's finally ready. You can store the hard brown fruits in a cool place for as long as several weeks at this stage. That enables you to wait until all your seed cukes are ready and then process them all at once.

GETTING OUT THE SEED: Cut each cucumber fruit in half, trying not to damage any more seeds than necessary as you do it. Spoon out the seed together with the surrounding pulp into a nonmetal container (glass or crockery). Let seeds and pulp sit and ferment at room temperature, stirring twice a day. After 2 to 4 days the jellylike pulp that had been clinging around the seeds will change into a thin liquid that lets them go. It's ready for the next step when most of the seeds are at the bottom of the dish and the liquid above is pretty much clear. Don't worry about the seeds that are still floating. They are doing that because they're hollow, no good, and wouldn't grow anyway. Skim and dump those. Don't get in a rush and skip this fermentation procedure because it destroys seed-borne disease—a very important step in saving cucumber seeds.

RINSING AND DRYING SEEDS: Finish the seeds by filling your container with cool water, letting the seeds settle to the bottom and pouring off what's left. Do that several times. Now spread out the seeds to dry, no more than 1 layer deep, in a place like a sunny window. Don't use artificial heat like an oven or a heat lamp, because that could hurt or kill them. Figure on at least 2 days for them to dry, and then you can store.

STORING SEEDS: Label them with the year, their variety, and the characteristics you selected them for. It's a long time until next spring or the spring after that, and you're liable to forget if you don't record it. Store seeds in a cold, dry place. Don't panic if they freeze. If the seed is dry, freezing not only won't hurt but may even improve the crop. Cucumber seeds can easily germinate for 5 years and maybe more.

Harvesting

Keep picking to keep your vines producing. Pick cukes while they're green and small for the best taste. Pick according to the size of cucumber that your recipe calls for. In general, 3–9 inches long is about right. You can actually pickle or eat any size, but cucumbers that are getting yellow and seedy are not nearly as tasty. All you have to do once the cucumbers are big enough to suit you is gently pluck them off the vine and carry them into the house. Store extras in the refrigerator while you're figuring out what to do with them.

Very young, tender cucumbers can be used peel and all. "Midgets" are those up to 3 inches. They go into your midget crock—a glass gallon jar will do. "Dills" are those 3 to 6 inches long. Cucumbers over 6 inches long are "slicers" to be used fresh or to make cucumber sandwiches (slice peeled cucumbers and mayonnaise on homemade bread) or instant pickles (put thinly sliced, peeled cucumbers in a salt-vinegar-water brine). Great big cukes don't make good pickles anyway because they get too hollow in the middle.

If you've seen only store-bought cucumbers you may not know about yellow ones, but the life cycle of a cucumber goes like this: blossom, tiny green cucumber, big green cuke, real big green cuke, yellow cuke, brown cuke. Yellow/brown is the proper stage for saving seed or feeding to cows, pigs, or chickens. But some people cook the yellow ones or make pickles out of them.

STORING AND PRESERVING: Store green cukes in a basket in a cool, damp place such as your root cellar. Storing at 45–55°F, 80–90 percent humidity, will keep them fresh as long as is possible for cukes—which isn't all that long. Then you'll need to shift to another method.

Freezing. I've been told that if you wrap individual servings of sliced cucumbers in foil and freeze them, they make a delicious dish that winter served unwrapped, thawed, in individual dishes. Mix heavy cream with a little dollop of lemon juice and pour it over them.

Drying. I used to think pickling was the only way to preserve cucumbers. As on many other points, my readers have educated me. Jeanne Weston from Durango, CO, sent me a lot of advice about home-drying foods, and she says you can dry cucumbers. She has done it and says they make good salad flavorings. She thinly slices them, dries them until brittle, and stores them until needed. Then she breaks up the dried cucumber into small pieces and scatters them over her winter salad.

Recipe Ideas

RAW CUKES: Cucumbers are good raw in salads and sandwiches. Or peel and cut into sticks or chips and serve plain or with dip. Or make a gourmet salad: sharp cheese, Greek olives, tomatoes, and cukes, all chunked and tossed with raw greens and salad dressing. Or serve cuke slices with chopped onion, tomato, raw greens, and blue cheese dressing.

Boats. If allowed to grow, cucumbers will get very large—as long as 10 inches or so. Such a fat cucumber makes a fine child's boat for the bathtub. Cut in half lengthwise, scoop out the seeds, and there's your boat. You can feed the other oversized, yellowed, or imperfect cucumbers to the chickens and pigs. When feeding them to chickens, first break cukes open. If the chickens aren't hungry enough to stoop to cucumbers, the cukes will still make fine compost.

Sandwiches. In summer we eat lots of cucumber sandwiches, a quick lunch at a time of year when cucumbers are abundant and time is not. Peel and slice fresh cucumbers. Spread homemade bread with mayo, layer on sliced cucumbers—maybe add slices of fresh garden tomato—and top with another slice of bread.

Instant Pickles. I usually feel like I'm making oh-so-many of these and then discover that by the time the meal is on the table, they are already two-thirds gone, thanks to snitchers and big ones (my husband loves them too). I just peel and slice several cucumbers as for sandwiches. Put them in a bowl with salt, vinegar, and water. Now you are going to ask: "How much of each?" Sigh. I never measure, just taste my way to success, so I don't know. It adds up to just barely enough liquid to cover. About half vinegar, half cold water, and maybe ½ t. salt. It is a salty dish. The salt pulls the bitterness out of the cucumbers. It needs to be made at least 15 minutes ahead of the meal to let the salt work. The longer ahead you make it, the less salt you should use. It won't keep; it gets too strong.

➣ *INSTANT SALAD Wendy Czebotar, Kennewick, WA, slices cucumbers across in very thin slices, sprinkles them with salt in between, and then lets them set in the refrigerator an hour. Then she takes them out; squeezes out all the excess water to make the cukes limp; adds chopped onion, vinegar, oil, salt, and pepper; and serves.*

➣ *SOUR CREAM CUCUMBERS Peel 3 cucumbers. Mix with ½ t. salt. While the cucumbers are being worked on by the salt, peel and slice 3 small-to-medium onions, and add. Make a dressing by beating together 1 c. sour cream, 1½ T. vinegar, and 2 T. sugar or the equivalent in honey. Pour dressing over and serve.*

➣ *YOGURT CUCUMBERS Jan Franco, Hamden, CT, says cucumbers are also great in yogurt with a bit of dill weed and salt. She just slices them up and tosses them in the yogurt; there's no need to soak them with salt. Or season them with fresh mint leaves and coriander.*

➣ *CUCUMBER JUICE Peel cukes, grate, and squeeze.*

Cooked Cukes: Cukes can also be eaten cooked, as you might a summer squash, in soups and vegetable dishes. See summer squash recipes for more possibilities; you can often substitute cukes for zukes.

➣ *COOKED CUCUMBERS AND TOMATOES Saute 2 peeled, chopped cucumbers with 4 chopped tomatoes. Season with salt, pepper, a few dill seeds, and a bit of lemon juice or vinegar. Or saute with tomatoes, onions, and bacon, and season with chiles.*

➣ *FRIED CUCUMBERS Edna Andrews wrote me from Ravensdale, WA, with this recipe—a new idea to me. She said, "I slice the cucumbers, take these thin slices, and salt, pepper, and flour them. I put a thin amount of butter in the skillet and fry them. They look like fried green tomatoes but taste somewhat different."*

➣ *STUFFED YELLOW CUKES Lane Morgan told me she'd heard about "big yellow cuke blimps seeded; stuffed with a meat mixture; browned in bacon fat plus cucumber juice, vinegar, sugar, and salt; and then served with boiled potatoes. I tried a baked version of that, with burger and I forget what else, and it was pretty good."*

➣ *CUKE SOUP Cook pork until done. Add turnip and cucumber chunks and brassica greens and cook until tender.*

Pickles

Lots of vegetables get pickled (or made into a relish), including other cucurbits—citron, summer squash, unripe

cantaloupe, and watermelon rind. But when I think "pickles," it's cucumbers that first come to mind. There are 2 basic pickle categories: "quick" pickles and "fermented" (crock) pickles. Fermented pickles are whole, but quicks can be either whole or cut.

SECRETS OF MAKING QUICK PICKLES

1. If you're planning to make both quick pickles and fermented pickles, make the quick (unfermented) pickles first. That way you make your crock pickles around September. This is best because it helps if they don't ferment at a warm temperatures. At 80°F or above they'll spoil.
2. Get the cucumbers into the brine quite soon after picking. If you have to hold them any time, refrigerate or at least keep them in the shade with a wet cloth over them. Cucumbers deteriorate rapidly, especially at warm temperatures.
3. Wash them well. Handle gently to avoid bruising, since bruised places decay easier. Remove any blossoms because they are a source of enzymes that cause unwanted softening during fermentation. Don't soak cucumbers in water before pickling. They will fill with water and won't soak up the brine.
4. Don't use zinc, copper, brass, galvanized metal, or iron containers or utensils. Don't use plastic containers that are not food-grade (such as a garbage can).

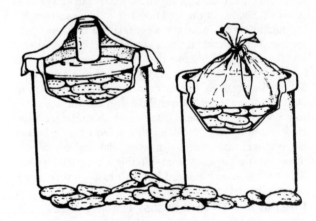

5. Use pure granulated salt ("pickling salt"), not iodized table salt, because the additive that keeps it free-flowing may make the brine cloudy. Don't use flake salt or rock salt.
6. For the best flavor, use fresh spices. Whole spices are best. Powdered spices may cause the pickles to darken and become cloudy. If you raise your own dill, by the time your cucumbers are ready for pickling, the dill should have matured its seed heads and be ready for cutting. You use stems, heads, and seeds, either dried or fresh from the garden. Dill heads give better flavor than dill seeds; 1 t. seeds equals 1 dill head. To use dill oil, substitute 1 drop for each head of dill.
7. Don't make the pickles using heavily chlorinated water. Hard water may cause cloudiness and off-colors. If only hard water is available, boil and let sit for 24 hours. Skim off scum and use water from the top of the container without disturbing any sediment.
8. Vinegar is the most important ingredient in recipes for quick pickles. Without an adequate amount of water, the pickles won't be safe to eat. Use vinegar with

LOWER-TEMPERATURE PASTEURIZATION

Here, for use in the recipes that call for it (and only those!), is a canning processing method that you can use for certain pickles to avoid a "cooked" quality. Processing at temperatures lower than the boiling point of water can give you crunchier, nicer pickles. But follow directions carefully to avoid spoilage.

1. Place jars in a canner half-filled with warm water (120–140°F). Add hot water to a level of 1 inch above jars.
2. Heat the water to 180–185°F and start a timer. Process for 30 minutes, checking with a candy or jelly thermometer to be certain that the water temperature is at least 180°F but not much higher (temperatures higher than 185°F may cause softening of pickles).
3. Immediately remove jars from canner at end of processing time.
4. Put jars on a rack or cloth so air can move freely around them.

5 percent acidity. Don't reduce the amount of vinegar or increase the amount of water in a recipe. For a less sour taste, just add a small amount of sugar. You can use white or cider vinegar. Don't use homemade vinegar unless you're sure of its acidity.

9. Cucumber slices are sometimes soaked in a lime-water solution for 12 to 24 hours before pickling. Lime contains calcium, which improves pickle firmness. *The lime should be food-grade. Don't use lime sold at garden centers or lumber yards.*

You may can your cucumber pickles whole or slice them into fourths, sixths, or eighths—depending on how big the cucumber is. Dill pickles are sliced lengthwise; bread-and-butter pickles are sliced crosswise.

The following recipes are courtesy of Pacific Northwest Cooperative Extension.

QUICK KOSHER DILLS: You'll need 4 lb. pickling cucumbers (4 inches long), 14 split garlic cloves, ¼ c. pickling salt, 2¾ c. vinegar (5 percent), 3 c. water, 14 heads fresh dill, and 28 peppercorns. Yield: 6 to 7 pints. Wash cucumbers and cut in half lengthwise. Heat garlic, salt, vinegar, and water to boiling. Remove garlic and place 4 halves into each pint or quart jar. Pack cucumbers into jars, adding 2 heads dill and 4 peppercorns. Pour hot vinegar solution over cucumbers to within ½ inch of top. Adjust lids; use water-bath processing and the "raw pack" times in the "Processing Times for Water-Bath–Canning Quick Pickles" table. Or use lower-temperature pasteurization.

PROCESSING TIMES FOR WATER-BATH–CANNING QUICK PICKLES

		Altitude (feet)		
Style Pack	Jar Size	1–1,000	1,001–6,000	Over 6,000
Hot	Pints/quarts	5 min.	10 min.	15 min.
Raw	Pints	10	15	20
Raw	Quarts	15	20	25

QUICK SWEET PICKLES: You'll need 4 lb. pickling cucumbers (3 to 4 inches long), ⅓ c. canning or pickling salt, 4½ c. sugar, 3½ c. vinegar (5 percent), 2 t. celery seed, 1 T. whole allspice, and 2 T. mustard seed. Yield will be 7 to 9 pints. Wash the cucumbers. Cut tip off blossom end, but leave ¼ inch of stem at other end. Slice or cut into strips. Place in bowl and sprinkle with ⅓ c. salt. Cover with 2 inches of crushed or cubed ice. Refrigerate 3 to 4 hours. Add more ice as needed. Drain well. Combine sugar, vinegar, celery seed, allspice, and mustard seed in 6-qt. kettle. Heat to boiling.

Hot Pack. Add cucumbers and heat slowly until vinegar solution returns to a boil. Stir occasionally to make sure mixture heats evenly. Then fill pint or quart jars, leaving ½ inch headspace.

Raw Pack. Fill pint or quart jars with cucumbers, leaving ½ inch headspace. Then add hot pickling syrup, leaving ½ inch headspace.

Processing. Adjust lids and process in a water-bath canner for the time appropriate to your altitude, as listed in the "Processing Times for Water-Bath–Canning Quick Pickles" table. Or use lower-temperature pasteurization. For the best flavor, store 4 to 5 weeks.

FIRMER (LIME-TREATED) QUICK SWEET PICKLES: Use liming solution and procedure for Firm Bread-and-Butter Pickles. For the rest of the procedure, use the preceding Quick Sweet Pickle recipe.

ONION-FLAVORED QUICK SWEET PICKLES: Add 2 slices raw whole onion to each jar of Quick Sweet Pickles before filling with cucumbers.

REDUCED-SODIUM SLICED SWEET PICKLES: You'll need 3 lb. cucumbers (3 to 4 inches long). Wash cucumbers and cut off blossom end. Cut cucumbers into ¼-inch slices. You'll need a canning syrup: Combine 1⅔ c. distilled white vinegar (5 percent), 3 c. sugar, 1 T. whole allspice, and 2¼ t. celery seed in a pan. Bring to a boil and keep hot until used. And you need a brining solution: In a large kettle, combine 1 qt. distilled white vinegar (5 percent), 1 T. canning or pickling salt, 1 T. mustard seed, and ½ c. sugar.

Now add the sliced cucumbers to your brining solution, cover, and simmer until the cucumbers change color from bright to dull green (5 to 7 minutes). Drain the cucumber slices. Fill *pint jars only*. Cover the slices with hot canning syrup, leaving ½ inch headspace. Adjust lids.

Use water-bath processing and the "raw pack" times in the "Processing Times for Water-Bath–Canning Quick Pickles" table. Or use lower-temperature pasteurization. Yields 4–5 pt.

BREAD-AND-BUTTER PICKLES: You'll need 6 lb. pickling cucumbers (4–5 inches long), 8 c. thinly sliced onions (about 3 lb.), ½ c. canning or pickling salt, 4 c. vinegar (5 percent), 4½ c. sugar, 2 T. mustard seed, 1½ T. celery seed, and 1 T. ground turmeric. Yield will be about 8 pt. Wash the cucumbers. Cut 1/16 inch off the blossom end and discard that. Cut into very thin slices ("3/16 inches"—those extension folks are so precise!). Combine cucumbers and sliced onions in a large bowl. Add salt. Cover with 2 inches crushed or cubed ice. Refrigerate 3 to 4 hours, adding more ice as needed. Drain. Combine remaining ingredients in a large pot. Boil 10 minutes. Add cucumbers and onions and slowly reheat to boiling. Fill pint or quart jars with slices and cooking syrup, leaving ½ inch headspace. Adjust lids.

You can use water-bath processing or lower-temperature pasteurization. For water-bath processing, process either pints or quarts 10 minutes at 1–1,000 feet, 15 minutes at 1,001–6,000 feet, 20 minutes above 6,000 feet. After processing and cooling, store your jars 4 to 5 weeks before serving to let them develop the best flavor.

FIRM (LIME-TREATED) BREAD-AND-BUTTER PICKLES.
Use preceding Bread-and-Butter Pickle recipe, except after your cucumbers are sliced, soak them in lime water. To make the lime water, mix 1 c. pickling lime and ½ c. salt per 1 gal. water. Use a 2- to 3-gal. crock or enamelware container. Avoid inhaling lime dust while mixing the lime-water solution. Soak the cucumber slices in the lime water for 12 to 24 hours, stirring occasionally. Then remove from the lime solution, rinse, and resoak 1 hour in fresh cold water. Repeat the rinsing and soaking 2 more times in fresh water. Handle carefully—slices will be brittle. Drain well. Proceed with the remainder of the Bread-and-Butter Pickle recipe steps.

SWEET GHERKIN (4-DAY) PICKLES:
You'll need 7 lb. of cucumbers (1½ inch long or less), ½ c. canning or pickling salt, 6 c. vinegar (5 percent), 8 c. sugar, ¾ t. turmeric, 2 t. celery seeds, and 2 cinnamon sticks. Optional spices: 2 t. whole mixed pickling spice, ½ t. fennel, and 2 t. vanilla. Yield will be 6–7 pt. Wash cucumbers. Cut off blossom end and discard, but leave ¼ inch of stem attached.

Place cucumbers in large container and cover with boiling water. After 6–8 hours, drain and cover with 6 qt. fresh boiling water containing ¼ c. salt. Repeat on the second day. On the third day, drain and prick cucumbers with a table fork. Combine and bring to a boil 3 c. vinegar, 3 c. sugar, and spices. Pour over cucumbers. After 6–8 hours, drain and save the pickling syrup. Add another 2 c. each of sugar and vinegar to the syrup and reheat to boiling. Pour over pickles. On the fourth day, drain and save syrup. Add another 2 c. sugar and 1 c. vinegar. Heat syrup to boiling and pour over pickles. Let sit and then drain 6 to 8 hours later, saving the pickling syrup. Add 1 c. sugar and 2 t. vanilla and heat to boiling.

Fill *pint* jars with pickles and cover with hot syrup, leaving ½ inch headspace. Adjust lids and process in water-bath canner using the "hot pack" times in the "Processing Times for Water-Bath–Canning Quick Pickles" table. Or use lower-temperature pasteurization. Or process using lower-temperature pasteurization.

FERMENTED ("BRINED") CUCUMBER PICKLES:
Not very many people make crock pickles nowadays—not because it's hard to do, but mainly because people are suspicious of the yucky-looking stuff on top that I will hereafter refer to as "scum." The scum is lactic acid bacteria that grow, change the pickle color and flavor, and produce a desirable acid. Old-fashioned crock pickles are cured by fermentation, and the scum is the fermentation agent. The bacteria have to be in the crock at least 3 weeks (longer if temperatures are cooler) to complete the process of fermentation. During that time, they will change in color from bright green to an olive or yellow green, and the white inside will become translucent.

To keep them in the crock all winter, which is what Great-Grandmother did and also the way they were stored in the pickle barrel down at the general store, they must be very acid and salty so as not to spoil. But that hasn't been necessary since canning was invented.

SECRETS OF MAKING FERMENTED PICKLES

1. You can't make crock pickles from waxed grocery-store cucumbers. The brine cannot penetrate the wax. So you'll be using cucumbers from your own or a friend's garden.
2. Don't let dirt in the pickle crock. The more beasties there are in the food at the moment you put it into the pickling solution, the greater your risk.

3. You'll need 1 gal. of container for each 5 lb. of pickles. A 5-gal. crock will hold 25 lb. of cukes. Or use glass or food-grade plastic. *But it's not safe to use garbage cans or other containers that are not made to come into contact with food that will be eaten.* For the container, a "crock" is traditional, but glass jars (gallon or larger) and unchipped enamel, plastic, or wood containers work fine.
4. Don't use a reduced-sodium salt. Fermented pickles need a specific amount of sodium to control bacterial growth and have a firm texture.
5. Alum is sometimes used to firm fermented cucumbers. But it isn't necessary. (Alum doesn't do anything useful for quick pickles.) I don't use it because I have a general principle of avoiding aluminum.
6. You need a weight to keep fermenting food under the brine. When using a crock, choose a dinner plate or glass pie plate that is slightly smaller than the crock. Weight it down with 2- or 3-qt. jars (with lids) filled with water. For a different kind of weight, fill a large food-grade plastic bag (either heavyweight or double-bagged) with brine (in case it breaks). The plate should be well below the top of the fluid so that your pickles are under 2 inches of brine. Your pickled food must always be kept completely covered by the protective brine, preferably by a safety margin of at least 2 inches.

7. Don't let the fluid get too low. The water will slowly evaporate. Keep a cloth over the top to keep bugs out.

8. *It's extremely important to wait until fermented pickles taste tart before canning them.* Use either water-bath processing or lower-temperature pasteurization.

Fermented Dill Pickles. For each gallon you want to make, you'll need 4 lb. cucumbers (about 4 inches long), 2 T. dill seed or 4 to 5 heads fresh or dried dill weed, 2 cloves garlic (optional), 2 dried red peppers (optional), 2 t. whole mixed pickling spices (optional), ½ c. salt, ¼ c. vinegar (5 percent), and 8 c. water.

Wash cucumbers. Trim off blossom end, but leave ¼ inch of stem at the other end. Place half of dill and half of the other flavorings on the bottom of a clean, suitable container (see "Secrets of Making Fermented Pickles"). Add cucumbers, remaining dill, and flavorings. Dissolve salt in vinegar and water. Pour over cucumbers. Cover and weight down cover. Store where temperature is 70–75°F for about 3 to 4 weeks. Temperatures of 55–65°F are acceptable, but the fermentation will take 5 to 6 weeks in that case. Your pickles will get too soft if temperatures are above 80°F during fermentation. Check the container several times a week. Skim off surface scum or mold. *If pickles become soft or slimy or develop a disagreeable odor, discard them.*

Fully fermented pickles may be stored in the original container for 4 to 6 months, provided you refrigerate them and remove surface scum and molds regularly. But canning is a better way to store fully fermented pickles. To can them, pour the brine into a pan, heat slowly to a boil, and simmer 5 minutes. Filter brine through clean cloth or paper coffee filters to reduce cloudiness, if desired. Fill pint or quart jars with pickles and hot brine. Leave ½ inch headspace. Put on lids. This is a raw pack. Process pints in boiling water bath 15 minutes at 1–6,000 feet above sea level, 20 minutes above 6,000 feet. Process quarts an extra 5 minutes.

NIGHTSHADES

Eggplant, peppers, and tomatoes (as well as husk tomatoes, ground cherries, and tomatillos) are all related. They're members of the big nightshade family (Solanaceae) and are also called "solanums." (I talk about potatoes and huckleberry, which are nightshades too, elsewhere in this book.) Martynia and okra are not solanums but are grown and bear fruit so similarly, and are so different from other plants, that I squeezed them in here too.

GENERAL INFO ON RAISING SOLANUMS: Eggplant, okra, peppers, and tomatoes share the same basic nature: All are tropical natives grown as annuals in the temperate zone. All refuse to germinate unless their ground is warm, grow slowly in cool weather, and may be badly and permanently stunted by exposure to a temperature below 45°F, so they're often protected by a cloche for the first part of their garden time. All take a long time to bear fruit, so northern growers must start them indoors. All do best of all when soil and air temperatures stay very warm. Try out species and varieties until you find the one that suits your climate and cooking best. But there is one group of nightshades that is easy to grow: the Physalis group (ground cherries and tomatillos). See "Planting" in the "Tomato" section for much more info on starting nightshades.

Soil. A good soil combination is 1 part each peat, sand, and garden dirt. If you are worried about disease or bug prob-

lems in the dirt, sterilize it in the oven at 180°F for 45 minutes. Put your seedbed dirt into shallow boxes, small growing pots, or big tin cans with drainage holes in the bottom. The dirt should come up to about ¼ inch below the rim of the container. (See "Planting" in the "Tomatoes" section for more information useful for planting any nightshade.) About 2 hours before planting, moisten your seedbed dirt well. Then plant, and let them grow. They'll do best in a really warm place, such as near your furnace. Water as needed. Before transplanting them to the garden, harden them off.

Hardening Off. Most nightshades, especially peppers and eggplant, should be "hardened off" before transplanting from house to garden. Start 10 days before they will be set out by taking them outside on warm days, bringing them in each night. Leave them outside (unless the weather gets unseasonably cold) the last 2 or 3 nights. Then plant them in the garden—in the evening if possible. Make sure they aren't shocked by cold soil or cold air. They can't go out if nighttime temps are below 50°F. Keep them growing inside until then.

Keep them well watered their first few days. After that, water when they're dry. In blistering hot weather, protect them from the worst of the sun. After the soil gets good and warm, you can mulch to help keep it damp, but don't mulch prematurely, because that delays the warming of the soil—and your harvest.

Storing. Don't cram fruit into airtight plastic bags. That will make them spoil sooner rather than later.

Eggplant

Eggplant (*Solanum melongena*) is a tropical perennial grown for thousands of years in China and India and since the 16th century in Europe. Technically and botanically, the eggplant is a "berry" (so is a pumpkin!). It takes up space and doesn't bear heavily, so it's not practical for a small garden. Most eggplant varieties are grown as an annual in temperate zones; to bear fruit, they need a growing season of at least 90 days, with hot days and warm nights. (Eggplant is the most temperature-sensitive solanum.) Disease or bugs may get it. On the good side, eggplants are pretty, they're in their element and produce well in both heat and drought, and garden-fresh eggplants are wonderful.

VARIETIES: Glecklers sells Louisiana Green Oval, which bears large (up to 4 lb.), light green, mild-flavored fruits; Snake-Eye mini-eggplant, which bears ½-inch fruits that can be mashed into a sauce; Small Ruffled Red, which bears 2-inch red fruits; and white Italian types. The familiar big, oval, purple variety is *Solanum melongena* var. *esculentum,* also called "aubergine" (especially outside the United States). It is the best keeper, and that's why you see it in supermarkets. However, aubergine needs a growing season of about 120 days, and it usually ripens a total of only 2 to 6 fruits, each weighing 1–5 lb. depending on climate, soil, care, and the plant itself. You can get hybrids and Orientals that fruit as soon as 55 days. Black Beauty, a disease-resistant non-hybrid, bears aubergine-like fruit in only 80 days.

Orientals. These are hardier and quicker to harvest than the aubergine. They produce about twice as many fruits and do so earlier, and they produce several fruits at a time. Lane Morgan says, "Short-season and cool-season growers should stick with the Oriental kinds if my experience is any guide." You can order Orientals from Burpee, Gurney's, Hudson, Johnny's, Kitazawa, Le Jardin, Nichols, Park, and Redwood City. But the seed companies are liable to call them anything, making the Oriental connection hard to recognize at times.

One Thai eggplant is round, white, and baseball-sized. Another Thai is tiny with purple streaks near its stem. The Japanese have a purplish black, cucumber-shaped, foot-long one called "black eggplant" or "nasubi." Nasubi has a delicate, edible skin, so it doesn't keep well and is more vulnerable to flea beetles. It doesn't cook up mushy like the aubergine, instead keeping a pleasant, crunchy texture. Chinese eggplant, grown there for millennia, is long, thin, and lavender/violet. The Indian type is long, deep purple, and club-shaped. Bitter Orange is the strangest Oriental eggplant, so bitter it spices up bland dishes. It resembles a small, flat green pepper.

PLANTING: Eggplants thrive in well-drained, sandy, really rich soil (2 or 3 inches of manure or compost worked in well). If bacterial wilt is a risk, make sure the soil hasn't been previously used to grow eggplant, peppers, or tomatoes. Plant in a seed flat in March or April. The best germination temperature is 75 to 90°F. Allow 12 to 15 days for sprouting. Transplant to peat pots after they get 2 inches tall. (Or you can buy plants at setting-out time.)

Transplanting and Garden Growing. Transplant 6 to 8 weeks later but not until at least 2 weeks after the last frost date; even then, they'll do best starting under plastic. A late frost will kill them, and they won't do anything in cold soil anyway except stand there weak and vulnerable to bugs and disease. (If you do get disease in your garden, pull out and burn affected plants.) Plant where sheltered from cold winds, ¼ to ½ inch deep, 18 to 30 inches apart, rows 2 to 3 feet apart (wider for longer, hotter growing seasons or bigger varieties). They produce better if you add more manure

during their growing. The water supply needs to be moderate but regular—about once a week at the most. In drought they seal up their pores like a cactus to save water, and they thrive anyway, but too much watering causes watery, bland-tasting fruit. Eggplants also do better if their roots aren't walked on.

Container Growing. Put 1 plant in each 12-inch pot (3 gal. soil). The container's dirt should be at least a foot deep. If multiple plants are in a large container, leave at least 18 inches between them. Eggplant does well in a tub on a patio and is easy to bring in before a chill. You can grow a lot of eggplant in a tub indoors because eggplant is self-pollinating and doesn't need insects to help it bear fruit. If you live in a subtropical zone or keep your eggplant warm year-round, it can live 6 years and get as tall as 8 feet!

SAVING SEED: Eggplant is a fruited, self-fertile (self-pollinated) annual. Its flowers have both male and female parts and its flowers can attract insects, so crossing with other eggplant varieties is technically possible but likely only if there's another variety within 20 feet. Select the best fruits on your best plants and identify them. Leave on the bush the eggplants destined to make seed—until they fall off, if possible, because that means the seeds inside are fully mature. But if frost is a risk and the fruit is ripe enough to be eaten, you can pick them and store them indoors. After about 2 more weeks, the seeds should be mature. Clean the seeds then, because if you wait too long, the fruit will rot—seeds and all.

Cut the fruit in half, and scoop out the seeds and the pulp that contains them into a glass bowl. Add water until you can easily work the seeds and their pulp around with your fingers. Knead and squish them around until the seeds have all been freed and have sunk to the bottom. Pour off the water. (You may have to squish and pour several times.) Now spread out the seeds to dry in a sunny spot at room temperature, gently separating them if they stick together. Eggplant seeds live about 5 years.

HARVESTING: Eggplants produce most in hot, sunny weather. Cool, rainy weather cuts your harvest to a fraction of that. Aubergines typically bloom in early July but don't have mature fruits until the end of August or even early September. You can start harvesting as soon as the fruits are shiny and as big as a large egg. If not picked, they'll continue growing slowly to their variety's size. Be sure to get aubergines before they get overmature—before the skin loses its gloss and the fruit is longer than 8 inches. These are signs the fruit has gotten bitter. The younger ones are more tender and have smaller seeds and no bitterness. And picking early results in more fruit being set. Cut fruit off using a sharp blade because the stem is tough and pulling can cause damage.

STORING AND PRESERVING: Eggplants store better on the vine than anywhere else, so it makes sense to leave them there until your menu calls for eggplant. Off the vine they store best if part of the stem is still attached. Or you can preserve by drying or freezing.

Drying. Peel and slice ⅛ to ¼ inch thick. You can dry those whole slices or further cut them down into ½-inch strips or 1-inch squares. *Steam-blanch* about 4 minutes for full-sized slices, 3 minutes for little ones. In a dehydrator or oven, dry at 120°F for about 18 hours. They're done when leathery and dry all the way to the middle. Or dry in

There are several edible *Physalis* species within the solanum category: *Physalis peruviana,* the ground cherry; *P. alkekengi,* the lantern plant (one of the few edible plants not covered in this book; you can read about it in Deep Diversity's catalog); and *Physalis ixocarpa,* the tomatillo (discussed a bit later).

For more info order "Ground Cherries, Husk Tomatoes, and Tomatillos," a 22-page booklet by C. Dremann, from Redwood City. For more on the ground cherry and tomatillo, also see *Unusual Vegetables: Something New for This Year's Garden* by the editors at Rodale Press.

---

a single layer in full sun and freely moving air. Takes 2 to 3 days. (Take trays inside at night.)

Using Dried Eggplant. Start by soaking dried slices or pieces in water for several hours or even overnight. Then use them in recipes as you would fresh eggplant. You can use dried pieces in long-cooking recipes without presoaking. Just add some extra liquid.

Freezing. Peel; slice or dice. Add 1 T. lemon juice per 1 qt. water, and put eggplant pieces in water to protect their color while they're waiting to blanch. Steam-blanch, or scald 2 to 4 minutes. Cool. Dip again into the lemon-juice solution, drain well, and freeze. Or precook eggplant, put wax paper between slices, and freeze.

Canning. Eggplant doesn't can well.

PREPARING: You can peel or not peel. *If you're not peeling supermarket eggplant, wash them well. They've been sprayed a lot!* Home-grown, freshly harvested fruits have a tender peel that you can remove with a potato peeler. White fruits generally are eaten skins and all.

Some people salt eggplant before cooking, no matter what the recipe (except if they're going to split it down the middle, scoop out the insides, stuff the halves, and bake). If you want to salt, slice your eggplant (peeled or unpeeled), sprinkle each slice with salt, stack them on top of each other, weight them down, and leave them for about 30 minutes. Then they pour off the liquid that has seeped out, rinse the slices, and proceed with the recipe.

Bitter Orange Recipe Ideas. This strong-tasting Oriental can be presoaked and then stewed Chinese-style with pork shreds, greens, and hot peppers. Or saute slowly with hot peppers and greens until soft. Or marinate in vinegar to pickle it. Or presoak and cook with tofu, vegetables, and hot peppers to make a soup.

Eggplant Recipe Ideas. Eggplant has only 19 calories per cup. Here are some ways to fry it: Dip thinly sliced eggplant into buttermilk and then in seasoned flour; fry coated pieces. Or dip into an egg-and-milk mixture and then into fine homemade bread crumbs; fry in oil, first on one side and then the other. Or (from reader Mary Debonis's Italian friend) dip into beaten eggs and then into flour; fry until brown, turning once; layer the fried slices in a casserole, alternating them with grated Italian cheese and Italian Gravy (see "Cooked Tomato Recipe Ideas" in the "Tomato" section); and bake 20 minutes at 350°F. Ruth's vegan "fried" eggplant: Marinate unsalted slices in lemon juice or tamari (and your choice of herbs), roll in bread crumbs, and cook in tomato sauce, covered, until tender.

BABA GANOUJ ("EGGPLANT CAVIAR") This is a Middle Eastern eggplant dip or sandwich spread. Cut off stem ends of 1 large or several smaller eggplants. Bake them whole on a cookie sheet at 400°F for 45 minutes—until they're sagging, wrinkled, and quite soft. Cool. Scoop out the flesh from the peel, and blend or mash with a fork with one or more of the following: ½ c. finely chopped onion, 2 crushed garlic cloves, 3 T. lemon juice, salt to taste, 1 T. minced parsley, and 1 T. olive oil. Vegan Ruth makes it with only eggplant, garlic, and enough lemon juice for consistency and flavor. Or she may add parsley or onion, or a scoop of tahini. She and her family use baba ganouj as a thick salad dressing or sandwich spread, and they also spoon it over baked potatoes. You can also blend it with ½ c. yogurt or sour cream. It's also good with dark bread or chips.

VEGAN GRILLED EGGPLANT STEAKS Remove stem end from a large eggplant and slice lengthwise into 4 equal slabs. Trim peel off each slab. Crush 2 or 3 garlic cloves and mix with ¼ t. oregano, 1 t. tamari, 2 T. lemon juice, and 2 T. water (or tomato juice). Poke a few shallow holes in each steak with a fork. Then drizzle on the marinade. Grill for 15 to 20 minutes over slow coals, turning and basting frequently. Place a slice of ripe red tomato on each "steak." Drizzle on more marinade, and cover with grill hood for a few minutes.

EGGPLANT AND PASTA Slice an unpeeled, large eggplant the long way into French fry–size strips. Saute them in a little olive oil about 15 minutes. Add a dozen sliced fresh mushrooms and fry 10 more minutes. Pour 4 c. of any kind of warm tomatoey sauce over 1 lb. of cooked pasta (penne is traditional). Now mix in the eggplant and mushrooms. Season with a little salt, pepper, and Parmesan cheese.

Ground Cherry

The ground cherry (*Physalis pruinosa* or *P. peruviana*) is also called the "strawberry tomato" and "husk tomato," but it's not a true tomato. This low, bushy plant bears fruit about the size of a small cherry. The fruit is round and yellow, and it grows inside a thin, paperlike husk.

VARIETIES: The ground cherry is a native of the Central and South American tropics; there are many wild and domestic species of it there. Deep Diversity's seed catalog divides the ground cherry into these varieties: *P. peruviana,* the basic 3- to 5-foot rambling plant with 1-inch berries, the most flavorful of all; the giant ground cherry, which is from Guatemala and is the biggest; and the Goldenberry (cape gooseberry), which is bigger than *P. peruviana* and matures earliest.

PLANTING AND GROWING: Seeds are available from Burgess, DeGiorgi, Henry Field, Hudson, Nichols, Shumway, and Thompson & Morgan. Follow procedures for planting and growing tomatoes. Plant ½ inch deep in full sun. The ground cherry will grow in poor soil and needs little care. In northern zones, you can start seed inside, harden off young plants, and transplant to the garden at 6 weeks or later, at least a week after the last spring frost. These plants grow across the ground like tomatoes, 1 or 2 feet high and off in every direction. So plant 3 feet apart. Water if the ground gets dry. Keep the ground weeded and cultivated so it doesn't pack around the plants. To grow in a greenhouse or container, start in peat pots; at 2 inches, transplant to 12-inch pots. You can squeeze 2 into a 10-inch pot. In a window box, space plants 18 inches apart. The trailing vines are nice in hanging baskets.

SAVING SEED: Even though the plants perish in the chilly weather of fall, seeds self-sown by the plants may survive and sprout spontaneously in the spring, providing an early crop. You may find wild ground cherries that migrated from somebody's garden and self-seeded. In a subtropical climate zone like southern California, the ground cherry grows easily and self-sows enthusiastically. To save seed, select the best plants and use the procedure for saving tomato seed.

HARVESTING: Figure about 75 days to fruit. Harvest your ground cherries when they have turned yellow and become a little soft. If any fruit has fallen onto the ground, it was dead-ripe. If you pick once a week, you'll have a good chance of staying ahead of them. Even if they do get onto the ground, they'll be good for several more days. You'll be able to harvest an average 2 lb. of ground cherries from each plant.

PRESERVING: If you spread them out in a cool, airy, dry place, they might last a couple of weeks, but the best way to preserve them is to cook and can, or freeze, or dry.

Ground Cherry "Citron." Cut the ground cherry into chunks, roll chunks in sugar, and dry in full sun or a dehydrator until thoroughly dried. Substitute for another dried fruit, such as raisins or citron, in baked goods or fruit cake.

Freezing. Peel off husk, scald 2 minutes, chill, pour a syrup over, package, and freeze.

RECIPE IDEAS: This veggie has a fruity taste that's tart and acidic yet sweet. Eat raw, dehusked and plain, or add whole to any salad with a sweet dressing. Or add to a stew, bean chili, or vegetable soup. Or cook with onions, garlic, parsley, and peppers; add vinegar and use as a sauce. Or boil in water; add mushrooms, onions, cilantro, and ginger; and add tofu at the last moment. Or treat like a fruit and substitute in any basic fruit sauce, fruit pie, or fruit preserve recipe. Or cook, sweeten, and serve as an ice cream topping.

Martynia

Martynia (or *Proboscidea*), of the botanical family martynacia, is a native of the southwestern United States. There are more than half a dozen types of this desert and plains species, which has bristly leaves and an edible seed pod. They are found in an area ranging from the United States south to Brazil.

VARIETIES: *Proboscidea fragrans*, a common Mexican type of martynia, has bright red flowers whose pods pickle especially well. *P. lutea* has yellow blooms and is from Brazil. *P. annua, P. parviflora,* and *P. louisianica* (a.k.a. *P. jussieus*) all also have edible pods. *P. louisianica* is considered the best risk for northern gardeners. Martynia seed is available from DeGiorgi, Park, and Shumway.

You need 120 warm days to get martynia from seed to a pod harvest. This is easy if you're gardening in the south. Northern gardeners must start martynia like a nightshade.

In the garden, plant 1 inch deep, rows 3 feet apart. Plant near the end of February or early in March. Set out your started plants in peat pots at the same time as the nightshades. Plant 4 feet apart in the garden, rows 3 or more feet apart. They need to be that far apart because, although they get only a few feet tall, they spread out widely. Plant in full sun and fertile soil.

HARVESTING: Martynia will start flowering about 6 weeks after germination. Its large (2-inch), lovely flowers grow in clusters of up to a dozen at the end of each stem. Each is followed by the edible seed pod, which somewhat resembles an okra pod (fuzzy and green) but has a curving rather than a straight shape. Harvest while still tender and green.

RECIPE IDEAS: Include either whole or sliced in soups and stews. Or pickle using a dill recipe. Or cook, chill, and serve with a vinegar-oil dressing. Or dry on the plant and then include that unusual double-forked tip in dried flower arrangements.

Okra

Okra (*Abelmoschus esculentus* or *Hibiscus esculentus*) is not a member of the nightshade family. But since it most resembles the nightshades in its growing requirements, I added it to this section. (Along with roselle and hollyhocks, okra belongs to the cotton family.) Okra grows wild in Egypt and Ethiopia and has been cultivated since prehistoric times. Ruth wrote me from her Caribbean desert isle of Bonaire: "Okra is one thing that will grow in this awful soil and horrendous heat." It's a famous Deep South garden annual and a beautiful plant. But it doesn't store or preserve very well. It's possible to grow okra outside the South if you have a hot summer.

VARIETIES: Many okra growers plant it in their flower rather than their vegetable area because the leaves can be as much as a foot wide. Okra grows from 2 to 9 feet high depending on the variety. There is a Red Okra variety that has yellow and red blooms, red stems, and red okra pods. Geneva Travis wrote me from Kell, IL: "Red okra is a beautiful red-maroon color. It bears more quickly, tastes better, and isn't nearly as slimy. I win a blue ribbon at the fair every year I enter it."

PLANTING: Okra will grow in any soil as long as the soil temperature is at least 60°F before planting, but it does better if the soil is fertile. If you live in an area with a hot summer but a short growing season, plant okra indoors a month before setting-out time. Start okra only in a pot that can be planted out in the garden as is; otherwise it won't survive transplanting. Four or five plants can produce enough for a small family. Soak the seeds in tepid water several hours before you plant them; otherwise they will be slow to sprout. For permanent container planting, choose a dwarf variety (dwarf okra pods are the same size as standards) and plant in a tub or box. A dozen plants will supply an average family.

Don't plant outside until you have dependably warm weather, for okra is very cold-sensitive. In a northern garden, plant in as much wind shelter as you can—but always in full sun. Set out or plant seed about the same time you would watermelon or squash, when you're sure the last frost has taken place and the soil has warmed up. Plant seed directly into the garden ½ to 1 inch deep, 3 inches apart (because okra germination rate is poor), rows about 30 inches apart, closer for a dwarf variety. Later thin to 12–20 inches apart. While the plants are young, keep them weeded but don't till deeply, because that messes up their root systems. Once they start to cover the ground, don't cultivate at all. Okra usually doesn't have pest or pestilence problems.

SAVING SEED: Okra is a self-fertile, insect-pollinated annual. Cross-pollination is possible if any other okra species is within a mile, but it's unlikely because of okra's self-fertilization. Let the pods stay on your chosen plant until they become completely mature: brittle, brown, and up to a foot long. In the late fall, gather the pods, break them open, and shell out the seeds like beans. Dry and store.

HARVESTING: Varieties differ, but in general you begin harvesting 50 to 60 days after planting. Before making fruit, okra bears lots of pretty blossoms that are either all yellow or yellow with red centers. A few days after the flowers come the edible seed pods. Severely hot, dry weather, a harsh change in temperature, or poor drainage can cause bud drop. But if growing conditions are halfway right, you'll be loaded with green, fuzzy, finger-shaped okra pods. Some varieties start bearing pods when only a foot high and will keep on from then until frost.

Okra leaves have spines that are almost invisible but can get into your skin and cause a miserable burning itch. So if you're going to be picking much okra, wear gloves and long sleeves, and don't pick unless the plants are completely dry.

Pick the long, green seed pods when they are 2 to 3½ inches long—not longer! Bigger ones are getting old and can be bitter and tough. Go through and collect pods at least every other day if possible, not only to get pods at their prime but also to keep the plants producing, because if you let pods mature on the plant, it will stop producing new ones. Cutting off the pods rather than pulling them off protects the plant roots from tugging. If you keep on picking, the plant will keep on making fruit until it's killed by frost, but the first part of the crop is the best. In the South, in midsummer when okra gets too tall to harvest, growers cut the plants down to about 18 inches. The plants quickly grow up again and provide another crop!

PRESERVING: Fresh okra will keep only 1 or 2 days. It does best if you occasionally sprinkle water on it and keep it where air can circulate. So preserve or eat the okra as soon as possible, because the pods will toughen quickly, turning woody the same way they do if left on the plant. Okra can be frozen, dried, or canned.

Freezing. If you start with young, tender pods, okra freezes well. Trim off the stems—but don't cut into the pods. Steam-blanch 2 or 3 minutes; chill. Leave whole or slice them. Package and freeze.

Frozen Half-Fried Okra. This tastes even more like fresh okra. Wash, trim off tips, slice, season with salt and pepper, and shake in a sack with cornmeal until all covered. (Or use in fried eggplant recipe ideas; see "Eggplant Recipe Ideas" in the "Eggplant" section.) Then fry only until barely half-fried. Cool to room temperature. Then package and freeze. To use, thaw and cook in the oven, or thaw and then finish browning in a skillet (with little or no oil).

Drying. The old-timers dried okra by stringing small, tender pods on a thread, hanging them over the stove to dry, and then giving them one last good heating in the oven before putting them into long-term storage. You can string up larger pods the same way. First wash them, cut off stem ends, and slice. Then string, and hang the strings in an airy

but shady place until dried. No need to blanch okra. Or slice okra and spread out it thinly on your drying tray in the full sun (take in at night). It takes only a day or two to sun-dry. Or dry inside: cut young, tender pods crosswise or lengthwise, ¼ inch thick, and spread thinly on trays. It takes up to 12 hours in a dehydrator at 120°F to dry them. They're done when brittle. To cook dried okra, add 2 c. boiling water per 1 c. dried okra and simmer. It's tastiest if you add onion, tomato, and seasoning.

COOKING: "Gumbo" means okra. A gumbo recipe means okra soup, a Creole specialty. Inside the okra pod there is a kind of "slimy" stuff. If you like okra but not the slimy part, cook it with tomatoes or in soups to cut it. Geneva Travis, Kell, IL, says boiled okra is less slimy if you "kinda steam it till barely fork-tender, drain, and then set it back on the turned-off burner till ready to serve. This dries it out a little. I fry okra kinda fast—no lid, stir often, and watch carefully." Trim off both ends of the pods before cooking. Very young and tender pods can be cooked whole. With pods of middling age and tenderness, slice them into about ½-inch lengths.

Woody Okra. To get some food value out of woody okra, add it to your soup or stockpot. The soft part will cook into the mix and add flavor and vitamins. After the cooking, fish out the woody part that's left so you don't have to eat it.

Okra Peas. The best okra is picked when its seeds are no more than half grown. But if the seed is still tender but fully grown, you can shell it out separately, discard the too-tough pod, and cook like peas. Okra peas combined with whole wheat flour or sesame seeds make a perfect protein.

Recipe Ideas. Okra is good with peas, tomatoes, onions, peppers, corn, squash, and eggplant—any or all. It's a natural thickening agent. Stew it with tomatoes and rice, and add filé powder at the last minute. Or cook over low heat in a spicy sweet-and-sour sauce. Or blanch and served with chopped tomatoes, green onions, greens, and a vinegar-oil dressing. Or cook and then soak in the liquid left from dill pickles, or use in a dill pickle recipe. Or dip in tempura batter and fry in deep fat. Or boil pods in salted water until tender; drain and add butter, seasoning, and a dash of vinegar, and simmer until butter is absorbed. Or cover sliced pods with hot water and simmer 20 minutes; add peeled, cut-up garden tomatoes and cook 10 minutes more; add butter, salt, and pepper, and serve.

Julia Reynolds, Galvin, WA, likes okra cooked, sliced, and fried with potatoes. Reader Ruth Miller cooks sliced okras in a mixture of tomato juice and water with chopped green pepper and onion; adds chopped tomatoes, frozen corn kernels (or sliced green beans), and a dash of cumin; and serves it over rice. Also see gumbo recipes under "Sassafras" in Chapter 5.

▷ *RUTH'S BONAIREAN GUMBO* *"Here's how to make Bonairean-style gumbo, 'sopi di giambo.' Cube ½ lb. salt pork, beef, or goat. Cover with water and simmer until tender. Add 1 lb. of fish like red snapper, and cook till the fish flakes easily. Remove meat and fish, and chunk them into bite-sized pieces. Cut about 4 c. of okra rounds and add to broth, along with sprigs of fresh oregano and/or basil and a bit of hot pepper. Simmer till okra is tender. Then use a whisk to break okra into tiny pieces, and simmer on till broth is thick. Return meat and fish; test for seasoning. (Bonairean cooks always taste and season!) Serve with funchi [cornmeal cooked in water to a mush, molded, and chilled]."*

Pepper (Hot)

The pepper family (the many species of the genus *Capsicum*) is huge and varied, ranging from mild green peppers to burning "hot" ones. Peppers have all sorts of shapes, colors, uses, and Latin names. Most are *Capsicum annum* varieties, subdivided into the Grossum group (mild-flavored sweets) and the Longum group (hots, which range from a little hot to very hot). The hottest ones of all come from related species: *C. chinense* (Habanero) and *C. frutescens* varieties (Tabasco, Red Chili, Thai). Peppers come from the Americas, where they've been domesticated for at least 7,000 years. They're perennial shrubs in the tropics (some grow as tall as 10 feet!), grown as annuals in temperate zones. Special info on hots is covered in the following text; sweets come after that, and growing info for both kinds is in the "Sweet Pepper" section.

Hot peppers, natives of the American tropics, are also called "chili" or "chile" peppers or "pequins" because they're all relatively small in size compared to the sweets. Compared to the sweet peppers, the hot peppers generally are easier to grow and give bigger harvests. They are usually larger plants with smaller leaves. Most are green at first, some have a yellow stage, and most end up red. Some get brown. Because of the bright colors, they are often grown as ornamentals as well as for their fruit. All the peppers are tropical perennials that must be grown as annuals except in subtropical climate zones. The smallest chilies generally like the hottest climates. New Mexico is where the most U.S. chili peppers are grown. And the farther north they grow, the less hot even the same variety tends to be.

HOT TOPICS: For more info, read *Peppers: The Domesticated Capsicums* by Dr. Jean Andrews (U. of Texas Press, 1984); "Taste Bud Burnout" by Jake Page in *Hippocrates*, May/June 1987; and the article in *National Gardening*, May 1988. You could join the National Hot Pepper Association for $20 at 400 NW 20th St., Fort Lauderdale, FL 33311; 954-565-4972; fax 954-566-2208. You'll receive a 28-page quarterly newsletter with recipes, growing tips, and knowledge in the field of peppers and pepper products. Or order *Fire & Spice: 200 Hot & Spicy Recipes from the Far East,* and other hot cookbooks, from the association.

What Hot Peppers Are Good For. Peppers are high in vitamins: They have more C than citrus, more A than carrots, and contain E and B1 too. But the quality of hots that you notice most is their heat. Is that good for anything? Well, hot peppers and other spicy foods raise the body's metabolic rate, for some reason, causing the eaters to burn as much as 25 percent more calories. Perhaps that's why a bowl of chili is great on a wintry day. It literally warms you. Chilies also stimulate saliva and gastric juice production, so in that way they aid digestion. Researchers have also discovered that a diet of blazing hot peppers helps dissolve blood clots and thus protects against stroke and heart attack. Hot peppers are also a medically sound home remedy for colds because they help relieve lung congestion and stuffy noses. The chemical that makes hot peppers hot is capsaicin, an alkaloid, and its presence is measured by the Scoville heat scale.

Scoville Heat Scale. Food scientists and commercial food processors use the Scoville heat scale (created in 1912 by Wilbur L. Scoville) to measure the comparative spicy-hotness of foods: the more Scoville units, the hotter it is. The scale ranges from 0, or no heat units (for sweet peppers of every kind) up to 600,000 of them (for the Tepin, the hottest pepper of them all). What the scale is actually measuring is the amount of the capsaicin: the more capsaicin, the more heat units.

Capsaicin. Your regular taste buds register sweet, sour, salty, and bitter—but not capsaicin. When chili lovers speak of the "burn," they're being precise. The way you "taste" capsaicin is that it literally burns the place on your body that it touches, and the pain receptors tell you it's there. You "taste" hot peppers via the pain receptors in your mouth rather than via taste buds. It's called a "nerve-irritating chemical" because it irritates nerve cells—on the skin and in the eyes as well as in the mouth.

Capsaicin Damage. In large enough amounts, capsaicin causes irritation and even bleeding in your stomach. If you have an ulcer, even smaller quantities will make the ulcer worse. The condition of large intestine irritation caused by capsaicin (epidemic among participants in jalapeno pepper-consumption contests) is called "jalaproctitis" by doctors. Long-term, heavy consumption of very hot peppers significantly increases your risk of colon cancer. It also results in some permanent nerve loss. Even though those organs are merely innocent bystanders and can't taste the capsaicin, they can get burned by it. When you eat spicy-hot food, the capsaicin literally causes a chemical burn of the inside of your mouth and on down your digestive tract. To a doctor, the results of Chinese red oil taken in a soup, for example, look like second-degree burns. Burned taste buds usually heal within a couple of weeks, but the nerve cells that actually register the presence of capsaicin don't always manage to recover from the damage they suffer. In fact, people who chronically consume capsaicin don't even taste it any more at low levels because some of their nerve endings have already been destroyed.

In effect, it works like a kind of addiction. The more you consume, the more you have to consume to taste the same amount because of the numbness caused by nerve destruction. So why do people eat it? Is it bravado, a sense of contest, the thrill of going to the brink of endurance? Researchers have noted that the pain receptors stimulated by capsaicin cause the brain to secrete endorphins, which are morphine-type natural chemicals that also cause the familiar "runner's high." They theorize that heavy-duty hot-pepper eaters are actually after those endorphins.

VARIETIES: Hot peppers can be classified according to "hotness." (You can mail-order a "Pepper Hotness Test" from Redwood City that tells you how, with simple equipment (gram scale, blender, etc.), you too can accurately measure hotness.)

Mild Hots. These are semisweet, semihot, or "mild" peppers. The banana pepper is mild, longish, and yellow. The Japanese mildly hot pepper, also called fushimi or long Asian, resembles a green bean with its long, wrinkled shape and curved tail. It dries well because of its very thin skin. It can be used in sweet pepper recipes or substituted for the hot chilies in Mexican and Cajun recipes; they'll give you some of the effect without so much of the punishment. Numex Big Jim is a foot-long mild from New Mexico State U. Anaheims range from mild to medium-hot, depending on the variety, averaging 1,000 Scovilles. They are long and pointed at one end. They are first green and then turn red, and they're popular in California and the Southwest. Anaheims are used to make chili powder and chiles rellenos and to string into ristras.

Hotter Hots. In this group, there is Chamayo (shaped like a green bean and smaller than most of the others), Hungarian wax (ranging from medium to hot), Negros/Pasilla (black when dried, used in mole sauce), and Poblano (hot; wide rather than long). Jalapeno peppers are small (about 1½ to 3 inches long) and very hot, rated at 3,500 to 4,500 Scovilles. Jalapenos are first green and then turn red, and they are often used to make salsa. Both Caribe and Guero are yellow, very hot, and the same size and shape as jalapenos. Fresno peppers, also jalapeno-sized, are red in color. Ancho may be mild or hotter-hot, depending on which type of "ancho" it is.

Hottest Hots. *When preparing peppers this hot or hotter, use rubber or plastic gloves.* Cayenne is first green and then turns red. It's thin, measures 3–12 inches long, and is much hotter than jalapeno—20,000 Scovilles—and is dried and ground to make cayenne pepper. Serrano, pale green and 1 to 1½ inches in length, may or may not be hotter than cayenne. Fresh serranos score at 7,000–25,000 Scovilles. Serranos are a traditional ingredient in Southwestern guacamole and tomato sauces. Other very hot peppers are de Arbol, pequin, and Pasilla.

Hottest of All! *Remember, use rubber or plastic gloves when preparing these peppers!* Tabasco peppers rate at 70,000. (Tabasco sauce is made from either serrano or Tabasco peppers; dry the peppers when they're yellow but turning orange-scarlet, and then grind them.) In this category are the Thai pepper (a *C. frutescens* variety at 70,000–80,000 Scovilles) and other very hot Asian peppers used in traditional Szechuan and Thai cuisines. Habanero peppers are native to the Yucatan peninsula but are now being grown all over the United States. These pale green, small (1-inch) peppers come in at an incredible 80,000–300,000 Scovilles. Red Chili is even hotter than that, however; it's a *C. frutescens* variety with small, bright red fruits that are 2 inches long and ½ inch wide. And the "Hottest of All!" title belongs to the Tepin pepper (*C. annum* var. *aviculare,* or "Chiltepin"), which is round, red, ¼ inch thick, as tiny as a fingernail, and twice as hot as a Habanero!

PLANTING: Burpee, Native Seeds, Nichols, Redwood City, Seeds of Change, Shepherd's, and Territorial all offer a good selection. The Pepper Gal, Betty Payton, offers 250 varieties! Contact her at 954-537-5540; fax 954-566-2208; PO Box 23006, Ft. Lauderdale, FL 33307; **peppergal@mindspring. com; www.peppergal.com.** If you live well north of the Mason-Dixon Line, look for varieties bred to produce even in northern zones. Lane Morgan says that at her home on the western Canadian border, hots grow more easily than sweets.

Plant like sweet peppers. Hot peppers usually do well in containers and in the house, where some, such as cayenne, will produce all winter. You can grow 1 of these small pepper plants per 8-inch pot if it has at least ½ gal. soil, 8 inches deep. In a larger container, space plants 6 to 8 inches apart.

HARVESTING AND PROCESSING

NOTE: Wear gloves when harvesting or processing hot peppers. Whenever working with cut chilies, keep your hands away from your face, especially your eyes. Keep all chilies—whole, cut, or ground—out of reach of small children!!!

NOTE: A child with chili in his or her eyes is having an unforgettably traumatic experience. For first aid, rinse and rinse and rinse with whole milk or a mild alcoholic beverage. Rinsing with water or drinking water won't help, because capsaicin does dissolve easily in fat or alcohol—but not in water.

The chili fruits start to get hot when they're about 4 weeks old; they make more and more alkaloid from then to full maturity. Ordinarily, you let them ripen completely before gathering—about 65 to 75 days to first harvest for most. *To prevent damage to the plants, cut off the pods, leaving 1 inch of stem on them. Don't pull them.* Keep the pods picked if you want the plant to keep producing at full capacity. There's no hurry about the final harvest. If a frost occurs, the peppers will probably still be all right because most chilies can survive even several light frosts.

STORING: Keep in a plastic bag in your fridge. They store best at 40–45°F. Green peppers will last in storage 3 times as long as red ones, which are fully ripe and ready to deteriorate.

DRYING: You can pull up whole plants by hanging them upside down in an airy place. To dry small individual chilies, wash them, remove stems, and slit with a knife; cut in half lengthwise; or cut into thin slices. Spread out and dry in an airy place in full sun, or in an oven or dehydrator at 120°F. Sun drying works best if day temps are at least 85°F. If night temps drop to the dew point, bring them in. They shrink and darken as they dry, eventually getting leathery or brittle and hard.

Ristas. These strings of dried chilies are best made from the most thin-skinned varieties: cayenne, ancho, Red Chili, pepperoncini, etc. String the pods on a thread by piercing them through the stem end with the needle. Hang by those strings in the sun or a sunny window to dry.

Chili Powder Recipe Ideas. Plain cayenne powder is made by removing the seeds and grinding dried shells of red cayenne or "chili" peppers. Or mix dried, ground cayenne peppers, cumin seed, and oregano in the proportions you prefer. Or combine 3 dried ancho chilies and 3 or 4 dried pequin chilies (stems removed, seeded, and crumbed), 1½ t. cumin seed, 1 t. oregano, and ½ t. garlic powder. Pulverize the mixture and store the powder airtight (in a nonmetal container). Use to season chili sauces and beef, hamburger, or meatloaf recipes.

FREEZING FOOD THAT CONTAINS CHILI PEPPERS: Remove the chilies before freezing, or the stuff will get hotter and hotter! To freeze chilies by themselves, chop them up first. The thick and fleshy varieties are best preserved by freezing rather than drying.

CANNING CHILIES: Wash; remove cores and seeds. Slash 2 or 4 slits in each pepper, and either blanch in boiling water or blister outer skin with heat. Pack loosely. Add salt as desired. Cover with boiling water, leaving 1 inch headspace. Pack in half-pint or pint jars only. Process half-pints for the same time as pints. Process in a pressure canner only for 35 minutes. If using a weighted-gauge canner, set at 10 lb. pressure at 0–1,000 feet above sea level; set at 15 lb. at higher altitudes. If using a dial-gauge canner, set at 11 lb. pressure at 0–2,000 feet above sea level; 12 lb. at 2,001–4,000 feet; 13 lb. at 4,001–6,000 feet; 14 lb. at 6,001–8,000 feet; or 15 lb. above 8,000 feet.

Pickled Hot Peppers. You'll need 4 lb. of hot, long red, green, or yellow peppers (Hungarian, banana, chili, or jalapeno), 3 lb. sweet red and green peppers (mixed), 5 c.

vinegar (5 percent), 1 c. water, 4 t. canning or pickling salt, 2 T. sugar, and 2 garlic cloves. Wash peppers. If small peppers are left whole, slash 2 to 4 slits in each. Quarter large peppers. Blanch in boiling water or blister skin to peel. Allow peppers to cool by placing in a pan and covering with a damp cloth. Peel after several minutes. Flatten small peppers. Fill half-pint or pint jars, leaving ½ inch headspace. Combine and heat other ingredients to boiling, and simmer 10 minutes. Remove garlic. Add hot pickling solution over peppers, leaving ½ inch headspace. Adjust lids and use boiling-water processing. At up to 1,000 feet above sea level, process 10 minutes; at 1,001–6,000 feet, 15 minutes; and above 6,000 feet, 20 minutes. Or use lower-temperature pasteurization, detailed in "Pickles" section under "Cucumbers."

Canned Mexican Tomato Sauce

CAUTION: Wear rubber gloves while handling chilies, or wash hands thoroughly with soap and water before touching your face. Wash and dry 2½ to 3 lb. chopped chili peppers. Slit each pepper along the side to allow steam to escape. Peel using one of the above methods. Discard seeds and chop. Wash tomatoes and dip in boiling water for 30 to 60 seconds or until skins split. Dip in cold water, slip off skins, and remove cores. Coarsely chop 18 lb. tomatoes. In a large pan, combine chopped peppers, tomatoes, 3 c. chopped onions, 1 T. salt, 1 T. oregano, and ½ c. vinegar (5 percent). Bring to a boil. Cover and simmer 1 hour. Fill jars, leaving 1 inch headspace. Adjust lids and process in a pressure canner: 20 minutes for pints, 25 minutes for quarts. If using a weighted-gauge canner, set at 10 lb. pressure at 0–1,000 feet above sea level; set at 15 lb. at higher altitudes. If using a dial-gauge canner, set at 11 lb. pressure at 0–2,000 feet above sea level; 12 lb. at 2,001–4,000 feet; 13 lb. at 4,001–6,000 feet; 14 lb. at 6,001–8,000 feet; or 15 lb. above 8,000 feet.

CHILI OIL: Heat 1 c. cooking oil until hot (but not until smoking hot!). Add 24 small (dried) red chili peppers. Cover and let cool gradually. When it is cooled to room temperature, strain out the solids. Chili oil is used in Asian recipes to add *heat!*

USING: Capsaicin is created in the fleshy white "placenta" that is the inner lining of the pod, but it can seep into the flesh and seeds too. So when you remove seeds and inner parts of the pepper, you cool it some. When you grind any hot pepper in a mortar, be sure you crush it really fine. Otherwise, if somebody gets an oversized chunk of that stuff in his food, it'll take off the top of his head!

Skinning Peppers

1. Place peppers in a 350–400°F oven and roast for 20 minutes or until you see even browning. Or place chilies under a broiler for 6 to 8 minutes until skins blister.
2. Put peppers inside a food-grade plastic bag for 5 minutes, or put them in a pan and cover with a damp cloth. This step makes peeling easier.
3. After several minutes of cooling, slip off skins.

✒ *HOMEMADE SALSA #1* Chop 3 fresh jalapeno or serrano chilies, 4 ripe big tomatoes, 1 globe (or 6 green) onion, 2 garlic cloves, and ¼ c. fresh parsley (or cilantro) leaves. Mix together. Stir in ½ t. salt.

✒ *HOMEMADE SALSA #2* Combine 4 fresh (split and seeded) red chilies, 2 c. boiling-hot vinegar, and 2 peeled gar-

lic cloves. Cover and let steep 2 days. Add 1 c. chopped tomatoes and blend thoroughly. Add 2 dried chilies. Cook half hour in double boiler. Strain out solids. Store in refrigerator.

✒ *CHILES RELLENOS* Use 1 or 2 mild, big peppers, such as Anaheim or Numex, per person. Roast, skin, and deseed the chilies. Cut a 2-inch opening at the top of each one, and remove the seeds and inner fibers. (At this stage you could flatten the whole chilies to remove air, package them with waxed paper between, and freeze for later use.) Rub the sides of a casserole dish with butter. For proper rellenos, the chilies are stuffed with cheese, but in this quick and easy version, you cover the sides of the casserole with the chilies and then cover all with about ½ lb. grated Cheddar cheese. Beat together 2 eggs, ½ c. flour, and 2 c. milk, and pour that mixture on top. Bake about 1 hour at 350°F. Serve with beans and guacamole.

✒ *CHILI VINEGAR* Add chilies (your choice of kind and amount) to white vinegar in a glass container. Optional: Add garlic cloves. Soak in dark, cool room for at least 2 weeks. Use to make salad dressing, guacamole, or salsa.

Chili Insecticide. The best use for the real hot stuff, I think, is as an ingredient in garden spray. Mix hot chili with soap powder and water. The spray works against a wide variety of insect varmints, including the tomato worm. Or dust your invaded plants (when wet with dew) with dry, ground chili pepper. Or spray plants with a 3-way punch: hot pepper, onion, and garlic!

Pepper (Sweet)

VARIETIES: The sweet peppers (*Capsicum frutescens grossum*) are basically bigger than the hots and come in many types: blocky bell peppers; heart-shaped pimentos; tomato-shaped "cherry" varieties; long banana-shaped peppers that are only 2 inches wide at the top but 6 to 8 inches long and produce heavily (30 or more fruits per plant); the long, curved, green Italian bull's horn pepper; Japanese sweet peppers; Lamuyo, the European sweet pepper; and yellow-green, thick-walled, 4- to 5-inch-long cubanelles that set fruit continuously once mature. You can grow the pimento (also spelled "pimiento"), an exceptionally sweet pepper when red-ripe, for salads or to make red strips for stuffing olive centers (see "Canning Pimentos"). In my opinion, bell peppers are for folks who've never tried the others. Sweets do well where there's a long, warm growing season; they're also a possibility if you have a hot summer and give them an early start indoors. Redwood City, Territorial, Shumway, and Nichols all have good sweet-pepper offerings.

PLANTING: Sweets like a light soil. (I have the heaviest clay imaginable. Our valley used to have a brick factory, and all the really old buildings on Main Street are made of Kendrick mud.) *Too much nitrogen in the soil makes tall, dark green plants that don't grow any peppers.* Small plants will set more peppers. In temperate zones, start peppers from seed indoors, about 50 to 70 days before your frost-free date. Plant between February and April, ⅛ to ¼ inch deep and 1 inch apart, more or less. During germination, keep them at 75 to 95°F; a soil temperature of 85°F is ideal. Keep moist until they've sprouted. *Water with warm water to avoid a possibly fatal cold shock.* After germination they can handle 70°F day temps and night temps as low as 60°F, but they'll grow faster if warmer. Below 55°F, they stop growing.

When peppers are about 2 inches tall, transplant to 2 inches apart. They need plenty of dirt for their roots! If you buy plants, be careful: Sweets and hots look exactly the same when young. To grow in a container, put 1 pepper plant in each 12-inch pot; to grow in a larger box, space 18 inches apart, soil at least 1 foot deep, 3 gal. soil per plant.

Wait to transplant peppers to the garden outside until they are at least 5–6 inches tall, 6 to 8 weeks old, and and last frost date is at least a week past (2 weeks is better). (They grow best when days are 70 to 75°F.) Plant 1–2 feet apart, rows 2 or 3 feet apart. Don't mulch cold ground.

SAVING SEED: Sweet peppers are self-fertile and bee-pollinated. They will cross with nearby plants, so don't grow another variety within 20 feet. Remove inferior plants before flowering happens so that any marrying that occurs is between your best. Thoroughly ripen before picking—until they actually begin to shrivel. If frost is a risk, gather just before frost and finish ripening inside. Then cut in half and remove seeds. Not much pulp will come along, so you can just dry and store them. You'll get hundreds of seeds per fruit. They live about 4 years.

HARVESTING AND PRESERVING: Night temps below 60°F and day temps above 90°F can cause blossoms to die and drop off. But with good weather, you'll harvest maybe 10 weeks after transplanting to the garden. Each bell plant ripens only 1 fruit at a time. You'll get 8 to 10 fruits per bell under ideal growing conditions, with steady picking and no frost. Be sure to harvest before frost. You can use the small peppers too (they're great stuffed). To pick, cut the stem an inch above the fruit. "Green" peppers start out green-colored and are generally picked green if they're to be shipped to market. But you can wait until they are ripe and truly sweet (the darker the color, the sweeter the flavor). They change in color to red (or yellow, dark purple, white, or brown for unusual varieties). When a frost is imminent, pull up the whole plant, hang it upside down somewhere, and the fruit will continue to ripen! Sweets will keep a while more off the plant and in the house, if it's cool and the air is not too dry.

Freezing Sweets. Cut in half; remove seeds and pulp. Freeze your nicest ones in halves for later stuffing. Dice or slice the others. No need to blanch. Package in small plastic bags, since you may want only a little at a time. To freeze pimentos, roast and skin as described under "Canning Pimentos," and then freeze. Frozen pepper strips of various colors make visually appealing dishes. Never thaw pepper before using. Use in strips in winter salads when only partly thawed and still crisp. Or add to soups, casseroles, and macaroni or chicken dishes.

Drying Sweets. Cut in ½-inch strips or rings. Remove seeds. Spread on drying frames or thread on a string. Spread rings no more than 2 layers deep, strips no more than ½ inch deep. Dry until crisp and brittle.

Canning Sweets. Cut out stem ends and remove seeds and cores as above. You can leave them whole or cut into any number or shape of pieces you fancy. Preboil 5 minutes. Then pack hot with hot liquid. Use procedure and times for canning chilies (in "Pepper (Hot)" section).

Canning Pimentos. First roast in a 450°F oven 5 minutes or until the skins blister. Then drop them into cold water. Then peel. Cut out stem ends; remove seeds and cores. Pack them flat in pint jars. Sprinkle in about ½ t. salt. Put on your jar lid. Pimentos make their own liquid—don't add any. Use procedure and times for canning chilies (in "Pepper (Hot)" section).

Sweet Red Pepper "Pimentos." Halve sweet red peppers. Take out seeds and pith. Cut into strips; steep in boiling water 5 minutes. Drain. Put into canning jars. Pour over a boiling-hot mix of 1 c. cider vinegar, 1 c. water, ½ c. sugar, 1 t. salt, and 2 t. olive oil. Cover and let soak like that 2 weeks in the fridge. Then either repackage into small bags and freeze, or use procedure and times for canning chilies (in "Pepper (Hot)" section).

❧ *RED AND GREEN PEPPER RELISH You'll need 3 qt. chopped cucumbers, 3 c. chopped sweet green peppers, 3 c. chopped sweet red peppers, 1 c. chopped onions, ¾ c. canning or pickling salt, 4 c. ice, 8 c. water, 2 c. sugar, 4 t. each of mustard seed, turmeric, whole allspice, and whole cloves, and 6 c. white vinegar (5 percent). Add cucumbers, peppers, onions, salt, and ice to water. Let stand 4 hours. Drain. Recover vegetables with fresh ice water for another hour. Drain again. Combine spices in a spice or cheesecloth bag. Add spices to sugar and vinegar. Heat to boiling and pour mixture over vegetables. Cover and refrigerate 24 hours.*

Heat mixture to boiling and fill hot half-pint or pint jars, leaving ½ inch headspace. Adjust lids and use conventional boiling-water processing. For either half-pints or pints: At up to 1,000 feet above sea level, process 10 minutes; at 1,001–6,000 feet, 15 minutes; and above 6,000 feet, 20 minutes. Or use lower-temperature pasteurization, detailed in "Pickles" section under "Cucumbers."

Recipe Ideas. Whether using raw or cooked sweet peppers, always get rid of the seeds and white pulp inside. There's really no need to skin a pepper except with pimentos, but if you want to, see "Canning Pimentos." Serve them raw, chopped in a green salad, or as strips with or without dip. Or add to casseroles, lay strips on pizza, skewer as part of a shish kebab, add to omelets, fry with just garlic, or stir-fry with other veggies and maybe meat too. Or saute with garlic and onion, adding tofu chunks at last moment. Or stuff with cheese and rice (see the following recipe). Or pre-cook with onions and green beans, and serve mixed with melted cheese. Or chop small and add to any stew or soup. Or dip in batter and fry.

❧ *RUTH'S VEGAN STUFFED PEPPERS Cut around the top stem with a sharp small knife as if you were going to make a lid for a jack-o'-lantern. Lift it out, and scoop out seeds and pulp. "Plunge 4 large, de-seeded green peppers into boiling water. Return to boil, remove peppers, and drain. Combine 2 c. corn kernels, 1 c. cooked dried beans, and ½ c. tomato sauce. (Actually, peppers can be stuffed with almost any bean or rice mixture.) Stuff into peppers, and sprinkle liberally with cumin. Place peppers in baking dish with a little water for moisture. Bake 20 minutes in a preheated 375°F oven."*

❧ *PIMENTO CHEESE From Judy Hohstadt, Cove, OR: "I've been trying to raise pimentos. They grow great except for turning red; that they will not do for me until after they're picked. By the time they're red there is not much meat left in them to can. We use them in this Pimento Cheese recipe— great in sandwiches or as a dip. Grate ¾ lb. medium sharp cheese. Add ¼ c. (or more) mashed, canned pimentos with juice, 1 t. onion juice, and a pinch pepper. Mix with enough mayo to be spreadable."*

➣ RUTH'S PIMENTO PEPPER PASTA SAUCE *"Cook a large chopped onion and 2 c. (firmly packed) chopped red pimento pepper in ¼ c. water until soft. Puree in blender with ¾ c. water until pulpy. Pour the puree back into a pot and add 1 T. lemon juice, 3 T. parsley (1 T. dried), and 1 t. each of oregano and basil (dried). Simmer 5 minutes and then serve over warm pasta."*

➣ PAPRIKA *Dry and grind the outer shell of the sweet red pepper. It's good sprinkled on a white sauce or white vegetables (such as mashed potatoes, cauliflower, or parsnips) to add color as well as taste. Or use in any meat, gravy, sauce, or veggie dishes. If made from sweet peppers, paprika rates 0 on the Scoville scale.*

Tomatillo

Tomatillo (*Physalis ixocarpa*), also called the "Mexican husk tomato," is closely related to the ground cherry (see "Ground Cherry"). You can get tomatillo seed (green or purple) from Nichols, Redwood City, Seeds of Change, and Shepherd's. Greens bear bigger fruit (2 to 2½ inches across), but the purples, although only 1 to 1½ inches across, taste and store better. This solanum grows anywhere, unlike its less hardy cousins. This sprawling plant can grow to 4 feet in diameter, so plant far apart. Jana Dean, Olympia, WA, says, "They grow like weeds and don't need water. They volunteer themselves."

HARVESTING: Tomatillos take 68 days to produce, and then they bear prolifically. They're ready more quickly than tomatoes and don't mind cooler weather. Tomatillos grow encased in a papery outer husk that looks like a Chinese lantern and splits when the fruit is ready for picking. Pick when the fruit is the size of walnuts. They may be sticky to touch. If left on the vine to continue ripening, they'll turn from green to purple or yellow (depending on variety) and get milder and sweeter in taste. Jana advises that to make great tomatillo green salsa, pick only green tomatillos, not yellow ones: "Harvest as soon as they nearly fill their husks." People usually get about 1 lb. fruit per plant.

Storing. To store, leave them in their husks and set only 1 layer deep in a cool and airy room, or keep them in the refrigerator. But don't seal or wrap in plastic or anything similar. They store better than ground cherries. The purple kind stores better than the green. If you pull back the husks of purples and string them like garlic, they'll keep for months.

Canning. Remove the husks. Rinse fruit. Boil uncut tomatillos in a covered pan for 10 minutes (or until tender). Drain. Pack hot into hot pint jars. Pour in boiling water, leaving at least ½ inch headspace. Add ½ t. salt and 1 t. lemon juice or vinegar. Put lids on and tighten. Follow instructions for canning tomatoes.

Freezing. Cook first; then freeze. You can use frozen tomatillos to make salsa verde or any other cooked tomatillo dish.

Recipe Ideas. Tomatillos are a south-of-the-border favorite, the basis for genuine Mexican salsa verde, the green mild-hot sauce used on tacos and chiles rellenos. Green tomatillos taste something like green tomatoes and can be substituted for them in recipes if you compensate for tomatillos being solid rather than open and juice-filled inside. You can substitute fully ripe (purple or yellow) ones in ground cherry recipes, but cooks generally prefer using tomatillos

when they're green, because dead-ripe tomatillos taste so bland. Serve sliced raw tomatillo in a mixed green salad, sliced plain, or with dip as finger food. Or use to make salsa verde or dip. Or cook and add to dishes (tomatillos add an herb-lemon flavor). Or slice and add to a veggie soup or bean casserole.

➣ TOMATILLO DIP *Combine 2 c. chunked, uncooked tomatillo, 1 c. chunked onion, ¼ c. dried epazote, maybe a little minced hot pepper, and 1 t. garlic salt. Churn in a blender until smooth. Add 1 c. sour cream. Serve chilled.*

➣ TOMATILLO SALSA VERDE *Make the above dip, but leave out the sour cream and add 1 T. lemon juice and 3 cloves garlic.*

Tomato

This tropical perennial, grown as an annual in temperate zones, is from South America. Natural tomatoes do best if they have a long, hot time to grow, but rigorous selection has developed early, more hardy varieties. Tomatoes have both fruit and veggie uses. Botanically they are fruits. In 1893 the U.S. Supreme Court applied its solemn expertise to the problem of tomato classification and decided that henceforth the tomato, *Lycopersicon lycopersicum* (a.k.a. *L. esculentum*), would legally be a vegetable rather than a fruit.

TOMATO INFO AND RESOURCES: You'll enjoy R. H. Shumway's *Totally Tomatoes* (and peppers!), an 80-pg catalog: 803-663-0016; fax 888-477-7333; PO Box 1626, Augusta, GA 30903-1626; **www.totallytomato.com.** Tomato Growers Supply Co. carries 200 varieties, and everything else for the tomato grower in its catalog: 941-768-1119; 888-478-7333; PO Box 2237, Fort Myers, FL 33902; **www.tomatogrowers.com.** *The National Gardening Book of Tomatoes* shares tomato-growing expertise from the National Gardening Association; 802-863-5251; 1100 Dorset St., So. Burlington, VT 05403; **www.nationalgardening.com.**

VARIETIES: Tomatoes are big business for the seedsman, the most popular garden vegetable in the United States (beans are the next most popular). New varieties and hybrids are easy to develop, so there are many, many kinds to choose from.

The original tomatoes were yellow; now you can have them in red, orange, pink, green, or white, with fuzzy or

HOW MANY TOMATOES?

It's easy to raise tomato plants from seed, and they transplant without difficulty. One ounce of tomato seed might produce 3,500 to 4,500 plants. (I didn't count 'em. I read that in a book—like a good share of the stuff in this book.) It's easy to accidentally get far too many started. If you can't bear to throw out the extras, you'll have to hit up your friends to please take a few dozen plants, or maybe a few hundred. Even 25 plants would give you a big crop of tomatoes, with lots to put up for the winter and some for the neighbors too—if you give them room, fertile soil, and plenty of water. With 100 plants, you can become a truck gardener and sell tomatoes. Just half a dozen plants gives you a good summer's eating.

Ricki Witz, Armstrong, IL, wrote me, "For the first 26 years of my life, I lived in the northwest suburbs of Chicago. The first time I saw a cow was in the petting zoo when I was 11! I had never even planted a seed when I married my husband. I thought I would go crazy living in his small country town . . . a nice house on 5 acres, small but affordable. When we moved in, I found that the previous owner had planted 21 tomato plants. I had never seen a tomato plant in my life. I couldn't imagine why there was horse manure all over the garden and *ick!* around the tomato plants.

"Well, they grew and grew with no attention from me until my husband started bringing in 40 or 50 lb. of tomatoes every 2 or 3 days. Soon my sink was full of rotting tomatoes. I made up my mind then . . . it was throw away food or learn to can it, so I bought a canner and jars and made taco sauce, spaghetti sauce, and tomato juice. Then our apple tree (that I didn't know was really an apple tree) started to do its thing too. After supplying my 'city' friends with crates of apples, I made the plunge there too and canned apple sauce (80 pints) and apple butter. I was glad when it was all over."

Ricki told me the next year she planted only 10 tomato plants! Just exactly how many is right for you depends on how much room you have in your garden, how large your family is, how well your variety will produce, and how hard you're willing to work at putting them up for winter. After growing them a few summers, you'll know the answer.

---

smooth skin. They range in size from supersized 1½ lb. tomatoes to the cherry (earliest to mature) and dwarf kinds, some of which are as small as a marble. They can be sweet or sour; round or oval; open-pollinated heirloom standards that you can save seed from or heavy-yielding hybrids; vines or bushes. The plants can grow anywhere from 18 inches to 6 feet tall. You can get early (sets fruit well even in cool weather; matures quickly), mid-season, or late-maturing (biggest individual fruits; 80 to 90 days) varieties. It may be 120 days before you have a big harvest from a late variety, but you can get 200 lb. of tomatoes from 1 packet of seeds or a 50-foot row, and that is worth the wait.

You can choose a variety that's resistant to verticillium wilt, fusarium wilt, or nematodes. Those resistances are coded in seed catalogs as V, F, or N. Other varieties resist cracking or tobacco mosaic (spread by people smoking in the garden or smokers who handle tomato plants). A tomato variety has either "determinate vines" that are bushy, stay short, and are probably best for container growing; or "indeterminate vines," the usual garden kind, which grow and bear until frost, sprawling across the ground and growing bigger and bigger unless staked, caged, or trellised. We just let that kind run.

You can choose juicy types, more solid types for making tomato paste and sauce, or even the hollow Burgess Stuffing tomato. You can get them seeded or seedless. Commercial gardeners grow varieties that ship better than they taste; gardeners can go for the most flavorful kinds. Florida growers, plagued with nematodes and blight, may get the best tomato crop by growing Celebrity or 5000 and remembering that tomatoes will produce best there if in a shady area. If you live in the cool, cloudy weather of the maritime Northwest, pass up the beefsteaks (which require heat) in favor of very early kinds such as Oregon Spring Tomato (Nichols) and cherry tomatoes. Your extension agent probably has a list of varieties recommended for your area. Or ask a gardening neighbor. My choice is a standard, red, average-sized, usual-shaped, high-acid type. But it's fun and good insurance to try 2 or 3 kinds unless you're saving seed.

PLANTING: Move your tomatoes around in the garden. To avoid disease, wait 3 years before planting tomatoes in the same place or in a place where potatoes or eggplants have grown. If you live in the southern part of Florida or Texas, you can plant tomatoes outside, right where you want them to grow. They need a soil temperature of 60 to 85°F for best germination. In the garden, plant ½ inch deep. Plant generously and thin later to the best ones for your crop. It will be 7 to 12 days before the seeds germinate. Thin to as much as 4 feet between plants and between rows unless you need to cram tighter.

Sheltered Starts. In somewhat more northerly but still mild-wintered areas of the South, start the plants outdoors in cold frames during cool weather, and then transplant to your garden proper from there. In colder climates than that, plant indoors or in a hot frame 10 to 12 weeks or longer before your average last spring frost date. Plant ¼ inch deep; cover with newspaper, plastic, or glass, leaving a small opening on a corner; and keep at least 70°F. Keep the dirt moist with a fine spray. When you can see seedlings, take off that cover and provide lots of light. Try not to wet the leaves while you're watering.

When the plants are 3 to 4 inches tall, repot into a deeper container, setting them down in the dirt right up to the leaves. When they've grown to about 10 inches high, repot again into a yet deeper container (such as a milk carton), again setting them as deep in the dirt as you can—right up to the leaves (you can pinch off the lower ones). Harden plants for at least 10 days just before transplanting.

Lazy Person's Indoor Start. If you don't want to bother with all that transplanting and covering in the garden, plant

353

in March or April and transplant to the garden in 6 to 8 weeks—after last frost. You'll harvest in July and August.

Transplanting to Garden. Move the first few to your garden 3 weeks before last frost date; then move a few more each week after that until all danger of frost is over. If the day isn't cloudy, wait to transplant until evening. Plant in a full-sun site with fertile soil. Water your tomato plants before transplanting. Their dirt should be wet enough to cling to the roots. Before you take the plant out of its former home, dig the hole or trench you're going to plant it in. Put plenty of water into the new hole.

Trench Planting. The best way to set the plant in is with its stem laid down under the dirt horizontally instead of vertically, until you come to the leafy part, which you should let stick up out of the dirt. Set the plant in right up to its leaves. You can pinch off the lower ones. It will grow new roots along the part of the stem that is underground. Tomatoes do better in trench than in vertical planting because the upper soil is warmer, and solanums need that warmth. Set the plants 2 to 6 feet apart depending on the variety and garden space available, in rows 3 feet or farther apart. But crowded tomato plants are no bargain—they produce less fruit. Once the plants are in the holes, firm up the dirt over them by gently stepping on it. Then give the area a good wetting. Don't mulch unless you use black plastic. Use a cover for windbreak, frost protection, and heat-gathering until the weather seriously warms up.

Cutworms. What to do? You set out your plants, you come back the next day, and all that's left is a little stem sticking out of the ground. Mae Wallace, Berwyn, IL, says she uses cornflake boxes or other similar boxes, cutting around them to make narrow cardboard collars for each plant. She makes the collars about 3 inches tall and pushes them down into the soil until the dirt comes to within an inch of the top of the band. The cutworms don't crawl over, and her plants are spared.

Container Growing. Tomatoes are great container plants and do well on a window sill or in a hanging basket. Cherry or dwarf bush types are good for small containers. When the seedlings have made it to 2 inches tall, transplant them to individual pots. To raise full-size tomato plants in a container, place only 1 in a container the size of half a whiskey barrel. You need 3 to 5 gal. of soil per tomato plant, and it should be at least 12 inches deep. In larger or longer containers, space plants at least 18 to 24 inches apart. With dwarf tomato varieties, you can squeeze one into a 12-inch pot and need 1 to 2 gallons of soil per plant, 8 to 10 inches deep. Plant small ones at least 12 inches apart.

OF STAKES AND CAGES: There are different varieties of tomatoes, but the typical one can be allowed to run over the ground like any vine plant. Or it can be staked up or caged to save room. Caged tomatoes produce up to twice as much as staked ones (which in turn may produce less than vines allowed to run free). I let mine run, but lots of people stake or cage. To stake them, plant a stake as high as your variety is expected to grow. Using an old stocking or rag or some such, tie a strip firmly to your stake and then make a loose loop with the cloth around the stem of the tomato plant. If you squeeze the stem, you'll really hurt the plant. To cage, buy a ready-made cage, or put a circle of woven wire fencing or something similar around your plant. You can fasten it down to the ground on each side with stakes.

WEEDS: One way or another you've got to fight weeds. You can put down a good 2-inch mulch or come through regularly tilling the ground between plants until the vines cover the ground and prevent weeds.

TOMATO WORMS: You may have to cope with tomato worms. I haven't ever had them, but I've had neighbors all around who did. I credit my chickens for allowing me to be spared. Chickens also like tomatoes, though, so I have a struggle either way. Shutting up the chickens from midsummer on seems to work fine. A tomato worm is about 1½ inches long; it's a very fat, hairless green grub with one horn sticking out of its tail. They can't sting with the horn, although folklore says they do; and they can't bite, but they are revolting to pick up with your bare hands. You find them deep in the plant and have to pick them off by hand, going out early each morning with gloves and a can. Personally, I'd rather cope with the chickens. A reader in Berwyn, IL, says she takes a green twig that will bend but not break and uses it as pincers to pick off the green tomato worms.

SAVING SEED: Don't save hybrid seed. Tomatoes are a self-fertile, insect-pollinated, temperate-zone annual. Although the chance of crossing is slight, it is possible if you have different varieties flowering, so plant them as far apart in your garden as possible. Choose the best fruits from the best plants—at least 3 of each variety you're saving from. Let the fruits stay on the plant until well past what you would consider overripe for table use. Then gather and follow the fermentation directions under "Saving Seed" in the "Cucumber" section. Tomato seeds will live 4 years or more.

HARVESTING: Your tomatoes will probably begin to ripen sometime in August. Pick them as fast as they get ready. Green, yellow, and red are the stages of ripeness for ordinary tomatoes. Vine-ripened tomatoes are so good! Pick them when red and ripe, when their taste is at its perfection. (Don't pick them early to ripen later yet. They have to do it that way in the commercial world, where picking green tomatoes is serious science and big business. Those tomatoes are picked once they're mature enough to finish turning red off the vine. Then they're treated with ethylene gas to help get them going and are shipped to supermarkets.) The time you do have to pick green tomatoes is frost time. Your tomato vines will keep bearing until frost kills them, so you should keep picking to eat, can, freeze, sell, give away . . .

GREEN TOMATOES: Green tomatoes extend your tomato season as well as become tasty dishes in their own right. Before you expect the first frost, either cover your tomatoes with plastic, old sheets, shower curtains, or rugs—anything to protect them—or give up and pick all the nice big green ones as well as the ripe red ones and bring them in the house for storage.

If you slice a green tomato with a sharp knife and you can cut one of its seeds in two, it isn't mature enough to make it off the vine. Tomatoes that are mature enough have seeds suspended in a jelly-like juice that will shift away from the knife so the seeds don't get cut. Once the fruit is at that stage, it's worth picking.

If a frost doesn't actually occur that night, wait until you fear one again. Then go through the same routine of covering or picking again. If you pick, you'll get all the ripe-enough tomatoes that have matured since you last picked. The day after a vine-killing frost finally does occur, harvest every tomato left on the vines—whether developed or not, frosted or not. Tomatoes that got touched by frost will have translucent spots. But deep inside the vines, if the frost wasn't too heavy, there will be lots of unharmed ones. The undeveloped ones can be used in green-tomato recipes, and both frosted and undeveloped tomatoes are good food for pigs or chickens.

Storing Greens. You are either going to eat them green, try to store them green until you want them to ripen, or try to get them to ripen. Green tomatoes stay green best around 45°F. They ripen best at around 70°F. Either way, store where the light is dim.

Storing on the Vine. Trudy Dorr, Lynden, WA, wrote me: "When freezing weather comes, I pull up the whole plant, root and all, and hang in porch, shed, attic, etc., and the tomatoes will ripen. This way I have tomatoes until at least Thanksgiving, and they taste the same as summer vine-ripened ones." Another reader has a similar system: "I cut the vines off at the ground and haul them indoors, cages and all, and pile them on a drop cloth on my basement floor. I pick them there in my basement until November or December, when they're gone. Then I clean up the mess. Even small ones ripen. I make these late ones into sauce."

Storing Off the Vine. You can also pull them off the vines to bring in. Anything that is big enough to have gotten to the glistening stage will eventually ripen. Spread them out in a place where they won't freeze and won't be damp. You can lay them on straw in cold frames (cover if needed) or on shelves. Tomatoes in storage will gradually ripen. They will taste like store-bought tomatoes rather than vine-ripened ones. But you'll have home-grown tomatoes for Thanksgiving dinner and fresh-sliced ones on the table, and that's worth a lot too. *To hurry ripening, put an apple in with the tomatoes.*

Checking on Them. Check the tomatoes every couple of days, especially at first. The reason you don't want to pile your green tomatoes in a box is that when they go bad, they do so suddenly and make a repulsive, slimy mess. A bad apple in a box just quietly shrivels and gets fuzzy. A bad tomato collapses all over its neighbors, spreading the infection. Spread them out so they don't touch each other; that way you can quickly remove any bad ones, and the rest will be unaffected. If a tomato has a translucent spot on it, that is where it got a touch of frost, and it will rot first from that spot. If you catch it soon enough, you can just trim out the spot and use the tomato in a green-tomato dish.

Recipe Ideas. For more green-tomato recipes, check out *The Green Tomato Cookbook* by Paula Simmons. Storey Communications offers a booklet, "52 Great Green Tomato Recipes!" Green tomatoes can be sliced and dried the same way as ripe ones.

⮞ *FRIED GREEN TOMATOES I like these, and this is the easiest way to fix green tomatoes. Slice your green tomatoes into about ½-inch slices. Combine flour, salt, and pepper in a pie tin. Dip the tomato slices in the mix to get both sides well coated. Fry them in hot shortening on one side and then the other. Serve hot and right away. Or you can use an egg-and-flour coating. A little basil in the flour is also good.*

⮞ *BAKED GREEN TOMATOES Cut your tomatoes in about ½-inch slices and arrange half of them in the bottom of a greased baking dish. Over that make a layer of small toasted*

bread cubes (use homemade bread), salt, pepper, and butter dots. Add a second layer of green tomatoes and then a second layer of everything else. Finally, sprinkle grated Parmesan cheese on top. Bake at 350°F until tender.

⮞ *GREEN TOMATO PIE This is a classic green-tomato dish. Cover 2 c. chopped green tomatoes with water, and bring to a boil. Drain. Add ½ c. brown sugar, 2 T. vinegar, ½ t. cinnamon, ½ c. chopped raisins, 3 T. melted butter, ½ t. salt, 3 cloves, and ¼ t. This makes a mock mince filling. Use a pie plate lined with a bottom crust. Add your mock mince. Put on a top crust, and slash to let steam escape. Crimp crust edge. Bake at 375°F about 40 minutes.*

PRESERVING

NOTE: *Don't refrigerate vine-ripened tomatoes unless you have to. Cold destroys their wonderful fresh flavor.*

Speeding Up Sauce-Making. Marie Oesting, Ocean Park, WA, says, "When making spaghetti sauce, paste, ketchup, etc.: Scale and peel, take out bad spots, slice or 'whunk' them up, and then let them set in a strainer, colander, jelly bag, or anything like that overnight. You'll be surprised at the amount of water you separate out—it's clear liquid, not at all red, and you save about half the cooking time. Incidentally, the quickest jelly bag is a kid's short-sleeve or sleeveless pajama top or a man's undershirt. Sew the waist shut and stick a broomstick through the arms to hang it up with, or put a string through the arms. I did this with one of my husband's old undershirts, rinsed it out, and put it in the laundry. I forgot about it and put it back into his undershirt pile. Boy, was he frustrated one morning trying to put that jelly bag on!"

Lane Morgan has a different system for the same purpose. She says, "Put your washed, stemmed tomatoes in a steamer with just a little water in the bottom. Heat slowly until the tomatoes start to give up some liquid, and then turn up the heat. Keep steaming until tomatoes are cooked. Then you pull out the basket, puree your cooked tomatoes however you like, add whatever else you like to put in tomato sauce, and cook until thick enough—maybe half an hour. Then can or freeze as usual. The watery juice that takes hours to evaporate by other methods is right there in the bottom of the steamer pot. And better yet, although it looks thin, it tastes great. I drink it straight or with a dash of salt and Tabasco sauce. Or else I put it in soup stock or bread dough. If you want to use it as a regular-looking tomato juice, mix in a bit of the puree. Leave a little liquid in the pot after the first batch of tomatoes to get the next one started."

FREEZING: Freeze tomatoes raw or cooked. To use, just drop the frozen chunk into the stew or whatever. That way it cooks up so quickly it can't spoil.

Frozen Whole. Lane Morgan says, "I freeze whole tomatoes. They thaw into mush, but it's great, fresh-tasting mush. It's good for salsa. Just put them straight into the freezer and bag them up later when they are hard. In my garden I seldom get enough tomatoes at a time to can, so this lets me build up a supply slowly. I leave the skin on—it peels right off as the tomato begins to thaw." For a salad, take them out just before mealtime, cut in pieces, and mix with your lettuce. They will be just right by the time you're ready to eat.

Frozen Stewed. Peel tomatoes and cut into quarters. Boil them 5 or 10 minutes. Cool, package, and freeze. You can freeze them in jars; I've done it and it works all right, but I like canned tomatoes better because you don't have to bother thawing them, and I think they taste better.

Frozen Tomato Mix. Liz Zellhoefer, Albany, CA, grew over 300 lb. of tomatoes in a 12 × 16-foot plot. She wrote me: "Well, I caught on real quick that if I canned all those tomatoes, I might go bananas. So I looked around for recipes and came up with this way to put up many pounds of tomatoes as easily as possible. In a huge kettle put 30–40 lb. of washed, halved tomatoes. Add 3 chopped celery stalks, 3 carrots, 3 onions, and a bunch of parsley, and boil. Boil hard until everything is mushy. Drain off water; puree through a ricer. Bring to boil and cook until thick. Pour into containers and freeze. I had so many containers that for 1½ years I didn't have to buy any tomatoes or tomato sauce!"

Frozen Tomato Juice. Low-acid tomato varieties and sound, well-ripened tomatoes will freeze best. Quarter them. Place in a covered pan. Crush lightly to provide enough juice to cover the bottom of the pan. Heat rapidly to 185–195°F (below boiling). Then put them through something to get the juice—a food press or a rotary colander, for instance. If you want seeds in your juice, use something with large holes. Then cool the juice quickly by setting the pan in ice water. Add 1 t. salt per 1 qt. juice. Pack in your containers and freeze immediately.

Frozen Tomato-8 Juice. This makes lots. Cook until soft ½ bushel of tomatoes, 10 large carrots, 4 green peppers, 4 large onions, ½ lb. green beans, 3 kohlrabies, a bunch of celery, and a bunch of parsley. Rub it all through a colander. Season with salt and pepper. Cool as quickly as possible, package, and freeze.

Frozen Green Tomatoes. Edna Andrews, Ravensdale, WA, wrote me: "I slice them thin, package, don't add anything to them, and freeze. Sometimes a few on top look dark when the package is opened, but they still taste good. Because of freezing, we can have fried green tomatoes all winter. They lose some of their hardness from the freezing, but when fried crisp they taste just like fresh ones."

DRYING: Drying tomatoes is harder than drying most other vegetables because tomatoes are mostly water. They're so wet that a dehydrator may not be able to release moisture fast enough, increasing the risk of mold. Yet it's easier to dry them in a dehydrator than in the oven or sun, unless you live where the humidity is very low and the sun's heat is very high. Starting with paste-type tomatoes helps a lot, because they're low-moisture types. The tomatoes must not be overripe, or they'll have an even greater tendency to mold. (You can make a leather from overripe ones.) Choose firm ones that are just at the peak of maturity. Peel and slice as thin as possible—⅛ inch thick. Drain off juice and seeds (which may cause a bitter taste). Optional: Sprinkle with salt.

Lay the sliced pieces directly on your drying tray, no more than one layer high, with a little room between slices for air circulation. Use only part of a commercial dehydrator so that it isn't overloaded with moisture. Gen MacManiman says to dry them at 110°F (it takes up to 30 hours). Some people who dry tomatoes dehydrate them at up to 140°F in a homemade dehydrator or at 120–200°F in an oven—with either dehydrator or oven door propped open several inches. If using the higher temperatures, check every 15 to 30 minutes because tomatoes scorch easily in the last stage. With care they can dry very nicely, keeping

their flavor and color. Dry until shriveled and slightly flexible yet not brittle. To make tomato leather, use the basic directions for making food leathers in Chapter 7.

Tomato Paste. Start with a paste-type tomato variety. Cook to softness, blend or process into a puree, and simmer until reduced in volume by 50 percent. (Stir often and don't let it scorch!) Now can in pint jars in a pressure canner using the times and directions for canning pumpkin (see "Winter Squashes"). Or spread a ½-inch layer of the thick puree onto a cookie sheet. Dry in dehydrator or sun until no longer sticky (maybe 2 days). Then make into balls, dip in oil, and store in a tightly lidded jar in a very cool place. Optional: Add basil, parsley, oregano . . .

Dried Tomato Recipe Ideas. Season with salt, basil, and oregano and marinate in olive oil in a dark place for at least 4 weeks. Or add to soup, stew, chili, or lasagna. Or pour boiling water over, simmer until tender, season as you would stewed tomatoes, and serve. Or grind to a powder and add that to meat loaf, casseroles, etc.

CANNING: I can tomato juice, sauce, and stewed tomatoes while they are in season. Literally bushels of tomatoes go through my canner. Then we have the green tomatoes all fall. The following tomato information and recipes are from Pacific Northwest Cooperative Extension and represent the state of the art:

BIG CHANGES IN TOMATO CANNING: Recent research has caused more changes in the tomato-canning process than in the process for canning any other kind of food:

1. Because tomatoes are the least acidic of all the foods defined as "high-acid," and because acidity varies so much, canners are now urged to *always* add citric acid or lemon juice to all water-bath–canned tomatoes in order to raise their acidity. Water-bath canning is okay for plain tomatoes, but they *must* be acidified.
2. Processing times have been lengthened.
3. Pressure canning can be used as an alternative to water-bath canning.
4. Recommended pressures now differ for dial and weighted-gauge canners. (This is true of canning *anything!*)
5. Altitude adjustments for both boiling-water canners and pressure canners have been revised. (This is also true for *all canning recipes.*)

Adding Acid, Sugar, and Salt to Canned Tomatoes. Add 1 T. bottled lemon juice per pint or 2 T. per quart. Or add ¼ tsp. USP citric acid per pint, ½ t. per quart. Some people add a little sugar to mask any sour flavor: 1 t. sugar per pint, 2 t. per quart. You can add salt to taste; it doesn't help preserve the tomatoes. On average, people add ½ t. salt per pint, 1 t. per quart.

Choosing and Preparing the Tomatoes. The amount of tomatoes it takes to make a canned quart ranges from as little as 2¾ lb. for crushed tomatoes to 3¼ lb. for tomato juice, on up to 5–6½ lb. for tomato sauce. Select firm, under-derripe-to-ripe tomatoes. Never use decayed or overripe ones because their presence can significantly lower the acidity. Don't can tomatoes from dead or frost-killed vines. Wash tomatoes in cool running water. Skinning is optional. To skin, dip into boiling water for 30 to 60 seconds or until skins split. Dip in cold water; slip off skins.

Crushed Tomatoes. To pack them hot without any added liquid, cut your prepared tomatoes into quarters. Heat them

NOTE FOR RECIPES

1 lb. mushrooms = 2½ c. sliced mushrooms	1 lb. onions = 2½ c. chopped onions	1 lb. peppers = 10 large peppers
		1 lb. tomatoes = 3–4 small tomatoes

quickly in a large pot, crushing the first layers with a wooden spoon to press out juice. Continue heating to a boil, stirring to prevent burning. Boil gently for 5 minutes after adding all tomatoes. Fill pint or quart jars immediately with hot tomatoes, leaving ½ inch headspace. *Add acid.* Adjust lids and process in a boiling-water bath. For quarts: At up to 1,000 feet above sea level, process 45 minutes; at 1,001–3,000 feet, 50 minutes; 3,001–6,000 feet, 55 minutes; and above 6,000 feet, 60 minutes. Process pints for 10 minutes less than the time given for your altitude.

To use a pressure canner, process for 15 minutes. If using a weighted-gauge canner, set at 10 lb. pressure at 0–1,000 feet above sea level; set at 15 lb. at higher altitudes. If using a dial-gauge canner, set at 11 lb. pressure at 0–2,000 feet above sea level; 12 lb. at 2,001–4,000 feet; 13 lb. at 4,001–6,000 feet; 14 lb. at 6,001–8,000 feet; or 15 lb. above 8,000 feet.

Whole/Halved Tomatoes Packed in Water.

Prepare as above, but leave whole or cut in halves. To raw-pack, fill jars with raw, peeled tomatoes. Cover with hot water, leaving ½ inch headspace. To hot-pack, add enough water to cover tomatoes in a large pan. Boil gently for 5 minutes. Fill jars with hot tomatoes. Cover with hot cooking liquid, leaving ½ inch headspace. *Add acid* to both hot- and raw-packed tomatoes. Adjust lids and process in a boiling-water bath. For quarts: At up to 1,000 feet above sea level, process 45 minutes; at 1,001–3,000 feet, 50 minutes; 3,001–6,000 feet, 55 minutes; and above 6,000 feet, 60 minutes. Process pints for 5 minutes less than the time given for your altitude. Process pints or quarts in a pressure canner for 10 minutes at the correct pressure for your altitude, as indicated in the preceding Crushed Tomatoes recipe.

Whole/Halved Tomatoes Packed in Tomato Juice.

Prepare tomatoes as in the preceding recipe and tomato juice as in the following Canned Tomato Juice recipe. To raw-pack, heat the tomato juice in a pan. Fill jars with raw tomatoes. Cover with hot tomato juice. Leave ½ inch headspace. To hot-pack, completely cover tomatoes with tomato juice in large pan. Boil gently for 5 minutes. Fill jars with hot tomatoes and cover with hot tomato juice, leaving ½ inch headspace. *Add acid* to jars of either hot- or raw-packed tomatoes. Adjust lids. Process pints or quarts in a pressure canner for 25 minutes at the correct pressure for your altitude, as indicated in the Crushed Tomatoes recipe. To process pints or quarts using a boiling-water bath: At up to 1,000 feet above sea level, process 85 minutes; at 1,001–3,000 feet, 90 minutes; 3,001–6,000 feet, 95 minutes; and above 6,000 feet, 100 minutes.

Whole/Halved Tomatoes Packed Raw Without Added Liquid.

Prepare tomatoes as above. Leave whole or halved. Loosely fill jars with raw tomatoes, pressing until spaces fill with juice. Leave ½ inch headspace. *Add acid.* Adjust lids and pressure-can pints or quarts for 25 minutes at the correct pressure for your altitude, as indicated in the Crushed Tomatoes recipe. Or process pints or quarts using a boiling-water bath for the times indicated in the Whole/Halved Tomatoes Packed in Tomato Juice recipe.

Canned Tomato Juice.

Wash, remove stems, and trim off bruised or discolored portions. Slice or quarter tomatoes into a large pan. Crush, heat, and simmer for 5 minutes before juicing. Press the heated, crushed tomatoes through a sieve or food mill to remove skins and seeds. Heat juice again to boiling. (If you made the juice in a blender or Squeezo strainer, cook it 5 minutes more to get out the bubbles so they don't pop off the jar lid.) Fill jars with hot juice, leaving ½ inch headspace. *Add acid*—especially if you used overripe tomatoes. Adjust lids and process pints or quarts in a pressure canner for 15 minutes at the correct pressure for your altitude, as indicated in the Crushed Tomatoes recipe. Or process in a boiling-water bath. For quarts: At up to 1,000 feet above sea level, process 40 minutes; at 1,001–3,000 feet, 45 minutes; 3,001–6,000 feet, 50 minutes; and above 6,000 feet, 55 minutes. Process pints for 5 minutes less than the time given for your altitude.

Tomato/Vegetable Juice Blend.

Prepare, crush, and simmer tomatoes as for making tomato juice. An average of 22 lb. of tomatoes is needed per 7-qt. canner load. Add no more than 3 c. of any combination of finely chopped celery, onions, carrots, and peppers to each 22 lb. of tomatoes. Simmer mixture 20 minutes. Press hot, cooked tomatoes and vegetables through a sieve or food mill to remove skins and seeds. Reheat tomato-vegetable juice blend to boiling and fill jars immediately, leaving ½ inch headspace. *Add acid.* Adjust lids. Process pints or quarts in a pressure canner for 15 minutes at the correct pressure for your altitude, as indicated in the Crushed Tomatoes recipe.

Canned Tomato Sauce.

Prepare tomatoes, heat, and press as for making tomato juice. Simmer in large-diameter pan until sauce reaches desired consistency. Simmer until volume has been reduced by about a third for thin sauce or by about a half for thick sauce. Fill jars, leaving ½ inch headspace. *Add acid.* Adjust lids. Process pints or quarts in pressure canner for 15 minutes at the correct pressure for your altitude, as indicated in the preceding Crushed Tomatoes recipe. Or process in a boiling-water bath using the times given in the Tomato Juice recipe.

Spaghetti Sauce Without Meat

NOTE: It is not safe to increase the proportion of onions, peppers, celery, or mushrooms in this recipe if you are planning to can the sauce!

Wash 30 lb. tomatoes and dip in boiling water for 30 to 60 seconds or until skins split. Dip in cold water and slip off skins. Remove cores and quarter tomatoes. Boil 20 minutes, uncovered, in large pan. Put through food mill or sieve. Saute in ¼ c. vegetable oil until tender: 1 c. chopped onions, 5 minced garlic cloves, 1 c. celery or green pepper (chopped), and (optional) 1 lb. sliced mushrooms. Combine sauteed vegetables and tomatoes. Add 2 T. salt (or to taste), 2 t. black pepper, 2 T. oregano, ¼ c. minced parsley, and ¼ c. brown sugar. Bring to a boil. Simmer, uncovered, until thick enough for serving. (The volume should be reduced by nearly half.) Stir frequently to avoid burning.

Fill jars, leaving 1 inch headspace. Adjust lids. Process in a pressure canner 20 minutes for pints, 25 minutes for quarts. If using a weighted-gauge canner, set at 10 lb. pressure at 0–1,000 feet above sea level; set at 15 lb. at higher altitudes. If using a dial-gauge canner, set at 11 lb. pressure at 0–2,000 feet above sea level; 12 lb. at 2,001–4,000 feet; 13 lb. at 4,001–6,000 feet; 14 lb. at 6,001–8,000 feet; or 15 lb. above 8,000 feet.

Spaghetti Sauce with Meat. Prepare 30 lb. tomatoes as in preceding Spaghetti Sauce Without Meat recipe. Saute 2½ lb. ground beef or sausage until brown. Drain off fat. Add 5 minced garlic cloves, 1 c. chopped onion, 1 c. chopped celery or green peppers, and 1 lb. sliced mushrooms (optional). Cook until vegetables are tender. Combine vegetables with tomato pulp in a large pan. Add 2 T. salt (or to taste), 2 t. black pepper, 2 T. oregano, ¼ c. minced parsley, and ¼ c. brown sugar. Bring to a boil. Simmer uncovered until thick enough for serving (till volume is reduced by nearly half). Stir frequently to avoid burning. Fill jars, leaving 1 inch headspace. Adjust lids and process in a pressure canner 60 minutes for pints, 70 minutes for quarts. If using a weighted-gauge canner, set at 10 lb. pressure at 0–1,000 feet above sea level; set at 15 lb. at higher altitudes. If using a dial-gauge canner, set at 11 lb. pressure at 0–2,000 feet above sea level; 12 lb. at 2,001–4,000 feet; 13 lb. at 4,001–6,000 feet; 14 lb. at 6,001–8,000 feet; or 15 lb. above 8,000 feet.

Stewed Tomatoes. You'll need 1 gal. peeled, cored, chopped tomatoes, 1 c. chopped onion, ½ c. chopped green pepper, and 2 t. salt. Combine those in a pan, cover, and cook over gentle heat for about 10 minutes. Then ladle hot mix into hot jars. Allow ½ inch headspace. Put lids on and tighten. Process in pressure canner: pints 15 minutes, quarts 20 minutes. If using a weighted-gauge canner, set at 10 lb. pressure at 0–1,000 feet above sea level; set at 15 lb. at higher altitudes. If using a dial-gauge canner, set at 11 lb. pressure at 0–2,000 feet above sea level; 12 lb. at 2,001–4,000 feet; 13 lb. at 4,001–6,000 feet; 14 lb. at 6,001–8,000 feet; or 15 lb. above 8,000 feet.

Basic Garden Vegetable Soup for Canning. Prepare 1 gal. peeled, chopped tomatoes 3 qt. peeled, chunked potatoes, 2 qt. snapped green beans, 2 qt. corn cut off the cob (about 20 ears), 3 qt. carrot chunks (about ½-inch), 1 qt. onion chunks, 8 crushed garlic cloves, 1 T. black pepper, and salt and other spices according to your taste and preference. Combine vegetables in a big pan; add 3 qt. water. Bring to a boil and cook 5 minutes. Dip hot into clean pint or quart jars. Leave 1 inch headspace. Put on lids. Process in *pressure canner only* for 95 minutes for pints or quarts. If using a weighted-gauge canner, set at 10 lb. pressure at 0–1,000 feet above sea level; set at 15 lb. at higher altitudes. If using a dial-gauge canner, set at 11 lb. pressure at 0–2,000 feet above sea level; 12 lb. at 2,001–4,000 feet; 13 lb. at 4,001–6,000 feet; 14 lb. at 6,001–8,000 feet; or 15 lb. above 8,000 feet.

RAW TOMATO RECIPE IDEAS: Our summer tomatoes are usually eaten fresh, mouthful by mouthful, juice running down grinning, happy chins. For meals, I serve the tomato cut in thick slices, skin and all. But if you dip the tomato in boiling water for 1 minute and then into cold water, you can easily slip off the skin. We also like tomatoes in sandwiches and salads.

Making Tomato Flowerets for Salads. Choose small tomatoes of equal size. Cut across 3 or 4 times not quite to the base. The tomato should open up like a water lily. You can put a little blob of mayonnaise in the center with a pinch of chopped parsley on top.

TOMATO JUICE RECIPE IDEAS: Tomato juice can be drunk plain from fresh, canned, or frozen sources. Or to 2½ c. tomato juice, add a trace of pepper, a pinch of salt, 1 T. lemon juice, ½ t. horseradish, and a pinch of celery salt. Or combine 1 part each celery juice and tomato juice, and season to taste. Or combine 1 part each grapefruit juice and tomato juice; then add a squeeze of lemon juice and a dash of salt. Or combine 1 part each sauerkraut juice and tomato juice; then add a squeeze of lemon juice, and spice it up with Tabasco and Worcestershire if you have an iron stomach.

GAZPACHO From Ruth of Bonaire: Combine in blender 4 c. tomato juice, 2 tomatoes, juice of ½ lemon, 1 peeled cucumber, 2 green onions, 1 celery stalk, 1 T. tamari, and basil, oregano, and/or parsley. Serve well-chilled."

RAW-TOMATO SPAGHETTI SAUCE Make the sauce at least 1½ hours before you're going serve it. After you have your sauce all made and it has rested 1½ hours to get the flavors well-merged, add your cooked spaghetti (well-drained), mix it up with the sauce, and serve right away. To make the sauce: Combine ½ c. olive oil, about a dozen medium-sized fresh tomatoes (sliced very thin), 20 leaves of fresh basil (torn across), 3 mashed garlic cloves, 1 t. salt, and a pinch or two of freshly ground pepper.

COOKED TOMATO RECIPE IDEAS: Briefly saute chopped tomatoes and stir into a pasta dish together with melted cheese. Or add to any vegetable and/or meat soup. Or saute with onion and cooked chicken strips; then toss with cooked noodles. Or saute chopped tomatoes with garlic, basil, chopped sweet peppers, and onions; simmer a bit and serve as a sauce over pasta or bread.

ITALIAN GRAVY Fry 1 medium chopped onion, 1 chopped garlic clove, and 2 T. chopped parsley in 4 T. olive oil until light brown. Add ½ lb. ground beef, 1½ t. salt, and a pinch of pepper, and cook until the meat loses its redness. Blend in 1 can tomato paste and 1 small can of tomatoes or puree. Simmer for 1 to 1½ hours (longer tastes better), stirring occasionally. Add chicken, sausage, meatballs, pork chops, steak, or wieners to the gravy while simmering.

STEWED TOMATOES Slice and peel into a cooking pan. Cook for 5 minutes and season with salt and pepper. Serve plain or on slices or cubes of toasted homemade bread.

INSTANT KETCHUP Put 3 t. cornstarch in pan over medium heat and make a paste by gradually adding 2 c. tomato juice. Flavor with ½ t. salt, 1 t. honey, a little onion, and garlic salt. Optional: Add a pinch of red pepper.

Seventh edition. Four days ago I had a baby, my sixth! On Monday I wrote the new version of the pepper section, which is mostly like writing from scratch because I've been expanding it so much. Tuesday morning I woke up and my water broke (in exactly that sequence—I was still lying in bed). My labor didn't start, but after a while Mike took me to the hospital anyway, because once before, with Rebecca, I had had the baby about 3 hours after the water had broken, which is fast as these things go. Even though Mike has tested a cow for pregnancy and delivered umpteen farm-animal babies, he doesn't want to get stuck delivering one of ours.

So he took me to the hospital labor room. I lay there all day wishing I could get to work on the potato section of this book. I felt very bored and sort of guilty because Mike had work to do too, and there we were and nothing was happening. Then at 5pm I had a contraction, at 5:15 another, at 5:20 another, and at 5:25 another. The nurse came in and I told her that I thought something might be happening. She said I'd have to be more regular than that, and then she left. Then everything stopped for 30 minutes. Then I had contractions for another half hour, then nothing for the next half hour. From 7 to 8pm the labor ambled along in a semiserious way. The nurse checked me and said I was 3 centimeters dilated. (I had been 2 cm that morning, when I had checked in.)

At this point, I asked her to call my doctor, Dr. Drury. He had repeatedly made me promise that I'd let him know when "labor started" because, he said, "I have a feeling it might go pretty fast once you get started."

The nurse thought the call was premature. "It's too early," she said. But I humbly requested again, and she made the call.

In the meantime, nothing happened: still no serious contractions, still no good dilation. At 8:30 Mike was seriously considering going for a walk. But then I had some harder contractions, and he decided to stick around. At 8:45 I asked him to please tell the nurse it was feeling more serious. She came in and checked me and said, sounding kind of disgusted by the nuisance of having to measure somebody who wasn't doing much, that I was dilated 5 centimeters. That was at 8:48.

Just as her shoulders were disappearing out the door, I said, "Mike, you better tell her I feel like I'm getting ready to bear down!"

Mike took me absolutely seriously. He jumped up and dashed out into the hall after the nurse. The two of them came racing back with a cart, got me loaded onto it almost as fast as I could say it, and wheeled me into the delivery room, which was directly across the hall. They moved me off the cart and onto the delivery table, getting me in place before that predicted next contraction hit me at about 8:55.

For as soon as I was on the delivery table, here it came. I was bearing down all right! That one contraction moved the baby out of the womb and well down the birth canal. The nurse was running around getting things ready and paging Dr. Drury over the intercom system in case he had already arrived at the hospital, telling him to come to the delivery room immediately. In the meantime she was also yelling at me, "Don't push! Don't push!"

But a few minutes later, I had another powerful bearing-down contraction. I pushed for all I was worth because that was what was happening. Just then Dr. Drury came in the door at a dead run. He threw his coat off onto the floor as he passed through it—just as the baby crowned, because the second bearing-down contraction had moved its head all the way to the opening of the vagina. The others could see the top "crown" and almost to the baby's shoulders—

out far enough so that Mike could see that it was as blue as blue ink. It was asphyxiating!

"Push! Push!" screamed the nurse.

I tried to push. With a bit of effort came a third, huge, involuntary bearing-down contraction. It brought the baby out all the way. As it came out, Mike, the nurse, and Dr. Drury could all see why it was blue. The baby had a loop of umbilical cord tightly wound around its neck and another around its chest. But Dr. Drury had the expertise that comes from having helped with hundreds of births. He expertly caught the baby as it slipped out, and in an instant, fluid motion as fast as the wink of an eye, he slipped his fingers under that loop of cord around the baby's neck, gently loosened it, and lifted it over the baby's head. Then he did the same for the other loop around its chest.

The baby gasped its first breath, coughed, cried, and turned a healthy pink!

I was sitting up, sobbing with joy and trying to see every part of the baby at once, trying to comprehend that the baby I had carried unseen for so many months really was, in every part and way, a fine healthy boy. And he was! It makes you believe in miracles.

Today is Saturday, 4 days later. I got home from the hospital on Thursday.

January 12, 1992. That baby—Jacob—is 15 now, almost 16. His brains are fine. He's graduating from high school in a few more months (yes, he's been accelerated 2 years), and he's eagerly awaiting the results of his applications to various colleges. It could so easily have been different. I still ponder that mysterious birth of his, so unlike those of my other children. Jacob was delivered in just 3 huge bearing-down contractions. The delivery time was 9pm on February 15, 1977—exactly 12 minutes after the moment the nurse had said I was merely 5 centimeters dilated. Jacob spent only about 5 minutes in his transit down the passage between the womb and the outside world. That's as long as you can hold your breath without brain damage.

Because of the cord around his neck and chest, if I had delivered that baby any more slowly, he surely would have been born permanently brain-damaged from lack of oxygen —or dead. He was fine as long as he was in the womb, but the moment the womb opened and he entered the birth canal, that cord tightened around his neck and chest; he then ceased to receive oxygen and began strangulation. The unique way that particular birth happened couldn't have been an accident. How did my body know exactly what had to be accomplished? Is there more capacity for communication with and inner direction of one's physiology than we consciously or scientifically understand? I'm so glad I didn't have any anesthetic in my system to mess up that subtle capacity for inner-directed birthing, if such was the case . . .

Herbs & Flavorings

HERBS & FLAVORINGS CONTENTS

INTRODUCTION

An herb lady once told me, "I used to think anybody who grew flowers in their garden was wasting space. Now I don't grow food any more—just herbs, mostly the herbs I use in my work. Herbs are ornamental, fragrant, and a pleasure to use." So herbs can be a necessity of life, depending on your convictions. For sure they're a pleasant luxury, a comfort so natural to country living that I'm including them in this book.

"Herbs" are the leaves or other parts of aromatic plants grown in the temperate zone. "Spices" are the stems, leaves, roots, seeds, flowers, buds, or bark of aromatic plants grown in the tropics. Here are some of the possible directions for your collection:

- Culinary herbs: basil, bay leaf, caraway, chives, mint, parsley, rosemary, sage, tarragon
- Stronger seasoning herbs: capers, dandelion, garlic, horseradish, hot pepper, mustard, nasturtium
- Decorative herbs: bergamot, lovage, rose, rosemary, tansy
- Scented herbs: chamomile, scented geranium, lavender, marigold, mint, patchouli, rose, rue, thyme
- Medicinal herbs: anise, horehound, hyssop, feverfew
- Herbs that are natural pesticides: pennyroyal, pyrethrum
- Herbs that thrive in containers: garlic, parsley, thyme, tarragon, marjoram, oregano, chives, mint, winter savory, geranium, bay leaf

- Edible flowers: marigold, lemon mint, borage, nasturtium, bean, chrysanthemum, cucumber, rose, squash, violet

You can also grow herbs for dyeing, making cosmetics, or attracting bees that make exotic flavors of honey.

Some people doctor with herbs, but not all herbs are as safe or effective as you might think. If you wish you knew what has been scientifically verified about healing herbs, what's hocus, and what's dangerous, read *The New Honest Herbal* (especially the "Remedies" section by Dr. Varro E. Tyler, a plant drug specialist at Purdue University).

Healthwise, I recommend a Seventh-Day Adventist doctor as providing the best of both worlds. On one visit to my Adventist doctor, Dr. Drury, when I was full of mysterious problems, he first wrote me a couple of prescriptions, then gave me some marital advice, and finally prayed for me. Now that's doctoring! The gist of his advice was that I should quit trying to write this book. He has continued to offer that same advice at every visit. I almost always throw away his paper prescriptions (I just want to hear what he thinks, not get pills) and, as you see, I didn't obey his advice about the book, so any health problems I end up with are no fault of his! Fact is, though, I feel great.

Dr. Drury was, I think, the last of the old-time country doctors. If you wanted to give birth in his office examining room with only him and his wife (a nurse) to help, he'd let you.

Then he'd move you and baby to a waiting room. Some of his waiting rooms had real beds, so sick people or women who'd just given birth could be genuinely comfortable. My daughter Esther was born that way about 2:30am (she was my seventh). After Dr. Drury got her and me all fixed up, he and his wife went back to their home, just a little way up the road. We stayed there for a while, my husband Mike sleeping on one bed in the room, precious baby Esther and me on the other. Mike woke up at about 6:00am and said, "Well, are you ready to go home?" I answered, "Yes." We took our new baby, let ourselves out the back door of the silent building, got in our pickup (which was parked out back), and drove home. We loved it—no hospital bill, no hassle! And the expertise of a doctor who had delivered hundreds of babies available if needed.

Dr. Drury had delivered most of the local babies for thirty-some years when the insurance company forced him to quit. Doc explained that they'd made a new rule: the more babies a doctor had delivered (so the more experience he had and the more women trusted him, went to him for their birthings, and told other women about him), the higher his insurance rates soared. Dr. Drury had delivered so many babies that his rates became absolutely unaffordable. He had to start telling women to go to a young city doc who had only delivered a few and thus could afford insurance.

HERBS

YOUR HERB GARDEN: Unlike spices, herbs can be used fresh from the garden because we temperate-zone dwellers can grow them ourselves. You can plant herbs in a border around your vegetable garden or give them a plot of their own. Kitchen herbs fit nicely into about a 3 × 5-foot area, ideally outside near your back, or kitchen, door! Herbs are grown in solid patches jammed up against each other rather than in rows like a vegetable garden, so you get lots for your space. Some herbs are enthusiastic self-spreaders, but wood, stone, or metal edging keeps them within your chosen bounds and can also serve as little footpaths of stones or slate. Some herbs you can start from seed, but many are propagated by division or layering. Some are temperate-zone perennials, but many do best if you bring them in for the winter. Some do fine in an ongoing window box or container setting. For herbs in the house, a southern-facing window in a coolish room is ideal.

PUBLIC HERB GARDENS

Brooklyn Botanic Garden offers herbs in their store, books on herbs and growing them, and videos ("Dyeing with Plants," 10 minutes); classes on herbs; and more: 718-623-4241; 1000 Washington, Brooklyn, NY 11225; **www.bbg.org.**

Lady Catherine's Herb & Wildflower Garden features medicinal and period gardens (Biblical, Shakespearean, etc.): 903-639-2254; 1487 County Rd. 2924, Hughes Springs, TX 75656.

Medicinal Herb Garden, founded in 1911, is run by the U. of Washington's Botany Department (Box 355325, Seattle, WA 98195). It's on the main campus, open to the public seven days a week, and admission is free. For $25/yr, you get their quarterly newsletter.

The National Herb Garden of the U.S. National Arboretum is the largest herb garden in the world. Founded by the Herb Society of America, it regularly offers teaching workshops: 202-245-2726; 3501 New York Ave. NE, Washington, DC 20002; **www.usna.usda.gov.**

Our Grandmother's Garden welcomes visitors to their greenhouses and gardens, which display culinary, decorative, aromatic, and medicinal herbs. These include a scented geranium garden and a 17th-century Elizabethan knot garden. Shop offers 450 varieties of herbs: 203-888-5649; 67 Christian St., Oxford, CT 06478.

Ozark Folk Center State Park offers herb vacations at the Ozark Folk Center's Lodge. Its Heritage Herb Garden does a yearly Spring Extravaganza with lavish herbal feast and various seminars: 800-264-3655; Box 500, Mountain View, AR 72560; **ozarkfolkcenter@arkansas.com.**

Well-Sweep Herb Farm, an old-time family outfit, has one of the largest collections of herbs and perennials in the U.S. They have more than 5 acres of display gardens, featuring common and unusual herbs, scented geraniums, and flowering perennials. They offer special events, courses, and lectures throughout the year. Free catalog. Contact: 908-852-5390; fax 908-852-1649; 205 Mt. Bethel Rd., Port Murray, NJ 07865; **herbs@goes.com; www.wellsweep.com.**

INFO AND NETWORKING: Online, try **www.herbworld. com, www.herbnet.com,** and **www.herbsociety.org.** The latter is a great site maintained by The Herb Society of America: 440-256-0514; fax 440-256-0541; 9019 Kirtland Chardon Rd., Kirtland, OH 44094; **herbs@herbsociety. org.** You can e-mail **herbworld@aol.com** with herb-related questions.

The Herb Growing and Marketing Network publishes *The Business of Herbs: International News and Resource Service for Herb Businesses* 6 times/yr: **www.herb-biz.com/bofh. htm.** It also publishes *(The) Herbal Connection,* a bimonthly that provides info on growing and using herbs. Their $20/yr membership fee gets you a newsletter, their industry herb directory, *The Herbal Green Pages,* listing hundreds of small growers with herbs to sell, and a cooperative herb buying program: **www.herbworld.com;** 717-393-3295; PO Box 245, Silver Spring, PA 17575-0245; **herbworld@aol.com; www.herbnet.com.** They're an "herb world" indeed!

Rodale's *Illustrated Encyclopedia of Herbs* (1987) is a print overview of kitchen and medical herbs. *Herbs: Partners in Life,* by Adele G. Dawson, is a guide to cooking, gardening, and healing with 70 wild and cultivated plants, written by a 76-year-old Vermont herbalist (available from Southern Exposure Seed Exchange). *The Harrowsmith Illustrated Book of Herbs,* by Patrick Lima, is helpful for northern gardeners. Storey Books offers many herb books, such as *The Art and Skill of Teaching about Herbs,* a teaching packet by Portia Meares.

OTHER HERB PERIODICALS

(The) Country Shepherd Herb News: Herbal News and Information for the Southeast provides a calendar of herbal events, listing of nurseries, etc.: 706-788-3116; Rt. 1, Box 107, Comer, GA 30629; $15/6 issues/yr.

Herbalgram is a sophisticated, fascinating quarterly collection of articles on the medicinal uses of herbs and other topics of interest to serious and well-educated students of *materia medica*. They sell a goldenseal data and grow packet. The magazine costs $25/yr: 512-928-4900; 800-373-7105; American Botanical Council, PO Box 144345, Austin, TX 78714-4345.

MEDICINAL PLANT INFO: To research medicinal herbs, you might attend the Southern Appalachian School for Growing Medicinal Plants: 828-649-3536; 300 Indigo Bunting Lane, Marshall, NC 28753; **robert@ncgoldenseal. com; www.ncgoldenseal.com.** Or read *The Encyclopedia of Medicinal Plants* (1996), by Andrew Chevallier; *Cunningham's Encyclopedia of Magical Herbs* (1985), by Scott Cunningham; *The Herbal Medicine Makers Handbook,* by James Green; *The New Age Herbalist* (1988), by Richard Mabey, et al.; *The Complete Medicinal Herbal* (1993), by Penelope Ody; and *Jude's Herbal Home Remedies* (1992), by Jude C. Williams. For an establishment medical view on what is scientifically verified about healing herbs, what's hocus, and what's dangerous, read *The New Honest Herbal* (especially the "Remedies" section), by Dr. Varro E. Tyler, a plant drug specialist at Purdue University. On the web, look up "Medical Plant Database," "Native American Ethnobotany," and the Southwest School of Botanical Medicine. More online info and a bibliography for medicinal herbs are in the ATTRA publication "Herb Overview" (800-346-9140; **www.attra.org/attra-pub/herb.html**). You'll find Steven Foster, author of *Herbal Renaissance* (1992), at **photography@stevenfoster.com; www.steven foster.com.**

The Business of Herbs

BUYING HERBS AND HERB PRODUCTS: Herb growing and use are enjoying renewed popularity both with builders of beautiful cuisines and fragrant potpourris, and with seekers after kinder, gentler, cheaper cures for what ails them.

Here's a list of places to buy herbs. Later in this chapter, as I discuss specific herbs, I'll note the firms that sell them. If you don't find their addresses below, look in the introduction to Chapter 2 (for firms that also carry vegetables) or the source list in Chapter 6 (for those that specialize in trees and fruits).

HERB PRODUCTS

Frontier Natural Products Co-op offers a wide selection of natural and organic foods and personal care products, plus bulk and bottled herbs, spices, and baking flavors, etc.: 800-669-3275; 2990 Wilderness Blvd., Ste. 200, Boulder, CO 80301; **www.frontiercoop.com.**

Indiana Botanic Gardens sells by mail-order dried herbs, essential oils, floral scents, potpourri, spices, etc. Free catalog: orders 800-644-8327; info 800-514-1068 or 219-947-4040; fax 219-947-4148; PO Box 5, Hammond, IN 46325; **www.botanichealth.com.**

LorAnn Oils sells essential oils, flavorings, and specialty ingredients for soap-, candle-, and food-crafters: 4518 Aurelius Rd., Lansing, MI 48910; 800-862-8620; 517-882-0215; fax 517-882-0507; **customercare@loran noils.com; www.lorannoils.com.**

Penzeys Spices offers 250+ spices and spice blends for gourmet cooks including arrowroot, vanilla beans, ajwain seed, annatto seeds, cassia buds, and gumbo filé: 262-785-7676; 800-741-7787; PO Box 924, Brookfield, WI 53008-0924; **www.Penzeys.com.**

HERB PLANT SOURCES: Herbs are sought after by cooks, decorators, and healers. For hard-to-find sources of seeds and growing info, order the 96-pg encyclopedic *Ethnobotanical Catalog of Seeds.* It's $1 from J. L. Hudson (see below). In the detailed description of each herb (alphabetical, later in this chapter), I usually name places to buy seeds or starts in addition to this general list. (Also see the list of seed companies in Chapter 2.)

Abundant Life Seed Foundation sells herb seeds and books, etc. Catalog, $2: 360-385-5660; PO Box 772, Port Townsend, WA 98368; **www.abundantlifeseed. org.**

Burnt Ridge Nursery specializes in unusual trees, shrubs, and vines that grow edible nuts or fruit: 360-985-2873; 432 Burnt Ridge Rd., Onalaska, WA 98570; **burntridge@myhome.net; landru.myhome.net/ burntridge.**

Cricket Hill Herb Farm, Ltd.: 978-948-2818; 74 Glen St., Rowley, MA 01969.

Dabney Herbs sells herbs, native Midwestern plants, books, etc.: 502-893-5198; Box 22061, Louisville, KY 40252; **dabneyherb@win.net; www.dabney herbs.com.**

Garden Medicinals and Culinaries offers 170 varieties of herb seeds, roots, tubers, and specialty garlics, herb books, and supplies/equipment for herb growers and herbalists. Many links to herb-related and phytotherapeutic sites from their website: **www.garden medicinals.com.** Catalog, $2: 434-964-9113; fax 434-973-8717; PO Box 320, Earlysville, VA 22936.

Herbal Advantage, Rte. 3, Box 93, Rogersville, MO 65742; 800-753-9929; **www.herbaladvantage.com.**

Horizon Herbs Seed Farm: 541-846-6704; fax 541-846-6233; **hhcusrserv@HorizonHerbs.com;** PO Box 69, Williams, OR 97544; **www.HorizonHerbs.com.**

J.L. Hudson, Seedsman, sells medicinal plants and herbs. No phone. Catalog $1: Star Rte. 2, Box 337, La Honda, CA 94020; **www.JLHudsonseeds.net.**

Le Jardin du Gourmet sells herbs and seeds: 802-748-1446; PO Box 751, St. Johnsbury Center, VT 05863-0075; **www.ArtisticGardens.com/.**

Linda's Garden offers a complete herb and herb line. 1436 Campbells Landing Rd., Virginia Beach, VA 23457, 757-426-5303; **herb@cyber9.com; www.cyber9.com/ herbs.**

Long Creek Herbs: Call/fax 417-779-5450; Rte. 4, Box 730, Oak Grove, AR 72660.

Mulberry Creek's Herb Farm offers a very large selection of certified organic herbs, stevia plants, etc. Free catalog: 419-433-6126; 3312 Bogart Rd., Huron, OH 44839; **www.mulberrycreek.com.**

Nichols Garden Nursery is an herb specialist that's been around longer than this book, selling a wide variety of herb plants and seeds; 1190 N. Pacific Hwy., Albany, OR 97321; **www.gardennursery.com/;** 541-928-9280; fax 800-231-5306.

Redwood City Seed has a great herb collection: 650-325-7333; PO Box 361, Redwood City, CA 94064; **www. ecoseeds.com.**

Richter's is an herb specialist offering 900+ culinary, medicinal, and ornamental varieties including stevia and yucca. Free catalog: 905-640-6677; fax 905-620-6641; 357 Hwy. 47, Goodwood, Ontario, L0C 1A0, CANADA; **info@richters.com; www.richters.com.**

Sandy Mush Herb Nursery offers 1,850 varieties of culinary and tea herbs; decorative, scented geraniums; dye plants, etc. Their $5 catalog fully describes all those plants, their growing conditions, and uses; plants for various purposes and places; growing and using herbs; recipes; herb books; and sample plans for kitchen, bee, butterfly, fragrant, and geometric culinary gardens: 828-683-2014; 316 Surrett Cove Rd, Leicester, NC 28748-2014; **brwn.org/sandymushherbs.**

Southern Exposure Seed Exchange uses organic/sustainable methods and has an extensive online catalog: PO Box 460, Mineral, VA 23117; **www.southern exposure.com.**

SELLING HERBS: This isn't necessarily easy. But you might do well selling herbs at a farmer's market, either in peat pots, in hanging pots, or cut for culinary use. Develop a personal clientele. Herb growers, by definition, are supposed to be 100% organic, because the Environmental Protection Agency has not authorized any pesticides for use on herbs. And wholesalers won't buy herbal products unless growers can certify they are chemical free. (However, spot checks have found poison residues in some commercial herb products.)

For good information from a pro herb wholesaler for both beginners and other pros, see *The Potential of Herbs as a Cash Crop* by Richard Alan Miller or *Profitable Herb Growing* by N. P. Nichols. *Growing and Selling Fresh-Cut Herbs* (1999), by Sandie Shores, covers crop production methods, including in a greenhouse (**www.freshcutherbs.com**). Lee Sturdivant's *Herbs for Sale* focuses on small-scale growers selling herbs. The ATTRA brochure "Herb Overview," including an extensive resource list, is available free (800-346-9140; **www.attra.org/attra-pub/herb.html**). The American Herbal Products Ass'n (AHPA) is at 301-588-1171; fax 301-588-1174; 8484 Georgia Ave., Ste. 370, Silver Spring, MD 20910; **ahpa@apha.org.** Their website posts news such as "German health authority has cancelled all registrations for products containing kava," and "New bill limits the use of the name 'ginseng' . . . to ingredients derived from the genus Panax" at their great website: **www.ahpa.org.**

If you're interested in the flower market, a valuable article on "Cut Flower Production" is at **www.attra.org/ attra-pub/cutflower.html.** And read Lynn Byczynski's 1997 book, *The Flower Farmer: An Organic Grower's Guide to Raising and Selling Cut Flowers* (Chelsea Green). It has info on varieties to grow, picking a site, harvesting, marketing, and arranging. Join the Association of Specialty Cut Flower Growers: 440-774-2887; fax 440-774-2435; P.O. Box 268, Oberlin, OH 44074; **www.ascfg.org.** Also, network with and learn from other herb sellers by joining the Herb Growing and Marketing Network **www.herbworld.com.** For local networking, just look in your Yellow Pages under "Herbs."

Harvesting Herbs

NOTE: *If you want to gather wild herbs, keep in mind that roadsides, fields, and even forests can get unannounced and unrecorded but heavy doses of herbicide or insecticide. Be cautious.*

WHEN TO HARVEST: Gather herbs on a dry day, early in the morning but after the dew is off. The season to harvest varies with the species. Parsley and chervil are dried in May, June, and July; burnet and tarragon in June, July, and August; marjoram and mint in July; summer savory and lemon thyme at the end of July and August. The tender young leaves that appear before the flowering are usually best. Get leaves before the plants show signs of going to seed. That happens after they blossom, when the blossoms turn into seed clusters and their energy goes into making seed. At best the plant is not at its prime; at worst it gets bitter.

HOW TO HARVEST: Cut the herbs with pruning shears or scissors and put them into clean pillowcases or some such. Don't cut to the ground; leave at least a 4-inch stem if you're topping an annual. If it's a perennial, leave at least two-thirds of the plant unharmed. Then take the herbs home and carefully pick them over. Rinse in cool water and drain.

Preserving Herbs

If you can't pick from your herb plants all winter long or bring some into the house in pots, you can either freeze or dry your herbs for winter use. Whether freezing or drying, label all containers. Frozen and dried herbs tend to look alike, and you may not be able to smell the difference.

FREEZING: Wash if needed, shake off excess water, package in small amounts in baggies or boxes, and freeze right away. Herbs that freeze well are anise, basil, chives, coriander, dill, lovage, marigold, mint, oregano, parsley, rosemary, sage, savory, sorrel, sweet marjoram, tarragon, and thyme. Take out of the freezer only the amount you intend to use.

DRYING

Outside. Spread individual leaves or leaves still on the stem (they'll be easier to get off once dried) on sheets of clean cloth to dry in the shade in an airy place, or dry in a very slow oven or dehydrator. Or put them in an outdoor dryer covered with cheesecloth and place where there's good air circulation all around. Direct hot sunlight ruins leaves by burning or browning; a little sun early or late in the day is OK. The aromatic herbs shouldn't be exposed to too much heat, and don't let them get rained or dewed on.

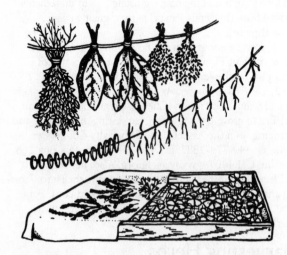

Hanging Bunches. Cut off the top 6 inches of the plant, or use whole plants, bunch them, tie the bundles with string, and hang them up with the root end upward in a shady, airy place. (They hold the flavor better when not powdered.) Allow at least 2 weeks for drying. Hanging works well with anise, basil, marigold, marjoram, mint, oregano, parsley, rosemary, sage, savory, tarragon, and thyme. If you dry your herbs whole like this, crumble them or rub them through a sieve to remove the stems and midribs when you're ready to use them.

In an Oven or Dehydrator. Spread in shallow pans at 110°F, with the door ajar if you're using an oven. Don't mix different kinds of herbs. It takes an average of 8 hours.

Big Leaf/Small Leaf. Some herbs are huge plants (as tall as 6 feet high) with real big leaves. Drying big, moist-leaved plants is harder than doing small ones. With comfrey, borage, and costmary, you can tear the midrib away from the rest of the leaf and then tear the rest of the leaf into smaller pieces. That helps the leaves dry better and prevents mold. Or hang these big leaves individually to dry.

Mint, lemon balm, and most other small-leaved kitchen herbs easily dry in the shade within 3 days. Tearing the small leaves away from the stem (which can then be discarded) speeds up the process. The problem with tearing the leaves is that they don't hold their flavor as well.

Turn all drying leaves once or twice a day. Keep good air circulation. Thick leaves tend to be better frozen than dried.

Roots. Herb roots are generally better fresh rather than dried. Dig in the fall after the leaves are dead and the roots are mature, or before they start growing again in the spring. Wash in cool water. Dry in a place that's warm enough to dry them soon but that's not exposed to the sun, such as an attic. Or slice and dry in a shady place where air circulation is good. Dry in the sun or oven only if you can't dry them completely the first way. Store when thoroughly dry and brittle. If protected from extremes of heat and cold, the roots will keep fine for years. Store so as to protect them from the air as much as possible.

Seeds. To save herb seeds, pick the entire stalk when the seedpods are fully formed but have not yet burst. Spread the pods on a cloth in the sun to dry. If it takes more than one day, stir occasionally while they are outside and bring them in at night. When your seeds are dry, shell and store them in a tightly covered container in a cool, dry place.

Flowers. Don't bruise or overheat. Collect just after they have bloomed. Don't pile them up; dry on a screen if possible. Harvest orange flowers and elderberry flowers in May, June, and July.

Storing Dried Herbs. To store leaves, seeds, or roots, I use baby food jars, cleaned, dried, filled, and with the lid on tightly. Keeping herbs in airtight containers helps prevent flavor deterioration. The fewer times you open the lid, the better they keep their strength. And try to keep them in a cool, dark, dry place away from heat—not on a shelf over or beside your stove! The cool storage inhibits evaporation of the flavoring oil in the herb, and the darkness protects the color, which fades when exposed to light.

Cooking with Dried Herbs. They are at least 3 times as strong as fresh. So figure 1 t. dried herb equals 1 T. chopped fresh herb. Another way to figure it is about 1 t. dried herb in a dish for four.

My head just does not want to work this morning. I have so many things to do, and my brains are moving like molasses in January. Mike said an angry word as he went out the door to work, and I'm not going to be right all day. Dear God, make that be a lesson to me to really watch my tongue and speak only kind and loving things. God, if I deserve it, make me a better person. Guide me, Lord. Sometimes things get so confusing. Sometimes I'm not sure what it is You really do want me to do. Help me to get everything done that I've got to do. Thank You for the joy to come.

PRODUCTS AND PROCESSES

BUTTER: To make herb butters, start with either salted or unsalted butter, as you prefer. Soften the butter and cream into it finely chopped herbs to your taste. Chives, minced garlic, or watercress are fine additions. You may want to add a little lemon juice. Use 1–2 T. (well-packed) fresh herbs or 1–2 t. dried ones per ¼ c. butter. Use the herb butter on bread or hot meats, or with eggs. Unsalted butter won't keep as well as salted, but it's best for people who are watching their blood pressure.

CANDYING LEAVES AND FLOWERS: Mint leaves, rose petals, and the blossoms of borage, orange, lemon, lilac, sweet pea, and violet can all be candied. Dip in an egg white that's been stiffly beaten, flavored, and colored to suit. Coat with sugar. Then dry in a 110°F oven (door ajar) or dehydrator.

CANDY, HERB-FLAVORED: For a basic recipe, see "Horehound" under "Alfalfa to Yucca—Garden to Table."

CRYSTALLIZING: To crystallize angelica stems, very thin slices of fresh ginger root, rose petals (damask and cabbage roses are especially good), etc.: Cover the item to be crystallized with water. Boil 5 minutes. Drain. Repeat that process 3 more times. Save the liquid used to boil the item the fourth time. After cooling, measure the liquid and its herb contents by volume and add sugar equal to its volume plus a half more. Boil the herb/water/sugar until the herb gets a translucent quality. Drain the herb, dry it, and roll in white sugar. This keeps well if stored in sealed jars. (For another recipe, see "Angelica" under "Alfalfa to Yucca—Garden to Table.")

DYE: Homemade colorings from herbs and other food products are more soft and subtle than artificial ones. Here's what you can use to make different colors:

- Black: barberry leaves
- Blue: blueberries
- Brown: nut hulls (walnuts are best), tea, coffee, rose hips, tobacco, hickory chips
- Green: beet tops, sunflower seeds, birch leaves, Spanish onion skins (outer leaves only), elderberry leaves, spinach, cabbage, rhubarb leaves
- Orange: orange juice
- Pink: cherries; beet and sassafras roots
- Purple: blackberries, cherries, huckleberries, cranberries, raspberries, grapes, purple cabbage
- Red: red onion skins, bloodroot, fresh beet juice, madder root, and logwood
- Yellow: the stem, leaves, and flowers of apple bark; barberry stems and roots; cinnamon; curry; ginger; the stems, leaves, and flowers of goldenrod; hickory bark; mustard; paprika; pear leaves; saffron; tanglewood stems; turmeric

For more information about dye plants, see *Weeds: A Guide for Dyers* and *North American Dye Plants* by Ann Bliss. There's also *The New Dyer* by Vinroot and Crowder, *I'd Rather Dye Laughing* by Jean M. Neal, *Hands-On Dyeing* by Blumenthal and Kreider, *The Dye Pot* by Mary Francis Davidson, and *California Dye Plants* by Marilyn Wilkins.

Natural Food Coloring. For a brown color, use a little browned flour, a little burnt sugar, or caramel. Pounded, uncooked spinach leaves make a rich green. Adding some spinach leaf puree makes a lovely deeper green. This green can also be used to tint icings, desserts, etc. Another way to make a cooked-spinach green coloring is by washing some spinach, boiling it until tender, and pouring off the juice for your coloring extract. For a stronger green, let the spinach cool, squeeze dry, mash by pounding, and then put through a sieve. Cooked green peas make a lighter shade of green; split pea soup makes a very pale green color. The coral of a lobster pounded and put through a sieve yields red, as does vinegar or water that has stood on sliced boiled beets. See "Easter Eggs" in Chapter 9 for more information.

Color Blending Chart. Commercial vegetable colorings can be varied like this:

- 2 drops yellow, 1 drop green, and 1 drop red = blue
- 1 drop red, 2 drops green, and 1 drop blue = gray
- 2 drops blue + 1 drop green = dark green
- 3 drops yellow + 1 drop blue = light green
- 12 drops yellow and 1 drop green = olive
- 2 drops red + 1 drop blue = orchid
- 3 drops red + 1 drop yellow = orange
- 3 drops red, 4 drops yellow, and 1 drop green = tangerine

Secrets of Dyeing Fabric with Herbs

NOTE: Dyes and mordants (substances used to set the dyes) are often poisonous. Keep them out of the reach of children. Don't use them in regular cookware.

1. Use an enamel kettle for dyeing. Don't dye in aluminum, iron, or tin pans; these metals can affect the mordant chemistry and color.
2. Herb dyeing is not an exact science. Plant colors can vary, even between one batch and the next. The soil the plants grew in, the amount of rainfall, the light intensity, and the time of year all can affect the color yield.
3. Flowers are the best bet for getting color from a plant, but stems, roots, leaves, fruits, and vegetables may make color too. In general, start with a weight of plant product equal to the weight of fabric you plan to dye.
4. Steep, heat, or even boil the plant until you have a heavily colored liquid; that is your dye. Experiment with a small amount to see if boiling improves extraction or if it makes the color dull.
5. A mordant sets the dye into the dyed substance, making it permanent and often brighter, even under the stress of machine-washing. Alum, acetic acid (from vinegar), and ammonia are mordants. Different mordants can give you completely different colors. Coreopsis plus alum results in a beautiful yellow. Coreopsis plus potassium dichromate (another common mordant) gives brick red. In a pinch you can use lemon juice, salt, or white vinegar as mordants.
6. Natural fabrics like linen, wool, and cotton, jute, silk, and rayon (which is cellulose-based) take herb dyes best.
7. Make your dye first and have it ready. Then wash the material to be dyed, soak it with the mordant, and finally dye it.
8. To dye fabric, heat it very gradually in the colored water up to almost the boiling point, and then cool it down equally gradually. *Don't actually boil it.* Or soak in the color for at least 1 hour. *In the case of silk, keep below 160°F.*

EXTRACT: An herbal extract is an herb's essence or oil in a solution, usually with alcohol. Extracts and pure oils are used to make scented candles, soaps, and cosmetics like peppermint-flavored toothpaste, and to flavor candies and baked goods. Certain ones are also used in mixtures to repel insects from people and plants. Gather fresh herbs and pound to a pulp with a mortar and pestle. Let the plant parts concerned stand in pure distilled vinegar, alcohol, or corn, sunflower, or olive oil. Getting 180-proof edible alcohol to make an alcohol-based extract isn't as simple for us as it was for Great-Grandmother, but you can substitute vodka—it's half water and half alcohol, equal volumes in 100 proof. Use 2 T. pounded herb to ¾ c. liquid. Or put your herbs, berries, etc. into a bottle and cover with liquid. The liquid then gradually absorbs the soluble parts of the plant. Shake daily for 3 weeks. Keep at a warmish temperature—in the sun, for instance.

➤ *CITRUS EXTRACT Peel away the fruit's outermost skin, called the zest. (There's a special tool for this at kitchen stores.) Don't use any of the white pith. Fill a wide-mouthed bottle one-third of the way up with zest. Pour in vodka for the other two-thirds. Soak 2 weeks, shaking twice daily. Strain and bottle your extract.*

FLOWERS: Edible flowers are fun. Learn more in the brochure "Edible Flowers," free from ATTRA (800-346-9140). You'll find recipes in Cathy Wilkinson Barash's 1993 book *Edible Flowers from Garden to Palate* and Coralie Castle's 1994 *Cooking from the Gourmet's Garden: Edible Ornamentals, Herbs, and Flowers.*

➤ *CLOVER-ROSE "HONEY" For this old-time homemade honey substitute, in the summer gather and dry about 90 white and 90 purple clover blossoms, plus 25 sweetbriar rose leaves. Add 10 c. sugar, 5 c. water, and cook together. Sieve out solids. Cook to a syrup consistency.*

GROUND HERB OR SPICE: Ginger root was once invariably sold intact, and people grated their own. The same cooks also crushed their cinnamon bark and ground their cloves. Now you can take your choice, but the more freshly ground, the better tasting. So when buying, figure the more whole the better, and grind it yourself at home as needed. Whole spices store well and keep their strength a long time. Once they're ground, though, they start to weaken. It's best to grind no more than a 6-month supply of spices at a time, preferably far less. If you don't believe me, I suggest the sniff test: Grind some whole allspice or peppercorns. Sniff. Then sniff your kitchen container of preground spice.

So equip yourself with an old-fashioned mortar and pestle, "spice mill," or pepper or salt grinder; or grind herbs in your blender or juicer. With those you can also mash seeds, crush dried herbs, and so forth. You grind in your mortar by crushing with the pestle—just pure elbow grease (available from 719-962-3228; **www.cfamilyresources.com**). The old-time spice mill was a little hand-cranked grinder with a box to catch the ground spice.

HAND LOTION: Immerse ¼ oz. gum tragacanth (from Indiana Botanic Gardens) in water and soak for several days. Combine 2 oz. glycerine and 1 oz. alcohol. Strain the gum tragacanth solution and add the liquid to the glycerine/alcohol solution. Scent with herbal or floral extract (rose, lavender, rosemary, etc.). Add enough distilled water to make it the thickness you want; 2 cups is about right. See also "Quince" in Chapter 6 and "Sheep, Lanolin" in Chapter 11.

JELLY: Basically you combine a juice (grape, orange, cranberry, etc.) with an herb or spice (or both). Tarragon, mint, sage, rosemary, and thyme are good for this; allspice, ground and whole cloves, ginger root, and stick cinnamon are good spices.

➤ *MODERN Prepare 4 half-pint jars. Heat 1 cup of your juice to boiling. Then pour it over ¼ c. fresh herb (or 1½ T. dried herb) or 2 T. whole spice. Let soak for half hour. Strain into nonaluminum pan. Add 2 more cups of juice, 2 T. vinegar, and 3 c. sugar. Mix and boil, stirring constantly. Now mix in ½ bottle pectin; boil another minute, still stirring. Remove from heat. Stir in food coloring at this point if you want it. Pour immediately into ½ pint canning jars. Put on lids. Process 10 minutes in boiling-water bath.*

➤ *OLD-TIME Prepare jars to hold 10 cups. Coarsely chop 6 lb. tart apples, put into non-aluminum pan, add just enough water to cover, and cook half hour or to softness. Then pour into jelly bag over bowl and let drain overnight. On the next day, measure the juice. Add 2 c. sugar for each 2½ c. of juice. Stir sugar into solution over low heat. Add herbs or spices, or a mix of them, tied into porous bag, and simmer until jelling point is reached. Remove bag and pour into jars. Process 10 minutes in boiling-water bath.*

OIL: Herbs get their flavors from their natural oils. When herbs are dried the oil is still in there, but it's concentrated, which is why it takes less in volume of dried herb to give the same amount of flavor. In general, one drop of an "essential oil" is comparable to one handful of fresh dried herbs. Rose, lavender, violet, and lemon balm make good oils. If you do it right, the oil will have a strong scent of the plant, and you can use it like perfume or add a drop to your potpourri or homemade cosmetics. To make an herbal "oil" or "essence," there are several methods. For any particular plant, one works better than another, so experiment. Best of all, read *Potpourri, Incense and Other Fragrant Concoctions* by Ann Tucker Fettner, a thorough, accurate collection of everything you need to know about perfume ingredients and the extraction of scents, including recipes.

➤ *SUN-EXTRACTED OIL Start with as much as possible of your fresh herb or flower. Lavender or lilac flowers, mint leaves, rose petals, rosemary, thyme, and basil all work well. Press them into a crock, using enough pressure to slightly bruise them. Carefully pour rain or distilled water over them until they are covered. Set the crock outside in full sun, in a place where it will be undisturbed. (Bring inside only to avoid rain.) It takes around a week for oily scum to develop on the water's surface. Using a small bit of cotton to absorb it, get that oil out of the crock. Squeeze it out into an appropriately small, dark-colored glass bottle. Don't put the lid on yet. The next step is to cover that container with cheesecloth to keep dust from getting in but allow all the water to evaporate. After a few days, you can go ahead and seal the bottle tightly.*

➤ *COOKED-OUT OIL Put your crushed ("bruised") plant materials—flowers, leaves, bark, or roots—into a bag. Put the bag into a kettle of water and simmer about 24 hours over a slow fire. Then slowly cool. Skim the oil that rises to the top of the water. The bag is used because it almost invariably floats, and it's easier to get the oil separated that way. Squeeze the bag to help get the oil out. You can even* put it through a clothes wringer or use a cider press. For pine oil use pieces of wood cut fine. For birch oil, use the inner part of the tree; for cedar oil, use the tips of the branches. To make sunflower seed oil, throw seeds in premashed to help the oil come out.

> **OIL BY EVAPORATION** *Boil your materials in a tea kettle. Strain. Boil more. The principle is that you are separating out substances that vaporize at a higher temperature than water; that's the oil. After the water evaporates, the oil is left behind because it hasn't yet vaporized.*

> **ALCOHOL-EXTRACTED OIL** *Soak the herbs in a capped bottle of pure alcohol for 10 days or so. Strain. Leave the alcohol and its contents in a wide, open container in a warm place. Put a cheesecloth over it to keep the contents clean. After the alcohol evaporates, your oil remains.*

> **CITRUS OIL** *You can collect citrus oil by turning rinds inside out to squeeze them just a little and then wiping the outside (now inside) surface with a bit of absorbent cotton.*

> **OIL INTO OIL** *Because the essential oil can be so minute in volume, here's another option if you have only a small quantity of herb to start with. Pulp your fresh herb thoroughly using a mortar and pestle or some such. Place it in a small bottle—about 2 T. herb for a 1-cup bottle. Pour a quality cooking oil over the pounded herb until the bottle is nearly full. Add 1 t. distilled vinegar. Cover tightly. Place where it will be in hot sunshine every day. Shake twice a day for 3 weeks. Strain and it is ready to use.*

OIL, HERB-FLAVORED FOR COOKING: Make the above oils by the pint or quart for wonderful herb-flavored oils for salad dressings and cooking.

OINTMENT: See "Salve."

PASTILLES: Also called scent balls. Same contents as sachets, herb pillows, and potpourri, except that they're melted together with a gum resin that makes them hard. Any size from a tiny bead up. Pound your ingredients in a smooth-sided mortar together with gum tragacanth, and moisten with a little rose water until you have a mixture that is like a dough. Shape and dry. Can be polished on a lathe. Can be sculpted into jewelry and so on; to make beads, pierce pastilles with a needle while they are still soft.

PHYSICK: An old-time word for any plant-based medicine.

PILLOWS, HERB: See "Sachets and Herb Pillows."

POMANDER: A mixture of aromatic or fragrant substances enclosed in a bag or box that has holes in the sides. A pomander is used to scent clothes or linens; in old-time usage it was worn on the body to guard against infection. The pomander ball was most often made of amber or a partially dried orange with cloves stuck into it. To make one, start with a thin-skinned, small orange and a handful of cloves. Press the point of each clove into the orange as you would a thumbtack into a wall. Continue until the orange is quite covered with cloves, with only their large "heads" sticking out. Now roll the orange in ground cinnamon, getting as much on it as you can. Set on paper in an airy place and let dry for 3 weeks. Then your pomander is done. It can be placed in the traditional box or hung by a ribbon.

POTPOURRI: That's pronounced "poe-purree" (it's French). The purpose of a potpourri is fragrance, but sometimes it can be very beautiful too. One formula is ⅞ any flower petals, ⅛ herbal leaves, and then just a few added spices and/or dried citrus zest. (For more potpourri recipes, see "Geranium" and "Rose" under "Alfalfa to Yucca—Garden to Table.") The container should be china or pottery with a lid you can close tightly. Keep that lid on tight after the potpourri is made, except when you want to scent a room; then uncorking for half an hour should do it. I don't recommend using a glass container because light deteriorates potpourri; on the other hand, I've seen beautiful potpourris in glass bowls that were wonderful to both see and smell. When they deteriorated, the potpourri was simply replaced.

Using Herbs. A tablespoon or two of fragrant leaves adds to your potpourri's interest, but be cautious of adding more, because they may get overwhelming. Try rosemary, bay leaf, marjoram, cedar or balsam needle, basil, mint, sage, lemon verbena, scented geranium, sweetbriar, lavender, southernwood, sweet cicely, lemon balm, bergamot, myrtle, costmary, eucalyptus, chamomile, thyme, or anything else that catches your nose's attention. Also consider adding the flowers of rosemary and thyme.

Using Flowers. Although potpourris may contain many different ingredients (flowers, fragrant leaves, and spices), traditional potpourris were at least four-fifths rose petals—especially damask, moss, or gallica roses. You can make the other one-fifth any kind of sweet-smelling flower, or just use straight rose petals, or create your own flower mixes. Suitable additional flowers are acacia, bergamot, calendula, carnations, heliotrope, honeysuckle, hyacinth, jasmine, jonquil, lavender, lemon verbena, lilac, lily of the valley, mignonette, myrtle, narcissus, lemon or orange blossom, pansy, peony, philadelphus, pinks, stocks, thyme, violet, wallflower—or any combination of flowers you want to try. Use any fragrant petals so long as they're thin enough to dry well. Patricia Wiley, Watsonville, CA, wrote me, "Don't forget to include some small buds, as they add their personality to the dried mixture."

Drying Herbs/Flowers. Choose a dry morning to collect the herbs and flowers—after the dew has dried. Pick blossoms that have just fully opened early in the day. Don't pick roses that have already been fully open for several days. Don't use roses that have been in a vase for a week; most of their fragrant oils will be gone. Collect about four times as much as you expect to need, because they shrink in drying. Use the petals and buds of flowers only. Pull them carefully from the rest of the flower, which you discard. Dry them away from light, spread them out in a shallow layer on clean paper or cloth, and stir a couple of times a day. Dry to a papery state.

Using Spices. Two or three teaspoons of crushed spices add fragrance, but be careful not to use too much. Good spices to use are cloves, cinnamon, nutmeg, mace, coriander, aniseed, or allspice. Or you could put in a slice of lemon or orange peel stuck full of cloves.

Using Liquids. Traditional potpourris were either dry or moistened with fragrant oil. You can add a few drops of a fragrant oil like eucalyptus, lemon verbena, peppermint, rose geranium, or rosemary oil, or another strong scent like brandy or attar of roses. Add 1 drop at a time, and stir with a wooden spoon.

Fixatives. The fixative both acts as a preservative and helps to hold the scent. Rose expert Patricia Wiley wrote me, "A modern fixative is isopropyl alcohol, sprayed on. *Do not use any fixative until potpourri fragrances have had time to sit and blend together, about 3 weeks."* Combine the scented materials with the fixative by layering—a layer of potpourri, then a layer of fixative. Pack into jars, seal tightly, and let rest 2–4 weeks. Your fixative can be a few dashes of orrisroot, or much more. You can grow and process it yourself or buy from an herbal supplier. An orris/salt fixative is made by mixing one-third orrisroot powder with two-thirds uniodized salt for your fixative. An antique Elizabethan fixative was made by combining ¼ oz. gum benzoin, 2 oz. orrisroot, and a spoonful of brandy. Gum benzoin can also be used alone for this purpose.

Using Potpourri. Stir it. Moisten it with a little rose water, add a drop of fragrant oil, use as is as a source of room fragrance, or pack it into little cotton sachet bags. Every couple weeks or so, stir the potpourri bowl a little to release new fragrance.

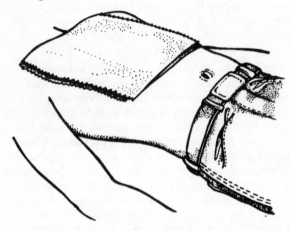

POULTICE: A poultice is a bag of hot herbs held against an aching or infected portion of the body. Comfrey leaves make a healing poultice. Another traditional one is a bowl of hops mixed with a cup of hot vinegar. A poultice of boiled mullein leaves is good for cuts on animals. Chop green leaves finely and soak them a bit in almost boiling water. Let them cool before you put them on so they don't burn the patient. Then put them on the hurt place. You can make the poultice stay on by putting a cloth over it or wrapping the leaves in a clean cloth. Don't leave a cold poultice on; have a fresh one ready to go on when you take off the cooling one. Don't reuse the herbs. This may sound spendthrift of herb, but comfrey (the #1 healing herb) grows huge, so you'll have all you want once it gets a good start in your garden.

☞ *LINSEED POULTICE To help aching bodies, scatter ¼ lb. linseed into 2 c. very hot water, stirring constantly. The mixture will gradually turn into a dough. Mix in ½ oz. olive oil. Spread that thickly over a piece of prewarmed cloth. Fold over the extra ends of the cloth to make a sort of bag, and place the poultice on the hurting part.*

POWDER: An herb powder is simply bark or dried herbs pulverized to a powder in your mortar.

SACHETS AND HERB PILLOWS: These are cloth "pillows" made to hold dried, crushed herbs and flowers. Sachets are tiny bags meant to be placed in a drawer or closet to scent clothing, sheets and pillowcases, or stationery. Herb

pillows are several times larger and are traditionally used to overcome a sickroom smell and soothe nerves.

You can experiment to get your favorite scent. Lavender is traditional, but don't be afraid to try other mixtures. Lilac, rose petals, sweet peas, mint, rosemary, and thyme are all suitable. Or use lavender, sage, peppermint, and lemon balm in some combination, or sage, peppermint, and lemon balm without lavender. (For more ideas, see "Potpourri.") If you are making sachets intended to keep moths away, try a mixture of the insect-repellent herbs: cotton lavender, mint, rosemary, rue, southernwood, tansy, and wormwood.

As in the case of potpourris, the scent, whatever its source, will not last. To renew scent, every couple weeks or so, crush the sachet bag a little between your fingers to break some herbs and expose a new supply of their fragrant oil for scent. The aromatics will eventually run out; potpourris need to be refilled at least every year.

Preparing the Contents. Follow potpourri instructions. Once your planned ingredients are harvested and dried, mix them and grind to a powder in your spice mill, mortar, or blender/food processor. Add a fixative like orrisroot. (See "Fixatives.") If you are making a quantity of powder at once—more than you need to fill your sachets or pillows—store in a small tightly-lidded bottle in a cool place and protect from the light.

Making the Sachet. Pack the powder into "pillowcases" of cotton, and sew up the open side. You can make a large herb pillow by sewing together two men's handkerchiefs. You can cover the inner pillow with velvet, gingham, percale, ribbon-trimmed lace, or any other scrap material you have. To hang or pin in place, sew a loop of ribbon or bias tape into one corner as the fourth side is sewn. Just make sure the material and the seams are tight enough so that dust from the contents doesn't leak out.

☞ *HEADACHE PILLOW A midwestern pioneer recipe. Mix together ½ oz. cloves and 2 oz. each of lavender, marjoram, rose petals, and betony rose leaf. Proceed as above. You're supposed to sniff it to cure your headache.*

☞ *TO-EASE-MELANCHOLY-AND-PUT-YOU-TO-SLEEP PILLOW Mix 2 oz. rose petals, 1 oz. mint, and ¼ crushed clove for pillow.*

☞ *HERB SACHET Mix 1 part each dried sweet basil, dried thyme, dried marjoram, and dried rosemary leaves. With this one you don't need any fixative.*

SALVE: This is a mixture of herb with a carrying agent that you rub onto the problem area. Gen MacManiman, who sells all sorts of food-drying information and supplies, is not only a food drying expert but also an herb lady! She wrote me, "For the base, salves and ointments use various wax/oil mixtures. An olive oil and beeswax combination is most commonly used. Freshly rendered lard is an excellent salve base. It has healing virtues and is just the right consistency. If stored in a cool place, it will keep a long time."

➣ *CHICKWEED OINTMENT Gen MacManiman's recipe: "Warm one cup lard in the dehydrator. (Lard becomes fluid at low temperatures—80–100°F.) Add ½ c. dried, powdered chickweed, and mix well. Return the mixture to the dehydrator and dry it for two days at 100–110°F. The fluid will then be quite green (the greener, the better) and ready to strain and place into containers. Store in the refrigerator or a cool cupboard. This is very healing for any abrasion or scratch, but best of all, it instantly takes the itch out of a mosquito bite! Try it on any itch."*

➣ *BALM OF GILEAD SALVE This is good for cuts, scrapes, and chapped hands. The main ingredient is the sticky, brownish buds of the black cottonwood (Populus trichocarpa), commonly called balm of Gilead. It grows wild, west of the coastal Rockies, from California to Alaska. Pick the buds in spring before the green leaves form. Make sure you get the buds at the sticky stage. Put them into a big tin can, because the container will be almost impossible to clean out and it will be easiest if you can just throw it out after you're done. Add enough lard to just cover the buds when the lard has melted. Don't use cooking oil—you'd get liquid instead of solid salve. Simmer the buds/lard mix on low heat 2–3 hours. Then strain into sterilized jars or cans. You'll end up throwing out the straining cloth, so make it something you can do without.*

SHAMPOO: You can make your own herbal shampoos. Start by finding a jar with a lid. Pour into it 1 T. olive oil, 1 bottle Castile soap, and 2–3 t. of your favorite culinary herb. Lemon verbena, rosemary, and thyme are good choices. Mix your ingredients well with a wooden spoon. Put the lid on the jar and let the contents rest in a dark, cool place for about a week. Then strain to get the solids out. What remains is your herbal shampoo. Or you can use it as a hand or body soap.

SIMPLE: A plant medicine.

SPIRIT: A solution of an herb made with brandy is called an herb spirit. The basic recipe for herb spirit is to use fresh herbs, picking just before flowering or when otherwise appropriate. Strip the leaves from the stems and pack lightly in a jar. Fill the jar with brandy and cover tightly. Let rest for a month. Strain and bottle.

➣ *HERB SPIRIT FOR SEASONING SOUPS Equal parts sweet marjoram, basil, thyme, savory, and parsley. Measure and mix before filling the jar. Proceed as above.*

SYRUP: You make an herbal syrup, used as a beverage or a medicine base, by adding simple syrup (sugar and water) to the herbal infusion when hot and somewhat evaporated. Bottle and seal when hot. Violet flowers make an excellent syrup.

TEAS: We gather wild mint for tea down along Brady Gulch Creek, which runs along the bottom of our canyon, and wild strawberry leaves from the tender little plants that grow in the timbered places. You can drink teas and coffees made from the dried leaves and stems of many plants, from barks and nuts, and from grains too. In colonial America, when tea drinking became unpatriotic during the Revolutionary War (remember the Boston Tea Party!), the conventional China tea leaves were replaced by raspberry leaves, loosestrife, hardtack, goldenrod, dittany, blackberry leaves, sage, and many others. Some other homemade drinks enjoyed on the frontier were teas made from wild rose hips, mint, oat straw, sarsaparilla, and the marrow from beef bones. Rye and chestnuts, ground and roasted, or roasted crushed barley alone, were made into "coffees." Those alternative teas and coffees contain no caffeine.

Of Infusions and Decoctions. Those two aren't exactly the same thing. A decoction is made by boiling an herb in water (an average of 10 minutes) and straining while hot. Coffee is a familiar decoction. An infusion is made by pouring hot water over an herb and then letting it steep. In general, leaves and flowers are steeped; roots and seeds are boiled. That's why flower/leaf drinks are "teas" and dandelion/chicory root drinks are "coffees."

Leaf Teas. They're easy to make. Just boil water and measure out your herbs: from 1 t. dried to 1 T. fresh herbs for a cup of water, or from 1 T. dried to 1 c. fresh for a quart, depending on the strength of the herb. Then use one of the following methods.

- Pour water directly over herbs in teapot. To serve, put a little strainer over your cup and pour through that.
- Put your leaves or flowers into a tea ball or into a strainer. Set that into the cup and pour the hot water over it. Pour over leaves and let set 2–10 minutes. You really must experiment to get it just right. Every herb is a little different, and so are tastes. On average, the leaves are steeped in the hot water for 5 minutes. Get to know your teas, and you'll be able to judge by the color when you have the desired strength. Too little soaking and the tea will be too weak; too much and it will be bitter. Sweeten with brown sugar or honey to complement the taste of herb tea. You can freeze your leftover tea to use for quick servings, but strain out the herbs first, or it will get too strong.
- For health tea, add to just-boiling water 1 handful fresh chamomile, 1 bunch lemon balm (or ½–1 oz. dried, or ¼ c. lemon juice), and 1 bunch peppermint. Cover and steep 20 minutes. Add honey to taste. (If lemon juice is used instead of lemon balm, add it before honey.) Stir well. Put in jug in the refrigerator and dilute to taste as you drink it.
- For herbed lemonade, add any concentrated herb tea to lemonade and chill for a nice, different drink.
- For sun tea, fill a gallon jar with water. Add your tea or herbs. Screw on a lid tightly. Shake a moment. Let set in the hot sun 4–5 hours—or more, like a day . . . or two . . . or three. Shake occasionally. Now strain out the tea leaves or herbs. Add honey or lemon juice. This is also a good way to fix dried fruit such as prunes, plums, or apples; just combine fruit, water, sweetening, and cinnamon, and let it set in the sun all afternoon.

I got these recipes from listeners to a phone-in radio program I appeared on in Wichita, Kansas, in January 1975.

Folks in Wichita also recommended mint leaves in lemonade, raspberry leaves for when you're in labor, and sarsaparilla for any fella who needs more manhood!

TINCTURE: Here's Gen MacManiman's expertise again: "Vinegar tinctures are inexpensive, easy to make, and will last for many years. I have many tinctures which are over ten years old. They are simple to make. Herbs can be used in combination or individually. I use either vinegar or vodka and always use the dried herbs, finely crumbled or powdered. Basic proportions are 1 pt. vinegar or vodka to 2 oz. powdered herbs. Sunlight energizes these tinctures. Set the jar in a window for two weeks and shake twice daily. At the end of two weeks, strain and bottle the mixture. Dropper bottles are great."

TISANE: An old-time herb tea, often used with medicinal intent. It's a strong brew given by the tablespoon several times a day.

VINEGAR, HERB-FLAVORED: Vinegars can be flavored with leaf herbs, seeds, spices, or combinations thereof.

Secrets of Making Herb Vinegar

1. You can start with store-bought cider or wine vinegar or with your homemade. Match strong-flavored herbs to red wine vinegar, mild-flavored ones to white wine vinegar.
2. In general, use 3 T. seeds, 1 c. fresh herbs, or ¼ c. dried herbs per 1 qt. vinegar.
3. Gather your herbs fresh, if possible—the flavor will be more pungent. Crush just before steeping.
4. If you must use dried leaves, moisten them with a little hot water in a bowl before steeping.
5. Heat vinegar to boiling. If you are using seeds or spices, crush them with a mortar and pestle (or crush them in a wide-mouthed jar with a wooden spoon). Boil them in the vinegar for 10 minutes.
6. Pour the vinegar and seeds/spices over the herbs.
7. Cover and let stand several weeks in a warm dark place. Shake the bottle gently twice a day.
8. At or before the end of the recommended period, taste the vinegar. If it doesn't seem flavorful enough, strain and start over with more seeds or leaves.
9. When straining, first use a sieve and then a cloth.
10. When the vinegar suits you, bottle it: Place a fresh sprig of herb inside your long-term storage bottle. Strain your steeped mixture in on top of that. Herbal vinegars are best stored at room temperature.

Here are specific recipes for herb vinegars (in alphabetical order by herb). Burnet (leaves or seeds), marjoram, dill, lemon balm, and chives are other possibilities. Mix and match to suit yourself. For chervil and tarragon vinegar recipes, see "Chervil" and "Tarragon" under "Alfalfa to Yucca—Garden to Table."

🍶 *BASIL VINEGAR* *Combine ¾ c. leaves and 1 qt. wine vinegar.*

🍶 *CARAWAY, CARDAMOM, CELERY SEED, OR MUSTARD VINEGAR* *Combine 3 T. seeds and 1 qt. white wine vinegar.*

🍶 *GARLIC VINEGAR* *Combine 4 cloves garlic, peeled and chopped, ½ t. salt, 2 t. ground cloves, 1 t. freshly ground peppercorns, 1 t. caraway seeds and 1 qt. wine vinegar. Give it 2–3 weeks before you strain and use.*

🍶 *MINT VINEGAR* *Combine 2 c. mint leaves, 1 c. sugar, and 1 qt. cider vinegar. Or pack the leaves into a pint jar and fill the jar with wine vinegar. Let stand 2 weeks or more, then strain. Bottle.*

🍶 *PLAIN ONION, GARLIC, OR CELERY LEAF VINEGAR* *Use 24 green onions (shallots are best if you have them) or 4 cloves garlic or 2 c. celery leaves, peeled and chopped. 2–3 weeks in 1 qt vinegar. Strain and use.*

🍶 *MULTI-SPICED VINEGAR* *Combine 1 qt. cider vinegar, ½ oz. celery seed, ⅓ oz. dried parsley, 1 clove garlic, 3 small onions, grated, 2 whole cloves, 1 t. peppercorns, 1 t. nutmeg, salt to taste, 1 T. sugar and 1 T. good brandy. Cover in jar. Let stand 3 weeks, strain, and bottle.*

🍶 *HOT, HOT VINEGAR* *Add horseradish, onion, paprika, pepper, chili peppers, cayenne pepper, curry powder—any or all as suits you. Strain and bottle when you like the taste. These aren't for me, but some people love anything that scalds their gullet.*

FOOD SEASONINGS

Seasoning Mixtures

Save your empty spice containers to hold your own mixes! Store seasoning mixes in an airtight container and in a dry, cool place—not over or beside your stove!

Spices tied in cheesecloth   **Tea ball**

PACKAGING SEASONING MIXES: Combine your favorite spices, dried vegetables, and herbs. Lay out squares of foil or small plastic baggies. Spoon 1 serving size of your mix into the center of each foil square or baggie. Seal foil packets by folding over the ends and rolling them. To store in plastic, press the air out and tie tightly shut.

Spice Bag. When a recipe calls for a spice bag, put the whole spices listed in the recipe into a handkerchief-sized piece of cheesecloth or some such, tie firmly, and cook right with the dish to be flavored. Remove the bag before serving. Or use a tea ball for the same purpose. It will prevent your friend with an ulcer from biting down on a peppercorn.

SALT MIXTURES

❧ **SALTY HERBED SALT** In a bowl combine 1 c. salt and 1 t. each dried parsley, chives, onion flakes, and summer savory. Store in an airtight container and use for roll or bread dough and to season salads.

❧ **LOW-SALT HERBED SALT** Combine ¼ c. salt, 2 t. dried basil, 1 t. dried tarragon, 1 t. dried chives, and ½ t. dried oregano. Get it all very fine and well mixed. Good on popcorn, etc.

❧ **HERB-SALT MIX FOR HAMBURGERS** Crumble until fine as possible 1 t. each of dried basil and dried oregano. Mix ¼ c. chopped parsley, the dried herbs, 1 t. paprika, and 1 c. salt. Keep in a salt shaker.

❧ **LOW-SALT SEASONING SALT** Combine ½ t. garlic powder, ½ t. dried lemon rind, ½ t. onion powder, 2 t. paprika, 6 T. salt, ½ t. dried thyme, 2 t. dry mustard, ½ t. curry powder, and ½ t. powdered cumin. Blend well. This is good with anything: veggies, meats, fish, or salad.

❧ **SESAME SALT** Put into a frying pan and heat gently until the seeds begin to brown (do not overheat): 8 parts raw sesame seeds and 1 part sea salt (available at health food stores). Remove and allow to cool. Mix well and grind. Sprinkle this on foods at the table—soups, salads, entrees—but when you do, leave out any other salt.

❧ **SALT/PEPPER MIX** Keep a shaker of 3 parts salt and 1 part pepper near the stove if you use salt and pepper in practically everything.

HERB MIXTURES

❧ **HERB BAGS TO SEASON SOUPS AND STEWS** In each of several 4-inch squares of cheesecloth combine ½ t. each basil and marjoram, 1 crumbled bay leaf, and 5 peppercorns. Tie the squares into bags with string. Store in an airtight container.

❧ **BOUQUET GARNI** This classic French herb mix is packed into little 4-inch packets of cheesecloth. Spread the cloth out flat. Measure into the middle of it 1 bay leaf, 1 t. marjoram, 1 T. parsley, 1 t. savory, and 1 t. thyme. Bring together the corners of the bag and tie them with a string so it looks like a miniature peddler's bag. Good in soups and stews. You can vary it to taste, adding or subtracting herbs as you please.

❧ **FINES HERBES** This is a standard herb mix for seasoning egg and other recipes. Combine ⅓ parsley, ⅓ chervil, ⅙ tarragon, and ⅙ chives—all gathered fresh and finely chopped.

❧ **HERBS AND PEPPER** In a bowl combine ¼ c. coarsely ground black pepper, 2 T. thyme, 1 T. each ground caraway seed and sweet Hungarian paprika, and 1 t. garlic powder. Store the pepper in an airtight container and use it to season roasts and steaks.

❧ **POULTRY SEASONING** For each 2 T. commercial poultry seasoning called for, substitute 1 t. sage, 1 t. marjoram, 1 t. thyme, and 1 T. dried parsley; or 1 t. each of sage, thyme, savory, rosemary, and marjoram.

SPICE MIXTURES

❧ **BEST NO-SALT SEASONING** Combine 1 T. garlic powder, 5 t. onion powder, 1 T. paprika, 1 T. thyme, ½ t. celery seed, 1 T. dry mustard, and ½ t. white pepper. Store tightly covered.

❧ **DESSERT SPICE BLEND** This blend is nicely balanced in flavor and is good for spice cakes, cookies, and pies. Combine 2 t. powdered cinnamon, 2 t. ground nutmeg, 1 t. powdered ginger, ½ t. powdered allspice, and ½ t. powdered cloves. Optional are ½ t. mace, ½ t. ground coriander, and ½ t. ground cardamom.

❧ **HOMEMADE PUMPKIN PIE SPICE** In a bowl combine ¼ c. ground cinnamon and 1 T. each ground ginger, allspice, nutmeg, and cloves. Store in an airtight container. Use 1½ T. per pumpkin pie. Or use to flavor gingerbread, pies, and other desserts.

❧ **PICKLING SPICE #1** In a bowl combine 2 T. each whole allspice and whole coriander, 1 T. mustard seed, 2 crumbled bay leaves, and a 1-inch piece of dried ginger root, peeled and chopped. Store the spice in an airtight container and use it for pickling fruits and vegetables, making preserves, and braising meats.

❧ **PICKLING SPICE #2** Combine whole cassia buds, white peppercorns, black peppercorns, allspice, bay leaves, mustard seeds, dried sliced ginger, and chili pods.

CURRY POWDERS: Curry powder is a mixture of spices—from just a few to as many as fifty. The curry powders sold in grocery stores are usually a combination of 15–20 herbs, seeds, and spices, but people who really know about curry have special combinations of spices to go with various dishes, some of which need mild, subtle seasonings and others hotter ones. The strength of a curry depends on how much chili powder is used. Coriander seed is considered to be the one traditional and most necessary ingredient; other possible ingredients include allspice, anise, bay leaves, caraway, cayenne pepper, celery seeds, cinnamon, cloves, cubeb berries, cumin seeds, curry leaves, dill, fennel, fenugreek (seeds and leaves), garlic, ginger, juniper berries, mace, mint, mustard, nutmeg, oregano, pepper (white and black), paprika, poppy seeds, saffron, salt, and turmeric. Have all ingredients well powdered, using a mortar and pestle to grind. Sift together and keep in a tightly corked bottle.

➢ *CURRY MIX #1* *Combine 3 oz. turmeric, 4 oz. coriander seed, 2 oz. black pepper, 1 oz. fenugreek, 1 oz. ginger, and 1/4 oz. cayenne pepper.*

➢ *CURRY MIX #2* *Combine 6 t. coriander seed, 1/8 t. cayenne pepper, 1 1/2 T. turmeric, 1/2 t. whole cloves, 1 1/2 t. fenugreek seeds, 1/2 T. cardamom seed, and 1 1/2 T. cumin seeds.*

➢ *FAVORITE CURRY MIX* *From Zubaidah Ismail, Penang, Malaysia: Combine 1 t. ground turmeric, 1 t. chili powder, 1 t. ground ginger, 1 t. coriander seeds, and 2 t. powdered cinnamon.*

MULLED BEVERAGES: You can mull any juice by adding sugar and spices and heating to a boil. Then simmer 10 minutes, strain, and serve hot. Grape juice, orange juice, cider, and red wines mull especially well. Spices invariably include cloves and cinnamon sticks. Whole allspice, nutmeg, and ginger are other possibilities. Lemon juice and lemon slices are good too. Sweeten with your favorite sweetener. Be sure to strain unless all will be consumed immediately. The longer the whole spices are in it, the stronger the drink gets—and it soon becomes too bitter to enjoy!

➢ *SPICED LEMONADE* *Put 2 qt. water, 4 T. sugar, 3 cloves, and about 2 inches of stick cinnamon into a pan. Bring slowly to a boil, strain, add the juice of 4 lemons, and reboil. Serve with a slice of lemon in each glass.*

➢ *MULLED RED WINE* *Use the cheapest red wine you can find (it will still be good). Heat 1 qt. wine and add 1 stick cinnamon, juice of 1 lemon, 1/2 c. sugar, 8 cloves, and 1/2 lemon sliced into sections. Strain. Serve with a slice of the lemon in each cup. Good for the old, cold, weary, and disheartened—a medicinal substance. Mull port or sweet wines without adding sugar.*

➢ *MULLED CRANBERRY CIDER* *Mix 4 c. cider (or grape juice), 4 c. cranberry juice, 6 cloves, 1 stick cinnamon, 4 whole allspice, and 1/2 c. brown sugar. Heat until the sugar dissolves, and serve hot.*

➢ *SPICED CIDER* *Mix 4 c. cider, 2 whole allspice, 2 whole cloves, and about 3 inches of stick cinnamon, and boil 5 minutes. Add 1/2 c. brown sugar, boil 5 minutes more, and serve hot.*

➢ *CIDER PUNCH FOR A CROWD* *Squeeze 1 orange and 1 lemon. Combine the chopped peels, 1/2 c. sugar, 1 stick cinnamon, 1/2 t. whole allspice, and 4 c. water. Boil gently 30 minutes. Strain; add the orange and lemon juice and 2 qt. cider. Reheat and serve.*

➢ *MULLED GRAPE JUICE* *Combine 4 c. grape juice (dilute if it is very strong), 4 sticks cinnamon, about 1/4 c. sugar, and a dash each of nutmeg, cloves, ginger, and powdered cinnamon. Bring to a boil and serve hot.*

➢ *HOT SPICED TEA FOR A CROWD* *Combine 3 qt. boiling water, 3 T. tea leaves, 2 sticks cinnamon, and 1 t. whole cloves. When your tea is strong enough, strain and add 3/4 c.*

sugar, 1/3 c. lemon juice, and 1 c. orange juice. Reheat. The "tea" leaves can be whatever kind you prefer—raspberry, strawberry, rose hip, etc.

SAUCES

➢ *WORCESTERSHIRE SAUCE* *Pour 1 qt. wine vinegar into nonaluminum pan and heat. Add 1/2 t. curry powder, 1/4 t. shredded and crushed pimento, 1 minced garlic clove, 4 t. cut and mashed green onions, 1/2 lb. brown sugar, and a pinch each of ginger, pepper, mustard, and salt. Stir into the vinegar, note how high in the pan the liquid is, put on a lid, and cook on very low heat for 1 hour, adding more vinegar occasionally to keep the liquid amount the same. When the time is up, add 2 c. sherry and let rest a week in a warm place. Then strain out the solids and bottle the sauce into sterilized, dark-colored glass. It tastes best if all your ingredients are fresh.*

➢ *KETJAP MANIS (SWEET SOY KETCHUP)* *From Ruth, Bonaire, Netherlands Antilles: "Ketjap manis is sweet sauce, and more common than ketjap benteng, or sour sauce. To make it, simmer together equal parts of water, strong Japanese soy sauce, and molasses, and jazz it up with fresh or ground ginger, coriander, and pepper. It's basically a sweetened, thick, and rather spicy soy sauce, like North American ketchup!"*

By the way, some years back I received a letter scolding me for using the word "catsup" to describe a thick sauce. The writer explained that the origin of the word "ketchup" was "ketjap," a Malay term for any thick sauce and *not* a trademark of Hunt's, etc. He wryly commented that the only meaning of "catsup" that he could figure out had to do with the position of a cat rather than a thick sauce!

After Ruth sent me that ketjap recipe, I knew he was right. The situation has gotten so far from the truth that even the dictionary calls "catsup" the real thing—and "ketchup" only a "variation." And it defines "catsup" as a *tomato* sauce, which is *so* incorrect it boggles my mind: "Ketjap" means all kinds of thick sauces, and "catsup" was also used by antique English recipe books to mean a thick sauce made out of any fruit or vegetable.

I like the sound of "ketchup," and I like knowing I'm using a word precisely—and that I'm now going to treat fairly all the great thickened, spicy sauces that may or may not have tomatoes in them! I always hated the sound of "catsup" anyway. It never felt right in my mouth or to my ear. "Cat's up . . . " Yuk. "Ketchup!" Yeah!

Which Herbs/Spices for Which Foods?

Lillian Reed, Kirkland, WA, typed the 685,000 words from the eighth edition of this book, plus addenda, onto computer disks for me so I'd have an easier time revising and expanding it for this ninth edition. As she neared the end of half a year of hard work, I invited her to add something she had created herself to the book—something that would help people. She brought me this!

APPLESAUCE: anise, cloves (ground)
ARTICHOKES: chervil, coriander seeds, fennel seeds, oregano
ASPIC: allspice

AVOCADO: ginger (fresh or ground)
BEAN SPROUTS: ginger (fresh or ground)
BEANS: mint, oregano, thyme; or 1 part each parsley, savory, and onion
BEANS, GREEN: chervil, dill seeds, dill weed
BEEF: allspice, marjoram, oregano, thyme, turmeric; or 1 part each basil, savory, and thyme
BEEF, BOILED: dill seeds
BEEF, CURRIED: saffron (threads or powder)
BEETS: allspice, anise, dill seeds, dill weed
BOUILLON, COURT: allspice, anise, bay leaf, chervil, coriander seeds, dill seeds, fennel seeds
BREAD: anise, cumin (ground or seeds), fennel seeds, saffron (powder)
BREAD, SPICE: cardamom (ground), ginger (ground)
BROCCOLI: nutmeg
BUTTER, HERB: marjoram
CABBAGE: dill seeds
CABBAGE, RED: allspice
CAKE: cinnamon (ground), mace, nutmeg, saffron (powder)
CAKE, SPICE: allspice, anise, cloves (ground)
CANDY: anise
CARROTS: allspice, anise, bay leaf, cumin (ground or seeds), ginger (fresh or ground), mace, marjoram, mint, nutmeg, tarragon
CAULIFLOWER: nutmeg
CHEESE: mint
CHEESE, COTTAGE: dill weed, thyme
CHEESE, CREAM: sage, thyme
CHEESE, GOAT: rosemary
CHICKEN: chervil, cilantro (fresh coriander), dill weed, ginger (fresh or ground), marjoram, nutmeg, oregano, rosemary, thyme; or 1 part each marjoram, parsley, savory, and tarragon
CHICKEN, CURRIED: cloves (ground), saffron (threads or powder)
CHICKEN, FRICASSEED: dill weed
CHICKEN SOUP: nutmeg, rosemary, tarragon
CHILI: cumin (ground or seeds)
CHOWDER: rosemary
CHOWDER, CLAM: marjoram, caraway seed, sage, thyme
CHOWDER, FISH: bay leaf, curry powder, dill, thyme
COLESLAW: chervil, dill seeds, tarragon, thyme
COOKIES: anise, cardamom (ground), cinnamon (ground), coriander, mace
CONSOMME: basil, marjoram, savory, tarragon
CRANBERRY JUICE: cinnamon, allspice, cloves
CREPE: cinnamon (ground)
CUCUMBER: dill weed, marjoram
CUSTARD: cinnamon (ground), mace, nutmeg
DIP: cloves (ground), cumin (ground or seeds), thyme
DIP, CHEESE: chervil, marjoram
DIP, CREAM CHEESE: dill seeds
DRESSING, SALAD: marjoram
DUCK: marjoram, rosemary, thyme
EGGPLANT: coriander seeds, oregano, sage, thyme
EGGS: basil, chervil, cumin (ground or seeds), ginger (fresh or ground), tarragon, thyme, or 1 part each chopped chives or green onion, marjoram, and parsley
EGGS, DEVILED: cloves (ground), turmeric
EGGS, SCRAMBLED: saffron (threads or powder)
EGGS, STUFFED: dill weed

FENNEL BULBS: fennel seeds
FISH: basil, bay leaf, chervil, mace, marjoram, mint, nutmeg, thyme; or 1 part each chopped green onion, dill, tarragon, and lemon juice (or lemon peel or a lemon-flavored herb)
FISH, BAKED: cumin (ground or seeds), dill weed
FISH, BROILED: cumin (ground or seeds), oregano
FISH, POACHED: cardamom (ground), dill seeds, dill weed
FISH, STRONG: sage
FRITTERS: cinnamon (ground)
FRITTERS, VEGETABLE: sage
FRUIT, COOKED: nutmeg
FRUIT, FRESH: ginger (fresh or ground)
FRUITCAKE: cloves (ground)
FRUIT COCKTAIL: rosemary, mint
GAME: bay leaf

GINGERBREAD: cardamom (ground), cinnamon (ground), coriander, ginger (ground)
GUMBO: bay leaf, filé, thyme
HAM: cardamom (ground), cinnamon (ground), ginger (fresh or ground)
LAMB: allspice, basil, cinnamon (ground), cloves (ground), marjoram, nutmeg, oregano, rosemary, saffron (threads or powder), tarragon, thyme. Or lamb seasoning 1: Combine ¼ c. dried onion flakes, 1 T. each ground cumin seed, garlic powder, pepper, and basil. Or lamb seasoning 2: Combine 1 t. each marjoram, parsley, rosemary, and thyme.
LAMB, CURRIED: turmeric
LAMB, ROAST: coriander seeds
LEEKS: chervil, sage, tarragon
LENTILS: cilantro (fresh coriander)
LIVER: basil, sage
MACKEREL: fennel seeds
MARINADE: allspice, bay leaf, ginger (fresh or ground), nutmeg, oregano, rosemary
MARINADE, GAME: coriander seeds
MARINADE, MEAT: cumin (ground or seeds)
MARINADE, PORK: fennel seeds
MEATBALLS: cardamom (ground), coriander seeds, fennel seeds

MEATLOAF: cardamom (ground), cinnamon (ground), cloves (ground), marjoram, nutmeg, oregano, thyme

MEATS, VARIETY: tarragon

MEXICAN DISHES: cilantro (fresh coriander) as topping

MINESTRONE: marjoram

MUSHROOMS: coriander seeds, oregano, rosemary, tarragon, thyme

MUSHROOMS, MARINATED: fennel seeds, marjoram

MUSHROOM SOUP: curry, oregano, marjoram

OMELET: marjoram, oregano

ONIONS: basil, sage

ORIENTAL DISHES: ginger (fresh or ground)

PAELLA: saffron (threads or powder)

PASTA: basil, cilantro (fresh coriander)

PATE: bay leaf, cinnamon (ground), tarragon, thyme

PEAS: chervil, mint, rosemary, sage

PEPPERS, HOT: cilantro (fresh coriander)

PEPPERS, SWEET: cilantro (fresh coriander)

PICKLES, DILL: dill seeds

PIE: cinnamon (ground)

PIE, APPLE: cardamom (ground), coriander

PIE, FRUIT: allspice

PIE, MINCEMEAT: ginger (ground)

PIE, PUMPKIN: cardamom (ground), cloves (ground), coriander, ginger (ground), nutmeg

PILAF: turmeric

PORK: allspice, basil, chervil, cinnamon (ground), cloves (ground), marjoram, oregano, rosemary, sage, tarragon, thyme, turmeric; or 1 part each basil, sage, and savory

PORK, CURRIED: saffron (threads or powder)

POTATOES: basil, bay leaf, chervil, nutmeg, oregano, rosemary, tarragon, thyme; or 1 t. each oregano, thyme, pepper, and rosemary

POTATOES, BOILED: dill weed

POTATOES, SWEET: cardamom (ground), mint

POULTRY: basil, sage, tarragon

POULTRY, CURRIED: cardamom (ground)

PUDDING, RICE: cinnamon (ground)

QUICHE: nutmeg

RABBIT: chervil, marjoram, rosemary, tarragon

RICE: cardamom (ground), cilantro (fresh coriander), ginger (fresh or ground)

RISOTTO: saffron (threads or powder)

ROLLS: cardamom (ground)

SALAD, AVOCADO: cilantro (fresh coriander), dill weed

SALAD, BEET: chervil

SALAD, CARROT: cinnamon (ground)

SALAD, CELERY ROOT: turmeric

SALAD, CHICKEN: basil, tarragon, thyme

SALAD, CUCUMBER: thyme

SALAD, EGG: cilantro (fresh coriander)

SALAD, FRUIT: basil, cardamom (ground), cinnamon (ground), cloves (ground), mace, mint

SALAD, GREEN: chervil, marjoram, mint, tarragon

SALAD, GREEN PEPPER: cumin (ground or seeds)

SALAD, POTATO: dill weed, fennel seeds

SALAD, SEAFOOD: oregano, tarragon

SALAD, SHELLFISH: fennel seeds

SALAD, TOMATO: basil, cumin (ground or seeds), thyme

SALAD, WALDORF: mint

SALMON: fennel seeds

SALMON, SMOKED: dill weed

SAUCE, CREAM: chervil

SAUERKRAUT: dill seeds

SAUSAGE: allspice, coriander seeds, cumin (ground or seeds), fennel seeds, marjoram, nutmeg, thyme

SEAFOOD, BROILED: tarragon

SHELLFISH: basil, dill weed, mint (garnish), turmeric

SHRIMP: allspice, ginger (fresh or ground)

SOUFFLE: chervil, nutmeg

SOUP: cilantro (fresh coriander) as topping

SOUP, TOMATO: tarragon

SPINACH: nutmeg

SPREAD: basil, cloves (ground), cumin (ground or seeds), thyme

SPREAD, CHEESE: chervil, tarragon

SQUASH: cardamom (ground)

STEAK: rosemary

STEW: chervil, cilantro (fresh coriander)

STEW, BEEF: cumin (ground or seeds)

STEW, CHICKEN: cinnamon (ground), cumin (ground or seeds)

STEW, FISH: coriander seeds

STEW, LAMB: bay leaf, dill weed, fennel seeds, mint, turmeric

STEW, PORK: dill weed

STEW, RABBIT: fennel seeds

STEW, SEAFOOD: saffron (threads or powder)

STEW, VEAL: bay leaf

STUFFING: allspice, chervil, cloves (ground), dill seeds, dill weed, ginger (fresh or ground), marjoram, mint, nutmeg, oregano, sage, thyme

TOMATO JUICE: ¼ t. dried basil per cup

TOMATO SAUCE: basil, oregano

TOMATOES: allspice, basil, bay leaf, chervil, cilantro (fresh coriander), dill weed, oregano, sage, tarragon, thyme

TOMATOES, STEWED: oregano

TURNIPS: dill seeds

VEAL: allspice, basil, chervil, nutmeg, oregano, rosemary, sage, tarragon, thyme

VEGETABLES, CURRIED: cumin (ground or seeds)

VEGETABLES, MARINATED: coriander seeds, oregano

VENISON: chervil, rosemary

ZUCCHINI: marjoram, mint, oregano, thyme

ALFALFA TO YUCCA— GARDEN TO TABLE

Mail-order sources for various herbs and spices are listed in specific entries. Look for the addresses of those firms in the source list at the beginning of this chapter. If they're not listed, look in the source lists in Chapter 2 (for firms that also carry vegetables) or Chapter 6 (for those that specialize in trees and fruits).

ALFALFA: This plant makes wonderful high-protein hay for winter feed for herbivores. Also, a tea can be made from the leaves or seeds. Sometimes it is combined with peppermint. Harvest your leaves when the plant is in early bloom. Separate out the stems and discard them. Cure in the shade. Pour boiling water over the dried alfalfa to make tea. You can also eat the young tips as greens.

Violet Stewart wrote me, "I go out in a field of fresh alfalfa where there is new growth. Cut an armload and bring home. Put into a tub and wash thoroughly. Shake water out and lay on trays to sun-dry. When dampness is gone I strip tender leaves off and lay the leaves on trays and dry in

200°F oven to kill any bug eggs left, and when thoroughly dry put into a tight can ready for tea making. I think it keeps arthritis in check. I drink it every day instead of coffee or tea." Available as "green manure" or hay crop. (See Chapter 2 for information about planting alfalfa.)

ALLSPICE: The berry of the 40-foot evergreen pimento tree (*Pimenta officinalis*), allspice tastes like cinnamon, nutmeg, and cloves rolled together. You can grow a little tree in your garden, even in a moderate temperate zone, if you bring it in the house to winter in a pot, but it will only bear fruit if you live in Guatemala, Honduras, Jamaica, or Mexico. The tree does not bear fruit until it is 7 years old—and then bears for maybe 50 more years. If you have a fruiting tree, climb it and pick the branchlets with green fruit about ¼ inch in diameter. Throw them down, strip the berries from the branch, and sun-dry them for about a week, or until they're one-third their original size and are dark brown in color. Then you have "berries," the whole allspice. Use whole or grind to make a powder. Use in fruit pies, cakes, sausage, cabbage, and curries. *Pimenta dioica* is hardy down to 26°F and is available from Pacific Tree Farms.

"Allspice" (*Calycanthus floridus*). This perennial shrub or small tree is no relation to the true allspice, but its leaves, when crushed, and its wood emit an aroma very similar to that of allspice berries.

ALOE VERA: This is one of the most highly regarded medicinal plants. Of the several *Aloe* species, the one you want is *Aloe barbadensis,* or Medicine Aloe. You can buy one from a florist or get a starter plant from a neighbor. Or order by mail from a source such as Merry Gardens. To use, snap off the tip of one of its fat, cactus-type leaves (they are smooth with no stickers at all). Squeeze out the natural salve from inside the leaf onto your burn, scrape, rash, or other skin problem. It's also good for sunburns. The plant will heal its broken tip and refill for the next time you need it.

AMBROSIA: See "Epazote."

ANGELICA (*ANGELICA ARCHANGELICA*): A hardy biennial with lush, 2–3-foot leaves when mature, angelica can get up to 8 feet tall—the largest herb that isn't a tree. Much like celery in its growing requirements, angelica does best in rich soil kept constantly moist and partially shaded.

Planting. Let the seeds mature on the plant; in August, gather and lay them in a flat or seedbed, uncovered by soil. (Seeds are viable for up to a year, but are best used right away.) Or just let the falling seeds self-sow and transplant. Young angelica plants grow slowly their first year, developing only a small leaf rosette. But in the second or third year, the plant begins growing rapidly. Consistently removing buds before the early spring flowers open—or at least before seed develops—turns your biennial into a perennial. Seeds available from Le Jardin du Gourmet, Nichols, DeGiorgi, and Thompson & Morgan.

Using. Use angelica root and leaves to flavor stewed fruit. They are a natural licorice-flavored sweetener for tart fruits.

> **CANDIED OR "CRYSTALLIZED" ANGELICA** *To make this Victorian delight, which can be used in fruitcake or as a decoration or confection: Cut young, tender stems (harvest only the topmost section for this purpose) into 2–5-inch sections. Using only a little water and a covered non-aluminum pan, boil to tenderness. Pour off the water, but save it. Peel off the tough outside layer of the stems. Return to the pan with the same water and cook over very low heat until stems are green. Drain once more. When the stems are dry, put them on a kitchen scale and weigh them. Then scatter them over a baking or drying tray or a sizable plate, and scatter over them an amount of sugar equal to the weight of the herb. Let them sit in a loosely covered container in the refrigerator or a cool room for 2 days. You want them to dry, but not harden.*

> *After 2 days, the mass will have toughened considerably and you'll have to scrape with a knife to get it off the plate and back into the pan. Add just a few teaspoons of water so it won't burn, and heat that just to a boil. Remove the stems and drain the liquid. When the stems have cooled, return them to the pan and pour over them a newly made syrup (1 c. water to 1 c. sugar), enough to completely cover. Simmer 10 minutes. Drain off most, but not all, of the liquid. Spread the stems on waxed paper on a drying tray, and let dry until they are no longer damp to the touch.*

ANISE SEED: There are 2 different, easily confused anise spices—anise seed (see below) and star anise. Anise seed grows on *Pimpinella anisum* (Umbelliferae), a native of the Mediterranean area and a favorite herb of Italian cooks. An annual, it is a relative of parsley that looks like dill, grows 18–24 inches tall, and bears decorative yellow flowers. The plant parts have a mild, sweet licorice flavor. Anise doesn't require fertilizing, weeding, or full sun. Available from William Dam, DeGiorgi, etc.

Growing. Anise is naturally a warm-climate plant; it needs at least a 120-day season to grow and produce seed. If you live in a cold, northern region, start seeds indoors in the fall in very moist soil in a fiber pot. Next spring, after the last frost, plant the whole pot in full sun, because anise doesn't transplant well. Or plant directly to garden, or just keep it in a container. Space plants 18 inches apart. You can save your own seed; it remains viable for 3–4 years.

Harvesting. Gather leaves while still young and tender. For your seed harvest, cut the plants off at ground level in August, when the seeds are fully formed and are drying on the plant. Dry the plants and store them inside a big paper bag (seed heads down) in a warm, dry place for further drying—or dry in oven or dehydrator at 110°F. Then loosen seeds, separate from chaff, and store in tightly closed jar.

Using. Anise leaves can be chopped and added to a salad or to fish dishes. Use seeds in cakes, cookies, and other sweet dishes, in curry mixtures, and in Italian anisette toast. Anise root is also edible; it can be chewed on or candied in very thin slices, like ginger. Oil of anise is used in commercial cough medicines. Anise tea is a valid home remedy for asthma, bronchitis, cough, and congestion.

ANISE, STAR: This spice is the fruit of a variety of evergreen magnolia tree.

> *CHINESE 5-SPICE BLEND In a blender or mortar combine 2 T. black peppercorns, about 40 whole cloves, 10 inches cinnamon stick, 2 T. fennel seed, and a dozen star anise. Blend or grind together. Store in an airtight container. Good in Chinese recipes and any chicken dish.*

ARTEMISIA: In my childhood I knew it as plain old sagebrush. It was my favorite plant. I loved the silver-gray leaves and their pungent sage scent. Sagebrush is not a true sage, but is actually in the sunflower family. Native Americans used to dry and burn the sagebrush leaves as a sacred incense. You can order big sage, *Artemisia tridentata,* and prairie sage, *Artemisia ludoviciana,* from Redwood City. (See also "Southernwood" and "Wormwood"; these are related sage species.)

ARUGULA: See "Rocket" in Chapter 4.

BALM, BEE (*MONARDA DIDYMA*): This North American hardy perennial herb (a New York native) is called bee balm because its splendid scarlet or pink flowers are strongly attractive to bees. (Hummingbirds like them too.) It's also called bergamot, Oswego tea, and Monarda. It is bush-shaped and grows up to 4 feet tall.

Planting. Bee balm is best started by root division in the spring or fall. Plant in fertile, moist soil. It tends to spread, but not invasively. Keep it under control and divide it at least every 3 years.

Growing bee balm from seeds is difficult. Try planting seeds in the spring or fall; growth will be very slow. Seeds remain viable 2–3 years and are available from Harris and Hudson.

Using. The heavily aromatic, lemony leaf is edible and makes a good tea (so used by the Oswego Indians). It's also good in fruit punches, fruit soups, and potpourri. Leaves picked right before flowering are the most scented, but they can be picked and dried anytime during summer. Good in poultry stuffing.

> *BEE BALM FANCY TEA Combine 1 part each dried bee balm leaves, dried basil (or sage), and dried citrus peel.*

BALM, LEMON (*MELISSA OFFICINALIS*): Also called sweet balm, lemon balm is another hardy perennial herb bush; it grows 2–3 feet tall and has little white flowers and lemony-mint–flavored leaves. There are several varieties. Seeds available from Hudson, Nichols, Redwood City, DeGiorgi, etc.

Planting. Lemon balm starts nicely from seed and will spread by seed drop in your garden as well as by runners. You can also propagate it by planting cuttings and root divisions. It will grow well in northern as well as southern zones, but plant in damp, fertile soil. It actually prefers partial shade, so plant near a tree or fence.

Harvesting. For preserving, pick whole stems just before the plant flowers. Dry quickly and package in an airtight container. For fresh use, just go out and pick leaves. Always use or preserve balm without delay; the flavor and scent quickly disappear into the air.

Using. Its leaves are so strongly flavored that they will give a lemony touch to any dish, and you can substitute fresh or dried balm for lemon in any recipe. Use fresh leaves in salads. Leaves are used commercially in perfumes and toilet waters and to flavor Benedictine. Balm makes great herb tea and is famous as a headache relief. Serve as an iced tea in summer and hot tea in winter. Balm is also good for scenting your soap. Fresh balm is best for cooking; dried leaves are good in potpourri or sachets for linen storage, being somewhat insect-repellent.

> *PARTY BALM-MINTADE Combine ½ c. balm that has been cut fine, ½ c. mint also cut fine, ¼ c. honey diluted with ¼ c. water, ½ c. lemon juice, and ¼ c. orange juice. Let stand an hour. Now add 4 qt. ginger ale—homemade or store-bought.*

BASIL: Another favorite annual herb, basil is a basic Italian seasoning with a clove-like scent that's easy to grow, in or out of a container (although a frost will kill it). There are many varieties, ranging in color (green, dark purple), size (dwarf basil is smallest), flavor (cinnamon basil, lemon basil), and zone hardiness (bush basil is hardiest). Sweet basil (*Ocimum basilicum*) is the traditional variety. All grow 1–2 feet tall in an erect bush shape and are very fragrant.

Planting. Basil starts easily from seed as long as your soil is warm. (Seed remains viable 2–3 years.) If you plant indoors, start about a month early, and then set out after frost danger is over. Space 6 inches apart. Basil prefers partial shade; plant near a tree or fence if possible. Basil grown in poor soil has more strongly fragrant leaves. Water regularly. Plant every 2–4 weeks through spring for best continuing supply of nonblooming plants, because fresh basil is so much better than preserved. Or grow in containers, where it does well, for a fresh supply year-round. Seeds are widely available; Redwood City offers 8 varieties; DeGiorgi, 10.

Harvesting. Cut both leaves and buds when buds appear. The flowers are edible cooked or fresh, and pinching off developing blossoms keeps the quantity and quality of the leaf crop going. (If you don't pinch the buds and the plant succeeds in fully flowering, it will seed and then die.) Basil will grow a second crop if you don't cut all the way to the ground.

Cut leaves will keep in the refrigerator for several days; frozen ones, for up to 6 months. Use fresh or frozen leaves in a salad, or substitute for dried basil in recipes. To dry basil, tie in bunches or spread on trays out of direct sunlight. Or dry in oven or dehydrator (110°F) until leaves crumble. Basil must be dried quickly to prevent molding. Now crumble the leaves off the stems, discard stems, and store leaves.

Using. Dried basil is weaker and different than fresh or frozen, but is still useful. Make a medicinal tea; flavor vinegar, tomato dishes, eggs, fish, cheese, soups, stews, meat pies, lamb chops, squash, peas, green beans, or salad dressing. Or use in potpourri—or pesto . . .

> *PESTO* *In your blender, mix 4 cloves garlic, 2 c. freshly picked basil, ¼ c. nuts (pine nuts or walnuts are good), 1 t. salt, ¼ t. pepper, and ¼ c. olive oil. As you blend, gradually add another ¼ c. olive oil. Pour into a bowl. Stir in 3 oz. just-grated Parmesan or other firm cheese. Use pesto right away. If you must keep it, store in an airtight container (air exposure makes pesto turn brown). Pesto is great as a sauce for noodles or green beans, or as a flavoring for pasta, soups, or cooked fish. To freeze pesto, omit cheese, adding only when thawed and ready to serve.*

BAY: There are 2 varieties, sweet bay and California bay. Both are warm-climate plants, although sweet bay is hardier than California bay, which is subtropical (zones 8–10). Both are evergreen trees. Both can be grown either in sun or semi-shade. If you live in the desert, you'll need to water them once in a while. Keep the soil well drained, and let it dry out between waterings.

Sweet Bay. Sweet bay is the seasoning leaf you find in the stores. Also known as bay laurel (*Laurus nobilis*) and Grecian laurel, it grows 25–40 feet high. It can be clipped into almost any shape you want and thus severely limited in size, and it does well in containers. It's your best choice if you're in a northern climate (bring it inside for the winter). In a container, bay needs a coolish room; repot it once a year or prune it back severely. Outside, it needs to be in a partially shaded site if you have blistering sun; it's somewhat drought resistant. You can start it from seed (allow a month for germination at 70°F), or take a sucker cutting and root it (allow 6 months). Plants available from Nichols, DeGiorgi, and Thompson & Morgan.

California Bay (*Umbellularia californica*). Also known as California laurel, Oregon myrtle, and pepperwood, this bay grows wild on the California coast and in southwestern Oregon. It can get much taller than sweet bay—up to 75 feet high and 100 feet wide—but it's planted only from seeds and grows slowly, so you're not likely to see that size outside of the forest. It is naturally multi-stemmed and drought-resistant. Fruits are inedible. Plants available from Pacific Tree Farms and Raintree Nursery.

Using. The flavor of the California bay leaf is similar to that of the sweet bay but is significantly stronger. Both are used to perk up soups, stews, and meats. Both can be gathered any time of year, but late summer is preferable. Choose small but mature leaves. The leaves should not be crumbled, so handle them carefully. Discard any broken ones. Dry outside away from direct sunlight, turning once, until brittle. Or dry in oven or dehydrator at 110°F. Store in airtight jar. Add 1, 2, or 3 whole leaves at the beginning of the cooking process to any dish you want to flavor: stews, soups, spaghetti sauce, any meat or fish dish. Do not eat the leaf itself; remove it before serving, or warn the unknowing to discard it if found in their portion. A wreath for the head made of sweet bay leaves was a Roman award of honor.

BEE BALM: See "Balm, Bee."

BERGAMOT: See "Balm, Bee." The bergamot oil used by the perfume industry is extracted from the Italian bergamot orange.

BORAGE (*BORAGO OFFICINALIS*): This is an easy-to-grow, ornamental and edible annual herb with hairy cucumber-flavored leaves and numerous lovely bee-attracting, intensely blue flowers. Grows up to 2 feet tall—more in heavily manured soil. Does well in a container, and can handle partial shade.

Planting. Plant seeds in spring, early summer, or fall. Plant several seeds per spot, and then thin to 1 plant. Plant in succession to keep prime plants available. Doesn't like wet feet. Once established, it will self-sow and create a dense clump, so allow room for that when planting. It grows quickly whether in a bed, row, or pot; it's nice to have indoors in winter. Available from Thompson & Morgan, William Dam, Redwood City, DeGiorgi, etc.

Harvesting and Using. Both flowers and leaves can be eaten. In general, preserve and use like basil. Leaves will be ready in about 6 weeks. They're best harvested before flowers appear—while the leaves are still young, tender, not too hairy, and about 2½–5 inches long. Mince them fine and add to an early spring salad or to cool drinks. Or cook like spinach (the hairs will cook away) or add to soup. Flowers are best harvested when they are just opening. Add them to salads and lemonade.

> *BORAGE TEA* *Soak a handful of borage leaves in water that has been boiling. Then chill, sweeten to taste, and add ice. Serve with a borage flower floating atop!*

> *CANDIED BORAGE FLOWERS* *You can actually do this to any tiny flower. Dip the flower in egg white and then into sugar. Dry and use plain or as cake decorations.*

BURNET (*POTERIUM SANGUISORBA* OR *SANGUISORBA MINOR*): This herb perennial with cucumber-flavored leaves and lovely flowers is also known as salad burnet. A wild variety called great burnet (*Sanguisorba officinalis*) can be used in the same way as salad burnet.

Planting. This very hardy plant is a creeper, easily grown from seed or by root division in early spring. Seeds or plants are available from Comstock, DeGiorgi, William Dam, Hudson, and Park. But I don't recommend burnet because it's not that important as an herb, and is so likely to become a weedy nuisance in your garden.

Harvesting. Burnet doesn't dry well, but it can be picked off the plant even in winter, so that doesn't matter. Pick center leaves; older, outer ones are tough and taste unpleasant. Leaves (only!) are used in salads, as garnish, as flavoring for vinegar, in any cream soup, as a sandwich topping (minced and mixed with butter), or as a tea.

CALENDULA: See "Marigold, Pot."

CAMOMILE: See "Chamomile."

CAPERS: *Capparis spinosa* originates in the Mediterranean area of Europe. The plant is grown for the unopened flower buds, or capers, which can only be eaten pickled but are considered a delicacy. They grow 3–5 feet tall. (Nasturtium is used similarly but is *not* the real thing.)

Planting. Plant seeds or cuttings in full sun. The plant is easy to grow if you have a dry, mild climate. It thrives in sandy or rocky ground, relatively poor soil, and on hillsides—in a sunny, warm, well-drained site. It will be an evergreen perennial in the warmest zones (9–10), but will winterkill in zones 6–8. Grow it there as an annual, starting indoors if your summer is on the short side. Seeds available from Park and Pacific Tree Farms.

Harvesting. In summer, harvest the flower buds just before they open. They will look small and green. Keep them in the dark 3 hours; then pickle them. The fruit of the caper is also edible and can be pickled.

> *PICKLING CAPERS* *Have ready clean, hot pint (3) or cup (6) canning jars. Divide 1 qt. washed capers between the jars. In a stainless steel or enamel pan, mix together ½ c. brown sugar, ½ c. water, 1½ c. wine vinegar, 1 crushed clove of garlic, and 1 t. each mustard seed, salt, dill, and celery seed; if you wish, add mace, green onions, garlic, nutmeg, or peppercorns. Boil the pickling solution hard for 10 minutes. Pour it through a strainer to get out the solids and then boil once more. Pour the almost-boiling liquid over the capers. Pack in ½-pint jars. Process in boiling-water bath 15 minutes. Keep in a cool, dark place and wait at least 10 days before using to allow capers to pickle. Use pickled capers in soups, stews, vegetable dishes, salads, sauces, fancy sandwiches, and poultry stuffing. (See "Nasturtium" for more recipes.)*

CARAWAY (CARUM CARVI): This plant comes in 2 varieties. The old-timer is a biennial: You plant it one year, and it grows that first year and makes seed the next. Now there's an annual kind too.

Planting. Plant 8 inches apart in the spring (or fall) in a well drained, sunny place where you can leave it for 2 years, such as the border of your garden. Mulch roots in the fall to avoid freezing. It grows about 2½ feet tall. Once you've got it, it tends to self-sow. Caraway seed is viable for 2 years and is available from DeGiorgi.

Harvesting. When seed clusters ripen the second year (turning brown), cut off flower heads. Dry away from direct sun in a warm, dry place, laying flat on screen, paper, cloth—a surface from which you can easily gather spilled seeds. Once the seeds are dry, finish threshing by rubbing the heads with your hands. Blow off chaff and store seeds for planting or eating.

Using. The seeds make good additions to rye bread, biscuits, sauerkraut, and cottage cheese. Or cook them with cabbage and cauliflower. The flavor of caraway stems and foliage is similar to the seeds but milder. Use them in cheese and fish recipes and salads.

> *CARAWAY-STUFFED CELERY* *Mix cream cheese with caraway seed and stuff into hollow side of celery. Cut into 2-inch sections. Sprinkle with paprika.*

CARDAMOM (ALSO CARDAMON): *Elettaria cardamomum,* whose seed is an aromatic spice, is a relative of ginger and a native of India. It grows on a shrubby little tree, 8–10 feet high, also known as the cinnamon palm. You can grow it in a temperate-zone garden if you move it to a pot and bring it into the house before winter. The leaves are deep green with a spicy ginger-like scent. It bears fruit only when 3 years old.

Planting. Cardamom is propagated 2 ways, by seed and by transplanting the plant just after harvest. That causes the top part to die, but the roots send up a new one—which fruits after 2 years. Available from Merry Gardens.

Harvesting. Pick it whole (seeds inside their pods) and grind before using, pods and all. The pods will disintegrate as a result of the cooking but will enrich the flavor. Also use pod and all in pickling mixes. Use ground to flavor puddings, pies, ice cream, and Danish pastries.

CASSIA (*CINNAMOMUM CASSIA BLUME*): This is a Chinese flavoring agent, reminiscent of cinnamon and cloves. And no wonder, for the plant is a close relative of cinnamon. Cassia bark is sometimes sold as cinnamon; it is indeed the same flavor, but stronger. It's raised and harvested in the same way as cinnamon. Cassia "buds" are sold for use in pickling. They are the unripe fruit of the cassia, dried.

CATMINT: See "Catnip."

CATNIP: There are 2 kinds, similar in many ways and frequently confused. Both are perennials of the mint family. Both are energetic spreaders that like full sun and regular watering. Both are used in old-time medicinal remedies for humans. But in a cat's opinion, the true catnip is *Nepeta cataria,* which grows 2–4 feet tall. This is the one that makes cats go crazy. It has gray-green, downy leaves and either lavender or white flowers at branch tips in spring (June).

Catmint (*Nepeta faassenii,* a.k.a. *N. mussinii*): Catmint also has grey-green leaves and bee-attracting, lavender-blue flowers in loose spikes. The word "catmint" used to mean both types of catnip; more recently, catmint is used as the common name for *N. faassenii* only. It is much more ornamental but weaker in the cat-crazing element.

Planting. First plan how you're going to keep the little plants safe from cats. That means a catproof barrier all around the plants. Otherwise cats will discover them and roll on or eat them. Once the plants grow larger than the cats, they don't need protection any more. For either catnip or catmint, start the seed inside, or outside once the ground is really warm. Or plant in late fall, plant a cutting, plant in a container, or divide existing clumps of older plants and replant in sandy soil in full sun. Provide fertile soil and shelter from cold winds. They can grow in a semi-shaded spot, although they like sun. The flavor will be stronger if the plants grow in sandy rather than clay-type soil. Catnip seed available from Redwood City and DeGiorgi.

Harvesting and Preserving. Cut off the tops when the plant is in full blossom. When drying catnip, keep it in shade and high above the ground, or you'll have every cat in the neighborhood coming to call! (They don't seem to smell it if it's high off the ground.) Or dry indoors at 110°F. Dry and discard the stems. To freeze: gather, wash, pat dry, and pack leaves in layers with waxed paper between. Take out a few at a time to make a happy cat.

Using. Make a tea from the leaves (fresh or dried). It is a traditional remedy for menstrual difficulties. Adding a few fresh leaves to your salad is a good way to greet spring. Or sew little gingham or felt mice come winter, stuff them with catnip, and give them as Christmas presents to all your cat-owning friends!

CATTAIL: The fibers of cattail down make excellent cushion stuffing. Start with a sackful and use in your pillows as you would any other stuffing.

CHAMOMILE: Half the time you'll see it spelled "chamomile," half "camomile." And are we talking about garden (Roman) chamomile or sweet false (German) chamomile? The two plants are unrelated, although they have similar leaves, blossoms, and uses. They look very different: Garden chamomile is a low-growing creeper, while sweet false chamomile is tall and upright. The blossoms look like those of feverfew. And for the first 8 editions of this book I got it confused with yet another lookalike, dog fennel, and gave wrong information. Well, I'm straight at last!

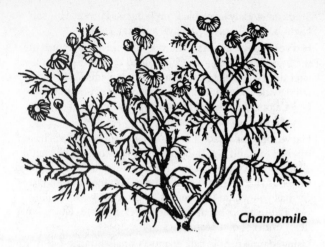

Chamomile

Roman/Garden/True Chamomile (*Chamaemelum nobile,* a.k.a. *Anthemis nobilis*). This small evergreen perennial is grown either from seed or by root division. It makes a good ground cover and can survive in partial shade and without fertilizer. Available from Redwood City and Thompson & Morgan.

Sweet False Chamomile (*Matricaria recutita*). This 2–2½-foot-tall annual is propagated only by seed. Plant 1 foot apart in full sun and well-drained, light soil. It germinates easily, self-sows, and has pineapple-flavored flowers. Available from DeGiorgi.

Harvesting, Preserving, and Using. The little daisylike flower heads are the usable parts of both types of chamomile. Gather when in full bloom and dry at 110°F. True chamomile is the best for medicinal and tea use.

❧ *CHAMOMILE TEA Pour 1 pint boiling water over 3 t. dry flowers and steep to make tea. It's bitter medicine; Peter Rabbit had some when he got back home. It's supposed to be good for indigestion, chills, and nervousness, and he had all three. It's also used as a rinse for blonde hair and as a treatment for plant diseases.*

CHERVIL (*ANTHRISCUS CEREFOLIUM*): This hardy annual grows 1½–2 feet tall. Delicate and ferny in appearance, it is easy to grow and does well in poor soil as long there is water. The 2 basic varieties are "curled" and "flat."

Planting. Chervil does best shaded from hot afternoon sun. Plant in spring or late fall in the garden; it doesn't transplant well. Don't cover the seed; it requires light to germinate. Plant every few weeks thereafter until midsummer to keep it coming prime. Available from William Dam, Thompson & Morgan, Redwood City, DeGiorgi, etc.

Harvesting. For freezing, use tender young leaves cut from seedlings at least 6 weeks old. You can use older leaves for drying (at 110°F until brittle). Cutting off seedheads promotes leaf growth. It you allow the plants to flower, they will self-sow but basically stay in the same area.

Using. Chervil is the gourmet's parsley. Use it fresh as you would parsley, as a garnish and in salads, especially when you want a milder flavor than parsley. Use frozen or dried in soups, salads, poultry, fish, and egg dishes. Its flavor is mild; use 1 T. dried herb for salad, 2–3 T. for cooked dishes.

❧ *CHERVIL VINEGAR It's good in salad dressings. Half-fill a bottle with fresh or dry leaves. Fill the bottle with good vinegar, and heat it gently by placing in warm water. Bring water*

to boiling point. Remove from heat; when cool, cap. Let steep 2 weeks. Then it's ready.

❧ *HERB SOUP Seasoned with chervil, this can be varied indefinitely as to the green vegetables. For a start, pick sorrel, spinach, and lettuce fresh from your garden, and get rid of any tough midribs. Wash and shred. Use 1 c. finely shredded spinach, ½ c. shredded sorrel, and ½ c. of the white heart leaves of head lettuce. Use about ¼ c. butter and saute (don't brown). Add 4 peeled potatoes, 1 T. salt, and 2 qt. boiling water. Let the soup simmer gently for 1 hour. Crush the potatoes, add 1 T. chervil, and simmer 5 minutes more. Add a cup of croutons before serving.*

❧ *SOUR CREAM AND HERB DRESSING Mix this in a jar and serve on green salads as you need it. Mix 2 c. sour cream and 1 t. each chopped parsley, chives, tarragon, and chervil. Add 2 T. brown sugar, ¼ c. vinegar, ½ c. oil, a grind of pepper, a dash of salt, and 1 t. dry mustard. Mix well.*

CHICORY: See "Coffees that Aren't Coffee" under "Cocoa, Coffee(s), and Tea" in this chapter, and "Leaf Vegetables" in Chapter 4.

CHILIES: See "Peppers, Hot" in Chapter 4.

CHINESE PARSLEY: See "Coriander."

CHIVES: See "Allium" in Chapter 4.

CILANTRO: See "Coriander."

CINNAMON: This is the bark of a tropical evergreen bush (*Cinnamomum zeylanicum*) that only grows in India and Sri Lanka. There are several other varieties of cinnamon tree. Cassia cinnamon (see "Cassia") and Ceylon cinnamon are most common. The tree is hardy down to only 30°F. The bark can be burned as incense, turned into scented bath oil, and used to season food. Available from Pacific Tree Farms. For detailed instructions on harvesting cinnamon, see the herbal section of Rodale's *Encyclopedia of Organic Gardening.*

❧ *MAKING COARSELY CRUSHED CINNAMON Break sticks into pieces, put them into a bag, and pound with a hammer.*

❧ *CINNAMON SUGAR Combine ¼ c. sugar with ½ t. ground cinnamon. Mix well and store in a covered jar. Use on toast, etc.*

CLARY SAGE: See "Sage, Clary."

CLOVER: This is wonderful stuff. All the varieties of clover are legumes, can be planted for a green manure crop, and should be inoculated. There are other fun things you can do with the clover blossoms! Redwood City offers *Trifolium pratense,* a red clover variety whose dried blossoms make a sedative tea and whose seeds make good salad sprouts.

❧ *ALASKA HONEY Larry Malcom wrote me from Eagle River, AK, to supply this recipe "for people who for reasons cannot have bees but still want to make honey! Boil together 10 c. sugar and 2 c. water for 10 minutes. Remove from heat and add 1 t. alum and 25 fireweed flowers, 45 pink clover flowers, 45 white clover flowers (or 90 clover of any color). Let stand 5 minutes. Strain and pour into jars. Simple, isn't it? And it comes out nice and thick and wonderfully good! We're having a taffy pull this weekend. Hooray! Went dog-sledding yesterday for the first time. Beats sno-machines hands-down! So quiet, with a full moon!"*

CLOVER BLOOM VINEGAR *Combine 6 lb. brown sugar, ½ bushel clover bloom, 4 qt. molasses, and 9 gal. boiling water. Let cool. Add 3 T. dry yeast dissolved in ¼ c. water. Let stand 14 days, strain, and store until it tastes like vinegar.*

CLOVES: These are actually the unopened flower buds of an evergreen tree. The tree grows wild in the Molucca islands, the West Indies, Sumatra, and Brazil. To harvest, gather the purplish buds (growing on those familiar little clove stalks) before they open. Dry. The drying will turn them from reddish to dark brown. Use whole or ground. Powdered cloves can be used as a louse or flea powder on small animals.

COMFREY: Comfrey is controversial. It used to be considered totally harmless, a traditional cure for anything, food for anything. Well, it's not *deadly* poison, but modern chemistry has identified a poisonous substance in it, pyrolizzidine, so the up-to-date recommendation has to be that it *should not be eaten in any form.*

Too bad, because this is a deep-rooting, hardy perennial with lush green leaves that can grow 3 feet high and come back quickly after being cut back. (The same hardiness has been known to result in a comfrey-turned-weed problem.) *Symphytum officinale* is widely available. Russian comfrey (*Symphytum peregrinum*) is slow-growing, is a source of compost material for organic gardeners, and is used to feed animals. Comfrey cannot be raised from seed. It has to be propagated by root cuttings. Plant a 2-inch root cutting 4 inches deep any time of the year—3 feet apart, because they get really big.

CORIANDER (*CORIANDRUM SATIVUM*): This herb is a hardy annual, a member of the dill family. It's also called cilantro, Chinese parsley, and Mexican parsley.

Planting. Plant in spring or fall, ½ inch deep, 6 inches apart, in full sun or partial shade. (Don't transplant.) Keep seedbed moist until germination. It grows 2–4 feet tall. Let 1 head go and it will self-seed for future years. Plant every 3–4 weeks for an ongoing supply of choice leaves for flavoring. Northern gardeners should buy only non-bolting kinds (Johnny's Seeds and Nichols have them), which can handle the long days that trigger bolting in other varieties. Lane Morgan, who lives in northern Washington, says, "The standard kind bolts as soon as it's out of the ground up here."

Seeds are widely available from Burgess, Burpee, Hudson, Nichols, Park, Redwood City, DeGiorgi, etc.).

Harvesting for Leaves. The very first leaves to appear are the best for cooking—the fan-shaped ones rather than the later dill-type ones. Start picking when plants are 6 inches tall. Divide your patch into plants for leaves and plants to be let alone to make seed. Don't dry the leaves; they must be used fresh to have value.

Harvesting for Seed. Do this when some seed pods have ripened (around 2 months after you planted). Don't wait for all the pods to ripen, or you'll go out there one day and find the pods shattered and seed scattered on the ground. Proceed as you would for caraway. Mash seeds with a rolling pin. Put in apple pie and apple butter; also see "Curry Powders" under "Food Seasonings" for recipes.

Using. Some people hate cilantro's smell. Strange but true: When cooked, the flavor of the plant will be milder and more pleasant than its odor in your garden. Use the pungent leaves to flavor salsa verde, guacamole, soups, stews, salads, stir-fries, egg, fish, pork, hot dogs, etc. It's great with anything tomatoey and is used in Mexican and Indian cooking and in pickling mixes. Just don't use too much!

CILANTRO CHICKEN TOMATO SOUP *Shelley Dalen, Pasco, WA, sent me this. "My husband's grandmother gave it to him. It's quick, easy, one-pot, cheap, delicious, and can be changed around. It also can use lots of tomatoes when your garden is going nuts. Turn your burner on medium. Put a cut-up fryer, or just chicken pieces, in a Dutch oven (on the burner). Cover the chicken about 3 inches deep with tomatoes (canned or sauce is OK but fresh is best). Use more if you want more broth. Stir once to get a few tomatoes under the chicken and to prevent the chicken from sticking to the bottom of the pan. Put 1 large peeled and chopped onion on top of the tomatoes. Put ½ c. snipped fresh cilantro (or any other fresh or dried herb you like, in the amount you like) on top of the onion. Cover tightly, and let cook for 30 minutes. I serve with corn tortillas."*

CRESS: Pepper grass is the most peppery of the cresses and the easiest to grow, given its ability to tolerate more dryness and heat than the others. It grows fast to 4–5 inches high. Another variety of seasoning cress is Upland, also with peppery-tasting leaves. Add chopped cress to a green salad or potato salad, or sprinkle over sliced tomatoes with a dash of vinegar/oil dressing. Cress is a good winter pot plant too. Available from DeGiorgi.

CUMIN (*CUMINUM CYMINUM*): This annual plant, an ancient Mediterranean herb, resembles fennel. It blooms with pink and white flowers and is raised for its seeds.

Planting. Plan for the 16 weeks of growth necessary to mature seed. So if you live in the northern United States, start indoors and transplant only after the soil is warm. Plant in light soil. The seeds will grow on the flower head and by late summer, they will be too heavy for the plant to hold; instead it will sprawl over the ground. Let the seed pods dry on the plant until they are just about to burst and be scattered. Then harvest, shell, and dry. Cumin seeds are good mixed with any cheese, in bread, beans, rice, sausage, pork, or wild meat sauces. Ground cumin is used in curry, pickling, and chili powder mixes. Available from Redwood City and DeGiorgi.

DAYLILY: Originally from East Asia, the many species of *Hemerocallis*, the daylily, have long since become local weeds. They are perennials with bright flowers, sold in a multitude of named varieties; they also live in the wild. The entire plant is edible: spring shoots, summer buds, flowers, leaves, and the small tubers. Like weeds, they do well in any soil and in either sun or shade. Some varieties need occasional dividing; some need almost nothing at all. Daylilies (or seed) available from Burpee, Park, Thompson & Morgan (seed only), etc. The best selection of all is from Gilbert H. Wild and Son, who is a daylily specialist and offers a huge number of kinds: P.O. Box 338, Sarcoxie, MO 64862, (417) 548-3514.

Using. Harvest young outer leaves in early spring when 3–6 inches long. Steam, saute, or stir-fry. The flower buds and blossoms are all edible. They have a sweet taste and an okra-like, mucilaginous quality. Closed buds can be pickled like capers, prepared as tempura, or cooked into omelets. To gather the little tubers, wait until fall or even winter, when they have had a chance to store food all summer. While you're dividing too-dense clumps, you can harvest the daylily tubers. Wash, peel, and prepare like potatoes; eat raw or in a salad like Jerusalem artichokes; or prepare like salsify fritters.

DANDELION: See "Leaves We Eat" in Chapter 4.

DILL (*ANETHUM GRAVEOLENS*): This common garden herb is an annual with little yellow flowers and feathery leaves.

Planting. Available from almost any catalog, dill doesn't transplant, but will grow from seed (viable for 2–3 years). Plant ½-inch deep, spaced 3 inches apart, in garden in spring or fall, or in 6–8-inch pot indoors. Needs moist soil, especially before germinating. Germinates slowly. You need only a row about 1½ feet long to meet your needs. It can be interplanted with any member of the cabbage family, or cucumbers. Dill can get up to 4 feet tall but doesn't shade its neighbors because of its fine, ferny leaves. When harvesting, leave 1 plant to self-seed; it won't become a problem weed. For winter use, dig up little 2–3-inch plants grown from self-seeding in the fall and pot them.

Harvesting. If dill is allowed to dry out completely, it may flower prematurely. The leaves (dill weed) and seeds and flower heads (dill heads) are all used to flavor foods.

To harvest dill weed, cut off what you want any time after it gets 1 foot high. It's strongest in flavor just before flowering, so you can plant some early for seed at pickling time and some late for milder "weed," because once the plant flowers the weed isn't as good.

To harvest dill heads, pick before the seeds have formed, and pick only the heads. Plants are likely to make a second or third crop of heads. These are nice added to each jar of dill pickles.

To harvest dill seed, cut the plants before the seed heads turn dark brown, because after that seeds begin falling. Harvest on a dry summer day. Tie in bunches and hang in an airy but shady place. Have something underneath to catch seeds that drop, or just lay them on a clean paper. When the heads are dry, shell off the seeds and store in covered glass jars, or fold up stalks and all in your paper (they'll keep fine). One school of thought says the seed is better dried off the heads; I can't tell the difference. You can also freeze dill or grow it in a kitchen pot through the winter. It's amazing stuff. A friend of mine poured the brine from a jar of dill pickles on the ground by her garbage cans, and—"lo!"—a crop of dill grew there.

Using. Use fresh or dried. Dill weed is milder than the seed. Add it to vegetable dishes, salads (especially macaroni and potato), and soups. Heads, seeds, and stems can be used to make dill pickles or any recipes involving raw cucumbers. You can put a whole dill head in a jar of homemade pickles or dill vinegar. Dill also goes well in bread, yogurt, cheese, sour-cream vegetable dips, mashed potatoes, eggs, and mustard mixes; with fish; and with sauerkraut or cabbage in any form. Dill seed tea is a traditional treatment for adults with indigestion. A tea made from the branchlets is a traditional solace for babies with colic or gas.

> ✒ *DILL VINEGAR Crush 1½ t. dill seeds; then soak in 1 pt. cider vinegar for 2–3 weeks. Strain, and it's done.*

> ✒ *DILL SOUP Ellie Allers, Eureka, MT, wrote me, "This recipe for dill soup is my grandmother's wash day standby. I have eight grandchildren myself so it's no recent one. This consisted of every vegetable available, plus tomato sauce or ketchup, a handful of rice or some other grain, 2 or 3 sprigs of dill, salt, pepper, 2 or 3 hefty T. bacon fat carefully saved from day to day and, if you had it, a bit of chopped bacon. It simmered on the stove all morning. It sounds horrible, tastes marvelous. My husband loves it, and I have canned it for future emergency needs. Best served with hefty chunks of homemade bread and butter."*

ECHINACEA: There are many varieties. All are of some medicinal value. Available from Seeds of Change, Richter's, J. L. Hudson, and Southern Exposure Seed Exchange. ATTRA's info on this subject is at **www.attra.org/attra-pub/echinacea.html.**

EPAZOTE (*CHENOPODIUM AMBROSIOIDES*): This ancient herb (pronounced "eh-pah-SO-tay") grows wild throughout the United States and is a close relative of the grain quinoa. It was used by the Aztecs and is used by modern-day Mexicans as well as Europeans and others. Epazote and cilantro are possibly the two most characteristic spices in genuine Mexican cooking. It's also called ambrosia, Mexican tea, and wormseed. Epazote looks like a bush, grows about 3½ feet high, and is noticeably odorous. It's an annual where winters are cold, a perennial elsewhere. (In marginal areas, cut it to 12 inches high and lay mulch over it.)

Planting. One or two plants will meet a family's kitchen needs. It will grow under almost any conditions (it's sand-tolerating and drought-resistant). Hardship simply makes it more aromatic. If you start with nursery plants, set them out in your garden after the last frost, 2 feet apart. Or plant seed ¼ inch deep. Available from Redwood City.

Using. Like cilantro, epazote should be used fresh for cooking purposes. And like cilantro, it cooks up milder than it smells in your garden. It will keep up to a week wrapped in a wet towel in the fridge. Unlike cilantro, though, you can dry some to make epazote tea in the off-season. Pinching back the stem ends not only supplies greens, it also keeps the plant from flowering and going to seed. Use in almost all Mexican recipes, especially those containing beans, such as black bean soup. (Mexicans believe that epazote diminishes the gas effect of beans.) Use about 3 chopped epazote leaves per 1 gal. of food. Add when beans are about three-fourths cooked. Also good in cheese and chicken mixtures. But don't use too much, or you'll get the medicinal rather than the culinary effect. Epazote got its folk name of "wormseed" because native Americans took it to remedy intestinal worms.

EUCALYPTUS: This family of trees and shrubs has over 500 species in its native Australia, about 150 of which are now thriving in Arizona and California, since it is a natural for deserts. Some have leaves with odd colors, such as blue; many have beautiful flowers. Some species have lemon, peppermint, or medicinal scents. The leaves of some species are always fragrant; others must be crushed to release the scent (use their leaves in potpourris and sachets).

Eucalyptus plants are extraordinarily fast-growing, as much as 10–15 feet/year while young, and they can live a century. All species are tender, so if you have one in a planter, keep it in the house in cold weather and move it outside only for warm weather. Doesn't transplant well; don't change it from container to ground or back again. For more information, see the *Sunset Western Garden Book*.

➤ *EUCALYPTUS COLD REMEDY From Clara Magers, Modesto, CA: "We had eucalyptus trees out in front. My mother took some leaves and boiled them in a saucepan with some water and then let it simmer. We who had a cold would stand over the stove with a towel over our heads and breathe the steam. It clears your head."*

FENNEL: This herb comes in a confusing number of varieties. Chapter 4 discusses sweet fennel (stalks eaten) and finochio or Florence fennel (bulb eaten). The herbal fennel for flavoring, *Foeniculum vulgare*, is a hardy biennial. It can become a weed in your garden, hard to control. The answer to that is Bronze fennel, a less aggressive variety. Available from Redwood City.

Fennel vs. Dill. Fennel is different from dill in that it prefers slightly alkaline soil, but it resembles dill in growing 3–5 feet tall, with feathery branches and yellow flowers. The resemblance is familial, for the two are relatives and shouldn't be planted close together due to the risk of cross-pollination. Plant and harvest as you would dill, but don't interplant as you can with dill; instead, put fennel at the back of your herb garden, since it has a reputation for inhibiting vegetable growth.

Using. Fennel weed or seed can be substituted in any dill recipe, but it's on the strong side, so just use a pinch or two. Fennel is also used in apple recipes and to flavor candies.

Fennel Seed Tea. Straight fennel tea is an old-time remedy for baby colic. For an interesting combo, try fennel-mint tea: half peppermint leaves and half fennel seed or weed.

➤ *BENGALI CRACKERS Crush ¼ t. fennel seed and ½ t. black peppercorns. Mix with 1 c. whole wheat flour and 1 t. baking powder. Add 1 t. tamari, ¼ c. lemon juice, and water as needed; work into a dough. (Be careful not to overwork.) Roll out one half of the dough at a time, 1/16-inch thick, cut into 2-inch squares. Bake 8–10 minutes. (Cover half of dough while working with other half.) From Ruth Miller of Bonaire in the Caribbean.*

FENUGREEK (*TRIGONELLA FOENUMGRAECUM*): Also called bird's foot or Greek hayseed, this legume grows a wheat-sized pea in a long, yellow, beaked pod. It's easy to grow, has a sweet clover scent, doesn't take up much room, and is good for the soil. Once started, it self-sows.

Planting. Plant ¼-inch deep, 3 inches apart. Keep well weeded. It will grow about 2 feet high. In summer weather, fenugreek matures and makes seed quickly. In warm zones you can plant in fall as a leguminous green manure to plow under before spring planting. Seeds available from Park, Redwood City, DeGiorgi, or William Dam.

Using. Use leaves in salads, stews, or soups. A few leaves go a long way. Use seeds in honey as a dessert, or steep to make tea. The seeds are pretty bitter taken straight. Dried seeds, until you cook them, are hard as rocks. The seeds are also good for sprouting, or grind them and mix with spices to make curry.

FEVERFEW (*CHRYSANTHEMUM PARTHENIUM*): I just discovered that for the first 292,500 copies of this book, the following description was listed under "fennel" instead of "feverfew"! I deeply appreciate Marie Oesting, who obviously knows her herbs well and took the trouble to call the error to my attention. Feverfew is an annual that grows like a weed. It has foliage with a strong, medicinal odor and small, midsummer-blooming, daisylike white flowers resembling those of chamomile. It got its name from old-timers who believed that a tea of its leaves would reduce a fever.

Planting. Seeds need to be chilled before planting for 3–6 weeks. Seeds available from Redwood City.

Harvesting. Harvest the plant when the blossoms are just starting to open. It's a close relative of chamomile and is a traditional folk medicine for colds, fever, and flu. Combine with sage for a sore throat. Old-time feverfew was single-rather than double-flowered. A strong feverfew tea on your skin is reputed to have insect-repellent value. Feverfew has been closely studied by pharmacologic researchers, who have established that its use has no risks and that it helps prevent migraine headaches! It wouldn't hurt to try it on a fever.

FILÉ: See "Sassafras."

GERANIUM: There are many kinds of genus *Pelargonium*, family Geraniaceae. The "scented" or "sweet-leaved" geraniums are tender perennials originating in South Africa. They have very minor flowers compared to their beautifully blooming unscented relatives. What they do offer is fragrance of every sort—you choose the variety: almond, anise, apple/nutmeg, apricot, balm, balsam, cinnamon, clover, eucalyptus, filbert, ginger, lavender, lemon, musk, orange, peppermint, pine, rose, strawberry, southernwood, or violet. The plants vary extremely in the intensity of scent. Usually the leaves must be in the presence of the hot sun or else lightly rubbed in order to release their fragrance, but some are extremely fragrant without that help. The rose geranium (*Pelargonium graveolens*), which has a spicy rose scent, is one of the oldest and still one of the most popular kinds.

Planting. Geranium bushes grow 1–4 feet tall: only up to a foot if grown in a pot in the north, up to 4 feet if grown outdoors in a subtropical zone. They can be grown in the garden in summer in a moderate temperate zone, but must be moved inside in a container before frost. They're most often kept permanently in a container; they actually do better when pot-bound and will keep thus for years. Don't move the pot outside until the sunny days of early summer. Propagate by making stem or root cuttings from new young shoots. They can be planted from seed, but since you cannot depend on the seeds to grow true to type, you're better off starting with a plant. Plant in dry, sandy, fertile soil. Place in full sun. Keep on the dry side.

Using. Good in sachets and potpourris, as floaters in finger bowls, and for making perfumes, scenting cosmetics, and flavoring drinks. Make a tea out of the leaves, or flavor a compote or pound cake. To flavor any cake, put a leaf in the bottom of your cake pan and pour the cake batter over it. To flavor jelly, put a leaf of rose geranium in the bottom of the glass. Oil of geranium has some insecticidal value.

> *GERANIUM POTPOURRI Combine 8 c. geranium leaves, 2 c. geranium flower petals, 1 c. leaves from your choice of a fragrant mint (all pre-dried), and 1 T. each of powdered coriander seeds and powdered cardamom seeds. Use gum benzoin (1½ oz.) or orrisroot as your fixative. From Janice Lamp, Port Orchard, WA.*

> *GERANIUM-ROSE POTPOURRI Combine 3 c. rose petals, 3 c. geranium petals, 1 c. peppermint leaves, 1 c. lavender petals, 1 T. powdered nutmeg, 1 T. powdered cloves, and powdered orris or 2 oz. gum benzoin for fixative. (See "Potpourri" under "Products and Processes" for additional recipes and instructions about fixatives.)*

> *ROSE GERANIUM CAKE Sift together 2 c. flour, ½ t. salt, and 1 t. baking powder. Cream ½ c. butter and 1 c. sugar. Add alternately the flour and ⅔ c. water. Finally, add the unbeaten whites of 4 eggs. Whip hard for 5 minutes. Line a loaf pan with buttered paper and rose geranium leaves. Pour in batter. Bake in a 350°F oven for 30–45 minutes. Pull the leaves off with the paper when the cake is done.*

> *ROSE GERANIUM JELLY Make by flavoring apple jelly. Wash the apples, but do not peel or core. Quarter the apples and barely cover with water. Simmer until tender. Get the juice and put it through the jelly bag, measure apple juice, and return it to the stove. When it is boiling, add ¾ c. sugar per 1 c. juice. Boil on to jelly stage. When almost done, put a few rose geranium leaves into the boiling jelly. They quickly give off their flavor. Dip them up and down until you have the desired taste and fragrant smell. Use 2 or 3 leaves for each pint. Tint a rose color with food coloring. Remove the leaves. Pour the jelly into your jars and seal.*

GINGER (*ZINGIBER OFFICINALE*): This is a tropical Asian native; it can grow outside in Puerto Rico or Florida, but north of that needs a greenhouse or comparable hot, humid room in your home to thrive. Cold wet dirt kills ginger. Ginger is grown for the root, which is not really a root but a "rhizome," an enlarged underground stem. Ginger root is spicy. An old-time horse trading trick was to poke some ginger up the tail end of a tired old horse right before sale time; it would prance around and act very young!

Planting. Ginger does well in a medium-sized container. Plant in well- and regularly fertilized dirt—but not sandy, pebbly, or gravelly soil. Water well and frequently. If outdoors, it needs partial shade. The stems grow 3–4 feet tall, leaves almost a foot long. Outdoor tropical plants are harvested in December and planted in February; you can actually harvest anytime after 5 months, but the longer you wait, the bigger the root gets. When purchasing, make sure you get *Zingiber officinale* and not an ornamental ginger variety. You might be able to get one from the store to grow, but best would be to order root from Exotica or Gurney.

To propagate, save a rhizome out from the harvest. Like a potato, it has "eyes." Wait 2 months; then divide the root and plant the eyes 3 inches deep and 14 inches apart. Multiple plants can grow from the knobby root, one from each place where it bulges and gets closer to ground level.

Fresh Ginger Root. If in good condition, the root will be firm, with a light-brown outside skin that is papery. Wash, dry, and bag. It will keep in your fridge for 2 weeks. If you substitute grated or minced fresh ginger (or sliced ginger, or ginger put through a garlic press) in a recipe that calls for ground ginger (as in gingerbread), be prepared for the fact that fresh ginger is stronger and also has quite a different taste.

Preserving. Fresh ginger can be candied, crystallized, or preserved in syrup. If peeled and immersed in sherry, it will keep a long time, and you can use the sherry for flavoring too. For one of these sweet methods of preservation, ginger should be harvested at 8 rather than 10 months. To freeze ginger root, just wash a whole piece, dry, wrap in freezer paper, and freeze. Don't blanch it. To cook with your frozen ginger root, just take it out, grate or slice off as much as you need, and put the leftover part back in the freezer.

Using. To make fresh ground ginger, trim off the leaves, cut the root into pieces, wash in very hot water, spread the pieces outside, and dry in the sun. When totally dry, grind. Ginger root has been discovered by researchers to counter motion sickness, so give your children gingerbread or pumpkin pie to take on a long drive! Or serve ginger-flavored preserves, fruit pickles, Chinese dishes (anything with soy sauce in it!), Indian food, or applesauce. Ginger is also a time-honored home remedy for worms and nausea.

> *GINGER SUGAR Into a bowl, sift together 2 c. sugar and ¼ c. ground ginger; combine well. Transfer the mixture to an airtight container, and let stand for at least 3 days. Use to flavor cakes, puddings, squash, and applesauce and to glaze hams.*

> *GINGER ALE Ginger ale is a good base for lots of other drinks when mixed with various fruit juices. If you like it stronger, just add more ginger. If your weather is cold, add more yeast. If it's hot outside, be prepared to refrigerate it as soon as you have the desired amount of fizz. It takes only a couple of days for it to work enough to be a real "pop" beverage.*
> *Dissolve 2½–3 c. honey or 5¼ c. sugar in 2 gal. water. Add the beaten whites of 3 eggs and 1 T. ginger moistened with water. Put into a large pan and bring to the boiling point. Skim and set aside to cool. (You'll think you're losing all the ginger, but don't worry. Even though a lot of it gets caught in this skimming, the flavor is there.) When lukewarm, add the juice of 4 lemons and ¼ t. dry yeast. Stir well. Let stand a few moments. Strain through a cloth. In 48 hours it will be ready to drink.*
> *NOTE: Don't seal ginger ale into anything unless you then heat it enough to kill the yeast, or you'll have an explosion from the gas pressure, and somebody could lose an eye or something awful!*

> *ANOTHER GINGER ALE RECIPE Pound 3 T. ginger root. Pour 4 qt. boiling water over it. Add the juice of 1 lime, 3 c. sugar or the equivalent in another sweetening, and 3 T. cream of tartar. Cover with a cloth so flies don't drop in. Cool to lukewarm. Add 1 T. yeast. Let rest 6 hours; then chill and serve.*

> *UNFERMENTED GINGER ALE Cut 4 oz. ginger root into small pieces and mix with 4 lemons. Cut into strips as thin as you can manage. Pour 2 qt. boiling water over the mixture and let set 5 minutes. Strain out the solids and chill your liquid. Add 2 c. lemon juice and sweeten to taste. Dilute*

with cold water if it tastes strong or if intended for small children. Serve with ice and mint leaves in the glass for a hot weather special.

⮞ *MINT GINGERADE* *Pour 2 c. sweetened boiling water (with a dash of salt in it—helps draw out the mint flavor) over 2 c. finely chopped mint leaves. Let stand until cool. Strain out the leaves. Add 2 qt. ginger ale or gingerade and serve very cold, garnished with a pretty mint sprig.*

Now here are some recipes for nice beverage mixes you can make once your ginger ale is done. (Or start with store-bought ginger ale or fizzy water.)

⮞ *GINGER SPICED APPLE* *Combine 1 qt. apple juice, 6 cinnamon sticks, 16 whole cloves, and ¼ t. nutmeg, and bring to a slow boil for 10 minutes. Strain. Chill. Add 1 qt. chilled ginger ale.*

⮞ *GINGER GRAPE* *Combine 4 c. ginger ale, 2 c. grape juice (or grapefruit or orange juice), 3 T. lemon juice, and a sprig of mint (optional). Add the ginger ale just before serving over ice.*

⮞ *GINGER, GRAPE, GRAPEFRUIT* *Combine 3 c. ginger ale, 2 c. grapefruit juice, and 2 c. grape juice.*

⮞ *GINGER MINT LEMON* *Gather a bunch of mint, discarding the stems. Bruise the leaves and cover with ½ c. water and 1 c. lemon juice. Let soak an hour. Add 6 c. ginger ale, sweeten to taste, and serve over ice.*

⮞ *GINGER PUNCH* *Cook ¾ c. sugar (or ½ c. honey) in 4 c. water for 3 minutes. Add ½ c. lemon juice, 1 c. orange juice, grated rind of ½ orange, and 1 T. grated lemon rind. Cool. Add 1 qt. ginger ale (or 1 qt. tea).*

GINKGO BILOBA: You'll find much about the amazing ginkgo biloba tree at **www.xs4all.nl/~kwanten/.**

GINSENG (*PANAX QUINQUEFOLIUS*): This herb can be grown outdoors in many parts of the United States. More than 90 percent of the crop is exported. This is a great commercial crop if you can grow it, the most expensive herb in the marketplace, prized by Asians for its effects on both women and men.

A great info resource for ginseng growers is back issues of the bimonthly newsletter *Northwest Ginseng News,* which was published from 1992 through 1999. All back issues are available, with subject index, in a 3-ring binder. This is the complete reference guide to the markets, history, establishment, maintenance, disease management, weed control, harvesting, and drying of ginseng. The cost is $115, plus $5 shipping: 360-887-3128; fax 360-887-0320; Pacific Rim Ginseng, 1600 NE 236th St., Ridgefield, WA 98642; **ginseng@e-z.net.**

Ginseng roots are expensive, however, and they need a northern habitat to grow. In its fourth season, each plant will produce 20 seeds—unless you've already lost them to rodents of all sorts, who devour both root and tops. Even having seeds isn't an easy answer. Ginseng seed, even if viable when grown or purchased, takes as long as 18 months to germinate. If it dries out before that, it is likely to die. Don't plant ginseng in an ordinary greenhouse; it will probably die or do poorly. What it needs is well-drained, highly organic forest soil in a shady area. Plant your roots or seeds spaced 12–18 inches apart, weed conscientiously, and mulch with fallen leaves.

Harvesting. If you can avoid climate and rodent problems, you can indeed do well financially from a few acres of ginseng—if you can afford to wait long enough: The roots are not harvested until mid-October of the sixth or seventh year after planting! Dig the roots out with their forks intact; don't scrape or scrub! To cure, dry them at 60–80°F for 3 days and then at 90°F. Roots over 2 inches in diameter will need 6 weeks at 90°F to cure, smaller ones less. Have them well-ventilated and spread thinly; turn frequently to prevent mildew.

Using. Ginseng is a stimulant. Much of the commercial stuff is only mildly effective, but fresh ginseng can be very powerful, so use discretion.
NOTE: Prolonged use of ginseng can result in nervousness, insomnia, and high blood pressure.

GOLDENSEAL: You can get 200+ varieties of herbs, including goldenseal, from Herbal Comfort; 573-857-2727; Hwy. 160, 7 miles E. of Doniphan, MO; HC1 Box 717, Fairdealing, MO 63939 (they also sponser a May herb festival). Steven Foster, of Frontier Natural Products Co-op, sells goldenseal root (bulbs) and buys its product: **www. frontiercoop.com.** Meeks Farm & Nursery, 37305 160th Ave. SE, Auburn, WA 98002; 253-735-0245; **bmeeks92@ ix.netcom.com;** provides goldenseal roots and growing instructions to interested persons. Steve Edwards sells starts of ginseng, goldenseal, and other medicinal plants at Aspen Hill Farms: 231-582-6790; Box 750 Anderson Rd., Boyne City, MI 49712. Or buy whole plants, large or small, and a goldenseal growing video (30 minutes, $30) from NC Ginseng & Goldenseal Co.: 828-649-3536; 300 Indigo Bunting Lane, Marshall, NC 28753; **robert@ncgoldenseal.com; www.ncgoldenseal.com.**

The Herb Growing and Marketing Network, **www. herbworld.com,** offers a report, "Goldenseal: A North American Treasure! Will It Disappear in Our Lifetime?" Jeanine Davis or George Cox of the Mountain Horticultural Crops Research and Extension Center, Fletcher, NC, provide a production guide and list of sources on their website: **www.ncherb.org;** 828-684-3562; fax 828-684-8715. A free brochure, "Agroforestry Notes: Forest Production of Goldenseal," is available from the USDA National Agroforestry Center: 402-437-5178; East Campus, UNL, Lincoln, NE. ATTRA provides info on growing ginseng, goldenseal, and other native roots in a "Horticulture Technical Note" and in personal consultations: 800-346-9140; **www.attra.org/ attra-pub/ginsgold.html#commercial.** Read "Commercial Production of Ginseng and Goldenseal" at **www.hort. purdue.edu/newcrop/NewCropsNews/94-4-1/ginseng. html.**

Goldenseal is listed by the Convention on International Trade of Endangered Species, so be cautious when exporting. A general permit can be obtained from the USDA, Animal and Plant Health Inspection Service, Division of Plant Protection and Quarantine, 4700 River Rd., Riverdale, MD 20737-1236.

HEMP: For more info, read *Comeback of the World's Most Promising Plant* (Chelsea Green); and *Hemp Culture,* by Chas. Richards Dodge (1895), available from Caber Press (call/fax 503-735-3942; **tcl@teleport.com; www.teleport. com/~tcl).**

HENNA (*LAWSONIA INERMIS*): You can grow the henna bush, a well-known source of cosmetic and hair products, even in the temperate zone—if you dig it up, pot it, and bring it inside for the winter. It's an Old World tropical shrub or small tree of the loosestrife family. It bears aromatic white flowers and small leaves. The famous dye is made from those leaves and is used to make paint for skin designs in India or as a rinse that gives hair a reddish tint. In quantity, you can give yourself a serious dye job. Available from Hudson.

HOPS (*HUMULUS LUPULUS*): Once every farm had a few of these hardy perennial vines. The light green flowers of the female plant, which look and smell like pine cones, bloom in the summer and are harvested in the fall. Speaking precisely, those flowers are your "hops." They are used commercially to flavor ales and beer and can also be used to season food. Because of its alkaline qualities, hops were also used by some pioneer bread bakers to help leaven the sourdough. Publications on hops are available from ATTRA (800-346-9140) and WSU (**pubs.wsu.edu/**).

Planting. Hops are usually started from root division of female plants, although you could start with seed. Plant in full sun. They need well-drained, fertile found, and regular and generous watering. They must be helped to grow where you want them. Their natural inclination is to grow straight up and very high. They can be trained over an arbor, up a trellis or support post, or out of a pot. And they grow fast—15–25 feet in a summer. Chop them back annually to keep them from taking over the place. They shed their leaves for winter, like grapes, but come back in the spring.

Harvesting. Gather the hops before they get to the shattering point and before they get frosted. Dry in an airy but shady place.

⧁ *ZHEDAHOOBLO* *This spring specialty of the American pioneers is still an epicurean treat in Europe. Cut off the top 6 inches of the earliest spring shoots of hops, and cook just like asparagus. Because of their thinness, you'll need a lot for a meal. Adding lemon juice to the cooking water helps them hold color. Serve with a white sauce. Eating the shoots helps thin the crop, for once established, the hop vines will send up twice as many shoots as they should.*

HOREHOUND (*MARRUBIUM VULGARE*): This is also called white horehound because the leaves and stems are covered with thick silky hairs that make it look frosted. (There is a Spanish horehound, *Marrubium suppinum*, which is not the one you want.) It's a small, hardy perennial bush that gets around 15 inches tall. It's a medicinal herb that has been used for centuries to treat coughing and bronchial congestion. Because of its extreme bitterness, it has usually been administered in association with sugar, as in the famous horehound candy (cough drop) of Victorian times. Either in tea or cough drops, it's still considered a good treatment for a cough or asthma.

Planting. To propagate, plant a clump division in the spring, or plant seeds 1 inch deep early in the spring in a sunny, well-drained place with light soil. Thin later to 8 inches. Although horehound is hardy, it tends to die if a harsh winter is also a soggy one. Place it in a well-drained site, and mulch the roots. Available from DeGiorgi.

Harvesting. Just before flowers open in late summer, cut off smaller stems near the ground, and cut off just the tops of larger stems. Break into 3–4-inch sections. Dry in a

warm, shaded, airy place or in an oven or dehydrator at 115°F until brittle. Store in covered glass.

⧁ *HOREHOUND TEA* *Bring 3 pieces horehound just to a boil in 4 c. water; then steep 15 minutes. Serve hot and sweetened. If unbearably bitter, dilute some more.*

⧁ *HOREHOUND CANDY* *These are basic instructions for making saltwater taffy.*

1. Prepare the herb: Combine 2 heaping t. dried horehound and 1 c. water in a non-aluminum pan. Gradually bring to a boil. Take off heat and let steep 30 minutes. Strain. Put the horehound in a cloth, and press or twist to get every last drop of flavor. Boil juice down to concentrate. (If you want, you can also boil to make tea. The medicinal component in horehound is not hurt by boiling.)

2. Make the candy: Mix 1 c. sugar and 2 T. cornstarch in a 1½ qt. non-aluminum pan. Now make the candy: Stir in ¾ c. light corn syrup, ½ c. water, 2 T. margarine, and ½ t. salt. Cook over medium heat, stirring constantly, until sugar completely dissolves. Continue cooking, without stirring, until temperature reaches 260°F, or until a hard but shapeable ball is formed in cold water. Remove from stove.

3. Combine and finish: Stir in horehound flavoring concentrate. At this point you could substitute 1 t. of any herbal or commercial flavoring extract, plus coloring, instead of horehound.) Pour onto lightly greased cookie sheet. Let stand until cool enough to handle. Grease hands and pull until it has a satin-like finish and a light color. Cut into 1-inch pieces. To store, wrap in waxed paper.

HORSERADISH (*ARMORACIA RUSTICANA*): Because this is strong stuff, a comparatively few plants will suffice for your family use. It is a perennial relative of mustard, not of the proper radishes. Tender, young, early-spring horseradish leaves will add a mustard-like taste to a ham or cheese sandwich with their hot taste, but most commonly it is grown for the roots. It's a good plant for a cold climate.

Controlling. You can grow horseradish in a container. In fact, that might be the best way, since it can be hard to control once started in your garden; any bit of separated root will grow into a new plant. Or plant outside with edging, such as a bottomless bucket or a trench lined with plastic or slate. Give manure occasionally and water once in a while.

Planting. Horseradish is propagated from a root cutting. Any root has several side roots growing from the upper part of the main one. Cut those off straight-sided where they join the big root. Trim off the tip of the root at a slant. The time to do this is in the fall, when you are harvesting your horseradish crop. Store your root cuttings in damp sand in your root cellar until late winter or very early spring, when you can get into the garden. Dig 6-inch-deep trenches in fertile, heavy, well-tilled soil. You can make horseradish rows just a foot apart and space the plants also a foot apart. (These instructions are for commercial scale.) Lay the root cutting in at something approaching a 45° angle, straight-cut (thicker) end to the topside. Cover with dirt so that the top of the root is about 3 inches underground. Pack soil firmly around the roots.

Making "Straight" Roots. Commercial growers clean off the lateral roots by digging away the dirt from the top 4 inches of the horseradish root when it's 9–12 inches long and stripping off the lateral roots from that area. Then they replace that dirt.

Harvesting. Some people insist that horseradish roots are tastiest when little and that harvesting should commence as soon as the roots are well started. Some are positive that horseradish is at its best only in the fall after experiencing several frosts. You can dig up the thick, white roots the fall after you planted them, any time from September until the ground freezes. You can also dig up the roots in the early spring before the leaves start. But keep in mind that horseradish makes its greatest growth in late summer and early fall, so you'd get the biggest harvest in the fall. (You could dig all winter if the ground isn't frozen and you want to.) Harvesting horseradish also keeps the plants from spreading beyond where you want them. (Any root, or piece of root, left in the ground will grow again.) About 4 days before harvesting, remove the tops of those you plan to harvest as near to the ground as possible; that makes them die back. Dig up; after digging, use them very soon, or store them.

Storing. Folks usually just dig as they need roots, because they keep best right in the ground. If you must dig and then wait, store them layered in damp sawdust or sand in a root cellar or outdoor pit. If roots are stored at 32–40°F and 90–95 percent humidity, they'll keep 4–6 months.

Preparing. It's a good idea to wear gloves when you are preparing horseradish. Keep juice away from your eyes! The hot flavor comes from the "mustard oil" they contain. Scrub roots clean. Don't be disturbed about how they look; homegrown horseradish roots are more crooked than those raised for market, which are uprooted, trimmed, and then replanted. Peel off the brown outer skin with a vegetable peeler. Drop them into cold water right after peeling to prevent discoloration. Then put in a blender, through a food grinder, or grate. (Makes you cry worse than onions.) Put the ground horseradish in a half-pint, pint, or baby-food jar.

Preserving. Add vinegar to moisten your grated horseradish and prevent it from turning color: white wine vinegar (unless you want pink horseradish) or distilled vinegar. (Cider vinegar causes the grated horseradish to turn dark within a comparatively short time.) Add ½ c. vinegar per 1 c. grated horseradish. Optionally, add ¼ t. salt (or sugar), or a little beet ground in to make it red. Mix, pack in jars, and tightly cap. It is important to get the grated root finished and bottled as quickly as possible. Refrigerate the prepared horseradish to keep it "hot." It's preferable to just make it as you need it, since over long usage, the vinegar will gradually evaporate and need replacement. After a month or so, your horseradish may be turning brownish and have less flavor even though kept in the fridge.

◈ NO-TEARS HORSERADISH *From Lois Rumrill, Forks of Salmon, CA: Scrub and cut roots into pieces. Pour 1–2 c. vinegar into blender pitcher. Put in several pieces of horseradish and turn blender on. Keep adding pieces of the roots until the vinegar just covers them. Pour all into clean, small jars, cap, and refrigerate. For additional batches, just repeat the process.*

Lois wrote me, "I like the horseradish in the vinegar a lot better than in water, and making it this way I don't shed any tears when 'grinding' it. But if you prefer water, use water in place of the vinegar in this process. The thing you can't do with horseradish is heat or can it, because that weakens it."

Drying. Dry the root, grind to a powder, and put up in bottles in dry form. Prepared this way, it will keep much longer, but it does not make as good a relish as when grated fresh.

Serving. Serve horseradish with hot roast beef or any cold meats; or hot; or in salad dressing, with fish, or just on homemade dark buttered bread.

◈ SIMPLEST HORSERADISH SPREAD *Mix grated root with a little bit of vinegar and a big bit of thick cream.*

◈ SOUR CREAM HORSERADISH *Chill ½ c. sour cream thoroughly, and then whip it until stiff. Add ½ t. sugar (or pinch salt) and whip some more. Fold in 2 T. of your prepared horseradish. Serve with meatloaf or ham.*

◈ FANCY SOUR CREAM HORSERADISH *To the above recipe, add 1 T. chopped chives, or parsley and 1 T. vinegar, or a pinch cayenne pepper, or ½ t. prepared mustard, or a dash Tabasco, or ¼ t. pepper, or a combination thereof.*

◈ HORSERADISH SANDWICH FILLING *Mix equal quantities of finely grated horseradish and mayonnaise. The horseradish can be topped with thinly sliced tomato, cucumber, radish, or chopped watercress. Spread between thin slices of buttered brown bread.*

◈ HORSERADISH SAUCE *Melt 1 T. butter. Blend in 1 T. flour. Add 1 c. soup stock or water. Cover and heat to boiling. Stir in ½ c. freshly grated horseradish, 1 T. lemon juice, and salt and pepper to taste. Simmer 2 minutes and serve. This is especially good with tongue.*

◈ HORSERADISH MILK SAUCE *In the top of your double boiler, combine 3 T. butter and 3 T. flour. Make a paste. Gradually add 1½ c. milk and then ⅓ c. grated horseradish. Cook over simmering water 20 minutes. Add ½ t. salt and a pinch pepper, and you have your sauce.*

HYSSOP (HYSSOPUS OFFICINALIS): This unusually attractive, hardy perennial herb grows 1½–2 feet high and provides an old-time medicine for sinus/chest problems. Great for bees, since it blooms profusely all summer (July–Nov.) with lovely, intense blue flowers. (There are also white and pink varieties. Grows like a low shrub (cut it back to keep it blooming), and leaves stay on most of the year, so it makes good edging for your herb garden. Birds like the seeds.

Planting. Plant seeds (viable 3–4 years) indoors and cover. Germinates easily in 10 days, if warm. (In garden, hyssop tends to self sow.) You can also propagate by division or tip cuttings of young shoots. Set out 10 inches apart in slightly alkaline soil, full sun or partly shaded spot. Can handle some drought. Available from William Dam and DeGiorgi.

Harvesting. Cutting back the plant regularly makes it keep producing the tender young leaves you'll want for harvesting. Dry as you would basil.

Using. You don't need many leaves. Hyssop is bitter, strong stuff. Use it to flavor sausages or any stuffed meat or pork, or use it in any strongly flavored meat dish, soup, stew, or vegetable juice. The tea, especially sweetened with honey, is a traditional treatment for colds, coughs, asthma, and sinus problems. Gourmet restaurants put anise hyssop leaves in salads.

IRIS: There are a multitude of varieties of iris, but old-time orrisroot powder is made from the "white flag" kind (*Iris florentina*). It's a perennial that grows 2 feet high, blooms early in summer, and is cultivated for the dried root, which is fragrant (violet-scented) and is powdered to make a fixative for potpourris and sachets. *NOTE: All parts of the iris plant and the orrisroot powder made from it are poisonous!*

Planting. Rhizomes (underground stems that look like roots) are planted lying horizontally with the upper side showing just over the ground level. They prefer light soil and partial sun. The plants propagate rapidly at the root and need to be dug up in late summer (August) and divided every few years. To divide, cut them apart, leaving each piece some roots, a stem, and a fan of leaves above that. After they bloom, cut off the flower stems. That will improve the quality of the root.

Preparing. Use your surplus roots to make orrisroot powder. Wash the dirt off the roots with running water. Dry them like other roots. When absolutely dry and brittle, cut them into very fine chips. Dry those chips about 3 more days, stored in a paper bag in a dark, dry place. They will then keep fine for years. You'd better label them "Poisonous!" The orrisroot chips (or a powder made from them with a mortar and pestle) keep potpourris and sachets fragrant for years. Orrisroot also absorbs the general fragrance of the other substances in there and holds it. Use ¼ c. chipped or powdered orris to 4 c. fragrant materials (see "Potpourri").

JOJOBA: This plant does well in a dryish situation. The oil extracted from the seeds is used in shampoos, etc. Available from DeGiorgi.

JUNIPER (*JUNIPERUS COMMUNIS*): This shrubby perennial conifer grows to only 6 feet at most—even less in the windswept areas to which it's naturally adapted. It's hardy and will grow just about anywhere it can get sun. The plants are male or female. The females bear berries, which ripen extraordinarily slowly—2 to 3 years. As they ripen, they change color, from green to black with a bluish cast. Wait until fully ripe to pick. Dry and then store. Before use, crush lightly. Juniper is used commercially to flavor gin. You can use it to flavor sauerkraut, stews, wild meat sauces, or casseroles. But go easy on it—it's strong stuff.

KENAF: This is an annual non-wood fiber plant from central Africa. Related to okra and cotton, it can grow to 12–18 ft. in a 6-month growing season. It's the great new hope for a pulp plant to replace trees in papermaking: "Kenaf Production" is at **www.attra.org/attra-pub/kenaf.html**. The American Kenaf Society promotes products and uses of this plant: 520-741-0840; 250 E. Valencia Rd., Tucson, AZ 85706; **www.kenafsociety.org.** For seed and growing info contact The International Kenaf Ass'n at 903-367-7216; 101 Depot, PO Box 7, Ladonia, TX 75449; **bledso@ koyote.com; www.kenafseed.com.**

LAVENDER: This semi-hardy perennial blooms from June to August with fragrant blue and purple bee-attracting flowers—possibly the most wonderfully scented plant, fresh or dried. It grows 1–3 feet high (trim back after harvest of flowers if you want it shorter). Catherine Shirley wrote me, "The true lavender is a small shrubby plant native to southern Europe. The plant thrives best in hot sun and light and rather dry soil well supplied with lime. On low and wet land it is certain to winterkill. It also should be loosely covered to prevent the snow from getting inside the branches which freeze and thus winterkill."

There are many different varieties: English lavender (*Lavandula vera*), spike lavender (*Lavandula spica*), and French lavender (*Lavandula stoechas*). *Lavandula angustifolia* is another name for all three. English lavender is the hardiest, and mulching can get it through a winter. Dwarf kinds grow 12 inches tall and are suited to a pot life, 1 or 2 plants in a 6–8-inch pot. More tender varieties are best brought in for the winter.

For more info request ATTRA's free brochure, "Lavender as an Alternative Farming Enterprise" (800-346-9140; **www.attra.org**). Read Virginia McNaughton's book, *Lavender: The Grower's Guide* (Timber Press, 2000). And visit **fletcher.ces.state.nc.us/staff/jmdavis/lav.htm.**

Planting. Be choosy about the plants you buy. Some lavenders are not of commercial quality and do not produce quality oil. Lavender seeds can live 2–3 years. The plant can be started from seed, but it grows very slowly. It is more readily propagated from stem cuttings (6 inches long), by layering, or by division. Plant deep. Cuttings should be set in well-prepared soil in early spring, 12–15 inches apart, in rows spaced to suit the cultivation intended.

Lavender can be grown as a hedge to give plenty of flowers for harvesting. Frequent and thorough cultivation is desirable. Growth is slow, and plants do not produce any considerable quantity of flowers for several years, but full crops may be expected for some time thereafter if the plants are given proper care. They should not be watered very much. Lavender grown in poor soil that is limy and gravelly produces the most strongly scented flowers. Available from William Dam and DeGiorgi (3 varieties).

The Sequim area of Washington state has many lavender specialists who offer plants, products (aromatherapy, sachets, dried lavender, lotions, fragrance, etc.), and/or volume plugs. Here are some specifics:

Cedarbrook Herb Farm: 50+ varieties; 360-663-7733; **cedbrook@olypen.com; www.lavenderfarms.com/ cedarbrook;** 1345 S. Sequim Ave., Sequim, WA 98382.

Lavender & Herb Growers of Franklin County, MA: 413-772-0858; fax 413-772-8858; 56 Glenbrook Rd., Greenfield, MA 01301; **www.laverland.com.**

Olympic Lavender Farm: 360-683-4475; 1432 Marine Dr., Sequim, WA 98382; **www.lavenderfarms.com/ olympic/main.htm.**

Purple Haze Lavender Farm: Mike Reichner; 888-852-6560 (orders); office 360-582-3088; fax 360-681-5427; 180 Bell Bottom Rd., Sequim, WA 98382; **purphaze@olypen.com; www.purplehazelavender.com.** Great website and links!

Rancho Allegre has 5,000 lavender plants and produces essential oil, dried flowers, 20 lavender varieties, and plugs: 650-879-1876; PO Box 538, Pescadero, CA 94064; **ditz@earthlink.net.**

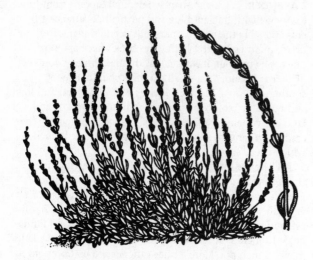

Harvesting. Gather the flowering tops or "spikes" as soon as the first buds on a spike begin to open. That's when the flowers have their strongest scent. Catherine wrote me, "A lot of fragrance can be lost if they're left standing too long, especially if rain falls on them. If the plant got wet already, cut without waiting for all buds to bloom. For production of oil, the leaves are generally used rather than the flowers, and they are distilled at once without drying. (To prevent plants turning woody, prune them back sharply every year after harvest.) If dry flowers are wanted for sachets, shake the spikes over spread-out paper, as some buds will fall off. Carefully hang the spikes up to dry in an airy room (in the shade). Takes about 3 weeks. Once dried the flowers are stripped from the stems by hand."

CAUTION: Inhaled lavender can cause sneezing, tearing, and even vomiting, so wear a dust mask or respirator while working with it, and keep animals out of the room!

Using. Old-timers kept it simple; they just hung some bunches of dried lavender from the ceiling or placed them between folded clothes in a drawer. But the dried flowers and buds can be used in bath water, potpourris, fragrances, and sachets for scenting linens; as a tea herb; as a scent for soap and commercial cosmetics; and in jellies and wine vinegar. They'll keep moths out of the cupboard too. You can also get a good and useful lavender oil that improves with age.

LAVENDER BOOKMARKS Catherine wrote, "Real short lavender spikes with flowers and buds can be artistically arranged between 2 small squares of nylon tulle, nylon organdy, or any stiff transparent material in a sandwichlike fashion. Secure the spikes with glue that dries clear or a few small staples so the spikes do not move around. Then sew patches of pretty braid or tapes around the edge on all sides to suit your fancy. Good gift for people who read a lot."

LAVENDER SACHET POWDER Mix ½ oz. dried powdered lavender flowers with ½ t. powdered cloves. Sew them up tightly in a little cloth pillow and leave the pillow in a bureau drawer to perfume the clothes. That's old-time elegance.

LAVENDER WATER Dissolve 3 drops oil of lavender in 2 c. distilled water. Age at least a week. It's better with a lump of sugar in it, but then it has a tendency to ferment and go bad. A perfume.

LEMON BALM: See "Balm, Lemon."

LEMONGRASS (*CYMBOPOGON CITRATUS*): This tender Asian native looks like a green onion, but the leaves are greyish green and spearlike. It's not pretty. It can be grown in the temperate zone but must come indoors in a container for the winter because frost kills it.

Planting. One way to get started is to find it at an Oriental grocery. Look for some with the root still on it. Put it in water in a glass jar. Set the jar by a window that gets lots of sun. The roots will grow. Once the roots have expanded a good bit, plant it where it can get 4–6 hours of sunshine each day. Water only once in a while, but water thoroughly when you do.

Using. Lemongrass needs to be harvested. Cut the long blades, wash, and drain. To use fresh, cut into short sections. Or dry those sections at 110°F until crisp and crumbly (6–8 hours). You can powder and store it, but it will lose its flavor quickly. Its peculiar citrus flavor is great in Mexican and Asian cuisine. Some people like a tea made from its steeped dry leaves. Soak dried lemongrass in hot water for an hour to get the flavor out.

LEMON VERBENA (*LIPPIA CITRIODORA*, FORMERLY *ALOYSIA CITRIODORA*): This is an attractive perennial shrub (up to 6 feet tall) with pink flowers.

Planting. Plant after last frost, and bring back in before the last warm summer evenings are over. To propagate, make cuttings of shoots early in the summer and plant in light, well-drained soil.

Harvesting. The lemon verbena leaves are at their best during early apple harvest season. You can dry leaves for winter use or use fresh (finely chopped) to make a soothing tea, good at bedtime. For lemon flavoring, add fresh lemon verbena leaves to drinks, fruit desserts, fruit salad, and jellies. The leaves are also good in potpourri or sachets.

LICORICE: *Glycyrrhiza glabra* is the plant from whose root licorice flavoring comes. It's a perennial. Plant seed in spring, or do root division in spring or fall. To harvest, wait until the roots are 3 years old. Licorice has a mild laxative effect, a very sweet taste, and a tradition of flavoring cough syrups and candies.

LOVAGE (*LEVISTICUM OFFICINALE*): This Mediterranean-originating hardy perennial resembles angelica, grows 6–7 feet high, and is considered by some to be one of the loveliest herbs.

Planting. Plant seeds (they won't keep) in fall or spring, or do root division. Plant in moist, fertile soil, in sun or light shade, 12 inches apart. You need only a few plants. Dies in winter, but comes back from roots in spring. Available from William Dam and DeGiorgi.

Using. You can harvest and use in your kitchen lovage leaves, seeds, stalks, and roots, fresh or dried. They all taste somewhat like celery and can be used to flavor salad, soups, or meats. (Go easy; they're strong.) You can save the seeds and use them anywhere you would celery seed. To harvest roots, give them 3 years to get well-grown.

MACE: This spice comes from the seed (nutmeg) of the tropical nutmeg tree (see "Nutmeg"). It has an outer shell that is covered by a lacy red network called aril. The peach-like fruit of the tree is edible. Save the kernel. Remove the aril and sun-dry. The dried pieces of aril are called blade mace. When ground, the powder is called mace and is used to flavor meats, fruit, sweet baked goods, and jams—but nutmeg is considered the better choice for sweet dishes, with mace the better choice for meat.

MARIGOLD, POT (CALENDULA OFFICINALIS): This hardy annual flower has a bold and pleasant golden color. Of all the varieties of marigolds, the pot marigold (also known as calendula) is the most important. The flowers and leaves of all marigolds can be used in salads or soups, but the pot marigold also yields an ointment used by traditional healers to treat ulcers and wounds. Plant in fall or early spring in full sun. Because pot marigold repels many garden insect pests, organic gardeners like to grow lots of it around or in the garden. Petals are good in salads; you can also add petals (or a strong petal tea) to casseroles, soups, cakes, and puddings.

MARJORAM: This is one of the main branches of the Origanum family (the other is oregano). Some marjorams are merely ornamental. The culinary varieties are pot marjoram (*Origanum onites*) and sweet marjoram (*Origanum majorana*). Sweet marjoram, the generally preferred type, comes from the Mediterranean area and is "semi-hardy," unable to withstand frost and snow, so in zones 1–7 it must be grown as an annual or taken indoors. It grows 1–2 feet high, and has small gray-green leaves and small lavender or white summer blooms. If your climate allows it to grow as a perennial, it will enlarge each year to a 2–3-foot-wide bush shape. That one plant will probably be enough to meet your kitchen needs for marjoram.

Planting. Start marjoram from seeds (viable for 2–3 years), cuttings, division, or layering. Seeds germinate easily but slowly (2 weeks). It helps to soak seeds in water overnight before planting and keep planted areas moist until they're up. Plant after frost or, for most northern gardens, start inside and then transplant after last frost. Allow 5–6 square inches per plant in solid block plantings, or 9 inches in rows. Marjoram is easy to grow but is happiest in a fertile, neutral pH, well-drained, well-watered and -mulched situation. Plants also prefer partial shade. Once established, they self-sow. Marjoram is a good container plant for a windowsill that gets sun (it has a naturally shallow root system). Or just stick it in the basement for the winter; it will go dormant. Prune to avoid woodiness. Available from William Dam, Redwood City, DeGiorgi, etc.

Harvesting. For fresh leaves, cut marjoram year-round, anytime after the plant is at least 5 inches tall. When the plant begins to bloom, take the top 4 inches and dry. You can harvest again in the fall by cutting the whole plant off and drying. Don't wash; just sort the leaves and dry like basil. Marjoram is unusual in that its flavor is improved by drying!

Using. Marjoram is a basic herb in Italian cooking (spaghetti sauce! poultry stuffing!) and sausages. It makes one of the best herb butters. In the kitchen, use on hot vegetables, especially zucchini, potatoes, lima or green beans, and peas. Use fresh or dried in egg dishes, stews, soups, and gravies and with fish or meats. Orange juice flavored with marjoram makes a nice herb jelly. And you can make a good herb vinegar with it. Also good in sachets.

MARTYNIA: This unusual annual from the botanical family Martynacia is a native of the southwestern United States and is also called Proboscidea. There are more than a half-dozen types that come from various regions, from the United States south to Brazil. A desert and plains native, the plant has bristly leaves.

Varieties. *Proboscidea fragrans,* a common Mexican type, has bright red flowers whose pods pickle especially well. *P. lutea* has yellow blooms and is from Brazil. *P. annua, P. parviflora,* and *P. louisianica* (a.k.a. *P. jussieus*) all also have edible pods. *P. louisianica* is considered the best risk for northern gardeners.

Planting. You need 120 warm days to get martynia from seed to a harvest of pods. This is easy if you're gardening in the south. Northern gardeners should start martynia in a protected place. In the garden, plant 1 inch deep, rows 3 feet apart. In either case, plant near the end of February or early in March. Indoor plants in individual peat pots should go to the garden about the same time as your nightshade fruits (tomato, pepper, eggplant). Plant them in the garden 4 feet apart, rows 3 feet or further apart in full sun and fertile soil. They need to be that far apart because they spread out widely, although they get only a few feet tall. Seed available from DeGiorgi, Hudson, and Park.

Harvesting. Martynia will start flowering about 6 weeks after germination. Its large (2 inches across), lovely flowers grow in clusters of up to a dozen at the end of each stem. Each is followed by an edible seedpod that somewhat resembles an okra pod (fuzzy and green) but has a curved shape. Harvest while still tender and green. They are good cooked (either whole or sliced) in soups and stews, pickled using a dill recipe, or cooked, chilled, and served with a vinegar/oil dressing. Flower arrangers like to let them dry on the plant because of their unusual double-forked tip, which they use in dried flower arrangements, etc.

MEXICAN PARSLEY: See "Coriander."

MEXICAN TEA: See "Epazote."

MIGNONETTE (RESEDA ODORATA): Its name means "little darling." This plant is *not* for culinary use, but it dries well and is useful for potpourri because of its intense musky scent. Available from Thompson & Morgan, William Dam, etc., it's easily grown from seed and is not particular about soil. Mignonette is best suited to a dryish place with a warm summer.

MINT (MENTHA): The most important thing to understand about mint is that it is a large family of plants with various characteristics and uses. There are purely ornamental mints that are not good in the kitchen. There is an insecticidal mint, pennyroyal, that can be deadly poisonous and should never be consumed in any form. (See "Pennyroyal.") Mints are just about the easiest herb to grow—very hardy perennials that can be overly aggressive in the garden. Other than lemon balm and horehound (which have their own entries elsewhere in this section), the main culinary mints are listed below.

Apple Mints. These are a whole family in themselves. *M. rotundifolia,* called "apple mint," "wooly mint," or "Bowles

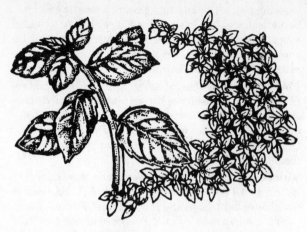

variety," is popular in English and Italian kitchens but is not considered the best culinary mint in the United States, where it grows wild. The American apple mint (*Mentha gentilis variegata*) is preferred in the United States.

Ginger Mint (*Mentha gentilis*). Also called "Golden Apple," this has a spicy mint scent and mixed gold and green leaves. It grows on the tall side for a mint, to 2 feet.

Peppermint (*Mentha piperita*). This grows 3 feet high and has small purple blooms and dark leaves with toothed rims. Peppermint has been scientifically proven effective in treating digestive problems. It's also reputed to have soothing effect, so chew on a peppermint leaf! For a good tea, mix half peppermint and half rose hips. Peppermint and spearmint are sizable commercial crops. Peppermint oil is used to make candy and medicines. It isn't an important culinary mint, but it is *the* important medicinal mint.

Orange mint (*Mentha piperita*, var. citrata) is a variety of peppermint. It's also called bergamot or eau de Cologne mint. It has light blue flowers and nice minty fragrance. It's good for scenting bath water. Available from William Dam, Thompson & Morgan, DeGiorgi, etc.

Pineapple Mint (*Mentha suaveolens* 'Variegata'). This kind has variegated foliage, soft leaves, and a pineapple scent and flavor.

Spearmint. There are several varieties, including *Mentha spicata* and *Mentha viridis*. This is the most commonly grown mint; it has pointed deep green leaves and grows 1½–2 feet high. Spearmint is good with new potatoes and green peas and is used to make mint jelly and mint sauce. *Mentha spicata* is available from DeGiorgi.

Planting. Planting from seed is one option. Or to get new plants from old, just dig up and replant runners, plantlets, or root divisions. The little plantlets grow just below the dirt surface. Be careful to cut between rather than through any baby or adult plants. Or plant a 6-inch piece of root 2 inches deep in fertile soil in spring. Mints can handle semi-shade (as little as 4–6 hours of sun per day), but they are more aromatic in drier, brighter situations. Supply lots of water to get them going. Once established, they'll thrive on neglect, but they need to be divided regularly. Thin by using. Having the right climate helps too. Gayle Lowery, Phoenix, AZ, wrote me wondering why she can't get mint to survive when grown from seed, and her store plants started by division don't thrive either. Trade them in on a cactus? *NOTE: Mint spreads ruthlessly by those creeping underground stems. To keep it where you want it, sink 12-inch boards outside its assigned growth area, or plant in a sunken, bottomless*

5-gallon bucket, tub, or plastic-lined hole. Do not try to get rid of mint by rototilling it. Each piece will grow into a new plant!

Container Mint. An 8–10-inch pot is a good choice for a tall variety in a container, a 5-inch pot for a dwarf one; a wide, shallow pot for mint grows out rather than deep down. But mints can be left out through the coldest winter, and even harvested in winter! Not everybody has boisterously growing mint, though. You can use regular dirt, but the more clay in your soil, the less likely the mint is to be able to handle waterlogging. Put enough stones or broken crockery in the bottom of the pot for good drainage. Choose a shallow pot rather than a narrow, deep one, since mint is a surface spreader rather than a deep grower.

Harvesting. Cut off plant tips; wash, dry, and cut off the leaves with your scissors. Mint can be harvested anytime, even after blooming. The more you cut, the faster it will grow. Use fresh, frozen, or dried.

Preserving. Frozen mint keeps its strength better than dried. To freeze mint, just wash, dry, and wrap a few tips of mint at a time in freezer paper or a baggie. To dry it work quickly, or the mint leaves' color will turn black. Gather only as much as you can dry in 1 batch. Spread leaves thinly over surface and dry in shade or in oven/dehydrator at 110°F. Two tablespoons fresh chopped mint are equivalent to 1½ t. dry mint or 1 t. mint extract.

Using. Good in Greek cooking and potpourri and sachets. Mint goes especially well with lamb or mutton, peas, baby potatoes, little carrots, and parsnips, and in salads, cucumber sandwiches, or a cup of tea. Crush fresh leaves just before using to release flavor. Chopped mint is good in a drink made with fresh tomatoes plus salt and pepper to taste.

BASIC PEPPERMINT TEA *Pour boiling water over a handful (4 T.) of peppermint leaves. Steep 5 minutes (less if desired less strong). Strain, pour into serving cups, sweeten to taste. Serve with affection.*

MINT SYRUP *Boil ½ c. water and ½ c. sugar for 5 minutes. Add 6 T. chopped mint leaves and ⅔ c. lemon juice. Let stand overnight. Strain. If you want it greener, color with food coloring. Put into jar and store in refrigerator. Add to iced tea, lemonade, punch, and the like for mint flavor. Garnish drink with a fresh sprig.*

MINT JELLY *You'll need 1 c. fresh mint leaves, ¼ c. boiling water, 2¾ c. sugar, and 1 qt. apple juice. Wash mint leaves; strip from stems. Add boiling water and 2½ c. sugar. Let stand a few hours. Bring to boiling point and strain through several layers of cheesecloth. Add the remaining ¼ c. sugar to apple juice and stir until it reacts to jelly test. Skim and pour into hot, sterilized jelly glasses. Seal with paraffin. If the color is too pale, add a little green food coloring.*

ICED MINT TEA *Peel and quarter a lemon. Combine 4 sprigs mint, juice of the lemon, 2 T. sugar, and 2 c. hot water and let steep a half hour. Strain. Add strips of the lemon peel. Chill and serve.*

MINTED GREEN PEAS OR NEW POTATOES *Add some sprigs of mint while boiling. Figure about 6 leaves per 4 c. vegetables plus 1 t. of butter.*

PINEAPPLE-MINT DRINK *In a blender, combine 1 c. mint leaves with 1 c. pineapple juice. Add more (about 3 c.) pineapple juice to dilute to taste. Serve over ice cubes.*

> **MINT VINEGAR SAUCE** *For roast lamb or chops. Wash and then chop very fine 1 c. mint leaves. Dissolve 1 T. sugar in 1 c. vinegar. Add the mint and let stand in the liquid 1 hour. Optionally, add 1 T. lemon juice and a dash each of salt and pepper.*

> **MINT JELLY SAUCE** *Combine 1 T. chopped mint with 1 c. currant jelly in a saucepan over low heat. Serve hot with lamb or mutton.*

> **BAKED PEARS WITH MINT** *Place 3 large, thinly sliced pears in rows in a greased baking dish. Sprinkle with ¼ t. salt and 2 T. sugar. Dot with butter. Cover and bake at 300°F for 30 minutes, or until tender. Garnish with mint sprigs and serve hot.*

> **FRUIT SALAD DRESSING** *Combine 2 T. mint vinegar, 2 T. cream, and 1 c. mayo.*

> **RUTH'S MINTY TABOULI** *Pour 4 c. boiling water over 1¼ c. cracked wheat and let stand until fluffy (about 2 hours). Drain well; then mix with 1 c. cooked garbanzos, 1¼ c. minced fresh parsley, ¾ c. minced fresh mint, ¾ c. minced scallion or onion, and 3 chopped tomatoes. Dressing: 1 c. lemon juice, ⅓ c. water, dash tamari. Chill dressed salad well before serving (at least 2 hours), and serve on lettuce leaves.*

MUGWORT (*ARTEMISIA VULGARIS*): Also called *Lactiflora*. Do not eat. Plant this perennial by seed outdoors. When dried, makes a good homemade moth repellent in cedar chest and closet. Available from Redwood City.

MUSTARD: There are 2 basic mustard varieties (black and yellow) whose seeds are used for seasoning. They are ancient and important culinary plants, their usage dating back at least to the Greeks. In addition to that spreadable yellow product, their unground seeds can be used to add a spicy hotness to recipes. Indian mustard, spinach mustard, and "mustard greens" are close relatives. Mustard seed can be viable as long as 6 years. Seeds for various mustard varieties available from Hudson, Redwood City, and DeGiorgi.

"White" or "Yellow" Mustard (*Brassica sinapelis alba*). This variety gets about 1½ feet tall. *Plant it away from your garden patch because it freely self-sows and can become a problem weed.* It's not the wild mustard we know in the Oregon and Idaho valleys. Yellow prepared mustard is made from it, and the whole mustard seed is used in pickling mixtures and to add spicy hotness to recipes. Available from DeGiorgi.

Black Mustard (*Brassica sinapelis nigra*). This hardy annual herb can get 4 feet tall. Plant in fertile, moist ground for best seed production. Has smaller blackish-red seeds. The seeds are a good flavoring and preservative for mayo, curries, and salad dressings. In France this is the prime ingredient for mustard paste. In the US it's used as a pickling spice. Available from DeGiorgi.

Harvesting and Processing. Harvest when pods have turned yellow but before they have finished ripening: once dead-ripe, they shatter and the fine seed is lost onto the ground. The harvested pods should then be spread out to dry—outdoors in the sun is fine. Once pods are thoroughly dry, smash them to free their seeds and sift to separate seeds from pods. Now work with the seeds in a mortar to loosen the hulls from the seeds. Sift and discard the papery hulls. The seeds can be used as condiments as is. Or grind your mustard seed to make wet mustard recipes. The finer you grind it, the smoother your mustard will be. But there is an

important element in the processing of commercial dry mustard that I haven't been able to find out for you, so your homeground mustard won't be quite the same as the commercial kind.

Using Leaves and Buds. Add mustard leaves that are very young and tender to soup, and cook. Or add them, in small amounts, to a salad and eat raw. Mustard buds are edible too. Gather unopened mustard buds in the early spring and serve them like broccoli with a cheese sauce.

Mustard Plaster. These were used in traditional medicine. I well remember my mother's mustard plaster remedy for a chest cold. Mix 1 part mustard with 8–10 parts flour. Add lukewarm water until you have a smooth paste. Then spread between 2 pieces of cloth, such as muslin or old sheets of flannel. Rub the chest well with Vaseline before applying to prevent blistering, and don't leave it on after the skin is well-reddened. Keep away from mouth and eyes.

Wet Mustard Recipes. Wet mustard is ground dry mustard moistened with vinegar or water, and sometimes with other seasonings added. For a thickening agent, cook your mustard mix together with beaten eggs, or evaporate to a spreadable state. Note: Commercial mustard powders vary in their ingredients and therefore also in their hotness and ability to absorb liquid. If any mustard is too spicy-hot, steaming it in a heatproof container for 15 minutes may make it milder. For more gourmet homemade mustard recipes, see *Better Than Store-Bought* by Helen Witty and Elizabeth Schneider Colchie (Harper, 1979).

> **HOMEGROWN MUSTARD** *In a blender combine unground mustard seeds with enough wine vinegar to moisten, a bit of allspice, some peppercorns, and a pinch salt. Here's a more precise recipe: Combine ¼ c. mustard seeds, ¼ c. red wine, and ⅓ c. wine vinegar, and let soak overnight. Then put in blender. Add ¼ c. water, ¼ t. allspice powder, pinch pepper, 1 minced garlic clove, ½ t. salt, 1 broken-up bay leaf, and 1 t. honey. Blend on slow. Then move mixture to the top of a double boiler and simmer over boiling water until the mix has thickened. Store in fridge.*

> **BASIC WET MUSTARD** *Mix 1 part dry mustard powder and 1 part wine vinegar. Add to taste: salt, mustard seed (cracked or whole), turmeric, garlic, other herbs, sugar or honey, etc. Then use your choice of thickening agent or process.*

> **SWEET-HOT MUSTARD** *Combine 2–4 oz. dry mustard (how much depends on how hot you like it!) and 1 c. vinegar. Cover the bowl and let rest in cool place overnight. In the morning, beat together 3 eggs and ½ c. sugar. Add to mustard/vinegar mix. Cook over medium heat, stirring constantly, until thickened (about 8 minutes). Refrigerate 2 days for flavor to ripen before using. Optionally, combine the mustard you just made with 2½ c. mayonnaise for a milder, delicious mix.*

> **SPICED MUSTARD** *Make by first spicing the vinegar and then adding other ingredients. Put 2 T. finely chopped onion, 3 bay leaves, and 1 chopped clove garlic into 1½ c. vinegar. Cover and heat in a moderate oven (325°F) for about 20 minutes. Strain out the solids. In another container, mix the amount of dry mustard you want to make up with a pinch each of powdered cinnamon and cloves and a bit of sugar. Gradually stir in the hot vinegar until the mustard is the consistency you want. Save the rest of the spiced vinegar for*

making salad dressing or more spiced mustard when you want it. Pack your mustard mix into small jars and cover when cooled.

🐝 **DIJON MUSTARD** Combine 1 large chopped onion, 3 minced cloves garlic, and 2 c. dry white wine in non-aluminum pan. Cook on low heat 10 minutes. Then let steep 15 minutes. Strain and discard solids. To your flavored liquid, now add 4 oz. dry mustard, ¼ c. honey, 1 T. plain-flavored cooking oil, and salt to taste. Simmer again, stirring constantly, while you evaporate it until it's thick enough to spread.

MYRRH: See "Sweet Cicely."

MYRTLE (*MYRTUS COMMUNIS*): This tender perennial fragrance herb gets 3 feet high when grown outside in a warm enough climate. Its leaves and flowers are useful in potpourri and sachets.

NASTURTIUM: This annual, one of the easiest plants to grow, originated in Peru, traveled back to Europe with the conquistadores, and is now known on most continents. Its pretty, brightly colored summer flowers (cream, yellow, orange, red), leaves, seeds, and stems are all edible and have a peppery taste. There are 2 basic species, the tendril-climbing (*Tropaeolum majus*) and the dwarf (*Tropaeolum minus*), which is nice in a flower border.

Planting. Start these tender annuals from seed in late spring and warm soil. They need full sun and well-drained soil. For your plants to be loaded with blossoms, their soil must be poor; fertile soil results in more leaves but fewer flowers. Plant ½ inch deep, rows well spaced apart. Nasturtiums do well in pots (2–3 seeds in a 6-inch pot). The climbers are lovely in a hanging basket. Or plant to climb around a window casing or up a fence or trellis. It tends to reseed itself. Seeds available from William Dam, Redwood City, De-Giorgi, etc.

Harvesting. Any and every part of the nasturtium plant is edible. Pick leaves and flowers fresh anytime you want them. Nasturtium plant parts, however, are not dried. The small green seed pods are picked green and pickled like capers. Pick just after the flower has dried off and *before the seed dries*. If your nasturtium seeds are appearing during an inconvenient period of time, pick them as they are ready and keep in a brine of ½ c. salt to 4 c. water. Change it every 3 days. When you have all the seeds you are going to get or that you want, you can go ahead and pickle them.

Using Flowers. Add the fresh flowers to salads and sandwiches, plain and fancy. Add leaves to sandwiches and salads. To make nasturtium blossom sandwiches, wash and dry the blossoms. Lay on buttered white or brown bread; if you wish, add mayo. Fresh seeds are also good in sandwiches or added to chutneys or pickles. Cut in fancy shapes and add a blossom to the top of each sandwich.

Pickling Nasturtium Seeds. Below are some recipes for pickled seeds. To preserve, pack in ½-pint jars and process in a boiling-water bath 15 minutes. To use, sprinkle on pizza or add to soups, stews, veggie dishes, salads, sauces, sandwiches, and poultry stuffing.

🐝 **PICKLED NASTURTIUM SEEDS (PLAIN)** Brine seeds in salt water for 2 days, then in cold water for 1 day; drain and pack with a hot vinegar solution.

🐝 **SPICED** Put 1 c. white vinegar in a pan. Add ½ t. salt, 1 bay leaf, and a few peppercorns, and boil. Remove from heat and let steep 2 hours. Strain. Pour over nasturtium seeds.

🐝 **SWEET** Combine ½ c. cider vinegar and ½ c. sugar and pour over seeds.

🐝 **FANCY** In a pan bring to a boil 1 c. vinegar, 2 sliced cloves of garlic, ½ t. each dill seed and mustard seed, and 1 t. each peppercorns and salt. Strain and pour liquid over 2 c. nasturtium seeds.

🐝 **CAPERED** Pickle using the recipe for capers. (Or you can pickle capers using these recipes!)

NETTLE (*URTICA DIOICA*): A common perennial weed, this is also called the common stinging nettle because of its leaves, which have fierce little stingers that poke through your skin at the slightest touch. Then you get red welts that burn and itch like crazy, on and on. (An old-time remedy for nettle stings is crushed mullein leaves pressed on the welts.) I used to have to navigate around a dense patch when I was a little girl hauling buckets of water up from the "crick" to fill the porch water tank. Miserable stuff. I'd just as soon never have anything to do with nettles again. But they are edible once cooked—worth considering if you're starving for food or looking for a dish that's also a conversation piece ("How I captured the nasty nettle").

Planting. I wouldn't plant it on purpose. It self-sows and thrives under most conditions. However, seeds are available from William Dam.

Harvesting. *Don't touch nettles with bare skin until cooked!* The points are tiny silica needles that inject formic acid. Use gloves to pick, clean, and work with them in the kitchen! Use the tops of young plants in spring, when they are about 6 inches tall. Otherwise, take *only* the top rosette of just-growing leaves and the topmost bud plus the few leaves just under that. You can go on harvesting to mid-June.

Using. Don't let them sit around. Pick and then boil them. The cooking disarms them. Serve sprinkled with caraway or dill seed. Nettle leaf tea, sweetened with honey, is an old-time remedy for a stuffy nose or a sore throat. Nettle root makes a yellow dye. A nettle poultice is an old-time remedy to stop the bleeding from a wound.

Nettle Fabric. The fully mature nettle plant (a hemp relative) can be used to make a fiber that can be woven into a fine white linen-type fiber nearly as strong as flax and comparable to cotton in its uses. Nettles were commonly used to make a linen-type fabric in Europe years ago. American Indians used the nettle variety *Urtica gracilis* for that purpose.

🐝 **NETTLE RENNET** Combine 6 c. very strong nettle tea with 4 c. uniodized salt. Use just enough to get the curdling action for your cheese-making.

🐝 **CREAM OF NETTLE SOUP** Steam 4 c. young nettle leaves until soft. Puree. If they need more liquid, add a little meat or vegetable soup stock. Melt 2 T. butter. Cook 2 T. grated onion in the butter. Add 2 T. flour to that and cook, stirring, until mixture is turning brown. Now gradually add 2 c. more stock, salt and pepper to taste, and the nettle puree. Simmer on low heat 10 minutes. Add 2 c. milk and heat just warm enough to serve. Good with grated cheese sprinkled on top.

NUTMEG: Nutmeg and mace both originate from the same tall East Indies evergreen tree, *Myristica fragrans*. The edible, peach-like fruit of that tree has a shell and inside that a brown seed, which is the nutmeg. The nutmeg trees are male or female. They take about a decade to bear but then continue for a half century more. Eat the peachlike fruit. Strip away the "aril" (mace) from the outside of its seed and dry. Sun-dry the pit a few weeks. This will cause the nutmegs inside to shrink enough so you can hear them rattle in there. Take off shell, finish drying the nutmegs, and store for use.

Using. Grind as needed. It's always better when fresh. Burn as incense or use to flavor desserts, sausage, or pickles.

OREGANO: Be choosy about which oregano you buy. There are several varieties, but only one is of culinary quality. Wild marjoram (*Origanum vulgare*) is weak in flavor. If a plant is called *Origanum* spp., that means no one is sure just what it is. Hold out for Greek oregano (*Origanum heracleoticum*), which is the real stuff.

Planting. Buy and then, after last frost, transplant to a sunny place in your garden that's well drained. Plant about 10 inches apart. It gets 1–2 feet high. Greek oregano is a winter-hardy perennial. It's also drought resistant once mature.

Container-Grown. The flavor of leaves grown outside is much better than that of those grown inside, but oregano can also thrive potted. You could use 4–5 plants. Start in 8–10-inch pots. If you don't repot to larger pots by at least the end of the third year, the plants will stop thriving. Eventually the stems get woody; then you need to replace the plant. Propagate from cuttings or root divisions.

Using. Harvest and dry like marjoram. Dried oregano is as good as, or maybe better than, fresh. Rub it to a fine powder before storing. Keep it cut back by adding it to any Italian, Mexican, or Greek dish. Use fresh or dried in chili, tomato sauce, salad dressings, pasta, hamburgers, wild game, broccoli, and eggplant. The leaves can also be used to dye.

ORRISROOT: See "Iris."

PAPRIKA: See "Peppers" under "Nightshade Fruits" in Chapter 4.

PARSLEY: There are several varieties of this easy-to-grow, popular herb, a dark green, semi-hardy biennial that does well just about anywhere. Curly parsley (*Petroselinum crispum*), the one restaurants use because it keeps its freshness longest, gets 8–10 inches tall. Its cousin, the stronger-flavored flat-leaf or plain-leaved parsley (*Petroselinum hortense*), is a little hardier to both cold and wet weather than curly, and gets much bigger—3 feet tall. Celery-leaved (or Neapolitan) parsley grows stalks that can be eaten like celery. (Both plain- and celery-leaved parsleys get called "Italian parsley.") Mitsuba is a perennial Japanese parsley. For parsnip-rooted or Hamburg parsley, you harvest and use the tops like parsley and also have a sizable edible root. (See the root section in Chapter 4.) Parsley doesn't inhibit the growth of other plants and may help repel insects.

Planting. Plant ½ inch deep in any fertile soil in early spring (April–May), or in August for growing in a cold frame (parsley is much nicer fresh than dried). Plant in sun or partial shade (it can manage on a half day of sunshine), directly in the pot (2–4 plants per 8-inch pot) or in a cold frame or garden. Allow 4 square inches per plant in a bed, one plant every 6 inches in a row. Allow 20 inches between rows.

Once well-started it doesn't transplant well, because of a long, sensitive taproot, but hardier varieties can stand some freezing weather, so consider starting it outside. Germination takes 3–8 weeks (a 1–14-day pre-soak in cold water helps). Parsley seed is viable for only 1–2 years and has a high failure rate in germination, so overplant it. Keep the soil moist during its early period. Parsley takes about 90 days to mature. Time your plantings if possible, so you have it fresh year-round. Most seed houses carry some parsley; good variety available from William Dam, etc.

Container-Grown. Parsley does well as a potted plant and can even be dug up in the fall, potted, and brought in for fresh winter parsley—if you make sure to get all the roots, don't let them get exposed to air, and settle plants in a big, deep pot because of the roots. Let soil dry between waterings. Two or three parsley plants will be enough for a family.

Harvesting. You can expect a yield of 50 lb. per 50-foot row by commercial standard. Harvest all you want anytime after the plants have had a good start. Take leaves from the outside of the plant just as they mature. Let the center leaves finish maturing. If you are in a warmer climate zone where you can leave parsley out all winter, you can harvest it right on through its first year and first winter, until it starts to flower in its second year. In harsher zones (even quite northern ones), your plants may survive outside year-round, but they won't grow leaves in frigid weather. Survival depends on the parsley variety, your climate, and how well they're mulched (cover with thick hay or leaves after first few frosts). The second year you must either let it make seed (cuttings from a parsley plant going to seed are bitter and worthless for cooking), or else cut off the flowering stalk as soon as you recognize it. If you do that, you can keep on cutting it for culinary use. Once parsley goes to seed, just yank the plants out and put them on the compost heap unless you're saving the seed.

Saving Parsley Seed. Parsley is a biennial. In its second year, uncover mulched plants in the spring. Parsley flowers have both female and male parts and are pollinated by insects. They do need isolation from other varieties. Once some seeds have turned brown, which means they are mature, go out periodically and rattle the parsley flower head around inside a paper bag. The ripe seeds will fall off, while unripe ones will stay on. When most of the seed head is brown (around September) you can cut the head off and spread it on cloth or paper to finish drying. Seeds are viable only about 2 years.

Chopping Fresh Parsley. Pinch the tufts of parsley tightly between the thumb and forefinger of your left hand; then cut finely with your kitchen scissors. Try adding parsley to fresh corn in place of salt.

Drying. Cut off parsley tops with new leaves. Dry either whole or chopped. Spread thinly over your drying surface. Dry in oven or dehydrator at 110°F. Drying parsley bunches outdoors is risky; they don't dry easily. They're done when crisp. Put the dried leaves or powder in a glass jar with a tight lid, and keep it in a dry place. Drying destroys most vitamins and flavor in parsley.

Freezing. The easiest way to preserve parsley is to shove a bunch into a quart jar, put a lid on, and freeze. Remove as needed. Or roll a bunch up tightly like a cigar, wrap in foil, and freeze.

Using. Parsley is grown for its low-calorie, attractive, edible leaves, which contain lots of vitamins and minerals, including lots of vitamins A and C. Add to meat, stew, soup, salads, vegetables, carrots—anything but fruit—just before you serve it, for parsley shouldn't be cooked.

Or use a pretty sprig as an edible garnish beside food on a plate, or as a bouquet in the center of the table. Eating boiled parsley is said to be helpful for a urinary stone and for eye inflammation. It's also said to be a breath sweetener, a natural antidote to garlic and onion breath.

➤ **PARSLEY BUTTER** *Add the juice of 2 lemons, drop by drop, to 1 c. softened butter. Keep stirring as you add it—it takes quite a while. Then add 2 T. crumbled dried parsley. Good as a clam dip.*

➤ **PARSLEY-DILL POTATO SALAD** *Peel and cook 5 lb. potatoes in boiling water with 1 t. salt until tender. Drain and cool. Dice or slice. Add ¼ c. parsley, chopped. Combine 1 c. sour cream with ¾ c. mayonnaise. Add 2 T. dill seed and 2 T. vinegar. Combine potatoes, parsley, and mayonnaise mixture. Chill. Optionally, add 6 chopped hard-boiled eggs.*

➤ **QUICK PARSLEY FLAVOR** *When you have lots of extra parsley, grind it and make ice cubes out of the juice. Wrap each cube separately in foil or in a baggie and store in freezer for flavoring soups, sauces, and gravies.*

➤ **PARSLEY SALAD DRESSING** *Mix thoroughly together ½ c. buttermilk, 6 T. mayonnaise, 1 T. vinegar, ½ c. fresh chopped parsley, 3 T. grated Parmesan, and 3 minced cloves garlic. If it's too thick, add a little water until it's the consistency you want. Use for pasta and cooked vegetable salads, asparagus, and artichokes. It's also good spread on bread and broiled until the top bubbles and starts to get brown. From Monica Ipswich, Salt Lake City, UT.*

➤ **PARSLEY TABOULI** *Combine ½ c. soaked raw bulgur wheat, 3 chopped tomatoes, 1–1½ c. chopped fresh parsley, ⅓ c. chopped green onions, ½ c. lemon juice, ½ c. cooking oil (sesame or olive is best), 2 T. chopped fresh mint, ½ t. salt, and a pinch paprika. Mix well and let rest in fridge several hours. Taste. Add more seasoning if wanted. Optionally, add chopped black olives or other chopped greens.*

PATCHOULI (*POGOSTEMON PATCHOULI*): This is a shrublike mint from India. Its aromatic oil is a powerful perfume. Even in a temperate zone, you can grow patchouli if you dig it up, pot it, and bring it into the house for the winter. Available from Merry Gardens.

PENNYROYAL (*MENTHA PULEGIUM*): A potentially deadly variety of mint, this semi-hardy plant prefers moist soil and has a low, creeping growing style, reproducing by runners.
NOTE: Do not give pennyroyal to humans in any form or for any purpose. It contains a powerful abortifacient, which means it causes miscarriages, but don't take it for that purpose, because it also causes permanent liver and kidney damage and can cause death! In book after book on herbs I see pennyroyal tea recommended for something or other. That horrifies me. Please don't believe these books.

Pennyroyal is a fly repellent when planted around doors and windows because mosquitoes, ants, and fleas all avoid it. Powdered pennyroyal will take care of your cat's fleas. Available from Redwood City, William Dam, DeGiorgi, etc.

PEPPER: The familiar partner of salt is made from ground peppercorns, which grow on a vine (*Piper nigrum*) that thrives on the Malabar coast of India (and nowhere else!). Use whole, coarsely ground, or powdered.

For green peppercorns, harvest fruit while still unripe, soft, and green. Preserve them in salt water or vinegar, or dry in the sun. For black pepper, pick somewhat more mature berries and sun-dry until they turn black. For white pepper, let the peppercorns stay on the plant until they have a pink-red cast, which means they're fully mature. Then pick, pack in quantity, and let set until they ferment some. Then wash them well and dry. White pepper is milder than black. To most Americans, "pepper" means black pepper, but many European cooks prefer white pepper. It's good with gravies, vegetables, and soups.

PEPPERMINT: See "Mint."

PINEAPPLE SAGE: See "Sage."

POKE SALET (ALSO CALLED POKE SALAD): My friend Hazel, in Georgia, wrote me, "Poke salad is a wild plant with large dark berries which are poison. Gather in early spring around wet swampy places. Use the first tender green leaves. It's the first thing 'fresh' we can get around here so when we see it in the early part of the year, we know spring has arrived. The stems are good fried like okra."

I've got another friend who loves poke salad greens. She's Violet Stewart, a woman of Native American descent from Okay, Oklahoma, who says ripe poke salet berries make a deep red dye. They are ripe in the fall. And the Native Americans in Oklahoma still use them to dye clay, wood, cloth, wool, and feathers.

Dee of Hopewell, VA, also of Native American decent, wrote to warn that poke salet leaves are also "somewhat poisonous—unless cooked a long time through several changes of water, more trouble than they're worth."

➤ **POKE SALET DUMPLINGS** *Make dumplings with cornmeal. Shape into balls and drop into the pot of boiling poke salet. Be sure to use hot water for the dumplings. I've heard another way to fix poke salet greens is to mix them with mustard leaves, cress, or other greens. Add a dash of salt and some ham or bacon. Keep covered while cooking. Gardening in the South, a great book, has a section on poke salet.*

POPPIES: There are numerous varieties. The California poppy (*Eschscholzia californica*) attracts birds who love its seeds, but it is entirely different botanically from the "poppy" whose seeds are used as a bread topping. That's a species of Papaver used since the Stone Age for the food value in its seeds. The seeds have a mildly spicy taste and are good used whole, pressed into the dough, to top breads, rolls, cakes, or cookies. Because one variety of poppy is also the source of heroin, a disgusted friend told me that one day Drug Enforcement Agency agents came stomping through all the front and back yards in her north Idaho neighborhood, yanking out every poppy they saw. (The seeds have no narcotic qualities; only the milky exudate from the opium poppy's green seed pod does.) Redwood City offers several varieties, including "Breadseed," a good one for growing those baking seeds.

Growing. This plant is best adapted to a Mediterranean or southeast Asian climate. In northern zones the seeds won't have time to mature in your garden unless started indoors. Plant in peat pots to avoid overt transplanting, which usually fails. Plant 6 inches apart in fertile, damp soil and full sun.

Harvesting. Let the seed pods ripen on the plant until that golden moment when they are fully ripe but have not yet turned their salt-shaker top openings toward the ground and dumped out the seed. Take the pods indoors to finish drying. When dry, thresh by rubbing between your palms.

Then put the pod/seed mixture into a strainer and shake onto a cloth. The tiny seeds will fall through. The coarse pod pieces will be caught and can be discarded.

Using. Add poppy seeds to any baked goods. Poppy seed is also used in birdseed mixes and can be crushed to make an oil used like olive oil.

PURSLANE (*PORTULACA OLERACEA*): This Brassica relative is also known as poupier, pussle, verdolaga, carti-choy, and portulaca. Purslane is a common weed in the United States and many other places. It can endure drought and thrive in any soil. It will reseed itself.

NOTE: Purslane is a risky plant to start in your garden. It has a neat trick of being able to make and mature seeds even if pulled out of the ground and left for dead! The joints of purslane stems root down and make new plants any place they contact soil. Many gardeners swear that purslane must have three or four more, still unknown, ways of spreading. If you choose to grow purslane, grow only in a container!

Varieties. Wild purslane has jointed, purplish-green stems and fleshy reddish-green foliage; it's a creeper. The cultivated variety that Europeans have grown for hundreds of years grows taller; it has larger leaves that are golden yellow instead of reddish green. The cultivated French purslane has a milder flavor than the weedy wild one. Plant after frost danger has passed. Seeds for French purslane are available from William Dam and Le Jardin du Gourmet.

Using. Best to harvest before flowering, for after that stems get tougher. Use young shoots and leaves raw in salads, stems in pickle mixes, and leaves and stems in any cooked form. Purslane stems are thick and fleshy and, when cut, ooze a mildly acid fluid that will thicken a recipe much as okra does.

PYRETHRUM (*CHRYSANTHEMUM ROSEUM*): This perennial is a related species of insecticidal chrysanthemums. It is a powerful natural insecticide that grows up to 2 feet tall. *NOTE: Pyrethrum is poisonous to people. Do not eat it.*

Pyrethrum blossoms are daisy-like and pink, white, or red. Propagate by root division or seeds. Plant in well-drained, slightly alkaline soil, in full sun. The plant gets about 18 inches tall. Plant them 1½–2 feet apart. To harvest, gather the flower heads and dry them. Make a spray of fresh or dried flowers by blending with water, or make a powder of dried blossoms. The spray will repel soft-bodied insects such as aphids. The powder is a good flea control for your animals. Two varieties available from Redwood City.

ROSE: These fragrant, hardy perennials grow 2–8 feet high. Most have thorns. Modern roses are more varied in color than wild or old-fashioned roses, but as hybridizers have moved the species toward more photogenic blooms, their fragrances have weakened and even disappeared in the process. The scentless rose is a modern reality. That's why, to grow roses for use in potpourris, rose jars, beads, and food, you can't start with just any of the vast variety of roses; you need an "old-fashioned" rose. (Lovers of old or new roses might enjoy *American Rose Magazine,* published by the American Rose Society. Annual dues are $37, Canadian $42, international $47, and include a subscription. Contact: PO Box 30,000, Shreveport, LA 71130-0030, 800-637-6534; **ars@ars-hq.org; www.ars.org.** They also offer a *Handbook for Selecting Roses,* in which members rate more than 3,000 commercially available roses.

Old-Fashioned Roses. The heritage roses are usually more winter hardy, more able to handle hot summers, and more strongly scented than the moderns. Patricia Wiley, owner of Roses of Yesterday and Today, reviewed this rose section, and made valuable corrections on my facts.

She added: "There are roses dating back to the time of Christ and before. An 'old' rose was discovered/introduced before the date of the first Hybrid Tea, which was La France. Most old roses are overpoweringly fragrant. The fragrance intensifies with drying the petals and buds. The old-fashioned roses vary in their bloom time. Some bloom only once in the spring, but there are many that bloom again and again throughout summer and fall. Much more interesting and lovely than the modern roses, each of the old roses has its own personality. Beyond the ease of care, there are many reasons for planting them: mass of bloom, fragrance, foliage color that varies from pale green to grey, and even leaves that change color in the fall of the year.

"Most old-fashioned roses shed their old bloom cleanly and do not have to be constantly clipped back. Just shape up the plant after it blooms in the spring and then leave it alone. Its beauty is in the large plant with masses of flowers. It should never be pruned severely.

"The most fragrant types of old roses are the Damasks, Bourbons, Centifolias, Moss roses, Albas, and Gallicas. Many hybridizers are bringing fragrance into the modern roses by combining them with the old roses for new varieties, so you must use your nose in discerning fragrance. Choose rose varieties with petals varying from deep pink to deep wine if you want to make the most colorful potpourri. The Hybrid Perpetuals are old roses of Grandma's time and she called them 'cabbage roses.' There are many varieties of these roses, and most are very fragrant: 'Paul Neyron', 'Heinrich Munch', 'Prince Camille de Rohan', 'American Beauty', and 'Henry Nevard', all excellent for making potpourri, and all good garden roses."

Planting. Buy young plants. Set out in a sunny, absolutely weed-free bed of somewhat heavy soil, with plenty of compost or manure worked in. It's best to plant early in spring, when the soil is no longer frozen. Water and add more manure or compost regularly, as the rose grows. Lay a thick mulch over the roots to suppress weeds, hold in moisture, and protect the roots through severe winters. Old-fashioned roses don't need much pruning, just cutting away of dead wood.

Rose Sources

High Country Roses specializes in one-year-old old-fashioned and hardy roses (tested in Colorado at 8,000 ft.) grown on their own roots. They offer 200+ varieties, shipped in 1-qt. pots; free catalog: 800-552-2082; 435-789-5517; PO Box 148, Jensen, UT 84035; **www.highcountryroses.com.**

Jackson & Perkins calls itself "one of the foremost producers of new roses in the world," especially floribunda: 800-292-4769; **www.jacksonandperkins.com;** PO Box 1028, Medford, OR 97501.

Roses of Yesterday and Today does mail-order retail sales of old, rare, and unusual roses—more than 240 varieties; catalog $3; 831-728-1901; 803 Brown's Valley Rd., Watsonville, CA 95076; **www.rosesof yesterday.com.**

Susannah Garden & Nursery is an antique rose (and herb) specialist: 281-288-5835; 20120 Kuykendahl, Spring, TX 77379.

Using. The petals are the part of the rose where the fragrant oil for scent or flavor is concentrated, so that's the part you work with to make sachets or to flavor jelly, cake, etc. You can do more with roses than perhaps you ever guessed! But first let's consider the fruit of the rose, used not for its fragrance but for its huge vitamin C content.

Rose Hips. A rose hip (or "hep") is the round orange-to-reddish "fruit" (also called "haw") formed after the flower of a rose has bloomed. The hip is the seedpod of the plant. Some hips are better-tasting and bigger than others. *Rosa rugosa*, the Japanese rose varieties, flower with large and lovely blooms in almost every color. They also grow the largest rose hips, about 1 inch across, which are much easier to work with. Sweetbriar eglantine (*Rosa eglanteria*) also has good hips. The sweetbriars have the extra gift of aromatic leaves that smell like ripe apples and can be added to your potpourri. Wild rose hips are also good. There are wild roses in every state except Hawaii. The rugosa has escaped and gone native in some areas.

Rugosa Rose Varieties. These sucker profusely, so it's wise to plant in a big container or some other kind of root-limiting structure. Or buy grafted plants, so you don't get a forest of roses that takes over the yard. It isn't a good idea to plant them near wide open spaces either, because birds are likely to disperse their seeds and create thorny rugosa thickets out in your pasture. They do make a great 6-foot-tall, impenetrable hedge, the kind Sleeping Beauty had. They are easy to grow, exceptionally hardy, and can endure wind, seaside exposure and drought conditions (once established). They can be planted from seed in either full sun or partial shade and almost any well-drained soil. They have almost no problem pests or pestilences, and actually produce hips better with little to no pruning. *Rugosa* does need winter chilling and won't grow in subtropical climates. *Rugosa* or *eglanteria* available from Gurney's, Raintree Nursery, Farmer, Roses of Yesterday and Today, or High Country Rosarium.

NOTE: *When picking rose petals or hips to eat, be sure they have not been sprayed by you or anyone else. Those growing along railroad tracks and major highways probably have been sprayed and should be avoided.*

Harvesting Hips. Some people gather hips any time after they have turned from yellow to orange and on to scarlet.

Some wait for the first frost, convinced they taste better after that. If allowed to get soft, they're definitely not nice anymore.

Processing. We're talking vitamins here. That means keep them cool until you can use or preserve them, and the sooner you do that the better—same day, if possible. Stew, dry, or freeze. Wash and cut off both ends of hips with scissors. Cover if you cook them. Use wooden spoons and earthenware or china bowls. Cook in glass or enamel pans or stainless steel. Hips are so high in vitamin C that they are valuable for winter use to supply that vitamin in tea, etc.

Cooking. Process into jelly; combine with honey to make a syrup; make granita, jam, extract, cold rose-hip soup, or hot tea.

Freezing. Just toss them into plastic bags and freeze until needed. Or make sugarless rose hip syrup by pouring boiling water to cover the hips and cooking on low heat 15 minutes. Let that cool and steep 24 hours. Strain and freeze. When needed, use your sugarless syrup to enrich soups, toppings, teas, etc.

Drying. For large hips, wash, cut open, take out seeds, spread, and dry in oven or dehydrator at 110°F until they are hard and brittle. For small hips, you can dry whole without cutting or removing seeds, or you can cut into slices and dry, also without removing seeds. When thoroughly dry, store in airtight jars. (If not very dry, they will mold.) When ready to use, cover with water and simmer until soft. Use the pulp to make jam or jelly. Hips mix well with other fruits like apple or cranberry.

☞ *ROSE HIP TEA Boil dried coarse-ground rose hips with water, about 1 T. for each cup of tea. The longer you boil, the stronger your tea. Mash the hips with a spoon to get out all the juice, and strain. Sweeten with brown sugar or honey.*

☞ *DORIS'S HIP MIX TEA Rose hips are not strongly flavored, although they are nourishing, so a hip mix makes for a tastier tea. Stem the hips, dry them, and grind. Mix dried ground hips with mint and well-dried strawberry leaves: ¼ rose hips, ¼ mint, and the rest wild strawberry leaves. Or leave out the mint, or combine hips with lemon balm, etc.*

❧ **ROSE PEAR GRANITA** This recipe is from Lane Morgan's Winter Harvest Cookbook (Sasquatch Books, 1990), an excellent little collection of gourmet recipes for homely vegetables that you might have in your field, garden, or root cellar in the winter: "No special equipment is required for this simple ice from Le Gourmand. The rose hips give the crystals a bit of tartness and a gorgeous red-gold tint. This makes a good digestive as well as a deceptively simple dessert. 1 quart pear juice. ½ cup rose hips, cut in half and seeded. Pour juice into a saucepan, add rose hips, and simmer, covered, until liquid is reduced by half. Put through a food mill and pour into a shallow pan. Freeze. Stir when mixture starts to get slushy and return to freezer until time to serve. Makes 1 pint."

❧ **ROSE HIP SYRUP** Wash 2 lb. fresh hips and remove stems. Put through food chopper using medium blade. Cover with 6 c. boiling water and boil 2 minutes. Strain through sieve and put solids in a jelly bag to drain. There should be 1½ pints of liquid. If more, boil it down. Add ¾ c. sugar and boil for 5 minutes. Bottle.

❧ **ROSE HIP JAM** Try to preserve the hips the same day you pick them. Boil 4 c. hips with 2½ c. water until the hips are tender. Put through sieve to remove seeds. Add 1 c. sugar for every 2 c. pulp. Add 1 t. lemon juice. Mix thoroughly and bring slowly to a simmer. Cook about 20 minutes. Seal.

❧ **ROSE HIP EXTRACT** From Lila Morris, Beavercreek, OR: "Add it to breakfast juice, gelatin, desserts, meat sauces, soups or sherbet for lots of vitamin C. Gather rose hips, chill, and remove blossom ends, stems, and leaves. Rinse off. For each 1 c. hips bring to a rolling boil 1½ c. of water. Add the rose hips. Cover and simmer 15 minutes. Mash with fork or potato masher and let set 24 hours. Strain off liquid part. That's your extract. Bring extract to a good boil. Add 2 T. vinegar or lemon juice for each pint. Pour hot into jars and seal.

❧ **ANN MARIE'S EXTRACT** For each 1 c. hips, pour over 1 c. boiling water. Let soak 48 hours. Strain off the juice. Add ¼ c. honey per quart of juice. Heat to boiling point. Pour into clean hot jars and seal. Take 2 t. per day in winter for your vitamin C.

❧ **ROSE HIP JELLY** Wash, stem, and chop your hips. For every 4 c. hips, boil 2 c. water for 5 minutes and then let hang overnight in a jelly bag to get the juice. For every 1 c. rose hip juice, add 3 c. apple juice. Boil 10 minutes. Gradually add 1 c. sugar for every cup of juice you are working with, and boil until it jells.

Harvesting Rose Petals. Gather just when the rose has fully expanded. If you wait a day longer, until they start to fade, they will have lost some of that precious fragrance. Gather in the morning after the dew has dried, but before they have gotten really warmed by the sun. Dry before proceeding by pressing them gently between layers of cloth. Dry them in a dehydrator or on a muslin cloth laid over a screen in an airy, shady place.

❧ **ALL-ROSE POTPOURRI** This potpourri has a prettier color, but it doesn't stay near as fragrant as long as the moist one. Gather your fragrant roses in the early morning just after the dew is off. Use roses between three-quarters and full bloom. Simply hold petals together with the tips of your fingers and twist. They will usually all come off in your hand. Gather small buds too. Dry your petals and buds on a screen or cloth or in a dehydrator, out of direct sunlight. When dry, combine with powdered orrisroot and set out in an open-topped jar. Or use in a sachet.

❧ **A DAMP POTPOURRI** Dry the rose petals just until they feel leathery—8 hours or overnight. Use ice cream-type salt that is coarse and not iodized. Layer salt and rose petals in the bottom of a glass jar, ¼ c. salt to 2 c. petals. Add some orrisroot, too. Keep a lid on the jar and open only when you want to let out some fragrance.

❧ **ATTAR OF ROSES** "Attar" is rose petal oil. The damask rose varieties (Rosa damascena) are good for making attar. I'd heard that Rosa damascena trigintipetala is the most highly regarded variety for making potpourri and attar. But Patricia Wiley says the best is Rosa damascena bifera, the rose of Castile. Pure attar of roses is extracted from fresh petals. The finest potpourris are made by spraying attar on dried, mixed petals and buds.

Fill a large glass jar with rose petals, carefully separated from the rest of the plant. Add just enough water to cover them and let the jar set in the sun 2–3 days, bringing it indoors overnight. At the end of the second or third day, small particles of yellow oil will be floating on the surface of the water. In the course of a week, they will have increased to a thin scum. The greenish-yellow scum is attar of roses. Take it up with a little cotton tied to the end of a stick, and squeeze it into a small container. Or use a feather. On the commercial market, attar of roses is very pricey stuff, a valuable ingredient of perfumes. It takes a whole lot of roses to make even a tiny bit of attar: approximately 5 lb. of petals for 1 oz. of oil!

❧ **ROSE EXTRACT** Put petals into a wide-mouthed bottle and pour over them some pure alcohol. Let stand a month, and then strain. The liquid is rose extract, or essence of roses.

❧ **ROSE WATER** Combine 1 part attar with 1 part alcohol and 10 parts distilled water. Or 1 t. extract mixed into ¾ c. distilled water. Or combine 1 oz. attar with 1 gal. distilled water. Age 2 weeks. You have to shake a long time, slowly at first, to get a solution.

❧ **ROSE BRANDY** To flavor sauces for cakes and puddings, gather rose petals while the dew is on them. Fill a bottle with them. Then pour into the bottle a good brandy. Steep 3 to 4 weeks. Strain and rebottle.

❧ **ROSE VINEGAR** Boil 2 c. white vinegar in non-aluminum pan and pour over 1 c. rose petals. Add ½ t. lavender or rosemary. Cover and steep 10 days. Strain and bottle. Patricia Wiley wrote me, "You can use 2 cups vin rosé wine for a light wine vinegar—pretty, too!"

❧ **ROSE PETAL HONEY** This recipe was a favorite of Martha Washington's. Bring 2 pints of honey to a boil. Add 1 pint rose petals. Let stand 4 hours. Heat again. Strain into jars.

❧ **ROSE PETAL JAM** Chop the petals into pieces and pack firmly into a measuring cup. You'll need 2 cups for this recipe. Cover the 2 c. petals with 2 c. boiling water in a pan and simmer for 10 minutes. Strain, keeping the liquid. Add 2¾ c. sugar and 3 T. honey to the water in which the petals were cooked. Simmer, uncovered, for 30 minutes. Add 1 t. lemon juice and the chopped petals, and simmer 30 minutes more. The rose petals will have dissolved. Have ready your clean, hot jelly jars. Pour hot liquid into the hot jars and seal.

❧ **SARA'S ROSE PETAL JELLY** Corean Morgan, Sweet Home, OR, wrote me about her friend Sara, "Dear Carla, The recipe book I bought has been given to a friend—who lives on top of Green Peter Mountain, and who shot a bear (a real, live bear) that was getting honey from the hives. Not only did she shoot it, she skinned it and put both hide and meat into the deep freeze. Perhaps you would like to have this recipe of hers:

"Combine 2 qt. pink rose petals, 3 c. boiling water, 3 c. sugar, ¼ c. lemon juice, and 1 package MCP pectin. Gather rose petals in early morning just after the dew has left. Yellow petals may be added if you are short of your quarts. Red rose petals may also be used, but be careful, since they have a much stronger flavor. Pour the boiling water over the petals and steep until all color is absorbed. Measure sugar into a dish to add later. Measure rose water and lemon juice into a 6- or 8-qt. kettle. Add pectin and stir well. Place on hottest fire and bring to a boil. Add measured sugar and mix well. Continue stirring and bring to a full rolling boil. Boil exactly 2 minutes. Skim and pour into prepared glasses and seal."

❧ **ROSE PETAL BREAD** Add to a regular 2-loaf white bread recipe 1 c. lightly packed rose petals, 1 t. rose extract, 3 t. lemon extract, and extra sweetening.

❧ **PETAL-SCENTED TEA** The Chinese use cabbage rose petals and/or jasmine flowers to float on and scent a cup of steaming tea.

❧ **ROSE AND RHUBARB SYRUP** Simmer 1½ lb. chopped rhubarb about 20 minutes. Strain. It's the liquid you want to save. To that rhubarb juice add 1 lb. sugar and petals from about 8 red roses. Simmer 20 minutes more. Strain again, this time discarding the rose petals. Bring the syrup back to boiling. Simmer until it thickens. Pour into small (for it will ferment soon after opening) hot bottles and seal them. To use, add to a milk shake for flavor or to hot water to make a tea.

❧ **CRYSTALLIZED ROSE PETALS** From Catherine Shirley: "I pick a few first roses. They are dark pink fragrant ones of the old-fashioned kind. They have thorns. This project is rather tedious and time-consuming, but makes nice gifts when put in nice containers at Christmas time. They are also pleasant to eat. I picked a few roses with short stems. This makes the roots get stronger. I cut off the white part, which is the base of the rose, because it is bitter. I take the petals apart and wash each carefully under running water; if water is not plentiful, I swish each petal in a pan of water and change the water quite often. Put on paper towel to dry. Then take an egg white, add a little cold water, and beat slightly. I dip each petal in the egg white, lift it out with a fork, and lay on granulated sugar, press gently, and carefully turn it over and treat same way and lift and lay on piece of waxed paper. Let dry thoroughly, turn over, let other side dry thoroughly. Then pack in a dark jar so they will keep their color. P.S. I make crystallized pinks or carnations called 'pinks,' and they taste nice, like clove-flavored candy."

❧ **ROSEBUD ICE CUBES** Freeze a tiny rosebud in each cube to float in special summer drinks.

Rose Beads. A curious thing about rose petals: You can make them into beads. The first people to do this were monks making "rosary" beads. The beads smell fragrant and get darker and harder when aged. First you make the dough. Then you shape it.

❧ **PURE PETALS BEAD DOUGH** Blend 8 c. fresh rose petals with a little water. You can do a few at a time and freeze until you accumulate a total of 8 or more cups. Now put petals in a cast-iron pan and add several rusty nails too. Add enough water to no more than just cover the petals. Cook over lowest heat, uncovered, for several hours. Once in a while, stir (wooden spoon only!). Don't worry about the disgusting odor. Take off the heat, cover, and let rest until the next day. The next day, cook it just like before. Add a little water as needed. Then let set overnight. Do the same thing again the third day and the third night. By now (or maybe it will need yet another day and night), you should have a black pulp. Soak out the extra water from the pulp using paper towels. You'll be able to start bead making when you've got the pulp dry enough to hang together. Store the pulp in the refrigerator until you can make the beads.

❧ **PETALS/SALT BEAD DOUGH** Combine an amount of firmly packed rose petals with an equal amount of salt. Mash together and add half as much distilled water or rainwater as you have salt. Mix in an enamel or iron pan. If in enamel, add a drop of oil paint if you want artificial color. Heating them in a rusty iron skillet will make the beads velvety black. Bring it up with low heat to just under simmering stage. Stir constantly until you have a smooth mixture.

❧ **PETALS/FLOUR BEAD DOUGH** Combine 1¾ c. flour, ¼ c. salt, and enough water to shape a dough. Add 3 c. rose petals that have been chopped very, very fine. Work the petals thoroughly into the dough.

Shaping the Beads: The hardest dough to work with is the all-petals one. It will also stain your hands, so use rubber gloves or else plan to wash your hands a lot for the next few days. Measure the pulp for one bead with a melon baller—one scoop will make one bead. (All petal pulp will shrink by two-thirds.) Be patient with the shaping. For salt and flour rose beads, roll the dough out on a floured bread board to ¼ inch thick. Use a thimble to cut out sections, because those will be a good bead size. Roll each bead like clay in the palm of your hand to make it smooth and round.

Stringing Beads: To make holes in the beads so you can string them, string the finished beads onto florist's wire (#24 or #26). Hang them on the wire in a dark room until dry, shifting them around once in a while so they won't stick. For your final necklace, string beads on cord or dental floss. For a very special rosary, string with gold or crystal beads or both. For a final scenting, you can dip the pin you use to make their holes in a rose oil, or dab a little onto each bead.

ROSEMARY (ROSMARINUS OFFICINALIS): This decorative, tender perennial has leaves somewhat like soft green evergreen needles. Rosemary has the widest range of uses of any herb. Bees love it. The plant can be used as a hedge (2–3 feet high) if you start with the upright variety, 'Collingwood Ingram'. The other varieties of rosemary are trailing in nature, beautiful in a hanging basket or cascading over a wall. Delicate blue flowers bloom on branch tips in early spring. Rosemary looks like a tiny pine tree, but it can't survive a serious winter; move it into the house in a pot for the winter, or keep potted all the time (start in 6-inch pot), for it does fine on a windowsill. Or keep in a 12-inch container outside in the summer and inside in the winter. Do note that dry indoor heat will cause leaves to drop.

Planting. You can propagate by seeds, but they germinate so slowly and unreliably that stem cuttings are preferable. Spring cuttings can be started in water and then planted. Or take cuttings of non-flowering shoots in early fall and plant in a cold frame to get through the winter. Or layer. Plant in well-drained, alkaline (add lime regularly), light soil in full sun, but sheltered from cold winds. Rosemary can handle dry conditions, but it needs at least several deep waterings each summer. Plant the upright species 12 inches apart. You can dig up and divide an older plant. Two or three will be enough to meet a family's needs. It handles pruning well.

Harvesting. Pick rosemary needles anytime to use fresh.

Drying. Pick needles that are mature enough to have developed aroma but still relatively young and tender. You can cut foliage several times a summer. Remove poor-quality needles. Don't wash. Spread thinly and dry in shade or slow oven/dehydrator at 110°F to crispness. Crumble before using.

Using. Called "the herb of remembrance," rosemary has been used both at weddings to symbolize fidelity and at funerals, placed on graves, to signify remembrance. More mundane uses: in perfumes, as a hair rinse (leaves hair scented and shining), in potpourri, as an insect repellent where food and clothing are stored, and, of course, as a fresh or dried seasoning for food (a little goes a long way). Pluck some needles to add to boiling potatoes, summer or winter squash, turnips, broiled lamb chops, pork roast, and rabbit. Add some to spaghetti sauce. Rosemary and cranberry juice combine for a good herb jelly.

❧ *HERBAL HAMBURGER Melt I T. butter with ½ t. dried rosemary in a frying pan. Stir a bit to let rosemary flavor butter. (Don't brown butter.) Add about I lb. hamburger shaped into patties, and cook. Remove hamburgers when done. Add another I T. butter to pan drippings together with ½ t. dry mustard and a dash Worcestershire sauce. Stir a minute. Pour over hamburgers.*

❧ *ROAST POTATOES WITH ROSEMARY Use 2 lb. really fresh new potatoes, scrubbed and cut into I-inch cubes. Preheat oven to 425°F. Place potatoes, leaves from 4 large sprigs of fresh rosemary, and 4 large cloves of peeled and crushed garlic in a roasting pan. Pour ½ c. olive oil over that. Sprinkle in salt and pepper. Now bake, stirring occasionally, until potatoes are browned and crisp on the outside, tender on the inside, 30–40 min. Sprinkle with parsley and serve. From Winter Harvest Cookbook by Lane Morgan.*

❧ *ROSEMARY TEA/HAIR RINSE Pour boiling water over the needles, and steep until to your liking.*

RUE: *Do not drink or eat this plant; it is toxic.* Propagate by stem cuttings or seeds. Plant in well-drained, light soil in full sun. The plants are only a foot high. Both the stem and leaves can be used. Rue is avoided by the Japanese beetle. Its smell is unpleasant. In hot weather, handling rue can cause poison-ivy type blisters on sensitive skins. Use only as an insect-repellent or decorative plant. Available from William Dam, DeGiorgi, etc.

SAFFRON (CROCUS SATIVUS): This strongly aromatic crocus gets only 4–6 inches high. It has thin, grasslike leaves. It's easy to grow, but takes 3 years to produce flowers from seed, so it's much quicker to start with plants, propagating by planting divisions of "corms" (enlarged underground stems) called "offsets" in late summer.
NOTE: The autumn crocus (Colchicum autumnale) resembles saffron crocus but is not a true crocus and is poisonous.

Planting. Plant 3 inches deep in rich, well-drained soil, full or partial sun, 3 inches apart, outdoors (zones 6–9) or in a container. Saffron corms available from Nichols Garden Nursery.

Harvesting. The saffron crocus develops purple flowers in the fall. Saffron is the most expensive spice because of the effort, tedium, and small return of harvesting the red-or-ange, edible stigmas—the "threads" at the center of the flower. Gather the stigmas using tweezers. Dry them in a warm and airy but shaded place. You can buy either ground saffron or whole dried stigmas or "threads." It's safest to get the threads because ground saffron may well be adulterated.

Using. Saffron colors sauces (or dyes fabrics) a golden shade and adds a unique flavor to foods. It is essential for making bouillabaisse, Spanish rice, paella, and saffron breads.

SAFFRON, MEXICAN: This is an imitation sold in some Latin American outlets; it's made of dried, ground safflower petals. For more information, see Chapter 4.

SAGE: This herb is a semi-hardy perennial that grows to 2 feet high and has light-bluish flowers. It has numerous varieties—narrow-leaved, broad-leaved, purple- and red-leaved, and dwarf, which is good in a pot. (For information about the fragrant sagebrushes of drylands in the western United States, see "Artemisia.")

Broad Leaf Sage (Salvia officinalis). This is the historical medicinal variety, but it can also be used at table. It's a perennial that needs direct sunlight. Available from DeGiorgi.

Clary Sage (Salvia sclarea). This 3–4 foot biennial is valued for both its attractive, aromatic flowers and its use as a fragrance fixative like orrisroot. It originated in the Mediterranean. Plant seed every year to get flowers. Plant in full sun and average soil. Plant outdoors 1 foot apart, or in shelter and transplant later. Clary sage leaves are used fresh to flavor drinks and egg dishes. Dried leaves are good with rose petals, lavenders, and mints in potpourris or sachets, or added to soups or stews. Dried clary sage flowers make a fine herb tea. Clary sage seeds, like quince seeds (see Chapter 6 for recipes), release a mucilaginous material when soaked in water. This paste was traditionally used to bathe eyes. Available from Redwood Seed.

Pineapple Sage (*Salvia elegans*). This is a tender perennial, the last herb of the season to bloom. You can add its red flowers to fruit punch or salads for a pretty color and a nice fruity flavor. The leaves are edible too, and have a mild pineapple flavor. Use them in fruit dishes and to make an herb jelly. This plant has to be transplanted to a pot and brought inside to survive a real winter. It is different from scarlet sage, which is an inedible ornamental.

Planting. Sage grows easily from seed and transplants easily. Seed is easy to find and is viable for 2–3 yrs. Or use stem cuttings, or root division in the early spring. Fine in average-to-poor, well-drained soil (let dry between waterings) and full sun. Plant 2–3 plants for family use in 6-inch pots or a foot apart in the garden. Plant it away from your annuals, since it will inhibit their growth. Broad-leafed sage and clary sage freely self-sow. Because sage grows well in a pot, some people bring it in for the winter. Too much fertilizer or water weakens the aroma of the leaves. In the spring, prune away the old, dead, woody parts, or thin by removing 3–4-year-old plants because of their developing woodiness. Sage naturally dies after about 5 years.

Harvesting. If you want just a few leaves, go out and pick them anytime after your plant is 8 inches high. The best leaves are newly grown from the tips of the branches, or stems, cut just before flowering. But you can cut off whole stems to dry even at the last moment in the fall, and they'll definitely be sage. Sort them over. Don't wash. Tie in bunches and hang up to dry, or dry in the sun, dehydrator, or very slow oven at 110°F until crisp. Sage has a dryish quality even on the plant, and once dried, it stays dry. To store, rub off the stems and pack into airtight jars.

Using. Chopped fresh sage leaves add flavor to pickles, cheese, and sausage. Dried sage is best in poultry or pork stuffings; if you are using fresh sage, soak it 5 minutes in boiling water, dry, and then chop.

➤ *SAGE BREAD This is a good sandwich bread. If your milk is raw, scald it first. Use 2 c. milk, ¼ c. sugar, 2 t. salt, 2 t. celery seed, and 1 t. powdered sage. Add ¼ c. cooking oil, 2 eggs, and 2 T. yeast. Mix well. Add enough flour to make a kneadable dough. Knead, let rise, punch down, and divide into 2 loaves. Put loaves into greased bread pans, and let rise again until they double in bulk. Bake at 400°F until loaves sound hollow when rapped.*

➤ *SAGE TEA Steep fresh sage leaves or 1 heaping t. powdered sage in 2 c. boiling water. Strain. Sweeten to taste. Drink hot. For a medicinal gargle, brew until dark green in color. This is a traditional comfort for the cold victim as well as a good hair rinse.*

Salad Burnet: See "Burnet."

Salt: Salt is sodium chloride. Just ¹⁄₁₀ t. salt per day is necessary to keep you alive. But too much more of it day in and day out will give you high blood pressure and put you at risk for stroke and heart disease. A person who does little physical labor and spends the summer in an air-conditioned office doesn't need much salt. However, if you spend your summer days working hard out in the sun, and in the evening come home to a hot house, you need as much salt as you hunger for as well as plenty of water or diluted, unsweetened fruit juice to compensate for all that perspiring.

The secret is not to let salting become a habit, because salt needs vary according to the time of year and your activ-

ity. In the old days salt was used to preserve food, but now there are healthier ways of preservation. Most foods naturally contain sodium, as do some water supplies. Almost everybody in a grocery-store, restaurant-eating lifestyle gets too much salt in their diet.

How to Lower Your Salt Intake
1. Don't salt your cooking water.
2. Don't eat "processed" foods. Cook from scratch so you can leave the salt out of the recipe (or greatly reduce it). The worst offenders in the grocery store are canned soups, lunch meats, canned vegetables, and all "snack" foods. Fast-food restaurants typically serve high-salt meals, and virtually all restaurants use some salt.
3. Avoid beets, carrots, shellfish, cheese, and celery, because those foods are naturally high in sodium.
4. To flavor your food, use herbs, spices, flavored vinegars, wine, and garlic instead of salt. Thirteen-year-old Ruth, doing her best to wean me entirely from the salt habit, advised me, "Try things like finely chopped onion, tomato chunks, sweet pepper, lemon juice, and various herbs instead of fostering that salt taste. There is such a thing as low-sodium tamari, but don't become dependent on that either."

And read *Cooking Without a Grain of Salt* by Elma W. Bagg (1971).

Sassafras: *Do not eat products made with sassafras bark or root. The sassafras tree can be grown in mild climates like Texas and Arkansas. The leaves are made into filé, a traditional gumbo ingredient. In the past the wood, root, and bark have all been used to make beverages; however, the FDA has taken the bark (which was an old-time root beer ingredient) off the market because of its risk as a carcinogen.*

Filé. Pick young, tender sassafras leaves in the spring. Spread over your drying surface and dry outdoors in an airy, shady place or in oven or dehydrator at 110°F until they are crisp. Then pulverize them to make your filé powder. When added to soup (gumbo), they give it a distinctive flavor and have a thickening effect. Note: Never boil the gumbo after adding the filé powder. If you do, it becomes ropey, stringy, and disagreeable. For this reason, reheating leftover gumbo can be a problem, so just make enough for 1 meal at a time.

Filé Variations—Mix filé with a few leaves of sweet bay. Or, if you don't have sassafras, substitute young okra pods for the filé.

➤ *SASSAFRAS BEEF GUMBO Add 1 large spoonful of dried and powdered sassafras leaves to a pot of beef soup after taking it off the heat.*

➤ *FROM-SCRATCH OLD-TIME SASSAFRAS GUMBO Start with 6 squirrels or 2 chickens. Cut up small and cook until flesh falls from bones. Add 1 qt. okra, 2 onions cut fine, 6 diced white potatoes, grated carrot, a little cabbage, pepper, and salt. Add pod of red pepper and filé just before serving.*

Savory: There are 2 basic varieties of savory, summer savory (*Satureja hortensis*) and winter savory (*Satureja montana*). They are used the same way in cooking. Both grow fine in a pot. Both attract bees, prefer full sun, do well in poor, stony soil, and prefer soil to dry out between waterings. But they have significant differences.

Summer Savory. This savory is an annual that gets about 18 inches tall and is grown from seed planted in the early spring (allow 4 weeks to germination). Transplant 2–3 plants to a 6-inch pot, or plant outside, 10 inches apart. Seeds stay viable for only 1–2 years. Plant in April to May. Prefers light soil. The beauty of summer savory is that it's so easy to get going. Space plantings at 3-week intervals for continuous prime leaves. Thin when 3 inches high to be about 6 inches apart. Summer savory's flavor is sweeter and finer than that of winter savory. Available from Redwood City, Thompson & Morgan, DeGiorgi, and William Dam.

Winter Savory. This hardy perennial survives down to 10°F with mulch and a sheltered position. Compared to summer savory it's a little smaller and much prettier, with its little lavender summer flowers. Winter savory seeds are so slow to germinate that it's easier to propagate them via cutting or root division in the fall. Grow in 6–8-inch pots, or plant 1 foot apart outside. The flavor of winter savory leaves is similar to but stronger than that of summer savory. One plant is enough. It will die after 5 years, so figure on replacing it. Available from William Dam and DeGiorgi.

Harvesting and Drying. The flavor is strongest when the plants are in flower. Summer savory leaves can be harvested in mid-summer or can be pulled out by the roots in the fall for drying. Winter savory tips can be cut 2 or 3 times a summer. Don't wash. Dry in shade or at 110°F. Done when crisp.

Using. The leaves of both types of savory have a peppery quality that goes well in salads, soups, and sauces. Dried leaves are good in poultry stuffing and with meats, fish, cheese, eggs, and green beans. It's also used in sachets. Crushing and rubbing summer savory leaves on a bee sting can help make it better.

SESAME (*SESAME INDICUM*): This annual does best in full sun, grows to be about 2 feet tall, and blooms with pretty trumpet-shaped white flowers. In late summer the flowers wither and a seedhead develops that contains the small nut-flavored seeds we know as sesame seeds. These must be harvested before fully mature; otherwise, they will shatter onto the ground. Use fresh or toasted.

SLIPPERY ELM: Old-timers would break the inner bark of slippery elm into bits to make the famous tea. They would pour 1 c. boiling water over 1 t. slippery elm bark and let it steep until cold. When cold, it was strained, and lemon juice was added to sweeten it to taste. But since the elms are having such a hard time now anyway, I'd leave them alone and try something else. If you do have an eco-harmless source, slippery elm is an edible herb with thickening ability. It's good for thickening edible leathers (dried food paste). Use 2 T. slippery elm for each 1 c. pulp and soak 5 minutes; that will do it.

SORREL: Sorrel originated in Eurasia. The variety called garden sorrel now grows wild in many places in the United States. All true sorrels are very hardy (zones 5–9) perennials, members of the buckwheat family. They all have a similar taste and can be used as leafy flavorings for salads and meat, fish, or egg dishes.
NOTE: Oxalis acetosella or wood sorrel, although it has a similar name, is not related and is not safe to consume!

Varieties. There are several true sorrel varieties, wild and domesticated. The preferred eating kind, French sorrel or oseille, is easily confused with its wild relative, sheep sorrel. The various sorrels are also known as sourgrass. The other domesticated sorrel is garden sorrel or Grande de Belleville

(*Rumex acetosa*). Its leaves get up to 2 feet long, compared to the 6-inch French sorrel. Available from DeGiorgi.

Sheep Sorrel (*Rumex acetosella*). Also known as dock, this is a common weed. It is related to, looks somewhat like, and is as delicious as French or garden sorrel, and it can be used in exactly the same way. But I don't recommend letting sheep sorrel into your garden, because it propagates by underground runners (like morning glory) that tend to be terribly difficult to control in the garden. If you want a sorrel, plant French or garden instead. If you must plant sheep sorrel, do so inside outer barriers that will safely stop those roaming roots from taking over.

French Sorrel (*Rumex scutatus*). This one propagates slowly by developing clumps on its perimeter (which you can divide and move) as well as by seed. In fact, it's a good idea to pinch off all developing seed heads, for French sorrel will self-sow and can become a weedy garden nuisance in that way. Pinching off seedheads also keeps its energy going into making leaves for flowering and cuts way back on, or even ends, leaf production. Still, French is more controllable than sheep, and that's why it's the sorrel variety of choice for gardeners. Available from DeGiorgi, etc.

Planting. French sorrel prefers somewhat acid soil and does not grow in quite alkaline soil. Being perennial, it needs a permanent location and appreciates nitrogen. If you have scorching hot summers, choose a site with partial shade. If your summers are frequently cloudy, plant in full sun. Otherwise, it is easy to grow, a bush that will become between 18 inches and 3 feet high. Once started, it will basically make it on its own, although it produces leaves best in moist soil. Sorrel has relatively deep roots and so can handle dry spells better than some other plants. Plant from seed in March or by root division, directly outdoors, in either spring or fall. Plant ½ inches deep in 6-inch pots or outdoors a foot apart. Keep the dirt moist until the plants appear. Thin to 6 inches in a dry climate, 12 inches in a wet one. French sorrel runs out of "oomph" and needs to be divided, moved, or given generous nitrogen feedings at least every 3–4 years. Wherever sorrel has been growing, the nitrogen will be depleted. Sorrel has a chronic problem with Japanese beetles.

Harvesting. French sorrel will be the first green to appear in your spring garden. The arrow-shaped leaves can be harvested in spring, fall, and winter. Choose fully formed leaves, 3–7 inches long. Take only the outer leaves so the rosette heart will be undamaged and able to continue growing new ones. Harvesting those outer leaves, whether or not you need them, is desirable because it keeps the tender new ones coming. Basically, you harvest in spring, give it up for a while in summer, and trim back the dense summer growth around September; then you'll get a fall crop of tender leaves that continue to come until a really heavy freeze stops them for the winter.

Preparing. Discard tough, overmature leaves, unless they're to be pureed. Sorrel wilts unusually quickly, as greens go, and must be moved promptly from garden to table. If you're harvesting sorrel for a cooked recipe, pick lots, because it shrinks! And never cook sorrel in aluminum or iron pans, because the sorrel leaves will turn an unappealing brown or even black. Carefully rinse off and drain the leaves.

Sorrel Recipes. The leaves have an acid, lemony, tart flavor that is surprising and pleasant in small quantities—when slivered thinly and added to the milder lettuce-type greens of a salad, for instance, or used like parsley to garnish fish or tossed in to help flavor a soup. Or use some chopped sorrel with your favorite other ingredients (tomato, cheese, etc.) as an omelet filling. Or blend with mayonnaise for added zip and green coloring. But sorrel is one of those plants that is high in oxalic acid, a substance that both prevents calcium uptake in your system and in quantity is a carcinogen, so it's best used sparingly (unless well cooked before use, which totally disarms it).

In larger quantities, sorrel's strong flavor can be disagreeable unless covered, as in a cream soup recipe, or heavily balanced, as in combination with fish, chicken, or game. For example, saute sorrel with butter and chopped olives and serve with fish. Or cut the sorrel into small pieces, cook with trout or salmon, and serve with a white sauce or lemon juice. Or puree 1 lb. sorrel, combine with shredded, cooked chicken and chicken stock, and serve with lemon juice or cream. Or sprinkle chicken or fish with lemon juice and basil or pesto, wrap it inside large sorrel leaves, and bake.

SOUTHERNWOOD (ARTEMISIA ABROTANUM): This close relative of wormwood is a decorative perennial bush 2–3 feet high with small yellow flowers in late summer. It's not hardy and needs a sheltered planting where severe frosts won't affect it. Plant in full sun in well-drained, heavy soil. Propagate by seeds or semi-ripe summer stem cuttings. Southernwood leaves are insect repellent and can be made into mothproofing sachets to be stored with clothing. They're also used in potpourris. Because they taste so bitter, they are not used in the kitchen. Harvest and dry sprigs as you would wormwood.

✑ *A SHAKER CLOSET BAG From Janice Rebstock, Boonville, IN: Combine 2 c. southernwood, 1 c. tansy, 1 c. lavender, ½ c. orange peel, and 2 T. crushed cloves.*

STEVIA: Stevia (*Stevia rebaudiana*) is a small shrub from Paraguay, Brazil, and Argentina that sweetens anything without adding sugar or calories or raising blood sugar levels. *How to Grow Stevia* can be bought at **www.uconect.net/~guarani/s-bookl.htm.**

SWEET CICELY (MYRRHIS ODORATA): Also called "myrrh," this perennial herb has ferny foliage, grows 2–3 feet high, and is a serious self-sower that can become a weed in your garden.

Planting. Plant the black seeds in fall or spring, or root pieces with a bud on each. Sweet cicely thrives in light shade and any type of damp soil. Allow 8–10 square inches per plant. Seedlings can be transplanted. To save your own seed, note that seeds should be chilled in damp peat for about 2 months (at least 40°F) for good germination. Seeds available from Thompson & Morgan and DeGiorgi.

Harvesting and Using. It's best not to harvest the first year unless you plan to treat the plant like an annual and expect it to die off at summer's end. The plant parts all have an anise scent and flavor. Use leaves in salads and desserts. Sweet cicely can be cooked with very acid fruits like rhubarb and gooseberries. It sweetens any food it's cooked with, reducing the need to add sugar, and is thus favored by diabetics. Harvest and preserve leaves as you would dill. The seeds have a spicy taste. Pick while still green, after the flowers fade. The taproot is remarkably large and can be cooked and added to salads or used as a vegetable.

TANSY (TANACETUM VULGARE): *Do not eat tansy.* This medieval herb is now used only in dried arrangements and as an insect repellent. Propagate by seeds or plant division; it can be transplanted. The problem is usually over-propagation; tansy can become a problem weed in your garden, especially its running roots, which you have to constantly pull out to keep the plants from taking over the entire garden. Plant in average, well-drained soil, in full sun, about 3 feet apart. Available from DeGiorgi.

Tansy in various forms, especially the oil, has been effective against flies, mosquitoes, ants, and some intestinal worms. It was used in the middle ages to flavor puddings, cakes, and in medicinal teas, to scent cosmetics, and to make perfumes, but it is now considered poisonous.

TARRAGON: Originally from Siberia, tarragon is a perennial that comes in 2 basic varieties. French (also called German) tarragon (*Artemisia dracunculus*) is called "little dragon" for its pungent taste. It is not very hardy; if your winters are severe, mulch or bring in. It is a smaller plant (2–3 feet) that is most difficult to propagate, since it never makes seed, but is better tasting.

Russian tarragon (*Artemisia dracunculoides*) grows to 5 feet tall and will make seed, but it has poorer flavor. It's preferred only where French can't make it. Available from DeGiorgi.

Note: Mexican tarragon (*Tagetes lucida*) is a perennial marigold whose leaves have a distinctive tarragon flavor and can be used as a substitute. Available from Redwood City.

Planting. Because French tarragon produces no seed, propagate it by layering, stem cuttings, or root division in the early spring (divide before growth is 2 inches tall). Plant in well-drained, fertile, light (sandy) soil, in full sun or semi-shade. Divide large plants every 2–3 years. Grows well in a pot (use part sand).

Harvesting. Cut off fresh leaves any time through summer.

Drying. Cut off leaves and tops of young plants just after their dew has dried. Dry away from sun or in oven or dehydrator at 110°F until crisp. Or harvest whole stalks in early fall by cutting them off several inches above the ground and hanging them loosely to dry.

Using. A favorite with French chefs for its wonderful flavor, fresh tarragon leaves are good in oil and vinegar salad dressings and with beets, sauces, and any meat, seafood, or cheese. Also used to make perfumes. Dried tarragon is good in tomato juice or any tomato dish. If you're using Russian tarragon, use more, since its flavor is weaker. Grape juice and fresh tarragon make a good herb jelly. You can saute tarragon leaves in butter or oil and baste meat or poultry with it.

✑ *TARRAGON EGGS A mixture of finely chopped tarragon, onion, and parsley is good in an omelet or scrambled eggs.*

✑ *TARRAGON VINEGAR Tarragon keeps its flavor better if preserved in vinegar rather than dried. Gather the tarragon just before it blossoms. Discard the larger stalks. Mash the leaves some. For a plain tarragon vinegar, place two 5-inch sprigs of fresh tarragon in 2 c. white wine vinegar. Or make a fancy one by combining 4 c. tarragon leaves and smaller stalks, 1 qt. white wine vinegar, 3 cloves, and 1 small clove garlic (remove garlic after 24 hours). Takes 2 months to get really good.*

THYME: This popular, semi-hardy, low-growing (to 4–12 inches) Mediterranean perennial has a host of varieties. Common thyme (*Thymus vulgaris*) is easily grown, 6–12 inches tall with grey leaves and lavender blooms, great in the kitchen, can be used for fragrance, makes exceptional honey, and is an antiseptic. Lemon thyme (*Thymus citriodorus*) grows 4–12 inches high, has green leaves and lavender blooms, is good in salads, is superior for poultry stuffing, but is not as hardy as common thyme. Other types such as dwarf thyme and creeping varieties are grown as ornamentals and used in perfumery, but for kitchen use, what you want is common or lemon thyme. Almost every seedhouse carries one or more kinds.

Planting. Thyme grows slowly, so you're best off starting with a plant. Or plant seeds (viable for 2–3 years) in spring. Plant either indoors (1–2 plants per 4-inch pot, or 3–4 plants per 6-inch pot) or out—good in a rock garden or as a border—slightly alkaline soil. Thyme can handle full sun or part shade. Poor soil and infrequent watering actually improve the flavor. You can easily propagate creeping varieties by cuttings in spring or summer, or by root division or layering of lower branches starting in the second year. Thyme grows well in a pot. Bring in for the winter if weather is harsh. Creeping kinds are nice in a hanging basket.

Harvesting and Preserving. Snip some off and use fresh as seasoning, or dry for future use. Thyme is the easiest herb to dry, dried thyme is as effective as fresh, and harvesting makes your plant more bushy and attractive. If you are harvesting from an outdoor, creeping variety, wash the thyme thoroughly, because it tends to contain dirt. If harvesting from common or lemon thyme, which are bushy, cut down as far as the stem remains tender, and you won't need to wash it. Harvest anytime for fresh use. To preserve, cut when thyme has flowers, but snip only the non-flowering shoots. Dry at 110°F until crisp.

Using. The dried leaves are a seasoning ingredient for many soups and sauces, the herbal equivalent of pepper. You can make tea from the dried leaves or flavor vegetable juice, meats, soups, peas, poultry, clam chowder, and gravies. Use fresh leaves in salads. The only rule is to go easy; it's strong stuff. A pinch will usually do, or else you risk the thyme overwhelming the other flavors. Use flowers or foliage in potpourri. Or combine a strong thyme tea with honey and take for a sore throat, or use with a poultice because thyme contains thymol, an oil of proven antiseptic value. Old-timers also gave thyme as a wormer.

TOBACCO: Check with your local USDA and U.S. Treasury Dept. (Bureau of Alcohol, Tobacco and Firearms) so you can comply with any rules or regulations regarding the cultivation, production, or manufacture of tobacco or tobacco products before planting any tobacco seeds. *Nicotiana* species are one of the great natural insecticides. Just keep in mind that it's highly addictive, and don't smoke it. Redwood City sells 3 varieties as well as copies of an 1892 USDA instruction booklet for tobacco cultivation. You can buy seeds from Southern Exposure, Hudson, Seeds of Change, Native Seeds/SEARCH, Eden Organic Nursery (954-455-0229; **www.eonseed.com**), or Jim Johnson, 3421 Bream St., Gautier, MS 39553. Virtual Seeds Co. offers 30+ varieties (530-686-9735; **www.virtualseeds.com**). The U. of Kentucky College of Agriculture offers an 80-pg booklet titled *Tobacco in Kentucky.* ATTRA's brochure, "Organic Tobacco Production," is at **www.attra.org/attra-pub/tobacco.html**. Start in pots as you would plants of the nightshade family (see Chapter 4). Transplant 1–2 feet apart to well-fertilized soil in full sun.

NOTE: Uncured tobacco can be much stronger than commercial cigarettes and dangerous to smoke. Curing lowers the nicotine content.

TURMERIC (*CURCUMA DOMESTICA*, A.K.A. *CURCUMA LONGA*): This relative of ginger can be grown and harvested as you would ginger. It originated in tropical Asia and is now commercially grown in Haiti. Plant the root pieces 2 feet apart. Harvest the roots; wash them, sun-dry them for about 10 days, and then grind to a powder. The spice is used to make curry powders, as a food coloring and dye agent to make a golden shade, to season Far Eastern recipes, in wet mustard recipes for both its color and flavor, and as a saffron substitute. The dictionary says it's also used as a "stimulant." Available from Pacific Tree Farms.

VANILLA: Vanilla beans are the fruit of a Mexican climbing orchid (*Vanilla fragrans planifolia*). The orchid fruits naturally there, but anywhere else on the planet it has to be hand-pollinated. Vanilla begins fruiting at 3 years old, dies at about 10. If you don't live in a tropical climate, this is a greenhouse plant, wintering at no less than 60°F.

Processing. The skinny, 6-inch green pods and their beans don't have the sought-after flavor when picked. They have to be sweated and fermented for days while wrapped in a blanket. Next they are dried in the sun until thoroughly cured. The total time for fermenting plus sun-drying can be several months. They're done when vanillin, an aromatic substance, has developed in the beans; then they have that characteristic, wonderful flavor and fragrance and can be used in perfumes, potpourris, and cooking. By then they are dark brown in color.

Using. Cooking with the whole bean and pod results in remarkably better flavor than just using the extract. The seeds are edible. The pod adds to the flavor if tossed in too, but should be tossed back out after using and not eaten. That outer pod is good for flavoring baking custards and puddings. A 3-inch section of vanilla pod stirred into your mixture equals the flavoring of 1½ t. vanilla extract. To cook with the pod, first split it; then scrape the beans into your food mixture. They can be boiled, or you can make your own extract. Use vanilla or its extract to flavor desserts of any sort.

➣ *OLD-TIME VANILLA EXTRACT Use 4 oz. vanilla beans, 16 oz. edible alcohol, and 16 oz. water. Slice the beans and cut into fine pieces with a sharp knife. Thoroughly powder them in a mortar with 1–2 oz. granulated sugar. Put the powder into the alcohol and water mixture. If you don't have pure alcohol and are substituting a strong whisky blend or brandy, use correspondingly less water. Let the vanilla soak in the liquid for 4 weeks. Strain. The liquid is your extract. Old-time imitation vanilla extract was sometimes made using half or all tonka beans in place of vanilla beans to make it cheaper.*

➣ *EASY VANILLA EXTRACT Violet Stewart, Okay, OK, wrote me that she simply takes 1 qt. of any good 80-proof brandy, splits 2 vanilla beans, and drops them in. She corks it and lets it sit for 2 months before using.*

➣ *NONALCOHOLIC VANILLA EXTRACT Mrs. G. Goodman, Randallstown, MD, wrote me, "Cut up vanilla bean into* small pieces, place in a bowl. Pour ¼ c. boiling water over them; cover bowl, allow mixture to steep overnight. Blend mixture. Strain and return juice to the blender. Add ½ t. liquid lecithin, 1 T. honey, and 1 T. vegetable oil. Blend, pour into a bottle, cap, and refrigerate. Before using, shake well. Use same as commercial vanilla extract in recipes."

VERBENA, LEMON (*LIPPIA CITRIODORA*): This semi-hardy, perennial, fragrant bush has crinkly, pointed leaves and tiny mauve blossoms growing in spikes. It is sometimes confused with lemon balm, which is the one you want for culinary use. Lemon verbena has non-culinary usages such as perfume making and potpourri. (See also "Lemon Verbena.")

VIOLET: There are several varieties of violet. *Viola tricolor* has edible flowers and leaves and is pretty in your garden or salad. Most violets are great in a potpourri because of their heavy perfume.

WINTERGREEN (*GAULTHERIA PROCUMBENS*): This is a very hardy (to −30°F) little evergreen plant with small white flowers. It grows wild, ground-cover style, in coniferous forests of Minnesota, Wisconsin, New York, and Connecticut. Or you can order from Richter's or Raintree Nursery. The berries are bright red and edible raw; nice in a fruit salad. Both leaves and fruit have that wintergreen flavor. Good ground cover.

Planting. It's difficult to grow wintergreen in a domesticated setting. It will grow between 1,000 and 3,000 feet above sea level, but 2,000 feet is ideal. It is naturally adapted for a forest setting of open shade and acid soil. You'll have better luck starting with nursery plants than with wild ones. Propagate by root division in the fall before frost or spring. Plant 12 inches apart in acid (its natural habitat is pine woods), well-drained, light soil. It's a good idea to grow it in a lathe shelter, since it must have full or partial shade to grow well. Or fake the woods to make it happy: Plant on a wooded hillside with a heavy pine needle mulch.

Using. Wintergreen or its extract is excellent in homemade root beer. Wintergreen flowers are edible and can be added to fruit salads or ice cream. Wintergreen leaves are nice to chew on fresh. Dried or fresh leaves make a fragrant tea. Harvest both berries and leaves in early September or October. Use 1 c. fresh leaves per 1 qt. water. The extract is used commercially to flavor gum and candy. The bright red berries are edible, sweet, and tasty. Neither berries nor leaves are dried. Make oil of wintergreen for out-of-season flavoring and fragrance uses.

WITCH HAZEL (*HAMAMELIS VIRGIANA*): This slow-growing shrub (10–15 feet) native to eastern North America has yellow flowers that bloom in October and November. An alcohol extract of witch hazel bark is sold commercially as an astringent lotion. Available from Thompson & Morgan, Richter's, etc.

WOAD (*ISATIS TINCTORA*): *Do not eat.* This European herb, also called dyer's woad, is grown for the blue dye that can be extracted from its leaves. Seedpods are used in arrangements. It reseeds. "Woad" also refers to the dye itself. In 1861 a whimsical Orson Fowler wrote of "singing woad" which, when boiled, results in a "bird-pitched warbling and whistling that issue from the pot." Available from Richter's, etc.

WORMSEED: See "Epazote."

WORMWOOD (*ARTEMISIA ABSINTHUM*): This hardy perennial grows 2–14 feet high. Propagate by root division or fall-planted seeds (viable for 2–3 years). Plant in poor, light soil, in partial shade. It gets several feet tall. Give it a spot by itself. Wormwood is strong stuff. It has a strong, disagreeable smell and can inhibit the growth of nearby plants, even herbs such as caraway, fennel, and sage. If you have harsh winters, cut it back and mulch heavily in the fall for protection.

Wormwood is usually harvested in fall. Dry the sprigs and use to make moth-repellent sachets. A strong wormwood tea can be used as a fleakiller bath for your pets. It is used in flavoring absinthe and was traditionally used to treat worms (hence its name). A wormwood spray can protect against some pests. Available from Redwood City, Richter's, etc.

YUCCA: The roots of yucca contain saponin, a natural sudsing agent, good for washing delicate fabrics.

Planting. It takes 1–2 months to germinate at 65–75°F. Even after that, its growth tends to be slow and erratic. It needs easily draining soil. If in a pot, it actually does better if a little pot-bound. It's not very hardy. Available from Richter's, Thompson & Morgan, etc.

Using. Chop roots, soak in water, and stir to a lather.

COCOA, COFFEE(S), AND TEA

COCOA: Cocoa trees (*Theobroma cacao*) originated in the tropical lowlands of Central America and southern Mexico. The tree seeds are cocoa beans. Foods made from them contain theobromine, a mild stimulant; caffeine, a stronger stimulant (in a much smaller amount than tea or coffee); and possibly also phenylethylamine, a mood lifter. So for medicinal purposes, chocolate can help the lethargic, the depressed, and the lovelorn. It can also make your toddler temporarily hyperactive. Hardy only to 32°F, cocoa trees are available from Pacific Tree Farms.

Cocoa to Drink. The original beverage made by ancient Native Americans by steeping the crushed bean in hot water was bitter but treasured. The Spanish tried adding sugar to sweeten it, and that helped. They also mixed ground cocoa beans with cinnamon and used them to create a wonderful meat sauce.

Cocoa Butter. In its natural state, the cocoa bean is about half fat, or cocoa butter. Because of all that fat, it is hard to dissolve cocoa. A Dutchman discovered a way to remove half the fat; the resulting product, our familiar cocoa powder, is much more soluble and pleasant to drink. An enterprising Swiss entrepeneur discovered a way to use the cocoa butter removed in the process of making cocoa powder. He perfected a method by which machines rolled and kneaded the beans and at the same time doubled their fat content by adding the surplus cocoa butter from the powder-making process. The result was confectioner's chocolate.

Milk Chocolate. Another Swiss man added milk and so created milk chocolate, a less concentrated and more pleasant product. Since then, chocolate has been selling by the ton.

White Chocolate. This is pure cocoa butter (all the rest of the bean removed) with sugar to sweeten it and vanilla to flavor it.

Basic Cocoa Bean Processing. Harvest the pods that hold the cocoa beans. Then split them open, shell out the beans, and let them ferment for a period. Then dry them and roast them. The familiar scent and taste of chocolate will not emerge until after the roasting. The beans actually consist of 2 layers, the outer shells and the inside "nibs," which are the central "heart" of the bean. After the roasting, crack open those outer shells and discard them (they make great mulch). Grind the nibs enough to create some heat. The heat melts the cocoa butter portion of the nibs into a thick paste, referred to as the "chocolate liquor." That liquor mixture is then poured into molds, square or bar-shaped, and cooled. After cooling, you now have unsweetened baking chocolate, the same stuff you can buy in the store!

Making Cocoa Powder. You have to get rid of half the fat and grind. To make fondant chocolate, add extra cocoa butter and knead it in. If you add sugar, vanilla, and powdered milk and knead them in, you'll have milk chocolate. Results are affected by the varieties of cocoa beans you start with, the nature of the roasting stage, how much cocoa butter and sugar you add, and how long you knead it. More detailed recipes are manufacturer's trade secrets that I couldn't find out for you.

> *❧ HOT FUDGE SAUCE Break 8 oz. unsweetened or semisweet baking chocolate into chunks. Combine chunks with 1 c. light cream in a heavy pan set on very low heat. Once the chocolate begins melting, stir constantly until the fudge is smooth and thick. If it's too bitter for your taste, mix in sugar. Then take the pan off the heat source and stir in ½ t. vanilla. This is traditionally served over vanilla ice cream. Pour surplus sauce into a jar, cover, and refrigerate. It will keep at least several weeks. When you want to use it again, just reheat, again constantly stirring.*

> *❧ BASIC MOCHA "Mocha" means flavored with a mixture of chocolate and coffee. Combine 2 c. strong black coffee (instant is OK), 3 c. hot milk, 4 heaping T. chocolate powder, and 3 heaping T. sugar. (If chocolate powder is already sweetened, skip sugar.) Beat until foamy.*

> *❧ SPICED MOCHA MIX Combine 1 c. dry nondairy creamer, 1 c. cocoa powder, ⅔ c. instant coffee, ½ c. sugar, ½ t. cinnamon, and ¼ t. nutmeg. Keep it in a jar in a cool place. To serve, add 3–4 heaped t. to 1 c. very hot water. Nice served hot with a dollop of whipped cream on top, or cold with ice chunks in it, or with a big scoop of vanilla ice cream in it!*

> *❧ COCOA INSECTICIDE Soaking poultry with a strong tea made from cocoa leaves will clear them of lice. Cocoa shells are also lice-repellent and are useful mixed with animal bedding.*

COFFEE (GENUS *COFFEA*): The coffee plant is native to east Africa. It looks like a small tree or shrub and grows up to 8 feet tall in a pot (up to 15 feet outdoors). A dwarf variety gets only 3 feet tall. Coffee can be grown in a temperate-zone garden if you transplant to a container and bring inside for the winter. The coffee plant is quite ornamental with its scented white flowers and shiny dark green foliage. The coffee plant can't survive a frost and needs some shade to protect it from excessive sun. It can be grown outdoors in the California coastal area from about Santa Barbara on south. Pacific Tree Farms says their variety is hardy to 28°F.

Plants or seed are available from Richter's, Pacific Tree Farms, Banana Tree, and Colin Westwood (who also offers growing instructions): 02-6677-6003; 196 Farrants Hill Rd., Condong, NSW, 2484 AUSTRALIA; **coli7@bigpond.com**.

Planting. Keep seeds dry before planting. Plant coffee seed on the soil surface in a sand-peat or half-organic mix. Keep warm (about 85°F) and allow a sizable time (a month or more) for germination. Once well started, transplant outdoors or to 4-inch pots. Grow potted coffee in well-drained soil; situate in a sunny window. Young coffee plants grow best at 70–75°F. If you have trouble with brown leaves, it means you've been watering too much, need to move the plant to a larger pot, or both.

Harvesting. For flowering and fruiting, the plants need 55–58°F night temperatures. Without those conditions, the plant will just grow bunches of lovely dark green glossy leaves—no flowers, no beans. Also be cautious with pruning. Cutting off the top does no harm, but trimming branches eliminates your crop, since flowers and beans grow there. The white flowers evolve into ½-inch fruits that are first green and then red, purple, or scarlet when ripe. When ripe, harvest them.

Using. Each pod contains 2 coffee beans, which you rescue from the outer pulp, dry, roast, grind, and soak in very hot water to make your beverage. (You can mail-order a coffee grinder from Lehman's, 888-438-5346; **www.Lehmans.com**.) Coffee contains a lot of caffeine. An occasional cup can be a helpful sustainer in an emergency, but I know too many people who are addicted: They drink 30–40 cups a day, desperately wish they didn't, and can't stop. Heavy coffee consumption is definitely linked to pancreatic cancer.

Coffee Grounds. These, on the other hand, are a first-class, environmentally harmless deterrent to ants. To keep ants out of your house, or any other building, just lay a solid 3-inch layer against your foundation all the way around. To deal with an anthill, surround it likewise with a sizable ring of grounds. Grounds will also prevent cutworms (as do wood ashes). Just dig a shallow ditch around vulnerable plants and pour grounds into it. As they break down, they'll also add fertility to the soil. Grounds are also great in your compost pile; earthworms love them and will quickly turn them into rich humus. And a manure/grounds/leafy mulch mixture added to poor soil will practically instantly make it fertile. No need to strain your pancreas! To get enough grounds to accomplish all this, just contact a business that brews coffee in quantity, and ask them to let you take all those unwanted coffee grounds off their hands!

COFFEES THAT AREN'T COFFEE: You can buy them at the store: Postum, Kaf-free Roma, etc. Mike and I have drunk Postum for years and enjoy it. It's made from ground and roasted grain. Mike drinks a heaping teaspoon of Postum in a cup of hot water. That's too strong for me. I like a level teaspoon with honey and milk, about one-third or one-fourth milk. I often make a whole coffeepot of it that way and share it with the children for breakfast. Unlike real coffee, "coffees that aren't coffee" can safely be shared with them. It's more comfortable than saying to children, "That's not good for you; you can't have any," while they stand there watching me drink it. The wise psychologists say our children imitate what we do and not what we say. In their innocent devotion, they try to follow the truest form of our behavior.

You can drink Postum in all milk, in milk with a dash of cocoa, made into an eggnog with milk, or with milk flavored with molasses. Another store-bought non-coffee product is called Yannoh. It is made from barley, wheat, soya, chickpeas, rice, dandelion, and burdock roots. You perk it just like coffee. If your grocer, co-op, or health-food store doesn't have it, ask them to order it for you.

➤ *ROASTED GRAIN COFFEE Combine 8 c. wheat bran, 3 beaten eggs, 2 c. cornmeal, and 1 c. molasses or sorghum. Spread the mixture on a cookie sheet and bake slowly at about 200°F, stirring often. Boil with water to serve.*

➤ *ACORN COFFEE Select plump, round, sweet acorns. Shell and brown in oven. Grind in a coffee mill and use as ordinary coffee. Or hull ½ c. small sweet acorns. Add ½ c. cracked wheat. Mix. Roast in your oven. Pound in a mortar. Boil with water to get your coffee. Add honey, molasses, or brown sugar to sweeten.*

➤ *DANDELION ROOT COFFEE Dandelion coffee makes a surprisingly good substitute. Gather roots in the fall (October) or in the early spring before blooming. Scrub unpeeled roots with a stiff brush. Use the big part for a root vegetable (see "Dandelion" in Chapter 4). The skinny side roots are what you dry, grind, and roast. Dry them in the oven (150°F) until they are brittle and snap easily. Then roast them at about 375°F for 15–20 minutes or until they are dark brown inside. Grind in blender until they look like coffee, or use a rolling pin to grind to a coarse powder. Store in glass jars and use just as you would coffee. Boil about 1 t. per cup and stir it in. Your brew will have a flavor all its own, vaguely chocolaty and pleasing. You'll like it better every time the price of coffee goes up. But bear in mind that dandelion root is a powerful diuretic, so it may not be the best choice if you're pregnant.*

Chicory Coffee. The mature roots of the Magdeburgh chicory variety (available from William Dam) can be dried, ground, and mixed with coffee to stretch it. Added to oven-browned barley, it makes a coffee substitute that has been very popular in Europe. (See "Chicory" in Chapter 4.) You can also make a chicory coffee from Witloof or wild chicory roots, but Magdeburgh is the specialist.

Unlike the other chicories, this is a perennial and needs a permanent corner of your garden. It has broad, smooth-edged, dark green leaves that grow in loose, upright (edible) heads. But what you're after is the 14–16-inch roots. Grow those roots an entire season long, at least 100 days. Or better yet, let them grow 2 summers. Then cut off the green tops (make salad). Scrub or scrape the roots, slice them, and string your little circles or strips of chicory on a thread. Hang up to dry. When completely dry, spread on a cookie sheet and roast at a low temperature until a very dark brown—they start to smell like chocolate cake. Taste to detect the moment of roasted perfection. Now cool the chicory. Grind it with mortar and pestle or some other means.

To brew chicory coffee, first boil a pot of water. Then drop in a spoonful of ground chicory, stir, let steep a few minutes, and there you are. Chicory is stronger than coffee, so use less. Serve plain or with honey and cream. You can make more chicory coffee out of the same grounds.

TEA: Tea leaves come from tea trees (*Thea sinensis*). They still grow wild in a few parts of the world, but they've been domesticated since ancient China. Tea handles pruning well and makes a fine hedge. It blooms in fall with small, fragrant, lovely white or pink flowers. The stimulant, caffeine, is a natural component of tea leaves. For more information, read *Tea Growing* by C.R. Harler (London: Oxford University Press, 1966), *All About Tea* by William H. Ukers (New York: The Tea & Coffee Trade Journal Co., 1935), or *Tea for Home Use,* a USDA pamphlet on how to cultivate and harvest home-grown tea, available from Redwood City.

Climate. Tea is a subtropical, evergreen plant of the camellia family that can't handle frost or snow and also dislikes high winds. If your climate has blistering sunshine, plant in partial shade. If you have a relatively cloudy, cool weather pattern, plant in full sun. Tea does best where there is warm, humid weather, temperatures don't drop below 24°F, and quite a bit of rainfall falls evenly distributed throughout the year. Morning fogs are wonderful for it. Tea will grow in southern California and the deep South. In colder areas, your tea trees can thrive and produce leaves in a container.

Varieties. There are about 30 different varieties. Unpruned wild teas grow 30–40 feet tall and belong to a large-leaf group. The domesticated teas are small-leaved, pruned to be shrubby, and allowed to grow only 4–15 feet high for easier harvesting. The tea tree has a round, dense nature. In the Far East you'd have many named varieties to choose from, but here you don't.

Planting. Tea plants are hard to find. Plant a half dozen to meet the tea-making needs of a family. You can mail-order seed from Park. Almost any soil, from sand to clay, will do, but tea needs acid soil with lots of organic material in it, a pH of 4–6, and good drainage (and no saltiness!). Plant tea seeds with their "eye" face down. Once you've grown a plant from seed, layering is another possible way of propagating, as is planting a cut branch or grafting. Water young plants regularly enough that their roots never dry out. Keep thick mulch over the roots. Be patient; tea plants grow very slowly. It will be years before your plant gets even 4 feet tall. Mature plants can get along with less regular watering.

Harvesting. In commercial tea plantations, the trees are fertilized, seeded, pruned, and harvested—all mechanically. (Pruning is done to cause new small leaves to grow as well as to shape the plant.) You'll be doing it by hand. Wait until your tea tree is at least 2–3 years old before you start. Then in early spring, when the weather gets warm and new leaves start to grow on the plant, pick just 2 or 3 leaves from the very tip of each branchlet. Those make the best tea. Harvesting doesn't hurt a tea plant's growth because you take only the new, outside leaves. Tea leaves can be harvested from spring to fall—as long as you always choose the new leaves. Specialty teas may have special harvest times. Green tea and Pao Chung tea are harvested in spring and autumn. Certain black teas and oolong tea are harvested in the summer. "Green" and "black" teas refer not to tree varieties but to the result of different processing methods.

Making Green Tea. Place your just-plucked leaves in the top pan of your double boiler as is, covered but with no water over them. Fill the lower pan with water, bring it to boiling, and boil about 10 minutes. The leaves will now be much softer.

Pre-Drying: Spread them out thinly on a drying surface. Place your leaf-covered tray in an airy but shady spot. You want them to get limp, but not brittle! After 12–24 hours (you'll learn the golden moment from experience), the leaves will be ready to roll.

Rolling: Lay out 1–2 cups of leaves on a clean rolling surface, roll firmly with a rolling pin, and then knead with your hands, just like bread dough. Spend about 10 minutes on this stage. Now evolve your kneading motion to incorporate a twisting, rolling movement that will gradually transform those leaves into a tight roll. By now some moisture should be coming out of them. If it isn't, you dried them too long, and you need to add about 1 T. water. Veteran tea-makers say that the tighter and longer the leaves are rolled (at least 30 minutes, please!), the more flavorful the tea.

Final Drying: After that, distribute leaves over a drying tray and dry in oven or dehydrator at a very low temperature and with good ventilation (oven door open). Toss and turn the leaves around once in a while to help the drying process. Continue drying at that very gentle heat until they become totally dry (brittle).

Making Black Tea. Pick your leaves. Skip the heating process and go directly to the pre-drying and rolling. Then, before the final drying, add this curing step.

Curing: Press the leaves together into a dense ball shape. Wrap the ball tightly with plastic or a faintly moist cloth, and let rest in a somewhat cool room for about 8 hours. By now the leaves are distinctly fragrant and have changed to a copper color. Now do the final drying.

Storage. Have ready airtight containers for storage. Keep them in a cool place.

🍃 *EAST INDIAN TEA Make black tea; add milk and honey. Keep heating. Add ginger, cinnamon, and ground cardamom to taste and serve.*

🍃 *HOMEMADE SPICED ORANGE TEA Crush 2½ t. whole cloves and five 2-inch cinnamon sticks to a chunky but not powdery stage. Combine with 1 lb. orange pekoe tea, 4 T. candied ginger (chopped fine), 4 T. dried orange peel, and 1 t. nutmeg. Just 1 t. of this tea makes 1 cup for serving. Steep about 10 minutes before drinking. For company, serve with an orange slice and sweetener.*

The oldest sections of my book were written before my readers got the message through to me that I was supposed to sound like myself instead of a book. I figured that out later. With the first 2 issues of the book that I mailed out to "subscribers," I also sent cover letters to explain a few things (make my excuses). So many people wrote back to say my book would do, but what they really enjoyed was the cover letters! After that, I tried to do all my writing the same way as those cover letters. I've been leafing through those old letters. Here's part of one I wrote in February 1971:

"Thank you very much for your check and order for the *Old Fashioned Recipe Book*! I will send it as soon as possible, but I must beg your patience because that may be as long as a month yet."

No kidding, I said that. At that time I had no understanding of the real size and nature of the job I'd gotten myself hooked into. It wasn't until 3 years later, in 1974, that I actually finished that first edition.

DO-IT-YOURSELF COSMETICS

Here's another whole category of environmental poisons that we could do away with. In Japanese the words for "pretty" and "healthy" are the same. Once when I was bemoaning my adolescent imperfections, my mother said, "To be young is to be beautiful." At the time I thought she was talking nonsense. Now I'm the age she was then and I understand the truth of it. The lily doesn't need to be gilded. My father taught that beauty was on the inside, that it consisted of glowing good health and a fine character. On the other hand, maybe I lean too far toward being unconscious of appearances. I could have won the worst-dressed prize every year of my life. And somebody else had to tell me to put natural cosmetics in this book.

I'm glad she did, for once I got started looking for these formulas, they turned out to be great fun to try! Experiment and see which ingredients suit you best. But don't forget that your skin's condition is influenced most of all by your diet, age, amount of exercise, and amount of sleep. Too much stress in your life, too little humidity in your air, too much exposure to sun, and too much fatty, sweety, junky, chemicalized food can be doing your appearance far more harm than these treatments by themselves can relieve. *NOTE: To prevent allergic reactions, test a small quantity of any unaccustomed substance by rubbing it on the underside of your arm. Then wait 24–48 hours to see if a rash develops.*

FOR YOUR FACE

Analyze Your Skin Type. What you put on your skin should be appropriate for its type. Only very oily skin should be dosed with highly acid treatments like citrus fruits (lemon, lime, grapefruit), Concord grapes, strawberries, or apples. If you don't have very oily skin but want an acid skin treatment, use fruits that are a little less acid than the previous list—peaches, apricots, grapes other than Concord, and tomatoes. If you want a beneficial fruit treatment whose acidity is about the same as that of normal

POISONOUS PLANTS

Here are some poisonous plants to look out for. This list was sent to me by my dear friend Violet Stewart. She wrote me, "I hope you can find a space for this in your book. I'll feel I may have had a part in saving one life." I did find space—and since then I've learned and added more.

Aconite: All parts.

American False Hellebore

Anemone (wind flower): Nemerosa is poisonous.

Angel's Trumpet (*Datura*): All parts poisonous.

Arrowgrass

Azalea: All parts very dangerous—nausea and vomiting, depression, hard to breathe, prostration, fatal coma.

Baneberry: Berries, red or white, are poisonous.

Black Locust: Flower is edible; rest is poisonous.

Bleeding Heart: Leaves and roots may be poisonous in large amounts.

Bloodroot

Bouncing Bet

Butterflyweed

Castor Oil Plant (*Ricinus communis*): One or two castor bean seeds are a near fatal dose to an adult, let alone a child.

Celadine Poppy

Chokecherry: Leaves and seeds are poisonous.

Christmas Rose (*Helleborus*): Seeds and all plant parts are poisonous.

Cockle, Corn or Purple: All parts are poisonous.

Columbine (*Aquilegia*): Seed/all plant parts poisonous.

Crocus: Autumn crocus bulbs can be dangerous.

Daffodil: Bulb causes nausea, vomiting, diarrhea, and may be fatal. Sap makes your hand swell up if it gets into a cut.

Daphne: A few of the berries can kill a child.

Datura: See "Angel's Trumpet."

Daylily: Roots are poisonous.

Deadly Nightshade

Death Camas

Desert Rose (*Adenium*): The milky juice may be a heart poison.

Dieffenbachia: All plant parts cause intense burning and irritation of mouth and tongue. If the tongue swells and closes the throat, no air can get through.

Digitalis: See "Foxglove."

Dutchman's Pipe (*Aristolochia*): All plant parts are poisonous.

English Ivy

European Bittersweet

Foxglove (*Digitalis*): All plant parts poisonous. Leaves contain digitalis, a heart stimulant. In large amounts it can be fatal.

Frangipani (*Plumaria*): Poisonous sap.

Garland Flower: Poisonous berries.

Hemlock: Read the story at the end of this chapter.

Horse Chestnut, Horse Nettle, and **Horsetail**

Hyacinth: Eating the bulb will cause nausea, vomiting, diarrhea, and may be fatal.

Iris: Entire plant is poisonous.

Jack in the Pulpit

Jessamine: Berries are fatal.

Jimson Weed

Larkspur (annual delphinium): Poisonous seeds and leaves.

Larsonia: The seeds can be fatal.

Laurel: All plant parts can be fatal, producing nausea and vomiting, difficulty in breathing, prostration, and coma.

Leafy Spurge

Lily, Flame: All plant parts are poisonous.

Lily, Glory: The tubers are highly poisonous.

Lily of the Valley: The leaves and flowers disrupt heartbeat, stomach, and mind.

Lobelia: Poisonous.

Lupine: All plant parts, including seeds, poisonous.

Marsh Marigold

Marvel of Peru (*Mirabilis*): All plant parts poisonous.

Matrimony Vine

Mayapple: Poisonous; fruit is also poisonous if too much is eaten and must be yellow, totally ripe,

and smell sweet.

Meadow Saffron

Mistletoe: Berries can be fatal to children or adults.

Monkshood (*Aconitum*): All parts, including roots, are poisonous.

Morning Glory (*Ipomoea*): All plant parts poisonous.

Mountain Laurel

Narcissus: Bulbs are poisonous—cause nausea, vomiting, diarrhea, and may be fatal.

Oleander: Leaves and branches are poisonous—affect heart, cause severe digestive upset, have killed.

Pennyroyal: Poisonous.

Poinsettia: Even one leaf can kill a child.

Poison Ivy

Poison Oak

Pokeweed: Young shoots up to 6 in., if free of purple coloring, are edible if boiled in a sequence of two discarded waters. Rest is poisonous.

Poppy, Horned (*Glaucium*): Roots are poisonous.

Poppy, Iceland: All plant parts are poisonous.

Poppy, Somniferum: Fruits and sap are poisonous.

Privet

Rhododendron: All parts can be fatal—nausea and vomiting, difficulty in breathing, prostration, coma.

Rhubarb: The leaves, even cooked, can cause convulsions and coma, soon followed by death.

Rosary Pea: A single seed has caused death.

St. Johnswort

Skunk Cabbage

Snowdrops

Solomon's Seal (*Polygonatum*): The seeds and all plant parts are poisonous.

Star of Bethlehem

Tobacco (*Nicotiana*): All species/plant parts poison.

Wisteria: Poisonous.

Yew: Berries and leaves (more so) are fatal. Death is sudden—no warning symptoms.

skin, use bananas, green peppers, cucumber, watermelon, or persimmon. If you want a treatment that will moisturize dry skin using substances very low in acid, go with carrots, iceberg lettuce, cantaloupe, avocado, or honeydew melon.

Steaming. This is a good treatment for skin problems and a general pick-me-up. I've enjoyed it many times. It deep-cleans your facial pores. To experts, steaming means putting your face in a hot towel tent. To me, it means spending 5–10 minutes with a few hot washrags on my face. When you're done, wash out any dirt that's left; then close those pores with cold washrags or an astringent. *NOTE: Don't use this or any other heat treatment on a face that already has broken veins, because it can make them worse.*

Face Masks. A mask consists of a "binder" (which makes it adhere) and other ingredients mixed in with the binder. Choose your binder according to whether your skin tends to be oily or dry. For oily skin, use yogurt or egg white as a binder. For dry skin, choose lanolin, honey, sour cream, or egg yolk. Experiment with the other ingredients. You can blend vegetables and fruits and combine them with your binder, or use any of the recipes below. Wash your face clean before applying the mask. Don't ever put a mask onto the area around your eyes. Rinse off after a half hour or as soon as the mask dries. (While you're waiting, it's a good time to take a nap.) To remove the mask, use a washrag and warm water. Then use cold water to close your pores. *NOTE: If you feel any irritation, rinse off immediately!*

➣ **EGG WHITE MASK** *This helps drag blackheads and whiteheads out of your pores. Slightly beat an egg white and spread it fairly thickly over your face. Let it dry. Do the same thing with another egg white right on top of the first.*

➣ **OATMEAL MASK** *Mix together ⅔ c. oatmeal and enough honey to make a pasty consistency. Optionally, add 2 t. rose water.*

➣ **HONEY/LEMON MASK** *Mix 2 T. slightly warmed honey with 1 t. lemon juice. Put the mixture on your face and leave for about a half hour.*

➣ **BREWER'S YEAST MASK** *Mix yeast with enough water to create a paste. Smooth it over your face (not into eyes!). Let dry. Then remove with warm water. Do this 1–2 times a week. For dry skin, add 1 T. wheat germ oil or 1 egg yolk to mask. You can also add 3 t. brewer's yeast to milk or fruit juice and drink it daily.*

Skin Cleansers

➣ **INSTANT SKIN CLEANSER** *Get a lather up with mild soap. Sprinkle some kitchen cornmeal into the lather and rub and scrub your face with the mixture. See "Elderberry" in Chapter 6 for more recipes.*

➣ **YOGURT CLEANSER** *Mix yogurt with a tiny dash of salt. Not for dry skin.*

➣ **CLEANSING CREAM** *In a double boiler, melt and mix together ½ c. safflower (or sweet almond) oil, 1 T. cocoa butter, and 1 T. anhydrous lanolin. Take off the heat, beat until partly cooled, and store in a jar. Shake before using.*

➣ **FRUIT CLEANSER** *Sliced tomato or cucumber.*

➣ **HERBAL STEAMING FACIAL** *Moisten your hot washrags with an herb tea—chamomile, nettle, rosemary, or peppermint.*

Other Treatments

➣ **ASTRINGENTS** *Use peeled cucumbers, lemon juice and water, or rose water.*

➣ **SKIN FRESHENER** *Try a strong mint-tea facial.*

➣ **PEACHES AND CREAM MOISTURIZER** *Blend together 1 ripe peach and heavy cream. Refrigerate. Massage onto your skin wherever needed once per day.*

➣ **TREATMENT FOR LARGE PORES** *Put 4 T. bran mixed with the chopped skins of 2 lemons into a jelly bag. Dip it into boiling water. Apply to face with enough pressure on bag contents to squeeze out a little of the lemon quality. Repeat for a while.*

➣ **FOR OILY SKIN** *Try cold parsley tea dabbed on several times a day.*

➣ **HOMEMADE LIP GLOSS OR ROUGE** *Mix a drop of food coloring with a fingerful of petroleum jelly. Kids have fun with this, and it won't hurt their skin.*

FOR YOUR BODY

For a recipe for herbal hand lotion, see "Products and Processes."

Herbal Bath. Make a strong tea by pouring boiling water over your chosen herbs. Let steep while you draw your bathwater. Then strain into the water. Or just put herbs right in your bath water—either loose or in a little cheesecloth bag. Let them steep 10 minutes; then join them in there. Good herbs for bathing are chamomile, lemon verbena, mint, peppermint, and rosemary.

➣ **HERBAL BATH SALTS** *With Epsom salts, mix sage, thyme, and pennyroyal; lemon balm and peppermint; lavender, rosemary, and pennyroyal; or another herb or herbal combination that pleases you. Or use Epsom salts with a few drops of your favorite fragrance or herbal oil mixed in. When bottled attractively, this makes a nice gift.*

FOR YOUR HAIR

➣ **HEALTHIER HAIR** *Take vitamin A and D supplements daily, plus 1 t. brewer's yeast.*

➣ **VINEGAR HAIR RINSE** *Mix 3 T. vinegar per ½ gal. water.*

➣ **HERBAL HAIR RINSE** *Rinse your hair in herb tea. Chamomile is best for blondes, rosemary for brunettes.*

➣ **BALSAM HAIR RINSE** *Pound 1 qt. balsam fir needles with a hammer to release the oils. Then soak them in cold water overnight. Rub in 2 T. of your balsam rinse after shampooing and rinsing. Rinse well again.*

➣ **CHAMOMILE SHAMPOO** *Barb Ingram, Santa, ID, says she uses this formula: Put 1 T. soap flakes, 1 t. borax, and 1 oz. powdered chamomile flowers into a basin. Add ½ pint hot water. Heat until thick lather is formed. Wet hair with warm water, massage, rinse, and wash again. (For a general herbal shampoo recipe, see "Products and Processes.")*

FOR YOUR TEETH

➣ **HOMEMADE TOOTHPASTE** *You can use common table salt for a toothpaste. It's rougher on your teeth and mouth and doesn't taste as good, but it's cheap and available. Takes care of bad breath too! Or use plain baking soda; baking soda with a drop of oil of spearmint, peppermint, cinnamon, or cloves in it; a mixture of 3 parts baking soda and 1 part salt; or, best of all, a mixture of 4 t. baking soda, 1 t. salt, 1 t. mint flavoring, and just enough water to get a toothpasty texture (about ½–1 t.). Keep any moist* homemade toothpaste in a covered container so it won't dry out.

☙ **BREATH FRESHENER** *Chew up some mint leaves!*

WILD FOOD FORAGING

May 25, 1976. Last summer a forest ranger near here sat down to eat his packed lunch out in the woodsy open. He spotted an interesting-looking plant nearby, broke off a leaf, added it to the inside of his sandwich as an experiment, and ate his lunch. He was dead within 2 hours. A little boy 25 miles down the road from us at Lapwai, Idaho, spotted a big reedy plant that looked just right for whistle making. He carved himself a very fine whistle out of it, blew on it to see if it worked . . . and died.

Those are true stories. They both happened in the summer of 1975, and in both cases hemlock was the cause. Hemlock is one of the most poisonous plants in the world. It belongs to the same family as the plant substance that killed Socrates when it was fed to him in a cup. That was water hemlock, which is native to Greece and causes death within 5 minutes. Hemlock has migrated from Europe to the United States and is spreading all over North America. It likes to grow in shady places and spreads along river and creek banks. The North American kind takes ½–2 hours to kill you.

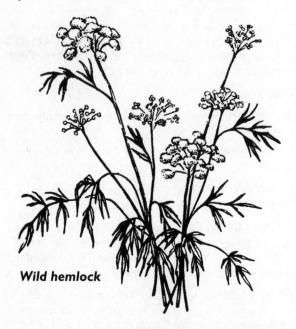

Wild hemlock

Hemlock is a biennial and a member of the carrot family. The first year it grows low and has a very carrot-like top; its energy goes into making a sturdy root, which is its most poisonous part. The next year, energy from that big root pours up into building a sturdy, tall stalk, 5–6 feet high—perfect-looking whistle material. Then it flowers and makes seed at the top of the stalk.

Its flowers and seeds are poisonous too. Some neighbors down the road with a lot of the stuff chopped it all down, gathered it into a pile, and set fire to it. The smoke made their whole family sick. The county weed control agent, Homer Fudder, told them that fumes from burning hemlock were also poisonous. Homer has a personal campaign to try to stop the hemlock and to stop people from

dying of it. He told me you can even die if you try to pull out the plant and have a cut on your hand that hemlock juice gets into.

But you say you've got a book that tells you which wild foods are edible and which aren't. Well, right in front of me I have an article called "Principal Food Plants of the United States," published in an utterly respectable wilderness and country living magazine. It says, "HEMLOCK—(all year) young tips used for tea and formerly in root beer; inner bark used for breadstuff; sap, potable." It doesn't distinguish between the nonpoisonous hemlock tree and the poisonous hemlock plant. If that one entry in a list of a couple hundred "food plants" is so potentially misleading, how much can others be trusted? What about the books that describe plants that have "medicinal uses"? I found hemlock in one of those, too. It said it was "good to strengthen male potency."

Take it from a professional author. Don't believe everything you read. So often authors end up simply collecting information already in print—with the ever-present danger of passing on somebody else's error. Or they have to put the ideas in their own words so it isn't plagiarizing, and they end up restating something in such a way that the facts become distorted. Or they write down hearsay that simply isn't true. That's scary when the results could be fatal. That's why this book doesn't have a real wild-foods section. You'll find wild foods mentioned here and there within it: nettle tea, poke salet from the South, dandelion root and greens, elderberries and chokecherries—but only when I know from personal experience or from common experience of friends and neighbors that at least part of the plant really is edible, and when it's commonly known and easily identified.

I don't mean to put down the bulk of the wonderful research that has been done on wild foods, but be cautious what you put in your sandwich. A good program on wild foods comes from Miriam Kramer at Wilderness Leadership International: 909-796-8501; 24414 University Ave. #34, Loma Linda, CA 92354; **outdoorsurvival@yahoo.com**; **www.outdooreduquip.com**. They sell correspondence courses in edible wild plants, using herbs, and wilderness survival. "Dining on the Wilds" is a 6-hr. video set with two manuals.

The Wild Foods Forum is published by Vicki Shufer, Virginia Beach, VA; 757-421-3929; **wildfood@infi.net.** Goosefoot Acres: Center for Resourceful Living publishes a *Directory of Edible Wild Plant Educators,* sells books, sponsors contests, and publishes a newsletter on using wild foods: 216-932-2145; orders 800-697-4858; PO Box 18016, Cleveland, OH 44118; **petergail@aol.com; www. edibleweeds.com.** Peter is a Ph.D. ethnobotanist, author of eight books, 250 articles, and inspiration of the National Dandelion Cook-off (first weekend in May; Dover, OH)! For $35/yr, join Defenders of Dandelions, and get Peter's book, *Dandelion Celebration: A Guide to Unexpected Cuisine,* plus T-shirt or tote bag and newsletter, *Dandelion Doings.*

Could a rancher who had lived in the country all his life make a mistake in his plant identification? Just a month ago, I happened to be standing close by when three innocent visitors to the School of Country Living (Julaine Konselman, a young widow; her 12-year-old only son; and Jack Clark, a local businessman) ate hemlock after a local pointed out a plant he called "Indian celery" and urged, "Try it." (The showing-off-his-"knowledge" local didn't himself partake.)

I wish I'd managed to stop them before they swallowed the stuff. But I did break up their idyllic stroll through a pasture immediately after they ate it, rushed them to town, ran to the drugstore, bought Ipecac (the stuff that makes you throw up), and made them drink it. Jack and Julaine's son threw up, but she didn't. "I'm sorry," she apologized miserably. "I never throw up." Then I recruited friends to rush them the 28 miles to the emergency room of the Lewiston hospital, where all three got their stomachs pumped.

After a night's sleep, they all felt okay—good enough, in fact, that Jack kept wondering if I'd put him through all that misery for nothing. The Ipecac and the stomach pumping was enough to make a person feel lousy, he figured. And the rancher kept insisting it really was just "Indian celery."

So a week later, Jack returned to that pasture, picked a specimen of the exact same stuff he and the others had eaten, and took it to the office of a poison weed specialist at the University of Idaho. When he walked into the professor's office, it was noontime and the gentleman was reading at his desk. Jack set the plant down in front of him and said, "I ate some of that."

The scholar looked up from his book at Jack, and at the plant. His eyes widened. He half-rose from his chair. "How long ago?" he nervously asked.

"A week ago," Jack coolly replied.

There was a long silence. "You ought to be dead," the professor finally muttered. "You're very lucky."

"What is this plant?" Jack asked.

"Hemlock . . . deadly poisonous."

POISON CONTROL CENTERS

Alabama: Poison Center, Tuscaloosa: 800-462-0800 (AL only); 205-345-0600. Children's Hospital, Birmingham: 800-292-6678 (AL only); 205-933-4050.

Alaska: Anchorage Poison Control Center, Anchorage: 800-478-3193; 907-261-3193.

Arizona: Poison & Drug Info Center, Tucson: 800-362-0101 (AZ only); 520-626-6016. Good Samaritan Regional Medical Center, Phoenix: 800-362-0101 (AZ only); 602-253-3334.

Arkansas: Poison & Drug Information Center, Little Rock: 800-376-4766; TTY/TDD: 800-641-3805.

California: Poison Control System: 800-876-4766 (CA only); TTY/TDD 800-972-3323.

Colorado: Rocky Mountain Poison & Drug Center: 800-332-3073; 303-739-1123 (Denver metro).

Connecticut: Poison Control Center: 800-343-2722 (CT only); 860-679-3456; TTY/TDD 860-679-4346.

Delaware: Poison Control Center, Philadelphia: 800-722-7112; 215-386-2100.

District of Columbia: National Capital Poison Center, Washington, DC: 202-625-3333; TTY/TDD 202-362-8563.

Florida: Poison Information Center, Jacksonville: 800-282-3171 (FL only); 904-244-4480; TTY/TDD 800-282-3171. Miami: 800-282-3171 (FL only); 305-585-5253. Tampa: 800-282-5846; 404-616-9000; TTY/TDD 404-616-9287.

Georgia: Poison Center, Atlanta: 800-282-5846; 404-616-9000; TTY/TDD 404-616-9287.

Hawaii: Poison Center, Honolulu: 800-362-3585; 808-941-4411.

Idaho: Rocky Mountain Poison & Drug Center, Denver: 800-860-0620 (ID only).

Illinois: Poison Center, Chicago: 800-942-5969 (IL only); TTY/TDD 312-906-6185.

Indiana: Poison Center, Indianapolis: 800-382-9097 (IN only); 317-929-2323; TTY/TDD 317-929-2336.

Iowa: Statewide Poison Control Center, Sioux City; 800-352-2222; 712-277-2222.

Kansas: Mid-America Poison Control Center, Kansas City; 800-332-6633; 913-588-6633; TTY/TDD 913-588-6639.

Kentucky: Regional Poison Center, Louisville: 800-722-5725; 502-589-8222.

Louisiana: Drug and Poison Information Center, Monroe: 800-256-9822 (LA only).

Maine: Poison Control Center, Portland: 800-442-6305 (ME only); 207-871-2950; TTY/TDD 877-299-4447 (ME only); 207-871-2879.

Maryland: Poison Center, Baltimore: 800-492-2414 (MD only); 410-706-7701; TTY/TDD 410-706-1858.

Massachusetts: Regional Center for Poison Control and Prevention, Boston: 800-682-9211 (MA & RI only); 617-232-2120; TTY/TDD 888-244-5313.

Michigan: Regional Poison Control Center, Detroit: 800-POISON1; 313-745-5711; TTY/TDD 800-356-3232. Grand Rapids: 800-POISON1 (MI only).

Minnesota: Hennepin Regional Poison Center, Minneapolis: 800-222-1222 (MN only); 800-POISON1 (SD only); TTY/TDD: 612-904-4691.

Mississippi: Regional Poison Control Center, Jackson: 601-354-7660.

Missouri: Regional Poison Center, St. Louis: 800-366-8888; 314-772-5200.

Montana: Rocky Mountain Poison & Drug Center, Denver: 800-525-5042 (MT only).

Nebraska: The Poison Center: 800-955-9119 (NE & WY only); 402-955-5555.

Nevada: Oregon Poison Center, Portland: 503-494-8968. Rocky Mountain Poison & Drug Center, Denver: 800-446-6179 (NV only).

New Hampshire: Poison Information Center, Lebanon: 800-562-8236 (NH only); 603-650-8000.

New Jersey: Poison Information & Education System, Newark: 800-POISON1 (NJ only); TTY/TDD 973-926-8008.

New Mexico: Poison & Drug Information Center, Albuquerque: 800-432-6866 (NM only); 505-272-2222.

New York: Central Poison Center, Syracuse: 800-252-5655 (NY only); 315-476-4766. Rochester: 800-333-0542 (NY only); 716-275-3232; TTY/TDD 716-273-3854. Sleepy Hollow: 800-336-6997 (NY only); 914-366-3030. Mineola: 516-542-2323; 516-663-2650. TTY/TDD 516-924-8811; 516-747-3323. N.Y.C.: 800-210-3985; 212-340-4494; TTY/TDD 212-689-9014. Buffalo: 800-888-7655; 716-878-7654.

North Carolina: Poison Center, Charlotte: 800-848-6946; 704-355-4000.

North Dakota: Poison Information Center, Fargo: 800-732-2200 (ND, MN, SD only); 701-234-5575.

Ohio: Central Poison Center, Columbus: 800-682-7625 (OH only); 800-762-0727 (Dayton only); TTY/TDD 614-228-2272. Cincinnati: 800-872-5111 (OH only); 513-558-5111. Cleveland: 888-231-4455 (OH only); 216-231-4455.

Oklahoma: Poison Control Center, Oklahoma City: 800-POISON1 (OK only); 405-271-5454; TTY/TDD 405-271-1122.

Oregon: Poison Center, Portland: 800-452-7165 (OR only); 503-494-8968.

Pennsylvania: Central Poison Center, Hershey: 800-521-6110, 717-531-6111; TTY/TDD 717-531-8335. Pittsburgh: 412-681-6669. Philadelphia: 800-722-7112; 215-386-2100.

Puerto Rico: Poison Center, Santurce: 787-726-5674.

Rhode Island: Regional Center for Poison Control: 800-682-9211 (MA & RI only); 617-232-2120; TTY/TDD 888-244-5313.

South Carolina: Palmetto Poison Center, Columbia: 800-922-1117 (SC only); 803-777-1117.

South Dakota: Hennepin Regional Poison Center, Minneapolis: 800-POISON1 (SD only); TTY/TDD 612-904-4691.

Tennessee: Poison Center, Nashville: 800-288-9999 (TN only); 615-936-2034; TTY/TDD 615-936-2047; Memphis: 800-288-9999 (TN only); 901-528-6048.

Texas: Poison Center, Temple: 800-POISON1 ; 254-724-7401. Dallas: 800-POISON1 (TX only). San Antonio: 800-POISON1 (TX only); TTY/TDD 800-POISON1 (TX only). Galveston: 800-POISON1 (TX only); 409-765-1420. Amarillo: 800-POISON1 (TX only). El Paso: 800-POISON1 (TX only).

.Utah: Poison Control Center, Salt Lake City: 800-456-7707 (UT only); 801-581-2151.

Vermont: Poison Center, Burlington: 877-658-3456 (toll free); 802-658-3456.

Virginia: Poison Center, Charlottesville: 800-451-1428 (VA only); 804-924-5543. Richmond: 800-552-6337; 804-828-9123.

Washington, DC: Poison Center: 202-625-3333; TTY/TDD 202-362-8563.

Washington State: Poison Center, Seattle: 800-732-6985; 206-526-2121; TTY/TDD 206-517-2394; 800-572-0638 (WA only).

West Virginia: Poison Center, Charleston: 800-642-3625 (WV only).

Wisconsin: Poison Center, Milwaukee: 800-815-8855 (WI only); 414-266-2222. Madison: 800-815-8855 (WI only); 608-262-3702.

Wyoming: Poison Center: 800-955-9119 (NE & WY only); 402-955-5555.

NATIONAL ANIMAL POISON CONTROL CENTER: 888-426-4435; 900-680-0000.

Tree, Vine, Bush & Bramble

Tree, Vine, Bush & Bramble Contents

INTRODUCTION

The bulk of what follows used to make up the "Sweets" chapter, and there was a lot more in it about how to make apple butter than about how to grow a tree. Now, as I sit down to write this new edition, I am more worried about preserving the topsoil, maintaining our atmospheric oxygen, and reducing the earth's carbon dioxide level (and risk of a disastrous "greenhouse effect") than I am in making sure you can cook apple butter. Apple butter is still here, but I've added as much as I could (not as much as I wanted) about trees. Trees are the single most important answer to those 3 most critical challenges for the future of life on earth.

The massive, semipermanent root networks of trees forestall erosion and make possible a form of long-term agriculture that can sustain humans and their livestock without the loss of topsoil and the desertification of their agricultural land, which is the great risk of annual tillage for generations. The leaves of trees both yield oxygen and remove carbon dioxide as part of their natural chemistry. And, as if that isn't good enough, you can plant entire forests, or plantations, or farm crops of trees that also provide food. Fruit, yes, of course. But not just fruit. Tree fruits are wonderful: apples, pears, peaches, and nectarines from the temperate zones, and avocado, banana, persimmon, guava, and a long list of others that grow in warmer climates. In Central Asia there are forests made up entirely of various kinds of fruiting trees, all growing wild—gardens of Eden. In the United States before 1900 there were vast wild nut forests, mainly chestnuts, which made up a third or even a half of the total tree population, and under which the pioneers' pig herds roamed untended—reproducing and flourishing until their surplus was needed for table meat. But the magnificent, towering hardwood forests of walnut and such have long since been cut down to make dressers and coffee tables. The Eastern chestnuts all died in the terrible epidemic of a new disease (some Western ones survived!)—chestnut blight—that struck the forests in the early 1900s.

There are trees that build up the soil—nitrogen fixers, exactly like beans, peas, and alfalfa in your garden and field. Mesquite is one, for example, and it also has the gift of being able to live in desert conditions. There are bread trees, bean trees, sugar trees, protein trees, chocolate trees. Some of each broader category are suitable for any major climate zone. You could feed your family and all your livestock entirely from trees (and some people do!). And, of course, the dead branches and overage trees are a practical fuel source and building material. All these possibilities exist so long as trees aren't cut down to clear land for the plow, or carelessly killed off by the burning of high-sulfur coal, which then causes the atmosphere to rain sulfuric acid down on them.

In certain areas of the Mediterranean, farmers for centuries have practiced a "2-story" agriculture. Tall trees are the upper story: carobs for stock fodder and olives for the delicacy of their fruit or cooking staple of their oil, or some other tree. Underneath the trees they may let pigs or cattle or goats roam to fatten on the tons of nourishing foodstuffs seasonally cast down from the generous tree branches above. Trees whose leaves and fruits are edible and relished by meat, milk, and egg producers are called "livestock fodder trees." These trees are important because such an agriculture is virtually permanent and totally nondestructive. The trees and the pasture beneath them stay put so there is no soil erosion from tilling multiple times each year, no bare fields of dirt to blow or wash away. And the dense tree foliage and pasture beneath maximize the contribution green stuff makes to good air, as well as to meat supply. The Mediterranean farmers have a garden space, too, but it doesn't have to be very big.

There are farmers in the United States who also do some variety of 2-story farming. They can turn swampy, marginal land into an almost effortless wealth producer by planting a forest of stock-feed dropping trees—not just accidentally this kind or that, but a carefully planned layout to provide as nearly as possible a year-round fall of fodder for the animals: one tree crop raining down its bounty early in spring, another that fruits in mid-summer, still another in fall, and another for late fall feeding. And the animals in turn nourish the trees by their manure. That's how it has to be for this ecosystem to be permanently healthy. The cycle has to be complete: plants give what animals need; animals return what plants need. Or underneath and between their trees (which are perhaps 40 feet apart), these 2-story farmers raise annual crops of grain or vegetables. Because of the partial shade of the trees, their tilled crop doesn't yield as much as it would in full sun. But the Mediterranean communities of which I spoke have been doing this for centuries, and the depth of their topsoil and its fertility is undiminished, whereas in far too many neighboring countries there is bare rock or desert now where centuries ago fertile farms provided the basis of ancient civilizations. The success of their 2-story farming is due to the trees, which hold soil in place and perpetually enrich it with their annual generosity of falling leaves and fruits. (Did you ever hear of terrible famines like those of Ethiopia and Somalia happening to people who live in the middle of a dense forest? I haven't.)

Another form of 2-story farming is described in the Tilth organization's visionary classic *The Future Is Abundant* ("Chopaka Nut Orchard," by Michael Pilarski, p. 106): a nut orchard with 2 heights of trees. "The upper story of the nut orchard consists of walnuts, Chinese chestnuts, heartnuts and a few Turkish tree hazels (*Corylus colurna*). The middle story is composed mainly of filberts, with some pears, peaches, and plums. The south side of the orchard is planted to peaches and nectarines to take advantage of the warm, sunny exposure. On the west side grapes have been trained along the high deer fence which surrounds the orchard. . . Bill [the grower] has found that spacing the walnut trees 60 feet apart and the filbert trees 25 feet apart is ideal." On the ground story of his orchard, Bill raises yet another crop, peacocks

and peahens, which protect his trees from insects and also provide a cash crop from feathers that Bill collects during their molting seasons, plus sale of live birds. He also raises bees, which feed themselves from the tree blossoms, perform pollination duties, and make prime honey.

So we need to keep the trees we have. And we need to plant more. In England farmers love their pastures, and I've heard they fence them not with posts hacked from the bodies of dead trees but with ingeniously devised barriers made of closely growing and intertwined living trees called "hedgerows." Their hedgerows, made of ash, elm, heather, holly, ivy, and willow, provide some winter food for livestock, summer and winter harvests for people and animals, shelter for some wild critters, privacy, and a guaranteed role on their land for trees. For how to create one, refer to *Hedgerow* by Eric Thomas and John T. White (New York: Morrow, 1980).

We need to shut down or convert the high-sulfur coal-based industries and replant the forests that have been poisoned. We need to replant as much as possible of all the earth's lands that were once forested. In areas where natural rainfall supports forests, we need to make a conscious agricultural evolution from an open-field–based agriculture to a tree-based or 2-storied agriculture. That's the next great agricultural revolution.

I have an insistent vision of a wonderful earth thousands of years from now, with healthy air and water and healthy, happy, cultured, literate humans living on it. They survive and thrive in carefully maintained balance and companionship with and humble service to the plants and animals that

sustain them. In those places where trees can naturally grow, I see people living contentedly under a canopy of green leaves.

I like the idea of planting trees for grandchildren—or for generations to come. As each year goes by, other people's children look more like my children to me. The older I get the more it feels like I'm related to everyone I meet and that the children and their children to come are all somehow my offspring, too. I'm understanding at last in a fully integrated way that all humans are ultimately family, and beyond them, we are connected to all animals, too, and beyond them, with all life. Yes, related to a tree. And not so distantly as we might think. Trees and people are far more closely related to each other than either is to a rock!

Choosing trees to plant can be very exciting. How about a Dawn Redwood, one of the ancient species that dates back to the Upper Cretaceous era, 100 million years ago? How about the honey locust, a wonderful drought-resistant cold-hardy tree that will grow hundreds of pounds of pig and cattle fodder each year for winter feeding and also, being a legume, enriches the soil? Plant a tree for your anniversary, or your birthday, or Arbor Day, or . . . It's actually good to mix your species. Get the right combination and you have an ideal permaculture.

NOTE: For easier reference, most recipes in this chapter are grouped together with a particular nut or fruit. However, preparation details are not repeated each time if they are covered in Chapter 7. If your recipe seems incomplete or vague, refer to that chapter to find the rest of the processing information.

PLANTING A TREE

Someone asked Martin Luther, "What should I do on the last day of earth?" Luther replied, "Plant a tree."

It's a wonderful, spiritual thing to plant a tree. Each tree is a living thing that can share the rest of your life. It will grow and give you shade, elegant beauty, food to eat, and branches for birds to nest in and children to climb in and for you to hang your hammock on and take a well-deserved nap. No matter what, plant one or more trees every year. And plant as many—or more—as what you take out. If you're planting various kinds of trees your harvesting will be staggered because they grow at different rates and you may be harvesting different sorts of products from them. You can sell Christmas trees, nuts, maple syrup, firewood, fence posts, sawlogs, and fruit. If you have livestock fodder

trees, you can get rich selling pork, because pigs can more easily get a total diet from tree crops than any other animal. So plant some nut, fruit, sugar, stock forage, timber, or woodlot trees every year on your land. And if you don't have land, or have no more room, then plant them on someone else's land, doing your share to guarantee our mutual future.

NETWORKING: To network with other dedicated tree planters, contact TreePeople: 818-753-4600; fax 818-753-4635; 12601 Mulholland Dr., Beverly Hills, CA 90210; **TreePeople@TreePeople.org; www.TreePeople.org.** Friends of the Trees, based in Bellingham, WA, seeks solutions to world deforestation and offers programs, seminars, and info at local, regional, national, and international levels (**geocities.com/RainForest/4663/**).

For more tree information, contact American Forests: PO Box 2000, Washington, DC 20013; 202-955-4500; fax 202-955-4588; **info@amfor.org; www.american forests.org; www.treestories.org; www.historictrees.org.** And The National Arbor Day Foundation; 402-474-5655; fax 402-474-0820; 211 N. 12th St., Lincoln, NE 68508; **gbrienzo@arborday.org; www.arborday.org.**

Read *The Theory and Practice of Agroforestry Design,* by Paul A. Wojkowski (1998); *Tree Crops: A Permanent Agriculture* (1987), by J. Russell Smith; and *Temperate Agroforestry Systems* (1997), by Andrew M. Gordon and Steven M. Newman, eds. The Association for Temperate Agroforestry (AFTA) encourages use of permaculture know-how in temperate North America, combining trees and shrubs with crops and/or livestock to increase and diversify farm and forest production while conserving natural resources. They publish a quarterly newsletter, *The Temperate Agroforester,* cosponsor a biennial conference, and supply tree crop info: 573-882-9866; fax 573-882-1977; 203 ABNR Bldg., U. of Missouri, Columbia, MO 65211; **afta@missouri.edu; www.missouri.edu/~afta.** And see "Agroforestry Overview" at **www.attra.org/ attra-pub/agroforest.html** or order a print copy (it's free) from 800-346-9140.

The USDA's National Agroforestry Center offers info, too (Alley Cropping; Forest Farming; Silvopasture; Windbreaks; etc.): **www.uni.edu/nac/.** Rodale's Agroforestry Articles & Resources has an article on "Little-Known Acacias [such as *A. baileyana*]: Promising Agroforestry Species" at **fadr.msu.ru/rodale/agsieve/txt/agrofor.html.** Plants for a Future (a database of 7,000+ useful species of plants, worldwide!, with details on how to grow and uses) has a website section on "Edible Trees and Shrubs" at **www.scs. leeds.ac.uk/pfaf/index.html.** The Australasian Tree Crops Sourcebook is another amazing online resource, listing all sorts of nut, fruit, and timber tree crops (and plant sources of useful oils) with links to plant sources: **www.aoi.com/au/ atcros/.**

Guerrilla Tree Planting

I'm for it, urban, or rural: guerrilla tree planting. Choose the right species for the climate and suitable sites: a neglected space on private land, or an open one on public land. Then you sneak up and plant your tree there. Trees can handle a lot of crowding; 15 feet apart is fine in a forest setting. During the planting seasons of spring and fall, plant trees on your weekend outings. Plant trees on your holidays. Don't leave town without some seeds or seedlings in your back seat. Don't go picnicking or backpacking without a few gifts to the earth in the form of seeds or seedlings: evergreens, or fruit or nut trees. You can start them in a nursery bed in your yard, or in a flat or pot in your window. Plant in the morning sun or by the full moon. Keep a private tally: how many trees you've planted so far. Take pride in it. Go back and visit some of them years later and say, "Hi, I'm your parent. My, but you're looking good!" Expect some losses; it's okay.

If people are the whole problem, people can just as easily be the whole answer. All they gotta do is do it. A guerrilla tree-planting friend, ex–Viet Nam vet, proposed with a crooked grin and a twinkle in his eye, "Let's cluster-bomb the planet with trees!"

Amen.

It takes a long time for a tree to grow, and some of them may not make it. And, sooner or later, grown trees, like people, die of old age. But then they can be fuel or building material, or a home for wild things until they finally decay and become food for other trees in the fullest completion of their life cycle. In the space where they once lived, plant new trees, continuing their spirit of hope. Plant a tree for your housewarming, and one for each anniversary, one for farewell—any excuse will do, the more often the better!

Hopefully you'll end up with a big, diversified nut and fruit orchard, and vine and berry plants, too. You'll probably be surprised at the amount of fruit and nuts your family could use if they had all they wanted. I canned 100 qt. of cherries last summer, and here it is the first day of February and I have only 1 qt. left. But I still have apricots, plums, grape and tomato juice, apple plum butter, and a lone jar of applesauce, so we aren't clear to the end. The cherries are my family's favorite fruit, and I haven't been too strict on the rationing. As the year wears on and the favorite fruits like cherries, peaches, and pears are eaten up, the others start looking better and tasting better to them. Your local extension agent or nursery can advise you what varieties do best in your climate, when they ripen, what pollinators they need, etc.

Climate

Is your climate subtropical or tropical, or temperate? What fruits you grow depends mainly on climate unless you're doing greenhouse farming. The farther north you live, the higher in altitude you are, the shorter your frost-free season. In colder areas you may be limited to apples and cherries, and colder than that to crab apples. Colder yet, and chokecherries or sand or bush cherries, gooseberries, and maybe a few other berries are your only possible fruit crops. The farther south you live, the more fruits you can add to the list. But temperate-zone fruits won't do well where bananas grow. Deciduous trees need a cold winter for their normal annual cycle. Each temperate-zone species usually needs a specific number of hours spent below a certain temperature in order to break its dormancy and make it resume growing and bearing fruit normally again in the spring: its "chilling requirement."

If you live in a hot zone, here's a letter from Ella Hupman, Fort Lauderdale, FL, that's bound to set you dreaming. "Dear Carla, We decided that it was just as easy to raise vegetables as flowers and grass, and fruit trees instead of shade trees. We took out all our areca palms and planted about 10 varieties of bananas. Also put in orange, grapefruit, tangerine, avocado, mango, Key lime, lemon, calamondin, and carambola trees. After 3 years of gardening, we know what vegetables we can produce with greatest success. Our tomatoes have been most successful and I've canned them in every form. Rabbits are our source of fertilizer besides a source of meat."

She didn't plant any apple, cherry, apricot, plum, peach, nectarine, or pear trees. Those are temperate-climate fruits. So you can be blessed with fruit wherever you live—but not necessarily the same fruit. However, there are some tropical fruits you can grow in a tub and bring in when it's too cold for them outside: banana, pygmy date palm, everbearing fig, pineapple, pomegranate, and dwarf citrus.

Choosing Your Plants

You need expert advice about what combinations to buy.

POLLINATORS: Some nut and fruit trees, and vines (such as kiwi), can't make fruit alone; they can be either male or female, and they need another tree to be a pollinizer for them. Other trees are "self-fruitful" or "self-fertile" or "self-pollinating." There are trees that are kind of in-between; they'll produce some harvest, but only a small crop unless they get cross-pollinated by a different plant. Trees that are to be wind-pollinated should be planted within 100 feet of each other.

LATE FROSTS: If there happens to be a freeze while fruit or nut flowers are blooming, there will be no crop of fruit. Having as large and diversified a fruit patch as possible guarantees that, although frost will probably catch some of your trees in bloom (and pests and diseases may take a toll on others), lots more will still make it through, because different kinds of fruit and different varieties of the same fruit have different blossoming dates—earlier and later. Furthermore, if late frosts are a problem in your area, you can avoid trouble by seeking out varieties that bloom late enough to be fairly safe.

SIZE: DWARF, SEMI-DWARF, AND STANDARD: One of the main questions you have to ask when shopping for a tree is, "How big will it get?" Little seedlings can grow into awesome 100-foot giants. Don't choose a size you'd have to keep amputating to live with. Better to go with a genetically smaller one. You'll often have a choice between dwarf, semi-dwarf, and standard-sized trees. The big difference in the trees is the rootstock. If you decide to do your own grafting, you will be offered a choice of dwarf, semi-dwarf or standard rootstocks, and as the rootstock is chosen so the tree will grow.

Dwarfs are, of course, smaller, so most growers can spray, prune, or pick fruit easily. Dwarfs don't need nearly as much room to grow as standards. If you have a small yard in a city, the obvious choice would be to divide the area among different kinds of dwarf fruit trees for as much variety as you could get for the given area. Many years ago dwarf trees were more expensive. That was when they were becoming popular and demand was greater than supply. Now at the nursery I go to, dwarf, semi-dwarf, and standards are exactly the same price.

Production Time/Amount. Somebody wrote and asked me, "What trees produce the fastest and largest quantities?" The answer is: not the same ones. That's the big decision in dwarf versus standard. Dwarf trees bear fruit sooner. A standard apple tree may not produce fruit for 6–8 years, while a dwarf may in 2–4 years. (Apple takes the most time.) The fruit is the same size on either tree. However, standards produce the largest quantities of fruit per year per tree once they get going, and they will live longer than dwarf varieties. A dwarf tree will live for maybe 25 years, a standard tree for maybe 40. Semi-dwarfs are a compromise between the extremes. You have to make your own decision based on goals for your family and your orchard and then get the appropriate kind of tree.

TRANSPLANTING "WILD" TREES: Evergreen seedlings can usually be transplanted. In fact, curious but true, forest conifers that have already been transplanted once tend to have stronger roots and grow better when transplanted a second time. At the other extreme, most nut trees, wild or domesticated, have a central taproot that grows straight down. Any tree with that sort of taproot will not transplant successfully if the taproot is cut or broken off, or even bent over, when replanting. Thus nut trees over 6 feet are a high risk to transplant—whether from the wild or the nursery.

Tree/Fruit Propagation

PLANNING YOUR ORCHARD AND BERRY PATCH: It takes a few years to get production going (unless you inherit mature plants). In the meantime you can compensate by scavenging for wild fruit and berries. Find out where they are and when. The general rule is to freeze berries and can fruit, but you may also can berries, or dry any of them. You'll want a good supply of canning jars. Figure on at least 80 qt. of fruit annually for a couple and 40 more for each child, and that's a desperate minimum. That's only 1 qt. a week per person during the 9 months when fruit is out of season. Then you can use rhubarb, strawberries, raspberries, cherries, and early apples to carry you until the later, larger fruits are ripe again.

SEEDLINGS VS. GRAFTING: Nursery and mail-order trees may be seedlings or grafted trees. Seedlings have some definite drawbacks compared to grafted, or "named," trees. Grafting gives you the hardiness of a "native" (near-wild) rootstock combined with the fruiting ability of a highly selected variety of branch. So grafted trees usually have better weather or disease resistance, bear larger nuts or fruits, may bear more regularly, and yield heavier crops than seedlings, and are totally predictable in performance. With seedlings, you never know for sure what kind of tree or product you'll get because of its wide range of inherited possibilities; only about half, or less, of the progeny will probably be top-notch. You could wait a long time to find out if your tree is worth keeping. You can avoid that problem by choosing grafted (or budded) trees.

GRAFTING AND BUDDING: To plant an orchard you may plant seeds, but usually you'll start by buying young trees from a local nursery or by mail-order. Eventually you might get involved enough to want to do your own grafting and budding. The main principle of grafting is that if you graft a Golden Delicious branch onto the rooted stub of another young tree, the future tree will produce Golden Delicious apples, even though the rootstock may have been from a different variety. Grafting techniques go back to the Romans, or maybe earlier.

To do your own grafting, you can buy rootstocks from a nursery or mail-order house. Or grow your own from seed. You could get prunings from neighborhood fruit trees to graft onto them. Any twig will do it. But the twig will fruit like the tree it came from. So you're probably better off buying top-quality plants for grafting or select from your own good-quality stock.

Grafting and budding are easily learned. Get a neighbor who does it to show you how or you could order the booklet *Grafting Fruit Trees* from Storey's, Schoolhouse Rd., Pownal, VT 05261. A wonderful book on this subject is *Plants-a-Plenty* by Catherine Osgood Foster (Rodale Press, 1977). Someone in your area probably offers a grafting course. Ask your extension agent, or ask around at nurseries. In this case, watching somebody doing it is the best way to learn. But in general:

To graft, cut off the top of a young rootstock tree. Rootstocks are selected to get roots that are resistant to disease, and hardy against cold winters, early frosts, poor soil, lack of moisture, etc. You can grow your own from seed or order it from a fruit specialist such as Adams County Nursery, PO Box 108, Aspers, PA 17304, which carries a large selection of rootstocks.

The fruit-tree part is usually chosen for abundant production of quality fruit. Select a whip or branch that has one or more buds. Cut off the bottom of that young fruiting tree. Make the cuts for both top and bottom in a matching zigzag so the fruiting top and rootstock will fit together tightly and firmly. Now fit the top into the bottom and bind them in place. Eventually they'll grow together.

If you're budding, the difference is that instead of cutting off the whole top of the rootstock, you place just one bud of the fruiting selection into and beneath a slit cut in the bark of your chosen rootstock. As new branches grow, prune away any that are from the rootstock rather than from the bud, or graft.

GRAFTING AND BUDDING DEFINITIONS: A top (scion) from a plant with good heredity for fruiting is patched onto a bottom (rootstock) with good root and trunk qualities so they'll grow together and give you the best of both. Here are some other relevant definitions:

- Multi-stemmed: The plant will have more than one trunk.
- Rootstock: The bottom, root part of a graft combo.
- Scion: The top of a graft combo.
- Spur: This is a short special-purpose twig that certain fruit trees (apples, pears, etc.) grow flowers and fruit on.
- Stone Fruits: Apricots, cherries, nectarines, peaches, and plums have a hard cover over their seed—so they're the "stone fruits" or "drupes."
- Sucker: When the rootstock (or root) decides it wants to grow a top of its own and sends 1 or more new stems up, those are suckers. Suckers must be promptly cut off from a grafted plant or they'll take over. Some plants sucker a lot naturally (pawpaw and jujube), and will form a thicket if you don't keep the suckers cut back.
- Taproot: Certain trees have a large central root growing straight down from its center—way down. This is the taproot. The opposite of a taproot tree is one with a spread-root system. Taproot trees can pull up water from the water table so they're drought resistant, but they're hard to transplant once that root gets very long.

PROPAGATION BY CUTTINGS: A "cutting" is a piece of a parent plant that when planted on its own can develop into an independent plant. You can plant a cutting taken from the branches (a "stem cutting") or a piece of root ("root cutting") or in some cases you can even use a single leaf ("leaf cutting"). You can take a cutting from a dormant plant or from one that is actively growing in the spring and early summer. Later than that you are past the time for planting cuttings. Your planted cuttings need halfway agreeable weather, protection from getting dried out—keep them well watered until they take—and protection from curious children who would pull them up to see if they've got roots yet!

In general, for a shrub or tree-type plant, you cut off an entire branch of the previous season's growth (1–2 feet), or the end of a branch, or a sucker. Don't cut it off until the plant is in thorough dormancy, its leaves all dropped if it's deciduous. Plant the cutting, half underground and half above, in suitable soil for the type of plant in the place you intend for its permanent home, since transplanting is risky and stressful for the plant. When you want some berry or grape plants, or more berry or grape plants, you don't plant a seed—you plant a "cutting" of some sort.

PROPAGATION FROM SUCKERS: Many berry runners travel under the ground like the nuisance lilac "suckers" and then pop up anywhere to reach for the precious light. Various trees and shrubs put out suckers too. Any plant that suckers from the roots is a good bet for propagation by this method. In the spring you just dig up these nearly independent sticklike shoots, replant them where you want them, and with luck and care they'll go ahead and grow.

TREE SEED? If yours is a grafted tree, this is not a good idea. If you plant a pit from your prized cherry or apple tree, the chances are significant that the offspring will have little in common with the parent. The offspring fruit, if any, might be very small and sour. The reason fruit seeds from grafted stock don't breed true is because the top of the tree is usually grafted onto a hardier rootstock, but one whose seed may not have the fruiting capacity of the top part.

GROWING TREES FROM SEED? The answer is that sometimes you can, and sometimes it's practical. When it works, it's certainly the cheapest, easiest way to get a tree. You just plant the seed wherever you want the tree to grow. There's no expensive purchase, no transplanting, no early pruning needed. Growth from seed is how the great wild nut, fruit, etc., forests of the earth got planted and re-planted—by squirrels who buried nuts and forget where, or fruits that were carried away by hungry critters who consumed the tasty flesh and left behind the unwanted seed. Growing from seed does mean a few years longer to wait before bearing—and 99 percent of the time, growth from seed results in a plant not as high in quality as one you might obtain through grafting or budding from a plant with known, superior abilities. A tree that was grown from a seed is called "a seedling."

In general: Wait to take seeds from the fruit until it is fully ripe, but don't let them stand in fermenting juice an overly long time; that might kill the embryo. Dry the seeds and store them until late autumn. Plant 3 inches deep. The winter chill and freezing will break the seeds' dormancy, and next spring they will grow. (Specifics are found below under each fruit.) Or order fruit tree seed to plant. You've a better chance of getting good heredity doing that.

Buying Tree, Vine, Bush, or Bramble

If you can, avoid buying fruit trees mail-order. Or buy mail-order from nurseries that are near where you live—or located in the climate zone where you live. The catalog salesmanship is great, but in the long run I think you'll be happier with what you buy in person from a local nursery. The mail-order trees are cheaper. They are also smaller and in worse condition and get off to a much poorer start. Your local plant nursery knows expertly what trees are already acclimated, and if your tree should die they will quite likely replace it for you at no charge if you ask (save your receipt!). Buy the biggest (oldest) trees you can afford. It takes them long enough to grow anyway.

BARE ROOT: These are plants sold with no soil around their roots. They are usually deciduous perennials, dug while dormant. Bare root is an affordable and healthy way to buy.

GENETIC DWARF: This plant is a natural shortie and not a standard plant grafted or budded onto dwarfing rootstocks. Genetic dwarfs are smaller than plants on dwarfing rootstocks.

CATALOG SOURCES

NOTE: These sources primarily carry trees and fruits. General seed and plant suppliers are listed in Chapter 2. Very specialized nurseries are listed with their plant entry but are not listed here.

California

Exotica: Rare Fruit Nursery ships one of the world's largest selections of fruit trees worldwide. Their list includes acerola, Asian pears, bamboo, bananas of many sorts, carob, cherimoya, Surinam Chercitrus, coffee, curry leaf, figs, ginger, guavas, jujube, kiwi, loquat, longan, lychee, mango, mulberries, palms, papayas, passion fruit, persimmon, pineapple, quince, pomegranates, sapotes, star fruit, sugar cane, tamarind, pine nut, cashew, chestnut, ginkgo nut, Italian stone pine, jojoba, and macadamia; 760-724-9093; fax 760-724-7724; PO Box 160, Vista, CA 92083. Visit them at 2508-B E. Vista Way, Vista, CA; **www.bonusweb.com/exotica/**.

Pacific Tree Farms offers an amazing choice of subtropical and tropical plants and seeds: banana, citrus, guava, kiwi, mango, pomegranate, sapote, Surinam cherry, tea, etc.: 619-422-2400; 4301 Lynwood Dr., Chula Vista, CA 91910; **www.kyburg.com/ptf**.

Midwest

Seed Savers Exchange offers a 40-pg color catalog of heirloom vegetables, all open-pollinated. A truly unique selection of outstanding vegetables, flowers, and herbs: 297 varieties produced by networking home gardeners: 3076 N. Winn Rd., Decorah, IA 52101; **www.seedsavers.com**.

Southmeadow Fruit Gardens offers a very large collection of old, new, regular, and rare fruits. Free price list: 616-422-2411; Box 211, Baroda, MI 49101; **www.southmeadowfruitgardens.com**.

Northeast

Adams County Nursery is a wholesale/retail operation that serves the northeastern U.S.: Michigan to Maine, south to Virginia. Their free catalog offers a large selection of rootstocks: apple, plum, sweet cherry, nectarine, and peach; and detailed, good instructions on pruning apple trees: PO Box 108, Aspers, PA 17304; 717-677-8105; fax 717-677-4124; **acn@cvn.net**; **www.acnursery.com**.

Brittingham Plant Farms sells strawberries, blueberries, raspberries, blackberries, and grapes. Great service!!! 410-749-5153; fax 410-749-5148; PO Box 2538, Salisbury, MD 21802-2538.

Miller's Nursery offers berries, grapes, apples, nuts, and plums. Catalog: 800-836-9630; West Lake Rd., Canandaigua, NY 14424; **www.millernurseries.com**.

Nourse Farms specializes in small fruit plants: strawberries, raspberries, blackberries, blueberries, currants, etc.: 413-665-2658; fax 413-665-7888; 41 River Rd., South Deerfield, MA 01373; **www.noursefarms.com**.

F. W. Schumacher Co. specializes in seeds of trees and shrubs such as Christmas trees, etc. Good, conscientious folks. Details to plant each seed species on their website: **www.treeshrubseeds.com**; 508-888-0659; fax 508-833-0322; PO Box 1023, Sandwich, MA 02563-1023.

St. Lawrence Nurseries is an apple specialist, offering 100+ varieties and also specializing in fruits and nuts for northern climates (pears, plums, cherries, Juneberries, grapes, blueberries, lingonberries, mulberries, raspberries, edible ornamentals, nuts, and timber trees, all raised in their own nursery). They also sell books, tools, and tree tags: 315-265-6739; 325 State Hwy. 345, Potsdam, NY 13676; **trees@sln.potsdam.ny.us.**

Northwest

Burnt Ridge Nursery specializes in unusual trees, shrubs, and vines that grow edible nuts or fruit: Carolyn and Michael Dolan; 360-985-2873; fax 360-985-0882; 432 Burnt Ridge Rd., Onalaska, WA 98570; **burntridge@ myhome.net; www.landru.myhome.net/burntridge/.**

C & O Nursery is a wholesale/retail fruit-tree specialist; catalog: PO Box 116, 1700 N. Wenatchee Ave., Wenatchee, WA 98801; 509-662-7164; **tree@c-o nursery.com; www.c-onursery.com.**

Cloud Mountain Farm is a demonstration garden par excellence, a nursery that sells young fruit trees, and also a teaching facility: 6908 Goodwin Rd., Everson, WA 98247; **info@cloudmountainfarm.com; www.cloud mountainfarm.com.**

Columbia Basin Nursery sells fruit trees and rootstock, wholesale/retail. Brochure: 800-333-8589; 509-787-4411; fax 509-787-3944; Box 458, Quincy, WA 98848; **cbn@televar.com.**

Raintree Nursery offers 500 varieties of fruit, nut trees, bamboo, and berries: aronia, akebia, sweet gooseberries, currants, figs, persimmons, mulberries, lingonberries, alpine strawberries, pawpaws, etc. Free 88-pg catalog: 360-496-6400; 391 Butts Rd., Morton, WA 98356; **info@raintreenursery.com; www.raintree nursery.com.**

Van Well Nursery sells fruit trees wholesale or retail; catalog: 509-886-8189; 800-572-1553; fax 509-886-0294; PO Box 1339, 2821 Grand Rd., Wenatchee, WA 98807-1339; **vanwell@vanwell.net; www.van well.net.**

South

Vernon Barnes & Son Nursery offers fruits, nuts, and berries mail-order at bargain prices and good service. Free catalog: 931-668-8576; fax 931-668-2165; PO Box 250, McMinnville, TN 37110.

Cumberland Valley Nurseries sells fruit trees, wholesale and retail. Free catalog: 931-668-4153; PO Box 471, 394 Shaffie Lane, McMinnville, TN 37110; **fruitrus@ blomand.net.**

Hidden Springs Nursery offers organically grown unusual and disease-resistant varieties including apple, pawpaw, mulberry, persimmon, and quince; catalog $1; 170 Hidden Springs Lane, Cookeville, TN 38501. No phone. No e-mail. Conscientious service from Annie!

Ison's Nursery and Vineyard offers fruits, nuts, berries, and grapes, wholesale or retail; catalog: 800-733-0324; 404-599-6970; PO Box 190, 6855 Newman Hwy., Brooks, GA 30205; **www.isons.com.**

Lawson's Nursery offers a free b/w catalog. Jim Lawson does his own grafting/budding. Trees: delicious quince, butternut, filbert, plum, fig, peach, pear, apple, grapes, gooseberry; walnut cracker, pecan trap (roll it across the ground and it picks up anything round!). Old-fashioned and unusual apples (more than 100 varieties): 770-893-2141; 2730 Yellow Creek Rd., Ball Ground, GA 30107; **lawsonsnursery@aol.com.**

Patrick's Vineyard/Orchard Nursery specializes in nuts, fruits, and berries for Southern growers: 229-388-9999; 800-972-2101; Pomegranate Blvd., Ty Ty, GA 31795; **www.tytyga.com.**

West

Pikes Peak Nurseries sells retail and wholesale fruits, nuts, berries, grapes, etc.: 719-632-4751; fax 719-630-8902; 630 Abbott Lane, Colorado Springs, CO 80905; **leland ppn@aol.com; www.pikespeaknurseries.com.**

TREES TO REJECT

1. Any tree that can't stand up without support.
2. Any tree with bark wounds on its trunk. (Look under the tree wraps.) Such a tree has a much lower chance of survival.
3. Any big tree in a small pot. An 8-foot tree with a trunk that's 1 inch in diameter needs a rootball about 1½ feet in diameter to be healthy.
4. A tree with kinked or girdling roots. However, it's hard to detect these because they are often deep within the rootball.
5. Species that are known to cause problems with dropping limbs, by raising sidewalks, getting pests and diseases, or perishing from climate extremes.
6. Look out for varieties that are merely ornamentals—such as "flowering almonds" or "flowering plums, quince, pears, etc". They grow flowers, but not necessarily nuts or fruit.

How to Plant a Tree

In general, the best time to plant a tree is in the early spring or the late fall, but research your specific plant in case of exceptions. Where to plant is the spot where the tree will have the amount of sunshine it needs—full or partial, as specified; full if not specified. And, if it isn't hardy, plant it where it will have shelter from the wind. Plant big deciduous (shade) trees on the south side of the house where they will shade in summer and let warming light enter your windows in the winter. Conifers do well as winter windbreaks on the north or windy side of the house. (Wisely placed trees can improve your home's heating/cooling situation a lot!)

SITING URBAN TREES: Proper siting of trees that must compete in an urban setting is a challenging art and science and something landscapers do for a living. A tree that lives 200 years in the forest has an average urban life span of only 20 years. (Incidentally, the more urban your dwelling, the shorter *your* probable life span also.) Above all, plant where the tree will have enough room, both for its above-ground growth and its rooting area. Imagine the full-grown tree 10 or 20 years from now. How close are walks, driveways, windows, houses, and cars?

- Keep in mind that fruit and nut trees can be a problem in the middle of a lawn. Mowers frequently damage young trees; or the droppings from mature and fruiting trees (especially nut trees) can damage mowers. The moistness of lawns can contribute to fungal disease in the tree. And the dense grass planting competes for food and water with your tree and will probably reduce the size of the harvest you might otherwise have from it. On the other hand, if the lawn is the only place you have, then do it anyway. Plant that tree!

- Don't plant under telephone lines unless the expected mature maximum height will be substantially less than the height of the wires (usually 25–30 feet).

- Watch for fire hydrants; sewer and water lines; and underground gas, electric, and cable lines. Most cities will send someone out to locate underground utilities for you for at no charge—and be grateful that you cared enough to ask. Your phone directory or operator will tell you whom to call.

- Don't plant your tree where it will obscure a stop sign or make it impossible to see around a corner, or otherwise impair drivers' visibility. A big tree close to a street can risk impact between trucks and branches.

- Sidewalk planting strips less than 5 feet wide are not big enough for any but the smallest (mature height shorter than 30 feet) species of trees. Near a sidewalk branches can be a problem to pedestrians. And powerful roots can eventually buckle the pavement. Plant any larger-sized tree in the yard.

- There is a long-standing notion that tree roots don't go out beyond the drip line on the outer circumference of the branches and that they go very deep under the trees. Certain kinds of trees (nuts) do have very deep taproots. But all the trees tend to root more spread out, wider, and shallower than imagined. A lot of tree roots are in the top 18 inches of soil. Deep digging around them can harm those roots. That's why herbicides laid on a lawn may harm a tree at the edge of the lawn.

DIGGING A HOLE: Dig planting holes wide and shallow, no deeper than the rootball's size, and make them wider than needed to accommodate the tree's spreading roots. The larger the area that you dig up around the hole in preparation for planting the tree, the easier it will be for its roots to spread and find food and water. Remove any grass for 3 feet in diameter.

Testing for Clay or Compacted Soil. Dig a hole about 10 inches deep (a shovelful), and fill it with water. Check it again in 10 hours (overnight). Is it empty? If it has drained less than an inch an hour, you have a serious drainage problem.

Soil. Any kind of tree that needs "well-drained soil" is at risk to drown within 2 years if it's planted in compacted and clay-type soils—those that are poorly drained. Instead, plant tree varieties that are adapted to poor drainage— hardy plants that don't specifically need "well-drained soil." Or else rebuild the soil in a very large rooting area for your tree by working lots of organic material into the top 12 inches of dirt; or bring in better soil from somewhere else

and create a large planting mound out of it. And dig wide: every inch of diameter dug out to the side before planting literally increases your tree's chances of survival in such difficult soil. It may also help to set the tree higher than usual in the planting hole. The sides of a hole in clay should be left with a rough surface rather than slick-cut by the digging tool. Don't work clay or saturated soils on the day you plant. Do your digging a bit ahead for the most normal soil structure to put the tree into.

Built-In Special Drainage. This is an option if you want to put a whole line of trees into a poor-draining area. Install "perf" pipe, or drain tile in gravel, and connect it to a storm drain. But don't put gravel under the roots!

PLANTING THE ROOTBALL

1. Unpot the Tree. Speed matters. Don't let the roots or rootball dry out. Care matters also. Don't let the roots or rootball break. Your plant either will be "bare-rooted" and wrapped in some sort of protective substance or will come with the roots in a ball of dirt in some kind of container to hold it together—a peat pot, burlap, wire basket, or bag. If it's a metal pot, cut off the pot with tin snips. Tear it off if it's made of paper. You have to get as much of the wrapping off as possible without actually harming the rootball. This may have you struggling with knives, wire cutters, etc. Untreated burlap can, if necessary, be planted with the tree.

2. Double-Check Hole Depth. Do this by setting the tree in the hole to see how it fits. The "collar" (or "crown" or "root flare") should be just at soil level or a little above (to allow for mulch). Usually it's easy to see because you'll be looking for the same soil line that the tree had at the nursery. Trees planted too deep can die within a few years, or develop problems as many as 15 years later.

3. Set Tree in Hole. Then spread out the roots. If you see any girdling, damaged, or circling roots, cut them off. Try to lay the roots out in a way that they make good, straight contact with their new soil.

4. Fill in Dirt. Place dirt over and around it. Don't add anything to the dirt you're going to put back into the hole to cover the tree roots—not peat moss, not fertilizer. It does more harm than good to spot fertilize a newly planted tree. This is because it tends to make the soil around the tree roots of a significantly different composition from the soil next to it. Water doesn't move normally across the difference. The result is a tree that's liable to be abnormally wet, or too dry. Don't bury incompletely decomposed organic litter around the seedling tree either. This can mess up the pH, the nutrient balances, and the populations of microscopic soil creatures. On the other hand, fully composted organic material that is evenly distributed across the top of the ground in your young tree's area could be helpful. Stomp dirt all around it to be firm and create a depression into which water can settle.

5. The First Soaking. When soil is dry, watering the tree as soon as possible after planting is critical for its survival. Use water also for the final settling of the soil. If additional settling occurs, add more soil, but *don't step on the wet soil around the tree.*

6. Mulch. Mulching the surface of the soil around your newly planted trees 2–4 inches deep does help them by controlling competition and gradually releasing nutrients. In nature, trees mulch themselves every fall. By keeping weeds away, retaining water, and moderating the soil temperature, mulch improves the chances of survival for your tree. But *never let mulch pile up against the trunk.* After mulching the planting pit, brush back the mulch that is in contact with the trunk.

7. Avoid Staking. Natural flexing is necessary for the plant to develop a normally strong trunk and roots. Use staking only if needed to hold the tree up until the roots have become established (usually within a year). To stake, use 1 or 2 wooden stakes (pipe or rebar are too hard to pull out), which have been pounded firmly into undisturbed soil. Place the tie about a third of the way up the tree in order to allow maximum trunk movement. Use soft, flat tie material (inner tube, flat soaker garden hose, commercial products). Never use straight twine or electric, or any other type of wire, against a trunk. Remove stakes and ties as soon as possible. Trees are frequently girdled by ties that people forgot to take off.

8. Prune. But do not prune the tree top to "compensate for root loss." That's a myth. You may prune to take off broken, rubbing, and weak branches, but try not to remove more than ⅓ of the branches.

9. Dirt Dam. Build a circular dirt dam to create a basin effect around the outer edge of your tree planting area to retain water. Trees need water that soaks in deeply to establish good root systems. Water trees a lot the first year or two and during a drought. Let the root zone dry out between waterings unless your tree is a swamp variety. Five to 15 gal. a week is typical.

10. Care After Planting. Young trees benefit if they are irrigated, fertilized, and weeded, being a crop like any other. Water them at least twice a week. Regularly rescue them from weed and grass competitors. Or, easier and better yet, mulch around them so thoroughly the competition doesn't get through. If your trees don't grow well and aren't an obviously healthy green color, they need fertilizer. Spread some manure from your barnyard. However, there's such a thing as too much nitrogen, so spread it in reasonable amounts. For long-term care, young urban trees are most at risk for being bashed by cars or lawn mowers, or vandalized.

TO SPRAY OR NOT TO SPRAY: I think spraying is a vicious habit. It just creates ever more resistant insects and diseases, exactly the same way that super gonorrhea and super tuberculosis have been created by antibiotics. In a few decades fruit growers have gone from spraying once in a while for a specific problem to spraying regularly as many as 30 times a season. The pests they spray to kill just get more and more resistant because there are always a few that survive—the toughest, of course—and they pass their toughness on. Even organic fruit-growers tend to fall into the trap and call themselves "organic" because they spray only, maybe, 6 times a year. And they may spray on only petroleum ("dormant spray"), plus perhaps even some truly biodegradable and environmentally nontoxic botanics. It's hard to roll over and play dead when something is eating your fruit crop.

The pendulum is swinging back now, with people more willing to accept some scars on the sides of the fruit and an occasional worm. If you can accept a reasonable amount of damage you can usually manage by using nontoxic control measures such as predator birds and insects, and planting resistant species. Another organic option, if your crop is getting wiped out anyway, is to take out the plants and burn them and plant other kinds of fruit that you can get a crop off of without poisonous chemicals.

I'd like to see that both government and private-party buyers adopt that policy. If a crop can't be grown without massive use of poisons, it should be unrewarding to grow it. Environmental costs need to be charged as part of the product cost. If the pests are denied their usual diet, maybe they'll become extinct. And anyway, then we won't be poisoning the field workers, our air, water, and soil, and the fruit eaters on down the food chain. We won't be messing up the balance of nature and breeding super pests trying to get a fruit crop past them.

So if your peaches can't make it without spraying, I suggest you switch to persimmons and figs and kiwi and nuts and hardy berries. Same for apples, pears, or whatever. If everybody plants the same fruits and the same varieties of those fruits, a huge opportunity opens for any predator organism. There are so many lesser known fruits and varieties of fruits deserving of cultivation, which are not so troubled by pests. Give them a chance to perform for you!

PRUNING

In the first edition of this book, I was both very scared of pruning and very ignorant about it. Frank Reuter, Berryville, AR, wrote me these reassuring words: "A friend once told me, after planting several new apple trees, 'Pruning just doesn't seem natural.' Having obtained the bare-rooted trees from a local nursery, she had dug them into the ground on a crisp, late autumn day. Then she hesitated. 'There's so little to start with, and I paid so much. I'd hate to cut anything away.'

"'Look,' I said, 'do you want puny little apples seven years from now, or would you like to sink your teeth into a juicy, large apple in just a few years? I know cutting away branches on something you want to grow fast seems crazy, but experience has taught fruit producers again and again that careful pruning really does increase production.'

"'But I don't know how,' she worried. 'I'd botch it for sure.'

"That's the problem: knowing how. Pruning itself is not a difficult task, but it is complicated by the fact that there are so many different pruning situations. You don't prune an apple tree like a plum, nor do a grape vine like a raspberry cane. I had another friend who put in about 15 blueberry plants and waited the long 6 or 7 years until they came into full production. For several years, blueberry pies and muffins literally spilled from his house on a year-round basis. And then he noticed a gradual decrease in his crop. He started asking experienced gardeners and got the same advice from every source: 'Prune harder. Some of those canes look mighty tired. Your stand is losing its vigor.' He took the advice and in just a few years he had a growth of new vigorous canes bending under the weight of their load of fruit. If he hadn't changed his ways and started pruning more heavily, he might have destroyed the entire stand.

"Point number one about pruning: in almost all cases, the problem is not in pruning too much, but in pruning too little. On the other hand, it is possible to prune too much. The results of excessive pruning can be disastrous."

Frank's right. I saw a yard full of adult trees that had been pruned by a professional yard-care person, and it was just heart-breaking how severely they'd been cut back. A year later some of them had actually died from their injuries; others would clearly need several years more before the damage would be concealed by fresh growth and their beauty recovered.

A wonderful lady named Cass Turnbull has made herself the advocate for those who cannot speak, the trees. Her beat is an urban one, Seattle. Her self-defined mission is to fight pruning excesses and unnecessary killing of trees. Cass founded an organization, PlantAmnesty, which puts out a "newsletter published for the fertile minds of PlantActivists—people who don't beat around the bush." PlantAmnesty's goal is to "end the senseless torture and mutilation of trees and shrubs caused by malpruning." It carries "Adopt-A-Plant" and "Eco-Exchange" information. This award-winning little quarterly paper (16 pages, printed with soy ink on recycled paper!) can be yours for $20 per year regular, or $10 if you have limited income.

Cass never stops trying to get the facts out: "Most of us who have horticultural knowledge are frustrated that those who do the work, either pruning or planting, don't have the same knowledge." So she's also the author of a book on how to do this necessary evil of pruning right: *The Complete Guide to Landscape Design, Renovation and Maintenance: A Practical Handbook for the Home Landscape Gardener.* Join PlantAmnesty or order her book ($17.50 postpaid) by contacting Cass Turnbull, 906 NW 87th St., Seattle, WA 98117, (206) 783-9813.

So the secret lies in between: some pruning, but not too much. And then again it depends on the plant, because some plants need a lot of pruning and some shouldn't be pruned at all; and it depends on the time in the plant's life, because plants are most likely to need "training" when they are very young, and then some should be left pretty much alone after that, but others need frequent attention. Plus no 2 people prune alike. So there are specific pruning instructions in the how-to-grow it section for each plant. And here are some basics.

Pruning Tools

Back to Frank: "When you shop for pruning tools, be forewarned: there is a lot of cheap stuff on the market. But bargain tools are likely to get dull in almost no time. Pruning requires you to cleanly remove a limb or cane, sometimes in a very tight space. If your equipment is not razor sharp, you will slash and tear your plants, leaving wounds or scars which invite disease and insects. With some garden tools, you can get by with less than first-rate equipment. But for pruning tools, be sure you are buying quality. When you are

finished pruning, your plants should not look as if one of those whirring, mechanical, roadside-clearing tree slashers had a shot at them. Cuts must be made cleanly."

Cass would approve of that!

Experience helps you know which tool to use for each cutting situation. Always use the smallest tool available. Only if it is not doing an adequate job do you move on to the next larger one.

BASIC PRUNING EQUIPMENT

1. Snips: Hand-pruners, "snips" (also called "pruning shears" or "hand clippers") are your basic and most important tool. Be sure not to confuse this tool with a grass trimmer or a scissors-type shears. A hand pruner is an anvil-type instrument consisting of a sharp blade that snaps against a piece of metal.
2. Lopping Shears: Also called "long-handled pruners," these are necessary for reaching higher limbs or for heavier cuts.
3. Saw: A pruning saw (a bow saw or a narrow, curved pruning saw) is used for thick wood that can't be handled by the lopping shear. Such a saw can have a straight or curved blade, be fine- or coarse-toothed. A bow saw has the advantage of giving you leverage; a narrow curved pruning saw is better for getting into tight places. Incidentally, the saw will be your least-used tool. Never cut large branches unless you have a good reason. A "good reason" would be because a branch is diseased or dead.
4. Pole Pruner: This tool is useful if you have standard or semi-dwarf trees and you find it necessary to prune beyond the reach of your lopping shears. These are clippers mounted on top of a pole, activated by rope and spring.
5. Here is what is *not* a pruning tool: For home fruit-tree pruning, don't use hedge clippers or a chain saw. Hedge clippers are intended only for very fine twigs, and chain saws produce too rough a cut.

SHARPENING PRUNING TOOLS: Frank says: "In general, always keep them sharp and clean. Sharpen pruners or shears as needed the same way you sharpen a pocket knife: Use an oiled whetstone. Place the blade on the edge of the stone with the cutting edge facing away from you. Tilt the dull side of the blade toward you, making sure that the cutting edge stays in contact with the sharpening stone. Then draw the blade toward you. Repeat until nicks and cuts disappear and the blade again is sharp to the touch. If your whetstone is fairly large, you may have to disassemble a pair of hand pruners. If you must, do what all smart mechanics do when they take anything apart: make a sketch of all the pieces and their position relative to each other so you can put your shears back together again. Saws, of course, are a special case. If your saw gets dull, either purchase a new one or pay a professional to sharpen it."

WINTER TOOL STORAGE: "To prevent rusting and corrosion of your tools, lubricate them lightly with oil, especially if they have to be kept in a damp place." If your tool becomes gummed up with sap or pitch, use kerosene sparingly to clean it.

How to Prune

Cass let me borrow heavily from her book on pruning for this section. So, if it sounds like I know what I'm talking about, that's the reason. In addition to the information here, you'd find Cass's entire book helpful. Also you can get bulletins from your local extension service, get other books, and take classes. Pruning can get really complex, and pruners don't necessarily agree with each other about even basic principles. There's a lot more to it than learning how to spread open young limbs (some people use clothes-pins) or to shore up old limbs with 2 × 4s to keep them from breaking.

TREE SURGEON'S HYGIENE: With fire blight in mind, Frank advises: "Certain plant diseases can be passed from one plant to another on your pruning tools, so clean them periodically while you work. Use a rag soaked with a bleach and water solution (1 part bleach per 10 parts water) to . . . wipe the cutting surface of your tools. For small jobs, you can use a paper towel soaked in isopropyl alcohol, which is the ordinary rubbing alcohol and available in a drug store. If you are making cuts on plants which are clearly diseased [like fire blighted], clean your tool after each and every cut to prevent spreading the disease to healthy plants. And, of course, after every pruning job, clean your tools with your cleaning rag before storing them away. Also clean them with your sterilizing solution before beginning any job; someone else may have used your tools on a diseased plant without you being aware of it."

HOW A TREE HEALS: Research suggests that none of the "wound healers" on the market really help much. A tree does its own healing, and it heals by creating a barrier against the injury that rot won't get through. A tree doesn't fill in the wound with replacement living tissue the way people do. It just puts a wall in there and does the best it can with what's left at that site. So leave a "rotten" hole in a tree alone. Don't gouge at it. Because under the rot is the layer that stops it, and you don't want to cut that open.

PRUNING AWAY FIRE BLIGHT: Fire blight is a misery of a disease that can afflict many temperate-zone fruit trees. If it's a problem in your area, prevention of fire blight is a 3-part program: First, avoid feeding excess nitrogen to fruit trees because succulent young growth makes them more likely victims. Secondly, avoid any but the most necessary pruning. Finally, avoid unnecessary watering. Keep an eye on your trees, especially from bloom until fruit, because next to prevention, early detection to bring fire blight quickly under control is the best.

If blossoms, twigs, and leaves on your tree die and turn black but stay on the tree, you have a case of fire blight. You may also see mummified fruit and cankers. The cure is a radical pruning away of all the infected wood. Inspect care-fully to identify all branches that are infected. They are a total loss. In addition, cut a foot beyond the infection because the bacteria tend to be working somewhat ahead of where their damage is visible. Keep in mind that the branches, leaves, even twigs that you're taking off carry the problem organism, so don't handle the blighted areas and then touch the healthy tree. Keep the blighted cuttings away from the tree. As soon as you have them off, move them well away from any orchard trees. Burn them in a hot fire so they won't spread disease. And disinfect!

But hopefully, all your pruning will just be routine procedures.

PRUNING DEFINITIONS

Whip. This is a young tree that has no branches, or one that someone made to look like that by cutting back all the branches to the main stem, leaving the top intact but no side branches.

Pinch. It is less stressful for a tree to have new sprouts pinched off as they form rather than pruned off when they are larger. Pinching maintains all the leaves possible, which helps to feed the tree, yet halts all unwanted new growth. But this method takes much more time than pruning since you have to pinch regularly during the first few weeks of new growth.

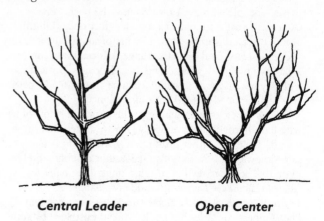

Central Leader   *Open Center*

Central Leader. The single, central tree trunk that grows straight up is your "leader," sometimes created artificially by pruning. The goal of creating a strong central leader can be assisted by "training" the tree while it's very young. But, sooner or later, you have to quit the struggle and let the plant go as it will.

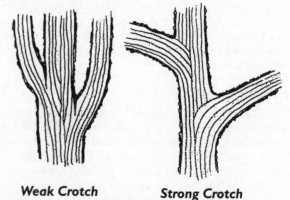

Weak Crotch   *Strong Crotch*

Crotch. This is where a branch connects with the central leader. If a branch is very upright, making quite a narrow

428

angle between it and the trunk (less than 40 degrees), it's called a "bad," or "weak," crotch and is a candidate for pruning because bad crotches are weaker and more likely to break when laden with fruit than branches that leave the tree at a wide angle. The pruner knows that heavy, long, very horizontal limbs, especially when fruit-laden or heavily blown, are more likely to break off than more upright ones, so such branches are also candidates for pruning.

Lateral Scaffolding. The "lateral" or "scaffold" branches are simply the side ones that grow off the central leader. In general you prune a tree in its first few years, allowing only 4 or 5 main branches to come off the leader. You want them to be spaced nicely on the trunk, not to be on exactly opposite sides of each other, and not to have too acute an angle (weak crotch). You do that pruning only once and you're done. A "well-trained" tree is good for climbing. On the other hand, if you want eventually to put a tree house in your tree, train for several branches that grow out near the same spot.

Head Back. To cut off the end of a branch or the top of a central leader is to "head back."

Sucker. Some people use this word to mean both suckers, which grow from the underground or bottom trunk part of a grafted tree, and watersprouts, which grow straight up from higher portions of the tree. (Cass uses it to mean both.)

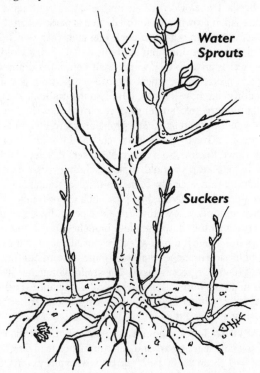

Apical Dominance. The last bud on the end of a branch is called the "terminal bud." It releases a chemical that travels by gravity and keeps the other buds on down the line rather subdued. It's the boss bud. That's called "apical dominance." When you cut off the terminal bud (or even pull it over), the chemical flow is disturbed. That causes the other buds to begin to grow.

TIMING: Here's Carla's simple system for pruning: Don't prune any the first year. After that, you can prune once in the spring and again in the fall. Prune when the leaves are off the tree. Don't remove the lower branches of dwarf trees;

there won't be any higher ones. Here's Cass's much better simple system for pruning!

Pruning of young fruit trees (under 6 years) is done to develop strong, low framework branches and not much else. In fact, it may take a while longer for your tree to fruit. Go easy in the early years. Don't prune too much (no more than ¼ total leaf surface) in any year. Old trees can be invigorated by heavy pruning to produce new wood and spur systems, although you may experience a temporary drop in production when you cut off older and lower limbs. But don't try to fix it all in 1 year. If you have a tree of any age that needs a lot of work, do it over several years.

Summer pruning of fruit trees is all right if the tree is vigorous and healthy and well-watered. Summer pruning can be useful for spotting dead wood (no leaves). It can be useful in reducing the spread of fungus-bacterial diseases that like damp weather, and it will help reduce suckering. It generally slows the growth rate and will help restrict the size of your tree. But summer pruning is harder on the plant, so go easy.

NOTE: Never prune during a drought.

BASIC PRUNING

1. First, and always, take out all of the dead wood.
2. Take out the worst crossing, rubbing branches.
3. Take out the worst wrong-way branches. These are the ones that start on one side of the tree, head the wrong way through the center, and come out on the other side.
4. If you have a grafted tree, carefully prune off any suckers growing up from the roots or out from around the base of the main stem below the graft line.
5. Take out some, not all, of the suckers and waterspouts. (Fruit trees can develop a whole bunch of shoots—suckers or watersprouts, reaching for the sky.) Cut some out altogether. Leave some alone (don't cut off the tips), since they will flower and fruit and be pulled over and produce more spurs later. Head back some suckers to thicken them up into second-story branches. Try to head back to another upright side branch and not to a horizontal branch that would sucker back madly. Thinning back some of the branches, especially toward the top (even a few big branches) increases light penetration and lowers your tree. This helps ripen the fruit lower down. It increases air circulation, too, which is important in order to discourage the numerous bacterial and fungal diseases that spoil the fruit.
6. The conventional wisdom for regular pruning is to remove weak crotches. Both horizontal connections and very narrow crotches may be vulnerable. The preferred connection is wider than a 45-degree angle, but less than a 90-degree one.
7. But to encourage more fruiting on your apples and pears, prune for more horizontal branches. Horizontal branches bear more fruit than vertical branches. You can head back laterals to force more spurs to form.
8. Mature fruit and nut trees can be pruned to let more light into the tree. That will make for larger, better harvests.
9. Too much pruning can weaken your fruit tree enough to result in sickness.

Removing a Tree Limb. First find the "branch collar." That's a little doughnut-shaped bulge at the base of the limb. Don't cut so flush that you cut through the middle of the branch collar. Cut just out from it. That will end up being almost flush, but not quite. The reason it's important not to cut the collar is because cutting it opens up the tree trunk to rot. If you can't see where the collar is, just leave a little space for an assumed presence of one.

Pruning for Fruit Production. Certain kinds of branches make more fruit buds or spurs than others. These are the ones that are situated in a not-too-horizontal position. You can pull or push new branches into such a position, or you can just start cutting out the ones that aren't in the right place and leave the ones that are. Nature makes fruit by sending up a young, straight-up soft branch. It flowers on the tip, and the flower turns into a fruit. The weight of the fruit pulls this supple branch over. As a branch gets older, it stiffens in a more horizontal position. As the branch tips over, the apical dominance of the terminal bud weakens, and buds farther down the branch are released to form nice little side branches (laterals) and on them, teeny, tiny ¼-inch branches called "spurs." These spurs have fat flower buds (fruiting buds) rather than skinny leaf buds. We want the laterals and spurs.

In the winter, it is the fat-budded spurs that you see on trees that make you think what you're looking at might be a fruit tree. You can encourage some, but not all, of your side branches (laterals) to make spurs by heading (also called "tipping back") to 2 or 3 buds. This works on pears and apples, but it doesn't work on cherries.

If your main branch gets pulled too far over—past 90 degrees—apical dominance is diminished, too many buds are released, and those miserable suckers start charging back up. In some senses pruning fruit trees breaks all the rules for ornamental tree pruning. You try to keep your tree small, something that should never be done to other trees. Pruners often reduce fruit trees dramatically, which would be extremely bad pruning on a maple or oak. We also head a lot. We head side branches (laterals) to force them to make spurs. We shorten major scaffold branches with heading, especially young ones, so that they won't swing in the wind and lose fruit. Heading causes these branches to get fatter or stouter. We need stout branches to hold up heavy fruit. On apples and pears, especially, we do a lot of heading. Peaches, nectarines, and Japanese prunes really like it when we whack and whale. However, don't do it to your cherries or European plums.

CASS'S PRUNING CATEGORIES

Prune Hardest: You can, and should, both head a lot and prune most on your peach, apricot, nectarine, and Japanese plum trees.

Prune Medium: Cass suggests that good trees to practice your pruning on are apples and pears "because these trees are so forgiving." Keep young apple and pear trees short, she says, head laterals to encourage fruit spurs, and prune medium.

Prune Least: Cherries and European plums are hard to keep short with pruning. No topping, no heading of lateral is appropriate for these. Love them as they are or train early by bending branches.

PRUNING ERRORS: The most common errors when pruning fruit trees are, first, topping and, second, creating umbrella trees. Topping is bad for any tree, including fruit trees. The suckers that shoot back up from a topped fruit tree not only will be ugly; they are also too busy trying to get enough leaves back in order to feed the tree to make much fruit.

Dealing with Suckers. You may have a forest of suckers that are the result of previous bad pruning. If you remove all of the suckers, they all come back. So leave some to dominate the rest, shorten some to create a second story up, and thin out the rest. The reason why you "leave some to dominate the rest" has to do with that botanical phenomenon of apical dominance.

Reducing the Height of an Apple or Pear. As you work, keep in mind apical dominance. Thus, it is a good idea to cut back a tall vertical branch to a shorter branch that also faces upward. Basically you are not trying to eliminate all vertical branches; you are simply replacing them with shorter, younger, and fewer vertical branches. This retains some apical dominance and allows the tree to grow a little every year. It's like a volleyball game—you rotate out a few of the tallest old suckers every year.

Instead of topping, many orchardists choose to reduce the height of apple and pear trees using the "drop-crotch" method of lowering trees. Drop-crotching means you selectively head back to a side branch of a decent size, say one-half the diameter of the parent stem. This is hard on the health of old trees and opens them up to rot. Trees 15 years or younger withstand this height-reduction better. Drop-crotching reduces the amount of sucker growth, as compared to topping, but does not eliminate it.

Umbrella Trees. Don't create umbrella trees with ugly, sucker-laden crowns. An umbrella tree is made when the pruner cuts to an outside branch year after year, which is called "bench-cutting." But the typical state of many old fruit trees is an umbrella, which is all right if the umbrella is low down on the tree where you can get the fruit, and if you don't care how it looks. But often the umbrella occurs high up on the tree, shading out the fruit below. In that case, you'll want to fix it. The problem is terminal buds that are too low. Gravity prevents the chemical from reaching buds down the line, so a crown of suckers develops at the top. To help keep your old apple tree from excessive crown suckering, thin back low branches to get a branch facing more up and out. To do that, pick out a major (scaffold) branch and follow it with your eyes. Does it dip down quite far, crossing other, lower scaffold branches and cluttering things up? Then you may selectively head back (prune) to one of its side branches that faces more upward and outward (40–60 degrees is ideal). The scaffold branch now ends in a boss bud with greater apical dominance. This will reduce the number of returning crown suckers farther back as well as improve the looks of your tree.

GRAFTING: To learn how, watch a neighbor do it, take a grafting course, hang around at a nursery, or read *Grafting Fruit Trees* (Storey's: 802-823-5810; **www.storey.com**); or *Plants-a-Plenty,* by Catherine Osgood Foster.

SUGAR TREES

MAPLE VARIETIES: You can gather a sweet sap from just about any maple variety although the sugar maple, *Acer saccharum,* is most frequently tapped. If you live in a state bordering any one of the Great Lakes or in the Northeast, you should be able to grow sugar maples and tap them. You can grow them other places too, but tapping won't be as successful. Your altitude is an important factor. Between 600 feet and 2,500 feet is best for sugar maples. For good sap production your climate has to have a big difference between day and night temperatures in the spring. Maples don't produce much sap where winters are mild.

There are other sweet-sapped maple varieties besides the sugar maple that will grow from California on north to Alaska, and they grow over much of the eastern United States south to Alabama and north to southern Ontario and Quebec. The black maple is almost as good to tap as the sugar maple. The Norway maple comes in right behind the black. The sap of red maples has only half as much sugar as that of the sugar maple, and the syrup isn't as fine, but it can be used. The Rocky Mountain maple, big-leaf maple, silver maple, and big-tooth maple all may also be tapped.

Sugar maples are excellent summer shade trees and glorious in the fall with red, yellow, and orange leaves that make the ground look like it's covered by cool fire. They're hardwoods that grow 50–100 feet tall.

Sugar maples aren't the kind of crop you cash in on in a hurry. They are planted more for your successor than for you because they take so long to grow—about 30 years or more to get large enough for tapping. And if competition for space is tight in your planning, also keep in mind that each maple tree will produce only about 1 or 2 qt. of finished syrup per year. So it may not be worth it to you—or to your successor.

PLANTING AND GROWING: Sugar maple seed is available from William Dam Seeds (905-628-6641; **www.dam seeds.com**), and it's okay to grow them from seed. Or propagate by budding. Country Heritage (PO Box 536, Hartford, MI 45057) sells 4–5 ft. started trees. In the West, Burnt Ridge Nursery sells them. Don't prune your sugar maples much. They produce best if they have lots of branches. Trees spaced 35–45 feet apart produce the most sap, but keep some young ones coming in between there as eventual replacements. One way to thin maples is to use a portable sap tester, which tells you the sugar content of each tree. Then you can thin out the less-sweet trees. Another option is to plant your maples both for tapping and for timber. In that case put them 20 feet apart. Less sap but more trees to tap will add up to the same sugar harvest, and you'll have a bigger eventual timber harvest.

MAPLE SUGARING INFO/SUPPLIES: Storey's offers a booklet, "Making Maple Syrup," and a book, *The Maple Syrup Cookbook* (802-823-5810; **www.storey.com**). Check out *The Maple Sugar Book,* by Helen and Scott Nearing, and *Syrup Trees,* by Bruce Thompson (1978). Sugaring supplies of every sort, books, and a free catalog are available from Leader Evaporator Co.: 802-524-3931; 802-524-4966; fax 802-527-0144; 25 Stowell St., St. Albans, VT 05748; **sales@leaderevaporator.com; www.leaderevaporator. com.** A person can spend almost nothing or thousands of dollars on sugaring equipment, depending on your inclination, how many trees you're trying to keep up with, and whether you are producing for home use or for commercial sale.

Incidentally, don't expect your homemade syrup to taste just like store syrup, which is merely flavored with the real thing. Maple syrup is the most expensive natural sweetener on the market—because it takes so much sap to make a gallon of syrup (33–40 gal. at 3 percent sugar content), the tapping season is short, and the trees give but not copiously. But if you have maybe 14 or 15 trees to tap, you can have a nice home-sugaring operation.

IDENTIFYING SUGAR MAPLES: Since you're most likely to be tapping from trees that you didn't plant, you may not even be sure if you have sugar maples and which of your trees they are. In yards, you'll have to distinguish the sugar maple from the Norway maple. In the woods you'll have to distinguish it from the red (or soft or swamp maple). In that case get somebody who knows to point them out to you and put a splash of bright paint on each designated tree so you don't forget. Even an experienced mapler, however, may have difficulty distinguishing sugar maples in winter and spring. Fall is the easiest time. So be sure and get your trees to be tapped marked before fall is over, while their distinctive foliage is still on.

TAPPING MAPLES

When to Tap. You tap your maple trees in early spring, around the first March thaw, generally mid-March to mid-April. Be careful not to tap prematurely. Some old-timers suggest to tap 1 month before your snow is usually gone. You can get some sap in the fall or any warm winter day but not nearly as much as you will during the spring run. The important determinant isn't the calendar; it's the thermometer. The right weather is a freezing night followed by a sunny day, with a temperature of at least 40°F. Take wind-chill into account: more wind requires a higher temperature. It's traditional to try to get all your buckets up in one day.

As soon as you have tapped, the tree goes to work healing the wound and closing off your supply—takes it about 4–6 weeks. If you accidentally tap before the weather has really settled into a spring pattern and the days turn freezing again, your sap supply will temporarily stop and you'll lose some tapping time once it does start to run again.

How to Tap. In addition to tapping the right kind of tree, you need to tap a tree of the right size. Don't tap a maple that is less than 10 inches in diameter. For each 6–8 inches of tree diameter more than 10, you can add 1 tap, as many as 2. (Newest research shows you should limit yourself to 2 taps per tree.) The hole in the tree is bored with a hand drill about 2 feet up from the ground (the lower, the better) and about 2 inches deep. (The hole has to be deep enough and the spout placed in it firmly enough so that even a heavily loaded bucket won't pull the spout out.) If the hole into the tree is angled slightly upward, it will help the sap run out. Sugaring suppliers sell $^7/_{16}$-inch bits, which match the size of most commercial spouts. But a $^3/_8$-inch or $^1/_2$-inch bit can be made to do. New tapholes are drilled every year.

Ann Moran wrote me: "Sap shows in the end of the twigs, usually in late winter if the winter was mild or in the earliest spring. The hole in the tree is bored with an auger. New tapholes are drilled every year and into each hole you insert a hollow metal spout and from that you hang a bucket. A really big old tree can have as many as four buckets on it. So the sap goes up the tree trunk and out the spout and down into your old-time bucket and then every day you should collect the drippings from each tree and take them to the sugarhouse for boiling down. If you've only got one tree go ahead and tap it. Boil the sap down on your kitchen stove and you'll have about a pint of maple syrup. It takes a lot of sap to make syrup."

Into each hole you hammer in a hollow metal spout with a sequence of light hits, and from that you hang a bucket. Be careful not to hammer so hard you split the bark. Sap would leak out through such a split and be wasted. This spigot can be homemade out of wood or a piece of metal pipe or purchased quite inexpensively from a sugaring-equipment source. Manufactured spouts are made with built-in hooks to hold a bucket firmly on. Your first taps should be on the south and east sides of the tree. Then tap west and north. (North-side taps are last to begin flowing, but they'll also be last to stop.)

If you are tapping from a tree that has been tapped within the previous 10 years, place any new tap holes at least 3 inches to the side of and 6 inches above or below the old holes. That's because a tap hole causes death of the inner bark in an oval pattern around it, the oval being a couple inches to each side of the hole and a few inches above and below it. It takes 10 years for the tree to heal that place completely.

How to Collect. So the sap goes up the tree trunk and out the spout and drips down into your bucket. What can you use for the bucket? A coffee can, plastic milk jug, or a specially designed bucket. (If buying used buckets, beware of beat-up or rusty ones—they probably leak.) A larger container will need to be emptied less often. A commercial bucket will hold 4 or 5 gal. of sap. The bucket needs to be protected from sugar-loving animals, and from rain, snow, and wind-blown debris like dirt, leaves, and bugs. The easiest protection is a lid, which is an attachment you can buy for a commercial bucket, or you can devise your own.

Then every day you should come by each tree with your gathering pail into which you'll empty the spout buckets. Take the full gathering pail to your chosen site for boiling down. You may need to collect more than once a day on the best days.

A modern collection system for trees that are reasonably close together and uphill from the boiling place is plastic pipeline that picks up the sap at the spout and carries it directly down to a holding tank. It's inexpensive and easy to collect with but inconvenient to clean after the season's end. It's also difficult to notice a tree sending in bad sap, and the set-up is attractive to wild critters who'll like to take a bite and help themselves to the sap.

Freezing can shut down a plastic pipeline that has a slack and low place in it. It doesn't hurt the sap at all to freeze, either in the bucket or elsewhere, before you get around to boiling it. An interesting thing about partly frozen sap is that as the sap freezes, the sugar tends to stay in the liquid part. A bucket of sap half frozen would have a sugar concentration in the liquid part of twice the usual, the equivalent of half your boiling time accomplished already.

But the frozen lump does have some sugar in it, although a proportionately lesser amount.

WHEN TO STOP TAPPING
1. Before the leaves go into bud (see step 4).
2. If you get tired of boiling sap before that (just pull the spouts out of the trees and you're done).
3. If the sap stops flowing.
4. If some sap is a pale to bright yellow color (a sign that the tree is ready to bud and no good for syrup-making).
5. If the finished syrup is dark brown rather than amber, with a strong, unpleasant flavor (it's edible, healthy, but not the kind of syrup you can give for a present).

THE BOILING DOWN: At your boiling center all the individual buckets are emptied into a holding tank—maybe a big plastic garbage can. This should be outside in a cold place (north side of a building). Or pour directly into your big kettle, like a canning kettle, or one of the large, flat-bottomed pans specially designed for this process. Galvanized pans are not recommended. You can boil the sap down in any pot and on any source of heat. But if you use your kitchen stove and if you are boiling very much of it, it makes the house damp and steamy. Large producers boil in a "sugarhouse," which is a separate building—as simple as four corner posts with a roof or as fancy as a wooden building with windows that open and/or a steam vent in the roof. It's helpful to make it large enough to keep a dry wood supply right in there, too. Holes in a sugarhouse wall help to let the steam out. Either way it's nice to have a level floor. Another choice could be a fireplace or outdoor stove in your yard, possibly made of cement blocks. It helps if your boiling place is near the maple trees but at a lower elevation.

The sap you've collected looks and tastes like sugared water. In fact you can drink it straight, or use it to sweeten other drinks or in cooking.

Beginning the Boiling. Boiling down the sap is a long process, and it takes a lot of sap to make syrup. It takes a 6-gal. kettle of sap 4–5 hours of boiling to turn from sap into syrup—about a quart of it. Thirty to 35 gal. sap would boil down to 1 gal. of syrup. Jean Nance wrote me from Neoga, IL: "We make maple syrup in small batches, from 10 maple trees. If you have 8 qt., you are going to get about 8 oz. of syrup. Until the volume is down to perhaps 16 oz., you are essentially boiling water and don't have to watch it at all. The last bit of boiling down does have to be watched carefully. The main problem is steaming up the house—everything drips!"

A rule of thumb is that while boiling down from the start to $\frac{1}{10}$ the original volume, you don't need to watch it. From $\frac{1}{10}$ to the final stage ($\frac{1}{35}$) though, you do have to pay attention. At this stage later sap begins to develop a layer of thick white foam on the top. (Beginning-of-the-season sap is less likely to foam and boil up.) Skim off that foam with a strainer and discard it; wear a leather or rubber glove while skimming. Boiling up (and possibly over) is a problem related to the physics of surface tension; just add a drop of cream and it will go back down. (Without the drop of cream, you won't be able to boil it as hot and fast for fear of the boiling up.)

Once begun, the boiling-down process should proceed promptly. Sap that stays in the pan too long darkens in color and gets a heavy flavor. But it is fine to add more sap to a batch that is already in the process of boiling down.

Testing the Syrup. You can test your boiling sap for density with the regular sugaring tests or with a hydrometer, sugaring thermometer, or candy thermometer. Boil until your candy thermometer shows 219°F at sea level. For every 550 feet above sea level where you are, add 1 degree Fahrenheit to that temperature. An easy old-time test: Unfinished sap will drop back into the pot off an ordinary spatula that has been dipped into the boiling sap, but finished syrup will cling to the bottom of it.

If you intend to sell your syrup you need the equipment to get it to exactly the correct density and labeled with its grade, available from a sugaring supplier. For commercial markets maple syrup is graded by established standards for color and density. The lighter amber the better grade. Dark-colored syrups have a caramel flavor rather than a maple flavor.

Maple Sugar. *You will make maple sugar if you don't watch the boiling sap carefully in its last stages.* If allowed to get even slightly too dense, the syrup will gradually, over the succeeding months, precipitate out rock-sugar crystals, which will collect on the bottom of your jar. These crystals are hard and tasteless. It's safer to stop a little short of the ideal density than to let your syrup go a little past it.

On the other hand, if you deliberately want to make a maple candy, then pour some of it onto clean snow. When it's close enough to done it will cool on the snow into a glasslike rock sugar. To make the whole amount into rock sugar candy, heat your syrup to 32°F more than the boiling point of water at your altitude. Then cool slowly back down to 155°F, stirring constantly. Then pour it into molds.

Straining the Syrup. If you skip this step, you'll have debris in the bottom of your syrup that you'll have to discard after the clear syrup above it has been poured off and used. So, after the syrup is completely boiled down, strain it through flannel or a paper coffee filter to remove that debris. Or use a commercial felt strainer.

MAPLE RECIPES

✎ *CANNING MAPLE SYRUP If you filtered it, you have to put the syrup back on the heat and bring it back to a boil. Then pour it boiling hot into clean jars or any other sterilized container that you can get a really tight lid on. Pints are a good size for this precious stuff. Fill to very near the top of the container. Then lay the sealed container on its side so the top gets sterilized too. Some people use a paraffin dip. If your syrup isn't carefully canned, it will get moldy. Refrigerate after opening.*

✎ *MAPLE SNOW CANDY Marlissa Carrion wrote me from New York about her childhood in Ohio: "When Mom and my aunt would be heating maple syrup, we used to run out in the yard in the winter with a big roaster pan and scoop up fresh-fallen snow in it. Then we'd trail ribbons of maple syrup into the cold snow. It would harden to a kind of candy."*

✎ *CANNED MAPLE-WALNUT ICE CREAM TOPPING Mix together in a saucepan 1 c. maple syrup, 1¼ c. corn syrup, ½ c. water, and ½ c. sugar. Boil, stirring once in a while. After it has commenced boiling, add 2 c. walnut pieces, stir in well, reduce heat to a simmer, and let cook 15 minutes or until thick enough to suit you. Then ladle hot syrup into hot jars. Leave ¼-inch head space. Put on lids. Process 10 minutes in a boiling water bath canner.*

✎ *MAPLE CREAM SAUCE Combine 1 c. maple syrup and ½ c. cream. Boil to soft ball. Beat 1 minute. Add 1 t. vanilla.*

✎ *MAPLE-HONEY SYRUP Combine ½ c. maple syrup, 1 c. honey, and ¼ c. butter.*

OTHER SUGAR-SAP TREES: Sugar maples are the best known, but not the only sweet-sap trees.

Palm Sap. Palms are the tropical-zone sugar-sap tree. In the blooming stage they send energy to the flowering and soon-to-fruit high part of the plant in the form of a rich, very sweet sap. To tap it, you must climb the trees all the way up to the flower stalk, which is located high in the palm's crown. Cut it open and establish a drainage arrangement. The flow of sap can be continued for weeks by cutting open the flower stem each time it heals shut. Pounding on the tree can help, too. A palm tree being tapped for sweet sap will not produce nuts as long as it's being tapped for sap.

Butternuts and Birch. Butternut trees can be tapped in the spring just like maple trees and their sap boiled down to make a sweet syrup. Birch trees (even in Alaska!) can be tapped for syrup. Black (sweet) birches give lots of sap. Tap in April, same as for maple. Birch sap is less concentrated than maple sap, but if you boil it patiently enough you get your syrup. Use same directions as for the maples.

NUT TREES
Enter the Wonderful World of Nuts!

If you live where nut trees grow wild, you can bring home bags of nuts for free. But there are fewer and fewer wild nut trees. So consider planting some. Nuts provide fat, protein, and, in the case of acorns, carbohydrates. Most seedling nut trees take 5–10 years, or longer, to bear, but once started they continue producing crops year after year with practically no care—as well as providing a bonus of beauty and shade. World-wide there are nearly 1,000 kinds of nut trees, but in North America there are relatively few types, each with distinct climate requirements. So what nut varieties you can grow depends above all on where you live.

CLIMATE: If you live in Southern California you can raise macadamia nuts. In North Central California, almonds and Persian or Carpathian walnuts are primarily grown. If you live in the Southwest, you can grow pine nuts; in the Southeast, pecans. California, Oregon, and Washington grow fine filberts, hazelnuts, and Persian or Carpathian walnuts. The Northwest is excellent for chestnuts. Black walnuts can be grown well in the central and eastern United States. Nut tree nurseries, agricultural universities, and individuals are constantly working to develop improved varieties of each nut. Incidentally, peanuts are not technically a nut, but rather a southern-suited legume, a member of the pea family.

NUTS FOR SALE: The best-selling volume market nuts from wild trees are pecans and black walnuts. Statistically, almonds are the number 1 nut grown and sold in the United States in terms of volume produced, followed by Persian walnuts, with pecans coming in third. Chestnuts and pistachio nuts are right up there too. Commercial nut growers must invest in expensive machines that shake trees and other machines that pick up nuts, as well as drying and storage buildings, grading, shelling, and packing equipment. But there are also nut growers who make a living using very old-fashioned production and processing methods.

NUT TIMBER: Some nut varieties, especially black walnut, are grown for their valuable timber. To do that, plant closer than for an orchard and prune to a strong central leader. As they grow taller, every fall cut off several of the lower branches until you have an 18–20 feet trunk or "bole." Allow at least 2 times as much branched area on the trunk as limb-free trunk. It's better to cut those lower limbs (making a straight, valuable trunk) while the tree is small and young rather than later when the wound may be larger and may never properly heal over, resulting in a scarred trunk. Butternut, black walnut, chestnut, and pecan woods are particularly prized for making paneling and furniture.

NUT BOOKS: Look in your library for *Nut Tree Culture in North America* (Richard A. Jaynes, editor), which offers a wealth of information for serious nut growers. "The Annual Report" (1910–present), put out by the Northern Nut Growers Association, contains lots of nut culture info. Other good sources are *Nuts for the Food Gardener* by Louise Riotte (Garden Way, 1975), and *The Improved Nut Trees of North America* by C.A. Reed and J. Davidson (1958).

I'll describe only about 20 nuts in this book, a fraction of the world's nut-bearing plants. Read about the rest of them in *Edible Nuts of the World* by Edwin A. Menninger.

NUTWORKING: These organizations welcome questions from amateurs.

Illinois Nut Tree Association: Robert Adams, Treasurer; 309-367-4650; RR 3, Metamora, IL 61548-9310.

Kansas Nut Growers Association: William Reid, Secretary; 620-597-2972; PO Box 247, Chetopa, KS 67336.

Nebraska Nut Growers Association: Todd Morrissey, Treasurer, 402-472-3674; 122 Mussehl Hall, East Campus, U. of Nebraska–Lincoln, Lincoln, NE 68583-0714.

Northern Nut Growers Association: members include commercial nut growers, nut scientists, and amateurs. Visit their website for nut tree info and to ask questions of an expert: **www.nutgrowing.org.** NNGA's Membership Directory, quarterly newsletter, *The Nutshell,* "Annual Report," access to the lending library, and an invitation to the annual meeting—all for $20/yr: Nancy Pettit, Treasurer; 302-659-1731; fax 302-659-1732; PO Box 550, Townsend, DE 19734-0550; **chestnutsunltd@email.msn.com.**

Pennsylvania Nut Growers Association: Tucker Hill, Assistant Secretary, edits PNGA's quarterly newsletter, *The Nut Kernel,* and is the person who answers questions. I am indebted to him for reading this section, painstakingly correcting my errors, and supplying valuable info: call/fax 717-938-6090; 654 Beinhower Rd., Etters, PA 17319-9774; **tuckerh@epix.net.**

Society of Ontario Nut Growers (SONG) is a Canadian association of nut growers interested in hardy nuts and good publications: Ernie Grimo, Treasurer, RR 3, Niagara-on-the-Lake, Ontario L0S 1J0, CANADA.

Getting Started

PLANTING NUT SEED: Nuts are very perishable and can easily lose their germination ability if they dry out or mold in storage. It works best to plant nuts very soon after you harvest them. Plant in a cold frame or directly into your orchard. But this presents another problem since squirrels and rodents are likely to dig up the nuts and make a meal of them. The answer is to plant with some sort of cage over the seed. A good technique is to put the seeds between layers of sand in a wire-screen covered box. Or to make an individual cover that you can leave until the seedling is developed: a tin or aluminum can with its bottom cut out and its top slit and folded back enough to let in light but not enough that a critter could get through. Push a can fixed like that down on top of each seed you've planted. Seed nuts need time out in the cold outdoors in order to stratify and be able to germinate come spring. It doesn't hurt them to freeze. *NOTE: Grafted trees will produce much sooner than seedlings. Only quality trees are grafted, so if you buy grafted trees you're guaranteed good nuts.*

NUT NURSERIES: These are only a few of many, but all these are recommended. More entries may be at the individual nut listing.

Burnt Ridge Orchards offers hardy almonds, pine nuts, ginkgo nuts, monkey puzzle nut trees, hazelnuts, walnuts, chestnuts, northern pecans, and oaks that grow edible nuts! 432 Burnt Ridge Rd., Onalaska, WA 98570; 360-985-2873; fax 360-985-0882; **burnt ridge@myhome.net; landru.myhome.net/burnt ridge/.**

Campberry Farm sells seedlings of hardy pecans, sweet chestnuts, hardy almonds, heartnuts, kingnut hickories, Carpathian walnuts, sweet kernel apricots, persimmons, pawpaws, filberts, hazelnuts, etc. Catalog $2, payable to R. D. Campbell: 905-262-4927; RR 1, Niagara-on-the-Lake, Ontario L0S 1J0, CANADA.

Exotica Rare Fruit Nursery will send Bunya bunya, cashew, chestnut, ginkgo nut, Italian stone pine, jojoba, macadamia, and Ecuadorian black walnut plants to CA, NV, or AZ only: PO Box 160, Vista, CA 92083.

John Gordon Nursery offers a few grafted nut trees and many kinds of seedlings, nut seeds, and scion wood: 716-691-9371; 1385 Campbell Blvd., Amherst, NY 14228-1404; **nuttreegordon@hotmail.com; geo cities.com/nuttreegordon.**

Grimo Nut Tree Nursery: John and Lisa Brittain spring-ship grafted and seedling trees—Persian walnuts, black walnuts, heartnuts, butternuts, apricots, Korean pines, hazelnuts, chestnuts, hickories, pecans, and fruits—to the U.S. or Canada: phone/fax 905-934-6887; RR 3 Lakeshore Rd., Niagara-on-the-Lake, Ontario L0S 1J0, CANADA; **nuttrees@grimonut.com; www.grimo nut.com.**

Grinnell Nursery: Sid ships custom-grafted hazel, Persian walnut, and black walnut by UPS or US Postal: 517-625-7176; 14495 Morrice Rd., Perry, MI 48872-9548; **grinnellnursery@tds.net.**

Lennilea Farm Nursery sells grafted trees and seedlings: 215-845-2077; RR 1, Box 314, Alburtis, PA 18011.

Nolin River Nut Tree Nursery is a small family-owned outfit that offers custom grafting and 200+ varieties of budded or grafted black and Persian walnuts, buartnuts, northern pecans, hicans, hickories, butternuts, Chinese chestnuts, heartnuts, pawpaws, and persimmons. Free catalog: 207-369-8551; 797 Port Wooden Rd., Upton, KY 42784; **john.brittain@gte.net; www. nolinnursery.com.**

Pacific Tree Farms offers varieties for the Southern zone. Specialty in new and rare trees: 619-422-2400; 4301 Lynwood Dr., Chula Vista, CA 91910.

Raintree Nursery: For the backyard grower, they offer Ennis and Butler filberts, filbert hedges, trazels, filazels, beaked hazel (*Corylus cornuta*), Chambers and Spurgeon black walnuts, Layeroka and Colossal chestnut, Titian almond, and the Goldenhorn tree (Chinese edible nut): 360-496-6400; 391 Butts Rd., Morton, WA 98356; **www.raintreenursery.com.**

Nut Crop Management and Recipes

STORAGE: Nuts need protection from both air and heat to prevent the oil in them from becoming rancid. They keep best in the shell—best of all at 32–36°F, at 60–70 percent humidity. And use them up within a year. If you have shelled nuts, they'll keep better whole than chopped. They'll keep better unroasted than roasted. Shelled nuts, if stored in a tightly closed container in the refrigerator, will keep for several months, which isn't bad if you can spare the refrigerator room. You can also freeze either shelled or unshelled nuts. They'll keep up to 2 years there.

Dry nuts at least 2 weeks before storing. It doesn't hurt nuts to freeze, so they can be stored outdoors. But don't store nuts where light, heat, mice, or moisture can get at them.

CRACKING: To crack 1 nut or a bushel of nuts, the basic procedure is the same: Lay the nut on a hard surface and hit it with a hammer. Hard shells will be easier to crack and nut meats less fragile and liable to break if you first soak the nuts in warm water. After the soaked nuts are cracked, spread out the nut meats to dry for several hours before you put them away. For very hard-shelled nuts, try freezing them first, then crack them while they're still frozen.

But gadget-makers have invented wonderful aids to this chore, not only the old-time hand-held nutcracker, but also modern techno marvels like the famed Potter Walnut Crackers from 918-224-0567; PO Box 930, Sapulpa, OK 74067. They crack both hard- and thin-shelled nuts (hickories, hazels, pecans, almonds, butternuts, Brazils). Burnt Ridge Nursery offers the Asuite Nutcracker, a hand-cranked tool that cracks more than one nut at a time and is easily adjusted for English walnuts, hazelnuts, pecans, and almonds. The large 10-in. hopper will crack nuts nearly as fast as the hopper is filled, as much as 50 lb. of hazelnuts (90 percent whole) in about 1 hour. Their Top Cracker will shell all your pecans, walnuts, almonds, filberts, even Brazil nuts. Or get the Amish-made "Our Best" nutcracker from Lehman's (it can crack black walnuts): 888-438-5346; **www.Lehmans.com.**

ROASTING: Bob Keene, Amboy, WA, who is also the food columnist "Cousin Grace," sent the following note and recipe: "Carla, the so-called 'roasted' nuts people buy are not roasted, but deep fat (French) fried. That can be avoided."

> *ROASTED, UNSALTED NUTS* Here's his recipe: Place about ½–1 lb. of raw nuts in a 9 × 12-inch cake pan or on a cookie sheet or pizza pan, and place it in the oven. Use a gas oven set on low, which is about 180°F, or an electric oven set on 200°F. "Anything over this temperature is unsafe, as the nuts will burn unless watched carefully," he says. "Keep an eye on them. They'll probably be done within 30 minutes.

If not, check again after 5 minutes. Watch them carefully or you risk badly burnt nuts. With dark-colored nuts such as pecans, almonds, walnuts, and filberts (hazelnuts), it is difficult to tell when they are finished."

> *QUICK STOVETOP NUT "ROASTING"* Roast the nuts in a heavy frying pans or Dutch ovens on top of your stove. It will take 10–15 minutes on very moderate heat. Add 1 t. salad oil per cup nut meats. Mix the oil in well before starting. It will help you get even browning. After the nuts are done, sprinkle salt over them if you want. If oiled, cool on absorbent paper.

> *COUSIN GRACE'S (BOB KEENE'S) TRAIL MIX BALLS* "Use about 1 part any dried fruit to 3 parts nuts. The fruit—dates, raisins, figs, berries—acts as a binder. The nut portion can be any kind of nuts: pine nuts, sunflower, walnuts, pecans, filberts, peanuts, pumpkin seeds, etc. First chop the fruit and nuts in a food processor or meat grinder. If you don't, the stuff won't stick in balls. After the mixture is run through the food processor, pick some up in a teaspoon and make it into a ball. To prevent the balls from sticking to each other, roll them in sunflower seed meal, rice flour, or whatever. They can be stored and carried in Ziploc bags or empty margarine tubs."

Thank you, Cousin Grace, for your great recipes, and say "hi" to your wife from me.

> *RUTH'S NUT CANDY* "Grind 2 c. any kind of dried fruit. Combine with ¾ c. any kind of nut butter. Optional: add the juice and grated peel of 1 lemon. Mix thoroughly, then form into any sort of shape. Or use cookie cutters. Roll in coconut if you like coconut."

> *BASIC NUT/SEED BUTTER* Blend a cupful of nuts or seeds to produce your butter. If they seem lacking in spreadability, add a little more oil. Sesame seed butter is called "tahini" and is good spread thin on a cracker.

> *MIXED NUT BUTTER* Prepare ¼ lb. almonds, ½ lb. pecans, ½ lb. filberts (hazelnuts), and ½ lb. roasted peanuts. Put them all through a grinder and then mix well. Pack in a glass or some other straight-sided container and chill. When wanted for use, dip the container in hot water and the contents will more easily slip out. Cut into slices. Good for vegetarians.

NUTTY MEASURES

Nut	Ounces/ Cup (to Nearest Oz)
Almonds, whole	5
Brazil nuts, whole	5
Coconut, shredded	3
Filberts, whole	5
Peanuts, roasted	5
Pecan halves	4
Walnuts, chopped black	5
Walnuts, halved English	4

Nut	1 Pound in Shell Equals
Almonds	1–1½ c. shelled
Peanuts	2 c. shelled
Pecans	2¼ c. shelled
Walnuts	2 c. shelled

Through the Nut Alphabet

ACORN: The little acorn grows on the mighty oak (you knew that). Oaks can grow to be very old, over 200 years! They can reach a very large trunk diameter and a crown spread of up to 50 feet. (Crown spread is measured from branch tip to opposite branch tip.) A wonderful book called *Acorns and Eat 'Em*, by Suellen Ocean, provides a field guide to 18 kinds of oak trees and their acorns, plus recipes. Yes, it tells how to harvest, prepare, and cook acorns! Send $15 for the book ($15.91 CA residents), or $19.95 for her video version ($21.25 CA residents) to Ocean-Hose, PO Box 115, Grass Valley, CA 95945.

Oak Varieties. The 2 main categories of the some 300 varieties of oak are the black (and red) oaks and the white oaks. Most unprocessed acorns aren't immediately edible for people—too bitter from the tannin content. (But tannin is used in tanning hides into leather.) Black oak acorns contain so much tannin, they're scarcely worth the effort to make edible. But acorns from the white oaks (they have rounded lobes on the ends of the leaves and no bristles) contain less tannin and what is there can be gotten out by leaching. White oak varieties that are good for acorn-growing are the "white oak," "swamp oak," "bur oak," and "chestnut oak." The bur oak (*Quercus macrocarpa*) grows wild in eastern North America. The Oregon or Garry white oak (*Q. garryana*) is another suitable choice. Burnt Ridge Nursery sells 6 different oak varieties, including the cork oak and ones with good acorns for human or stock feed.

Oak Timber. Among the oaks suitable for the Northwest climate are the cork oak (*Q. suber*), which has an edible acorn plus a bark that is used for cork. In old-time Europe these trees were grown on cork estates in Portugal. Oak timber is valuable. White oak is also considered the world's best wood for holding liquids and is ideal for making barrels because of the reddish-brown "gum" that blocks the wood pores. Varieties vary considerably in growing speed, time to bearing, and acorn production.

Climate. Oaks can grow from Alabama northeast to New England, north to Minnesota, and east to Texas. The Ohio and Missouri areas are fine for oaks.

Harvest. Young oaks typically produce a couple bushels of acorns per tree. Old ones can produce prodigious harvests of acorns, even as much as a ton per mature tree, but more likely about a third of that. Oaks vary hugely in the amount of acorns they will produce from variety to variety, and from year to year. Some oak trees have alternate-year bearing cycles; some give a light harvest one year and then a heavy bounty on the alternate year; or a partial crop for 2 years and a full crop on the third. The ilex (holly) oak bears as much as 900 lb. of acorns on alternate years. Some bear significantly only every third or fourth year but give 500–600 lb. of acorns at that time. The emory oak, however, is said to bear almost every year, at least 4 bushels. One of the reasons for delayed bearing may be acorn crops that are lost to early frosts. But the tree tends to make up for lost time when it does get a crop past the frost risk. The larger the tree, the larger the acorn crop it can bear. Grafted oak trees generally yield at least double the acorn harvest of wild ones.

Acorns for Livestock Feed. Acorns provide food for both humans and their livestock (especially pigs, which will feed themselves off the acorns that drop and get fat on them)—a tradition that goes back to antiquity. Acorns are the best keepers of any of the nuts. They'll lie under the tree for a long time without rotting, which makes them perfect for a forage crop. Pigs will roam happily under the oaks, eating nuts as needed. Chickens love acorns that have been broken up so they can get at the nutmeats.

☙ *ACORN MEAL Fortunately, tannin is very soluble in hot water. So, peel the acorns. Grind them up. Soak the "flour" in very hot water. The water will turn brown, because of the tannin coming out. Throw away the water and repeat 4 times. Another way to do this is to line a colander with a straining cloth, put the ground acorns in, and gradually pour a gallon of water, as near boiling hot as you can manage, through. There will still be some dark chocolaty color to the paste, but after exposure to a gallon of hot water, you can be confident that enough tannin has been removed to render the acorn meal edible. Spread the acorn paste on a baking sheet and bake at a low temperature until thoroughly dry. If it has caked, grind again, and you have your acorn flour. You can substitute acorn meal for cornmeal in any recipe, or use part acorn meal and part cornmeal, or ⅔ acorn meal and ⅓ oatmeal.*

ALMONDS: Almond (*Prunus amygdalus* or *Prunus dulcis dulcis*) trees are related to peach and plum trees and are similar in habits. They grow 15–30 feet high with an equal spread of branches. Some varieties are bushy, others more treelike. Almonds start to bear nuts after 3 years of growth, but they don't achieve full-scale production until they're about 12 years old. But once your almond is mature and bearing nuts, it will yield for another 50 years, if kindly cared for.

Climate. The sweet almond does best with a long, warm growing season (zones 7–9), plus low humidity. Most almond orchards are on the West Coast, principally in California. Almond's tendency to bloom a month earlier than peaches means that although the trees can survive in northern areas it's hard to get a nut crop during any year you have an early frost.

Varieties. Almond extract is made from the bitter almond tree, which grows in Europe and whose nuts contain enough prussic acid that you couldn't eat more than a few. Bitter almonds are hardier than sweets and can be raised anywhere that peaches can. There are dwarf almonds that can be grown in containers. There have to be 2 different cultivars, but the almond is pollinated by bees rather than wind so the pair doesn't have to be planted really close together. New Halls have received a lot of publicity, but Tucker Hill wrote me, "I've spoken to a number of people who were disappointed with this almond."

Planting. Soak dried seeds a day, then stratify at 40°F. Or simply plant the seed in the fall where you want it to grow. Choose well-drained soil. Protect seed from being dug up by squirrels by placing a "cage" over it until it is well-started. Or bud graft on a seedling rootstock. Good stocks are bitter almond, peach, peach–almond hybrid, plum (if resistant to oak fungus), or any other almonds. Nemaguard and (peach) Lovell are good for waterlogged or irrigated areas. Good scions are Bartre, Nonpareil, and Mission. Plant the smaller (15-foot) varieties 20 feet apart. Avoid unnecessary pruning of the young tree because that will delay nut production. Train like a peach.

Harvesting. Your almonds will be ready for harvest in August or September. *How to Grow Vegetables and Fruits by the Organic Method,* edited by the Rodale staff, available from

Rodale Press (see Chapter 1) has a good description on page 850 of how to raise and harvest this and other nuts grown in the United States: "The outer hulls of the nuts split open in fall when almonds are ripe. When most of the hulls in the center of the tree have split, nuts are shaken or knocked out of the branches and gathered from the ground. Heavy rubber mallets may be used for jarring the nuts loose without injury to the bark. After the harvest, almonds should be shelled and dried to prevent mildew. Kernels are spread for drying in a partially shaded place and are left until the meat is crisp. They are then stored in airtight containers in a cool place until used."

➣ **BLANCHED ALMONDS** *To blanch an almond means to get the papery outside skin off. Pour boiling water over the nuts. Let them stand 5–10 minutes, or until the skins wrinkle. Drain away the water. You can easily slip off the skins by just squeezing the nut between your thumb and index finger. (If they don't want to give, go with another boiling-water treatment.) Dry.*

➣ **ALMOND SALAD DRESSING** *From Ruth of Bonaire: "An interesting salad dressing can be made with 2 c. carrot/cucumber juice and 8 oz. fresh almond butter. Blend till smooth."*

➣ **ROASTED ALMONDS** *"Roast" in a fry pan by pouring the almonds, blanched or unblanched, in with 2–3 T. hot oil. Fry, stirring, until evenly browned. Drain. Sprinkle salt on them. Or do them in the oven by spreading on a baking sheet and roasting at 350°F 5–12 min. Stir them occasionally while baking.*

➣ **SLIVERED ALMONDS** *Lay the nuts, flat side down, on a cutting board and cut lengthwise with a sharp knife into slivers.*

➣ **TOASTED ALMONDS** *Put on a cookie sheet in a 350°F oven until golden, about 5 minutes. Or mix in 1 T. melted butter and 1 t. salt per 1 lb. almonds and bake until lightly browned and crisp, stirring often. Or you can do it on top of the stove by first blanching, then heating butter in a small pan over low heat, adding nuts, and frying 5 minutes, or until lightly browned. Then drain on absorbent paper.*

➣ **ALMOND PASTE** *This Victorian gourmet ingredient was used to make macaroons, crescents, and marzipan. To make it yourself, grind in a mortar or in a chopper, or blend in a blender, shelled, skinned, and dried almonds (not roasted). If need be, run through the grinder several times until the nuts are really fine. Then, method 1: For every 2 c. almonds, dissolve 1 c. sugar in ½ c. orange juice and then mix thoroughly with almonds. Method 2: Mix 1 lb. ground almonds with 1 lb. sugar and 1 c. water (sugar and water cooked to the soft-ball stage). Then add ½ c. orange juice. Almond paste improves with some storage. Wait a week at least before using. If you have lots of time and use white sugar, consider taking up the art of marzipan-making. You can buy marzipan molds for making fruit shapes from kitchen specialty outlets.*

➣ **OLD-TIME MACAROONS** *Blanch ½ lb. almonds and pound them to a paste in a mortar, or put several times through a grinder set on "fine," or blend. Add ½ lb. powdered sugar and 2 stiffly beaten egg whites. Work it all together, then form balls about the size of a whole nutmeg. Bake at 250°F until light brown.*

➣ **MACAROONS WITH ALMOND PASTE** *Add gradually to ½ lb. of almond paste, ¾ c. sugar and 3 beaten egg whites. Mix well and add ¼ c. powdered sugar and 2 T. flour. Put teaspoonfuls on a paper on your cookie sheet. Flatten the shapes a little. Bake at 250–300°F for about 30 minutes.*

➣ **MARZIPAN** *In the old days marzipan was also known as "toy candy," a traditional holiday treat. To make it, mix 1 c. almond paste, 1 c. powdered sugar, and ½ t. orange or vanilla extract, or rose water (the traditional flavoring). Knead it a long time—20 minutes maybe—and then set it on a rack to dry. After drying, it can be shaped into tiny replicas of fruits, or whatever takes the cook's fancy.*

Coloring: After drying your molded shapes at least overnight, paint them with food-coloring using a small paintbrush. Or dip them into the color Easter-egg style. Then give them time to dry. You can also give them accessories such as cloves for stems and leaves made of bits of angelica.

Glazing the Figures: Leave them covered with heavy sugar syrup 8 hours. Make the syrup by cooking 5 lb. sugar and 2½ c. water to the soft-ball stage — 234–240°F. Remove syrup from heat and let it cool. Add marzipan in a single layer. It is important throughout to avoid disturbing the syrup as much as possible. Then drain your candies and let them dry again.

BEECHNUTS: Beech trees can live very long, well over a century, and grow very large. Although the Beech was originally wild, domestic varieties have been developed that yield larger-sized nuts than the wild or seedling trees. Brown beechnuts are good to eat. The American beech grows to 50–75 feet high. Beech trees are very hardy, suitable for zones 4–9, and only rarely lose a crop due to spring frost. They have good disease resistance and no insect problems. They are self-fertile. Plant them 80 feet apart. The tree produces a crop of triangular nuts covered with a burr.

BRAZIL NUTS: This tropical nut grows wild in the Amazon forests of Brazil. It can't be grown unless you have virtually tropical conditions, including heat, lots of rain, and fertile soil. The most southern tip of Florida might be suitable. Mature Brazil nut trees are big and beautiful. Their nuts grow inside hard wooden outer husks about 4 inches across, 18–24 nuts to the husk. They're delicious eating—rich in fat, protein, a little carbohydrate, and a lot of calcium!

BUTTERNUTS: See "Walnuts."

CASHEWS: The cashew, *Anacardium occidentale*, is a little evergreen tree that comes from the West Indies and can't grow outside the tropical zone. Trees bear only after 4 or 5 years. You can plant seeds, which grow reasonably soon, or graft.

The fruit, called "cashew apples," is ready to harvest in early summer. Sticking out of the base of each cashew apple is the cashew nut inside an outer shell. But the nut is protected by a substance similar to poison ivy, released to do its damage if the shell is broken by some would-be cashew eater. The solution is to roast the nuts before shelling because that disarms them. The cashew apple has no such problem. You can eat it raw or cooked or juiced or anyway you would a regular apple.

CHESTNUTS: The chestnut (*Castanea*) tree produces abundant flowers from which honeybees love to gather pollen and nectar. A single tree can produce 250 lb. or more of nuts every year. Chestnuts are specialty nuts that are especially popular at Thanksgiving and Christmas time.

Varieties. There are chestnut varieties that bear early (Meiling Chinese chestnut), middle, and late. By planting some of each you can prolong your harvest season. The other big factor to consider is blight resistance.

Chestnut Tree and Nut

American. The splendid American chestnut was a relatively fast-growing tree, reaching up to 60 feet tall with trunk diameters of over 3 feet in less than 60 years. And that chestnut timber was an excellent hardwood with many uses. But those native American chestnuts (*Castanea dentata*) of the eastern and southeastern United States all died as a result of the terrible air-borne blight disease that arrived from the Orient in 1904 in a shipment of plants—and still attacks any vulnerable chestnut. Before that, the American chestnut, a superior variety both for timber and nut production, grew huge and wild, making up as much as half of the natural forests in its area. There were also large commercial chestnut orchards, the chestnut being an economical and valued "tree corn." Although new suckers continue to try to grow from the stumps of some of the old giants, they are struck down by the blight after reaching 20–30 feet.

The chestnut blight, incidentally, presents a very clear example why we should always maintain genetic diversity, even at the cost of supporting some obviously less desirable varieties of a species!

Hybrids. The few American chestnuts that have survived have been propagated and hybridized with European (the Spanish) or Asian (the Chinese) chestnuts. Burnt Ridge offers many chestnut varieties. Chestnut Hill Tree Farm sells bare-root Dunstan seedling chestnuts through the U.S., January to April. Dunstan is a blight-resistant American–Chinese hybrid. (Actually, not one person has ever died of the blight, and this is the most widely planted chestnut in the U.S. today.) They have large nuts, timber tree form. They have been grown successfully from Maine to Florida, west to Illinois and Texas, and on the Pacific Coast from Washington to California: 386-462-2820; 15015 NW 94th Ave., Alachua, FL 32615-6709; **www.chestnuthill nursery.com.**

Chinese Chestnut. *Castanea mollissima*, the most blight-resistant and most popular chestnut variety, grows about 35 feet high and bears tasty nuts. It is hardy as a peach, rarely suffers frost damage, and lives a long time. Most nut trees prefer neutral or slightly alkaline soil, but this one favors a slightly acidic one. Its wood is very brittle. Head back long branches to avoid breakage.

Chinquapins. These are a small, native-American, Southern chestnut, which is basically resistant to the blight.

Japanese Chestnut. There are several varieties of this one (*Castanea crenata*). Mostly they grow into a large bush or small tree, but some grow into trees as tall as 30 feet. In the past, this tree hasn't been as blight-resistant as the Chinese, but the folks at the the Connecticut Experiment Station (New Haven) have managed to create some promising new crosses of the American chestnut with the Japanese that are quite blight-resistant: Essate-Jap and Sleeping Giant. This variety is more suitable for the warmer zones, hardy only in zone 7 or south of it.

Native Northwest Chestnut. The *Castanopsis chrysophylla* species hasn't been hit by the blight. The Northwest is now one of the best areas in which to grow chestnuts because of fertile soil and moderate climate—and because the chestnut blight has not yet found its way into the area.

Planting. Chestnuts are not self-pollinating; plant 2 or more. Open-pollinated European or European–Chinese hybrids are for dual-purpose timber plantings, blight-resistant Layeroka seedlings for nut orchard pollinators, grafted Layeroka and Skookum for nut orcharding, and others. Nanking, Kuling, and Abundance are older favorite varieties.

Fall planting is possible, but chestnut seeds (nuts) must experience at least 3 months at temperatures 40°F or below in order to germinate. They will grow best if planted lying on their sides, in humus-rich soil of pH around 5.5, protected from nut-eating predators. Or you can store your seed in a very cool place. With luck chestnuts retain germination ability for as long as 3 years. Or you can graft or bud. Serious chestnut growers almost all use grafted trees.

Pruning. Chestnut wood is brittle, so prune early for a strong central leader, horizontal crotches, and balanced branch arrangement. Prune only when leaves and nuts have fallen and the tree is dormant. Chestnut pollen is carried by wind or insects.

Harvesting. On the tree, the chestnuts grow inside of burrs. When ready in the fall, the burrs split and spill out the nuts inside onto the ground. You must pick them up before they have a chance to get moldy, wormy, or eaten by squirrels or 4-legged furries.

Storing. If you put chestnuts in water, bad ones will float. When you refrigerate them, give them air by packing them in loosely covered containers or in plastic bags that have holes in them. Unshelled chestnuts will stay fresh for several months if refrigerated, and for much longer in the freezer.

Cooking. Human food for some 6,000 years, chestnuts are an unusual nut because they are mostly starch with only a little fat, so you can do vegetable kinds of things with them. Prepare like a vegetable main dish; grind into a flour; prepare in a soup or sauce; add them to pasta, pastry, or desserts; and, of course, roast them over an open fire.

Shelling by Roasting. Roast in an oven 15–20 minutes at 375°F. Then peel.

Shelling by Boiling. With a sharp knife, cut a crisscross gash on the flat side of the shell of each chestnut. Simmer until they are quite soft, about 15 minutes. Remove nuts from water, shell, and remove brown skins with a sharp knife. Then go ahead with any of the following recipes. It helps to lift the nuts out one at a time and peel off both shell and inner skin while the nut is still damp.

Freezing. *Shelled, blanched chestnuts should be frozen if you won't be using them within a few days. Just pack any chestnut puree recipe in containers that can be closed tightly. Use in cooking without thawing ahead of time.*

❧ *CHESTNUT–MEAT-STOCK PUREE Cook peeled chestnuts in meat stock, or in a half-and-half mixture of milk and water until they're tender. Puree nuts in a blender or some such. Make a soup by mixing some of the puree with the stock.*

❧ *CHESTNUT–SQUASH PUREE Mix chestnut puree with squash or pumpkin puree for a special side dish. When freezing this puree, prevent separation by mixing in either 1 T. butter or 1 T. honey to each cup of puree before freezing.*

❧ *PLAIN CHESTNUT PUREE Boil peeled chestnuts in lightly salted water until tender. Then mash and add a little butter, salt, and pepper.*

❧ *CHESTNUT POULTRY STUFFING To the puree, add bread crumbs, beaten eggs, and a little of the juice in which the chestnuts were cooked.*

❧ *CHESTNUTS AND SPROUTS Sliced chestnuts are good with Brussels sprouts.*

❧ *PLAIN CHESTNUT CHICKEN SOUP Chestnuts go well with chicken soup. Cook 1 c. peeled chestnuts in 2 c. chicken soup until tender. Add about 6 c. more chicken soup. Season with salt and pepper and serve.*

❧ *FANCY CHESTNUT CHICKEN SOUP Heat 1/4 c. butter in pan. Fry a half dozen chopped green onions or 1 small chopped globe onion until golden. Add 1 lb. fresh, simmered, peeled chestnuts. Fry 1 minute, stirring constantly. Add 1/2 c. chopped celery or celeriac and 2 c. chicken stock, and cook 30 minutes or until chestnuts are quite tender. Strain solids out of the broth and puree them. Then stir back into the broth. Reheat just to a boil. Add salt and pepper to taste, a pinch of nutmeg, and 1 c. light cream (or half-and-half). Do not boil!*

❧ *DIFFERENT CHESTNUT SOUP Puree 2 lb. fresh chestnuts, or use 1 lb. unsweetened chestnut puree. Heat puree in 1 qt. vegetable stock. Add 1 c. finely grated carrot (or salsify) and cook on low heat about a half hour. Melt 2 T. butter in a separate pan. Add 2 T. flour and cook, stirring constantly, until it begins to darken. Add the hot chestnut soup in slowly, stirring to keep it blending. Add 1/2 c. red wine, 1/4 t. nutmeg, 1/4 t. cayenne, and salt and pepper to taste. Cook 10 minutes more over low heat (stirring often!). Sprinkle a little paprika over each bowl you serve.*

CHINQUAPIN: See "Chestnuts."

COCONUT: There are many different varieties of palms, all tropical species. The beautiful coconut palm (*Cocos nucifera*) grows in both the East and West Indies, the tropical Americas, the South Pacific, Southern California, and Florida. They can grow as high as 100 feet tall. It has no branches, but there's a cluster of large leaves at the very top. Those few leaves are 12–18 feet long and useful for braiding into things or thatching houses. One tree will produce 40–75 coconuts per year (depending on soil fertility), with fruits maturing all year round. Coconuts are salt tolerant. Ocean sprays, wind, flooding, or even an occasional covering with salt water doesn't hurt them. Palms can also be tapped for their sweet sap. But they need lots of humidity, a frost-free climate, 40–60 inches of rain fairly evenly distributed through the year, and a minimum average temp of 72°F.

Planting: A coconut husk high on the beach may have dropped from a tree into the ocean and floated for thousands of miles before washing ashore. Under natural conditions, eventually it will sprout and grow. To plant the seed yourself, place an unopened coconut into a partially shaded nursery bed. Leave the top half of the shell outside the dirt. Keep it moist. If you plant while the nut is still a bit soft it will germinate in only a few weeks. Once the nutshell gets fully hardened, it may take as long as 4 years to germinate.

Harvesting. Dwarf trees bear in 3–5 years, standards in 5–10 years. Once the tree starts, coconuts will continually ripen year round, more every year—from 50, when it's young, increasing to maybe 200 when the tree is fully mature at 15–20 years. The fruit is covered with an outer husk that is made of tough fibers that are very resistant to saltwater. It changes from yellow or green (depends on variety) to brown as it ripens. Those husks are used to make fishing nets, doormats, rope, and brushes. The nutmeat is inside a tough shell, which itself is inside the husk. The shell can be used as a bowl. You can harvest using a knife fastened to the end of a long pole.

Opening a Coconut. Pound something sharp through one of the 3 "eyes." The shell is thinnest there. Then drain the coconut milk into a cup. Next, whack the shell with a mighty hammer blow and it will crack wide open so you can get at the nutmeat. It can be eaten fresh or dried.

❧ *MAKING COCONUT MILK The store product called "coconut milk" or "mix" for making alcoholic drinks is not the real thing and can't be substituted for genuine coconut milk in tropical cuisine. The clear liquid at the center of the coconut is sometimes called "coconut milk," but usually coconut milk for cooking is produced by the following method: Cut fresh coconut meat up into cubes about 1 inch on the side. Measure out an equal amount of hot water. Place water and coconut in your blender and blend at a high speed for a couple minutes. Let rest 30 minutes. Set a strainer over a bowl and pour the puree into it. Squeeze out as much "milk" as you can by pressing on the pulp. Giving the coconut milk an extra straining through an even finer mesh makes it nicer. Coconut milk will keep fresh only a few days in the refrigerator. If you need to store it, freeze it. Real coconut milk can be used to make sauces, soups, desserts, and curries.*

❧ *SHREDDING COCONUT Open a hole in your coconut, and pour out the milk. Drink the milk or save it for cooking. Grate the coconut meat or shred it with a vegetable shredder.*

❧ *TOASTING SHREDDED COCONUT Put the shredded coconut in a flat pan and put the pan in the oven at about 200–300°F. Stir occasionally until it is dried. You can also sun-dry coconut. All you have to do is cut the meat into thin slices, spread it on your trays, and put it in the sun to dry. Dried coconut is called "copra." Store copra in airtight cans or jars. Add copra to pudding, eat it as a sweet, or use it in any recipe in place of nuts.*

❧ *COCONUT MILK MADE FROM DRIED COCONUT Combine 1 c. natural (unsweetened) dried coconut with 1 1/2 c. hot water. Let rest 5 minutes. Puree and strain.*

❧ *COCONUT CREPES WITH POLPANI FILLING Sift together 1/4-lb. sorghum flour and 1/4-lb. wheat flour 3 times.*

Place flour in a bowl. Add salt to taste, and the yolks of 6 eggs. Add 3½ c. thick coconut milk. Mix with a wooden spoon. Gradually add 3½ c. more of thick coconut milk. Beat the whites of the 6 eggs to a very stiff foam and fold them into the batter. Set the crepes batter aside and prepare polpani. (You can substitute any crepe filling for the polpani.)

To prepare polpani (brown sugar and coconut filling): Place 4 oz. unrefined brown sugar in a pan. (The original recipe calls for 4 oz. "jaggery," which is an unrefined brown sugar made from palm sap!) Add 2 T. water and a ½-inch piece of cinnamon stick. Stir and cook over heat until syrup thickens. Add 4 oz. fresh coconut scrapings and a pinch of salt. Keep on low heat a few more minutes, until mixture thickens.

Now put your pancake pan on the heat and melt a little butter, margarine, or coconut oil in it. Pour enough batter into the pan to make a pancake about 5 inches wide and very thin. When it is cooked on one side, turn it over. When both sides are done, slip the crepe onto a plate, put a spoonful of the polpani in the middle of it, and then roll it up.

➢ *COCONUT BREAD* Combine 2 c. shredded coconut, 1 c. mashed other fruit, and 5 eggs. Mix well. Sift together 2 t. salt, 2 t. baking soda, and 4 c. any flour (doesn't have to be a wheat flour!). Add 1 c. brown sugar and mix all ingredients well. Let rest 20 minutes. Stir once. Pour into a greased pan. Bake at 350°F. Cool, then serve.

➢ *COCONUT OIL* When dried coconut is pressed, it yields coconut oil.

Green Coconut. You don't have to wait until a coconut is fully ripe to eat it, although that is the proper stage at which to harvest if you want to press from it. The immature coconut flesh is soft: "green coconut." Eat it with a spoon. It's delicious, nourishing food, traditionally given to infants, the elderly, or ill people.

FILBERT FAMILY: Hazelnuts and filberts aren't the same thing, but they are related. The hazelnut (*Corylus americana*) is a native American filbert. It's a small bush that can grow up to 8 feet tall. The filbert (*Corylus avellana*) is a large bush that can be pruned to take the shape of a small tree. Filberts grow up to 15 feet tall. Both filberts and hazelnuts are relatively quick growing and produce nuts early. But both also have a relatively short life span of only about 20 years, so plan for replacement trees as they age. Both prefer neutral soil, have no serious insect pests, and need 2 or more trees for cross-pollination. The hazelnut has the best disease resistance, the best chance of escaping frost damage, and the best general hardiness. There are many other species.

FILBERTS: The filbert is a long-domesticated, much-hybridized, and improved plant, one of the nuts with the distinction of regularly appearing in holiday nut mixes. This nut is popular as a yard-grown tree, being easy to grow, hardy (zones 3–6), and naturally on the small side. In Washington and Oregon filberts are grown commercially. You can grow filberts in colder climates if you get the late-blooming kind. Filberts occasionally lose a crop to frost (again, hazelnuts are hardier).

Propagating. You can reproduce filberts easily by layering. To layer, bend a low filbert branch clear to the ground, cover the middle portion with dirt, and put something heavy on top to hold it down like that. Soon that covered (layered) section will have taken root on its own. Eventually you can cut it loose from the parent tree, and later yet you can transplant the new start to wherever you want it. The filbert doesn't have the long taproot of the walnut family, so it's easier to transplant. Grafting and budding are another option. Good stocks: Turkish tree hazel (*C. colurna*); and *C. americana* and *C. cornuta*, both disease-resistant Americans. Good scions: Barcelona and Nonpareil.

Filbert Tree and Nut

Growing from Seed. Growing filberts from seed can be difficult if you're doing it on purpose. On the other hand, volunteers from careless birds or forgetful squirrels may grow generously. To grow, seeds must have been successfully pollinated, then chilled at 40°F or below for at least 3 months. If your seed doesn't germinate the first spring, don't despair, because sometimes it will after 1 or 2 years or even longer. If you plant numerous seeds in pots, flats, or a nursery bed in your garden, you can hope for better success. In their permanent location, plant filberts 20–25 feet apart.

Pollinating. Barcelona is a good pollinator for Daviana. Filbert trees have unusual blooming patterns. The trees do not have a natural dormant period. They can be loosely classified into early bloomers, mid-bloomers, and late bloomers. Early bloomers start about November and continue into January and February. Mid-bloomers bloom mostly in the winter months. Late bloomers start later and continue until March. To make it even more murky, sexes may bloom at different times. The males of some varieties bloom first; within other varieties, the females bloom first. You're fortunate if you can get them both to bloom at once, which is what you need for fertile seeds.

Pruning. Easterners usually let filberts grow as a large bush (limited to 5 or 6 stems so the center doesn't get too dense), but on the West Coast, they are often pruned to a single main stem to make them look like small trees. Prune mature plants in a way that lets more light into the center of the tree. Prune only during winter.

Cooking with Filberts. Filberts may be toasted, ground, and so forth. For baking they are usually left unblanched, for the pinkish skin adds much to their flavor and food value.

Removing the Skins. Spread the nuts on a cookie sheet or in a shallow baking pan. Bake at 300°F for 15 minutes, stirring occasionally. After they have cooled enough to handle you can rub the skins off with your fingers. If you plan to chop filberts, toast them after chopping. Store toasted nuts in an airtight container. Filberts make a great nut flour.

Harvesting. Filberts that are pollinated in January or February will grow in spring and drop in September and early October. The female flower has already been growing a year and a half when the filbert nut, which has been attached to it almost 8 months, finally drops. Pick up the nuts as soon as possible to prevent mold and to reduce loss to birds and squirrels. Give them the water test—floaters are not good. Dry them by spreading them out in a dry room and stirring them occasionally. Store in the shells in a place where mice and rats won't be tempted.

HAZELNUTS: These trees differ from filberts in that their smaller size allows you to plant them only 10 feet apart. The nutmeats are good-tasting but tend to be smaller than those of the filbert. Winkler is a good variety. Hazelnuts make a nice raw nut butter. You can mix it with vegetable or fruit juices to make a salad dressing.

HEARTNUTS: See "Walnuts."

HICKORIES: Hickories (*Carya*) grow wild in the central and eastern United States. They naturally grow into straight, very tall trees (maybe 50 feet) and are sold for their unusually strong wood, used to make tool handles. Hickory wood is also a prized firewood, and the bark is excellent for smoking meat. It takes a hickory tree an average 5 years to start bearing nuts. When mature, they'll produce 4 or 5 bushels per year. They can be stored in the shell for months in a cool dry place.

Hickory Varieties. Hickories include pecans, bitternuts, shagbark, water hickory, mockernut, shellbark, and pignuts. There are still other varieties that are natural hybrids, and more that have been developed by plant breeders for the big commercial pecan market. The value of the nuts depends on the variety.

Bitternut. The bitternut is practically inedible. Bitternut is the hickory that can grow farthest north, even in southern Canada, though the shagbark, shellbark, and mockernut hickories are also very hardy.

Shellbark and Shagbark. The pecan is the prime culinary and market variety; the shellbark and shagbark compete for second-best. The shellbark bears a large, white, 4-cornered nut with a sweet kernel. The shellbark hickory grows wild from Tennessee north to New York and is a good nut tree, especially for northern states (zones 5–8). Hicans are hybrids made by crossing pecans with shellbark hickory. Tucker Hill says the McAllister hican is unreliable for nut production though a good shade tree; the others are good producers. All the hickories have good disease resistance; the shagbark is most free of insect problems. Shellbark nuts have thick shells. One method that helps in cracking them is to freeze them overnight, then crack with a hammer blow on the nut's edge. You'll learn to swing with just enough force to crack the nutshell without smashing the nut. Or some readers say a hot-water bath beforehand helps make shelling easier.

Pecans. Pecans (*Carya illinoinensis*) are a hickory variety—a good tree that is easy to grow, does fine in yards, and bears a nut that is easy to shell. Some small varieties have been developed that are more suitable for a small yard. A paper-shell pecan tree can give you 100 lb. of pecans a year. One way to choose your varieties is between southern early-bearers (Candy, Elliott, Shoshoni, Success, Western, etc.)

and southern late-bearers (Curtis, Mahan, Schley). Read ATTRA's "Sustainable Pecan Production" at **www.attra.org/attra-pub/pecan.html.**

Climate for Pecans. Big pecan crops are possible all over the southern and southwestern United States and in California. The southern pecan is the least hardy and requires a long growing season, so commercially they are usually grown only from Georgia on south. However, northern pecans are grown in Kansas and Nebraska, as well as Illinois, Indiana, Ohio, and Pennsylvania. The variety you buy needs to be exactly chosen for your climate zone. Tucker Hill warned me to beware of Southern pecan propaganda. "Northern pecans are smaller but higher in flavor. Both Kansas and Nebraska are producing outstanding pecans. We do quite well here in Pennsylvania."

Planting Pecans. You can plant seeds, graft, or bud. But seeds can't be depended on to breed true. In the South, plant seeds in the ground any time following the nut drop and before the next spring, as long as the contents of the nut haven't dried out. Northern varieties need to be chilled in the ground or in your storage area at just above freezing for about 2½ months in order to germinate. To bud pecans, large varieties should be selected for stock. Seedling trees take years to reveal what you've got—8 or more. Grafted trees usually take about half as long. Plant orchard pecans 30 per acre. Grow 2 different varieties near each other in order to have pollination.

Harvesting. If you have trouble getting your nuts off the tree you can knock them from the branches with a pole. In the shell they will keep best in the refrigerator.

VEGAN PECAN BURGERS From Ruth of Bonaire: "Combine 1 c. ground unroasted pecans, 1 c. wheat germ, 1 c. bran flakes, 1 c. grated onion, ⅔ c. grated carrot, 1 T. tamari, and water enough to moisten, if needed. Shape the mix into patties. Fry on a nonstick or potato-rubbed skillet. Serve on buns together with your favorite toppings."

PECAN MACAROONS Beat 1 egg white until stiff. Then gradually beat in ⅓ c. pecan nut meats (chopped fine). Drop mixture by teaspoonfuls onto a baking sheet covered with buttered paper. Make smooth rounds of your drops. Sift powdered sugar over the top. Bake at about 350°F.

PRALINES Combine 1⅞ c. powdered sugar, 1 c. maple syrup, and ½ c. cream. Boil to the soft-ball stage. Remove from heat, and beat until creamy. Add 2 c. chopped pecans (or any other nuts). Pour into a buttered pan and cut into squares.

Planting Hickories. Plant a nut, or a seedling, or grafted/named variety. But this tree has a long, strong, early-developing taproot, so don't consider transplanting unless it's a very, very small tree and then plan carefully and put that small tree where you'll want to keep it. And if the taproot is cut or bent while transplanting, prune it just above the injured part.

Pruning. Prune after the nuts have fallen, in early fall. Take off a few lower limbs each year while the tree is young until you achieve a 6–8-foot bottom trunk. After that, mature trees don't usually need any pruning.

MACADAMIA: This nut tree is a good-looking evergreen that's native to Australia where it's known as the "Queensland nut." Later grown also in Hawaii, they are now getting started in California and Florida, too. In Australia where the soil is fertile and the moisture abundant enough, they can get 40–50 feet tall.

Planting. Macadamias need to root in deep soil to keep themselves from being blown over, and they seem to do best in an acidic soil. Stratify the seeds during your coldest season; then plant them in individual pots in a greenhouse-type situation. They are slow to germinate. When you transplant be careful not to disturb the root mass. They can be grafted to better cultivars. Warm climates only.

Harvesting. For some reason, only a few of the hundreds of tiny macadamia blossoms produce nuts, but there are so many flowers to start with that your crop can still be generous. The nuts mature inside a husk and require more than half a year's time. The husk ruptures itself when the nuts are mature, allowing them to fall to the ground. During the harvest season (about a month long), go out at least twice a week and gather up all the nuts off the ground. Then dry them thoroughly.

Using Macadamias. You need a special tool (such as vise-grip pliers) to crack the shells because they are so hard. Before you use the nutcracker, spread the nuts on a baking sheet and roast at 200°F for 1 hour. Cool slightly; then shell. Store shelled nuts in the refrigerator in a covered container.

🐝 *MACADAMIA SALAD DRESSING Ruth of Bonaire combines 1 c. of apple/celery juice or carrot juice with 3 oz. macadamia butter made from unroasted nuts. Or, she suggests using orange juice for a tropical flavor.*

🐝 *MACADAMIA WALDORF Also from Ruth: "Dice 6 tart apples. Pour the juice of 2 oranges and 1 lemon over. Chop 4 stalks celery. Drain the juice off the apples and blend juice with 3 oz. macadamia butter. Mix dressing by hand with apples and celery. Serve in lettuce-lined bowls."*

PEANUTS: These are a variety of the legume, pea family (see Chapter 4).

PECANS: See "Hickories."

PINE NUTS: Pine nuts are also called "piñon nuts" or "pignoli." The evergreen trees (*Pinus*) that bear them are easy to grow and hardy across a wide range (zones 3–10), but all pines are harmed by smog so they don't belong in the city. Piñons can thrive, however, on dry, rocky hillsides in desert climates. Pine nut trees range in appearance from a large shrub about 10 feet tall to a shade tree up to 100 feet tall. The smallest nut pine can be grown in a pot but won't produce very many nuts in a container. Being pines, these trees have needles rather than leaves, varying in length from 3 to 12 inches depending on the variety. How much sun is needed also depends on the variety: some can thrive in partial shade. For more information, read Ronald M. Lanner's book, *The Pinyon Pine: A Natural and Cultural History* (Reno, NV: University of Nevada Press, 1981).

Varieties. The Mexican piñon pine (*P. cembroides*), which tends to be short, grows bonsai-fashion into odd, gnarled shapes and is often planted as an ornamental. The Italian stone pine (*P. pinea*), another good nut-bearer, takes 25 years to get old enough to start its regular and generous production, grows tall (60–75 feet) and straight, is very hardy even to –35°F, and makes a good windbreak. The best variety for the desert is the Mexican piñon. Other species that produce seeds large enough to be called nuts are the Korean stone pine (*P. koraiensis*), which grows taller than

any of the others (up to 100 feet); the Swiss stone pine (*P. cembra*); Siberian stone pine (*P. sibirica*); sugar pine (*P. lambertiana*); digger pine (*P. sabiniana*); limber pine (*P. flexilis*); whitebark pine (*P. albicaulis*); piñon pine (*P. edulis*); and single-leaf pinon (*P. monophylla*).

Pine Tree, Cone, and Nut

Planting. You can buy started pines from nurseries, collect them from the woods, or plant seed. Plant in well-drained soil (moist is okay). Don't fertilize. This is naturally a desert plant, and once the tree gets going, it doesn't need much watering. It doesn't need pruning either, unless there is dead wood needing to come off or it's growing somewhere that's definitely forbidden.

Harvesting. You'll have to wait 10–20 years for your tree to mature enough to bear nuts. In the meantime you could gather wild ones. In different years your tree may bear very different sizes of crops. You can market pine nuts for a good price, and enjoy them for the rest of your life once the trees get started producing. Pine nut time is the fall. Race the squirrels for them and win by going out and collecting the pine cones after they have ripened, but before they have fully opened. Store them in a big shopping bag, or some such, in a warm place in your house. The pine nuts grow snugly placed at the base of each scale. As the cones open inside the bag, the nuts will fall freely to the bottom of it.

Eating. Pine nuts are hard to crack open. Once you do get the nuts out you have top-notch food. Store them in something airtight, frozen if you want to hold them more than a month. To use: roast, salt, and eat out of hand. Or add to any rice, stuffed cabbage, Italian, or pesto recipe.

PISTACHIO: This deciduous nut tree (*Pistacia vera*) can be grown as a single tree or in a group—several make a great hedge because of the tree's tendency to grow densely. But pistachios thrive only within rather narrow climate limitations. They need some winter chilling, about 30 days of cold, but are likely to die if the temp gets below 10°F. They need a hot summer, 100 days of that. They need dry air; high humidity can be a problem. In general, you could try pistachios in zones 7–9, especially if you live where olives grow. California's Sacramento Valley is just right. In southern Turkey, ideal conditions are also present; there, pistachio trees grow wild. Within its climate zone, the pistachio is hardy and able to thrive despite thin soils; they can root even into rock crevices.

Pollination. Pistachios come female or male. You must have both female and male trees in order to have any nuts, although if you absolutely have room for only 1 tree, a length of male branch can be grafted right onto a female tree and will accomplish the job that way! The females grow to be 20–30 feet high, males even higher.

Planting. There are 2 female varieties available: Red Aleppo and Kerman. A male pistachio has got to be Peters. Few nurseries carry them, and then only in containers rather than bare root. The male and female must be planted within 50 yards of each other for pollination to be certain. Plan on planting a few: you want both sexes, and individual plants produce nuts only every other year, so to get annual production you need several plants.

Growing. They grow well from seed, or by bud-grafting, so long as they have the right climate, full sun, well-drained alkaline soil, some pruning, some manure fertilizing, and organic mulching. Once your pistachio pair is well-started it will be quite resistant to water shortages. However, if you give the trees more water, they will bear more nuts.

Pruning. Pistachios crave to be bushes. If you want trees, train to a central leader with a scaffold of 4–5 lateral branches starting 4–5 feet above ground. An unpruned pistachio can grow really dense.

Harvesting. Your pistachio tree won't be mature enough to bear nuts until it's about 10 years old, and it will be 15 years before it's going well. Once bearing, in the fall the fruit will be apparent as heavy bunches of yellow or red nuts hanging prettily from the ends of branches. The color change of the shells to those pretty, bright shades signals that the nuts are getting ripe. When the nuts come away easily when picked and when the shell separates easily from the inside when squeezed, it's time to pick the nuts from your tree. If you don't get right at it, squirrels may do it instead. Expect 10–20 lb. of harvest from a newly producing tree. As a pistachio tree gets older, it steadily increases nut production.

Storing and Using. After picking the nuts, remove their hulls right away, for nuts in a pile in the hull tend to start spoiling almost within hours. Dry the unhulled nuts spread out in a single layer in the sun for a week. In the shell they will keep in a cool place for many months. They're hard work to shell. If you keep running into empty shells, that means your summer was too chilly for this plant, or else that pollen wasn't transported successfully. After shelling, they must be stored tightly covered, preferably in the refrigerator. Eat raw, or roasted. Pistachios are fun to put in ice cream or scatter on top of any other desserts.

SWEET-PIT APRICOTS: These relatives of the apricot (which is related to the almond) can grow in areas that are too cold for almond nut production, if it's moderate enough for apricots. A variety of sweet-pits is the Hunza-cot, a fruit with an edible nut-seed that has been grown and eaten for centuries by the famous long-lived Himalayan Hunza people. Most apricot "nuts" contain cyanide and are bitter at best, potentially fatal at worst. But the sweet-pits don't contain cyanide and taste like almonds. They also can provide fruit and wood. You can order them from Raintree Nursery.

WALNUTS—GENERAL: English walnuts, Carpathian walnuts, black walnuts, butternuts (and the filbert–hazelnut family, too) are all related (Juglans). Choose the variety best for your climate. There are suitable walnuts for almost anywhere, from the Gulf of Mexico (*J. nigra*) and California (Placentia, El Monte), to the Pacific Northwest (*Eureka*) and Canada (*Carpathian, Broadview, Colby, Gratiot, Hansen, Somers*). The black walnut and butternut are native North Americans.

Planting. Space these trees, when grown for nuts, 30–40 feet apart. The bark of young Juglans trees tends to sunburn. Whitewash or use a tree wrap until it is several years old. And either coax rodent-hunting birds to live near your orchard or wrap young walnut trunks with something to keep rodents from chewing on their bark.

Grafting. Grafting any Juglans is risky because some crosses of black walnuts (and butternuts) get graft failure after 12–15 years. That's a terribly long time to wait only to learn it didn't succeed. Growing from seed is satisfactory for timber production, but a combination of growing from seed followed by grafting is best for nut production. The grafted tree also produces timber. If you are planting walnuts, check on the sex life of your variety. Some are self-fertile, but some need a partner. It matters, because it's quite likely you don't have space for two of them!

Pruning. Walnut wood is so strong that there is no need to worry about weak crotches. Basal-prune and train for a strong central leader while very young. If branches are producing so heavily that they are at risk of breaking, prune back some length. Make your pruning at a fork. Prune only after nuts have dropped, in early fall. You may also cut back old unproductive wood to stimulate new fruiting branches. Walnuts pruned in spring bleed severely.

WALNUTS—BLACK WALNUT: Native to North American zone 4, black walnuts do everything slowly and grandly. They bear late, unless grafted, but once started, a mature black walnut tree can produce nuts generously. They grow slowly; it takes them 100 years to get near full growth and 30 more to start feeling middle-aged. They get wonderfully big. The largest of the walnuts are the largest of any nut tree, except maybe the beech or pecan. They are beautiful in your yard. However, keep in mind that roots of both black walnut and butternut defend their space by manufacturing a toxin that is deadly to some other plants. The black walnut is afflicted with few diseases or insect pests. When they do get old enough to die, they're worth a fortune for furniture making. Plant some for your grandchildren! Or great-grandchildren? Read *Black Walnut for Profit* by B. Thompson (1976), for more information on walnut for timber and commercial nut sales.

Planting. Varieties vary as to hardiness and pest resistance. Plant 80 feet apart in neutral soil.

Harvesting. Black walnuts only rarely lose a crop to frost. Commercial walnut growers use mechanical shakers to harvest the nuts and have to prune the trees in such a way that their machines will work, but private parties devise their own shaking systems, or wait for the walnuts to fall naturally off the tree at summer's end. At that time there is a thick yellowish-green husk covering them. Before they fall from the tree, it's a grass-green hull. There are recipes for a ketchup made from those green walnuts in all the old-time recipe books. I never had the nerve to try one. I chomped into a green walnut once and was puckered up for the rest of the day. If they aren't poisonous, I can't understand why not.

Dehulling. Best way to get those hulls off is to gather up all the walnuts in their hulls and transport them to your driveway. Use rubber gloves. The juice in the hulls that have been mashed by being walked on or some such will stain

443

your fingers (it also makes a great home-grown furniture stain). So use rubber gloves to handle them. Spread them out and let the cars run over them for a while. The tires will mash those husks away without harming the nuts. In about a week the job will be done. Get out your rubber gloves again and move the walnuts indoors for stage 2 of their treatment. Don't leave them lie in the sun and wind. It will hurt the nutmeats inside. Don't dawdle around and delay harvesting them until the husks turn black—bad for your walnuts. (Don't be surprised by maggots in black husks. They are there before, just more obvious in the black husks, and a routine, harmless situation.) A cement floor of a sheltered building where you can spread them out and stir them around once in a while will be perfect. A cool, darkish, well-ventilated attic would work very well, too. It's important to dry them not too quickly and not too much.

Cracking. Black walnuts are comparatively difficult to crack and the nut meats are hard to get out whole from all the little chambers. But they sure do produce. (Heartnuts are relatively easy to crack.) The ideal is to hit the walnut hard on that sharp point enough times so that it splits from top to bottom into 4 neat sections. However, Tucker Hill, my nut consultant advises: "This is next to impossible. With a hammer in the hand of an amateur, not smashing the nut to smithereens will be sufficient accomplishment!" Practice helps. Once the shell has been cracked, Tucker advises: "Use a wire cutter to clip away the shell from the kernel. That is easier than digging out the kernel with a nut pick."

In the December 1992 issue of *The Nutshell,* Tucker wrote about visiting a gentleman whose system was that he "husks them with a board and a slightly deflated back car tire, cleans them in a wringer washing machine, dries them on 5 × 10-foot wire frames, and hand-cracks enough nuts to pick out roughly 100 lb. of kernels . . . his homemade nut cracker was of his own design and one of the heaviest crackers I have ever seen . . . effective, efficient, and easy to use."

Storing. In the shell, properly cured, walnuts will store until the next fall. You can bake the nutmeats right after cracking in a 215°F oven for 15 minutes, and they'll keep a good long while. Or you can freeze them, or merely keep them in the refrigerator.

WALNUTS—BUTTERNUTS: These are *Juglans cinerea,* a medium-sized variety of walnut also known as "oilnuts" and "long walnuts." In addition to bearing nuts, they can be tapped for their sap like maple trees. They are the hardiest of the walnuts, thriving in zone 3, and the least likely to lose a crop to frost damage. Butternuts are one of the most northerly in range of the nut trees, growing well across the northern United States and also throughout southern Canada, zones 4–9. Of all the nut trees, butternut wood is the strongest and lightest in weight, once used to make windmill blades. Butternuts have a shorter life span than any other walnut, a relatively heavy shell on the nut, and somewhat smaller kernels than some other walnuts. They prefer neutral or slightly acidic soil. Their roots give off a poison that kills evergreen trees, so butternuts and evergreens can't be grown near each other. Keep butternut trees in good health with plenty of compost feeding, mulching, and water during dry seasons.

Planting. Butternuts are self-pollinating, so a single tree can produce a nut crop for you. When planting butternuts for a nut crop, place them 30–40 feet apart. To plant for a timber crop, plant 15 feet apart. You can mail-order them from Vernon Barnes & Son Nursery.

Pruning. Butternuts have a bushing tendency, so if you want a treelike appearance, pinch and prune to a strong central leader during the first few years. Prune a nut-bearing tree only in early fall after all the nuts have fallen off. Don't worry about weak crotches; butternuts have such strong wood that there is little tendency to break.

Harvesting and Shelling. Your tree will start producing about the third year. The nuts grow in clusters inside a spongy, hairy husk. The husk is easy to get off. Butternuts are really hard to shell. You can wear a glove to protect your hand and stand the butternut on solid iron, like an anvil, then hit the pointed end with a hammer. In half an hour you might have a pint of nut meats. They are a little easier to shell if you first cover them with boiling water and let them soak for 15 minutes. Inside the hard shell that you hammer off, the nut parts are almost, but not quite, separated by woody membranes, like a black walnut. You have to pick the nut meats out, and they break in the process. Butternuts can be stored in a cool dry place for several months (longer if refrigerated).

Cooking with Butternuts. They are the fattiest of all nuts, good in cake or homemade bread. Just add to any recipe and cut back the shortening a trifle.

WALNUTS—ENGLISH (PERSIAN) WALNUT: *Juglans regia* is the botanical name for the Persian walnut—the more correct of the common names since this tree originated in Persia and then arrived in the colonies via English boats. So it originally needed a relatively warm climate to thrive. But now there is a Carpathian variety from Poland that can grow almost anywhere in the temperate zone up to the northern tier of the United States and even in southern Canadian provinces. English walnuts bear younger than black walnuts. And then there are hybrids in which Persian walnut tops are grafted onto black walnut bases.

Planting. English walnuts are usually self-fertile so you need only one. However, some Carpathian and black walnuts need 2 trees to make nuts. To save seed from English walnuts, harvest nuts while still in the hull. They must be chilled 6–8 weeks at 35°F or so before they'll germinate. Plant 1 inch deep in flats to see which germinate. Transplant only during the dormant season. Or to plant seed directly outside, plant under protection from wild nut-eaters. To graft, cut scions from proven cultivars when they are at least 1 year old. Patch bud in summertime or whip graft. Stocks are best if 2 years old. You'll find the least risk of *Juglans* dying back with these stocks: California black walnut, English walnut, Eastern black walnut, and the Paradox.

WALNUTS—HEARTNUT: *J. sieboldiana,* or heartnut, is the smallest walnut, growing only 35 feet tall. It rarely suffers frost damage, lives long, has good disease resistance, the mildest-tasting kernel of all the walnuts, and nuts that crack unusually easily.

TEMPERATE-ZONE FRUITS

"Fruit" means different things to different people. To a plant scientist, a "fruit" is a plant's seed container. So acorns, pea pods, apples, and ears of corn are all equally fruits. But to others, fruits mean delicious, soft things that grow on trees, vines, bushes, or brambles—and which usually have seeds inside them somewhere: apples, bananas, grapes, berries, and so on. And fruits are sweet.

Maybe seeing a grumpy, tired, teething baby close its eyes in sleep is really the sweetest thing in the world. Maybe it's hearing the man you've been married to for many years say "I love you," and mean it. Maybe it's finding out that something you've been worried sick about is going to be all right after all. I'm sure it isn't anything in the recipes in this chapter.

Most true sweets have their bitter side. The sweet is so sweet because it's such a relief after what's come before. When I think of food sweets, my favorite thing to think of is fruits and berries. Those are the best tasting of all to me, never caused a cavity that I know of, and don't need a thing extra in season to make them a joy to eat.

On the subject of bearing fruit, a reader sent me this quote from a Native American spiritual leader called Black Elk. I taped it to my computer (yes, now I use one and what a help it is!) until I knew it by heart.

A vision without a task is a dream.
A task without a vision is drudgery.
But a vision with a task can change the world!

I do have a vision, and I do have a task—several visions in fact, and thus several tasks. One of them has to be to tell how to grow all the temperate-zone fruits!

INFORMATION AND NETWORKING: *The Harrowsmith Book of Fruit Trees* by Jennifer Bennett is good on temperate zone fruits. Any library has lots more references. The Home Orchard Society is dedicated to promoting the growing of fruit-bearing plants and to preserving historic fruit varieties. Write for their newsletter and info about pruning workshops, scion exchanges, orchard tours, and rootstock training: PO Box 230192, Tigard, OR 97281-0192; 503-639-6250.

PEACH TREE BORERS: These are a bad problem for peach, apricot, cherry, and plum trees in places like Pennsylvania, readers tell me. They not only attack peach trees but also wild and cultivated cherry, plum, prune, nectarine, and apricot trees. You've got them if you find masses of tree gum that contain red-brown larval droppings and sawdust on the tree trunks near the ground. The borers eat on the roots and the inner tree bark from below the soil surface to 10 inches above it. The trees first do poorly and the leaves get off-color. Then, often, they die. The borers themselves are about an inch long. They look like worms that have brown heads and cream-colored bodies. They eat in late summer and fall, then winter in their burrows in the tree. In spring they feed again until their pupal stage, which they spend in the top inch of soil around the tree. The adult insects emerge about June. They have long black bodies except for a broad orange band (female) or yellow stripes (male). The female lays eggs on the tree and in the nearby soil. After hatching, the larvae begin boring and feeding.

The best cure is prevention. Paint your newly planted trees with exterior white latex and add a sticking agent for longer-lasting protection. Keep the tree growing at the proper rate with plenty of water and fertilizer. Any tree weakened by injury, drought, hunger, or sunburn will be more susceptible to attack by borers. If your tree does get infected you can worm it by digging up the dirt surrounding it down to 6 inches. Find the wormholes by making cuts around the damaged areas. Use a flexible wire in the burrows to skewer the worms. Do it again in 2 weeks. Fill up the holes and replace the dirt. Put mothballs or lots of ashes on the ground around the tree trunk to discourage a return visit.

Apples

These are the most popular temperate-zone fruit. They grow easily, store well, and have many uses. The modern apple tree is available in a wider range of sizes than that of any other fruit: from 30-foot standards down to 6-foot dwarves. However, the modern apple is also, in apple-growing areas, plagued by many pests and diseases, especially where summers are wet. It's important to choose trees that will be most resistant to whatever pest problems are prevalent in your area. Last I heard, the Liberty was about the most disease-resistant variety available, but the heroic folks who develop trees may have an even better one now.

VARIETIES: There are more than 1,000 apple varieties and many nurseries that specialize in apples, some just in "antique," old-time apple varieties, some in the most modern cultivars, some that carry both. Both Lawson's and St. Lawrence Nurseries carry 100+ varieties. You can get a free list of "Disease Resistant Apple Varieties" from ATTRA at 800-346-9140. They also offer "Considerations in Organic Apple Production" and "Organic and Low-Spray Apple Production." At Applesource, the wise and wonderful Tom Vorbeck sells not trees, but mail-order apples. His website, **www.applesource.com,** includes a grower section with Tom's suggested apple varieties for central Illinois backyard growers: 800-588-3854 (LUV-FUJI); 1716 Apples Rd., Chapin, IL 62628. You can choose apple varieties to ripen early, middle, or late in the season; apples with specialized resistance to a particular disease or to all of them; or apples with low-chilling needs suited to southern California and Florida. In fact, there are apple varieties suitable for every temperature through the temperate zone (even to -40°F!). There are apples grown especially for eating out of hand, or for cider, or for cooking, or for winter storage. And green, red, or yellow apples. And short-lived or long-lived apple trees. And tall or "standard" (a large tree that gives a large harvest), shorter standard, semi-dwarf (12–18 feet), or dwarf (6–12 feet) apple trees. The semi-dwarf and dwarf apples will fruit in containers. Standard apple trees are bigger—up to 30 feet—and thus take more room than any other standard fruit tree. And you'll have your choice of trees that are 1, 2, or 3 years old.

Pollinizers. Each variety of apple has its own specifications that you'll learn when you're shopping for it. Suffice it to say that most regular apples need a pollinator, but most crab apples don't. But even the "self-pollinators" will produce better if planted near a pollinating variety. So plan to plant 2 varieties—at least unless your neighbor has an apple tree already.

Crab Apple. This is an apple species distinct from the regular apple. It is unlike any of the others in many ways: It has the smallest fruit and is the only apple that is not comfortably eaten raw because of its extreme tartness. On the plus side, crab apple trees are the hardiest of all apples and thus are a treasure for frigid areas. They have by far the showiest spring blossoms, they are usually self-fruitful, and their fruits make excellent jelly, good pectin, and unforgettable pickled fruit. Crab apples come in both standard and dwarf sizes. When shopping, beware of ornamental varieties; their fruits are as edible as any, but usually smaller. Transcendent is a good edible crab apple. Adams and Robinson are good for disease resistance. Dolgo is the most cold-weather hardy variety. No need to thin crab apple fruits.

☙ *SWEET PICKLED CRAB APPLES Wash the crab apples and remove the blossom ends. You'll need a peck (about 2 gal.) of them. Make a syrup of 1 qt. vinegar, 3 lb. brown sugar, 1 t. whole cloves, and 1 stick cinnamon. Boil. Add apples and cook them in this syrup. Remove apples, put them in a jar, and pour the syrup over them. Seal. Additional good-tasting things to add to your syrup are cider, allspice, ginger, nutmeg, and lemon juice.*

☙ *CRAB APPLE PRESERVES Core the crab apples with a sharp knife through the blossom-end, leaving the stems on. Use 1 lb. granulated sugar and 1 c. water per 1 lb. of prepared fruit. Put sugar and water over the heat, and boil it to dissolve the sugar. Skim, and then drop the apples in. Let them boil gently until clear and the skins begin to break. Take the apples out with a perforated skimmer and pack them in jars. Pour the syrup over them and seal. Optional: slices of lemon boiled with the crab apples, 1 lemon per 3 lb. of fruit.*

PLANTING: First the seeds must experience a period of chill. At least 2 months on damp paper, covered with more damp stuff, in a jar in the refrigerator should have them stratified enough to sprout. Then move them to a nursery bed. But most apples grown from seed will bear only small, sour fruit and not be worth the space. That's why apple trees are almost always propagated from cuttings, or by grafting or budding. Standards need to be spaced 40 feet by 40 feet. Dwarfs are spaced 8 feet by 10 feet. Plant in well-drained soil. Allow full sun for strongest disease resistance and sweetest apples.

GROWING: Maintain organic mulch plus a yearly spread of manure or rich compost for feeding. Make sure young trees get regular watering. Once they're several years old, apple trees can make it just with summer rain if your climate provides that reasonably often. Otherwise give them a thorough, deep soaking at least once a month. Prune only while dormant. Some growers do no pruning for 2 years after planting, then prune only minimally to keep the center open. Thinning out to get better air circulation helps combat mildew in your tree. The apples grow on "fruiting spurs"—little branches that grow off bigger ones. When you prune, don't take these out, because in the case of the apples, the fruit is grown year after year on these same spurs rather than on new wood. If you thin the young fruit to get bigger individual fruits, thin to 6–8 inches apart.

HARVESTING: Standard apples take 5–8 years before the first fruiting and take up to 10 years to get into full production, yielding 5–20 bushels per tree per year. Once mature, however, your trees can live and fruit for as many as 30 more years. Dwarf apples fruit in 2–4 years and yield 1–2 bushels per tree. For best storing, pick them before they're dead ripe. Don't pick right after rain; they should be dry. You can use a ladder, but it's safer to use an apple picker, which is a long pole with a stiff wire loop and basket on the end of it. I sort the apples while picking—setting aside bruised, very ripe and soft ones, and ones with wormholes to make into applesauce or give to the animals. When storing green apples, put the very greenest and soundest ones into storage. Don't throw them around. If an apple falls off the tree instead of being picked, put it into a box for quick use since even if it doesn't show, it has been bruised and will spoil more quickly. You can make good cider out of the "windfalls." In fact, if it's cider you're making, harvest by shaking the tree! If wasps are active around your tree, pick late in the day to avoid grabbing a wasp along with the apple.

PRESERVING YOUR APPLE HARVEST

Root Cellar Storage. The keeping qualities of raw apples vary. The best apples for storing are said to be Yellow Newtown, Winesap, Arkansas, and York Imperial. In our orchard we have early apples that come on at the same time as the apricots, and, of course, we don't worry about raw storage for them. What we don't eat we can as applesauce or apple butter. They are better applesauce apples than storing apples anyway. Ditto for the next crop of apples. The last crop consists of apples that don't turn red until fall is really on, and they aren't picked until after the first frost. It is October as I write this, and I have only just begun to harvest these red apples. These are the ones we store for winter. Obviously, the later you put them into storage, the later you have them. They keep better on the tree than in the basement. Only when they really show a determination to fall from the tree do I pick in earnest. We also have a big green late apple. It gets very large, never does turn red, and is very good. These apples are so good we always just eat them up.

Cool storage is vital. It just amazes me how fast the apples start to shrivel, lose that nice crisp texture and flavor, and plain old rot when we bring in a box from the storage shed to the kitchen—literally within a couple days. The secret is keeping them cold but not frozen. In warmish weather they tend to rot first at the bottom of the box. Adjacent apples won't catch the rot very fast but eventually they'll soak up a noxious rotten flavor, so picking over the apples—but carefully not to bruise them—is a good idea once in a while. Apples on top that have been touched by frost will be brown and then bad in the frosted place.

A way to help keep your apples cold is to give the cellar access to frosty night air and then shut it up tight during the daytime. With the best of luck they will even keep until spring. But the apples shouldn't freeze. You could insulate your boxes under straw in the barn, or inside barrels underground, with a straw and dirt covering. Another way to store apples is in a big box lined with crumpled newspaper and then a heavy quilt or some such. My apples are stored in cardboard boxes in the bunkhouse under an old mattress. The children enjoy fresh raw fruit so much when it is out of season. I bring apples into the house as needed. We generally eat them peeled—with breakfast or between meals. Or baked, served with thick cream.

Exactly how long they can last depends on the variety and storage temperature. Eventually, they get softer, then mealy in texture, then hopeless. Keep checking them and shift to another preservation system before that happens.

Invest in an apple peeler, corer, and splitter. You'll be so glad you did (Back to Basics Products; **www.backtoba-sicsproducts.com**). If the tree was sprayed, peel the apples.

❧ *CANNING APPLES Wash, peel, core, and quarter or slice your apples. Drop into a solution of 2 T. salt and 2 T. vinegar per 1 gal. of water. That prevents darkening. Then drain, rinse, and boil them for 5 minutes (in either thin sugar syrup or plain water). Then pack your hot fruit into hot, very clean jars, leaving ½-inch headspace. Pour boiling liquid from the cooking over up to your headspace limit. Put on lids. Process in boiling water—for either pints or quarts: 20 minutes at altitudes 1,000 feet and lower; 25 minutes at 1,001–3,000 feet; 30 minutes at 3001–6,000 feet; and 35 minutes at above 6,000 feet.*

❧ *CANNED APPLESAUCE (AND OTHER FRUIT PUREES) I make lots of applesauce. It's a good way to preserve apples that wouldn't keep otherwise. Cut large fruit into pieces. Simmer until soft. Add a small amount of water, if needed, to prevent sticking. Put through food strainer or mill. Add sugar to taste. Reheat to simmering (185–210°F) and pack hot into hot jars, leaving ½-inch headspace. Adjust lids, and waterbath can. From sea level to 1,000 feet altitude, process pints 15 minutes, quarts 20 minutes; from 1,001 to 3,000 feet, process pints 20 minutes, quarts 25 minutes; from 3,001 to 6,000 feet, process pints 20 minutes, quarts 30 minutes; above 6,000 feet, process pints 25 minutes, quarts 35 minutes.*

❧ *FREEZING APPLES FOR PIE For apples to use in making pies and so on, just wash, peel, core, and slice them. About 50 lb. of apples will make about 35 frozen pints. To keep them from turning dark, quarter (or slice) them into a solution of ½ c. salt per 1 gal. water. Or else dunk them into boiling water for 1½–2 minutes. Then drain the apples, rinse them under cold water, and drain again. Method 1: Scald, drain, chill, cover with a thin syrup (1 c. sugar per quart of water plus ½ t. ascorbic acid), leave headspace, and freeze. Or Method 2: Mix 1 qt. apple slices evenly with 1 t. ascorbic acid and ½ c. sugar. Then put into plastic bags or freezer boxes, seal, and freeze. Or Method 3: No sugar. Just pack 'em plain. The slices break apart quite easily while still frozen for making apple pie or crisp, or you can add a small amount of water and make applesauce. Or Method 4: Freeze whole apples, unpeeled. Just wash, put into plastic bag, seal, and place in freezer. To use frozen whole apples, thaw under cold running water until they can be peeled. Then remove the core and slice. (Work fast; an apple that thaws before peeling darkens.)*

❧ *FREEZING APPLESAUCE Applesauce turns out nicer, I think, canned than frozen, but you can freeze it by just making it, then cooling, packaging, and freezing.*

❧ *PINK APPLESAUCE Use red apples and leave the skins on while cooking. Proceed as above. Strain.*

❧ *APPLE-RHUBARB SAUCE A real treat! Make cooked rhubarb sauce in the spring and freeze it. When the apples*

come on, take it out, combine half and half with applesauce, and enjoy.

❧ *DRYING APPLES You have to slice them; they aren't dried whole. Fully ripe sweet apples are ideal. Usually they are peeled and cored and what's left is made into doughnut-type rings about ¼-inch thick to oven dry, ⅛-inch to sun dry. Let the slices fall into cold water while you are working to prevent "rusting," ¼ c. lemon juice or 1 t. ascorbic acid per 2 c. cold water. If your apples are small, wormy, or too mealy to make into doughnut rings, cut into slices of whatever shape you can. Old-timers then strung them on a thread and hung them in the sun, but now we usually just spread them out on a surface. Using an oven or dehydrator, dry them at 140°F on a cookie sheet—turning once in a while—until they are leathery.*

❧ *APPLE LEATHER If apples need sweetening, add it. Cinnamon or coconut are good mixed in: ¼ t. cinnamon or ½ c. coconut per 2 c. puree. Start by peeling, coring, sectioning, and grinding the apples in your grinder. Be sure and catch the juice that runs out. Add 2½ c. cider (juice) per gallon of ground apple, and then cook the whole mixture over low heat. When it is boiling and has cleared some, sweeten it if needed, and then spread it out in sheets to dry.*

Cooking. Apples are one fruit that you will have raw for a very considerable time out of season. That gives you so many great possibilities for ways to use them. I like apples in salads, apples in puddings, apples in any dessert, fried apples, and baked apples.

❧ *BAKED APPLES Peel and core the apples (or don't peel if they're on the small side or never sprayed). Place in a shallow pan with a piece of butter and a dab of honey in the center of each apple. Sprinkle with cinnamon. Add 3 cups water to the pan and bake, covered, at 375 F. until tender and juicy. Or, if you bake uncovered, baste often. The apples will be nearly transparent when done. Serve with whipped cream. Or the traditional "hard sauce" of hot brandy, butter, and sugar. For a really special dish stuff the apple center before baking with pitted, mashed dates. Or raisins. Or nuts. Or both.*

❧ *"APLETS" CANDY You'll need 2 c. cold homemade, unsweetened applesauce, 2 c. sugar, 2 T. unflavored gelatin, ½ c. cold water, 1½ c. chopped nuts, a few drops of orange extract, and some powdered sugar. Sprinkle the gelatin into the cold water and let it stand. Put the applesauce through a sieve to make sure it's fine, then add the sugar, and cook until it gets very thick. Remove it from the stove and add gelatin. Stir well. Add nuts and flavoring, mix, and pour mixture into a buttered 8-inch-square pan. Let stand overnight but do not refrigerate. Next day cut into squares and roll them in the powdered sugar. This keeps well and can be made a week or more ahead of the holidays.*

❧ *"COTLETS" CANDY Use the Aplets recipe, substituting the same quantity cooked and sieved dried apricots for the applesauce.*

❧ *APPLE–PLUM BUTTER Use from 2 to 3 times as many apples as plums. Cut up the fruit and cook in a little water until tender. Then put it through the colander. Add sweetening. Continue cooking until the butter is thick enough to deserve the name. This is Mike's favorite. He likes it on waffles or pancakes or toast, and so do I and the children.*

🐝 *APPLE KETCHUP* *Peel and quarter a dozen round, tart apples. Stew until soft in as little water as possible. Sieve them. For every quart of sieved apple, add 1 c. sugar, 1 t. pepper, 1 t. cloves, 1 t. mustard, 2 t. cinnamon, 2 medium-sized onions—chopped very fine, 1 T. salt, and 2 c. vinegar.*

MAKING CIDER: You'll need about a bushel of apples to make each 2–2½ gal. cider (or "juice"). Any kind of apples can be used, and you can try different blends for the sweetness–tartness qualities you prefer. Professional cider makers or serious hobbyists can get really picky about how much of what kind of apple, but hey, it's all apple juice. The important thing is to find a way to make use of what you have. In general, good eating apples are also the best cider apples. The only apples you seriously shouldn't use are sprayed apples, partly rotten apples, or apples that have been lying on the ground very long.

🐝 *UNPRESSED CIDER* *Even if you don't have a cider press you can make cider. Clean and cut your apples. Put them through a grinder or chopper, saving all the juice, and then squeeze your grindings through a strong cloth bag.*

Cider Presses. In these modern times you may already own an electric, centrifugal juicer, which may be fine if you want to make just an occasional 2–3-gal. batch. It may or may not be heavy-duty enough to make large amounts of cider. And then again a cider press doesn't require electricity. Companies that carry supplies for home wine-making carry fruit presses. The press can also be used for crushing large amounts of other heavy fruits to make juices: grapes, peaches, pears. For larger batches you can get ever-larger sizes of presses, more expensive as they get bigger. Or you can make an apple press out of a screw or small hydraulic jack (a 1-ton jack for a bushel-press). A typical old-time press that holds a bushel of apples produces about 2 or 3 gal. cider for each pressing.

Cider presses come in various sizes. The smallest one may be called a "fruit press" and can be used to make cider only if the apples are preground. The fruit press is also good for juicing berries, cherries, soft fruit, or precrushed fruit. This is often sold as a "cider press." A big cider press has an electric motor that can make 30 gal. of cider an hour. A

grinder is part of that machine. Or you can get a manually operated cider press with a grinding attachment (also manual). Pre-grind them. Whole apples tend to tear up the press. Happy Valley Ranch specializes in mail-order cider presses; free catalog: 16577 W. 327th St., Paola, KS 66071; 913-849-3103; fax 913-849-3104; **hvr@micoks.net; www. happyvalleyranch.com.**

Preparing the Apples. Wash (!) your apples and cut out the wormholes. Usually it's handiest to cut all the apples in 2 pieces as you go, in order to get at the wormholes. Cut out rotten spots or scarred places where the apple rubbed against the tree. But it isn't necessary to take out the seeds.

The Pregrinding. The press I have will not extract juice from apples very well if they are whole or even in chunks. If you have a press or pressing system that requires a pre-ground apple, then the apples should be chopped to a fine pulp or mashed before squeezing. You can use a hand food chopper, a meat grinder, a food processor, or a special electric grinder for making large quantities of apple pomace (the ground apple is called "pomace"). Grind it twice if you can't get it fine enough the first time through. Save the juice that results from grinding to add to the cider later. You also need a wooden pestle to use for a follower on the grinder contents rather than risking your fingers. You put the mashed fruit in a cheesecloth or nylon mesh bag and then put the bag into the press. Or else line the press with that cloth.

Pressing Out the Cider. Put the cleaned and cut apples into the metal cylinder and press. There is a crank device to put the pressure on. Have a nonmetal container ready to catch the juice. This process can't be rushed. Apply pressure, and then wait until the juice stops coming. Now apply still more pressure. The more patient you are about pressing and waiting, the more cider you'll get, and the clearer it will be. You can drink it the moment it comes out of the press if you like. Or heat a cup of freshly pressed cider, and add a dash of powdered spice to it!

The Filtering and Settling. You could use it strained or unstrained. If you don't strain it, the bottom couple inches will collect a visible pulp. If you want to strain it, just pour the juice through a couple thicknesses of cheesecloth. Rinse your cloth whenever the holes clog.

Before canning or freezing cider you can let the freshly pressed juice stand, and the pulp will gradually settle out. To start, pour the juice through a cheesecloth or diaper or such into its settling container. This should be a pan, bowl, jug, or bottle made of crockery, stainless steel, glass, or unchipped enamel—never regular metal because the juice is acidic. Keep the juice below 40°F for 12–36 hours—long enough to get the cider clear enough to suit you. (It takes about 4 days to get it absolutely clear, and by then you're risking some fermentation.) But some people prefer their apple juice with some sediment in it so maybe you won't want to bother with this step at all.

Storing Cider. Cider doesn't need any sweetening. You can drink it fresh. If you keep it refrigerated, below 36°F, it might stay fresh as long as 2 weeks. But store cider is pasteurized, treated with chemicals for preservation, and then canned. If you don't either freeze or can the cider, sooner or later, depending partly on the temperature but maybe as soon as 3 days, you will have first fizzy cider and then "hard cider." You need to preserve it before that stage unless you're making apple wine—and to do that you need more instructions than what I'm providing. You can freeze it, use it as the liquid when canning other fruits, or can it straight. When you can with apple juice, you can reduce or eliminate the sugar.

Freezing Cider. You don't need any heat treatment. Just pour it in containers and put in your freezer. Figure that it will expand about 10 percent when frozen, so you don't break your container. Plastic containers or glass jars with plenty of headspace are all right. You can line tin cans by putting a plastic bag inside them. Twist and tie the bag over the top of the juice and freeze it that way, too. It will keep frozen as long as a year.

Canning Apple Juice in Jars. This recipe is also good for citrus, grape, or pineapple juice. Make your juice. Add 1 c. sugar to 1 gal. juice, if desired. Heat to simmering (185–210° F). Pour hot juice into hot jars. Leave ½-inch headspace. Process in boiling water bath. Process pints and quarts for 5 minutes at altitudes under 1,000 feet, for 10 minutes at 1,001–6,000 feet, and for 15 minutes above 6,000 feet. If you are packing it in ½-gal. jars, and that is an option with these fruit juices, then you process 10 minutes at lower than 1,000 feet, 15 minutes at 1,001–6,000 feet, or 20 minutes if above 6,000 feet.

Pasteurizing Apple Juice. Use your dairy thermometer to get the temperature right. Heat it to 170°F and keep it there for 10 minutes. If a scum forms, skim it off. You don't want to get it hotter or keep it hot longer because you'll get a cooked flavor, and it won't be cider to be excited about. Have ready your spotlessly clean bottles, jugs, or whatever, and caps. Pour the hot cider immediately from your pan into the preheated, sterile bottle and lid or cap at once with scalded lids or caps. Now set the bottle into a hot water bath of 165°F for 5 minutes. Next move the bottles to a tub or sink containing lukewarm water for 5 minutes. Then cool them down some more under cool running water. The reason for such gradual heating and cooling is so your containers won't break. The best caps are screw caps fitted with rubber gaskets rather than cardboard linings. The rubber gaskets give you a much better seal.

☙ *CIDER TEA Half cider and half tea, this drink is flavored with lemon juice and sweetened to taste. Or combine 4 c. cider, 2 c. tea, and the juice of 2 oranges and 1 lemon. Sweeten to taste.*

☙ *CIDER BLENDS Mix cider half and half with plum, pear, cherry, or raspberry juice. Combine before freezing if possible.*

☙ *CIDER ALE Combine 1 c. orange juice, ¼ c. lemon juice, 2 c. cider, and 2 c. ginger ale. Sweeten to taste.*

☙ *CIDER PUNCH Combine 8 c. cider, 2 c. cranberry juice, the juice of half a lemon, and 4 c. ginger ale. Sweeten to taste.*

☙ *CIDER ICE Dissolve 1½ c. sugar in 4 c. cider. Add 1 c. orange juice and ¼ c. lemon juice. Mix and freeze.*

☙ *OLD-FASHIONED APPLE CIDER BUTTER This is the traditional apple butter made of pared apples boiled down with cider. Boil 6 c. apple cider in an enamel or stainless-steel pan. (Optional: For extra redness start with 12 c. cider and boil it down to 6 c.) While the cider is boiling down, core and quarter about 10 lb. of apples. Add apples when the cider is ready and continue cooking slowly until they're tender. Put it through your colander. Put your butter back into the pan and add 1½ c. brown sugar (or more to taste—it depends some*

on the sweetness of your apple variety). Optional: add ½ t. ground cinnamon, ¼ t. allspice, ¼ t. cloves, and a pinch of salt. Continue cooking over very low heat, stirring a lot, until the cider and sauce do not separate when a spoonful is placed on a plate. Then pour into containers for canning or freezing.

Apple-Pear
See "Oriental Pear."

Apricots

This wonderful fruit tree gives a large harvest of fruits that are somewhat like small, orange-colored peaches. Apricot trees live long; old ones look gnarled and wise.

VARIETIES: Like apples, apricots tend to have disease and pest problems. Plant the most resistant varieties. They come in either standard (20–25 feet), semi-dwarf (12–15 feet), or dwarf (4–8 feet) sizes (which will fruit in containers). The fruits of all varieties are very similar; the differences are in chilling requirements, etc. with one big exception: the edible-kernel apricot or "sweet kernel." All apricot kernels (the nut inside the pit) are high in cyanide and basically poisonous except for these varieties, which have an almond-like edible nut, and are also listed here under nuts.

CLIMATE: There are apricot varieties suited to a range of temperate zones. Because they need winter chilling to break dormancy, no apricot varieties will grow in subtropical climates. Manchurians are shrubby types that are the most cold-hardy. Choose a type hardy enough for your area and one that blooms late enough that most years your crop will be safe from frost-kill (29°F or lower). Zones 4 and 5 are marginal for apricots unless you use the Manchurian, have an ideally protected planting site, or grow dwarfs in containers, which you can bring in during severe cold or during untimely spring frosts.

PLANTING: Accomplish this by cuttings, budding, or grafting. Planting the seeds just won't pay off. Plant in well-drained soil where each tree can get full sun: standards 20 feet by 20 feet, dwarfs 12 feet by 12 feet. Keep in mind that apricots tend to grow as wide as they are tall. Don't plant on land that has had melons, peppers, potatoes, raspberries, strawberries, or tomatoes growing there for the past 5 years, as the apricot can pick up a disease from those plants. Like other temperate-zone fruit trees, apricots bloom in early spring. Some apricots need a pollinizer tree and some don't, but even the ones that don't usually bear better with cross-pollination, so plant 2 varieties.

GROWING: Apricots can usually make it without many amenities. You can choose not to prune, not to thin, and not to mulch, and probably still get a crop. Moderation is the secret to apricots. An organic mulch including some compost helps keep the roots warm in winter and cool in summer and nourished always, but too rich a diet can result in diseases and splitting. If your summer is dry, they need a monthly deep watering, but too much water if your soil doesn't drain well can make them sickly. Like apples, apricots bear their fruits on "fruiting spurs" that produce for 3–4 years. The conventional wisdom is that some conservative annual pruning will increase harvest, and that hand-thinning will give you larger fruits. I've missed pruning and gotten fruit anyway, and I don't think the thinning is worth the effort if the fruit is for home use rather than competing in a supermarket produce aisle.

Scab. Apricots are subject to a fungal disease called "scab." That's what it looks like, and all unsprayed trees have more or less of it—domestics often more than wild trees for some strange reason. You can trim off the scab to eat the fruit raw. To can it, either trim the blemishes or go ahead and can the fruit, scab and all. Given a good cooking your apricots will be just as delicious as if the scabs weren't there. The scab is not harmful to eat, softens up, and is hardly noticeable for family use. Beats eating poisons. This is called peaceful co-existence.

HARVESTING: Apricots take about 3 years to begin fruiting. Harvest time is a wonderful crisis that usually comes in July. Mature standards yield 3–4 bushels, dwarfs 1–2 bushels. The fruit ripens all at once. You know it's ripe when the color has gotten bright and the fruit is soft. Once ripe, apricots are highly perishable, so the next challenge is a crash effort toward eating up or preservation: by canning, freezing, drying, making jelly or jam, or juicing into "nectar." You can't get ahead of the game by picking green fruit, because apricots won't ripen off the tree (they will just shrivel and get bitter).

CANNING: Wash the apricots, cut them in half, and take the pit out. (If you leave in the pit—which contains cyanide—your syrup will get cloudy and the fruit won't taste good.)

Raw Pack. Pack your halved apricots into overlapping layers, cut side down, in clean jars. Add boiling syrup (or any fruit juice or plain water). Leave ½-inch headspace. Put on lids. Process in a hot-water bath. At altitudes up to 1,000 feet, process pints for 25 minutes, quarts for 30; at 1,001–3,000 feet, process pints 30 minutes, quarts for 35; at 3,001–6,000 feet, process pints 35 minutes, quarts for 40; at 6,000 feet and higher, process pints 40 minutes, quarts for 45.

Hot Pack. Heat the halved apricots in your chosen liquid thoroughly through to boiling. Boil 5 minutes. Then fill hot jars with the hot fruit, and immediately process in a boiling water bath. At altitudes up to 1,000 feet, process pints for 20 minutes, quarts for 25; at 1,001–3,000 feet, process pints 25 minutes, quarts for 30 minutes; at 3,001–6,000 feet, process pints 30 minutes, quarts for 35; at 6,000 feet and higher, process pints 35 minutes, quarts for 40.

FREEZING: Wash the fruit, cut in half, take out the pit, peel or not as you prefer. Twenty pounds of fresh apricots will make about 25 pt. frozen apricots. Method 1, halves: Cover with syrup (or any fruit juice, or plain water) and freeze. Method 2, mashed: Steam the pitted apricots about 4 minutes, mash, sweeten to taste, pack, and freeze.

DRYING: Wash fruit, cut into halves, remove pits. Do not peel. Optional: Preserve color by dipping into a solution of 1 t. ascorbic acid per 1 c. cold water. Now soak 10–15 minutes in mildly salty water (2–4 T. salt per 1 gal. water). Drain. Lay on tray with the pit side up. They're done when they look and feel leathery and no moisture comes out when you squeeze.

> **APRICOT LEATHER** Wash and pit the fruit. Puree your apricot halves (leaving the skins on). To each cup of mashed apricots, add 1 T. honey and ¼ t. cinnamon (or any other sweetening or spice that suits you, like a dash of nutmeg or nothing at all). Spread the drying tray (or whatever you use) with plastic, or oil it. If you use plastic, make sure some hangs off the edges. Spread your fruit paste on the surface and set it out to dry. When it's done you can just peel the plastic backing away.

> **APRICOT LEATHER AND JUICE** Steam or cook slightly 1 gal. pitted apricots. Add 1½ c. pineapple juice. Drain off the juice—the more juice you get off, the quicker what's left will dry. Sweeten the pulp that's left if you want. Almond extract is a good flavoring; add 3 t. Can the leftover juice. Spread out your pulp to dry.

> **DRIED APRICOT SAUCE** Chop 1 c. of dried apricots. Cook with about 2 c. water until tender. Then add 1 t. lemon juice, and sweeten to taste. Add a little more water if it turns out too thick, or cook some more if it's too thin. Or use any other dried fruit.

> **APRICOT JUICE** Pit and quarter the apricots. Bring to a boil in just enough water to prevent scorching. When tender, mash with a potato masher and then press through a sieve or colander. This is a "puree." (Optional: add 1 T. lemon juice per 3 c. puree.) For juice, strain again through something finer. Sweeten, if desired. Incidentally, 1 lb. apricots is approximately 10 whole ones or 2 c. chopped or crushed apricots. To can the apricot nectar, use applesauce processing times. Apricot juice dilutes to taste very successfully, same as grape.

> **APRICOT–CITRUS JUICE** Combine half apricot puree and half orange or grapefruit juice.

> **APRICOT PUNCH** Combine 1 part apricot juice or puree with 2 parts any other juice.

> **APRICOT NECTAR FROM CANNED APRICOTS** Blend or puree 1 qt. canned apricots. Add water to thin, if needed. Serve right away.

Cherries

This fruit in all its varieties is a favorite of mine! Cherries grow in zones 4–9. Sour cherries are hardier than sweet, able to handle more cold, and do well in the northern half of the United States. Sweet cherries appreciate a mild, even climate, such as that around the Great Lakes or in the Pacific Northwest. But if you have a bit of sheltered land you can sometimes sneak them into harsher zones. Chokecherries are wonderfully hardy, growing on mountain sides and in Canada where almost no other fruit tree can make it.

VARIETIES: Cherries come in several basic varieties: sweet, sour, and hardy. In general when people say "cherry" they mean sweet or sour. Among the sweets and sours, you can also choose among early, midseason, or late-fruiting trees. Better yet, plant a series, and have fresh cherries for months!

The Sweets. These fruits can be black, yellow, or red in color. The standard-sized trees take 6–7 years to first fruit, need 25 feet by 25 feet orchard space, and get 25–35 feet tall (make good shade trees!); semi-dwarfs 10–15 feet tall; dwarfs 6–8 feet tall. Sweet cherry dwarfs take 4–5 years to fruit, and can be grown and will fruit in containers. Sweet cherry trees tend to grow right and need little pruning.

The Sours. Compared to sweets, the sour varieties, also called "pie cherries," are more disease-resistant, more hardy for cold climates (hardy enough to make it "wild"), fruit a couple years sooner, and require less room. The bad news is that the fruit is sour-tasting, not so pleasant for eating any way except in pies or preserves. Sour standards grow 15–20 feet tall, the dwarfs, 8–10 feet. "Dukes" are hybrid sweet–sour cherries, less sour than the sours, hardier than the sweets.

The Hardy Cherries. These are the chokecherry, sand cherry, and bush cherry. The importance of them is that they can be cultivated in places where so few other fruits can. All 3 are very tart. You can use the same recipes interchangeably for any of them. Can and freeze according to sweet or sour cherry recipes. (Recipes follow.) The bush cherry grows on bushes that are 4–5 feet high. Like the other 2 hardy cherries, it can be grown where sweets and sours can't, even in the Dakotas and Alaska. Sand cherries can grow in Alaska, Canada, and the northern United States.

Chokecherries grew wild where I lived in Montana as a little girl. They're a native, wild cherry tree. People who haven't grown up with chokecherries generally don't appreciate them much at first. They grow on a bushy sort of tree in places cold enough that you really appreciate any kind of fresh fruit. They come on in the fall after the frosts, and for weeks on end on the way to and from school, walking or riding my pony (it was always one or the other for the 2-mile stretch) a pause to refresh at the chokecherry grove was my pleasant stop along the way, for the fruit stays on the tree quite a while. The chokecherry pit is very large in relation to the tiny cherry-like flesh around it. You spit out the pits.

NOTE: The seeds are poisonous (contain a cyanide). Don't ever grind or use the chokecherry seeds or can chokecherries with the seeds in. The leaves of the tree are also quite poisonous, so don't try making tea with them.

The flavor of chokecherries is so sour ("choke") that it will pucker you up, but, once you've learned to endure and even love chokecherries, you eat them anyway, pucker up, spit out all the seeds, and reach for another handful! You can buy started chokecherry trees from some mail-order nurseries and hometown nurseries.

PLANTING CHERRIES: Graft or bud. Cherries need a pollinizer tree except for the sour cherries, which can usually self-pollinate. The pollinizer needs to be a different variety of cherry—and make sure you have 2 that bloom at the same time. But not all varieties will pollinate all other varieties. So before you buy, consult about the pollination aspect! Prune the young cherry once for good shape. Keep in mind that if it's a standard, it needs to be climbable. After that, prune in mid-June, if at all.

HARVESTING: Standard cherries start bearing 3–5 years after their final transplanting, but they'll keep growing and increasing their harvest for another 10–20 years. The yield of a mature standard sweet could be up to 3 bushels; sours, 2–2½ bushels. There's no such thing as a really dwarfed cherry though. So if you raise cherries, you're going to be doing some "cherry picker" picking. Pruning off the top of a cherry tree won't increase cherry production down lower, so don't try it. Let the birds have the high ones and you take the low ones. Harvesting cherries is work, but they're worth it.

Birds. I take my biggest losses to the birds. They love cherries. It helps to have predator birds to keep a balance in

your ecosystem; in so many places birds of prey are nearly extinct. And some growers plant mulberry trees around or among their cherries because birds like that fruit even better. Commercial cherry orchards have automatic, periodic "cannon" noisemakers. Private folks sometimes throw bird-proof netting over the cherry tree and that works the best of all if you don't mind the look of it.

PRESERVING: Sweet cherries are wonderful canned, frozen, in jam or jelly, dried, or eaten fresh. Sour cherries are rather sour for raw eating, but they make great pies and jam. The cherry pitter is an excellent invention, especially for those of us who like to dry cherries! A typical pitter can pit a pound of cherries in less than 5 minutes. You can order one from Lehman's, Box 41, Kidron, OH 44636.

CANNING CHERRIES (SWEET OR PIE): Cherries can be canned with or without pits. I used to think it was insane to go to all the work to take out the pits when the kids could spit them out so easily and the flavor was fine with them in. But with those newfangled cherry pitters, it's a more realistic option. I still prefer them whole though. I put up over 100 qt. of cherries last year. They contained an occasional stem or leaf because I put the children to work packing for me, but despite that, they looked very attractive and tasted fine. Cherries can more easily and nicely than any other fruit except maybe peaches. I give canned cherries as gifts sometimes to visitors—I'm that pleased with the product. That's sweet cherries. Canned sour cherries are . . . sour and not pleasant unless you do something extra with them, like stick them in a pie.

Hot Pack. Add ½ c. water, juice, or syrup per quart cherries. Bring to a boil in a covered pan. Pack hot cherries into hot jars. Cover with cooking liquid, allowing ½-inch headspace. Process in boiling water bath. At altitudes to 1,000 feet, process pints for 15 minutes, quarts for 20; at 1,001–3,000 feet, process pints 20 minutes, quarts, 25; at 3,001–6,000 feet, process pints 20 minutes, quarts, 30; at 6,000 feet and higher, process pints 25 minutes, quarts, 35.

Raw Pack. Pack cherries into jar. Shake jar to settle them down. Cover with boiling syrup. Process in boiling water bath. At altitudes to 1,000 feet, process pints or quarts for 25 minutes; at 1,001–3,000 feet, process pints or quarts 30 minutes; at 3,001–6,000 feet, process pints or quarts 35 minutes; at 6,000 feet and higher, process pints or quarts 40 minutes.

✒ *MARASCHINO CHERRIES Wash 2 lb. good ripe, but not overripe, Royal Ann cherries. Combine 1 c. limewater (from a drugstore) and 4 c. cold water, pour it over the cherries, and let them soak 6 hours. Now drain cherries, rinse well, and pit them. Combine 3 c. sugar, 1–½ c. hot water, and 2 T. red food-coloring. Heat to boiling and add the pitted cherries. Let them cook on low heat for about 10 minutes. Cool and let rest in the refrigerator until the next day. Now reheat to boiling and stir in 1 T. almond extract. Then hot-pack the cherries in hot, sterilized jars—half-pints only—together with enough syrup to cover. Use cherry canning instructions.*

✒ *CHOKECHERRY JELLY To 3 c. chokecherry juice, add the juice of 2 lemons and 3 c. sugar. Boil at least 25 minutes, or until a drop of juice on a saucer will jell. Pour into jars and seal. Half crab apple, half chokecherry also works nicely. And those are 2 fruits that go together; those and gooseberries will grow in the high mountain country where other fruits won't.*

QUICK CHOKECHERRY JELLY You'll need about 9 half-pint jelly jars for this. Combine 3 c. chokecherry juice and 6½ c. sugar, and bring to a boil, stirring constantly. Stir in 1 bottle liquid fruit pectin. Bring to a boil again and boil hard 1 minute, stirring nonstop. Take off heat. Stir and skim 5 minutes. Now pour into jars. Adjust lids. Process in a waterbath canner for 5 minutes.

VIRGINIA'S CHOKECHERRY SYRUP This wonderful, unusual-tasting pancake and waffle syrup was one of my mother's specialties. Here is my friend's recipe for it: Combine equal parts of berries and boiling water. Mash berries thoroughly with a wooden mallet or spoon. Squeeze pulp through a cloth supported by a colander. Combine equal parts juice and sugar. Bring to a boil. If you like it thicker, boil it down to the density you want. Another way is to combine water and berries and cook a few minutes, then mash with a mallet and proceed as above. Some cooks add pectin to the pulp—½ box to 6 c. juice—boil and then add sugar. It hastens the process. Get it thick enough and you'll have jelly.

CHOKECHERRY-APPLE BUTTER Combine 4 c. apple pulp and 2 c. (seedless) chokecherry pulp. Mix well and heat to a boil, stirring carefully. Add sugar to taste and ½ t. almond extract. Ladle into hot jars. Put on lids. Process by applesauce times.

SAND CHERRY JELLY Use 2 c. sand cherry juice, 1 c. tart apple juice, and 1½ c. sugar. Use the chokecherry jelly directions.

SAND CHERRY JAM Cook fruit with water to cover until soft. Put it through a sieve. Measure. Add an equal quantity of sugar. Simmer until thickened.

FREEZING CHERRIES: First wash them. Pit cherries you'll want for salads or cooking. Leave some unpitted for eating. You can even freeze them plain with the stems on! For cherries frozen in a syrup you can freeze covered with apple or pineapple juice, or any sweet syrup (such as 2 c. sugar per 1 qt. water plus ½ t. powdered ascorbic acid), or a sprinkle of sugar. Lemon juice is good in there, too.

FREEZING SOUR CHERRIES FOR PIES: Pack 1 qt. sour cherries with ¾ c. sugar, thoroughly mixed until sugar dissolves. Fifty pounds of cherries make about 35 pt. for freezing.

DRYING CHERRIES: Wash, pit, and halve the cherries or chop or leave whole as you prefer. Place halves or sections sticky side up, spread out. Dry at 115°F in your dryer or at 140°F in your oven. Stir once in a while. They don't need to be turned. They will be chewy when dry. Drying cherries takes up to 36 hours in the oven or dehydrator, possibly significantly less, or 1–2 days in the sun. They come out sort of like raisins. And, in fact, you can substitute dried cherries in any recipe that calls for raisins, or add to any baked goods, or stew them up like stewed prunes.

CHERRY ICE Pit 1½ qt. cherries. Mash them with a potato masher as well as you can. Add ¼ c. honey and the juice of 1 lemon. Mix well. Freeze, stirring occasionally since it freezes first on the sides of the bowl and you'll want to pull that to the center. Serve with homemade whipped cream, slightly sweetened.

CHERRY JUICE Stem, sort, and wash your cherries. Drain and pit. If the cherries are red, crush them, heat to 165°F (don't boil), and strain the juice through a jelly bag. If they are a white variety, grind and press them for juice without heating them. Cool, let stand overnight, and pour off the juice to be your cherry juice or else strain it through a bag. Sweeten it if you think it's necessary. Sweet cherry juice doesn't have the flavor and tartness of sour cherry juice. Adding some sour cherry juice will improve your product if you are working with sweet cherries.

QUICK CHERRY DRINK Mash through a colander 1 qt. very ripe pitted cherries. Add 1 qt. water and the juice of 1 lemon. Sweeten to taste. Strain and chill. Serve with ice.

OLD-TIME CHERRY PUNCH Combine 9 c. water and 9 mint leaves. Simmer 5 minutes and strain. Add sweetening and cook 5 minutes. Cool. Combine the mint tea, 2 c. orange juice, 2 c. lemon juice, 2 c. cherry juice, 2 c. pineapple juice, and 4 c. regular tea. Mix and let rest an hour. Serve chilled. It makes a lot.

SAND CHERRY–RHUBARB PIE Combine 1½ c. pitted sand cherries and 1½ c. diced rhubarb (or blueberries). Mix in 1 c. sugar and 1 T. flour. Place in pastry-lined pie dish. Dot filling on top with 1 T. butter. Cover with pastry. Bake at 425°F until done.

Elderberries

These resemble chokecherries, only they are even smaller. There are lots of elderberry trees around here. Under natural conditions elderberries grow at lower elevations, chokecherries at higher ones, but they both like mountains and the sides of canyons. Elderberries are on the sour side. They have a lot of seed, which you sort of collect in your mouth until there are enough to bother spitting out. Or go ahead and swallow them. Elderberry blossoms are listed in Chapter 5 for tea-making. There are red elderberries and blue ones. The blue are best. They grow up to 30 feet tall. *NOTE: The sap of the red elderberry is very poisonous. Even the berries taste foul to the point of being inedible. And some varieties of elderberries must be thoroughly cooked or they're poisonous. Consult an old-timer if in doubt.*

Here's what Criss Wilhite, from Fresno, CA, wrote me about elderberries: "Another thing we dry is elderberries. We go to the mountains in August and cut bushels of elderberries and elderblow. We dry the elderblow for tea. We dry the berries on their stems. It takes only a few days. Then we remove the woody stems and forget about the smaller ones. The berries this way are great in home-grown and ground cornmeal mush or muffins or any baked goods. Elderberry juice is great to mix with apple juice or sauce. We also make elderberry–gooseberry juice." "Elderblow" is the flower petals.

ELDERBERRY JELLY Remove large stems from elderberries. Place about 3–½ lb. ripe berries in a large pan. Crush, cover with water, and cook on low heat about a quarter hour. Strain to get elderberry juice. Measure juice. For each 3½ c. juice (you can stretch it with apple juice), add ½ c. fresh lemon juice (strained). Heat that combo. Add 7½ c. sugar, and boil, stirring constantly. Add 1 package powdered fruit pectin and boil hard 1 more minute. Take off heat. Skim off foam, pour into hot, clear jars. Cover with paraffin immediately. Or put lids on and process in boiling water bath 5 minutes.

ELDERBERRY TEA Use 4 c. fresh ripe berries and 2 c. water. Stir, mash well, and strain, squeezing to get all the juice you can. Freeze or can. When wanted, let simmer a bit. Sweeten with honey. Dilute to taste.

❧ **ELDERFLOWER LEMONADE** *Gather elderflowers in June or July when they are in best bloom and remove from the stalks. Slice a whole lemon thinly into a pitcher. Place 4 large heads of elderflowers face down in there, and pour 4 c. boiling water over. Cover with a cloth and let rest and cool about 12 hours. Next day, strain off the solids, add sweetening to taste, and serve.*

❧ **ELDERFLOWER TEA** *Pick blossoms in full bloom. Use fresh, or dry and store. (See Chapter 5.) At cold or flu time, put 1–2 t. in a cup. Pour boiling water over. Strain. Add honey to sweeten.*

❧ **ELDERFLOWER FRITTERS** *Start with 10 elderberry blossoms with stems. Dip the blossoms in clean water for a few minutes. Shake off the water. Mix ¾ c. flour, ¼ t. salt, 3 beaten egg yolks, and ½ c. milk. A tablespoon of rum or brandy adds flavor. Heat frying pan with 1 inch of oil. Dip each blossom into the flour and egg mixture, fry, and serve. Good with a green salad.*

❧ **ELDERFLOWER CLEANSING CREAM** *These flowers have an ancient fame for being good for the skin. You can dry them to have year-round. Drop a few in your bathwater or make this special cleansing cream: In a double boiler heat 1 c. homemade buttermilk with ¼ c. elderberry flowers for half an hour. Remove from heat and let rest for a few hours. Heat again. Strain out the flowers. Add 2 T. honey. Store in a very cool place.*

❧ **ELDERFLOWER SOOTHING, PROTECTING, HAND AND FACE CREAM** *Melt either 1 lb. pure (clarified) lard or the same of petroleum jelly. Then pack in as many elderflowers (stripped from stems) as you can get in and covered. Maintain the flower–lard mix on a very slight heat (don't boil!) for 60 minutes. Then strain out the flowers and pack your cream into jars.*

Jujube

This fruit tree is hardy in zones 6–10, but it's filed in this book with "Subtropical and Tropical Fruit."

Mulberry

There are many species of mulberry growing around the world. *Morus alba* is a shrubby Chinese variety, 6–8 feet tall, whose leaves are relished by silkworms. Commonly called the "white mulberry" (or often mistakenly called the black), it is common in the South. Its berries can be black or red. *Morus nigra*, the "black mulberry," is a semi-hardy tree (zones 5–10) that can get 30 feet tall and can survive north to Virginia in the east or Seattle in the west. There are also named varieties that have big, sweet berries in black, red, or white, instead of the rather insipid-tasting old-time tree mulberries. Weeping mulberries are a decorative variety that fruits, but their fruit is of very low quality.

PLANTING: Most "mulberry" trees in nurseries are fruitless ornamentals. You can get edible types from Raintree Nursery, Burnt Ridge, or Hidden Springs. Once started, you can grow more trees from cuttings or from seed. Cuttings transplant easily as long as you keep them moist. Nature plants mulberries via the birds. To grow a mulberry orchard as some old-time pig farmers and chicken farmers did as a source of livestock feed, plant them 25–30 feet apart. They'll grow on almost any soil, even gravel or rocks. Mulberries don't need fertilization but will benefit from mulching their first year. Most mulberries are self-fertile. Pests are not a serious problem. Mature plants are able to endure drought quite well.

HARVESTING: Mulberries resemble blackberries in shape and size and also have many seeds. They're fully ripe when black and soft. The almost-but-not-quite-ripe berries are red and tart and can be used in anything you'll add sugar to. Late June and July are harvest time for birds, beasts, and people. They are less tart and less pleasant-tasting than blackberries, but are healthy to eat. One way to harvest them is to spread a sheet of cloth or plastic underneath the tree, then shake the branches until the fruit falls. Or let the berries fall naturally and gather them regularly. Mulberries stain something fierce. Pros handle them with thin plastic gloves (order through a beauty shop) on their hands. You can use them in the recipes below . . . or grow silkworms! Silkworms eat mulberry leaves. You can buy silkworm eggs and get info about growing them from Karen Emery, Royal Hare; 707-579-2344; 946 Lodi St., Santa Rosa, CA 95401.

PRESERVING: You'll have to deal with the fruit immediately since it doesn't keep. Make pies or jelly, or freeze.

❧ **SPICED MULBERRY JAM** *Stem a mixture of ripe and green mulberries until you have a quart. Cover them with cold, salty water (¼ c. salt per quart of water). Let set 5 minutes. Then drain, and rinse in cold water several times. Now crush the berries. Add 3 c. sugar, ¼ c. lemon juice (or ¼ c. cider vinegar like the old-timers), and ½ t. cinnamon. Cook over low heat, stirring until the sugar dissolves. Then boil hard, stirring constantly, until it arrives at the jellying point. Take off heat. For the next 5 minutes, alternately skim and stir. Have ready clean, hot jars. Ladle your jam into them, and put on lids. Process in a boiling water bath for 5 minutes.*

Freezing. Wash and dry the berries, and lay them on a tray for quick freezing. Once hard, move them into freezer containers. If you have both gooseberries and mulberries, try freezing them mixed half and half, unsweetened. They go well together baked in a pie, etc. Or try freezing mulberries with sugar (½ c. sugar per 4 c. mulberries).

❧ **(FROZEN) MULBERRY CREAM** *To serve, thaw for almost an hour, then prepare sweetened whipped cream and stir the fruit into it.*

Drying. Lay mulberries spread thin in a single layer outside on a screen, out of the sunshine, in a warm, dry situation. Don't let birds rob you. It takes 4–5 days to dry them like that—less in a food dryer.

Nectarines

See "Peaches."

Pawpaws

This fruit is a North American relative of the South American custard apple (cherimoya). The fruit doesn't survive shipping, so it's not a commercial crop, but for the home gardener this can be a wonderful choice. A deciduous shrub (with leaves up to a foot long), the pawpaw can also be pruned into a single-trunked tree and grow as tall as 20–30 feet high, but it's more naturally inclined to be the sort of plant you'd use as a screen or hedge. They can grow in either full sun or a somewhat shaded location, and they adapt well to being in the middle of a lawn. Once established they are hardy, usually pest- and disease-free, and expand vigorously.

CLIMATE: The wild pawpaw is classified as both a subtropical and temperate-zone plant, for it grows from Florida to Texas and as far north as Michigan. Pawpaws need some winter chilling (they're hardy to −30°F), prefer hot summers, and are suitable to try in zones 5–9, especially in midwestern areas. They need at least 30 inches of rain per year or the equivalent in irrigation.

VARIETIES: There are both inedible and edible varieties, and the edible ones can be hard to find. If the fruit has white flesh it's a bitter, inedible variety. If the fruit has dark-colored flesh, it's an edible one. Most "pawpaw" trees sold by regular nurseries are seedlings intended merely to be ornamentals. For your edible pawpaw look for named varieties that are specifically edible.

PLANTING: The easiest way to get started is to plant a grafted tree from a nursery. If you're transplanting a grafted nursery plant, prune back to just a foot beyond the graft point. Pawpaws do best in well-drained, well-mulched, and well-fertilized, deep and slightly acidic loam, but no matter how good your care they tend to be very slow-growing. Keep their soil slightly moist. Growing wild, a pawpaw prefers a fertile bottomland site along a stream or a hillside. You can use the "cuttings" or "layering" methods, or you can try to bring home a wild one by transplanting, but pawpaws are notoriously hard to get started in those ways.

Transplanting a Wild Pawpaw. Pawpaws are not easily domesticated. They grow wild but are hard to transplant. There's a theory that pawpaws need the action of a symbiotic fungus and that you should add soil from near the base of an already established plant to your planting hole. Surely, you should try transplanting only a very young pawpaw, and try to get the entire root system and keep the roots thoroughly moist during transition (and for the first year after the move).

Pawpaws from Seed. To use your own seed, keep the seeds damp or else plant them immediately after removing from a fruit. To hold pawpaw seeds indoors over winter, store in a plastic bag in the refrigerator. They are very slow to germinate. Your spring-planted seed may not germinate until mid-summer and may even wait a whole year to come up. An alternative, easier method is to do it nature's way and plant the entire pawpaw in the fall. Cover the fruit with only a very thin layer of dirt. When the seedlings come up, remove all but the best-looking ones. Exotica carries pawpaw seeds.

Planting for Pollination. Pawpaws bear lovely maroon flowers in spring. They blossom early enough that the bees may not be active enough for thorough pollination. Old-time pawpaw lore has it that if you lay a hunk of rotten meat close to the blooming trees, the meat will attract flies that will help pollinate. Pawpaw pollination is rather unpredictable, with some needing cross-pollination and others not. Plant more than 1 tree for best results.

Pruning. Once your pawpaw gets going, pruning and cutting off suckers will be necessary every year. If you want a tree, prune away all suckers and lower branches to create a single trunk. If you want a hedge, let the suckers grow that come up in the area where you want the screen to grow; otherwise clip them out. If you have a grafted pawpaw, re-

move all root suckers, since they're not the part you want to proliferate. An unpruned pawpaw grows into a dense thicket.

HARVESTING: In fall your pawpaw crop gradually turns from green to yellow and on to brown (ripe). Harvest when they're slightly soft. Just exactly when to pick them from the tree depends on how sweet you like them. If you harvest a couple weeks earlier than dead ripe, they will be much less sweet than later, but pleasant in another way. If you leave them on the tree too long, they get mushy and are likely to fall off on their own and be damaged. Look out for late-ripening fruits from late-blooming flowers and leave them on the tree to finish. Handle them gently, and bring them into the house to finish ripening.

EATING OR PRESERVING: The flesh of a ripe pawpaw is yellow-orange with a mild banana-like flavor and a custard-like texture. Pawpaws keep only 1 or 2 days. Use pawpaw fruit in a custard pie recipe, make jam or jelly from it, eat it raw, bake it into bread, make dried fruit sections or a leather, or freeze (eat frozen pawpaw immediately after thawing). *NOTE: Don't eat pawpaw seeds. They are classified as "mildly poisonous."*

Peaches (and Nectarines)

Peaches and nectarines are my favorite fruits in the world to eat out of hand. I have a little nectarine tree growing in the orchard. Last year a neighbor ran over it with his pickup and practically broke my heart, but one branch survived, and I have hopes for it yet. A nectarine is a variety of smooth-skinned peach. I used to think it was a cross between a peach and a plum, but now I know that's wrong. Nectarines have existed for centuries and sometimes mysteriously appear growing on a peach tree branch. You can sometimes grow a nectarine from a peach tree seed if that peach has some nectarine in its ancestry and was pollinated by a nectarine.

Peach trees are short-lived, bearing only 10–15 years. If you have trouble growing peaches, try genetic dwarf peaches—they are easiest of all. From California to Georgia, in North and South Carolina, Colorado, Utah, these fruits can grow. They're a little more tender, though, than apples or pears. They need well-drained soil. Peach leaf curl is a big problem in damp climates.

VARIETIES: Peaches were grown in China 4,000 years ago. There are hundreds of varieties. When you choose yours, look for disease-resistant kinds whose climate adaptations are a perfect match for your site, such as the very winter-hardy, spring-frost–resistant, and disease-resistant RedGold nectarine if you live in a chilly place. Among peaches, you can get a very early one, such as Harbinger, or a medium one, such as Red Haven, a late one, such as Loring, or a very late one, such as Stark Autumn Gold—and have peaches constantly coming on from summer through fall. And you can choose between "clingstones" that have a pit to which the peach flesh adheres (best for canning) and "freestones," easiest to eat raw.

POLLINATION: Peaches bloom early, before their leaves come out, so the crop is always at risk of early frosts. Nectarines don't need a pollinizer, but most peaches do. Consult about pollination needs when you buy.

CANNING PEACHES: Wash them and dip them in boiling water, then quickly into cold water. That loosens the skins so you can slip them off. Now cut the peaches in halves and take out the pits. If you're slow you can drop the fruit into water containing 2 T. each salt and vinegar per gallon water to prevent darkening. But I just work fast.

Raw Pack. Pack your halved peaches into overlapping layers, cut side down, in clean jars. Add hot syrup (or any fruit juice or plain water). Leave ½-inch headspace. Put on lids. Process quarts in a boiling water bath for 30 minutes at altitudes under 1,000 feet, 35 minutes at 1,000–3,000 feet, 40 minutes for 3,000–6,000 feet, or 45 minutes above 6,000 feet. You can process pints 5 minutes less.

Hot Pack. Heat the halved fruit in your chosen liquid thoroughly through to boiling. Boil 5 minutes. Then fill hot jars with the hot fruit, and immediately process. Process quarts in a boiling water bath for 25 minutes at altitudes under 1,000 feet, 30 minutes at 1,000–3,000 feet, 35 minutes for 3,000–6,000 feet, 40 minutes above 6,000 feet. You can process pints 5 minutes less.

CANNING NECTARINES: Do just as for peaches.

➢ *PEACH KETCHUP My husband's favorite. He likes it with game or ham, as a dipping sauce, or in the gravy. Combine 1 qt. stoned, sectioned peaches, 1 chopped onion, 1 c. sugar, ½ c. vinegar, ¼ t. salt, ¼ t. allspice, ½ t. cloves, and ½ t. cinnamon. Boil 1 hour. Fill clean, hot jars. Process in water bath 15 minutes and seal.*

➢ *PICKLED PEACHES OR PEARS You can easily skin peaches by dipping them quickly into hot water and then sliding the skins off. Pears have to be peeled. For about a gallon of peaches or pears, boil 3½ c. sugar with 2 c. vinegar and a ½-oz. stick cinnamon. Put a few peaches or pears at a time into the syrup and cook until tender. Then pack the fruit into jars, putting a few cloves into each jar. Pour the hot syrup over them and seal.*

FREEZING NECTARINES OR PEACHES: Go through the same preparation as for canning, only you put them in the freezer with cold syrup instead of processing. Or you can freeze whole peaches. Freeze first and then pack in plastic bags for long-term storage. To serve these frozen whole peaches, hold them under running water until the skins will slide off. Slice. You won't need sugar. They'll keep their natural sweetness. Or you can freeze peeled, sliced peaches in pineapple or apple juice with a little ascorbic acid or lemon juice added. Best of all are sliced peaches frozen in orange juice! Don't try to freeze overripe nectarines— they're, well, yucky. Fifty pounds of peaches will make about 35 pt. to freeze.

DRYING NECTARINES: Follow the directions for apricots.

DRYING PEACHES: Freestones are best for drying, and they're best dried if ripe enough for eating, but not dead ripe. Peel, halve, cut again into fourths, or thinner, and remove the pit. Optional: To prevent darkening, dip into a solution of 1 t. ascorbic acid (from a drugstore) per 1 c. cold water. A further option: Now soak 5–15 minutes in a solution of 2–4 T. salt per 1 gal. water. Drain, spread, and dry. Turn occasionally to keep the dampest side up.

➢ *PEACH LEATHER For general instructions about making fruit leather, see Chapter 7. Get the fuzz off the peaches either by washing or peeling. Cinnamon and nutmeg add a nice touch. Peaches are so sweet you certainly don't need to add any sugar.*

➢ *PEACH SAUCE Use about ⅔ c. water per 1 lb. peaches. Cook only 5 minutes or so. Optional: add cinnamon and nutmeg.*

➢ *PEACH JUICE Heat the peaches before extracting juice. (But my preference is to can rather than juice peaches because they are the perfect canning fruit.)*

➢ *PEACH SPECIAL Combine half peach juice, half orange or grapefruit juice.*

➢ *PEACH BUTTER Scald, peel, stone, and slice 7 lb. of whole peaches. Cook in ½ c. water very slowly until soft— about 3 hours. Then sieve. Add 1½ c. brown sugar.*

Pears

These trees are less hardy than apples, more so than peaches. You can lose them to a blight, a drought, an early freeze. But when you get them past the pests and diseases and weather problems, pears produce abundant, delicious fruit.

VARIETIES: Pear trees come in many sizes. The standard trees at 30–40 feet are one of the tallest fruit trees. Semi-dwarfs get 15–20 feet tall, dwarfs up to 15 feet. The dwarf pears will fruit in containers. Match your variety carefully to your climate. All need some winter chilling, but the amount varies. Plant varieties resistant to local pests and diseases. There are so many to choose from: early, midseason, late, and very late ripening varieties; various colors: yellow, green, russet, or red; various sizes and shapes. Harvest date varies from August to October, depending on variety. Zones 4–9 are suitable for your familiar, "common," or "European" pear. Zones 5–9 are suitable for the "Oriental" or "pear-apple" or "sand pear."

Oriental Pear. This is very distinct from your familiar pear. It's from Japan, pear-colored and pear-tasting, but apple shaped, crisply apple textured, and very fire blight resistant. It will grow where apples and pears will, is harvested in the fall like them, and stores well. The remarkable Keiffer pear is an Oriental-common hybrid. It stores well, cooks well, is fire blight immune, and can grow almost anywhere.

PLANTING AND PRUNING: Pear seed can't be depended on to produce good fruit. Propagate by grafting a branch or bud onto a young, strong seedling. Remove any root suckers that grow. Prune to shape until the tree begins to bear, after that very little. A northern slope holds back your pear from blooming too soon. A site there in full sun is best. Pear tree branches grow up rather than out, so you can fit a lot of tree into a comparatively small space. Provide organic mulch, but don't fertilize because of fire-blight risk. In dry weather, water mature trees deeply once a month, young ones more often. Pears don't need any special pruning. But if you must prune them, it's better to do an annual light pruning (no more than 10 percent of the branches!) rather than an infrequent heavy one (you'll risk fire blight). Heavy pruning will also reduce your harvest the next year.

POLLINATION: Pears tend to bloom early and so are always at risk from frost. They are pollinated by bees and other insects. Almost all varieties will cross-pollinate and need a pollinator. Some Oriental pears will cross-pollinate with commons. But Seckel and Bartlett won't cross-pollinate each other. Make sure you get same-time bloomers, or at least ones that overlap. *Consult about pollination requirements when buying pears.*

HARVESTING: Pears fruit on long-lived "spurs," which are short special fruiting branches. Oriental pears, like apples, should be left on the tree until ripe. But common pears are always picked green and stored to ripen. If you leave them on the tree to ripen they tend to go bad at the center or fall off and rot on the ground. Standards produce 3–5 bushels per year, dwarfs less than 1. Pick the pears when they are fully grown but still hard and green—when they change from deep green to pale green and a slight tug will separate them from the tree. Once off the tree, they'll ripen best at 65°F and 85 percent humidity. Bartlett pears ripen the quickest—in a couple weeks. Keiffer pears are fast, too. Keep below 75°F. Oriental pears never get truly soft like the common pear will. When the pears get ripe you need to go ahead and eat them or preserve them some other way.

PRESERVING

Root Cellar Storage. Pears will not keep in storage unless picked early and stored then! Don't put any bad ones in the storage box. Box them shallow rather than deep. It helps to wrap them individually in paper (not newsprint unless you're going to peel them). Keep them where it's cool. The ideal is 32–40°F, 80–95 percent humidity. How long they'll keep depends on the temperature and the variety—maybe 2 or 3 months, maybe even 5. Use up or can up because pears stored overly long won't ripen normally when taken out.

Drying. Use sweet pears. Wash, peel, and slice them into halves. (Optional peeling method: Boil the fruit until the skins will slip off. Cool. Remove skins.) Scoop out the core with a teaspoon. Lay out the pear halves, or halves cut into slices, on trays or cookie sheets. In oven or dehydrator, dry at 115–140°F with the oven door propped open ½ inch. Stir or turn once in a while. It takes 12–24 hours, or 2–3 days if drying in the sun. They're done when they're leathery and the center isn't moist (cut to see). Store these dried pears in the refrigerator or freezer.

➤ *STEWED DRIED PEARS Pour 4 c. boiling water over 2 c. dried pears. Mix in ¼ c. sugar or other sweetening, 4 whole cloves, and 2 t. grated lemon peel. Cook on low heat a half hour. This serves my tribe; divide recipe in half for a smaller family.*

➤ *PEAR LEATHER Peel the pears and core them. Don't sweeten. Use usual leather-making procedures, as explained in Chapter 7.*

Canning Pears. It's best to use them while ripe but still quite firm. Wash, peel, cut into halves lengthwise (or quarters), and core. Work fast or else keep them in a salt–vinegar solution (2 T. salt and 2 T. vinegar per 1 gal. water), and then drain well before canning. Use packing process and times for canned peaches. Add syrup, fruit juice, or plain water (a diabetic friend raves about how delicious his pears are canned in just water!). Optional: add 1 t. lemon juice per quart.

➤ *GINGER PEARS To make this "spiced fruit," peel and quarter 2 lb. hard late pears, removing cores. They shouldn't be too ripe for best results. Slice thinly. Grate the rind of 1 lemon, and squeeze it to get its juice. Combine lemon juice, lemon rind, ½ c. water, and 2 lb. sugar in a kettle. Add 2 oz. ginger root or crystallized ginger and simmer about 45 minutes, by which time the fruit should be transparent. When the syrup is thick, pour it into jars. Process 10 minutes.*

Freezing. Consider first that pears don't freeze very well. They're much nicer canned or dried than frozen. Fifty pounds of pears will make about 45 pt. to freeze.

➤ *PEAR JUICE Follow directions for apple cider under "Making Cider."*

Persimmons

Diospyros varieties grow over a wide range of temperate climate zones and can handle the competition of a lawn. The tallest kinds can get up to 40 feet tall; the shortest are shrub-like. Persimmons are always ornamental, some for extraordinary leaf coloring (Hachiya), and especially in fall and winter, because the brightly colored fruit stays on the tree long after its leaves have dropped. The plant gives a generous harvest, and its wood is valued by carvers. In the western United States, the persimmon is virtually disease- and pest-free. Borers may go after its trunk in the East, but they can be picked off by hand.

Persimmons are memorably puckering (tannin)—just like biting into a walnut hull, until they ripen; don't even try it. Then they make a sudden, miraculous transformation, and become the sweetest—and one of the most delicious—of all fruits. Some varieties get sweeter than others; some have more tannin, and hold it longer, than others. When the usual persimmon becomes very soft, the stage at which it becomes edible, it will be very high in sugar content.

VARIETIES: Worldwide there are hundreds of persimmon species, varying in every conceivable way. Because of great variation in time of fruit ripeness, you can select to have them ripening in succession. There are 2 basic types, American and Oriental. In either case, it is a good-looking deciduous tree.

American. This is a newly domesticated native (*Diospyros virginiana*), available as a tree or shrub. Its tree form is taller than the Oriental at 30–40 feet. It has a myriad of sub-species varying in size, color of fruit, harvest time, presence/absence of seeds, size, and shape of tree. Its fruits, in general, are smaller, from ½ (wild) to 2½ inches across, and fig-like. It grows suckers that will need to be pruned away regularly unless you want a persimmon thicket.

Oriental. The commercial persimmons (*D. kaki*) are the result of centuries of careful plant selection. They are always a tree, 25–30 feet tall. Hardy to 0°F, they need only 100–200 hours in winter below 45°F to fulfill their genetic chilling requirement and enable fruiting so they do well in southern states. The fruits get large: Fuyu, as wide as 4 inches across and tomato-shaped; Hachiya, 4–5 inches in length. The Fuyu tree is on the small side and is the only type that loses its tannin early enough to be eaten while still crisp, like an apple.

CLIMATE: American persimmons are a little hardier than Orientals, good in zones 5–9, as far north as the Great Lakes and Rhode Island. But persimmons are risky in the more northern areas, because a hard frost that hits before the fruit is ripe can ruin it. In general persimmons can't survive in the northern plains or northern New England. However, once the fruit is ripe, frost, or even freezing, doesn't harm it. So the challenge is to find a variety that will ripen before frost hits in your area, as well as a plant that is itself hardy enough to survive your winters. Wild Americans grow in southern Indiana, Virginia, Alabama, and points between. Orientals are better in hot areas, zones 6–10, for they are only hardy down to around 0°F. In the United States,

Orientals are suitable for areas south of Ohio, continuing on down to Florida, and the West Coast.

Mature trees of either category can handle about 10 more degrees of cold than young ones (up to 3 years old). In a marginal area, plant against a south-facing wall. That will help warm your plant in winter and get its fruit ripened. Note that not every young persimmon that looks dead from frost really is. The top growth may be gone, but well-mulched roots can live to come back and thrive.

PLANTING: The persimmon is best propagated by budding, grafting, or cuttings. Start with named varieties if possible. Purchase them as very young trees to avoid problems with the long taproot. It could be a temptation to try to transplant wild persimmon to your garden, but older trees simply cannot be transplanted. To transplant young ones, cut the top way back, and try to get as much of the root as possible. (Some nurseries grow their seed on top of a wire mesh that cuts off the tap root.) Plant allowing a growing space of 20 square feet or what is recommended. Move only during the December to February dormant season.

Seeds. You could plant seeds and make them grow, but their resulting type and harvest would be unpredictable. Or use them as grafting stock. Plant them in the fall in a potting mix (such as part sand, part peat moss). Leave outdoors during the winter for the chilling requirement, in a cold frame if your climate is northern.

Growing. The American persimmon is extraordinary in its ability to make it in poor soil—sand and clay, even in clay where all the topsoil has washed away. Persimmons need good drainage, but some Americans will grow in muck. All appreciate full sun. Prune young trees to 3–5 main branches, widely separated. After that, let it be, except to take out American suckers. All grow on the slow side, 1–4 feet per year the first 2 years, less after that. Mulch lightly to keep the roots warm, but avoid excess nitrogen. Too much may cause premature fruit drop. Water young trees regularly, but once they get going, persimmons are quite drought-resistant and can get along on only an occasional (monthly) deep watering.

Pollination. Persimmon flowers come male, female, or bisexual. An individual tree can have one kind, or another, or any combination. So some female trees will make fruit without cross-pollination. If they do that, you get seedless fruit. But some trees will not bear fruit without cross-pollination—and their fruit is seedy. Americans are normally sexed trees with males that produce pollen (but no fruit) and females, which will produce the fruit. Unless you see wild trees close to your orchard, plant both. Orientals are usually self-fertile. Find out when you buy just what your persimmon's pollination habits are, and match accordingly.

Harvesting. Persimmon fruit grows on new wood, so it forms on the outer tips of the branches. There's no need to thin the fruit. On the tree, persimmons are first green, then yellow, then, when ripe, orange. Totally ripe persimmons, unless somewhat dried, can be so soft that they're hard to handle.

Harvesting American Persimmons. Fruit from a variety of wild American trees will ripen gradually over a long period of time, storing themselves well on the tree, even after frost has stopped the actual growth. Even lying under the tree, they'll keep a month or longer in cool fall weather. Hanging on the tree, they gradually undergo a natural drying

process. Thus the fruit you pick, even in the wintertime, is still delicious and healthful! Just pick it from the tree, even if it's frozen. Thaw it, eat, and enjoy. Persimmons start bearing soon after planting and often bear in abundance (the average tree produces 25 lb. of fruit per year), some types in alternate years, some annually. If you're anxious to harvest, wait at least until after the first frost. Then gather the ripe fruit, sort, wash, and drain it.

Persimmons for Livestock Fodder. Virtually every animal on your place loves persimmons. Old-timers fed them to mules and calves together with grass or good hay for a winter diet. Some pastured their pigs on mulberries in June and July, then let them eat persimmons from September to December, gathering their own as the fruit gradually fell so the animals could get it.

Harvesting Japanese Persimmons. Some grow in clusters, like grapes—only their fruits can be many times larger than a grape. Growers usually pick these about October, before the first frost, then store them in the refrigerator, or at room temperature. Don't eat until they soften, unless you have a Fuyu! They'll ripen around December.

Ripening Persimmons in a Hurry. Put them in a plastic bag together with a few ripe apples. Close the bag so that it is airtight. Leave at room temperature for as long as 4 days. The apples release a gas that has a ripening effect on the persimmons.

Using and Preserving. Low-tannin persimmon varieties can be eaten while still crisp, like an apple. For high-tannin types, wait until the fruit is very soft, then eat it with a spoon; or substitute it in any recipe calling for applesauce or bananas. Persimmons are traditionally eaten either raw, dried, or in a pudding. A dried whole American persimmon resembles a dried fig except there are no seeds inside (if you have a seedless fruit). In modern times, we also freeze them, or even can them.

Drying. Dry the softer kinds of persimmons at that golden moment when they're soft enough to eat but not too soft to handle easily. Firmer kinds can be dried at a riper stage. Peel. With a stainless steel knife, cut in ¼-inch to ½-inch slices. Spread them out to dry in a single layer, none touching. Dry at 115°F for 18–36 hours (or 3–5 days in the sun)—until there is no more moisture, even in the center. Your dried persimmons will be brown and chewy, leathery. Turn twice during the drying. You can serve dried persimmons as a candy. Or use them to make a homemade trail mix in combination with other dried fruits, plus some nuts and seeds. Or substitute for "raisins" in any recipe, add to any baked goods, or sprinkle over fruit. Persimmon pulp can be made into a good leather (sieve out the seeds).

☞ *DRIED PERSIMMON "SUGAR" You can make a pure fruit sugar out of the highest-sugar kinds, which, when dried, are very sweet! Dry as above. Then chop the dried fruit into sections and dry a second time—until very hard. Then blend or grind in a mortar to a powder. That powder is your persimmon sugar. Use it in place of sugar.*

Freezing. Freezing is suitable for the soft, sweet kinds of persimmons. (The crisp Fuyu that lasts and lasts, is best eaten fresh.) Method 1: A thoroughly ripe, seedless persimmon can be frozen unpeeled and whole. To eat, thaw and spoon out of its skin somewhat like a sherbet. Or peel (the skin will slip if you hold the fruit under running water), dice, and serve with cream. The cream freezes as the fruit thaws. Method 2: Blanch your persimmons, peel them, and put them into individual plastic bags. Seal, and freeze. Method 3: For persimmon puddings, mash the soft pulp out of the skin (discard it) or put it through a food mill or colander, package in something moisture-proof, and freeze.

Canning: This is the least popular way to preserve persimmons, but it's possible. Start by making a persimmon pulp, sieving out the seeds. Can the pulp in small jars, no bigger than a pint. Process in a hot water bath for 30 minutes.

➤ *CANNED PERSIMMON PUDDING Phyllis Bates, Tangier, IN, invented this, and her husband, Allan, learned how to can it. "It's yummy." For every 2 c. persimmon pulp, add 2 beaten eggs, 1 c. of either dark or white sugar, ½ t. double-acting baking powder, ½ t. baking soda, ½ t. salt, ½ c. melted butter, 2 c. milk, 2 t. cinnamon, 1 t. ginger, and ½ t. nutmeg or allspice. To eat right away, bake the pudding in a 9-inch-square greased baking dish, at 325°F for 1 hour. To can it, fill pint jars only two-thirds full. Can at 15 lb. pressure for 25 minutes.*

➤ *PERSIMMON ROLL CANDY Start with 2 c. fresh or frozen persimmon puree. Mix in 1 c. sugar, ½ c. brown sugar, 1 lb. smashed graham crackers, 1 c. chopped nuts, and ½ lb. miniature marshmallows. Lay out a sheet of waxed paper and spoon ⅓ of persimmon mixture onto the paper in a roll shape about 3–4 inches wide. Roll it up in the waxed paper, with a sheet of aluminum foil or plastic wrap on top of that, and freeze it. Do the same with the rest of the mixture. To serve, partially thaw a roll, and cut about 8 slices, each of which will be an individual dessert serving. Top the slice with vanilla ice cream or whipped cream.*

➤ *PERSIMMON FRUIT BARS Combine 1 c. chopped dried persimmon with 1½ c. of a combination of other chopped, dried fruits (apricots, cherries, peaches, figs, or what have you). Add 1 c. chopped nuts, and ⅔ c. flour that has been thoroughly mixed with 1 t. baking powder and ¼ t. salt. In another bowl cream together ½ c. butter and 1 c. sugar until fluffy. Add 2 eggs and 1 t. vanilla to butter–sugar mix and mix well. Now add the fruit–flour mix to the rest, a cup at a time. Blend thoroughly after each addition (with a spoon, not a mixer). When finished combining, spread it into a greased 9-inch-square pan and bake 45 minutes in a 350°F oven. When done, cool completely before cutting. Slice into 1-inch by 3-inch bars. Roll bars in powdered sugar.*

Plums

These are an easy fruit to grow. My family, though, will ask to eat cherries, peaches, nectarines, pears, apricots, or berries before they will plums. Sad but true. Personally, I'm grateful for anything that grows without poisons—and I love Greengages!

VARIETIES: Plums come in so many different colors and sizes—purple, red, green—from as small as a cherry to almost as big as a peach. Standard plum trees have a height and width of 15–20 feet, dwarves 8–10 feet. Take your choice. "Europeans" bear mostly oval, usually blue fruit, and are hardy in zones 5–7. Damson is a tasty blue European. Greengages are wonderful old-time European plums that are good eaten raw, or in pies and puddings and sherbet. "Japanese" plums are mostly round and red and hardy in zones 5–9, which makes them better for the South. Santa Rosa is a good red Japanese plum; Shiro is an early-ripening

yellow one. "American" plums are small, hardy wild natives. But they have been crossed to create better fruiting hybrids that will bear in zone 4. The "plumcot" is a hybrid between the plum and the apricot.

SO WHAT'S A PRUNE? A prune is a kind of European plum, a freestone. It is blue-black and oval, with firm flesh. The sweetest varieties of plums make the best prunes. Blue Stanleys are the usual commercial choice. So, you dry prune kinds of plums and you have prunes. You dry any other kinds and you have dried plums. There are yet more mysteries to prune production (see "Drying Prunes").

POLLINATION: Japanese plums and European plums won't cross-pollinate. Most European plums are self-fertile. All Japanese plums need cross-pollination, but they are limited to another variety of Japanese plum to do the job. Consult when you buy.

PRUNING: Japanese plums need heavy pruning with the strong upper wood whacked back to weaker branches. European plums should not be pruned so severely.

HARVESTING: It takes 3–4 years after planting to get your first plum crop. Plums fruit on long-lived spur branches, so don't prune those all away. For bigger plums, you can thin the fruit to 3–4-inches apart, but I don't think it's worth the trouble. Let them ripen on the tree. Pick them when they're soft and they separate easily.

PRESERVING

Canning. Choose ripe, but still firm plums that are only just beginning to get soft. Among the best varieties to can are Greengages and similarly "meaty" kinds. Wash and drain them. Experienced plum canners prick the skins of the plums a couple times with a fork if they're to be canned whole. That helps prevent the fruit from splitting. Freestones are easily halved and pitted and nice that way.

Hot pack: Add plums to hot syrup and boil 2 minutes. Cover pan and let stand 20–30 minutes. Fill jars with hot plums, cover with cooking syrup. Raw pack: Fill jars with raw plums, packing firmly. Cover with hot syrup. For either hot or raw pack, process in a boiling water bath. At altitudes under 1,000 feet, process pints 20 minutes, quarts for 25; at 1,001–3,000 feet, process pints 25 minutes, quarts for 30; at 3,001–6,000 feet, process pints 30 minutes, quarts for 35; at over 6,000 feet, process pints 35 minutes, quarts for 40.

➤ *PLUM JUICE Tree-ripened plums of deep color are best. Wash and mash. Simmer until soft in just enough water to cover them. Press and strain. Sweeten if the fruit is tart enough to need it. Can by instructions for apple juice (see "Making Cider").*

Freezing. Wash, remove stems and pits, and cut in half. Method 1: Spread out on cookie sheets and freeze like that to get them frozen as quickly as possible. Then move them into freezer bags or boxes, seal, and store in the freezer. To serve the frozen plums, rinse them off and slice them into dishes, letting them defrost enough so you can get your teeth into them. Or eat them whole like fresh fruit. Method 2: Freeze the plum halves in a fruit juice (white grape or apple are good), or syrup, or plain water. These will be best cooked after thawing. Freeze as quickly as possible. Fifty pounds of plums with make about 40 pt. of fruit for your freezer.

Drying Plums. Cut plums in half and remove the pit. Optional: Now blanch the halves by steam for 15 minutes.

Then dry your plum halves (or quarters) the regular way. Some dry them whole, but they're a lot easier to get dry halved than whole. Dry when pliable and leathery. Plums dried without pits are good for pies.

Drying Prunes. For results that look somewhat like store prunes, pick the proper variety of fruit when very ripe, and dry it whole. The first secret of prune making is that "very ripe" part. Some expert prune makers even hang a cloth under the tree to catch the plums at that moment of maximum sweetness when they fall from the branch. Another prune secret is to presoften the skin, either by soaking them 20 minutes in very hot water before drying or by soaking them in a lye bath—a solution of 1 oz. lye crystals in 1 gal. water (in a nonmetal container!)—for several minutes. Then rinse them well in cool water. Then dry them on trays. To oven-dry prunes, start at 120°F for 15 minutes, and very slowly and gradually increase the heat to 160°F. If you raise the temperature too fast they may burst. Turn them occasionally. It takes about 2 days. A last prune secret is to paint them with a honey solution before their final drying.

➥ *PLUM SAUCE Cook plums in about ½ c. water per 1 lb. plums. They'll need 7–10 minutes. Put through a strainer. Sweeten to taste. Add 1 T. lemon juice.*

➥ *SPICED PLUMS Decide how many plums you want to spice and weigh them. For 1 lb. of plums use 1 lb. of sugar (1¾ cups) and ⅔ cup vinegar. For every gallon of plums use ½-oz. each of ground cinnamon, cloves, mace, and allspice. Prick each plum in several places with a needle. Add the spices to the syrup and boil it. Pour the boiling mixture over the plums. Let them rest 3 days; then pour off the syrup and reboil it. Boil it down until it's thick but there's still enough to cover your plums. Pour it hot over the plums in the jar in which they are to be kept. Cover the jar well to keep out the dust and insects. Makes plums very special.*

➥ *PRUNE RYE BREAD This is a favorite of mine. The recipe makes 2 small loaves. It is very heavy and moist. It keeps well and my children love it as much as a "sweet." First put your dried prunes on to cook, enough to make 1 c. when they're cooked enough to be able to cut out the pits. Sift together 6 t. baking powder, 2 c. rye flour, 3 c. wheat flour, ½ t. salt, and ½ c. honey. Add 1 egg and 1¾ c. milk and mix it well. When your batter is mixed, add the 1 c. chopped prunes, and stir just enough to distribute them. Pour into 2 small (6-inch by 3-inch) greased loaf pans or 1 larger one (11-inch by 3-inch by 3-inch) and bake at about 350°F for about an hour. After baking, when the bread has cooled enough, wrap it in foil, a cloth, or plastic for a tender crust.*

Quince

Quince is an ancient, deciduous fruit, Asian in origin, and a distant relative of the pear. The fruits are yellow, hairy, baseball-sized, and come in several varieties, some round, some pear-shaped, ripening in September. Quince naturally grows as a shrub and makes a good hedge because of thorns and that shrubby style of growth. Or you can prune it (in winter only) to a single trunk and make it grow like a small tree, usually only getting to be about 12 feet tall.

CLIMATE: In general, quince is hardier than peaches, but a little less hardy than pears. The growing range is wide, from California to the Midwest to the Northeast, zones 5–9. A special cold-zone advantage is quince's blooming time,

which is late in spring. In warm, humid areas, quince is more likely to get fire blight and other diseases.

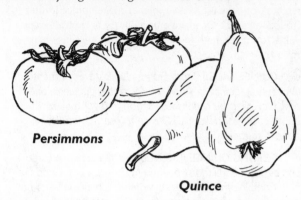

Persimmons

Quince

VARIETIES: When ordering plants be sure you get the edible or "orchard" variety (*Cydonia oblonga*). Orange, Pineapple, and Smyrna (probably the best) are good edibles. All quinces are self-pollinating so you need only one. Don't get one of the many ornamental flowering quinces, although they are much hardier than the edible. The ornamentals can be deceptive because some produce fruit, but it never ripens and doesn't have the delicious taste, when cooked, of the edible. The fruit of some ornamental quinces will make sauce okay.

PLANTING: Use layering, cuttings, or division rather than planting seed, as seedling quinces are unlikely to grow true. To reproduce by layering, simply force a branch down on the ground in spring and fasten it there somehow. Cover the part that's on the ground with dirt and wait until fall, by which time it will be growing roots. Then cut it off where it connects to the parent plant and transplant to your chosen site.

GROWING: Quince does best in moist, well-drained soil, but it is quite exceptional among the fruits in that it can endure some wet feet from poor drainage. Quinces fruit best in soil of a medium type rather than either very heavy or very light, and they appreciate full sun. If you want your quince to look like a tree, you'll have to sometimes take out suckers. Prune only in the winter and as little as possible because pruning may result in fire blight. Fertilize only with an occasional mulch or helping of manure because excess nitrogen weakens resistance to fire blight. Quince blooms after apples, in late spring.

HARVESTING: The fruit is produced on the tips of current growth. It ripens late in October or even November. Don't harvest until they are almost ripe. You can tell because the quinces turn yellow and smell fragrant when they get ripe. They don't drop from the tree just because cold weather arrived, so you've plenty time to get them. Pick somewhat before full maturation, being careful. They seem firm, but quinces actually bruise easily. Store in a single layer and they'll stay good for 2–3 months. If you store quince in the refrigerator or with apples and pears, everything else will end up smelling like quince!

COOKING: The reason you've probably never seen a quince is because quinces are sour-tasting and hard, absolutely inedible while still raw. However, when cooked they are good. The Greeks, Romans, and American colonists enjoyed quince dishes: a jelly, or quince blended with other fruit dishes, such as an applesauce made of half-cooked quince and half applesauce (a good choice to can!). Or can quince, or spice or chutney it (use basic fruit recipes), or bake it like an apple, or make quince leather (rolled in sugar). Or make quince–berry or quince–grape jellies (quince is high in pectin). Or quince–orange marmalade.

🌭 **QUINCE SAUCE** *From Frances Dallosta, Sacramento, CA: "Cut up quince in small chunks, add sugar, cook, and cool. Never let the chunks lose shape and get mushy! It's like applesauce, just delicious!" Quince mixed with apples or pears also makes a great sauce.*

🌭 **GETTING QUINCE JUICE** *Cut out the cores and stem and blossom ends (don't peel) from 3 lb. quinces. Grind the fruit. Combine fruit with 4½ c. water in a nonaluminum pan and heat to boiling, then simmer for quarter hour. Now squeeze out the quince juice in a jelly bag or some such.*

🌭 **QUINCE JELLY** *Combine 4 c. quince juice, 7½ c. sugar, and ¼ c. lemon juice in a pan. Stir together and then heat to boiling. Don't stop stirring! Now add in ½ bottle liquid pectin, and boil as hard as possible another minute—still stirring constantly. Then skim off the foam and pour the jelly into your jars. Cover them immediately with ⅛-inch of hot paraffin. Or make jelly using 2 parts apple juice to 1 part quince, or 1 part cranberry juice, 1 part quince, and 1 part apple juice. Use two-thirds as much sugar as juice. In any case, save the pulp for a quince butter. Or make quince jam.*

🌭 **SPICED PICKLED QUINCES** *Peel about 10 large quinces, cure, and cut them into ¾-inch sections. Put fruit in a pot. Pour 2½ c. boiling water over it. Cook around 5 minutes. Drain (save the liquid). Measure 1½ c. of the liquid back into the pot. Add about 15 whole cloves, 2 oranges cut into very thin slices, 6 c. sugar, and 2½ c. white vinegar. Boil 10 minutes. Add quinces back in. Boil a half hour more (better stir once in a while). Pour into sterile pint-size canning jars. Process for 15 minutes in a boiling water bath.*

🌭 **QUINCE SEED HAND LOTIONS** *When quince seeds are soaked in warm water they soften and separate into a "goop" and what's left of the seed. Good, gooey, soothing hand lotions made from this goop were both homemade and commercially produced by the old-timers.*

Country poet Dallas A. Sall got this recipe for me from his mother. Soak 2 oz. quince seeds in a pint of warm water for 30 minutes. Strain through a cloth, squeezing well to get the goop off the seeds. To that goop, add 2 oz. bay rum, 2 oz. glycerin, and enough water to make a pint. Add fragrance if you wish.

🌭 **WITCH-HAZEL CREME** *Sherry McGuarrie of Pouris, Manitoba, Canada, who does chemistry demonstrations, kindly sent me this old-time commercial recipe plus advice that this author should be "editing your Recipe Book to a more manageable size by deleting most of the chatty bits that don't add to the helpfulness of the text." So, straight down to business: Soak 4 oz. quince seed in 16 oz. hot water. Dissolve 6 oz. boric acid in 128 oz. witch-hazel water. Add 32 oz. glycerin and the witch-hazel water/boric acid solution to the quince seed-water mix. Let that stand for 2 days, stirring occasionally. Then strain and add perfume.*

SUBTROPICAL AND TROPICAL FRUITS

That eastern Washington widow Florence Merrifield, who retired in Jalisco, Mexico, keeps sending me tantalizing progress reports: "My banana tree has a bunch of bananas ready and 2 other hands forming. Papayas are getting ripe and some have fallen. And mangos . . . there must have been a ton on the seven large trees in my garden. At last they are all about gone. I also have a large vegetable garden. Some green beans and cukes ready now. Planted 5 more banana trees Saturday . . ."

In general, "southern" or "subtropical" fruits can't handle freezing or temperatures close to it. Hawaii, southern California, and southern Florida are the most tropical U.S. zones. Northern gardeners can sometimes grow these plants in containers, moving them indoors during cold weather, or in greenhouses, or simply in the house in a sunny window.

TROPICAL FRUIT INFORMATION: If you can't grow them, but long to eat organically grown tropical fruits, you can order mangos, bananas, avocados, grapefruit, oranges, and honey from David Starr, a mail-order distributor of organically grown tree-ripened Florida tropical fruits. Free catalog: Starr Organic Produce; 888-262-1242; fax 305-818-6972; PO Box 551745, Ft. Lauderdale, FL 33355; **starrorg@msn.com; www.starrorganic.com.**

Warm-Climate Gardening, by Barbara Pleasant, covers fruits, vegetables, and herbs for the subtropics. *Growing Unusual Fruit,* by Alan E. Simmons, covers 100 fruits. Pacific Tree Farms has a terrific book list for subtropical growers, including *All About Citrus & Subtropical Fruits,* by Moore and Sweet; *Fruits of Warm Climates,* by Morton; *Malaysian Fruits in Colour* by Chin and Yong; *Manual of Subtropical Fruit,* by Papenoe; *Tropicals,* by Courtright, etc. *Florida Gardening: The Newcomer's Survival Manual* is also good. It's $11.20 from Betty Mackey, publisher, who also offers *Herbs and Spices for Florida Gardens* ($15.50), and *Creating and Planting Garden Troughs:* 610-971-9409; PO Box 475, Wayne, PA 19087-0475; **bbmackey@prodigy.net.**

Join the Rare Fruit Council International for $40 and you'll get a subscription to *Tropical Fruit News,* a monthly magazine: PO Box 561914, Miami, FL 33256. Or subscribe to *Pacific Horticulture: Journal of the Pacific Horticultural Foundation,* $25/yr; 510-849-1627; PO Box 680, Berkeley, CA 94701. *The High Value Fruit Crop Newsletter,* put out by Claude Sweet, offers detailed info on individual exotic food crops, plus a computer system to predict specialty crop profitability for you. Sample $4: RIM Corp., PO Box 370, Carpinteria, CA 93014.

AVOCADO: This is an evergreen tree, 20–40 feet tall in its standard form, 8–10 feet tall as a dwarf. There are 3 basic varieties of avocados. They can be grown in California, Florida, and Hawaii. They need reasonable watering and fertilizing and have a few disease problems. Grafting or budding is far better than planting that big seed. A plant started from the seed will grow foliage, but no fruit.

Preserving. You are going to get an abundant harvest of perishable fruit. Eat it, give it, sell it, or make guacamole and freeze it! Or freeze puree for making guacamole later.

🌭 **GUACAMOLE** *Peel, remove pit, and mash 4 avocados. Thoroughly mix in 1 chopped tomato, ½ t. garlic powder, 1 T. lime juice, plus hot sauce to taste if you're so inclined (I prefer* *it without). This is great in almost any sandwich combination or with chips, in a salad, or as a side dish (without the hot sauce). It can be frozen.*

⋙ FROZEN AVOCADO PUREE *Choose avocados that are ripe and soft but have no dark blemished places. Peel, slice into halves lengthwise, discard pits, smash pulp. Option 1: Add ⅛ t. powdered ascorbic acid per quart puree; it will taste and keep better. Option 2: Add 3 T. lemon juice to each quart puree. When thawed, use for sandwich spread, dips, or in salads.*

BANANA: Bananas have been a domesticated plant for tens of thousands of years. A dried part of banana root that is planted in a warm, moist place will grow again, even after some time. Over the millenia, human selection developed the banana from a fruit with big seeds into a seedless one. Bananas thrive in Central and South America, Pakistan, India, the Philippines, Thailand, and similar climates. Technically, the banana is not a tree. Its trunk is made up not of wood, but of stalks grown up around each other from the roots in a way that forms a hollow tube.

Planting. The Banana Tree offers a big selection of bananas, plus brief growing instructions (catalog on Internet): 610-253-9589; fax 610-253-4864; 715 Northampton St., Easton, PA 18042; **faban@enter.net; www.banana-tree.com.** Bananas are planted with pieces of root. Each banana "rootstalk" has buds that resemble potato eyes. Make sure your piece has a bud. Plant about a foot deep. It will soon send up several shoots. By the time a banana plant is about a year old, it will be 15–30 feet tall. Then a purplish flower bud pushes up through the hollow leaf stalk and emerges at the top. It gradually droops and clusters of flowers grow out of it. After the flowers finish blooming and fall off, little fingers of fruit grow from where they were. Each banana is a "finger." The banana fingers are clustered around the stem in bunches of 10–20, called a "hand." It takes 3–4 months for the flower bud to evolve from just becoming visible to being a mature bunch of bananas.

Harvesting. Pick them green. If bananas are allowed to ripen on the plants, they spoil. Cutting down a banana bunch is a 2-person job. One person, with a knife on the end of a pole, reaches up and partly cuts the stem several feet below the bottom of the hanging banana bunch. The cutter is careful not to cut all the way through because he wants the cut to be just great enough that the weight of the bananas makes them bend over so his partner can just get under them and catch them on his shoulder. Then the cutter trims the stem off the bananas and cuts the "tree" off at the ground. When the bananas have finished growing the plant dies anyway. A banana "tree" will never grow more than just the 1 bunch of bananas. But after the next good rainfall a new banana plant will grow up from the same roots.

Using. In food value, bananas are very like potatoes. In tropical countries they are typically steamed, boiled, fried, or baked. For cooking, the firm, green ones are preferred. They are peeled, wrapped in banana leaves, and immersed in a pot of boiling water to boil. When cooked, the fruit may be mashed before serving. To bake, the bananas are chosen green, or slightly ripe, and left in their skins. Or the green bananas may be grated, wrapped in a banana leaf, and baked like that. Or grated green banana is mixed with coconut milk into a paste, and then baked. Bananas are fried plain, or mixed with sugar, flour, and a dash salt, and

fried. Or a bread pocket is filled with banana and then fried. Banana "figs" are considered a dessert treat. To make "figs," ripe bananas are dried in the sun and then sliced. They turn out dark-colored, stock, and sweet. A banana flour is made by grinding dried bananas. The big banana leaves have many uses, too: umbrellas, wrapping "paper," plates, roof thatching. They can also be made into twine and used to weave mats and baskets.

Drying. Perfect bananas for drying are still firm, but flecked on their peels with brown. To prevent darkening, dip sections for drying into pineapple juice (undiluted), ascorbic acid, or a solution of ¼ c. lemon juice in 2 c. water. Method 1: Peel and slice ¼-inch thick onto a drying tray. Method 2: Using a coarse shredder, shred right into your drying pan. Cook 1 minute under the broiler, if you have one. Method 3: Cut in half crosswise, quarter each half and dry.

Spread sections, shreds, or quarters on your drying trays, only 1 layer deep. Dry at 115–125°F in a dehydrator or 140°F in an oven. Turn them over after 3–4 hours, rotate trays occasionally, and stir occasionally. Dry until crisp, about 6–10 hours. Sun-drying bananas takes longer—2 days or more.

Freezing. Put ripe fruit through a food mill or mash very thoroughly. Add powdered ascorbic acid or lemon juice to prevent darkening. Freeze. Thaw your puree to use in banana breads or cakes or for baby food.

⋙ BANANA POPSICLES *Linda Crabtree of Kettering, OH, sent me this recipe on February 11, 1976. You'll need firm but ripe bananas and popsicle sticks or popsicle-type sticks; some chilled, strained honey; and chopped salted peanuts. Cut the bananas in half crosswise. Stick a popsicle stick into the end of each banana half as a handle. Coat each one with honey and then roll it in the nuts. Freeze unwrapped until solid.*

BREADFRUIT: This is the fruit of a very large Polynesian tree *Artocarpus*. Since its juice hardens on contact with air, natives to the tropics have used breadfruit to waterproof canoes. Breadfruit is similar to chestnuts and potatoes in nutritional value; it provides carbohydrates as well as vitamin C. Just 2 or 3 breadfruit trees can keep a shipwrecked sailor alive.

Preparing. Breadfruit is large, as much as 8 inches in diameter, round, with a thick, bumpy outside. *This fruit must be cooked before being eaten.* The fruit's flesh is an off-white color and tastes honestly like bread. It's better when prepared on the unripe side rather than being overripe. You can prepare it by boiling it, then mashing and seasoning it with herbs and garnishing it with nut slivers. Or cut it into slices; combine it with sliced onions, carrots, or other vegetables; wrap them in an edible leaf; and barbecue it. Or steam breadfruit until cooked, then scoop the flesh out of the rind, mix it with pineapple chunks, flavor it with molasses, and serve with baked squash. Or cut the breadfruit center into chunks and stuff a bird with it and roast them together. Or boil the fruit, then serve with a pasta sauce. Or bake the fruit until very well done, then serve it with an herb butter.

CACTUS: See "Prickly Pear."

CARAMBOLA: The carambola tree (*Averrhoa carambola*) will grow only in southern Florida, Hawaii, and points south. The leaves are sensitive and fold up when touched. It blooms pink flowers, 3 sets a year: spring, summer, and fall. You can choose between a sweet-fruit or a sour-fruit kind. Or try *Averrhoa bilimbi,* the "cucumber tree." It's closely related and similar in needs to carambola, though even less cold-hardy.

Planting. Pacific Tree Farms carries it. You can grow these from seed. Graft good scions to seedlings if you want more control of fruit type. Baby trees are more vulnerable to cold than their elders, which can live at temperatures down to 28°F—provided it doesn't stay there very long.

Harvesting. The carambola fruits are the size of a large orange, good-tasting, and good for juicing.

CAROB: The carob tree (*Ceratonia siliqua*) is an evergreen leguminous tree that grows 20–40 feet high. Carob is a prized shade tree, windbreak, or screen plant because of its dense foliage. Carobs can't live where temperatures get lower than 20°F. They also don't appreciate high-precipitation climates. They are perfect for mild-wintered Southwestern areas as long as they are away from the coast.

Planting. Carob is easy to grow. If you don't have a full-sun site for it, plant where there's light shade, and it will get along. Carob can be started from seed or by budding, but carob seedlings are unpredictable in their fruiting performance. Many trees offered in nurseries are seedlings intended only for ornamentals with no attention to fruiting and no identification of gender. You can get carob seed from Exotica or from Redwood City. Starts are available from Exotica. Dwight Roberts (3111 Victoria Dr., Alpine, CA 91901-3679) will swap carob seed for your regional seed. (He also has acacia, loquat, and yucca seed.) There are some named varieties, some immune to worms.

Pollination. A few varieties are self-fruitful, but most carobs are not, and you need at least 1 male and 1 female tree to get fruit. It's safest to plant at least 5 if you're growing them from seed because you need good odds to get at least 1 of each sex. You won't know what sex they are until after 3 or maybe even 5 years.

Growing. Carob gets along in any well-drained dirt—sand or clay being equally acceptable. They don't need fertilizing. The mature tree doesn't need watering although some watering will increase your carob bean harvest. Carob can be allowed to grow its natural way into a multi-stemmed shrub or pruned to be a tree (but prune as little as possible). With no pruning it will eventually get about 40 feet high and 40 feet wide. Carob roots are extraordinarily efficient at finding their own water so this plant is a natural for desert homes.

Harvesting. The flat, long (about 10-inch), edible "bean" pods ripen during October and November. When they have turned dark brown, they are ready for harvest. You can eat them right off the tree out-of-hand. If you have a problem with moldy or wormy pods, it means there was too much rain during the pod-ripening time. To deal with the worms, you must pick up and somehow destroy every ground-scattered pod. Carob beans can be fed whole to any of your livestock and will delight them.

Making Carob Powder. You'll find carob pods sweet-tasting and chewy, resembling a date. They contain little black seeds. Commercially, the pods are roasted and then ground to create carob powder, a healthy chocolate substitute. But that kind of processing simply is not possible at the household level. If you want to try making a powder of them, first wash the pods, then pressure-cook 20 minutes at 15 lb.

The purpose of the cooking is to soften those pods enough that you can split them open to get the seeds out fairly easily. After the seeds are removed, chop pods into pieces, and put them through a drying process. Once they are good and dry, grind into a powder in a blender or with a mortar and pestle. You'll be able to process only a little at a time. Use your powder in general as a chocolate substitute.

CHERIMOYA: *Annona cherimoya* is a small tree from the American tropics. Called "cherimoya" or "cherimoyer," it will grow in the south of California and Florida. The fruits are egg-shaped and can weigh more than a pound. The texture is smooth and the flavor is a combination of peach, pineapple, and banana. The tree grows quickly and fruits after only 2 years, but the flowers have to be hand-pollinated (use a paintbrush) in order to get fruit from the flowers. This fruit is delicious fresh and not preserved.

Varieties. The custard apple (*Annona reticulata*) is closely related to cherimoya. These trees are deciduous, frost-tender, and grow up to 20 feet tall. The fruit ripens in late winter. You can plant from seed. Custard apple makes good rootstocks from grafts of cherimoya, soursop, and sweetsop. Its fruit is terribly sweet, best when eaten chilled. Sugar apple is another related variety. They all need high humidity, well-drained soil, and neither too much cold nor too much heat.

CITRUS: For more information, read *Citrus—How to Select, Grow, and Enjoy* (Tucson, AZ: H.P. Books, 1980)—very thorough. A Red Flame grapefruit tree can live to be at least 40 years old!

Citron. There is a "citron" fruit that looks like a large lemon and grows on a small shrubby citrus tree (*Citrus medica*). The preserved rind is used to flavor cakes and puddings. (Don't confuse with the "citron" that is a small hard-fleshed watermelon variety that is made into pickles and preserves.)

Citrus Juice. Tree-ripened citrus fruit (oranges, grapefruits, lemons, limes), if you can get it, makes the best juice. Don't heat citrus juice and don't strain it. Just halve your fruit and extract the juice on a juicer or what-have-you. Don't press the oil from the rind, and do remove the seeds. Don't sweeten the juice unless it is for lemonade and limeade. I've heard that navel oranges don't make good juice for canning or bottling but I don't know why. Cut away the navel ends before you juice them. If you want to strain the juice use something with big holes. To get the maximum juice from the fruit, quickly heat it in hot water for several minutes before squeezing or roll it to soften.

☞ *JUICING ORANGES* You can figure that a dozen large oranges will give you 7 or 8 (8-oz.) glasses of juice. A dozen medium-sized ones would give you 6 or more glasses, and a dozen small ones would give you 4½–5 glasses. It's a good idea to work as rapidly as possible to preserve nutritive values.

☞ *LIMES* These are more acidic than lemons. They can be substituted in almost any recipe calling for lemons, using two-thirds as much lime juice as lemon juice.

☞ *CITRUS COMBO* Two-thirds grapefruit or orange juice combined with one-third other juice: it can be apricot, peach, nectarine juice or purees, or any other juice you want to experiment with.

☞ *GRAPEFRUIT-GRAPE* Combine half grapefruit juice and half grape juice. Serve over ice cubes.

≫ *ORANGEADE Combine 2 T. sugar or other sweetener, 1 c. water, and the grated rind of 1 orange in a saucepan. Boil 5 minutes. Cool. Add 2 c. orange juice and 2 c. cold water. Serve chilled over ice.*

≫ *LEMONADE For each serving mix 4 T. lemon juice, 2 T. sugar or other sweetener, and 1 glass ice water. For a batch, juice 5 lemons. Add 5 c. water and sweeten to taste. Serve with a slice of lemon in each glass.*

≫ *PINK LEMONADE Add to a pint of lemonade prepared in the usual way, 1 c. or less of strawberry, red raspberry, currant, or cranberry juice. (A little cranberry juice goes a long way.)*

≫ *LIMEADE For each glass use 3 T. lime juice, fill with water, and sweeten to taste. Serve a slice of the lime in each glass.*

≫ *ORANGE SYRUP Strain the juice of 24 oranges and 6 lemons. For each pint of juice add 1¾ c. sugar. Boil the juice-sugar mixture, skim, strain and chill.*

≫ *IRENE'S LEMONADE SYRUP Combine 2 c. sugar, 1 c. water, and 2 lemon peels cut into small pieces. Boil 5 minutes. Add the juice of 6 lemons. You can either strain the syrup or just leave the cooked peel in it. Keep it refrigerated.*

≫ *ORANGE FLOWER WATER Combine 1 lb. orange flowers and 1 oz. grated orange peel (no white pulp) with 4 c. water. Let soak 24 hours. Concentrate to 2 cups. Or dissolve 1 oz. orange essence from an herbal supplier in 1 gal. distilled water.*

≫ *SIMPLE ORANGE MARMALADE Cut 6 oranges into quarters and then cut each quarter into thin slices. Discard the seeds. Measure your resulting fruit and then add 3 c. water per cup fruit and let soak overnight. The next day simmer until the rind is tender. Then add 1 c. sugar for each cup of fruit. Cook until fruit is clear and the syrup sheets from a spoon (222°F). Pour into glasses and seal.*

Rinds. If your rinds are unparaffined save a reasonable amount, grate, and store tightly covered in the refrigerator for appropriate dishes. It's called "zest." Don't include the white inner pulp!

COCONUT: See "Nut Trees."

DATES: The date palm is one of the oldest food-bearing trees to have been cultivated and also is one of the most useful. Dates grow on a palm with feathery foliage that light passes through easily, so beneath the branches of a 100-foot palm there is enough sun to support another layer of plants. Cultivating a date palm takes a lot of effort, but dates are so healthy and delicious that it's worth it. Date palms are very particular about where they will grow. They require a hot climate with little rainfall (as in Southern California or Arizona).

FIGS: Commercial fig orchards are grown in Southern California and Texas. In the tropics the fig tree can get 40 feet tall. But individuals grow figs farther north. A woman in Seattle has one. Northern figs tend to be shorter, 25–30 feet tall. Southern-growing figs sometimes have pest and pestilence problems. Once established, fig trees are long-lived.

Varieties. Careful selection of figs is constantly extending their growing range north. They come in several varieties, most best suited for subtropical and tropical zones, but at least 1 type can be grown as far north as New Jersey or Michigan, and several do well in greenhouses or containers.

The fig family is a large one, and the different types of fig can be extremely unlike. Not all are even edible. Pollination is totally different and sometimes very complex and difficult, depending on the variety. Some figs are self-fertile, some are not. Plants are available from Burnt Ridge. The California Fig Advisory Board offers lots more info: 559-224-3447; 800-588-2344; fax 559-244-3449; 3425 N. First St., Ste. 109, Fresno, CA 93726-6819; **info@californiafigs. com; www.calfreshfigs.com.**

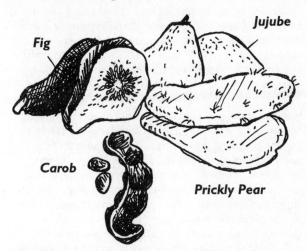

Common Fig. These varieties bear both male and female flowers, so can mature fruit without a second plant.

Caprifigs. These are inedible "wild" figs, but they have both sexes of flowers and thus are pollinators for edible figs, and provide a home for fig wasps.

Smyrna Figs. These types bear only females. To grow Smyrnas you also have to grow the fig wasp (which actually develops inside the caprifig!), their only possible pollinating agent, which means, of course, that you must grow the caprifig; otherwise the Smyrnas won't get pollinated and their fruits won't mature. Smyrnas figs are large and delicious, and they dry well (they're familiar commercial dried figs).

Others. Dwarf figs are sold in tubs from nurseries. This is one of the best varieties for container planting. Kadota figs are the best to can. Mission and Kassaba figs dry well. Turkey figs are good eaten fresh off the tree.

Planting. Don't start from seed; you may get a plant, but you're taking a chance on its fruiting capacity. Propagate by buddings, cuttings, grafting, or layering.

Planting from a Cutting. Cut off a 10–24-inch length of previous season's growth. Don't cut it off until the fig is thoroughly dormant, its leaves all dropped. Bury the cutting in sand and store it in a cool place for the winter. In the spring, plant the cutting half underground and half above, in well-drained soil of any type in the place you intend for its permanent home, since transplanting is risky. Plant it where it can get plenty of sun, since less light results in less fruit.

Planting in a Container. Start your cutting in a 4-inch pot. When the roots have filled that size, move the plant to a 6-inch one. But if you started your fig in the garden in the spring, but want to shift it to a container in the fall for safety, it will need a still larger pot or a small "tub." A wonderful thing about figs in pots is that when winter comes you can simply take them inside and store them until spring. They'll be fine in a cellar, or a basement. To winter a fig that is growing in the ground in a marginal area or to get it through a cold snap, you can wrap and/or bury it; bend the branches over and heap dirt over them and the trunk. Your bundled/buried fig can survive the cold fine that way, too.

Growing. Fig roots grow unusually close to the surface, and mulch helps keep them moist. Avoid soil cultivation around fig trees. Don't fertilize excessively. Figs in too rich a soil tend to grow branches rather than fruit. Be careful of the bark while you're picking fruit or doing anything else to a fig, as it's fragile and easily damaged. Don't prune it unless the leaves have dropped and the tree is fully dormant, since otherwise figs tend to bleed severely. Brown and white figs bear fruit only on new wood, so every year each branch needs to be pruned back extensively for best fruit production. This is not true of black figs.

Harvesting. Figs grown from cuttings sometimes bear fruit as soon as the second year. They don't blossom. The fruit just appears along the branches; that's because the fruit actually is an enlarged stem end that contains the flowers. Temperate-zone fig trees bear 2 crops, usually the first in June and the second in August. The second crop is usually larger. Farther south, you can pick figs longer, usually from June to November. Leave figs on the tree until they're thoroughly ripe because they won't ripen any more once picked. While picking, wear gloves to protect your hands because the fig tree's white sap will irritate them. When picking the fresh fruit, handle it with care; the skin is delicate and any tiny tear in the fruit's skin is likely to result in its spoiling. Depending on the variety and which crop, ripe figs may be yellow, brown, purple, black, or anything in between. If you are planning on drying the figs and your weather is suitable, leave them unpicked to dry on the tree until they naturally drop off. The important thing to keep in mind when harvesting figs is that they don't keep well fresh and need to be preserved somehow as soon as possible.

Preserving. You can candy, pickle, or spice figs, make them into jam, freeze, can, or dry them. Substitute dried small fig pieces for raisins in any recipe.

Drying. Gather tree-dried figs that have dropped and continue their drying process in the sun. Stir them once in a while, covering them with cheesecloth if insects are a problem, and take them into the house at night. Or, for indoor drying, gather figs that are a few days short of dead ripe, and cut off the stem and blossom ends. Steam them for 20 minutes or dip them into boiling water for just 30 seconds. Drain and dry. For quickest drying, poke holes in each fig using a fork, or even cut them in half—or chop them into small pieces. In a dehydrator or oven, dry at 120°F, 36–48 hours for whole figs, 12 hours for pieces. To store dried figs, brush outside lightly with honey. Pack in plastic and keep in refrigerator or freeze.

Freezing. Black Mission and Kadota figs freeze well. Wash them in ice water, take off the stems, and peel. Pack unsweetened, simply stacked in your container or with water poured over. (Add ¾ t. ascorbic acid per 1 qt. water.) Or pack covered with a light syrup with ascorbic acid added. Leave head space. Or put fully ripe figs into food-grade plastic bags and freeze. After thawing they must be used immediately.

Canning. Black Mission, Celeste, Kadota, and Brown Turkey figs all can well. Select firm, ripe, uncracked figs. *Do*

not can overripe fruit with very soft flesh. Figs have very low acid anyway. Wash thoroughly. Drain. Do not peel or remove stems. Hot pack only. Cover figs with water or syrup and bring to a boil. Let rest a few minutes. Pack into jars hot. Add 2 T. bottled lemon juice per quart, or 1 T. per pint to the jars. Cover as needed with more hot water or syrup. Leave ¼-inch head space. Adjust the lid. Fill jars with hot figs and cooking syrup. Process in boiling water bath: At altitudes to 1,000 feet, process pints 45 minutes, quarts 50 minutes; at 1,001–3,000 feet, process pints 50 minutes, quarts 55 minutes; at 3,001–6,000 feet, process pints 55 minutes, quarts 60 minutes; above 6,000 feet, process pints 60 minutes, quarts 65 minutes.

➤ *BAKED FRESH FIGS Wash about 2 dozen large figs and cut off both ends. Set them in a glass baking pan and pour a nice fruit juice over the top—apple is best. While they are baking (in a moderate oven) stir the juice every once in a while to moisten the figs and roll them over occasionally. Cook them at least 40 minutes. Good with whipped cream.*

➤ *SPECIAL FIGS Put in the oven as for baked figs (350°F) with the contents of a 16-ounce can apple juice concentrate. After 40 minutes, turn the heat down to 150°F and dry them for 30 minutes more. They come out "candied."*

For more info contact the California Fig Advisory Board, PO Box 709, Fresno, CA 93712; 800-588-2344; **www.californiafigs.com/.** Or Valley Fig Growers, **www. valleyfig.com/.** Or read *Organic Gardening,* "Discover Figs for Your World," Sept./Oct. 1991, pp. 30-34. Or *National Gardening Magazine,* July/Aug. 1996, pp. 35-40, "Fabulous Figs."

GUAVA: This tropical American native, *Psidium guajava,* a.k.a. the "Florida peach," is an evergreen shrub or small multi-stemmed tree (about 20 feet high) that is now grown in subtropical and tropical areas all over the world. To grow guava you need a frost-free zone and warm weather. The fruit has a strong smell that some people don't like. Guavas easily freeze out, but then resprout from the old roots and will be fruiting again in a few years. These trees handle soils that are unusually acid or alkaline but need lots of fertilizer.

Varieties. The common guava belongs to the Myrtle family. For eating out-of-hand, people prefer the uncommon guavas such as the "white" guavas, popular in California and Florida. And there are others:

Strawberry Guava. This close relative, *P. cattleianum,* a.k.a. "Cattley guava," has round, purplish-red, 1-inch-long fruit. It actually does taste like a strawberry. This one is a little hardier than the common guava and, once fully grown, can survive down to 22°F for a bit.

Pineapple Guava. *Feijoa sellowiana* is another close relative with similar characteristics—hardy to 15–20°F—but it prefers a cool summer and won't set fruit in a desert, or in the deep south of Florida. It does tolerate some salt in the soil, is disease-resistant, and thrives wild in Hawaii. Pineapple guava is exceptionally good eaten raw. Let it get entirely ripe though; the flavor improves much with the final ripening. The basic rule is that they aren't completely ripe until they actually fall off the tree. To serve, cut in half and spoon the fruit flesh out of the skin like you do a cantaloupe. Good in any fruit mixture.

Planting and Growing. Modern orchard guava trees are the result of extensive selection for commercial quality. Make sure you start with a type bred for good fruiting rather than ornamental talents. Don't plant from seed; they will grow but you could end up with anything. (If you must plant seeds, plant straight from the fruit into your planting site; germination will be in a few weeks.) Plant just before your rainiest season. Most varieties are self-pollinating, but a few are not. Find out when you buy. Guavas do best in deep sandy loam and need good drainage. You can propagate by layering, root cuttings, or grafting. Full sun or partial shade is okay. Pinch to thin. Guavas start to fruit as soon as 2 years after planting. Starting then, fertilize with organic manure or compost 4 or 5 times a year, as long as fruiting continues, and it may do so year around. Weeding is best done by mulching. Winter pruning of old branches will stimulate fruiting. If you have a dry season, you'll have to irrigate then.

Harvesting and Using. Guava fruits are a true berry, and the tree bears a lot of them. The shape of the fruit varies with variety from round to pear-like; size varies from walnut- to apple-size. Harvest season is about a month and a half in the summer. Unripe guavas are literally green. As they ripen they turn yellow, perhaps with some red. Inside the thick outer skin, the pulp contains many seeds. Fresh guava has a musky quality, but improves greatly when cooked. Guava fruit can be eaten fresh—they're rich in minerals and vitamins, especially C, but they are more often used to make jelly (guavas are high in pectin) or conserve.

Freezing. Peel the fruit, cut off the portion between the peel and the seeds. Freeze that.

JUJUBES: The jujube is an Asian fruit tree with weeping-willow–type drooping branches. They are thorny, beautiful plants with shiny deep-green leaves.

Climate. Jujubes are very hardy trees that will survive in almost any climate (zones 6 to 10), but they require long hot summers to bear fruit and cannot do without full sun. They also like dryness.

Varieties. There are both shrub-like and tree varieties—15–30 feet tall—and both evergreen and deciduous varieties. But the Lang and Li varieties are the only 2 kinds of jujubes generally available in the United States, though the Mu Shing Hong and Sui Mon can sometimes be found, too. These are all Chinese jujubes, deciduous trees with clumps of thorns. There are also, if you look hard enough, Indian or Malay jujubes (*Ziziphus mauritania*). They are evergreen trees with broad thorns along the undersides of their branches; they are hardier plants with a smaller fruit than the Chinese jujubes. They need cross-pollination, so plant 2 different varieties. Jujube starters can be difficult to find, but Pacific Tree Farms lists both Chinese and Indian/Malay varieties in its catalog.

Planting. These can be planted from seeds or propagated by grafting. Jujubes do best in high-quality, well-drained soil, but will make do with almost anything. They don't require fertilizing or special care, and are resistant to most diseases, although in very wet climates they may catch funguses. They have suckers that can break through pavement, though. To discourage those powerful wandering roots, water the plants infrequently and deeply.

Harvesting. The fruit is harvested in the fall. Jujubes are shaped like huge roundish olives, reddish-brown in color, and crisp to bite into and mild when just coming ripe, but softer and much sweeter when dead ripe.

Drying. Jujubes can be eaten fresh, dried, or candied. For drying, harvest very ripe, riper than you would usually eat them fresh. Dried jujubes resemble dates in taste.

LOQUATS: This fruit, also known as "Japanese medlar," *Eriobotrya japonica*, grows on an evergreen tree. Some people like the taste, some don't. They do well on a beach and near the ocean, full sun to some shade. "Champagne" has a big fruit with the best flavor. The leaves are large. Loquat is an evergreen of the rose family! The fruit is juicy with an acid-sweet flavor and yellow flesh, and it contains a few dark seeds—sort of like eating super-sized rose hips.

Climate. Loquats come from southeastern China and are grown in quantity in Japan and Taiwan. There are loquat orchards in California and some grown also in Florida. They're semi-hardy, okay down to 15–20°F, but the fruit crop is ruined by a freeze so they do best in California or the Gulf states. Loquats are harmed if the temperature falls below 32°F. Loquats grow 15–25 feet tall where it's warm and wet, 20–40 feet under the best conditions, shorter than 15 under least favorable conditions. They can handle drought once well-started, but you won't get much of a fruit crop unless you water.

Planting. Make sure you get a grafted, named variety, not an ornamental whose fruits would not be as good. But most nurseries just have seedlings rather than the grafteds. You need only one; they're self-pollinating. Plant them where the drainage is good because they can't handle wet feet. They do best in gravelly loam or clay on slopes. If you prune, a modified vase form or hollow round headed form is traditional. This tree can get fire blight. Organic manures are considered essential for a good crop in the Orient, applied at a very young stage of the fruit and again after harvesting. Flowers and fruits are both thinned. You can do your own propagation by aerial layering.

Harvesting. Loquat flowers appear in September and October. The fruit ripens from January to April of the following year, depending on your variety. The variety called "Early Red" is ready to eat in January. "Advance" ripens March to May. (Loquats are the earliest fruiting fruit in their areas.) The fruits are small, loosely clustered, and yellow. They have top flavor when fully ripe but make better jelly and preserves when somewhat on the green side. They're ripe when fully colored and somewhat soft.

→ *CANNED LOQUATS Remove stem and blossom ends. Cut fruit in half and take out seeds. Cook about 5 minutes in water or syrup. Pack hot. Cover with the hot liquid you cooked them in. Leave ¼-inch head space. Put on lids. Process pints 15 minutes, quarts 20 minutes in a boiling water bath.*

→ *LOQUAT JELLY Remove blossom ends from about 10 lb. loquat fruit and cut fruit in half. Add 2 c. water and 1 c. lemon juice. Simmer until tender. Strain and measure juice. Add ½ c. more lemon juice. Boil juice 5 minutes, then add 5 c. sugar. Cook until jelly test works, or add 1 package powdered pectin. Then pour into jars, adjust lids, and process in a water bath for 5 minutes.*

→ *TROPICAL FRUIT CUP Mix ½ c. sugar and 1 c. water, boil 5 minutes, chill, and add ¼ c. lemon juice. Gently mix 3 peeled, sliced kiwi fruits; 3 peeled, sectioned sweet citrus fruits; and 3 c. fresh, sliced loquats (or 1 c. canned). Pour syrup over fruit. Chill and serve. Fancy: Add some sliced ginger root to syrup before boiling. Remove the ginger before adding fruit.*

THE OLIVE CLIMATE

1. Zones 9–10. (See the planting zone map in Chapter 2.)
2. No spring or summer temperatures of 28°F or lower. Those damage blossoms and fruit.
3. Preferably no temperatures below 15°F; those damage the tree itself. At 10°F or below the tree will die.
4. Altitude not above 2,000 feet.

Olives won't grow at higher elevations.

5. Winter is cool enough that there are at least 2 months of chilling when temperatures average 50°F.
6. Pollination doesn't go well in high humidity.
7. A long summer with high heat is needed for fruit to mature.

8. The tree can handle drought (8–10 inches water per year), but will fruit better with deep watering once during blooming and once again in early fruiting. Its long taproot is made to pull up water from the water table. Too much rain and humidity above ground makes it more disease-prone.

LYCHEE NUTS: The following was written by my son Jacob at age 16: "My mother spent a year and a half in Taiwan (although it seemed like forever), and according to her, lychee nuts were one of the best features of her stay. However, my friend Ross described them as being 'Disgusting. Like a grape, except really gross,' so it would be best to be sure that you like the fruit before you commit yourself to growing it. Lychee nuts can be found canned or dried in Chinese specialty stores and in many supermarkets. The trees are tall, beautiful, rounded evergreens and are practically free from care. They originate in southern China, and the fruit is shaped like an eyeball with a pebbled, paper-thin shell and a grapelike flavor. To preserve, dry or make into preserves."

Growing. The lychee nut will grow only in areas with cool, dry winters and cannot withstand extremes of temperature. In the United States it's grown in Southern California and Florida. It will grow easily in loamy, fertile soil, especially if it is given compost or manure in early spring. It has almost no problems with insects or diseases, though you may wish to spray it with Malathion if it becomes infested with aphids.

Planting. The lychee nut can be planted from seed, air layer, cuttings in sand, or grafting. Air layers work best because the plants reach maturity much more quickly. Transplanting is best done in winter, though you can get away with it in any season.

Varieties. There are a number of Taiwanese varieties, the most popular of them being "Black-Leaf." None of them vary widely from each other. But you may wish to consider the Longan, which is a close relative of the lychee nut. Its skin is yellowish-brown rather than red, and it is a hardier, shorter (35 meters) tree—those are the only real differences.

MESQUITE: This multiple-trunked desert native, *Prosopis fuliflora*, is a nitrogen-fixing legume, a distant relative of carob, and is amazingly well-adapted to desert survival. The long, sugar-rich bean pods provide a food both humans and animals can eat. Stock also enjoys munching on young mesquite. Mesquite roots go amazingly deep and far and are a good source of wood in the desert.

➤ *MESQUITE (OR CAROB) BEAN DRINK Soak the seeds in water for several hours to get a sweet lemon-flavored drink. Or grind the seeds and mix that powder with water to get your beverage.*

OLIVES: The mango and *Olea europaea,* the olive, are the most long-lived of domesticated fruit trees. They both can live to 600 years! Despite its age, an olive grows only 15–35 feet high. It's an evergreen with pretty silvery leaves and abundant, fragrant flowers in May and June.

Climate. Olives will grow in the interior valleys of California, southern Arizona, New Mexico, and Texas.

Planting and Growing. Olives need good drainage and fairly fertile soil (not very alkaline!), and *full sun.* Give the tree about 30 square feet of its own. The fruit drop is messy so the trees are best situated over a lawn or other ground cover or mulched ground rather than a patio, walkway, or driveway. These are the kinds in order of size of fruit, smallest to biggest: Sevillano, Manzanillo, and Mission.

Buy a fruiting, rather than ornamental, variety. Ornamentals do fruit some, but not nearly as much.

Most, but not all, olives are self-fertile, but cross-pollination gives you more fruit. They tend to bear every other year, so plant more than one. Plant bare-root nursery trees in winter months only. This tree has a long taproot. Coat or paint trunks of your newly planted olive to protect it against sunburn. Keep strawberries away from your trees since they may carry verticillium wilt, a risk for olives. Don't fertilize until fruiting starts, and if then not much.

Olives will grow from ripe (black olive) seeds if you chill the seeds first (3 weeks in the ice-cube tray freezer), but seedlings are genetically unpredictable. So plant from cuttings: just cut off and stick in the ground. Or graft cuttings onto seedling roots.

Olives naturally drop their leaves every 2 or 3 years, in the spring.

Harvesting. The tree takes 4 years to bear. The fruit develops on new wood from the previous year's growth. Thinning gives you larger fruit. Olives are easy to grow but the harvesting and curing is work. *Don't harvest olives from public ornamental plants unless you're sure pesticides and herbicides haven't been applied.* Olives are first light green, a pale straw color, or rosy red. When fully ripe they're black. Pick green for a "green-ripe" curing. Pick reddish-black for a Greek cure. Pick fruit for curing off the trees gently so it isn't bruised or skinned. You can hold the olives for curing in a salt brine (¾ c. salt per 1 gal. water) in a cool place for just a few days. But if you haven't started curing by then, they'll be too soft. To harvest olives for oil pressing you can leave them on the tree as long as desired, and hit the branches to bring them down onto tarps or plastic you've spread under the tree.

Curing Olives. You can't eat olives straight off the tree. When fresh they're loaded with tannin and, so, very bitter. They have to be "cured" before eating. Lye neutralizes the acid as part of one curing process, but that lye is even more of a risk to you than uncured olives so be very careful when using it.

Green-Ripe Cured Olives. These instructions are from the University of California, Agricultural Sciences Department.

This process will produce straw-yellow to green or brown olives. Choose fruit that is green, straw-colored, or cherry-red. Do not use black-ripe fruit because it is likely to become soft when pickled. *Start early in the morning. This is going to be a 12-hour work day.*

1. Prepare a solution of 2 oz. (about 4 T.) of lye to each gallon of water. (An easy way to do this is to dissolve a 12-oz. can of flake lye—household lye—in 6 gal. water.) Use a wooden, glass, heavy plastic, or stoneware container. Never use an aluminum container because the zinc will dissolve and may make the olives poisonous. Stir the solution until the lye is well-dissolved. Then let the solution cool to a maximum of 65–70°F.

2. Cover the olives with the lye solution early in the morning. Place a towel or cloth over them and push it down tightly to keep the olives submerged. Stir the olives with a lath or a wooden or stainless steel spoon every 2 or 3 hours until the lye reaches the pits. This usually takes 10–12 hours. You can judge the amount of penetration by cutting sample olives to the pit with a sharp knife at intervals of 1 or 2 hours. The lye solution discolors the flesh to a yellowish-green color. Test the biggest ones. The olive's inside will be a yellowish-green color where the lye has penetrated, but it's hard to see the line of separation between that which has been penetrated and that which has not. Keep an uncured olive handy to compare colors. How long it takes the lye to reach the pit depends in part on the weather

and the temperature. It can be from 8 to 48 hours.

If the lye has not reached the pits by bedtime, remove the lye solution and cover the olives with water. The reason for such caution is that if the lye gets into the olive pits, it's next to impossible to get it out again. Next morning, pour off the water and cover the olives with a solution of 1 oz. (about 2 level T.) of lye per 1 gal. water and let stand until the lye reaches the pits completely. This may take as long as 30 hours if the fruit is quite green.

Frequently, this lye treatment is insufficient. Some olives neutralize most of the lye so that it fails to penetrate to the pits. In such cases, prepare a fresh solution of 1½ oz. (3 level T.) of lye per 1 gal. water and allow it to cool. Then discard the used solution and pour in the fresh. Let the olives stand until the solution reaches the pits, then follow the procedure in steps 3 to 5.

3. Pour the lye solution off the olives and throw it away. After the lye stage, you have a long rinsing stage. Then comes the brining period. And then you eat or can them.

4. Rinse the olives twice in cold water, then cover them with cold water. Change the water 4 times each day until you can no longer taste the lye in the olives. This may take as long as 7 or 8 days. (For commercial packers, it takes about 4 days.) *Expose the olives to the air as little as possible during the lye treatment or this rinsing.*

5. Prepare a salt brine containing 4 oz. (about 6½ level T.) of salt per gallon of water. (If the solution seems too salty, reduce the amount of salt to 3½ oz.) Dissolve the salt thoroughly, and cover the olives with the solution. Let stand for 2 days.

The olives are now ready to use. Store them in a cold place, preferably in a refrigerator. They are susceptible to spoilage. Refrigerate and use within a short period of time (2 weeks). Or you can make them last longer by brining.

6. If you do not plan to use the olives within 2 weeks, prepare a brine using 8 oz. (about 13 level T. or slightly more than ¾ c.) of salt per gallon of water. Store the olives in this brine for 1 week. Then replace the brine with a solution of 1 lb. (26 level T. or about 1⅔ c.) salt per gallon of water. After 10–12 days, put the olives in a fresh brine of 1 lb. of salt per gallon of water. In this strong brine, it may be 2 months before your olives begin to deteriorate.

Freshening from Holding Solution. Remove olives from holding solution and soak them overnight in fresh, non-salted water. By then they should be nice. They won't keep now. Use them up within 3 days. *If at any time your olives seem mushy, moldy, or bad smelling, don't even taste them. Throw them out.*

Canning Olives? Since green olives will keep for months simply refrigerated, it makes sense not to can them. Olives are quite low in acid. A food specialist told me that in California the 2 most common sources of botulism poisoning are home-canned taco sauce and home-canned olives.

Anonymous Olives. This letter wasn't signed. "Home-cured olives are such a treat. They are easily done, but you have to follow instructions closely or you will fail. First have everything you're going to use ready and clean. The olives should be freshly picked and I always make the green ones. I worked in an olive curing plant and the black ones are more difficult to get just right. The olives should be graded so all are the same size so as to cure at the same rate. Throw away all bruised or cut ones. This recipe is to cure 40 or 50 lb. of olives. A wooden keg is best but you can use a crock jar. Only you need a drain hole at the bottom and you do not naturally have that in a crock. I used to use an old wooden washing machine. Dissolve 1 can of lye in 5 gal. cold water. (Soft water works better. Do not use fluoridated water.) Stir with a long wooden stick so the lye fumes don't burn your hands. Now gently pour olives into lye solution. Water will cover olives. Stir gently every few hours to get them all well soaked in the solution. Keep them in there until the lye almost reaches the pit. The water turns lighter. You can cut one in half and see if it is still bitter. You can taste it but do not let it stay in your mouth. Spit it out and rinse your mouth. When the lye has almost reached the pit, drain and cover with fresh water. Change the water every 12 hours for 2 days and be careful not to bruise any of the olives. If you see slick or cut ones take them out.

"Now place your olives in a second lye solution using 1 lb. lye to 6 gal. water. Always use cold water. Allow olives to remain in this solution for 4 to 5 hours, or until the lye reaches the pit. You will know when you cut them open.

"Drain off the lye and cover with cold water. Change water every 12 hours for a week. Then cover with brine. To make the first brine, use 2 T. salt per 1 gal. water and let stand 1 day. For a second brine, use 2 T. salt to 4 gal. cold water. Allow to stand 1 day. For your third brine, use 2 T. salt to 6 gal. water and allow to stand 2 days. For your fourth brine, use 2 T. salt to 8 gal. water and allow to stand 3 days. Now make a final brine using 10 T. salt to 10 gal. water. Bring this to a rolling boil. Skim scum, let cool, and cover the olives. Have the last brine ready to go over the olives right after you drain them of the next to last brine."

Keep these olives in a holding solution, same as step 6 in the method above.

Process for Dark-Ripe Olives. This process is more complex than the one for green-ripe olives. The purpose of it is to make the olives dark-brown or black. Start with green, straw-colored, or cherry-red olives. It is best to use fruit that is all the same color (the same degree of ripeness) and nearly the same size.

1. First Lye Treatment: Prepare a solution containing 1½ oz. (about 3 level T.) lye per gallon of water. (Follow above directions for preparing the lye.) Pour the solution over the olives and let stand until it penetrates the skins. (Start checking the olives after 3 hours, and then check them every 30 minutes.) Remove the lye solution and expose the olives to the air in the container in which they were treated. This helps give the olives their dark color. Stir the olives 3 times during the first day they are exposed to the air.

2. Second Lye Treatment: Prepare a lye solution of the same strength as for the first lye treatment. Pour this over the olives and let stand until the solution penetrates ¹⁄₃₂–¹⁄₁₆-inch into the flesh. Remove the lye and expose the olives to the air for 1 day, stirring as before.

3. Third Lye Treatment: Use a lye solution that is the same strength as the first lye treatment. Pour it over the olives and let stand until it penetrates ⅛–³⁄₁₆-inch into the flesh. Pour off the solution and expose the olives to the air for 1 day, stirring as before.

4. Fourth Lye Treatment: Make a solution of the same strength as for the first lye treatment. Pour it over the olives and let it stand until it penetrates ³⁄₁₆–⁵⁄₁₆-inch into the flesh. Pour off the solution and expose the olives to the air for 1 day, stirring as before.

5. Fifth Lye Treatment: Make a lye solution using 2 oz. (about 4 level T.) of lye to 1 gal. water. Pour this over the olives and let stand until it penetrates thoroughly to the pits. Pour off the solution and expose the olives to the air for 1 day, stirring as before.

6. Rinsing: Cover the olives with cold water. Change the water 4 times daily until the olives no longer taste of lye (up to 7 or 8 days).

7. Holding Solution: Cover the olives with a holding solution and store as described for green-ripe olives.

Freezing Ripe Mission Olives. You can preserve pickled ripe Mission olives by freezing, but other olive varieties soften badly when frozen and thawed. You can freeze Mission olives processed either by the green-ripe or dark-ripe method. Cover them with a brine made with 4 oz. (about 6½ T.) of salt per gallon of water. Boil for 10–15 minutes. This will lessen the softening from freezing. Discard the brine and chill the olives in cold water.

Pack the olives without brine in rigid cartons, glass jars, cans, or used coffee cans. The package should be moisture–vapor resistant to prevent drying out. Seal coffee cans with freezer tape. Tightly seal other types of containers in the usual manner. Quick-freeze the packaged olives and store in the freezer.

Before serving, let the olives thaw thoroughly. If desired, roll the thawed olives in olive or salad oil mixed with chopped garlic or other seasoning and let stand overnight.

Drying Ripe-Processed Olives. You can dry processed green-ripe or black-ripe olives in a home dehydrator or in the sun until bone dry. If you use a dehydrator, dry at 145–150°F. The dried olives will keep well in airtight food-grade plastic bags, glass jars, or metal containers. However, they keep best when refrigerated or stored in a home freezer. You can eat the olives out-of-hand without soaking, or use them in cooking. Do not prepare more olives by this method than you can use within 3–4 months because they'll become very rancid during storage.

Brined Greek-Style Olives. Always use mature, full-colored (dark-red to purplish-black) fruit to prepare this style of olive. You can use any variety, but be sure the fruit is firm and harvested before frost. It is most common to use the Manzanilla and Mission varieties. The cured olives may be more or less shriveled because of the high salt brine used to preserve them. Some of the olives may fade in color during curing. In general, they tend to darken again when exposed to air.

How to Prepare Greek-Style Olives

1. Sort out defective fruits.
2. Place good olives in a container that can be made airtight. A 1-qt. glass jar is the smallest size recommended.
3. Cover the olives with a brine containing 8 oz. of salt per gallon of water (see step 6 under Spanish-Style Green Olives, below). Fasten the lids loosely. Store the olives at 60–80°F.
4. At the end of 1 week, replace the original brine with one containing 1 lb. of salt per gallon of water, again leaving the covers loose.
5. After 15 days, replace the brine with one containing the same concentration—1 lb. of salt—and seat the covers firmly.
6. If pressure forms, carefully loosen the cover to release the gas. Then close it firmly.
7. If brine spews out, replace it with more containing 1 lb. salt per 1 gal. water.
8. If you prefer less bitter olives, you can replace the brine at 1 month intervals for 2 or 3 months after step 4.
9. If you keep the olives airtight in brine, you can store them for at least 1 year, if the container cover does not corrode. There is no danger of spoilage or possible toxicity because of the high salt concentration of the brine.
10. You can eat the olives within 2 months after preparation if you like fairly bitter olives. In any event, after 2 months in the strong brine, you can use them for cooking in tamale pies and similar dishes. It is desirable to soak the olives in water overnight to reduce the saltiness before eating them out-of-hand.

Store any desalted, uneaten olives made by this method in the refrigerator, in a solution containing 1 part red wine and 1 part red wine vinegar, with a layer of olive oil floating on the surface. Before serving, since the olive oil may congeal in the refrigerator, allow the olives to sit at room temperature until the oil has melted.

Black Olives. The black olive procedure takes longer. The big difference is that the olives have to be exposed to the air as part of the process.

1. Mix 3 level T. lye per gallon of water and soak your olives in it until it merely penetrates the skins. As little as 3 hours may do it. Check often so you don't have an overdose.
2. When the lye has just penetrated the skin and not the flesh, pour off the lye solution and let the olives lay out in the air for a day. Stir them every few hours.
3. Now give your olives another lye bath until the lye has soaked in another $1/36$–$1/16$ of an inch. Then pour off the lye water and let the olives lie in the air again, stirring every few hours.
4. Again lye bathe them until the lye has gone in $1/8$–$3/16$ inch. (No wonder everybody thinks this procedure is too hard!)
5. Now give them a new solution of 4 level T. lye per gallon water. Leave them in there until it soaks to the pits. Pour off the solution and give the olives another day of fresh air.
6. Now cover them with fresh water, changing every few

hours all day long until the lye taste is gone. Freshening will take about a week.
7. Now give them the brining treatment and can them like green olives.

Oil-Cured Greek-Style Olives. Make Greek-style olives from mature olives that are dark-red to black. Mission olives are commonly used, but any variety will do. Use smaller olives because larger ones get soft. The olives will become shriveled since they are salt-cured. These olives are salty and slightly bitter, and you may have to acquire a taste for them.

1. Cover the bottom of a wooden box with burlap. Weigh out 1 lb. salt for each 2 lb. olives. Mix the salt and olives well in the box to prevent mold from developing. Pour a layer of salt over the olives to a depth of 1 inch. *Place the box outdoors so the brine that forms won't ruin the floor.*
2. After 1 week, pour olives and salt into another box, then back into the first box to mix them. Repeat this mixing process once every 3 days until the olives are cured and edible. This usually takes about 30–35 days. Stir things up as gently as possible. Remove any olives that have gotten soft or broken.
3. Sift out most of the salt through a screen. Dip olives in a colander into boiling water for a few seconds, drain, and let dry overnight.
4. For storage, add 1 lb. salt to each 10 lb. olives. Mix olives and salt and put the olives in a cool place. Use within 1 month, or store in a refrigerator (they'll keep up to 6 months) or home freezer (they'll keep up to a year) until used.

Just before using, coat the olives with olive oil by dipping into olive oil. Or put them in a large pan or box and sprinkle a little olive oil over them. Work the olives with your hands to coat them with oil. But don't oil if you plan to use the olives for cooking.

Don't worry because they look all shriveled up and wrinkled. That's how Greek olives always look! This type of olive is useful for flavoring stews, tamale pie, spaghetti, and as a relish eaten out-of-hand.

Using Olives. Use olives to decorate main dishes or eat as finger food. Add to pasta sauce, chopped, to salads, or any meat soup, or baked meat, or omelet mix.

☞ *STUFFED OLIVES Remove the seed. In its place put a strip of pickled pimiento, a nut, or some other tasty morsel.*

Homemade Olive Oil. Many people have asked me how they can make their own cooking oils. This is the only system I've ever been able to find that seems halfway possible for people to do on their own. The recipe was written by the late W.V. Cruess, who was Professor of Food Technology at the College of Agriculture, University of California, Berkeley, CA.

There are 2 ways you can make homemade olive (or any other) oil: by grating, simmering, and skimming, or by pressing it out. By these processes, you get only two-thirds as much oil as from a commercial press. Still that isn't bad for homemade.

Grate/Simmer/Skim Extraction. Ordinary lye will be needed. Make up a solution of $1/2$ lb. lye per 1 gal. water, using an agate-ware or iron pot (not aluminum!). A small basket of wire screen such as is used for making French-fried potatoes will be needed, or a piece of cheesecloth can be used. Heat the lye solution to boiling and while it is boiling, dip the olives in it for about 20 seconds. The time needed will vary with the toughness of the skins. Leave the olives in the lye until the skins are softened—that is, practically dissolved. Then plunge them into cold water for a few seconds to stop the action of the lye. Place the lye-treated olives on a piece of fly screen tacked to a frame over a large dishpan. Rub them on the screen until the flesh has separated from the pits and dropped through the screen into the pan. A heavy pair of rubber gloves is necessary in this process to prevent your hands from becoming badly stained and roughened by the lye and olive juice.

Place the pulp, which should now be of a pasty or mushy consistency, into a pot with about 2 or 3 times its own volume of water. Heat to simmering, stirring constantly, for about ½ hour. Set it aside for several days to permit the oil to rise to the surface. Usually a fair yield of oil can be obtained by skimming it from the surface of the pulp. The pulp may then be boiled a few minutes with more water and allowed to stand again. The process should be repeated several times. The secrets of success are to rub the olive flesh to a fine-grained pulp and always use a large excess of water with the pulp. The yield of oil is also sometimes increased by adding about ¼ lb. salt per gallon of water used with the pulp.

Oil obtained by this process must be washed and should be filtered as described later.

Pressure Extraction. The simplest way to prepare olives for pressing is to place them in a strong sack, then hammer the sack with the broad side of an ax or with a heavy board until they are thoroughly crushed and broken up. The olives will crush even better if boiled a short time beforehand to soften them. Now press them in your store-bought or homemade olive press.

Homemade olive press

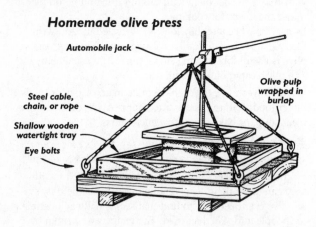

Automobile jack

Steel cable, chain, or rope

Olive pulp wrapped in burlap

Shallow wooden watertight tray

Eye bolts

Making a Homemade Olive Press. Materials needed: a heavy auto jack, 2 lengths of steel cable or chain or heavy rope, 1 shallow wooden watertight tray, 1 piece heavy burlap material to hold the crushed fruit, a pair of 2-inch by 10-inch by 16-inch boards for the bottom, a pair of 2-inch by 4-inch by 20-inch boards for braces, and 4 threaded eyebolts with nuts. Start by nailing the bottom together. Put the 2-inch by 10-inch boards side by side and nail them onto the edge of the 2-inch by 4-inch boards as shown. Next build a tray or simple box and caulk all joints to insure watertightness. And set this on the bottom. Then drill holes for eyebolts in

the 4 corners of the bottom as shown, and insert eyebolts. All that is left is to set the jack up and measure and attach the cable.

The Pressing. You can press either green or black olives for oil. Green makes the best quality oil, but less of it. *For kitchen oil, don't press hard enough to crack the pits. There's oil in them, but it's good enough only to make soap with.* The oil from a first pressing is highest quality and called the "virgin oil." Green olives press best if first dried a week out of direct sun.

Place the crushed fruit and pits in a piece of heavy burlap and fold the edge of the burlap in to give a pressed cake about 10 inches square and about 4 inches thick. Make 2 of these and place them in the press. Press slowly until no more juice can be obtained. Save all juice and oil pressed from the fruit. The pressed pulp should now be boiled with an equal volume of water and pressed a second time. Repeat boiling and pressing again. Usually a fourth heating and pressing will pay. Combine all of this pressed liquid and allow it to stand in a tub or barrel overnight. The oil can then be skimmed off.

Clearing the Oil. Oil obtained by either of the above methods will be bitter and not clear. Use any of the following methods to clear it.

Method 1, Water Washing. Prepare a bucket or a 5-gal. can with a hole and faucet or cork near the bottom. Place the oil in this container and add an equal quantity, or more, of warm water. Mix oil and water by stirring for several minutes. Allow water and remaining solids to settle for several hours. Draw off the water and replace it with fresh warm water. Stir, let it settle, and draw off water and solids again after several hours. Repeat until the oil no longer has a bitter taste. Usually 2 days' washing will be sufficient.

The oil will be cloudy and mixed with a little water. Now pour it through filter paper from the drugstore or a coffee filter placed in a funnel over a bottle or jar. Oil filters slowly. Do not become discouraged if it requires several days for it to run through the filter. A way to hurry it would be to filter it through several layers of cheesecloth—again and again. Then bottle as below. Some oil makers swear that the oil needs aging for several months to have the proper flavor. Method 2 has aging built-in. For method 1, age in bottles away from bright light. Too much light will cause it to lose color and flavor. But a warm room will help it age more rapidly. The oil will also age faster if the bottles are only ¾ full, and if a small piece of cotton is used to close the bottle.

Method 2, Siphon System. In this case you take the oil off the top instead of the water off the bottom. Start by straining the oil through several layers of cheesecloth into glass containers (the glass is an advantage of this system). Let it settle a couple weeks. Then siphon the oil off the top, stopping before you get near the sediment. (Plastic tubing works well.) Strain again, settle again, siphon again. Five such cycles will give you quality oil. Now pour into sterile jars (don't heat), and add lids or cork to seal.

Once you break the seal on a jar of your olive oil, refrigerate it to prevent rancidity.

PAPAYA: The papaya is the most tropical of tropical fruits. Even the tree has an exotic look of the jungle about it. It isn't actually a tree. It is more of an overgrown 20-foot herb. It produces vast amounts of a delicious fruit that is also very nutritious. In appearance and taste it is much like a melon.

Varieties. There are a number of papaya varieties, different in sweetness, hardiness, and pollination requirements. Mexican varieties are less sweet and more hardy. If you're going to grow only a few, I'd recommend the Solo Papaya, which is small and sweet and will pollinate itself.

Growing. The most important factor in growing a papaya is climate: they cannot abide chill. In the United States, the only suitable climates are in Hawaii, along the Southern Californian coast, and the Gulf coast. Temperatures below 30°F, even for only a few hours, will damage the plant and/or prevent fruiting. Luckily, the plants can be grown in containers and brought indoors for cold spells. Most types of papayas need both male and female plants to fruit, and only the females bear papayas. The soil should always be kept moist but never wet. Fertilize frequently. Plant from well-washed seeds, 2 or 3 of them in a pot filled with a mixture of manure, sand, and loam.

POMEGRANATES: These can be grown from seed, by cuttings, or layering. Or order them from a nursery. They look like small trees. They are hardy in the Las Vegas area and have no insect problems. They flower beautifully for a good 2 months—brilliant coral trumpet-shaped blooms. The pomegranate is ripe for sure when it starts to split. (You can't tell by the outside color.) Pomegranate juice will severely stain your kids' clothes. Rosalind Creasy, in *The Complete Book of Edible Landscaping,* has recipes for pomegranate jelly, grenadine syrup, and pomegranate juice.

PRICKLY PEAR: *Opuntia ficus-indica,* prickly pear cactus or "Indian fig," is the best known cactus fruit, but there are numerous edible cacti in the *Opuntia* and *Nopalea* cacti species. In general they will grow from zones 5 to 10. They grow well in containers so you can bring more-tender ones inside for cold weather if your weather gets below 20°F.

Varieties. Choose your species thoughtfully. Some are more hardy than others; *O. opuntia* is the hardiest. (See *Cactus and Succulents,* published by Sunset.) Edible types include *N. chamacuera* (fruit and pads), *N. dejecta* (fruit and pads), *N. cochenillifera* (fruit), *O. engelmanii* (pads eaten fried), *O. leucotricha* (pads and fruit), *O. ficus-indica* (pads and fruits), and *O. basilaris* (flowers can be steamed and eaten).

There are new spineless varieties available, which cattle like to eat and which can grow in deserts where little else thrives, doing well in a well-drained rocky or sandy soil. Starts are available from Jim and Electra Elliott at Arizona Cactus Sales, 1619 S. Arizona Ave., Chandler, AZ 85248; 480-963-1061; **www.arizonacactussales.com.** Or Arizona Cactus: 520-432-7040; **azcactus@primenet.com; www. arizonacactus.com.** John and Vickie Dicus offer a "nearly spineless" *Opuntia ficus-indica* var. *Burbanks Spineless,* a rapidly growing variety called *Opuntia ficus-indica* var. *Santa Maria,* and the "Dinner Plate" cactus (*Opuntia robusta*), whose edible "almost spineless" leaves can grow as large as 16 in. across: Rivenrock Gardens, PO Box 196, Nipomo, CA 93444; **www.rivenrock.com.** Or shop at GreenDealer: 502-459-9054; PO Box 37328, Louisville, KY 40233-7328; **king@adept.net.**

Planting. You can start a plant from either seeds or pads. If you live where cactus grows wild, just broadcast seed, cover with ¼-inch sand, and wait. Otherwise, plant in flats. It takes the seed months of a little dampness and a little sun to get going. Planting a pad goes faster. Let it cure a few days in sunshine, then plant right-side-up in moist sand. No fertilizer is needed, but they do need water at least once a month their first year. Not too much water, though; excess results in mildew or rot of these desert naturals.

Harvesting. It takes several years for the plant to get big enough to fruit. In spring, nice yellow (or orange) flowers bloom. The leaves are thorny, thick green extensions called "pads." They're edible and taken in spring. The flowers are followed by fruits, ready in the fall. The pads and fruits both have needles. Be careful not to get punctured. Old-timers pick fruit and pads with leather gloves.

Nopales. "Nopales" is the Mexican name for prickly pear pads served as a vegetable. To use, first get rid of the bristles on the pads by scraping them off completely or singeing or cutting them off like you're cutting out "eyes" from a potato. Then peel and cut into large chunks, then boil in water. (Cooked nopales are still firm.) Drain and serve with salt, pepper, and butter. Or serve raw and sliced. Or add to a basic meat and vegetable soup or stew. Or fry sections.

Prickly Pear Fruits. These can be eaten fresh if you're willing to spit out the seeds. Marion Stick is a woman of Native American descent who lives in Phoenix, AZ. Marion says Native Americans pick the fruit from cactus and make jelly and candy. The following recipes tell you how.

❧ *CACTUS CANDY Marion makes this from the small barrel cactus. Take off spines and outer skin. Cut pulp across in 1-inch slices. Soak overnight in cold water. In the morning cut into 1-inch pieces and boil until tender. Drain and cook slowly in a syrup until syrup is almost gone. Watch so the pieces do not scorch. To make syrup for about 2 qt. cactus pieces, combine 3 c. sugar, 1 c. water, 2 T. orange juice, and 1 T. lemon juice. Bring to a boil and add cactus. When syrup is almost gone, remove cactus pieces. You may cover with powdered or granulated sugar.*

❧ *PRICKLY PEAR JELLY Pick prickly pears with leather gloves. Take off spines. Rinse the fruit and place in kettle, adding enough water to cover. Boil until quite tender, then squeeze through a jelly bag or jelly press. To every 2½ c. of juice add 1 (1¾ oz.) package powdered pectin and boil for couple of minutes. Then add 3 T. lemon juice and 3½ c. sugar. Stir often and boil hard for 5 minutes. Pour in jelly glasses. Adjust lids. Process 5 minutes.*

ROSELLE: This attractive, tall (4–5-foot) annual, *Hibiscus sabdariffa,* also called "Florida cranberry" or "sorrell," is grown for the fleshy cranberry-flavored red calyces that develop from the bases of its yellow flowers. It needs subtropical or greenhouse conditions with a long, hot summer. It grows fast and can be used in the South as an annual hedge. Plant like tomatoes, spaced 1½–2 feet apart.

Harvesting and Use. The plants are triggered to begin flowering when the days shorten, but too soon a frost will prevent the roselles from maturing. The roselles will be ready for harvest around 15 days after the flowers bloom. To harvest, just snap them off. The red calyces, called "roselles," can be used fresh or made into a fruit sauce, or used to flavor jelly, iced drinks, or hot teas. Roselle juice is like cranberry in color and taste, but lacks cranberry's bitterness. Dried roselles, or "Jamaica flowers," can also be used as flavoring. Young roselle leaves and stems can be cooked and eaten same as spinach.

> *ROSELLE JELLY* *Cover the roselles with water and cook them until tender. Strain through a jelly bag. Measure the juice. Boil it 5 minutes. Add 1½ c. sugar and 2 t. lemon juice per 2 c. roselle juice. Cook until it sheets from the spoon. Skim. Pour into your jelly jars and seal.*

SAPOTE: Sapote (*Sapotaceae*) is also known as sapota, sapodilla, and the "chocolate pudding fruit." Mamey Sapota, var. "Pantin" (*Pouteria sapota*) is a grafted plant that needs tropical conditions such as a heated greenhouse, available from Pacific Tree Farms: **www.kyburg.com/ptf.**

TAMARILLO: The tamarillo (*Cyphomandra betacea),* or "tree tomato," is grown in sub-tropical areas around the world. It's a beautiful plant with large leaves and a sweet smell that grows only about 8 feet tall.

Planting. Choose a wind-protected, warm site and well-drained, light soil. Provide reasonable watering. Tamarillo will grow from seeds (available from Southern Seeds).

Harvesting and Use. Your plants start bearing smooth, bright fruits in 2 years. They are sweet and acid and make good preserves and sauces, or can be cooked as a vegetable —good stewed or baked with any meat. They have tough outer skins that help them store well, but they must be peeled before eating.

VINE, BUSH, AND BRAMBLE FRUITS

The Complete Guide to Growing Berries and Grapes by Louise Riotte (Garden Way) pulls together most of the basic details about small fruits. For good readable advice on grapes see *Organic Gardening,* February 1972, p. 72. You can also get a lot of useful information on grapes out of the Henry Field Seed Company catalog.

This section is divided into 2 parts: the vine fruits are listed first.

Grapes

(For information in this section I am heavily indebted to Cass Turnbull, who knows so much more about grapes, their training, and their pruning, than I do.) Quite likely you can get started with grapes with cuttings from a neighbor who has them. You cut in the early spring before the sap has started to run, when it looks all dead. Don't prune grapes after the sap is running because they'll bleed like crazy. Cut off a length of stem with at least 5 bud spots on it. This is where the leaves will develop later. Stick it in your chosen place with 2 or 3 spots underground and the other 3 above. Roots will grow from those underground, and leaves from those above. Keep the ground soaked around them all that first summer. You may have grapes from them even the first year. If you're planting in a row, set cuttings about 2 feet apart. They can be by the side of a building if you want, but pick a sunny side. Supply a pole for climbing. When choosing grape starts, be careful to take slips off a good productive plant rather than just anything.

VARIETIES AND PRODUCTION: Green grapes make nice table grapes, but purple salad grapes are better for preserves and juice. Ours are some little green kind with seeds. Don't get in a hurry for production. Generally you'll have no grapes the first year you plant, very few the second, more the third, and then in the fourth year you'll start to get into

real production—depending on how you prune. That's true of cold-weather grape types. You see, there are 2 basic kinds of grapes. One is your vinifera or California wine type. They are most common in warm climates. Thompson Seedless, also this type, is a good table grape. With these warm-climate grapes you can have grapes growing by the second year after planting. The labrusca varieties have slip-skins and are cold-weather kinds of grapes. Concord is one. The Concord grape is a good producer. These do better in cold climates where they will give you a heavier production than warm-weather types will. Cold-weather types will do fine in New York. But they take at least 3 years to bear fruit. They bear fruit from the third, fourth, and fifth buds from the base of the vine. When you are pruning you have to be careful you don't cut away that fruiting wood. You'll find lots more info on commercial aspects under "Organic Grape Production," at **www.attra.org/attra-pub/Grape. html.**

GRAPE PRUNING: Cass wrote up this subject to help me: Grape pruning is daunting to the novice, especially to one who has inherited someone else's old, overgrown vine. Don't worry. In grape pruning, as with most pruning, there is a large margin of error. If you avoid the big mistakes you can do a decent job until time and experience teach you the rest. The 2 most frequent mistakes I see are not pruning at all and simply shearing or whacking all canes back to the arbor or trellis and leaving a big, tangled clump.

A Grapevine Story. An early settler planted a grape vineyard. It grew fine for several years, but eventually the settler moved on and the vines were left unpruned and neglected. Eventually they grew out of site and rambled along the ground. The grapes were poor in quality and out of reach. A new owner bought the property with the intent of raising livestock and pack animals in the forgotten fields. A year or two later the animals had nibbled back all of the vines. Thereafter the vines returned and fruited magnificently. The moral: Any ass can prune a grapevine.

Controlling Grapevine Size. If you have planted or acquired grapevines, you will soon have a lot of experience pruning them. That's because the primary reason for pruning grapevines is to keep these "rampant plants" from growing up and covering nearby houses and trees. This extensive annual growth is the *modus operandi* of most vines. Don't take it personally. Furthermore, if you neglect to prune, you will find that all the grape clusters appear way out of reach at the ends of your enormous vine.

Maximizing Production. On old, let-go vines, you will find many, many clusters of grapes, but they will be small and of poor quality. Shortening and thinning allows more energy and light to reach fewer buds, making the fruit bigger and bigger.

How Much Grape Pruning Is Enough? Take off between 60 and 80 percent of the foliage and old canes every year. That looks like a lot, but really it isn't for a grapevine. Yes, it is possible to overprune. The plant won't die, it will simply stimulate rapid and rampant regrowth. Such growth has bigger than normal leaves and fewer fruiting buds, meaning fewer grape clusters. This is one reason that severe pruning, which is commonly done to renovate an old vine, is often spread over several years.

When to Prune. Most grape pruning is done in the dormant season, meaning mid-winter. If you prune too late (late February or March, in Seattle), your grapevine will "bleed." This means it will ooze sap from every cut end. Bleeding doesn't hurt the grapevine, but it will scare you. If you have a bleeding grape, don't put on a tourniquet. Just wait. It will stop once the leaves have emerged.

Thinning Grape Clusters. Early in the growing season, you may want to thin out clusters of young grapes. Just cut some clusters off, or parts of clusters off, to channel more energy into what's left. Here again this is not essential, but it will make the remaining grapes bigger and better. I like to do a little touch-up pruning in the summer to get more light to the grape clusters.

GRAPE-PRUNING DEFINITIONS

Shoot. New supple, 1-year-old, green growth.

Cane. A 1- or 2-year-old shoot. On it are buds that never grow out unless they are pruned back, buds that become new shoots, and buds that become flowers and fruit. A good, young cane is about pencil thickness and is smooth and tan, not brown and shaggy.

Spur. A cane shortened to 1 or 2 buds, about 3 inches long.

Fruiting Arm. An older spur that is cut a little farther out each year until it becomes a thicker, older, more permanent feature a few inches long. When a fruiting arm becomes too old, pick a new cane originating on the truck or scaffold and train it as a replacement (spur prune). Then cut back the old arm.

Scaffold. Main side branches. Originally these were the canes arising from the trunk that you trained along the wires or across the arbor. They have been cut back to be 6–10 feet long and kept year after year as framework. They are now fatter, browner, and shaggy.

Head Prune. A system of pruning in which canes are cut back to the trunk, not scaffolds.

Trunk. The main trunk. Wood is thick and shaggy.

TRAINING A NEW GRAPEVINE

Support for a New Vine. The first 4 years of pruning are done to create a strong, compact framework for your vine. Too commonly I see grapevines being trained on thin posts with wire trellises. Be sure your main framework is sturdy: Use 4 x 4 posts or 3-inch pine buried deeply in the ground (or perhaps even set in concrete). Remember that it will eventually support the weight of a large, old, heavily grape-laden (as in, "oops, it got away from me") vine. Unless the vine rests on top of an overhead arbor (using a system of 2 × 4s), it will also need wires around which to wrap its tendrils and onto which you tie canes.

Space for a Grapevine. Give your vine a lot of room. Even with annual pruning they require at least 6–10 feet in which to grow. Early training of grapes doesn't make sense to the logical mind. The first winter after planting you cut the poor tiny thing down to as few as 2 buds from the ground (3–6 inches). This is done to force rapid regrowth and a strong trunk. The next spring it zooms up and sends out side branches. In the spring or summer you cut off the side branches and keep tying the main stem (or sometimes 2 stems) onto the stake to hold it up. Don't tie too tightly, or the ties might girdle the vine.

During the next winter, whack it back to half of its present size (about 2 feet). Really this is the way it's done! Let it grow through the summer. Gently tie it every 6 inches or so, as it grows up the post or stake. Again, remove side branches (shoots) and basal shoots (those coming from the base or ground level). When the vine finally reaches the lowest of the wire supports, allow 2 shoots (one on either side) to grow along the wire, tying them in place temporarily if need be.

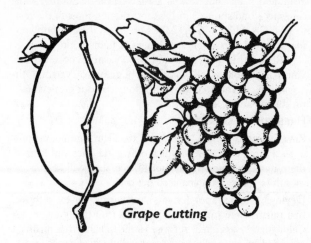
Grape Cutting

You now have a "trunk" and 2 scaffolds. They are the main framework for your plant. You will need to cut back your scaffolds the first year to about 10 buds (2 feet or so) just like you did the trunk. This forces them to become thick and sturdy and causes them to set up more buds close to where you'll want them. The shoots arising from the scaffolds are similarly cut back, becoming "fruiting arms" an inch or so long. Arms should be spaced about 6 inches to a foot apart on the scaffolds.

SYSTEMS OF PRUNING

Spur Pruning: When you spur prune, you cut back a cane until it has only 2 or 3 buds from the scaffold or fruiting arm. Do this in the winter. Spur prune canes, which are spaced every 6 inches or so apart along the scaffold, and cut off all other shoots and canes entirely. This keeps crowding down. The 2 buds will grow into new canes and set fruit next year. The next winter cut off the outer one of the 2 canes and shorten the other cane to 2 buds. Repeat annually.

This is the method used for most European varieties except Thompson Seedless (the most common supermarket grape). European grapes are Red Malaga, Ribier, Perlette, Muscat, Cardinal, Tokay, and California wine-type varieties.

Cane Pruning. This is also known as "renewal pruning." Some varieties won't set fruit if you spur prune all canes annually. These are the American grapes such as Delaware, Concord, Niagra, and Pierce, as well as the Thompson Seedless. These fruit form growth farther out on the cane. Therefore, you cut back half your canes (the newest ones) about 2–4-foot lengths (8 to 14 buds) every year. Wrap or tie the canes gently around the support wires. Cut the other half (meaning the older canes that bore fruit this last summer) way back, making them into spurs. This type of spurring is done to ensure a continued supply of canes that are close to the trunk or scaffolds.

The Shotgun Method. If you're like me, you are probably faced with an old tangled mop of a grapevine monster, and you have no idea what type it is. Try the shotgun method. Cut out 60 percent (or more) of the shoots and canes entirely back to bigger scaffolds or to the trunk. You follow each chosen victim with your eyes, cutting it in many places and unthreading it from the tangled mass. Keep an eye out for old, dead canes and cut them out too. Dead canes look, well . . . they look dead and dry. They have no live, plump buds along them, and they are light-weight.

What's left is the big fat trunk, the scaffolds you wish to keep, and many (but now far, far fewer) canes. Shorten some canes to 2 bud spurs (3 inches) and shorten most of the rest to 10 or 14 buds (2–6 feet). If it's on an overhead arbor, you may care to leave some canes longer as framework.

Repeat this procedure annually. By careful observation you may be able to tell which type of grape you've got. Otherwise this method should suffice to keep your grapevine producing and in check.

PRESERVING GRAPES

Raw Storage. Grapes, like pears, are a late summer crop—at least around here. If you pick only good ones and keep them in a cold, moderately moist place, they will keep a month or more. Catawba keep the best.

Drying. When grapes dry you have raisins. I used to think that raisins were some kind of tropical fruit that grew in California. It was a real surprise to me to learn that raisins are dried grapes and prunes are dried plums! Grapes are one of the harder fruits to dry—more difficult than any of the large pitted sorts, which are the easiest. Any sweet grape can be dried. Seedless varieties are obviously preferable. Good raisin varieties are the Thompson Seedless, Black Malaga, Black Thompson Seedless, and Muscat.

Making Raisins. Let your grapes ripen on the vines until they are sweet as you'd expect them to be before they start going bad. Then pick the branches, cluster by cluster. Spread them out in the sun to dry and turn them over occasionally. It may take a couple of weeks or so. Once the raisins are dried you can remove them from the stems for storage or store them on the stems as you prefer. Or you can dry seedless green grapes at 170°F for at least 24 hours in an oven.

Criss Wilhite, of Fresno, CA (the "raisin capital of the world"), wrote me: "We cut the grapes, lay them on [a lead- and dioxin-free] paper next to the vines. Then, days later, we turn them over. Then days after that, we roll them up in the paper. Since there is no dew here in summer, we don't have to cover them up. The hard part is stemming them! Last summer, we dried so many grapes that we ended up with 100 lb. of raisins. I put the raisins in baskets and sorted them out from the big stems and stuff. Then I bagged them in 2-lb. bags and stuck them in the freezer. (Since this is the agribusiness and grape center of the country, every grape-loving, pesticide-resistant bug imaginable winters over in raisins. Freezing is easier than oven-heating.) Whenever we need raisins I spill a bag out and empty it into a colander. I sort of knead the raisins around in it and the stems rub off and fall out. I do this until about 70 percent are stemmed. Then, I put them in a damp terry cloth towel, roll them up, and rub them around a bit. I do that twice. It gets a few more stems out, washes, and moistens the fruit. It all takes 20 minutes maximum. We eat 3 or 4 lb. a week! A hundred pounds a year isn't enough for us."

➣ *RAISIN SAUCE Cook ½ c. raisins in a little over ¼ c. water. When the raisins are soft, strain and reserve ¼ c. water drained from them. Combine ¾ c. brown sugar and the raisin water and cook together 5 minutes. Then add 2 t. butter and ½ t. vanilla. Mix, add raisins or not as you prefer, and serve warm.*

➣ *GRAPE JUICE The Concord and Catawba varieties are especially fine for juice, but you can make it from others, too. The key to enjoying homemade grape juice is knowing that you want to dilute your juice with water to taste when you serve it. The floating crystals are tartrate (cream of tartar). In grape juice you have a natural concentrate. If the grapes are ripe and sweet you don't need to add sugar. If you add more sugar to your grape juice you get the equivalent of a syrup.*

Use only sound, ripe grapes. Let them ripen on the vine, and after you pick them keep them out of the sun until you have a chance to pick off the stems and wash them. Mash the grapes with a potato masher or in a press. Cover the red grapes and Concord grapes with water and heat to 145°F. Don't heat white grapes. Put the pan contents in a cloth or fruit press. Work the sack gently so that you extract all the juice or just let it hang all night. If you want clearer juice let the extracted juice stand overnight in a cool place. Then pour off the top. The pulp will have settled to the bottom. If you have white grapes be careful not to crush the seeds. To can grape juice, use the recipe for canning apple juice. When serving the juice I dilute half and half with water. Early in the season the children don't care much for grape juice, but by about February when the apples are gone they really start to relish it, and I do too.

➣ *HOMEMADE FRUIT COCKTAIL Green grapes can be made into homemade fruit cocktail. Just cut your fruits small. Use whatever you have—strawberries, peaches and so on. Combine with a honey syrup and can or freeze. Although you never see grapes listed in regular canning lists they can be canned.*

Canning Grapes. Just remove the stems, pack in your jars, pour over hot syrup or even plain water. Process in a hot-water bath 15 minutes. I have a friend who has no freezer and whose family lives off their own produce. She cans quarts and quarts of whole grapes, strawberries, and raspberries every year.

➣ *SIMPLE CANNED GRAPES Into a clean sterile quart jar put 1 c. any kind of grape. Add 1 c. sugar or ½ c. hot honey. Fill the jar on up with boiling hot water and seal it. Takes about a month to be ready. Tastes good.*

Freezing Grapes. I used to think you couldn't freeze grapes because that's what I'd read, and I'd never tried different. Then a friend told me he freezes grapes and they freeze very well. He said he takes the grapes off the stem, washes them, and bags them up with no other treatment in plastic bags. He said that they were practically like fresh when thawed.

➣ *GRAPE PUNCH Combine the juice of 2 lemons and 1 orange, 2 c. grape juice, and 2 c. water. Sweeten to taste.*

➣ *GRAPE ICE Pulp 3 lb. grapes. I like the little green seedless ones. Then you can keep the pulps and skins in the syrup. If you are using seeded grapes you'll have to pick the seeds out and put the grapes through a sieve, in which case you'll lose a lot of good stuff and good time, too. Add ¼ c. (or more) honey and mash well. Freeze, stirring occasionally. It takes quite a while to freeze. Serve when it is barely beyond the "slush" stage. This is nice with a whipped cream topping, or plain.*

Kiwis

These have also been called "Chinese gooseberries." Kiwis started out in China, then got to New Zealand, and finally to California. Commercial size and quality patches can grow even in northern Washington. Kiwis grow on a grape-type vine, are large as a lemon, and have no connection with the regular gooseberry. The first importers of the fruit renamed them "kiwi fruit," and that's what they are called in American supermarkets.

Here's Cass's wisdom again: An interesting thing about kiwis is that most varieties are dioecious, meaning male and female flowers are on different plants. You need 1 male plant to service about 7 females. Of course, only the females will fruit. (Some newer cultivars are self-fruitful. Finding and planting one of these may save you a lot of room.) It may take from 2 to 8 years for a vine to begin producing. Kiwis also need a long summer to ripen on the vine. In short season climates like mine [Pacific Northwest], we pick the fruit after the first frost and ripen it inside in a cool storage area.

PRUNING KIWI VINES: Kiwis are like grapes in many respects—only more so. Their growth is so extensive that summer pruning is essential, as often as once a month, to keep the vine from running down the block and covering your neighbor's house and trees. They need even more room to live than grapes (10 by 16 feet on an arbor, 3 by 16 feet as an espalier). Prune them in the winter as well.

Early training for kiwis is similar to that for grapes. Prevent the main stem from twisting around its support stake. Once mature, kiwis are pruned a lot like "spur-type" grapes. In the winter cut back all of the new rampant growth to the original spur system, only a little farther out. This means that you will cut to 2 or 3 buds beyond where it last fruited. However, your spur system will eventually get old and crowded. You will need to renew it by cutting it back severely or starting it over by cutting back to the scaffolds.

Passion Fruit

This wonderful perennial and evergreen vine from Brazil will grow only in a hot, humid subtropical zone. It can endure a brief light frost, but that's it. Because it will grow in a container you have that option also, pruning to keep it the size you need. The flowers are unusual and very beautiful. It grows quickly and generously produces fruit in 2 years. The vine can climb as high as 30 feet. There are several varieties, some better for flowers, others for fruit. The fruit will be mature about 3 months after the flower bloomed. *Passiflora edulis* fruits from summer through fall. Passion fruit has an outer juicy orange pulp and seeds in the middle. You can juice it for any juice use: punch, syrup, jelly. Seeds are available from Southern Seeds. Several varieties, guaranteed down to 25 or 26°F, are offered by Pacific Tree Farms.

Bramble, Bush, and Other Tiny Fruits

It's a good idea to have several varieties of berries, as well as a good orchard. Your first strawberries will bear in June. Raspberries mature in July. Blackberries and wild berries are on in August and September. You will have berries all summer long.

BERRY PICKING: When you pick berries that have thorns, wear long stockings with the feet whacked off—not nylons—or some similar heavy protection on your arms so you won't get too badly scratched. A leather belt around your waist with a half-gallon can hanging on it is handy, and then you can empty the berries into a big bucket when the little one is full. Don't worry about leaves and such when you're picking. You can put the berries in water when you get home, and leaves will float to the top; you can just scoop them away.

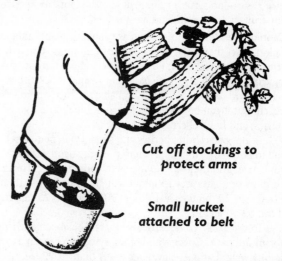

Cut off stockings to protect arms

Small bucket attached to belt

RUNNER REPRODUCTION: Strawberries and many other berries reproduce by "runner." Strawberry runners travel on top of the ground, then stop about a foot away from the parent plant, put down roots and become a new, independent strawberry plant. You just whack the connection, dig up the independent plant, and reset it in your ground where you want it.

BERRIES FOR FREE: When gardening neighbors are cleaning out unwanted berry runners in the spring and cutting back perennials, they can give you all the good starts you'll need if you just give them advance notice that you would like to have them. They have to dig them out anyway from between their rows, and if they didn't give them to you then they would throw the starts away. Berry plants planted from suckers bear no fruit the first year; they will bear fruit the second year.

NURSERY STARTS: If you can't get berry and grape starts from neighbors, buy from your local nurseryman rather than by mail-order, unless you live someplace where there are no plant nurseries and mail-order is the only answer. Almost all the big catalog seed houses carry a wide selection of berry cuttings, but some specialize in them.

BASIC BERRY AND TINY FRUIT RECIPES: If you have some unusual kind of berries or small fruit for which you can't find specific recipes (there are umpteen different kinds of berries), just substitute in recipes that call for a similar fruit because they are very similar except for the sweetness/tartness, which you can taste-test and add more or less sweetening as needed. For preservation methods, experiment! It may be better to freeze or can. Or make leather. You have to find out.

DRYING BERRIES: Dried berries may not be as agreeable to eat out of hand as the larger fruits, especially seeded berries. Even unseeded ones may turn out quite tough, dry, and full of seeds. But there's an old man who lives near here who dries lots of berries just like his mother did before him when they wintered mostly on dried food. He soaks his dried berries in water and then they make fine pies!

❧ BERRY LEATHER Puree your berries some way or another. Putting them in a blender works. Add 1 T. honey per 1½ c. berry puree and proceed with drying.

Freezing Berries. For nicest taste and texture, I like my larger fruits canned, and my berries frozen. I just pick, bag, and freeze—no syrup or liquid at all. Same for any berry or tiny fruit. It saves work and mess too.

Canning Berries. Process them as soon as possible after picking. Get them ready by hulling or stemming. *Can only firm berries with no mold.* Put in a sieve and wash by swishing them through a pan of cold water several times. Strawberries tend to lose their color and aren't as nice canned as frozen, but it can be done. Blackberries, blueberries, gooseberries, and huckleberries can nicely.

To hot pack, bring berries and sugar (½ c. per quart) to boil in covered pan. Shake pan to prevent sticking. Pack hot berries and their juice. Process in boiling water. Times for pints or quarts are: 15 minutes at elevations lower than 1,000 feet; 20 minutes at 1,001–6,000 feet; and 25 minutes above 6,000 feet.

To raw pack, pack berries into jars. Shake jar gently to obtain full pack. Cover with boiling syrup. Process in a boiling water bath: At elevations lower than 1,000 feet, 15 minutes for pints, 20 for quarts; at 1,001–3,000 feet, 20 minutes for pints, 25 for quarts; at 3,001–6,000 feet, 25 minutes for pints, 30 for quarts; at 6,000 feet or higher, 30 minutes for pints, 35 for quarts.

❧ BASIC BERRY JUICE The general rule—except for strawberries (which aren't heated)—is to wash, crush, heat to 175°F and extract the juice. Can by instructions for apple juice.

❧ BASIC BERRY JAM Weigh hulled and washed berries. Weigh out an equal amount of sugar. Mash berries and set to cook over low heat—but not in an aluminum pan. Bring to boil slowly with frequent stirring. Add sugar. Simmer until thick, stirring often enough so jam doesn't start to stick and burn on the bottom. Pour into hot clean jars. Process in a boiling water bath 5 minutes.

❧ OMELETS WITH BERRIES Beat up 2 or 3 eggs until just blended but not frothy. Melt 1 t. butter in a clean frying pan. Pour half the egg mixture into skillet for your first omelet. Stir around once and then stir by shaking the pan. When the omelet is done put it on a serving dish. Pour ½ c. fresh berries onto it. Fold over. Top with whipped cream and a few more berries, and do your other omelet with another ½ c. berries and whipped cream.

❧ BASIC BERRY SYRUP In a nonaluminum pan, mix together 2 c. berry juice and 3 c. sugar. Cook over low heat until all the sugar is in solution. In a separate small saucepan combine ½ c. water with ½ bottle liquid pectin or ½ box pectin. Boil 3–5 minutes, stirring constantly. Stir pectin mixture into the juice mixture and refrigerate until ready to use. Your result will be a basic pancake-type syrup.

❧ BUSY WOMAN'S BERRY JUICE (Blackberry, raspberry, gooseberry, and the like.) This stretches the berries as far as possible. Put your berries in a kettle. Cover with water and boil 5 minutes. Drain off the juice and save it. Cover the

berries again with water, boil 5 minutes. Drain off the juice and save it. Cover the berries again with water, boil 5 minutes more, drain again and save the juice. Squeeze the seeds and stuff left if you want. Boil again if you think it would help. You can use your busy woman's berry juice as a base for jelly or for juice. Each successive boiling will make a lighter-colored juice. Sweeten to taste.*

❧ WONDERFUL BERRY DRINK Boil 2 qt. water with 1½ c. sugar or ¾ c. honey for 3 minutes. Then crush 2 qt. raspberries, blackberries, or strawberries and pour the hot syrup over the fruit. Cool. Strain. Add 1 c. lemon juice and ice cubes, and serve.

Brambles: Red and Black Raspberries and Blackberries

PRUNING BRAMBLES: The pruning of brambles is different from that of trees. Since new fruit grows on new canes yearly, you do a fair amount of complete pruning: that is, removing entire canes that have already produced their crop. Every year blackberries send up new shoots from their root systems. The size of these canes by the end of the summer depends on local conditions: soil, moisture, and light. But fruit is borne on these canes only in the following year, largely on lateral branches, which grow during the spring of the second season before flowering. In the wild, after these canes finish bearing, their leaves die and discolor, and the dead canes stand in place until they slowly fall over, decay, and rot. If a stand is particularly thick, it will soon become choked with those used up canes. If you keep the berry patch clean of dead and dying canes, you can significantly extend the life of a good stand. And the amount of fruiting wood available can be increased significantly by pruning. If you head back the top of the canes the first spring, the plant will put all its energy during the second season into the lateral branches, the ones that produce the fruit. Furthermore, blackberries under cultivation can be spaced and trained in such a way that a careful picker will not be so scratched up by the thorns. When pruning out at the end of a season, cut the canes on the ground, but do not pull them down to remove them. Cut them all off in an area at once, then stand up and lift out the canes—less tearing of leaves on the new canes that will bear next year's fruit.

BLACKBERRIES: They grow wild and they grow tame. They are called "blackberries" and they are called umpteen other names like "dewberry" and "thimbleberry," "black raspberry," "flymboy," "wineberry," "nagoonberry," "cloudberry," "wild raspberry," "salmonberry," "blackcap," and "bake-apple." The line of distinction between blackberries and raspberries in the wild isn't very clear, and there are so many different varieties with so many different sizes and colors—suffice it to say they are all good to eat. If you live where they grow abundantly you have a wonderful ready-made free source of small fruit. Blackberries make good out-of-hand eating and good jam and jelly. You can make a hedge of blackberries. If you pick them prematurely they won't be as sweet as later on. Let them stay on the bush until they are really, really ripe, and then they will be sweet and not sour tasting. The "dewberry" variety of blackberry has huge beautiful berries but it isn't as winter hardy as some others. You can propagate blackberries by the volunteer suckers that grow or by root cuttings. Vine-type blackberries like youngberries, boysenberries, dewberries, and loganberries seldom sucker but can be propagated by leaf bud cuttings, except for some fancy thornless varieties. If you took a root cutting of an improved thornless variety, the new plant would revert to the old thorny kind. A 2-inch segment is enough of a root cutting to plant.

❧ *BLACKBERRY SYRUP Crush well-ripened blackberries and add one-fourth as much boiling water as you have berries. Let stand 24 hours, stirring frequently. Strain. Add 1 c. sugar for each quart of juice and boil slowly for 15 minutes or until you have the density you want, and then can it.*

❧ *LOGANBERRY ALE Combine 1 c. loganberry juice, the juice and grated rind of 4 lemons, 1 c. sugar, 2 c. ginger ale, and 3 c. water. Let stand a couple hours to mellow. Garnish each glass with a mint sprig and a lemon slice.*

❧ *LOGANBERRY SPECIAL Combine 2 c. loganberry juice, 1 c. raspberry juice, 1 c. lemon juice, and 3 crushed mint leaves. Mix and serve over crushed ice.*

RASPBERRIES: These, like blackberries, are a very soft berry. The soft berries do better frozen than canned because they cook up so easily. They make good jam, jelly, sauce, and juice, too, but are nicest of all fresh. Raspberry plants don't last forever. A started raspberry row will last 7–10 years. So after the fifth year start a new row so it will be growing berries when the old one starts slowing up. Raspberries now come in black, red, or yellow. Most varieties will bear only once on a cane so you prune by cutting out old canes after they have fruited. But there is one kind of raspberry now that will bear fruit 2 years in a row before stopping on any particular cane.

❧ *RASPBERRY JUICE Use fully ripe, juicy berries. Wash in cold water and drain. Crush and heat the berries slightly to start the flow of juice. Strain in a jelly bag to get the juice.*

❧ *RASPBERRY-APPLE JUICE Combine half raspberry juice and half apple juice.*

❧ *RASPBERRY-MINT DRINK Combine 1 c. sugar or ½ c. honey, 1 c. water, and the grated rind of 2 lemons. Cook, stirring over low heat until your sweetening is dissolved. Boil 5 minutes more. Cool. Add 2 c. crushed raspberries, 1 c. lemon juice, and 4 c. water. Serve with some mint leaves in the bottom of the glass (and in the pitcher) and a mint leaf on top.*

The Non-Bramble Berries

BARBERRIES

❧ *BARBERRY JUICE Use cranberry juice recipe.*

BLUEBERRIES: These need an acidic soil. If they have that, you have a wonderful berry that may bear fruit the first year and for the next 50, but if they don't have that soil they will die and that's all there is to it. St. Lawrence Nurseries offers numerous varieties of half-high blueberries. You can prune blueberries only very lightly. Blueberries don't really have "canes," just twigs. In all but the far north, do what judicious cutting you must in late winter. You'll find lots more resources in ATTRA's "Organic Blueberry Production" at **www.attra.org/attra-pub/blueberry.html.**

❧ *BLUEBERRY SAUCE Start with 1 c. blueberries. Put half the blueberries and ½ c. water into a pan. Simmer 3 minutes. Add 1 t. cornstarch and stir thoroughly. Continue cooking, stirring constantly, until thick. Then add the other half of the berries and cook 3 minutes more. Add 2 T. lemon juice.*

❧ *BLUEBERRY SYRUP Combine 1 c. fresh (or frozen or canned) blueberries, ½ c. water, and ¼ c. sugar, and bring to a boil. Crush berries. Simmer 2 or 3 minutes more. Serve this syrup hot.*

Drying. Dry blueberries out of doors 2 sunny days in a row, then in the oven at low heat until they are rubbery and look like raisins.

CRANBERRIES

❧ *CRANBERRY JUICE Cook 1 lb. cranberries in 1 qt. water until soft. Crush and drain through cheesecloth for a nice clear juice.*

❧ *CRANBERRY COCKTAIL Grind 4 c. cranberries in your food chopper. Add 1 c. sugar to 6 c. water. Add the ground cranberries and their juice and boil all for 5 minutes. Cool and strain. Add 1 c. orange juice and the juice of 1 lemon. Chill.*

❧ *CRANBERRY ICE Heat 1 qt. cranberries and 2 c. water together, boiling until the cranberries are soft. Run through a sieve. Add 2 c. brown sugar to puree. Heat again, stirring until the sugar is dissolved. Add the juice of 1 orange. Remove from heat. Cool. Pour into tray and freeze firm. Remove to chilled bowl and beat until light. Return to tray and finish freezing without stirring. Serve at slush stage.*

❧ *CRANBERRY KETCHUP Wash and pick over 2½ lb. cranberries. Cover with vinegar and cook until they burst. Force through a sieve. Add 2⅔ c. sugar, 1 T. cinnamon, and 1 t. ground cloves. Return to heat and simmer until thick. Pour into hot sterilized jars and seal.*

❧ *SWEET CRANBERRY "RAISINS" Saute cranberries in brown sugar and butter until the skins break. Add a little honey and stir. The secret is the broken skin that allows the sweetness from the brown sugar and honey to get inside the cranberry. Then dehydrate. It takes a lot of cranberries to make a little bag of cranberry raisins.*

CURRANTS: This small fruit went through a time of trouble in the 1920s when bushes were uprooted and became very rare as a result. Certain varieties of currants and gooseberries were supposed to carry white-pine blister rust, a disease that destroyed white pine trees. Many states passed laws banning currants and gooseberries, and seed catalogs stopped carrying them. Now currants are making a comeback. Legal restrictions on them are being lifted, and increasing numbers of nurseries are carrying them again.

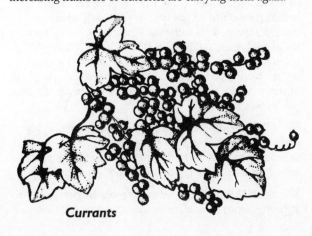

Currants

That's good news, because currants and gooseberries are among the hardiest of the berries and are important to folks who live on mountainsides. Currants are a firm berry as compared to the blackberry. They are easy to propagate by stem cuttings, and I know people who have raised them from seed. Take cuttings about 8 inches long anytime during the fall, winter, or very early spring. They won't do quite as well if you start them after growth has got going in the spring. They do well in a clay soil. It's still a good idea not to plant currants if there are white pines (pines with needles growing in clusters of 5) within 300 yards. And check your local laws to make sure you aren't in an area where it's still illegal to plant them.

Drying. Put your currants into a large bowl and add some flour (about ½ c. per 1 lb. of currants). Mix the flour with the currants and then rub the currants between your hands to get the stems off. After the stems are off, put the currants in a colander and let water stream through them until you have nothing left but currants. Then scald them a half minute, and chill by drenching again with cold water. Drain. Spread on pie dishes, trays, and so on, and put out in the sun or on your screen or into the oven to dry. They are like little raisins when done.

❧ *CURRANT JUICE Choose fully ripe, bright red currants. Wash in cold water and remove stems. Crush the currants and warm to 165°F to start the flow of juice. Don't boil. Press the hot fruit in a jelly bag to extract juice. Sweeten to taste.*

❧ *BLACK CURRANT PUNCH To each cup of currant juice add 2 c. weak green tea. Sweeten to taste. Serve in glasses half filled with chopped ice and garnish with a sprig of mint.*

❧ *CURRANT SYRUP Boil 3 c. sugar with 4 c. water until the sugar is dissolved, then add 4 c. cooked, strained currant juice and the juice of 6 lemons. Cool and bottle. This is nice to add color to other drinks.*

❧ *CURRANT KETCHUP Combine 4 lb. ripe currants, 2 c. vinegar, 1 T. cinnamon, 1 t. salt, 3½ c. sugar, 1 T. cloves, and 1 t. pepper. Mix, boil down to a thick sauce, and bottle.*

GOOSEBERRIES: These went through the same thing as currants and became very uncommon. Berry gooseberries grow on a low berry-type bush. For "Chinese gooseberries," see "Kiwi" in the vines section. Regular gooseberries are another tiny berry-type fruit.

Harvesting. When gooseberries are green they are still underripe. They turn kind of purple red at the moment of ripeness. There is a wide variety of sizes, from tiny on up. In my experience they either have to be picked before the berries get too ripe or you have to cope with worms in them. It's the same as with peas. The insects "sting" them—make black spots on the outside, which, if left long enough, hatch into worms. If you have a sturdy stomach you can use the wormy gooseberries. I set them on to cook in plenty of water. As the berries heat, the worms rise to the top and can be skimmed off.

❧ *GOOSEBERRY SAUCE Stew ½ lb. gooseberries in ½ c. water until soft. Rub through a sieve. Return to pan. Add sweetening to taste and 1 T. butter if you are planning to serve it as a relish with roast goose, duck, or mutton.*

❧ *GOOSEBERRY FOOL Simmer green gooseberries, starting with cold water, until tender, adding a little salt (optional)*

to preserve the color. Strain and puree. Put the puree on the heat with sugar to taste and cook until sugar is dissolved. To serve, mix with cream.

❧ *GOOSEBERRY JAM Cook 4½ c. gooseberries in 2 T. water over medium low heat until yellow. Add 2 c. sugar. Bring to a boil again and boil 5 minutes. Pour in jars and seal. You'll get 2 pt. jam.*

❧ *GOOSEBERRY PIE Cook 3 c. fresh gooseberries just long enough so they pop. Add 1½ c. sugar, ½ t. ground nutmeg, and 4 T. flour. Pour onto a prepared unbaked piecrust. Put second crust on and seal well to keep from boiling over. Put slits on top. Brush top with cream and sprinkle sugar on it. Bake about 45 minutes at 425°F, or until it looks cooked. Good with plain cream.*

HUCKLEBERRIES: These are cousins of the blueberry—a small, firm berry.

Canning. These can nicely. Use basic canned berry recipe. If you can huckleberries, make sure your jars are sealed and you wash the outsides because they tend to give off an odor that other foods pick up.

❧ *BASIC HUCKLEBERRY SAUCE You'll need 1 c. huckleberries, ¼ c. sugar, 1 t. water, 2 T. light corn syrup, 2 T. berry juice, 1 T. cornstarch, and 2 t. lemon juice. Place berries in a pan. Add sugar, water, and corn syrup. Bring to a boil. Blend berry juice and cornstarch and add to berries, stirring constantly. Cook until thickened. Stir in lemon juice and remove from heat. Chill. Good for jelly roll, open-face pie, cooked pie shell, or topping for ice cream.*

❧ *HUCKLEBERRY PIE Make dough for a 2-crust pie. Boil, drain, and rinse 2 c. huckleberries, then cook again with a very little water until tender. Add sweetening to taste and 2 T. flour. Bake in a 425°F oven.*

❧ *HUCKLEBERRY CAKE Barbara Stone, Stites, ID, wrote me: "I don't care for huckleberries raw but in a cake is something else. Separate 3 eggs. Beat the whites until stiff and set aside. Beat the egg yolks and blend with ¼ cup milk. Blend in 1 cup sugar and ½ cup butter or other shortening. Sift 1½ cups flour with 1 teaspoon baking powder, ¼ t. nutmeg, ½ t. cinnamon and add to egg yolk mixture. The batter will be unusually stiff. Put berries into flat dish and roll in flour. Up to this point an electric beater can be used, but now the berries are folded into the batter with a spoon. Then fold in the beaten egg whites. Bake in a greased and floured [8-inch square] pan. A loaf pan is better so the batter doesn't spread too thin. Sprinkle the entire top of the cake with a thin coating of sugar. This will form a glaze. No frosting is necessary. Bake in a moderate oven (350°F) until done. Depending on the oven it usually takes 50–60 minutes."*

SALAL: This Pacific Coast native, *Gaultheria shallon*, is an evergreen shrub, 2–6 feet high, and can thrive in either sun or shade. It can grow from mid-California to British Columbia. It needs moist soil.

Planting. Plant seeds, cuttings, or divisions. You can get plants from Raintree Nursery, 391 Butts Rd, Morton, WA 98356.

Harvesting. Pick the small bluish-black berries in the fall when the whole cluster has finished ripening. You can substitute in any blueberry recipe or use to make a jelly.

SALAL JELLY *You'll need 1 c. salal juice, 1 c. tart apple juice, and 1 c. sugar. (See "Jelly-Making" in Chapter 7.)*

SARVIS BERRIES OR SASKATOON BERRIES: Eaten fresh, these are bland and flavorless, but put them in pancakes. When the heat hits them, the flavor comes out. Or use them as a filler with other berries. Or add lots of grated orange and orange juice to add flavor.

STRAWBERRIES: These plants want lots of moisture and a sort of shady location, like on the shady side of your house or under an orchard. Next edition I'm going to say more about them, but no time now. Krohne Plant Farms is a mail-order strawberry specialist: 616-424-5423; fax 616-424-3126; 65295 CR 342, Hartford, MI 49057. If you're interested in growing them for sale, you'll find much more info in "Strawberries: Organic and IPM Options" at **www. attra.org/attra-pub/strawberry.html.**

Preserving. Imogene says, "Just let them boil up once, then pour into jars and seal." That's Imogene's way and she cans umpteen quarts every summer. To can strawberries the regular way, pack them hot, cover with hot juice, and process 15 minutes. I freeze them. Dried strawberries are delicious tasting, despite the fact that they turn very dark and look terrible.

STRAWBERRY JUICE *Use fully ripe berries. Wash in cold water. Drain. Remove anything green. Crush and strain the juice through a jelly bag.*

STRAWBERRY PUNCH *Mash 1 qt. strawberries. Add the juice of 1 lemon, 2 T. orange juice, and 6 c. water, and let the mixture stand 3 hours. Strain. Sweeten to taste. Serve with ice.*

STRAWBERRY-PINEAPPLE JUICE *Combine 2 c. strawberry juice, 1 c. pineapple juice, 4 c. water, ½ c. lemon juice, and ⅓ c. honey. Mix well and serve with ice.*

OVERNIGHT STRAWBERRY PRESERVES *Wash and hull firm, choice berries. Combine 2 c. sugar with 1 c. water and boil until you can spin a thread when you hold a spoon up that has been dipped into the liquid. Now gently add 4 c. strawberries, ¼ c. lemon juice, and 2 c. more sugar. Boil 12 minutes without stirring. If you get a scum, skim it off. Pour the mixture out into a shallow pan and let set 24 hours. Put into jars cold and seal with paraffin. The berries keep their shape and color.*

MODERN PRESERVES *Prepare 4 half-pint jars. Heat 1 c. of your juice to boiling. Then pour it over ¼ c. fresh herb (or 1½ T. dried herb) or 2 T. whole spice. Let soak for half hour. Strain it into a nonaluminum pan. Add 2 c. more of juice, 2 T. vinegar, and 3 c. sugar, mix, and boil (stirring constantly). Now mix in ½ bottle pectin, and boil another minute, still stirring. Remove from heat, and stir in food coloring at this point if you want it. Pour immediately into sterilized jelly glasses. Adjust lids. Process 5 minutes.*

OLD-TIME PRESERVES *Prepare jars to hold 10 cups. Coarsely chop 6 lb. tart apples, put into nonaluminum pan, add just enough water to cover, and cook a half an hour, or to softness. Then pour into jelly bag over bowl and let it drain overnight. Next day, measure the juice. Per 2½ c. juice, add 2 c. sugar. Stir sugar into solution over low heat. Add herbs or spices, or a mixture of them, tied into a porous bag, and simmer until jelling point is reached. Remove bag and pour into jars.*

STRAWBERRY SHERBET *Soften 1 envelope unflavored gelatin in 1 c. orange juice in a small pan. Combine 1 qt. washed, hulled, and crushed strawberries with ½ c. sugar, and then stir in gelatin–orange-juice mixture. Pour into your freezer tray. Freeze, stirring once or twice, until almost firm. Remove to chilled bowl, break up with a fork and then beat until smooth but not melted. Fold in 2 stiffly beaten egg whites, blend, and return to refrigerator. Freeze, stirring once in a while with a fork, until firm.*

WOOD HEAT
Managing an Existing Stand of Trees

If you are starting your forest or orchard management career with an existing stand of trees, the first thing to do is to get acquainted with them. What kind are they? What are their uses? You may choose to leave them exactly as is. Or, to do some tree weeding, taking out some in order to replace them with more needed ones, yet retaining a mixture of trees for many different purposes and products. Or you may want to take the existing trees out and start over, specializing and growing a plantation of all the same kind of tree. When you are planting a tree crop, you're usually planting for a maturity date or a market year one or more decades away, so think long-term.

Horse logging does the least environmental damage to big tracts. Read *Work Horse Tales: Adventures in the Forests of Appalachia*, by Anita G. Mannon, for glimpses of the life-style of folks working with draft horse partners in the forests of the Blue Ridge Mountains today: 888-795-4274; PO Box 689, Floyd, VA 24091; **www.xlibris.com/book store.**

Reforestation

You don't have to prepare the soil by cultivation to plant forest-type trees. If trees are planted 5 feet apart (right for a 6-foot-high tree), you can grow 1,000–1,300 per acre. Each tree needs sunlight to live, so plant in the open spots. Two people can plant a huge number of trees in just a single long, hard-working day, using no more equipment than a spade. (There is such a thing, however, as a mechanical tree planter.) But don't expect all of them to survive; a percentage won't make it and will need to be replaced (maybe up to 30 percent, but probably much less).

MULCH COLLARS: You can raise the survival rate dramatically (up to 90 percent) by installing a heavy cardboard circle (available from printing-press shops) at least 36 inches in diameter, with a center cut out plenty wide for the tree, around the tree base. Or make a mulch out of newspaper or weed-block mats. But the heavy cardboard circles do the best job of protecting seedlings from competition from weeds and brush. Just make sure that what you install isn't in a position to girdle the tree (cut a seedling hole in the middle), is of a material that will eventually decompose (cardboard or paper), and has a system to let water through (cut slots for that). The mulch mat must be anchored using wood slash or rocks heavy enough to keep it from blowing off or slipping over on top of the baby tree. If the mulch protection lasts 3 years, by the fourth the tree is usually far enough developed to survive no matter what. Shaded lower branches may wither, die, and eventually fall off. That's okay. Actually, a long "clean" trunk is desirable for lumber.

WOODLOT GROWING INFORMATION: To grow enough wood to stay even with the appetite of a wood-burning stove is a grand achievement in itself. For more help, read *The Earth Manual* by Malcolm Margolin, an inspiring book about how to work with wild land without taming it. It covers tree-felling, tree-doctoring (why not to), erosion control, seed collecting and planting, pruning, etc. You can order the pamphlets "Woodlot Management" and "Fast-Growing Firewood" from Storey's, 802-823-5810; www.storey.com. *Working with Your Woodlot* by Mollie Beattie, Lynn Levine, and Charles Thompson covers hardwood forests in the northern U.S. and mountainous South.

GROWING CHRISTMAS TREES OR TIMBER EVERGREENS: If you don't need pasture and your land is on the poor side but still gets enough rainfall or can be irrigated for evergreens, a market option is to plant Christmas trees. They'll grow on cool, north-facing hillsides that fruit trees might not do so well on. They'll be harvested while still reasonably small so no big equipment is necessary. And your investment can be quite reasonable. Plan to space your Christmas trees an average 5 feet apart for a 6–7-foot harvest size. (If you will harvest smaller, plant closer.) To make more efficient use of your space, plant small trees between each pair of large trees 2 years before harvest time for the big ones.

GATHERING TREE SEED: You can gather cones, dry them, shake the seeds out, freeze them for conditioning, plant in seedling pots, then transplant them when they're bigger. Or you can plant seedlings . . .

COLLECTING SEEDLINGS: You could collect these from forests (but don't steal). Gather in early spring when they are 5–15 inches high. Dig or pull out (only when the ground is very moist), being careful to preserve their root system. Bundle, transport, and replant in your field. It's best if you can pull and replant them in the same day. You may want to save space and grow them for a couple years in a nursery bed before setting them out in the field.

NURSERY SEEDLINGS: Or you can buy seedling trees from a nursery. Buy locally if possible, or from a nursery in your same climate zone. Trees grown in a warmer climate than yours will tend to start growing in the spring by their old calendar rather than your new one and possibly be killed by frosts. To buy seedlings, learn what kind of trees are available, how much they cost, and how many years they've grown in the seed bed and then in the transplant bed. Some states have tree nurseries and sell seedlings reasonably from them. (A state extension agent can inform you on this.) Here are nurseries that specialize in woodsy seedling trees:

Carino Nurseries specializes in seedling Christmas trees and other evergreens: 800-223-7075; fax 412-463-3050; Box 538, Indiana, PA 15701.

Musser Forests: 800-643-8319; fax 724-465-9893; PO Box 340, Indiana, PA 15701-0340.

Pikes Peak Nurseries: 412-463-7747; R.D. 1, Box 75, Penn Run, PA 15765.

Why they're all in Pennsylvania is a mystery to me.

Harvesting Wood

Foresters harvest trees for their wood before they become over-mature or die. Plain folks find good uses for dead wood in the stove. Either way, every block of wood represents a concentration of sunlight's energy ready to be released by fire.

February is an awful time to be out scouting for wood. The wood is best gotten during the fine dry days of mid-summer and early fall. Old-timers say that if you fell the tree while the sap is still in the leaves, the trunk will be dryer and easier to cut.

Finding Your Wood. Any tree is owned by somebody—a rancher, a homesteader, a corporation, or a government agency and, by extension, the public. Anywhere outside your own property, you need permission before you cut firewood. The U.S. Forest Service and the Bureau of Land Management look after a lot of the public woods and will, in many areas, readily grant you a permit to cut 10 cords or so, if you give them $10. You can get your permit at any Forest Service District Office or at any B.L.M. office. Some states (e.g., Montana) will give you a free permit to cut firewood on land managed by them. Be sure you know exactly where the state-owned trees are before cutting it. To cut wood on privately owned land, ask permission first. Owners can become very angry, and justifiably so, if you enter and cut without permission. That's trespassing and theft. If you can't find the owner, leave the wood alone. Large corporate landowners often offer paid permits available at the corporations' offices. There will be a strict set of guidelines you must follow when cutting their wood.

Choosing the Tree. Every variety of tree is different. They look different and are of differing hardness, burning style, sawing and splitting quality, even aroma in the forest and in the fire. Softwoods, such as pine and cedar, have a coarse fiber that burns quickly. They make good kindling. Pine is very pitchy. You can tell a pitchy wood in the fire because it does a lot of noisy popping. For a long-term steady fire, especially for oven-baking, hardwood (or coal) are nicest. It really depends on what trees are available to you. Some woods provide you with beech, yellow-birch, maple, and black-cherry, and those all make fine wood, too. Another consideration might be ease of sawing if you're working by handsaw rather than chain saw . Balsam is especially hard to hand-saw. Yellow birch takes less effort to saw than maple. Or consider ease of splitting; maple splits cleaner than the birch. Or whether it will burn green or has to be well dried; yellow birch will burn green.

Tree felling is dangerous if you aren't experienced, so proceed cautiously. First find the one you want. Standing dead tamarack, red fir, or black pine are the best in this part of the country. White and yellow pine are fairly good. Cedar's good for a hot quick fire to set off harder woods but it doesn't last. Bull pine, white fir, or any spruce are not very good firewood but will do if you can't find anything else. It's ideal to find a snag (dead tree) that still has bark and branches on it. The bark and branches show that it hasn't been dead too long and hasn't had time to rot. Or a blow-down with bark and branches will be all right if it's not too wet. Use green wood (live wood) only if you have cut it and let it season at least 6 months to dry out well.

Chain Saws. To cut down a tree it's most convenient to use a chain saw. You can do it with an ax, but if your tree is big enough to bother cutting down at all that's a pretty big struggle. A 12-inch chain saw is cheaper, lighter, and easier to handle than a 16-inch one, but it won't cut as big a tree. In general, a chain saw can handle a tree with a diameter almost twice the length of its blade, though if you really know what you're doing you can stretch that. You've got to oil it all the time you're sawing by a squirt attachment. You get a round file that is the same size as the teeth on your saw and file them sharp between sawings. The rakers on the chain also have to be filed down regularly. Different wood conditions require different heights for the rakers. Sawing frozen wood is different, too.

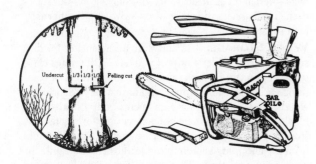

You need a manual or somebody who knows what he's doing to help you get started with a chain saw. Hang on to your chain-saw warranty. They break down a lot, especially the cheaper brands. The big ones are used by sawyers who are felling trees on a professional scale. The chain saw runs by a gasoline motor. Once in a while you can get a new one on sale for as low as $125. The lighter saws are cheaper and won't wear you out near as fast. For more information, see *Chainsaw Savvy* by Neil Soderstrom, which covers cutting, sharpening, and repairing a chain saw. Great on safety, cutting form, kickback protection, safest refueling, felling, limbing, bucking, and moving logs. Also read *The Good Woodcutter's Guide,* by Johnson, which covers chain saws, portable sawmills, and woodlots (Chelsea Green). Log splitters, chain saws, heaters, and more are available from Northern Tool & Equipment Co.: 800-533-5545; fax 952-894-1020; PO Box 1219, 2800 Southcross Dr., Burnsville, MN 55337; **www.NorthernTool.com.** A portable sawmill can cut a tree into 2 x 4s or 4 x 6s. Cost is about $12,000. I know four families who each put in $3,000 to buy one and soon earned their money back.

Cutting Down the Tree. A personal safety guideline for you to hold is to never go into the woods to fell trees alone, no matter how good you are. People get killed that way, or

they get hurt and have nobody to help them. If you've never cut firewood before, the best way to learn how is to go out together with somebody who has done it a lot.

Decide which way you want the tree to fall. You'll have to take into consideration which way it's leaning already. I don't know any way to make a tree fall uphill from a decided lean. If possible, you want to knock it down toward the road so you won't have to haul the pieces so far. Try not to fell it uphill because it might bounce back downhill when it hits and hurt somebody. Cut a wedge from the side of the tree where you want it to fall, sawing up toward the center of the tree from the ground angle and down toward the center of the tree from the sky direction. The V-shaped cut should have its point one-third of the way into the tree. That's important. The wedge should be about a 30° angle. Remove the wedge of wood.

Now saw from the opposite side of the tree with your cut on a line to meet the point of the "V." Go slowly the last few inches and when things start to creak and clatter get the heck out of there. The tree should be starting to topple over toward the "V."

You'll be about one-third of the way in from the other side when it starts to go. On trees over a couple feet in diameter you should use a wedge. Hammer the wedge in after you get the cut deep enough to take it. As you saw deeper, hammer the wedge in deeper. When you get one-third of the way in, take the saw out and keep hammering the wedge in until the tree falls. Usually the fellows here use a regular "felling" plastic wedge. You can buy them at a saw shop.

Bucking. Once the tree is on the ground you can finish wherever you want to. First you take off the limbs—"limb" it. Sawing it up into chopping-size segments is the next step, and that's called "bucking." If you have a big logging truck you can load the whole log up and take it home, or you can saw it up on the spot and take chunks home. Know how long a piece your stove takes (a little shorter than the length of the firebox). That's how long your segments should be. You can buck with a roaring chain saw and it'll be done in a jiff. Or you can do it with an old-time 2-man crosscut saw together with a friend, spend a little more time, and have a pleasant conversation while you work. The rhythm of working with a 2-man crosscut saw is something you learn with experience. After the bucking, folks usually leave the chunks in a big heap to dry some more before chopping.

Chopping. Before the wood is stove-ready, the segments have to be split with an ax—double-bladed or single. Save a couple of blocks of really good hard wood with wide diameter to be chopping blocks. They're indispensable for woodmaking and for slaughtering poultry, too, if you do it the old-time way. Maybe taking such an interest in ax technique is unwomanly; I don't have to chop wood now much, thank heavens—there's plenty else. But I was the only kid at home all my adolescence, and I chopped it aplenty for my mother (as well as hauled water by the bucketful up the creek bank to keep the porch tank full).

Chopping Safety. Strive for accuracy before you strive for force—at least enough so that you don't hit your foot. Then, once you're sure you can put the blade onto the wood, you want to give it all the power you can. Use a good big ax, a heavy one, because you can get a lot more force with it. *Wear heavy boots in case you miss.* Chips can fly up into an eye or the ax blade can hit a knot and be deflected, so *don't let children, or anybody, stand near when* *you're chopping.* My little boy got an ax blade in his forehead when he got too close behind another boy who was chopping. No harm remains than a little scar, but it's a lesson. If you want to be really safe, wear goggles, a hard hat, and steel-toed boots!

Chopping Technique. Everybody's got his or her own way of chopping. A friend of ours only lifts the ax to shoulder height, then brings it down with a big grunt and the wood splits. Another friend raises it straight over his head. Mike holds the ax strong in his left hand, loose in his right hand, and then brings it down kind of pulling with the left hand and pushing with the right hand. The best stroke for me uses both hands on the ax—as if you were holding a baseball bat, only farther apart. To do it my way, if you're right-handed, start the ax out back of your right shoulder behind your head with your back arched backwards just a trifle (or you can alternate shoulders with every swing) and then bring it forward and down, moving your shoulder and chest forward at the same time.

Try to hit your block of wood right in the center. Mike says you don't want the ax absolutely perpendicular to the stump when it strikes. I aim to get it square on. If your wood doesn't split from the center you can try taking slabs off the edge awhile before you tackle the heart. If you can get your ax into the tree but not out the other side, pull it out and try again. Look for a natural crack to strike into. There usually is one in old wood. If you're still finding it hard, use wedges and a wood-splitting maul or sledgehammer instead of the ax.

Knots. A "knot" is where a branch grew out of the trunk. That branch extends like a holding pin all the way through the trunk to the center. It prevents the trunk from splitting naturally. With tamarack or red fir you won't have too much trouble with knots. With cedar they're impossible. Split away from the knot and just throw the knot away unless it's small enough to burn by itself. But big cedar knots are too huge for anything but a bonfire. Cedar blocks make dandy furniture though, so if you see a knot in the block you could just reserve it for a stool or something.

Kindling. Some of the wood has to be split and re-split into very slender sticks called "kindling" for starting fires. You need really dry wood for kindling. Wood on the green side burns okay in a big fire, but it makes terrible kindling because it is so damp. To make kindling out of it you have to

split it into small kindling-size sticks and then dry them out some place like in your warming ovens—and then it will work to start a fire.

Kindling is made with a hatchet because those little sticks won't stand up by themselves. You have to hold them up with your left hand and chop up with your right hand using the short-handled hatchet. The thing with using a hatchet is not to cut your fingers off. Either learn unbelievably good aim or learn to let go just before the hatchet blade strikes, so the fingers are out of harm's way. I keep the hatchet back of the wood range, hanging on the wall by its neck—a nail on each side, high out of reach of the children. That's where the other wood-stove implements are kept too.

WOOD STORAGE: Cut and store under shelter inside a shed or at least under a tarp. If you have 2 buildings close together you can roof over the gap with tin sheets or something cheap, put a back on it, and have a very adequate woodshed. Or you can have an open woodpile for the blocks outside somewhere and a large area for drying and storing wood on your porch. I carried wood to our porch from my chopping station in the yard by the woodpile. But we lived in a relatively dry climate. A wet one would need covered outside storage too.

My father always insisted on a very neatly arranged stack of wood inside our front porch. The wood supply on my parents' porch was enough to last about 10 days and was arranged by graduated sizes with the real small kindling on the left end and the wood pieces getting bigger as it moved to the right. That way my mother could easily find whatever size sticks she wanted. Now my husband and I have a similar system: a pile of tree chunks outside by the chopping block, a porch storage area for chopped wood, and a kitchen wood box near the stove. It has to be filled once a day in cold weather. It's 2½ feet wide, 4 feet long, 3 feet high, and bottomless so I can pick it up and sweep up the sawdust come spring. I toss all the paper-type garbage in it in wintertime for starting fires.

The Technology of Wood Piling. Split your wood before stacking; this increases the exposed surface area and reduces drying time. Stacking the wood in alternate directions row by row further helps the drying process. Protect your wood supply from rain and snow by keeping it in a woodshed if possible. That's better than stacking it against the side of the house or under trees in the yard. If you must store wood on the ground, stack at least 6 inches off the ground to protect the lower part of the woodpile from ground moisture. Simply lay 3 parallel poles under the pile and then set the wood on top of them.

SHARPENING HAND TOOLS: It takes practice to master tool-sharpening. Find someone in your area who regularly sharpens tools and watch how it is done. No edge remains sharp after being used. The edge dulls as the metal wears. The sharper the edge to start, the more quickly it wears and the more often you'll have to sharpen if you want to keep such a sharp edge. Corrosion caused by rust or fruit juices also dulls blades. If you cut something acidic (even with stainless steel), it helps preserve your blade's sharpness to wipe the knife dry afterwards.

COAL: Bituminous coal doesn't make as hot a fire as anthracite, and it's dirtier and smokier. If you are using coal, it has to be stored where it won't get wet. Coal requires more shelter than wood. To bring the coal to the stove from its storage place in your woodshed, or a corner of the garage or cellar, the coal scuttle (a strong bucket with a wide pouring spout on the end and a bale handle, about as big as what a person can stand to carry) is traditional. Any bucket will do, though. You usually need only a bucket at a time in the kitchen if you're mostly using wood. The coal is to get a hotter fire than wood will give you and a longer-lasting one; you put in the coal the last thing before going to bed. Tamarack holds a fire about as well, though.

Burning Wood

Burning wood seems easy and natural to me. But I live in a timber-producing area, have timber here on the farm, and a sawmill and wood products plant both just down the road. Correspondents tell me that in the East, wood is very scarce and very high-priced, that wood stoves are hard to come by, and that insurance companies won't insure a home that is heated with wood. Anyway, if you haven't got dead trees around then a wood cookstove isn't necessarily right for you.

WOOD HEAT REFERENCES: I have been urged to position the references at the very end of the topic. I know that's how other people do it, but I prefer to put them right after my introduction to a subject. That's because I believe the references are potentially more important to you than what I have to say. They're written by specialists in the field who have spent years experimenting and gathering information on just a single topic. By putting them up front I'm urging you to start with them and maybe even skip what I have to say, or heavily supplement my material.

When it comes to using chain saws, felling trees, and installing a stove, you need more expert and in-depth advice than mine! Get *The Wood Burning Stove,* by Geri Harrington. Older classics on this subject are *Solid-Fuel Furnaces and Boilers* by John W. Bartok; and *The Wood Stove Handbook* by Wilburn W. Newcomb (1978). *Solid Fuels Encyclopedia,* by Jay Shelton, is encyclopedic on this subject. *Mother Earth News* often ran articles on wood heat (Sept./Oct. 1982; Sept./Oct. 1985). Storey's has 32-pg pamphlets ($3.95) on these subjects: "Curing Smoky Fireplaces," "Buying & Installing a Wood Stove," "Build Attractive Hearths," "Catalytic Combustors for Your Woodstove," and "Chimney & Stove Cleaning." The cutting edge of research these days is into clean combustion and efficient woodlot management.

THE ECONOMICS OF WOOD HEATING: If you are considering switching to wood heat, calculate your total fuel bill for last year and then figure your bill for next year.

If you install a wood stove, how much of your previous fuel do you still expect to use, either for supplemental heat or for uses other than space heating (water heating, cooking)? What do you expect to pay per cord of wood? If you don't know, look in the classified section of the local newspaper. Multiply the price per cord by the number of cords you will need per year. A cord of dried softwood such as pine, larch, or Douglas fir provides about the same amount of heat as 19.3 thousand cubic feet of natural gas, or 5,276 kilowatt hours of electricity. So, if you now heat with gas, divide the number of MCF of natural gas by 19.3 to estimate equivalent cords of wood. If you heat with electricity, divide kwh by 5,276 to estimate equivalent cords of wood.

I've seen numbers suggesting that you might save only, for example, $75 per year by switching from gas to wood if you got your wood for $50 a cord. However, if you are switching from electric heat to wood, your savings might be $700 or more a year. If you cut the wood yourself, you could save more money. But there would still be expenses involved. Is it your wood? And how far do you have to drive to get to it? On average, you'll spend $12.50 a cord on gasoline for cutting and hauling, plus the wear and tear on your truck and chain saw and you. And don't forget the cost of your wood stove and its installation, and the chimney, and the chimney-cleaning. Some states offer state tax credits for switching to wood, but only if you buy a clean-burning stove that meets their standards.

OF WOOD BURNING AND AIR POLLUTION: This is a problem with wood stoves, both for the individual home-owner and for the environment in general. Wood stoves make a considerable contribution to an area's smog if there are lots of them in a small area. Air inversions and still air can keep that pollution hovering right over you. Or your next door neighbor, an elderly asthmatic, may literally be dying from your burning. So, if you want to burn wood, be considerate of others. And if you're in an area with regulations, obey the laws. Oregon regulations began in July 1986 and national standards patterned after Oregon's went into effect in July 1988. The stoves that I've described down below wouldn't pass the emission laws in Oregon.

FIRE PREVENTION: How would you cool your fire quickly if a pipe or your box gets red hot and you become worried about a fire? In an emergency you could just pour water on it. On the other hand, that could cause cracking of the stove parts! During the winter months chimney fires in the northern Idaho community of Coeur d'Alene averaged 1 a day between November 1 and January 1. In Coeur d'Alene about half of the homeowners heat with wood. Fires from wood heat devices make up almost 60 percent of the residential fires in the nation. You have to install these devices, use them, and maintain them correctly. Many fire departments will make a courtesy inspection of your wood heater.

Wood Stove Safety Products. You might also want to buy a special chimney fire extinguisher and keep it handy. And any wood-heated home needs a smoke detector. The smoke detector will warn you if your stove develops a back draft during the night or if there's a fire out of control. Installing and operating a wood stove in a mobile home requires special vigilance. You can order numerous products that assist in woodstove safety from Lehman Hardware (888-438-5346; www.Lehmans.com), such as Soot Destroyer, a stove and stovepipe thermometer, and a chimney fire extinguisher.

Creosote. The primary danger is creosote, a waste product that collects on the surfaces of the stove and pipes. Anything over ¼-inch thick of creosote build-up is dangerous. Creosote burns at about 2,300°F, hot enough to melt stainless steel. If you simply knock the creosote off the smoke shelf and down into the chimney, you can ruin your catalytic converter. A common problem is buying a stove that's too large for your house size, then letting the fire burn low inside it to save money. One last log smoldering | is what makes the chimney thick with creosote. A good way to clean up is once or twice a day, when you first build your fire, let it free burn freely and cook for a few minutes. The intense heat will clean out the pipes. You can also slow down the build-up of creosote by burning only well-seasoned wood, being sure your fire has an adequate supply of oxygen, inspecting your flue often, and cleaning your chimney at least once a year. If you do this yourself, you need a metal brush with a long extension rod, designed for the job. Your stove-dealer can provide these.

Chimney Fires

NOTE: Read this if you see a cherry-red stovepipe and hear the roar of a chimney fire! Shut off the air supply to the stove and get everyone out of the house. Call the fire department. Then use your hose to cool the roof, but don't spray water directly into the chimney. That could result in even more damage, by causing the overheated flue to contract too quickly. Once the fire is out, have the chimney thoroughly cleaned and closely inspected before using it again.

WOOD-STOVE SHOPPING: When I first started writing this book, there were no such things as stores specializing in wood stoves. And stove design was traditional and hadn't evolved for a hundred years. Then there was a burst of attention to wood-stove technology coming from alternative energy scientists, and now wonderful stores are scattered all over the areas where wood is convenient to burn, selling these much improved stoves. The new stoves are cleaner, safer, more efficient, and bewildering in number—some 450 different models to choose from. So many of the modern wood stoves are amazingly high-tech. Some are computerized, many are the result of thousands—tens of thousands—of dollars spent on research and development. They're more efficient: efficient at combustion and efficient at heat transfer capability. You need both kinds of efficiency.

So check in your yellow pages to find stores that specialize in wood-burning stoves and related products. A door/stovepipe/legs kit for a barrel stove is available from Lehman's (888-438-5346) for $59 or $79, and from some hardware stores.

The next cheapest wood stove is a small "outdoor" or "camping" type. It can heat one room. The largest size can heat a house. They usually have flat tops you can cook on. A Chinese import in this category is the Boxwood Heater/ Stove, $170: 800-423-2567; international 805-388-3000; toll-free 800-444-3353 or 800-237-4444; **www.harbor freight.com.** Cabela's, a camping mail-order outlet, offers one brand of this stove type, made in Utah, for $150 to $639 (depending on size); free catalog: 800-237-4444; One Cabela Dr., Sidney, NE 69160; **www.cabelas.com.**

For nicer stoves, prices go up . . . to $4,000 and anything in between. How about an outdoor wood furnace? Central Boiler Classic is installed away from your home. It has thermostatically controlled heat to a possible several buildings. A water jacket surrounds the furnace firebox,

and heated water is pumped to the buildings through insulated underground pipes: 800-248-4681; **www. centralboiler.com.**

A mail-order wood heat specialist is Vermont Castings: 800-227-8683; CFN Majestic Product Co., 474 Admiral Blvd., Mississauga, Ontario L5T 2N1, CANADA. Or check out Energy House, 3902 S. Main, Salt Lake City, UT 84107; 801-261-3210; 877-440-6481; **www.transoceanltd.com.** You can find a local dealer for the Norwegian manufactured wood stove, Jotul, at their website: **www.jotulflame.com.** These specialists routinely carry wood-stove accessories, books, and pamphlets, as well as stoves. And they'll give you good advice on what to buy. You need guidance in your wood-stove shopping now because the Environmental Protection Agency has adopted regulations that strictly limit emissions from all wood stoves. Your stove dealer is probably certified by the Hearth Education Association and has worked hard to become knowledgeable on this subject.

Fireplace? A fireplace fire can make you warm if you're sitting within 6 feet or so of the radiated heat, but it's not an efficient way to heat the entire room. A fireplace can be modified with fireplace screens and tubular grates or fireplace inserts or stove-like inserts to improve its efficiency.

Stove Material Choices. You'll buy a stove made of cast iron, plate steel, or sheet metal (or even soapstone or porcelain). In general, the thicker the metal, the more it costs, but the longer the stove will last. Plate steel and cast iron are about equal in their heat retention ability and cost about the same. A sheet metal stove is cheaper, but will burn out faster and need to be replaced sooner than a heavier one. A sheet metal stove with reinforcement from firebrick or metal plates in the firebox will last longer than one without.

Stove Designs. Radiant stoves have a single-walled firebox. These stoves heat by simply radiating the heat out into the room. A convection stove has a firebox to contain the fire and another metal layer surrounding the firebox, with an air space in between. This stove heats by circulating the air from this space, thus heating the room with warm air. There may be an electric fan to circulate the heat away from the stove. You can position a circulating stove at about half the distance from combustible materials as that required for the radiants.

Some think that wood-pellet stoves are the wave of the future as wood gets scarcer and more expensive and air-quality regulations on emissions of wood-burning stoves increase. Pellets burn cleaner, and there are special stoves designed for them such as Welenco. A ton of pellets costs about $125 and will last 6–8 weeks of average winter weather. Pellets are made not only from wood, but also from corn, walnut, and almond shells.

Catalytic Combustor. This isn't a wood stove but is used to increase the overall efficiency (it can help up to 20 percent) of almost any wood stove it's attached to. But the combustor is a rather fragile item and not cheap. Also you'll have to be careful not to burn anything but wood in your stove, since the lead found in nails and in the newsprint on magazines and newspapers can destroy the converter.

You are likely to need professional help installing one of these sophisticated stoves.

WOOD STOVES AND AIR POLLUTION: Anytime you burn something, you're putting more carbon dioxide into the atmosphere, exacerbating the Greenhouse Effect. Wood fires also produce dozens of different gases, particles, and other airborne odds and ends, many of which, if inhaled too much, are even carcinogenic. Cigarette smoke and wood smoke are identical in many ways. The wood-smoke particles are small enough to get deep into your lungs and accumulate there, aggravating asthma and bronchitis, making you cough, or giving you a sore throat, runny nose, or headache. A hot, clean fire produces some pollution; every wood stove—even the airtights—let some pollutants escape into your house. If you have a chronic heart or lung problem of any sort, wood-heating can be a health problem. From that point of view, solar, geothermal, wind, and hydroelectric are the winners of the clean-energy-source contest. Ah, if only more of us individual home-owners could be users of them—and not of environmentally damaging energy sources.

Of Wood Cookstoves

I remember the wood stove we had when I was a little girl. It was our only heat and a much-appreciated presence on winter days. Mother raised bread behind the stovepipe. The spring chickens first lived in a box on the floor back of the stove before they graduated to the bathtub. Hot water came from a tank attached to the right-hand side of it with a circulating pipe rigged up to pass near the firebox. I started out cold mornings sitting on top of the stove. As it got warmer I scooched away from the firebox. Then I leaned on the stove. When it got hot enough so I couldn't lean on it anymore I was thawed out enough to function anyway. I never could understand how my mother managed to get up in that icy house leaving my father and me in our warm beds and make the fire. Now I understand better. Necessity is the progenitor of toughness. I mean, when you have to, you can.

Now I have an electric stove and 2 old-fashioned wood ranges in my kitchen. I use my younger Montag Duchess white-enameled stove in winter as a cupboard and the top as a work area. In summer it moves to the backyard under a canopy to be my canning stove. I like to bake in the electric stove, and it's a blessing on hot summer days because I can cook a meal on it without heating up the kitchen too much. But I prefer the wood stove for frying, stewing, such delicate businesses as making cottage cheese and cream cheese, and for its friendly and practical warmth on cold days since it heats the kitchen area. That stove is a big black box with the name "Monarch" on it in 9 places, warming ovens on top, and lots of fancy metalwork. It's a good stove too.

INSTALLING A STOVE: The old-style wood-and-coal range is a large iron box, which may or may not be on legs. It should be placed well enough out from the wall not to be a fire hazard and set on a fire-retardant sheet to protect your wooden floor. Stove pipes need to be assembled carefully and cleaned regularly. Chimneys must be insulated properly. A spark arrestor on top of the chimney will protect your roof. You may be concerned about how to keep squirrels and birds out of a fireplace chimney and about creosote build-up.

Leveling a Stove. When you first set up a wood cookstove it's important to get it level. Put a frying pan on top with a few drops of water in it for an indicator. The drops of water should go to the center of the pan.

GETTING ACQUAINTED WITH YOUR STOVE: The firebox is usually on the left. At the bottom of the burning area is a movable grate—an iron grill with interlocking fingers—which is opened by a special handle to let ashes fall down into the ash pan, a trap that occupies the lowest level under the firebox. You can keep the grate shaker hung near the stove along with the scraper, poker, pot holders, hatchet, and lid lifter. The poker is a long metal rod with a handle used to move chunks of wood away from the sides of the firebox, or to do whatever poking you need to in the fire without burning your hand.

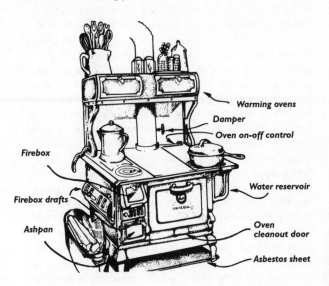

About Dampers and Drafts: In addition to fuel, fires have to have oxygen to burn. The range is connected with the chimney vent by means of the stovepipe. There is a damper in the pipe and probably another at the front of the grate and another at the back or side of the firebox. Technically, the ones that are above the fire are "dampers," the ones in front of it are "drafts." The dampers and drafts are used to control the amount of air flow. A new fire needs lots of air. The 2 lower dampers are probably shifted by metal handles to open or close air holes into the firebox. The stovepipe damper is a plate just the diameter of the pipe with an outside handle. It may be adjusted to obstruct the pipe and slow (dampen) the fire by limiting the airflow (draft). The "flue" is the hole inside the chimney or stovepipe through which your draft flows. If you let your fire get big and roaring a little bit before you damp down, it will help burn up and blow out the cinders in the stove and stovepipe that can't be reached so easily any other way.

Of Stoves, Air, and Weatherization. No matter what you burn for heat, you'll save money and the environment if you burn less, and you'll burn less if you insulate your house. Find out where you're losing heat and try to stop those leaks. Drafts are a major culprit. You can buy a helpful pamphlet ("Cut Those Energy Bills") from Storey's or Vermont Castings. But don't cut off your oxygen supply completely! Keep in mind that if your house is very tightly sealed, there may not be enough natural leakage into it to provide adequate air for your stove. That would result in a weak draft, smoking, difficult starting, and poor performance. (Test to see if cracking open a nearby window solves the problem.)

Here's another problem with weatherization in a wood-stove–heated home: in a home that is just leaky enough to provide a good, fresh draft for the stove and a frequent exchange of room air, the pollutants that leak from the stove can't stay around long enough to concentrate in the room air. But as you tighten your house against drafts, air exchange from outside air happens less often; indoor pollutants have time to accumulate, and this can be a health problem. Not all the pollutants—notably carbon monoxide—can be smelled or seen. So, if you are burning wood, the room where you keep your stove has to have a conscious system to vent and renew the air with an air-intake system that will feed your fire with outside air instead of recirculated room air. And always burn a hot, clean fire to minimize the amount of pollutants produced in the first place.

STARTING A FIRE: On very cold mornings, if there is no other heat, I let the children build the fire. It keeps them occupied while the house is warming up. Otherwise, they just stand around the cold stove and complain. The basic idea is this: You strike a match to get heat enough to light paper, which will burn and create heat enough to light kindling, which will burn and create heat enough to ignite bigger, and then bigger, hunks of wood, which will burn with enough heat to kindle coal. That's because each thing has its "kindling point," meaning the lowest possible temperature at which it will catch on fire. So you start with the thing that has the lowest kindling point (the match) and work your way up.

Starting Clean. Before starting a new fire, you first need to clean out the ashes from the previous day's burning. Shake the grate with the shaker to get all the old cold ashes down into the ash pan. Take the pan out and empty it onto the garden or into the lye barrel, compost heap, or garbage. If you were using coal yesterday, be thrifty and pick out any half-burned chunks to save and finishing burning later. Having all those old ashes out helps the new fire get air. Besides if you don't empty your ash pan now it will be overflowing by noon with ashes and hot cinders. Then you will have to empty it and the tray will be burning hot and very unwieldy to carry anywhere.

Laying Burnables into the Stove. Separate sheets of newspaper. Wad them up individually and put them into the firebox. Or use any discarded papers or paper containers. Add some of your most finely cut kindling on top of the paper, then a few bigger chunks of wood on top of that, then a couple of yet larger sticks on top of that. Arrange all the wood in as open a style as possible, not pressed together so that lots of air can get in there. Not only does the fire in general need air, but at first every individual stick needs an air supply. I carefully arrange them log cabin or teepee style to ensure this. Once it gets going you needn't be so particular. And start with plenty of sticks. One stick of wood never burns well alone. (There's some profound philosophy there if I ever get time to ponder it—a sermon even.) Now light the paper with a match as near the bottom as you can.

Adjusting the Dampers. Fire travels up. Always start your fire with all the dampers wide open. As the fire gets going, keep it supplied with fuel of the appropriate size for the stage it's at. As it gets going better you can gradually cut back on the draft. You will waste fuel and have a hard time heating your stove and oven if you let all your hot air go directly up the chimney, which is what it will do with all the dampers left open. So when your fire is going really well, cut back the draft—by turning the damper in the stovepipe—until it starts smoking. Then turn it back

enough so you have no smoke. If the chimney damper is shut too tight, you'll have smoke all over the place. If it's open too wide, the fire will roar and consume like crazy—but it won't make the room warm. Close the damper at the back or to the side of the firebox, shut or almost shut. Adjust your front damper to the point that the fire's health seems to require. The hotter your fire the more dampening it can stand. If your fire is too slow, give it more air. If your fire still isn't burning well, try loosening up the pile of fuel.

COOKING ON A WOOD STOVE

Shopping for a Wood Stove's Needs. Lehman's carries an excellent line of wood-stove items: cast iron (enamel-lined) or stainless steel tea kettles, enameled frontier coffee-makers, old-time flat irons that heat on the stovetop, pokers, lid lifters, scrapers, lids, books . . . and stoves themselves; 888-438-5346; **www.Lehmans.com**.

The Top of the Stove. The oven of a wood stove is hard to work with but the top more than makes up for it. The heat on top of a wood stove is more even and potentially milder than that on an electric or gas stove. You will be delighted with your fried eggs because the texture of eggs cooked alone or in mixtures is directly affected by the temperature at which they are cooked. Cooked below the boiling point of water the egg white is firm but tender, and the egg yolk is tender and like a salve. Eggs cooked at too high a temperature are first tough, then leathery, then crispy. Fry your eggs in a little butter in a cast-iron pan on the right-hand side of the wood range.

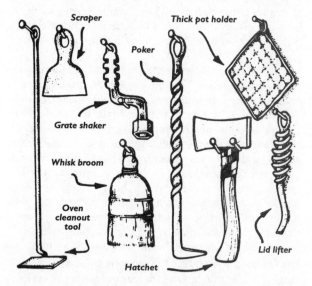

It's basic knowledge that the different parts of the stove top have different temperatures. The hottest area is usually just to the right of the firebox. (If the draft isn't good, the hottest may be right over the firebox.) You can adjust your cooking temperature just by moving the pan to a suitable place on the stove top. Start it boiling over the hot part, then settle it down to the rate you like by moving it over some distance to the right. The far right is the traditional place for making cottage cheese and keeping dishes warm when a meal is waiting for the eaters.

Pot Handles and Holders. This kind of stove is hard on perishable pot handles—wooden or plastic ones. The stove top is hot all around the pan as well as under it and a wooden handle such as that on a coffeepot may even catch fire. The traditional handles are metal and you pick them up with a pot holder. You can make a pot holder by folding an old washrag in half and the folding it in half again and sewing down all around the edges. Or you can sew down enough layers of cotton rags to get a manageable thickness and then attach a loop to hang it up by. It can be round or square, about 7 inches across is nice. Crocheted ones burn you through the holes unless they have an extra cloth filling or you use them several at a time stacked like pancakes. Keep the pot holders hanging on nails handy to your stove. You'll be using them a lot.

Stirring on a Wood Stove Top. You need long-handled wooden spoons. You can use a clean stick if you haven't wooden spoons. Wood doesn't conduct heat. The long handle helps you keep your arm away from the heat. Any metal spoon will quickly heat up and burn your fingers. Then you'll drop it in the pot. The old-fashioned flat irons, griddles, waffle pans, and other "hot air" pans—including the kugelhupf (apple-dumpling pan)—are meant to be put right on the hot range top. (If you want to use these pans on an electric burner, put a metal pie pan over the burner—otherwise they'll get too hot in one spot.)

➤ *POTATO LEFSE This Scandinavian dish was traditionally baked right on top of a wood range although you can use a pancake griddle. Boil 5 large, peeled potatoes, then mash them and add ⅓ c. cream, 3 T. butter, and 1 t. salt. Beat until the mixture is fluffy. After it has cooled, add enough flour to roll out thinly, as for pie crust, or even thinner, using your rolling pin. Start with walnut-sized balls. Roll out to tortilla-sized pancakes. Use the center panel of the stove or you can bake on a grill or in a heavy skillet. Clean and oil it and then bake there, turning as often as you need to keep from scorching.*

➤ *WHEAT LEFSE Mix ½ t. salt with 3 c. whole wheat flour. Add ¼ c. oil and 1 c. water; mix and knead. Roll dough thin as for Potato Lefse. If your dough is sticky, add a little more flour. Cook like the Potato Lefse. You can eat plain, or buttered, or like pancakes, or like tacos with a filling rolled up inside (keep them hot) like mashed dry beans, green onion, and tomato.*

➤ *WELSH STOVETOP COOKIE Jennet Gray, age 10, Fruitvale, ID, gave me this recipe. It was passed down from her namesake, Jennet Havard, born November 30, 1875, in Wales—Jen's great-great grandmother. Mix 4 c. whole wheat flour, 1 c. brown sugar, 1 T. baking powder, 1 T. freshly ground nutmeg, and ½ t. salt. Cut in 1 c. butter. Add 1 c. raisins or currants. Add 2 eggs mixed with ¼ c. milk. Roll out ¼-inch thick and cut into large circles. Cook them on the stovetop in a frying pan (or in an electric fry pan at 350°F). Brown one side. Flip over and brown the other. Jen's mother is a remarkable lady who worked every summer for years out in the woods for the U.S. Forest Service—until she got so disturbed about timber overcutting that she went back to college for an M.A. in political science and guidance about finding a way to influence and limit the unfortunate industry-dictated policies she knew so well.*

The Oven. The oven of a good wood range is beside the firebox and is heated by hot air circulating from the firebox over, down the far side and under the oven. If your oven is not heating or is heating unevenly, the problem may be accumulated soot in those areas. My mother taught me to clean them out once a week. You can lift off the top of the

range to clean the top area and sides. The bottom is reached through a little door under the oven. There is a special tool for cleaning there called a "stove scraper."

Ovens vary among stoves and with the kind of fuel you are using and the weather. You'll have to get to know your individual oven and fuel. Throw away your former standards for baking. Just be grateful if it isn't raw and isn't burnt. Disregard suggested cooking times. Your oven may be faster or slower or both. Keep an eye on what's happening in there. If the oven doesn't have a built-in thermometer, by all means go out and buy one of those little portable oven thermometers that you can hang or set inside. That way you'll never have to bother with the famous flour or paper tests. The problem isn't finding out the temperature—it's controlling it!

If your oven is too cool, stoke up the fire with more fuel. If the oven is too hot, leave the door open a crack and ease up on feeding the fire. If one side is obviously getting more heat than the others, the oven is hotter there and you will need to rotate your baking pan occasionally during the baking. If you have several pans in the oven, rotate them all to take turns in the hot spot. If the top is browning too fast, cover it with greased or wetted brown paper or aluminum foil. You can put a whole pie into a paper bag. Old fashioned cast-iron frying pans, Dutch ovens, and gem (iron muffin) pans are helpful, since the cast-iron absorbs heat and distributes it evenly throughout the surface of the pan.

WOOD COOKSTOVE REPAIR: Assuming you don't lose a lid lifter, or, worst yet, one of your stove-top lids, the first problem likely to come up is that the stove liner (the firebrick material that lines the inside of the firebox and protects the metal) will first crack and then gradually crumble away. This takes years, but it eventually happens.

I didn't know how you could replace these worn-out firebox parts. Barbara Ingram told me of a way to reline any stove that has a firebrick-type liner using something called "refractory cement." Buy a can of it and a small putty knife. Apply a very thin layer to the part to be relined. Let it dry until hard. Then apply another very thin coat. Keep it up until that area is built up to match the rest. Refractory cement will resist temperatures up to 8,500°F and is the stuff they use in blast furnaces. Katya Morrison, Mount Airy, MD, shared her experience too. "After using our wood stove a while, the lining of the firebox cracked. We tried plain cement made with just sand and it has lasted beautifully and was easy to do."

Karen Prahl, Washington Island, WI ("an island 7 miles out in Lake Michigan off the NE tip of Wisconsin"), says: "Some brick and block companies sell a dry powder mix that, when mixed with water, can be used to lay a liner to protect the metal surfaces. We have not had a chance to pursue this item and see how it works."

Now that's really putting our heads together!

I wrote the above paragraphs 20 years ago. Now (2002), you can go to your local wood-stove store. Or mail-order furnace cement, firebox inserts, or obsolete stove parts from Lehman's (888-438-5346; **www.Lehmans. com**) or The Cumberland General Store (#1 Highway 68, Crossville, TN 38555; $4 for their 289-pg catalog; 800-334-4640; fax 931-456-1211; **www.cumberland general.com**).

Of Green Leaves, Courage, and Foolishness

In my front yard, outside my front door, there's a foolish little almond tree. Perhaps it's appropriate—this foolish little almond tree living outside my door. Because this is the same winter that so many people are calling me foolish. Again.

I bought the tree for 6 dollars down in Lewiston at Garden Square Nursery. And maybe it was a foolish thing that I bought it because almonds don't belong in cold climates. Some people have managed to raise them at Lewiston, but I'm about 500 feet higher. I'm always trying to grow things that can't be grown (my nectarines are doing well though the fig tree died), so I bought and set out 2 little almond trees. They were practically alike—about 4 feet high with 8 twiggy branches. We pruned them both when we set them out, cutting off the tip of each branch. I winced when we did that. I hate to hurt anything, but the nurseryman said it would help them—that there wouldn't be so much tree for the roots to support while they were just getting started. They both grew nice green leaves and made a fine start for themselves this summer. Then I had to go away and spend months traveling and selling books. While I was gone fall came. Then winter.

I'm back. I've been back 6 weeks. And here in my yard is this foolish almond tree. Right outside my front door. I don't know whether to laugh over it or weep. Time and again I jump up and run to the window to look at it—can it be real? Yet it is; all my visitors have seen it too. Right this moment, in December, I am in my kitchen and my wood cookstove is burning with the hearty fire inside that we need to keep warm. Outside snowflakes float steadily down, piling up on the ground where the little almond trees stand rooted. And there is the one tree, looking just the way it ought to in a December snowstorm: its leaves long since shriveled, changed color, and fallen away, the narrow whip of its lean young trunk waiting patiently for spring to come and transform winter's boredom into another frenetic season of growth like all sensible farmers and plants alike must accomplish. And then there is that other, foolish, tree.

I just got up and looked out the window again. There is the foolish tree, there in the snow, in the snowstorm. Its branches aren't 6 inches long like those of the wise tree. They are over 2 feet, though there aren't quite so many of them. And there are 47 lovely, spring-like, green leaves on that foolish almond tree. I went out and counted them. I stood shivering without my coat in the storm and gently touched the smooth green perfection of each one. Snow and ice were clinging to some so I gave the little tree a gentle shake to try to free it of that chilling burden. Then I looked down and saw 3 of those perfect leaves lying on the snow. Had I done that by shaking it, even so gently? I hurt for them. I felt so guilty for what I'd done. Yet, even on the snow and separated from their tree, they didn't look in the least wounded, not in the least dead.

I've been watching that foolish tree ever since I got home from my months on the road selling books. I've been waiting for it to give up and cut off the flowing sap to those green leaves like all the other deciduous trees in the orchard have, but it doesn't do it. And I'm starting to cling to the image of those green leaves in my heart as a symbol of Hope.

Has God given me a mutation? Or a miracle? An accident? Or a promise? Or just a foolish almond tree? Is the tree going to make it through the winter? Are 47 leaves enough if 3 fall each snowstorm? So many times God has pruned me, and I've lost green leaves and whole branches, but I knew He was shaping me for better things. That little tree is mocking the annual death we all accept so calmly: out there being summer in winter. Is it some genetic freak, lacking the inner knowledge to accept a winter's hibernation? Will it die completely after having made such a magnificent struggle not to sleep at all?

I'm the foolish one. Because I get weary. Discouraged. Because I consider, just for a moment, that maybe it would be possible to agree with everyone else and say, "Yes, it's too hard—it can't be done" about all the things I dream of, that I work and struggle to make happen. It would be kind of a relief to agree with them. Or am I foolish? Because I believe that life can be full of wonderful joyous miracles . . . if we only stretch out our arms, our living branches, and let life flow through us unceasingly, no matter what the weather report.

God has set a foolish almond tree outside my front door. My beloved, wonderful, foolish almond tree isn't a figment of literary imagination. Nothing in this book is. Sometimes I have wild thoughts of running out and wrapping it in my big warm winter coat and in my arms till spring. Or I get up on a new morning and go to the window thinking: Now, finally, it will have accepted the inevitable and dropped those leaves. But no, there it stands. Green. I remember my pastor saying that he will die only at God's appointed hour for him to do so and no mere disease will change that fact. Oh, foolish tree. God's perfect thing. Reminding me that the Valley of the Shadow of Death is just that, only the valley of the shadow of death.

CHAPTER SEVEN

Food Preservation

DETAILED STEP-BY-STEP DRYING INSTRUCTIONS

LONG-TERM FOOD ARRANGEMENTS

TWELVE LIFE-SAVING CANNING RULES

WATER-BATH CANNING AND PRESSURE CANNING

ROOT CELLAR CHECKLIST

SUMMER ICES AND FROZEN FRUITS

JAM/JELLY RECIPES

BASIC SPICED FRUIT

MAKING VINEGAR

FOOD PRESERVATION CONTENTS

7 | FOOD PRESERVATION

INTRODUCTION

➤ *HOW TO PRESERVE A HUSBAND*
Be careful in your selection; do not choose too young and take only such as have been reared in a good moral atmosphere. Some wives insist on keeping husbands in a pickle, while others put them in hot water. This only makes them sour, hard, and sometimes bitter. Even poor varieties may be made sweet and good by garnishing them with patience, well-sweetened with smiles and flavored with kisses to taste. Keep warm in a steady fire of domestic devotion and serve with peaches and cream. When thus preserved, they will keep for years.

➤ *PRESERVED CHILDREN Take I large field, a dozen children, 2–3 small dogs, a pinch of brook, and some pebbles. Mix together children and dogs; sprinkle the field with flowers; spread over all a sky of deep blue and bake in the sun. When brown, set away to cool in the bathtub.*

Once upon a time, in the bad old days when the Communists and the Western countries were poised on the brink of mutual nuclear annihilation, many of us in the back-to-the-land movement were poised to repopulate the barren earth by managing to be the only survivors of that holocaust. I built a fallout shelter in the backyard. It was very carefully designed, for I'd studied the subject thoroughly—enough to understand that the shelter could solve only part of the problem. But I had children to worry about, and although I couldn't do anything about nuclear proliferation, I could, at least, build a concrete hole. And I managed to do it quite economically for the quality of concrete I used. Thank God it was never put to the test.

All we have to worry about now are local nuclear conflicts, and nuclear power plants blowing up one at a time, and forever-deadly nuclear wastes piling up and leaking away into the planet's circulatory systems.

Another critical issue back then for would-be survivors was how to be self-sufficient, foodwise, if normal supply systems broke down and the grocery stores were empty. Unlike building a fallout shelter, growing your own food and having a good backup supply in storage is still a worthwhile endeavor. The one thing that does not change is the fact that there will be changes. You can be certain there will be more crises. Most prophets of doom are right . . . if you wait long enough. How long? Centuries? Millennia? Which crisis will be next? Which will be worst? My bet is on some sort of "environmental" disaster.

In 1991 the United States imported more than half its oil, which accounted for 65 percent of our trade deficit. I recently saw a news item about how Cuba couldn't get any oil and was suddenly having to harvest sugar cane by hand and with oxen. We had a few generations to make the switch away from animal power to petroleum power. It is likely the switch back would happen as it did in Cuba—suddenly, unexpectedly, in an atmosphere of crisis. If what I've heard is true about the oil supply being expected to run out in 50 years, or 100, or 150, there are some big adjustments—or reversals—ahead. Even though it seems inconceivable, we may have to remember how to do things the other way, the way we did them before "progress" happened. (In some ways I would consider that a huge blessing.) But it's more complicated than that.

Modern nations almost literally sow oil to produce food. If there were no oil, there would be no artificial fertilizers, no herbicides, no pesticides, no gas for the $50,000 ($150,000?) tractors that help us grow our food supply. If there were no petroleum, there would be no crop—except for what the organic farmers could produce without mechanized equipment. Our modern food supply is also utterly dependent on the petroleum products used to create the electricity that runs milking machines and electric egg incubators.

Other things have changed too. In the old days, there were no seed catalogs; people saved their own seed from year to year. There was no artificial insemination; farmers knew where to find a bull for their cows, because otherwise there would be no milk and no calf for meat the next year. There were no electric egg incubators; poultry species brooded, hatched, and reared their own young. Preserving food didn't require electricity or metal. If people's labors were fruitful, they put away a long-term food supply as a matter of common sense. And their food was wholesome, hearty, and free of carcinogens.

Thus, until about 70 (or fewer) years ago, families harvested in the fall and stored enough food to get them and their livestock through until the next harvest. Milk, butter, and cheese from dairy animals, along with meat and the stored foods, were important winter foods. Old-timers stored food mainly by root cellaring, drying, salting—or feeding to livestock, which returned the food as milk, meat, or work. The old-timers never let anything go to waste. After canning came along, most country families canned many, many jars of fruit, vegetables, and meats every year. When freezers were invented, some preserving, especially of fruits and meats, was shifted to that system.

ORGANIZING FOOD PRODUCTION, STORAGE, AND USE

City Food Preservers

You don't have to have your own orchard and garden to reap the benefits of home food preservation. You can make an arrangement at a roadside stand, farmer's market, or U-pick to get organically grown food in bulk. It's best if you make arrangements the previous fall, so the grower can make sure to plant enough for your needs.

Plan Ahead

If you haven't previously raised your own food, I would guess it will take more food to keep your family going than you now realize. In general, can or freeze only the amount your family will use up before the next harvest season. In your first year, you may have trouble figuring out how much. But by your second, you'll know what ran out fast and what was left over. With that info you can fine-tune your plan.

Do you know how many cows, goats, chickens, sheep, etc., you need for one year's supply of milk and meat? How many bushels (or acres) of grain? How many heads of cabbage and sacks of potatoes? You can find out to a certain extent by keeping records and then by experience. You'll need a lot of food, because people doing hard outdoor work have bigger appetites, because you have animals to feed too, and because you have to allow for loss by crop failure or spoilage in storage.

With pumpkins and fruit, you have to figure from harvest to harvest—a full 12 months. You store greens from fall to spring because you'll have them fresh the rest of the time, from dandelion greens in the spring to your last cutting of Swiss chard or mustard greens in the fall. Meat is a crop you can harvest in winter but not in summer—except for very small animals like poultry and goats. Milk is available fresh year-round—providing you have more than one animal milking and stagger the time they come fresh. You have to store enough winter feed for them. A hungry cow won't just loyally grow lean. She'll either go way down on the milk, or she'll go through the fence and range onto the neighbors' land. (She is also likely to leave in search of a bull when she needs one—fences hold only contented cows.)

All spring I try to plant something every day—from late February, when the early peas and spinach and garlic can go in, on up to midsummer, when the main potato crop and the late beans and lettuce go in. Then I switch over and make it my rule to try to get something put away for the winter every single day. That lasts until the pumpkins and sunflowers and late squash and green tomatoes are in. Then comes the struggle to get the most out of the stored food—all winter long. It has to be checked regularly, and you'll need to add to that day's menu anything that's on the verge of spoiling, wilting, or otherwise soon becoming useless. Or preserve it a new way. If a squash gets a soft spot, I can gut it out and cook, mash, can, or freeze the rest for a supper vegetable or pie, or add it to the bread dough.

You have to ration. You have all the good food you can eat right at arm's reach and no money to pay . . . until you run out. You're likely to have either no elk at all or a lot of it (meatwise, an elk is about as much as a whole cow). Rotate

---

A MEASURE OF YOUR FOOD SELF-SUFFICIENCY

See how your ability to feed yourself and your family measures up by the old-timers' standards. There are no right or wrong answers to this "test." Its purpose is just to help you evaluate where you are right now—and think about what direction you might want to expand in.

Do you grow your own vegetables?
Yes ____ No ____ Percent ____

Do you grow your own dairy foods (milk, butter, cheese, yogurt, etc.)?
Yes ____ No ____ Percent ____

Do you grow your own meat?
Yes ____ No ____ Percent ____

Do you grow your own fruit, berries, honey, and sorghum syrup or maple sugar and use them for the sweets in your diet?
Yes ____ No ____ Percent ____

Do you grow your own cereal and bread grains?
Yes ____ No ____ Percent ____

Do you save your own seed from garden and grain patch?
Yes ____ No ____ Percent ____

Do you have males for dairy and meat breeding or easy neighborly access to them?
Yes ____ No ____ Percent ____

Do your orchard and nut and berry patches include young plants?
Yes ____ No ____ Percent ____

Do you replace every tree you harvest?
Yes ____ No ____ Percent ____

Is the land on which you grow food:
Borrowed? ____ Rented? ____
Being bought on contract? ____
Paid for? ____

Do you preserve vegetables for year-round use?
Yes ____ No ____ Percent ____

Do you make cheese from your extra milk?
Yes ____ No ____ Percent ____

Do you preserve your family's food supply by salting?
Yes ____ No ____ Percent ____

By drying?
Yes ____ No ____ Percent ____

By freezing?
Yes ____ No ____ Percent ____

By canning?
Yes ____ No ____ Percent ____

By root cellar storage?
Yes ____ No ____ Percent ____

Do you use cloches, a cold frame, or a greenhouse to prolong your growing season? Yes ____ No ____

Do you have enough food on hand to feed the family 1 week? ____
2 weeks? ____ 1 month? ____
3 months? ____ 6 months? ____
9 months? ____ 1 year? ____
Longer? ____ How long? ____

Do you have enough seeds on hand to grow your food supply next year?
Yes ____ No ____ Percent ____

---

when you have a variety. If you have elk, beef, and some odds and ends of chicken, trout and ham, eat elk on one night, beef on the next night, and alternately chicken, trout, and ham on the night after that. Garden crops have a tendency to either fail completely or overwhelm you with abundance. Fruit comes by the barrel but for only a short time—unless you can preserve it.

Plan ahead. Breed your milker 9 months before the time you'll want milk. If you butcher 30 chickens in June and have chicken every Sunday, you'll have no more after Christmas until next summer. And did you save layers? They may not lay in the winter, but hens that have rested will make up for it in May. Did you preserve eggs during that period when the hens lay like crazy—from May to October (or sooner)—just in case you don't see another egg until spring? I'll confess that I never manage to do all the food preserving correctly. But we keep struggling toward the ideal.

For information about planning a garden, see Chapter 2; planning an orchard, see Chapter 6; planning your meat supply, see Chapter 8; planning your dairy supply, see Chapter 10.

PRESERVING NOTEBOOK: Keeping one makes it possible to learn from experience. If you've the time and the patience, you can put down even more detail than this. Record in the notebook:

1. When you butchered what and about how many pounds of meat you put into the deep freeze.
2. How many chickens you have and how many eggs you get.
3. How many goats you're milking and how much milk you get, and the same for cows or other dairy animals.
4. How many seed packets of what you planted, or how many pounds of potatoes. At harvest time write down how many bushels of spuds, etc. you had to go into storage.
5. How much you're spending every week on store-bought food and where you're spending it.
6. See if you can bring that down by using more home-grown ingredients.
7. How many mouths you're feeding and what age they are.
8. How much you preserved of what and in what way.
9. When you ran out.

A very organized reader named Lin Shoemaker, Pullman, WA, even records what recipes she used in her food preserving, and if she added to or subtracted from the basic recipe. She refers back to that the next year to see if she wants to change or to do the same.

You'll get used to planning ahead for an entire year—from garden to garden, from slaughter to slaughter—in order to avoid a feast-and-famine cycle. Then in the long winter evenings when you're planning for next summer, adjust where needed. Not enough eggs? Save more hens from the chopping block this year. Couldn't eat all those pickles? Don't give so much garden space to cucumbers next year.

Menu Making: 365 Independence Days

For supper tonight we had kidney beans, helped along with some head meat fished out of the kettle where I'm cooking up some from a pig we butchered last weekend. With the meal I served milk and a dessert made of whipped cream, crumbled heels of homemade bread loaves, and some home-canned cherries and apricots.

It put me to thinking. Certainly wasn't a gourmet dinner. People have sometimes eaten at our home and really gone away raving—for instance, when they happened onto us when we were having sirloin steaks, or homemade ice cream made the old-fashioned way (mostly whipping cream and fruit), or homemade bread with so much applesauce in it that it was about half "cake" (only no sugar). But I imagine most folks would turn up their noses at a meal of kidney beans, head meat, and recycled bread dessert. Yet it was really special to me because all the ingredients came from our farm.

Just this afternoon I read an article in the women's section of the newspaper about a lady who grew much of her own food. I was impressed. But then it went on to give her recipes, and only one ingredient per recipe could possibly have been home-grown. The others were things like margarine, brown sugar, vanilla, baking powder, exotic nuts, cake mix, confectioners' sugar, miniature marshmallows, cocoa, and so on.

This noon for lunch we had a soup made of carrots, potatoes, onions, and milk, along with hamburgers (homemade bread and cut-up onion added to home-grown beef). Breakfast was homemade bread and butter and an eggnog (eggs from our chickens, milk from our cow) flavored with store-bought molasses. My grocery bill for the last few months has been averaging around $20 a month [1974], and that's not bad for a family of 7. (We rack up other expenses in producing the food, of course.) It's that cheap when everything on the farm is producing just perfectly—corn, chickens, garden, orchard, cow. Any slip sends the bill soaring—for instance, if the cow dries up, then I'm short on dairy products. None of us can stand reconstituted powdered milk, so suddenly I'm spending for dairy products.

If you have to buy all your food at the store now [1993], the USDA figures it will cost a family of 2 adults $220–400 per month, and a family of 2 adults and 2 children $365–700 a month. Gardening, if you have a place to do it, is one of the best ways to save money.

My favorite month, foodwise, is June: new potatoes and peas, turnips and lettuce, fresh strawberries, raspberries, and cherries, lots of milk and eggs. The winter food bill depends precisely on how much food is in the deep freeze and other forms of storage.

People have to choose what they're going to struggle for. Life is always a struggle, whether or not you're struggling for anything worthwhile, so it might as well be for something worthwhile. Independence days are worth struggling for. They're good for me, good for the country, and good for growing children. I think being married to a fine man, raising children, and raising food are the most important worldly things there are. And the most rewarding.

I think the best food product is the one you grow or make yourself, starting with ingredients that are as natural as possible (or, if you're stuck in the city, the ones in your grocery store labeled "organic"). The results may not look or even taste the best, but they really are the best. That's what I believe. When it comes to believing, you just have to believe whatever you believe and let it go at that without more fuss.

My ideal woman milks a cow or goats, gardens, and cares for her children herself. She hasn't got time for fancy cake decorating and vegetable dishes with 10 ingredients. And my ideal woman wants to use as few store-bought ingredients and gadgets as possible. She's looking for from-scratch recipes or making up her own.

Use What You Have: There are a few basics to cooking in any food category. Some cooks use a recipe only to guide them through the first few times. Then they know the recipe by heart—or, better yet, know the principles involved and can strike off on their own to do variations on the theme. I don't want to be a slave to recipes with ingredients that are unreasonable, inappropriate, and expensive—recipes that would have me running to the store way too often to search for strange ingredients. On the other hand, it's interesting to learn about new foods, new seasonings, new cuisines. But ingredients are most exciting to me if I might be able to grow them.

The wonderful magic at the heart of a food-growing household is the magic that turns your home-produced turnips and cream, apples and meat into your meals. The moment of triumph is when you say to the family: "Here's what we worked so hard to grow, and isn't it good!" I think you cook most happily, freely, and independently when you make good things out of what the Lord is giving you!

Lane Morgan, author of the *Winter Harvest Cookbook* (Seattle: Sasquatch Books, 1990), says, "I agree entirely that cooks are spending too much time and money at the supermarket and the gourmet supply store. But I think we would profit by spending more time looking at cuisines of other cultures, to help us better use what our particular gardens can grow. Country people around here will eat canned green beans and carrots all winter, which are considerable work to put up, because that's good American garden food. Meanwhile they could be eating fresh kale and leeks and Japanese mustards from that same garden, which would be tastier, more nutritious, and easier all around, but they don't because that's foreign stuff and they don't know the Greek or Indian or Japanese techniques to make them wonderful. They'll make clam dip from a package, but they won't consider an Indian chutney made of garden mint and garlic, served with garden spinach and potatoes. Too strange."

Making menus out of what you can grow is the way Great-Grandmother did it. Each week she looked in the larder and the cellar and took a walk through the garden to see what she had to work with. Then she made menus. When she had eggs and milk aplenty, a little honey, and some stale bread, the family had a bread pudding. In May she served rhubarb in it, in June strawberries over it, and in September peaches—because that's the way they grew.

To have 365 days of independent eating, you've got to learn to eat what you can grow, and you've got to learn to grow what you want to eat. At first it will be hard, but stick to it. If you don't like what you have, eat it anyway and use the energy of your distaste to figure how to get what you'll like better. If your only meat is elk, eat elk until you can raise something else. If you miss bacon, get four little pigs. In six months they'll be 200-pounders, and you'll have a year's supply of bacon plus a sow to breed and keep the bacon coming. If you're still living in the city and you don't have anything but dreams, try for fun buying only what you imagine you could grow—in a natural unprocessed state—like whole grains, and see if you can learn to live off it.

When lettuce is in season, have a salad every day—you can't preserve it. If you miss it in the off-season, contrive a way to raise winter lettuce in the house. If you miss sweets, learn beekeeping. If you have barley and corn, make your bread, pancakes, and pie crust out of barley flour, cornmeal crust, and a bear-meat filling. If you have

some tough old hens past their laying prime, 3 extra male goats, and 100 rabbits, then learn good ways to cook tough old hens, goat meat, and rabbit.

Seasonal Eating: At any particular time of year you'll have a different set of fresh foods coming out of the garden and root cellar to complement what you have frozen and canned. Winter, cloche, cold frame, and greenhouse gardening enable you to have at least a few varieties of garden-fresh vegetables year-round. Even in chilly November, in a basic temperate-zone garden and with some attention to protection, you might be able to harvest broccoli, brussels sprouts, cauliflower, collards, cabbage, Chinese cabbage, carrots, escarole, kale, leeks, lettuce, parsnips, salsify, spinach, rutabagas, turnips, and winter radishes.

Homestead Menus Through the Year: Here are some menus from back in '72 and '73. Those were my banner years for home growing and good cooking. It wasn't "gourmet" or "health food" cooking. But we raised it ourselves without poisons and had plenty of food and plenty of variety. We dried fruit in our front yard. Mayonnaise was homemade. Butter was from our own churn and bread from our oven. Bacon or ham was home-cured, and sauerkraut was out of our crock, as were pickles. The root beer and ginger ale were homemade, too. We always had milk and usually an herb tea on the table.

Breakfasts. If your chickens aren't laying, leave out the eggs.
1. Cornmeal mush; bread, butter, honey; soft-boiled eggs
2. Toasted sourdough bread; pork chops; applesauce; scrambled eggs
3. Homemade grape nuts with cream; sliced fresh peaches; poached eggs
4. Cornmeal mush; home-canned fruit; elk sausage (⅓ pork meat); fried eggs
5. Leftover boiled potatoes (sliced and fried); elk sausage; home-canned tomato juice; fried eggs
6. French toast (bread sliced and dipped in an egg-milk mixture and fried); honey and butter to go on the toast; fried pork side meat; wild plums
7. For a summer breakfast cooked outdoors: pancakes; goat's butter, honey; stewed wild apples; fried pork side meat

Lunches
1. May lunch: scrambled eggs; leftover boiled potatoes fried with chopped green top-set onions; cooked, buttered asparagus spears
2. Fried leftover cornmeal mush with butter, molasses, or honey; blackberries; fried meat; bread and butter
3. Hamburger; sliced fried leftover boiled potatoes; tomato ketchup; bread, butter, jelly

4. Leftover stew, extended with some fresh vegetables; bread, butter, wild plum sauce; mint tea with honey

5. Ground leftover ham and pickle sandwiches; cottage cheese (we eat it with milk and honey—except Mike, who prefers it with salt and pepper)

6. Sandwiches of herb bread and sliced cold venison roast; canned juice; pickles

7. A special lunch: cold leftover steak sliced in strips; fried potatoes and onions; hard-boiled eggs; canned applesauce; bread and butter; iced wild strawberry leaf tea

Spring and Summer Suppers

1. Potatoes; bread; creamed onions; stewed dandelion greens; raw fresh asparagus

2. Dandelion greens and (real) bacon bits; roast ham and gravy; potatoes; stewed rhubarb; radishes

3. Leaf lettuce salad; radish roses; potatoes; fried meat and milk gravy; strawberries on leftover bread with cream

4. Leftover sliced cold roast; bread and apple pudding (crumbled bread crust baked with milk, sliced cored apples, beaten egg, honey, cinnamon); warmed-up leftover gravy extended with milk (to go on the meat); boiled Swiss chard

5. Chicken stew (made from an old layer, with carrots, potatoes, onions, turnips) and dumplings; blackberry-apple bread pudding (berries, apples, milk, bread crust, and honey, baked and served with cream); iced herb tea

6. Corn on the cob; sliced fresh fruit; roast; mustard greens; potatoes; half-cured crock pickles

7. Carrot sticks; boiled peas; boiled new potatoes; fried chicken and gravy

8. When you're hot and tired: potato salad (made ahead and chilled); barbecued meat (cooked by husband); tossed green salad (made by children); raspberry ice (made ahead); bread and butter

9. Picnic: Fried chicken; potato salad; leaf lettuce salad; raspberries in whipped cream; ginger ale

Winter Suppers

1. Boiled sliced turnips; roast and gravy; baked potatoes; pickles; bread and butter; junket pudding

2. Elk roast and gravy; sage dressing; baked squash; spinach; mashed potatoes; mincemeat cookies

3. Pork chops; gravy; boiled peas; yeast biscuits; boiled potatoes

4. Steak and gravy; mashed potatoes; cole slaw with homemade dressing; cream-style corn; crumb bread and cherry jelly; canned apricots

5. Stew made with meat, tomatoes, carrots, cabbage; raw turnip slices dipped in herbed sour cream

6. Leftover sliced cold roast; bread and apple pudding; mashed boiled turnips

Snacks. Snacks are for company, for husband or children famished between meals, for an afternoon tea break or a bedtime family treat. Lots of old-time farm families have a regular midmorning and midafternoon mini-meal for the working men in summer, when they are putting in long days. Maybe we take sandwiches and a gallon of cold tea out to the field and the work stops for a few minutes.

I blacklisted store-bought cookies, potato chips, pop, and candy. But I don't fight snacks that are home-grown and home-prepared: fresh, canned, or frozen fruit; dried fruit; pickles; popcorn; homemade popsicles; homemade crackers; jerky; bread with homemade jam or honey.

Leftovers like cold sliced roast or cold boiled potatoes are good with some salt or butter. My husband Mike doesn't like to eat leftovers, except potatoes and meat, so if somebody doesn't snack them up, the chickens or pigs get them—except for bread, which metamorphoses into bread pudding or lunch dishes that I serve when it's just me and the children.

Feasts. Holiday feasts are wonderful rituals that bring a family closer, a time to pull out all the stops and load the table with everything good you can think of.

Thanksgiving 1972. Gander (the one that bit our son Danny twice) stuffed with sage dressing; sliced tomatoes (last of the fresh ones—picked green just before frost and stored to ripen gradually); cooked pumpkin mashed with butter; boiled green beans with onion and bacon; boiled potatoes with giblet gravy; sweet crock pickles; bread and cheese; brandied peaches (buried in September and dug up for Thanksgiving); root beer.

Thanksgiving 1973. Roast goose stuffed with sauerkraut; giblet gravy; mashed potatoes; baked acorn squash halves (a dab of butter and honey cooked in the heart); boiled Swiss chard; brandied peaches; mincemeat pie.

Christmas Dinner. Turkey and dressing; peach ketchup; potatoes and giblet gravy; boiled green beans; carrot and dried fruit salad (grated carrot tossed with chopped dried fruit and mayo); bread and butter; pumpkin pie.

A SYSTEM FOR MENU PLANNING: My mother taught me the following basics of menu planning. I've heard of other systems, but this is the one I grew up with. It has served me well enough that I'll pass it on. To me, if something works, then it was obviously made in Heaven. This worked for me and my mother and, for all I know, for Great-Grandmother, too. But it's sort of like Infinite Goodness; I'm always striving after it and often falling short. Still, if you're striving after a good thing, usually even your failure will be a sort of success.

Breakfast. My mother's rule was to include a fruit or fruit product, a meat, a starch, eggs, and a beverage. That was a huge country-style breakfast for men who were going to do hard physical labor all day. Modern, more sedentary and health-conscious folks are cutting back on cured meats and high-fat and high-sodium foods. So I now suggest you omit the meat or eggs—or both! Anyway . . .

A "fruit" can be a glass of fruit juice, sliced orange sections (cut orange on the equator; then get about four sections out of each hemisphere and eat with fingers), a grapefruit half, a half-cantaloupe or muskmelon, stewed or canned fruit, fresh sliced fruit on cereal or in pancakes, berry syrup hot for breakfast bread, or preserved fruit on bread.

A "meat" can be bacon, link sausage, patty sausage, ham slices, breakfast steak, pork chops, or fried trout.

A "starch" can be leftover boiled potatoes, maybe fried in butter with a little chopped green onion or green pepper added (saute first), or grated and fried (that makes hash browns). For potato pancakes, make patties with leftover mashed potatoes mixed with egg and milk (chopped onion optional), and fry in a little butter. Or have homemade bread, plain or toasted, or biscuits, pancakes, waffles, crepes, or corn bread. Or any hot cereal, or a cold one like homemade grape nuts. Or leftover rice warmed with hot milk and honey.

"Eggs" can be an ingredient in the breakfast bread, or they can be fried slowly over low heat in butter or boiled, poached, scrambled, souffled, or used in an eggnog.

Lunch. This varies so much depending on who is eating. If you feed a man who works near enough home to eat lunch with you, then you may even want to reverse the lunch and supper menus. If your man can't get home for lunch, lunchtime is handy for using up leftovers for you and the toddlers—or the cat. That's what I do. Mike takes a packed lunch to work. It usually consists of two sandwiches of leftover sliced meat on homemade bread plus some variety of extras such as hardboiled eggs, pickles, a ripe tomato, or carrot sticks. In the winter he takes Postum (made with milk), soup, or tea in his thermos; in the summer, cold tea, root beer, or ginger ale. On weekends we often grind leftover meat to make sandwich spreads. Then we have sandwiches, milk, and fruit.

Supper. Your menu should include a meat, a starch, and 2 vegetables. One of the vegetables should be raw. One should be green and the other should be a yellow, red, or white one. For a special dinner, have 3 vegetables—one green, one otherwise, and one raw—and add something sweet (jam? dessert?) and something sour (pickles? relish?) to the menu.

A "meat" can be any kind of meat prepared any way.

In my meals, a "starch" usually means bread, dumplings, noodles, or boiled, baked, or mashed potatoes. In Taiwan it would mean rice.

A "green vegetable" can be peas, beans, Brussels sprouts, broccoli, cabbage, collards, spinach, lettuce or any of the many other leafy greens, green onions, green peppers, and so forth. A "yellow, red or white vegetable" can be carrots, turnips, squash, sweet potatoes, cauliflower, parsnips, pumpkin, corn, radishes, beets, tomato, eggplant, and the like.

"Something sour" can be anything of the pickle, relish, spiced fruit, or vinegar family. "Something sweet" to me usually means fruit or a pudding sweetened with honey.

The "beverage" in summer is homemade root beer or ginger ale, cold water, iced tea and milk for the small children. In winter it's tea or honey and lemon with hot water, a mulled beverage, eggnog, or milk lassie made with hot milk.

Food Preservation Methods

This section describes general methods of food preservation. For detailed canning, freezing, drying, or root cellar storage procedures, look in the chapter that covers that food—for grains, Chapter 3; for herbs, Chapter 5; for fruits, Chapter 6; meats, Chapter 8. For vegetables, look in Chapter 4; pickles are mostly discussed under "Cucumbers" and sauerkraut making under "Cabbage" in that chapter.

IN-GROUND STORAGE: Some people say you should leave most of the root vegetables in the garden during the winter, even after they're grown, rather than using other preserving methods. Parsnips and salsify are about the best for that; they're often left in the ground over winter with a mulch over them. But I tried that and despaired. Every time I wanted something out of the garden, the ground was either frozen so solid that I couldn't dig it up, or it was so wet and muddy that I could barely manage to pull my legs back out of the garden soil, much less bring an armload of vegetables with me. If the ground freezes down far enough to freeze your vegetables, they will get soft and be no good anyway (except for leeks). I guess it depends a lot on where you live or what your garden storage system is. For more information, see "Extended Season Gardening" in Chapter 2.

DETERIORATION IN STORAGE: We share this wonderful world with myriad invisible but ravenous little critters who love to eat exactly the same things we do. The food preservation game is to get a move ahead of them and "enzymes," which are chemicals contained in the food itself that can cause undesirable changes. Salt, sugar, alcohol, sodium benzoate, and sulfurous acid are "chemical" preservatives

that, in effect, poison or make the food yucky to the beasties. Drying food makes it impossible for them to grow and reproduce in it. Freezing puts them into hibernation except for the most cold-hardy, which can then double their number only in months, perhaps, rather than in hours. Canning, when you do it right, kills every last beast in the food and seals it up tight so that no more can get in. Cellar storage takes advantage of certain living foods' natural defenses against spoilage.

All stored foods, no matter how they are stored, slowly but steadily lose quality and nutritional value as time goes by. Some foods deteriorate faster than others. If a food was on the verge of spoiling when you started, it may lose quality more quickly in storage. Some storage methods, such as canning and drying, hold the food better than others. The biggest single risk factor for most stored foods is warmth, which causes the loss of both nutrition and palatability. With few exceptions, the cooler it is (above freezing for nonfrozen foods), the better they keep. For every 20 degrees' increase in storage temperature, you lose one half of the possible shelf life of most stored foods. The ideal storage temperature is 38–40 F.

THE BASIC METHODS: There are 6 basic methods of food preservation: canning, freezing, drying, pickling (for salt, vinegar, and spices), sugaring (for jams and jellies),

and root cellaring—underground or even in the garden (live storage). Root cellaring is the oldest method, but not all foods store well using that method; in fact, most don't. Freezing is the most popular method and the next easiest, but it's also the most expensive, and you have to own a freezer and have electricity. Canning takes the most time and effort, but the food can be safely kept (if you carefully follow the rules) and stay delicious.

PRESERVING MEAT: Our family of 7 (and very often extras) can use 2 big calves, 4 pigs, maybe half an elk, and 50 or more chickens a year. The pigs supply cooking grease as well, which can be canned or stored in the deep freeze. Without electricity to run a deep freeze, you can't keep meat frozen, except if you live where there is a really bad winter—and even then, only during that winter. In most places, your outside temperature will be below freezing sometimes, but you'll also get off-season thaws that could spoil the meat. So, without electricity, you'll have to either rent a locker in a nearby town, which doesn't cost much, or can most of your meat right after butchering. That's what the old-timers did, and they ate well. You can also dry the lean meat in small strips—jerky. But that isn't as tasty or chewable as canned meat. You can can the meat from any kind of animal; just bone it out first. Another food preservation system for meat is making mincemeat at the beginning of the cool season. It will keep during the winter months in a cold, outdoor place.

COST COMPARISON: Another way of comparing preserving systems is by their cost. From that point of view, in-the-ground in your garden is cheapest. Root-cellar storage is next, because you build the cellar and then have no additional expense. However, drying can be cheaper than root-cellar storage if you have to factor in the cost of a root cellar, for if you're drying with simple sunshine, drying is free. If you're using an oven or dehydrator, it isn't.

Canning is a bit cheaper than freezing—even taking into account the cost of new jars, some sugar to add to your fruit, and the electricity it takes to heat your canner. If you live where electricity is expensive, the cost of canning can be as little as half the cost of freezing. On average, the electricity to keep 2 cubic feet of freezer space cold for 1 year in the Northwest will cost $7.68. On the other hand, electricity to can the equivalent amount of food (assuming peaches here) on high heat for 1½ hours would be only 13 cents. But electric costs vary wildly depending on where you live. Here in the Northwest, we have just about the cheapest rates in the country. If you're canning on a wood stove and have your own wood supply, then you don't even pay for electricity, and once you have your basic jar collection, new lids are your only expense. Electricity to dry that amount of fruit would cost about 40 cents. Freezing is the most costly method because you have to buy a freezer and pay for electricity and wrapping material or containers to freeze the food in.

NUTRITION LOSS IN STORAGE: But also consider, according to the USDA, that foods lose 60–80 percent of their nutritional value when they are canned, because of the high canning temperatures and water soaking. (Storing canned goods in a dark place minimizes the loss of riboflavin, which is caused by exposure to light.) Canned goods also lose vitamins from exposure to warmth. Frozen foods lose only vitamins E and B6, but if stored above 0°F, they can also lose a considerable amount of vitamin C and other nutrients, up to 40–60 percent of their food value. Blanching before dehydrating helps hold vitamins. Dehydrating using very low heat levels is less destructive of nutritional value than sun drying. However, dehydration results in more nutrition loss than any other form of food preservation. Live storage (in a root cellar) is the best of all for holding nutritional value, so long as the food doesn't freeze, the storage is cool, and the food is an appropriate one for this method. Heat, oxygen presence, and passage of time all cause losses.

Nutritionists are most concerned about what happens to vitamins A and C. Vitamin C is totally lost after sun drying foods (80–90 percent is lost after drying in a dehydrator) but is 100 percent retained in freezing. In canning, 25 percent of C is lost from fruits and 50–90 percent from vegetables. So they recommend that you dry or can high-vitamin A foods but freeze high-vitamin C foods.

SUMMING UP NON-FOOD FACTORS: Root cellar storage is cheapest of all and will retain most of the nutritional value. Of canning, freezing, and drying, freezing is quick and easy, but the most expensive; drying and canning are both cheap, but drying is by far the worst in terms of loss of nutritional value.

THE FOOD TO BE STORED: Yet another factor is that there are one or two best methods of keeping any single type of food. Sometimes even a particular variety of plant will keep better by one method than another. In my opinion, tomatoes, large fruits, syrups, fruit butters, and juices are all best kept canned. Cucumbers and cabbage are best pickled (preserved in salt). Green beans are good either canned or frozen. Corn, greens, peas, baby turnips, baby carrots, extra bread, meat, and hides waiting to be tanned are in my freezer. Berries are better frozen than canned. Fruits, except berries, are also very good dried. Apples are good made into sauce or butter and canned. Or you can dry apple rings or freeze slices in syrup for pie making. Onions, beets, green tomatoes, potatoes, winter squash, pumpkins, big turnips, big carrots, and celery will keep best in the root cellar. I didn't include drying in this list, but if you live where there's lots of dry, hot sunshine, this is also a wonderful option. Even if you don't and have to use an oven or dehydrator, it still may be a great option!

Books, Containers, and Equipment

FOOD PRESERVATION BOOKS: *Stocking Up III: The All-New Edition of America's Classic Preserving Guide,* by Carol Hupping, covers canning, drying, freezing, root cellaring, plus preserving meat and dairy products. A similar, good, big, conservative, encyclopedic book on food preserving is *Putting Food By,* by Ruth Hertzberg, Beatrice Vaughan, and Janet Greene; it also covers making sausage, cheese, lard, and grits. *The Busy Person's Guide to Preserving Food* by Janet Bachand Chadwick (1982) and *The Big Book of Preserving the Harvest* by Carol W. Constenbader would also be helpful. For commercial level postharvest technology, see the *Wiley Encyclopedia of Food Science and Technology* (4 vols., John Wiley & Sons, NY, 2000).
NOTE: The USDA says be careful of any canning recipes published before 1990! Before then, all canning recipes were based on research completed in 1942, but USDA studies completed in 1990 found numerous errors in the old research.

EQUIPMENT: If you are preserving foods gathered from your garden, orchard, and home butchering, you are periodically faced with preserving large amounts of the same thing—a mountain of apples, tomatoes, peaches, beans, etc. There are gadgets for sale that can make almost any food preserving process easier: cherry pitters, bean splitters, pear corers. And then there are the larger slicing, dicing, squeezing, and juicing types of machines. A "food mill" purees food and can also separate pulp and liquid; it's good for making sauces, fruit butters, and leathers. An electric blender or food processor is great for making smooth-textured sauces and spreads, and for chopping finely. These are all wonderful if you can afford them, but are not absolutely necessary if you can't. Everybody can afford some gadgets, though, even a humble one like a paring knife! A kitchen scale that weighs amounts up to 5 lb. is nice for making old-time recipes given in pounds. For heavier weights, use your bathroom scale.

C. F. Resources offers all kinds of food preservation stuff: vegetable strainers and juicers; canning funnels; a wide choice of pressure canners; American Harvest dehydrator; gamma seal lid to go on grain/bean storage buckets; opener for plastic pails; pasta makers; sprouting trays; grain grinders; 1-lb. dry yeast packages; and much more. Free catalog: 719-962-3228; **www.cfamilyresources.com.**

Over the years you'll find ways to acquire such gadgets. They save you time and energy and make food preserving more fun. Make sure you have a special place to keep directions for use, parts ordering info, and warranties—an envelope in a special drawer, maybe, or a photo-type album kept with your cookbooks.

PLACES TO BUY CONTAINERS

Basco, 2595 Palmer Ave., University Park, IL 60466; 800-776-3786; **www.bascousa.com;** food and water storage containers and seals.

Container Store, Melvin Selcer, 314 S. Main, PO Box 263, Agra, OK 74824; 918-375-2601.

Drumco/WaterTanks.com, PO Box 340, Windsor, CA 95492; 901-396-6484; 877-655-1100; **sales@water tanks.com; www.watertanks.com.**

Major Surplus & Survival, 435 W. Alondra Blvd., Gardena, CA 90248; 800-441-8855; offers gamma seal lids, etc.

NITRO-PAK Preparedness Center, 475 W. 900 S., Heber City, UT 84032; 800-866-4876.

The Wheat Bin, 620-345-2611, offers 5-gal. buckets, $3.65, or 6-gal. buckets, $4.

USING SAVED CONTAINERS: Back when I first wrote this book, public recycling was barely getting started. Back then thrifty housewives saved things like containers and found good uses for them at home. That principle can still apply.

NOTE: Polyvinyl plastic may cause cancer, so do not use plastic garbage cans, wastebaskets, or garbage bags that are not "food-grade" to hold food.

Cans. The 46-oz. juice cans are good lard holders. You can just fit a baggie over the top to make a fairly tight cover before putting it away in the freezer. Or put the right size "food-safe" baggie inside to line the can and fill it with liquid or food. Then tie, or wire shut, the baggie at the top and use it as a freezer container. One-gallon cans are good lard containers, too, and good grain holders to feed the chickens. Punch a few little holes in the bottom of your small cans, and you can start plants in them indoors. Cans make the best plant pots I know—except for peat pots, which aren't reusable or as sturdy, and you have to buy them.

Glass. Any gallon jar (glass or plastic) is good for many things—holding milk, pickling, anything you need a "crock" for. Widemouthed jars can be used as drinking glasses, or to hold seeds, crayons, Scrabble letters, or other odd things. In the summer, the children need jars with holes punched in the lid for grasshoppers, spiders, and so on. Small jars can hold dried herbs and spices, dried jerky, dried fruits, and crackers.

Paper. I wouldn't store (or eat off, or wipe with) white paper, because much white paper is bleached and has traces of carcinogenic dioxins in it. But brown paper bags are healthy to store in, as long as the food is dry and you don't heat the bag.

NOTE: Don't ever put a paper bag in a microwave or regular oven though, because bad chemicals will leach out of the paper when it gets hot.

Found Toys. There are 3 places in my kitchen where children are especially welcome. One is the box that holds their toys, coloring books, and so on. The second is the special drawer where I keep my collection of lids, which double as toys. They think of their own games to play with the lids, and the possibilities are practically infinite. Toddlers love the clunky bright metals, especially the doughnut-shaped canning screw-tops. Bigger children make up matching games. The woodbox is their other favorite kitchen toy box. All kinds of forts, houses, barns, highways, railroads, and towers go up on my kitchen floor. They all end up in the stove, of course, but then the children are very willing to haul in more wood for me.

DRYING

Sun drying is the oldest method of food preservation. Nowadays it is the least common form. Too bad, because drying is a cheap, easy way to preserve, and everybody loves the results. You can dry fruits, vegetables, meats, fish, herbs, berries, edible flowers, nuts, and eggs. For directions, look in the entry in this book that tells you how to grow them. Small, thin, leafy herbs are the easiest foods to dry. Apples, apricots, cherries, and coconuts are the easiest fruits. Easy vegetables are mature kidney, mongo, pinto, red, black, and soybeans; green lentils; chili peppers; parsley; celery tops; mature sugar, cow, chick, pigeon, and other peas; sweet corn; sweet potatoes; and onions. You can make jerked meats, vegetable chips (corn, potato, zucchini, etc.), and much more. Dried foods require less space and weigh less than foods preserved in any other manner.

LOW MOISTURE: Dried foods are preserved by their very low moisture content, so if in doubt, it's better to get them too dry rather than leave them too moist. The moisture

content of a well-dried food varies with the food, from as little as 5 percent for leafy vegetables up to 25 percent for acid fruits. Most microscopic beasties won't grow in a low-moisture environment. The beasties aren't dead, however—they're just waiting. Research on drying and dehydrators is going forward at a marvelous speed, so your drying results can be better all the time. Recent problems with canning lids, shortages of jars, and threats to public power have really impressed on me the importance of knowing how and being equipped to dry. Friends who fed me their home-dried foods eliminated my last shred of prejudice against dried vegetables. They were delicious!

DRYING INFO AND SUPPLIES: Get the latest extension service bulletins on home drying, probably free or at least cheap. Horizon Publishers (801-295-9451) specializes in dehydration books. They offer *The ABCs of Home Food Dehydration* and *New Concepts in Dehydrated Food Cookery—*

Hundreds of New Ideas and Tested Recipes for Enjoying Home Dehydrated Foods, both by Barbara Densley; *Fun with Fruit Preservation—Leather, Drying and Other Methods* by Dora D. Flack; *Home Food Dehydrating—Economical Do-It-Yourself Methods for Preserving, Storing, and Cooking* by Jay and Shirley Bills; and *Just Add Water—How to Use Dehydrated Foods and TVP* by Barbara G. Salsbury. There's also *Making and Using Dried Foods* by Phyllis Hobson; *Food Drying at Home* by Bee Beyer (300+ recipes for dried foods); and *How to Dry Foods* by Deanna DeLong. ATTRA's booklet, "Options for Food Dehydration," is at **www.attra.ncat.org/attra-pub/ dehydrate.html.**

Dry It—You'll Like It by Gen MacManiman (75 pp., $10) is a fun drying book—the first of them, and still a good one! Gen, now 86 and still going strong, offers her book, her personal line of Living Foods Dehydrators (your choice of three sizes, plus kits for those three sizes, plus they sell parts to make your own), and a free basic catalog of drying supplies: Living Foods Dehydrators; 425-222-5587; 3023-365nd SE, Fall City, WA 98024; **www.dryit.com.** From Gen's catalog you can order heat-fused polypropylene tray screening that is nonstick, absolutely food-safe, and easy to clean. You can get dryer thermometers and an electric food grinder specially adapted to powder dried herbs and vegetables, which you can then use to make your own instant soups and teas. (Powdered dried vegetables and meats are also nutritious additions to pet food or baked goods.) She also sells guar gum, a natural, excellent thickener for fruit leathers. Her growbox attachment turns a food dryer into a little hothouse for germinating seeds or sprouts. She offers Teflon sheeting—a permanent, nonstick, wipe-clean base for drying fruit leathers.

"FREEZE DRYING": This isn't something you can do at home. Food is freeze-dried by being spread on trays and then frozen there. Then the tray is put into a vacuum chamber. All the air is pumped out and the chamber is heated. The heat melts the ice, which turns directly into water vapor in the vacuum and is then pumped out of the chamber. Freeze-drying gets food drier than other drying systems; moisture is below 2 percent. So freeze-dried food stores longer and more safely.

Detailed Step-by-Step Drying Instructions

1. HARVEST: Harvest your fruit or vegetables at the peak of flavor. They'll taste better when slightly immature than when overripe—unless you're making leather. You can make fruit leather out of overripe fruits, but you're better off raising chickens and pigs on the overripe vegetables. Get started on the drying as soon as possible after picking the harvest. For sun-dried foods, start early in the morning. Then you've got the entire first day to get them started drying. Start on a day that promises to be dry and hot.

2. CLEAN AND SLICE: Wash off any dirt. Scrub if necessary. Dry off. Do the necessary shelling, peeling, slicing, or what-not. Vegetables to be dried are generally first cut up very thin, unless they are already small, like peas. Slice about ¼ inch thick—a little thicker for peaches, tomatoes, and zucchini. An important rule of drying is that smaller pieces dry faster and have better color and taste. If you slice peaches rather than merely halve and pit them, it takes more time at the start, but it saves time and struggle later on.

The same goes for your other foods, especially vegetables.

Because vegetables are low in acid and spoil more easily, they need to be cut thinner than fruits so they will dry quickly enough that no microscopic beasties can get going. On the other hand, you've got a point of diminishing return on the thin slicing. Carrots, zucchini, pumpkin, sweet potatoes, squash, and turnips, thinly sliced and dried, make wonderful snack chips—good plain or with a dip. But if you slice them too thin, some foods, such as tomatoes and zucchini, tend to stick to the tray. (Unless you're using Gen MacManiman's wonderful nonstick liners.) But then again, almost everything sticks to some degree or other, and that cures itself as the food continues drying.

3. PRE-DRYING TREATMENTS FOR FRUITS: Fruits do not get blanched, but some people believe that the larger, lighter ones are improved by dipping in ascorbic acid, salt water, fruit juice, or honey solution before drying. The dips are useful for apples, pears, apricots, peaches, and other light-colored fruits that turn brown (an oxidation reaction) if exposed to air. A mere change of color would be no big deal, but oxidation also damages flavor and destroys some of the vitamins A and C. Most dark-colored fruits, such as figs, prunes, and grapes, don't oxidize. For those that do, here are harmless ways (unlike sulfuring, which is harmful) to prevent or minimize oxidation. The ingredients for these solutions are available in various places; try your grocery store—or your drugstore.

Salt-Water Dip. To keep fruits from darkening, you can slice or chop them directly into a gallon of water that contains 6 T. flaked pickling salt. Soak no more than 5 minutes so it doesn't get mushy with water content or too salty-tasting.

Ascorbic Acid Dip. Ascorbic acid is a form of Vitamin C. To make it, crush 5 one-gram Vitamin C tablets, or add 1 or 2 T. ascorbic acid crystals or powder to 1 qt. lukewarm water. Slice or chop your fruit right into this solution. Remove the fruit from the dip before it gets soggy. Drain and dry.

Commercial Fruit Preservative. This is a powdered mixture of L-ascorbate, sugar, and maybe also citric acid. Just follow directions on package.

Sulfuring (or Not). The "sulfur" used for this purpose isn't usually pure sulfur. It's one of several preservative compounds containing sulfur that prevent darkening of light-colored fruits and repel insects. I don't give a hoot or a howl what color things are—dark skins are just as good as light ones, and vice versa. And I think that what insects would consider inedible probably wouldn't be healthy for my kids either. And I hate using chemicals unnecessarily. And unsulfured food tastes much better to me and digests easier. And 5 percent of asthmatics are sensitive to sulfites (some non-asthmatics may be also). The USDA says, "Those persons who are sensitive to sulfur dioxide and sulfiting agents have experienced sudden attacks of asthma, difficult breathing, nausea, diarrhea, and even death" after eating sulfured food. *NOTE: Sulfur fumes are injurious. If you sulfur, you must do so outside and avoid breathing the fumes! But I'm not going to tell* *you how to do it. Gerald Lehman, supplier of food dryers to the Amish, gets the last word here: "There is no need for chemicals or additives. Dried and properly stored dried foods will last as much as five years. Simply slice, dry, place in jar, and store in cool, dark area."*

4. PRE-DRYING TREATMENTS FOR VEGETABLES:

Blanching is a hot water "dip" or a period in steam. It is used for vegetables to be dried or frozen. Vegetables should be blanched to reduce the risk of spoilage of low-acid vegetables; to halt enzyme action, especially the enzyme that causes first ripening and then over-ripening; and to tenderize them. However, drying slows the enzyme action anyway. Those who research in this field say that most vegetables will retain more flavor, color—and possibly also nutrients—if they are blanched before drying. Not everybody blanches, but many do, especially if the veggies are old, have been gathered too long, or were grown under very dry conditions. Chili peppers, onions, celery, zucchini slices, thinly sliced mushrooms, and garlic need not be blanched.

The Non-Blanchers. Crystal Glenn (beautiful name!) of Aspen, CO, has lived on a farm most of her 52 years and made soap, bread, butter, cottage cheese—and raised chickens and dried foods too. She wrote me that she has never steamed her fruit before drying it, nor has she blanched her vegetables. She said, "I've never had anything spoil or get wormy." Catherine Humes wrote me that the only food she ever steams before drying is potatoes, "so they won't turn black." Farmers' Bulletin 841, put out by the USDA in 1917, agrees: "Blanching of vegetables is considered desirable by some housekeepers, but it is not strictly essential to successful drying."

Steam Blanching. You need a heavy pot or double boiler that has a tight-fitting lid, plus a wire basket that can be suspended over about 2 inches of hard-boiling water. The chopped or sliced vegetable in the wire basket shouldn't be more than 2 or 2½ inches deep. That way the steam flow will stay strong enough for all the food to blanch properly. Put the vegetable in over the boiling water, and cover tightly so your steam doesn't escape. If you don't have a steamer, put a sieve in the pan (hanging over the boiling water) or suspend a bag with the food in it over the edge of the pan. The important thing is to keep the food out of the boiling water so you actually steam rather than boil it. Blanch for the suggested number of minutes. Or just estimate: leave veggies in there until they are heated clear through and wilted, or until they look translucent when cut, tender but not completely cooked.

Boiling-Water Blanching. Start out with the kettle, but use lots more water. Put the food in the wire basket, but in this case you dunk the basket right down until the vegetable is all covered by the boiling water. Start counting as soon as the water starts boiling again and leave it in there for the recommended amount of time. You can use the same water over and over. Use at least 1 gal. water per 1 lb. food. You need plenty of water so water will boil again soon after immersion and for best heat distribution into the food mass.

After Blanching. Pull out the vegetable, drain, chill by plunging into ice water or under cold running water, and drain again. Merely draining doesn't get it dry enough to go into a dehydrator. Blot vegetable dry with cloth or paper towels.

5. SPREAD ON TRAY:

Spread your vegetables or fruit on the drying trays, one layer only in thickness, except for leafy stuff like parsley or herbs, which can be loosely mounded a couple inches deep. Don't dry very moist foods together with almost-dry ones. Dry strong-flavored (or -odored) foods by themselves. Set each piece separately (not touching) with air space between it and the next one. When drying look-alike herbs and fruit leathers, label them before drying.

6. SET TRAYS IN HEAT:

Set them out in the sun, in your attic, or in your solar or oven or electric drying situation. Dry at a low temperature for better flavor and color, safer storage, and no risk of burning. *The drying temperature must be high enough that the food will dry before it spoils, but low enough that the food doesn't cook or get hard on the outside while damp inside.* Within those limits, the faster a food dries, the better its final quality.

7. STIR OR TURN FOOD:

Turn the food often enough to keep it from sticking. Turn big-hunk kinds of food at least 2 or 3 times a day to speed drying and prevent sticking. Stir small pieces of food. Using a dehydrator, move most-nearly-dry foods to the bottom trays and put new and moist ones into the top. As foods shrink, you can consolidate to save tray space.

8. DONE WHEN?

Fairly dry food may last a month or two. For longer storage, it needs to be completely dry. When is that?

Dry vegetables until they are brittle and will shatter when struck by a hammer, or until the dried slices crumble or break when bent. Fruits are dry enough when between leathery and brittle. Some fruits such as figs, cherries, raisins, and dates, are always sticky, no matter how dry. But even though still pliable, fruits must not produce any beads of moisture when squeezed.

Drying Methods

SUN DRYING: You can dry either by sunshine, in an oven, or in a dryer ("dehydrator"). I prefer sunshine drying over oven drying. Taste is good, there's no expense or risk of burning or scorching. Sun drying is the basic commercial method too. Most apricots, raisins, figs, peaches, etc.—your grocery-store–dried fruits—were sun dried. Read Stella Andrassy's 1978 classic, *The Solar Food Dryer Book,* and Joseph Radabaugh's exciting updates in *Heaven's Flame: A Guide to Solar Cookers* (**www.homepower.com**).

Climate. For sun drying, your climate matters a lot. I live in a region where the days are very dry and very hot when fruit is in season. Hot days when the sun shines brightly all day long are perfect for sun drying. So outdoor drying is easy here in northern Idaho and in the dry Midwest and Southwest. It's harder in the rainy, humid, coastal Northwest.

Nights. Bring trays indoors at night because cool nights put moisture back into the food. Drying in the daytime but re-moisturizing at night can result in moldy food.

Bugs. If the sunshine holds, insects are the biggest threat in open-air drying. If you are drying early in the season before the flies and wasps are about, you can simply put the food out on trays. Sun drying works best if the wasps aren't around yet. Once August arrives, we are afflicted by wasps, with some child or other getting stung almost every day. I intensely dislike wasps, as does everyone else. Wasps especially eat meat and fruit. Fruit set out to dry not only attracts hordes of them, which is dangerous for the children, but the wasps actually will eat it up themselves. Cherries and apricots usually come before the wasps, so I can just lay them out plain with at most a porous cloth over the top. They'll go ahead and dry underneath it. Once the bugs are about, you must dry under a cheesecloth or nylon net, using something to raise it so that there's no chance of it blowing onto the food, especially into a sticky leather. Or else put the food outside in a screened bug-proof setup.

Flies are the other possible problem. A fly now can mean a maggot later in some types of food, especially meats. That's the real advantage of drying inside the house in a sunny window spot, or up in your attic, which is probably warm, dry, and bug-free. Another good spot is in the rear window of your car with the windows rolled down only ½ inch.

You can make a screened-in sun dryer by starting with something wooden with four legs and a vaguely box-like structure, such as an unused rabbit hutch. I have a neighbor who did this. He replaced the top and bottom of the hutch with screen. He hinged the top and, just like that, he had a wonderful dryer in which to put the food trays. You can even design it so that more than one level of trays can be loaded in at once. Mike made me an outdoor dryer from an old wooden table: a screen on the top replacing the original tabletop and a screen on the bottom. The top was hinged to lift up, and the food trays went inside. But I have to confess that this nice dryer made from a table later evolved in the other direction and ended up becoming a rabbit hutch for Becca's two Christmas bunnies.

Secrets of Sun Drying

1. Don't dry outdoors where there is traffic pollution to avoid possible airborne lead contamination!
2. Don't ever lay food to dry directly on galvanized screen. The screen contains zinc and cadmium and will contaminate food.
3. Fruits can be dried nicely at 85°F or higher, but a temperature of 100°F or more is best for drying vegetables.
4. Always dry in full sun in a place where the air is moving as freely as possible.
5. Begin your drying with the trays covered with cheesecloth or some gauzy cloth (propped up to keep it from touching the fruit) in order to protect it from insects.
6. Fruits can get dry enough to store in a couple days. Vegetables may need as long as 3 or 4 days. It usually takes about 3 times as long to sun-dry as to dry in a dehydrator or oven.
7. Researchers have discovered that if you keep the drying process continuous by using an artificial drying system during the night, your food dries much faster and there is better quality, less loss of nutrients, and less risk of mold.
8. At the end of each day, turn your drying pieces and take your trays inside the house for the night to avoid dew. Set them out again the next sunny morning until the drying is done.
9. If insect eggs may have been laid on your food, "pasteurize" before storing (discussed later in this chapter).

Homemade Drying Trays and Outdoor Dryer. You can make portable drying trays by making square (more or less) frames of soft lumber. Across the top, staple or thumbtack a single thickness of curtain netting or some other strong but very porous cloth or Gen MacManiman's plastic screening—

not metal, which may badly contaminate your food. The drying rack will resemble a window screen with a wooden frame. If you make your frame at least a couple inches smaller than the inside of your oven, you can also use these trays for oven drying. If the cloth sags, reinforce it underneath with string stretched from side to side. These screens are best when set up on posts or some such outside, so that air circulates through the mesh and all around your food. Inside the house, you can arrange a stack, with 3 or 4 inches between each tray, over the rear of your wood cookstove or heater, and dry food that way too. Allen Dong offers plans for a farm-scale food dehydrator at PO Box 413, Veneta, OR 97487. John Vivian published "How to Build a Food Dryer" in *Mother Earth News,* Feb./Mar. 1993.

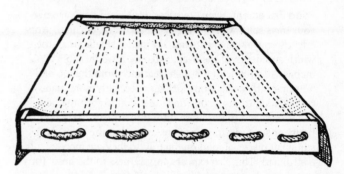

DRYING IN AN OVEN OR DEHYDRATOR: Food dried in an oven or dehydrator generally has more color, flavor, and nutrients than sun-dried ones (except for leather). And there's no bug problem.

Any very hot, dry area such as your attic, your car's rear window, or around your heater or cookstove is a good drying environment. So is your oven, but oven drying, unlike sun drying, means you have to be on hand to keep an eye on what's going on. Using a dehydrator is more like sun drying in that it's usually foolproof; you can walk away and forget about it. Low-wattage dehydrators work well on electricity from alternative power sources and are still cheaper than canning. Dehydrators are the easiest to dry in. In your oven or dehydrator, you can dry year-round. Most, of course, during harvest, but . . .

More Dehydrator Uses. A dehydrator is good for more than dehydrating fruit! In a dehydrator, you can make fruit leathers, jerky, and crackers; dry vegetables and herbs; rejuvenate limp crackers or chips; dry bread sticks to use with dip; and dry homemade pasta. It's also good for raising bread and decrystalizing honey. Use it to dry flowers, dyed wool or wool sweaters, and lingerie. In some you can start seedlings, grow sprouts, and make yogurt.

You can dehydrate food leftovers (remove and discard all fat) to later toss into a stew, soup, or casserole or munch for a snack: peas, sliced carrots, even leftover spaghetti casserole! Dry the food you salvage from your root cellar storage, such as half a squash whose other half spoiled and went to the pigs, chickens, worm bed, or compost heap.

Temperature. The biggest problem with oven drying is that it is often hard to get a steady enough heat at a low enough temperature. The ideal drying temperature is 120–150°F. Over 150°F is potentially disastrous. Judging temperature can be a problem. Some ovens don't have a thermometer. If you don't have an oven thermometer, you can buy a portable one and put it in there; toward the rear of your top tray is best. If you can't get an oven thermometer, you can judge temperature by feel. The food should feel cooler than the air in the oven. If it feels warmer to you, either you need less heat or the oven door should be open wider.

Disengage, remove, or do not light the top heating element of the oven. Preheat it at its lowest setting.

Air Circulation. This is also a problem in the oven if you have a tight-fitting door. You want the air to circulate around the food to absorb the moisture and carry it away. So prop the oven door open at least ½ inch. Gas ovens need to be open at least 4 to 8 inches. It helps to put a fan at one side of the open door to drive the air through the oven. While drying, occasionally change the fan's placement from one side of the oven door to the other.

Food Placement. Don't overload trays, and don't arrange your trays solid wall to wall, or the air won't circulate properly. Use trays that are at least 1½ inches smaller than the width and depth of the oven. Separate trays by about 2½ inches. Allow at least a 3-inch clearance from the top and bottom of the oven. Don't load an oven with more than 6 lb. of food to dry at one time; the food nearest the heat will scorch and that farthest from it won't dry. Every couple hours or so, swap tray positions around in the oven. And stir small pieces of food on the tray so they are more evenly distributed. This also exposes any wetness to the heat. Turn over large chunks individually.

Done? Oven drying is much quicker than attic, on-a-string, or outside drying. Vegetables may be done in as little as 5 to 12 hours, fruits in 6 hours or so. Pieces around the tray edges tend to dry first. Remove them first. Watch carefully near the end of the drying; it's easy to scorch food that overheats at the end. When drying is almost done, it's safest to turn off the heat and open the oven door wide.

Homemade Dehydrator. There are plans for making an electrical dehydrator in *Dry It—You'll Like It* and in Gen MacManiman's catalog.

Ready-Made Dehydrators. Among the many brands of electric dryers available, the Excalibur is very popular. It comes in three sizes, including a "family size." It's a real workhorse. For a free color catalog with recipes and drying tips, write: 6083 Power Inn Rd., Sacramento, CA 95824-2381; **www.excaliburdehydrator.com.** Look for a dehydrator that has a thermostat and is made of something better than the cheapie plastic that tends to break off after a few years. Magic Mill is of middling quality. Gen MacManiman sells a good one, the Living Foods Dehydrator. The American Harvest dehydrator has useful side venting.

Fruit Leathers

Another way to dry fruit, as well as certain vegetables, is to leather them. Leathers are lightweight, high in nutrition, and easy to store and pack for hikes and camping. They are a good way to make use of overripe fruits, a good healthful "candy" for the kids, and a good liner for a cobbler. Apricots and peaches make the nicest leathers, but you can make good ones from pears, plums, rhubarb, unseeded berries, and many other foods or combinations of foods.

OVERRIPE FRUIT LEATHER: All the rule books advise starting with only the best produce when preserving, but fruit leather is a blessed exception to that. If fruit is too ripe or bruised but not yet rotten, you can still make it into wonderful leather. In fact, slightly overripe fruit actually makes a sweeter, better-tasting leather! You just wash it, cut out the worst, mash, and dry. Bananas, even if almost brown, make fine fruit leather.

STEPS TO "LEATHER" MAKING

1. For any fruit, basically you just rinse it off and grind or force it through a sieve, mash with a potato masher, put through a food mill, or blend. Remove the peels, especially with pears, or you'll get a disagreeably grainy leather. Take pits and seeds out at whatever stage is appropriate. Too many seeds can really spoil a leather. You can store the mashed fruit in the freezer until you get around to making leather, and it will be all right. Even if it has started a wine-type fermentation, it will still make good fruit leather!

2. To make vegetables (squash, sweet potato, pumpkin, etc.) into leather, you have to precook and then sweeten and/or spice them to taste. You may like the final results of your fruit leathering better if you add 1 or 2 T. of sweetener per batch, and 1 t. lemon juice to light-colored fruits. You can vary sweetening and spices as you please, but you don't need to sweeten as much as you might think because as the leather dries and gets more concentrated, it gets sweeter and a chemical change occurs that causes the creation of more sugar.

3. The fruit or vegetables need to have the consistency of a smooth puree that is thin enough to pour. Add more fruit juice (any fruit juice will be great) or water if thinning is needed. (Apple and pumpkin tend to need thinning.) But too much water makes a puree that's too thin; thin puree tend to make a leather that sticks to the drying surface. (Grape and berry purees tend to be too thin.) If the puree is too thin, thicken by combining with a thicker sort of fruit puree; by slowly cooking it down over low heat to evaporate some of that water before you start drying; or by adding a thickener. There are lots of possible thickeners out there: guar gum (1 t. guar gum per 1 c. juice; let rest 10 minutes before you proceed); psyllium seed husks (1 T. per 1 c. juice; let soak 5 minutes before proceeding); slippery elm (2 T. per 1 c. juice; let soak 5 minutes); wheat or oat bran; or chia or flax seeds.

4. If you're making leather from light fruits (apple, apricot, peach, or pear), heat puree to almost boiling (about 180°F) before drying. That will retard the browning.

5. Line a drying rack or cookie tray with food-safe plastic. *Don't dry leather on wax paper or foil. The leather will hopelessly stick to them.* Low-pectin fruits naturally stick more than high-pectin fruits. Combine with apple if you want to raise the pectin amount. If you're expecting a sticking problem, lightly coat the drying surface with a nonstick vegetable spray or vegetable oil. If your plastic is flimsy stuff and likely to blow into the leather, tape or clothespin the loose edges to each side of the pan. A 12 × 17-inch cookie sheet will be just right for about 2 cups of puree. For larger quantities, one system is to cover the top of an outdoor table with plastic wrap fastened at the sides and ends with tape. Pour your puree onto that. To ward off bugs, you can make a cheesecloth tent over it.

6. Pour your puree in and get it spread an equal depth by carefully tilting the tray one way and then another. The

thinner your layer is, the quicker and easier it will dry. I recommend ⅛ to ¼ inch. Get it too thick and you'll have trouble with spoiling, or you'll just plain get tired of having it around before it finally dries. If you get it thicker in the center than at the edges, you'll end up with leather that's brittle around the edges while still sticky in the middle.

7. You can dry by sun, oven, or dehydrator. Even home economists say that sun drying makes the best fruit leathers! They taste better and keep longer. When oven drying, try not to get the heat above 130°F and definitely not over 140°F! Oven drying with insufficient air circulation or excessively high heat tends to make a brittle leather. High heat also runs the risk of scorching the fruit or even melting the plastic! It takes longer to oven-dry fruit leather than plain fruit, but your leather could be done within 6 hours. In a dehydrator, dry at 120°F. Rotate pan or shelves often. When top side is dry, pull fruit off its backing. Dry with the down side up for about an equal time, and then you're done. Drying time in the sunshine depends on how hot and how humid it is. As few as 8 hours is possible.

8. Fruit leathers that are still slightly sticky to the touch but peel readily from the plastic are dried enough if they'll be eaten within a month or so, or frozen. They're nicer for finger food, but will store only up to 3 months or so at room temperature; if dried until no longer sticky, they'll store indefinitely (a year or more). Leather that is completely dried is mold-proof but tends to crack, crumble, and not roll. Pear, pineapple, and rhubarb leathers just naturally get more brittle during drying and storage than other kinds.

9. When your fruit leather is dry, cut it in strips about 1¼ × 2 inches, or into squares. If you made strips, roll each one up, tightly layered between waxed paper or plastic wrap. Wrap with plastic or paper on the outside. Or store in flat sheets with something between them. Enclose in a tightly covered moisture- and bug-proof container. Or you can just bag them up in plastic and store in the freezer. If the leather is not adequately protected from light, air, warmth, and moisture during storage, it will tend to darken and deteriorate.

10. To serve, you can cook up the leather like dried fruit, but children enjoy snacking on hand-held chunks so much that's generally the way mine goes. Children love them as much as candy. Other options are to dissolve the leather in water and use as a pie filling, serve as a dessert topping over a pudding or ice cream, or stir in yogurt to flavor it.

⤷ *APPLESAUCE LEATHER COMBOS Mix applesauce with berries, or any strong-flavored or scarce fruit, to stretch it.*

Then use this mixture to make the leather, following the leather-making instructions above.

⤷ *CRISP FRUIT WAFERS Add ½ c. wheat bran per 1 c. thin fruit puree. Mix well, and proceed immediately as if to make a fruit leather. What you'll get is a delicious snack wafer. You can use oat bran the same way (especially good with tropical fruit juices), only it needs to soak for several hours before drying.*

⤷ *FRUIT LEATHER "CANDY" Sprinkle a breadboard with powdered sugar and work the leather strips on it, patting and rolling until about ⅛ inch thick and powdered.*

⤷ *LEATHER-JUICE COMBO The essence of this method is that you steam or precook your pitted fruit, then pour the panful into a sieve. What stays in the sieve gets made into fruit leather by the above recipes. What runs through (without a struggle) gets made into juice. The more juice you get, the quicker what's left will dry. This is really a great way to make your fruit juice without struggle and without waste!*

⤷ *FRUIT PASTE CANDY The pulp of two or more kinds of fruit can be combined for this. You can start from scratch with fresh, or use canned fruit. Just put the pulp through a fine strainer. Then measure it. For each pint of pulp, add 1⅓ c. sugar. Cook, stirring constantly, until thick and clear. Then turn out on an oiled platter. Let dry until a good tough film is formed on the top. Then turn it out onto a plastic screen to finish drying. Dry until it loses its stickiness. The sooner you can get it dried, the better. I recommend open air and sunshine for the job.*

⤷ *SUNSHINE PRESERVES This is actually a partially dried leather. This is the way to proceed if you want to keep the shape of the individual fruit sections in the preserves rather than work with a pulp. Dry fruit only until it has a "jam" consistency; then stop. Try this with apricot halves, nectarine or peach slices, or whole berries. The fruits keep their shape and color well. Use 3 c. sugar and 2 T. lemon juice to 4 c. fruit. Combine fruit, lemon juice, and sugar in a pan. Stir gently to blend the ingredients. Now cover and let set at room temperature 1 hour. This is to extract some juice to cook it in. Now put it on the heat and stir until it boils. Then let it boil hard 4 minutes without stirring. Now cool, uncovered. Pour your preserves out into glass or plastic pans or trays, ⅓–¾ inch deep. Set out in direct sunlight. If bugs or dust are a problem, cover with a pane of glass or clear plastic, leaving a 1-inch opening along the side. Once every hour stir a little bit. They are done when the fruit is plump (turn as needed) and the juice is about as thick as corn syrup. Your preserves will get thicker when cold.*

⤷ *UNCOOKED SUGAR-DRIED FRUITS To make this half-dried crock preserve, pit, peel, and cut up peaches, apples, sliced pineapple, or whatever. Dry partly. Then pack in a crock with sugar spread thickly between each layer. Another way is to halve peaches, remove the pits, sprinkle the cavities with granulated sugar, and dry in an oven. Currants and cherries can be boiled with ½ lb. sugar per 1 lb. fruit for 15 minutes and then spread out to dry.*

Storing Dried Food

CONDITIONING: The Number 1 problem in storing dried foods is mold. The risk is highest in a damp climate. So conditioning is very important, because it equalizes moisture so there are no damp spots where mold can get going. Conditioning allows excess moisture from some pieces to be distributed among and absorbed by drier ones.

After you finish the drying, put the food into a wide-rimmed, open-topped bowl for about a week. Give it a stir 2–3 times a day. Keep it covered with a screen or porous cloth fastened around the rim with a rubber band or string to keep out bugs. Then, if you wish, you can repack more tightly.

THE PASTEURIZATION OPTION: Some dryers heat up their dried foods once after they're done drying (and before storing) to "pasteurize" them. Other home dryers consider this step unnecessary and never do it. It's basically a final line of defense against bug problems. To pasteurize, heat the dried food before storing in a 175°F oven for 15 minutes, or in a 160°F oven for 30 minutes. Or else put in your freezer for 48 hours.

PREVENTING STICKING: Before bagging up sticky dried fruits, you can reduce sticking by shaking them in a bag of dusting material. Gen McManiman suggests dusting bananas with powdered oats, apples with cinnamon, pears with nutmeg, tomato slices with garlic powder or chili mix, and pumpkin pie leathers with pumpkin pie spice.

MORE TIPS ON STORING DRIED FOOD

1. Store in small batches because even one small still-moist piece can cause the whole container's contents to mold, and because dried foods are best if used within a short time after their container is opened.
2. If you live in a moist climate, put the dried food inside the jar, and screw the lid on tightly as soon as you've finished drying, so it can't accumulate moisture again.
3. The lid does not have to be a perfect-sealing canning-style lid; save your money. On the other hand, it's nice if the container is moisture-, bug-, and dust-proof. But the reality is that you can use almost anything for a while—and we do: even a paper bag, a recycled mayonnaise jar and lid, or a plastic box with a tight-fitting lid.
4. Don't store in glass jars or clear plastic bags. It's nice to easily check and see just what's going on in there, but where there's light, there's oxidation; and when there's oxidation, there's nutrient destruction. If you do use a glass jar, line it first with a brown paper bag. If you

must use glass and clear plastic, be sure to store it in the dark. Or you can store in paper bags.

5. In a humid climate, if your plastic or paper bags aren't airtight, you could put them inside a larger glass or metal container and put a tight lid on that. The outer glass or metal will also protect against }insects or rodents. *Dried food should never be stored in direct contact with metal!* (Line containers with plastic or paper.)
6. Label jars and packages with the name of the food and date you dried it. An easy system is to just put a strip of masking tape on the container and write on that. Freezing and thawing doesn't hurt dried food.
7. Store out of direct light and in a dry, cool room. You can keep it dark enough by storing the jars inside a cardboard box or under a sheet of black plastic.
8. Check once or twice a week for the first several weeks, and occasionally after that. *If you see moisture beads inside the jar, the food should be dried some more!* Mold is the result of food that's too moist when stored or that is packaged so openly in such a humid environment that moisture is absorbed.
9. Dried food should stay in prime condition for at least 6 months and may last up to 5 years, but there will be slow but steady deterioration in the meantime.
10. If bugs get into your dried food, you can salvage it by removing them and then roasting the dried food at 300°F for 30 minutes. Repackage and store the food again in containers that don't allow air circulation or insect passage. It should be all right, but check again after a few weeks. If there are signs of bugs, give the food yet another heat treatment. Bugs are not poisonous, just visually unappealing.

Using Dried Food

You can eat dried foods straight or "rehydrate" ("refresh") them by soaking or cooking in water, broth, or fruit juice. The warmer the water, the quicker the food will soak it up. Don't add sugar or salt to the rehydrating fluid; they both hold back water absorption.

Eat dried fruits out of hand for snacks at home, on the trail, or in lunch boxes. Or use pieces of dried fruit in cookies, cakes, puddings, breads, etc. Reconstituted dried fruit makes nice stewed fruit or sauce served plain. Or add it to bread, gelatin, stuffing, homemade ice cream, milkshakes, or cooked cereal. Soak before cooking—6 hours or more.

Unlike fresh fruit, dried fruit needs little or no sugar. That's because the drying process changes the starch in the fruit to sugar. The dryness and the sugar content were the forces that combined to preserve it. A little lemon juice, though, usually improves the flavor.

Add dried vegetables to stews, soups, or sauces. Or make a basic soup mix by powdering them in a blender. Add herbs or spices and package for quick soup. Combine with dried milk for an instant cream soup mix. Use in meat pies and other main dishes or add to gelatin or vegetable salads.

➤ *BASIC STEWED DRIED FRUIT Pour 1 c. boiling water over 1 c. dried fruit. Add ¼ t. cinnamon, ¼ t. nutmeg, and a pinch of ginger. Let set until it softens to your taste. Tastes good sweetened with honey or mixed with yogurt.*

➤ *FRUIT GRANOLA Chop dried fruit into small chunks; half raisins and half other fruit such as apples, apricots, or peaches is good. For every 2 c. chopped dried fruit, add 7 c.*

rolled grain (all one kind or a combo such as half oats and half wheat). Optional: peanuts, sunflower seeds, or other nuts and seeds. Stir together until well mixed.

❧ *DRIED FRUIT AND RICE* *Pre-soak 1½ c. brown rice. Then cook. Add lots of dried fruits, pumpkin pie-type spices to taste, perhaps nuts, and a pinch of salt. Serve with your choice of milk, butter, or honey. This is great warmed up with hot milk for a quick, good breakfast.*

❧ *DRIED FRUIT JAM* *Use dried fruit in any combination that suits you. Add extra sweetener if you like; ½ c. dried apricots with ¼ c. dates, for example, is good. Make this in a blender and moisten with a fruit juice to enhance spreadability. One cup pineapple juice is about right in that apricot-date combo. It helps to soak the dried fruit overnight in the juice before blending. This dried fruit jam makes a nice syrup on pancakes and waffles too.*

❧ *DRIED VEGETABLE SLICES AND DIP* *Slices of dried carrot, cucumber, eggplant, and tomato are good with a dip.*

❧ *INSTANT SPAGHETTI SAUCE* *To a basic tomato puree, add dried onion, dried green pepper, dried basil, and oregano.*

❧ *VEGETABLE POWDER* *You can grind any thoroughly dried vegetables in a blender or in Gen's special powdering machine. Store in tightly sealed, small packages. To use, just add to boiling water. You can create your own formulas for instant soups or extra nutrition and flavoring for casseroles or stews.*

FREEZING

Freezing is the most popular food preserving method. There is no risk of botulism. It's simpler and far faster than canning. And it retains more nutrients than any other form of food preservation. Freezing is a wonderful system for preserving meat.

The foods that freeze least well are the ones that you are accustomed to eating crisp: celery, lettuce, cucumbers, green onions, green peppers, and radishes. But even these can be frozen and used in cooked dishes. Food varieties have become very specialized; the fruits and vegetables that freeze best of all may now be distinct varieties developed especially for that quality. Check with gardening neighbors or your county extension agent.

After the home freezer was invented, people soon froze more than they canned, and they still do. However, you need a real freezer. You can't do serious food storage by freezing in that small space above the refrigerator. It isn't big enough, it isn't cold enough, and its temperature fluctuates too much for safe long-term storage. Upright or

chest-type freezers will keep food in a good state for months or longer, though it will lose quality.

To sum up, freezing is great and most foods do wonderfully well in the freezer, even over long periods. But there is a big difference between food that has been in the freezer two weeks and food that has been in there a year!

BOOKS: See *The Complete Book of Home Preserving* and *The Home Freezer and The Complete Book of Freezer Cookery*, both by Ann Seranne. The new *Ball Blue Book Guide to Home Canning, Freezing & Dehydration* is available from Alltrista, Direct Marketing, PO Box 2005, Muncie, IN 47305. But there's no substitute for experience. There's no way you can kill yourself eating frozen foods. So don't worry. Plunge in, start doing it—and you'll learn how as you go.

LOCKERS: A "locker" is a box-like space that you can rent in a public walk-in freezer. They are wonderfully cold. You can rent all the space you need. They're so cold that they're good for quick freezing both meat from hunting or butchering and a mountain of vegetable harvest that you will sooner or later move to your home freezer. They're good for holding a harvest overflow, and they're priceless if your power or freezer conks out and won't be operational again for a while. To find one, look in the Yellow Pages under "Lockers," "Frozen Food Locker Plants," or "Cold Storage." Lockers are inexpensive to rent. Get the size you need. You furnish your own pad-lock, and you can come and go as you please to add or remove food.

ONCE-A-MONTH COOKING: As the owner of a freezer, you have the option of this exciting new concept in food preparation! Once a month, in 1 or 2 hard-working days, cooks prepare 30 or more meals at a time, then package them in portions and freeze. The rest of the month, they just pull them out of the freezer, thaw, and serve. (Thaw in fridge 24–48 hours. Then bake, if not pre-cooked—most of these are casseroles. Or microwave.) Once-a-month cooks say it helps them get the food budget under control, saves having to figure out what to fix for dinner every night, avoids excess visits to the grocery store, enables them to supply a meal on short notice with very little effort, and saves washing pots and pans every night. When a friend is sick, you can take her a meal from your freezer. And this system frees up a lot of time for things other than cooking.

Actually, not everybody who cooks this way makes 30 dinners at a time. Some cooks prefer to do it every 2 weeks and make 15 at a time, or to just double or triple the recipe every time they cook and put the surplus in the freezer. Some prefer to do 45 at a time! Learn once-a-month cooking with **www.simplemom.com**, the website of Deborah Taylor-Hough, author of *Frozen Assets Lite and Easy*. Or read *Once a Month Cooking* (also published as *Dinner's Ready*) by Mimi Wilson and Mary Beth Lagerborg.

Buying and Installing a Freezer

CONVENTIONAL OR RADICAL ALTERNATIVE? There are some amazing new appliances out there in the rapidly developing area of alternative energy products. Consider checking out the sources listed in Chapter 1 that specialize in these, and see what they've got. When you buy these pioneering products, you finance people who are doing urgently needed research and help test their innovations. Even more energy-efficient versions of standard mass-market freezers are a good investment. They're likely to cost maybe

10 percent more up front, but you'll save money in the long run because a typical freezer will last for at least 20 years.

FROST OR FROST-FREE? Frost-free freezers use more energy and tend to dry out food. With the other kind, you'll have to defrost once a year.

CHEST OR UPRIGHT? The upright freezer takes up less floor space, is easier to see into and find stuff in, and you're less likely to lose stuff into the bottom until it is so old it no longer tastes good. In all other categories, the chest type is superior (and it is the most popular). The chest type is cheaper, won't need defrosting as often, and gives you more room for your money because you can pack it practically solid without everything falling out every time you open the door. It's also more heat efficient and better at keeping the food at the needed steady cold temperature because the cold air doesn't fall out every time you open the door. We have the biggest chest type there is. It cost about $250 [1974]. The freezer is a low-maintenance appliance. The guarantee probably won't be an issue for years.

SIZE? Chest freezers range in capacity from about 5 to as much as 28 cubic feet. Uprights can be just as small or even larger. On average, 1 cubic foot of freezer space will hold 35 pounds of frozen food. The size most often bought by families is the 16-cubic-foot capacity. The largest size freezers, 18 to 25 cubic feet, work well for large families that are doing major gardening, home butchering, and/or advance meal preparation. A family that uses its freezer a lot can make use of just about all the space they can get, as much as 7 cubic feet per family member. A bigger freezer can inspire you to do more food preserving, more baking and cooking ahead, and more shopping for bargains.

Some big families I know use 2 chest freezers. But I think one can do it for most families if you stagger the input. Vegetables and berries are frozen in season. Canning your fruit saves room. Wait to butcher until the weather is quite cold and there is increasing room in the freezer because the vegetables are being eaten up. On the other hand, if you have, say, two 10-cubic-foot freezers instead of one 20-cubic-foot one, you can use one for long-term storage and the other for frequently used items. The long-term foods will store better because the lid isn't going up and down all the time. And when you defrost, you can keep frozen goods in one while you defrost the other, and then switch and do the same thing to clean the other.

CORD AND PLUG: When you are setting up your freezer, put the cord and plug in a place that's as protected as possible from little gremlins. All they have to do is pull that plug to bring on a terrible disaster in the freezer. Since the first edition of this book came out, several people have written to tell me that you can buy a special attachment for a plug that makes it childproof. Sounds like a great thing.

WHERE TO PUT IT? It would be nice to have it close to your kitchen, but freezers generally aren't in the kitchen. That's because the cooler the location you put it, the less the freezer will have to run, which saves on electricity. On the other hand, don't ever put a freezer where the temperature goes below freezing. Oddly enough, they're built to cope with heat (up to about 110°F) but not to endure that much cold. So consider putting it on a back porch or in a basement, attached garage, or any relatively cool part of the house. Set it out of direct sunlight and in a well-ventilated space. A 50–65°F room is good. Don't put it near your wood stove or furnace, or in a humid area; that hastens frost accumulation.

NOTE: Figure out where your freezer will go before you buy! Check to make sure doors and turns are wide enough to get it in there. Allow for a 4-inch space between the back of the freezer and the wall (to vent condenser-coil heat).

IDEAL FREEZER TEMP: The ideal temperature at which to set your freezer is −5°F. You can double-check the freezer temperature with a mercury-type thermometer. Food will keep longer at lower temperatures, but your electric bill will be proportionately higher; 0°F will keep it long enough. *NOTE: Don't set it any higher than 0°F. Above that, food deteriorates much more quickly, even though it is still frozen.*

Yes, I know that 32°F is the temperature below which things freeze, but though food stored even at 15–20°F seems solidly frozen, it just won't keep as well as food stored at 0°F or below. Even at a few degrees above zero, the freezer life of your food is cut in half! Those low-temp-specialist microbes are really something. If your freezer or freezer compartment can't keep food at 10°F or below, try to use it up within 2 months.

Also consider that the top center of a chest-type freezer tends to be a few degrees warmer than the bottom. In an upright freezer, the storage area inside the door tends to be the warmest. Adjusting the freezer compartment of your refrigerator to store food at 0°F will tend to keep the refrigerator section underneath below 37°F (the ideal temperature for preserving nonfrozen foods).

So if you want to save on the electric bill, a better way than turning up the temperature is to keep the freezer at least 70–80 percent full. Keeping air cold requires more electricity than keeping food cold! Keep the freezer door shut except when you absolutely have to get in there, and make it fast when you do open it. That helps keep it cold. Be especially careful when the air is hot and humid. If your freezer is old, make sure it's staying well-sealed around the door. Gaps allow cold air to leak out and warm, moisture-carrying air to get in.

Milk Carton Tip. From Jan Grant, county extension agent, Seattle, WA: Fill up your extra freezer space with empty cardboard milk cartons full of water. Once they are frozen, they will help keep your food cold longer in case the electricity goes off. And you can use the block of ice when blanching vegetables for freezing: Put it in your chilling water. It's also an emergency water supply; just melt and drink.

Steps to Freezing Food

The four most most important factors for success in freezing food are food quality to start with, speed in processing, airtight packaging, and temperature control.

1. FOOD QUALITY: Start with only high-quality, truly fresh-from-harvest food. You'll have best results if you choose young, tender vegetables. When I thin the carrots, I wait until I have some "baby" size—finger size, you can say. I pull those out and freeze them. That way I don't have to throw away any plants. I come back and get more later if the garden needs more thinning or my freezer needs them. Big carrots don't freeze well. They are better kept in the ground or in the root cellar, or sliced thin and dried. But those baby carrots can be frozen whole. The same goes for the baby beets. Beans for freezing should be no more than half grown, in the long, slender stage before they have gotten fat and tough with the beans inside too well developed. Full-grown vegetables are better off canned or stored in the root cellar. Lettuce, onions, cucumbers, and radishes don't freeze well.

2. Process Quickly: Get food, especially vegetables, from the garden to the kitchen counter as rapidly as possible. If vegetables are sitting, they're losing both nutrition and flavor. If they must wait, store them in a cold place.

3. Prepare Food: Wash the food thoroughly in cold water in a colander or sink filled with cold water. Scrub as needed with a medium-stiff bristled brush or a plastic or nylon-net scrubber. Lift the food out of the water when you're done to leave behind the grit that has settled to the bottom of the sink. If you want to freeze slices of vegetables such as broccoli, cut them before blanching, except for corn—cut it off the cob afterwards.

4. Pre-Treat (Blanch) Vegetables: Blanching destroys enzymes that cause food spoilage. Don't blanch chopped onions, green peppers, sliced mushrooms, sliced zucchini, or fresh herbs. It also isn't necessary to blanch vegetables that are to be stored less than 3 months. For longer storage it's not a matter of life or death, but color and texture will turn out better if you blanch. At first there's no difference, but after 4 or 5 months, blanched foods are much nicer.

Non-Blanchers. Not everyone blanches before freezing. Ione Thompson of Colusa, CA, wrote me, "We do not care to blanch many of the vegetables we freeze, as they lose flavor and crispness. With peas and beans (also all fish) we clean them, put into plastic cartons, and cover with water. When frozen, take from carton, put in baggie, and return to freezer. We wrap corn and asparagus tightly in foil, then put in baggies or freezer paper and freeze." Indeed, many vegetables can be frozen without blanching, but their storage life won't be as long. Other than those named above, the best vegetables not to blanch are celery, corn in husks, cabbage, sugar snap peas, summer squash, and broccoli. To see what you prefer, run an experiment. Blanch some of your vegetable and don't blanch some. Label the packages and compare the results.

Equipment. You need a deep kettle that contains boiling water; a colander and/or big sieve (to hold vegetables to be blanched) that can be immersed in the kettle without having the rim or handles go under water; and 2 buckets or double sinks full of ice and water.

Blanch. Immerse the vegetables in hot water. Time the scalding starting from the moment the water returns to a boil. (The time needed to blanch a food is given under the entry for that food in this book.) Add 1 minute to the blanching time if you live 5,000 feet or more above sea level.

Chill after Blanching. Immediately after the blanching is completed, remove from the hot water. Sometimes I put larger vegetables directly into the kettle of water, as you do with corn on the cob. When they are blanched, I fish them out with 2 potato mashers, one held in each hand. Smaller vegetables are fished out with a sieve, which then holds them under cool running water from the sink faucet. The ideal procedure is to put the blanched vegetable into an ice bath or to cool in a colander under a stream of cool running water until you have its temperature down as low as possible. The immediate chilling reduces as much as possible the period of lukewarm temperature during which

the bacteria quickly build their numbers. The thicker the vegetables, the harder it is to get them frozen (beets and whole carrots take longer than peas, for example), so you should have them cooled as much as possible before packaging. The only exception to chilling before freezing is if you're working with only a small amount that you can put in small packages for the freezer to cool.

Sample Blanching Procedure: Peas

a. Put shelled peas in the colander and sink colander, peas and all, in the boiling water.

b. Leave it there just long enough for the water to return to a boil. Then start counting. If it takes longer than 2 minutes for the water to boil again, you're trying to blanch too much at once. You can time the vegetable or do it by experience. When the peas change color, they're ready—"blanched."

c. Lift out the colander full of peas and let it drip a moment. Immerse in a first bowl of ice water. Stir with your fingers to help it cool.

d. In a minute or two move it to a second bowl of ice water.

e. When the peas are thoroughly chilled, drain, package and put in freezer. You'll have terrific-tasting peas using this system.

5. Pre-Treatments for Fruits: Fruit can be packed for freezing without a sweetener or a liquid. Fruits that will be eaten raw or used for pies or jams after thawing will be fine without a sweetener. Just slice or crush in them in their own juice, or even freeze them whole.

Anti-Oxidant Treatment. To prevent discoloration of light-colored fruits and other deteriorating effects of oxidation, fruit can be briefly soaked in a solution of ascorbic or citric acid (or a combination of the two)—about ½ t. per 1 qt. water. Or some lemon juice can be added to their water. You can buy the acid at any grocery or drugstore under a trade name.

Sugar and Syrup Packs. Fruits deteriorate in color, texture, and flavor less quickly if packed in a sugar or syrup pack than if frozen unsweetened.

Pectin Pack. Fruit is frozen in a syrup made by mixing powdered pectin, sugar, and water. Combine 1 package (1¾ oz.) powdered pectin with 1 c. water. Boil 1 minute, stirring. Add ½ c. sugar and stir until dissolved. Remove from heat. Add enough cold water to make a total of 2 c. syrup. Cool before using.

Dry Sugar Pack. Just mix sugar and fruit until the sugar dissolves in the fruit juices. Use 1 part sugar per 4 or 5 parts fruit, measured by weight. Or sprinkle ½ c. sugar per 1 lb. fruit.

Honey Pack. Honey will work if your freezer faithfully stays at 0°F or below. If the temperature gets higher, the honey is likely to crystallize.

Syrup Pack. The fruit is prepared for freezing by immersing it in a sweetened syrup. Syrups may be called light, medium, or heavy, depending on how much sugar they contain. A light syrup is made by mixing 2 c. sugar with 4 c. water. A medium syrup is a mix of 3 c. sugar and 4 c. water. A heavy syrup is 4¼ c. sugar and 4 c. water.

6. Package: Use vapor-resistant or vapor-proof packaging materials. Package in such a way as to remove as much air as possible and seal the package airtight. Be sure to label the outside of the package with the date and name of what's inside! I like to package in plastic bags because it saves freezer space. Paper containers with only a thin layer of wax, and the thinner plastic bags and wraps, are not suitable containers.

Plastic Boxes. Best are plastic containers that are intended as freezer containers. You should be able to seal the cover airtight. You can use waxed cardboard cartons (cottage cheese, ice cream, or milk cartons) only with a polyethylene bag liner, because alone they are not moisture/vapor-resistant. If you put a plastic bag inside the plastic freezer boxes before you pour in fruit, the fruit keeps better and the outer plastic container lasts better. You can use regular zip-top plastic bags from the grocery store for this. Don't use hard plastic containers such as cottage cheese, yogurt, or margarine tubs at all—or at least only with an inside bag—because they tend to crack at low temperatures.

Jars. The best jars for freezing are wide-mouthed freezer jars with straight sides. The best shape for rigid glass or plastic containers is square, so they fit close together and don't waste freezer space. To pack food into a wide-mouthed container, allow ½ inch headspace at the top for pints, 1 inch for quarts. If it's a narrow-mouthed container, leave ¾ inch headspace for pints, 1½ inches for quarts. This is to allow for expansion of the liquid while freezing. You can freeze in nonfreezer-proof jars if the contents will be relatively loose and dry rather than liquid.

Bags. The non-rigid containers that you can use are boilable plastic bags and plastic freezer bags. Boilable bags are constructed of heavy-duty, food-safe plastic that can handle both cold and heat. (If you are using boilable bags, you can blanch, cool, freeze, and later cook the vegetables, all right in the same bag.) Polyethylene film and bags are good for freezing. You can get them at grocery outlets. For freezing, it's best to use only plastic bags labeled "food safe." I bag all my vegetables. If the bags aren't sturdy, especially when holding peas and beans, I pack them into a larger, stronger plastic freezer bag. A chicken will fit into one big bag.

Freezer Wraps. We wrap other meats with butcher paper ("laminated paper" or "locker paper") fastened with freezer tape. Your butcher can tell you how to get such paper if your grocer can't. Or you can wrap in polyethylene or Vinylidene chloride film (Saran) sheets. Heavy-duty foil ("locker"- or "freezer"-grade) is another option, though I dislike putting aluminum next to food. Regular kitchen waxed paper is not enough protection for long-term freezer storage. When using a wrap, press it around the food to shut out as much air as possible. You want your package to be moisture/vapor-proof. The best wrap is the one that is most tightly sealed. To package food using rolled material, cut it to size, wrap around your food in about three layers, press to get out all the air, and seal with freezer tape.

Sealing Boilable Bags. Seal by placing the top of the bag on the small, heated sealing strip inside the bag sealer. Some bag sealers and bags are designed to use a continuous-roll bag that you custom-seal to whatever size bag the situation calls for. There are various brands of bag sealers, such as the Oster Automatic Bag Sealer, Dazey Seal-A-Meal, and Krupp vacuum sealer, all modestly priced. Or you can seal by filling the boilable bag, laying it on a heavily padded board, covering the bag with a damp cloth, and sealing the open edge using an electric iron at its low setting. This is more trouble than the regular bag sealer, but it works.

Foods Containing Free Liquid. For foods that are mushy or runny, you'd appreciate something sturdier than a plastic bag. You could line with a plastic bag a tin can, an odd-sized jar that can't be used for canning, or a jar with a chipped rim. (The bag also makes air space in the bottom of the jar that prevents the jar from breaking when the frozen liquid expands.) Pour in the liquid and close off at the top. Leave 1 inch headspace in glass jars, ½ inch for plastic containers. Freeze it in the upright position; once frozen, it can go any which way. You can also freeze using freezer jars. In that case, pour the food in your jar, put on the lid, and screw the band down tightly. That is probably the best freezer container because it's an airtight, leakproof, moisture-proof, odor-proof container. Be sure and leave headspace at the top to allow for expansion during freezing.

Vacuum Sealing. Vacuum sealers for individual users are a recently developed product. You can buy them at Costco for $250 or so.

NOTE: After you vacuum-seal food, it must be refrigerated and eaten soon—or kept frozen or canned. Otherwise, vacuum-sealed food can kill you from botulism, just as underprocessed canned food can! People see shrink-wrapped foods in the store that are keeping well and assume all the packager did was wrap them. But those foods were packaged and sealed and then heat-processed, much like canned foods!

7. FREEZE: Speed is important! Quick freezing minimizes ice-crystal formation and spoilage.

Secrets of Speed Freezing

1. Twenty-four hours before you're going to be doing a major freezing project, turn your freezer temperature to –10°F.
2. Small packages freeze faster than big ones.
3. You can freeze food most quickly by spreading it out on a tray and putting it in the freezer. When frozen, gather up the food and bag it for long-term storage. Not only is this style quick, but you can also freeze food loosely so that a little can be removed at a time rather than it all coming out in one big frozen hunk.
4. Put the packages of unfrozen food right next to the freezing plates or coils in the coldest part of the freezer. Or place unfrozen food against the freezer wall, and in a single layer across the top of your freezer, with space between packages. After they're frozen you can re-arrange for long-term storage.
5. For big quantities, you can quick-freeze in a locker and then bring home to your freezer.
6. Once the food is all frozen, turn the freezer back to 0°F.

Freezing a Lot at Once. The bigger your freezer is, the more food it can handle freezing at once. But don't overwhelm it. The manufacturer's booklet that comes with the freezer will tell you the maximum amount that you can freeze at one time. If you have half a beef, perhaps it would be best to take it to a locker for quick-freezing first. The more unfrozen food you put into a freezer at once, the longer it will take the machine to get it frozen. Worse, having a bunch of warm food in there may raise the temperature of the frozen food already in there. It's more at risk than the fresh food, because frozen food whose temperature increases can quickly spoil. So be conservative in adding new food—in general no more than 2 to 3 pounds of food per cubic foot of freezer space. For example, a 16-cubic-foot freezer should not have more than 35 pounds of unfrozen food put into it in one 24-hour period of time.

Freezer Storage Times for Good Quality

Fish and Meat

Fish	2 to 3 months
Oysters, crab, roe, lobster	4 to 6 months
Raw meat	8 to 12 months
Fried meat/poultry	1 to 3 months
Roast meat/poultry	2 to 4 months
Meat dishes, cooked/combo (stew, etc.)	3 to 6 months
Meat loaf	3 to 4 months
Meat, ground	3 to 4 months
Pork, cured	1 to 2 months
Pork, fresh	6 to 8 months
Poultry (chicken, turkey, etc.)	12 months

Dairy and Eggs

Butter	5 to 6 months
Cheese, hard or semi-hard	6 to 12 months
Cheese, soft	4 months
Cottage cheese	1 month
Eggs	12 months
Ice cream/sherbet	1 to 3 months
Milk	1 month

Baked Goods

Biscuits, baking powder breads, rolls	6 months
Cakes (angel, chiffon, sponge)	6 months
Cakes, shortening (chocolate, nut, spice, etc.)	6 months
Cheesecake	4 months
Cookies, baked	6 months
Cookies, unbaked (except meringue)	6 months
Cupcakes	6 months
Fruitcake	12 months
Muffins	6 to 12 months
Pastry crust, unbaked	6 to 8 weeks
Pie, baked pastry	2 to 3 months
Pie, chiffon	1 month
Pie, fruit or nut	3 to 4 months
Pie, mince	6 to 8 months
Waffles	1 to 2 months
Yeast breads, baked	6 months

Fruits

Fruits, citrus	12 months
Fruits, non-citrus	12 months

Vegetables

Onions, uncooked	3 to 6 months
Vegetables, cooked	1 month
Vegetables, uncooked (except onions)	12 months

Other Foods

Appetizers containing mayonnaise, sour cream, egg whites	3 to 4 weeks
Dips and spreads (no mayo, sour cream, or egg whites, but may contain cheese, cold cuts, fish, or egg yolk mixes)	1 year
Nuts	6 to 8 months
Pasta (macaroni, spaghetti, etc., cooked)	1 month
Soups, stews	6 months

It's best to use all frozen foods within a year, and most of them in less time. These recommended keeping times for frozen foods are based on quality loss. You could have a turkey in there for 14 years and, if it never defrosted, it would still be safe to eat, though not very tasty.

Using Your Freezer

LONG-TERM FOOD ARRANGEMENT: I try to arrange food in up-and-down columns so I always have something of everything on top. Meat takes up a lot of room, so it goes on one whole side, with the vegetables and fruits on the other. When I have only a little of something—like packages of butter, cream cheese, or bread—it goes into the baskets on top so it doesn't get lost down among the rest.

RECORDS: It's a good idea to keep an inventory taped to the outside of your freezer of what's in there. It should be a list of all the food inside and when you put in each item. That will help you plan meals and use food within its recommended storage period. Cross off items as you take them out.

DETERIORATION OF FROZEN FOODS: Each bag holds the amount we would use at one meal. That isn't always the same, though. As the year wears on, it takes larger portions of the frozen food to satisfy our hunger. Even when it still looks and tastes good, your frozen food is losing some food value and you have to eat more to get your hunger satisfied. Over the months, the frozen vegetables and fruits slowly but steadily lose taste, texture, and nutritional value. There is a big difference in the green beans, for some reason. What that means is that in the early spring, when cooking and serving, you have to serve—and eat—a bigger portion of those beans (or other frozen foods) in order to get the same amount of nutrients as you did when you first froze them in the fall. The "Freezer Storage Times for Good Quality" table gives guidelines on how long different kinds of foods will keep.

Deterioration of frozen foods can come from four sources: growth of low-temperature microbes; "freezer burn," which means dehydration and oxidation from air contact; ice crystals, which puncture cell walls, turning food into mush; and those ripen-then-rot enzymes doing their thing.

Microbes. Yes, some microbes are functional at even below-freezing temperatures, and they can reproduce even in the freezer, although very, very slowly. At that low temperature, mid- and high-temperature microbes can't grow at all, and even the low-temperature-specialist beasties can't grow very fast. They may double in number only every couple months instead of every few hours, as they would outside the freezer.

That growth of low-temperature bacteria is why food, even in the freezer—especially rich, moist foods like ice creams and gravies—will indeed slowly but eventually "spoil," although it takes 1–24 months depending on the food and the freezer. To keep low-temp bacteria under control, it really matters what temperature your freezer is set at and whether it remains constant or fluctuates up and down. To keep bacteria almost perfectly inactive, the food has to stay at 0°F or lower. Anything warmer, even for a while, is a marvelous window of opportunity for those cold specialists.

Freezer Burn. If your container isn't securely closed, the food will, over months, dehydrate and deteriorate. You can see freezer burn on the food; it will look kind of faded and dried.

Mushiness. Frozen water inside the food forms tiny ice crystals that can puncture cell walls. You know that has happened if, when the food thaws, the juices run out and the food seems mushy. But the faster the food freezes, the smaller the ice crystals will be; that helps preserve your food quality. Partial thawing and refreezing double the cell damage and diminish food quality that much more.

Enzyme Deterioration. If your vegetables aren't blanched or your large fruits aren't packed in syrup, the action of natural ripen-then-rot enzymes inside them will cause undesirable changes in color, flavor, and food value.

WHEN YOUR ELECTRICITY GOES OFF: When you have a freezer, there is always the nightmarish possibility of the power going off. For sure, sooner or later it will, or the freezer will break down. Plan what you will do when that happens. Locate a nearby freezer-locker plant or a place that sells dry ice. Your only other emergency option is to can or dry the food immediately as an alternate preservation method. The food would lose some, but certainly not all, of its quality in the processing.

1. If you know ahead of time about a possible or certain upcoming power loss, turn your freezer to the coldest setting. The colder it is to start with, the longer it will stay cold without electricity.
2. Keep the door closed!
3. Cover the freezer with blankets, except for the motor vent openings if there's a possibility the power might turn on again (that could overheat the motor if the vents are covered).
4. The more full your freezer is, the longer it can hold out without electricity. Food in a full freezer will stay frozen for about 48 hours without electricity, but food in a half-full freezer may keep only 24 hours; a quarter-full one, only 12.
5. If the power is likely to stay off longer than your freezer will stay frozen according to Step 4, wrap it in blankets and/or newspapers and move it to a locker. Or . . .
6. If you know where you can buy dry ice *and if you can get it fairly soon after the power failure,* 25 pounds of it would keep a full 10-cubic-foot freezer below 32°F for 3 to 4 days. Fifty pounds would do the same for a 20-cubic-foot one. If the freezer is only half full, the ice will keep it below freezing only 2 or 3 days. But you have to get the dry ice in there as soon as possible, before the contents have started to thaw. Don't open the lid if you can help it, to avoid letting out the cold air.

NOTE: When working with dry ice, don't put it directly on the packages. Lay a piece of heavy cardboard on top of the food packages. Put the dry ice on top of that. Wear gloves! Don't touch the dry ice with bare hands. After that, open the freezer door only to take out food or add more dry ice.

WHEN POWER RETURNS: SAVE/TOSS WHAT? Food that still contains ice crystals has not gotten warmer than 40°F. If there are no ice crystals left in the food, it is technically "defrosted."

Bread Products. Even if defrosted, these can be re-frozen.

Cooked Foods. *Do not refreeze any dishes containing meats, fish, or poultry.*

Fish and Shellfish. *Never refreeze these* because they spoil very, very easily; also, they normally stink, so you can't use their smell as an indicator of dangerous spoilage.

Fruits and Fruit Juice. Even if defrosted, they can be refrozen (or canned or dried). There will be loss of quality. If fruits didn't thaw out completely and still have some ice crystals in them, they will refreeze without much loss of quality. Concentrated juices can be refrozen. They will lose quality, though, and may not reconstitute as well. Plain fruit juices will probably refreeze fine.

Ice Cream. *Do not use.*

Meat. *Do not refreeze cooked meats.* When my raw meat has thawed partly but not "defrosted," I've refrozen it and then used it up as soon as possible thereafter. It looked and smelled fine, and I gave it a very thorough cooking to make sure. But any meat that thawed and didn't look and smell fine, I gave to the animals. Spoiled meat looks and smells odd. "When in doubt, throw it out!" Technically speaking, if the meat has not heated above 45°F, it should still be fine.

Vegetables. If vegetables get even a little thawed out, they really go downhill fast—much faster than fruits. When this happens to me, I just throw them to the chickens or pigs. Or you can compost them. The experts agree: Don't refreeze them.

DEFROSTING THE FREEZER: Our electricity has never been off long enough to matter. What invariably happens is that some child pulls the plug and it takes me a day to find out, although I try to maintain an unconscious habit of glancing at that light that indicates the freezer is on as I go by. This seems to be a spring phenomenon, so I haven't yet had to set up a special time for cleaning out my freezer. When the accidental spring thaw comes, I just say "Praise the Lord" and very quickly finish emptying the freezer. Then I wash it clean, plug it back in, put back in what I dare, and threaten the children with horrible vague happenings if they ever do that again.

If I don't defrost accidentally, then I defrost on purpose once a year. Ideally, you should defrost every time as much as ½ inch of frost builds up over a lot of the inside of the freezer, and when frost starts to collect even on packages stored only a few hours. Frost buildup is a problem, but taking all that food out of its protective cold can be viewed as even worse. The ideal time to defrost is in early spring, when the freezer is getting toward its emptiest and before the new produce is ready in the garden. The frost has to be gotten rid of for several reasons. It acts as an insulator, preventing heat inside the freezer from getting removed by the condenser coils. The more frost you have, the less space you have. It also tends to absorb and hold foul odors. And the more frost you have, the more electricity the freezer must use to maintain its coldness.

Steps to Defrosting

1. Turn off the electricity.
2. Move the food to another freezer or to a well-insulated situation, wrapped in blankets and/or newspapers.
3. Scrape off what frost you can using a wooden or plastic (not metal!) scraper.

4. Place big pans of very hot water inside the freezer; then close the lid.
5. After the frost is all melted, scrub out the inside of the freezer with a mix of 3 T. baking soda per 1 qt. water.
6. Rinse.
7. Dry.
8. Turn electricity back on.
9. When the remaining dampness in the freezer has frozen, it's ready for the food to be put back in.

Defrosting Food for Cooking

NOTE: Always defrost meat, fish, and poultry in the refrigerator, not out on the kitchen counter. These products can be defrosted in a microwave oven, but if you do this, the food must be cooked immediately, because a microwave leaves hot spots in food. Do not microwave-defrost and then let stand for several hours before cooking. The USDA advises that cooked meats, vegetables, soups, ice cream and sherbet, frozen "dinners," and meat, poultry, and fish dishes that have thawed and have been at room temperature longer than 2–3 hours are unsafe and should be thrown out.

The above warnings are given because when you freeze foods, you don't kill the beasties; you just put them to sleep. So it's important to thaw and cook the food in as fast a sequence as you can. Foods that have been frozen, especially vegetables, are subject to very fast deterioration once thawing has set in. For vegetables, I peel off the baggie and put the frozen hunk directly into a little boiling water. I serve as soon as it is thawed and hot. I drain the cooking liquid into the gravy or the pig bucket. Put a big glob of homemade butter on the vegetables and serve.

I thaw frying meat in the refrigerator on the morning I plan to use it. Frozen roasts and roasting meats, like ribs, are put into the oven still frozen. It takes about 1½ times the usual cooking time if the food starts out frozen. It takes a while to thaw a quart of frozen stuff like stew. I put it in a pan of lukewarm water and *very, very gradually* raise the water temperature as the contents of the jar start to liquefy. *Never plop a jar of frozen food directly into hot water. Glass containers are likely to crack if exposed to sharp changes in temperature.*

Improving Thawed-Out Stew. When I reheat a thawed-out stew, I usually add some fresh vegetables from the root cellar or garden to make it taste better.

Stir-Fried Frozen Veggies. Melt 1 T. butter per serving in a cast-iron frying pan. Add your frozen veggies. Stir-fry in hot pan until the water has evaporated and it's done enough.

Long-Stored Green Beans. When string beans are in really bad shape, I can make them most palatable by putting the icy hunk directly into a frying pan with a little bacon grease or a smear of oil. I stir them as they thaw, adding a few previously fried onion chunks or green spring onions out of the garden (the top-set onions are ready by March).

Long-Stored Meat. It will be dry and of poor flavor, but you can still get use out of it. Cook it well, and cook it in a soup or sauce to mask the off-flavor.

CANNING

A favorite neighbor of mine, Imogene, is about 60 years old. One of her arms is sort of paralyzed from a childhood case of polio, and she sees only well enough to read newspaper headlines. She lives on about 3 acres with her husband, who has been a total invalid with a bad heart condition for several years now, and with her widowed mother, who doesn't get around too actively due to arthritis. She was not blessed with children. Imogene milks goats and has a big garden. Of all the families I know, hers comes closest to living totally off their own produce.

But the important thing about Imogene is that she is the most cheerful, friendly, giving person I know—I'd even risk saying "in the whole world." She's always got a big smile and a sincerely happy-to-see-you "Hello!" She loves company on any day but her precious Sabbath, which she withholds for rest and prayer, as she feels God wants her to. Seems like she's always calling me up wanting to give me something—a big sack of carrots and another of spuds or some such. I'd rather eat Imogene's vegetables than my own. Hers are raised with such love there just have to be more vitamins in them!

When the fruit is ripe in our orchard I can from morning to night using 2 big enamel water bath canners. It keeps me moving because as soon as I have loaded with fruit and juice the 8 jars that each canner will hold, it's time to take out the last batch and load in the new ones. That's because of the handling involved in getting the fruit ready—like washing, picking out the leaves, and pulling out the stems for cherries. When I can every day, even only 4 or 6 quarts, I have a lot of jars by summer's end. But many days I can more than that.

KEEPING THE HOUSE COOL: Most canning is done in summer. A lady wrote and asked me if it's possible to can on a wood stove. It sure is; I do. It's quite an experience to keep that fire roaring all the time on those hot summer days, because the big thing about safe canning is that *you can't let the water stop boiling for even one minute during your processing time. You have to watch it closely so the heat doesn't drop.*

One smart lady I know has her wood canning stove in the basement. I'm even more impressed with the ones who have a summer (canning) kitchen built outside, away from the house. If you have to can in the house, how can you cope with the extra heat? Especially if you are choosing to do without air conditioning anyway, which many fine people are doing as an eco-sound choice, even in the South. So if you are able, use a summer canning kitchen and do your summer cooking, especially canning, out there so you don't have to heat up the house. Basically all you need is a stove, even just a stove top, plus some counter space for working. Of course, it would be wonderful to have a screened-in outdoor kitchen equipped with water and electricity.

The Science of Canning

Drying and salting were the basic preservation methods until Nicholas Appert, a French baker, tried cooking food in tightly corked glass bottles in 1809. Napoleon had asked Appert for a system to preserve food for his far-flung troops. Appert continued his experiments for 15 years. His basic system was to put food in a widemouthed glass bottle, close it with a cork stopper, and then heat in boiling water 5 hours or more. Some of his jars kept and some spoiled, but Appert's efforts proved that heat treatment of a sealed container could preserve the food inside. That was the beginning of canning.

The heat kills beasties that are invisible to the naked eye. But they're there, everywhere, always: in your water and air, on all the surfaces around you, on the food, and especially in the soil in which it grows. There are 3 types of invisible competitors for your food: molds, yeasts, and bacteria. They are present either as the adult form or as seed, or "spores." The spores are tiny, very tough particles that, when dry, float up into the air and travel thus. When they happen to land on something edible, their life cycle starts again.

You can clearly see when you've got a major crop of mold on something. Bacteria aren't visible in the same way. Like molds and yeasts, there are many different kinds of bacteria that could make a home in your food. Some bacteria thrive at a low temperature and are a problem in your freezer. Some are most comfortable in middle-range temps. For canners the important bacteria are the "thermophiles," which actually reproduce contentedly at a range of 130–150°F and whose spores can handle boiling awhile and still be okay. That's why you have to be so careful when canning.

Five basic factors are involved in safe canning: number of micro-organisms in food to start with, density of the pack, acidity of the food, canning temperature, and processing time.

1. NUMBER OF BEASTIES: The more beasties your food contains to start with, the more heat treatment it takes to eliminate them all. So start with fresh, unspoiled food. Remove any spots of decay. Wash food thoroughly in clean water. Chill freshly killed meats and poultry immediately after killing, and keep them chilled until canning.

2. DENSITY OF JAR CONTENTS: I know home canners who long to can in half quarts or gallons for the efficiency of it. But they don't, because it isn't safe. Heat during canning travels inward toward the center of the jar. The last place in the jar where the beasties die is in the center, because that's the last place to heat up. If the center doesn't get hot enough long enough, the contents will spoil. A factor in how long it takes to kill all the beasties in there is the nature of the jar contents. Pure fluid is the easiest to heat up and heat through, so juice is easy to can. A loosely packed food heats much faster than a jar whose contents are tightly packed, so green beans with liquid between them heat

much faster and easier than a solid pack of squash. And a jar whose contents have a liquid cover heats through more quickly than one without, so that's why the liquid covering the food in your jar is there. The densest foods, and thus the slowest to heat, are corn, meat, and "dried" beans. Foods like apples and pears are loosely made and conduct heat easily and quickly through to the center.

3. ACIDITY OF THE FOOD: The more acid a food is, the less heating time is required to destroy bacteria. The pH is a way of measuring that acidity. The standard pH scale uses the number 7 to mean the neutral point. Foods with a pH smaller than 7 are more and more acidic as the pH number gets smaller; foods with a pH above 7 are more and more alkaline as pH gets larger. The "pH of Foods" table tells you the pH of some common foods; every food has some pH.

pH OF FOODS

2.8	Plums
3.0	Gooseberries
3.1	Prunes
3.3	Apricots
3.4	Apples
3.5	Blackberries
3.5	Peaches
3.6	Sour Cherries
3.8	Sauerkraut
3.8	Sweet Cherries
3.9	Pears
3.5–4.6	Tomatoes*
5.0	Okra
5.0	Pumpkin
5.0	Carrots
5.2	Cabbage, Turnips
5.3	Beets, String Beans
5.5	Spinach
5.7	Asparagus, Cauliflower
6.0	Lima Beans
6.3	Corn
6.9	Peas
8.0	Lye Hominy

* *Researchers at Washington State U. discovered that the acid content of tomatoes ranged this much and depended on the climate where they were grown as well as on their variety and ripeness.*

As you see, tomatoes are the lowest in acid of the high-acid foods, so they deserve special care. Pickles are high-acid because of all the vinegar in them. Salsas and taco sauces need the same processing times as tomatoes. "Hotness" of a food doesn't protect it from spoiling. Acid content is why fruit and other high-acid foods may be canned using a water bath, but vegetables and meat *must be pressure-canned* for safety.

4. CANNING TEMPERATURE: The standard canning instructions are that foods from tomatoes on up through plums can be processed at 212°F, but that foods from okra on down must be processed at 240°F—meaning in a pressure canner, which is the only way you can get them that

CANNER'S PLANNER				
Food	Times/Week	Serving	Jars/Person	Jars/Family (4)
Meats, poultry, fish	4/week, 36 weeks	½ c.	36 pt.	144 pt.
Soups	2/week, 36 weeks	1 c.	18 qt.	72 qt.
Jams, jellies, preserves	6/week, 52 weeks	2 T.	40½ pt.	160½ pt.
Relishes	3/week, 52 weeks	1 T.	5 pt.	20 pt.
Greens, carrots, sweet potatoes, winter squash	4/week, 36 weeks	½ c.	18 qt.	72 qt.
Pickled vegetables	2/week, 52 weeks	2½T.	13 pt.	52 pt.
Citrus fruits/juices and tomatoes	7/week, 36 weeks	1 c.	63 qt.	252 qt.
All other fruits/veggies	14/week, 36 weeks	½ c.	76 qt.	304 qt.
Pickled fruits	2/week, 52 weeks	2½T.	13 qt.	52 qt.

hot. That temperature is required to kill the spores. The adult forms all die more easily.

5. LENGTH OF PROCESSING TIME: The higher the temperature, the shorter the time needed to kill those tough spores. For food with a pH of 7, for example, one test showed the spores could endure boiling for 330 minutes before they croaked. Boiling, of course, happens at 212°F. If the temperature was held at 220°, they could hold out only 100 minutes; at 230°, 33 minutes; at 240°, 11 minutes. A pressure canner is supposed to get up to 240°F. The rules allow it a little margin for error.

Old-timers used to can meats and low-acid vegetables using the water-bath method, boiling for as long as 6 straight hours, before pressure canners were invented that could achieve the higher temperatures. Because a lot of things can happen in 5 or 6 hours, including a temporary drop in temperature you don't know about, to say nothing of the waste of fuel energy, that long-cooking method is no longer recommended for low-acid vegetables. On the other hand, water-bath canning is still very desirable for high-acid foods, because even in a water bath, their processing time can be faster than waiting for a pressure canner to heat up and then cool down again, and just as safe.

Whether you do "hot pack" or "raw pack," meaning whether you put the food into the jars pre-cooked and still hot or uncooked and still cold, affects your processing time. If hot pack is specified, it's important to process that way, because the hot-pack precooking is figured into the processing time. Hot pack is also beneficial because the food shrinks, and you'll get more into every jar. And the precook releases air, which helps your seal.

About Botulism

OF CANNING, BARGAINS, AND SAFETY: Canning is a bargain compared to buying store food. Being a frugal-minded person, in previous editions of this book I used to look for ways to make canning even cheaper. No more. I understand better now the risk of botulism. Over 700 people have died of botulism since folks started canning in this country. (In 1992 in the United States, 10,000 persons were killed by handguns, which puts that in some perspective.) Last year [1976] in the United States, there were 20 reported incidents of botulism involving 30 persons and resulting in 7 deaths. One death from botulism is one too

many, because they could all be prevented by following proper canning procedures. In this new edition I've painstakingly given you only the safest procedures, and the canning instructions scattered throughout the book have all been reviewed by true experts (which I am not) and either approved, changed so as to be approved, or dropped.

HOW BOTULISM GROWS: Botulism poisoning is caused by a certain kind of bacteria (*Clostridium botulinum*) that is practically everywhere in the soil. The food poisons specialists call the beastie "bot" for short. You're safest, and most likely correct, to assume that bot is present on your garden food too. The bacteria themselves are not poisonous. But it's a good idea to keep your baby out of the dirt because children under age 1 don't handle them as effectively as older people do. Bot won't grow in the refrigerator. When cooked, bot bacteria die easily, but their seed forms, called "spores," are extraordinarily resistant to heat. They aren't resistant to *high* acid and sugar, however; those inactivate the bot spores. (We're beginning to learn that botulism can survive in mildly acid products.) That's why high-acid foods, sweet preserves, and pickled foods can be canned using a boiling-water bath.

But if bot spores get a combination of insufficient heating, no air, low acid, and low sugar content, then they are in bot heaven. The area inside a sealed jar is a no-air place. And if it isn't jam or pickles or fruit, it's a low-acid food. In that case, you have to pressure-can. That extra heat is the only remaining line of defense. Bot spores can resist a lot of boiling, but they are reliably killed by the 240°F temperatures achieved by heating under pressure— "pressure canning."

"HIGH ACID" OR "LOW ACID"? Different foods naturally contain varying amounts of acid. As the acid strength increases, the temperature or time needed to kill the beasties decreases. High-acid foods can be processed more quickly than low-acid foods. High-acid foods can also be processed at a slightly lower temperature—merely the boiling point of 212°F—whereas low-acid foods must be processed at 240°F to be safe. And only inside a pressure canner can you get a sustained temperature that high. So low-acid foods such as beans and corn must be pressure-canned to destroy the spores of the bot bacteria. Spores are the most resistant seed form of the beasties. Unless you roast to death *all* the spores of the *bacillus botulinus* in low-acid foods, the remaining spores grow. As they grow they give off an invisible, tasteless, but powerful toxin (poison).

"BOT" TOXIN: This toxin is one of the most deadly poisons known on earth. If you merely touch a finger to it and touch that finger to your lips to taste, you could get enough to kill you. It is said that 16 ounces of bot toxin would be enough to kill the entire world's population. The toxin itself doesn't trumpet its presence. You can open the jar and it may look and smell fine. It is, however, destroyed by heat. That's why it is recommended that all low-acid home-canned foods be boiled 15 minutes with the lid on before tasting or serving.

The symptoms ordinarily appear within 18 to 36 hours of poisoning but have been known to take as long as 8 days to become evident. What are the symptoms? At first nausea and vomiting, later blurred vision, dry throat, and difficulty swallowing. Then comes progressive weakness that can paralyze the respiratory tract as well as the limbs. The poison does that because it affects the nervous system, breaking down communication between motor nerves and the muscles.

The botulism cases that I've heard about involved pickled beets, tomatoes (for which pressure canning has not in the past been recommended), spicy tomato products such as salsas and taco sauce (the problem being the false assumption that the "hotness" will preserve the food), mushrooms, olives, asparagus, beans, cabbage, carrots, and peppers. In rare cases, it has also happened with pressure-canned food.

Researchers are just now discovering that bot bacteria can survive in the presence of more acid than had previously been believed. Some standard canning directions used to say to simply bring pickled beets, for example, to a boil and then hot-pack them. Some people got bot poisoning from doing that. Now we know it's not safe to can pickled foods without a water-bath canning time. So therein lies the risk of using old recipes. Some cooks thought that because salsa was so hot, it could be canned without much processing. Again, now we know better because of a bot case. Spicy hot doesn't bother bot.

Now that I've practically scared you to death, let me revive you with success stories. Many's the family that cans 700 or more quarts a year, year after year, with great success. Florence Ward, Quilcene, WA, wrote me, "I have canned for over 50 years. When we lived on a dairy ranch for 17 years, I used to can around 600 quarts of fruit and meats each year. Pickles too. We had five children—all married long since. Fruit, such as peaches and apricots, cherries and pears—I've canned thousands of quarts of them."

Sandra Oddo, Hurley, NY, wrote me, "A year ago I got a pressure canner from Sears for $24 (can 4 quarts, hold 8) and now I wouldn't be without it. It's too small for mass canning, but perfect for what's left of the lentil soup after we've had a ham—canned soup heats faster than frozen, too—and for food deliberately mass-cooked so there will be leftovers for pressure canning, which saves later work. It saves enormously on fuel. Would you believe that 45 minutes turns a 3-year-old rooster into a tender stew?"

From Maureen Darby, Leslie, AK: "The cost of the canner is easily offset by the fact that it requires far less fuel to operate than it would to can in boiling water. I even can fruit under pressure. I do have to watch it closely, but it's better than waiting to boil the quantity of water needed to cover the jars in a water bath. We don't own a freezer. The initial cost and the cost of the electricity to run them make them impractical—besides the constant worry of power shortage."

So be careful when you can. But bot poisoning is rare—an average 7–30 cases a year nationwide among about 100 million canners. It's rare because of all the careful home canners who read the rules that come with canning equipment and in good canning books, and follow them, and use pressure canners. Still, that's 7–30 too many sick people. Those safety rules are all very clearly stated here, too. Please, better safe than sorry. Follow them!

Canning Methods and Supplies

Get ready for your food preserving ahead of time, because when the harvest is on you'll be frantic. Good supply sources for home canners:

Cumberland General Store: 800-334-4640.

Gardener's Kitchen (old-fashioned no-phone lifestyle; great lids and prices); PO Box 322, Monument Beach, MA 02553; gkitchen@cape.com; www.gardeners kitchen@cape.com.

Home Canning Supply offers a free catalog: 800-354-4070; 760-788-0520; 1815 La Brea St., Ramona, CA 92065; **sales@homecanningsupply.com; www.home canningsupply.com.**

Lehman's Non-Electric: 888-438-5346; **www.lehmans. com.**

BOOKS

NOTE: Recent discoveries about canning safety mean that no canning recipe from an old book (including older editions of this one!) can be fully trusted. Get your canning recipes from up-to-date sources. Until recently, all canning recipes were based on USDA research completed in 1942. In 1986 the USDA asked Pennsylvania State University to repeat that old research to double-check their results. By 1990 they were finished, and the news was out that there were numerous errors in the old research.

Current canning recipes are in recent books or university extension bulletins. For a free booklet, "Home Canning Made Pure and Simple," write Consumer Products Co., PO Box 2005, Muncie, IN 47307. This company now owns and markets both Ball and Kerr (another disgusting example of complete marketplace monopoly, the trend). For answers to food preservation questions, or to order the *Ball Blue Book Guide to Home Canning, Freezing and Dehydration* ($6), call them at 800-240-3340.

SUMMARY OF METHODS: Here's a basic summary of methods to illustrate what supplies you'll need. You'll either be doing water-bath canning or pressure canning—or both, depending on what foods you choose to can. The old-time "open-kettle method" is no longer recommended, even for jam making! Jams are now processed 5 minutes in a water bath. Paraffin is no longer recommended for sealing them because it isn't considered reliable enough—just use a regular jar lid!

Water-Bath Canning. James R. Coffey, Elkton, MD, wrote me that it's "known as cold packing in my area." Water-bath canning is only for fruits and high-acid tomatoes, *not for vegetables or meats.* Water-bath canning preserves food because the prolonged heat combined with the high-acid content of the food effectively kills botulism and other bacteria.

For water-bath canning you need jars, lids, rings, a canning kettle, a rack, and a jar lifter.

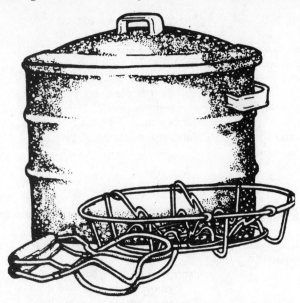

You put the prepared fruit is in sterile, clean jars, covered with water or syrup. Then you put the lid and ring on and tighten. You lower the jar(s) into your kettle of boiling water. You need a perforated rack in the bottom of the pot for the jars to rest on. This ensures that they won't break if they sit on the bottom of the kettle itself. The water needs to be able to move freely around the outside of the jars. The kettle must be tall enough so that water will cover the jars by at least 1–2 inches at all times. During long boilings, have another kettle boiling nearby from which you can add water as necessary. Once the correct amount of time has gone by, remove the jars with a jar lifter. Set them on top of a towel or wooden board on your counter to cool. You start timing when the water comes to a boil again.

Pressure Canning. This method works to preserve low-acid foods such as vegetables and meats because low-acid foods have to be heated to at least 240°F in order to kill any botulism spores present that enjoy a low-acid environment, can live indefinitely through mere boiling, and thrive in the oxygen-free environment of a sealed jar.

To do pressure canning, you need jars, lids, rings, a pressure canner, a rack, and a jar lifter.

Follow the recipe for the food preparation. Put on the softened lids and rings. Set your canner on the heat with the lid off, with 1 to 2 inches of water in the bottom of it, to start heating. Make sure the rack is in there. Set the jars onto the rack in the pressure canner. Put the lid on. The water boiling in the canner will cause steam to escape from the vent on the lid of the canner. Once the steam release is constant, start timing and wait 10 minutes. By then all the air will have been removed from the inside of your canner. Shut the stopcock, or put your weight on. Watch the canner gauge. Wait until it shows the correct pressure has been reached (usually 10 lb. for low-acid foods and 5 lb. if you're canning high-acid foods, but a little more if you live at a high altitude—see "Altitude Adjustments for Pressure Canning" table later in this chapter). Now start timing your canning process.

Once the processing time is over, take the canner from the heat. Let it cool naturally and slowly. (The natural cooling time is part of the recipe!) When you're pressure cooking, you can run water over the canner to cool it quickly, but don't do that when pressure canning. The manual for your particular canner will tell you how to know when the canner is cooled. Once it is cooled, open the canner lid. Remove the jars using a jar lifter.

CANNING JARS

Getting Jars: If you plan to can, get your jars, lids, and screw bands ahead of time. You can buy new canning jars at big grocery outlets, but they're not cheap. Nathan D. Justus, Fair Haven, NJ, wrote me, "For one dozen quart jars in my area, it costs approximately $8, but I feel this is inexpensive, particularly since the jars can be reused many times, if they are treated with proper care." It's best to buy them by the case a year ahead of time, since stores sometimes run out at the peak of the season. Or look (or advertise) for used canning jars, usually a good bargain.

How Many? How many jars you need depends on how large your family is, how much of your preserving is by canning, and how many months a year of fresh garden produce you can grow. If you put up 100 quarts of green beans, your family could eat 2 quarts a week all year round; the same for corn or fruit. So you can figure out what you think you'll need. An average family of 4 in an average climate might want to can 300 quarts. Alice Flanigan, Blackstone, IL, wrote me of her neighbor with a family of 7 who cans 700 quarts a year.

You can also refer to the "Canner's Planner," the USDA's attempt to take the guesswork out of planning for the coming year. In the Planner, the phrase "36 weeks" means that item is canned only for the out-of-season weeks of the year. The Meats category assumes you also have 10 other servings of meat, poultry, food-from-water, or eggs. A sizable old-time family with no meat preservation system other than canning, no modern refrigeration, and lots of animals on the farm canned as much as 400–500 quarts of meat per year. (Canning made it possible for them to have meat besides chicken in the summer months.) Any individual family will want some variation on this estimate based on their family's personal preferences.

What Type Jars? The size jar you want depends on how much your family can eat at a meal. For my family, it works best to put up butters, jams, jellies, and taco sauce in half pints to minimize spoilage before that food gets used up. All stews, vegetables, and fruits go into quarts. (It is possible to can your family's most loved high-acid fruit in half-gallon jars—but *only high-acid fruit.*) Pint jars are best for ketchups and vegetables, except string beans and tomatoes, which do well in quarts. You'll have a choice of regular jars, widemouthed jars, can-or-freeze jars, and jelly glasses and jars.

If you wonder whether a jar is the right size for canning, test it with a screw band. If one of the three sizes will fit, it's okay. The glass isn't quite as heavy as in regular canning jars, but if you are careful that the food you put into the jars is hot or has hot water or juice poured over it before you put it in the hot canner, it won't break.

NOTE: Don't use antique canning jars, either the zinc-lidded jars or the old 2-piece glass-lid type, because their seals are not dependable, and replacement rings are getting impossible to find.

On the other hand, wonderful fancy jars are available from The Cook's Garden (800-457-9703; **www.cooks garden.com**) and other outlets. They offer stylish glass

Apples: Hot-pack, cover with hot liquids.

Applesauce: Hot-pack.

Apricots: Wash, halve, take out pits. Pack in jars. Add liquid.

Berries (except strawberries/cranberries): Wash, stem, pack, add liquid.

Cherries: Can with pits, pack, cover with liquid.

Cranberries: Wash, stem, boil 3 minutes in heavy syrup, pack.

Currants: Wash, stem, pack, add liquid.

Figs: Cook 2 minutes, make syrup, cook 5 minutes in syrup, pack.

Fruit juices: Make your juices, pour into jars.

Nuts: Pack, oven-process at 225°F for 45 minutes.

Peaches: Peel, pack, add liquid.

Pears: Peel, pack, add liquid.

Plums: Pack, add liquid.

Preserves: Prepare according to your recipe, hot-pack, process at 180°F ("simmer").

Rhubarb: Cut in chunks, precook, hot-pack, add liquid if needed.

Strawberries: Stem, hot-pack, cover with hot juice.

Tomato juice: Hot-pack.

Tomatoes, whole: Scald, peel, core, quarter, heat. Hot-pack.

PACKING LOW-ACID FOODS FOR PRESSURE CANNING ONLY

Meats: Pack raw or precooked, salt 1 t. per qt. unless presalted in recipe (sausage, ham). Do not add liquids to meat packed raw. Pack loosely.

Fish: Pack raw, no liquid. Use only fresh, firm fish.

Vegetables

Asparagus: Hot-pack, add liquid.

Beans, snap (green or yellow): Snap, hot-pack.

Beans, lima: Shell, hot-pack loosely.

Beets: Wash, boil, skin, pre-cook, hot-pack.

Broccoli: Hot-pack.

Brussels sprouts: Hot-pack.

Cabbage: Hot-pack.

Carrots: Hot-pack.

Cauliflower: Hot-pack.

Corn: Cut off cob, hot-pack loosely.

Greens: Wash, hot-pack loosely.

Hominy: Hot-pack loosely.

Mushrooms: Hot-pack loosely. (*Don't can wild ones.*)

Okra: Hot-pack.

Onions: Hot-pack.

Parsnips: Peel, chunk, hot-pack.

Peas: Shell, hot-pack.

Peppers, green: Cut out seed pod, hot-pack.

Peppers, pimentoes: Bake/boil, peel, remove seeds.

Potatoes, white: Peel, hot-pack.

Pumpkin: Peel, chunk, precook (don't mash), hot-pack.

Rutabagas: Peel, slice or cube, hot-pack.

Squash, winter: Peel, chunk, precook, hot-pack.

Sweet potatoes: Precook 20 minutes, peel, hot-pack.

Turnips: Peel, chunk, hot-pack.

---

herb jars, hexagonal French jars, and imported German jars with the old-fashioned glass top, rubber ring, and small steel clips—all okay for canning homemade chutneys or jams.

Widemouthed Jars. The widemouthed jars are good for large whole fruits, such as peaches and pears, and for meat and pickles. They are easy to fill and clean because you can get your hand inside for thorough washing, but the lids are a little more expensive.

"63" Jars. The "63" jars (small size) are hard to fill, especially for hot-pack canning. Very liquid items like juices, or small fruits such as cherries, berries and apricots, go into them best.

Recycled Mayonnaise Jars. The cheapest way to get jars is to have everybody save their mayonnaise jars for you. I know that numerous other writers say this is awful. But I have the assurance of Jan Grant, King County extension agent and founder of the Master Food Preserver program, who carefully reviewed all the contents of this book, that there is no safety problem with these jars if all your other procedures are correctly followed. However, these quart and pint mayonnaise jars should be used for *only water bath—not pressure—canning* because they aren't as sturdy as regular home canning jars. And use them *only if you use a regular home canning-type Ball or Kerr lid set, not the store lid, with them.*

Avoiding Jar Breaks. Glass expands with heat and contracts with cold. If you pour something hot into a cold jar, the inside might expand enough to crack the outside, and blooey—food all over your table and no jar. When working with glass jars, keep that in mind. But you already knew that, I'm sure.

LIDS: Brand-new metal jar lids are reasonably priced and are virtually your only expense when you're canning garden produce and already have the jars. So don't even consider reusing jar lids. They are made to work only once. Make sure the lids you buy will fit the jars you have. There are 3 standard lid sizes: "63" (which is small), "regular," and "widemouthed."

SCREW BANDS: These come in the same 3 sizes as the lids. Match the sizes! Screw bands, like jars and unlike lids, can be used over and over—unless they get bent. If a screw band is rusty or bent, it can prevent a safe seal. Throw away bent screw bands and use new ones.

About Reusing Lids and Screw Bands. Actually, you can reuse them *if you are canning only high-acid fruits.* That's because you never have to worry about botulism with high-acid fruits. As F.E. Pennington of Kelso, WA, wrote me, "Who cares how rusty the rings are? They never touch the product. And if you hold a bunch of lids together, you can detect any bent lids. They can be used same as new lids—that is, the Ball dome lids. Reusing does not work well with Kerr lids. I get at least a 90 percent seal."

UTENSILS FOR CANNING

Funnel. A widemouthed canning funnel is available from kitchen specialty stores and homestead mail-order outlets. If you don't have one, you'll wish you did, because you'll be always burning your fingers. They also prevent spilling, so the jar rim stays clean. They are especially necessary for hot-pack canning.

Canning funnel

Screw bands

Lids

Soup Ladle. You can use a cup, but you're less likely to burn your fingers using a ladle if you're filling jars hot-pack style. F. E. Pennington says, "I find a funnel a nuisance. I ladle the fruit into the jar."

Slotted Spoons. Big spoons with long narrow holes inside are wonderful for lifting fruit out of a dip, and so on.

Canning Tongs. This tool is valuable for lifting lids and empty hot jars out of hot water.

Jar Brush. This is used for cleaning inside regular (narrow-topped) jars.

Hot Pads, Mitts, Heavy Potholders. Use so you don't burn your fingers.

Jar Lifter. You need this to get the hot jars out of the hot water. It closes around the jar and tightens as you lift. No risk of dropping hot jars with this! A funnel, jar lifter, kitchen tongs, lid lifter, and jar wrench are available as a set from The Cook's Garden (800-457-9703; **www.cooks garden.com**).

TIN CANS: Seems like everybody knows somebody in Alaska who cans in real cans. (The rest of us are actually "jarring.") Lane Morgan says, "I have friends in Alaska who do subsistence fishing. They can lots and lots of salmon and they use commercial-style cans, not jars. I think they like the cans because they use the canner space more efficiently. I don't know how they put the lids on. They can their salmon with a teriyaki marinade and it really is sensational. Their other meats—mostly moose and bear—they freeze." People who can in metal fill the can, seal it, and then toss the can into boiling water and leave it there, boiling non-stop, for the designated number of hours. This method is the most common one used in commercial canning, but the equipment is not easily available to home canners. The cans are actually made of steel plated with tin or enameled on the inside. The can and lid are supplied as separate items, and you need a special can sealer. You can't reuse metal cans, and they're much more expensive than jars. *NOTE: When using metal cans, do not use procedures or processing times given here.*

WATER-BATH CANNING KETTLE: These come in 22- to 26-quart sizes (which hold 4 or 6 quart jars at a time) and aren't expensive. The kettle is enamel and equipped with a jar-holding rack to keep jars on the bottom of the pan. Hardware and kitchen stores have them. But actually, any container large enough to hold jars covered with boiling water can serve as your water-bath canning kettle. You can make a big canner out of an old-fashioned copper washtub. Put it on 2 burners at once. It will hold 16 quarts at a time. You can get a stainless-steel canning-size kettle from Lehman's; 888-438-5346; **www.Lehmans.com.** You can use a pressure canner as a water-bath canner if you don't fasten the cover down and are careful to leave the petcock wide open.

Steam Canners. Steam canner manufacturers have never done the very expensive testing necessary for USDA approval, so this cannot be an extension-recommended method. *However, if all you can in it is high-acid fruit, you may end up with spoiled fruit, but nothing that can kill you.* But you may safely use a steam canner in place of a water-bath canning kettle *only to can the most high-acid fruits,* because this method does not kill critters as dependably as a regular boiling-water bath. You especially can't use it in place of a pressure canner!

One model resembles an upside-down pot. There is a shallow bottom pan with a tray over that. Your jars of fruit go on the tray. Water goes in the pan. The tall, tightly fitting top covers the jars and holds in the steam from the heated water. *Don't let it boil dry.*
NOTE: A microwave oven cannot be used for canning because it doesn't heat evenly enough.

PRESSURE CANNER: These cost more than the other items on this list, but it's a one-time cost because they last a lifetime, and you absolutely must have one to can low-acid foods. A pressure cooker is not the same as a pressure canner. Incidentally, follow the manufacturer's instructions for proper washing and care of the pressure canner after using it. Be careful not to nick or chip its sealing edges.
NOTE: Pressure canners are potentially dangerous. Make sure a manual comes with yours. If you lose the manual, write to the manufacturer to get another one.

Dial Gauge vs. Weighted Gauge. When shopping in many outlets, you'll be asked to choose between a "weighted-gauge" and a "dial-gauge" canner. They are both safe, good canner types. The dial-gauge pressure canner is nice for high-altitude canners because it can fine-tune adjustments of pressure, even as little as ½ lb. It's also quieter than the weighted-gauge style. But you have to take in the dial gauge every year to be tested for accuracy, and it must be watched to maintain pressure. Being more complex, it also has a few more parts to get lost.
NOTE: When the Penn State canning research was done, they discovered that in a dial-gauge canner, the ideal temperature of 238-240°F for killing bot was achieved not at 10 but at 10.5. So it is now recommended that every time you see a recipe that says "10 lb. pressure," you should actually use 11 lb. if you're using a dial-gauge pressure canner. On the other hand, the weighted gauge is manufactured to reach the 10.5 pressure even though set for 10. Based on that research, the weighted gauge is safer and preferable. In addition, its accuracy is guaranteed for the lifetime of the product.

The weighted-gauge style of canner, on the other hand, has an annoying, noisy nature and adjusts pressure by only

5 lb. at a time. On the good side, it's simple to use, has fewer parts, doesn't need to be tested every year because it cannot be made inaccurate unless the weight is damaged (very unlikely and hard to do!), and doesn't have to be constantly watched. But I prefer the weighted-gauge type. You can train yourself to recognize what its noises are saying, and it allows you freedom to do other things while canning. However, high-altitude canners who need added pressure may be wiser to choose the dial-gauge style.

James Coffey of Elkton, MD, a very serious home canner, wrote me, "I have 2 water-bath canners and 2 pressure canners. I prefer the dial gauge for most canning, but I use weighted gauge for tomatoes especially. I am a baker by profession and can at home as a hobby and to save on the food bill as well."

Sizes range from 7-qt. liquid capacity (holds only 4 pint jars for canning) up to the 22-qt. size, which holds 20 pint jars, and the 30-qt. size, which holds 19 pint or 14 quart jars. Lehman's also sells pressure canner parts such as knobs and gauges. Secondhand canners are a bargain and have been a blessing. But they can also be big trouble. Make sure yours comes with a little booklet about burns and explosions, unless it's identical to your other one or you can write to the manufacturer and get the right manual for it.

Gasket. Your old pressure canner needs a new gasket if steam persistently escapes around the rim and pressure fails to build up. An overage gasket either may get hard and slippery or may stretch and no longer fit easily and well.

Hard Water? If your area has water so hard that it leaves a mineral deposit on the outside of jars, add ½ c. vinegar to each cannerful of water to prevent that.

Twelve Life-Saving Canning Rules

Canning low-acid food is the only preservation method that can be deadly, so with canning instructions you must follow the rules closely and not experiment. You will hear from people who insist that they canned food in less time or with methods that are not recommended and haven't died of it. Because so many factors enter into what makes food safe, with good luck you might be able to get away with it for a long time. But then again, that luck could run out at any time, and the unthinkable of botulism poisoning could occur. These canning instructions are designed to always provide you such a wide margin of safety that poisoning is simply impossible. You follow the directions, and then you can be confident.

Learn and follow these rules absolutely!

1. Don't use jars larger than a quart. Home canning technology cannot guarantee that larger quantities will be sufficiently heated through for enough time. Rather, the food on the outside will overcook, while that on the inside won't get hot enough. Botulism spores can boil awhile and still be fine.
2. Use water-bath canning only for high-acid foods. High-acid varieties of tomatoes, fruits, rhubarb, sauerkraut, pickles, and jams/jellies are the only high-acid foods. All others (vegetables, meats, stews) must be canned using a pressure canner.
3. Use only modern canning recipes from reliable sources.
4. Never reuse jar lids. Used lids aren't reliable for sealing correctly. If a screw band is rusty or bent, it won't work right and should be discarded and replaced.
5. Don't use antique or "French"-type canning jars. They aren't as safe as the modern, regular (Ball, Kerr) type.
6. Check the jar rims carefully every year by running your finger over the top of the rim and checking for nicks. Even the tiniest nick makes a jar unusable for canning. A nicked jar rim won't seal reliably.
7. Raw pack is not safe for certain foods: beets, all kinds of greens (spinach, etc.), white potatoes, squash, okra, a tomato/okra combination, and stewed tomatoes!
8. You must allow the correct amount of space (headspace) between your food, together with the liquid that covers it, and the jar lid.
9. Don't begin counting the processing time until after the water with the jars in it comes to a good rolling boil if using the water bath method, or until after steam has vented for 10 minutes from your pressure canner.
10. Process the full recommended time. If canning on a wood stove, watch your fire carefully to make sure it stays hot. If your boil or your pressure fails at any point in the process, you must start over and reprocess for the entire recommended time.
11. Lift out each jar individually (not inside the rack) using a jar lifter; keep it upright and not tipped.
12. If a jar didn't seal, discard the lid, put on a new one, and reprocess. Or put the jar that didn't seal in the refrigerator and use the contents within a week or so.

General Canning Instructions

This section explains the canning process. First you prepare and pack the food; then you process it using either a water-bath method or a pressure-canning method; and then you cool the jars and store them. (And finally, if all goes well, you eat your good canned food!)

PREPARING AND PACKING

1. Run your finger around the rim of each jar to check for nicks. A nicked rim can't be depended on to seal properly.
2. Wash jars in hot soapy water till clean. If you can't get a jar clear-clean, don't use it to can. Get a head start on this part by getting the jars thoroughly clean after you take food out of them, so they'll be all ready for the new year. Store them upside down or covered with old lids to keep out dust and the like over the winter. Then wash each jar before using it again, and rinse thoroughly.
3. Give jars a scalding rinse and turn upside down to drain on a clean folded cloth. A dishwasher is not a necessity, but if you have one, you'll find it a real help and time-saver when canning. You can use it to wash batches of canning (or freezing) jars and to keep them hot until needed. If you are doing a hot pack, keep the jars hot *so they won't break from the contact with hot food.* Never pour boiling water or hot food into a cool jar, and never place a cool jar directly into boiling water. You can keep jars hot by soaking in a big kettle of hot water until you're ready to remove and fill them.

   NOTE: For food products that will be processed less than 15 minutes by either water-bath or pressure methods, it is recommended that you use a sterilized jar. A sterilized jar is one that has been boiled for 10 minutes.
4. If you are canning high-acid foods with the water bath method, now fill the water-bath canning kettle with water two-thirds full, and put it on to boil. You need a very big, hot burner or a very hot stove top to can with

this method. If you have trouble with your water boiling down in a water-bath canner, keep an extra pan of water boiling on your stove and add boiling water from that to the canner.

5. Put a pan that holds about a gallon of water on to boil to make your canning liquid.

6. Follow your recipe for food preparation. You'll find canning instructions for specific vegetables and fruits under their entries in Chapter 4 and Chapter 6, respectively. You can add or omit salt in any canning recipe as it suits you; it will not affect the processing time except for brined pickles, where salt content is critical for safety!

   The food to be canned should not have bruise spots or decay and should be as freshly gathered as possible. If you can manage 2 hours from garden to jar, you'll be a wonder and have the best-tasting canned food possible. Be especially careful not to let any dirt into the jar or food mixture, because bot bacteria live in soil. Thoroughly wash all food to be canned. The best results come from washing small batches at a time under running water, or in and out of several changes of water. Lift the vegetables out of the water so that any dirt gets left in the bottom of the pan. But don't soak the food, because then it loses vitamins and can get soggy. Scrub root vegetables especially well.

   Here are more fruit-canning hints and options:
   - To easily remove the skins of tomatoes and some fruit, drop them into boiling water for a minute or so, until the skins peel off freely.
   - To prevent discoloration when peeling large, light fruits for canning, keep them in a brine (2 t. salt per quart of water, or 2 T. salt and 2 T. vinegar per gallon water). Remove the fruit within 15 minutes. Or you can not worry about darkening and just work fast, which is what I do; keeps down the salt intake.
   - To prevent darkening and loss of vitamins, add ascorbic acid (a form of powdered vitamin C). Use ½ t. powdered ascorbic acid per quart of fruit. Mix it in with the water/syrup that will cover the fruit in the jar.

   For other fruit pre-treatments, see the "Freezing" and "Drying" sections on fruit pre-treatments.

7. Fill your clean jars with the fresh-cut food, leaving at least ½ inch headspace (see Step 9). Food can be packed raw in the jars (called "raw pack"), or the food and its liquid can be preheated first and then ladled hot into hot jars (called "hot pack"). For packing instructions for the specific vegetable or fruit you're canning, see its entry in Chapter 4 or Chapter 6. For a quick reference, see the tables "Packing High-Acid Foods for Water-Bath Canning" and "Packing Low-Acid Foods for Pressure Canning Only." If packing halved large fruit, pack it with the inside down to get more in.

If you are canning juice, tomatoes, or something else that doesn't need liquid added, skip the next step and go to Step 9.

8. Prepare canning liquid by adding sugar, honey, or a combination to hot water. Sugar helps fruit hold its shape, color, and flavor, but you don't have to add it to safely preserve food. You may can food in plain water

or use much less sugar than the usual recipe says. Or you can use a honey solution, can in fruit juice, or use no sweetening or water at all! Refer to the table "Standard Syrup Mixtures" for suggested combinations. See "Freezing" section for syrup recipes. Or you can add sugar directly to hot-packed juicy fruit. Use ½ c. per quart of fruit, heat to simmering, and then pack.

For info on honey canning, see *You Can Can with Honey* by Nancy Cosper. Or use plain hot water. Sorghum, molasses, or brown sugar are other possible sweeteners but are less preferable because they tend to overwhelm the flavor of the fruit.

After mixing the ingredients for your syrup, heat and stir until in good solution.

STANDARD SYRUP MIXTURES (IN CUPS)

	Sugar	Light Corn Syrup or Honey	Water or Fruit Juice*
Thin	2	0	4
Medium	1	1	4
Medium	0	1	4
Heavy	4	0	4
Heavy	0	4	4

Any combination of water and juice (from the fruit you're canning or from another kind) is OK.

9. If hot packing, pour liquid over the fruit in the jars. Leave enough headspace between the food and the jar lid. Too little headspace doesn't allow the food inside room enough to expand when hot and boiling during processing. Too little headspace can result in liquid being forced out of the jar during processing, and a failure to seal. Usually your recipe says how much headspace to leave. But here are the guidelines that recipe writers follow:

   Jellies, fruit syrups: ¼ inch headspace

   Jams, preserves, pickles, relishes, syrups, juices: ¼ inch

   Canned fruits: ½ inch

   All meats, poultry, fish, and low-acid vegetables (except limas): 1 inch

   Lima beans: 1¼ inch (pints), 1½ inch (quarts)

10. Release any air trapped in the jar by running a thin flat *plastic or wood (not metal)* utensil around the side of the jar. This will cause air bubbles to come to the surface. A thin plastic spatula works perfectly for this. (Metal may crack or chip the jar.) *Be especially careful to get the bubbles out if you have a product that has been in a blender. You do this because trapped air can emerge later and ruin the seal.* Add more water if needed to maintain the proper headspace.

11. Wipe clean the rims of your jars before putting on lids. Use a wet cloth for syrupy contents, a dry cloth if there may be fat droplets.

12. Get your lids ready by heating them to simmering in a pan of water. Then remove from heat. Don't let them boil.

13. Put the flat metal lid on the jar, "composition" side next to the glass. Screw the metal band on over it. Screw down firmly by hand. Don't use a jar wrench for screwing down bands because lids must be loose enough so air can escape in the canner.

If you are water-bath canning, proceed by the following directions. If you are pressure canning, skip to "Pressure Canning Procedure," which follows "Water-Bath Canning Procedure."

WATER-BATH CANNING PROCEDURE

1. Load your jars into your rack. (You can load jars with the rack either inside or outside the canner, but when it's time to take them out, leave the rack inside the canner and take the jars out one by one to avoid accidents with boiling water.) If you loaded outside the canner, holding the rack by the two handles, lower it into your canning kettle. Adjust the water level so that it is at least 1 inch above the tops of the jar lids. Work quickly enough so that your jars are still quite hot from the hot liquid being poured in; otherwise, they may crack when they hit the boiling water. (Commercial jars, like mayonnaise jars, crack more easily than regular canning jars.)

2. When the water in the kettle returns to a cheerful boil (don't confuse the bubbles of air escaping from the inside of the jars with a boil), start timing and boil it the recommended processing time, being careful that it never drops below a boil, in which case you'll have to start your timing all over again. The "Processing Times for Water-Bath Canning" table shows how many minutes to boil various high-acid foods. If you live more than 1,000 feet above sea level, adjust the processing time as indicated in the "Altitude Adjustments for Water-Bath Canning" table.

PROCESSING TIMES FOR WATER-BATH CANNING

	Minutes	
Food	Pints	Quarts
Apples	20	20
Applesauce	20	20
Apricots	25	30
Berries	15	20
Cherries	25	25
Cranberries	15	15
Currants	15	15
Figs	45	50
Fruit Juices	5	10
Peaches	25	30
Pears	25	30
Plums	10	10
Preserves	20	20
Rhubarb	10	10
Strawberries	15	15
Tomatoes	35	45
Tomato juice	35	40

ALTITUDE ADJUSTMENTS FOR WATER-BATH CANNING

Altitude (feet above sea level)	Processing Time
Under 1,000	Time called for in recipe
1,000–3,000	Time called for plus 5 minutes
3,001–6,000	Time called for plus 10 minutes
6,001 or more	Time called for plus 15 minutes

Now skip to "Cooling, Storing, and Using."

PRESSURE CANNING PROCEDURE

This is the bot-safe method for canning low-acid foods: meats, poultry, fish, and vegetables (except rhubarb and tomatoes). Technically you can also pressure-can fruit, and some people do. But the canning times are so short that most people think a pressure canner is a pure nuisance to use for canning fruit, because fruit requires only about 8 minutes or less of pressure canning, and it gets frustrating to wait for the thing to heat up and then cool down so you can get on with the next batch. That's why we prefer to can fruit water-bath–style.

NOTE: If you have a dial-gauge canner, have the gauge tested every year before canning even one batch! Call your cooperative extension office to find out where to get this done. Even a brand new one must be tested before use, since shipping can make it inaccurate. When your canner lid is tested, you'll also get information about any recommended changes in time and pressure and procedure of canning.

1. Put wire basket in your pressure canner.
2. Follow instructions for your particular size and style of canner as to the amount of water to put in—probably enough to cover the bottom 1 to 3 inches deep, maybe 1 or 2 quarts. *Read the manual. Follow its instructions. You have to keep your mind on a pressure canner! They can be very dangerous!*
3. Put filled jars with tops screwed on into canner on the wire basket. (Setting jars directly on canner bottom will break them.)
4. Put lid on pressure canner and screw on until it is tightly closed.

5. Check petcock valves with a toothpick if you haven't used the canner lately, if you have that style.

6. Turn up the heat. *Watch for the steam—when you hear it, start timing. Watch for a steady flow of steam coming from the vent for 10 minutes.* This is air leaving the jars and canner. It's called "exhausting" or "venting" the canner. You want the air trapped in the canner to escape through the petcock or steam valve. If the canner isn't properly exhausted, the air will cause the reading on the gauge to be inaccurate, and your canning temperatures may be too low to be safe.

7. After the canner has exhausted for 10 minutes, close the vent or place the weight control over the steam valve.

8. Watch for the pressure gauge to reach the correct pressure for your altitude (see the "Altitude Adjustments for Pressure Canning" table). Then set your timer or look at the clock and begin the designated processing time, as shown in the "Processing Times for Pressure Canning" table. If you are processing food in jars of a half pint or smaller, use the time listed for pints.

PROCESSING TIMES FOR PRESSURE CANNING

Food	Minutes	
	Pints	Quarts
Meats	75	90
Fish	100	100
Asparagus	30	40
Beans, snap (green or yellow)	20	25
Beans, lima	40	50
Beets	30	35
Broccoli	25	40
Brussels sprouts	45	55
Cabbage	45	55
Carrots	25	30
Cauliflower	25	40
Corn	55	85
Greens	70	90
Hominy	60	70
Mushrooms	45	NO!
Okra	25	40
Onions	40	40
Parsnips	20	25
Peas	40	40
Peppers, green	35	35
Peppers, pimentoes	35	35
Potatoes, white	35	40
Pumpkin	55	90
Rutabagas	35	35
Squash, winter	55	90
Sweet potatoes	65	95
Turnips	20	25

ALTITUDE ADJUSTMENTS FOR PRESSURE CANNING

	Processing Pressure	
Altitude	Dial Gauge	Weighted Gauge
Below 1,000 feet	11 lb.	10 lb.
1,000–2,000	11 lb.	15 lb.
2,001–4,000	12 lb.	15 lb.
4,001–6,000	13 lb.	15 lb.
6,001–8,000	14 lb.	15 lb.
8,001 or more	15 lb.	15 lb.

9. Adjust your heat source so the gauge stays at your determined temperature. If it's showing a higher temp, turn down heat a little. If lower, turn up heat. If you have a gauge that has to be watched, turn it so you can keep an eye on it as you do your other work in the kitchen.

10. When the jars have been processed the correct amount of time, take the pressure canner off the heat (use dry potholders or heavy towels) and let it cool. Let the pressure go down of its own accord. Don't try to rush it. On the average it takes 45–60 minutes for the pressure to go down in a pressure canner.

11. *The steam and heat inside even a "cool" canner can be dangerous.* Wait until the pressure gauge has gone down to zero, or until steam isn't visible rushing out when the regulator is nudged (*with a pencil or long-handled fork, not your finger!*). You will hear a hissing sound whenever you nudge the regulator, but if you don't *see* steam, it's ready for you to remove the lid.

12. When you can see no more steam, first open the petcock or remove the weighted gauge (not with your fingers!). Open the petcock valve slowly. Let the canner cool further. Then unlock the canner lid. Slide lid across the top of the canner toward you, thus letting steam escape from the far side of the canner. Leave lid sitting loosely on top of the canner for two more minutes. Remove canner lid. Take your jars out after 10 minutes. If you leave jars in the canner too long, they may not seal and they may overcook.

COOLING, STORING, AND USING

1. For proper sealing, the jars must be removed from the water while still hot. Use your jar lifter to take out each jar *one by one*. You should use a jar lifter because it helps you keep them upright as they are moved from canner to cooling place. This is a dangerous time. Have the children out of the way of scalding hot drips. Don't wear shoes with slippery soles.

2. Set jars aside to seal on a surface warm enough that they won't crack because of a temperature contrast—a board, a cooling rack, or several layers of newspaper or towels—not a cold surface. *Turning jars upside down is no longer recommended, for jam or any other food.* Leave a couple inches between them for air to circulate. Don't cover them. *Don't tighten the lids.* That could break a seal which has already formed. Let them finish sealing on their own.

3. The beginning of the cooling causes a vacuum to develop inside the jar that sucks the lid down tight. You can often hear the pleasant "ping" popping sound as it seals. Test for the seal when the jar has cooled off. Most seal almost immediately, but some seal a little later on.

The sealing takes place when airflow between the jar and the outside is cut off. The air inside the jar contracts because it is cooling, so you have a vacuum effect inside the jar, which pulls the lid downward and reinforces the seal.

You can sometimes tell whether or not the jar is sealed by looking at the lid. You can feel the seal too, the downward-to-the-center (concave) curve of the lid. Whether the lid moves when you press it down is also an indicator. If it stays down when pressed, the jar is sealed. But if the lid pops back up, it's not sealed. Some lids have a "safety button" in the center. When this button is flat, the jar is sealed. If it is popped up or later pops up, the jar is not sealed, or the seal has broken.

And you can hear it! If it is sealed, you'll hear the difference for sure if you tap it with a fork or spoon. A sealed lid makes a clear ringing sound when tapped with metal because of the tension on it. The only exception to this would be if the jar is too full and food is touching the lid. Then you can't know if it's sealed so must assume it is not, because it wouldn't make the canner's famous and beloved "ping." If the lid is not sealed, the sound is lower-pitched and not musical or prolonged. After you've heard the difference a few times, you'll never mistake it. (However, hearing isn't as reliable as seeing and feeling the seal.)

If a jar does not promptly seal after processing, re-process for the full canning time using a different lid, or leave off the lid, put jar in fridge, and use within a week. But reprocessed foods will be distinctly overcooked.

4. Let sealed jars cool undisturbed 18–24 hours. *Don't move them or tighten the rings any more because that can cause the seal to be broken.*

5. After at least 18 hours have passed, take off the rings (screwbands) so liquid under them won't cause rusting. Wipe any stickiness off the outside of the jars. Label them with type of food and date.

6. Store in a dry, cool, dark place. A root cellar or regular cellar is ideal. You have to store the food someplace where it can stay cool but can't possibly freeze. Freezing would break your jars as the water expands. In general, the cooler the storage, the better the quality retention. Leaving at least ½ inch headspace in the jar protects it from freezing to a certain extent but not entirely. That's why canned food should be stored together with root vegetables in your root cellar, if you have one. Otherwise it needs a cool, dark place such as a basement. The coolness helps hold down enzyme and microbe activity in stored food, and the dark helps protect the color. If you live in an earthquake-prone area, canned food arranged on shelves is very vulnerable to the slightest tremor. In that kind of area, store canning jars in boxes flat on the floor, with cardboard strips as cushions between the jars. When you run out of floor space, use strongly attached shelving with edging strips to prevent the jars from falling off.

7. When you open a jar, check for signs of spoiling. *Do not taste if you have any doubts. If you don't hear air rush in, that indicates it was not sealed; discard it. If the cap bulges upward or the food has a strange smell or look, don't taste it; discard it.* Some bacteria produce "flat-sour

spoilage"—sour spoilage with no gas—in canned goods. Some cause gas formation, and you get a bulging lid. Spoilage can make food either more acid or more alkaline, depending on the beastie. Some, such as botulism bacteria, leave no sign of their presence at all—no taste or smell—but nevertheless make the food poisonous.

On the other hand, if the underside of your metal lid has turned dark, don't worry about it. The natural acids and salts in certain foods can interact with the metal and create those harmless brown or black deposits under the lid. They are not harmful to you.

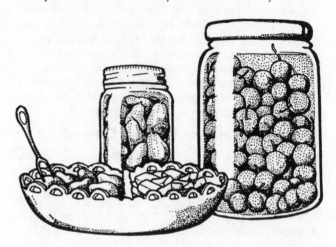

8. *If in doubt, throw it out.* Don't throw it to the animals, because if there is really bot toxin in there, it would poison them. The USDA says, "Due to the risk of botulism, low-acid and tomato foods that are not canned according to . . . USDA . . . recommendations should be boiled before eating, even if you detect no signs of spoilage. Boil foods for 10 minutes at altitudes below 1,000 feet. Add an additional minute of boiling time for each additional 1,000 feet elevation. This is because bot toxin breaks down when heated. Boiling it covered gives you a higher temperature in the pan. If a canning procedure is not USDA-recommended, it says so in this book. If you followed the recommended processing times and all the rules, if your pressure canner was in good condition, and if the pressure gauge was accurate, your food is safe."

But I repeat, *if in doubt, don't taste it; don't try to salvage it by boiling; just throw it out.*

How Long Will Canned Food Keep?

Safety is one measure. Quality is another. As long as your seal lasts—which can be for years—canned food is safe to eat. But every year it sits on the shelf, you lose quality. You lose color, texture, taste, and nutritional value even though it's still safe to eat. With the passage of years, jars may lose their seal and the contents truly spoil, although they can last surprisingly long.

I think the best way to proceed is to plan so you eat up during the winter everything you canned the fall before. That way you can eat from your garden in the summer and from your garden via your various food-preservation systems, including canning, during the winter and have all your preserved food of the very best quality. If you manage correctly, you'll polish off the last jarful as the new garden is starting to produce.

May 18, 1976. I've been writing this book for 6 years now. I don't have a baby anymore. Sara just had her third birthday, and Luke is 4. Becca is ready for the first grade next fall, and Dolly will be 12 in a few weeks. Danny is a dignified young man of 8. This seventh edition has been a long time coming, longer than any of the others. This year and the year before, it seems like I've done everything but write. Last summer was my first attempt at a School of Country Living. Afterwards I had a lot of bills to pay.

I went back on the road with all 5 children and me living in the van and going from town to town all around the whole United States. Julaine was setting up appointments for me from Los Angeles, and we kept in close touch on the telephone. Darlene, Diann, Ivy, Kay, and the crew back at the Living Room Mimeographer in Kendrick were standing by to make and mail the books they hoped I'd create orders for. Mike was lonesome at home taking care of the big zoo of domesticated animals we had developed for the School and the stock cows that were to eat the grass crop. I didn't get on any big national shows because I wasn't that important, but Julaine could generally get local TV, radio, and newspaper interviews for me in the smaller towns, where big-star types didn't bother to go.

So I'd do about 5 cities a week, working all day. A typical day would be maybe 2 TV shows, 2 radio shows, and a newspaper interview. I'd get done about four o'clock and then in the evening drive a few hundred miles to the next town, with laundromat and grocery store stops as needed. We were so desperate for money to pay the bills I'd run up over everyone's dead body, trying to make my School go, that I just couldn't ask them for money back in Idaho. So I literally peddled my way. When I had a live show, I'd suggest that folks could meet me at the public library or a downtown park or some such, and I'd show them my books for sale and pictures of the School and pass out my free brochures. When I got low on both gas and cash and had no live interviews, I'd set out with a couple of books and knock on bookstore doors or pass out brochures to whoever was around until somebody bought one. I traded books for gas in gas stations, sold one to a stranger whom we asked for directions, and got a bath when somebody invited us home.

Many a morning I washed my hair in the sink of a TV station bathroom before the show. The plumbing plugged up in the van, and all through the Midwest we stunk worse than a load of upset skunks. And we practically died of asphyxiation from the fumes when I ignorantly mixed ammonia and lye trying to clean the toilet. Finally we completely quit using the thing, and it composted naturally and was done. I was grubbier and tireder as every day went on. "Sparkle, Shirley!" I'd remind myself as the lights came on. And in true show business style, I'd sparkle through the show as best I could and then drag myself back to the parking lot.

But now the poor old van was getting sick. And without Mike, who had always changed my tires and oil and fixed engines for me, I was helpless. I barely made it through the Holland Tunnel, and the engine died at the intersection of Sixth Avenue and something-or-other street right in downtown Manhattan. I gave my next-to-last dollar to some fellows to push it out of the intersection onto the curb. Somebody stuck their head in the window and asked, "What are you going to do?"

"I'm going to sleep," I answered.

He looked dumbfounded. I was too tired to care. It was the middle of the night and I'd been fighting that engine all afternoon. It had taken me 3 jump starts with long waits between to get into New York City, where I had a show to do the next day. I crawled in the back and we went to sleep. In the middle of the night, somebody tried to crawl in a window of the van. When I raised myself up and stared at him, he looked more scared than I and ran away. I went back to sleep.

The next day there in New York City, we got to do the "To Tell the Truth" show, and that was a good respite. They fed us and bought us a room in a fine hotel. The children bounced on the beds and played in the bathtub and drove the hotel staff crazy. There was only one other show to do in New York, because nobody else had wanted me. That was a sort of blessing, for on the whole this trip was much busier than the one before had been.

ROOT CELLAR STORAGE

Root cellar storage keeps vegetables and fruits fresh (live!). And because of the cellar's coolness, they keep longer. It also protects your live foods, and jars of canned food, from freezing if you live in a cold zone.

Planning for this type of storage starts with planning your garden. You plant foods that store well in a cellar. Beets, late cabbage, carrots, celery, parsnips, potatoes, sweet potatoes, salsify, and turnips can be stored without canning, freezing, or drying in a root cellar. Carrots and potatoes in particular may stay crisp and nice until May. So you don't need to can late fall apples, onions, and big winter squash. To make it easier on the food preserver in the family and reduce dependence on electricity and the availability of jar lids, do fresh vegetable storage. If you want to do this, plant a larger portion of your garden with these kinds of foods.

My cellar is my favorite room in the house next to the kitchen. (Well, in wintertime I also love that big bed in our

Live Storage Guidelines

Food	Freeze Point	Place to Store	Temp.	Humidity	Time Stored
Dry beans/peas	N/A	Any cool, dry place	32–40°F	Dry	As long you want
Late cabbage	30.4°F	Pit, trench, outdoor cellar	Near 32°	Moist	Late fall and winter
Late celery	31.6°	Pit or trench; roots in soil in storage cellar	Near 32°	Moist	6 to 8 weeks
Endive	31.9°	Roots in soil in storage cellar	Near 32°	Moist	Late fall and winter
Onions	30.6°	Any cool, dry place	Near 32°	Dry	Through fall and winter
Parsnips	30.4°	Stay in garden, or in cellar	Near 32°	Moist	Through fall and winter
Peppers	30.7°	Unheated basement or room	45–50°	Moist	2 to 3 weeks
Potatoes	30.9°	Pit or storage cellar	35–40°	Moist	Through fall and winter
Pumpkins and squash	30.5°	Home cellar, basement	55°	Dry	Through fall and winter
Root crops	Various	Pit or cellar	Near 32°	Moist	Through fall and winter
Sweet potatoes	29.7°	Home cellar, basement	55–60°	Dry	Through fall and winter
Tomatoes (mature green)	31°	Home cellar, basement	55–70°	Dry	4 to 6 weeks
Apples	29°	Cellar	Near 32°	Moist	Through fall and winter
Grapefruit	29.8°	Cellar	Near 32°	Moist	4 to 6 weeks
Grapes	28.1°	Cellar	Near 32°	Moist	1 to 2 months
Oranges	30.5°	Cellar	Near 32°	Moist	4 to 6 weeks
Pears	29.2°	Cellar	Near 32°	Moist	3 months

bedroom with all the thick quilts that I hate to rise from on cold mornings.) The walls are lined with shelves, on which rest the canned goods plus all our typical needs. I try to shop only once a month and buy things ahead as much as I can, so when we need something I can head for the cellar rather than the store.

On the floor are the pickle crocks, jugs of vinegar, cooking oil, honey and so on. On a wooden platform on the floor are cans of oatmeal, flour, and wheat. The deep freeze is in another part of the basement. But not everything can be kept in our basement because it doesn't have a dirt floor, and that's bad for vegetables. And in winter it's too hot for them once we have the furnace going.

MORE INFO: *Root Cellaring* by Mike and Nancy Bubel (1979) is a treasure of a book. It covers everything—how to store vegetables and fruits, recipes, etc.—but its strong point is its presentation of a multitude of various root cellar designs. There's a good article on this in *Backwoods Home Magazine,* Nov./Dec. 1992. On the web, see **www.post harvest.com.au** for an Australian website with postharvest handling and storage info and links to other sites. And order "Postharvest Handling of Fruits & Vegetables," free from ATTRA; or online at **www.attra.org/attra-pub/post harvest.html.** North Carolina State University offers a terrific series of fact sheets on postharvest cooling and handling of apples, strawberries, peppers, sweet corn, etc. Order print copies from 919-515-2861; Box 7603, Raleigh, NC 27695-7603. Or read them online at **www5.bae.ncsu. edu/programs/extension/publicat/postharv/index.html.**

Storage Places

You can store vegetables and fruits in an attic, unheated basement room, cellar, outdoor pit, etc. To figure out what food to store where, use a thermometer to learn temperatures. Any place that is dependably 32–60°F can be used to keep some kind of food; the temperature and humidity of each location determines which kind. A room 4 × 4 × 6 feet is large enough for most families. A room 6 × 7 × 7 feet will hold about 30 bushels of produce—5 bushels per month for 6 months. An 8 × 10 × 7-foot room will hold about 60 bushels of produce—10 bushels per month for 6 months.

A WARM ATTIC: In the fall, dry herbs, beans, walnuts, or hickory nuts here.

PANTRY OR UNHEATED ROOM: This is good for short-term storage of potatoes and long-term storage of onions, spices, vegetable oils, nuts, and commercially canned foods. Low storage temperatures extend the shelf life of dried foods such as dried beans, herbs, dried fruits and vegetables, coffee, flour, rice, pasta, and cereals. Be careful that the room doesn't get below freezing.

FOR ROOT VEGETABLES, CABBAGES, APPLES, PEARS: These need very cool, moist conditions. They store well without refrigeration in basements, cellars, outbuildings, and pits, but then you need cool outdoor air to provide the refrigeration. The kind of storage place you need depends much on your climate. Typical root cellar instructions assume outdoor temperatures during winter that average 30°F or lower. You can make do with a combination of cellar, attic, and outbuildings, but nicest of all is to have a "real" root cellar. A proper root cellar can be a little building sitting by itself or adjacent to another building, or it can be a real dirt cellar under an outbuilding. It should be near the house because you will be going there a lot in very cold weather and you don't want a long hike. *NOTE: Don't store live food in or near a garage, unless it is wrapped so that it will be fully protected from car emissions, which produce will absorb.*

HEATED HOUSE BASEMENT: A well-ventilated basement under a house with central heating generally is dry and has a temperature range of 50–60°F. It is fine for ripening tomatoes and for short-term storage of pumpkins, winter squash, potatoes, sweet potatoes, and onions.

Insulated Basement Storage Room. To store vegetables and fruits over winter in a basement that has a furnace, you would have to partition off a room and insulate it from the heat source. Build the room on the north or east side of the basement, if practicable, and don't have heating ducts or pipes running through it. You need at least one window for cooling and ventilating the room. Two or more windows are desirable, particularly if the room is divided for separate storage of fruits and vegetables. Shade the windows in a way that will prevent light from entering the room. Equip the room with shelves and removable slatted flooring. These keep vegetable and fruit containers off the floor and help circulation of air. The flooring also lets you use water or wet materials (such as dampened sawdust) on the floor to raise the humidity in the room. It's safest to store vegetables and fruits in wood crates or boxes rather than in bins, although my friend Imogene winters her carrots all in a big barrel and they do fine.

CELLAR UNDER HOUSE WITHOUT CENTRAL HEAT: Cellars under houses without central heat have long been used successfully for winter storage of fruits and vegetables in colder parts of the United States. These cellars usually have an outside entrance and a dirt floor. The door is a means of ventilating the cellar and regulating the temperature. Some cellars have no windows. If there is a window, it aids in ventilation and temperature control. If the cellar has separate compartments for vegetables and fruits, then you need at least two windows, one for each compartment. Shade the windows in a way that will prevent light from entering the cellar. Light causes potatoes to turn green and become bitter. Insulate the ceiling so cold air will not chill the house.

Out-of-House Storage

IN-GARDEN STORAGE: It is possible to leave some root crops, such as carrots, turnips, and parsnips, in the garden where they grew, for part or all of the winter. Parsnips, horseradish, and turnips actually get a better flavor after light freezing—between 28° to 34°F—because that cold causes their starch to change to sugar. After the ground begins to freeze in the late fall, cover the root crops with a foot or more of mulch—straw, hay, or dry leaves. Do not place mulch on warm soil, because doing so will cause vegetables to decay rapidly. Wait until the ground is cold. Root vegetables can be hard to dig out of the frozen ground, but will not be harmed unless the temperature around the roots gets down to 25°F or lower. Carrots are damaged at about 25°F, but parsnips can stand lower temperatures. But if rodents are a problem, it is wiser to store these in a buried closed container or in a rodent-proof indoor storage area. One gopher can chomp away a whole row of carrots.

Certain other cold-hardy crops such as beets, cabbage, Chinese cabbage, cauliflower, celery, endive, cos or romaine lettuce, kale, leeks, and onions can endure the early light frosts and can be stored in the garden for several weeks more under a heavy mulch. (See growing details in Chapter 4.)

PITS: Foods that need a cold moist place (see "Live Storage Guidelines" table) can be stored outdoors. An advantage of pits is there's no buildup of rot spores, as there may be after a year or two in a cellar. But any outdoor storage has the disadvantage of sometimes being inconvenient or impossible to access, and rodents and other beasts may come to share. Pick a site that is well-drained so it doesn't collect water. You need lots of insulation to protect the food from frost and fluctuating temperatures. People use straw, hay, dry leaves, corn stalks, wood shavings, and plain dirt for insulation. (Dirt is best as a layer over other insulation.) Be sure your insulation isn't contaminated with chemicals or pesticides. Pits should be made in a different place every year because leftovers in used pits are contaminated.

Buried Can. One type of pit is made simply of a wooden barrel covered with several layers of straw and dirt. Or you can use an insulated wooden box or ice chest (but not a plastic "garbage" can!), buried in the ground. This makes a convenient and cheap storage place for your vegetables. Metal cans are most rodent-proof. The opening of the can should sit about 2 inches above ground level. Make sure the container hasn't held anything that would poison or give an off flavor to the food. *Never use drums or containers that might have held pesticides or other chemicals.* Make several holes in the bottom to allow drainage. Dig your hole deep enough so you have room for a layer of rocks in the bottom of it for drainage. Set the can on top of the rocks. The vegetables go into the can in layers with straw or other mulch between each layer. Cover the top of the can with a mound of insulating material that is at least 1 or 2 feet deep and that extends at least a foot on each side of the can.

Cone-Shaped Pits. Cone-shaped outdoor pits are often used for storing potatoes, celeriac, kohlrabi, rutabagas, winter radishes, carrots, beets, turnips, salsify, parsnips, and cabbage. They are sometimes used for storing winter apples and pears. The pit may be built on the ground or in a hole 6 to 8 inches deep in a well-drained location. Build the pit as follows:

1. Select a well-drained location.
2. Spread a layer of straw, leaves, or other bedding material on the ground at least 3 inches thick. Or dig a shallow hole 6–10 inches deep; this gives better frost protection (but increases the risk of water collection). Lay insulation in the bottom of the hole.
3. Stack the vegetables or fruits on the bedding in a cone-shaped pile up to 12 inches above ground level. Don't store apples and pears in vegetable pits, for they'll pick up odors.
4. Arrange them around a beanpole that will stick up through the top of the mound, high enough to be seen through snow cover, so you can find your food in winter.
5. Cover the vegetables or fruits with more bedding.
6. Cover the entire pile with 3 or 4 inches of soil.
7. Firm the soil with the back of a shovel to make the pit waterproof.
8. Dig a shallow drainage ditch around the pit.
9. Small pits containing only a few bushels of vegetables or fruits will get sufficient ventilation if you let the

bedding material over the vegetables extend through the soil at the top of the pile. Cover the top of the pile with a board or piece of sheet metal to protect the stored food from rain; a stone will hold the cover in place. To ventilate large pits, place two or three boards or stakes up through the center of the pile of vegetables or fruits to form a flue. Cap the flue with two pieces of board nailed together at right angles.

Removing Pit-Stored Food. It's hard to get food from a pit in a frozen, snow-covered garden. *Once a pit is opened, its entire contents should be removed.* The vegetables that were in the pit will now keep only 1 or 2 more weeks. Though they look the same, pit-stored vegetables won't keep as long as freshly harvested ones. So you'll need to eat them up or shift them to another method of preservation. For this reason, it's better to construct several small pits rather than one large one. Put a small quantity of different vegetables in each pit. Then you can open only one small pit and get a variety of vegetables. When several kinds of vegetables are stored in the same pit, separate them with straw or leaves.

ROOT CELLARS: Outdoor storage cellars may be attached to your house or located in your yard or under an outbuilding. But they should be convenient to your kitchen. Outdoor storage cellars can be constructed entirely or partly underground. Cellars constructed below ground stay at the best temperature longer and more uniformly than cellars that are above ground. The secret to a good root cellar is the combination of insulation where it contacts the air and a design that allows it to absorb warmth from the ground. That's why the more earth there is around your root cellar, the better it functions.

Water. It's important to dig a root cellar and not a well. Find out your water table level. Avoid a site that gets a lot of runoff from rain or spring thaws. Make the floor plan slope just a bit downward for drainage. If you have a water problem, ditch with drainage tile or gravel under it. Or if you end up with water 2 feet deep, make your floor out of planks over supports. You'll have plenty of humidity.

Outer Room. Some folks have an anteroom built outside the entrance to their cellar. That helps with insulation and provides a great place to store garden tools, empty canning jars, etc.
NOTE: Don't build using pressure-treated wood. The phenols used to treat it are dangerous poisons that will tend to vaporize into the air in your cellar.

Roof. Cover your roof with a waterproof material, and then put the dirt over that.

Underground Cellar. The walls and roof of an underground cellar must be strong to support the weight of earth over the roof. Stone and masonry block in combination with concrete can be used, but a cellar made of reinforced concrete is better. A typical underground cellar design has the whole structure, except the door, covered with soil. Wire screen over the outside ends of air intakes and ventilators keeps out birds and small animals. This kind of cellar can also serve as a storm cellar (or fallout shelter).

Partly Underground Cellar. This type of cellar is used in colder parts of the country. First you look for a small hill that you can dig into—or plan to haul dirt. This cellar has walls of masonry that are partly underground. Soil is banked around three walls, and one wall is left exposed. The exposed side has an insulated double door. If you have

more than one storage compartment, an air inlet and a ventilator are needed for each one.

Bill Rogers lives in Wheatland, WY, one of the coldest places in the United States. He wrote me, "Your description of the double house, insulated, is great, but let's come back to the real ranch and mountain vegetable cellar. Most of us in the mountains have caves. We dig them in the mountainsides and it is extremely laborious, although not so laborious as you might think, going into rocky mountainsides—usually not blasting. Often your caves amount to no more than a slice into the hillside, walled up and roofed over. My own is inadequately insulated, but it became much more usable and dependable when I built a toolshed in front of the door—keeping it always sheltered and shaded. It never freezes, so I am inclined to believe I could not better my cave if I did insulate expensively."

More Types. Bill wrote me, "Some people in more level country shore up a huge mound of earth covering a specially constructed storehouse. An entranceway with a dead air space 3–4 inches thick between the inner and outer doors is really necessary in the way of insulating. This type of construction is necessary where the water table is relatively high throughout the year. Some people excavate a cellar and have done so since the days of the first pioneers. Two doors are necessary—one on the surface and one at the bottom of the steps. Ventilators are necessary for all types of vegetable cellars. Much more care is necessary in vegetable storing than most people realize. I lost my potatoes last winter due to the lack of air circulation through them. Cabbages keep fresh in bushel baskets, however! One of our garden problems is that in our short growing season everything ripens with a rush and you cannot use it—unless you can put the surplus in storage. Frost comes and everything will be lost unless you can move wheelbarrow loads into storage."

Mostly Above-Ground Cellars. Storing vegetables and fruits in outbuildings is practical only where the climate is consistently cold *but* the average temperature is not below freezing. Even in these climates, temperatures may drop to 0°F or below, and supplemental heat may be needed on very cold nights to keep your food from freezing. Thermostatically controlled heat can be used if the building is wired for electricity. Only a small amount of heat is necessary to prevent below-freezing temperatures in a building unless the cold outside is extraordinary. But you'll have to watch the storage temperature closely whenever low temperatures are predicted.

Storage outbuildings can be made of masonry or lumber, but they must be well insulated. Hollow-block walls, regardless of thickness, don't insulate much. Put vermiculite or some other dry granular material in the channels of hollow blocks as each layer of block is laid. If you use cinder blocks, scrub them on both sides with cement grout to make them less porous. Then paint them on the inside with aluminum paint; the paint serves as a moisture barrier. Lay tar paper between the ceiling and joists as a moisture barrier, and spread at least 12 inches of dry sawdust or other granular material in the attic above the ceiling.

A frame building can be built of 2 × 4-inch studding and rafters. Make walls tight by sheathing the inside and outside of the frame with matched lumber. Insulate the space between the walls with loose fill or mineral wool blanket. Put laminated kraft paper (with asphalt between layers), aluminum foil, or polyethylene between the insulation and inside walls as a moisture barrier. Put building paper over the outside sheathing before you lay shingles or siding to make the building tight. Paint the inside of the building with aluminum paint or whitewash. To ventilate above-ground storage buildings, you need intake and exhaust vents.

Imogene's Cellar Design. Here are her directions for building one like hers. The floor should be dirt, because root vegetables keep much better on a natural ground floor than they do on boards or concrete. The floor should be

then a gently sloped roof above that (the outside house) with a considerable overhanging eave. (That makes possible a good depth of insulation across the entire inside area of the cellar, except where your air vents go through in summer. They reach up through the insulation to the free air above.) The roof does not need to shed snow; snow is itself a good insulation. The door area should also be insulated by making two doors, one for the outside wall and one for the inside. You can add hanging blankets inside the door area for additional insulation.

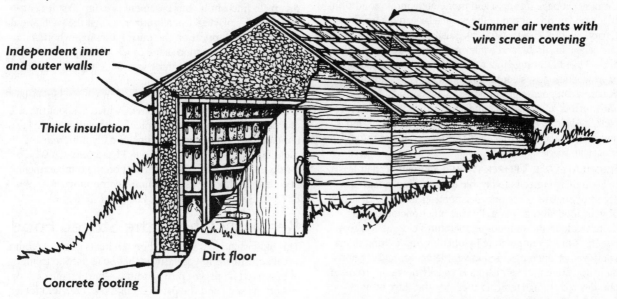

Independent inner and outer walls

Thick insulation

Summer air vents with wire screen covering

Dirt floor

Concrete footing

dug down at least a foot below natural ground level (more is better) so that you actually step down into your root cellar. This puts it below the level to which the ground generally freezes in winter.

Build your storage cellar as large or small as you like. It could be as small as 6 × 6 feet inside, but larger is nicer, especially if you have a large family. It will be mighty full in the fall and have lots of room in the spring. The walls are usually double and wooden and best set on a concrete footing. Build the concrete footing to go down a couple feet on the very outside to prevent rodents digging under. There are no windows, but the roof has summer air vents with a wire covering to keep out rodents. There should be at least two of these ceiling vents. They should be square, about 12 × 12 inches. After the freezing weather comes, stuff them up. Most people keep their canned goods in the root cellar too, so they cover the wall space from floor to ceiling with wooden shelves for holding jars. The vegetables sit on the floor.

There is a space of 2 feet between the inner and outer walls all the way around, which is filled with a good insulation like wood chips or sawdust (free around here, since we are a land of sawmills). There can be a layer of plastic between the wood and insulation. If the outside boards are done tongue and groove, that makes it even better insulated. In your construction, it's also important to make the outer and inner walls as independent of each other as possible, because any connection between them will draw frost into your root cellar at that place. You have to connect them around the door, but you don't have to anywhere else, so don't. What you are building is a house inside a house, with insulation between the walls. The roof consists of a flat layer of boards (the inside house), 3 feet more of insulation, and

Maintaining Your Storage

KEEP THE STORAGE SPACE CLEAN: Keep storage facilities for vegetables and fruits clean. *Get rid of vegetables and fruits that show signs of decay.* At least once a year, remove all containers from your storeroom. Then clean them and air them in the sun. Wash the walls and ceiling before you put back the containers.

HARVEST FOR LIVE STORAGE: Harvest during dry weather, not too soon after a rain, and let the surface of the product dry, since wet produce is much more susceptible to disease in storage. Handle food carefully to prevent skin cuts and bruises, which also invite decay. Containers should have smooth inner surfaces. Protruding wire staples in baskets and hampers, for example, damage food. Vegetables or fruits with skin breaks should go directly to the kitchen or another preservation system. Make sure there are no crushed, cut, or decaying foods mixed in with those to be stored. They'll cause their neighbors to soon decay also. Harvest in early morning, or let crops picked in daytime heat cool outdoors overnight before you store them. *Don't wash produce before storing.* Just leave the garden dirt on; it helps them keep. Some commercial foods are waxed to reduce moisture loss and appeal to potential buyers. Home folks don't do that and have better food because of it.

Containers. Sturdy *food-quality* plastic cans with or without handles and with airtight lids are useful for holding grains, beans, flour, honey; making sausage; hauling produce and milk; and curing pickles and sauerkraut. You can reuse any plastic container from store-bought food. But don't make the mistake of putting food in regular plastic garbage cans or bags, because they may be made out of a kind of plastic that is very carcinogenic! It's safe to use a big enamel or stainless-steel kettle (enamel is cheaper, but it doesn't last as long because the enamel will chip). Crocks are romantic and healthy and unlikely to tip over, but a 20-gallon crock can be expensive.

Cans made for food storage are fine. Wooden bins are fine as long as the wood hasn't been "treated" in any way. Dried beans, peas, soybeans, and the like can be stored in airtight cans in your cellar. Squash, pumpkins, and onions need dry storage. Potatoes, late cabbage, cauliflower, and Chinese cabbage like cool and moderately moist conditions, so a wooden box or bin in the root cellar is okay for them. Carrots, endive, beets, parsnips, salsify, rutabagas, turnips, late celery, kohlrabi, and winter radishes need to be quite cool, 32–40°F. Storage in a wooden box under moist sand, or in wooden boxes containing sawdust, is best for them. Potatoes can go straight into the bins. That may be okay with carrots, etc., also. Try and see.

NOTE: Apples give off a gas that stimulates potatoes to sprout and shortens the keeping of other root veggies, so don't store fruits with veggies.

REGULATE THE TEMPERATURE: You will need at least 2 reliable thermometers to be able to carefully regulate storage temperature. Place one thermometer in the coldest part of your food storage place. Put the other one outdoors. Watch indoor and outdoor temperatures closely. You regulate the storage temperature by opening and closing doors, windows, or openings used as ventilators. In most regions, daily adjustment of ventilators is usually necessary to maintain desired storage temperatures. See the "Live Storage Guidelines" table for the freezing points and the best temperatures for long-term storage of your foods.

Outdoor temperatures well below 32°F are necessary to cool storage air to 32° and to maintain that temperature. Once cooled to 32°, the temperature will rise again from earth warmth if ventilators are closed, even though outdoor temperature is about 25°. Close ventilators tightly whenever the outdoor temperature is higher than the storage temperature. Be careful during subfreezing weather so that the stored food doesn't freeze. For example, in an insulated storage cellar partly above ground at Beltsville, MD, full ventilation both day and night was necessary to maintain a temperature of 32°F if outdoor temperatures ranged between 18° and 30° during the day and dipped to 10° at night. But if the minimum temperature at night was 8° for 5–6 hours and ventilators were still fully open, the storage temperature dropped to 30°—below freezing. During a night of high wind, even a minimum of 12° cooled the cellar to 30°.

For a more sophisticated postharvest storage system, consider buying a used, reconditioned cooler, freezer, or refrigeration system from Barr, Inc., "world's largest inventory": 920-231-1711; fax 920-231-1701; 1423 Planeview Dr., Oshkosh, WI 54904; **info@barrinc.com; www.barr inc.com.**

MAINTAIN NEEDED HUMIDITY/DRYNESS: Without enough moisture in the air, stored vegetables and fruits may shrivel, lose quality, and eventually become unfit to eat. (See the "Live Storage Guidelines" table for specific humidity needs.) You can add moisture to storage air by sprinkling the floor, by placing large pans of water under fresh-air intake vents, by covering the floor with wet materials such as damp straw or sawdust or by any combination of

those. Humidity of 95 percent is almost rainfall and is difficult to achieve indoors. Humidity of 90–95 percent is very moist and good for storage of potatoes and other root crops. Too much humidity encourages mold and other decay critters. (Excessive humidity is present when water droplets form on the surface of the food.) A humidity of 60–75 percent is dry and good for storage of pumpkins and winter squash.

Testing for Dampness. But pumpkins, squash, and onions need a very dry but not cold place for their best storage. So they don't belong in your basement or root cellar at all if it's damp. To find out if your basement is damp, test for condensation by placing a small mirror against the wall. Should droplets or fog appear on the mirror after a few hours, it means that condensation is the cause of dampness. Ventilation fans might help but aren't worth it. Store those particular foods upstairs.

You can install a humidity gauge in your cellar. Delta Track sells a "Hygro Thermometer," which is about the size of a deck of cards, battery operated, with a digital display of temp and humidity and recording of daily min./max. of each: 800-962-6776; PO Box 398, Pleasanton, CA 94566. Or do this simple test for condensation in your basement. Spectrum Technologies sells humidity monitors: 800-248-8873; 23839 W. Andrews Rd., Plainfield, IL 60544.

Regularly Check the Stored Food

This old-fashioned way of food preserving is going to require a real adjustment in your attitude if you're used to thinking of preserved foods as a near absolute—putting the cans or jars on the shelf and the packages in the freezer, and forgetting about them until needed. It isn't so with storage of fresh vegetables and fruits, nor is it so with dried, salted, sugared, spiced, or alcoholed foods. These items require upkeep—regular, faithful attention all the while you have them.

ROOT CELLAR CHECKLIST

1. Tour your root cellar at least once a week, carefully looking for problems. You'll be in a race with decay all winter long, just as you were in a race to preserve nature's abundance from your garden and orchard all summer long.
2. Be ready to make a switch from this method of preserving to another if it looks like you're going to lose some food. That means if there's a problem, you salvage what is possible and can, dry, pickle, freeze, or quickly eat it. You also want to remove any and all spoiling vegetables or fruits because the rot spreads to others if you let it go.
3. Green tomatoes and apples: If they have begun to spoil, check them every day or two. Remove bad apples and tomatoes. Take tomatoes that have turned red for kitchen use. If the apples start going in quantity, make a lot of pies or applesauce or freeze apple slices in syrup for pies.
4. Check crock pickles for excessive scum (or mold) on top. If they have it, pour off the brine, boil it, add another cup of vinegar and an extra handful of salt, and then pour it back onto the pickles.
5. Check dried fruits and vegetables for signs of mold. If you have mold, heat in your oven and then repackage.
6. Check grains and grain products for insect infestation. (See Chapter 3.)
7. Check for mold or bugs in your home-dried fruits. If bugs are present, put the food in a small cheesecloth

bag and dip into boiling water for 6 seconds. Dry again and then store in something bug-proof. Or freeze for a few days.

8. Jams and jellies may develop surface mold. If one does, throw it out.

9. If a squash or pumpkin has developed a soft spot, cut out that spot and give to the animals. Cook up the rest to use, can, or freeze.

If you are interested in storing large quantities of food for a very long time (like years), make some Mormon friends. They have made a complete study of this and have lots of practice too. I am blessed with a Mormon mother-in-law who is a dear and precious mother to me and has guided me to a lot of learning. They'd rather be called "Latter-Day Saints," but you probably already knew that.

I think the biggest single principle of cellar-type storage is that you should put away more than you expect to need in order to allow for losses during storage. The thing that makes root-cellar storage really pay off is owning a pig or chickens, so you can recycle the food that doesn't keep into bacon and eggs. By late March, seven-eighths of your winter squash either will have been brought up to the kitchen for cooking or will have spoiled or be near enough spoiled so that you have fed it to the animals. In other words, if you let all your squash set on the shelves all winter long in whatever condition it was (and that would hasten spoilage of the remainder), only seven-eighths of it or less will make it to March. If you do end up with good food left over, you can share it with your neighbors (or the animals).

When you have made your major weekly inspection, sorting out what's bad and should be fed to the pigs and chickens (which is good for them) and setting aside what needs to be cooked up next week for the family, then stop a moment. Admire your shelves covered with home-canned food, your deep freeze full of vegetables and meat, the boxes of apples in the garage, the crocks of pickles and boxes of root vegetables covering your cellar floor, and the cabbage waiting in trenches outside in the garden. Feel good about what your family accomplished and secure about the future, and give thanks to your Good Lord for it.

SUGARING—AND FRUIT PRESERVATION

Sugar, salt, and alcohol were the original "chemical" preservatives. At sugar concentrations of 50–60 percent, sugar's preserving action begins to work. Above 70 percent, nothing grows. Because 15 percent salt and 70 percent sugar don't appeal to human taste, in the old days the former brine and the latter syrup were diluted before use. Pickles were removed from the brine for a day and soaked in several changes of clear water. Syrups were diluted with water to taste.

My favorite food "preserved in sugar" is pure honey, which will keep literally forever. You can make any jam into a self-preserving recipe by altering the amount of sugar used to the required 70 percent. But it's healthier to dry fruit, make fruit leather, or can fruit for a winter sweet, because those are naturally sweet without adding the empty calories of sugar.

In colonial America, dried pumpkin, maple sugar, and honey were used as sweetening agents. My mother bought plain old white sugar in 25- or 50-lb. bags and then transferred it to a bin in the kitchen. There was a bin for flour, too. They didn't go to town too often from the ranch. It was a long day's proposition, so when they did, the car really came home loaded. The sugar lasted a long time. Mama didn't often make desserts, though when she did they were delicious. Fudge and divinity at Christmas time was her candy repertoire. Oven-baked custard, apple pie, or oatmeal cookies were her everyday desserts.

I've got a real sweet tooth, and I practically ruined my teeth with candy bars and pop once I got away from Mama. Now I'm a mother too and fighting the same battle. I prefer using honey, and I can make a 5-gal. can last all winter.

There are four kinds of sugar. Fructose is found in fruits and honey. Glucose is also found in fruits and in the blood; it's the sugar they give in hospitals. Lactose is a kind of sugar found in milk; the whey from cheese making is rich in it and will sweeten your bread. If you boil down the whey, you get a more concentrated lactose syrup. Sucrose comes from sugar cane and sugar beets.

Fruit is a wonderful natural sugar. In summer when the fruit starts, the children and I quit cooking breakfasts. We just get up in the morning and head for the orchard. Who needs any other start to the day when there are trees loaded with heavenly ripe cherries waiting to be eaten? It's fun to gather 'round the tree, big ones handing down fruit to the smaller ones, Mother pulling down low-hanging branches for smaller children to hang onto and strip. That's the easy part. Then we've got to put up the winter's supply.

SUGAR ALTERNATIVES

Honey. Some people substitute honey for sugar in food preservation recipes. This doesn't reduce the sugar content of preserved foods because 2 types of sugar—fructose and glucose—are the major components of honey. Honey can be substituted for sugar in canned and frozen fruits. The flavor of honey is sweeter than that of granulated sugar, so it is advisable to use less honey than the amount of sugar specified in the recipe. In jelly recipes without added pectin, honey can replace up to one-half of the granulated sugar. With added pectin, honey can replace up to one-fourth of the sugar. Be sure to use light, mild-flavored honey if you don't want noticeable flavor changes in your preserved food.

Corn Syrup. Light corn syrup can replace up to half the amount of sugar in syrups for canned fruits. Be sure to use light corn syrup. Dark corn syrup, sorghum, and molasses are a problem to use because their flavor overpowers the fruit flavor and may darken the fruit. On the other hand, if that's what you have, it won't win a county-fair prize, but it's good food.

Artificial Sweeteners. This stuff isn't good for you, but diabetics and desperate dieters may resort to it sometimes. You'll generally get better flavor if you can or freeze without any sweetener than if you use saccharin or aspartame (Nutrasweet or Equal). Saccharin may become slightly bitter when heated or frozen. Aspartame should not be used in canning because it breaks down when heated, but it can be added to food to be frozen. The best way is to add either of these just before eating the preserved food. If you do add them, it is better to undersweeten the fruit than to overdo it.

Fruit Juice and Juice Products

The quickest and easiest way I know to keep working men and women happy in hot weather is to keep gallon jars of cool liquid in the refrigerator and a plastic gallon jar of ice cubes in the freezer compartment. I make lots of tea (wild strawberry leaf is Mike's favorite, and wild mint is mine). I sweeten the tea with honey, chill it, and serve it plain or with ice cubes for a special treat. I also keep some of our spring water chilled in the refrigerator in summer for drinks. And the children enjoy the juices canned up from the previous summer's fruit crop, thinned with cold water.

Way back when this book was first getting made, I had hopes of finding a young woman to come and work with me in return for room and board. I advertised. The first answer was somebody's sister, whose sister I think was more enthused than she was. She called me up long-distance from Michigan, and when I told her we worked about a 12-hour day in the summer, she decided she wasn't interested. Then an Oregon woman drove all the way here to look us over. She stayed an hour, declared, "Your place is just like my mother-in-law's," and left. By the next summer I was getting some real solid inquiries, but by then Mike and I had decided not to take on any extras. But it's really not so bad around here in the summer—12-hour days and all. Part of what makes it tolerable is having good things to drink.

JUICE EXTRACTOR AND BOTTLING EQUIPMENT: You don't need special equipment to make fruit juices. Cider, grape juice and other juices in quantity are fairly easily extracted with the aid of a fruit press or a Mehu-Maija, which is the brand name of a very fine Finnish steam process juice extractor. Or you can buy a juicer. A juicer or fruit press makes juice without cooking the fruit. *The Juicing Book,* steamers, a press for juicing citrus fruits without heating, a juice extractor for other fruits and veggies, a food strainer/sauce maker, etc., are available from Back to Basics: 801-571-7349. You make juice in the steamer, simmer for 40 to 70 minutes (still in the steamer), and then empty the hot juice directly into soda pop or wine bottles, or half-gallon or gallon cider jugs.

JELLY-BAG JUICE EXTRACTION: Cook the fruit (some berries can simply be mashed) and put it through anything from a cloth to a colander (good for liquids like tomato juice with some seeds). A modern one can be a fine-mesh nylon bag suspended somehow for juice to drip through. Prop the bag/sieve up in a pan and go do something else while it drops, or use a rotary colander and rub the pulp around with your wooden pestle. If you are using a cloth, make it a sturdy one. You can "wring" out the juice, or pin the cloth to the sides of the colander with clothespins and let it drop. A first treatment often yields juice with pulp floating in it. If you want clear juice for jelly making or a beverage, give the juice a second straining through a clean cloth, or let it set overnight and pour off the top. You can often get extra juice from berries by taking the pulp of your first squeezing and putting it back on the stove with some water. Boil 5 minutes and then squeeze again.

Crushing Fruit. When directions call for crushing the fruit, you can use a wire potato masher, pastry fork, or slotted spoon for soft fruits. Firm fruits can be crushed with a food chopper. A colander, food press, or strainer will give you a puree. Don't use galvanized ware in direct contact with fruit or fruit juices because the acid in fruit forms poisonous salts with the zinc. Metallic off-flavors may result from the use of iron utensils, chipped enamelware, or tinware that is not well-tinned.

NECTARS: Juices like apricot, berry, melon, peach, pear, and plum are categorized as the ones that make "nectars." They are best thinned with water or added to other juices.

MIXED JUICES: Home-grown fruits vary widely in sweetness and flavor. Fully ripe fruits are best for making fruit juices. Use your judgment as to the thinning and sweetening desirable for your own juice. Berries, sweet cherries, apples, melons, pineapples, peaches, and apricots have relatively sweet juice. Cranberries, plums, currants, rhubarb, sour cherries and tart grapes have tart juice. The tart juices can be drunk sweetened and make fine additions to other juices or ginger ale. The amount needed to dilute sour cherry, plum, grape, and berry juices is generally one-third to one-half; you can use water or a bland juice or ginger ale to dilute. The "citrus" juices are orange, lemon, lime, and grapefruit. These are generally thinned with water and sweetened, and are often combined with other juices.

Preserving Juices

Your juices, once extracted, can be easily canned (water-bath time is 5 or 10 minutes), frozen, drunk on the spot, or made into syrup or frozen concentrate to be diluted later.

FREEZING JUICE: Freezing liquids isn't hard. Put a plastic baggie into a pint or quart jar or tin can you've saved. Pour in the fluid and fold the baggie over the top of the fluid. The air space at the bottom of the baggie protects jars from breaking. If it is a widemouthed jar or if you don't fill it near the neck, you can freeze liquids in glass without a baggie. When the juice is thawed out again, it will probably be more diluted near the top and oversweet near the bottom. Just stir it up.

Although you can freeze juice in almost anything, you'll have a better-tasting long-term product if you manage to make it something you can seal. If you freeze in a canning jar, leave plenty of headspace:

Widemouthed pint jar	½ inch headspace
Narrow-mouthed pint jar	¾ inch headspace
Widemouthed quart jar	1 inch headspace
Narrow-mouthed quart jar	1½ inches headspace

Homemade Frozen Juice Concentrate. Many recipes assume you have frozen fruit juice concentrates, since there are so many fun things you can do with them. To make a homemade frozen juice concentrate just like the store-bought kind, you need only a large, narrow-necked container, such as a gallon jug, and a freezer.

Pour your juice into the container. Food-grade plastic works well. If you aren't using plastic, be sure to fill no more than three-fourths full so you won't risk breaking the jug when the liquid expands in freezing. Cap and freeze. After it is all frozen, remove the cap and turn the jug upside down. Suspend it by the "shoulders" over a lower container, such as a widemouthed gallon jar, so the drips won't make a mess and because the drips are the good part. Don't try to rush the draining process with heat. That would mess up the process because the ice melts, runs down, and dilutes the juice concentrate.

The reason it works is because the juicier bits melt before the plain water crystals do. When the drips running off are no longer sweet and colored, take away the jug. Finish melting the ice. Throw out the ice water. Now repeat your freezing and dripping procedure 2 more times (3 total). You now have a fine concentrate. Store it in the freezer.

CANNING JUICE: Heat high-acid fruit juices—from apricots, berries, red cherries, red grapes, peaches, plums, and rhubarb—to 190°F to inactivate enzymes and deepen color. If you do it in the top of a double boiler, you'll get a fresher fruit flavor. Don't let the temperature reach the boiling point. Once it has reached 190°F, cool it quickly to keep the fresh flavor. If you have a choice, don't heat apple, light-colored cherry, light grape, or citrus juices. Heat destroys vitamin C. Store in freshly sterilized bottles. (Sterilize by boiling, covered with water, for 20 minutes.) Cap with cork-lined metal caps and turn upside down for 5 minutes. Leave bottles in a dark place. If you haven't one, put the jars in paper bags or cardboard cartons. To hold flavor, color, and vitamins, have a storage place that doesn't get above 70°F.

Capper

Old-Time Sealing Wax for Bottle Corking. Use 1 lb. resin, 2 oz. beeswax, and 1½ oz. tallow. Warm and combine. First cover cork using a brush, and push it into the bottle. Then dip the entire corked end of the bottle into the melted wax.

Summer Ices, Frozen Fruits

An "ice" is a frozen beverage. A "frappe" is a dessert ice that is basically a fruit sauce frozen only to a coarse mushy stage. A "sherbet" can be a water ice with a little dissolved gelatin or beaten egg white added. (For milk-based sherbets, see Chapter 10.) And then there are popsicles. Actually, you can use any popsicle recipe to make a frappe and vice versa. To make a frappe, just eat it out of a bowl before it is frozen clear solid. If you get a dessert ice frozen too hard to serve, let it thaw again until it has the consistency of thick mush. Then serve. Feel free to change the sweetening type and amount to suit your preference. You don't have to have a crank freezer for any of these, although if you do, then by all means use it.

An electric ice shaver turns ice cubes into soft, fluffy snow. You can pour flavoring over it to make snow cones, slushes, etc. Shavers are available from Back to Basics for $29.95 (801-571-7349). They also sell lime, raspberry, grape, kiwi, etc., flavor concentrates (powdered—add water and sweetener, or liquid), dispenser bottles, ice molds, and recipe booklet.

HOMEMADE POPSICLES: These are cheap, easy, and even more fun for the children than going to the store. Children like strong, sweet juices like grape and cranberry for popsicles—but when kids are hot, anything will do. My little ones enjoy goat's milk popsicles. Popsicle making is a nice way to use leftover juices from canned fruit, too.

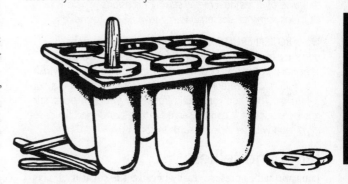

Of Handles and Molds. You can use wooden sticks for handles and sturdy small bowls or cans for containers—work up a collection. Or buy popsicle molds; Tupperware and Back to Basics carry them. If you have a big family or lots of small friends, I recommend getting at least 2 molds so you can have one freezing while they are consuming the other. You can even make parfait popsicles by freezing a layer of one color and then a layer of another color. My plastic holders soon got lost or fell apart, but then we substituted sticks in a bowl or can and were fine. Fill the molds not quite full, insert your holder, and freeze.

Unmolding. Don't let the gremlins pull the holders until you're sure the center of the popsicle is solidly frozen and you have loosened the sides by running hot water over the back of the mold. Otherwise they might pull out the holder prematurely, leaving a hole that it won't freeze back into. You don't have to unmold all the popsicles at once. Just loosen as many as you need. Refill the emptied units and return to the freezer.

BASIC FRUIT POPSICLES *Puree 1 c. any kind of fruit or a mixture of fruit and mix with 1 c. water. Pour into your ice cube tray. When they are starting to freeze, add a wooden stick or toothpick to each section.*

PUDDING POPSICLES *Susan Staley was in Germany when she sent me this recipe. She said, "If your children love the Fudgsicle-type popsicle, you can easily make them. Just make up a batch of pudding and freeze it in your popsicle molds. They're delicious and you can make different kinds besides chocolate. Butterscotch is very good. In fact, any flavor of pudding your children love hot, they're bound to like cold in hot summer weather."*

ANY FRUIT ICE *You could juice pomegranates or barberries or red currants, or cook and strain quinces, or grate pineapple, or boil and pulp apples or rhubarb—whatever you have. Sweeten to taste, add lemon juice if the flavor needs it, and freeze.*

GINGER ALE ICE *Combine ¾ c. sugar and 2 c. water. Heat and boil 5 minutes. Cool. Add 1 c. orange juice, ½ c. lemon juice, and 2 bottles ginger ale. Freeze.*

ROOT BEER ICE *Combine 1 bottle root beer, 1 T. lemon juice, 1 T. brown sugar, and a few grains salt. Freeze.*

STRAWBERRY OR RASPBERRY ICE *Remove the green stem end from fruit, enough to make 3 or 4 cups. Pour ½ c. honey over the fruit. Mash the mixture with a potato masher until you have it pulped as finely and mixed as well as you can. (If you like, strain out the seeds.) Add 1 c. water and the juice of 1 lemon. Freeze, stirring occasionally. This is a delicious summer dessert and my favorite ice to make.*

FROZEN FRUITS *Strawberries, raspberries, fresh peaches, or crushed pineapple (as well as canned fruits, especially pears and peaches in syrup) can be frozen. Mash the fruit, add sweetening to taste, and let stand until a syrup is formed. Then use your crank freezer or freeze in trays, stirring occasionally. It can be served in slices or dished up casually. Good with whipped cream on top.*

Jams and Jellies

Jams and jellies preserve easily because the sugar itself acts as a preservative. Jam is fruit boiled thick with sugar. Most jam recipes call for a 2:1 ratio of sugar to fruit by weight or volume. Some jam recipes that are really trying to hold down the sugar content call for a 1:1 ratio. Jelly generally has a 1:1 ratio, 1 c. juice to 1 c. sugar. Jelly making depends on having proper amounts of fruits, pectin, acid, and sugar. Jellying is a chemical change based on the presence of pectin and acid.

JAM/JELLY RECIPES: Canning books always have jam and jelly recipes. You can get free ones with any package of commercial pectin that you buy or from your extension agent, and you'll find lots here and there in this book. You can personalize recipes with your own flavors and spices, but stay close to the recipe for the essential pectin/sugar/acid proportions.

PECTIN: Pectin is the key to jelly. It's a natural substance in some fruits, especially underripe ones, that "jells" when heated and combined with acid from the fruit and sugar. Apples are usually rich in pectin. Natural ripening causes the pectin to break down. So if your fruit is overripe, your jelly will never get firm no matter how long you boil it. Peaches, strawberries, and cherries don't have much pectin. You can combine pectin-rich fruits with pectin-poor fruits, use commercially prepared pectin, or make your own.

No-Sugar Pectin. Pomona Universal Pectin sells low-methoxyl pectin. That's a pectin which jells fruit without using sugar in the recipe. In this way, jams, jellies, and fruit spreads can be made without sugar or long boiling times: 413-772-6816; PO Box 1083, Greenfield, MA 01302; **aggie-horticulture.tamu/plantanswers/recipes/sugarless.htm.** For more ideas, see *Canning and Preserving without Sugar* by Norma M. MacRae. Her recipes for canned fruits and jams use honey, frozen juice concentrate, canned juice, date sugar, and dried fruits for sweetening. But keep in mind that *every time you reduce the sugar, you're reducing the time the jam or jelly can be safely kept out of the freezer before mold grows on it.*

Homemade Pectin From Apples. To make this, use skins and cores of cut-up apples or whole apples, or apple pulp. Boil 2 lb. apples with 4 c. water for about 45 minutes. Extract the juice through a cloth or jelly bag without using pressure. Boil the resulting juice 15 minutes and can it if you won't be using it right away. Use a cup of this apple pectin per 1 c. pectin-weak fruit juice. When making jellies using this combination of apple pectin juice and other fruit juice, ¾ c. sugar per 1 c. liquid is usually correct.

Old-Time Test for Pectin. Here's a way to tell whether you have enough pectin present for good jellying: Into a glass container put 1 T. juice; with this mix 1 T. alcohol. If you have enough pectin, the fruit juice will turn into a jelly-like mass that you can gather up with a spoon. If not enough pectin is present, it won't jell when you add the alcohol, and that tells you to add some more pectin.

Modern Test (Jelmeter). Or you can buy a modern pectin tester from Lehman's, Box 41, Kidron, OH 44636, and have perfect jelly every time. It's called a Jelmeter. In 60 seconds it tells exactly how much sugar must be added to your juice and whether or not pectin is needed. Comes with instructions and 50 recipes.

Short of Pectin? Add sour apples, crab apples, currants, lemons, cranberries, sour plums, loganberries, or green gooseberries. Ripe apples, blackberries, oranges, grapefruit, sour cherries, and grapes have a sort of average pectin content. Fruits that don't jell well on their own because of low pectin content are apricots, peaches, pears, strawberries, and raspberries.

ALTITUDE AFFECTS JELLY MAKING: Martha Mohan, who lives over 6,000 feet up near Hotchkiss, CO, wrote me, "To make jelly from wild berries at altitudes over 6,000 feet, I have found that the wild berries should be boiled at least 3 times and preferably 4 times as long. At 6,500 feet I cook all jellies 3 times as long as cooking charts show, until it sheets off the spoon. An old-timer, a lady we know, who lives at 8,300 feet elevation, told me this and it works for me. These jellies are really worth the extra effort and are great with any wild meat."

ACID CONTENT: You must have enough acid content to jell. Taste the juice for tartness. If it isn't very tart, add lemon juice for extra acid.

JELLY MAKING, OLD-TIME DIRECTIONS: To make jelly, the fruit has to be cooked; cooking brings out the pectin in the right form for jelly making. Only with commercial pectin can you jell uncooked fruit. To jell with natural pectin, the fruit is generally cleaned, cooked, mashed, and put through a jelly bag or two to get the juice that is the jelly base. If you squeeze the bag you will get pulp too, which is okay unless you want a clear jelly—in that case, don't squeeze the bag.

JELLY MAKING WITHOUT ADDED PECTIN: These are USDA instructions. Use only firm fruits naturally high in pectin. Select a mixture of about ¾ ripe and ¼ underripe fruit. One pound of fruit should yield at least 1 c. clear juice. Do not use commercially canned or frozen fruit juices because their pectin content is too low. Using peels and cores adds pectin to the juice during cooking of the fruit and increases jelly firmness.

Wash all fruits thoroughly before cooking. Cut firm, larger fruits into small pieces. Crush soft fruits or berries. Add water to fruits as needed. Put fruit and water into a large saucepan and bring to a boil. Simmer, stirring occasionally, for the amount of time listed or until the fruit is soft.

When fruit is tender, press lightly through a colander. Then let juice drip through a double layer of cheesecloth or a jelly bag. Excessive pressing or squeezing of cooked fruit will cause cloudy jelly.

Using no more than 6 to 8 c. extracted fruit juice at a time, measure and combine the proper quantities of juice, sugar, and lemon juice and heat to boiling. Stir until the sugar is dissolved. Boil over high heat, stirring frequently, until the jelling point is reached. Here are some recipes.

➤ *APPLE JELLY Add 1 c. water per 1 lb. fruit. Simmer 20 to 25 minutes before extracting juice. To each 1 c. strained juice add ¾ c. sugar. Optional: add 1½ t. lemon juice. If you start with 4 c. juice, your jelly yield will be 4 to 5 half pints.*

➤ *BLACKBERRY JELLY Add 0–¼ c. water per 1 lb. fruit. Simmer 5 to 10 minutes before extracting juice. To each 1 c. strained juice, add ¾ t 1 c. sugar. From 4 c. juice, your jelly yield will be 7 to 8 half pints.*

➤ *CRAB-APPLE JELLY Add 1 c. water per 1 lb. fruit. Simmer 20 to 25 minutes before extracting juice. To each 1 c. strained juice, add 1 c. sugar. Jelly yield from 4 c. juice will be 4 to 5 half pints.*

➤ *GRAPE JELLY Add 0–¼ c. water per 1 lb. fruit. Simmer 5 to 10 minutes before extracting juice. For each 1 c. strained juice, add ¾ to 1 c. sugar. Jelly yield from 4 c. juice will be 8 to 9 half pints.*

➤ *PLUM JELLY Add ½ c. water per 1 lb. fruit. Simmer 15 to 20 minutes before extracting juice. To each 1 c. strained juice, add ¾ c. sugar. Jelly yield from 4 c. juice will be 8 to 9 half pints.*

➤ *NO-SUGAR JELLY To 1 c. fruit juice, take 1 to 2 T. unflavored gelatin that has been dissolved in 1 to 2 T. cold water. (Stir the gelatin into the cold water until well dissolved. Let stand a few minutes.) Now add hot juice steadily and stir well. Set aside to cool in your refrigerator. Because there is no extra sugar in this kind of jelly, it won't keep without refrigeration and you must use it up within two weeks.*

➤ *HONEY-FRUIT JELLY Combine 2 c. high- or medium-pectin fruit juice, ½ c. mild-flavored honey, and 2 t. lemon juice. Bring to a boil and stir in all at once 2 T. powdered pectin. Let boil 10 minutes and pour into your jelly glasses.*

For low-pectin fruit juices, use 4 t. lemon juice and 3 T. powdered pectin. If you want to use homemade pectin, substitute 2 c. homemade pectin for both the lemon juice and powdered pectin.

MICROWAVE JAMS AND JELLIES: Use only recipes developed specifically for the microwave (see your librarian). And consider that recipes developed for one microwave may not work in another because of differences in power output between the ovens.

TESTING JELLY DONENESS

Temperature Test. Use a jelly or candy thermometer. Boil to a temperature of 220°F at sea level, 218°F at 1,000 feet, 216°F at 2,000 feet, 214°F at 3,000 feet, 212°F at 4,000 feet, 211°F at 5,000 feet, 209°F at 6,000 feet, 207°F at 7000 feet, and 205°F at 8,000 feet of altitude.

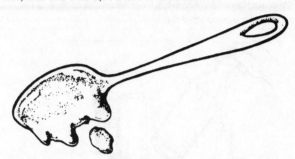

Sheet or Spoon Test. To see if the jelly is ready for canning, dip a cool metal spoon into the boiling jelly mixture. Raise the spoon about 12 inches above the pan (out of the steam). Turn the spoon so liquid runs off the side. The jelly is done when the syrup forms 2 drops that flow together and sheet or hang off the edge of the spoon.

If your jam or jelly doesn't jell, here's a tip. Thin jam or jelly is often caused by lack of pectin, or too much or too little acid. The best way to fix it is add gelatin. Just pour the non-jelled stuff back into the pan. Heat to boiling. Shake a package of gelatin out over the top and then stir it in until all dissolved. One envelope (1 T.) gelatin thickens 4 c. runny jelly or jam. Now pour it into jars. To can, put on lids and process in boiling-water bath 10 minutes.

WHEN JELLY IS DONE: Remove it from the heat and quickly skim off foam. Using a widemouthed funnel, ladle the jelly into sterile jars, leaving ¼ inch headspace. Adjust lids and freeze or can.

Freezing. If you use commercial pectin you can freeze your jams and jellies. Use plastic freezer containers. Good instructions for both canned and frozen jams and jellies come with each package of Sure-Jell or Jam and Jelly Pectin. Frozen uncooked jam keeps that delicious fresh fruit flavor but will be softer than cooked jams.

Canning. Pour hot into sterile half-pint or pint canning jars, leaving ¼ inch headspace. To sterilize empty jars, put them open side up on a rack in a boiling-water canner. Fill the canner and jars with hot (not boiling) water to 1 inch above top of jars. Boil jars 10 minutes. Remove and drain hot sterilized jars one at a time and fill with food. Food residue should be removed from each jar's sealing edge with a clean, damp paper towel. New 2-piece canning lids prepared according to manufacturer's directions should be put on.

After screw bands are tightened, process jars in a boiling-water canner. Fill canner half-full with water and preheat to 180°F. Load sealed jars into the canner rack and lower with handles, or load one jar at a time with jar lifter onto rack in canner. Add water until you have a level of 1 inch above jars. Cover. When water is boiling vigorously, lower heat to maintain a gentle boil. Process all jellies and jams in half-pint or pint jars for 5 minutes if you live at 1–1,000 feet; for 10 minutes at 1,001–6,000 feet; or for 15 minutes above 6,000 feet. After the processing time is over, remove jars from the canner with a jar lifter and place on a towel or rack. Do not retighten screw bands. Air-cool jars 12 to 24 hours. Remove screw bands and check lid seals. Jelly and jam are best if consumed within a year.

NOTE: Here a few jam/jelly precautions. Don't put a jam or jelly into a quart jar; it won't jell. Don't double a recipe. Open-kettle canning is no longer recommended for jams and jellies; they need at least a 5-minute water bath. Paraffin sealing is no longer recommended because it's not reliable enough, and the contents are more likely to mold.

MAKING A WINE BOTTLE INTO A JELLY GLASS:

Old-timers made narrow-necked wine bottles into preserve holders by tying strings soaked in kerosene around the shoulders. Then they set the strings on fire. That cracked the necks so they could be knocked off and the edges filed smooth. The bottles were washed and sterilized, the hot jam poured in—and then the bottles were sealed with paraffin. You let your jelly set up (jell) and cool clear down first, before you added the paraffin.

SEALING JELLY WITH PARAFFIN:
Doing this enables you to use odds and ends of jars other than regular canning jars, thus stretching your jar supply. You simply pour a ¼- to ½-inch layer of melted paraffin onto the top of the jelly after the jelly has cooled enough to set up. And you can wash these little disks of paraffin as you use the jelly, toss them in a box, and melt them down again the next year for reuse.

The USDA, however, now recommends canning with a 5-minute processing time instead of sealing with paraffin, because research has shown that paraffin-sealed jams and jellies—especially low-sugar ones—are more likely to mold.

JAMS WITHOUT ADDED PECTIN:
For best flavor, use fully ripened fruit. Wash and rinse all fruits thoroughly before cooking. Do not soak. Remove stems, skins, and pits from fruit; cut into pieces and crush. For berries, remove stems and blossoms, and crush. Seedy berries may be put through a sieve or food mill. Measure crushed fruit into large saucepan.

➣ *APRICOT JAM* Use 4–4½ c. crushed fruit, 4 c. sugar, and 2 T. lemon juice. Jam yield is 5 to 6 half pints.

➣ *BERRY JAM* Use 4 c. crushed fruit, 4 c. sugar, and no lemon juice. Yield is 3 to 4 half pints.

➣ *PEACH JAM* Use 5½ to 6 c. crushed fruit, 4–5 c. sugar, and 2 T. lemon juice. Yield is 6 to 7 half pints.

JELLIES AND JAMS WITH ADDED PECTIN:
Fresh fruits and juices, as well as some commercially canned or frozen fruit juices, may be used with commercially prepared powdered or liquid pectins. The order of combining ingredients depends on the type of pectin used. Complete directions for a variety of fruits are provided with packaged pectin. Jelly or jam made with added pectin requires less cooking, generally gives a larger yield, and has more natural fruit flavor. In addition, using added pectin eliminates the need to test for doneness. The following recipes are usually available with packaged pectins.

Jellies. Apple, crabapple, blackberry, boysenberry, dewberry, currant, elderberry, grape, mayhaw, mint, peach, plum, black or red raspberry, loganberry, rhubarb, and strawberry.

Jams. Apricot, blackberry, boysenberry, dewberry, loganberry, red raspberry, youngberry, blueberry, cherry, currant, fig, gooseberry, grape, orange marmalade, peach, pear, plum, rhubarb, strawberry, and spiced tomato.

NOTE: Buy new packaged pectin each year because old pectin may not jell well.

PACKAGED-PECTIN RECIPES

➣ *GRAPE-PLUM PECTIN JELLY* You'll need 3½ lb. ripe plums, 3 lb. ripe Concord grapes, 1 c. water, ½ t. butter or margarine (optional ingredient to reduce foaming), 8½ c. sugar, and 1 box (1⅔ oz.) powdered pectin. Wash and pit plums. Do not peel. Thoroughly crush plums and grapes, one layer at a time, in a pan. Add water. Bring to a boil, cover, and simmer 10 minutes. Strain juice through a jelly bag or double layer of cheesecloth. Measure sugar and set aside. Combine 6½ c. juice with butter and pectin in a large pan. Bring to a hard boil over heat, stirring constantly. Add the sugar and return to a full rolling boil. Boil hard for 1 minute, stirring constantly. Remove from heat, skim off foam, and quickly pour into sterile half-pint jars, leaving ¼ inch headspace. Adjust lids and process. Yield will be about 10 half pints.

➣ *PEAR-APPLE PECTIN JAM* You'll need 2 c. peeled and crushed fully ripe pears, 1 c. peeled and finely chopped apple, ¼ t. ground cinnamon, 6½ c. sugar, ⅓ c. bottled lemon juice, and 6 oz. liquid pectin. Wash, peel, and core pears. Crush well and measure 2 c. into a large pan. Wash, peel, core, and finely chop 1 c. apples. Add apple to pears and stir in cinnamon. Thoroughly mix sugar and lemon juice into fruits and bring to a boil over high heat, stirring constantly. Immediately stir in pectin. Bring to a full rolling boil; boil 1 minute, stirring constantly. Remove from heat, quickly skim off foam, and pour into sterile half-pint jars, leaving ¼ inch headspace. Adjust lids and process the jars as above. Yield will be about 7 to 8 half pints.

➣ *STRAWBERRY-RHUBARB PECTIN JELLY* You'll need 1½ lb. red stalks of rhubarb, 1½ qt. ripe strawberries, ½ t. butter or margarine (optional to reduce foaming), 6 c. sugar, and 6 oz. liquid pectin. Wash and cut the rhubarb into 1-inch pieces and blend or grind. Wash, stem, and crush strawberries, one layer at a time, in a large saucepan and simmer 10 minutes. Strain juice with a jelly bag or double layer of cheesecloth. Combine and mix 3½ c. juice and sugar. Add butter if desired. Bring to a boil over high heat, stirring constantly. Immediately stir in pectin. Bring to a full rolling boil; boil hard 1 minute, stirring constantly. Remove from heat and quickly skim off foam. Pour into sterile half-pint jars, leaving ¼ inch headspace. Adjust lids and process as above. Yield will be about 7 half pints.

Syrups

Homemade syrups can be beverage-based syrups or sweet pancake-type syrups meant to be used straight and poured over another food.

BEVERAGE-BASED SYRUPS: These are handy for making drinks on camping trips and at picnics. They keep well in the refrigerator, and a little syrup poured into a glass three-quarters full of cold water or soda water and ice makes an easy, quick drink the children can fix for themselves. Just about any fruit juice can be made into a syrup—cherry, raspberry, and the like. Add ice, if possible, when serving. Dilute with ginger ale or various clear bubblies for variety. You can store unsealed syrup in bottles or a fruit jar. Store in a cool, dark place.

☞ *PLAIN SUGAR SYRUP ("SIMPLE SYRUP")* Boil 2 c. sugar with 2 c. water for 5 minutes. Chill and store in a covered jar. Or water-bath process this for 15 minutes, and then it can be stored on the shelf for the long term. This was popular with Great-Grandmother for sweetening summer drinks, because the sugar was already in solution and she didn't have trouble with sugar settling in the bottom of the glass.

☞ *STANDARD FRUIT SYRUP RECIPE MEANT TO BE SEALED* Wash currants, black or red raspberries, blueberries, grapes, elderberries, and so forth. Simmer in water to cover until soft. Drain juice and strain it. For every 2 c. juice, add 1¾ c. sugar. Boil 15 minutes. Skim and pour into sterilized bottles. Bottle hot and seal or cork, making sure the bottles are airtight. Tie plastic or foil over the top, wrap around the top with sticky tape, or tip the tops of the bottles into sealing wax. Because syrups may ferment after being open for 2 or 3 days, use small bottles.

☞ *STRAWBERRY SYRUP* Take ripe strawberries, crush in a cloth, and press out the juice. For each 2 c. strawberry juice, add 2 c. Plain Sugar Syrup (recipe above). Boil gently for 15 minutes. Bottle.

☞ *RASPBERRY SYRUP* First extract the juice from the raspberries. (See "Fruit Juice and Juice Products.") Measure the juice, pour it into a pan, and bring to a boil. For each 1 c. juice, add 1 lb. sugar, bring to boil again, and let boil for 1

minute. Skim off the scum. Pour into sterile bottles and seal. Optional: Add some whisky to the syrup.

☞ *PLUM SYRUP* Cook 3 lb. plums and 3 lb. sugar with a little water for 20 minutes, stirring often. Drain without squeezing. Measure your syrup. For each 2 cups, add ½ t. almond flavoring. (Optional: Add whisky or brandy, from ½ t. up to 1 qt.) Use the leftover plum pulp to make a fruit pie or butter.

☞ *LEMON SYRUP* Put 1 c. water and 1 qt. sugar into a pan. Simmer, stirring constantly, for 3 minutes. Skim if needed. Add 1 c. lemon juice and 1 T. grated lemon rind, and simmer another 2 minutes. Pour into sterile bottle and seal.

PANCAKE SYRUPS: Homemade syrup was one of the delights of my childhood. Usually it was chokecherry syrup poured over pancakes. Sometimes it was honey syrup, for we allowed bees on the place and the bee man repaid us in honey, more honey than we knew what to do with.

The first money I ever made was peddling buckets of chokecherries in our local metropolis—Livingston, Montana. I rode my pony, Shorty Bill, laden with empty buckets a couple of miles on up the mountain from our home to a little canyon where the chokecherry bushes were thick. I worked hard all day picking berries and filling those metal buckets. Rode home, tired but satisfied, with the fruit of my labors. The next day was Mama's day to drive the 30 miles into town to do a few weeks' shopping. She took me and my buckets of chokecherries. I went from door to door, knocking on doors, offering my chokecherries for sale. I think I charged about a dollar a bucket. Those housewives were really pleased to see buckets of chokecherries like the ones they had picked when they were little—something that wasn't sold in stores.

The old-time syrups were used not only on hot breads like biscuits and pancakes and on ice cream but also on puddings and pound cakes, as flavorings in sauces and sherbets, and as beverage bases. One or two spoonfuls of a fruit syrup in a glass of cold water with shaved ice makes a nice summer beverage. Most of the recipes below call for white sugar, but you can substitute honey. The trouble with using honey is that it has such a distinctive flavor of its own that if you use it in everything, you get tired of honey's flavor pretty soon.

☞ *BASIC FRUIT SYRUP* Fruits vary in natural sweetness or tartness, chokecherries probably being at one extreme and dark sweet cherries probably the other. So the amount of sugar to add involves your judgment. But in general, get the juice from the strawberries, raspberries, currants, grapes, or what you want as directed for fruit juices. After the juice is brought to a boil, add sweetening and boil down to the density you want. Then can.

☞ *WHOLE FRUIT SYRUP* Wash, core, and pit the fruit; peel if you think the peels wouldn't make it through the blender or wire-mesh strainer or wouldn't be nice. Now blend or force through a wire strainer. For every 1 c. mashed fruit, add ¼ c. water, 2 t. lemon juice, and ½ c. honey. Boil together 5 minutes, stirring constantly. Now take your syrup off the stove. Skim off the foam. Pour into hot jars and seal or cool for serving.

☞ *QUICK BERRY SYRUP* If you haven't time for all the boiling down, do this. For each 4 c. berry juice, stir in 2 c. sugar and 2 c. light corn syrup. If it is strawberry or raspberry juice, add 2 T. lemon juice (the others don't need it). Boil. Skim if needed. To can it, process 10 minutes for pints or quarts.

❧ **RESOURCEFUL WOMAN'S SYRUP** *Take any leftover fruit syrup or juice. Sweeten as needed and boil down until it is syrup-like.*

❧ **PHONY MAPLE SYRUP** *Boil 1 c. dark brown sugar with ½ c. water for 5 minutes. Add ¼ t. maple flavoring and 2 T. butter. Serve warm.*

❧ **CREAM AND SUGAR SYRUP** *Mix in a pan ½ c. cream, 1 c. brown sugar, and ½ c. dark corn syrup. Bring to a boil and serve warm.*

Fruit Sauces

If you have a batch of fruit that is going bad, and you want to get it put up the quickest, easiest, cheapest way possible—sauce it! Applesauce isn't the only member of this family. You can sauce cherries, peaches, rhubarb, cranberries, etc. Berries make fine special sauces to go on desserts. Apricots and even prunes can be made into a sauce. The sauces aren't meant to be supersweet. Sweeten to taste. The right amount of sweetness depends on you—and on the fruit.

❧ **BASIC SAUCE** *Prepare your fruit (peel, core, or whatever is appropriate). Add it to boiling water (a third part or less of your fruit amount). Cover and simmer gently until tender. Remove from heat. Put the fruit through a strainer to make a smooth sauce, or use as is. Add sweetening and mix well. Always use a wooden spoon to stir and a really heavy (non-aluminum) pan to cook it in.*

❧ **BASIC FRESH, RAW-FRUIT SAUCE** *Crush fruits such as peaches, raspberries or strawberries. Sweeten to taste and serve over ice cream, pudding, or cake.*

CANNING A HIGH-ACID SAUCE: Follow Basic Sauce recipe (above). Return to a boil again. Have jars ready. Boil some lids in a pan of water. Using a widemouthed funnel, quickly pour the very hot sauce into the jar. Put on the first lid and then the screw one. Now give it 15 minutes of hard boiling in a water bath. Lift out, tighten, and set aside to cool.

FREEZING A FRUIT PUREE OR SAUCE: If needed, cook or steam your fruit in water until soft. Then mash or press through a colander or strainer, or blend. Add sweetening and/or lemon juice to taste. Heat to boiling; then cool as rapidly as possible. Pack into freezer containers. Leave headspace for expansion from freezing.

Other Sauces

Great-Grandmother was strong on sauces. She made her own and made lots of different kinds. Her "pudding" (really a steamed bread) was always served with a sauce. The calf's-foot jelly also usually had a sauce. I like coffee jelly with a simple brown-sugar-dissolved-in-rich-cream sauce. Sauces generally run in three types—sauces for fruit, meat, and pudding. My sauces for fruit generally are based on whipped cream. To go with meat at table, it's usually a homemade fruit ketchup for me. The other kind I make a lot is a barbecue sauce, which to me means some form of tomatoes, plus molasses, a dash of vinegar, and some chopped onion, which I mix together and pour over the meat when it's about one-third to one-half done. Barbecued

meat is a favorite with the children. (Anything sweet is a favorite with the children.)

❧ **FRUIT AND CREAM SAUCE** *Whip 1 c. cream and sweeten with about ¼ c. honey. Put the whipped cream on your pudding or shortcake and then pour a spoonful of fruit on top.*

Fruit Butters

A "butter" is a thick, smooth sauce made by straining fruit or vegetables. You can use a butter just like a jam, to spread on pancakes or bread, but it doesn't have nearly as much sugar in it. Just cook up the food with enough sweetening to suit you, add any other seasoning you want, can it, and you're done. Personally I think the tarter fruits make better butters. Peach or sweet cherry butter turns out almost too sweet. But apple and apple cider butter made with a tart variety of apple is good, and apple-plum butter is our alltime family favorite (recipe under "Apple" in Chapter 6).

We first started making apple-plum butter at our first home in Juliaetta, 4 miles down the road from here. The nearest thing that place had to an orchard was a big walnut tree in the front yard—so when fruit season came, I scavenged up and down the highways and byways. This region is unusual in that everywhere, throughout the years, pioneers and others have stopped to lunch or picnic and have left apple cores and plum pits. The volunteer apple and plum trees generally have a smaller fruit, but they are loaded almost every year and free for the picking. So the children and I would drive down the road with a back seat full of cardboard boxes and then go home and make apple-plum butter, one-third plum to two-thirds apple.

MAKING A BUTTER: It basically takes long cooking over very mild stove-top heat. You have to watch it closely and stir very frequently. For fruits, cook in an enamel or stainless-steel pan and use a wooden spoon to stir. Cook on low heat slowly for a long time. If you are very busy, cook it in the oven instead, in a covered kettle at a temperature of 300–350°F. Then you don't have to stir it, and it doesn't burn on the bottom. If your sauce doesn't get smooth enough to suit you, put it through a rotary colander after cooking. Season your finished butter with cinnamon, cloves, nutmeg, allspice, or whatever you like.

FOLEY MILL OR ROTARY COLANDER: This is a cone-shaped colander with a wooden mallet to help work the stuff through. You fill it with goop and then turn the wooden mallet, rolling it around the sides of the colander. Don't just stomp with the mallet—that gets you nowhere.

CANNING A FRUIT BUTTER: Have the butter boiling on the stove and proceed by my directions under "Canning" in this chapter. Use the times under "Applesauce" in Chapter 6. Be careful, because the thick sauce is hard to heat clear through.

FREEZING: Just pour into a container, cool, and put in the freezer. Can or freeze butters in half pints or pints because a butter that isn't heavily sweetened will mold in a couple weeks, even if refrigerated, unless you can depend on your family to eat it up faster than that.

Ketchups

A "ketchup" is a fruit or vegetable pulped and preserved with some combination of salt, vinegar, spices, and sugar. Just which of those and how many can vary a lot. It can be made out of tomatoes, grapes, cucumbers, peaches—lots of things. Tomato ketchup is the best known and most popular version of this type of sauce. To make a ketchup, the food consistency is the key. It's a cooked, strained fruit or vegetable that is highly spiced to make a smooth, thick sauce. Don't worry about color. Homemade ketchups won't turn out like the commercial ones, but color isn't everything. The spices can be varied to your taste; add or subtract as you please.

APPLE, PLUM, OR GRAPE KETCHUP: Start with 1 qt. applesauce. Or for grape sauce, cook grapes in an enamel kettle slowly until soft (about 25 minutes). Then put through colander to get the grape puree. Cook plums and colander them for plum sauce. Combine 1 qt. of any of those sauces with 1 t. ginger, 1 t. cinnamon, 1 t. cloves, 2 c. vinegar, 1 t. pepper, 1 t. mustard, 1 t. onion juice, and 2 t. salt. Simmer slowly until thick. Pack into pint jars. Adjust lids. Process in boiling-water canner 15 minutes. If you like sweet sauce, add brown sugar or molasses to taste.

APPLE KETCHUP: Peel and quarter a dozen round, tart apples. Stew until soft in as little water as possible. Sieve them. For every quart of sieved apple, add ½ c. sugar, 1 t. pepper, 1 t. cloves, 1 t. mustard, 2 t. cinnamon, 2 medium-sized onions chopped very fine, 1 T. salt, and 2 c. vinegar.

For some reason I'm having a hard time concentrating this morning. Dolly is playing the piano. She had a little sleighing accident day before yesterday and still isn't able to walk. We tried to get her to the doctor yesterday, but it is the first week in January, with unusually heavy snows. After struggling about an hour we gave up and decided to wait until today. I'll try again this afternoon. The pickup is all chained up (no heater in the beast), and then Dolly and I will try to get to Troy and our wonderful Dr. Drury. Maybe by then the sun will have melted some of the snow and black ice off the highway. Looking out my living room window right now, I see the highway where it runs along the other side of the canyon, and it is still snow-covered.

The worst is getting off our personal mountainside and down to the highway. Worse still is trying to get home again up our mountainside. About a week ago Mike and I were driving in, and we literally started to slide off the cliff. It's a good 200 feet to the bottom. I chickened out first, opened the car door, and said, "Mike, I'm leaving." He lasted about 10 seconds more, and then left too. The car hung there until the next day. He got our crawler tractor (a Cat with tracks instead of wheels) going and recovered the vehicle.

In a way I enjoy the snow. It reminds me of winters when I was a little girl. On the sheep ranch in Montana, we were really on top of the world. The lowest point on the ranch was 6,000 feet. The buildings were located at that point. If I rode my horse on up to a high point, I could easily see 75 miles on a clear day, and days were mostly clear in summer. ("Oh, give me a home where the buffalo roam, and the deer and the antelope play, where seldom is heard a discouraging word and the skies are not cloudy all day.")

So today I have all five of them home instead of the usual four. I'm trying to keep them usefully occupied. Danny and Dolly are working in arithmetic workbooks. Becca is working in a pre-primary reading workbook. Luke is in the basement playing with the pumpkins, and Sara is discovering she can crawl under chairs. When I was a little girl, I spent a lot of time studying at home with my parents—usually January and February. When I did go to school, I rode horseback the 2 miles each way.

It wasn't really a "one-room" school, for it had a cloakroom in front and a teacherage in the back. The teacher slept and cooked there when the snow got too deep for her to drive back and forth from the ranch where she lived with her husband, in the Shields River Valley below, between Clyde Park and Wilsall. Our creek, school, and community were all called Bracket Creek. That is home in my heart, though long gone in the world of reality. On cold days like today, Mrs. Carroll would fix us some hot canned soup on top of the potbellied wood stove that heated the classroom to complement the cold lunches we brought from home.

Everybody rode horseback to school. Some rode 5 miles each way. You can make fast time when you have a good horse and when you're used to it. There was a little barn behind the schoolhouse where the animals waited patiently for school to be out, and then the merry race to the crossroads began. I always lost. I rode a not-so-young half-Shetland gelding called Shorty Bill.

He was my closest friend. I would go out to the field to get that horse after breakfast—a little kid running with bridle in hand. He would run across the field to meet me. We'd go down to the big red barn with its vast mow full of hay and its underparts full of a complicated wonderland of stalls, pens, grain, and harness rooms, where Shorty would have his breakfast of rolled oats, and I'd saddle him up.

On summer days, when the business at hand wasn't serious, I would often ride him with no saddle or bridle. I could pull myself up by a handful of his mane. (It got sparser and sparser at the point where I grabbed.) I'd push on his neck to show him the direction I wanted him to go, kick him to make him go, and slide to the side to tell him I wanted to stop. In summer there was hard work to do on horseback, though, and Shorty had no part of that. That was for the 5 big horses we had, the largest being a great big pink-eyed Appaloosa that could pick his way down a cliffside with 200 lb. of pack rattling on his back like there was nothing to it.

Once every week we had to take the Appaloosa and the other horses, all loaded with food and general supplies, up to the sheep camp to help move it. We'd take down the tent and sack up the pots and pans and sleeping bag and gun. Then the horses would carry it all to the new grazing site. The ride was generally miserable. Big biting horseflies drove everybody crazy, man and beast. They are the meanest fly in the world, I think, with a bite so hard it leaves a bloody mark. If they happen to get your horse in a tender place, you've suddenly got a very insecure seat.

Well, that ought to be enough digression to get my head organized. Digressions are easier and more fun to write than the rest of this.

Spiced Fruit

Spiced fruit doesn't have to be canned or frozen. The real old-time recipes don't spoil—they just get spicier and spicier. In small amounts they are very tasty—like the spiced crab apples that you can get in the store, only much more spicy. This is not a method of preserving a staple food, just a holiday goodie.

If your fruit does show signs of fermentation, pour off the liquid, boil it awhile, and then pour back over the fruit. Brandied fruit has an alcohol content, but spiced fruit doesn't. For a milder version, you can cut back on sugar, vinegar, and spices and then can the results. The real thing can be left in a bowl with a plate on top all winter. I've done it. Whenever you want some, just fork it out. Don't be bothered by floating mold or scum. Your fruit is below the level of the fluid's surface. Rinse the fruit before serving, in case any top glop came along as you fished it out (like when you make crock pickles).

BASIC SPICED FRUIT: Use 7 lb. fruit, 4 lb. sugar, 2 to 4 c. vinegar, and 1 T. each of cinnamon, cloves, and allspice. Pare peaches and pears. Prick plums and tomatoes with a needle in several places to help the preservatives get inside. Boil the fruit in the syrup 5 minutes. Remove fruit and boil the syrup until it has thickened some. Put the fruit in jars and pour the boiling syrup over it. You can spice blackberries, currants, gooseberries, peaches, pears, plums, tomatoes, cherries, crab apples, watermelon rind, pieces of almost-green cantaloupe, apricots, nectarines, prunes, quinces, citron, and so on. Let your spiced fruit stand at least several weeks before using it.

HONEY SUBSTITUTION: My spiced fruit recipes all use sugar. But in the Middle East, fruit is preserved in a syrup made of honey and vinegar, and I'm sure you could convert any sugar recipe and do the same thing.

Becca (short for Rebecca) just crawled down from my lap to go hold a bunny. Santa brought her two little half-pounders for Christmas. They make great pets. Fearless now, they hop all over the place. Makes January a little livelier for the at-home folks. Luke, his silver pistol, and his little toy crawler tractor are now all in my lap (replacing Becca). And on we go to brandied fruit.

Brandied Fruit

Foods preserved in alcohol are "brandied." Wines and foods containing over 14 percent alcohol by volume are self-preserving. Wines and foods with a weaker concentration of alcohol can become sour and vinegary. Brandied food should be kept cool and airtight. Burying it deep in the ground works well. The trouble with preserving food by brandying is that it will give you a hangover. I'd hate to have to get drunk to eat.

Incidentally, many people hold very strong opinions for or against the use of alcohol. Some of my best friends wouldn't let the stuff in their homes in the form of tutti-frutti or anything else. I have sympathy with that point of view. I don't see any excuse for debauching, because it is invariably damaging to something. So for me the most significant thing about brandied fruit, for better or for worse, is that it has an alcohol content. It makes a heady dessert—and not one that children can have very much of—so you don't need much for a winter's supply. Tutti-frutti is the most common and versatile sort, because you can eat it straight, use it for an ice cream or general dessert topping, or make a sort of fruit cake out of it (actually better than eating it straight).

Incidentally, baking or boiling evaporate most, but not all, of the alcohol in any recipe. Despite the cooking, 10–15 percent of the alcohol will remain. You can indeed get intoxicated from fruit cake—if you eat enough of it.

➤ *EARLEN'S TUTTI-FRUTTI* You can start with 1½ c. fruit and 1½ c. sugar. For your first mixture, half-drained crushed pineapple and half-drained chopped canned peaches are good, along with 6 chopped maraschino cherries. (Peaches brandy best, and after them cherries.) A package of dry yeast stirred in helps to get the fermentation off to a quick start. Stir it several times the first day. At least every 2 weeks after that, add 1 more c. sugar and 1 more c. fruit. Alternate your fruit so you don't end up with all the same thing. Don't put it in the refrigerator, but don't have it too near the heat either.*

Once you get it going, you can give a cup of "starter" to friends, who can soon work up their own supply of tutti-frutti from it. The mixture is at its best after 4 weeks have passed. You can take out fruit to use as needed, but try not to let what's left get below 1 cup. To have more, just add more fruit and sugar ahead of schedule. You can use fresh, canned, or frozen fruits such as Bing cherries, raspberries, blueberries, apples, pears, or fruit cocktail as well as the first ones I mentioned. But if pears and fruit cocktail are used, treat them gently so they don't become too mushy. Don't use bananas.

Be sure to keep the fruit under the liquid. You can use a weighted saucer to hold it down. Fruit exposed to air will darken in color and taste too fermented.

➤ *OLD-TIME TUTTI-FRUTTI* The first recipe I gave you is quite common around the country now and implies some city-type living with the maraschino cherries and pineapple.*

Here's a way to make tutti-frutti from your own garden and orchard, a sack of sugar, and a cup of brandy.

Start this at the beginning of the fruit season. Strawberries are probably the first fruits you'll have and are great for this purpose. You can start in a jar and transfer to a crock as your supply grows. I'd suggest keeping it in the coolest place you can find during the summer. As the season goes on, add cherries, apricots, plums, nectarines, and peaches. Avoid apples, pears, melons, and blackberries.

Into the jar put 1 c. very good brandy, rum, or cognac, 1 c. sugar, and 1 c. fruit. Stir and let rest. Don't refrigerate. Cover to keep the dust out but don't seal. As each new fruit comes along, add it and more sugar, at the rate of 1 c. sugar per 1 c. fruit. You don't need more brandy. Cut large fruit into small pieces and stir well at each addition. Take out pits and seeds where appropriate.

If you figure 3 months for it to mature, it will be about ready by Christmas time. Serve over plain pudding, cake, or ice cream. Or make a fruit cake or a holiday fruit bread with it.

➢ **ALMOST-INSTANT BRANDIED FRUIT** Use canned fruit. Apricots, peaches, pears, and so on are all right. Save the juice from the fruit and boil it down to half the original amount. Add 1 part brandy to 2 parts of your boiled-down syrup and pour that over the fruit. Let it rest at least 24 hours before serving to let the fruit absorb the flavor.

➢ **RUM-BRANDIED FRUIT** You can also make brandied fruit using rum. Mix 2 c. well-drained fruit with 2 c. sugar. Cover well with rum. It takes about 1½ cups. Just as in the other recipes, you then can add more fruit and sugar every week or two to keep it going.

➢ **TUTTI-FRUTTI ICE CREAM** Soften store-bought vanilla ice cream or make your own. At the very end, add tutti-frutti and refreeze or freeze.

➢ **TUTTI-FRUTTI FRUITCAKE** Mash ½ c. butter together with 1 c. sugar until well mixed. Add 4 eggs, 3 c. flour, 2 t. soda, 1 t. cloves, 1 t. allspice, 2 c. your brandied fruit of any sort, 1½ c. applesauce, 1 c. raisins, and 1 c. nuts. This bakes best in an angel food-type pan because it is very moist— a buttered 9-inch tube pan would be right. It takes a long time to bake—70 or 80 minutes or more in a moderate oven (350°F).

➢ **COMBINATION SPICING AND BRANDYING OF PEACHES** Peel about 4 lb. peaches. Dissolve 4 lb. sugar in 3 c. water. To spice with cloves alone, insert 2 whole cloves in each peach. To spice with cinnamon and cloves, put 1 T. stick cinnamon and 1 T. of whole cloves into a spice bag and boil with the syrup. Put in the fruit a little at a time and boil each 5 minutes. When done, remove the fruit to jars and boil the syrup about 10 minutes, or until thick. Pour syrup over the fruit to fill the jar two-thirds full and then finish filling with brandy. Remove the spice bag when syrup suits your taste test for spiciness.

➢ **RUMMED BLACKBERRY JUICE** Steam 4½ qt. blackberries until the juice starts to flow. Strain in a cheesecloth bag until you get all the juice you can. Add the juice of 3 lemons and 4 oranges to the blackberry juice. Bring to a boil what you have left of the blackberries with 6 c. water; strain again and add that to your juice. Add 2 c. sugar. Now bring juice just to a boil and add 2 c. rum. Can or bottle it. (You could substitute brandy.)

➢ **BRANDIED CHERRIES** Boil 5 c. sugar with 2 c. water for 12 minutes, or until you have a clear syrup. Pour that syrup over 5 lb. cherries (the small sour kind) and let stand overnight. Drain off the syrup and boil it again. Add cherries and boil about 5 more minutes. Take out cherries with a skimmer (the kind with holes in it to let the juice drain away) and put the cherries into canning jars. Boil the syrup down 15 more minutes. It should be getting pretty thick. Add 2 c. brandy. Remove from heat. Pour over cherries and seal.

➢ **BURIED BRANDIED PEACHES** I think the very best brandied fruit of all is made by this recipe. I found it in an antique book, and Mike and I tried it out of curiosity. I imagine it would work with any fruit, although we used peaches. This recipe needs no brandy, only fruit and sugar. Choose fine, ripe, very sweet peaches. They must not have bad spots. Peel them. Cover with whole peaches the bottom of something you can bury. Pour in enough sugar to cover them. Add more peaches and then more sugar in the same manner, until you are out of peaches or room in your container. Cover very tightly, but not absolutely airtight, and bury in the ground for 4 months or more. We put ours about 3 feet down, which made the top of it about 2 feet down. Mark the spot so you'll know where to dig it up.

I was really afraid dirt would get into it, but not one speck did. We put it down in peach season, just outside the back door, and dug it up for Thanksgiving (which isn't a full 4 months). The floating top layer, the part that was out of the liquid, was discolored and yucky-looking from oxidation. We threw that away. What was left was brandied peaches of a quality the likes of which I'd never seen before. The peaches' color was perfectly preserved; they looked just as they had the day we put them in.

But they darkened very fast when exposed to air; within 24 hours we could see and taste the difference as they commenced to deteriorate. Apparently exposure to air was causing the trouble. If I had it to do over, I'd reseal them in smaller jars as soon as we dug them up and just open them as needed, so there would be as little exposure to air before serving as possible. You absolutely must keep any brandied (or spiced) fruit below the liquid and out of the air, but this stuff was even affected by the exposure of the liquid to the air.

I think the temperature control also helped make it good. I imagine if you sealed a crock of tutti-frutti and buried it the same way for 3 months, it would do as well, because the temperature underground is evenly cool but not too cold— especially early in the season, when above ground it's hot. Brandied fruit made from scratch needs a cool temperature, since you don't have the help of the preservatives that are in store-bought foods.

February 1975. Dolly had hurt her knee, went to the doctor, and got a crutch. I thought then she'd soon be fine. I had no idea that the next morning she would be unable to walk on the remaining good leg. Subsequently, both arms went bad, then neck and back. It all turned out happily in the end, but the end was much longer in coming than I had expected. She's much, much better now than she was in the middle of January, when there were days when she could not use her hands even to turn the pages of a book or to feed herself. In fact, she seems very nearly well again.

The doctors predict she is almost certain to suffer another, worse attack within a relatively short time. But that's doctor thinking for you. As far as I'm concerned, it's over and done. Dolly is well now, and she's going to stay well. I'm going to take such good care of her that the old bug, whatever it is, doesn't have a chance. And this isn't the first time my opinion parted company with the doctor's and I won. There's too much at stake here for me to agree with something like that. God will guide my hand in nursing her, and He's the greatest Physician of them all. [She never did have an attack of arthritis again. Dolly's nearly 30 now, married, with children of her own.]

I used to have a section about making candy—but I had to cut it (not enough space). It had the basics like taffy, and some fancier things too. But making hand-dipped chocolates and marzipan and other fancy candies belongs more to arts and crafts than to cooking, I think. I can't really reconcile myself to the notion of spending all that time and labor to make something so beautiful and then opening my mouth and wiping it out. Same for cake decorating. I enjoy the fancy decorated cookies the grandmas around here make for Christmas. But when people have the creative urge, you just have to get out of their way and let them go. I used to write poetry, and maybe that's just as useless a product as a cookie or cake decoration—and maybe more so because it isn't even edible. I tried to sell my poems by mail once. Out of a mailing of several hundred, 2 dear people responded—more to keep my morale up, I think, than for the sake of the poems.

When Mike was a student in the big city, I used to take my poems down to a street corner in Greenwich Village (along with a baby or two), put on a great big sandwich board that said "Poems for Sale" on each side and sell copies for 25 to 50 cents apiece. (Mike priced them for me.) I barely made enough to pay my bus fare and buy lunch, but it was really beautiful just standing there sharing my work all day with people who came to read my notebooks and pick out one or two poems that would really go home and live with them and become a part of their lives. That was the only thing I've ever missed about New York— selling poems. I never was one to write in an ivory tower. I needed people to react to what I was writing. Their reactions provided a sonar for me as I swam through the literary waters, guiding me to a better and better result—better because it meant more to them. Though I've always written something or other, it's best when there is a real human being on the receiving end who can laugh and care and learn something they really want to know.

PRESERVING WITH VINEGAR, SALT, AND FAT
Pickles

The "Cucumber" section in Chapter 4 has lots of information on crock and canned cucumber pickles. But you can actually pickle just about anything using different combinations of salt, sugar, vinegar, and spices. Cured meats like ham, bacon, and corned beef are made using salt and sugar, with the addition of saltpeter (makes foods red and helps preserve them). Dill pickles use salt and vinegar, leaving out the sweetness. Spiced fruits leave out the salt and put in sugar, vinegar, and spices. Krauts and salted-down vegetables are vegetables and salt only. (See "Cabbage" in Chapter 4.) These ingredients aren't there just for flavoring. Salt,

vinegar, and (under certain circumstances) sugar are the original chemical preservatives.

There is a nearly infinite number of different ways to pickle different foods, depending on your choice of picklers, how strong they are, which vegetables you choose to pickle, and just how you go about it. There are some great books on pickling in your library or bookstore.

Vinegar

Vinegar is high-acid and thus is the basis for another sort of natural "chemical" food preservation. I've never managed to make it—not for lack of trying, and not because it can't be done. A dear old lady in Juliaetta named Mrs. Eggers took my recipe and made wonderful vinegar from it, absolutely the best wine-type vinegar I ever tasted. And she ended up with a "mother" (a thick substance that vinegar-making critters live in) that was like a colored firm-but-clear gelatin, just like you're supposed to. She even gave me the mother after she got done making vinegar. I brought it home and tried to make vinegar out of it: still no luck. For the time being, I've given up.

My last attempted batches were in the living room. One was a jar of mixed grape and peach wine. One was a big crock of malt stuff that I hoped would become malt vinegar. And, oh yes, there was also a yet larger crock of rotting apple peels and cores on the way to becoming cider vinegar. They all smelled so bad it got to be a social problem. Like the day Dolly's music teacher got a funny look on his face and gave a very short lesson (the piano was in the same room, and I never explained about the crocks). One fine day soon after that, Dolly was sitting on top of the (unused) stove, playing, and she fell off *splat* right into the biggest crock of all. She gave out an anguished cry—half embarrassment and half pain. By the time we got her fished out of there, all 3 containers were either spilled or contaminated, so I called it quits for the time being. So I'm going to tell you how Mrs. Eggers makes vinegar.

To get the right cultures (and home boiling gear), check the Yellow Pages under "Beer Homebrewing Equipment & Supplies" or "Winemaking Equipment & Supplies." Or get a list of suppliers from The American Homebrewers Association, Box 1679, Boulder, CO 80306. Or . . .

Alternative Beverage, 114-0 Freeland Lane, Charlotte, NC 28217; 704-527-9643.

Beer & Winemaking Supplies offers hard-to-find mead vinegar cultures: 413-586-0150; 154 King St.,

Northampton, MA 01060; **stout@map.com; www.
beer-winemaking.com.**

The Cellar Homebrew: PO Box 33525, Seattle, WA 98133;
800-342-1871; **staff@cellar-homebrew.com; www.
cellar-homebrew.com.**

Seeds Blum offers four kinds of vinegar culture, including
malt red wine, white wine, and cider: 800-528-3658;
HC 33, Idaho City Stage, Boise, ID 83706-9725.

Also see *Super Formulas, Arts and Crafts: How to Make
More Than 360 Useful Products That Contain Honey and
Beeswax,* by Elaine C. White. Available for $14.95 from Val-
ley Hills Press, 1864 Ridgeland Dr., Starkville, MS 39759;
800-323-7102. Free brochure available. Just ask.

HOW TO MAKE VINEGAR: Making vinegar is a two-
step fermentation. First, one kind of organism turns the
sugar into alcohol. Then another takes over and turns the
alcohol into acetic acid. Acetic acid is the textbook name for
vinegar, only what we put on the Swiss chard at dinnertime
isn't nearly as strong as what they use in the laboratory.
Adding yeast makes the alcohol stage get going faster.
Adding the mother helps the acid formation from the alcohol, because it adds the right kind of organism for that
change. If you don't use either yeast or acid, eventually
the right kind of critters will just fall in from the air. Mrs.
Eggers did it that way.

A lady who read what I had written before this wrote
me, "When I was a child some 50 years ago, the apples
were ground in an old outside cider mill; then the juice
was pressed out with a wooden press, yielding 50-gallon
barrels. They were wooden barrels with wooden lids. A
large cloth was tied over the top of the barrel and the lid
propped open to let in air. The barrels were stored in the
smokehouse to ferment all summer. The smokehouse
was made of hewn oak logs, with a solid door and one cat
hole large enough for the family cat to enter to catch all
the mice that might enter. It had no windows and a dirt
floor. It was always cool and damp even on the hottest day.
An old iron pot was in the middle of the building where a
fire was built to cure the ham and sausage in winter. The
fire was always smothered to a smoke and Daddy watched
it very closely.

"Before cold weather the vinegar was stored in big
barrels that lay on their side with a large stopper in a hole
in the top side. We sold gallons of vinegar to everyone in
the community year-round. The barrels were never used
for anything but vinegar and were washed with fresh
well water each year, removing the mother, and refilled
with fresh apple cider. All the kraut and salt pickles were
made in the same building. There was an attic above
the smokehouse with a ladder to climb. We stored apples
and Keiffer pears and jars of canned fruit and vegetables
in the attic. Daddy always brought a small barrel of salt
fish for the smokehouse every winter, and we had a leg
of dried beef."

You want to know how they make "cider vinegar"
nowadays? Commercial cider vinegar starts with apple
wastes (peels and cores), which is really not bad. You can
do the same thing. The cider company presses the apple
wastes to get out the juice. It adds water and sugar, heats
it to cause fermentation, and then rapidly oxidizes it to
produce the acetic acid content. The vinegar is diluted and
labeled and takes less than 48 hours from apple core to
finished product.

Well, back to how you can make vinegar like Mrs.
Eggers . . .

WHAT'S IN VINEGAR: You can't use store-bought
vinegar to hurry your vinegar making, because if you add
vinegar in the first step, while you are making wine, the
vinegar will tend to mess up or stop that reaction. Adding
it to the second stage, when you want the wine to turn to
acetic acid, will do you no good because the store vinegar
is all pasteurized so the needed beasties in it are dead.
You can use unpasteurized homemade vinegar for that
purpose, however.

Starter Foods. Vinegar flavors and acidities vary according to the kind of juice you start with. You can make
vinegar from any fruit juices, even from the leftovers
from your fruit canning—the peelings and corings of
peaches, pears, apples, grape hulls, and whole cherries.
Mrs. Eggers made hers from apple peels and cores. *Cider
vinegar* means you started with apple juice (cider) or some
apple product like peels and cores. *White vinegar* starts
out from grain. *Malt vinegar* is made from barley. You can
make vinegar from any homemade wine but not from
cheap store-bought wines, because those contain preservatives that would prevent the second-step fermentation you
need. Some expensive imported wines can be used because
they don't contain preservatives.

FERMENTATION STAGE 1: MAKE ALCOHOL: This is
identical to the process involved in wine making except that
to make vinegar it isn't necessary to have perfect fruit, and
for vinegar you won't want as much sweetening, although
you could add sugar or molasses to beef it up. Or anything
sweet—leftover sweetened tea, leftover canned fruit juices,
jellies, sugar-bowl rinsings.

Container and Cloth. Put your starters in a crock,
wooden or stainless steel container, or glass jar. *Never ferment in aluminum or chipped enamel containers.* Leave from
a half to a fourth of your crock space empty for later additions—you can add more makings every day for a while,
adding a little more water each time—and general bubbling
up. Cover with a clean cloth and tie it firmly around the
neck of your container with a string to keep bugs from
falling in and dying. That crock is going to be sitting there
a long time, and if you aren't careful the contents will get
dirty. Wash and replace the cloth once a week. Set the crock
in a warm place—80°F is a good temperature. It will work
at a cooler temperature, but the cooler the temperature, the
longer it takes.

Bubbles. During the first fermentation stage, it bubbles.
As long as that stage is going on, you'll be able to see the
bubbles coming up if you hold a match over the surface.
If it won't bubble for you, or if you want to hurry it up, or if
you want to be sure the right kind of microbes move in,
add 1 T. yeast to get it working. While it's bubbling, it's
"working." When it gets done bubbling, it's ready for the
second stage.

FERMENTATION STAGE 2: ALCOHOL TO ACID:
When the sugar-to-alcohol (primary) fermentation is totally
completed, you're ready for the secondary fermentation,
which changes the alcohol to acetic acid. Vinegar is a dilute,
household-use solution of acetic acid.

Transfer. Siphon, dip, or strain the liquid from your
fermentation crock to a (dark-colored) glass, enamel,
wood, stainless steel, or pottery container, *leaving behind*

the sediment. A wide-topped container is helpful because acetic bacteria need oxygen to do their work. Fill no more than three-quarters full. Use a cloth cover, same as before. While it's working, store your becoming-vinegar container in faint light (sunlight holds the change back) and warmth.

Getting the Vinegar Beasties. Now I know why Mrs. Eggers could make vinegar and I couldn't. She caught the acetic bacteria, without which you can't make vinegar. They're carried both through the air in general and on the feet of vinegar flies! But you're always at risk of getting your crock infected by one of the bacteria and molds floating in the air that do *not* change sugar to alcohol or alcohol to acetic acid. In that case you could end up with a disgusting mess, which is what happened to me—unless you start Stage 2 with a fairly high-alcohol solution, which would protect it from just about everything except the acetic bacteria. But it's easiest, quickest, and surest if you can start by putting some mother in there.

Mother. This thick, clear, jellylike amber substance is made by the kind of beasties that make vinegar, and they live in it. If you've got some to add to your crock when you're ready to get Stage 2 going, you'll soon have the nicest vinegar you ever tasted. If you don't have it, you may be able to buy it from a health food store or a winemaker's supply house. Using mother can make a big difference in time as well as taste. If you don't have any mother to add, it could take as long as 6 months to complete your first batch of vinegar, because you must wait for the right kind of beastie to be brought by the vinegar flies.

When that does happen, the crock surface will gradually start to show a thin graying film floating on top. This is your mother getting started. Don't disturb it. It's important that the mother stay on top until its work is done. It will settle to the bottom of your crock, heavy and thick, later on. Taste occasionally to see how sour your vinegar-to-be is becoming.

How Long? The length of Stage 2 can vary greatly. It depends on whether you have some "mother" or have to wait till you catch some vinegar microbes, and on the temperature during the fermentation. In general, at 75–90°F cider should turn to vinegar within 4 months, but it can happen in as little as a few weeks or take as long as 6 months.

Care of Mother. Don't lose your mother now that you've got her! Strain it off. To store, just put it in a jar, cover with vinegar, and put a (non-metal!) cover on the bottle. Or keep a batch going continuously.

BOTTLING: Strain off the vinegar and put it away safely. Strain the vinegar out of your crock until it's "clean" enough to suit you; 3 layers of cheesecloth are about right. If the vinegar is sufficiently strong (made from full-strength hard cider), you can bottle in sterile bottles, seal, and store as is. If the vinegar was made from incompletely fermented cider, pasteurize it before bottling to avoid the possibility of it making more bubbles and blowing the bottle. When capping any container of vinegar, *don't use plain metal lids, because vinegar corrodes metals!* So seal with a cork, a cork-lined cap, or some such.

From the time of sealing, the vinegar will gradually grow more mellow and more distinct in flavor, although you can use it immediately if you want. This homemade

vinegar can be used as a "starter" for your next batch. But it will keep best if you pasteurize it.

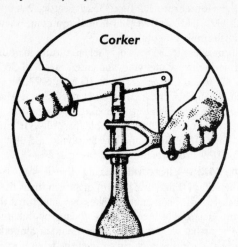

Corker

Pasteurizing (or Not). If you pasteurize your vinegar, it can't be used as a starter. If you don't want to pasteurize the vinegar, strain it through a wet, doubled cheesecloth before bottling and then store in a cool dry place.

But pasteurization will keep your vinegar from clouding due to formation of mother. Put the bottles or jugs of vinegar into a pan filled with cold water. Heat the water gradually. Be sure the bottles are loosely corked or unsealed while pasteurizing. Then heat until the vinegar is about 145°F and hold it at that temperature about 30 minutes. Then cool it.

🐝 *PIONEER CIDER VINEGAR Put 1 gal. good sweet natural cider and 1 qt. molasses into a crockery or glass container. Cover the top with cloth and set it in the sun. Cover it when it rains. When it stops bubbling, add some mother if you can. In a month or so it should be good strong vinegar. You can dilute it if it is stronger than you want.*

🐝 *CIDER-SEDIMENT VINEGAR Lois Rumrill, Forks of Salmon, CA, described her vinegar-making system for us: "When we make cider, I let it set in jugs for at least 24 hours and siphon the clear juice off the top of each jug, which leaves 1–1½ inches of sediment. [Lois doesn't mention the time for Stage 1; I'm sure it was in there.] I then pour the sediment into glass gallon jars, add mother to each, cover with cheesecloth and a cocked lid, and let it go to work. Lo and behold! In almost a month . . . vinegar! I remove the mother (to another gallon jar containing vinegar), siphon the vinegar into ketchup bottles, and pasteurize: I pour the vinegar into a large pan, turn on heat, heat vinegar to 170°F, and hold at that temp for 10 minutes. Pour it into hot jars, seal, and store. Or sometimes I don't pasteurize—just let the bottles of vinegar keep forming mother. When I use those unprocessed bottles of vinegar, I just put the mother into that gallon jar with the rest of my mother. My vinegar tastes so very much better than store-boughten."*

🐝 *FRUIT-HARVEST LEAVINGS VINEGAR When you are processing a bunch of apples, peaches, pears, grapes, or cherries, wash them thoroughly before preparing for use and save the peelings, hulls, cores, or seeds as appropriate. Place these in a crock. Sweeten well. Add enough water to cover them. You can sweeten with honey, molasses, or sugar. Let stand several days, keeping the top covered with a cloth. You* can add fresh peelings now and then. The scum (mother) on top will gradually thicken. When the vinegar tastes right, strain and bottle. Another method is to let your peelings, water, and sweetening stand several days; then strain and let the resulting juice stand until you have table vinegar.

⟫ *PURE CIDER VINEGAR* *Sylvia Nelson, Hillsdale, WY, wrote me, "I've made both malt and apple cider vinegar. The trick to making good cider vinegar is to start with cider, not apple parts. I sweetened it somewhat (white sugar does fine), added a few grains of yeast (I'm impatient), put a cloth over the jug, and left it in a warm place until done. The more sugar, the stronger the vinegar."*

⟫ *WINE VINEGAR* *You can make your own wine vinegar by starting with homemade grape or dark berry juice. Dilute; sweeten and mix, if desired, with a lighter juice such as peach. Keep in a warm place, covered. First it will ferment. You'll see the bubbles of carbon dioxide rising poetically as it works. Then it will go flat and your vinegar making will begin; that takes much longer and is less dramatic. You don't have to have mother to start. It speeds things, but unless you live in the frozen north, mother is all around us. In the South you may end up with father, aunt, and uncle too.*

⟫ *APPLE COMBO VINEGAR* *Combine a fruit juice with a tart apple juice. Pear is good. If you don't have a juicer, it will be easiest for you to just wash and mash the fruit by stomping with your kraut stomper. Then let it work until you like the vinegar flavor. Strain and store in glass in a cool dark place.*

USE OF VINEGAR: It has a multitude of uses. In general, wine vinegar makes the best salad dressings, while apple cider vinegar is used to make pickles and ketchups—and an old-time beverage, "shrub."

Strength of Homemade Vinegar. Commercialized vinegars have a standardized acid content; they are diluted to a predetermined strength and then pasteurized and bottled. Homemade ones vary in strength. A plain hard cider with no sweetening added will develop about 6 percent alcohol, which in turn will become about 6 percent acetic acid, which is a good strength for kitchen use. If you start out with sweetened liquid, your vinegar will be stronger. Take that into consideration when you are cooking or pickling

with it. Or dilute to the strength you want with distilled water. To strengthen the vinegar, let it freeze on top. Then take the ice off the top, since only the water portion freezes.

Shrub. The base for the beverage called shrub is a vinegar-fruit mix. To serve, dilute it to taste with water or ginger ale. Great-Grandmother liked it served hot for coughs and colds in winter and as a chilled beverage in summer. When bottled, it will keep for years.

⟫ *BLACK CURRANT, RASPBERRY, OR BLACKBERRY SHRUB* *Wash 2 lb. berries. Remove stalks and stems. Put into a crockery bowl and crush very thoroughly with a potato masher or pestle. Pour over the fruit mush 2 c. white vinegar and let stand for 5 days, stirring every day. Strain through a cloth. Measure the resulting juice and for every 2 c., add 1 lb. sugar. Boil very gently for 10 minutes, removing any scum. Strain again. Pour into bottles, cork, and seal with paraffin. (Stores that handle beverage-making supplies carry corks. The grocery store has paraffin.)*

⟫ *RASPBERRY OR STRAWBERRY SHRUB* *Add enough vinegar to cover 1 gal. red raspberries or strawberries. Let them stand 24 hours, scald, and then strain. Measure the juice. Add 1 lb. sugar per 2 c. juice. Boil 20 minutes and bottle.*

⟫ *SPICED RASPBERRY SHRUB* *Put your raspberries in a crock or jar. Cover with cider vinegar. Mash. Let stand overnight. Strain. For every 2 c. juice, add 2 c. sugar, 1 cinnamon stick, and 6 whole cloves. Boil 10 minutes. Bottle and seal while hot.*

Salting

Salting is another method of food preservation. A 5 percent salt solution reduces bacterial activity, 10 percent stops most of it, and 15 percent stops anything. See "Cabbage" in Chapter 4 for instructions on making sauerkraut, a basic salted, fermented food whose formula can be applied to other vegetables (corn, green beans, turnips). Carrots, beets, and turnips keep well if peeled, shredded, and salted. They also do well in a root cellar. String beans and corn cannot be stored in a root cellar, but they salt well. Peas and onions do not salt well, but peas dry well and well-cured onions store well if put away on a shelf where they won't freeze. Peppers, green beans, and asparagus salt well but need to go into a brine rather than be put down in dry salt. For more information, see *Making Sauerkraut and Pickled Vegetables at Home: The Original Lactic Acid Fermentation Method* by Annelies Schoeneck.
NOTE: Never use galvanized containers for pickling—acid or salt works on zinc and makes a poison.

DRY-SALTING VEGETABLES: Any root vegetable should be peeled and then sliced or chunked. Corn should be cut off the cob and string beans snapped into sections. Use a glass, crockery, or wood container to store the food—nothing made of metal, unless it's stainless steel. You'll need about 1 lb. salt for every 4 lb. vegetables.

Put a layer of salt on the bottom of your container, then a layer of vegetable, then salt, and so on until it is full. You can add more at later dates as your crop in the garden is ready for harvest. When you have as much vegetable in there as you want (don't go clear up to the brim), pour a in final layer of salt. Lay a plate on top, weighted down with a boiled stone, a jar full of water, or some such. Lay a cloth over the whole thing to keep flies from dying in it.

Let rest 2 weeks, changing the cloth weekly. The salt will draw the natural juices out of the vegetables and create a brine. When you need food, take some out and replace the plate. You must keep your vegetables out of contact with the air. Add more water as it evaporates to make sure that the water level is always higher than the vegetables.

Brine Salting Vegetables. With peppers, green beans, and asparagus, lay vegetables whole in your crock. Pour over a brine of 3½ lb. salt per 1 gal. water. Then follow the rest of the dry-salting instructions above. You can salt down in canning jars too. For example, pack green beans down in jars between layers of salt and then close up the jars.

SERVING: Any salted vegetable must be freshened by soaking overnight in several changes of water and then promptly cooked. A vegetable that has been preserved in salt will spoil amazingly fast once the salt is rinsed off, so you must be very efficient in getting it from your brine crock, through the freshening waters and the cooking, to the table.

Larding

Another old-time method of food preservation is "larding." The French call larded bird meat a "comfit." Julia Child's *The Art of French Cooking* has a chapter on this process, using goose fat. The fat seals the air out. August Bartelle, San Diego, CA, remembers: "After slaughtering a hog, the fat was rendered into lard. Those cuts of the hog that were not cured for smoking or made into sausage, like the shoulder, were fried. While still hot, these slices of pork steak were preserved through the winter by larding. In a large crock, layer on layer of the fried steaks was covered with hot lard. This meat was then used through the winter by scraping the lard off each layer. The amount necessary for a meal was removed and reheated. The used lard was reused in pies or other baking or cooking and ultimately for soap."

F.E. Pennington, Kelso, WA, wrote me about her pioneer childhood: "I was raised on a stump ranch in western Washington. We grew what we ate and ate what we grew. If we didn't grow it, we didn't eat. We let nothing go to waste. Once Daddy killed a fat bear and larded it in its own grease. We ground the meat up and cooked it in balls, then packed it in a 4-gal. stone crock which was set in the spring. The spring was as cold as ice water where it emerged from the hillside. It worked."

NOTE: *If you try this, make sure the food is stored under refrigeration, because there could be a botulism problem in that air-free, low-acid environment. The old-timers larded only in winter and stored it outdoors, where it was really cold.*

February 1, 1974. I have to write up the "Butters" section, the "Beekeeping" section, the introduction to this chapter, the "Fruits (Apple to Pomegranate)" section, and the middle of the "Dairy" chapter—and then I'm done with this [first edition of] the book.

If you think that because I've written a book and I'm a Christian and I don't use white sugar (not to imply equality among these various qualities), I never had my troubles, let me tell you different. You don't know the half of it. But I've had my miracles too. And that's the important thing. And just making it—just having gotten one foot in front of the other and kept moving all day long no matter how heavy the foot and the heart felt—can be miracle enough in some situations.

Being this near to finishing the first draft of the book seems a miracle. A year and a half ago I made up my mind not to take it up again. My husband's preferred choice with regard to the book from the very start has been that I refund the money on all those early orders I took. I would have, only I never had the money again.

Then we came to one of those great marital shakeups that have to happen once every 5 years or so, I guess, and I got thoroughly shook up and swore off everything except what could make me a better housekeeper, wife, and mother. Not a bad decision. I did need strengthening in those directions. So I swore off the book and regarded it as a selfish desire and any further involvement with it on my part as in the nature of being tempted into sin. For one full year, I never touched the manuscript. For most of that year, I didn't think about it much because I was busy just trying to get the housekeeping in my head done and become somebody that God and I could be satisfied with.

But around last August, thoughts of the book started coming to me again—first, in terms of responsibility to the people whose money I had taken and spent, to whom I had promised so much by sending them, first of all, that ambitious table of contents. I had already sent parts of the book in three separate mailings to them all, and most of them were willing to consider that good enough, but a few were still holding me to that original table of contents. I'd left them all hanging now, without any further word, for a year. I've always been an almost painfully responsible person and, although I've had my fantasies of disappearing in the Underground or becoming a waitress in Tahiti, I don't expect it will ever happen. So I started to try to plan how to refund the money and get a letter out to everybody explaining why I had given up. But I just couldn't seem to get that done, even though it meant typing only one stencil and mimeographing it and mailing it out.

And the notion of finishing the book kept cropping up in my head more and more often, no matter how hard I tried to put it down. I regarded that oft-upcropping thought with almost tearful frustration: We had less money than ever; Mike had been laid off from the part-time job he had been working at in addition to his full-time one. I had less time than ever because when I started the book, I had 2 children, but I now have five. How could I buy paper with no money? How could I get the mimeographing done since I no longer had access to the machine at Mike's office I'd been borrowing (because I had broken it)? How could I pay for postage?

But the urge to write again just got worse and worse, even though just getting through the chores I had seemed to take all my strength. I'm not a lazy or puny person. (I had my fifth baby, Sara, on a Thursday morning, left the hospital Friday evening, and went home and commenced to catch up on the dishes and laundry.) But it seemed like I was at my limit, and being nagged by the urge to write seemed to make me even more tired. (That's a curious thing, because once I actually started writing, the sensation of weariness gradually left.)

But was the desire just mine? In my one year of experience with God's way of leading me, a thought that nags me, patiently, relentlessly—the "do this, do this, do this"—is one way God has of showing me His will. And that's the way the thought of finishing the book came to me, more and more.

One day I literally broke down. Kneeling on my living room floor, crying out with lifted hands, I said, "Okay, Lord. I submit. This seems to be Your will. I can't see the way it's possible, but if it's Your will, I know You have a way through for me if I just go ahead and trust You."

The next day, secretly, I went back to work on the book. I constantly sought for God's leading with regard to the project and followed it explicitly. I had no hope outside His Power to accomplish miracles. I worked on it during daytime hours, while my husband was at his job. I did the displaced housework in the evenings: scrubbing floors and ironing shirts, usually until 11:00 at night. God gave me the strength. That was His first miracle for me. I was able to accomplish twice as much work as before.

When, weeks later, I finally felt it was time to tell Mike, he was good about it. That was a second miracle: Over the years past, Mike had grown to hate with almost a passion everything relating to the book and my work on it, but ever since then he's been very patient.

Introduction to Animals

Introduction to Animals Contents

INTRODUCTION

Domestic animals are basically human-created, symbiotic species. Most have been companions to people, caring for and being cared for, for literally millennia. For example, all but about 2 percent of the chicken varieties now sold in North America are breeds whose characteristics have been affected by careful selection by human breeders. Wild chickens, though they still run about in the jungles of Southeast Asia, are scarcely available for purchase elsewhere and would be impractical to own. The chicken as it now exists is dependent on its keeper to survive.

But in return for the responsibility you take for domestic animals'

care, feeding, housing, and doctoring, your animals eat your garden waste, kitchen surplus, and the field plants that humans can't eat, like grass and brush; and they turn it into high-quality protein foods for your diet (eggs, milk, meat). They also contribute manure to renew your pasture, field, and garden soil, and they devour insects. They can be used as pack animals; they can provide transportation, pulling power, and by-products such as wool, feathers, hides, and horns. Truly, they are benevolently symbiotic species that have been carefully evolved by fine farmers throughout the world over thousands of years to be the best possible companions,

economic and social, to food growers. They are *not* imprisoned wild animals! Most would quickly become extinct if not cared for by people.

My humble friend Stephen Scott (who makes a living growing pork, chicken, and organic vegetables for mail-order and his local farmers' market) has a wonderful way of putting things. He wrote me, "What raising pigs is all about, aside from the meat, is getting back to our roots as providers in a way that is much more important than just working at a job to put food on the table. I believe that the act of raising and caring for our own animals makes us more human."

RESOURCES

BOOKS: There's info about raising animals for meat in *Raising Your Own Meat for Pennies a Day,* by Will Graves (1983); *Raising Animals for Fun and Profit,* by the editors of *Countryside* (1984); *Barnyard in Your Backyard,* Gail Damerow, editor; and *Small-Scale Livestock Farming: A Grass-based Approach for Health, Sustainability and Profit* (1999) by Carol Ekarius (last two from Storey Books, address in Chapter 1). *Organic Livestock Handbook,* Anne Macey, editor, is a project of Canadian Organic Growers Inc. (**www.cog.ca**).

MAGAZINES: *Ranch and Rural Living* is a monthly about sheep, goats, and cattle: $25/yr; free sample; 915-655-4434; PO Box 2678, San Angelo, TX 76902. The *High Plains Journal* covers the livestock scene, too: 800-452-7171; fax 316-227-7173; PO Box 760, Dodge City, KS 67801; **journal@hpj.com; www.hpj.com/**.

MAIL-ORDER SUPPLIERS OF LIVESTOCK EQUIPMENT

Brower Equipment for Poultry, Livestock, Pets: Highway 16 W., PO Box 2000, Houghton, IA 52631; 319-469-4141; 800-533-1791; fax 319-469-4402; **brower iowa@aol.com; www.browerequip.com**. Free catalog of equipment for poultry, pigs, and cattle; mousetraps; high-tech incubators.

Jeffers Livestock sells vaccines, cattle and goat supplies, fencing systems: 800-533-3377; **www.jeffers livestock.com**.

Klubertanz's Equipment specializes in welded wire and hex mesh, 1 x 2 in. spacing and smaller, and supplies for small animals. Free catalog: 1165 Hwy. 73, Edgerton, WI 53534; 800-237-3899; fax 608-884-7509; **www.klubertanz.com**.

Modern Farm sells farm and ranch supplies. Free catalog: 800-443-4934 or 307-587-5946; 1825 Big Horn Rd., Cody, WY 82414.

Premier1Supplies offers goat/sheep supplies, fencing, clippers: **www.premier1supplies.com**.

Sheepman Supply Company provides a wide range of

supplies to sheep, goat, cow, horse, llama, alpaca, and horse farmers, including shearing gear, health care products, books, and videos. Free catalog: 800-331-9122; 301-662-4197; fax 301-662-0361; PO Box A, Frederick, MD 21702; **info@sheepman.com; www.sheepman.com**.

LEARNING LIVESTOCK CARE: 4-H, your extension service, and agricultural college classes are all resources. All the counties of western Washington state have a program that produces "WSU Extension Livestock Advisers" after training in animal care, "from how to feed a llama to how to eliminate goat horns." Although "master gardeners" are everywhere, right now that is the only livestock master program in the country; I hope others will soon start up elsewhere. For info, contact the program founder and guiding light: Mike Hackett, Skagit County Cooperative Extension; 360-428-4270; 306 S. First St., Mt. Vernon, WA 98273-3805; **hackett@wsu.edu; www.skagitcounty.net/wsu.htm**.

Heifer Project International is a charitable worldwide organization that provides a female animal to a poor family in return for their gift of a female offspring to another family to pass on the help: 1015 Louisiana St., Little Rock, AR 72202; **www.heifer.org**. They seek donations in rich countries and donate animals in poor ones.

Considerations About Keeping Animals

Home-grown meat and eggs will always taste better and probably be healthier for you. They may even be cheaper to produce than store-bought eggs. You may hope to sell surplus animals for a profit as meat, breeders, or pets. Or you may just want to keep the animals as food sources for your family, as pets, for their beauty, or to show at judged poultry events as a hobby—or any combination of those.

RESPONSIBILITY: A basic question to ask about raising any livestock is whether you can afford the space, time, nuisance, and expense of adding them to your family. They may not be permitted by your local zoning. They may cause odors and noise and attract flies, mice, and rats. You won't be able to take vacations unless you can arrange caretaking. No matter why you want to keep poultry or any other livestock, start small enough so that you can try out your management ideas without too much stress on either you or the animals, which will be dependent on your expertise, faithfulness, and ability to provide for them.

One of your most important responsibilities is simply being around your animals. You won't be able to leave home without considering their needs. You can limit the responsibility and tied-downness of animal keeping by just raising a spring crop: buy a flock of young ones in the spring, raise them to butchering weight, transfer them to the deep freeze, and you're done for the year. Your schedule may determine whether you choose a small egg flock of hens to raise year-round, or have a big meat-chicken production operation for just a few months a year—or do both. You can stay away from most egg flocks for a few days and they'll be fine, but a bunch of meat birds requires daily tending.

Carol Caple, Neosho, MO, wrote me, "It really boosted my ego to read that someone else has troubles from time to time and that some other woman has had to chase escaped livestock while her husband was at work in his clean, air-conditioned office. People (me included) thought we had done something wrong when our one and only goat died of pneumonia. I now realize that nature takes its course and things like that happen."

Your Animals' 4 Basic Rights
1. Treatment when injured or diseased.
2. Freedom from extreme physical discomfort.
3. Sufficient and nourishing food and water.
4. Care that minimizes fear and stress.

ANIMAL PSYCHOLOGY: Animals are different, but they're all heavily endowed with instinct and subject to habit. You have to work with their instincts and instill good habits in them. Once your animals have gotten their routine established, you must patiently subject yourself to their rules. Take time to listen to them and learn what their noises, expressions, and behaviors communicate. They listen to you. They may not understand all your words, but they'll understand some, and your voice's tone, facial ex-

pression, and body motions will communicate eloquently to them whether you're pleased, angry, insistent, or indifferent. Rule them like you do children: you must have a history of 8 or 10 true kindnesses before you will have earned the privilege of a moment's needed educational discipline. When you come to see them, bring a treat. When you get an animal someplace you want it to go—the stanchion, pen, or pickup truck—reward with a treat. Animals you've handled since they were young will be more friendly and less fearful than those bought as adults.

ZONING: Before investing in any farm animals, small or large, check your local zoning ordinances. Animals make smells and noises and occasionally escape from custody, and the very ones you love may be regarded by your close neighbors as unbearable nuisances. Chickens and turkeys, in particular, smell because of the high concentration of ammonia in their droppings. So choose where to live with your farm family in mind, or choose your farm family keeping in mind where you live. I have had the experience of being visited by the town police officer and told I must either get rid of my animals (goats) or move (I moved).

CHOOSING YOUR ANIMALS: You'll be concerned with the hardiness of the varieties you buy, suitability for your situation, and length of time to slaughter. For example, broiler chickens go into the deep freeze after 8 weeks at about 4 pounds each; ducks go into the freezer after 8 weeks at 7 pounds each. Turkeys will weigh more at slaughter (15–20 lb.) but must be cared for longer (5 months) and fed more, and they're not quite as hardy. Some animals can forage better than others and thus cost less to feed. For birds destined for a commercial meat market, white-feathered breeds are preferred because their pinfeathers (small, immature feathers that tend to remain in the flesh) are white and don't show up. Every situation has individual angles you'll want to consider. You may want just one kind of animal, or you may want an assortment.

Shawn Trumble, Ionia, MI, wrote, "When I first bought your book, we were living in a little apartment in town. The landlord wouldn't even let us plant a few tomato plants. Now we have 3 acres (not enough!), a big garden, the start of a small orchard, 30 or so assorted hens, a pig, 4 assorted Jerseys including a cow we milk, a veal calf (good use for extra milk!), a few geese, and a turkey! The kids raise and sell broiler chickens in the summer and have a waiting list of people for the next batch. We also sell eggs. So we raise our own beef, pork, poultry, dairy products, eggs, fruit, and vegetables!"

ANIMAL ECONOMICS: A lot of people who raise animals end up complaining that it costs them more to home-grow eggs and meat than to buy them from the store. They generally qualify that by adding that the meat tastes much better, and they usually believe home-grown is healthier. But cheap is desirable, too, and sometimes is necessary. With good management it's possible to home-grow at a profit. To raise any animals, your basic expenses will be the animals (or their parents), their feed, their housing, and the equipment you need to raise them, such as feed and water troughs and a brooder lamp. Some things you can buy used at a bargain. Most housing and equipment can be used over and over again so that it becomes a minimal expense.

Farming is the only industry in which you buy retail and sell wholesale. It's hard to make a profit, although the organic market has been growing and becoming more competitive. If you can afford only a small piece of land that

Any mammal that is trained to wear a halter and act appropriately on the other end of a lead rope is easier to live with than a halter-ignorant one.

1. Start as young as possible. Younger ones are easier to handle and easier to train. Be patient and gentle.

2. Start by getting up to and putting a halter on the animal's head.

3. Next, just tie up the animal for a couple hours to an immovable object. This gets them used to the idea that they can't get away and accustoms them to the feel of the halter. Tie up the animal with just a foot length between its head and the fence, or whatever it's tied to, so it can't get its legs tangled in the rope. If possible, tie it to a fence rather than an isolated post so it can't wind itself around it. Have a sharp knife handy so that if something goes wrong, you can cut the animal loose.

4. Repeat every day until this lesson is learned. Don't leave it alone at first. It might fight and choke itself. Grooming it while it stands there helps reassure and gentle it.

5. Take the animal into a small, totally enclosed space like a pen or corral (to keep it from escaping; an animal that has gotten away once will be twice as hard to train the next time). Practice leading it counterclockwise around and around. Don't tie the lead rope around your arm or body so there's no risk of being dragged. Keep the animal's head up and bent a little toward you. Practice about half an hour. Stop the practice for six hours or so. Then practice another 30 minutes. (Same-day practices really help!) Practice every day until it gets easy.

6. For a difficult large animal, it may help to first tie the animal to the back of a vehicle (a "leading gate"), which is then moved to lead the animal. Or tie the trainee firmly to another animal that already knows what it's all about, and lead them both in that way.

7. For your first out-of-corral leading, let your animal get a little thirsty, and then lead it to water.

won't run enough animals to support your family in a commercial operation, and yet you want to be a full-time farmer, there are two other ways to do it. One is raising organic meat; you get paid much more for the carcasses than you would otherwise (so you can make it with fewer animals). The other is raising registered animals. But both of these are somewhat risky, like all farming, and both depend a lot on your ability to sell yourself and your animals. It's also important to get into, and along with, the groups that promote these special products and breeds.

You'll have a vastly different approach to raising animals depending on whether you want to make money on them. If you have a few animals to help provide healthy food for your family, you'll know them well and be friends with them. But to profit from livestock, you have to operate like a business and view the animals more impersonally. Know what's possible: for instance, a calf can grow 100 pounds of meat for you in only 3 months (more meat quicker than any other animal), but it takes 10 years to develop a herd of 30 cows, even if you start with 3 beef cows with calves. On the other hand, one bred sow can have 700 descendants in three years. But also consider rabbits . . . and chickens . . .

Then set goals. Try to continually increase the quantity or quality of your product and have better cost control. Keep track of all you spend and earn, and regularly reconsider the project according to those numbers.
NOTE: P. Wells of Smallholder, *the English homesteaders' magazine, wrote me: "Tell people to check local laws. There are several new guidelines on selling, processing, and producing foodstuffs, eggs, and dairy produce." That applies equally to readers in any country—or U.S. state, for that matter.*

THE AUCTION RING: Cull cows generally go to the auction ring; some good cows do too. The Lewiston auction ring handles hundreds of animals every time it's in session: cows, pigs, sheep, and sometimes others. It's a sight to see. I was there once when they brought a Charolais bull through. Charolais is one of the new beef breeds, off-white and very big—a bull can be over 3,000 lb. This was a big bull, and he had horns and was in a horrible mood. It really had us nervous for a while because he was charging everybody in

sight and they couldn't even get into the ring to open the gate to let him out. Finally a brave man dodged out into one side of the ring and let the bull charge him (he got away) while another person just managed to get the gate open at least partway before the bull saw him and charged him too.

TRAVELING WITH ANIMALS: You need to be prepared to travel with your animals. Even if the person you buy it from agrees to deliver the animal, 2 days later you may need to take it to the vet, or you may be mad enough at it to want to take it back to the previous owner. A half-ton pickup can hold any smaller animal, including a small cow like a Jersey. (It can hold a bigger cow, but it's a real struggle.) You'd have to bend a big Shorthorn cow pretty near to an S-shape to get it in. A ¾-ton pickup bed will hold any cow or bull easily. You'll need stock racks, of course, to haul cows. You can make your own. A 1-ton truck can transport 3 big cows plus 1 or more calves tucked in around the sides.

You can transport a goat in the back of a pickup most comfortably by tying a rope to each side of its collar and fastening the ends to each side of the pickup. That holds it in the pickup so it cannot jump over the side. Or you can tie it to the middle, right behind the cab, on a very short lead. You can tie the legs of a calf or goat and put it in a car trunk with the door a little open, but I don't care much for that method. If you can spread out a big sheet of plastic so your upholstery is perfectly protected, you can move one or more goats, small pigs, or sheep in the back of a car. (Just don't try to eat anything in the front seat during a trip with goats, or you'll have goats in your lap.) You can bring a newborn calf or smallish pig home in a gunnysack tied around its body that leaves its head outside the sack.

I once traveled 60 miles in a small car with 5 goats, 3 young children, and myself very largely expectant. The humans and goats made it fine, but it took the car a while to recover.

Genetics

There are distinct genetic lines of poultry (and other animals) that go by the same name and yet have inherited differences, some of which are beneficial and some of which can be a problem. That's why it is helpful to always buy stock from a breeder you trust. Genes matter. They define what your animal's ancestors were and what your animal is capable of becoming—what its strong points and weaknesses will be.

For example, the modern hen lays about 7 times as many eggs per year as does a wild hen. This achievement is, above all, the result of farmers' careful and continual selection of her predecessors for many generations. You can decide what characteristics you want your poultry to have and then obtain birds with those traits. If you decide to become a breeder yourself, remember that good breeders ruthlessly eliminate stock that doesn't meet their standards.

OF PEDIGREED ANIMALS: A pedigreed, or registered, animal is one with known genetic characteristics. Its parents, grandparents, and so on have been recorded. When it is bred to another animal with known characteristics, you know what sort of offspring you are going to get. There is a long, valuable tradition of exhibiting the best breeding animals at the annual local county fair. So that's a good place to go to study the breeds.

If you decide to raise registered animals, you will pay a sizable price for your start of breeding stock. To start with, you just breed and build up the numbers of your herd. You don't eat any of the offspring. The registered stock is much too valuable financially to be wasted on your dinner table. You'll have to raise some cheaper animals for your family's food. And you can't sell your registered animals through the regular outlets—like a stockyard for cows on regular sale days. You'll have to wait for a special sale of registered animals, and you might have to truck your animals quite a way to get there. Or you sell them through ads in specialty magazines. To sell pricey registered animals, each animal must be carefully and throughly halter-broken and in tiptop condition. And it's almost a must to take your best ones around to all the stock shows you've got the time and money to go to, because the more ribbons they win, the higher the prices you can charge for them or their offspring.

You'll also join your state and national associations for your particular breed of registered animal. You'll get a monthly publication, and part of your dues will be applied to the cost of the advertising that keeps up the national, or even international, image of your breed. These associations also usually put out a directory of members and sometimes a handbook on caring for their breed; many sponsor an annual convention or meeting. Many have affiliated state groups that meet more frequently. If you happen into a breed whose central organization has troubles, one that isn't really meeting the competition in the national advertising market, you may have trouble getting the top price for your animals. To locate the society for any particular breed, look in the *Encyclopedia of Associations* at your local library.

Who will you sell to? To people who think that a registered animal is so much better that they are willing to pay the higher price. And to people like you who hope to make money selling registered animals and are trying to get their own start of breeding stock. And to parents of 4H'ers and FFA teenagers looking for an animal that might win a prize at the county fair. (They'll favor breeds that have recently been winning.) And to people who have money and think of owning registered animals as an upper-class thing. And to large-scale livestock raisers who want to introduce particular characteristics into their herds. (For example, a dairy owner may buy a purebred big meat-type bull (or artificially inseminate with its semen) so the bull calves will sell at the higher prices that beef with those characteristics brings.) And to commercial operations that want to start with the best or upgrade the stock they have. And to plain folks who want a guarantee of no bad genes in the offspring.

BAD GENES: We had a problem once with a herd of purebred cows that every so often produced a naturally sterile heifer. (Now I know why they were cheap and the owner was getting out of the business!) We have a heifer out here now that was born without a tail and missing the last couple of humps of her backbone. Otherwise she's fine, but we won't use her for a brood cow, since the trait might pass on. I had a 4-titted nanny goat once (they should have 2; cows have 4) who had 4-titted nanny kids. I wouldn't keep her offspring for breeding either, since they might pass it on. Some people say never to mate 2 animals that have the same fault, but that's not good enough. If an animal has a serious fault, don't let it mate at all. You don't want that trait to continue.

ARTIFICIAL INSEMINATION: In some cases, you can

make more money selling semen from your animal than selling the animal itself. That's because it's cheaper to buy as many females as you can afford and artificially inseminate (A-I) them than to buy a champion male. You do that by buying frozen semen from the champion male of your breed. But even the semen may be very pricey. This method is sometimes used by cow breeders. You probably can take an A-I course somewhere in your area to find out how to do it. Check with your local extension agent or 4H leader.

If you set out to buy a registered animal, keep in mind that you're being exposed to an expert at person-to-person salesmanship. And be alert to the possibility that the animal is being misrepresented. Owners have claimed that their animals were bred when they weren't, and that they gave more milk than they really did. At such a high price, it pays to be very, very careful. Remember also that the owner is selling his or her own culls. An owner of registered animals is trying all the time to improve the characteristics of the herd: how much milk the animal gives if it's a dairy herd, how fast the calf gains weight if it's a beef herd. The animals offered for sale are the ones that don't meet the breeder's standards. You can't buy the best ones, unless you're prepared to pay fantastic prices.

A final summing up and advice from Carolyn Christman, program coordinator of the American Livestock Breeds Conservancy: "You can choose purebred animals or animals of unknown breeding. An advantage of purebred animals is predictability: you know exactly what the offspring will be when they grow up. If you choose purebred, you can then choose registered animals. Registered animals cost more. This cost is worthwhile if you are at all interested in the sale of breeding stock or in the development of a breeding herd. If you are making this kind of investment, shop around and find reputable breeders from which to start your herd. An auction can offer a bargain, but because things happen so fast, you can't do very careful buying. Don't assume that because an animal is stated to be a particular breed, it is. Look at the papers and make sure that they match the animal (check brands or tattoos if possible) before you pay extra for that registration! And make sure that the registry is a legitimate outfit. In short, do your homework!"

Heritage Breeds and Exotics

These aren't the same thing.

HERITAGE LIVESTOCK BREEDS: These are old-time livestock breeds. Some are still popular, but many are quite rare and some have vanished forever. Back in the old days they were regular farm livestock, an essential part of rural life and agriculture. Years ago there were far more breeds of the 9 basic livestock species (asses, cattle, chickens, ducks, horses, geese, sheep, swine, and turkeys) worldwide than there are now. Back then, every area of the earth where people lived was a distinct eco-niche in which those humans and their specifically adapted animal breeds sustained each other. Modern times and agribusiness (mass) production of a very limited number of the most profitable breeds have caused the extinction or near-extinction of most of those other old-time domestic species. The mass-market producers tend to choose just one or a very few breeds and let the others approach or cross the line to extinction.

The preservation of these heritage livestock breeds happens on family farms that have a use for or an interest in such critters as pigs that thrive on pasture rather than in

confinement (such as the Tamworth breed); poultry that will set and hatch their eggs; and a cow that is small in size and moderate in milk production (the Jersey). The Florida Cracker cow is adapted to the hot, humid climate of the Deep South. The horned, spotted Jacob sheep is a good survivor.

Commercial agriculture has zillions of the one breed most suited to agribusiness' mass production: Holstein for the dairy industry, Leghorns for the chicken industry, etc. But homestead-type folks keep the others going. The old-time breeds of livestock are worthwhile for their genetic uniqueness as well as their historic value. For example, someday there might be a disease in pigs equivalent to the hybrid corn blight. Rare breeds also may produce lovely colored wool, unusual cheeses, astonishing feathers, etc. And heritage breeds are typically better suited than industrial ones for the free-range, chemical-free homestead family's needs.

Carolyn Christman of the ALBC again sums it up: "These animals have better forage efficiency on pasture, maternal abilities, disposition, longevity, parasite and disease resistance, and general health. Their animal services—such as brush clearing, pest and waste control, production of manure, and grazing to improve pasture—are also quite valuable on the homestead farm."

I hate to spoil the fun, but I can't end this without sourly adding that some less common species have been left behind for good reasons, and the ALBC says only the good things about heritage livestock. Do your homework so you aren't disappointed.

NOTE: Before shopping for livestock, know exactly what you want your animals to be able to do in your particular eco-niche, or what market you are aiming their production toward. Then choose the most suitable species.

By the way, the American Livestock Breeds Conservancy works to protect nearly 100 endangered breeds of American livestock and poultry from extinction. They take a periodic census of all varieties of domesticated livestock in the United States. They name those at risk of extinction and encourage people to buy and breed them. If you join ($30/yr), you get a bimonthly newsletter, annual breeders directory, and access to a long list of reports and publications on rare and endangered livestock: ALBC; 919-542-5704; Box 477, Pittsboro, NC 27312; **albc@albc-usa.org; www.albc-usa.org.** Their newsletter contains classified ads for heritage breeds as well as a calendar of events like these:

Country Fair and Crafts Festival, Hancock Shaker Village: Eric Johnson; 413-443-0188; PO Box 927, Pittsfield, MA 01202.

19th Century Agricultural Fair: Patty Warren, Genesee County Village and Museum; 585-538-6822; Flint Hill Rd., Mumford, NY 14511; **www.gcv.org.**

EXOTICS: An exotic breed is one that is either newly created, a once-wild native (such as buffalo!), or recently imported and new to the United States. For instance, have you considered raising butterflies? Contact Rt. 1, Box 447A, Mathis, TX 78368, **www.butterflyrelease.com** for more info. The Asclepias Seed Co. provides milkweed planting seed for nurturing monarch butterflies and larvae: 800-621-3696; 218 Prospector Dr., Ogallala, NE 69153.

You'll find listings of many rarer breeds of livestock at www.ansi.okstate.edu/breeds. Their scarcity, the media interest in them, and speculators' hopes for profit make for risky business. The exotic market has on occasion seen speculators making large profits — and the unaware taking large losses. The beefalo (a cow-buffalo cross) was once the center of bidding excitement, as were a relatively useless rabbit variety called the Belgian hare and later the ostrich. It's safest to pay a price for an animal based on its potential to produce meat, work, hide, fur, or feathers rather than its potential as a breeder (rather than speculating, that is, that since you were willing to pay a mint for an animal, that means you'll be able to sell its many offspring for a mint each too). That get-rich scenario runs into trouble when there are no more well-heeled speculators available to buy your animals — or when the media interest shifts to some other unfamiliar creature.

Nevertheless, there are good profit possibilities in raising exotics, so I'm not trying to totally talk you out of it; I just want to instill a healthy caution. Do consider raising breeds such as buffalo, ratites (ostriches, emus, and rheas), caribou, elk, antelope, water buffalo, red or fallow deer, cattalo (another buffalo-cow hybrid), and South American humpless camels ("camelids") such as llamas, alpacas, guanacos, and vicunas. You can sell to restaurants that want unusual meats on their menu and to people who want the meat or an unusual pet. You can sell exotic fibers (such as camelid wool). You can sell the animals for packing (the camelids, **www.packllama.org**), or performing draft work (river buffalo). In South America, guinea pigs (raised on a diet of corncobs, grass, alfalfa, and lettuce) are butchered when they are 6 months to a year old. Their meat is an Andean special treat: "cuy."

Exotics include breeds such as yak (International Yak Ass'n; **www.yakpage.com**). Also, there are now miniature breeds of cows, horses, goats, pigs, etc. Miniature horses, for example, stand 19 to 38 in. high. They're too small to be ridden, even by children, but they can pull a cart. (Available from 520-682-8009; fax 520-616-7022; **wowworks@aol.com**.)

Humpless Camels. For expert advice on the medical problems of South American camelids, especially guanacos and vicunas, contact Dr. William L. Franklin: **billfranklin1@juno.com**.

Llamas are said to be useful as livestock guardians. Doesn't make sense to me that one could handle a bear, cougar, pack of wolves, or coyotes. (I recommend you get one or more Great Pyrenees dogs for this: **www.c-c-farms.com**).

Here are lots more camelid info resources:

Alpaca Discussion List is for alpaca owners and those interested in them. The mailing list serves 700+ persons and is moderated by John L. Pinkowski (Pine Ridge Alpacas; 330-849-6435; **Alpacasite-owner@onelist.com**; subscribe at **www.onelist.com/group/Alpacasite**.

AlpacaNet includes files about alpacas, their fiber, and directories of products and ranches; **www.alpacanet.com**.

Alpaca Owners and Breeders Association sponsors an annual convention: 970-586-5357; fax 970-586-6685; PO Box 1992, Estes Park, CO 80517; **alpacainfo@aol.com; www.aoba.org/; www.AlpacaOwners.com**.

Canadian Alpaca Breeders Ass'n: www.caba-alpaca.org.

Canadian Llama and Alpaca Ass'n: 800-717-5262; 403-250-2165.

Llama Information Exchange Newsletter is info about llamas and their issues, written by owners: **members.aol.com/lamainfoex**.

Llama Search's site contains farm listings, info links, products, etc.: **www.llamasearch.com/**.

Llamapaedia was written by vet students. It covers husbandry, breeding, care, etc.; **www.llamapaedia.com; www.llamaweb.com/**.

Pack Llama Trail Ass'n: PO Box 25, Meridian, ID 83680-0025; **ccllamas@mindspring.com**.

Rocky Mountain Llama Ass'n maintains a research library and holds many public llama events: 303-241-7921; 593-19 3/4 Rd., Grand Junction, CO 81503; **www.rmla.com**.

Suri Alpacas are unique in the camelid family for their fiber, which hangs in long, separate locks rather than being woolly: **surinetwork.org**.

Useful Llama Items is a catalog for llama and alpaca owners offering halters, leads, medications, grooming and farm and training supplies, books, videos, shearing equipment, packs, harnesses, carts, wormers, specialty clothing, etc.: 800-635-5262; fax 815-234-7684; 5458 N. Rizoville Rd., Byron, IL 61010; **www.usefullama items.com**.

Camelids of Delaware sells guanacos: 313-545-2820; 130 E. Nine Mile Rd., Ferndale, MI 48220. Mettowee Valley Farm sells alpacas: 802-325-3039; fax 802-325-7023; PO Box 55, Rupert Mountain Rd., Pawlet, VT 05761; **jcallen998@aol.com; www.mettoweevalleyfarm.com**. Seldom Scene Farm raises both llamas and alpacas: 606-873-8352; fax 606-873-1622; 1710 Watts Ferry Rd., Frankfort, KY 40601; **sscene@lex.infi.net; www.seldomscenefarm.com**. Or contact Spa Alpacas: 518-885-0585; 7 Paisley Rd., Ballston Spa, NY 12020; pjzanella@aol.com; www.spaalpacas.com. Or Tia and Peter Rosengarten: 802-824-8190; Mountain Pond Farm, 74 Obed Moore Rd., Weston, VT 05161.

Deer/Elk/Reindeer Farming. Deer and elk farming is big business in New Zealand, which exports, and in the former West Germany, which consumes venison second only to beef and imports more than 25,000 tons per year [1989] and produces at least the same amount within the country. Commercial venison production is doing well in the United

States too. The first deer farm ever in this country was the Lucky Star Ranch in Chaumont, NY. An extension bulletin says Lucky Star Ranch raises 3,000 deer on 1,500 fenced acres and has done well with its own USDA-inspected slaughter and processing plant on the premises. Owner Joseph von Kerckerinck, founder of the North American Deer Farmers Association, sells fresh and frozen venison cuts directly to consumers by mail, but most deer and elk ranchers make arrangements with a cattle slaughterhouse to do that work.

Von Kerckerinck wrote me that the big start-up expense for raising deer or elk is a fence between 6 feet 3 inches and 8 feet high, which is a necessity. He says if you are raising fallow deer, you can keep 4 deer per acre; wherever you can pasture 1 cow, you can keep 6 to 7 fallow deer. Coyotes and domestic dogs are a problem for deer ranchers, but there are ways to make your pastures predator-proof. And for meat that may sell at $5–$10 per lb., the risks may well be worth it. He sells a videotape on the subject: 315-649-5519; Lucky Star, 13240 Lucky Star Rd., Chaumont, NY 13622.

The H & A Ranch offers bison bulls, bred bison cows, elk bulls, and bred elk cows: 731-845-5671; 411 Redbud Lake Rd., Lexington, TN 38351; **dlautry@pchnet.com.** For more info, order the *Bison Breeder's Handbook* and *The Buffalo Producer's Guide to Marketing and Management* from the National Bison Ass'n: 303-292-2833; fax 303-292-2564; 4701 Marion St. #100, Denver, CO 80216; **david@bison-central.com; www.bisoncentral.com.** ATTRA's article on "Bison Production" is at **www.attra.ncat.org/attra-pub/bison.html.** You can subscribe to the *North American Bison Journal:* 800-253-3656; fax 605-347-2525; bisonjournal.com. They have years of archived issues on their website.

Want to raise reindeer? Ethel Evans is Corresponding Secretary for the Reindeer Owners and Breeders Ass'n: 303-841-4098; 10190 Bayou Gulch Rd., Parker, CO 80134; **moondeerranch@aol.com.**

Ostrich. Ostrich hides make good boots, and ostrich meat is plentiful and good, but these birds can live for as long as 70 years and will keep producing beautiful plumes all their lives. You can't determine the sex of ostrich chicks until they're at least 8 weeks old. Ostrich chicks are liable to have nutritional problems and pneumonia unless kept well fed, warm, and dry. An ostrich hen can lay as many as 30 to 50 eggs a year, but not all the eggs will hatch. Abuse or teasing stresses the birds. They should not be left alone with small children, for they don't understand the strength of their peck. Their big bills snatch up a wristwatch, glove, ring, or buttons in an instant. Their strong forward kick protects against coyotes or stray dogs. Young ones can be crowded, but adults need space—½ to 1 acre per adult pair of ostriches. Fence height depends on age; for adults you need a 5-foot fence. Ostriches don't fly or jump, but they will lean into a fence. As long as it doesn't fall over and they don't fall over it, it will hold them.

Dale Coody offers a 36-pg manual, *Ostriches: Your Great Opportunity,* for $12.50 and a video for $59.95 from his 4-C Ostrich Farm: 580-353-3078; Rt. 1, PO Box 71A, Lawton, OK 73501. He also sells ostrich-scaled incubators and brooders. A subscription to *Emu Today & Tomorrow*—$25/yr for 12 issues—is available from phone/fax 580-628-2011; 11950 W. Highland Ave., Blackwell, OK 74631.

MORE EXOTIC INFO

Animal Finders' Guide is "The Magazine Devoted to Animal Lovers," covering current animal issues, reader letters, classified ads, 18 issues/yr, $25, $2 for sample copy: PO Box 99, Prairie Creek, IN 47869; 812-898-2678.

Animal Market Place is a periodical of classified and display ads and articles featuring rare, unusual, and hard-to-find animals, pets, and alternative livestock: $24/yr from Kyle E. Blankenship, PO Box 35784, Canton, OH 44735; 877-879-6527; **urbann@prodigy.net; www.animalmarketplace.com.**

Animals Exotic and Small is a big international bimonthly magazine for breeders and owners of miniature, exotic, and unusual animals. Each issue is 100+ pages; $25/yr; sample $5 USA: 1320 Mountain Ave., Norco, CA 92860-2852; 909-371-4307; fax 909-371-4779; **aes@linkline.com; animalsexoticandsmall.com.**

Heart of America Game Breeders' Assn., annual dues $10, offers twelve 8-pg newsletters with free ads for members and a Breeders' Directory listing about 475 members in 27 states: Terry Smith, 14000 W. 215th St., Bucyrus, KS 66013.

Rare Breeds Journal, "The Digest of the World of Alternative Livestock, Wildlife, Animals and Pets," offers an exotic market review, a global connection to the exotic animal industry for $25/yr,: Box 66, Crawford, NE 69339; 308-665-1431; fax 308-665-1931; **rarebreed@bbc.net.**

Wings & Hooves Magazine, "covering all animals since 1988," is $16/yr for 12 issues, sample $2; write Rt. 1, Box 32, Forestburg, TX 76239-9706; 940-964-2314; **wingsandhooves@ntin.net.**

Predators

When you raise animals, especially small stock like poultry and rabbits or vulnerable stock like sheep and goats with kids, you're likely to soon find out if something's out there that likes to kill and eat—or merely kill—your kind of animals. The predators may be wild animals like hawks, owls, mink, skunk, raccoon, coyote, foxes, weasels, and ferrets, or they may be domestic dogs. Dogs are much worse than coyotes. While coyotes kill only to eat, dogs may kill a whole flock of sheep.

IDENTIFYING PREDATORS: Your first problem is to identify the problem animal. Each variety of predator has a characteristic modus operandi, and if you discuss the details of what happened with old-timers in the neighborhood, they'll give you good advice. Mammals will take small stock of all ages and can be a big problem if you live far from town. Rats usually kill only very young or very small poultry, but they can wipe out a hatch of chicks or ducklings in one night and can consume or ruin a lot of feed. Hawks hunt by day; owls, weasels, raccoons, and foxes hunt by night. A weasel may suck the blood or take only the head of even a mature small animal. The predators may be domestic animals gone wild, like uncared-for cats; or they may turn out to be domestic animals that should be under better control—possibly even your own pet.

Since knowing what you're dealing with is important in planning a defense, check out *Tracking and the Art of Seeing: How to Read Animal Tracks and Signs* by Paul Rezendes, a good book that covers 46 mammals.

PREDATOR-PROOFING: If the problem is your own pet, you must train it not to kill livestock, physically control it by fencing in or tying up, or destroy it—or you give up on that type of livestock and get something too big for it to kill—like a draft horse! You can predator-proof confined small animals by housing them in well-built quarters that predators can't squeeze or dig into. You can protect against night predators by confining your animals in predator-proof quarters at least at night. Covering the top of your birds' or bunnies' outdoor runs keeps out both flying predators and disease-carrying wild birds. Some counties trap wild predators as a public service.

Rats can be a problem. Keeping feed grains in rodent-proof containers helps. Both rats and mice are attracted by poultry feed. It's best to keep feed in covered metal containers like metal garbage cans. Keeping a mousing cat, trapping, or putting out poison grain are more combative approaches.

To protect animals in a herd, get a guard dog (918-967-4871; C&C Farms, Rt. 3, Box 6815, Stigler, OK 74462; bcoate@cwis.net; www.c-c-farms.com/). Read ATTRA's article "Predator Control for Sustainable & Organic Livestock Production." It's free from 800-346-9140 or downloadable at **www.attra.org/attra-pub/.**

FIRE ANTS: An especially ugly and growing problem is fire ant predation. These newcomers to North America are gradually spreading through the southern United States. They are expected to spread eventually to western Texas, most of California, and through the Oregon and Washington coasts. Fire ants sting like a bee with a formic acid poison, are very aggressive, and will swarm over unmoving victims, possibly giving a fatal number of stings. They eat meat as readily as vegetable products. They attack anything alive and are most able to destroy young, slow, or otherwise vulnerable animals. So they can kill setting hens, baby chicks, and mother and baby rabbits. They've been known to attack calves, starting with their eyes. (They're hard on wild animals too.) They basically eat everything from their victim but the skin and bones. Boiling water kills them.

CHICKENS AND PREDATORS: Make sure your chick area is safe from predators: dogs, cats, rats, weasels. Rats and weasels have been known to squeeze through 1-inch chicken wire. If you're covering holes with wire mesh, the holes should be no more than ½ inch in diameter. Baby chicks can easily be squeezed to death by a carelessly tight grip. And, like other animal babies, they do best with a schedule that allows a lot of rest and a minimum of stress.

The facilities you plan for your poultry will reflect your judgment about what risks you care to take—as well as what existing housing there is, what you can afford, and what the individual species' needs are. Living any life requires balancing the joy of freedom against the wisdom of precaution. Chickens love to roam, but then they're more likely to get run over, carried off by a hawk, killed by somebody's dog (maybe even your own), or afflicted by parasites. You may have to lose a few to find out just what the perils and limits to practical freedom are in your particular environment. You also have to consider the neighbors, because free-roaming chickens do not observe property lines.

DOGS: Dogs often are allowed to run loose at night, and sometimes they form packs that will chase and even bring down fairly large animals. If you see this happen or catch an offender in your trap, you have legal recourse and should use it, because it is never right for someone else's animal to hassle or destroy your property—which includes your animals. A Havahart trap will capture, without injuring, 4-footed night prowlers, including somebody's pet. You can order one from Rocky Top (865-882-8867; **www.rockytopgen.com**).

After the capture or identification, the next step is to tell the animal's owner what happened. The owner should agree to control the pet in the future and offer to repay your losses. You bill him/her a just amount, the owner pays, and it's done. If the owner will not cooperate, or if you do not know the owner, call the local animal control officer. Of course, if your animal causes damage to your neighbor, then you also have to do the right thing. It works both ways!

Dynah Geissal, homesteader and country-topics writer, suggests, "If at all possible, raise your dogs in contact with your livestock. You certainly don't want to have to worry about your own dogs harming your animals. Unless you know for certain that your neighbor's dog is good with livestock, do not allow it near your animals. Call or visit your neighbor immediately and make it clear that you will not tolerate their dogs on your property. Every livestock owner understands this.

"The trouble usually comes from people who think they can let their dogs run loose because they live in the country.

"The best defense against feral dogs and coyotes is a dog of your own. I'm talking about a farm dog, not a dog that spends its time in the house. It should be a dog that willingly and naturally protects your livestock. With a good dog on guard, a predator will usually look for easier pickings. (I have a Great Pyrenees and they are tops.) A gun is a last, but sometimes necessary, resort."

BARNS AND FENCES

Do a bunch of thinking before you start building. The design needs to be just right for the purposes it will serve.

Building a Barn

Homestead writer Don Fallick said, "Truthfully, most livestock need little protection from the elements, except for the wind and direct sunlight. They will need more feed in cold weather, though, if poorly sheltered. Of the many considerations involved in planning a barn, two of the most important, and most often neglected by novices, are animal control and manure handling. If you design your barn right, your animals will go just where you want them to, with very little effort on your part. Do it 'wrong' and you'll be fighting your livestock several times every day. This can range from inconvenient, with goats, to hilarious, with chickens. With cattle and horses, which are bigger than you, it can be downright dangerous." Wise words!

MORE INFO: For building animal shelters, I recommend *Building Small Barns, Sheds and Shelters* by Monte Burch, *Practical Pole Building Construction* by Leigh Seddon, and *Build It Better Yourself* (Rodale Press, 1977). Ashland Barns offers 100+ barn plans . . . stables, garages, workshops, homes, country styled. Also, weather vanes and signs: 541-488-1541; 990 Butler Creek Rd., Ashland, OR 97520; **www.ashlandbarns.com.**

SITING: Where will you build your barn? You want a

place where water won't be running into it and where there's good drainage. Allow for unusually heavy rains. Make it strong enough to withstand the amount of snowfall you typically—and might atypically—get. Make it able to stay dry even when all that snow is melting in an off-season warm wind. Site where it will be easy to bring water and power to it. Don: "I know people who've been milking cows for 30 years in a barn with neither electricity nor running water. It can be done, and done well. But there will be times when you really wish for good, strong light or plenty of running water."

BUILDING MATERIALS: My friend Stephen Scott and I are firm believers in recycling where possible. He said, "Many times you will be able to pick up building materials where you work. A lot of people won't bother with 5-foot 2 × 4s or ones of any length that are sawn. Talk to the people who work in the shipping and receiving areas. Many times junk lumber will be thrown back in trucks or rail cars. Usually people will save some of it for you for the price of a cup of coffee. If this is not your situation, you can buy new lumber as a last resort. Think about places in your area where you may be able to get some construction material for free."

FLOORING MATERIALS: Your barn will likely have a concrete, wood, or dirt floor. Each has pros and cons.

Concrete. Don: "Horse stables should *not* have concrete floors, even though this would make manure handling much easier. Impervious concrete keeps the urine trapped in the bedding and can cause hoof problems, even if the bedding is changed daily. One solution to this problem is to use sand for the floor. The sand soaks up the urine in the top inch or so, which can be shoveled out and replaced as needed, like cat litter. Eventually, it all needs to be removed and replaced, though, and this can be a very big job."

Wood. Don: "A more traditional solution is to make floors of wood, 3 or 4 inches thick. This allows for raking as well as shoveling of the bedding, which is placed on top of the wooden floor. The problem with wooden floors is that they, too, eventually need to be replaced, which can be quite expensive."

Dirt. Don: "The cheapest solution, and the least satisfactory from the standpoint of hygiene, is bedding directly on an earthen floor. The earth gets compacted by the horse walking on it and becomes as hard as concrete. It turns to mud where the horse has scraped away bedding material, which horses all do. It catches pitchfork tines and shovels nearly as much as wood, and needs to be removed periodically like sand, but must be broken up with a pick before it can be shoveled out. It makes for very heavy compost, which can be a real pain if you are handling manure without benefit of a tractor. But it's literally dirt-cheap, and horses like it. Whichever method you decide to use, plan your barn so the flooring is easy to replace and level with the rest of the barn."

DESIGN: Don: "If you are going to keep several kinds of stock in the same barn, it is not necessary to design a special room just for each species. The same room that serves as a lambing pen in the spring can be used for raising goat kids or foals. The important feature of a properly designed barn is that every room opens onto a common hall, with doors or gates big enough to completely block the hall when opened outward. This makes it easy to separate species by driving the whole herd down the hall and simply opening and closing gates to make each critter go where it's supposed to go. Then you can separate animals by species, even separate kids and calves from their mothers, without having to drag them or entice them with grain or treats.

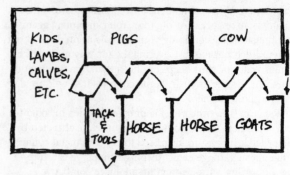

"For example, suppose you have a horse, a cow, and a few goats. The dominant animal, usually the horse, will go into the barn first, followed, perhaps, by the goats and the cow. You open the door to the horse stall so it blocks the hall, and beyond it, you open the gate to the goat pen. Then you open the main barn door at the end of the hall, and all the animals enter in order. Close the barn door before the cow enters. The horse will go right into its stall. Close the horse stall door, and the goats have nowhere else to go but into their pen. You can open the cow pen gate and the main barn door and drive the cow right into its stall."

For Goats. Don: "The same principle applies when building a milk parlor for goats. To eliminate the hassle of trying to get only 1 goat at a time into the parlor, build it with 2 doors—one for the goats to enter the parlor by and another for them to leave by. These work best if they are goat-sized, in which case you'll need another, larger door for you. The entrance door opens in while the exit door opens out, and both lock from the inside. With a setup like this, it's easy to train the goats to come into the parlor one at a time and leave after they've been milked, especially if you feed them grain while milking and "free choice" hay afterward. The principle remains the same: allow the animal nowhere to go but where you want it to go, and you won't have to 'convince' it every time."

For Horses. Don: "Horses present special problems for the barn builder. They're as big and heavy as cattle, they kick things, and they frequently 'crib,' or chew on wood. Any horse barn or stall simply must be built of pieces of lumber no smaller than 2 × 8, as high as the horse can kick. All boards used as dividers should be screwed to their posts, not because nails won't hold (they will) but because this makes it easier to remove and replace the pieces of the old boards after the horse breaks them. Stall walls should be planned with large, long-span horizontal boards to minimize the number of nails and screws, for two reasons: horses will crib around the nails and may hurt their tongues, lips, and teeth; and long boards are more flexible and therefore more durable around horses than short boards. Replacing bedding for even one entirely confined horse every day can quickly become a real chore if the barn is not arranged to make this easy. If you design a door from the stable directly to the yard, the bedding can be forked out of the stable and out of the barn in one operation.

"Some people who have never kept horses might think it would be cheaper to run horizontal stringers at the top and bottom of the wall, and maybe even in the center, than screw vertical boards to the stringers. This is false economy, because it places the bottoms of the vertical boards where they are subject to rotting from the wet bedding. And you dare not use pressure-treated lumber in a stall, where the horse may be inclined to crib on it. It also places the center stringer right where a horse that is inclined to crib can best reach it."

For Cattle: Loafing Sheds. Don: "In many parts of the country, including the mountains of Colorado and the upper Midwest, it's quite common for cattle to sleep in three-sided, concrete-floored 'loafing sheds' and enter a barn only to be milked. The manure is scraped out by a tractor with a blade on the front or back; it is pushed into piles to compost or loaded directly into manure spreaders. In the milk parlor, the cow stalls are arranged so any manure or urine released during milking can be hosed easily into a manure channel and then out of the barn. I have even seen horses kept in loafing sheds quite successfully. Sheep are rarely kept in anything more substantial, except around lambing season. Goats and pigs need more protection although, in warmer climates, goats too can sleep in a loafing shed."

Design for Feed Handling. Don: "After handling of the stock themselves, the most important aspect of a barn to the animal keeper is ease of handling feed and manure. In the Midwest, most barns are built with an earthen ramp leading up to the hay mow, usually in the center of the barn. This makes it easy to back a truck up to the haymow and unload hay and other feeds, which can be pitched down to the animals on the lower story as needed. Often feeders are arranged so grain can also be fed directly from the hay mow. Similar patterns of barns can be found all over the country."

Feed Storage. Store hay up off the ground and with a roof, tarp, or plastic sheet to cover it. Openly available grain feeds attract rats and mice and can result in foundering. Most barns are designed with a separate room for feed storage. Inside that, make your storage containers or areas as rodent-proof as possible. Good possibilities are *food-grade* plastic cans or buckets, or metal drums that have never held poisons. And they must all have lids! Lacking a true lid, you can make do with a piece of flat, sturdy wood held down with a big rock.

You can also protect your stored livestock feed by making the habitat uninviting for rodents. Carefully clean up any spilled feed. Piles of lumber and junk are favorite nesting places for rodents, so try to keep those cleaned up and off the ground. Similarly, if your chicken houses, etc., are constructed up above the ground, you'll eliminate the dark, moist, sheltered spaces under them that rats enjoy. And a couple of big, tough mouser/ratter cats will help too. You can also set traps.

Design for Manure Handling. Every animal creates manure, and all their manure has to be dealt with regularly. How will you get the manure out? If you're working by hand, plan for a downhill run from the barn to the compost pile. Don: "It's okay to carry it uphill to the garden. Composted manure is *much* lighter than fresh, wet manure. Your best manure-handling system depends on the species of livestock, your method, and your intended use of it. Cattle produce copious amounts of manure, which is sloppy and must be shoveled, hosed, or scraped away frequently.

Horses produce drier manure but equally large amounts of urine, which must also be frequently dealt with. Goats and sheep produce small amounts of very dirty dry manure, which can be left to accumulate for a long time if they have sufficient clean bedding to sleep on. Pigs are very clean animals and will not drop manure in their bed area if there is room for them to walk 12 feet away from it upon arising."

See "Manure" in Chapter 2 for more!

Fencing

A basic fencing principle is to get it right the first time. Be sure and put the fence exactly on the line if you and your neighbors (talk to them first!) agree on where that is. They may even be willing to share costs or labor. Otherwise, put the fence at least a foot inside your boundary to save a legal hassle. Find out if there are any county restrictions on fences, such as setback rules or height limits. Make the fence strong enough. If animals get the idea that they can go through a fence, they're that much harder to keep in. In fact, once they've tested a fence and won, they're likely to ram their way through a fence that otherwise would have held them. Another basic principle is that the type of fence has to be tailored for the type of animal.

Don wrote me, "Fences can be used to fence animals in or out, to cross-fence pasture, to define spaces, for ornamental purposes, or even to use up rocks in a field. Construction of fences depends on their purpose and on the materials available. Common materials are barbed wire, woven wire, welded wire, electric wire, rails, slabs, milled lumber, stone, and combinations thereof. The overwhelming factor in deciding what type of stock fencing to build is the type of livestock to be fenced in or out. Cattle require very strong fences. Deer and goats need high fences; pigs and sheep, very tight ones. The old-timer's adage about building all fences 'horse-high, bull-strong, and pig-tight' applies only if you don't know what you're going to be keeping behind it, or if you have an unlimited source of labor and materials. It's far cheaper to build a 4-foot tall, 4-strand barbed wire fence for horses, a 4-foot high, 3-strand fence for cattle, a solid wood fence for goats, and a pen of welded "hog panels" for pigs, for example, than to try to build one fence that will do for all of them."

Here's the rebuttal from William F. McCamman, president of New Zealand Fence Systems, a guy who sells fencing for a living. He makes a good point and wants you to always have the best (though he isn't giving any away). "That paragraph advocates building a fence for only the animals you know you will have rather than the full range you might expect. It is very expensive and laborious to raise a fence height later. A dime saved now might well cost a dollar later. Using barbed wire for horses is very short-term economy until the veterinary bills start accumulating. Fence designs vary due to topography, animal characteristics, pressure on the animal, consequences of failure, and the owner's mental satisfaction."

FENCING BOOKS: For specific info on fencing for chickens, turkeys, goats, pigs, etc., see this book's sections about those animals. The latest and possibly greatest fencing book is *Fences for Pasture and Garden* by Gail Damerow (Garden Way, 1992), especially useful for goat people. Or see John Vivian's *Building Fences from Wood, Stone, Metal, and Living Plants* for complete how-to on every imaginable type of fence and hundreds of drawings and photos; *Build It Better*

Yourself, edited by W.H. Hylton; G.A. Martin's *Fences, Gates and Bridges*; S. Schuler's *How to Build Fences, Gates; Walls, Fences, Gates and Walls* by Chamberlin and Pollock; *How to Build Fences and Gates* by D.W. Vandervort; *How to Plan and Build Fences and Gates,* edited by by J. Barrett and D. Rutherford; *Fences and Gates, Walkways, Walls and Drives* by E. A. Proulx; and J. Russell's *Walks, Walls and Fences.* Pennsylvania State U., College of Agriculture, Cooperative Extension Service, University Park, PA 16802, offers *Smooth-Wire Tension Fencing—Design and Construction* by Mark Mummert, et al., which gives info on design and building of New Zealand-type fencing. The Small Ruminant Page at www.sheepandgoat.com/fencing.htm contains many links to publications on fencing, as well as to many fencing vendors.

FENCING PRODUCTS AND SPECIALISTS

Kencove Farm Fence, 344 Kendall Rd., Blairsville, PA 15717; 724-459-8991; 800-536-2683; **www.kencove.com; farmfence@kencove.com.**

Max-Flex Fence Systems: U.S. Rt. 219, Lindside, WV 24951; 305-852-2465; fax 305-852-0889; **sears@maxflex.com; www.maxflex.com.**

Premier Fencing: 319-653-6631; 800-282-6631; 2031-300th St., Washington, IA 52353; **www.premier1fence.com.**

Southwest Power Fence & Livestock Equipment specializes in electric fence systems and solar-powered automatic gate technology: 800-221-0178; 830-438-4600; fax 830-438-4604; 26321 Hwy. 281 N., San Antonio, TX 78260; **www.swpowerfence.com.**

ABOUT ELECTRIC FENCES: Don: "If you have 15 or 20 acres of rich grass per cow, almost any kind of fence will do for cattle, as long as it's stout and strong, 4 feet high, and visible to the cattle." (Note: Don lives in the eastern Washington desert. Lane Morgan, who lives in the rainy Pacific Northwest coastal zone, says, "We have an acre per cow. That's plenty around here.") Don: "Most ranchers who keep cattle have found that electric fences work best. Cattle quickly learn to respect the fence, especially if rags are tied to it every 10 feet, so they can see it. Cattle don't have very good eyesight, but after a few shocks, they'll learn to avoid the area. It's not a good idea to depend entirely on the live wire, though. If the juice is off for some reason, or a cow or bull breaks the wire, there will be nothing to restrain your animals from going wherever they please. It's amazing how much damage even 1 cow can do in a very short time. Three or four strands of barbed wire strung with the electric wire can prevent a lot of grief. Use wooden posts set 8 feet apart, with the electric strand set about 3½ feet high, between the top 2 strands of barbed wire. Many ranchers build 2 fences—an electric fence set about 2 feet inside a stout barbed-wire fence. There are different kinds of electric fences and fence chargers, even solar-powered ones that require no electric hookup.

"'New Zealand' fence chargers seem to be getting more popular. They give a stronger shock than the traditional kind—too strong, some folks believe. I've never heard of one killing a cow, but I have seen one kill a mule deer. My personal feelings are that anything that can kill a large deer is not safe to have around dogs or children." Lane Morgan adds, "New Zealand fencing has been very big around here in recent years, especially for horses, but lately I've been hearing about some problems. This is a windy area, and it turns out the tape shreds in the wind and shorts the fence. The shorts are very difficult to locate since the tape may still look intact."

For specific instructions on building and testing an electric fence, see Chapter 11.

WIRE FENCING—BARBED AND WOVEN: Don: "If you are not going to use electricity, you'll do your cows a favor by using 9-gauge woven wire fencing. Cows sometimes develop the habit of scratching themselves on fence posts, and barbed wire can tear up their udders. It has even been known to entangle and kill horses. Woven fence with 12-inch wide rectangles is fine for cattle and horses but *not* for goats or sheep. They'll get their heads stuck in the fence. Sheep are so dumb they may not think of pulling their heads back out, and they can starve to death! Goats will chew on the wire until it breaks and pokes holes in their cheeks. The experts recommend 6-inch mesh for goats and sheep."

POSTS: Don: "Posts of cattle fence absolutely must be the strongest you can afford. If you are using metal posts, use only the heavy-duty kind. They can be driven into most soils with a driver made by cutting the end off a truck drive shaft. The hollow shaft fits over the post, to be lifted up and slammed down repeatedly until the post is driven. Round wooden posts are not generally suitable for cattle. They are usually made from small-diameter trees, which have a high percentage of the soft heartwood. Use splits or other hard posts. Quartered sections of old telephone poles make adequate fence posts, though they have to be replaced after a few years.

"Just how long such posts will last depends mostly on how moist the ground is. In fairly dry soil, an untreated softwood post may last 3 to 5 years. The strongest wooden posts are triangular sections split from large diameter trees. Osage orange, black locust, catalpa, northern white cedar and red cedar will all last 20 years or more in average soil. In general, the softer the wood, the shorter the time it will last. Pressure-treated wooden fence posts, available in lumber yards or farm supply stores, cost about as much as metal posts but don't last as long. They look nicer, though."

Making Fence Posts. A "wedge" is a piece of metal shaped like an ax blade, flat on top—like a single-bladed ax head with no handle. Wedges are sharpened a little bit but not too much, because they tend to get stuck if they're too sharp. You need at least 2 wedges to make fence posts ("splitting rails"). Cedar is the most popular wood to make wedges from because it is wonderfully easy to split and is slow to rot. Cedar is a nice wood in general; it has a good smell and a pretty appearance.

Pick a point on the side of the pole, up toward the "top." Try to make that point a natural crack if there is one; there usually is in old wood. Tap the wedge in. Then drive it in with a sledgehammer as far as it will go. Take a second wedge and start driving it in where your pole still isn't split apart farther down the line. That will loosen up the first wedge and put it at the farthest point of the split from the second wedge (you're working your way from the top down). Keep going this way until you've finished splitting it.

Another way to get fence posts is to start by felling the tree; long, straight pines are good. You want regular posts to be about 3 or 4 inches across, so that's what the diameter of your tree should be, because trees other than cedars don't split well. After felling, cut them across to be the length you want. For uprights, the length should be how high you want your fence to be plus how deep you want it to go in the ground. Corner posts need to be really husky: more than 4 inches in diameter is good. The poles to lay lengthwise can be longer.

Now you want to skin your pole. You smooth off all the knots and then strip away the bark. A flat-headed shovel is a good bark stripper. Hardwood doesn't need a preservative treatment, but softwood does. That's to keep bugs from lunching on it until your fence collapses in a heap of dust. So soak those poles for 2 months in a vat of used motor oil, and they'll last longer than you will. If you haven't got that kind of time, soak them in a mixture of pentachlorophenol and oil for a couple of days. If you have neither the time nor the money, use red fir, cedar, or black pine because they are the most rot-resistant. You'd get 15 years out of an untreated cedar post around here—less in a more southern or wetter climate. It also depends on soil acidities, and that gets complex.

STRETCHING WIRE: Back to Don: "Wires can be stretched tight with a ratchet fence stretcher, available at farm and ranch supply stores, or even by tying or chaining them to a tractor or pickup truck. The idea is to grab onto the wire several inches before it reaches the corner post, so there will be enough slack wire to wrap around the post and twist around the tightened wire. Then go back and staple the wire loosely at each intermediate post. This supports the wire while allowing for future stretching and retightening.

"Woven wire fences can be stretched the same way, but you may need to use a couple of fence stretchers together. One way is to wrap the end of the fence around a board or short post and then pull the post with fence stretchers, tractor, etc. After stapling the fence to the corner post, the horizontal wires of the excess fence can be cut free with pliers and wrapped around the post and themselves. Fence pliers are very handy for dealing with wire fencing, but very heavy wire cutters and a couple of claw hammers make an adequate substitute."

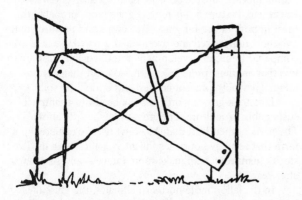

Bracing and Corner Posts. Don: "Wire fences for horses and goats need wooden rails at the top, or the animals will break them down and just walk over them. And any kind of wire fence needs special bracing at the corner posts. These should be the stoutest posts you can get. Used railroad ties in good condition make good corner posts. They are treated against rot and can be purchased for $5-10. Stout as they are, they still need bracing. One way to do this is to brace the corner post on the diagonal, with a short post notched into the top of the corner post. The other end of the brace can rest on a flat rock on the ground. A variation of this, which I think is stronger, is to place the first line post 4 to 6

feet away from the corner post and notch the bottom of the diagonal brace into the line post near the ground. A double strand of wire is then wrapped around the top of the line post and the bottom of the corner post. A stick is thrust between the two strands, twisted tight, and secured. Protect the tops of corner posts from rain and snow by tacking sheet metal flashing over the ends, or at least cut them at an angle, so water will run off."

Wire Fence Upkeep. Don: "Since cattle like to rub against fence posts, the posts must be checked regularly and replaced when needed. A broken post can be jerked out of the ground by tying or chaining it to a horizontal post, which can then be used as a lever. Sagging wires can be tightened temporarily by crimping them into a zigzag with the claws of a hammer. Two framing hammers can be used to permanently tighten a strand of barbed wire. Hook the claws of one hammer over the line at one of the barbs, and use the handle as a lever to pull the wire tight, just like pulling a nail. While holding the wire tight with one hammer, use the other to pull the free end around the post and wrap it around the tightened strand."

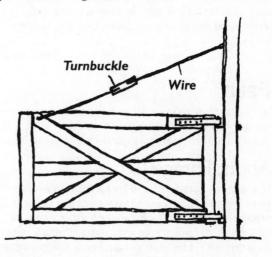

GATES: Don: "The simplest gate for a wire fence is one made as a freestanding panel of wire, secured to the gateposts with removable loops of wire. The gate can be stretched to a reasonable degree by making it just a bit too short to reach. The bottom of the gate endpost can still be hooked in the bottom wire loop by leaning the endpost at an angle. The top of the endpost can be pried toward the gatepost with a short stick and attached to the gatepost with a short length of wire. Even the shortest wooden gate is too heavy for normal hinges. The best kind of hinge for wooden gates is the kind that has a single metal loop on the gate and an L-shaped hinge pin that screws into the wooden gatepost. It'll last forever, and you can easily compensate for sagging gates by lifting the gate off and screwing the pins in or out. Metal gates are light and strong, last forever, are readily available in many sizes, and cost plenty. You get what you pay for."

WOODEN FENCES: Don: "Nothing beats wooden fences for keeping horses or goats. For horses, you need three or four 2 × 6 rails, equally spaced, with the top of the top rail 4 to 5 feet high, depending on the height of the horse. The top rail should be capped by a 2 × 8 rail laid horizontally, for strength. The horses *will* lean on it. Posts should be 8 inches in diameter or 6 × 6 square stock, every 8 feet. If you're going to spend this kind of money on a wooden fence, it's silly not to buy pressure-treated posts and top rails. They'll have to weather for a year before you can paint them, though.

"That's the ideal fence for horses, but few horse owners can afford that kind of expense. Peeled poles 3 to 6 inches in diameter will do fine for fence rails, if they are inspected often. Lumber mills sometimes sell 'slabs' (the outside portion of the tree, with the bark still on) really cheap. They look 'rustic' and may be plenty strong. Watch for thin spots, though. Trees work really well as fence posts. Nail the rails to the inside side of the post or tree with 20d nylon-coated sinker nails."

STONE WALLS: Don: "Much of rural New England is divided up into picturesque fields surrounded by stone walls. The walls, for the most part, began simply as something to do with the stones that constantly surfaced in the fields. The farmers had to haul them to the edge of the fields anyway, and building walls there served as a boundary and used up the rocks without having to cart them further. If you are cursed with such a field, you might adopt the same plan for dealing with the stones. I can't honestly recommend any other good reason for building stone fences."

For more on stone fences, see "Fencing" in Chapter 8.

FEED

You'll either buy your animal feed or grow it. You can feed animals with live food that's growing in the field, such as pasture, or feed them from stored food such as hay and grain.

About Forage Crops

You can grow forage crops to feed animals in northern zones where you can't grow many fruits and vegetables. In practice, that means it's natural to eat a diet largely based on milk and meat (which your animals manufacture from the grass they eat) in the cold-climate places, where you can't grow enough vegetable-type foods to keep you going. Cheat grass, which grows on rocky hillsides (and is thus useless for vegetable gardening), is that sort of forage crop; there are much better ones. But cows can eat cheat grass in the spring and get fat. (Goats get abscesses from it, though.)

A reader named Tom asked me if any special feed or type of pasture was necessary for animals. The feed question is really complex. I've tackled it in the section on each animal in this book. For the most chemical-free food possible, the best economy, and a good feeling of self-reliance and the adventure of it all, it's nice if you can raise as much of your own animal feed as possible (as long as you have unpolluted ground on which to do so). The old-timers raised food for their livestock as well as their kitchen, and so can you, although some feed companies do their dangdest to discourage you from doing so, for obvious reasons. Animals raised on home-grown feed typically gain weight a little more slowly and give fewer eggs and less milk. This doesn't mean you're an abusive owner. It means you aren't pushing production to the max as a factory farmer would. The value you gain in self-sufficiency, reduction in cost, and healthiness of your product can more than outweigh that extra production.

For more info on forage crops, see Richard Langer's *Grow It!* (1973) and D.A. Miller's *Forage Crops* (1984).

VEGETABLE FEEDS: The old-timers extended the forage season in pasture by planting special crops that the animals would harvest themselves in the fall, when the grass started dying back, or that the farmers could feed to confined animals during the winter. In fact, the following foods, together with hay, were generally used where grain is now used in animals' winter diet: sugar and mangle beets (the mangle, or "mangle wurzel," also known as the "stock beet," is a very large, nourishing beet), marrowstem kale, thousand-headed kale, turnip, rutabaga, carrot, forage radish, Swiss chard, Jerusalem artichoke, comfrey, beets, kohlrabi, and parsnips. These should be fed in combination with hay.

If root vegetables are to be your animals' basic winter feed, plan to supply about 40 lb. per day to a milking cow, 3–4 lb. per day to a sheep. But the best diet is a combination of various vegetables and hay, since too much of one thing in the vegetable line, especially beets, can be bad for animals—even make them sick. Horses winter better on carrots than on beets, and most animals do better on turnips, carrots, etc., than on beets. You can feed root vegetables whole to pigs (though they like them best cut and cooked), but you should cut them into pieces (or even grate or pulp them) for other animals. Fresh beets tend to cause diarrhea, so store your crop at least 4 weeks before feeding and then ease into this diet. Never feed moldy or partly decayed roots!

ABOUT RUMINANTS: Of the common domestic animals, the cow, sheep, and goat are "ruminants." A ruminant is specially adapted to eat much food quickly and then go elsewhere to digest it. And it is an animal inside an animal, because it digests food in a private fermentation vat where microscopic beasties transform the food so that the ruminant can digest the cellulose. Every ruminant is alive because it's in lifelong symbiosis with the tiny digesters in its rumen.

Pasture

Ruminants are capable of being nourished by grasses, leaves, etc. Pasture is a perennial grass crop, probably the most important use for grass. Tree crops and pasture are the two most underrated and overlooked ways to use land. Yet, compared to urban development and tilled soil, they are the two that are most protective of the soil and the environment. They both prevent erosion and enrich the soil.

Livestock growing on grass is a beautiful example of sustainable agriculture. The grass nourishes the animals. The parts of their feed that they can't use are excreted in a form that actually nourishes the grass, which uses the livestock's manure to help make more forage—and so on, year after year.

In the fall in more northern climates, the grass dies back and, during the months of winter, hay has to be fed. When spring comes, the grass grows again, the hay-feeding season ends, and the grazers can feast on that green stuff and get fat. But every pasture is different, and some are worse than others. Making a good pasture from a bad one or even from bare ground takes some effort. And it takes good management to maintain a proper animal/grass balance in order to avoid overgrazing and thus causing holes in that protective grass cover.

GRASS MAGAZINES & BOOKS: Here's the competition to factory farming techniques! *Graze* is a monthly publication with articles from and about graziers on pastured dairy, beef, sheep, hogs, and poultry. Subscription is $30/yr; $54 for 2 yrs. Free sample: 608-455-3311; fax 608-455-2402; PO Box 48, Belleville, WI 53508; **graze@mhtc.net.** Another magazine focused on pasturing is *The Stockman Grass Farmer,* a monthly devoted to the art and science of turning grass into cash. It costs $28/yr; $50 for 2 yrs. To subscribe, or for a free sample, contact: 800-748-9808; 282 Commerce Park Dr., Ridgeland, MS 39158; **sgfsample@aol.com; www.stockmangrassfarmer.com.** They also sell great books with titles like *Pa$ture Profit$ with Stocker Cattle; Grass Farmers; Quality Pasture: How to Create It, Manage It, and Profit from It;* and *Paddock Shift: Changing Views on Grassland Farming.* Those are all by Allan Nation, founder (1975) and guiding hand at *The Stockman Grass Farmer.*

Other good grass books are Rebecca Lewis's *Making Pastures Produce* (Rodale Press, 1980); *Grass Productivity,* by Andre Voison (1988); *Why Grassfed Is Best!* by Jo Robinson (206-463-4156; **www.eatwild.com/**); and *Holistic Resource Management,* by Alan Savory. David Schafer's new book, *Just the Greatest Life,* is available from him at 760 SW 55th Ave., Jamesport, MO 64648; **sales@schaferfarmsnaturalmeats.com; www.schaferfarmsnaturalmeats.com/.** (He also sells natural beef, lamb, chicken, and pork.)

American Farmland Trust provides info on grass-based farming systems plus many links at **www.grassfarmer.com.** The American Forage and Grassland Council offers info at 800-944-2342; **www.afgc.org.** Another website with extensive info on raising animals on pasture is **www.Eatwild.com.** Their site includes a state-by-state directory of pasture-based farms so you can buy meat, eggs, butter, or cheese from pastured animals just a pleasant country drive away! ATTRA's look at "Nutrient Cycling in Pastures" is at **www.attra.ncat.org/attra-pub/nutrientcycling.html.**

SEEDING PASTURE: If there's nothing left out there but brush and weeds, plow it up and replant to a good pasture mix of grains, grasses, and legumes. If there's something there but not enough, or if your land is hilly, don't plow it up to plant; just add new growth. To do that, plant in early spring, when the most bare ground is exposed. Go over it with a shallow-set disk and then broadcast seed, use a no-till drill, or just toss the seed out there in the spring, when raindrops have already softened the ground and future rain will splash soil over the seed to cover it.

Pasture Seed Mixes. The most nourishing pasture should include legumes (clover, alfalfa, lespedeza) because grasses don't provide as much protein and sugars for the animals. Pasture needs a soil pH of 6.5–7.0 and some nitrogen to thrive. Usually folks plant a mixture: a few grasses, a few legumes. Usually a few kinds of weeds are in there too, and that can be a good thing, since the more kinds of plants in your pasture, as long as they aren't poisonous, the better balanced in vitamins and minerals your animals' diet will be. It is possible to seed in some additional desirable plants for a pasture without actually tearing up and reseeding the entire thing.

Choose very hardy plants that are well suited to your area's soil and climate conditions. Drive around and look for a beautiful pasture. Then ask the owner what's in it. It'll probably have some grasses and some legumes (clovers). Bird's foot trefoil is a good combo livestock pasture plant and ground cover because animals can graze it to the bottom, but it always comes back. Good legumes are vetch, sainfoin, peas, trefoil, alfalfa, and the clovers—red clover, white Dutch clover, yellow sweet clover, and subterranean clover (or "subclover"). Legumes, of course, build up the soil at the same time as they provide protein-rich food for the animals. Some farmers rotate periodically between grass and legumes, plowing up grass and planting legumes every 3 to 5 years for a hay crop or green manure, and then returning to a grass mix meant for years of pasturing. But Luane prefers a closely managed permanent pasture for economy and topsoil retention.

OF WATER AND PASTURE: This last spring we planted 50 acres to a combination of peas and oats. We mixed the pea and oat seed and planted it together. We were raising the mixture to be winter feed for the cows and chickens. Well, there was a terrible drought, and most of it never germinated. In August we were having to feed our cows hay to keep them alive because there was no grass. It literally didn't rain one drop all summer. The price of hay shot up from the normal $45 per ton to $80 and more per ton. When the rains came at last, in the fall, the field finally turned green. The seed hadn't died; it had just waited. But December is no time to make hay. You have to get your forage planted before the good spring rains have stopped coming and hope there will be enough summer rains to finish the job. Or irrigate.

HARVESTING PASTURE: Grass needs to be mowed occasionally for best health, but your grass-eating animals will accomplish that without any effort on your part. They'll also fertilize the pasture for you. Ideal pasture harvesting is done consciously and carefully: it's a planned, intensive grazing that maximizes your crop's forage-producing ability. Grass is the cheapest feed for animals that can live on it. Making the most of your grass as feed can mean the difference between an operation that goes broke and one that makes a profit. Expert grass farmers use controlled rotational grazing, which means they have their grassland divided into smaller paddocks of as little as 1½–3 acres, usually by electric fencing. Stock growers using rotational grazing keep a close eye on the grass height and frequently change their stock from one paddock to another as often as every day. (This also reduces or eliminates having to search for lost animals.) An experienced animal owner can pretty much look at the grass in a paddock and know how long and how well it's going to feed the animals. Move the animals after the grass is eaten but before it is overgrazed and its comeback ability is damaged.

NOTE: Pasture plants are most nourishing for the animal when they're fresh and green. That means spring pasture—or pasture that hasn't been grazed for a while, has gotten water, and has had a chance to renew itself.

Regular shifting of animals plus a relatively short grazing period maximizes the ability of grass to come back and make more. Grass needs to be left alone to grow for at least a month after having been grazed down. This is time enough for the root system to recover its health and be able to store enough food to be able to grow back quickly from yet another livestock feeding. Grass with healthy roots grows, on the average, ⅛ inch per day. But if you let the animals keep it too short, the roots lose their recovery ability and can't manage that maximum rate of growth any more. As a stock grower, that costs you money because then your land is no longer producing the maximum amount of forage, and your animals can put on only as much weight as

the amount of food they can get.

The number of animals has to be suited to the amount of grass. In a drought, you'll have to sell some grass eaters, because your pasture won't be able to feed as many as usual.

Another way to get the most from your pasture grass is to use more than one tier of grass eaters: use animals that clip it closer to follow animals that eat just the top. But don't let the grass get eaten down so close that its ability to recover is harmed. A third method is to keep the animals out foraging in the pasture as late in the year as possible before resorting to hay feeding. It might surprise you how long the grass and animals can keep each other going.

Pasturing Green Hay. Alfalfa is even better pasture for cows than grass if you can spare it for them. But don't start animals on alfalfa if they aren't used to it; they'll bloat. Wet alfalfa is the most dangerous of all! We've got that situation now: a whole field of wet—soaking wet for 3 weeks—alfalfa with a layer of bleached hay on top of it. My husband Mike says we'll just give up and turn the animals in there. But they aren't used to alfalfa—to say nothing of wet alfalfa. So first we must wait until it dries off. And then we'll let them in there for an hour, and for a couple of hours the next day, and so on until they get used to it. And we'll buy hay from somebody who had better luck with this winter's feed. If very many people had the kind of weather we did in haying time, the price of hay will be up this fall!

Hay

"Hay" means a harvest of grasses (carbonaceous hay) or legumes—such as alfalfa, clover, or peas. Hay is dried plant food, preserved to serve as a winter food supply for herbivores.

WINTER FEEDING: To winter an animal, you'll need a certain amount of food stored: the kind of food that's right for each animal, or a combination of such foods, and enough of it. For grass-eaters, "winter" means the number of days that the ground is covered with snow or that, for some other reason, there is no grass. But a summer drought may dry up all the grass and have you feeding hay in summer too, long before the snow comes. Or your pasture may be too small to supply enough grass for the number of animals you have. In that case, you'll have to supplement with hay even in summer.

HAY PLANTS: Plants are grown specifically to be cut and dried for hay. Red and white clover and timothy (both brought over by pioneers from Europe) were old-time hay crops. Those are still valuable, but now there are other good hay species. The best hay is green, with leaves on the stems. This green, leafy hay is great feed for any herbivore. Just what you grow (or buy) for hay depends . . . Here are some possibilities.

Legume Hay. Best-quality legume hay is 12–14 percent protein. Possible plants to grow for legume hay are alfalfa, clover, lespedeza, peas, and vetch. The pioneers planted hay by scattering hay chaff as well as barn and haymow sweepings. Now you plant it by buying seed. You plant red clover or sweet clover at 10 lb. per acre. Weight per bushel of both is 60 lb. Ladino clover and white clover are planted at 2 lb. per acre but also weigh 60 lb. per bushel. But the most popular legume hay of all is alfalfa.

You don't need a big farm to grow good, high-protein alfalfa hay for your animals' winter feed. You can grow clover or alfalfa in your yard, as a garden rotation, or on a couple of spare acres. Just cut and dry well, and store under cover.

Plant alfalfa at 15 lb. per acre; weight per bushel is 60 lb. Here's my friend Stephen Scott on growing alfalfa for part of his pigs' feed: "If you plant a legume, you will be providing your pigs with protein. Protein supplements are the most expensive part of your balanced ration, so if you plant some legumes, you can eliminate the supplements. Alfalfa is a legume—capable of fixing nitrogen from the air. Nitrogen is the critical building block for the production of proteins.

"I have an Esmay seeder that I picked up from a rummage sale for 25 bucks. It is a push-type seed planter. It has an aluminum frame, two plastic wheels, and a little hopper for the seeds. You can get one from most seed catalogues, but they are quite expensive there. If you plant a very big garden it may well be worth the price, as it works well on almost all types of garden seeds.

"I plant alfalfa in early May, after I have worked the ground well. I plant it in rows about 10 inches apart. When it starts to come up, I go between the rows with my old high-wheel cultivator. Alfalfa grows slowly; it would be overwhelmed by the weeds if I didn't cultivate. Just for good measure I go through the patch a few times a year as needed and pull weeds in the rows. If weeds are not a problem in your fence, you can broadcast the alfalfa seed and rake it in with a garden rake. You will need about ½ lb. seed per 1,000 square feet. You can buy small amounts of legume seeds from garden seed catalogs, but you can save money by buying the seed from places that sell whole bags of it to farmers. Usually they will have an open bag from which they will be glad to sell you a couple of pounds. The very best alfalfa seed goes for about 4 bucks a pound from a farm seed store; it will be about twice as much from the seed catalogs.

"I plant alfalfa in the field that the pigs will not be in during the year that I plant it. That is the case because the alfalfa plant will not be established and ready to provide much protein in the first year. It gets itself started and mainly grows the root system that it will need in order to provide grazing in the next year. If you have only 1 field, then alfalfa will not work for you [as a rotation forage crop for pigs]. But you can still harvest to feed to animals."

GRASS HAY: "Carbonaceous" hay means grass—not legume—hay. Native grasses provide good pasture but ordinarily do not grow luxuriantly enough to make good hay for winter feed. They also tend to be low in protein compared to legume hays. The best carbonaceous hay plants are probably bluegrass, oats, sudan grass, timothy—and any grass grain. If fed to animals, these hays always need a grain supplement.

Grain Stubble. You can cut (or pasture) the straw stubble that is left after grain crops are harvested. It can be part of your winter feed for big animals. The straw provides roughage, which they need, but you'll have to supplement it with better feed because straw doesn't have protein, which they also need. If the grain is harvested with the seed heads on, and before the straw is all bleached out, it's a different situation.

Oat and Pea Hay. This is a mixed legume and grass (including grain!) hay. For winter hay we use part alfalfa and part oat and pea hay. We plant a mixture of oat and pea seed and then cut it for hay when it's grown up. It's very nourishing for the animals, and I like it because it has grain right in there for the cows and chickens. This year the chickens got in there and scratched around for their own grain all winter long and did fine. I didn't feed them this winter except for that, and they're giving me 15 eggs a day now, plus the ones being set on. Harvest mixed oats and peas just as the oats start to turn. If you wait longer, the oats will be too ripe and won't make good hay. Peas and oats are good protein, and the pea vines and oat straw are good roughage.

MAKING HAY: There isn't anything complicated to it: you make hay while the sun shines. Hay is just dried grass or other green leafy stuff that is food for animals. But it's really vital to have, because with hay you can keep your cows, goats, sheep, rabbits, horses—and chickens, too, if the hay contains some grain heads—alive through the winter. And the animals will be making milk, meat, and eggs for you during the time when vegetables and fruit don't grow. You can cut any grass for hay; in time of terrible drought, I've seen farmers get out and mow every open field an owner would give them permission to mow, trying to get something together to keep the animals alive through the winter.

Mike and a neighbor may hay all summer. Mike has a baler and Doug has a mower. They get our hay and Doug's, and then put up hay on shares all up and down the valley for people who don't, or can't, do it for themselves. When the hay has grown high enough again, it's time for the second cutting, and they go through all the fields making hay again.

So we've usually had plenty of hay for ourselves, some to sell, and some to trade. With the cost of machinery and everything else nowadays, you just can't afford to own everything yourself for one farm. So neighbors here trade machinery and labor, too. And they don't make a big deal out of what they're going to get out of it. It's more like a giving contest: "I can do more for you than you can do for me." It's a good game that works to the benefit of everybody, but it really baffles some people. They have notions of capital and labor and how they're supposed to be at each other's throats.

I've seen people come out here and be given a job more out of charity than because they were needed and then turn around and act vicious because they thought they got paid 2 dollars less than they should have been. Then they wonder why they couldn't find another job. The bush telegraph is almost as inexorable as credit companies' files for carrying ratings on people's characters. City people are used to anonymity, but that doesn't exist in the country. You are what you are, and everybody knows what you are—for better or for worse.

The important thing with hay making is not to let the hay get rained on. Cut the grass when it is tall, rich-looking, and green, before the stalks have turned real tough, and when no rain is expected. For the very best hay (the kind you can feed your cows and need no grain supplement at all), grow it on a well-manured field, cut legumes when they are beginning to blossom, and cure it as fast as possible.

Mowing. When you know there's a lengthy spell of hot, dry weather coming up and your hay crop is tall enough to be worth cutting, you come through with a scythe (see "Mowing" in Chapter 3 for details) for small amounts of hay or a tractor-driven mower for a big field. Or you can mow hay with a horse-drawn mower. To scythe hay, the old-timers had a special kind of cradle that put the hay in a windrow, which is a long pile of hay for drying. Their scythe was a steel blade mounted on a crooked stick. (Frequently sharpen the blade—that razor edge is important! And get rid of stones in the field so they don't ruin the blade.) In general, to put up more than an acre of hay, you'll be glad for a tractor-driven mower and a rake.

Here at Kendrick, Idaho, on unirrigated land, 2 hay crops is a good year. On irrigated land here in the river valley with plenty of good hot sunshine, I've seen an enterprising farmer down the Potlatch River harvest as many as 5 cuttings of hay off a single field. In irrigated country in California, where they grow hay year-round, they can get 10 crops. It takes both moisture and heat to make hay.

Raking. The cut plants are then left lying right where they have fallen. Or the cut hay can be gathered using a horse-drawn dump rake, which then dumps it in a windrow. Or it can be forked by hand up into piles or rows by hand to dry. It cures in the sunshine until nearly dry. Then you come back and, by hand or by machine-pulled equipment, rake the hay into windrows.

Drying in the Field. You let the hay lie in the sun for a few days until it has dried out (it doesn't have to be all bone-dry). You probably haven't got it safely dry yet if you twist a wisp of hay and it feels tough, if you break a stem and it feels tough, if you break a stem and there is evidence of moisture, or if you can scrape the epidermis off a stem with your fingernail. It is probably cured enough when the hay is acting sort of brittle, and there's no wetness when you twist a stem, and the epidermis doesn't peel off the stem when you scrape it with your fingernail. Then gather it up and get it under cover.

From the time you cut it until the time you can get it under cover, you pray that it won't rain. If it rains all the time, you can't harvest hay. You want rain when the stuff is growing, but when you are ready to harvest, you want sunshine. If you have good hot sunshine, you should be able to get your hay cut and out of the field in 4 days. Then it can rain again, and you'll be glad because that gets your next crop started growing. If you're rich and can afford a swather, you can harvest hay even more quickly. You could swath on a Monday and, if it's hot, you could bale on Wednesday.

The reason I'm moved to make these remarks is because this summer it has rained practically 3 weeks in a row (we normally have hot, dry summers), and our first hay cutting is ruined. If hay is cut and then lies on the ground in the rain (and you can't finish harvesting if it is wet), the rain washes out the color and a significant amount of food value. You'll have to wait again for it to dry out, and it'll take longer this time because it's lying in a mass on the ground. Instead of being nice and green, it then looks yellow like straw. Such hay is called "bleached," and it's no good. Even so, you've got to get it up off the field so the grass can grow back again. If you left it lying there, it would act like a mulch and stifle the plants underneath. So now we've got that bleached hay to get rid of—whenever it dries out enough so we can get into the field and work.

MOVING HAY: The old-timers, after raking hay into windrows and curing it, loaded it with a pitchfork from the windrow into a wagon—literally "pitched" it up there—for moving to an outdoor haystack or indoor storage in the barn's haymow. Then they pitched the hay from the wagon into a big net that hung from a rope on the end of a derrick. Then they turned the derrick around and pitched it from the net into the haymow.

Baling. Baled hay is so much less work to move than loose hay. For a large field, you must consider hiring somebody with a baler to come and bale it. A baler picks up the cured hay from the windrows, presses it into a rectangular block, and ties the block firmly together with wire or twine. Those bales then are dropped in the field. You'll have to come back to pick them up, load them onto something, haul them somewhere, and stack them there. There's a newer type of hay baler that rolls the hay into huge, heavy, round bales that are like mini-haystacks in themselves, each weighing about a ton. The stacks can be left in the field and used as feed right where they lie.

Hay Hooks. These are invaluable at haying time if you're working with 50–100-lb. bales. I've used them on untold hundreds, ever since I was a little girl. You'll soon get the knack of slipping that hook into the bale and lifting the bale wherever you want it, bracing the other end of the bale against your body.

STORING HAY: Gather up your dried loose or baled hay and pile it to make an outdoor haystack, or move it to the haymow of your barn. But be sure it's dry.

Of Damp Hay and Fire. Another reason for wanting your hay dry before you bring it in is that damp hay has a little trick of setting itself (and your barn) on fire by spontaneous combustion in a composting heat-up. Hay has this tendency if it is piled up in storage incompletely cured—that is, too wet. I know it doesn't make any sense that damp hay is more likely to catch on fire than dry hay, but it's true— heavy, leafy legume hays are more likely to do that to you than is grass hay. Stacked hay (or unthreshed grain) makes heat in its early stages of curing.

To get an idea of how hot your stored hay is, push a 4-foot wooden stake deep into the stack but still reachable from outside. Leave for a while. Then suddenly pull it out and feel the inner end of it. That will give you a sense of the temperature.

Bale Storage. For bales out in the open, use sturdy plastic or tarp; tie it firmly down so it doesn't blow away. Unprotected hay is likely to mold. To get the bales off the ground, stack them on crisscrossed boards to allow some air circulation under the bales.

Making a Haystack. Haul the hay from your field to the place where you're going to build your stack. Now create a haystack that is at least 12 feet tall, with a diameter at the base of around 14 feet or more. The general shape is round at the base and as conical as possible at the top. The idea is to build a pile so dense and so conical in shape that although the outer layer will probably be ruined by weathering, from a few inches on in, the hay will stay green and delicious for your livestock.

FEEDING HAY: The best hay for horses is what's left over after you've fed the other animals, like cows and goats and rabbits. That's because horses can get by with almost anything, but the others can't. Horses even like timothy hay. But don't give them moldy hay; that gives them a condition called "heavey horse." Milk cows won't hold up so well on grass hay, and goats and rabbits need good green alfalfa. Hay gives cows 2 important foodstuffs, protein and roughage. Protein feeds them, and there's lots of protein in alfalfa and pea hays (not so much in clover hay). And they need roughage, provided by the grasses or stalks, to make their systems work right. Alfalfa hay is good hay because it has both. If you're feeding a low-protein hay like clover or grass, then you need to supplement that feed with grain to supply the needed protein.

Silage

Crops for forage (livestock feed) are preserved by either drying (hay) or ensiling (silage). I'll take a time-out here to tell how you can salvage a crop that will never get dry by making it into silage. There are parts of the country where during many years, grains never get dry enough in the field for normal curing. There are occasional years in other areas where that happens too. If it does, the grain can't be saved for people food, but it can be salvaged for livestock feed by a natural fermentation (and preservation) process called "ensiling." Grain silage is a sort of hay-based sauerkraut. It will smell awful and be a disgusting brown color. And your animals will love it and survive the winter on it.

MAKING SILAGE: Start with any moist green plants: grains, grasses, legumes, hay mixtures . . . But not too moist. To reach the ideal dampness for a non-corn silage, wait to harvest until the leaves and stems are wilted and limp-looking. You can make it from any or all parts of the plant—including the roots, if you want to take the trouble to pull them out. To make good silage, the green stuff must be well compacted and stored in a dark, confined, airtight container. Under those circumstances, it undergoes fermentation, creating organic acids that preserve the silage as long as the container is airtight.

Chop. To speed the compacting and fermenting, chop or grind the plants. Inch-long sections are ideal. You're making salad for animals.

Moisture. If the chop is too dry, you need to add water to produce the bacterial fermentation. But usually the plants are plenty moist, unless they've been harvested after a frost. If corn is let dry on the cob, right on the plant, and then the whole thing is dried, pulled up, bundled, and made into silage, it will need moisture. Chop the corn, mix it with some water (and possibly also stock-grade molasses), and then let it ferment.

Too much moisture is also a problem. Too much water can cause a partial failure of the preserving process, yielding bad-smelling, poor-quality silage. At worst, there must be a hole in the bottom of the sack or a drain in the bottom of the silo to allow excess liquid to run out. For good silage, the greens or grains need to be damp but not submerged in liquid. If you drain, then close the hole to keep out air.

Airtight Storage. To make small-scale silage, pour that chop into plastic sacks, packed in as tightly as possible. For large-scale silage, you put the chop into a giant plastic bag that looks like a huge sausage casing or into a special building made of hollow tile, concrete blocks, or reinforced concrete, or into a glass-lined steel cylinder called a "silo." To make large-scale silage without the special building, you can use a trench or pit in the ground called a "pit silo." Simply bulldoze a ditch, put the silage in there, and pack it down as tight as possible. If there's no cover, the top foot will spoil. It helps to cover any silage pile with plastic.

The fermentation process that preserves this feed will occur only if all the oxygen is used up by the fermentation process and no more oxygen can get in. So when packing, avoid air pockets and pack as tightly as possible. The silage will pack tighter if you pack a large amount over several days, giving each layer time to wilt and settle before you add another one. If air gets in, an equivalent amount of the silage will be spoiled. (You can still use spoiled silage as organic manure.)

CAUTION: The gases that accumulate in a silo can be fatal to breathe. Operate the blower for a few minutes to remove them before entering the silo.

FEEDING SILAGE: Silage that contains grain is a more nourishing feed than silage that doesn't. Supplement a silage diet with some form of protein (a dairy product, good alfalfa hay, commercial protein concentrate, or some such), because that's one thing silage is comparatively short on.

Of Grain and Grain Sprouts as Food. All the grains are good food for both human and beast, although some need to be husked or ground for better digestibility. Baby poultry need small cracked grain at first, like what you could make in your blender, but they can manage larger grains within a few weeks. A livestock feed of half wheat and half corn is great. All the grains will sprout. The best of the old-time

farmers regularly fed some sprouted grain to all their livestock in wintertime. Do that and you won't need to use "all-vitamins-included" commercial feeds! (See Chapter 2 for more on sprouting.)

Animal Feeds You Buy

For every animal you are feeding, you can go one of three routes:

- Go to a feed store and buy pre-mixed rations.
- Go to a feed store and buy foods that you have them mix, or mix yourself, to the formula of your personal choice.
- Raise your own feeds for your animals, making your own choices about what to grow and what proportions to feed it in.

FEED MILL FEEDS: The good thing about these feeds is that they are assembled according to formulas devised by expert animal nutritionists, and all feed elements the animals could possibly need are present in ample amount. The bad news is that although people doctors and, yes, animal doctors too must write a prescription if they want to administer drugs, feed mills have no similar restrictions. Thus animal feed companies can put into the feed whatever antibiotics or other drugs they choose, in whatever amount they choose. There is no supervision of what they put in. They have a huge loophole, and they use it.

Because animal antibiotics and people antibiotics are exactly the same drugs, this is a serious problem. Every factory farm that is feeding antibiotic-laced feeds year in and year out is potentially breeding yet another antibiotic-resistant supermicrobe. These bugs then can sicken humans, for all too many human diseases have started by crossing over from animals (most recently, the AIDS virus), and this potential will always be there. Low-level, permanent antibiotic drugs are most commonly used (as of 1993) in the feeds for poultry and for feed-lot cattle (not cows/calves on grass). Drugs are used not only because they keep the cows well but also very much because animals on an antibiotic diet grow faster and larger. That side effect makes feeding antibiotics profitable to the grower.

But I think that antibiotics should *never* be given to animals as a routine lifelong or long-term dietary supplement. Instead the animals should be raised with such a nourishing diet and healthy environment that they are able to naturally resist disease. And farmers should do without the extra growth caused by the antibiotics. If such an animal actually does get sick, it could be treated; if there is a risk of transmission of the illness to the herd, the animal could be briefly given a preventive treatment. But that's it.

Just recently [1993] a U.S. senator introduced a bill calling for regulation of the feed mills' practice of adding drugs to animal feeds. It didn't pass. He'll try again. This is much-needed legislation. I hope he receives more support next time!

FEEDS GROUND TO ORDER: With these, you buy the feed ingredients you want and have them mixed and ground to order. This way you can include what you want —and omit what you don't want. Shawn Trumble of Ionia, MI, wrote me, "We try to stay as far away from chemicals as possible. The feed store can never understand why we have our feed ground with no antibiotics or other strange stuff in it! We do, however, vaccinate for everything we can. We figure we're money ahead!"

Growers who are striving to produce certified organic meats are now looking for organic livestock feed suppliers. They need grains that are organically grown in their feed mixes with no antibiotics, growth promoters, or hormones of any type. ATTRA's list of such feed suppliers is at **www.attra.ncat.org/attra-pub/livestockfeed.html**. You can find another list of organic feed suppliers worldwide at **www.dba-sw.com/ppoultry/osuppliers.html**. For example . . .

Buckwheat Growers have a farmer-owned cooperative that grinds and mixes alternative grains as feed for livestock: 218-631-9212; 218-445-5475; 206 Aldrich Ave., PO Box 492, Wadena, MN 56482; **www. buckwheatgrowers.com/**.

Modesto Milling: 209-523-9167; Modesto, CA.

Organic Feeds.com: 800-767-4537; 570-374-8148; fax 570-374-2007; **info@kreamerfeed.com; www. organicfeeds.com**.

Organic Unlimited is a NOFA-NJ certified feed mill: 610-593-2995; fax 610-593-2155; PO Box 238, Atglen, PA 19310; **www.organicunlimited.com**.

Petaluma Poultry Processors: 707-763-1904; 707-763-3924; 2700 Lakeville Hwy., PO Box 7368, Petaluma, CA 94955; **www.healthychickenchoices.com/ index1.html**.

Valley Ranchers: 800-354-4503; **eggscvr@pacbell.net;** Arcadia, CA.

Willow Brook Feeds, 707-795-7190; PO Box 750818, Petaluma, CA 94999.

ANIMAL DOCTORING

Ask neighbors or your vet what diseases are prevalent in your area so you can take preventive measures or be on the lookout for the ailments. Keep your animals well by providing good living conditions, giving whatever immunization shots are needed in your area, and checking on them daily.

SOURCES OF MAIL-ORDER MEDICINES AND SUPPLIES

Grazier's Supply & Management specializes in American Holistic Livestock Ass'n animal health products: 507-237-5162; fax 507-237-2343; **www.grassfedisbest.com**; 25303 461 Ave., Gaylord, MN 55334; **www.holisticlivestock.com**.

Jeffers Vet Supply: 205-793-6257; 800-633-7592; Box 100, Dothan, AL 36302.

Nasco Farm and Ranch offers general equipment, including dairy and A-I supplies: 920-563-2446; 800-558-9595; fax 920-563-8296; 901 Janesville Ave., Ft. Atkinson, WI 53538; **www.nascofa.com**.

Omaha Vaccine Co. offers everything for pets (dogs, cats, birds), and for horses and large animals (not just vaccines); 800-367-4444; fax 800-242-9447; Box 7228, Omaha, NE 68107; **www.omahavaccine.com**.

PBS Animal Health offers thousands of products for pets, livestock, and horses at everyday low prices. Free catalog: 800-321-0235; fax 330-830-2762; PO Box 9101, Canton, OH 44711; **www.pbsanimalhealth.com**.

Spalding Laboratories sells beneficial insects for fly control! Call or write for fly or flea control catalog: 800-845-2847; fax 805-489-0336; 760 Printz Rd., Arroyo Grande, CA 93420; **www.Spalding-Labs.com**.

UPCO sells pet supplies of all kinds and wormers for some farm animals. Free 200-pg catalog: orders 800-254-8726; fax 816-233-9696; inquiries 816-233-8800; PO Box 969 (3705 Pear St.), St. Joseph, MO 64502; **sales@upco.com; www.upco.com**.

Valley Vet Supply offers wormers, calving supplies, sheep and pet supplies. Your choice of the 72-pg free Equine (horse), Pet, or Farm and Ranch catalogs: 785-562-2484; 800-468-0059; PO Box 504, Marysville, KS 66508; 1118 Pony Express Hwy (East Hwy 36); **www.valleyvet.com**.

Wiggins & Associates offer 3,000+ items of international vet and animal care supplies: 503-667-0716; fax 503-667-4701; 800-600-0716; 503 SW Victoria Court, Gresham, OR 97080-9265; **jpwiggins@att.net; www.wigginsinc.com**.

HOME VETTING BOOKS: Most books about livestock have a vetting section. *Animal Husbandry and Veterinary Care*, by Guy Lockwood, DVM, and *The Merck Veterinary Manual*, by Merck and Co. (1986), are especially useful. *Handbook of Livestock Management Technic*, by Battaglia and Mayrose (1981), covers procedures, not diseases, and is very professional, but usable by an amateur. Rural Bookstores carries *Cattle Lameness & Hoof Care* by Roger Blowey; *Horse Foot Care*, by Doug Butler; *How to Be Your Own Veterinarian (Sometimes)*, by Ruth B. James, DVM; *The Lame Horse*, by James R. Rooney, DVM, etc.: 931-268-0655; fax 931-268-5884; **ruralheritage.com**. *Keeping Livestock Healthy* (revised/updated 4th edition), by N. Bruce Haynes, DVM, focuses on prevention and covers nutrition, housing, and care, plus livestock disease and treatment (Storey Books, address in Chapter 1).

The Complete Herbal Handbook for Farm and Stable, by Juliette de Bairacli Levy, pioneered herbal veterinary medicine. First published in 1952, now a classic in its field, it has been revised, updated, and enlarged. The American Holistic Veterinary Medical Ass'n does "holistic veterinary medicine, acupuncture, chiropractic, herbal medicine, homeopathy, nutritional therapy & other complementary or alternative modalities." The website contains listings of manufacturers, practitioners, publications, suppliers, links, treatments, etc., none guaranteed: 410-569-0795; fax 410-569-2346; 2218 Old Emmorton Rd., Bel Air, MD 21015; **www.AHVMA.org; or www.altvetmed.com**.

Common Home Vetting Procedures

The most important is the daily lookover you give your animals. You get to know who they are and how they are. Then your observation and gut instinct will tell you when something isn't right.

GIVING SHOTS: Practically everybody who's any sort of a farmer gives their own shots. It is cheaper and more convenient. You can buy vaccines in bulk from vet suppliers that specialize in mail-order business to farmers. But it's better to buy from your own vet or vet supply center because of all the free advice you'll get with your purchase and the promptness with which you can get it home. Another disadvantage of mail-ordering vaccines is that there's no way to know in advance for sure who is going to be sick with what. You can also get needles, antibiotics, and immunizers from your vet or supplier.

Combiotic is a veterinary antibiotic that will store in

your refrigerator and is a good thing to have on hand, and it keeps for a few years anyway. Sick animals that need an antibiotic get shots—usually one a day for 3 days, or more if necessary—2½ to 3 cc. for a baby calf. Penicillin and its descendants are very precious stuff for man, beast, and even insect. (There's a variety of Terramycin in an edible powder that's for bees.) Boil your needles between uses. Plastic needles can be boiled too.

Filling the Needle. Peel off the little foil cover in the middle of the metal cap on the medicine bottle. That exposes a rubber area. Just force the needle point right through the middle of the rubber into the bottle. (Turn the bottle upside down.) Force the air out of your needle before you put it in the bottle by pushing the plunger clear down. Fill your needle with as much as you need, measuring by the calibrations on the body of the needle as you pull back on the plunger. (If you accidentally pull it all the way out, you have to start over.) Pull the needle back out of the bottle. Look at it to make sure that you don't have air in it. Squeeze a drop out of the end to make sure. Air inside a cow is unhealthy.

Bobbi McCollum, a Pietown, NM, nurse, wrote me, "When you pull medicine out of the bottle, do this first—draw plunger back to where you want to fill and inject an equal quantity of air into the bottle whose medicine you're removing. If you don't, you create a vacuum in the bottle. I assisted in a surgery of glass removal from a nurse who had had a bottle shatter in her face for just this reason."

Fill your needles on the site. Don't let children carry them with bare tips. I've had the experience of falling with a needle in my coat pocket. It rammed right into my innards. I was lucky it wasn't an eye. So get your animal ready first; then get the needle.

Sticking. Cows don't like shots any more than you do, and they have a lot more fight. Lock their head in a stanchion with the lure of some grain. Hobble or tie at least one hind foot very securely. With goats you can have someone sitting on the head and someone on the behind; same for a calf. If your cow isn't gentle and won't come into a stanchion, you need the kind of squeeze chute used for loading cows (a tight corridor that can be locked off in front of and behind the animal so it can't go anywhere). Or you will have to rope and tie it, unless you're so expert that you can give a shot practically on the run. (The needle is liable to bend or break out.)

Find a bulge of pure muscle in the front shoulder or rear thigh. Don't stick into a bone. Aim that needle right in the middle of the muscle. You won't have to jab as hard as you think—the needles are really sharp. The hard thing is to get the plunger pushed carefully all the way down and the needle removed if the animal is carrying on like crazy. But it may stay calm. Lane Morgan says, "I've never had trouble giving shots to cows or horses. When I was a kid the vet taught me to punch the horse 3 times on the chosen muscle and jab in the needle on the third punch. Usually it takes me several more punches to get up my nerve. Maybe the punch is a local anesthetic because they usually don't even twitch. With cows I do the same (in a stanchion), and it has worked so far."
NOTE: Don't let a needle break off at the neck. If you do, you'll have to get the needle out of the cow to prevent it from bleeding through the hole in the needle.

FEEDING A PILL: Cow pills seem huge. Here are the ba-sics for giving pills to calf, cow, goat, or horse. For a calf, have somebody help you hold it. For a cow or goat, put it in the stanchion. A good horse should just stand there and accept anything, but you may need help. Push your fingers into the mouth, up at the corner where there are no teeth, and the animal will open up the teeth part. (You open a horse's mouth to put the bit in the same way if it won't just do it for you.)

Put one arm firmly around the neck and, with the hand you've got in its mouth, just push that big bolus pill right down the animal's throat hole as fast as you can. Don't worry about choking it. You won't. Don't worry about making it uncomfortable. If the animal is sick enough to need the pill, a moment's discomfort is unimportant. When you think the pill is shoved down far enough, pull your hand out and with both hands try to hold the animal's mouth shut.

Bolus Gun. From Lane Morgan: "In my wimpy opinion, you'd have to be nuts or desperate to give a cow a pill without a bolus gun. You stick the pill in the slot at the end of the plunger and then push it down the beast's throat. Use the nose holder to keep her head pointed up until the pill is swallowed. We've had 3 milk cows. Two have been Holstein/Hereford crosses—bigger and not as docile as our one sweet little Jersey. I could dose them myself with the bolus gun and nose holder. Without it I wouldn't want to try. If you have two people, you can substitute someone's fingers for the nose twitch."

Down or Out? Now the animal will try to get the pill up and spit it out. One of 3 things will happen. It will either swallow the pill. Or it will burp it up, chew a moment, swallow half of it back down (that's why you're holding the mouth shut), and spit out the other half when you finally let the mouth open. Or it will spit the whole thing out. If it spits out half or all, you simply have to start again and try to poke it down farther this time, over and over, until you finally get that pill down your animal. The usual beginner's problem is not poking it far enough down. That's one of the reasons that a bolus gun is so helpful.

ELECTROLYTE DOSING: Lane Morgan says: "If you're raising a lot of calves, especially bought calves, I think it's worth it to buy the rig for dosing them with fluids. It has a bottle that you fill with your electrolyte solution or whatever and hang from something high. That's attached to a hose that you put down the critter's throat. The hose has a clamp so you can release the fluid when the time is right. All the parts are easy to sterilize and reuse. Of course, you could make your own. The point is to have something that works with minimum struggle and maximum cleanliness. I brought a far-gone scouring calf back from the brink with one of these, so I'm a believer. One saved animal will more than pay for it."

BODY TEMPERATURE: *Use a vet thermometer with a string or clip, or tie a string on a drugstore thermometer if you don't want to go in after it, because they tend to get sucked in!* You put the thermometer up the animal's rectum, just like you do with a baby. A vet thermometer comes with an attachment so you don't lose it into the animal. Or use a baby thermometer with your version of the attachment.

The usual rectal temperature of a goat is 101–102°F. For a calf it's 98–102.5°F; for a cow it's 101.5°F, but can range from 100.4–102.8°F normally. Sheep temp is 100.9–103.8°F. A pig's is 101.6–103.6°F. Rabbits are normally 102.5°F. The normal body temperature of any baby poultry is 102–106°F. For any adult poultry in the daytime it's 107.5°F!

Managing Livestock Reproduction

DEFINITIONS

Freshen: To give birth and start milk production

Gestation: Pregnancy

In heat, in season: When the female is ovulating and will stand still to receive the male and get bred

Service (v.): To breed an animal; to get her pregnant

Settled: Pregnant and out of heat

Spring: When the lips of the vulva swell, a sure sign that the birthing is coming

Udder: Her "breast" milk bag

HEAT PERIODS: A mare (female horse) stays in heat for 2–11 days, usually around 6, and comes in about every 22 days. She will be in heat again in 3–15 days after giving birth to a colt. A sow comes in heat again 1–8 weeks after pigging (which means to have a litter of babies). A ewe (female sheep) comes in heat for about 35 hours every 16 days. A lady dog will stay in heat for 9 days, more or less, and a cat can stay in even longer. After a large animal is bred and out of heat, she is said to be "settled." She won't feel that good again for a long time.

ARTIFICIAL INSEMINATION (A-I): A-I enables you to breed a cow when you can't manage or don't want to provide a bull. Instead, the cow is given bull semen through a metal tube while she is in a chute. Ask around to find somebody in the A-I trade in your area. Or ask the nearest vet; he or she will know for sure. Or take a course and learn to do it yourself!

GESTATION PERIOD: A "gestation period" means how long an animal is pregnant before giving birth. People take about 9 months. These periods vary somewhat, but in general, a cow will calve 285 days from her date of service, a goat will kid 151 days after, a mare will foal 336 to 340 days after, a sow will pig 112 to 113 days after, a ewe will lamb 150 to 152 days after, a dog has her litter 60 days after, and a cat has hers 64 days after. In other words, a mare bred on September 4 would be due to foal on August 7 of the next year. A sow bred on September 4 would be due to pig on December 25.

HELPING WITH BIRTHING: This is a delicate matter

where experience means a lot. If you pull a baby, such as a calf, out too fast, it can turn the womb inside out, which is very serious and requires vet treatment to keep the cow from dying. It's best if nature can take its course unaided. However, sometimes help is needed.

The moment when the baby's head and shoulders push out is the time when tears are most likely. If you are pulling to help the baby come out, *pull only very gradually* to prevent or minimize tearing. And don't get involved too early, before cervical dilation is complete, because that can cause tearing too. Don't pull on both protruding legs at once. Pull first on one, then the other. This allows the shoulders and hips to move out one at a time instead of both at once, making the baby less wide, so it will come out more easily. A calf that is coming out backward, rear end first, may be a hard delivery.

CARE OF NEWBORN'S NAVEL: For the offspring of large mammals such as pigs, goats, sheep, and cows, the baby gets its navel cord coated inside and out after birth with iodine. There'll be a few inches of cord hanging under the animal's abdomen. An infection from germs that entered through the navel is prevented by grasping the baby firmly while it is lying on its side and dipping that end of the cord inside a bottle of iodine. Then tip the bottle up against the baby's tummy so that some of the iodine runs up into the center of the cord. For best protection, this should be done within minutes after birth. To be safest, do it again 2 days later.

VACCINATIONS: This depends on the kind of animal and what diseases you have in your area. Ask a livestock-raising neighbor or a local vet. We give all our calves immunity shots. Much as I hate to stick a needle in anything (I really have to pray hard to get the courage), it's better than seeing them sick.

Once I didn't practice immunization of my children. After almost losing a child to whooping cough, I've totally changed my mind on that issue, and now my babies get shots against diphtheria, tetanus, and whooping cough (the famous DPTs); the oral medicine against polio; and the 3-in-1 against hard measles, German measles, and mumps just as soon as the doctor allows.

Now it makes me so upset to see advice in otherwise sensible and useful books and newsletters telling women that immunization is more risky than the disease. That's totally false! And it makes me furious to read that for whooping cough, you're supposed to give a "decoction of garlic and thyme" and "apply clay poultices on the back of the neck, wheat bran-climbing ivy poultices on the solar plexus," etc. What baloney! Absolute, total baloney! I *know* these writers never had a child with whooping cough, or they'd have offered more realistic advice. How irresponsible of them to presume to give advice that's not based on experience to trusting young mothers faced with the true risk of their child getting a desperately serious disease.

What you do for whooping cough is give up peace of mind and sleep. Your child of any age—infants can get this! —will have a literally life-threatening coughing attack, desperately battling to dislodge the constant dangerous buildup of the most thick, copious, ugly masses of phlegm you can imagine, every 8 to 18 minutes, day and night, for the next couple *months*—and longer. The child can drink light liquids like 7-Up. There won't be much other eating going on because the constant battle with phlegm predisposes to vomiting, though you have to try to get food down. But milk curdles the phlegm and makes it worse. You have to be present for every coughing attack to get the child sitting up and leaning slightly forward so the exhausted victim can get the phlegm out of their mouth. Literally scoop and pull the long strings of phlegm out of the child's mouth with your fingers if the child is choking on them and is unable to get them out without help.

There is no medical treatment for whooping cough, even in these modern medical-wonder times, although perhaps intravenous feeding could help. Once the child has the disease, all you can do is practice unending vigilance and tender nursing until the next spring, when it will finally completely go away. You'll need somebody to bring you whatever you need because you'll have to stay constantly at home with the sick child until the disease has run its course. You cannot possibly leave even for a moment. It's extremely contagious, so you'll have to practice quarantine. If a medical person knows your child has whooping cough, they will insist that the child be hospitalized, even though they have no treatment. With luck and faithful nursing, in or out of the hospital, your child will live. But not all do. The younger they are when they get it, the more risky it is for them.

Nor is measles a routine, harmless disease in the way that chicken pox is. Measles can have horrible results: brain damage, deafness, blindness, etc. Mumps can result in permanent male sterility. German measles can result in a dead or brain-damaged baby if you're pregnant at the time. When I was young, polio was the mysterious scourge of the summer season, and I personally knew people who died or were heartbreakingly crippled from it. I can't imagine why anybody would invite these illnesses upon their child and themselves for the sake of avoiding the so-called "risks" of immunization, which are something like 1 in a million. Nursing my 14-month-old baby Danny through whooping cough was one of the most terrifying, exhausting—and instructive!—experiences I ever went through.

The technology of immunization is not witchcraft. If this book could be long enough and you took time to get the lab tech training and could afford the lab equipment, you could be told how to make and administer vaccines. Pasteur invented the process way back in the 1800s and began saving lives right away, vaccinating against rabies and the scourge of smallpox.

Well, back to animal immunizations. Around here newborn calves get 2 cc. of vitamin A and D solution and 2 cc. of Bose (the immunizer against white muscle disease) as soon as possible after they are born. At 3 months they each get 5 cc. of black leg vaccine.

TEACHING BOTTLE DRINKING: To give a bottle to a resistant kid or calf or other young mammal who doesn't know what it's supposed to do: Force its mouth open. Put in the nipple. Hold its body to prevent it from backing away from you. Once the nipple is in, hold your hand around the sides and bottom of its mouth to prevent it from spitting it out. Once it gets some swallows of good milk, it'll get the idea. Kid goats are easier to bottle-break than calves.

Castration and Dehorning

REASONS FOR CASTRATION: Castration is worth considering with sheep, pigs, or goats and almost unthinkable with calves and horses unless you specifically want to use a male for breeding. There are good reasons for castrating.

Aggression. The following section focuses on cows, but the same principles apply to other large species. (And if you think human males aren't aggressive, just read a history book—or the newspaper. Or study anthropology. One study of bones from a dig found that those of females had 25 percent more fractures than those of males. The conclusion was that the prehistoric ladies had suffered those injuries at the hands of their not-so-gentle men. Thank God we're more civilized now.)

Bulls have very reckless, aggressive instincts and the size to easily do harm. But even ram sheep and buck goats have hurt people. The male is said to be willing to risk itself at the slightest provocation. I got a letter only a couple of weeks ago from a friend homesteading in Mexico whose 8-year-old boy was run down by a Charolais bull that escaped from his pen. The boy's leg was broken. The list of animal owners who've been harmed, even killed, by uncut (not castrated) male animals is tragically long.

Bulls with horns are even more dangerous. Horns and testicles are no joke when your bull calves are in the alfalfa and you are trying to chase them out before they bloat themselves to death. The next thing you know they are taking the whole thing wrong and have decided to charge you.

The reason the word "steer"—the term for a castrated bull—has become practically synonymous with "beef" is because extra bulls are so hard to manage. Bulls, with horns or without, can be dangerous. They are more aggressive than cows, more likely to attack if they think they have been provoked. Bull calves grow big enough to become dangerous well before the age of butchering. Nature meant the bull to protect the herd from predators as well as to compete with other bulls for dominance in breeding.

Don't think that because milk cows are so gentle, milk-breed bulls will also be gentle. In fact, it is just the opposite. For some reason, the bulls with the worst disposition of all are those of the dairy breeds.

Premature Breeding. A bull calf (or a male of another species) is ready to breed well before he is ready to butcher. If bull calves would only mature to butchering size before they mature in sexual capability and aggressive instincts, this problem wouldn't exist. Unfortunately, when they are less than half-grown, they think and act like any full-grown bull. So if you have a lot of young bulls around, you are liable to get 5-month-old heifers bred.

If a heifer (a young female cow) gets bred too young, she is bound to have trouble in calving, possibly meaning a choice between her life and that of the calf, or even a dead calf. Even if she calves successfully, she may not be able to make much milk, and her full growth may be stunted by the premature calving. The same is true of other species.

Fence Busting. Cows are very strong and can go through fences if they want to badly enough. A bull—even a very young one—is a big, husky animal. They quickly reach sexual maturity, and the first time they smell a cow in heat it doesn't matter whether they've ever been near a cow before. The fact that there is a fence between the bull and the cow in heat is no more important to the bull than if it was 2 garden stakes with a string between them. He will be inclined to just walk through, over, or under the fence, scarcely showing bewilderment at why that thing happens to be there just then.

Control of Herd Genetics. Genetically speaking, you have a lot more control over what's happening in your herd if you are breeding only from known sires at known times. If you have a Jersey bull calf and your neighbor has registered Herefords, and your bull calf goes through the fence and breeds some of his cows, he is going to be just furious! And that is bound to happen if you are keeping bull calves anywhere but locked up in your barn or in a real tough corral. He would owe you the same consideration if your situations were reversed. Cattle ranchers, as a matter of routine, make steers out of all their bull calves except the few they mean to raise and keep or sell as breeding sires.

HOW TO CASTRATE: So you see, the alternative is worse than a brief surgery at a young age for male calves and young males of other species in which these problems are possible.

Age When Castrated. On big ranches, the calves get cut and branded and have their shots all at once when they are moved. The February calves go to spring pasture in April (more or less depending on where you live), and that's when they are handled. The fall calves are done when the animals are brought back to their winter feeding place. So the typical age is 6 to 8 weeks on a calf. It is important to do the castrating after the animal is well established but before it is too old. Don't castrate too late. I've heard of people who had 5 or 6 big yearling calves bleed to death because they were too old when it was done. A year is way too old.

Nowadays there are several different ways to castrate.

With the Knife. Castration by the knife is a technology that has been around a few thousand years. It is a bloody and disgusting business and the most traumatic for the animal. Cowmen did it at branding time. They branded, gave shots, and steered, and so got all that stuff over with at one time. The first time you do it, get help from somebody who has done it before. If there isn't anybody to help, I'll give the best directions I can.

You have to first throw the animal, of course, and tie its legs and have plenty of help with sitting on it to hold it still. Slit the scrotum right down the middle belly line. There are about three layers of tissue, one of which is pretty hard to get through. Have your knife razor-sharp. Now put your hand around the outside of the scrotum so you squeeze the testicles clear out. There's a cord attached to each one. You cut that away and it's done. Have the gear ready to give a shot of Combiotic or some other animal antibiotic. Some Blood Stop helps, too; it's a purple powder available from your vet.

◆ *ROCKY MOUNTAIN OYSTERS Save those round balls in a bucket. Then you can be like the old-time cowboys and have them next morning for breakfast with eggs. In country talk, they're called "Rocky Mountain oysters." To cook them, just bread and fry like oysters. Store in the deep freeze like any other meat while you're working up your nerve.*

Docking Tool. The docking tool is, if anything, an even bloodier business than the knife, but it is also very fast and efficient. The tool is a round circle with sharp blades around the inside. You put it up over the scrotum and squeeze. The blades close in a pincerlike action and take the whole thing right off. You have to use it on a young calf because an older one will bleed too much. This tool is sold by Sears, Montgomery Ward, Ranchrite, and so on. It also dehorns. It's the quickest way to do it, but they bleed the worst. Don't use it on a very big calf—one over 250 lb. He'd bleed to death.

Elastrator (Emasculator). You buy this from a veterinarian or vet supply house. Ask advice on using it when you buy it. It's used for docking sheeps' tails as well as for castrating various animals. It's a better method for a beginner—maybe better for everyone. It's simple, there is not a drop of blood, and the animals don't seem to suffer excessively. The elastrator is a special tool that holds open a tough rubber band. You pull the testicles through the held-open rubber band. Put that tough rubber band around the base of the animal's scrotum, right where the scrotum joins the abdomen. Then you release the band and it remains on the calf, choking off the blood supply to his testicles. Elastrate a bull calf when it's about 1 week old. Don't wait.

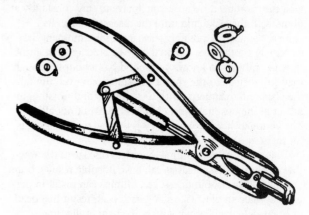

Yet even this system is not perfect. This last year both we and a neighbor had calf trouble using the elastrator. I don't know if the manufacturer tried to make the band out of some new rubber that wasn't as good, or what. So watch for infection. Eventually the testicles (or tail) drop off for lack of blood.

DEHORNING: I always used to just let my goats that were going to grow horns go ahead and grow them. I reasoned that a fine set of horns is a glorious sight and that because of our predator problems, the goats needed their horns for self-defense. We had goats come home with blood on their horns and spots of blood on their heads—and it wasn't from fighting each other! And no goats were missing. That's absolute proof that the predators got the worst of it! Mike says when goats are attacked by coyotes, they get in a circle with the kids in the middle and their horns facing out.

On the other hand, if you want to show goats at the fair, if your goats will be playing with small children, or if you have a buck you intend to keep, there are arguments for dehorning. My children never have been hurt by a goat, but I've been lucky. Cows of both sexes can be much more dangerous than goats. Naturally hornless animals are called "polled." A lot of the breeds now have polled strains. So the easy alternative to dehorning is to buy "muley" goats or "polled" animals. Otherwise, you can burn, nip, or saw off horns. Burning is the easiest method.

Age at Dehorning. If you're going to dehorn, it's much, much better to do it when the animal is 3 days old rather than later on, when the horns are big. You can dehorn a baby goat using a caustic paste or a burning treatment. Goats with horns that have already started to grow are dehorned by nipping. Baby muley goats have straight hair around their horn buttons; don't do anything to them. A baby that is going to grow horns will have curly hair there.

Dehorning by Burning. You can buy a special tool for this, the "bell-shaped dehorner," or use any make-do iron rod as long as the base is equivalent to the size of the horn. Commercial hot irons for this purpose come in a set of sizes to be matched to the horn. You can use this method on any young animal as long as their horn is shorter than ¾ inch. Calves can be dehorned this way up to 4 months of age.

Heat the electric dehorner as instructed. Heat the rod dehorner in a fire, branding-iron style, until it is really hot. Then press the hot end to the horn button. You have to have an extremely solid hold on the young animal so it can't wiggle. Having it in a stanchion that holds its head tightly is best. Hold the heated dehorner over horn, button, and horn base. Keep it there until you see a circle of copper-colored skin become visible around the horn's base. It takes only about 10 to 20 seconds. You'll smell the burning skin and hair. Do this once for each horn, and you're done forever with the problem. You can turn the animal loose right away.

Dehorning by Caustic. Caustic comes in sticks and in a paste. The sticks are easier to use. Caustic is a problem either way because it eats indiscriminately wherever it lands. A kid goat with caustic on can't be allowed out in the rain because if the caustic runs into its eyes, it could go blind. It you're going to use caustic, you have to do it on a very young goat, like 3 days old, before the horn has started to grow out. And you've got to do it right, or what you end up with is ugly, deformed horns—but horns anyway. To apply caustic:

1. Have your Vaseline and dehorning stick handy.
2. Restrain your animal. A miniature stanchion works well, or use a box with just space for the head to stick out.
3. Trim off hair from around horn buttons as completely as possible.
4. Cut off the horn button's tip using a sharp knife. This ensures that the chemical can get to the tissue that builds horn. If the horn button hasn't yet grown out through the skin, you'll have to cut the skin that's over the horn button with a knife to allow the chemical to get at the horn.
5. Lay Vaseline around the skin near the base of the horn button to protect that area from the caustic. It helps to stick adhesive on the button to protect it. Take adhesive off the button after you get the Vaseline in place. The Vaseline is to protect the animal's skin and eyes.
6. Dampen a caustic stick. Then apply using leather gloves or with stick enclosed in a paper towel. (Don't get it on your skin. It really eats.) Put caustic on exactly as the directions tell you. It's important to get on exactly the right amount. Too little results in a stub horn. Too much overflows the Vaseline. If using paste, apply to the thickness of a dime. Apply stick caustic to horn button with circular motion. Also apply to area right around the horn. Rub the stick on the horn button until you see blood.
7. You're going to have to figure out something for the next several hours until the caustic dries so the animal doesn't spread that stuff around itself or get it on its mother. You could have somebody sit and hold it for that time. Or keep it in the very confining cage you used for restraint.
8. You've got to go through this every day until you're sure you've won. If the horns get ahead of the paste, forget it. Go on to "Nipping."

Nipping. Young goat horns can be cut with nippers. You can get proper dehorning nippers affordably. *Pruning shears*

won't work. Get some Blood Stop from your vet too. The animal will struggle, scream, and bleed. Have help to sit on it while you're nipping. Make sure the edge of the nippers is almost even with the skull. Put the nippers carefully where you want them and then do it quickly and firmly.

Sawing. Big, old horns have to be taken off by sawing with a meat saw. It's a hard job. You need at least three men to do a goat—two sitting on the goat and one sawing. They bleed like the dickens, but Blood Stop will lessen the blood. The hole in the horn goes right down to the nostrils. You can look down there and see them breathe. But Blood Stop seals it up in a hurry. Shake the powder on the horn right where you have cut. The wound will seal in a hurry. If you have a goat who is making itself dangerous with horns, this treatment will solve that.

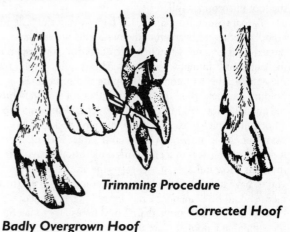

Trimming Procedure

Corrected Hoof

Badly Overgrown Hoof

FOOT PROBLEMS

Hoof Trimming. Some animals grow more toenail than others. You may be able to get away with no trimming, but sometimes regular trimming is the only way to keep hooves from getting so long in front that the animal can't walk normally. An overlong hoof can even split, and infection can get into the crack. Before you trim hooves, watch somebody with experience while they do it.

A horse will let you pick up its foot (usually) and work on it to trim or shoe it. A horse's hoof is first trimmed and then filed with a horse's hoof rasp. A cow is harder to trim. She won't pick up her foot for you as a horse will. Won't. Period. If she's a sedate and friendly animal, she will allow you to do her hoof trimming while she's lying down. Second best is to trim her hooves while she's standing on them. You need a special cow hoof trimmer to do that. Put her into a stanchion so her head is held still, and have her stand on a clean board so you can see what you're doing. (The only other way is to put her in a squeeze chute or rig a body sling under her belly and raise her off the floor.) See Chapter 10 for how to trim goat hooves.

NOTE: Trim hooves a bit at a time. If you cut too short, you will temporarily, or even permanently, lame an animal! Don't draw blood! If hoof color is getting pink—or if it's feeling soft—you're getting close to blood and must quit!

Foot Rot. If your cow gets swollen feet and acts as if she has pain in her legs, the cause is probably foot rot. "Foot rot" means any bacterial or fungus infection (swelling, redness, etc.) in the soft tissue between a cloven-hooved animal's toes or in the hoofhead. It's a misery for the animal, makes it lame, will reduce milk production in a milker, and will cripple a draft animal.

It can happen anytime and under any conditions, but it usually happens when animals stand in muddy or wet ground. They're also more likely to get it if standing on frozen ground, in gravel, or on other ground types that raise the possibility of a cut on the foot where an infection can start. To prevent foot rot in stabled animals, keep bedding and pen clean and dry. Hoof trimming also protects their feet. If you have a case, it's best if you can notice and treat it soon. Not every lameness is from foot rot. The animal may have a puncture wound or hoof abscess instead. Carefully cleaning the hoof so you can clearly see what is actually going on there is the necessary first step. Cows with foot rot can be treated with injected antibiotic and/or a dipping of the foot into copper sulfate.

Barbara Stone from Stites, ID, has a wonderful "Glenn's grandpa" who has been around cows all his life and has passed on this remedy through her. "Foot rot can happen to just about any animal with hooves. This is quite painful to the animal. The symptoms are limping and sometimes holding the foot up off the ground. Either rope or stanchion the animal before beginning the treatment. Using a stick or a horse-hoof pick, clean off all the manure, rocks, and whatever else is in the area between the toes. Pick up the foot and just stick it in a pail of used motor oil. Leave it in there for a few minutes or as long as the animal will allow you to have it there. Sometimes it is not too easy. This treatment should be done once a day for as long as needed. Usually it won't take more than 2 or 3 times. Try to keep the animal in a floored place that is not too wet or full of manure so the hoof can dry off. If nothing else, lock it in the barn."

Digestive Ailments

BLOAT: See Foundering.

CONSTIPATION: Sometimes an animal becomes plugged and cannot have a bowel movement. To check on a cow's digestion, a vet listens at the hollow behind the ribs. One vet said that when a cow's gut is working right, it sounds "like a spring storm." Give mineral oil for constipation. Contact your vet to find out the proper dosage for the specific animal.

FOUNDERING: Foundering happens to ruminants (cows, goats, sheep) and horses. It's serious indigestion—quite often fatal. Not too long ago I accidentally left both the door to the grain room in the barn and the outer people door of the barn open. My enterprising milk cow, Buttercup, went in that people door, walked down the corridor into the grain room, and there nearly polished off a 50-lb. bag of chopped barley. Needless to say, she promptly foundered.

She was a big cow and used to grain in lesser quantities, which is what saved her life. But when I found her she was suffering terrible diarrhea and looking very, very sick. Foundering affects cows in one of two ways—diarrhea or bloat. Diarrhea is better. We got her to the vet right away, and he dosed her and sent her home with follow-up pills for us to give her. She took the pills nicely for 2 days. The third day she was feeling better than we realized. When Mike tried to give her the pill, she turned her head suddenly and firmly pressed him between her head and the stanchion, breaking three of his ribs. We pronounced her

well enough. She never did get that last pill.

But that wasn't the end of the troubles from Buttercup's foundering. She got so dehydrated from her diarrhea that she dried up. I had to abruptly wean her little calf. After more time, her milk did come back a little but was still way down from where it had been. I sold her and used the money to buy a fresh cow.

Cause of Foundering. Foundering and hardware sickness are the 2 most common large animal ailments I've seen. Both are due to human carelessness rather than to germs. Animals depend on our good management; they have no natural judgment about what to eat, how much, or when. They will eat as much of the richest feed they can find, as fast as they can gulp it down.

Foundering is caused by a sudden, great change in diet from less rich to more rich food. In other words, if I started Buttercup on a cup of grain a day and gradually worked her up, she could digest big quantities without harmful effect (although probably still not 50 lb. of grain per meal). When we had an alfalfa field and kept the cows pastured in it from the very earliest spring day, they got fat on alfalfa and thrived. They were there when the first little starts of alfalfa came on slowly in the early spring, and they ate them. As more alfalfa plants grew, the cows got accustomed to their feed getting richer every day. That's why, when the alfalfa was waist-high and chock-full of food value, the cows could eat a bellyful of it as often as they wanted and be fine.

When alfalfa is cut and dried in the sun, it turns into hay and no longer has a potential bloating effect. Green alfalfa is the dangerous kind. If those same cows had been pastured in the field next to the alfalfa, on plain old grass, or on dry baled hay, and a child came to tell me they were through the fence into the hay (the green alfalfa), I would run, knowing time was precious and hoping they hadn't already been in there long enough to eat themselves to death!

Bloat can also be caused by grazing on frosted or wet, lush, spring pastures. If you buy an animal, ask how much grain and what green feed it has been eating. Drill it into your children that animals may slurp up grain like crazy, but grain in amounts the animal isn't used to can kill. Prevention is by far the best cure.

We've had all our bloat cases from over-graining. We had a nice 5-month-old billy kid. Company came to visit the farm. The children thought it would be nice to give grain to the little goat. Unbeknownst to me, they gave it a terrible quantity. That goat was not accustomed to grain in its diet at all. That evening it could not stand up. The following morning it was dead. You'll find "Tips to Avoid Bloat" at **www.dairyherd.com/nutr73.htm.**

Symptoms of Foundering. Foundering kills all sizes of animal. Bloat can take a 3,000-lb. bull just as easily as it did my billy kid. It kills quickly. You have to identify and treat it fast. You're usually certain of the diagnosis because you know when your animal was overfed. They usually founder from eating either grain or unaccustomed green alfalfa in the field—or other rich green food when they are used to hay.

The worst foundering is a "bloat." The animal's sides swell up and up. At first it belches quantities of gas. If it is still swelled up but stops passing gas, the disease is turning fatal. You know what really happens in a bloat? All that rich food ferments inside there and makes gas. The problem is how to get the gas out before there is so much that it squeezes the animal's lungs and causes suffocation.

Step-by-Step Treatment for Foundering

1. For any mild bloat keep the animal moving, and don't let it lie down. That helps it belch, which is what's needed.
2. If the animal belly continues to swell (especially on the left side) instead of getting smaller, get the front feet higher than the rest of the body, such as in a loading chute. Again, that's to help it belch. Or use some other system to get the front feet 6 inches higher than the back ones. Keep it standing.
3. Raising the front feet works even better if you force the animal's mouth to stay open by tying a length of hose with a rope threaded through it into the animal's mouth, over its tongue, and from side to side at the rear of the mouth, like a bit. This helps belching too.

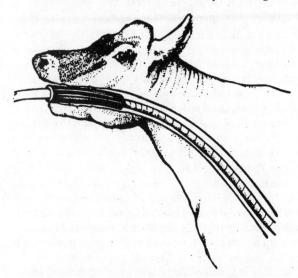

4. If the animal isn't belching effectively yet, you'll have to resort to a stomach tube ("hosing"). Barbara Stone, Stites, ID, wrote me, "Here is the method to use in 'letting the cow down,' letting the gas out of its stomach. First, get a piece of garden hose approximately 4–5 feet long. If possible, use a ¾-inch rubber hose rather than plastic hose. Next get a piece of 1½–2-inch black plastic pipe, the kind used for irrigation. Make sure both pieces are thoroughly cleaned. If the hose is the hard plastic kind, take a bucket of boiling water to the area where you are working. Take the garden hose and put it in the pail of water, let it set for a few minutes, and then drain completely. Take the end of the hose and carefully cut off all the rough edges. It may hurt the animal if left sharp.

   "Place the black pipe in the mouth and carefully put the garden hose through it down the throat. The black pipe in the cow's mouth prevents the animal from chewing on the hose, so you can get it down. How far down you go depends on the size of the animal; on a cow you may have to go 3–4 feet before hitting the air pocket. When you hit it, they will immediately start burping and belching. Keep the pipe out of line of your face, or it will just about knock you off your feet. Keep the hose in the stomach until all the gas is out. By putting the hose to your ear, you can hear if there is any more left. Take the hose out. The animal should be on its feet in just a few minutes. If not, work with it until you can get it up. If the cow has her head lying flat on the ground, try to get her on her knees; otherwise it doesn't go in the right places. Sometimes if the animal is in the barn or is up on its feet, you can use the same method, but hold the head back slightly so the hose will slip down easily. This works on calves as well as cows.

   "If you don't have a hose handy, you can use a regular rope. Stanchion the animal and take the rope in both hands, placing it sideways in the mouth over the teeth. Put this as far back in the mouth as possible. This makes the animal chew and gag and start belching. Continue this until the gas is out. But as in the other method, stay out of the line of fire. Don't put the rope down the throat."

5. Give mineral oil (or salad oil) or turpentine. For a cow-sized animal, give 1 pt. to 1 qt. oil or 2 oz. turpentine mixed with 2 c. cold water. The oil or turpentine acts to reduce foaming in the animal's stomach and so helps the gas escape through belching.
6. If the animal is down and you can't get it up, its legs are extended, and it's gasping for breath, there isn't time to call a vet. Bloat kills when it causes the animal to suffocate. You have to try "sticking," since once it cannot rise, it will soon die. For this very last resort, you stick a pocket knife in the gut to let out gas. Stick the knife into the *left* side exactly equidistant between the animal's last rib, and hipbone, and loin area of the backbone. That's right behind the rib cage, below the spine, in that swayback spot where it sort of caves in naturally. Have the knife point pointing forward toward the right front knee of the animal. It isn't good enough to just get a blade in there. You need to then turn the blade to make space for gas to come out. (Get your eyes out of the way of the gas, digestive juices, and food that may blow out!) Turn the blade or follow it with a small tube that will hold the cut open and allow the gas to escape. Keep the tube in place until no more gas is coming out.
7. If you stuck the animal and saved its life, great. But now it's at risk for peritonitis because of your non-antiseptic sticking. So check with your vet about further treatment.
8. For a recovering foundering case, it's best to give grass hay rather than alfalfa hay for the next few days. And no grain!

HARDWARE SICKNESS: That's what the old-timers call what happens when your cow eats a piece of metal. Our vet tells me that he gets around 200 cases a year. Cows, unlike goats, aren't picky about what they eat. They munch mechanically along, and if there is a nail in or near the food, it goes down too. I had a neighbor whose cow ate baling wire. That's bad. She eventually had to be operated on by the vet. But cows can survive eating nails, bolts, and even hinges if you know how to help them. The old-timers came up with a remedy for hardware sickness that's still used. Of course, prevention is the best remedy of all, so check your feeding places, keep your eyes open when you're walking around in your pasture, and pick up any small, loose metal pieces you see. Once in a great while, a goat gets hardware sickness too.

Symptoms. The animal stops eating. It gets a miserable look in its eyes and will stop going out to browse with the herd. It just lies around by the barn being reluctant (but not unable) to get up. There is no fever.

Treatment. The old-timers went to town, bought a magnet, and forced the animal to swallow it. If the metal has not progressed beyond the big stomach region, this will save your cow. The magnet grabs the metal and pulls it to the bottom of the cow's stomach. It doesn't ever pass out. She has a magnet and metal inside for the rest of her life. But the important thing is that she doesn't die. When she starts eating again, you can relax and feel safe. Veterinary suppliers sell small, very heavy, smooth, oval-shaped magnets for this very purpose.

Getting to a vet will make treatment easier. In the first place, a vet can make a surer diagnosis than you can. First take the cow's temperature. The above symptoms with no fever may lead you to suspect hardware sickness. But the animal doctor will have a metal detector. Doc can put the earphones on and run the rod around under her belly. If it screeches, Doc knows for sure that it is hardware sickness and also knows the location of the metal. If it goes untreated for too long, the metal can tear up her insides. The vet will probably give her a dose of medicine to stimulate her bowels, since hardware sickness makes them stop moving. It will make her have diarrhea for a couple days, but in this sickness that's a good thing. Then the vet will make her swallow the magnet. And Doc may give her a shot of antibiotic and send some home with you to give to her for 2 more consecutive days.

Our vet tells me that they have to operate on only about 2 of those 200 cows a year with hardware sickness. If the cow doesn't recommence eating and doesn't seem perfectly all right by 5 days after the onset, take her for surgery, which is expensive but maybe not as expensive as a cow. Ask and see.

Diseases/Infections

NOTE: Any animal that does very poorly—and you don't know why—is not meat you want to eat.

ABSCESS: An abscess is a localized infection, usually right under the skin, like a big pimple. Dynah Geissal wrote me advising, "Leave an abscess alone until it is ready to lance. At this time the hair will pull out easily near the head of the abscess. After lancing, treat with iodine. Abscesses are sometimes caused by dirty needles, so be scrupulously clean when giving shots."

CANCER: If it's where you can see it, there'll be a hard protruding lump that just grows and grows while the rest of the animal does poorly. Make sure it's a cancer lump and

not merely an infection. You do this by jabbing it with a knife. An infection runs pus; a cancer is hard clear through. If it is a cancer, take the animal away, shoot it, and dispose of the body.

CUT: Clean and then treat the cut with a product called Bag Balm, which is available from veterinary outlets. Bag Balm is also good for humans, and other cuts on your animals can be cleaned and treated with it. But use separate cans of Bag Balm for man and beast. For badly infected wounds, inject antibiotics.

INFECTIONS: Lance the wound by cutting it to let it drain. Put a healing salve like Bag Balm on it. If that isn't good enough, use antibiotic shots.

MASTITIS: For this udder infection and other dairy problems, see "Dairy Vetting" in Chapter 10.

PINKEYE: People pinkeye, kitten pinkeye, and rabbit pinkeye are all disagreeable. We take the kids to the doctor for a prescription or get some Murine eyedrops; that works for kittens and baby rabbits too. Dynah Geissal says goat pinkeye is "usually caused by dusty feed but sometimes by bacteria. Treat with diluted lemon juice twice a day. This usually works, but if it doesn't, you will have to resort to the more radical treatment of injecting antibiotics into the eyelid! Pinkeye must be treated because it may lead to cancer eye, which causes blindness, severe emaciation, and death."

Bovine Pinkeye. We have a lot of this ailment around here—it starts right after the face flies do, in late June or so, when the weather dries out and starts to turn hot. The face flies hang around a cow's eyes and drive her crazy. We try to help by soaking rags in a face-fly discourager and hanging them up on a rope so the cows can scratch themselves on it. But the best prevention is choosing a pinkeye-resistant breed of cow. Breeders have paid a lot of attention to resistance to this disease. Black Angus cows can list among their fine selling points that they are pinkeye-resistant. Shorthorns are not; I know from personal experience. Charolais are supposed to be resistant, but some still get it. Herefords are more susceptible than Black Angus.

Bovine pinkeye comes on very fast. It generally happens on only one side at a time. The eye turns white all over and looks ulcerated and awful. You'll know the instant you see the cow that something is terribly wrong. If you don't have pinkeye-treating experience, or even if you do, the best thing to do is load up the sick animal and get her to the vet immediately, because every hour really matters with this rapidly progressive disease. If you're in doubt, phone the vet first to discuss if it is what you think it is. It's a good idea to check all the cows' eyes each morning and evening in face-fly season, as a matter of routine, to catch any pinkeye when it's just getting started. In some cases, with quick action, the vet may be able to save the eye. Or you may lose that eye but prevent the disease from spreading to the other eye. Then you've got a one-eyed cow, but otherwise she will be functional.

If you lose both the animal's eyes to pinkeye, you'll have to sell the cow for hamburger or eat it yourself, because it'll starve anyway. I know an old-timer who says the way to treat it is to get a handful of salt and rub the affected eye with all your might. Lane Morgan says her vet gave them something in a spray can (the spray was purple) that worked.

PNEUMONIA: Calves and goats get pneumonia. The symptoms are similar to the human disease. Animals with pneumonia have a very snotty nose and maybe runny eyes. They run a fever, are weak, and are obviously very sick. Their breathing is unnatural—raspy, maybe with coughing. The treatment is to keep the animal in as warm and dry a place as you can, feed frequently, and give Combiotic shots for 5 days. Coddle it a while more, because they can relapse.

Preventing Pneumonia in a Down Cow. From Barbara Stone, Stites, ID: "Our big Holstein cow went clear down during the night over the holidays, and she was down for almost 3 days. She had somehow hurt herself and couldn't get up. If you have a cow down, it's important to prevent her from getting pneumonia. It was awful cold at that time. We couldn't get her in the barn. We just had to keep old blankets and straw around her for the time she was down. We put feed and water in front of her, and she ate and drank. She finally did get up, to everyone's joy."

RED WATER: Dynah Geissal wrote me, "This disease is named for the way the urine looks when cows have it because there is blood in their urine. In goats it is detectable only with a microscope. I had 3 goats autopsied by livestock vets, one of whom told me the goat had starved to death. In fact, they do look starved. A pet vet did a fourth autopsy and found blood in the urine and then discovered the cause. After losing half my goat herd, I started inoculating and have never lost another goat to this disease. Red water is caused by liver flukes, which are carried by snails. If your goats graze or water in places that the fluke-carrying snails inhabit, they could get it. Ducks help to keep this problem under control by eating the snails. Having well-drained pastures and not allowing the goats to use natural watering places cuts way down on the problem—but inoculating eliminates it."

RINGWORM: Ringworm is a fungus. Supposedly the animal kind can't spread to humans, but I know better. First I got a spot on my arm. It kept breaking out again on my arm. We couldn't figure out where it was coming from. Then we discovered patches on Marietta, our milk cow. I'm the one in the family that milks. (Mike runs them in at night and feeds them, and I come along with the bucket and do my thing.) So it had to be more than coincidence that Marietta and I had ringworm at the same time. The doctors have a new treatment now for people ringworm, a one-shot painting that wipes it out. The ringworm eventually spread to all the cows. It took the hair off in (usually) roundish areas, leaving a kind of whitish, scaly surface.

Dynah Geissal treats goats that have ringworm with lemon juice, applied 3 times a day. I've found that iodine dissolved in glycerin is a good medicine for ringworm. You can get ringworm medicine from your vet. You paint it on once, and that's fine until you find the next spot. In the old days, they just left it alone. It was a winter affliction that the cows sloughed off in their spring molt. Another old-time remedy was to get an old rag and tie it on a stick. Dip the rag into a can of used motor oil and run it over the ringworm areas (not near eyes).

SCOURS: Scours means animal diarrhea. Usually it's the babies who get it. Chilling, a change of food, or a bacterial infection can cause it. For treatment of a kid or calf with scours, see chapter 10. For older animals with mild scours, Dynah says she treats "with ginger fed with grain. More severe scours is treated with Kaopectate."

WHITE MUSCLE DISEASE: Dynah says, "The symptom is stiff hind legs. It occurs in selenium-deficient areas. It is prevented by feeding a mineral mix that includes selenium."

Parasites

LICE: Lice can turn up on practically anything, man or beast. And don't let anybody kid you and tell you that animal lice leave human beings alone. I know several people whose whole households have gotten horrible cases of lice from animals, in one case from a neighbor's milk cow. Animal lice don't generally make the jump to people unless you get really intimate—like leaning your head against the cow. But once you've got 'em, you have a fight on your hands. If you can help it, don't go home. Take a hot shower. Wash your hair with a strong soap. Wash all the clothes you were wearing in detergent and hot water. If still in doubt, buy a can of garden spray that's good for flying bugs (terribly strong stuff, I know, but nothing lesser that I know of is really effective) and spray your car. Take off your shoes and spray them.

If the infestation of lice is in your whole family or your house, you're going to have to go through this battle again and again. It won't be easy, but in the end you'll win. I've been through it. Wash all the clothes and bedding. Shampoo and bathe the children. Fumigate the house thoroughly. If it doesn't work, do it again. And you have my sincerest sympathy. This is one of the most miserable afflictions I can think of—and it's the same for the cow or chickens or other critters that have 'em. Malathion is an effective spray, but it's terrible inorganic stuff. A new treatment of whitewash in your animal shelter and crankcase oil on the roosts, in the case of chickens, has been known to work. Makes me itch and scratch just to write about it.

MAGGOTS: Maggots are caused by flies that lay their eggs in a wound. When the eggs hatch, the little worms live in the animal's flesh. It is a terrible sight. When I was little we had a lot of trouble with bears getting into the sheep. Often the bears succeeded only in getting part of a sheep. I remember vividly helping my daddy. He would hold the wounded sheep down while I poured the dark, thick anti-maggot medicine all over where the worms were writhing in the exposed flesh. So be forewarned. If your animal has an open wound in the fly season, you must keep a salve on it or else pour an antimaggot solution over it.

WORMS: Medicine for worms can be given via an animal's food or drink, or in a shot. It depends on the animal and on the worm—the varieties of which are legion. Don't treat unless you actually have the problem.

INTRODUCTION TO BUTCHERING

For specific species butchering instructions, also see the section in this book dealing with that animal.

The tiger naturally eats nothing but meat. Man naturally can thrive on a diet of part meat which, like the tiger, we have to kill to get. I don't think much of people who say they like to eat meat but go "ick" at the sight of a bleeding animal. Doing our own killing, cleanly and humanely, teaches us humility and reminds us of our interdependence with other species. My husband adds that there would be fewer wars if people were doing their own killing and knew what it was to have to cause death to a living creature. I'm sad, humble, and grateful for each creature that perishes for the sake of nourishing my family.

I grew up on a farm and in a climate where meat and dairy products were naturally an important part of the diet. By "naturally" I mean that as you go farther north, or farther up in altitude, you get into climates where fruits and vegetables are harder to grow, but forage crops—food for animals—like brush, grass, and hay can still do well in season. In such areas your diet naturally tends to lean away from fruits and vegetables, which become ever more limited in selection and in season as it gets colder, and toward meat and dairy products—foods that can be harvested even in snowdrifts, foods manufactured by animals that can eat grass in summer and hay in winter, 2 food sources that humans can't eat.

Killing that provides for the ample continuation of the species is acceptable to nature. In other words, we eat the extras—especially the extra males. No one wants an adult male of these domesticated species except for meat. No one, that is, with the exception of the female (if only for a moment), so there have to be enough males for breeding. The other exception is castrated males that are work animals, namely oxen. Uncastrated males don't make good pets, are expensive to feed, and don't produce the milk or babies that make the females a valuable part of the farmstead ecosystem.

We also eat the females that are past reproductive age —or even younger females, if the herd has grown to a size where its natural environment couldn't support it anyway. And we may kill to improve the genetic heritage of our surviving breeding stock—thus eliminating less hardy or less productive individuals. Killing purely for the sake of sport is wasteful unless a species has over-reproduced to the point where its ecosystem can't support it anyway. Don't kill members of a species that doesn't have extras.

Custom Slaughter and/or Cutting

Some people send their animals to a custom-cutter to be butchered, cut, wrapped, and quick-frozen. The cost is figured per pound and is often waived in part in return for the hide, so many pounds of the hamburger, or some such. My friend Stephen Scott wrote me: "I take the sissy way out and send them off to a professional butcher. It is not an inexpensive proposition anymore to ship pigs, have them butchered, cut up, and wrapped, and have the hams and bacon smoked, but I prefer it to the alternative. We are lucky to have a few places left that do this kind of thing in our area. Twenty years ago there were at least 10 places that would do custom butchering; now there are just 2. One of them comes out to pick the pigs up with his own truck. For the other one, you have to haul the pigs to him—haul them yourself or hire a livestock trucker to haul them for you. I don't have a trailer that will haul livestock, so I have to pay 15 bucks to have the butcher come and pick them up. We raise three pigs: one for ourselves and two that we sell. We split the hauling fee so that each one of us has to pay only 5 bucks apiece. Not a bad price considering the trouble that you can have on the road with 3 scrappy 200-lb. porkers."

Another possibility is custom slaughterers who work from a mobile rig and will visit your place for the day. If you want to hire out some or all of this work, make arrangements in advance with a local person, find out what the price will be, and make an appointment for a particular place, day and time.

CUSTOM CUT AND WRAP: Some people do their own butchering but send out the carcass to be cut and wrapped. It's easier on the animals to be slaughtered on-farm, and you'll get the organ meats fresh. Or you can hire a commercial butcher to come and do the job on-farm. In either case, you get to eat your own carefully nurtured meat, but you avoid the mess and labor of slaughter and cutting up. If you take the complete carcass to a professional butcher or to a meat locker, you can have it cut to look like the cuts at the supermarket. If you're planning on driving somewhere else with the butchered quarters in the back of your pickup, you'll want some clean old sheets to wrap the meat in, so it doesn't get dirty.

Instructions for the Meat Cutter. He'll package it just right to serve your family's size. Tell him how thick you want the meat cut, how much you want your roasts to weigh, how many steaks, chops, etc., you want wrapped in each package, what percentage you want made into burger or sausage, and if you want any of the meat cured. You may want to get the bones back. A reader wrote me, "When we send a beef to the butcher to be cut and wrapped, we request that they give us all the bones too. We pressure-cook them, let them cool, and then pick the meat off them (there's a lot!). We can the stock with some of the picked-off meat and some onion slices in each jar. It makes a great stew base and makes the budget stretch farther."

Home Butchering

QUALIFICATIONS AND PREPARATIONS: Unless you've had a college course in comparative anatomy or dissected a cat or two in a zoology course, you may not be able to distinguish one muscle bundle from another. When I was a little girl, my mother believed that every situation could be made to have educational value. As the teachers of subjects like "Hellenistic Marketing" and "Music of Ancient China" say, it's bound to be useful sooner or later; you might be surprised just when. So whenever Mother cleaned a chicken, she would call me over and have me identify all the various abdominal organs. Eventually, I struggled through 3 years of pre-med at the University of Illinois at Chicago. But chemistry, trigonometry, and physics were my downfall. So I didn't become a doctor. But I got straight A's in all the anatomy and dissecting-type subjects. I have just listed for you my credentials for writing about meat cutting—above and beyond having done it.

"Butchering" is when you kill, skin, gut, and quarter the animal. Then you hang the quarters up to age, in the case of most animals, or merely to cool overnight, in the case of pigs. This book does not describe professional butchering; it assumes that you can probably tell bone from meat from fat—and not necessarily much more. Its essential goal is to enable you to get your meat from hoof to pan yourself, and I trust it will accomplish that. There are cuts here that you don't see in the store, but a professional butcher has lots of expensive power-cutting equipment that you don't want or need to buy. You'll understand any procedure better after you try it a few times. The school that best teaches you something is the one where you actually do it enough times to get comfortable with it. The biggest hurdle is getting started—getting the confidence that you really can do your own butchering.

I've tried hard to make the directions that follow clear and dependable. It would be even better than reading this chapter, however, if you could butcher and cut up an animal with somebody who is experienced. If you are inexperienced and must be on your own, it's a good idea to start with something small—such as a chicken or rabbit—and gradually work up, rather than trying to learn on a 1,200-lb. cow. The basic principles are the same.

In general, if you are careful with your basic preparation (don't shoot the animal if it's excited, get it thoroughly bled out, don't spill intestinal contents on the meat, get it cool, keep it clean, and don't let the meat spoil), you really can't go too far wrong. You're going to eat the meat yourself. If your steaks are triangular, they will just give you a good laugh every time you eat them.

Jacki Robinson, Reddick, FL, wrote me, "Fifteen years ago my husband and I decided to move out of the city into the country . . . We bought a 5-acre postage-stamp farm that was already set up with garden space, barn, root cellar, and chicken house. After some repairs we were ready to start, and we did. We got a milk cow, a beef calf, goats, chickens, geese, guineas, ducks, bantams, pigs, and bees.

"When it came time to butcher our pig, we could get no help from any neighbors. (They were sort of close-knit and related to everyone but us. The consensus was that we would never make it.) So we went to the library. Our beautiful librarian loaned us a copy of your book . . . My husband butchered our pig while I sat on top of the truck with your book telling him what to do next. The pork chops looked like triangles, and there were many unnamed pieces of meat, but it sure tasted good. After that, the neighbors were a little friendlier. I checked out your book so much that I finally bought it. Living out here is so precious to me. Growing a child and the food we eat are enriching my soul."

Once you have gotten the animal killed and the meat cut, you need to preserve it (or have a big barbecue and eat it immediately). So before you commence slaughtering, be sure to decide how you are going to preserve the meat, and be prepared to get that meat processed within the necessary time limit. This chapter contains a section describing every possible way of preserving meat, including freezing, canning, and drying. The last section tells how to make homemade soap from surplus animal fat and how to tan skins. (Candle-making info is in Chapter 1.)

BOOKS AND SUPPLIES: A good one is *Basic Butchering of Livestock and Game* by John J. Mettler, Jr., D.V.M. (1991). It covers beef, pigs, sheep, deer, poultry, rabbits, small game, goats, horses, and also buffalo—as well as pickling, smoking, and curing meat, and how to build a smokehouse and make sausage. *Butchering, Processing and Preservation of Meat* by Frank G. Ashbrook contains material from USDA bulletins. Texas A&M offers meat science info and training seminars such as "Beef 101" and "Sausage School"! Contact the Rosenthal Meat Science and Technology Center, Dept. of Animal Science: 409-845-5651; fax 409-847-8615; **meat.tamu.edu.** The American Meat Science Ass'n lists classes, such as Pork 101, on its website: 217-356-3182; fax 217-398-4119; **info@meatscience.org; www.meatscience.org.**

Forschner knives ar German products that are very good. They are available only from butcher supply houses. Recycled professional (Chicago Cutlery's Biocurve) processing knives are available (bargain!) from Tim Shell: 540-885-4965; 407 Mt. Solon Rd., Mt. Solon, VA 22843-9718; **tschell@fristva.com.** To cut up something large like a beef, a band saw really helps, but they are very expensive. We don't have one. Sometimes you can find a small saw secondhand for a bargain price. Some people make their own.

FIT TO EAT?

What's Live and Fit to Eat. Don't choose an unhealthy animal for slaughter. If you suspect an animal of being unhealthy, get it checked by a veterinarian and treat it until it's healthy again. (Then wait for the antibiotic to wear off.)

What's Dead and Fit to Eat. If you know an animal has just died, and you know why, here are your rules: don't eat an animal that died of a disease (other than a non-microbial-type disease, like foundering). Do eat an animal that died of an injury, like getting hit by a car. It would be a shame to waste the meat. If you don't know why the animal died, or if it has been dead awhile, definitely do not eat it. (When in doubt, throw it out.) As soon as possible, as much of the blood as possible must be drained out. Getting that accomplished is very important and very necessary if you want the meat to look normal and keep normally. Don't butcher or eat any animal that has received any kind of medication within the last 2 weeks or that has been been recently wormed or treated for external parasites. Check the directions on the medicine container for the precise withdrawal periods after which butchering is safe. The time varies according to the particular treatment.

YOUR MEAT INSPECTION: After the slaughter and evisceration of any animal, examine the internal organs and the carcass carefully for any visible abnormalities that might suggest the unfitness of the meat for food:

1. Local bruises and injuries, enclosed abscesses, and single tumors are conditions that the professionals simply cut away and discard; the remainder of the animal is fine to use.

2. Worms in the intestinal tract are routine and don't disqualify the meat.

3. If you find inflammation of the lungs, intestines, kidneys, inner surface of the chest or abdominal cavity, or (in the case of sheep) numerous yellowish or pearl-like growths scattered throughout the organs, call your vet and discuss whether you should use the meat! (When in doubt, throw it out.)

4. If a liver has many white-filled spots on it, you have coccidiosis disease on your farm. The livers need not be fully spotted. Any slight discoloration is a sign of infection. Chickens can get it; so can various other varieties of poultry, rabbits, and sheep. Do not eat the meat of infected animals! Burn the carcass.

Butchering Meat for Sale or Trade. The Federal Meat Inspection Act requires that some meat that is to be sold or traded for human consumption must be slaughtered under inspection in an approved facility under the supervision of a state or USDA meat inspector. For more details about these regulations, see the Chapter 9.

Radioactive? If they ever drop the bomb, or if a nearby nuclear power plant or nuclear waste dump blows up, don't eat any internal organs, bone marrow, or animal skin. The muscle meat will be safe if you keep it absolutely dirt-free. Milk from dairy animals will be contaminated if your animals ate contaminated feed or drank contaminated water. It will be okay if they ate clean feed and drank clean water.

Other Poisons. Relative to the industrial-chemical era in general, if there are any poisons in the animal's system, they will wind up getting concentrated in the brain, liver, and kidneys and in the fat. *So minimize your eating of animal fat not only because of cholesterol but even more because of DDT and other chemicals!*

WHEN TO BUTCHER: Around here the best months for butchering are late October, early November, and late February. That's because then the weather is cold enough so the meat will keep, but not so cold that everything keeps freezing on you. An outdoor temperature of around 35°F is ideal, since spoilage bacteria do not grow well in such a cold environment.

Another factor in the timing of slaughter is food supply. There is often a time that's economically best for killing. For grass eaters it's when the grass gives out in the autumn, which is around the same time as when the weather gets cold enough so the meat will keep. Another economically determined time is when the critters will no longer put on much extra meat relative to the food they eat, when they're basically done growing. That's why ducklings are ready after about 10 or 12 weeks.

Small animals like rabbits and poultry that will go straight to the refrigerator or the table can be butchered under any weather conditions at any time of year. Larger animals that will be quickly barbecued whole, like small pigs, lambs, or kid goats, can also be butchered in summertime, even without refrigeration. But for larger animals, you'll have to consider how long it will take you to get the animal butchered, how long you want to hang it, how long it will take you to cut it up, and what plans or facilities you have to store the meat (canning, freezing, locker storage, drying, etc.).

Avoid slaughter in high winds, when dirt might be blown into the workers' eyes or dust onto the carcass. Most people avoid slaughter in hot weather, except of a small animal such as a goat. Hot-weather slaughter is best done in the late evening hours. In most families the men butcher and cut up and the women wrap, but I know some country women who take great pride in cutting up the meat themselves. Wear old and very washable clothing to butcher. Most people get blood, etc., on their clothes. Wash your hands and arms frequently.

PREPARATIONS FOR SLAUGHTER: All large animals are typically killed, skinned, and eviscerated outside and then cut up on an inside counter. Small animals may also be cleaned inside the house.

Checklist Before Large Animal's Slaughter

1. Choose ahead of time a site with clean running water handy.

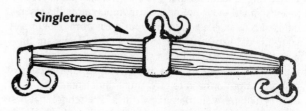

Singletree

2. Locate a tree with a high, healthy limb or a building with a high beam strong enough to hang the carcass from. You'll also need a block and tackle or strong rope or singletree and hoist to raise the animal's rear end.

3. Have ready a gun or pistol (.22-caliber or higher rifle or pistol with cartridges) and know how to use it.

4. Collect a few very sharp knives and means to sharpen them again (a steel knife sharpener or Carborundum whetstone), and a meat saw. Razor-sharp knives minimize waste by enabling you to trim closely and precisely.

5. Gather buckets to hold liver and heart (you need a 4-gal. bucket for one cow's organ meat) and clean cloth or food-grade plastic to cover the animal after the carcass is skinned and eviscerated.

6. If you're butchering a larger animal, you'll also need a regular wood-cutting saw for cutting the animal in halves. The meat saw blade is too thin for that job.

7. It is also helpful to have a bucket of warm water with a heavy dash of vinegar in it for washing your hands when they get sticky, especially after you've been handling the innards and before you go back to work on the meat.

8. It's a good idea to clean and defrost your freezer before putting a large amount of meat in it. And check whether you have enough space available in your freezer. If you have a small freezer and a large animal, consider boning it out and cutting away and discarding the fat.

9. If possible, pen the animal the day before slaughtering. Do not feed it for 24 hours before killing, but do provide ample access to water during all that time. Withholding feed helps because then the guts are less bulky. Access to water helps complete bleeding out, results in brighter-colored lean meat, and makes skinning easier. But if penning isn't possible, don't worry. Your meat will still be all right.

10. The offal (butchering residue) can be awful if you don't have a plan to deal with it. See below.

11. Plan how you'll age the meat. See below.

12. If you're planning to freeze the meat, you'll need

freezer paper and freezer tape, which you can get at a grocery store or from a local butcher. Have handy a crayon or marker to label your freezer packages with date and contents.

OPTIONS FOR THE AWFUL OFFAL: You could bury it in the garden, give it to the chickens, push it over a cliff, feed it to the pigs, or compost it.

Feed It. It takes chickens a long time to eat up cow innards. Pigs can take care of them right quick, but for either pigs or chickens there's a concern that eating innards reinforces the animals' parasite supplies. You can solve that problem by boiling the innards at least an hour, and preferably several, before feeding them to the animals. In that case, you need a huge pot and an outdoor place to get a fire under it. That's probably the best solution. In warmish weather, innards can get stinky pretty fast.

Compost It. Another solution is to compost the waste—innards, extra bones, hides, and blood (but not fat). Add them to your yard clippings, manure, peelings, food leftovers, feathers, and anything else organic. Mix everything with a layer of soil. Let it set a few weeks and then stir it again. But then you have to cover it in a way that guarantees some critter won't dig it up. Since some of these items decay very slowly, the delayed action continues to feed nutrients into your garden for a long time.

Remember: If not thoroughly bled out, the meat won't be pale in color. It will look "funny" and won't keep as well. And be careful to tie off rectum and to not let contents of the intestines spill onto the meat. That's how it can get contaminated with the likes of E. coli.

GENERAL PRINCIPLES OF AGING MEAT: Aging, a bacterial breakdown of complex proteins in the muscles that adds to flavor or tenderness, naturally begins when the meat is cool. If you choose to age the meat, keep it at about 40°F. Warmer temperatures increase the danger of spoilage. Colder temperatures slow down the process. Aging large animals for about 10 days should be sufficient. Deer will age in a week. Antelope should not be aged longer than 4 days. Very lean carcasses are not suitable for longer aging because they dry out too much. If the animal was less than a year old, the meat doesn't need aging at all. Don't age pork and pork-type meats (bear, wild boar, etc.).

Aging is done after skinning and gutting and before cutting up—except into halves or quarters (whichever is suitable for the size of the carcass). The aging process helps tenderize the meat and mitigate wild flavors. Small animals may be wrapped in a damp cloth and aged in your refrigerator for a day if they are young, for up to 4 days if they are old. Somewhat larger carcasses may still be small enough to be cut up and aged a while in your refrigerator. How long or whether you age large animals will probably depend a lot on the age of the meat and the temperatures the meat will be exposed to.

Wild hoofed game is often hung about 10 days; it needs to be kept at 35–40°F for that period. If you have a walk-in cooler where you can hang your meat and keep the temperature above freezing but below 40°F (meat will actually turn out more tough if frozen within 24 hours of butchering), you could age it for 1 week, or 2, or as much as 3. If the weather is cool enough, let the meat hang in one of your own outbuildings with the door shut, to prevent wandering canines from helping themselves and to protect

it from freezing at night. If you don't have facilities to hang the meat that long, or if the temperatures are getting too hot, by all means go ahead and cut it up. It may not be as tender as it might have been, but at least it will be edible.

About Cutting Up

CUTTING TERMINOLOGY

Chop: Lamb, veal, and pork terminology for what's called "steak" on a beef or elk

Cut up: To take the quarters into your house, onto the table, and cut them up into cooking-type pieces

Inside: Inside the chest and abdominal cavity

Outside: On the side where the skin was attached

Tips: Mini-steaks, possibly literally the tip of the muscle bundle

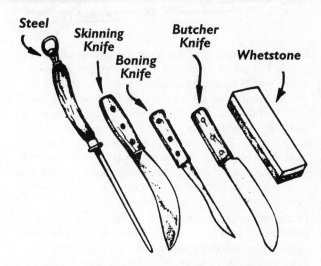

CUTTING-UP OPTIONS: Basically, you'll go one of 3 ways, or some combination thereof, with your cutting up:

1. Cut meat into chops (steaks), roasts, stew meat, and hamburger/sausage according to the part of the animal. This is the conventional way to cut meat.
2. "Bone out," which means to remove all the muscle bundles from the bone. If you have limited freezer space, if you plan to can all your meat, or if you can't stand working with a meat saw, boning out is the way to go.
3. Bone out and then grind the meat of the entire animal for hamburger/sausage. This is a frequent farmstead choice when an older animal that might be tough needs to be cut up. It gives you a good use for the meat without creating a struggle for the cook to make it usable.

THOUGHTS BEFORE YOU START CUTTING: Ask the cook about his/her preferences. Your animal is going to become spareribs, hamburger, stew meat, steaks, roasts, and soup bones. But spareribs can also be soup bones or can be cut into smaller chunks for stewing meat. Stew meat—even steaks and roasts—can be made into hamburger or sausage. Roasts can be cut into steaks by just cutting them into slices across the grain. The usual practice is to make the more tender cuts into steaks. You can learn to tell the difference. The best meat for steaks is a lighter color. It is sad but true that the least desirable cuts require the most work.

Cutting Technique. Always try to cut either outside the muscle bundle or across the grain of it (across the muscle fibers). A commercial butcher works with frozen meat and power saws. He or she can saw out all the cuts. It's best for you to first cut with the knife through the meat part and then saw with the meat saw across the remaining bone if you want to include the bone. Meat is almost impossible to saw because it's wobbly and won't hold still. If you freeze it before butchering, that problem is eliminated, but then it will be a lot harder to find your way around in the carcass and harder to cut it with a knife.

Meat Saw

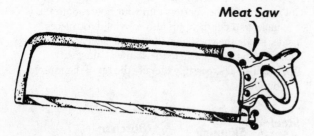

Cut Portion Sizes. The thickness of your steaks or chops is truly and purely a matter of the cook's preference, anywhere from ¼ inch to a full inch or more. Personally, I like goat and venison steaks ¼ thick (wild meat is usually cut about half the thickness of beef), beef ½ inch, and lamb ¾ inch thick. The ideal size of your roasts depends on the size of your family. Figure out how much meat per person per meal an average roast needs to supply (½ lb.?) and multiply that by the number of people in your family. If some of your people are small eaters, lessen it accordingly. Add an average ½ lb. per person for roasts that contain a bone.

Preparations for Cutting Up. Have ready 3 containers—such as cardboard boxes, enamel or stainless steel dishpans, or plastic buckets or pans—and a fourth if you plan to set aside some of the meat for jerky. One container is for the unusable trimmings you will give your cat, dog, chickens, or pigs to eat. The second is for pieces of meat that you intend to grind up for hamburger or sausage. The third is where you put the bones and ribs, which are bulky and would crowd your tabletop, until you have a chance to wrap them and put them away in the freezer. The fourth holds long, lean strips (at least 3 inches long) without too much gristle and with every bit of the fat cut away; these make the best jerky. (Note that you can't make jerky from pork because of the trichinosis threat.) You can sort these out from among the general to-be-ground-for-hamburger or sausage pile.

A big sturdy table is a good place to do the work. Everybody I know uses the kitchen table. We have a piece of plywood cut to fit the top of it for cutting-up days. You may want to also cover that with butcher paper before starting.

ORGAN MEATS: Don't age organ meats. They don't keep as well as the muscle meat. Brains, sweetbreads, kidneys, and tripe are the most perishable. Cook any or all of them within 24 hours of slaughter. The tongue, heart, and liver can last longer but should not be deliberately aged. You can store liver, heart, and tongue in your freezer.

Sweetbreads. "Sweetbreads" are the thymus gland. It looks pinkish grey and sort of spongy. I haven't included them in the regular butchering directions because most people ignore them, but the sweetbreads of calf and lamb (not pork) are edible. Lane Morgan says they're delicious. Sweetbreads are situated at the base of the neck near the heart.

Tripe. "Tripe" is the lining of the first and second stomachs of calves. I didn't mention it in the coming butchering section either, but it's also edible. "Plain tripe" means the lining of the first stomach. "Honeycomb tripe" means the lining of the second stomach and is considered better-tasting than plain tripe. You get the tripe by cutting the stomachs away from the rest of the intestines, cutting them open, and turning them inside out. Wash and rinse at least 3 times in clean water. To prepare tripe, boil at a low temperature, covered with water, until tender (4 hours or more). Then refrigerate until wanted for a recipe.

OF SUET: Suet (also called tallow) is the hardened fat around the kidneys and loins of sheep and cows. You can use hogs' intestinal fat and all sheep and calf fat for making soap and candles and for bird feed. Suet is used in many recipes, and it's also good to feed to wild birds in cold weather. Many wild birds (especially insect-eating birds, which you want to keep around) love to get suet during the winter months. These birds can metabolize the energy in suet more efficiently than that in seeds. Be careful, however, to leave out all salt, as it will kill most small birds. You can offer suet to birds by freezing it until winter and then setting a lump in a hanging container (a wire basket or a perforated plastic bag works well for small clinging birds) or sticking it to tree bark or cones. Woodpeckers enjoy suet poured into a hole in a log. Suet poured into a coconut shell half will be eaten by all sorts of wild birds. Or you can mix in corn, seeds, or peanuts for a bird pudding!

➤ BASIC BIRD PUDDING *Spread seeds, grains, popcorn, cracked corn, peanuts, granola, cornmeal, cheese, oatmeal, dry cake, or what-have-you in a container. Heat suet in a double boiler and pour hot fat (½ to ¾ lb. of fat to 1 lb. of mixture) over mixture until it is covered. Birds need grit; ordinary sand will do. Add ½ t. sand to 1½ c. suet. Let set. Turn out onto a table unless you have prepared it in a tit-bell or coconut holder. In spring, when insects, worms, and new growth appear in the softened ground, stop suet feeding. For more wild bird feeding recipes, consult* The Bird Table Book in Colour *by Tony Soper or* My Recipes Are for the Birds *by Irene Cosgrove.*

About Cooking and Eating Meat

Being faced with eating an entire large animal may require quite an adjustment. Maybe in the past you've learned only to cook hamburger 365 ways and are uncertain about coping with many different cuts. Don't worry: the ways to prepare and cook meat are infinite. Big hunks are roasts. Little tiny hunks are stewing meat, shish-kabob meat, or slicing meat for Chinese cooking. Medium-sized flat pieces of meat are steaks or chops. Very thick flat pieces are roasts. Bones with very little meat on them are soup bones. The ribs are "spareribs" that you bake with barbecue sauce on them. With a Dutch oven and a frying pan or wok, you'll have no trouble consuming even an entire cow. Cook the roasts and ribs in the Dutch oven with the lid on, the soups and stews in it with the lid off. Cook the flat meat in your frying pan.

RATIONING: Don't eat steaks every day the first three weeks—you'll end up eating hamburger every day the last three! Rotate. Have steak one day, then hamburger, a roast the next, then a stew, soup, or ribs. That system will make the various cuts come out about even. Or, if you want to consume less meat than that, spread the system out so you're eating the meat only every other day in the same rotation. You can be using the leftover supper meat on your off-meat days for cold cuts, hash, or ground-meat sandwiches. If you have a pig in your freezer too, add pork to your rotation. Most of the pig makes good breakfast meat. Or you can limit your meat consumption to once per day and add a couple of nights of pork roast, ribs, or chops, or add the "breakfast" pork meats to your evening meal rotation. If you use about as much pork as you do beef, you can eat up about 4 pigs while you are eating up 1 cow using this system.

TENDERNESS: Home-grown and wild meats may vary in age at butchering time and thus in tenderness. If you can't butcher your animal young, you could make hamburger or sausage out of the whole thing. The quick, hard-working old-fashioned way to tenderize is to pound the meat with a wooden meat mallet or a special steel hammer with a corrugated pressure-surface made for pounding meat. Or you can precook the meat, covered with water, for about 15 minutes. Discard that water and proceed with your regular recipe. (This process both tenderizes and floats away some of the wild, goatey or muttoney tastes.) Or cook the meat longer, or cook it a short time in a pressure cooker (15 lb. pressure for 15–20 minutes). Or marinate it, which may improve flavor as well as tenderize it. Popular marinades include a mixture of vinegar and lemon juice; grated onions and oil; tomato juice, water and lemon juice; water and vinegar; French dressing. The meat is typically soaked in the marinade in the refrigerator for 24 hours and turned in the liquid several times during that period. Or use a commercial tenderizer, which is made from a natural enzyme and will soften the toughest meat in a few minutes.

Coffee Tenderizer. Frank Womack, Jr., Pomeroy, WA, wrote me, "Coffee is a means of tenderizing about the toughest meat you can get. You do not need a knife to cut roast cooked in this way. It falls apart simply using a fork. I use it making stews, also. Simply substitute leftover or fresh coffee for an equal amount of whatever fluid you use in cooking the roast. There is no taste of coffee in the meat, and the remaining fluid after cooking makes excellent gravies. Or you can soak the meat overnight in the coffee; then discard the liquid and cook in your recipe."

SECRETS OF COOKING STRONG- OR STRANGE-TASTING MEATS: Some meat may be objectionably "strong" or "strange" tasting for some eaters: older, uncastrated males, goat and mutton of any age or sex, and all wild meats. There are many ways to moderate or cover such tastes.

1. Any marinade helps.
2. Trim away all fat. This is important because the fat tends to be even stronger-tasting than the meat. Baste and fry instead with cooking oil, margarine, butter, or lard. A roast can be larded with fatty pork strips or basted with sauce to keep it from becoming dry and tough.
3. Also make sure there are no hairs on the meat; hair too carries a strong "off" taste. If you need to clean the meat, do so with a cloth dipped in vinegar. Vinegar helps dissolve clotted blood and pick up stray hairs.
4. It helps to presoak from half an hour to an hour in a solution of salt and/or vinegar.
5. Or precook 15 minutes, covered with water, and then discard water.
6. Wild-meat recipes tend to include rich marinades,

stuffings of sliced onions and/or orange halves (discarded after the baking), or tasty stuffings that are served together with the meat.

7. A couple tablespoons of a tart jelly—like currant, barberry, or wild plum—in the gravy or on the plate helps any strong meat. Or serve the meat plain with a fancy fruit ketchup, such as peach. Or use other types of flavorful gravies, sauces, and heavy seasonings in general. Any recipe that involves a barbecue sauce will also camouflage an unfamiliar meat.
8. Another way to soften a strong meat's flavor is to combine the strong meat with a milder one, as in a wild meat/pork sausage combination; with potatoes, as in hash recipes; or with other bland vegetables like cabbage, cauliflower, asparagus, or breaded tomatoes.

COOKED OR RARE? Most people know about the possibility of trichina in underdone pork or *E. coli* from undercooked beef, but few know about toxo from underdone lamb. Toxoplasmosis is a parasite that can be carried in any animal, including humans, but it reproduces in cats. *Wash your hands after contact with cat litter.*
NOTE: All meat should be cooked enough to reach 160°F and change color throughout. Also wash hands after handling raw meat. When you are eating in a restaurant, check every burger or other meat. Open it up and make sure there's no pink meat at all to protect yourself and your children from toxo, E. coli, and other diseases carried by raw meat.
NOTE: Toxoplasmosis can give anybody a "flu," but pregnant women have to be especially careful not to eat rare or raw meat. Toxo is very serious to a fetus. It can cause blindness, retardation, or death.

Other animals besides cats can get toxo in their meat by eating cat poop that's in a grain bin or on grass. This can result in sheep with toxo cysts. Toxo cysts are killed by freezing, but the meat has to be frozen for a very long time at a very low temperature, not in the freezer compartment of your fridge. However, cooking takes care of them quickly and finally.

WILD CRITTERS

Porcupine is one kind of animal my daddy never hunted. He said that was the only kind of meat that a man who was lost in the forest without a gun had a chance of catching, because they are so slow-moving. He wanted to save them so they'd be plentiful for such a desperate man. In the years since I started this book, I've seen the numbers of various animals fall—and sometimes rise to the nuisance level again! So obey your current hunting laws, because they're carefully tuned to your local situation and needs.

I like wild animals, and I like a certain wildness in people too. I'm bothered by the extent to which writers think they have to write only what editors want, what publishers will print. I think writers have a special function and social obligation to their human community to be on the cutting edge. We need writers with bold new visions—ideas that are controversial or seemingly impossible at first glance yet may map the future. Farsighted writing that challenges the status quo tends by its nature to be unacceptable to Establishment publishing, yet it's essential to society because it articulates options. Some options are radical, some bad; but hidden in the confusion of choices is a new path—perhaps a hitherto unconsidered route, perhaps a revalued treasure of traditional living—that is the best one of all. So much important thinking appears first in small magazines or is self-published. We need to keep the doors open to these voices. And it's terribly important for our freedom of speech that people be able to publish magazines and books without submitting them to government review first, even to get a "copyright" or bar code/ISBN number to facilitate marketing.

The bottom line has to be courage. There's a plaque on my wall that I've treasured for years: "Anybody who says something is impossible is always being interrupted by someone doing it." "Impossible" is merely a relative term. One person's "impossible" is another person's "possible"—if the second person is willing to invest in the project an amount of dedication, time, and effort that the first person couldn't even imagine, much less put forth. Now, back to the topic . . .

Hunting Birds with a Shotgun

Don't! As many as 3,000,000 water birds now die every year from lead poisoning, according to the Nov. 22, 1992, issue of *Awake!* magazine. Lead poisoning from waterfowl hunting is a tremendous environmental problem. The U.S. Department of the Interior estimates that for every bird that hunters kill, half a pound of lead pellets from their shotguns ends up in the ground and water. Wildlife biologists testing wetlands have discovered as many as 100,000 lead pellets per acre in the top few inches. (Lead fishing weights lost by fishermen litter the bottom of popular fishing areas.)

Waterfowl frequently eat lead pellets during their search for food. In a bird with lead poisoning, the poison reaches the heart, liver, and kidneys 3 to 10 days after it eats the lead; after another week, it is so sick that it enters a coma and soon dies. Bald eagles acquire lead poisoning by swallowing waterfowl that contain lead because they have been shot. At least 120 bald eagles have died from lead poisoning since 1966, and the rate of this type of death is increasing. Since official statistics include only eagles whose carcasses were examined for cause of death, obviously they represent only a small part of the total.

Lead-polluted land is also permanently ruined for agriculture, because any human or animal fodder that grows on it will have a high lead content. People may grow food or fodder there, not knowing of the lead, and thus risk further

poisoning. I'd like to see lead-pellet shotguns made illegal. I'm totally serious. They aren't worth the environmental costs. I'd also like to see lead fishing weights made illegal. In fact, just about all uses of lead need to be outlawed. Lead poisoning is currently a worldwide long-term epidemic affecting people of all ages from conception to old age because lead is entering our bodies from our drinking water, air, and food. At best, lead exposure "merely" permanently lowers I.Q. At worst, it causes death.

PREPARING WILD BIRDS: If you do kill a wild bird for food, proceed as you would if it were a domesticated breed. Pick or skin the bird, and then remove the entrails. The bird will pick easiest while it still has as much body heat as possible, before the feathers have had a chance to set tight. See the discussion of ducks in Chapter 9 for details. Cook as you would a domesticated bird. To cook a game bird in a camping setup, you can roast it by turning it on a spit slowly over a campfire, or cook in a slow to moderate Dutch or camper's oven, or (easiest of all) boil to tenderness in a stew. Wild birds are leaner than domesticated ones, and it may help a roasted one to turn it frequently, basting with margarine or a basting sauce.
NOTE: Before you cook a wild bird, consider a moment: what has that bird been eating in these polluted times? Mercury-treated seed grain? Then don't eat it! Fish from waterways polluted with dioxins, heavy metals, or radioactivity? Then don't eat either bird or fish!

Large Wild Mammals

Stay within the hunting limit. Mike and I didn't get any wild meat this last year. We were going to keep the deer on our place as pets, but we got a rude awakening. Somebody came on our place and shot them. The same guy got the buck, the doe, and the fawn. We know because he bragged about it to a friend of ours. Kind of makes you feel that posting your property isn't such a wicked and unsociable thing to do after all!

BE PREPARED: To avoid waste (hunting is harvesting of a wild food), be prepared to deal properly with the meat. A good reference about hunting and wild meat is *Enjoy Your Game Meat: From Planning the Hunt to Eating the Bounty* by Neal Blair and Judy Hosafros (Wyoming Game and Fish Department, 1974). Another one is *Getting the Most from Your Game and Fish* by Robert Candy.

Start by taking a good sheath knife or a substantial folding knife and a small whetstone. Your folding knife blade must lock in the open position so it can't snap shut on bare knuckles. A belt ax or small hand saw will be handy. There are a number of saws on the market for the hunter. Some fold into the handle; some come in leather sheaths. Pick one of good quality. Elk bones dull a poor-quality saw in a hurry. A small block and tackle hoist can be a real timesaver. Some of these weigh as little as 2 lb. and can hoist an elk. Pack some cheesecloth sacks to put the quarters in. You can buy them at sporting goods stores or make them. Take salt too—not iodized salt but pickling salt—because even if you don't want the hide, you can give it to someone who can use it or sell it to a buyer.

Always carry fire-making equipment or matches in a waterproof container when hunting. Even in wet weather, you can always chop away some of the outside layer of a dead stump or whittle some dry kindling from pitch wood inside the soggy exterior. If you get lost late in the day, don't stumble around in the dark. Build a fire in a sheltered spot near available wood and make the most of it till daylight.

Wild meat generally has more lean than fat; the big exception is bear in the prehibernation season. And the lean of such animals as deer, elk, antelope, moose, caribou, reindeer, and small game is of greater density than the flesh of domesticated animals, maybe because they get more exercise. The age range is greater too, since domestic animals are almost always butchered in their young prime—except for hamburger-type cows or sausage pigs, whose meat is ground up, so you can't tell its age.

So wild meat may be on the tough side. Another reason for that: more care is generally given to the meat when butchering domestic than when butchering wild. What I mean is, a wild animal may have been running for, say, 2 hours during a peak hunting day as it encounters hunter after hunter. It is then cut down with a whole batch of bullets that hit it in prime meaty places, such as the front shoulder or hind hip. The animal lies for a couple of hours before being gutted, and the gutters forget to remove the testicles. Then it waits another 5 days or so in warmish weather, while the rest of the hunting party has a chance to get "theirs," before being cut up and taken to the freezer. Is it any surprise that the meat may not compare very favorably to beefsteak?

To minimize the meat's wild flavor, hunt early in the season, or else kill a female. In the large game animals, the meat of the males becomes stronger in taste as the mating season advances. Try to avoid handling the musk glands of deer, which are between the hocks and hoofs. Try to avoid killing the animal when it has been running and is very upset; such meat might be "bloodshot," not bleed out well, and thus have an off-taste. Be sure to gut it completely and as soon as possible, and don't forget to remove a male's testicles. Then halve and quarter and hang up to cool, if you aren't going anywhere for a while. The meat of any antlered game animal is called "venison."

APPROACHING A DOWNED ANIMAL: Never assume an animal is dead, even if it appears to be. Approach cautiously with your rifle ready and from a direction that will enable you to stay away from flying hoofs and flaying antlers. Once you are sure the animal is dead, do whatever is necessary to mark the kill as yours, according to the local hunting laws.

BLEEDING OUT LARGE GAME: Any large animal—deer, elk, caribou, antelope, moose, etc.—has to be bled out, and thoroughly. Head, neck, and spine shots do not allow enough bleeding. And if the animal has been shot in the chest or abdomen, it probably won't bleed more than a little because, in that case, its blood has already run into those body cavities. So you have to cut the throat as soon as you can get to a downed animal. Beginners may find it easiest to do a side-to-side cut at the base of the neck. Pros prefer a breastbone to upward cut. Now move the animal to have its head downhill so as much blood as possible can run out the hole you made.

DEALING WITH PORKY GAME: This category is boar and bear.

NOTE: Like domestic pig, wild pig (boar) and bear meat must be cooked well done before eating.

Boar. Butcher boar, a kind of ancient wild pig, by the directions for pigs in Chapter 11. Boars are comparatively lean

and, because they get so much more exercise, their meat has a "wild" flavor. So consider using boar meat in wild-meat recipes (see "Recipes for Wild or Gamey-Tasting Meats").

Bear. The old-timers cleaned a bear by sticking one hand in his mouth, grabbing his tail with the other, and turning him inside out. Nowadays we lesser mortals have to go the more mundane route of slitting and skinning off the hide—unless you find a bear without his skin. I did once.

As a little girl, I was walking down a little canyon near my home and came upon a large bear lying on the ground. I could see no wound. He appeared to be asleep. The strangest thing, though, was that he was minus his hide. I touched one leg tentatively and uncertainly. He kicked me! Well, I took off for the house yelling. My daddy was there, sharpening his knife blade. I said, "Daddy, Daddy, there's a bear alive in the canyon and he hasn't got his skin on." My daddy laughed. Then he explained that there are reflexes in animals' limbs for a little while even after they are dead.

There are now only 4 or 5 states in the Union where you can kill a bear (or an elk) any more. If you do kill a bear and want to save the fur, turn it on its back and cut the skin in a very straight line from its tail to under its lower jaw. Then cut from the lower inside of one front paw straight across to the lower inside of the other paw. Cut from paw to tail and from paw to tail on the belly side of each of the hind legs. Then peel off the bear's hide. You can gut and quarter it and then take the meat to a custom cutter to be cleaned and cured. Or you can do it yourself, following my directions for pigs in Chapter 11. "Bear grease" means bear lard, and some people declare it's better grease than any other you'll find. You render it the same as pork lard.

You treat bear as you do pork. You can't make jerky out of bear meat because it can carry trichinosis, just like pig meat, and must always be well cooked before eating. A female bear is called a "sow." A young bear is a "shoat." The important thing about female bears and young bears, though, is not their name but their disposition. The only animal that I would tell you outright is aggressive and dangerous is a female bear with cubs. When I was a little girl, we had a man walking around town on one leg, and he was lucky to be walking at all. He made it up a tree with that one leg. Bears have the capacity to keep coming even with a bullet in the brain. You don't want to shoot one unless you're sure it can't get to you before it drops. Don't ever be one of those foolish Yellowstone Park tourist types who tries to get close and photograph that kind of bear.

If you want to thoroughly recreate an early colonial Thanksgiving dessert, make a mince pie with a filling of bear meat and dried pumpkin. Sweeten it with maple sugar and use a cornmeal crust.

> **ROASTED BEAR MEAT #1** *Rub a bear roast with sorghum on the top and sides, and roast in a Dutch oven with about ½ inch water. This is my favorite way of making plain old pork roast, too.*

> **ROASTED BEAR MEAT #2** *Rub a bear roast with vinegar and then dry with a cloth. Rub with a mixture of bacon grease, ½ t. poultry seasoning, ½ t. savory salt, ½ t. garlic powder, and ½ t. salt. Put the meat in your Dutch oven or roaster with a little water. Cover tightly and bake at medium heat until tender. That's if you want to be able to taste everything but the bear.*

> **TERIYAKI SPARERIBS BARBECUE** *From Lane Morgan, who reports that her Alaska friends marinate bear spareribs in teriyaki sauce and then cook them suspended over a fire. The sauce tenderizes the meat and cuts the wild taste. The ribs are less greasy because the fat drips out. "Great dinner!" she says.*

DRESSING DEER, ANTELOPE, ELK (AND GOATS): These animals are all more or less closely related and similar to butcher. Remove the innards ("dress it") as soon as possible. Removing all viscera promptly will speed cooling and prevent spoilage so you'll have better-tasting meat. Arrange the animal on its back, hind legs spread. It may help to use a stick, rock, etc. to prop it in the right position. Now you have to cut the critter open from stem to stern, from neck to rear.

Of Sex and Scent. In some states, the law requires that sex identification be left attached to the carcass. If you've got that rule, cut around the scrotum or mammary gland and leave that skin attached. Sex organs won't harm the flavor. However, the scent glands may reinforce the wild flavor unless you remove them. They're on the hind legs, right below the "knee" and toward the inside (belly side) of the legs. Pros remove them carefully: secretions still on hair around the openings could get on your hands or knife blade and from there onto the meat. But most folks just settle for the wild taste.

Basic Gutting. Cut the skin in a straight line from the lower end of the breastbone down to the anus. Be careful not to cut into the intestines. You accomplish that by holding them away from the knife with your non-cutting hand as soon as the opening is large enough for you to get a hand in there. If your animal is a female with milk-filled mammaries, circumvent those and continue cutting to the rectum, but not into it. Then go back and lift and cut away the mammaries. Cut around each side of the sexual organ of a male and around each side of the rectum. Be careful not to cut into the sex organ or rectum. (Any contaminated meat would have to be cut away.) Tie off the rectum so that no contents can escape. Let it drop into the body cavity.

 *Wrong*

 *Right*

You will have to cut around the edge of the muscular diaphragm that separates the abdominal cavity from the

chest cavity in order to get at the lungs and heart. On an elk or moose, you may well need to use your ax or saw. Carefully reach forward in the chest cavity to cut the windpipe and gullet, which are in front of the lungs. Cutting those will free up the lungs and heart so you can pull them out of the chest cavity. Once all the contents of the chest and abdominal cavities are free, turn the animal on its side. Split the pelvic bone by inserting your knife blade into the seam between the 2 halves of the pelvis, tapping on the end of the handle and then prying downward. Again, on moose or elk, the hand ax may be necessary. Carefully roll out all the intestines, bladder, and genital organs. Also make sure any accumulated blood there is drained away. Slit the muscles holding the windpipe and gullet and pull them out.

Removing the Edible Organs. Cut the heart free from its membrane pouch. Carefully cut away the gall bladder from the liver. You'll have to throw away part of the liver to do this without cutting into the gall bladder. Then remove the liver and the 2 kidneys. You may wish to save the sheets of abdominal fat. To get the tongue, cut through the underside of the jaw deep enough so the tongue can be pulled through the opening and cut off near its base. (Don't remove the tongue if you're planning on having the head mounted.) To get the brains, the easiest way to open the skull is with a meat saw, although you can do it with an ax too. A waterproof bag is a good idea for carrying these back to camp or home. Use the organs for camp meat, if you aren't going home right away, since they won't keep as well as the muscle meat. See "Recipes for Wild or Gamey-Tasting Meats" for camp-type recipes for organ meats.

Cooling the Meat. Wild meat needs to be cooled quickly to avoid spoiling. If you intend to leave the carcass for a while, arrange it in the shade on some rocks or logs with the cavity propped open so that air can circulate through it and the body heat can dissipate. Throw a few fresh branches over it loosely to keep out birds. If you split the backbone between the shoulders with an ax, the cooling process (especially for moose or elk) will be greatly expedited. In warm weather, skin before cooling and cover the carcass or quarters in cheesecloth or cotton bags to protect it from flies. Avoid cooling in plastic or other materials that do not allow air to circulate; they could cause spoilage.

SKINNING, QUARTERING, AND PACKING: First comes a decision: To skin or not to skin? The answer is: It depends. Here are some factors to consider in this judgment call.

"Yes" to Skinning. There are practical reasons why you should skin the carcass quickly. In above-freezing weather, the meat will cool much more slowly with the hide on. In below-freezing weather, you want to finish skinning because the more recently the animal has been killed, the easier it is to skin off the hide. You also want to skin before the hide has time to freeze on, which makes it much more difficult to get off. And meat stays fresh better when the air can get to it.

"No" to Skinning. Alternate thawing and freezing will reduce meat quality. If the temperatures are fluctuating from day to night, you may want to leave the hide on to keep the meat at a more uniform temperature. If you are going to age the meat, leaving the skin on prevents excessive drying.

How to Skin. Hanging up the animal makes skinning it easier. A "skinning knife" has a curved blade, but you can make do with any sharp hunting or butcher knife. Have some flour or cornmeal handy; if you accidentally cut into the flesh and blood starts to get onto the fur, you can apply flour or meal to the freshly cut areas to stop the blood. Skinning should be done before the skin is set on firmly. On a warm, freshly killed carcass, the skin can almost always be pulled away, and it takes just a few minutes. The skin on a cold animal must be cut away, and that greatly increases your risk of accidentally getting holes in the hide.

To remove the hide, cut around each of the 4 knee joints. Then slit along the inside of the leg clear up to the center cut from which you took out the viscera. Extend the belly incision on up to the neck just below the lower jaw. Take off the head by cutting completely around the neck, right behind the ears, jaws, and antlers (unless you want to save the head for mounting, in which case the directions are very different and you should come prepared with instructions from your taxidermist as to how he or she wants it done.) Slit the skin on the underside of the tail and then begin cutting the skin from the body. Like mutton, venison has a thin white layer between skin and flesh. You cut through this layer in long easy swipes with a very sharp blade. It helps to have someone pulling the skin taut while you are cutting it loose. If you intend to tan the hide, see the instructions on scraping and caring for the hide in the "Tanning" section.

Skinning Antelope. Antelope is a little tricky to skin and dress. The meat can develop a strong, gamey taste if the animal was run hard or was crippled before being killed. Pronghorn antelope should be cleaned and skinned immediately, right on the spot. Remove the entrails first; then skin. Do not get hair on the meat. Hang the carcass to allow air to circulate for at least an hour before you load it up.

Quartering. This is necessary with wild game unless you can drive to the carcass. Split the body completely in two

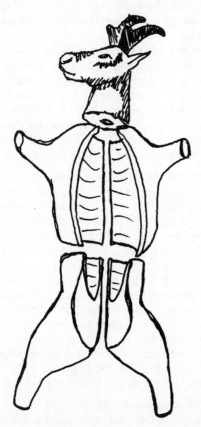

along the backbone, working quickly to help cool it and avoid any spoiling. Quarter by cutting between the second and third rib from the rear and the vertebrae. To do this quartering, you need a meat saw or sharp ax. Place the quarters in cheesecloth sacks. If you won't reach home for more than a day or two, salt the hide. Rub the salt all over, more on thicker places, and get into all the corners. Roll the hide and get it to the person who will tan it as soon as you can.

Packing It Out. A big buck deer will dress out to about 200–225 lb., an elk to 800 lb. You can usually pack an elk out 2 quarters to 1 horse. You probably need 3 horses for a large moose. Some people bone out the meat to get the weight down. Balance the meat on the horse's back to spare the horse from serious injury. This is no problem as long as you pack the 2 front quarters or the 2 hindquarters from the same animal on one horse. Pack one on each side of the saddle, and fasten them down with a diamond hitch.

If you have to pack the meat yourself, don't drag it. Cut it up into smaller parcels and make several trips carrying it on your back.

Until you can get the meat home, keep it as cool as possible. Quartering and hanging it with air circulating around it will help. On the way home your animal is better off on the trunk of the car than over the hood because the engine's heat promotes spoilage.

SECRETS OF TRIMMING MEAT

1. Chill meat as much as you can before cutting up. Any meat is easier to cut when it is cold because cold fat is firmer. Wild meat, being so lean, is especially wobbly.
2. It helps to have one person trimming fat, etc., off the cuts as another carves them off.
3. Trim away all fat because wild game fat quickly becomes rancid.
4. Unless you're lucky and the hunter got the animal in the head, wherever the bullet passed through it the meat will be messed up—torn and bloodshot (meat containing hard black bits is "bloodshot"). You must trim out all bloodshot meat, or else throw away the whole piece. Bloodshot meat doesn't look or taste good, and it spoils very easily.
5. Get rid of all the black bits. A well-bled animal shouldn't have too many.
6. If some of the meat has started to spoil, trim off the moldy areas or the parts that don't smell good. Go ahead and wrap and freeze the rest. *Such meat, however, must be cooked very promptly and thoroughly upon thawing.*
7. On wild meat, you trim away the tough paper-like outer skin from your steaks. You can cut it at each end and just rip it off across the middle.

BONING OUT: This means removing all the meat from all the bones, period. It's most feasible with a relatively small game animal. But this method, like most "methods," is rather extreme. We bone out only a few appropriate cuts. You can save the fat for candle or soap making.

CUTTING UP THE HINDQUARTERS: These directions are for deer, elk, antelope, moose, and goat.

Haunch. This is the quarter containing the Achilles tendon, by which you were hanging the animal, and the big rear "haunch." "Haunch" means the whole hind leg of the animal. Cut off the haunch at the hip joint. It begins just below where the ribs end, and you'll have to guess at just the right spot. You'll need your meat saw to get through the bone.

Now cut across the haunch in 2 places to make thirds from top to bottom.

The top (widest) third is your round steak. To make big round steaks, cut right across the grain and through the bone of the entire haunch. An easier way, which avoids having to saw across that bone for every steak, is separating the muscle bundles. The largest bundles are the "top round" and "bottom round" cuts. You can separate these two bundles if you want, and cut across into steaks or leave them attached together and cut into steaks (depending on the size of your animal and your preference). The other muscle bundle is the sirloin. Cut across the grain for your sirloin steaks.

The middle third of the haunch is generally made into a roast. Some people, however, strip it off the bone and make hamburger or jerky out of it. The long, nice strips are good for jerky. The bottom third is generally stripped of meat and the meat put into the hamburger or jerky pile. The bone can be a soup bone.

Ribs and Backstrap. What you have left of the hindquarter is the ribs and backstrap. There are 2 strips of muscle along the backbone. The strip along the outside is the backstrap (tenderloin) and is the choicest, most tender meat in the animal. You can either "bone out" these 2 muscles by cutting them away from the backbone and slicing them into steaks, or you can cut across the backbone for each steak and have both muscles represented in each steak.

If you sawed each one out you would have these cuts (using beef terminology), starting from the front end of the animal: club steaks, then T-bone steaks, and finally sirloin steaks. You can see the "T"shaped bone in the T-bone steaks. As a general guide, the first third of the backstrap will be club steaks, the middle third T-bone, and the last third sirloin. Some people make a roast of the last third instead of cutting it up for steaks; to make a roast, just leave it in one piece.

On a small animal such as a deer (a deer has about one-fourth the meat of an elk or cow), all that sawing is not worth the amount of meat you get out of it, so the 2 long muscles are generally boned out. The small inside strip is the one that would be the small piece of meat on the inside of your T-bone steak. If you bone it out, you can slice and make "tips" of it, which are fine floured and fried. You lose a little but not too much on your chop size from the boning-out process. Cut as close to the ribs and backbone as you can to minimize loss. If you decide to bone out the tenderloin, then just cut across it to make the steaks. From a small deer, the steaks are very small but good. Allow 2 or 3 for each person per meal. Some people make a roast of the sirloin instead. If you want 2 roasts, just cut it across the middle.

You can saw across the ribs and backbone to suit yourself for soup bones, spareribs, and dog food. A small deer doesn't make very good spareribs—there is so very little meat on the ribs—but you can try.

CUTTING UP THE FRONT QUARTERS

Arm. Cut the front leg from the ribs as you would a chicken thigh, pulling the bone away from the body in the joint as you cut until it is severed across the line where it joins the chest. It should pop right out of the joint. In butchering terminology, the front leg is called the "arm."

Saw the arm into thirds from top to bottom with your meat saw. The top third is called "blade roast." Some people make it into hamburger because it's a hard roast to serve and eat, especially if the animal is small. The middle third is

made into an "arm roast." Trim what meat you can from the bottom third of the leg and put it into the pile for hamburger or jerky. Put the bone of that bottom third into your bone box.

Remainder of Front Quarters. The meat along the outside of the backbone is the extension of the tenderloin muscle. Slice steak or tips out of it just like you did on the hindquarters. The rest is pretty much bone. Saw off the backbone and make it into soup bones or whatever you want. Section up the ribs for spareribs or stew meat, using the meat saw where needed.

Recipes for Wild or Gamey-Tasting Meats

For people who aren't used to wild, "strong," or unusual-tasting meat and want to disguise that taste, the following recipes will be helpful. They are most likely to suit small and large wild mammals but are also tasty recipes for domestic meat. In addition to these recipes, Oregon State U. Extension will sell you a booklet, "From Hunt to Home," for $2.50. Order from 541-737-2513; OSU, Ad S 422, Corvallis, OR 97331.

STEAK: I was raised in large part on wild meat, and our deerburger was all deer, but there are more gourmet ways to fix wild meat, starting with a simple canned deer stew, which was a childhood favorite of mine, and going from there. One fall my father was hurt in a logging accident in Oregon and had to be laid off for the rest of the winter. The little cash my folks had went for baby milk, and the rest of the diet was venison. So we never knocked venison!

A possible problem with wild meat is that its tenderness varies greatly. Tame meat is usually butchered relatively young. But wild meat might be any age—and correspondingly tough or tender. You'll soon know the kind you have and will be able to make cooking adaptations accordingly.

Tender Ones

☙ *FRIED WILD MEAT WITH JELLY GRAVY Sprinkle the meat with salt and pepper or garlic salt on both sides, and then dip it into flour. Fry quickly over moderate to low heat in a little butter or oil. After 1 side is cooked, turn to brown the other side. Remove the meat from the pan. Thicken the pan drippings with 1 T. (or so) flour. Add water until it is of a suitable gravy consistency, and add 2 T. currant (or other tart) jelly. Season the gravy if your taste buds say it is needed.*

☙ *WILD STEAK, ORIENTAL Mix together ½ c. cooking oil, 2 chopped garlic cloves, and 2 T. soy sauce. Cut about 1 lb. wild steak into cubes or strips. Let first mixture rest about an hour to get well flavored. Remove and discard seeds from 1 green pepper; then cut it into strips. Chop an onion, add 1 c. chopped celery if you have it, and get ready a couple of fresh tomatoes by slicing into chunks. This is a good one to make near the end of the garden season, when you have this stuff. Now brown the steak bits in your oil mixture; then add green pepper, onion, and celery; and cook about 7 minutes more. Dissolve 1 t. cornstarch in a little water and stir it into the mixture. Salt and pepper to taste. Add a little homemade ketchup or tomato sauce, if you have it; your fresh tomatoes; and a little more water if needed to give the mixture a manageable consistency. Serve with cooked rice.*

☙ *WILD MEAT, HAWAIIAN Cube or cut into strips about 1 lb. wild steak. Shake the meat in a paper bag with some flour until the pieces are all coated. Brown them in enough* butter to do the job. Then add ½ c. boiling water, salt to taste, and simmer until tender. Hollow out and slice 2 green peppers. (Optional: add ½ c. pineapple chunks.) In a separate pan make a sauce of 2 T. cornstarch, ½ c. vinegar, 2 T. soy sauce, 2 T. brown sugar, and ½ c. pineapple juice if you are using pineapple or water if you aren't. When the sauce is thick, pour it over the meat. Cook the entire mixture about 3 more minutes and then serve with rice.

Tough Ones

MUSTARD STEAKS Brush both sides of 4 good-sized wild steaks with about 2 T. mustard. Sprinkle both sides of the meat with salt and pepper, and then dip both sides in flour. Brown in melted butter in your Dutch oven. Set aside. In a saucepan combine 2 T. brown sugar, 1 t. salt, 2 T. mustard, and a dash each chili powder and cayenne — and, if you have have a strong digestive tract, 2 T. Worcestershire sauce, ½ c. vinegar, ½ c. water, and 1 c. tomato juice or ½ c. tomato ketchup and ½ c. water. When the sauce seems well mixed, pour it over your meat. Put the lid on the Dutch oven and bake at 350°F until done.

WILD STEAK, HUNGARIAN Start out with enough steak for 6 people. Dip it lightly in flour; shake off the excess. Brown in a little fat. Pour into your Dutch oven. Brown several large onions, sliced, in some oil. When they're cooked to transparency, pour them over the meat. Add 1 t. salt, ½ t. paprika, ½ c. sour cream, ¾ c. water, and 1 bay leaf. Bake at 325°F about 2 hours.

STEAK AND WATER Brown steaks in 2 T. shortening. Remove meat from pan. Make a gravy by adding 2 T. flour, salt and pepper to taste, and 2 c. water, after your flour has absorbed all the drippings and browned. Return steaks to pan in gravy. Cook, covered, in the oven at 300°F until tender (about 45 minutes).

ROASTS: I usually cook these in a Dutch oven, usually with the lid on, usually at about 350°F but sometimes less, and I usually brown the meat in a little fat in a frying pan to just sear and seal the outside before commencing roasting. You can substitute your favorite roasting pan for my Dutch oven. Trim all the fat away from a wild roast before commencing.

If your meat is from a comparatively old, tough animal, you may prefer a first stage of simmering in a large pan of boiling water, 30 minutes per pound, or until tender. Then drain and finish "roasting." A quicker way to precook is in your pressure cooker. You may have to cut the roast into several pieces to fit. Pressure-cook for 15 minutes at 15 lb. pressure. Then go ahead and "roast." It won't take long after the precooking. Your results will be both delicious and tender.

WILD MOCK HAM Bake in an airtight cooker like a Dutch oven at 350°F, 30 minutes per pound. When meat is tender, take it out. In a separate container combine ½ c. brown sugar, 1 t. mustard, and 1 c. orange or pineapple juice (or available juice of your preference). Score outer layer of roast with knife, and pour juice mixture over it. Stud with cloves. Bake uncovered for an additional half hour, basting frequently with pan juices. Good served hot or cold.

SPICY OVEN-BAKED WILD MEAT Combine ½ c. flour with 1 t. salt, 1 t. curry powder, ⅛ t. pepper, and ⅛ t. paprika, making sure the seasonings are well distributed in the flour. Cover meat pieces (cubes, tips, small animal parts—

whatever you want to cook) on all sides with the flour-seasoning mixture. Fry meat in oil or fat until well browned on all sides. Then move meat to a baking dish, add 1 c. water, cover, and bake an hour. If you like, you can make a gravy before serving by adding flour and water to thicken liquid.

BARBECUE-SAUCE WILD ROAST This recipe is good for 1 entire small animal cooked whole or for a chunk of a bigger one. Cover meat with cold water, add salt, and 1 small hot pepper. Cook over low heat until just tender. Pour off the water; place meat into baking pan. Roast at moderate heat, basting often with barbecue sauce, until it looks done to suit you.

ONION-SMOTHERED ROAST Mix together ½ c. flour, 1 t. salt, and ½ t. pepper. Flour your meat pieces thoroughly in that and then fry them until browned in just enough oil. Move meat to a baking dish. Add 3 large chopped onions, and 2 bay leaves. Bake in a moderate oven until tender.

WILD ROAST WITH DRESSING Brown your roast in a little bacon grease or other fat. Sprinkle it with salt and pepper to suit yourself. Bake in a Dutch oven, covered for 2 hours at 300°F (assuming about a 2½-lb. roast). Make about 1 lb. bread crumbs. Combine them in a bowl with 1½ t. sage, 2 eggs, ¾ c. chopped onion, and 1 bay leaf. Add enough milk to moisten the mixture, and mix it well. Take your roast out of the oven. There will be juice in the bottom of the pan. Skim off any grease floating on top of it as best you can. Then spoon your dressing right down into the meat juice all around the roast. Cover and continue baking at 350°F for 1 hour more. To serve, remove the roast and carve it. Serve the dressing in a separate bowl. This is a favorite of mine.

COFFEE WILD ROAST In a wild roast, make slits big enough for sliced onions. Slice 2 onions and fit them into the slits. Make a marinade of ⅓ c. vinegar and ⅔ c. water; pour that over the roast. Marinate overnight in the refrigerator or other cool place. When ready to cook, drain off the marinade, brown roast in bacon fat or other oil, lay a few bacon strips across the top, sprinkle salt and pepper over, and set in your Dutch oven or roaster. Add a mixture of half coffee and half water (about 2 c. of each); keep the lid on your roaster and cook at 350°F until done.

GREEN PEPPER WILD ROAST I like this one a lot too. Put your wild roast, a sprinkle of salt and pepper, and 4 chopped garlic cloves (or fewer if you aren't a garlic lover) into your Dutch oven. Pour in 1 c. water, cover, and cook until done. Remove the seeds from 3 green peppers, cut them into slices, and saute about 10 minutes in a little cooking oil. Add some of your homemade tomato ketchup, canned tomatoes, or tomato juice if you like the flavor. Pour the green pepper sauce over the meat; carve and serve.

HERBED WILD ROAST Combine ½ c. flour, 2 t. marjoram, 1 t. thyme, 2 t. rosemary, and 1 cut-up clove garlic. Rub your wild roast with a little cooking oil. Sprinkle salt and pepper on it; then apply your herb mixture to it. Put the roast into your Dutch oven; add 1 c. water and 1 c. apple juice. Bake, basting occasionally, until done.

MOOSE POT ROAST WITH MUSTARD AND TARRAGON From cookbook author Lane Morgan! Marinate meat a few hours in red wine, raspberry or blueberry vinegar (if available), and a little soy sauce. Brown meat in a little oil. Then add a few chopped garlic cloves, a chopped onion, and 2 tomatoes (fresh, canned, or frozen). Reduce heat. Add a pinch of tarragon, 2 T. Dijon mustard, and salt and pepper to taste. You can also pour in some of the marinade, but you don't have to. Cover tightly, and simmer or bake until meat is done. The meat will make its own juice. Pour the sauce, which is fantastic, over the sliced meat and barley or rice.

HEART, LIVER, KIDNEYS, BRAINS, AND TONGUE RECIPES

➤ *WOODSMAN'S LIVER Slice liver ½ to 1 inch thick. It will grill quickly over a campfire on the end of a pointed stick or over a rack made of green wood. Eat plain or with salt and/or butter. A method that's a step less primitive is to brown it in a frying pan in fat. Optional: add chopped onions.*

➤ *LIVER AND ONIONS Cut liver into thin slices and soak in salted water for 1 hour. Dry slices and dredge in flour; fry in butter and add sliced onions. Fry until tender.*

➤ *WOODSMAN'S HEART Cut heart ½ inch thick, season, baste with margarine, and broil over campfire about 3 minutes per side. A less primitive method is to fry in a pan in a little fat and season with salt and pepper. For tougher meat, roast in a Dutch oven until tender. Add vegetables (potatoes, carrots, onions) to boiled heart for a campfire stew.*

➤ *STUFFED HEART Prepare your favorite stuffing or combine instant rice, mushrooms, chopped onions, celery, salt and pepper, and beef bouillon. Cook all the stuffing ingredients in the bouillon. Clean the heart and remove membranes. Stuff the heart and bake, loosely covered, at 325°F for 15 to 20 minutes per pound of meat.*

➤ *KIDNEYS Strip away the connective membrane. Cut kidneys into walnut-size chunks. Simmer covered with water in low heat with butter, salt, cloves, and some chopped onion. Discard liquid and serve meat with mashed potatoes and/or fresh bread.*

➤ *WOODSMAN'S BRAINS When the fresh brain arrives in camp, salt it lightly and keep overnight. The next day, dip it into hot water. The outer membrane will peel off easily. Dip the brains into beaten eggs and then in crumbs, and fry in a little oil slowly until crisp outside and hot all through. Season to taste. Or mince them, add chopped green-onion tops and beaten eggs, and scramble the whole works.*

➤ *TONGUE Cover with cold, salted water and boil thoroughly, spooning off any scum that comes to the surface. When the tongue is tender, cook it; then peel off the outer skin. Good sliced thin and served with mustard or horseradish with or without bread. The tongue of a very young wild animal is so tender that it will cook up to a mush if you're not careful.*

➤ *CAMPFIRE MARROW BONES Heat them in the campfire, break them open to get at the marrow, and eat the marrow.*

Small Wild Mammals

Lane Morgan suggests that I "mention the animals that are most realistic for hunting in most areas of the country—squirrels and raccoons and possum, I suppose. We could certainly use fewer possums around our place." The wise and knowledgeable Gene Logsdon, one of my favorite authors, wrote in *Gene Logsdon's Practical Skills* (published by Rodale Press, listed in the book source list in Chapter 1): "Eating wild rabbits, squirrels, groundhogs, and raccoons

seems distasteful, even to those who are gulping down steak and hamburger every day. As civilization 'advances,' that part of its society that eats meat tends to restrict itself to fewer and fewer species of animals, which is quite wasteful. Earlier societies ate many more kinds of meat than we do today: in medieval Europe all manner of birds and small game were kept in captivity for meat, occupying various niches in the food web." So here are some tips to help you expand your food resources if you so choose.

HEALTH RULES FOR SMALL-ANIMAL EATERS

1. Never eat a small animal that is already dead.
2. Don't hunt an animal that isn't acting lively.
3. Even if you personally kill the animal, if, once you have a chance to inspect it more closely, it looks somehow in poor health, don't even touch it. (When in doubt, throw it out.)
4. Wild rabbits and some other small mammals may be sick with infections that can be contracted by the hunter (less likely during winter). Don't cut yourself while cleaning such animals. It's recommended that you wear rubber gloves when skinning or cleaning any small game animal, especially wild rabbits.
5. Check the animal's liver. White cyst-like spots in the liver, pea-size or smaller, indicate tularemia or coccidiosis. If you have handled an infected carcass, clean hands thoroughly with strong soap and discard the meat. *Do not eat the meat of animals with white liver spots.*

KERNELS: Some small mammals have small waxy or reddish glands, like kernels, situated under the forelegs, along the lower part of the backbone, and/or under the lower part of the abdomen. They are often pulled away with the skin. If not, they must be carefully cut out so as to be removed intact because if one gets cut, it will give a strong, musky taste to the meat.

DRESSING: Small game should be dressed as soon as possible and allowed to cool thoroughly. Remove the entrails and let the blood drain. To clean a rabbit in the field, make an incision down the belly from the vent to the breastbone, taking care not to puncture the intestines or stomach. Grasp the front feet and the head in one hand and swing the rabbit sharply downward, snapping the entrails out of the body cavity. Then reach into the chest and pull out the lungs, heart, and liver. Cut off the head and wipe the body cavity out with a cloth or dry grass.

Beaver: Cook beaver tail in the skin. Beaver tail meat is gelatinous. Use like ham with baked beans or pea soup.

Muskrat: Remove scent glands situated under both hind and forelegs.

Opossum: When skinning, remove scent glands in the small of the back and inside the forelegs.

Porcupine: Skin by starting with the unquilled belly.

Rabbit, Wild: *Wear gloves.* Remove glands from under forearms.

Raccoon: Carefully remove the brown, bean-shaped kernels under each front leg and on both sides of its backbone, similar to opossum.

Woodchuck: As part of the skinning process, carefully remove the small red scent glands located between the forelegs and the body. Because of its exceptionally strong flavor, boil woodchuck for 20 minutes in salted water (then discard the water) before using it in any recipe.

BASIC SMALL-MAMMAL SKINNING: These directions are for when you want to use the skin. Any small game—muskrat, wild (or domestic) rabbit, squirrel, opossum, porcupine—may be dealt with as follows. Cut off the head, tail, and forepaws. Hang up the torso by the hind legs. Have those hind legs separated far enough so you'll be able to easily work between them. Cut on the backside of the leg in a straight line from the hock on one side up to the tail hole. Do the same thing on the other side. Now cut the skin from foreleg to the neck opening on one side, and then do the same on the other side. Starting from the hind end of the animal, now peel off the skin. Using pliers can help you get a better grip on the skin so you can pull hard enough to get it off. Squirrels have tough skin that clings more.

After cutting through the tail (keeping it attached to the back of the skin) and slitting the skin from the base of the tail down the back side of each hind leg and around the hocks, peel the skin off the back legs. Now stand on the tail and pull upward on both of the squirrel's hind legs. This may take a little practice, but eventually you'll be able to peel off the hide over the head and front feet. For more info and suitable recipes, see the section on rabbits in Chapter 11. You can leave the skin on a wild rabbit until you cook or freeze it.

COOKING A SMALL MAMMAL: Any small game may be cooked whole or cut into pieces. Use in wild-meat recipes, rabbit recipes, chicken recipes, or any meat recipes that you feel like trying it in. See "Recipes for Wild or Gamey-Tasting Meats" for more ideas.

➣ *BRUNSWICK STEW This is a classic old-time small animal dish. Start with 2 lb. meat; a medium-sized bird, a large rabbit, or several squirrels will do it. Brown the meat in fat along with 1 chopped onion. Cover and boil with water or bake until meat is tender. Then add water (if more is needed), corn, tomatoes, and beans. There are infinite variations: the corn can be canned or on the ear, the beans can be lima or green, the tomatoes can be fresh or canned. Season to taste with salt and pepper. Eat when the vegetables are cooked.*

Snail, Snake, Turtle, and Frog

Here's how to prepare these critters that are neither bird, mammal, nor fish.

SNAIL: There's a lot to know about collecting and eating snails. Some are not good to eat. Some need special treatment. There are land and marine snails too, and each are

different. California is good snail hunting country. Here's the necessary info (thanks to the Division of Agricultural Sciences, U. of California) for preparing the edible European brown snail or brown garden snail (*Helis aspersa*), which is called "escargot" in French but is the same as the common garden snail considered a pest in the gardens and yards of California. Also known in France as the *petit gris* or vineyard snail, it was probably first brought to the North American continent around 1850. Another edible snail found in some parts of California is the white Spanish or "milk" snail (*Otala lactea*), which is preferred by many people of southern European stock. (Ask an Italian!)

Snails have been used as food throughout the world for centuries. Edible types can be cultivated in cages placed in dooryards, basements, and even in dwellings. Snails are close relatives of the abalone, a sea snail that's also a table favorite. But the U.S. escargot is generally thought of as a garden nuisance rather than as a free, low-calorie meat crop (about 90 calories per 100 grams [3.5 oz.] of snail meat) that's also rich in protein and minerals. It would be much better to harvest and use snails for food than to poison them.

Harvesting. The brown garden snail (escargot) is about 1 to 1½ inches in diameter and ½ inch wide when mature. Mature snails are the best for cooking—there is more and tastier meat, and the shells are easier to get off. Immature snail shells are thin and hard to work with.

NOTE: Don't collect snails in areas where poisons have been used for snail control. Instead, water down the area thoroughly and wait at least 6 weeks before collecting snails.

Snail hunting is best about 2 hours after dark because snails are night creatures. Take only moving snails: that's a sign of good health. Light watering in the late afternoon before your hunt helps bring them out of hiding. You may be able to harvest them more easily during dry weather, when they seal themselves to any surface available; in citrus groves, for example, tree trunks are often covered with hundreds of snails.

Purge. *Snails collected for eating must be purged of any off-flavor or toxic materials from previously eaten food.* Put about ½ inch of damp cornmeal in the bottom of a container such as a plastic wastebasket, metal pan, or crock. Put snails in the container and cover with a ventilated top; a wire refrigerator shelf, hardware cloth, cheesecloth, or nylon netting provides plenty of air and let you observe the activity of the snails. The cover should be weighted with bricks or tied securely so the snails do not escape. Place the container in a cool, shady area and let snails purge themselves (by eating the cornmeal) for at least 72 hours. Snails can be kept in containers for a long time if the cornmeal is replaced every other day to prevent it from molding and souring. The snails will feed and then crawl up the side of the container to rest; use only active snails. *Throw away without eating those that remain inactive on the bottom.* After 72 hours the snails can be removed from the container and washed thoroughly with cold running water to remove the cornmeal from their shells. They are now ready for blanching, another essential procedure.

Blanch. Plunge the live snails into boiling water and simmer about 15 minutes, as is done in preparing live shrimp, lobster, crab, or crawfish. (A bay leaf in the cooking water will give this operation a pleasant aroma.) The water will foam as the snails cook, so heat should be controlled to prevent the kettle from boiling over. After blanching, turn snails into a colander to drain. Then, with a toothpick, nut pick, or pointed knife, pull the snail meat from the shell. Save some shells for later use.

Remove Gall. Remove and discard the dark-colored gall, about ¼ inch long, which is found on the tail end, where the snail is attached to the shell. Wash snail meat several times under cold running water.

Frozen Snails. After purging and blanching snails, the meat may be packaged and frozen for later use or prepared according to your favorite recipe.

Preparing the Shells. Boil the empty shells for 30 minutes in water to which about ¼ t. baking soda per pint of water has been added. Drain the shells, wash them thoroughly in cold running water, and then dry them. Use them to serve snails in recipes calling for cleaned shells.

NOTE: Avoid or minimize salt and vinegar in snail recipes, because they make snail meat tough.

Snail Recipes

❧ SNAILS IN TOMATO SAUCE *Saute 1 chopped medium onion, 2 crushed cloves of garlic, and ½ c. chopped bell pepper in 2 T. oil. Add 1 lb. canned tomatoes, salt and pepper to taste, and simmer until bell pepper is tender and flavors are blended. Add 1 pt. cleaned and blanched snails and simmer 10 minutes. Serve over hot toast wedges, hot cooked rice, or hot noodles.*

❧ BAKED SNAILS *Simmer cleaned, blanched snail meat for 10 minutes in water seasoned as desired with onion, garlic, allspice, bay leaf, etc. Toss cooked snail meat in melted butter or margarine and roll in bread or cracker crumbs seasoned with salt, pepper, and garlic powder. Place in greased shallow pan and bake in a hot oven (450°F) until brown. Sprinkle with lemon juice before serving.*

❧ STUFFED SNAIL SHELLS *Simmer cleaned, blanched snail meat in salted water until tender. Chop snail meat, mix with minced garlic, and saute in olive oil or margarine about*

5 *minutes. Stuff cleaned shells with the chopped, seasoned meat. Seal shell opening with garlic butter. Place under broiler for a few minutes until butter bubbles. Serve immediately.*

❧ FRIED SNAILS *Simmer cleaned, blanched snail meat for 10 minutes in water seasoned as desired with salt, bay leaf, parsley, thyme, allspice, etc. Roll cooked snail meat in fine cracker or bread crumbs seasoned with salt, pepper, and garlic powder. Fry in oil until browned, as you would fried oysters. Sprinkle with lemon juice to serve. These may be served as an entree or, pierced with toothpicks, as hors d'oeuvres.*

❧ SNAILS IN WINE SAUCE *Combine in a casserole dish 18 cleaned and blanched snails, 2 diced slices of bacon, 9 small boiling onions or ½ c. chopped onion, 1 crushed clove garlic, 1 T. minced parsley, a pinch thyme, ¼ t. pepper, and 1 c. red wine or grape juice. Cover and bake 1 hour in a slow oven (275°F). Just before serving, thicken with a butter and flour mixture and serve over crisp toast wedges or croutons. (Serves only 3 people.)*

❧ SNAILS IN GARLIC BUTTER *Start by creaming together until thoroughly blended 1 crushed large clove garlic, ½ c. butter or margarine, 3 T. finely chopped parsley, 2 t. finely minced green onions with tops, ¼ t. salt, and ⅛ t. pepper.*

SNAKE/EEL: These instructions are for snake, but you can prepare eel the same way. Kill the snake by cutting off its head. If it's a poisonous snake, be careful not to touch the fangs, since they contain poison that can enter the bloodstream through a cut or scratch in your skin. There is no poison in the meat, which is typically very white and tender. To skin the snake, nail it down or have someone hold it by the front end with a pair of pliers. Peel off the skin as you would peel a banana. Cut open the body and take out the innards. Cut the skinned meat into 2–5-inch portions. You can split them down the backbone to make them lie flat.

❧ FRIED SNAKE *Dip pieces into beaten egg. Roll in seasoned flour (garlic, salt, pepper) or cracker crumbs. Pan-fry or deep-fat-fry the snake. Or wrap to keep from drying out, and bake.*

TURTLE: Freshwater snapping turtles are good eating but dangerous to catch. Grip the shell behind the head, so you can't get bitten. Or get it biting on a stick and then cut off its head with an ax. Let it hang head downward after beheading until bled out. Cut off all the claws. Then skin the hide down the legs to the feet, which you cut off at the joint. Small turtles can be cooked in the shell until the meat cooks free. Another school of turtle cuisine prefers to proceed by dropping the live turtle into a pan of boiling water, cooking it for about 10 minutes, and then moving it to ice-cold water for 10 more minutes. After this treatment, it will be possible to rub the skin from head, tail, and legs.

Whether you skin or boil your turtle, the next step is the same: you cut through the shell part connecting top and bottom shells. You can use a sharp knife if you have a snapper, but you'll need a saw or ax for a tougher-shelled turtle. Then pry off the bottom shell. Once the shell is off, you can easily remove the innards. After you get the turtle shelled and cleaned, cook it whole, cut it into quarters, or cut it up as you would chicken (depending on its size and the size of your cooking pans).

There's a good section on the diamondback terrapin in Gene Logsdon's *Getting Food from Water.*

🐟 **DORIS'S TURTLE** *Soak turtle meat 8 hours in cold salt water (important). Flour it in a mixture of unbleached white flour, salt, and pepper; brown in a frying pan; and bake 4 hours in a slow oven. Or, after browning, add 2 sliced onions and enough water to cover, and simmer until tender. Make gravy with pan juices and serve with mashed potatoes. For turtle soup, Doris does the same as above and then cools the meat and removes the bones. She chunks the meat and cooks it together with small whole new potatoes, corn, peas, carrots, celery, a bay leaf, a little curry powder, lima beans, and fresh snap beans. She adds additional seasoning to taste and sometimes tomatoes too.*

FROG: The front and hind legs of bullfrogs, leopard frogs, and green marsh frogs are all edible; the rest is discarded. In Oregon the bullfrog is classified as a game fish, and there's a specific bag limit of so many per day. To prepare frog's legs, cut off the legs, remove the feet, and peel off the skin.

🐟 **GOURMET FRIED FROG'S LEGS** *Season the legs with salt, pepper, and lemon juice. Dip legs into beaten egg and then into crumbs of flour. They will fry very quickly—about 3 minutes in deep fat (a wire frying basket preserves their crust). If you are pan-frying them, turn the heat low and cook 5 to 10 minutes, turning as needed, until the meat separates easily from the bones. You may substitute frog's legs in any gourmet or regular chicken or rabbit recipe.*

PRESERVING MEAT

SANITIZER: You can use 1 T. chlorine bleach to 1 gallon of cool water to make a basic sanitizer with which to clean equipment, hands, and work surfaces that you have worked with raw meat on. It's important to have all those surfaces cleaned before you use them for cooked meat.

Freezing

NOTE: If you want to store meat in your freezer a long time, keep in mind that unsalted, unseasoned, unground meat keeps the longest and best.

Gone are the days when smoking, salting, and canning were the only alternatives to eating meat as soon as it was slaughtered. Freezing is perhaps the best way to preserve meat. It has virtually no effect on flavor or texture and gives you the convenience of having a variety of fresh meats in all seasons. Freezing won't keep meat forever but, estimating conservatively, at 0°F beef and lamb can be stored up to 9 months, veal keeps for 6 months, and ground meats and pork are good for 4 months. Some think that several weeks of freezing has a tenderizing effect, but a tough steak is pretty much always going to be a tough steak. Plan ahead for your freezing needs. Despite the number of home freezers that are crammed with meats and animal products, the home freezer was not designed to quickly freeze hundreds of pounds of meat at a time. If you are butchering that much meat, I would advise you to get a freezer storage locker and just keep enough meat at home for a week's meals. Or else butcher during very cold weather and let nature help with the quick freezing.

WRAPPING AND FREEZING MEAT: Immediately after cutting, meat must be properly wrapped, quickly frozen, and stored at 0°F. You'll want to freeze the meat at −10°F or lower, if possible. Put in only the amount of meat that will freeze in 24 hours, and allow ample air circulation by not overpacking the freezer. "Proper wrapping" means using moisture-proof wrap, such as heavily waxed freezer paper, and wrapping meat closely in order to keep out as much air as possible. Air in your package can result in freezer burn and rancidity of the fat.

Freezer Paper. It is shiny on one side, plain on the other. Have ready a pile of sheets of your freezer paper. To cut across the big roll of butcher paper, take a few good snips with your sharp scissors. Then, holding the paper firmly, just push the scissors on across, and it will cut like a razor. An even faster way is to measure out the length of paper needed. Then place the rolled paper on the edge of the kitchen counter or tabletop and pull the paper across the table edge. It will tear straight across.

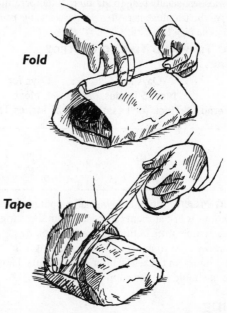

Fold

Tape

Wrapping Procedure. Figure out how many steaks or chops your family needs per meal, and wrap just that number into each package. Place 2 layers of butcher paper or ordinary waxed paper between the individual steaks or chops. That way they'll come apart easily when you need them. Also figure out how much stew meat and how many pounds of ground meat you should put in a package. Ground meat can be stored in rolls, blocks, or ready-to-cook patties, with 2 layers of paper between. You can season meat before you freeze it, but if you expect to keep it frozen longer than 2 weeks, wait to salt it until after you thaw it. Put the meat on the shiny side of the paper—that's to keep it from sticking and from soaking the paper. Put the meat in the center of the sheet, a little nearer one corner. Fold that corner over the meat, fold in both sides, and roll the meat over and over until the paper is used up. Fasten the loose end with a strip of freezer tape. (Freezer tape is needed because regular tape doesn't hold well under freezing temperatures.) Write on the package the kind of animal (elk, beef, or whatever), the kind of cut (steak, stew, or the like), and the date.

Here is a way of double-wrapping meat that some people use. We don't because we're frugal of paper and use up the meat relatively quickly, but for an excellent wrapping method that pushes out the air and protects your meat from freezer burn over the long term, do this:

1. In center of paper, put enough meat for one meal.
2. Wipe hands clean.
3. Bring paper tops together and fold over. Tuck under ends as if wrapping a gift.
4. Get second sheet of paper. Double-wrap.
5. Tape it closed.
6. Write on the outside what is inside and how many of them.

ABOUT FREEZING AND TRICHINAE: Does freezing kill parasites? Yes, if the meat is frozen long enough—and at a sufficiently cold temperature. The kind of parasite that is hardest to kill by freezing is trichinae, which may be in bear or pork meat. The "Freezing Temp. and Time to Destroy Trichinae" table shows how to kill it by freezing. But trichinosis can always be avoided by cooking meat, especially pork and most especially *bear,* to an internal temperature that destroys the trichinae parasites. *Fully cook to the point where there is no pink left at all!*

FREEZING TEMP. AND TIME TO DESTROY TRICHINAE

Freezer Temp.	Days for Meat 6 Inches Thick (or Less)	Days for Meat 6–27 Inches Thick
5°F	20	30
−10°F	10	20
−20°F	6	12

THAWING MEAT: You can thaw small amounts of frozen meat in various ways: at room temperature, in the refrigerator, at a low temperature in the oven or the cooking pot, or in the microwave. At room temperature, thawing 1 lb. meat takes 2 to 3 hours; in the refrigerator, 5 to 8 hours. Large slabs of meat should be thawed in the refrigerator.

Canning

My mother canned a lot of meat when I was a little girl, and one of my most pleasant childhood memories is of the taste of her canned venison stew. You can can any kind of meat. Chicken and rabbit may be canned on the bone, but all the bigger meats, of course, are cut away from the bone before canning. Canning is a good way to handle tough cuts because they get cooked tender in the process. *Can only fresh meat that was chilled immediately after killing and kept chilled until canning.* Don't can any meat that has turned dark or smells like it's starting to spoil!

See the canning directions in Chapter 7 for info about supplies and safe methods.

PREPARING

Large Pieces of Meat. Chill the fresh meat immediately after slaughtering at 40°F or below (but don't freeze it, or you lose quality). You can hold the chilled meat for several days or can it as soon as the body heat is gone. Don't wash meat; if needed, just wipe the outside with a damp, clean cloth.

Frozen Meat. Canning frozen meat is a second-best option but if you have to, it can be done. *Don't thaw it.* Just cut into pieces with a saw and soften them in boiling water until they are soft enough to pack in jars. Cutting across the grain, remove most of the fat and reduce the meat to pieces that fit into the jars. Smaller, less tender cuts should be canned separately for stews and casseroles. Bones simmered

in water make fine broth both for canning and for soups.

Strips, Cubes, or Chunks of Meat. Choose quality chilled meat. Remove excess fat. Soak strong-flavored wild meats for 30 minutes to an hour in brine water containing 1 T. salt per quart. Rinse. Remove large bones. Then hot-pack or raw-pack.

PACKING MEAT IN JARS: You can either raw-pack or hot-pack.
NOTE: Always leave 1-inch free space ("headspace") at the top of each jar to assure a good seal.

Raw Pack. Add 1 t. salt per quart to the jar, if desired. Pack raw meat loosely in clean hot jars, without adding any liquid. Wipe the sealing edge dry.

Hot Pack: Precook meat until rare by roasting, stewing, or browning in a small amount of fat. To brown, just place the meat in a large, shallow pan with a little water. Cover and heat until it is medium done (the pink is gone from the inside). Add 1 t. salt per quart, if desired. Loosely pack hot meat in jars with the juice, or add about 4 T. broth, water, or tomato juice (tomato juice is especially good with wild game) per quart jar. You don't need much liquid, since canning cooks more out of the meat.

PROCESSING: *Pressure-can only.* Place lids on jars and process pints 1¼ hours, quarts 1½ hours. Process at 10 lb. pressure (weighted gauge) or 11 lb. pressure (dial gauge). Increase pressure for higher elevations according to the "Altitude Adjustments for Pressure Canning" table. Consult your pressure-canner manual for specific meat-canning directions. *Don't underprocess meat!*

USING: When using meats you have canned, always make sure the seal is good (listen for a rush of air, similar to the sound when you open a sealed coffee can). If you don't hear that sound, or if there is dryness, discoloration, or a bad smell, throw away the meat.

OTHER CANNED-MEAT VARIATIONS

Ground or Chopped Meat. This recipe is good for bear, beef, lamb, pork, sausage, veal, venison, etc. Use fresh, chilled meat. With venison, add 1 part high-quality pork fat

ALTITUDE ADJUSTMENTS FOR PRESSURE CANNING		
	Processing Pressure	
Altitude	Dial Gauge	Weighted Gauge
Below 1,000 feet	11 lb.	10 lb.
1,001–2,000	11 lb.	15 lb.
2,001–4,000	12 lb.	15 lb.
4,001–6,000	13 lb.	15 lb.
6,001–8,000	14 lb.	15 lb.
8,001 or more	15 lb.	15 lb.

to 3 or 4 parts venison before grinding. Use freshly made sausage, seasoned with salt and cayenne pepper (sage may cause a bitter off-flavor). You can add additional spices when you cook the meat for serving. Use ¾ lean meat to ¼ fat. Shape chopped meat into patties or balls or cut cased sausage into 3–4-inch links. Cook until lightly browned. Ground meat may be sauteed without shaping. Remove excess fat. Hot-pack only; fill jars with pieces and add boiling meat broth, tomato juice, or water, leaving 1-inch headspace. Add 1 t. salt per quart to the jars, if desired. Pressure-can using "Processing" directions.

Meat Patties. For ground meat, remove fat and keep meat cool while you are working. Add 1 t. salt per 1 lb. meat that you grind. Form ground meat into thin patties that will fit into jar without crumbling. Precook them in the oven at 350°F until they are medium done. Drain off the fat drippings and place patties in jar. Add enough boiling broth or water to cover them. Make sure there are no air bubbles trapped under the patties. Pressure-can using "Processing" directions.

Canned Soup Stock. A way to keep from wasting the bones is to boil them up for a soup stock and can that. Soup is a great thing to have on hand for general cooking purposes. Cook your bones, chicken, etc., until tender in lightly salted water. Then chill. Remove fat and bones. Keep the meat and sediment. Reheat and pour your boiling soup into jars. Don't use burned pieces or bones from pork, smoked or corned meats, or fatty lamb to make stock. You can also freeze your stock, in which case you can lift the frozen fat from the top and have very lean stock. Before canning your meat or soup stock, season it with salt, a few vegetables and onion, celery leaves, bay leaf, or whatever you like. Hot-pack. Adjust lids and pressure-can using "Processing" directions.

Variable Vegetable and Meat Soup. For this soup, you use a mixture of vegetables, dried beans or peas, meat or poultry, and broth. Select, wash, and prepare dried beans or peas, meat, and vegetables as follows. Dried beans or peas: For each cup, add 3 c. water. Boil 2 minutes, remove from heat, and soak one hour. Reheat to boiling; drain. Meat: Cover with water and cook until tender. Cool and remove bones. Vegetables: Simmer several minutes until barely cooked. Broth: Meat broth, canned tomatoes, water, or a combination may be used. Season to taste. *Do not add flour, cornstarch, or any other thickening agent.*

Combine meat, vegetables, and drained beans or peas. Add sufficient broth to cover. Boil 5 minutes. Pack jars half-full with hot soup mixture. Add more hot broth to fill jar, leaving 1-inch headspace. Adjust lids and pressure-can using "Processing" directions.

Basic Canned Meat Stew. Cut up about 5 lb. meat (beef, venison, chicken) into about 1½-inch cubes. If you wish, brown in a little fat in your frying pan. Add ½ gal. chunked carrots, 1 qt. chunked onion, and 3 qt. peeled potato chunks. Add 1–2 T. salt, and pepper or other seasonings to taste. Mix together; add boiling water and heat until food is heated through. Pack hot into hot jars. Allow 1-inch headspace. Put lids on and pressure-can using "Processing" directions.

Wild Meats. Use the methods in this section, but soak the meat in a brine solution for 30 minutes to an hour before placing it in jars.

➤ *HOME-CANNED MEAT SANDWICH Open jar. Take out meat. Slice meat. Lay on bread. Add mustard, mayonnaise, and/or sliced pickle.*

➤ *ALMOST INSTANT CANNED BEEF DINNER Cook 1 lb. rice. Open a jar of canned beef (or other meat). Add barbecue sauce. Heat. Serve beef sauce over the rice.*

Drying

There are 2 basic ways to dry meat. The modern way is to precook, cube, and dry by sun, oven, or dehydrator. The other way—drying thin strips of raw meat, combined with salting—produces jerky.

MODERN MEAT DRYING: Prepare the meat by trimming off all the fat, boiling it until it is tender (or pressure-cooking it for 20 minutes at 15 lb. pressure), and cooling. Cut into fairly small cubes and spread on trays. Chunks larger than ½ inch square may not dry thoroughly. Dried meat is about two-thirds its original size.

Reconstituting. Pour boiling water over dried meat cubes and then simmer them for 45 minutes to return them to a tender eating consistency.

Heat Sources. You can dry it in the sun if the weather cooperates. Just place trays of cooked meat cubes in a well-ventilated place, covered to protect from insects, where the sun will shine directly on them. It may take 2 or 3 days to get the cubes hard and dry to the center. Turn the cubes several times to get all sides dry. You can also use a commercial dehydrator, a homemade dehydrator, or your oven if you have good control over the lower temperatures. The method for all these devices is the same: keep the temperature at 140°F for the first 4–6 hours, and turn and stir the cubes frequently; then reduce the temperature to 130°F and continue at that heat until the cubes are hard and dry.

Storage. Keep in an airtight jar. Remember that each time you open the jar, moisture in the air gets in. *Dried meats, especially jerky, keep only a short time at room temperature because any fat on the meat will turn rancid.*

JERKING: Indian- and pioneer-style dried meat is called "jerky." In this case, strips of raw meat are seasoned in a salt-and-pepper brine and dried (or smoked). Some Indian tribes soaked meat in sea water to salt it before drying. Or they hung strips over a slow-burning fire to smoke-dry it.

Jerky is a homemade snack that anyone can enjoy. It's tasty and nourishing cold, and it can be cooked into stews. I send Grandpa Emery a big jar of jerky with a red ribbon around it at Christmas because he really likes that kind of thing. It's good for company. But like many other old-fashioned arts, you have to practice a couple of times to get comfortable with the procedures and to find out just how dry and how spicy your family likes its jerky. Modern commercial jerky is so heavily treated with seasonings and preservatives that trying to eat it as a basic food would make you sick. Meat jerked to use as a basic food should be cut in very thin strips, prepared without any salt or spices, and dried in the sun a couple of days. Good to eat, snack on, and use in stews and soups. *Freezing is the safest way to store it.*

Meats to Use. The original jerky was made of unsalted raw beef, but you can make jerky from other raw meats as long as they don't carry parasites. But so many meats are at risk for carrying parasites that beef, deer, elk, or moose are basically the only choices you have. Use lean red meat. You can jerk any well-cooked meat. Cooked turkey and chicken make tasty jerky. Veteran meat jerkers use the poorest meat for sausage and better cuts such as the loin and round steak for jerking. Frozen meat can be thawed and jerked at any time in its locker life, if it was put into the locker fairly promptly in the first place. About 5 lb. raw meat yields 1 lb. jerky.

Preparing Meat for Jerking. First remove all fat, bone, and visible connective tissue. Cut the remainder into strips about 5 inches long, 1 inch wide, and ½ inch or less thick. (Or 6 inches long and ¾ inch across, or 9 inches long, or whatever you like—but remember that any piece thicker than ½ inch will be hard to get dry.) Cut lengthwise along the muscle, not against the grain, to make the long strips. Partially frozen meat will cut more easily into proper-shaped slices. Some cooks then parboil the strips for 13 to 30 seconds, just long enough for them to change color. Some people then marinate the strips.

Seasoning. After the strips are cut but before they are dried, you season them. There are as many possible ways to do this as there are recipes for jerky, and really, they all work okay. You'll probably experiment. Mike and I never have agreed about it. The simplest method of "seasoning" is to dip the meat into salted (*not iodized*) water, but people usually want a stronger flavor. Some people use soy sauce or Worcestershire sauce as a marinade. You can soak the meat in a seasoned brine for 24 hours; then rinse briefly and hang up to dry. Or else rub or pound the seasoning in by hand, let the seasoned meat rest a few hours, and then rinse it off under the faucet. Jerked meat usually takes more seasoning than you might think because the heat of the drying process weakens the spices. Sugar, allspice, oregano, marjoram, basil, thyme, garlic powder, and Tabasco are all possibilities. Some people, when making oven-dried jerky rather than smoked jerky, fake it with that store stuff called liquid smoke.

Here are a few seasoning recipes to get you started.

❧ *PURE SALT BRINE Make a brine of ½ to 1½ lb. pickling salt in 1 gal. water. Proceed as below.*

❧ *SWEET BRINE Dissolve 1 lb. pickling salt, 1 lb. brown sugar, 1 t. ground allspice, and 2 T. black pepper in 1 gal. water. Use a granite canner, crock, or plastic bucket. Soak the jerky strips in the brine for 12 hours. Weight the meat with a plate and a quart jar of water on top of the plate so that the liquid stays over it. Then rinse off in clear water. My husband prefers this recipe, but I think it is very strong. To weaken it, leave the meat in the seasoned brine a shorter time. Also, marinated meat is likely to take longer to dry than dry-seasoned meat.*

❧ *FANCY FLAVOR Combine ¼ t. pepper, ¼ t. salt, 1 t. lemon juice, and ½ c. soy sauce. Marinate the meat in the mixture 1 hour or longer, turning occasionally.*

❧ *FALSE SMOKED JERKY In a bowl, combine 1 c. soy*

sauce, ¼ c. brown sugar, and a few drops of liquid smoke for your dip.

❧ *TAMARI MARINADE Mix 1 t. ground black pepper, 8 T. tamari (or other soy sauce), 16 crushed cloves garlic, and 4 t. wine vinegar with enough water to cover 2 lb. sliced meat. Soak meat for 4 to 6 hours in the refrigerator.*

❧ *AN EASY DRY METHOD Have ready a suitable-sized granite canner, crock, or plastic bucket. Sprinkle the bottom with salt, pepper, garlic powder, and brown sugar. Put in a layer of meat and sprinkle again. Put in another layer, and so on until you are done. Place the container in the refrigerator or some cool place and let rest 18 hours. Then remove, drain the meat thoroughly of the extracted juice, and proceed to dry it. For a mild jerky, rinse the meat before drying it. This is my favorite recipe. It makes a comparatively sweet jerky.*

❧ *ANOTHER DRY METHOD Lay the meat strips on a towel. Mix thoroughly ⅓ c. brown (or white) sugar, ¾ c. salt, and 1 t. crushed black pepper. Or use ½ c. salt and ⅔ c. brown sugar. Rub in the seasoning. Juice will be coming out. Turn the strips over and repeat on the other side. Some people do this on a wooden board and pound it in. Then roll the strips in a damp (wet and then wring out) towel and leave them in the refrigerator for 8 hours. Take them out of the towel. Rinse each piece thoroughly under running water. Lay on a dry towel for 2 or 3 hours.*

DRYING: After the strips of meat are seasoned, they are ready to dry. This can be done "in the field," by the heat of the sun during the day and the smoke of your campfire by night; in your smokehouse; or in your oven, depending on your preference and facilities. Just exactly how dry you want the jerky is also a matter of preference. For simple food preservation, the dryer the better, but the jerky should be dark, fibrous-looking, and slightly flexible but yet brittle enough to break apart when bent. You can stew the jerky to eat it, but people usually make it for smoking and plan to use it up soon, so they don't dry it clear out. As a snack it's nicer with some moisture left in. If some moisture is left, you'll have to keep it stored in the refrigerator. If you get your jerky too dry to suit you, you can wrap it in a damp towel and keep it in a tightly lidded gallon jar in the refrigerator to recover a little moisture.

In the Field. The meat strips can be spread on rocks or bushes on a hot day. If insects are a problem, you can cover the meat with a fine-mesh cloth, or build a smudge fire, or stand there waving your arms all day, praying for a wind. If the weather changes to rain before you're done, you'll have to take your meat indoors and wait until the sun shines again to finish. It will take about 3 days to do it this way, more or less, depending on the dryness and heat of your weather.

Wood Stove. Drying meat strips over a wood stove is a fine method for wintertime, when you use the stove a lot. Just run wires like clotheslines above the stove, so the meat can be suspended in the hot air around and above the stove. The little metal fasteners sold for hanging Christmas ornaments work fine for fastening a strip of jerky to a clothes hanger or wire.

❧ *ROBERT'S OVEN-DRIED JERKY This is for lean cuts of beef, cooked ham, venison, chicken, or turkey. Trim off all fat and connective tissue. Cut 1½–2 lb. meat into thin slices. In a bowl, combine ¼ c. soy sauce, 1 T. Worcestershire, ¼ t. pep-*

per, ¼ t. garlic powder, ½ t. onion powder, and 1 t. hickory smoke-flavored salt. Stir until the seasonings are well mixed; then add meat and make sure all surfaces are coated with the seasonings. Cover and let stand at least 1 hour. Shake off excess liquid. Arrange strips close, but not touching, on oven racks or cake racks set in shallow baking pans. Dry at 150– 200°F until meat turns brown, feels hard, and is dry to the touch. Poultry will take about 5 hours; beef and venison, 4 to 7 hours. Pat off beads of oil, cool, and store in airtight containers or plastic bags in refrigerator. Makes about ½ lb jerky.

☞ *DEHYDRATOR JERKY* Place meat strips on trays without overlapping. Dry 4 hours at 140°F. Rotate the trays and turn the strips over. Continue drying for another 6 to 8 hours. Place aluminum foil or some such below the trays to catch the drippings.

☞ *MICROWAVED JERKY* This recipe is from the National Live Stock and Meat Board, which warns that microwaved jerky does not have the same long-keeping qualities of traditionally prepared jerky but will keep 4 weeks or more. Prepare your jerky as usual, cutting lengthwise with the grain into ⅛-inch-thick strips. Mix thoroughly together 3 t. salt, 1 t. garlic salt, and ½ t. black pepper. Sprinkle seasoning over strips and mix in order to distribute spices as equally as possible. Arrange a load of strips flat and close together on a microwave-safe bacon rack, and cover with wax paper. Microwave on low for 22 minutes (strips keep better and dry more evenly when cooked at "low" temperature rather than at a higher setting). Now turn strips over and redistribute the driest ones to the center. Rotate rack a half turn and microwave on low again for another 22 minutes, or until jerky is dry but slightly pliable. Take out the finished jerky and repeat the same procedure with the rest of the strips until you finish them all. Let meat dry still more in open air for 24 hours before storing it in a covered container. Store in an air-tight jar or sealed plastic bag (or frozen for long-term storage).

STORING JERKY: For long-term storage, jerky that's completely dry will keep very well if stored in an airtight container. I use quart jars. Just screw the lid on tight. Salt and sugar have the same preservative effect in jerky as they do in old-fashioned home-cured hams and bacon. The dryer and more heavily seasoned the jerky, the better it will keep, but I would still try to use it up within 6 months.

PEMMICAN: Real old-time pemmican was made by the pioneers from lean portions of venison, buffalo, or other meat. It was an Indian trail food that was light to carry and didn't spoil. It contained all the food elements a person needed except vitamin C, and if berries were in it, it had that too. To make it as they did, cut away the fat from the lean. Sun-dry the lean meat in thin jerky-like strips. Then pound up the jerky until you have shredded jerky. Cut the raw fat into small chunks. (This works best, of course, with a fairly firm fat.) Gradually melt them in a pan in the oven or over very low heat. Don't ever let this grease boil up.

The proportions should be 1 part lean to 1 part fat by weight. Since it takes about 5 lb. lean beef to make 1 lb. fully dried jerky, you'd start this recipe with proportions comparable to 5 lb. lean to 1 lb. fat meat. When the fat is all melted, pour it over the jerky bits; then mix the two together. It will look quite a bit like regular sausage. No salt at all should be included. Dried berries are optional. Package the pemmican in commercial sausage casings or some other waterproof container such as plastic bags. When you need it, cook it like sausage or eat it in chunks or slices like dried beef.

MEAT PRODUCTS

Here's an alphabetical list of some basic meat products you can make at home the old-time way.

Gelatin

By "jelly," the old-time recipe writers meant gelatin. Now we call pectin-jellied preserves "jelly" and animal jellies "gelatin." To Great-Grandmother they were both "jelly." "Stock" means soup broth. Homemade gelatin is strained, clarified meat stock flavored any way you like. It sets up (jells) when it is chilled. It melts when it gets warm. To firm it, just chill again and it will set up again.

Gelatin is made from bones and ligaments. Commercial gelatin is made from skins, bones, and sinews. Feet are the boniest, ligamentiest part of the animal and not good for anything else in the kitchen. If you don't have "4 calf's feet" for a recipe, substitute 2 lb. or more of soup bones. "Calf's foot jelly" is a traditional old-time dish, but you can actually make homemade gelatin from cow's heels (the same as feet, only grown up); beef soup bones; sheep or goat legs; pig's feet or backbone; chicken necks, heads, backs, feet; or any other bony pieces you've got.

I make homemade gelatin as often as I can get the

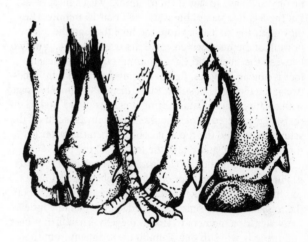

makings. We butcher here at home fairly often, and friends who butcher often let me have the feet. You can't buy feet to make jelly. Our local custom butcher is compelled by law, in the name of "health," to put all cow's feet from the knee down into a barrel and pour creosote over them, so he can't sell them to me to make gelatin or even give the bones to a neighbor lady's dog for gnawing. (That law is stupid and wasteful. By the time you've boiled the feet 4 to 7 hours to make gelatin, I'm sure no germs can survive.)

After trying my first homemade gelatin, I really noticed the contrast between it and the acid bite and heavy sweetness of the presweetened, preflavored commercial gelatin powder. Homemade gelatin hasn't been bleached, preserved, or sugared. Its taste is very mild with a hint of meat flavor. I like beef and pork jelly best. My chicken jelly is a bit too chickeny, although adding extra flavoring helps disguise the chicken.

Learning how to make gelatin was a real research job for me. I started out with an antique recipe and had to experiment for a long time to figure out what was meant. Here, for you, is everything I learned about making homemade gelatin.

COOKING THE MAKINS: After butchering, you can keep feet (skin and all) and other bones for jelly making in big paper bags in your freezer until you have time to work with them. Start your jelly at least the day before you plan to use it. I'll forewarn you — you don't get an awful lot for your work. This is a rare and precious delicacy.

Here's an outline of how to proceed:

1. Prepare bones. (If you're the independent type, that means "butcher.")
2. Cover them with water and simmer until reduced by at least one-half (4 hours or more) to get concentrated stock. (For specific directions for each kind of animal, see the following paragraphs.)
3. Chill enough to set up firmly. Remove fat from top and sediment from bottom of gelatin.
4. Clarify (complete directions given later).
5. Flavor to suit yourself (recipes later).
6. Reset, serve, and enjoy!

Calf's Foot (or Cow's Heel) Gelatin. Start with 4 calf or cow legs (or 3 or 5, if your cow is odd that way). Cut the foot off each one at the first joint above the hoof. Use a sharp knife and a lot of elbow grease (depends on how good you are at finding joints). If you cook the leg bones, too, you'll have even more gelatin, but you'll need a big kettle or you'll have to saw them in chunks with a meat saw. Put the feet in a pan of hot water and boil 15 minutes. Remove. Stir the skin away from the hoof through the top portion of the hoof, which you'll discover is soft. Cut in two between the "toes" and right on up through so that each foot is now in 2 pieces. Remove as much of the fat from between the toes as is possible. Rinse them. Put into a big pan with a gallon of cold water. Bring it gradually to a boil. Gently boil, uncovered, 6 or 7 hours. Several times, skim off the scum that rises to the top as it cooks. When the water is down to about 1 quart, take the feet out of the pan.

Strain the liquid through a cloth or fine sieve. Measure it. Put it in the refrigerator or in a cool place and let it set up. In the morning take off the fat that has accumulated on the top and quickly rinse the outside of the pan in a little hot water for a moment to loosen the jelly. Then turn it over and the jelly will slip out. Trim off the sediment from the bottom. Clarify.

Pig Gelatin. For some reason I think you get more gelatin from pig bones than from any other animal. Use the whole foot from the knee joint down. The backbone is very good for jelly making too. Leave the skin on if the hair has been scraped off. Otherwise, skin the feet. No need to cut or trim. Cover with water and boil gently 4 to 7 hours: skin, toes and all. Skim off scum and fat several times while it cooks. Strain through a sieve to get out the bones and meat (save that for other dishes). Chill overnight. If your broth doesn't jell firm enough to suit you, boil it down some more.

Mutton or Goat Gelatin. Boil leg (shank) bones of sheep or goat for 6 or 7 hours.

Chicken "Foot" Gelatin. Use the head, feet, necks and backs, if you don't need them for something else. Or if you're a purist, use just the smooth legs of birds less than a year old. With luck, about 3 pairs of feet will make a pint of jelly. Scald with boiling water and cook slowly a long time.

CLARIFYING: The clearer you can get your jelly, the more attractive the final result will be and the better it will combine with other foods in recipes. Clarifying also reduces the animal flavor. But homemade gelatin, even when well clarified, is still a little on the milky order and not crystal-clear like store gelatin. For every quart of gelatin in your pan, add ½ c. sugar (white or brown) or honey, along with the shells and slightly beaten whites of 5 eggs (less if you're short, but it won't turn out quite as clear). Stir in the sweetening, shells, and egg whites as soon as the jelly is melted. You can leave out the sweetening if you want; it will still clarify. The following recipes are based on sweetened gelatin. Don't stir the jelly after it begins to get really warm. Let it boil 10 minutes, add ½ c. cold water, and let boil 5 minutes longer. Take the pan off the fire, cover tightly, and let stand for ½ hour in a warm place. Strain through several thicknesses of cloth. Dipping the cloth in hot water and wringing it out helps prevent the jelly from setting in the cloth during the straining process. Strain while hot; otherwise it will jell in the bag. You'll probably have to apply some pressure. Wring the loose ends of the bag to force the broth through. If it isn't clear enough the first time, you can put it through the cloths again.

SETTING UP: The stiffness of your jelly depends on what part of the animal you make it from, how long you boil to concentrate it, and how much liquid you add while preparing it for table consumption. The stiffer you make it to start with, the more possibilities you have for adding flavoring later. Once you have your jelly you can divide it, using 1 part in 1 recipe and 1 part in another. If you're tasting as you go, be reassured: it tastes more like a proper gelatin after it has set up.

For the following jelly recipes, set up the jelly in your final serving molds, preferably individual ones like custard dishes, because it doesn't transfer well once set; it tends to lose shape and shine. Use cold sauces only. It melts easily. Serve chilled; it melts at room temperature. If it starts to melt on you or gets broken up, just finish melting, return it to the refrigerator, and it will again set up very nicely for you.

SECRETS OF GOOD GELATIN MAKING

1. If your gelatin does not set up, you used too much liquid for the amount of gelatin. A scant tablespoon of powdered commercial gelatin will jell with 2 c. liquid.
2. Some ingredients prevent gelatin from setting up. Pineapple, papayas, mangoes, and figs have enzymes that react with the protein in the gelatin and cause it to stay soft. Use these fruits or their juices in gelatin only if they are cooked first.
3. To keep solid ingredients from settling to the bottom, wait until the gelatin is partially set before adding them and mix them in gently, distributing evenly. Banana slices, strawberry halves, and chopped nuts and apples tend to rise to the top of gelatin. Fresh grapes, canned fruits, and orange slices tend to sink to the bottom. Use these tendencies to create layered desserts.

🐾 *MY FAVORITE GELATIN* Let jelly melt over low heat in pan. Add grape or orange juice frozen concentrate (I can make my own frozen concentrates) and lemon juice to taste. Cool the jelly. Add chopped, peeled apple and let set up again.

🐾 *COFFEE JELLY* Melt 1 c. jelly. Combine 2 t. instant coffee with 2 T. water. Add to jelly. Pour into mold and let chill to set. To make this with regular coffee, combine a very firm jelly with enough strong coffee to flavor. Add extra sweetening, if desired.

LEMON JELLY *Combine 1 c. jelly and the juice of 1½ lemons. Strain the lemon juice through a cloth before adding it to keep the gelatin as clear as possible. Chill.*

OLD-FASHIONED WINE JELLIES *Start with a very stiff jelly. Add lemon juice and either red or white wine to taste (I prefer red). To a white wine jelly, you could add some orange juice and grated (unparaffined) orange and lemon peel. To red wine jelly, you could add red berries such as raspberries, strawberries, and currants.*

FRUIT JELLY *A thick gelatin can take the fruit directly and it will remain in suspension. Let it partly set up, and then add the fruit. In a diluted gelatin, the fruit sinks to the bottom. In that case, chill a bottom layer until firm; then add a layer of fruit and then more melted gelatin. Chill until firm again, add another fruit layer, and so on. Fresh peaches, apricots, plums, and apples are good if cooked in a little sweetened water before they go into the jelly. (Drain thoroughly before adding.) Strawberries, raspberries, grapes, cherries, chopped peeled apples, and currants can go in raw. Your own sun- or oven-dried fruits and brandied cherries are fine too. Cut up large pieces before adding to the jelly.*

JELLIES AS SAUCES FOR MEAT: Great-Grandmother served animal jellies with a sauce when she was able (the same way she served the bread varieties she called "pudding"). The easiest sauce is whipped cream. For salad-type jellies (make with raw vegetables, home sun-dried fruit, and fruit juices), serve homemade mayonnaise, sour cream, or yogurt dressing.

VANILLA SAUCE *This is nice on a dessert jelly and uses up egg yolks left from clarifying. Scald 1 c. milk. Add a little sweetening, 2 or more egg yolks, and ½ t. cornstarch. Cook, stirring constantly, in your double boiler until it thickens. Add a bit of real vanilla flavoring. Stir until cool.*

Substituting Your Gelatin. In modern recipes, use 2 c. homemade gelatin for "1 envelope" commercial gelatin, and cut back on the fluid by 2 cups.

OTHER GELATIN PRODUCTS

Homemade Meat Glaze. This adds color and flavor to soups, sauces, and gravies. To put on meat, melt the glaze over hot water and apply with a pastry brush. To make it, start with your bone stock as for homemade gelatin and boil it until greatly reduced, keeping it well skimmed. Do not clarify. Figure on boiling 1 qt. bone stock down to a cup or less, transferring it to a smaller pan as it reduces. To get a darker color, simmer the concentrated stock with caramelized sugar until it becomes like a syrup.

Bouillon "Cubes." Make your stock and concentrate, but do not clarify. Whatever type of meat you used will be the flavor of the cubes you get. Remove fat but not sediment. When you have a well-jellied stock, you're ready to make bouillon cubes.

1. Melt the jelly.
2. Season it strongly with your favorite soup seasonings.
3. Pour the seasoned jelly 1 inch deep into some containers you can get along without, like cans—the smaller the better.
4. Set the cans in a water bath that reaches about one-third up the side of the can. Cook on low heat at least 8 hours more, refilling the water bath as needed.
5. Chill.

6. Separate concentrate from container.
7. Wrap in foil or in paper squares cut from grocery bags.
8. Pack in jars with tight-fitting lids. Keep out of dampness.

Gravy

Good gravy to go on the potatoes can be made any time you fry or roast meat. When your meat is done, remove it from the pan. Estimate how much gravy your family can use. If you want 1 cup, pour off the grease until you have about 2 T. left, 4 T. for 2 cups, and so on. If you don't have that much, add a little melted butter, bacon drippings, or lard. Loosen all the good brown bits in the bottom of your pan (assuming you don't have a burnt mess, in which case salvage some grease by pouring off the top and start over in another pan), and add 2 T. whole wheat or unbleached flour per 2 T. grease.

For heaven's sake, don't stop to actually "measure" the hot grease and flour. You can learn to estimate close enough by looking at it, and it really doesn't make that much difference if you use a little more or less of either. Just don't have a whole lot of extra grease, because it will float on top of your gravy and look and taste yuk!

Over medium heat make a paste of the brown bits, grease and flour with your fork, and let cook a couple minutes, stirring constantly. This accomplishes the browning and cooking of your flour and gives you almost an "instant" gravy. Your mashing action with the fork will break up potential lumps. Now pour in a little liquid. Stir it in until the lumps are gone; then add more and stir again until the lumps are out. Repeat until all your liquid is added. You can add more liquid each time, but start with very little. Stop adding liquid when your gravy is as thin as you want it.

For liquid, use your potato water, water from another cooked vegetable, or milk. Or juice from a pot roast or stewed chicken, if you have it. I drain the vegetable waters into the gravy (or else add them to the animal pail) and then cook that down to the wanted density. Pork-chop gravy is good with half milk and half water or all milk. Chicken gravy is good with half or all milk. Beef gravy is good with part milk or just your vegetable water. Deer, elk, and other game gravies don't get along with milk. Game gravies are much improved by adding a couple tablespoons of currant, wild plum, or some other tart jelly. For roast turkey, duck, or goose, use no milk, but add the chopped cooked giblets and the giblet broth for a delicious gravy.

If you get the gravy too thin and watery, you can boil it until it thickens enough to suit you. Finally, salt and pepper to taste. Taste it until it seems right, but don't burn your tongue! Good gravy seasonings are black pepper, onion powder, thyme, sage, marjoram, and basil. For a final garnish, sprinkle freshly chopped parsley, dill, chives, or scallions on top. Then serve to pour on your meat and mashed potatoes, rice, or thick slices of bread in a sturdy bowl with a good dipper. And put the pan to soak in the sink, so it won't be a chore to wash.

Gravy Trick. Put flour in a jar with a tight-fitting lid. Add cold water, about 1½ times by volume. Shake by hand. Never fill jar over three-fourths full. Add to the gravy or stew slowly, stirring the whole time. From Howard Perkins, Pennsauken, NJ.

Roux. From Virginia Boegli, my high school friend who drew some of the illustrations for the early editions of this book."I've discovered a great little French technique that really simplifies gravy. It's called roux (pronounced "roo"). A roux is a paste of about equal parts fat and flour. The fat may be drippings or butter or so forth. A roux can be blended into hot liquid without all that lumpiness. When my roasting pan has a hard brown coating after roasting meat, I like to put water in it and simmer to get all that good stuff. Then stir in a roux and seasoning—voila, it's gravy. If you want you can make a jar of roux and keep it in the refrigerator. A glob the size of a walnut thickens about a quart of gravy or a large pot of stew. If in doubt, it's easy to add a little at a time."

White Sauce. This is a meatless white gravy. It's good poured over bland vegetables such as boiled onions, cauliflower, or asparagus. I mix white sauce with diced leftover ham (omit the salt for home-cured ham) to get an extra meal out of it. To make white sauce, melt some butter in your frying pan. Soak it up with an equal measure of flour and brown a couple minutes, stirring constantly. Now gradually dilute with milk, stirring constantly. Season, and it's ready to be poured over your vegetables. Also good with cheese grated into it.

Hash

The basic hash recipe is to grind or cut into small pieces cooked meat (mutton, beef, corned beef, or what-have-you) and add diced cold boiled spuds. The usual proportion is half meat and half potato. Some people stretch it with more potato. You can add chopped onion too. Moisten with leftover gravy, soup stock, egg, or even milk or water. Season with salt and pepper. I usually make it with leftover gravy.

When you want to eat it, turn it into an oiled frying pan and bake in a hot oven until brown, or fry on top of the stove, turning once. Slightly beaten eggs mixed with the hash will make it stick together better if you don't use gravy. If you cook an especially moist hash slowly in a covered pan for about half an hour, until there is a rich crust on the bottom, you can fold it like an omelet and serve that way. Hash is a good breakfast (or lunch) dish with eggs on the side, and it's good for using up leftovers.

☙ *GERMAN HASH Mix 1 c. chopped cooked beef, 1 c. chopped tart apples, 1 c. chopped boiled potatoes, 1 t. salt, and a pinch of paprika. Saute 1 small onion, chopped fine, in 3 T. butter until transparent. Add the other ingredients to the onion and butter and heat until very hot, stirring often.*

☙ *GROUND MEAT HASH Fry 1 lb. lean ground meat with 1 T. oil until the pink color is cooked out. Add a small chopped onion and continue frying until the onion pieces are transparent, stirring as needed to separate meat. Stir in ½ t. salt, ⅛ t. garlic powder, ½ t. pepper, and 4 T. soy sauce. When this mixture is thoroughly cooked and mixed, add a layer of shredded raw potato or sliced cooked potatoes. If you use the raw potato, cover pan and cook on low heat, stirring occasionally, until the potatoes are done. If using precooked potatoes, just get it hot and then serve with ketchup.*

☙ *SHEPHERD'S PIE This old English recipe was traditionally made with sheep meat but will work with any variety, including ground meat. Have ready about 1 lb. mashed potatoes that were originally made with plenty of butter, salt, and pepper. Cut ½ lb. cold, cooked meat into thin strips. Oil a baking pan or dish, put one-third of the potatoes into the bottom of the pan, then a layer containing half the meat,*

then a layer with the next third of the potatoes, then a layer with the rest of the meat, and a final layer on top with the last third of the potatoes. If needed, sprinkle more seasoning on each layer as you add it. Optional: dot top of pie with butter bits, or arrange slices of tomato or bacon on it. Bake at 325°F about ½ hour or until well heated all through. Will heat faster if you preheat the potatoes with some melted butter, stirring in a frying pan until hot, before you layer them.

Mincemeat

Mincemeat belongs to the same family as fruitcakes and plum pudding—meaning that a little goes a long way. The old-timers made their crock mincemeat in late November or whenever the weather turned cold and would stay that way a few months. They kept it through those cold months in a cold place. Homemade mincemeat doesn't taste like store mincemeat at first, but the more it ages, the more it does. It's a good idea to add a little more liquor or a juice such as grape or orange just before baking a mincemeat pie. "True" mincemeat is probably the variety containing beef and suet —specifically the kind made from beef neck—but mincemeat can also be made from pork or wild meat. There are also mock varieties made from green tomatoes and raisins, or rhubarb and raisins.

Any mincemeat recipe can be stretched by adding chopped apple when you want to bake with it. A tart apple such as Winesap, Transparent, or Jonathan is best. Old-time crock mincemeats are very concentrated for the sake of easy preservation. A cup or more of chopped apples mixed with a pint of mincemeat really improves the mixture when you bake with it.

PRESERVING MINCEMEAT: Old-time crock mincemeat contained sugar, spices, vinegar, molasses, and alcohol, alone or in such combinations as to make it self-preserving. The more modern recipes I've given below aren't as strong and must be immediately canned or frozen after you make them unless you're going to eat up the mincemeat right away. To freeze mincemeat, just put in cartons and place in the freezer. If you have leftover crock mincemeat and spring is coming, just package it up and freeze.

☙ *PORK MINCEMEAT If you are doing your own butchering, this is one good way to use the hog's head (headcheese is another) and backbone. Boil until tender. Then skin the head, bone out the meat, and grind it up. Don't use all the fat. For each 8 lb. pork add 2½ lb. dried apples (ground and then cooked) and 3 lb. green apples, if you can get them (or 3 lb. fresh tart apples). Put 4 whole lemons and 4 peeled oranges through the grinder. Combine ground fruit, pork, 3 lb. raisins, 1 qt. vinegar, 2¾ lb. sugar, 1 T. allspice, and 1 T. cinnamon. Cook for 1 hour.*

RECIPES USING MINCEMEAT
☙ *THANKSGIVING PIE Mix 1 pt. mincemeat with 2 c. peeled, cored, chopped tart apples. Fill an unbaked pastry shell. Top with pastry. Bake 10 minutes at about 450°F and then 30 minutes at a lower temperature.*

☙ *FILLED MINCEMEAT COOKIES Blend ½ c. soft shortening, 1 c. sugar, and 2 eggs. Stir in 2 T. thick cream and 1 t. vanilla. Sift together 2½ c. flour, ½ t. soda, and ½ t. salt. Add to shortening mixture. Gather dough into a round ball and chill for 1 hour. Then roll out to about ⅟₁₆ inch thick. Cut into 3-inch rounds or squares. Put a rounded teaspoonful of* mincemeat on each dough round. Fold the dough over, pressing edges together with the floured tines of a fork or with a fingertip (a square would thus become a triangle). Put the filled cookies on a greased cookie sheet. Bake at 400°F 8 to 10 minutes.

❧ **MINCEMEAT COOKIES** Cream 1 c. shortening. Add ½ c. brown sugar and blend well. Add 2 eggs and beat thoroughly. Mix ½ t. salt and 1 t. soda with 3 ½ c. flour. Alternately add 1½ c. mincemeat and the flour mixture to the liquid mixture. The liquid amount determines how liquid your mincemeat will be. You might want to add a little more or less flour to get the right cookie consistency. Finally, add ½ c. chopped nuts (more or less depending on how many you have). Mix. Drop with a spoon onto your greased cookie sheet. Bake 10 minutes at 375°F.

❧ **MINCEMEAT JELLY ROLL** Combine 2 c. sifted flour, ½ c. sugar, 1 t. salt, and ½ c. milk. Add 1 T. dry yeast dissolved in ⅓ c. lukewarm water and a beaten egg. Let rise. Punch down. Let rise again. Divide dough in half. Roll out each half to a ½-inch thickness. Spread a layer of your mincemeat over each half. Roll it up jelly-roll style. Pinch edges to seal. Let rise once more. Bake at 350°F about 30 minutes, or until nicely browned and crusty on outside.

❧ **MINCEMEAT MUFFINS** Beat 1 egg with 1¾ c. milk. Add 2 t. melted butter. Combine 3 c. whole wheat flour, 3 t. baking powder, 1 t. soda, 1 T. sugar, and 1 t. salt and then add to liquid. Add 1 c. mincemeat and 2 t. fruit juice or water. Mix it all together well. Grease your muffin tin and fill the cavities two-thirds full. Bake at 375°F for 25 minutes.

❧ **CRANBERRY MINCEMEAT PIE** Combine 1½ c. mincemeat-chopped apple combination, 1½ c. cranberry sauce, ½ c. orange juice, and 3 T. flour. Pour into an unbaked shell. Cover with a top crust. Pinch sides and brush the top with milk. Bake at 400°F 50 minutes.

❧ **MINCEMEAT-OATMEAL COOKIES** Sift together 1½ c. plus 2 T. flour, ¾ t. soda, and ½ t. salt. Cream ½ c. lard and then gradually add 1 c. brown sugar. Add 1 well-beaten egg and 1⅓ c. mincemeat. Add flour mixture gradually and then 1½ c. rolled oats. Drop by spoonfuls onto greased cookie sheet. Bake at 350°F about 15 minutes.

❧ **MINCEMEAT APPLES** Try baking apples with the cores out and the cavity stuffed with mincemeat.

❧ **MINCEMEAT BROWN BETTY** Make 2 c. bread crumbs, preferably from homemade whole wheat bread. Butter a bread pan. Put one-third of the crumbs in it. Add a layer of 2 peeled, sliced apples and then a layer of ½ c. mincemeat. Sprinkle over a pinch of cinnamon. Add another layer of

crumbs, 2 more sliced apples, another ½ c. mincemeat, another sprinkle of cinnamon, and the remaining crumbs. Pour ½ c. orange juice over all. Dot with butter. Bake at 350°F for 30 minutes. Good with cream.

Sandwich Mixes

These sandwich fillings are meant to be spread on homemade bread. Store-bought bread is too salty and generally "strong"-tasting for them. Any leftover meat can be made into a fine sandwich filling. Just remove bone and fat (except for old-time potted ham). Slice or grind the meat. Moisten the grindings with a salad dressing, such as mayonnaise or tartar sauce. You can make plain meat fillings this way or with the variations that follow. Croquettes are another good way to use meat leftovers. So is sliced meat warmed up in leftover gravy and served with rice or sliced boiled spuds that have been sauteed in a little butter with some chopped fresh green onion.

❧ **HAM AND EGG** Grind the ham with chopped hard-cooked egg. Moisten with mayonnaise or cream dressing. Add finely chopped red or green pepper and mustard.

❧ **HAM AND PICKLE** Grind 2 c. ham. Mix smooth with 1 small ground pickle, 2 t. prepared mustard, 2 T. butter, and ½ t. pepper.

❧ **HAM AND EVERYTHING** Mix together 1 c. chopped ham, 1 chopped hard-cooked egg, 2 T. chopped green pepper, 2 T. chopped sour pickle, and a pinch of pepper. Moisten with mayonnaise. Add thin pickle slices and strips of green pepper, if desired.

❧ **OLD-TIME POTTED HAM** Grind one-third fat and two-thirds lean meat to a smooth paste. Add salt and cayenne pepper to taste. Heat and pack in small pots.

❧ **HAM AND CHICKEN** Grind 1 c. cooked chicken meat, white or dark, and ½ c. cooked ham. Mince ½ c. celery and 1 T. green pepper, and mix with meat. Moisten with about ½ c. mayonnaise.

❧ **CHICKEN SALAD SANDWICH FILLING** Grind cooked chicken and moisten with mayonnaise. Add crumbled crisp bacon or chopped celery.

❧ **CHOPPED VEAL** Grind about 1½ c. veal and season with 1 t. salt, 1 T. lemon juice, and a little pepper and mustard, if desired.

❧ **CHOPPED MUTTON** Grind until fine about 1½ c. cold mutton or lamb. Season with 1 t. salt, 1 T. pickled nasturtium seeds if you have them, 1 t. chopped fresh mint if you have it, a pinch of pepper, and 1 T. lemon juice. Good on whole wheat bread with lettuce.

❧ **BEEF SANDWICH SPREAD** Grind the meat, add mayo to moisten, salt and pepper to taste, and stir in some chopped green onion or green pepper or pickle. Doesn't keep well, so eat it all up.

HOMEMADE LUNCH MEAT LOAF RECIPES: From Gertrude Johnson, Lamont, WA, a rare and splendid lady who says these homemade lunch loaves have no chemicals or nitrates and are inexpensive to make and very tasty.

❧ **TURKEY SANDWICH ROLL** This recipe makes lunch sandwiches for a week for a family of 3. Place 2 turkey drumsticks (or 2–2½ lb. meat), 3 carrots (scrubbed and cut into chunks), 3 ribs celery (including the leaves, scrubbed and cut into chunks), 2 medium onions (peeled and cut into chunks), 4 whole peppercorns, and salt to taste together in a large, heavy pot. Fill with enough water to cover the contents plus 1 inch more. Bring to a boil; cover and simmer about 2 hours or until the turkey is no longer attached to the bone. Remove meat and set aside until cool enough to handle.

Strain turkey broth into a bowl through a cheesecloth-lined strainer. Set the bowl aside. Discard the cheesecloth and its contents. Remove and discard the skin from the drumsticks; then remove the meat from the bones. Use your fingers to shred the meat and to check for any stray bones. Put the shredded meat into a clean saucepan. Add just enough turkey broth to pan to moisten the meat without making it soupy. Set the pan on low heat and stir to further shred the meat as much as possible. Add salt to taste. Very gradually, add enough broth to keep the meat generously moist but not soupy.

When this is heated through and seasoned to your liking (try including 2 T. dried parsley flakes or ½ c. fresh parsley and 3 thin slices of lemon), remove from heat and sprinkle 2 envelopes of unflavored gelatin on top. Stir constantly for 3 minutes. Pour mixture into a deep quart-sized, lidded container or into an 8 × 4 × 2-inch loaf pan. (Greasing is not necessary.) Cover and refrigerate overnight. When set, remove the roll from its container and cut it into slices for sandwiches. It will keep (refrigerated) for about 2 weeks. Do not freeze!

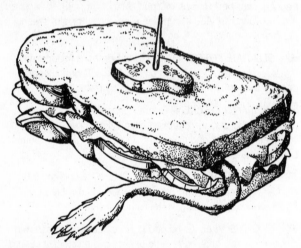

➣ **BARBECUED BEEF SANDWICH LOAF** You'll need 1½ lb. stewing beef, 1 large onion, peeled and quartered, ½ t. salt, ⅛ t. pepper, ⅔ c. barbecue sauce, 2 c. water, and 2 envelopes plain gelatin. Cut beef into ½-inch cubes. Place meat in heavy pot with onion, salt, and pepper. In a separate bowl, combine barbecue sauce with water. Pour two-thirds of this mix over meat cubes. (Set the rest aside.) Bring meat mix to boil and simmer, covered, over low heat for 1 hour or until beef is very tender. Then shred beef and onion in blender, using all of the pan juices and the rest of the barbecue and water mixture. Finish as above with the gelatin, etc.

➣ **HAM AND CHEESE LOAF** Make this when you have leftover ham (or other meat) that is in shreds and bits, unsuitable for serving. You'll need 1½ c. leftover cooked meat, water, 1 envelope (1 T.) plain gelatin, and ½ c. diced cheddar cheese. Shred, mash, and then chop ham into very small pieces in a small saucepan. Gradually stir in enough water to

moisten, plus 3 T. more. Bring to a boil, remove from heat, and sprinkle gelatin on top, stirring for 3 more minutes. Let mixture reach room temperature. Then stir in cheese and pour into a lidded 2-cup plastic container. Cover and refrigerate overnight. When set, remove from container to slice for sandwiches. Do not freeze.

Sausage and Hamburger

NOTE: In the following recipes, there are no chemical preservatives, so as a safety measure, follow these instructions:

1. Use only fresh rather than aged meats.
2. After making your sausage, immediately store in a freezer that is set at 0°F or below.
3. Or preserve by canning. (Follow the directions in the "Canning" section for ground or chopped meat.)
4. Cook frozen sausages thoroughly before eating.

SUPPLIES AND BOOKS: To shop for casings, ask the custom butcher in your area. Larger cities may have stores that specialize in sausage, or your local market might order them for you from their wholesaler. If that doesn't work, check the Yellow Pages under "Meats, Custom Cutting" and "Meats, Wholesale." The Sausage Maker sells everything you need for making sausage and curing meats, including spices, tools, casings, equipment, and an instructional video/book combo deal for $39.95. That book, *Great Sausage Recipes and Meat Curing,* by Rytek Kutas, contains 175+ sausage recipes: 888-490-8525; 716-824-6510; 1500 Clinton St., Bldg. 123, Buffalo, NY 14205; sausmaker@aol.com; www.sausagemaker.com. Luhr Jensen offers a "Home Sausage Kit" with a booklet of instructions and recipes, as well as sausage-making supplies: 800-535-1711; 541-386-3811; PO Box 297 (400 Portway Ave.), Hood River, OR 97031. Order *Home Sausage Making: Healthy Low-Salt, Low-Fat Recipes* (including poultry and fish recipes), by Charles Reavis, from Storey Books, address in Chapter 1. You can buy sausage mix that does not contain MSG from the KOCH company: 800-456-5624. Meat grinders and sausage makers are also available from 719-962-3228; www.cfamilyresources.com.

GRINDING AND MIXING THE MEAT: Sausage making is an important country art in this part of Idaho, maybe everywhere in the country. The arrival of late fall and butchering time on the farm means sausage time. Often it is made twice a year: in late fall and again in early spring, when some more butchering is done. In most of the small towns around here, it is a public operation as well as a private one. The communities have an annual sausage-making bee followed by a big sausage feed.

Hamburger Making. "Hamburger" is ground meat with whatever percentage of fat added or left out that you prefer. The precise point at which ground meat stops being "hamburger" and becomes "sausage" is vague. If pork is added, the result is generally called "sausage." Hamburger and sausage are basic meat foods, a way to make use of all your meat scraps. When you butcher wild animals and small animals like goat, you get so many odds and ends of meat pieces (especially if you are boning out the meat), that ground-meat recipes are the answer. Grinding also solves the problem of using tough, old animals. And ground meat is easy to heavily and thoroughly season, so it also can solve the problem of what to do with strong-tasting meats. Hamburger and sausage can be heavily or lightly seasoned—

whatever you prefer. Besides the seasoning, you can add water and fat. Ground meat that is all lean can often benefit from a little added water, about 1 T. water per 1 lb. lean meat. *NOTE: The following sections usually refer to "sausage," but some of it applies equally to hamburger.*

Adding Fat. To any hamburger or sausage, you have the option of adding fat. If you choose to do so, choose a soft, low-cholesterol fat such as pork fat. Don't use a strong-tasting (high-cholesterol) fat like venison or goat. *Don't use mutton fat.* You don't have to add fat. You can make all-lean hamburgers, and they will be delicious and cook fine. But in the past it has been popular to add pork to nonpork meats because the pork seems to bind the meat together while cooking and improve its flavor. If you add fat, make sure the fat and meat are well mixed before you package the hamburger or sausage. You can knead the mixture with your hands until the fat and lean are distributed equally.

Grinding. To make sausage, one thing you must have, or have access to, is a meat grinder. The best grinder for sausage is one with a choice of coarse (½-inch holes) and fine (⅛-inch holes) plates. Don't plan on using one of those small home-style meat grinders to make your sausage. I made that mistake. They just can't handle the job. Even if you keep the screw as tight as it will go, which helps, you end up getting some steel flavor in your meat. You have to keep tightening the screw because it keeps slipping. And sooner or later the grinder starts getting stringy ligaments wound around the outlet, and finally it gums up completely and is immobilized. It helps some to trim out as many of the ligaments as possible, but there's no way to get them all.

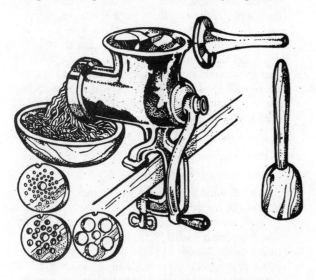

Better than trying to grind sausage in a little home grinder is to take a dishpan or two of it to your local butcher. But check first to see if the butcher feels able to do it for you. There are so many new laws now that discriminate against home-butchered meats that he or she may not want to take the chance.

It helps to use a larger model of meat grinder (Food Grinder Pro, $100, or Stainless Steel Meat Grinder, $150, from Back to Basics, 801-571-7349). Or mail-order a sausage grinder and stuffer from Lehman's (888-438-5346; **www.Lehmans.com**); they sell other sausage-making equipment, too. A typical bargain grinder has the 2 disks for fine or coarse grinding and a 7/8-inch stuffer attachment. It's crank-operated. Power grinders are the nicest of

all, if you have the kind of handyman who can hook up a washing-machine motor to anything.

Before you grind the meat, trim it from the bones and cut away all gristle and blood clots. Cut it into strips, whether it is fat or lean. Put your fat in one pile and your lean in another to help you have a notion of proportions. You're supposed to use one-third fat and two-thirds lean, and you can kind of judge that with your eye. I don't see much use in the fat part, however, so I generally just use whatever fat comes along of its own accord, and the fat that I can easily cut out goes into the rendering pail.

Seasoning. Some people grind their meat coarse and then add the seasoning and grind again. But it's too much struggle to grind more than once, and it's easier to mix the seasoning with the meat before grinding than after. So do it like this. Cut the meat in strips. Lay it out on a mixing surface, such as a sheet of freezer paper with the wax side up. Sprinkle the seasoning over and mix with your hands. Sprinkle again and mix again until you have it well mixed. You can season about 20 lb. at a time this way. It's much easier than working with it ground.

Now grind. If you have a very good grinder, you can form your ground sausage into fist-sized balls and put them through the grinder again. It really helps to have a wooden "follower," which is a basic cylindrical meat pusher, so you don't grind your fingers but do hold the sausage in the grinder.

If you aren't sure of your seasoning amounts, make a little sausage cake up on the spot, fry it, and eat it. Then you can adjust the seasoning of the rest accordingly. Don't taste raw pork because it's been known to carry trichinae, a parasite that causes a horrific disease. A woman at my college got it after eating several hot dogs in Chicago. She got really sick and had to quit school. I can't imagine our home-grown pork having any such thing because pigs get it from eating infected meat, and I know where everything that our pigs eat comes from. Nevertheless, it's a good idea not to taste raw pork.

If you decide to add more seasoning to your already ground meat, mix it in a big kettle. Get ready by washing both hands clear up to your elbows, and then plunge in. Knead as for bread dough, picking up from the bottom, pulling up over the side to the top, and punching into the center. In a moment give the kettle a quarter turn and continue. Some people grind the meat coarse, add the seasoning, and then grind it fine. That's okay if you have a good power grinder.

The seasoning can be as simple as salt and pepper. Or it can be a very, very complex mixture. Morton Brothers (the salt people) makes a sausage seasoning that's sold in our local grocery stores. Some people add a little Tenderquick to their seasoning; some make it all from scratch. The commercial seasonings contain a lot of spices blended with salt as well as monosodium glutamate and preservatives. Use 8 oz. seasoning per 24 lb. meat for strongly seasoned sausage. For a milder sausage, use 8 oz. for 35 lb. meat. I've tried just grinding and freezing the sausage plain and then seasoning it right before I cook it, but it doesn't have the best flavor that way. The seasoning needs a chance to work in.

ABOUT CASINGS: You travel one of 2 basic routes, the easy one or the hard one, in shaping the ground seasoned meat into sausage. The easy way is to make patties. Sausage that is seasoned and frozen in breakfast-sized packages, which you can simply thaw, shape into patties, and fry (or sausage-fry and then can), is just as much sausage as the kind that's stuffed into casings, and it's a lot easier to make. The harder option is to stuff the mixture into casings. Stuffing casings is extra work and expense (or time if you clean your own casings). At home I usually just wrap my sausage in freezer paper, enough per package for a meal, and that's it. But at the big hog-butchering and sausage-making bees, I've enjoyed the adventure of doing the real thing. At these bees, while the men butcher the hogs, the women clean the small intestines, and those become the sausage casings. They make sausage and stuff the casings and then smoke them in a little smokehouse right there.

Homemade Muslin Casing

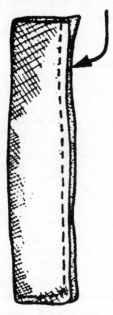

You can use plastic, muslin, or gut casings. Casings are sold by the "hank," which is a 1½-lb. package that is supposed to stuff about 100 lb. of sausage. You don't eat the plastic casings, of course, or the muslin ones. But when you make sausage with casing made from the natural gut, you eat the casing too. Plastic casings used to be readily available but are hard to get now. They were sold in 1-inch, 2-inch, and 4-inch sizes. Two-inch was generally the most satisfactory.

Making Muslin Casings. *Don't dry sausage in these. You have to strip the muslin off first.* Sew 8 × 18-inch strips of muslin. This allows for a ½-inch seam. Fold and sew up 1 end and turn inside out. Firmly pack the sausage in there. Be sure there are no air pockets, because air pockets may cause mold to grow on the inside of the casings. Tie the top with a heavy cord and give it a loop to hang up the sausage. Be sure to dip your muslin casings in water and wring them out before starting to stuff them. If you don't have a sausage stuffer, you can spoon sausage into big casings like these.

MAKING NATURAL CASINGS: There are 3 kinds of natural casings, and a really good sausage stuffer has 3 nozzle sizes. Little-pig size (what they call link sausage) is about 2 inches long and ½ inch wide and is a sheep casing. Beef casings are used to hold salami-type sausages. Pork casings make traditional "sausage" sausages. A hank of pork casings is supposed to stuff 100 lb. of pig—but about 85 lb. is more likely. Sheep casing will take 50 lb. Beef casing will take a lot. You can buy natural casings in quantity and keep them in your freezer. I have a friend who kept hers there for 3 years before they were all used up, and they kept fine. Soak them in warm water before stuffing.

Making natural casings is cold, tedious, hard work, and it's not for the squeamish. You need a fairly low faucet or hose that runs water on the ground, a knife to cut the gut when it shows a hole or tears, and a set of knitting needles. If you are going to clean casings, it's doubly important that the animal not be fed for 24 hours before butchering. The casing is made from the small intestine of the animal (sheep, cow, or pig). If there is food in there, it makes a lot of extra work to get it out.

If you are planning to save casings, it's a good idea to keep your pigs especially well wormed. (Worm medicine is a liquid that you mix with a gallon of water and have them drink.) Not only is it disagreeable being in the same vicinity as a bunch of 6-inch-long, husky, writhing, white roundworms, but they also make holes in the intestine. A really infested pig will have a gut like a sieve.

1. Cut the small intestine off where it starts below the stomach, and cut it on the other end where it is about to connect up with the large intestine. You'll have to rescue it from the general pile of innards. Put it in a big dishpan.

2. Carry it over to your faucet or hose. Strip it between your fingers or between knitting needles to remove as much of the contents as possible—food, worms, or whatevers. Just let them spill out on the ground. Then rinse them off under running water. This is where the agony starts, because sausage and butchering weather is cold weather, but you have to do all this work with your bare hands because the gut is delicate and so is the job. Your cold, wet hands will be in a state of near-paralysis after the first 10 minutes. It's not so bad if you're doing just 1 gut, but if you're doing more than one, it's nice to have somebody working with you so you can take turns freezing your hands working with the casings or thawing them out over the nearest fire.

3. You have the gut contents stripped out as best you can and the outside rinsed off under your faucet. Now you're going to turn the entire gut inside out. There's a neat trick to this turning. Practice beforehand in the house with something like a sock, when your hands are warm and dry, till you feel you'll be able to do it even with wet, frozen hands and a slippery gut:

   a. Take a sock.

   b. Hold it upside down.

   c. Start turning it inside out.

   d. Keep in mind that if it was a gut rather than a sock, it would be about 25 feet long and slippery. The way to get it turned inside out is by water pressure. The hard part is getting it started. Returning to the sock, if you turn socks inside out like I do, you have your thumbs in a sort of pocket you've made all the way around. Now you're going to run your water into that pocket. Since the gut is waterproof, the water pressure going into the pocket will push on it and draw more and more of the gut inside out until you're clear to the end. If you run into a wormhole or the gut starts to tear, you lose your water pressure as the water starts to leak out the hole. In that case, cut the gut at the point of the leakage and start over again with the part that hasn't been turned yet.

4. Put your turned, cleaned casings in a pan. Now get 2 knitting needles. Put 1 end of the cleaned gut between the knitting needles. Have somebody hold the needles tightly together while another pulls the casing through between them.

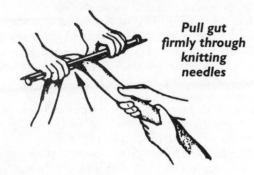

Turn gut inside out using water pressure

Pull gut firmly through knitting needles

5. Rinse them some more.
6. Store in cold water if you're going to use them soon. Otherwise freeze them. Soak in warm water before using.

☞ *CHITTERLINGS This is a Southern name for casings used as a meat dish. Having gotten them this far, you soak them in vinegar to remove the smell and then cook.*

STUFFING THE CASINGS: The stuffer is basically a nozzle with a container on top, fixed so you can put pressure on the contents. The pressure forces the sausage out through the nozzle and into the casing. The simplest sort is just a funnel. You hold the casing under the funnel and push it through with your hand. The usual sausage grinder has a stuffer attachment. Using the attachment, you turn the crank to force the sausage out of the nozzle into the casing until it is full. Pack the casing as tightly as possible. At the sausage-making bees they have a special big crank-operated sausage stuffer, but that's not practical for one individual or family.

If you're going to have only one stuffer size, it's better to have it too small than too large. Really nice stuffers have 3 nozzles for the basic casing sizes, but ordinary ones have just one size, ⅞ inch in diameter. It has to be small enough that the smallest casing can easily slip over the end of the nozzle.

Step-by-Step Guide to Stuffing Casings

1. Separate out a length of casing.
2. Put the entire casing over the nozzle of the stuffer.
3. Pinch the free end shut with your left hand.
4. Have a helper run the stuffer. The casing will unfold itself as the sausage is forced into it. To make a round sausage, fill about an 18-inch to 2-foot length. To stop the stuffer, crank it quickly backward a half turn of the crank.
5. Pull off a little empty length of casing. Cut the casing.
6. Put the 2 loose ends of the sausage casing together, forming a ring. Tie the ends together with twine or a stout soft white string. If you plan to hang the sausage to smoke it, tie another knot between the 2 free ends of your twine so you have a little ring of string for hanging it up. Your sausage should be long enough to make a comfortable circle and touch end to end. Round

sausages smoke best because they can't stick together, twist, or flip.

If a casing breaks with sausage in it, set it aside for the time being and restuff it later.

To make short links rather than rings, start as before. Let fill about 5 inches, or as long as you prefer. Stop filling. Twist casing several times around to make a thorough obstruction. Commence filling again, and so on. Cut off when you have enough to tie in a circle. (Takes about three.) Tie as before. If you don't tie them in a circle, you'll have to tie between each link. Three inches long is nicest, but you have to be pretty good at it to make them that short.

A butcher doesn't even need to stop the machine but can just keep the links flowing across the table.

Another way to do it is to make very long links and freeze them. Then you can just break off what you need.

Stuffing Using a Funnel. Use a funnel with a ¾-inch opening. Put the wet casing over the funnel end. Push meat down the funnel into the casing, regulating the thickness as it goes in. Make 5 inches long. Twist funnel around to form link. Continue pushing meat in until used up. Puncture with a skewer to let air out.

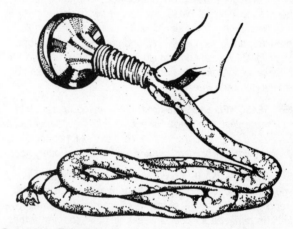

SAUSAGE RECIPES

NOTE: Sausage made from these recipes should be preserved by freezing or canning.

☞ *HEALTHY HOMEMADE SAUSAGE For the healthiest sausage, omit salt and reduce fat. Using a mortar and pestle or your blender, make a powder from your spices and add that spice mixture to the ground meat.*

☞ *CLASSIC SAUSAGE Simply grind your meat scraps and add one-fourth to one-third pork fat and seasonings (salt, pepper, sage, optional red pepper) or one-third preseasoned pork sausage. Classic all-pork sausage is made of pork trimmings—one-third fat to two-thirds lean.*

☞ *CARLA'S DIGESTIBLE SAUSAGE I'm always in a rush, so we just grind the sausage, season it, bag up in the usual meal-sized lot, and put it in the freezer. Just grind up the pork trimmings, using only one-fourth fat. Add hefty amounts of salt, garlic salt, onion salt, dried parsley, sage, and thyme. Leave out the pepper, red pepper, cinnamon, allspice, and so on. This tastes absolutely sausagey and has no bad aftereffects for even the most sensitive eater. I never seem to be able to keep sausage on hand. It gets used up faster than any other part of the pig.*

☞ *PLAIN PORK SAUSAGE Take 10 lb. fresh pork, 5 T. salt,*

2 T. sage, and 2 T. black pepper. Grind together. Mix thoroughly some more afterwards to make sure the spices are evenly distributed.

❧ **OLD-TIME GARLIC SAUSAGE** Combine 20 lb. beef, 40 lb. pork, 1 ground onion, 4 T. garlic juice, 2 c. salt, ½ c. brown sugar, and ½ c. pepper. Mix thoroughly. Set out overnight so part of the liquid can evaporate. Stuff in casings. Smoke with apple wood 12 hours or until casings are somewhat dry.

❧ **BREAKFAST HERBIE LEAN SAUSAGE** For every pound of lean ground meat add ⅛ t. pepper, ½ t. marjoram, ½ t. thyme, ¼ t. sage, and 1½ t. savory or ½ t. coriander seed. Mix all together thoroughly. Let rest in refrigerator overnight to help seasonings get well absorbed. Shape into patties, fry, and enjoy.

❧ **SPICY SAUSAGE** Sample recipe: combine 4 lb. pork (one-third fat, two-thirds lean), 5 t. salt, 4 t. sage, 2 t. pepper, ½ t. red pepper, ½ t. cloves or 1 t. nutmeg, and 1 t. sugar. Full-scale recipe: combine 100 lb. pork, 1¾ lb. salt, 3 oz. sage, 3 oz. pepper, ½ oz. red pepper, and ½ oz. cloves or 1 oz. nutmeg.

❧ **MARJORAM-MACE BULK SAUSAGE** Take 85 lb. lean pork, 15 lb. beef, 1½ lb. salt, 4 oz. pepper, 1 oz. red pepper, 1 oz. marjoram, and 1 oz. mace. Cut all meat into small pieces, sprinkle seasoning over, and grind with small plate. Store for 24 hours. Add enough water so you can knead the mixture well. Make into patties; stuff casings and freeze; or smoke and then freeze.

❧ **SEASONED SAUSAGE** First mix your seasonings; then mix seasonings into meat. For each 2½ lb. ground meat, combine 2½ t. sage, ½ t. thyme, ½ t. cayenne, ¾ t. pepper, ½ t. garlic powder, ½ bay leaf, crushed, and a dash of celery seed.

❧ **PIZZA SAUSAGE** Combine 10 lb. pork, almost all lean if you can manage it, ½ c. salt, 1 t. pepper, 1 t. crushed chili pepper, and 3 t. fennel seeds. Mix in seasonings. Grind. It will keep in refrigerator about 2 weeks. To cook, cut into patties and fry slowly or bake at 350°F for 45 minutes. Good with tomato sauce and spaghetti. Crumble as it fries to put on pizza.

❧ **BOLOGNA** This traditional sausage is made of a mixture of ground beef and ground pork. You could make it if you were butchering both a beef and a pig. That's a pretty natural thing to do come weather cold enough for slaughtering. By then we're low on all kinds of meat. You can substitute mutton or lamb for beef in this type of recipe. The proportion of pork lean and fat to beef can vary, according to taste and convenience, from as little as 5 lb. pork to 20 lb. beef to as much as 15 lb. pork to 20 lb. beef. So to a certain extent, it can just be a matter of how many pounds of beef and pork scraps you have. You might want to save a lot of your beef hamburger, though, to be plain old hamburger, and the same with pork. The nicest mixture is probably 2 lb. lean beef to 2 lb. lean pork with some fat pork (not more than 1 lb.) thrown in.

Season with sausage seasonings and grind. Use 1 t. seasoning per 1 lb. meat. If you want to put together your own seasoning, try salt, pepper, garlic, onion, coriander, and mace. Water is added in the proportion of 3 or 4 pt. per 25 lb. meat. Bologna is traditionally stuffed into beef casings, smoked, and then cooked. Remember to soak the casings before stuffing them. Smoke the bologna for 2 to 3 hours. Then simmer the bologna just below the boiling point until it

floats—15 to 30 minutes. Chill in cold water and hang to drip in a cool place. Then you can freeze it.

❧ **LIVER SAUSAGE** Along with seasoned pork sausage and blood sausage, this is one of the most popular country sausage recipes around here. Boil 5 lb. pork liver for 1 hour. Strain and discard broth. Cover 5 lb. lean pork and 5 lb. pork skin with water. Add 3 bay leaves, 6 whole cloves, and 1 onion. Boil for 2 hours. Skim the fat from the broth. Remove the meat and cool the broth. Grind the liver and the meat. Add salt, pepper, and garlic salt to taste. Add enough of the broth to moisten the mixture well. Stuff into casings and boil 1 hour. Then keep in refrigerator or freezer. This recipe makes enough to stuff only about 6 casings. Don't smoke liver sausage.

The above recipe is pretty heavy on the liver side. Most liver sausage contains only 10–20 percent liver. You can add your pork head, tongue, and the like to it. In that case, go ahead and cook all the meat except the liver just the way you would for scrapple—until it can be easily separated from the bones. Then cut the livers deeply with a knife and add them for the last 10 minutes. Don't overcook the variety meats. It all gets cooked again in the casings anyway. For 100 lb. meat use 2 lb. salt, 2 oz. pepper, 1 oz. sage, ½ oz. red pepper, and 1 oz. allspice. Mix in the seasonings and grind the meat until it's ready to stuff into the soaked casings. Stuff, tie, and simmer in water until it floats (10–30 minutes). Cool, chill, and hang up to drain. Freeze.

❧ **SALAMI** This is made from meat that might be tough and need grinding or that tastes like a wild meat you aren't used to. The spiciness covers the taste. Don't use any fat from wild meat, except bear, since the wild flavor is generally concentrated in the fat. Wild sausage that's part pork or pork sausage makes a fine breakfast sausage. Wild meat is generally extremely lean, so you can combine it with really fatty pieces of pork and it will benefit. You can use one-fourth to one-third pork. Season and grind up. Then I just bag it up, tie with the wires, and freeze. Each bag holds enough for a breakfast. When we have plenty of wild meat and pork, I make salami by the kettleful. Season with commercial seasoning, 1 t. per pound, or use your own formula. You can add black whole peppers after your grinding to make it authentic. Sage, allspice, garlic, ground cardamom seed, and onion salt are all good in it. After the meat is seasoned, you can stuff it into casings if you like. Smoke about 48 hours (smoking is no substitute for cooking, however). Freeze it and cook it when you are ready for a sausage meal.

❧ **POTATO SAUSAGE** This recipe was sent to me by the Johnsons of Wheaton, IL. Use 4 lb. ground beef and 2 lb. ground pork. Peel and grate potatoes until you get about 1 qt. grated potato. Use some of the liquid that drains off the grated potatoes so that the mixture is like a soft meat loaf. Grind 3 large onions and add. Add salt, pepper, and ground allspice to taste—½ to 1 t. The flavor should be subtle. Put this mixture in sausage casings. Don't pack too tightly. Tie the ends. Simmer in salted boiling water for ½ to 1 hour. Freeze. To cook, put in a shallow pan in the oven and brown at 375°F for about 10 minutes.

❧ **BLOOD SAUSAGE** This recipe makes about 30 lb. sausage. Take 7 lb. fresh pork (cook the day before and save broth), 1 bundle casings (well washed and soaked in water), 3 lb. rice (cooked almost done), 2 lb. barley (also precooked the day of use), ½ c. cinnamon, 1 t. cloves, 1½ t. allspice,

½ c. marjoram, 3 T. pepper, ½ c. salt, and 2 qt. fresh beef or pork blood.

It is probably better to use beef or lamb casings, and the sausage will taste better if you use beef blood. The meat used should be mostly pork; a little beef can be added. Fresh pork hocks, shanks, shoulder, or meat from the hog's head works great. Fat must be left with it, since it is a necessary ingredient. All ingredients should be ready ahead of time.

Blood should be caught in a manner that keeps it clean. Add a little salt to keep it from setting, or stir it. The best way to get a cow or pig's blood is to shoot the animal and then quickly hoist it. Cut the jugular vein in the neck—or, if you're a real expert, go straight to the aorta coming out of the heart. Press the neck of a jar to the animal's neck to catch the blood as it pours out. To get blood from an unhoisted beef or pig, just hold the pan so as to catch blood after cutting it open. One hog will give about 1½ to 2 gal. blood. Don't get blood from nose or mouth. Keep pan under animal, and keep stirring for at least 5 minutes; otherwise the blood will congeal into a lump, and you want to keep it liquid. If you have snow, pack the jar with snow to cool it.

Grind meat and fat. Warm broth. Mix meat, broth, warm rice, barley, and blood. If blood has set, grind it and then mix in. Add spices. Mix thoroughly. Mixture must be quite warm to put in casings. Don't pack casings too full. Have a kettle of water boiling. Tie casings, leaving room for expansion. Drop a few at a time into the water. Cook about 10 minutes. Test by pricking it with a needle. If juice is clear, take out and cool. Wrap for freezer.

My family enjoys this fried crisp or put on a cookie sheet or shallow pan in a hot oven until crisp. We use it for either breakfast or dinner. It is very expensive to buy, and what we do buy never seems very good.

➤ **GERMAN FRANKS** Take 5 lb. veal without bones, 5 lb. pork (no fat), 8 lb. lard, 13 grams (½ oz.) salt per pound of meat, 3 grams (¹/₁₀ oz.) pepper per pound of meat, and ½ nutmeg per pound of meat. Grind meat very fine together with salt, pepper, and seasoning. Mix well after the grinding. Put into clean intestines and make 6-inch pieces. Prick with fork. Franks will keep a while in refrigerator.

➤ **KIELBASA (POLISH SAUSAGE)** Combine 1½ lb. pork loin or Boston butt, ½ lb. veal, salt and pepper, 1 clove garlic (crushed), and 1 t. crushed marjoram, if wanted. Run meat through coarse grinder. Add 3 or 4 T. water, garlic, salt and pepper to taste, and marjoram. Mix thoroughly and stuff casing. It is now ready to smoke. Or just place in baking dish and cover with water. Bake at 325 to 350°F until water is absorbed.

➤ **DRY ITALIAN SAUSAGE** Take 5 lb. freshly butchered ground pork butt, 2 t. black pepper, 1 clove garlic (chopped), 1 wine glass of red table wine, 1 T. salt, 1 T. fennel seed, and 1 t. ground hot pepper. Blend well and store in refrigerator overnight. The next day, stuff in casings. Then freeze, or hang up to dry in cool, ventilated room for 1 week and then freeze. Some people add ground onions to sausage.

➤ **ROSEMARY SAUSAGE** Take 1 lb. pork, 1 lb. beef, 1 lb. veal, 1 lb. suet, 1 T. salt, 1 t. black pepper, 2 t. rosemary (ground or chopped), ½ t. thyme, ½ t. marjoram, ½ t. freshly grated nutmeg, and casings. Finely grind first 4 ingredients. Add remaining ingredients and mix well. Put into casing and tie every 4 inches, or form into patties and refrigerate.

➤ **DUTCH "POUTDEN"** Use a Dutch oven or a large pan with a cover. Cut or chop up the following ingredients, working from the bottom of the pan to the top. On the bottom make a layer of potatoes, then carrots, then onions, then apples, then cabbage (cut in chunks), and then mettwurst or any good smoked sausage (cut in small pieces). Add 1 to 2 c. water, salt, and pepper. Boil until mushy. Can be served as it comes or mashed together.

➤ **SWEET AND SPICY SAUSAGE** To 4 lb. pork trimmings, add 5 t. salt, 4 t. sage, 2 t. black pepper, ½ t. ground cloves, and 1 t. sugar.

Canning Sausage. See the Ground or Chopped Meat recipe in the "Canning" section.

Preparing Hamburger or Sausage to Be Frozen. Mix together your desired meat, fat, and seasoning ingredients. Then decide if you want to freeze it in clumps, patties, or rolls. For clumps, divide into the sizes you want, wrap, label, and freeze. For patties, divide meat into ½-lb. balls and press into flat patties (or use a hamburger press). Package for freezer the desired number of patties per package. Separate the patties by a double thickness of wax paper. Wrap, label, and freeze. When thawed, these patties can be broiled, pan-fried, or baked in gravy. For rolls, shape meat into cylinders of a diameter and length that will feed all of your family for 1 meal. Wrap, label, and freeze; when you defrost a roll, cut into slices. Rolls slice better if they have some fat content or if all-lean meat is mixed with a little water.

Soups from Meat

CONSOMME: Prepare for the pot a chicken that weighs about 4 lb. Saw about 2 lb. worth of beef bones into pieces. Cut up 2 lb. beef. Put everything in a covered kettle and add water to cover. Let it all soak an hour; then put over the fire and bring quickly to the boiling point. Reduce heat at once to simmering and cook 6 or 7 hours. In the last hour of cooking, add 1 T. salt, ½ c. carrots, ½ c. onion, ½ c. celery, 1 t. peppercorns, 2 whole cloves, 1 allspice berry, 1 small bay leaf, 2 sprigs parsley, 1 sprig thyme, 1 sprig savory, and 1 sprig marjoram. Cut the vegetables into reasonable-sized pieces. At the end of the last half hour of cooking, strain the soup. Then chill it. When it's cold, remove any fat that has solidified on the surface. Clarify by reheating with 2 slightly beaten egg whites, stirring constantly until it boils. Boil 5 minutes. Then let stand until it settles. Strain through 2 thicknesses of cheesecloth.

BOUILLON: Use 3½ lb. beef. Put in a pan with water and let stand an hour. Then put over heat in covered pot and bring to boiling point. Skim off scum. Reduce heat and simmer 3 hours. Chop 1 onion, 1 carrot, 1 sprig parsley, and 2 stalks celery and add to soup with ½ bay leaf, 2 cloves, 6 peppercorns, and 1 t. salt. Let simmer an hour more. Strain into a bowl and chill. Remove fat when it is firm and clarify for consomme.

BONES: No matter how closely trimmed, bones can be cooked for a delicious and nutritious broth. Fill a large pressure cooker or canner with trimmed bones, half-fill it with water, and cook at 15 lb. pressure for 1 hour. After the pressure has dropped, strain the broth into another kettle and pick off any meat still on the bones. Chill the broth and remove the fat from the top. The remnants of meat and broth can be either frozen or canned. Use the bones as dog treats or bury them in the orchard or garden, where they will serve as time-released fertilizers.

By-Products: Soap and Tanned Hides

There's no need to waste anything from your animals.

Soap Making

Soap is nothing more than a mixture of fats or oils with lye and water. Although soap has been a part of human life for at least the last 2,000 years, its commercial history is very short. Before people learned the connection between bacteria and disease and figured out that soap killed bacteria, cleanliness was not a popular concept. But by the mid-19th century, innumerable fat-lye soaps were on the market, some made with animal fats and others with palm kernel oil, which lathers more easily than tallow soap. These days, commercial soaps and detergents are so plentiful that homemade soaps are a handicraft.

The idea of making one's own soap is attractive for several reasons. First, it is the only way to really know what you are rubbing on your hands or soaking your clothes in. Makers of commercial soap detergents don't list all their ingredients on the package. Those of us who are concerned about ecology have to dislike the detrimental effects of the commercial synthetic detergents that have been widely used since just after World War II. (Although soaps in large concentrations can poison marine life, this rarely happens because the soap decomposes readily.) Second, soap is another use for the by-products of slaughtering your animals, making the proposition of raising stock that much more economically efficient. Third, the cost of making homemade soap is much less than that of buying commercial soaps.

Homemade soap leaves clothes with a lovely clean smell. (Use about 1½ c. per load, or more if you're planning on putting a lot of clothes through the same water.) I like homemade soap for dishwashing, too. Here's my testimonial: my glasses have been shinier and my silverware sparklier since I started washing them with homemade soap. I can also see the soap in the rinse water for the dishes because it turns gray very quickly—an advantage over detergents, which are so clear that you think you have washed them away, but you end up eating them! Homemade soap works okay in lukewarm water if you can give a halfway

ample hot rinse. It's also fine for human bodies if it is properly aged. You can wash your face and take baths with it. You can use the leftover water to irrigate garden or flowers, since the soap has no additives that harm the environment. And homemade soap is a bargain!

If you wonder what using homemade soap flakes is like, just buy some White King. As far as I can tell, it's identical to homemade! Of course, homemade soap doesn't contain the bleach that is present in so many detergents now, so your clothes won't look "white" unless you add a bleaching agent separately to the water. Or you can make your soap with bleach. Homemade soap won't work well in a very hard water unless you use some borax to hold down the "curding." You can put borax in when you make the soap. Using liquid bleach will also help hold down the curds.

BOOKS ON SOAP MAKING: *The Art of Soap Making: A Complete Introduction to the History and Craft of Fine Soapmaking,* by Merilyn Mohm (1979); Dorothy Richter's *Make Your Own Soap! Plain and Fancy* (1974); and *The Natural Soap Book,* by Susan Miller Cavitch, are available from 719-962-3228; **www.cfamilyresources.com**. *Milk-Based Soaps,* by Casey Makela; *The Soapmaker's Companion,* by Susan Miller Cavitch; *The Handmade Soap Book,* by Melinda Coss; *Making Natural Liquid Soaps* and *Making Transparent Soap,* both by Catherine Failor; and *Melt & Mold Soap Crafting,* by C. Kaila Westerman, are available from Storey Books (address in Chpater 1).

The most recent is Elaine C. White's *Soap Recipes: Seventy Tried-and-True Ways to Make Soap with Herbs, Beeswax, and Vegetable Oils.* Order her book from Valley Hills Press, 1864 Ridgeland Dr., Starkville, MS 39759 ($24 postpaid).

SOAP-MAKING SUPPLIES: A homemade bar of soap can be a work of art and/or a way of making money.

K & W Popcorn ships 5-gal. coconut oil or 35-lb. bags: 816-359-2030; PO Box 275, 710 E. 24th St., Trenton, MO 64683.

Liberty Natural Products, 8120 SE Stark St., Portland, OR 97215, 800-289-8427; fax 503-256-1182; **www.liberty natural.com**. Wholesale only; $50 minimum. They sell essential oils, soapmaking fats, herbs, clays, etc.

Lorann Oils offers molds for soap and candies, essential oils, flavorings, and specialty ingredients for soap-, candle-, and food-crafters: 4518 Aurelius Rd., Lansing, MI 48910; 800-862-8620; fax 517-882-0507; **customercare@lorannoils.com; www.lorannoils.com**.

SunFeather Natural Soap Company, 1551 State Hwy. 72, Potsdam, NY 13676; 800-771-7627; fax 315-265-2902; **www.sunsoap.com**, offers soap-making books, supplies, and equipment. Free color catalog.

HOT WATER, COLD WATER, HARD WATER: Homemade soap is good for washing if you are able to wash in hot water. It isn't good for washing dishes or clothes in cold water, though, because it doesn't dissolve easily, even if you make it into soap flakes. If you use it to wash dishes in hard water, it leaves a ring around the sink. Hard water contains calcium, magnesium, and iron, which, with soap, form compounds, or "curds," that resemble sticky gum. Use borax or washing soda to soften hard water before adding soap. Make sure the soap is dissolved before you add clothes or dishes. Otherwise you risk having little particles of undissolved soap left among your clothes. A really good hand rinse will easily get rid of those particles, but automatic washers aren't built to handle that. You'll have to agitate the water to dissolve the flakes into solution and produce suds. Use water as hot as your hands can stand—or hotter. Great-Grandmother literally boiled her clothes with homemade soap in a big iron pot over a fire in the backyard on washday. But then, practically everything her family wore was cotton.

SOAP JELLY: You can solve the dissolving difficulty by heating, or adding hot water to, a concentrated soap mixture, stirring it into solution, and then cooling. The old-timers called this dissolved soap "soap jelly" and made it ahead. They used it in washing machines and for washing dishes because soap jelly easily melts in hot water and makes thick suds. To make soap jelly, you cut 1 lb. hard soap into fine shavings and add 1 gal. water. Boil about 10 minutes and then cool. Keep soap jelly covered to prevent drying out. A reader told me an even easier way. She puts homemade soap bars into a few gallon glass jars and pours hot water over. Every day or so she drains off the liquid into a plastic pail, and that liquid is soap jelly.

Buying Lye. You can buy lye from the cleaning agents section of a regular supermarket. If they don't carry it, ask. They can order it for you. It may be called sodium hydroxide or caustic soda. Store lye is sold in cans, usually containing about 13 oz., under several different brand names. Note the sodium hydroxide content. It should be 94–98 percent. Lye for soap is different from the lye used for drain openers, which has nitrates and other additives. There is usually a soap recipe on the lye can. Most lye companies will send you further information on soap making upon request.

Making Lye. Use ashes from hardwoods, if possible, such as oak, walnut, or fruit wood, since they make a stronger, better lye. Pine, fir, and other evergreens are soft woods. Put the wood ashes in a barrel with a small opening near the base to let the water "leach" through. Set the barrel so that you can put a container under the hole. If your wooden tub or barrel doesn't have a hole, bore one with a drill on the side near the bottom of the barrel. Before putting in your ashes, put several clean rocks or bricks inside the container by the hole and then add a generous layer of straw, if you have it—hay or grass, if you don't. Then you can add your ashes. You can just let them accumulate until you want lye or until your container is full. The most efficient way of proceeding is to then add soft water to your barrel until water begins to run from the tap (this may take awhile). Then plug the tap hole with a cork plug (home brewer's supply houses have them) or something, and let it soak a few days. If you have extra ashes, you can add more ashes and water as the first layer settles in the barrel from the wetting. In 3 days, open the plug and have a wooden tub, crock, or glass container ready to catch the trickle of lye water emerging from the opening.

Lye Concentration. Store lye is just fine if you follow the directions. For homemade lye, put in an egg or potato. If it floats enough that a piece about the size of a quarter is exposed on the surface, the lye is about right for soap making. If it sinks, the lye water needs to be leached another time through fresh ashes or else boiled down until the concentration is strong enough. If your lye isn't strong enough, you'll make soft soap as the pioneers did. Knowing how much homemade lye to use in soap making requires experience. Excess lye makes a coarse, flinty soap that will crumble when shaved and burn you when used. Soap should have a smooth, velvety texture that curls when shaved. If any free lye is present, the soap "bites" when touched with the tongue.

Lye for Cleaning. You can use lye as a cleaning fluid for washing garbage cans; hog, dairy, and poultry housing; and other problem areas. Use about 2½ c. liquid lye or 1 can commercial crystals per 10 gal. warm water, or as you like it. In days past, lye was poured down rat holes and also used in making hominy.

FATS FOR SOAP: Since soaps and candles both use tallow, pioneer families often produced both at the same time. The grease must be pure, clean, and fresh (or frozen) to obtain soap with a clean, wholesome odor. By "toilet" soap, the old-timers meant soap using fat from butchering rather than drippings; it was a whiter, better-quality soap. "Saddle soap" meant an all-mutton or beef tallow soap. Such a soap was valuable as a cleaner and preserver of leather.

Six pounds of fat and 1 can of lye will make about 9 lb. of soap. Mutton (sheep) or goat tallow (fat) is the hardest of all animal fats, having the highest melting point. Used alone, mutton or goat fat makes a hard, dry soap unless you add extra water or mix the hard fat with softer ones like lard, goose grease, or chicken fat. Beef tallow, once the preferred fat for soap, is next in hardness and also should be mixed with softer fat or additional water. One pound of untrimmed beef fat will get you 1 c. tallow. Lard (pig fat) makes fine soap, giving you 2 c. fat for every pound of meat, although it may be a little soft. Poultry fat is too soft when used alone, so it should be mixed with harder fats. Meat fryings, cracklings, meat trimmings, and other refuse fat must be first clarified and desalted.

You can use any animal or vegetable fat (even salad oil), but not mineral oil. Tallow alone produces a hard soap without much lather. Adding vegetable oils improves the texture. The best vegetable oil by far is coconut oil, which produces a fine sudsing soap similar to a "shaving" soap. (All-lard soap is similar; you can use the coconut oil soap recipe to make it.) Soap made from vegetable oils or soft fats requires less water and needs to dry longer than soap made from tallow. Cottonseed oil is difficult to work with and results in a soft soap, while olive oil is better for soap making than other vegetable oils.

Store your fat in a cool, dry place while you accumulate enough for soap making. When you do have enough,

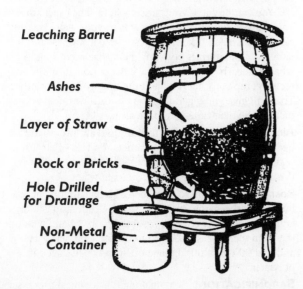

Leaching Barrel

Ashes

Layer of Straw

Rock or Bricks

Hole Drilled for Drainage

Non-Metal Container

make it into soap promptly, because fat will become rancid over time, and rancid fat has to be cured of that problem before it can be used (more on that later). Soap improves with age; fat doesn't.

To accumulate fats, each day save your fats of all kinds. If you boil meat, cool the pot of liquid and remove the fat. Then put the accumulated fat on and melt it. Cook long enough to get all the water out (if you don't, it will mold or spoil). Then fold several thicknesses of cheesecloth or any loose-weave cotton, and strain the melted fat. Always be careful when handling hot fat, since it can burn you. Keep all fat in a tightly lidded pan, away from any strong-smelling stuff, until you are ready to make soap. You may want to freeze it, but if you can store it in a cool place, it will keep for several weeks.

Rendering Fat. Render any surplus fat from butchering or fatty trimmings from cutting up. Grind the fat or cut it into pieces. Put it into a large kettle on top of the stove or in a large pan in the oven. Add about 1 qt. water for each 10 lb. fat. Use a moderate temperature and stir occasionally. When the fat is liquefied and the solids (cracklings) are brown and settling, carefully strain the fat. You may want to do this more than once. Your soap will be as white as your fat is. If your fat is not pure enough, you may end up with yellow soap with an unpleasant odor. If you do not want to strain the fat, scrape the sediment off its bottom, pour off the liquid, and repeat as necessary. Years ago, old-timers had a "fat press" for pressing out lard or tallow. It was an iron kettle about 1½ feet in diameter, with a sieve in the bottom and a big dasher that fit over it and could be screwed down tight to put pressure on the cracklings.

Clarifying Drippings and Removing Salt. Put the leftover cooking grease into a kettle with an equal amount of water. Use a large pot so it won't be likely to boil over. The day before soap making is a good time to do this. Bring to a boil, stir, and add 1 qt. cold water for each 1 gal. drippings. Stir to break up any lumps. When the water boils, let it set and settle. Then cool and skim fat from surface with skimmer, or refrigerate and clean the cake of fat as described above, or strain. Repeat these procedures until you are satisfied with the condition of your grease. I would advise not even bothering with leftover grease that has absorbed strong smells, but sometimes you can cut the effect by adding a little lemon or vinegar to an amount of water equal to half the amount of fat and boiling them together. (Soft fats that won't get firm even when refrigerated have to be skimmed, of course.)

Removing Rancidity. Boil the sour or rancid fat in a mixture of 5 parts water to 1 part vinegar. Cool and skim fat, or refrigerate and remove fat cake. Remelt the fat; for each gallon of fat, add 1 qt. cold water. Stir slightly. Cool and skim fat or remove fat cake. Repeat as necessary. Fat that is rancid is fine for soap making but not for eating ever again.

OTHER SOAP INGREDIENTS

Water. Water is a basic ingredient of soap making. You need pure water, free of chemicals that can combine with the lye. Don't use hard water unless you neutralize the chemicals in it with washing soda. "Hard water" means water with minerals dissolved in it. Rainwater isn't hard, but almost all water from springs, wells, or rivers is, in varying degrees. Measure the water into enameled, wooden, or crockery containers that are easily handled.

You can test how hard your water is by making a solu-

tion of denatured alcohol or wood alcohol and pure soap. At room temperature, mix in soap a bit at a time until the solution is nearly thick. Then find 2 identical small medicine bottles or spice containers. Put rainwater or distilled water in one and the test water in the other. Use an eye dropper to add soap solution to the distilled water. Shake frequently. The idea is to get suds to cover the water surface for 1 minute after the bottle is laid on its side. If you then add the same number of drops to the test water, shaking, you can see how long the suds last there. Soft water will produce a minute's worth of suds; hard water will not.

Perfume. Perfumes like oil of sassafras, oil of lavender, and oil of lemon may be added to soap. They used to be cheap, but not any more. Oil of citronella is sometimes suggested, but I wouldn't use it. It's an excellent insect repellent, however. Never use perfumes containing alcohol—they will not last and may cause separation. Experiment to learn just how strong you want your soap to smell. For a start you might use, per 15 lb. tallow: 4 t. oil of sassafras; 2 t. oil of lavender; 1 t. oil of lemon; 1 t. oil of cloves; 1 t. oil of almond; 2 t. oil of pine; or ½ t. rose geranium oil.

You can make your own rose geranium perfume by making a tea of the rose geranium leaves and adding it to your soap. All soap readily absorbs odors, desirable or undesirable, so it can be perfumed simply by placing with it the petals of any favorite flower or perfume, if you have yet not added a scent.

Coloring. Uncolored soap is fine. A light yellow or marbled effect can be made with liquid butter coloring. You can make your own pink coloring by adding an extract of the blossoms of pink roses or tulips. A green color can be had by pounding the tops of beets (or spinach, parsley, etc.) to extract a few drops of the juice and adding it to the water. (For more ideas, see the section on making food colorings in Chapter 5.)

Borax. Borax quickens the sudsing action of soap because it helps to hold down homemade soap's tendency to curd in hard water and it's a natural fabric softener. Because they used borax, the old-timers could hang their clothes on a line and they'd come out soft.

Since chemically, borax doesn't play any role in the soap recipe—it's just a physical additive—using more or less doesn't affect the quality of your soap a bit. I've seen recipes with anywhere from 2 T. to 3 c. borax per can of lye. You can buy it at your grocery store. The exact amount you should add depends on how hard your water is. You can make a batch one way and see how it washes, and then either add or subtract borax the next time according to what you learn. Or you can leave the borax out of the soap recipe completely and add it at the time you wash clothes. That will give you a good notion of just how much borax to include the next time you make soap.

Air. If you want your soap to float, fold air into it when it begins to have a creamy consistency. You fold in air just as you would fold an egg white into a cake mixture. Test for floating by flicking a few drops on cold water.

Rosin. Adding rosin to soap increases its lathering ability but makes the soap darker and softer. Rosin soap is okay for laundry. Add 8 oz. crushed rosin to 5½ lb. fat and heat until the rosin melts or is dissolved in the fat. Cool fat to 100°F and add 90 lye solution made of 1 can lye dissolved in 2½ pt. water.

SAPONIFICATION: Soap making is a chemical process.

When lye and fat are brought together under the right conditions, they react to make soap, which is an alkali salt of fatty acids and glycerin. The process is called "saponification." It may take several weeks for complete saponification to take place. This is one reason that aging is so important in soap making. Soon after it is made, soap actually contains some free lye, but the longer it ages, the less likely it is to contain any free lye. Soap made from lard or soap that has been boiled requires longer aging before it becomes hard and ready for use. Once it is saponified, the soap will never separate into fat and lye again. In homemade soap, the glycerin is left in. In commercial soap making, it is separated and sold.

LYE TO FAT TO WATER

To make good soap you need correct proportions of these basic soap ingredients.

Lye	Fat	Water
2 T.	1 c.	½ c.
¼ c.	2 c.	¾ c.
¼ c. + 2 T.	3 c.	1 c.
½ c.	4 c.	1½ c.
½ c. + 2 T.	5 c.	2 c.
¾ c.	6 c.	2¼ c.
¾ c. + 2 T.	7 c.	2¾ c.
1 c.	8 c.	3 c.
1 c. + 2 T.	9 c.	3½ c.
1¼ c.	10 c.	3¾ c.
1¼ c. + 2 T.	11 c.	4 c.
1½ c.	12 c.	4½ c.
1½ c. + 2 T.	13 c.	5 c.

Cold Process. The process I use to make soap is the cold process. To make the very best soap (mine is not), use exact weights, measures, and temperatures. A dairy (floating) thermometer and household scales are useful. Soap has to have the right proportion of fat to alkali. Too much fat makes for an ineffective emulsifier, but too much alkali will make soap that's too harsh, especially for skin. The saponification has to be nearly complete. Free fat can become rancid, smelly brown spots on your soap. Free bits of lye can burn the skin.

Combine lye, water, and fat (see "Lye to Fat to Water" table for proportions). First add the lye slowly to your water when making a solution from the lye crystals, and then add the lye solution slowly to the melted fat. Stir evenly, preferably only in one direction. Rapid addition of the lye to your fat, or of the fat to the lye, can cause separation. So can jerky, uneven stirring. Boiled, or hot-process, soap is probably superior to the kind I describe here, but it's a lot trickier to make. Use an enameled kettle, never aluminum.

Confused already? This will help.

The Basic Steps of Soap Making

1. Slowly add 1 can lye to 5 c. cold water in an earthenware or unchipped enameled or "ceramic on steel" container. Steel or aluminum under the enamel is okay. Don't use cast iron. Ask at a kitchenware store or at a homesteader's supplier if you are not sure what pot to use.

   Mix lye and water outdoors or near open windows, because the mixing produces heat. There will be strong fumes that you can see. Try not to breathe them; they'll make you cough. Don't use anything but a wooden spoon to stir. Be careful not to splash it on your skin. Stir constantly until the lye crystals are all dissolved. Now let it cool. Cool the lye solution to 70–75°F if your fat is lard (pig fat), 90–95°F for an all-tallow soap.

2. Heat 10 c. melted fat. A relatively large proportion of fat gives you a milder soap. If the temperature of the lye water (including borax if it's in your recipe) is about 75 to 80°F at the time of mixing with the melted fat, the fat should be heated to the appropriate temperature, as shown in the "Heating Fat" table. Too high a temperature darkens the color of the soap and may keep it from setting.

HEATING FAT

Type of Fat	Temperature
Vegetable oil	110–115°F
Bear	115°F
Goose	115°F
Pork	120°F
Beef	130°F
Deer	130°F
Sheep	130°F

3. Pour the fat slowly into the lye water when you have each at the right temperature.

4. Add your borax, perfume, coloring, or other extras at this point.

5. Stir in one direction until you have soap. This usually takes about 15 minutes, but it could happen in 5 minutes or take an hour, depending on temperature. If you have waited for your ingredients to cool, you should have no problem. If you're having a setting problem, you might try setting the mixing container in cold water. If, on the other hand, the soap starts setting on the edges, stir faster or even beat it. Soap starts out dark-colored; as you stir, it gets somewhat lighter in color. When all the lye gets mixed with all the fat, saponification happens. You'll notice a cloudiness first. It's ready to pour when it is like thick pea soup, and drops that are trailed from the spoon stand momentarily on the surface of it. It's also ready if the stirring spoon will stand by itself in the middle. If you pour too soon, the soap may separate into 2 layers, the bottom hard and brittle and the top greasy. But if you wait too long, you'll end up with incomplete, odd-shaped bars with air pockets.

6. Pour into molds. Scrape all the mixture out of the bowl. Your soap will be a little dark when first made but will turn white in a week.

This sounds like a lot of work, but it isn't after you make a couple of batches. All these little things will soon come naturally. There are infinite variations on this procedure, but it's the one I know best and it's relatively simple. It makes a good basic raw (cold, not cooked) soap for soap flakes with which to wash dishes and clothes. But later on, I have some even easier ones for you that readers have sent me.

SOAP MOLDS: What you can best use for a mold depends on whether you're planning to make soap flakes or bar soap. For soap flakes, you can use anything except metal containers for a mold—serving bowls, enamel pans, wooden boxes, plastic containers, and cottage cheese cartons (handy because you can cut them off when you're done). Avoid containers with paint or dyes that the soap could absorb. Have your molds ready before you start, and expect to dispose of them once the soap hardens. Grease

1. Lye is caustic soda. It burns, even in tiny flakes. Lye in the eyes or on skin or clothing can cause severe burns. Obviously, you should not swallow it.
2. Keep children and animals away from lye.
3. The fumes of lye in water can burn your throat and chest. Work in a well-ventilated space, outside or near a window. Don't breathe the fumes!
4. Keep newspapers handy to sop up spills.
5. Don't keep lye or a lye solution in metal; lye reacts with metal. Don't put it in aluminum, because it will react with the aluminum. Don't put it in tin, iron, or stainless steel. It's best contained in plastic, glass, stoneware, or unchipped enamel.
6. Be careful with glass. Water and lye can heat enough to break glass.
7. Measuring spoons of stainless steel are okay, but cups should be glass or heat-resistant plastic. Utensils exposed to lye should be enamel, crockery, glass, or wood—and they should never be used for any-

thing else. Rinsing utensils after they have been in a lye solution makes them safe to handle, but remnants of lye in cracks can contaminate foods.

8. Use only wooden spoons. A slotted spoon is good for stirring. Better yet, stirring with a piece of kindling will save spoiling a good wooden spoon.
9. Never add hot, or even warm, water to canned store-bought lye crystals. They heat up anyway when combined with water, and the hot water will cause spattering.
10. For protection when making soap, wear rubber gloves and keep a bowl of vinegar nearby, so if you spatter lye on your hands or arms, you can dip them immediately into the vinegar to neutralize it.

First Aid for Lye Burns

Be extremely careful when working with lye. If lye comes in contact with human skin, it causes a chemical burn. Flush immediately with water. If it is not flushed, it will continue to burn. If possible, add a little salt to the water. If water is not available, use soda water or

soda pop—they're better than nothing. If, after 5 to 10 minutes your skin is still red and painful, seek burn care in a hospital emergency room.

If lye is swallowed, call 911. Swallowing lye can be fatal. When swallowed, it burns the esophagus, so vomiting (which may be inevitable) should be avoided. Take milk or ice cream to help neutralize the lye's chemical reaction. Although vinegar, orange juice, and so forth also neutralize lye, they should *not* be ingested because the combination creates heat. This rise in temperature will burn physically in addition to the chemical burn.

If lye gets into the eye, call 911. Flush the eye immediately with water; add salt to the water if possible. Again, use milk if available, to neutralize the chemical reaction. Most likely you should get to an emergency room as soon as possible. Do *not* use vinegar or boric acid solution.

But the best advice is: Be Careful!

---

the molds with Vaseline and then pour the soap carefully into the mold. Smooth the top surfaces with a plastic spatula.

Keep setting soap away from the heat. It takes from a few hours to several days for the soap to harden enough to be removed, and it shrinks as it hardens. Soaps with higher amounts of soft fats will take longer to dry. To get it out of the mold, slip a paring knife around the edge and pry some. The longer it sets, the easier it is to get out. The Vaseline gives the soap a nice surface finish. Let the soap dry at room temperature for about 2 weeks, but keep it from freezing, since

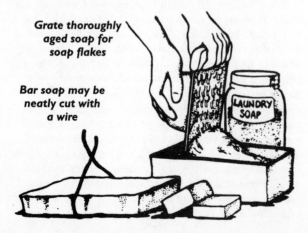

Grate thoroughly aged soap for soap flakes

Bar soap may be neatly cut with a wire

that stops the curing process and produces a too-soft soap.

To make flakes, use a grater with medium holes, or put the soap through a food chopper, or shave with a knife. Once the flakes are completely dry and hard, you can store them in a cardboard box, paper bag, or what-have-you.

Although the soap is soft and easy to flake immediately, let it age as long as possible before making flakes. The longer the soap has aged, or cured, the more complete the saponification and the less the risk of free lye. Five-year-old soap crumbles into something very much like detergent in consistency. Age soap in an open box in open air for 8 or 10 months or a year if you can. Don't allow the soap to freeze for at least the first 2 weeks. The best curing is at room temperature. If you're desperate, the soap can be used after a month has passed. If you grate it prematurely and find that it still has so much moisture in it that it comes out lumpy, you can rush it by first flaking and then drying it in a 150°F oven. When thoroughly dry, pulverize it.

To mold bar soap, pour soap that is ready to mold into a soaked wooden box lined with a cotton cloth that has been wetted and then wrung as dry as possible. Or you could use Plexiglas or glass pans lined with wax paper, or milk cartons. If you have molds the size of soap bars, those are most convenient of all. You can construct an open wooden grid that fits into a box and makes several bars of soap at the same time. Cover with cardboard and then with a rug or blanket to retain heat while the soap is texturing out. Some people cut the blocks into bars only a few hours after pouring. If you do this, be careful. The saponification is probably not complete, and the lye in the solution can still burn you. Some people prefer to leave the soap molds undisturbed for at least 24 hours before cutting and piling. Others take a knife and score the soap into bars a few hours after making, let it sit overnight, and then turn them out on a board and finish breaking the cuts so the bars will separate nicely. When well set, remove the soap and cut into convenient-sized cakes. To remove the soap from a mold made of a damp box lined with cotton, just lift the soap by the ends of the overhanging cloth lining. Pile the bars on top of each other so air circulates around each cake. The soap can be neatly cut by wrapping it once with a fine wire such as piano or guitar wire, crossing the ends, and pulling.

Many of the commercial molds for decorative candles can be used to make soap too. Just avoid the metal ones. Those molds that shape the top of the soap must be pressed tightly since soap hardens more slowly than wax, especially in a closed mold. Remove the soap before it is completely hard so you can smooth the edges and fix any small flaws. Remember that the soap is still fairly caustic at this stage.

Soap on a Rope. Double a washable cord and wrap the ends with thread for 2 inches. Stick this end into setting soap and let harden.

STORING BAR SOAP: After the soap has completely dried, you can wrap it in wax paper, tissue, plastic wrap, or paper envelopes. Colored papers may stain the soap. Aluminum may interact with the alkalis. Scents will fade from soaps unless they are wrapped.

➣ GERTRUDE JOHNSON'S BOILED SOAP WITH BLEACH
Gertrude Johnson of Lamont, WA, wrote me, "I've made soap for years, but mine never turned out to my satisfaction until I ran across this recipe. Start with 10 c. melted fat (lard and suet is a good combination), and stir in 1 c. liquid bleach until well blended. Dissolve 1 can lye in 6 qt. water (don't use aluminum pan). Do this outdoors, being careful not to breathe the fumes or splash any liquid on your hands, face, or arms. Stir with wooden spoon or paddle until well dissolved. Stir the bleach/fat mixture into the lye solution and stir well again. Set aside for 4 to 6 days, stirring frequently.

It will start out thin and watery, but by the fourth or fifth day it will be solid to the bottom of your old canner (my soap kettle). Put on the stove and melt, and then boil over medium heat, stirring all the while, until melted and thick like honey. Pour into molds, cover, and let cool. Cut into bars. Store in a dry place for several months to cure. I just grate this and then melt it in water to make thick suds to use in my automatic washer, and it makes my clothes clean-smelling and white. Besides, the suds don't ruin the soil and water as detergents do." Since I first published Gertrude's recipe, lots of people have written to tell me what good soap it made for them.

➣ VIOLET'S SOAP-MAKING TECHNIQUE
Violet Stewart is a wonderful pioneer lady from Okay, OK, who has helped me a lot with the writing of this book. She wrote me, "Weigh fat. I make only small batches at a time since it is easier to handle. Granite pots are best to use. Do not use glass or aluminum. Aluminum will turn soap dark—besides, it ruins the aluminum; lye eats it. Melt the fat and do not let it get hot, just melted. Set aside and measure out 2½ pt. cold water for 6 lb. melted fat. Measure water into pot large enough to hold

the amount. Slowly add 1 can of commercial lye and stir with a wooden stick that's long enough so that lye doesn't spatter on your hand. Stir gently until lye dissolves. Pour in your 6 lb. melted fat, stirring gently while pouring the fat. Fat must never be hot or it may explode when added to lye. Keep moving gently for about 20 minutes, and it will get about like honey. The fat should feel warm to the hand. Have molds ready. Pour soap into molds and put where draft will not hit it. Each batch makes 9 lb. finished soap. I make it every time I get 6 lb. clean fat."

➣ ABRASIVE SOAP
To make a regular mechanic's soap, add pumice stone, emery dust, or Tripoli powder. Castor oil or some other light mineral oil is also needed to prevent the abrasive from settling. Dissolve 3 lb. homemade soap in 6 c. water (more if the soap is very dry). Add 1 T. borax and 3 oz. castor oil or other light mineral oil. When cooled to a creamy consistency, work in 5 lb. pumice stone powder. Pour into widemouthed jars or cans, cover tightly, and use as a paste. Or pour into a mold and, when hard, cut into cakes. Or you can add 5 to 6 lb. of the abrasive to the regular soap mixture when it thickens, and stir until thoroughly blended.

➣ FLOWER SOAP
Take 4 packed c. fragrant flowers (such as rose, cherry, or apple), 4 c. rendered tallow, 2 c. cold soft water, vegetable oil, and ½ c. plus 2 T. lye flakes. Gather flowers just before you make the soap. Immerse them in the melted tallow. Heat for an hour just at the melting point. Allow to harden overnight and then remelt (don't overheat) and strain. Add enough vegetable oil to flower tallow to total 5 cups. Cool. Stir lye into cold water until dissolved. Grease molds with vaseline. Proceed to cool, mix, and mold as for any other soap.

➣ "CASTILE" SOAP
This one is a very high-grade soap: use 24 oz. olive oil, 38 oz. good tallow, and 24 oz. coconut oil. Have fats at 90°F. Use 1 can lye and 2 pt. water cooled to 90°F. Follow basic soap-making procedures to complete.

➣ COCONUT OIL SOAP
A pure coconut oil soap gives a very profuse but thin lather. For a thicker lather, use part tallow. Pure coconut oil soap is made by using 1 can lye, 4½ lb. coconut oil, and 2½ pt. water. Have lye solution at 70°F, oil at 130°F. Follow basic soap-making procedures to complete.

➣ MYSTERY PALM OIL SOAP
This recipe was sent to me by Randee Greenwald, a Peace Corps volunteer working in Cameroon, a country in western Africa. Like many Westerners in non-Western settings, Randee wrote me to say this

book had been useful and to help me make it more so. She shared her soap recipe, adapted to the local village economy. This recipe requires 5 liters water, 5 liters palm oil, and 500 grams (17.5 oz.) caustic soda. (A liter is just a bit more than a quart.) "Palm oil can be produced in the villages. The oil has to be cooked first. It takes anywhere from ½ hour to an hour to cook out all the impurities. It then must be allowed to cool awhile. The caustic soda must be bought in town. Using a plastic bucket, add the caustic soda to the water and stir until it's dissolved. Let it cool for a couple of minutes and add the oil."

Now here this recipe runs into a problem. A mouse chewed off a bit of the edge of the letter during the years I stored it waiting to write this new edition. After the gnawed-away place, it continues: "... ached [be bleached?] first—and takes anywhere from ½ hour to an hour to cook out and stir ... [another mouse-eaten chunk, blank?] with a wooden stick. This takes quite some time—an hour or more. You know when the soap ... [is done?] when your arms break or when you stop and it does not separate. You can leave the mixture in the plastic bucket or pour it into molds. It takes about 3 weeks to dry." (Anybody who can supply the mystery words, I'd love to hear from you!)

NATURAL SUDSING AGENTS: A number of plants (mostly tropical) produce a substance called saponin that can enhance the sudsing quality of handmade soap. Saponin is commonly obtained from soapbark, a South American tree, but a few saponin-yielding plants grow in the northern United States and Canada as well. *Saponaria officinalis,* a common weed known as chimney pink, soapwort, bruisewort, bouncing bet, or latherwort, has an abundance of saponin in its roots. It has dense pink and white flowers in late summer and early fall. Although all parts of the plant have saponin, you can dig up the roots and crush them in water to obtain a foam that is good for cleansing silk and wool. Another plant that has saponin is *Saponaria ocymoides,* a small pink-flowered perennial. Sweet pepper-bush, a species of white alder, grows along the coast in the United States and in lower Canada, mostly in swamps. Lamb's quarters, a summer weed, also has the soaping agent. And finally, quinoa growers have to get rid of the saponin before eating their grain. To extract saponin, crush or grind the plants, boil them in alcohol, and strain the hot liquid. While it's cooling, it will produce a white crumbly powder that easily sudses in water.

Tanning

Animal skin, when fresh and unworked, has 3 layers. The outer skin is called "scarf skin" by tanners; it comes off with the hair. The middle skin is called "grain." The underskin is called the "flesh." The scarf skin peels off naturally. The flesh you scrape off. The grain is what, combined with tannin or other substances, produces leather. Grain is made up of interlaced bundles of gelatinous fibers more or less filled with fluid matter. In the tanning process the fluid is eliminated, leaving only the fibrous portion that can be affected by the tanning substance(s). The loss of this fluid is what reduces the weight of the skin.

Tanning is a long, hard process. Sometimes you may be more successful than others. Some techniques may suit you better than others. The ways to do it are as varied as the end products. When you tan a skin, you're converting an easily decomposed substance, skin, to one which resists putrefaction—leather.

TANNING SUPPLIES AND SERVICES: To ship a hide, put it into some sort of mailing container and send by motor freight, parcel post, or UPS to the tannery of your choice. Include instructions for what you want done to it.

Braintan.com equals Matt and Michelle Richards. They sell books, tanning supplies, tools, and info on making buckskin, leather, and furs. 10398 Takilma Rd., Cave Junction, OR 97523; **matt@braintan.com; www.braintan.com;** 541-592-3693. Their amazing website contains 250+ pages of articles, tutorials, an online, ongoing forum, sources for tools, books, videos, finished skins, and more traditional tanning info than you knew existed.

Bucks County Fur Products tans to order (send SASE): PO Box 204, Quakertown, PA 18951. No phone, but good service.

Eagle Feather Trading Post offers pre-1800 patterns for homemade buckskin clothing, Indian craft supplies, Mountain Man, rendezvous, and survival supplies: **egicrafts@aol.com;** 801-393-4555; 6756 North Fork Rd., Liberty, UT 84310; **www.eaglefeathertrading.com.**

Hanson's Leather sells supplies, tools, patterns, and books for making traditional leather clothing and goods: 6900 Andressen Rd., Sheridan, CA 95681; 530-633-0844; fax 530-633-0193; **hansons@succeed.net; www.hansons.net.**

The Leather Factory sells leathers, tools, books, saddle and tack hardware, supplies for repairing shoes, etc.: PO Box 50429, Ft. Worth, TX 76105; **www.leatherfactory.com;** 800-433-3201.

Stern Tanning Co.'s Jeff Stern will gladly tan your hides: 920-467-8615; fax 920-467-8694; PO Box 55, 334 Broadway, Sheboygan Falls, WI 53085; **sterntanning @powercom.net.**

Tandy Leather Co. sells leather-working supplies: leathers, tanning kits, tools, dyes, hardware, and books, including Stohlman's encyclopedia series on the manufacture of leather products: 808-890-1611; PO Box 791, Fort Worth, TX 76101; **www.tandyleather.com.**

Van Dyke's offers a wide variety of tanning chemicals, oils, softening and pickling agents for home or commercial use, plus a complete line of tools, fleshers, leather, felt, and accessories. Free mail-order catalog: 800-843-3320; Woonsocket, SD 57385; **www.vandykes taxidermy.com.**

INFO ON TANNING: Subscribe to *The Leather Crafters & Saddlers Journal* to network and learn about serious leather-working: supplies, patterns, machines, step-by-step instructions, etc.: $29/yr for 6 issues: 715-362-5393; 331 Annette Ct., Rhinelander, WI 54501-2902; **journal@newnorth.net.** You'll find good directions for tanning sheepskins in the Spring 1984 issue of *The Black Sheep Newsletter,* available for $1.95 from *Shepherd* magazine (address in Chapter 11, "Bee, Rabbit, Sheep, and Pig").

Good books on tanning include *Home Book of Taxidermy and Tanning* by Gerald J. Grantz (1969) and *Leather Makin'—A Manual of Primitive and Modern Leather Skills* by Larry J. Wells. A good book on making things from leather is *Brendan's Leather Book* by Brendan Smith (Outer Straubville Press, 1972). *Home Tanning and Leather Making Guide* by A. B. Farnham (1959) is a guide to home tanning of leathers using chemicals or old-time bark tanning. *Leather: Preparation & Tanning by Traditional Methods,* by

Lotta Rahme, describes the traditional tanning methods of Canadian Native Americans and the Sami Laplanders in northern Sweden: $19.95; call/fax 503-735-3942; 7549 N. Fenwick, Portland, OR 97217; **tcl@teleport.com; www.teleport.com/~tcl.** *Primitive Wilderness Living & Survival Skills,* by John and Geri McPherson, describes dry-scrape brain tanning in chapter 1 of their excellent book.

The Shoe Trades Publishing Co. publishes and/or sells the *Leather Manufacturer Directory* and many books on leather processes such as *Manual of Shoemaking. The Fundamentals of Leather Manufacturing* by Prof. Dr. E. Heidemann is a new book that covers the great extension in tanning knowledge of recent years: collagen, keratin, and elastin chemistry; mechanisms of enzyme action; microbiology; chemistry of vegetable and synthetic tanstuffs, fat liquors, and dyestuffs, etc. The *Leather Technician's Handbook* by J. H. Sharphouse is the newly revised text for England's famous "Leathersellers College" written by world-renowned leather scientists, dealing with all steps of the tanning process. Shoe Trades Publishing Co. also offers *Theory and Practice of Leather Manufacture* and the *Complete Handbook of Leathercrafting:* 617-648-8160; PO Box 198, Cambridge, MA 02140-0002.

THE BASICS

Vocabulary

Bating solution: A solution for neutralizing the hide after dehairing in limewater.

Buckskin: A dehaired leather tanned by Indian methods.

Dehair: To remove hair from the hide. You have a choice of several dehairing methods.

Flesh (v.): To scrape off every bit of meat, fat, and "flesh" from the hide. (See "Fleshing" section.)

Green hide: An untanned hide.

Hide: The skin of a large, adult animal.

Hide-relaxing compound: A do-it-yourself formula is to wash and soak hide in hot borax solution until you can feel it's not so stiff.

Neat's-foot oil: Fat skimmed off after hoofs and hide trimmings have been boiled down in water for so many hours that they set solid as a "gelatin." (You can get it from a shoe store.)

Pelt: A sheepskin.

Prime: Of skins that you want to keep the hair on, from an animal killed during the cold months.

Rawhide: A leather produced without chemicals—not truly tanned, because it is never very pliable except when wet.

Salinometer: An instrument that measures the salt concentration in your solution.

Scarf skin (striffin): The outer layer of the skin. It cannot be tanned.

Scores: Cuts.

Skin: The skin of a smaller animal (the skin of a larger animal is called a hide).

Sleeker: An instrument for smoothing the hide.

Unprime: Of skins that you want to keep the hair on, from animals killed during the warm season.

Skin Weights.
The kind of leather that you can make depends on the size and weight of the skin you start with. Commercial tanneries have equipment that can split a heavy hide into layers of lighter leather, but you can't do that without a special shaving tool available from tanning suppliers. So if you want light leather for gloves, bags, or garments, you have to start with the skin of a small animal such as a sheep, calf, goat, or deer. The finished leather is generally just a bit thicker than an untanned hide. The hide of a full-grown cow will start out weighing 60 lb. or more (which is a word to the wise about just what sort of a job it is hefting one of those around to tan it!). To make heavy belting, shoe-sole, or harness leather, you must start out with a hide weighing over 50 lb. Lace leather, small belting, and straps are made from a hide of 20 to 40 lb., which would be the skin from a light- to medium-sized cow. Calfskins, which average around 7 or 8 lb. in weight, are used for boot and shoe uppers and heavy gloves.

Season.
The season affects the ultimate use of the skin, too. The best leather comes from animals taken in the summer and fall. Winter hides are less firm and are weakened by having grown all that hair, and the hair is just an extra chore if you don't want it. On the other hand, the best hair-on skins are those taken during the winter, when the animal has its heavier winter coat of fur. A fine, fur-bearing skin would be tanned to take advantage of the fur.

Species.
Deer is not recommended for hair-on tanning because its hair becomes brittle and sheds. Angora goatskins are often tanned with the fleece on for rugs. With the hair and scarf skin off, they make fine light leathers. As for cowhides, rather than struggle with such a heavy hide all in one piece, tanners traditionally make big cowhides into 4 separate strips for tanning. The hide is cut down the back to make 2 halves. Then each half is cut again in the nose-to-tail fashion. The back strips are a heavier leather when finished than the belly strips. The splitting of the back strip from the belly strip is generally done at the break of the flank, which makes the back strip about twice as wide as the belly one.

A BASIC OVERVIEW:
Start small—for instance, with a few rabbit hides. It will take around 2 weeks to finish them. Here are the basic steps:

1. Soak in fleshing solution.
2. Carefully scrape off all bits of flesh, fat, and membrane without tearing the skin.
3. Soak a week in a tanning solution.
4. Dry them slowly at the same time as you work them by hand so they don't get stiff (too quick a dry means you must rewet and start over).
5. Oil hide with neat's-foot oil.
6. Store flesh side to flesh side for a month. Then they'll be soft and ready to sew.

Skinning and Storing.
Making leather or fur starts with properly skinning and storing your animal. If you plan to make a rug, the traditional way is to first cut the animal's skin down the center of the belly, from the throat (below the mouth) to the base of the tail. Then cut along the inside of each leg, from the foot straight up to the belly cut, and remove the skin in 1 piece. (See "Skinning, Quartering, and Packing" under "Wild Critters" for skinning instructions.) If you want to do hair-on tanning, be careful not to get blood on the fur. If you are skinning in the woods in winter, you can wipe bloody places on the fur with snow to get them clean.

Fleshing.
Once the animal is skinned, you must scrape all pieces of flesh and fat from the skin. If they are left on, the salt won't penetrate and the hair will slip while in the later curing process. Special tools are advertised in tanning-supply catalogs, but you can use a knife. Just be careful not to

make holes in your hide. This is a preliminary, superficial operation, as distinguished from the more serious scraping that comes later.

Freezing. If you have a deep freeze, just pop the skin in there until you're ready for the next step. You can store a hide at 0°F for a month.

Salting. If you are planning to make home-cured rawhide or buckskin, don't salt the skin; otherwise, spread it out flat, fur side down. Dampen the hide if it has dried. Rub salt liberally into the flesh side of the skin, about ½ inch all over the hide. Be sure and get salt into all the crannies and especially in places where the hide is thick. If you have several hides, you can salt them in layers—that is, you can spread out a hide, salt it, then put another on top, salt it, and so on. You can use any kind of salt; fine table or dairy salt is best. The basic principle of salting is that you can't use too much salt. Then roll the skin(s) up tight and let cure. The salting sets up the skin so that you can get right down to the hair roots when you flesh. *Always roll hides destined for hair-on tanning fur side in.*

For skins that you are planning to send to a mail-order tannery, just leave them rolled up to cure for a few hours. Then turn the scalp flesh side out, resalt, stretch, and partly dry in shade. *Never let skins destined for fur-on tanning dry in folds, as the hair will slip.* When partly dry, roll up flesh side out and ship at once. *Roll before skins get too dry and hard to roll.*

For skins to be tanned at home, store in a cool, dry place and leave the salt on at least 4 days. Seven days is better to hold the hides a second week. Shake, drain, resalt, and reroll. Don't store them too long. If they spoil, you've lost that skin, because it's just about impossible to get the bad smell out again.

Drying. Do this step if you are planning on storing your hide even longer, or if you are planning to send it to a mail-order tannery. Otherwise, skip it. For hair-on tanning, don't ever let the sun get on your hide, and don't let it dry in folds. Give the salted skin a good shake to get off the excess salt. For hair-on tanning, hang the skin to dry somewhere under cover. You can hang your hide by making a hole in it and putting a rope through it, or just by hanging it over something. After it has hung to dry a while, it turns white and gets progressively harder. The salted skin stores better if it is dried completely in the sun, but if you do that, when you get ready for the next step, you must resoak it from 1 to 6 hours in water and then give it a good scraping on the flesh side to remove the glaze that otherwise would prevent your tanning solution from soaking into the hide. Scrape with a dull knife or broken glass.

TANNING RECIPES

Bark-Tanned Leather. Old-fashioned bark-tanned sole and harness leather is the finest leather known, but it requires 120 lb. of finely ground oak or hemlock bark for each cowhide treated. I don't have the recipe, although I've heard it was in USDA Farmers Bulletin #1334.

Unslaked Lime and Sulfuric Acid. After a preliminary fleshing to remove large hunks of flesh and fat, the skin should be rolled up in salt (see "Skinning and Storing" section) for 2 weeks in warm weather, 3 in winter.

Then flesh it right down to the root hairs to remove all the tissue paper–like membrane. If you want your hide tanned without the hair, the next step is to remove the hair or fur. Otherwise this step can be skipped. Remove hair by soaking the pelt in a milk of lime solution. Put 6 to 8 lb. of unslaked (caustic) lime in a wooden barrel or plastic garbage can. Slowly add 1 qt. water and stir. Do not add so much water at one time that it stops the slaking action, and don't let the solution splash on your skin or eyes. (That will cause a burn.) If working in a plastic can, don't let the heat build up enough to melt the container. After slaking is complete, add 2 gal. clear cold water, mix thoroughly, submerge hide, and cover container. Stir 3 or 4 times daily and test hair each day. When the hair can be rubbed off (not pulled off), the process is complete. A deerskin requires about 3 days.

Remove the skin from the solution and scrape in the direction of the hair with a square-edged tool, such as the back of a knife. Scrape the hair uniformly, and wash out all the lime with fresh water. You cannot overwash it at this point. If you don't get the lime solution out, it will continue to eat up your hide. If you live along a creek, the ideal way to get rid of the lime is to hang the hide out in the riffle for 3–4 days. You can further neutralize it by soaking in a solution of ½ gal. vinegar to 20 gal. water.

The pickling solution is prepared by first filling a plastic container with as much water as necessary to cover the hide without crowding it. While stirring, slowly add 1½ liquid oz. commercial sulfuric acid (65–70 percent) for each gallon of water in the container. (The Indians used urine as a pickling acid.) Do not pour water into the acid; it causes a violent reaction. (If any acid splashes on you, wash it off immediately.) Now stir in all the rock salt the solution will dissolve. Place the hide in the solution and move it around so that the solution reaches every part of it. Let it soak, stirring it daily for 4 or 5 days or as long as necessary to bleach the skin white. Test by cutting off a small strip of the hide along 1 edge to see if it is white clear through. Then wash it thoroughly and press it dry. (You can squeegee it out on your fleshing beam.)

Now take the amount of water that will completely cover the hide, and mix in as much baking or washing soda as the water will hold in solution. Soak the hide in this for an hour to completely neutralize the acid. When this is done, rinse out the soda solution thoroughly, and wring the hide out as much as possible by hand. Thoroughly rub the flesh side of the hide with a mixture of neat's-foot oil and beef tallow. Then wash the skin with cold water and detergent, and hang to dry again. When it is almost dry and still somewhat flexible, work the skin back and forth over the edge of a board or square iron bar, flesh side down, to soften it. Pull and stretch the leather in every direction until it is white, dry, and pliable. If the skin feels too oily, fine hardwood sawdust can be worked into it and then brushed off. Charlie Wilkes of Hillside, NJ, sent me that recipe, and I appreciate it.

Salt-Alum Tan. Before tanning a large hide, split it lengthwise down the center to make 2 easily handled pieces. Soak and cleanse the sides in a wooden or fiberglass tank (or a 30-gal. plastic trash can). Allow them to soak for 18 hours. Flesh the skins thoroughly, removing every bit of flesh, fat, and gristle. Remove the hair by soaking the skins in a solution of 10 lb. hydrated lime in 5 gal. water. Add more water to completely submerge the hide and soak the skins for 10 to 14 days. Move the skins around and stir several times a day. When the hair slips off easily by hand rubbing, remove the skins and lay them over a beam. Now you can take off the rest of the hair along with the thin top layer of skin in which the hair grows.

The salt-alum solution is widely used to tan leather. But if you don't do it correctly, the leather may be stiff and hard; if so, repeat the process. Dissolve 5 lb. salt and 2 lb. alum in 5 gal. warm water, and then cool the solution before immersing the hide. Stir several times a day for 6 to 10 days. Tanning is complete when a thick sliver of skin cut from the edge shows the same light color throughout its thickness. Rinse the tanned hide thoroughly and hang to dry. Work the flesh side vigorously over the fleshing beam or the edge of the board. Keep the hide damp, and roll it up until it is pliable. This must be done several times until the hide is flexible as cloth. The final step is to rub a little warmed neat's-foot oil into the dampened leather. Then work it over the beam once more. The product will be a leather than stays supple even when it gets wet.

Salt-Alum Dry Cure for Small Pelts.

To get a long-lasting fur, you had best send your pelts to a professional tanner. But if you just want a simple home cure to give you a usable small skin, rub fresh skins (only the flesh side) with a mixture of 1 part salt and 1 part alum. Dry for 3 days in a cool shaded place. Remove all the dried fatty tissue and trim the edges of the pelts. Wash in a mild soap and rinse out suds. Don't twist or wring. Hang the wet hides over a clothesline with the fur inside. Keep them out of the sun; it can stiffen them by drying them too quickly. Fluff the fur several times over the 2 or 3 days they take to dry. Rub neat's-foot oil or saddle soap onto the skin side. The more you rub, the softer the pelt will be.

Salt-Alum Brine Cure for Small Pelts.

Rub each skin thoroughly with salt. In a container, cover the skins for 4 days in a cool place. Take the skins out and scrape the skin side until all fat and gristle are gone. Mix 2 lb. salt, 1 lb. alum, and 2 gal. water to make the brine. (Double or triple if necessary.) Soak the skins in the brine for 2 weeks. Then wash them in soap or detergent and dry them on a line in the shade for 2 days. Fluff the fur several times and be sure the hide is completely dry before rubbing neat's-foot oil or saddle soap onto the skin side.

Tanning a Snake Skin.

Young Missy Kolb of Mt. Airy, MD, wrote me of shooting a copperhead that lay coiled up in her horse barn. She noticed this book didn't tell how to tan a snakeskin, so she sent me her instructions! "To tan a snake, split the skin along its stomach from head to tail (unless you *want* the belly to show, in which case you split along the spine). Peel the skin like a catfish (except use fingers, not pliers). Scrape it out as much as possible with a spoon and let it dry out a little. Mix 1 part denatured alcohol and 1 part glycerine and paint it on both sides. Then spread skin out flat on a pine board. Put another pine board on top and weight it heavily with rocks or blocks. Paint both sides every day *at the same time each day* (meaning you leave 24 hours between paintings) for 7 days. On the eighth day it is ready to be a belt, hatband, etc.!!" Thank you, Missy!

Tanning Kits.

If you want to try one of the sophisticated chemical tans, probably the best way to start is with a mail-order tanning kit. But please note . . .

NOTE: Many tanning chemicals are very dangerous. Don't breathe the dust. Keep them off your skin and out of your mouth. Some have very pretty colors—don't let your children get hold of them!

HAVING A SKIN COMMERCIALLY TANNED:

If you plan to have the actual tanning done elsewhere, the hide should first be fleshed, salted, and dried according to the directions at the beginning of this section and then mailed to the tannery. The finished hide will be returned to you for final cutting and sewing into your rug, vest, or whatever. Many commercial taxidermists use these mail-order tanneries rather than doing their own tanning. Some places are also willing to make "buckskin," which in this case means hairless leather suitable for making gloves and the like. The price depends on the size and type of hide. For example, a bear cub hide would be cheaper to tan than a big bear hide. The wholesale price is generally a third less than retail.

Shipping Hides.

Put the hide into some sort of mailing container and send by motor freight, parcel post or UPS to the tannery of your choice. Be sure to include instructions.

USES FOR HAIR:

Hair from hides is removed by the lime process described under tanning. If you want to use the hair for upholstering, wash it through several waters until clean, and then dry in a warm place. It may then be used to stuff cushions and couches as desired.

RAWHIDE:

Rawhide and buckskin tanning (see next section) are the 2 processes most appropriate in a really primitive situation. The biggest drawback of rawhide is that after you're all done, it can lose its shape if it happens to get soaked again. The biggest problem with home-tanned buckskin is that it smells bad.

You can make rawhide entirely of easily available natural materials. (You can't use a skin that has been salted to make rawhide.) Properly speaking, rawhide isn't "leather," but it is potentially very useful. It is shaped when wet and then dried. Once it dries, it holds that shape and will be tight and hard. If something made of wood cracks or if you want to fasten wood pieces together with a nonmetal material, bind them with damp rawhide and then let it dry. Rawhide can be made into a rope by cutting in strips and plaiting. To plait rawhide, first soak the strips until soft. Keep them damp while you're plaiting, and grease the rope after you're done to keep it from getting too stiff.

You can also make buckets, baskets, or other containers from rawhide. Cut the rawhide to the shape you need. Then soak until soft and sew up, using thin strips of rawhide for thread. Fill with dry sand and let dry, or put over a wooden form that is the shape you want it to be and let dry. When dry, your rawhide container will be really sturdy.

Now that you know what rawhide is good for, you might want to make some.

1. Get your hide. It's most convenient to work with that of a small animal such as a calf. If the skin has already been dried, you'll have to soak and scrape it until soft before proceeding.
2. Trim off unwanted flesh and fat with a sharp knife (don't cut the skin!). Then use either the paste or container method to get the hair off. With the paste method, lay the skin, hair side up, on a clean surface and sprinkle about an inch of dry wood ashes over every part of it. Work the ashes well into the hair and then wet by sprinkling with the softest water you can get hold of—rainwater if possible. Fold the hide, ash paste and all, hair side in, into a tight bundle. Tie the bundle with a rope. Wrap with wet burlap that you can keep wet, or bury your hide bundle in moist earth. It will take about 3 days for the hair to get loose enough for the next step.

If you have a wooden or crockery container big

enough for the job, you can soak the hide instead of making paste. In that case, soak in caustic lime or a weak lye made by mixing wood ashes and water. Leave it in the solution until the hair is slipping.

3. Rinse the hide thoroughly. Proceed to dehair and flesh it. You need a surface to put the hide on and a scraper. You could buy a fleshing tool or make one. A table knife blade is the right kind of blade. If you can remove the knife from its handle and set it into a piece of wood, so you can have a handle on each side of the blade, you have a perfect fleshing tool. Lacking that, even a rib bone will work as a scraper. But if you're going to get serious about tanning, a good farrier's tool for fleshing is worth having.

Fix yourself a beam to work the hide on. A log or

half log (the round edges are the really important part) or even a 2 × 8-inch plank, rounded off, will do. Set the beam on legs at a 45° angle, bracing it well. One end can rest on the ground. Equip yourself with a bucket of water for rinsing. Throw the hide over the beam with the end falling off the tip, so you can press your body against the hide and hold it on the beam while your hands are occupied with the fleshing tool. Have the tail end of the skin toward you as you scrape to avoid catching your fleshing tool on the hair roots and cutting into the skin. Wear a waterproof apron and scrape downwards. Scrape the flesh side with your scraper, moving the hide around as necessary to flesh it all. Then turn it over to the hair side, now with the neck end toward you, and scrape off the hair and scarf skin at the same time.

4. Wash the dehaired hide thoroughly, stretch it to its full extent, and fasten for drying. You can nail it to the side of a building if you do it high enough so animals can't get at it. If you're planning to make a lot of rawhide or buckskin, rig yourself up a frame to lace it on. Make the frame out of wood strong enough to hold up against a good bit of pull and big enough to go around the outside of your stretched-out hide with room to spare. Then thread a ¼-inch rope or what-have-you through the edge of the hide, then around the outside of the frame, back in and through the hide, around the frame again, and so on until you have the whole skin stretched. Keep your framed hide where animals can't get at it. If you find the hide stretching, keep taking up

the slack until it is tight as a drum. Don't dry your rawhide in direct sunlight. Find a shady spot where air can circulate around it for best results.

5. When the skin is bone-dry, you have rawhide. For an extra, optional finishing touch, you could go over both sides of the skin with sandpaper, pumice, or sandstone to smooth down rough spots and give it an·even texture. When you want to use some, just cut off what you want, soak 10 to 12 hours until workable, and shape as already described. Another way to soften rawhide is by making a mixture of 1 part neat's-foot oil and 1 part tallow, or use any animal grease and work it into the rawhide as you work it on your beam.

BUCKSKIN: The best information on buckskin making is available from Matt Richards in his recent book, *Deerskins into Buckskins: How to Tan with Natural Materials, a Field Guide for Hunters and Gatherers* (10398 Takilma Rd., Cave Junction, OR 97523; **www.braintan.com**; $15 plus $3 s/h). Take a buckskin tanning class from River Spirit School of Natural Living, PO Box 173, Mad River, CA 95552. Like rawhide, buckskin is not, properly speaking, either "tanned" or a "leather." It's useless for harness or binding because it stretches so badly if wet. It tends to have an odor. On the other hand, it can be made relatively quickly without any store-bought stuff. It's soft as chamois but stronger and warmer than cloth, and it protects your skin against briars as well as denim does. You can wash it like cloth, squeezing the soapy water right through. Indians, hunters, and pioneers wore buckskin moccasins and clothes year-round, but it was considered low-class stuff.

You can make buckskin from deer, calf, sheep, or goat, but sheep isn't too desirable because it doesn't wear as well as the others. Deer and elk are the easiest to handle. Technically, "buckskin" means skin in which the grain fibers have been separated and softened by continuous pulling and stretching while drying, rather than by chemical action, and are preserved in that separated and softened condition by grease and by having been smoked. If buckskin gets wet it stiffens up again, but it can be resoftened by working with the hands.

1. Don't salt skins to be made into buckskin. Soak them in plain water until the hair rubs off easily. Keep the water in a warm place, if possible, and keep an eye on the skins so you'll know when they're ready. Stir at least once a day. If your hair won't slip, add wood ashes to make a weak lye solution. In this case, remember to rinse well before proceeding (see warnings about lye under "Soap Making"). Don't try to take the hair off until it comes off easily. You won't rot your hide by soaking it a little longer. When it's ready, you should be able to just rub the hair off with your hand.

2. When the hair is slipping, throw the skin over the beam that was described under "Rawhide" and commence working with your fleshing tool. Have the hide's neck up toward you, and work the flesh down the beam away from you.

3. You can use either the brains or soft-soap method for this stage, as follows:

   Brains method: Make a paste with warm water and the skull contents (the brain) of the animal. You can add any animal grease if you're afraid you won't have enough for the job, but generally each animal has enough brain to treat its size of hide. The brain paste is applied warm to both sides of the hide. If you are worried that the brains won't keep while the hide is soaking, mix them with moss, make into patty shapes, and dry out by sun, fire, or oven. To get the paste on both sides, you'll need to lace the skin in a frame the same way you do with rawhide. Apply paste. Remove from frame, roll flesh side in, and store in a cool place for 2 days. Rinse well and wring as dry as possible. For detailed info, order the 52-minute video *Brain Tanning Bison Robes the Native American Way* by Larry Belitz (who is also a tipi expert: "Sioux Replications"). Or order his illustrated booklet, "Step-by-Step, Brain Tanning the Sioux Way": HCR-52, Box 176, Hot Springs, SD 57747; 605-745-3902.

Soft-soap method: Soft soap is soap made with a weak lye solution. If you aren't a soap maker, shave up a bar of yellow laundry soap and dissolve it in water. Use 2 c. soft soap or 1 bar of laundry soap to about 2½ to 3 gal. hot water. Begin by rinsing your hide well. Then work it as it dries. Grease it with animal fat. Then put it into the warm soft-soap solution. Soak the skin in it for 4 or 5 days. Remove skin and rinse again. Work while drying again, according to direction in step 4 under "Rawhide." The hide must now be continuously worked while it is drying. If you let the hide get dry in the middle of the job, it will get stiff and you'll have to dampen it again. Try not to get it too wet or you'll have to wait for the extra water to dry out. It can be pulled over the end of your beam or a stump and scraped with sharp stones or shells if you don't have metal tools. Or pull back and forth over a fence post with a wedge-shaped top. A small hide can be worked entirely by hand. A large one just about requires some kind of system, such as 2 people pulling it back and forth over a beam. The important thing is to somehow pull, twist, and stretch that hide in every possible direction to loosen the fibers of the grain. It is this procedure that makes the skin buckskin. You're done when the buckskin is almost as flexible as cloth. It should be easy to squeeze water right through the skin. If it isn't soft or you have hard spots, moisten and work while drying again until you are satisfied.

4. The final step is to smoke the buckskin. Before smoking, it's optional to go over the flesh side with sandpaper for any roughness. The smoking improves both the durability and appearance of the buckskin. There isn't any one absolutely fixed, correct way to do it. If you have a regular smokehouse, spread out the skin in there by stretching it horizontally. You can smoke several skins at once by arranging them in layers. Or you can fasten large hides together in a tent shape and build a small fire right under them. For the "tent," make a cone of small poles tied around the neck at the top, tipi style. Then arrange your hides over that. Burn green hardwood if you can get it. Don't use soft (pitchy) woods. Willow, birch, and alder are okay. The Indians used green willow, which makes the buckskin yellow. The smoking process will take 1 or 2 days. Don't scorch the skin. You'll have to turn it over and smoke the other side when the inside is done. The buckskin is finished when it is colored a deep yellow or light brown.

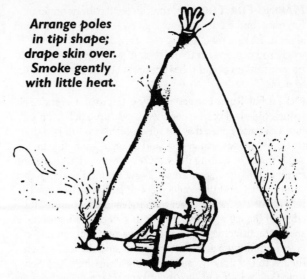

Arrange poles in tipi shape; drape skin over. Smoke gently with little heat.

Blankets, Rugs, and Clothes from Skins

CUTTING SKINS: If the hair is on, always cut from the hairless side and let the knife ride through the hair so you don't shorten it. Use a sharp knife or scalpel depending on how heavy your hide is.

SEWING SKINS: You can hand-sew leather seams with a "glover's needle." You can hand-sew using silk, heavy-duty mercerized nylon thread, heavy waxed linen thread, or dental floss. In general the thicker the leather, the tougher the thread you'll use. Some leather workers sew their thread through a cake of beeswax to help it slip through the subsequent leather. For fancy work, where it will show, use the clear nylon that is like a fishing leader; when sewing a skin onto a backing of felt, use a heavy, colored thread to match the felt color.

Machine-Sewing Leather. Rabbit hides that have been worked to soft enough can be machine-sewn. For bigger or less-soft hides, you must sew by hand or use a special needle designed for piercing leathers, called a "leather-point" or "15 by 2" needle. It has a wedge-shaped point rather than a round one and makes a clean cut. There are different sizes of leather-point needles for leathers of different weights. It's advised to use size 11 for light leather, 14 for medium, and 16 for heavyweight. Homemade skins tend to be medium to heavyweight leathers.

To sew thick leathers on your sewing machine, you also will benefit from loosening the presser foot so it doesn't press down too hard. The thicker the skin, the fewer stitches you set it for: 12 per inch on lightest leathers, 7–10 on mediums, 7–8 on heavyweights. There are special heavy-duty sewing machines for large-scale leather working. Or you may be able to have the sewing done for you; check with shoe repair shops, taxidermists, or saddle shops.

Mending Cuts. Check the skin for cuts and mend them. If you have a bullet hole, cut away enough skin to change the shape of the hole from a circle to a diamond; it will look better after it's sewn up. If the fur has a bad spot, you can patch it using a baseball stitch over the top and back through again.

WASHING LEATHER OR SHEEPSKIN: Wash in lukewarm water and pin on a clothesline to dry. It might get stiff, so start when half-dry and rub to soften. *Don't dry in a dryer.*

MAKING FUR THINGS: You can lay a pattern on your fur, trace, and cut it out. You can sew together several small skins to make a robe, parka, vest, cap, or whatever you want. You can sew fur to the back of woolen mittens for extra warmth. Rugs and robes are probably the easiest things to make.

Make a Fur Rug. The easiest way is to just use a crude salt-tanned hide laid on the floor, wool side up. Such simple hides can also be used as lap robes, blankets, bed pads, truck and tractor seat covers, and so on. A more finished rug is made by cutting the skin to your preferred shape and trimming off the ragged edges. Draw around the skin to get your pattern, and then cut a piece of felt (or whatever material) about 1½ inches larger than the skin all around. The edges of the felt are generally cut in a zigzag with pinking shears for attractiveness. For extra warmth you can put in a layer of quilting batt between the skin and the felt. Attach the felt to the skin by catch-stitching along the edges. Sew from the back. If you can, try to keep your stitches from going clear through the hide. If your rug has a tail with it, that is usually not bordered unless it is short.

A Robe. This is usually around 60 × 70 inches. One horsehide, one cowhide, 2 or 3 yearling cowhides, 8 calf hides, or 6 to 10 sheepskins or goatskins will give you a robe. You can use either sheared or unsheared sheepskins. You'll want to make sure that the fur or wool is clean and that tangles and burrs are brushed out. A robe can be unlined, but it is always nicer with a flannel or felt lining sewed on the way you make a fur rug.

Fur Slippers. Choose or cut out a piece of fur or sheepskin at least 4 inches longer than your foot and wide enough so that when you stand on the piece with 1 foot and fold the sides upward on each side of that foot, they reach at least 2 inches above your ankle protrusion. Now sew the backside of your slippers up where the backside of your heel will be. Cut to fit, and sew together the part that will go over the front of your foot. Hem down a 2-inch "collar" around your ankle, and run a leather thong or elastic through the opening to help hold your slippers on.

Woven Fur Blanket. You can make a blanket from many small skins, such as rabbit skins, by tanning them and cutting into strips about 2 inches wide. Sew together end to end until you have strips long enough to form the warp and woof of a basket-style woven blanket. Join the ends with the overhand baseball stitch and make sure that the fur is running the same way along each strip. The more strips you have, the bigger your blanket can be. When you have enough, fasten into place on a frame the strip that will form the warp. Interweave the woof, but not too tight. Put a piece of outing flannel on the back, and stitch together as if you were making a quilt.

Other Fur Products. You can make mittens, moccasins, shoes, and sheepskin coats. Leather-working manuals and other books can give you more patterns. There is probably a leather-crafts shop in your region where you can find guidance.

Horns

Horns are composed of a hard material that can be turned into a variety of useful and decorative objects. You can ex-

periment and turn pieces of horn into buttons, beads, decorative inlays, knife handles, and even zipper pulls.

FOOD FROM WATER

As public oceans and rivers more and more double as toxic dumping grounds for every city or country that can get at them, regular commercial water creatures are ever riskier to eat. The so-called FDA seafood inspection program actually inspects only 1 lb. of fish for every 160,000 lb. we eat. And the FDA seal of approval is false security anyway because the FDA has toxic limits for only a dozen or so modern poisons—even though biochemists know there are hundreds that today's fish may carry. And as increasing numbers of the world's people chase fish, the supply grows ever shorter.

The answer is growing your own food from water—in water you know is pure, using food you know is safe to enter the food chain—or buying the equivalent. Growing food from water, or "aquaculture," has been part of family farming in many places around the world for centuries. But now small-scale fish farming is booming more than ever, and rightly so. You can grow more of this healthy, low-fat, heart-protecting protein in a smaller space than any other variety of animal on your homestead! Water farmers grow clams, mollusks, catfish, yellow perch, bluegills, bullheads, crayfish, bass, trout, carp, tilapia, mosquito fish, and others. They market them as human food, bait, or as stock for other people's food-growing or ornamental ponds or fishbowls. As always, it's best to start small and get experience before you invest heavily.

Almost anybody can do some water farming. You can raise catfish in just a barrel! If you have as much as 10 acres and a water supply, you have room for several fish culture ponds. Fish can be part of the natural ecosystem on your homestead, with meat-eating fish eating discarded innards and algae-eaters profiting from pig and poultry manure used to fertilize the pond. Or you can feed them commercial fish feed made from residues of the agricultural industry. Or both.

HELP FOR SICK WATER CRITTERS

Alabama Fish Farming Center; William Hemstreet, Fish Health Specialist; 334-624-4016; fax 334-624-4050; 529 Centreville St., Greensboro, AL 36744; **whemstr @acesag.auburn.edu.**

Southeastern Coop. Fish Disease Lab; Dept. of Fish & Allied Aquacultures, Auburn U., Auburn, AL 36849; 334-844-4786.

UAPB Cooperative Extension Program; Larry W. Dorman, Extension Fisheries Specialist; 870-265-8055; fax 870-265-8060; 523 Hwy 65 & 82, Lake Village, AR 71653; **ldorman@gw.uaex.edu.**

ONLINE INFO

aquanic.org takes you to the Aquaculture Network Information Center (AquaNIC).

agebb.missouri.edu/mac leads to the Missouri Alternatives Center website.

MAGAZINES: *Aquaculture Magazine* serves "the international aquaculture industry" with 45 non-ad pages per bimonthly issue, an *Annual Products Guide* each summer, and the *Buyers Guide and Industry Directory* each December. Coverage includes all water-grown species: abalone, alligator, baitfish, bay scallop, blue crab, bowfin, carp, catfish, freshwater lobster, hybrid striped bass, mollusks, mullet, oyster, paddlefish, prawn, rainbow trout, salmon, shrimp, soft-shell crabs, striped bass, sturgeon, tilapia, trout, whitefish, and aquaculture science. It's $24 for 6 issues/yr: PO Box 2329, Asheville, NC 28802; 828-254-7334; fax 828-253-0677; **comments@aquaculturemag.com; www. aquaculturemag.com.** The website includes an online discussion forum, archives of back issues, calendar of events, and weekly updated news items.

Austasia Aquaculture magazine promotes aquaculture in the Australasian and Asian regions. It covers all aspects of this vast industry in that region, including regular columns by industry specialists. Their delightful website is at **www.aquaculture.com/au/.**

Northern Aquaculture is "The Voice of Cold Water Aquaculture in North America since 1985." It's a monthly magazine (Canadian-based): $30/yr. Subscribers also receive a free weekly e-mailed newsletter. The website has Buyers' Guide, Events Calendar, and Aquaculture Jobs sections, etc.: **www.naqua.com/.**

UNIVERSITY AND EXTENSION HELP: Aquaculture, like the rest of modern agribusiness, is spurred on by university Ph.D.s and USDA researchers and specialists providing tech services to corporate and also independent food growers. It is a huge, profitable, and often very technical part of the food-producing industry. Subscribers to *Aquaculture Magazine* also get a yearly *Buyer's Guide and Industry Directory* (300 pp.). This is a great resource for anybody interested in aquaculture, beginner to expert. For example, it lists name, phone number, and often the e-mail address of all the Extension Agent aquaculture experts! There are one or more in every state, beginning with Jeff Allred of the Alabama Fish Farming Center (529 Centreville St., Greensboro, AL 36744; 334-624-4016; fax 334-624-4050), and ending with Joe Hiller, U. of Wyoming (PO Box 3354, Laramie, WY 82071-3354; 307-766-5479; fax 307-766-6403; **jhiller@uwyo.edu**).

Want to learn this business? Study at the School of Fisheries at the University of Washington, the U. of Idaho, Louisiana State U., Auburn U., or Texas A&M at Corpus Christi (361-825-2676; **www.sci.tamucc.edu/pals/mari.html**). All have outstanding aquaculture programs.

Since 1980, the U.S. government has heavily funded aquaculture research and development. There are five regional centers from which these funds and services are administered:

Center for Tropical and Subtropical Aquaculture: The Oceanic Institute, 808-259-3168; fax 808-259-8395; 41-202 Kalanianaole Hwy., Waimanalo, HI 96795; **library.kcc.hawaii.edu/CTSA.**

North Central Regional Aquaculture Center: Michigan State U., 517-353-1962; fax 517-353-7181; 13 Natural Resources Bldg., East Lansing, MI 48824-1222; **ag.ansc.purdue.edu/aquanic.ncrac.**

Northeast Regional Aquaculture Center: U. of Massachusetts Dartmouth; 508-999-8157; fax 508-999-8590; 285 Old Westport Rd., Research 201, N. Dartmouth, MA 02747-2300; **www.umassd.edu/specialprograms/ NRAC.**

Southern Regional Aquaculture Center: 662-686-3285; fax 662-686-3569; 127 Experiment Station Rd., PO Box 197, Stoneville, MS 38776; **www.msstate.edu/dept/srac/.**

Western Regional Aquaculture Center: 206-543-4290; fax 206-685-4674; School of Fisheries, U. of Washington, Box 357980, Seattle, WA 98195; **www.fish. washington.edu/wrac.**

BOOKS AND PAMPHLETS: *Fundamentals of Aquaculture,* by James Avault, Jr., is a 900+-page step-by-step guide to commercial aquaculture covering pond construction, feeding, disease control, etc., available from AVA Publishing (see book dealers). Two British books are *Fish Farming,* by C. F. Hicklin, and *Backyard Fish Farming,* by Bryant, Jauncey, and Atack. Gene Logsdon's *Getting Food from Water: A Guide to Backyard Aquaculture* is an American classic. He covers beach harvesting, pond building, stream management, pond fish management, waterfowl, garden pools, etc. *Aquaculture: The Farming and Husbandry of Freshwater and Marine Organisms,* by Bardach, McLarney, and Ryther, is an older, in-depth book. *A Fish and Vegetable Grower for All Seasons,* by Robert E. Huke and Robert W. Sherwin, covers the aquaculture/solar greenhouse (raising vegetables) combo.

Other books: *Farming the Waters* by Peter Limburg; *The New Field Book of Freshwater Life* by Elsie B. Klots; *World Fish Farming: Cultivation and Economics* by E. Evan Brown; *Trout Farming Handbook* by S. Dumond Sedgwick; *Koi of the World: Japanese Colored Carp* by Dr. Herbert Axelrod; *Creative Fishing* by Charles J. Farmer; *Fish and Invertebrate Culture* by S. Spotte; *Home Aquaculture: A Guide to Backyard Fish Farming* by S. D. Van Gorder and D. J. Strange.

AQUACULTURE BOOK DEALERS

Aquatic Eco-Systems: 407-886-3939 or 800-422-3939; fax 407-886-6787; 1767 Benbow Court, Apopka, FL 32703; **www.aquaticeco.com.**

Aquatic Promotions: 305-247-0460; PO Box 700166, Miami, FL 33170-0166; **www.cichlidnewsmagazine.com.**

AVA Publishing: 225-763-9656; fax 225-766-0728; PO Box 84060, Baton Rouge, LA 70884-4060; **AVApub@aol.com; www.AVApub.com.**

Miami Aqua-culture: 305-262-6605; fax 305-262-6701; 4606 SW 74 Ave., Miami, FL 33155; **www.miami-aquaculture.com.**

Seacoast Information Services: 401-364-9916; fax 401-364-9757; 135 Auburn Dr., Charlestown, RI 02813; **www.aquanet.com/aquastore.**

AQUACULTURE CAN BE DONE IN THE CITY TOO! Read *The Integral Urban House,* an account of a 2-story Berkeley house that the Farallones Institute turned into a center to demonstrate "urban-scale appropriate technology" —including a 2,000-gallon concrete pool in the backyard containing black bullhead catfish, bluegills, and Sacramento catfish, with the power for water filtration and recycling provided by a windmill-operated pump.

Mariculture

This word refers to harvesting food from beaches—from the "intertidal zone" where sometimes the land is covered by ocean water and sometimes it isn't. Lots of algae, shellfish, and sea vegetables grow there. If you don't have a pollution risk in your area, this area has tremendous food potential. See *The Sea Vegetable Book* by Judith Cooper Madlener for info on gathering and using sea vegetables, and try *Sea Vegetable Recipes from the Oregon Coast* by Evelyn McConnaughey (2 volumes!) for ways to use them. *Seaweed in Agriculture and Horticulture,* edited by B. and G. Rateaver, describes traditional seawood use in Europe, how to make seaweed extracts, etc. Nori seaweed can be grown on nets suspended under a raft in shallow sea water. Its culture also can be combined with raft culture for shellfish and fish.

RAFT CULTURE: Raising shellfish using rafts and/or floating pens is big business now. The first raft culture was done by a shipwrecked Irish sailor. He suspended a net into the water between 2 poles to catch sea birds, left it there, and then found out that mussels had fastened themselves to it while it was under water at high tide. Now the Washington State Department of Natural Resources, which supervises many acres of tidelands, leases sites to individuals and provides aquaculture advice. The techniques for farming shellfish have been around for only the last few years. It's an exciting new field for small growers.

SHELLFISH: For growing shellfish, it's handy to live right on the edge of the ocean. Or you can lease a few acres of open water from the Department of Natural Resources and tether a raft over it.

Red Tide. *Don't go out to gather shellfish without knowing about red tide and being sure that the critters are safe to eat.* "Red tide" is an algae bloom that can occur from late spring to fall. It's toxic to humans, although shellfish thrive on it. Shellfish on a diet of red tide are no good for human eating until they've gotten it out of their systems. Any filter-feeding shellfish—oysters, mussels, etc.—can have this problem. *Harvest only when the government in your area says it's safe to or, if without expert advice, harvest only in winter.*

Mussels. You start out by buying mussel seed (there is a specialist in northern California who grows oyster, clam, and mussel seed under laboratory conditions). Seed for about 1 million mussels costs about $1,000 and can be contained in a coffee cup. After "planted," only about 10 percent survive predations of flatworms, starfish, and other dangers to baby mussels, but that still leaves 100,000—so many that thinning may be necessary. They're ready in a year and can be harvested from September to June. They'll keep well, even out of water, as long as a week if kept cold and damp. To cook, remove the byssus (silky filaments by which they attach themselves to rocks), scrub the shells clean and drop them, shells and all, into boiling water. Or steam. (Don't overcook.) Then make a chowder of mussel meat in tomato juice. Or combine chopped mussel meat with pasta. Kamilche Sea Farms is a commercial mussel-growing operation: 360-427-5774; fax 360-427-0610; SE 2741 Bloomfield Rd., Shelton, WA 98584-8640; **Kamilchesf@aol.com.**

Oysters and Clams. You harvest these with a shovel at night, by lantern light, at extra low tide. Best results in windy, cold, rainy weather. But worth it! Aside from the harvesting method, oysters and clams are similar to mussels. You could model your oyster farm on the Jolly Roger Oyster Co., which grows bottom-cultured oysters: 360-665-4111; PO Box 309, Ocean Park, WA 98640.

Greenhouse / Hydroponics / Aquaculture Combo

Water can be used in a greenhouse for supplemental heating and cooling. It's cheap and readily available, and it stores more heat in less space than any other commonly available heat-storage material. Greenhouse water can be recycled to raise edible fish or to do hydroponic gardening. *Fish Farming in Your Solar Greenhouse* by William Head and Jon Splane explains how to use greenhouse water as a heat-storage material for growing fish and how to use the leftover food and body wastes of fish to grow vegetables. Thus all you must buy or obtain is fish food (for tilapia and catfish), and your crop is both vegetables and mature fish. William Head also wrote *Gardening Under Cover,* from which I quote (pp. 100–103):

"In this system, fish supply the fertilizer for the plants in the form of uneaten food and nitrogen-rich waste by-products, and the plants help to keep the water clean by absorbing nutrients from the fish water. Ideally, additional fertilizers are not needed and equipment costs may be minimized. We have had both success and failure, trying to make the concept work . . . [after failure] we redesigned the entire hydroponic system, incorporating a method called the Nutried Film Technique (NFT).

"NFT can grow crops on much lower nutrient levels than are required in other hydroponic systems. This is particularly important for hydroponic designs that use only the relatively low nutrient levels of an aquaculture system. A shallow stream of nutrient water is circulated through a dense mat of plant roots. The upper roots in the mat are exposed to moist air. This provides both abundant nutrients and oxygen to the roots . . .

"The aquaculture tank was stocked with 60 small channel catfish (*Ictalurus punctatus*) and 120 African perch (*Tilapia mossambica*) . . . The fish were fed twice daily with a commercial fish pellet (Purina trout chow). The plants were irrigated entirely with the aquaculture water. During a 7½-month testing period, 90 pounds of edible fish were harvested, and each of the 24 tomato plants had an average yield of 9 pounds of tomatoes. Tomato plants of the same variety that were raised in the greenhouse soil yielded about 7 pounds of fruit per plant . . . this design required less labor than crops growing in the soil beds, and we never had to worry about watering the plants. Water flowed freely along the pipes throughout the testing period."

For more information, see the sections on greenhouses and hydroponics in Chapter 2. The New Alchemy Institute has done particularly useful research in this area. In the above-quoted book, Head wrote (p. 103), "New Alchemy's best hydroponic trial has produced about 2.3 pounds of vegetables per pound of fish food, plus the edible fish."

Pond Fish Farming

Some raise them for fun and family food, some as a business. A pond can provide irrigation water for your garden and orchard and a place for the kids to catch frogs and turtles, swim in summer, and skate in winter. If you plant a pond's banks with nuts, fruits, and Christmas trees, you get an extra dividend. And you can have waterfowl enjoying the top of the water. There are more than 2,000,000 farm fish ponds around this country. Stephen Scott wrote me, "I have, just this past year, begun to raise fish in very small ponds. I feed them worms and frogs, which we have in abundance. The ponds are hand-dug affairs, 24 feet in diameter and about 5 feet deep. They are spring-fed, and the fish seem to be growing surprisingly fast."

On the other hand, Lane Morgan carps, "Farm fish may be fed subtherapeutic doses of antibiotics, like other livestock. Farm fish and hatchery fish are crowded and stressed, like 'factory farm' livestock, and they suffer health problems and may be medicated accordingly. Also, the farms cause pollution problems, not to mention that the escapees that breed with wild fish can mess up the intricately adapted genetic responses of the wild species. I guess fish farms have their place, but I'm not a big fan."

STEP-BY-STEP POND BUILDING

1. Assess Soil, Water, Topography, Etc.. For a good fish pond, you need a reliable supply of clean water and a situation where either it doesn't flood or you can arrange drainage to compensate for flooding. Your soil must be capable of holding water on both the proposed pond bottom and the sides, or else you'll have to line it with Bentonite or some such. You need enough spring flow, well water, or runoff to fill the pond in a year or less and to replace water lost from seepage and evaporation.

The ideal water source is a well, because then you will have no unwanted fish, no flood problems, and no

muddiness. Well water, however, is no guarantee against pesticide pollution. Your well flow should be fast enough to fill your pond in a week or so, to replace water lost through evaporation in hot weather, and to supply oxygenated water. A problem with springs is that they often fluctuate seasonally—check on that. If oxygen level is not adequate, you just aerate the water. Water source also affects water temperature, which affects the fish species you can grow. In summer temperate zones, a surface runoff water source means warm water. Water from a well or spring means "cold" water. If there are fish in the spring water, you just filter it to keep them out. Stream water needs to be filtered to keep out other fish too.

2. Get Permits. Check with the local branch of the USDA Soil Conservation Service. Your land must contain a site considered suitable for impounding water. On most sizable places, there are one or more sites that can pass muster. Your pond can be viewed as a water storage or even wetlands restoration. If you have a swampy area that's growing cattails, you can use that. But first you need to get an appropriate permit or, more likely, permits.

3. Plan Size. Don't be easily discouraged. You can raise channel catfish in a barrel! But bigger ponds are easier to manage and succeed with. A warm-water pond for bass and bluegill fun fishing needs be at least an acre in size. Trout

ponds are recommended to be at least ⅓ acre, though I've seen a very good one that was smaller. But surface area is vital relative to depth because it helps oxygen, which fish need to breathe, get into the water. At the other extreme, 15 acres is considered to be the maximum desirable size.

4. Plan Depth. Shallow water is a problem because weeds grow in it. In ponds stocked with bass and bluegill, those weeds protect small fish from the bass. Shallow water also causes mosquito problems. A pond is easier to manage if it has no shallow water. Deepening and/or filling will eliminate those shallow edges. A minimum depth of 2 feet is good, but 3 feet is better. So your pond needs deep sides to discourage plant growth but a smooth bottom if you plan to harvest by seining. Water 10 feet deep—or more—will allow the fish population to stay comfortable in winter. Where the pond will be covered with ice for a month or more and winter fishkills are frequent, water depth may need to be as much as 20 feet. If your pond depends on seasonal rains for its water supply, water should be at least 10 or 12 feet deep over a fourth or more of the pond area. A shallow bottom is desirable for bluegill and bass to nest in. Throughout most of the South, an average depth of 3 to 4 feet is adequate for fish growth; no more fish can be grown by providing additional depth.

5. Plan Spillway and Drainage. The emergency spillway to prevent floodwater from going over the dam should be dsigned to keep the flow shallow. This prevents big fish from swimming out and unwanted fish from swimming in. To prevent unwanted fish from entering the pond from downstream, a 24- to 36-inch vertical overfall in the emergency spillway should also be used. A drainpipe is useful and is required by law in many states. It should be large enough to drain the pond in 5 to 10 days. An overflow pipe or trickle tube connected to the drainpipe keeps the normal water level a few inches below the spillway. This reduces erosion of the spillway and prevents excessive loss of fingerlings soon after the pond is first stocked. A device to take outflow from the bottom rather than the top helps warm the pond early in the spring, may save fertilizer, and may permit fertilizing in spring when the flow is heaviest. Plan your water cycle if the water will be aerated or filtered.

6. Clear Trees/Brush. Most trees and brush should be removed from the area to be covered with water. If possible, remove stumps and snags from the pond bottom. This leaves the bottom smooth for seining, which may be required for good management. Clearing trees and brush from a strip 20 to 30 feet around the pond reduces the amount of leaves that fall into the pond. Leaves discolor water and encourage growth of algae, and decaying leaves may cause oxygen depletion in the water. A cleared strip also provides a grassy bank for fishing.

7. Dig/Fill. A demolition expert could dynamite out some deep holes in it for you. Or if you have a meandering river on or beside your property that has left a former meander now abandoned, part of the meander might be blocked off for a waterfowl area for you. Or you can dig a pond from scratch with a bulldozer. There are many different ways to build a new water area or develop an existing one. A "raceway" is one nice way to raise trout; water flows downhill from one pondlet to another.

8. Stock Pond with Fish. Before stocking, eliminate all wild fish from your pond and drainage area to keep them from competing with the stocked fish for space, oxygen, and food. Draining the pond does it. Choose your fish species to stock based on the temperature of your water, its depth, what you have to feed, and what you want to eat. You can stock with a single species such as trout or with a combination of species, such as bass with bluegill. Private and certain state and federal hatcheries provide fish for stocking. You can get info on sources of fish for stocking from the Soil Conservation Service, Extension Service, Fish and Wildlife Service, and your state fish and wildlife agency. How many fish depends on the species you choose, your water, and whether you want to do supplementary feeding. Prices are reasonable; for example, tilapia fry (50 will fit in a teaspoon) are about 17 cents per 1,000, 14 cents per 5,000 [1992].

9. Do Long-Term Fish Pond Management. Intensive management with carefully figured and faithful fertilizing and supplemental feeding gives you the maximum harvests, but it can also be costly and time-consuming.

10. Breed Fish. This is an optional step. Hatching and raising fingerlings takes knowledge and attention. I'm not going that deep here, but if you want to learn how, the info is out there. You can even get a degree in fisheries management from the University of Washington!

A CHOICE OF FISH TO STOCK

Large-Mouth Bass and Bluegill. Every imaginable fish combination has been tried by fishery scientists. This is the one that works best. These are the species most commonly stocked in warm-water (80°F or more) ponds. Red-ear sunfish may be added for variety and to lessen the risk of the fish population getting unbalanced. The bluegill and red-ear sunfish provide food for the bass. The bluegills eat insects that eat pond plankton. The bass eat bluegills (and baby bass). With this combo, properly managed, you'll have good fishing for years. Alabama ponds that won't be supplementally fed are generally stocked with 50 bass and 500 bluegill per surface acre. With supplemental feeding you can stock with 100 to 150 bass and 1,000 to 1,500 bluegill per surface acre.

To keep your pond species in balance, the first year return all fish caught. The second year you can take out 80 lb. bluegill per acre, but still no bass. From the third year on, take 80 lb. bluegill per acre and 20 to 25 lb. bass per acre. When handling fish that will be returned, wet your hands to preserve the slimy protective coating of the fish.

Carp. These warm-water (80°F or above) fish don't need running water and are very good to eat. If the water gets too cold for their liking, they will hibernate at the bottom. Originally from China, carp has been a domesticated fish for millennia. There are several varieties. The grass carp is a vegetarian. It prefers green grass and vegetables—all kinds of freshly cut land grasses, weeds if not too tough, leaves of some trees, all kinds of fresh vegetables, rice bran, and bean meal. The others are carnivorous but are not the biting, chewing sort; they suck in food from the pond bottom. The black carp needs a diet of snails. The silver carp eats plankton. You drop manure or night soil into a carp pond. The fish don't eat it, but other critters do, and then the carp eat them.

☙ *BROILED CARP Clean carp and cut into pieces. Sprinkle the pieces with lemon juice. Broil, turning once, for 25 minutes. Sprinkle salt on it and serve.*

Catfish. Catfish are warm-water fish that prefer 80°F and above. They're good in more southern areas and do well in farm ponds. They grow well in water 70°F or more, slowly in 60–70° water, hardly at all in water colder than 60°F. They do well in a pond about 2½ feet deep at the shallow end and sloped to 4 or 6 feet at the outlet. You can stock with blue, channel, or white. Channel are easy to raise and easy to manage because they seldom reproduce in a farm pond. Catfish that do reproduce can result in pond overpopulation—more and more fish that are smaller and smaller in size. You can raise catfish in a combo. If your pond tends to become infested with unwanted fish, the answer is actually to also stock it with large-mouth bass and fathead minnows. The minnows feed the bass, which get big enough to eat up the undesirable fish; thus you get the maximum yield of catfish.

Once your pond is stocked with fingerlings, the fish come up at feeding time and compete for the feed you

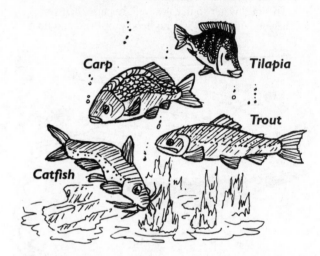

throw them. They can get to be 6-pounders. Harvest by regular fishing pole, seining, traps, or lift nets. Four to six feet deep is good for them.

Crayfish. These taste like lobster, are ready for harvest in less than a year, and will thrive in almost any pond, lake, stream, or swamp anywhere in the continental United States. They can live on hay supplemented with garden-cull roughage. There is a growing commercial market for them.

Although known as "crawfish," these are correctly called "crayfish." They are fresh-water crustaceans that resemble the lobster but are usually smaller. Little creeks around here have them. To catch them, you grab the crawdad in the middle with 2 fingers. Press the front pincers together and drop it into a bag. They're usually quite small, so it takes a lot—several dozen or so—to make a meal. For plain crawdad, just drop the live crawdad into boiling salted water and boil 5 minutes. Then serve. You pick off the shell and pick out the meat using toothpicks—sort of a poor man's lobster. For larger ones, pull out tail fin and intestinal vein. For tastier crawdad, add a chopped onion and chopped dill weed to the boiling salt water and serve with a garlic-seasoned melted-butter dip on the side. Crawdads are good served with biscuits.

Tilapia. Tilapia are very easy to raise. They can even survive in water without oxygen because they can come to the surface and gulp air. They are very disease-resistant and gain about 1½ lb. in 6 months if generously fed. Tilapia are algae feeders. The female holds her fertilized eggs in her mouth and broods them there for 3 weeks until her fry hatch out. She doesn't eat during that time. For about 3 weeks after hatching, the fry will hide in mum's mouth when afraid, so during that time she still doesn't eat much and loses weight. So tilapia raisers try to prevent spawning by hand-separating males from females. Tilapia taste good and sell well to pricey restaurants and grocery stores.

Trout. Rainbow and brook are the trout varieties usually stocked in ponds because they're available, easy to manage, and easy to catch. You need a dependable supply of year-round good-quality water—from a well, spring, or stream. You need good water circulation—a minimum flow of 450 gallons per minute. You can stock either kind or both. If you're stocking trout, don't put in any other species of fish. Trout just aren't able to compete successfully. This is a cold-water (70°F or less) fish. Stock a natural pond with no more than 500 half-pound trout per surface acre per year. With supplemental feeding you can stock 2,000 per year. With good management, your pond should reach its carrying capacity in pounds of fish within a year after stocking.

During the second year, trout don't grow much unless the pond is fished enough to make room. Fishing is good for the crop! Each fish you take out lets the remaining ones gain weight faster. You can start fishing as soon as the trout are 6 to 8 inches long—about 6 to 10 months after stocking the pond with fingerlings. By early in the second year, they'll be 12 to 14 inches long and weigh about 1 lb., and they'll continue to gain weight. But only a small percentage of the trout you stock will live more than 2 years. At the end of 3 years, just a few large trout will remain, a number far below the carrying capacity of your pool. Time to start over.

Cleaning Trout. Keep the trout out of the water and away from the bank long enough to make sure it is dead. There are various ways to clean it. Start from the 2 fins behind the anal vent. Cut them off around the vent and cut forward to the neck. Then pull out and discard the internal organs and scrape out the bloody membrane tissue along the backbone with your fingernail. That tissue is the fish's kidney. Rinse in water.

The head is handy if you want to carry the fish with you on a forked stick, with one branch through the gill flap and out the mouth, or if you have an almost-too-small-to-be-legal fish. If you want to take off the head, cut it right back of the gill flaps. There is no need to scale a trout. Put it on ice, if possible, while you're waiting to either cook or freeze it.

Wilderness Trout. I once fried 3 small trout on a flat rock heated in my campfire. I had no salt, pepper, flour, or anything else to add, but I remember those trout from an isolated mountain lake as one of the best meals of my life. I was 16 years old. I had ridden 15 miles before that meal and had 15 miles yet to go. Makes for a good appetite!

⊜ QUICK TROUT *Season inside and out with salt and pepper. Roll in flour or cornmeal until coated inside and out, or dip in beaten egg and crumbs. Fry in oil or lard. It will cook very quickly. Turn once. Watch to prevent burning.*

⊜ DUTCH OVEN TROUT *Partly precook 5 slices of bacon in a frying pan. Preheat your Dutch oven and pour the bacon grease into the bottom of it. Put the trout in a layer to cover the bottom (about 4 medium-sized ones). Sprinkle with salt and pepper to taste. Lay the bacon over the trout. Put the lid on and cook in the oven at medium heat about 15 minutes.*

Serve with lemon wedges, if you can get them.

⊜ PLANKED LARGE TROUT *A Victorian delight. Place fish whole on hot greased plank (hickory, oak, or ash—1½ inches thick). Sprinkle with salt, pepper, and melted butter. Bake at 400°F an average of 15 minutes per pound for whole fish. When almost done, arrange a border of hot mashed potatoes around it. Brown under broiler. Surround with hot vegetables. Garnish. Serve on plank at the table.*

Eating Trout. Peel the skin off the top side (it's tasty too!). Very carefully, and in the best light you have, separate meat from bones—each person for himself. But do it for the smaller children, and don't give any trout to toddlers lest you goof and get a tiny bone in it, on which they might choke. Peel the meat slowly and carefully from the side using your fingers for best results, or a fork if you're squeamish. Peel from the head toward the tail and from above the backbone moving down, and cut along the ribs in order to avoid dislodging the fine rib bones from their connection with the backbone. If they do get loose with the meat, it's a real nuisance trying to pick them out one by one, and it's very easy to miss one. With practice, you can lift the whole side of flesh up off the little rib bones. Do the same to the other side of the fish, and you have your good eating ready.

Other Fish. Other cold-water (70°F or below) fish you might want to raise in your pond are muskellunge and northern pike. Another possible warm-water (80°F or above) fish choice is buffalofish. There are other varieties, like the bluegill and redeye sunfish, that are stocked to feed not humans but fish that will then be human food.

FISH FOOD: As with feeding any other livestock, there's a choice ranging from home-grown to ultracommercial feeds. Even among commercial feeds there are choices. You can choose feeds that have no preservatives, artificial colors, fixatives, synthetics, or pesticides.

Fertilizer. "Fertilizer" feeds the algae, which feeds the fish. You fertilize before the growing season for warm-water fish. In the extreme South, fertilizer can be applied year-round, but the fish-growing season decreases progressively toward the North, so fertilization is less effective in the northern states and may even do more harm than good. Too much fertilization can cause oxygen shortage and fishkills, especially if you also have an ice cover. Where fertilization works, ponds need refertilization any time during the growing season that a white object can be seen 18 inches or more below the water's surface. (If the pond is fertile enough, the resulting algae bloom will obscure an object at that depth.) As many as 12 fertilizer applications per year can be of benefit to maintain that fertility. You fertilize with animal or people manure or other organic products.

Supplemental Feeding. In trout ponds, this can raise production from 100 lb. per acre to 1,000–2,000 lb. per acre. Feeds are sold as finely ground mash and as floating or sinking pellets. Or you can make home-grown feed by offering chopped meats, wheat, whey, greens, and earthworms; watch what they take and what they don't, and be guided by that.

OTHER POND MANAGEMENT TASKS: Keep an eye on what the waterweeds are doing. Maintain a balanced fish population if you're keeping a combo. Be aware of the possibility of fish diseases. Maintain good water quality.

Preserving Food from Water

Use top-quality, fresh meat. Process for preservation as soon as possible after you catch (or buy) it. The longer you wait, the poorer the quality will be. To prevent spoilage, keep fish and shellfish cold—on ice or in your refrigerator. Handle raw seafood safely. Raw seafood may contain microorganisms that cause food poisoning. These bacteria are destroyed by heating the seafood before eating. Make sure that you wash your hands, utensils, and work surfaces (such as cutting boards) after handling raw seafood. Don't let raw seafood come into contact with cooked seafood.

Keep live shellfish (clams, oysters, mussels) moist and cold. Place them in a bowl, cover with a wet cloth, and store in the refrigerator. Keep fish on ice. Avoid rough handling. Don't stack fish on top of one another—this causes crushing and bruising, which speeds up spoilage. Keep live crab cool. *The Great American Seafood Cookbook* by Susan Hermann Loomis (New York: Workman Publishing, 1988) has good illustrations of filleting and cleaning and good info on wild seafood.

FREEZING FISH: Fish may be frozen whole as they come from the water, or whole but "drawn" (with the entrails removed). Drawn fish are best for freezing because they take less storage space.

Cleaning Scaly Fish. Soak the fish for a few minutes in cold water. Next, hold it down so it can't slide, and scrape using a dull knife from the rear end toward the head. The scales near the base of the fins and head are trickiest to get.

Removing Entrails. Switch from the dull knife you used for scaling to a sharp knife. Slit the belly from vent to gills. Remove the head by cutting above the collarbone. Scoop out and discard the innards. Break the backbone over the edge of the cutting board or table. Remove the dorsal or large back fin by cutting the flesh along each side and pulling out the fin. Never trim off the fins with shears or a knife because the bones at the base of the fin will be left in the fish. Wash the fish thoroughly in cold running water. You can leave the tail on a small fish. It will ordinarily be cooked whole. Rinse your scaled and cleaned fish in cold, running water. Your fish will keep better if you don't soak it in water after cleaning.

Steaks and Fillets. Large fish are cut crosswise into steaks or lengthwise into fillets for cooking. Cut steaks about ¾ inch thick. Fillets are a bit more complex. A fish's side bones are inside next to its cavity. So you make a boneless fillet by cutting the meat away from the backbone, tail to head, with a sharp knife, until you can lift the meat off the bones in 1 piece. With a sharp knife, cut down the back of the fish from the tail to the head. Then cut down to the backbone just above the collarbone. Turn the knife flat and cut the flesh along the backbone to the tail, allowing the knife to run over the rib bones. Lift off the entire side of the fish in 1 piece, freeing the fillet at the tail. Turn the fish over and cut fillet from the other side, resulting in 2 fillets—one from each side of the fish.

If you wish, you may skin the fillets. To do that, lay a fillet flat on your cutting board, skin side down. Hold the tail end with your fingers, and cut through the flesh to the skin. Flatten the knife on the skin and cut the flesh away from the skin by running the knife forward while holding the free end of the skin firmly between your fingers.

Preparing Catfish. Nail the fish through the head to some-

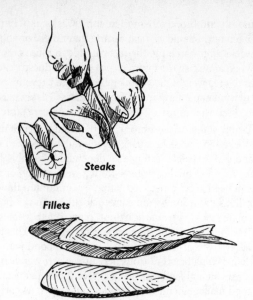

Steaks

Fillets

thing firm. Cut through the skin around the front end. Pull the skin down to the tail. Pliers can help you get a good grip on it. Then cut off head and tail and remove entrails.

Brine Dip. Commercial packers give fish steaks and fillets a 30 second dip in a 5-percent salt solution (⅔ c. salt per 1 gal. water) before wrapping and freezing. It helps preserve them.

Wrapping Fish for Freezing. Wrap in a covering that's resistant to water vapor. Try to make the package airtight to prevent drying. Place 2 layers of waxed paper between individual chops, steaks, and fillets so that individual frozen pieces can be separated easily. Wrap in freezer paper on the outside. Or put them in a milk carton or similar container full of water and freeze fish and water together. The water keeps them from drying out.

The Freezing. Spread packages. Turn control to coldest position. For quickest freezing, place packages against freezing plates or coils or in fast-freeze section of freezer. Store at 0°F or below. You can cook without thawing; it will just take a little extra cooking time. Or thaw first and then bread and fry, or stuff. Cook immediately after thawing.

STEP-BY-STEP FISH CANNING: This info is from Pacific Northwest Extension.
NOTE: Do not can smoked seafood; freeze it instead.
1. When you catch fish, remove viscera at once. Chill the cleaned fish until you're ready to can.
2. Before you can, remove head, tail, and fins.
3. Wash fish carefully, removing all blood.
4. Split fish lengthwise. Cut into lengths suitable for jars. (About 1 lb. of fish will fill one half-pint jar.)
5. Pack fish tightly into pint or half-pint jars, leaving 1-inch headspace. *Do not can fish or shellfish in quarts.* You may add 1 t. salt per pint. You can also add lemon juice, vinegar, salt, or oil (1–3 T. vegetable oil or fresh-type dressing per pint) as you wish.
6. Adjust lids. Wipe jar rims clean with a wet paper towel before putting on the lid. Moisten towel with vinegar when you pack fatty fish such as tuna and salmon.
7. Process half-pints and pints for 100 minutes *in a pressure canner* at 10 lb. pressure (weighted gauge) or 11 lb. pressure (dial gauge). Increase pressure for higher elevations as shown in the "Altitude Adjustments for Pressure Canning" table in "Preserving Meat."

Eating Home-Canned Food from Water. *Before tasting home-canned seafood, examine for spoilage.* Bulging jar lids, spurting liquid, an "off" odor, or mold show that the food is not safe to eat. *Do not taste or eat questionable food. For an extra margin of safety, heat any home-canned seafood before you eat it.* Boiling the seafood, covered, for 10 minutes will destroy bot toxin. Or you can preserve texture by baking. To do that, remove lid and insert a meat thermometer upright into the center of the jar. The tip should be at the approximate center of the fish. Cover the jar loosely with foil and place in an oven preheated to 350°F. Remove the jar from the oven when the thermometer registers 185°F. You'll need about 30 to 35 minutes. Let the jar stand at room temperature for about 30 minutes. This will let the temperature become uniform throughout the jar. Serve the fish hot or refrigerate immediately for later use.

NOTE: *If you prepare canned fish in a casserole, bake at 350°F and check the internal temperature at the end of the cooking time as described above for jar.*

My favorite animal in my whole long life was the half-Shetland pony I rode as a child, Shorty Bill. I'll never forget the night that horse saved my life. Or was it my father who did?

Shorty Bill was half the size of a regular horse. I rode him every day to a country school 2 miles down the road, there and home again after school. One late fall day I took a notion to ride him from school directly over the mountain instead of going by the road. I let myself through the gate across from the little schoolhouse, and Shorty and I didn't have another fence from there to home. We were on what you might call open range. We slowly moved up out of Bracket Creek Canyon, where the school was, into the treeless exposed top of the mountain that lay between the school and my home.

As I rode, dusk fell early. Then, without warning, out of the gray sky came a true blizzard. The snow began to fall thicker and thicker—big white flakes, and with them utter black darkness. The wind howled and whined in my ears, pushing against my pony's body and mine. I couldn't even see my pony's ears ahead of me. Though I was warmly dressed, as always, I started to feel a real chill on my face.

There was no light, no road, no fence to follow. No sound but the wind. I was a little girl of about 8 with no hope in the world but my pony. I knew those blizzards. It might snow for days and nights, and when it stopped there could easily be 4 feet of snow on the ground. I had gone out with my father the morning after a band of freshly sheared ewes and lambs had gotten caught in a blizzard. I'd watched as he frantically searched for rounded mounds in the surface of the snow and then dug down through its smothering, chilling blanket. But the sheep and lambs he found were all dead.

I remembered that and, for a moment, I was very frightened. What could I do? Who would help me? There was nobody.

Then I remembered my daddy once saying to me, soon after he gave me my horse, "If you ever get lost with Shorty Bill, just let him have his head." (That means let him choose and go where he wants.) "Horses have senses that people don't, and can't even understand. He'll take you home." I heard those words again in my mind just as clearly as if he were there with me, saying them for the first time. I was so grateful that Daddy had bothered to give me the bit of advice that now was the only hope I had. It had to be my answer. There was no other way. It had to be Shorty Bill who took me home. But was Daddy right? Could Shorty Bill find his way even in this storm? The storm wouldn't kill him even if he didn't find his way home. His body was so big and strong and warm. But it could kill me.

Nothing to do but trust and obey. Obey my father. In a sense, obey Shorty Bill. So I let him have his head: I simply let the reins hang slack instead of putting pressure on his mouth and neck to inform him which way I wanted him to go. Now he could go any way he wanted to. He would soon realize that.

Having given up the "steering," I instead concentrated all my efforts on keeping warm and hanging on. I made myself as small a target for the freezing wind as I could, hunching over my pony's back with my head low, my chin snuggled as deep into my coat as I could get, trying to shelter my face from the wind.

We went a very long time like that. Shorty wasn't one to hurry. He was old as horses go. He moved along steadily, though, and I felt soothed by his steady rocking motion, almost sleepy, except I had to make myself stay awake enough to hang on tight. I don't know how long it was, some hours . . .

Suddenly he stopped. That did scare me. As long as he was moving, I could still hope that he was taking me home. Now I peered up and out from my coat collar's shelter to a wonderful sight: I could just barely see the shine of a light. It was the one outside the barn. My daddy was there, standing out in the freezing cold, right under the light, right by the barn door. He must have been waiting for us. He walked quickly over and lifted me off Shorty Bill with one great swoop of his strong arms. He hugged me wordlessly to his chest for a long moment. Then he took Shorty Bill into the barn's wind-sheltered warmth, took off his saddle and bridle, and gave him an extra-big serving of oats for his dinner.

Whenever I remember that journey on Shorty's back, lost in the storm, I think about trust. Who you trust. How you trust when there is nothing else to do. And how that trust can bring you safely home. Whenever I think of that, I think that going home to Heaven must be like that. You trust because there is nothing else to do anyway. And your trust brings you safely home. I've felt that I was in darkness many times since that ride. But there's a hand that holds mine and an invisible light that goes before me. Guiding, guarding all the way. Though it be even the valley of the shadow of death.

Poultry

Poultry Contents

INTRODUCTION

Although my mother could turn out good food on the old wood cookstove and wasn't discouraged by all sorts of country problems, no part of the barnyard was ever really her thing except the chicken house. She loved her chickens and they seemed to love her. I love all the animals, including the big ones, but Mother was terrified of them. I remember one time Daddy had to be away overnight. Mother assured him that, just for once, she could manage to milk the cow. Well, I awoke the next morning to hear her hollering desperately outside the window. I ran to look, and there she was, perched on the very top of a fence post, balancing up there in some mysterious way while our gentle milk cow stood close by, patiently waiting to be taken on into the barn. Mother was convinced she was under attack.

I'll never forget that scene because, although I'm lean like the Harshbarger side of the family (my full maiden name was Carlotta Louise Harshbarger; "Carla" is a nickname), Mother always packed quite a bit of weight, and her getting on top of that fence post was an achievement. If you don't believe me, just go out and try to stand on top of a wooden fence post—no matter how much you weigh.

Every spring Mother had baby chickens living in a cardboard box

back of the wood stove. One year Daddy added a bathroom with a bathtub in it on to the house. Afterwards, Mother moved the spring chicks to the bathtub once they outgrew the cardboard box, until it was warm enough for them to be outside. We took our spring baths in a big round metal tub

on the kitchen floor, just like we'd done before we had plumbing.

Mother had a wonderful healing touch with sick animals. I saw her revive an almost-dead baby chick that had suffered some crisis of illness or injury. She would work the stiff little legs and wings up and down until circulation was restored. Then she'd wrap the chick in a soft white dishtowel (white from being boiled in lye

water on top of the stove) and put it in a little box near the stove, wherever a wave of her experienced arm told her the brooding temperature was just right.

The chickens loved my mother. They got all her kitchen scraps. Daddy could feed the pigs on whatever else there was—the chickens had first rights. And they appreciated this. They laid eggs aplenty for us. If Mother went to town shopping and stayed away too long, the chickens would get restless and manage somehow to get the front door open. Mother would walk in and find chickens roosting all over—on the kitchen stove, the table, in cupboards. And they would all fly up and squawk at the sight of us, feathers and droppings going every which way.

I'll never forget the taste of Mother's fried chicken. First she'd have me go out and catch and kill a couple birds (she never could bring herself to come out of the house until that part was over). Then she'd appear with a big bucket of scalding water, and we'd pluck, clean, and cut up the birds together. That very night for supper we'd eat them. Mother turned up her nose at chicken that was over 12 hours from the hoof to the pan. She didn't have a deep freeze. She canned lots of venison, but her chicken was always absolutely fresh.

CHICKENS

NOTE: The following section on chickens contains basic information relevant to all poultry varieties. In the other poultry sections that follow, only data that is different from the information in this section is covered.

Getting Started: Information and Supplies

POULTRY PERIODICALS: Most U.S. rural-living magazines have occasional articles on poultry—the most common homestead animal. And also . . .

Feather Fancier Newspaper is a Canadian newspaper focused on purebred poultry, pigeons, waterfowl, pheasants, etc.; $20 US/yr; sample $2; 519-542-6859; fax 519-542-4168; 5739 Telfer Rd., Sarnia, Ont. N7T 7H2, CANADA; **featherfancier@ebtech.net**; **www.feather fancier.on.ca.**

National Poultry News is "the Country Paper Country Folks Love to Read," a homespun 32-pg quarterly, largely reader-written. It covers show birds, homestead flocks, and often other homestead animals and homestead topics too! Cost is $10/yr; sample issue $2 USA; $5 overseas. Contact Glenda L. Heywood, Editor: phone/fax 864-855-0140; PO Box 1647, Easley, SC

BASIC PRINCIPLES OF ECONOMIC CHICKEN MANAGEMENT

1. Start your flock with quality chicks, bought from a local hatchery or mail-ordered, or incubate your own eggs.
2. Choose your best caretaking schedule: a small egg flock year-round, or a big meat-production for a few months a year (or both). Choose a broiler breed for your fryers, a good laying breed for your layers, or a quality meat–eggs breed and eventually raise your own.
3. Feed your cockerels or capons only long enough to get them to the eating size you want, butcher them yourself, and then can or freeze them, so that you won't have to feed them any longer than necessary.

4. Use home-grown feeds when possible: pasture, household, and garden scraps; surplus milk; garden squash and mangel beets raised and cooked for your birds' winter veggies . . .
5. Feed your birds a generous (and diversified) diet. To a real extent, the more they eat, the more they grow, and the more they lay. Make sure your birds have adequate ventilation, space, sunshine, and gravel for their gizzards.
6. Buy or raise some new pullet chicks every year; periodically cull your existing flock of layers carefully and send to the stew pot any birds that are performing poorly.

7. Shovel out the chicken house at least twice a year, age the manure in your compost heap, and then use it to enrich your garden soil.
8. Sell your surplus eggs direct to other householders at a reasonable profit to help pay for the cash expenses of poultry-keeping.
9. Preserving eggs evens out the spring surplus with the winter shortage and enables you to get along feeding fewer laying hens.
10. Keep basic records so you know where your greatest expenses and best profits are.

29641-1647; **frizzlebird@yahoo.com; www.national poultrynews.com; poultryconnection.com; www. g-kexoticfarms.com.**

New Zealand Poultry & Pigeon News Digest is a bimonthly journal sent air mail; 20 A4 pages on "interesting topics from constructive breeding to show reports." Price $15 US/yr. Back issues and book list available: PO Box 133, Inglewood, NEW ZEALAND.

The Poultry Press is available monthly from 765-827-0932; PO Box 542, Connersville, IN 47331-0542. Cost is $21/yr; $59/3 yrs; sample copy $3.

Poultry Times: If agribusiness concepts don't stick in your craw, to understand the commercial poultry production scene, and for good disease articles with solutions, spend $9 for a year's subscription to *Poultry Times;* 770-536-2476; fax 770-532-4894; 345 Green St. NW, PO Box 1338, Gainesville, GA 30503; **ptedit@mind spring.com or ptpub@mindspring.com.** A commercial farm poultryman in your neighborhood would be a breeder (who sells eggs to hatcheries), a hatcheryman (who sells just-hatched birds to growers), or a grower (who sells eggs and/or broilers to processors and distributors). But *Poultry Times* will ask further: whether you're a broiler processor, egg packer and processor, hatcheryman, broiler or layer producer, commercial egg producer, turkey producer, feed manufacturer, flock serviceman, hatching egg producer (breeder), supplier to the poultry industry, turkey processor, started pullet raiser, ag college, veterinarian, government, financial advisor (banker), or nutritionist (poultry feed component specialist). Its calendar lists poultry specialty conventions, conferences, seminars, and short courses—all aimed at the for-profit, large-scale poultry operation.

POULTRY CLUBS, MUSEUMS, AND TOURS: The American Poultry Association offers membership, quarterly newsletters, and an annual yearbook and show awards for $10/yr. Contact Lorna Rhodes, Secty-Treas; 508-473-8769; 133 Millville St., Mendon, MA 01756; **apanetcontact@ home.com; www.amplrya.com.** The Society for Preservation of Poultry Antiquities promotes endangered and rare poultry worldwide and also unites collectors of antique poultry equipment. Get a Membership Breeders Directory and four bulletins for $12.50/yr: Glenn Drowns, Sec.; 1878-230th St., Calamus, IA 52729. The Maine Alternative Poultry Association (MAPA) organizes growers with less than 2,000 laying hens or less than 10,000 meat birds: Dr. Opitz, 207-581-2771.

The National Poultry Museum at Bonner Springs, KS, is part of the National Agricultural Museum. It displays thousands of antiques representing the poultry industry's heritage. Or visit the American Poultry Historical Society: Dr. Lou Arrington, Secretary, 260 Animal Sciences Bldg., 1675 Observatory Dr., Madison, WI 53706. Overseas, visit the Dutch Poultry Museum in Barnveld, Holland.

For the ultimate guided tour, join the 16-day annual Stromberg Poultry Fancier Tour. You'll visit Sweden, Poland, Holland (International Flower Auction, poultry museum, and a private fancier), England, and Germany (the Thuringer Poultry Museum and the famous Hanover Poultry Show displaying 20,000+ birds of every type, plus dealers and suppliers), and more. For tour schedule, details, and price contact Loyl Stromberg: 218-543-4228; 8302 Big Whitefish Narrows, Pine River, MN 56474.

POULTRY SUPPLIES: For small flock service, look in your local Yellow Pages under "Feed Dealers" or "Poultry." Your local feed salesperson can be an invaluable source of advice to help you get started and keep you going, as well as supply information on commercial feeds and basic components of build-it-yourself feed rations and general livestock supplies. Hatcheries, local or mail-order (listed below), often sell specialized books and poultry equipment for family flocks.

Brower Equipment offers a free catalog of brooders, bulbs, cages, waterers, and feeders: 319-469-4141; 800-553-1791; fax 319-469-4402; Hwy. 16 W., PO Box 2000, Houghton, IA 52631; **broweriowa@aol.com; www.browerequip.com.**

EggCartons.com sells poultry supplies, especially egg cartons (pulp or foam) sized for chicken or duck eggs, $37.50/250, etc.: 888-852-5340; fax 877-455-4647; 24 Holt Rd., PO Box 302, Manchaug, MA 01526-0302; **info@EggCartons.com; www.EggCartons.com.**

Foy's Pigeon Supplies sells general poultry supplies. Free catalog: 877-355-7727; 3185 Bennett's Run Rd., Beaver Falls, PA 15010; **www.foyspigeonsupplies.com.**

G & M Sales of Virginia sells poultry feeders, etc.: 800-296-9156; 540-433-9156; fax 540-433-4818; 4562 S. Valley Pike, Harrisonburg, VA 22801; **sales@gmsalesofva.com; www.gmsalesofva.com.**

GQF Mfg. Co. Quail & Poultry Equipment offers incubators, brooders, waterers, candlers, and much more! 912-236-0651; fax 912-234-9978; PO Box 1552, Savannah, GA 31402-1552; **sales@www.GQFmfg.com; www.GQFmfg.com.**

Inman Hatcheries offers a free color catalog of ducklings, goslings, turkeys, gamebirds, chickens, incubators, brooders, waterers, medications, books: 800-243-1962; 605-225-8122; PO Box 616, Aberdeen, SD 57402-0616.

Rocky Top General Store sells poultry and gamefowl supplies, antique tools, coal/gas/wood stoves, farm/pet supplies, grain mixtures, kerosene heaters, etc., by mail-order or in-store: 865-882-8867; fax 865-882-9056; PO Box 1006, Harriman, TN 37748; **rockytopgen@msn.com; www.rockytopgen.com/.**

Smith Poultry and Game Bird Supply sells poultry books, incubators and brooders, medications, vitamins, wormers, and watering supplies; 14000 W. 215th St., Bucyrus, KS 66013; 913-879-2587; fax 913-533-2497; **Smith@PoultrySupplies.com; www.PoultrySupplies.com.**

Stromberg's Unlimited sells poultry-keeping supplies, poultry stock, incubators, chicken pickers, books. Free catalog: 800-720-1134; 218-587-2222; fax 218-587-4230; Box 400, Pine River, MN 56474; **info@strombergschicken.com; strombergschicken.com.**

Val Products is a multinational manufacturer in this field: 717-392-3978; fax 717-392-8947; PO Box 958, Lancaster, PA 17608; **chick@valproducts.com; www.valproducts.com.**

POULTRY BOOKS: *Raising Chickens* by Cynthia Haynes (1985) is fairly recent and carefully researched. *Raising Poultry the Modern Way* by Leonard S. Mercia (updated 1990) is a long-time classic for those who want a commercial operator's approach. If your interest is in a few chickens kept as pets or show stock in a suburban setting, read *Bantams: A Complete Pet Owner's Manual* by Helga Fritzsche (1985), translated from its original German edition. Other useful books are *Chickens in Your Backyard* by Rick and Gail Luttmann; *Raising Poultry Successfully* by Will Graves (1985), which covers chickens, ducks and geese; *Starting Right with Poultry* by G.T Klein (1973); *The Complete Handbook of Poultry Keeping* by Stuart Banks (1979); *Raising Turkeys, Ducks, Geese, Pigeons and Guineas* by

Cynthia Haynes (1987); *The Family Poultry Flock*, edited by Lee Schwarz (1981); *Raising Small Meat Animals: Efficient Home Production of Cornish Game Hens, Chicken Broilers, Turkey Roasters, Rabbits and Squabs* by Victor Michael Giammattei; and *Producing Eggs and Chickens with the Minimum of Purchased Feed* by Ed Robinson (1972).

Chicken Breeds

Here is a description of the different kinds of chickens, sorted out in various ways to help you make sense of it. To me, the most important aspects of a chicken are ranging, mothering ability, and climate suitability. But there's a bird for everybody's needs here. Browse until you find your perfect match. But first a useful definition: "sex links."

Wyandotte

Sex links exist in various breeds and are always worth considering. Sex links are the offspring of the crossing (mating) of a "gold" (red, buff, brown . . .) male with a "silver" (Wyandotte, Plymouth Rock, Sussex, Brahma) female. The chicks will be sex differentiated by color: males, cream or white; females, buff or red. The sex links generally belong to the "heavy" size category (see "Heavy Chickens" below). Keep in mind—if you are planning to incubate your own eggs—that they are hybrids, and crosses do not breed true. That means the chicks will not turn out like the parents. (Only pure breeds breed true.) The Black Sex Link is a meat–eggs hybrid gotten by mating a Rhode Island Red rooster to a Barred Plymouth Rock hen. The Red Sex Link has a Rhode Island father and a White Leghorn hen mother. Hatcheries like to see sex links because of the fact that cockerels and pullets are different colors at hatching, and that saves the hatchery time, which is money, in determining the sex.

GOOD EGG LAYERS: The most efficient layers of all come from carefully selected genetic lines of chickens that have been developed for commercial egg production. The Leghorn is the old-timer in this field. White Leghorns are the best known, but Leghorns also come in brown, buff, red, and the black-patterned Columbian. Other modern breeds that lay as well as, or even a little better than, the Leghorn, are the New Hampshire, Golden Sex Link, Whelp-Line, and Barred Plymouth Rock. All these breeds, including the Leghorn, will lay between 245 and 255 eggs per year under good management. The best egg-laying breeds grow relatively slowly and eat a lot relative to the weight they put on. You can't have both top egg production and most efficient meat production from the same line of birds. It is also worth noting that at least 2 duck breeds, the Khaki-Campbell and the Indian Runner, lay eggs as dependably as these chickens.

Leghorn

EGG COLOR: Brown eggs are exactly the same inside as white ones. To find out what color egg a breed lays—if no one tells you and you care—just ask. In most places, brown eggs sell for 2–10 cents a dozen more than white eggs. In general, the smaller (Mediterranean-derived) breeds—Leghorns, Minorcas, Anconas—lay white-shelled eggs; the larger (American) breeds lay brown. The major English-developed breeds—Cornish, Orpington, and Sussex—are brown-egg layers, as are the Asiatic chickens—Brahma, Cochin, Langshan. Pure-bred Araucanas, chickens from South America, lay eggs in the purple to pink range. If an Araucana is mated with a brown-egg layer, half the offspring will lay eggs with dusky shells. If an Araucana is mated to a white-egg layer, half the offspring will lay eggs with light blue shells. An individual hen won't change colors. Whatever color she first lays will be what you'll always get from her.

SIZE: Chickens come in broiler, giant, heavy, light, and bantam weights. The concept helps sort out most of them, though many breeds now have both a large variety and a bantam variety.

Broilers. These are your basic meat birds. The ideal broiler is now expected to gain 4 lb. in 8 weeks and then go into the deep freeze. It used to be that meat birds were either extra roosters or culled hens. Then came a period when caponized cockerels were the popular meat birds. Now extra male chicks of egg-specialist breeds are frequently

destroyed at the hatchery because, even at bargain-basement prices, they aren't the bargain that broiler chicks are if what you want is meat. Broilers grow phenomenally fast because they've been carefully selected from genetic lines that have maximum feed-to-flesh conversion ratios. That means with a broiler, 2 lb. of feed turn into 1 lb. of meat in just 3 weeks. The best laying breeds, on the other hand, would have to eat around 6 lb. of feed to gain a pound, and it would take longer than 3 weeks. Another way to put it is that your broiler will eat twice as much feed as the other breed, but you'll be done and putting it in your deep freeze 3 months sooner than you would the regular heavy breed. Probably the maximum farm efficiency is to have a good egg-laying dual-purpose (American) breed and raise some extra broiler chicks every year for the bulk of your meat birds. Don't let broilers grow older than 12 weeks because by then they've put on all their meat and mainly acquire fat.

Any "giant" or "Cornish" or "Cornish cross" or "jumbo" or "broiler" is a broiler. The hatchery catalog will make it clear to you which of their breed names means "broiler." The Cornish-Rock is a hybrid of a Cornish rooster and a White Plymouth Rock hen. A friend who raised a batch told me they dressed out between 7 and 8 lb. at 12 weeks old. She said they made good roasters because of that sizable cavity to stuff and had huge breasts and lots of white meat. Hubbard Roasters are another rapid-growing, large-breasted bird. None of these breeds makes good layers because they eat so much more per egg they lay than a good layer does, and they don't lay as well.

Giants. Many sources rate Black Giants and Jersey White Giants as "heavy" chickens, but to me they fit best here, along with Cornish. Their capons may grow to 15 lb. The giants and Cornish are a little slower to mature than heavy breed birds or broilers. If you want to breed your own broilers, a purebred Cornish rooster mated to heavy-breed hens will produce acceptable meat-type offspring. Hatchery broilers come from carefully developed genetic lines that are protected, sometimes even patented. These birds do mate naturally, but only if they're on a lean diet, eating only about 70 percent of what they'd like to have. Cornish roosters do have a problem breeding because of their top heaviness. You have to pick your roosters carefully and not let them get too heavy. The small birds that you see in grocery store meat displays called "Cornish game hens" are Cornish Rocks that were butchered at 4 weeks of age. Butcher them at 2 lb. live weight to get the proper "Cornish game hen" dressed weight (1½ lb.). Pure Cornish are available from large fowl breeder Ken Herring, President of the Cornish Club: KB4R@aol.com. Or from Billy Grimes, Secretary: bgrimes@fanninelectric.com.

Heavy Chickens. These also make good fryers and roasters and stay put behind a fence. Your extra roosters and over-age hens are meaty enough to make butchering worthwhile. They ordinarily eat more and lay slightly bigger eggs than lighter breeds. It is among the heavy chickens of "American" descent that you find your good combination meat-and-eggs barnyard breeds. They don't grow as much meat as the giants, nor as fast, but their size is not shabby, and many of them are top-of-the-line egg-layers, too. Butcher these breeds at 16–20 weeks of age.

Rhode Island Reds, Production Reds, Plymouth Rocks, White Rocks, Barred Rock, Wyandottes, and New Hampshires fall into this category. Chicken breeds that were developed in England and fit in this weight group are the Australorp, Dorking, Orpington, and Sussex. The Buff Orpington is an exceptionally gentle bird that is a good bet to set when the warm weather comes. The non-bantamized Asiatic chickens—Brahma, Cochin, and Langshan—belong here because of their characteristically large bodies; they also have feathered shanks and heavy bones, and they lay brown eggs. Hen weights range from 6½ lb. for a mature Wyandotte, Rhode Island Red, New Hampshire, or Black Australorp hen, to 7½ lb. for a mature Barred Plymouth Rock, White Plymouth Rock, or Black Minorca hen. (The Black Minorca is the largest member of the Mediterranean group of egg breeds, but by weight it belongs here.) The naked-necked Turken grows to be 6 lb. or more.

Light Breeds. These are the Leghorn and other Mediterranean-derived chickens, plus the Araucana—which is as lean as the Leghorn and still has all its brooding instincts—and the American-developed WhelpLine, a 5-lb. hen. The Houdan is an old-time French-developed light breed. California Gray, Sicilian Buttercups, Minorcas, White Faced Spanish, Blue Andalusians, and Anconas are other light breeds. The Sicilian Buttercups and Houdans are especially good layers. The lights are somewhat more nervous in temperament than the heavy breeds, which are better with children. The high-strung lights don't tame easily. A hen typically weighs 4–4½ lb. Leghorn roosters make passable fryers, though they are smaller than Reds or Rocks. Leghorns, or Leghorn varieties, are the general favorite of commercial egg operations. The white eggs sell better and color better at Easter. The smaller size means the chicken eats less per egg produced (though the eggs are slightly smaller). The production-oriented Leghorn gets a lot of bad press among homesteaders, but the fact remains that half a century of selection effort has gone into those birds to achieve ideal cost-efficient egg production. Lane Morgan, writer, gardener, and chicken-raiser, summed it up for me nicely: "Leghorns might be a good choice if you are raising a flock in confinement, on commercial food. I've had a Leghorn laying flock, and they certainly do lay, but I just didn't enjoy their company much. Incidentally, I find Araucanas much calmer and more sensible than Leghorns; I personally wouldn't lump them with other hysterical light breeds."

Bantams. A "bantam" is the bantam weight—a very small bird, smaller even than a Leghorn and about one-third to one-fourth the size of a large chicken. There are dozens of types and colors of them with wonderfully varying size, color, and plumage patterns, and they are popular as show birds for the county fair. There's a considerable size range among the different varieties. La Fleche is the heaviest with a 3-lb. cock. Silkies and Faverolles are a little over 2 lb. (cock); Chochin and Ancona cocks are a little over 1½ lb. The hen typically weighs slightly less. The black Silky was domesticated in China 4,000 years ago, the Chabos and Cochins 1,000 years ago. In addition to these ancient breeds, there are many new breeds of dwarfed commercials and other modern chickens, as well as ever-evolving new varieties of selections and crosses being developed for the hobby and show markets, mainly selected for their lovely or interesting feathers.

Bantams require less room and less feed than larger chickens. They provide less meat and their eggs are small, though actually large in proportion to the bird's body weight. (In a recipe, 3 bantam eggs equal 2 regular eggs.) Some breeds will lay almost as many eggs as a commercial chicken (La Fleche, 200/year; Amrock, 200/year; Ancona, 180-200/year), but most lay less than that; the Sebright and Game varieties rank at the bottom for egg-laying (50–80/year). These breeds are not the most efficient egg-layers, nor do they offer the most efficient feed–growth conversion ratios, but there is one important quality about some of them that merits consideration: many of these chicken varieties will readily brood and be good mothers. The majority of the modern bantam breeds, like the modern breeds from which they were dwarfed, do not reproduce naturally—they must be incubated. The traditional bantam hen, on the other hand, will virtually insist on becoming a mother, and is such fun to watch, and such a good mother, you'd probably be willing to allow it. To own such a bantam hen, choose a variety that has high ratings for broodiness, mothering, and foster-mothering ability: Ancona, Cochin, Silkies, Brahma, and Faverolle. Silkies and Cochins are also outstanding for their tranquil dispositions.

You can start out with just 2 bantams, male and female, and they'll do the rest. Or start out with just a bantam hen, and a regular-size rooster. Then, with genetic luck, her pullet offspring will have the mothering ability of a bantam and grow to more nearly the size of a large chicken. The older bantam breeds are also typically healthy (they can make it through almost anything) and cute, with lots of personality, and are great foragers, as well as good incubating machines for their or any other chicken's fertile eggs. A disadvantage to running bantams (which many folks call "banties") together with a general flock, if you're hatching your own eggs, is that the bantam roosters are so wonderful at doing their thing that soon you'll have all half bantams—which is not good from the meat point of view. You can avoid that by eating the bantam roosters. Bantams are too small to be proper fryers, but they stew okay. A risk with these born foragers is that they'll become totally independent of you and roost in places you disapprove of, and you'll only be able to catch one with a .22.

Orpington

You may want to join the American Bantam Association and get their quarterly newsletter: PO Box 127, Augusta, NJ 07822; 973-383-6944; fax 973-383-8633; **fancybtms@Skylands.net; www.Bantamclub.com.** They publish 19 books on bantams.

CLIMATES: If you live in the frozen North, the heavily feathered, heavy-breed Brahmas, Cochins, Orpingtons, Black Giants, and Wyandottes are worth considering because they are heartier and lay better in cold weather than more lightly feathered breeds. In general, the heavy breeds are the best for cold climates. Neither the broilers nor the light weights tolerate cold well. Frozen combs are a special hazard for cold-climate flocks. In unheated housing, large combs can tend to freeze, which causes lowered egg production from hens and a temporary end to the fertility of roosters in breeder flocks. So avoid buying such large-comb birds as the White Leghorn. A cold-climate bird is best adapted if it has a very close-fitting "rose" comb. The Mediterranean-derived breeds adapt well to warm or hot climates.

BREEDS FOR RANGING: In general, don't buy any white birds if you have predator problems and expect your chickens to range free at least part of the time. They stand out too much. An alert, active variety handles predators better. Regular size Anconas, Brown Leghorns, and Dark Cornish, and old-time bantam breeds are well spoken of in this regard. Araucanas, too.

SETTERS AND NON-SETTERS: Most chicken breeds have had the instinct to set and mother completely bred out of them, but some still have it. If your basic interest is egg production, broody hens are a nuisance. If you like the tradition of a natural chicken family you have to pick one of the breeds that can still handle that assignment. Breeds that will set are Orpingtons (Buff are best mothers), Turkens, Partridge Rocks, Buff Rocks, Speckled Sussex, Dark Cornish, Columbian Wyandottes, Buff Cochins, Partridge Cochins, and Light Brahmas, and any of the good bantam mothering breeds.

BREEDS FOR FLY-TYING AND FEATHER-JEWELRY: Raise Barred Rocks for the Grizzlies, Blue Andalusians for the Duns (only half of their offspring will be blue, even when breeding true), Silver Penciled Rocks or Wyandottes for the Badgers, and buff, brown, and red breeds for other lovely feathers.

RARE BREEDS: The American Livestock Breeds Conservancy (Box 477, Pittsboro, NC 27312; 919-542-5704) classifies as "rare" those poultry breeds with 500 or fewer females and fewer than 3 sources. As of 1993, Ancona, Black Minorca, Delaware, Dominique, White Jersey Giant, White Wyandotte chickens, the Pilgrim goose, and the (unimproved) Bronze turkey were "rare." The AMBC classifies as "minor" breeds those with 2,000 or fewer females, and 5 or fewer sources, or a concentration of the breeding population in fewer than 3 sources: Black Jersey Giant, Brown Leghorn chickens, and the Khaki Campbell duck. They classify as "watch" breeds those with 2,000–20,000 females, but fewer than 10 sources, or a declining number of sources. "Watch" poultry breeds are Barred Plymouth Rock, Black Australorp, New Hampshire, Rhode Island Red (old-type), Rouen duck, and Toulouse goose. In addition to the ALBC and regular mail-order poultry-outlet offerings (listed below), you can locate unusual breeds by asking around locally. Or contact the American Poultry Association, which publishes *Standard of Perfection*,

a show-oriented guide to chicken varieties; 503-630-6759; 133 Millville St., Mendon, MA 01756; **www.ampltya.com.**

Starting by Buying Adult Birds

The cheapest way to start a flock is to order chicks from a hatchery and raise them yourself. That virtually guarantees you a disease- and parasite-free flock to start with. And it eliminates the possibility that somebody is selling you their culls. Furthermore, moving from one home to another tends to throw adult layers into a molt, which will end laying for a while. Nevertheless, you can buy adult birds from neighbors, local commercial sources, and mail-order sources—and there may be circumstances under which so doing will be your best choice. This type of transaction is most likely to occur with fancy breeds and breeding stock in general. I'll tell you how to do this now and later describe how to obtain and manage baby chicks, or hatch your own chicks by incubator or mother hen.

HEALTH: Buy only healthy individuals. To make sure of that, check out the following points before you buy:
1. Look to see if they have skin or feather parasites. Do this by taking along a little magnifying glass and peering among the underarm feathers down by the skin.
2. Combs and wattles should be shiny red (unless the hen is broody or mothering). Eyes should be alert and bright. Feathers should be smooth and shiny.
3. Droppings should be well-formed rather than loose, and without the pinkish tinge of blood.
4. The birds should be busily eating, dusting, or preening—generally active and curious. If they are quiet, with feathers fluffed out, they are not healthy.

BRINGING NEW BIRDS HOME: If you have no other chickens and the new ones are healthy, and if you give their housing a good lye-cleaning before they are moved into it, and if you make sure they don't run on ground that other poultry have used within the past 3 years, there's a good chance the new birds will stay healthy. If possible, bring your new birds home near sundown. No matter what time of day you end up bringing them home, confine them in your chicken house until they've gone to roost there. Then keep them penned up for the next few days with plenty of food and water available. After a few nights of requiring them to roost where you want them to, their habit will be set and they'll consider it home. Then you can open the outside door.

INTRODUCING NEWCOMERS TO AN ESTABLISHED FLOCK: Birds can be very cruel to unknown individuals. To bring in such a stranger, he/she would have to be approximately the same size as the rest of the flock's members. Pen the new one(s) where the old ones can see them for about 3 weeks. Then "accidentally" leave the cage door open and keep a distant eye on what happens next. Lane Morgan said, "When I have to introduce new birds to an established flock, and I don't have the option of keeping them separate but in view for weeks, I do 2 things. I put the new birds in at night, so they have roosted together before they have a chance to fight, and for a few days I evict the old birds into their yard every morning, leaving the new one or ones in the inside pen with the food and water. The new ones get a chance to eat in peace and to take possession of the new space, and when the established birds are let back in, they are too busy eating and drinking to make a lot of trouble."

TAMING BIRDS: To tame new birds, get them to eat from your hand. And pet them on cheeks, head, and neck, and get them accustomed to being gently carried by you. But you may not want to tame birds whose life cycle will be strictly utilitarian.

Starting by Buying Chicks

The subject of raising chicks is so complex I scarcely know where to begin: With the chicken who lays and sets on and mothers her own? With the egg that you collect and incubate artificially and then raise the resulting chicks like a batch from the mail-order hatchery? Or with the chick that has just arrived in the mail and first of all needs the warmth of a brooder? I am guessing that most people nowadays get their chicks mail-order, so I'm starting with that. Afterwards, I'll tell you how to hatch your own in an incubator, and, last of all, how to let a mother hen do it the old-time way.

MAIL-ORDER CHICKS: These are incubator chicks that have been grown at commercial regional hatcheries and are sent through the regular mail to you if you've placed an order for them. It takes 21 days to hatch chicks, so you order and pay for them ahead of time. The earlier you get your order in, the better. Some hatcheries give price breaks for early ordering. Some get booked to capacity in the rush season and can't accept more orders. Some rarer species get sold out way ahead of time. Hatches are scheduled for early in the week. You may want to order all your chicks at once—or to work with a smaller number at a time in a smaller brooder space and raise several batches—maybe one in February, one in April, and one in October. To start a large number of chicks and not have to worry so much about chilling in colder climates, the ideal time to get them is around July 15. At that time of year you could probably raise any number of chicks without even a heat lamp, if your nights are warm.

HOW MANY? You should always have at least a pair of poultry—chickens, or any other domesticated birds—and a trio (a cock and 2 hens, preferably) is better; they really get lonely and don't thrive without the companionship of another bird. But you'll probably start with more than that if you start with chicks. Most hatcheries won't ship fewer than 25 chicks at a time. That's because it requires at least that many to create enough body heat to keep the chicks warm enough during their journey from the hatchery to you. Chickens get along best if they were raised together, so it would simplify your life to start your intended flock all together and at the same time.

CHICKS FOR LAYING HENS: An average hen will lay 220 eggs per year. A typical family needs 2 laying hens per family member to supply them with plentiful eggs. So you'll order 25–50 chicks of a breed that lays well and has good food–egg production conversion efficiency. After the ninth edition of this book, Lane Morgan took me to task: "In these cholesterol-conscious days, that number seems high to me. We have done fine with one layer per person and have had enough extra eggs to supply a neighbor. With a 60-watt bulb on a timer, they lay all winter—not a lot but enough." She's right.

When placing your order, you'll also have to choose whether you want to buy all pullets, "straight run," or cockerels. Sometimes called "hatch run," straight run means mixed-sex chicks. If you buy specifically one sex or the other, pullets of good egg-laying breeds may cost you from 2–8 times as much as cockerels. But, if your main interest is in eggs, they'll be worth it. If you buy straight run, you've got to figure out for yourself when they get big enough what sex each is and treat them accordingly. (All, or most, of the cockerels would go into the meat count.) You'll get about 50 percent of each sex. You'll probably lose a few of the chicks you order to general hazards of the growing-up process. The remainder will become your flock of laying hens. So buy 50 straight-run chicks for every 20 laying hens you want. If you already have a flock of layers, the most economical practice is to replace around two-thirds of the poorest layers of them each year with new pullets. If you like keeping old friends around though, there's nothing in the rules to prevent you.

Pullet Chicks and Time of Year Hatched. If you buy pullet chicks in January, February, March, or April, they will mature while the days are still getting longer, and that will stimulate them to mature sexually and promptly commence laying. They will continue laying through winter and on to the end of the next summer. Or they may have a late molt that first year. Such pullet laying, though they'll at first lay smaller and fewer eggs than more mature birds, can compensate for the molting time of older birds. Pullets that come into full production at a relatively young age do have a statistically greater tendency to prolapse (part of the tube comes out with the egg). But you'll probably never encounter that in a small flock. Usually they will be fine and finish up their growth normally, together with their egg-laying. Pullets that mature after the days have stopped getting longer will not commence laying until the following spring. These late-laying pullets do lay more eggs, bigger ones, and more fertile eggs with less chance of poor health because they have come to full maturity before commencing laying. In that case, you would order chicks to come in July.

CHICKS FOR MEAT: How many days a year do you want to eat chicken? Once a week? Order 50 quick-growing birds to be raised and processed for the freezer as soon as they reach the target weight. Twice a week? Make that 100 of them. Or, if you're not used to thinking of it by the bird or have a small family, 15 chickens per year per member of your family is a conservative estimate. Remember to include the cockerels from your laying stock (if you're getting straight run) in your count. Lane Morgan again: "A 10–12-week-old Cornish cross is big. Our family of 4 gets at least 2 meals out of it, which affects menu planning and butchering quotas."

If your interest is to get birds for roasting and frying, the broiler breeds are a shortcut to that end. Or try a straight run of a heavy breed. You may get offered a great bargain in cockerels (generally Leghorns). Don't jump at it unless you have lots of virtually free food to give them. It might be called something like "Super Bargains" or "Assorted Surplus." It takes so many more pounds of feed to grow a Leghorn to eating size than it does a broiler breed that the money you save on Leghorn cockerels at the outset is more than offset by the extra feeding expense. Such light-breed cockerels, if not bought by the uninformed, will end up in dog food or livestock food or ground up for fertilizer.

HATCHERY SEXING: Sex-classified chicks are sorted at the hatchery by vent-sexing specialists who work with a lighted magnifying glass strapped to their heads. Accuracy is not absolute—only about 90–95 percent—which is really very good, considering how little they have to base a decision on.

OF DEBEAKING AND DUBBING: The hatchery may offer to "debeak" and "dub" the birds for a small additional fee. I would decline, on the grounds that the expense to you and trauma to the bird is not necessary if you are going to raise them in a halfway humane manner. Nevertheless, here's the data on debeaking and dubbing.

Debeaking. Debeaked birds have about half of the top beak cut off and the end tip of the lower one. At the hatchery this is done with an electrical device that cuts and heat-cauterizes at the same time. You can debeak birds yourself with wire cutters, goat nail trimmers, pit-tooth nippers, or some such. The reason many big production operations have their chicks debeaked is because the natural end of a chick's top beak has a sharp down-curving extension with which they can peck other birds and with which they are said to fling some food out of the trough, causing waste. Objections to debeaking are that debeaked chicks are not as able to drink water and eat food, that they look mutilated and ugly, and that the beak is likely to grow out again anyway, requiring a repeat of the debeaking process. Most small holders, whose birds will not live with the extreme stress and crowding of huge commercial flocks, do not have their chicks debeaked.

Dubbing. "Dubbing" is cutting the bird's comb off close to the head. If it is done to older birds, both comb and wattles will be dubbed, but with mature birds considerable bleeding is a problem. The argument is that this prevents frozen combs. Since frozen combs occur only in severe cold and inadequate housing, and in certain large combed breeds, it really is a rare problem. Furthermore, it is mainly the cock who is at risk from a frozen comb, because his comb stands up. Large-combed hens have a comb that folds over on itself and that helps keep it warm. Dubbing prevents the bird from naturally making enough Vitamin D from the sunlight to be independent of artificial rations—because they do that in their comb, their only unfeathered, unscaled part. Furthermore, if you don't like a large comb, choose one of the many breeds with a small, close-to-the-head "rose" comb. You can do the dubbing yourself using an ordinary sharp scissors to decomb baby chicks. (Dub older birds using tin snips or commercial dubbing shears.) Better yet—to dubbing—just say, "No."

ARRIVAL AND INSPECTION: The ordered birds, after hatching, are immediately shipped by whatever method will get them to the destination within 36–48 hours. Stay in touch with your postal carrier when you're expecting. You may get a phone call from the post office with a background of melodic cheeping. Open your parcel at once in the presence of a postal employee. Count all the live birds. If there are dead birds or if the number you received is not equal to the number you paid for, have the problem verified by the postal employee in writing to the hatchery immediately. They'll make good on it with replacement stock for you.

Places to Buy or Order Poultry

FEED-STORE CHICKS: At Kendrick, the feed store doesn't sell chicks, but apparently in many other places it does. Lane Morgan said, "You don't say much about buying chicks from the feed store, but that's what I do. Find out what day their birds will arrive, and make your purchase several days later. That way someone else, probably with better equipment, has fed and sheltered the babies through those first touchy days. I've gotten 2-week-old birds for the same price as newborns, which saves a lot in food and hassle. This is a specially good deal for turkeys, since they are expensive and accident prone."

MAIL-ORDER SOURCES, MIDWEST

Cynthia Dick sells roller pigeons, ringneck doves, call ducks, mandarins, four kinds of chickens, 12 bantam breeds, etc.: 1054 Fulton Rd., Hedgesville, WV 25427; tillysbarnyard@aol.com; www.tillysbarnyard.home stead.com.

G&K Exotic Farms offers chickens, turkeys, peafowl, guineas, and pheasants: 865-674-6318; fax 865-674-2870; 1061 Leadmine Rd., White Pine, TN 37890; kimbro@worldnet.att.net; www.g-kexoticfarms.com.

Inman Hatcheries sells goslings, ducklings, pheasants, turkeys, chickens: orders 800-843-1962; info 605-225-8122; PO Box 616, Aberdeen, SD 57402-0616.

Eugene W. Leffelman offers chickens, peafowl, pheasants, ducks, geese, turkeys, rabbits, pigeons, and white-tailed deer: 815-857-3607 (call after 6pm); 1785 Lee Center Rd., Amboy, IL 61310.

Murray McMurray Hatchery sells chicks, bantams, ducks, geese, turkeys, guineas, and pheasants. Good source for rare and exotic varieties. Extensive poultry equipment selection for sale. Free color catalog: 515-832-3280; order 800-456-3280 (24-hr); fax 515-832-2213; PO Box 458, Webster City, IA 50595-0458; www.mcmurrayhatchery.com.

Pilgrim Goose Hatchery sells 13 duckling breeds, chicks (specialty Rhode Island Reds and giants), goslings, poults, guineas. Color-illustrated catalog and book list, $1. B/w catalog, free: 216-293-7056; Creek Rd., Williamsfield, OH 44093.

Ridgway Hatchery sells meat-type broilers, white rocks, hamps, reds, barreds, sex links, white leghorns, white pekin, rouen, mallard, khaki-campbell, Indian runner ducklings; embden, toulouse, and Chinese goslings; large white and bronze turkeys; ringneck pheasants; and guineas. Free catalog: orders 800-323-3825; info 740-499-2163; fax 740-499-2828; Box 306, LaRue, OH 43332-0306; www.ridgwayhatchery.com.

Schlecht Farm & Hatchery offers 12 breeds of geese, 15 of ducks, and a large selection of rare breed chicks. Free brochure. Contact: 563-682-7865; 9749 500th Ave., Miles, IA 52064; Schlecht@netins.net.

Joe Schukar offers poultry, pheasants, doves, ducks—eggs, chicks, and adults in the fall: 308-468-6152; PO Box 507, Gibbon, NE 68840.

Welp Hatchery offers 100+ varieties of chicks, turkeys, ducklings, goslings, bantams, guineas. Cornish-Rock broilers available all year. Cordial, efficient service. Free catalog: 800-458-4473; 515-885-2345; 515-885-2346; PO Box 77, Bancroft, IA 50517-0077; www.welphatchery.com.

MAIL-ORDER SOURCES, NORTH CENTRAL

Bob Streich offers pheasants, wild waterfowl, peafowl, swans, chickens, emu, pheasants, geese, cochins, bantam silkies, etc.: 605-338-6797; 26704 481st. Ave., Brandon, SD 57005-7203.

Stromberg Chicks and Gamebirds Unlimited sells chicks, bantams, ducklings, guineas, goslings, turkeys, pheasants, quail, swans, peacocks, and "exhibition birds." Wide selection of rarer breeds. Full range of poultry equipment, books, Havahart traps, incubators: 800-720-1134; 218-587-2222; fax 218-587-4230; Box 400, Pine River, MN 56474; info@strombergs chickens.com; strombergschickens.com.

MAIL-ORDER SOURCES, NORTHEAST

Clearview Stock Farm & Hatchery ships goslings, ducklings, bantams, chickens, turkeys, guineas, gamebirds: 717-365-3234; fax 717-365-3594; Box 399, Gratz, PA 17030.

Hoffman Hatchery offers goslings, ducklings, chicks, guineas, turkeys, bantams, pheasants, quail, chukars, swans, peafowl, books, and equipment. Free catalog: 717-365-3694; PO Box 129, Gratz, PA 17030; www.hoffmanhatchery.com.

John Marth Jr. offers pheasants, chukars, chickens (including Silkie bantams), jungle fowl, guineas, peacocks, doves, and pigeons: 570-676-0435; RR #1, Box 25B, Newfoundland, PA 18445.

Moyer's Chicks offers incubators, fertile eggs, chicks. "Selling over 200,000 per week." Free brochure: 215-536-3155; fax 215-536-8034; 266 E. Paletown Rd., Quakertown, PA 18951-2831; www.moyers chicks.com.

Rainbow Feather Farm offers pheasants, doves, waterfowl, pigeons, and chickens. Send long SASE for complete breed list to Don and Roseann Woodward: 717-734-3625 (evenings); RR 1, Box 339, Honey Grove, PA 17035; birds54@hotmail.com.

Cathy Smith offers pheasants, blue peafowl, chickens, and doves: 717-933-5438; 336 Long Rd., Myerstown, PA 17067; Cathsmith@Paonline.com.

MAIL-ORDER SOURCES, SOUTH

Double R Discount Supply offers 150+ breeds and varieties of chicks (poultry, waterfowl, gamebird), plus incubators. Free catalog: 321-768-1912; 4036 Hield Rd. NW, Palm Bay, FL 32907; Sales@DblRSupply.com; www.DblRSupply.com.

Ideal Hatchery is the only place that offers capons. They also sell the commercial-type white Cornish roosters, etc.: 254-697-6677; fax 254-687-2393; PO Box 591, Cameron, TX 76520; chickenorders@ideal-poultry.com; www.ideal-poultry.com.

Larry Miller offers peafowl, turkeys, cochins, doves, quail, pheasants, etc.: 817-558-0606; 716 Many Oaks, Joshua, TX 76058; lmiller@cniinternet.net.

Gerald Smith offers ducks, geese, turkeys, pigeons, standard chickens and bantams, etc.: 478-934-4286; Rt. 3, Box 2100, Cochran, GA 31014.

Unicorn Woods Hatchery ships chicks, chickens, bantams, cornish, cochins, turkeys, pheasants, ducks (eggs, meat, or exhibition breeds), Saipan jungle fowl, quail, peacocks, etc., by U.S. mail to any U.S. address: Carla J. Quataert; 870-895-4212; HCR 87, Box 832-N, Salem, AR 72576.

MAIL-ORDER SOURCES, WEST

Harder's Hatchery sells "old favorite breeds" of baby chicks, turkeys, ducklings, goslings, guineas, bantams, and gamebirds. Free catalog: 509-659-1423; Ritsville, WA 99169.

Phinney Hatchery, whose motto is "cheepers by the dozen," offers all sorts of standard chicken breeds, turkey poults, ducklings, goslings, and some gamebirds. Free price list: 509-525-2602; 1331 Dell Ave., Walla Walla, WA 99362.

MAIL-ORDER SOURCES, CANADA

Frey's Hatchery hatches eggs mid-March to mid-July: chickens, large white turkeys, broilers, crosses, Barred Plymouth Rock, Rhode Island Reds, ducks, pheasants, and ready-to-lay hens. Contact: 519-664-2291; 80 Northside Dr., St. Jacobs, Ontario N0B 2N0, CANADA; www.freyshatchery.com. *No shipping to U.S.*

Brooding Chicks

If you wait to order your young birds until local temperatures are quite stably warm—and if you have a draft-free place for the chicks—you can make do with a minimal source of heat their first week or so at night and that's it. This is the closest thing you could have to a non-brooding option. If you're going to raise chicks, you've got to learn at least a little about brooding them.

INTRODUCTION TO BROODER STRUCTURES: Newborn chicks are tiny, fragile, and fluffy. The basic characteristics of an adequate brooder setup for your chicks are warm, dry, draft-free, clean and cleanable, escape-proof, safe from predators, and expandable. But it doesn't have to be expensive. Lane Morgan advised, "Distinguish between the ideal and good-enough reality. I've had good results with very funky setups, but then I never raise very many at a time." My mother started her chicks by the wood stove, then put them in the bathtub, then moved them to a shed. Many small growers start them in a basement or garage for 3–4 weeks, then finish them in a garage or shed. Big commercial growers may be brooding in narrow 100-foot brooder houses, one end blocked off by a plastic curtain, which is gradually moved down to make more room.

Whether you have borrowed chicks, bought them, or home-incubated them, your first concern, once they appear in your life, is to supply a mother's warmth. That's what brooders are all about. If your chicks are to be brooded in a special room or small building, it should be tightly constructed, insulated, without drafts, and able to hold a uniform temperature. And yet there should be ventilation enough to move moisture and waste gases out without losing too much heat. If you choose a room (or build a room) in an outbuilding that doesn't have electricity, you can use a heavy-duty extension cord to get power out there. If there is a risk of transmitting disease or parasites in your brooder house, give it a thorough cleaning about 2 weeks before the chicks arrive. Then let it air out a while; fresh, strong, cleaning agents can burn chicks' feet and eyes.

You can buy various styles: a battery brooder that is like a lidded box with a thermostat and heater, or a hover-type brooder that hangs from a ceiling in a brooder room and can handle large numbers of birds of any size. (The "hover" is a very large reflector around the bulb that keeps the heat focused down at the floor level.) Or you can make a homemade brooder. Or you can take the minimalist option.

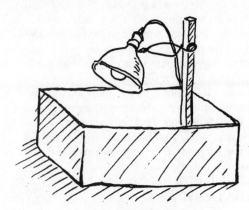

Homemade Brooder

Homemade Cardboard-Box Brooder. The typical homemade incubator involves a light with foil focuser, or heat lamp (or a box just the right distance from a heat source for the temperature you need if you have no electricity). If a bulb is used for heating, keep in mind that infrared is better than white-light because the birds are less likely to pick at each other under infrared. A cardboard box 30 inches square with high sides, situated in a room where the temperature doesn't drop below 65°F, with a 69-watt light bulb shining from overhead could handle 50 chicks to start. Make sure you're not using the type of bulb for indoor suntanning. Chicks can sunburn, too. And don't use a high-wattage bulb, like a 100-watt, because that could be too hot, and bright light in a brooder can result in excessive picking. Such a heat-box arrangement is your brooder. Covering a half to a third of the box top will also retain heat in the hover area. It's ideal to have a 6- by 8-foot space for 100 brooder chicks to allow some growing room.

Adding a "Room." You can add space for chicks who have started out in a cardboard box by cutting out one side of the box and taping on other boxes, as needed, to create additional "run" space, and to provide space in which to offer food and water. Where you cut away the side of the box, hang a piece of cloth. That helps keep heat in the hover box, and the chicks will run in and out of its warmth through the inch or two you leave between the bottom of the cloth partition and the bottom of the box, just as if they were running to and from the warmth of a hovering mother hen.

NOTE: Don't start a fire! This may happen if you have the light bulb too close to flammable litter. Check on this by putting your hand about 2 inches above the brooder floor under the heat. If your skin feels uncomfortably hot, lower the wattage or raise the light or some such. Don't completely cover a brooder. The heat will build up in there and can kill chicks or cause a fire. Overheated chicks will pant.

The Brooder House. A 250-watt infrared lamp, suspended about 18 inches above the floor level, will brood 75 chicks. Large brooder operations use a row of such bulbs with their individual hover areas. An advantage of using more than one bulb is that if one burns out, there is an alternative source of heat in the room. Inside this warm, draft-free building, arrange a little pen with sides made of whatever you want to rig up, and over it hang your heat light from the ceiling.

Chick Fencing. The chicks need boundaries to limit their area at first, help them find their food and water, and keep them from wandering very far from the source of heat. Naturally, you need chick fencing only if you're brooding in an otherwise open area. If you're brooding a small number of chicks in something like a box, it already has sides. Baby chicks can't be put behind chicken wire; they're so little they'll walk right through it. You can buy a wire with finer mesh if you want to use that in your brooder design. You can't use anything very low to fence them in. Baby chicks can fly over short obstacles by the time they're a week old. One good system is to cut cardboard boxes into long sections at least a foot high, then tape or staple the sections together in a circular shape. Make it sturdy enough so it can't possibly fall over. The circle is so the chicks won't have a corner to crowd in, which could result in smothered chicks if you have more than a few in there. And it prevents drafts and keeps them close to the warmth, which should be focused at the center of the circle. Start out with the fencing 3–4 feet out from the heat source. Day by day, as they grow in size and endurance, you can keep adjusting their "fencing" outwards. After a few weeks, your chicks have outgrown the need for fencing and you can remove it and let them run all over their pen's area.

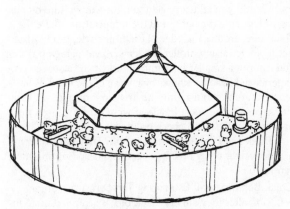

Hover-Type Brooder

Commercial Brooders. You can purchase a ready-made brooder in the size that is practical for you. There is wonderful brooder equipment sold: infrared heat lamp brooders, or big commercial gas brooders and other non-electric styles. The most common and inexpensive style for small-scale brooding is an infrared light with a metal reflector to focus the light and prevent ceiling condensation from dripping on the bulb and exploding it, and a heavy guard wire under the bulb so that if the light fell the bulb wouldn't touch litter and start a fire. Another common brooder-style is the hover-type brooder, which looks like a small flying saucer suspended from the brooder room ceiling on a chain. Larger brooders are equipped with thermostats to control their heating. The principle of a brooder's operation is simple, and directions will come with your equipment.

Wood Stove Brooding. If you have no electricity or fossil fuels, you can still keep chicks warm. Put the chicks in a cardboard box. Put that cardboard box into a larger cardboard box that has a layer of hay, or some other similar insulating material along the bottom; insulate between the walls, too. Cover most of the top with a cloth or some other insulating layer (allow ventilation!). Put the box at a suitable distance from your source of heat. If that isn't warm enough—and in cold weather, or on cold nights— fill a large jar full of very hot water. Wrap it in a towel to prevent burns, and place in the center of the box. Refill with hot water as needed. Check your baby chicks often, including several times a night, until they have outgrown that necessity.

Solar Brooding. The concentration of America's poultry industry in Sun Belt states is partly because of chickens' dependence on warmth, more so than any other livestock. Solar poultry brooding research has been done by the government, and solar brooding has been found to be technically feasible. For details, see *Raising Chickens* by Cynthia Haynes (see "Poultry Books").

TEMPERATURE CONTROL: Turn on the brooder the day before its occupants are to arrive and check to see if you can get the desired temperature.

Checking the Brooder Temperature. To control the temperature in any style of brooder, first you have to know what it is. Use a drugstore human-type oral thermometer or a brooder thermometer (mail-order from poultry suppliers for about $3). An oral thermometer is the most accurate sort. (Be sure and shake it down and wait long enough for the temperature to register fully.) Lay the thermometer just at the edge of the brooder's heat circle. When using a light for warmth, you adjust to get the right temperature by raising or lowering the light until the temperature where the chicks are, around the edge of the heat circle, is 95°F (but not if you're raising broiler chicks; see next paragraph). (Or you can put a smaller bulb into your light-heat socket.) An experienced brooder knows by a wave of the hand if the temperature is about right. The first week or two, while the chicks are at their most fragile, it wouldn't hurt to get up 2 or 3 times a night and check on them.

Broiler chicks should start at 85°F. They don't tolerate heat as well as other breeds—need less brooding and more ventilation.

Chick Behavior and Estimating Temperature. Chick behavior, after they are one week old, is a very accurate indicator of temperature conditions in your brooder (before one week use a thermometer). If it isn't warm enough, they'll huddle directly under the heat source (or in a cold corner). Comfortable chicks make contented chirps. They may signal chilliness with a shrill peeping that says, "Mother, I need you!" If it's too hot in the heat circle under the lamp, they avoid it. They may also spread their wings and pant. Under ideal conditions the chicks will form a circle around the edge of the brooder heat. They won't be in the absolute center. If they are gathering at one side of the brooder, the problem may be a draft. Keep in mind that whenever a door opens, cold air may rush in at floor level—which is where the chicks are. And that draft can instantly and invisibly sweep away the accumulated heat from under the brooder.

Decreasing the Heat. As the chicks grow older, they need less warmth. You decrease the heat 5 degrees a week by raising the heat source, say, 2 inches per week, until it gets down around 70°F. With an electronic brooder, you lower the temperature by changing the setting of the thermostat. Thus their second week you'll have them at 90°F, their third at 85°F, their fourth at 80°F, their fifth at 75°F, and then their sixth at 70°F.

Weaning Completely from the Heat. After the 70°F point (they'll be 6 weeks old), your brooder temperature depends to a large extent on your outside weather conditions. Probably you'll start to turn their heat-source off during the day, but put it back on at night. At this stage, with warm weather outside, you won't be needing the brooder any more at all, except perhaps if the nights are cool. Chicks come out of the egg with fuzz, then gradually grow feathers. In prolonged heat, they actually feather out a little more slowly. Their first feathers are a transitional set; they grow the "real" ones later. Exactly when you turn their heat completely off depends on what the weather conditions outside are and how completely your birds have feathered out— probably a few weeks after you began to turn the heat off in the daytime; it's a judgment call. But I'm getting ahead of the story here. Let's go back to what those baby chicks need.

CHICKS AND LIGHT: For the first week it will help your chicks to be in a lighted area 24 hours a day. It's during this period that they learn where the food, water, and warmth areas are. But make the night light only about 15 watts, since bright lights for brooding tend to create a pecking problem (they are also an inefficient and expensive heat source). Keeping chicks in a dimly lit place and using only small wattage green or red light bulbs in brooders will relieve a pecking problem. Chicks who have been raised under a brooder light, white or infrared, have to be gradually and gently introduced to true darkness when the time comes. They've been accustomed to associating light with warmth and safety, and they may be frightened when the light is gone and pile up and smother one another.

OF FLOORING, CHICK LITTER, AND SPRADDLE LEGS: You don't want the chicks to eat their own droppings. And you don't want them to eat the litter. And you don't want them to slip on their flooring. In the first few days of a chick's life, it is quite vulnerable to developing spraddle legs from slippery flooring. Long-legged varieties are most susceptible. Those early days their leg cartilage has not yet hardened and can easily be gotten out of position. Straw and flat newspaper are the slipperiest surfaces and the most likely to cause spraddle legs; their legs begin to turn sideways at the joint until finally they are turning straight out from each side. There is no cure for spraddle legs.

Safe Flooring. The shipping pads in the bottom of chick mail-order boxes are designed to prevent spraddle legs. For the first week or so you'll want to come up with your own system. Thus, a good covering is clean burlap sacking. Put clean sacking down daily. Or clean rags. (If you wash these, don't load them with bleach. The bleach could interact with material in the feces and result in poisonous gases.) If you are using a battery brooder with a wire bottom and the chicks are so small their legs are slipping through, cover the floor of it with your clean rags for the time being, changing it as needed for sanitation. If you use rags, make sure there are no loose threads that could get wound around a chick and kill or cripple it.

Newspaper Floor Covering. Later, once your chicks have definitely learned what is and isn't food, and their legs have grown strong, you may want to evolve to a thick layer of newspapers. This helps prevent them from eating feces since every day you roll up and take away as many layers of the paper as necessary to make their flooring clean and dry again. Don't use any colored pages as they are loaded with lead. Don't let the newspapers get wet and slippery. If you put a layer of shredded newspaper on top of the flat newspaper it will be more absorbent and will eliminate the slippery factor. Just tear the newspaper in strips, stir it up, and lay it down.

NOTE: Don't ever use newspapers as floor covering for ducklings, goslings, or turkey poults.

Loose Litter: Another option is loose litter, about 2 inches deep. It should be an organic, absorbent material—not straw, which is not absorbent. Don't use sawdust or sand as litter. Sometimes the birds will eat too much of it instead of their food and get an impacted crop and/or gizzard and starve. Sawdust also can become wet and moldy and cause disease. Hay or wood shavings, 2 or 3 inches deep, are good. The basic rule is to use litter pieces that are too big to fit into a chick's mouth—that way you're safe from them eating it—unless it's something utterly harmless, like potting soil, and that actually does work fine. If you use loose litter, turn it daily and remove wet areas. Small chicks are at risk from diarrhea organisms that thrive in wet litter. Large ones that cannot roost and must bed down in their litter (Cornish crosses) especially need it to be kept dry, clean, and fluffy to prevent them from developing dirty breast feathers and breast skin irritations. Once the chicks are 4 weeks old you can keep them safely on almost anything. *Note: Some disinfectant and fragrance sprays will kill chicks.*

Chick Dust. If your initial brooder arrangement is inside your home, soon you'll be wanting to move them elsewhere, for the sake of cleanliness and your health. Baby chicks create a powdery, disagreeable dust that gets everywhere in their environment and is difficult to live with and to keep up with. Small traces of bird protein exit with the bowels. The droppings dry to a powder. Those droppings also tend to contain a microorganism that can cause problems for humans and other creatures who breathe it. Also, chicks molt twice while they are growing up. The first molt is their loss of the fine down they wore at hatching. Shed down, dried droppings, and chick feed all contribute to the chick dust. People who work with birds a lot are subject to hypersensitivity pneumonitis (an allergic reaction in the lungs), also and variously known as bird fancier's, pigeon breeder's, breeder's, or handler's lung disease. Bird feces may also carry an irritating microscopic life form that if it dries, turns to dust, and becomes airborne, can put longtime handlers at higher risk for cancer and any lung disease. This is true of all birds, from parakeets and parrots on; in fact, this latter problem is associated with birds that are kept in the house rather than with barnyard fowl.

NOTE: If you are at all concerned about this possibility or bothered by the chick dust, don't keep birds in your house, and please do wear a dust mask while in the same room with and working with your chicks or adult birds.

SICK AND DEAD BABY CHICKS: It's important to observe your young poultry closely every day. Professionals expect a 2–3 percent mortality rate for chicks. If you find a sick one, separate it from the rest and try TLC (tender, loving care), isolation, and warmth in its own private little hospital box. If you find a dead one, remove it from the pen and bury or burn the body.

HOUSING FOR THE OLDER CHICK: Brooder chicks grow rapidly, and as they grow they require more space. So your chicks will likely go through a series of different brooder arrangements. One common plan is 3-step housing: full-scale brooding for day-old to 6-week-old chicks (6-week-old chicks need twice the space day-olds do); less protective brooding arrangements from 6 weeks to 2 months; then a final shift to your regular chicken house for the pullets. The precise transition ages can vary a lot with your own particular situation. One option is to use a portable coop as a transition home for young birds that have outgrown the brooder, but are not yet ready for the chicken house. In experimental new housing arrangements, you can tell if they're chilled by watching to see if they huddle. If they are acting cold, you need to change something to provide more heat, like with a light bulb. Broilers will go directly from the transition housing to your deep freeze. They'll be ready at 7–10 weeks—whenever they reach 3–4 lb. (the exact weight goal and length of time to get there depends on your breed of bird and its diet). That will probably take about 8 weeks on commercial feed, a few weeks longer on home-devised diet.

Roosting Chicks. Chickens have the urge to roost from age 5 weeks on, and will hop up on a perch to sleep if it's available. Roosts (a long pole works well) 6 inches apart with about a 4-inch space for each bird will be suitable. Their first perch can be as high as a foot. They can hop farther as they get older. Roosts slanted from floor to wall like a ladder help them gradually make the grade. Some growers don't provide broilers with roosts because they say some birds scrape those big breasts on the roosts. They let them sleep on a floor. But Lane Morgan disagrees: "Even my Cornish stupids will roost if I give them a low enough roost. I encourage their roosting because they stay cleaner and it conserves space in their house at night."

Moving into the Chicken House. It's best to delay the chicks' joining of the regular flock until they're big enough that getting picked on won't be a risk to life and limb. Somewhere between 10 and 12 weeks after hatching, you can put them out with your other chickens, depending on their size, the weather, and how well insulated or warmed your chicken house is. Move pullets into the hen house before they begin to lay to prevent throwing them out of the mood, as any major change is likely to do that to chickens. Pullets that are moved after laying has commenced may stop laying and go into a molt. To move larger birds from one housing to another, do so at night, placing them on the roosts in their new quarters so they'll have slept there a night before they go out the door in the morning. That helps them know where home is. If they're still not sure the next night, shoo them in there again, and shut them in for the night. If they're reluctant to go in, let them get a little hungry, then feed them in there.

CHICK AGE AND APPEARANCE: When the chicks are a little more than 4 weeks and a few days old, you'll be able to distinguish the cockerels, who have grown pink combs and clearly visible wattles, from the pullets, who grow and color their decorations slightly later. The final adult plumage starts to grow when the bird is 12 weeks old and will be finished coming in by 16 weeks. To make a pet out of your bird, this 12–16-week period is a good time to carry and pet it frequently. Be gentle, and the fowl will learn to trust you and be your friend.

Chick Water

WATERER TYPES: To make a homemade chick waterer, fill a quart jar with water. Put a shallow bowl upside down over the open mouth of it like a cover. The bowl's diameter should be only a little more than that of the jar top. Quickly turn the whole thing upside down outside the chick pen. The jar will slop for a moment. Slip a match or toothpick under one edge of the jar to keep the water flowing as the chicks need it. Set it down in the chick pen like that. There are also well-designed commercial waterers (and feeders) available mail-order from poultry specialists or from your local feed store. You need a minimum of two 1-gal. waterers per 100 chicks. By the time they're a month old, you'd find it convenient to be using a 5-gal. waterer per 100 chicks. Lane Morgan advised me, "You can buy a plastic base that works with a quart jar. If you use commercial plastic gallon waterers, I'd say get the kind with prongs and slots, not the kind where the top screws all the way onto the base. The screw kind never screws on right."

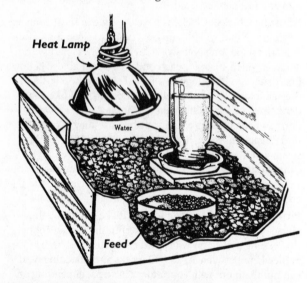

Heat Lamp

Water

Feed

TEACH THEM HOW TO DRINK: Give mail-order chicks food and water immediately after they arrive. Water first—it's most important—then feed. (Unless the chicks arrive to you chilled, in which case warmth is the first priority.) At first your chicks may not realize what to do with the water. When you move them from the mail-order carton into their brooder house arrangement is a good time to teach drinking. Gently and briefly dip their beaks into the water, one by one. They'll quickly catch on. Then others will imitate the ones you showed how. They dip their beaks in, then tilt their heads back and slightly open their beaks to swallow. Separate the ones who have learned how from the ones who have yet to learn and give the slow learners another dip. If the chicks arrived to you chilled, warm them and then serve them lukewarm water with just a little sugar dissolved in it.

KEEP THEIR WATER CLEAN: Chicks drink a lot (about 2½ times as much water by volume as the food they consume), so make sure that drinking water is always available

to them, and that their water supply is kept clean. To do that you'll need to clean and change their water supply at least a couple of times a day, and disinfect the containers once a week in some hot and soapy water or—most powerfully—by boiling them. Put their water supply as far as possible from their food supply so they don't get their feet gummed up with spilled chick food that has gotten damp and stuck to them. Change the newspapers lining the bottom of their housing once or even twice a day to keep their floor dry from water spills and droppings. Be careful you don't spill water into the chick pen, because eating wet food or droppings at this age can make them sick. If they do get into wet food and it sticks onto their feet, or if droppings cling to their rear ends, you need to clean it off very gently. Apply Vaseline where you cleaned them and keep an eye on those chicks after returning them to make sure they don't get into difficulties again.

WATER SUPPLEMENTS: You can buy vitamin and electrolyte supplements to add to your chick water. You don't have to have these, but they don't hurt and may help. There is a special home-grown supplement for the fast-growing broiler chicks, which is helpful to them. The broilers need extra Vitamin D_3 to avoid rickets and crippled legs because of their extremely speedy growth. Cod liver oil added to their drinking water from day 5 to about 4 weeks does the job. Just pour a few drops on the surface of their drinking water daily. You'll need about 4 oz. to supply 25 chicks for that 3-week period. Don't give before day 5 because that might cause diarrhea. After that, if you're giving too much and they get looser bowels, cut back. Or make sure they get lots of direct sunshine.

CHICK WATER DON'TS

1. Don't give water in containers with edges over an inch high.
2. Don't use a container deep enough that a chick could fall in and drown. (If they can, they will.)
3. Don't use a container that chicks could tilt or tip over by jumping up and perching on the edge.
4. Don't have an arrangement that allows any chick droppings to get into the water.
5. Don't give ice-cold water. (Serve it lukewarm, baby-bottle temperature.)
6. Don't let chick drinking water run out.
7. Don't put the water (or food) directly under the heat lamp.

Chick Food

If you have hatched your own chicks, rather than bought them, they won't be hungry right away and shouldn't be fed prematurely. Once you see them start pecking at their litter or flooring, it's time to feed them. (They should be watered before they are fed.) Have feed ready when you put mail-order chicks into their first brooder. And have their litter (if you are using organic litter) covered with newspapers, which are covered with cloth the first 4 days—until they've learned what's food. Mail-order chicks may have been hatched 3 days when they arrive and be ravenously hungry and start eating litter in their instinctive, but uninformed, search for nourishment—which at best would cause them indigestion and at worst, death. Young chicks instinctively peck at anything that is at the same level they're standing on. So, for the first few days or week, feed them on paper plates, pieces of cardboard, newspapers, or in the bottom part of egg cases or small box tops to maximize access to proper feed and encourage them to learn how pleasant eating the right stuff is.

Once they learn to eat food, you can feed them in tuna-size cans or jar lids, or shift them to commercially made trough feeders or other suitable containers. Don't place feeders right under the heat center. Instead, place them like spokes on a wheel, with their main portion out of the central heat area and waterers between them. Plan one inch of feeding space per chick. But by the time they're a month old they'll be needing 3 inches of feeding space per bird, so you'll need double the amount of feeder length they required at the beginning. At any time, you want an arrangement they can get at, but not walk in. And one that won't allow them to waste feed by scratching it out of the container. They also have a tendency to toss it out with their beaks. It will help in that regard if you don't fill their troughs over half full. Research has shown that any poultry, given full-to-the-brim feeders, will waste about ⅓ of the contents! If their feeders are only ¾ full, waste drops to about ⅒ of the contents. At ½ full, waste is down to more like ⅟₂₀. They should clean out one batch before you give them another, so stale feed won't accumulate at the bottom of their feeder. The birds will be put off by the presence of stale feed and won't eat as much, and it could end up causing them diarrhea. Keep feed before them virtually all the time, for at least the first 6 weeks and preferably longer. Check the food supply several times a day.

DIET OPTIONS: When feeding chicks you have 3 choices. You can use commercial feed all the way; feed commercial chick starter at the beginning, phasing into a home-devised diet; or use home-formulated feed all the way. Chickens also need pebbles (grit) to help their gizzards digest food. It's not necessary at this time to feed grit with commercial mash; chickens of any age being fed an all-mash ration can make it without grit. If the feed includes some coarse material or is a home-devised diet, add a very little sand sprinkled over the top. Or you can buy a product called "chick grit." You'll have to increase the size of their grit as they get older. Warning: Consuming too much grit and/or litter will impact the chick crop and gizzard, causing the chick to starve.

Commercial Chick Feed. Whether there is something intrinsically evil about buying feed ready-mixed is a matter of opinion. It's true you can never be completely sure of what's in there. The feed industry considers listing complete amounts of ingredients to be giving away trade formulas, and it doesn't do so. The feed's true "protein" could be from ground cull baby chicks, feathers, slaughterhouse discarded poultry heads and feet, and so forth.

Commercial feeds must be bought in bulk for greatest economy. Industry sources say they shouldn't be stored for more than 3 weeks, but in the real world people store them longer. If you can buy your commercial feed only in 100-lb. quantities, as is frequently true, and you have only a few young birds, you may have them ready for grower ration when you still have half a sack of starter left. The practical wisdom in that situation is to keep on feeding the starter until the sack is empty, and then move them to growers ration. Starter rations are actually the highest in protein of all the types.

Commercial feed comes in 3 sizes: mash, crumbles, and pellet. Chicks tend to scatter and waste the mash, and it's so powdery it's difficult for them to swallow. The pellets are too large for them, so crumbles are best. (You can feed pellets if you mash them.) Feed all they'll eat. Most people have the best success using the commercial starter. Chicks will eat heartily and grow fast. You can continue feeding your chickens with commercial products, moving from the "chick starter," when they are 5 or 6 weeks old, to "growing mash," and from that to the "laying mash," according to directions on the package or feed-store advice. When you move the chicks from one ration to another, take a week to do it, thus making the change gradually: 25 percent new feed at first, phasing into 50 percent and, finally, 75 percent. There is a particular formula of high-protein feed for the fast-growing broilers. Don't feed laying mash too early to your pullets; feed it from about 5 months on.

Starter-Feed Antibiotic. The starter feed contains antibiotic. Chick starter feeds are available at 2 levels of antibiotic content: low and high. If you are able to get prepared chick feed that doesn't have any antibiotic at all in it, it would be less expensive. That antibiotic and expense are 2 reasons why many chicken-owners wish to shift their birds to home-based feed quickly. You can shift any time. Lane Morgan uses antibiotic-laced feed only the first week, then shifts. By then the chicks have more natural resistance to infection. The longer you use the medicated chick starter feed, the more you risk birds becoming antibiotic-dependent and unable to be healthy on their own. "Growing" and "finishing" commercial feeds do not ordinarily contain antibiotics. To be sure, read the feed bag label. Your bird should be off antibiotics for at least 5 days before slaughter, and preferably more.

From Commercial Feed to a Home-Based Diet. Anywhere from the chicks' fourth day on, begin to offer fresh, finely chopped greens as part of their diet, along with finely cracked grain. Barley, wheat, and oats are good. The plain grain should be no more than 5 percent of the diet at first, but you can gradually increase it, and increase the size of the grain bits. Supply sand for grit, then shift to a larger size grit when they are about 8 weeks old. By this age also you can have them completely shifted to the diet described under "protein" in the chicken-food section that comes in a few pages.

Home-Grown Diet All the Way. A young chick eats only a thimbleful of food per day, and that small quantity must supply all its different and complex dietary requirements. Supply a menu made up of 2 parts finely ground wheat, corn (not too much corn), and oats, combined; one part protein—such as fish meal, meat meal, a daily small portion of canned cat food, chopped hard-boiled or scrambled eggs, clabbered milk, yogurt, cottage cheese, or worms, bugs, and grubs (a combination of these is best of all; from variety comes nutritional adequacy); and one part a variety of greens: alfalfa meal, alfalfa leaves, or fresh green stuff—comfrey, chard, clover, lettuce, dandelion, cress, chives, grass, spinach, weeds (finely chopped). Other good diet components for your chicks could be wheat germ, sunflower seeds, powdered seaweed, powdered milk, and linseed meal. Their diet should be about 20 percent protein. To collect worms and bugs for them, lay boards on the ground in your garden, or wherever the harvesting is best, at evening. In the morning pick them up and serve what's alive and gathered underneath them to the chicks. Never mind how disgusting it looks to you. The chicks will love it.

Their necessary Vitamin A comes in the green stuff. They'll also need ground eggshells and/or oyster shell (unless there is another source of calcium in their diet), fine grit or sand for their gizzards, and a sprinkle of salt. As they grow they'll need coarser grit, and can handle coarser grain. After their fourth week, they can eat their grain whole. If they aren't getting any sunshine from which to manufacture Vitamin D, they'll have to have cod-liver oil, or some other form of D. You might ask how this chick diet differs from that suggested for mature birds: it doesn't—except that chicks need proportionately a little more protein and calcium, and they need their grain broken up to start with. (A mother hen breaks it up for them.)

When your weather is warm and sunny, you can let them out to pasture on clean ground after the sun has dried all the dew off the grass—briefly, at first, longer as they get older. Small chicks tire easily and need to rest and get warmed again. Watch carefully as a mother hen would that they don't get chilled or become a meal to a bird of prey or a domestic cat. And perhaps provide a box on its side for shade and coziness.

But keep in mind that chickens, like any other critters, can get spoiled and picky as to what they will and won't eat.

CHICK HEALTH PROBLEMS

Chick Diarrhea, or Coccidiosis. This is a widespread problem for young poultry but is much less common in home flocks than in commercial ones. Coccidiosis is caused by a protozoan parasite that birds pick up from feces. There are many varieties of *Coccidia,* some of which make birds sick and some of which don't. Most varieties trouble only one type of bird and not the others. Symptoms of a serious attack are blood in the droppings and an obviously sick bird. To prevent it: avoid overcrowding, feed a balanced diet, keep food available. Commercial, medicated feeds contain medicine at a low level to permit the birds to develop immunity, or at a high level to control the disease completely. In the absence of such medication, manage your chicks in such a way as to minimize the possibility that they will eat litter or droppings. Refill water containers more than once a day, and sterilize the water containers once a week. Keep the litter dry; remove any portions that have gotten wet. Coccidiosis is more likely to strike in damp, chilly weather, so keep young birds dry and warm.

A home remedy for coccidiosis is to add 1 T. plain vinegar per quart drinking water for 3 days or until the chick droppings look normal again. (Don't give cod liver oil while giving vinegar.) Conspicuously sick or weak chicks that are being persecuted by stronger siblings should be separated into a special hospital-brooder box until they can get their strength back. Dead chicks should be removed from the pen immediately and burned or disposed of in a way that couldn't spread disease to the others.

Pasted Vent. This can be caused by chilling when the chicks are being shipped, although the pasted vent occurs a few days later. You'll notice a chick whose hind end is glopped up with droppings stuck to the vent area. It needs to be cleaned off gently. You can pick it off dry, but it is easier to hold the chick's hind end under lukewarm running water and gently massage loose the dried feces. The fluff around the vent will pull away too, which is a bit hard on the chick, but that can't be helped. After the cleaning, apply Vaseline to the area. Dry the chick's down with a hair-dryer or some such before you put it back with the others.

Picking at Each Other. Penny Anderson of Aitkin, MN, advises me: "If you have chicks picking at each other, cover the picked area thickly with Vaseline so when they pick they get a beak full of goo. Easiest to just put Vaseline on all the chicks' tails when the feathers are starting to come out. I've only had this trouble a couple of times. Haven't figured out why since they have always had a big pen, plenty of light, etc."

Hatching Eggs in an Incubator

The most productive modern chicken breeds (in terms of meat and eggs) are carefully selected genetic strains that won't go broody. So if you want more of them, you have to buy them again from the commercial hatchery—or incubate their eggs yourself. Home incubation is actually a practical option, especially with the inexpensive, but functional, small incubators available for sale. Even the smallest size, which will hold about a dozen eggs, can keep them adequately warm, humidified, and turning. Nevertheless, you're bound to have some eggs that don't hatch. Fifty percent is a poor hatch rate, 70 percent about average, and 85–90 percent is very good. If you have an incubator and can buy fertile eggs locally for reasonable prices, it's probably cheaper than mail-ordering.

OF EGGS AND HEREDITY: Look carefully to see whether one end of the egg is pointy or round. Pointy-ended eggs make roasters, says Ellinor Nurnberg of Ontario, Canada. Round-ended ones make hens. This method is 90% accurate. If you collect eggs from hybrids and crosses the offspring will not be like the parents. Raise purebred chickens of a kind you like. Then you know what you have, and you know what you're going to get. To raise crosses you'd have to do your own crossing by finding out what 2 kinds of chickens result in the cross you want, and then breed them. Whatever roosters, hens, and eggs you choose, choose the best: birds that conform to their established breed characteristics for fancy breeds, and birds that carry desirable traits of egg-laying, egg size, good health for egg–meat production breeds. If you're breeding from birds who are in their first laying season ever, wait to begin storing eggs for incubation until the hens have been laying several weeks. The first eggs tend to be smaller and less uniform in size, with lower fertility rates.

GETTING HATCHABLE EGGS

Diet. For prime hatchability of your eggs be sure to feed your breeding birds a diet high in protein with plenty of greens and comparatively little grain. The bird, if offered excessive grain, tends to fill up on it, like a kid with junk food, when what she really needs are the protein and greens. Laying mash is not a suitable feed for birds you want to hatch chicks from, but there is a special commercial feed for them called "breeder's ration." Free-running birds will do fine, or you can offer the home-based diet (see "Protein"). Both the roosters and hens involved also need to be fed regularly and generously since a rooster's reaction to loss of body weight from short rations can be sterility, and a hen's reaction is to quit laying for a long time. In general, the more eggs a hen is laying, the more likely her eggs are to be good hatchers, because she's in such prime health. The lighter the yolk, the less hatchable your eggs will tend to be.

Rooster. If you don't have a rooster among your chickens, none of the eggs will hatch; you need that daddy chicken for fertile eggs. This is elementary birds-and-bees data, but I've met city folks who've never stopped to consider such details. Furthermore, the younger the rooster, the more likely his eggs will be fertile. (And the younger the hen, the more likely her eggs will be fertile.) A young light-breed rooster can fertilize a harem of 10–20 hens, while an old rooster can keep up with only 5–10 hens. A heavy-breed rooster, even a young one, shouldn't be assigned more than 8–12 hens. A bantam rooster is best matched with a harem of from 2–5 hens. Getting the right number of roosters for your hens takes delicate guesswork. Too many roosters causes the egg-fertility rate to go down, because then they spend more time fighting with each other than they do courting—or the egg production can go down because the hens are getting hassled too much. If there is only 1 hen per rooster, she can end up in really bad shape from too much mounting. And your hen must be compatible with your rooster, because some hens, to some roosters, will say "No."

A rooster with a frozen comb won't be sexually active until his comb heals up, which can take several weeks. A molting rooster isn't interested either. Birds in batteries basically don't reproduce naturally, because of the low ceiling. You have to raise the roof, or artificially inseminate (see "Artificial Insemination" under "Turkeys").

For a fertile egg the hen needs to have been inseminated no sooner than 24 hours before laying, and no later than 2 to 3 weeks. There is no way to look at an egg and know if that egg's mother has had a passionate embrace from a rooster in the required time frame. You'd just have to hope for the best and proceed. Once incubation has begun you can tell if the egg is fertile by candling it (see "Candling the Eggs"). But if you have actually seen the rooster mounting hens, you can start collecting eggs. A rooster has no penis. He breeds by simply pressing his vent to the hen's and extruding semen into it.

Daylight. No matter what the age of your rooster, he will be more fertile between March and May than he is during the other months of the year. More daylight causes his semen output to increase. Commercial egg-laying breeds may lay year-round; more natural breeds begin laying in February and will have fertilized eggs by March or April. That's because it takes the rooster longer to get going and become fertile than it does the hen. You can cause a rooster to get fertile earlier by extending his hours of light to 14 hours per day and warming him to 60°F. Five weeks after that change, approximately, he will get in the mood. It takes the hen 2 or 3 weeks after the days get long enough to have fertile eggs.

Handling and Labeling Eggs-in-Waiting. Gather them before night, if your nights are chilly, to keep them from possibly harmful low temperatures. Handle the eggs very gently and keep them either on their side or with the large end up—never with the small end up as that may cause the air cell located in the large end to rupture. Choose normal shaped, normal sized, uncracked ones. Don't wash eggs-in-waiting. The water could carry the very bacteria you're trying to avoid through the shell's pores and into the egg. If something on the egg shell is a real problem, buff it off gently. Yet very dirty eggs have been washed by desperate owners (less than 3 minutes in water 110–115°F), and the chicks lived to peep the tale. If you are incubating eggs from a variety of poultry breeds, it may help you to write on each egg—in pencil—a code designation for the breed. Write on the small end of the egg, because the large end

gets broken away in the hatching process. You might write, for example, "M" for mallard and "L" for Leghorn. If you are keeping track of different genetic lines of the same breed you can give each pen a different number. In that case, you might have L1, L2, and L3, for eggs from 3 different pens of Leghorns.

Storing Eggs-in-Waiting. Placing the eggs in egg cartons works nicely, at a temperature of 45–60°F, in a place that has at least reasonable humidity. That temperature won't kill the embryo, but it will keep it from commencing development. Don't store them in an air-conditioned room. Air conditioning removes moisture, which is bad for the eggs. The temperature of your household refrigerator is probably lower than desirable and would reduce hatchability. Don't let the eggs that you plan to incubate go below 40°F, which will kill the embryo, or above 80°F, which would cause a slow growth of the embryo that weakens and eventually kills it. Actually, the embryo starts to develop at any temperature above 68°F, but the growth rate becomes a major risk above 80°F. Eggs that are going to be incubated should be turned or tipped 3 times a day. The easy way to accomplish that is by raising one end of the egg carton. Then, next time, raise the other end. Start incubating eggs from 1 to 14 days after laying, better in the first week than in the second.

INCUBATOR TYPES: You can order incubating equipment to handle almost any number of eggs—from a dozen to 75,000. Most incubators are electric, but there are non-electric (kerosene, oil) models available. Each incubator comes supplied with detailed directions, and they'll work best if you follow those instructions very carefully. If you have a new incubator, set it up and level it. Run it a couple days to be certain it's working as it should. Test to see if it's keeping the temperature you want. Make sure the moisture pan has water. Before using an incubator that has been used before, clean it carefully. Or you can make a homemade incubator.

Drawer from Incubator

Homemade Incubator. The proper brooding temperature for almost all varieties of eggs is 99.75°F (which is just exactly the temperature under a mama hen). The most primitive homemade incubator is something like a bucket with eggs in it. The eggs are wrapped in a cloth and a light bulb is suspended over the top. This is the least likely to work, and yet I know of people who have hatched chicks with exactly such an arrangement. What you're striving toward is a heat source that can keep about a 2- or 3-square-foot area at approximately that 99.75°F. You can make a better box-style incubator out of a Styrofoam cooler, or a cardboard or plywood box. If you make the top side of glass, you'll be able to watch the hatching. A plywood incubator with a 40-watt light bulb should be about 11 inches high, 11 inches wide, and 16 inches long, with a hinged front side for a door. With ⅜-inch ventilation holes on each side—near the top of 2 sides, near the bottom of the other two—you get a natural air circulation inside your incubator. The eggs should be placed in a tray made of wire mesh fastened to a wooden frame 2 inches off the bottom. A water pan should be placed on the bottom of the incubator underneath the eggs. To test the temperature of the incubator lay a human oral thermometer among the eggs. It's all quite adjustable: the wattage of your bulb, the material and size of the box—so long as you end up with the temperature you want in the place you want it.

Commercial Incubators. If you're buying an incubator, you must first choose between a still-air incubator and a circulated-air incubator. The still-air incubators are the smallest—with capacities of about 1,100 eggs—and least expensive. Still-air incubators depend on gravity to move air through vents on the top and bottom of the incubator. The operating temperature of a still-air incubator is always set a little higher than that of a forced-draft machine—101.5–102.75°F, depending on the variety of egg. (If you don't know the recommended temperature, go with 102°F, and you'll probably be fine.) You have to be home every day at certain times to turn the eggs. The cheapest, smallest models of all do not have a thermostat and are poorly insulated. Just as with incubating with a light bulb, this is not as cost-efficient or reliable as using more sophisticated equipment. The Hova Bator Incubators are well thought of for hatching small batches of eggs. Incubators that turn the eggs for you generally use either a mechanism that rolls the eggs or actually physically turns them. Avoid the "rollers" because eggs tend to get cracked.

Circulated or "forced" air incubators are used by large commercial hatcheries. They have fans that move air around the eggs. They cost more but give you better hatching percentages because of the improved control of the incubator environment and because the eggs are turned in a tray rather than rolled. With automatic egg-turning you are a lot freer to be away from home. Big models can hatch very large quantities of eggs. Humidaire incubators are expensive but give high-quality service. If you are planning to hatch very small eggs such as quail, ask your supplier for special advice on your incubator model.

HUMIDITY: During incubation eggs lose some weight due to evaporation of the contents. The presence of humidity helps control that loss. Humidity helps your eggs to hatch. Too much humidity, however, results in a chick too large to work its way out of the shell. Too little humidity results in a chick that is glued in there.

Measuring Humidity. Measuring incubator humidity is done with a wet-bulb thermometer. "Relative humidity" is determined by comparing the difference between the dry-bulb temperature reading and the wet-bulb reading. If the recommended relative humidity is 62 percent (correct for large turkey eggs during the first 25 days), then at a dry bulb reading of 99.5°F, the wet-bulb reading will be 87.5°F. If you have a hygrometer you can measure the humidity in your incubator air. You're aiming for a wet-bulb reading of 85–87°F the first 18 days of incubation (60 percent relative humidity), and 89–90°F the last 3 days (70 percent relative humidity).

Increasing Humidity. Incubator operators generally try to raise the humidity the last few days of the process. If the relative humidity wanted is 70 percent (correct for the last 3 days of turkey eggs) then the machine will be set at 99.5°F, and you'll be looking for a wet-bulb reading of about 90°F. Humidity in still-air incubators usually comes from an evaporation pan in the bottom of the machine. A soaked sponge sitting in the pan can increase humidity. If the weather is dry or the incubator is opened frequently you can supplement humidity by using a sprayer that emits a fine luke-warm water mist. Humidity is added by increasing the amount of evaporation area or by changing the ventilation; reducing the ventilation increases the humidity, and, in turn, increasing the ventilation decreases the humidity.

INCUBATOR TEMPERATURE: The room in which you keep an incubator should be well-ventilated and at a temperature of around 60–70°F. Incubators (and brooders) are engineered to raise normal room temperature of about 70°F up to the required temperature, and they don't work properly in an unheated building and/or in cold weather. So don't let your incubator sit in the sunshine, or near a heater, near a window, or in a draft because any of those might be more than the heat control system can handle. Don't let the eggs ever get over 103°F. That would probably kill them. A forced-air incubator should be set for 99.5°F; a still-air model is set for 102°F.

ADJUSTING TEMPERATURE SETTING: Each variety of bird has a specific number of days needed to hatch its eggs. If your eggs hatch in fewer than that number of days, it suggests that the incubator temperature was set a little too high. Lower that setting 0.5–1°F and incubate another batch of that variety of egg. On the other hand, if your eggs took longer than the predicted number of days, then you should raise the incubator temperature the same amount. After several trial runs of this sort, you'll know the best temperature to set your incubator at in your particular environment.

Cooling. Most incubators are modeled on the original hen, and they cool the eggs 15 minutes a day—for 5 minutes at a time—which may or may not help. Circulated-air incubators are equipped with cooling systems. So if the heat system gets turned off for a while, don't panic. Maybe it was like a mother hen leaving the eggs once a day to get food and water. Quite likely the eggs will be all right, though maybe a day later in hatching. If the electricity should go off for a long time while you're incubating, try to keep the eggs warm anyway, by enclosing the incubator in a down sleeping bag, or moving it near an alternative heat source.

TURNING THE EGG: Faithful, frequent turning is essential to the embryo's proper development. A hen on the nest instinctively does that too. Not turning the egg regularly can result in a crippled or deformed chick, the death of the embryo, or a chick that can't hatch out properly (this is because turning prevents the embryo from sticking to the surrounding membrane, which can happen if it stays in one position too long).

1. Turn the egg from a fourth to halfway around at least 3 or 5 times a day. This helps the network of fine blood vessels through which an embryo breathes to finish developing. Some incubators automatically turn the eggs once an hour.

2. The odd number of turns will ensure that the eggs will be on opposite "sides" during the long nights, rather than always resting in the same position.

3. The way to tell where you're at is to mark an "X" on the egg and turn the mark up one time and down the next.

4. Any time you write on an egg, use a pencil, not a ballpoint pen or marker pen. Ink may be absorbed through the shell pores and may harm the embryo.

5. Be extremely careful not to cause shock or jarring to the egg when you turn it, especially in its first 24 hours, when certain delicate blood vessels are just forming. Some incubator operators skip that first day completely, not even opening the incubator door once, and start the turnings with day 2.

6. After the eighteenth day of incubation, quit turning the eggs. If you are hatching the eggs of a species other than chickens, quit turning 3 days before their expected hatching date.

7. From the tenth day on, make sure that the large end of the egg is at least somewhat up. Around the twelfth to fourteenth days, the chick takes a lengthwise position in the egg. If the small end of the egg is up at this stage the chick develops with its head in that end. With its head in the small end, a chick may manage to pip (peck a hole in) the shell, but it's practically impossible for it to hatch clear out. In a broody hen's nest, under natural circumstances, an egg lying flat will just naturally have the larger end a little more elevated. In the incubator you consciously have to make sure it's like that.

VENTILATION: Whether you're using a homemade incubator or a commercial one, you need ventilation for it, because the developing baby chicks are taking in oxygen and breathing out carbon dioxide right through tiny holes in the shell. Without an adequate air supply, the embryo will suffocate.

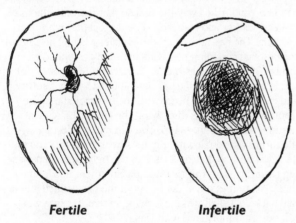

Fertile   **Infertile**

CANDLING THE EGGS: Candling, once done with a candle, is achieved by shining a powerful light through the egg in a dark room. Specific designs vary widely. You can use a slide projector, or a small box with a 40-watt light bulb enclosed in it, the insides covered with black paper, and just 1 opening, slightly smaller than egg-sized, through which you view the egg. You can buy a commercially designed candling box. Any method that enables you to thus examine an egg against a bright light in a dark room will work for white-shelled eggs; brown-shelled eggs take a longer

time, but you can eventually identify an embryo in them too. The darker the egg's color, the harder it is to make out what is going on in there. To test eggs, hold each one up against the opening through which the light is coming, broad end upward (always!), and peer through it.

There is no way to know for sure that an egg is fertile without candling it. (Or opening it.) Some growers candle after 72 hours of incubation, when the fertile eggs have a typical blood vessel formation that looks like a spider. Some growers don't candle until 3 days before the scheduled hatch. (Eggs removed for being infertile at 72 hours or at 9 days can still be eaten.) Eggs in which the embryo has died and is now rotting must be removed because that process releases harmful gases and uses up incubator oxygen, and the spoiling egg may explode and scatter bacteria-loaded glop on normally developing eggs. If you're candling the eggs of a setting hen, do it while she's on her daily break. You may candle at any time you're concerned that the chick embryos might have been harmed by something. In such a case, wait several days after the trauma, to give the egg a chance to recover or perish, then candle.

Candling Signs. When you candle an egg, you will see one of the following: A clear egg means the egg is infertile or the embryo's development stopped very early. Remove it from incubator. A dark haze or grayish clouds mean the egg is rotting. (Note: At 2 weeks of incubation, fertile and normally developing eggs will be nearly dark throughout.) A dark red circle with no veins means the embryo has died. A fine network of veins radiating from a dark center means the embryo is developing normally.

If you candle a few days before hatching is expected, the fertile eggs will permit light only through the large end of the egg. The rest of it will appear dark or black in color.

THE PIPPING: Somewhere between the 19th and 22nd day of incubation, your egg will hatch—if it's going to. The chick has been getting food and water from the yolk, and oxygen from the air that comes in through the shell's pores. It took in calcium from the shell to help form its bones. The last thing the chick does before pipping (to "pip" is to make a hole in the shell) is to, over the last several days before hatching, draw the yolk into its body. The yolk goes in through its connection (like an umbilical connection) to the chick's lower abdomen. The drawn-in yolk makes the chick's abdomen bulge. The chick has to finish pulling the yolk sac into itself through its umbilical opening, and then grow that opening closed. At the same time, the chick swallows what is left of the egg's white. (That's why chicks can be sent by mail—that yolk can nourish them for as long as 72 hours after hatching.)

Starting as early as the eighteenth day, the baby chick may begin picking at its shell from the inside. It pecks its way through to the egg's air space and takes a breath. Once the chick's head is in the air space you can hear it loudly peeping inside the shell. The ready-to-hatch chick has an "egg tooth," which is a sharp little extension on the end of its beak. (A few days after hatching, the egg tooth drops off.) On the 21st day, or thereabouts, depending on if the incubation was a little cooler or warmer than normal, the chick pecks a small hole in the shell. It has pipped. Incidentally, it's important that you leave the eggs completely alone during this pipping and hatching period; avoid even opening the incubator.

THE HATCHING: Making the hole to the egg's air space was hard work for the chick. It's tired now and goes to sleep for hours. When it awakens it goes back to work on the hole, pecking eagerly. As it pecks, it is gradually rotating its body inside the egg. The effect is that the crack it is creating gradually comes to extend in a straight line, which gets longer and longer until it is almost all the way around the egg. Then the chick gives a powerful kick with its big feet and it is out of the shell. It takes the chick from several hours to a day or two to get from pipped to clear out of the shell, and then a couple hours more, once it gets free, to finish drying off. When the chick is first out of the shell it is wet and tired. Don't try to help it free or rush the process. If you peel the shell off for the chick, thinking to help, the chick will probably be even worse off. It may still be in the process of drawing the last of the yolk into its body. (Note: Helping a chick out of the egg has been done, but it's a delicate business needing a knowledgeable person.) If a significant number of your chicks pip, but don't finish coming out of the egg, your humidity was too low. (Raise the humidity level the last 3 days before the hatching.)

The just-hatched chick rests on its stomach for a little while, and if you didn't know better, you might think it was sick. When the chick first tries to walk, it can't. It hobbles, using its wings to help. The chick gradually dries and gains strength. After they hatch, leave chicks in the incubator until they finish drying off and get fluffy (12–24 hours). They don't need food yet, and it can actually harm them to be fed too soon. Baby chicks can scamper about as soon as they are rested and dried off from hatching. Then you can move them to your brooder. Clean the incubator thoroughly before storing it.

SEXING DAY-OLD CHICKS: To get started at doing your own chick vent sexing you need a magnifying glass and the book called *Sexing,* compiled by Mr. Stromberg, published and sold by Stromberg Publishing Company, Pine River, MN 56474. It's very thorough, covers sexing many varieties of poultry, and includes diagrams and photos.

Chickens That Hatch Their Own Eggs

"Setting" or "brooding" are words that mark that dramatic turning point when a hen decides to start her family. Then she stops just laying her eggs and walking away, and instead she stays to sit on them, keep them warm, and so incubate out a family. It's desirable or undesirable—depending on whether you want chicks or eggs. Or whether you want her to incubate or your machine to incubate. You can recognize a broody because her manner of speech changes from the everyday sing-song to a lower-pitched "come here" cluck that she will use to call her chicks. There's no known way to force a hen to get broody. A dimly lit, private, comfy nest with several eggs in it may help incline her that way. When I was young, several of the hens in my mother's flock would be broody at any one time. Five years ago you might get 5 hens that would go broody from a flock of 50 commercial-breed layers. Now scarcely one out of a 100 of them will try. And the one that does is likely to forget all about it after a few days on the nest, get up, walk away, and not return. If you want a hen to hatch out some eggs, you'd be best off choosing one from among the breeds that are known to still have genes for that behavior. (See the breed descriptions at the beginning of this chapter.)

A good reference on this subject is *Bantams: A Complete Pet Owner's Manual* by Helga Fritzsche.

THE BROODING: Just as soon as the weather starts to get nice, your broody-capable hen begins to want to set. A roaming chicken may make a nest in some secret place where she thinks it will be dry and safe and far from all the fleas and mites that may infest a chicken house. (Young birds are extra vulnerable to ectoparasites.) Or, in a hen house, she may choose the place where she is used to laying her eggs. She begins to lay eggs in the nest, an egg a day. Each day, before and after her laying, she sits a little longer on there. Under natural conditions a good setting hen will lay 10–14 eggs in her nest. There may be more than 1 hen laying in the same nest. Or you may not want every one of those eggs to be set. In that case, mark with a pencil the ones you're going to let her set and take the rest. When she's ready to incubate the eggs seriously, she may perfect her nest by picking feathers off her breast with her beak; these feathers will help insulate the nest. By exposing breast skin she is also able to share her body heat more efficiently with the eggs.

Once a hen has begun to set, you can, if she is in an absolutely unacceptable place, try to move her (carefully!) to a more suitable brooding nest that you have prepared. But brooding hens need to be undisturbed, and the move itself may cause her to give it up because of the disturbance. If you have more than 1 hen setting at a time, it helps if they are reasonably far from each other, perhaps in separate portable coops. But, again, it's risky to move them. Another preparation might be to sprinkle the setting hen with a louse-repellent powder, once you separate her from the rest of them.

Nest Design. The brooding nest should be roomy enough that the hen can turn around in it and turn her eggs, and near enough to the ground that the chicks won't take a disastrous fall overboard once they hatch—although they are very light and tend to survive such falls well. (After they are hatched you'll take away the nest so that then the chicks can easily enter and leave their shelter together with their mother.) The typical human-designed egg-laying nest is not the best egg-brooding nest. Chickens are descended from ground-nesting species, rather than tree-nesting ones. An ideal nest is a little wooden house about 15 inches square and at least 16 inches deep, with the top roofed and the front side open. It sits directly on the ground. The ideal nesting material is grass turf. You can make a nest by laying the turf grass-side down, or grass-side up, or you can make a thicker nest by cutting 2 turfs of the right size, then placing their dirt sides together and placing them inside. In either case, pound down the center of the nest sufficiently to make it into a shallow saucer-shape so that the eggs won't roll out. And moisten it with water.

Eggs Per Hen. A large hen that can cover and keep warm 14 regular-sized eggs will have to be given proportionately fewer if some of them are exceptionally large: 6–7 turkey eggs, 9–11 duck eggs, 4–5 goose eggs. Those numbers are not absolute but average: it all comes down to how large—and well-feathered—the bird is, and how large the eggs are. Insofar as possible, match egg size to bird. A small bantam hen finds a goose egg awkward to sit on; large birds are likely to break very small eggs (like quail). A bantam hen that isn't heavily feathered may be able to cover only 8 eggs or so. Don't give a hen more eggs than she can adequately cover. If you do, you may lose the whole clutch, because she rotates eggs from the inside to the outside of the nest, so they'd all get chilled sooner or later. You can try the clutch on for size so to speak: give the eggs to her, and then look to see if she can cover them all. If you have goose eggs under a hen, you'll have to turn them 3 times a day yourself, because they are too big and heavy for a chicken to get properly turned.

Eggs-in-Waiting. Some chicken-owners, anxious to assist nature, collect the eggs and care for them as with incubator eggs-in-waiting until the hen actually commences setting. Since it's impossible to predict exactly what day she'll go broody, such eggs are marked with pencil stating the date collected. When the hen does commence setting, you supply her with a clutch selected from the eggs fresh enough to be the best bets for hatchability.

Egg Adoption. After a hen has begun to set, on one of the first few nights she stays on the nest, slip the eggs to be adopted under her late at night. It can be disastrous to put eggs under her after she's already been setting very many days because after 23 or more days of faithful egg-attendance, the hen may say "to-Hell-with-it" and leave the nest. On the other hand, many modern hens have such a weakened broody instinct that they are not dependable brooders and will soon give up and leave the eggs anyway. If you're worried your hen might not be dependable, let her set on fake eggs for a few days. Take her off the eggs a couple times. If she gets back on the nest each time, she's a good bet and deserves some real eggs to hatch. While she's setting, she will be very protective of her eggs and upset with you as soon as she realizes you're planning to do something under her. She'll peck at you with her hard little beak, and it can do damage. Wear a heavy shirt with long sleeves. You could wear a mitten, but I'd rather take a peck than take a chance with fumbling the eggs. Place them carefully under her, one by one, giving her a chance to receive and arrange to her satisfaction each individual one.

Inter-Species Brooding and Mothering. If you have commercial breeds as well as ones that will go broody, you can put their eggs under the broody hen. Setting hens of breeds that are good broodies and good mothers will hatch and try to mother even large eggs like those of ducks or geese, although they will get quite unhappy when those "chicks" jump into water and swim. If you want an egg to be adopted, follow the rules for eggs-in-waiting. Rare eggs that you're eager to try hatching can be kept for 4–5 weeks—until you have a broody hen that's just starting to set a clutch of eggs. The long wait will lower hatchability, but you might still get offspring. If there are eggs hatching at widely varying times, the hen may choose to follow an existing family and give up on the unhatched eggs. (It may help to take the first few hatchlings into the house for nurturing.) If all the eggs are low hatchers, she may give up before they're done. As you get to know your hens better, you'll learn which you can count on to stay with it for a long incubation.

Days to Hatch. Chicken eggs, all breeds, take an average of 21 days to hatch. That's exactly 3 weeks. But the length of time for a specific egg can vary from 19 to 22 days or more. If the hen continued laying eggs for a few days after she started setting, chicks may appear for a day or two. Or maybe another hen laid eggs in the nest during some of the

brooder's time off the nest. Those will also hatch later. Any eggs left after the brooder gives up probably aren't going to hatch at all. A difficulty of inter-species egg adoption is that various eggs will have varying days to hatch. Pheasant, Bobwhite quail, and Chukar partridge eggs take 23–25 days to hatch. Guinea eggs take 26–28 days. Turkey, duck, and peafowl eggs take 28 days. Goose eggs take 29–31 days. Muscovy duck eggs take 33–35 days, and swan eggs take 35–37 days.

Human body warmth is just right to hatch eggs. Women of ample mammary endowment have incubated eggs kept between their breasts for the necessary number of days!

The Brooding Routine. Now your hen has her final clutch of eggs to brood. She sets on the nest for 3 weeks. On the first night she stays on the eggs, you can start counting toward 21. Many times a day she turns each egg in her nest very carefully halfway over and rotates eggs on the outside of the nest to the inside—which ensures equal sharing of the warmest and coolest locations in her nest by all the eggs. The broody hen is a willing martyr. She eats very little. She loses weight and her feathers get duller. She's very irritable toward visitors: she clucks, ruffles her feathers, even pecks at them. Now that she's seriously setting, she leaves her nest only once a day for food and water. She'll be gone only about 15 minutes, or maybe a half hour, if the weather is warm and the sun is shining so she doesn't worry as much about the eggs' chilling. Like a chick in the egg, a setting hen is receiving nourishment independently because, once she starts to set, she stops laying and instead begins to absorb the food energy stored in her conveyer belt of formerly developing eggs. Yet it's a friendly, helpful act to also leave fresh food and clean water close by for her. Her feeding excursion is a good time for you to peek and see what her nest looks like. But don't handle her eggs or nest while she's gone. Too much of a foreign scent around could cause her to leave that nest and refuse to return to it again.

She talks to her chicks while they're still in the egg and has a good sense of what's going on with them in there. If something like a severe thunderstorm or a prolonged chilling kills all the chicks in their eggs, the hen will know it. Be careful you don't accidentally shut a setting hen away from her eggs. She'll be frantic, and with good reason. Nevertheless, eggs that have been uncovered a night are not necessarily dead, though it may set the hatching back a day. The last 24 hours before hatching, she won't leave her nest even for the usual food and water recess.

Humidity Assistance. You can help keep the humidity right by keeping the earth between the 2 turfs damp. If the weather is seriously dry, you can also help the hen by adding humidity. Some growers do that by spraying her eggs with a light mist of luke-warm water once a day, while she is on her break, starting on the 16th day. Other growers believe that spraying water on incubating chicken eggs promotes fungal growth and embryonic death and suggest instead flotation of the eggs—on the 19th day of incubation—in water that is exactly 97°F and for only 1 minute. But in real life it doesn't have to be that exact. Certain other species require even more humidity and even stronger measures. (See "The Waterfowl: Ducks and Geese.")

THE MOTHERING

Taking in the First-Hatched Chicks. A newly hatched chick is wet and could be fatally chilled if the mother isn't sitting on it to dry it and keep it warm. Some folks feel it's best to take the first-hatched chicks into the house—once they're safely separated from the egg and dried off. That's to save the hen the conflict of wondering if she should sit on the remaining eggs or follow lively chicks that have jumped out of the nest and are out in the cold peeping mournfully and maybe dying of chill. For just a few chicks that soon will be returned to the mother, keep them in a warm, dark place in the house—maybe in a box lined with newspaper and partly covered with warm cloth. Put the box where the brooding temperature is right, near a heater or under a light. Give them food and water using the general directions for chick care. It can also be a favor to the hen to pull out from under her the abandoned shells of fully hatched chicks.

Returning Chicks or Adoption. Return your borrowed chicks, if possible, the first night after the hatching is finished and the hen has been moving about with her chicks. This is also the time to give her any chicks you want adopted. A hen can mother more chicks than she can hatch. She can mother as many as she can hover over and cover when they need warmth. She doesn't literally sit on top of them; instead she stands and covers them—a blanket of warm feathers fluffed out all around them—plus dispenses the heat coming directly off the bare spots on her breast where she pulled out her feathers. Hens have been known to bring up as many as 25 chicks. So, if you have access to orphan chicks, or your own incubator chicks, or mail-order chicks, and if the timing is right, you can add them to the hen's family at this stage. The important thing is that your chicks, to be successfully adopted, have to be the same age as the hen's own chicks—preferably just 1 or 2 days old. Older chicks won't be as likely to obey the hen, and the hen will be more likely to reject them.

Putting Chicks Under a Hen. To accomplish the return or adoption of chicks is just like adding eggs-in-waiting to a hen's clutch. You wait until late at night, then slip each chick under her. The chick will be attracted to her warmth and will nestle under her. She'll fluff up more as needed and cuddle the new ones together with her others. To give chicks to a hen who has been allowed to set on fake eggs, put the chicks under her as above, taking away a dummy egg after each chick has been placed under her. You can't get a chicken to adopt chicks unless first she has become broody and set for 3 weeks or so. That's when she gets her mothering instinct activated. She might kill chicks given to her prematurely. These things have to unfold naturally, and there's a time for this and a time for that.

Chick Rejection and Obedience. Check the next day to see if she's rejected a chick. She does that by pecking at it whenever it comes near. It will soon give up and go hide its head because she won't peck at it if its bright eyes aren't showing. You can try to put the outcast chick under another hen, or raise it yourself in the house. You can't change chicks from one hen to another if their original mother is nearby in the same poultry flock. The chicks will remember the sound of their own mother's voice and always want to go back to her. And if you did inter-species brooding, you can't count on the young of very different species—guineas, wild ducks, peafowl—to follow and obey a hen mother. You have to watch and see if the babies are successfully bonding to the adoptive parent. If not, you'll have to mother them yourself.

Chicken Mothering, Food/Water. Hens, especially ones who are descended from a line of mothers who hatched and mothered their own chicks, can be very wise mothers. After only a few hours, the chicks know their mother. She teaches her chicks to come when called and to eat and drink. (Make food and water available. If it seems like it's taking time for the chicks to get started, remember they are equipped at hatching for 3 days in a desert. But if she's an inexperienced or inadequate mother, you can help by showing the chicks how to nourish themselves, same as for brooder chicks.) An experienced mother cracks seeds that are too large for the chicks in her beak and feeds them the small pieces. She teaches them what is and isn't good to eat. She'll find a bug, put it down where she wants them to gather, call the chicks, and tell them if it is or isn't good food.

Chicken Mothering, Protection. She watches carefully to see if the chicks are getting chilled and need to be called under her for a warming up, and to make sure she hasn't lost track of one. She can be fearless in defense of her babies. She can be dangerous to pet rabbits or guinea pigs that might happen to be in the area. An angry bantam fluffs out her feathers to the max to make herself look much bigger than she really is. She'll stand her ground against a far larger animal, making little pecking charges to try to drive it off. Unfortunately, a mother hen's blindly aggressive behavior may also extend to other mother hens—in which case chicks sometimes get trampled in the conflict, or may even be pecked by the other mother. (That's why it's wise to establish such families on opposite sides of your barnyard, or in separate coops.) She teaches her babies to be careful when cats come around and to look out for hawks.

Separation from Mother. A lost, scared chick sounds the alarm with a very distinctive, loud, "Peep, peep, peep." That's their S.O.S., and whoever is mother—you or the hen—better hurry and see what the problem is. A common serious problem occurs when 1 chick gets trapped somehow away from the group. The hen is torn; she doesn't want to leave the rest of her chicks unprotected, unwarmed, and alone, yet she doesn't want to abandon the separated one. In a case like that, you should interfere. It's generally as simple as lifting the isolated chick over some kind of barrier.

HOUSING FOR A HEN AND CHICKS: Keep the chicks away from the chicken house to start with, both to protect them from vermin and to prevent them from being pecked by larger birds, who can be very cruel. Or a predator, such as a roaming cat, might get a chick. You have 3 choices for housing: leave them alone to tough it out and hope for the best, start them in a big cardboard box or A-frame and then gradually set them free, or start them in a chicken coop or subdivided pen and keep them living like that quite a while. Chicken coop containment is especially wise with a chicken mother who is just learning the ropes herself, not having been raised by a natural mother. She may not know enough to encourage her chicks to keep warm. Leaving them alone is the riskiest option.

Cardboard Box or A-Frame Housing. You can place hen and chicks in a large cardboard box with a chicken-wire cover. Such a box should have appropriate litter, food, and water. It doesn't need a heat source. The hen will hover over the chicks when they need it to warm them. The big problems with box-housing are the small size and fragile construction. Instead, you may want to build an old-time A-frame chicken coop, the size of which is about 4 feet by 4 feet. It has no bottom, and no nest in it; anything else is too difficult for the chicks to get in and out of. There are slats across the opening, close enough together to keep the hen in, and aviary netting or a 6-inch board across the bottom to keep the chicks in. You can gradually phase some freedom into this setting by leaving hen and chicks shut in there for a couple of days, then letting them out together in the daytime and shutting them in again at night. In the A-frame, make available water in a chick-waterer and baby chick starter food. Arrange things so the babies don't get their feet wet. After 10 days or so you can let the cooped hen and chicks do whatever they want and they'll probably be fine.

Chicken Coop. The last option is a classic chicken coop. A coop ensures that the mother and her chicks don't get separated (unless a chick squeezes through the wire and gets lost). Move the family into the coop at the end of a week in the cardboard box or the A-frame, or, better yet, situate the A-frame right inside the coop and at the end of the first week, or whenever weather is suitable, just pull the board or netting off that keeps the chicks and their mother inside their house and let them have the freedom of the coop. A coop can be created by subdividing space from a regular chicken house or large bird pen or by creating a special portable unit. Ideal is a portable ground pen enclosing a little roofed box house (A-framed or rectangular) in which the hen can hover over her babies.

Good dimensions are 4 feet wide by about 6 feet long and 2½ feet high, with a wooden frame and a hinged roof. The house for such a coop can be built onto the end of it. If it has a low wooden floor and a swinging door, you can just shoo the family into it and shut the door when you want to move them. That way the coop itself doesn't have to have a bottom, which helps keep the grass under it nicer and more accessible to the birds. In good weather, put the coop right outside, moving it whenever the grass underneath seems significantly soiled or trampled. The coop should allow sunshine to enter, yet have spots of shade, and the little house should be rain-proof and heavy enough not to blow over in a wind. If the weather is cold, damp, or uncertain, put the coop in a sheltered place—inside your barn or in a shed. A coop of this design has other uses too. You can use it to isolate purebred birds for controlled breeding, or to isolate a sick bird, or to isolate newly purchased birds that are still in their quarantine period, or to house transition-size young birds.

A SECOND FAMILY: It's almost unheard of now for chickens to set more than once a year, and that's a shame. The old-time hard-working bantam hens used to have as many as 4 families a year. After raising one family, when the early spring chicks were about 2 months old and could find their own food and get along without their mother, she chose a new nesting place, pecking and scolding the youngsters if they came near her. They would give up on being mothered and join the general flock. (Even if she doesn't want to set again, feel free to take the mother away when the chicks are 8 weeks old, or older. They will now be fine without her and can be treated like transition-age chicks from the brooder.) Such a talented chicken mother would begin laying again. When she had enough eggs she'd get broody, set again, and start another family. If I were a breeder of household poultry, I'd select for that characteristic alone!

Chicken Housing

Chicken houses—and all the features that go into and around them—are a big topic. Some chickens have to spend their lives in very cramped quarters.

BATTERIES: Some commercial operators keep their birds in small, individual, stacked wire cages called "batteries." A battery-housed bird is never threatened by anything except boredom and inactivity. Batteries can't be used unless they're inside a warm building, even if they have a self-heating component. The baby chicks live in pens 5 tiers high; when they've grown larger they're moved to somewhat bigger cages stacked 3 tiers high. Food and water are provided in troughs at the edge of the tray. Battery cages can be bought ready-made or you can make them. They're certainly economical of space, but many people consider them an abomination because they don't allow a chicken to do the things chickens normally do—like scratching, dusting, sunning themselves, roosting at night, and moving around in the daytime to explore, socialize, and mate.

But even the freest ranging chickens need, and want, shelter from bad weather and night-roaming predators, for chickens are sound sleepers to the point of helplessness.

HOW MUCH HOUSING SPACE PER BIRD?

If your chickens will be roaming free during the day, they need only a relatively small shelter in which to sleep at night—big enough to hold their roosts. Totally confined birds, on the other hand, need much more space to avoid overcrowding them. Larger breeds need more space than smaller ones. Many birds need more space than few birds. Your bird population may be cyclical: a large crop of broilers in the spring plus your layers, but only the layers in wintertime. Figure 5–8 square feet per bird for fully confined birds in a small flock, 4 square feet per bird for a larger flock. By using a temporary chicken-wire partition, you can divide a chicken house into 2 parts during its busy cycle: one-half for the broiler crop and spring pullets being raised for replacement layers, the other half for your layers.

USING AN EXISTING CHICKEN HOUSE: Check first for rodent holes; nail metal over them. Check the roof for leaks and fix as needed. Sweep the dirt out. If the building has been used to house birds in the last 3 years, give it a good cleaning before you move your own birds in. (Follow directions under "Cleaning Your Chicken House.")

ADAPTING AN EXISTING OUTBUILDING: To renovate an outbuilding, choose one with a rat-proof floor, walls, and roof, that can keep out rain and has windows or some kind of openings for light and air. In a cold climate, it should not be drafty. In a hot climate, it should have good ventilation during the summer. You can put your chicken house inside a larger building—a large shed or barn—using existing walls where suitable and adding new ones as appropriate. Or you can build it against the outside of a larger building such as a lean-to shed (on the south side if possible).

BUILDING A CHICKEN HOUSE: Keep in mind that you want a short walking distance from your home to the chicken house, because you may be going there several times a day. Situate the building so that it will be convenient for you when cleaning day comes and you want to cart the accumulated manure and litter away. Plan where you will store the feed. Art Boe is an ex-Alaska fisherman, off-and-on building contractor, former high-school science teacher, South Dakota farm boy, cow milker, and friend. His wife is a second-grade teacher and has had an Emery in her class about every other year. Here are Art's directions for building the ideal chicken house:

You'll probably need a local building permit to build a from-scratch chicken house. You can get very detailed plans from chicken books, magazine articles, state agricultural colleges, etc. A simple pole or frame building, shed type, is adequate. You can manage with a space as small as 6 by 8 feet for a dozen chickens, or 10 by 12 feet for 30–40 of them, or 20 by 40 feet for 250, which is a commercial-sized operation. Plan ahead for how you're going to clean out the manure. That means you'll probably want the roof high enough so you can get inside and shovel manure out comfortably. Slope the roof, say from 7 feet in front to 6 feet in the back, to help water run off. The rule of thumb is 1 foot of drop for each 8 feet of roof—more if you live in snow country where piled-up snow could collapse your roof.

Of Windows and Light. You'll want windows on the south side in northern climates, with enough roof overhang to keep out the hottest summer sun. To be most effective the roof overhang must slant down over the windows, creating a "V" (upside-down) or "cowl." Such a window-overhang combination will keep out the summer sun, let in the winter sun, and protect the front wall from rain. Install windows across a third to a quarter of the wall on the south side, made so that you can remove the glass in summer for additional ventilation, or easily open and close them from the outside. Windows are especially important for poultry because the male's fertility and the female's egg production are both affected by the presence or absence of light—so you want to maximize their exposure to light.

Ventilation. The more chickens you have in a house together, the more warm and moist the air is going to be in there. Chickens, especially confined ones, suffer in very hot weather and may die if the temperature in their house gets too high. They have a high respiratory rate and a high body temperature—they need proportionately more oxygen. They do not excrete sweat or urine (though their droppings are moist). A chicken breathes out her excess moisture. Moisture that doesn't have a chance to circulate out of the chicken house causes wet litter, which in turn can result in breast blisters and manure burns. In a warm chicken house, the ammonia from the manure becomes very strong, and in a very short time can result in ammonia blinding and serious respiratory damage if adequate ventilation for a confined flock is not provided. Ammonia poisoning can also retard growth, reduce egg laying, cause foot pad burns, and encourage staph infection.

So the chicken house needs ventilation enough to get oxygen in and also to get ammonia and moisture out. You will need some ventilation even in winter—windows that drop down or tip in and can be opened at least a crack. In cold weather it's best to have the ventilation on one side, to the south, to prevent chilling cross drafts. In warm climates or hot weather, you'll want to be able to open up both sides of the chicken house to get cross-drafts. Chicken wire on the inside will hold in the chickens and keep out predators and wild birds, which can carry parasites and diseases that chickens can contract. Don't use fly screens to cover the chicken house windows; they don't let enough air through to do the job in hot weather.

Climate Zones and Chicken Housing. In very warm climates like southern Texas, the southern Gulf states, and Florida, chicken houses typically have wire walls that can be covered with tarp or plastic curtains in case of windy or cool weather, and they are located under a shade tree. In the rest of the southern United States and on the extreme west coast, chicken houses are typically uninsulated and have large front openings that can be covered with plastic or windows in stormy or cold weather. (Or you can construct a more "regular" house for them—but have a screen door, screened windows, and extra screened openings in both peaks of both walls for ventilation in hot weather.)

Eastern, Midwestern, and Rocky Mountain-area chicken houses need to be well insulated (double walls with a 1½-inch insulation layer between them), tightly constructed, and protected from the wind. You can insulate your chicken house cheaply—by gluing Styrofoam to the walls and ceiling. In yet colder climates—such as Montana, the Dakotas, the Great Lakes area, and northern New England—the chicken house can benefit from even thicker insulation and electrical heating (at least a light left on) during severe winter weather. In interior Alaska, chicken houses may be built underground!

Of Insulation and Electricity. The birds will be warmer in winter if you insulate your chicken house and if it is small enough with a low-enough roof to keep the warm air near the chickens, who make quite a bit of heat themselves. Insulate by building the walls in 2 layers with air space in the middle. Air is an insulator. Or put commercial insulation material in the middle. Or fill that wall space with some different, available insulating material. Don't spend a fortune on a chicken house unless you have it to spend. For cold climates, one or more light bulbs burning at night can prevent frost-bitten combs and wattles on the roosters and help keep drinking water from freezing. With electric warmth in the chicken house, young birds can leave the brooder and be moved into the big house at earlier ages. You'll also find electricity useful if you live where winter nights are long and you want to push your chickens to maximum year-round production by leaving the lights on. On the other hand, you don't have to wire the chicken house. It's cheaper and simpler not to, and you'll still get eggs.

The Floor: Dirt, Wood, or Concrete. For a dirt floor, first level your ground, and then just build your house on top of that. You may be able to get along with a dirt floor, but they're hard to clean, hard to keep dry, and vulnerable to weasels and rats tunneling in; also, parasites in the ground can be harder to get rid of. Another option is a wooden floor. Building it up off the ground prevents rats from hiding underneath and gnawing through it. If rats do gnaw a hole in the floor or wall, nail sheet metal—or a tin can lid—firmly over the hole to block it. A wooden floor is warmer than dirt and dries from underneath. Chickens make a lot of moisture. But wood can warp and rot. You could reinforce a wood floor by making it of 2 layers, with building paper or insulation board between them. The other option is a concrete floor. Slope a concrete floor about 4 inches from back (where the roosts are) toward the front of your chicken house.

LITTER: You can go 3 different ways with this: Use a foot of litter to start with. Or build up litter by starting with 2 or 3 inches and then gradually adding more throughout the year in layers atop of what's already there to a total of as much as 2 feet. Or use a thin layer, which is cleaned out and replaced every week or two. This litter is very important—don't skip it. It gives the chickens something to scratch and prevents their droppings from adhering to the chicken-house floor. The litter dilutes the "strength" of the chicken manure. For chickens in a cold climate, built-up litter insulates their floor, and the decomposition and fermentation processes inside it actually provide heat for them. For the same reason, when warm weather comes the chickens will be cooler and more comfortable if you get the old litter out of there and provide fresh.

Litter Materials. Soft wood shavings, peat moss, sugar cane fiber, or some such shredded organic material is best. You can use hay, preferably that rejected by the cows. But not sawdust because it tends to be so dusty it is hard on your chickens' respiratory systems. And do not use oak shavings because they are toxic.

NOTE: Don't let the litter mold! Moldy litter can result in a serious poultry disease in which the mold organisms actually move into the birds' respiratory and digestive systems and live there. The mold organisms can also damage your health.

Stirring the Litter. Some chicken-raisers stir together the shavings and manure every couple weeks with a rake. That stirring prevents the litter from packing and promotes drying since the litter has to absorb a lot of moisture from the chicken droppings. Then when it comes time to clean out the chicken house, the litter is already more than half-composted. Other owners just let it stack up until they can't stand the sight of it any more, or the garden is going to be wanting it, and then they take it all out in a big 1-day ordeal. If you leave it alone more than a few months, the manure gets quite compacted, and it will be like spading a garden to cut it loose and get it out of there.

NESTS: This is something (anything) like a wooden box, about 10 inches square, with a top and sides, but open at 1 side for the hen to enter. A slit in the top helps ventilate the nest. A slanted top prevents roosting on the nesting box with its attendant manure collection. Cover half the open side with wood, or cover all the open side with a curtain of cloth that's slit to let a chicken hop through. It should be relatively dim inside. Hens like dark, comfy, private places to do their thing in. An instant nesting place can be made by leaning a sheet of plywood, or anything similar, against the chicken-house wall. They'll lay between the sheet and the wall. Put hay, chopped straw, wood shavings, or some such, in the nesting place for the hen to nestle down in. Change the nest litter occasionally, when it gets dirty. Nail a nesting box, 2 feet high or so, up on your chicken-house wall. You can put them in a row. Supply 1 nesting box for each 4 layers—more or less. Pullets, just laying their first eggs, are liable to drop them anywhere, and that can't be helped. Some hens may be tempted to make a nest in a corner of your hen house on the floor. That is a problem because it may result in the development of egg-eating. Stop it by picking up the eggs and clearing away the "nest."

ROOSTS: You'll want roosts in your chicken house. The chickens will fly up there and perch, curling their toes around the roost to hang on. (That's why it's handiest for them if you use a pole or round the top edges somewhat.) If you don't have a chicken house, your chickens will fly up onto rafters or into trees—if they can fly—as soon as they get big enough to fly that high. Since they sleep unbelievably soundly, chickens have an instinct to pick a very protected place to do it in.

Building Roosts. Basically, the perch is a long pole, 2–3 inches in diameter, set 2–4 feet off the chicken house floor. The best perch isn't made of really smooth material; the birds would have trouble hanging on. And it would be firmly nailed in place, so it can't turn. An easy-built roost is just a 2 × 4, about 12 feet long, nailed across 1 or more corners of the chicken house, as needed. But don't put roosts right on top of each other. Birds drop feces in the night. Arrange the roosts in such a way that the droppings have a clear fall to the floor. The roosts are best when they are no closer than 18 inches to a wall. Allow about 18 inches perching room per adult, heavy-breed bird. In cold weather they'll crowd and take less room as they huddle together to keep each other warm. The area right under the roosts will collect more chicken manure than all the rest of your chicken house combined. Some growers recess the area under the roosts to separate the deposits there from the rest of the litter. That arrangement is called a "droppings pit." Some growers fence the pit at top and sides with chicken wire to keep the birds from getting into it.

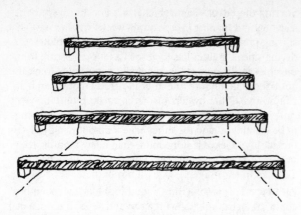

Roost Height. The height needs to be right for your particular birds. High-flying bantams will like it on the high side. (If unconfined, such high-flying bantams are likely to perch in your orchard instead of the chicken house. If you let them do that a few nights, they'll want to keep doing it. It's just a matter of your preference, whether they should or not.) Yokohamas, with their lovely long trailing tails, need high perches to keep their tails out of the droppings. Bantams that don't fly much, feather-footed breeds, and Chabos need perches no higher than 1 foot. For average meat–eggs breeds, if you have enough birds to need more than 1 roost, you can put them one behind the other in rising order, like separated staircase steps, at 2-, 3-, and 4-foot levels.

PEOPLE DOORS: You need a people door from the outside into the chicken yard, and a people door from the chicken yard into the chicken house. Or a people door from the outside into the chicken house directly, and then one from the chicken house into the chicken yard. Another useful door is a lengthwise one along the floor right behind the chicken's roosting area. That one would allow you to frequently rake out the manure from where it builds up under the roosts. Some classy chicken houses have special hinged doors that open directly into nesting boxes and allow you to gather eggs without entering the chicken house. It's all a matter of your preference.

CHICKEN DOORS: You'll want separate doors for your chickens: little bird-sized doors (about a foot square) that are shut easily from the outside. That way, in chilly weather you can leave their doors open but close the people-sized door to minimize cold drafts. Also, for free-running chickens, such a small door keeps out large stray dogs. As an extra protective measure, close that little door at dark, after they've all gone in to sleep—because some night-predators are small enough to slip in through it and can make a dreadful carnage of the sleeping chickens. On the other hand, unless you leave plenty of food and water inside the chicken house before you go to bed, you'll need to get up early in the morning (chicken time is early indeed!) and open it again.

Chicken-Sized Door Design. It should be about half a foot above floor level so litter doesn't escape from it. One handy style of door is a plain flat piece of wood that slides up and down in wooden grooves. Another style is attached at the top by nailed-on leather straps or metal hinges and is held up during the daytime by a loop of twine that can be hooked on a nail situated at just the right height above. Yet another style combines a door and walkway down. You make it by sawing out your door and letting it fall to the outside, drawbridge style, during the day, then drawing it back and fastening it shut at night. If you don't have that style chicken-door and your chicken entrance is not at ground level, then you could make a separate walkway by providing a board for the birds to walk up from ground to door level. Strips of wood nailed crosswise on the board an inch apart will help them get traction in wet weather.

CHICKEN-YARD OPTIONS: Basically, you have 4 outdoor options: a sun porch, a fenced dirt yard, a fenced pasture (regular or rotated), or free-running.

Sun Porch. Most chicken owners don't have the option of letting their poultry run completely free, but they want them to have some outdoor time. The most protective choice would be a sun porch. This is an outside pen or an inside pen with an attached outside run. The outside part is built at least a foot off the ground, and it has chicken-wire sides and top, and a floor of small wire mesh or wooden slats—which allows manure to fall through onto the ground below. This allows poultry to get sunshine and fresh air and prevents them from eating feces or dirt. Such a pen can be dependably sanitized. The use of a sun porch is best if you have very disease-vulnerable stock or are in a disease- or parasite-ridden area. Chickens usually don't require that much protection. Turkeys sometimes do. (See "Sunporch" under "Turkeys" for more information.)

Fenced Yard: Yarding reduces confinement stress problems: cannibalism, feather-picking, egg-eating. And chickens just plain enjoy basking in sunshine (to make their Vitamin D) and benefit from exercise. Your chicken yard should be planned so that it has a portion that will be shaded and a portion that will be in the sunshine. In coldest climates, they'll be using their yard in the warmer months. Then, in extremely cold, stormy, or snowy weather, you shut the door to the chicken yard and keep them completely inside. Feed them inside the chicken house. Or, if you choose to feed them in the yard, use a covered-style feeder to keep out rainwater. A small chicken yard is a dirt yard. If it wasn't dirt to start with, it will be soon. A dirt yard is nicer if you cover it with litter. Chickens love to scratch in litter; scatter some kind of mulching material. That will also help keep it nice looking and good smelling and will inhibit possible health problems associated with wet, muddy yarding. Straw, tree leaves (not black locust—poisonous), or ground corn stalks and cobs, are cheap, fine sorts of yard litter. You then periodically add the yard litter to your compost pile, together with its nitrogen load.

Pasture. This is an excellent option. See "Water and Food for Chickens (and Other Adult Fowl)." Free-ranging is covered there, too.

Fencing for Chickens. "Chicken wire" has smaller holes than the "woven wire" you use to fence in larger animals. Chicken wire isn't as stiff as woven wire, so it takes more structure to hold it up. Posts set in the ground will corner the chicken yard. On the sides place a post about every 5 feet. Then stretch the wire around the outside, tightening it by pulling on the 3 or 4 reinforcing wires woven into the mesh for that purpose. Staple or nail (nail halfway in, then bend the nail over the wire and hammer it down) the reinforcing wire to the post. If there is any risk of predator invasion by tunneling—and to prevent birds from slipping out through holes created by dusting pits right next to the fence—bury about 6 inches of board all around the bottom of the fence and staple the wire to the top edge of the board. Or dig a trench all around when you are building the fence and bury a foot of the chicken wire. If the chickens have a larger pasture—say a whole orchard to run in—don't worry: it could probably be less painstakingly fenced.

How High a Fence? The rule is this: The smaller the chickens, the higher the fence you'll need. In general, heavy chickens need a 4-foot fence, light breeds need a 5-foot fence, and a 6-foot one may or may not hold bantams. If you are troubled with birds that fly out over the top of your fence, make the fence higher by adding more chicken wire—another foot or two at the top as needed. (Or "clip the wings" of the flyers. You do that on one wing, the outer row of feathers only. Those will be large primary wing feathers. Cut with a sharp scissors. That ruins their aviation balance. But feathers will grow back and have to be cut again after the next molt.) Or fasten chicken wire over the top of the run, and that settles the problem forever. If your chicken run has a covered top it need not be higher than 2 or 3 feet. Then you also never have to worry about birds of prey snatching a bird, or wild birds robbing chicken feed and bringing disease or parasite problems—like pigeons that may carry avian cholera, deadly to a chicken flock.

CLEANING YOUR CHICKEN HOUSE: It's a good idea to clean your chicken house at least once a year, in the spring when the heat-producing litter is no longer needed and will become more of a problem than a help. Or you can do it twice a year: in the early spring and 6 months later in the fall. Or time your cleaning to occur after 1 group of chickens has gone to the freezer and a new batch, now outgrowing your brooder facilities, is about to arrive. Incidentally, this between-flock cleaning policy helps keep your birds healthy, if you're troubled with disease or parasite problems. Clean a chicken house that you've just bought before you move your own chickens into it. Infectious agents—disease or parasite—can live months in the dirt of a chicken house, in the soil around it, in nearby fields—anywhere the infected poultry roamed.

Chicken-House Cleaning Day. You need a warm, dry day to do this job. If you are cleaning a house that is not vacant you'll have to get the job completely done between dawn and dusk, because the chickens will want very much to go home and sleep when the sun goes down. This tends to be a day to remember. There are 4 steps possible in your cleaning process. Do any or all as your individual preferences and situation suggest, but in the following order:

1. Give your birds their insect (external body parasites) or worm (internal parasites) medication, if such treatment is on your agenda. But don't treat for both internal and external parasites the same day—kills the chickens. Then turn them out or move them from the quarters to be cleaned.
2. This step has to be accomplished: Shovel all manure and litter off the floor. Scrape manure off the roosts. Clean old litter out of the nest boxes. Most chicken diseases and internal parasites are transmitted through the feces.
3. This step can be skipped, or done to any degree you think appropriate: Hose down, soak, and scrub the walls and floor with a high-pressure hose, steam cleaner, or elbow grease and basic soap or a disinfectant solution. An ideal disinfectant is a lye–water mixture: 1 oz. lye/1 gal. water. This is most effective if

applied hot but is also effective when applied cold. Lye water is effective against parasite eggs and disease germs, but only if the litter and droppings have first been thoroughly swept away; litter and droppings neutralize the lye, and then it can't work against bugs. Bleach can also be used for this purpose, as can a special-purpose disinfectant available at most feed stores. Some disinfectants are sprayed on. Read and follow disinfectant directions exactly. Some poultry-owners prefer liming the house out once a year by mixing a paste of lime with water and brushing or spraying that on. Make sure you clean the roosts, in cracks and crevices, and under loose boards with a bristle-coated brush or broom. Then let it dry out.

4. This step can be skipped: Paint the lower walls, dropping boards, pits, roosts, nests, and where the roosts and nests touch the wall, with a mite-killing solution. Follow directions carefully.
5. Let dry. Put fresh litter on the floor. Move in the old or new tenants.

Chicken Injuries, Diseases, Parasites

The Chicken Health Handbook (1994) by Gail Damerow will help. Also, download "Sustainable Poultry: Production Overview" from **www.attra.ncat.org/attra-pub/poultry overview.html.**

INJURIES THAT CAN BE FIXED: A bird with any of these problems is injured but not diseased, and is fine to eat. So you could choose not to bother with the following remedies and send the animal straight to the deep freeze. But they often can recover, if given the chance.

Broken Leg. A chick's leg can be splinted with Popsicle sticks and masking tape. A larger bird's leg can be splinted in the same manner with heavier-duty materials.

Egg-Bound. The chicken squats, strains, maybe spends all day in the nest looking constipated. Treatment: Pour warmed olive oil into her vent. Feed her castor oil. Then gently try to maneuver the jammed egg out.

Prolapsed Vent. This is most likely to happen to pullets who began to lay before they were fully grown. A mass of tissue will hang from the vent. It can be fixed more easily than it looks. Wash the protruding mass with warm water and a gentle antiseptic. Lubricate it with medicated Vaseline or mastitis ointment. Then push the prolapsed mass very gently back into the vent. In cold weather, dry the wet feathers with a hair dryer or some such. Isolate the recovering hen from the rest of the flock (which might be tempted toward cannibalism). Feed her drastically reduced rations for a week to slow up the egg laying. But supply plenty of greens and fresh water. Clean her vent area each day and apply ointment. By the end of the week she will probably be fine again and able to return to the flock. Later she will begin to lay normally. If, however, she prolapses repeatedly, turn her into stew.

Impacted Crop (Crop-Bound). Birds of any age that have eaten too much litter; or long, very dry, once-green feed; or other unfortunate things (like a burlap bag), can get their crop packed with it in such a way that it can't go down, and it blocks them from eating anything else. The bird will have a distended, doughy-feeling crop and convulsive movements of the neck. The treatment is to pour a teaspoonful of olive oil down the bird's throat and then gently massage the crop, gradually working its contents up and out of the bird's mouth. Fortunately, unlike humans (who are adapted for speech), a bird has its windpipe and esophagus completely separated, so you don't have to worry about them not getting air while you're doing this job. When you have the crop emptied give the bird water, but not food, for 24 hours. It should return to normal after that. However, sometimes the muscles of the crop have been injured, and the condition frequently repeats. In that case you give up and send the bird to the dinner table.

THE DISEASED BIRD: Most families growing only enough poultry for their own needs don't experience the variety and scale of poultry health problems that intensive growers with large numbers of the same breed and age in a small area do. So this section attempts to compromise between saying nothing and telling it all. To prevent disease and parasites, don't let your poultry go where infested bird manure from past years is located, such as in your compost pile or your garden.

If You Have a Sick Bird. Isolate it in smaller quarters to prevent it being literally picked on. Keep it warm (the Number 1 priority!) and provide dietary TLC with special bug and greens offerings. If the bird dies, burn or dispose of it in such a way as to avoid spreading the disease. Don't eat such a bird.

Disposing of Dead, Diseased Birds. Dead poultry, especially baby chicks, can be completely burned in a burn barrel. Make sure you destroy all the remains. A heavy grate on the top of the barrel can ensure that pets or predators don't drag them away. That's better than burying the carcass of a sick animal because of the possibility of it being dug up and/or of the disease organisms remaining in or spreading through ground water.

State Poultry Veterinary Lab. If you have several sick birds and they seem to have the same problem, consult your local agricultural extension agent or agricultural university extension poultry specialist. That person may refer you to your state poultry veterinary diagnostic laboratory. Every state has at least one, and many states have more than one. Call the lab to find out if they prefer you to send a couple live sick birds or one or more dead ones and what they suggest to be the method of delivery. If they will be studying a dead bird, they probably will want you to chill and freeze it as soon as possible after death. If you do have a communicable poultry disease problem, you need a prompt diagnosis, treatment for the rest of your flock, and advice on how to prevent the problem in the future.

Giving a Pill to a Bird. Open the bird's mouth, put the medicine on the back of its tongue, close its mouth, hold it closed, and wait for it to swallow.

Vaccinations. For small home poultry flocks, vaccination isn't usually necessary. Poultry diseases are much more likely to be a problem in big, commercial farms with many birds confined in a small space. Vaccines are available from poultry suppliers for a number of different bird diseases, including fowl cholera, erysipelas, Newcastle disease, laryngotracheitis, fowl pox, and Marek's disease. If you do vaccinate, give the vaccines that are recommended for your geographical area. You can buy them and the necessary equipment to inject, spray, etc., and do your own bird doctoring. To give a shot or eye- and nose-drop vaccines, hold the bird between your legs. Some of these vaccines—such as that for infectious bronchitis—use a live virus, which is given in the birds' drinking water. Be careful when giving any vaccine, especially a live one. The vaccine used for Marek's disease—a live turkey herpes virus—must be given at age 1 day to be effective. Some people are allergic to vaccines.

Pullorum Testing. That same state veterinary laboratory will test your breeders free-of-charge for pullorum and typhoid. All reputable hatcheries can advertise that their breeders have been tested and are pullorum-free. At one time pullorum disease was widespread in both chicken and turkey flocks. An infected hen lays pullorum-infected eggs that hatch pullorum-infected chicks or poults. The infected young birds spread the disease to others near them and many of them die. Some recover and will carry the bacteria that cause this disease on to the next generation. In order to break that infection cycle, responsible growers began to blood-test all their breeding stock. Infected birds were butchered. (Their meat was all right to eat.) Only uninfected stock was kept for breeding. There is no medical treatment for pullorum disease. Prevention is the only way to go.

SOME POULTRY DISEASES

Blackhead. (See also "Blackhead Disease" under "Turkeys"). Blackhead disease, which is the most widespread and destructive problem of turkey growers, is caused by a protozoan that spends part of its life cycle in the cecal worm. This is why raising chickens and turkeys together can be a problem. If your chickens don't have cecal worms—or if their cecal worms don't carry the blackhead organism—you're okay. Blackhead seldom makes chickens sick, even the ones that are hosting it.

Coccidiosis. About nine different species of *Coccidia*, a host-specific protozoan parasite, afflict chickens, of which three cause the problems. About six afflict turkeys, of which only two make the birds visibly sick. Most likely to be a problem for brooder chicks.

Fowl Typhoid. It's caused by a bacterium and affects many species of birds including chickens and turkeys. Because prevention and control against fowl typhoid are about the same as for pullorum, buy pullorum–typhoid-clean birds.

Paratyphoid. As with pullorum infection, there is no treatment for this. The birds start dying very young, and half to three-fourths of an afflicted flock may die. It is not possible to separate out infected birds as it is with pullorum. If this disease shows up in a flock, all the breeding birds must be disposed of and a new start made with completely healthy replacements. Paratyphoid is also called "Salmonellosis" and can be a public health problem because humans (as well as reptiles and all other animals) are also susceptible to these bacteria. Humans usually encounter them as salmonella food-poisoning. Chicks suffer with them as a blood-poisoning disease. This organism can be spread by just about anything it gets on, animate or inanimate.

Infectious Bronchitis. This is a viral chicken disease that is highly infectious. When it afflicts young birds it damages the reproductive organs, and they will not lay normal eggs, either by exterior or interior qualities. There is no treatment, but it can be vaccinated against. The vaccine can be administered individually by nasal or eye drops, or to poultry groups in drinking water, or by dust or spray. This vaccine is frequently administered together with the Newcastle vaccine.

Newcastle Disease. This is a widespread, serious, very contagious viral respiratory disease that afflicts almost all species of poultry, especially chickens and turkeys. It could come into your poultry by wild birds or by tracking, bird purchases, equipment, feed, etc. from other poultry farms. There is no effective treatment. It is easy to vaccinate birds against Newcastle disease. The vaccine can be given in drinking water or dusted or sprayed. If you are concerned, ask your extension agent if vaccination is advised in your part of the country.

BUGS ON BIRDS: There are chemical remedies to all these problems, which I have described with reluctance. I don't like poisonous chemicals. Parasite treatments done during molting can interfere with the bird's healthy feather development. Never treat for internal parasites and external parasites simultaneously. It will kill your birds. Wait at least 5 days between such treatments. I don't like environmental pollution. But when my kids got head lice I went straight down to the drugstore, bought some head-lice–killing stuff and used it on them (following directions carefully). Nobody likes parasites. These are hard decisions. You could burn down the chicken house, wait 3 years, and start over. You can tell me what you did that worked that didn't pollute the world, and I'll gladly add it to these methods.

Bedbugs. This brown or yellow-red insect hides by day under roosts and in nooks and crannies of the chicken house. It comes out at night to feed on the birds. Its bites cause such itching that the birds pull out feathers trying to relieve it. Use Sevin or Co-Ral.

Chiggers. These critters afflict bird and human alike. Chiggers tend to cluster on a bird's skin on its neck and back and under the wings. Too many can even kill a bird. It helps if grass and weeds are kept short.

Fowl Tick (Blue Bug). Night blood suckers like the red mite, these flat, reddish-brown, egg-shaped insects look like ticks, and like ticks, they cause loss of blood, carry diseases, and may cause paralysis. The chemical remedy is malathion spray in the chicken house.

Lice. There are 7 basic varieties of lice: the body louse, which lives on the bird's skin; shaft louse that eats its feather shafts; large chicken louse; brown chicken louse that lives on feathers and prefers southern climates; head louse on the bird's head and neck; wing louse on its wing feathers; and fluff louse in its fluff.

These parasites are common, especially the body louse. These insects are either chewers or biters, and they spend their entire life-cycle right on the bird; off a bird, they die

within a few hours. They lay eggs on the feathers and stick them there with a sort of glue. Depending on the variety of louse, the eggs (nits)—which are laid on the breast, the back, and under the wings—will hatch in a few days to 2 weeks. Lice eat skin scales and feathers. Chickens acquire them from being exposed to a bird or rodent, wild or tame, that has them. Lice increase faster in warm weather, but are there in the cold season, also. Too many lice can cause a decline in egg production and in the hatchability of the eggs.

Birds that are completely confined are far less likely to get them than birds that run loose. You can help your chickens in their fight by maintaining good hygiene according to the chicken-house cleaning directions. Dig in their chicken yard enough to get them started in a new, clean, dust-bathing place occasionally (see "Dust Baths"). Dust clogs louse pores. Crumbling a handful of tobacco leaves in each nest and in bird dusting sites will help. Rotenone and sulfur (from plant nurseries) in the dusting site will also help. Since roosters don't like to dust as much as hens, they may have a worse problem with lice. To dust a bird with rotenone powder hold her by the legs with head downward. This way her feathers will open and you can easily sprinkle in the dust. Don't get it in the bird's eyes.

Lane Morgan told me, "I dust my birds with diatomaceous earth and also put some in their feed. It isn't perfect, but it helps." Another friend told me she dusts her birds with wood ashes and that controls their lice.

Insecticide powder in the feathers of a mother hen will kill her chicks when they huddle under her, so don't dust a mother. If you're going to dust her, do it well before the hatching dates. The tender skin and feathers of a chick are especially vulnerable to louse predations, and large infestations can quickly kill chicks and young chickens. Insecticide treatment will kill the lice but not their eggs, so you have to apply it again in 10 days to kill the newly hatched lice. Time the chemical treatment to match the timing of your cleaning and disinfecting the chicken house. Stronger chemicals used to treat lice are carbaryl, malathion, coumaphous (brand name: Co-Ral). Follow the directions carefully. All this effort may or may not actually succeed in eradicating a louse population.

Mites, Depluming. A severely infested bird may be nearly naked because it pulls out feathers trying to relieve the itching caused by this mite that characteristically burrows into the skin at the base of a feather. Control it by dipping the bird into 2 oz. of sulfur and 1 oz. soap dissolved per gallon of water. Be sure and get the solution down to skin-level of the bird. Repeat in 3–4 weeks if the first dip doesn't solve the problem.

Mites, Northern Fowl. This one is reddish to dark brown and is found around tail, vent, and breast. Like lice, these mites live their entire life-cycle on the bird. They suck blood and can reduce a bird's productivity and general good health. Sevin or Co-Ral can kill them.

Mites, Red. To check your hen house for these mites, look for little creatures moving in the cracks and crevices of the chicken house walls, perches, etc. You're also looking for small "salt and pepper" deposits that make a "trail" under the roost perches. If the mites are there, they hide in those cracks by day and come out at night and crawl up chickens' legs while they're sleeping to feed on them. Knowledgeable chickens will avoid sleeping on such perches, preferring uninfected places. To find out for sure, pluck a bird off the roost at night, and examine between the feathers of its legs and elsewhere. If the mites are there, you'll see them. And if one bird has them, they all do. When you leave the chicken house you're going to feel like a shower. Take one. And put your clothes in the washer. Treatment for Red Mites is Sevin or Co-Ral unless you want to use an old-time remedy:

The old-time remedy, an effective one, was to brush or dab used crankcase oil, perhaps diluted 50 percent with kerosene, on the crevices and roosts of the hen house. Start after daybreak by chasing the birds out of the house and shutting the door. Smear the stuff with a paint brush or a rag tied to the end of a stick all over the perch, especially underneath where the mites hide all day. Don't let the birds back in until as late in the day as possible. Give the treatment again in 2 weeks, and again in 6 months. Penny Anderson of Aitkin, MN, wrote me, "A few years ago when it got really cold here, I ended up with a lot of sparrows in the barn, and they brought red mites. My great-aunt Marie told me to provide a pan of wood ashes to let the chickens dust in. That and coating the roosts and bottoms of the nest boxes (under the straw) with old oil cleared them up in no time."

Mites, Scaly Leg. These are another common type of mite spread by wild birds. They cause scales on the chickens' shanks (the bare-looking "ankle" to "knee") which protrude and may flake off. You can't see these because they are microscopic in size and burrow into the leg skin, under the scales. Sometimes they also get into the comb and wattles. Severe infestations cause an abnormal gait. You kill these by dipping each bird's feet into a mixture of two-thirds oil and one-third kerosene. It helps if you clean the chicken house together with the treatment. Two weeks after the first treatment, dip again. Some people dip a third time, 2 weeks later. An alternative treatment is to wash the shanks and rub with Vaseline. Yet another treatment is to dip the bird's legs in salad oil or baby oil, up to the shanks weekly for 6 weeks.

Tropical Chicken Flea. These beasties can cause blindness and even death simply by their clustering on the comb, wattles, earlobes, and around the bird's eyes. The chemical remedy is carbaryl (Sevin) in dust or spray.

WORMS: To some extent worms are routine in poultry and can be tolerated, though they lower the flock's general disease resistance. Chicken growers in southern states have the worst problem with worms. If wild birds that have them get in to share your chickens' food, they leave droppings in the chicken pen. Chickens that pick at those droppings then acquire their parasites. Or the dropping of wild birds may be eaten by insects. If your chickens eat those particular insects, they acquire that worm variety. It helps to keep confined poultry well supplied with grit or gravel so they're less likely to peck at droppings to acquire new grit. If worms do get started in your flock the problem will spread. The worst off birds may have diarrhea and emaciation, be weak, and lay less.

Testing for Worms. You test for worms by having an expert examine the bird's manure. Some owners do this twice a year—in January and in July. Some owners combine the feces of several chickens to send in as a sample—on the theory that if one has them, they all will soon anyway. To send a fecal sample to a distant laboratory, put it on a piece of aluminum foil and fold the foil carefully over it. Put that into a small jar or metal container and close the lid. If the examining veterinarian identifies a parasite, he'll suggest what to do. Or you can worm the birds yourself . . .

Worming. Garlic, in any form, fed to the flock may help suppress worms. Some growers routinely add garlic to the flock's drinking water. Other growers feed diatomaceous earth in the same way: 2–3 T. D.E. per 1 lb. (0.45 kg) of bird feed, or about 2 c. per 50 lb. (22.7 kg) of feed, and for the same purpose. D.E. is available from Glyn Miller: 318-793-4950; 1008 Hwy 465, Sieper, LA 71472-9774; **glgl miller@aol.com.** Steam-cleaning a chicken house at a high temperature can help kill worm eggs. Pharmaceutical worming preparations are available. Some growers believe in regular de-worming, every 6 months. Some fancy- and pet-bird owners advise feces tests, followed by worming if advised. That's expensive. Some growers are against giving chemical treatment unless the birds are definitely appearing unhealthy. Or you can hang in there with "organic" methods. If you want to use chemical treatment, you really would be best off with expert advice about which one, or combination, to use. Follow directions carefully. Overdosing with worm treatment will kill your birds. Withhold all food the night before your morning chicken-worming event.

Here are some common poultry worms:

Roundworms. The worms are 1½–3 inches long and live in the bird's intestine. A light infestation doesn't seem to be a problem, but too many is not good. Piperazine preparations are effective against roundworms. They can be given to the bird in water, feed, or in a capsule form. To prevent or limit roundworms, avoid using a dirt-floor chicken house and properly clean out and disinfect the chicken house floor. It can also help to manage poultry so that they are let loose on a particular range only once in 3 years. This is the most common chicken internal parasite.

Cecal Worms. These are also known as "small roundworms." They are very small and are not considered a problem themselves. Their problem is that they are the carriers for the Blackhead organism. (See "Blackhead Disease" under "Turkeys.")

Tapeworm. Actually there are a variety of different tapeworm species. The smallest are microscopic; the largest can be 7 inches long. These flat, white, segmented worms live in the bird's small intestine and can be quite a drain on its (and your) resources. Tapeworm eggs can live in the ground for more than a year. Infestation can be controlled by rotating poultry ranges, using an area only once every 4 years. The tapeworm uses intermediate hosts—snails, beetles, worms—in which to complete its life cycle. Poultry acquire the tapeworms by eating the infected insects.

Others. There are also capillaria worms, acquired by eating infested earthworms, and gizzard worms, acquired by eating the grasshoppers, beetles, weevils, and other insects serving as intermediate hosts. Neither parasite is treatable once acquired.

Roosters

At 3–8 weeks of age, you can distinguish the young cockerel chicks by their slightly larger combs—that red decoration on top of the head—and wattles, the one that hangs under the chin. Roosters grow their decorations and get color in them first. Roosters are usually larger than pullets. When they have grown, you eat most of them and save a few for breeding; you don't need to keep very many roosters back from the butchering process to have fertile eggs. Three could take care of a flock of 50 chickens very nicely; figure 1 rooster per 15 hens. The extra roosters should be culled from the layers by the time the pullets are 20 weeks old if you want the best egg-laying and breeding performance. Extra roosters may hassle the pullets excessively.

CROWING: Roosters crow very early in the morning, in the night if they get disturbed, and at other times when the impulse takes them. In some places there are zoning laws against crowing. You can't stop a rooster from crowing; you can only stop having a rooster.

FIGHTING: Young males who are growing up together may look fierce but generally there are no injuries from their combats. These are ranking fights and once the issue is resolved there will be peace. Even fighting game breeds are peaceable if they have grown up together. The serious fighting happens when strange males are brought together at adult ages. Serious injury or death can be the result. The best book on the language and sociology of chickens is *Bantams* by Helga Fritzsche.

NOTE: Roosters are aggressive and may chase and peck small children in the eyes.

Many a time I've run out of the house because I heard a small child screaming in the yard, and there was a rooster flying up toward the child's face. I wondered if somehow it was my private nightmare until I received the following letter from another mother, Becky Jacobson of Felton, DE: "Dear Carla, We had a small rooster who would fly at people once in a while, but we never though much about it. Our few chickens are usually kept penned up in the chicken yard. One afternoon they were out, and my 20-month-old daughter was playing and following her father around. She walked past the rooster and must have stopped in front of him. Before we knew what happened he flew up and spurred her in the eye. She is now blind in her left eye and the eyeball is disfigured. It's cost us thousands of dollars and much heartache to learn this lesson."

Roosters won't bother a larger child; it's your toddler or 2-year-old they would go after. Roosters raised to be fryers, that are butchered as soon as they achieve sufficient weight, don't get old enough to be a problem in this regard. And you don't need roosters to have eggs. Hens will lay eggs even if there isn't a rooster at all on the farm. The eggs won't be fertile, but they're fine to eat, just as good as fertile eggs. If you have a rooster that acts like he might be a danger, have him for dinner, and consider cutting off the spurs of your roosters. Or make capons.

MAKING CAPONS: Roosters can be castrated. It's called caponizing them. Here's a letter I received: "Dear Carla, How do you make capons from roosters? It seems to be a lost art. Seems such a waste to kill them small, when I understand somewhere under the right wing you cut . . . and remove something and they grow as big as a turkey if you desire. If you have this information, whatever cost, please let me know." Well, in case you, too, are that vague about it, and also want to know the details as much, here's the caponizing nitty-gritty.

This is indeed an old-time art; it was invented in ancient Greece. You can get a caponizing outfit, including complete directions for using it, from mail-order poultry ranch suppliers. The things you're removing are the male sex glands that are located in a young cockerel's abdomen. Caponizing will solve the pecking and aggressiveness problem, and the roosters will grow sometimes as much as 50

percent heavier than they would otherwise—maybe to 10 pounds. Generally, the birds have no ill effects from the operation. Caponizing is in the process of going out of fashion. It involves virtually major surgery on the bird, which may go awry. The operation results in a heavier bird, but a significant proportion of that weight is fat. The capon market is now being displaced by the new "giants," which are large without the nuisance of the operation, and whose weight is proportionately more meat than fat.

Caponizing can be done by hand instruments or an electronic gadget. You operate when the birds are 8–10 weeks old. Operate in bright light and with the bird firmly held down onto a board or table with straps, its left side down, right side up. Pull enough feathers out to expose the lower rib area. The incision is made between the 2 last ribs from the bird's head end. With traditional hand tools, you need a knife to make the incision, a spreader to hold open the cut, a hook to tear the membrane covering the intestines, a blunt instrument to press the innards back out of the operator's way, and a forceps-style extractor to remove the 2 testicles, which will be located, one somewhat above the other, just in front of the kidney and near the backbone. The testicles are white and oval-shaped. A large artery runs between the two, which mustn't be punctured.

On to a more pleasant subject: your laying flock!

Laying Hens

OF BUYING GROWN BIRDS FOR LAYING: It's best if you buy pullets from 3 to 6 months old, so that their full egg-laying career is ahead of them. There's many a horror story of what happened when a novice bought somebody's worn-out cull hens. Growers don't let go of their best chickens—unless it's your mother, and maybe not even then. Be very careful and gentle whenever you are handling birds that may have eggs inside them. If they are birds that have already begun to lay, moving is quite likely to throw them into a molt and stop their egg-laying for the time being, because chickens are strongly creatures of habit. They'll go into that molt whether they were just starting a laying season and at full production, or whether they were near the end of it anyway. That's why it's so much better if you buy pullets that have not yet begun to lay—or chicks.

EGG RECORDS: To calculate if you're making or losing money, keep track of the values. In total, the original cost of your laying flock, plus their feed and any other expenses incurred on their behalf, is subtracted from the value of the eggs laid and the meat value of the stewing hens. Small growers generally find that if they use commercial feeds they enjoy their home-grown eggs but lose money on them. If they use home-grown foods and/or foraging, they come out ahead. Exactly how many eggs your layers will produce for you is extremely variable, depending on what breed they are, how well you feed (the more they eat, the more they lay), how much protein is in their feed, how you house them, what time of year it is, and how old they are. Commercial breeds in the 1940s averaged around 180 eggs a year. Now if a bird is laying about 20 eggs per month in her first 10 months of egg-laying, she's doing average; 300 eggs the first year is excellent. The urge to lay is fragile and can be thrown off by moving, changing feed, weather change, broodiness, or molting. And there are other factors to be considered besides pushing for egg production: feeding economy and electricity conservation.

EGG-LAYING ANATOMY: When you butcher an egg-laying chicken, you'll see the eggs-in-making inside of her. There will be tiny little yellow ones, no bigger than grains of sand, clustered together with small pebble-like ones, graduating on up to larger and larger yolks. (She builds the yolk first.) When the yolk-of-the-day is ready, it enters a long passageway where it is fertilized (if she has had the company of a rooster) and gets the white wrapped around it. Further down the assembly line, her egg gets 2 membranes added to the outside of it that hold the yolk and albumen in place. Then it goes to her shell-building station where the outermost layer is added. When she has finished building the shell, the egg moves on out to where her oviduct meets her digestive tract, just inside her vent (or cloaca). She then lays the egg, which she has spent approximately 24 hours building. When an egg is laid, its passage out is eased by a slimy, wet coating—the "bloom." When she decides to lay an egg, it generally doesn't take her long. As soon as the egg is laid, the bloom commences to dry into a thin, invisible membrane that protects the outside of the eggshell, and she cackles with the joy of accomplishment.

OF LAYING AND AGING: You can guess a bird's age by looking at its shanks: young chickens have smooth ones; older birds have larger, rougher ones. A pullet normally starts laying when she is 20–24 weeks old. She starts out making very small eggs occasionally and gradually increases egg size and frequency of laying until she is in full production. It takes her about 7 weeks to work up to full production. She's called a "pullet" until she has her first adult molt that will follow her first season of laying. After that she's called a "hen." Hens average about 20 percent fewer eggs their second season of laying, but the eggs tend to be larger, and the hen will have put about an extra half pound of weight on herself. Plan for enough replacement pullet chicks to keep the number of your eggs averaging up where you want it. A flock that is 75 percent pullets and 25 percent yearlings and older will operate at peak efficiency. On the other hand, if absolute money-efficiency isn't such a big issue for you and your hens are as much friends and pets as financial investments, you can expect them to live as long as

14 years, and to lay tolerably for maybe 7–10 of those years. The hen's lifestyle can make a big difference. If on a natural schedule and not pushed to lay, she doesn't suffer "egg burnout"—and produces somewhat less but somewhat longer.

LAYING AND BLEACHING: As a hen lays she loses her yellow coloration. If all her yellow is there, she hasn't started laying at all. After a few weeks of laying the yellow will be faded around her vent, eye, and ear lobe. After producing for a couple months her beak's yellow will be faded also. After 6 months of egg production her feet, toes, nails, and shanks will also be faded. When hens quit laying, the color will come back—in the same order in which it left. A parasite infestation can also cause bleaching.

"SEASONS" OF LAYING. A hen that laid 240 eggs her first season will thus lay about 190 in her second season and about 150 in her third, although her feed consumption remains the same all 3 years. For peak laying efficiency, the longest you'd keep a hen is 3 laying seasons. Then you stew her. How do you define a "season" or "year" of laying? Under natural conditions, the first egg-laying season begins (depending on when the pullet hatched) between August and March. That first season will end with a molt in September or October. Her second season starts when she begins laying again after that molt, sometime between November and January. She'll lay until her second molt begins the following September or October. Some growers cull all layers at the end of their second season. Some let them have 3 seasons. Some give them longer yet.

DUST BATHS: Roosters don't care much for dust-bathing, but hens love to dig into warm, loose, clean dirt and take a dust bath when the weather is warm enough so they won't get chilled by doing so. They look for a fairly new place that hasn't yet acquired a flea population. They scratch there until the dirt is fine. They'll find gizzard grit at the same time. They then roll in it with their eyes closed until the feathers are full of the dirt right down to the skin. Then they shake it all out and feel purified. Instinct or experience somehow informs them that dust clogs the breathing pores of the tiny parasites that tend to afflict poultry and is therefore a perfect, natural (nonpolluting) insecticide. You can provide hens that are totally confined with dust bath facilities by furnishing a deep pan or tray with loose dirt or hardwood ashes in it. Or you can build them a "sand box" using 1-inch-thick boards, about 6 inches wide and 20 inches long. Put such an artificial dusting spot where it won't get rained on in summer and where it will be in the warmest place they have as the season cools off. They'll appreciate that. A good dust-bathing material is half fine dirt and half dry sand. Such a human-made dust bath needs to have the droppings cleaned out of it periodically and the contents changed every few weeks. You don't give chickens water baths. If you want them super-clean, supply a dusting place with pure sand in it. They'll do the rest.

DISCOURAGING A BROODY BIRD: You could try taking away all her eggs. But a hen really in the grip of instinctive broodiness may stay on her nest even if there are no eggs in it. If you let her sit there 3 weeks, then separate the hen from the nest, she'll adjust in a day or two. Or you could let her set just 3 or 4 days and then give her the treatment. Or you could act the moment you notice her acting broody. Put her in a pen where there is no soft, suitable nesting place and no straw or litter of any kind with which to try to make a nest. Don't put the cage on a litter floor or she'll obtain litter and that will make her nest-minded again. Put the cage in a brightly lit area. Supply her with plenty of food and water. If you put a rooster in there with her, he'll hassle her and that will help get her mind off brooding. Modern hens will generally pull out of it in only a few days, and will soon be acting normal again. Production-minded poultry growers object to setting because a hen that sets has stopped laying and will not lay again for about 10–12 weeks unless her broody mood is "broken up." Even if the setting is broken up she'll probably be out 2–4 weeks from when it started.

My mother used to dump buckets of cold water on such a broody hen to try to get her to quit it and lay again. Another modern method is to put her in a swinging cage suspended from the chicken house ceiling—a tiny box that has wire sides so she'll get lots of light. It has a slatted bottom that she won't like to set on. A broody hen that won't quit no matter what may be a problem to you but might really be appreciated by another family.

MOLTING: Hens from typically very good egg-laying lines generally molt late and fast, beginning between September and October, lasting 2–3 months. Or not at all. For many chicken generations now, growers have been culling birds who slack off on their laying to molt as determinedly as they've been getting rid of ones that choose to turn broody, and the results are new genetic lines of egg-producing breeds that will lay right through the molting period. So the following discussion will be more relevant to chicken varieties of the old-fashioned sort. With them, your strongest egg-production will typically be from early spring when the days start to get long until molting time.

Chickens molt once a year. Your chickens will molt in late summer, fall, or early winter. Molting is important to chicken-raisers because when the hen molts she quits laying. When a rooster molts, he quits breeding. For chickens on a totally natural cycle, springtime brings a rush of egg-laying, followed by broodiness—when she quits laying—motherhood, repeat of egg laying, broodiness, motherhood—maybe for a total of as many as 4 families a season. And then the molt. With the onset of her molt, such an ancient-rooted bird would stop laying for the year, then lose its old feathers and grow new ones for winter warmth.

The modern hen, if she is of a commercial egg-laying breed, begins to lay eggs when she's 5–7 months old. She skips the broody period, skips the molt, and lays more or less continuously for 12–15 months. Then she finally does stop or slow up for a major molt. She may stop for 3 or 4 months. At this point most commercial or very cost-conscious operations would cull her out for stewing chicken. The average chicken reaches that point at about a year and a half of age. That's why some people simply send the older crop of layers off to the freezer as soon as they molt. There's a middle ground to that. This hen begins to lay when the days lengthen in late winter (January, February) and gradually increases her laying to a peak in April and May. Then she gradually reduces productivity again through July and August. Around September the shortening days stimulate her to cease laying and use the extra nourishment thus available to grow her winter feathers. After 6–10 weeks spent in her molt, she may start laying again in October or November, or she may stay out until January or February. This is a more typical pattern.

The Molting Sequence. Molting occurs first on the head, then neck, then breast, then body, then wings, and, finally, the tail. The new feathers push the old ones out, just like children getting grown-up teeth. It takes a hen 6 weeks to grow one of those big, primary feathers. If she loses and replaces only one such feather at a time, she'll be a long time finishing the molt and returning to lay. Under natural conditions, a very gradual molt helped survival. A chicken that lost large wing feathers only very slowly kept its ability to fly during the molt. Hens that lost several primaries at a time got it over with fastest. While the hen is molting her comb becomes less bright-colored and full-shaped. Then, when the molt is over and she's ready to lay again, the fullness and color return to her comb.

Hens that molt the latter part of July, or the early part of August, are considered good candidates for culling, because they will probably wait until December or January to start laying again, whereas birds who wait to molt until September or later, also begin lay again in December or January (when days start to lengthen). Feeding your hens lots of good green stuff may help hurry them through their molt and get them back to laying within a couple months. If you have young pullets hatched in early spring, they'll be starting to lay at this fall molting time and that will compensate in your egg production. Then they may go into a molt in early winter. It all depends on a combination of the particular heredity of your hen, her age, and stress factors.

Stress-Triggered Molting. If you want all your hens to go into a molt at the same time, you can easily cause that. Just shut them up in the chicken house in the dark, especially when they've been used to running loose, and for 3 days give them water, but no feed at all. Then provide a poor-quality feed. That will do it. You won't have to worry about eggs for a while. Most often owners accidentally throw their birds into a molt by creating some of these conditions. But some owners prefer force-molting. Natural stresses can cause molting, too. After a serious disease, the recovery phase of a bird is typically characterized by molting.

OF TEMPERATURE, LIGHT, AND LAYING: Although different breeds of chickens can be quite different about when, or if, they lay, in general, the light breeds shut down at freezing temperatures. So if you have Leghorns and you want them to do their best, set your thermostat-controlled heater in the chicken house for at least 40°F. They'll also need 14 or more hours of daylight to start laying and stay at peak productivity. Incidentally, chickens can see most colors, but not true blue; so you can use a blue light for their night warmth without disturbing their rest in the least, or to create light for night inspections.

Daylight Hours. Chickens go to roost and go to sleep when the sun goes down—as early as 5pm in winter at my latitude (see "Hours of Daylight by Month" table). Chickens have a built-in system to measure hours of daylight and lay best when days are long—14–16 hours. The long days stimulate a pituitary hormone. In a local university experiment they were fed that hormone generously, and they not only laid all winter—they laid 2 eggs a day! If a pullet becomes sexually mature while the days are lengthening, she will begin laying eggs even before she has finished growing. If a pullet becomes mature enough to lay eggs when the days are shortening, she may not begin to lay eggs until the days lengthen again the following spring. If you choose to go natural and give your chickens a winter vacation with no

Month	45°N Lat.	40°N Lat.	35°N Lat.	30°N Lat.
January	9hr, 09min	9hr, 39min	10hr, 04min	10hr, 25min
February	10hr, 26min	10hr, 41min	10hr, 56min	11hr, 09min
March	11hr, 53min	11hr, 54min	11hr, 57min	11hr, 58min
April	13hr, 29min	13hr, 15min	13hr, 04min	12hr, 53min
May	14hr, 51min	14hr, 23min	13hr, 59min	13hr, 39min
June	15hr, 35min	15hr, 00min	14hr, 30min	14hr, 04min
July	15hr, 07min	14hr, 34min	14hr, 07min	13hr, 44min
August	14hr, 06min	13hr, 46min	13hr, 29min	13hr, 14min
September	12hr, 33min	12hr, 30min	12hr, 26min	12hr, 22min
October	11hr, 01min	11hr, 12min	11hr, 20min	11hr, 28min
November	9hr, 34min	9hr, 59min	10hr, 21min	10hr, 41min
December	8hr, 48min	9hr, 22min	9hr, 50min	10hr, 13min

HOURS OF DAYLIGHT BY MONTH

more light than what nature supplies, they'll definitely lay fewer eggs in winter—like 2 eggs per week per hen. Then spring will come and they'll all start to lay maximum at once—like 5 eggs per week per hen. Suddenly you'll be up to your ears in eggs.

Light-Stimulated Laying. It may not be a good idea for you to put electricity in the hen house or use it if it's already there. Lights will increase egg production but they also raise your electric bill, raise your feed bill (because laying chickens are eating more), and invite egg-laying burnout in your chickens. (Once again, I'm trying to give you all sides of the argument, and all requisite data to make your own decision and proceed on it.) In the northern United States, days are too short for maximum egg-laying during many of the fall and winter months. If you want to buy electricity for

egg-making, exactly when you begin supplementing light and how many extra daylight hours you will need to provide depend on your latitude. At an average northern U.S. location, you would start supplementing about August 15. During November, December, and January, the months when days are shortest, you'd need to supply about 5 extra hours of light. You can add the hours to their day at sunset, or you can turn their light on a sufficient number of hours before daybreak and achieve the same result. You can leave the light on all night and still get the benefit to egg-laying, if turning it off is a nuisance to you. Modern timer devices that take care of turning it on and off for you simplify that problem and save electricity. If you supplement light, it's important that you do it regularly. A lighting period that is irregular, or stops, will promptly result in irregular or reduced laying, reduced rooster fertility, and hen broodiness. And it's important that you continue it until your artificial lighting neatly phases into the days of naturally increasing light.

Use a 40–60 watt bulb with a reflector to enhance the wattage. Brighter light isn't necessary to get the effect. If you have a sizable chicken house, one such bulb with a reflector every 10 feet will do. An Alaskan reader wrote me that she hangs a kerosene lantern in her hen house just about dusk during the winter. She leaves only enough oil in the base to burn the needed number of hours to supply 14 hours of daylight. Some growers, with a more sophisticated system, use a small transition light to resemble dusk. That allows the chickens to go to their roosts for the night in a natural kind of way. Bright light, suddenly shut off and leaving the chickens in pitch darkness, can create a problem as chickens may have trouble finding their roosts and steering well enough to fly up and get on them.

HENS TO CULL: Cull non-layers and maybe also the early molters. A pullet who has never yet laid an egg has a very yellow beak and feet. As she commences laying the yellow gradually bleaches out of beak and feet. So your first culling will be of hens who for some reason do not lay eggs at all.

Early Molters. Some people think the first birds to molt should be culled, because they are often the last to return to laying. You can check your flock for culls whenever you want a chicken dinner, or periodically every few months. A pullet or hen with feathers missing from the top of her head is not molting. A bald head and bare back are the result of too many attempts at mating by one or more roosters. (The rooster grabs the top of her head with his beak in order to steady and balance himself and places his feet on her back to hold her down.) To catch early molter culls, check during July and August. Hens that are laying lots of eggs have bright eyes, a warm, fully developed, bright red comb and wattles, and a comparatively large, moist rectum. You can fit 2 knuckles to 2 to 3 fingers between the pubic bones on each side of her rectum. (The easiest time to catch and handle chickens to do this test is at night when they are on the roost.) That's the good girl and you spare the chicken that fits that description. The chicken to be culled has dull eyes, a cold, dull-colored, shriveled comb, a small, round, dry vent, and you can only get one finger between her pelvic bones. That chicken is either a simple non-layer, or she is a layer that is in molt. You can't judge them by the feathers. A good layer may well have ragged, worn plumage because she's putting so much of her energy into egg-laying, whereas a low producer may have better looking feathers.

But that was then. This is now. Genetic lines have been selected for hens that can get through their molt without a break in laying.

Avoiding Culling. Put all your flock on the same in-and-out schedule, not bothering to check for non-layers, and butcher them all and replace with a fresh crop you've raised—say at the end of their third laying season.

Water and Food for Chickens (and Other Adult Fowl)

WATER: You must have a constant supply of clean drinking water available. Even a short period of water shortage can slow growth or egg production, and chickens can take a distressingly long while to come out of such a slump. Grown chickens need twice as much water as they do food. Chicks need even more. In very hot weather, chickens pant to cool themselves (water evaporates from their lungs). That form of air-conditioning may double their previous level of water consumption. Chickens can be left for a weekend alone, but not unless you've made arrangements for an adequate supply of water while you're gone. They can do without food a lot better than without water. In winter time, frozen water can be a problem. My mother used to go out in freezing weather several times a day carrying hot water for her chickens. They'd start to drink as soon as it got reasonably cool and it would be long enough before it froze for them to drink their fill (this was in an unheated, uninsulated chicken house).

You can water adult birds in any sort of container, but something they can't tip over is best. Figure a 1-gal. capacity waterer for every 12–15 hens, filled at least once per day. You can make a homemade waterer out of the bottom of a plastic jug, and then cover that with a wooden-sided box that has a chicken-wire top. The birds can drink through the chicken wire, but they can't tip the plastic over. If the water freezes in the jug, one sharp rap gets it out and re-placements, if needed, are cheap.

FOOD: Poultry have no teeth and swallow their food whole. They have 2 stomachs. The topmost one is their crop, which stores food. The second, lower one is their heavily muscled gizzard, which "chews" the food by grinding it against small stones the bird has swallowed for that purpose.

Train your fowl of any variety to come when called by rewarding them with their food. Use a characteristic sound, whistle, hand clap, whatever. That way you can gather them when wanted and lure them into their pen when needed.

Food Containers. You can buy fancy food containers. The ones that hang from the ceiling are to prevent the chickens from scratching litter into their food or food out of the container. Or you can make a food container, like a wooden trough, for them. Or you can throw the food on their litter or on the ground and let them get exercise hunting for it. Or some combination of the preceding. Thoroughly clean and sterilize food and water containers once a week for chicks, once a month for adult birds—more often if the containers get visibly disgusting. To do this remove any clinging manure with a scrub brush, then wash the container in a sink or tub that holds 2½ c. regular liquid bleach per 5 gal. water along with some laundry soap. Let them drip dry. Refill and serve. Don't pour fresh feed of any sort on top of uneaten older feed ever. Rotate your feed containers so that one is picked clean before you refill it. Don't feed your poultry moldy food.

Of Food and Egg Production. The better your layers are fed, the more eggs they'll produce. To make a laying flock pay, feed them to the hilt. For every 12 percent you cut back on their food, they'll slack off on laying 25 percent. And they must have a balanced diet to grow well or lay well: carbohydrates, protein, calcium and phosphorus, trace elements, and vitamins. Old-timers say the time of day you feed them matters, too: that for best production you should feed them amply twice per day, once before they go to bed, and again have food and water waiting for them when they rise in the morning. (Since chickens are such early risers, you'd probably want to set that food out the night before, after they've gone to sleep.)

Commercial Feed. It's available in differently formulated offerings for baby chicks, growing fryers, growing pullets, layers, and breeders. There are also all-purpose feeds available: for young birds (up to 5 months) and for the older flock. An adult chicken eats 85–110 pounds of feed per year. If you're wondering how much food is enough simply take note of how much they're eating. If there is no food at all left over at night or in the morning, give them more. If they are not eating up all their food, decrease it. That same principle works with home-devised diet.

Commercial vs. Home-Grown Feed. The notion that you must have modern, commercially prepared, or mixed-by-formula chicken feed to own chickens is an insult to the intelligence and honor of thousands of years of chicken farmers who domesticated the animals and kept the genetic lines going right up to the time-line doorstep of our present era. That notion is, however, good business for commercial feed sellers. And it is certainly true that their feeds are carefully researched, carefully prepared, and more foolproof than your own. It is also true that, using commercially prepared feeds, you can grow your meat-bird to the desired weight faster and on less pounds of feed than you can on home-devised or foraging diets. And it is also true that commercial feed is much more expensive than whole grain you purchase directly from a farmer you know, and far more expensive than the grain and other foods you can raise yourself on a small plot of ground. Using commercial feeds is a luxury that risks bankrupting your operation. On less concentrated, cheaper, home-devised diets, poultry will ultimately achieve their target weight, albeit slower and with perhaps less fat, which you don't need anyway. Layers may not lay the absolute most of which they're capable, but they may not burn out as fast to become culls either. I'd hate to see society come to some kind of crisis and not have the know-how to keep their livestock going without centralized poultry-feed processing and packaging plants.

Feeding Table Scraps.
Chickens will eat all your peelings, sour or sweet milk, pickles, meat scraps, and rancid lard. They love all sorts of overripe or damaged vegetables, cull fruit, pea pods and vines, thinnings from the garden, general table scraps, and refrigerator throw-outs. They're not so keen on onions, green peppers, cabbage, or citrus fruits. And don't feed them moldy food. (Feed those to pigs or compost.) Marilou Heath of Rialto, CA, wrote me: "We were out to dinner today. The waitress looked odd when we asked for a doggie bag—all we had left was banana peels, melon rinds, and French fries, nothing that any self-respecting dog would eat. Had to explain it was actually for the chickens. And the bunny loves banana peels."

Grain.
A chicken's gizzard is ideal for grinding grain—as long as the bird can get grit. So you don't need to grind it (or have it ground) for them. An exception to that might be for small bantams who sometimes have trouble eating very large grains and prefer them to be ground. Young chicks also need it broken up. A mixture of grain is better than a single grain. Coarser grinds are better than flour or mash grinds, which may stick to the beak or get wasted. Corn is probably the easiest to grow at home. A traditional feed called "scratch" consists of a rather flexible mixture of grains—such as field corn, buckwheat, and sorghum heads. Or corn/oats/barley. Or corn/oats. Or corn/wheat. Or corn/oats/wheat. Or corn/wheat/sorghum. Or your own formula. But corn can be a peril as well as a blessing. Birds love corn, but it's a high-fat, low-protein food. Fat roosters don't breed as well. Fat hens don't lay as well. To a real extent, what you feed them will be reflected in what you get out of them. If you want protein out of them, you have to put protein into them.

Contrary to popular impression, a chicken does not have to have grain to live, though grain is a rich food that certainly encourages them to grow well and lay generously. The most essential time of year to feed grain is winter, when chickens need extra nourishment to keep themselves warm. The best time of day to feed it is just before they go to bed. That encourages them to come home to roost, and to lay an egg at home in the morning. An old-time way of fixing the quantity of grain to feed was to feed only the amount of grain the chickens would clean up in about 30 minutes. In winter they made that 30 minutes in the morning and then another 30 minutes at night. The grain can be fed in a trough or scattered in the litter or on the ground. Hopper feeding keeps confined birds out of their droppings. On the other hand, tossing the grain into the floor litter gives confined birds something interesting to do and reduces the tendency to pick at each other, satisfies their instinct to scratch, and provides them more exercise.

Feeding Chickens in Winter.
You can't get something for nothing. When there are no or few natural foods for the chickens outside, or the weather is too bad for them to get out, they need commercial feed, plus grain, water, and grit. Or, if their menu is to be home-devised, feed them protein, grain, and greens. In winter they'll enjoy vegetable peelings; cooked cheap bulky vegetables like squash and mangel (stock) beets; warm, cooked cull potatoes; and sprouted grain. They'll also benefit from a source of calcium. They'll eat some good alfalfa hay and get all the grass and weed seeds mixed in there. If they aren't on commercial feed, make sure they can get some sunshine or Vitamin D. Chickens that are allowed to be out all winter, freely ranging, don't lay as many eggs as confined (deep-litter or battery-style) chickens. Still, such a hen, if she's of a good-laying breed, may still lay 200 eggs or so, which is not shabby. The lower the temperature, the more food your poultry need to consume just to be okay. Each degree of temperature drop in their environment forces chickens to eat proportionately more food to maintain themselves. In a below-freezing environment 100 heavy breed layers would require an extra 375 pounds of feed per month. For the same cost you could insulate the chicken house better and you'd get more eggs, as well as saving some feed expense.

SUNSHINE: In the dead of winter my mother used to feed both me and her chickens cod-liver oil, which contains Vitamin D. Modern research has explained what old-timers knew from trial and error: chickens, like people, make Vitamin D from sunshine. If they can't get out to have sun shining on them, they'll have to be given cod-liver oil (or some other D supplement) or commercial chicken feed. If chickens are low on D, they won't thrive and they won't lay, or they may lay thin-shelled eggs. Young ones may grow with weak bones that result in leg deformities. The easiest solution is to provide them with an outdoor run since sun shining through glass panes doesn't do the job. But if you live in northern Alaska and in winter being outdoors is not an option, then give the vitamin.

FREE-ROAMING VS. CONFINED CHICKENS: Most chicken growers don't have room enough for roaming chickens, dogs, goats, or anything else. Such are these modern, crowded, times. Chickens that roam, at least some of the time, look the happiest and healthiest. Farm-raised chickens that were mothered by real chicken mothers are most knowledgeable about foraging. Bantie breeds tend to take to it naturally, but most chickens can learn to do some. In summer my chickens range all over the farm, looking for weed seeds and insects. Chickens don't understand about property lines. If you have close neighbors, perhaps you can compromise by just letting the chickens out the last few hours before sundown, so they won't have time enough to get too far from home. No matter how good at foraging your poultry are, don't leave them completely on their own. Chickens can get into insect baits and rodent poisons, and they should not feed near where crops or orchards have recently been sprayed. Give them some food in the chicken house to remind them where they are supposed to lay their eggs and where home is. The best food supplement to free-ranging chickens' diets, besides table scraps, is plain old grain, offered morning and night.

Of Roaming Chickens in a Garden.
They'll take a toll by pecking tomatoes and strawberries. You have to decide for yourself if the bug patrolling is worth the price you pay in

sharing your produce. You'll definitely want to keep chickens out of the garden just after planting corn, beans, peas and beets, until the young plants are well started and no longer have the remnant of a seed at their roots. Otherwise, chickens will dig up and eat the seeds. Some people let only a select few of their chickens (banties usually) do the garden patrol. It really depends on how many chickens you have, how big a garden you have, what type of produce you're growing there, and how bad your bug problem is. To keep them out, you'll either have to fence the chickens in somewhere else, or fence them out of the garden.

Green Food for Confined Chickens. They love green food of any kind, from plain grass to dandelion greens to even chopped nettles. In summer, feed them from your garden: carrot tops, pea shells, surplus Swiss chard. If you serve confined birds their greens in a wire basket hanging from the ceiling they'll be entertained. It's the green feed in their diet that makes egg yolks from farm chickens darker than those from commercial chickens (more vitamins make darker color). If chickens have the opportunity, they can and will use greens for 20 percent of their diet. An easier plan any time but the dead of winter, however, may be to pasture them. There is a limit to the good chickens can get from any bulk food with high-fiber and low-nutrient content like greens. If you try to push that type of food in general and limit other types, their health will suffer because a chickens' system is made for eating a significant proportion of protein (grubs, worms under natural conditions) and grain (weed seeds under natural conditions). The goose or cow will do better on greens than the chicken.

Fenced Chicken Pasture. For chickens that must be confined in good weather, you can create a portable chicken coop holding, say, about a dozen hens, with a little night shelter at one end and a wire-enclosed and wire-covered pen and an open bottom so they can graze. Move that about every 2 or 3 days onto fresh grass. Don't leave it in one place until the grass is totally killed. Or you can build sizable, fenced runs that are connected to your chicken house. Three is the perfect number of runs for this system (with a possible fourth enclosed run in which you feed and water them). Plant the 3 green runs to some kind of hay or cultivated grass, and then alternate your poultry from one to another—about every 2 or 3 weeks—so they don't stay long enough to eat down to and kill the plant roots. Swiss chard, chicken kale, and chicken lettuce are other good plants to grow at least a little of in the chicken runs. The general rule is this: the larger and greener your chickens' pasture area, the better it will be for them. If you can fence in an entire orchard for them, or some similar territory, better yet. Geese are natural grass-grazers. Chickens are not. The domestic chicken is derived from an East Asian jungle fowl that scratched in the dry leaves and rotting vegetation of a forest floor looking for insects. You have to work out what will work in your particular circumstances. Milkweed, nightshade plants and berries, and leaves of the black locust tree are poisonous to chickens.

Andy Lee's book *Chicken Tractor: The Permaculture Guide to Happy Hens and Healthy Soil* (1998) is about raising chickens on grass in a movable chicken coop. Just out is his *Day Range Poultry: Every Chicken Owner's Guide to Grazing Gardens and Improving Pastures* (Good Earth Publications: 540-261-8874; **goodearthpublications.com/**). Joel Salatin's book *Pastured Poultry Profits: Net $25,000 in Six Months on*

Twenty Acres (Chelsea Green) covers raising pasture-grazed chickens from building pens to processing. His books (and seminar schedule!) are available in print or video from Acres, USA's bookstore: 512-892-4400. More at **sunsite. unc.edu/farming-connection/grazing/pastpoul/resource. htm.** *Free-Range Poultry* (1997) by Katie Thear is a British book with lots of attractive poultry skid housing designs. Alanna Moore wrote the Aussie entry on this subject: *Backyard Poultry Naturally* (1998).

Robert Plamondon is both a tech writer and a free-range poultry grower. His website provides FAQs, a description of his own setup, and reviews of recommended books: **robert@plamondon.com; www.plamondon.com.** ATTRA's info on pastured poultry is at **www.attra.ncat.org/ attra-pub/pasturedpoultry.html.**

Herman Beck-Chenoweth's *Free-Range Poultry Production and Marketing* (1996; 740-596-4379) presents info on production and direct selling for the producer/processor. His system is 8 x 18 ft. wooden skid houses enclosed with chicken wire and with gabled tarp-covered roofs and litter-covered wood floors (300 birds per house). He opens the house doors every morning and shuts the birds in every night. He uses a strong perimeter fence around the field to contain wanderers, but usually the birds forage close to home and return there at night. He harvests continuously. The system is described in more detail at his website: **www.free-rangepoultry.com.**

Join **www.pasturepoultry@yahoogroups.com,** and the American Pastured Poultry Producers Association (membership $20/yr; good-quality newsletter, *Grit*); for more info: PO Box 1024, Chippewa Falls, WI 54729; **grit@apppa.org; www.apppa.org.**

You can buy or make movable cage/shelters. Henspa offers a wide choice of backyard-sized chicken-house/yard combos with wheels hidden inside, ice-free water supply, feeders, and nests inside: Henhotel (25 hens); Henhaven (5 hens); Henspa (10 hens). There's also the Henspa Deluxe or a vertical garden and portable poultry/swine paddock-fertilizer generator, the Foodspa: **www.henspa.com/.** Robert and Cindy Pellet build their Forsham Cottage Arks (dovecotes and chicken dwellings) suitable for a small backyard at 44 (0) 1233 82-157; fax +44 (0) 1233 820157; Goreside Farm, Great Chart, Ashford, Kent TN26 1JU ENGLAND; **www.forshamcottagearks.co.uk/.**

Brower sells a PVC pastured poultry hoop pen that rests easily, moves around freely, and lets birds graze yet stay cool on scorching hot days and dry on wet days. Brooder flaps/wind blocks are available at additional cost: 319-469-4141; **www.browerequip.com.**

PROTEIN: Protein is essential for chickens. Free-running chickens, in suitable weather, gather their own from bugs and worms. Commercial feed supplies it. If you are using a home-devised diet, include milk, meat, or bugs in season for their protein. You can feed chickens butchering scraps, including innards, and they'll appreciate them. If you have plenty of freezer space, you can stretch such meals by freezing meat scraps in reasonably sized packages. You can also get protein supplies for them from a feed merchant—meat, bean meals, sunflower seeds, lupine seed, linseed, coarse ground peas or beans, and alfalfa meal or good-quality alfalfa hay. These vary in the amount and completeness of their protein, so you are safest offering a variety, or choosing an animal-derived protein. I would avoid feeding them fish in any form, because of rampant water pollution these days. Don't feed soybeans unless they have been heat-treated because raw soybeans contain compounds that can be poisonous to chickens. Don't feed them cottonseed meal because it contains gossypol that will poison chickens.

Milk Protein. Chickens love sweet milk, sour milk, or buttermilk. If you're offering milk for protein, make sure you give enough. Chickens on a completely noncommercial diet would love a minimum of 1 gal. milk per day per 30 birds, plus all the grain they'll eat (or other substantial food like baked squash and mangel beets), plus ample access to pasture, or being fed cut greens daily (or good leafy, green hay in wintertime). Powdered milk cannot fully meet this need because it is missing the whey (liquid), which contains a part of the nutrients the chickens need. Don't serve milk in a galvanized container because of its tendency to turn acidic. Serve it in plastic, enameled, glass, ceramic, pottery, or stainless steel feeders.

CALCIUM: Growing chickens, like children, need calcium to make bones. Laying hens need calcium to make strong eggshells. If your layer's diet becomes calcium deficient, she'll quit laying within 2 weeks. You can supply a partial calcium supplement by drying eggshells until they're brittle, breaking them up thoroughly with a rolling pin, and then feeding them back to the chickens. (Lane Morgan told me she bakes them because baking makes them easier to crush and, she figures, changes the taste enough to make the chickens less likely to become barnyard egg-eaters.) But a chicken needs more calcium than what she can get from just her own recycled eggshells. Ground oyster shells or ground limestone are good for the calcium content, too. The chicken partially grinds the oyster shells in its gizzard and absorbs what calcium is released that way. The old-timers met this need by feeding surplus dairy products, which are rich in calcium and phosphorus. There can't be such a thing as too much calcium in a chicken's diet, so offer oyster shells, milk, etc.

Egg Eaters. Overcrowded chickens, with insufficient space to run and insufficient gravel in their diet, are more likely than others to develop into egg eaters. Make sure there's plenty of calcium in their diet, provide nests that are quite dark inside, and gather eggs frequently, even as often as 3 times a day. A chicken who has learned the habit might learn differently if you plant an egg filled with red pepper to give an experience she won't forget. A drastic treatment if you see a chicken eating an egg, or notice egg yolk on its beak, is to cut off the end of the bird's beak, or butcher it. To try to identify the culprit, you might set an egg out in the open and watch and see what happens. Darken the chicken house windows and reduce the wattage of light bulbs, if you are supplementing light. Penny Anderson of Aitkin, MN, advises, "To cure egg-eaters, get plastic or one of those decorative marble eggs and set them out in the nests. Make sure to collect the good eggs as soon as possible."

OF GRAVEL AND THE GIZZARD: Chickens have to have a chance to pick up pebbles (grit) for their gizzards. A chicken has no teeth. It swallows down into a first stomach, the "crop," at the base of the neck. Then, as needed, the bird swallows on down from there into its chewing stomach, the "gizzard." In that tough gizzard, grain is pushed around amongst those pebbles until it is literally ground to powder. Chickens constantly suffer a certain attrition for

their gizzard's gravel supply. Confined chickens can suffer a real digestive crisis if you don't take adequate care of them in this regard. Without fresh tiny little rocks to eat, they'll scratch in the manure, find, and eat the old ones over again, which can be comparatively unhealthy. But they have to have them (unless they're living on mash). So, supply confined chickens with a container of fine gravel, river gravel, or pebbles. Or you can buy and give them commercial "grit." Figure 1 lb. of grit per month per 3 adult chickens. Supply an appropriate size of grit. Very small birds can't eat large grit; large birds can't keep very small grit in their gizzard—it tends to just pass on through. Feed-store grit comes in 3 sizes: start, for chicks; grower, for bigger chicks; layer, for adult birds. Limestone can't be used as grit: It's soluble.

CANNIBALISM: Sociologists have been interested in the pecking order (literally) that chickens create among themselves: who pecks whom signifies who outranks whom. Of more practical concern is the bird at the bottom. If it starts bleeding, dab iodine or pine tar onto the hurt place, and isolate it until it's healed, because chickens are likely to devour an injured bird if it can't get away on its own. For minor problems the iodine alone may do the job, as chickens hate the smell of iodine. Or use the commercial product, "Anti-Pick Lotion," for this purpose. You apply that to the feathers and the picked areas of chickens. It encourages healing of the wound and is so distasteful to chickens that it discourages the other birds from further picking. Put your anti-pick substance on as soon as you spot a problem.

Picking is less likely if the birds' diet is adequate with plenty of protein and salt. Crowding can make it worse, and boredom contributes. The combination of bright lighting and confinement can cause it. That's why free-ranging birds are much less likely to cannibalize than closely confined ones. Keeping feed before the chickens helps keep their beaks productively occupied. Giving them opportunities to scratch grain out of their litter may distract them from paying so much attention to each other and keep them occupied. To stop an individual pecker who is worse than most, clip the little sharp end part off the tip of that bird's beak with a fingernail clipper. (See "Debeaking.") Or send it to the stew pot. The best thing is not to let cannibalism get started because, like all chicken habits, once they learn it, it's hard to stop.

NOTE: Birds can get very sick from consuming even small amounts of gasoline, engine oil, or polish. This sort of thing can float on top of a puddle and be taken in by a bird drinking puddle water. Even a small amount can cause chronic gastrointestinal illness to the bird. Antifreeze, rat poisons, insect poisons, plant poisons—any or all of these could be deadly to your poultry.

Eggs

Have you ever watched a chicken lay an egg? It's rather a private act, I suppose, but when I was a little girl about 6 or so, I got a great desire to see the egg come out. I patiently waited, every morning that I had the chance, hanging around for days behind a little red hen who laid her eggs in a rather exposed nest. Finally one day it happened: I saw the egg come out! Not as dramatic as watching kittens, puppies, or baby goats come out, but a wonderful moment nonetheless. I was impressed with the serious effort the act required from the hen and her immense relief when it was all over. She jumped up from her nest and walked in a

happy and excited way all about, cackling her head off over the joy of it all. So, if you want to meditate on where eggs come from, that's where, and you can rightfully be grateful to the hen because she worked at it.

FINDING EGGS: A basic principle for gathering eggs from any poultry is this: the more you take, the more they lay, and the less they go broody. And you should gather every day to make sure the eggs are fresh. If your birds are confined in a hen house, it's easy to gather regularly and gather often. If not, it can be an adventure. All hens like to lay where there are already eggs. That's helpful. But they'll often pick a new nest spot if you keep emptying it completely of eggs. Then you'll have to discover it all over again. So leave an egg in there marked with a pencil so you won't let it get too old before gathering that one and using a new one. Homestead mail-order suppliers often offer wooden or plastic "eggs," or a smooth white stone can serve the purpose.

The biggest trouble with letting chickens run loose is that sometimes you never do find the eggs—until mama shows up with a family, or you discover a heap of woefully overripe ones. The best way to keep free-running chickens laying in the hen house (besides shutting them up completely, which would probably throw them into a molt and decrease production), is to feed them in there generously last thing in the afternoon when it is about their bedtime (well before true dark), and then shut them up for the night (keeps out night predators, too). They will tend to lay their eggs first thing in the morning. Waiting a few hours after their rising hour to open their door gives you extra security. Then you can let them go on their foraging way. It also helps if you have a roomy, nice chicken house with lots of nesting boxes made the way hens like them, and plenty of clean straw bedding inside.

VARIOUS EGGS: Your home-grown eggs may vary considerably in size, color, and freshness. Pullet eggs are smaller than those the hen will lay later. You can tell when a pullet starts to lay eggs because she gets broad across the behind (same thing happened to me having babies). If you have a small and varied flock you'll learn to recognize each hen's egg—they are a unique combination of size, shape, and color. Then you'll know who's laying and who isn't. (But the heredity will be an undesirable mish-mash.)

BIZARRE EGGS: You may get an egg with 2 yolks. It's fine to eat—just trying to be twins. You may get an egg covered with chicken poop—just wash it off. Your egg yolk may be darker in color and stronger in taste and the egg white thicker and firmer—the whole egg held together more firmly—than store eggs. That would be because your chickens have had access to a richer, more natural diet than commercial layers, which are required to do their most with the

least (and the egg shows the difference). Your home-grown egg may have a speck of blood. That's a hereditary characteristic in some chicken lines and doesn't affect the edibility in the least. The egg may have a distinguishable white speck. In that case, it was a fertile egg and, given the right conditions, could have become a chick. Such an egg is also fine to eat. Your egg may have a weirdly shaped shell. It's good to eat, but don't incubate such eggs because you don't want that hereditary trait passed on—besides, they are less hatchable. Your egg may have an egg inside an egg, a curiosity caused when an egg backs up in the oviduct for some reason and thus goes through the last couple production stages twice. The only obviously undesirable egg is one that has a half-developed chick in it or is full of rotten gunk. Otherwise, if you're in doubt, you have to test for freshness. *NOTE: Use cracked eggs only if it's just the outer shell that is cracked and the inner membrane is okay. The membrane is okay if there isn't any egg oozing out the crack. But just to be on the safe side, cook such eggs thoroughly or use them in foods that will be cooked.*

FRESH OR ROTTEN? If you discover a nest where some hen(s) hid and laid 25 eggs, then the problem is to distinguish which eggs are still fresh enough to use:

The Bowl Test. The simplest way to determine freshness is to put eggs on the menu. Start by examining the eggs carefully. Usually you can tell a bad egg without even breaking it clear open. It's hard to crack because the membrane inside the shell has become tough. It may smell bad, and if you just start to crack the shell, yucky stuff may come oozing out. Okay, those you toss. Then come the marginal cases. You have to shell them into a bowl to find out for sure. You're bound to get surprised sometimes: an egg that looks dirty and old will turn out to be just fine, and vice versa. If the egg in your bowl doesn't have a funny smell and looks average, I'd say go ahead and use it. So pour it out of the small bowl into your mixing bowl, and go on to the next egg. Incidentally, if the last egg was a rotten one, be sure and rinse your testing bowl well before you pour another egg into it.

Float Testing. If you want to know about the egg without opening it—which, once you've encountered hydrogen sulfide, is understandable—use the float test. Put the eggs in a pan of water. Fresh eggs will lie on their sides on the bottom of the pan. If an egg's a few days old, one end will tip upwards. If stale, an egg will stand on end. If plumb rotten, it will float. This is all because an egg contains an air cell at the large end of it. Eggshells are perforated through by tiny holes that would be needed by the chick for breathing. Thus, with time, a part of the liquid content of the egg evaporates, the white and yolk shrink, and the resulting new space is filled by an enlarged air space. But, like life, this float test is not 100 percent dependable.

Candle Testing. A more sophisticated system is to "candle" the eggs. (See "Candling the Eggs" for details.) If the contents do not fill the shell, the egg is not perfectly fresh. As with the float test, the larger the airspace (which is now made visible), the older the egg. The yolk should be perfectly clear and round in outline. Another candling sign for freshness is yolk movement: in an older egg the yolk moves about more freely. An egg that has been stored a while will show some shrinkage, however, even if it has been kept chilled and fresh.

SELLING YOUR EGGS: In general, government regulations permit you to sell eggs to friends, neighbors, and at a roadside stand without a license or supervision. If you acquire 3,000 birds or more and sell to licensed outlets like restaurants, bakeries, and grocery stores, then you will need to comply with state and federal laws and should inquire to find out what they are.

NOTE: *The USDA, because of increasingly frequent cases of food poisoning from salmonella in some commercial eggs all over the country, now advises against eating raw eggs in any form. I was asked to delete from this book every recipe containing raw or undercooked eggs, and I have done so. But I did it sadly and reluctantly, because egg nogs, egg drop soup, and uncooked eggy ice cream were favorite recipes of mine, and because salmonella in eggs has not been a problem for people with a small family flock and their home-grown eggs. Salmonella poisoning from eggs is most likely to be a problem when 4 conditions are present:*
- *Commercial eggs are used.*
- *Many eggs have been combined, as in a scrambled egg mix.*
- *The eggs are then allowed to sit at room temperature for an hour or more before cooking.*
- *The eggs are undercooked.*

These 4 conditions give one bad egg a chance to contaminate the whole batch—followed by a perfect growing environment for the salmonella bacteria. Poisonings of this sort have occurred, for example, in scrambled eggs prepared ahead for a church breakfast. But for absolute safety, the USDA urges you not to eat uncooked or undercooked eggs in any form, because to kill salmonella, the egg or food with egg in it must be heated to 140°F for at least 3½ minutes—no more soft-boiled eggs. How does the salmonella get into the egg? Last I heard, they still weren't sure. The USDA info number about this is (800) 535-4555.

Salmonella: This variety of food poisoning has been a problem in the northeastern United States now for more than 10 years. Recent research has traced it to commercial Grade A eggs. To be precise, a report by the Centers for Disease Control (CDC) states that cases rose sixfold between 1976 and 1986, from 549 to 3,579, and that during the last 2½ years prior, 77 percent of the salmonella outbreaks that could be traced to any particular food source were found to have been caused by eggs that had contained salmonella. It used to be thought that the problem was cracked or dirty eggs. The latest CDC study has caused researchers to hypothesize that the bacteria are actually being transmitted to the eggs before the shell is formed. To kill salmonella, the internal temperature of the egg must be raised to 140°F for at least 3½ minutes. It is extremely unlikely that your personal flock of birds has this problem.

EGGS AS DEER REPELLENT: Margie Minard of Mt. Vernon, OH, told me eggs help those who have problems with deer in their gardens. Her husband read that one of the huge lumber companies found out that deer hate eggs and had developed an eggy spray for their seedlings. She said "We've just been throwing our used eggshells out here and there in the garden and among the berry bushes and the deer don't come near any more!"

EGG-USING RECIPES: When eggs are in season (spring), you can make scrambled eggs, deviled eggs, pickled eggs, French toast, puddings, crepes suzettes, eggnogs, ice cream, homemade mayonnaise, potato salad, or put plain old hard-boiled eggs into packed lunches. If cholesterol consumption is a worry in your family, feed some or most of the yolks (that's where all the cholesterol is) back to the hens or pigs and shift the recipes to use pure or mostly egg whites. In other words, you could make scrambled eggs for a family using 6 whites and, for example, only 2 yolks. Chicken eggs are 10.5 percent fat. Eggs should be cooked at a low or moderate temperature because a higher temperature makes the egg tough. When eggs are used to thicken liquids, the mixture is generally cooked over hot water kept just below the boiling point to prevent curdling or separation of the liquid.

➢ *HARD-BOILED EGGS Fresh eggs, unlike cold-storage eggs (grocery store), are hard to peel when hard-boiled. That's because they haven't lost any fluid to evaporation—the inside of the egg doesn't have any space between it and the shell—so part of the white layer tends to come off with the peel. The way to avoid this problem is to let the eggs destined for hard boiling get at least 5 days old before they hit the hot water. Then put your eggs into cold water (not more than 2 or 3 dozen in one container), bring to a boil, then simmer, covered tightly, for 10 to 15 minutes. Cool on the stove for half an hour. Put into very cold water and leave for 5 minutes. They should now peel easily. If the egg forms a greenish colored layer around the yolk, the egg has been cooked too long or at too high a temperature. This color can also develop if you store the cooked egg. It is unattractive, but harmless.*

➢ *SHIRRED EGGS Melt 4 T. butter and distribute it among 6 small custard dishes or muffin containers. (There used to be a regular product for this called an "egg shirrer.") Dust the buttered bottoms with dry bread crumbs. Break 2 eggs into each hole. Don't stir. Sprinkle with salt and pepper and set them into a moderate oven until thoroughly set.*

➢ *EGGY CREPES Combine 6 eggs, 1½ c. unbleached or whole-wheat flour, ½ c. loosely packed brown sugar or a couple tablespoons honey, and 1 c. milk. Beat until there's air captured in it for lightness. Pour just enough to make a large, thin pancake onto a greased frying pan or griddle over medium low heat, turning when one side is done. Serve flat or rolled up with butter and honey, fruit sauce, syrup, Devonshire cream, or cream cheese inside.*

➢ *OLD-FASHIONED RICE PUDDING Boil 1 c. uncooked rice in 2 c. water (with a pinch of salt) over strong heat until water is absorbed. Then add 5 c. milk and continue cooking over low heat until milk is absorbed, stirring occasionally. Beat 5 eggs, add 1 c. sugar, and 2 t. vanilla. Move rice to an oven casserole dish. Fold in egg mixture. Add 1 c. raisins (optional) at this point. Sprinkle cinnamon on top, and bake at 350° F for 45 minutes.*

➢ *SCRAMBLED EGGS FOR A CREW Beat together 1 dozen eggs, 1½ c. milk, 1 t. salt, 1 rounded T. flour, ⅛ t.*

pepper, and 4 T. butter. Fry in butter over low to medium heat. Enough for 8 people.

⊛ **DEVILED EGGS** *Cut hard-boiled eggs neatly into halves lengthwise. Remove and mash the yolks and season them with salt, pepper, mustard, grated onion, or what you prefer. Roll the mashed, seasoned yolk into balls of the appropriate size and put one ball into each half egg-white. Serve spread out on a platter.*

Omelet Secrets To avoid sticking to the pan, use enough oil to flow around the pan. And use a skillet with flared sides, rather than a straight-sided one.

⊛ **VEGGIE OMELET** *4 eggs, pepper, 2 T. butter, chopped vegetables (such as onion, tomato, green pepper, mushrooms, broccoli, shredded sprouts), grated cheddar cheese. Beat eggs. Melt butter in skillet and add egg mixture. Add your choice of vegetables to one side of the omelet and season with pepper. Cook slowly till underside is barely brown, then sprinkle on the cheese and fold the plain side over the vegetables and cheese. When the egg has fully cooked, serve.*

Separating Eggs. Separate whites from yolks by cracking the egg over a bowl and gently breaking the shell in two, keeping the yolk in one half of the shell. Let the white drain into the bowl by pouring the yolk from one shell to the other.

Beating Egg Whites. To get the highest peaks, separate the whites and yolks while the eggs are still cold, but wait until they are at room temperature to beat them. (Keep the yolks for other cooking.) Beat the whites with an egg beater at a steady, high speed. They will get frothy and gradually thicken. You can quicken the process by adding a pinch of salt or cream of tartar. The whites are "stiff" when they form peaks that stand by themselves. First you get soft peaks, then harder ones. Home-grown egg whites whip much faster than store-bought ones.

Custard Secrets
1. Custard should come out firm rather than runny.
2. Check for doneness by inserting a thin knife into the center of the custard. If it comes out clean, the custard is done. If any egg clings to the knife, the custard needs more cooking.

3. If it's cooked, but still runny, there weren't enough eggs for the amount of milk. (Most recipes are based on large-size eggs.) Or you used too much sugar, which can also cause the custard not to set up properly. Or the cause of runniness can be that your custard was stirred during baking.
4. If you want a soft custard, stir the mixture from time to time as it cooks. If you want a firm custard, leave it alone. If you want it extra firm, use more eggs.

HOMEMADE EASTER EGG DYES: Wilma Litchfield, my Utah pen pal for years now, wrote me about this. She says safflower (plus 1 t. vinegar) gives pale yellow; orange marigold petals make yellow; turmeric (plus 1 t. vinegar) makes golden yellow; yellow marigold petals make greenish yellow; red onion skins make a rusty red; sandalwood gives a salmon color; cranberries (plus 1 t. vinegar) make a pale gray-purple; blueberries make a bluish purple; raspberries make a pale lavender; walnut hulls cause a nice chocolate brown. Dyeing with red cabbage leaves gets the best color if you add 1 T. alum.

To begin, wipe egg with vinegar, rinse, and pat dry. Put each egg on a cheesecloth square together with the dyestuff you want to use for that egg. Put egg in center of dyestuff. Pull up sides of cloth around egg, tying ends with a rubber band. Put egg packages in a pot of cool water deep enough to cover them completely, heat the water to boiling, and continue cooking at a slow boil for at least 10 more minutes. Take eggs out of water, and cool packages under cool water. (Use white vinegar to avoid adding unwanted color.) (See Chapter 5 for more information.)

No matter what it is, or how unimportant you may think a particular item is, somewhere somebody collects it. And no matter what the subject, somewhere somebody has written a book about it. At least, that's my theory. On this subject a good reference is *Natural Dyes and Home Dyeing* by Rita J. Adrostco (Dover, 1971).

Here are some specific Easter egg recipes.

⊛ **ONION SKIN PACKAGES** *Wrap eggs in onion skins, then in a cloth, and then tie with string. Onion skins are a natural dye, and the string presses the skin against the egg, making patterns also. Boil these eggs in the cloth package (they can start out uncooked), and then unwrap for lovely surprises. (Can be dyed again with food coloring for further decoration.)*

⊛ **FOOD COLORING AND VINEGAR** *Submerge a hard-boiled egg in a cup of water that has a little vinegar in it. (Vinegar sets the color.) Using a dropper, drop the food color onto the egg. It spreads and makes amazing patters. Rinse the eggs afterwards to remove excess color. From Carol Kahn, Vernonia, OR.*

⊛ **PRECOOKED DYES** *From Mrs. Linda Crabtree, Kettering, OH: "Natural dye colors turn out much softer looking than commercial egg dyes and often give you a spotty or speckled finish. Dyes should be cooled before using, preferably overnight. Add just a little vinegar to fix the color. (Don't boil vinegar in aluminum.) Examples: 5 red cabbage leaves plus 4 c. water equals aqua color and an egg pattern like tie-dye material. Or boil the outer dry skins of 2 medium onions for an orange dye. Orange peel gives you a light yellow dye. Yellow Delicious apple peelings make lavender with soft rust flakes. Thyme boiled makes a pale graying yellow-orange dye. The possibilities are only limited by your imagination and willingness to give it some effort."*

❧ *DANDELION AND PINE NEEDLE EGGS* *"First send the children out to gather lots of daffodils, dandelions, needles from fir or pine trees, and big, strong leaves. Then take your uncooked eggs and wrap them with the leaves, pulling in the flowers and needles against the eggshell under the leaf. Cover the egg by wrapping more leaves around the whole thing. Tie string around the leaves to hold them on. Boil until the eggs are hard-cooked. Remove from water, take off the string, and unwrap the leaves. The pine or fir needles will have produced a design on the egg. The green leaves produce yellow. Daffodils and dandelions produce deeper orangish-yellow coloring. For deep dark blues and purples, squash blackberries or blueberries on the egg and then cover with leaves or onion skin. The leaves can be used again and again. Boiling longer produces richer, darker shades. The eggs are beautiful and each is different. We also like to dye the big goose eggs. The geese lay about Easter time and it's fun to have the big eggs."* All this information is from Nancy Dyer of Corbett, OR.

❧ *FLOWER-PATTERNED EGGS* *"My great-grandmother taught my mother this. You need brown onion skins, small spring flowers like buttercups, grass flowers, uncooked white-shelled eggs, small squares of soft cloth, and string. Lay flowers next to eggs, petals spread out. Next, position onion skins on top of flowers. Wrap gently in soft cloth and tie with string. Cook in gently simmering water about 25 minutes. Unwrap cloth, peel off onion skin and flowers, and they are truly beautiful."* From Karen Hayes, St. John, WA.

PRESERVING EGGS: Under natural conditions, more hens' eggs are laid during the months of March, April, May, and June than during the other eight months combined. So you tend to have egg shortages from December to January, and an egg glut in April and May. Preserving eggs evens that cycle out somewhat. The eggs you preserve should be the ones that you are most sure are fresh—not over 4 days old, less if possible. Eggs from hens that have no roosters running with them (infertile) will keep longer than fertile eggs. But you can store fertile eggs, too. There are many storage methods. Choose what suits you best.

About Washing Eggs in the Shell. Don't wash any egg that is to be stored in the shell unless you're doing a mineral-oil seal, or unless you follow the instructions below. If the egg is dirty, it's better to just put it into the daily supply to be used up soon. Not washing helps eggs keep, because an eggshell is naturally covered by a gelatinous film, which

washing removes. That film helps seal the shell pores. Without it, the egg is more susceptible to bacteria and evaporation. You can assume that a dirty egg is covered with bacteria. A rotten egg is one that bacteria have gotten into. The washing dilemma exists because it is a fact that bacteria can be more likely to get inside the shells if dirty eggs are washed in the wrong way than if the dirt is simply left on there. That is because adding moisture to the dirt will encourage the bacteria to breed and increase; liquid carrying the load of surface bacteria, under certain circumstances, can penetrate through the shell pores into the egg; and washing the "bloom" off the egg removes its outermost shell-pore protecting layer.

Safely Washing Eggs for Preserving. Washing eggs in cold water simply causes them to spoil more quickly. You can make it easy for yourself by simply washing dirty eggs in warm water; use within a week and they'll be fine. Or, first scrape off big chunks of dirt with a table knife. Then prepare your water. It must be at least 20°F warmer than the eggs (minimum 90°F; maximum 120°F). Use a cleaning mixture made of 2 T. detergent plus 4 T. chlorine bleach per 1 gal. water. Use a soft cloth to wipe away dirt. Rinse with clear water that is slightly warmer than the wash water was. Do not wipe eggs dry. Let them air dry in the open on a towel or in a rack.

Cold Storage. The commercial method of preserving eggs is to store them at between 35 and 40°F. At that temperature they'll keep fresh for 100 days. A high humidity is helpful. Don't store eggs near smelly things like kerosene or onions because they easily absorb odors through the shell pores. Old-timers did a sort of cold storage by packing eggs in a barrel or crock (nowadays in a plastic can) in sawdust or oatmeal, small end down, and keeping them in a cool place comparable to cold-storage temperature. For you that could be your refrigerator, root cellar, or basement.

For cold storage, it's best to gather the eggs every day or even several times a day and store them right away in your cool place. A chicken's body temperature is about 107°F. To stay fresh, a freshly laid egg needs to cool to around 60°F reasonably soon. The cooling rate will depend on how soon after being laid you collect the egg, what the air temperature was while it was waiting to be collected, and what you did with the egg after it was collected. Eggs put into egg cartons don't cool quickly because the Styrofoam or cardboard is a good insulator. Freshly laid eggs left together in a bucket keep each other warm. In very hot weather you may want to collect eggs at 10am, 1pm, and 5pm. An ideal place to store eggs is a basement or root cellar that is cool and damp and doesn't have much fluctuation in temperature or humidity. Self-defrosting refrigerators are not very good for long-term egg storage because they pull moisture and will gradually dry out fresh eggs. Don't store eggs near where they could pick up strong odors—from onions, chemicals, paints, oil or gas products, and so on. They're most likely to pick up odors if they've been washed. Any poultry eggs can be refrigerated for up to 6 weeks. Always store them in a clean container. Scald it first if there's any doubt. If you seal freshly laid eggs in a plastic bag the eggs can keep in the refrigerator 2 months. When using stored eggs, rotate to use the oldest first.

Pickled Eggs. These come in many varieties. Poking the eggs a few times with a toothpick will help curing (not beet reds—see below). Figure about 7 days to complete curing.

These pickled egg formulas all may be doubled, tripled, etc., as needed. For storage, make in larger quantities and keep in the juice, refrigerated. The pickled eggs will keep months that way. Or you may can them.

🥚 *EASY RED PICKLED EGGS* *Hard-boil the desired number of eggs. Shell eggs and cover in half pickle juice and half beet juice. Keep in refrigerator 3 to 4 days. Drain and serve with garnish.*

🥚 *MUSTARD PICKLED EGGS* *Boil the eggs, cool, and remove the shells. Boil together 1 qt. vinegar, 1 t. dry mustard, 1 t. salt, and 1 t. pepper. Pour the cooled brine into your pickling jar and add the eggs. Cover and let them cure at least 10 days before they're ready.*

🥚 *SPICED PICKLED EGGS* *Hard-boil the eggs, cool, and remove shells. Make a brine of ½ c. salt to 2 c. water. Soak the eggs in the brine 2 days. Then pour off the brine and make a new brine by heating 1 qt. vinegar, ¼ c. pickling spices, 2 cloves garlic, and 1 T. sugar to boiling. Pour it over the eggs.*

🥚 *CLOVE PICKLED EGGS* *Stick a few cloves in each egg in either recipe above.*

🥚 *BEET RED EGGS* *Start with 1 c. of strongly colored beet juice, either from canned beets or the homemade equivalent. In a small pan, combine beet juice, 1 c. cider vinegar, ½ c. sugar, and 1 t. salt. Bring to a low boil and hold there for 5 minutes, stirring constantly. Pour over 6 peeled, hard-boiled eggs and refrigerate, tightly covered. Halve to serve. You can add a few slices of cooked whole beet to the mixture.*

🥚 *SOY EGGS* *Combine ½ c. soy sauce, ½ c. chicken broth (or water), 6 T. sugar, ½ t. sesame seed oil, and 1 T. minced onion in a pan. Bring to the boiling point. Add 4 peeled, hard-boiled eggs, cover the pan, and simmer 10 minutes. Remove from heat. Allow eggs to cool in the mixture for 30 minutes. Turn the eggs during the cooking and cooling to ensure that they are colored evenly. Drain the eggs and cut into quarters lengthwise to serve (may be served either hot or cold). The beet and soy egg recipes are from Eileen Draper, Pullman, WA—belly dancer, artist, writer, wife, mother.*

🥚 *DILLY EGGS* *In a pan combine 1½ c. white vinegar, 1 c. water, 1 t. dill seed, ½ t. white pepper, 3 t. salt, ½ t. mustard seed, ½ t. onion juice, and ½ t. minced garlic. Bring to a slow boil. Boil 5 minutes, stirring frequently. Add peeled, hard-boiled eggs. Cool, cover tightly, and refrigerate.*

🥚 *CANNED PICKLED EGGS* *Fill a sterilized quart jar with hard-boiled, peeled, cooled eggs. (You can fit about a dozen eggs in per quart.) Add to the eggs in the jar 1 sprig of dill, 1 chopped clove of garlic, 1 dried crushed red hot pepper, and 1 t. peppercorns. In an enamel or other noncorrosive pan combine, for each quart of eggs you are canning, 3 c. white vinegar and 2 T. sugar. Bring the solution to a boil and simmer 5 minutes, then pour hot liquid over eggs and spices to within ½ inch of the jar's top. Put on the lid and seal it. Process in boiling water bath 20 minutes.*

Frozen Eggs. The freezer life of an egg is 8 months to a year. Eggs that have been frozen should be well cooked before being eaten. Use only fresh, nest-clean eggs. Don't ever refreeze thawed eggs. Decide how you will use the eggs: whole, as for scrambling, or yolks and whites separated.

(Frozen whites don't whip into a stiff mixture.) Or maybe you could use some of each kind. Well, then what percentage of each? Now decide how many of these eggs, whole or separated, you want per package. You have to use your frozen eggs within 12 hours of thawing, so you don't want to pack more than a day's worth per package or they will be wasted. Be sure and label each container as to what's inside: whole eggs, whites, or yolks—and whether the whole eggs and yolks are sweet or salty. Use sweet egg mixtures for baking, salty egg mixtures for other cooking. Be sure and adjust the other ingredients to compensate for the added sweet or salty flavor. Equivalents: 1½ T. thawed yolk equals one fresh egg yolk; 2 T. thawed egg white equals one fresh egg white; 3 T. thawed whole egg equals one fresh egg (sort of, because home-grown eggs aren't all that standardized anyway).

Freezing Whole Eggs. Take them out of the shell and pour them into your freezer container, as many as you decide you want in a package. Stir them together, but don't whip in air. For each cup of whole eggs, add 1 T. sugar or ½ t. salt. If you freeze whole eggs in an ice cube grid, each cube is equivalent to half an egg.

Freezing Whites and Yolks Separately. If you are freezing egg whites, don't include even a speck of yolk and don't add anything else. In the case of the egg yolks, freeze them together with either salt or sweetener, depending on the use you intend for them: 2 t. sugar or corn syrup or 1 t. honey, or ½ t. salt per ½ c. yolks. If you don't add the salt or sweet to the egg yolks, they'll get gummy or lumpy. Baby food jars are good containers for them. Freeze egg yolks promptly. They sour easily. When they are thawed, use within 48 hours or discard.

Brined Eggs. This was an old-time egg preservation method, but the resulting eggs aren't as nice as those from cold storage or freezing. Nevertheless, here's the recipe: Put clean eggs in a crockery, wooden, or plastic container. Cover with a mixture of 3 gal. water, 1 pink quicklime (from lumberyard or drugstore), and 1 c. salt. Put weight enough on top of a plate to hold eggs under the solution. You can add more eggs later, but be careful they don't crack going in. Store in a cool place.

Eggs Made into Noodles. You probably haven't thought of noodle-making in this way before, but it's an excellent way to preserve eggs! Use any egg-noodle recipe from Chapter 3 or your own. Make them, dry them thoroughly, and store them in a dry place. Or else package and store them in your freezer. Or make them into a soup and can them.

Dried Eggs. Dried eggs won't keep more than 3–4 months before the yolk fat goes rancid, but up to that time, they can be useful. Ruth Miller found this recipe for dried eggs in a really old recipe book: "Break perfectly fresh eggs onto large plates—making just a layer on the bottom of each; place in the sun to dry. It will take about 5 days to dry them thoroughly so that they break very easily when touched. Then crumble them finely and leave another day. Then roll with a rolling pin to a fine powder and store in clean, dry tins with airtight lids. A good teaspoonful equals 1 egg. The powder should be soaked in cold water or milk for an hour before use and then be used in scrambled eggs, omelets, puddings, cakes, and so on, with perfect success."

Here's a modern way to dry them: Beat very fresh, whole eggs thoroughly (use an egg beater or the equivalent). Pour beaten eggs to make a very thin layer (maximum

⅛ inch) on drying surfaces that have been precoated with plastic or foil. In an oven or dryer, dry at about 120°F for 24–36 hours. When the egg layer is dry on top and firm all through, peel away the plastic or foil layer, turn the egg layer upside down and dry that side 12–24 hours more. Then break it up and dry it a few more hours. Then turn your dried egg into a powder using a mortar and pestle or a blender. These eggs work fine in baked goods. Make scrambled eggs by combining the powder with an equal amount of water, such as ¼ c. dried egg powder with ¼ c. water.

To substitute dried eggs, use 1½ T. dried egg plus 3 T. water for each large fresh egg called for in the recipe. Dried Eggs or Dried Egg Whites are available in a 20-oz. can from **UrbanHome@aol.com.**

Larded, Salted Eggs. The old-timers used many variations of this method to preserve eggs. The eggs were packed in a crock of lard, or greased with lard or pure butter and then packed in sawdust or oatmeal. They were then stored in the coolest possible place, short of freezing. However, *The Mother Earth News* experimented and learned that eggs in lard will keep several months even when temperatures are 65–70°F. But cold is always better. An Ohio lady, Yolanda Breidenbaugh, wrote me of "a good, cheap way to preserve eggs. It works wonderfully well. Over a year later the eggs still aren't rotted. Here it is: Take freshly laid clean eggs and dip them in melted lard and pack in salt! I put them, not touching each other, in a 5-gal. bucket and set the lid on and put it in a cool cellar. I got 'feed grade' salt at the feed mill. When I want to use one, I just rinse it off with warm water. Even a year later, they're still okay. Certainly good enough to cook with."

Lime/Salt Preserved Eggs. Make a solution containing 16 parts water, 1 part pickling salt, and 2 parts food-grade lime. For example, 1 part could equal 1 cup. Submerge the eggs in that. *The Mother Earth News* tested this one and found it also would preserve eggs several months, even at 65–70°F.

Laws on Home Poultry Processing

Under federal law, there is no inspection if you process fewer than 20,000 chickens (or 5,000 turkeys) per year (Poultry Products Inspection Act, Section 15), so long as the poultry is sold in your state. Local and state regulations may be more restrictive. Here follows a summary of the laws in each state, inspired by and indebted to "Legal Issues for Small-scale Poultry Processors," compiled by Janie Hipp for Heifer Project International. (It's free from NCAT/ ATTRA: 800-346-9140; **www.attra.ncat.org**).

Alabama has a state law controlling meat and poultry inspection, administered by the Commissioner of Agriculture and Industries: Meat and Poultry Inspection; 334-240-7210; fax 334-223-7352; 1445 Federal Dr., PO Box 3336, Montgomery, AL 36109-0336.

Alaska's small-scale poultry processors may need to get a state permit and comply with state laws on food safety and sanitation. For more info: Dept. of Environmental Conservation, Food Safety and Sanitation; 907-289-7501; 555 Cordova St., Anchorage, AK 99501; **www.state.ak.us/ dec/deh.**

Arizona law exempts processors of under 20,000 birds if they are processing according to recognized religious dietary laws; or for personal use; or who label the home-grown and home-butchered product with their name and address before sale to individuals or to restaurants, hotels, or boarding houses: Arizona Dept. of Ag, Meat and Poultry Inspection Branch; 602-542-6398; fax 602-542-4290; 1688 W. Adams, Phoenix, AZ 85007.

Arkansas follows federal guidelines as to exemptions: Arkansas Livestock and Poultry Commission, No. 1 Natural Resources Dr., PO Box 1069, Little Rock, AR 72205. Or U. of Arkansas, School of Ag, PO Box 490, Pine Bluff, AR 71611.

California law lets persons who process poultry on their farm be exempt from inspection requirements so long as they sell to persons who are not going to resell the birds: Dept. of Ag, Meat & Poultry Inspection Branch; 916-654-0504; fax 916-654-2608; 150 N St., Room A-125, Sacramento, CA 94814.

Colorado follows federal guidelines in exempting small-scale poultry processors from inspection, but all small-scale processors must have their processing facilities licensed by CDA: Colorado Dept. of Ag; 303-477-0086; fax 303-480-9236; 2331 W. 31st Ave., Denver, CO 80211.

Connecticut's poultry processing is supervised by the Commissioner of Agriculture: 860-713-2500; 860-713-2514; 785 Asylum Ave., Hartford, CT 06105.

Delaware's Secretary of Agriculture is responsible for poultry inspection. State law is based on the federal guidelines but requires a decision by the Secretary as to any particular exemption: Delaware Dept. of Ag; 302-739-4811; fax 302-697-4463; 2320 S. DuPont Hwy., Dover, DE 19901.

Florida's Animal and Animal Production Inspection and Labeling Act requires that anybody who processes birds for sale must have federal or state permits: Florida Dept. of Ag and Consumer Services, Division of Food Safety; 850-488-5772; fax 850-487-0703; The Capitol, PL 10, Tallahassee, FL; 32399. Or U. of Florida, Meat Processing Center; 352-392-1921; fax 352-392-7652; PO Box 110910, Gainesville, FL 32611.

Georgia rates as a misdemeanor the offering for sale, or possessing for sale, of any poultry product made, transported, or stored under unsanitary conditions. Their definition of "unsanitary" is very broad. All poultry processing plants must have a license and keep records of all birds slaughtered on site: Georgia Dept. of Ag, Meat Inspection Division; 404-656-3673; fax 404-657-1357; 19 Martin Luther King Jr. Dr., Rm. 108, Atlanta, GA 30334.

Hawaii exempts persons who slaughter poultry for members of their own household and if the product is wholesome and sold at home direct to the consumer (not for resale). Exempt operators must register with the Board of Agriculture and get a permit for exemption (which may be refused): Hawaii Dept. of Ag; 808-973-9560; PO Box 22159, Honolulu, HI 96823-2159. Or U. of Hawaii at Manoa; 808-956-6564; fax 808-956-8663; 1920 Edmondson Rd., Honolulu, HI 96822.

Idaho follows the federal regulations, including exemptions for small-scale processors, and has no state inspection system for poultry processors: Idaho Dept. of Ag; 208-332-8500; fax 208-334-2170; 2270 Old Penitentiary Rd., Boise, ID 83712. Or U. of Idaho, Dept. of Animal & Veterinary Science; 208-885-7390; fax 208-885-6420; Moscow, ID 83844-2330.

Illinois producers may request, in writing, an on-farm processing exemption. If granted (two years at a time), they must keep records of the number of poultry processed per year (no more than 5,000 to keep the exemption). They must sell only from the farm (no deliveries), and must be sanitary (periodic inspections may occur): Illinois Dept. of Ag; 217-782-2172; fax 217-785-4505; State Fairgrounds, PO Box 19281, Springfield, IL 62794.

Indiana's State Board of Animal Health, under the Indiana Humane Slaughter Act, is required by law to exempt a processor who would be exempt under the federal guidelines: Commissioner of Ag; 317-232-8770; fax 317-232-1362; 140 W. Market St., Ste. 414, Indianapolis, IN 46204. Or Indiana State Board of Animal Health, Division of Meat & Poultry; 317-227-0359; fax 317-227-0330; 805 Beachway Dr., Ste. 50, Indianapolis, IN 46224.

Iowa's poultry inspection is under the Meat and Poultry Inspection Bureau, which exempts processors who handle fewer than 1,000 birds per year and sell all products to the final consumer or use them at home: Iowa Dept. of Ag & Land Stewardship; 515-281-5322; fax 515-281-6236 (or 515-281-5597; fax 515-281-4282); Wallace Bldg., Des Moines, IA 50319.

Kansas exempts poultry producers who slaughter for home use and under certain other conditions: Kansas Dept of Ag, Meat & Poultry Inspection; 785-296-3511; fax 785-296-0673; 901 S. Kansas Ave., 7th Floor, Topeka, KS 66612.

Kentucky producers must follow rules of the Kentucky Cabinet for Health Services: Kentucky Dept. of Ag; 502-564-5126; fax 502-564-5016; Rm 188, Capitol Annex, Frankfort, KY 40601. Or Market Services Office; 502-564-4696; 502-582-4291; Capital Plaza Tower, 7th Floor, 500 Mero St., Frankfort, KY 40601. Or Benjy Mikel; 859-257-7550; 205 WT, Garrigus Bldg., U. of Kentucky, Lexington, KY 40546.

Louisiana's Dept. of Ag and Forestry's Meat and Poultry Division does inspections for operations of fewer than 20,000 birds and grants exemptions upon written request of the processor (quarterly compliance checks on persons with exemptions): Dept. of Ag & Forestry; 225-922-1234; fax 225-922-1253; PO Box 631, Baton Rouge, LA 70821-0631.

Maine established new guidelines in 2002 that are said to be friendly to small-scale producers and processors: Commissioner of Agriculture, Food and Rural Resources; 207-287-3419; fax 207-287-7548; Deering Bldg (AMHI), State House Station #28, Augusta, ME 04333. Or U. of Maine; 207-581-3449; fax 207-581-3212; 5717 Corbett Hall, Rm 303, Orono, ME 04469.

Maryland exempts from inspection any poultry processed for home use, or for sale from your home if healthy and labeled with your name and address: Maryland Dept. of Ag; 410-841-5880; fax 410-841-5914; 50 Harry S. Truman Parkway, Annapolis, MD 21401. Or U. of Maryland College of Ag; 410-651-9111; fax 410-651-9187; LES/REC Princess Anne Fac., 11990 Strickland Dr., Princess Anne, MD 21853.

Massachusetts exempts poultry processors from inspection at the discretion of its Commissioner of the Massachusetts Dept. of Public Health, so long as exemptions fit under federal guidelines. Thus the processor must be selling birds he raised himself. They must be shipped in boxes that bear the grower's name, address, and the word "Exempted." He may sell to households, restaurants, hotels, and boarding houses: Mass. Dept. of Ag; 617-626-1700; fax 617-626-1850; 100 Cambridge St., Boston, MA 02202.

Michigan uses the federal guidelines: Michigan Dept. of Ag; 517-373-1052; fax 517-335-1423 (517-373-8200; fax 517-373-6015); 611 W. Ottawa, PO Box 30017, Lansing, MI 48909.

Minnesota also follows federal guidelines except that direct farm sales are allowed only to households (not to hotels, restaurants, and institutions). To deliver products off farm or sell them at a farmer's market you must get a state license and comply with state inspection rules, no matter how few the birds being processed: Minnesota Dept. of Ag; 651-296-2627; fax 651-297-5637; 90 W. Plato Blvd., St. Paul, MN 55107.

Mississippi follows federal guidelines: Dept. of Ag and Commerce; 601-359-1100; fax 601-354-6290; 121 N. Jefferson St., Jackson, MS 39201. Or Meat Inspection Division; 601-359-1189; fax 601-354-6502; PO Box 1609, Jackson, MS 39215.

Missouri must exempt from inspection laws any facility that would be exempt under federal guidelines, but persons with such exemptions are subject to regular reviews. The Director of the Missouri Dept. of Ag is allowed, after giving notice, to withdraw any exemption if conditions have changed under which it was granted: Missouri Dept. of Ag; 573-751-3359; fax 573-751-1784; PO Box 630, Jefferson City, MO 65102.

Montana's Board of Livestock (under Montana's Dept. of Livestock) does poultry inspection. Persons slaughtering for home use are exempt. Custom butchers are exempt so long as the meat is kept separate from meat prepared for sale, is plainly marked "Not for Sale," and is handled in a sanitary way: Montana Dept. of Ag; 406-444-3144; fax 406-444-5409; PO Box 200201, Helena, MT 59620-0201. Or Meat, Milk & Eggs Inspection Division; 406-444-5293; fax 406-444-1929; PO Box 2021001, Helena, MT 59620.

Nebraska follows the federal guidelines: Bureau of Dairies & Foods; 402-471-2536; fax 402-471-2759; PO Box 95064, Lincoln, NE 68509.

Nevada's State Board of Health does not permit the sale of uninspected poultry products. Federal exemptions don't apply here. Anybody who wants to process and sell poultry must have a state permit. The permitting process requires inspection of your place by the state Board of Health and that there be an inspector present when birds are processed. However, owner/operators may be tested and certified as inspector at their own place: Nevada State Board of Health; 775-687-6353; fax 775-687-5197; 1179 Fairview Dr., Carson City, NV 89701. Or Nevada Dept of Ag; 775-688-1182; fax 775-688-1178; 350 Capitol Hill Ave., Reno, NV 89502.

New Hampshire's policy follows the federal guidelines: New Hampshire Dept. of Ag, Markets and Food; 603-271-3551; fax 603-271-1109; PO Box 2042, Concord, NH 03302-2042. Or U. of New Hampshire, Cooperative Ext. Food Safety & Nutrition; 603-862-2496; fax 603-862-3758; 129 Main St., 219 Kendall Hall, Durham, NH 03824.

New Jersey allows uninspected processing of home-grown birds for home use: NJ Dept. of Ag; 609-292-3976; fax 609-292-3978; PO Box 330, John Fitch Plaza, Trenton, NJ 08625. Or Rutgers U., Dept of Food Science; 732-932-9611; fax 732-932-6776; 65 Dudley Rd, New Brunswick, NJ 08901.

New Mexico does not allow any exemption from inspection for poultry slaughtered on the farm: New Mexico Livestock Board; 505-841-6161; fax 505-841-6160; 300 San Mateo NE, Ste. 1000, Albuquerque, NM 87018.

New York exempts by federal rules up to 1,000 birds per year: NY Dept. of Ag and Markets; 518-457-4188; fax 518-457-3087; 1 Winners Circle, Capitol Plaza, Albany, NY 12235. Or Cornell U., Dept. of Food Science; 607-255-3262; fax 607-254-4868; 11 Stocking Hall, Ithaca, NY 14853.

North Carolina's Dept. of Ag and Consumer Services inspects poultry products. Exemptions are given for processors of less than 1,000 birds or 250 turkeys; or those operating according to religious dietary laws; or if the birds are home grown for home eating; or custom slaughter of birds intended for the customer's home use. Small growers may process and sell their home-grown healthy poultry if packaged under a label identifying the name and address of the producer. They may sell to households or distribute to restaurants, hotels, and boarding houses: Dept. of Ag and Consumer Services; 919-733-7125; fax 919-733-1141; PO Box 27647, Raleigh, NC 27611. Or Meat and Poultry Division; 919-733-4136; fax 919-715-0246.

North Dakota's Health Dept. gives no exemptions from inspection requirements for farm-slaughtered poultry: ND Dept of Health; 701-328-2213; fax 701-328-4567; 600 East Blvd., Bismarck, ND 58505-0020. Or ND State U.; 701-231-7682; fax 701-231-7590; 5727 Hultz Hall, Fargo, ND 58105.

Ohio exempts growers processing for family use, and grower/processors of fewer than 1,000 birds per year who sell to other household consumers (no resale expected). You are still subject to laws on licensing, sanitation, labeling, etc.: Ohio Dept. of Ag; 614-466-2732; fax 614-466-6124; 8995 E. Main St., Reynoldsburg, OH 43068-3399. Or Division of Meat Inspection; 614-728-6260; fax 614-728-6434.

Oklahoma allows certain exceptions for small producers or religious processing, etc.: OK Dept. of Ag; 405-521-3864; fax 405-521-0909; 2800 N. Lincoln, Oklahoma City, OK 73105. Or Meat Inspection Program; 405-521-3741; fax 405-522-0756.

Oregon follows federal guidelines. Inspection is also not applied to fryers that are sold to ultimate customers at the farm where they were produced: Oregon Dept. of Agriculture; 503-986-4552; fax 503-986-4750; 635 Capitol St. NE, Salem, OR 97310-0110. Or Oregon State U.; 541-737-3414; fax 541-737-4174; Withycombe Hall 112, Corvallis, OR 97331.

Pennsylvania's Dept. of Ag and various municipal departments can enact and enforce regulations: Dept. of Ag; 717-772-2853; fax 717-772-2780; 2301 N. Cameron St., Harrisburg, PA 17110-9408. Or Bureau of Food Safety & Lab Services; 717-787-4315; fax 717-787-1873; 2301 N. Cameron St., Harrisburg, PA 17110.

Rhode Island poultry growers who do their own processing for either home use or sale must register each year with the Director of the Department of Health during the month of January. Slaughter premises must be approved by the Department, and the Director of the Department can make rules about those premises and can inspect them as he wishes: RI Dept. of Ag; 401-222-2781; fax 401-222-6047; 235 Promenade St., Room 370, Providence, RI 02908-5767. Or ESN Research Center: 401-874-2972; fax 401-874-2994; 530 Liberty Lane, West Kingston, RI 02892.

South Carolina allows exemptions from getting a permit to persons who butcher according to religious dietary laws; persons processing home-grown poultry for home use or doing custom slaughter on somebody's home-grown birds for home use; persons selling to households, restaurants, hotels, or boarding houses home-grown poultry that have been raised healthy and are labeled with the grower's name and address (up to 20,000 birds or 5,000 turkeys): SC Meat & Poultry Inspection Division; 803-788-1747; fax 803-788-8114; PO Box 102406, Columbia, SC 29224-2406. Or Clemson U., Meat & Poultry Inspection: 803-788-2260.

South Dakota's Livestock Sanitary Board runs their inspection program and allows no exemptions from inspection: SD Dept. of Ag; 605-773-3375; fax 605-773-5926; 523 E. Capitol, Pierre, SD 57501-3182. Or SD Animal Industry Board; 605-773-3321; fax 605-773-5459; 411 S. Fort St, Pierre, SD 57501.

Tennessee's Meat and Poultry Inspection Act is administered by their Dept. of Ag. Growers report that the rules are confusing, unevenly applied, and not always administered according to the written law: TN Dept of Ag, Ellington Ag Center; 615-837-5100; fax 615-837-5333; PO Box 40627, Melrose Station, Nashville, TN 37204.

Texas accepts the federal guidelines and exempts small-scale processors from inspection. However, low-volume livestock processing establishments must register with the Texas Dept. of Health (TDH) and must develop a Sanitary Operations Procedures Plan that you keep on file for government review in case anybody gets sick from your animals. If anybody does get sick, they may shut you down: TX Dept. of Ag; 512-463-7476; fax 512-463-1104; PO Box 12847, Capitol Station, Austin, TX 78711. Or Meat Safety Assurance Division, Bureau of Food and Drug Safety; 512-719-0205; fax 512-810-0240; 1100 W. 49th St., Austin, TX 78756.

Utah follows federal guidelines: UT Dept. of Ag and Food; 801-538-7101; fax 801-538-7126; 350 N. Redwood Rd, PO Box 146500, Salt Lake City, UT 84114-6500. Or UT Dept of Ag; 801-538-7117; fax 801-538-7169; PO Box 146500, Salt Lake City, UT 84114-6500.

Vermont's Commissioner of the Dept. of Ag, Food and Markets may exempt from inspection any person who could be exempted under the federal guidelines. But Vermont's rules are more strict than federal ones, applying only to processors of up to 1,000 birds. Any meat served in hotels, restaurants, or institutions must be from a state or federally inspected source: VT Dept of Ag, Food and Markets; 802-828-2426; fax 802-828-2361; Drawer 20, 116 State St., Montpelier, VT 05620-2901.

Virginia law follows the federal guidelines, but the state does require producers who want to operate under exemption to get a state permit: VA Dept. of Ag and Consumer Services; 804-786-3501; fax 804-371-2945; PO Box 1163, Richmond, VA 23209.

Washington's Dept. of Agriculture is in charge of inspections. Slaughter of birds by religious dietary laws or for home use is exempted. Inspection is unnecessary for poultry growers if they are under 250 turkeys or 1,000 birds of smaller species per year. But some city and county agencies have additional rules and do not recognize these exemptions (King County/Seattle area requires all poultry sold therein to be processed and stored in a state-licensed facility); WA Dept. of Ag; 360-902-1801; fax 360-902-2092;

PO Box 42560, Olympia, WA 98504-2560. Or WSU; 509-335-2880; fax 509-335-1082; 123 Clark Hall, Pullman, WA 99164.

West Virginia exempts producer/processors of up to 1,000 home-grown, home-slaughtered birds per year, but has no application process to get the exemption: WV Dept of Ag, Meat and Poultry Inspection; 304-558-2207; fax 304-558-1882; State Capitol, 1900 Kanawha Blvd. E., Charleston, WV 25305; **JCharminski@ag.state.wv.us.**

Wisconsin exempts poultry processed on the owner's farm, up to 1,000 birds per year. Birds must be labeled and tagged with name/address of the grower and marked "NOT INSPECTED"; WI Dept. of Ag, Trade and Consumer Protection; 608-224-5012; fax 608-224-5045 (or 608-224-4725; fax 603-224-4710); PO Box 8911, Madison, WI 53708.

Wyoming has no exemptions from inspection. The Ag Dept. does inspections: 307-777-6569; fax 307-777-6593; 2219 Carey Ave., Cheyenne, WY 82002. Or 307-266-1203; fax 307-266-3701; 473 Trigood Ave., Casper, WY 86209.

Butchering Chickens

Once you know what you're doing and have your system worked out, 2 people can kill, pick, and cut up about a half dozen chickens an hour—or even more.

OF AGE AND STAGE: Home-grown chicken to eat comes from 2 basic sources: the broilers or cockerels you raise to butchering age and then put in the freezer, and the hens whose egg production is declining or stopped, that you cull out of your flock. The broilers or cockerels are your young, tender birds. At 8–12 weeks of age, they'll weigh from 2 to 8 (or 12 or even 15) pounds, depending on the breed. They can be cooked as a "broiler," or a fryer. From 14 weeks to 6 months of age, and from 4 pounds and up, the bird will make a fine roaster. If you want to know exactly when your bird is at the desired weight, put it inside a sack. That will keep it still long enough for you to get an accurate measure on a scale. A bird 6–9 months old is a judgment call. Older than that they are stew birds for sure. Culled laying hens have lived long enough to get really tough, so they are your classic "stew hens." You can tell relative age by feel. A young chicken has soft cartilage at the end of the breastbone and pinfeathers. An older, stewing-type chicken has a rigid breastbone and long hairs on its skin.

DARK MEAT, LIGHT MEAT: The color of muscle meat is a result of the exercise that muscle has experienced. Home-grown chickens tend to have relatively darker meat because they lead more active lives. A bird that flies will even have dark breast meat.

CATCHING A CHICKEN AT NIGHT: Enter the chicken's sleeping quarters well after dark, equipped with twine or a burlap bag. Carry a flashlight. Quietly grasp the bird you want by its 2 skinny legs (make sure the 2 legs are from the same chicken), and tie twine firmly around them. Or put it in the bag and tie the mouth of that. Or haul it out with a firm grip around those 2 ankles and leave it for the night in an empty rabbit hutch, where you'll be able to easily reach in and grab it in the morning. Actually, holding a bird by its legs can be a bit of a struggle because they're not crazy about being upside down and will flap their wings and try to get righted. Avoid that wing flapping. Better yet, carry it the polite and friendly way, which is to hold the wings down and put it under your arm with one hand on a leg or two, just in case.

CATCHING A CHICKEN IN THE DAYTIME: If the chicken can't be walked up to when you feed it (or cornered in the chicken house), make a chicken hook out of a length of wire. Unwinding a clothes hanger gives you a good length. Or use a 4-foot piece of heavy wire. Make it single rod except for a miniature shepherd's crook at the chicken-catching end—narrower than a chicken's foot, wider than its skinny lower leg, which is the part you hook it by. Or loop around the other end to make a better handle. Then you set out to pursue your quarry with the wire in hand. Pour a heap of grain on the ground. The chickens will all gather, heads down, backsides to the outside of their little crowd.

When you get within reach of the one you want with the wire, suddenly stretch it out and hook the chicken's leg in the crook. Pull the chicken toward you and transfer the leg from the crook to your hand and get the other one, too. That works, but it's so much easier to catch a chicken while it is sleeping that I always do that. And if you can isolate the chicken the night before you butcher it, by leaving it in the gunny sack or, better yet, in a wire-bottomed rabbit cage or something similar, you won't have to contend with such a full crop when cleaning it.

MEAT CHICKENS TO SELL: Joel Salatin's 1993 book, *Pastured Poultry Profit,* is the classic in this field. Herman Beck-Chenoweth's *Free-Range Poultry Production and Marketing* (1996) shows a set-up to process 200 broilers per hour (cost about $15,000).

New poultry processing equipment is available from Stromberg's (218-587-2222) or Pickwick (319-393-7443; **www.pickwickmfg.com**), or Brower's Pastured Poultry Division, which advertises a 150 birds/hr system for under $4,000 with rotary kill line, scalder, spin picker, evisceration table, chill tank, aprons, knives, etc. (800-553-1791). You can buy used equipment from Tom Neuberger's South Dakota Poultry Headquarters: 605-296-3314; Rt. 1, Box 303, Canistota, SD 57012. Contact ATTRA for info on homemade scalders and pluckers: 800-346-9140. Kenneth King of Jako, Inc., builds a low-cost batch dunker/scalder, and plucker. He travels to help other area producers on slaughter day with a mobile processor mounted on a trailer (killing cones, scalder, plucker, eviscerating table, etc.), which he also builds and markets: 620-663-1470; 877-525-6462; 6003 E. Eales Rd., Hutchinson, KS 67501; **kenking@ jakoinc.com; www.jakoinc.com/.**

Some producers have built their own state- or federally approved processing plants. (See Patrick Slattery's "Small-scale Processing Offers Large-scale Profits" in *Acres, USA,* Sept. 1995; or Keith Richards' article on "Adding Value to Chickens on the Farm," in *Southern Sustainable Farming,* March 1996.) ATTRA's info on this topic, "Processing & Marketing Chicken Products: Meat & Eggs," can be downloaded at **www.attra.org/attra-pub/process& market.html.**

KILLING A CHICKEN: When I was a little girl, chopping chicken heads off for my mama, I used to say a prayer for the chicken before I raised my axe. I would pray that if God had a place in Heaven for the souls of chickens, He should please take this one. In the animal graveyard beside our garden, where beloved, departed cats, dogs, and mice lay planted, brother Dick and I also buried not a few chicken heads with full honors. There was a certain fascination to staging a really good funeral.

By then the feast would be ready, and Mama would call us to dinner. Oh, Mother's fresh fried chicken! With mashed potatoes and lots of gravy made with milk! Dick and I would eat and eat, the pile of bird bones beside each plate heaping steadily. The wishbones were saved and dried on top of the topside cupboard of Mother's wood cook stove for a week or two, until they'd become properly brittle. Then Dick and I each took hold of a side, got our wish in mind (you couldn't say out loud what it was or the magic wouldn't work), and pulled at the count of three. The one who ended up with the longest piece of wishbone would get his or her wish—or so we claimed.

"Chop and run" is how I killed chickens for Mama and how I did it when I was writing the first edition of this book, but it's not the best way because it's messy. These following methods are approximately in order from worst to best because that's the order in which I heard about them as I accumulated material for this book. To avoid gory details you could just skip to the end of the list. But first read this next paragraph.

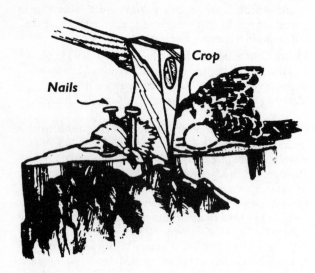

Blood. However you get the unfortunate task accomplished, be sure and let the bird bleed out thoroughly, since this will improve its eating and keeping quality. Wear old clothes, have a container ready—a bucket or some such— and don't let go of the chicken's legs and wing tips after the head is severed. Then get the chicken neck down into that container as soon as possible to minimize the mess. If you just drop the bleeding body and run, it will flop around, scattering blood from the severed neck over an amazingly large area.

A Chopping Block Demise. You grasp the bird firmly by the ankles and both wing tips with the left hand (assuming you're right-handed), and place its body on the chopping block so that the neck is stretched out across the block. (A chopping block is a large flat-topped and flat-bottomed piece of tree, with the grain running perpendicular to the ground.) A heavy-headed ax is better than a hatchet for the job, I think.

Getting the chicken to lie still with its neck stretched out across the top of the block while you aim the blade may require a bit of maneuvering. The chicken may retract its head just when you're all set. [Note: Since I wrote that, I've gotten some interesting advice from readers on how to make that chicken hold still while you're trying to chop its

head off. One writer told me that she "hypnotizes" the chicken by putting the chicken's head under its wing, then swinging it around, and only then chopping its head off. Betty Lawrence, White Swan, WA, wrote me that she hammers 2 nails about one inch apart on the surface of her chopping block. She leaves part of the nails sticking up. She lays the chicken's neck between the nails and pulls back gently until the head is next to the nails. If you use this system, you'll have to be careful not to hit those nails—hitting nails is very bad for ax blades—as well as not to hit the crop.]

Anyway, have a sharpened ax or hatchet ready in your right hand for that moment when the bird is in the right position, and then, quick before it moves, with one hard blow bring the blade down and sever the head from the neck. Hit the chicken's neck clear across so you don't cut off just half of it with the first blow. (I've had to try twice to finish the job more times than I'd care to admit.) Cut it off as near the head and as far from the body as you can in order to save the neck for cooking, and to avoid cutting the crop, which is located at the base of the neck.

Wringing the Chicken's Neck. Some people prefer this method. It may be done by grasping the chicken firmly by the upper part of the neck or head. Then get the body swinging rapidly as you would twirl a heavy object on the end of a string. You swing once, swing twice, swing thrice, and then *snap*—like you're doing "Crack the Whip" with the chicken's body. Then the body separates from the head you're holding. It will.

Death by Shooting. A BB-gun won't do it. A .22 will.

By "Hanging." Mrs. George Huckabey, Athens, TN, doesn't like dead chickens flopping around on the ground. "Find a low-hanging tree branch; loop a twine string around it firmly. Place loop around the legs of the chicken. It will be hanging head down. Now grasp the head firmly and with a sharp knife, cut the chicken's head off just at the top of the neck." This way the chicken doesn't go flopping around, leaving a trail of blood on your property, and you can control the bleeding mess by having a container ready to put the bird in and making sure it gets in there and stays in there. Lane Morgan uses this system too.

By Severance. This popular professional method is to pierce the brain with a knife turn through the roof of the mouth, then sever the blood vessels, which are in the neck behind the earlobe. With this method, the bird doesn't flop about either, but it takes some know-how and experience to get it right.

Killing Cone. You can mail-order a commercially produced killing cone from a poultry supplier or from a local farm-supply store or make your own. To make a homemade killing cone, cut off the bottom of a 1-gal. plastic bottle. Cut about 2 inches from the top and handle. Nail the bottle to a wall or tree—or hang it by a rope or hook upside down. To use the killing cone, grab your bird by the ankles and put it, head downward, into the killing cone. Make sure the head and neck extend through the smaller end that you cut. Now proceed with either the "hanging" method or the "severance" method, or by grasping the head with one hand and pulling just firmly enough to create a small amount of tension on the neck, then cut into the neck on the left underside, just back of head and beak—which will sever the jugular. When you do it the latter way the head stays on; you just cut the throat. Have something ready in which to catch the blood, and this is the most manageable and least messy way. Commercially manufactured killing cones are not expensive and come in 3 sizes: one for broilers, pheasants, and fryers; one for roosters, ducks, and guineas; and the largest for turkeys.

Hiring Out. Lane Morgan wrote me that "lots of communities have backyard chicken butchering entrepreneurs. You bring them live birds in the evening and pick up dressed, bagged, chilled chicken the next morning. Or sometimes they'll come to your place. Or you can rent their equipment and have a butchering bee with friends. When both partners work off the farm, which is more and more likely, it isn't easy to find a solid stretch of time to butcher 50 chickens with less-than-efficient equipment."

PICKING THE CHICKEN: There are those who just skin the bird. In that case there's no scalding, no plucking, no disagreeable wet feather smell, no singeing. If you have no use for the feathers and remove the skin anyway to keep the fat low, this may be your best choice. Otherwise, following tradition. . .

You need to choose between dry picking and scalding before plucking out the feathers. Dry picking is more difficult than picking after scalding, because the feathers are harder to pull out. I think it's crazy to dry pick when you could scald. So skip to the next paragraph. But then again, maybe you want the feathers. But you can use the feathers plucked from a scalded bird, too. But connoisseurs say they prefer feathers that have been dry-picked rather than scalded and then picked.

Dry Picking. If you're going to save the feathers, have bags ready. Start immediately after killing—even before the bird stops bleeding—before the flesh has a chance to become cold, which will set the feathers in tightly. Pick up the breast and up the side. Then do the wings, back, and finally the pinfeathers, which can be removed with tweezers or with a knife blade (you catch the pinfeathers between the blade and your thumb and pull). You'll clean the feathers later and make them into nice things. Right now you need to get on with the butchering. Go to "Singeing."

Scalding and Plucking. Put water in a metal bucket or a big pan (like a canner or roaster) on to boil before you go out to kill the bird. While the chicken is flopping and bleeding, adjust the water temperature to about 130-180°F. Better to start out with your water too hot than too cool. Too hot will loosen the feathers plus cook the skin a little. Too cool won't accomplish anything. And your water will be cooling all the time, especially as you do a series of birds in it. If it gets too cool, stop and resupply with hot enough water. (Rebecca Coufel wrote me that she and her husband do 70 or 80 chickens at a time by pre-wetting the dead birds with a hose or bucket of cold water before scalding. She believes the hot water gets under their feathers better for the presoaking.) Spread out newspapers on which to do the picking. You can roll them up afterwards with the feathers inside to keep them from flying all over your yard.

Now, grasping your bird by the ankles (the unfeathered legs and feet don't need to be scaled), immerse it in the hot water. If you are using a flatter-styled pan, like a roasting kettle, you soak the breast of the bird in the hot water, then turn it over and hold the backside in. Try to manage in such a way that every feathered part of it has nearly equal time in the hot water. Make sure you get the legs that you're

holding in far enough to scald the feathered "knees." Make sure the wing and tail feathers get a good scalding, because they are the toughest to pull out. Overscalding any part of the bird will cause the outer surface of the skin to rub off—which doesn't hurt the meat any. Less than 30 seconds should to it. Hotter water does the job quicker; with cooler water you'll have to keep the bird in there a bit longer.

How long you need to scald also depends a good bit on the size of the bird. Little birds like pigeons and quail need less scalding time. Bigger birds need more. A turkey requires the most of all. Older birds will take a higher temperature and a longer time than younger birds. You can scald several birds, one after the other, in the same water, so long as it doesn't cool below about 130°F. If your water gets too cool, add hotter water to bring it up. If the first dip doesn't loosen the feathers enough, you can give the bird another pass in the water. You have to have the bird in there long enough and with enough motion to get the hot water penetrated clear to the skin.

Then take the bird out, let it drain just long enough so you can get your hands on the biggest feathers and start yanking. Have newspapers or some such spread out to pick the bird on so that cleaning up will be easy—but don't let the bird's body actually contact the newspaper because you don't want lead in your diet (causes brain damage). It can help with the requirement to do the picking while the bird is still as hot as possible, if one person scalds and another picks. Commence picking immediately after pulling the fully soaked bird out of the hot water, starting with the wing and tail feathers. Then do the body feathers, and finally the pinfeathers. Purists insist that feathers must be pulled out in the direction in which they are growing. That's certainly true of the biggest ones. I pull short ones any way I can get them.

Singeing. After the pinfeathers have been removed, you will still have down and very fine long hairs, especially on an older bird. These are burned off by singeing. Do it someplace where you won't set anything else on fire. Hold your bird by the ankles over a flame. If you don't have a gas stove, you can use a candle, propane torch, small alcohol burner, or a rolled cone of newspaper or other paper (not with color)—rolled tight at one end (to be the handle), and wide enough at the other to flame readily. A burning paper bag won't blacken the bird as much as a newspaper, but a newspaper cone is probably actually the worst way—probably gives them a lead content or some such and it certainly risks setting something else on fire. Don't touch the paper to the bird in this process, since that would dirty it with ashes. With practice you can do several chickens with one paper cone. Have all the chickens you plan to singe right there at hand when you light the paper. That's the way my mother and I used to singe them. Constantly change the bird's position over the flame, holding the bird with one hand and the cone with the other, until all parts having these hairs have been exposed enough to singe them completely. It won't take long to singe the whole chicken.

CLEANING THE CHICKEN: Now your chicken is ready to be cleaned or "drawn." That means you'll remove the head, feet, and innards. First, put the bird into very cold water in order to cool the entire body quickly. Get ready a bowl of clean, cold water to rinse pieces in (or you can rinse them under the faucet), a very sharp knife, and an empty container to hold the cut-up pieces. Have ready a wooden cutting board to cut up the chicken on. Don't cut the chicken on newspaper because the ink could get on the meat. Have something ready to hold the disposables, like a wax-paper–lined box, or a bucket.

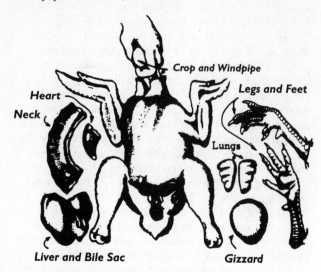

You can dispose of innards by burning, composting (but not where varmints will scatter the compost pile), or feeding them to the pigs. Your chickens would be delighted to recycle the chicken butchering scraps—if you have no fear of parasite or disease transmission. Do not feed these raw chicken scraps or any other poultry innards to your dogs and cats, lest they become tempted to obtain more of the same by killing a few birds for themselves.

Poultry Tuberculosis (TB). Incidentally, there is a variety of TB that chickens can get. The older the bird, the more likely it is to have this—or any other problem. On the other hand, I've never had TB in a flock and most family flocks never do. But if you did, the bird would feel very light, wasted, and the innards would look weird, would have abscesses on them (bird TB attacks the digestive tract and their intestines get abscesses on them). If you suspect TB, don't eat the bird.

Head, Feet, and Oil Sac. You need a small, but very sharp knife to do the next steps. If the head is still attached, cut it off and discard. If the head was chopped off and the chicken flopped on the ground and got dirt on the stump, cut the dirty part off and discard. Carefully feel for the knee joint right at the top of where scaly leg meets feathered knee. Bend the knee and cut across each joint until the foot is off. Some authors tell you to cut off the small oil sac at the end of the chicken's back on the "north end going south." That isn't necessary. Its presence doesn't affect the taste. It is necessary with certain other birds (goose and duck and game birds).

Outing the Innards. Place the chicken on its back with its hind end closest to you. Carefully cut across the abdomen from thigh to thigh (or from below the breastbone to just above the anus—it doesn't matter which), making sure you do not cut into any of the intestines in the cavity. Reach inside carefully between the intestines and the breastbone until you reach heart level. Loosen the membranes between the innards and the body wall and gently pull out the entrails in one mass. The gizzard, heart, and liver will come out with it. Be especially careful of the

gallbladder, a greenish sac embedded in the undersurface of the right lobe of the liver. If it should break, the bile that it contains will make bitter and undesirable any part of the chicken that it touches. You'll probably have to make a special effort to scoop out with your fingers the light pink lungs, which adhere inside the ribs.

To finish extricating the innards, cut carefully around the outside of the excretory vent, allowing plenty of room so as not to cut into it or the attached intestine, so that it can now be discarded along with the intestines. The kidneys in the back cavity adhere closely and should now be at least partly removed. Just scoop out what you can with your fingers of the soft, brown kidney tissue. It's impossible to get all the kidney out. Don't worry about what's left. It will be cooked along with the rest of the bird. Now, finish up the front end of the chicken: cut the skin the length of the back of the bird's neck. The crop tears very easily. The crop is a thin-skinned round pouch off the bird's esophagus that serves as a first stomach. You must gently pull it apart from the skin next to it. Then carefully pull crop, esophagus, and windpipe out of the bird and discard them.

Removing Giblets. "Giblets" means heart, liver, and gizzard—usually the neck, also. To get the liver, cut off the part of it that contains the gallbladder—allow plenty of leeway (better safe than sorry), and discard the gallbladder along with its attached liver section. Rinse the remaining liver and put it into your giblets bowl. Cut the gizzard open along its narrow edge. Continue the cut to three-quarters of the way around. Inside the gizzard there will be food and grit. Empty that out onto your newspaper. Carefully peel off and discard the yellowish inner lining of the gizzard. If you can get that lining separated from the gizzard proper at some point along your cut edge, the rest of the lining should strip out, easily connected to it. If it tears and does not all come out the first time, you'll have to work it loose at some other point, then pull again. When the lining is all pulled off, discard it. Rinse and save the gizzard. Cut the heart away from its attached arteries, rinse, and put in your giblet bowl. Cut the neck off at the base and add it to your loose pieces in the bowl.

Outing the Innards: Poultry Shears Method. An alternative system popular with owners who must butcher many small birds (like game birds), duck owners, and efficiency lovers in general, is to cut off the oil-gland on the bird's tail, then carefully cut around the vent until the anus and attached intestine are separated from the rest of the bird, and then use the poultry shears to cut all the way up the back on one side of the backbone. The bird is then opened out from that cut and the innards will basically just drop out. Sort out and deal with heart, liver, gizzard, and neck as above. (Poultry shears are wonderful. You can also use them to simply halve and quarter the bird and be done with the cutting up process, too!)

Dealing with the Garbage. At this point you have feathers and innards. You can make use of the small feathers (see "Cleaning and Using Feathers"). Or you can bury the whole works in your compost bin. Make sure no creatures can dig it up again.

Washing the Bird? June Scherer, Eastman, WI, wrote me that she washes and scrubs the chicken's skin with dish soap at this point. "It's surprising how dirty they are, and the soap leaves no taste. Just rinse good."

Marketing Your Poultry. You could go into the poultry business. Lane Morgan wrote me, "People (at least city people) will pay a lot for humanely raised, nonmedicated poultry." She's right. I have a cousin who does well taking orders for broilers. She merely grows them and then contracts out the butchering. Takes only prepaid orders. She charges $8 per bird [1992]. Many families order their year's supply of chicken from her and then store it in their deep freeze to eat year-round. It's true that there is an amazing, clearly discernible difference in the taste of "real" chicken like hers and factory-produced supermarket chicken. And she, as Lane Morgan suggests, can indeed guarantee her customers that her chickens' lives, though short, are pleasant, and that they bear no antibiotic or other chemical residue. She never has advertised. She got started because people asked her to and her business has grown by word of mouth.

A reader in Missoula, MT, became a serious chicken rancher in a similar way: "I sell 100 chickens every 7 weeks. There is a large population of Hmong [Vietnamese] people in Missoula. One day this teacher friend called to ask if I had any chickens to sell. At the time, my husband and I annually raised fifty chickens for ourselves and fifty to sell. Joan asked me if she could tell her Hmong friends about my chickens and I willingly agreed. I remember Joan saying, 'You may have a lot of people coming out.' That turned out to be the supreme understatement.

"The next morning we started getting calls at 8am. It didn't stop all day. Whole families came out. Usually only one person in the group had English. It was wild. When all the chickens were sold, except for ours, the people still came. They insisted that we had too many chickens. 'Please, sell only 3 more!'. . . In the end we had only 25 for ourselves. Still more Hmong people came. They pointed to my chicken house where my laying flock lives. When I told them that I had no more chickens to sell, they said, 'Yes, you have many chickens. You sell me some!' I'd say, 'No, those are my layers.' They'd say, 'You sell me 3 layers!' Then a young man came who had excellent English. I explained the situation to him, and we came to an agreement. My husband built a brooder house in which I can raise chicks all year. The Hmong would buy even more than what I have now, but one hundred at a time is all I care to manage."

Killing, plucking, cleaning, and singeing is not an issue at all for the above writer. She told me that one of the big reasons the Hmong were so eager to buy live chickens from her is because it's a matter of conviction with them to do their own butchering! But if you're willing to butcher as well as grow the birds, there are exemptions for small producers in the Poultry Products Inspection Act. Check with your state Department of Agriculture for more information.

MAKING USE OF UNUSUAL CHICKEN PARTS

Cooking Giblets. If your bird is a roaster, you can use the giblets (except for the liver) in the stuffing or gravy. (Precook and dice them, then mix them in.) If your bird is to be a fryer, fry the giblets right along with the rest of the pieces. If it's a stew bird, use the giblets (except the liver) right with the rest. Another way to use giblets is to grind them up for taco and pizza meat. When chicken is canned, the hearts and gizzards are canned separately, and the livers are not canned at all.

⮞ *FRIED LIVERS AND HEARTS Sift together 1 c. flour, ½ t. salt, and ½ t. baking powder. Add enough water so you*

have a thin batter. Dip the separate hearts and livers one by one into it. Then fry them in hot (350°F), deep fat until the batter changes color to a golden brown. Remove from fat, drain off excess fat, and serve.

About Bird Livers and Pâté. The liver gets left out of most recipes because its flavor is just too distinctive to blend successfully. From extra livers you can make the gourmet delicacy called pâté. The livers of about 5 or 6 average-sized chickens will give you ½ lb. of chicken livers. If you just do in a couple every Saturday for Sunday dinner, you could add the fresh livers to your supply in the freezer until you have enough to make pâté. You can make pâté out of any bird livers; recipes are by weight of liver, and variety of bird doesn't matter. If you have a food processor or blender, that helps to get the pâté perfectly smooth. After the pâté is made, it's stored in a small crock or bowl in the refrigerator. Old-timers kept the vulnerable pâté from contact with air by smoothing the top and pouring clarified butter over it until it was completely covered. Nowadays you can cover it with plastic wrap pressed close over the top of the mixture.

Make pâté in small amounts because it doesn't freeze successfully and needs to be eaten up within a few days to a week at most. Pâté is good with a taste of mustard or tart jelly—red currant or crab apple—or with chutney. It's good served cold with sliced apples, crackers, toast fingers, or melba toast, or to make fancy sandwiches.

⮞ *PLAIN PÂTÉ Cook ½ lb. livers slowly in 2 T. butter with 2 chopped onions until the onion is soft and the pink in the liver has disappeared. Remove the liver, mash with a fork, and force it through a sieve, or blend until smooth. To the sieved liver, add ½ c. sour cream. Salt and pepper to taste.*

⮞ *GOURMET SEASONED PÂTÉ Saute 1 large onion, chopped, and 2 minced cloves of garlic in ⅓ c. butter until vegetables are limp. Add 1 lb. chicken livers and saute until pink has thoroughly disappeared. Add tarragon (1 T. if fresh or 1 t. if dried), 1 t. salt, ½ t. freshly cracked black pepper, 1 t. dried thyme, ½ t. cayenne pepper, ½ t. cloves, and ½ t. allspice. Process mixture until smooth. Add 3 T. dry sherry, and blend again until smooth. Pour into bowl, cover, and refrigerate overnight before serving.*

Unfinished Eggs. When butchering cull hens, eventually you're going to encounter one with a cluster of eggs of all sizes—from the size of grains of sand to soybeans size to almost-regular-egg size. They look like little egg yolks. That's what they are, for the addition of an egg white and a shell are the last 2 steps on a hen's ovarian conveyer belt. The sight will give you awful pangs of guilt, as you will have obviously goofed in your culling and butchered a hard-working egg layer. At least you can avoid wasting the unborn eggs. Carefully remove them, rinse, and save. Use fairly soon. They are good food. You can cook them in the chicken broth for soups, scramble them together with regular eggs, or stir into any rice-vegetable mixture that you want to turn into a fried rice.

⮞ *CHICKEN-FOOT SOUP Scald feet with boiling water until the skin and claw cases will peel off. Then place cleaned feet in cold salted water and cook slowly with stew-type veggies and seasonings to taste.*

⮞ *BARBECUED CHICKEN WINGS You'll need 20 chicken wings, ¼ c. soy sauce, ¼ c. honey, 1 T. vinegar, and ½ t.*

ginger. Mix all the ingredients and marinate the chicken wings overnight. Bake at 400°F for ½ hour, turning chicken occasionally while baking.

SERVING THE BIRD WHOLE

About Trussing. A roasting bird is "trussed" by drawing the thighs and wings close up against the body and fastening them securely with skewers or tying them with a string. Trussing keeps those appendages from drying up while the thicker parts of the bird are still baking.

Roasting a Bird (Chicken, Duck, etc.). Roast 2–2½-lb. chickens at 400°F for 1–1½ hours, and they will brown well. Roast 2½–4-lb. chickens at 400°F for 1½ to 2½ hours. (If cooked at a lower temperature they will require a longer time to cook and won't be as brown.) Roast 4–8-lb. chickens at 325°F for 3–5 hours. If your bird is stuffed with a dressing, allow 15–20 minutes additional cooking time. (See "Cooking a Turkey" under "Turkeys" for instructions on larger birds.)

About Stuffing. The bird may be stuffed through both the opening you made to remove the crop and in the abdominal cavity. Stuff sufficiently to fill it, but loosely, since stuffing expands when cooking. When the body is full of stuffing, sew up the skin or close with a combination of skewers and thread. If the sides are very slack, skewers alone could do the job. The loose skin of the neck is drawn over the stuffing in that neck cavity and sewn or skewered. A bird for roasting may be frozen with the stuffing in it for up to 2 months. Make the stuffing ahead and prechill so it is thoroughly cold before you stuff and freeze the bird. (See Chapter 3 for stuffing recipes.)

☙ *BARBECUED BIRD You'll need 1 whole (4–5 lb.) chicken or duck, salt, and pepper. Have plenty of hot coals ready. Season inside cavity. Fasten bird securely to rotisserie rod (or a pole over an open pit). Salt and pepper the outside of the bird. Position bird 6–12 inches from the coals. Enjoy the aroma as the bird sizzles for 2½–3 hours. When it's done, serve it piping hot.*

CUTTING UP THE BIRD

A Halved Broiler. Traditionally, you start with a bird in the 1 to 1½-lb. range. Split the bird into 2 halves, down one side of the backbone and along the breastbone. If you want, you can also cut it along the other side of the backbone and remove the bone completely. To freeze the broiler, place 2 pieces of freezer paper between the halves to make it easy to separate them, then wrap well in a plastic bag or freezer paper. Label with date of freezing and "broiler."

Quartered Bird. You just cut each half in half again so that you end up with 2 breast–wing pieces and 2 thigh–drumstick pieces.

Making Old-Time Frying Pieces. I cut off both the legs and wings before opening the abdomen to remove the entrails. But a person can cut them off afterwards, too. You may leave the drumstick connected to the thigh and serve the resulting larger piece as one, or you can find the joint by wiggling it with one hand and feeling for it with the other and then cut them apart. To get the thigh off the body, place the chicken on its back. Pull the thigh away from the body. Cut through the skin that is thus exposed, between the thigh and the abdomen. Now bend the thigh sharply away from the body cavity until the ball of the thighbone

pops from the hip socket. Cut between ball and socket and finish separating the thigh from the body. Do the other leg the same way.

Next comes the wing-joint cut to make a big piece. You press the top bone of one wing against the body. Feel for the shoulder ball-and-socket joint. Cut through the joint, pull wing outward from body, and cut it from body. By this technique a portion of breast meat will come away with the wing. (It makes the wing piece more significant than it is otherwise.) If you prefer just wing and no breast meat with it, pull one wing upward to expose the joint connecting the outer wing to the body and cut through that joint. Do the other wing the same way.

The last step is cutting up the body. Insert knife blade into the cavity of the bird. Cut parallel to the backbone, slicing through the ribs at approximately the halfway point. Do the same thing on the other side. Pull apart the breast and back. You'll see the meat-covered shoulder blades that unite them. Slice down through these bones to separate the breast section completely from the back. Cut across the backbone where the chicken's rib cage ends to divide the back into 2 pieces. To finish, place the breast skin-side up and cut down the length of the breastbone to divide it into 2 equal pieces. If this were a very large bird, like a turkey or goose, you could cut across extra times to get more breast pieces.

FREEZING, CANNING, OR DRYING POULTRY AND OTHER SMALL STOCK MEAT

Freezing a Roaster. Trim away and discard the excess fat. Cool bird in the refrigerator or soak it in ice water until it is well cooled. This may take 6–8 hours. Then drain thoroughly, for 20 minutes (the dryer it is when it goes into the freezer, the better it will keep). Wrap the giblets in freezer paper. Put the giblets into the bird's empty cavity, then slip the bird containing giblets into a plastic bag. Lower the bird in bag into a pan of lukewarm water. Be careful not to let any water get inside the bag. The water will press the plastic against the bird and expel all air. Twist tightly the part of the bag remaining out of the water. Then loop the tag end of plastic double and fasten with a wire twist or a strong rubber band.

Freezing Cut-Up Chicken. Chicken in pieces is more compact than a roaster, and so takes up less freezer space. The freezer life of a chicken is about 6 or 7 months. If you freeze cooked chicken, it will stay prime only 2 or 3 months.

Canning Poultry, Small Game, or Rabbits. Use cut-up pieces. Remove as much bone as possible so it will pack more compactly. You can include the neck, but do something else with the gizzard, heart, and liver. You could can the gizzards and hearts separately. Or make broth with them and the wings and use it to cover your canned meaty pieces. Or, instead of canning the wings, which are bony and don't have much meat, use them for old-hen recipes, soups, or dog biscuits. Boil chicken pieces 1 hour to precook. You can bone them and can the meat pieces for creamed chicken, sandwiches, or chicken a la king. Or can on the bone.

☙ *HOT PACKING, ON THE BONE Precook until no pink color is left, even at the center of the pieces. Add 1 t. salt per quart jar. Pack clean quart jars loosely with precooked, hot pieces. Pour hot chicken broth over the meat. (You'll need ½–¾ c. per quart.) Leave 1 inch of headspace. Put on lids and process in pressure canner at 10 lb. for 65 minutes for* pints, 75 minutes for quarts. Take jars out of canner and complete the sealing.

➤ **CANNING GIBLETS.** Precook in pan until cooked through. Add ½ t. salt per pint. Pack hot. Add broth to cover giblets, leaving 1 inch headspace. Process in a pressure canner at 10 lb. for 75 minutes (for pints).

➤ **HOT PACK, NO BONE** Precook. Remove bones. Fill jars immediately, leaving 1 inch head room. Process in pressure canner at 10 lb. pressure for 75 minutes for pints, 90 minutes for quarts.

➤ **RAW PACKING ON THE BONE, NO LIQUID** Wash pint or quart jars in hot soapy water, then rinse. Pack raw chicken pieces into jar, drumsticks and thighs against the outer glass, breasts in the center. Add 1 t. salt per quart sprinkled over chicken, no liquid. Wipe jar rim dry. Put on lid. Process in pressure canner at 10 lb. pressure, 80 minutes for quarts.

Drying Chicken. Start with freshly butchered chicken. (Or turkey, but not fat poultry such as duck or goose; fat poultry meat doesn't dry well.) First precook. Cool, remove skin, bones, and all fat. Cut all remaining meat into equal-sized cubes no more than ¼–½-inch square. Distribute these cubes across your drying surface in a very thin layer. Dry in oven or dehydrator 4 hours at 140°F, then continue at 130°F until drying is finished. It helps to stir once in a while and turn trays occasionally. If sun drying, it will take 2 or 3 days. You're done when the meat cubes are dry all the way to the center and so hard they can't easily be cut with a knife.

GOOD RECIPES FOR OLD HENS! You can use these recipes for other small, tough old creatures (like rabbit) simply by substituting "creature" for "chicken."

➤ **CHICKEN AND NOODLES** This recipe is delicious and warms up well. Put your stewing hen in a deep pan. Add all giblets except liver. Cover with water and add ½ t. salt for each pound of chicken. Add 1 carrot, 1 small onion, 1 clove, and 3 peppercorns. Bring to a boil, reduce heat, and simmer until the meat will come off the bones and is very tender. That will require at least several hours or more, depending on how tough your old bird is. Cool it down enough to work with. Take the chicken off the bones and discard bones, skin, and cartilage. Return the meat to the broth. Mash the vegetables in the broth. When you're almost ready to serve this, heat it to boiling. Pour in noodles and cook, frequently stirring to make sure nothing is sticking, until the noodles are done. Serve. I always make this with homemade egg noodles.

➤ **CHICKEN STEW** Prepare the chicken as for "Chicken and Noodles" (above), but instead of adding noodles, add potatoes, more carrots and onions, and peas (or any other vegetables you have and enjoy in stew). Cook until tender.

➤ **"CREAM" OF CHICKEN SOUP** Prepare the chicken as for "Chicken and Noodles" (above), but instead of adding noodles, puree vegetables and add them to the chicken and broth.

➤ **CHICKEN POT PIE** Make "Chicken Stew" (above) or use leftover chicken stew to make this. Brown 7 T. flour in a frying pan with 4 T. butter. Gradually add enough chicken broth to make a good gravy (about 2½ c.). Butter a baking dish. Put the vegetables and meat from your chicken stew

into the dish. (Hold back any excess broth to use in another recipe.) Pour the gravy over it. Make a dumpling dough by your favorite recipe (see recipes in Chapter 3). Drop the dumpling dough by marbles or teaspoonfuls (depending on how you like to make it) on top of the meat and gravy. Bake at 350°F until the dumplings are done.

➤ **CHICKEN AND DRESSING** Cook the chicken and giblets (except liver) until you can easily separate the meat from the bones. Let cool and remove bones and cartilage. Then grind the chicken skin and giblets and add to the meat. The chicken meat is nicest sliced thin. Make a bread dressing base from (preferably homemade) bread plus egg, seasonings, and chicken broth and milk (see recipes in Chapter 3). In an oven pan put a layer of dressing, then a layer of chicken, a layer of dressing again, and so on. Bake, covered, for 40 minutes at 350°F.

➤ **IVY'S CHICKEN LOAF** Ivy Issacson is a beautiful person, a real old-timer. Her husband, Dick, has experience driving oxen and knows how to make an ox yoke, starting with the right sized tree. Here's her recipe: First, boil your old hen by the "Chicken Noodle" recipe (minus the salt), until it is so tender you can pick out the bones and discard them. Keep the chicken meat and broth. Mix 1 small loaf bread torn into pieces with 4 c. corn bread and add enough of the chicken broth to moisten the breads thoroughly. Now add ½–1 c. chopped celery, ½–1 c. chopped onion, salt, pepper, and sage to taste. Place mixture in a buttered 12 × 15-inch pan. Cover with the chicken meat. Mix ½ c. melted butter with ¾ c. flour. Add 2 c. milk. Cook same as any white sauce until thickened. Cool. Add 6 eggs, beaten. Pour over chicken. Sprinkle with buttered bread crumbs. Bake at 350°F for 1 hour. This will give you 15 to 20 servings. Good to take to a potluck!

GERTRUDE JOHNSON'S CHICKEN SPREAD *Cut a stewing chicken of at least 2 lb. into pieces, and place it in casserole that has a tight-fitting lid. Dot with 4 T. butter. Add 1 onion, peeled and quartered; 2 carrots, halved; 2 ribs celery, halved; and 4 peppercorns. Lay 3 lemon slices on top. Cover casserole tightly and bake for 3 hours at 325°F or until chicken is very tender. You might want to just serve the chicken for supper right at this point in the recipe! Otherwise, remove chicken and cool. Discard the vegetables, spices, bones, and skin. Run meat through a meat grinder 2 or 3 times, or whirl it in a food processor until smooth. Put chicken in a mixing bowl and blend in 4–8 T. of softened butter. Stir in ½ t. Worcestershire sauce, salt, and pepper to taste. Press your chicken spread into small jars. Pour a ½-inch layer of clarified butter over the spread in each jar. Cover tightly and refrigerate until wanted to make sandwiches.*

DOG BISCUITS *You can use the excess broth from any old hen recipe to make this, or you could cook the chicken specially to get broth, use the meat in another recipe, and use the broth for dog biscuits. (Actually you can make this recipe with other types of meat broth, too.) This recipe will yield 60 medium-sized dog biscuits which your pet will consider a great treat. Mix together 3½ c. unbleached flour, 2 c. whole wheat flour, 1 c. rye flour, 2 c. cracked wheat, 1 c. cornmeal, and ½ c. skim milk powder. On the side, dissolve 1 T. (or 1 pkg.) yeast in 3½ c. lukewarm chicken broth. The richer this broth is, the more your dog will like the biscuits. Let yeast-broth mixture sit 10 minutes, then stir in the flour mixture. Roll resulting dough out ½ inch thick. Cut dog biscuit shapes from dough. Brush biscuits with egg wash. Bake on greased cookie sheets at 300°F for 45 minutes. Then turn oven off and leave biscuits in there overnight to finish hardening.*

Cleaning and Using Feathers

Now that you've taken care of the meat, you can get back to the feathers. You can make and sell jewelry, art objects, and trout lures from feathers. Or clothing. Or a quilt. But first you have to clean them.

CLEANING FEATHERS

Cleaning Nice Feathers. Wash them in warm water with a little detergent in it, then wash them again in a fresh tub of water with detergent (or washing soda or borax). Then rinse them, and place them into a clean cheesecloth bag or gunny sack and slowly dry. Fluff the feathers several times a day. If you hang them out on the line, dry them in the shade because the sun will bake the life out of them. Or you can dry the feathers by putting them into a slow oven for about half an hour, then removing them, then putting them back into the oven 2 or 3 times. The oven must not be too hot. Or you can suspend the bags from the ceiling of a warm kitchen, or some similarly very warm place.

Cleaning Not-So-Nice Feathers. Ducks and geese are not generally subject to the kind of feather parasites that afflict chickens. You could just throw away the feathers and resolve to trade in your dirty-feathered poultry variety for waterfowl. Or you can struggle on. You won't get good results from what are called "dead" feathers. Those are the ones that the chickens lose in their regular molting process and your children find in the yard or on the chicken-house floor. They will be hard to clean and not as lively and nice as freshly plucked ones.

Pat Woods, Sedro-Woolley, WA, wrote me that a neighboring chicken farmer just presented her with 6 great big sacks of feathers in this condition, and what should she do? Personally, I wouldn't bring home a batch of feathers that had critters, because next thing you'll know they'll be all over your own farm. Just tell your well-intentioned neighbors to keep their feathers. So I'm writing to her and writing up her situation for the book at the same time. (I'm always glad to get questions from people. It tells me what people are needing to know and helps me make this book a more useful one for its readers.)

If somebody gives you a mess of feathers that are not in good shape (and that's the way you'll usually get them)—I mean, containing lice and other creepy-crawlers along with the dirt, droppings, and so on—and you want to keep them, here is what you do.

You'll have to pick out rocks, straw, sticks, and major globs of flop by hand. If there are no bugs, go ahead and strip the wing and other large feathers to get those big quills out of the way. It takes a long time to strip feathers. And cut off the sharp tips on the shorter feathers. If there are bugs, you'll want to give it all a very antiseptic laundering first. Sew or tie the feathers into a bag. If you've got something like old scrim curtains, the kind you can look through, that's perfect, because they let the dirt out. But any loosely woven cloth will do. Then you put the whole thing in the washing machine, and wash it repeatedly until you're satisfied. Or wash the bag by hand, squeezing it and letting it fill, again and again. You can use a soap suitable for wool, even some bleach, and warm, but not boiling hot, water unless the bug problem is bad. In that case, a dose of boiling water in a pan on the stove may be the only answer for your "presoak" cycle.

So if you've got questions too, do write me—don't feel embarrassed about it. If I don't know, I'll just tell you so, or maybe I can find out, and then we'll both learn something. If you have a question, suggestion, or need another copy of this book, or want to know about other books I've written, or the latest edition, find me at **www.carlaemery.com**.

Drying Feathers. If you have a dryer, put your washed sack of feathers inside a pillowcase for extra coverage, then just go ahead and dry them on a very low heat setting. If not, hang the feathers inside a very loosely woven bag in the shade on your clothesline or some place where it can get lots of air. Give the bag an occasional shake. Or you can spread them on screens placed above the floor, or even on the floor itself, if you make sure to turn them over often enough for thorough drying. The main thing is to get them dry as quickly as possible without exposing them to direct sunshine. If the feathers don't dry quickly enough, they will start to deteriorate in quality, becoming fibrous and, ultimately, decomposing.

USING FEATHERS: Whatever feathers you use to stuff, they must be absolutely dry. The higher your percentage of the more down-type feathers, the better. Don't use the quills (wing and tail feathers) at all, unless you strip the fluffy part off the quill base and use it without the quill. You can sell well-washed waterfowl down. It takes about 5 ducks to make a pound of down. Or you can make something of your own with it. Make pillows. Or a quilt.

Making a Feather Quilt. Lay the feathers, still in their cheesecloth bags, upon the bottom layer of the quilt as it is stretched out on your quilting frame. Then put your quilt

cover on, tack it down, and sew or tie it. Or the feathers could be placed directly between layers of cheesecloth, and then the quilt made over that. If this method is to be used, stitch over the entire cheesecloth and feather layer (and quilt, too, if you wish) to create an effect of "diamonds" or "squares." This will keep the feathers from shifting out of place and bunching. Another technique is to sew 2 layers of cloth together around 3 edges leaving the top open, and then sewing from the head to the toe of the quilt, creating long pockets into which you stuff the feathers and down, then sewing the top edge closed. Such quilts can be washed very occasionally if care is used, but it is preferable to have removable covers, and thus protect the feathers from washing as much as possible. To make pillows and ticks, use commercial ticking and fill them as slack or full as you like. But the first time, make them fuller than you think you want, because they will gradually pack. Use a ratio of about ¼ small body feathers to ¾ down to get a resilient pillow. Sew double-stitched seams to keep the feathers in. Make sure you have the feathers in a special inside layer, because you don't want to have to pull a needle through the feather section as you quilt the top. It will pull feathers out with it every time.

Making a Feather Bed. Use regular twill ticking to contain the feathers. Sew double seams so you won't have feathers creeping out. Leave one end open. Pour in 10 to 20 lb. of dry, clean feathers and sew it up. Feather quilts go on top of you; feather mattresses beneath you. With feathers above and below in that manner, you can sleep warm, even in temperatures 50°F below zero, and I kid you not. That's what the settlers in places like Vermont—where they had no heat in their homes at night—used for bedding.

Feather-Stuffed Clothing. Items such as down jackets can be made by creating 2–3-inch channels in the garment to keep the feathers evenly distributed. For clothing use a higher percentage of down, up to 90 percent. Use a down-proof lining, and sew double seams everywhere.

Making Old-Time Quill Pens. The second, third, and fourth quills of the wing are the best for this. If you want them to be clear, put the feather into boiling alum water for 5–10 minutes, then scrape its outer "skin" off. After this, dry the quills in hot sand on a stove, or before the fire.

There exist strange, believe-it-or-not life paradoxes: you get by giving; risk can provide safety; and great, break-through understandings that change a person's life and set them back on the right road can come in lulls between episodes of fierce struggle, born of action. I have a theory that you can't go and contemplate dandelions and have anything important happen in your head—unless you are first bone tired from doing something you think is important. But, on the other hand, I don't think you can get along on pure action either. So spend some time with the dandelions. Or in the garden. Or with the milk cow. Or watching your chickens. In those lovely, quiet times your head gets a chance to tell you a few things you were needing to be told. Your own head can be your best friend, if you listen.

TURKEYS

Don't buy just 1 turkey. Turkeys don't like being alone, and a solitary one may refuse to eat and, consequently, die of starvation. Or the lonely bird may adopt a human. Margie Minard of Mt. Vernon, OH, wrote me: "We have a pair of bronze turkeys. I love them! Their names are Ben Franklin and Betsy Ross. Betsy has been sitting a nest for nearly 3 weeks. Ben has been lonesome since Betsy has been so busy and has become my buddy. He goes to sleep every night on his perch in the barnyard, but every morning he's waiting for me to get up and go out on the porch and have my coffee with him. I talk to him, he peeps back, and we share an apple. Our pair of turkeys seems to be very sweet and very gentle creatures." (A word of caution, here: I wouldn't recommend getting to be that good friends with any farm animals unless you're planning to keep them for breeding.)

Dynah Geisel of Missoula, MT, reported: "I used to keep adult turkeys in the hope of raising my own babies. However, the females wanted to be pets, following me everywhere, trying to come into the house, wanting to sit in my lap outside, etc. The males at around 1 year of age became so mean that they terrified grown men and were a real danger to little children." Indeed, these big turkey toms (a tom is a male) can be very aggressive and dangerous. Once I had a band of gobblers that sneaked up and attacked my husband, Mike, when they were free-ranging. (They didn't stay free-ranging!) Yet I've also had free-ranging turkeys that got along fine with everybody.

Turkeys, like the other poultry, come in different kinds and sizes, but even the small ones are sizable birds. If you're going to raise turkeys, you'll need to invest in a large deep freeze and, even so, be cautious that you don't raise more than you can use. Turkeys have received a lot of bad press about being hard to raise. They are a little slow to learn how to drink and eat, and a little more vulnerable to disease than other poultry, if kept in large numbers. (Crowded birds in general are more vulnerable to disease and parasites.) Other important issues are the initial high-cost of poults, the large amounts they will need to eat (expensive if they are on all-commercial diet), and the large amount of turkey meat you will end up with. Most families would want to raise 6–12 turkeys per year for family use. For commercial growing, 1 acre of land supports between 100 and 150 turkeys.

All turkeys have brightly colored, bizarre-looking folds of skin hanging down from their heads called "wattles." Somebody asked me what wattles are for. I don't know. A full-grown gobbler is an amazingly ugly creature, or handsome, depending on your point of view. Mature toms gobble noisily when strangers approach.

Turkeys by G.T. Klein is a classic on the subject, first written in 1946 and updated in 1972. For a more modern treatment of the turkey subject, see *Raising Your Own Turkeys* by Leonard S. Mercia. Or *Turkeys: A Guide to Management*, available for $22.95 from David Bland, 800-423-4525.

For my summary of the most important things about growing turkeys (that aren't already covered under "Chickens"), here goes.

Turkey Breeds

THE BROAD-BREASTEDS: The biggest of the turkey breeds (also known as the "heavies") are the broad-breasteds, either the traditional Broad-Breasted Bronze or the newer Broad-Breasted White. The Broad-Breasted Bronze is the brown- or black-feathered turkey, but since dark-feathered birds end up looking "dirty" when plucked, the white varieties are becoming the commercial choice.

Broad-Breasted Whites grow large, even larger than Bronzes. These birds grow very fast, have exceptionally large, meaty breasts and may ultimately dress out to 25 lb. (hens) or even 45 lb. (toms). (Other poultry breeds don't have such a striking difference in ultimate weights between the sexes.) You can reasonably send one of these to roast any time from 12 lb. on up. Both Bronzes and Whites make good large roasters at 24–28 weeks. As turkeys (and other poultry) get larger, their feed conversion efficiency and rate of gain decreases. The usual goal is to grow an 18-lb. tom (12-lb. hen), in about 5 months, or a 25-lb. tom in 6 months. Hens can be butchered at only 13 weeks as fryer–roasters or at 20 weeks to make medium roasters (about 14 lb.). If left to full maturity, they get heavier yet. Toms can weigh 50 to 60 lb. at maturity, but by then the meat is toughening. Because the Broad-Breasteds can put on more flesh weight than the others they should be started a month earlier than a medium or light breed.

Many formerly abundant turkeys breeds are now extinct or very near extinct due to the extent to which the market has become dominated by the 2 broad-breasted breeds. But some still exist.

NOT BROAD-BREASTEDS: If you want a turkey variety that can be fertilized without human assistance, and has good setting and mothering instincts, it keeps getting harder as more and more genetic lines are losing that ability. You can get small-sized Beltsville Whites that will reproduce naturally. And you can get naturally mating Bronze turkeys from Wish Poultry, Box 862, Prairie City, OR 97869, spring hatch only. The Bronze is a large bird that does relatively well either in confinement or on range.

Beltsville Whites. These are smaller turkeys; they make good broilers at 15–16 weeks and good medium-size roasters at 24 weeks. Beltsvilles do not convert feed as efficiently as the Broad-Breasted varieties, but they are usually cheaper to buy as poults.

Bourbon Reds, Royal Palms. The reds and palms are both medium-sized turkeys. The Royal Palm is the only major turkey breed whose hens are dependable brooders.

Others. Some sources sell Wild Turkeys. These are hardy, good flyers, and smaller than the commercial breeds—a "light" variety. Because they are being raised in order for the bird to make a comeback in the wild, check with your state game regulatory agency before ordering any. You may need a permit. The Wild Turkey breed needs a high-protein feed, like game-bird starter. Other turkey breeds are Black Spanish, Narragansetts, Blue Slates, and a rare Guatemalan turkey, also called the "ocellated turkey."

Turkey Reproduction

Most people start by mail-ordering turkey poults just as is done with chicks, but you can breed your own. Keeping turkey breeders over winter is expensive because of their sizable food consumption. A broad-breasted tom can eat as much as 250 lb. of feed per year. Letting a bird hatch its own eggs is an iffy method of building a flock because sometimes hatchability is not good. On the other hand, it's nice to know that at least some of the domestic turkey species could survive without artificial insemination and electricity. Growing the better part of your turkey food keeps the expense down. And if you are well-informed about what you're doing, you can avoid the pitfalls.

A good time to buy poults being reared to be breeders is 8 months before you'll want the eggs. Use only the birds that best represent the characteristics you want to breed for. For light-breed turkeys, 1 tom per 20 hens can do the job. Medium-heavy breed turkeys need 1 tom per 18 hens. Heavy-breed turkeys need 1 tom per 16 hens. But you should have at least 2 toms to ensure fertility and performance since one may die or just not have the right stuff. Commercial breeders get the birds started early by stimulating the toms with extended light hours 4 weeks before mating, and hens 3 weeks before egg production with 13–14 hours of at least 50–watt lighting or sunlight.

TURKEY SEX: When hens begin to lay, they begin to mate. The toms strut and court them. The hen chooses the tom she prefers, squats near him, and with luck, he responds and mounts her. If he doesn't respond she loses interest in males for a while. (I can relate to that.) Males that have been "pre-lighted" tend to respond more effectively. Sperm then stored inside her will fertilize her eggs for somewhere between a few days and a few weeks.

Artificial Insemination, or AI. The breeds that are not heavy-breasted and are old genetic lines can usually reproduce naturally. The commercial, heavy-breasted breeds of turkey are not as fertile because that body type selected for by growers, with its very large breast, has some technical difficulties in achieving fertilization naturally because that big meaty breast is too much in the way. So heavy-turkey growers either inseminate artificially completely or attempt to raise the fertility rate by supplementing nature with AI. Inseminating turkeys is not as hard as it sounds.

Milking the Tom. First you capture the tom and the lady and have them close by because turkey semen must be used within 30 minutes of collection. The ideal AI schedule is to inseminate once, wait 4 days, and inseminate once more; after that, do it once every 2–3 weeks while the egg-laying season is on. Toms can donate 2–3 times/week. You need at least 2 people to do the job. You "milk" the tom by flipping him on his back (or you can have him upright and work on him with his legs spread a little from his backside) and stroking his abdomen and pushing his tail up and toward his head. His organ enlarges, protrudes a little bit and then someone must grab it high up and stroke downward just like you're milking a cow. That's it. Have something ready in which to collect the semen. You'll get only a half cubic centimeter or less of it—less than ⅛ teaspoon.

How to AI the Hen. Get her into position by flipping the hen on her back, flipping up her tail, and everting the cloaca. Now pour the tom's semen into it. But for best results, it's not that simple. Ideally, you will expose the opening of the oviduct and use a glass or plastic straw or a small needle-less syringe to place the semen about 1½ inches into that oviduct. If you can't find the oviduct you may have a hen that's not in lay, in which case it's all a waste of time anyway.

EGG PRODUCTION: Have available nests that are 24 inches high by 18 inches wide by 24 inches deep with comfy litter in them in a dimly lit area before laying will start—1 nest for every 4 or 5 hens. For a lot of hens you could supply a 3 × 6-foot community nest. One of those can accommodate about 20 hens. Supply litter generously and gather eggs frequently during the laying season because turkeys like to lay together and tend to step on and break each other's eggs. Heavy hens may lay 50 eggs, medium hens 50–70 eggs, light turkey varieties 85–100 per bird. Turkey eggs are good to eat, but are generally too valuable as the progenitor of another turkey to waste in an omelet. As with chickens, turkey egg production is best the first year and then each succeeding year decreases about 20 percent. Like chickens, egg size increases the second year.

NATURAL BROODING: Broodiness is common among turkeys, but full-fledged mothering ability is not. At least, among the most modern breeds, the turkey hens simply don't have the best sense about the care of poults. Ideally, your turkey would lay 15–20 eggs, then stop and brood them. At least take the eggs until you have a reasonably sized clutch for the hen to sit on. Or let chickens, ducks, or geese brood the eggs. A medium-size chicken can cover 6–7 turkey eggs. The incubation period will be 28 days.

I think the retention of breeds that have the requisite instincts and experience to reproduce on their own is important, and the people who raise these are doing the homestead market a valuable service. If you have a mothering turkey, provide a turkey-sized A-frame inside the pen, 1 for each hen, with straw inside to make into a nest. The nest can be about 14 by 24 inches, on the ground. She'll lay eggs in there and brood them. Some growers slaughter the breeders as soon as the poults are independent of them so as not to have to feed them over winter. Old breeders can be cooked like any other turkey—only longer.

INCUBATING TURKEY EGGS: If you're planning to incubate, broodiness is a problem and you'll want to chase broodys off the nest and treat them like you do a chicken with unwanted broodiness (see "Discouraging a Broody Bird" under "Chickens"). The growers who incubate eggs feel that it makes more economic sense to keep those hen turkeys laying and they will, of course, stop immediately if allowed to stay broody. Incubate turkey eggs for 28 days at 102°F in a still-air incubator or 99.5°F in a circulated-air incubator. Relative humidity during the first 25 days should be about 62 percent (dry bulb reading 99.5°F; wet bulb reading 87.5°F). During the last 3 days it should be about 70 percent (dry bulb 99.5/wet bulb 90°F). Which brings you to the directions for raising poults.

Brooding Poults

A "poult" is a just-hatched turkey.

MAIL-ORDER POULTS: Order your poults to arrive after the weather has turned warm. Or you may be able to buy them at your local feed store. They cost $3 to $5 each, depending on the breed. To mail-order turkey poults you need to get your order in early, by midwinter. Check on delivery schedules since they are hatched during only a few months of the year—about March to July. Poults delivered to you in late May or early June will have just the right amount of time to reach finished weights before Thanksgiving. If you begin your brooding after warm weather has arrived it will be easier and cheaper.

SANITATION: Do make sure you clean the brooding area, disinfect it, then let it stand empty for a month before the turkey poults move in—if it has previously held chickens. This precaution is because turkeys are susceptible to coccidiosis and blackhead disease, both of which are carried in chicken droppings. Still, the most severe turkey disease problems occur in large commercial flocks. Small numbers of turkeys raised and then put into the deep freeze seldom have communicable disease problems.

BROODING: See "Brooding Chicks" under "Chickens" for further information, because the basics are the same. You can brood in a cardboard box with an electric light or a shed-room or in a penned-off space in a barn. If you are using a thermostat-controlled brooder, brood Broad-Breasted Whites at 100°F the first week and Broad-Breasted Bronzes at 95°F the first week, and then reduce 5 degrees a week just as with other young poultry. Depending on your climate and the time of year you start them, they may need supplementary heat as little as a few days or as much as the full 8 weeks. If poults get wet and chilled, they must have heat to recover. As with other poultry, most of the work and worry with turkeys comes in the first 8 weeks. It's important to check on poults frequently and observe them closely, even after the first few days, to see if there is some problem.

Teaching Poults to Drink and Eat. You can use chicken feeding and watering equipment for turkeys. As soon as your mail-order poults arrive, take them one by one out of the shipping container, dip their beaks into their proper

drinking container (which should be filled with lukewarm water). Then dip their beaks into their proper feed trough (which should be filled to the brim). Do this same thing morning, noon, and night for each poult for the first few days, or until they learn how to eat and drink and can do it on their own. Some people put a few chicks in with the poults to show them how; chicks are quicker learners than poults.

But don't count on that technique working. There are reports of poults having died of starvation while standing on their food. (Anyway, it's unhealthy for them to eat food that has been spread on the floor or ground and gets mixed with feces.) Unlike chickens, turkeys seldom scratch to find food. Instead they peck at something that catches their attention. So an additional good teaching technique is to put strips of aluminum foil or some brightly colored marbles both in their feeders and waterers to catch their attention and encourage them to start picking at it. Or you can lay their food out on clean sheets of white paper towel. Or put it in low-sided box tops like oatmeal carton lids. Another technique to help them find that feed and water is to supply intense light, such as 150 watts, 24 hours a day for the first 3 days.

After those first 3 days or so, you can take away the chicks so they won't get trampled. Move the feed from paper towels or box tops into the regular metal feeder, and fill the trough only ¾ full.

Commercial Turkey Food. Most local feed stores don't carry turkey starter mash, although that is a very suitable food for the poults. So, the poults can be fed chick-starter rations with plenty of water. In either case the feed will contain a coccidiostat (antibiotic to prevent coccidiosis). They'll eat the starter ration for their first 8 weeks. Then gradually shift them to a grower's ration. At about 16 weeks of age they are gradually shifted to a finishing ration. Growing and finishing rations are not usually medicated. Supply grit. If you are using any medicated feeds for older birds, be sure and stop offering them at least a week before slaughter and preferably longer.

About Antibiotic Withdrawal. Food writer Lane Morgan, who reviewed this book, complained that in the chicken section it says to withhold medication for 5 days, and here it says a week. Actually, never medicating them is best. Or, lacking that, stopping as long before slaughter as possible. Or 7 days. Or 5. How desperately hungry are you? Starvation is worse than a little antibiotic in your protein. These things are judgment calls, not absolutes. The basic principle here is that the less antibiotic you feed your animals, the better—for them and for you. Routine antibiotic-feeding results in an animal whose own immune system is underdeveloped and under-functional. That's true whether it's livestock or your children. Antibiotics are a quick fix for which we pay a long-term price in the development of antibiotic-resistant varieties of whatever we were fighting in the first place. Livestock diseases often transfer over and become human illnesses too, and this can also happen with antibiotic-resistant varieties of livestock illness. Simply speaking, the more you use antibiotics (or pesticide, herbicide, fungicide, etc.), the sooner they won't work any more. Basically, if you have fed your animals antibiotics, the longer between that feeding and your consumption of the meat, the better.

Home-Devised Poult Diet (or Diet Supplement). It helps to supplement the chick starter at first with scrambled eggs or chopped hard-boiled eggs because the fast-growing poults need a lot of protein at first and, like broiler chicks, can develop leg problems without it. Or you can start them on home-grown food using the same rations as for geese (see "Feeding Goslings" under "The Waterfowl"), only leaving out the water poured over the food. They like crumbled cornbread, too, and can make good use of fresh whole or skim milk served from their first week on. Other good foods for them are eggs scrambled with milk and mixed with any kind of flour or fine grain—ground or rolled oats, barley, or corn, etc. They love bugs, especially maggots. They'll eat boiled meats, including butchering leftovers. A liquid mixed with any fine grain makes a home-grown mash for them.

Birds on a home-devised diet need to be able to get out and forage when weather permits. Later they can handle more coarsely cracked corn and wheat if they have grit. Large-scale growers may plant special crops of soybeans, alfalfa, rape, or kale for them. For just a few birds you can let them find their own food so long as it's not something forbidden. They can benefit from greens like Swiss chard, rape, alfalfa, cabbage, lettuce, and so on for about a quarter of their diet. Gradually add a combination of cracked corn, wheat, oats and greens. (See the chicken section for more on useful home-devised diet options.) Or you can supplement commercial rations with such combinations. The birds must have insoluble grit to be able to make use of whole grains and other fibrous foods.

Of Turkey Housing and Yards

TURKEY SPACE: Until they're 8 weeks old, the poults can get along on a square foot of space per bird. But they'll grow fast and need more square footage per bird before butchering time. A peculiarity of turkeys is the great difference in size between toms and hens. In an all-tom flock, you'd eventually need 5 square feet of floor space per bird. An all-hen flock could manage with 3 square feet per bird. Another consideration is that some turkey breeds are considerably smaller than others. Those smaller breeds could grow in even less space. Breeders require more space than birds simply being grown for slaughter: 6–8 square feet per bird. In general, the more space you can provide, the better your poultry will do.

TURKEY YARDS: You can raise turkeys in complete confinement, but providing their house with an attached fenced yard would be nicer. The yard should be well-drained ground with no puddles, or pavement, or gravel, or fenced pasture, or rotated pastures. Their shelter house has its uses, too. Confining young turkeys during rainy weather will keep them out of wet grass. Wet poults can easily get chilled, weaken, and die. Or they can be raised in an off-the-ground sunporch for exercise and sunshine. You don't walk into a sunporch pen. You build it so that you can feed and water from outside the cage. That way you don't carry in any blackhead disease on your shoe soles. The sunporch is the ideal way to raise turkeys in areas where they are very likely to catch diseases.

Blackhead Disease. This is very serious for turkeys. Chickens very seldom get blackhead though they may act as a carrier for the cecal worm that hosts the blackhead protozoan. Blackhead is the most common and destructive disease afflicting turkeys, and it can strike them at any age if

they happen to pick up cecal worm eggs that contain the organism. Blackhead-afflicted turkeys are droopy and their droppings are brownish-colored and foamy. Their heads may look dark. The liver of a blackhead-affected turkey may have ulcers, and inflammation of the intestine may be present. If you live in a blackhead-afflicted area you'll want to be careful to keep your turkeys completely away from places where chickens go. If your birds have the disease, they can be treated with drugs. It also helps to keep them on a sunporch.

Sunporch. A typical turkey sunporch arrangement is a pen 5 × 12 × 2 feet high, entirely supported 2–3 feet above the ground on legs, with half of it roofed over and 2 sides covered or next to another building. You can keep 1 turkey for every 5 square feet in such a sunporch. The floor can be a problem. The smaller varieties and those that will be butchered by 12–16 weeks can manage the wire floors. Large turkey varieties that are destined to be heavy roasters need a wood slat floor, or some other firm arrangement to avoid developing leg problems. Wire or slat floors do solve the sanitation problem nicely. The droppings fall through, and the birds don't pick up any parasites and are safe from predators. However, turkeys in a sunporch do suffer the usual confinement-associated problems of feather-pulling and cannibalism. To prevent this behavior avoid overcrowding the birds, and keep them busy with food and water, roosts, fibrous foods like oats, and greens or a cabbage hung by a string for them to peck at.

Range Arrangements. Or you can let older birds out completely in the daytime and pen them in only at night. If shade is provided for the yard—even a row of sunflowers or corn—the birds grow faster and feather better. It will help prevent parasitic infections if this ground has not had poultry running on it for a year—or more. Like geese, turkeys can be very hard on your garden if they are not confined. Turkeys are good foragers and can find a good part of their diet if they are allowed to hunt for greens. In reasonable weather turkeys that are well feathered-out over the hips and back (about 8 weeks old) can sleep out in the open on the ground, and you can plan to have them in the deep freeze before the cold weather sets in. Adult turkeys being kept for breeders don't need as much warmth as chickens and are quite hardy against cold weather. I once had a tom whose nose decoration froze off, but the rest of him survived a bitter winter fine.

A good design for a turkey pen is a long run with posts set into the corners to hold up high wire sides. Ground-running turkeys can be fenced in with 4–6-foot hog wire or heavy-gauge poultry wire with reinforcing barbed wire at the bottom outside of the fence. Or you can use temporary fencing moved once a week or so to keep them on clean, dry ground.

Moving Turkeys to Yard or Range. If you are planning to range your turkeys, be careful with the transition. Turkeys are slow learners, and if they have been previously kept in complete confinement and are suddenly set loose in the open, they will not know the use of shade to protect them from sunlight or of shelter to protect them from rain and storms. They are likely to pile in a corner and smother or not know to eat out of their new feeding arrangement. Poults in a new environment are as vulnerable as when they are a day old and must be watched as carefully and helped as carefully to learn the necessities in their new environment. Make sure they do have shade available. Make the move on the morning of a good day. Move their feeder and waterer as needed to avoid the creation of a muddy spot that could harbor disease and organisms.

Gapeworm. This parasite can dwell in turkeys' bronchi and trachea. An infestation can result in a sort of pneumonia, shortage of breath, or suffocation. Birds acquire gapeworm by eating infected earthworms. The gapeworm is "6"-shaped, red-colored, and you can sometimes see them simply by opening an afflicted turkey's mouth and looking down its windpipe. If your turkeys have 'em, check with your vet. There is a treatment.

POULT AND TURKEY FLOORING: Poults don't do well on a dirt floor. Cover litter the first week to keep them from eating it. And don't put them on newspapers because they'll slip and develop bad legs. Distribute the litter very evenly and then put some sort of rough paper on top of it. Turkeys produce an exceptionally wet, copious manure. Remove wet or dirty litter daily, and add dry, clean litter. You can expect to gain about 100 lb. compost from them before the season is over.

Turkeys That Sleep on the Floor; Piling. Turkeys have a problem with "piling." That happens when something frightens them, like sudden light, unexpected noise, or strange animals. Fireworks and sonic booms can cause piling. They are most likely to pile when frightened at night. Then they tend to all run and pile up in the nearest corner of their building or fence. If you see them piling you need to unpile them as soon as possible to prevent injuries and smothering of the innermost ones. A low-wattage night-light is said to help prevent piling.

Turkeys can get along permanently without roosts. If they don't have them, like broilers, they will just sleep in the floor litter. In that case, keep the litter relatively clean and dry to prevent breast blisters and dirty feathers.

Turkey Roosts. Supplying roosts of either the step-ladder sort or just flat frames with perches helps avoid night piling. Flat roosts can be 1½ feet off the floor with 9–12 linear inches of roost space for each bird. Turkeys will begin to use roosts when they are about 4–5 weeks old. Older turkeys that are being raised out of confinement, with a pasture to roam in and a minimal shelter to sleep in, can benefit from roosts made of 2-inch poles or 2 × 4s laid flat. These are good when spaced about 2 feet apart and built 1½–2½ feet up off the ground, allowing at least a foot of perch space per bird.

Butchering

By 12–16 weeks of age turkeys can become "broilers" or "fryer roasters"; by 22–26 weeks of age they should weigh enough to be heavy roasters. If you're not sure if the turkey is heavy enough for butchering, weigh it. Broiler–fryers are considered ready at around 4 lb. If it's a tom and weighs 18 lb. or more, that's good enough. (Those numbers are for Broad-Breasted Whites—lighter breeds could be considered ready to roast at lighter weights.) If your turkey is not yet up to the weight you desire, turn it loose and continue feeding it another couple of weeks, then weigh it again. If you keep turkeys longer than 6½ months, the hens may start to lay. Both toms and hens tend just to acquire fat after that age rather than to grow. And soon they'll go into their first molt, which means many more pinfeathers to fight with. Turkeys are quieter than chickens to have around while they are young, but once the toms reach maturity (at 5 or 6 months) they will start to gobble noticeably. If you send your turkeys out to be butchered, Lane Morgan suggests scheduling will be easier if you don't do it around Thanksgiving. Beat the rush.

KILLING A TURKEY: First, catch the bird and tie its legs. (If you can first herd the turkey into a confined area, especially a small, dark room, it helps.) Then grab its legs and tie them together. The butchering process with a turkey is basically the same as that with a chicken except that your bird is approximately 5 times bigger. It will take you about half an hour to kill and pick 1 bird, and another half hour to finish it up freezer-ready. The turkey may then be beheaded with an ax (a 2-person job, one to hold the turkey and one to chop). Another method is to suspend a cord or wire from a beam, so that the lower end comes even to about your shoulder. Hang the bird from this by its legs—head downward. Give it a sharp blow on the back of its head to stun it, then reach a sharp knife through its mouth and cut crosswise to sever the arteries in the throat. Or use a turkey-sized killing cone. And/or cut the throat just back of the jaws. Allow the bird to bleed out thoroughly.

PICKING: To dry-pick, begin doing it immediately, while the bird's still warm. Be careful not to tear the flesh. Pull the wing feathers and the main tail feathers by yanking them straight out. Remove the breast feathers next because the skin of the breast is tender and likely to tear if it's cold. Jerk them straight outward from the bird as it hangs, a few at a time. After plucking the breast, move up over the body and then to the back. Finish on the neck.

Scalding is easier than dry-picking, once you've figured out how to manage the logistics. A metal garbage can is an easy answer. Scald the bird at 140–180°F for 30–60 seconds. (See "Scalding" under "Chickens.") Turkey pinfeathers are probably easiest to remove under running water with pressure and a rubbing motion, or with a dull knife by applying pressure between knife and thumb, the way teenagers squeeze pimples. Then singe and eviscerate, same as chicken. Remove the oil sac on the tail as for waterfowl.

Cooking a Turkey

➣ *TURKEY BROILER Prepare, quarter, and barbecue the same as a chicken broiler. Turn frequently and baste with a good sauce each time you turn a piece.*

➣ *PAN-FRIED TURKEY Start with a 4–9-lb. turkey that has been cut up according to the directions for chicken frying pieces (see "Cutting Up the Bird" under "Chickens") or as you prefer. In a bowl toss together ¾ c. flour, 1 t. paprika, ½ t. oregano, and 1 t. salt. When the flour and spices are* well mixed, pour them into a bag and shake the turkey pieces in there, 2 or 3 at a time, until each is well-coated. Fry the turkey pieces just like you would chicken, first browning them well, then cooking them covered on top of the stove or in the oven until all meat is tender and cooked through (about 1–1½ hours). Remove lid and continue cooking until pieces are crispy again. Remove them. Make gravy in the drippings with the leftover flour/spices mixture, and serve.

❧ **TURKEY BURGER** *If you have a lot of turkey meat, you can vary the menu by making burger out of some of it. Grind it and add flavoring ingredients such as ketchup, onion flakes, lemon juice, Worcestershire sauce, paprika, salt, pepper, etc. Shape patties and cook in your preferred manner until the meat is completely done.*

❧ **TURKEY SAUSAGE** *1 lb. ground turkey, ¼ c. seasoned bread crumbs, 2 T. chicken broth, 2 T. minced onion, 1 T. minced fresh parsley, 1 t. vegetable oil, ¼ t. ground sage, ¼ t. ground thyme, ⅛ t. ground black pepper, 1 egg white. Combine and blend well all ingredients, except egg white. Beat egg with a fork and add. Shape patties and place on nonstick or oiled cookie sheet. Broil 3–4 inches from heat 4–5 minutes (until light brown). Turn and broil other side 2–3 minutes (or until cooked through).*

❧ **BOILED TURKEY** *You'll need 12 c. water, 2 large carrots, 3 stalks celery, 1 quartered onion, ½ c. coarsely chopped parsley, 4 t. salt, 1 t. dried thyme (½ t. if you use powdered), ½ t. peppercorns, and ½ t. whole cloves for this recipe. You also need a very large kettle with a rack in the bottom, so the turkey won't stick. For a 12–14-lb. turkey use a kettle that will hold at least 12 qt. water. A canning kettle will work, although the metal it is made of does not heat particularly evenly. Cutting the bird in half lengthwise through the breast bone will allow you to cook it in 2 smaller kettles by dividing the other ingredients. Put the turkey and the giblets (except the liver) into the kettle and add the water. Add all the vegetables and spices. Cover and bring to a boil. Reduce the heat and simmer about 15 minutes per 1 lb. turkey. Cool the turkey in the broth for 30 minutes then cover and place in the refrigerator overnight.*

The next day, take the turkey from the broth, and remove the skin. Remove the meat from the bones, starting with the large pieces of breast meat. Wrap the meat well and either refrigerate or freeze. A whole breast will slice beautifully, and the other meat can go into casseroles, sandwiches, soups, etc. You could return all of the bones and skin to the stockpot and simmer for 4–6 hours to get additional broth. Chilling will allow the fat to rise to the top of the broth; remove it before storing broth in refrigerator or freezer.

❧ **ROASTED TURKEY** *You must first figure out how you're going to get it into the oven, if you let it grow to a humongous size. Then rub the outside with oil or butter, stuff it if you want, and truss. It will cook faster if you don't put the stuffing into the bird, but bake it separately. But a problem with roasting turkey is keeping it from drying out. So it helps— and is delicious!—to have a nice moist dressing inside it, and gravy to pour over when you serve it. For dressing, giblet gravy, and seasoning, proceed as you would for chicken, except everything is on a larger scale.*

Set the bird on anything that will hold it, fit into your oven, and won't burn—like a cookie sheet. Set it down on top of a couple slices of buttered bread to keep it from

sticking to the pan. Some cooks roast them breast down, but I prefer breast up. Some cooks, especially for a very large bird, bake it for an hour and a half, take the bird out, turn it over, and continue baking with the other side up. But I think that's unnecessary extra struggle.

Roasting Temperatures and Times. The following baking times tend toward the maximum rather than the minimum. It's hard to be precise because you may have started with the bird more or less chilled from the thawing, and ovens vary in their true temperatures, and stuffings vary in their density and temperature. So your bird is quite likely to be done an hour or so sooner. That's okay. It's easy to keep a roasted turkey warm in the oven before dinner. It's impossible to hurry one up while your hungry would-be diners are waiting for it to finish baking. Note also that fresh turkeys take a little longer to roast than ones that have been frozen—about 5 or 10 minutes longer per pound.

Roast at 425°F for half an hour, then finish at 325°F. Continue roasting until it has turned a nice shade of brown. The larger the turkey, the more baking time. With stuffing, figure on cooking a 6-lb. turkey, 3–3½ hours at 325°F; an 8-pounder, 3½–4 hours; a 12-pounder, 4½–5 hours; a 16-pounder 5½–6 hours; a 20-pounder, 6–7 hours; and a 24-pounder, 7½ hours.

Eating Up a Whole Turkey. This can be a real challenge for a small family. This is not a one-time happening, so you might well do some advance planning. Figure on roast turkey for its first appearance at the table. Serve it with baked or mashed potatoes, stuffing, and maybe a green vegetable, hot giblet gravy, homemade bread, and dessert. A real feast. Now it's not so simple. For the second appearance you could offer turkey a la king with a "white" sauce that substitutes chicken broth for the milk. Add pieces of turkey, pimento, and peas and serve over toast. Next time have turkey sandwiches with mayonnaise, salt, pepper, lettuce or whatever. Or turkey (taco) salad. Or turkey pizza. (Marinating leftover turkey in olive oil and rosemary prevents drying.) Or turkey and rice. The last time serve Turkey Bone Soup.

❧ **LEFTOVER TURKEY AND RICE** *Spread out 4 c. cooked, chunked turkey meat in a large skillet or shallow baking pan. Mix together salt and pepper to taste, ½ c. honey, ½ c. prepared mustard, 1 t. curry powder, and 1 T. turkey drippings from the roasting. Pour the sauce onto the turkey meat and mix it all together. Heat thoroughly on top of the stove, stirring as needed, or bake until hot (about 30 minutes at 350°F), stirring once or twice during that time. Let your family spoon this over cooked rice. A sprinkle of chives over all adds more color and flavor.*

❧ **TURKEY BONE SOUP** *Break up leftover cooked turkey when you're seeing more bony skeleton than meat on the carcass. Put bones, meat, and your leftover stuffing along with carrot chunks and some onion and maybe celery into a kettle with plenty of water. Add a few peppercorns, salt, and a bay leaf. Cook an hour or until you can get the remaining meat easily off the bones. Then sort out and discard the bones. Now add about ½ c. rice or barley, and cook on low heat until the grain is ready.*

❧ **CANNING TURKEY—OR RABBIT, OTHER SMALL GAME, OR OTHER POULTRY** *Cut the bird up enough to be able to precook it in a big pan or pressure cooker. Cook until you can easily remove all the bones, then discard them. Place the hot meat pieces into quart jars. Add 1 t. salt per jar, put* *on lids, and process at 240°F (10-lb. pressure) in a pressure canner for an hour and a half. When the cooker is opened, remove jars and fully tighten lids.*

✍ **CANNED TURKEY SOUP STOCK** *The water that you precooked the turkey meat in is a good basic soup stock. Cool and skim to remove the fat. Pour stock into pint jars. Add 1 T. barley, rice, or other soup-grains to each jar, plus small pieces of the gizzard and heart and marginal bits of meat scavenged from the bones pile. Do not add liver. Fill to within ½ inch of the top. Put on lids, process for 35 minutes at 240°F (10-lb. pressure). Tighten lids.*

Turkeys never have to ponder the mysteries of life and love. Reality can be harsh and hard, full of pain you can't escape—but it can also be joyful and marvelous, like falling in love. You can love your plants and animals and feel in control. When you fall in love with another human being, you must trust them to care for you. You're no longer in total control (although I've seen some people manage to come darn near it—loving and being in control of their own life and now their partner's also: a stressful lifestyle). There is a time to love, when it's very hard not to love. Yet you could resist. Would it be better to say no this time and hope for a better match next time? There will be another chance.

THE WATERFOWL: DUCKS AND GEESE

Many of the principles of waterfowl care are the same as those for chickens and are covered in that section. This section covers cases in which duck and goose care are the same for each other but different from that for chickens. Following this combined section, there are individual duck and goose sections.

In general, ducks are small waterfowl, and geese are big. (The Muscovy is a bird that fits into both categories. I've seen it grouped with the geese, but it's more often categorized with the ducks, and that's what I've done, too.) Ducks and geese often form strong attachments to their owners. On the average, ducks are noisier than geese, especially White Pekin females. Muscovy ducks don't quack, but they do hiss like a goose. The waterfowl are actually hardier in resistance to poultry diseases than chickens and seldom suffer disease when kept in small flocks. However, when waterfowl are raised in very large numbers in a small area, they, like all animals under those conditions, are more likely to be affected by disease. Egg-specialist duck breeds lay as many eggs as egg-specialist chicken breeds. Duck and goose eggs are 14.5 percent fat, as compared with chicken eggs, which are 10.5 percent fat; in both cases the fat is located in the yolk. Some shade and shelter are preferable, and fencing will keep birds in and predators out.

FURTHER DUCK AND GOOSE INFORMATION: For more info, read Dave Holderread's *Raising Ducks* and the *Book of Geese: Successful Duck and Goose Raising*, by Darrel Sheraw (Stromberg Publishing: 800-720-1134; **www.strombergschickens.com**); *Ducks and Geese in Your Backyard*, by Rick and Gail Luttmann (1978); *Waterfowl: A Guide to Management and Propagation*, by Simon Tarsnane; and *Modern Waterfowl Management and Breeding Guide*, by Oscar Grow.

To join the American Pheasant and Waterfowl Society ($25 annual dues and you get the *APWS Magazine* with classified ads, breeders directory, annual convention, lending library, free "wanted" ads, etc.), contact Lloyd Ure, Secretary-Treasurer: 715-238-7291; fax 715-238-7623; W2270 US Hwy. 10, Granton, WI 54436; **lloydbevbirds@tznet.com; www3.upatsix.com/apws**. Another good waterfowl website is **members.tripod.com/~QuackersHomePage/index.html** or **QuackersHome.com**.

WATERFOWL BREEDERS: Also see "Places to Buy or Order Poultry" under "Chickens" in this chapter for other waterfowl addresses, because most chick hatcheries offer some waterfowl.

Clearview Hatchery offers a free catalog: 717-365-3234; Gratz, PA 17030.

Johnson's Waterfowl offers 21 breeds of ducks and 12 of geese: 218-222-3556; 36882 160th Ave. NE, Middle River, MN 56737.

Metzer Farms sells ducklings, goslings, guineas, pheasants, wild turkeys; 35 breeds in all; also equipment. Free catalog: 800-424-7755; 831-679-2355; **metzinfo@metzerfarms.com**; 26000 Old Stage Rd., Gonzales, CA 93926; **metzerfarms.com**.

Phinney Hatchery offers ducklings, goslings, etc. Free price list: 509-525-2602; 1331 Dell Ave., Walla Walla, WA 99362.

Windchime Lakes: Dan Bishop is a swan specialist. Contact 402-359-4444; 4820 Dodge St., Omaha, NE 68132; **swan@swan.net**.

TOE-PUNCHING: Because they have webbed feet, and because their feet have no nerves, ducklings and goslings are sometimes marked to record sex, breed, genetic category, etc., with small holes punched in the web between the claws, or with a certain number or location of notches cut into the edge of the web between toes: for example—1 hole for a goose, 2 for a gander.

Of Water and Waterfowl

For best health, these birds need at least to be able to get their heads and feet wet. You don't need a pond to raise waterfowl, but they do like at least a small tub in which to splash. Frequently changed swimming water for them in something like a shallow hog pan or a child's swimming pool can be sufficient. Adults can be kept in a pen with just a bucket or tub of water that is refilled a couple times a day. A water container with a float valve works well—sunk into the ground so that the edge is level with the ground, it is perfect. Or you can make a cement pool, maybe 3 feet across and 12–18 inches deep. Put gravel around the edge of the swimming pool to keep the area from being muddy

and help keep the water clean.

Once started, ducks require little commercial feed if they have enough foraging space, eating a combination of grain, green stuff, worms, and bugs in season—grasshoppers, caterpillars, crickets, and slugs. Geese can live on grass, but you may not want them in any lawn area since their droppings are very messy (not a treat for children's bare feet). Both ducks and geese are among the most efficient animals at converting feed to meat, and they tend to get fat if overfed. Ducks are ready for the deep freeze faster than geese: 8 weeks of feeding yields 7 lb. of duckling; 13 weeks of feeding yields an average 12 lb. of young goose (live weight). These are the healthiest of the fowl (with geese being even hardier than ducks) and are rarely afflicted with diseases or parasites, and they require little or no shelter, even in winter.

OF WATER AND MATING: In such a pool as described above, the waterfowl that can't mate effectively on land can accomplish what must be done. The heavy duck and goose breeds—Giant Toulouse, Aylesbury, Rouen—need swimming water in order to mate successfully. Wild ducks and geese mate on the water. Domesticated birds closely related to the wild also need water to mate: Mandarins, Wood Ducks, and Canada geese. Ducks or geese that are sitting on a nest always need access to water; a shallow pan of it can suffice. The birds must dampen their feathers daily to add required humidity to the eggs' environment.

POND LIFE: If you have a pond, about 25 ducks and 6 geese is the maximum population per acre of water surface that you'd want to carry. You wouldn't want them swimming in a place you use for people swimming because they poop copiously into the water—which is good fish food—and on the banks of it. They like to eat water lilies and small frogs. A reasonable-sized flock of ducks will clean up a pond full of green filamentous algae because their droppings encourage microscopic pond life that hold back the algae. Those droppings can also be food for certain species of fish. Ducks eat water weed roots and will clear the shore of a pond, widen and open up streams. Waterfowl do not effectively control tropical water plants such as water lettuce and water hyacinth. An overpopulation of ducks will muddy water and cause bank erosion as they dig up the edge looking for worms and roots. It's always best to look for balance in an ecosystem.

DUCK PLAGUE: Ducks and geese in commercial flocks in the eastern United States have a problem with acquiring duck virus enteritis (duck plague) from migratory waterfowl that stop over on their ponds. Birds without such attractive open water avoid the disease.

PREDATORS: You may lose ducklings and goslings to underwater predators, snapping turtles, pike, otter, or some other aquatic creatures.

STICKY EYES: Their water should be at least 8 inches deep so the waterfowl can get their heads in there, yet shallow enough (or with a ramp supplied) so they can easily go in and out for swimming. (Exhausted waterfowl have been known to drown, especially ducklings and goslings that are not fully feathered.) Clean the water container thoroughly at least once a week to prevent mud sludge and bacteria build-up. Waterfowl that haven't been able to dip their entire head into water to rinse it off sometimes develop sore or sticky eyes, an infection that may cause permanent blindness.

Grossly dirty water can also cause sticky eyes in your waterfowl. Treatment for sticky eyes is astringent eye ointment.

WATERFOWL ON SALTWATER: Ducks thrive in saltwater too. But if your wetlands are salty, be sure you supply adequate amounts of fresh water for drinking.

RAISING YOUNG WATERFOWL: It would be wise to start with only about a half dozen birds, at least until you better understand what you're doing and how the fowl are going to fit in with your environment and lifestyle. Don't overcrowd your waterfowl. Consider that you need about 13 square feet of housing and about 40 square feet of run area for 1 goose or 2 ducks. You can mail-order ducklings and goslings, but these larger birds are not cheap. Ducklings cost about $3 each. The care of young ducklings and goslings is distinctly different from that of chicks in some important ways, although the basic principles are the same. Or, if you have breeder birds, you could let them raise the babies.

Incubating Waterfowl Eggs. Use all the guidelines for chicken eggs-in-waiting, plus: In the incubator you'll want holders suitable for eggs larger than chicken eggs. Serious waterfowl hatcheries use incubators that are specially adapted for hatching these eggs. Set the temperature control for 99–100°F for a forced-air style incubator, 101–102°F for a still-air incubator.

Incubator Moisture. Waterfowl keep their eggs very moist. In a dry climate, even in an incubator, high humidity is not good enough. There are several ways to supply this extra humidity: Give a light spraying of lukewarm water to the eggs once a day. Or, do as a friend of mine does and remove duck and goose eggs from the incubator twice per day and dunk them in warm water. The way the parent bird keeps them wet enough is to get off the nest, get her breast feathers all wet, and then return to the nest. Finally, you might enhance the water pan's evaporation ability by resting a piece of sponge in it that rises a couple inches out of the water, and each time you turn the eggs, spray them gently with warm water.

The Hatching. On the 25th day quit turning the eggs, but keep on dunking or spraying the water until the ducklings pip their eggs. The pipping should take 28 days after incubation began for most ducks, but Muscovy eggs require 35 days. Give 1 last spraying and/or dunking when the pipping occurs. Then you hope for the best. Day-old ducklings can be vent-sexed in a manner similar to chicks.

BROODER SHELTER: Although they are hardier than chicks or poults, ducklings and goslings must also be kept from chilling for the first month. Their shelter can be simple, but it should be dry and not drafty. The flooring of your brooding space can be wood, concrete, or dirt. An 8 × 10-foot southeast corner of a barn would make a fine spot in which to start ducklings. If you are using a brooder setup that was designed for chicks, you can expect that it can handle half as many ducklings as it could chicks, or a third as many goslings. Plan for about 1–1½ square feet of floor space for each duckling or gosling, increasing the space to 2½ square feet for each bird at 7 weeks. Waterfowl grow faster and develop warm feathers earlier than baby chicks. Some people use unheated boxes insulated with 2–4 inches of rags, straw, sawdust, or grass, covered with burlap, with a small entry hole in the side. The young ducklings' body heat can keep them warm in this close environment. Although this is less expensive than a heated brooder, you have to be careful that the babies don't suffocate.

Brooder Heat. If you are using infrared brooders, every 25 goslings or 30 ducklings should have their own 250-watt heat lamp. You'll want to raise the heat source a few inches higher than what you use for chicks for these larger babies. Having enough separate heat sources for the number of young birds eliminates overcrowding around the heat source, which could result in smothering. Leaving the light on all night can also discourage crowding. Try for a starting temperature of around 90°F at the edge of the heat circle. Each subsequent week, reduce the heat 5 degrees until you get to 70°F. Brooder temperatures that are chronically too high cause the birds to grow and feather out more slowly than normal. Panting birds are a good indication also that the heat is too high. Huddling birds are not warm enough. After 4 to 6 weeks you can turn the heat off, unless your outside temperatures are outrageously low. By 4 weeks of age ducklings have begun to grow a covering of heavier feathers for their backs and can go outside in the daytime in good weather. As early as 10 days, goslings are ready to abandon the brooder.

Duck-Raised Ducklings: For those ducks that make good mothers, the ideal circumstance is to let the mother duck manage her own ducklings. Duck-raised ducklings learn faster to forage for themselves and how to swim. There are, however, some cautions. Ducks with broods should be separated from the rest of the adult flock and confined at night until the ducklings are 6–8 weeks old. Even 2 hens with broods should be kept separate, as they often react with hostility toward any but their own ducklings. If you are planning on hatching more eggs than you have brooding mothers, you can incubate.

Waterfowl Mothering Chicks. If you give a duck chicken eggs to sit on, she'll do a good job, but once the chicks hatch out, it can be a very risky business. Most owners take duck-hatched chicks away and brood them separately, because the duck mother may lead her chicks to the deep water, and the chicks are likely to get wet or drown as she goes about her necessarily sloppy way of drinking. You can have chickens or turkeys set on duck eggs, but if you do, be sure to confine the foster mothers for the first 2 weeks so they won't desert their charges. If you set duck eggs under a chicken hen, keep the number down to 8–9. Unless a chicken has set and hatched ducklings, don't trust ducklings to her care.

Of Ducklings and Goslings, Food and Water

Strangely enough, you have to be just as careful to keep these babies dry as you do baby chicks, at least for the first 2 weeks. Chilling after becoming wet is the most frequent cause of duckling deaths. Waterfowl raised by their parents learn to swim early, but hatchery goslings and ducklings can't swim until they feather out at about 6 weeks. Even after they can swim, young birds can tire easily and drown, so be sure they can easily get out of water containers and ponds by providing a ramp or gently sloped banks.

DRINKING WATER: Always keep drinking water avail-

able, and in generous quantities. When mail-order babies first arrive, dip their bills, one by one, in lukewarm water several times. Then dip each bill in the feed trough. *NOTE: Make sure they drink before they eat, or they can choke on the dry stuff. Be sure the water you supply at all times is deep enough for them to get their entire head into. They need more water than chickens in order to clean the dry feed out of their breathing holes, located in the upper bill near the head.*

Drinking Containers. A suitable water container for young waterfowl could be a narrow trough about 2 inches deep by 1 inch wide. They would be able to submerge their heads in that. (Young Call ducks have a tendency to chill, soak, or even drown themselves in their water containers and need special supervision.) Ducks can be extremely messy with their feed and water. Use a watering device that they can't get into and splash from because you want to keep your brooder house floor dry. A piece of clean burlap bag spread over the floor surface would be a good beginning flooring. Or, if they're on a cold floor, cover it with a litter layer—about 4 inches of shavings, ground corn cobs, peanut hulls, peat moss, or almost any other sort of organic dry litter. If places on their flooring do get wet, shovel them away and add dry material. Or move the water pan frequently and stir the litter as needed to keep the top reasonably dry. *NOTE: Do not put newspapers down for water-slopping babies. Newspapers become a slippery surface, which can cause the birds to become spraddle-legged and crippled.*

STARTER FOOD: For goslings and ducklings, food should be ready when they arrive. Keep food in front of them all the time. But fill their feeder only half full to prevent waste. They'll also need very small gravel for their gizzards. Because of the shape of their mouths, you can't use chick feeders for these birds. To start with, offer food in small box tops scattered near the heat lamp until they learn to eat. Later you can supply food on rough paper, like the bottom of open grocery store bags. Don't feed them on smooth paper; they can slide around on it and get hurt. Older birds can be fed from pans or troughs or from self-feeders that hold pellets and have small openings.

HOME-GROWN STARTER FOOD: Commercial chick

feed is not good for young waterfowl. The protein content is too high, and some of the medication in such feeds can harm them. I worked up the following system to start goslings on home-grown food, and they liked it. I suppose this sounds bizarre to people who are used to feed that comes from the store in sacks. All I can say in my defense is this: they thrived. I fed them 3 times a day, all they would eat of the following: For breakfast, cooked oatmeal covered with a little water. Lunch: scrambled eggs covered with a little water. Supper: homemade whole wheat bread covered with a little water or milk.

I supplied greens at all 3 meals—not grass or tough stems at the beginning—but very tender green leaves. They enjoy finely chopped onion greens and dandelion greens and practically any others that are fresh. Ducks thrive on watermint and cresses. I cut the greens up for them with a knife or scissors. If you are supplying water in a trough, sprinkle the green bits in the water. After the first week, I offered more and more greens. Young waterfowl won't pick each other to death, but, if short of green foods, they may pull and eat each other's feathers, which isn't very good for either the eater or the eaten.

I gradually shifted from cooked food to grain. Their bills were stronger and they could manage weeds better. In good weather they went outside to pasture with my daughter as goose girl. Grass is a very important part of a gosling's diet. Protein is the eggs-and-milk part of their diet. Feed about 20 percent protein. At 2 weeks on a home-devised diet, supply or allow them to get some grit. They're well fed if they have 2 or 3 feedings a day of all they can consume in 5–10 minutes.

COMMERCIAL STARTERS: If you can't get a duck-starter ration or goose-starter (either one would be fine for either species), you can use *unmedicated* chick, turkey poult, or game-bird starter for the first week or two (then switch to grower feed) if the feed is also recommended for ducklings and goslings. That's because some types of chick starter and growing feeds contain drugs for coccidiosis control that can cause lameness or even death if fed to the water birds. Yet some folks have fed medicated starter and layer feeds to waterfowl and gotten away with it; maybe they were feeding starter medicated at a low level. Crumbles are the best consistency. Fine mash feeds are more likely to cause the birds to choke.

After 2 weeks for ducklings, or 4 weeks for goslings, gradually shift to a pelleted grower ration. Ducklings and goslings being raised for the commercial market are usually given turkey finishing rations or some similar food their last couple weeks. By using genetically fast growers like the White Pekin, placing high-protein commercial rations constantly before them, and ensuring the inactivity of confinement, you can have freezer-ready ducks at 7 lb. in 7 weeks. Goslings for the commercial meat market are usually finished in the fall months when they're 24–30 weeks old.

HOME-GROWN FOOD FOR ADULT WATERFOWL: They can make it on mixed grains and greens. Aim for variety and some ranging if possible. You can get ducks and geese accustomed to eating whole corn off ears that you've broken in two—that helps them get started. Feeding them ear corn is easier for you—if you have it—and prevents more aggressive birds from hogging the food supply. If you're going to feed them oats, feed it before the

corn, or instead of it. Wheat is probably the best single grain for waterfowl. Oats and wheat are a good combination. They can eat nonmedicated rabbit pellets. Feed round, firm fruits and vegetables (apples, beets, turnips, potatoes) by crushing them first, as under a board, because the broad-billed waterfowl can't peck like c hickens and need some help getting started with them. Waterfowl on a home-devised diet may produce about half as many eggs as those on a commercial laying mash— so the laying-mash people say. But those birds can give you residue-free meat and eggs!

Housing for Post-Brooder Geese and Ducks

If you have just a few adult waterfowl, you may be able to keep them with your chickens. Unlike chickens, ducks and geese don't roost but like to sleep on the ground or floor. On the other hand, chickens may peck at ducklings and goslings, so provide them with some small pen within the coop that the chickens can't get into.

There are 3 distinct schools of thought on the subject of shelter for waterfowl. One is no shelter at all, or only a windbreak of bales of straw. A second concept is shed-sheltering, allowing them a place with 3 sides and a roof, but an open front. The third concept is a complete building—which may be a small, possibly portable, mini-dwelling—with or without attached pen or yard, in which they can be confined just at night or all the time.

NO SHELTER: Waterfowl always need access to shade, but once they are 6 weeks old they can do without other shelter (unless there is a long spell of chilling rain or stormy weather). By 8 weeks of age they can pretty well take care of themselves. Adult waterfowl seldom require shelter. This is because their outer coat of closely packed feathers has been waterproofed. Ducks in the wild build their nests near water on the ground. A flock of ducks can do well and lay without formal houses or nest boxes.

Nevertheless, some fancy breeds are less hardy or less disposable than others, and some climates have worse winters than others. Ducks, who do not roost but sleep on the ground, have been known to become frozen to the ground by their own moist droppings. (Ducks that have access to open water may spend the night there.) Unconfined ducks (especially the breeds with poor mothering instincts) are likely to lay eggs all over the place—on the ground, even in the water. If you have foraging, unsheltered waterfowl, be vigilant against predators, keep them in the territory where you want them, and consider shelter at least from severe storms. If baby ducks are being raised by you or their mothers near any body of water that is halfway natural, you may take some hard losses. Bullfrogs and other critters like to eat baby ducks. You might do better bringing the young ones into the house to raise until they've attained a good size.

A 3-SIDED SHELTER: Some waterfowl raisers prefer this system that protects the flock from wind and rain but otherwise allows them freedom. Waterfowl dislike wind, and such a shelter (built broadside against the prevailing wind direction) can at least protect them from wind and precipitation. Waterfowl like fresh air and dislike poorly ventilated quarters. They are nervous and like to be able to see what is going on about them at night. And if crowded into a small house they may startle and pile in a corner. There's no need to make the 3-sided (with a roof) shelter any taller than the birds it is designed to protect (which saves on lumber). Waterfowl confined indoors a lot may not be as healthy as those allowed to live outdoors. Like Chinese geese, African geese are susceptible to frozen or frostbitten knobs (on their beaks) in winter and would be better off with at least this minimal shed-type shelter. If it will be below 20°F, these knobbed fowl need even more shelter to protect their knobs. If, however, the knobs do freeze, it merely results in a discoloration of the bill and knob, which will return to normal by the following fall.

TOTAL SHELTER: Waterfowl can be housed just at night or all the time. Ducks adapt well to housing at night only because their egg-laying habits are so precise (almost all lay their eggs before 8am, 9am for sure), and because their habits are so regular (they can be trained to return home to be fed and be confined at a precise time). Duck and goose owners in areas where night predators such as rats, raccoons, skunks, weasels, and ferrets are active prefer to confine their birds at night—or even all the time—in a building similar to a chicken house. Call, Mandarins, and Wood Ducks are not as hardy as the others and do need winter shelter, though they can go outside and get in the water at 40°F and warmer. African, Chinese, and Egyptian geese benefit from winter shelter (in temperatures below 20°F). Ducks will start laying earlier in the year if housed; it does not make any difference to geese. If you do confine ducks at night, be aware that they are nervous creatures and can damage themselves by panicking and running in circles. If you leave on a low-wattage night light, you will minimize this danger.

Waterfowl housing can be small and portable and frequently moved to keep the ground underneath tolerable. Such housing may be set into sizable, well-drained, well-shaded fenced runs that (ideally) have access to clean, running water. Small ducks such as Calls, Indias, and Mallards can be raised sun-porch–style. A graveled duck yard that can be cleaned when hosed daily at high-pressure and is sloped somehow to drain, can help keep clean the quarters of a large spring flock being raised for butchering. Without gravel or concrete, you risk a sea of mud.

TOTALLY CONFINED WATERFOWL: Allow 4 square feet of floor space per duck for ducks that are let out during the day. If ducks are kept confined at all times they'll need 6–8 feet of floor space per bird. If you limit the total number of fowl and have a loose, deep (1-foot) litter layer, you can keep them confined and it can be manageable. Large (15 inches square), shallow nesting boxes located on the floor in the corners of their housing will attract the egg-layers. Confined ducks need excellent ventilation in hot weather and plenty of water, always. Shutting them up together with chickens can be a problem if there are too many birds for the space, because ducks have such exceptionally copious and liquid droppings. If the waterfowl housing is to be permanent, the ground underneath should slope to one side for drainage and the floor should be made of pea gravel, which can be hosed and drained, or concrete with a center floor drain. Waterfowl kept completely on hard, dry ground, however, can sometimes develop bumblefoot, which is a warty local infection of the foot that causes limp-

ing. Isolate such a bird in a place with a soft straw flooring. Treat the foot with antibacterial ointment. After the skin has softened some, lance and drain if appropriate. The birds don't get bumblefoot on grass pasture.

OF FLYING AND WATERFOWL: The flyers are Muscovies, Indies, Calls, Mallards, Canadas, and Egyptians. To keep these at home you'll have to clip the long feathers on 1 wing side with heavy scissors when the feathers first develop and after each molt, if you keep the birds that long. Or you can "pinion" them—which means to amputate the tip of the wing (the part below and outward from the "claw" extension just beyond the last wing joint) on 1 side. The pinioning operation is done when the duckling or gosling is a week old. The cutting is done with a sharp knife, razor blade, or debeaking machine. And use 4-foot-high fencing.

About Feathers

The feathers and down from geese and ducks can be used to make pillows, comforters, insulated jackets, and other outdoor clothing, and you don't always have to kill the birds to get their feathers. In the spring, geese grow lots of lovely little feathers and then pull them out themselves and use them to create wonderful downy nests. These goose feathers are very soft and warm. Duck feathers have the problem of an odor which is difficult to remove completely. Nevertheless, either duck or goose feathers are softer, fluffier, and more moisture-proof (so they don't absorb sweat) than chicken feathers. A general rule is that the feathers from 3 geese or 5 ducks will amount to 1 lb. of feathers. You can sell goose feathers if you have enough to make it worthwhile. Mature ducks have more down than young ones and also more down in the fall when cold weather has set in. So what human beings might try to do is share in the feather crop that's going to come off anyway.

LIVE PLUCKING: In Colonial days, goose feathers were obtained 2 (spring time and harvest time), 3, or 4 times a year, by stripping them from the live birds—except for the quills, which were used for pens and were never pulled but once from a goose. The first time is when the geese are between 9 and 11 weeks old—when they start molting. After that they are plucked about every 8 or 9 weeks. The best feathers of all, however, are said to come from geese that are fully grown, from October on for spring-hatched geese. In Europe and in some areas of Canada such live plucking is still done. But times aren't so grim now, and I don't know anybody who plucks their geese until after they've been butchered and scalded.

Live-plucking causes momentary discomfort and stress to the bird and does reduce egg productivity. But if you must try this, wear old clothes and tie a cover over your hair, because the down flies everywhere. Have paper or cheesecloth bags and string ready before you start. Pull a stocking over the bird's head to keep it from biting. Pluck the down and short body feathers in a season the birds would normally be shedding them, at which time the feathers release a little easier than at other times. Pull the feathers the "wrong way"—against the grain, firmly and quickly. In small pinches, pull the feathers from the underside of the bird, removing not more than half the feathers from any area. Don't leave bare patches and keep the plucked birds from swimming for a couple weeks so they can regrow sufficient feathers to stay water-proof. They say the birds get used to it, but it seems to me that the small gain in feather quality is not worth either the stress to your birds or the extra work for you.

A good further source is "Producing Your Own Down," by Ken Bernsohn, in *Organic Gardening and Farming,* Vol. 25, No. 3 (March 1978), p. 114.

DRY-PICKING A DEAD BIRD: If you're planning to save the feathers, have bags ready before killing the birds. Pull in the direction they grow. Working over a large garbage bag or in a confined area will keep the down and small feathers from floating away. Be careful to free the feathers of any skin or flesh that adheres, or they will be tainted. Pull the large flight feathers first, then the outer layer of feathers second, and finally pull the soft under-layer of down. If you want to get some stuffing from the feathers over 2 inches long (especially the large wing and tail feathers), cut with a scissors, or strip off and discard the quill. But most people don't bother with that. After the feathers are taken off the bird, remove the down by brushing the body with your hand moistened in water. The bags full of feathers can be closed at the top with string or staples or folded tightly. The next step is to clean and dry the feathers. (See "Cleaning and Using Feathers" under "Chickens.")

CHICKEN-STYLE SCALDING AND PICKING: This, of course, you do to a dead bird. In a large container, heat water—enough to cover your bird completely—to 140°F or higher. Add a little detergent (or shampoo) to the water and stir it in—this is so the hot water can get past the bird's preening oil. Holding the bird by its feet, submerge it completely and swish it forcefully around for about 1½ minutes (much longer than for a chicken)—until the hot water has penetrated the bird's skin and done its job of relaxing the feather follicles. Older birds may need more time. Then, right away pull out the feathers, big ones first. If you have trouble getting them out, your water wasn't hot enough and/or the bird wasn't in there long enough. (Try it again.)

WAXING METHODS: The disadvantages of these methods are that you need to buy and melt the wax, it ruins the feathers, and it takes a lot of wax to do the job—especially on a goose. Nonetheless, some growers think it's easier this way. Use paraffin, a combination of half paraffin and half

beeswax, or a commercial mixture that you get from a poultry supplier. The wax takes out the feathers easiest immediately after butchering. The wax should be heated to between 160 and 200°F in a double boiler. Higher-temperature wax penetrates better but doesn't adhere in as thick a coat. A wax coat that's overly thick may not cool and harden as well. *NOTE: Do not heat the wax by itself. Do not let the double boiler run out of water.*

Hold long-necked birds by the head in one hand and the feet in the other to dip them. The dryer the birds when dipped into the wax, the better the wax will cling to the feathers you're trying to remove. You can keep dipping and stripping until you're satisfied. Commercial growers scald and pick first, then dip and strip to get whatever's left over. The wax can be recovered by heating (in water) to melt it and then straining or screening out the feathers, etc. It can be reused for this purpose again and again.

HOT WATER/HOT WAX/COLD WATER: For this technique you need 3 pots, 2 hot and 1 cold. You dip the dead bird first in hot water and do a full chicken-style scale, then dip the bird in hot, melted wax. Then dip the bird into cold water to solidify the wax. Then you can strip wax, feathers, and pinfeathers all together from the bird.

COMBINED HOT WATER/HOT WAX-HEAT: Save your scalding water. Add paraffin to the hot water, which will melt and form a thick floating layer on the top of it. Put the bird into the hot water and swish to scald the feathers loose. Then pull it out very slowly so that a layer of the wax will cling to all the feathers. Allow the paraffin to solidify and then pull wax and feathers away.

Once the feathers are off, singe off the filoplumes (the remaining long, hair-like feathers) over an open flame of alcohol, and cut off head and feet at the first joint. Some people like to skin the carcass to remove all signs of feathers, but this can cause the meat to be dry and less flavorful when it's cooked.

Cleaning Ducks and Geese

Remove the oil sac on the tip of "the north end going south," including all the yellow oil-producing area around it. That's where birds get oil to preen themselves, and that of water birds is strong tasting enough that it would be a problem to leave it on. Clean as you would a chicken. The esophagus and windpipe of ducks may require some force to remove.

Of Ducks in Particular

DUCK FEATURES: When the duck preens, it spreads the oil from an oil gland at the base of its tail, over its feathers. A layer of insulating down under larger contour feathers that are lubricated with this oil enables the duck to swim in near-freezing water. Even the webbed feet are made to withstand cold because there are neither nerves nor blood in them. Most domestic breeds are earthbound, but Muscovies, Calls, East Indies, and Mallards can still fly to some degree. Ducks can live up to 30 years; however, few make it to that age because their ability to produce eggs drops off after 3 or 4 years. If you are buying adults for breeding stock, choose birds 6–7 months old with evenly colored bills and legs, and make sure they are healthy. The male duck is called a "drake." The female is called the "duck" (which, of course, also means the species in general) or "hen."

DUCK TEMPERAMENT: Of all the varieties of poultry, ducks—male and female alike—are the gentlest and least likely to act aggressive. Drakes seldom fight unless females are present. (This might be an incentive for you to choose them if you have small children.) Ducks are notoriously nervous and noisy at night and will make a commotion over the slightest deviation in their environment's characteristics, benign or dangerous. Because ducks are so nervous, announce yourself when you are coming to them, move slowly, and talk to the birds to calm them. If a duck does display aggressive activity, it is best to remain calm and ignore the behavior.

Ducks tend to be either good egg layers or good meat producers. Meat producers are calmer, easier to confine, and grow faster and bigger. The feed conversion ratio for ducks is about 3:1, which makes them a good economical choice whether you pick a breed for meat or eggs. You may also want to consider the noise level, coloration as a defense against predators, and expense and difficulty of obtaining the birds. And then there are the eggs–meat combination breeds to consider.

DUCKS IN PRINT: *Raising the Home Duck Flock,* by D. Holderread (1978), is a helpful book. *The New Duck Handbook: Ornamental and Domestic Ducks* by Raethel Heinz-Sigurd, translated from the German (1989), has everything about housing, care, feeding, disease, and healing, with a special chapter on commercial uses of ducks.

DUCKS FOR EGGS: Don't buy ducks for eggs until you try eating duck eggs. Duck eggs have a ducky flavor, all the more so if the birds do a lot of scavenging in the bottom of a muddy pond. Also keep in mind the pollution problems of various bodies of water. So if you're going to let your ducks feed in water, be sure it's not polluted water. You can hide duck eggs in an omelet with chicken eggs and use them in baking. If you have trouble eating duck eggs straight because of the unfamiliar "strongness," make bread and custards out of them. Or, like the people in countries where duck eggs are a staple, you could get used to the taste and learn how to cook with them.

Becky Coleman of Charlo, MT, wrote me: "I kept Khaki Campbells for eggs once and found that, except for a certain toughness, they couldn't be told from chicken eggs. They had the run of the yard and a pond, but were mainly fed a chicken layer crumble. I wonder if the strong flavors people talk about come from what the ducks have been eating, rather than being intrinsic to duck eggs." Thank you, Becky! I haven't personally kept ducks for eggs, and there are real perils for me in passing on lore I've read and never experienced, so I appreciate it when somebody straightens me out. (The trouble with trying to cover everything in a book is that it's not possible for me to try it all myself.)

Duck eggs do not fry nicely by chicken-egg techniques—best to use a different process. (See "Frying a Duck Egg.") Incidentally, duck hens often lay more copiously if they haven't mated with drakes, and nonfertile eggs keep better than fertile ones. So if you need eggs in quantity, consider segregating your layers from your breeders.

Of Duck Laying and Setting. Light-breed ducks (egg breeds) will begin to lay at about 6 months of age. Heavy-breed ducks are mature and will begin to lay eggs at about 7 months. An egg-laying duck's commercially useful laying period is considered to be 3 seasons. Actually though, they will lay longer than that. Most ducks lay their eggs at night, so it's a good practice to confine them then. Ducks begin to lay in the spring, in the morning. It's customary to let them out after 10am, by which time they will be done laying. You can maximize egg production by providing at least 14 hours of light (use a 40–60 watt bulb) daily. Some people leave the lights on all night, as it also keeps the ducks calmer. If you want a duck to go broody, leave her eggs and let them fill up a nest. Free-ranging ducks will build nests of twigs, leaves, grass, and their own down, on the ground. Muscovies, Indies, Calls, and Cayugas are likely to be good brooders. Cayugas are good at incubating goose eggs. Among the Blue Swedish, Aylesbury, and Rouen breeds, some individuals may be good brooders.

EGG BREEDS

Indian Runner. There are many varieties of Indian Runner ducks of which the White Penciled, Fawn, and White are said to be the best egg producers (225–325 eggs per year). The Indian Runner originated in Asia (as did the rarer Bali to which it is related). Runners are a nervous, light breed (drakes are 4 lb. at butchering age, ducks are 3½ lb.) that stand quite erect, nearly perpendicular to the ground. They can move quickly, which helps protect them against predators. Their feed-consumption-to-egg-production ratio is very good, and they lay equally as well as the other best duck layers—the Khaki-Campbell. And their eggs are larger. They are exceptionally good foragers but make poor mothers.

Khaki-Campbell. This duck is a quiet, healthy, good foraging, hardy breed that will continue laying in cold weather—as many as 300–325 eggs a year. The Khaki-Campbell duck is khaki with bronze highlights, has a green bill, and weighs only about 4½ lb. They don't go broody, and they are the least interested duck when it comes to swimming. Their eggs are creamy white and large, considering that this is one of the smaller breeds of duck—smaller than Pekins or Rouen. Khaki-Campbells were developed by an Englishwoman (Mrs. Campbell) out of Mallards, Indian Runners, and Rouen ducks. Crossbreeding has diluted many strains. To get a good egg-laying bird, be sure you get a Khaki-Campbell selected for high egg production. Authentic Khaki-Campbells are said to lay well 3–4 years and do well in winter, as long as they're sheltered from extreme cold. Butcher young Khaki-Campbells at 4 lb. to get a meat that is lower in fat than most ducks.

Welsh Harlequin. These ducks are said to have laid as many as 300 eggs annually. Duck egg production of these egg-specialist breeds is right up there with the best chicken layers. It's interesting to note that, like the egg-specialist chicken breeds, the egg-specialist ducks are also lighter in weight, more high-strung in temperament, slower growing, and non-brooding.

MEAT BREEDS

Aylesbury. These ducks are a British strain considered by the English to be the prime meat breed of duck. They are noted for being less nervous than Pekins and exceptionally friendly toward humans. They are also less hardy. They have white feathers and skin and light orange legs and feet. Aylesburys eat grass quite well and will be ready for slaughter at 7 lb. at around 8 weeks. The males will grow to 9 lb., the females to 8. For breeding, use a single drake to 2 ducks and provide water for a mating surface. Aylesbury ducks are not the best egg-layers. You may get anywhere from 35 to 125 eggs a year. In pre-incubator England, broody hens were used to raise the Aylesbury young.

White Pekin

Chinese White Pekin. This is the most popular meat duck. The White Pekin is a blocky, extra-heavy duck, disease- and stress-resistant. The Pekin is probably the best bird to raise if your main interests are efficient meat production for home or market and white pin feathers. They are an extra large duck and grow very fast with an efficient growth-per-pound-of-food ratio (2½ lb. of feed required per pound of gain). The White Pekin can be ready to eat at only 7 weeks of age, weighing 6½–7 lb. The bird is then perfect for roasting (although fairly high in fat content) and is technically called a "duckling." Adult Pekin drakes weigh 10 lb., hens, 9. The Pekins come in numerous different genetic strains, as developed by different competing breeders. In general, Pekin drakes are very fertile; the Pekins' large, white eggs are quite hatchable; and 1 Pekin drake can handle 3–5 ducks.

Although they are high-strung and poor setters, free-ranging pairs have been known to raise up to 20 ducklings a year. Don't mate a younger drake to older ducks. Pekins are a poor choice for a foraging duck, and the females are noisy. The Pekin is considered a good layer—between 125 to 175 eggs per year, if they are well-managed, and so could be used as a meat–eggs breed. When Pekin ducklings are being raised on a commercial scale for meat (and not being kept for breeders), they are referred to as "green ducklings." Green ducklings are kept confined to limit their exercise and kept under continuous light because that stimulates growth. Feed-conversion efficiency drops off after 7 weeks, and green ducklings are butchered shortly after, when their wing feathers develop. That's pure agribusiness for you.

Muscovy. This is a large white or colored (depending on the variety) lean duck with well-muscled breasts. They often have a darkening, like a mask, around the eyes. The Muscovy duck is the only domestic breed not of Mallard derivation. They originated in South America, come in White or Colored, are slower growing than Pekins or Rouens, but are a first-class forager. Muscovies are also different from other ducks in the nature of their feathers,

which are not as downy, are harder, and don't oil as well as those of other ducks. They can actually drown, if unable to get out of the water for too long—especially heavy, long-winged males. The good news about Muscovy feathers is that they're easier to pick than those of other ducks. An adult male can weigh 16 lb., but is more likely to be around 12. The much smaller females weigh 7 lb. Their meat is best if they are slaughtered before 17 weeks. The big ones can get quite fat if confined and overfed.

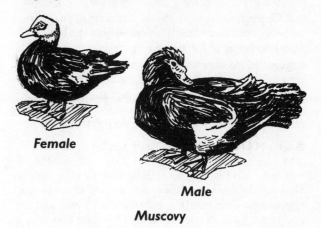

Female

Male

Muscovy

The Muscovy is said to be resistant to diseases that the Pekin and the Runner (when kept in large numbers) are subject to. It is noiseless, which your neighbors might appreciate, but hens fly quite well when fully grown. Unlike the other ducks, the Muscovy roosts at night like a chicken, preferring a fence or tree so they're safer from predators. But the flying can be a problem; for example, they might get into your orchard—or your neighbor's. But if you put Muscovies in your deep freeze shortly before full adulthood, the flying problem won't come up. Or you can clip 1 wing.

Muscovies have sharper claws on their feet than other ducks, and the big drakes can become temperamental, so be cautious when handling them. The Muscovy hen may lay as many as 100 eggs a year. It is probably the best for reproducing itself, as the hens are excellent layers and brooders, with excellent fertility and hatchability. The hen will lay 20–25 eggs and then brood them. She may produce and care admirably for 2 broods each season. She'll even face and drive off dogs and foxes. The ducklings are hardy, but they take a month more than other ducks to grow full feathers. Most duck eggs hatch at 28 days, but Muscovy eggs require 35 days.

Rouen. This duck breed is large, like the White Pekins, which makes it a good roaster, and colored as prettily as the wild mallard from which it was adapted several centuries ago. Fly-tyers say that Rouen feathers make good trout flies and streamers. The Rouen doesn't fly, and it has a quiet, friendly nature, which is nice if you have small children. They lay 35–150 eggs a year, some blue-green as Easter eggs, some creamy white. Rouens are slower growing than Pekins. They can be butchered anywhere between 2½ and 6 months. Rouens tend to stay very near home. Genetic Rouen lines vary in egg-laying powers—some are excellent, some poor. A reasonably light drake can take care of 4 or 5 ducks. Look for the trait of continuing to produce fertile hatching eggs past 3 laying years. Rouens do well on farm ponds and near wooded areas where a rugged duck with good survival instincts is required. A 3–foot-high fence will keep Rouens (and most other non-flying ducks) in.

DUAL-PURPOSE DUCK VARIETIES

Blue and Black Swedish. This duck is rare in the United States (but more popular in Europe). It's a good insect-eater, lays 100–150 bluish to grayish white eggs a year, and has been said to be less prone to predator attacks because of its protective coloration. Crested drakes weigh around 7 lb., the ducks, 6 lb. They make good mothers and forage well.

Buff Orpington. These ducks are another rare dual-purpose (eggs and meat) breed. Drakes weigh 8 lb., hens 7. They may lay up to 250 eggs a year.

Cayuga. In the same weight class as the Swedish, Cayugas are a rare, rugged black American duck that can stand extreme cold very well, are good foragers, and lay 100–175 eggs a year. They are very quiet, but to avoid an unattractive carcass, it's necessary to remove the skin and pinfeathers.

BANTAM DUCK BREEDS: There are also the bantam duck breeds—the Call, the Australian Spotted, and the East Indie, all of which are excellent foragers and brooders. Most people keep them as novelties, as they do not produce eggs in great quantities (not more than 125 a year) and are comparatively small (usually under 2½ lb.) for a good meat source. But their meat is of very fine quality, and they do lay well in the spring, if the eggs are gathered daily.

Call. These are the best-known of the bantams. They are noisy little birds, either gray or white, favored as live decoys in England, where they originated. You'll need some patience to raise Call ducklings. They may do well on a diet of rolled oats and ground greens mixed in with their water. You can buy them from Shane Risner at Prickeree Pines Gamebird Farm: 616-868-6015; 12410 64th, Alto, MI 49302; **X95risner@email.com.**

Male   **Female**

Mallard

Mallard. These are relatively small (male, 2.8 lb.; female, 2.4 lb.) ducks that can fly. They prefer living where there's water to fly from and alight on, and they frequently dive and swim underwater. They are a wild species (believed to be the progenitors of many domestic ducks), are perhaps the best duck foragers, and are natural mothers. The Mallard does not fatten as well or ship as well as the Pekin, and they have gamey-tasting meat. The drake has dramatic feathers, while the female is a demure brown. Check with your state game regulatory agency before ordering Mallards—you might need a permit.

DUCK FOOD: By the time they're a month old you can have your ducklings on a diet of grain, household scraps, and food from foraging. Liquid milk, mixed into their dry food at feeding time, and hard-boiled eggs can promote egg production and add shine to plumage. Adult breeder ducks being fed over winter can make it on a home-devised diet suitable for chickens. Ducks, like chickens, need calcium from some source for eggshell making and grit for their gizzards. Like chickens, they should not eat decaying vegetation or spoiled feed because they can get botulism poisoning from that. Most grains, including millet and rice, are popular with ducks.

The Duck-Foraging Option. Because of their foraging ability, ducks can be a bargain to raise, plus they help control bugs and slugs. At 4 weeks of age, your ducks can go on range. Foraging birds grow more slowly and are leaner at butchering time but will ultimately (in as many as 12 weeks perhaps) reach the same target weight. They are naturally good foragers and will hunt for and consume tender grass, clover, and green leafy plants in general—as well as insects, slugs, snails, and all their ilk. The most natural foraging territory for ducks is wet, low marshland. But a year-round large flock can make excellent use of a pond plus plenty of foraging space on shore. If given the opportunity, they'll eat weeds, berries, and seeds; will glean for fallen grain and fruit; do bug patrol in alfalfa fields and under rabbit hutches; and will clean out algae from ponds. Ducks enjoy Japanese beetle larvae. When liver flukes are a problem to cattle, ducks sent into their pasture will devour the snails that host those parasites and make the land safe for the cows again.

Ducks are not as good grazers as geese. Unlike geese, ducks must have young grass, so it helps them if you mow their foraging area to encourage new growth, or put some geese in with them. Some duck growers help by locating 1 or more electric lights near ground level, turning them on only at night. The ducks can then feed on the insects attracted to the lights. Foraging ducklings need adequate space for the number of them. Confined too closely they'll simply end up killing all vegetation in their space and creating a foodless mud hole. If you have wandering ducks and live near a road there may be a problem. Ducks travel together, they are fearless, and they don't move fast. Ducklings raised by a mother duck learn to find their own food very young.

By allowing your birds to forage you can cut back on the amount of their commercial ration or even completely do without it if you regularly supplement with such grain as cracked corn, wheat, milo, oats, etc., during seasons when they can't forage as well, or year-round if their foraging territory is limited.

Commercial Food. Ducklings do better on crumbles than mash, which they are very wasteful of. Ducklings need more niacin than chicks; lack of it stunts their growth and causes weak legs. So if your ducklings are not on a duck starter you could add a soluble vitamin from the feed store to their water. Their crumbles should be sprinkled occasionally with fine gizzard grit. Don't feed cracked or whole grains until the ducks are at least 4 weeks old. Once they get big, feed only once a day except in the dead of winter. Feed in the evening—about what they'll clean up in a quarter hour. Confined birds will need more feed, more often than foragers, such as twice a day. Confined ducks in winter can get along on cheap grains supplemented with greens or quality hay. Don't throw grain for ducks on the ground; offer it in a trough. Confined birds will enjoy greens or vegetable throwaway parts cut into small pieces and put into their water. Add ground eggshells to their food for calcium. Even if you're feeding all commercial duck formula, it's good to supplement with fresh greens.

DUCK REPRODUCTION: Ducks are sexually mature in 5–7 months. A drake in his first year is called a "drakelet," and a duck in her first laying season is called a "ducklet," corresponding to a pullet. Don't raise male ducks or geese without the company of females. This can result in birds that bond to other males and will never mate with females.

Telling Drake and Duck Apart. With ducks it can be difficult to figure out which sex is which when you want to slaughter or sell some of your fowl and keep others for breeding. The Rouens can be distinguished by color, but most other domestic ducks cannot be sexed by color. You can sex ducks that are old enough for slaughter by voice. By then females will have developed a raucous, raspy-sounding call, whereas the male is comparatively hoarse and quiet. That doesn't work with the Muscovies, but adult Muscovy males are considerably larger than females, so you can tell that way. Another way to sex mature ducks of all the Mallard-derived breeds (doesn't work with Muscovies) is by tail feathers. Males have about 4 curly feathers on the upper side of the tail that form a loop back toward the bird's head. Those are called "sex curls." Females don't have them. Duck hens with yellow or orange bills may develop dark spots on their bills when they begin to lay. An experienced person can identify the sex of a duckling by 2–3 weeks of age, by examining the duckling's vent, but this requires care as ducks injure easily. To do it, you'll need good strong lighting since the sex organs inside the vent are very small.

Duck Mating. Under natural circumstances, ducks mate on the water. The smaller breeds can also accomplish this on land as can smaller pairs of the bigger breeds. So pondless duck breeders select small drakes and large ducks. In general, heavy breeds should have 1 male to every 3–6 females. Light-breed drakes can service 4–7 duck hens. It's smart to have an extra 1 or 2 avian studs for backup. If you are raising several duck breeds, keep them separated to assure the ducklings are of purebred status. Provide each breeder bird with 5–6 square feet of floor space inside and 40 square feet outside. Commercial breeders feed a breeder developer ration, about ¼ lb. morning and evening, until about 1 month before egg production, at which point they switch to a breeder ration—as much as the birds want to eat.

Hatchability. Fertility is greatest when egg production is highest. Hatchability declines after the first few settings. It's uncertain how long your drake breeder will remain fertile. One Runner drake is on record for having fertilized eggs 20 years, but most duck growers don't take a chance and retire drakes after 8–10 years of age.

BUTCHERING A DUCK

When. If you're not sure if a duck has hit the 7-lb. slaughter weight yet, weigh it. But some breeds never get near that weight, no matter how much food and time they have. If you're planning to butcher a duck, it's best to do it at 8–12 weeks, before 5 months for sure. After that the meat is tougher. In addition, ducks in molt are unsuitable for butchering. Pin feathers from the coming plumage make the plucking a formidable task. They molt at about 10 weeks of age, so butcher either before that or well after it. Or skin the duck.

Catching a Duck. First try to corral it in a small pen or fence corner so you won't end up chasing it. With one hand right under the head, grasp it by the neck, and with your other hand, bring its body close to you, wrapping your arms around its wings so it can't flap them. Ducks are easily hurt, especially their legs and wings, so you have to capture them without a big fight. Once you have hold of the bird like this, you can carry it with one hand under its body and the other holding its wings down. You can carry it with the head pointing to the back of you or to the front. Keep the bird away from your face and take special care with Muscovy claws.

Killing a Duck. Chop off its head. Or stun it with a sharp blow on the head and then stick it through the throat or just behind the eye with a narrow-bladed knife. Or hang it by both its legs and cut the throat back of its bill. Or use any of the same directions as found under "Chickens" in this chapter. Bleed the bird thoroughly. For picking directions, see "About Feathers." A 7-lb. duckling will dress out to about 5 lb. of meat. For fried duckling some people prefer to peel off the skin and fat from the body and legs (the wings will be hard to do). If the duck is to be cut up (rather than roasted whole), any of the chicken methods can be used. Chill the carcass to 34–40°F as soon as possible.

DUCK RECIPES

Frying a Duck Egg. You can't fry a duck egg the familiar, chicken-egg way and expect it to be tender. So lightly grease and heat a frying pan that has a lid. Break your eggs into it as for frying chicken eggs. Pour a little hot water about the edges of the eggs. Put the lid on the skillet and cook like that until the egg-white is firm (a few minutes). Serve promptly.

✒ *ROAST DUCK WITH ORANGE JUICE Rub the duck inside and out with salt and pepper. Put a whole onion and some chopped celery inside the duck or stuff it with a bread stuffing. Rub the outside skin with cooking oil or butter. Pierce the skin of a fat duckling in multiple places to allow the fat to render out. A duckling can be roasted at 450°F for 15 minutes, then at 350°F until done. A full-grown duck should be roasted at 350°F for about 25 minutes per pound, uncovered. When the skin is turning brown, begin to baste the bird once in a while with freshly squeezed orange juice or with the pan drippings. Optional: When the duck is done roasting, make a sauce by adding 2 T. flour to the drippings in the pan. If you burnt the bottom, pour the drippings into a frying pan and add the flour there. Add a cup each of water and orange juice. Don't let it boil. Pour the sauce over the duck and garnish with orange sections.*

✒ *FRIED DUCK Cook the gizzard, heart, neck, and rib bones the same as to make Seasoned Giblet Gravy (see recipe under "My Favorite Goose Recipes"). Or fry the first 3 along with the other pieces. If you saved the skin and fat from the body and legs when you were cleaning the bird, cut them into small pieces and render out the duck grease. Remove the cracklings. Beat 1 egg with a fork and add 3 T. milk, and salt and pepper. (You may need more dipping batter than this.) Dip each piece of duck into the batter, then roll* it in fine, dry bread crumbs. Brown the duck pieces in the rendered duck fat. When browned, pour off most of the fat, add 2 T. water, cover and bake at 350°F for 45 minutes in a Dutch oven. Remove cover during the last 10 minutes.

Doris' Duck Tip. If your duck has a fishy or wild flavor, put the whole duck in salt water and add onions. Bring just to a boil and drain off water. Then prepare the duck as usual. Another lady told me her system was to stuff the duck with an apple and an onion, each chopped, and seasonings.

Geese

Although their primary value is as a meat bird—a good roast and *paté de foie gras* (goose liver spread)—many people keep a couple of geese on their farms as pets. They act as "watchdogs," honking loudly whenever a strange person or animal approaches. Although some geese lay fairly well, none will lay as well as the best duck and chicken breeds. On the other hand, some duck breeds are practically burnt out on laying after 3 years, and some commercial chicken breeds have a similar decline. Your goose is healthy, long-lived, and intelligent. They can thrive on no more than grass, can be a cash crop, and will lay eggs for an amazing number of years. (This perhaps can be an example to us on the benefits of plain living and moderation.) Most goose owners brood the eggs to maximize meat production and get table eggs from ducks or chickens.

Your geese will appreciate a grassy field; they need grass in their diets. In fact, except in winter, geese fare quite well with very little care. It's not unusual to see them foraging through snow. They are extremely resistant to disease and parasites, and they need only a little shade in summer and a bit of shelter against extreme cold. Young geese are relatively quiet animals, which may be a factor if you have irritable neighbors. The "goose" is the female, "gander" the male. A group of them is called a "gaggle."
NOTE: Be careful when handling big geese, even docile ones. Their wings may be longer than your arms and they have clawed feet. Their strong wings can break an arm and they have serrated bills that can tear flesh. An adult goose's charge, complete with loud hissing and flapping wings, can frighten anyone, especially a small child. However, if you are raising goslings just to freezer size, they won't get mature enough to become that aggressive.

Sylvia Nelson, Hillsdale, WY, wrote me, "Our first batch of geese, gray Toulouse, imprinted on me and just worship me. We also have a few white Embdens and 2 cross-breeds, hatched out last season, our first successful hatching. Toulouse and Embdens are supposed to be gentle, but a couple of years ago we learned how fierce they can be. My husband woke up one night, with a terrible ruckus going on in the duck and goose yard. He looked out, and saw a fox in the yard. We had seven geese at the time, and each one had a mouthful of fox, and were each pulling in a different direction. The next morning we found a couple of scratches on the geese, no missing geese or ducks, and chunks of fox fur all over the yard, plus a 1-inch-square piece of hide. The fox never returned!"

A gander will be particularly aggressive during the reproductive cycle. Dynah Geissel of Missoula, MT, wrote me, "The female geese are not mean but will bite if you mess around with their nests. There is always a dominant male who is ferocious during breeding season. He will even bite me at that time—even when I'm feeding him. The rest of the year he's not exactly friendly, but he keeps his distance, except if I approach a nest. Sometimes if there's not a goose in sight, I'll check to see how many eggs are in a nest. The geese seem to have a sixth sense, for out of nowhere one will come running to bite me."

GEESE IN PRINT: You'd benefit from reading *The Book of Geese* by D. Holderread. See also the section earlier in this chapter, "Further Duck and Goose Information."

GOOSE BREEDS: There are about 15 breeds of domesticated geese. Basically, the goose is raised for meat. Personally, I like goose meat much better than turkey. Whatever breed of goose you prefer, you'll probably want to separate breeds or choose only one, because purebred geese are more marketable than those that are crossbred. An exception is the cross between the White Chinese gander and an Embden goose, a match that produces a goose that matures quickly to market weight.

Chinese. The closest thing to an eggs-and-meat goose breed is the White Chinese, which is almost as lovely on the water as a swan, gives noisy warning like a watchdog, and is a good forager and weeder. But they are less hardy than some geese in winter. The Chinese need shelter at below-freezing temperatures and heat at 20°F or lower. You'll at least need to provide them a south-facing lean-to with a straw-covered floor. They are about half the size of the larger breeds—10–12 lb.—but still big enough for a Thanksgiving dinner, though connoisseurs complain that the Chinese's carcass configuration is not as good as that of the larger breeds. But, the Chinese has a naturally leaner meat. The Chinese is the smallest bird and the best egg-layer among the goose breeds with quite good fertility. They produce from 40 to 65 eggs per year. Their eggs are large, white, and—like any other bird egg—just fine for cooking and baking. Some strains of Chinese have lost much of their broody urge; others still have it.

Pilgrim. This is an interesting, more recently developed breed (developed before the Second World War). The adult male is white with blue eyes. The adult female is gray and white with hazel eyes, which makes it easy to distinguish it from the male. Even day-old goslings are sex-linked to white and gray. The Pilgrim ganders are said to be friendly to humans and diligent in helping rear their goslings.

Pilgrims are cold-weather hardy, being able to do without shelter even in sub-zero weather. Pilgrims are smaller than Embdens, rating as a medium-sized goose, and weighing 14 lb. (goose) to 16 lb. (gander).

Toulouse. These geese have broad bodies of dark gray with white abdomens. They have reddish-orange legs and toes and orange bills. They are hardy in winter and are basically meat birds that grow fast—a pound or more a week for the first 12–14 weeks—and end up quite large. Toulouse are meat specialists. A Toulouse will have fall weights from 20 to 25 lb. Some Toulouse males grow quite large, up to 26 lb., if allowed to grow to maturity—which requires a full year. Toulouse geese have another advantage: they are the best goose for reproducing themselves, though the White Chinese and Embden geese also go broody very well. Although the female will lay about 25 eggs over a month, let her set on only 15. Giant Toulouse geese are an extra-heavy variant of the Toulouse that has the reputation of being a quiet breed, which may be kept unfenced because they won't wander far. Giant Toulouse geese will lay about 60 eggs per season, but hatchability runs only a little over 50 percent. The Giant Toulouse is said to be a relatively poor brooder and mother.

Embden. These geese are pure white, have very nice feathers, and are also hardy in winter. Like the Toulouse, they grow fast, although they are slightly smaller. The White Embden is the commercial grower's favorite. A gosling can go from 4 oz. at hatching to 11 lb. in 10 weeks. At the end of 12–14 weeks you can put 10–12-lb. birds in your freezer. Or let them grow longer. An Embden will have fall weights of 18–20 lb. Embden geese go broody very well and will lay between 35 and 40 eggs a year.

African. The African goose is not as heavy as the Toulouse or White Embden, but it matures earlier. It is light brown with dark brown accents and a black knob on its head. The dressed carcass is on the lean side, with an abundance of pin feathers. The African goose is a heavier relative of the Chinese, weighing 14 lb. (goose) to 16 lb. (gander) at butchering stage, a couple pounds heavier as a breeder. It also is a relatively good layer. African geese are significantly noisier than other breeds.

Royal Chinese. This rare breed is the largest goose in captivity. They can exceed the adult weight of most other breeds when they are only 10 weeks old.

Buff and Sebastopol Geese. Both are unsuitable for meat and egg production. The Sabastopol does have beautiful curly feathers, making it fine for showing or to keep for a pet.

Canada or Wild Geese. These are best left wild. Although you can keep one from flying off by penning it or clipping its wings, they give you neither plentiful eggs nor good meat and you need a permit to keep one.

CARE AND FEEDING OF GEESE

Care of Goslings. A good time to get mail-order goslings is when you have really warm weather. Order from the supplier who can get them to you quickest, and make arrangements to pick them up immediately upon arrival. Goslings will be about $5 apiece. An average family could eat 5 or 6 a year. (Plan to have that many disposable goslings a year once your flock gets going.) It's important to get your order in well before early spring, or the mail-order sources will be sold out. That's because a lot of these birds lay only in the spring, and if you don't get your babies then, you won't. For more detailed information on raising goslings, see chick-raising information under "Chickens" and the water-fowl section.

Feeding Goslings. Provide green grass to goslings as soon as they will eat. Although you can feed goslings the same diet as ducklings, you can also offer them bread or corn bread moistened with milk. Provide a fine grit. For the first week, feed them all they can eat in 15 minutes, 4 times a day. You can gradually reduce the number of feedings until the fourth week. By then they should be surviving well at pasture, supplemented with a little grain.

PASTURE FOR GEESE: When you are raising goslings, plan to provide them with green stuff, starting in the first week. Lawn clippings are fine for them so long as the grass hasn't had any chemical treatment. If the weather is mild, and you make sure they don't get either chilled or over-heated, you can literally let them out to graze, from a few days of age on. This saves you a lot of money on other feed. The best kind of grass for them is tender and green, not long, dried up, and coarse. Same for weeds—they can't eat high, coarse weeds until they are older. Don't let them get rained on or be in wet grass until they are at least a month old, especially when the weather is cool. And if there is no natural shade for them, they'll need to be able to find shade under trees, or under a shelter—maybe a sheet of plywood nailed a few feet up on top of 4 corner posts.

At 5 or 6 weeks of age your goslings can survive entirely on pasture if they can get enough of it, although it's helpful to their diet if you continue the supplemental grain and/or pellet feeding until they're completely feathered. For serious, large-scale goose raising, goslings enjoy fields of ladino clover, other white clovers, alfalfa, and almost any grass such as bluegrass, orchard grass, timothy, and brome-grass. They can eat grocery store culls of lettuce, cabbage, endive, and celery leaves. They also like barley, wheat, and rye, especially for fall pasture. For best results, plan on 1 acre of prime pasture for each 20–40 geese. The larger the goose, the more grass it will eat. The poorer the quality of the pasture, the more space will be needed per bird. You can compensate for poor pasture by feeding supplemental grain. It will help keep your pasture in good shape if you rotate the birds from section to section, so they don't have a chance to eat any of it down so far it can't grow back quickly. In winter, your geese will try to forage and may be able to discover some dried grass and weed seeds, but they'll also need some good (*not moldy!*) alfalfa hay, corn fodder, grain (they like cracked wheat and rolled barley), or whatever you're feeding your chickens. Geese enjoy warm, cooked cull potatoes and can thrive on them. Feed any poultry such warm food toward evening. Then they will face the night's chill full of inner warmth. You can train them to enter shelter at night or during the winter in response to that feed.

Geese as "Weeders." Geese love green stuff. It's their natural food. Grown geese can thrive on grass and weeds alone, if the plants are tender (they don't get good nutrients from tall, tough, stems). Feeding geese grass gives them cheap nourishment and keeps them healthy. They love to eat dandelions, morning glory, pigweed, thistles, and burr weeds, which can be a blessing. Unfortunately, however, their favorite foods in my experience seem to be lettuce, chard, young peas, beans, and corn. They'll even eat onions. If they get into the garden very often they can wipe

you out, so you either have to fence your garden away from the goslings and geese, or fence the goslings and geese away from your garden. If you put them into a corn field after the corn is grown up tall and the ears are almost ready to pick, they'll get the weeds and leave the corn. But if you put them in there with the young corn plants, the geese will wipe them out. They are the same in a field of sunflowers. And beware of small trees in your orchard. Geese have been known to strip tender bark.

Before herbicides came into standard usage there was a goose-glorious period of agricultural history, when commercial growers rented young geese by the truckload in spring as weeders—12 geese considered equivalent to 1 person with a hoe. If you are buying geese to function as weeders in cotton fields, orchards, vineyards, berry patches, etc., figure 7 geese per acre. The geese should be at least 6–8 weeks old, and the weeds can't be so far ahead of them as to be high and coarse. Water and shade placement control the movement of the weeders. Geese can survive and thrive on clover, alfalfa, grasses, and weeds alone, but if their greens diet is limited in quantity or quality, some supplemental feeding in the evening is a good idea. Geese aren't so reliable in commercial fields of strawberries. If weeds are scarce, they'll eat the berry plants, and they like strawberries both green and ripe. Unlike chickens, geese don't scratch off the mulch looking for worms.

CONTROLLING GEESE

Fencing for Geese. As with 4-legged herbivores, you can turn the geese into a fenced pasture to graze. Goose-fencing keeps them in and it keeps them safe. Geese are quite vulnerable to large predators. My last summer's batch went down to the creek, and something got every one of them. Unfenced geese tend to wander away down a creek into the woods and will most likely be gone by the next day. Skunks, raccoons, or weasels will do the job, although I have heard of a case in which the geese killed a skunk. Two-inch poultry wire netting works fine for younger birds, and it need be only 18–24 inches high, since these birds don't usually fly. For birds 4–6 weeks or older, regular woven-wire fencing will work—3 feet high is good. Or even single-strand electric fencing. They'll stay in pretty well behind minimal fencing, except a henless gander may occasionally fly over and need to be caught and returned. The latest thing in goose-fencing is an electrified net, powered by an optional solar/battery system. I've talked to a grower who had such a system, and he was very enthusiastic about it. (Your hardware dealer could tell you more.) If you want to manage your geese without fencing, the best alternative is to make one of your children into a goose-herder to take care of them, as geese actually herd pretty well.

Controlling an Aviator Goose. Take the tips off the wing feathers 5 inches on one side. Just cut with scissors. It off-balances the goose. If you were to cut off both sides, he could still fly because he would be balanced. Be careful not to cut the wing, and if the bird is molting, just cut the tips of the feathers. (During molting, a thick sheath of blood vessels nurtures growing feathers. If you cut through that, your goose could bleed to death.)

OF GOOSE AND GANDER: It's easier to tell a young goose from an old one than to tell a female from a male. A young goose has soft, yellow down on its legs, an older one does not. But determining sex is difficult. Domestic geese are all to some extent polygamous, so it's efficient to eat the surplus males. But adults all look alike except in size—except for the color-differentiated Pilgrims. There usually isn't much difference in size either, yet with sharp attention perhaps you can discern the ganders, which not only are larger, but also have a broader head, longer neck, and more upright carriage. And ganders are more aggressive. If a strange dog comes along, the ganders will be the ones to take it on. A gander also has a somewhat louder and shriller voice than a goose. If any mounting is going on, that tells you. The one on top is male. Otherwise, if you're determined to know, you have to do a rabbit-style close anatomical observation.

Sexing Adult Geese.
Get somebody to help you. Pick the goose up, turn it upside down and start hunting around. There isn't much to see, but with practice you can learn the difference. Lubricate a finger. Stick it in the cloaca about half an inch and rotate gently several times. Now press around the outside of the vent gently to squeeze out the sex organ. It's difficult to get the penis visible, so if you get a round hole with a twisted nubbin sticking out, you know you have a male, but if you don't see a nubbin you may or may not have a female. If you can get a friend who has done it before to help you the first time, it's easier. See *Sexing*, published by See *Sexing* (Stromberg Publishing: 800-720-1134; **strombergschickens.com**) for more details.

The easiest way to differentiate the sexes is to wait until spring. You may not know, but the geese sure do. The one who ends up laying eggs and sitting on the nest is the female.

Breeder Ages.
Geese do not mate well if the goose is older than the gander. A goose produces eggs for many years, the most between ages 2 and 5. However, if she eats too much and gets obese, she won't lay as many eggs, and those she does lay aren't as fertile as they would be after a diet. The gander ain't what he uster be after about 10 breeding seasons but is still good for some offspring. Geese will breed even up to 40 years of age. (101 is claimed to be the record.) If your geese don't breed their first year, don't panic: Geese sometimes don't start until their second year. Frequently, that first family may not be as numerous or hardy as later hatches. But after their trial run, most geese, left on their own, will brood and raise about 15 goslings a year.

Gander-Maturing Ages.
The age of maturation varies. In some breeds, ganders are not mature enough to mate effectively until they are 2 years old—3 if they are of the Egyptian or Canada breeds. Slower breeds may be pushed into becoming productive earlier if exposed to increased artificial light.

Possible Breeding Ratios.
These vary with the breed. The Canada and Egyptian geese mate only in pairs. Ganders of other breeds may pair exclusively with one female, but polygamous groupings are common. Embden, Toulouse, and African geese can suitably be grouped 1 gander to 2 or 3 geese. The Pilgrim, Buff, and Sebastopol ganders can each handle a harem of 3 or 4 geese. The smaller White Chinese gander can manage a harem of as many as 6 geese. For breeds that are capable of polygamy there should be at least 2 or 3 geese per gander for best tranquillity in the gaggle. However, there have been cases in which, as individual ganders grew older, they became monogamous and grew indifferent to all but one mate. But Chinese ganders not only accept a larger harem than any other variety, they also will not revert to monogamy.

Goose Conservatism.
Geese generally choose partners in the fall. Once the groupings are established, it is difficult to add more geese. Geese do not mate on first encounter like so many other animals. If your proposed partners are new to each other, you'll have to allow them time to get acquainted. Many ganders do not change partners easily. Previous companions have to be completely absent for as long as a month before such a gander will accept one or more new ones. How did "goose" ever become synonymous with "stupid"?

LAYING AND NESTING

Breeder Foods.
Geese lay best when they're getting grass, even in winter. If you are serving feed-store food, begin feeding them 15–25 percent breeder feed or mash and some good-quality hay in January, a month before egg production. A calcium supplement will assure eggshell hardness. It would also help to feed breeder geese a chicken-laying mash, if you're giving commercial feed. Whatever's in that, it does indeed push females to lay.

Egg Laying.
Don't let overeager birds go broody in January, because none of the eggs will hatch. The way you prevent that is by taking the eggs every day, leaving just one (not the same one). Unlike the duck (which dependably lays early each morning), the goose will lay her egg any old time of day. Goose eggs are used the same way you would use a chicken egg. They taste just the same to me, but are much bigger. One goose egg will make an omelet; fry one and it fills the pan. Goose eggs are also prized in decorative eggshell arts. Becky Coleman of Charlo, MT, wrote: "My pair of Embden geese were 'mature' when 1 year old. They hatched 8 goslings out of 9 eggs. That pair was hatched one spring and started breeding the following spring. I took away the first couple dozen eggs and then let the goose set with results as stated. The one egg that didn't hatch was cracked."

Goose Nest.
Free-ranging geese will lay their eggs on the damp ground. If you have predators in the area, it is best to restrict your laying geese, but they will still prefer to nest outside. A good nest for a goose is an old tire with straw or hay in the center of it or, better yet, an old doghouse or something similar with clean straw inside of it. Smaller breeds prefer a smaller "house"—a box or barrel. Keep a little distance between nests to discourage squabbles. When the goose starts laying, remove all but 2 eggs until you have accumulated a nest full. The eggs can be stored in a cool place up to 2 weeks. (Wild goose eggs should not be gathered.) When you feel the weather has improved enough for her to raise a family, leave the eggs. When she has filled up her nest with a dozen or so eggs, she'll begin to set. A broody goose, in proper season, can raise up to 20 goslings.

Wherever she nests she'll lay her eggs there and brood them, and then both parents will help raise the family. Once the young are hatched the mother will provide the needed warmth for them, but it will be helpful if you provide food and water in appropriately sized containers for the young ones.

Chicken-Brooded Goose Eggs.
If you have a breed that will lay more eggs and you wish to hatch them all, you can put fertile goose eggs of a non-broody layer under a setting hen and let her raise them. Take the excess goose eggs away before you let the goose accumulate her nest. Choose foster hens that are completely free of lice and ticks. A hen can cover 6 goose eggs, but they're too big for her to turn. You'll

need to mark them and turn them yourself every day. Sprinkle them with water daily, too. Expect a hatch in 28–35 days. Or you can put orphan birds from a mail-order source under a hen who has a new family (see instructions at "Inter-Species Brooding and Mothering" under "Chickens"). When the goslings hatch, you may be able to slip them into the goose nest, but watch carefully. If the goose rejects them, the chicken hen may raise them.

Incubating Goose Eggs. Like duck eggs, goose eggs need a high humidity to incubate. While the eggs are waiting to go in the incubator, use all directions listed in "Eggs-in-Waiting" under "Chickens" with the addition of a light spraying of lukewarm water every time you turn the eggs and a once-a-day dunking. (See "Incubating Waterfowl Eggs.") Large-breed geese hatch in 30 days, Chinas in about 28, Canadian and Egyptians in 35.

BUTCHERING: If you have an old goose, I'd let it die with its dignity intact rather than trying to eat it. I wouldn't eat one over 3 years old. They get tough as shoe leather.

Catching a Goose. A good time is very early in the morning. When he comes hissing at you, bend toward him, reach out, and grab his neck behind the head. Then you can hold his head away from you with that hand, so he can't bite, and with the other arm, just scoop up his body, pinning the wings by tucking him under your arm and pressing him to your side. Hold him backward—with the head under your arm and coming out behind you and the bird's rear end on your front side. Otherwise the bird can stretch out that long neck and bite you in the face. That way—holding his neck in one hand and his body with wings pinned under your other arm—you can carry him safely where you need to go. The usual goose-slaughtering time is in the fall, when they are 5–6 months old, although you can kill heavily fed birds at 12 weeks if you don't mind dealing with more pinfeathers. At 5–6 months, they'll weigh 10–15 lb. and pinfeathers won't be a problem. Over age 10 months, their meat becomes tough.

Killing a Goose. You can hang it by the feet, stun it, cut the throat, and bleed it out thoroughly. Or . . . some friends have been continuing my education about geese. They say they shoot a goose in the head with a .22, and then skin it out rather than pick it. Well, meat's meat.

Scalding and Picking a Goose. Heat the water to 155°F— you'll need a *big* pot of it for a 20-lb. goose. You can heat water in a big canner to boiling and then pour it into the bottom of a metal garbage can and repeat as needed until you have enough accumulated to get the bird entirely under water somehow. Follow directions under "About Feathers." Soak the goose as long as 4 minutes (in 140°F water with lots of agitating), depending on its size—long enough to get the feathers loose. The bigger a bird is, the longer you have to soak it to loosen the feathers. Follow directions under "Butchering a Duck" to cut up the bird. You can save the blood as well as the entrails for other stock.

SOME OF MY FAVORITE GOOSE RECIPES

BRAISED GOSLING This is a delicious way to prepare a bird that has just reached roasting size. Use a roaster with a rack at the bottom of it. Put a chunked carrot, an onion, a turnip, a pared and cored apple, and a stalk of celery on the grating. Lay the bird on that. Rub salt, pepper, and a little sage on it. Pour some boiling water in the side. Cover and roast at 350°F, 15 minutes to the pound. Baste with butter.

To make the gravy, remove the gosling when done, and mash the vegetables by pouring them and the cooking liquid through a sieve into a bowl. Skim away as much of the grease as possible after it has set a moment. Chop the cooked giblets (except the liver, which you discard), and add them to the broth. Put about 3 T. of the goose grease into a frying pan. Thicken with flour, then add the broth gradually, stirring the lumps out before adding more liquid, until it has all been added. Season your gravy to taste. Serve the bird on a platter, the gravy in a bowl. Have mashed potatoes ready to pour the gravy over. Applesauce, and green peas or lima beans will complete a wonderful meal.

SEASONED GIBLET GRAVY This is a variation of the above. You roast your goose without the vegetables in the roaster. Precook the neck, gizzard, and heart (again discard the liver, or do something different with it—like make paté de foie gras, for which I don't know the recipe, only that it's made out of goose livers) by boiling them until the gizzard is fork-tender. Allow enough time, because it often takes just as long to cook that gizzard tender as it does to roast the entire rest of the bird. (If you wanted to use the giblets as part of your bird's stuffing, instead of in the gravy, you'd cook them the night before.) Season the giblet water with 1 t. salt, 2 peppercorns, 1 clove, a bit of bay leaf, a sectioned carrot, a sectioned celery stalk, and an onion.

After the giblets are cooked, cool them. Remove the neck bones, and cut the meat into very small pieces. By now your roast goose should be done. Make a gravy as in the recipe above, using grease from your goose roast, flour, and the broth the giblets were cooked in along with the mashed vegetables from it and the minced giblet meat. Make lots of the gravy. For your second (and third?) meal from this food reheat your leftover gravy, adding sufficient water to get it the right consistency again since it thickens some while stored. Add sliced leftover goose meat to the gravy and serve over slices of bread or with potatoes.

GOOSE STUFFED WITH SAUERKRAUT This is a good fall dish, when the geese and the sauerkraut are both at their prime. Fill the goose with homemade sauerkraut. Sew up, tie into shape, and place in a large kettle. Cover with about 2 qt. more of sauerkraut and add boiling water. Simmer gently for 3 hours. At the end of this time, take your goose out of the pan and put it in your roaster. Rub the skin with butter. Bake in a 400°F oven about 1 hour, or until nicely browned. Serve the boiled kraut seasoned to taste with salt, pepper, or butter, since the boiling weakens the flavor.

Life is a river. Lived right, it's a quick, clear river rushing over and around the rocks in a long straight path down to the sea. But I sometimes see someone allowing his or her beautiful river to turn into a sluggish, muddy swamp with a multitude of mosquitoes growing on top. Getting out of the swamp requires change. There's a basic rigidity of life: that it's hard (or impossible) to change him, or her, or it, or that. The place where you've got room to maneuver, to manage a healing of the swamp, is to change you. That's something always within your power to do.

But first you have to get the vivid and important realization that you are in a swamp—and you want to get out!

Ain't that something. For umpteen pages I give instruction, then I preach. It's a good thing I have teenagers to keep me humble. In this new edition I've tried to reduce the burbling and stay with the subject better than I used to. But then wonderful readers write me and say they loved thus and such in my book—and it's frequently a burble rather than a how-to they're talking about, though it's also surprising how many people have written to thank me for prosaic things such as chicken-butchering directions. So I don't really know which is most important. Guess I'll just keep doing like I'm doing.

GUINEAS

What is not considered a game bird but acts a lot like one, comes from Africa, and roosts in a tree if you don't keep it penned up? It's a guinea, called the African chicken, although it is more closely related to the pheasant. They're noisy, quarrelsome with other poultry, and probably not practical to own unless you're going to keep them penned up (because unconfined guineas hide their eggs, lose their babies, and are difficult to catch) or unless you have a major insect problem and lots of room for them to roam. But they are hardy, do have a tasty meat, and lay rich eggs.

Dynah Geissel, Missoula, MT, wrote me about guineas, "I wouldn't say that guineas are useless. They announce the arrival of a hawk by screaming and standing their ground while the chickens run for cover. They also broadcast the arrival of other visitors. They are excellent and persistent setters, but they lay their eggs in the fields where they become easy prey to predators such as skunks. They are terrible mothers who will lead their 12–15 keets through puddles, wet grass or anything else in their way. The best bet is to take the eggs and let a hen hatch them. If a guinea does manage to hatch her clutch, take all but two and raise them yourself. Turn them loose when they're 8 weeks old. Butcher them in the fall (shooting them out of the tree where they roost is your best bet). Be sure you shoot the babies and not the adults. This partly for the sake of tenderness, but also because a guinea dramatically mourns the loss of its mate. The meat is wonderful—like pheasant."

You can get more information on guineas in the handbook *Guinea Fowl,* available from Inman Hatcheries (see "Poultry Supplies" under "Chickens" in this chapter).

Guinea Attributes

SELF-RELIANCE: Guineas have been companions to human beings since the ancient Greeks, yet they can never be called more than "semi-domesticated." Guinea fowl will be less dependent on you for care than perhaps any other type of animal you raise. They are able to search out their own food—except in winter—and as a result they are one of the less expensive birds to raise. They are both hot-weather and cold-weather hardy, being adapted from northern Canada to the torrid south, but will need some protection during extremely cold weather. They are less prone to disease than any other poultry, clean in habits, and are not associated with the familiar "poultry" smell.

INSECT-EATING: If allowed to roam, guineas will consume more insects than other fowl. Unlike the grain-loving fowl and unlike the plant-eating fowl, guineas are insect eaters. And they will work hard to get bugs. Guineas eat ants and will wipe out ant hills. They eat potato bugs and Japanese beetles. They do not scratch and will not harm garden or flowers; they go there looking only for insects. They chase flies, and catch them. They will ride on larger animals, picking insects and catching flies. The guinea is naturally an open-range feeder, but no matter how far it travels in daytime bug searches, it always returns home by evening.

GUINEA PATROL: Like geese and watchdogs, guineas make a loud frightened shriek when they notice strangers coming around—human or animal. They have been known to chase away wild birds like robins and waxwings from berry bushes and fruit orchards with their noise, flying into the trees and darting at the other birds. The guineas themselves are not fruit eaters and will not pick at fruit even if it falls on the ground. Guineas are on guard at night, too, and their noise can be a real problem to you and your neighbors. One of the flock, by turns, stays alert all night, ready to give the alarm. But owners have complained that they simply make noise all the time, rather than making useful noise, and they may be eaten by the very creatures they're supposed to give the alarm about. This new generation of guineas, hatched in incubators and raised in a brooder, doesn't live up to the reputation of its more naturally brought-up ancestors. When you eliminate old-time mothering and the survival lore that is thus passed from parent to offspring, you forsake education, and raise a helplessly ignorant species.

GUINEAS FOR MEAT AND MARKET: Guineas produce excellent meat. The guinea usually weighs 2–3 lb. at 16 weeks. Birds for market are butchered at 2½–3½ lb. The weight is mostly meat because of their small, flying-bird bones, a little smaller than a roasting chicken. The best time to butcher is at 4–6 months of age. The meat is all dark and tastes like a game bird's, so there is a market selling guinea meat to elite restaurants. As with other birds, young guineas are tender, while old ones are best as stew birds. You may substitute guinea in any recipe calling for grouse, partridge, or pheasant. You can also substitute guinea in any recipe for chicken, keeping in mind that the bird is the size of a light-breed chicken and is typically leaner than chicken and thus benefits from ingredients that add fat or moistness.

Low-Cholesterol Eggs: Guinea eggs are brown-shelled and are the lowest in cholesterol of all poultry—or so I've heard. They have a flavor all their own. The exceptionally light yolks are excellent for souffles, mayonnaise-making, and baking. Their eggs are small, banty size. If you're making angel food cake, 16 guinea whites equal 11 hen whites. Guinea eggs keep well because of an unusually heavy shell. However, since they're such poor layers and hide what they do lay, you're lucky if you get very many of those wonderful eggs.

Getting Started

There are several varieties of guineas, but the main difference between them is color of feathers. Basically, a guinea is always a guinea. The 2 most commonly available varieties in the United States are the Pearl and the White African. Pearl Gray guineas have lovely feathers. The Whites, with their lighter skin, are sometimes preferred by restaurants, where they may be served in pheasant dishes. They're said to be not quite as loud as the Pearls, and you can see them better to follow to a hidden cache of eggs. Thomas G. Horan, RR 4, Box 417, Tamaqua, PA 18252, 570-467-3683 (evenings best), is a guinea specialist. He offers nine varieties: pearl, white, lavender, dun dotte, coral blue, royal purple, buff, opaline, or porcelain. Ralph Winter, 21357 White Pine Lane, New Vienna, IA 52065-9728, 319-853-4195, **www.guineafarm.com**, offers 20 colors of guineas to choose from (also 10 varieties of peafowl and blackneck swans).

Start your flock with day-old chicks from eggs set under chickens, or mail-order keets, because adult birds, when moved, are likely to wander, even if they've been penned for as much as several weeks. Your keets can be adopted and raised by your hen, or in a brooder.

Guinea Feed: Besides insects, the free-ranging guinea will pick up seeds of grasses, weeds, and grains. A dense patch of blackberries or such undergrowth is heaven to a guinea. If you want them to stay close to home, you can let them out only in the late afternoon to range. Completely fenced-in birds kept in a rotation setup need to be shifted every 3 weeks, but fenced range won't work for unfed guineas unless it's large enough. They need enough territory for adequate insect-hunting, since that is their primary diet. When guineas are close-penned, or cannot range because of weather or snow cover, you can feed them high-protein turkey or game-bird feed, chicken or turkey laying mash, or a home-devised chicken diet. If using a home-devised diet, they need less grain than other birds, and more protein—corn, wheat, oats, milk curd, and meat scraps. They appreciate oyster shells and limestone grit.

Guinea Shelter: Adult guineas are certainly happy roosting in an orchard, all year round. But some owners prefer to teach them to roost in a poultry shed. This solves the problem of having to shoo them inside in extremely bad weather (guineas intensely dislike snow). They don't need a heated or insulated shelter. To teach a guinea to sleep indoors, you start when they're about 2 months old and getting the urge to roost somewhere high. Each night, drive them into the place where you want them to roost. They can be taught the habit. Or you can let them roost outdoors in the summer. Then each evening of the fall feed them nearer the place you want them to roost, so that by the time really cold weather comes it won't be so difficult to get them to sleep in there. But for easiest and best management they should be confined in bird runs. (See "Pheasant Housing" under "The Game Birds.")

Guinea Pens: At least 1 cock and 3 or 4 hens should be penned together. The pen size should be a minimum of 6 × 10 feet for this group. Sides 5 feet high on a pen that small will prevent the birds from flying out. If they are to be penned during laying season, place the pen in such a way that at least 1 corner contains brush or tree limbs, deep grass, or hay. Guineas do not like nesting boxes. The hens will lay their eggs on the ground where they feel securely hidden. Make a special egg-door in the fence by the nesting place, so you can gather eggs without coming into the pen. Another good argument for letting the birds roam, at least once a day, is to help you gather the eggs unseen. What guineas see, they remember, and they don't make a mistake more than twice.

Worms: The primary health problem a guinea can suffer from is worms, round and tape. It is possible, but risky, to worm them.

Guinea Reproduction

Male and Female: It's difficult to tell the sexes apart. Baby guineas cannot be vent-sexed. After the keets are 12 weeks old, a cock's comb is just a little larger than the female's. The adult cock's comb and wattles are just a little more developed than the female's, and the white on his neck extends farther down. The cock's call is one-syllabic, while the hen's is either a 1- or a 2-syllable call, variously rendered as "put-rock," "buck-wheat," or "good-luck." If one bird is separated from the others, you can tell by its call what sex it is. Males are the ones that rush about with wings lifted a little, an expression of avian courtship. Under natural circumstances guineas are monogamous. But they will accept harem life. You can maintain egg fertility with as few as 1 cock to every 4–6 females. The social grouping so formed will be permanent. The cock always remains protectively near his hens. If the hens have 1 wing clipped and are kept in a pen, an unclipped cock won't fly away and leave them. Guineas can mate with chickens. The resulting offspring, like the mules that result from horse–donkey matings, will be sterile.

Nests: Since guineas are known for laying in out-of-the-way places, its a good idea to confine them each day until they've laid (until 3pm if you've got a number of hens). If your guineas are free-roaming, you will have trouble finding their eggs. Guineas are seasonal egg-layers, and they hide their nests. There's an art to finding those nests. When the laying season begins (late March to mid-May, depending on your climate), watch to see where they go. The flock will go together to lay between about 11am and 1pm. A guinea nest will be a shallow hole scratched in the ground. All the hens may lay in the same nest, even at the same time. The cock stands nearby to guard them. You must see without being seen. Guineas are easily upset and may quit laying, or move the nest. So don't ever come near while they're laying. Just mark the spot visually, and then, after they've gone on their way, go find it. The laying season will be over sometime between August and October.

When you take out eggs, leave from 1 to 5 (opinions vary) marked ones. Never let them see you take the eggs. A guinea hen will set when she gets an accumulation of 12–24 eggs. So, you'll get a greater total of eggs from which to hatch keets (under a hen or in an incubator) or for eating, if you mark and leave those 1–5 eggs in her nest and take the others to put under setting hens. Rotate the ones you're leaving, and don't worry about their freshness—remember that guinea eggs are the best keepers. With you taking more of the eggs, the guinea won't get broody until late summer. If you want to break her from the notion to set, just take all the eggs. Guinea broodiness breaks up easily.

INCUBATING GUINEA EGGS: Guineas lay far fewer eggs than commercial chicken and duck breeds. A hen will lay maybe 45–55 eggs a year, in the period from May to September. The good news is that guineas live a long time, and, like geese, lay as many eggs when they're relatively old as they did their first year, and their eggs remain as fertile.

HATCHING GUINEAS: You may return 12–15 eggs to a guinea hen for setting, set 20–28 guinea eggs under a brooding chicken hen, or incubate the eggs. The eggs take 28 days to hatch. Brooding guinea hens have been known to give up on the rest of their eggs once 2 or 3 keets have hatched. The remaining eggs can be saved if you move them to an incubator or chicken hen. Forced-air incubator setting should be 100°F; during the last 3 days of incubation it should be 99°F. Still-air temperature would be 101–103°F. Humidity: 83–85. Do not turn eggs after 25 days. Humidity is essential because of the hard shell. Humidity during the last 3 days should be 90–94. For eggs incubated under a hen in a dry climate, or in dry weather, it will help the keets hatch out of their thick-shelled eggs if you occasionally sprinkle them with warm water. If you're hatching only part of the eggs, choose the larger ones, because larger eggs tend to hatch out larger birds. Because of keet susceptibility to lice, if you plan to hatch guinea eggs under a hen, she needs to be louse-free, and sitting in a clean nest. The last week before hatching, give her an anti-louse treatment, and put her on fresh sod for nesting material. A little pinch of fine-cut tobacco mixed in the nest litter helps. Banty hens are better for the job than a heavy-breed hen, because they're less likely to cause heavy-footed harm to the fragile-boned guinea keets after they hatch.

KEETS: The guinea chicks, or "keets," are tiny and vulnerable. They are available from hatcheries from about April through August for about $1.50 each. For the first few weeks, you'll want to keep them penned up and feed them frequently. Start with 6 meals a day for the first month. Then give them 4 meals a day for 2 weeks. After an additional 6 weeks of 3 meals a day, you can feed guineas much like turkeys. They'll grow twice as well on turkey starter feed than on chicken starter, but they can make it on (non-medicated!) chick starter. If their feed is to be home-devised, it should be high in protein, with chopped hard-boiled eggs, crumbled cornbread, and cottage cheese or clabbered milk, as well as bread crumbs, oatmeal, and a few greens, with fine grit. Keets cannot eat a coarse feed.

They need a 95°F brooder warmth and to be in groups no larger than 25. They can get through 1-inch holes and fly by the end of 2 weeks. They can drown in chick-size waterers. During the first 2 weeks water them from very small, shallow containers with marbles or rocks in them, devised so they cannot possibly get wet. The keets will stand on the rocks and drink the water. Lice will kill them. Make sure your brooder area is clean in this regard. Wood shavings are a good litter for keets. If you bring up the young keets with chickens of the same age, they learn to come in at night, with no work on your part.

GUINEA MOTHERS: Guinea hens are not the best mothers for their young, so it's really preferable to raise them with a chicken or in a brooder. Modern guinea mothers don't have good judgment about how far a keet has the strength to go, or under what conditions. Keets mothered by a chicken tend to be less wild and more manageable. Guinea keets that are to be mothered by a hen should be penned for the first few days with the hen, until they learn to recognize her "come-here" call. For the first 2 weeks they mustn't roam in wet grass or get caught in the rain. Use a portable coop and move it every day to fresh range. By the time guineas are 4–6 weeks old, when they begin to develop adult feathering, hen and chicks should be completely free to wander. Keets raised in a brooder can be shifted to range and range shelters when 6–7 weeks old. Once on free range the keets need no more supplemental feeding. Guineas are herd creatures, and keets raised with a hen will stay with her until they are fully grown, which may deeply upset a banty hen who wants to go off by herself and set privately on a new clutch of eggs. But the guineas will want to stand guard, guinea-style, while she lays her eggs, and roost with her at night.

Catching a Guinea

My helper, Pam (a treasure: a grown woman with a husband and a beautiful baby, who volunteers her time for the cause of making this a better book; God bless her!), at first kept trying to upgrade my language. She wanted me to say "Administering a Pill to a Bird" rather than "Giving a Bird a Pill" and "Guinea Capture" rather than "Catching a Guinea." I've been fighting for the right to use Plain English on the printed page for 25 years. So I had a talk with her. I asked, "Why must we have a 2- or 3-syllable word when a 1-syllable word can do the job? Why must we make the reader of a how-to book feel like the writer is so-damn-smart and been-to-college?" I explained that my big worry is how to manage to get that reader, you, to truly believe that you—whether amateur, city-raised, Ph.D. or only 6th-grade graduate—can do all this stuff, too. Doctors "administer" medicine. You and I give pills! Right?

Plain language empowers plain people. That's the whole idea: that you, too, could do any or all of the stuff in this book. And it's okay—it's great!—whatever you choose to try. When you give knowledge to people, you empower them. So many times some beautiful person has come up to me and said something like, "I love your book because I can understand what you're saying! You write like people talk!" I do that on purpose. I wish I did it better, and more. Using Plain English in a book doesn't mean the writer is dumb. My IQ is awesome. If I wanted to write more obscurely, more formally and distantly, in the usage of the literati, I could. But I don't want to. Talked Pam into my point of view, too! Like I said, she's a neat lady. And well on the way to recovering from that college degree!

So, to catch (or "capture") a free guinea . . . you can make anything work once or twice: shine a spotlight in her eyes, teach her to feed in an open coop and then sneak up and shut the door, or run her into netting supported by stakes. Using a net on the end of a long handle is a good technique. Be careful when handling guineas, though—their bones are fine and their legs easily broken. It's helpful if they've been taught to sleep indoors. And shooting them in the head always works, if your aim is good!

THE GAME BIRDS

Pheasants, partridge, quail, grouse, and peafowl—the "game birds"—vary a lot, but in general they all are fragile, they typically do not reproduce efficiently or at all in confinement, their eggs must be incubated, they are raised in total confinement (either in runs or cages), and they are chronically nervous. The main argument for keeping them is the extraordinary beauty of some varieties (the pheasants in particular), the small size of some (particularly the quail) that make "garage ranching" possible, and their market value as specialties. Game birds are usually fed commercial game-bird starter/grower/finishing/breeding rations. Whether you can make them pay or not depends on your knowledgeability and skill as a handler and the quality of your facilities—as well as the current state of the market and your ability to network with it. For highest egg-laying rates, many growers send older birds continually on to market, replacing them with their offspring as breeders. That way they're assured of having young, vigorous breeders all the time.

GAME-BIRD BOOKS AND SUPPLIES: There are lots of books on raising game birds in general and on each specific game bird, too. Inman Hatcheries (see "Poultry Supplies" under "Chickens") offers game-bird books: *Raising Game Birds, Game Bird Propagation, Pheasant Breeding and Care,* and *Partridges—Their Breeding and Management* by G.E.S. Robbins. Other useful game-bird references are *Pheasants—Their Breeding and Management* by K. C. R. Howman (helpful to newcomers) and *Raising Game Birds.*

Join the North American Game Bird Association, run by and for game-bird breeders, for $45 ($55 Canada) per year. You get a directory of members, listing in a hunting preserve directory, and *Wildlife Harvest,* a news magazine covering new and proposed regulations, meetings, courses, and ads for birds and equipment: 803-796-8163; PO Box 2105, Cayce-West, Columbia, SC 29171. Or subscribe to the *Game Bird Gazette* ($23.95/yr). It covers breeding, hatching, brooding, feeding, and housing of game birds such as quail, pheasants, guineas, partridges, doves, ducks, and swans. There's a large classified ad section in every issue: 801-575-1111; PO Box 171227, Salt Lake City, UT 84117-1227; **www.gamebird.com.**

SOURCES

B & D Game Bird Farm is where Bert and Dianne Tumey offer bobwhite, Tibetan, and Pharoah quail, ringneck pheasant, chukar junglefowl, guineas, books, videos, supplies, and a free brochure: 405-964-5235; Rt. 1, Box 812, Harrah, OK 73045; **info@bdfarm.com; www.bdfarm.com.**

Bayou Bird Farm offers many varieties of pheasants, junglefowl, and peafowl: 318-949-2294; 846 Elsie Dr., Princeton, LA 71067.

Cutler's Pheasant Supply: 810-633-9450; 1940 Old 51, Applegate, MI 48401; **cutlers@greatlakes.net; www.cutlersupply.com.** Free 56-pg. catalog lists incubators, brooders, feeders, waterers, ringers, netting, catching nets, coated wire, books, medicine, blinders, and much more.

Cottonwood Grove Bird Sanctuary offers quail, pheasants, partridge, junglefowl, and peafowl. Contact David Bauer: 308-893-2707; 5480 W. 85th St., Kearney, NE 68845; **bauerd@unk.edu.**

Stanley Downey offers many varieties of pheasants (also bantams and pigeons): 863-646-5410; 4725 Old Gov't Rd., Lakeland, FL 33811.

Thomas G. Horan, RR 4, Box 417, Tamaqua, PA 18252; 570-467-3683 (evenings), offers pheasants, chukar partridge, French red leg partridge, Barbary partridge, bobwhite quail, mallards, Hungarian partridge, Gamble quail, blue scale quail, and valley quail.

George Irons offers many kinds of pheasants (also peafowl and ducks): 508-252-3148; fax 508-252-3992; 117 Hillside Ave., Rehoboth, MA 02769; **tragopan9@yahoo.com.**

Jarvis Farms offers various pheasants and quail, including bobwhites: 330-549-3536; 9649 Detwiler Rd., Canfield, OH 44406.

Thomas R. Kent offers to ship various kinds of pheasants and partridge: 912-433-5172; 1070 Kent Smith Rd., Pinehurst, GA 31070.

Oakwood Game Farm hatches 50,000 ringneck pheasants and chukar partridge weekly. Established in 1966. Free price list: 800-328-6647; fax 763-389-2077; PO Box 274, Princeton, MN 55371; **oakwood@sherbtel.net; www.oakwoodgamefarm.com.**

Quailco Game Bird Farm offers chukar, quail, pheasant, and wild turkey day-old chicks. Contact owner Mikel Hays: 505-477-2397; Box 368, Dora, NM 88175; **quailco@yucca.net; www.quailcogbf.com.**

Reston Gamebird Farm ships eggs and adults: 14 pheasant varieties, three of quail, three of partridge. Contact: 541-679-0844; 3621 Reston Rd., Roseburg, OR 97470; **www.restongbf.com.**

Game-Bird Housing

GAME BIRDS AND STRESS: Because of their natural wildness, game birds are easily stressed by life in captivity. Stress makes them more susceptible to disease. Crowding, poor nutrition, changes in their diet, changes in their housing, and handling of any sort tend to be stressful to them and must be managed as carefully as possible.

PENS FOR SMALL GAME BIRDS: It's best if you separate birds by species and age. The smaller game birds, such as quail, are usually raised in tiered metal battery-style pens or in homemade off-the-ground pens that have a wood frame with poultry-netting sides and small-mesh flooring. A basic homemade pen uses 2 × 4s for the frame and 4 legs, which support a 2 × 2 × 4-foot cage. The floor of the cage is made of hardware cloth (a rugged galvanized screening). The wire floor allows droppings to fall through to below the pen where they can be gathered up for the compost pit. The sides are of chicken wire. The top can be made of chicken wire if the pen is inside, wood or metal if it is outside. Such pens can be on tall legs with a back-sloped roof and can be fixed on posts or portable.

HOUSING FOR LARGER GAME BIRDS: Pheasants, for example, are usually kept in sizable cages that have a chicken-wire top and sides. Such a cage could be partitioned off inside an existing building—about 6 × 12 feet—or built outside. Outside ground pens can be built to include brush, one or more trees, and shrubs; that provides a more comfortable and natural environment for the birds. Dimensions can be adjusted according to the variety of bird, number of birds, and the space you have. Height should be 6 feet. Outside ground pens need a south-facing shelter to protect the birds from sun and storm. If your climate is cold, the shelter needs to be a little house with a bird-size door to get into it. The ground in a pen needs to be kept clean, either by spreading a heavy litter, such as that of tree leaves, which are regularly stirred and occasionally changed, or by regularly raking and removing bird droppings. Game birds, like chickens, can become afflicted with external parasites such as mites and lice.

GAME-BIRD BREEDING: Separate your breeders in the correct ratios of males to females for your particular species about 4–5 weeks before you will begin gathering eggs. Both males and females will be stimulated to produce if you supply 17 hours of light a day and maintain a temperature of at least 60°F.

Here is information on the specific game-bird varieties: first pheasants, then partridge, then quail.

Pheasants

Pheasants are large, colorful relatives of the other game birds—partridge, quail, and grouse. The males are the most colorful as well as the largest. Pheasants are not good egg producers, but they are, in many cases, beautifully feathered birds. They aren't the most practical for home food production, but they might make money for you.

PHEASANTS FOR HUNTING: Some pheasants are raised for hunting. Raising sports-variety pheasants is under the control of your state game commission. In the states I know of, you must have a permit to raise them in captivity. In Idaho there are unannounced visits by an inspector making sure that certain requirements with regard to their housing and so on are met. So talk to your state game commission and find out the rules before you order a game variety. They don't regulate the "show" pheasants—the goldens and silvers, for example.

Ringneck Pheasant

PHEASANT HOUSING: Pheasants are the most timid domesticated bird there is. Free-running Chinese Pheasants will mate with chickens, resulting in an impractical hybrid. Pheasants will absolutely suffer in crowded quarters with lots of commotion. They need to be in a big, long pen where they can get away from you. It has to have a roofed top to prevent them from flying away. If they get out after belonging to you awhile, they may hang around, roosting on a board fence or some such until hunting season. Then they will disappear. They can generally take care of themselves in the wild okay, but to harvest them you may need luck and a .22.

DEBEAKING: Not necessary, says Tracy Haan of Sioux Falls, SD. Use a special pheasant lamp, plus mix baby chicks with the baby pheasants: "It works wonderfully." Separate the species when grown. "Adult pheasants won't pick each other if they have ample flying and roosting space (especially roosting space)."

PHEASANT REPRODUCTION: Pheasants are polygamous. For maximum economy, pen 1 cock with 4 or 5 hens. Don't put more than 1 cock in the same pen. Game hens have a tendency to leave the nest after their first few chicks hatch. You can take the abandoned eggs into the house and incubate them to finish up the hatch. Then add the remaining chicks to their mother's family. Or you can collect the eggs and do all the hatching in an incubator.

Incubating Pheasant Eggs. Pheasant eggs will hatch in 23–26 days, varying with the exact variety of bird. Forced-air temperature is 100°F, but the temperature in the last 3 days of incubation should drop to 99°F. Still-air temperature for incubation would be 101.5–102.5°F. Desirable humidity is 86–88. Do not turn eggs after 21 days. Humidity during the last 3 days should be 92–95.

Raising Pheasant Chicks. Chicks are available, May to August, from hatcheries. You can't tell ringneck pheasant chicks apart by sex until 6–8 weeks, when they finally develop distinguishing plumage. For a method of sexing day-old ringneck pheasant chicks, see *Sexing* (Stromberg Publishing; **info@strombergschicken.com**). Use turkey starter or game-bird starter to feed them. (Or you can feed them a home-devised diet as you would for chickens—heavy on the protein side.) Young pheasants are easily stressed and need calm and routine. They are also highly cannibalistic and often use their very sharp beaks on each other, requiring an ongoing struggle with debeaking and anti-pick lotion on your part. Interesting food that needs a lot of picking at, like crisp fruit and vegetables and grain, also helps divert the birds from picking at each other. Pheasants mature in 26–28 weeks and will dress out at 2½–3½ lb. They start their own laying career at 7 or 8 months of age, or the next spring. Commercial growers bring them into production earlier using artificial lighting to create a long day.

Partridge

Before ordering partridge, check with the state game-bird regulatory agency in your area that controls wildlife management. You may need a permit. Chukar partridge come from India, weigh about 1½ lb., and are raised for meat. They have a beak that grows so fast, it must be trimmed (debeaked) frequently or it will become difficult for them to pick up feed. Males and females look the same, but the males are a little larger. Adult chukars are sexed on the basis of the leg nubs. The male has short nubs on both legs. Hens may have the nubs, but never as large as the male ones.

Vent sexing is the surest way to tell. Chukars are not monogamous. They reach breeding age at 26–28 weeks, but hens will wait to begin laying until the next spring after hatch unless forced with artificial light (17-hour days).

SHELTER AND FOOD: A 2 × 2 × 4-foot pen could house 15 chukar. One 8 feet long could hold 30–35 chukar. Breeders are usually housed in a colony pen (2 × 2 × 1 foot) with 1 male to every 3 or 4 females. It's better to house these polygamous birds in separate families to avoid cock fights. Young chukars are easily stressed by rough handling, changing pens, changing their food, or changing their feeding routine. They do best if kept in the same pen from hatching to maturity, after which their nerves get calmer. Chukar do well on a game-bird ration, starter until 3 months old, then grower mash until butchering. For your breeders there's a game-bird breeder mash. After 6 weeks of age, supplement with grain and crisp fruits and vegetables to reduce cannibalism.

INCUBATING CHUKAR EGGS: The incubation period will be 23 or 24 days. Forced-air temperature for incubation is 100°F, dropping the last 3 days of incubation to 99°F. Still-air incubating temperature should be 101–102°F. Humidity is best at 80–82. Do not turn eggs after 21 days. Humidity during the last 3 days should be 90–94. For information on vent-sexing chukar chicks (and other fowl) see *Sexing* (Stromberg Publishing; 800-720-1134; **strombergschicken.com**).

Quail

These, and pigeons, are the smallest of the domesticated birds. Quail require the least space of any food-producing domesticated animal and can be raised in an apartment. A 2 × 2 × 8-foot pen could hold 50 quail. Coturnix and Bobwhites are the most commonly raised quails. Bobwhite quail are raised to eat as dressed birds and for shooting preserves. Coturnix are raised for their eggs (says my friend Lee, "Quail eggs are a son of a gun to peel"), as well as for meat. Blue Scale and Gambel quails are some rarer varieties. Bobwhites are the most difficult quail to sex. The vent system has to be used. Quail eggs are small. An incubator that will hold 90 pheasant or chukar eggs can hold 200 quail eggs. If the incubator can hold 300 of the larger eggs, it will hold 800 quail eggs. For more information consult *Albert F. Marsh's Quail Manual* (Garden Grove, CA: Marsh Farms, 1976) or *A Quail in the Family* by William J. Plummer (Henry Regnery Co., 1974).

Quail

COTURNIX QUAIL: After centuries of foreign cultivation, Coturnix quail were imported to the U.S. There are various breeds of Coturnix quail: Pharaoh, Tuxedo, Manchurian, Golden, British Range, English White, Australian Fawn, and Giant Brown. The Giant Brown was developed at Texas A & M Univ. by Dr. Fred Thornberry, Poultry Science Dept. It's a wide-breasted variety that reaches a tasty 10 oz. at 6 weeks. They're available from Bear Bayou Quail Farm, PO Box 514, Channel View, TX 77530; 281-452-5407; **bearbayouquail@ flash.net.**

SEXING COTURNIX: In 2 varieties, the Pharaoh and the Manchurian Golden, the sexes can be color-distinguished once the chicks are 2 weeks old, at which time they grow new feathers with their distinguishing colors. Males have a reddish breast tint; females have a gray-mottled and more speckled breast. The other breeds are the British Range black quail, the English White, and the Tuxedo breeds, and they can be sexed only after 6 weeks, when they are sexually mature and the hens have started laying. A laying hen will have an enlarged vent of a more bluish color. The sexually active male has a ball-like appendage immediately above its vent. If the ball is squeezed, foam will run out. If the male does not have the ball, he will not breed. Coturnix females grow to be about 20 percent larger than the males. Females may be heavier yet because of the developing eggs in their bodies, so comparative weight can be another way to sex them. They also have different calls. The hen says, "whee-whee-whe." The cock says "grr-rrr-rrr-rrr."

Coturnix are rather sensitive to handle. Some people do very well with them; other people have a hard time getting very many eggs—and the egg is the basic purpose of raising them. They are a small bird with a very small egg, but those eggs are almost identical in flavor and nutrient content to chicken's eggs. And the Coturnix needs far less feed to produce the same weight of eggs. They start laying eggs when they are a little over 7 weeks old. They can be very productive egg-layers with high fertility, hardy, and fine to eat, though the dressed weight of a mature Coturnix is only about 4 oz. The hen quail averages 6 oz., the cock, just a shade less. Males can be eaten at 6–8 weeks. Coturnix quail are characteristic of their game-bird relatives, elusive and alert. If they escape—and it's possible—they will be gone forever. Low cages prevent injury from the quail's tendency to fly straight up. These quail require plenty of water because the egg the hen lays almost every day is ⅕ her body weight, and a good part water. Adult quail can eat turkey laying mash, or home-devised diet for confined guineas. You can experiment with other foods to see what they enjoy.

COTURNIX REPRODUCTION: To select breeders from a batch of chicks, choose at 6 weeks of age healthy, active birds that have the proper breed characteristics. The ideal sex ratio is considered to be 1 cock per 2 hens, though they can be raised as monogamous pairs or in a ratio of 1 cock to 3 hens. Don't keep a solitary bird; they need a mate or the single may die. The young are mature and in full egg production by 35–50 days and will be fully grown at 10 weeks. The hens will lay 5 or 6 eggs per week, so 20 to 30 hens can lay about 1,250 eggs—which may be hatched or eaten—in 10 weeks. So their potential reproduction rate is phenomenal. Laying birds are fragile (egg inside!) and should not be handled unless absolutely necessary, and then very carefully. The Coturnix quail lays a large egg for its size, and, if not allowed to set, a lot of them—200–300 per year.

INCUBATING COTURNIX EGGS: The eggs should be incubated 16–18 days, 99.5°F (forced-air) or 101–101.5°F (still-air), at 85 percent humidity, turned a minimum of 4 or 5 times per day. Temperature the last 3 days of incubation can drop to 99°F. Do not turn the eggs after 15 days. Humidity during the last 3 days is best at 90–94. Regular incubator trays won't be suitable for the small quail eggs but can be adapted by using an upside-down egg tray in there to hold them. Using an incubator, your quail production, because of their rapid maturation and prolific egg-laying, can be extraordinary. For quail to set their own eggs, supply extra space and nesting material of soft grass. Each hen will produce at least 4 families per year, each of 10–14 young quail.

BOBWHITE QUAIL: These birds are monogamous and usually pair for life. The male has a white eye-stripe and brown throat. Females have a buff line through the eye and a buff throat. They are physically mature at 16–20 weeks and, if mated, will start laying eggs at 24 weeks. The mature birds weigh ½ lb. If dressed out for eating, a Bobwhite will weigh a little less—about 6 oz. Bobwhite normally mate mid-May to mid-August and lay from 50 to 60 eggs (varying with climate and weather conditions). However, if provided 17 hours of light per day and kept in a temperature over 60°F, the bobwhite hens, once they reach the breeding age of 6 months, will lay eggs the year round—200 or more per year. Bobwhite quail will not set their own eggs in captivity. To incubate these quail eggs allow 23–24 days. Forced-air temperature should be 100°F, dropping the last 3 days to 99°F. Still-air temperature should be 101–102°F. Humidity should be 84–86. Do not turn the eggs after 21 days. Humidity during the last 3 days should be 90–94°F (wet bulb). In the brooder the Bobwhite chicks should start at 100°F, gradually reducing to 70°F when they are nearly grown.

QUAIL CHICKS: These are so tiny that if you use a regular poultry waterer, you must put rocks or marbles in the waterer to keep them from drowning. There is specially designed chick and adult equipment marketed for quail raisers. G.Q.F. Mfg. Co., P.O. 1552, Savannah, GA 31498, and Rocky Top General Store (see "Poultry Supplies" under "Chickens") are among those. Raise Coturnix quail chicks by "Chickens" directions with "Guineas" refinements. Or they can be fed game-bird starter to 6 weeks, grower to adulthood, and breeder ration for breeders. The chicks will die of dehydration before they'll drink dirty, stale water.

QUAIL HOUSING: A 2 × 2 × 8-foot pen could comfortably house 20–25 quail. If such a pen is divided into eight 1-foot-wide compartments, you could keep them in individual colonies; a pair of Bobwhite; a trio of Coturnix. When birds are housed in smaller groups it's easier to identify less productive and/or disruptive ones. A water trough in the back and a feed trough in the front is considered ideal. A wire floor allows droppings to fall through. If the floor is slightly tilted to one side, it allows the eggs to roll gently out of the pen to an outside gathering place—which keeps them clean and makes them easy to get.

USING QUAIL MEAT AND EGGS: The young birds are fine eating, either roasted whole (for ½ hour), halved and broiled, or substituted in any squab (young pigeon) recipe.

The eggs are a delicacy in the pickled form. Butcher at 6–14 weeks of age. (See "Pigeons and Doves" for directions on the slaughter of small birds.) Coturnix eggs are said to be "rich, mellow and usually served fried, poached, boiled, or pickled, are delightful decoratives in salad dishes, and make interesting appetizers and hors d'oeuvres." That information was from Fred Frey, Missoula, MT. He also wrote, "Their meat is all dark, no white meat on the breast. Recipes include browning in a heavy fry pan followed by 45 minutes of baking. Some include sauces or baking along with a dressing. Very good if not allowed to dry out, which a small bird like this can easily do."

Peafowl

If you join the United Peafowl Association (US $25, Canada $30, others $35 per year), you'll get the bimonthly *Peafowl Today*; Dennis Erdman, Treasurer; 570-425-3364; PO Box 24, Klingerstown, PA 17941; **derdman@ruralife.net**; **www.peafowl.org.** Bill and Monte Haney offer 30+ varieties of peafowl: Box 612, Angelton, TX 77516; 409-848-0407 or 409-849-7464; 409-239-1931. Visitors by appointment only. Roughwood Aviaries offers 17 kinds of peafowl and is "Home of the Purple Peafowl": PO Box 71, Austin, IN 47102; 812-752-2799; **ln@scottsburg.com.** Bayou Bird Farm has seven varieties: 846 Elsie Dr., Princeton, LA 71067; 318-949-2294. There's more info in *Keeping Peafowl* by James Blake. D. C. Townsend offers more info on raising peafowl at **www.voy.com/28388/1151.html.**

PIGEONS AND DOVES

Both pigeons and doves are technically members of the pigeon tribe, but doves are smaller. There are many varieties of pigeons that vary considerably in size, color, and weight. Most pigeons are raised for meat because they grow so fast. In fact, during the 1930s depression, pigeons were the primary source of meat for many families. All of the pigeon and dove varieties are monogamous, raise young called squabs, and feed them "pigeon milk." Pigeon milk is an interesting substance that is secreted by the lining of the parents' (both sexes!) crop. The milk is rich in protein and fat and the parents pump it out of their mouths into those of the squabs. Caged pigeons must be confined as permanent pairs, but only a few pairs can produce enough squabs to vary your menu. You can keep them in wire cages or in ground runs.

BREEDS: Pigeons have been domesticated for thousands of years. There are squab recipes dating back to the Romans. There are many types and colors of pigeons to choose from. When you purchase your starting pair, be careful to distinguish between the squabbing breeds and the exhibition breeds—they are very different. The exhibition types don't raise as many squabs, their squabs are not as large, and they have a longer molting season and fewer squabs in the winter. The Runt (a breed unchanged since Roman times), White King, Giant Homer, and Mondaines are the premier squabbing breeds. They are big and healthy, and require only casual attention. To buy birds, consider Dynamite Lofts, which offers rollers and spinners: 631-395-3249; PO Box 167, Shirley, NY 11967. Herb Schull offers 19 breeds of pigeons: W8744 Park St., Pembine, WI 54156. James M. Feasel offers several breeds: 419-639-2935; 2373 County Rd. 181, Clyde, OH 43410; **jfeasel@glis.cc.**

PIGEONS IN PRINT: *Making Pigeons Pay: A Manual of Practical Information on the Management, Selection, Breeding, Feeding and Marketing of Pigeons* by Wendell Mitchell Levi (1946) is a classic on the subject. Also try *Pigeons* by B. Hunt and B. Waldman (Prentice Hall, 1973); *Doves and Dovecotes* by Peter and Jean Hansell (Millstream Books, 1988); *Raising Turkeys, Ducks, Geese, Pigeons and Guineas* by Cynthia Haynes

Join the American Dove Association ($20/yr) and get their bimonthly *DoveLine* newsletter with free classified ads for members, dove show info, and membership directory: ADA Sec., Kathy Hildreth; 7775-15 Montgomery Rd., Cincinnati, OH 45236; **info@doveline.com; www.dove line.com.**

Feathered World is the U.K. pigeon paper: phone 01772-250246; fax 01772-562569; Winckley Publishing, 5 Winckley St., Preston, PR1 2AA, ENGLAND; **feathered. world@winckley.u-net.com.**

PIGEONS GONE WILD: Pigeons bought to be pets or food animals will go wild, if they are neglected—or encouraged to be independent. If a pair move out of your cage, you'll have pigeons in your chicken house, pigeons in your barn loft, pigeons in your garage, pigeons in your machine shed. You can pat yourself on the back because the pigeons are foraging and making it quite well on food they steal from your other animals and neighbors. But if they are roosting over your car, you will have a fresh set of droppings on the hood every morning.

They will turn every building they sleep and nest in into a chicken house full of smelly droppings—"guano." They reproduce really effectively: in a few years your homestead may have more pigeons than are welcome. Cities are famous for their downtown pigeons, which is exactly the same situation, only a public problem rather than a private one.

Dealing with the Independents. If you get pigeons where you don't want them, you'll have to wrestle with the situation until they are all dead or back where they are supposed to be living. The adults can be caught, with effort, in traps. But it's not an easy matter to harvest squabs from the kind of places pigeons choose for their nests. (Best done in the dark with a flashlight and a bag to plop them into. Don't break your neck, leg, etc.) You can always invite your friends in for a shotgun hunt, if you live isolated in the country. Any pigeons are edible, but the old ones, like all old poultry, are only stew birds. Moral of that story: keep them in their cages.

Free-ranging Pigeons. These roam to eat, but come home to roost. There are 2 very big arguments for their freedom. One is monetary: free pigeons will find much of their own food, yet come back home to roost, and you can still collect the squabs. (Independent pigeons will raise only about 5 squabs per year.) The other has to do with time: free pigeons will subsist with only quite casual attention. So free-roaming pigeons are worth considering. When times are tough, it's hard to argue with a proposition like that. With luck, and occasional forceful management, you can insist that your pigeons live where you prefer them to, meaning a place where you can collect the guano, and where it will be wanted (in your pigeon loft) rather than on walks and roofs. Pigeon guano, like all poultry manure, is exceptionally good garden fertilizer.

Feed. To keep roaming pigeons coming back home, you feed them. They are generous about what they will eat and gratefully return home for—whole wheat, alfalfa leaves, or vegetables. They also like corn and peas. Purchase some grit specifically made for pigeons. Such foraging pigeons find insects and gather spilled feed from the pens of other animals. Confined pigeons are not efficient feed-to-meat converters. A breeding pair can consume 100 lb. of grain in the time it takes to produce 10–12 squabs. But if you do keep confined pigeons, feed them twice daily with a commercial pigeon ration or a high-protein diet, heavy on the grain and legumes side, together with grit and salt—and vitamin D (cod liver oil) every 2 weeks if they're getting inadequate sunshine. Temporarily confined pigeons have also done well on a combination of grains and legumes. Be sure all feed is dry and free of mold. Pigeons need plenty of clean water, both to drink and to bathe in.

Shelter. Free-roaming pigeons will appreciate a small home with at least enough room for nesting and eating your offerings. It can be like the shelter for confined pigeons, only with an outside landing perch next to a doorway for them to enter and leave. Their dwelling should be designed so that cats and other predators cannot enter. Build it so you can keep their loft dry and well ventilated. In cold weather your pigeons will need some extra warmth to keep their quarters above freezing, since they will still be incubating eggs or raising squabs. Confined pigeons need more room than you might think—they're not like Coturnix quail in this respect. A pair of pigeons will appreciate a dovecote (pigeon house) at least 4 feet square in floor area, about 2 feet high, with a chicken-wire partition to make 2 apartments. Provide a window for the front side of the dovecote, which you should place to get maximum sunlight. If you have the space, a 10 × 15 × 7-foot flying pen would be an ideal completion of the arrangement. Clean out the guano once a month. Provide a large pan of water for bathing as well as for drinking.

THE NEST: Each pair needs a nest. Use an old-time wooden orange crate sitting on the floor of their room. Some pairs will maintain 2 nests, 1 with newly laid eggs and 1 with still growing squabs, which is why the dovecote needs 2 apartments. Provide straw, pine needles, or other fibers for nest-building material.

Getting a New Pair Settled In. You'll probably start by buying a pair or two of pigeons from a poultry dealer or a nearby pigeon owner. At least, you hope you have a pair.

Pigeons are difficult to sex accurately, even by experts, especially when the birds are young. Be sure they are healthy. Swellings on the necks or near their mouths are probably canker disease. Have their shelter ready before you bring them home. Let them loose in it. Keep them there for 3 weeks. It must be a place where they can see out, if you intend to let them loose eventually and want them coming back. Feed them well. At the end of the 3 weeks, if you want them to be free, open the door to their flight deck, give them a little grain or other food every day, and that's all there is to it.

Domestic Relations. Sexing some breeds of pigeons is very difficult. Males are a trifle larger, act more aggressive, coo more actively at other pigeons, and may at the same time "dance" (strut and turn completely around). Males will fight other males. The male pigeon chooses the nest site, chooses his mate, and nudges her to his nest. Young pigeons first take a mate at 6 months. If you see a bird mounted momentarily on the back of another, you have a pair. At night, pairs roost side by side. Pigeons mate for life, but if widowed or divorced by humans, a pigeon will accept a new mate. The time to mate a pair is during the molting season, between February and July. Place the new cock next to the hen, but divide them in the center with chicken wire. The male will court his lady, billing and cooing in classical dove style. He also proves his practical abilities by feeding her partly digested grain. If she accepts, you can take out the partition and consider them a pair.

On the Nest. About a week after the molt is over, the hen will lay an egg, then another in a day or so. If the female lays more than 2 eggs, remove the extras. Two healthy squabs are all that can be expected at one time from a pigeon family. Once both eggs are laid, the pigeons will incubate them—both parents sitting in shifts on the eggs. Usually the female is sitting on the eggs from about 3pm, through the night, on until about 10am the next morning. Then the male takes over until afternoon when the female is back on. That's one way to sex your pigeons. The one on the nest at noon is probably the male. The one on the nest in the evening is probably the female.

Incubating Pigeon Eggs. To incubate pigeon eggs, allow 17 or 18 days to hatch. Use a forced-air temperature of 99.5°F; the temperature the last 3 days of incubation can be 99°F. Use still-air temperature of 101–101.5°F and wet-bulb humidity of 85. Do not turn the eggs after 15 days, and raise humidity during the last 3 days to 90–94.

Pigeon Parenthood. The eggs will hatch usually within a few hours of each other. The adults will do all the work of caring for the young, but you should make sure they have what they need. When a pair of squabs are about 3 weeks old, a good hen will begin laying more eggs. When the adult birds begin to incubate the new eggs, it is imperative that you remove their fledgling squabs to your table or deep freeze. Squabbing breeds have been developed with this expectation in mind. The squabs are very dependent on and demanding of the parents; it is too difficult for the adult pigeons to try to incubate eggs and care for squabs at the same time. But some, less prolific, pairs will wait 6 weeks to lay more eggs. If you are not rushed by the presence of new eggs, take the squabs when they're feathered out under the wings; they'll be about 4½ weeks old. You can slaughter then or feed them out to 6 weeks old and then slaughter. Your breeding pair will live to be about 7 years old, laying all the while.

Lice. Infestations of lice can be dealt with by adding small amounts (not more than 1 T. per 2½ gal. water) of sodium fluoride to the pigeons' bathing water.

How to Kill, Pick, and Clean a Pigeon

Squab size is anywhere from 14 to 28 oz. Most breeds will attain this size in 25–35 days. Break the neck with a sharp, twisting pull. Cut off the head, hang by the feet, and let bleed. Or place the bird on a chopping block and sever its head with a very sharp knife. Now scald and pluck away the feathers (see directions in the "Chickens" section), or skin the bird. To skin a small bird, you tear open the breast skin and then pull skin together with its feathers upward and outward. Pull the skin off over wings, legs and back. To clean the bird, see instructions under "Chickens." The poultry scissors method is easiest with small birds.

COOKING PIGEON: Preparing squab shouldn't be confused with preparing gone-wild pigeons captured in the field, forest, or your barn. Exercise results in dark meat and the gamy flavor of wild things—which is not necessarily distasteful. But squab, since it has never done anything but sit and swallow, has pale meat and a mild taste. It will weigh ¾–1 lb. Squabs can be fried, roasted, or broiled. Older birds can be pot roasted, made into the traditional pie, or stewed.

☙ *BROILED SQUAB Split the bird and flatten the resulting pieces. Rub them with butter, and sprinkle on salt and pepper. Place them on the broiler, breast side to heat. Serve each half-bird on a thick slice of buttered, toasted homemade bread with a sauce poured over—either gravy or heated condensed mushroom soup.*

☙ *PIGEONS ROASTED IN GRAPE LEAVES Brush the birds inside and out with melted butter and dust lightly with salt and pepper. Wrap each bird tightly and thoroughly in grape leaves—2 should do the job. Place the wrapped birds side by side in a baking dish, about 1 bird for each person you are feeding. Bake at 350°F until they are cooked through and tender. To serve, remove and discard the grape leaves. Make a sauce with the pan drippings, 2 T. butter, and the juice of a lemon, mix well, and then pour it over the birds on their serving platter.*

☙ *TRADITIONAL PIGEON POT PIE Stuff birds (4 serves an average-sized family) with the stuffing of your choice (see recipes in Chapter 4). Sew the cavity shut with a needle and thread. Brown birds in butter. Place them in some sort of covered baking dish or pan. Add several onions, large carrot chunks, and whole potatoes—as many as your container will comfortably hold and your family can be expected to eat. Add 2 c. hot water, cover tightly, and bake at 325°F until the meat is tender (about 1½ hours). Cook giblets (not liver) separately. When giblets are tender, cut into small pieces and add them to the pot pie. When the pot pie is almost ready to serve, take out the meat and vegetables, and thicken the remaining liquid by adding 3 T. flour that has been premixed with ½ c. cold water. When your gravy has thickened, pour it back over the birds and vegetables and serve—or serve the gravy separately.*

ROAST SQUAB *Stuff the bird's whole cavity with the poultry stuffing of your choice. Rub the outside of the bird with celery salt and pepper. Place in roaster, cover, and bake at 400°F for 45–60 minutes. During roasting, frequently baste the bird with drippings. At the halfway point, turn so that both sides will have a chance to brown.*

I've been doing fairs every weekend this fall, sitting behind my card table laden with copies of my book, working hard on this new edition while waiting for customers for the older one. People who don't know me are skeptical, hesitant when they see my hand-lettered, scavenged-cardboard sign, and multicolored, ringbound books with unprinted green cardboard covers.

Couldn't be worth much, they reason, a homemade book.

If they're curious enough to give me eye contact, I hand them the one-sheet brochure. Maybe a person pauses long enough to leaf through a sample copy. Perhaps he or she even buys one and carries it away—the expression on his or her face showing surprise at its weight. I watch the person going and I have to chuckle. Maybe I'll be sitting here years later and we'll meet again.

There's such a big difference between the new readers and the old ones. The old ones notice my table, creep up, and study the situation and me. Maybe they begin, "I have this book. . ." talking so because they doubt that the dumpy, aging woman behind the table could possibly be the Carla they had imagined—so rumpled (from sleeping in the car) . . . and where are all her little kids? (My kids are too grown-up now for tagging along with me to fairs. They're living with their own families, or off at college, or have their own weekend plans.) Eventually she, or he, hesitantly asks, "Are you . . . Could you be . . . ?"

I say, "Yes, I'm Carla."

Or maybe they are able to recognize the person in the old photos of a younger me, now concealed behind aging flesh. Some people do. They greet me with a shout of acclamation, rushing up eagerly to tell how they got their first copy of the book, and their land, and what they learned to do on it, and what happened then. Often they buy the new edition and ask me to autograph it, or they go home and get their old one for that purpose.

I think of this book's readers as "my people." They're my readers, at least, the people who live my (our) dream in all its tawdry chicken-plucking day-in-and-day-out fine print. They're the people I've worked my writer's lifetime to serve. I want to touch these precious, truly beloved readers—real beside me at last. So we clasp hands across the table. Or, if they look like huggable sorts, I come around the table and put out my arms, and we hug each other with genuine feelings of love. I know that a particular reader is someone who already knows me well and cares about me. She or he's the person I've worked so long and hard to serve, visualized in my mind's eye, talked to as I wrote and wrote and wrote this book over the lonely days, months, and years.

Those meetings with loving readers are always a beautiful experience—my reward! Then I know it's all been worth it. And I'm again astonished, and humbled, to discover that a mere book can mean so much to people. The job of writing is indeed a special one. And the work truly is greater than the workman!

An extraordinary encounter of that kind happened one unforgettable day a couple years ago at the Missoula (Montana) County Fair. That time I did have several children with me, but they were all off watching the pig races. A couple came in the door of the Culinary Arts Building, where I'd just wound up a chicken-butchering demonstration. They were carrying a copy of the book, holding it together, out in front of them. They were both silently crying, unashamed, walking slowly toward me.

The audience for my chicken-butchering lesson had been very small. There'd been an article in the newspaper that I was at the fair, and the demo was in the fair schedule, but it obviously didn't hold nearly the attraction of the pig races. Just as well. It was embarrassing to realize that most of the people I was talking to knew more about chicken butchering than I did. But there were also a few genuine novices there, for whom I was so grateful. They were the ones I'd hoped to help when I put the event on my program. I knew it wouldn't be fun, but I'd been determined to do it. I knew nobody but me would ever have the gall to teach a chicken-butchering class. And that's among the things people tell me they most often have to do for the first time, depending only on what it says in the book.

Before it started, while my audience waited inside, I had to remove the poor "subject" from its wire carrying cage and dispatch it out back of the building with a few of the "students" observing. As I had arrived in what I imagined would be a proper alley, I observed to my horror there were hundreds of dressed-up fair attendees strolling by the site. And the knife I'd been provided turned out to be so dull it was a considerable achievement merely to draw blood, to say nothing of managing an elegant and humane execution of the bird. I was also trying desperately to keep my bird's head *way* down in the 5-gallon bucket I had available, so it wouldn't escape to do a flopping, blood-splattering extravaganza before all those noncomprehending and curious eyes. That achievement by the bird would probably have gained it the sweet revenge of landing me either in jail or in an asylum.

Well, I did finally manage to get the job done and brought my headless bird back into the exhibition hall. There I demonstrated its immersion in scalding water, picked off its feathers, singed away the remaining hairs, and finally demonstrated how to cut it into frying pieces. I felt so relieved when it was all over. I sat chatting with some of the people who'd come to watch, autographing books, answering a few last questions about the fine points of chicken butchering.

That was when I saw the couple come in the door and head straight for me, bringing their beat-up old book for an autograph. They hadn't bothered dressing up, or maybe they didn't have any better clothes. They slowly approached, eyes fixed on me. I stepped away from the people I'd been talking to and waited until at last the middle-aged couple stood before me. They were a decade or two younger than I, but still gray and dusty, shabby, holding that frayed green-covered book out toward me as if it were their ticket to enter—as if it were something so precious to them. The tattered book was darkened by years of . . . Was it smoke from a wood cookstove in a small, poorly ventilated cabin? Did their lungs look like that inside? I wondered.

I smelled dope. They were both just reeking of marijuana. They were both looking at me, silently crying, tears running furrows of wetness down their dusty cheeks. What to do?

Like me, I thought, they were once so young and handsome, so full of hopeful dreams. Looking at them, I already knew the story: how they'd left a big city together years ago when they were young and moved to some version of the rural outback with such an optimistic, beautiful vision. How they'd struggled, worked, raised food, raised children, been scorned by some of their neighbors and their kids' teachers—and finally, perhaps, even by their kids. But they never gave up. And they still did have their acres—I hoped—and each other, obviously. And that beat-up, much-used old book.

Well, they were definitely more "my people," aroma and all, than those who sometimes show up—real-estate agent types, dressed to the nines, beaming at me, able to buy several more books to take with them, tickled pink with my role in their prosperity and, clearly, lifetime straight.

The couple stood crying before me.

I felt a sudden crushing emotion of shame. They'd taken it all literally, I thought. They actually went out and tried to live it—all of it. They stayed with it, never wised up, never went back to town as so many of the others had—others who bought the book and wrote me a Hooray-Carla-we're-back-to-the-land letter, but later—a year or two, or five—the book was in their garage sale. They were outta there.

I felt so guilty, so sorry for this couple. I started crying too, looking in their eyes and knowing all that, all the suffering they'd gone through because of keeping so loyal to the Dream. Always raising and butchering the dang chickens themselves instead of buying them ready-to-fry at the supermarket.

Should I be punished for articulating and promoting so hard, so costly, a lifestyle? Maybe I should be horse-whipped, tarred-and-feathered, dragged forever through a field of organic mud behind a stubborn mule in just retribution for setting their feet on that more rural path. How their parents who, years ago, must have planned an easier, more prosperous, more respectable life for them, must have been disappointed. Their parents probably hated me. I felt so guilty.

But I took a step toward them, toward the beauty inside them that radiated from under the shabby cloth, the aging skin, the trappings of poverty, the smell of burnt grass. Then they took the last step forward toward me. We, all three, put our arms around each other, and cried and cried. We cried together with the bittersweet intensity of summing up a life's meaning in a moment: mine as writer, theirs as readers. We were three people made one through the mysterious magic of a stack of printed and bound sheets of paper. We were so close, and it was so beautiful.

After a moment, whatever it was we were doing was done. The tension broke. Our wordless solemnity and tears suddenly turned to easy chatter and laughter, the way people act when they're coming out of church after services. Then they told me their story. Sure enough, it was all just as I had figured—except they didn't want me to feel guilty. They were grateful for the vision and the guidance I'd given them!

Then the woman confided that she wanted to be a writer like me and asked my advice. I gave my blessing and what wisdom I could, for that's another hard path.

I autographed their book. I gave them the latest edition (they couldn't afford to buy it) and was promised some home-grown food in trade (which they later sent to me). Eventually it all wound down, and they left. But I'll never forget that day . . . that meeting . . . them. They left me a gift of canned jam and a searing emotional memory I'll never forget and never escape. Sometimes it's scary being that involved in people's lives.

Five years later, I see the woman's articles in homestead-genre magazines quite often. It makes me happy and proud for her. She keeps getting better. She'll be doing her own book someday, I reckon.

CHAPTER TEN

Goats, Cows & Home Dairying

MILK A SHEEP? COW? GOAT?

GOAT FACTS OF LIFE

FENCING, HOUSING, AND FOOD

FACTORS IN CHOOSING YOUR CATTLE BREED

COW PSYCHOLOGY AND SENSES

SECRETS OF DAIRY COW FEEDING

BUYING A YOUNG CALF

COW BUTCHERING

MILKING PROBLEMS AND PROBLEM MILKERS

BOOKS FOR CHEESEMAKERS

BUTTER CHURN TYPES

GOATS, COWS & HOME DAIRYING CONTENTS

10 | Goats, Cows & Home Dairying

INTRODUCTION

This chapter is dedicated to the discriminating woman who would rather own . . . a cow or a goat!

September 1993. Almost done with the ninth edition. I am amazed at the sophisticated and widespread knowledge that exists these days among home-dairying people. Once, perhaps, I had a lot to offer here. I'm not so sure any more, but I've done my best to catch up on things and to update this section while staying within my time and space limitations. There are so many good books written about this area, so many opportunities for education and self-education, and so many dedicated dairy extension agents with information to offer. This chapter can now be thought of only as a place to begin. (Actually, the same can be said of every chapter in this book.) My hope is that I can still be of use—by providing a little information on just about everything and leads about where to find more.

Marietta, the shorthorn cow, got mastitis Christmas Eve. So from then until now [April 1974], we had no milking cow. We finally squeezed out enough money—$350—to buy a Jersey carrying her third calf, due to calve in August. She was number 108. I had a notion I'd go out and milk her for the first time and tell about the experience for the introduction of this chapter. I figured it would really be rapturous and poetical.

Well, that morning I couldn't get out the door without an entourage of Becca, 4, Luke, 2, and Baby Sara, 11 months. And for some reason they were all in bad moods and Sara was crying more on than off. We arrived at the barn accompanied by our dog, Thor, who not only chases chickens but also thinks he must impress milk cows with his importance. A cast of about 30 chickens were with us, too, pursuing the grain can I was holding, figuring on sharing the cow's feed.

Number 108 apparently had never been in the presence of whining children, a barking dog, or cackling, crowing, thieving chickens. She

wouldn't move a foot when I tried to chase her, and she turned out to have a solid distaste for stanchions. Fifteen minutes later I was squatting in the middle of the barn holding crying Sara with one arm, trying to milk with the other, and admonishing the children and Thor by turns to be quiet. The chickens were in the manger eating the cow's grain. At that moment Dolly yelled from the house that I

was wanted on the telephone, and I thanked God for mercifully giving me a release from my suffering.

When I returned to the barn after the phone call, I was alone because the baby was asleep in her crib and the other children were happily occupied elsewhere. The chickens had their tummies full of the cow's grain, so they were off looking for something more exciting—fat bugs perhaps. And I'd locked the dog in the house. By the time the milking was over, number 108 had developed such an affection for me that she followed me back to the house and walked around it for the next 2 hours, mooing longingly.

The homesteading literature is somewhat slanted toward goats. Goats are small, and they are playful, mischievous, and fun. But I've had experience with both cows and goats and let me tell you—cows may not jump around, but still water runs deep, and they sure enough have an emotional life. This morning I was getting ready to milk number 108, now called Nelly. I've submitted to her disinclination for stanchions and discovered it a blessing. I finally realized that I couldn't

drive her anyplace because her notion is to follow me, and if I get behind her she just stands there. There's always a period of adjustment when a new animal joins your family. A cow has a different mentality from a goat. Cows are very steady animals. Once a cow gets a notion of how things are supposed to be, that's the way she's going to proceed, and it's unreal for any mere human to try convincing her otherwise. But if you learn to yield a little to a milk cow's preferences, she can be really loving and giving in her own way.

So now I gather up the milk bucket. I use a plastic bucket because it's so much quieter—doesn't rattle and ping and startle the animals or me out of our reveries. And I fill a jar or pitcher part way with warm water and put a rag in it, for udder-washing and seduction. Then I go directly from the house through the gate into the field. Nelly sees me and comes right away. It's not good for milk cows to run. My father drilled that into me—never, never run a milk cow. Nelly used to run to me when she saw me, but that was when she was new and so nervous. When a 700-lb. cow runs up to you, that's too much love. You'd really rather she walked up—just in case her brakes slip. But now as soon as Nelly sees me she starts coming, following me to wherever I decide to stop. That will be a flat spot inside the barn or in the field, depending on the weather. If I bring grain and the chickens follow, Nelly starts eating the grain along with the chickens. She's used to them now. She has a much bigger mouth than they do, so they don't really get away with that much. I take my bucket and go to the rear and start milking.

It's so nice out in the sunshine. The children may be near, and the dog too, but Nelly is used to them now. Nelly, being a Jersey, isn't very high off the ground. I can even sit on the ground to milk. She's very careful not to move around while I'm milking. Instinct tells her she must be still. Her whole psychology is such a beautiful mixture of inborn wisdom about how she will take care of me (or a calf) and how I will take care of her (she's descended from millennia of "domesticated" human companions) that it's virtually a spiritual experience being near her. Her belly is hanging low because she's full of calf again. I think any animal—whether it be a goat, cow, sheep, reindeer, or yak—that goes through being pregnant, bearing young, and then using her own body to make food, enough food for her baby and mine too, deserves a lot of respect and affection. When I started writing this book I had goats. Now I have cows. They're both wonderful.

Dairying

SELLING DAIRY PRODUCTS: There's a big difference between home-dairying and dairying in order to sell your products. Even in places where milk can be sold raw, licensing is required, and the nannies or cows must be carefully tested and kept free of brucellosis and tuberculosis. Do you have money to invest in a special outbuilding for dairying, or a cheese-making place? (You could sell stocks for financing.) Can you write a 5-year business plan? Have you studied your state's dairy laws? (In at least 21 states, for example, goat milk when retailed must be pasteurized—requiring an investment in equipment.) Have you talked to your dairy extension agent? That's somebody who's willing to explain everything, shepherd you through all the preparatory steps, guide you through the legal requirements for your building and equipment, and later regularly inspect for cleanliness and test your milk samples to be sure they don't contain bacteria or antibiotics. (Dairy production is the most heavily regulated and supervised food business there is.)

If so, then you're ready to start your dairy business. You could sell milk, cheeses, yogurt, maybe even meat and sausage products. But the more products you sell, the more start-up money you will need to build approved facilities. You'll also need a lot of marketing time and know-how—especially for selling goat's milk. Usually, the hardest part is finding the money to pay for everything you need for the start-up of a commercial operation. The easiest commercial dairy areas to get started in are cheese-making in particular, and the special services and specialty products markets in general. (For example, whole milk with cream that rises to the top and that is home-delivered in bottles is coming back in some areas.)

But to sell fresh dairy products (as opposed to processed ones), you must have the highest possible sanitary standards. Milk direct from a cow is 100°F. In a commercial dairy the milk moves through hoses directly from the cow to a plate cooler that in just a few seconds chills the milk to about 38°F. Then it probably goes to a stainless-steel tank, then to a pasteurizing unit where bacteria are killed and enzymes are neutralized. Then it is separated into skim and butterfat. Then a sophisticated system mixes butterfat in again but only in the amount right for the particular product: nonfat, 1 percent, 2 percent, etc. Then the milk is homogenized, a process that breaks big fat globs into ones so tiny they can't get together and float to the top but remain evenly distributed in the milk. Then the milk is piped to a machine and put into containers. Some dairy farms can't afford all that equipment and prefer to be part of a co-op, so they can truck the milk from their holding tanks to a center for the rest of the processing. But, one way or another, most dairies get their milk from the cow to the grocery store within 48 hours.

Dairying, like many kinds of farming, is a hard business to survive in and an easy one in which to lose your shirt. Between 1981 and 1991, the amount of money that farmers in Washington State received for milk decreased by more than 20 percent, even though the retail price of milk at the store increased 27 percent. During that period a lot of the Washington's dairy farmers left the business.

Dairy farming has changed a lot since my grandfather's day, when cows ate grass in meadows and were milked by hand. The basic trend has been to get big or lose out. Washington is one of the top dairy states and one where there are still many medium-sized herds harvesting the rich coastal mainland grasses. Here an average dairy farmer markets $350,000 worth of milk each year from an average of 210 milking cows. That same farmer also has maybe 200 more calves, to be sold for beef, and heifers not yet come to milking age. Each year, the farmer will buy $175,000 of feed, especially hay. Washington's dairy farms are small compared to the average California dairy operation, where 1,000–5,000 cows are the industry standard.

So you can see why commercial dairying tends to be a sophisticated big business, and why so many small dairies have gone under. The industry, nationwide, is increasingly dominated by mega-dairies, each with over 1,000 cows—almost always Holsteins—bred for maximum production, fed for maximum production, and living computer-monitored lives designed to wrest every possible ounce of milk out before the cow goes to the hamburger line.

They work hard for a living—the cows and the dairy farmers. And their product, milk, is a wonderful food, a high-protein food that is far, far more pure (as best I can figure it) than almost any captured-in-the-wild food. Milk is the most monitored food in the food chain! And if you have a bit of land with enough room for a couple goats or a small cow, you can have your own organic milk, butter, ice cream, etc., from animals who were fed organic foods. Because what comes out is as pure as what goes in!

DAIRY INFO AND SUPPLIES

Caprine Supply offers a huge free goat supply catalog, including cheesemaking supplies: 800-646-7736; fax 800-646-7796; 913-585-1140; Box Y, 33001 W. 83rd St., DeSoto, KS 66018; **caprinesup@aol.com; www. caprinesupply.com.**

Cheesemaking Supply Outlet: call/fax 440-968-3770; 9155 Madison Rd., Montville, OH 44064; **rmhcso@ alltell.net.**

CreamLine: This quarterly newsletter for small-scale dairy owners interested in on-farm processing also contains useful info for folks just making dairy products for family use. It's packed with hard-to-find sources for small-scale equipment, facts on pasteurization, cheese-making, packaging, etc. It profiles successful small dairies and provides recipes for dairy products. Cost is $40/2 yrs; $2 sample copy. Contact: Vicki Dunaway; call/fax 540-789-7877; PO Box 186, Willis, VA 24380; **ladybug@swva.net; www.metalab.unc.edu/creamery.** Vicki has also published *The Small Dairy Resource Book,* a 56-pg. annotated bibliography of books, periodicals, videos, etc., on farmstead dairy processing: cheese, ice cream, butter—both production and marketing—which is *first* in providing small dairy info! To order a print copy ($8), go to **www.sare.org/san/htdocs/ pubs/** or call 802-656-0484. Vicki also publishes *Home Dairy News.*

Dairy Center Inc.: PO Box 2564, Ontario, CA 91762-6690; 909-628-4784; fax 909-627-8781.

Glengarry Cheesemaking & Dairy Supply offers equipment, supplies, etc., for making cheese, including molds, ingredients, and courses: 613-525-3133; fax 613-525-3394; RR #2, Alexandria, Ontario K0C 1A0, CANADA; **morris@cnwl.igs.net; www.glengarry cheesemaking.on.ca.**

Hoegger Supply Co. offers all a goatkeeper could need, reasonably priced: 800-221-4628; fax 770-461-7334; PO Box 331, 160 Providence Rd., Fayetteville, GA 30215; **hoegger@mindspring.com; www.Hoegger goatsupply.com.**

Lehman's Hardware sells ready-made or custom goat and cow bells, each with a unique tone; milk pasteurizers; carved butter molds; milk cans; strainers; cream separators; butter churns; cheese presses; milk funnels and strainers; anti-cow kickers; milking stool, etc.: 888-438-5346; **www.lehmans.com.**

Nelson-Jameson is a "food and dairy supplier": 800-826-8302; **www.nelsonjameson.com.**

New England Cheesemaking Supply offers equipment and info to make and sell cheeses. Free catalog: 413-628-3808; fax 413-628-4061; PO Box 85, Ashfield, MA 01330; **www.cheesemaking.com.**

Small Dairy Project/Second-to-None Dairy Supplies sells and loans customers small-scale dairy equipment: 603-927-4176; HC 65, Box 45, Bradford, NH 03221; **nunsuch@conknet.com; www.nunsuch.org.**

Milk a Sheep? Cow? Goat?

If you're just getting started, your first big decision is what kind of animal to milk. Around the world not only cows and goats are milked, but also sheep, reindeer, camels, water buffalo, and others. Any dairy animal is a miracle of efficiency. Grass, vegetables, grain, water, and salt go in one end. Milk, baby animals (meat), and manure to build up your garden soil come out from various other locations. There is no waste. She can be purchased reasonably, moved from location to location—and will love you! But what kind to buy?

SHEEP: How about dairy sheep? Yes, you can milk sheep! They have wonderful milk. See Chapter 11 for more on this. Nevertheless, most home dairyers will choose a goat or cow.

GOAT OR COW? Worldwide, goats are milked more than cows. Figured by percentage of body weight, a goat is more efficient and produces much more milk than a cow. On the other hand, cows produce much more meat from

their surplus calves and can get along better on a basic pasture/hay feed. Any cow eats much more than a goat does and requires hay in quantity in winter, whereas goats can get along on less hay and quite a bit of vegetable food and brush. Cows give more milk per animal by far, and their cream can be more easily separated to be made into butter, whipping cream, or plain cream. A milk cow can be bred annually to a beef-type bull in order to have a beefy calf for eventual slaughter.

Expenses. You can keep about 5 goats to 1 milk cow as far as the expense of feeding goes. You won't have near the struggle keeping the cow out of the garden as you would with the goat. On the other hand, if 1 goat dies you haven't lost everything. Around here, a home-dairy–type Jersey could sell for $800. A Holstein would cost much more—$1,000 for an average dairy-quality Holstein, $1,800 for a good cow that's bred-back to a good bull. If you get offered a cow for $500 or less, it's somebody's cull, giving maybe 2 gal. per day. The least expensive cow would be a first-freshening ("to freshen" means to calve and give milk) heifer, but if it's your first time, you might be best off starting with a cow with some experience.

The best cow is one that isn't too old and is already re-bred and trained to milk. How much milk should she give? Twenty years ago when I was first writing this book, a cow who gave 6 gal. per day was super. Dairies now have cows that are giving 12 or 13 gal. per day. That's how much dairy cows have been selected upward. But these super Holsteins are more prone to mastitis now than they used to be. And that's a ridiculous amount of milk for a family cow unless you're going to raise other animals on the surplus. Dairies usually sell off a cow as a cull when she gets down to 4 or 5 gal., and that's still a lot of milk for a family. One of the small, old-time home-dairy breeds, like a Jersey, may be more what you want. It's simplest for you if she's bred and in at least her second lactation.

Incidentally, by the time you get a cow or goat home, through the period of adjustment, and allow for exaggerations on the part of the seller, she may turn out to be giving a little more than half what you were promised. Which still can be a lot of milk.

Dairy-type bull calves now sell for $140–$185, a beef-type calf for $185–$250. If you bought from the dairy itself, you might get one for $95–$110. It's hard to find a young heifer calf for sale. People hang on to them. A cow grows up to weigh between 700 and 1,500 lb., depending on the breed. A bull can weigh around 3,000 lb. That's a lot of meat compared to a goat.

The price of goats is much less than that of cows, but is still much more than it was 25 years ago. Back then, a non-purebred milking nanny changed hands for as little as $5, when you could get somebody to take one. Now a registered show-type milking nanny might sell for $100–$150, a grade milker for $70–$75, a young grade doe for $35–$65. Kids back then were generally given away. Now at the livestock auction, a 2- or 3-month-old buck may sell for meat for $25, a doe for $35. A year-old goat for butcher might bring $75–$110 from the ethnic meat buyers.

But livestock prices are volatile, responding mercilessly to the laws of supply and demand. I've lived long enough to have seen them take amazing crashes several times. I remember one such time—February 1, 1974—when the bottom dropped out of the beef market, and beef-type bull calves were selling for under $10, others up to $35. When prices are like that, what a great time to invest in some animals for yourself! Milk cow prices hold fairly steady if the cows are in good health and sold privately. But when sold in the livestock auction ring, they are affected by the great fluctuations in beef cow prices and sell for per-pound prices, which can be low.

The Land Factor. Whether you have a cow or a milk goat (or goats) is a very individual matter and depends a lot on what kind of land you have, as well as on how much money you have to get started and your personal preferences. Some people get really hot arguing one against the other. I started out with goats because I started out poverty-stricken on 3 acres and had a chance to get the goats at $5 a head. I've had as many as 20 at one time.

If you have a brushy cliff behind your house and just enough flat land for a vegetable garden, I'd say get a goat—it will thrive. If you are planning to homestead in dense timber where there is no open, grassy meadow, don't buy a cow. You'd have to buy hay year-round for her because you wouldn't have enough grass. Get goats. Their instinctive feeding habits are like those of a deer. By preference they eat twigs instead of grass, so they'll be delighted with a forest and will help make a clearing for you. They like to eat the young tips of trees and bushes—just the way you'd prune—but beware: they don't know when enough is enough and can kill the plant or tree. That's fine if you're afflicted with lots of dense brush. They'll keep it back. But protect your orchard!

If you have a nice alfalfa pasture and plenty of capital and you'd like to raise baby calves and pigs and lots of chickens, a cow would be very sensible. If you get a cow, you raise calves and dine on beef-steak instead of goat-burger. But how much land for a cow? You need at least 1 well-watered, good green acre for her grazing, either all at once or divided for rotation. Another lush acre will grow her winter feed, since an acre can grow almost 2 tons of hay and that's how much winter hay she'll need. With luck you can also graze her on her hay field—maybe the month of March before it seriously gets going, and then after your last hay cutting is off in August and September. A further eighth of an acre of garden will grow lots of winter veggies for her.

Goat's Milk vs. Cow's Milk. Like I said, I think any animal that shares the fruit of its body with us, be it milk or meat, is wonderful. I think it's disrespectful to cows to get too prejudiced toward goats. And by the time you're done reading this dairy section, you'll see that I love goats, too, just as much as any confirmed goat-lover does. The fact is that milk is milk, and it's food, and that's the important thing.

A poor goat in her first lactation may give only a couple of cups a day. A prime milk goat may give as much as 5 quarts a day. A small Jersey cow will give 2–4 gallons a day. Really fresh goat's milk tastes very like cow's milk. It does develop a strong taste more rapidly after that, but there's no need to drink old goat's milk unless you're trying to get cream to rise to the top of it. In that case you need to let it rest a few days. Don't judge fresh goat's milk by canned goat's milk. That stuff is pretty awful.

Goat's milk is prehomogenized like store milk, although given enough time some cream will finally rise to the top. You can skim it off with a dipper and have it on something for a real treat. Cow's milk is fun because the cream rises fast and clearly to the top, so you just skim it

off and there's your whipping cream and cream for butter-making and cream to go in a pitcher on the table to pour over the strawberries. Some people struggle to make butter from goat's milk. I did, too, and made it. But I think the most sensible thing, if you're going to use goat's milk, is to just plan the menu around whole milk the same way you would if you were living on reconstituted powdered milk and you couldn't afford to buy cream or butter—only this way is so much better because the cream and butter is there—you're eating it—it's just not separated out so you can see it.

GOATS

You can raise goats for fun, for milk and/or meat, or to make a living. Here are some commercial options for goat keepers:

1. Use nanny goats to raise calves (25 goats can raise their own offspring plus 25 to 35 calves).
2. Sell milk from a goat dairy (you need pasteurization and bottling equipment, a big market reasonably nearby, and a willingness to work hard and constantly). You can get extra income by selling kids for meat at Easter time. There are hundreds of prospering 50–150-doe goat dairies in the United States, even some 500–900-doe dairies.
3. Manufacture goat cheeses: blue, caerphilly, camembert, cheddar, chevre, feta, semi-aged, soft-ripened, shepherd's, tomme, and capriano are all classic goat cheeses.
4. Sell fresh goat's milk curd (used in sauces and for making cheese—in 1988 goat curd sold in New York City for $6.98/lb.), and goat yogurt (sells for more than regular cow yogurt).
5. Sell goats for meat (to the fancy restaurant trade) and for fine leather. This works well for people with a going grassland operation of sheep and/or cattle because meat (and/or Angora) goats eat some plants that sheep and cattle don't, and the three animals pasture well together.
6. Raise goats for fiber—angora or cashmere. In 1988 mohair sold for $1.75 to $7.25/lb. (depending on the quality). That same year, cashmere "down" sold for from $39.68 to $77.93/kg. Fiber-goat raising comes under the Wool Act.
7. Train wethers (castrated male sheep) to pull, either alone or in a team. One can pull a small cultivator or a light wagon loaded up to 2 times his weight. He should be taught to lead at 2 months, be halter-broken by 6, harness-broken by 8, pulling loads by 10. Use

verbal commands as with oxen. Dairy-goat suppliers sell goat harnesses and carts.

GOAT INFO: *Raising Goats for Milk and Meat,* by Rosalee Sinn, is available from Heifer International: 1015 Louisiana St., Little Rock, AR 72202: 800-422-0474: **www.heifer.org**. This spiral-bound training manual has been used worldwide to teach goat care. It's suitable for 4-H. You might also read *Practical Goatkeeping* by Jill and John Halliday (1990); and *Raising Milk Goats Successfully* by Gail Luttmann (1986). Older classics are *Raising Milk Goats the Modern Way* by Jerry Belanger; *The Goat Owner's Scrap Book* by Dr. C. E. Leach; *Management and Diseases of Dairy Goats* by Samuel Guss, DVM; and *Fundamentals of Improved Dairy Goat Management* by Robert A. Jackson, DVM, updated by Alice G. Hall. *One Day with a Goat Herd* by C. J. Stevens is good for beginners. *Your Goats* is G. Damerow's 172-pg. guide to raising and showing goats, including how to buy, raise, choose a breed and equipment, etc. *The Illustrated Standard of the Dairy Goat* by Nancy Lee Owen covers buying, breeding, showing, and milking.

English books are *All About Goats* by Lois Hetherington (1992) and *Goat Farming* by Alan Mowlem (1992). Mowlem's book covers goat keeping in developing countries and exotic/tropical goat diseases. It's available from The Smallholder Bookshop (44-1366-500466; **www.small holderbooks.co.uk**).

The Pack Goat, by John Mionczynski, explains the use of goats as pack animals. These bright, cooperative animals are good for rough trail hiking. A goat can carry a load that's 20 to 40 percent of its body weight. *Life in the Goat Lane* by Linda Fink covers shows, breeding, kidding, etc.

MAGAZINES, NEWSLETTERS, STORES, CLUBS

Alpine Haus specializes in mail-order goat and farm books: 40110 N. Hardesty Rd., Elk, WA 99009; 509-292-8191; **www.alpinehaus.com**.

American Dairy Goat Association offers a wide choice of books and videos on goats, and it's the biggest registry for the six major dairy breeds. It publishes a directory plus info handbooks and has a question-answering service: PO Box 865, Spindale, NC 28160; 828-286-3801; fax 828-287-0476; **adga@adga.org; www. adga.org**.

American Goat Society also registers main dairy and pygmy goat breeds and trains judges: 543-349-4709; PO Box 330, Broad Run, VA 20137; **office@american goatsociety.com; www.americangoatsociety.com**.

Boer Goat and Meat Goat On-Line Magazine is a busy commercial site with announcements, advertisements, a breeder's directory, and articles: **www.boergoats.com/**.

Cornell University's web info at **www.ansci.cornell.edu/ extension/marketfact1.html** advises on starting a meat goat operation. Additional info is offered at two other Cornell sites. (To access these sites use the same address, substituting "fact2" and "fact3.") They also offer an Ethnic Calendar and the Empire State Meat Goat Producers Ass'n: **www.ansci.cornell.edu/extension/ esmpga.html**.

"Cyber Goats," at **www.cybergoat.com/**, is a busy website that offers classified ads, breeder's links, auction notices, list of caprine vets, breed lists, online auctions, national breed show announcements, and links to various breed talk lists.

Dairy Goat Journal has served goat owners since 1916: 800-551-5691; fax 715-785-7414; W11564 Hwy 64, Withee, WI 54498; $21 for 6 issues/yr; $35 for 2 yrs (12 issues); **csymag@tds.net; www.dairygoat journal.com**.

Goat Droppings is a meat goat info website: "Supplemental Winter Feeding of Goats," "Meat Goat Production & Marketing Handbook," "Meat Goat Marketing in Greater New York City," "Upstate South Carolina Meat Goat Producers Newsletter," etc.: **goats.clemson.edu/**.

(The) Goat Farmer calls itself "the largest circulation goat magazine in the world," the only professional magazine dedicated to goats only, and the one magazine which takes an international overview of the goat industry, largest collection of goat articles on the web, online A–Z of goat diseases, poisonous plant list, and free entry in their breeder directory: PO Box 641, Whangarei, NEW ZEALAND; **thegoatfarmer@caprine.co.nz; www.caprine.co.nz**.

(The) Goat Magazine is an all-breed goat periodical "for the serious goat breeder as well as those with just a few goats." Topics include goat health, beginner's basics, goat nutrition, pack goats, guardian animals, reader experiences, breeder directory, and upcoming goat events. Cost is $24 for 6 issues/yr, each 72–76 pp. A sample issue costs $5: 830-789-4268; fax 830-789-0006; 2268 CR 285, Gillett, TX 78116; **editor@goat magazine.com; www.goatmagazine.com**.

Goat Rancher covers the meat goat scene: 662-569-9529; 731 Sandy Branch Rd., Sarah, MS 38665; **www.goat rancher.com**.

Homesteader's Connection is a 24-pg, newspaper-format bimonthly. It covers homesteading and simple living, featuring dairy and meat goats, small livestock, gardening, alternative energy, etc. Cost is $18/yr; sample $2: Andy Oliver; 915-653-5438; PO Box 5373, San Angelo, TX 78902; **www.homesteadersconnection.com**.

Institute for Goat Research offers courses and demonstrations: Box 730, Langston, OK 73050; 405-466-3836.

Jack & Anita Mauldin Boer Goats is a website that shares Boer goat info and some general goat info also. Articles on "Goat Birthing from Beginning to End," "State and Federal Scrapie Requirements Program," etc.: 2400 County Rd 100, Georgetown, TX 78626; **jack@jack mauldin.com; www.jackmauldin.com**.

Meat Goat Monthly News and/or *Ranch & Rural Living Magazine* ($25 for 12 issues/yr) covers meat goats, the wool and mohair industry, and goat shows: 915-655-4434; fax 915-658-8250; PO Box 2678, San Angelo, TX 76902; 915-655-4434; **info@ranchmagazine.com; www.ranchmagazine.com**.

GOAT VET RESOURCES: *Fundamentals of Improved Dairy Goat Management,* by R. A. Jackson, DVM, and Alice Hall, combines the know-how of a goat keeper with the expertise of a vet. *Goat Health Handbook* provides diagnosis/ treatment info for goat diseases. Both are available from Winrock International Institute for Agricultural Development, 38 Winrock Dr., Morrilton, AR 72110; 501-727-5435; **receptionist@winrock.org**, $8.50. *The Goatkeeper's Veterinary Book* by Peter Dunn, B.V.Sc. (an English book), and *The Management of Diseases of Dairy Goats* by Sam B. Guss, DVM, an older book on this subject, are available from Caprine Supply. You may find *Natural Goat Remedies,* by Karen Ray, also helpful: 616-621-6000; 59520 Springdale Dr., Hartford, MI 49057; **www.karenelizabethray.com.**

DIETARY SUPPLEMENTS: I deeply appreciate the nutritional supplements I take. Your hard-working dairy animals may benefit from some, too. You can buy herbal supplements, books, vitamins, minerals, colostrum, milk replacers, medications, etc., from Nutritional Research Associates (800-456-4931; Box 354, South Whitley, IN 46787) and Vita Stress (360-794-9663; 12119 Bollenbough Hill Rd., Monroe, WA 98272).

A footnote: I enjoy noting a resemblance between people and their favorite animals. (I've always had Border Collies, or a Collie/Husky cross—strictly working animals for this workaholic woman!) Is that true of the chosen milk animal also? Goat keepers do seem to produce far more books and magazines than cow keepers! Is that because goat keepers, like their inquisitive charges, are a more paper-loving (literary?), or more social and lively group? Are cow keepers, like their bovine milkers, more sedate and reserved, with less appetite for newsprint?

COURSES ON GOAT KEEPING: You can study "Dairy Goat Production #225" by correspondence. Write Independent Study, University of Guelph, Guelph, Ontario, Canada N1G 2W1. The course teaches breeding, feeding, housing, herd health, and kidding. Slides and tapes included. Incidentally, this is the best mail-order education I know of on food production skills in general. The program is managed by the Ontario Agricultural College, (519) 767-5050, fax (519) 824-9813. You can take courses just to learn or for a diploma. There are dozens of possible choices from "Making Maple Syrup" to "Greenhouse Management" to "Livestock Biology and Butchering" to "Marketing for Small Rural Enterprise." Their program combines manuals, videos, tapes, assignments, and a telephone counselor.

You can also enroll in the Dairy Goats correspondence course from Pennsylvania State University, 307 Agricultural Administration Bldg., University Park, PA 16802, for 9 lessons covering dairy-goat origins, characteristics, feeding, care and management, breeding, housing, and equipment. In-person courses and demonstrations are offered by the Institute for Goat Research, Box 730, Langston, OK 73050, (405) 466-3836; the Dairy Goat Research Facility, University of California at Davis, Animal Science Dept., Davis, CA 95616, (916) 752-6792; and also at the International Dairy Goat Research Center, Prairie View A&M University, Box 4079, Prairie View, TX 77446, (409) 857-3926, fax (409) 857-2325.

Barney Harris, Jr., Extension Dairyman at the Florida Cooperative Extension Service, 203 Dairy Science Building, University of Florida, Gainesville, FL 32611, (904) 392-1958, is eager to send people goat information. Or you could study there in the Dairy Science Dept., where he is a professor, and get a degree in dairying!

GOAT ASSOCIATIONS: There's the American Dairy Goat Association, Box 865, Spindale, NC 28160, (704) 286-3801, a registry for the 6 major dairy breeds (the biggest). It also puts out a directory plus informational handbooks and has a question-answering service. Canadians can join the Canadian Goat Society, Box 357, Fergus, Ontario, Canada N1M 3E2. If you want to research goats, try the International Dairy Goat Registry, Rt. 1, Box 265-A, Rossville, GA 30741, which registers all breeds and also offers a library and archive.

GOAT-KEEPERS' SUPPLIES: Hoegger Supply Co. has a $1 catalog that offers everything the goat keeper could possibly imagine needing. Write P.O. Box 331, Fayetteville, GA 30214, (404) 461-4129, or (ordering only) (800) 221-GOAT. There's also Caprine Supply, Box Y, DeSoto, KS 66018, (913) 585-1191.

GOAT WORDS: I've heard you shouldn't use "billy" and "nanny"—you should use "buck" and "doe" instead. But "nanny" is also commonly used and the goats don't care! I hate to hear a non-pedigreed goat called a "scrub" though. It really puts her down unnecessarily. The word "chevon" means a goat intended for meat, or goat meat itself. A "wether" is a castrated male goat. "To kid" is to give birth, when speaking of a goat.

Getting Started with Goats

HOW MANY GOATS? Let me deal in conservative figures in case your goats turn out to be average or worse. Such a goat gives about 3 qt. milk per day. You'll need 1 qt. per day to feed her kid, and more later, leaving only 1½ qt. or so for your family. Yearlings won't give even that much. They aren't as large as full-grown goats and their teats and bags are smaller. At one time I milked 2 mature nans and 2 yearlings. I got only about 1½ gal. per day, and that barely supplied the 2 nan kids that I was feeding plus our 4 children, me, and Pa. Now, as I write this section about goats, I'm milking 7 goats and that includes some really good ones. I get about 6 gal. per day. With this supply I always have plenty for the family, for making butter and cheese, and for raising 2 pigs. You really can't have too many does. You can get them to adopt a calf or a bum lamb or let them raise their own kids for meat or market crop if you don't want to bother milking them. If you feed a milk goat really well, including vegetables and grain, she'll give more milk and can be milked for as long as 2 years on one freshening. The basic rule of thumb though is that you need 1 goat per person in your family in order to have all your dairy product needs met.

COMPANIONSHIP: Goats need companionship to be happy. But it doesn't have to be another goat. A sheep, a cow, or your children can serve the purpose. Chickens can't, though. A chicken just does not have it—except to another bird. Dynah Geissal, whom I am honored to call friend, and who regularly writes for many of the best homesteader magazines, advises: "A goat is a herd animal. If she must live alone, you will become her herd. This can be fun sometimes and maddening the rest of the time. She will get along with other livestock, or even a dog, if there are no other goats, but she is happier being one of a goat herd."

By the way, Dynah generously shared her wisdom for many parts of this section on goats. You'll find that she and I don't always agree on the details, but she may be right and I wrong, and I wanted you to benefit from her experience.

WHAT AGE TO BUY? Says Dynah Geissal: "Buying a kid has some advantages: you learn while she learns, but you'll wait a long time for milk. An older doe who is past her prime, but still in good health, may be a good bet. If a goat owner shows you an older doe who has been a special favorite, a good milker, and a good mother, you may have found a goldmine. You may be inexperienced, but your older doe is not." Let me add that a yearling usually doesn't produce well, but if she has good genes, she probably will.

Your goat will give more milk each freshening up to age 6 or 7, with the years 4–6 being usually her highest production time. But with good care she'll keep freshening and milking well right on to age 10 or older.

BREEDS: I won't state a preference among the full-size dairy goat breeds. They're all wonderful. But individuals vary. There are more than 50 goat breeds (more than 200 worldwide). Visit the website at Oklahoma State U. for profiles on each one: www.ansi.okstate.edu/breeds/goats/kinder/index.htm.

MEAT GOATS: Read Sylvia Tomlinson's 1999 book, *The Meat Goats of Caston Creek,* and *Meat Goats: Their History, Management and Diseases,* by Stephanie Mitcham (a veterinary pathologist) and Allison Mitcham, a good coverage of diseases and treatments. "Meat Goats Make Money" is an audio from *The Stockman Grass Farmer:* 800-748-9808; PO Box 2300, Ridgeland, MS 39158. You'll find ATTRA's "Sustainable Goat Production: Meat Goats," at www.attra.ncat.org/attra-pub/meatgoat.html.

Boer. These stocky, muscular, meat-type goats were developed in South Africa in the '30s. They came to the U.S., by way of New Zealand, in 1993. They are most common in the Ozarks, Southwest, and Texas where they clean up brush and are marketed for butcher (best prices near Moslem holidays and in winter). International Boer Goat Ass'n (IBGA) membership info is available from Casey: 877-402-4242; PO Box 310, Bonham, TX 75418; ibga@netexas.net. Boer Goat Breeders' Ass'n of Australia offers literature and info, registration, etc.: (02) 6773-5177; fax (02) 6772-5376; c/o ABRI, Univ. of New England, Armidale, NSW 2351, AUSTRALIA; boergoat@abri.une.edu.au; boergoat-une.edu.au.

You can buy Boers from Bill and Nancy Hatton: 719-683-2556; 25945 E. Garrett Rd., Calhan, CO 80808. Or Mary Sherwood: 417-995-4691; RR 1, Box 1100, Dadeville, MO 65635; sherwoodfarms@tri-lakes.net; www.sherwoodfarms.net. Or James and Julie Mabrey: 11880 SE 975 Rd., Humansville, MO 65674; turtlerock@tri-lakes.net; www.turtlerockboergoats.com. Or Tri-Quest: 417-754-8135; 3326 S. 1st Rd, Humansville, MO 65674; triquest@tri-takes.net; www.triquestboergoats.com. Or Troy and Mary Powell; 800-817-2010; Box 168, Benjamin, TX 79505.

Kiko. This New Zealand meat goat was imported to the U.S. in 1991. Dr. An Peischel has an outstanding herd: 530-679-1420; fax 530-679-1430; PO Box 29, Rackerby, CA 95972; kiko@inreach.com; www.home.inreach.com.

Spanish. This is the goat equivalent of the beef cow, a meat rather than dairy breed. Spanish goats are tough, thrifty, and hardy. They may be kept in flocks of 350 to 400 does if you have lots of pasture and some Pyrenees dogs or equivalent to keep coyotes and wild dogs off. Available from 8-Mile Ranch, Jim Willingham, PO Box 1828, Uvalde, TX 78802-1828; 830-278-3884.

DAIRY GOATS

Alpine. Alpines come in a variety of colors and patterns. French Alpines were very good milk producers for me. Alpines are Dynah's favorite breed: "They are independent, quiet, hardy, and give large quantities of milk. They are friendly and affectionate, yet go about their business when you are not working with them." Hazel McTeer raises both Alpine and Saanen dairy goats: 1753 E. Farm Rd. 48, Springfield, MO 65803; 417-833-3790. Or Merryl Winstein, Sunnytimes Dairy Goats, PO Box 19875, St. Louis, MO 63144; rhibbs@msn.com. Or Sheradee Peyton, 4496 N. 172nd, Walkerville, MI 49459; scottpeyton@hotmail.com.

La Mancha. No ears and full size means it's a La Mancha, a great milking breed. Saanen, French Alpine, and Toggenburgs have a similar size and milk production, erect ears, and are of Swiss origin.

Nubian. Nubians are the same on size and milk production as LaMancha, but have long, drooping ears. They're from Africa and withstand heat well. They have good dairy temperament. Available from Vickie Liguori; 540-377-2530; 334 Old Providence Rd., Spottswood, VA 24476; meadobrk@cfw.com.

Oberhasli. This is a relatively new breed of full-size Swiss dairy goat. They're available from Kim Emery, PO Box 478, McEwen, TN 37101; 931-582-3134; emery@mcewen.net. Or from G'day's, 2600 Phipps Rd., Applegate, MI 48401; 313-633-9528. Or Audrey K. Hallowell, 2479 Newcomer Rd., Chambersburg, PA 17201-9397; 717-264-4786.

Saanen. These are among the largest and most popular of the Swiss breeds. Mature does weigh 135 lb. or more and stand from 30 in. at the withers. Bucks weigh from 185 lb. and are a little taller. The Saanen's hair is quite short and all white. Saanens are terrific milk producers, and also good-natured, patient, long-suffering, people-loving goats! I had one called "Angel" and it was a fitting name. Contact: National Saanen Breeders Association, Justine Gilchrist, 8555 Sypes Cyn Rd., Bozeman, MT 59715; $15 to join. More info is in *Saanen Roots,* by Allan L. Rogers (available from Caprine Supply).

Toggenburg. Toggenburgs are always some shade of brown with white markings on the face and rump. Among the goat breeds that I've had experience with, Toggenburgs far and away impressed me the most. Mine were persnickety aristocrats. It was an old Toggenburg that usually bossed the herd. Toggenburgs had very definite notions as to how I ought to handle them and were more independent than the rest, but, wow, did they ever give milk. They were also in the front line when it came to fighting coyotes. The Toggenburgs always got the most blood on their horns.

FIBER GOATS

Angora. Angora goats originated in the Himalayas. At this point I am interrupted by a polite but testy letter from writer-about-Angoras Sue Drummond, who did me the favor of stating: "I have no idea where you got your information on Angora goats, but most of it is way off base. The following is what I would suggest you print about Angoras." So, yours-truly-always-and-humbly-grateful-to-be-corrected cut out all the "off-base" stuff, and here's the word from a true expert instead! Bruised feelings aside, I'm honestly grateful anytime somebody who knows better takes the trouble to straighten me out. Now here's Sue:

"Angora goats originated in the Himalayas and have been kept for their luxurious fiber for centuries. They are white, long-haired goats that produce mohair. Angora goats are not kept for their milk. Their hair grows around one inch a month all year round. They are the most efficient producers of fiber of all animals except for a few breeds of wool sheep. Angora goats are sheared twice a year in the spring and the fall. An adult doe produces from 10 to 16 lbs. per year.

"Mohair is valued for its properties of sheen, loft or fluff, strength, fire resistance, soil resistance, and its ability to take dye brightly. Raw mohair can be processed for hand-spinning by washing and rinsing it in 140°F water using dish-washing liquid. Care must be taken not to agitate the hair too much during washing and it must not be dried in a dryer. The mohair can be carded and spun and dyed in the yarn or dyed before spinning.

"Texas is the largest producer of mohair in the world after South Africa. Texas is the home of around 2 million Angora goats. Other states such as Oklahoma, Arizona and New Mexico also have substantial Angora goat populations and Angoras are found in nearly every state in the United States.

For more info on Angoras, contact the American Angora Goat Breeder's Association: 830-683-4483; PO Box 195, Rocksprings, TX 78880. *Ranch Magazine* prints articles about Angora goats: PO Box 2678, San Angelo, TX 76902. And check out *The Complete Angora Goat* and *The Angora Goat Book & Guard Dogs,* a guide for beginning Angora goat raisers by Jean Ebeling, $26 (postpaid): 5443 CR 401, Marble Falls, TX 78654. And the Northeast Angora Goat Breeders Ass'n, Bob Ramirez, Pres.: Keldaby Farm; 413-624-3090;

12 Heath Rd., Colrain, MA 01340. Cerulean Farm offers Saanen dairy goats, Angoras, Anatolian shepherd guard dogs, and spinning equipment: PO Box 100, Harrah, OK 73045; 405-356-2612; **bluemohair@earthlink.net.**

Cashmere. These goats are another fleece type. They produce "cashmere," which is not the same thing as the mohair that angoras produce. Cashmere is a fine underdown that cashmere goats grow between the longest day in summer and the shortest day in winter. Their body hormones are triggered by shortening day-length to grow it. They shed the cashmere in the spring, unpredictably any time between January and May. You can't comb the down out until it becomes loose. If you leave combing too long, you'll lose it. The finest cashmere goats are said to be in China, but they're also grown in Turkey, Iran, Iraq, New Zealand, and Australia. Some are being imported into the United States.

Cashmere goats are available from Cashmere Goat Registry of America: 219-784-2989; 22819 Stanton Rd., Lakeville, IN 46536. Or Flying M. Manor, Sarah Mace; 920-836-2769; 3788 W. Breezewood Lane, Oshkosh, WI 54904. For more info, contact Northwest Cashmere: Carole Laughlin; 503-625-8816; 21935 SW Lebeau Rd., Sherwood, OR 97140. Or International Cashmere Co.: 614-493-2401; 614-493-2595; PO Box 845M, Piketon, OH 45661. There are three cashmere processing plants in the U.S. (eight in the world). One is the Forte Cashmere Co.: 21 Eliot St., South Natick, MA 01760; **www.Cashmere.com.** Forte prefers clean white cashmere fiber, the longer and finer the better. More info is in the *Cashmere Goat Manual,* which started as a project for the El Paso County 4-H Club. It's $10 from Jim Osborn, 3585 Spaatz Rd., Monument, CO 80132; 719-488-8860. And read *Angora Goats the Northern Way* (1988), by Susan Black Drummond; and *Angora Goat and Mohair Production* (1993), by Maurice Shelton. Or contact the Australian Cashmere Growers Association: call/fax 03-9629-2390; PO Box 380, Kellyville, NSW 2155, AUSTRALIA; **cashmere@acga.asn.au; www.cashmere.cx.**

Nigerian Dwarves. These little spotted or patterned, naturally horned, dairy goats come from West Africa. If milked, they give about ½ gal. per day. They will mate all year round and can be bred every 8–10 months. Kathy Claps wrote me: "This is a small breed, as small as the Pygmy, but has a more refined, dairy-type conformation. They are found in a great variety of colors and milk quite well for their size." The American Nigerian Dwarf Dairy Association is the national breed club: PO Box 96, Monticello, NM 87939. Or contact Penny J. Tyler: Tupence Nigerian Dwarf Goats, PO Box 799, Allyn, WA 98524; 360-275-4236; **tupence@hctc.com.**

Pygmy. An adult goat that never gets more than 20 inches high is a Pygmy. They can be milked but only give about ⅓ as much as a full-sized goat.

Or you could have a cross between any 2 or more of the above breeds.

MOVING YOUR NEW GOAT: When you buy a goat, find out how the current owners get her places. Do they lead her with a rope or shake a can of grain in front of her nose? This information immediately becomes very important. It's nicest if she's broken to lead. All my new or naughty goats wear collars with a short rope attached. It makes it easier to grab them and get them started leading. I don't like the grain-can bit because with a big herd and some calves and horses in there too, I'm liable to get trampled. But for just a few goats it's a good technique to train them to follow as you walk along holding the can, occasionally shaking it so they can hear the scrumptious noise. Stop and give them just a bite before they start or whenever they look like they're losing faith in you and the can. Or you can grab the horns and just drag them along with somebody behind to push—a time and place when horns are useful, but still a desperation measure. Or you can carry them—another desperation measure.

THE BUTTING ORDER: Goats are rough on each other. They occasionally even bite each other. A big goat with big horns will bully a new goat, especially a small one, and keep it away from the food. If you're planning to have just 2 goats and have small quarters for them to live and eat in, it would make sense to get 2 goats that are dehorned or naturally hornless. And make that either 2 yearlings or 2 adults while you're at it. There are exceptions, though. I had a yearling once that was so mean to the big goats I had to sell her. Generally, though, once a herd gets established and used to one other, they all live together fairly peaceably. Given time, any combination of goats will become pals. A boss goat always emerges, too, usually a big, older nanny. She will lead the herd out to feed in the morning and back home at night. But goats aren't necessarily charitable to the weak. If a goat seems hurt or sick, put it in a pen by itself with water, straw or hay bedding, and good food. The other goats probably wouldn't let the sick one get its share of food and might persecute it to boot.

Fencing, Housing, and Food

FENCING FOR GOATS: The biggest problem with any goats, male or female, is controlling them. They can jump over, crawl through, or squeeze between—and they can do terrible damage terribly fast if they get where they don't belong. Wrap the trunks of your fruit trees with chicken wire 6 feet high if you have goats. This keeps the goats from eating the bark. If the goats are sticking their heads through and getting stuff they shouldn't, fence them in with chicken wire. Keep them well fed so the garden won't look so tempting. Even so, they may get out just for the principle of it.

Dynah Geissel wrote me: "Just as you would prepare a place for a new baby, preparing a place for your new livestock will save a lot of anxiety and confusion when you bring them home. First, check your fences. Each goat should have access to ¼ acre. The minimum fence height is 4½ feet. A determined goat can clear a 6-foot fence, but if she is properly cared for and has not established bad habits, 4½ feet will generally restrain her. Obviously the fence should not lean out. Also, if the top is wire, there will be no 'step up.' There should be no vertical gap greater than 14 inches and no horizontal gap greater than 8 inches. You'd be surprised what a goat can slip through."

Don Fallick wrote me: "Rail fences for goats don't work well, unless the rails are so close together that a goat just can't get through. Even then, the goats can see through, and may jump right over even an 8-foot fence. But goats (and deer) won't jump a fence they can't see through or over. Many goat breeders have found a solid wood fence 5 feet tall keeps their goats at home. If you decide to build a solid goat fence from slabs, nail the vertical slabs to horizontal stringers, with the bark side away from the goats. Goats love to chew on bark and can loosen up even the hardest driven nail just to get at the tiny piece of bark under it. If you intend to fence goat kids, make the top panel inward-sloping, or make it of chicken wire, to prevent them from caroming off the corners and flying out.

"Goat fences need gates that hook shut with spring-lock hooks. Besides being able to jump unbelievably high, goats have prehensile tongues, and can unlock most standard latches, even including spring hook latches. Goats have prehensile lips and can reach and unlock latches that many people have trouble with. I once rigged such a latch so the hook was inside a coffee can, which made it difficult for me to let myself out of the pen when I was working inside it. After I got it finished, I tested it by going inside, unlocking the latch and letting myself out. The goats watched in fascination. Then I went out, locked the hook, shook it to make sure it was latched—and got less than 3 paces from the gate before a goat nudged me. That's how quick they figured out how to unlock it! So if all else fails, use a chain and padlock!"

Curing a Fence Tester. If a young goat starts going through (or over) fences, Mike finds a forked tree branch shaped like a "Y." The goat's neck goes into the "V" and the ends of the stick are tied above its neck with leather or something. It can't squeeze through fence holes anymore, and jumping isn't convenient either. If a goat grows up thinking it can't do those things, it will give up trying. After 6 weeks you can take off the yoke and there won't be a problem again. If the goat does jump again, just put the yoke back on as a reminder. That's how to raise goats that don't test your fences.

Picketing a Goat. If a goat knows it can and wants to, it can jump over a 5-foot, or even a 6-foot fence. If I get a goat that has a bad jumping habit, I sell it to somebody who has the kind of situation where they have to picket a goat anyway. To picket the goat put on a collar or halter and attach a light-link chain. The chain is attached to a metal stake that you can drive into the ground with a mallet where you want her to browse. Or use a "stay." That's an old tire or a heavy piece of iron instead of a stake. You can move the stay around occasionally without the trouble of pounding in the stake. None of my goats have to be picketed because we have plenty of room here.

Catching a Goat. How do you deal with a goat that jumped the fence and is happily eating your neighbor's roses and doesn't want to be caught?

1. Try the grain-shaken-in-a-can bit. Turn the grain so he can see it.
2. If he's leery, walk past him carrying the grain but completely ignoring him. Go pick up some curious object beyond him and examine it. Then put down the object and walk back past the goat, still carrying the grain, and still carefully ignoring it. Whistle if you can. The goat will be overcome with curiosity and follow you. Slow down. At a point of closest approach dive for legs or horns, whichever you think you have the better chance of grabbing. I love horned goats because in desperation I can usually catch them by those handles. Then yell for help.
3. If that didn't work, rope him, and put him up for sale.
4. If you can't rope him, shoot him and make goat sausage.

GOAT SHELTER: Goats don't need fancy quarters. Just a good dry place to get in out of the rain or snow. An indoor home with an open door to pasture is perfect. Goats or cows both have plenty of sense to know when to go in and are happiest choosing that for themselves. But Dynah Geissal, who lives in Montana, pointed out 2 important exceptions: ". . . kidding and extreme cold. Goats can tolerate very cold weather if their shelter is dry and draft free. When the temperature drops to around 20 degrees below however, there may be problems. Newborn kids are especially at risk, as are unprotected udders. At this temperature I add extra bedding, close the barn door to maintain as much warmth as possible, leave a light on to encourage movement even at night, and feed extra hay."

Goat Shed. A quick and easy shelter from rain and sun can be made by putting 4 posts in the ground, adding a sheet of tin for roofing, and wrapping some tin around 3 sides.

Dynah Geissal wrote me: "There should be deep bedding, which is changed once or twice a year, fresh air but no drafts, and at least 6 × 6 feet per goat. Never allow ammonia to form. One door may be left open without creating a draft. Bedding should be dry at all times. In case you're wondering—no heat. If your barn is heated, your livestock will not be acclimated to the outdoors. Keep them dry and draft free, and they will be fine. You will also need a keyhole feeder for hay and a method for giving them fresh, clean water. A milking platform or stanchion is also required."

Don Fallick: "Goats love to push on anything handy, so I've learned that goat barn walls must be sturdy. To build a goat shelter, I have the wall boards nailed onto the walls from the inside of the barn, not the outside. I frame 2 opposite walls and slide them from the inside, then scab studs to the corners and frame the other 2 walls. Also, since goats in the wild do not live in caves, they'll never be comfortable in a barn that has no windows, and you'll want light to see by when examining kids, or milking. But windows can be a problem, as goats, and especially kids, jump around so much. There is real danger of them breaking the glass unless it is protected with expanded metal mesh, if you can get it, or 2-inch mesh welded wire fence (not woven wire—it's not strong enough)."

Goat Hutches. This is ready-made, portable goat-sized housing. You can buy molded plastic huts for kids from the Pet Castle Co.; 915-643-2517; 800-381-1363; PO Box 1059, Brownwood, TX 76801. VIC offers fiberglass hutches, both small and large: 507-498-5577; 800-537-7145; 111 Maple Dr., Spring Grove, MN 55974.

However, Don warns: "It's tempting to make a goat barn no taller than goat height, to conserve materials and heat in winter. This is false economy. You will eventually need to get into the barn to remove composted manure. Goat manure, with a little bedding thrown in, composts into an extremely dry, tough layer of felt-like substance that must be cut before it can be shoveled. If you don't have room to swing a pick or a mattock, you'll wish you did!"

Sleeping Platforms. Says Dynah Geissal: "A nice addition is one sleeping platform for each goat. Some use them; some don't, but the ones that do will really appreciate them. Each platform should be 12 inches wide, 2 feet off the ground, and 4 feet long.

GOAT FOOD AND WATER

Water. Like other animals (and you), your goats need fresh, clean water available all the time. Freely available water helps goats have good health and do their best milk-giving.

Food. I've just read a book that said goats could starve on grass. True, but it's not that simple. Goats need some brush in their diet, but they can get along on brush plus grass and a wide variety of weeds (herbs) and/or vegetables just fine. The vegetables can take the place of brush. They don't do as well just on grain and grass—say, oats and hay. They need some veggies, too. Goats can eat grain, stock beets, corn fodder, carrot tops, lettuce, nice second-cutting alfalfa (they don't care for the coarse stuff), melon rinds—anything from the garden. They like brush, rose bushes, and apple branches, so if you have fruit trees, roses, and berry bushes, you'll have to protect them. Chicken layers' mash will kill goats. Grain or alfalfa will bloat them if they aren't used to it. (If you live near somebody's alfalfa field, install especially good fencing.) In fact, any major sudden change of diet can be rough on your goats.
NOTE: Some plants are poisonous to goats, such as azaleas, laurel, milkweed, and wild cherry. Ask your extension agent about problem plants in your area.

Wintering Goats. I know that in a pinch you can winter goats purely on hay because I've done it. But to keep milk production up and to keep them happiest they need some vegetables, a grain ration, and access to brush. Just what quantity it takes to winter goats depends on the quality of your feed and the method you use to feed. A good winter ration in an average winter around here—which is not a real rough winter—is 6–9 bales of good hay (second-cutting alfalfa) for the whole winter. You ration it out to them —plus a handful of chopped grain apiece per day. They like squash, mangel beets, and carrots, too. That's a good liberal diet for a milking doe. Goats that aren't being milked don't need any grain at all.

Feeding System. Feeding in a manger does go farther than throwing feed on the ground. Dynah says a "keyhole feeder" is best of all. And have your hay stored so they can't get in and walk around on top of it because they've no judgment, and will get it in such foul condition that they won't want to eat it.

Goat-Feeding Myths. I read recently in a very popular book that goats are "wasteful" eaters. That same book instructed its readers to give them what seemed to me an amazing quantity of grain per day. Well, if you gave any goat that much grain, of course it would "waste it," because they can't eat that much. It also described goats as "finicky" eaters. They can be. Goats are a lot like cats and dogs.

Everyone has heard of Aunt Minnie's tiger tomcat that won't touch anything but chopped liver and she has to buy it fresh every day for him—or some such. You can do that to a goat if you work at it.

But not everybody has a large range area with a large variety of plants, which is the way goats would naturally meet all their nutritional needs. Consider Dynah's feed-store–based system.

Dynah's System. Dynah Geissal has published "20 or 30 articles" on food-growing subjects. I am so grateful she shared her experience in this goat section. This longtime goat-keeper recommends: "Obtain some top-quality alfalfa, 3-way, a mineral salt block, a dairy mineral mix (and a box in which to feed it).

"Her main feed should be top-quality alfalfa—second or third cutting. Feed her free choice in a keyhole feeder. Don't continuously feed more than she will eat or she will pick out the tastiest bits and leave the rest. A goat is fastidious and will waste any feed that is soiled, and a keyhole feeder will minimize waste. Grain should be fed 1 lb. for each 3 lb. milk produced. Three-way is a good feed for goats and may be mixed half and half with ground barley. Top off the grain with 2 T. apple cider vinegar for each goat. This will aid in preventing mastitis and in keeping down the parasite problem. In the spring, introduce fresh pasture gradually. Feed plenty of hay first and only leave the goats on pasture for a short time. Never turn them out for their first spring grass onto wet or frozen pasture, for this may lead to bloat.

"In addition, provide . . . a mineral salt block and . . . a good dairy mineral mix. It will probably have salt in it; if not, mix it half and half with salt. If your area is deficient in selenium, it should be provided here. Put this mineral mix in a feeder high enough off the floor that it isn't easily soiled. And . . . provide a natural cattle block. This is a protein mineral supplement. Be sure it has no urea. Urea is poisonous to goats and should never be fed to them. This block should contain molasses, which is good for them any time but is necessary during the winter and 2 months before kidding. They will eat whatever they need of these additives. If they have not been provided previously, they may devour them at an incredible rate at first. After they have obtained what they need, this will drastically decrease."

Goat Reproduction

GOAT FACTS OF LIFE: Goats are in their prime generally from 3 to 6 years of age. It is best to breed young does from 15 to 18 months, or at least 10 months old. Too early breeding will stunt growth and heighten risk for dead babies and poor milk production. The usual number of kids for a mature doe is 2—or 1—or even 3 or 4. Keep records on your does. They will tend to repeat themselves.

GOATS IN HEAT: Young goats may vary about when they come into heat the first time—breeding them for the first time at about 10 months is ideal. Older ones that birthed in the spring won't come into season again until fall. In that case, the first chill frosts of September will bring it on. Don't bother looking for heat signs in summer unless the goat went through the fall and winter without a chance to conceive. Goats come into heat from September to January for 1, 2, or 3 days. So, you have to notice them fast and get them bred fast. The period between heats is 17–21 days.

October and November are the months she's most likely to conceive. Dynah Geissal: "Some does come into heat in August. You may want to let your buck run with the does early in the season to allow any early breeding to take place. Winter milk is usually scarce."

Detecting Heat. You can tell when a nanny is in heat because she bleats all day long, runs up and down the fence looking longingly out, and wiggles her tail provocatively and constantly. She is spotting blood if you look closely, and the labia of the vagina are swelled up and red. Dynah Geissal: "Rub a rag on the most fragrant buck available and store it in a lidded jar. In October, display the rag to your doe each day. When she comes in heat, you'll know! Keep track of each heat so you'll know her cycle. Then plan for her breeding. After breeding, watch for her heat to be present or absent so you'll know if she's bred. A doeling may be bred at 7 months if she is well grown, approximately 70 lb."

THE BUCK: You can keep a buck of your own, or maybe take your nan to someone who has one when she needs him. Or artificially inseminate. Twenty-five years ago artificial insemination for goats ranged from uncommon to unheard of. Now it's a third good option. Goat breeds are basically the same size except for the pygmies. You can breed a goat of any breed to a goat of any other breed, and the results will be goat and will get born fine (that isn't always true of cow breeds, which vary greatly in size).

Keeping Your Own Buck. The buck is always ready. All you have to do is put them together and he does the rest. A half hour should do it. Bucks are unpopular inside city limits and in crowded neighborhoods because a mature buck goat has a tremendously strong odor. Every time you handle him you'll walk away with a tremendously strong odor, too. If they aren't always handled carefully and gently, they can develop some very bad butting habits. If horned, they can be quite dangerous to small children, because a point of one of those horns could come up and get an eye. I rescued my 2-year-old from being butted against the chicken house wall after a friend played at "wrestling" with our buck and awakened his butting instinct. I had to get rid of that buck. Unfortunately, no matter how careful you are, sooner or later bucks will get that butting instinct awakened.

To get your own buck, you can buy a young one fairly cheaply in the spring. He'll be able to do the job by fall breeding time. Some folks keep the billy goat in a special little house—but I let mine run with the herd. That way I don't have to worry about trying to tell when the nannies are ready for him.

Dynah Geissal wrote: "Once a year the services of a buck will be needed. Keep a buck, [artificially inseminate], or take your does elsewhere. With 1 or 2 does, a buck would be superfluous; but with a larger herd, a buck would be a significant part of the natural order of herd life. Whether you are buying your own buck or renting the services of one, find out his reliability as a stud and the milking and mothering history of his mother. If possible, obtain a purebred buck, and one that the owner assures you is easy to handle. Inexperienced people should consider a hornless buck.

"The best bet may be to raise your own. In this case, breed the best doe (preferably purebred) to the best buck obtainable. Hopefully, she will produce at least one buckling who will be left with his mother. You don't want him thinking that you are mother. Start working with him as soon as possible, but don't make a pet out of him. It could be dangerous if he thinks you are part of the herd. Be firm, even more so than with your does. Put up with no rough-housing, and always let him know that you are boss. Never allow him to get away with challenging you. Teach him early to lead and stand quietly for grooming, shots, hoof trimming, etc.

"Your buck may be used to breed a limited number of does at seven months. He should be separated from the does during breeding season. Otherwise the does will be bred indiscriminately. I once left a 3-month-old buckling with the herd because he was quite small; but surmounting a great difference in height, he managed to breed the entire herd, producing fourteen kids who looked amazingly like him and quite tiny.

"I have never had trouble with the smell of the buck getting into the milk, but it will if the does and buck are closely confined. With plenty of space and fresh air, it shouldn't be a problem. I wouldn't want to separate the buck for most of his life, for he's an important member of the herd."

Rent-a-Buck. If you can tell when your doe is wanting the buck you can take her and bring her back the same day with fair confidence of success. But it may be expensive. If too pricey, that's a good reason to keep your own buck, or check into the availability and price of artificial insemination.

Artificial Insemination. Artificial insemination for goats was uncommon or even unheard of 25 years ago. Now it's a third good option. Ask your county extension agent or local goat folks about local bucks. Or ask Buck Bank about semen, breeding supplies, collection, and training. They offer your choice of champion Alpine, LaMancha, Nubian, Oberhasli, Angora, Boer, Cashmere, Nigerian Dwarf, and Saanen bucks: 541-826-2729; fax 541-826-9717; 2344 Butte Falls Hwy., Eagle Point, OR 97524; **dheaney@jeffnet.org.** Or contact Wayne and Carol Rhoten; Magnum Semen Works: 301-374-2927; 2200 Albert Hill Rd., Hampstead, MD 21074. To read up on the subject check out *Artificial Insemination and Genetic Improvement of Dairy Goats* by Dr. Harry A. Herman; or *Artificial Insemination Handbook* by Vaughn Solomon and Donna Forsman.

GESTATION: The gestation period ranges from 146 to 152 days (about 5 months). So wait 5 months minus one day, and then watch for her to spring. Dynah Geissal: "If she has little milk, stop milking when she has 2 months left until kidding. If she has a lot of milk, feed her well (not to fatness), and keep milking her. I've had goats who milk well for 3 continuous years with no problem, but they need top quality feed. If she isn't milking, don't give any grain the last 2 months before kidding, for a fat goat may have birthing problems. Give shots, worm, and trim hooves 6 to 8 weeks before kidding."

Ketosis. Stress, overfeeding, underfeeding, and lack of exercise can all be contributors to this pregnancy-related illness. Dynah: "Symptoms are dullness, disinterest in feed, pressing head against something, teeth grinding, and aimless walking. *To prevent ketosis, provide blackstrap molasses during the last 2 months of pregnancy.* Detection is by using Ketostix to see if her blood sugar is low. The cure is to feed glycerin, exercise her, and keep her eating."

KIDDING: We had a white Saanen buck goat named Miracle. His mother's name was Mary. He was the first goat born on our farm. He was Mary's first baby and neither she nor I had gotten into the farm kidding routine yet. She gave birth to him on a miserable rainy day in late February on the manure pile. Mike and I had been through a birth rather recently ourselves when he was with me in the delivery room, and I cried with the wonder of it when he and I found them, and that's why I named the kid "Miracle." There isn't that much difference in the basics. The miracle of life is the same whether it begins among sterile sheets and bad-tempered nurses or in the rain on a manure pile. And I always cry with joy when it's over, whether it's a goat, cow, or me.

Signs of Near Birthing. When the lips of the vulva swell up and the opening becomes longer and larger and the nanny is springing, delivery is nearing but not imminent. When hollows appear under the tail above and to the left and right of her vagina, delivery will take place within 2 hours. Dynah Geissal: "Kidding may occur as many as 5 days before or after the doe's due date (5 months, 1 day after breeding). Signs of an imminent birth are a full udder and a thin, clear mucous discharge. This is different from the thick yellow mucous pus which may appear as much as a month before kidding."

The Kidding Place. When you know a free-running goat is near kidding, check on her every morning. *If she doesn't show up, go find her.* If your goats run free in the open, you need to discover the mother with her kids as soon after kidding as possible. Goats, in my experience, aren't super picky where they have their kids. If she kids in cold weather out in the open, the kids will die if you don't help them. And we have lost newborn kids to predators. So I would advise that, especially if you live near the woods, keep a goat about to kid near the buildings or in protective custody until she has kidded and her kids are able to run as fast as the rest of the herd. (Kids develop jumping and running abilities very quickly.) Predators are less likely to come in where the human smell is heavy.

Provide a sheltered place—inside a shed or barn. Cover the floor of her shelter with dry bedding such as straw, hay, or sawdust. Dynah Geissal adds: "A lead goat will choose an appropriate place to kid, but a lower one may not because of being harassed. So be sure to isolate her in shelter before kidding. When it's been determined that your goat will be kidding within a few hours, isolate her in a place that is familiar to her. Be sure that it's dry, draft-free, and has plenty of bedding. Provide fresh, clear water in a small bucket (to minimize the chance that she will drop her kid into the water). Give her plenty of good hay."

The Birthing. Kids are usually born in the early morning hours. The mother probably won't need any help from you with the birthing itself. But if she does, here's Dynah Geissal's expert instructions on what to do:

"Generally speaking, a goat should be left alone to kid. If she is very attached to you, she may be reassured by your presence. Most goats, however, prefer to be alone, although they do seem to be more at ease if they are able to see their herd sisters. Be sure to check on her frequently during her labor. It may be many hours before hard contractions start. If she seems at ease and eats or chews her cud, all is well. When hard labor begins, your doe may lie down, pant, and call out during a contraction. Between contractions, she will get up and resume cud chewing in the early stages. This may last several hours.

"When the kid is showing, check to see which part is presenting. If the front feet are first, with the head resting on them, everything should proceed normally. This stage may last as long as an hour. Unless things proceed rapidly, clean the kid's nose and mouth before it is born."

Assisting in Kidding. Dynah, again: "There are certain circumstances where you will have to aid in the birth or get someone else to help you: . . . If the water breaks and more than 2 hours have elapsed and there is no kid in sight, your goat probably needs help. . . . If she seems to be in great pain, wait no more than half an hour before assisting her.... If she seems exhausted, wait only a few more minutes—maybe fifteen.

"If the kid is presenting, you may have to do no more than pull gently downward with each contraction. This is sometimes necessary with an especially large kid. When the kid is presenting, but in an abnormal position, you will have to enter the vagina. Scrub your hands and arms thoroughly, paying special attention to your nails. Oil your hands and arms. A presentation that is normal except that the head is turned back is easy to correct, but almost impossible to give birth to if not corrected. The same is true if one or both feet are tucked underneath the kid. A kid that is presenting normally but upside down may be turned. A breech birth may proceed successfully if the feet come first; but there must be no delay once it is presenting. The cord may be constricted in the birth canal. When the kid is coming rump first, it may be born with some help from you during contractions if it is fairly small. Otherwise, you will have to push it back and bring out the feet first.

"If the kid is not showing, but you have decided that your doe definitely needs help, reach in very carefully to prevent rupturing the vagina. In a situation where you cannot feel the kid, the cervix may not be open. In this case, you should consult a vet. Assuming you can feel the kid, determine its position and reposition if necessary. This is probably all that is necessary. On the other hand, when her water has been broken for a long time or if she is exhausted, or if the kid is very large, you may have to also pull the kid during contractions.

"A goat who has serious birthing problems 2 successive years should be butchered. I once had a goat who seemed to be giving birth normally: 2 feet were out but then nothing. When I began to examine her, I found that one leg was much larger than the other; 2 kids were trying to be born at once! I had to push one back to free the first. Then the process repeated itself, and 3 healthy kids were born."

Sue Bradford, Kansas, IL, wrote me: "My best milker, Storm, almost died giving birth. I knew she was in trouble. Phoned my boss, explained, and was told, 'She's only a 2-dollar goat and you're going to lose a day's pay!' She's a pure bred Nubian, but that doesn't matter. She was in pain and any animal in my care will not be left to die. Anyway, this was my first experience delivering. She had delivered a kid hours before. I found she had the next kid sideways. I got him out and of course he was dead, but then out popped a beautiful little girl kid! I gave Storm a pail of warm water with blackstrap molasses to drink. She drank it all, but wouldn't stand up. She wouldn't even look at her kids and wouldn't stand up. I still don't know how I did it, but I lifted her up enough to get enough milk to get both kids started on the bottle. It was a few days before Storm could stand without help, so I held her up every day while my husband milked her. Her next kids were born without problems. I love this life! I was raised in town, but my husband, Lee, and I have lived on his family farm (90+ acres) for 26 years now. We now have a ¼ acre garden, fruit trees, goats for milk and meat, and chickens for eggs and meat. I've learned to sew, make quilts, can and freeze garden get, make jelly, milk goats, make cheese. I even cut up a deer and goat and made salami."

Doe's Post-Birth Feeding. Dynah Geissal recommends: "Feed mother 1 lb. grain plus warm water containing molasses." That drink of warm water with some molasses in it is a real help to a goat that is kidding. She may drink as much as a gallon. If she seems chilled and seems to be having difficulty expelling the afterbirth, the drink of warm water also helps.

Afterbirth. The afterbirth comes out after the kid. It may take a long time to finish coming out. Leave it alone. I know how miserable it is when the doctor gets in a rush about afterbirth. It will come out in time. You put her more at risk by pulling on it, because that may make her bleed! When she gets done passing the afterbirth naturally, she may or may not eat it. If she does, it's recycling. If she doesn't—well, after all she's not a meat eater by nature.

CARE OF THE NEWBORN KID: Carry a towel with you and dry the newborn as soon after birth as possible (getting born is a wet business). There is no reason for you to tie the cord. My advice would be, in fact, don't. Leave that part of it up to nature. I usually don't find the babies until after nature has taken care of that part anyway.

Dynah Geissal's system: "Have dry, clean towels ready and either iodine or alcohol. When the kids are born, clean the faces immediately. Let mother take over, but if she doesn't do a good job, you should. Dip the cord into an iodine solution as soon as possible (don't dab it on). The cord is a wick to bacteria and infection. 'Navel ill' is an infection of the umbilical cord which spreads to the kid's entire body, especially the joints. It is prevented by dipping the cord in iodine or alcohol immediately after birth. It is treated by antibiotics or sulfa."

Helping Kid Nurse. Dynah: "There are usually 2 kids born and 3 is not unusual. The kids should be up almost immediately. Be sure the kids receive colostrum right away—hopefully within 15 minutes of birth. If not, help them up at least to nurse. If the kids have a strong sucking response, hold the teat and the kid until its initial hunger is satisfied. When the sucking response is weak, get some milk into the kid and then try in a couple hours. If a kid is not nursing on its own, you'll have to help. If the kids are weak, or there are multiple kids, you may have to help for as many as 3 days. You will learn quickly how often they are hungry—usually every 3 to four hours. Once you are certain that a kid has nursed on its own, it won't need your help any more.

"If there is no sucking after several hours, you will have to bottle feed the kid, if you want it. Once is usually enough to get it strong enough to nurse. Give the bottle as few times as possible so the kids learn to nurse the mother rather than depending on the bottle. Don't keep the kid in the house or its mother may reject it and it won't have adapted to the temperature of the barn. If the kids are bottle fed, they tend to become pets. You're their mom and, personally, I don't think livestock should be pets. I have dogs and cats for that. A pet goat is usually intractable and as obnoxious as an untrained dog. My goats are friendly and affectionate, but they are members of the herd, not the family."

Chilled Kid. If a goat kids outdoors in cold weather and the kid seems to be inactive, it's probably chilled. You may even find a kid that's weak, or prostrate from the cold. Just pick up that little baby in your arms and carry it into the warmest room of your house. Keep it wrapped in warm cloth and put it in a cardboard box near the heat source until it dries off and gets warm and is thoroughly recovered. When the kid climbs out of the box and wobbles all over the house nuzzling at everybody optimistically, it is doing fine for a 6-hour-old baby. Its little tail will wag and its disposition already demonstrates the incurable curiosity of goat.

Separation of Kid and Mother. One school of thought advocates taking the kid away from the mother immediately so she won't get attached to it and be harder to milk later. Another is to leave the kid with the mother for 3 days and then separate them. But since the latest research has shown that animals nursed by another animal are more respectful of humans and much safer to have around when mature, owners are trying harder to find a way to keep the kid on the goat. You can't change your mind in the middle because, if the kid is taken away from its mother for the first 6 hours or more, on its return she may well butt it viciously and refuse to mother it. Here's Dynah's system for leaving the kid nursing its mother:

"Kids should stay isolated with their mother for 3 to 5 days or until they are strong, active, and nursing well on their own. Then turn them out with the herd. The only time I have had a problem with this is when a yearling calf crushed 2 kids behind a door. So if you have large livestock sharing their barn, keep them separated a few extra days.

"Check the mother's udder twice a day to be sure it isn't too full. She will probably need milking after 3 days, but if not, you could wait up to 5 days. Except for the grain fed immediately after kidding, don't feed any more grain until your regular milking has begun. That prevents her milk from coming in too fast.

"Let the kids stay with their mother and continue to nurse her until they have grown husky and are eating regular food well. This is usually 2 months for single and twin kids, but closer to 3 for triplets. At this time, begin to separate the kids from their mother all night. That way you have the morning milk but let them take the rest during the daytime. The kids will learn the routine in a few days. Then they will stop crying and will even run into their own

sleeping area when you come into the barn at night to shut them away."

Bottle-Feeding. If the kid will be bottle-fed (or disposed of), give mother some grain and milk her. If you haven't milked or handled her much before, you'll find birthing has made her completely gentle and she'll cooperate fine with you. Save that colostrum milk to feed her baby if you will be bottle-feeding. Take the milk to the house, put some into a small pop bottle, using a lamb nipple on the end of it, and feed it to the baby. Just get the nipple in its mouth and it'll get the idea. Never feed cold milk. After a few feedings and a really good warming the baby goat will be fine and can go back out to the barn to live. Or if it still seems to be doing poorly, you could keep it in the house until you feel sure it's strong. If the kid is too weak even to nurse the long, soft lamb nipple, you can feed it with an infant syringe (the rubber bulb you use to clean a newborn baby's nose), available at drugstores or a spoon.

Don't use a human baby bottle. It's the wrong style nipple. You should have several "lamb" nipples on hand (baby lambs are treated exactly the same way) well before the birthing. It's terribly important to get that first good nourishment into a chilled newborn animal. You'll be amazed at the change. I've found kid goats that looked almost dead. But after they were warmed up and had a meal in their tummy, they stood up, bleated, and wagged their tails. After 2 hours and another meal they were just fine.

Lamb nipples don't have an internal air supply like baby bottles that feed air in through the rim. The kid has to learn to let go of the nipple every so often so air can rush in and equalize the pressure; otherwise the milk will stop coming.

Timing the Feedings. Feed every 2 hours the first day, 4 hours the second day, 8 hours the third day, then morning, noon and night for about 10 days, and from then on morning and night after you milk. Notice how much they are able to take at a feeding. At first they take only an ounce or so. By the end they'll empty a big pop bottle.

Scours. The turds of goat kids should be round and firm, miniatures of mama's. When goat kids (or calves) get a loose diarrhea; it's called "scours." Chilling and overfeeding are the 2 greatest dangers. Sometimes they scour a while and finally get over it, but sometimes it kills them. Goat kids have a hard time on any milk but their natural milk. That powdered fake stuff is the worst thing I know of; powdered milk is next; and cow's milk is best for them. (Bigger kids can handle cow's milk better than little ones.) If a goat kid on anything but goat's milk is scouring, then a half bottle, a bottle, or all goat's milk for several feedings will usually clear it up. I am always very reluctant to sell unweaned kids to people who don't have goat's milk to give them because I know they'll have a hard time keeping the kids healthy.

If you are milking goats and have yearlings, or a poor milker, or they all have triplets—you don't have much choice. You're going to have to kill some kids to insure your family milk supply or else find homes for them elsewhere. You can't afford to buy milk for them. They are worth only a few dollars, if you can find somebody to take them. They aren't as important as having milk for your own children. If you try to raise them on that cheap milk substitute they'll be scouring and sick most of the time, and you'll spend whatever you saved on Kaopectate and antibiotics trying to help them hang on.

Surplus Newborn Kids. I try never to kill a nan kid because it is a waste, but when I have more billy kids than I have extra milk for, and nobody wants them, I kill them. This is hard to talk about and hard to do, but I'm going to tell you how because I'm writing this book for people trying to do real things in difficult situations, and sometime you may need to know this. Dynah Geissal says on this subject: "Before your kids are born, decide how many doelings you will keep and stick with it."

If I'm going to kill the kid I get there as soon after birth as possible. I check for sex. Then I take the little billy out of earshot of the mother and hit it as hard as I can on the head with a hammer. That blow probably suffices. The newborns don't have much stamina, but I hit it a couple more times to make sure. Better have it quick, certain, and complete if it has to be done.

Calf Adoption. It takes about 2 good goats to support 1 calf. Get your goats milking well first, and then you can acquire the calf. One really good goat can support a calf if she can be persuaded to adopt it and let it nurse her.

Kids for Meat. If you do have extra milk, then by all means raise your extra bucklings and cull doelings for meat. If you don't have a market for them, you might as well eat them yourself. Since goats typically have more than 1 kid at a time, and they can even kid twice a year, you have extras pretty fast once you get started. The animals can be butchered when they're big enough to suit you. Even a kid 6 weeks old will add 15 lb. of meat to your supply. But the longer you wait the more meat you'll get—up to a point. Calves keep growing until they are about 2 years old, and the same with goats.

Sexing Kids. What you plan for the kid may depend on its sex. Boy kid goats have small testicles hanging from their tummy, just to the front of their hind legs. They pee from the middle of the tummy so it runs straight down as they stand. Girl goats don't have those testicles and they pee from the rear, squatting backwards as they do so.

Of Big Kids and Weaning. Incidentally, big babies that are still nursing tug so hard they are liable to pull a rubber nipple off a bottle. You'll have to hold it on the bottle as they suck. A goat can be tapered off when he is eating other feeds well, weaned completely at about 4 months.

Castrating. Male kids, like bull calves, are usually castrated for easier management. Dynah says, "Male kids should be castrated by one month of age. I use an elastrator and have never had a problem. Don't wait any longer than a month or it will be too traumatic. I castrate the males so they can run with the herd. If they aren't castrated, they must be separated from the does by four months."

GOAT MANNERS: Dynah Geissal: "Goats are very smart and can be taught manners. Don't allow your goats to jump on you or to jump up to get feed you're carrying. A slap on the nose and a loud "no" will save a lot of irritation and hassle. Don't allow loose goats to butt or to steal food from a goat who is confined in a stanchion."

Goat Vetting and Grooming

See the general section in Chapter 8, "Introduction to Animals." Dynah Geissal: "Disease is not usually a problem with goats if they are fed top-quality feed and additives, get their shots on time and are well maintained."

TOENAILS: Some goats never seem to have toenail problems. Others have toenails that grow and grow, and you have to cut them off to keep the goats from becoming virtual cripples trying to get around with all that nail on each hoof. A young goat has fairly soft hooves and you can trim them with a knife. Make them look like a newborn's hooves, but *don't go far enough back to get into the quick.* Though it may make them nervous, it doesn't hurt. On an old goat the hooves are very hard, and you'll need a meat saw or regular hoof nippers to do the job. I bought an old doe once who had 5 inches of toenail that had to be sawed off from the front of each hoof. The best way to keep up with it is to trim once a month. But don't trim hooves right before or right after kidding.

PARASITES: Dynah Geissal says, "If other goats come to your farm, assume they have parasites and act accordingly. Never loan out your buck, but have the does brought to him."

Worming. Dynah, again: "Worming should be done 3 times a year. The whole herd should be done together (within a few days of each other) at least one of those times. Does should be wormed 6 to 8 weeks before kidding. Other times could be before confining for the winter, before turning out in the spring, before breeding, etc. I use TBZ, which can be used during pregnancy and during lactation."

Lice. Dynah: "You will probably need to dust for lice each year in the spring. Choose a dust that is safe to use on lactating dairy animals and poultry. These are the safest as well as effective. Dust immediately after the morning milking and do it outside. Kids under 8 weeks should be dusted with ashes."

SHOTS: Dynah: "The best time to inoculate goats who have been confined for the winter is just before turning them out and no closer than 6 to 8 weeks before kidding. Don't forget your buck. If red water is a problem in your area, you will need to give 8-way. Ask neighboring ranchers or your local extension service. If they vaccinate their cattle for red water, so should you vaccinate your goats. If not, use 7-way."

HORNS: Dynah: "Horned goats will tend to scatter, then stand and face the predator. Hornless will just run, which encourages chasing and may lead to injury or death." For dehorning see Chapter 8.

BLEATING: Some goats are very noisy. If your choice is to have a silent goat or no goat at all, get a goat, and if the bleating becomes a problem you can have it debleated at the vet's. Keeping the kids and mama out of sight of one another and separating them before they have a chance to get really attached helps. A nan in season will be noisy, and actually that's a convenience because it lets you know when she is ready to be with the billy. To me, debleating is a last resort, but I know some of you have special constraints, living with lots of neighbors and critical municipal authorities.

DESCENTING: At the same time that buck kids are disbudded, they can also be at least partly descented by burning out the scent glands on their heads. Or those can be surgically taken. (Ask a vet.) Castrated bucks won't develop the odor, but the one you're keeping intact for breeding will. Dealing with the head glands doesn't solve the problem entirely; there are also leg glands that produce scent.

Goat Butchering

We've eaten a lot of goats. Goat meat is "wild" flavored, resembling venison in taste. I've made goat stew, goat steaks, and goat burger. I prepare those all pretty much on the same basic plan as other meats. If serving goat meat to a guest who isn't used to the taste, I might camouflage it in a wild meat recipe. We never have cut roasts off our goats. I'd rather serve and eat the meat fried, or in burger, or made into sausage, so it's always either sliced or ground. Goats are easy to butcher and cut up. If you've ever done a deer, it's the same thing. Goat meat is technically called "chevon"—and in the Southwest market, "cabritos" or "cabrito meat" means young goat, just like pig meat is "pork" and cow meat is "beef."

OF GOAT AGE AND BUTCHERING: You butcher a kid goat the same way you do an adult, basically—only the whole thing is quicker because there is less of everything. If you need milk more than meat, it makes sense to butcher kids at birth. Use the rabbit butchering directions for that size. Most people don't butcher before 12 weeks of age because you don't get much meat. There is quite an Easter/Passover market for milk-fed kids that are about 20–30 lb. To maximize their meat production from a buck kid, however, most homesteaders butcher surplus kids at 5–9 months old. That way you have an animal big enough to make small steaks and even small roasts.

After the kid is skinned and gutted you can roast it whole on a spit, barbecued, like for the Fourth of July when you have lots of guests. Or you can quarter it for barbecuing or roasting, a quarter at a time for a regular meal. The other age at which goats are most frequently butchered is "old"—mostly cull does. These are nans that can't be bred, or don't give enough milk to bother, or can't be milked or can't be controlled. Older goats are generally boned and the meat ground for goat burger or sausage, appropriate uses for strong-tasting, nontender meats.

Goat for the Meat Market. Young goats for the Easter (March) market generally range in weight from 17 to 38 lb. If not sold then, they are usually marketed at 8 months of age. Worldwide about 1.2 million tons a year of goat meat is sold (more than cattle or hogs!).

KILLING A GOAT: Aim from behind it with your gun, at a spot just below the ear, while the goat is preoccupied with a pan of grain, because it probably has some experience with guns and might otherwise be frightened. Or use a hammer, particularly if the goat is a young kid. If you are planning to stun the animal with such a blow, keep in mind that the back of the head is most vulnerable, and that most of the skull is solidly built; these are animals that depend on butting as a defense. Deliver a sharp hit to the head, more if necessary, until the goat is unconscious. In either case, you then cut the throat with a sharp knife to bleed the

animal out thoroughly. Hang head down for thorough bleeding out.

This particular set of directions has you skin the goat first, then eviscerate. But it would also work to eviscerate first, and then skin. The skinning directions are here. For details on how to manage the sex organs or mammary gland, see the section about wild mammals in Chapter 8. The information there will apply. For the gutting, use the directions later in this chapter under "Gutting the Cow."

SKINNING A GOAT: Try not to cut into the meat while you're working. Cut a slit from the midpoint between the hind legs up to the throat. From the center cut, cut along the insides of all 4 legs. The skin will be firmly attached at the tail. Cut around the rectum, pull it out enough to tie off the connecting intestine with a length of string, then let the tied-off intestine fall into the body cavity. Continue cutting off the skin. Skins to be saved for tanning should be cut off the head as close to the ears as possible. Otherwise, you can simply cut off the head at the base of the skull. Finish removing the hide.

EVISCERATING A GOAT: Follow instructions under "Gutting the Cow."

CUTTING UP: To cut up a goat, follow the directions given in Chapter 8 for cutting up a deer. You have to use your own judgment and cut your meat according to the size of the animal and the use you need of it. How you cut it up also depends on whether you have power meat-cutting equipment available. If you have a band saw, cutting meat is so easy that mini-steaks (the kind you'd offer about 3 to a serving) are fine. But if you have to saw out each one the hard way (sawing through the bone by hand), there is scarcely enough meat on them to make it worth the trouble.

GOAT RECIPES: Use any recipe from the wild mammals section in Chapter 8, especially if it's suggested for deer. Goat meat is so much like that of deer, antelope, moose, elk, etc. Or get *Chevon Recipes* from Caprine Supply, for more than 70 good goat-meat recipes. And get the *Dairy Goat Cook Book* by C.A.V. Barker, available from *Dairy Goat Journal*.

CATTLE

Cows and humans go way back, at least to the Sumerians in the ancient Middle East, who recorded their relationship in stone, and probably back to the Stone Age. Since a dairy cow can live 20 years or more, producing a calf each year and milking most of that time, she can be in your life for a long time. You use her male calves for beef, her female calves either for beef or raise them to be milk cows, too. With a dairy cow in your life, except during her annual rest for late pregnancy, you'll have more milk than at first you know what to do with. You can use the extra milk in the sorts of recipes I've collected here. You'll still have too much. So use some to raise her calf, and young pigs for your meat supply, and to help feed the hens. Or make cheese, and feed the pigs and chickens the whey that is left from cheese making.

Getting Started

Before you buy your cow you need to consider: Do you want such a large animal, one that must be fed proportionately large amounts of food? Do you have at least 2 acres of

good pasture? A large enough outbuilding for her to shelter in and you to milk her in? A place to store a few tons of hay and straw for winter feeding?

CATTLE WORDS
- Bull: A mature male.
- Calf: A young 'un; sometimes they're called calves until they are nearly 1½ years old.
- (To) Calve: When a cow gives birth to a calf.
- Dam: A mother cow.
- Heifer: A female cow before her first calving (or, according to some, a female cow before her second calving).
- Sire: A bull.
- Steer: A castrated male, raised for beef or draft service.

FACTORS IN CHOOSING YOUR BREED: Here are the factors you might take into account: foraging ability; longevity; disease-resistance; food-conversion efficiency; polled or horned; calving ease or problems; gentleness; northern–southern adaptation; amount of milk; size; length of lactation period; amount of muscle ("beef characteristics"); draft usefulness; availability; salability (is there a breed association?); cream content of the milk; price; and risk of genetic defects. That list can be used to judge a beef, a dairy, or a dual-purpose breed.

BREEDS: Worldwide there are literally hundreds of beef, dairy, and dual-purpose breeds, and at least 35 common ones—including both dairy and beef—in the United States. In addition, there are many variations of the cow-related water-buffalo–type animal most common in Asia. In the most heavily populated parts of the world, cattle are the main source of power. They pull the plow and furnish power for grain production to keep people fed. Milk production is incidental, and the meat often is not used at all. In the Western world, cattle are used for milk and meat, rarely now for draft animals. If you are interested in all these different cattle breeds, you'd enjoy the 2-volume set, *World Cattle* by John E. Rouse (Norman, OK: University of Oklahoma Press).

Beef vs. Dairy Breeds. There are 3 big differences between beef and dairy breeds: (1) Gentleness: Beef-breed cows are not usually to be milked by ordinary mortals. Angus, for example, are very excitable animals. You'd never be able to catch one to milk her. If you want to milk a cow, you want one that is born with dairy-cow genes. (Yet somebody somewhere has made a milk cow at some time out of every beef breed there is.) (2) Milk production: The main difference between beef and dairy breeds, besides gentleness for milking, is milk production. A good beef cow has enough milk to raise 1 healthy calf without a grain supplement. A dairy cow can easily raise 2 or 3 fine calves (which you can generally persuade her to adopt by shutting them up in the barn together for a while), with a grain supplement. (3) Difference in build: "conformation." The dairy cow is lean, bony, has less muscle in places that would make high-priced steaks and roasts. When you buy a dairy-type animal you're buying a greater percentage of bone, but the lower price will compensate for it.

Dual-Purpose Breeds. A "dual-purpose" breed has a beef conformation with a dairy-type ability to produce milk. The Shorthorn is a large cow in this category—the "milking shorthorn" more so than the "beef shorthorn." The Brown Swiss is another beef–dairy combination cow. The river buffalo is a triple-purpose breed: milk, beef, and draft!

Dairy Cattle

Cows, at their best, are really multipurpose animals. They make meat and manure as well as milk. From the beef point of view, milk and all its wonderful by-products like yogurt, cheese, butter, and ice cream, are just an extra added bonus. And then you can also use the extra milk to raise more meat and eggs by feeding it to the pigs, baby calves, and chickens. I think the most efficient way to get your beef is to have a milk cow and use the extra milk to raise a couple calves a year. You'll get them cheapest if you buy them at 1 day old.

DAIRY COW INFORMATION: Check out Joann Grohman's *Keeping a Family Cow* (1984); Phyllis Hobson's *Raising a Calf for Beef* (1976) (good up to 6 weeks old); and Dirk van Loon's *The Family Cow* (1975). For a periodical, if you're interested in commercial milk-production from cows, subscribe to *Hoard's Dairyman,* 920-563-5551; fax 920-563-7298; PO Box 801, Fort Atkinson, WI 53538-0801; **www.hoards.com.** Hoard's also offers dairy books such as *Calf Care, About Cows,* and *Dairy-Related Careers.* A word of caution: There is a lot of baloney in cow/calf books written for the family farm. Even certain ones I've recommended here have some really stupid misinformation mixed in with the good information.

DAIRY COW AGE: A cow can bear calves annually and be milked until she is 10, 12, 14, even older. The old-timers sometimes kept one going to age 20. But, sooner or later, you'll find it impossible to get her bred again. So a 4-year-old cow is a fine buy.

"Heifer" used to mean a female cow that had not yet had a calf; now some folks use the term to mean a female cow that hasn't calved a second time. Heifers sell cheaper, but they may be unaccustomed to the calving and milking routine—which could be a problem if you are too. They may have trouble calving if it's their first time, and cows, like goats, give only half as much milk the first year they are fresh as they will later on. One way to avoid this calving difficulty is to breed the heifer with a bull of a small dairy breed, like a Jersey, or with a bull of a small beef breed, like a Black Angus, which are deliberately selected for small calves—hence easy calvings.

DAIRY BREEDS: Jerseys and Shorthorns have the reputation of easiest calving. Jerseys, Guernseys, Brown Swiss, and Holsteins are the gentlest and friendliest breeds I've known. Jerseys are the smallest breed, half the size of Devons (and so eat half as much). Guernseys are next bigger. Milking Shorthorns, Brown Swiss, and Holsteins are next up in size. Red Poll and Devon cows are also dual-purpose breeds. They are exotics and the biggest I'm going to mention. To a certain extent your cow will be priced by the pound, and that makes the larger breeds more expensive. Rare breeds are likely to be the highest priced of all. Milking Shorthorns and Brown Swiss are among the dual-purpose breeds, stocky builds for meaty calves, plus easy calving and good milk production, which are dairy characteristics. The amount of milk you get from an individual cow is a result of her breed, plus how much and what richness of feed you give her.

Ayrshire. Another fine basic dairy breed. For more info, contact the Ayrshire Breeders' Association: 614-882-1057; fax 614-895-3757; 267 Broad St., Westerville, OH 43081; **www.usayrshire.com.**

Brown Swiss. A Brown Swiss is large, tan-colored. Brown Swiss may have some calving difficulty on the first calf because they have large calves. Brown Swiss Cattle Breeders' Association: Box 1038, Beloit, WI 53511; 608-365-4474.

Dexter. The Dexter is a small dual-purpose (meat and milk) breed from Ireland. For more info, contact the Dexter Cattle Association, 404 High St., Prairie Home, MO 65068; 660-841-9502; **info@dextercattle.org; www.dextercattle.org.**

Guernsey. A Guernsey is yellow and white. Only Jerseys are smaller than Guernseys. The Guernsey has a lower cream percentage to its milk than the Jersey, but more than the Holstein. Guernseys have a reputation for being very docile and manageable, as do Jerseys. Their milk has a slightly yellow tint. American Guernsey Association: 7614 State Ridge Blvd., PO Box 666, Reynoldsburg, OH 43608-0666; 614-864-2409.

Holstein. The Holstein cow is a big, lean, black-and-white animal—a bony, pure-dairy type. It used to be that they gave up to 6 gal. per day, but now that's up to 10–14. Their milk has the lowest butterfat percentage of any dairy breed. Because of typical Holstein size, there is actually a lot of beef on a Holstein bull or steer. So a Holstein bull calf could actually be a good choice to raise for a beef calf. Holstein owners wisely breed their heifers to Herefords (a small, beef animal) for easy calving, and later, to a larger-breed bull. Almost the only dairy cow being used these days for commercial operations is the Holstein. Holstein Association USA: 1 Holstein Place, Brattleboro, VT 05302-0808; 800-952-5200.

Jersey. The Jersey is a small, dairy-type cow that gives lots of milk with a high butterfat content, the highest of any

breed. They are wonderful family cows. A Jersey gives about 3 or 4 gal., 4 in her prime—which for almost any family would be plenty. The Jersey costs less to keep than larger dairy cattle because she is smaller and eats less, but she gives less milk, and the bull calf (your meat) doesn't grow as large as most others. Jersey bull calves sell especially cheap because Jersey fat is yellow. On the market this is confused with old bull fat, so feeders won't touch them. But for homestead use they make fine meat. Jersey and Milking Shorthorn are the 2 most popular in our area for home milk cows. Although Holsteins are the dominant cow in the United States numerically, I've heard that worldwide the Jersey is most common. American Jersey Cattle Club: 6486 E. Main St., Reynoldsburg, OH 43608-2362; 614-861-3636; **www.USJersey.com.**

Water Buffalo. This misunderstood and underestimated Asian bovine has extraordinary potential. It's large and not particularly good looking, but very gentle. The 2 major types of water buffalo are the swamp buffalo, or carabao, and the river buffalo. Both are good draft animals and good meat producers. The carabao is rarely milked, but the river buffalo is an excellent dairy animal. River buffalo are now being used in Latin America, working in tropical mud that would bog down a tractor. Their working life as a draft animal can be 20 years.

Mozzarella cheese was traditionally made from the milk of river buffalo. River buffalo milk has more butterfat (7–9 percent) and more nonfat solids (18 percent) than cow's milk. River buffalo are the basic milk producers (70 percent) for India, Eastern Europe, and many Middle Eastern countries. Both river buffalo and carabao produce meat that is leaner than beef (50 percent cholesterol), and just as tender. They do better in hot weather than cattle, but still need access to shade or a pond.

Shorthorn. Milking Shorthorns can be fine dairy animals too. But pure white Shorthorn heifers sometimes have an inherited defect that prevents them from conceiving. And in our experience they were somewhat more disease-prone than the average, especially to pinkeye. Shorthorns give plenty of cream. Their butter is white, rather than yellow. American Milking Shorthorn Society: 608-365-3332.

Crosses. Gardening and food writer Lane Morgan, who reviewed the manuscript of this book, says their milk cow is a Holstein–Hereford cross and a very good family cow!

You just have to decide what is best for you.

Beef Cattle

For raising these animals practicality has to be the bottom line. A beef cow has to raise a calf each year or . . . become hamburger. You can't afford to keep beef cattle if it costs you more to raise their only product, the meat calf, than what you can sell it for. Expenses come from feed, medicine, and vet visits, fencing, and the cost of the grassland you pasture them on. As with any business, you have to keep production up and costs down. Rotation grazing on a good pasture works well.

BEEF COWS IN PRINT: *The Cattleman Magazine* comes from the Texas and Southwestern Cattle Raisers Association: 817-332-7064, ext. 131; **www.texascattleraisers.org.** Membership is handled by Lisa Walker: 817-332-7064, ext. 138; **lwalker@texascattleraisers.org.** *Farm Journal* offers "Beef Today": **sking@farmjournal.com;** 800-331-9310; **www.farmjournal.com.**

A Primer on Cattle Marketing Practices That Will Increase Your Bottom Line (1995), by Jay Nixon, is available from 830-780-2455, 302 E. Buchel, Karnes City, TX 78118. *Acres USA* offers lots of great books on cattle raising.

BEEF BREEDS

Angus. If you're worried about pinkeye, get the Black Angus breed. They're as good at foraging as Herefords, plus very disease-resistant. Angus are as wild as the proverbial March Hare, so they don't make family milk cows. They're not big, so there isn't as much meat per animal. And their small build causes calving problems; you'll have to get good at recognizing and helping with calving problems.

Beefalo. This is a buffalo-cattle cross with, some feel, the best of both breeds.

Buffalo. This close relative of cattle is a low-cholesterol, low-fat, high-profit meat animal (producers can get $18 a pound for buffalo tenderloin, $28 a pound for jerky). If there are plenty of boys and girls, food, and water, and you're lucky, they may stay inside your fencing. They can be fed a grain and hay diet just like a feedlot cow and be kept under similar circumstances. One lady keeps 9 buffalo on 10 acres. Eighty percent of this country's buffalo are now privately owned (Ted Turner and Jane Fonda have the biggest buffalo ranch: more than 5,000 head). However, these animals can be hard to control.

Exotics. Charolais, Limousin, Simmental, and a whole list of new breeds called the "exotics" are simply huge beef animals. Charolais cows tend to have trouble with their first calves because their calves are so big. A farmer nearby who raises them loses about 1 calf in 5 born to his Charolais heifers.

Hereford. The famous red-and-white Hereford cows are small like Angus, with a terrific foraging ability. Their small-boned structure is comparatively efficient at food conversion. A Shorthorn would starve to death on the deserts of southern Idaho and Wyoming, where Herefords can wander and grow fat. But, as with Angus, the smallness also brings less meat and more calving problems. A breed of miniature Herefords is now also available: (08) 8388-8393; **info@oradala.com; www.mini-hereford.com.**

Miniature cattle breeders have a society and registry. They provide info on all 24 breeds of these mini-cows and also publish a newsletter: *International Miniature Cattle Breeders Newsletter* (6 issues, $25): 253-631-1911; fax

253-631-5774; 25204-156th Ave. SE, Kent, WA 98042; **info@minicattle.com; www.minicattle.com.** For example, there are Lowlines . . .

Lowlines: These black miniature cows were created in Australia. A 14-month-old may weigh 314 kg live. Lowlines are docile, polled, with marbled meat: **info@oradala.com;** (07) 3202-9414; (02) 6226-5222; **www.lowlinebeef.com.au.**

Longhorns. If you want dramatic (scary) big horns on animals who can look after themselves very well, thank you—get Longhorns.

Scottish Highland. These cows have horns resembling the longhorns, but also coats of long, shaggy hair which makes them very hardy against both weather and predators. Joyce Hetrick gives tours of her operation and sells registered breeding stock, halter-trained and gentle: PO Box 667, Greenbrier, AR 72058; **Joyce@Heifercreek.com; www.Heifercreek.com.** The American Highland Cattle Association is the national breed association, offering info, a nice quarterly magazine, and breeder's list: 200 Livestock Exchange Bldg., 4701 Marion St., Denver, CO 80216.

Oxen: Cattle That Pull

Any bovine that has been trained to pull is a "draft ox" or "bullock." If you have 2 or more of these trained cows, you have a "yoke" or "pair" of "oxen." Technically, a steer calf, yearling steer, 2-year-old, or 3-year-old can be pulling, but it's not until the animal is practically mature at 4 years that it fully qualifies to be called "ox."

DRAFT BREEDS: Any gentle breed of cow can be trained to pull. Usually people work with steers from a large dairy breed, such as Holstein, because they're easy to get hold of. The Charolais, a French variety, are very large, powerful animals that were traditionally used as oxen in that country. They aren't terribly bright but are of a peaceable nature. Best of all are the water buffalo.

OXEN VS. DRAFT HORSES: Farmers argued for generations over whether bovines or horses were better as draft animals. Jared von Wagenen, Jr., wrote in *The Golden Age of Homespun* of "great patient brutes with hooves that grip the earth, mighty shoulders, heaving flanks, and drooping heads, placid eyes, and spreading, gleaming horns—the glorious ox team." Draft horses are more popular in the United States, to the point where the knowledge of how to train cows for draft work has teetered on the brink of extinction. A wonderful book called *Animal Traction* by Peter

Watson (1981, revised 1983) offers solid information on every aspect of using oxen for cultivation.

ADVANTAGES OF OXEN FOR DRAFT WORK

1. Many a pioneer family whose cow pulled their 2-wheeled oxcart or wagon were grateful that she also gave milk and gave birth to calves.
2. Oxen use a far less complex and less expensive, less perishable, harness than horses. They simply have their wooden yoke which is low-cost and easy to make and lasts a lifetime. The yoke gets directly attached to the tongue of the farm implement or wagon, or to a chain that is attached to their load. In the woods, there is no need for whiffletree or trace chains, only the chain going to their yoke. The traditional wooden ox yoke is cheaper than horse harnesses, although the old-timers sometimes harnessed with leather rather than yoked their oxen—and considered them less hard on harnesses than horses!
3. Oxen are generally less likely to jerk and startle than horses, more gentle and docile by nature.
4. A typical ox is heavier than a typical horse, with more pulling power. Von Wagenen wrote, "It was in the rough, hilly sections that oxen were found in the greatest numbers and lingered longest." But that is hotly disputed; I've heard elsewhere, "It takes 2 yoke of cattle to do the work of one 1,200-lb. team of horses."
5. The pioneers considered oxen to be better among stumps and stones than horses.
6. Oxen can be shod, but aren't as needy of it as horses. And don't shoe your oxen until they're at least 4 years old because before that their hoof isn't strong enough yet for a nail. And, once shod, an ox holds a shoe longer than a horse. (If oxen are worked a lot, they *need* shoes. A horse takes a single shoe per foot. An ox requires 2 shoes on each foot, 1 for each half of their cloven hoof. A horse will allow its foot to be picked up and held; an ox usually won't easily cooperate, but it can be done.)
7. Oxen are claimed by their owners to be healthier than horses. The old-timers believed oxen could do more work on a diet of plain hay and pasture than a horse.
8. The price of a potential draft cow is less than that for a draft horse—bull calves are cheap to get if you have milk cows.
9. Oxen are good in deep snow.
10. An old, or retired ox can be converted to hamburger for the family. Old horses get sold for dog food, but are not eaten at home.
11. Oxen are more patient and less likely to injure themselves. (Horses are faster.)

(For all the good things about draft horses, see *The Draft Horse Primer* by Maurice Telleen.)

RESOURCES

Association of New England Ox Teamsters works to preserve New England traditions: Linda Wilbur, Secretary; 603-357-4197; 989 Old Walpole Rd., Surry, NH 03431; **lhwmoo@earthlink.net; home.attbi.com/~cynthia123.**

BerryBrook Ox Supply sells ox equipment: new and used yokes, bows, ox shoes, goads, whips, logging equipment, horn knobs, horn weights, yoke hardware, books, videos, etc. Their newly manufactured logging/farming fore cart and logging scoot are of good

quality and reasonably priced: 603-335-4475; 394 Meaderboro Rd., Farmington, NH 03835; **berry brookoxen@aol.com.**

Drew Conroy teaches dairy farm management at the U. of New Hampshire, Thompson School of Applied Science, 291 Mast Rd, Durham, NH 03824-3562; 603-862-2625; **oxwoodfarm@aol.com.** He's the expert on training and using oxen as draft animals who wrote *Oxen: A Teamster's Guide.*

Mid South Ox Drovers Ass'n is for people interested in cattle trained for draft purposes (oxen). Demonstrations and newsletter available.

Midwest Ox Drovers Ass'n holds a wonderful annual meeting and has a regular newsletter ($10) focusing on education and sharing info: c/o Jeff Hieb, 1119 Portier St., Green Bay, WI 54301; 920-468-6420; **oxdrover@execpc.com; www.execpc.com/~hiebej/.**

Tillers International: Take a "Yoke Building and Fitting Workshop," the "Ox Driving Workshop," or one of the many other relevant classes in nonelectric skills offered by Tillers International; 616-344-3233; fax 616-344-3238; 5239 S. 24th St., Kalamazoo, MI 49002. They also sell ox-power publications and products: *The Pride and Joy of Working Cattle,* successful techniques for ox training, by Ray Ludwig; and *In Praise of Oxen,* by Terry James and F. Anderson, photos of Canadian teams. Membership in Tillers gets you the *Nigh Ox,* their newsletter. Other ox books from Tillers include *Advanced Training of Oxen; Training Young Steers; Selecting and Teaming Oxen;* and info on how to build an ox yoke, cart design, single-cow yoke design, yokes, yoke rings, and training videos.

TRAINING OXEN: Begin training with calves, so they have a long time to get used to all that is involved. The old-timers looked for an animal with ambition and that "light-footedness." True draft breeds or dairy breeds are preferred for their docility, once steered. The old-time English Devon was treasured for its draft ability. Von Wagenen wrote that "the breed had a certain snappy activity and light-footedness." Nowadays Devons are rare; and Holstein steers make fine oxen, too. Oxen are normally used in a set of 2.

Oxen can be trained to work by voice commands, combined with a prod or whip used by a driver who walks next to them, or to work using a harness and bit and driven with reins like a horse team. In either case you start by getting them used to wearing a halter and teaching them to lead. To drive using a bit and reins, train like a draft horse. Work with them at least half an hour a day. If you work right before their dinner, it ends their labor with a food reward.

Voice Commands. Traditional names for a yoke of oxen are "Tom and Jerry," or "Buck and Bright" or "Pat and Mike," or "Duke and Dine." The traditional voice commands are "gee, gee" for "go right" and "haw, haw" for "go left." "Whoa" means "stop." "Ged-dup" means "go." ("Go" sounds too much like "whoa" to use.) "Back" means reverse, back up. You can habitually combine a command with the animal's name: such as "Gee Pat" to go right, "Haw Mike" to go left. Training them, like horses, to wear a bridle with bit, combined with the yoke, allows the driver more precise control, but the beauty of using voice commands is that it leaves your hands free and you don't have to worry about reins.

It takes considerable time and effort to get those 4 terms drilled into them. Teach them to obey voice com-

mands using ropes that force them to do what the voice command means. Or to teach "whoa," step right in front of the animal while pulling hard backward on its halter at the same time you say the word. You repeat that over and over until the animal does it without the halter pull or the rope (classic Pavlovian conditioning). Cows are brighter than you might think, but, still, they are creatures of extreme habit. What they've learned is what they know. That's why from the first day you assign 1 of your pair to be the nigh (left) ox, and the other to be the off (right side) ox. From then on you *always* yoke them that way. Otherwise they're "backwards," and oxen yoked backward will be very confused! If your nigh ox, for example, dies, replace it with another trained nigh ox—or train a green steer. Don't try to use an off ox there. The old-timers in New England usually called that nigh ox, "Buck," and the off ox "Bright." That way they knew which side an ox was trained for by his name.

Gad. The voiced command is supplemented by the "gad" or "whip," traditionally a 4- or 5-foot length of narrow hardwood sapling with 2-3 feet of thin leather strap attached to the end. Let me make it clear that the gad is used for touches to get Buck and Bright's attention, to direct and manage them, rather than to punish. Some teams, in some circumstances, work fine with only voice.

Yoke. The traditional hitching system is based on the yoke, a large carved wood shape that fits over each animal's neck and is held there from underneath by a U-shaped bow under the cow's neck. To see how a yoke is made, check your local pioneer museum! You can make a yoke by cutting it out of a block of wood with a chain saw and trimming with a knife. The bow under the cow's neck can be made of any strong, flexible wood, steam-bent into that U-shape.

You'll be putting them into a series of yokes, of ever-increasing size, as they grow. To fit them properly with a yoke, start by tying them up standing parallel and with their sides 6 inches apart. Measure the distance between their necks and build their yoke accordingly. When they've grown enough that their sides are rubbing, it's time for a bigger yoke.

A modern variation is a bridle and bit on the animals by which they are directed from behind with reins just like with harnessed horses, but combined with a yoke.

Training Oxen to the Yoke. At the center of the single yoke that binds them together there is a metal ring. You fasten the tongue of the farm implement that they are to pull there, and that's it. While still young, they can pull a pole with something noisy attached to it to help them develop calm nerves—later a light sleigh or cart. At 18 months old they can start more seriously working. For tough work like plowing, even 4 yoke of cattle might have been combined in the old days.

Cattle Handling

Cows vary wildly in gentleness from a sweet pet of a Jersey family milk cow to a huge, mean, wild range bull. The following wisdom is specially applicable to working with range beef cattle, but there are wise reminders here for any handler.

COW PSYCHOLOGY AND SENSES: Your cow's closest relative on the farm is the sheep. They're both herd-oriented, humble animals. (For least stress and best production keep 2 or more calves or cattle.) There will be a boss cow, same as the boss goat described in that section. Large cattle herds will form smaller subherds with an order of dominance in each group. A cow's best sense is her smell. She can smell her calf 3 or 4 miles away. A bull can smell a cow in heat that is miles away. Cattle have good hearing, too. They dislike high-pitched sounds like the crack of a whip.

Cow psychology is influenced by the design of a cow's body. A cow has 360° panoramic vision. That means she can put her hind foot into the bucket or kick it over on you, and it's not a lucky accident for her. She can actually see beside and behind herself without turning her head. But cows can't see color. Everything is black and white to them, so it doesn't matter what you wear. They are very sensitive to stark black and white contrasts, though, and have poor depth perception. White lines painted across a road can look like a cattle guard to them. It's hard for a cow to tell the difference between a shadow and a hole in the ground so a dark shadow can scare her into going around it.

SECRETS OF SAFE CATTLE HANDLING

1. Move your cattle patiently, quietly. Avoid exciting or hurrying them because a running cow does its own unpredictable thing whereas a slowly walking one is likely to go where you want.
2. Cows follow the leader. If you can coax the first 1 or 2 through a gate, etc., the rest are likely to follow naturally.
3. To turn a cow you can make some noise and make yourself look large by waving your arms widely, but do this from an angle, not right in front of the animal because you may lose. Being straight ahead in the cow's way invites you getting knocked down and hurt.
4. Teach your cattle to come to a certain familiar call to get a treat of grain or a bale of hay. When you feed them frequently and handle them gently they learn to trust and depend on you. Then you can call and lead them where you want. (Always follow the call with the food reward or they'll lose faith.) This, of course, works best if they're hungry.
5. Cows are frightened of new places and made nervous by change in their daily routine. They don't take easily to learning anything new. They resent being forced to do anything. The best approach is true patience and a plan to outsmart rather than outfight them.
6. Build good fences and keep them repaired.
7. Build a corral and a loading chute.
8. A knowledgeable horse or dog can help a lot.
9. Keep a docile, hornless breed.
10. When dealing with a cow–calf pair, have a means of escape available, such as a pickup that you could run around or vault into; the cow's protective instinct might get aroused, in which case she would attack using her head. She's most likely to charge you if her calf bawls. (The strong maternal instinct of beef cattle is a usually good thing. They've been known to protect calves successfully even against lions and bears.)
11. Before you help a calving cow, first halter her and tie her to a fence post, tree, or (worst choice) pickup bumper.
12. Be careful around a cow in heat. She may try to mount you.
13. Be even more careful around a bull. Never forget its potential danger. Never come near it without having an escape route in mind. Never turn your back on it. If possible always have a second person with you. If a bull does become threatening, hamburger it. *Never let children into a pasture or pen that has a bull in it.*

Cattle Housing

Don Fallick, Davenport, WA, wrote me: "Cattle lean on things. And they're heavy. Anything built for use around cattle simply must be very sturdy."

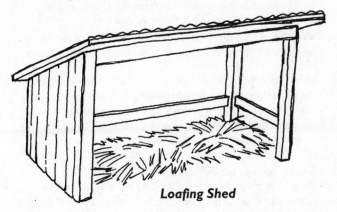

Loafing Shed

LOAFING SHED: A loafing shed for cattle should be anchored by posts at least 8 inches in diameter, extending below ground at least 3 feet. Old telephone poles work well. The phone company pulls poles when they get too rough to climb safely, but they may still be sound from a structural point of view. The posts can be connected by 2x8s set 2 feet on center. Skin the outside with exterior grade plywood, no thinner than ⅝ inch, though ¾ inch is better if you can afford it. Particle board will weather better than plywood, but will never stand up to the punishment cattle will give it. Corrugated metal roofing is so good and so cost-efficient, it has virtually become standard. Such a loafing shed is cheaper than one built of cement blocks, and much cheaper than one with concrete walls, but it won't last nearly as long. A good compromise is to build the bottom 4 feet of the walls of reinforced concrete or reinforced cement blocks. Then build the top of the walls of wood.

MILK PARLOR: Your "milk parlor" is an outbuilding where you will milk your dairy cow(s). Don Fallick says: "A milk parlor for cattle should be built similar to a barn, but for cleanliness I favor walls of concrete, at least at the bottom. If you use cement blocks, painting them will make them easier to clean. To fasten the frame tops of the walls to the concrete or cement blocks, set L-bolts in the top of the concrete, or fill the cement blocks with sand where the L-bolts will be set, except for the top course. Then fill with cement and set the L-bolts in every third block. The L-bolts will be used to bolt down the bottom plate of the frame portion of the wall. A slick way to position the L-bolts exactly is to drill the bottom plate first and install the L-bolts in it loosely, then use it to position the bolts in the wet cement. After the cement is dry, the bottom plate can be removed and the wall framed, installed, and bolted down." Believe you me though, says Carla, it can be simpler than that.

Feeding Cattle

Any cow needs grass or hay, water, and salt. (There's lots more about pasture, hay, and silage in Chapter 8.) Cows that are giving milk have special nutritional considerations

(see below). They all always need water and salt. Mature cattle are true symbionts, in that they cannot live without the help of millions of microscopic critters that live in their rumen and do their digesting for them! A cow's stomach is literally a big fermentation vat in which their friendly bacteria and protozoa are constantly digesting the food and fiber they eat.

NOTE: *A cow is designed to eat with her head down. If your feed trough isn't low enough, her saliva won't run well.*

WATER: Cows need lots of clean water. If you have trouble with it freezing in winter, you can buy an electric heater that keeps the tank warm enough so the water doesn't freeze. Mike just goes out twice a day and chops a hole with the ax so they can drink and hopes for warm weather and a thaw. It's nice if you have a way to warm their water in winter, but it doesn't have to be warm. And, given a choice, cows would much rather drink unchlorinated water and will drink more and produce more milk on it.

SALT: You can get various kinds of salt blocks. Some of them have minerals added. There is even a kind that contains a medicine to help fight the burrowing flies that cause worms in their backs. (Can't give that kind to milk cows.) Your block will last the longest if you keep it sheltered from the weather.

FEED FOR BEEF COWS: You don't need to give beef animals any grain. In general, beef fat is one animal product there just isn't much use for. You can take some beef tallow on the end of a fork and use it to grease a pancake griddle. You could make soap with it. You can grind a little bit in with your beef hamburger, but it's a comparatively high cholesterol fat. Our cows for eating are entirely grass-fed: grass in summer, hay in winter. They've never tasted grain.

SECRETS OF DAIRY-COW FEEDING

1. Provide lush pasture—or the equivalent in hay and supplements. In an average temperate zone your cow can be well-fed on pasture from early May to late November.
2. Pasture is most nourishing when it includes legumes (clover, alfalfa, lespedeza), several kinds of grasses, and a variety of herbs (natural, healthy "weeds" or fenugreek, lavender, marjoram, mustard, rosemary, sage, thyme, etc.).
3. Feed hay during winter: tender, green, cut just as it blooms.
4. Every day feed 2–3 lb. good hay per 100 lb. body weight of your cow, as much as she'll eat during winter. If you're feeding silage, give 3 times that much, since it isn't nearly as nourishing as good hay. If you do feed silage or green chop, best feed some hay too.
5. Feed only an amount of hay that she'll eat up before the next milking. Cows don't like stale feed and the surplus will be wasted.
6. You have the option of feeding your dairy cow only such good hay and/or good pasture. She will still produce plenty of milk for an average family.
7. When pasture or hay quality falls, your cow will give less milk.
8. If you supplement with grain (oats, barley, corn, wheat) and other high-protein foods (peanuts, soybeans, legumes, sorghum, milo, kafir, soybeans, peas), you can increase her milk production by 30–40 per-

cent and prolong her production period. You can buy this type of supplement from a feed store or provide it home-grown. Store feed grains in a covered, metal container to prevent losses to rodents.

9. Feed supplements morning and evening at milking time.
10. If your cow isn't used to them, add them gradually, increasing the amount slowly to avoid bloat.
11. Start feeding supplements after calving and increase gradually as she produces more heavily, then taper off gradually as she slows in production, nearing the end of her lactation. Thus you match your supplementing to her milk production since the reason you're giving supplements is to replace the protein lost in her milk production. She normally peaks in production a month after calving, stays high for the next 3 months or so, then tapers down until the end of her 10 months lactation when it's time for you to stop milking her.
12. Every cow has a maximum ability to give milk, beyond which extra feed is just wasted on her. You can learn that by increasing supplement until her milk supply stops increasing. Then stop increasing—give her a little less than the peak amount for her 8-month production high. An average cow can use up to 1 lb. grain per 3 lb. milk produced. But with quality pasture or hay and ½ lb. grain each day, she'll give about 90 percent of her capacity. And that may be more than enough for your needs.
13. If you choose to supplement and/or winter her only on home-grown food, the easiest system is to give her corn and cornstalks starting in late summer. As long as the corn is still somewhat soft you won't need to grind it for her. Starting in about November add supplemental hay. Starting in December feed as much good hay as she'll eat, plus several ears of corn, ground, at each milking until the pasture is ready again in late spring. You can also give her root vegetables (carrots, beets—washed and sliced), crushed beans and peas, whole sunflower heads, cabbage, turnips, beet pulp, squash, pumpkins, buckwheat—actually, any grain (see animal-feeding instructions under that grain), and winter-growing green leafies such as comfrey and kale. It takes a lot of root vegetables or leafies to supplement for a cow. Figure about ⅛ acre of garden per cow to grow her supplementary feed at 25 lb. per winter day.
14. If pasture is overgrazed or the hay is poor-quality, she'll need extra-rich supplements.
15. Or, if she is gentle enough to wear a halter and be staked out—and many family milk cows are—you can put her out to graze on unfenced patches of good green grass in summer and make good use of feed that would otherwise be wasted. A staked-out cow needs a large water container nearby kept filled, especially if the weather's hot; or else somebody must lead her to her drinking place at least 3 times a day.
16. Know your cow's normal appearance. If she's fat, cut back on supplements. She could have calving difficulty from being overweight. *If she's getting thin, give her more feed! If she refuses to eat, call the vet!*

ABOUT ROUGHAGE AND PROTEIN: A dairy cow needs 2 kinds of food in her diet to be healthy: roughage, which can be supplied by any kind of grass, even straw; and protein. Alfalfa hay has both. Straw is high in roughage, low in protein. You have to supplement straw with grain or good alfalfa hay, which is a high-protein hay. Straight grain isn't a good feed because there's not enough roughage. If you can supply your cow good green leafy alfalfa hay, almost any mixture of home-grown grains will be a fine protein supplement.

MORE ABOUT GRAIN FOR YOUR MILK COW: Grains differ in food value. Barley is richer than oats, but more expensive than oats. A good grain treat feed for the milk cow is a mixture of half-chopped oats and half-chopped barley. Any grain that you buy for your animals should be chopped or ground before you bring it home. They can digest it better that way, so they'll get more food value for your dollar. If you raise your own grain, rigging up your own chopper is almost a must. Or you can use the coarsest grind on your home flour grinder. Whole grain is cheaper, so you can save yourself money by doing your own grinding. I give our milk cows about a half gallon of grain morning and night. That's really more than necessary. Oat-pea hay is a good winter feed for them. That, plus some alfalfa, contains everything they need—including enough grain.

ABOUT HAY FOR COWS: It takes a lot of hay. You don't need to give anything else but water and a salt block to nonmilking cows, but cows that are milking or getting ready to come fresh are grateful for some grain every day. Cows have the kind of digestive tract that needs a lot of roughage but also some protein. Alfalfa hay is ideal for them because it has both. But if you haven't got or can't afford alfalfa hay, you could use a poorer hay with a grain supplement to supply protein. Or a straw, alfalfa, grain combo. If you use straw, such as barley straw or oat straw (the stalks left after the combine has taken the grain heads), you should also give them some higher-quality food value in it to keep them in good shape. To winter a cow you figure about 2 tons of hay per cow per average winter.

Cow Reproduction

SCHEDULING: A milk cow can very neatly be put on an annual schedule. Keep your cow pregnant 9 months out of the 12. Dry her up about 2 months before calving time. (If her feed is mostly grass rather than grain and supplements, it's wise to dry her up 3 months before her due date.) The second time she comes into heat after calving (about 18–22 days after the first heat she'll be in heat again), put her with the bull or A-I. That way you are milkless only about 8 weeks of the year, and she is producing beef calves and replacement heifers about as fast as bovinely possible. Gestation is 285 days, about 9½ months. So she will calve again at about the same time next year, and you get 1 calf a year from her plus all that milk.

HEIFERS: It's better to not let a heifer get bred as soon as she is capable of it or you risk a difficult birth, a cow stunted for life, always a poor milk producer. They can conceive as young as 3 months. Don't let them conceive until they're at least 13 months old. To minimize calving problems, don't grain a heifer before she has her first calf.

COW HEATS: Usually her heat period is every 21 days, but individual animals can have a cycle as short as 18 days or as long as 24. Her first heat period after giving birth will be in 30–60 days. A cow stays in heat from 8 to 30 hours, on the average about 16 hours. If you notice heat, get her bred immediately, because the next day may be too late!

SIGNS OF BOVINE HEAT

1. Restlessness, stamping around, twitching her tail an unusual amount.
2. She'll be doing a lot of bawling.
3. She may drop a little in milk production.
4. You may see redness and swelling around her vulva, plus maybe a mucous discharge there.
5. If you have other cows (even females), they'll be riding her in the manner of a bull.
6. If a normally peaceable heifer goes through your fence, it probably also means she's in heat.
7. If the neighbor's bull comes through your fence and breeds her, that's an absolute proof.
8. Lane Morgan warns, "Be alert. She may also try to mount you."
9. If she lies down any time in the latter part of her heat period, she'll go out of heat.

BREEDING: From the time of her first post-calving heat on, she'll have monthly heats until she's bred. A less frantic way of arranging her breeding than trying to get the A-I techie there her first heat is to simply mark down her date, then make tentative arrangements for the next heat, which you now know the approximate date of—it will arrive in 18–22 days. Cows can thus conceive—and calve—at any time of year. The best schedule for cheapest food production is to time it so her calf comes in very early spring. Her first breeding may not take. (About 1 in 3 tries don't.) If not, try it again the next "month," and that probably will settle her for sure.

Bull. You don't want to keep a bull unless you're running a serious cattle ranching operation. If you do, the bull needs more feed than a cow, but can make it on grass in summer and hay and roughage in winter. A bull for breeding should be at least 18 months old. *A bull must always be handled with care. They are always potentially dangerous.*

A-I. If you artificially inseminate, you can have a calf that's half anything. A heifer that hasn't had a calf before, or for safety's sake, that hasn't had 2 calves yet, shouldn't be bred to a bull of a larger breed than her own. Cow breeds vary too much in size. An unbred Jersey cow might weigh 600 lb. or even less before her first calving. On the other hand a Devon cow could weigh 1,600 lb. So you see, you wouldn't want to breed your Jersey heifer to a Devon bull because the resulting calf would probably be so big she couldn't bear it naturally. Breed her to a Jersey bull the first couple of times. Then you could try something bigger. Shorthorn is fine later on, because although the Shorthorn cow weighs about 1,200 or even 1,500 lb. on some of the Australian Illawarra exotics, the calf is not large.

The people who artificially inseminate are certified by the state after taking an A-I course. You can pay the inseminator to come, or you can take a course and do it yourself. The inseminator brings a kit in which he or she carries all kinds of frozen semen for you to choose from. Very fancy stuff—it can be from champion bulls of any breed you choose. The semen will cost an additional fee per ampule, price depending on the source. The cow has to be in heat for the A-I to take.

GESTATION: The length of pregnancy varies somewhat, but in general a cow will calve 285 days from her date of service—in about 9½ months. If you don't dry up your cow that last 6 weeks it's hard on her, and the milk may get "strong" tasting.

CALVING: The same principles apply as with goats. Prevention of problems is the best cure. The dairy breeds of cows all calve easily anyway, as they are selected for that. It's some of the smallest and largest beef breeds that have the reputation of calving difficulty.

Because a cow's birthing instinct is to go hide in a woods and do it all by herself, it's wise to bring her into a pasture near the house in summer or into the barn where you're providing a warm stall with lots of clean bedding if the weather is awful. Do that at least a couple days before her calving date so you can keep a close watch on her. You'll know calving is getting near when her udder swells with a milk supply, her vulva swells, and the flesh seems to loosen around her tail bone and fall away.

After that point, check on her several times a day. You have a big investment at stake here and will want to help or call the vet if she has calving trouble. But ordinarily your cow will calve, and you'll find her standing there nuzzling her baby, and you won't have to do a thing except provide the usual necessities of food, water, and shelter. She may very likely calve in the open. That isn't nearly the problem it can be with goats and sheep because calves generally are hardier at birth.

If your cow is obviously in trouble and you live in the country near experienced neighbors, the first thing I'd do is ask them for advice. Most knowledgable cow people can help you judge what is happening very competently. *If she isn't able to give birth after 3 or 4 hours of hard labor, call the vet to come.* A cow is worth a lot of money and well worth what you'd pay the vet to get her fixed up. And then you save the value of the calf, too. A calf normally is able to stand, though awkwardly, soon after birth and nurse from its mama. If you're there when she calves, stay long enough to make sure that the calf indeed makes it onto its feet and found a teat.

Cow Down. Barbara Stone, Stites, ID, wrote me: "We had a cow that had just calved, but she had lain in such a position that she couldn't get up. She was in the middle of the field, but she found a place where she had her head downhill and her back area uphill. This had never happened to us before, so we didn't know exactly what to do, but we knew she couldn't stay there too long. With the help of a neighbor we got her feet dragged around with both areas on the same level. Put her on her knees and held her so she'd stay there. Within just a few hours she was up as if nothing happened. If this happens again, and it probably will sometime, we'll know what to do. If no one is around to help, use the tractor or the pickup, tie a rope around the front legs and carefully roll them around until they are straight. Watch the neck that it doesn't get hurt. All of these things a person has to learn sometimes the hard way. After the animal is up, make sure it stays up."

A cow might be down if she's been injured from slipping on a slick surface, or had a blow from another cow, or by calving, or by disease. A "downer cow" is indeed a crisis. She needs to be kept comfortable, fed, watered, and treated as needed. Pro cow operations use a "downer cow skid" to move her if moving is needed. (It takes at least 2 or 3 strong people to roll a downed cow onto even the lowest skid.) *NOTE: But if a cow goes down and can't get up just before or right after calving, I'd start by calling the vet quickly in case she has milk fever.*

Newborn Calves

Take out a big towel or blanket to dry off the newborn calf with a good rubbing. Check to make sure it's in a relatively nice place. Calves are tougher than kids. If you want the cow and calf moved, just pick up the calf and carry it in your arms. The cow will follow. She'll try to hide the calf as soon as she can. That's called "brushing up," and it's an instinct cows have. She'll go to the hiding place several times a day to feed and check on it. (Goats, on the other hand, will stay right by their babies.)

We usually give the newborn calf its Bose vaccine and maybe some A and D and Combiotic and hang around until it stands and finds its first meal. Even if you leave the calf with the cow you've still got to milk the mother out yourself at least once a day. That's because any milk cow in her second (or more) lactation gives much more milk than a newborn calf can use, and she will be miserable and risking mastitis if you don't help by taking the extra milk.

BUYING A YOUNG CALF: You can often buy a calf from a nearby dairy or farm. If you just want a calf to raise for meat, a male calf of a dairy breed is probably the cheapest to buy. A dairy-beef cross would give you a little more beef; they grow faster and have a meatier carcass. Be sure you have a healthy one. A thriving young 'un holds up its head —back straight, tail out a little. A calf that won't stand or huddles in a corner with its head hanging, back hunched up, and tail down between its legs is probably sick. A bargain calf that brings disease, parasites, and vet expense to you—or even dies—is no bargain. It's best to take care and a little time in buying, though it will cost you more. Ask: When was the calf born? How many days of colostrum has the calf received? What vaccinations has the calf received? What diet is he on right now? How much milk per day? How many feedings per day? How much grain or hay?

AUCTION CALVES: If you buy a day-old calf at a livestock auction you have special problems. Maybe the calf has never eaten. Ranchers may take a calf to the sale ring while it is still practically wet if the sale day happens to fall that soon after it is born. Or the brood cow might have died in calving, and he doesn't want to bother with an orphan. By the time you get such a calf home it will seem weak and listless. You may find that a calf you buy at auction that has been nursing the cow is better started health-wise but is not pan or bottle broken.

Taking Your Calf Home. The best time of year to get a calf is late winter. (Then, about the time it's weaned, it can go on grass and live on that until late-fall butchering time.) If you plan to buy a baby calf at auction and the weather is cold, take an old blanket to the sales yard or provide some straw bedding. A long chilly ride home in the back of a pickup is going to weaken your calf even more. Put a halter on him and fasten it tightly near where you want him to ride. When you get your calf home give him a place indoors —in the barn with lots of hay or straw bedding and a blanket over if he is shivering or wet or weak. Give an antibiotic "calf starter" pill if he can't have mother's colostrum.

Calf Shelter. A calf born in late-spring or summer outside in a pasture will do fine. A late-winter auction calf needs to have a home inside your barn where it's dry and sheltered from the wind. A mid-spring calf can go to a more humble outdoor shelter consisting of an open-front shed or some such. Provide warm bedding and frequent feedings of warm milk. Later add a water supply and a hay manger if hay will be fed.

White Muscle Disease. We had a calf die of this. It was very stiff in the joints, moved little, slowly, with obvious difficulty, and was in poor health, generally. It couldn't follow its mother and so didn't get enough to eat. There is a lot of white muscle disease in our area, and it's important that we get a calf immunized against it as soon as possible after birth because it's just about impossible to cure once it sets in. We try to give the immunization shot the same day the calf is born. You can mail-order these and other serums or buy from your vet or vet supply.

Chilled Calf. If you find a calf prostrate, shivering, with tongue slightly protruding and eyes sunk in—one that cannot get up or eat due to the chill on an unseasonably cold night—carry it into the house. Lay a towel in the bathtub. Lay the calf on the towel and a blanket on top and draw in enough hot water to stop the shivering. In the meantime get a hot place ready for after it comes out of the tub so it doesn't get chilled again. Keep the calf warm even when it seems to be pulling out of it. A chill may give it a fatal setback.

Surplus Calves. These are never just killed and discarded like kids may be. Even a newborn calf is worth at least $75 or can be butchered for meat. But a normal cow gives plenty of milk to meet both your needs and the calf's.

MILK FOR CALVES: You can take a calf from the mother anytime from birth on. If you take the calf away immediately, you get it without prejudices about how it should eat and without too much energy to fight your ministrations. If you wait 4 days, however, it has been well-started by the mother, but the mother's milk production in the long run may benefit more if you take the calf off her immediately and milk her out twice a day.

Colostrum. Feed the calf all the milk you get from its mother for the first 4 days of milking after calving. You can refrigerate surplus until needed. Don't use it yourself since it's brownish-yellowish and not very appetizing looking for people food, and more importantly it contains antibodies the calf urgently needs. After that the colostrum taste is out, and you can use the milk, too. The colostrum milk is fine for pigs and chickens as well as the calf, so you don't need to throw any away.

Calf Adoption. A dairy cow can easily raise 2 or 3 calves. To put a calf on a cow that's not its natural mother, it works best to restrain the cow while the calf nurses until it learns how to sneak a meal from behind. Some folks put vinegar on the calf and on the cow—on their noses and other places—to try to fool the cow into accepting the calf more readily.

Milk Formula for Calves. If you have no colostrum, give the calf warm milk with egg yolk beaten into it. Cold milk can kill a calf. The egg yolk makes the first meal a little richer and thicker. Continue to give the milk and egg yolk mixture for several meals and return to it if the calf does poorly after that. After that, feed milk from another cow, just as it comes from the cow. If you don't have that, you can feed fresh goat's milk, diluted 1:1 with water. Lacking that, feeding reconstituted dried whole milk is next best. Dried nonfat milk is not as healthy but can work.

How Much Milk? A quart or so per day to start with, then work up to 2 qt. per day at 2 weeks, then 3 qt. per day at 3 weeks. It depends also on how much the calf will drink.

You can give more of the cow's milk than of a powdered milk–water mix or goat's milk. Calves of different breeds, hence different weights, will take relatively more or less. A larger calf will be drinking 2–2½ qt. at each of its 2 daily feedings. The older the calf, the more it will take. Too much causes scours. A big calf would happily drink much more milk than it is ordinarily given. We force the calf to share his milk with us because we need it too.

Temperature. The milk should be warmed to body temperature, about 100°F.

Calf Bottle/Feeder. You feed them either out of a pan or from a calf bottle, calf feeder, or a calf group feeder (a box with several nipples). A calf feeder is a bucket with a nipple attached to the bottom. If you're going to use the calf feeder you've got to start with it—the very first time you try to feed the calf. He'll get a fix on whatever he is sucking when he gets his first good swig of milk and will be hard to change over. You coax the nipple into his mouth the first time. Same with a calf bottle, which is a big plastic bottle with the right-sized nipple. Try to stay with small calves drinking out of a calf bottle. Otherwise, they may yank the nipple off, end up inhaling their dinner, and get clinical pneumonia. The calf group feeder is the latest and greatest thing, especially for mass production of beef calves. Let's say you have 5 calves in a pen. At feeding time you bring their milk in a big bucket and pour it into the group feeder. The group feeder sits on legs on the ground or is hung from or attached to the wall. It has 5 equal-sized compartments to hold milk, each of which is attached to an outside calf-sized nipple. The milk-holding part has marked lines on the inside like a measuring cup so you know how much you're feeding. You pour the milk into the little trough; the calf sucks it out through a nipple. Have the group feeder high enough so young calves suck in the natural head-up position.

Pan Feeding. Or use a stainless-steel pan (but any kind will do) about 6 inches deep and about 1 foot across. I warm my milk and egg mix right in the pan. Make it a little extra warm to compensate for chilling on the trip to the barn. The calf has 2 strong natural instincts that you have to consider when you're breaking him to a pan feed: one is to reach up to feed; the other is to suck on a nipple-type object.

So do this: Cup your left hand slightly. Dip your hand in the warm milk. Slip your middle fingers into his mouth. With your other hand scoop up milk and pour it into your feeding hand. Some of it will run down the grooves between your fingers and get into his mouth. You need some-

1. Time: It takes about 3 hours for us to butcher a cow and 2½ hours longer to cut up each quarter. If we took the cow to a custom butcher he would charge and also keep the hide and organ meats. It's a lot of work, but it does save money to do it yourself.
2. The work will go faster and be much easier if you have a way to get the animal up off the ground.
3. It helps, too, if you've had experience skinning and gutting some smaller animals like goat or deer. I'd hate to see somebody start on an 800-lb. calf.
4. Butchering a cow is very hard work. The more experienced help you can call in the better. Cow hide is tough—leather in the making. Cows are big and hard to shift around. Even the innards are heavy, and there is such a weight of them it presents quite a challenge. So before you start have a few friends on hand.
5. Have ready too, a gun to shoot the animal.
6. And a bucket or pan to hold the heart and liver.
7. You'll need sharp hunting knives or skinning knives or butcher knives—plenty of them, plus the stone you rub the blade edge across to sharpen it. You will have to stop occasionally and sharpen your knife.
8. You need a big washtub for the guts. Even so, they will have a tendency to overflow it. And have a plan for what you're going to do with all those innards. (See Chapter 8 for suggestions about handling the awful offal.)
9. You also need a meat saw for making the halves and quarters. You could use a chain saw, but it is far from necessary, maybe not even preferable. The saw you use is a regular crosscut or carpenter's-type saw.

body to hold the pan while you are doing this. And the calf needs to be lying down to make it easier for you. You may have to spend a long time just doing this. Now try to gradually lower your hand into the milk. He'll suck up the milk and it will go into his mouth. Wiggle your fingers in his mouth a little if he seems to be losing interest. It takes a little effort to get him pan-broken, but once he is, all you have to do is take his pan and set it down and get out of the way. That's helpful when he grows to 200 lb. Note: It's actually healthier for a calf to nurse with his head up than down because that's the way he's designed—so there's another advantage to the bottle method.

Frequency. Feed the calf every few hours (5 times a day) until you're sure you are getting food down it. Then go to 4 times a day for a few days. Then feed him morning, noon, and night for a few days. Then only twice daily. He will be a ravenous glutton, but don't give him all he can drink, as it will make him sick. Twice a day continues until you're ready to start weaning.

Calf Scours. When we have a baby calf with scours we put him in the warmest, driest place possible, give him an extra calf starter pill if it's very bad, and give him half a 12-ounce bottle of Kaopectate. Kaopectate is a mixture of real fruit pectin and kaolin—a natural clay. It really helps. Then I give less milk and sometimes make it less strong by watering it. You just have to experiment to figure out what the individual animal needs. If calves scour on a diet of goat's milk you can't change to cow's milk—the change in formula will make them even sicker. Just give Kaopectate and give them less of what you're giving them. Some baby cereal or scorched flour with the Kaopectate may also help. And so will shots of vitamins and antibiotics.

WEANING: When calves are raised to set records for weight gain and final size—registered championship-type animals—they are usually left on the mother because the plain fact is that given all the milk they desire on a demand schedule, they gain faster and end up being bigger and better-looking than they do on the bucket. Their competition is animals that have had a lot of grain pushed into them from as young as they'd take it. You can wean a calf from milk completely at a surprisingly young age. The bottom line is usually your personal farm economics and convenience. The weaned calf should have a source of water, and a salt-mineral block to lick. To commence weaning a bottle baby, you cut down to one feeding so he's getting half as much milk as before. Then give that every other day. Then not at all.

Late Weaning. If the cow gives plenty of milk for your needs as well as the calf's, you can let it nurse until time to butcher it for veal or baby beef or until she dries up to have her next calf—and save money and hassle. This is basically demand feeding. The calf is shut away from Mum either at night or in the daytime, so the family gets at least one milking a day for their use. The calf eats grass or hay as wanted, and grain for treats and teaching and taming but not a regular diet of it. You can do the same thing with a bucket- or bottle-fed calf when you have abundant milk —wait to wean until they are 6 or even 7 months old. After Mum dries up in preparation to calve again, the naturally nursing calf will give it up forever (in case you have a calf that makes a liar of me and continues nursing, you can buy an anti-sucking device from Nasco), and will be physically ready to, even though still in the same field. Beef calves naturally nurse on this schedule, and thus don't get weaned until about 6–8 months of age.

If you have a mother cow and a pasture of nice grass, you have the most economical way to raise beef. You don't have to pay for the milk or the grass. A calf born in late winter will make the most of the spring, summer, and fall grass. By the time the pasture is going dormant or getting snow-covered it will weigh 800–1,000 lb. You can butcher then and have no winter feeding bill and lots of meat.

Average Weaning. Watch to see when the calf starts taking substantial amounts of other kinds of feed. Then cut back on the milk proportionately. A calf can be weaned partially when he is eating other foods and completely when he is able to sustain himself on other foods. A husky growing calf will need an acre or more of pasture, or less pasture plus several pounds of good hay each day. On this system he gets more and more milk at first—and then gradually less and less, until he's finally weaned at about 4 or 5 months.

Early Weaning. When grain is cheaper than milk, producers tend to push calves to early (premature) weaning. In this case, you start feeding chopped grain and hay and pasture to calves as soon as they will take it. As soon as they are eating this other food, the milk is cut back. Some growers take pride in a calf that's weaned by 6 or even 5 weeks of age. But be careful of trying this because too abrupt a switch from milk to solid food can result in temporarily stalled growth. *Don't stop the milk ration until the calf has been eating grain for at least a month.* The calf on a grain-based diet will grow fast, but only when mature enough to digest it efficiently. You can gradually increase the amount of grain and hay, if not pasturing, until a 6-month-old calf may be eating 4 or 5 lb. grain a day.

Winter Feed for Weaned Calves. Feed as much good hay as they'll clean up, about 2 lb. per 100 lb. of their body weight each day. Or give corn stalks and cobs; 3 lb. of that equals 1 lb. of hay. Or grain; figure 1 lb. of grain equals 2 lb. of hay. The important thing is to feed what you naturally produce or can economically buy nearby; plant byproducts of almost every sort. But if you want organic meat, of course, then you have to be careful what goes into him. The easiest thing is typically to feed good hay plus some grain.

HALTER-BREAKING: Break an animal to lead while it is a baby, small enough to manage. You can't break an 800-lb. bull to do anything. So put a collar on it. Let the children tie something to the collar and lead it around and around and around until it gets the idea. Keep this up regularly and when it's big you will still be able to put the rope through the halter ring, give it a little tug, and your 800-lb. beast will follow docilely.

HEEL FLY: I just discovered a new one here. It's a fly called the heel fly that lays eggs in summer under the heel of a cow. The eggs hatch and the larvae crawl clear up the leg of the cow through blood vessels to live on her back. The next summer they bore an opening, change into flies, and leave the cow to find another host. I've got one cow that has this (she had it when I bought her), and the vet tells me at this stage there is nothing to be done. The preventive, an internal medicine, has to be given in the fall of the year. He says anything strong enough to kill them at this stage would kill her too. Oh, yuck!

Cow Butchering

AGES: What you'll call the meat depends on what age the cow was when butchered.

Veal. A calf that is butchered at 8–10 weeks will weigh about 180 lb., dress out to about 100 lb., and be called "veal." Veal is light colored and mild flavored and very tender compared to beef. Veal goes well in recipes for young chicken. In Victorian days when they really went in for a big variety of exotic meats for the tables of the rich—blackbirds in a pie and the gamut to a haunch of venison—veal was a delicate and delicious regular. But from the point of view of somebody raising their own meat, veal is an uneconomical meat because in that last 8 months your calf will put on so much weight that to butcher him before is to be

woefully inefficient. However, you can butcher a calf any time from the day he's born, and meat's meat.

Baby Beef. Breeds vary considerably in size, but, on the average, a calf 6–8 months old will weigh 300–400 lb. and about 60 percent of that will be edible. A calf that age is called "baby beef," a meat about halfway between veal and beef.

Beef. A yearling may weigh from 800 to 1,000 lb. An older animal may weigh 1,200–1,500 lb. or more. The butchering principles are entirely the same—only the scale is different. But I would recommend butchering no earlier than 15 months. Let's assume you get a spring calf. You give him milk that spring and summer and he's costing you milk and trouble. Throughout the winter you have to feed him hay, and that's money and trouble again. If you butcher him the next spring, well OK—but wait. If you let him go, he'll feed on all that good free summer grass all the second summer of his life, on through the fall, up to the time you would have to start feeding hay again, when the ground gets covered with snow. That's the natural time to butcher him. He'll put on weight at an amazing rate now that his basic frame is built, and that grass feeding is cheap and easy for you. If you let him go even to 24 months (when he is finally mature in build), he will continue growing all that time.

NOTE: Read "Introduction to Butchering" in Chapter 8 before you begin butchering your cow.

KILLING THE COW: If the animal is gentle enough, or if it is halter broke, maneuver it to where you want to butcher, preferably right beside the hoist you have in place for hanging it, because with that kind of weight it's a lot of work to move it. Hopefully a heap of grain or a salt block will persuade it to go where you want it. *Don't kill the animal when it is excited or has been running.* If you've just had a big struggle getting it moved to where you want to kill it, go away for a few hours and let it calm down before shooting. That will help the final quality of your meat.

You could use a .22 but a .30-.30 or bigger is surer. *Try very hard to get it right with the first shot.* If you miss with the first shot, the animal may either go on a rampage and hurt somebody (come right through the side of your corral), or it may just turn around and that will make it even harder to get another shot into the right place. We had a really wild Angus heifer that Mike had to shoot 3 times to get down. She turned just at the last and wrong moment on the first shot. So you see, it can happen to anybody, even to a great shot like Mike.

Anyway, shoot your cow by mentally making an "X" with the top points on each ear and the bottom points on

Shoot here

each eye. Shoot where the lines cross. Tie the cow up if you can and 1 shot will be enough. Shoot straight in. You'll have to move around to do it, or wait until the cow turns to face you. Take your time and do it right. If you get it right the cow will drop to the ground instantly, exactly where it was standing when you shot it.

STICKING: As soon as the cow drops, start running toward it with your best knife to cut the throat. (Don't fall on it!) You want to *open up the throat while the heart is still beating so it will pump the blood out well.*

I used to think you were supposed to cut across the throat from side to side, under the ears or an inch or so back, clear to the backbone on either side of the esophagus, until the head was about half off. It helps if the head is slightly downhill. That's how we did it. But I've since heard that a better way is to cut the throat lengthwise, from the jawbone to the breastbone, and then push the knife under the breastbone and between the first ribs into the chest cavity to cut the carotid arteries. Try not to cut the heart, so it will continue to pump out blood as long as it works.

Work the front leg back and forth for a while as if the animal were walking to help expel the blood. Wait until it gets completely quiet. Kicking reflexes will go on for a while and could hurt somebody. Keep the head downhill and the flow of blood unobstructed while you're waiting.

MOVING THE COW: If the cow didn't drop where it was handiest for you, and you have a tractor or other strong vehicle, use that to drag the body where you want it. Use a towing-type chain. Fasten one end of the chain to the cow around its cut neck, the other end to the vehicle. Then drag the cow to the place you want to skin and gut it—preferably a place where you have a way to hoist it.

HOISTING THE COW: A tractor with a fork-lift (hoist) is the handiest thing for moving and raising your carcass. Cut a place to hook the singletree ends under the tendons of the rear legs. Cut on each hind leg just inside the back of the "knee." Do it just above the first joint. You will be over 2 feet up from the hoof. Don't cut the tendon. Hook up the singletree with the tendons.

Fasten the singletree chain to the fork-lift and raise the animal. If you are working with a pulley or a "come-along," which is a 1-person pulley, hook that up to your singletree and haul away to get that animal raised off the ground, upside down, to a height at which you feel comfortable work-

ing. From 18 to 24 inches above the floor is good.

IF YOU DON'T HAVE A HOIST: It's hard to do what needs to be done with the animal lying on the ground—but it's not impossible. We've done it that way. It's the same as when you kill an elk (a cow-sized game animal) in the woods. If the cow is lying on the ground, first cut the head off. When you have the skin and meat all cut through, give the neck a hard twist around and around until you feel it break. Then finish cutting it off. Now maneuver the animal onto its back, exposing the full extent of belly topside. Doing that to a big cow is hard. Propping up one side with a stick for a brace may help. Then use the directions given below, except with the cow on the ground the innards will not fall out by themselves—you'll have to help them out. Proceed to "Gutting the Cow."

CUTTING THE HEAD OFF: Usually a cow is gutted before being fully skinned, whereas sheep, rabbits, or goats are skinned first. Finish cutting around the neck. Turn the head with a hard twist around and around until you feel the neck break. Then cut it all off. You'll have to finish with the saw. Some people use beef head meat to make sausage. Most people discard it except for the tongue. Cut out the tongue and put it in your organs bucket.

(After having already sold 1,500 of these books, I discovered to my awful embarrassment that at this point I left out how to remove the innards of the cow! Bad enough printing pages upside down, but that was worse. All those people depending on me—and I told them to get the animal raised up off the ground and then directly to commence sawing off steaks!)

GUTTING THE COW: If you have a male you start by cutting around the genitalia, including a patch of skin around it. Then you slit up the midline (I'm assuming the animal is hanging by its heels so "up" means toward the hind end), cutting the hide first and then around the anus so that you free the gut for tying off with a twine, so nothing in there will come out. You lift free the genitalia along with the cord and then proceed to open the hide on down the belly line. The animal isn't skinned. You'll skin it after you gut it. Most folks run their hand inside the skin as they are cutting down from the outside to push back the intestines and prevent the knife accidentally cutting them open since they are right underneath. If you hear a hiss you did it. But don't despair. That happens a lot to amateurs. It's happened to us, and it needn't harm the meat. Just struggle on. Saw through the H-shaped bone, which is called the "aitch" bone. It's between the hind legs in front of the rectum. Cut all the way down the front before starting to pull the innards out. Have your washtub ready; they are big and heavy. After they are halfway out and the part that's out is in your washtub, you can take time out to find the liver and heart.

Beef Heart. This is really good food, but to find it you'll have to look hard. It's encased in tissue and fat. Cut it free and put it in your organ pail. (Later, back at the house, I give it a good rinsing under cold water, slice, and bag for freezing.)

Beef Liver. This is big and easy to see. Remember to get the gall sac off the liver. You have to cut it out plus discard the part of it by the liver to do it safely, but there will be plenty of liver left. Back at the house, give the liver a good rinsing under cold water and then slice it very thinly and freeze in meal-size bags. Remember to eat up the heart and

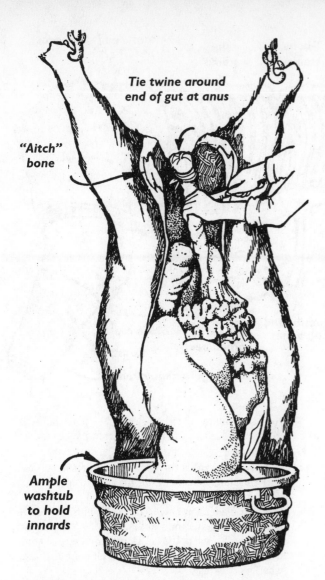

Tie twine around end of gut at anus

"Aitch" bone

Ample washtub to hold innards

liver fairly quickly because they don't keep as well as the rest of the meat. If you don't have refrigeration, you'll have to have beef liver for dinner that night and every meal thereafter until you use it up, because it doesn't cure or can well.

Finishing the Gutting. Cut through the breastbone now on down to the throat to finish opening up the belly side of the animal from tail to throat. That will make it easy for you to finish taking out all the innards and the tongue, which is very good to eat.

After you have the innards all out, stop and give your hands a good washing in the bucket with vinegar water. Sharpen your knives, if they need it. Now go back to work. Skinning is next.

SKINNING THE COW: This is the hardest single butchering job I can think of—a long job. But stick with it because the cooler the animal gets as the body heat leaves, the harder it is to skin. The reason you butcher a cow first and skin it afterwards is that if you skinned first, those innards might wait in there too long for the meat's good. Use the goat-skinning instructions. There are good directions for handling your hide in the tanning section in Chapter 8.

HALVING, QUARTERING, AND AGING THE BEEF: If you cut the tail off and skin the top part of it, you have the makings for oxtail soup! For the rest of it, read on.

Quartering the Beef. Pork is usually hung in halves and

best left just overnight because aging doesn't improve it, but beef is so big you need smaller sections just to be able to carry it around and to help it cool quicker, and aging does improve it very much. If you do the quartering right, each quarter will turn out to be from 90 to 140 lb., depending on the age of finishing—and all 4 pieces will be nearly of the same weight.

Saw down the middle of the backbone to divide the animal into equal halves. Use a wood saw or a chain saw or whatever you can lay your hands on. It's a mean job, and it helps if there is more than 1 person so you can take turns —one resting while the other is working. Now standing on the "belly" side and starting with the rear end of the cow, look inside the chest cavity to see where the ribs begin and count them. Cut between the third and fourth rib from the rear. When you get the 2 ribs cut part way apart, make a slit between the fourth and fifth ribs and tie a rope through there. That's preparation so the front quarters can be hung by that rope in whatever place you have ready for hanging the quarters. Have someone else hold the front quarter off the ground while you finish separating it, then carry it to the hanging place and hang there by your rope from a rafter or whatever. Get the other front quarter the same way. Now let the hoist down enough so you can untie the hindquarters, and then move them to your hanging place for aging.

The Hanging Place. This should be someplace cat-proof, dog-proof, and fly-proof, if possible (you can use meat bags —even make your own out of old sheets or some such— to help with the fly problem, or, better yet, butcher out of fly season). You need a cool place, too, and if you haven't butchered in cool weather you'll want to put the animal in a neighbor's or butcher's walk-in cooler. But a lot of butchers won't let you use their walk-in cooler now because federal laws have made it illegal to have uninspected homestead-type meat in there with the high-class fast-food-type meat.

Aging the Beef. Tenderizing the beef improves the taste. How, I don't know, but it really does. Age it at least a few days and preferably a week or even a little more. Aging just means letting it wait before you go ahead and cut it up, wrap, and freeze or can. The meat doesn't rot right away because there aren't any microbe seeds in there. It was just alive. When it does start to go bad, it'll start from the outside and work in, so you have plenty of warning and can trim off any bad parts. But handle the tallow (fat that you want to make special use of—maybe for soap) and hide promptly. Once they start going, it's impossible to get the bad odor out.

CUTTING UP

Timing. When the time does come for cutting up the quarters, it's a good idea to do it no faster than a quarter at a time. I mean a quarter per day. Another day of aging will improve the remaining beef, and defrosting could be a disaster for food already in your freezer when you put the meat in. Defrosting is what happens if you suddenly put a whole beef in there. In my experience it takes nearly 24 hours to get 1 quarter of beef all frozen in a large chest freezer. Or rent a locker or make arrangements to have it quick-frozen and then move it all to your freezer.

Making Cuts. If you're a pro you know exactly what you want. If you're not sure what you're doing, cut steaks off the wide ends, make roasts out of the narrow ones, and hamburger out of the mistakes. Mike thinks that ¾ inch

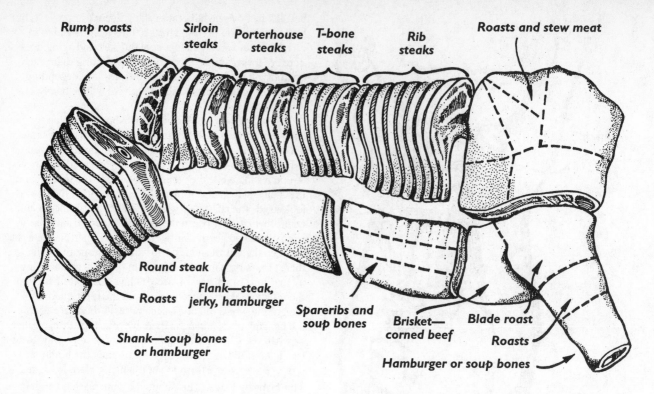

Rump roasts · Sirloin steaks · Porterhouse steaks · T-bone steaks · Rib steaks · Roasts and stew meat

Round steak · Flank—steak, jerky, hamburger · Spareribs and soup bones · Brisket—corned beef · Blade roast · Roasts

Roasts · Shank—soup bones or hamburger · Hamburger or soup bones

is a perfect thickness for steaks. I like ½ inch, but he thinks that's really too thin for any beef steak except maybe round. He says any steak with a bone in it should be at least ¾ inch thick. Some people do cut them an inch or even an inch and a quarter, but I think that's way too thick. But, bottom line, how thick you cut is entirely a matter of personal preference. Or economy—a thinner cut yields more steaks!

To saw out steak, cut with your knife all around the bone. Then saw through the bone. The tenderloin is the most tender steak. The round is the toughest. The muscles the cow uses the most (round, hind leg) are the toughest. Don't trim off all the fat—you want some around the edges of your steaks for flavor.

Hindquarters

1. Cut the leg from the body.
2. Starting from the top of the leg, slice off the round steaks clear down to the "knee" joint. When packaging, if you cut the round steaks in half, they will be easier to thaw.
3. The next portion of the leg (working down) will become roasts. If you make them about 2 inches thick or more it's fine. You are slicing the same as a steak only much thicker, and that makes it a roast. If you trim out the bone that can be a soup bone for you.
4. When you get down to where there isn't so much meat, cut the rest of the lower leg into chunks for soup bones that are called "shank boil." Or you can trim off the meat and put it in your hamburger pile, if you want.
5. Cut the belly abdominal muscle flap away from the rest. That goes into the hamburger pile.
6. On the piece that's left you can start from the "front" end, taking odd rib steaks. There will be 11–14 inches of rib steak on a big beef, 6 or 7 on a smaller one. The big hind end of the loin is the rump roast. Saw it off. It will have something of a triangular shape.

7. Now start taking off sirloin steaks. The porterhouse is in the middle. The T-bones are clear to the front.

Front Quarters

1. Remove the "arm" at the joint. Have 1 person cut from underneath as the other pulls the arm upwards. You've got to force it on up and out, under and around that shoulder blade. You now have an arm plus the rest.
2. Cut off the top one-third of the arm for a "blade roast" and trim off some of the fat. Don't trim the roast completely clean either. Some fat around it helps the taste when it's cooking.
3. The next 6 inches can be a roast. And so can the next. Make it into what you like. It could be a big roast or a small one plus some stew meat.
4. You can make the rest of the leg into stew bones or trim the meat away from the bone for hamburger.
5. With the meat saw, separate the ribs from the backbone and its accompanying muscle bundles—the tenderloin and backstrap. Saw about 8 inches from where the ribs connect with the backbone.
6. You can see what your steaks are going to look like now. Cut off the steaks. You waste less if you saw each one out, but that requires tremendous time and effort. If you're not up to that you can bone out the 2 muscle bundles and make rib eyes of the larger muscle and tips from the smaller backstrap.
7. The neck end, which you can identify because it curves a little upwards, can be made into roasts and stew meat.
8. The remaining rib area is a vast ordeal of spareribs and soup bones. Here you have the most work for the least desirable cuts. Starting from the rear, cut between one rib and the next all the way until they are completely separated. Then between the next and the next all the way and so on. Then saw across the individual ribs at 6-inch intervals or as your cook likes them. You'll end up probably sawing each rib thus into thirds.

BEEF RECIPES

☙ DRIED BEEF Use the jerky recipes in Chapter 8.

☙ MOCK TURTLE SOUP (CALF'S HEAD SOUP) Boil a beef or veal head (and feet, if you want) until the meat separates from the bones. Remove bones. Cut meat into 1-inch pieces. Boil an hour more (until tender) with an onion and bay leaf. Add 8 sliced small onions and 1 T. parsley, and season to taste with mace, cloves, and salt.

☙ BASIC BEEF STEW Cut 4–5 lb. of beef stew meat into 1½-inch cubes and brown them in a small amount of fat. Add 2 qt. small carrots (or 8 chunked large ones); 3 c. onions, quartered; and 3 qt. peeled potatoes, quartered. To this very basic stew, add your own favorite seasonings, cover with boiling water and simmer until all the meat and vegetables are tender.

☙ CANNED BEEF BONE SOUP Saw or crack fresh, trimmed beef bones to release their flavor. Rinse bones and place in a large stockpot or kettle. Cover bones with water. Cover pot. Simmer 3–4 hours. Remove bones. Cool broth. Pick off meat. Skim off fat. Add meat removed from bones to broth. Reheat to boiling. Fill jars, leaving 1 inch headspace. Adjust lids. Process in pressure canner only: pints 75 minutes, quarts 90 minutes. If using a weighted-gauge canner, set at 10 lb. pressure at 0–1,000 feet above sea level; at higher altitudes, set at 15 lb. If using a dial-gauge canner, set at 11 lb. pressure at 0–2,000 feet above sea level; 12 lb. at 2,001–4,000 feet; 13 lb. at 4,001–6,000 feet; 14 lb. at 6,001–8,000 feet; or 15 lb. above 8,000 feet.

What's the Beef?

There are more myths out there regarding cows than regarding any other domestic livestock. Why do cows get picked on? Is it because of their size that they're less likely to be part of a family operation and more likely to be in a commercial ranch setting? Because they aren't cute like goats? Cuddly as rabbits? I am astonished to find outrageous untruths/ignorance, even in a how-to book that says it's going to tell you how to raise a calf for beef. Here's a partial debunking.

MYTHS AND TRUTHS ABOUT COWS AND THE BEEF INDUSTRY

No.1: It is best to use land to raise cereal grains for people, rather than using it to feed animals.

The answer is . . . not that simple. Not all land can raise cereal grains. The most efficient and productive use of land is to raise meat animals off the parts of your land you can't cultivate—hillsides, woods, really dry places, or places with really short growing seasons. Those are natural forage areas. It would be truly wasteful if there were no grazing animals for the natural forage areas that grow enough cheap grass to fatten a cow in spring or enough brush to maintain goats. Even if all your land is tillable, you may not want to expend the time and labor to garden or farm intensively more than a portion of it. You may want to have a wood lot or to leave the land as near a natural state as possible. Your grazing livestock will do the work for you and harvest and put to good use the plants growing on that uncultivated land.

No. 2: If you don't feed grain to a growing beef animal, it will take 5 years to mature enough for butchering—and then be tough.

False. I can't believe I'm looking at that in a book about cow-raising, but I am. The truth is, beef animals, like other animals, don't grow as fast on natural as on concentrated feed; they don't get as big; they don't give as much milk. But they grow almost as fast (not counting fat) and mature at the usual time. And if you want tender beef, butcher a young animal, age 1–1½, not a 5-year-old! It's that simple, grain or no grain. The "tenderness" created by excess grain-feeding is a false tenderness created by the presence of fat inside the muscle.

No. 3: Steers for beef are raised in feedlots under crowded, inhumane conditions.

Again . . . it's not that simple. It used to be that most farmers had a few calves and finished them on their own grass and grain for home use and market. Now family farms still may raise 1 or 2 calves for beef, but overall the beef industry has become very specialized, divided between brood cow–calf and feeder operations. I think it's important to understand that cows are not ordinarily fed grain in the cow–calf operations. These cows eat grass in summer and hay in winter. The herd of brood cows stays on the farm and calves every year. The farmer sells the calves when they are between 400 and 800 lb. They are sold at so many cents per pound through the auction ring.

The calves sold by the cow–calf operation at auction may either be bought by a middleman or by a feedlot operator. The middleman is somebody who has surplus grass and wants to make his land pay by getting those calves onto it to eat the grass and put some more weight on before their return to the auction ring. Typically, the middleman doesn't keep brood cows, or doesn't have enough to eat up all the green bounty of his summer pasture. By buying extra calves in the spring, when his grass is starting to come on well, and selling them off in the fall just as his grass is dying back for the winter, he gets a profit from his grass crop. The difference between what those calves weigh when bought in the spring at the auction ring, and what they weigh in the fall, multiplied by the price per pound paid for them, equals the middleman's gross profit for that summer's operations.

Then, unless they go to the grass-fed beef market, which exists but is still comparatively (pathetically) small, they go to the feedlot. *But it doesn't have to be that way. The calves could continue to feed, like their mothers, on grass and hay, to butcher weight.*

No. 4: Trees are being cut down to grow beef.

Not that simple. A good bit of the U.S. landscape once was forested, but now isn't. Cows may or may not be what now grows there. It would be nice if those trees could be replaced. Everywhere trees are being cut down at an appalling rate—to make toilet paper, paper towels, book paper, etc. After the quick profit from timber sales the land is then either tilled or ranched unless it is reforested. In Central America, tropical forests are indeed being cut down by cattle ranchers who want the cash profits of selling beef to fast-food restaurant chains. (This isn't a large issue in the United States, because we've already cut down most of our original forests and forgotten they were ever there.)

Logging isn't the cows' fault. The cow—of all animals —is the one best suited to take the roughest of all feeds— native grass—and turn it into quality human food. Like the buffalo, the cow is most naturally a dweller on grassy plains. Cow–calf operations are best situated in good, natural-grass forage areas. There, feeding your cows grass is no problem and they'll make the milk to feed their calves. If you have even a few acres of decent pasture, you can get a lot of nice milk and meat off it for your family by means of a cow or cows, anywhere. For untillable, or untilled, grassy land, cows are also an excellent and ecologically appropriate choice. Cows can also graze among growing trees.

No. 5: Cows are fed grain that could end world starvation.

Not that simple. Cows are fed a lot of grain, which, as said, they don't actually require. But if cows weren't eating it, it probably wouldn't go to poor, starving people either because the first problem would be: Which poor, starving people? And the second would be: Who pays the grain grower for it? It costs money to grow every bushel of grain. Grain growing, like all farming, is a business—nowadays a petroleum-based business. The commercial farmer buys seed and makes his payment on the land and machinery and, if it's not an organic farm, also buys nitrate fertilizers, pesticides, and herbicides. When he finally harvests his crop, obviously he can't give it away or he'll not make his land payment, and some more practical farmer will be working it instead. So his grain crop gets sold to nearby bidders with money to buy—among them feedlot operators.

Woody Bernard, the Dairy Agent in Washington State who kindly reviewed this chapter, adds another good point: "Animals utilize byproduct feeds that people won't eat." That's so true. They eat the leftover from pressing seeds for oil, the corn cobs and stalks left after the corn is harvested, the beet pulp after sugar is extracted, seed hulls after the seeds are removed, and so on. Cows are wonderfully complementary to human beings because they can digest and change their food into good foods for us— milk and meat —all from food sources that people cannot eat.

No. 6: Cows have to be fed grain.

Not that simple. You can raise a calf for beef, and a cow for milk, and never feed a mouthful of grain, using instead quality pasture, good hay, and winter vegetables. Beef animals raised this way are called "grass-fed beef," and they're the best that money can buy: best for the environment, best for your health. But cows are generally fed a little grain even on a homestead operation because they love it so much. It helps gentle them. It's a wonderful way to get them to do what you want. They are natural grass eaters, and it's natural for them to love grain, which is grass seed: the goodness of grass in a concentrated form. Grain provides extra nourishment if you want to build up the health of an animal near to calving, or keep a milker going longer, or stimulate maximum milk production. If other foods are in short supply, and grain is ample, then grain is obviously a way to go. And dairy cows will give up to 40 percent more milk if fed a generous grain supplement! But grain doesn't have to be fed. Many buffalo ranchers now feed grain daily to those animals. You think buffalo have to have grain? Of course not. It's just that they love it, so it gentles them, it's a convenient concentrated feed, and they're less likely to get restless and walk through your fence.

No. 7: Feedlots feed animals beyond their normal growth into forced obesity.

True. The feedlot operator buys calves either directly from the cow–calf operation or from the middleman. He keeps the animals confined to a small area called a "feedlot" and gives them a grain-based, rather than a grass-based, diet. He wants to put more weight on them as fast as possible and get them up to profitable size and an acceptably fat grade of beef. The animals are in the feedlot from 2 to 6 months. Then the feedlot operator takes them back to the auction ring where this time they are sold to the meat

packer. Some feedlots use the cow manure from the feedlot to feed pigs in an associated swine-growing operation, because the pigs can get food value from the surplus grain that is passed through the cow's system. If the cows were fed only up to a normal growth, the feedlot could be viewed, I suppose, as a space-efficient, work-efficient operation for growing meat so long as the grain is cheap and available. But I see 3 big problems with them: stress for the animals; feeding of antibiotics; and overfeeding to create marbled meat.

No. 8: The USDA meat-grading system protects consumer health.

False. The USDA meat-grading system protects the grain growers who want the feedlot operator's business, and it protects the feedlot owners. It's the big reason feedlots exist, the big reason why supermarket beef isn't good for your arteries.

The trend toward feeding cows beyond their normal growth developed largely in response to the USDA meat-grading system. Up to a certain point, the cow's body keeps its muscle and its fat separate, with the fat on the outside of the muscle. But if calories are forced upon the animal—if, as in the feedlot, physical inactivity is combined with a high-calorie diet—eventually that natural barrier is overwhelmed. Fat begins to appear inside the muscle, between the muscle strands. When this happens to beef muscle (meat), that cut of meat is called "marbled." "Marbled" beef is what the law and the supermarkets call "choice beef." But "choice" beef really isn't the best for you. A normal beef animal has red meat with no fat inside the muscle tissue. This is a good thing for humans because beef fat is high in cholesterol, higher than any other domestic meat, and we don't want to eat that cow fat. But according to the law as established in USDA grading standards, beef should be fat, and the fatter the better. The fatter an animal is, the higher its meat will be graded by the USDA inspector. So feedlots pour the grain into them to make them fat.

There's a historical reason for this attitude. During the 1950s there was so much more grain being harvested than there was a market for it, that there was talk even of throwing grain in the ocean to get rid of it. But then certain cowmen bought that cheap grain. They built feedlots and there finished calves cheaper and faster on that grain than they could have otherwise. And the feedlot operators got a meat-grading system put through that favored their product over the grass rancher's beef product. The grain farmers backed that new grading system, too, because it in effect legislated a couple of hundred extra pounds of grain into every cow destined for the supermarket. Thus feedlots and grain for cows got written into the law of the land: marbled beef. Forty years later, it's still there. Through advertising, "choice" beef became commonly accepted as the best beef, and more than 1 generation of people who must eat out of supermarkets have never seen anything else.

Woody Bernard says: "The meat grading system has been changed to reduce the fat in beef. Also, the more exotic breeds don't marble like the old ones."

No. 9: Feedlot operators feed antibiotics daily.

True. To compensate for the crowding and stress, and because of its growth-enhancing effect, feedlot operators routinely feed low-level antibiotics as part of the cows' daily ration.

No. 10: Beef from commercial slaughter houses is always safe to eat.

Not that simple. Usually it is, but not necessarily. Under the Reagan administration, slaughter houses were deregulated. Now a big operation that once was limited to processing 60 cows an hour may be processing 300 cows an hour. At that pace, it's easy for accidents to occur. *E. coli* naturally occurs in the intestines of all animals. If that animal/ cow is butchered and the contents of her intestines accidentally get on the meat, the meat will be contaminated.

NOTE: It's important, whether in home or commercial butchering, that the contents of the intestine never get on the meat.

If a batch of contaminated meat is mixed in a big vat with the hamburger from many different cows, the problem spreads. That's how hamburger for fast food places is prepared—and how it can become contaminated.

NOTE: Always look and make sure your—and your child's—restaurant hamburger is well-cooked, not pink inside, before eating it. If it's pink, send it back to finish cooking.

No. 11: Cows give off methane gas that contributes to the greenhouse effect.

True, but it's ridiculous to take that source of methane seriously. Other related animal species contribute to the problem, too. But the big reason this particular greenhouse gas is pouring into the atmosphere in unnaturally great amounts is the use of natural gas. Natural gas is mined from "wells" and then piped into homes and industries to burn. Some of the gas inevitably leaks out of pipes into the atmosphere. In fact, it's people who make most of the gases that cause most of the greenhouse effect. I cannot comprehend this ranting against cows. What a convenient scapegoat. They contribute only a tiny percentage—far, far less than what the once-mighty herds of 60–100 million buffalo did. It would do far more good to reduce the numbers and improve the exhaust systems of cars, ban fossil fuel burning of all sorts, and restrict belching industrial plants. Those are the biggest source of greenhouse gases.

No. 12: Cows drink a lot of water.

True, but not as much as humans use. People use (waste?) on the average 77 gal. per day per person. The drinkingest cows, of course, are lactating dairy animals of the largest breeds. They produce as much as 14 gal. milk per day for human use. They drink as much as 30 gal. water per day. The more milk they produce, the more water they must drink. Beef cows drink much less. An average 400–700-lb. steer (a typical size growing for the meat market) drinks 5–10 gal. per day. And cows, if uncrowded and on natural pasture, recycle their water back into the ground as nutrient-rich urine, which help grows their feed. People waste theirs into sewer systems.

No. 13: Cows destroy salmon spawning habitat.

Again, a joke. You try swimming from the ocean up any river and see what happens: industrial and urban pollution running into the water, dams and more dams, development up to the water's edge. And somebody is begrudging a cow drinking at the streamside? The cow, being closely related to the buffalo or elk or moose, is the most natural part of the equation. If there were only cows living in the United States, the salmon would be doing fine.

I can't help but wonder if there isn't some deep human need to identify and pick on a minority and persecute it. All varieties of human beings now being off limits for prejudice, the homely bovine tribe and their keepers are being subjected to these arguments for extermination.

No. 14: Nobody will buy cattle that have been only grass-fed and raised without growth stimulants or antibiotics in regular feed at the price it would cost to raise them.

False. You'd be surprised how many people who can't grow their own are desperately looking for just such meat, from every kind of meat animal! Now you can at least get leaner hamburger everywhere. And in organic-type food stores you can get "grass-fed beef." What is grass-fed beef? It is a normal animal that hasn't crowned his preslaughter experience by standing in a feedlot being inactive and getting obese. When a grass-fed cow goes to regular market, he is the same age as the corresponding "finished" or grain-fed cow—18–20 months, up to 24 months. And no 18–20-month-old cow is going to be tough, grain or no grain—don't let anybody kid you about that! Grass-fed meat is what the country people who raise their own calf for beef have usually eaten, tender and delicious.

You can either advertise privately and take orders for your meat, or market it through the kind of co-op that's always looking for organic food for their customers. Here are some sources of grass-fed beef:

Colman Natural Beef: 800-442-8666; 5140 Race Court, Unit 4, Denver, CO 80216; **www.colemannatural.com.**

Cordonnier Meats are free-range, homegrown, corn-fed, but no drugs. They sell freezer beef (half, quarter, or by the steak); beef summer sausage; their own *canned* beef, chicken, turkey, and pork; chicken fryers, roasters, and farm-fresh eggs; vegetables and fruits: 937-295-2297; 3333 Russia-Houston Rd, Russia, OH 45363-9736; **BertCordonnier@yahoo.com.**

Ervin's Natural Beef: 928-428-0033; 128 E. 19th St., Safford, AZ 85546; **www.ervins.com.**

Homestead Healthy Foods: 830-997-2508; Rt. 2, Box 184-A, Fredericksburg, TX 78624.

Kay's HomeFarm Beef is tender and lean, raised without using synthetic hormones, maintenance antibiotics, or processed feeds. 262-377-7292; fax 262-377-5002; 8707 Kaehler's Mill Rd., Cedarburg, WI 53012; **slc@execpc.com; myexecpc.com/~slc/HomeFarm.html.**

Larsons' Greenfarms sells certified organic beef: 800-762-2092; fax 608-879-3900; 13246 W. Sagen Rd., Brodhead, WI 53520; **www.larsonsgreenfarms.com.**

Lasater Grasslands Beef offers cattle that are finished on grass, never confined in feedlots and fed grain, no growth hormones, no antibiotics, no pesticide treatments: 719-541-2855; PO Box 38, Matheson, CO 80830; **www.lasatergrasslandsbeef.com/.**

Tom and Martha Mewbourne sell pasture-raised Angus at Thorntree Farms, 276-479-3057; Rt. 2, Box 776A, Nickelsville, VA 24271.

Rob and Alanna Reed offer all grass-fed Angus and Angus-crosses at Overlook Farm; 724-756-0540; 233 Spruce Rd., Karns City, PA 16041; **www.greatbeef.com.**

The bottom line is that real change for the better has to be market-driven—people who spend the dollars for food have to demand and pay for organically grown vegetables and fruit and grass-fed beef. Then ag chemicals and cows supposedly fed too much grain won't be a problem anymore!

How to Milk

When you milk an animal, you're getting into her emotional life. You can't help it, so adjust gracefully. If she's upset about anything, if something scared her, if she doesn't know you or doesn't like you yet, she won't have the contractions that bring her milk down. If in the midst of milking something scares her, or if she has a sore teat and it hurts when squeezed, the milk may momentarily stop coming down.

EQUIPMENT: It's best to milk your dairy animal in an outbuilding, or in a part of one—a place that is special for milking and cleaner than where she sleeps.

Stanchion. If yours is a gentle, experienced animal, you can tie her up to milk her (have a halter on her) or even eventually you could walk up to her in the field and milk her as she stands. I've done it. But usually a stanchion works best. A stanchion is a frame that holds a goat or cow firmly by its neck while it's being milked. Stanchions always have a manger or platform for a bowl in front so the animal can eat a treat while you're milking. (Give and you'll be given unto.)

You can fashion a goat stanchion out of one made for a cow just by nailing a board on it to narrow its grip. There is a manger where the animal's head will be, in which to place grain or hay. The animal sticks its head in to feed in the manger. Then the movable slat is moved over at her neck and fastened so she cannot pull her big head back through until allowed to. Some animals just hate stanchions and will let down their milk better if you milk them in the open. But if you're milking a big herd or have nervous animals, a stanchion really helps.

Stool. A stool for you to sit on is needed to milk a big cow. A sturdy stool about a foot high will suit you and you can milk into a bucket—one with a bail (handle) for easy carrying.

Goat-Milking Platform. Goats are built nearer the ground, so some people have little goat stanchions (or a place to tie her) built on a special raised platform about 12–18 inches above the ground. It has a little manger up front or maybe just a place for you to set a low-sided can with her treat in it. Then you can comfortably sit on a stool, which may or may not be built onto the goat's platform. If your barn floor is nice and clean, you can just sit on the floor to milk. Or you could squat to milk the goat. But it's nicest and cleanest to sit on an extended side of her platform made for that purpose.

SCHEDULING: Milking is done every 12 hours. It works well to milk early in the morning, before the animals scatter to feed. Twelve hours later you'll milk early in the evening; in winter you'll still have some daylight to do it. Either that or you need to carry a lantern to the barn or have electricity in there. If you milk a very heavy producer 3 times a day, you may get even more milk if you need it. Milking is usually done all by hand, but some

ABOUT MILKING
A Review of Dairy Sex

You can't just buy an animal, walk out to the field, and milk it. Milk comes only from female mammals that have recently given birth and have either been continuously milked or nursed since then by their young or some other species. (For example, you can put bum lambs or a calf on a goat.) So for a cow to be a milking cow, there has to have been a bull in her life about 285 days ago—likewise with a goat, 5 months ago. Even if you buy an animal that is already "fresh" (milking), time is going to run out on you. You can't just keep milking her forever. She will gradually dry up. You have to again give the cow access to the bull or the artificial inseminator at a time when she is receptive (in heat). (You probably knew most of that, but I'm trying to assume nothing. I've had people ask me if they should pasteurize the eggs, or why their chickens won't sleep in the nests but keep climbing up to the hen house rafters, or if a heifer and a Hereford are the same thing.)

Then she has a gestation (pregnancy) of 9 months, calves, and comes fresh (gives milk). Your cow is milking again, but you also have a hungry calf. A cow usually has plenty of milk for everybody, though if it's her first calf she won't be giving as much as she will after subsequent calvings. You can separate the calf from the cow, do all the milking yourself, and feed the calf its share out of a bucket, then turn the cow in with the calf until your family runs out of milk again. Or you can keep the calf shut away from the cow all night, milk in the morning, and then let them run together the rest of the day—meaning there will be no evening milking for you.

people raising a calf or goats leave baby and mother together all night. Then you can separate them in the morning and milk for the household supply in the evening. Or separate them in the evening, and then the morning milk is for the house.

NOTE: If you're late milking, the animal's udder hurts her severely. You lose production and increase her risk of mastitis.

STEP-BY-STEP PREPARATIONS FOR MILKING: First you call your milker to where you want to meet and accomplish this. You put her in the stanchion, offer a treat to eat, groom as needed, wash her udder and teats, and then commence seriously milking, from let-down, to stripping, to her release from the stanchion.

Calling. A good milk cow is a gentle creature. After a while she'll come when she sees you or knows that you want her. Once she has decided to adopt you, she'll call out and run to you when you call her. You're her baby and she's going to sustain you. Have a can of grain handy. She'll follow you to the barn.

Putting Her in the Stanchion. You have to start by getting your milker in a situation where you know she'll stand still and where you can comfortably work at her teats for 10 or 15 minutes. You could tie her up or have somebody hold her, but a stanchion is best of all for this. She'll soon learn to come voluntarily, even eagerly, when you call and stick her head right in there if you scatter some grain or other treat in the stanchion feeder area. (Don't expect her to eat all her feed in the 10 minutes you're milking. Her regular feeder will be elsewhere.) Once her head is in place, you close the stanchion so she can't back out again.

Grooming. I'll confess I looked 'em over for problems, but I never groomed a dairy animal. If you're a groomer, then maybe once a day—before 1 of the 2 milkings is a good time—brush to remove dry skin, loose hair, and parasites. Dynah Geissal says they love it.

Washing. Wash and dry your hands before milking. Take a pot of quite warm (120–130°F) water and fuzzy rag to the barn with you when you go out to milk, so you can wash her udder and teats. You may get more milk if you wash the udder and teats, and if she's been lying in the mud it keeps the dirt out of the milk. Debris in the milk means a high bacteria count—which means it sours quicker and is likely to get an off-taste. An udder that hasn't been washed isn't as easy to grip as a damp one either. And mud that got into the milk, even just dust, will go right through your straining cloth. You'll discover it as a sort of dark sediment at the bottom of your milk jar after it has set 12 hours or more. Woody Bernard, the Dairy Agent for Pierce, King, and Grays Harbor counties in Washington, reviewed this chapter and gave me much excellent advice for which I'm very grateful. He adds here: "Washing stimulates let-down. Wait 1 minute after washing." Then milk.

Let-Down Contraction. Each teat is like a syringe bulb, and the bulbs are empty when the milk is held up high as it is before the let-down. No matter how you squeeze, none will come out. Your stimulation of the teat (pronounced "tit") causes a contraction reaction called "let-down" to occur in the milk-storing area of her bag. This let-down is an involuntary response under both hormonal and nervous system control. That's why when you first handle the teats of a nervous goat maybe nothing happens. It helps if you keep barking dogs and romping, noisy children away at milking time. And that's why some dairy farmers play sweet, soothing music to their ladies. If your animal is happy and relaxed, and expects to give her milk to you anyway, as soon as you handle her teats the upper part of the udder contracts and forces milk steadily down. Then when you squeeze the teat, something comes out.

First Squirts. The teat ends are a hole into her body, and the first milk right there tends to be higher in bacteria. So dairy sanitarians urge us not to use the first 2 or 3 squirts from each teat. Just milk them onto the ground or better yet into a cup for examination for mastitis signs (later discard). The strip cup is a neat little invention: a cup with a screen on top that really makes the strings or flakes or lumps of mastitis milk show up clearly. (You can make a homemade strip cup by putting a small tea-strainer over a cup.)

NOTE: If you suspect mastitis, don't use the milk, and get her under treatment.

MILKING—THE MAIN ACT: This milking can be done by machine or by hand.

Milking Machine. Both goats and cows can be machine-milked. Managers of huge dairies appreciate them. You can buy milking machines from a dairy supply house. But with a few animals being milked for home use, a milking machine is as impractical and unreal as a 200-gal. bulk cooling tank would be. The machine is expensive and has to be washed after each use. You can hand-milk a goat as fast as you can machine-milk, and it's simpler and far, far quicker when you include milking machine wash time.

Hand-Milking. Now you've got to milk for all you're worth. The contraction reflexes in the bag won't go on forever, and you've got to get the milk out while it is on. Empty the filled cavity of the teat by squeezing the milk in there out the hole in the end. Then open your hand long enough to let it fill up again from the pressure above, and squeeze it out again. On one of my goats it took about 167 squeezes on each side plus stripping to get all the milk out. In effect, you block off the space above the teat with your fingers so it doesn't go back up, and then squeeze on the rest of it to empty it out the hole. Then open up at the top again to let more milk down. Once you get going, you can really move the milk out if the hole is big enough. The reactions on each side are separate. After you've milked a teat, you might still have to work a little to get the next one going.

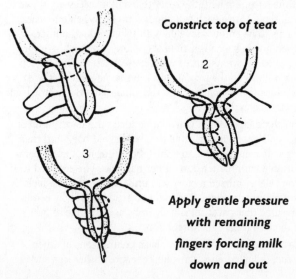

Grab high on teat near udder

Constrict top of teat

Apply gentle pressure with remaining fingers forcing milk down and out

Squeezing Technique. A cow has 4 teats whereas a goat has 2. Just how you squeeze the milk out of them depends on the shape of the teats. A yearling goat with very small short teats is hard to milk and it takes a long time—even though she doesn't give much. You milk those short teats by blocking off with your thumb and index finger and then adding your next 2 fingers (one at a time) to force the milk on out. Or you can "strip" by starting at the top of the nipple and pulling your hand down to force it between your thumb and forefinger. This will also help to enlarge a small nipple.

You have to keep your hand above or away from the nipple hole or the milk will go everywhere but the bucket. On a good-sized teat you can use your whole hand, and then it's easy. Just block with your thumb and index finger as high on the nipple as you can get, and then add your other fingers one at a time to force the milk out gradually. *NOTE: Don't grab hold above the teat on the udder tissue because that's not natural to her, and it can harm the udder attachment and milk-producing tissue inside.*

Within a few days you can be pretty fast and comfortable with it, though at first your wrists will get tired. My son Danny could milk a goat when he was 4. He fired both barrels at once. Then sat and waited for them to refill. But the usual way is to alternate hands, squeezing with one while the other is filling with new milk. So while your left hand is blocking off at the top and then squeezing, your right hand is relaxing. Then your left hand is relaxing while your right hand is blocking off at the top and then squeezing. Try to develop a smooth rhythm. Speed will come later. Eventually it should take only about 10 minutes total to milk a goat.

Stripping. Dynah Geissal wrote: "'Butt' the udder gently with your hands several times (light slaps), especially when the milk flow slows, to encourage complete let-down." Woody Bernard writes: "I disagree. Gentle massage is better."

Before milking, her bag and teats will look full and round. As you milk, the teats get a wrinkled, shriveled appearance and a cow's udder develops 2 big folds on the backside. When the flow of milk slows very perceptibly and the teat takes longer and longer to fill, it's time to switch to a stripping motion. Use your thumb and index finger and pull them down over the teat so the teat is pulled through your fingers from top to bottom, and you have the last few drops. (Some owners support a goat's udder with one hand while stripping with the other to avoid unnecessary downpull on it.) Strip each teat about 5 times. When one teat seems to be empty move on with that hand to another. Then go back a couple of times before you finish stripping again to get what's left. If you get every last bit you'll keep her milking to the max. If you leave some milk in, she'll produce that much less next time and may never come back up to that earlier level.

Finishing Up. When you're done, open the stanchion. Pat her and say a kind word like, "Thanks, old bag," and then chase her out of the barn. She'll be feeling a lot more comfortable with the tension off her bag since you emptied it. If you've ever nursed a baby, you understand how she feels. A full mammary gland (breast on you, udder on her) is misery. One that's overfull is hell. She was desperate to be milked to relieve the discomfort.

Barnkeeping. Milking stimulates contractions of other parts. Be prepared when your cow spreads her legs and starts to squat, and get yourself and the milk bucket clear away fast, because it tends to splash all over. Goats are so much nicer that way. At regular intervals, like every few days, shovel the scrapings out of the barn into a pile to age and ripen for the garden. It makes the barn nice to scatter straw on the barn floor after you have it shoveled out.

Milking Problems and Problem Milkers

Phyllis Vallette, missionary in Djibo, Burkina Faso, wrote me: "At our semi-desert latitude, the Africans manage their cattle and goats with absolutely no barns, and very limited use of pens. The Fulanis here do make a calf-pen, which they use at milking time—they corral the calves, then a child is posted to let them out one at a time on call. The calf starts to nurse, then the milker-woman takes it off the udder and ties its neck to the cow's front leg (both an anchor and a distraction to keep her occupied). She squats, no stool, and milks into a wooden bowl, then lets the calf free to finish off—and calls for the next calf. If a cow is likely to gouge, a second person holds the head with a long stick and loop around the horns. Goats are milked by taking a hind leg and tucking it into the crook of your knee as you squat! The Fulanis keep the kids around the house and yard all day while the adults are sent off to the bush (without a goatherd, usually) to browse. They cut small branches of leaves to bring to the kids as necessary. About 5 pm the goats return, and the air is filled with the high and low bleats of the kids and goats as they reunite. The Mauritanians keep all the kids and goats together, but they fashion a little bag for the udder and tie it over the back when they want to limit the kids' nursing!"

CHANGING A MILKING SCHEDULE: If you bought a cow that is used to being milked at 6 am and you sleep until 9 am, that's okay. Milk her 15 minutes to a half hour later each morning and evening until you get her on the schedule you want to keep. That way you minimize the drying-up tendency. And give her lots of grain in the meantime to help keep up the milk production.

MILK PRODUCTION FACTORS: Lots of things can affect her milk production. If she is standing out in a cold rain with no shelter, not only might she get pneumonia but her milk production will go down. Goats must have shelter available. If she isn't getting a variety of good food—ample brushy range and a little grain supplement in summer; hay, grain, and vegetables in winter—her milk production will go down. She's a wonderful conversion machine. Grass goes in one end and meat, milk, and garden manure come out at various other points, but if you don't supply her with adequate raw materials, she can't do her thing.

The biggest effect on her production is reliable, by-the-clock milking. Her ability to give milk is a long-term investment, and if you skip a milking she starts to dry up—to say nothing of her suffering and pain. If you don't milk her regularly, or if you don't milk her completely dry each milking, you trigger partial drying up. Nature makes automatic adjustments for the "baby's" demands. If you milk your cow completely dry regularly (twice a day), Nature says to that udder that her baby is growing and hungry—he's eating all you have and wants more, so keep making that much, and more if you can. So she produces as much milk as she possibly can. On the other hand, if milk is left in the udder, Nature says to her the baby is eating other food and isn't so hungry now: make less milk. So the next day she produces less milk.

Teat and Udder Size. The speed with which you can milk a goat is—other factors being equal (her state of mind and the quantity of milk)—probably directly proportionate to the size, both length and width, of her teat. It takes a long time to milk a yearling or a goat that hasn't been hand-milked before because her teats aren't enlarged. A good family milker isn't a natural thing. Her udder is abnormally large to cope with saving all that milk for 12 hours when nature meant her to feed her calf or kid much more frequently. Her teats are long and large from hours of being pulled on during hand-milking. So when you see a goat with a big udder and big long teats, she'll probably be a good family milk goat. One reason she's so expensive is because she didn't get like that overnight.

Extra Teats. A 3-teated goat—with 1 normal side and the other with 2 nipples instead of 1—isn't uncommon. Nor is a 4-teater with 2 nipples on each side. You can use them just for brood goats. That means you let them rear kids and don't try to milk them, or you can try to make them into a family milk goat anyway. The third nipple may or may not release milk. If it does, you may have to develop a special way of milking that double-teat to compensate for the problem of 2 nozzles. I had one that I milked from behind, between her legs, because somehow when I grabbed her from

that angle I had more luck getting both squirts in the bucket. I wouldn't use the son of such a goat for a breeding billy for fear the trait could be passed on through him.

Nervous Milkers. Nerves can really affect the amount of milk she gives you. You may get some, but not as much as you'd expect. Feel her udder. You can tell if it's still round and not slack as it should be when emptied. Try milking into food-grade plastic because it is less noisy. Keep everything routine and keep children and strangers away from her, especially at milking time. If other animals are harassing her, isolate her. Speak softly to her, if at all, and be patient. An animal gives milk when a brain signal results in the release of the hormone oxytocin into their system. (Same as humans.)

How to Turn On a Reluctant Milker. Sharon Koskela, Troy, MT, wrote me: "Did you ever have a problem cow that no matter what you do, she just won't let her milk down? We have to inject her with oxytocin every milking—that means no breeding back until she's off that. We've tried milking 4 times a day, bag balm, and hot packs, massage, etc., all to no avail. Just wonder if you've any suggestions. Sure could use some!!!"

A cow that gets a shot of oxytocin to turn her on is going to be less likely to have a normal let-down because the injection has become the let-down stimulus instead of the normal routine of udder washing, gentle massage, and squeezing (sucking). The oxytocin should never have been started.

So how do you turn on a goat or cow that doesn't want to be milked? The answer is: You seduce her. Do a good job with your warm water and cloth washing of her udder and teats. The combination of warmth, wetness, and manipulation (like the baby that would naturally push on her udder) goes a long way toward overcoming hostility and nervousness. If that didn't work—you're still squeezing and nothing is coming out and you're afraid she's going to dry up—I know an absolutely surefire way to get her to relax and let that milk down. Maybe she's upset because she's new in your family, or has just been separated from an old buddy, or because you just knocked her kids in the head and she heard them cry out.

Just take the teat in your own mouth and suck a little. She can't resist that—it's too real. Nature will get her and the milk will come. Once the bag contraction is started, you'll have no need to resort to that again. If you'd rather find some more artificial technique, use a syringe from a snakebite kit, and it will have somewhat the same effect. So as soon as you taste the milk coming or can tell it's started, just go ahead and finish the regular way.

But some cows never get easy to milk. You have to squeeze hard and work hard for each stream of milk instead of having a good let-down contraction helping you. She's called a "hard milker" and should be sold off or eaten up and replaced.

Switching a Goat with an Older Kid to Hand-Milking. If somebody sells you a doe with a kid 6 weeks old and keeps the kid, you are going to have a very hard time switching her over to hand-milking. It's much better to plan ahead and do it all one way or the other. The doe with kid at side probably gets milked out a minimum of 8 times a day. By the time the kid is 6 weeks old she is producing a lot of milk, but she never has very much in her udder at any one time. Her teats are short and small because that works fine for the kid. He sucks it out instead of manipulating it out

1. Did you use something other than seamless stainless steel, food-grade plastic, or glass to milk into, strain into, or store milk in?
2. Was there exposure to sunlight or fluorescent light? That causes oxidation and off-flavor.
3. Is the drinking water for your milker extra high in iron or copper?
4. Did you add warm milk to chilled milk or let chilled milk turn warm?
5. Is it late in your milker's lactation?
6. Did you feed onions, garlic, cabbage, turnip, or other strong-flavored vegetables or silage closer than 7 hours to milking time? Most of those foods work fine to feed if given right after a milking. But don't ever feed onions or garlic!
7. Are there other strong-tasting weeds in your animal's pasture that she's eating?
8. Did the doe smell strong odors within the few hours before milking, such as from a buck? Or was the buck near the milk?
9. Are you milking in a dirty, manure-filled, ammonia-reeking barn? (The milking place is best separated from more fragrant parts of your barn by doors.)
10. Did any manure, dirt, or hair get into the milk? (It helps to brush your milker before you milk.)
11. Did you wash your hands and her udder and teats, then dry them, before you started milking?
12. Are you smoking around the milk?
13. Do you daily wash milk containers with homemade soap, then rinse with boiling water? Do you boil your straining cheesecloths in water with a little lye before reusing, or else dry them at high heat in a dryer?
14. Are you getting your milk cooled to 40°F or less within an hour after milking and then keeping it cool?
15. Did you serve the milk within 24 hours?
16. Is there something wrong with your milker's health?

the way we have to. If you try suddenly to milk her every 12 hours, she's almost certain to abscess on you or at least be terribly sore and miserable. Her udder isn't used to holding all that milk that long. By the time you're ready to milk, she'll be so tight and sore her teats will be hard as rock, and she'll jump and tremble every time you touch her. By the time you've tried to milk out a half gallon, 10 cc at a time, she'll be bruised—and have a very bad attitude. If it has to be done, phase her over gradually by milking rather frequently at first and then making it less and less often all the time. It's a good idea to plan on milking 1 or 2 new nans every year, along with the rest of your herd. It takes about 6 months to get them well broken in. Then let them conceive and kid again, and you'll have a good milk goat.

Yearling Milkers. Dynah Geissal says: "Some does start off slowly, and for the health of the [not yet full-grown] goat, I think this may be best. A yearling milker may give only ½ gal. and ¾ gal. a year later. That's O.K. She'll come around later. The best doe I've ever had produced a stillborn kid her first pregnancy. I tried milking her, but her teats were half the size of my little finger and her milk supply was meager. I kept her because her mother had been a fantastic milker and this doeling had excellent conformation. Her second pregnancy produced live kids and a decent supply of milk. Also her teats had grown to small but manageable size. Her third lactation was excellent and her fourth incredible. She's eleven now, only producing one (healthy) kid a year, but producing milk in excellent quantities for 10 months a year. From ages 4 through 8 her production was phenomenal. You can coax a young goat into producing huge quantities of milk by feeding lots of grain, but it makes no sense financially and is probably harmful to her health."

Training an Inexperienced Milker. It helps if, even before the first birthing, you teach the animal to enter the stanchion to get a treat in her manger and then shut her in there and handle her for a bit. Put her through the grooming and udder-washing routine. Gently touch her udder and teats enough to help her get used to the idea of it. Goats soon learn to jump up on the milking stand. All animals learn to put their heads through the stanchion opening without a struggle. Once their bags are filling with milk they learn that going to the stanchion spells R-E-L-I-E-F from the pressure plus a food treat—and so meet you there happily.

How to Dry Her Up. Usually your milker will gradually dry herself up, but some generous animals will go on and on until you make them stop. If you want annual kidding, then you dry her up after 10 months of milking. But you don't have to. You could continue milking her until she dries herself up. My friend Imogene has milked goats as long as 3 years without a new freshening (kidding). (So she only needed to get them bred every 2 or 3 years.) But if you do choose to dry her up . . .

NOTE: It's important to dry up your animal gradually and correctly to avoid udder damage and unnecessary suffering for her. (As somebody who nursed 7 babies and stopped dead out of several nursings due to ignorance and reasons beyond my control, I have personal experience and strong feelings about this!)

The way you dry up an animal is to stop milking her all the way out. For her to stop producing milk, you have to leave enough milk in there that there's some pressure. Heavy milkers are harder to dry up. The secret is to allow enough pressure to slow her up more and more without causing so much that she is in pain and her udder bruised, even infected. You (1) stop feeding grain or rich supplements. (2) Temporarily reduce water drinking (don't eliminate it completely!). (3) Don't take all the milk as you milk twice a day. Then (4) milk less and less often, dropping to a once-a-day milking for a week, then to every other day, then to every few days, then once more after a week, and that should do it. (5) Watch her carefully for signs of mastitis; this is a high-risk time for that.

NOTE: If you want to give a worming or a lice treatment, her dry time, when there's no risk of poisons getting into the milk, is the best time to do it.

To dry up a cow, if she is milking more than 2½ qt. per milking, start gradually taking less about 3 months before her due date for calving. Time it so that you stop milking completely by 8 or even just 6 weeks before she is due to calve.

Culling. I used to be more forgiving, but Dynah Geissal says: "Don't even consider keeping a kid from any but your best does. It is vital to cull ruthlessly and to not be sentimental. Be sure to check for extra teats on any kid you are considering keeping. I wouldn't keep any mature doe (or her kid) who didn't provide at least ½ gal. milk per milking throughout spring and early summer. Near breeding season, production will drop, but there should be a reasonable amount, gradually tapering to about a quart 2 months before kidding."

COPING WITH BAD ATTITUDES AND BAD HABITS:

If your cow or goat puts her manure-caked foot right in the middle of your milk bucket just as you are finishing milking her, don't kill her. You aren't the first one it ever happened to.

Kicking. You might think the front end is so far away it couldn't know what the hind end is doing, but a mad cow can kick with hind foot forward, to the side, or back, and she can put that foot right where she aims it; it can really hurt. Some of them really make a habit of it. In that case you'll have to develop a defense. If she does succeed, just consign any contaminated portion of the milk to the animals and try again. A big, tall flat-bottom bucket is more stable, and it's harder for them to get a foot into it.

Bodily Restraint. If she kicks or is otherwise hard to control, you'll have to milk in a stanchion for sure. In the case of a goat you can hold 1 foot while you're milking with the other hand. For a cow, use hobbles on the hind legs of any animal that kicks the bucket or dances around. There are various styles of them. Lane Morgan says, "Another thing we've done with a kicky cow is to have one person hold her tail up while the other one milks. You have to grab it right at the base or you risk injuring the tail. Cows can't kick with their tails held straight up—I don't know why but it's true! After a few days—with luck and kindness—the cow calms down and forgets about kicking."

Some goats kneel on their front feet when you try to milk them. Some have the habit of trying to lie down completely. In the former case you can learn to milk her on her knees. In the latter, you can either rig up a body sling or make hamburger out of her. Part of breaking her of any bad habit is to refuse to stop milking—even if you have to milk on the ground. Then she may give up resistance as ineffectual.

Tails of Woe. One thing that a cow can do to you that a goat can't is switch you right in the eye with a manure-caked tail. If she's got that habit just include her tail in the hobble or get it under your arm and keep it there for the duration. In October you can trim it as short as possible for the winter but let it grow out again by summer to help her defend herself against the flies.

Self-Suckers. Goats are limber enough to do this, and if they get started self-sucking it can turn into a dreadful habit. The cure, unless you sell her or make hamburger, is an "Elizabethan collar" or "side-stick harness." Either one prevents her neck from turning. The collar is just a firm wide collar of metal or wood and wire. The harness is a halter plus a chest strap connected by a wooden stick between her front legs stretching from the chin loop on her halter to a connection located on the belly-side of her chest strap. Some cows can self-suck too. In their case there's an anti-sucking nose ring you can order from Nasco (livestock supplies).

MASTITIS

NOTE: Stop drinking the milk until you get the animal cured. Throw it away. But be careful where you throw it, because it is full of infection. Remember to wash your hands very thoroughly after you milk a mastitis-infected animal, and before you milk another animal, or you can spread the mastitis germs to every animal in your herd.

Cause. Mastitis is an infection of the tender udder tissue by bacteria that have entered through the cow's teat hole or through a cut on the udder. Mastitis is not due to any particular bug—at least 20 different organisms can cause it. Under normal conditions the cow has enough resistance to these microscopic bugs that are all around her to always avoid infection. Unfortunately it's common in both goats and cows. Mastitis is not just a threat to the animal's milk-producing capacity (any lactating female can get it, women also), which is threat enough. I've seen animals near death because it went into a general systemic blood poisoning.

Prevention. Prevention is the best management for mastitis. Best prevention is regular milking. *Mastitis is more common in machine-milked animals than hand-milked ones, and more common among animals pushed to their absolute production limit.* But sometimes it happens for no apparent reason. An overfull udder bruised from the outside or the internal bruising caused by her not getting milked out when she needs to be, makes her more susceptible. Dynah Geissal says feeding apple cider vinegar in their grain also helps prevent it. Woody Bernard says, "Not likely."

Mastitis Symptoms

1. Check the udder for tumors or abscesses. If there are tumors, you can feel them as large, very hard areas. Goats frequently have benign tumors that don't seem to do any harm. However, an abscess is a red, tender swelling of the entire side.
2. But usually mastitis first shows up as flaky, lumpy, or ropy milk. At least once a week examine her milk closely. A strip cup is designed to check the first few squirts of milk from each teat. Or you can just squirt onto a cloth so you can examine the milk closely.
3. The infected quarter of a cow's udder, or half of a goat's, will feel warmer than usual from the fever in it and be harder than usual.
4. It will seem hard to milk out and you won't get as much milk as usual. As the mastitis worsens, the milk will become thicker and thicker until it is a struggle to squeeze it out, and it comes out like toothpaste out of a tube.
5. As mastitis worsens the fluid will turn from milk's pure white to a yellowish color, which reveals pus in it—or brownish or pinkish, which is blood in it.
6. A part of the udder that has had mastitis before will be especially susceptible to it again.
7. Mastitis can also happen in dry (nonmilking) animals, so if you have a sick female see what you can squeeze out of each teat even if you expect her to be plumb dry.

Early Diagnosis. As you milk, morning and night, be alert for mastitis symptoms. *If you can't prevent it you can at least catch it early.* Mastitis will happen only one quarter at a time (a cow's udder has 4 separate quarters, each with its own faucet-teat). If you can catch it while it is confined to one quarter you can prevent it spreading to the others.

Cure. Mastitis is very hard to cure even using antibiotics, which are about the only hope you have. For a suspected case, the vet can test a milk sample. Daily shots of antibiotic give me the best results. Check with your vet by telephone for the kind and amount. *Knock out the infection as quickly as possible before the animal's current and future milk production is jeopardized. Get on it the day you detect or suspect mastitis, and stay on it until it's gone.* Your animal will more than likely have dried herself up a lot before it's over though. Rich feed may help bring her back if she's recently fresh. If she is severely abscessed, you'll have to dry her up, and she'll have a tendency to abscess again next time around. Dynah Geissal says she won't keep a goat who has it twice.

NOTE: Mastitis can spread from one dairy milker to another. Always milk mastitic animals last. Don't throw their milk away where other milkers might contact it—onto the floor or bedding in the barn. Always disinfect your hands after milking a mastitic animal. Don't give that milk to people or baby animals.

DAIRY VETTING: Mastitis is the biggie, but here are other possible problems, too. Here they're listed in alphabetical order.

Bang's. This is a disease. Cows that carry it don't show it. But their babies are born dead, and you and your children can catch a human form of Bang's called undulant fever, which is a very grim disease. A friend of mine in the dairy business nursed one of her daughters through it. To prevent Bang's, give your heifers shots at 4–8 months to vaccinate them.

Blood in the Milk. Dynah Geissal says, "May be caused by mastitis, a cut teat, chapped teats, rough milking, or the udder being too full causing small blood vessels to break."

Cuts. Bag Balm is a wonderful product that heals cuts or chapped skin on man or beast quickly. Just rub it into the problem area several times a day.

Chapped Udder. Rub Bag Balm on her after milking.

Cut Teat. Cuts occur often on the teats. Clean the cut. Don't break your milking schedule—even if it takes a long time to milk that cut teat, and the cow suffers, and you agonize in sympathy. She'd suffer more if the milk built up, swelling in that teat under the cut and abscessing above it. You may have

to hobble her to keep her from kicking if it hurts.

Milk Fever. This is a disease of pregnant or just-delivered animals. A goat with milk fever, according to Dynah Geissal, "lies down with her head turned back against her side. Other symptoms are muscle tremors, walking unsteadily, and subnormal temperature. The disease is prevented by a good daily mineral mix to maintain a proper calcium/phosphorus balance. The disease is hypocalcemia. The cure is to inject calcium gluconate and works almost miraculously."

Tuberculosis. Nowadays this isn't a very common dairy disease because of the long vigilance practiced by dairymen. But it's still smart to have your dairy goats and dairy cows checked for TB by a vet because the animals can get it from coming into contact with an infected wild animal. It's worth the money to be sure the milk is safe. *But, according to statistics, you're far more likely to get TB from living in crowded quarters in the inner city than from a dairy animal.*

ABOUT MILK AND MILK PRODUCTS

Milk Types

COLOSTRUM MILK: It's very important to get the mother's first milk into the kid, calf, etc. The general rule is that the milk for the first 4 days is for the baby. Either let the baby nurse those days at least, or milk her yourself and bottle-feed it to her baby. That milk has a special name, "colostrum," and it looks special—thicker and darker in color than regular milk. Colostrum contains precious immunizations and vitamin concentrates the mother is passing on to her kid, and the kid is likely to be sickly without it. Don't heat colostrum more than barely lukewarm because it will turn hard as cheese and be useless.

You have to go out within a couple hours after the goat has kidded, take the kid and put it in a warm dry place, milk the nanny mother for her colostrum, and then get her comfortably settled if you are planning to separate them. You can freeze extra colostrum milk (it's best frozen in a sterilized glass container). Then you can thaw and warm it to feed multiple births or an orphan that may appear later.

➤ *COLOSTRUM MILK CUSTARD The Swedes, Lane Morgan, and Kim Carlson (who helped edit this chapter) enjoy this specialty! Lane writes, "Mix 1 c. regular milk with 2 or 3 c. colostrum (second, third, or fourth milking). Add ½ c. honey or sugar and stir. Season with cinnamon and bake or cook in double boiler. The colostrum will thicken and set without eggs because it's high in albumen. It tastes very rich." But Woody says, "The milk shouldn't be used for human consumption for 4 days after birth."*

WHOLE AND SKIM MILK: "Whole milk" is milk in which the normal amount of cream is mixed throughout the milk by shaking it up. This is always a temporary situation with home milk, as you can't duplicate the dairy homogenization that shakes it up never to separate. If all the cream has been skimmed or separated out of the milk it is called "skimmed milk" or "skim milk." Skimmed milk is fine food for chickens, pigs, and the like.

SWEET OR SOUR: Sweet milk is fresh milk. As the days go by, especially at warmer temperatures, the bacteria do their natural thing and your milk (or cream) turns sour. When thoroughly soured, or "clabbered," it "sets up" and separates into a thick part (curds) and a thin clear liquid (whey). You can make cottage cheese out of this or feed it to the animals. Sour milk can be achieved naturally by waiting, or hurriedly by adding 1 T. lemon juice or vinegar per cup of milk.

The old-timers didn't feed their chickens very much, if any, grain. They fed them clabbered milk! Chickens do very well on a steady diet of this sour milk. Or you can give them fresh milk. But it's easier for them to get at the milk protein if you clabbered it before feeding. The clabbered milk is also somewhat more digestible for them. (They need plain water in addition to the clabbered milk.)

CHANGING MILKS: Goat's milk does not taste like either raw or store-bought cow's milk. You may have trouble changing your family over from any one kind of milk to any other. I can remember as a child how awful the store milk tasted to me when we sold our last cow and then how awful the raw milk seemed to taste for a while when several years later we again had a milk cow.

First serve the new milk in eggnogs, Postum (⅓ milk), and such. Once your family gets used to drinking it in mixtures, drinking it straight will soon follow. Give babies an especially gradual transition, starting out with one-fifth of the new type and working up gradually. There may be a period of either constipation or looseness until they make the adjustment.

Switching Baby's Milk. If you try to switch a baby over without this gradual introduction, your child can end up in terrible distress. Cow's milk is very constipating for babies who have been on canned formulas. If you try to make a sudden, total switch, your baby might not be able to have a bowel movement—even need surgery. So be gradual when you set out to change a baby's milk type—even one you think is a "big" baby, even a toddler. Watch the subsequent bowel movements carefully. Give that one-fifth part of the new milk. Wait to see how the next few bowel movements are. Then increase the mix one-fifth more, and so on. If there's a problem, reduce the new milk. Some children never do tolerate cow's milk.

Milk Handling

You need a stainless steel or food-grade plastic container to milk into, and quart, half-gallon, or gallon jars to store milk in; Bag Balm for treating teat and udder chapping and nicks; and cheesecloth or another system to strain the milk. There are other possible items but they're optional. Stainless steel is expensive but it lasts a lifetime.

CLEANING HOME-USE MILK UTENSILS: Quick-cooling the milk and using clean utensils can vastly improve milk flavor.

1. Prerinse with lukewarm water as soon as possible after their use. Lukewarm is important because cold water forms solid, hard-to-clean-off butterfat, and hot water coagulates milk protein and makes it stick to things.
2. Wash with an *alkaline* soap: 1 t. washing soda dissolved per quart of water, or homemade soap, or "dairy detergent." *Don't use regular detergent.*
3. A scrub brush helps.
4. Then rinse.
5. Give a final scald with boiling-hot water.
6. Air dry on a rack upside down because if you wipe them with a cloth, you're just rubbing bacteria back onto them.
7. Before you take your milk bucket out in the morning, you could rinse it out with boiling water from your tea kettle.

STRAINING THE MILK: You'll have less to strain out if the udder is washed before milking—or at least wiped off to get rid of dried mud and manure that might fall into the milk. Your next chance to prevent contamination is at the straining, when you bring the milk into your house. Straining helps to get rid of hair, dirt, and so on, which cause off-flavors and a high bacteria count. Milk with a high bacteria count will sour fast. You'll help avoid strong-tasting goat's milk if you strain and refrigerate right after milking.

Strainers. A regular commercial milk strainer looks like a big metal bowl with holes in the bottom. A ring fits in the bottom to hold down a paper filter disk. The gunk is trapped on the disk, which is thrown away after the straining. For a homemade strainer, pour your freshly milked milk through 4 thicknesses of dish towel, clean diaper, or cheesecloth laid over a large strainer. This won't catch soluble impurities. They settle as a kind of "dust" in the bottom of your jar and do no harm I know of. Or you can buy that specially designed milk strainer and use throwaway strainer pads. But there's no throwaway involved if you strain through cloth. Rinse and boil the cloth afterwards to clean it. That's my preferred system.

CREAM SEPARATION: See the section on cream. In this case you separate after straining but before bottling.

RAW OR PASTEURIZED? Raw milk does not taste like pasteurized milk from the store. The more raw milk ages, the more pronounced the difference becomes. If you're going to pasteurize, do this after straining (and separating if you choose), and before cooling.

Pasteurizing. Pasteurization is a germ-killing process achieved by the temperature you heat the milk to and the length of time you keep it there. The higher the temperature, the shorter the time. You can pasteurize cream, milk, or any combination thereof. There are pros and cons to this decision.

If you're selling milk, you usually are required to pasteurize. But if your animals are tested against tuberculosis and brucellosis and clear, pasteurization isn't needed for healthy home milk and just makes more work and more stuff you have to wash for no reason. I like the taste of raw milk. The process does destroy a goat milk enzyme, which causes it to eventually develop that goaty flavor. But if you're getting plenty of milk twice a day there's no need to have it fresh-tasting longer. Pasteurization doesn't hurt the food value of milk except it decreases vitamin C and thiamin—but milk doesn't have much of those anyway. *NOTE: Boiling milk or over-sterilization harms the nutritional value of milk.*

Machine Pasteurization. If you're doubtful about the health of your milk source (pasteurization will kill TB germs and won't affect flavor much if done right), or just want to pasteurize anyway, the easiest route is to buy a home milk-pasteurizer, which will pasteurize up to 2 gal. milk at a time, for $225 from New England Cheesemaking Supply (413-628-3808; **www.cheesemaking.com**).

Flash System. Set a pan (only glass or quality stainless steel) inside another with water between them, double-boiler style—because milk burns so easily. Put the milk into the top pan, cover, and heat to 161°F. Hold at that temperature for 15–20 seconds, then cool. Don't let the temperature get higher than 165°F, and don't keep it up there more than 20 seconds or you risk a cooked taste. Judge the temperature using a floating dairy thermometer. (Another system is to heat the milk quickly in an open-topped container, stirring constantly with a stainless steel spoon.) Then cool the milk fast as possible by setting it in ice water or under cool running water. Stir constantly until it gets down to 60°F, then once in a while until it gets down to 50°F.

Slow System. Create a double boiler as above. Heat milk to 140–150°F and hold it at that temperature for 30 minutes. Stir once in a while with a sterile, stainless steel spoon. Cool as above.

Bottling. Pour the milk into clean, scalded, jars or bottles, and cool it. Cover with lids.

Cooling. You milk the animal, take the milk into the house, strain it, and cool it—all in quick sequence. That's because warm milk is perfect food for bacteria, and so you want to get it cooled as fast as possible. Fast cooling avoids off-odors from bacterial growth. You can put it into prechilled *quart* glass jars, and put them in the coldest part of the fridge. But milk will cool even faster if it's sitting under running cold water, or in a pan of ice water with more ice added as needed. *Your basic goal is to cool it down to 40°F within 1 hour.* If you pour milk into a jar that's at room temperature and just set it in the fridge it won't get that cool that fast. It won't be bad to drink, but it will be more likely to develop an off-flavor if cooled too slowly. Fresh milk keeps best if stored around 34°F.

FRESH OR AGED MILK? On the farm you should drink both goat's milk and cow's milk fresh. When you've got it coming every 12 hours there's no reason to use milk over 24 hours old for plain table milk. You can use older milk for baking, cheese-making, etc.

PRESERVING MILK: Sometimes you will have more milk; spring and summer are peak months for milk, as well as eggs. Late winter may find you really short of milk. Cheesemaking is a way to preserve milk from your surplus times for your lean times. See the section on cheese storage for how to shelf-store or dry cheese. Other ways are to can it or freeze it. Or have enough milkers that you always have plenty—and when you have too much you can raise an extra calf, colt, pig, flock of chickens, etc., with it.

Canning Milk. Strain your fresh milk and cool it. Then pour it into clean jars to within ½ inch of the jar top. Put on your lids firmly. Process in a pressure cooker for 10 minutes at 10 lb. of pressure or 60 minutes in a water bath canner.

Freezing Milk. Pour fresh (as soon as cooled and before the cream has a chance to rise!) milk into straight-sided, lidded containers, quart or half-gallon size, or into food-grade plastic bags. It keeps well for 6 months or more. Don't thaw and then refreeze milk.

Foods Made from Milk

There can't be too much milk. You'll find that in order to get enough milk in the winter for household use, you'll have to live with a surplus of milk in the summer. That's okay. When your family doesn't need it all, you can raise calves, pigs, and chickens on it, feed the dog and cat, and make butter, cheese, and many other wonderful dairy foods. I separate the cream out for butter-making, refrigerate whole milk for cooking and table use, and separate out the curds from the rest for cheese, which you can make and store. The animals get the whey. My recipes use real cream and butter in them because you are milking and have these. Here are ideas for good ways to use, preserve, store your milk.

MILK SOUPS: Soups made with milk are so easy to make, good-tasting, and good for you. We just finished a lunch of tomato soup. I made it by thickening some of my V-7 juice with flour. Then I added salt, a little pour of molasses, and gradually stirred in milk. I was going to add some soda but couldn't find any. It came out good, anyway.

As a general rule, milk or cream soups shouldn't be boiled. Boiling hurts the flavor and makes a mean scum to clean out of the kettle. Always add the hot milk to the other ingredients at the last minute. You can make a milk soup out of any vegetable using the same general formula as in the following recipes. They're mostly called "cream of whatever" but are really made with milk.

☙ *CREAM OF FRESH MUSHROOM SOUP The old-timers around here go out in the spring and come back with pans of mushrooms. They saute them in butter and eat them right away, can them, or make soup: Wash ½ lb. fresh mushrooms, bruising them lightly if necessary, but do not peel. Chop rather fine. Brown slightly in 6 T. butter. Then blend in 4 T. flour, and gradually stir in 6 c. milk. Cook in the top of a double boiler for 20 minutes, stirring frequently. Season with salt and pepper. Serve with crackers.*

☙ *ONION SOUP Chop about 1 lb. onions. Cook the onions with a couple of tablespoons butter over a gentle heat for a few minutes without browning. Add 4 c. chicken stock and salt and pepper to taste, and cook 30 minutes more. Add a little flour and milk paste for thickening and 2 c. milk. Cook, stirring, until thickened. Good with bread and cheese.*

☙ *CREAM OF ONION AND POTATO SOUP Boil about 4 cubed potatoes and 4 sliced onions together in water until tender. Drain, saving the water. Rub the vegetables through a coarse strainer or blend them into a puree. Melt 2 T. butter and then mix into it 2 T. flour, ½ t. salt, and a pinch of pepper. Gradually add 3 c. scalded milk and the potato water. Stir constantly as you add the liquids. Add the potatoes and onion puree, stir, cook 3 minutes, and serve.*

☙ *CREAM OF SPINACH SOUP Puree ¾ c. cooked greens in a blender or chop fine or rub through a sieve. Combine 2 c. milk, 1 bay leaf, 2 sprigs parsley, and 1 t. minced onion, and heat to boiling. Melt 3 T. butter, blend in 3 T. flour, a pinch of paprika, 1 t. salt, and the milk mixture. Simmer 5 minutes, stirring constantly. Add the spinach to the mixture* and ¼ c. cream. Reheat and serve.

☙ **CREAM OF TOMATO SOUP** Peel about 6 tomatoes and cook, or use about 2 c. canned tomatoes. Simmer for 15 minutes after you have mashed them to break up large pieces. Now cool and then puree in a blender or just finish mashing. Add ½ t. soda, 1 T. honey, and 1 t. salt. In a separate pan melt 2 T. butter. Mash in 2 T. flour. Then gradually stir in 2 c. milk, stirring constantly until it thickens. Now stir in your tomato mixture, 2 c. more milk, and 1 T. finely chopped parsley, if you have it. Heat and serve.

MILK BEVERAGES

☙ **HOT FLAVORED MILK** Combine 1 c. or more scalding hot milk and a pour of molasses (or some instant cocoa, or a little honey and vanilla). Beat it up with the eggbeater or put into the blender. Pour into a glass. Sprinkle nutmeg on top. Serve with toasted homemade bread.

☙ **BANANA MILK SHAKE** Slice 2 bananas and beat until creamy, or put through a coarse sieve, or blend. Add 2 c. cold milk, mix thoroughly, and serve at once.

☙ **GOAT MILK SHAKE** From Sonya Lizarraga, Salome, AZ: "You just freeze the goat milk in small containers (neighbors give me their plastic cottage-cheese cartons). When you want your shake, you cover the blades in your liquifier (blender) with just cold milk, then put in 2 big spoons of carob powder (a good protein) and a banana. Then add as much frozen goat milk chunks as will make it thick, blending to mix up well. Fun to experiment with other flavors too, but banana is our favorite."

☙ **REAL STRAWBERRY MILK SHAKE** Crush about 1 qt. strawberries, and press through a coarse sieve in order to get at least 1⅔ c. puree. Or blend. Combine the strawberry puree with 5 c. milk and ½ c. cream. Add ½ c. honey, ½ t. salt, and 2½ t. lemon juice. Mix well and chill. Top each glass with a spoonful of whipped cream.

☙ **BANANA-STRAWBERRY SHAKE** Mash 2 medium-ripe bananas and combine with 1 c. slightly sweetened, crushed strawberries. Mix in 1 T. lemon juice, 1 qt. milk, and 1 qt. slightly softened vanilla ice cream with a whisk. You could garnish each serving with a fresh strawberry.

☙ **APRICOT MILK** Put 1 c. cooked apricots and their juice through a sieve, or blend. Mix the pulp with 3 c. milk. Put ½ pint vanilla ice cream in a pitcher and pour the milk mixture over it. Stir slightly.

☙ **PRUNE MILK** Pit and mash the prunes until you have 1 c. pulp. Add that to 3 c. chilled milk, and beat them together or shake in a jar. Pour into glasses and top with whipped cream.

☙ **PEAR AND GINGER ALE MILK** Press 1 c. cooked or canned pears (not the juice) through a sieve, or blend. Mix with 1 qt. milk. Pour into glasses, and to each glass add a splash of fizzy ginger ale (recipe in Chapter 5).

☙ **MAPLE AND GINGER ALE MILK** Add ½ c. maple syrup to 1 qt. milk, and mix well. Pour the milk into tall glasses and add ginger ale to taste.

☙ **MILK LASSIE** Stir 1 T. molasses into 1 c. milk, hot or cold. Easy and nice.

☙ **BANANA LASSIE** Mash 1 ripe banana until smooth. Stir in 1 T. molasses and a pinch of salt. Add ¾ c. milk and mix well.

☙ **ORANGE JULIE** Combine ⅓ c. frozen orange juice concentrate, ½ c. milk, ½ c. water, ¼ c. sugar, ½ t. vanilla, and 6 ice cubes in a blender, and whir until smooth. Serve right away.

☙ **SHAKER SYLLABUB** The Shakers heavily sweetened 1 gal. warm apple cider with maple sugar or syrup and grated a nutmeg on top, then milked the cow right into the mixture and served it at the table while still hot and foamy. Some winter I'm going to try that just for adventure!

CUSTARD: Custard can be made by baking or boiling, or can be thickened with rennet, which causes a yogurt-like result. Custards have to be cooked at a low temperature and not too long or they will curdle. But frankly, I'm always in such a muddle my custards "curdle" more often than not, and they are still delicious. All "curdle" means is that some water separates out. I just pour it off and serve what's left. The best way to regulate the cooking temperature of baked custards is to surround the pan with water. Set the individual custard dishes in a pan of hot water. Make all boiled custards in the top of a double boiler. Milk that is a little sour can also cause curdling.

If the custard does start to separate, remove it immediately from the heat, set the custard pan in a pan of cold water, and beat to redistribute the particles. Any acid such as lemon juice would reinforce the tendency to curdle. Baked custards come out firmer than boiled custards. You know it is done when the blade of a knife run into the center of the custard comes out clean. The firmness of the custard is also a result of the amount of egg in it. The more egg in your custard, the firmer it will be. Two eggs per cup of liquid is a good general guide. One egg per cup of liquid makes a soft custard, all right for baking in small cups.

☙ **BAKED CUSTARD** Combine 3 lightly beaten eggs, ¼ t. salt, and ⅓ c. sugar. Add 3 c. scalded milk slowly, stirring constantly. Add ½ t. vanilla. Pour into custard cups. Sprinkle with nutmeg. Place the filled custard cups in a pan of hot water and bake in a moderate oven (325°F) for 45 minutes, or until a knife inserted in the center of the custard comes out clean.

For chocolate custard: Add 1½ oz. (squares) of chocolate to the milk and heat until melted. You can't use that instant chocolate stuff.

For coconut custard: Add ½ c. shredded coconut to the mixture.

For coffee custard: Scald 2 T. ground coffee with the milk, strain, and proceed as for the baked custard.

For date custard: Add ½ c. chopped dates to the custard before baking.

For honey custard: Use ½ c. honey instead of sugar.
For rum custard: Leave out the vanilla and add 2 T. rum.

☙ **BOILED CUSTARD** *Combine 2 lightly beaten eggs, ⅛ t. salt, and ¼ c. sugar. Add slowly 2 c. scalded milk, and cook in the top of a double boiler until the mixture coats a spoon. Add ½ t. vanilla and chill.*

For almond custard: Use almond extract instead of the vanilla, and top with shaved, toasted almonds when ready to serve.

For caramel custard: Use brown sugar instead of white.

For chocolate custard: Melt 1 oz. (square) chocolate in the milk.

Custard making is so simple and yet such an art. My mother's custards were carefully made in little individual dishes. They always came out just perfect, and were such a gift of love it makes me both hungry and homesick just to remember them.

RENNET PUDDINGS: Rennet puddings made from scratch turn out like yogurt. When Little Miss Muffet was sitting on a tuffet, eating her "curds and whey," I figure it was a junket rennet pudding. They used "essence of pepsin" or "liquid rennet" or a "junket tablet" to make them. That's the same rennet that is used in cheese-making. (See "Cheese" for how to make rennet if you don't buy it.)

☙ **BASIC RENNET PUDDING** *Just stir in the acid, let the milk stand at room temperature for about 20 minutes, then refrigerate. Serve with cream and sweetening, or fruit. It's very bland.*

☙ **VANILLA RENNET CUSTARD** *Combine 2 c. milk, 2 T. sugar, and a dash of salt in a small pan. Cook, stirring constantly, over low heat, until lukewarm. Remove from heat, and add 1 t. vanilla. Crush 1 rennet tablet in cold water in a cup, stirring until dissolved. Add it quickly to the milk mixture, stirring only once or twice. Pour immediately into a quart dish or into individual dishes. Let stand at room temperature until the mixture is set (do not move) then chill. The custard will set in 10–30 minutes, depending on the temperature of the room. The higher the room temperature the more time is needed. Sprinkle top of custard lightly with nutmeg or cinnamon just before serving. Rennet is sometimes available at grocery stores.*

FLOUR-THICKENED MILK: Mrs. Lillie R. Balph, Beaver Falls, PA, wrote me: "My mother served this to us as a breakfast cereal. It isn't a soup. She used flour to thicken the milk to a pudding consistency. She put butter and salt in it and heated it until it was very smooth and creamy. She served it in cereal bowls. She ate it with sugar and more butter, but Father and us children used cream and sugar. My aunt made hers lumpy as did other women in the community. Sometimes I make it for myself."

Kat Atkins, Coquille, OR, speaking of goat milk, wrote me: "I keep a quart made and in the fridge, and I add at least 2 eggs to each quart and thicken with 3 heaping T. flour. Then I just make toast and pour the milk over, after rewarming, add some nutmeg now and then and Instant Breakfast. Also great over oatmeal. Good for people with queasy stomachs. Good frozen. Makes soup and a good base liquid for any cooking. I make it ahead when I'm not busy. It lasts about 3 days. 'Thickened milk' made with a dash of vanilla, poured into a bowl with granola topping even pleases and fills my husband at breakfast."

CULTURED MILKS: Store-bought buttermilk, kefir, and yogurt are the 3 common cultures in use, but they are not the only ones. For more information on these quick milk cultures, read *Making Your Own Cheese and Yogurt* by Max Alth (1973) (also good on cheese-making); and *Yogurt, Kefir, and Other Milk Cultures* or *Fermented Foods and Beverages,* both by Beatrice Trum Hunter. You can order the appropriate culture starters from dairy or cheese-makers' suppliers, or start with some grocery-store product. Kefir grains and other specialized products for yogurt and kefir-making are available from GEM Cultures: 707-964-2922; 30301 Sherwood Rd., Fort Bragg, CA 95437; **www.gemcultures.com.** GEM also sells a culture thermometer ($7), cheesecloth, and Kombucha Tea Fungus.

CULTURED "BUTTERMILK": Real buttermilk is the liquid left over after you've churned butter. It is delicious and good to use in cooking or to drink straight. Commercial dairy "buttermilk" or homemade cultured "buttermilk" never was near a butter churn. It is made by adding a culture to milk to thicken it. At the dairy, sometimes dots of melted butter are sprayed into the cultured milk to make it look "buttery" (real buttermilk doesn't have any butter in it). They add 1 or 2 percent butter that way—whatever they think the customers want. Then the "buttermilk" is ready for sale.

So dairy-type "buttermilk" is skim milk that has been cultured with a variety of bacteria in the same way you make yogurt. It sets up (thickens) 12–14 hours after the culture is introduced. Then you stir to break up the mass. That's why it doesn't have a yogurt-like consistency. *NOTE: To substitute in a recipe for store buttermilk, you can use your homemade yogurt plus a dab of butter.*

☙ **BUTTERMILK-CULTURED MILK** *Mix 2 c. raw milk or home-grown milk with ¼ c. store buttermilk. Cover and set in a warmish place for 24 hours. (Read instructions under "Yogurt," because it's the same procedure.) You can use ¼ c. of your resulting thick milk to start a new batch and so on. You can make cottage cheese out of the results. Both curd and whey are good and nourishing to eat if you want. Any little mold that forms on top can simply be scraped off and given to the animals. Buttermilk culture is the least sour tasting of the three. Sourness also depends on how soon you eat it. The sooner you eat any of these 3, the less sour they will be. The longer you wait to eat your cultured milk the more sour it will be—up to a certain point. You can keep the culture going until it gets contaminated in the same way yogurt does.*

YOGURT: This is milk soured by a selected variety of bacteria. Yogurt is thickened because the bacteria consumes the milk sugar and changes some of it to lactic acid. Once you have made a yogurt culture at home you can keep making more by using a little of your last culture to make each new batch, but eventually the mixture gets invaded by an off-breed of bacteria. In that case you could start over with some dairy yogurt. This happens about once a month. Once you learn to make this wonderful stuff, consider getting *The Stonyfield Farm Yogurt Cookbook* by Meg Cadoux Hirshberg, available from Harrowsmith (see magazine list in Chapter 1) for 300 yogurt-using recipes. Garden Way offers *Cooking with Yogurt,* Bulletin A-86: yogurt gravy, salad dressing, soup, frozen, etc. Electric yogurt-makers are nice but not necessary.

Getting Your Culture to Start. An easy way to get started is to buy a pint of yogurt and add 3 T. of that to a quart of your own milk. You can use cow, goat, or soybean milk—even powdered skim milk. Or use a commercial yogurt culture for a starter. You can't make your own culture (starter) unless you're a bacteriologist, because that involves isolating a batch of 1 kind of invisible bacteria from all the others and growing it alone.

Yogurt Thickness. The thinnest yogurt is made from nonfat dry milk liquefied with water. Mixing it with skim milk gives you a thicker yogurt. Starting with whole milk makes it thicker yet. Making the yogurt from whole milk with some nonfat milk mixed in gives you thicker yet. If you add evaporated milk, or light or heavy cream to whole milk you get the thickest yogurt of all!

Secrets of Great Yogurt

1. Start by pasteurizing the milk.
2. Cool milk to 105–110°F.
3. If you start from store-bought yogurt, make it an unflavored, additive-free one: 2 T. per quart of your milk.
4. Keep the mix as near 105–110°F as possible while it's working.
5. It takes more than twice as long for yogurt from a freeze-dried culture to get going, as for starts from active yogurt culture.
6. Move from the warm "incubating" place as soon as it has thickened, and chill at least 12 hours; keep refrigerated until used up.

Heat milk to 150° to pasteurize, cool to 110°

Add milk powder if desired for extra thickness and nutrition

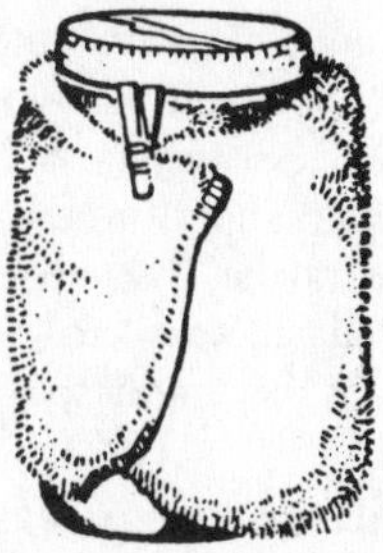

Stir in starter and maintain at 110° until thickened. Disturb as little as possible

🐦 **BASIC YOGURT** From Connie Hughes: "Use 1½ c. canned milk, ⅔ c. skim milk, and 1 t. unflavored gelatin. Put the milk in a 2-qt. pan and sprinkle on gelatin. Let soak 5 minutes or so, then stir with a wire whisk while heating to almost boiling (to pasteurize). Cool to warm (I set the pan in a dishpan with cold water and watch it until it's just warm). Add ¼ cup commercial yogurt (unflavored) and whisk in well. Rinse out small jars with hot water and fill with warm yogurt mixture. Set in a warm place overnight until set. Taste it to see if it's ready or not. Then refrigerate." To thicken this recipe add anywhere from 2 T. to 1 c. powdered milk. From scratch with powdered milk, use 2½ c. dry milk powder with 3¾ c. water.

🐦 **CHRISTINE'S YOGURT** From Christine Roelke of Manchester, PA. "I have a yogurt maker/warming tray. Use 1 qt.

whole or skim milk and add ⅓ or ½ c. powdered milk (optional for a firmer or pudding-like consistency). Scald, then let cool until it feels lukewarm to the touch. Add vanilla (1 t.) and honey (less than 1 t.). Mix in 2 to 3 T. plain yogurt. Let sit on warm surface for 2 to 4 hours. Cover the containers with a cookie sheet to keep the warmth down where the yogurt is."

🐦 **HEATING PAD YOGURT** From Kat Atkins, Coquille, OR: Heat 10 c. goat's milk to 162°F. Cool to 110°F. Add ½ c. noninstant milk powder, 8 oz. Dannon brand plain yogurt, ½ t. honey, and (optional) a dash of vanilla. Pour into 1-qt. sterile jars. Cover the top of each jar with plastic. Put a heating pad into a canning kettle (36-qt.) and turn pad on to high until the kettle is warm inside. Put a down pillow on top of pad, then the jars—wrapped in towels—then another pillow. Don't leave airspace. Change heating pad temperature to medium and wrap kettle in a blanket. Let go 3 days. Unwrap and put jars of yogurt in fridge.

For Your Next Batch. Save about ¼ c. of your first batch. Keep it in the refrigerator or in a covered container. Use it within 5 days to start another batch of yogurt. And so on until your yogurt gets that off-taste that shows you that some sort of bacteria has moved in on the original variety. That's when you have to get some of the store kind again. You could also buy yogurt culture direct from a dairy supplier if you have use for so much at once.

More Yogurt Recipes. There are so many good things you can make from yogurt.

🐦 **FLAVORED YOGURTS** Blend in with the finished yogurt berries that have been put through a sieve or blended, or any fruit juice. Use about ¼–¾ c. flavoring per 2 c. yogurt. Sweeten with honey or sharpen the flavor with lemon juice as you prefer. Rhubarb sauce and yogurt go well together. Or serve it with any whole fruit. Use it for a vegetable salad dressing combined with seasoning—parsley, horseradish, tomato juice, onion, or Roquefort cheese.

🐦 **VANILLA YOGURT** Mix ½ t. vanilla flavoring into your quart of milk that's going to be yogurt. Sweeten to taste.

🐦 **YOGURT AND CUCUMBERS** Peel 3 large cucumbers and slice into ⅛-inch-thick pieces. Combine 4 c. yogurt, 1 clove garlic—ground or finely chopped—and 1 t. salt. Pour over the cucumbers and serve cold.

🐦 **YOGURT-FRUIT DRINK** In a blender combine 1 c. fruit juice, 1 c. yogurt, a little honey, if you need more sweetening, and ½ c. ice, if you want it really cold.

🐦 **BANANA-YOGURT DRINK** Combine in a blender: 1 c. yogurt, ½ c. milk, 1 banana, and honey to taste. Ice is optional.

🐦 **YOGURT SALAD DRESSING** Combine 4 cloves finely minced garlic, 4 T. lemon juice, ¼ c. cooking oil, and 4 T. grated onion with 2½ c. yogurt, 2 t. salt, ¼ c. chopped parsley, and a pinch of red paprika. Serve chilled.

🐦 **FROZEN YOGURT** Soft frozen yogurt is good topped with nuts, honey, granola, fruit, fruit juice, or any other sweetening. Mix yogurt with fruit (1 c. yogurt to 1 c. fruit). Use fresh fruit, finely cut. The procedure is to freeze your yogurt to a soft mush, then beat it up with fruit, freeze again, and serve.

🐦 **CARDAMOM FRUIT YOGURT** Mix 3 c. yogurt with 1 c. any fruit; add 1¼ t. ground cardamom.

⋑ YOGURT CHEESE See "Yogurt Cream Cheese" in the "Cream Cheese" section.

KEFIR: This is very similar to yogurt except it is a little different in taste, more fluid in consistency, and made a little differently. To a dairy bacteriologist, kefir is a symbiotic association of certain organisms: a gum-producing microbe that manufactures the polysaccharide grain, a lactose-fermenting yeast, and several lactose-fermenting bacteria (*Lactobacillus bulgaricus*, *Lactobacillus acidolphilus*, and *Lactobacillus kephiri*). In plain English, it's a variety of cultured milk, like yogurt. Yogurt is firm and eaten with a spoon, but kefir is liquid. That's because it has very low curd tension, unlike yogurt in which the curd holds together. So you drink kefir. Kefir is a great tradition in Caucasia and the Eastern Mediterranean. It's nourishing and healthy stuff and is supposedly more digestible than yogurt because of the smaller particles. It's good to drink mixed with fruit juice or fresh or frozen fruit, or sweetened with honey, sorghum, or molasses.

For success make your kefir by stirring the grains (see below) into your home-grown raw milk and let stand at room temperature overnight.

⋑ EASY KEFIR *Combine 2 c. raw milk with ¼ c. unflavored store-bought kefir. Cover and let rest for 48 hours.*

⋑ KEFIR MADE FROM "GRAINS" *Mrs. George O. Nordmann, Topton, NC, wrote me this recipe for kefir: "First, obtain some kefir grains. The surplus may be dried, frozen or held over for a short period in the refrigerator. The grains may be used with any good quality milk: powdered, skim, goat's, cow's, or soya milk. When using powdered milk, avoid chlorinated and/or fluoridated water. Place the grains (after rinsing in cold water) in the amount of whatever kind of milk you use in a quart jar and let set at room temperature overnight. Next day, strain out grains, rinse them and place in more milk in another container. The milk from which the grains were removed is now ready to drink. The sourness depends on the length of time the grains were allowed to stand in the milk. Always rinse the grains in cold water before reusing. The proportion of grains to milk should be about 1 c. grains to 1 qt. milk. They multiply fastest in skim or low-fat milk at about 68–70°F."*

⋑ KEFIR FROM A BLOB *Alan Clute, Sunnyvale, CA, got some kefir culture from a friend: "Ours is a gelatinous blob, about ½ inch across, which we recently got from a friend. You just plunk it into some barely warm milk and let it sit, covered and wrapped, at warm room temperature—no need for special heat as with yogurt. Next day you fish it out and repeat, sort of like milking a cow. When the blob grows big enough, it can be divided and shared. Our friend said the culture needs to be used every couple of days or so, which means that, as with a cow, somebody else has to care for it while you're away."*

KOUMISS: A popular old-time fermented milk beverage, this was originally of mare's milk. Put milk fresh from the cow into a scalded pop or small wine bottle. Fill it almost up to the top and cork tightly. Shake it up thoroughly every day for 10 days. At the end of that time it is koumiss and ready to drink.

CHEESE

Welcome to the world of cheese-making! It's easier than you think. In fact, cheese is simply naturally or artificially coagulated milk with the whey poured off or pressed out. The importance of cheese viewed as a traditional food is that it's the only way to preserve milk when you have no refrigeration. Even so, this is a temperate-zone preservation system. In the tropics the temperatures are just too hot except for storing ghee (see "Butter"). Old-time dairy animals didn't milk as many months a year as ours do now. And milk in the form of cheese tastes better—rather than worse—with the passage of time! Milk in the form of cheese, after 60 days, is guaranteed free of bad germs because the cheese-making process kills them; so where pasteurization was impossible and there were health problems with the milk, cheese was the safe way to eat it.

CHEESE NETWORKING

Online. Cheesemakers-L is a list group with a great website. It's for serious cheesemakers and also folks with dairy animals who just want to make good homemade cheese and dairy products: **members.xoom.com/cheesemaker/ Cheesemakers-L.htm.**

Books. When I first wrote about cheese, in 1971, I couldn't find recipes anywhere. Now there are lots of them. The best to date are in *Goats Produce Too!* by Mary Jane Toth. Her recipes will usually work for either goat or cow milk. She also has recipes for goat milk soaps, chevon (goat meat), and goat milk ice creams, sherbets, and fudges. Price is $12.95 plus $2 s/h: 517-465-1982; 2833 N. Lewis Rd., Coleman, MI 48618; **mjt@voyager.net.** New England Cheesemaking Supply (413-628-3808; **www. cheesemaking.com**) published *The Making of Farmstead Goat Cheeses* by Jean-Claude LeJaouen, an expert on French sheep and goat cheeses (70+ goat-cheese recipes, and how to build a cheese room); and a beginner's text, *Cheesemaking Made Easy,* by Ricki and Robert Carroll (60 cheese recipes for both goat and cow milks). *Goat Cheese: Small-Scale Production,* by the Mont-Laurier Benedictine Nuns, covers making mold-ripened cheeses. Older books are *Cheese Making,* by Charles J. Hunt; and *Cheese Making at Home: The Complete Illustrated Guide,* by Don Radke (1974).

Demonstrations. Mary Jane Toth gives cheesemaking and cooking demonstrations. Call her to schedule a class (see books). Ricki Carroll (co-author of *Cheesemaking Made Easy*) offers all-day cheesemaking workshops on how to make gouda, fromage blanc, creme fraiche, queso blanco, mascarpone, ricotta, whey, mozzarella cheeses, etc. ($100; spring, summer). Get more info from the American Cheese Society.

CHEESEMAKING MAGAZINES, INFO, AND SUPPLIES

Ag-Innovations sells imported cheese vats, molds, and draining bags. Dr. Larry Faillace and Linda Faillace teach cheesemaking classes: 802-496-3998; **aqinnov@madriver.com.**

American Cheese Society schedules cheesemaking courses, conference panels and presentations, tours, a big annual convention with cheese-judging, and a list of American cheese producers: 502-583-3783; 304 W. Liberty St., Ste. 201, Louisville, KY 40202. Their website posts conferences, articles, and their latest newsletter: **www.cheesesociety.org.**

The Basics of Making Cheese is a terrific British website that describes in downloadable detail the science and procedure of cheesemaking: **www.efr.hw.ac.uk/SDA/ cheese2.html.**

(The) Cheese Reporter Magazine website has a searchable supplier directory, a wide choice of books and videos, and many links: **www.cheesereporter.com.**

The Cheesiest Site on the Net aspires to be the most comprehensive guide to cheese online, plus special reports on exceptional cheesemongers, dairies, and cheese-makers. It covers Cheeses, Essential Vocabulary, Links, Cheesemaking, and Cheese Retailers: **www.erols.com/auraltech/index2.html.**

Jaybee builds and sells "The Vat," a 7–15 gal., 150-lb. stainless steel heater/mixer/pasteurizer for liquids to be marketed ($8,000): 603-744-6644; PO Box 231, Bristol, NH 03222-0231; **www.jaybeeprecision.com.**

Kusel Equipment sells 3A vats, finishing tables, air-veyors and curd elevators, presses and molds (such as 40-lb. "Wilson" hoops), submersible brine systems, and cottage cheese systems for large commercial producers: 920-261-4112; fax 920-261-3151; 820 W. St., Watertown, WI 53094; **www.kuselequipmentcom.**

CHEESE MARKETING: Selling cheese is about the easiest way to start selling dairy products off your homestead. You can use raw milk and age the cheeses 60 days, which will kill off the bad germs, or start with pasteurized milk (heat milk to 145–150°F for 30 minutes, then cool to 70°F and make the cheese). You can sell your cheese mail-order, from the farm, or through stores. *American Country Cheese* tells the start-up stories of 30 cheese companies.

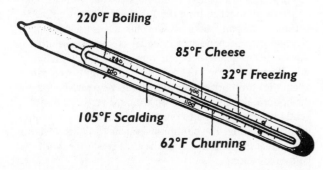

220°F Boiling
85°F Cheese
32°F Freezing
105°F Scalding
62°F Churning

DAIRY THERMOMETER: All through this section you'll be reading instructions to have your milk or curds at a precise temperature. For that, you need a "dairy thermometer." This glass thermometer is made to float upright in liquid and be easily readable. It reads a range from about –10° to 220°F. Some are also marked in degrees centigrade. Available from any dairy or cheese-makers supplier.

CHEESE TYPES: There are 5 basic types of cheese: soft, semi-soft, firm, hard, and processed.

Soft cheeses are unripened, fresh ones: cottage, cream, pot, ricotta, gjetost, Neufchatel. The soft cheeses that ripen naturally in just a few days include Brie, Camembert, and the double and triple creams, which have thin white crusts and almost fluid insides.

The semi-soft cheeses are ripened using specific types of helper bacteria and yeasts or molds: Basic Swiss, Brick, Muenster; Liederkranz, Limburger, Port Salut; Roquefort and Gorgonzola. These are among the most difficult for homestead cheese-makers because of the special organism culture you need and the special "ripening" conditions needed to control how they grow.

Firm cheeses are Cheddars, Cheshire, Lancashire, Caciocavallo, Swiss Emmenthal, Gruyere, Jarlsberg, etc.

Hard cheeses are made like the firm cheeses but are matured to a grainy texture for grating: Asiago, Parmesan, Romano, Sapsago, etc.

Processed cheese is called "American" cheese and comes from factories, and thank God if you don't have to eat it. It's made of chemicals, artificial flavor and color, and a wide variety of other nondairy items with some milk thrown in. Your homemade cheese is just milk plus curdling agent.

FLAVORED CHEESES: Any cheese, hard or soft, can be varied by adding more or less salt, herbs, chili peppers, onions, chives, caraway, cumin, dried tomatoes, garlic, fennel, star anise, lavender, pink peppercorns, dill, rosemary, and savory. You can mix a crumbly cheese with nuts and dried fruit. Or wrap chunks of aged strong-tasting cheese in grape or chestnut leaves. Cheese can also be smoked.

WHEY: Any time you make cheese, you get "whey," which is the clearer fluid that you pour off from the curds. Don't throw it away. Whey is terrific for animal feed, especially for pigs. In food value, 1¼ gal. of whey equals 1 lb. of ground barley. *NOTE: Don't use galvanized containers for any cheese-making.*

Making Soft Cheeses

Your homemade soft cheeses—cream and cottage, etc.—will seem different from the store product of the same name. If you read the ingredients on the store container, you'll see why. For example, store cottage cheese may contain various additives, stabilizers, and preservatives, and is usually saltier than homemade. It also may have a creamy substance mixed in.

CREAM CHEESE: Cream cheese and yogurt are actually very similar. Yogurt is cultured whole or skim milk. Cream cheese can be made from more or less rich cream—even from skim milk!—which gives you, in turn, a higher or lower calorie cream cheese. "Cream cheese" made from milk instead of cream is called "Fromage Blanc" (instructions available from New England Cheesemaking Supply Co. Cream cheese will soon spoil, unlike your hard cheeses, and so after it's made, it has to be protected from air, refrigerated, and eaten relatively soon.

You can substitute your homemade cream cheese in all those good recipes. A 3-oz. package equals 6 T. of your own; the 8-oz. package means 1 c. of your own. Don't store cream cheese in your freezer. You'll cause weeping and destroy the texture, because when the ice crystals form they break up the fine consistency. This cream cheese takes 15–18 hours to set up. You can use yogurt culture or a regular cheese culture or a cultured buttermilk.

You can make cream cheese from regular cream, which contains 24–35 percent fat, but it improves it to add skim milk powder to increase the milk solids and reduce the fat. Pure cream cheese is very buttery. Store cream cheese doesn't contain so much cream. Instead, dairies add a gelatin "stabilizer."

Here are some of the old-fashioned ways to make something like cream cheese without using gelatin or powdered milk.

➤ *YOGURT CREAM CHEESE Pour freshly made yogurt into a cheesecloth-lined strainer or colander. Gather the 4 cloth corners and sides in your hands and tie firmly. Hang this yogurt-filled bag where it can drip in a cool, airy place for 6–48 hours (sooner is safer). Then scrape what you have left from the cloth and place it in a jar. Use plain as a spread or flavored with your choice of salt, chopped chives, fresh dill, garlic, oregano, etc. This is a kind of "cream cheese."*

☙ *SOUR CREAM CHEESE 1 Salt sour cream to taste and stir well. Pour into a cloth that has been wrung out in cold water and proceed as above. This has a really sour taste.*

☙ *SOUR CREAM CHEESE 2 Take 1 qt. of cream (the lighter the better, to avoid the buttery taste). Set the dish in a pan of hot water, and warm it almost to the boiling point. Remove and cool to lukewarm. Add rennet. Let stand until thick. Break the curds slightly with a spoon and then tie up in a cloth. Press the cloth lightly with a weight for a half day so the pressed-out whey will drain away. Then re-tie in a clean cloth, rub salt over the outside, and let hang to drip for a day or so more.*

☙ *DEVONSHIRE OR "CLOTTED" CREAM This is just delicious, and I really recommend that you have lots of milk and cream to play with. Combine 2 qt. milk and 1 qt. heavy cream and refrigerate overnight. The next day heat to a temperature of about 90°F and hold it there for 3–5 hours, or until a wrinkled, leathery look appears on the surface, containing little pockets filled with a liquid resembling melted butter. Don't stir or shake the }contents. Don't let it get too hot. When it is very wrinkled and drawn-looking, cool and again refrigerate overnight.*

The next day, skim off the thick top cream. This is your Devonshire cream. It is good with canned fruit or fresh strawberries. You'll get about 1 pint of Devonshire cream.

COTTAGE CHEESE AND FARMER CHEESE: These can be made of skim milk, buttermilk, whole milk, or goat's milk, but not very well of pasteurized milk because the natural souring process is key to good cottage cheese. If you must use pasteurized (store) milk, warm it to about 75°F. Then add 1 c. cultured buttermilk from the store. It will help also to use rennet (½ tablet to 1 gal. of milk), or, even better, a junket tablet, which has a milder action than rennet. Goat's milk does not thicken as easily and has a softer curd than cow's milk, so to make cottage cheese with it, it helps to mix in one-half or one-third cow's milk. Otherwise it takes about 5 days to get goat milk sour enough for cottage cheese.

One qt. of milk will make about 1 c. of cottage cheese. You can work with any convenient amount since there are no other ingredients except salt "to taste" in the final stage. The best container in which to "set" the milk is a wide, coverable one. Sour the milk in the same container in which you will make the cottage cheese. A covered enamel roaster, a canning kettle, heavy crockery, or a stainless steel bowl would all be fine. Do not use aluminum.

The larger volume of milk you work with, the easier it will be to control the temperature; 75–85°F is the temperature to strive for through the clabbering (thickening) process. Leave the milk on the warming shelf of your wood stove or some other warm but not hot place, similar to one you would use to raise yeast bread. (If you are using milk that is already sour, you would skip this step, of course.) Temperatures that are too low allow the proliferation of less-desirable bacteria. Temperatures that are too high will kill your bacteria and stop their creation of the lactic acid you need to clabber the milk. They will also toughen the curd.

The clabbering may take a few hours or a few days, depending on temperature and bacteria count. When the milk is "set," it will have a jelly-like consistency. The solids will have formed one large curd, which floats on whey in the bottom. When the milk is sour and clabbered, you are ready to cut the curd.

Cut the curd using a clean butcher knife with a blade long enough to reach from the surface of the curd to the bottom of the pan. Make parallel cuts across the curd one way and then perpendicular parallel cuts across the other way to create squares between ½ inch and 1 inch on the side. If you are using a deep pan, rig up a galvanized wire to cut the curd horizontally at intervals between the top and the bottom of the pan. Now stir the curd very slowly and gently, endeavoring not to break up the curd but preventing it from clumping. The clumping tendency will be most pronounced at first and less so as the curd gets firmer with your final heating.

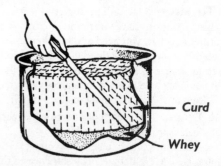

Curd

Whey

Cut clabbered curd into ½-inch to 1-inch squares

Now the curd is heated a little more to get it to just the right firmness. This is more art than science and depends on how you like your cottage cheese. The lower the temperature at which you stop, the softer your cheese curds will be. The higher the temperature, the firmer your curds will be. Don't let the milk heat over 110°F for traditional soft-curd cheese. Up to 120°F gives you the tough-curded "farmer" style cheese. One system is to take a half hour heating at the rate of about 2 degrees every 5 minutes to a final temperature of 100°F or so, and then hold it at that temperature until it has developed the desired firmness. That's the laboratory ideal and really can't be duplicated in the kitchen. But have courage—many a fine bowl of cottage cheese has been made under less than perfect conditions!

Heat very slowly to desired temperature, stirring gently

To test the curd, pinch a little between thumb and finger. If a tiny bit remains on the ball of your thumb it is about ready. When you are satisfied that all the curd would pass the pinch test, you are ready to drain the whey. Dump the curd and whey into a cheesecloth-covered colander or a colander having very coarse holes and substantial interstices to hold back the curd as the whey drains away (save the whey for your animals). You can make something suitable by punching holes in a metal pan or can from the inside out.

If the milk is very sour you can rinse the curd with cold water and drain again. At this point you may want to break up the curd with cold water and drain again. Sprinkle salt over the curd, work it in thoroughly, and let the cottage cheese continue to drain for at least an hour. You could tie the end of the cloth together and hang it from a nail until all the whey has drained off.

You now have dry cottage cheese. It will keep about a week or 10 days in the refrigerator (covered). The usual commercial product is "creamed." You can add cream to yours at this time or before serving, but it makes more sense to do so shortly before serving because creamed cottage cheese does not keep nearly as well as the dry.

If you blend some "dry" cottage cheese with water and add tomato sauce and seasonings, you can make a salad dressing. With blue cheese in it, it's blue cheese dressing; with vanilla and sweetening added, it's a low-calorie imitation whipped cream.

Other ways to serve the cottage cheese are to press it into a dish and then cut off slices or roll it into balls. You could add ½ t. each: grated onion, minced green onion tops, or minced chives per cup of cottage cheese. Or you could mix in ¼ c. chopped stuffed olives, and 2 T. mayonnaise per cup. We like it with cream and honey and grated nutmeg on the top, but I've seen the horrified faces of enough cottage cheese-with-salt-and-pepper eaters to know it's all a matter of preference. You can also serve it mixed with celery seed or caraway seeds. Health-food fans might like their cottage cheese mixed with sea salt, garlic, and chives.

Drain whey from curd; salt to taste

≥ **EASY CURDS AND CREAM (ONE OF INFINITE VARIETIES)** *Set your milk in a bowl until it becomes clabbered. Pour the clabbered milk slowly into a curd press (see "Making Semi-Soft, Firm, and Hard Cheese"). Let the press drain overnight. Turn the curds out into a flat dish. Grate nutmeg freely over the top, and serve with heavy sweet cream, more grated nutmeg, and sweetening.*

≥ **DORIS GRONEWOLD'S GOAT MILK COTTAGE CHEESE** *You'll need 1 gal. of freshly drawn goat's milk—should be at 100°F. Dissolve ⅛ of a cheese rennet tablet in 2 T. warm water. Stir in the milk. This will set in 30 minutes. Stir the mixture to break the whey from the curds. Squeeze. Salt, chill, and serve. I sometimes add chives to mine.*

≥ **DRY CURD COTTAGE CHEESE** *Sirniki and some other recipes below, call for "dry curd cottage cheese." That means natural cottage cheese with nothing added—no cream, no sour cream. To change store cottage cheese back to dry curd, rinse the "small-curd" type in cold water, then place in a sieve and squeeze the water out.*

≥ **SIRNIKI** *From Ann Moran, Vancouver, WA: For this Russian entree, mix 3 c. dry-curd cottage cheese, 2 eggs, 2 T. sour cream, ⅔ c. flour, and 1 pinch salt. Shape that mixture with your fingers into golf-ball–sized masses. Sprinkle or roll some more flour onto the outside of the ball. Then press it down to a ¾-inch thickness. Dust more flour onto it. Fry in a generous supply of melted butter, first on one side, then on the other. Set this on the table with a container of sour cream and another of fresh or cooked fruit chunks or sauce for people to combine as they please.*

≥ **COTTAGE CHEESE BLINTZES** *Blintzes are a Jewish pancake. Beat 1 egg with a rotary beater until white and yolk are blended. Sift together 1 c. sifted all-purpose flour and ½ t. salt. Alternately add flour and 1 c. water, a little at a time, to the egg. Beat until smooth and free from lumps. Break the surface air bubbles with a fork. Heat a 6-inch skillet over medium heat. Grease lightly. Using a ¼-c. measure, pour 3 T. of the batter into the pan all at once. Tilt the pan quickly so that the entire bottom is covered with a thin layer of the batter. Cook on one side only. Invert on a clean tea towel. The pancake will slip out easily when it is done. Place a heaping tablespoon of the filling (recipe below) on the pancake. Fold the 4 sides over the center and invert on the cloth. Continue with the remaining batter and filling, and grease the pan from time to time as needed. This much preparation may be done in advance, and the blintzes wrapped in a tea towel and stored in the refrigerator; or they may be wrapped in foil and frozen.*

At serving time, heat 4 T. oil in a large skillet or shallow baking pan. Place the blintzes in the pan, side by side without crowding. Brown over medium heat or bake at 350°F for 30 minutes (allow slightly longer if the blintzes were still frozen when placed in the pan). Turn over once during cooking, to brown both sides. This makes 11.

For the filling, mix 1 lb. dry cottage cheese, 1 slightly beaten egg, 1 T. sugar, ½ T. ground cinnamon, and ¼ T. salt until blended. This makes 2 c., enough for the above recipe. If served as a dessert, ½ t. vanilla extract and ½ c. seedless raisins may be added. Serve with sour cream, or both sour cream and jam.

SAVE-THE-SOUR-MILK VINEGAR-CLABBERED CHEESE
This is a Sloppy Carla's quick-and-easy money-saver that works for city people, too. You have a container of milk and your kid says, "Yuk, it's sour." Do you throw it out? Not unless you have pigs or chickens, who'll love it. You can salvage it by pouring it into a microwaveable or ovenproof bowl. Toss in a slug of white vinegar. Let set undisturbed until it clabbers— 30 minutes or so. Then heat in microwave or oven until the curds are nice and firm and the whey is seriously separating out. Pour off the whey and—if you don't eat the curds on the spot because they're so delicious—use them in cooking any way you would melted cheese, such as in a lasagna. But only make this from just-recently-soured milk, which is still really good food— not truly rotten milk with 3 colors of mold on it!

VINEGAR-CLABBERED SALTY CHEESE FROM FRESH MILK
Here's how to do it right. You can do this with the above milk also. Heat milk to about 185°F. Add (about) 1¼ T. vinegar per 1 qt. milk. Stir vinegar in thoroughly. Let rest until it clabbers. Drain off whey through cheesecloth. Add ½ t. salt per 1 qt. of milk you started with. Mix well. Let drain several hours more. It's ready to use.

COTTAGE CHEESE SANDWICH SPREADS
Mix cottage cheese with finely chopped beet pickles; or nuts and cherries; or chopped green beans and green peppers; or finely cut nuts and pimento bits; or cucumber and celery bits, onion and paprika; or finely chopped Swiss chard and onion and pickle; or tomato chunks and chopped olives; or lemon juice and lettuce; or cucumber slices and tomato slices!

COTTAGE CHEESE PANCAKES
Sent by Bobbi McCollum from Canyon Country, CA: Combine 4 beaten eggs, 1 c. sour cream or yogurt, 1 c. cottage cheese, 1 c. flour, a dash of salt, and 1 T. sugar or honey. Fry on medium hot griddle same as any pancake. You can thin it down and add fruit, or add vanilla to make it cakier tasting.

Homemade Cheese Spreads. American cheese, the familiar processed cheese from the store, is a blend of fresh and aged cheeses that have been melted, pasteurized, and mixed with an emulsifier. This makes the texture uniform and soft and also destroys some of the flavor. The pasteurization discourages further ripening. Commercial cheese spreads also usually have extra moisture and a "stabilizer" added.

FROM HOMEMADE CHEESE
Grate 1 lb. of basic cheese, like Cheddar. Combine with ½ c. butter, 4 T. dry mustard, and ¼ c. milk. Cut up some pimentos to mix in, or stir in caraway seeds, or shake in garlic salt or onion salt for your flavoring.

CUP CHEESE
Start with about 4 qt. of thick sour milk. Cut the milk through several times with a long sharp knife, then heat slowly to 90°F, or scald until the curd is very dry. Remove from the heat and place in a wet cheesecloth bag. Press under a heavy weight for 12–24 hours, or until the cheese is dry. Force through a cheese sieve or grate fine. Place in a wooden bowl, cover with a heavy cloth, and keep in a warm place for 3–7 days, or until soft and ripe, stirring occasionally. Then place in a frying pan and cook, stirring constantly, until all the lumps are dissolved. Add 1 t. salt and 3 T. butter, mix well, and pour into cups or bowls. It will make about 3 c. of cheese.

DUTCH CHEESE SPREAD
Pour 1 qt. of milk into a crockery bowl and let stand in a warm place to thicken.

When the milk is quite thick, pour boiling water over it, place in a cheesecloth bag, and let drain for 12 hours. Rub the cheese through a fine sieve. Work in 2 T. milk and 2 T. cream with a spoon until it is all the consistency of apple butter. Season with ½ t. salt and a very little pepper, if desired. Serve on buttered bread with apple butter.

POTTED CHEESE
This is an old recipe that a friend sent me: "Cheese that has gone dry or begun to mold can be turned into a very delicious compound by the following process: Remove all the moldy portions. If dry, grate it. If not, pound smooth. Add a wineglass of sherry and 1 t. of white sugar for each pound. When the whole is a smooth paste, press down tight in small pots or jars and lay a paper dipped in brandy on the top or turn hot melted suet over it until the surface is completely covered. One [tablespoon] butter added to each pound of cheese, while rubbing smooth, will make the compound rich. It will keep several years. This cheese is better when a year old than when freshly made. Keep in a cool dry place."

EASY LONGHORN
From a reader in Willow Springs, MO: Scald 3 gal. clabbered milk (makes 3 lb.). Stir occasionally. Drain and press dry the curd. Place in mixing bowl. Mix 8 T. butter and 1½ t. soda. Mix very well; the better mixed, the better the cheese. Let sit 2½–3 hours. Place in double boiler on stove. Add 1⅓ c. sour cream and 3 level t. salt (and food coloring, if desired). Cook until it looks like melted cheese. Turn into buttered container. Wait 24 hours, and slice.

NEUFCHATEL CHEESE
Recipe from Mrs. Carl Sandburg and Doris Gronewold: You'll need 1 gal. freshly drawn goat's milk, ½ junket or rennet tablet thoroughly dissolved in ¼ c. cold water, and ⅓ c. smoothly coagulated sour milk (you can use sour cream or kefir or yogurt starters). Also: nuts, olives, onions, chives, etc. Cool milk to 75°F. Add ⅓ c. sour milk. Stir for 1 minute. Add rennet tablet and stir again for 1 minute. Do not disturb again, and keep in a warm room for 18 hours. Dip the curd into cheesecloth and hang to drip. Drain, but not until the curd looks dry, as the mixture doesn't seem to stick together when pressed. Put curd in bowl, salt to taste, add nuts or whatever you like. (Doris loves it with olives and nuts.) Press in a cheese press (if it's a homemade press, be sure the rough edges of holes in the bottom and sides are to the outside). Line with cheesecloth and ladle in cheese. Draw cheesecloth over the top. Place a wooden follower on the cheese, and apply a 50-lb. weight. The length of time required to press the cheese depends on the temperature and weight (12–24 hours).

Making Semi-Soft, Firm, and Hard Cheeses

The 2 parts of this book about which I feel the greatest sense of accomplishment are the descriptions of home-butchering and this cheese section of the dairy chapter. The home-butchering is described as a homesteader would do it, using simple language—something I simply wrote down as we did it. The cheese-making was a different sort of hunt. Professionals wouldn't tell me. They said things like, "You couldn't make cheese without a big factory and lots of expensive equipment and very controlled conditions."

I ordered a government book called *Cheese Varieties* that is full of what appear to be cheese recipes. But every time friends and I tried them—and in total that was a lot of times and a lot of different recipes in the book—it turned out to be a moldy disaster. (A commercial publisher reprinted this book word for word, calling it *Cheeses of the World,* and it is still just as useless from the cooking point of view.)

Finally I got a recipe from Mary Simeone, who at the time was 9 months pregnant and living in a tent two-thirds up the side of an Idaho mountain, while her husband built a log cabin. She was milking 2 goats, and her finished cheese tasted very much like the good strong Greek and Italian cheeses that you can usually find only in city gourmet shops. Her recipe is the one I called "Basic Farm Cheese." I like it because it spares you all the useless detail of the rennet company recipe. She aged her cheese by hanging it on the end of a string under the biggest bull pine she could find. That should encourage any of you who think you can't make cheese without a factory. The fact is, from a historic view, factories are very recent arrivals on the cheese scene. Mary and her husband are from an Italian section of New York City, and they are making it fine now in Elk River, which is really out of the way, even for Idaho.

But my biggest breakthrough was in meeting John E. Montoure, Associate Professor of Bacteriology-Biochemistry at the University of Idaho, at a meeting of the Idaho Purebred Dairy Cattle Association, where my husband and I sort of stuck out like sore teats. A speaker got up and told us how we should be counting our blessings because we belonged to the upper classes and were in the lap of luxury. He must have meant all those guys with 150 head of milking Holsteins home in the dairy barn. I thought of our 3 head of registered Shorthorns that we traded hay for to a desperate man and got hysterical giggling, and practically fell out of my chair.

Anyway, that's where I met John Montoure, who was head of probably the biggest and best university-type cheese-making laboratory in the country before somebody in the Idaho state capital decided to cut the funding and eliminate the program.

When I talked to Dr. Montoure and asked about making cheese homestead style, he didn't say, "Oh no, you have to have a factory." That man just sat down and started calculating. He knew every recipe I asked for by heart. On each recipe he'd have to start out figuring from 1,000 lb. of milk, because that was what he was used to working with. Then he'd convert every ingredient down to household quantity for me in proportion. I spent 2 long afternoons with him, writing as fast as I could. And he hadn't the slightest hesitation about sharing his information with me though I told him it was for publication, and he wasn't getting paid anything for it.

RENNET: Rennet is used to make these cheeses; you don't rely on the natural souring that you use for cottage cheese because the use of rennet allows you to get out more water and that gives you a different kind and a nicer cheese. Even 3 percent less water makes a big difference in the final product. You can order rennet from the addresses I gave above. Your basic store rennet rule is to dissolve ¼ rennet tablet for each 2 gal. milk in ½ c. cool water. Add to milk that is 86–90°F. Stir well. Cover and let it rest an hour, or until the curd is well-formed. If you have trouble clabbering your milk, use more dissolved rennet. Better too much than too little.

Homemade Animal Rennet. If you cared to, or had to, you could make your own rennet, since it is the salt extract of a suckling calf (that means one that has eaten no grass or solid food). You just take the biggest stomach of a suckling calf (or pig or lamb) that never has eaten anything but mother's milk. The suckling calf has all 4 stomachs, but its rumen is underdeveloped and that fourth stomach, its abomasum, is relatively big; rennet comes from the abomasum. Add salt to it, cut it into strips, and dry it as if you were making jerky. To make cheese with it, cut off a 1-inch square and add it to milk. That would be the equivalent of 2 drops of liquid rennet.

Vegetable Rennet. Yes, you can make this from various plants. It never acts as fast as regular rennet. At best it will curdle milk overnight. You can make veggie rennet from yellow (lady's) bedstraw, nettle, lemon or common sorrel, fumitory, unripe fig sap, or the giant purple thistle. Nettle and thistle are the best. All species of Compositae thistles have the milk-curdling magic. It's best in giant, thorny kinds. Regular purple thistle will work. Globe artichoke is a Compositae thistle variety, and can be used also. Cardoon is another option.

To harvest thistle for rennet, gather the thistle flowers when they have turned brown. If you see thistledown, the plant is over-mature. Get it right after the end of bloom and before the stage where down blows away. Air dry the flowers. You can store them in jars to wait until needed for cheese-making.

To use your veggie rennet, a quick way is just to tie a bundle of thistle flowers together with string and leave it in the milk until it clabbers. But the more professional way is to pound and extract. You take out enough—5 heaping t. of pounded dry herb will be needed per 1 gal. milk to be curdled. Pound in a mortar with your pestle until quite crushed. Then pour just a little warm water or whey over, just enough to cover. Let soak 5 minutes. Pound 5 minutes more. Repeat the soaking, and repeat pounding until you've pounded at least 4 times total. You should be seeing a dark (brown) fluid. Strain. Add the fluid to your milk. Be careful not to add too much of any veggie rennet herb because ex-

Because the finished product may be ready months after the critical first steps, this will help you remember how you got what you have.

Type of Cheese: _____

Quantity of Milk: _____

Starter Added? ☐ Yes ☐ No
    Type: _____ Quantity: _____

Temperature of the Milk: _____

Length of Time Milk and Starter Set: _____

Amount of Rennet Added: _____

Time to Cutting of the Curd _____

Temperature of Milk from Adding of Starter
    Until Cutting: _____

Size of the Cut Curd: _____

Length of Time Curd Is Drained: _____

Is Curd Recut or Ground? _____

Amount of Salt Used: _____

Is Curd Hooped to Drain? _____

Time: _____

Is Curd Pressed? _____

Pressure ☐ Light ☐ Medium ☐ Heavy

Is Cheese Bandaged at Pressing? _____

Length of Time Cheese Is Pressed: _____

Is Cheese Salted in Brine? ☐ Yes ☐ No Time _____

Is Cheese Paraffined? ☐ Yes ☐ No

Temperature Cheese Is Aged At: _____

Length of Time: _____

How Often Turned: _____
    Cleaned: _____

---

cess can, at best, be unpleasant-tasting for the cheese-eater at the end of the line, and at worst, actually cause indigestion.

CULTURE: You're familiar with that word from making yogurt, cultured buttermilk, and cultured cream cheese. Culture is a bacterial organism that you can order in a dried form from the addresses given above. Before 1940 they thought you couldn't make cheese with pasteurized milk. They soured milk the natural way, like for cottage cheese. The result was that some cheese-makers made good cheese, but some didn't. That's because their luck depended on what kind of bacteria happened to be plentiful in their cheesery. Some organisms will make a bitter cheese. Bad ones break down protein; good ones make an acid. The enzymes will break down some protein, but in a desirable way—so you get the flavor you want.

After 1940, cheese makers learned to pasteurize the milk to destroy the bad bacteria, then to add good bacteria—exactly the ones they wanted—to their "culture." When you use culture you have a choice to add or not to add rennet. That's because, given time, the good organisms will clabber the milk anyway. Factory cheese operations order frozen cultures, which are shipped by express in an ice chest with dry ice around them. You can also order freeze-dried cultures, and that's the kind you would prefer. Consult with your cheese-makers supplier about what cultures you need if you want to make any specialty cheese.

Maintaining Your Cheese Culture. After ordering the dry culture grains, you can keep your cheese culture going, same as you would yogurt. In fact, make yogurt with it and then you have both! Add some to 1 qt. of milk. Let set at 70°F. Every 2 or 3 days, take out 1 t. and add it to another quart of milk to keep it going. Use a clean container and pasteurized milk.

But most homesteaders avoid all this struggle and use cultured buttermilk from the store dairy case to get their starter. They add ¼ c. buttermilk starter to 1 qt. milk. Let

work 24 hours at room temperature. Add your quart of home-cultured buttermilk to 3–5 gal. milk, warmed to 86–90°F and let ripen 1 or 2 hours. Now you're ready to add rennet. If you skip this step, your cheese may swell and not ripen properly. These are the "good" microorganisms that you want to ripen your cheese. If you don't fill your milk with them, you will have less desirable ones.

COLORING: Adding this is optional. But do not use butter; it colors only the fat.

MOISTURE CONTENT: Most cheeses are made of the same thing—milk, usually skim milk. The different results are achieved by slight differences in dryness, acid content, or temperature. The temperature at which you cook it and the length of time you cook it controls the moisture content. More moisture gives you a softer body, a sharper taste, and a faster cure, but there is a tendency to develop off-flavors.

CHEESE-MAKING PROCEDURES

Temperature. This is really important! If you can't control the cooking temperature, you're going to end up with a different cheese each time. This doesn't mean it will be bad cheese though. In making these hard cheeses if you go much above 100–102°F, you will kill off the good organisms, which you don't want to do—ever. This is where hard cheese is different from cottage cheese. Hard cheese is made as much by the curing process as by what you do at the beginning, and it's the organisms working gradually in there that give you the cure.

Pressing. The traditional press for homemade cheese used to be a coffee can with nail holes punched through the bottom and sides. *Now we know not to use coffee cans because some have lead solder. The acid in the whey may leach out the lead into the cheese.* If you get your press from a cheese-maker's supplier, it will be lead-free. It's important to get the curds into the press (wrapped in a cloth) while they are hot. Then put your round wooden follower on top, and weights on that. The combination of heat and pressure drives off the whey and causes the curds to change from individual pieces to a solid mass that won't spoil inside.

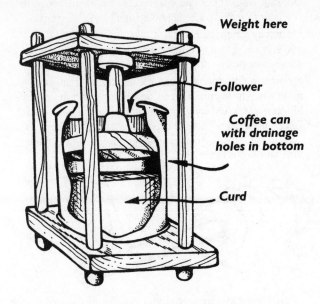

Weight here

Follower

Coffee can with drainage holes in bottom

Curd

🐝 *WHEY LEMONADE Wherever you have cheese-making you have surplus whey. Lane Morgan tells me she makes a whey lemonade by adding juice of 2 lemons to 1 qt. of strained whey. Sweeten to taste with honey or sugar.*

Salting the Curd. It's a good idea to add the salt in 3 portions. Add the first third, stir, add the second, stir again, and so on.
NOTE: Salt in your cheese adds flavor, but also helps release the whey and discourages growth of microscopic stuff that might spoil your cheese. If you want to make salt-free or low-salt cheese, you can do it, but your cheese won't keep as long.

Wrapping the Cheese. Professionals use a foil coated with wax into which the cheese ball is sealed. You could use foil inside of butcher paper. A cloth soaked in vinegar is easiest though. You have to freshen the vinegar at intervals. Paraffin dip is a good mold preventer. Just melt your paraffin, dip the cheese all around into it, and cool.

Storage of Curing Cheese. Curing temperature matters —45°F is best. At 45°F, a Cheddar cheese will have the right kind of flavor in 6–9 months. Curing at 48–52°F can give you an entirely different cheese. Turn your cheese over every day or so for the first month. Grease the bandage and rub it when you do that.

Storage temperature is the place where making cheese at home is rough compared to having the "factory conditions," which means having controlled temperatures and humidity. So just don't worry about getting your cheese precisely like the store version. It will still be good food and good cheese. Second, do your major cheese-making in the fall after the worst of the heat is over. Third, figure out the coolest place you have—the most nearly suitable. (Same problem as with storing apples.) For good-quality cheese, 60°F is too high. Your root cellar might be a good place, although you risk the cheese picking up an off-flavor from the vegetables there. The vital thing about a root cellar is that it remain dark as much as possible and maintain a constant and correct temperature and humidity. That means no windows and a door opened as little as possible. So if you wait until late enough in the summer so your root cellar

won't be above 60°F, you could use it. Before then you could use your refrigerator. You must be very careful to keep all flies out of your curing place or you may get maggots in the cheese.

The size of your cheese also matters. Smaller cheeses have a greater tendency to dry out. Starting with at least 5 gal. of milk will help you here. But the milk shouldn't be more than 2 days old if you can help it. It's okay to skim it. *NOTE: Resist the temptation to cut into and taste aging cheese until it's done. Under-aged cheese is drab in flavor compared to properly aged cheese, and your cheeseball needs an intact rind.*

Storage of Finished Cheese. Cheeses with high fat content are the poorest storers. Shelf-cured cheeses will keep a while more on the shelf. Or you can keep any cheese for a while in the refrigerator, much longer in the freezer.

Drying Grating Cheeses. Low-fat "firm" or "hard" cheeses are best for drying. Grate or shred the cheese. In a dehydrator or oven, spread the cheese bits over your drying tray. It helps to lay the cheese on something absorbent like cloth or paper towel to absorb melted fat. Dry at 120°F, stirring once in a while for 6–8 hours or until hard. If you are sun-drying, dry in full sun in an airy place. This will take a day or longer. Use dried cheese like Parmesan to sprinkle over casseroles or spaghetti sauces. You can store as is dried, or pour into plastic bags and freeze.

Hard Cheese Recipes

BASIC FARM CHEESE: This process works fine with cow's or goat's milk.
1. Fill with whole milk a 9-quart enamel or stainless steel bucket (never aluminum!) to within about an inch of the top.
2. Warm it to 86°F. Use a dairy thermometer.
3. Add ¼ rennet tablet (or a whole junket tablet), crushed, with 1 t. of water. Stir it in. (Your drugstore can order rennet for you.)
4. Let set quietly until it curds, about 20 minutes.
5. Cut into approximately ½-inch squares by cutting one way and then cutting the other (to make a pattern of squares on the top) and then by reaching in to cut across from top to bottom of the bucket.
6. "Bathe" the curds for 2 minutes with your hands. That means to move the curds around in the whey gently and slowly.
7. Set your enamel bucket in a dishpan of water back on the stove. Keep it covered with a cloth so specks and flies won't fall in or crawl in.
8. Slowly warm to 102°F (dairy thermometer again), stirring occasionally to keep contents at an even temperature. It will tend to get hotter at the bottom of the pan.
9. Take it off the stove and let it set an hour, stirring occasionally very gently.
10. Put cheesecloth over a colander. Fasten the edges with clothespins. Pour the cheese in there. Save the whey. You can feed it to the animals or make bread with it. All the vitamins are in the whey now.
11. Add 1 T. salt and mix with hands. Add another 1 T. salt and mix again.
12. Tie ends of cheesecloth together to make a bag. Hang it up where you can let it drip for the rest of the day.
13. Put a holding band around the edge of the cheese bag made of cheesecloth like a headband or belt. Put a

paper plate with the fluted edge trimmed off over the cheese and one under it, and a heavy weight over it and a hard flat smooth thing underneath, and let it press like that all night. Something flat and iron is good to press it, or use a piece of wood with bricks on top.

14. After it has been pressed all night, let it dry in an airy, cool place, turning it every few days until it forms a hard rind. If it molds, cut the mold away.

15. Paraffin it. To do that you heat a block of store paraffin in a pan almost to boiling (210°F), then brush the hot wax over your cheese or dip parts of the cheese in until you have it all covered. Attach a string in there and you can hang it up in a cool place to age. At first your cheese will be tasteless and have the consistency of a rubber eraser. The flavor comes with aging. Give it 2 months at least. Be careful you have it thoroughly paraffined, or it may get wormy.

COLBY CHEESE: Pasteurize 12 gal. of milk. Cool to 88–90°F. Add 2 c. of your culture (from "Maintaining Your Cheese Culture"). Let it set for 30 minutes. Now add 2 drops of liquid rennet that has been diluted in 1 c. of water. If you use tablets follow the manufacturer's directions. They'll say how much for 12 gal. Mix the rennet into the milk thoroughly for 3 minutes and then stop. It will take about 30 minutes to set up.

Put your finger into the milk at a 45-degree angle. If the curd breaks cleanly, in a nice straight line, it is ready. Your finger won't have goop on it, and the curd can be picked straight up. Now cut the curd. The more uniform the pieces you cut it into the better, because small ones will cook too fast and big ones will be undercooked, meaning they will still be fragile and will shatter. Cut as for cottage cheese.

Let it rest 15 minutes. This is to "heal" the curd so it doesn't break up when you start to stir it. Now heat it very slowly. The professionals go up 1 degree the first 5 minutes, 2 degrees with the second 5 minutes and so on (100–102°F is the very highest you should go). If you heat higher, your organisms will start to die, and the cheese won't develop as you want. Use a cheese thermometer (same as a dairy thermometer). It will take about half an hour to get the temperature up if you are doing it just right. Set up some kind of a double boiler—like a 5-gal. pail inside a canning kettle with enough water to come halfway up the sides. That will keep the temperature right.

After you have gotten the temperature up to 100°F in this gradual way, drain off the whey, and stir the curd so it doesn't form a single mass. Add salt to taste—maybe 3–4 T. for 10 lb. of curd. If you are on a low-salt diet you can substitute a potassium salt. If you didn't salt at all you would get a bland cheese and a different type of fermentation because the salt holds back some organisms. Thoroughly mix. Put it in a sterilized cheesecloth and press. Start with 5 lb. of pressure for the first half hour to give it a chance to knit together. Gradually increase the pressure to 20–25 lb. It will be of a spongy texture now, not solid like a Cheddar. The cheesecloth closes up the surface of the cheese and gives you a nice product. (Resist the temptation to nibble.) The cloth also acts as a wick and draws moisture out of the inside giving it a path to travel out of the press. So, use a cloth whatever else your pressing arrangements. Press overnight—12–16 hours. Wrap the cheese as above.

Now cure the Colby below 45°F. Curing above that temperature speeds up the process, but you risk a poor taste. If you cured it in your refrigerator it would take 9–12 months, assuming the temperature in there is 38–42°F. For the first month it would taste like "green curd." At about 3 months you start to pick up a reasonable amount of Colby taste.

Monterey Cheese. Same as Colby, only you "cook" at 100°F, holding it at that temperature for 1 hour and 45 minutes before proceeding.

Montoure Cheddar Cheese. "Cheddaring" removes even more whey from curd after its first heating and draining. Monterey Jack and longhorn are cheddared cheeses also. Cheddaring helps cheese because it makes them have an even lower moisture content. Dryer cheese can age a longer time and keeps better.

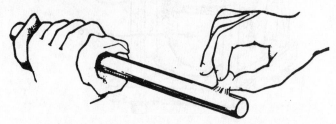

To make Montoure-system Cheddar cheese, proceed as directed for the Colby-type cheese until the end of the curd-heating process. The curd should be contracted to about one-half the starting size, firm, and without a tendency to stick when pressed together. Use an ordinary flat-iron to make a hot iron test. The curds, when rubbed on the clean hot iron and then drawn away, should show fine threads about ⅛ inch long. When the curd passes this test, dip or pour off the whey, keeping the curd stirred with your hands as you do so.

When the whey is off, put the curd in a deep, more or less rectangular pan that has a hole punched in the bottom to let whey escape. The top or bottom of an old fashioned roasting pan will work fine for a moderate amount of curd. Don't let the curd cool off while you are draining and transferring it. Pile it evenly in the roasting pan and cut a channel through the cheese to help the whey drain toward a hole at one end of the pan. Keep the pan slightly tilted.

Put the pan in your oven. You'll want just enough heat in the oven to keep the cheese at a temperature of 98–100°F. Put a pan underneath to catch the whey. This is the Cheddaring process and will probably require some experimentation for you. Avoid too much heat. After about 20 minutes the curd will be firmly matted. Then cut the curd into blocks 6 inches long. Then turn them over so that what was the top of the curd is now underneath and next to the bottom of the pan. Continue the heating. All during your heating, try not to let the temperature of the curd get below 90°F. You'll need a thermometer inserted in the curd to keep you informed. Turn the curd pieces about every 15 minutes. At the end of the third turning, pile the curd blocks 2 deep. In 15 minutes pile them again—but 3 deep if they seem dry enough. The Cheddaring process is done when the hot iron test shows you strings from ½ to 1½ inches long. (There is an easier acidity test, but you would have to use special equipment.)

Next cut the curd with a butcher knife into small pieces about ½ inch wide and 1½ inches long. Then stir thoroughly for about 15 minutes before salting. Add 2 or 3 oz. of salt for every 5 gal. of milk that you started with. The best salt is cheese salt, obtainable from a dairy supply or maybe from your drugstore. Its coarse, flaky consistency makes it more readily absorbed by the cheese. Spread out the curd, sprinkle the salt on, let it cool to 86–90°F, sprinkle on another bit of salt, stir thoroughly, and wait for the salt to dissolve. The curd isn't ready for the press until it is dissolved. Maintain your temperature throughout, and when you're ready to press, put the curd in the press at a temperature of about 85°F. Now turn back to the directions for Colby cheese and press and finish the cheese according to that. This Cheddaring process will take about 2½ hours in all. When you're done, the curd is all in little strings that look almost like a cooked chicken breast.

W.S.U. Extension Cheddar Cheese: Use fresh, clean, high-quality, whole milk; 10–12½ qt. (20–25 lb.) whole milk will make 2–3 lb. cheese.

Equipment. You'll need:

A container that will hold 10–12 qt. of milk, such as a pail, kettle, or canner (rust-free)

A dairy thermometer

A long-handled spoon

A knife or spatula with a long blade (to reach the bottom of the container)

Measuring cup and measuring spoons

Dishpan or container for draining curd

Cheesecloth for draining curd (large enough to fit over pan for draining)

A cheese hoop: a straight-sided, 1-gal. container (punch about a dozen holes in the bottom with a nail)

Cap cloths, the same diameter as the hoop, made of flour sack or muslin

A follower: a round piece of wood, 2–3 inches thick, slightly smaller in diameter than the hoop, so it will fit down into the hoop (be sure it is made of seasoned lumber that is not gummy!)

Weights: bricks or something similar that weigh 30–40 lb.

Bandage: cheesecloth or gauze for wrapping cheese

Paraffin to cover the cheese

Ingredients. You'll need 10–12 qt. pasteurized or raw milk; ½ c. cultured buttermilk for a starter; ½ t. liquid rennet (or tablets); ⅛–¼ t. cheese color; and 1¾–2 T. salt.

Pasteurize. Heat milk to 145°F, and hold it there for 30 minutes. If the temperature drops, reheat slightly. Stir constantly to avoid scorching. Cool the milk rapidly to 86°F by setting the pan in a container of cold running water or in water chilled with ice. (If you use already pasteurized milk—just heat milk to 86°F.)

Add Starter. Add about ½ c. cultured buttermilk for 10–12½ qt. milk. Get buttermilk as freshly cultured as possible. Allow milk to ripen at 86°F for 30–60 minutes. Maintain temperature at 86°F. Apply slight heat if necessary.

Add Color. Optional. Cheese made in the winter without color added will be white. Dilute ⅛–¼ t. liquid cheese color in ¼ c. cool water. Stir thoroughly.

Add Rennet. Maintain milk at 86°F and add rennet: about ¼–½ t. liquid rennet diluted in ½ c. cool water. If using rennet tablets, follow directions. Stir in rennet to mix thoroughly. Cover and maintain at 86°F. Let milk remain undisturbed for about 30 minutes to coagulate. (If disturbed, curd may break and become grainy, and the whey will separate before the curd is ready to be cut.)

Cut Curd. Test the curd to see if it is ready to cut. Insert your forefinger at an angle in the surface of the coagulated milk. If the curd splits cleanly, and clear whey fills the opening, the curd is ready to cut. With a clean, long-bladed knife or spatula, cut the curd into ⅜-inch pieces. Cut straight down across curd from one side of the container to the other, being sure to cut to the bottom of the container. Cut several times in each direction, making right-angle cuts. Then turn the knife blade at about a 45° angle and slash at that angle several times in each direction to cut the strips into shorter pieces. After cutting, stir occasionally, being careful not to break the pieces of curd.

About 15 minutes after you finish cutting the curd, heat slowly to 100–102°F (takes about 30–40 minutes). Hold at this temperature until the curd reaches the desired firmness.

Test for Firmness. Squeeze a handful of curd, and release suddenly. If it breaks apart easily and shows little tendency to stick together, it is at the desired firmness. If it is soft and pasty, hold longer. If too firm, the cheese will be dry and corky.

Remove Whey. Allow the curd to settle to the bottom of the container and dip off most of the whey. Pour the curd and remaining whey over cheesecloth that has been stretched over a large container. Allow the whey to drain off. Stir occasionally to keep lumps from forming.

Salt. When the curd has cooled to 90°F and is slightly rubbery in texture (squeaks slightly when you chew it), sprinkle on 1¾–2 T. salt.

Hoop. Place 1 cap cloth in the bottom of the hoop. As soon as the salt has dissolved and the curd reaches about 85°F, place the curd in the hoop. Be sure the curd is not below 85°F. If cooling rapidly, begin with curd at 88°F. Place the other cap cloth on top of the curd.

Press. Place the wooden follower on top of the cap cloth and add 12–15 lb. of weight for 5–10 minutes. Increase the weight to 25–30 lb. and press for 30–60 minutes.

Dress. Remove the weights and follower, and turn the hoop upside down so the cheese will drop out on the table. Remove the cap cloths and dip the cheese in warm water (about 100°F) to remove any fat from the surface. Cut a bandage 2 inches wider than the cheese and long enough to wrap around the cheese with a 1-inch overlap. Wrap the cheese tightly in the bandage. Replace the cap cloths and put the cheese back in the hoop. Replace the follower and press the cheese with 30–40 lb. weight for 16–20 hours.

Dry. Remove the cheese from the hoop and wipe away any surface moisture. Be sure there are no cracks in the surface. If there are, remove the bandage and dip the cheese in warm water again to soften the surface, rebandage, and put back under weights for about 1 hour. When the surface is smooth, put the bandaged cheese on a shelf in a dry, cool room. The temperature during drying should be 50–60°F. Turn the cheese and wipe it daily. As soon as the surface feels dry and the rind begins to form—in 3–6 days—paraffin the cheese. (If a rind has not started to form by 6 days, the cheese should be put in a drier place.)

Paraffin. Heat paraffin to 210–212°F in a pan deep enough to immerse half the cheese at a time. Be sure the surface of the cheese is dry. Do not remove the bandage. Hold the cheese in the hot paraffin for about 10 seconds. Let dry, then immerse the other half.

Cure. After paraffining, the cheese is placed again in the dry room at 50–60°F. Turn the cheese often to keep it clean and free from mold. Wash the shelf under the cheese, and dry it to keep mold from forming. Cheese cured for 6 weeks will have a mild flavor. If you want a sharp flavor, cure for 3–5 months longer. The cheese will cure more slowly if the temperature is below 50°F.

GRATING CHEESE: This is a firmer cheese that you grate and use the way you do Parmesan. Make it from skim milk. Clabber, cut, and cook in the whey same as Colby. Only don't cook just a half hour; cook for 2 or 3 hours. After it is nicely cured, go ahead and grate it. You can add additional seasoning to suit yourself.

PROFESSOR MONTOURE'S DEEP FAT FRIED CHEESE: Fry chunks of pressed curd. The pieces are cut ½–1 inch long, similar to French fries. They keep their shape and have a nice flavor. Do this with "green curd"—freshly made cheese. You can't do it with aged cheese.

ROQUEFORT CHEESE: You can't make genuine Roquefort unless you have sheep's milk. You can blend sheep's and cow's milk and still get the right flavor. Even 1 part sheep's milk to 9 parts cow's is okay.

BLUE (OR BLEU) CHEESE: Blue cheese is very similar to Roquefort, except you can use cow's or goat's milk to make it. Blue mold is the most common one. You may have some around the house right now. It's a penicillin-type mold. It is also used to develop Tilsit, Roquefort, and Gorgonzola cheeses. This is another case in which you can't be afraid of mold. Unless it's unbelievably foul, you don't discourage the mold. One problem with making this, though, is the mold tends to spread and you may find it on other things besides your blue cheese, especially if you have a humid environment. A cloth soaked in vinegar discourages it. Use a fairly heavy cloth, like good cotton flannel. But the vinegar will evaporate, so you must keep it freshened. This is to protect your other cheeses. Paraffin would protect them completely; mold must have air to grow. If another kind of cheese does get moldy, scrub the mold off with vinegar. Wait until it dries. Then dip into paraffin and it should keep. Some mold on the outside doesn't hurt the inside a bit, even if it is in a thick layer.

Start to make your blue cheese with 5 gal. milk. That will give you 3½–4 lb. of cheese. Use raw milk—don't pasteurize it. Shake part of the milk to get air bubbles in it. You can put a quart in a blender for 5 seconds and then add it to the other milk. Or shake some in a half-gallon fruit jar or use an electric mixer. Just a portion of it thus shaken will do. Now add your culture. The same as with Colby. Use 1 c. of culture. Now have your milk lukewarm and add rennet —1 drop of the liquid or an appropriate amount of the tablet kind, or ½ square inch of the calf's stomach. When it has set up, cut the curd. Mix well but don't agitate more than 3 minutes. Cut 1-inch-square chunks. These are larger than for Colby. You want a softer curd in this case. Let set 15 minutes. Now turn the curd slowly. You don't want to break up the curds. You don't want dry blue cheese.

Now bring the temperature up gradually and cook for 2 hours at 100°F in your double boiler. Drain. Add your blue mold. You could buy a pound of the freeze-dried mold from a dairy supplier. It will keep practically forever. All you need to make your batch of blue cheese is just a pinch stirred in.

Now mix in ½ t. salt and get ready to drain the cheese. In this case you don't wrap in cloth. And you don't put

pressure. Make a cheese hoop by taking a straight-sided can that is about 6 inches in diameter and 6 inches or so deep, like a 6-inch stovepipe, and poke nail holes in the sides from the inside out so you won't have rough edges inside. Make the holes about every 1 or 2 inches on the sides. Make a follower for each end. Any piece of board that was the right size and shape to barely fit into the can or pipe would be fine. Now put the first follower on the table. The pipe goes on top of that. The cheese goes into the pipe. And put the last follower on top of the cheese and turn the whole thing upside down. Keep doing this every half hour for 2 hours. The cheese will be cooling off. Water will be running out. The central mass will be holding its shape well enough.

Take the cheese off the follower and set it instead on heavy burlap, a towel, or 3 or 4 thicknesses of sheeting. But not on paper—that would cause the cheese to get soggy on the bottom. And let it set like that for 12–16 hours. Now rub 1½ T. salt on the surface (iodized table salt is fine). It won't all go on at first. Do it once a day for 5–7 days. You're salting the curd from the outside. The moisture will come out, grab the salt, and go back in. After the week of salting comes the poking.

Take a ⅛-inch knitting needle and poke holes in the side of the cheese, 1 inch apart all over the surface and deep enough so you come clear out the other side. Then tip over the cheese and do the same from the other side. This is to allow air inside so mold can grow inside (because mold must have air). Then let the cheese set at 45°F in a humid place. You don't wrap it, of course. If you set it in the refrigerator everything else would probably mold. Incidentally, this blue mold won't make you healthy eating it—it's different from the one the doctor prescribes. It takes 4–6 weeks to be properly cured. You want mold on the surface as well as in the center. The mold colors will vary from blue to gray. If you get black, wash that off with vinegar and then let it go again. Or use a mild salt solution and a soft brush. At a higher temperature it would be ready even sooner. After it has arrived at the flavor and ripeness you like, you can wax it or put it in a cold place to store. But if you freeze it, it will turn crumbly.

Growing Bleu Mold Starter. Or you could grow your own by getting some blue cheese or Roquefort from the grocery store. Then you set some of the cheese on a damp slice of bread. Any kind of bread will do. And put it in a jar with holes punched in the top lid or with a cloth over the top. In 1 or 2 days, or maybe even as long as a week, your bread with the cheese on top will also be good and moldy. Then you remove one-fourth of your slice of bread, dry it, crumble it, and you have enough blue cheese mold to make a batch of this cheese. Save the other three-quarters and each of them could make a batch, too. Remember, when you dry the bread, don't do it in an oven. Just leave it out at room temperature because you don't want the mold spores to die. You can keep your culture going by taking one-quarter of the molded bread and putting it on a fresh damp slice of bread again. In the good old days, even commercial dairies used this method for growing mold spores.

ITALIAN CHEESE: This is a cheese made especially for grating. Heat 10 qt. fresh milk to 85°F. Add ½ rennet tablet dissolved in cold water. Wait 40 minutes to let the curd get firm, then break up the curd with your hands, and heat it in the whey until it is as hot as your hand can stand. Gather the curd with your hands, and mat it together until it is firm. Remove the curd from the whey and put it in the cheese press. Press one side, then reverse it in the press and squeeze some more. Put the curd in its sack back into the whey and heat (don't let it boil). Remove from the heat and let the cheese stay in the whey until all is cold. Remove and let drain for 24 hours. You could now eat the cheese, but for the proper grating cheese rub it with salt and let dry in your curing room for 3 days or so. When it is dry, put it in a jar of salt brine for another 3 days. Make the brine so strong that there is salt undissolved in the bottom. Then put the cheese in your curing room to dry again for 3 days and rub the cheese lightly with salt every other day until dry. Put the cheese in a crock. Cover the crock with a cloth. Rub it lightly with salt once a week for a month. Then just leave it in the crock for 3–6 months. Now your cheese is completely cured and ready for grating.

TWENTY-MINUTE CHEESE: (This and the next recipe are from "Home Cheesemaking with Goat Milk," a pamphlet available from *Dairy Goat Journal.*) To 3 qt. fresh goat's milk at blood heat (98.6°F), add ½ t. liquid rennet. Stir gently. As it thickens, which is almost immediately, add 1 qt. boiling water and continue to stir gently, separating the curd from the whey and firming the curd so it can be handled at once. Place a reed cheese basket in a colander and dip the curd into it, pressing down. When all the curd is in the basket turn the basket over, dump the curd out, and put it back in with the bottom side up. Thus the reeds will mark the cheese on all sides. If an unsalted, uncured cheese is wanted, it may be eaten now.

To cure the cheese, leave it in the basket for 36 hours, or until it is firm enough to keep its shape. During this time keep it in the kitchen or any other warm, dry place, and slip it out of the basket twice a day and turn it over. When firm enough, remove from the basket and keep on a plate in the kitchen or pantry. Sprinkle dry salt on the side that is up. Continue to turn as before, each time salting the upper surface and the rim and using a dry plate. When no more moisture sweats out, it can be placed in a stone crock in the cellar. If it molds, wipe with a cloth dampened with salty water. While the cheese may now be eaten or kept for a year, it is perhaps at its best when it's about 6 months old. The color is white, but a yellow cheese may be made by adding a few drops of cheese coloring when the rennet is added to the milk.

CHEESE À L'OBISPO: Get a bottle of rennet tablets for cheese (not junket). Use about 8 lb. milk; put in rather more rennet than suggested in the instructions that come with the rennet. Let it set an hour. Cut curd, and heat to 98°F, no higher. Stir gently every few minutes. Cover and set away for an hour longer. Drain on a sieve lined with muslin and pack into a mold, salting away for 24 hours. A circular piece of stout tin should fit inside the can for a follower. Now for weight, use a quart jar filled with sand. Line the mold with thin muslin. Take out of the mold and set it on a screen tray in an airy place, with a soft folded cloth under the cheese, and a bit of muslin over it to keep off the dust. Press, turning daily for 10 or 12 days, changing the cloth underneath each time. It is now sufficiently cured to eat. Melt paraffin in a tin lid and turn the cheese carefully in it until it is well coated.

Your cheese can be eaten now, or cured for as long as 6 months. In damp weather the cheese will mold on the outside before fully cured. If it molds, clean off with a cloth dampened in vinegar and wipe dry.

ABOUT SWISS CHEESE: This is a very delicate cheese for which everything has to be just right. To get good eye formation (the holes) you need a very large cheese. They cut it up in little pieces to sell it, but if you make a ball of less than 40 lb. (that would require 60 gal. of milk), the eyes won't form right. You also need very little temperature change—the other thing that is difficult to manage at home. Sometimes, even in the factory Swiss cheese goes a little wrong and the gas inside explodes—cheese blows all over the room! Other times it makes no eyes at all.

Swiss cheese makers use a special culture, not the general Cheddar culture but a half and half mixture of *Streptococcus thermophilis* and *Lactobacillus bulgaricus*. They may also add another bacteria, an "eye former" (*Propiono bacterium shermanii*) during the cooking operation. The "eye former" has to be kept refrigerated. The genuine outer rind is really tough on a Swiss cheese in the making.

CREAM

This is where goat's milk and cow's milk are so different. Technically, cream is just the globules of fat that have been held in suspension throughout the liquid.

COW'S CREAM: In cow's milk the globules soon rise to the top due to their comparative lightness (oil floats on water). The longer the milk sets quietly, the more cream there will be—for the first 48 hours. But it isn't worth waiting all that long. You get most after 12 hours, and most of the rest after waiting 24. The heaviest cream, which is called "whipping" or "spoon" cream, is nearest the top in a thick layer. I prefer cow's milk because I enjoy homemade butter and whipped cream. I like having a little pitcher of cream to pour over strawberries, or a big one to make ice cream.

GOAT'S CREAM: You find goat's cream on the top in the same way, only it takes longer to rise and there is never as much. There is butterfat in goat's milk—in fact, it averages 3.5–4 percent! But goat cream doesn't come nicely to the top for skimming like cow's cream does. You can get some goat cream if you let it set long enough, but by then it's almost sour. So to get goat's cream you have to use a mechanical separator. Or you can get goat's butter by churning the whole milk.

Separating the Cream

SKIMMING: I keep my milk in gallon jars or 5-gal. buckets (when I have that much) in the refrigerator. I skim the cream off at the end of 24 hours unless I need it sooner. The best thing is a regular skimmer. Mine are antiques. I don't know if you can still buy them or not. A skimmer is a long-handled utensil with a cup fastened on the end. You set the cup into the cream so that the rim is just barely below the liquid's surface. That way the part of the liquid that flows over into the cup of the skimmer is the top cream and not the milk underneath.

When you get used to it, you can do a very precise job of separating the cream from the milk and getting the cream out. Your jar, of course, has to have a wide enough mouth so the skimmer can easily fit in and out. Old-fashioned recipe books often say to let the cream rise in a shallow, wide container. I can't understand why. I find the cream is much easier to skim off from a tall, deep container. When you skim cream, you never get it all because the lighter portion stays mixed in with the milk—though if it sets longer, a greater percentage rises and can be skimmed. So a 48-hour sit yields more cream than a 24-hour sit. But the first cream is denser and better for whipping and butter-making.

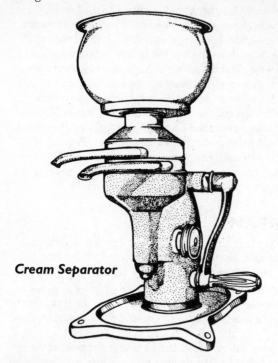

Cream Separator

SEPARATORS: These separate cow's milk from its cream content very thoroughly. The separator is set to deliver cream at a certain percentage of butterfat—for example, 30 percent. Some people like them. Mostly they're the people who milk a lot of animals and sell their milk and cream. Or else it's people who have numerous goats, because their separator makes it possible for them to enjoy goat cream and butter. You have to take them apart, wash all the parts, and dry them after each use. It's a lot of work. My separator has 18 disks, 17 other parts, the wrench—plus jars and milk pails to wash morning and night. Because of all that cleaning, it's much easier for me to get cow's cream by just letting the milk set in a gallon jar for 24 hours and then skimming. I used to separate but don't bother now.

Buying a Separator. For years it was impossible to find a hand-cranked cream separator except at an auction. Now you can order one from any dairy supply company. Lehman Hardware offers a hand-cranked model whose bowl holds 11½ qt., very like the one my parents used. You can also get them from New England Cheesemaking Supply Co. (413-628-3808; **www.cheesemaking.com**). Separators can be adjusted to manage the percentage of butterfat you remove from the whole milk.

Using a Separator. Separators work on a centrifugal principle. The milk is supposed to be put through while still warm, at least 90°F. For separating in winter, you could flush some warm water through the separator first. But I know people who put it through cold and it seems to work all right. A table-type separator has to be bolted to a very sturdy tabletop. The hand-cranked ones won't separate properly unless you have the crank moving at the proper speed. It is supposed to click. You keep going faster until it just quits clicking and stays at that speed. If you crank too

fast you're going to throw away a rather high percentage of your cream. Don't go by the clicks of somebody else's separator unless it is the same model and the same make. Different ones require different speeds.

Separating Goat's Milk. Goat's milk is hard to separate even with a cream separator. Make sure you have a model that can be set specially for goat's milk. Otherwise it won't work. You can save your milk for several milkings, and then separate it all at once. It even works with cold milk if you have the right setting on the cream percentage. The special thing about goat's milk is that the fat globules are so much smaller.

☙ *CARAMELS Combine 3½ c. sugar, 2½ c. white Karo syrup, 6 c. cream, and 4 T. butter. Cook to hard-crack stage, stirring constantly (it's okay to get this cream hot!). Add 1 t. vanilla and cool several minutes. Beat hard until it loses the glossy quality. Then pour out onto a large, buttered baking sheet. Cool. Cut.*

CREAM CHEESE: See "Making Soft Cheeses."

COOKING CREAM: Cream added to a highly acidic dish —one with fruits or tomatoes—is likely to curdle, especially if it's overheated. A dish with lots of cream in it that will be cooked should be cooked slowly and at a low temperature, best in a double boiler.

PRESERVING CREAM: The cream does have a tendency to get ahead of me when the milk is really in season—in spring after the babies come. Cream can be frozen. But I prefer to make butter and then freeze the butter; takes up less space. (For tropical living, see "Ghee: Hot Climate Butter Storage.")

Sour Cream

Home-cured cream is different from dairy soured cream the same way home-soured milk or buttermilk is different from dairy yogurt or cultured buttermilk. Home-soured cream has more of a tendency to separate into curds and whey. Just pour off the whey or stir it up and proceed with your recipe.

☙ *QUICK SUBSTITUTE FOR SOUR CREAM If you are baking and the recipe calls for sour cream and you don't have any, you can make a substitute by adding 1 T. lemon juice or vinegar per cup cream and mixing well.*

☙ *REAL SOUR CREAM Most recipes today mean dairy sour cream when they call for sour cream, and you can't always substitute home-soured cream with success unless you have a very smooth, mild-flavored one. You get that by pasteurizing your cream. (Heat in a double boiler to 185°F, stirring constantly. Move to a pan of ice water, and stir until cool.) Pour into a clean (scalded) jar. Add 2 T. cultured buttermilk per 2 c. cream. Put lid on. Shake well. Let stand in warm place 24–48 hours. By then your cream will be thick and sour.*

☙ *SOUR CREAM GRAVY Use this as a basic "stroganoff" sauce with "chicken paprika" Hungarian style. It is also good with chicken, veal cutlets, liver, kidney, tripe, rabbit, or any game. Cook a chopped onion or more in butter or in the grease left from cooking in your pan. Blend in flour enough to take up the grease. Season with salt, paprika. Add mushrooms, if you have them, and their juice, if canned. When the base is ready, add sour cream gradually, stirring constantly. Heat just to boiling. Don't overcook! Stir while you are heating and as it is thickening. Then remove, pour over the meat, and serve immediately.*

🐝 *SOUR CREAM COOKIES Combine 1 c. real sour cream, 1 c. sugar, 1 egg, 1 t. vanilla, and 1 t. soda, with enough regular flour to make a dough. The dough should be thin enough that the cookie will spread out a little as it bakes, but not pancake-flat. Optional: Add nuts, chocolate chips, raisins, or chopped dried fruit. Drop dough by teaspoons onto an oiled baking sheet. Bake at 350°F, 10–15 minutes.*

Whipping Cream

SECRETS OF WHIPPING CREAM

1. Success partly depends on your dairy animal. Milks—and creams—are different. Store-bought "whipping cream" is different yet, containing the likes of "mono and diglycerides, guar gum and carrageenan." But you can whip your home cream without those added ingredients.
2. If your top cream seems too thick to whip you can add some milk before whipping—but not too much, because cream has to have at least 30-percent fat, or more, to whip properly.
3. Fresh cream doesn't whip well. Age it from 12 to 24 hours before whipping.
4. Forty percent butterfat or higher, pasteurized, freezes best, and will still whip up after freezing.
5. Whip chilled cream because warmth thins it.
6. Use a big deep bowl to whip in so it won't splash all over.
7. Stop whipping when the cream gets firm enough to hold a peak when the eggbeater is pulled out. If you keep going, it makes butter—which happens quickly and can't be reversed.
8. One-half cup whipping cream gives you about 1 c. whipped cream.
9. With a very sweet dessert you can use unsweetened whipped cream, and it will taste fine.
10. Don't add your sweetening if it is a liquid, like honey or molasses, until you have your cream all whipped. Then stir it in gently. A couple drops of vanilla improves whipped cream's flavor.
11. You can make ahead a stabilized whipped cream by sprinkling ½ t. unflavored gelatin over 1 T. cold water in a small bowl. Set that bowl into hot water until gelatin dissolves. Let cool. Whip 1 c. cream to almost stiff. Add dissolved gelatin, and finish whipping to stiffness. Cover. Keep in refrigerator. Mix with a spoon right before you serve it. Optional: pinch salt, ½ t. vanilla, 1 T. sugar.

🐝 *QUICK CREAMY CHOCOLATE FROSTING Whip 1 c. cream. Gently stir in ¼ c. instant cocoa or chocolate milk drink powder.*

🐝 *LEMON CREAMY FROSTING Combine 1½ c. heavy cream, ¼ c. sugar, 1½ t. grated lemon peel, and several drops yellow food coloring. Beat to stiffness.*

Butter

To churn butter, you shake, beat, or agitate the cream until the butterfat has separated out and formed a big glob. Goat's butter is white rather than yellow and has a different taste than cow's butter—doesn't taste as buttery to me. There's a difference among cows' milks, too, but not nearly so much as between cow's and goat's. Butter-making is also affected by your cream's whipping ability. You may find that your particular cow's cream is harder than the average to

make butter from. Sometimes the farther a cow gets into her time of milking, the harder it is to get the butter. *NOTE: The latest medical research has established that people who eat real butter over a lifetime live longer than margarine-eaters! I have that directly from 2 friends who are medical doctors and who are now urging everyone they know to switch back to butter.*

BUTTER CHURN TYPES

Plain Jar. If you don't have a butter churn, the simplest way to make butter is probably to put your cream in a quart or half-gallon jar and give it to the children to roll back and forth across the floor. It takes 15–30 minutes for the butter to churn.

Rotating Barrel. You can buy one of these from Lehman's Hardware (888-438-5346; www.Lehmans.com). It is sold as a "pressure washer" for washing clothes (and it is useful for that), but if you have more than a little cream, it also makes a great butter churn.

Drill Churn. There is an electric drill attachment for stirring paint that could also churn butter if you simply put an electric drill through a hole in the metal top of a wide-mouthed gallon (or larger) jar and rigged up paddles to fit, and then fastened on the drill.

Electric Mixer. Butter can be churned using an electric mixer, but you have to watch carefully and remove the mixer just before the butter starts to come. Finish by beating it with a spoon or churning it in a jar as first mentioned. Otherwise the mixer would shred the butter and it would be very hard to gather together again.

Blender. Food writer Lane Morgan says, "I think a blender is the way to go for small batches of butter. It's easy and *fast*—4 or 5 minutes instead of 20 or so. Also, you can see what's happening. You just pour in the cream and turn it on a low setting. Scrape down any of it that whips and pretty soon it will separate into butter and buttermilk. I've made many a pound that way. (And I'm with you; I like sour milk best for butter.)"

Crank-and-Jar Churn. Our Sears and Roebuck's Farm Catalog carries 2 sizes of electric churn: a 1-gal. jar (it will churn 3 qt.), or a motor and dasher, which can be fitted on a 2-, 3-, or 5-gal. jar, or used on a crock. You can get an electric or nonelectric jar churn from Lehman Hardware.

Dasher Churn. A familiar sight in antique stores is the tall, upright crock churn with a lid through which is run a wooden dasher. You stand or sit by the churn and work the dasher up and down until the butter comes.

CREAM CONTENT: Anything from whole milk to "spoon cream" (so thick it won't pour), either sweet or sour, can be churned for butter. However, churning whole milk is hardly worth your while, since a quart of milk makes only about a teaspoon of butter.

CREAM TEMPERATURE: About 60°F is ideal. If the cream is too warm, the butter is long in coming and is too soft to handle. If it is too cold, it also takes too long to come, and only part of the butterfat separates from the cream, leaving a very thick buttermilk. The cream may churn easier if you wait until it is not too sweet. The taste of your butter is affected also by how sour the cream is that you use. I prefer butter made from sour cream, but not so sour that it has 3 colors of mold on it. I've heard that the feed your cow has been on can also affect the churning, that cottonseed meal and timothy hay for some reason are trouble. Sweet cream takes longer to churn and doesn't give as much butter proportionately.

THE CHURNING: Don't ever fill up a container in which you want to churn, because as it whips it doubles in bulk and will slop out the top. Leave it at least half empty. It churns easiest when the container is only one-third full. So for the average paddle churn of 3-gal. size, use about 1 gal. cream.

The churning should be done at a set rate and not too fast. It takes about 20 minutes of steady churning until you first hear the splash of butter and feel the stiffness in churning. It is best to churn past the first coming of butter to be sure you get all the butterfat from the cream. If you are using a big barrel churn with a bunghole to let out the buttermilk, stop turning when the granules are the size of wheat grains. You can tell with experience because the sound of the cream in the churn changes. Let the buttermilk out through the hole and run it through a strainer to catch any particles of butter.

WASHING AND GATHERING: The next step after churning is to wash and gather the butter. Some wash first and gather after. Some do both at once. If you are working with a large churn that has a bunghole, you could add pure clean water and twice as much buttermilk as you drew off after replacing the cork. Rotate the churn about 4 times, then drain that wash water, and repeat with clean water. Then commence to work the butter. About ¾ oz. of salt is added per pound of butter, or according to your taste.

To work the butter by hand pull the bung on a paddle churn and drain off the buttermilk. With a spoon remove the butter to a bowl, and scrape the butter from the paddle. Remove pieces of butter in the buttermilk. You will get 2½–3 qt. buttermilk and about 1 lb. of butter from 1 gal. cream. If the temperature is 80°F or so, you can't work butter until you've chilled it. Pour cold water on it to chill it. Now gather it into a ball, press it into a thin layer, and then gather into a ball again, *ad infinitum,* until all the salt is well worked in and the buttermilk is worked out. There is an old-time machine called a "worker" that you rinsed with hot water and then with cold, and then used to press the butter into a thin layer, fold it into a pile, and press again. It was great for large quantities of butter and for mixing the salt into the butter.

To wash and work the butter at the same time, put the butter from the buttermilk into a large bowl of ice water,

and squeeze it gently between your fingers until it feels smooth and waxy. It should go through several bowls of cool water. When the water stays clear, repeat 1 more time. Then shape into a cake and pat to remove the extra water. Next salt to taste and work the salt in well. The habit of salting butter originated from the preserving power of salt. Unsalted butter does not keep as well. In some countries like Australia all butter is unsalted. Butter can absorb odors if it isn't kept covered. But ours usually doesn't last that long.

COLORING: The color of cow's butter may vary. There is a coloring product on the market for butter and cheese. It isn't the kind that is dangerous to health. But color never did matter that much to me.

STORING BUTTER: Make sure all the buttermilk is out. You can brine the butter first by making butter balls the size of a baseball. Cover them with brine strong enough to float an egg. Cover and store in a cool place. This is good for months or even longer under cool temperatures. If you have the salt you can cover them with layers of pure salt.

Ghee: Hot Climate Butter Storage. Certain volatile fats in butter can get rancid. If it is heated enough that they're driven off, then it doesn't taste like butter any more, but it keeps much better. This is what folks on the Indian subcontinent and in Africa do. You heat the butter at simmering about an hour. Don't let it brown. Skim off the scum that rises to the surface again and again. At the end you'll see a clear yellowish fluid in your pan. Pour through a few layers of damp cheesecloth to remove the sediment that went to the bottom. More strainings give you greater keeping power. Pour into a scalded container. Cover to keep air out. It will store nicely now for months, even at hot temperatures.

➤ *ETHIOPIAN SPICED GHEE Gradually melt 1 lb. butter (unsalted) in a pan and then bring to a simmer as above. When foaming begins, add 4 T. chopped onion, 1½ T. chopped garlic, 2 T. grated fresh ginger, ½ t. turmeric, 2 crushed whole cardamom seeds (or ½ t. ground cardamom), 1-inch stick cinnamon, 2 or 3 whole cloves, and ⅛ t. ground nutmeg. Simmer, uncovered, until solids have gathered on bottom and the middle liquid is clear. Strain 3 times through damp cheesecloth for longest keeping.*

SHAPED BUTTERS

Butter Molds. Before using a butter mold, scald it, then soak it in cold water for an hour. Pack it solidly with butter and level off the top surface. When the butter is molded it can be pressed out.

Butter Balls. Scald a pair of wooden butter paddles, then soak them in cold water for about an hour. Measure the butter by teaspoonfuls so the butter balls will be about the same size. Have the butter firm but not hard, and roll each spoonful lightly between the paddles to form the balls. Drop onto a chilled plate, onto cracked ice, or into ice water. Or press each ball slightly to make it round on the side and flat on the top and bottom.

Butter Pats. Shape your butter into a rectangle the shape of the commercial quarter pound. Let it cool to firm. Cut neat squares off the end to be your pats. To decorate you could dip a fork in hot water and draw on them or put a little sprig of parsley on each one.

Butter Curls. These were traditionally made with a "butter curler." It was dipped into hot water and then drawn lightly and quickly toward you across the butter. This made a thin shaving of butter that curled up. The butter curler was dipped into hot water after each curl.

Whipped Butter. For a soft, fluffy spread, bring ¼ lb. butter and ¼ lb. water to room temperature. Whip them together with the mixer. You might need more water. That's all there is to it.

FLAVORED BUTTERS

✑ *LEMON BUTTER Cream butter until fluffy and add a few drops lemon juice. Use for sandwiches, canapes, and fish.*

✑ *HERBED BUTTER For each ½ c. butter add about 1 t. of your choice of dried herbs (basil, thyme, marjoram, dill are fine) or chopped fresh herbs. A dash of garlic salt is good, too.*

Buttermilk

CHURNED BUTTERMILK: This is the milk substance left after you have churned your butter. It may have an acidic flavor and it may not. It depends on how sour the cream was when you churned. Sour cream makes a sour-flavored buttermilk. If you want nice buttermilk, don't let your cream get too rank before you churn. The "dried buttermilk" that you used to be able to buy in the grocery store was the real thing—dried.

BUTTERMILK RECIPES: There are so many great things you can do with buttermilk. In any of the following recipes you can use store-bought buttermilk or the yogurt–butter mix I mentioned, or your homemade buttermilk left over from churning if it's nice-tasting. In baking you can use even a pretty strong-tasting buttermilk, and it will still turn out deliciously. It makes a fine gravy.

✑ *BUTTERMILK CHEESE Go through the usual steps. It will make the best cottage cheese or hard cheese of all!*

✑ *STRAWBERRY-BANANA BUTTERMILK Mash and beat together 1–2 c. strawberries, 1 banana, and 2 c. buttermilk. A very special beverage.*

✑ *ORANGE-HONEY BUTTERMILK Combine 4 c. buttermilk, the juice of 2 oranges, and 2 T. honey.*

✑ *BUTTERMILK COLESLAW DRESSING Combine 1½ T. sugar, 1 c. cold buttermilk, ½ t. mustard, 1½ T. lemon juice or vinegar, and ¼ t. salt.*

✑ *BUTTERMILK VEGETABLE SOUP Slice 2 medium-sized cooked potatoes. Chop 3 green onions (the white part very fine, the green part not so). Mix with 1 qt. churned buttermilk. Add salt and pepper to taste. Heat to the serving temperature and serve (don't boil it). You can use big onions instead of the green ones by chopping and prefrying them. Bacon bits are good, too.*

✑ *BUTTERMILK RAISIN SOUP Moisten 1 T. flour with 1 T. buttermilk, and heat 1 qt. buttermilk to scalding temperature. Add the flour and beat with your eggbeater until it is well-distributed. Add ½ c. seedless raisins, 1 stick of cinnamon, and a pinch of salt. Cook until the raisins are puffed. When it's ready to serve, add sweetening and ¼ c. heavy cream, whipped.*

✑ *BUTTERMILK PORRIDGE Boil ½ c. barley slowly in 3 c. water for about 2 hours. Add 1½ qt. buttermilk, stirring until it boils, cook a few minutes, then add ½ t. salt. Serve with syrup or other sweetening.*

✑ *BUTTERMILK BISCUITS From Ruth Brant, Stayton, OR: Combine 2 c. flour, 2 t. baking powder, 1 T. sugar, salt to taste, and 1 c. buttermilk. Mix, roll out, cut. Let stand 15 minutes. Bake 12 minutes in a 450–500°F oven.*

✑ *BUTTERMILK WAFFLES Sift together 2 c. flour, 2 t. baking powder, ½ t. salt, ½ t. baking soda, and 3 T. sugar. Combine 2 beaten egg yolks, 2 c. buttermilk, and ¼ c. melted butter. Add liquid to dry ingredients and beat well. Fold in the 2 stiffly beaten egg whites and bake on your waffle iron.*

Ice Cream

The old-time name for ice cream was "cream." Old recipes usually contained lots of cream and eggs. It was considered a confection and was manufactured by the same people who made bonbons. If you like to make ice cream, you'd love *Ben & Jerry's Homemade Ice Cream & Dessert Book* by Ben Cohen and Jerry Greenfield.

INGREDIENTS

The Cream. If you get a buttery taste it may be either that the cream was overwhipped or that it is too rich in butterfat. You can fix that simply by using a more thorough skimming so the cream won't be quite so rich. It is better not to use absolutely fresh cream. Good cream will double in bulk while freezing.

Fruit. Fresh fruit for frozen desserts should be very ripe. If it doesn't seem ripe enough, cook with a little water. A fruit "puree" in a recipe could be cooked fruit put through a sieve or raw fruit grated or pulped, as with the ripe fleshy fruits like apricots and strawberries.

Ingredients for Lightness. Refrigerator ice creams usually contain whipped cream and/or beaten egg white to give them their lightness. Crank freezer ice creams gain a light consistency from the cranking process.

THE FREEZING: Ice cream can be made in your refrigerator's freezer compartment or in a crank freezer. The stirring breaks up ice crystals and improves the texture. "Refrigerator" ice cream contains so much cream, eggs, and/or gelatin that ice crystals and texture aren't a problem. But even if the dessert is to be frozen in the refrigerator or freezer, it helps to remove it when it is at the mushy stage, put it in a chilled bowl, and beat it vigorously. A second beating later on would improve it even more.

In a Refrigerator. In the freezing compartment the amount of time needed to freeze depends on the mixture, its depth, and the refrigerator; the average time is around 2 hours. The temperature should be under 20°F. It helps to use cold ingredients and to chill the mixture well before putting it in the freezer. Don't try to make ice cubes at the same time. The sweeter the mixture the more difficult it will be to freeze. It's best to freeze at the coldest setting you have—the quicker the desserts freeze the better they hold their lightness. But after freezing is accomplished they are improved by resting to mellow for a couple of hours. It helps the flavor and the texture.

In a Crank Freezer. If you buy a crank freezer (Lehman Hardware sells them), directions will come with it. The crank freezer will consist of a wooden or metal bucket that holds the ice-and-salt freezing mixture and a nonrusting metal can with a tight-fitting lid for holding the cream to be frozen. The ice cream is stirred by a paddle inside the can, which is turned by a crank on the outside—or in some

cases by an electric motor.

You usually need about 12 lb. of ice for a batch. You could freeze milk cartons full of water in your freezer and then dump out the ice into a bag and pound it to chips with a wooden mallet. You need rock salt, too, for the freezer. The recommended proportions vary. Usually you can use just 1 part rock salt to 8 parts crushed ice during the freezing process. Alternate layers of ice and salt to a point higher than where your ice cream will be in the can. After freezing the ice cream you can repack it for mellowing—use 4 parts ice to 1 part rock salt. Then cover the freezer with newspapers or a piece of rug. In winter you could use snow instead of ice. If the salt doesn't act rapidly enough on it, add a cup of cold water.

But I never bother mellowing our homemade ice cream. The children are so anxious and it tastes fine enough to me when it's first done. I don't worry about measuring proportions of salt and ice either. I just pour in ice and then pour on salt. The can shouldn't be more than two-thirds full. Turn the crank slowly at first until the ice cream is mush, then more rapidly until it is too stiff to turn. You might want to take off the lid occasionally to scrape the harder ice cream off the sides of the can and back into the middle. Be careful to wipe off the top of the freezer can each time you open it, since even a little of the rock-salt brine getting in could spoil your batch. If your recipe contains nuts or fruit, it will work better if you don't add them until the mixture is mush.

STORING ICE CREAM: A good temperature is 0°F. Use it within 2 weeks. Don't let it thaw and then try to refreeze because it will get hard and not be nearly as nice. To keep your ice cream, repack it in nonmetal containers; it deteriorates very rapidly in metallic ones.

BPO ICE CREAM *My favorite for big occasions is a mixture of 1 mashed ripe banana, 1 c. crushed pineapple, and 1 orange (peel and seeds discarded). More fruit makes it better. Stir in maybe ¼ c. honey, if the fruit needs it. Then I fold in 1 c. of cream that has been whipped into the fruit mix. More of that doesn't hurt either. This really doesn't make very much. I usually double it.*

VANILLA ICE CREAM *Here's the family recipe for vanilla ice cream from Margaret Kerrick, West Roxbury, MA: Mix 1 qt. light cream, 1½ T. vanilla, and ¾ c. sugar. First put the cream mixture into the freezer can, set the can in the freezer, adjust the top, and fill in around the can with ice and rock salt in layers. Use 3 parts of ice to 1 of rock salt. Then turn the handle of the crank, slowly at first, then faster as it begins to freeze. This makes for a smoother ice cream. When you feel that it is becoming harder to turn, you can open it up and see if it is done. "Then you can lick the paddle. Pull it out and gather around with spoons and dig in. If there isn't enough for everyone to have a taste from the paddle, let them eat from the freezer. We always made the ice cream before we went to church. After we had our licks, my father packed it, poured off the water from the melting ice, added fresh ice and salt and covered the freezer with a burlap bag with the remains of the ice in it. Then after we came home from church and had our dinner, we unpacked the freezer and ate huge dishes of ice cream."*

FRUIT MOUSSE *Whip 2 c. heavy cream. Combine with 1 c. of any pulped fruit. Add a trace of vanilla, sweeten if needed, and freeze.*

ICE CREAM SANDWICHES *Between thin slices of devil's food cake (or whatever you like) place a serving of vanilla ice cream (or whatever you like). You can make your own paper cases and store them in the freezer.*

NEAPOLITAN ICE CREAM *Pack a mold in salt and ice or have ready a mold to go into your freezer. You'll need to have ready your 3 preferred varieties. Strawberry, vanilla, and chocolate are traditional, but you can vary that. Spread the first variety of ice cream smoothly over the bottom. If it is not very firm, cover, and let it freeze a few minutes. Then spread a thick layer of the next variety on it. As soon as this hardens, spread over the last kind. Cover and freeze.*

APPLESAUCE ICE CREAM *Combine 1 c. applesauce, a pinch of cinnamon, a pinch of nutmeg, 1 t. melted butter, and 2 t. lemon juice. Chill. Fold in 1 c. whipped cream and toasted flaked coconut or chopped nuts, if you want it extra rich, and freeze until firm.*

MILK SHAKE *Mash fruit, fresh or frozen, such as strawberries. Add ice cream and some milk and continue mashing. Add more milk and mix gradually until your milk shake is thinned as much as you like it.*

LOW-FAT ICE CREAM *From Oregon State University, via "Gertrude": "Dissolve 1 T. plain gelatin and 1½ c. sugar in 1 qt. warm water and bring to a light boil. Cool to 100–110°F. Add 1 c. instant nonfat dry milk and mix well. Chill mix to below 40°F. Add 3 c. chilled whipping cream. Pour all into freezer tub. Add 2 T. vanilla. Stir and freeze in ice cream maker until desired firmness is acquired. It will be ½ gal. to start. Should make, with air added in the freezing, nearly 1 gal. ice cream."*

FROZEN YOGURT *From Phyllis Vallette, spouse of a Wycliffe Bible Translator, Djibo, Burkina Faso: "You tell in the yogurt section how to serve frozen yogurt with fruit. I wish you had a cross reference to it in the ice cream section. For us it fills the same function as ice cream, but is easier, cheaper and less rich. I make a nice 'ice cream' of yogurt and* *guava sauce, about 50-50, sweetened to taste. When I'm not in Africa I do the same with apple sauce (cinnamon optional). For some reason yogurt seems to freeze smooth without long ice crystals, and I don't bother to mush it up at the halfway point."*

HOMEMADE SNOW CONES *My neighbor Kay Morey, a very dear friend who has dug me out of many a hole, gathers clean snow and packs it into cups. She pours fruit juice or syrup over this, and the children love it.*

I used to think that bottle-fed animals would just naturally be the most gentle and manageable for their humans. I was so wrong. After numerous tragic farm incidents of injury by animals, veterinary researchers now say this:
For males you plan to keep for breeding and for females of large species, use natural nursing by the animals' own mothers or adoption by goats, another cow, or other mammal. Bottle-fed males and females of all species think people are their species, and later, when they're old enough to mate and show instinctive dominance behavior, they may harm a person. An animal raised by another animal ends up being safer to have around people than a bottle-fed one!

But two other old principles are still true: Be gentle and kind to your animals, and be patient. Don't force a bottle into the mouth if you can help it. Don't drag or carry the animals if you can help it. Take the time to coax and teach good habits. Make your animals respect you, and don't ever let one win a battle if you can help it, because you don't want them to think that it's possible.

A goat or cow with good manners, who has friendly feelings toward human beings and is well-trained in what is expected is worth the top price. An angry (mean) animal that won't cooperate is a cull and is worth only the bottom price—to say nothing of all the grief it's going to cause you.

The principles you live by shape the outcomes of your life. Principles, definitions, and measures can be applied to human beings as much as to elements in a laboratory. How do you define yourself? What do you measure yourself by? A lot of how well you do in life depends on the wholesomeness, soundness, and success of your own standards and design for your life—and your self-applied definitions and measures. If you have been defining yourself in one way for a long time and then are suddenly forced to change your self-definition, it's hard.

I went through several major changes in the 24 years since I began this book, including separation and divorce from my husband Mike after 18 years of marriage. I had to change from defining and measuring myself as Mike's wife and the mother of his children. I learned that in every ending there is also a beginning—small and curled up, like the promise of a flower's bud—that must be sought out and nurtured. I learned how to let go when you have to, even if that means letting go of a lot of your self-definition, hanging loose for a while, and waiting to see what your new self is going to be. A major change of self-definition like that leaves you like a child, born—reborn—new into the world. You need time to grow and gradually become acquainted with your (new) identity. I had to do that after Mike left: slowly discover who I was going to be without him, gradually learn that I could be okay without him.

Nine years after that divorce, 9 years spent devoted to doing the best job I could of raising our 7 children, and that task is almost over too. I can look back on both being a wife and being a mother with a clean conscience, for in both cases I honestly gave all I had, my very best every day, for all those years. Now a new time of redefinition, remeasuring, is upon me. Within a few more months the 2 youngest children will be off to college, and I'll be alone in a whole new sense. I won't be a "mother" in the old occupational way any more. It's an exciting next transition.

As with the divorce, at first I was horribly depressed about this and cried a lot. But then I shook myself out of that and realized I was entering a whole new era of exciting options I didn't have before. The kids are all going to be fine without me. Totally unencumbered now for the first time in 30 years, suddenly I can plan to travel freely, visiting old friends and making new ones. I'll be free to research new books where I choose, as I choose. I'll be free to join a club, or clubs, take up hobbies . . .

With nobody needing me at home, I'll be free to spend more evenings out at various interesting events than I spend at home. I've already made myself free enough to devote some effort and money to a major improvement in my appearance, freely answered an ad in the personals that intrigued me, freely chose to accept a dinner invitation from a handsome gentleman . . .

When other people demand their freedom, by default you get yours back too!

Bee, Rabbit, Sheep & Pig

BEE, RABBIT, SHEEP & PIG CONTENTS

INTRODUCTION

January 1994. Today I'm writing the last page for the ninth edition of this book. It's a funny feeling. I've been working on this book for 24 years—and it's finally finished. So many years have passed since I wrote the table of contents (which is still basically the same) . . . It's taken me this long to get it right. But I always had the same dream: to create a one-volume reference work in the field of family food production that would tell people how to grow every kind of food, every step of the way, and would include all the logical supporting information.

There are now almost a million words between these two covers, and that's just huge. I wanted to create a book so fundamental, so complete, and so dependable that it would be considered essential to have in every home, whether in the city or country. I wanted to make the book as reliable, standard, and useful as a dictionary.

Was it really God who was speaking to me, wanting me to write this book? I'll never know for sure. The older I get, the more I know I don't know, and the less I take for granted. Maybe it was something deep inside me, something I had to make happen to meet my own personal needs. That's

the theory I find most convincing. Or maybe I'm just the kind of person who sees a need, envisions a way to meet it, and accepts fulfilling that need as their personal responsibility and life's duty.

At the time that I made my life-long commitment to completing this book, I felt that God was responsible for the thought that kept coming to me, insisting that I should and could accomplish this task. There were two reasons I thought this: because our church's minister and my friends in the church told me that a thought that keeps returning is from the Lord, and because I couldn't see any earthly way I could do something so clearly impossible. Now I'm much more sophisticated, and I understand that a person can have a strong inner urging that expresses itself in a repeated thought, an urging that is simply a personal mechanism for achieving a personal goal. I know I do have another agenda that this book serves; this book is not my final task. With luck, and God willing, I'll get to the ultimate finish line.

This latest edition has some unique contents. It presents the latest, safest USDA-approved canning instructions and extension-approved canning recipes for every sort of food

and pickle—the updated methods the USDA issued after researchers discovered that all the old canning instructions had problems. Other material that's unique or hard to find elsewhere includes the detailed, accurate growing information about wild rice and Asian rice; the very complete procedures for harvesting grain without using any machines or petroleum products; the directions for having a baby if you're all by yourself; the instructions for training a team of oxen; and the procedures to follow if your child eats something that looks like a mushroom but isn't one. Also, this new edition tells how *E. coli* can get into a fast-food hamburger and how to make sure a restaurant hamburger is safe for your child if you go out to eat. It tells how to cope with a changing climate and where not to build a house. And more: It provides herb-growing instructions and recipes; how to make quince seed hand lotion; how to turn your garden snails into your supper; how to cure olives; and which simple kitchen item, if mixed with water, will kill and/or drive off even African bees.

Which brings me back to business here: the subject of beekeeping. Read on . . .

BEES

If you are buying honey rather than producing it, try to get it wholesale, direct from the beekeeper. Buy it by the 5-gal. pail. You'll save money, and that amount will probably be a whole year's supply for an average family. If you want to produce your own, read on. I hope to have lots of honey this summer. I even have a batch of bees living 2 feet away from the back door, in an old refrigerator that used to be a smoker. It's a beehive now since they moved in. I kind of enjoy their neighborly buzzing. But I've had high hopes before, and sometimes they get dashed. Beekeeping is a very special sort of livestock-raising, and getting your bees to produce isn't all that easy. It's easiest if you have a long flowering season and mild winters, and definitely no drought that keeps the flowers from blooming. A severe winter, a dry summer, an epidemic of some unfortunate bee disease—and they can all die on you. Even if you do get started with bees, figure that they probably won't be able to spare you a significant amount of honey until the third year. That allows them 1 year to get going and you 1 year to make mistakes. Without mistakes, you'll be there by the second year. Bees are essential to agriculture and to flowering plant life in general because of their function as pollinators. Beekeeping for a living can be an economic roller coaster, even worse than the usual for farming. Professional

beekeepers have to study their small subjects for years—their biology and the plants they can gather food from—plus learn how to market their product. But beekeepers have less control over market prices, weather (drought, extended rain and flood, prolonged freezing), neighbors who spray pesticides that kill bees, or sudden onslaughts of disease or parasites in the colony.

There are rewards, too. If you learn what to do and pay close enough attention to your bees so you can do what needs to be done, they'll provide the sweetest of all foods—and do so at a bargain—as well as produce a crop that there's always a good-paying market for! You'll be welcomed into the very exclusive ranks of local beekeepers and have lots to tell as well as ask about at their meetings. You can keep a few bees because they're interesting and you want honey for your own family, and, if you're lucky, you'll still have some to give away: Raise 1–12 colonies.

In a temperate zone, with your still-limited experience, you should count on only 1 or 2 gal. of honey per hive per summer—though with practice and luck you'll come up to the average of 4–5 gal. Then you could keep more hives and sell surplus honey for a side income—say from 12 on up to 200 hives. Or you could go into beekeeping as a full-time occupation, in which case you'd expect to handle enormous quantities of bees and make all your living at it. Kim Flottum, editor of *Bee Culture* (who very helpfully reviewed this section, corrected my errors, and added important new information; I am truly grateful to him!), advised, "You need about 700 to 1,000 colonies to make a living full-time." A pro beekeeper who lives in a prime beekeeping area may average as much as 200 lb. of honey harvest per colony, but the national average is less than 50 lb. per colony. With bees, the uncertainties of harvest are greater than with most other crops.

The commercial beekeeper has to produce as much honey as possible with the least possible expense and then sell that honey for the highest possible price. Beekeeping on this scale is very hard work. Before setting out to sell honey, find out what the local, current regulations are. And you'll have to plan for what containers you'll package it in. You can probably sell wholesale or to retail stores. If you live on a well-traveled highway, a produce stand is a means to sell your honey at a maximum profit.

There are about 150,000 beekeepers in the United States. They keep about 3,000,000 honeybee colonies. They keep bees as a hobby or as a profit-making business, selling honey, pollen, beeswax, propolis, or royal jelly—or bees. They may rent bees for pollination service or move their hives onto land in summer in exchange for a share of the honey. It's possible but very, very rare to find a self-contained operation in which the beekeeper plants the crop (such as rapeseed) that the bees will make honey from. Beekeepers, even more than most farmers, need to network and stay informed about the ever-evolving bee diseases and parasites and matters relating to African honeybees, as well as new types of equipment, marketing opportunities, and regulations. If you're a newcomer to beekeeping, you have even more work ahead of you.

Learning to Beekeep

Raising bees is a lot trickier than the manuals make it out to be, and I speak from sad experience. My general impression is that people usually expect more honey than they actually get. Maybe in the South it's better, but in these more northern climates it takes a couple years—at least—to get built up to where your bees will be keeping you in honey. *Above all, you can't just install and then ignore this tiny livestock.* Professional beekeepers visit their bees at least every 3 weeks to check for signs of trouble.

Of all the subjects in this book, beekeeping is the one I feel is hardest to learn from a book—mine or anybody else's. You really need to learn it in person. So try to find a local beekeeper who will let you visit, take you through a hive, and show you the workshop where hives are made and how extracting is done. Watch the technique. Learn to see and recognize the different kinds of cells and bees. You'll catch the professional beekeeper's calm. If a pro gets stung, he or she takes a half minute out (or maybe not even that) to cuss and then proceeds with the job. You'll need to learn a bunch of facts and procedures . . .

MAKE SURE YOU ASK AND LEARN:
1. What is the organization of brood and honey?
2. What does each type of bee look like (queen, drone, worker)?
3. What does each type of bee cell in the frame look like?
4. How do you find the queen?
5. What do the eggs and larvae look like?
6. Where and how is the honey stored?
7. How does the system of movable frames work?

8. How do you use a smoker to quiet the bees?
9. What other types of equipment does a beekeeper use?
10. How do you check the strength of your colonies?
11. How do you clean dead bees and debris out of the hives?
12. How do you make sure the queen is okay and laying well in the spring?
13. How do you add supers (the upper hive compartments in which your bees will store honey)?
14. How can you minimize swarming (which would halve the size of your colony)?

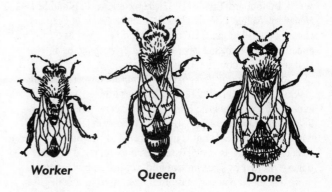

Worker   **Queen**   **Drone**

CLUBS: There's too much to grasp in a single casual visit with a beekeeper. Clubs: Beekeeping has to be both studied and practiced. Many areas have a local beekeepers' club. That's your best place to look for help to get started. Nowadays beekeeping is a highly organized, closely supervised occupation. Don't let that discourage you. The club will tell you the laws affecting apiculture (beekeeping), about possible inspection of hives, local zoning regulations, state registration requirements for beekeepers, and labeling regulations for honey you plan to sell. Your county agricultural extension agent may be able to put you in touch with local beekeepers. Or ask a bee supply outlet for local names. Or look in past issues of *Bee Culture.* Or network with beekeepers on the internet at the bee discussion lists: **bee-1. com/index.html.** Or write or call one of the following organizations.

American Beekeeping Federation, Troy Fore, Executive Director; 912-427-4233; fax 912-427-8447; PO Box 1337, Jesup, GA 31598; **troyfore@abfnet.org.**

American Honey Producers Ass'n, Lyle Johnston; 719-254-6321; **www.americanhoneyproducers.org.**

Eastern Apicultural Society of North America, Inc., Loretta Surprenant, Sec., Miner Institute, Chazy, NY 12921; 518-846-8020.

Western Apicultural Society of North America, Nancy Stewart, 2110 X St., Sacramento, CA 95818; 916-451-2337.

Florida State Beekeepers Ass'n, Eloise Cutts, Executive Secretary, 2237 N.W. 16th Ave., Gainesville, FL 32605; 904-378-7719. (Local beekeeping clubs meet more often.)

BEE BOOKS: Go to a beekeepers' (apicultural) school. Your local extension service can guide you to a class or program. If hands-on training from a neighborly beekeeper is not available to you, there are convenient alternatives: books, videotapes and slides.

First Lessons in Beekeeping by C. P. Dadant and *Starting Right,* a basic manual that's been in print for 70 years and is regularly updated by editors at the A.I. Root Co. (120 pg, $7.99), are a good place to begin. This is where Kim Flottum works, editing current editions of the famous Root publications for beekeepers. (Kim helped me with this bee section.) Kim also recommends *The Beekeeper's Handbook* by Sammataro and Avitabile (1988), and says that *Hive Management* (1989) and *A Practical Guide to Beekeeping* by Dick Bonney (1993) are also good. Other useful books are *The Complete Guide to Beekeeping* by Roger A. Morse (1980, reissued 1994), the *How-to-Do-It Book of Beekeeping* by Richard Taylor (1984, reissued 1994), *Beekeeping for Gardeners* by Richard Taylor (1982), *How to Keep Bees and Sell Honey* by Walter T. Kelly (1991), and the *Guide to Bees and Honey* by Ted Hooper (1976). Sue Hubble wrote two fun anecdotal bee books. Also, *Plants and Beekeeping*, by F .N. Howes (1979), covers forage plants for bees.

Also check out *Beekeeping: A Complete Owner's Manual* (1986), a user-friendly book by Werner Melzer, a German expert who presents the European bee scene. *The Honey Bee: A Guide for Beekeepers*, by V. R. Vickery, a Canadian, reads like a textbook but is up-to-date and thorough. *The Hive & the Honey Bee*, newly revised and enlarged (1,324 pages!), edited by Joe Graham and published by Dadant, is more advanced reading, has often been used as a college entomology and apiculture text. The *ABC and XYZ of Bee Culture*, edited by Kim Flottum and Roger Morse, first published in 1897, was in its 40th edition last I heard. It's encyclopedically complete, including history, anatomy, hive styles, etc. Also check out *Bees and Beekeeping: A Year in the Life of an Apiary*, by Keith S. Delaphane. *The Beekeepers Handbook* (1998), by Diana Sammataro, Alphone Avitabile, and Roger Morse, covers the life history and behavior of bees, bee management, disease control, and honey removal and processing.

MAGAZINES

American Bee Journal is an excellent monthly, $20.95/year, from Dadant and Sons. Free sample copy: 217-847-3324; fax 217-847-3660; 51 S. 2nd St., Hamilton, IL 62341; **abj@dadant.com; www.dadant.com/journal.**

APIS is an entomology newsletter, now out of print, but archived on the web at **APIS.ifas.ufl.edu.** The new configuration of the APIS newsletter is found at **groups.yahoo.com/group/APIS_newsletter.**

Bee Culture: The Magazine of American Beekeeping appears monthly. They offer a free sample. Also, "Who's Who in Apiculture," a list of bee organizations and government bee specialists, is published every May in *Bee Culture* and available at **www.airoot.com.** (Then click on beekeeping.) It's $21.50/yr from the A.I. Root Co.: 216-725-6677; 800-289-7668; 623 West Liberty Street, PO Box 706, Medina, OH 44258-0706; **beeculture@ beeculture.com.**

Bee World, the *Journal of Apicultural Research*, and *Apicultural Abstracts*, are all published by the International Bee Research Ass'n: international tel. 44 2920 372409; international fax 44 2920 665522;18 North Rd., Cardiff CF10 3DT, UNITED KINGDOM; **info@ibra.org.uk; www.ibra.org.uk.**

Canadian Beekeeping offers news, interviews, features, and ads, both in the text version and on the website where there are also current and back issue samples; $21.40 in Canada; $20 in U.S.: 905-936-4975; Box 678, Tottenham, Ontario, CANADA L0G 1W0;

editor@canadianbeekeeping.com/; www.canadian beekeeping.com/.

New Zealand Beekeeper comes from the National Beekeepers Ass'n of New Zealand; 11 issues per year (Feb.–Dec.). Overseas air mail costs U.S. $38; ship $31: 07-838-2589; fax 07-838-2960; PO Box 447, Hamilton, NEW ZEALAND; **magazine@nba.org.nz; www.nba.org.nz/.**

The Speedy Bee, "The Beekeeper's Newspaper," is a monthly for $17.25/year. Free sample copy is available from Troy Fore, Jr.: 912-427-4018; PO Box 1317, Jesup, GA 31598-1317.

BEEKEEPING SUPPLIES

Blossomland Supply sells both beekeeping and candle-making supplies: 616-473-3917; 800-637-5262; PO Box 74, Berrien Center, MI 49102; **katherine@ blossomland.com; www.blossomland.com.**

Brushy Mountain Bee Farm offers a free 84-pg catalog of beekeeping equipment and supplies, protective clothing, candle- and soap-making supplies, books, beekeeping videos, etc.: 800-233-7929 or 336-921-3640; fax 336-921-2681; 610 Bethany Church Rd., Moravian Falls, NC 28654; **www.beeequipment.com.**

Dadant is the largest bee equipment supplier. Ask for their dealer subsidiary in your area: 800-637-7468; 51 S. 2nd St., Hamilton, IL 62341; **dadant@dadant.com; www.dadant.com.**

Mann Lake Ltd. offers a free 84-pg catalog of beekeeping and candle-making supplies: 800-880-7694; fax 218-675-6165; 501 S. 1st St. Hackensack, MN 56452; **beekeeper@mannlakeltd.com; www.mannlakeltd. com.**

Rossman Apiaries sells supplies for beekeepers, including package bees: 800-333-7677; PO Box 905, Moultrie, GA 31776; **rossman@surfsouth.com; www.gabees. com.**

Western Bee Supplies manufactures and sells a full line of bee equipment. Order online, or request a catalog: 800-548-8440 or 406-883-2918; PO Box 190, Polson, MT 59860; **www.westernbee.com.**

About Bee Stings

The notion that you can work with bees and never get stung is a kind of romantic fiction perpetrated by bee handlers for fun. Two beekeepers in the presence of an innocent have a traditional conversation that goes like this: First beekeeper: "Have you ever been stung?" Second beekeeper: "No, never. Have you?" First beekeeper: "Never."

The fact is that even with the best preparation, you're almost certain to get stung about once for every trip to the beehives you make—and much more if you aren't wearing the right kind of bee costume. Some people get almost immune to the stings, and then the stings don't bother them much more than a mosquito bite.

But suddenly that can reverse. Some people, even after years of beekeeping, become allergic to bee stings. Benadryl is a treatment for this allergic reaction, but Benadryl by mouth can't solve a severe crisis. It doesn't get absorbed in time. You need a shot. If you have a severe allergic reaction, you can die within 20 minutes of the sting. *If you suspect an allergic reaction, head to the closest hospital right away!*

Three steps toward prevention: First, if you're considering beekeeping, get tested for allergies to bees or bee stings. If you're allergic, obviously you want to take up a different hobby or occupation. Next, wear your protective costume, especially around your head and neck, which are the most dangerous places to get stung, and don't get any more stings than you can help. Finally, work together with somebody else so that if one of you gets sick, the other can drive; a person in anaphylactic shock is confused (lack of blood to the brain!), very sick, and not fit to drive.

Kim's clarification: "A 'sting' is the organ (pointed) that enters the skin. A 'stinger' is the insect inserting the sting." Okay. So the place where a bee stung you itches like crazy because of the sting in it, which is full of venom. If stung, scrape the sting out quickly with your fingernail or a hive tool. Honeybees are good guys (girls?). They don't usually sting unless you are actually opening up the hive, moving around the frames, and harvesting honey. If you are merely peacefully watching bees come and go in their doorway, there's very little chance of being stung.

OF BEES AND "BEES": So, first of all, please clearly distinguish between honey-making bees and the yellow jacket/wasp/hornet tribes. It really isn't correct or fair to call all of them "bees" and teach children to be afraid of all equally. Honeybees can sting only once because when they sting, they leave their sting mechanism in you. They've given their life for that cause. So bees are much less likely to sting than wasps.

Wasps, on the other hand, will sting at the slightest provocation and can sting again and again. Wasps and hornets don't gather nectar from flowers as bees do. Instead they are aggressive scavengers that like to eat fruit, sweets, and meat. I used to say that if they were to become extinct, I'd shout, "Hooray!" But Kim taught me this: Wasps like to eat bugs and, in fact, live mostly on them. Kim wrote, "A yellow-jacket nest will consume 1,000–10,000 vegetable pests in a home garden in a season. Better, much better, than pesticides!" (Incidentally, do you want to hang out with pesticide haters? That's one more reason to join the bee club! They've suffered mightily from the modern delight in bugicide.)

BEE BREEDS: In North America alone there are more than 3,500 species of wild bees. They are helpful for pollinating, but they don't store honey at all. There are only 3 basic "races" of bees that beekeepers choose among: the "Italian," the "Caucasian," and the "Carniolan." The Italian bees are yellow and black, hardworking, and don't like their hive opened on a rainy day. Caucasians are considered to be less likely to sting than Italians. Carniolans are said to be the gentlest kind of all. You can also buy a hybrid queen, a cross of 2, or even a cross of all 3.

AFRICAN BEES: The Africans are another race of honeybee. When they breed with domestic bees, all their aggressive qualities tend to get passed on. Because of this genetic dominance, an African–domestic bee cross equals an African in outcome. A true African-domestic hybrid just doesn't exist.

How aggressive are they? The African bees are some 30 times quicker to take offense than regular bees, sting 10 times as often, and tend to attack *en masse,* having a stronger chemical system for calling their brethren to the project than do regular honeybees. Having thousands of bees attacking you all at once would be disconcerting, to say the least. Wherever there have been African bees, there have been deaths of people and livestock. They have been steadily migrating northward since the originals escaped from a research lab in Argentina. The African bees have made it north to Texas, New Mexico, Arizona, and California. They are expected to ultimately spread throughout the southern third of the United States but no farther north than that.

If African bees move into your neighborhood, you'll find out suddenly and traumatically as you're being chased down the road. Incidentally, the first line of defense against African bees is running away. If you can run 15 miles per hour for 5–7 minutes, you can get away from them. (That's 8–10 city blocks.)

If you encounter a nest or hive of African bees, don't try to be a hero and attack them. Kim Flottum explained to me that if you were to go in there in full bee regalia with a couple cans of Raid, the Raid would accomplish no more than to ensure that thousands of furious and still-healthy bees would attack you within seconds, and significant numbers would succeed. If there is even the slightest flaw in your outfit, say a loose legging, you'll have 200–1,000 stings within seconds. *If you encounter a nest of Africans, don't try to eradicate them yourself; call for help from authorities.*

There is a silver lining to this. Turns out Africans are vulnerable to something: soapy water. A fire truck loaded with soapy water can wipe out a colony.
NOTE: If a person is being attacked by African bees, spraying them with soapy water helps—it kills the bees. If there are African bees in your area, make a bee bottle (soapy water in a sprayer) part of your basic vehicle, tractor, and picnic pack. Mix 1 c. powdered or liquid detergent per 1 gal. water. Shake it up, and spray. A 2½-gal. Hudson sprayer is good for family-level defense. This has been tested, and it really works.

In this new era we must adapt to African bees as just another of the problems beekeepers have always routinely, and successfully, dealt with. Beekeepers, by definition, are not fearful persons!

Southern-Area Beekeepers. Winston predicts that the government will probably eventually be imposing a mandatory quarantine, so that colonies possibly infected with African- bee heredity do not travel out of the area. It would be a good idea to also do annual hive inspection for genetic infection, and annual requeening from a source of guaranteed pure honeybee line. All this means a higher level of training for old-time beekeepers. It also means that "hobby" beekeepers are going to have to be much more expert and involved with their bees than used to be necessary—or they'll have to give it up. Also, in these areas there needs to be a wider distribution of bee-sting kits and information about how to use them.

Northern Beekeepers. Some Canadian bee experts advise northern beekeepers that their self-defense against Africans is to stop importing queens and bees from southern areas, instead sticking to their own, or other safe northern, stock—or keeping queens alive over winter so the keepers won't need to buy new ones. This would be difficult to implement, though. The current practice is that, in addition to the mail-order queen-and-bee-package business from southern suppliers, every spring thousands and thousands of bee colonies are moved north for the pollination season.

All this spells not just risk but also opportunity. Basic agricultural economics suggests that the best time to go into a business is when others are leaving it. Agriculture *must* have bees. So there *must* be beekeepers, despite the newest hardship—the perpetual fight against African bees!

Getting Started

As with all livestock, it's vital that you have a suitable place for these critters to live.

SITING THE HIVES: Obey your local zoning regarding beekeeping. And place the bees in such a way that they don't bother your neighbors. Bees, like airplanes, take off and land in front of their hive. This is their flight path, and they guard it. So don't place the bees where their flight path will cross a place where your neighbors are likely to be—their garden, swimming pool, or sidewalk. Bees are also irritated by vibrating noises, so don't place them where somebody will be coming within 10 feet with a lawnmower or similar source of noise. (A.I. Root offers a free pamphlet about beekeeping in residential neighborhoods.) Place them where the early morning sun will reach their hive and stimulate them to get out and find nectar.

It doesn't matter if your own yard is very small or in the city; bees will fly for miles to find appropriate blossoms and will bring back the nectar. But it's not wise to crowd too many bee colonies into a small area. About 25 colonies per "bee yard" is the maximum if you live in the city. In the country, limit it to 60. You don't have to own the land your hives sit on, but you do need to have the permission of the person who does. Most farmers will be agreeable to letting you set your bees on their land in exchange for a share of your honey crop each year.

BEE/EQUIPMENT INSPECTION: State laws vary but it is against the law to sell used equipment for beekeeping in Florida, for example, without a certificate issued by the Florida Apiary Inspection Service. And every Florida beekeeper is required to register with the Florida Department of Agriculture. But some states don't have any inspection service at all and have fewer laws applying to beekeepers. For bee inspection or questions regarding it, contact your state's department of agriculture to get the name of your state apiary inspector, if there is one. He or she will help you contact a local inspector. An inspector is a good person to look over a colony of bees or any used equipment that you're thinking of buying. The bees can be examined for disease; the equipment can be tested for it. Contagious disease is such a huge problem for beekeepers these days. Some states (Washington and Ohio) have very good inspection services; some have none at all. You need to find out what the laws and services are in your particular state. Are the bees you buy going to be inspected where they come from, or after they arrive where you are, or at the border (California)? To sell bees, you want a certificate from an inspector guaranteeing their health. This service sometimes costs (Californians pay for mileage as well as an hourly rate for inspections) and is sometimes free (in Ohio, for example).

MOVING A HIVE: You could plug up the door of the hive with cloth or grass, but folded window screen stays put more reliably. Be sure to use something that's porous; if you plug it airtight, you'll smother the bees. If the plug comes out while you're moving the bees, you'll have a really, really big problem. Don't let this happen!

GETTING BEES: It's easiest to start small (with 1 or 2 hives) and expand gradually. You have to choose and order your bees and choose and order the hive you'll install them in. You can find bee producers from which to order in any popular bee magazine. Southern or California growers typically supply bees to northerners in the spring or sell "NUCS," which are colonies of about 1,000 bees that have queens that are already laying. Order package bees early, several months before you want them delivered. Orders are filled on a first-come, first-served basis, so if you order too late you may not get any bees at all. You want them delivered at your local fruit-tree blooming time. Package bees won't give you much of a crop the first year because of the low starting population. The alternative, buying a hive together with the bees in it from a neighboring beekeeper, is also best done in the early spring. In fact, I recommend that you start by buying hives from a nearby beekeeper. Then you'll get an already established hive in which everything is going right—one that has lots of workers ready to go and a fine producing queen. Buying from a neighboring beekeeper has another built-in advantage: neighborly advice if something doesn't seem to be going right.

Homemade Hives/Local Bees. Professional beekeepers used to make their own hives, but now they usually assemble them from pieces purchased from suppliers. If you start purchasing from a particular supplier, you may have to stick with him or her because components from one line often won't fit with those from another. So study and shop carefully before your first start-up. If you buy from a neighborly beekeeper, the bees will cost you from $25 to $50. You will have an already established hive in which everything is going right, one that has lots of workers ready to go and a producing queen. You'll probably get the bottom 2 boxes—your brood chambers—and would have to pay extra, around $8–$15 each, for supers. But in these disease-ridden times, you may prefer—or be required—to buy only inspected, certified disease-free bees and equipment.

Mail-Order Start-Up. You can get a good hive going by ordering bees from Montgomery Ward's catalog. But Kim says you're wiser to "order from a bee equipment supplier whom you can call and get help from. Ward's won't help you. A 3-lb. package of bees gives you 9,000–10,000 bees—not a bad start!" The hive comes disassembled, and you put it together yourself. Nothing to that. You don't have any finished comb to start with when buying mail-order; that's the drawback. But, given time, good conditions, and good care, mail-order bees will establish themselves and do fine.

Catch-a-Swarm Start. You can't get a hive going just by putting out a hive and hoping to get a swarm to move in. I've tried that too. If you're a beginner, catching a swarm is asking a lot of yourself—not that it's hard, but when you see a swarm of bees and everybody nearby in a panic over them, and you've never handled bees before, it often doesn't seem easy.

Starting Additional Hives. Once you have a start of bees, you can get all the other hives you want off your own bees. An old-time beekeeper would think it foolish to buy more when you could start your own. To start another hive, prepare a brood chamber around May 1. Now go into your best-established hive, the one with the most bees; it will be on the verge of swarming anyway.

Take 4 frames out of that well-established hive. Choose frames that have brood cells (which worker bees will hatch out of), some honey, and some bee bread (pollen), which means cells filled with a sort of yellowish grainy stuff. The frames will almost certainly have some workers crawling

1. Wear white-colored, smooth-surfaced clothing. The more white you wear, the better. White and smooth doesn't irritate bees as much as dark and rough-textured clothing. (Above all, don't arrive in a dark-colored, deep-pile coat, which would for sure set off your bees' instinctive bear alarm!)
2. Make sure *all* entrances to your body are safely closed off (bees crawl into dark crannies!).
3. If possible, work with your bees during sunny, warm weather near midday, when most are out of the hive harvesting from flowers.
4. Use a smoker to quiet the bees.
5. Raise a gentle breed and take all possible precautions against African bees.

around on them; if they don't, dump lots of worker bees in there, or scrape them off other frames. The frames will almost certainly have queen cells, too. There is usually at least 1 queen cell per frame if the bees are making queen cells at all. If need be, you can cut one out from a frame and stick it into a new frame. You can start a new hive with every queen cell.

Install the frames in the new hives. Put on the lid and stuff up the entrance loosely with grass to give the bees a chance to feel at home. Then go away and leave the bees alone. The workers will do the rest, including making a queen out of one of the eggs if you didn't give them a queen cell.

Protective Clothing

You can buy your outfit ready-made or make your own. I recommend the ready-made, which sounds out of character for me. But it's really important to have a good bee costume so you don't have to be nervous. That way you can just go in there and do what you have to do. The worst things that can happen when working with bees are for you to panic or for your nose to itch. A really safe bee costume on a hot day is hot inside. There's no escaping that. It helps to wear as little underneath as possible. I know a lady beekeeper who goes naked inside hers. It makes her less at risk for heatstroke, and she's not in danger of attack bending over a hive of bees from anything but a bee!

HOMEMADE BEEKEEPER'S COSTUME

Protecting Hands and Arms. Wear gloves. Kim advises: "You don't need very thick gloves. Some use rubber gloves. If too thick, you can't pick up frames or manipulate the hive tool." Gauntlets protect the area over your wrist and forearm. You can make a homemade gauntlet and sew it at the top of the work gloves. Make it long enough to reach high above your elbow, with elastic at the top to hold it firmly on. Use canvas that is thick and stiff and bags out well. The bagging out is your best protection. A favorite spot the bees sting is right at the top of your gauntlet, where the elastic presses them close to your arm. And they'll really try to sting your hands. Getting gloves of even the toughest leather isn't absolute protection. Sometimes they can sting through leather, too. The bees will crawl around on you and keep poking their sting down, trying to hit pay dirt.

Protecting Feet and Ankles. Wear work boots or cowboy boots. Both are absolutely beeproof, but work boots are better. Tie your pants tightly to the outside of the boots with a strip of inner-tube rubber or elastic so the bees can't crawl up your legs. Or use the top cut away from an old army combat boot—the canvas wraparound that straps tightly to hold your pant leg close against your boot. Bees crawl up.

They won't just sting you on your ankles if they get in; they'll go way up so fast it'll amaze you. This is the voice of experience talking. Don't assume they can't find the gap; that's really underestimating bees. Early in my beekeeping, I went out to the hives with my pant legs tied down, but I was wearing a winter coat rather than coveralls. I figured that would be good enough. Suddenly they found a way under that coat clear up under my shirt, and I ran all the way back to the house slapping bees. I had about 12 stings around my waist and above it on my back and chest.

Protecting Your Body. Wear white, 1-piece, baggy coveralls, complete with gloves, gauntlets, boots, and a firm fastening on your pant legs outside your high footwear to protect your body. If you make the 1-piece, zipper-in-front coverall out of rip-stop nylon, the stuff they make tents from, you'll avoid stings because bees can't get a foothold on it. It's far better than cotton in that regard because cotton has fibers the bees can get into with their feet. And if bees can get their feet dug in, then they can sting.

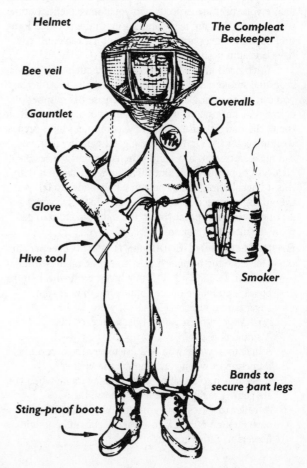

Helmet
Bee veil
Gauntlet
Glove
Hive tool
Sting-proof boots
The Compleat Beekeeper
Coveralls
Smoker
Bands to secure pant legs

Protecting Head and Neck. Use a tropical-type helmet (a construction hard hat) or a beeproof straw hat. Whatever type of hat you wear, it should have a firm, wide brim. You'll also need a bee veil, which you can mail-order. The bee veil top fits around the upper brim of your hat. The crown of the helmet fits up through the top hole of the bee veil. You tie it firmly around the crown with a drawstring. Now turn up your inside collar. Tuck your hair inside it. Draw the bottom drawstrings of the veil tight around the base of your collar. Make sure there isn't even a small hole. Then bring down the strings, cross them over, draw them around to your back, cross them there, and bring them on around to your front again, where you tie them firmly. Why? So that when you lean over, your bee helmet doesn't flop off, taking veil and all with it. Wearing all that in hot weather is bad enough.

Order in Which to Put It All On. 1. Coverall. 2. Boots. 3. Elastic to hold pant legs down. 4. Bee helmet and veil. 5. Gloves and gauntlets. (Dishwashing gloves work, too.)

STORE-BOUGHT BEEKEEPER'S COSTUME: These you buy from a beekeepers' supplier. Their bee gloves come equipped with gauntlets. You can buy a white coverall with helmet/bee veil that zips into place around the neck. It's worth the money if you can afford it. They come in all sizes and various styles.

Equipment

New, as opposed to used, bee housing and equipment is expensive, but it helps you understand what the ideal format is. The argument for starting with good stuff is that the lifetime of bee equipment is very long, easily 20 years and possibly 50. The hives should be purchased or built months before your bees are expected, so you'll have plenty of time to be certain they are ready and set up in the planned location before the bees arrive. You have a big problem if you have bees and no hive.

You'll need hive-working equipment such as your bee costume, smoker, and hive tool. Then each following year you can try to upgrade somehow: Increase the number of colonies or improve your efficiency. Or you can buy with an eye to the budget and not buy new equipment but purchase working colonies. Or, if you are a good woodworker, you can make your own hives and purchase package bees or NUCS to populate them. But there's much more to it than this. I haven't the space or personal knowledge to tell you everything you need to know. All I can do is give you a basic orientation and point you in the right direction to get more detailed information.

BASIC BEEKEEPING EQUIPMENT: Most beekeeper suppliers have a basic beginner's assortment along these lines.

1. One (or 2) standard 10-frame hives, each with bottom board, entrance reducer, foundation, frames, inner cover, and outer cover.
2. A package of bees, with a queen for each hive.
3. A smoker.
4. A hive tool, which you will use to pry the hive and frames apart when you examine the bees.
5. A bee brush to brush bees off a honey frame when you are getting ready to take it away from the hive.
6. A feeder to feed sugar syrup to your bees until they have enough numbers to gather nectar and enough flowers to gather it from.

BEE-GO-AWAY ITEMS: These all gently, diplomatically, make bees go away.

Smoker. The smoker has a burning chamber with an attached small bellows that you can pump. A. I. Root says that most beekeepers consider the smoker to be "their most important piece of equipment." The smoker is valuable because the presence of smoke triggers a bee instinct to drop everything else and fill up their honey stomach with honey. That keeps them peacefully busy, quiet, and not paying attention to you. Smoke also interrupts the communication of alarm signals between bees. But there is such a thing as too much smoke. Use only as much as you need.

Start your fire with a piece of crumbled paper, which you light and drop into the smoker's canister. Then add your solid fuel such as pine needles, dry grass, dry wood, wood chips, a piece of burlap bag (not one that has been treated with insecticide, which would kill your bees), corn cobs, or a piece of cotton rag. You want a fuel that will smoke rather than burn fast, so don't use fuels that create high heat in there, as charcoal or chemical fluids would. If you slowly pump the bellows, it will help your fuel get going well. Once your fire is burning, add the rest of your fuel and close the lid. Ideally the active fire will then stop, but your fuel will still be smoldering. Light the fire just before you're ready to go to work on the hives (after your bee costume, except gloves, is on). Even after your fire is started, give the bellows a little pump now and then to keep the fire from going out.

At the hive, stand to one side of the entrance (out of the flight path—bees instinctively react to obstruction of their flight path, especially the last few feet of it before the hive entrance)—and blow some smoke into the entrance. After a minute, take off the hive cover and blow more smoke through the hole in the center of the inner cover— if you use one (many beekeepers don't). Blow more smoke into the hive. Especially before you examine a bee-filled section, waft smoke over the tops of the frames. Then remove frames to look closely at them. Blow the smoke at the bees whenever they seem overly concerned with you rather than being about their own business.

Whenever you need to blow smoke at the bees, slowly pump the bellows. (Pumping too fast gets your smoker fire too hot and would pump out burning ash.) Experience teaches you how to best use your smoker to keep the bees under control.

Bee Brush. You can use the bee brush at honey-harvest time to brush any remaining bees off frames of harvested honeycomb that you want to take to your house. Brush them off gently near the hive entrance so they can easily find their way back home. At all times, avoid pinching or crushing bees when moving frames in and out. An injured bee releases an alarm odor that arouses other bees to sting.

Bee Escape. The bee escape is an inexpensive product that is used to eliminate bees from the honey-laden supers before you harvest them. It's a one-way exit that you can put in; then you come back in 24 hours and harvest your bee-free honey supers.

Bee Go. This trademarked product is sometimes used by beekeepers when they get ready to take the supers for extracting the honey. Directions for use come with the product. It's important not to get any of it on the honey or wax; that would ruin it.

If I were to say much more about your purchase options, I'd just be repeating what the catalogs will tell you.

PARTS OF A HIVE: The start-up structure before the bees arrive consists of the floor of the hive (bottom board); the sides of the first box; which are fastened together at the corners somehow; and the top cover. These parts are detachable from each other just by lifting them apart. Inside that box there are "frames." Most beehives are now made to hold 10 frames. There are ridges on the inside of the walls to set the wooden top bars of the frames on the hive box. The frames hang in there at an equal distance apart, all across the inside of the box. Each frame starts out holding a layer of beeswax "comb foundation" onto which the bees build full-scale comb for raising brood or storing honey. The whole thing needs to sit on a "hive stand," which is a platform.

Hive Stand. This platform is needed under your beehives if tall grass is interfering with the bees' flight patterns; it's also used to level the hive and keep out ants. If you can help it, don't put hives in the same pasture with horses or cows because sooner or later, one of the big animals will get rambunctious and knock over a hive. If this happens in cold weather and you don't notice right away, you'll have a hive of dead bees. They need the shelter their hive's enclosure provides. Skunks will take bees. They get outside a hive and scratch the front door. As the bees come out, the skunks eat them.

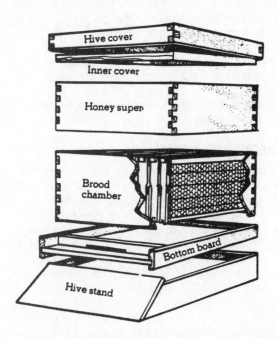

Brood Chamber. The bees live in the bottom box, which is usually called a "brood chamber." There the queen stays and lays eggs; most of the cells in there have baby bees in them rather than honey. The next layer up usually ends up being mostly brood cells, too, with maybe some honey around the sides and top. A layer is called a "super." Those 2 bottom boxes are what you get when you buy bees from a beekeeper, and you never want to break up that comb to try to get any honey. Just leave it alone.

Supers. The supers are (usually) shallower boxes that you set on top of these bottom 2 brood chambers. They are the ones that the bees store extra honey in. The bees work from the bottom up, and that's why you need more supers in a

good honey year and fewer in a bad one. Supers that you buy come in your choice of heights. The deeper ones aren't really desirable because if they do get full of honey, they are almost too heavy to carry. Each super or brood chamber holds 10 parallel frames, hung vertically so that they don't touch the bottom or sides of the box. Bees build beeswax cells on the frame to contain brood, honey, or pollen (bee bread).

Foundation. Beekeepers usually buy their comb foundation from a beekeepers' supplier. Foundation is a thin sheet of beeswax already pressed into the 6-sided shape of the bottom of a bee cell. All the bees need to do is build the sides and top (cap). When you put the foundation into the frames, you use wire to support it and add strength. Professional beekeepers have a choice of 2 special tools for heating the wires so they'll easily sink into the foundation. One sends a jolt of electricity through the wire that heats it.

You can make do with nylon fishing string (or even plain string if desperate). Put it through the hole and draw tight. If you don't use wire or string, the foundation will wilt in the summer heat and get out of place. If the foundation is not exactly where it's supposed to be, exactly the correct distance apart from the next layer of foundation, the result will be that you can't raise frames efficiently to look for the queen or queen cells because the frames will get stuck together by the bees where the frames are too close. If you put the foundation in right, the bees will build a neat sheet of cells along each side of the foundation and leave themselves an open-air walkway between each and every frame. That makes it easy for you to pull out an individual frame and look it over. If all goes well, at the end of summer, the frame will be covered with brood cells by the bees in the brood chamber or built into comb in the supers and filled with honey.

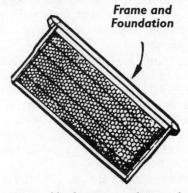

Frame and Foundation

Experienced beekeepers may harvest the wax comb, which can be sold profitably in addition to the honey, or they may return it to the bees for refilling with honey. Beginning beekeepers sometimes don't realize that they can't have honey until they have honeycomb. Every day the bees spend making the honeycomb is a day they can't be gathering and making honey. But Kim says that since bees can make comb even faster than honey comes in, there's no delay problem.

If beekeepers choose to reuse the comb, they just slice the end off the chambers and make the honey pour out of the inside by centrifugal force in an extractor. Then they give the comb back to the bees for them to refill.

Homemade Foundation. The old-timers used to make their own. In those days the Root Company made rollers for rolling the wax into foundation. Now you can't buy the rollers anywhere that I know of, unless you can find one as an antique. You can buy the foundation only from various supply companies. The old-time rollers were made of hardwood maple and were carved by hand. The roller has to be carved or built with a hexagonal impression pattern in it; otherwise the bees won't build it into comb. The way the old-timers made the sheets of wax for rolling was by taking an 8- or 10-inch board, dipping it into hot beeswax once or twice, and then letting it cool. When the wax was firm, they slit it on the side and peeled it off. They rolled that with their patterned roller, and that was their foundation. Kim Flottum says it worked okay but was expensive—lots of wax wasted—and slow.

Plastic Comb. This is a 1-piece, frame-foundation, completely drawn plastic honeycomb. Kim wrote, "Plastic foundation is like wax foundation—embossed with the 6-sided cell but made of plastic and coated with wax. The bees draw the cells from the plastic base, fill them with honey, and then cap them with wax. You take these in and out like the regular frame and foundation. They can go into an extractor."

Working with Your Bees

I know this is inadequate. There's really no substitute for going to the hives with an experienced beekeeper—no matter how well written or illustrated your manual.

WHEN YOU LOOK AT A FRAME: The cells that are capped dark-brown are brood cells. Those are the ones the bees hatch from. The ones that are capped light-colored contain honey. The cells will be in sections of either one or the other. Queen cells are very easy to find, about an inch long, kind of hanging away from the rest of the comb. They look like a peanut shell. Drone cells stick out too but not nearly as much as queen cells. Drone cells stick out like little lumps with bullet-shaped tops. The worker cells are just exactly level with the rest of the comb. In short: the queen cells are the biggest, the drone cells are next in size, and worker cells are the smallest.

The Queen Bee. Before you start moving stuff around, find the queen in the hive—so you'll be sure not to hurt her and you can have her end up where you want her. To do this, pull out frames and look them over carefully one by one until you locate her. She doesn't look like any other bee at all. She's about an inch long and tapers clear from her front to her tail. The other bees will be somewhat spread out away from her. They don't crowd her.

A queen bee might sting you if you grab her, but usually the only stinging she does during her life is directed toward other queen bees. When the first new queen hatches out, she'll go around and sting the others to death right in their cells. There can be only 1 queen in a hive. The drones haven't even got a sting. Only the workers sting you. The drones are big, fat bees with very large eyes. Their only function is to compete with one another on the queen's mating flight and earn the privilege of fathering the new hive offspring. A queen bee is a marvelous creature that can live 7 or 8 years—a long time for an insect! They are really good for only about 3 years, though, and that's why beekeepers talk about "replacing" the queen. Your honey crop depends in part on the vigor of your queen. It takes 21 days for workers to hatch, 16 days for a queen to hatch, and 24 days for a drone to hatch. The more eggs the queen lays, the more workers there are to make honey. But it also depends on the weather.

Queen Excluders. Excluders are made of a wire grid that allows a worker through but is too small for a queen. Kim wrote, "An excluder is used to keep the queen from moving into honey supers and laying eggs. You do not want brood in your honey supers. Excluders should be used for cleanliness and sanitary honey production." He also told me that excluders can't be used to separate queens because queens can and will sting each other through an excluder.

GOING INTO THE HIVE: This means to open up the hive and carefully remove and look over every single frame to find the queen, look for queen cells (but only in the spring), and generally assess how many bees there are, how many and what type of brood cells, how much honey is coming, and whether the bee colony needs more supers. You want to give them plenty of supers if they need them because overcrowding leads to swarming. (Sometimes they swarm anyway.) If you're very lucky, you may need 5 or 6 supers by summer's end—but more likely you'll need fewer. It will depend on the hive. Each hive has its own history each summer; there are seldom any 2 just alike.

Get into your bee costume and get your smoker going. Take either a hive tool or a screwdriver. (Kim: ". . . only if nothing else is available. They really wreck a frame.") Use it to pry apart the lid from the hive and supers from brood chambers. The nearer you get to the bottom, the harder it will be to get things apart as the comb gets bigger and firmer. You can set the supers on the grass while you are working in the brood chamber. Kim: "Set your cover (top down) down first, and set supers on this. That way if you miss the queen and she falls off, she won't get lost."

To put a super back on the brood chamber, do it so as to kill no more bees than necessary. Start it at one end and slide the super slowly onto the brood chamber so that you slowly shove the bees that are on the edge off the sides. They'll find their way around to the door again.

Water and Food

WATER: The bees should have a nearby source of water. In an urban setting, be sure and provide their water so they don't habituate a neighbor's swimming pool. The water supply should be fresh and running. Stagnant water has been named as a factor in bee disease. Bees bring water in to evaporate and cool their hive in hot weather and to dilute honey for feeding brood. If you don't have a nearby creek, let an outside faucet drip down onto a board set slantwise. If you have a heavily populated hive, the weather is hot, and you see bees clustering outside the hive entrance, they have a heat problem inside beyond what their water-carrying can handle. In southern states, hives are typically placed where they will have shade during the worst heat of the day. Or you could put the hive under slatted lath. Or make the hive entrance larger, or stagger the top supers to create a half-inch ventilation space.

BEE FOOD: Shakespeare said, "Where the bee sucks, there suck I." To me that means honeysuckle. It's a wild vine with pretty trumpet-shaped orange flowers. It grows up the trunks of trees and flowers among their branches. The children love honeysuckle time. To get the nectar, you pick some of the pretty, long, orange flowers when they are fully developed. Pick them with the tiny green bulb on their base intact. Then nip off that green bulb with your fingernail. Put your mouth to the opening you made at the base of the flower and suck. You will get a tiny taste of nectar. Some honeysuckle flowers have more of it and some less. Nectar is bee food, too. It's the only food they can eat. How much honey your hives yield for harvest is basically a result of how much and what quality of flowering plants were available. But bees are very good at finding, collecting, and storing it!

Bees gather flower nectar and carry it back to their hive, where they change it to honey. They like herb flowers—such as basil, bergamot, borage, catnip, fennel, hyssop, lavender, lemon balm, marigold, marjoram, oregano, rosemary, sage, savory, and thyme. They like almost any fruit blossoms. An orchard is a good place for your hives in the spring—*as long as it doesn't get sprayed with pesticide.* In southern California, where bee pasture is available nearly year-round, bees can make honey from flowers on the eucalyptus trees or from citrus and other trees that are in flower in winter, like the lemon.

Flower Flavors. Whatever type of flower your bees are gathering nectar from, that's the flavor the honey will have. Buckwheat honey is very dark in color and heavy in flavor. Clover and alfalfa blooms make a light-colored honey of delicate flavor. But if your bees get their honey from wildflowers, carob trees, and oxalis, it's likely to be rich, dark honey that the USDA would grade "Number 4"—meaning not fit for human use. Which is simply ridiculous. But commercial standards favor the sort of honey you get from a big sweet clover or alfalfa field, which is pale. "Number 4" is edible, and some people get along fine with weird-tasting honey. Food and gardening writer Lane Morgan says, "I have heard that people with allergies can use honey from the allergen-making plant to lessen their sensitivity. It's sort of a homeopathic treatment." But she also told me about "cabbage flower honey—which really is pretty much inedible."

Insecticides. Don't use pesticides yourself. Ask your neighbors not to use them. Even a shot of spray here and there on plants or gardens will kill a few bees. When entire fields and orchards are sprayed or dusted, the resulting loss to a bee colony can be devastating. The beekeeper sees a large accumulation of dead and dying bees at the hive entrances. If spraying is to occur in your area, you need to know about it in advance. If possible, work with the farmer and the pesticide applicator so their efforts will safeguard these valuable pollinating insects. Your risk from spraying comes not only from blossoms on cultivated crops but also orchards, orchard ground covers, and sometimes uncultivated areas such as roadsides.

Ask that insecticides not be applied to open blossoms. Be sure the sprayer knows that the safest time to apply insecticides is late afternoon, after bees stop foraging. (Early-morning applications are less dangerous to bees than those in midday.) Finally, persuade the sprayer to select an insecticide that has the least impact on nontargeted insects and animals.

If you're not successful getting these assurances but you can get a few days' warning of a spraying that you know will harm the bees, move the hives at least 2 miles from the spray area. If notice is short and the spray plane is coming right over your hives, drape them with damp burlap. That protects against a direct hit. Then you'll have to remove it and accept some loss of bees. But if a bee colony is repeatedly exposed to pesticide, there will be fewer and fewer living bees until at last the remaining ones can't survive.

If your bees are suffering due to pesticides or herbicides, tell your beekeepers' association, the state extension agent, the person or business that did it, and the spray inspector if it's a conspicuous wipeout. Kim Flottum wrote that no insurance compensation is available for this. "Don't even try. If you are able to prove neglect, however, you can sue the applicator."

Herbicides. These aren't good for bees either because they tend to kill flowering plants. Public spraying of herbicides around road edges and shorelines to fit some artificial notion of which plants are okay and which are not unnecessarily kills flowering plants that could support bees.

Weather and Climate. Bees gather what they find. They can work only when flowers are in bloom. So they have more chance to gather honey in climates where flowers blossom during more months. In northern climates the heaviest honey flow is usually in June. But a summer so dry the flowers can't grow or don't bloom well is a bad one for bees. I've seen dry summers when the flowers didn't bloom until the fall rains came, and the bees made hardly any surplus honey at all. Southern bee growers have a longer flower season and so tend to get larger honey harvests. In southern California it's not unusual to take as much as 100 lb. of honey from one 10-inch super twice a year. In an exceptional summer or in an exceptional climate (like Hawaii), each of your hives might yield 200 or even 400 lb.! An extra-cold, long winter shortens their harvest season and lengthens the time they must live on stored, or owner-supplied, food.

Winter Food. To get your bees through, a colony needs a young queen, a large cluster of adult bees, 50–100 lb. of honey, and a few combs of pollen. They should be in a 2-story standard hive with 1 brood chamber and 1 honey super (the removable top section where the bees store honey). Starvation—not cold—is the biggest risk for your bees! Bees don't hibernate during the winter. They are very much awake inside the hive, clustered in a ball in which they generate heat for each other. But they have to eat all winter long to have the energy to make that warmth, or they'll die. If they get low on honey, you'll have to provide supplementary sugar. Feed them a syrup of 2 parts granulated sugar to 1 part water. You can buy a substitute for pollen from a bee-supply dealer. Feed them that after the honey harvest in the fall, before winter sets in.

As long as there are blossoms, the bees will make honey. Around here they are done with most of their honey-making by the end of August, when everything dries up. That's the time to get the honey. We use 2 brood chambers and 2 supers, taking 1 super for our use and leaving the bottom honey super for the bees to winter on. You have to estimate how much honey they need to winter on—different parts of the country have a longer or shorter cold season—and take only what's surplus beyond that. If the bees don't have enough honey over the winter, they will die of starvation. You'll go out in the spring to look at them and just find a bunch of dried-up little bodies.

So check them in cold weather, too. You won't even need your bee suit. They'll be huddled in the brood chamber trying to keep alive by buzzing to make warmth.

Sugar Feeding. If they seem short of food, dump in a bunch of white sugar. Never, never feed them brown sugar. Dump sugar on an inner cover (not directly into the hive), between the frames, or onto the outside. They'll survive on it. A dear friend of mine who is an experienced beekeeper told me, "Big honey producers nowadays feed their bees thousands of pounds of sugar every winter to carry them through and also through dry seasons. If you aren't feeding your bees sugar, it takes them a lot longer to accomplish anything." So even under bad flowering conditions, a beekeeper can feed sugar to the bees and have a good honey crop. But honey from sugar-fed bees can be only for home use. If you sell honey made from sugar, you are breaking the law! Commercial beekeepers may feed sugar to build up their bee population to take advantage of the coming nectar flow but *not* to make honey for sale.

I've been working on this book for over 20 years, and I'm making some major additions or changes now for the eighth time. I tell other authors that I meet, people with a string of fine titles to their credit, "All my life I've written one book." That's generally good for a shared laugh, but there's a bittersweet private sadness to the fact for me. I have indeed come back to this book again and again, trying to make it more thorough and more accurate, and it makes me happy to see it improve. On the other hand, I have written, or tried to write, other books. None of those others have ever yet made it into print. Maybe some day. I've tried so hard. I read that a writer needs to write the first million words just for practice. Well, I've accomplished that. In fact, I think I'm somewhere in the second million. The breakthrough should be coming any day now! There's something else I want so much to say.

DEALING WITH SWARMING: This is common in the first half of June here in Idaho, earlier in the south—as early as March! There can be only 1 queen in the hive. If extras hatch out, many of your bees will fly off with the young queen to make a home and a new hive wherever they can; what's left of your hive won't give you much of a crop. If you don't want to start new hives, pinch out all the queen cells to prevent swarming. The more workers populate your hive, the more honey they will bring home. If you go into a hive and find queen cells but no queen, it probably means the old queen swarmed.

Then you'll hear from the neighbors. Sometimes bees move into house walls. They can get between the outside walls or between upper and lower floors. If they do that, don't poison them. Kim Flottum wrote: "You can trap them out using a funnel-shaped screen. The bees can leave a space between walls, etc., but can't return. An empty colony is placed outside and the bees move in. Eventually the old nest is empty, and you can then fill in the entrance solid so it can't happen again."

There's really no way to determine who owns the bees after they've left the hive, but once you've acquired a reputation as a beekeeper, the phone is sure to ring around swarming time. There'll be a hysterical voice on the other end yelling something like, "Your bees have swarmed to a bush in my yard, and nobody dares leave the house." You can tell the caller that swarming bees don't sting. It's almost always true. (If you see a photo of somebody whose face is covered with bees, they're probably swarming bees.) In fact, putting the word out to extension agents, police and fire departments, beekeepers, and anybody else in your area who might receive a "swarm!" call is a good way to build up your bee population on the cheap.

When swarming bees cluster, they all just hang there—solid bees, a little over a foot long, with lots of extras flying around outside. Well, if they swarm onto a branch, they are easy to get, all clustered up like that. You can even do it without your protective gloves on. Just cut off the branch with the bees on it. Hold it over a brood chamber or even an empty cardboard box, anything that will hold all the bees and can be closed up after they're in. Then shake or lightly brush the bees off the branch into the brood chamber. You can do it with a brush or a leafy limb. You can set the hive on a stepladder if it's a higher branch. Bee professionals carry around an extra brood chamber in the pickup just in case they see a swarm they can catch.

At least, that's how it's supposed to work. But bees are very independent. I remember once a swarm was clustered on a branch only a few feet off the ground. The beekeeper set up a hive that was left open on top right underneath the swarm, even put some honey in it. He gently brushed the swarm with a limb into the hive. Then he went away for the night. The next morning all the bees had taken off for who knows where. (If they had been in the hive, he would have put the lid on, blocked the entrance, and taken them home.)

On the other hand, I know a case where the swarming cluster was on a limb 40 feet high. The property owner was pretty insistent about getting rid of them, though, so the beekeeper—mostly to oblige her—left a hive sitting underneath the limb and, by throwing a rope with a weight on the end over the branch, managed to shake a few off and get them scattered on the ground below. Then he went home, fully expecting the problem to have flown far away by the next day. But he got a phone call early in the morning to tell him that—Lo and behold!—the swarm of bees had moved into his hive.

Bee Diseases, Parasites, and Pests

Like any other form of farm livestock, your bees can have these problems. You need to stay in touch with other local beekeepers to know what is currently going around, what the symptoms are, and what the prevention or treatment is. Most states have an "apiary inspector." They're listed in "Who's Who in Apiculture" and they, or a local inspector, can help if you suspect disease. And there is probably an expert in your beekeepers' group. That person can tell you whether your problem is one that legally must be reported and what treatment is advised or legally required.

BASIC BEE HYGIENE: *Don't introduce disease into your hives!*

1. Don't buy honey for feed from an unknown source because honey may carry American foulbrood disease.
2. Buy bees and queens only from reputable dealers.
3. Buy used bee equipment only after consulting with your apiary inspector.
4. It helps avoid disease if the bees draw new combs from foundations every 2–4 years for the brood chamber.
5. Learn to identify and treat diseases, parasites, and pests by taking a course or working with an experienced beekeeper, so you'll be able to detect a problem quickly and take appropriate steps.
6. Be alert for those signs of disease each time you open a beehive.

BROOD DISEASES: "Brood" means the eggs and larvae of the colony. The "brood nest" is made up of all the combs that have eggs and larvae in them. "Brood diseases" thus are ones that strike the immature bees inside their cells. U.S. beekeepers currently have to be on the lookout for American foulbrood, European foulbrood, and chalk brood. A healthy brood nest has few unsealed brood cells. The cell caps are slightly convex. Their color is a uniform pale brown. Normal larvae are plump, a lovely mother-of-pearl color, and have no odor.

Chilled Brood. This is the most common reason for a dead brood. It happens in early spring, if the population is rapidly expanding and then there is a period of very low temperature. The problem isn't disease in this case. It's that there is more brood than there are bees to keep them warm. The bees do their best, but the outer edges of the brood are just too far from the heated area, and they get too cold and die. This is different from an actual disease problem in that you will find dead brood in *all* stages, both very small and very large. With disease, the dead are all at one particular growth stage.

Chalkbrood. A fungus is the problem here. The cell caps will look either light or dark, and some will be punctured. The dead larvae in sealed cells are first white, then grayish black, hard, and chalklike. You should cut away and burn infected combs. Other than that, there is no treatment except that it helps to move the hives to an area with better air circulation, and the disease will then run its course and subside.

American Foulbrood. This is the worst of the brood diseases. A bacterium, *Bacillus larvae,* causes larvae to rot in their cells. Foulbrood can be contracted by your bees if they invade an infected colony of wild bees in some nearby old building or tree.

The cell caps look off-colored, sunken instead of convex, and punctured. There are dark scabs at the base of the cells. The larvae look brown, slimy, and dead. If you stick a straw or match into a cell and draw it out, you'll get only stringy substance. There is a gluey, rotten-egg smell. *American foulbrood must be reported to the state bee inspector.* Treatment must be as mandated by the state.

Last I heard, foulbrood is prevented with a medicine the bees eat twice—once in the fall, after you take out the honey, and again in the spring. It is a Terramycin powder that you sprinkle on the outside edges of the frame tops. In the fall, after you take out the honey, you sprinkle 2 T. of the stuff on each brood chamber; then do it again in spring. (But read the label in case it says something different.)

European Foulbrood. When you examine the brood nest, you'll see discolored cell caps, sunken and punctured as you would find with American foulbrood. The larvae also look brown or dark brown and something from doughy to slimy. Odor is sour rather than gluey. But the real big difference can be determined by the straw test. In this case—and with sacbrood—the straw does *not* pull up stringy filaments. There is no treatment for European foulbrood. The disease will run its course during that brood season.

Sacbrood. This is a rare brood disease caused by a virus. Cell caps look dark, sunken, and punctured. Larvae turn gray to black, die head up, a mix of watery and granular in consistency. No filament from straw test.

Stonebrood. This very rare problem results from a fungus that causes cells to look greenish and mildewy. Larvae cling to cell edges and look greenish-yellow, hard, and shriveled.

There is a musty odor. The bees can treat this disease themselves by chewing off and throwing out the diseased cells, and they will defeat it.

ADULT BEE DISEASES: For adult bees, Nosema disease is one of the most serious. Two parasitic mites, *Acarapis woodi* and *Varroa jacobsoni,* cause the most serious bee ailments.

Acarine Disease. *Acarapis woodi* bores into the air passages of bees that are 1–8 days old and sucks their blood. The bees are unable to get enough air and can't fly; they just hop in front of their colony home. The best treatment is to keep your bees out-reproducing the parasites; that works really well in the South but not so well in the North. For northern beekeepers there is a Terramycin treatment. A few years ago this disease was uncommon. It's very common now and is still deadly.

Nosema Disease. Most bees carry a single-celled parasite called *Nosema apis* in their intestinal tract. If bees get run down from lack of pollen (their protein source), the nosema can increase to the point of killing their hosts. Affected bees have swollen abdomens and crawl about with trembling wings outside the hive. Nosema disease is most likely to strike in the spring, when pollen supplies are running out. Prevention is easy: Make sure your bees have sufficient pollen, and use a preventive medicine called Fumidil-D.

Varroatosis. *Varroa jacobsoni* is an immigrant mite from India, where it coexists with some kinds of bees without seriously damaging them. For European bees, however, it is deadly and will kill untreated colonies in a single season. It is visible to the naked eye. The mites are light brown, oval, and measure 1×2 mm. (Males are round and 0.8 mm in diameter.) There is a 6-legged bee louse that is harmless. Varroa has 8 legs. Varroa mites seek drone cells for a critical stage of their life cycle. Kim Flottum wrote: "Treat with the plastic, pesticide-treated strips. If you don't treat, your colony will die. Count on it!"

OTHER PESTS

Birds. They do eat bees, but only sick or dead ones—unless they catch a young queen on her mating flight.

Mice. These can be a fall and winter problem. The prevention is to narrow the entrances in the fall to just ¼ inch wide.

Wasps. These predators kill honeybees and can enter and rob a small or weak colony. A bigger problem is when fall hunger hits and wasps try to get into the hive because, like bees, they too love honey. A strong hive will defend itself successfully. But you can help the bees by blocking off part of the entrance at summer's end so wasps can enter only one at a time. They're easier for the bees to kill that way.

Waxmoths. These offenders lay eggs on combs, inside the hive. The larvae (caterpillars) that hatch out eat the material in the comb left by the bees, and they burrow through the comb while doing it. They will wreck combs. You can be sure the problem is waxmoth if you see fine gray webs lining paths eaten into the comb. If you have a strong, well-populated colony, the bees cope by murdering each hatching waxmoth larva. Store unused combs where light and air circulation are good to keep these pests to a minimum.

Bears. Kim Carlson, one of the editors who worked on this book, asks, "What about bears? My father stopped beekeeping after bears ruined the hives for the second time. Maybe there's not much you can do to stop them (short of installing electric wire). This was in the Bitterroot Valley of western Montana, though—probably not much of a problem for most readers."

HARVESTING THE HONEY

Beekeepers usually have 1 big annual extraction. This involves taking the honey-filled supers from the hives and removing the frames. Slice the tops off the wax chambers in the comb of those frames. Then, using an extractor, force the honey from the insides of those storage chambers by centrifugal force—or cut and package the comb directly for comb honey. Extracted honey must then be strained—and bottled and marketed if you plan to sell it. If you've already made the acquaintance of a commercial operator, she or he may be willing to extract and strain your honey for you for a reasonable fee. Then either return the emptied comb in its frame back to the bees, or give the bees fresh foundation on the frame on which to build new comb.

When to Harvest?

Harvesting takes place in the fall when the crop is taken off and packed. All those pounds of honey have to be removed from the hives. That means carried away in the supers in which they've been stored by the industrious bees. Professionals wait to harvest until the major nectar flow is over. That's when the flowers are mostly gone—about August. You can begin as early as late June or as late as mid-September. But too late a harvest risks leaving the bees with too little honey since they have less time to replenish their stores.

How Much Honey to Take?

An average-sized family can use about 5 gal. of honey a year. Our large one uses about 10. To harvest that amount of honey, a family needs 2 or 3 hives. But don't take that much (or any at all) unless you can leave the bees with enough honey—60–100 lb. per colony, depending on how long and cold your winters are—to survive until the next flowering season. *Bees can gather food only when there are flowers. The rest of the time they must live on their stored food.*

COMB HONEY: You can eat your harvest right out of the frame, in the comb, just as the bees made it. The wax is fine to eat—not really food for humans, but not harmful to eat. You can spread comb honey like any thick spread. Eating comb honey avoids the expense and struggle of the extraction process. All you need to eat your harvest comb honey is a sharp knife to cut blocks of it out of the frame. If you want to learn more about producing this gourmet market item, read Richard Taylor's *The New Comb Honey Book* (1982). To preserve honey in the comb, save your nicest combs with the caps on, stand them edgewise in a crock or metal can, and cover with extracted honey. For commercial sale of comb honey, beekeepers used to put little wooden square boxes into the hive instead of regular frames. The boxes for comb honey were made out of basswood because it bent easily. But that sort of comb honey is seldom sold any more.

UNCAPPING THE COMB: The beekeeper's equipment probably consists of an electric knife to uncap one side of the frames, or else a hollow knife with steam run through it so the knife is hot. Either one slices the caps off the honey cells very nicely and easily. You can mail-order an electric knife from your beekeepers' supplier that is perfect for that uncapping. Keep the frames in a warm room before extracting so the honey will flow out easier when the centrifugal force is applied.

Processing Caps. I watched an expert beekeeper do this. He had a special vat for the slicings to fall into. They are valuable as beeswax as well as for the bit of honey still clinging. Heated coils help separate the slicings in the vat from the honey sticking to it. A little stream of melted wax comes out one side and the honey comes out the other. That is the only wax a professional beekeeper harvests— just the caps. He keeps the rest for the bees to use again.

MACHINE EXTRACTING: Then the beekeeper put the entire uncapped frame into the extractor. The commercial extractor is a big round drum that will hold 30–140 frames at once. (I've also seen a small manual style that holds just 3.) The uncapped frames are set into holders inside the extractor, their uncapped side facing the outside of the extractor. Then the extractor is made to whirl them around very fast, which causes the honey to flow out by centrifugal force (the force flings it against the wall of the drum). It flows down the wall and is collected at the bottom, being piped directly to a big holding tank. Smaller versions of an extractor can be bought through the Root Catalog, among others, but you don't have to have one.

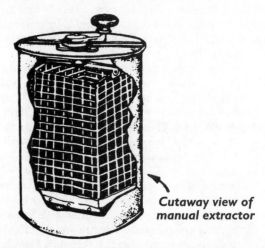

Cutaway view of manual extractor

HAND EXTRACTING: I have heard of squeezing honey out from the wax by hand, but that is an awful waste of drawn comb. A better system is to cut off the tops of the honey cells, and hang the frames up over a heat source like a wood stove. The honey will melt and drip down. Have something under there to catch it, of course. You have to do one side of the frame, and then the other. Or make a Rube Goldberg contraption with an electric drill top and a "barrel" bottom that will grip and spin your uncapped frame.

If you need the wax for candle-making anyway, the easiest method of all to get honey without an extractor is to melt the whole thing down together. Just make sure you use frames that are clean and don't have baby bees in them— they'll mess up the taste of the honey. You need frames that are solid honey. Leave the frames with some baby bees in them to feed the bees in winter. Cut the honey, comb and all, into chunks in a great big stainless steel fry pan. Melt it. Skim the whitish wax off the top and strain it into a separate pan. Strain the rest of the honey through a cloth set over a deep pan. Pour that strained honey into quart jars. You can let the honey with all the wax in it cool until the wax rises to the top. Then you can easily take it off. The honey that was with the wax can be reheated and poured into another jar. It's all that simple.

NOTE: Don't heat honey in an iron kettle. That will cause it to darken.

WAX IN THE HONEY: If the honey looks messy, heat and strain it. It wouldn't hurt you a bit to eat wax, but there are better things to do with it. Melt the honey-wax mixture in a double boiler over gentle heat. Take off the scum with a skimmer as it appears. You can sell the wax, make new foundation with it, or make candles. Pour your now wax-free honey into widemouthed jars and seal.

CLEANING BEESWAX FOR CANDLES: Beekeepers sell unfiltered wax for $1–2/lb. You can get it by the 10-lb. chunk. Or prepare your own. To make candles out of beeswax that has come fresh from the hives, a good way to do the first step of cleaning is to place it in a box on top of a beehive. The bees will promptly come and within a day they'll have every last speck of honey cleaned off it and carried back into the hive. But don't leave it there after the bees have it cleaned off because then wild animals will carry it off. Take it back in the house and finish cleaning it by melting and straining the wax. The very best filter for beeswax is sweatshirt material. Cheesecloth is much too porous. In factories they force it through canvas under great pressure, but sweatshirt material is better. Wrap the filter around the beeswax; as the melted wax drips down, the impurities are left behind. Beeswax melts at 130°F. A very gentle heating can be accomplished in a solar wax melter.

Here's another system to clean and lighten your wax if it's dark and dirty looking: Add a little cider vinegar to the wax and some water and hold it at 135–140°F for 2 or 3 days, if possible. The dirt settles to the bottom, and the honey collects in a layer just below the wax, which floats on top.

Storing Honey

Honey keeps easily—better than just about anything else. It doesn't need to be frozen, canned, or even refrigerated. It keeps just fine in glass, plastic, pottery, or metal, inside or outside. Don't refrigerate honey because that hastens the granulation process, and, unlike many other foods, it doesn't need to be kept cool. But store where it won't get warmer than 75°F since above that temperature it may lose flavor and color (the higher above 75°F, the faster the change).

A wide-topped container that you can scoop out of is handier than a 5-gal. can with a 2-inch opening. If the contents of a narrow-necked container crystallize, you have to melt the whole supply every time you need a quart—and each time you heat it up you may lose nutrition and flavor. Honey that isn't frozen will crystallize, eventually. And a 5-gal. can of honey weighs 60 lb. and thus is too heavy to accomplish much with easily. Best of all, pack your honey in widemouthed 1-gal. jars. Then keep a quart container of honey in your kitchen for current use. And keep your kitchen honey in a fairly warm place. Chilly, stiff honey won't mix with other ingredients very easily.

CRYSTALLIZED ("GRANULATED") HONEY: Any liquid honey may crystallize into a stiff, whitish texture if stored in a cool place. Sometimes this happens after only a week or so, sometimes after several months. This process is called "granulating" and is normal. It doesn't harm your honey a bit. It doesn't change it at all, once you've remelted it. Or you can use crystallized honey as is. It won't affect your recipe, except in that you've added a bit less liquid.

Re-Liquefying Crystallized Honey. When my honey in the can gets sugary on top, I just put the can on the back of the wood stove or on very low heat on the electric stove, and the sugars will go back into solution as fast as it warms; 130°F (water no hotter than you can bear your hand in) is a perfect temperature for the job. You can warm a quart jar of honey in a double boiler. Honey in a glass container can be reliquefied in a microwave oven. (Remove the cover first! Then cook on high 30 seconds or until clear.) No matter what your method is, be careful not to overheat. *Don't boil the honey because that ruins the delicate flavor.* Just keep it at about 130°F until it reliquefies—it may take hours, or days, depending on how much honey you're working with.

Storing it in a warmer place will help avoid a repeat. Unlike most food storage, storing honey at a warm temperature, in a closed bottle, does not result in any loss of flavor.

OTHER BEE PRODUCTS: Pollen, propolis, beeswax, and royal jelly can also be sold. Propolis is the resinous substance bees use to fill holes and gaps in the hive. It takes a lot of work to produce royal jelly, and there isn't much market for it. Beeswax sells well, but you need many hives to produce much.

Using Honey

NOTE: Don't feed your baby honey. Botulism spores can be in it. These don't harm adults when directly eaten, but in the intestines of infants under 1 year of age—especially under 6 months of age—they can grow. This was discovered in 1976 and is now thought to account for at least some cases of Sudden Infant Death Syndrome. Keep these small babies out of soil (where botulism spores are) in general.

HONEY AT THE TABLE: Get 2 small syrup pitchers. Fill one with honey and one with molasses or sorghum. If you grow it, or can afford it, you could keep a third with real maple syrup in it. Keep the honey pitcher in a warm spot in your kitchen—over the pilot light or on the warming shelf of your wood stove. Serve both pitchers whenever needed at your meals. Honey complements the taste of any herb tea just perfectly, helping to bring out the flavor. Basically, you can use honey anywhere you can use sugar: to sweeten any beverage (tea, coffee, warm milk), stirred into plain yogurt, dribbled onto cold or warm cereal, mixed with margarine or butter, or blended with any nut butter to make a spread.

COOKING WITH HONEY: Honey has been around longer than refined sugar. Honey is composed of simple sugars, mainly fructose and glucose. Plain white sugar adds sweetness to a recipe, but honey adds flavor as well as sweetness. The sweet taste of honey tends to be more concentrated than that of sugar, so you can substitute ⅔–¾ c. honey for any 1 c. sugar and end up with it equally sweet-tasting. You can substitute honey for sugar in any recipe, but because honey is a liquid you then decrease the liquid in the recipe by 2–3 T. per ¾ c. honey, or by ¼ c. per 1 c. honey. Honey is easiest to measure if your measuring container has first held the oil or other fat for the recipe, or if you first coat the spoon or cup with oil (or with nonstick pan-coating spray). Then the honey won't stick in the measuring container and you'll be able to get it all back out easily. Combine honey with other liquids in the recipe.

PRESERVING WITH HONEY

Freezing Fruit with Honey. Don't make a heavy syrup. Use 1 c. honey to 2 c. water. That will give you what the recipes call a "medium" syrup. For a "thin" or "light" syrup, use 1 c. honey with 3 c. water. Then allow ¾–1 c. syrup per 1-qt. freezer container. Measure your syrup into the container. Slice fruit directly into it and freeze. You won't need any ascorbic acid when you freeze fruit in honey syrup. The syrup itself will prevent the fruit from changing color. Add a crumpled piece of freezer paper to keep the fruit forced down under the syrup. Peaches and strawberries are especially good this way.

❧ *HONEY FRUIT JAM   To make Doris's gooseberry jam combine 3 c. green gooseberries and 2 c. clover honey. Cook slowly until mixture jellies on a cold dish. Put in jars and seal. This is simple and very good, and you can apply the same principle to other fruits.*

❧ *UNCOOKED BERRY-HONEY JAM   Mash fresh berries (raspberries or strawberries are very good in this). Put the mashed berries in a blender with a package of pectin and blend. Taste. Now add as much honey as you think it needs to be sweet enough, and blend again. You can make only a little bit of this at a time because blenders don't hold much. Store it in the refrigerator.*

❧ *LEMON-HONEY JELLY   From Nanci Falley, Lockhart, TX: Combine ¾ c. lemon juice and 2½ c. honey. Bring to a full rolling boil. Add ½ c. liquid fruit pectin, stir vigorously, and boil about 2 minutes. Pour into hot sterilized jars and seal.*

Canning with Honey. Honey can be used as the sweetening agent in canning, jelly-making, and other preserving. Since different types of honey vary in darkness, so do honey syrups, but they're invariably at least somewhat darker than a sugar syrup. This darker syrup will tend to darken light-colored fruits like pears and peaches. But the flavor will be delicious, so don't worry about the color. Honey syrups, compared to sugar syrups, have more of a tendency to foam when heated; use a larger kettle and watch it carefully to avoid boil-overs.

❧ *HONEY SYRUP FOR CANNING   When canning apples, tart cherries, plums, and strawberries, try 2 c. of honey per 3½ c. water. For syrup over blueberries, black cherries, peaches, pineapples, and raspberries, try 1 c. honey per 2–3 c. water. These proportions can be experimented with and varied according to your personal taste and need. It is entirely up to you how much or little honey you use. You can use plain water or pure honey or anything in between. The canning process and times are the same no matter what the type and amount of sweetener.*

Prepare your fruit for canning. Place it in a pan, cover with the syrup, and heat thoroughly. Put into prepared jars, filling to within ½ inch of the top. Put on lids, tighten them, and process in a boiling water bath the appropriate amount of time for your size of jar and type of fruit.

❧ *HONEY-FRUIT JELLY   Combine 2 c. high- or medium-pectin fruit juice, ½ c. mild-flavored honey, and 2 t. lemon juice. Bring to a boil and stir in all at once 2 T. powdered pectin. Let boil 10 minutes, and pour into your jelly glasses. For low-pectin fruit juices, use 4 t. lemon juice and 3 T.*

powdered pectin. If you want to use homemade pectin, substitute 2 c. homemade pectin for both the lemon juice and powdered pectin.

BAKING WITH HONEY: Marilyn Gordon and her husband raise and sell honey at Boone, CO. She wrote to me: "To substitute honey for sugar in a baking recipe use ¾ c. honey for 1 c. sugar and reduce liquid in the recipe by ¼ c.—like in cakes. If liquid isn't called for in your recipe, add 4 T. additional flour for each ¾ c. honey used in cookies. Bake at a temperature 25 degrees lower than called for, as baked goods with honey will brown faster. Cakes, cookies, and breads will be moist and stay fresh longer because of honey's moistness."

Honey is acidic. If there is as much as 1 c. of honey in the recipe, you can add ½ t. baking soda (per 1 c. honey) and get a leavening action as well as neutralize the acidic quality.

These next few recipes were presented to me by Shawna Marie Thurman, 1988 Montana Honey Queen, courtesy of Western Bee Supplies.

❧ *BEEHIVES   In a mixing bowl combine ¼ c. honey, 1 beaten egg, and 1 t. vanilla. Beat until well blended. Stir together 2 c. shredded coconut, 1 c. chopped walnuts, and 1 c. chopped dates that have been coated with 2 T. of flour. Now add them to the honey mixture. Drop your beehives by tablespoonful onto a greased cookie sheet. Bake at 325°F for 12 minutes or until done.*

❧ *HONEY-APPLESAUCE COOKIES   Cream together 1½ c. honey and 1 c. shortening. Add 2 beaten eggs and beat mixture until smooth. Add 2 t. soda to 2 c. applesauce. Sift in 2 t. cinnamon, 1 t. nutmeg, 1 t. salt, and 3½ c. flour. Stir in 2 c. quick-cooking oats (or rolled wheat), 2 c. raisins, and 1 c. walnuts. Drop on cookie sheet with a spoon. Bake at 325°F for 10 minutes.*

❧ *HONEY-FUDGE BROWNIES   In a saucepan over low heat, melt together ½ c. butter, 2 squares unsweetened chocolate, ½ t. salt, and 1 t. vanilla. Mix well. Remove from heat. Blend in 1 c. honey, ½ c. unsifted flour, and 1 t. baking powder. Add 2 well-beaten eggs. Beat the mixture well. Pour into a thoroughly greased 9-inch-square pan. Bake at 325°F for 35 minutes (or until done in center). Cool on wire rack 15 minutes before marking in 16 squares.*

OTHER HONEY RECIPES

❧ *CARAMEL CORN   Combine ⅓ c. honey with ¾ c. brown sugar and 2 T. margarine. Heat until sugar is melted and bubbling around edges. Pour over large bowl full of popped, salted popcorn, and mix well.*

❧ *STRETCHED HONEY   You can stretch your honey by mixing 1 c. honey with ½ c. sugar and ¼ c. water. Heat and mix together. Serve warm. Stretch it even further, if need be, by combining ½ c. water and 1 c. brown sugar per 1 c. honey.*

❧ *HONEY SYRUP   To use straight honey for syrup, warm in a pan of hot water before serving so it will pour easily, or else mix with about one-fifth water. A honey-butter syrup for immediate use can be made by melting about 3 T. butter per ½ c. honey. Serve while hot, and stir when necessary to redistribute butter, which will tend to float. Or swirl before each pouring to mix.*

❧ *HONEY LEMONADE   Stir ½ c. honey into a quart of very hot water. Add fresh lemon juice (from about 4 lemons)* or some form of lemon juice concentrate, to taste. Serve warm for a wonderful winter treat, or chill to serve in the hot summertime.

❧ *HONEY-CREAM SAUCE* Whip ½ c. cream, then beat in ½ c. honey and 1 t. lemon juice.

❧ *ORANGE SAUCE* Combine ½ c. butter, ⅔ c. honey, 1 T. orange juice, and 1 t. grated orange rind.

❧ *HONEY TEA* A bee man taught me this one. Put water on to boil. When it's boiling, add 3 t. honey per 4 c. water and boil a few minutes more until thoroughly in solution. Add tea leaves to make tea. Steep, strain, and serve. For iced honey tea, make as above, then chill.

❧ *HONEY DRESSING FOR FRUIT SALAD* Combine half honey and half lemon juice. Add a bit of yogurt and some cinnamon. Store, covered, in the refrigerator.

❧ *CRACKER JACKS MADE WITH HONEY* From Marilyn: "Blend ½ c. melted butter with ½ c. honey. Heat until well blended. Pour over a mixture of 3 qt. popped corn and 1 c. chopped nuts. Mix well. Spread over cookie sheet in thin layer. Bake in preheated 350°F oven for 10 to 15 minutes until crisp. Be careful, mixture is very hot."

❧ *BROILED HONEY TOPPING* Also from Marilyn: "Mix ¼ c. soft margarine or butter with ½ c. honey, ½ c. shredded coconut and ½ c. chopped walnuts. Spread over top of hot 9-inch-square cake. Broil until topping is bubbly. Tastes best served warm. Or heat ingredients in saucepan, thin with several spoonfuls of milk, and serve over ice cream or pudding."

RABBIT

I'm used to living way out in the country, and that is where I went through my rabbit period and quickly raised 30 or so rabbits with no neighbor problems (it was the goats we had complaints about). But that was near a community of 300, and we had 3 acres. In town, even for just 1 rabbit, learn the zoning rules first. Usually, there's no problem keeping a few rabbits, but sometimes the law specifies how many or where the hutches must go. Of course, some folks keep illegal rabbits, even enough for meat or marketing breeding stock. Being small and silent—unique and wonderful in that way among livestock—rabbits are the easiest of all to hide.

I used to think rabbits were rodents like rats and mice, but now I know they belong to a different group of mammals. They are "lagomorphs." Whatever you call them, rabbits are lovable, docile, quiet, small animals. They make good pets or can be raised for meat. They are so gentle even a child can manage them, so unobtrusive that even a covert backyard farmer can raise them. So you can raise rabbits almost anywhere: in town or country, in backyard or garage, in a house—even in an apartment!

Rabbits, of course, are also famous for their reproductive abilities. Lane Morgan says, "My elder daughter wants a pair of bunnies so she can raise babies. I told her the only way we were raising lots of baby bunnies was if we were going to butcher them, so she is brooding over this hard bargain." Yes, that's how it has to be. If you're going to make rabbit part of your meat production—or if you're going to keep 1 or more for pets—here's what you need to know.

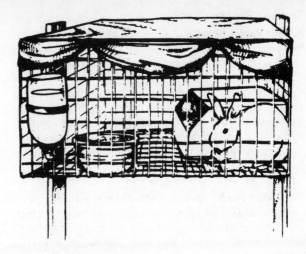

Getting Started

MAGAZINES: *Domestic Rabbits* comes out 6 times a year from the American Rabbit Breeders Association, c/o Glen Carr, PO Box 426, Bloomington, IL 61702; **arbapost@aol.com; www.arba.net.** The magazine, *Standard of Perfection*, and breed guidelines are available to members—$15/yr for adults, $8 youth. Send $2 for their beginner's booklet, $5 for their rabbit cookbook, or $1 for a bumper sticker "Get into the Rabbit Habit." It's a good place to find local rabbit clubs, rabbit products, and basic breeder stock.

BOOKS: Check out *Rabbit Feeding and Production* by Peter Cheeke (1987), *Rabbit Production* by Peter Choate (1987), *Raising Rabbits Successfully* by Robert Bennett (1984), *Practical Rabbit-Keeping* by Katie Thear (1981), *The American Rabbit Breeders Association Official Guide to Raising Better Rabbits*, *Rabbits and Hares* by Robert Whitehead, *Rabbits: A Complete Pet Owner's Manual* by Helga Fritzsche, and *The Book of the Domestic Rabbit* by Carl Naether. Older classics in this field include *How to Start a Commercial Rabbitry* by Paul Mannell, *Domestic Rabbit Production* by George Templeton (1968), and *Raising Rabbits* by Ann Kanable (1977). *Raising Small Meat Animals* by Victor M. Giammattel, D.V.M. (1976) has a terrific rabbit section.

RABBITRY SUPPLIERS

Bass Equipment offers the "world's most complete line of rabbit and small stock equipment": PO Box 352, Monett, MO 65708; 417-235-7557; fax 417-235-4312; **www.Bassequipment.com.**

Care Zap's It sells an Odor Digester and rabbit care products; send long SASE for brochure: 11727 Leader, Houston, TX 77072.

VOCABULARY

Buck: male
Bunny: a baby rabbit, also called a "kit"
Crib: to chew on a wooden cage
Doe: female
Droppings: rabbit feces
Hutch: a rabbit cage
Kindle: to give birth
Junior: young rabbit of either sex
Rabbitry: where your rabbits live
Run: group housing of a "natural" sort
Senior: an adult

BUYING STARTER STOCK

Finding Rabbit Breeders. You could probably arrange to buy your first rabbits from someone exhibiting at the fair, or ask advice of the fair superintendent or extension agent. They may know of rabbitries close enough to visit. In addition, good places to inquire are the local newspaper's stock-for-sale section, especially if you live in a rural area, and the local feed stores. Look over the feed store bulletin board and ask the clerk for advice. Because most rabbit owners buy feed and/or vet supplies, feed store clerks know who has what—and also have an idea how well cared for the animals are.

Get Good Stock. No matter whether you're buying papered or mixed-breed stock, get healthy animals—the best ones you can afford. You'll have a better idea which ones are best cared for and the best stock after visiting several rabbitries. Be cautious, even suspicious. A good rabbitry is clean. The animals look alert and happy—not listless and droopy. Ask what the rabbits are being fed and about other aspects of their care. A good match would be a rabbitry where the animals are fed and managed very like you intend to do.

Try to catch any problem before you put your money down. It's normal for the rabbit owner to want to unload a cull rather than the best rabbit. Why a cull and how bad a problem are your questions to answer. And all are not necessarily problems; a discard from a classy operation could be a great start-up animal for you. On the other hand, that cull might have a truly unfortunate condition such as a disease or bad genes that could doom your operation.

What to Start With. The minimal option is a single rabbit for a pet or a single bred female to start your rabbitry. You can go from that one pregnant doe to having enough rabbit for dinner every day and some to sell within 6 months. Rabbits are famous reproducers. But most people choose to start with more than 1, such as 2 bred does and the mature buck that bred them. These rabbits know what to do. Or choose a mature buck and pregnant doe, plus a junior buck and doe. This protects in case of failure by the older rabbits who may have been sold because they were close to stopping reproduction. Or get just a buck and a pair of does, all fairly young. Your trio will probably be plenty to start your own rabbitry.

Changing a Rabbit's Diet. Most livestock arriving new at your home will make the transition better if they don't have a sudden change in diet. Before you take them home, ask the previous owner what the rabbits have been fed, what feeding schedule, and how much of it. Ask the previous owner to sell you enough feed to help them make an easy transition, gradually switching from old to new if you will be feeding them differently.

You change a rabbit's diet by adding a little larger part of new feed and a proportionately smaller part of the old every day until the changeover is fully accomplished. Check their feed container to make sure they're eating the new rations okay. They may refuse a new food. Rabbits can be picky and opinionated. And going from an all-pellet diet to a home-grown one, for example, is a big transition; give it several weeks.

Quarantine. Any time you bring new animals onto your farm, it's a good idea to quarantine them away from other animals of their kind for 2 weeks or so. You may never run into a problem of a new animal getting sick. But if you do, you'll be glad you didn't let the other animals get it.

Rabbit Breeds

A good way to start getting acquainted with your many choices in rabbit breeds is by attending the rabbit exhibit at your county fair. It will be with poultry and other small stock. For a pet, pick any breed that catches your eye. Basically, a rabbit is a rabbit, but for anything beyond a few pets, you'll want to choose your breed carefully.

You have 5 things to consider: (1) Commercial meat breed with good food-to-flesh growth conversion ability and fast growth—or a noncommercial "fancy" breed? (2) Color? The Harlequin is a "calico." The chinchilla has a "ticked" fur. Many other rabbits come in 1 or more solid colors, such as the white, red, or black New Zealands. (3) Pelt type—long or short fur? Angoras have long, fluffy hair. Rex have a short, velvety fur. And you can find almost anything in between. (4) Size—dwarf, medium, or giant? (5) What appeals to you personally?

OF RABBITS AND PEDIGREES: "Mixed breed stock" may look like some breed or other, may be in fact purebred, but without the paper proof they aren't "pedigreed" or "registered." There are 45 recognized rabbit breeds. One listing of rabbit breeds is the *Official Guide Book of the American Rabbit Breeders Association,* free if you join the ARBA. The registering of rabbits has some unusual rules. It isn't good enough just to have the pedigreed parents and grandparents, and to be a member of ARBA. In order to be registered, the animal must also be an adult. Babies or young rabbits cannot be registered. And rabbits can't be registered through the mail. They have to have an inspection by an ARBA representative, a "registrar." The registrar checks your rabbit for physical defects and to see if it measures up to breed standards.

MEAT BREEDS: Rabbits produce more meat for less feed than any other livestock. And rabbit is the leanest land-grown meat. There are only 2 solidly commercial rabbit breeds, the New Zealand White and the California. Those have the best meat-to-bone ratio, good pelts, and have been selected for fast, efficient growth. New Zealand Whites and Californians both make white pelts (Californians have black spots on their ears, feet, nose, and tail, but they don't show up on the pelt proper). Commercial breeds are white because fur-market buyers prefer white skins—they take a dye. Other meat breeds are Champagne d'Argent, Chinchillas, New Zealand Reds and Blacks, and Satins. Commercial meat rabbits are available from Aspen Hill Farms, Box 753 Anderson Rd., Boyne City, MI 49712; 231-582-6790.

RABBIT SIZES

Dwarf. "Dwarf" rabbits usually have fairly short ears and a stocky build, and grow to weigh only 3 or 4 lb. You could raise a dwarf breed and get meat from them, but there isn't much meat on one, and their feed-to-flesh conversion ratio isn't as good as the standard meat breeds. There are some breeds that have always been small. Others are small versions of some medium-sized breeds, such as the dwarf lops. Popular dwarf breeds are Dutch, Himalayan, Netherlands Dwarf, and Polish.

Moderate-Sized. The 2 commercial breeds described above, as well as Angoras and many of the so-called "fancy" breeds, all weigh from 6 lb. to 10 lb. as adults.

That's average "moderate" rabbit weight, with the dwarf breeds coming in lighter and the giants heavier. Other medium-sized breeds are the Angoras, Champagne (and Creme) d'Argent, Chinchillas, English Spot, Harlequin, the various lops (they have long, flopped-down ears), Rex, and Satins.

Giant. I used to believe that the best kinds for meat were any of the giant varieties: Checkered Giant, Flemish Giant (up to 14 lb.), and Giant Chinchillas (the chinchilla rabbit coat plus giant size). But I've since learned that others make far better use of feed to make meat. Giants are relatively big when they're born and, like any rabbit, grow up fast. With luck, a breed like Flemish Giants might butcher out to a 3-lb. carcass at 10 weeks. If you wait and keep feeding, shortly later they'll make a 5-lb. carcass. They are impressive looking. You can get Flemish Giants in various colors. Checkered Giants are a little smaller with a distinctive black-and-white spotted coat.

SHOW BREEDS: How people tend to run after anything they think is new or will make them quick and easy money! In the rabbit field, the Belgian "hare" (actually a true rabbit) was a fad that made early investors profit but caused latecomers to the buying spree heavy losses. They are long and lanky in build, not good meat animals. The Belgian hare is a perfect example of a "fancy" breed show rabbit. These breeds, of course, are fine pets and enable their owners to play the win-a-ribbon game. That's good clean fun but not what this book is about.

Angora

Dwarf

Lop

ANGORAS, THE WOOL BREED: "Angora wool" comes from Angora rabbits. You pull it off them just as they pull it off themselves to make wonderful nests to have babies in. It's fine for spinning or stuffing, but it takes a lot of rabbits to accumulate enough fiber to work with. They are cute, cuddly things but must be plucked or brushed out to get wool for spinning. You can't shear them like a sheep. Plucking is work. Whether you have a use or a market for their wool or not, you still have to keep them brushed for the sake of their health and cleanliness.

Angoras are not a good choice if you live in a hot climate. They suffer in heat. The cage of an angora is harder to keep clean because of the tendency of their sheddings to build up on the cage floor, blocking feces from falling through the wire and trapping urine in the cage. So you have to watch angoras carefully for any signs of hutch burn or skin diseases. They're more likely to get these than regular rabbits, and beginning skin problems are harder to detect under all that fur. Water your angoras from a sipper bottle because they soak their neck fur when drinking from a more open container. When butchering them, you must take care to keep their long hair off the meat.

ABUNdance Acres Fiber Farm offers both French and Giant Angoras, plus black-and-blue Giants: 9713 Crystal Falls Dr., Hagerstown, MD 21740; 301-791-1110; **Osbunny@aol.com.**

Housing

NOTE: Plan rabbit housing to protect against heat and predators.

OF RABBITS AND HEAT: An important thing to know about rabbits is that they can't stand heat. Too much will kill them. Rabbits like some sunlight as long as they don't get too hot. If you get into terribly hot "dog days" in July or August, take your hose and soak the roof of the rabbit hutch a couple times each afternoon. During the hottest weather, make sure your rabbits always have plenty of water, but feed them only a little during the day, mostly at night. It will help if you set the hutch under a big tree or where a large building will shade it from afternoon sunlight. If you haven't taken these precautions against overheating, you can lose a batch of very nice rabbits real fast. When they die of heat, they look fine in the morning and in the evening when you look again, they are dead. I've had that happen to me.

PREDATOR PROTECTION: The biggest danger to your rabbits, however, is not temperature or disease, but predators. Rabbits have long done service fairly low on the food chain, and the predators around you instinctively know that. You have to consciously and carefully and diligently protect your rabbits from carnivores, whether you live in town or country. Predator protection starts with the good fence around the place where your hutches are, whether yard, garage, or outbuilding.

The common predators are dogs and cats, both wild and tame, as well as big birds of prey, coyotes, and wildcats. Wandering dogs may actually rip at cages trying to get a rabbit, or bite the feet of young bunnies if they step through the rabbit wire flooring the cage. Dogs have even managed to bite through wire net and kill a rabbit. Even if they can't get at a rabbit in a well-built cage, the scare from the dog trying could cause a doe to kill her babies. Children have to be viewed as possible predators, too. Like the dog, they may upset a new mother and cause cannibalism, or leave a cage door open, or feed a poisonous plant.

HOUSE RABBITS: Rabbits can be litter-box trained! Rabbits have dwelt in houses, apartments, condos—even (secretly, of course) in college dorms. Some house rabbits are kept caged. Others run free, at least in 1 room—when not confined to a paper-lined cage/house on the deck or some such. The biggest problem with house rabbits is that you have to be careful about taking them outdoors, since they're accustomed to house temperature and comfort.

They are more likely to get sick if moved outdoors than an outdoor-raised rabbit would be. To housebreak, just keep papers down where you want the rabbit to potty. The first time, it helps to demonstrate by putting some rabbit feces and urine on the paper. Your rabbit has an instinct to use the same place over and over as its toilet.

RABBIT RUNS: I got a letter from a lady who has about 80 rabbits living in her garage. The garage has a dirt floor. That living arrangement is called a "rabbit run." Most rabbit runs include an outside, fenced area. Advantages of a rabbit run are low stress, potentially less feeding, better meat because of exercise, better pelts from colder air, and healthier rabbits in that fresh-air environment. The very natural setting for the rabbits reduces their stress. They need less feed because they will eat some grass or whatever good forage is growing in their area. The disadvantages are that they're harder to catch, less likely to act like pets, and harder to keep breeding records on.

Rabbits are communal by nature and not inclined to fight much. People have had up to 100 of them in this arrangement without losing more than 2 or 3 to fights. The letter-writer said most of her does run loose on the floor, and each time they kindle they get a burrow in the dirt ready. Her system of raising the rabbits in an enclosed building is one sort of rabbit run. This housing plan has been around since the time of the ancient Romans, who kept rabbits in walled gardens, and the long-ago Chinese, who kept rabbits in grassy, fenced areas. How high a wall? Might surprise you. Rabbits can sometimes jump a 3-foot fence if they take the notion, so a 4-, 5-, or even 6-foot fence would be better.

The top can be either open or roofed. Rabbits in the open will become alert to predatory birds and develop places to hide. Or you can put a roof on. One modern variation is a fenced pit with loose hay for bedding and a plastic roof overhead to keep off rain. A variation on this system has breeding stock in cages only a foot above ground level, and the weaned offspring of the caged does running about in the fenced compound below. Besides a wall or fence that goes enough below ground level that rabbits won't burrow under, you need a door to get yourself in and out, and water, food, and bedding for the rabbits. To catch rabbits in a run, regularly feed them in the same corner. Then when you want to catch them, have somebody hold a solid gate across from side to side of the corner behind them. Inside that small space it will be easy to catch rabbits.

Flooring for Rabbit Runs. The rabbits will be happy in any building if you don't mind the floor being covered with manure. You can keep them in a floor run or in wood hutches, or metal cages in a garage, shed, or any outbuilding. A very good floor management system is to place plenty of organic bedding such as straw under the cages to collect the urine for your garden. Once in a while you'll have to shovel out that soiled bedding. If the floor is cement, you can then wash it after shoveling out. Rabbit hutches on wood floors eventually rot the floor. You can delay that by laying heavy plastic over the floor. Extend it so the plastic goes up part way on the side walls. But better flooring for rabbits in or out of cages is dry dirt. Or best of all, put them on pasture!

Portable Pasture Runs. This may well be the ideal way to manage rabbits in any season when you have green things growing. The cage looks like a long A-frame. It has a solid

wooden shelter at one end to protect from bad weather. The remaining sides are wire and let in sunshine, which, incidentally, rabbits need to be healthy. There is no floor to the cage. You place it over the green growing stuff, the day's grazing for your bunnies. This way you won't need to feed them as much other food.

RABBITS IN CAGES: Cages can be made of wood or wire. They can be single or built as units in a row, 2 or any number more. Multiple wooden cages are easy to build, but you'd better make them where they're going to stay because they're very difficult to move. No matter whether you're building with wood or wire, space needs and design features for rabbits are the same.

Cage Size. First decide how many rabbits you're going to keep and how large a breed they will be. (The housing, of course, should be prepared before the rabbits arrive.) In general, plan 1 square foot of floor space per lb. of rabbit that will be living there. The minimum though, even for a bachelor buck or pet is 2 × 2½ feet. Then figure out how your rabbits will be divided up into separate cages. A buck lives by himself and doesn't need as much room as a breeding doe, who will need space for a nesting box and her growing family. Your 9-lb. bunny would be content in a 3-foot square cage, but could you reach her? Don't make any cage so big that you can't reach every corner of it from the doorway with your arm. Otherwise you may be groping in vain for a reluctant bunny that has placed herself just out of your reach. Build either a narrow cage with a wide door, or a big roomy cage with a lid that lifts off when you need to get in there.

OUTDOOR HUTCH: Another housing option is a hutch out in the open. These cages are built solidly enough that they can stand alone outdoors and still keep the occupants warm enough in winter. If you have wood and a little inclination toward carpentering, a wooden hutch is easy to build. Wire hutches can actually be put together fairly easily too, once you get the hang of it. You can make a small hutch for a single occupant or construct multiple units. A good hutch style is a large, airy one set up on legs or posts so air can circulate easily under and around the hutch through its chicken-wire sides and bottom. But if your climate is cold, or during cold times of the year, you may want to protect the rabbits from bottom drafts by adding a wood or cardboard skirt surrounding the legs of the hutch. You could skirt only the sides and front or back, thus leaving one side open for cleaning manure out from under. In the coldest weather you could put a temporary skirt on that last side too.

Hutch Roofing. The hutch top can be made of wood covered with metal or asphalt roll roofing or even sturdy plastic. Include overhanging eaves that extend far enough over the sides of the hutch to shelter your rabbits from excessive sun and all rain, including what might fall on the outside portion of feeders if you have the style that extends to the outside of the cage.

Hutch Sides. This depends on your climate or season. You can have wire all around, or a solid (wooden) back and wire at the sides and front, or solid 3 sides round and wire only at the front. The wire sides are usually made of 1-inch poultry netting ("chicken wire"). Chicken wire is not the sturdiest of wires. You'll have to check it regularly for tears (a determined rabbit can make a hole in it with its teeth). Also, keep in mind that wire ages. The older it gets, the weaker it gets.

Hutch Flooring. Wooden floors will be chewed on by rabbits, soak up urine, smell, and are considered not as healthy as wire. On the other hand, rabbits can be happy on them so long as they're in good repair and you provide plenty of clean bedding to go over the wood such as sawdust, straw, hay—and clean as needed. The floor will be hardware cloth or "rabbit wire" (½-inch mesh). Be careful when putting in the rabbit wire because it has a "right" and a "wrong" side. The wrong side has a galvanized coating that can develop sharp points that hurt even furry feet. Another problem with rabbit wire is that the holes are so small that droppings mixed with hair may not fall through. You could use wire with bigger holes to floor the cage. That decision depends in part on what breed you're raising—how big their feet are! Rabbits with small feet need bottom wire with smaller holes.

Most hutches have a wire floor so the droppings can just drop right on through. The wire keeps the cage clean of feces, but sometimes it's hard on rabbit feet (see "Vetting"). Galvanized wire, 1 × ½-inch, is usual for medium or dwarf breeds. For larger rabbits, use 1 × 1-inch, 14-gauge. In summer, clean out the hutch if the manure starts building up in it instead of falling through. In winter, the manure in an outdoor hutch may help keep the rabbit warm.

ALL-WIRE CAGES: Compared to wooden hutches, these are more exposed to the weather and so must be enclosed in a protective outer building. Other than that drawback, they last well and are easy to clean and to move about. You can buy them ready-made in various sizes, or make your own. Commercial rabbit feeders and water bottles attach easily to the wire.

An Enclosing Shelter for Wire Cages. Your rabbit building should be draft-free for warmth in winter and yet have the option of lots of ventilation for coolness in summer. You can put hutches into almost any kind of ramshackle shelter, and it will probably be good enough for these naturally fur-coated critters. For example, corner poles with cardboard and/or plastic fastened to make sides and roof can work for a while. Don't forget to leave a doorway. For a more proper hutch shelter, screen in the windows helps to keep flies out in the summer.

Water

Rabbits must be kept supplied with plentiful and clean water. Clean out the water dish regularly, for hair and droppings will get into it. It is important to keep it in a well-roofed place so that droppings from wild birds don't get into it—which could give your rabbits coccidiosis.

HOT WEATHER: Supply as much as 1 gal. of water per day for a cage containing a doe plus her family. The minimum size for a rabbit water dish for them is up to a half-gallon, and you fill it twice a day. In very hot weather, check their water twice a day also—or more often. Heat is a big risk for rabbits, and having plenty to drink helps them stay cool.

COLD WEATHER: In the winter when their water freezes, go out twice a day with warm water to give them a chance for a drink. If their water dish is full of frozen water, you'll have to take it in the house to thaw first, or pour hot water on top to thaw it. The easiest system is to have 2 water containers for the hutch in freezing weather: 1 to be inside thawing, 1 to be outside serving water.

WATER CONTAINERS: A good size is 3½ inches deep and 6–8 inches wide. Hanging water bottles, like those pet stores use in gerbil cages, can work for a single, indoor rabbit. They are sanitary but have to refilled often and can't be used for an outdoor hutch in winter because of the freezing risk. Rabbit water and food containers either must be too heavy for them to pick up and dump over (a favorite rabbit trick) or attached firmly to the cage. Crockery drinking vessels don't rust, are too heavy to be dumped, are easy to clean, and have sloping sides and a rounded bottom that causes ice to rise as it forms instead of staying put and breaking the container. Or you can use the bottom half of a coffee can, or some such, cut down with a tin snips and wired to the side of the hutch so it can't be tipped over. Another homemade waterer is a large pop bottle wired on to hang upside down with its opening in a small can that extends on into the cage. For big operations with hundreds of rabbits an automatic watering system saves hours of time.

Food

In the wild, rabbits eat a wide variety of plant foods, but there they have experienced parents to teach them "right" foods from "wrong" foods. Domesticated rabbits depend on their keepers to know the difference. Rabbits have been domesticated for many centuries. The pellet is a very recent invention. So obviously it's possible to raise rabbits on inexpensive, home-grown feed. This does not require great skill in math or an agricultural degree, nor does it take a lot of extra work. Some folks choose to follow the path of home-grown rabbit feed, and they and their rabbits thrive on it. They are rewarded with inexpensive meat, totally free of pesticide residues, which is something you can't get feeding pellets (unless somebody came out with an organic rabbit pellet since I last looked—a great idea that wouldn't be that difficult and would be enthusiastically and gratefully received as would other livestock feeds guaranteed to be free of pesticide-residue.)

FEEDERS: You can set hay right on the cage floor or build a "manger" to feed it from. Cages that are in a row can have a built-in common hay manger between each pair of cages. You can set pellets, grain, or other small food in as is or put it in a bowl. Or use commercial metal feeders. Some styles

SECRETS OF RABBIT FEEDING

- Rabbits need a regular feeding schedule: same time each day, same number of feedings per day, and same order in which various feeds are given. Most people feed them twice a day—in the morning and afternoon.
- Rabbits are physically unable to eat fine foods such as a powder or a finely ground "meal."
- Cut hay-type feed with a hay knife or fine-toothed wood saw into sections no more than 3 inches long for rabbits.
- Rabbits don't like oily foods. They may enjoy the meal left after oils are extracted—such as from cottonseed, linseed, peanuts, sesame seeds, and soybeans.
- Rabbits are exceptionally vulnerable to insecticide residues on food. Don't feed them sprayed foods.
- Wash garden foods before feeding them to rabbits because

an accumulation of eaten dirt can make a rabbit sick. Slice root vegetables into sticks like carrot sticks. Don't feed soggy, rotten portions.

- Introduce any new feed—especially a garden one—gradually, by starting to feed a little, then feeding more and more.
- Don't feed potato sprouts, eyes, or peels.
- Cow parsnip is as good nutritionally for rabbits as alfalfa and can be substituted for it.
- Fresh greens should be clean, cool, fresh but slightly air-dried, and normal colored—not yellowish.
- To store greens for winter rabbit feed: Pick or cut the greens, then sunshine-cure them in thin swaths 2–4 days. They'll be ready when they're sun-bleached (a light green color) and dry (but not yet brittle). Pack in stacks or sacks in a dry place.

- Eating spoiled—yellowish or fermented—greens can make rabbits very sick.
- A rabbit on a natural, home-grown diet needs some exposure to sunlight in order for its body to manufacture a needed vitamin.
- It is normal and necessary for rabbits to eat their own night feces. They do this in the late night and early morning hours. Their droppings at this time are different from day ones. They're soft and light green, while day feces are harder and brown. The night feces are loaded with B vitamins, especially thiamin, which are produced by certain bacteria that live in large numbers in the rabbits' intestinal tracts. Rabbits eat the night feces to get the vitamins in them. If you prevent a rabbit for 3 or 4 weeks from eating its night feces, it will die of malnutrition.

---

extend through the side of the cage so you can put feed in from outside the cage without having to open the door. You can make a homemade feeder from the bottom of a metal coffee can. Cut it down to where it's only about 2 inches high. Bend down the sharp top edge to make it smooth. Punch holes (from the inside toward the outside!) down through the bottom of the can if you are feeding pellets. The useless dust that comes along with pellet feed will sift out through those holes. Make 2 side holes to put a wire through and fasten the feed can to the side of the cage.

HOW MUCH FEED? Like dogs and people, rabbits vary in the way they relate to food. Some will take just what they need and just the right foods. Some will eat themselves to illness on a single food, or overeat to a state of obesity if you don't limit them. Overweight does do have a harder time getting pregnant and have more risky kindlings. Obese bucks may lose interest in mating the does. So you need to keep an eye on their weight. How to tell if your rabbit has a weight problem? Well, the flesh should be firm anywhere on her except the belly, which is naturally flabby no matter what. In fact, the more litters she's had, the more loose skin you can grab in your hand on the belly of a normal-weight doe. Younger does, like young human girls, are firmer in the belly area. The older doe who doesn't have some loose tummy skin is the one who needs to go on a diet. Reduce her food amount.

CONTROLLED FEED AMOUNTS: About the easiest way to keep rabbits in normal weight is to feed them hay, all they want. Rabbits very seldom overeat on hay. Then just give small, measured amounts of the richer foods, if wanted. Rabbit scientists say the average nonpregnant,

nonlactating doe can eat 3.8 percent of her weight each day. For a 10-lb. nonbreeding bunny, that translates to a daily ration of 6 oz. pellets, or 2.5 oz. grain plus 3.5 oz. hay. Breeding bucks and does get 6.7 percent of their weight: 10.7 oz. pellets; or 3.5 oz. grain plus 7 oz. hay.

Pregnant and nursing does, as well as young bunnies, are generally allowed to eat all they want. The young rabbits maintain that good life at least until age 6 months (or until butchering weight of 4–4.5 lb.). If fed longer, they could weigh up to 10 lb. or so, but after 4 lb. they gain weight slower relative to feed consumption, so they're costing you more to keep.

PELLETS-ONLY DIET: I've heard that rabbits raised for meat will gain faster on a diet of rabbit pellets. The bulk of the pellet is a finely ground and pressed together mix of alfalfa hay and a blend of grains. Other minerals and vitamins are added. Pellets have many fans because of convenience. It makes feeding a 1-step operation—no guessing, no need to look around for various diet components and put them into the cage one by one. You can buy them "medicated" or "nonmedicated." But you still don't come out money-wise, because of the price of the pellets. Plain alfalfa pellets—which contain no grain—can be used to feed dry does and bucks that aren't breeding but not breeding males, pregnant or nursing does, or growing young rabbits. Feeding hay and grain is cheaper than feeding pellets, even if you don't grow any of it yourself.

HAY AND GRAIN DIET: A diet of mixed grains provides better nutrition than any single grain. Feed mixed grains (just what combination is up to you) for 30 percent of the rabbits' diet by weight. Oats, soft wheats, and grain

RABBIT FOOD

Edible for Rabbits		Not Good for Rabbits!
Acacia: has no food value, but twigs can be entertainment	Knotgrass	*These range from deadly poisonous, to hard-on-a-bunny, to having no nutritional value.*
Alfalfa: fresh or hay	Kohlrabi: all parts of plant okay to feed	Amaranth
Apples: all parts	Kudzu	Arrowgrass
Barley	Lettuce: all kinds	Bracken fern
Beans and bean vines (not soybean)	Lespedeza	Bromweed
Beets: both top and root of regular, sugar, or mangel	Malva (cheeseweed)	Buckeye
Bermuda grass	Meadow fescue	Burdock
Blackberry bush leaves	Milk: fresh or sour, as well as milk products	Castor beans
Bluegrasses	Millet: foxtail and Japanese	Chinaberry
Bread: dry, or soaked in milk	Milo	Chokecherry leaves or pits
Buckwheat	Napier grass	Comfrey
Cabbage: some okay, too much causes health problems (goiter)	Oats	Fireweed
Canadian bluegrass	Oranges: all parts (don't feed too much)	Foxglove
Carpet grass	Orchard grass	Goldenrod
Carrot: root and tops.	Panicgrass	Hemlock, poison/water
Cereals (if fat-free and fresh)	Parsnips	Horehound
Cheeseweed (malva)	Peas and pea vines	Jimson weed
Chicories	Plantain	Johnson grass
Clovers: any but sweet clover	Poplar	Larkspur
Coltsfoot	Potato: but not peelings or sprouts or leaves	Laurel
Corn	Prairie grass	Lima beans
Cow parsnip	Redtop grass	Lupine
Crabgrass	Rhodes grass	Mesquite
Dandelion	Root vegetables	Milkweed
Dogwood	Rye, rye grass, and Italian rye grass	Miner's lettuce
Fescue: red, etc.	Sheep sorrel	Moldy bread: or moldy anything
Filaree (stork's bill)	Sorghum grains	Oak
Grains: all types, unless dirty, damp, or moldy	Sprouted grains	Oleander
Grapefruit: all parts (don't feed too much)	Sudan grass	Pigweed
Grass/lawn clippings, grass grains: as long as they bear no insecticides	Sumac	Poppy
Hazelnut leaves	Sunflower leaves or seeds	Potato leaves, sprouts, or peels
Jerusalem artichokes: tops, stems, or roots	Sweet potatoes: vines or tubers	Rhubarb leaves
Kale	Timothy	Soybeans or soybean vines
Kentucky bluegrass	Turkey mullein	Spinach
	Turnips: all parts of plant	Sweet clover
	Vetch	Swiss chard
	Wheat	Tarweed
	Willow	Tomato leaves

sorghums are rabbit favorites among the grains. Protein is a small but extremely important necessity in a rabbit's diet. They can get some from grain and some from good legume hay, but they can't get any from nonlegume hay. Chopped grain is better than whole grain, but any grains may be fed whole except barley and oats, which should be rolled, mashed, or ground. Dry corn kernels should be also cracked or some such. Don't get it too small. And don't feed dirty, damp, or moldy grain.

So feed good alfalfa hay for the remaining 70 percent. "Good" hay for rabbits is very leafy, has thin stems, and is clean of mold or dirt. It will smell fresh. This kind of alfalfa hay, if analyzed, would show around 12–14 percent protein. To buy that kind of hay ask for "second-cutting alfalfa." With some grain, or bread, or dairy products added, your rabbit's protein needs will be met. You can

serve it in its natural form except that it should be cut into sections less than 3 inches long.

Thus, when you go to the feed store, get a 70-lb. bale of alfalfa hay and 30 lb. of a combination of grains. Another option is the hay–grain diet, plus about 10–20 percent pellets. One lady I know feeds her rabbits ½ lb. of grain and 1 lb. of that legume hay each day.

HOME-GROWN RABBIT FOOD: The old-timers who wintered their rabbits on food they'd grown themselves fed them such things as stock beets and cabbage in winter as well as their grain and hay. So can you. Pea and bean vines can be cured like hay and make an excellent hay substitute or supplement.

In season, rabbits like anything green, but you must be careful not to feed them plants that are outrightly poisonous, such as chokecherry or rhubarb leaves, or potato peels with sprouts or ones that have been in the sun long enough to get even the slightest touch of green. Other greens are only mildly poisonous in the uncooked state such as pigweed, amaranth greens, spinach, comfrey, and Swiss chard—but for a creature with a small body weight like a rabbit, especially a young rabbit, these can be a problem, too. Much of the reason that people develop fear of growing their own rabbit food, or have bad experiences with home feeding of rabbits is because they don't understand how very many greens, wild or domestic, are not fully safe to feed rabbits, and which are. Before feeding a leafy green or herb for the first time, check the list under "Edible for Rabbits," below, to see if there is a warning of any sort about it. Stick to feeding them human-type salad greens unless you know for sure a wild one is safe. If cooking is advised for a green or category of greens (the amaranth family), don't feed it to rabbits who, of course, would be eating it raw. If it's in the least toxic, don't feed it to them. If it might have chemical residues on it, don't feed it to them.

I plant extra rows of lettuce for them. And when I weed in summer, I take along a bucket to put the pulled edible weeds in for the rabbits. Feeding this way you never have to buy a rabbit pellet and they do fine. When fed home-grown stuff, they'll grow a little slower (and more normally) to that 2-lb. butchering size. But it's far cheaper, and I have organic meat because from conception on, they've been nourished with home-grown foods and greens, or hay and grain from a source I know is chemical-free.

Vegetables/Greens/Fruits. A combination of grains is better than a single one. A combination of veggies and greens plus grain and hay is better yet. Let your rabbits do some picking and choosing. They'll choose what they need. They'll love much of what you offer of this sort, and it's a nice way to tame them—hand-feeding some veggie treats. For pregnant and nursing does, variety is especially important. Offer the vegetables or leafy greens in season (the longer the season, the better). Garden and kitchen vegetables and fruit scraps can be included also, as long as they're not on the unhealthy list. If you're just starting to supplement a rabbit's diet in this way, go slowly at first until your bunny gets used to it. Limit what you feed so that surplus doesn't rot in the cage. Rotting surpluses are good for chickens or pigs, but not rabbits. In fact, rabbits can get sick from eating partly spoiled greens. Garden vegetables for rabbits, as for people, are mostly water. Greens are water plus lots of minerals and vitamins. Root vegetables are higher in energy supplied, lower in the mineral-and-vitamin department.

SALT: Rabbits enjoy a salt-and-mineral block in the hutch. They'll lick it for the food value. Rabbits with a block seem less likely to gnaw on their cage. You can just break a chunk off a cow-size salt block for them, or give them a lump of canning salt. But don't give them iodized table salt. Some rabbits prefer plain salt and some like the commercial salt-and-mineral mix.

"BONES" AND "TOYS": If rabbits have something to chew on, they are less likely to chew on wood parts of their cages and generally seem more content. You can combine a chew-on toy with a salt source by soaking a chunk of 2 × 4 in very salty water for about 3 days. Air dry it, and then give it to your rabbit. Rabbits also like to gnaw on a hunk of Sheetrock. They like to knock a tin can around in their

cage, but, because they're nocturnal, that kind of play may keep you up at night. In that case give them a toy that won't make so much noise.

Rabbit Reproduction

SEXING: The first thing that can go wrong with rabbit reproduction is having 2 bucks or 2 does instead of 1 of each. In determining the sex, it's easy to make a mistake, especially if you looked when they were young. The younger the rabbit, the harder it is to figure out which is which. If they're less than 2 months old, it verges on impossible. After that age the males get a penis you can see, and maybe testicles too. Once the buck is fully grown his testicles will be easy to see. To sex a rabbit, hold it on its back with one hand. The holding hand also has hold of its tail and is keeping the tail out of the way of where you want to look. With your other hand's thumb and first finger press down firmly but gently around the sex organ. With practice you'll learn the difference between male and female. If it's a buck, the sex organ looks more round; the female's looks more like a slit. As the male gets older, its penis will protrude and be plainly visible when you press and you'll see his testicles.

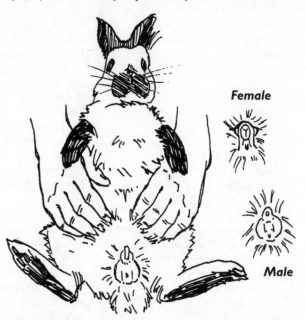

Female

Male

BUCKS: For a few does you need but a single mature male to keep the supply going. If you have more, you can eat the others. Or you can keep 2—just in case. If you're doing large-scale rabbit-raising, you need about 1 buck per 10 does. Use a buck up to 3 times a week.

BREEDING: Just put the doe into the buck's cage. *Don't put the buck in with the doe.* It's a fast way to lose a good buck, since the doe will fiercely fight him. This is because the doe has a motherly instinct to be protective of her hutch. After she has lived in there a while, she may attack even if another doe is put in there.

If your doe is not pregnant she will let the buck mount. It happens in a moment—about 1 minute to be precise—and then is over. The buck may tumble over on his side at the conclusion. That's normal and nothing to worry about. In about a minute more he will have recovered and be ready to mate again. If the doe is receptive, you can allow a second mating, but then get her out of there and back to her own cage. It's important to stay there and watch while they're mating. You watch so you know for sure it happened and that the doe is now pregnant. (Write down the date for future reference. In 30 or 31 days, she'll be a mother.) You also watch so you can remove the doe from the buck's cage as soon as possible. *Don't leave them alone together. The doe may come to resent the buck's attention and fight—even injure—him. Or the buck may hurt the doe.*

Human women typically ovulate 1 egg exactly midway between the first day of one menstrual cycle and the first day of their next one—the 14th day of an average 28-day cycle. Rabbits, however, don't ovulate until they have sex, and then they ovulate multiple eggs. That's rabbit rhythm. (That's how I got pregnant with Becca. Hadn't seen Mike for about 6 weeks and then we got back together. Well, it was a rapturous reunion and, even though it was the day before my period was due, I got pregnant. So I can testify from experience that rabbit rhythm can happen to people too!) Because of this, some rabbit-keepers bring the doe back to the buck 6 hours after the first visit to make sure that the eggs she ovulated in response to that first breeding are all fertilized by the buck.

MATERNITY CAGE: When does aren't bred, they can room together. But a doe who is expecting needs separate quarters in a pen that provides her with a nesting box and plenty of room for the growing litter: 7 to 8 square feet, minimum. Make sure the door is big enough to get the nest box in and out and that this cage is sized and shaped so that you can reach into all the corners.

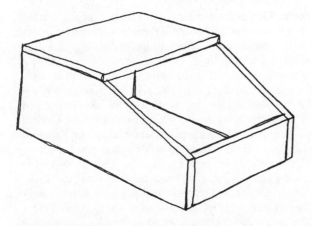

Nesting Box. The nesting box should be like a separate little room inside the larger cage the doe lives in, with its own top, bottom, and sides. If you don't provide her with a nesting box, the babies will fall through the wire, and she'll be so nervous and upset at being out in the open with them she is liable to eat some of them. Fixing her up with the box allows her to pretend she's in a burrow, and that's what her nature needs. You can set a wooden box inside the hutch to be her nesting box or make one out of wire. It should be roofed at least partly for warmth and to provide a sense of privacy for the nervous mom. The box should have its own floor, which also keeps the occupants warmer. It should be entirely separate and separable from the outer cage. There are cages with built-in or "integral" nesting boxes. Experienced rabbit-keepers complain, however, that they don't stay clean and tend to be unsanitary, hence, unhealthy. It's easy to make a passable nesting box with some boards, a saw, hammer and nails. Or start with an existing wooden

box, nail a top on it and cut out the doorway. If your climate or season is warm, you could create a wire nest box out of "rabbit wire." In cooler weather, one of those can be lined with cardboard. Make sure the nesting box will block drafts and won't leak. For cold weather, it should have a nice tight construction.

Dimensions. Commercial-breed–sized rabbits need a nest box about 12 inches by 18–24 inches and 12 inches tall. There should be a doorway just the right size for the doe to go in and out. The entrance to the box should be raised from 2 to 6 inches off the box's floor (higher is better, highest is best) so that the blind, helpless young don't accidentally roll out the doorway. When they have grown big enough to hop over that barrier on their own, they'll be all right out there anyway.

KINDLING MANAGEMENT DAY BY DAY

Gestation. To test for pregnancy you can put the doe into the buck's cage when she's supposed to be 2 weeks pregnant. If she stands still and lets him mount her, she probably wasn't really pregnant. But if you do this "check breed" you better be poised to get her out of there at a moment's notice, because if she is pregnant she'll fight him. Even if she did let him breed her, go ahead and put in her nesting box because there are does, though rare, that will accept the buck even when they're pregnant. Another way to test for pregnancy is by feeling her abdomen. The babies inside feel like marbles. The problem with that, however, is that the only way to feel them is to press so hard that you're likely to harm them. Best not to.

Check the doe for being overweight since an obese doe may die during kindling or deliver dead babies. A too-lean doe is not as much of a risk to herself or her babies. Put her on a diet if needed, early in the pregnancy. A few days of short rations generally does it. Rabbit pregnancy lasts 28–35 days, but most rabbits kindle on day 31 or 32. As her pregnancy progresses, gradually increase the amount of protein you're feeding. Toward the end, when the babies inside her are growing fastest, let her eat all she can clean up. If she doesn't get enough food at this stage, some of the babies may die inside her and she'll abort them. A doe who doesn't get enough (and nourishing enough) food has a smaller litter. Get her moved into a maternity pen with nesting box well before the delivery date.

5 Days Before Kindling. About 5 days before her due date, move a nest box into her hutch. Provide the mother-to-be with ample straw, hay, maybe even some cotton rags if the weather is cold—plus a calm environment. She'll make those nest-building supplies into just a dandy little nest in there. She'll pull out some of the fur off her own body to line it. In cold weather, it will help her if you also supply some extra rabbit hair, or wool. (As you care for your rabbits and find bits of rabbit fur, stash them in a paper bag in a dry place.) From those she can make an even warmer nest. Some first-time rabbit mamas don't catch on in time. If you have one who is failing to pull fur for her nest, it may help to provide her with that soft nesting material even if it isn't cold. With a good box and plenty of soft working materials with which to build her nest, she will herself create a shelter in which her young can survive even the coldest weather.

Also check over the cage, keeping in mind the young rabbits that will soon be romping and exploring in there. For a maternity cage a shared manger isn't a good idea unless it's built so the babies can't possibly crawl into the next-door cage. Make sure there are no holes a little rabbit could fall or crawl through.

From 4 Days Before, Until Kindling. When she is near to her birthing time, keep things around her as quiet as possible and basically just leave her alone. Rabbits are jumpy critters anyway, and even experienced mamas can go hyper around their kindling time.

Kindling: Day 1. First-time mothers are the biggest worry. If she made a nest but doesn't give birth inside it, the babies will die of exposure or fall through the wire. Or she may birth some babies inside, but some outside of the nest. If you find them and they're still alive, there's hope. In that case, old-time rabbit managers rub a chest salve such as Mentholatum or Vapo-Rub lightly onto the mother's nose while she's outside of the nest and gently return the outside babies before she goes back. The rub helps prevent mom's rejection of them by deactivating her smeller for a bit.

Check if there's enough fur for a warm nest. If there isn't, add more from your rabbit fur bag.

If a mama at kindling time gets very emotionally upset (it happens easily to rabbits), such as by a dog, or a drastic change in feed, or a water shortage, or too much handling, or just is quirky that way, she may even cannibalize the babies. In that case, give her 1 or 2 more chances to raise a family. If she repeats the crime and she's a stock rabbit, eat or replace her. If she's a pet, then get her to a nunnery for a life of pampered celibacy.

Day 2. If all the babies appear to be in the nest, wait 24 hours and check them on day 2 for the sake of mom's nerves. The babies are hairless, blind, and furless. Get the doe out of there, dab salve on her nose, and go to work on the nest. Count the babies. Rabbits may have as many as 16, but usually fewer. Since most does won't successfully nurse more than 8 or 9 babies, more than that are best fostered out. Remove any dead ones from the nest. Healthy babies are squirming restlessly in there. See if they're nursing well. Well-fed babies have bulging tummies. You can actually see the milk through their thin skin. Check to see if mom's breasts are doing okay. Check to make sure the nesting box is not leaking. It should be absolutely dry in there. Make sure the doe has plenty of nourishing food to eat. Otherwise her babies won't be their largest possible size at weaning time.

Day 3. Check again, as above.

Day 6. Check the babies again. If you find any dead ones—and it happens—remove the bodies.

Day 10. Check again. The little bunnies will be opening their eyes about this time and becoming active and fun. You don't need to supply any food for these young babies. The rabbit is a mammal and feeds her babies milk from her own body until they are large enough to come out and share her feed.

Day 21. The bunnies can start eating something besides mother's milk now. Milk-soaked bread is a good first supplement for them. Very young rabbits have delicate digestive tracts. Be careful. Add new foods gradually, watching for difficulties, just as you do for a human infant. Avoid foods that are harsh in content or texture. For example, oat husks can damage their intestines. To feed home-grown grains to young rabbits, crush them and remove the husks. Bigger young rabbits and their parents like to eat very green, leafy hay, as well as grain.

Day 56. Meat breeds weigh about 4 lb. and are ready to butcher as fryers at this time. Average-sized rabbits, butchered at 2 months, will each dress out to an adequate-for-a-fryer 2 lb. It's definitely time to rebreed the doe. Rabbit lore has it that a doe left unbred for too long may forget how and turn sterile. As for the offspring, there's a very sound reason for butchering at that magic number of 56 days, because if they aren't sent to that fate but rather are left in the cage, you'll have all those little boy and girl rabbits growing together, right? Okay. The simple fact of rabbit life is that an 8-week-old female rabbit housed with a male is about ready to get pregnant and will do so very soon, probably within days. So if you want to keep some of those bunnies to be mothers or fathers themselves, that's the age at which you can start breeding them—or they will start breeding themselves. If that's what you want, instead of butchering them, you give them their own housing, and proceed as above with the cycle of rabbit reproduction. If you want them to continue eating and growing some more but not producing offspring, you had better house the sexes in separate dorms. Unfortunately, the younger they are, the harder it is to tell what sex they are.

Any rabbit you don't want to keep for breeding should be butchered at least by 13 weeks of age, because after that the feed conversion efficiency really goes down.

ORPHANS: Once I had a mother rabbit jump out of her hutch and get killed by a dog when her litter was very young. I saved them by feeding them regularly with milk out of an eyedropper until they were big enough to lap milk out of a saucer like kittens.

Foster Mothers. Another way to handle orphans or babies from a too-large litter is to put them in with another litter of close to the same age. To get the new baby successfully adopted you do 3 things: (1) Lure mom rabbit out of the nesting box and over to the farthest-away end of her cage by feeding something there that she loves enough to give it her full attention for a moment. (2) While she's eating, gently sneak the new baby (babies) underneath those already in the box. The underneath placement is important because there they'll have a chance to pick up their new family's identifying odor before she catches on. Then gently pull the nesting material back over the babies. (3) Get some chest rub on mom's nose before she makes it back into the nesting box and repeat for several days so she can't smell the strangeness of the extras. Even so, some does can't be outsmarted and will just say no.

Rabbit "Vetting"

Rabbits are comparatively healthy and simple to manage as far as their health care goes. If you take good care of them and provide good housing and plenty of nourishing food, you probably won't have much sickness. If you do have sickness, it may be best just to replace the rabbit. They aren't worth what a vet would charge and many vets don't know much about rabbit ailments anyway.

HANDLING: *Never hold a rabbit up by its ears.* A rabbit's ears are tender and sensitive. If you are handling a small rabbit (less than 5 lb.), lift it up with 1 hand placed securely under its behind. Lift a large rabbit with 1 hand under it the same way and the other hand grasping the loose flesh at the back of its neck for security. Rabbits prefer to be carried with their head tucked beneath your arm so they feel hidden.

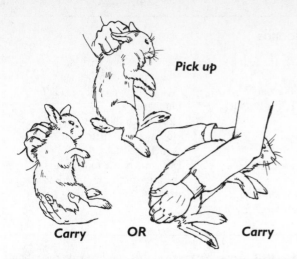

Pick up

Carry **OR** **Carry**

NAIL CLIPPING: Clip to minimize the risk of being scratched by hutch rabbits whose claws are too long. Use a dog-sized nail clipper.

GIVING MEDICINE BY MOUTH: First get the medicine into an eye dropper. Get yourself seated with the rabbit held firmly between your legs or in your lap. Now put the dropper into the back of the rabbit's mouth. Slowly squeeze the medicine out back there.

TAKING A RABBIT'S TEMPERATURE: Use a regular baby thermometer. Be careful, whether for your child or the rabbit, because those darn glass bulbs break off so easily. Put a little grease on it to make it slide better, and insert only about 1 inch up the rabbit's rectum.

USUALLY NONCONTAGIOUS CONDITIONS

Conjunctivitis (Weepy Eye). If your rabbits look like children with pinkeye—with stuck-together, goopy eyes, this is what they have. Use an antibiotic eye ointment and apply once or twice a day. The best ointment is one with an anesthetic so the animals will stop scratching and rubbing their eyes.
NOTE: To prevent conjunctivitis, don't use sawdust for bedding, and keep dust down in the rabbitry.

Hutch Burn/Vent Disease. This resembles diaper rash in that you'll see red and irritated, even scabby places around the rectum and genitals of the rabbit. At worst it's vent disease, which is a very contagious sort of rabbit syphilis. Only your vet can truly tell the difference. Rabbits with vent disease, left untreated, get well from their symptoms and simply become carriers of the sickness, which they give to unborn young. Injected antibiotic cures vent disease.

But your problem is far more likely to be hutch burn, which is merely caused by urine-soaked bedding on rabbit housing with solid floors. The ammonia generated by the urine irritates them. The treatment for true hutch burn is to clean out the soiled bedding and provide better conditions in the future. Or else change the rabbits to wire-floored cages. Treat by smearing Vaseline on the afflicted places. That protects them against ammonia. If the "diaper rash" has gotten infected, treat instead with an antibiotic salve. At its worst, hutch burn can become a blood poisoning of the whole system.

Sore Hocks. Because they often live on wire, rabbits can suffer from hocks that have gotten bruised or even infected. If your bunny's hock loses its hair, or looks red, swollen, or has a scab, it needs treatment.

NOTE: To prevent sore hocks, support a wire floor for heavy breeds so they don't sag, be sure wire flooring is the right side up, and keep flooring wire clean, disinfected, and free from sharp things. Minimize stress and keep bucks out of sight of one another, because rabbits may thump hard when excited and hurt their feet.

Constipation. Rabbits, like you and I, can suffer from this. The cause may be lack of roughage (hay), cribbing, or eating fur. The first symptom is some very small, very hard feces. Later, a constipated rabbit may lie on its side, obviously in pain. Treatment is making it drink 2–8 cc of mineral oil 3 times per day. Pineapple juice helps them digest hair balls. Giving a rabbit with a severe case an enema might cure it—or it might kill this easily stressed animal.

Abscesses. These lumps full of pus are caused by a streptococcus infection. Usually one starts when the rabbit gets a skin puncture in a fight or from something sharp in its cage. *Cages should not contain sharp, protruding objects.* Unless you seriously want to play doctor, you might just want to replace this rabbit. In any case, don't let it infect other rabbits, or you (wear rubber gloves when vetting).

"Buck" or "Wolf" Teeth. These are genetic (recessive) defects that some rabbits carry. "Buck teeth" are extra long upper incisors. "Wolf teeth" are extra long lower incisors. Eventually, the rabbit can't close its mouth and can't eat normally, and its teeth grow painfully into the flesh. Buck or wolf teeth are hereditary. Don't let an affected animal breed.

Cribbing. Rabbits like to chew. They'll chew on wood in their hutches, even tear holes in their wire. It helps to give them toys to play with, and something okay to chew on, such as pieces of Sheetrock. It also helps to have a salt block in there.

Mastitis. Any milking mammal can get this inflammation of the "breasts." It can be caused by a bruise or bacterial infection. A doe suffering from mastitis acts listless. Her mammary glands feel hot and swollen. Her temperature may be up. The treatment is an antibiotic. If a doe gets mastitis, her babies are usually taken out of the nest and dealt with like orphans with hand feeding, at least until their mother is well.

PARASITES

Coccidiosis. The best approach to rabbit coccidiosis is to emphasize prevention. The disease is caused by wild or domestic birds roosting above your rabbit pens and leaving disease-bearing droppings in the rabbits' water. This is a good reason for having a roof over the hutch (as well as to keep it cool in summer). Symptoms of coccidiosis in your rabbits are weak, listless behavior; weight loss; pot belly; loss of appetite; diarrhea; thinness.

However, most people don't discover they have coccidiosis disease on their farm until they butcher and find a liver that is filled with white spots. Chickens get it as well as many other kinds of poultry, sheep, and rabbits. The treatment for rabbits is to give them a medicine in their water. Make sure rabbits under treatment are in wire-bottom cages so they don't get reinfected by eating their night feces, which rabbits typically do. Don't butcher for at least 14 days after that treatment.

Ear Canker/Ear Mites. Ear mites are the beasties that cause ear canker in rabbits. Examine your rabbits' ears. If you see brownish discharge and crust, mites are likely the cause. Isolate the infected animals to prevent spreading of the problem, and treat them as soon as possible. After

If you want to make a profit on any livestock, you need to keep records. Some people scribble in a notebook or on a calendar. Some have slick computer systems. If you have caged rather than communal rabbits, you'll want to note breeding and kindling dates. That way you can have nest boxes available on schedule. A good system is 1 page for each rabbit and on that page you answer the following questions:

1. What's the animal's name?
2. How many were in the litter it was born into?
3. Who was it bred to?
4. When did it give birth?
5. How many were born? Alive? Dead?
6. Any problems with kindling and mothering behavior?
7. Were there any birth defects?
8. How many were weaned?
9. What date were they ready for butchering?
10. How much did they weigh?
11. How many of them were does? Bucks?
12. Did you choose to keep any of the litter for future breeding stock?

applying medicine, massage the ear's base to get the medicine well spread. To try to prevent reinfection, use something like rotenone on the pen and the cage. Be careful that you don't spread the infection.

Lice. Fortunately, rabbits don't often get lice—or mange either. If they do get lice, it will most likely happen in winter. A louse infection can be so severe as to make the rabbit anemic, even result in death. A louse powder is the treatment.

Mange. Mange can spread quickly from one animal to another and is not easy to treat. Sometimes diagnosis is difficult. True mange is caused by tiny mites hiding under matted hair. But fungal or bacterial infections can resemble mange. A vet can identify mange by examining a skin scraping. If you suspect mange, an organic response is to butcher the animal and burn its pelt because treatment involves insecticide, costs money, and is likely to not be successful at least the first time. An animal with mange is a source of infection to other animals.

Fungus Infections. Commonly known as "ringworm." Some rabbit-keepers immediately isolate, even kill and burn or bury any infected rabbit. To treat, cut the hair around the infected area quite short and apply fungus powder or ointment (wear rubber gloves). Sun shining on the affected area can help also.

Worms. Rabbits can get them—most usually the tapeworm—from other farm livestock, dogs, cats, birds, or rodents. Tapeworm can spread by infected cat or dog manure getting into rabbit cages or feed. A rabbit with tapeworm has dull fur and maybe blood or mucous in its droppings. For suspected worms, you can take the rabbit and a droppings sample to your vet, who will examine the feces under the microscope and know for sure. However, there's no treatment for tapeworm that wouldn't kill the rabbit, too.

Rabbit Butchering

Rabbit meat is the leanest of all nonfish meats—and delicious! It is often compared to chicken, but each has its own distinct flavor and texture. After all, one is a mammal, the other fowl. Precise weight at proper butchering age varies wildly because rabbits' weights can vary so much according to breed, sex, and age. The meat you end up with will be about half the live weight. Young rabbits are distinguished by their soft ears and paws—stiffness is a sign of age. An old rabbit can be stewed like an old chicken. Rabbit meat is almost fat-free.

KILLING: Some recommend that you first stun the rabbit with a hard blow on the head, right behind the ears, then chop the head off on your chopping block as close to the head as possible. Other rabbit owners find it very difficult to get a well-placed, effective blow in and prefer to begin by snapping the animal's neck by stretching it with the hands.

To do that, hold the rabbit's hind legs about chest-high with your nondominant hand (the left for me) and hold the rabbit's head firmly around the neck with your dominant hand. With the dominant hand you are now doing 2 motions at once: pulling the body down in tension against your other hand's grip, and bending the rabbit's head up and back as far as possible at the same time as you pull its body down. Keep pulling the rabbit's head up and back with a steady, firm motion until you feel the neck break.

Then proceed, as above, to cut off the head with an ax on a chopping block, or with a sharp knife, cutting through the spinal-column cartilage. To get the rabbit properly bled out, hold it upside down for a few minutes, or hang it. (You can save a mess by catching the blood in a garbage sack).

HANGING: Now prepare the animal for skinning (if it has not already been hung) either by nailing the 2 hind feet about body width apart to a board or skinning table, or by hanging it up. The hanging procedure is the same as that used with larger animals. Cut the skin off just toward the body from the hock joint of each hind leg and peel it back enough to expose the 2 Achilles tendons. Insert the hooks, ropes, chain, or whatever between the bone and Achilles tendons just above the hocks. It will be handy if you have ready a gambrel (hook), suspended about chest high. You can make one out of a piece of stiff wire about 1 foot long. Make a hook at each end to hook the exposed Achilles tendons of the rabbit (which are strong enough to hold the animal's weight even under considerable pulling pressure) and suspend from a tree branch or some such. Or a rope thrown over a tree branch with a hook at each end will work. Or you can just tie a couple loops around each leg las shown in the illustrations.

SKINNING: With the rabbit on the gambrel, you cut off the front feet and the tail. (Later, you can give the tail to the children to enjoy.) Slit the skin between the legs with a very sharp small knife. Start with the hock joint on the inside of one hind leg, cut down to the crotch of the rabbit and the back up the inside of the other hind leg to the other hock joint. Cut the skin from each front leg to the neck. (Do not cut down the belly centerline at this time.) Then peel then skin down off the body, beginning at the hind hocks, like

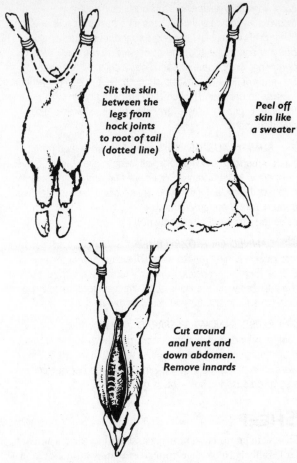

Slit the skin between the legs from hock joints to root of tail (dotted line)

Peel off skin like a sweater

Cut around anal vent and down abdomen. Remove innards

you would take off a banana peel or a sock. Cut around the anal opening and any place the skin is not coming off freely. Pull the skin off like that, inside out, clear down to the front feet, and then it will be completely off. If you have taken the skin off cleanly, you may want to use the very soft rabbit fur. See "Tanning" in Chapter 8.

Easy Skinning. If you don't care about the skin, skinning is easy. Just hold the rabbit by a hind leg and with your other hand pinch the hide at the hock joint and pull downward. The skin will tear at the point of the pull and you can peel it off without a knife. Or remove the head and feet, then pinch up the hide in the middle of the back and cut through it with a knife. Then grasp the hide on either side of the cut and pull in opposite directions. Pull the front half toward the head and the rear half toward the tail. Peel the skin off, rolling it down over the legs. Cut off the head, feet, and tail, and you're done with that.

CLEANING ("DRESSING"): You may either take the animal off the skinning board or down from the hanging position and place on a cutting board, or continue to work with it where you already have it. Cut around the anal vent and then toward the breastbone along the midline of the abdomen, being very careful not to sever any intestines. As you are cutting you might keep your finger inside to hold the intestines away from the knife. You may or may not cut right on through the breastbone, or "brisket," to the neck. Then pull out the intestines. If you didn't cut the breastbone, reach up into the chest and get the heart and lungs. You will have to help the lungs out since, unlike the intestines, they stick in the cavity. Save the heart. Pause to look carefully at the liver.

NOTE: *If the liver has white coccidiosis spots, dispose of the carcass. Do not eat the meat. The liver need not be fully spotted. Any slight discoloration is a sign of infection.*

If the liver tissue has white streaks or there are small, white cysts attached to the stomach or intestinal membranes, that's tapeworm. Don't feed the uncooked intestines to other animals (that would pass the infection on). You may eat the animal, but it must always be thoroughly cooked, like pork.

If you are going to save the liver, carefully cut away the gall bladder part of it. Don't spill any of the dark green bile that is stored in that gall bladder. If you do get bile on any of the meat you'll have to cut away and discard that part of the meat. Rinse the outside of it to wash away any adhering blood or hair or dirt. If you still have it up on the gambrel, take it down now.

CUTTING IT UP: First, cut off both front legs at the shoulder joints and both hind legs at the hip joints. Cut through the ribs on both the left and right sides, parallel to the backbone, to cut free the breast piece of the rabbit carcass. Divide the remaining back piece into 2 or 3 pieces (depending on how large the rabbit is and how large you want your pieces). The big meat pieces are found on the hind legs and the haunches (loins) where they are easy to cut from the body. The loin pieces are the choicest on the rabbit, great for stews. It's a good idea to bone the thigh, leaving the shank intact. The forelegs of a rabbit have very little meat and are better off in the stock pot.

FREEZING: Washed and chilled rabbit or cooked rabbit can be wrapped in plastic freezer bags or freezer paper. If you are including gravy or sauce with cooked rabbit, pack it in plastic containers with tight lids. Fresh rabbit will keep in the freezer for 4–6 months, but use the frozen cooked rabbit before 2 months. Thaw rabbit in the refrigerator and never refreeze. It will take up to 16 hours to thaw a whole rabbit, but smaller pieces will be ready in 4–9 hours. Or you could be modern and put it in the microwave—and be done in a jiff.

COOKING: Fry, boil, bake, roast, or barbecue the rabbit meat, or grind it for rabbit burger or rabbit sausage. Frying is the most common cooking method. Many recipes ask for rabbit meat to be browned. This can be done in a hot skillet for a few minutes then evening out in the oven at 350°F for 5–8 minutes. To preserve rabbit meat, freeze it, can it, or make jerky. Although almost any chicken recipe (and some for veal, too) can be adapted to rabbit, keep in mind that rabbit meat is very lean and delicate. Don't over cook it or let it dry out. To can rabbit, use directions for chicken.

☞ *OVEN-FRIED RABBIT Brush pieces of 1 rabbit with ¼ c. melted butter or margarine. Sprinkle with salt and pepper and place in a flat baking pan. Cover with foil or a tight-fitting lid and bake at 350°F for an hour or until tender. Occasionally brush on more butter or margarine until the top is light brown.*

☞ *BUTTERMILK RABBIT Place your rabbit pieces in a casserole dish. Pour 2 T. melted butter over 2 c. bread crumbs, and spread the buttered crumbs over the rabbit in the casserole dish. Add salt, pepper, and paprika, if you like it. Cover rabbit and crumbs with 2 c. buttermilk. Top with 3 bacon strips. Bake at 350°F for 1½ hours.*

☞ *SOUR CREAM RABBIT Cut rabbit as for frying. Brown in butter. Add 2 c. sour cream, and simmer until tender. You can*

819

season with salt, pepper, minced onion, and parsley that has been cooked in butter 2 minutes before being added. Add a little cayenne, if you like things hot.

☙ **DORIS'S RABBIT STEW** Cut up rabbit. Dredge in flour. Brown all sides. Fry until tender. Cool. Remove bones and chunk meat. Dice white potatoes and cook with thinly sliced carrots. Season. When partially done, add peas, parsley and sliced onions. Cook very slowly for 2 hours. Now take your skillet with the rabbit drippings (where you previously fried the rabbit) and make a light gravy. Pour this over your done, but not too juicy, stew. Add 2 T. butter and finish seasoning, if needed. This eliminates all wild taste in rabbit.

☙ **FRIED RABBIT** If the rabbit is very big, boil 10 minutes, drain, and then proceed when cool enough to handle. Dip in egg, then in crumbs, and sprinkle with salt (or into salted flour) and place in hot frying pan that contains plenty of fat. Cover and get the rabbit well done on the first side before you turn it to brown on the other side. If you want to make gravy, 1 c. of milk or cream will go well in it.

☙ **RABBIT AND BISCUITS** Cut up the rabbit, cover it with cold water, and put it on to boil. Add 1 t. salt and cook until tender. Have biscuits ready (buttermilk biscuits are wonderful!). Break open a biscuit on each plate. Put a piece of rabbit on the biscuit. Thicken a reasonable amount of the broth with flour, add 1 c. of milk or cream, stirring, and pour some over each piece of rabbit and biscuit. Serve at once.

☙ **ROAST RABBIT** Stuff the rabbit with a regular stuffing or line with sausage. Sew up and truss the shoulders and legs closely to the body or they'll cook to a crisp. Rub the skin with butter, add a little water to the pan, and baste often with butter unless you are using a Dutch oven with a tight-fitting lid. Make a gravy of the drippings with a little currant or wild plum jelly added and serve with mashed potatoes.

☙ **BARBECUE SAUCE RABBIT** Brown your cut-up rabbit in a heavy frying pan that has a lid. Make a barbecue sauce of 1 t. salt, pepper to taste, ½ c. water, 1 small onion (chopped), a shake of garlic powder, ¾ c. tomato paste, ½ c. catsup, ¾ c. brown sugar, ½ c. vinegar, and 2 T. prepared mustard. Pour the barbecue sauce over the browned rabbit, put the lid on the pan, and bake in a 350°F oven until done (an hour or so).

☙ **POTTED RABBIT (OR CHICKEN)** Brown meat in small amount of oil in skillet or Dutch oven. Add onions, tomatoes (stewed or fresh), wine, mushrooms (if on hand), and carrots or other vegetables as desired. Cook until tender and sauce is thick.

These recipes are from Nancy Cramer, Kent, WA:

☙ **BASIC SWEET AND SOUR SAUCE** Dissolve 1 bouillon cube in 1 c. boiling water. Add 2 T. vinegar and 1 T. brown sugar. Heat. Thicken with a flour and water paste (thin) or whatever to desired thickness. Can be used with baked chicken or rabbit.

☙ **RABBIT AND DUMPLINGS** These are even better than chicken and dumplings. Cook rabbit pieces in water (almost to cover) with salt and a bay leaf until tender. Remove bay leaf. Forty-five minutes before serving, add 2 large onions and 4 or 5 (however many you need for your family) carrots in thick slices (½ inch or thicker). Also add a couple of pinches of sweet basil and parsley. When done, drop

dumplings (any recipe) on top and cook until done—enough to avoid gumminess. I like dumplings best that rest on the meat and vegetables, sticking partly above water to cook. But you can make good dumplings in a broth too. When dumplings are done, fish them out with a slotted spoon. Serve dumplings and rabbit in one bowl, the carrot and onion mixture in another. Thicken the remaining broth with flour to make a gravy to serve over dumplings. Makes a nice one-dish meal.

☙ **BUNNY SAUSAGE** You'll need 6 lb. uncooked rabbit meat, ground; 2 small onions, minced; 2 level T. salt; 2 level t. pepper; ½ c. ground cracker or bread crumbs; ¾ c. milk; ½ t. paprika; 1 bay leaf, ½ t. ground sage; and 1 or 2 eggs, well beaten. Mix the ingredients well together. Mold into small cakes and fry until nicely browned.

☙ **CANNED OR FROZEN BUNNY SAUSAGE** Pack sausage into clean canning jars to within 1 inch of top of jar and add 3 or 4 T. of the grease in which the cakes were fried. Put on the cap, screwing the band tight. Process according to regular directions for meat. Or you could freeze it.

☙ **RABBIT SANDWICH SPREAD** Mix together 1 c. cooked, cooled, boned, and ground rabbit meat with ½ t. salt. Add mayonnaise or salad dressing as needed to moisten. If you want a spicier spread, add a pinch of white pepper, celery salt, or a seasoned salt. This is great on toast.

SHEEP

Sheep are grand lawn mowers and land fertilizers and are far less likely to damage your trees than goats are. A lamb is a cute pet that will delight any child's heart. "Lamb" (young sheep) is delicious, healthy meat. Ewes are mellow creatures to have around, and rams are pretty good as herd males go if they were treated kindly while young and were naturally mothered rather than bottle-fed. Sheep are easier to handle and transport than horses and cows. A small flock of sheep is a relatively easy livestock project for a beginner. If you have a well-fenced pasture with a minimal shelter for them, they requires only a few moments a day of feeding and watering time—except during lambing and shearing times.

They produce a wool crop as well as a meat crop, both of which can provide cash income. If your choice is between sheep and beef calves, consider that sheep aren't as expensive to buy as cattle. It is possible to milk them, and their milk makes good cheese. You can feed about 7 or 8

- Thin—this may be caused by worms
- Hard or lumpy udder—she may have mastitis
- Udder that doesn't have the proper number of nipples: 2
- Sore feet, lameness—possible infection with foot rot
- Broken or missing teeth

sheep on the amount of pasture that could support only a single cow. The meat crop will be ready 6 months after birth, instead of the year and a half it takes to get a calf to slaughter size, and the smaller animal will be easier to butcher. A general rule-of-thumb is that—in dressed meat—8 sheep equal 1 cow.

Sheep can get most cattle or goat diseases, but they are more able to survive them, and they get fewer diseases than pigs. If sheep fall in a stream, they often can't get out because their wool gets waterlogged. They are more susceptible to predators than the other large stock. Huge flocks on open range are notoriously vulnerable. When my daddy switched from the wheat business to raising cattle and a big herd of about 1,000 sheep on a high mountain ranch, sheep catastrophes sadly became routine: sheep with their flesh torn by predators and maggots crawling around in the wound, freshly sheared sheep and their little lambs dead under mounds of unseasonable snow, sheep crawling with summer ticks.

Yet I have also many lovely memories of my days among sheep—like when the Mormon shearers came up to shear in our long, tin-roofed sheep sheds. How they wrestled with the animals to give them that barber job, sweating in their trousers and long underwear tops. How the wool was packed into long cloth bags hung from a special tall tripod, and 1 man worked inside the bag stomping the wool down until he could walk on top—a very "ticky" job. Every evening Daddy would take off his long underwear, very privately in the bedroom with Mama, and she would pull the day's accumulation of ticks off him. Ticks really thrive on sheep in the mountains in the spring.

I remember in summer the weekly trip Daddy and I made up into the mountains riding horseback and leading a string of packhorses laden with supplies for the sheepherder. Sheepherders caring for a flock of sheep on a big, open range are a very special sort of people—not cartoon characters. There are lots of jokes about them, but the herders I knew in my childhood were real people, working a difficult and desperately lonely job in the mountains for low wages.

Getting Started

In general, learn as much as you can before you get started, and then begin on a small scale.

American Sheep Industry Association offers market, legislative, news, links, etc.: 303-771-3500; 6911 S. Yosemite St., Ste. 200, Englewood, CO 80112-1414; **info@sheepusa.org; www.sheepusa.org.**

Black Sheep Newsletter is a great quarterly for small-flock and colored-sheep owners. $14/yr in U.S.; $18 outside U.S.; 25455 NW Dixie Mountain Rd., Scappoose, OR 97056; 503-621-3063; **bsnewsltr@aol.com; www. blacksheepnewsletter.com.** They also offer *The Black Sheep Newsletter Companion: Writings for the Shepherd*

and Handspinner, a collection of the first five years of the magazine, and a lamb cookbook.

Montana Sheep Association offers it all: a terrific website with news, an online magazine, and a supply sales catalog! 406-442-1330; **www.mtsheep.org/.**

Sheep! gives practical advice for small flock owners, articles for small and commercial flocks on wool and related issues, plus an extensive breeders' directory and listing of breed associations and a regular feature on dairy sheep. It costs $20 for 10 issues/yr. Contact: 920-648-8285; fax 920-648-3770; PO Box 10, Lake Mills, WI 53551-0010; **www.sheepmagazine.com.**

The Shepherd, a monthly magazine for both small and commercial flocks, costs $20/yr: 419-492-2364; 5696 Johnston Rd., New Washington, OH 44854; **shepmag@brightnet.com.**

BOOKS: For sure, get a copy of *More Sheep, More Grass, More Money,* an 112-pg book by Peter Schroedter, owner of a large commercial sheep flock in Manitoba (available from *Sheep!* Magazine, $10 postpaid). The long-time (now updated/revised) classic is *Storey's Guide to Raising Sheep,* by Paula Simmons and Carol Ekarius. It includes breed descriptions, info on predators, herding with dogs, health, etc. *Sheep!* magazine often has pages listing books on sheep production. Other useful books are *The Sheep Raiser's Manual* by William Kruesi (1985); *Sheep: A Complete Owner's Manual,* by Gunther Marks (tr. from German and very good); and *The Sheep Production Handbook,* a comprehensive text from the ASI (1990) (303-771-3500; **www.sheep usa.org**).

ATTRA's booklet, "Sustainable Sheep Production," is at **www.attra.org/attra-pub/sheep.html.** Maryland Small Ruminant Page is a great website info center for both sheep and goat growers with articles plus links: **sheep andgoat.com.**

SUPPLIES

Sheepman Supply Company provides a wide range of supplies to sheep farmers, including shearing gear, health care products, books, and videos. Free catalog: 800-331-9122; 301-662-4197; fax 301-662-0361; PO Box A, Frederick, MD 21702; **info@sheepman.com; www.sheepman.com.**

Wiggins & Assoc. offer a nurser bucket for lambs, etc.: 800-600-0716; **www.wigginsinc.com.**

Vocabulary

Lamb—a young sheep
Bum—a bottle-fed lamb
Cosset—another name meaning bottle-fed lamb
Ewe—an adult female sheep, pronounced "you"
Ram—an adult male sheep
Wether—a castrated male
Yearling—sheep that's around a year old

BREEDS OF SHEEP: Marilyn Jones wrote a classic to help you sort them out: *Breeds of Sheep,* available from her at Jones Sheep Farm, 1556 E. 59th, Peabody, KS 66866. Or go to Oklahoma State U.'s livestock breeds page: **www. ansi.okstate.edu/breeds/sheep.**

What do you want the sheep for? Pets? To keep your grass mowed? To raise meat for your table—or to sell? To show at the fair? For sheepskins or leather? Or to grow wool that you will shear, card, and spin?

Do you want fast reproduction? Finn sheep have 3–6 babies at a time. But be careful you don't let a Finn ewe get bred by a ram of a larger breed. It could result in dead babies or a dead mama. Or do you want naturally polled or horned sheep? (Dorsets come either way.)

You do want always to select "open-faced" sheep, on which the wool naturally does not grow around the eyes. "Wool-blind" sheep can't avoid predators because their wool actually grows down their faces onto their eyes. So even in a wool breed you want an open face. Otherwise you must periodically clip around the sheep's eyes.

And what about personality? Breeds differ and individual sheep differ. Choose a style that suits you. A calm and pleasant disposition is easier to live with than a tense or aggressive one. On the other hand, Mouflon sheep are the only breed that is said to protect their young aggressively from predators, and that's good.

Crossbreeds. In the United States there are 9 major breeds of sheep—many of which used to be crossbreeds but now have become accepted as breeds in their own right—and innumerable crossbreeds. There are more people doing homestead-level independent and experimental cross-breeding with sheep than with any other farm species. They are frequently selecting for particular wool colors, but many other characteristics can be selected for also. Unless the crossbreed is obviously a real winner and a sheep of the future, crossbreeds may be less expensive than purebreds.

Wool Breeds. If your interest is wool, what climate do you live in? Fine-stranded wool (from the merino breed of sheep) traditionally comes from breeds suited to warmer climates like Spain. Medium-stranded wool breeds live in the temperate zones like England. The coarsest grades of wool (Lincoln breed of sheep) are associated with the cooler, damper climates. "Coarse" wool means a thick strand. Coarse wool spins faster for hand spinners than fine wools. In any case, when buying sheep for wool, look for a pink skin and a dense coat. A good wool breed like Corriedale should provide you about 10–14 lb. of wool per clipped ewe. (Enough to knit 2 sweaters.) A nonwool breed such as the Suffolk will produce only about a 5-lb. fleece.

Homespun wool has more life and strength than com-mercially spun wool. It has water-resistance, manageability, flexibility, durability, and warmth. You can choose your wool according to your purpose since wool from different sheep breeds can be quite different stuff, varying in length from 1½ to 10 inches, and in number of crimps per inch, from ½ to 30. Fine wools (such as Rambouillet) yield a softer product (suitable for a baby's blanket, for example), but are more difficult to spin. Coarse fibers (such as from Karakul or Lincoln sheep) spin more easily into a very durable product, such as a rug. Coarse wools are consid-ered too itchy to be made into clothing that would be worn next to the skin. The medium wools (Hampshire, Suffolk, Cheviot), with fibers averaging 3–4 inches long, stand be-tween these 2 extremes. They are manageable for beginning

spinners and can be made into blankets, sweaters, and fabric for other clothing.

Wool Colors. White sheep wool is the standard. Black wool is discounted in regular markets but more valued in specialty spinners' outlets. Black sheep wool can't be dyed. White and silver wool mixed comes from an old black sheep and can be dyed. Wool in other natural colors, other than white, is of interest only to hand spinners. But there are lots of hand spinners! Get more info from the Natural Colored Wool Growers Ass'n: Barbara Kloese, Registrar; 219-759-9665; 429 W. US 30, Valparaiso, IN 46385-9207; **kloese@gte.net; www.ncwga.org.** And from American Black Sheep Registry: 4714 Glade Rd., Loveland, CO 80538; **bmerino@concentric.net.** And the *Black Sheep Newsletter* (see "Getting Started"). If you want white, then make sure your sheep has no dark fibers mixed in. Suffolks are a black-faced sheep with white wool and the most com-mon registered sheep. They usually have a little black color matching their faces around their lower legs but no wool around their lower legs so they have cleaner, dainty looking feet. Hampshires are second most common, followed by Corriedales. Dorsets are all white, available either polled or horned, and are considered to be exceptionally good mothers. Karakul and Corriedale sheep are white sheep with a higher quality wool for hand spinning that you can get a premium price for.

Meat Breeds. Meat breeds have wool, too, but they are also bred for good meat production. Suffolks, Columbias, and Shropshires are good meat-wool breeds. Don't think that just because a breed is noted for good meat carcasses, it isn't also fine for wool production. Suffolks, for example, grow a nice spinning wool.

Milk Breeds. You can use sheep for milk. Sheep often have inconveniently short teats and a limited lactation period, and younger ones hate to stand still. But their milk tastes good, and it makes wonderful cheese with a dense curd. Try some Romano and see! Sheep don't give as much milk as goats. American sheep produce 1 pt. to 1 qt. of milk a day, but French dairy sheep give up to 3 qt. per day, so Americans are working now to upgrade their sheep dairy herds for productivity. Nevertheless, pound for pound, a sheep's milk will give you 2 or even 3 times more cheese than a cow's milk because it's that much higher in solids. Sheep butterfat is also different in a good way although there is twice as much of it; it's 45 percent polyunsaturated fat. Sheep milk is richer in calories than cow's milk. It pro-vides much more calcium, riboflavin, and thiamin. With all this good stuff in it, don't be surprised that it's yellower and thicker than cow's milk. Sheep milk is naturally homoge-nized because of the sort of fat in it, even harder to make butter from than goat milk, but it makes super ice cream and yogurt.

Cheesemakers' Journal regularly offers good articles on sheep dairying such as "Sheep Cheeses," "Milk Production in the Ewe," and "Yoghurt from Sheep Milk," in issue 18/19; "Sheep Dairying" in 24; "Sheep Cheesemaking in Poland" in 25; and "Sally Jackson of Washington State—Sheep Milk Cheeses" in 30 (available from 413-628-3808; **www. cheesemaking.com**). Yves Berger is the shepherd at the U. of Wisconsin's Spooner Research Station, working on dairy sheep research: 715-635-3735; W6646 Hwy. 70, Spooner, WI 54801.

David Major organized a group of Vermont folks to milk sheep. He now makes Vermont Shepherd, a sheep's milk cheese, in his curing cave from wheels of week-old sheep cheese that farmers bring him: 802-387-4473; 875 Patch Rd., Putney, VT 05346; **vtsheprd@sover.net**; **www.vermontshepherd.com**. Willow Hill Farm (**www.sheepcheese.com**) also makes sheep's milk cheese. Sheep cheeses are common in Europe but a fairly new industry here. Roger Steinkamp is president of the North American Dairy Sheep Association, and also a sheep cheese maker in Hinckley, MN. Roquefort, feta, and kasseri are all made from sheep milk, as is Italian-style Romano.

Sizes. Sheep come in different sizes. Bigger sheep require more feed and you can pasture fewer per acre. I've heard that smaller sheep actually produce more meat per acre of pasture, but I don't know if it's been proven.

Specific Breeds. There are so many breeds of sheep, I can't give you info on all of them, but here's a good start.

Border Leicester: American Border Leicester Association, Nila Swzeda, Registrar, PO Box 162, Crown Point, NY 12928; **hilltop@bluemoo.net.**

Cheviot: American North Country Cheviot Sheep Association, Edward Racel, Exec. Secy., 8708 S. County Rd. 500 W., Reelsville, IN 46171; fax 765-672-4275.

Clun Forest: North American Clun Forest Association, 21727 Randall Dr., Houston, MN 55943; 507-864-7585; **bramble@acegroup.cc; www.clunforestsheep.org.**

Coopworth Sheep Society of North America, Marcia Adams; 360-297-4485; 25101 Chris Ln. NE, Kingston, WA 98346; **rainfarm@tscuet.com.**

Corriedale: American Corriedale Association, Marcia Craig, Secy., PO Box 272W, State Rt. 182 E., Upper Sandusky, OH 43351; 740-482-2608; **columbiasheep.org.**

Cotswold Breeders Association; Tony Kaminsky, Registrar; 410-374-4383; fax 410-374-2294; PO Box 441, Manchester, MD 21102.

Damara "fat tail sheep" are called "low maintenance meat sheep for mowing, weeding, and fertilizing": (07) 5464-0533; **www.damaras.com.**

Finn: National Finnsheep Breeders Association, Elizabeth Luke, Secy., HC 65, Box 495, DeRugter, NY 13052, 887-USFINNS; **stillmeadowfinns@hotmail.com.**

Friesians are European dairy sheep that arrived in the U.S. in 1996. They're available from Willow Farm. **wsmart@together.net.** Or contact the North American Dairy Sheep Ass'n. c/o Tanya Gendreau; 608-582-4746; N20712 Thompson Lane, Galesville, WI 54630.

Hampshire: American Hampshire Sheep Association, Karey Cieghorn, Secy., 1557-173rd Ave., Milo, IA 50166; 641-942-6402.

Icelandic sheep are available from Susan and Rex Mongold, Tongue River Farm; 406-232-2819; HC 40 Broadus Stage, Miles City, MT 59301; **trf@mcn.net; www.icelandicsheep.com.**

Jacob Sheep Conservancy Registry and Breed Association, 1165 E. Lucas Rd., Lucas, TX 75002; 972-727-0900. Or PO Box 10427, Bozeman, MT 59719; **spotted sheep@yahoo.com.**

Karakul: American Karakul Sheep Ass'n; Leslie Johnson, 405-771-3072: 7001 N. Air Depot, Oklahoma City, OK 73141. Or Letty Klein; 616-381-0980, evenings; Pine Lane Farm, 6881 N. 25th St., Kalamazoo, MI 49004. American Karakul Sheep Registry: 660-838-6340; fax 660-838-6322; 11500 Highway 5, Boonville, MO 65233; **AKSR@mid-mo.net; www.karakulsheep.com.**

Katahdin Hair Sheep International, PO Box 778C, Fayetteville, AR 72702; 501-444-8441. Or Laura & Doug Fortmeyer: 785-467-8041; 2285 Falcon Rd., Fairview, KS 66425.

Lincoln: National Lincoln Sheep Breeders' Ass'n; Roger Watkins, Secy.; 1557-173rd Ave., Milo, IA 50166; 515-942-6402.

Merino: The American and Delaine-Merino Record Ass'n can provide breeder listings (AK, Canada, most states), detailed info on the breed, and registration paperwork: c/o Elaine A. Clouser, Secy.; 419-281-5786; 1026 Co. Rd. 1175, Rt. 3, Ashland, OH 44805. This breed, first developed by the Spanish from the 14th through early 19th centuries, is now raised also in America, Australia, Russia, and South Africa. Both polled (hornless) and horned varieties are available. Rated as a medium-sized sheep (rams 175–235 lb.; ewes 135–180 lb.), its "productive lifespan" is 10+ years. Merinos have a tendency to stay together (easy to herd), ability to breed out of season (lets you decide when lambing will happen), and very fine wool. Twins 50 percent of the time. Lambs weigh 100–120 lb. in five months.

Montadale Sheep Breeders Association, PO Box 603-H, Plainfield, IN 46168; 317-839-8198. Mary HaWaaboo has bred Montadales for 15 years at 3710 A St. SE #3, Auburn, WA 98002; 206-714-3257.

Navajo-Churro Sheep Association: Connie Taylor, Registrar; 505-737-0488; **churro@taos.newmex.com;** Box 94, Ojo Caliente, NM 87549.

Rambouillet: Bluestem Farm is where Walt & Wanda Martens raise both white and natural-colored Rambouillet: 502 Cash Spring Rd, Ozark, MO 65721; 417-581-7485; **bluestemfarm@hotmail.com; www.bwoolmercantile.com.**

Romanov: North American Romanov Sheep Association, 614-927-3098; Don Kirts, Secy., PO Box 1126, Pataskala, OH 43062.

Romney: American Romney Breeders Ass'n offers quality fleeces on large-framed sheep: **www.americanromney.org.** Larry & Gail Bullock have raised purebred white and natural-colored (range of black to oatmeal or champagne colors) Romneys for 20 years: 360-825-5613; 38815-272nd Ave. SE, Enumclaw, WA 98022; **lgbullock@aol.com; www.bullockromneys.org.**

Scottish Blackface Sheep Breeders Association; 417-962-5466; Richard J. Harward, Secy., 1699 Hwy. HH, Willow Springs, MO 65793; **sbsba@pcis.net.**

Shetland: North American Shetland Sheep Association, Secretary, 265 Truway Rd, Luxemburg, WI 54217; 920-837-2167.

Shropshire: American Shropshire Registry Association; Dale E. Blackburn, DVM, Secy.; 815-943-2034; PO Box 635, Harvard, IL 60033.

Southdown: American Southdown Breeders Association, Gary Jennings, Secy., 6226-100 Cornerstone Rd., Fredonia, TX 76842; 915-429-6226; **southdown@ctesc.net.**

Suffolk: United Suffolk Sheep Ass'n; Annette Benson, Secy.; 435-563-6105; PO Box 256, Newton, UT 65201.

Texel Sheep Breeders Society: Bonnie Davis, Secy.; 815-998-2359; fax 815-998-2113; 24001 N. 1900 E., Odell, IL 60460; **jbdavis@fcg.net; www.usatexels. org.** Or North American Texel Sheep Ass'n; Linda Gayle Smith; 601-426-2264; fax 601-428-2274; 740 Lower Myrick Rd., Laurel, MS 39443; **natsa@c-gate. net; www.usatexels.org.**

Tunis: National Tunis Sheep Registry, Judy Harris; 413-589-9653; 819 Lyons St., Ludlow, MA 01056.

Wiltipoll: This polled meat breed, derived from the British Wiltshire Horn, was recently developed in Australia. They're available from Rita Hough, (02) 6862-6363; Hebron Park, Parkes, NSW 2870 AUSTRALIA; **ritahough@hotmail.com.** Or David Oakley; (03) 5438-3036; 82 Brooke St., Inglewood, Victoria 3517 AUSTRALIA; **www.wiltipoll.com.** John and Glenyes Pickering; (08) 8536-0023; fax (08) 8536-0038, RSD 484, Clayton Rd, Finniss. via Strathalbyn. SA 5255 AUSTRALIA; **JandGPickering@glengrovehighlands. com.au.**

WHERE TO BUY: You are probably best off buying out of a healthy-looking flock nearby, so that you can drive the animals home yourself. Auction sheep are generally cheaper, but they may be the culls from somebody's flock, going by fast enough that you don't have a chance to find out their problems until too late. It's safest to take your time, take a sheep-knowledgeable friend along, and buy from a reputable breeder. If you want to show at a fair or to go into serious breeding, then you want to buy purebreds from an appropriate breeder.

NUMBER OF SHEEP: You will need to get more than 1 sheep or provide some other companionship because they're herd creatures by instinct. A sheep can be content in a field with a pony or even goats, but a lonely sheep will be miserable and annoy you by bleating all the time. At the other extreme, the more sheep you have, the more sheep problems you have; in other words, a small flock is easier to care for than a big one. A typical-sized year-round family flock consists of 6 or 7 ewes. A good way to get started is to buy ewes that have been recently bred in the fall. After lambing every spring, you'll have the extra lamb population for your good grass season until the fall when your lambs will be sold, butchered, or kept to increase your herd.

AGE OF SHEEP: You can start with any of 3 different age groups:

Bum Lambs. You may be able to get a couple of tiny, bottle-fed lambs for a small price, feed them milk until they can be weaned to grass, then butcher them in the fall, or keep them for breeding. If you have goats or cows and thus plenty of cheap, surplus milk (and children who will be enthusiastic about doing the work), this can be an economical way to get started. If you have to buy the milk, even using a special product from the animal feed store, it can get expensive.

Weaned Lambs. This is the easiest, least risky system of acquiring sheep as far as animal problems go. Start by buying a couple of weaned lambs. They'll be several months old as compared to the day-old bummers, past the risky stage for scours, and well started on a grass diet. If they are strictly for meat, you get them in the spring, pasture them all summer, and butcher them in the fall when the grass dies back. Or you could keep them for breeding stock. The problem with starting with yearling breeding stock is that they are slightly more likely to have difficulty lambing, and they may be reluctant to let their babies nurse—even reject them completely, which you can deal with when you have experience, but it is more difficult to handle when you're all learning together.

Pregnant Ewes. In the fall—October or November—buy pregnant 2- or 3-year-old ewes that have experience with lambing. When you buy them, be sure and ask the seller when they got bred; you need to estimate their lambing date. Feed them through the winter and lamb them out come late winter; by spring you have a sizable flock. Odds are for every 2 ewes you have, you'll get 3 lambs because of common twin or even triplet births. This is considered a relatively cost-efficient way to get started.

Whatever age sheep you start with, if you buy from a nearby breeder that you feel good about, you'll have somebody to go back to with future questions. In general, look for a large animal compared to others of the breed, with proper conformation if you're buying registered, and good health. Here are signs of poor health:

Teeth. An experienced sheep person can capture a sheep, gently lay it down, open its mouth, pull down its bottom lip, and see what shape its teeth are in. The teeth in a sheep's mouth tell its age. A lamb has 8 "milk" teeth—and they're all in its lower jaw. Somewhere between 12 and 18 months the center pair will be replaced by the sheep's first pair of permanent teeth. You can distinguish permanent teeth from the milk teeth because they're longer and wider. A 2-year-old has 4 permanent teeth. A 3-year-old has 6. A 4-year-old has 8, and that's the most it will get. In the 4-year-old sheep's mouth, all the baby teeth are replaced by the permanent ones. A sheep with those 8 permanent teeth has a "full mouth." The usual sheep produces well until it's 6 or 7 years old and may live until age 12, although after age 6, it's considered to be getting "old." As the sheep continues to get older its teeth gradually slant forward, spread out, grind down, even break off. A "broken-mouth" sheep, meaning one with teeth broken off or missing, is past its prime and not a good buy. If it lives long enough, all the teeth will be gone; that's called a "gummer."

TRANSPORTING SHEEP: You can move a sheep in the back of a pickup. Simply lift it up there! If the pickup bed has side racks, you can leave it loose in there. If the sheep is halter-broke, you can put a halter on it and tie the halter rope to something in the pickup bed. Or you can tie the sheep's legs so it can't walk and transport it that way. When moving sheep, you'll notice what size your sheep is. Transporting is one time you'd be glad for a smaller breed over a larger one.

Foods and Feeding

PASTURE

What Plants Are in Your Pasture? Ask your county extension agent if there are local plants that poison sheep, like lambkill or ragwort. Learn to identify them, and find out how other area growers avoid losses from them. Don't require sheep to clear out brush; that is a job for goats. On the other hand, be open to the possibility that a herd of sheep might well clean up a particular weed problem you have—for example, knapweed. This nasty green pest takes over very fast, kills off the other plants, reseeds itself generously, is a perennial, and is resistant to herbicides. But sheep eat it, get fat on it, and can eat it to near extinction, certainly down to a very controlled state. (In *The Sheep Raiser's Handbook* there is an excellent chapter on reclaiming brushy, weedy, abandoned pastures using sheep.) Straw and seeds in the fleece are no problem to a spinner, but burrs are a misery, so keep burrs out of your sheep pasture. Any grass is fine. Sheep are natural grass eaters and can live entirely on good green grass. Weaned lambs can grow to market weight on grass alone. Native grass is fine. If you're planting pasture for them, alfalfa, ladino, orchard grass, sweet clover, and timothy are all fine.

Keeping Wool Clean. If your wool is for you or other home spinners, you have a "spinner's flock"—and that means you'll want to take care with their pasture. Minimize burdock growth because its seed hulls are nearly impossible to get out of wool. The burdock plants are annuals. You can kill them by a hard chopping blow about 2 inches below ground level. Get to it before the plants have a chance to drop seeds. Sheep eat burdock, but not if they can find anything better. Chickens, however, will enjoy your thrown-away plants. Thistles, fleabane seeds, Spanish nettles, even the tiny timothy and bluegrass seeds, will be a problem if they get into the wool. (Chickens will enjoy all these discard plants.) Some people mow their pasture twice a year to keep weeds down. Some people bundle their sheep in actual jackets!

When you provide bedding for the sheep, it's best to select straw with long strands—it can be cleaned out of the wool relatively easily. Straw that has been chopped, wood chips, or sawdust all tend to get into the sheep's wool and become a problem to the spinner.

When to Turn Them Out. Some owners wait until the grass is 3–4 inches high before turning the sheep out to eat it. But sheep that have not been on pasture, when freshly turned out to it, may temporarily get loose bowels. It helps to give the sheep and lambs a generous portion of hay in the morning before you turn them out on the green grass the first time.

How Many Sheep? You can put out as many as 6 (or more!) ewes, plus their lambs, per acre if you have top-notch grass; 4 per acre if you have poorer grass; maybe only 2 if the pasture is full of brush and weeds, unless the weeds are a kind sheep thrive on, such as knapweed.

Rotating Pastures. This helps prevent worms. The easiest way to set up pasture rotation is to divide the pasture exactly in half. (Provide water on both sides.) When the grass on one side is eaten down, shift the sheep over to the other side.

Pasturing with Other Species. Because of the specialized shape of their teeth, sheep do eat grass down closer to the ground than cattle can. However, if they're not too crowded, cattle and sheep have been known to share a family pasture successfully. On the other hand, cows—and hogs, too—are much larger than sheep, and there have been cases when a pregnant ewe running with them got injured.

Other species pasturing with sheep have been used in the role of protectors. A donkey in with sheep is quite likely to turn the tables on predator dogs and chase them. Some goats will also stand up to dogs.

WATER AND SALT: Sheep need a reliable supply of clean water and a source of salt. You can buy the salt as a 50-lb. block at the livestock feed store.

WINTER FEEDING: As with all grass-eating livestock, the longer winters are in your locale, the more expense you'll have providing feed, and the more labor you'll have feeding it, and cleaning out the barn come spring. Some good winter feeds are almost free. Sheep enjoy being allowed to glean in harvested corn fields. The old-timers also fed them root crops from the garden in winter to supplement their hay. Some grain is traditionally fed at least in the period before and after lambing. Hay will be the bulk of their winter feed: 2–4 lb. of legume hay per day per sheep. On a basic hay and grain diet, each sheep will need about 10 bales of hay and about 75 lb. of grain to get through the winter.

SUMMER SUPPLEMENTS: To get good wool and normal growth, sheep have to eat. So hay and/or grain are used in summer to supplement if their pasture is poor: anywhere from ¼ to ½ lb. of grain per animal per day.

Housing and Fencing

HOUSING: Consider what your climate is and what the climatic origin of your particular sheep breed is. If you are raising only a couple of weaned lambs for meat to make use of your grass crop, you don't need to provide more than shade from the sun—either trees or a shed. Sheep have warm fur coats and don't mind rain a bit. If you are wintering over pregnant ewes, you do need some shelter for them in very cold weather (when temperatures fall below freezing), and at lambing time, and right after they are sheared if the weather turns cold. Other times they can live out in the open. Just about any old building will do, even a 3-sided one—except for during lambing, when pens are also necessary. You can even lamb on pasture ("Spring Pasture Lambing" audio, by Janet McNally; 800-748-9808). A creep (a feeder designed to allow young sheep but not adults to get the food) is advisable.

Don Fallick, my fence and barn expert, agrees: "Unless you live in a polar region, sheep don't really need a barn. A loafing shed to keep off the sun in the summer and protect from wind the rest of the year works fine. Some folks like to bring their sheep into a pen in a great barn during lambing time. With the advent of electric sheep clippers, it has also become common to see sheep brought to the barn for shearing."

HAY RACK AND GRAIN TROUGH: It makes your hay go farther if you provide a hay rack in which to feed it—and the same applies to a feeder trough for the grain. A trough is easy to make by just nailing boards together in a rectangular shape.

MANURE: When you have confined sheep you have sheep manure. I hear it's excellent for lawn or garden because it "does not burn" and can be scattered right onto field, garden, or lawn without harm. Or it can go directly to your compost pile and from there wherever it's wanted.

OF PREDATORS, PROBLEMS, AND FENCING: Of all the big domestic animals, sheep are most vulnerable to catastrophe. They have no natural defense against predators, not much good sense about things in general, and a frequently disastrous instinct to follow the leader, no matter what. That means if you have 1 sheep in trouble, you likely have more than 1 in trouble. One sheep grower told me, "I've lost over 100 head of lambs to coyotes in the last 8 years." I asked, "How big a herd was that out of?" I was hoping he'd say something like "thousands." His reply, however, was, "That was from about 60 head of ewes."

Sherrie Campos wrote me: "A pack of dogs ran through our back pasture and Sunday morning we found a literal blood bath in our pond. Our mama sheep, Abby, and her 4-month-old lamb were standing in the pond. We had to go in and pull them out. In horror we found huge chunks of flesh missing and her bare bones exposed, gashes all over her neck and back. Abby died in our arms. Her little lamb almost died. Thor, our precious bottle baby was dead with no mark on him. The vet said he was scared to death. We had 2 funerals that Sunday and another just 2 days later. The children had horrible nightmares for months."

Your well-built fence stands between these lovable innocents and all the bad things out there that could happen to them. Sheep need fencing to keep them out of gardens—and to keep predators away from them, especially bears, coyotes, wolves, and wild or uncontrolled dogs. Even when dogs don't mean to kill a sheep they can; if they run it for the fun of it, the sheep dies of exhaustion. Sheep and goats require similar fencing. If you have to build a fence, that will probably be your biggest start-up expense with sheep. Check the fence line occasionally. Sheep will find and enlarge small holes; and if 1 leaves, being groupies, they all will. The most predator-proof fence for them would be 6-feet-high woven wire with a single tight strand of barbed wire at its base and above its top.

Herd Dogs. Sheep owners may be interested in 2 very different types of sheep dogs. One type is the sheep-herding breeds. These dogs literally "drive" or chase the sheep to put a flock, large or small, where it needs to go. Sheep don't have high IQs. Sheep-herding dogs do. I've read that Border Collies are the most intelligent of all dog breeds. I've owned and loved them for years. They helped me raise my children and saved a little kid's life more times than I like to remember. Mike and I lived on a ranch that was afflicted with rattlesnakes, and that's what our dog (which herded young humans rather than sheep) protected them from. The dog always knew the snake was there before the kid did. It would get between child and snake and bark and carry on, barking and jumping around, until an adult came out of the house and solved the problem. Sheep magazines carry ads offering trained collies. A mature Border Collie is very like having another human being to work with, within 4-legged limitations, of course. All the collies are herd dogs.

Guard Dogs. The other type of sheepdog breed is the guard dog. A good guard dog does not chase or kill sheep. It remains with the herd day and night, following it everywhere, living in the field with it rather than in the house with you. Unsupervised, they will protect the flock from predators, from coyotes, wild dogs, wolves, etc. The typical guard dog is big, about 100 lb., placid and aloof in

temperament, able to live and work alone at their post. They typically respond only slowly to human command, but in a battle they move quickly to accomplish their job. Guard dog breeds are Anatolian Shepherds, Great Pyrenees, Maremmas, Komondors, Kuvasz, and Shar Planinetz. The Great Pyrenees dog is the size, shape, color, and texture of a sheep. I kid you not. And the idea is that they live with the sheep, but act like a dog protecting its family if a predator comes around. The guard dog is effective because it's big and it barks. It defends against other dogs because the larger guard dog easily establishes dominance over a possible predator dog, and the predator gets distracted in dog interactions rather than chasing sheep. Guard dogs also will threaten, even attack sheep predators, although they do not pursue a predator if it leaves, remaining instead with the herd. The best guard dogs are mature rather than young and playful. Not every member of a guard-dog breed makes the best guard dog. One traditional way of raising the best of these is to have a puppy of the breed be adopted by and nurse from a ewe.

For more info, look up "livestock guarding dog" or "working dogs" on the Internet. The Maryland Small Ruminant web page has many articles on predator behavior (coyote, wolf, bear . . .), identification ("Something's been killing my sheep, but what?") and defenses (fences, management, guard animals): **www.sheepandgoat.com.** "Using Guard Animals to Protect Livestock" is at **www. conservation.state.mo.us/documents/landown/wild/ guard_animals.pdf.** The book . . . *May Safely Graze: Protecting Livestock Against Predators,* by Eugene Fytche, has chapters on various guard animals.

Anyway, if you're serious about sheep, you may well want to get serious about a sheepdog too. Our sheepherders couldn't have made it without the dogs who would move the herd at the proper signal from the herder. Or try a guard llama. My friend Janice Willard says coyote predation on her flock stopped after she acquired an adult male, not-castrated llama to stay with them.

Reproduction

THE EWES

Fat Ewes. Overweight ewes are difficult to get pregnant. So if your ewes are too plump, they should be dieting starting at least 6 weeks ahead of the expected breeding date. Obese ewes are also at risk for pregnancy toxemia. In that case the heavily pregnant ewe acts listless, walks aimlessly. Her muscles twitch. She grinds her teeth. Then comes a coma followed by death. Obese ewes that are pregnant with twins or triplets and who have been underfed in late pregnancy are most likely to develop this (also called "twin-lambing disease" or "lambing paralysis" or "Ketosis"). There's no cure, only prevention—the diet before getting pregnant. Then take them off the diet and flush them in the usual way.

Flushing the Ewes. This is done about 2 weeks to 10 days before breeding, when the sheep is ovulating the eggs that will be fertilized by the ram when she is bred. The idea is to persuade her body to make as many eggs as possible, because twins and triplets are extra profit for the grower. And most growers figure that just barely to make it at least half the ewes must have twins—a "150 percent lamb crop." So the ewes are "flushed" by putting them out on the lushest pasture, or feeding the best legume (alfalfa) hay—as much as they will eat, or by adding a grain ration, or increasing the grain ration by about a half more. Ewes flushed this way do "shed" more eggs and thus have more multiple births.

Breeding-Time: Eye, Tag, and Foot-Check. If the breed is not open-faced owners may "eye" the sheep, which means clipping wool away from around the eyes. At the same time, they typically prepare for the breeding by cutting wool from around their animal's vaginal opening. That's called "tagging" or, at more length, "clipping wool from around the dock." The argument for doing it is that it keeps the animal cleaner and prevents wool from getting in the ram's way when he's trying to connect. And while the owner is at it, the sheep's feet get checked and trimmed as needed. Sheep hooves are trimmed the same as goat hooves. Use a sharp knife, pruning shears, or hoof trimmers from a livestock supply store.

Breeding Season. Except for a few breeds, most sheep have a natural mating season that extends from early September through December. During that breeding season your ewes will go into their sexually receptive, fertile "heat" phase lasting from 3 hours to 3 days on a cycle of about every 13–19 days, 17 on the average.

Because the gestation time is 5 months (143–151 days to be precise), a ewe bred in September will lamb in chilly February. A ewe bred in December will lamb in balmy May, which reduces the risk of a chilled lamb. On the other hand, lambs born in February will be husky enough to go out in the weather and eat grass as soon as it's coming on well, and thus be able to take advantage of the entire grass season for their growth. And they'll be ready for market sooner than May lambs. So either way has advantages. Some growers just leave the ram in with the ewes and let him service them whenever. In that case the ram decides— and he will probably breed them early rather than later. Then your lambs will arrive in January, or possibly February.

Age of Ewe at Breeding. A ewe that is at least 9 months old can be bred. She is a little more likely to require assistance during lambing, but statistical studies have shown no likely damage to her body, and by breeding her that first season, she'll produce 1 extra annual lamb crop over her reproductive lifetime.

THE RAM: Most sheep farmers who have a half dozen ewes or more keep a ram, or else they use artificial insemination. A mature ram can impregnate or "service" as many as 30 ewes. A ram that was born just the previous spring can also service ewes, but not as many—maybe a dozen. However, if you have a small flock, a yearling ram can be a good way to accomplish your breeding. You can buy a yearling ram from off your farm to avoid in-breeding. After he has bred your ewes, you might eat or sell him. That way you don't have to pay to winter him. If you do decide to keep a ram, he will be able to continue doing his job for years, but the number of ewes he can service and the comparative fertility of his sperm will start gradually dropping after around age 5.

People with only a few ewes are more likely to consider the drawbacks of keeping a ram. A ram tends to be larger, more grumpy, even dangerous. For example, a Dorset ewe weighs 125–150 lb., but a Dorset ram will weigh 175–200 lb. Since a ram has to work only a few minutes a year to do his job, some small flock owners avoid the expense and bother of owning one by renting a ram when needed, or

taking the ewes to a ram, or by artificially inseminating.

PREGNANCY AND LAMBING

Pregnant Ewes. Make sure that your pregnant ewes are getting enough nourishing food, especially during the last half of pregnancy when the fetus is growing fastest—particularly the yearlings because they are themselves still growing, too. Good legume hay fed free choice as the grass supply dwindles is essential. Growers who feed grain give it to sheep who are pregnant, lactating, or being prepared for the show ring or meat market. They gradually increase the grain ration for pregnant ewes from about ¼ lb. at the beginning of gestation to ½–1 lb. per day in the last 6 weeks of pregnancy. During these last 6 weeks of pregnancy the ewe especially needs generous feeding plus plenty of exercise. This regimen is thought to help prevent pregnancy toxemia.

Lambing Shelter. Your pregnant ewe will carry her lamb(s) for about 5 months, and then give birth. It's important to be prepared for that lambing event. The most dangerous period in a sheep's life is its first 48 hours. Planning ahead for good shelter can help minimize problems.

Lambing Pens. Your lambing pens should be in a place that's roofed at least enough to where it will be absolutely dry inside and thoroughly protected from wind. An easy way to create (and dismantle) pens as needed is to have a supply ready of what looks like gates without fences (about 8 feet long by 3 feet high), plus some baling type wire. When you need to create a pen you take 2 "gates," arrange them in an "L" shape against a corner pair of walls, and wire them into place. That gives you an instant square-shaped pen. Or you can arrange them against a flat wall and have a 3-sided pen. Make your "gates" ahead of time and use them year after year. Once you have them made, you'll probably discover some other good uses for them too.

Lambing. Because the lambs are typically born during cold weather, and because birthing is always a critical time for mothers and offspring, you need to be close by. I remember my daddy and the sheepherder making the rounds at night with a Coleman lantern and a big quart jar of iodine to dab on the babies' cord ends. When sheep have babies they tend to have them all at once. A flock of a thousand will all lamb out within 3 days or so, and it is bound to be a sleepless, exhausting time for the shepherd because he or she has to check the ewes every 2 hours, day and night, to give help where it's needed. Even when you own only a few ewes rather than hundreds, they will still lamb near the same time and need to be checked on that frequent schedule day and night until the birthing is accomplished and the lambs are on their feet, nursing, dry and obviously thriving.

LAMBING CHECKLIST

1. Birthing hang-ups: Sheep and goats are born the same way, so these instructions will work for either one. If the fetus is normally positioned you'll see the front feet and nose first. Usually the ewe doesn't need help, but once in a while you'll notice an overly long labor that isn't producing anything yet. In that case, wash your hands—and arms—well with a disinfectant soap and feel up her vagina. The fetus can get lodged in her birth canal sideways, or it may be coming out backwards, or a leg may be out of normal position and somehow preventing the normal delivery. You gently feel around and try to figure out what the problem is, and then figure out how to fix it.

2. Cord: After the lamb is born, pinch or cut off its umbilical cord 4–5 inches from its belly. Then dip its navel cord into an iodine solution or paint it with the iodine. That prevents infection.

3. Warmth: Have old towels, blankets, burlap bags, warm rags, or some such available in case you need to wrap a chilly lamb. Some growers even supply a heat lamp for drying off and warming newborn lambs right in the lambing shed. Chilling is the problem you're most likely to have. This is a big reason why at lambing time you check your sheep at least every 2 hours. If a lamb gets chilled, it can be quickly fatal. If you find a chilled lamb, even one that seems nearly dead, wrap it, get it into the house, warm it up, and then get it dry. For the worst cases, put the lamb into hot water for a few minutes—all but its head. Then dry it, wrap it in something, and put it in a thoroughly warm place such as a box by your wood stove, or under a heat lamp. A lamb in severe chilling crisis can also be helped by giving it warm milk to drink. Warm it thus for a few hours. Then it should be able to return to its mother.

   If the lamb has recovered from its birthing chill, has a mother that lets it cuddle up to get warm, and nurses regularly, it can endure temperatures that are even below zero—if you have it and its mother in a pen that is at least dry and sheltered from the wind.

4. Has the newborn lamb nursed on its own from the mother within half an hour of its birth? If not, move it gently close to the ewe's udder. Take one of the ewe's nipples in your hand, gently open and hold open the lamb's mouth with your other hand, and squirt her milk right into its mouth. This first milk is the antibody-containing colostrum, and the lamb needs it to thrive.

5. Did a ewe have twins or triplets? Is one of them visibly weaker than the other? If so, make sure that the mother is noticing both of them and nursing both of them, because it is possible she may not attend to the weaker one or may even harm it.

6. Overcoming lamb rejection: If you had to take the lamb away to warm it or if the ewe hasn't clicked into her motherly instinct with it yet, take some of her placenta and rub it across the lamb's body, especially right about the anus. That's the place a mother smells in order to identify her baby. After smelling her placenta on

it, she should be satisfied and cooperate in letting it nurse or letting you help it nurse. That system can work to get a ewe to adopt an orphaned lamb. Or adoption can be accomplished by skinning the dead lamb and then draping that skin over the orphan.

7. Pinning: A lamb's first feces tend to be sticky. Sometimes the tail gets literally glued to its body and it can't get out any more bowel movements. This will soon be fatal if not fixed. You just get it loose, clean up the lamb's rear, and give it a fresh start. (Most owners will cut off those tails a week after birth.)

8. Mastitis: Avoid this inflammation of the udder by not overfeeding the ewe. Ewes with access to good grass will do fine without any grain. Ewes being fed grain shouldn't get more than what they were eating before the lambing, as more would cause them to make more milk than their lambs can drink and the backup of milk can cause infection.

9. Does the ewe lack milk? This is rare, but it can happen. In that case you have a bum lamb and need to get it started on the bottle. But don't give up too soon.

BUM LAMBS: A bottle-fed lamb is known as a "bum lamb" or a "bummer" or a "cosset." It's perilously easy to turn a lamb into a bum lamb. To avoid this, just coax or force the sheep's nipple into its mouth. Reflex will do the rest. If you feed it its first meal from a bottle instead of managing to get ewe and lamb connected for the purpose, from that moment on it's going to look at you and follow you as if you were its mother—and bleat for you when it's hungry.

Bottle. Any glass bottle with a narrow neck can be a lamb bottle if you have a rubber nipple to pull over the neck of it. (Hold the bottle firmly by the neck to keep the lamb from jerking the nipple off with its forceful sucking and spilling the milk.) Or you can buy lamb feeding bottles from a livestock store—maybe even your local pet store.

Schedule. The lamb will do best if it is bottle-fed every 4–6 hours until it is 3 weeks old, and then every 8 hours or so for the next 2 months. At the beginning don't try to get the very young lamb to drink more than 2 oz. at each feeding. Its appetite will gradually build up.

Milk. You can feed a bum lamb spare goat or cow's milk once it's started, but it's important—if you possibly can—to get the mother's colostrum milk into it for its first few days. That may mean milking her by hand and then putting the milk into a lamb bottle for feeding. When the old-timers couldn't get the colostrum milk into a bum lamb, they would substitute a pint of cow or goat milk with an egg beaten up in it and a pour of dark corn syrup. Livestock stores can get you "lamb milk replacer," which is better food for them in terms of composition than goat or cow milk, but not cheap. But there's no substitute for the antibodies in natural colostrum.

Weaning. Lambs start out completely on mother's milk. By around 2 months old, or whenever the grass is sufficiently up, they'll start eating grass in addition to nursing. Gradually they shift to independent eating completely. Creep feeding is the practice of providing grain to the lambs in special feeders that the adult sheep cannot squeeze into. Creep feeding will cause lambs to gain weight faster than they would otherwise.

LAMB MARKETING: Lambs can be sold to 4-H members to use as fair projects, or kept to raise for family meat, or marketed as spring lamb to ethnic groups that have traditional lamb feasts for Passover or Easter. This market is generally located in big cities and wants a lamb under age 5 months. With the right contacts, it can pay off. Try not to make pets of lambs that will be eaten.

Sheep Vetting

TAIL DOCKING: Something most city folks don't know about sheep is that their tails are generally cut off when they are young—by the knife or by putting a very tight rubber band around its base to cut off the blood supply to it. The arguments for docking (cutting off) the tail are: If you don't dock the tail, fat accumulates in there and it gets pretty big. It also tends to get dirty with a collection of manure, burrs, and so on—especially if the sheep get the runs from a binge of too much grain or being suddenly put out on lush pasture. A build-up of manure under a tail can get maggoty and be a big problem—especially in a rainy, chilly climate. And some growers believe that a tailless ewe is easier for a ram to breed successfully.

The arguments against docking are that if you feed your animals carefully and avoid diarrhea episodes and plan to market or butcher them privately before breeding, there's really no need. A further argument is that long-tailed ewes actually breed fine, too. A final argument is that it's much ado about nothing because there are Mediterranean communities where a fat-tailed sheep is normal, and the big tail is a valuable product of butchering.

The more I know, the more I know I don't know. But as a personal preference, I favor the docking. There are several good ways to accomplish it if docking is your choice:

Elastration. The rubber band is a special type that is put on using a special tool called an "elastrator." The banded tail soon drops off by itself.

Cutting. To cut a tail off, first tie a tough twine very tightly around the tail's base. That cuts off the blood flow like a tourniquet. Choose a cutter that is strong, but not too sharp. (Sharper cutting edges actually make for worse bleeding.) Heat your cutter blades. That's for sterilization and because the hot blades cauterize the wound. Catch the lamb, hold it tightly between your legs with its hind end toward you. Holding it between your legs frees up your hands. Then simply cut off the tail with your nippers. Cut the tail off 1–2 inches from its base. If you cut shorter, it will bleed worse. Smear on wound-coagulant ("blood stop") and an antiseptic such as iodine. In an hour smear on wound-coagulant and antiseptic again. Done this way you'll discover that an hour later your lamb seems just as happy and healthy as if nothing had happened to it. Twenty-four hours later, take off the tourniquet twine and put on a final application of the coagulant.

CASTRATING: The old-timers believed that the meat of full males wasn't as good. That's true if you're going to wait over a year to eat it, but any male lamb that was born in the early spring and killed in the late fall will taste just as good castrated or uncastrated. Nevertheless, if you plan to market those male lambs, you'll get a lower price for them if they aren't castrated. A more serious argument for castrating males who are destined to be meat rather than kept for breeding stock is that the uncut males are more trouble to handle and will definitely breed the females among them if they are 6 months old or more. So if you have a planned

breeding program and incest isn't in it, then you'll have to get the males in separate quarters from the females by that age—or castrate. The usual time to castrate is 2 weeks after birth. For information about castration, see Chapter 8.

PARASITES AND DISEASES: Prevention is always the best approach. Buy from a healthy flock, give good feed, keep their shelter clean, rotate their pasture. Nevertheless, problems do happen. You can buy medicines for common health problems from your vet, or at your livestock feed store, or through a mail-order livestock-products supplier.

Worms. Having worms is the most common health problem that sheep may get. It's best if you can keep a worm problem from starting. The worms are picked up by the sheep from grazing on an infected pasture. Pasture rotation helps to keep them from grazing too close. If your animals do get worms, then you can give them a commercial wormer.

Foot Rot. Foot rot is fairly common, so if your sheep limps, the cause is quite possibly foot rot. It is treated by first trimming bad areas away from the hoof, then applying a medicine to the hoof. Prevent it by avoiding overcrowding among your flock and keeping their hooves trimmed neatly. A popular medical preventive is to drive your sheep through a footbath that has copper sulfate or formalin in it. The traditional dimensions for such a footbath trough are 1 foot by 6 inches by 16 feet long. Place portable fence sections on either side of the trough (tilted enough outward that the sheep can get through). Or you can paint the copper sulfate on their hooves with a big brush. In areas where sheep are common and sheep services are available, you may be able to get on the route of an itinerant sheep-dipper who will furnish the medicine, the vat, and the effort to run your sheep through it—for a fee.

Fever. Fever is a special problem with sheep because it affects the wool. When a sheep is fevered, the wool growing out of its skin at that time develops a weakness in the strand. Some growers deal with that by shearing the sheep after it gets well (no later than 2 weeks after the fever is best). That way the weak spot will be on the end of the strand anyway and the wool isn't ruined by having a weak spot in the middle.

WOOL: SHEARING TO SPINNING

WHY SHEAR? Do shear your sheep, even if you don't use or sell the wool and must throw it away. If you don't shear, the sheep shed some of it anyway and, unless you live extraordinarily far north or at high altitudes, are miserably hot wearing the rest through the summer.

WHEN? There is no absolute written-in-stone time you have to shear. It's a judgment call. Most sheep owners shear in the early spring. Or in the fall and spring. Most growers believe that if you don't shear them before the weather gets hot the sheep may feel hot or, worse, get worms or be sick. Growers generally wait for spring shearing until just before the sheep go off hay and onto grass pasture. One reason for that timing is that the new grass tends to have a laxative effect on the sheep, and that, of course, dirties the wool around their rear. Some old-timers also claim that warmer weather increases the amount of grease in the fleece, which makes cutting easier and the fleece heavier (it sells by the pound). Unless you have shelter for the sheep and have them in it, and if you live in a harsh climate, it's wise to wait until the warmer weather has arrived to shear because sheep have delicate health, and a night out in a storm immediately after shearing can take an awful toll. That one's from sad experience.

But a few growers shear only in the late fall just before the sheep are moved into winter housing from their pasture. If that housing is good shelter, the advantage of winter shearing is cleaner wool (outdoor living is cleaner) and a better wool market since you're selling in the off-season. Market lambs that will be butchered in the late fall can be sheared at about 5 months of age—or as part of a general fall shearing.

Who Will Shear?

Sheep-shearing isn't easy for an amateur. The goal is to get off the entire fleece in 1 piece, leaving the sheep looking neat—and do it with 1 swipe of the clippers in each place so that the shorn wool is of a maximum, and uniform, length. If you have to take more than 1 swipe to get the wool off your sheep, there will be wool of uneven lengths (called "second cuts"), and that diminishes the spinnability of the wool. You need somebody to do it for you, or show you how, if you've never shorn before. There are shearers who work for hire, going from farm to farm, and people with small flocks who do their own shearing and will also shear for hire. Your basic choice is to hire or learn how.

HIRE A PROFESSIONAL: So ask around of other sheep owners to find such a person. Many sheep shearers have a regular schedule during shearing season. The shearer may require a minimum number of sheep, or a minimum fee. In that case, you might be able to get permission to take your sheep to a place where the shearer is scheduled to visit and have them done there. But hiring a professional is possible only in areas that they regularly visit during shearing season. If you live in an isolated region, or are watching your budget closely, or simply want the adventure of learning this skill for yourself . . . read on.

DO IT YOURSELF: Shearing a sheep is challenging for an amateur, but anybody can learn how. It helps to watch somebody else do it first, although plenty of people have learned to do it without even that much help. You can order a 2-hr instructional video, "Shearing Techniques," from Rural Route Videos: 800-823-7703; PO Box 359C, Austin, Manitoba R0H 0C0, CANADA; **martin@ruralroutevideos. com; www.ruralroutevideos.com.** (They also offer videos on "Starting Your Border Collie on Cattle, Sheep or Ducks," "The Basics of Good Sheep Management," "Working Horses of the '90s," "Old-Time Farming," and "British Sheep Fairs." Price per video: $29.95 + $5 s/h.) Don't expect your sheep to look very great the first time. The important thing is just to give it that haircut, to get the essential accomplished somehow. You'll get better at it and more comfortable with doing it every time.

How to Shear

1. CHOOSE A SHEARING DATE: See "When?" above. Also, in very humid weather, the wool would be wet. It's best to shear after a spell of dry weather.

2. OBTAIN A CLIPPER: Hand clippers are cheap and can be made to do the job, as long as you don't have a large number of sheep. You could make do with garden-type shears. Have your shears really sharp. Electric clippers are expensive, but you have to buy them only once, and they're much easier to do a good job with. You can buy straight-bladed manual 6-inch sheep shears.

3. CHOOSE A SHEARING PLACE: Do your shearing in a small pen so that, if your animal does get away from you, you don't have to chase it all over creation to finish.

4. PREPARE A SHEARING SURFACE: Spread a tarp or plastic sheet on the ground, or shear on a clean floor well away from anything like straw or dirt that could get into the fleece. You want to keep the wool as clean as possible.

5. GET SHEEP: Herd or wrestle the sheep into the pen and onto your clean surface.

6. POSITION SHEEP: Have somebody else there with you to help hold the sheep. Keep in mind any time you handle sheep that you should not grab wool. Wool grabs can hurt your sheep—or mess up the natural appearance of the fleece. Get the sheep firmly between your knees on its side or back, with the head pointing toward your behind. Positioning the sheep on its rear minimizes the fight.

7. CULL CLIP: First you cut off any wool that holds fecal material, called "dung locks." Also cut off knots of matted wool, called "grease tags." Cull clippings are most likely to be from around the anus—and in the belly area. Owners of small private herds usually sell their wool to hand spinners, and these people want only clean wool. So people shearing for hand spinners are likely to discard the sheep's leg, belly, and head clippings if they are dirty or full of chaff, burrs, seeds, thistles, etc. After being cut off, the cull clips are thrown away.

8. DO THE WOOL CLIP: Now you're doing the serious shearing. Clip away, turning the sheep's body as needed. Clip as near the body as you can. The sheep's wool, if you work right, will come off all in 1 piece that holds together nicely, and that's the "fleece" or "wool clip." You will sort of twirl the sheep and shear it at the same time. With practice you'll soon get the moves right and know sheep anatomy blindfolded! The ideal is to shear off the entire fleece so that it remains 1 connected piece and the sheep looks neat and well-groomed when you're done. In order to accomplish this, here are the important points to keep in mind:

a. Start with the animal's head.
b. If you're using hand shears, clip across its body from one side, across its back, and across the other side. You work your way thus from its head end toward its rear end until you arrive at its bottom—and by then you have all its wool off.
c. If you're using electric clippers, make strokes from head to tail that are as long as possible. Pros can reach from one end clear to the other end of a sheep's body when shearing. In this case, another way to do it is (again starting with the head end) to first do one whole side (head to tail), then the whole back (head to tail), and then the other side (head to tail)—and then you're done.
d. Clip as close to the sheep's body as you can. The basic skill of shearing is learning to clip as near the body as possible, using a single cut only and without cutting the animal's skin. When you are just learning to shear, and if you are doing it with hand shears, aim to hold the cutter about ½ inch out from the skin. If you go

closer, you risk having a bleeding sheep. With clippers you can go closer. *Be careful not to nick your sheep's ears or teats!* But cut close, because if you cut the wool in the middle of its length, you get short wool that is not good for spinning.

e. A corollary of the "cut close" rule is: *No second cuts allowed.* That is, no going back and taking more wool where you've already cut once—for if you reclip (trying to get what you missed the first time), you just get loose, short strands that are no good anyway. If you do make a second cut for the sake of the sheep's appearance, just throw the short wool out. It can't be part of the fleece.

9. TREAT THE NICKS: Beginners—and old-timers, too!—inevitably make a few nicks, so forgive yourself. Treat each with a disinfectant before you turn the sheep loose again.

10. CHECK THE HOOVES: This is the same as the fall prebreeding check-up. Trim as needed.

11. BAG THE FLEECE: Have ready a bag such as a gunnysack. Gather up the fleece and put it into the bag.

12. ON TO THE NEXT: Turn that sheep out and grab the next.

13. PACKAGE THE WOOL: Each fleece should all be clinging together in a single piece. First lay it out and examine it. If you're selling to hand spinners, trim off any remaining dirty wool. For the commercial market, you can leave so-so dirty wool. Factory-handled wool gets a chemical treatment to dissolve dirt, etc. (which is why homespun feels better next to your skin). If the wool is damp or even wet, let it dry before the next step.

Gather up the fleece with the part that was closest to the sheep's skin now facing outside. Never tie a fleece with plastic twine, for those fibers can get mixed with the wool and create a problem at future processing stages. Paper twine—if you have it—is fine. To keep the fleece at home, store it in a loose state in paper bags or cardboard boxes. Never store it in a plastic bag.

14. LOOK FOR TICKS: Now you're done. Go someplace where you can strip naked and have somebody else check you all over for ticks.

Wool

WOOL MARKETING: Wool is sold by the pound. Some sheep keepers are into spinning and weaving, and they keep the animals mainly for their personal wool crop, which they'll card, spin, and weave themselves. Many sell to other hand spinners or to a larger wool buyer. In general, hand spinners like wool in interesting colors like black, silvery, brown, or blue, and will pay 2–10 times as much as commercial wool buyers, depending on how pretty—and how scarce—the color and texture of the wool is. Ask around to find out where other wool growers in your area are selling. You may find some willing to combine with you to make a commercial-sized shipment. The price of commercial wool depends on what is happening on the international wool market, which fluctuates and cannot be reliably predicted.

OF WOOL AND MARKET LAMBS: These will provide 3–5 lb. of fleece each at a 5-month shearing. After a private butchering, those sheep hides can also be tanned for sale. If the lambs had unusual colors or very nice wool, these tanned hides can be as profitable as the meat. (When sheep are sold for meat to commercial buyers the grower can't get the sheepskin.) Your county extension agent may be able to help in this marketing area.

CLEANING A FLEECE: A spinner can take a clean fleece and spin it before washing—it's called spinning "in the grease." But some people prefer prewashing. And many fleeces aren't that clean.

About Lanolin. Any "raw" wool fleece has a greasy feel from the natural sweat and lanolin wax. The older the wool gets before it is spun, the stiffer the wax on it gets, and the harder it will be to spin. Once you have your wool cleaned, it will weigh 30–60 percent less than it did before, because of the weight of the grease removed. But don't try or expect to get out all the grease. Leaving some permits easy spinning and creates a desirable water-resistance in your finished product. Since wool for dyeing must first have all the grease washed out to enable the mordant chemicals to take hold, many spinners seek out naturally colored wools: not just white, but also the shades of brown, black, and gray. Natural wool with some of its oil left in retains its water-repellent qualities. So don't wash all of the lanolin out of the wool. However, wool that you're planning to dye does have to have almost all the lanolin washed out or the dye won't set. To make homemade lanolin, boil a batch of sheep wool, and drain the oil. The lanolin is the oil. If you handle newly sheared wool you get your hands loaded with lanolin. It's very soothing and healing to the skin.

Degreased Wool. If you do remove all the grease in your cleaning process, or if you are working with purchased "scoured" (degreased) wool, you'll need to replace some oil. Sprinkle several drops of olive, mineral, or tanner's neat's-foot oil on your fibers, roll them up, and let them rest at least a quarter-hour before spinning.

Cautions When Cleaning Wool. A problem with wool is its tendency to be damaged by harsh treatment. When cleaning it, never agitate it in the water. Never wring or twist; it is all right to squeeze or press it. Always change

temperatures gradually. Never immerse it in any strongly alkaline solution: no bleach, no "super-cleaners" (use mild soap, mild detergent, or washing soda). Don't use too much soap. If the water is too hot, the wool will shrink and wad up into little knots and you can't even card it. Wool isn't that different fresh from the sheep or in the sweater. Remember you've got 100 percent wool! Dry the wool in the shade, not in the sun. Or if you choose to dry in the sun, minimize its exposure to a few hours. Don't let the wind blow it away.

Wool-Cleaning Steps

1. For this first step, you'll want to work with the wool over a newspaper outdoors. The fleece is probably dirty and has seeds and the like in it. Pull the strands gently apart and let that kind of thing simply fall out. While you're doing this you may want also to sort the wool somewhat. Any fleece contains more than 1 quality of wool. The shoulders and upper back tend to have the finest, softest strands.

2. Put wool in a tub or other container with warm water (95°F) and a very mild soap or detergent. Let it soak in warm water 10 minutes, drain, soak again, and drain again.

3. Add your cleaning agent to warm water, and make sure it is thoroughly dissolved before adding wool. Some people gently wash the wool, pulling it apart with their hands. Some just let the wool soak in this mixture another 10 minutes, drain, soak in fresh cleaning agent water again, and drain again.

4. Rinse twice using the same procedure as in step 2.

5. Dry by spreading the wool on paper or by hanging it in the shade.

6. At this stage you dye the wool, if you want to. Some dyes don't require a mordant (a dye fixative). All the lanolin must have been washed out if you use a mordant. You can mordant the wool before, during, or after dyeing. For further information on wool dyeing, see *Growing Herbs and Plants for Dyeing* (1982), and other books and magazine articles probably available in your local library.

7. An optional further cleaning and preparation step is working with the wool using cards.

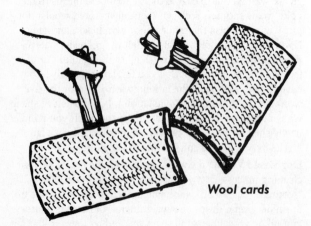

Wool cards

WOOL CARDING: Wool cards are rectangular pieces of thin board with a simple handle on the back, or at the side. To this board is fastened a smaller rectangle of strong leather, set thick with slightly bent wire teeth, like a coarse brush or currycomb. In the early days, the leather back of

the wool card was pierced with an awl by hand, the wire teeth cut off from a length of wire, slightly bent, and set one by one. The carder takes 1 card with her left hand and, resting it on her knees, draws a tuft of wool across it several times until a sufficient quantity of fiber has been caught upon the wire teeth. She then draws the second wool card across the first several times until the fibers are brushed parallel. Then by a motion, the wool is rolled or "carded" into small fleecy rolls, which are ready for spinning or to fill quilts.

MAKING A WOOL QUILT: Start with a layer of cheesecloth. Put the wool on the cheesecloth. It should be a ½-inch thick for a regular quilt, but for a thick comforter the wool layer can be 1, 2, or even 3 inches thick—or as thick as you wish. Put a layer of cheesecloth on top and coarsely stitch it into place with a pattern of diamonds or squares. This prevents the wool from shifting to the corner. The prepared layer can then be covered with cotton, sateen, outing flannel, satin, or whatever is desired. It can be tied with yarn or baby ribbon or coarsely stitched. The cover should be removable because you want to avoid washing the wool very much. I guarantee, if you keep the cover clean, the wool inside the cheesecloth won't get dirty in 25 years and will stay fluffy, light, and warm.

FELTING: This fairly simple craft turns wool into wonderful hats, boots, rugs, clothing, etc. Check out *Feltmaking* by Inge Evers; *Felt Craft* and *Felting by Hand* by Sue Freeman; *The Felting Book* from Louet Sales, PO Box 267, Ogdensburg, NY 13669; 613-925-4502; fax 613-925-1405; **info@louet.com**; **www.louet.com**; and *Feltmaking* by Beverly Gordon.

NOTE: For tanning and dyeing information, see Chapter 8.

SPINNING AND WEAVING: "Spinning" means making yarn, cord, or rope by twisting small pieces of fiber (cotton, straw, wool, hemp, etc.) around each other enough so that they then stay together; by spinning you create a far longer, stronger fiber than what you started with. It takes only a few hours, or less, to learn to spin, though the yarn produced by a beginner may have some imperfections. It's easiest to start learning on a hand spindle and only then shift to using a spinning wheel (which tends, at first, to whip the yarn out of the apprentice's hands disconcertingly fast). Incidentally, a sheep that was in very poor health at some time during the year may give wool that can be broken and thus won't spin well.

A spinner is concerned with basically a 3-step process: drawing out fibers to be spun, twisting those fibers together, and arranging the already-twisted fibers. A wheel supplies the twist and may also arrange the spun yarn. I'm not going to tell you more than this of spinning or weaving because, first, I'm not personally knowledgeable; second, on this subject there is a wealth of information in your library already; and finally, this is very much a living craft, with groups of dedicated spinners and weavers to be found in almost any community.

Weaving is the next step, wherein you set up threads on a loom and weave them into cloth.

You'll learn fastest and easiest from friends rather than out of books. To locate such friends, ask at your local "needle nook," or look in your yellow pages directory under "spinning," "weaving," or "crafts" for leads, or visit your county fair home economics exhibit, find the handmade fabrics section, and sleuth out names and addresses to contact from there.

Alden Amos wrote the *Spinning Wheel Primer* and *The Book of Spinning.* He makes custom spinning wheels and sells supplies: 209-223-3602; 1178 Upper Previtali Rd., Jackson, CA 95642.

Green Mountain Spinnery: 800-321-9665; 802-387-4528; PO Box 568, Putney, VT 05346; **spinnery@ sover.net; www.spinnery.com.**

Harrisville Designs charges $10 for their catalog, credited if you order: 800-338-9415; Box 806, Harrisville, NH 03450.

Louet Co.: Contact in the U.S. at 613-925-4502; fax 802-387-4841; 808 Commerce Park Dr., Ogdensburg, NY 13669. Their Canadian address is 3425 Hands Rd., Prescott, Ontario K0E 1T0, CANADA; **info@louet. com; www.louet.com.**

(The) Unicorn is the U.S.'s largest mail-order distributor of books on basketry, beadwork, crochet, dyeing, knitting, needlepoint, tatting, weaving, spinning, etc.: 800-289-9276; 1338 Ross St., Petaluma, CA 94954. Their 11 x 17 in., 75-pg *Unicorn Textile Book Catalog* is $3 and worth it.

Vermont Dept. of Agriculture lists fleeces, tools, patterns, etc., direct from Vermont homestead producers, online in the "Vermont Fiber Producers Directory" at **www. vermontfiberworks.org.**

Webs: America's Yarn Store offers a $2 weaving/spinning/knitting catalog. Contact: PO Box 147, Northampton, MA 01061-0147; 413-584-2225; fax 413-584-1603; **webs@yarn.com; www.yarn.com.**

Woodland Woolworks: Free catalogs: "Knitology" and "Spinology." Good prices on spinning wheels, books, etc. PO Box 850, Carlton, OR 97111; 800-547-3725; **info@woolworks.com.**

Yarn Barn sells supplies for weaving, spinning (spinning wheels, looms, books, etc.): 800-468-0035; 930 Massachusetts, Lawrence, KS 66044; **yarnbarn@ grapevine.net; www.yarnbarn-ks.com.**

Ashford Wheels and Looms offers a full range of fibercraft equipment. There will be an Ashford dealer near you. Their factory/showroom is at 415 West St., PO Box 474, Ashburton, NEW ZEALAND; phone 64-3-308-9087; fax 64-3-308-8664; **sales@ashford.co.nz; www.ashford.co.nz.** "Send for our FREE *Wheel & Loom* magazine." They also offer instructional books and videos.

Louet Sales Co.: 3425 Hands Rd., Prescott, Ontario K0E 1T0, CANADA; **info@louet.com; www.louet.com.**

Pat Green Carders manufactures quality drumcarders and wool pickers. "Sales are primarily to the U.S. The price list is in U.S. dollars with no tax, duty, or shipping charge. Free brochure." 604-858-6020; 877-898-2273; 48793 Chilliwack Lake Rd., Chilliwack, BC V4Z 1A6, CANADA.

Treenway Crafts sells spinning fibers and weaving, knitting and stitching yarns, especially silk! 250-653-2345; fax 250-653-2347; 888-383-7455; 501 Musgrave Rd, Salt Spring Island, BC V8K 1V5, CANADA; **silk@ treenwaysilks.com; www.treenwaysilks.com.**

Magazines: *Shuttle, Spindle & Dyepot* is an award-winning quarterly for members of the Handweavers Guild of America. Join for $35/yr: 770-495-7702; Two Executive Concourse, Ste. 201, 3327 Duluth Hwy., Duluth, GA 30096; **www.weavespindye.org.** Interweave Press publishes *SpinOff,* a quarterly magazine devoted to spinning ($24/yr); and *Handwoven* ($27/yr, 5 issues): 800-272-2193; 970-669-7672; fax 970-667-8317; 201 E. Fourth St., Loveland, CO 80537; **www.interweave.com.** *Fiberarts* (5 issues/yr) is available from 800-284-3388; 828-236-9730, ext. 702; 67 Broadway, Asheville, NC 28801; **www. fiberartsmagazine.com.**

Books: Interweave Press also offers a free, fascinating spinning/weaving book catalog, including *Spinning Wheel Primer,* by Alden Amos; *Hands-On Spinning and Linen: Hand Spinning and Weaving,* by Patricia Baines. Paula Simmons wrote *Turning Wool into a Cottage Industry* (1991) for home spinners who also raise sheep; and *Handspinner's Guide to Selling, Spinning and Weaving with Wool,* etc. For spinning info, read *Fleece in Your Hands,* by Beverley Horne; *The Art and Technique of Handspinning,* by Allen Fannin; and *Hands-On Spinning,* by Lee Raven. For weaving info, see *Hands-On Weaving,* by Barbara Liebler; *The Key to Weaving,* by Mary Black; and *The Weaver's Book,* by Harriet Tidball.

Directories and Websites: Buy a directory of festivals, spinners, supplies, associations, processing mills, tanners, etc., from Buynne Tramutola, PO Box 216-A, Fountainville, PA 18923. The *Organic Fiber Directory* lists companies that handle organic cotton, flax, hemp, and wool: Organic Fiber Council, PO Box 547, Greenfield, MA 01302; **smarquardt@ ota.com.** An Australian website tracks online info on wool, including markets, technology, spinning/knitting, conferences, and discussion groups: **www.dpie.gov.au/agfor/ wool_vl/whome.html.** The Association of Northwest Weavers' Guilds maintains a website of fiber-related links at **www.anwg.org/resources/links/index/html.**

Sheep Butchering

Because age makes such a difference in the taste and texture of sheep meat, there are different names for different ages. Carcasses are called "lamb" if the sheep was 14 months old or younger at butchering time. In general thinking, sheep could become meat any time after 3 months. They're considered ideal when they reach 50–70 lb. A 50-lb. lamb will dress out to about 30 lb. meat. Most growers aim for some golden moment when the lamb is as large as possible but still young—and not excessively fat. The meat is called "yearling mutton" if between 14 and 24 months at slaughter time. Mature sheep weigh up to 100 lb., about 60 percent of which will be edible. Sheep is called "mutton" if the animal was over 2 years when butchered.

Killing a Sheep

The following information is from me and from a USDA pamphlet called "Lamb: Slaughtering, Cutting, Preserving, and Cooking on the Farm": The animal should be tied to a tree or post in a place that you've prepared for the bleeding by laying down straw, leaves, or some such to protect the pelt. Stun the sheep with a bullet (.22 caliber rifle or pistol or larger) in the forehead, midway between and slightly above the eyes. Make the first shot right. As quickly as the animal goes down, bleeding should be begun. You do that with a straight boning knife. Hold the animal down with a knee on or behind the shoulder. With a hand on the sheep's lower jaw, pull the head back to better expose the throat. With the cutting edge to the outside, insert the knife as close to the neck bone (spine) as possible. Cut clear through, cutting from the inside outward, severing the windpipe, esophagus, and blood vessels. Alternatively, you can start the process without using a gun by simply attaching a rope or chain around the hind legs of the sheep, hoisting it off the ground to where its head is about the height of your waist, and there cutting its throat. Or you can accomplish the job with the animal lying on its side.

Skinning a Sheep

You'll need a bucket of cool water close by to help keep your hands and knife clean and the carcass clean. Dirt and wool on the carcass are very difficult to remove and usually have to be trimmed, so avoid that happening. At this point decide whether you're going to skin the sheep on the ground ("horizontal") or by hanging up ("suspended skinning"). You'll hang it up eventually, either before or after skinning (pelting), and there is a separate set of directions for either choice. It is a matter of your personal preference. (Personally, I'd recommend the horizontal method as being simpler and less hassle.) In either case, you're going to open the pelt around the legs and along the midline and breast.

THE FELL: In either case, make certain to cut toward the skin to avoid cutting through the thin membrane, the "fell" covering the outside of the carcass. If this membrane is broken, the lean muscles will bulge through and give the carcass an unattractive appearance. (It wouldn't really hurt the meat any though.) If the fell is broken, try to work around the break to get a new start. After the sheep has been cut up, remove the fell membrane from each sirloin, loin, and rib chop before cooking; the fell becomes hard in frying. When the chop is still cold, the fell peels off easily. Start peeling at the lower end of the chop. Leave the fell on the leg and shoulder roasts while they are cooking, to lessen the evaporation of meat juices. Clean fell on roasts, chops, or stews will not affect flavor.

"FISTING": This is done by pushing the fist under the pelt with the knuckles next to the carcass and the thumb over the first finger. Press the fist up against the skin, working it away from the carcass. Work slowly and avoid tearing through the fell and muscles. Fisting the pelt off is much easier if your hands are kept slightly wet.

THE PELT: For care of the sheep's pelt after it has been skinned off, see the tanning section in Chapter 8. *This care should start the day it is removed.*

CUTTING OFF THE FRONT FEET: They can be removed by cutting through the joint at the knee or by breaking them at the "break" or "spool" joints. To break the legs there, cut across the tendon between the knee and foot. Grasp the foot in one hand, the leg in the other, and break back and sideways. On young lambs the "break" joint will snap easily and the foot can be removed. On older lambs and old sheep, it will be necessary to cut across the pastern joint and twist the toes off. Don't remove them until the skinning directions tell you to.

HORIZONTAL METHOD: When the bleeding is finished, move the sheep to a clean working area, perhaps on top of a sheet of scrubbed plywood, concrete, or a clean floor. Standing to the side of the sheep, hold 1 front leg between your knees and allow the animal to lean away. Remove a

narrow strip of skin down the front of the foreleg, being sure to remove the skin over the knee. Turn the knife (with the cutting edge toward the skin) and make an opening to the neck in front of the breast.

Skin the opposite leg the same way, meeting the cut made in front of the breast. Open the pelt down the neck to the opening made by sticking for the purpose of bleeding it. This will form a V-shaped strip of pelt over the breast. Remove the pelt over the breast by pulling the pelt up and back. Once started, it is best to complete by fisting. After the pelt is loosened over the brisket (breast/chest), stop and skin out the rear legs.

To do the rear legs, stretch one out and remove a strip of skin down the back of the leg and over the hock (the "ankle" close over the hoof, which bends backward). With the leg still between your knees, turn the knife outward and open the skin from the hock to a point in front of the anus. Skin around the hock and "down" the leg. Remove the foot at the last joint, the one next to the hoof. Follow the same procedure on the other leg. Then fist the pelt off the inside of the legs and over the crotch. From the breast, fist down the belly and around the navel to the opening at the crotch. The carcass is now ready to be hung for evisceration.

SUSPENDED SKINNING METHOD: Tie a heavy string around one of the rear legs and suspend the carcass by that leg from a sturdy tree branch 8–10 feet from the ground or a strong barn beam equally high or some such. On the free leg, remove a strip of skin over the hock and past the dewclaws. Turn the knife outward and open the skin from the hock to a point in front of the anus. Skin around the hock and down the shank. Remove the foot at the last joint. Remove a strip of skin along the suspended leg and cut the skin from the hock towards the anus, connecting with the cut from the other leg. Remove the skin around the shank. Fist along the cut between the legs, removing the pelt around the back of the legs, in the crotch, and around the front of the legs. Suspend the carcass by the opposite leg and remove the foot on the loosened leg. Tie a heavy cord around both rear legs and suspend the carcass now with both hind legs tied.

Remove a strip of skin along the back of the front legs from the knee to the foot. Make a split in the pelt beginning at each knee and connecting at the neck in front of the breast. Open the pelt down the neck to the opening made by cutting the throat for bleeding. Remove the pelt over the breast by pulling the pelt up and back. Once started, it is best to complete by fisting. Fist along the belly and around the flanks, meeting the opening made at the rear legs.

Sides and Back. Open the pelt down the midline of the belly, and loosen the navel. Hold the pelt tight with one hand and fist off the sides. Work around to the back and up around the hind legs. Fist down past the shoulder, around the sides, and up over the rump. From underneath the hock, push up until the pelt hangs by the skin that is fastened to the tail and anus. It will be necessary to use a knife to remove the pelt around the tail. Carefully skin around the tail and allow the pelt to drop. Remove the front feet. Wash the carcass thoroughly before eviscerating.

Gutting a Sheep

PREPARATION: Whether you used a horizontal or suspended skinning method, now you remove the head at the joint closest to the head. If the animal is not suspended, suspend it now by tying a rope tightly around both hind legs and hanging it from a branch or beam 8–10 feet high. Rinse the carcass thoroughly with a hose or by sloshing buckets of water over it.

THE GUTTING: Loosen the large intestine by cutting around the rectum deep into the pelvic canal. Pull the rectum outward, cutting any remaining attachments. Tie a piece of string around the large intestine near its opening, and let it drop into the pelvic cavity. The pelvic bone is not separated. Locate the end of the sternum and split the breastbone with a knife or saw. Do not cut into the body cavity. Make a cut through the male's genital area (cod) or female's (udder) into the pelvic cavity. Make this opening large enough to insert your hand. Insert the knife handle inside the body cavity and, with the blade extended outward, open the body cavity to the opening made at the brisket. Allow the paunch and intestines to roll out and hang down. Do not let them fall, as the esophagus will tear and spill its contents onto the carcass.

Find the loosened large intestine and pull it down past the kidneys, leaving the kidneys intact. Remove the liver by reaching behind and pulling it, while cutting the connective tissue. Examine the liver for any abscesses (yellow or white pus) or scar tissue. Remove the gall bladder from the liver by cutting beneath it and pulling. Be careful not to allow its contents to spill on the liver.

Pull the paunch and intestines outward and cut through the diaphragm (the thin sheet of muscle and white connective tissue that separates the lungs and heart from the stomach and intestines). Make this cut at the edge of the thin muscle. Sever the large artery at the backbone and pull downward, removing the heart, lungs, and windpipe with the paunch and intestines. Cut across the top of the heart and separate it from the lungs.

Wash the heart and liver carefully in cold water and place them under refrigeration. Remove the kidneys and kidney fat, and wash the inside of the body cavity thoroughly.

Aging Mutton

PREPARATION FOR HANGING: Rewash the outside. Carefully trim away any pieces of adhering skin or wool, any bruises, hair, or manure spots. Lamb carcasses are not usually halved and quartered before cooling because of their relatively small size. In cool weather (28–35°F), the carcass can be wrapped in a sheet, hung, and chilled in a well-ventilated shed, but don't let it freeze. Freezing within 1 day after death may toughen the meat. One way or another you need to accomplish prompt and thorough chilling of the warm carcass. After it has been chilled 24–48 hours you can commence with cutting it up.

TIME TO AGE: Extended hanging (up to 3 weeks) tenderizes the meat but also risks spoiling. I recommend you aim for the middle range in aging that older sheep. Hang the meat only about 10 days—and that only if you have facilities to keep it above freezing and below 40°F.

Cutting Up

There are several "correct" ways to cut up a sheep carcass. No single method is required or even recommended. One old-timer told me, "The meat of either sheep or goat is cut up pretty much like rabbit. Peel the shoulders right off the body. Cut through the thigh joint to separate the hind legs from the body. If you are careful you can get some steak off the back from the strip along each side of the backbone—the tenderloin, from the hams (the hind 'thigh'), and the shoulders. Make big chunks into roasts, and grind odds and ends for hamburger."

Here are the USDA directions—a lot more complicated: Begin cutting the carcass by removing the thin cuts—the breast, flank, and foreleg. Lay the carcass on its side and mark a cutting line from the elbow joint of the foreleg to the front part of the hind leg. Most of the flank can be removed by starting the cut between the legs at the cod (or udder) fat where the flank begins. This cut is made in a straight line from the front of the hind leg to the elbow joint. More of the rear flank and lower ribs can be removed by making the cut higher, near the hind leg, if that's your preference. However, the cut across the lower shoulder should be as close to the joint on the foreleg as possible to leave the shoulder roast large.

After removing the thin cuts from both sides, remove the kidneys, kidney fat, and diaphragm, if not removed at slaughter. Turn the carcass over on to the cut surfaces and remove the neck. Cross sectional cuts make neck chops; or the neck may be cut off flush with the top of the shoulder and added to your stew or ground lamb bowls.

The trimmed carcass is separated into 4 primal cuts, each with different characteristics. A cut between the fifth and sixth ribs removes the shoulder. Another cut between the 12th and 13th (last) ribs separates the rib from the loin (the 13th rib remains in the loin). The loin and legs are separated just in front of the hipbones by cutting through the small of the back where the curve of the leg muscles blend into the loin.

Split the legs through the center of the backbone. Trim the flank and cod (or udder) fat off. Remove the backbone from the leg by making a saw cut approximately parallel to the split surface of the backbone and 1 inch below this surface. Saw approximately 1 inch deep, or until you feel a slight slippage when you cut through part of the hipbone.

Be careful not to saw all the way through the hipbone. Insert a knife into the saw cut, find the "slip" joint between the bones, and cut underneath the backbone to complete its removal. Cut off the lower shank bones by sawing where the tendon enters the muscle.

The leg may be further trimmed by cutting through the knee or "stifle" joint to remove the shank. This joint is located about halfway between where the muscles of the shank end and the muscles of the lower leg begin. Cut into the tissues over the bones until you locate the joint and work the knife through it. Continue cutting straight across the heel of the leg.

Several sirloin chops may be removed by knife and by saw cuts made parallel to the cut separating the leg from the loin. Split the loin through the center of the backbone and remove the flank about 1 inch from the loin "eye." Loin chops are made by cutting perpendicular to the backbone. Usually chops are cut ¾–1 inch thick. Doubles, or "English" loin chops, are made from a loin that has not been split. The flank portion may be ground or made into stew.

The rib should be split somewhat differently than the other primal cuts. The backbone is not split but is removed by cutting through the ribs along the ridge where they join the backbone. Continue cutting close to the backbone to separate 1 rib section. Repeat this cut along the opposite side of the backbone to separate it from the other rib section. Remove the breast portion by cutting approximately 2 inches from the rib "eye."

Rib chops are easily made by cutting between the ribs. The breast portion may be barbecued in a single piece or made into riblets by cutting between the ribs. After splitting, the shoulder may be roasted as is, made into chops, or boned and rolled to make a more easily carved roast. Arm chops should be made first by cutting parallel to the surface made when the foreleg and breast were removed. Only 2 or 3 arm chops should be made. Blade chops are made by cutting between the ribs and sawing through the blade and backbone.

BONELESS SHOULDER ROAST: First remove the ribs and backbone by cutting closely underneath the ribs following their curvature, then cutting along and over the backbone and neck vertebrae to remove them. Start at the rear surface and cut along the lower edge of the blade bone to lift the underlying muscles, exposing the blade bone and arm bone. Cut along the edges of these bones and then lift the overlying meat and cut close to the top surface of these bones to remove them. The blade bone has a ridge that runs close and nearly parallel to its shorter edge. Try not to cut through the skin surface when cutting over this ridge. The boneless meat should be rolled so that the shoulder "eye" is lengthwise in the roast. The shoulder eye is located under the flat surface of the shoulder blade. Roll the meat as tightly as possible, then tie securely with a strong twine or cord. The boneless shoulder may be made into a pocket roast and stuffed with ground lamb or other dressing. The edges of the meat are laced together after stuffing.

The lower shank bones of the foreleg are removed by cutting or sawing through the joint. The foreleg and hind shank are often barbecued, cut into stew, or boned and the meat ground.

Preserving Lamb and Mutton

FREEZING: Ideally, lamb or mutton cuts should be used within 6–9 months after freezing, ground and stew lamb within 3–4 months. They probably would last longer, but the quality wouldn't be as good.

CANNING: Be careful to remove the thin outer layer of skin, which has a strong flavor.

Cooking

Mike and some friends stole a sheep when they were foolish adolescents, butchered it, built a campfire, roasted quantities of the meat, and ate it on the spot. It made every one of them deathly ill. He hasn't been willing or able to eat sheep meat since. The moral is to start with a legal sheep, one that's not too old—*and don't eat mutton rare because of the risk of toxoplasmosis (see Chapter 8). Toxoplasmosis is more common in sheep than in beef.* For great recipes, order *The Black Sheep Newsletter Lamb Cookbook* (503-621-3063; **bsnewsltr@aol.com**).

COOKING TENDER YOUNG LAMB: This can be cooked with dry heat such as broiling, roasting, and pan-frying. *NOTE: Even tender lamb should be cooked to an internal temperature of 160°F to prevent any possibility of toxoplasmosis.*

COOKING THE OLDER SHEEP: Mutton has a very intense flavor, which some people love and some detest. You almost never see mutton sold in retail stores, except perhaps as soup stock or in processed meat mixtures. Bob Slover, North Las Vegas, NV, wrote me: "You mention that your husband doesn't like mutton. Well, I do, but I can't get any anywhere. The last time I had mutton was in 1948 in Brooklyn, New York. I refuse to eat lamb or veal because mutton tastes so much better. Here's a quote from *Humphrey Clinker* by Tobias Smollett (1771): 'As their feeding costs so little, the sheep are not killed till 5 years old, when their flesh, juices, and flavor are in perfection.'"

An older, tougher animal's meat should be cooked with moist heat slowly, as by pressure cooking or stewing, or ground into burger and cooked that way. If the taste is a problem for any of your family members, use recipes from the wild meat section of this chapter. Cooks with a lot of experience preparing sheep meat insist that burning the mutton fat is what creates the strong taste. They say, if you roast at no more than 325°F, that offensive taste can be avoided.

SHEEP FAT: *Trim away and/or cook away all the sheep fat.* It has the highest melting point of all the fats and so is high in cholesterol. It makes the best candles and fine soap, too, though better if mixed with softer fats. If you pressure-cook the meat until all the lean meat can be easily separated from the bone and fat, then use the meat in other recipes, you can eliminate the presence of fat almost completely. That's also a good way to cook tough meat.

Mutton Burger or Sausage. When making this *do not include any portion of sheep fat.* Make mutton burger out of 100 percent lean meat. Make sausage out of seasoned plain lean, or by mixing in a proportion (one-third is typical) of lard (pig fat).

Pressure-Cooking Tough, Old Mutton. Cut into pieces that will fit into the cooker. Soak 1 hour. Then cook 15 minutes at 15 lb. of pressure.

LAMB/MUTTON SEASONINGS: Lemon juice, rosemary, mint, tarragon, dill, and currant jelly are the ideal seasonings for lamb. Mutton is appropriately cooked with much attention to generous and interesting seasonings. Other possible good lamb-mutton seasonings are crushed mint leaves, fenugreek, marjoram, thyme, sage, savory, soy sauce, fresh parsley, beef bouillon cubes, chopped green pepper, Worcestershire sauce, chili sauce, ground allspice, nutmeg, sour cream, tomato sauce, green tomatoes and green tomato juice, Tabasco sauce, and red wine—used individually or in compatible combinations.

🖘 *LAMB/MUTTON SEASONING SALT This is excellent in mutton burgers (4 t. per 5 lb.) or in mutton casserole (mutton, peas, cream of mushroom soup, chopped onion, plus lamb salt) or other lamb/mutton recipes. Combine 1 c. fine salt (popcorn salt that dissolves instantly is best), 1 t. black pepper, 1 t. paprika, ½ t. ground ginger, ½ t. dry mustard, ½ t. poultry seasoning, ½ t. cayenne pepper, and 2 t. garlic powder. Mix well. Useful in the kitchen or packed in a shaker jar for table use with mutton dishes.*

RECIPES FOR UNCOMMON SHEEP PARTS: When you're doing home butchering you have all the parts to deal with, and most recipe books tell you only what to do with a typical roast or chops.

🖘 *APACHE TRIPE Francis Nuno, an Apache lady, told me her family doesn't season its meat except with salt, but they use everything! She gave me this recipe, as well as the next:*

Clean intestines really well. Coil them tightly around lumps of intestinal fat. Bake. Cut into sections and serve. The tripe will be crispy on the outside. The fat seasons and tenderizes it.

🐝 **FRIED BLOOD AND ONIONS** *Carefully save the blood. Cook it as soon as possible (within 24 hours) because it spoils quickly. Fry with onions in a cast-iron skillet. When cooled, it has the consistency of liver.*

🐝 **TRADITIONAL ENGLISH SHEEP'S HEAD** *Soak the head overnight in salted water. Then rinse thoroughly. Boil slowly for a couple hours with an onion. Cool, separate the meat from the bone, and use the meat in any suitable recipe (for example, any recipes for old stewing hens).*

🐝 **SHEEP TONGUES** *Soak in salt water. Rinse. Boil until tender. Bake in casserole layered with bacon and vegetables, until vegetables are tender.*

CONVENTIONAL LAMB/MUTTON RECIPES

🐝 **LAMB CASSEROLE** *Trim fat off of 1½ lb. stewing lamb. Cut meat into cubes. Heat 2 T. oil and saute 2 quartered onions until golden. Add meat and brown. Sprinkle with 4 T. flour and cook, stirring gently, for 1 minute. Add 2½ c. water, 1 t. salt, and ¼ t. pepper. Bring to a boil, then add 5 T. tomato paste, 1 clove finely chopped garlic, and a bouquet garni (bay leaf, thyme, and parsley tied in cheesecloth). Bake 1 hour at 350°F. Then add ½ c. fresh or frozen peas and bake another 20–30 minutes. Serve sprinkled with parsley. Serves 4.*

🐝 **SCOTCH BROTH (A MUTTON SOUP)** *Trim all the fat from about a 1½-lb. neck of mutton or some other piece. Put it in your pan, cover with water, and bring slowly to a boil. Skim off the scum and then add salt and pepper and about 2 oz. of pearl barley. Simmer 1 hour. Add 1 diced onion, 2 leeks (if you have them), some chopped parsley, 1 large carrot, 1 small turnip, and a few sticks of celery. Continue cooking another hour. Cool. Take out the meat, remove the bone, cut up the meat and return it to the broth. Reheat, add a little chopped parsley, and you have your soup.*

Here are 4 recipes from *The Good Food Guide to Washington and Oregon*, edited by Lane Morgan (Sasquatch Books, 1992). You can look at these and see how recipes really ought to be! But Lane says, "These recipes should be credited to Angelo Pellegrini."

🐝 **LEG OF LAMB ROAST** *"The preferred flavoring agents, in addition to salt and pepper, are garlic, fresh rosemary, capers, parsley, lemon juice, olive oil, and dry vermouth. For a leg of lamb roast proceed thus: Remove the bone. In the resulting cavity, spread 2 T. of the following all coarsely minced together: 3 cloves of garlic, a dozen capers, and leaves of parsley and rosemary. Salt and pepper. Sprinkle over the whole 1 T. olive oil and the juice of half a lemon. Add a sacramental spray of dry vermouth. Enfold the bone in the cavity; tie the whole securely with heavy twine. Roast it in a 350°F oven in a pan just large enough to contain it. Baste occasionally with its own juices enriched with a bit of vermouth."*

🐝 **LAMB SHANKS OR RIBS** *"Place lamb shanks or ribs in an iron skillet in the oven preheated to 375°F. When about half done, drain out all the fat. Sprinkle with olive oil; add coarsely cut garlic, a few sprigs of rosemary, a squirt or two of lemon juice fired with a squirt of Tabasco. Salt and pepper*

to taste. Give the skillet a shake, return it to the oven and reduce the heat to 300°F. In a few minutes the ribs will be done. The shanks will require more time."

🐝 **LAMB CHOPS AND LAMB STEAKS** *"For lamb chops and steak: Mince finely garlic and rosemary. Put in a small bowl, add olive oil and lemon juice. Remove what fat you can from the chops, rub them with this mixture, salt and pepper to taste, and cook them in a skillet rubbed with butter. When about done, spray them lightly with vermouth."*

🐝 **LAMB FRICASSEE OR STEW** *"For a fricassee or stew, cut neck bones and meat from the shoulder in small pieces. Dust them with flour flavored with salt, pepper, and curry powder. Using a heavy skillet, brown them in olive oil. Remove them with a slotted spoon onto a dish. In the same skillet, with no additional fat, saute onion, celery, carrot, and potato, all coarsely chopped and in what quantity desired. To 1 c. stock add a squirt of Tabasco, the juice of half a lemon, 2 T. tomato sauce, and 1 scant t. arrowroot for thickening. Stir well and pour over the saute. The sauce should be dense but fluid. If too dense, add some vermouth. If too fluid, add more arrowroot. Return the meat to the skillet, mix thoroughly, clamp on the lid, and simmer over low heat for 5 or so minutes."*

PIG

Pigs are the most civilized barnyard animal there is, yet probably also the ugliest. But Stephen Scott believes that pigs can look beautiful to those who love them and that caring for their welfare should be approached "from a spiritual perspective." My correspondence about pigs with Stephen started when I got his letter asking the price to mail-order a copy of this book. His letter was well-written, a pleasure to read—such an honest, down-to-earth guy—and in it he mentioned he was an organic pig grower. Staring at that letter, it occurred to me that this articulate man, who had raised so many more pigs than I, could probably teach me a lot! So I wrote and asked if he would add to what I already had about pig raising for the new book.

Stephen wrote back: "I got your letter as I was putting the final touches on, of all things, the new hog fence. Yes, I would be glad to deliver your readers from the folly of store-bought, factory-raised food into the wisdom of homegrown, raised-in-the-dirt food." And then Stephen seriously set out to explain in writing for me, and you, the things about organic pig growing he felt we really needed to know.

He wrote, "I believe that pigs are people too, and should be treated with respect. If you spend some time with your pigs, you will, no doubt, come to respect them as the magnificent creatures that they are. Watch them work out in the pasture for a while. They are unmatched for sheer brute strength, when they put down their snout and root in the ground. Aside from the good-natured squabbles at the trough, they exhibit a sense of togetherness that humans in confinement would be hard-pressed to match. They have individual personalities too, and my wife and I make sure to name them according to their personalities.

"We enjoy watching the pigs the whole while we have them, but when they are little we must watch them more—not only in order to detect signs of emerging personality but also to see if they seem content. The search for emerging personalities will insure that the right pig gets the right sister-in-law's name, and the search for contentment will insure that they will not go to bed hungry. You can tell contented pigs by the sounds that they make and by how they look. I should mention, at this point, that you should give them a week or so to settle in and become comfortable with their surroundings. After that, contented pigs will make mellow sounds punctuated with boisterous good-natured sounds. I realize that this is not a scientific evaluation of pig sounds, but, just listen to them. Dirt on the snout, as a measure of contentedness, depends upon where the dirt is. No dirt means not happy. Dirt half way up the snout means happy. Dirt up past the eyes means ecstasy.

"I have heard that it is not a good idea to name and make pets out of animals raised to be eaten. All that I can say on that subject is that if you have given the pigs a good life it is not a problem. Give them as much fresh air and fresh water and good food and respect and consideration as you would any other family member, and sending them off to the butcher will not be a problem. Consider the kind of life that they would have had. Everybody else I know of who raises pigs for a living these days raises them in confinement. The little pigs grow up never to see the sun. Never to feel the earth under foot. Never to put their snout into the ground. Agribusiness men raise pigs like this because they can raise more of them and make more money."

You'll hear a lot more from Stephen in the rest of this pig section. If you don't want to—or can't—raise your own pigs, and want organic pork, contact Allen Moody, who represents a marketing co-op of a dozen organic pork producers: 608-625-2602; Organic Valley, PO Box 159, La Farge, WI 54639; www.organicvalley.com.

Pig growers aren't necessarily male. It's interesting how many women have written me about how they began raising a pig for household pork—and eventually became commercial pig ranchers! Martha Wells of Normangee, TX: "My husband did not know anything about farm life before moving here. And, with his working off the farm, a lot of 'man things' are left to me. I want to let your readers know, a woman *can do* a lot more than she suspects! I knew how to string the hay baler and run the tractor, so guess who gets to do the hay baling each year! (After getting tired of having to fix the baler after the men used it, I took over that job.) I run commercial . . . cows. When they get penned and wormed, branded, or whatever, I do the penning and separating. Actually crawling in to castrate or give

shots—yes, I occasionally do lose my nerve and require help! I always assist in the delivery of my brood sows and castrate my own boar pigs also."

Nevertheless, everyone should be careful . . . *mature boars can be dangerous, and sows with litters should be treated with caution.*

Getting Started with Pigs

BOOKS: For the ag-biz view, see *Pork Production Systems: Efficient Use of Swine and Feed Resources* by Pond, Manes, and Harris (1991). Iowa State U. offers info on raising pigs in hoop structures at **www.ae.iastate.edu/aen189.htm** and **www.ae.iastate.edu/hoop_structures/home.htm**. *Hogs Your Way* (#BU-007641-GO) describes four growing systems. *The Swine Source Book: Alternatives for Pork Producers* (PC-7289-S) combines educational and popular press articles on sustainable hog raising, including hooped structures, pasture production, Swedish deep bedding, etc.: 800-876-8636; fax 612-625-6281; **order@extension.umn.edu**. *Fit for a Pig: Low-Cost Sustainable Strategies of Resourceful Hog Farms* (1991) looks at the methods of 10 growers. *An Agriculture That Makes Sense: Making Money on Hogs* (1996) describes and analyzes a 50-sow sustainable hog enterprise in Minnesota (651-653-0618; **www.landstewardshipproject. org**). Keith Thornton's 1990 book, *Outdoor Pig Production* (Diamond Farm, 800-481-1353; **www.diamondfarm.com**), also presents alternatives to factory rearing. *The New American Farmer* is a collection of interviews with American farmers, including hog farmers: 802-656-0484; **sanpubs@ uvm.edu**. The Gunthorps (**hey4hogs@kuntrynet.com**) are fourth-generation pastured pork producers. Their story is in "Pigs on Pasture—The Gunthorp Farm" at **grassfarmer. com/pigs/gunthorp.html**. *A Gentler Way: Sows on Pasture* presents inspiring testimonials from Minnesota and Iowa hog farmers: 507-437-3085; Dwight Ault, Rt. 1, Box 230, Austin, MN 55912; **baault@smig.net**. ATTRA's info, "Sustainable Hog Production Overview," is at **www.attra. org/attra-pub/hog.html**.

PERIODICALS: There isn't a folksy magazine specialized for small-scale owners and lovers of Ms. Piggy. But check out these more pro-oriented ones: *National Hog Farmer* costs $14.75 for 12 issues/yr: 952-851-4660; 7900 International Dr., Ste. 300, Minneapolis, MN 55425. The Pork Industry Group (PIG), a branch of the National Livestock and Meat Board, offers info on research, catalog, and free recipes: 312-467-5520; 444 N. Michigan Ave., Chicago, IL 60611. Kansas State Research and Extension: 24 Umberger Hall, Manhattan, KS 66506; **www.oznet.ksu.edu/library/** has a terrific swine research program and extensive pamphlet offerings.

VOCABULARY
Barrow—a castrated male pig
Boar—adult uncastrated male for breeding
Drift—herd or crowd of swine
Farrow—a sow gives birth
Feeder—a 40-lb. weaner pig that will be fed up to 200 lb.
Gilt—a female that hasn't had babies or has had only 1 litter (after getting pregnant the second time, she is called a "sow"; an "old gilt" is a female that got to be 1 or 2 years old and never bred)
Hog—grown pig arrived at butchering weight of 200 lb.
Piglet—newborn pig

Piggy—pregnant
Shoat—young weaned pig
Sow—adult female
Swine—one or more pigs
Weaner Pigs—little pigs that are big enough to leave their
  mother

ZONING: Stephen: "Local governments have rules concerning what animals can be raised in what areas. Some housing developments have rules that are stricter even than the zoning rules. Check with the local unit of government and find out if you can raise pigs where you live. Remember that the smaller the amount of space you have for pigs, the more concentrated the smell is likely to be. But if you have the means to build an attractive pen and fence, it may just be that your neighbors may become your customers. At least, talk it over ahead of time if you have a neighbor in close proximity to the prospective pen. If it turns out you can't raise pigs where you live, move."

BREEDS: Pig prices, like cow prices, fluctuate depending on supply and demand and whether they're generic pigs or brand-name and registered. There are different kinds of pigs, but they're all pig. So it's up to you if you want to buy pedigreed animals for a family meat plan. Names of some established breeds are Berkshire, Chester White, Landrace, Poland China, Duroc, Spotted Swine, Hampshire, and Yorkshire. If you want to have a breeding operation on pasture, you're best off with animals that were raised like that—no matter what breed they are.

Stephen: "We could go into a lengthy discussion of what breed of pigs you should buy, but I believe that would be an exercise in futility since almost all modern breeds will produce pork quite nicely. What will determine the breed that you buy is more likely to be what breed is raised in your area. . . . But don't buy novelty breeds, such as Vietnamese potbellied pigs. They are bred more for pets than pork, are quite expensive, and are not a good producer of pork as we know it. What will be more of a consideration is the type of pig that you like the looks of. If you don't like the looks of the little one, then you won't like the looks of it when it grows up.

". . . beauty is in the eye of the beholder. My aunt has raised pigs for many years. She raises many feeder pigs from 20 or so sows. She keeps sows for 6–8 years, and as each year goes by the sows get bigger and as far as I am concerned, uglier. But last time my wife and I went to see her, my aunt took us out to the pig barn and showed us her prize sow. It was a 600-lb. behemoth with an 18-inch-long snout and 12-inch-long ears that hung down over the eyes. She went into the pen and scratched this monster behind the ear and asked us, 'Isn't this the most beautiful pig you've ever seen?'

"Well, that sow had given her 12 little ones in each litter and 3 litters a year for the last 7 years. I admit there is a certain beauty in that. So find a pig you like the looks of and you will become more attached to it as time goes on."

Of Lean and Fat. Some growers are really concerned about the trend of selection that has taken animals that were brought to North America by the Conquistadors and after that traveled along with European pioneers—in essence, tough, independent, outdoors critters—and transformed them into dependent, sickly, hothouse animals. Part of the problem is that the latest thing in pig genetics is super-lean genetic lines. The problem with these is that they are so

lean they are not a good choice for pigs to go on pasture because they don't have that blanket of fat to keep them warm. And fat and reproductive hormones are linked. A sow must keep up a 20-percent body fat ratio if she is to be fertile and conceive, farrow a big healthy family, and give them plenty of milk. That's just how pigs are. Another problem with the modern pig is that it is descended from umpteen generations of hothouse pigs so qualities of hardiness and resourcefulness have often been lost. Indeed their requirements for food and care virtually demand a confinement lifestyle. But if you're going to raise sheltered pigs, then super-leans are not so bad. Tamworths are good old-time hardy hogs for pasture-raising.

FEEDERS: Most families raising a pig or more for their family pork supply buy feeder pigs in the spring or summer and raise them to butchering size off the summer garden surplus and fall harvest scraps as well as other feeds as needed.

Stephen: "Feeders are pigs that weigh around 40 lb. . . . a set weight that the pig-raising industry sets to provide a base price for feeder pigs. Many times you will be able to buy a 50-lb. pig for nearly the same price as a 40-lb. one because the farmer is docked in price for pigs that are over the standard 40-lb. weight. Large growers want all of the feeders at 40 lb., so that they will all reach 200 lb. at the same time when they sell them. . . . they will be docked some for pigs over 200 lb."

When to Buy. "Depending upon how you feed them, it will take about 4½ months to turn a 40-lb. feeder pig into a 200-lb. butchering pig. When it's best to buy your feeder depends on where you live. If you live in the north, then you will want them over the summer. Pigs have a hard time, in the northern climes, putting on weight and keeping themselves warm at the same time. Add to that the fact that they aren't able to go outside and forage for any of the food that they need, thus costing you more money to raise them. And winter pigs have to have a much more elaborate home and very likely need to be confined in a building, which may cause health problems. I live in Northeastern Wisconsin about thirty miles west of Green Bay. We buy our pigs in late June or early July so that they are ready to butcher in mid-November. If you live north of here you may want to consider buying them sooner and if you live south of here you may buy them later.

"If you live in the deep south, it may well be that you will want to raise them over the winter. In the south the hot weather of the summer may cause them to not be as happy as they would be in the cooler winter, and, as everybody knows, happy pigs will tend to be healthy pigs."

New Pigs. The time pigs are most likely to act weird and emotionally upset, to hide in a corner of the pig house and refuse to come out, or to take off and escape through your fences, are when you first bring them home. Stephen: "We know enough after 10 years of raising pigs to make sure that we stay home for the first few weeks after they have their little truck ride from the neighbor's place to ours. We lock them in the building for the first couple of days and feed and water them in there."

Runaways. Stephen: "This year everything went wrong. We got 3 pigs. Two of them had their transmissions lock up in forward gear and they burst through our fence. It took us 2 days to round up the 2 escapees and bring them back home. It cost my son a case of poison ivy, my wife

2 afternoon naps, and me—well, I had to listen to a lot of criticism about my choice of fences. No serious damage was done and the 2 recalcitrant porkers were soon back home. But then the third one must have heard from the others how great it was in the wide open spaces, because his transmission locked up in forward gear, and he too burst through the fence. He is not back home and it has been 3 months. I caught sight of him once this summer down by the woods, but he outsmarted the dog and me. Try as we might we could not get him."

To recapture a runaway pig, Stephen advises: "Bear in mind that pigs need water at all times. Check around in the area wherever there is water. Check for tracks and signs of rooting near water. If it happens to be a dry summer, you might have a chance of recovering your runaway. Unfortunately for us, this has been a wet year and it would appear we have lost this guy. No doubt, he has paid a price for his freedom already; it is unlikely that he will be able to survive the Wisconsin winter."

Home Sweet Home, For Pigs

Stephen on planning: "I had a farm background and so did my wife, and we had 20 acres and buildings, so we decided to raise some pigs. We were afraid of nothing in those days. We just went to the neighbor's and bought 3 nice white feeder pigs: 1 for ourselves and 2 to sell. Just a short while before we were to pick them up we realized that we hadn't thought of where we would put them: neither house nor fence did we have! That's how I learned that planning ahead eliminates mistakes. It is important to pick a good site. If you choose right the first time, you will not have to go through the hassle of moving the whole she-bang to another site. Think about it, take a walk around your place and consider different sites and different reasons to put them either here or over there."

So, combining the wisdom of Stephen with that of Mike and Carla, here are the essential points of pig housing site selection.

PIG HOUSING SITE SELECTION

1. Consideration of Neighbors—Put pigs where they won't offend a neighbor. Stephen: "If you live near a neighbor consider him or her in your plans as well. Life will not be too joyous for you if you have an irate neighbor to contend with."
2. Downwind from House—Stephen: "We started out with the pig field southwest of the house. And if you get any breeze at all in the summer here in Wisconsin, it will undoubtedly be a southwest breeze. So we got the full aroma of pig wafting over us all night long for 2 years until we finally moved the pen to the northeast of the house."
3. Shade—Pigs can sunburn. No matter how warm or cool it is, they must have the option of a shaded place to rest in.
4. Provide a Wallow—Pigs are also at risk for fatal overheating. Allow space for their mud wallow. The wallow can be a matter of survival for them. That's why, in hot weather, pigs roll in mud—it's to cool themselves. Some sophisticated pig operations provide a misty spray to cool the outside pig runs. But Barb advised, *"Never hose a pig with cold water when it is hot. It will put the animal into shock and it will die."* Don Fallick, Davenport, WA, explained: "Since pigs do not perspire,

their only method of cooling off is the pig wallow. Pigs do not actually prefer mud, and they will seek cool water to wallow in during hot seasons if given the chance. But you must give them some place to cool off, for their health. If your pigs are housed outdoors, in a hut, this is no problem, but if your sty is inside a large barn, some provision must be made for a hog wallow. If you don't have running water to the barn, at least in summer, you'll find yourself hauling an awful lot of water to the pigs."
5. Clean, Abundant Drinking Water—They must have a lot of water in their trough. When planning where to put them, if you make sure it's somewhere that you can get water to through a hose rather than by hauling it in buckets, you'll be glad for your foresight.
6. Consider the Lay of the Land—Because pigs like to play in their water and make mud, you should put their housing in a high, dry site, above their water, above their mud, so they'll be able to sleep warmly up out of the damp.
7. Shelter from Cold—If you have chilly, or outright cold, weather, they need a shelter such as a little house with a wooden floor or dirt with straw on it. The colder your weather will be, the better-built their housing needs to be. It could be one end of a shed or in a section of your barn.
8. Choose from Indoor/Outdoor Options—You have 3 basic variations to choose from: all-indoor, combined indoor-outdoor, or all outdoor with some shade provided. There are variations on those basic systems: You can either keep them confined in indoor quarters all the time, or just in bad weather. You can connect the indoor quarters chicken-yard–style with a door leading to a fenced outdoor run of whatever size is feasible for you, from a small run to a large pasture. An outdoor run 20 feet on the side would be fine for 1 pig. You could give more for more pigs. If you have a pasture for them you could just put their housing in the middle of their pasture. Or you could locate it along the fence side so there can be a people door on one side and a pig door to their pasture on the other. If space allows, pigs will choose 1 corner of their run or field for their pottying area.
9. Loading Facility—Plan and build a way to load them onto a truck. You'll need that for trips to the vet, or the meat cutter, or to a new owner. This should consist of a corral, which leads to a chute, which goes into a loading ramp. You can have one of these for all the livestock on the place with a system to get the pigs there, or 1 just for the pig housing.
10. Pastured Pigs?—Yes, this is an excellent option. Pigs give great weeding service. Is there a potential future garden spot you want de-weeded, plowed up, and fertilized? They're also good grazers. So you can put them where there is good stuff growing or where you've planted a fodder crop for them. Pigs on pasture will go far toward balancing their own diet, and will live in as nearly natural a way as they can manage. For parasite control they do best with a portable house like an A-frame on sled runners and rotated pastures—keeps pigs off a particular pasture segment at least 1 year before using it again. For example, there might be three 4-acre patches in your rotation, with crops grown on

the land in the years that pigs aren't on it. Or you can use modern wormers given by shots, or in their food or water. Obviously, you can produce pigs on pasture for a mere fraction of the start-up cost of a confinement operation. Sows can farrow out of doors from April through November even in temperate-zone areas, and all year round in the south. Supply a well-insulated hut with generous bedding for the cold-weather farrowing.

11. Squeezed-In Pigs—Or you could put them in a space that can't be used for anything else, because—bottom line—pigs are extremely adaptable and forgiving as long as they're fed and treated kindly.

12. Bedding—Wherever they live, provide the pigs with plenty of hay, straw, etc., for bedding. They'll know what to do with it. All you have to do is give them enough. They'll arrange it under themselves to make a warm comfortable bed. In cold weather, they'll have it over themselves also when they sleep, blanket style!

PIG HOUSING

Agribusiness Style. Stephen: "I don't pretend to be an expert in the new high-tech means of pork production, but I have talked to the people in this area who raise pigs in this fashion. They have 500 acres of corn, to which no cultivator has been set. Weeds are killed and crops are fed through the miracles of chemistry. They weren't making enough money selling the corn so they decided that if chemistry could help raise corn, it could also help raise pigs. I was not allowed into the pig-raising building while the pigs were in there, but I saw it and had it explained to me while it was in the construction phase.

"My brother-in-law showed me around. He was building it and marveled at the efficiency of the whole operation. Three rooms: in one the sows; in another, the nursery; in the last, the feeders. He showed me the shower room and the office. One man runs the whole thing. He takes a shower before he starts the day's work and, of course, a shower at the end of the day's work. He showers so he doesn't bring in any diseases with him.

"Paperwork is kept so that the sows that don't meet the average can be culled. Little pigs are born, nursed, and fed up to butchering size without ever seeing the sun or feeling the earth under foot. They are born in that building and they will spend their whole life there. It is a pork factory. My brother-in-law thinks that this system is slicker than snot on a doorknob. I do not. I think it is a disgrace that a sow can live her whole life without ever turning around. Animals are as much God's creation as we are. How we treat them while they are in our care says a lot about what kind of people we are.

"The pigs are given a balanced ration of feed, but it is not their choice what they eat. Their likes and dislikes are not considered. Profit is the only consideration. Also, the pork you eat is laced with antibiotics. [Pigs are fed more antibiotics than any other type of animal.] In nonorganic commercial operations, low doses of antibiotics are routinely fed to cows, pigs, and poultry, all of which are raised in confinement nowadays. It necessary to do this to insure that if a disease starts in one of these confined animals, it will not spread to all of them in the building. It is done also to increase weight gain, much of which is only extra water in the meat in my estimation. These days the only way you can get the good-tasting pork from

happy pigs is to raise it for yourself—or buy it from an organic pig grower."

Comfy Pig Housing. Don Fallick said: "Pigs need to be protected from the heat and wind, and, to a lesser extent, from the cold. Their subcutaneous fat does protect them from cold temperatures, especially if they are housed in a cabin small enough to trap their body heat. A proper pig cabin should be large enough for the pig to turn around in. 'A-frame' huts are quite common where pigs are kept outdoors. In an indoor barn, the pigs will still need a small enough sleeping area to keep comfortable."

Stephen described the building of his comfy pig housing to me: "I wanted a pig house with a dirt floor—no bottom on it—so it was important that it be situated high and dry. I wanted the house in a good permanent site, with a movable fence. So I took the tractor and disc and worked the area around where it was to be built . . . to make it easier to shovel the dirt into a mound about twice as wide as the house would be. Around the house I wanted the ground to gently slope away. If you have a slope, then when you dump out the water trough to clean it, the water will run away from the house. The pigs will tend to want to wallow in the discarded water and make a small sea of mud near the trough. If you plan ahead and do the extra work to make a mound like that, then you will have a neat and tidy feeding area and a dry sleeping area for your new friends.

"We raised our first pigs under a truck cap. The pigs didn't mind. They were just as happy as clams poking their heads out of the windows and the rear of the cap. But our second year's pigs, even though I'd reinforced the cap arrangement, enjoyed knocking their house around so much, they managed to reduce it to rubble by November.

"As luck would have it, the company I work for was throwing out some brand new 3-foot-square plywood pallets. I could not pass them up. I used 10 of them to make a 9 × 9-foot building with two 3-foot doors . . . on each end. That's 3 pallets on the side, and 2 on the ends, with the middle part open to make 2 doors. For the roof I used six 10-foot-long 2 × 6s for rafters, spiked to the pallets. To the rafters I nailed 2 × 4s laid the 4-inch way and covered this over, first with tar paper and then with rolled roofing. I tarred the seams."

Converting Existing Outbuildings. "If you have an existing outbuilding you can use that, and save yourself a lot of building problems. But if the pigs can get their noses into any holes near the bottom of the wall, they will eventually destroy that section of wall. So go in there and cover up any holes in the walls. If you are going to give them a fenced outdoor yard, they only need enough room in the building so that they can all lie down and stretch out. If space is tight, feed them outside.

"If you don't have a suitable outbuilding for them, assess your building skills, scrounging skills, financial situation, and ingenuity. Everybody can have a nice comfy pig building. It is up to you to decide if you're the building, scrounging, or buying type."

If You Can Build. Stephen: "You can build an A-frame affair that will suit your purposes nicely. Pigs don't mind what kind of a house they live in as long as it keeps them dry and cool, or warm, as conditions warrant. Most pig-raising books suggest that the building should have a floor in it. I don't agree. It can get quite cold and wet in Wisconsin in the fall, yet my pig house has never had a floor in it. Instead, I provide lots of straw, or old grassy hay that Jersey Belle, our milk cow, turns her nose up at. The pigs burrow into that. The pigs always make sure they don't get too close to the cold ground and still manage to cover themselves."

If Scrounging Is Your Skill. Pigs are indifferent to appearances. Function is all that matters. Stephen: "You can scrounge up a perfectly good pig building such as the old truck cap we used the first 2 years. I have seen pigs raised in a 1966 Buick LeSabre in a more rustic area of our fair state. When it comes to raising pigs on a subsistence level, the sky is the limit."

Buying Ready-Made. "You need not be ashamed to buy your pig house ready-made. In every rural area there are handymen who are not beneath building pig housing. If you can't find a handyman, go to the local high school and seek out the industrial arts teacher or the agriculture teacher. These guys don't make a fortune teaching and have the tools and the skills as well as the summer off in many cases and may welcome the opportunity to show off a little. In our area there are people who build gazebos and greenhouses and small storage buildings for the city folks. They build them at their home and then transport them to wherever the city folks want them. This would be high end housing for a pig, but if you have the money and don't want any of the hassle it is not a bad idea."

Your Pig Loading Set-Up. Stephen: "Our first year of pig-raising, we lacked a loading set-up. At year's end, after 4 hours of not a little chasing, diving in the mud, and considerable cursing, my family and the neighbor's managed to get 2 of them in the chicken coop. The third was a more serious problem altogether. It required brute force on the part of all 4 of us to physically drag the beast screaming and scratching, backwards, from the field to the loading setup.

"It's a well-known fact that pigs will do anything not to go in a direction that you want them to go. I figured out if we were to be successful in loading pigs on a truck they must be channeled into an area narrow enough that they can't turn around. I would never again try to load them in the middle of a field. So I built the pig house with 1 door that led into the fence and another to the outside world. I nailed boards over the outside door.

"When it came time to call the trucker to pick them up, it was a simple matter to go out at night when the pigs were sleeping and nail a few boards over the openings that led into their field. When the trucker arrived in the morning we took the boards off that covered the door that led to the truck bed. It would have worked great, too, if it were not for the fact that the pigs decided, since they had never gone through that door up until that day, that they never would! So loading was still really hard.

"The next year I dug in 8 cedar posts and bought 4 pieces of ⅝-inch plywood. The day before we were going to ship I nailed the plywood to the cedar posts, forming a corral as wide as the loading gate on the truck. We coaxed them out with a couple of cobs of corn and closed the door of the pig house behind them. It was a simple matter of finding a gate as wide as the corral and pushing them using it on up the ramp of the truck. This is the point that we are still at today. It has been 7 years and the system has always worked well."

Fencing For Pigs

You have to fence any area for a pig very carefully. Stephen agrees: "The pigs don't mind what kind of house, or fence, they have, but in this area it is important for you to care. Quality fencing is essential."

CATCHING A PIG: There's an old saying: "As independent as a hog on ice." If your pigs are used to the slop bucket, so that they know you and look forward to your visits with bucketfuls of that good garbage, all you have to do if they do get out is run get the bucket and they'll follow you anywhere—even right back into their pen! To catch a pig that isn't slop-bucket–broke—well, they're "as independent as a hog on ice" and as hard to get hold of as the one in a "catch-the-greased-pig" contest. You just find yourself a few neighborly football players and try to tackle the pig. Then you carry it, or drag it back by the heels, or whatever your imagination suggests. Even if your pigs will follow the bucket, it's still best to have good fences; if the pigs manage a few hours in the garden while you're not home they'll wipe out your root vegetables. A reader told me that on her wedding day, the hogs got out. She said, "When the hogs get out, you chase hogs . . . guys in tuxedos!"

PIGS ON PASTURE: Mike is a firm believer in having pigs preweed the garden. We suffer from morning glory, and after the stuff has taken over an area, he fences it off for the pigs to pasture in. Yes, you can pasture pigs instead of feeding them grains if you have enough land. If they are in a small area like your garden, they will plow and fertilize it for you as well as pasture in it.

Wherever they have ground they'll keep it thoroughly churned up, muddy, and manury. It makes no sense to give a pig a small grassy pasture. They'd ruin it for other grass eaters by rooting up and killing all the grass. On the other hand, if you can pasture your pigs on at least 1 acre per pig, and if the ground cover is lush enough (the more weeds, the better), they'll graze on grass and get fat, and have enough room so they won't ruin the pasture. But keep giving scraps, too. They need that food also.

Stephen agrees: "If you like the taste of real pork, then you should seek out organic growers who raise the pigs on the ground. Pigs find what they need from the earth in the way of minerals and other intangibles in ways that animal nutritionists don't even understand. That is why pigs raised on the ground have a much more well-rounded flavor. If you want to experience this flavor, buy some organic pork, or, better yet, raise your own pigs. You can make a small profit on them as well as provide your family with the very best tasting and most healthful pork available in the whole world. If you can't find organic pork in your neighborhood (or any other organic meat), there is a very good chance you can become a supplier of it. I have . . . gone from store-bought, factory-produced, unhealthful pork to frolicking, rip-roaring, snout-in-the-ground, tasty, healthful pork. You can do it too. It is no more tedious or time-consuming to raise your own pork than it is to mow, trim, edge, and fertilize your lawn in town."

The biggest problems with feeding pigs in groups, on pasture or elsewhere, are the chance of wasted feed, and also boss pigs that overeat and push away smaller, less aggressive pigs from the feed trough. An answer to that problem is using such long feed troughs that everybody gets a fair chance, or, if food is spread on the ground, spreading it over a large enough area that "pigging it" isn't possible. And you can use creep feeders for the piglets on pasture.

OF PIGS AND ROOTING: Pigs are rooters. The wild ancestors of our domestic pigs lived in the forest, eating roots, grubs, and bugs discovered by that excellent nose—as well as grass, and windfall nuts and fruits. That snout is pure bone and cartilage and it makes them happy to use it. Pigs on pasture with fruit and nut trees in it can be darn near self-supporting, especially in the south. In confinement though, the wonderful snout can be a problem for you. If you have an area of rocky ground, Mike says that would be a good place to put a small outdoor pig run since you can't use it for much else and they can't tear it up. Or another answer to this problem is to put a ring in the pig's nose. That inhibits rooting.

TYPES OF PIG FENCING

Steel Panel Fencing. This is the strongest of all, but the most expensive.

Stone. Stephen: "If you have the stone, the strength, and the time, a stone fence works well. Of course, you have to bear in mind that it is permanent. If you decide that stone is the way to go, you will want to choose some ground that is no good for anything else. You won't be able to make it large enough to use as a pasture, so you will have to provide all the pigs' feed. Its function will be to contain the pigs and not much more. It may require maintenance each year since the pigs will try to undermine the walls, and the frost will play havoc with them, too. If you are that special kind of person who likes to work with stone though, go for it. A stone fence can be a thing of beauty if it is done right. Since I have no skills in stonework, no time, no stone, and need to move their pasture each year, you are on your own as to how to construct it."

Wood. An entire fence made of strong wood panels works better than wire, but it's more expensive unless you can scrounge. Stephen: "I can tell you a little more about wooden fences. Like a stone fence, this is permanent; you will not be able to easily move it from year to year to change the pig's pasture area. You can cut down on the amount of wood you have to buy if you can do some scrounging. A friend of mine made a nice wood fence for his pigs by scrounging up wooden pallets and making a modular affair that worked pretty well. He scrounged pallets and nailed them top and bottom to scrounged 10-foot-long 2 by 4s. He had to put a post in every 10 feet because pigs can put a lot of pressure on a wood fence. He huffed and puffed to make the fence, what with posts every 10 feet. He had to do minor repairs on it *weekly,* and major

repairs between each new batch of pigs. That is the kind of guy he is—he loves his wooden fence. If that is the kind of person you are, think wood."

Woven Wire. Fence with "hog wire" if you're going to use wire. This is a woven wire. Pigs don't need as high a fence as other large stock, but their fencing must be stronger, and it must be protected below the ground. You can either dig a trench and set your fence in concrete, or bury the bottom part of your wire at least 6 inches underground. Or you can stretch barbed wire along the bottom of your posts. But I'll tell you from experience that even hog wire is liable not to work. The pigs will go through that wire more and more as they get bigger. They'll break holes even in the hog wire, and you'll have to go out with pliers to twist the broken ends back together.

The problem with breaking wire can be solved by putting a 2 × 10-inch board between the posts tightly right along the bottom. But if you've got soft dirt, your pigs can dig under the boards. If you can choose rocky or hard ground, it will help prevent that digging. Nail up a board also between the posts along the top of the fence. That way they can't pull the fence wire down by climbing onto it.

Here's Stephen on woven wire: "My mother used to make woven-wire fences in the beginning of her pig-raising days. She had the money to buy the wire and the time to dig the post holes. Woven wire is quite expensive unless you can scrounge used wire or buy it at auctions in your area. The advantage of woven wire fences over wood fences is that the posts can be placed farther apart, thus requiring less of them. The problem with woven-wire fences is that, no matter how stout the wire, pigs will eventually demolish it, or go under it. You will have to keep an eye out for places that the pigs have softened up. They always root near the fence first and will eventually manage to make a mini Grand Canyon in one place. The grass is always greener outside of the fence, and they keep rooting outward and eventually they will get their snout under the wire and squirt out of the fence. You can delay their escape by nailing old posts or planks to the bottom of the wire. A woven-wire fence is time-consuming to move each year, and it is expensive to make 2 of them if you intend to take advantage of their rooting by planting either food for them or a garden for you. But if you want a permanent fence that will require some maintenance each year, woven wire will do."

Electric. Stephen: "Electric fences are inexpensive to make and easy to move. I have 2 doors in my pig house—one faces north and one faces south. When the pigs are in their south pasture, they come out of the south door and I board up the north door—and vice versa. I dug 6 postholes and planted 6 posts; 2 form the north side of the north fence and 2 form the south side of the south fence. Halfway between them on the north and south side of the pig house and roughly in the middle of the pig house are the 2 posts that form the east and west side of the fence. We use cedar wooden posts, along with enough steel posts so that you have one every 20 feet or so between the wooden posts. I use smooth, lightweight wire rather than barbed because it is cheaper and easier to work with. You will need 8 corner insulators and 2 insulators for each lightweight step-in type post. Get the steel-post insulators where you get the steel posts so they will work together.

"Now take one of the step-in–type posts and step it in the ground near the first corner post. From the spool cut eight 2-foot long pieces of wire. Now take one of the 2-foot pieces and stick it through the hole in one of the corner post insulators. Then go behind the post and, keeping the insulator to the inside of the post, twist the ends of the wire together. This done, position the wire about the post with the twisted part to the back of the post and the insulator to the front. Take a staple and drive it into the post so that the 2 legs of the staple straddle the twisted wire. This should be done at a height of about 6 inches from the ground. Drive the staple into the post so that it sinks in a ways and holds the wire tightly. Follow the same procedure with the second insulator, but this time nail the twisted end of the wire to the post at about 18 inches above the first one. Do the same thing on all of the 3 other corner posts.

"Now go back to the spool near the first corner post and grab hold of the loose end of the wire. Walk toward the second corner post as the wire plays out of the spool, and when you get there, grab hold of the insulator and give 2 or 2½ turns to the right. The hole should be running up and down when you stop turning. Position the wire on the groove of the insulator, making sure that you put it on the groove and not through the hole. The wire may not want to stay in the groove, but don't be concerned about that just yet. Now proceed to the third and fourth post doing the same thing. Walk back to the first corner post with wire still in hand, and stick the end of the wire into the ground near the post. Take out your pliers and cut the wire from the spool, making sure that you will have enough wire to go around the back side of the post and meet up with the wire you stuck into the ground. (Always cut the wire a little longer than you think you will need it.)

"Now go behind the post and take hold of the 2 ends of the wire and twist them together to make the wire quite tight. You should kneel down while you do this because you will want the wire behind the post at the same level as the bottom insulator. Walk to the second corner post and see to it that the wire is in the groove of the insulator, then grab hold of the insulator and give it 2 or 2½ more turns to the right. Again the insulator should have the hole running up and down. Do the same thing on the third and fourth corner post. Now you go back to the first corner post and undo the twisted wire. Put the longest end in the groove and twist the ends to make the wire tight. Trim the ends of the wire off with your pliers. Go back to the insulator and, making sure the wire is still in the groove, grab hold of it and give it enough turns to tighten the wire, but not so many as to cause it to break. The wire need not be piano-string tight. Follow the same procedure with the second strand.

"Now that your wire is strung, take the step-in posts and step them in at about 20-foot intervals between the corner posts. When you have that done, take the step-in post insulators, and go to each post and fix the insulators to the wire and then to the posts. Your main goal will be to make sure that the bottom wire is about 6 inches from the ground. If the ground is uneven, it may be necessary to put in an extra one here and there to insure that the pigs can't get under the wire at any point. One last thing that is very important: cut from the spool a 2-foot piece of wire and attach the top and bottom wires of the fence to each other. I left this step out 1 year and it caused much consternation, and that is putting the situation in its very best light. Now to get the electricity to the fence will depend upon what kind of fencer you have. If it is a battery-powered one you

can build a little box to keep the water off from it and nail the box to whatever corner post is most convenient for you. If it is a 110-volt one, you will have to decide if you want to run an extension cord to it or put it in a building and run pig fence type of electricity to the fence.

"You will notice that there are 2 terminals on the thing. One is the hot one that will go to the wire, and one is the ground that must be placed into the ground in order to make the system work. It is best to have a copper grounding rod, but if you don't, almost any kind of clean, paint-free post or stake will work. You will have nothing but trouble with your fencer if it is not properly grounded. If you have a dry summer, it may be necessary to pour water around the ground stake. In any event, it is a good idea to make sure that the grounding stake to which you have attached a piece of wire cut from the spool is driven well into the ground.

"To test the fence to see if it is electrified, you could be a sissy and buy a fence tester, which consists of a probe and clear plastic handle with a little light on it. You touch the probe to the wire and if the light lights up you have current on the fence. I'm too cheap to buy one of these things so I use the old-fashioned way: Select a blade of nice green grass, the braver you are the shorter the blade of grass can be. Just flick the blade of grass on the fence. If you get a tingle, you have current. If you get no tingle, place the blade of grass on the wire and slide it on the wire until you do get a tingle. If you don't get a tingle at all, then you have to troubleshoot. When you troubleshoot, start with the most obvious thing first and proceed to the least obvious."

10-Point E-Fence Checklist

1. See if the fencer is plugged in.
2. See if it is connected to the fence.
3. See if the 2 wires are connected.
4. See if anything is touching the fence.
5. See if the wire that should be in the groove is touching the wire that goes around the post. These last 2 require you to walk slowly around the fence looking carefully at the wires.
6. If you can't find anything wrong with any of the above, it is time to check out the fencer. It should have a fuse in it; check that first.
7. Check the ground.
8. The regulator should be clearly visible on the front of the fencer. It is a little tin-can–type of affair. Pull it out and it should have 2 prongs on it. You should have a spare; put the new one in and test the fence with a blade of grass. If you still get no action take a deep breath and calm down.
9. Check each thing again.
10. If it is still a no-go, take the fencer to an expert.

Food for Pigs

PIGS RECYCLE KITCHEN SCRAPS: Pigs are important because they eat kitchen scraps—"garbage." We keep a slop bucket in the kitchen for the pigs. Into the slop bucket go peelings, leftovers, extra milk, spoiled foods from the root cellar, the contents from jars of canned fruit that got moldy, bread crusts—if I burned the bottom of the loaf or accidentally baked it 2 hours instead of 40 minutes—and so on. People have asked me if you can feed chickens scraps of chicken meat or pigs scraps of pig meat. Yes, you can. They don't mind a bit. They both eat meat leftovers, cooked or uncooked, although our cat and dog get first pick of the cooked meat scraps. They will eat leftover grease too. But I don't give pigs bones. The chickens can pick on them though. I do give fruit cores and seeds to the pigs when I'm working on fruit in the summer. Pigs are tremendously efficient food converters and they'll change all those throwaways into meat and lard.

Mike told me that in some urban areas there is a law that food scraps of that sort can't be fed to pigs. That just boggles my mind. It is so inefficient. Why throw out good food that could feed pigs, which in turn could feed hungry people? When food scraps are ground and poured down a sewer it increases the general sewage burden. When scraps are taken to a land dump and mixed with metals and papers and buried or burned, that's a disgraceful waste of a valuable recyclable material—food. Everybody should be saving their leftover food for recycling just like the country people do. A city could keep a whole army of pigs and chickens growing! Or that food waste could be composted and used to fertilize land from which more plant food will be grown.

The notion that kitchen scraps are unclean is nonsense. We feed our pigs and chickens the leftovers from our home-grown fruits and vegetables. That means our pork, eggs, and chicken have the same high standard of composition as the other food this family eats: "organic." Garbage only looks unpalatable because the peelings and the leftovers, gravy, and grease are all poured together in it. In the later summer and fall we carry the pigs on culls from the garden and root cellar.

So we get little pigs in the spring and feed them all summer on the leavings from canning and freezing. Come fall we butcher the spring pigs, which are just the right size for that, and buy more feeder pigs. We feed them on the food in storage that isn't making it—the green tomatoes that rotted instead of ripening, the apples that went bad prematurely, the spoiled pumpkins. About the time that source of food is really slowing down it is early spring and still cold enough for butchering if you pick the right day and the pigs are big and ready. We never need to buy them so much as a cupful of feed and feed them no grain at any time in their lives—milk and vegetables is it. So I take the pig's bucket with me to the cellar every few days to check the food in storage. A big pig gets nearly 5 gal. of this food each day as well as extra milk and table scraps. (There is no way I know to feed a pig more than it can eat.) If I fed it 10 gal. it would manage to eat all that too, but 5 is more than enough even for a big pig.

SPEED OF WEIGHT GAIN: Pigs gain weight very fast. If you get a little pig in the spring, 6 months later it will weigh 200 lb.—butchering size. If you feed a grain mixture they grow to 200 lb. in as little as 4 months. Corn is the richest food for them, but corn feeding makes for lots of fat. If you keep food in front of them constantly, that's when you get your fastest weight gain. They would go on up to 400 lb. if you let them, but, after 200 lb., the bacon just keeps getting fatter, and there is proportionately more lard and less meat. That is not what most people need or want.

OF PIGS AND FAT: How fat do you want your pig to be? If you pen an animal up and keep rich food like grain in front of it constantly (which is the commercial way to raise them), you're going to have more fat and softer meat than if you let your animal rustle by grazing in a weedy field.

Also, older pigs have relatively more fat on them. That's the reason for the practice of butchering at 200–225 lb. When you butcher at not more than 225 lb., you get more meat proportionately. More feeding will not be as efficient: above that weight per pound of feed, your pig will get fatter rather than meatier, and your pig will put on less weight per pound of feed than it did before.

Stephen: "Pigs are a lot like humans when it comes to eating. You will have to be like a good mother to them and see to it that they get what they need and not just what they want. The whole exercise is not to see how fast we can get them to butchering size; rather it is to keep them happy and healthy and put weight on them gradually. Pigs gain weight fast enough as it is. I can't imagine trying to rush them with 'high energy/high protein' feeds. But that is just what the experts at your local feed mill will want you to do. Don't allow yourself to be swept up in this whirlwind of salesmanship. 'Salesmanship,' you must remember, is a ship that transports money. The salesman wants to transport your money from your pocket to his. If you have some money that you want to take this scenic cruise between pockets, okay. But otherwise, build a coral reef around your pocketbook so that the feed salesman's ship of sales cannot dock in your peaceful little harbor and fill its hold with your money!"

CHEAP PIG FOOD: So, rather than feeding costly food for quickest weight gain (and nonorganic, antibiotic-laced food at that), I prefer using the cheapest possible pig feed for your area. Here that means household slop and oats, which aren't as rich as corn, and pea "screenings" (the weed seed the mechanical harvester separates out from the peas). Peas, barley, oats, weed seeds, etc., are all fine pig food. Some growers suggest that you soak all grains that have a husk, such as whole oats, for at least 2 days before feeding. (See the sections on the individual grains for directions on livestock feeding.)

Ruth Proctor wrote me from New Plymouth, ID: "Once I got the bright idea of asking a potato processing plant for their trimmings and peelings to feed to our 50 hogs and ended up getting 2 tons every day—the only catch being that we had to furnish the truck and keep the peels hauled off. We found out there is no way 50 hogs can consume 2 tons of spuds every day, but it made wonderful fertilizer for our fields—though somewhat sticky."

FOOD FOR NEWLY ARRIVED PIGS: Stephen: "You will want to buy a few bags of pig starter. It comes in pellet form and is like candy for the little feeder pigs. It will keep them happy and help them settle into their new surroundings. It might be worth asking the farmer you buy your feeder pigs from what kind of starter he uses, and then get the same brand. But I have found it unnecessary to get the same kind of starter because all of it is so good that the little oinkers can't resist it even if it is slightly different than what they are used to. Suffice it to say that you don't want the pigs to stop eating in the upset of changing homes, as that can lead to serious health problems. But get a pig starter that is unmedicated. The 'medication' would be antibiotics, which are unnecessary if you buy your pigs at the right time of year for your climate and have properly prepared their house for dryness.

"The salesman at the feed mill may tell you to give the pigs all that they want of the starter pellets. But since we have them out on the ground so that they can hunt for goodies with their snouts, we start out with three 40-lb.

pigs and three 50-lb. bags of pellets. Each pig gets about 4 lb. of pellets per day. You can divide this up into 2 meals, morning and night, or better yet, 3 meals, morning, noon, and night, just like people."

During the first 10 days the pigs are with you, you can gradually phase them into the home-grown diet that they will be on at your home. Or . . .

PARTLY COMMERCIAL DIET: Stephen: "When you open the last bag of pellets, it is time to go back to the feed mill. You should be about 10 days into the pig-raising experience. The salesman will now want you to buy concentrated feeds and corn (both expensive), but tell him that all you want is a couple bags of 'balanced ration': meaning some unmedicated concentrate (protein supplement), oats, and corn. Tell him you want oats and corn in a ratio of 2 oats to 1 corn *by weight not by volume*. (This should be ground fine and mixed thoroughly.) Feeding them this way, you will have to work a little to get what they need in the way of intangibles because they'll need to be on good ground, in which worms live and roots grow. Then they will do well without a lot of expensive additives to their food.

"To sum up: you get a balanced ration for them at the feed store consisting of a protein supplement, oats, corn, and minerals. Or you could substitute some other grain for corn, like barley. Any combination of grains will do, so long as there's enough natural variety in their diet. This year, having the pigs as usual on good ground with lots of greens, roots, worms, garden vegetables and sweet corn to eat, we omitted the feed-store corn and bought only oats and some protein supplement. *Caution: If you feed too much sweet corn, your pigs may develop the runs.* We fed about 4 cobs a day to each pig for the first part of the time we had them and 8 cobs a day per pig for the last half."

VEGETABLES: I feed vegetables to the pigs raw unless they happen to be kitchen leftovers, but Stephen cooks them! "I raise vegetables for the organic market in this area and always seem to have more than I can sell of one thing or another from year to year. One year it will be extra potatoes, the next year it will be extra carrots, and every year I have small cobs of sweet corn that I wouldn't want to sell. I can't see just letting this stuff go to waste, so I feed it to the pigs. I harvest the root crops with a potato digger that was manufactured in 1888, bring them into the barn, and put them into large wooden boxes. When I have time, I scrub up some of the veggies and put them into this large cast iron pot that I bought new a couple of years ago from a local foundry for $114. I build a fire under the pot and by dinner time the veggies are cooked through. I take a pail of them out and let it cool down some. It is usually starting to get cold here about harvest time and the pigs dive right into these warm cooked veggies. The pigs are happier with their bellies stuffed full of warm cooked veggies on a cold fall day.

"Before I bought my cast iron pot, I used to bring potatoes into the house and scrub them up and put them in a kettle on the wood cookstove. I did this as the last chore of the day and they would bubble away until we went to bed. The veggies would be cold in the morning when we got up, but by the time we got the stove going and a pot of coffee down the hatch, they were nice and warm, and the pigs relished them for breakfast. This is optional for you, but the pigs, after being treated to warm veggies for breakfast a few times, made it mandatory for me!"

FORAGE CROPS FOR PIGS: Stephen: "Remember that it is cheaper to buy seed than it is to buy feed. I have 2 different fenced in areas for my pigs. I used to plant garden vegetables in the one that the pigs would not be in, getting the advantage of their weeding and fertilizing, until I tried planting alfalfa 1 year. If you plant a legume you will be providing your pigs with protein. Protein supplements are the most expensive part of your balanced ration, so if you plant some legumes you can eliminate those too. I plant alfalfa in the field that the pigs will not be in during the year that I plant it. If you have only 1 field, then forage alfalfa will not work for you. But you can still plant something for your pigs to graze on. You can plant it the same year they'll eat it. That something is rapeseed, or the name I prefer, 'canola.'" (See Chapter 4.) Ladino is another popular legume for pig pastures.

Farm Equipment. Stephen: "Now, as you might have already gathered, it is going to take a large amount of feed and bedding to make this operation go. You will also have a considerable amount of manure to spread on your land. You will need at the very least a manure spreader and something to work the land with. You can buy the feed and bedding, but that will not leave you with much profit unless you are the type of person who can manage the whole thing well.

"You can grow some feed, but you will have to buy a pig starter to insure that the little ones grow rapidly and get proper nutrition. You will have to buy some protein supplement to make sure that you feed a balanced ration, in addition to all of the things mentioned . . . above. You can grow your own corn, oats and alfalfa and thereby cut your feed costs to a minimum. I believe that is the only way to go. You will have to have enough land and the right equipment to make it work.

"As the bare minimum you will need a tractor and a disc. This is a farm tractor; not a city-type lawn-mowing tractor. You might want to get a small used grain drill, but you can get by with a hand cranked broadcast seeder. They are still available from seed catalogs and farm supply stores. You will need an Esmay seeder to plant the corn with or an old farm-type corn-planter pulled by the tractor. You will need a corn-picker or you can pick it by hand. You will need something to cut down the hay and oats with, an old hay mower or one of the new walk-behind sickle bar mowers will do. I recommend that you cut the straw by hand and buy the oats to feed the pigs, unless you can find someone to come in and combine your oats for you. It would make your life easier if you had a baler to bale the straw and hay with but it is possible to get by without it if you are able to put the time in to pick up the hay by hand."

Crop Rotation. "Five acres of land should be enough to make the whole thing work. This depends, of course, upon how fertile the land is. You divide the land into 5 equal plots through which you will rotate the crops. In the first, which you have worked thoroughly in the fall, you plant oats and alfalfa seed . . . as early in the spring as you can get on the land to give it one final working. In the second, you have alfalfa planted last year, which you will cut for hay, and from which you harvested oats last year. In the third, you have alfalfa, which you will pasture this year, and from which you harvested hay last year. In the fourth you plant corn. It was last year's pasture, and you worked it last fall and again in spring until it dried out some and warmed up. In the fifth you will grow root crops for the pigs and vegetables for yourself. Last year it was corn and you worked it in fall and again in spring until it dried out and warmed up.

"This is all fine and dandy once you get the rotation going, but how do you start it? My brother worked all of the land in the fall. On one fifth he planted oats and alfalfa; on the second fifth he planted corn; on the third fifth he planted root crops and vegetables; and on the fourth fifth he pastured the pigs. The remaining fifth he worked every 10 days or so all summer long. The next year he planted oats and alfalfa on the one he worked all summer, pastured the pigs where the root crops were grown, cut the hay, planted corn where the pigs pastured, and planted root crops where the corn was the year before. Only in the first year did he have to buy extra protein supplement."

Keeping a Sow and Raising Piglets

Pigs are wonderful reproducers. Numerically, you could start with 1 sow and a boar. She will have 2 litters of average 10–12 piglets each year. If you keep all her female offspring, within a year her first babies will be farrowing also. And so on. Within 3 years you could have more than 700 pigs!

Keeping sows and raising little pigs is hard, harder than any other livestock breeding operation I think. Pigs can catch things pigs catch, plus practically every disease people get too. And they're most likely to get sick during the time between their birth and weaning. The first problem is birthing. At least 1 out of every dozen piglets is born dead. Even professional pig raisers lose an average of one-fourth of their piglets, counting those born dead. And feeding breeders is much more expensive than feeding a weaner pig, which is butchered at 200 lb. These are much bigger animals—maybe 500 lb. for a sow, up to 1,000 lb. for a boar. One of them will eat more than 2,000 lb. of feed per year. Infertility can be a problem also. About 1 out of 10 sows doesn't get pregnant. Costs can be brought down by keeping more sows—the average commercial operation keeps more than 50—but the more pigs you keep, the greater the risk of disease.

When breeding, consciously choose the genes you want to pass on. Cull pigs with problems of body or personality. You want a boar that can do his sexual job but is tame with you. You'll keep sows that have large litters of same-sized babies (runts are born dead or have trouble making it afterwards) and whose babies grow well and stay healthy.

Stephen: "It requires more planning and investment of time and money. It is as different from raising a few feeder pigs as swimming in the local swimming hole is from swimming the English Channel. At the local swimming hole you just plunge right in and flail away. In order to be successful on a swim across the channel you need to steel yourself against the icy waters and there are logistics to be considered.

"You will enter a business in which the price is set in Chicago. You can charge what you want if you raise organic pigs, but if you can't find enough buyers that are willing to pay your price you will have to sell at the market price. If you are forced to sell at the market price you will come up against the pork factory people. They can beat your head in with their cruel brand of efficiency. Pig prices fluctuate, at times wildly. You may have to take losses, which may cause you to want to get out of the business. As soon as you get out of the business, the prices may go back up and you may want to kick yourself for getting out. This happens all across America on a regular basis. The pork factories have

the capital and the information provided by the Pork Producers Association to which they subscribe, to aid them in making decisions. You will be alone. They are ahead of the game, and still from time to time even they get burned.

"You say that you will get into the pig-raising business on a small scale, and thereby be able to take the hits in the bad times and profit in the good times? But there are limits to how small you can go. My brother says you have to have at least 6 sows to make it worthwhile to keep a boar. . . . And you will also have to have an all-weather building, plenty of feed, lots of pasture—and straw bedding, which will have to be grown, and baled or chopped by you, or bought. You will have to handle tons of manure and must have a place to spread it and something to spread it with. You'll need a livestock trailer or some means to haul the pigs to market. In short, you will have to have a full pen and a thick checkbook, with the final question of profit and loss answered only in muffled tones. You will have to keep the books with a very sharp pencil over a long period of time to find out how you are doing.

"Well, I suppose if you had dreams of being a small-scale pig raiser, about now you are heading for the tissue box to dry your tears. Get a tissue . . . and then read on. There's still hope. You could raise pigs in a family herd!"

RAISING PIGS IN A FAMILY GROUP: "Pigs are raised almost everywhere in the world and there are many ways to manage them. In Europe, they are still herded into the oak woods each day to fatten on the acorns that fall from the trees. In Asia, they are still kept in bamboo hutches at night and allowed out to pasture each day. In some places in America pigs are still raised under strawstacks and in barnyards with beef cattle. . . . It is up to us to use our ingenuity to find out how to raise pigs in a fashion that we can morally live with—and with a little work and a little luck still make a profit.

"We had a neighbor who raised pigs using the strawstack method. [See Chapter 3.] He was the last one, besides us, who used a binder and a threshing machine to harvest grain. He pulled the threshing machine out into the barnyard and blew the straw into a stack over a 20 by 20 foot hutch that consisted of cedar posts dug into the ground and rough-sawn lumber nailed to the cedar posts. There was 1 door that faced to the south, and not much of a roof so that plenty of straw could fall through it onto the floor of the hutch. The pigs lived here year round, being let out onto pasture in the summer. Boars, sows, feeders, and weaners lived together under 1, sort of, roof.

"He raised corn, oats, and alfalfa for them. . . . the local cheese factory . . . gladly gave him whey, some of which he fed directly to the pigs and some of which he used to wet their feed. He had 4 huge wooden barrels to which he added finely ground alfalfa, oats, corn, and whey. When 1 barrel was empty, he just filled it again with layers of more dry feed and more whey and then allowed it to sit until it began to ferment.

"I'm telling you it was pig heaven. People who wanted pigs to butcher, or feeders to raise for butchering, came from miles around to buy old Harwood's pigs. It worked, and he made money on the operation. He has since died and with him went the last of the pig raisers who used the strawstack method in this area. I mourn his passing.

"That kind of an operation must be run by a special person. Harwood got inside his pigs' heads and understood what it took to keep harmony in the community of pigs.

He weeded out the potential troublemakers before they disrupted equilibrium in the family of pigs. It sounds crazy, but he was a real life pig psychologist.

KEEPING SOWS THE "MODERN WAY": Stephen: "For this system it takes harder work and more start-up money to have success. The hard work comes because we have to feed the pigs individually, fetch bedding for them, clean out their manure, and attend to their health. Money is necessary to build them a building, build pens in the building, build or buy farrowing facilities, grow or buy feed for them to eat—and from time to time pay the veterinarian to restore their health."

Keeping One Sow. Stephen: "If you are willing to go through all that to get her pregnant, you can raise a couple of batches of pigs from a single sow each year. You may raise the first batch of piglets up to butchering size for your family and sell the last batch as feeders. If you have a good sow and a little luck you could have 8 little ones each time your sow farrows. If you raise the first batch to butchering size, you can find buyers for the meat, and charge $1 a pound dressed weight; you can expect to make $1,240 on them. Add to that the 8 feeders from the second batch at $35 apiece, and you come up with a grand total of $1,520. This is, of course, before you subtract your costs. You might clear $500 a year."

Keeping a Boar and 6 Sows. Stephen: "If you want to keep a boar yourself, then you can get 6 sows, but you will either have to convert an existing building or build a building to house them. For this number of pigs you will have to build a building at least 20 × 30 feet. This allows for eight 4 × 8-foot pens in one room, and a nursery and feed room in the other room. The 4 × 8-foot pens are placed along the outside walls leaving a 4-foot aisle down the middle. The doors of the pens are 4 feet wide and must be made to swing out into the aisle. This is done so you can move pigs from one pen go the other as need be. The doors of the pens should have a hook on them to keep them shut and also so you can hook them to the pen across the aisle, and thereby block the aisle while moving the pigs around. The pens and doors should be made of at least inch-thick plywood or full inch-thick rough-sawn lumber. All of this has to be made very stoutly because pigs are very powerful and love to scratch themselves. Any weakly built pens will be reduced to kindling wood, posthaste." Amen to that. A determined boar is a half-ton, 4-legged, thinking power-sausage. You'd be amazed what he can just walk through if he decides to!

Feeders and Waterers. Stephen: "Each pen will have to be equipped with a feeder and a waterer. The feeders can be the dry self-feeder type or a trough in which you will feed moistened feed. The waterer can be a trough that is secured to the pen or floor or a self-waterer called a nipple. One caution about these self-waterers; they have a tendency to stick . . . your pig barn will become a very shallow swimming pool if this goes unnoticed. On the outside wall of each pen you may want to build doors so that the pigs can go from the pen directly out to the pasture in summer. Of course, the fences will have to keep each pig separate from the others so that they all get back to only their pen. A large walk-in door should be built at the end of the aisle to facilitate the loading of pigs when it is time to ship them. You will need a large barn fan to remove excess moisture both winter and summer.

The Nursery. Stephen: "On the other end of the aisle you will have another walk-in type door leading to the nursery. You should have 2 or 3 farrowing crates in the nursery. You can buy ready-made metal ones or build wooden ones. In the same room you will have space left over to put your feed and veterinary supplies. You will need a source of heat in the nursery to keep the newly born pigs warm in all conditions. My brother uses electric heat lamps . . . expensive to operate but they get the job done. I recommend that you store the bedding in the form of chopped straw above the nursery and have holes cut in ceiling above each of the pens in the other part of the building. If you can't get chopped straw you can use wood shavings. Growers can get shredded newspaper pressed into bales, but I would not use that because the ink will end up in the ground when you spread the bedding-manure mixture. I am an organic farmer and don't want heavy metals from ink in my ground."

Breeding Your Pig

THE BOAR: A boar matures sexually by 7–8 months old. *Boars are large, dangerous, and tusked. For safety most growers remove their tusks at 6-month intervals.* Fever, hot temperatures, and stress can cause a boar to become temporarily sterile. Stephen: "If you are going to have your own boar, you need 6 sows to support him. You can get by without a boar if you have a neighbor willing to let you use his boar."

HEAT: Most gilts have their first heat by 9 months old. But hog breeders may wait until she is a year old or has had 3 or 4 heats before breeding because then she'll produce more babies than if bred sooner. The first heat can be hard to detect. Once started, she will be in heat every 18–24 days for 2–3 days at a time. Signs of it are swollen, reddish vulva, possible discharge from it, and restless behavior including pacing around and noisiness ("barking"). An especially rich and plentiful diet right before breeding helps make her yield more eggs and have more piglets.

THE MATING: *"Don't put a strange boar in your sow's pen.* She will not be happy with an intruder in her home. You will have to use either a neutral pen at your place or take the sow to the neighbor's boar. If you don't have a livestock trailer you can borrow one or put the sow in a crate. If you put her in a crate you will have to lift her onto a pickup truck. She will have to stay with the boar until he has done his job. You can never be sure if she will settle and become pregnant, so you may have to repeat the process more than once."

Mating Systems: Pen, Hand, and AI. The boar can be in a pen with as many as 10 sows for a time to accomplish breeding (this is called "pen-mating"). But then you're not absolutely certain if the job got done. "Hand-mating" is surer. In this case you put the gilt or sow that's in heat into a pen with the boar and watch until they're done mating. Some growers give them a hand—literally—guiding the connection to target success. It's even surer if you repeat the encounter again the next day. With hand-mating you know for sure it happened and you know for sure when so you can put her due date on your calendar. The third possible system for breeding is AI. AI hasn't been as successful with pigs as with some other animals. Litters may be smaller, it's expensive, and it's difficult to manage the sow's cooperation. However, it's an option when you have no boar and a good way to introduce champion or exotic genes to your herd.

Pregnancy and Farrowing

After breeding is done, circle the calendar day 114 days away (3 months, 3 weeks, 3 days). With luck she'll have babies then. Since there's no way to know if she's pregnant until she delivers, you now have to wait to find out for sure, although you can usually tell by around the 80-day-point. As she gets farther along she'll get a larger belly and milk coming in. Failure to show heat signs suggests pregnancy but doesn't prove it. Pregnancy usually goes well.

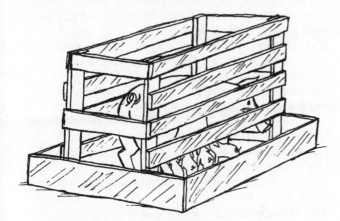

HOUSING FOR MOM AND PIGLETS: Your choice is a "farrowing crate" or a natural pen with plenty of straw for bedding, large enough for her to get some exercise, and to teach cleanliness, rooting, etc., to her babies. The "farrowing crate" is used by commercial producers—it's easy to work around because of its smallness, it protects the babies from being laid down on because of its special side structure, and it makes it easy to give shots, take a temperature, and take out and work with piglets. The bad things about a farrowing crate are that mom will be unable to make the traditional nest that her instinct is urging her to make, she can't exercise, and she can't teach her babies anything. A major argument for the farrowing crate is that it reduces losses from "overlaying," which is when piglets are unintentionally smashed by a reclining big mama. However, if you provide heaps and heaps of straw for her nesting instinct, she'll make such a deep nest that a squirmy little piglet can make its way safely out from under her through all of it. In cold weather a heat lamp that offers a 70–80°F area is nice for crated babies. In a natural pen situation, a heat lamp could provide it, but the piglets are likely to ignore your efforts and instead cuddle up to Mom for warmth.

THE FARROWING COUNTDOWN

1. Right before nest building, her mammary glands ("udders") become distended with milk. If you squeeze a teat, milk will squirt. She shows signs of nest-building. If she isn't there already, move her to where you want her to birth and live with her babies. Wash her.
2. In the 24–48 hours before birth the mother-to-be gets restless, tries to build a nest. Provide plenty of clean straw, which she will work hard biting into small pieces and piling up.
3. Labor begins. She is breathing faster. Her temperature rises. She discharges a little mucous and blood.
4. Before 2 hours the birthing of her sequence of piglets begins. It may take 30 minutes to as long as 5 hours, depending on how many piglets there are. She'll be delivering a piglet about every quarter hour. An average sow has 10–12 babies, usually no more than 14. A gilt in her first birthing is likely to produce fewer—maybe 6.
5. It's good for somebody to be there. The piglet comes out with a covering of thin individual placental skin. You can wipe it clean and dry or let it dry naturally. The wiping especially helps if the membrane or mucous are around the piglet's nose or mouth. Piglet birth survival rate is better with this human attention. Problems with the delivery itself are more likely if she's overweight, or if a baby gets caught in the delivery route. If that happens, pull on a rubber glove, lubricate it, and reach in and help. Most sows in labor will scarcely pay attention to what you're doing. (However, the occasional exception to that rule can be dangerous. Make her into sausage; don't pass on that trait!)
6. After she has delivered the very last piglet, the afterbirth will come out. Get it out of there.
7. Stephen: "Standard operating procedure is to cut and treat the umbilical cord, cut out the baby teeth, give each piglet an iron shot, castrate the boar piglets, and dock the tails." They dip the umbilical stub into a container of iodine. They may also weigh the piglet. (See below.) A shot of deworming medicine is another option for this stage. *However, some family growers skip all this and have fine piglets.*
8. The babies will naturally find her teats and begin to nurse. It's important that all the babies get some of the first few days' milk production—the colostrum.
9. A "runt" is any piglet born weighing under 2 lb. Not all the mother's teats are equal in milk supply. Those nearest to her head give more milk. A runt or weak piglet who is always pushed back to a hind tit by more husky siblings is going to fall even farther behind in growth. In fact, 60 percent of runts die. It can help a runt to give bottle supplements, but some don't make it anyway—or they live but remain smaller than average in size.
10. The piglets need iron or they'll get anemia. If you have a natural pen with an outside run (real dirt), mom will soon take them out to the dirt. They'll scamper and play there, and they'll instinctively get their needed iron by eating dirt. *Piglets raised without access to dirt have to get iron in a shot or as a feed supplement, or you can give them nice, clean dirt several times a week.* Another system is to paint an iron solution on the sow's udder—if she'll lie still for that.

NOTE: Mother will be protective of her babies, and come worriedly running if one hollers—possibly with a dangerous attitude. Be careful! To take piglets from a pen wear heavy boots and thick gloves, and act quickly.

RAISING ORPHANED PIGLETS: If you get orphaned piggies you can raise them in the house. Spread some straw in your basement and provide some dirt in a box the same way you would for a kitty. A pig will use his litter box just the way he's supposed to. Start out feeding the piglet with teaspoons of milk thickened with a little farina and sweetened with a little light corn syrup. Soon the baby can move on to cream of wheat and oatmeal. If your little pig isn't doing well on this diet, or if you have a sick one, the best special diet of all for little pigs is eggs—just plain shelled eggs in a bowl—anywhere from 2 eggs on up to 7 or so. Offer them 3 times a day. If you want to bottle-feed a pig, use any quart bottle with a lamb nipple, less for a smaller pig. But a plain milk will tend to make them sick. They really need some grain mixed in.

Margie Stroupe from Weingarten, MO, wrote: ". . . our mother sow had 15, came down with milk fever and almost died. She squashed nine because she couldn't handle herself and before I got nerve enough to get in with her and take the 6 living ones. Andy was down on his back and all he could do was storm because he was afraid she'd get me. But she couldn't even get to her feet. We called the vet and spent $15 for the sow's shot and the vet said if she wasn't better by morning to knock her in the head and put her on a brush pile. Well, his medicine did her no good and we wound up giving her 7 ccs. Combiotic [animal antibiotic] night and morning for 4 days. She got well, we fed her out, and on May 11, 1974, she butchered out 306 lb. without head, feet, skin and the like. So though we hated to do without a brood sow, she wound up feeding us almost a year. The baby pigs, well, that's another story. The milk I fed them wasn't the right formula and I lost 4 with scours [diarrhea] and getting them too hot."

But you don't want to keep pigs in the house too long. The lady who used to own this house told me how once she had an orphaned litter of 6 pigs living in the basement. One day a salesman came to call upstairs at the front door. She rushed up the stairs to let him in and forgot to shut the basement door behind her. The now-not-so-little pigs charged up the stairs behind her. When the door opened and the salesman saw her, and the 6 pigs charging up behind her, he looked really worried and sputtered, "Oh, I must have the wrong house," and literally ran away. You've got to be made of tough stuff to work door-to-door in the country!

A weaner-sized pig now needs other foods besides milk to be okay. Straight milk can cause them to bloat and die.

FEED SUPPLEMENTS FOR PIGLETS: Piglets can start eating supplementary "starter mash" at 1–2 weeks of age, but they'll never get a chance at it unless you use a creep feeder—a set-up where there's a hole to the starter mash supply big enough for piglets to "creep" through, but not big enough for mom to come and hog it—which she will if she can. Note: Commercial starter mash for piglets typically contains the antibiotic, sulfa. Pigs for slaughter fed the same thing would be condemned for sulfa residues.

WEANING AGE: It varies. Piglets would naturally nurse for about 12 weeks, or more, if allowed, but mom won't come into heat again while she's nursing, so commercial operations prefer to wean at 3–6 weeks. Early weaning can be hard, if not life-threatening, for young piglets, especially

for underweight, hind-teat types. So, first wean the biggest few piglets of the litter and let smaller ones continue nursing and growing. Don't wean piglets who are under 12 lb.!

Pig Vetting

Stephen: "To learn proper pig vetting I suggest that you develop a relationship with your vet. He will be glad to show you the correct way to do all of the things that need to be done to insure that your little ones and the sow are taken care of properly. Or you could get hold of a neighbor and have him show you how." In addition to birthing help and piglet procedures there's also:

NEEDLE TEETH CLIPPING: Clip the needle teeth with wire cutters, making them ½ inch shorter (don't crack teeth or cut gums!). Stephen: "A sharp pliers is used to cut the black teeth from the little pigs. These teeth are very sharp and will injure the sow's teats. If her teats hurt her too much the little ones will not get the nutrition they need because she won't let them nurse enough."

EAR NOTCHING: Ear notching is for pig outfits that can't keep straight who's who among their pigs. So they notch or tattoo ears for ID. (Follow your breeder organization guidelines.)

TAIL DOCKING: Tail "docking" means cutting off part of the tail with a wire cutter. The textbook argument is that the tail tip doesn't have many nerves in it, and docking prevents bored littermates from biting and chewing on it—which can result in infection. Stephen says, "For a happy pig, look for curly tails and fresh dirt on the snout. Curly tails, as a measure of contentedness, comes from a time before mass-produced pork. The agribusiness farmer generally has no choice in the matter. Either he docks the tails or he is docked in price by the guy who buys the pigs from him."

CASTRATION: Mike doesn't dock pigs' tails or castrate them. He says if a person is going to have just a few pigs, you're going to have them controlled, and if you're going to butcher at 200 lb., those procedures aren't necessary. If you're going to castrate, do it shortly after birth. An older pig bleeds more, and you can't pull the testicles off the same way. Make a cut on one side of the testicles with a razor blade, pull that testicle and its "tunic" (a white membrane) out of the hole, and continue pulling until it pulls off. (The piglets bleed less with pulling off than with cutting.) Cut an opening on the other side with your razor blade, pull out that testicle, and pull it off. Then apply antiseptic to both cuts and you're done.

WORMS: Whether your pigs have ever had worms or not, it's best to give worming medicine immediately upon bringing new pigs of any age to your property and every 6 weeks thereafter because pigs are so prone to worm problems. Get a bottle of liquid worm medicine from your veterinary products supplier. The exact instructions are on the bottle. You withhold food and water for 24 hours, then mix the appropriate amount of medicine with water and serve in their food through the next day. They drink it down willingly. But Barb Ingram from Santa, ID, sent me this different advice: "After bringing your new pig home, worm it. Then feed it all the slag coal it wants, and there is never any need to worm again."

Stephen gets the last word here: "Well, that is all there is to it. If this is your cup of tea, have at it. I hope to see you toiling in your own field some day. And remember, pigs are people too!"

BUTCHERING THE PIG

NOTE: Read all the relevant instructions over at least once before you begin.

Getting Ready

SEND IT OUT? Stephen hires his butchering done. "Our butcher doesn't smoke the hams and bacon; he sends them out to somebody else. So we make 2 pickup trips, 1 to get the unsmoked meat and 1 to get the hams and bacon. Pork doesn't have to hang for a week or so like beef, so 2 days after they butcher, the unsmoked stuff is ready to be picked up. It takes longer to make the smoked stuff, as much as 10 days to 2 weeks longer. I have the bacon cut thicker than store-bought, 5/16 of an inch. It fries up much nicer. You wind up with fewer pieces, but you have something to sink your teeth into. I like side pork, which is bacon that is not smoked. So we only have 1 side smoked and have 1 cut up fresh."

Even this can have pitfalls. Lane Morgan says, "Years ago our next-door neighbor was loading his 3 pigs for the ride to the butcher. Two went in the truck fine; the third had other ideas. So Bill's son, who was a state-champion high-school wrestler that year, put the hog in a headlock, and they heaved it into the truck. When they turned it loose, it was dead. The butcher legally can't take a dead pig, and they weren't set up to process the meat, so they bled it, gutted it, and took it to the barbecue pit at the rodeo grounds. Bill and a friend stayed up all night roasting it, and the next day they invited the whole town for lunch. What he lost in meat for the family, he certainly gained in goodwill."

WORKING ALONE? One person working alone will need 2–3 hours to complete the slaughtering process. It will take about 1½ hours to kill, scrape, and gut the pig if you have help—and about 4 hours more to cut it up. If you have only 1 person doing this you'll want either to scald the pig by the "barrel-at-a-45°-angle-in-the-ground method," or skin it. Best of all would be if you can work together with 1 or more neighbors at a hog-butchering bee in your area. Then you can use their facilities and learn from their experience.

HOG BUTCHERING BEE: Up at a ranch on a nearby "ridge," which means on the land up out of our canyon (where there is gently rolling ground called "ridges"), there is a big hog-butchering bee held each fall. Last year when we went, there were 19 hogs butchered in 1 day by 10 men. The women brought food for lunch, potluck-style, and in the tool shed where we lunched there was coffee and a fire going all day for hand- and food-warming. The men who scalded and scraped and sprayed the pigs (they had a hose attachment) wore rubber raincoats, rubber waders, and woolen hats, since they couldn't help but get wet in those freezing temperatures. (Hog butchering bees are usually held between December 9 and February 12.)

BUTCHERING AGE: Ideal pork comes from a young, healthy, meaty hog that weighs from 175 to 240 lb. In this we-love-lean era, people are leaning toward the low side rather than the high side. Heavier, fatter hogs produce proportionately less lean meat and more fat. The average hog produces as much pork as a family of 2 will eat in about a year. The meat from boars has a strong odor during cooking and an off-flavor described as being "soapy." So males are typically butchered before they reach sexual maturity. If old boars are to be slaughtered, this problem can be eliminated by castrating them ("Not a job for the timid," Lane notes!) and allowing them to heal and get the hormones out of their system before slaughter.

TIME OF YEAR: It is best to butcher pigs in weather cool enough to cool the meat naturally but not so cold as to freeze it. One of the most common problems with home-butchering of hogs is that improper cooling of the meat results in a rank and strong taste. The other reason for typical November killing is that the feeding of pigs is best timed to coincide with the growing season and conclude after the last of the harvest surplus is eaten up. Of course, if you have an artificial cooler, and are buying feed, then neither of those would apply and you could butcher in any weather. But it's nice and clean to butcher on the snow compared to dirt.

SKIN OR SCALD? First of all you must decide if you're going to skin or scald your pig. I'm going to offer you a choice of 3 ways to proceed with the pig, and 3 sets of corresponding directions: First, directions for team scalding in a barrel or vat; second, directions for 1-person scalding using a barrel on the ground; and third, directions for skinning the pig. Whether you skin the pig or scald it, keep in mind that pigskin, unlike the skin of other large animals, is edible. You can package and freeze it. You can add some pigskin to boiled potatoes or to milk gravy; a piece of it can be used to flavor baked beans. Or you can cook it with the cracklings when you make lard. Or cook it in the oven to get all the grease out, then eat what's left for a snack.

🐖 *PIGSKIN RULCHIS From Donna Joehn, Blaine, WA: "Of the skins, my folks made 'rulchis' (little rolls). They cut the skins in strips (all fat removed) approximately 2 × 6 inches, rolled them up tightly, tied with string, then cooked and pickled them with the pigs' feet. These were later enjoyed especially by us kids. If you wanted the crisp fried rinds you'd have to strip off all fat before frying them and cut in narrow strips. I do this with bacon rinds."*

Skinning Considerations. An inexperienced skinner is likely to lose a significant amount of lard and bacon because the bacon is right under the skin, and the skin does not strip away cleanly from the pig as it does from other animals. From a skinned pig, your bacons won't have a rind, your hams won't have a skin. And to skin a pig is a miserable job, especially around the head. There's nothing worse to skin than a pig. Well, not much.

GETTING READY TO SCALD: You must have yourself all set up and ready before you kill the pig. Make sure you've thought of a good way to get the pig into the hot water because if you let it lie too long in cold air before getting it into the vat, the body heat starts out. Start early in the morning to heat your water. You can use snow if it's clean. Use a good-sized scalding vat.

50-Gal. Barrel Vat. You can make do with this if it's clean inside, but sometimes they have held insecticides; you need to know the history of the barrel. Set it up so you can heat the water in it by means of a fire under or around it. To scald in a single barrel, you have to get the pig in, then pull it out, turn it around, and then get the other end in to scald it. That's almost impossible for 1 person to do alone and not easy for 2. A big hog won't fit in the barrel. About 240 lb. is tops.

Permanent Vat. The best thing is to make a permanent vat. The nicest ones are made out of sheet metal. This is set up with plenty of space underneath to build a fire and with a platform on each side, made of something like old bridge timbers, that won't catch on fire easily. The platform is for the men to stand on while they are rolling the pig in the water. An old steam-engine boiler also makes a good vat. Ours is made from half of an old steel hot-water tank. To make a really nifty vat, you can pick up some used firebricks (or even find some for free for hauling them away). Dig out a pit and line it with the brick; place your vat over the top. Be sure to leave enough room at both ends to be able to start your fire and to add more wood to keep the water hot.

Make a hole in the lower end of your scalding vat that you can plug with a whittled cork or some such. It helps mightily if the vat is located where you can get at it with a hose line from the house or some other water outlet. Rinse water through the cavity to clean it out a little. Then put water in it. You want to have a big enough vat and enough water in it so the pig is almost covered with water. Allow for losing some water by sloshing out at the side if you are doing more than 1 pig. You can't add more water because then it will be too cool for the next pig—unless you're willing to wait while it heats up again.

Test Water Temperature. It's handy to have a dairy thermometer to get the water's temperature. Between 150 and 165°F is right, but from 140 to 180°F works. The old-timers say that if you dip your hand through the water 3 times and on the third pass it feels so hot you can hardly stand it—it should be just right (if your hands are cold to start with). If the water is too hot, you'll cook the hog, and, worse yet, the hair will set and be very hard to get out.

Add Lye to Water. Put in about half a can of lye to 200 gal. water. Makes it clean up easier. The old-timers used a couple shovelfuls of wood ashes for their lye solution. (Stir well.) *NOTE: When the water is the right temperature, it's finally time to kill the pig.*

Killing a Pig

SHOOTING: Make a mental X from the pig's left ear to its right eye and from its right ear to left eye; where it crosses, shoot. It helps to wait until the pig looks at you before you shoot. Shoot straight in because the brain is small. A pistol is by far the best for this job (which is a good reason why country people don't want their pistols taken away). Get the right angle so you'll do the job the first time because it's much harder to get it right if the pig is wounded and jumping around. A .22-caliber is the most economic on meat because it doesn't destroy much and is still big enough to do the job (on a 200-lb. pig).

Shoot here

Patricia Kenyon, Castlewood, VA, disagrees: "Don't use the .22-shot-to-the-imaginary-X-on-the-face technique. Instead, do not feed the hogs their evening meal. The next morning, lay out a sumptuous hog feast for them, walk up behind the happy, munching hogs, place the gun behind the nearest hog's ear, aim toward the diagonally opposite eye and shoot the hog. A .22 does not make enough noise to spook the other hogs. The shot hog will keel over, having died in [ecstasy]. The other hogs will move into its vacated position and you can dispatch the next hog without moving. This works better than the front shot because the skull is much thinner from this angle. I developed this technique after annoying a 600-lb. hog with the .22 front shot. As the screaming hog began charging around the barn, snapping viciously, my helpers (2 farmer neighbors) shinnied up the nearest support posts in my barn and left the rest to me. After that ordeal, I went to the local college and studied the hog skeleton they had on display."

STICKING: Now immediately, using a long narrow-bladed sharp knife (at least 7 inches long) cut open the hog's throat about 3 inches in front of the end of the breastbone, then cut down inside and slightly back under the breastbone, until you get the jugular vein or the aorta. You'll know because then the blood will pour out. If you haven't got it just right, keep cutting until you do find it. Killing them is no fun, anyway. Do it right. The animal has to be well-bled, and the sooner it dies after you first shoot it the better for you both. For a knife you can use a large hunting knife or a good stiff butcher knife. The best place to cut is right back of the jaws in the center of the throat. Cut toward the pig's left side to get the aorta. Now wait and let it bleed. Adjust the head so the opening is downhill from the body and so the jugular opening is not covered.

MARKING OWNERSHIP: If several families' pigs are being butchered together, you cut an ear of the dead pigs to distinguish your own—1 notch for theirs and 2 for yours, for example.

MOVING PIG TO WATER: At the big butchering bee they have 2 tractors with fork-lifts ("farmhand," "front-end lift," "buckrake") working to move the carcasses around. The carcass is rolled into the hydraulically operated fork-lift on the tractor. You then raise the fork-lift and let the tractor take the hog to the scalding platform. If you don't have a fork-lift, the next easiest method is to use an old-time hay hook. Insert the hook point in through the open mouth, then out through the jaw so that it will be pulling against the strong jawbone. Drag the animal by the hook over to your scalding vat.

Scalding a Pig

USING ROPES: Lay the pig on the platform by the scalding vat. You now need two 30-foot (more or less) ropes. Half-inch rope is fine. You can make do with 1, but 2 are much better. Smaller rope is harder to get hold of and to work with.

Rope the pig up before you put it into the vat. With 1 rope this is a 2-man job. (With 2 ropes you use 4 people to roll the pig.)

1. Make each rope have a U shape.
2. Lay the pig on ropes across the U shape.
3. Bring the 2 free ends of the U over the pig and through the inside of the U.
4. Now take those free U ends back to where they were.

This would be a double half hitch if you pulled the ropes tight. Have 2 people take hold of the bottom of the U's, and 2 other people take the loose ends. You now have 4 people, each with a grip on the ropes, which cross the pig behind its front legs and in front of its hind legs. Two are on the platform on 1 side of the vat, and 2 are on the platform on the other side—with the pig inside the rope. This way you can let it into the vat, and roll it around in there.

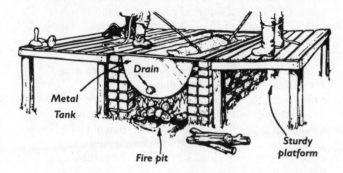

Put the pig into the vat slowly so as not to splash. Roll the pig gently back and forth. Now turn it over. Continue the rolling in the water. Keep the rope just snug enough to see if the pig's hair is "slipping" yet. "Slipping" means that you can pull it out. When both sides are scalded and the hair is slipping, then it's ready to scrape. Now haul the pig out. If this is a 2-man job, hand over both rope ends to 1 side so that both can haul the pig out from that side.

Knowing When It's Ready. If the hair is worn off where the ropes are around the pig, it's getting pretty close to being ready to come out. It will take 3–6 minutes of scalding to loosen the hair and scurf. The most difficult time of year to get the hair loosened is in the fall when the winter hair is beginning to grow. (That time of year you might benefit from higher water temperatures or longer submersion times.) If you can grab a handful of hair and the scarfskin comes off with it, it's ready. Or better yet, take a hog scraper, or a knife, and just scrape on part of it that's sticking out from the water while it's still in the vat. If the hair comes off, well, it's ready. If the dewclaws will snap off, the feet are scalded enough. If you start to scrape and find out you actually didn't scald the pig long enough you can put it back in to finish the process. If your water is too hot you can make it work by keeping the carcass in constant motion and pulling it from the barrel several times to prevent over-scalding. But if you leave the pig in the vat too long at too high a temperature the hair will set—which makes for quite a problem. The only answer, once the mischief is done, is to scrape as hard as you can and mutter a lot.

Hog scraper

SCRAPING A PIG

Scraping Tools. You'll need a hog scraper or several knives. The scraper is a 3½-inch-wide galvanized steel bell-shaped scraper with a 3¾-inch hardwood handle. If you have the sharpest scraping knife, you'll be the fastest scraper, but you'll also make the most cuts. It doesn't take long for a knife to get dull scraping on that hair though. Scrapers aren't as likely to make cuts. You can mail-order a hog scraper from Lehman's Hardware (also sausage grinders and butcher saws) 888-438-5346; **www.Lehmans.com.**

Extra Hot Water. Scrape your pig right by the barrel or the vat so that you can get hot water for pouring over it. Plan to have hot water to spare, because it helps, especially when scraping older hogs (which get really tough to scrape, especially red-haired ones). The last resort, if scraping doesn't work, is to pour more hot water over them out of a bucket, then pull hair out as if you were pulling chicken feathers.

Scraping Method. As you scrape you get not only hair, but also dirt and the scarfskin. Scoop more water up in your bucket and pour over to keep the pores hot and soft so the hair will keep coming loose. Try not to cut through the hide. Work over the whole body this way. The best scraping motion with a knife is to hold the knife on both ends. Don't pull the way you would slice; that cuts the skins. Pull across (sideways). Scrape the hot carcass as quickly as possible, because the hair tends to "set" as it cools. If you come to a patch of hair that is difficult to scrape because it didn't scald enough (like the mid-section of the pig), cover it with a burlap bag and pour hot water over it until loosens up. It will also help with the scraping if you place the legs or head so as to stretch the skin and smooth out the wrinkles.

Scraping the Feet. *The feet are hardest to scrape. If you are planning to save the pig's feet for pickling or some such, do them first, while they're hot.* You can pull the toe nails and dewclaws from the front feet by inserting a hook into the top of the nail and pulling. Do the same with the rear legs. Grip the legs with both hands and twist to pull off the hair. Leave the feet on for the time being. You can use the scraper on the rest of the carcass.

Scraping the Head. Do the head around the eyes, nose, and jaw next after the feet. On an old hog there will be bristles on the snout (whiskers). You can shave them off with a sharp knife, barber-style, or singe off as you would a chicken. More than 25 percent of your scraping time will be spent working on the head because it's hard to get around the parts of it. Save the ears. They are good to flavor a mess of beans or with kraut. There are a couple of pounds of meat in the jowl (cheeks) that will make good scrapple, headcheese, salt pork, or side meat. Most people leave on the ears.

Scraping the Body. After you're done with feet and head, do the rest. When you get one side of the pig done, roll it over and do the other side.

ONE-MAN SCALDING SYSTEM: This method is from a USDA booklet, "Pork: Slaughtering, Cutting, Preserving, and Cooking on the Farm" (Farmers' Bulletin Number 2265).

Read about scraping, above, before proceeding.

You'll need about 50 gal. of near-boiling water. Once you get the water into your scalding barrel, you can adjust to the more exact temperature (between 140 and 145°, recommended) by adding cold water. If you have 2 barrels, you can use 1, with a fire under it, for heating your water. You can have another one buried in the ground down almost to its lip at about a 45° angle. Having the barrel buried makes it humanly possible without any other machinery or equipment to maneuver the pig in there and out again by hand. You'll have to get it in and out at least twice, once for the head end, while holding it by the rear legs, and once again for the rear end, while holding it by the front legs. Then scrape.

Skinning a Pig

The skinning procedure used for a pork carcass is similar to that used for beef carcasses. Skinning requires less equipment and can be done faster than scalding and scraping. To begin, place the carcass on a clean surface (plywood, concrete, straw); wash any blood and dirt off, turn the carcass on its back, and hold it in place with blocks placed on each side. Cut the hide around the rear legs, just below the dewclaws. Make a cut through only the hide, down the back of the leg, over the hocks, and to the midline at the center of the hams. Skin around each side of the leg, removing the hide to a point below the hock. Open the hide down the midline from the point where the animal was stuck in the neck, around each side of the pubic area and continue to the anus. Make this cut by inserting the point of the knife under the skin with the blade turned up. This procedure is a sort of cutting from inside out and will, you hope, protect against puncturing the intestines.

Remove the hide from the insides of the hams. Be careful. It is very easy to cut through the fat into the lean. Continue skinning along the sides toward the breast. Grasp the loosened hide in the opposite hand and pull it up and out. This places tension on the hide, removes wrinkles, and allows the knife to glide smoothly. Holding the knife firmly, place it against the hide with the blade turned slightly outward. Skin as far down the sides as possible, but not around the front legs. Return to the rear of the carcass and remove the hide left on the rear of the hams. Do not skin the outside of the hams at this time. Remove the rear feet by sawing through the bone about 2 inches above the hock. Insert the spreader (see "Hanging a Pig") under the large tendons on the rear legs and secure the legs to the spreader.

Hoist the carcass to a convenient working height for skin removal from the outside of the hams. Skin around the outsides of the hams, leaving as much fat as possible on the carcass. Remove the hide around the anus, and cut through the tail at the joint closest to the body. Pull the hide down over the hips. The hide along the hips and back can be pulled off, leaving the fat on the carcass. Occasionally, you may need to use a knife to cut between the skin and the fat if large pieces of fat are being pulled off. Hoist the carcass to a fully extended position. Open the hide down the rear of the forelegs. Skin along the inside of the forelegs and neck. Skin along the outside of the shoulders and jowls to a point approximately halfway to the back of the carcass. Slowly pull out and down on the hide, removing it along the back. If the fat begins to tear, use a knife to correct the torn area, and then continue pulling the hide. Remove the hide as far down the back as possible. When it becomes difficult to pull along the top of the neck, complete removal with a knife. If the head is to be saved, skin over the poll and down the face. Remove the hide at the snout. Remove the front feet by sawing just below the knee joint.

Skip "Hanging" because you've already done that, and continue with "Gutting."

Hanging a Pig

After scraping, it's time to hang the pig up in order to gut it. (Of course, if you skinned it, it's already up.)

GAMBREL, "SINGLETREE," OR "SPREADER": This is what you hang the pig by. It can be any straight stick. Metal ones usually have metal hooks at each end. Wooden ones have a carved notch there. If you are making your own out of wood, basically all you need is a long enough, strong enough stick with a V-shaped notch on the topside near each end so the hamstrings won't slip off the end to the middle. A "singletree" is actually a piece of old-time horse harness that people found out made a great gambrel. Nobody around here knows what the word gambrel means. They all use a singletree and call it a singletree. We've used a neck yoke, too, and wired the legs onto it. One of these is an excellent investment if you are going to do home butchering of anything larger than a chicken or rabbit. The gambrel has to be long enough to spread the hind legs real tight, hence the other name of "spreader." For the average hog, that is about 30 inches.

WIRE, ROPE, OR CHAIN: You need something to hang the gambrel by. Use a wire, or rope, or chain around the center to hang it to your fork-lift, or to a tree limb, or a tripod, or a rafter beam when time comes to gut the animal after scalding. If you buy a ready-made gambrel, it will come equipped with something, usually a chain or rope, in the middle to hang it by.

GETTING THE HAMSTRINGS: The best system is to hang an animal by the hamstrings, or "Achilles tendons." They are located in the back of the hind legs. Make a vertical slit. Don't cut crosswise! There are actually 2 cords there. Get both of them, especially on a heavy hog. Use your singletree (gambrel) to hang the pig by the hamstrings. Put 1 hook from each end of the gambrel under each hamstring. If you are using just a stick, put each end of it through the space between the hamstrings and the bone.

After the pig is hung, now is your chance to put the final touches on your scraping job. Pour more hot water over where it is needed. Scrape up.

Gutting the Pig

When you butcher a pig you discard about 20 percent of its weight. This is the stage at which most of that goes. Have some twine ready or heavy string.

These instructions assume that the pig is hanging from its hind feet and that you are standing, facing the belly side of it.

It makes a difference in method whether you are butchering a male pig or a female.

A MALE: Cut around the penis, which is in the middle of the pig's belly, and slip the knife on up to around the rectum. Notice a cord running from the penis right under the skin up to the rectum. That cord runs right into the gut. Pick up the penis area and tie off the cord that connects to it with your twine. Cut the cord on out. Cut all around the anus to free the end of the gut and tie that. That's to prevent what's inside that part of the gut, which is not nice, from coming out on your meat at any stage of your work. When you cut around it, keep your knife sloping toward the meat and away from the anus so you don't cut the gut.

A Female: Start by cutting around the anus so you can get hold of the end of the gut and tie that off with twine the same as for a male.

Next, on Either Sex

1. Cut down the belly midline until you have the skin parted from up at the top to the jaw at the bottom. Be careful not to cut into an intestine.
2. Split the brisket or breastbone. Hammer on your knife to drive it through. The brisket is right in the center between the shoulder where the ribs join together in front of the heart, lungs, and liver. You're aiming to cut that pig into 2 separate and distinct halves, and the brisket ("breastbone") is the hard part in the front chest that you must cut through to accomplish that.

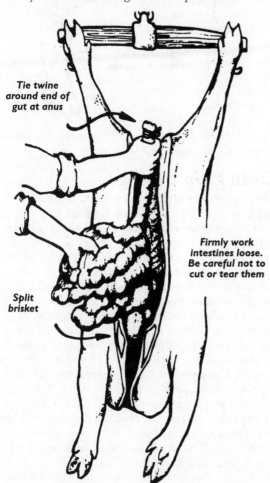

Tie twine around end of gut at anus

Firmly work intestines loose. Be careful not to cut or tear them

Split brisket

3. Cut between the hind legs starting on the midline.
4. Finish cutting on the belly by putting your hand inside, being careful that your hand is between the knife and the intestines. Believe it or not, it would be better to cut yourself than accidentally to cut the intestines, but you won't. Now bring the innards out of the hog, starting from the top. Have a big wash basin ready for the organs that you want to save: heart and liver.
5. Cut the diaphragm to bring out the rest of the organs. The diaphragm is a muscle layer separating the intestines area from the heart-lungs area.
6. Now deal with the organ meats: Trim off the top of the heart. Heart, trimmed, goes into a dishpan. Remove the gallbladder from the liver. If you are going to cut, then cut through the liver; if you accidentally cut into

the gallbladder the bile escaping will ruin your meat. Old-timers just peel it out and they follow the duct up a ways and peel that out, too. The sweetbread looks like brains. It is attached between the stomach and liver. Leave the kidneys in until you cut up the meat. The long narrow liver-looking thing is the spleen, and it isn't used.

"Aitch" bone

Ample washtub to hold innards

7. On a large, old, well-fattened hog the entrails will carry several pounds of fat, which you save for lard. Young hogs don't have enough to fool with. The "leaf lard" is inside the body cavity from midline to rear on each side. Peel it out. Don't leave it on the bacon because it's just pure lard.
8. When you're going to use the head, make sure that the cut is made clear down to the jaw. Then, when the innards fall out, you can pull out the whole mess from the neck, too—including the trachea, esophagus, jugular, and tongue. The last to come out will be the tongue as you bring out the windpipe and esophagus. Get the tongue out whether you plan to eat it or not, because if you don't, blood will collect there.
9. You have to cut the head off before you can make halves. Use the biggest, sharpest knife you have. Cut the head off about an inch behind the ears: Cut the meat down until you have exposed the bone all the way around the neck. Grab the head firmly and twist it around and around until it just snaps off from the body.

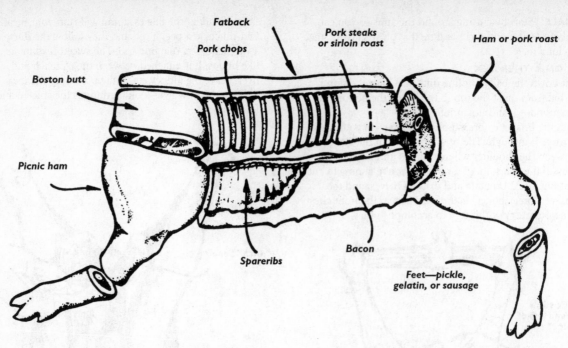

Fatback

Pork chops

Pork steaks
or sirloin roast

Ham or pork roast

Boston butt

Picnic ham

Spareribs

Bacon

Feet—pickle,
gelatin, or sausage

10. Make halves by sawing with a meat saw right down through the middle of the backbone from top to bottom.

11. Now let the meat hang to cool. Don't cut it up while it is warm, but pork, unlike beef or goat, is not aged. By the next day you could—and probably should—proceed to cut it up. It is not harmed though by a reasonable wait—even as long as 1 week if you have really cold weather. But it doesn't keep as well as beef.

Preparing Suckling and Barbecue Pigs

SUCKLING PIG: This is in case you have an extra piglet. By waiting 5 months you could have all the meat of a big pig, but your sow may have had too many babies to nurse manageably. You could bottle-feed the extra, or you could kill, scald, scrape, and gut it on the same principles as a larger animal. After cleaning out the innards, rinse the pig in warm soda water. Leave on the head, but clean the passages of the head and throat with a wooden skewer wrapped in a small piece of soft cloth.

Cooking a Suckling Pig. Fill with stuffing. To stuff a 12-lb. suckling you might use 3 c. diced celery, 2 c. chopped onion, ½ c. minced parsley—all fried in plenty of butter and then combined with about 7 c. dry bread crumbs. Sew and truss. Bend the forefeet backward from the knee and the hind legs forward. Make deep cuts in the skin in 3 places. Put a potato or apple in the mouth to hold it open. Roast at 350°F until the meat thermometer reaches 185°F (3–4 hours).

SPIT-BARBECUED PIG: This works best with a smallish pig, like about 40 lb. That will feed a huge family reunion or some similarly large group. Give it a good scraping, clean it, and scrape inside and out under running water an extra time. Optional: make a dressing to stuff it (about 2 gal.). Wrap feet and ears in foil to keep them from burning, and keep the pig turning on the spit. A motorized spit is the easiest. The roasting will take 5 hours for the 40-lb. pig, more if it is bigger. Use a meat thermometer to check on how done the pig is, deep inside.

Now back to handling the 200-pounder. This one definitely must be cut up.

Cutting Up the Pig

Before freezers, the pig's fat was rendered into lard, with cracklings used as a people snack or animal feed; as much as possible was eaten fresh, and the rest was heavily salted for preservation. When saltpeter came along, what had been salted meat was shifted to "cured" ("corned" if it was beef) and the amount of salt and spices could be lessened. Now that we know more about saltpeter (all bad) and have freezing and canning options, the healthiest choice for your family is obviously to freeze all of the pig, or to make sausage (which will be frozen) of part or all of it—especially if it's a predictably tough old animal. By not curing what could have been cured for hams you'll have roasts, and what would have been cured for bacon is "side pork," which you can slice and fry much like bacon.

Some people start cutting it up while it is still hanging, but we bring the carcass in, a half at a time, and lay it on our big plywood cutting board, which is scrubbed in the tub with a scrub brush and then laid across the kitchen table. A pig is actually easy to cut up. I'll theoretically divide it into thirds. The front third is figured as if the head were still on.

HAVE CONTAINERS READY: I use 4- and 5-gal. plastic buckets. One holds meat to be cured if curing is planned. Another holds pieces that are to be ground for sausage. Another holds bones for making gelatin, or to cook up with sauerkraut or beans. And one holds fat that will be rendered into lard. I also have ready meat-type wrapping paper and freezer tape with which to wrap the roasts, chops, and ribs that will go directly into the freezer after being cut.

FIRST, TRIM: Trim off the dirty and bloodshot spots—everything that doesn't look like what you would want to eat.

THE HEAD: There are numerous good ways to use the meat of the pig's head. They all require similar preparatory steps. Options:

- Prepare it according to the directions under "Head-cheese and Scrapple."

- Or cut off the jowl, which is the chin area, and make it into bacon, with the trimmings going into the sausage bucket (you want your bacon slab fairly neat-looking). Save the ears, too, to flavor a mess of beans, and you can discard the rest.

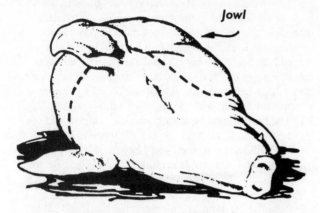

Jowl

- Or cut off all the meat you can get at and put into your sausage bucket—and discard the rest.
- Or cut off all the meat you can get at and use it to make pork mincemeat.
- Or cut of all the meat you can get at in thin slices, package, and freeze. You can fry the sliced scraps like side meat.
- Or clean out the ears, nose, and mouth passages well with a cloth on a stick or just a cloth on your finger and rinse well with water. Then, in a big kettle (I use my canner), cook the whole head for hours and hours and hours until the meat falls off the bones. Then remove the bones and the more strange-looking stuff like eyes and the lining of the mouth. Skim off every bit of the grease you can get to go with your lard renderings. Divide, package, and freeze what's left to go with kraut or beans. That is my favorite way of preparing the head.

THE HIND THIRD: This means one of the back legs.
NOTE: Instructions such as "front," "back," etc., are generally given as if the animal were standing up.

1. If you haven't done so already, saw off the hind foot through the ankle (hock) about a foot up from the hoof. You can either set aside the foot to make pickled pigs feet, or trim off the meat for sausage and put the rest into the gelatin bucket.
2. Now cut the hind leg (ham) away from the body. You'll have the tail end of the backbone included in your piece, which you can trim out later to make your ham look nice. You're cutting in front of the pig's hip bone and getting off all the hind leg with this cut. Cut the meaty areas with a knife. Finish going through the bone with a meat saw. On a sow you'll have 2 teats included plus about 2 inches. In person talk we'd call it the pig's thigh. On a young pig it will weigh about 20 lb.; on an old sow it will weigh about 30 lb.
3. Trim it around the top to make it look neat. Make sausage or lard of the trimmings (depending on whether they are meat and fat, or mostly fat). Sausage trimmings are generally cut into approximately 1-inch strips to go through the grinder better. If you are planning to cure the ham, the skin is generally left on. Put the ham into your curing bucket. If, instead of curing it, you want it to be pork roasts, trim the skin off (and

place the skin into your sausage bucket). Cut the ham into roast-sized pieces; the only rigid rule is that a roast has to be small enough to fit into your pan with the lid on. Other than that, a chunk of meat is a chunk of meat no matter what the experts say. Incidentally, if you plan to cure your hams and bacons with the skin on and you have a propane torch, you can use it to burn any remaining hairs off them.

THE FRONT THIRD: These directions are meant for a young pig, the 200-lb. kind. If you are butchering an old hog, then you take the whole front third and cut up most of the meat to go through your grinder for sausage.

1. If you haven't done so already, cut off the foot at the ankle—about 8 inches above the hoof. Put it in the same place you did the hind foot.
2. Now cut off the leg plus the front shoulder. You'll find the right spot by cutting behind the third rib. You'll need your meat saw. You're cutting it off just back of the shoulder blade, straight up and down the body. If you are making hams to be cured, take the big piece that you cut off (minus the foot) and divide it in half horizontally to the ground just below the lower edge of the shoulder blade. The resulting half that has backbone in it is called the Boston butt ham or shoulder roast and the lower half is called the picnic ham. If you would rather make roasts than hams out of your Boston butt and picnic hams, again cut them down into roaster-sized pieces.
3. Now trim out the backbone. Trim off the meat left around the backbone for sausage and put the backbone itself into your gelatin pile or bones pile.
4. The 3 front ribs that get included in the cut can be packaged for short ribs. Saw them away from the rest.
5. That flap of meat attached to the lower half of the front leg is bacon or sausage (or side meat if you'd rather). For bacon, cut away and make the edges nice. For sausage, cut it into strips. For side meat, leave plain and don't cure.

THE MIDDLE THIRD: That's what's left.
Separate the ribs from the bacon. You can see where the ribs are. The bacon is the boneless flap of "skin" behind the ribs. Stay out of the thick meaty pork-chop area along the backbone. You can peel the meat off the outside of the ribs, too, and make bacon out of it. Or leave it on for very meaty spareribs. That's what I like to do.

The "Bacon" or "Side Pork." You can take the skin off the bacon or not. (Personally, I like the skin off.) If you plan to cut the skin off, whacking the whole bacon section on the table as hard as you can, skin side down, several times before you start makes it a little easier. I like the bacon cut into squarish sections about 6 inches on the side. You can make them bigger—it doesn't matter. Put the trimmings into the sausage pile. I've made triangular bacon, but it slices up more nicely if it is square. Side pork is the same cut not cured; you can slice and fry it just the same for breakfast only it won't have the cured taste. Slice like bacon only thicker, season, and fry. Don't flour. Cook through.

The "Fatback." This is the fat on the back of the pig, which you trim off with the skin for your lard pail, leaving only just the amount you like on your pork chops—¼–¾ inch is plenty.

Chops. What's left looks like backbone. It includes the muscles that run right alongside of the backbone. You can either bone the chops out and have them with no bone, or saw them out and have a chunk of bone included with each one. I don't like bones out of chops, though that is easier to do. Boned-out chops don't look like chops anymore to me, and, though you only lose a little meat in the boning out process, on a chop that's a noticeable loss.

To bone them out: Cut the muscle away from the bone. Slice across the grain and package for the freezer in meal-sized numbers. The little muscle on the other side of the bone can be pulled out and cut across the grain into "tips," which means a mini-chop. The vertebrae can go into your bones department—the best thing I know for making gelatin.

To saw them out: The butcher does it with a power saw, which makes it easier for him, but you can do it by cutting the meat part with a knife and then finishing with a meat saw. Cut across the grain of the tenderloin the same way you would for boned-out chops.

The rear third of the "backbone" can be sawed into pork steaks (cut across the grain) or cut into a couple of sirloin roasts.

Headcheese and Scrapple

Headcheese is a homemade luncheon meat. It's quick and easy compared to scrapple. It's an all-meat product. You can add in the pig's tongue, skin, heart, and other scraps, if you want to. Headcheese makes a fine cold snack when cut in slices and served with hot mustard or horseradish. Or it can be dipped in egg and crumbs and fried like scrapple for your meat dish. Or you can make a kind of sausage out of it, if you know where to get casings (or how). Like all pork products it's on the bland side, so either while cooking or when serving you'll want to spice it up some.

SCRAPPLE: This, on the other hand, is a meat and meat soup mixture made firm by thickening it with a cereal and spicing it to taste. Almost everybody likes headcheese. Some people like scrapple and some don't.

If you'd like to make a trial run of something like scrapple, to see if you're going to like it, use some leftover ham to make it. Prepare 1½ c. ground cooked ham. Then mix together 1 c. cornmeal, ½ t. salt, pepper to taste, and 1 c. cold water. Boil 1¾ c. water and then slowly add the cold cornmeal mixture. Cook on low heat until the scrapple has thickened and is boiling, stirring all the time. Add the ground ham, mix it up well, and pour out into pans to set

up. That takes at least several hours in a chilly place. Then you can turn it out of the pan, slice off some, and fry as described earlier.

Now that you've decided whether you're going to make headcheese or scrapple, there's the problem of what you're going to make it out of. If you have, or are going to have, a hog's head, that's fine. Some farmers don't want to bother with their hogs' heads and will sell them to you. Heads vary considerably in size depending on how old the animal was. An old brood sow can have a head almost twice as big as that of a pig of the more usual butchering age. If you don't have a hog's head, you can actually make headcheese or scrapple out of any pork-sausage-type scraps.

1. The head should be already scalded, scraped, and separated. But if the head fate has given you to work with is a still-hairy one, then you'll have to skin it—which is an awful, tedious, frustrating job, and you have my sympathy. Or you can try singeing the hairs off with a blow torch.
2. Take the head out to your chopping block and split it in half with the ax. If it looks like mincemeat before you finally manage to get the halves separated don't despair—that won't hurt the final product. Just collect the pieces off the chopping block and carry them back to the kitchen.
3. Remove and discard the eyes, nasal passages, teeth, jaw, and eardrums. You can use the ears, lips, and snout if they are well-cleaned. Scrape the ears to get them clean. Usually the jowl isn't used because it's so fatty. The "jowl" is the neck-cheek area. Remove all the fat you can and save it to render for cooking lard or soap. Make deep cuts in the thick meat pieces.
4. Put the meat into your kettle. A cast-iron kettle is best because it heats most evenly (so is an old-fashioned wood or coal burning range for the same reason). For 1 hog's head you'll need the equivalent of a canner or big 8-qt. pressure cooker to make this recipe. Cover the meat with water and simmer until it is ready to fall off the bones.
5. Remove the meat from the broth. Pick it over and separate the meat from the most of the fat, from all of the bones, and from the broth. Grind the meat.

Up to this point the recipe is the same whether you are making headcheese or scrapple. Now it differs.

A Scrapple Recipe. Skim every bit of fat from the broth. Add to the broth one 2-lb. 10-oz. box of old-fashioned oatmeal. Don't use the instant kind since it won't make good scrapple for some reason. Or add enough cornmeal to make a soft mush. Or add half cornmeal and half buckwheat flour to make a soft mush. I prefer the oatmeal but you can vary the specific grain combination to suit yourself. If you are working with a large quantity of meat, rather than just 1 head, figure 1 part dry cereal and 3 parts soup to 7 parts ground cooked meat. If you use cornmeal, cool some of the broth and moisten the cornmeal with it before adding to prevent lumps.

Now season the scrapple. For the basic 1 pig's head and 1 box oatmeal recipe, add ½ T. ground pepper and 2 T. salt, or vary the seasonings to suit yourself. Marjoram, sage, nutmeg, mace, and onions are all good in it. (If you use onions, grind them first and add at the beginning of the time the cereal will cook.) After your scrapple is thickened and seasoned, it has to be cooked about half an hour very slowly. Don't let it burn on the bottom. When it is done, pour it into chilled, wet leaf-type (or other shallow) pans. That's all there is to it.

Scrapple makes a good quick breakfast or lunch. You can cut it into sections sized appropriately for 1 meal for your family, package it in a plastic bag, and freeze. To serve the scrapple, thaw it, and cut into ½-inch slices. Some people like it dipped in egg or in egg and crumbs before frying. Fry it like cornmeal mush in a lightly buttered pan, about 10 minutes per side, over medium to low heat until browned on each side and crisp. Serve with maple syrup.

Scrapple Without a Pig's Head. From Ellen Currans of Douglas, OR: "Start with 1 lb. pork sausage, browned in a skillet with 1 large onion, chopped. Add 3 c. boiling water and 3 c. oatmeal. Salt and pepper to taste. Cook, stirring, until oatmeal has absorbed the water and tastes cooked. Our family eats as is, or it can be packed in a loaf pan, refrigerated and then sliced and fried in butter for breakfast. Makes a great first breakfast to take on camping trips."

HEADCHEESE: Mix the ground meat mass with seasonings to taste: salt, pepper, red pepper, ground cloves, coriander, and sweet marjoram all are possibilities. Take a little sample, spice it, and then taste it to see if you like your combination. Keep testing until you get it right, and then spice the whole mass accordingly. Red pepper is good in it if you have a cast-iron stomach. I grind my own, but if you do too be sure you get it fine because if somebody bites into a speck-sized bit of it, it'll take the top of his head off.

Pack the seasoned headcheese tightly in a bowl or loaf pan and press into as compact a mass as you can in the bottom of the bowl. For extra firmness, cover it with a weighted plate. Refrigerate. When it is very firm it is ready to slice and eat.

Still another way to use the pig's head is a combination of headcheese and panhas. Go ahead and make your headcheese. After making headcheese you have a soup broth left over anyway to use as you please or throw out. Add cornmeal and seasonings to that meat broth just as for scrapple and you get the meatless scrapple called panhas.

Headcheese Sausage. This is a variation you can try sometime. After the headcheese is seasoned to taste, stuff it into casings instead of pressing it into a bowl. Then recook the sausages in the pork soup until they float, 10–30 minutes. After they float, chill them in cold water. Store in a cool place. You can add a smoke flavor by giving them 4 hours in the smokehouse.

Sylta Headcheese. From the Johnsons of Wheaton, IL: "This serves 20 to 25. Use ½ hog's head (5 lb.), 2 lb. lean pork and 2½ lb. veal shoulder. Clean and singe off hair and bristles. Clean teeth with a stiff brush and cut off ears. Soak in cold water for 6 to 12 hours, changing water. Place meat and hocks in boiling water to which has been added 4 t. salt, 30 peppercorns, and 20 whole allspice. Simmer 2 to 3 hours, or until tender. Remove meat from broth, save broth, and cut meat in slices. Spread cloth or towel, wrung out in hot water, in a deep bowl. Line with cooked rind from pork hocks, rind side down. To sliced meat, add 3 to 4 T. crushed whole allspice (measure after crushing with rolling pin). Add 3 to 4 T. salt. Arrange in cloth. Cover with rind if any is available. Pull cloth together tightly and tie with string. Put back in broth. Cook slowly 5 to 10 minutes. Lift out so it doesn't stick to the bottom. Remove to a platter,

cover with a board and put weight on for 24 hours. Set in a cool place. Remove cloth after that time and wrap in a fresh cloth that has been soaked in salted water. Put in a plastic bag and refrigerate. Serve slice thin with pickled beets."

Chitlins

This is the small intestine of the pig. Some people think these are the best part. Others think they're too much work to clean, slippery, fragile, and bad smelling. Pull all the fat off, rinse, and scrape as to make sausage casings until they're really clean. Then boil until tender with salt, pepper, and a potato. Serve chitlins hot with cabbage slaw or potato salad.

Making Lard

White, creamy lard comes from high-quality pig fat that was trimmed and rendered fairly soon after the butchering. The fats that you got from around the internal organs of the pig are called the "caul" and "ruffle" fats. If they were washed promptly, and if none of the contents of the innards were spilled on them, they can also be made into lard, except their lard is a darker color. Besides your own butchering, you could probably get fat from a butcher shop for a cheap price, if you want it; just leave word that you are interested in buying. (They'll probably give it to you.) But it wouldn't be residue-free. It's best to render lard during cool weather. Work with about 15 lb. or so at a time.

I render our lard in a big pan in the oven. It takes more than 24 hours of slow heat. The grease will separate more easily from the tissue fibers if the fat is cut into pieces before putting it in your kettle. Some people even grind it through a meat chopper using a 2- or 3-blade knife and plate with a hole ¾ inch or larger. But that ruins your chance for cracklings.

CRACKLINGS: These are the little pieces of meat tissue that are left after you melt out the lard, like frying bacon. Some people like cracklings and some don't. They are packaged commercially and sold as a snack called "pork rinds." I remember vividly as a little girl my father's hog butchering and lard rendering and how good those fresh cracklings tasted. My husband loves them, too. If you want proper cracklings, cut your lard into strips. I do that when I'm getting ready to render the lard. I cut the fat and skin into strips—any sort of shape but I try to get them not more than ½ inch wide.

THE HEATING: You can put pure fat in the kettle or else start out with a little water in the bottom. An iron kettle is fine. Burning is a problem. *Use only low to moderate heat.* It's safest to render with that kettle in the oven rather than on a burner. Or on the back of a wood cook stove, because there is such a gentle even heat back there. If you don't get done the first day, just let it set overnight and continue on the next day when you get the stove going again. *Don't stick your face in the kettle for a close examination.* There is an occasional "pop" as some moisture in the fat turns to steam, and you might get a grease burn in the eye. Remember the stuff is pure hot grease. *Make sure the pan is at the back of the stove and that the children stay away.*

Do not fill the kettle to the top so that there won't be any danger of it boiling over. Add ½ t. baking soda to the fat when rendering is begun, which will darken the cracklings but whiten the lard. Be careful not to scorch.

DEEP-FAT FRYING TIME/TEMPERATURE

Food to Be Fried	Time in Minutes	Temperature
Brown-off method to precook	5–6	350–375°F
Chicken, straight-through frying	15–20	300–325°F
Croquettes	3	370–375°F
Cutlets and chops, 1 inch thick	8	345–350°F
Doughnuts, cake	1½–2	375–390°F
Doughnuts, yeast-raised	1¼–2	360–370°F
Fish fillets	3–5	355–360°F
Maple bars, yeast-raised	2	375–390°F
Onions, French-fried	5	340-345°F
Oysters, large	2–4	355–360°F
Potatoes, blanching	8	380–385°F
Potatoes, browning	2–3	380–385°F
Potatoes, French-fried	8	380–385°F
Scallops	3–5	355–360°F
Vegetables (eggplant, cauliflower)	5–7	375–380°F

It happens so easily. The fat should be stirred frequently and cooking should be very slow until the fat begins to melt and the mass can be stirred easily in the kettle. If you have a dairy thermometer you can watch the temperature.

Early in the process of rendering, the temperature of the fat will be 212°F. As the water contained in the fat tissue evaporates, the temperature will rise slowly until it reaches 245–255°F—the highest it should be allowed to go.

Microwave Rendering. Lois Rumrill, Forks of Salmon, CA, wrote: "A microwave oven works just super for rendering fat of any kind. Use a 2-qt. Pyrex, Corning Ware, or other glass pan. Fill pan about two-thirds to three-quarters full of fat. Cover and place in microwave oven. Set time for 12 minutes. When time is up, remove pan from oven. Pour hot lard into jars. I put a doubled piece of cheesecloth over top of jar and secure it with a rubber band. I set the jars in a 13 × 15-inch baking dish. The jars really don't have to be scalded, just clean, and the lids should be hot. The grease is hot enough that when the lids and rings are put on the jars, they will readily seal. This method gives you a very clean, white lard. Also *no* smell, smoke from burnt grease, and almost no mess."

AGAIN, CRACKLINGS: As rendering proceeds, the cracklings will first float, then gradually sink to the bottom. This is where trouble can really begin because they go down there and scorch. If you stop the rendering while the cracklings are still floating you're safer. If you are saving the cracklings, scoop them out before they sink. As the lard renders out into a clear liquid in your pan the cracklings turn brown, shrivel, and float to the top. Don't stir excessively if you want them for snacking or they'll break up.

Be sure they're done—that all the grease is rendered out. When they get visible bubbles in them they're about done. Then scoop them out and finish them off separately. You can put them to drain in a hot place or in your oven in a colander set in a pan and they'll drip awhile more. I freeze them loose in plastic bags, about half a cup in each.

> *CRACKLING CORN BREAD Mix together 2 c. corn meal, 1 c. flour, 1 t. soda, and ½ t. salt. Add enough buttermilk to get a heavy gravy consistency. Fold in 1–1½ c. chopped*

cracklings. (Make sure that cracklings are broken into small pieces; you can make them more tender by soaking them in hot water then draining them.) Bake at 350°F until brown.

From Donna Joehn, Blaine, WA: "Cracklings are my very favorite breakfast accompaniment with eggs. Cracklings are not the skin or rind. They are what is left after rendering out ground-up lard. They are crumbly looking things—like coarse graham cracker crumbs. To eat, you reheat 'til bubbly and crisp, then press dry of fat in a potato ricer or with a spoon in a strainer. Salt, pepper, and enjoy in place of bacon. They sell them in British Columbia grocery stores; we live near the border where there is a large Mennonite settlement and people speak 'low German' on the streets."

WHITENING LARD: For the whitest homemade lard you can possibly make, add a raw potato in the bucket and stir it for a while. Then remove the potato.

SKIMMING LARD: The more water left in your lard the less well it will keep. If you want really water-free lard without struggling on to the bitter and potentially scorched end, skim your lard off the top with a dairy skimmer since the water will all be on the bottom. By "dairy skimmer," I mean a plain old soup ladle, which is what I skim the cream off my milk with.

STRAINING LARD: When your lard liquid is cooled down to only warm, it is ready to be put through a lard press, if you have one. They were common among the old-timers. I don't have one and don't know where you or I could find one except maybe as an expensive antique. I spread cloth in a wire sieve and strain through that into a bucket, and from the bucket I pour into the containers. When you get near the bottom of your rendering pan, the sediment gets thicker. You should stop and switch cloths, this time adding a couple extra layers. Then you can pour it all out and squeeze heartily to get every last drop.

COOLING LARD: When your lard is ready to store, get it cooled down as soon as you can. It should be protected from light, air, and moisture. So if you are storing plain, put your lids on as tightly as if you were sealing them. If your containers are glass, store them on shelves in a dark cellar or inside brown paper bags.

Antique Lard Press

LARD WITHOUT SKIMMING: If you want your lard to keep just as it is—without canning or freezing it—then continue rendering, stirring occasionally to make sure no sediment is scorching on the kettle bottom. In this case it is important that all the water be evaporated unless you skim your lard off, which is a disagreeable job. When the cracklings are a deep golden brown the lard should be done. You can test for moisture by placing a lid on the kettle to see if moisture will accumulate on it. Remove from heat and let the sediment get quiet.

ABOUT RANCID LARD: *Rancid lard should be discarded. It tastes bad and isn't good for you.* But rancid lard does make fine soap.

HOW TO AVOID RANCIDITY: Air and light cause the chemical changes that lead to rancidity. You can improve the storage life of lard thus by keeping it in the dark and in air-tight packaging. And/or you can add a commercial antioxidant (check with your local locker plant). Adding hydrogenated vegetable shortening to lard while it is cooling also helps preserve it. One part vegetable shortening to 16 parts lard is about right.

CONTAINERS FOR LARD: Get ready your containers in which to pour the rendered lard. Clean gallon tin cans are good, even if you don't have lids, or widemouthed jars, especially half-gallons and gallons. Or the tall juice-type cans. Chill it quickly (to get a fine-grained lard) and store immediately in the coolest place you have. Seal tightly and keep in the dark.

FREEZING LARD: Water in the lard doesn't matter if you're going to freeze or can it. I freeze it. It would probably keep okay outside the freezer, but I'm a shade surer that way. I take out 1 can at a time, and it lives on a shelf beside the kitchen stove until I've emptied it and am ready for another. Store lard in a dark cool place or in a freezer, inside a metal container or in a grease-proof freezer carton, sealed with a tight cover. I dip the melted lard off the top into bowls with my cream dipper and then put it into the refrigerator to chill. After the lard gets hard, I cut it into sections and put each one into a plastic bag and into the freezer. Or else, if I have enough coffee cans, I chill it in coffee cans. Then I put a plastic bag over the top of them for a lid and

put can and all in the freezer. You can freeze lard wrapped just in freezer paper if you can get it solid enough to wrap first. Cool it, for example, in a big metal bucket. Then cut and repackage in double layers of freezer paper or white butcher paper and freeze until wanted. It takes a lot of containers to store the lard from even one pig so be prepared.

USING LARD: A certain amount of lard is really very handy. You almost have to have lard to make pie crusts and good soap. You can use lard almost any place you would use oil once you get used to it. And if your animal was born to a residue-free mother and raised on all residue-free food, then you have fat that is pesticide-free and fairly low in cholesterol, and it makes a fine frying grease and baking fat. The only type of recipe I don't like to use lard as the fat in is salad dressings—except I like lard for wilted lettuce dressing. It's handy to keep most of it in the freezer, plus 1 large container in the refrigerator, and a small one by the stove, which you refill from the one in the refrigerator as needed.

LARD SUBSTITUTIONS: When substituting pure lard for "shortening" in baking, add an extra ½ c. flour for every ½ c. lard used because lard is "shorter" and needs more flour to take it up.

Deep-Fat Frying. Cheap homemade lard makes deep-fat frying a reasonable way to prepare some foods. Deep-fat fried foods are a favorite item with my family. My standard recipe is to batter whatever I deep-fry with beaten egg and flour and then fry it in grease hot enough to smoke. If the grease is hot enough before you start frying, the batter casing will immediately seal up and the food won't absorb excessive grease. It's frying at too low a temperature that results in greasy foods. See "Deep-Fat Frying Time/Temperature" table.

That lard for deep-fat frying can be used and reused. I sometimes just leave it in the kettle between uses. Or I strain it through a cloth or fine sieve to remove food particles and then store it in the refrigerator. After frying strongly flavored food, like fish or onions, a few slices of potatoes put in the cold lard and then heated until well browned will absorb the flavor. Then strain the hot lard.

Fat should never be heated above 400°F. Thaw frozen foods before you fry them to avoid lowering the fat temperature. Fry pieces of similar sizes at the same time. The kettle should about half full of fat and you should add fresh fat as needed. To avoid a greasy taste, don't overload the kettle, which would cause the temperature to drop and the frying time to increase. Test the fat's temperature with the fat-frying thermometer.

Accumulation of burnt particles will cause the fat to spoil sooner than it would otherwise. Remove this accumulation by straining the fat through several thicknesses of cheesecloth. For a clearer fat, draw it off into a separate container, and after it has cooled to below 200°F, sprinkle the surface with water. The water carries down to the bottom the particles of burnt food that have been suspended throughout the fat. The clear fat can then be poured off the sludge of water and burnt particles. Or the water, sediments, and thickness of fat can be drawn off the bottom of the container if it has an outlet at its base. Test taste fat before returning it to the kettle so you're sure it isn't rancid.

Meat, fish, and chicken pieces are usually dipped in a frying batter of seasoned milk, egg, and flour and placed immediately into the hot fat. Or dip them into a seasoned water-egg or milk-egg mixture, then roll in flour, crumbs, or cornmeal. Foods with a moist surface (such as oysters) are dipped in crumbs, then batter, and again in crumbs. Croquette mixture should be chilled, shaped, then rolled in crumbs.

Fritters. These are a food dipped in batter and then fried in generous fat. You can make fritters out of just about anything—chicken, oysters, vegetables (of any kind), or fruits such as bananas, pineapples, and apples. They were very popular around the turn of the century. If you've got lot of lard, these are fun to experiment with.

Use clear oil or lard for frying, about 3 inches deep, to cook fritters. Heat the fat hot enough that a bit of batter dropped in will immediately rise to the surface and begin to brown. Don't put in too many fritters at once. Brown first on one side and then turn and do the other. Drain well and serve immediately.

➢ *FRITTER BATTER Combine 1 c. flour and ½ t. salt; slowly add ½ c. milk, then 1 T. cooking oil, and, finally, 2 well-beaten eggs.*

➢ *BAKING POWDER FRITTER BATTER Combine 1 c. flour, ½ t. salt, and 1½ t. baking powder. Slowly add ½ c. milk, then 1 T. cooking oil, and, finally, 2 well-beaten eggs. This gets puffier, but I like the plain batter best for taste.*

➢ *VEGETABLE FRITTERS Cook, drain, and cut the vegetables into convenient-sized pieces before coating with the batter.*

➢ *APPLE FRITTERS Peel and core tart apples and cut them into round, thin, slices. If you want to give them the gourmet treatment, marinate them briefly in a mixture of brandy, lemon juice, and sugar. Drain and dust with flour. Fry on both sides in butter, drain, and sprinkle with powdered sugar and cinnamon. Serve hot.*

➢ *BANANA FRITTERS Peel bananas, cut in halves, and split each piece lengthwise. Sprinkle with lemon juice before coating.*

➢ *MEAT FRITTERS Use cooked, cold meats. Parboil oysters and other shellfish.*

➢ *CORN FRITTERS Combine leftover corn (1 c. more or less), 3 beaten eggs, 3 T. flour, seasoning, and 1 t. baking powder. No need for further batter; you've made your own. Drop by spoonfuls into the hot fat. You can substitute other leftover vegetables in this.*

➢ *LARDING MEAT Marie Oesting of Ocean Park, WA, writes, "We used to lard meat on the farm. I called my mom (she's 88) and asked her the details. Here goes. Beef cans good, but pork doesn't can well because it's so fat. So, they would take the pork chops and also the fresh pork sausage (seasoned but not smoked) and lard them down in a 20-gal. crock. Fry the meat thoroughly, so it's dry and extremely well done. Mother said she always salted the pork chops and sausage but doesn't know whether that's really required for preservation or not. When they are thoroughly fried, layer them into the crock, covering with melted lard (not the fat they were cooked in)."*

➢ *PIECRUST Basically, this is a mixture of flour and fat. The size of the bits of fat varies, as does the amount of water. For piecrusts, use 1½ c. flour sifted with ½ t. salt. Use 2 forks or knives to work in ½ c. lard. When the fat has been worked in until it is more or less of uniform texture, add 4 or*

5 T. cold water slowly until mixture becomes a stiff dough, which will hold together in one ball. Roll out and cut into the shape you need.

Pigs' Feet

Clean the pigs' feet. Be sure to remove the toes and dewclaws, the glandular tissue between the toes, the hair, and any dirt.

➢ *PICKLED PIGS' FEET Cover pigs' feet with boiling water and simmer until tender, 2½–3 hours. In a large enamel pan combine 1 qt. vinegar, 6 whole cloves, 2 bay leaves, 1 stick cinnamon, 2 T. salt, ½ t. pepper, ½ c. brown sugar, and 1 onion, sliced. Simmer 1 hour. Strain liquid to remove spices. Add 2–4 c. liquid in which pigs' feet have been cooked. Pour over feet and chill 2 days, if possible. This is right for 8 pigs' feet. (You can also use pig hocks or knuckle bones to make this.)*

The winter of 1946–47 we lived on a wheat ranch near Clyde Park, Montana. There I got my precious little goat, my first goat, on Christmas morning. That morning I heard a funny sound in the living room, jumped out of bed, ran in there—and there was a baby goat tied to the Christmas tree, trying to eat the tinsel. It was my beloved pet and pal from then on.

Late in January my birthday came, and I turned 8 years old. Later yet, spring finally came, the time of year when every few days we would hear the bleating baa-a-a-s as bands of sheep were hurried by up the blacktop highway a quarter mile away. The sheepherders were driving them off the valley bottom, where the sheep were wintered, up into the mountains, where the snow was now melting and the grass was coming on green and beautiful.

Every time we heard that sound, Mother gave me a bag of cookies and a thermos of hot chocolate (spring was by no means warm in Montana). Then I ran down our long lane to find the sheepherder who drove the flock. The herders always were happy when I came running up behind them with the cookies and cocoa. They never failed to share them with me. We'd sit inside their sheep wagon, that small summer home on wheels, or on its back steps. I'd eventually get around to asking if they had any bums.

I knew that herders of hundreds of sheep preferred not to be bothered with the ones that were orphaned and needed special feeding or that were sick or injured and unable to keep up with the flock's migration—that long walk up to summer pasture. I came home with so many bums that by spring's end, I had a flock of 7 lambs of my very own. I fed cow's milk to them in a pop bottle with a black rubber nipple pulled onto the end of it, and they all thrived. I had blind ones and lame ones, but they all knew who I was and loved me. I sure wasn't lonesome that summer. We were milking about 5 cows, so there was plenty of milk for them.

But those happy memories were followed by sad ones. In the hot August dog days of summer, a city-raised hired man who had just had his noon lunch in the house filled his tractor at our farm gas pump and then carelessly rubbed out his cigarette on the side of a tractor. As he pressed the hot butt on the place where gas had spilled time and again from the hose inlet above, the act instantly started a fire. In rapid succession, the fire burned the tractor, spread to the fuel-soaked ground in front of the pumps, and went on to the adjacent tool and coal-storage shed. From there it blew over to ignite our house's roof.

Because we had no phone and no car that day (Daddy and our single vehicle were away working in a far-off field), Mama sent me running down the lane as fast as I could to get help from our nearest neighbors, who lived not all that near. Mr. Steiner happened to be home, flagged down a car on the highway, told the driver to take me to town so I could spread the call for help there, and then left to help fight the fire. I ended up spending hours at Chet's Service Station in Clyde Park with the old man who was left tending the station after everybody else had jumped into vehicles and zoomed away to our ranch. I was hoping not to be forgotten—waiting to be taken back home and wondering about my pets.

When I had left, the fire had been burning only the tractor and the ground around it. But I could see from town the big column of black smoke over our place. And I got to thinking about how my 7 bum lambs and the goat always sheltered from the noon heat in the rear of that shed, napping away the hottest hours. It worried me a lot, but I hoped somebody had thought to open the back door of the shed and let them out. Surely Mama or somebody had done that. If I had been there, I certainly would have.

I refused to believe they had all—every last one of them—been dead for a long time. I climbed up the big butte in back of our house and called them, evening after evening. I hoped that the big fire had merely frightened them off. Finally Daddy took me to the blackened rubble where the shed had been, and with his boot toe he pointed out bones in the fire debris. It was the first time creatures I'd loved so much and cared for so well had died—and all of them at once. All I had left were lifelong memories that would always be dear. But learning to let go is part of having animals, or people, that you love in your life.

CHRONOLOGY OF THIS BOOK

December 25, 1969.

For Christmas, my mother-in-law gave my husband Mike and me a subscription to *Organic Gardening*, along with some back issues.

February 12, 1970.

Rebecca Neoma Emery was born.

Summer 1970.

"Old Fashioned Recipe Book" idea came to me.

September 1970.

Wrote the table of contents. (Believed I could finish the book in 2 months.) Placed an ad to appear in the November and December 1970 issues of *Organic Gardening*.

November and December 1970.

Received about 250 orders. Wrote all the people saying I'd send the book when done and promised them it would be only a couple more months.

March 1971.

First "issue" mailed to the "subscribers." It consisted of chapters on herbs, definitions and measures, and home industries except a still-to-be-written section on candles.

September 1, 1971.

Luke Carl Emery was born.

December 17, 1971.

Second "issue" mailed after I raised funds to do so by advertising to get more subscribers. About 200 more people ordered. The second issue consisted of beverages and half of a chapter on meats. Then I was sick for a while. We traded our 3 acres and a house as a down payment on 115 acres and a house.

September–December 1971.

Printed and mailed the third issue: chapters on oddments and food preservation and half of a chapter on dairying. Also sent larger binding rings because the book was turning out to be bigger than I'd expected. Then stopped writing.

May 17, 1973.

Sara Ann Emery was born. Sold goats on neighbor's request. Bought Nelly the cow.

November 1973.

After a long break I prayed, felt directed, and went back to work on the book.

January 1974.

Dolly became very sick. Sara was also sick.

February 18, 1974.

The book was finally finished. Dolly was better, Sara was well, and I was happy! But I still had to manage printing the book.

March 1, 1974.

The first edition (the one that came out in issues) and the second edition (the first whole book) were printed and put in the mail to my customers, thanks to Diann, Darlene, and the good collators.

By the late February, Diann had been mimeographing for weeks. Then there was a collating bee, organized by a librarian at the Moscow Public Library. I didn't know her, but she had heard of me. About 6 ladies came to the bee, which was in an empty apartment in the old folks' home that Viola Johns (Diann's mother) ran; I'd never met most of them before.

Diann introduced me: "This is our author." Everybody looked at me hard for a minute to see what an author looks like. I said, "Hello" and "Thanks for coming to help," and that was pretty much the end of it. They kept walking around that table collating, probably because they hadn't anticipated such huge piles of paper and they wanted to get home for dinner. We were doing 200 copies of what I called the fourth issue of the first edition, and then we put together 200 more of the "second edition," which would have the improvement of being an all-at-the-same-time book, to say nothing of the text additions and improvements I'd made in the earlier chapters.

My job was hauling boxes full of envelopes holding the fourth issue in the back of my pickup from the work area to the post office. When I got back for the next load and walked in the door, they nodded and kept going around the table. I saw they had already finished about 8 of the whole books. They had no way of knowing what was going on inside me. I had sort of thought I'd be the person to put the first whole book together. But no matter. I elbowed my way into the line that was going around and around the table and picked up the first of the 12 chapters. I couldn't say a word. I couldn't smile. The emotion in me was so intense and huge. I took a step, picked up the second chapter from its pile and laid it on top, and so on around the table until the last chapter, "Definitions and Measures," and then the back cover. And now I held it in my hands—a completed copy of the *Old Fashioned Recipe Book*. The first one I had ever held in my hands, a miracle!

I clutched it to me, turned, and walked back out the door alone, so full of feeling I thought I'd burst. Just up the hall I found an empty laundry room, went in, and closed the door behind me. There I knelt down, crying with gratitude, and talked to God and thanked Him.

There was more work to be done, hauling boxes to the post office. So then I went back to the collating place, and things just took up again as if nothing spectacular had happened. Only my heart knew better.

April 10, 1974.

Third edition finished. (As soon as I finished the first two, I thought of more things I wanted to include!)

I tried another classified ad in *Organic Gardening*—2 months at $200/month, and this time only one order. I tried selling to libraries and bookstores, working from mail-order lists, but they wouldn't buy at a high enough price to allow me a profit. There had to be another way to reach potential buyers with no middleperson. In the meantime, Viola rented her apartment. We moved the bookmaking to Diann's home, but it outgrew her living room. We had to find another place to do it. We rented an empty restaurant on Main Street in Kendrick for $75 a month. We collated on the abandoned counters and, with great care, settled in the precious new $1,200 mimeograph machine which, by the grace of God, had been allowed to us on time payments of $45 a month. Diann and Darlene started keeping regular office hours at the store, even though I owed each of them anywhere from $300 to $700 depending on which day or month you looked at, and the whole town was telling them they were fools. We painted huge, brave red-and-white signs on the outside of our new home advertising the *Recipe Book*, and did a little off-the-street business. I desperately needed to sell more books, and directly to readers. but how?

Then some college boys from the University of Idaho at Moscow visited me and urged me to take part in a craft fair they were organizing for Moscow's Main Street. I never turn anybody down, and as usual we were in a situation where if I didn't find $250 somewhere, we wouldn't be able to pay our paper bill and would have to shut down forever on the following Monday. So I took a folding table and all the children, and we set up shop there in the sunshine. I passed out hundreds of brochures and sold $300 worth of books at $9.95 each. It was a long day but great fun, and I had the money! From then on . . .

May 15–September 15, 1974.

The children and I were out every weekend at town fairs, art and craft fairs, and county fairs, peddling copies of the books and passing out brochures about how to mail-order them.

May 24, 1974.

Colored photos were added to the book, and that became the fourth edition. (We were constantly producing books. There actually were some fourth editions turned out before the fifth came along.)

May 26, 1974.

An index was added, and then we called it the fifth edition.

But the Idaho fairs just weren't big enough to support the kind of volume I needed to pay Diann and Darlene, the rent for the Livingroom Mimeographer, and the payment on the machine. Once again, it looked like the end. Then we heard of a 3-day craft fair 500 miles away, near the Pacific coast, in Bellevue, Washington (a suburb of Seattle). It was to take place on Thursday through Saturday. I said to Diann and Darlene, "I'll try it just this one more time. I'll go clear to Seattle. If I don't make it this time, I'll submit to the inevitable—I'll give it all up." That week's mail-order money was just enough to pay gas one way to Seattle. As usual, I took all 5 children (ranging in age from 1 to 10) plus blankets, a bag of groceries, and so many books I was afraid my poor old car wouldn't make it over the long, steep Alpowa grade over the Blue Mountains just west of Lewiston, Idaho. But it did. That night the children and I slept squeezed like sardines in the car, parked behind a shopping center. A policeman saw us, came over, and got very uptight about the whole idea of it, though he didn't arrest me.

The next day I found out I had the date wrong. The fair existed, but it didn't start until Friday. So I had Thursday to kill. I decided to try to get on TV. At a shopping center, I hunted for a phone. A nice secretary in a real estate office let me use theirs. I looked in the Yellow Pages for TV stations and called the "Seattle Today" TV show people to ask if I could get on that weekend. Meanwhile, my kids were kind of getting into things. At that moment, the bosses at the real estate office came in. The "Seattle Today" people told me on the phone they had an unexpected cancellation that day, and I should be there in 1 hour! The real estate people told me to please take my children and leave, and I did.

We headed for the KING studio; we'd never been there before. By a split second we found it in time. The children couldn't find all their shoes, so I made them stay in the car in the parking lot, looked after by the nice parking attendant. I rushed into the studio, and there you had a study in contrasts. The hostess of the live show was in an evening gown, her makeup expertly done, her hairdo lovely. I was in work clothes and tennis shoes, with bags under my eyes. The show was a smashing success!

Afterward, we headed back to the shopping center. The children had supper and I didn't, because we were getting low on food. The next day, bright and early, we set up for our fair. We sold $300 worth of books that Friday, plus I met some people who became my good friends before the summer was over—people who make quickie trips to Mexico and buy up goods there to sell at fairs here, and people who spend long winter months working in their basement craft shops (or some such places) painstakingly creating beautiful things and then, all summer long, weekend after weekend, take those things to one craft fair after another trying to sell them for enough money to get through another winter.

It's a very special way to make a living, and there's a

warm camaraderie among the folks who live that way. They took me in as a sister and began to teach me the things I so badly needed to know: when the big, good shows were; what you had to do to get into them; the fine points of just where to put your table to catch the best crowd flow; how to hawk your wares; and how to get along with the management. They told me that, although the fair there in Bellevue seemed so good, there was going to be an even better one Saturday and Sunday up in the Fremont district of Seattle. They were all going there, some leaving a friend to tend their tables in Bellevue. I went along, and Fremont was a whole new experience for me.

I thought I was arriving in Fremont plenty early Saturday morning at 6am, but *wow* was I late! There were hundreds of craftspeople already there—600, according to the brochure I saw later. Mobile TV cameras and reporters were already out getting stories for the morning news. All the good spots were already taken. I had to settle for a spot out on the edge of the fair. Nonetheless, I did $500 worth of business that day. The kids and I slept in the car again that night, and nobody minded. The next day, business was even better. I ran out of books, so then I took orders. So many would-be customers were crowding in wanting my book that I felt just overwhelmed. But then people appeared from nowhere to help me. They passed out brochures, took orders, and helped with the children. They begged and insisted until finally I went off and bought myself a 7-Up in a little nearby restaurant while they continued selling books back at my table.

I started to feel like a small sort of celebrity. People would come up and say, "Everybody's talking about your book." I walked back with my drink and saw them gathered here and there around one of my brochures, eagerly talking. That night the children and I slept in a motel, and we all had showers and reveled in our comfort. We bought a big bag of groceries—including luxuries like avocados and fruit juice—to celebrate. After the little ones were put to bed, my oldest daughter, Dolly, and I sat up and totaled the money we were taking home. We could scarcely believe our eyes— it was over $1,000. I remembered how once I had numbly apologized to Darlene because I still had no money to pay her, and I knew how much she needed it. She responded with words I'll never forget: "Oh, Carla, I just wish I had some money of my own so I could lend it to you." But now I could give Diann and Darlene all their much-deserved and long-awaited wages, and catch up on the other bills too!

After that I went to Pacific coast fairs every weekend. There was always one—or more—going on out in that heavily populated region. The biggest problem was getting over Alpowa while heavily laden with outward-bound books. Once when I was driving the family truck, it caught on fire. Flames and black smoke were coming up through the crack all around the outside edge of the hood, and I could see flames in the floorboard insulation around the brake and gas pedals. I stopped as soon as I could get over to the side of the road. I got out and raised the hood—and there was my engine burning merrily away.

I didn't know what to do next. I was no mechanic. I depended on Mike for things like that. Just then a Greyhound bus saw us and stopped right in front of us; the driver got out and ran toward us, holding a fire extinguisher. It shot a white powder all over the engine and put out the fire. We thanked him, and he drove off in his big bus.

Then we realized the fire had gotten going again, down in the floorboard insulation. We had no liquid; we tried to put dirt on it, but that was no good because the dirt couldn't get down to the places where the fire was smoldering. A farmer stopped, said he'd get us some water, and drove away. We kept moving the dirt, trying to hold down the flames until he could get back. He came back and soaked the thing out good and final. The truck engine was ruined. We ended up going over Alpowa in the wee small hours in the car, pulling a U-Haul trailer full of books.

That was the time we were going to do 5 fairs on the coast in the same weekend, so it was an extra heavy load of books. Darlene and her 5 kids in her car came along with me and mine and some extra young people to do the selling. Once we got to Seattle, I had to lead Darlene to the fair site in Tacoma where she was going to sell books. We happened to get on the freeway at rush hour. I had already been introduced to freeways and had learned how different they were from our 2-lane country roads at home, and I'd forgotten what a shock they could be. I found out later that Darlene drove down that freeway behind me crying all the way. But she hung in there behind me, and we got there okay.

From May 15 until December, I was home only 1 weekend. That was in August, when I was just too sick and exhausted to go out. That week Mike and I talked it over, and we decided to submit to the necessities. I had been leaving home just in time to get to the fair, generally on the late side because I had so much I wanted to do at home: time with Mike, working in the garden, all the canning and freezing, catching up with my milk cow. Mike tried to keep the cow going while I was gone, but she and Mike just couldn't get along. Then a pile of mail was always waiting for me, and there were people to call and decisions to make and, of course, I always had all 5 children with me whether I was at home or on the road. So I generally didn't get any sleep the night going to the fair, because I'd leave late and drive all night. And I generally didn't get any sleep the night coming home, because I was always so anxious to be with Mike again that I'd just drive straight home without sleeping.

But after I got sick, we talked it over and decided I wouldn't try to come home every week, as I had been doing. Instead I would go out for a few weeks at a time—or more. I did that, and my cow went dry, and the stock cows got into the garden about 3 different times and ate everything to the ground (everything that they didn't trample, that is). We had to get rid of some animals because no one could stay home with them, and some of my young fruit trees died for lack of water.

Sometimes I got home and felt like bawling because it all looked yellow with dryness, deserted, and rundown, as if nobody lived there. Here I was out telling everybody about the great country life and raising your own food, and there wasn't anything in my own cellar but the green beans, turnips, and peas I'd put up during the first part of the summer. But then I'd think about how people had come up to me and told me about the first garden they'd ever had, or their new home in the country and what a joy it was to them, and how my book had helped them. Then I'd feel so good, and I'd tell myself I'd have a milk cow and a garden again for sure the next year.

Oct. 1–Dec. 1, 1974.
First trip to California. We got a press agent, Julaine, and some TV and radio interviews—and a red-and-white van to sleep in when away from home.

December 31, 1974.
I publicly announced my plans to build a School of Country Living after Mike and I made the down payment on a beautiful 386-acre ranch nearby. I wrote the first schedule of classes and planned to open it in May.

January 1, 1975.
The children and I left for 4½ months on the road, circling the entire United States, doing radio and TV and newspaper interviews, telling people about the book and the School of Country Living.

Summer 1975.
First session of the School of Country Living.

Fall 1975.
Went back on the road until Christmas to sell books and recover expenses: another national tour with children in van.

January 10, 1976.
Sold rights to Bantam for $115,000 cash advance. With that money I planned to do a School of Country Living again.

Summer 1976.
Second school session. Flash flood washed away much of the school. I gave up.

Fall 1976.
Went back on road (pregnant) to pay off the debts—once more the big circle all around the United States.

February 15, 1977.
Jacob Michael Emery was born.

August–December 1977.
Toured to promote the Bantam edition (the seventh). Traveled with the 6 children and, for TV demos, a nanny, a milk goat, a turkey, a goose, and some rabbits. I was becoming a popular and sometimes paid performer on TV talk shows (Johnny Carson, Mike Douglas) with my comedic country-girl routines. Actually, I didn't so much deliberately set out to be funny as that's just how it happened. I was generally late and had no time to get nervous. And I'd have my baby in my arms. (I *always* had my baby.)

February 1978.
Mike Douglas's TV show flew me down to Los Angeles. Here's how it happened:

My fourth nationwide tour was the longest and most successful yet. Back home from that tour, I was still busy and still responsible for the Living Room Mimeographer's production, even though Bantam was now producing a commercial edition. I was still willing to do interviews and farm-girl comedy routines. The staff of Mike Douglas's show kept calling me up. I'd done several shows for them before, but I wasn't planning to tour again for a while. So they asked me to fly to Los Angeles and perform especially for them again. I agreed. After all, it's ever onward and upward, right? And they would pay me $250 a minute *and* foot the bill for my plane fare, hotel room, and a chauffeur and limousine while I was in town.

I certainly was climbing the ladder of success. It was flattering to realize I was good at something—TV comedy. That I could stand before all those cameras and be relaxed, interesting, and funny—even when I wasn't selling the *Recipe Book*. Fame, fortune, success . . . and back home we always needed more money. My husband had long since quit his town job. The girls at the Mimeographer . . . the kids . . . all expecting me to make money . . . more money. Like a monkey on my back . . . all those expectations and needs. Getting money was becoming the big thing in my life. Couldn't be poor.

The Mike Douglas staff was adamant about one thing: I couldn't bring my children, not even my baby. That hurt. I'd never left my children behind before. I didn't want to be separated from my baby, not even for 36 hours. But they wouldn't accommodate me on that point. "That's how it's done," I was told. I figured I'd better bend to fit them: $250 a minute. So I agreed. I left and flew in a jet to Los Angeles.

There were 2 big reasons why I had previously driven around the United States, again and again, in a van—above and beyond the fact that I wanted to get my books to people in towns of all sizes. First, I couldn't bear the idea of being separated from my children and needed a way to bring them along. And second, I am the ultimate white-knuckled flyer. But here I was, without even my baby, umpty-thousand feet above terra firma in a vibrating jumbo jet. I pulled a magazine out of my handbag. It had a feature article about me, written by a local journalist, a woman who'd followed the *Recipe Book* saga from the very beginning. I read it, and it's a wonder I didn't punch a hole in the aluminum floor of the airplane and fall through to Earth—all of a sudden I felt so heavy. The gist of her message was that Carla had gone Hollywood, turned hypocrite, apostatized her own dream of country peace and quiet. There was more truth to her angle than I was comfortable with. Lord, what a gift the press can give us, to see ourselves as others see us.

The plane landed. My chauffeur met me at the gate, and drove me in a long black car to an elegant hotel with a doorman. This uniformed character stood outside under a long, narrow, sideless awning that seemed determinedly pretentious. I was conveyed to my suite and left alone. Not just a room—a suite! Room after empty, elegant, Hollywood-gaudy room. In the bedroom was an enormous, triple-sized bed with a carved and gilded headboard. I could have fitted all the kids into it with me. There was a well-appointed kitchen; does a "star" bring her own chef? And a spacious, luxurious, outer sitting room. For the throngs of reporters? None present. For the throngs of fans? Mine wouldn't look for me in such a place. I was alone. It was deadly, depressingly lonely. I wasn't used to ever being alone. I didn't feel right. I wanted my baby.

Time to do my show. Chauffeur and limo again . . . . excitement . . . being fussed over by the show's staff. The make-up room to make me beautiful. The Green Room where I'd await my turn in the spotlight. I was brought out to wait just offstage early enough to overhear the last few minutes of the episode preceding mine. Mike Douglas was talking with 2 major female stars in the movie-theatrical sky. He asked one, "If you could live your life all over again and have it be any way you wanted, what would you do differently?"

She answered, "I'd be a man."

He asked the other, "If you could live your life all over again, what would you do differently?"

She answered, "I wouldn't have any children."

Her words chilled me to the soul. Like everyone else, I knew that actress through media reports. She had 5 children. I wondered if they were at home watching her performance on this live TV show, the way mine sometimes had. Or perhaps her children were bored with Mom as a celebrity and no longer bothered watching, as had later happened with mine. How might it affect them if they heard, or heard of, her words? What a chance she was taking.

Oh, I understood well enough. It was all the performance game. The conversation probably was sketched out ahead of time with the show's staff. Or the staff may have trusted those 2 professional women to do as required to put on an exciting show. Those words were the smashing finale, something shocking to get people's attention and keep them from switching channels. Attention equals success, fame, money. And that's show business, right?

But the chill in me wouldn't be explained away. It was my turn to go on, and I had to suddenly be upbeat and witty and whatever else it was that I can be that people can love and that was worth $250 a minute to the Mike Douglas staff. I can't remember what I did or what I said. I do remember that I was fighting a feeling that I had just seen the devil under the tinsel, the gaping maw of corruption and moral danger. I felt that, above all, I had to save my children from thinking that this was what I wanted, believed in, stood for, and wanted them to believe in and become.

Then it was time for the limo back to the celeb hotel and a sleepless night in that cavernous bed; next came white-knuckled flying back to Idaho. When I got home I told Mike it was all over for me, that what I wanted more than anything else in the world was to be a good mother and a good wife and to practice what I preached. I pulled the plug on the whole career thing and let it run down the drain. I folded the Living Room Mimeographer and let Bantam make all the books. Eventually sales slowed to a miniscule trickle because I did no more book-selling interviews or tours. Mike Douglas's staff soon quit calling after I steadfastly refused to come back. I heard from a Hollywood screenwriter interested in turning my book-writing and selling adventures into a movie. I said no.

Instead, Mike and I agreed to work on an exciting new personal project together: a seventh baby.

April 18, 1979.
Esther Marie Emery was born.

September 1985.
Mike left. Five days later, I began writing again—a diary this time.

Dec. 2, 1985.
I was divorced with custody of the children.

January 1986.
I began work on an eighth edition of this book and continued working on the diary.

January 27, 1988.
Last night I had to do some heavy deciding about the new edition of this old book that has been almost like a combination of life's work and diary to me over the years. In 3 weeks Mike is having a beautiful church wedding with a couple hundred invited guests. It's my job to make sure our 7 children are there, looking appropriately well-dressed and in suitably positive moods for a festive occasion.

The old-timers I've so revered got married, had big families, and stayed together until death did them part, maybe whether they were happy or not. I was born into a different era. I'm certainly not the only woman—or man—this ever happened to. Each of us then has to find our own way of adapting to the transition, of making a positive restructuring of our lives by discovering a new vision to live for and strive toward. Because you gotta have a dream.

What do I do about new editions of this book? After our divorce, the first time I was editing the book and came to a passage in which I spoke of my love for Mike, I deleted it. And then another such. But the next day I realized I had to put them back and not do that any more. My marriage to Mike is history and, in more than one sense, this book is history. You don't change history. That's dishonest. What I am free to change, or try to change, is the future. When Mike asked for his freedom, by default I also received the gift of mine.

What do I do about the future—of this book and of my life? Well, I keep on living for the positive, convinced that it is always better to heal than to wound, to love than to hate, to make peace than to make war. And yet I am now perhaps more aware of subtle and necessary distinctions in the practice of those ideals. I have a clean conscience about my marriage: over those many years, I gave it the best I could. I honestly put my husband and children first.

My younger children want me to go out and find another man, convinced that normalcy can be restored simply by creating another married-family unit. But life has stages, and I feel finished with that time for loving a man and bearing and rearing his children. I can't have children any more. I can't be young again. I can't go back to the beginning of a fullscale life's love and companionship the way you can go back to the starting point in a child's board game and play the course again. I'm 49. I can't be 26 again. For someone else it may be feel right—it may be right—to love once more, to serve again in the very real bonds of matrimony. But that's not for me.

Now that I no longer have the responsibilities of a wife,

and my mothering gets lighter all the time as my children grow older, I'm going to write! I want to write more books, print more books, sell more books, to travel and do fairs and say "Hello" to America again across my book-laden selling table. It's going to be a marvelous adventure. I'll love and be loved by so many unique, wonderful people—male and female, young and old—as I share my writing with them. It's a completely different thing from loving and marrying one man—I'm going to love and be loved by masses of people: these readers whom I want to serve. I'll give myself to my readers with the same fire, loyalty, and dedication with which I once gave myself to a single person—Mike. Yes, now I want to belong to you, as I once thought of myself as belonging to him.

With this transition I'm going to be freer to think than I was before. I want to daringly reconsider both the given and the forbidden, to live a challenging life of the mind, searching for both open and obscure facts, for I'm a lover of data. The coming years may well be the best, happiest ones of all my life. I'm truly looking forward to them.

July 1988.
Bantam lets the *Recipe Book* go out of print. All rights return to me. The book is now "out of print." But people still write and want copies.

January 1989.
I begin selling a copier-produced eighth edition by mail.

October 1989.
Three different universities have asked to be designated as the repository for my papers, manuscripts, etc. I choose the University of Idaho. I take them all my old newspaper-clipping and photo scrapbooks, copies of the old editions, etc. We create a separate, closed depository, its contents to be made public only with my consent or upon my death. I begin doing research for another book, related to the diary materials.

August 1992.
Chad Haight of Sasquatch Books, a Seattle publisher, wrote and asked me for permission to publish a new commercial

edition of the book. I agreed. From then until now I've been going to their office every Wednesday morning at 9:30am to turn in another chunk of revised or new text. I'm working with Lane Morgan, a fine author in her own right, who looks over the manuscript for problems; Anne Depue, editor-in-chief, who organizes the process; and Pam Milberg, intern, who helps sort material and keep the order of it sensible. Coming up, yet to be met, are a noble copy editor and a talented artist. I've never before produced the book with so much skillful help, and I think you're going to be impressed by the miracles that team effort can achieve! This new edition is definitely becoming the book of my dreams, the one I was trying to write from the very first day—after all these years.

Various Editions Described

If you're looking at an older copy of this book and wonder which edition it is, here are some hints:

First Edition. By subscription only, arriving in 4 consecutive shipments, mimeographed on Fibertint; 875 copies finished about March 1, 1974.

Second Edition. Mimeographed on Carlton and Mustang paper with an ivory Plastisheen cover; 185 copies finished April 10, 1974.

Third Edition. Contents expanded; 500 mimeo copies finished April 10, 1974.

Fourth Edition. Colored photos added; 1,000 mimeo copies finished May 24, 1974.

Fifth Edition. Index added; 13,000 mimeo copies started May 26, 1974.

Sixth Edition. Black-and-white photos added; 34,000 mimeo copies started January 16, 1975.

Sixth–Seventh Edition. Half new paging and half old paging; rewrites added. Index dropped due to confused paging; 4,000 mimeo copies started November 22, 1976.

Seventh Edition. All chapters fully revised and also now illustrated by Cindy Davis; 25,000 (?) mimeo copies started March 12, 1977.

The first 7 editions (before the Bantam edition) were 3-hole-punched and usually were bound with a bent length of plastic-coated copper wire in pretty colors or were Velobound (with a soft or hard cover).

Bantam Printing of Seventh Edition. A different set of drawings by Cindy because a better printing method allowed more detail; same contents. Bantam first printed on alternating sections of yellow and green; in later press runs, all pages were green. A total of 200,000 printed in 6 different runs—November 1977, December 1977, September 1978, September 1979, April 1980, and March 1981. Softcover only.

Eighth Edition. Chapters called "Poultry," "Meats," "Definitions and Measures," "Home Industries," "Vegetables," "Sweets," and "Oddments" were revised. Starting March 1990, about 3,000 copies were made by copy machine. Gradually upgraded through various printings; another 1,000 done by offset. Again 3-hole-punched, bound with 2-inch metal binder rings.

Proto-Ninth Edition. All 12 chapters thoroughly revised, updated, and expanded. Chapters called "Sours" and "Home Industries" integrated with other chapters. Chapters called "Introduction to Plants" and "Bee, Rabbit, Sheep, and Pig" added. "Sweets" chapter renamed "Tree, Vine, Bush, and Bramble," "Meats" now called "Introduction to Animals." First time book ever printed on white paper. Bound like eighth edition.

Ninth Edition. The one you're reading. Title and much of "Definitions and Measures" chapter dropped to make room for new information. Indexed and fully illustrated; *el supremo* version so far. And massaged by Sasquatch's editors to make my writing follow (most of) the rules that in the past I've been famous (infamous?) for spurning. No more world records for typos. Oh, well.

Updated Ninth Edition. More than 1,500 mail-order sources, checked and updated, with the addition of websites and e-mail addresses.

World Records This Book *May* Have Set

1. More typographical errors, run-on sentences, general horrors of composition, handwritten inserts, and inky fingerprints in the first edition and others than any other book on record. (I wrote the *Guinness Book of World Records* people and they said the number of typos did represent a world record, "but you have to count them." Never had time.)

2. Weirdest page numbers . . . Where else have you seen "½" pages? Or "26c"? That's because with each edition, I kept adding more material and didn't want to mess up the existing page numbering.

3. First author in history to have had 3 babies in the same 4½ years during which she gave intellectual birth to a 5-lb. book.

4. Biggest mimeographed book in general circulation: 936 pages at its largest. Then I discovered elite type! Then I discovered pica condensed. (The book stayed at 900-some pages; I just kept squeezing in more words.)

5. Most self-published copies sold. Even if it's not a record, it's a lot. And most copies of a mimeographed book sold: 88,000 (I'm sure that's a record). (That figure doesn't include the sales of the Bantam and Sasquatch editions.)

6. Most words (now over a million) by 1 person in 1 book.

7. Longest time spent writing 1 book (32 years).

YOUR ACHIEVEMENT CHECKLIST

1. Grind a handful of grain coarsely for cereal. _____ Grind finely for flour. _____
2. Mix, knead, raise, punch down, raise, and bake a loaf of bread. _____
3. Put on a bee suit and open a hive. _____
4. Make yogurt. _____
5. Start with cream and take it through every step until it has become a salted ball of butter and a glass of buttermilk. _____
6. Make cottage cheese. _____
7. Make a hard cheese. _____
8. Milk a goat. _____
9. Put a cow in the stanchion and milk her. _____
10. Feed the poultry and gather eggs. _____
11. Clean out a rabbit hutch. _____
12. Plan and cook a meal in which the food is 100 percent home-grown. Breakfast _____ Lunch _____ Dinner _____
13. Raise, catch, kill, scald, pick, singe, cut up, and cook a chicken. _____
14. Dry a batch of fruit or vegetables in a food dryer. _____
15. Take out the ashes. _____ Build a fire in a wood stove. _____ Adjust the dampers. _____
16. Freeze a batch of a fruit or vegetable. _____
17. Make a batch of sourdough starter. _____ Cook a meal of sourdough pancakes using that starter. _____
18. Make homemade noodles. _____ Crackers _____
19. Dry and save seeds from an annual. _____. A biennial _____
20. Separate milk. _____ Take apart, wash, dry, and reassemble the separator. _____
21. Make a batch of homemade ice cream using a crank freezer. _____
22. Harness a team of horses (or oxen). _____ Hitch them up to an implement or wagon. _____ Till a field with them. _____
23. Build housing for animals. _____ Repair or build a fence. _____
24. Correctly identify 10 different herbs from sprigs laid out on a table. _____
25. Make a pot of herb tea from herbs you have grown and harvested. _____

A FINAL EXAM FOR YOU

1. What is the basic bread recipe?
2. How can you start one beehive off another?
3. How do you make cottage cheese?
4. If you had no livestock feed store to buy commercial feeds at, what would you grow, and approximately how much of it or what proportions would you feed your goat every day in winter? Rabbit? Cow? Chicken? Pig?
5. What's a "potato onion"? How do you grow garlic? What prevents motion sickness?
6. What can you use to make a variety of home-grown, caffeine-free coffee?
7. If you have no electricity, gas, or other "modern" energy source, how can you preserve meat? Fruits? Root vegetables? Squash and pumpkins?
8. What do you use for potato seed? How do you plant potatoes?
9. What is the correct weight at which to butcher a broiler chicken? A rabbit? A pig?
10. State the advantages and disadvantages of keeping a goat or a cow for home dairy use.
11. What aspect of soap making is very dangerous, and how can you minimize that risk?
12. What can whole wheat be used for?
13. How do you make a homemade cheese press?
14. What is the best way to house an expectant doe rabbit?
15. How would you grow and harvest a grass grain without using any fossil fuel in the process?

The answers are all in this book!

INDEX

systems, 71–73
See also Water pollution
Water buffalo, 742
Water chestnuts, 326
Water oat. *See* Wild rice
Water pollution, 64–65
  agricultural chemical, 64–65
  hard water, 64
  water testing, 65
Water power, 28–29
Water spinach, 257
Water-bath canning, 522
Watercress, 271
Waterfowl, 694–709
Watermelons, 337
Wax beans, 283–85
Waxy maize, 159. *See also* Corn;
  Field corn
Weeds in gardening, 113–14
Wells (water source), 70–71
Welsh onion, 240–41
Wethers, 727
Wheat, 199–203
  bran, 203
  bulgur, 202
  cracked, 202
  graham, 202–3
  growing, 199–200
  harvesting, 200–201
  recipes for, 201–3
  resources, 199
  uses of, 201
Whipping cream, 783
White muscle disease, 579
White sauce, 602
Whooping cough, 572–73
Wild animals, 585–95
  resources, 586
Wild food foraging, 412–13
Wild rice, 182, 187–90
  growing, 187–88
  harvesting, 188–89
  processing, 189–90
  recipes for, 190
  resources, 187
Wine
  mulled red, 374
  vinegar, 545
Winged bean, 299–300
Wintergreen, 406
Wolf teeth in rabbits, 817
Wood cookstoves, 485–87
Wood heat, 479–88
  air pollution, 483, 484–85
  burning, 483–85
  fire prevention, 483–84
  harvesting wood, 480–83
  resources, 483
  stove shopping, 484
Wooden fence, 563–64
Wool
  breeds of sheep, 822
  colors, 822
  felting, 832
  fiberfest, 832
  quilts, 832
  resources, 833
  shearing sheep, 829–31
  sheep, 829–33
  spinning and weaving, 832
Worms
  in chickens, 662
  in guineas, 711

in livestock, 579
in pigs, 850
in rabbits, 818
in sheep, 829
See also Earthworms
Wormwood, 406

X, Y, Z

Yeast breads. *See* Bread, yeast
Yogurt, 768–70
  frozen, 786–87
Yucca as sudsing agent, 406
Yurt, 34
Zoning
  for animals, 553
  for pigs, 839